Guide to U.S. Elections

Congressional Quarterly's
Guide to U.S. Elections

FOURTH EDITION • VOLUME II

EDITORS

JOHN L. MOORE

JON P. PREIMESBERGER

DAVID R. TARR

CQ PRESS

A Division of Congressional Quarterly Inc.
Washington, D.C.

CQ Press
A Division of Congressional Quarterly Inc.
1255 22nd Street, N.W., Suite 400
Washington, D.C. 20037
(202) 822-1475; (800) 638-1710

www.cqpress.com

Cover design: Kachergis Book Design, Pittsboro, North Carolina

Printed in the United States of America

05 04 03 02 01   5 4 3 2 1

∞ The paper used in this publication meets the minimum requirements of the American National Standard for Information Science—Permanence of Paper for Printed Library Materials, ANSI Z 39.48-1984.

LIBRARY OF CONGRESS CATALOGING-IN-PUBLICATION DATA
Congressional Quarterly's guide to U.S. elections.—4th ed.
      p.   cm.
      Rev. ed. of: Congressional Quarterly's guide to U.S. elections. 3rd ed.
© 1994.
      Includes bibliographical references and index.
      ISBN 1-56802-601-3 (v. 1: alk. paper)
      ISBN 1-56802-602-1 (v. 2: alk. paper)
      ISBN 1-56802-603-X (set: alk. paper)
      1. Elections—United States—History—Statistics. 2. Political conventions—United States—History. 3. Political parties—United States—History.
I. Congressional Quarterly, Inc. II. Congressional Quarterly's guide to U.S. elections.

JK1967.C662   2001
324.973—dc21   2001037955

Summary Table of Contents

Contents

Tables, Figures, and Boxes

Guide to U.S. Elections

PART IV

Congressional Elections

CHAPTER 20

Introduction

AMERICANS ELECT A NEW CONGRESS on the first Tuesday after the first Monday in November of even-numbered years. Early the following January the elected representatives and senators begin their first session of that Congress. Those elected November 7, 2000, for instance, were sworn in January 3, 2001, on the opening day of the 107th Congress. They included many new faces—eleven new senators and forty-one freshmen representatives—as occurs in each Congress.

As an institution, Congress has suffered public criticism almost since the nation's beginnings. Alexis de Tocqueville, the astute French visitor of the late 1820s, observed the "vulgar demeanor" of the House of Representatives, where often he could not detect even one "distinguished man." In contrast, as he wrote in his classic *Democracy in America,* the Senate was "composed of eloquent advocates, distinguished generals, wise magistrates, and statesmen of note, whose arguments would do honor to the most remarkable parliamentary debates of Europe."[1]

Subsequent views of the entire Congress often have been no more charitable than de Tocqueville's opinion of the House. Gallup polls measuring American's trust and confidence in governmental institutions show Congress consistently ranking last among the three branches of the federal government. In December 1998 Gallup found that 63 percent of the Americans questioned expressed "a great deal" or "fair amount" of confidence in the executive branch, and 78 percent in the judicial branch. Yet 61 percent of those Americans polled stated their trust and confidence in the legislative branch, up seven percentage points from May 1997.[2] Related Gallup polls, asking whether Americans approve or disapprove of the way Congress is handling its job, have shown less enthusiasm for the legislative branch. In a February 2001 poll 53 percent approved and 32 percent disapproved. However, those results have been volatile over the years with the public at times giving approval ratings only in the 35 to 40 percent range. These and other polls over longer periods suggest that many Americans often view the legislative branch with a skeptical eye. But paradoxically, election results show that voters generally return incumbents to office, indicating a more generous attitude toward their own representatives and senators than the institution as a whole.

In the modern era the power of incumbency has remained strong with the turnover rate from deaths, resignations, and election defeats averaging about 10 percent or less, historically an exceptionally low level. An incumbent's appeal rests on more than the person's record in Congress and is significantly influenced by the public image projected through television, direct mail, telephone banks, and other devices used in election campaigns. But projecting that image, particularly through costly television advertising, is extremely expensive, requiring any candidate to raise substantial campaign funds. Incumbents are particularly well placed to raise money from special interest groups, whether business, labor, or ideological, as a result of their service in Congress and participation in important decisions that may affect the donors' organizations. This incumbency advantage generally tilts voter recognition toward the member and away from a challenger who often will have more difficulty raising money from the interest groups.

Incumbency during the 1990s, however, provided less protection, particularly in the House. In the 1992 and 1994 congressional elections more than eighty incumbents lost reelection bids. Voters were increasingly wary of long-service incumbents, labeled "career politicians" by their critics. Many challengers ran antigovernment campaigns presenting their absence of previous elected office as a reason to be elected. Some challengers vowed to serve only a limited number of terms to avoid becoming "career politicians" out of touch with the voters, although some winners by the end of their pledged terms were finding reasons to stay in office.

The anti-incumbent mood of the 1990s was clearly evident when the 107th Congress convened in January 2001. Almost two-thirds of the members of the House, 65 percent, were first elected in 1992 or later. Two out of every three representatives had never served in congressional office during any of the most momentous events of the post–World War II years. They had never experienced an economic recession, had not been part of the long twilight struggle of the cold war, were not in office when the Soviet Union broke up, and did not have to vote on waging war against Iraq in the Persian Gulf, Almost half of the House in 2001—48 percent—had never served in other than a Republican-controlled Congress, an enormous reversal of the Democratic dominance of the institution during most of the period since the New Deal days. Turnover in the Senate was less dramatic during the period but significant nevertheless. As the 107th Congress began, forty-five senators had been in the chamber for six years or less, a figure not matched since 1981.

In 1994 a landmark election swept Republicans to power in both chambers. Democrats had controlled either the House or Senate, and usually both, since 1955. Since 1933, when the Great Depression realigned political power, Republicans had managed to control both houses only twice—in the Eightieth Congress (1947–1949) and the Eighty-third Congress (1953–1955). Republicans also held a Senate majority from 1981 to 1987.

In 1996 the GOP maintained its majority, losing nine seats in the House, but gaining two in the Senate. It was the first time

that the GOP had won a back-to-back majority in the House since the 1920s. After the 1998 and 2000 elections the Republican Party again held onto both chambers but its majority was further trimmed to 221 Republicans and 212 Democrats (and two independents) in the House at the start of the 107th Congress and to an exactly even 50–50 split in the Senate. (Surprisingly the Senate would swing over to Democratic control in June 2001 with the defection of one Republican senator to the Independent ranks.) Moreover, there were signs that the power of incumbency had returned. In the 2000 House races, 97.8 percent of incumbents were reelected, only a fraction lower than in 1998. Although incumbency in the Senate was less powerful than in the House, nevertheless in the 2000 elections 79 percent of incumbents in that chamber won again.

Characteristics of Members

Whether the turnover is large or small, a certain uniformity pervades Congress. Congress has been dominated since its inception by middle-aged white men with backgrounds in law or business. Their levels of income and education have consistently been above the national average. But for many of the lawmakers today, business occupations are past activities. In recent years, ethics rules have limited the income that can be earned outside of Congress. Moreover, serving in Congress has become a full-time job. And since the 1970s it has attracted career politicians, whose primary earnings have come from government service.

Ever so slowly, other changes also have crept into the makeup of Congress. The numbers of women, African American, and Hispanic American members have increased in recent decades, although still not in proportion to their share of the total population. Of the 535 members of Congress at the beginning of 2001, seventy-two were women, thirty-six were black, nineteen were Hispanic, six were of Asian or Pacific Islands descent, and one senator, Ben Nighthorse Campbell of Colorado, was of Native American heritage. In addition, of the five nonvoting delegates sent to the House, two were black women, one was Hispanic, and two were of Pacific Island descent.

AVERAGE AGE

The average age of members of Congress went up substantially between the post–Civil War period and the 1950s but remained fairly constant until the mid-1970s. In the Forty-first Congress (1869–1871), the average was 44.6 years; by the Eighty-fifth Congress (1957–1959), it was 53.8. Over the next eighteen years, the average fluctuated only slightly. But when the Ninety-fourth Congress met in January 1975, the average age dropped to 50.9 years. (See Table 20-1, this page.)

The difference was made in the House, where ninety-two freshmen members reduced the average age of representatives to 49.8 years, the first time since World War II that the average in either chamber had fallen below 50. The Ninety-sixth Congress (1979–1981) was the youngest since 1949; the overall average age for both chambers had slipped to 49.5 years. It dropped again in January 1981, when the House had eight members under thirty, the most since World War II. The younger trend bottomed out in 1983 when the average hit forty-seven years.

Table 20-1
Age Structure of Congress, 1949–2001

Year	House	Senate	Congress
1949	51.0	58.5	53.8
1951	52.0	56.6	53.0
1953	52.0	56.6	53.0
1955	51.4	57.2	52.2
1957	52.9	57.9	53.8
1959	51.7	57.1	52.7
1961	52.2	57.0	53.2
1963	51.7	56.8	52.7
1965	50.5	57.7	51.9
1967	50.8	57.7	52.1
1969	52.2	56.6	53.0
1971	51.9	56.4	52.7
1973	51.1	55.3	52.0
1975	49.8	55.5	50.9
1977	49.3	54.7	50.3
1979	48.8	52.7	49.5
1981	48.4	52.5	49.2
1983	45.5	53.4	47.0
1985	49.7	54.2	50.5
1987	50.7	54.4	52.5
1989	52.1	55.6	52.8
1991	52.8	57.2	53.6
1993	51.7	58.0	52.9
1995	50.9	58.4	52.2
1997	51.6	57.5	52.7
1999	52.6	58.3	53.7
2001	55.4	59.8	54.4

Note: House and Senate totals reflect the average ages of members at the beginning of each Congress.

Source: Congressional Quarterly.

After that came a gradual increase, continuing through the beginning of the 107th Congress in 2001, when the average age climbed to 55.4. That aging trend was partly attributable to the aging trend of the nation's population. But low turnover in Congress was also a big factor. The youngest Congress of the 1990s was the 104th when the Republicans took control. The average age in January 1995 was 52.2, with House members averaging 50.9 years.

OCCUPATIONS

The legal profession has been the dominant occupational background of members of Congress since its beginning. In the First Congress, more than one-third of the House members had legal training. The proportion of lawyers in Congress crested at 70 percent in 1840 but remained high. From 1950 to the mid-1970s it was in the 55–60 percent range.

The first significant decline in members with a law background began with the Ninety-sixth Congress. Although sixty-five of the one hundred senators were lawyers in 1979, for the first time in at least thirty years lawyers made up less than a majority of the House. That situation continued through the 1990s. When the 107th Congress convened in January 2001, 156 of the 435 representatives and fifty-three of the one hundred senators were lawyers.

After lawyers, members with a business or banking background make up the second largest group in Congress. In the

107th Congress, 159 House members claimed such a background, the same as the 106th Congress but down from 181 in the 105th Congress.

Members of the clergy continue to be underrepresented in Congress. Only a handful of Protestant ministers have served in Congress, and no Catholic priest had done so until 1971, when Rep. Robert F. Drinan, D-Mass., a Jesuit, took a House seat. (Father Gabriel Richard was the nonvoting delegate of the Territory of Michigan from 1823 to 1825.) Drinan served five terms but declined to run again in 1980, the year that Pope John Paul II ordered priests not to hold public office. The pope's directive also prompted Robert J. Cornell, a Catholic priest and former U.S. House member, to halt his political comeback bid in Wisconsin. Cornell, a Democrat elected in 1974, had served two terms before he was defeated in 1978. Only three members of the 107th Congress listed their occupation as clergy.

A new breed of legislator emerged in the 1970s: the career politician whose primary earnings had always come from political office at the local, state, or federal level. This trend became possible because states and localities had begun to think of political positions as full-time jobs and had raised salaries accordingly. In addition, the demands of modern political campaigns left less time for the pursuit of other careers. This trend continued unabated through the following decades until the 2000 elections. In the 107th Congress 73 percent of new House members and 64 percent of new senators had held prior office, down from 83 and 78 percent, respectively, two years earlier.

New members of Congress also tend to lack military experience, continuing a trend prevalent in the 1990s. At the start of the 101st Congress in 1989, 286 members of Congress (seventy senators and 216 House members) cited military service. In 2001 at the start of the 107th Congress, only 171 of the 535 members claimed military service (thirty-eight in the Senate and 133 in the House). Thus the ratio of members with military experience dropped in a decade from slightly over half to under a third.

RELIGIOUS AFFILIATIONS

Among religious groups, Protestants have comprised nearly three-fourths of the membership of both houses in recent years. However, Roman Catholics form the biggest single religious group—a distinction they have held since taking the lead from Methodists in 1965. In the 107th Congress Roman Catholics made up the largest religious congregation in both chambers with a total of 149.

Among Protestant denominations, Baptists were the most numerous (73), followed by Methodists (66), Presbyterians (48), Episcopalians (40), and Lutherans (20). In all, the members listed affiliations with some nineteen religious groups, including Jewish (37), Mormon (16), Eastern Christian (6), Christian Scientist (5), Unitarian (3), and Pentecostal (3). Eight did not specify a religious preference, and forty-two simply listed "Protestant." No one was designated Moslem, Hindu, or Buddhist.[3]

Women in Congress

By January 2001 a total of 208 women had been elected or appointed to Congress and 205 actually served, starting with

Table 20-2
Women in Congress, 1947–2001

Congress	Senate	House
80th (1947–1949)	1	7
81st (1949–1951)	1	9
82nd (1951–1953)	1	10
83rd (1953–1955)	1	12
84th (1955–1957)	1	17
85th (1957–1959)	1	15
86th (1959–1961)	1	17
87th (1961–1963)	2	18
88th (1963–1965)	2	12
89th (1965–1967)	2	11
90th (1967–1969)	1	10
91st (1969–1971)	1	10
92nd (1971–1973)	1	13
93rd (1973–1975)	1	16
94th (1975–1977)	0	17
95th (1977–1979)	2	18
96th (1979–1981)	1	16
97th (1981–1983)	2	19
98th (1983–1985)	2	22
99th (1985–1987)	2	22
100th (1987–1989)	2	23
101st (1989–1991)	2	28
102nd (1991–1993)	3	29
103rd (1993–1995)	7	48
104th (1995–1997)	8	48
105th (1997–1999)	9	51
106th (1999–2001)	9	56
107th (2001–2003)	13	59

Note: House totals reflect the number of members at the start of each Congress and exclude nonvoting delegates.

Rep. Jeannette Rankin, R-Mont., elected in 1917. Her state gave women the right to vote before the Nineteenth Amendment to the Constitution enfranchising women was ratified in 1920. Of the 205 women, 176 served in the House only, twenty-two in the Senate only, and seven—Margaret Chase Smith, R-Maine; Barbara A. Mikulski, D-Md.; Barbara Boxer, D-Calif.; Olympia J. Snowe, R-Maine; Blanche Lincoln, D-Ark.; Maria Cantwell, D-Wa.; and Debbie Stabenow, D-Mich.—in both chambers. (Two women were never sworn in and one resigned her seat the day after she was sworn.) *(See Table 20-2, this page.)*

Certainly the most prominent woman to be elected to the Senate was First Lady Hillary Rodham Clinton, who won election in 2000 as her husband was completing his second term as president. Elected from New York, she was the first first lady ever to serve in the Senate.

In her 1996 book about women who had served in Congress, Rep. Marcy Kaptur, D-Ohio, wrote

From the first woman to serve in Congress—Jeannette Rankin of Montana, elected to the House in 1917—to the fifty-eight who serve today, their personal stories have varied tremendously. More than one-third of these women were widows who succeeded their husbands in office and went on to surpass them. Some were self-actualized women who either rose through the ranks of political parties and institutions or took them on and got elected to Congress on their own. Most encountered and rose above incredible adversity and tragedy; a few were blessed with vast wealth. All exhibited insight into the human condition, a persevering determination to overcome obstacles, and a conscience formed in the

knowledge that women have always been, and may always be, charged with nurturing, teaching and enlightening the human race.[4]

Several women served out unexpired terms of less than one year. Rebecca L. Felton, the first woman to serve in the Senate, did so for only one day. Felton, a Georgia Democrat, was appointed October 1, 1922, to fill the Senate vacancy created by the death of Thomas E. Watson. She was not sworn in until November 21, and the next day yielded her seat to Walter F. George, who had meanwhile been elected to fill the vacancy.

Gladys Pyle, a South Dakota Republican, was elected November 9, 1938, to fill the unexpired term of Rep. Peter Norbeck, who died in office. But his term ended the following January 3 before Congress convened and thus Pyle never took the oath of office.

In 1996 Kansas Lt. Gov. Sheila Frahm was appointed by Gov. Bill Graves to fill the Senate seat of Majority Leader Bob Dole, who had resigned from the Senate to run full time for president. Frahm held the seat less than five months. A special primary was held in August to fill Dole's seat, and Frahm lost it to a more conservative Republican, Sam Brownback, who went on to win the November general election.

THE WIDOW'S MANDATE

In many jurisdictions it became customary for the office-holder's party to run his widow for the seat in the hope of tapping a sympathy vote. Sometimes she filled the office by brief appointment until the governor or party leaders could agree on a candidate.

The "widow's mandate," as such, marked the beginning of political careers for some women. Edith Nourse Rogers, a Massachusetts Republican, entered the House after her husband died in 1925 and remained there until her death in 1960. Margaret Chase Smith filled her late husband's House seat in 1940 and went on to serve four terms in the Senate (1949–1973). Hattie W. Caraway, an Arkansas Democrat, who was appointed to the Senate seat of her late husband in 1931, was returned to Congress by Arkansas voters in 1932 and 1938.

Rep. Charlotte T. Reid, R-Ill., and Rep. Marilyn Lloyd, D-Tenn., became their parties' nominees when their husbands died between the primary and general elections (in 1962 and 1974, respectively). As women became more active in politics at all levels, the congressional tradition of the widow's mandate has weakened.

In the 107th Congress, three women held the House seats of their late husbands. Jo Ann Emerson, R-Mo., won a special election in 1996 to fill out the term of her husband, Bill Emerson. She later won the general election to win a full term in the 105th Congress. Two years later, Republican Mary Bono won the California seat that had been held by her husband, former pop singer Sonny Bono who was killed in a skiing accident. She won reelection easily in 1998 and 2000. Lois Capps, D-Calif., in 1998 won the Santa Barbara district of her husband, Walter Capps, who died in 1997 and was also reelected in 1998 and 2000.

Perhaps the most unusual case was that of Democrat Jean Carnahan of Missouri, who was appointed to a Senate seat in the 107th Congress that was won on November 7, 2000, by her husband, Missouri Gov. Mel Carnahan, who died in an October 16 plane crash while campaigning against incumbent senator John Ashcroft.

Marriages have also linked members of Congress. Rep. Emily Taft Douglas, D-Ill., was elected to Congress in 1944, four years before her husband, Sen. Paul H. Douglas, D-Ill., was. Another woman, Rep. Martha Keys, D-Kan., married Rep. Andrew Jacobs, D-Ind., in 1976. This marriage between colleagues was the first of its kind in congressional history. Rep. Olympia J. Snowe, R-Maine, in 1989 married the governor of Maine, John R. McKernan Jr., a former U.S. representative. In 1994 Rep. Susan Molinari wed her New York state colleague, Rep. Bill Paxon, joining together two House Republican leaders. In the 105th Congress, Molinari served as Republican conference vice chair and Paxon served as chair of the National Republican Congressional Committee. In 1996 Molinari gave birth to the couple's daughter.

Molinari earned another distinction as one of the few women in Congress who were daughters of representatives. She won the Staten Island seat of her father, Rep. Guy Molinari, who left the House to become Staten Island borough president. California Democrat Lucille Roybal-Allard also shared that distinction by winning the House seat of her father, Edward R. Roybal, whose congressional career lasted thirty years. California Democrat Nancy Pelosi, who entered the House in 1987, was the daughter of Thomas J. D'Alesandro Jr., a House member from 1939 to 1947 and then mayor of Baltimore.

SLOW GAIN IN NUMBERS

It has been a long, slow climb in women's membership since Rankin's election to Congress in 1916. Her seating was not followed by a surge of women members, even after women received the vote in 1920. The first notable increase came in 1928, when nine women were elected to the House. The number had scarcely more than doubled by 1961, when twenty women (two senators, eighteen representatives) served in Congress. After that women's membership declined slightly and did not regain the 1961 level until 1977. Another slippage followed until 1981, when the membership reached twenty-one for the first time.

The thirty women sworn in as members of the 102nd Congress in January 1991 represented a record number to be elected in a single election. Thirty women also served in the 101st Congress, but only twenty-seven of them were elected in the 1988 general elections. Three others—Ileana Ros-Lehtinen, R-Fla.; Jill L. Long, D-Ind.; and Susan Molinari—came to the House through special elections in 1989 and 1990.

The elections of 1992 found record numbers of women running for and being elected to Congress. The 103rd Congress, which opened in 1993, included forty-eight women in the House, an increase of nineteen, and seven in the Senate, an increase of four.

Several factors contributed to the success of women candidates in 1992. Many capitalized on an unusually large number of retirements to run in open seats. They also benefited from reapportionment, which created dozens of opportunities for newcomers in the South and West. Another factor was public dissatisfaction with Congress, which allowed women to portray

On the steps of the Capitol, Democrats Loretta Sanchez of California and Carolyn McCarthy of New York talk to reporters about their 1996 election to the House. In 2001 Sanchez and McCarthy were among the seventy-two women serving in Congress.

themselves positively as outsiders. The Senate's questioning of law professor Anita F. Hill's accusations of sexual harassment in the 1991 confirmation hearings of Supreme Court Justice Clarence Thomas also had an impact. The televised image of an all-male Senate Judiciary panel sharply questioning Hill brought home dramatically to many women their lack of representation in Congress.

By the first full Congress of the new century, the 107th in 2001, there was an all-time high of seventy-two women—fifty-nine in the House and thirteen in the Senate—on Capitol Hill. (The House total does not include two nonvoting delegates.)

The number of women elected to full Senate terms increased dramatically in the 1990s. By 2001 twelve of the thirteen women serving in the Senate were elected to full terms and the thirteenth (Jean Carnahan) was appointed to fill the seat won by her husband after he died during the fall campaign. Two states—California and Maine—were represented in the Senate solely by women: Democrats Barbara Boxer and Dianne Feinstein from California and Republicans Olympia J. Snowe and Susan Collins from Maine. Snowe and Feinstein were reelected in 2000.

In 1992 the first African American woman was elected to the Senate, Democrat Carol Moseley-Braun of Illinois. The daughter of a police officer and a medical technician, Moseley-Braun grew up in Chicago. She served in the state legislature from 1979–1988, where she rose to become the first woman assistant majority leader. She also served as the Cook County recorder of deeds (1988–1992). The outrage over the Senate's handling of the Thomas confirmation hearings propelled Moseley-Braun into the 1992 Illinois Senate race. She won that election with 53 percent of the vote, but lost in 1998 in her bid for reelection.

Before 1987, only four women ever won election to full Senate terms. They were Maurine B. Neuberger, D-Ore. (1960), Nancy Landon Kassebaum, R-Kan. (1978, 1984, 1990), Paula Hawkins, R-Fla. (1980), and Barbara A. Mikulski, D-Md. (1986). Kassebaum was the first woman ever elected to the Senate without being preceded in Congress by her husband.

LEADERSHIP POSITIONS

Although women have been entering Congress in record numbers, at the end of the twentieth century they still were finding it difficult to move to the top of the committee and party leadership ladders. In 1995 Kassebaum became the first woman to chair a major Senate committee, Labor and Human Resources. She was joined in the House by fellow Kansas Republican, Jan Meyers, who chaired the Small Business Committee. Before Meyers, no woman had chaired a full House committee since 1977, when Merchant Marine Committee Chair Leonor K. Sullivan, D-Mo., left Congress. Mae Ella Nolan, a California Republican who served from 1923 to 1925, was the first woman to chair a congressional committee; she headed the House Committee on Expenditures in the Post Office Department.

In 1989 Barbara Mikulski became the first woman to chair a Senate Appropriations subcommittee, the VA, HUD and Related Agencies panel. She became its ranking minority member when the GOP took control of the Senate in 1995. When the Senate unexpectedly switched to Democratic control in June 2001, Mikulski became the chair again. Three other Democratic women were also elevated to chairs of Senate Appropriations subcommittees after the 2001 changeover: Dianne Feinstein of California, and Mary Landrieu of Louisiana, and Patty Murray of Washington.

On the House Appropriations Committee, Barbara Vucanovich, R-Nev., chaired the Military Construction Subcommittee in the 104th Congress. In the 107th Congress, Ohio's Marcy Kaptur served as the ranking member of the Appropriations Agriculture subcommittee and California's Nancy Pelosi was the ranking member of that panel's Foreign Operations subcommittee.

In the wake of the 1998 elections, two women—Jennifer Dunn R-Wash., and Rosa DeLauro, D-Conn.—challenged their party's leaders for a larger role in running the House and each one was rebuffed. When the Republicans held leadership races for the 106th Congress, Dunn challenged Majority Leader Dick Armey of Texas for his job. Early in the 105th Congress, she had been elevated to an official leadership position, winning election as conference secretary. In July 1997 she moved further up in the leadership by winning the position of conference vice chair. But her effort to move Armey out of the second highest party slot failed. If she had won, she would have been the first woman majority leader.

During the Democrats' November 1998 organizational meetings, DeLauro challenged Martin Frost of Texas for the position of chairman of the House Democratic Caucus. Ten Democrats made nominating speeches on behalf of DeLauro, the caucus' outspoken chief deputy whip, but she still did not prevail.

Congress has been an important starting point for women seeking national office, however. Shirley Chisholm, a Democratic representative from New York, ran for president in 1972, and Geraldine Ferraro, another New York Democrat who served in the House, was her party's vice-presidential nominee in 1984.

Table 20-3
Blacks in Congress, 1947–2001

Congress	Senate	House
80th (1947–1949)	0	2
81st (1949–1951)	0	2
82nd (1951–1953)	0	2
83rd (1953–1955)	0	2
84th (1955–1957)	0	3
85th (1957–1959)	0	4
86th (1959–1961)	0	4
87th (1961–1963)	0	4
88th (1963–1965)	0	5
89th (1965–1967)	0	6
90th (1967–1969)	1	5
91st (1969–1971)	1	9
92nd (1971–1973)	1	12
93rd (1973–1975)	1	15
94th (1975–1977)	1	16
95th (1977–1979)	1	16
96th (1979–1981)	0	16
97th (1981–1983)	0	17
98th (1983–1985)	0	20
99th (1985–1987)	0	20
100th (1987–1989)	0	22
101st (1989–1991)	0	24
102nd (1991–1993)	0	26
103rd (1993–1995)	1	39
104th (1995–1997)	1	38
105th (1997–1999)	1	37
106th (1999–2001)	0	37
107th (2001–2003)	0	36

Note: House totals reflect the number of members at the start of each Congress and exclude nonvoting delegates.

Blacks in Congress

In 131 years, from 1870 to 2001 with the swearing in of the 107th Congress, one hundred and one black Americans served in Congress—four in the Senate and ninety-seven in the House. John W. Menard holds the distinction of being the first black person elected to Congress. But his 1868 election in Louisiana was disputed and the House denied him a seat in the Fortieth Congress. Hiram R. Revels of Mississippi, who filled an unexpired Senate term from February 1870 to March 1871, thus became the first black person actually to serve in Congress. The first black person to serve in the House was Joseph H. Rainey of South Carolina, from December 1870 to March 1879. (*See Table 20-3, this page.*)

Menard, Revels, and Rainey were elected during the post–Civil War Reconstruction era (1865–1877), when many white voters were disenfranchised and Confederate veterans were barred from holding office. During that period sixteen black men were sent to Congress from Alabama, Georgia, Florida, Louisiana, Mississippi, North Carolina, and South Carolina. But from the end of Reconstruction until the end of the century, only seven black men were elected to Congress, all from the Carolinas and Virginia. They, like their predecessors, were Republicans.

As federal controls were lifted in the South, literacy tests, poll taxes, and sometimes violence eroded black voting rights. From the time Blanche K. Bruce of Mississippi left the Senate in 1881,

no other black person served in that body until Edward W. Brooke, R-Mass., did from 1967–1979. In 1992 Illinois Democrat Carol Moseley-Braun was elected to the Senate, becoming the first black woman to gain a Senate seat. She served one term, losing her reelection bid in 1998.

The last black person elected to the House in the nineteenth century was Republican George Henry White of North Carolina; he was elected in 1896 and 1898 but did not seek renomination in 1900. For nearly three decades there were no black members of Congress—not until Oscar De Priest, R-Ill., entered the House in 1929 and served three terms. During the next quarter-century only three other blacks were elected to Congress: Arthur W. Mitchell in 1934, William L. Dawson in 1942, and Adam Clayton Powell Jr., in 1944. All three represented big-city black constituencies, in Chicago (Mitchell and Dawson) and New York (Powell).

Moreover, all three were Democrats, reflecting a switch in black voting habits. President Franklin D. Roosevelt had pulled a majority of black voters away from the party of Abraham Lincoln into a coalition of Depression-era urban laborers, farmers, and intellectuals. Mitchell, the first black Democrat elected to the House, was brought in by the Democratic sweep in the 1934 election.

That election also removed the Republican, De Priest, and marked the beginning of a fifty-six-year absence of black representation among House Republicans. That drought was broken

in November 1990 when Connecticut elected Gary Franks, a black Republican real-estate investor from Waterbury who had once captained Yale's basketball team. Franks was defeated for reelection in 1996.

House Democrats, in contrast, steadily gained black members. Only two were added in the 1950s—Charles C. Diggs Jr., D-Mich., and Robert N. C. Nix, D-Pa.—but after that the pace quickened. Five more were elected in the 1960s, and fourteen each in the 1970s and 1980s. The number of black Americans elected to Congress more than doubled during the 1990s—thirty-six were elected to the House—all but two Democrats—and one (Mosley-Braun) to the Senate.

The Supreme Court's "one-person, one-vote" rulings in the early 1960s, ratification of the Twenty-fourth Amendment in 1964, and congressional passage of the 1965 Voting Rights Act are credited with opening up the polls to black voters as never before. The Voting Rights Act provided for federal oversight in jurisdictions where black registration and voting was exceptionally low; the Twenty-fourth Amendment outlawed poll taxes and similar restrictions on voting; and the courts eventually ended a southern practice of diluting black voting power by gerrymandering voting districts. As black voter turnouts increased, so did black representation in Congress.

In 1968 Rep. Shirley Chisholm, D-N.Y., became the first black woman to be elected to Congress. She was joined in the House by Yvonne Brathwaite Burke, D-Calif., and Barbara C. Jordan, D-Texas, who both served from 1973 until 1979. In a 1973 special election, Cardiss Collins won the House seat previously held by her late husband, George W. Collins. Next came Katie Hall, D-Ind., the winner of a special election in November 1982, followed by two victors in the November 1990 general election, Maxine Waters, D-Calif., and Barbara-Rose Collins, D-Mich.

Jordan and Andrew Young, D-Ga., both elected in 1972, were the first blacks in the twentieth century to go to Congress from states of the Old Confederacy. Both Georgia and Texas later sent other black representatives, who were joined by black House members from Tennessee (Harold E. Ford), Mississippi (Mike Espy), and Louisiana (William J. Jefferson).

The 103rd Congress (1993–1995) had included several firsts for black Americans. In addition to Moseley-Braun becoming the first black woman ever elected to the Senate, for the first time since the Reconstruction era, the House delegations from Alabama, Florida, North Carolina, South Carolina, and Virginia included black members. Georgia elected its first black woman representative, Cynthia McKinney. The dramatic gains for African Americans in the 1992 elections was in large measure a result of redistricting aimed at increasing minority strength in Congress—a legacy of the civil rights era. This effort to draw so-called minority-majority districts, however, came under attack as the decade of the 1990s wore on. By the end of the decade, however, the Supreme Court in several decisions set new standards that limited this method of increasing black representation in Congress.

In 2001, at the beginning of the 107th Congress, all but one of the thirty-six black members in Congress were Democrats. The exception was Republican J. C. Watts of Oklahoma, a former

professional football player and youth minister. One other Democrat, Julian Dixon, was reelected in the fall but died December 12, 2000, before the new Congress began. His seat was filled in a June election by another black Democrat, Diane Watson, who had served twenty years in the California Senate and had been U.S. ambassador to Micronesia. In addition, Democrats Eleanor Holmes Norton of the District of Columbia and Donna M. C. Christensen of the Virgin Islands were elected as nonvoting delegates.

Despite the steady gains of blacks being elected to Congress and the growing power of senior black members, African Americans remained numerically underrepresented in Congress. In 2001 they made up about 12 percent of the population, but only 9 percent of the House and had no representation in the Senate.

As the number of black Americans continued to increase in the House, those elected earlier gained seniority and, in some instances, committee chairmanships. Dawson served as chair of the Committee on Expenditures in the Executive Departments (later renamed the Government Operations Committee) from 1949 until his death in 1970 (except for 1953–1955 when the Republicans controlled the House). Other notable black chairs included Powell (Education and Labor Committee, 1961–1967); William H. Gray III, D-Pa. (Budget Committee, 1985–1989); Augustus F. Hawkins, D-Calif. (Education and Labor, 1984–1991); and Louis Stokes, D-Ohio (Permanent Select Committee on Intelligence, 1987–1989, and Standards of Official Conduct, 1981–1985, 1991–1993).

In 1989 Democrats elected Gray to majority whip, the third-highest ranking job in the House. Gray held the post until 1991 when he resigned from Congress to become president of the United Negro College Fund. In 1991 Rep. John Lewis, D-Ga., a veteran of the civil rights movement, moved up into the House Democratic leadership as a chief deputy whip.

By the end of the century, a few black members of Congress had served in the House for more than twenty-five years. California Democrat Ronald V. Dellums, who retired from the House in the 105th Congress after fourteen terms, served as chairman of the Armed Services Committee in the 103rd Congress. In the 106th Congress, William L. Clay of Missouri, a former chair of the Post Office and Civil service Committee, served as the ranking member on the Education and Workforce Committee. He retired at the end of that Congress. In the 107th Congress John Conyers Jr. of Michigan, a former chair of the Government Operations Committee, was the ranking member on the Judiciary Committee; and Charles Rangel of New York, ranking member of the Ways and Means Committee.

The new generation of African Americans elected to Congress in the 1990s reflected the changes begun during the civil rights era. Many came to Congress with considerable experience in state legislatures and other local government positions. Bobby L. Rush of Illinois, a leader of the militant Black Panther movement during the 1960s, had served for a decade on the Chicago city council. Earl F. Hilliard, Alabama's first black representative since Reconstruction, was an eighteen-year veteran of his state's legislature. Cynthia McKinney had been a member of the Georgia state legislature, and Corrine Brown had served in

Jesse Jackson Jr., pictured here standing with his father, Jesse Jackson, said the blacks' recent gains in Congress should be viewed in the historical context: although he was the ninety-first African American elected to Congress in 1995, more than 11,000 other people had served by then.

Even though the black-majority 11th District in Georgia was invalidated by the Supreme Court decision, Cynthia A. McKinney, the district's black representative, scored a comfortable victory in 1996 in the newly drawn white-majority 4th District. Only one-third of the new district's voting age population was black, compared with 64 percent in her old district. In fact, all three of Georgia's black Democrats in the House were reelected to redrawn districts in 1996. Moreover, McKinney won again in 1998 and 2000 in the redrawn district.

The thrust of the Court's opinions threatened those who defended majority-minority districts as a way to empower minority voters. But the justices did not make sweeping determinations affecting all such districts, they seemed inclined to carve out new limits in a sequence of slightly different cases. The following states faced redistricting challenges between 1993–1998: Alabama, Georgia, Florida, Illinois, Louisiana, North Carolina, New York, Ohio, South Carolina, Texas, and Virginia.

Hispanics in Congress

The rapidly expanding Hispanic American population was expected to become a powerful voting bloc in Congress but by 2001 the group remained significantly underrepresented. At the start of the 107th Congress that year, nineteen members and one nonvoting delegate from Puerto Rico identified themselves as Hispanics—people of Spanish ancestry. However, the 2000 census showed the nation's Hispanic population continuing to grow rapidly, to 12.5 percent of the population—35.3 million persons—up from 9 percent a decade earlier. If Hispanics were represented proportionally in Congress they would hold fifty-four seats. Hispanic voter turnouts traditionally have fallen well below the national average, which group activists attribute to poverty, lack of education, language barriers, alienation resulting from discrimination, large numbers of young people, immigration status, and often a continuing attachment to their homelands. (See Table 20-4, p. 793.)

As of January 2001, a total of thirty-nine Hispanics had served in Congress—two in the Senate and thirty-seven in the House. Several other Hispanics represented territories as nonvoting delegates or resident commissioners. The 107th Congress included Anibal Acevedo-Vilá, the resident commissioner of Puerto Rico.

The growth of Hispanic representation in the House was in large part the result of judicial interpretations of the Voting Rights Act requiring that minorities be given maximum opportunity to elect members of their own group to Congress. After the 1990 census, congressional district maps in states with significant Hispanic populations were redrawn with the aim of sending more Hispanics to Congress, a goal accomplished by the 1992 elections. Before the 1992 elections, there were only thirteen Hispanic members of Congress.

No Hispanic candidate has been elected to the Senate since 1970 when Joseph Montoya won his second and last term. Dennis Chavez, his fellow Democrat from New Mexico, was the first Hispanic to serve in the Senate (1935–1962).

Rep. Romualdo Pacheco, R-Calif., was the only Hispanic to serve in Congress during the nineteenth century. Mexican-born,

the Florida legislature. The only new black member elected in the 2000 races, William Lacy Clay, Jr., had served in the House and Senate of his home state, Missouri.

In a 1995 special election, Jesse L. Jackson Jr., whose father, the Rev. Jesse Jackson Sr., was a civil rights crusader and two-time Democratic presidential contender, was elected from Illinois. He was thirty-one years old when he was sent to Congress. In 1996 Julia Carson of Indiana won the seat of her former boss, Democrat Andrew Jacobs Jr., and became the first black to represent Indianapolis in the House. She had served in both the Indiana House and Senate. Another African American woman, Carolyn Cheeks Kilpatrick won her House seat after serving seventeen years in the Michigan House. In 1998 the Cleveland district seat of retiring black Rep. Louis Stokes was won by African American Democrat Stephanie Tubbs Jones, a judge and prosecutor in Cuyahoga County.

REDISTRICTING BATTLES

Following the 1990 census, many states redrew congressional district lines under the provisions of the 1965 Voting Rights Act, which required that interests of minority voters be protected. Districts in which minorities made up a majority of the voting age population were known as majority-minority districts. As state mapmakers pulled districts this way and that to pick up minority voters, many old boundaries were tugged out of shape. In some states, oddly shaped majority-minority districts emerged.

Congressional remapping that went to extreme lengths to elect minorities quickly came under scrutiny by the Supreme Court. In 1993 in *Shaw v. Reno,* the Court ruled against North Carolina's bizarrely shaped majority-minority districts, inviting a new round of lawsuits challenging the constitutionality of districts drawn to ensure the election of minorities. Two years later in *Miller v. Johnson,* the Court struck down a Georgia redistricting plan that created three black-majority districts. The Court cast heavy doubt on any district lines for which race was the "predominant factor." In 1995 a panel of three federal judges imposed a new plan that reduced the black population share to about one-third in two of the districts.

with an English stepfather and an English education, Pacheco helped to bridge the cultural gap between the Spanish-speaking settlers of California and the newly arrived Americans. After California was taken from Mexico and given statehood, Pacheco moved upward in a succession of political offices to the governorship in 1875, filling out the term of his predecessor who resigned to become a U.S. senator.

The next year Pacheco ran for Congress and was certified the victor in a disputed election and took his seat early in 1877. But the House subsequently decided that his opponent was the rightful winner. Pacheco returned home and ran again—successfully—twice more. Upon leaving Congress he became ambassador to Honduras and then Guatemala. No other Hispanic American was elected to Congress until 1912. After that, only in 1927–1931 and 1941–1943 was Congress without any Hispanic American members. By 2001 Hispanic members had been elected from Texas (ten members), California (eleven), New Mexico (seven), New York (four), Louisiana (two), Florida (two), Arizona (one), Illinois (one), and New Jersey (one).

Sixteen of the Hispanics elected in 2000 were Democrats, and three were Republicans. In that year, only one additional Hispanic—Hilda Solis, a California Democrat—was elected. She won by defeating another Hispanic, Mathew G. Martinez. In the 1998 elections, Charlie Gonzalez of Texas succeeded his father Henry B. Gonzalez, a thirty-seven-year veteran of the House and the former chairman and ranking member of the Banking Committee. Other notable Hispanics who had long congressional careers were Rep. E. "Kika" de la Garza, D-Texas, a former chair and ranking member of the House Agriculture Committee, who served thirty-two years in the House; Rep. Manuel Lujan Jr., R-N.M., who served ten House terms before becoming President George Bush's secretary of the interior in 1989; and Bill Richardson, D-N.M., who left the House in 1993 after ten years to become U.S. Representative to the United Nations and then energy secretary in the Clinton administration.

Turnover in Membership

Congress experienced high turnover rates in the nineteenth and early twentieth centuries, principally in the House. The Senate experienced more stability because its members were selected for six-year terms and because state legislatures tended to send the same men to the Senate time after time. The Senate's turnover rate began to increase only after the popular election of senators was instituted by the Seventeenth Amendment in 1913. In the middle decades of the twentieth century, congressional turnover held steady at a relatively low rate. For a quarter-century after World War II each Congress had an average of about seventy-eight new members. An increase began in the 1970s; more than one hundred new members entered Congress in 1975. Turnover remained fairly high through the early 1980s, and then came a spell of strong incumbency and relatively low turnover that lasted through the 1990 election.

The 1988 election brought only thirty-three new faces to the House and ten to the Senate, the smallest turnover in history, both numerically and as a share (8 percent) of total membership. Another small turnover followed in 1990; the combined

Table 20-4
Hispanics in Congress, 1947–2001

Congress	Senate	House
80th (1947–1949)	1	1
81st (1949–1951)	1	1
82nd (1951–1953)	1	1
83rd (1953–1955)	1	1
84th (1955–1957)	1	1
85th (1957–1959)	2	0
86th (1959–1961)	2	0
87th (1961–1963)	2	1
88th (1963–1965)	1	3
89th (1965–1967)	1	4
90th (1967–1969)	1	4
91st (1969–1971)	1	5
92nd (1971–1973)	1	6
93rd (1973–1975)	1	6
94th (1975–1977)	1	6
95th (1977–1979)	0	5
96th (1979–1981)	0	6
97th (1981–1983)	0	7
98th (1983–1985)	0	10
99th (1985–1987)	0	11
100th (1987–1989)	0	11
101st (1989–1991)	0	11
102nd (1991–1993)	0	11
103rd (1993–1995)	0	17
104th (1995–1997)	0	17
105th (1997–1999)	0	18
106th (1999–2001)	0	18
107th (2001–2003)	0	19

Note: House totals reflect the number of members at the start of each Congress and exclude nonvoting delegates.

turnover for both chambers, including retirement, amounted to just 10 percent. The 1990 Senate incumbent reelection rate of 96.9 percent was the highest since direct elections began in 1914.

Several factors contributed to the turnover rates in the 1970s and early 1980s. The elections of 1972 and 1974 were affected by redistricting that followed the 1970 census; many House veterans retired rather than face strong new opposition. Those two elections also were the first in which eighteen-year-olds could vote. Probably the chief reason for change in 1974 was the Watergate scandal, which put an end to the Nixon administration and badly damaged the Republican Party. Democrats gained forty-three seats in the House that year, and the following January seventy-five of the ninety-two freshman representatives in the Ninety-fourth Congress were Democrats.

Most of those Democrats managed to hold their seats in the 1976 elections. The upheavals in that year's voting were in Senate races. Eighteen new senators took their oath of office in January 1977, marking the Senate's largest turnover since 1959.

An even larger Senate turnover came in the 1978 elections. It resulted in a 1979 freshman class of twenty senators, the biggest since the twenty-three member class of 1947. In 1978 ten incumbent senators retired, more than in any year since World War II. Three other incumbents were beaten in primaries, the most in a decade. And seven more were defeated for reelection, the second-highest number in twenty years. In the House a record

Limiting Terms

Although a push for term limits for elected officials became popular in the early 1990s, both the House and Senate in the 104th Congress failed to pass a constitutional amendment limiting the terms of members of Congress. When another try in the House failed in the 105th Congress, the momentum for term limits seemed to stall and the future for term limits at the end of the twentieth century looked uncertain.

The term limits movement was kicked off in 1990 when Colorado became the first state to seek to limit the number of terms that members of Congress could serve. A referendum approved by more than two-thirds of Colorado voters limited House members to six two-year terms and senators to two six-year terms. The measure also set term limits on state legislators and statewide elected offices.

By 1995 backers of term limits had won ballot initiatives or laws in at least twenty-three states. In 1995 the Supreme Court ruled in *U.S. Term Limits v. Thornton* and *Bryant v. Hill* that states could not impose limits on congressional terms. These rulings left term limits supporters only one solution: a constitutional amendment. But constitutional amendments are difficult to pass: they must receive a two-thirds majority vote from both chambers of Congress and then be ratified by three-fourths (thirty-eight) of the states.

Term limits supporters argued that mandatory retirement after twelve years was necessary to bring new people and viewpoints into Congress, to reduce the constant pressure to get reelected, and to control federal spending, which they said resulted from career politicians getting too close to special interest groups seeking federal funds. Opponents countered that term limits would strip Congress of experienced legislators, diminish the political power of less-populated states that were helped by their members gaining seniority, and would merely speed up, not solve, the problem of legislators getting too friendly with special interest groups. Depriving voters of the right to vote for an incumbent would be undemocratic, opponents added.

In the House the term limits constitutional amendment ran into trouble from the start. The House Judiciary Committee agreed on February 28, 1995, to send its version of the measure to the floor without recommendation. Committee Chairman Henry J. Hyde, R-Ill., staunchly opposed term limits, calling the concept "a terrible mistake, a kick in the stomach of democracy." He even filed a brief outlining his opposition when the Supreme Court took up the issue in its 1994–1995 term.

On March 29, the House rejected a term limits constitutional amendment that proposed a twelve-year lifetime limit on members of each chamber. The 227–204 vote fell 61 votes short of a two-thirds majority. Forty Republicans voted against the measure, and thirty of the forty who opposed it chaired a committee or subcommittee.

In the Senate, a term limits constitutional amendment limiting senators to two six-year terms and representatives to six two-year terms stalled on the Senate floor in April 1996. A vote to shut off debate on the measure failed, 58–42, two short of the 60 votes needed. All fifty-three Senate Republicans voted for cloture, even though some opposed limiting congressional terms, leaving the Democrats to take the heat for blocking the Senate from moving to an up-or-down vote.

Term limits supporters again tried to pass a constitutional amendment through the House in 1997. In February members voted on eleven versions of the term limits amendment based on different initiatives begun in nine states. The underlying broad measure—restricting House members to six years and senators to twelve—received a simple majority of 217–211. The tally was 69 votes short of the necessary two-thirds majority needed for passage. The House then considered ten proposals beyond the underlying measure. Some would have made the limits retroactive, given the states the authority to adopt stricter limits, or restricted House members to six or eight years. All were soundly defeated.

---

fifty-eight seats were opened by retirement, death, primary defeat, and other causes. Moreover, nineteen incumbents fell in the general election, giving the House seventy-seven freshmen when the Ninety-sixth Congress opened in January 1979.

In 1980, when Republican Ronald Reagan won the White House, the GOP took control of the Senate for the first time since 1957, ending the longest one-party dominance in that body in its history. They also netted thirty-three House seats, the biggest Republican gain since 1966. But the Democrats made a comeback in the 1982 midterm elections: of the eighty-one new representatives, fifty-seven were Democrats. Republicans lost twenty-six seats in the House, half of them held by freshmen.

As in the early 1970s, redistricting was an important factor in the 1982 election. The 1980 census shifted seventeen seats from the Northeast and Midwest to the Sun Belt states of the South and West. Democrats took ten of these seats despite the Sun Belt's propensity to vote for Republican presidential candidates.

In 1984, a presidential election year, Republicans gained fourteen House seats and Democrats two Senate seats in an election that resulted in little turnover. Forty-three new representatives and seven new senators entered the Ninety-ninth Congress. On only four previous occasions since 1914 had there been fewer than ten Senate newcomers. In 1986 Democrats regained control of the Senate, electing eleven of the thirteen freshmen senators.

The 1986 House elections were extraordinarily good for incumbents of both parties. Only six House members lost in the general election; two others had been defeated in the primaries. But enough seats were open from retirement and death to yield

a freshman House class of fifty members—twenty-three Republicans and twenty-seven Democrats.

In 1988 George Bush became the first Republican in sixty years to hold the White House for his party for a third consecutive term. But he also became the first candidate since John F. Kennedy in 1960 to win the presidential election while his party lost seats (three) in the House. Again in 1990, for the third straight election, Democrats gained House seats (nine). That feat had not been accomplished since the string of Democratic victories in 1954, 1956, and 1958.

In the presidential election year of 1992, voters opted to give the Democrats a chance to run both Congress and the White House by electing Democrat Bill Clinton, the former governor of Arkansas, as president. Clinton was elected with only 43 percent of the popular vote over Bush and independent candidate Ross Perot. Not since Democrat Jimmy Carter had relinquished the White House to Republican Ronald Reagan in 1981 had Congress been controlled by the president's party.

Heading into the 1992 campaign, there was grumbling that the American political system had lost its capacity for renewal—low turnover in the 1980s fostered a perception of Congress as an incumbency club, fueled by special interest cash that nearly always defeated any challengers. But 1992 redistricting as a result of the 1990 census dramatically reshaped many districts, prodding some members into retirement and forcing others to run in unfamiliar constituencies. Reports of lax management and overdrawn checks at the House Bank also contributed to a high congressional turnover.

All this tumult resulted in 110 new members entering the House in January 1993, an influx of freshmen exceeding anything Washington had seen in more than forty years. In the postwar era, only one House freshman class was larger—the 118 newcomers to the 81st Congress in 1949. And no other freshman class had so many women (twenty-five) and minorities, including sixteen African Americans, eight Hispanics, and one Korean American.

The Senate freshman class of the 103rd Congress was the largest since 1981, with nine men and five woman, including the chamber's first black woman (Moseley-Braun of Illinois) and its first Native American (Democrat Ben Nighthorse Campbell of Colorado) since Charles Curtis, a Republican from Kansas who stepped down in 1929 to become vice president under Herbert Hoover.

The midterm elections of 1994 brought even more upheaval as the Republicans gained control of both the House and Senate for the first time since 1955. The Democratic loss was truly national in scope. Republicans won 37 million votes in 1994—nearly 9 million more than the party had won in the 1990 midterm elections. It was the first time since 1946 that Republican House candidates received a majority (52.3 percent) of the total House vote. Democrats in 1994 drew almost one million fewer votes than in 1990, continuing a general downward slide in their congressional voting strength that had begun in the mid-1980s.

The GOP tide of 1994 was caused by large surges in voter support for the Republicans and voter apathy for the Democrats. The election marked the middle of Democratic president

Table 20-5
Longest Service in Congress

Member	Years of service	Total years[1]
Carl T. Hayden, D-Ariz.	1912–1927(H), 1927–1969(S)	57
Jamie L. Whitten, D-Miss.	1941–1995(H)	53
Carl Vinson, D-Ga.	1914–1965(H)	50
Emanuel Celler, D-N.Y.	1923–1973(H)	50
Sam Rayburn, D-Texas	1913–1961(H)	49
Robert C. Byrd, D-W.Va	1953–1959 (H), 1959- (S)	48[2]
Wright Patman, D-Texas	1929–1976(H)	47
Strom Thurmond, R-S.C.	1955–1956(S), 1957- (S)	46[2]
John D. Dingell, D-Mich.	1955- (H)	46[2]
Joseph G. Cannon, R-Ill.	1873–1891(H), 1893–1913(H), 1915–1923(H)	46
Adolph J. Sabath, D-Ill.	1907–1952(H)	46
Lister Hill, D-Ala.	1923–1938(H), 1938–1969(S)	45
George H. Mahon, D-Texas.	1935–1979(H)	44
Warren G. Magnuson, D-Wash.	1937–1944(H), 1944–1981(S)	44
Justin S. Morrill, R-Vt.	1855–1867(H), 1867–1898(S)	44
Melvin Price, D-Ill.	1945–1988(H)	44
William B. Allison, R-Iowa	1863–1871(H), 1873–1908(S)	43
Henry M. Jackson, D-Wash.	1941–1953(H), 1953–1983(S)	43

Note: H = House; S = Senate.
1. As of January 2001. Totals, based on exact dates of service, are rounded to nearest year. Minor differences in days or months of service determine rankings of members with the same total of years.
2. Service record as of January 2001. Byrd was reelected in 2000. Thurmond was reelected in 1996. Dingell was reelected in 2000.

Sources: Congressional Research Service, Congressional Quarterly.

Bill Clinton's first term, and the president's party had difficulty motivating its core constituency. Although Clinton had some successes during his first two years in office, most notably deficit reduction and the North American Free Trade Agreement, his failure in getting Congress to agree to comprehensive health care reform seemed to stall his administration's programs. In addition, Republican candidates reaped the gains they had anticipated from redistricting after the 1990 census. The remapping was largely favorable to the GOP.

Money also made the difference for some Republican challengers. According to the Federal Election Commission, Republican candidates had an easier time raising money from political action committees and other sources than in previous years. Conservative groups—from the National Rifle Association to term limit advocates—played active roles in several congressional races. Several GOP freshmen were elected with the prominent support of conservative Christian activists.

In 1994 Republicans gained fifty-two House seats, increasing their number from 178 to 230. The Democrats dropped from 256 to 204 seats. For the Republicans, seventy-three freshmen were elected, 157 incumbents were reelected, and thirty-four incumbents were defeated.

At the start of the 104th Congress, Georgia Rep. Newt Gingrich became the first Republican Speaker of the House from the South. His ascendancy accompanied the long-anticipated realignment of the South away from Democratic dominance to a Republican majority. For the first time since the end of Reconstruction in the 1870s, Republicans won a majority of southern congressional districts.

Republicans also swept the Senate in 1994, after eight years in the minority. The Republicans captured all nine open seats and ousted two Democratic incumbents, gaining control by a margin of 52–48 seats. Adding insult to injury, the day after the general election, Democratic Sen. Richard C. Shelby of Alabama announced that he was switching parties. The incoming Senate freshman class had eleven Republicans and no Democrats. Since 1914, when the popular election of senators began, there had never been an all-GOP Senate freshman class.

The 1996 elections also ended up in the record books. Never before had voters reelected a Democratic president and at the same time entrusted both the House and the Senate to the Republican Party. Clinton, who was almost written off after the disastrous 1994 midterm elections, scored a political comeback by winning handily in November 1996. And the Republicans won their first back-to-back majority in the House since the 1920s. The Democrats managed, however, to cut into the GOP's numbers. Democrats gained a net of nine seats, leaving a party breakdown in the House of 227 Republicans and 207 Democrats, and Bernard Sanders of Vermont as the lone independent.

In 1996 a total of twenty incumbents were defeated; all but three were Republicans. The heaviest toll in 1996 was among the mainly conservative and contentious GOP freshman class—eleven freshmen Republicans were defeated. The GOP held on to its majority in the House by its performance in the open seats. Of fifty-three open seats, Republicans won twenty-nine, ten of them given up by Democratic incumbents. Democrats won twenty-four, only four of which had been held by Republicans.

In the Senate, the Republicans built on their gains in the 1994 election. For the 105th Congress, the GOP had a solid 55–45 majority over the Democrats. That was the Republicans highest total in the Senate following any election since 1928.

By 1998 the turnover in the House and Senate seemed to have settled down. All but seven of the 401 House members seeking reelection were returned to office. The Democrats also regrouped in 1998—Clinton's second midterm election—and managed to close the partisan gap even further in the House. The Democrats picked up five House seats, giving the 106th Congress 223 Republicans, 211 Democrats, and one independent. This twelve-seat majority was the slimmest majority in the House since 1955.

The Senate's partisan breakdown remained the same in 1999 with fifty-five Republicans and forty-five Democrats. Just three of the thirty-four senators up for reelection in 1998 were defeated. Eight Senate freshmen joined the 106th Congress—four Democrats and four Republicans.

The pattern continued in the 2000 elections. Although the GOP maintained control in both chambers, its margin was reduced to nine votes in the House. In the Senate, an exact tie resulted: fifty Democrats and fifty Republicans. However, the Republicans retained control because their party won back the White House, which allowed Richard Cheney, the new vice president and presiding Senate officer, to vote to break a tie. This rare arrangement was short-lived, however, as moderate Republican James Jeffords of Vermont left the GOP to become an Independent in June 2001, giving majority control of the Senate to the Democrats for the first time since 1994. (*See Chapter 21, House Elections; Chapter 24, Senate Elections.*)

Shifts between Chambers

From the early days of Congress, members have sometimes shifted from one chamber to the other. Far fewer former senators have gone to the House than vice versa. In the 1790s, nineteen former representatives became senators and three former senators moved to the House. The same pattern continued through the nineteenth century and into the twentieth. By the end of the twentieth century, it was common to find House members running for the Senate, but senators rarely, if ever, returned to the House. Former senators were more likely to return home to pursue a race for governor, run as their party's vice-presidential candidate, or seek the office of president.

Although both chambers are equal under the law, the Senate's six-year terms offer the officeholder greater stability. That body also has larger staffs and more generous perquisites. A senator's opportunity to make his mark are undoubtedly better in a chamber of one hundred members than in the 435-member House. The Senate's role in foreign affairs may add to its luster, and senators enjoy the prestige of a statewide constituencies.

Perhaps the most notable shift from the Senate to the House was Henry Clay's journey in 1811. Giving up a Senate seat from Kentucky, he entered the House and was promptly elected Speaker, a position he used to prod the country to go to war with Britain in 1812. After five terms in the House, Clay returned to the Senate in 1823. Another prominent transfer was that of John Quincy Adams of Massachusetts; he served in the Senate (1803–1808), as secretary of state (1817–1825), as president (1825–1829), and finally in the House (1831–1848).

Only one other former president, Andrew Johnson, returned to Congress in later years. He had served in both houses of Congress (from Tennessee) before he entered the White House. As vice president in 1865, Johnson was elevated to the presidency upon Abraham Lincoln's assassination. He left office in 1869 a bitter man, having survived impeachment charges instigated by his own Republican Party. The Tennessee legislature sent him back to the U.S. Senate in 1875, where he served the last five months of his life.

Notes

1. Alexis de Tocqueville, *Democracy in America,* vol. l (New York: Vintage Books, 1971), 231.

2. The Gallup Poll: Public Trust in Federal Government Remains High, January 8, 1999. (From Gallup Organization Web site.)

3. Julie R. Hirschfeld, "Congress of Relative Newcomers Poses Challenge to Bush, Leadership," *CQ Weekly,* January 20, 2001, 178–182.

4. Marcy Kaptur, *Women of Congress: A Twentieth-Century Odyssey* (Washington, D.C.: Congressional Quarterly, 1996), 1–2.

CHAPTER 21

House Elections

THE AUTHORS OF THE CONSTITUTION recognized that the new government needed an executive to carry out the laws and a judiciary to resolve conflicts arising from them. But it was Congress, the lawmaking body, that the Founders designed to be the heart of the new Republic. There was little question that the new Congress should be bicameral, in accordance with the practice of the English Parliament, which was followed by most of the colonial governments and ten of the thirteen states. As George Mason put it during the Constitutional Convention in 1787, the minds of Americans were settled on two points: "an attachment to republican government [and] an attachment to more than one branch in the Legislature."

But little agreement existed over how the members of each of the chambers should be chosen. The nationalists insisted that the new government rest on the consent of the people rather than the state legislatures. So they held it essential that at least "the first branch," or House, be elected popularly. The government "ought to possess. . . . the mind or sense of the people at large," said one of the Framers, James Wilson of Pennsylvania. Those who were suspicious of a national government preferred to have House members be elected by the state legislatures. "The people immediately should have as little to do" with electing the government as possible, said Roger Sherman, because "they want information and are constantly liable to be misled." Election by the legislatures was twice defeated, however, and popular election for the House agreed to with only one state dissenting.

There was little support for the view that the people also should elect the Senate. Nor did the delegates to the Constitutional Convention think that the House should choose members of the Senate from among persons nominated by the state legislatures. Election of the Senate by the state legislatures was agreed to with only two states dissenting.

For the sake of convenience, the Senate is sometimes referred to as the "upper body" of Congress, and the House as the "lower body." But those terms were not used in the Constitution, and in fact the two chambers are equal in stature and legislative power. No bill can become law unless it is passed by both chambers in identical form and signed by the president (or passed over a presidential veto).

Representatives naturally resent having the House called the "lower body." Yet, from the earliest days of the Republic, the House has been generally regarded as less prestigious than the Senate. Indeed, the French scholar Alexis de Tocqueville wrote in the 1830s of being struck by "the vulgar demeanor" of the House as compared with the Senate.

Although a seat in the Senate continues to be held in greater esteem today, both chambers have been battered in public opinion polls over the years. (See box, Congressional Characteristics and Public Opinion, p. 800.)

The People's Branch

The House of Representatives was to be the branch of government closest to the people. The members would be popularly elected; the terms of office would be two years so that the representatives would not lose touch with their homes; and the House would be a numerous branch, with members having relatively small constituencies.

The lower houses of the state legislatures served as models for the U.S. House. All the states had at least one chamber elected by popular vote. Ten states had two-house legislatures; Georgia, Pennsylvania, and Vermont had popularly elected unicameral legislatures.

Article I, Section 2 of the Constitution set few requirements for election to the House: a representative had to be at least twenty-five years of age, have been a U.S. citizen for seven years, and be an inhabitant of the state from which elected. (See "Constitutional Provisions and Amendments on Elections," p. 1545, in Reference Materials.)

The Constitution left the qualification of voters to the states, with one overriding principle: the qualifications could be no more restrictive than for the most numerous branch of each of the states' own legislatures. At first, most states had some kind of property requirement for voting. Five states required ownership of real estate, five mandated either real estate or other property, and three required personal wealth or payment of public taxes. But the democratic trend of the early nineteenth century swept away most property qualifications, producing practically universal white male suffrage by the 1830s.

Over the years several changes in the Constitution also broadened the franchise. The Fifteenth Amendment (1870) extended the franchise to newly freed slaves; the Nineteenth Amendment (1920) granted the right of suffrage to women; the Twenty-third Amendment (1961) extended the presidential vote to the District of Columbia; the Twenty-fourth Amendment (1964) abolished the poll tax; and the Twenty-sixth Amendment (1971) lowered the voting age from twenty-one to eighteen. In 1965 Congress passed the Voting Rights Act to remove barriers several states and localities had erected to keep blacks and other minorities from voting.

TWO-YEAR TERM

Many delegates to the Constitutional Convention preferred annual elections for the House, believing that the body should reflect the wishes of the people as closely as possible. James Madison, however, argued for a three-year term, to allow repre-

Congressional Characteristics and Public Opinion

From the early days of the Republic until the present, the American public has criticized the abilities, ethical standards, and performance of members of Congress. Through the years the House has received more criticism than the Senate, perhaps because senators were not elected by popular vote until 1914.

An early but still familiar critique of Congress was written in the 1830s by Alexis de Tocqueville, the French aristocrat, scholar, and astute observer of America. After he had seen both chambers in session, Tocqueville wrote the following in his famous book of observations, *Democracy in America*:

On entering the House of Representatives at Washington, one is struck by the vulgar demeanor of that great assembly. Often there is not a distinguished man in the whole number. Its members are almost all obscure individuals, whose names bring no associations to mind. They are mostly village lawyers, men in trade, or even persons belonging to the lower classes of society. In a country in which education is very general, it is said that the representatives of the people do not always know how to write correctly.

At a few yards' distance is the door of the Senate, which contains within a small space a large proportion of the celebrated men of America. Scarcely an individual is to be seen in it who has not had an active and illustrious career: the Senate is composed of eloquent advocates, distinguished generals, wise magistrates, and statesmen of note, whose arguments would do honor to the most remarkable parliamentary debates of Europe.

Profile of 'Average' Member

A more modern—and charitable—description of the "average" member of Congress was presented in a popular textbook of the 1960s, *American Democracy*:

He is a little over 50, has served in Congress for a number of years, and has had previous political experience before coming to Congress, such as membership in his state legislature. He has a college degree, is a lawyer by profession, a war veteran, and, before coming to Congress, was a well-known and popular member of the community. He has been reasonably successful in business or the practice of law, although not so successful that he is sacrificing a huge income in giving up his private occupation for a public job. Congress is clearly not an accurate cross section of the American people but neither is it a community of intellectuals and technicians.

The description was accurate, even to the exclusive use of "he." Although the composition had changed some by the beginning of the twenty-first century, most members of Congress were male, Caucasian, and Christian, especially Protestant. Of the 535 members of Congress at the beginning of the 107th Congress (2001–2003), seventy-two were women, thirty-six were African American, nineteen were Hispanic, and eight were of Asian, Pacific Islander, or Native American heritage. Among religious groups, Protestants have comprised nearly 60 percent of the membership

of Congress, although Roman Catholic members have become more numerous than members belonging to any single Protestant denomination. Catholics took the lead from Methodists in 1965 and retained it in 2001 with a total of 149 Catholics. More than 70 percent of the Protestant members were affiliated with four denominations: Baptists led with seventy-three, followed by sixty-six Methodists, forty-eight Presbyterians, and forty Episcopalians. There were thirty-seven Jewish members. The average age for senators was 59.8, while the average for representatives was 54.4.

It was likely that a senator was a former House member but rare that a representative had served earlier in the Senate. Only two former presidents served in Congress after their terms in the White House: John Quincy Adams and Andrew Johnson. *(See box, Members of Congress Who Became President, page 000, Vol. I.)*

The legal profession had been dominant among members of Congress for most of its history, although most other occupations—including banking, business, public service, education, journalism, farming, law enforcement, and medicine—had been represented. It was not until 1997 that one of the chambers—the House—had more members from a business or banking background than from a law one. In the 107th Congress there were 156 lawyers and 159 bankers or businesspeople in the House, and fifty-three lawyers and twenty-four bankers or businesspeople in the Senate. The principal occupational groups underrepresented were the clergy, scientists, and blue-collar workers.

Public Opinion

Members' professional backgrounds notwithstanding, the American public shows little esteem for Congress as a whole. In Gallup polls taken from 1974 through 2000, it was rare for even half of the country to approve of Congress's performance. Its highest rating came in February 1998, when a Gallup poll found that 57 percent of Americans approved of the way Congress was doing its job, while 33 percent disapproved. The lowest rating came during an ethics scandal that erupted after revelations that hundreds of sitting and former House members had routinely overdrawn their accounts at the House bank. That March 1992 poll found Congress with only an 18 percent job approval rating—and a 78 percent disapproval rating.

But the American people are not nearly as hard on their individual representatives as they are on Congress as a whole. Indeed, since the end of World War II, House incumbent reelection rates have generally exceeded 90 percent.

The great chandelier is lighted as night falls in the old House chamber in this scene painted by Samuel F. B. Morse in the early 1820s. The House did not move into the chamber it occupies today until 1867.

sentatives to gain knowledge and experience in national affairs as well as the affairs of their own localities. The delegates compromised on two-year terms.

The two-year term has not been universally popular. From time to time proposals have been made to extend the term to four years. The movement to extend the House term to four years last gained momentum after President Lyndon B. Johnson urged the extension in his 1966 State of the Union address. His proposal received more applause than any other part of his speech.

However, the proposed amendment never emerged from committee. Opponents criticized the proposal's provision that the four-year term coincide with the presidential term. This would create a House of "coattail riders," critics said, and end the minority party's traditional gains in nonpresidential election years. This fear of diminishing the independence of the House appeared to be the principal factor that killed the proposal. *(See "Election Results, Congress and the Presidency, 1860-2000" p. 1569, in Reference Materials.)*

SIZE OF THE HOUSE

The size of the original House was written into Article I, Section 2 of the Constitution, along with directions to apportion the House according to population after the first census in 1790. Until the first census and apportionment, the thirteen states were to have the following numbers of representatives: Connecticut, five; Delaware, one; Georgia, three; Maryland, six; Massachusetts, eight; New Hampshire, three; New Jersey, four; New York, six; North Carolina, five; Pennsylvania, eight; Rhode Island, one; South Carolina, five; Virginia, ten. This apportionment of seats—sixty-five in all—thus mandated by the Constitution remained in effect during the first and second Congresses (1789–1793). (Seats allotted to North Carolina and Rhode Island were not filled until 1790, after those states had ratified the Constitution.)

By act of Congress (April 14, 1792), an apportionment measure provided for a ratio of one member for every 33,000 inhabitants and fixed the exact number of representatives to which each state was entitled. Congress enacted a new apportionment measure, including the mathematical formula to be used, every ten years (except 1920) until a permanent law became effective in 1929.

In 1911 Congress set the maximum size of the House at 435 members, where it has remained since the 1912 election (with the exception of a brief period after Alaska and Hawaii became states, when the number temporarily increased to 437). *(See Chapter 22, Reapportionment and Redistricting.)*

National population figures from the 2000 census showed that, on average, each House member represented about 647,000 persons.

MAJORITY ELECTIONS

Five New England states at one time or another had a requirement for majority victory in congressional elections. The requirement provided that, to win a seat in the U.S. House, a candidate had to achieve more than 50 percent of the popular vote. If no candidate gained such a majority, new elections were held until one contender succeeded.

The provision was last invoked in Maine in 1844, in New Hampshire in 1845, in Vermont in 1866, in Massachusetts in 1848, and in Rhode Island in 1892. Sometimes, multiple elections were necessary because none of the candidates could achieve the required majority. In the Fourth District of Massachusetts in 1848–1849, for example, twelve successive elections were held to try to choose a representative. None of them was successful, and the district remained unrepresented in the House during the Thirty-first Congress (1849–1851).

MULTIMEMBER DISTRICTS

In the early days of the House, several states had districts that elected more than one representative. For example, in 1824 Maryland's Fifth District chose two representatives, while the remaining seven districts chose one each. And in Pennsylvania two districts (the Fourth and Ninth) elected three representatives each, and four districts (the Seventh, Eighth, Eleventh, and Seventeenth) chose two representatives each.

As late as 1838, New York still had as many as five multimember districts—one (the Third) electing four members and four (the Eighth, Seventeenth, Twenty-second, and Twenty-third) choosing two each. But the practice ended in 1842 when Congress enacted a law that "no one district may elect more than one Representative." The provision was a part of the reapportionment legislation following the census of 1840.

ELECTIONS IN ODD-NUMBERED YEARS

Another practice that faded out over the years was the holding of general elections for the House in odd-numbered years. Prior to ratification of the Twentieth ("lame-duck") Amendment in 1933, regular sessions of Congress began in December of odd-numbered years. Because there was such a long period between elections in November of even-numbered years and the beginning of the congressional session, some states moved congressional elections to odd-numbered years. For example, in 1841 the following states held general elections for representative for the Twenty-seventh Congress, convening that year: Alabama, Connecticut, Illinois, Indiana, Kentucky, Maryland, Mississippi, New Hampshire, North Carolina, Rhode Island, Tennessee, and Virginia.

The practice continued until late in the century. In 1875 four states still chose their representatives in regular odd-year elections: California, Connecticut, Mississippi, and New Hampshire. But by 1880 all members of the House were being chosen in even-numbered years (except for special elections to fill vacancies). One major problem encountered by states choosing their representatives in odd-numbered years was the possibility of a special session of the new Congress being called before the states' elections were held. Depending on the date of the election, a state could be unrepresented in the House. For example, California elected its U.S. House delegation to the Fortieth Congress (1867–1869) on September 4, 1867, in plenty of time for the first regular session scheduled for December 2. But the Congress already had met in two special sessions—March 4 to March 20 and July 3 to July 20—without any representation from California.

SOUTHERN ANOMALIES

Many of the anomalies in election of U.S. representatives occurred in the South. That region's experience with slavery, Civil War, Reconstruction, and racial antagonisms created special problems for the regular electoral process.

Article I, Section 2 of the Constitution contained a formula for counting slaves for apportionment purposes: every five slaves would be counted as three persons. Thus, the total population of a state to be used in determining its congressional representation would be the free population plus three-fifths of the slave population.

After the Civil War and the emancipation of the slaves, blacks were fully counted for the purposes of apportionment. The Fourteenth Amendment required that apportionment be based on "the whole number of persons in each State. . . ." On this basis, several Southern states tried to claim immediate additional representation on readmission to the Union. Tennessee, for example, chose an extra U.S. representative, electing him at large in 1868, and claimed that inasmuch as its slaves were now free the state had added to its apportionment population a sufficient number to give it nine instead of eight representatives. Virginia took similar action in 1869 and 1870; South Carolina did it in both 1868 and 1870. But the House declined to seat the additional representatives, declaring that states would have to await the regular reapportionment following the 1870 census for any changes in their representation.

Part of the Fourteenth Amendment affected—or was intended to affect—Southern representation in the House. The second paragraph of the amendment states, "[W]hen the right to vote at any election for the choice of electors for President and Vice President of the United States, Representatives in Congress, the Executive and Judicial officers of a State, or the members of the Legislature thereof, is denied to any of the male inhabitants of such State, being twenty-one years of age, and citizens of the United States, or in any way abridged, except for participation in rebellion, or other crime, the basis of representation [in the U.S. House] shall be reduced in the proportion which the number of such male citizens shall bear to the whole number of male citizens twenty-one years of age in such State."

Designed as a club to force the South to accept black voting participation, the provision was incorporated in the reapportionment legislation of 1872. According to the legislation, the number of representatives from any state interfering with the exercise of the right to vote was to be reduced in proportion to the number of inhabitants of voting age whose right to go to the polls was denied or abridged.

But the provision never was put into effect because of the difficulty of determining the exact number of persons whose right to vote was being abridged and also because of the decline of Northern enthusiasm for forcing Reconstruction policies on the South.

As an alternative to invoking the difficult Fourteenth Amendment provision, Congress often considered election challenges filed against members from the South. When Republicans were in control of the House, several Democrats

from the former Confederate states found themselves unseated, often on charges that black voting rights were abused in their districts.

During the Forty-seventh Congress (1881–1883), five Democrats from former Confederate states were unseated; in the Fifty-first Congress (1889–1891), six; and in the Fifty-fourth Congress (1895–1897), seven.

Special Elections

When a vacancy occurs in the House, the usual procedure is for the governor of the affected state to call a special election. Such elections may be held at any time throughout the year, and there are usually several during each two-year Congress.

At times there are delays in the calling of special elections. One of the longest periods in modern times when a congressional district went unrepresented occurred after the death of Rep. James G. Polk, D-Ohio (1931–1941, 1949–1959), on April 28, 1959. An election to replace him did not take place until November 1960, when it was held simultaneously with the general election. Because different candidates were nominated for the two races, the winner of the special election, Ward M. Miller, R, had only two months remaining in his term.

In the days of the lame-duck sessions of Congress, elections for the remainder of a term quite often were held simultaneously with the general election, because the session following the election was an important working meeting that lasted until March 4. However, since the passage of the Twentieth Amendment and the ending of most lame-duck sessions, elections for the remaining two months of a term have become less common. Miller, for example, never was sworn in because Congress was not in session during the period when he was waiting to serve as a representative.

Usually states are more prompt in holding special House elections than was Ohio in 1959–1960. One of the most rapid instances of succession occurred in Texas's Tenth District in 1963. Democratic representative Homer Thornberry (1949–1963) submitted his resignation on September 26, 1963, to take effect December 20. On the strength of Thornberry's postdated resignation, a special election was held in his district—the first election was held November 9 and the runoff on December 17. The winner, J. J. Pickle, D, was ready to take his seat as soon as Thornberry stepped down. He was sworn in the next day, December 21, 1963.

Disputed House Elections

Occasionally the full House is called upon to settle disputes over the outcome of an election.

'MISSISSIPPI FIVE'

One of the most dramatic election disputes settled by the House in modern times was that of the so-called Mississippi Five in 1965. The governor of Mississippi certified the election to the House in 1964 of four Democrats and one Republican. The Democrats were Thomas G. Abernethy, William M. Colmer, Jamie L. Whitten, and John Bell Williams; the Republican was Prentiss Walker.

Their right to be seated was contested by a biracial group, the Mississippi Freedom Democratic Party, formed originally to challenge the seating of an all-white delegation from the state to the 1964 Democratic National Convention. This group, when unsuccessful in getting its candidates on the 1964 congressional election ballot, conducted a rump election in which Annie Devine, Virginia Gray, and Fannie L. Hamer were the winners.

The three women, when they sought entrance to the House floor, were barred. However, Speaker John W. McCormack, D-Mass., asked the regular Mississippi representatives-elect to stand aside while the other members of the House were sworn in. William F. Ryan, D-N.Y., sponsor of the challenge, contended that the regular congressional election in Mississippi was invalid because blacks had been systematically prevented from voting. A resolution to seat the regular Mississippi delegation was adopted on January 4, 1965, by a voice vote.

Later that year Congress enacted the Voting Rights Act of 1965, which contained strict sanctions against states that practiced discrimination against minority voters.

MCCLOSKEY-MCINTYRE CONTEST

The House easily dismissed two 1984 election challenges but fought for four months over a third race that an investigating panel said was the closest House contest in the twentieth century. Debate on the race took up far more time than almost any other issue the House considered in 1985.

Incumbent Frank McCloskey, a Democrat, appeared to have won reelection to his Indiana Eighth District seat by seventy-two votes. But correction of an arithmetical error (ballots in two precincts had been counted twice) gave Republican challenger Richard D. McIntyre an apparent thirty-four-vote victory. On that basis, the Indiana secretary of state certified McIntyre the winner. But when Congress convened in January 1985, the Democratic-controlled House refused to seat McIntyre, voting instead to declare the seat vacant pending an investigation of alleged irregularities in the election.

A recount completed in January showed McIntyre's lead had increased to 418 votes, after more than 4,800 ballots were thrown out for technical reasons. But a task force of the House Administration Committee, with auditors from the congressional General Accounting Office, conducted its own recount and, on a 2–1 partisan split, concluded in April that McCloskey had won by four votes. The House on May 1, 1985, approved a resolution to seat McCloskey, by a vote of 236–190, with ten Democrats joining the Republicans in voting against it. GOP members walked out of the House chamber in protest, accusing Democrats of stealing the election. Over the course of the four months Republicans had lost a series of votes to seat McIntyre, to get a new election by declaring the seat vacant, and finally to send the issue back to committee with orders to count controversial absentee ballots that the task force had decided not to count.

The Supreme Court May 28, 1985, refused to get involved in the dispute. Without a dissenting vote, it denied Indiana per-

Speaker Dennis Hastert swears in the 106th Congress in January 1999.

mission to sue the House in the Supreme Court. Earlier in the year, a U.S. district court judge in Washington, D.C., had dismissed a suit brought by McIntyre against House Democrats and House officers, ruling that the House had the constitutional right to judge its own membership. A federal district court in Indiana had dismissed a separate suit filed by McIntyre challenging recount procedures in two of the district's counties and had ruled that the House alone was responsible for determining the validity of contested ballots.

In a 1986 rematch, McCloskey handily defeated McIntyre.

SANCHEZ-DORNAN DISPUTE

In early 1998 thirteen months of contentious debate with ethnic overtones ended when the Republican-led House refused to overturn the defeat of California Republican Robert K. Dornan by Democrat Loretta Sanchez, a Hispanic woman. Dornan charged the 1996 election in California's Forty-sixth District was stolen by the illegal votes of noncitizens, mostly Hispanics. The House rejected his claim by a 378–33 vote on February 12, 1998.

A special three-member task force had said it found evidence of 748 noncitizen votes, not enough to offset Sanchez's 984-vote victory in November 1996. Republicans said the results nonetheless showed that Dornan's challenge had not been frivolous and that the GOP was not unfairly targeting Hispanic voters. But Democrats characterized the probe as a witch hunt, charging that Republicans sought to unfairly single out and intimidate Hispanic voters. Rep. Steny H. Hoyer of Maryland, the lone Democrat on the task force, supported the dismissal but criticized the process as contrary to the Federal Contested Elections Act and "an unprecedented intrusion into the privacy of hundreds of thousands of persons who did no wrong." He said the 748 included naturalized citizens and persons who may have inadvertently violated California's absentee voting law.

Dornan, an outspoken conservative who often clashed with Democrats during his eighteen years in the House, accused Sanchez and her supporters of impeding the investigation by noncooperation. Dornan's former Orange County district, once a Republican stronghold, had become a swing district through legal and illegal immigration. In the 1998 election, Sanchez kept her seat in a rematch with Dornan.

Party Control Shifts

The Republican Party dominated the House in the first three decades of the twentieth century and the Democratic Party controlled it for much of the balance until the Republicans returned to power late in the century.

The Republicans were the majority party in the House from 1901 to 1911 and 1919 to 1931, but, battered by the Depression, they lost the House to the Democrats in the November 1930 elections. Democrats briefly relinquished power in the House after losses in 1946 and again in 1952. But after the 1954 election, the Democrats held control for the next forty years. In all, they controlled the House for sixty of the seventy years in the period 1931–2001.

DEMOCRATIC DOMINANCE

In the history of Democratic control of the House, 1956 was the watershed year. In that year, Republican President Dwight D. Eisenhower was reelected in a landslide, but his party failed to recapture the House. It was only the second time that had ever happened—and the first since 1848, when Zachary Taylor was elected president while his Whig Party lost control of the House to the Democrats. Taylor won even though the Whigs were beginning to disintegrate over the slavery issue. Political writers said that the results of 1848 and 1956 were flukes caused by war

heroes whose support for president crossed party lines. But American voters went on to elect a Republican president and a Democratic House five more times in the twentieth century: in 1968, 1972, 1980, 1984, and 1988.

One theory offered to explain this pattern emphasized the role of the cold war, which seemed a permanent fact of life for nearly half a century. During those years the electorate as a whole seemed more comfortable having Republican presidents handle defense and foreign policy issues, while counting on Democrats in Congress to create and sustain popular domestic programs.

GOP RESURGENCE IN CONGRESS

But with the end of the cold war in 1991, national security seemed less salient as an issue, as Republican President George Bush learned in 1992. Despite broad foreign policy experience and his triumph in the Persian Gulf War, Bush lost the White House to Arkansas governor Bill Clinton. At the same time, the Democrats in Congress seemed beset by rising resentment of federal tax levels and increasing hostility toward government in general as expensive, overbearing, and inefficient.

Republicans were able to capitalize on this in the 1994 election, ending the Democrats' forty-year domination of the House and eight-year tenure in the Senate. The Democrats lost fifty-two House seats, the biggest loss by a president's party in the House since the 1946 midterm election. Other records were shattered as well. The election was the first since the end of Reconstruction in the 1870s in which Republicans won a majority of the congressional districts in the South. Democratic Speaker Thomas S. Foley of Washington became the first sitting House Speaker to lose reelection since 1862.

The 1996 election, in which Clinton won another term in the White House and the GOP remained the majority in Congress, was record-producing as well. Never before had voters reelected a Democratic president and simultaneously entrusted both chambers of Congress to the GOP. Moreover, the last time the GOP had returned a majority to the House was following the 1928 election. They had won a narrow majority of House seats again in 1930, but deaths of several Republican members created vacancies that allowed the Democrats to organize the House.

Republicans held on to Congress in the 1998 and 2000 elections but just barely. With the economy healthy and the nation at peace, Clinton's popularity remained high through the 1998 midterm election despite House Republicans' preparations to impeach him on charges that included lying to a federal grand jury about his affair with a White House intern. In what was

perceived as a backlash against impeachment, voters sent five more Democrats to the House, making Clinton the first president since Franklin D. Roosevelt in 1934 to gain House seats at midterm. Indeed, it was only the second time since the Civil War that the party not in control of the White House lost seats in a midterm election. The embarrassing setback prompted Newt Gingrich of Georgia, who had led the GOP takeover of the House in 1994, to resign as Speaker and leave the House.

In 2000 the GOP won a fourth term in the majority for the first time since 1924. But it was also the third straight election in which the Republicans lost House seats. The election resulted in a 221–212 party split, with two independents. It was the closest party split in a House election since 1952. This, combined with a 50–50 party ratio in the Senate, had politicians and pundits musing about the 2002 election before the dust had even settled after the 2000 races. (The Senate would later swing to Democratic control as early as June 2001 when Republican senator Jim Jeffords became an Independent.)

The table (Results of House Elections, 1928–2000) beginning on p. 1574 in Reference Materials shows the results of House elections state by state since 1928, the last election of the Republican era that preceded the Great Depression. It goes through the 1930s, when the Democrats gained seats in four consecutive elections from 1930 through 1936; a long period of competitive equilibrium in the House (1938–1958) between New Deal-Fair Deal national Democrats and a loose coalition of Republicans and Southern Democrats; the longer period of dominance by liberal-to-moderate national Democrats, marked by landslide victories in the congressional elections of 1958, 1964, and 1974 that echoed the earlier 1930–1938 period; and the Republican return to majority status in the 1990s but with a declining margin of control through the 2000 election.

REGIONAL SHIFTS

The figures also show significant shifts in the two parties' regional distribution of seats since the 1960s. The South, once called the "Solid South" because of its solidarity with the Democratic Party, ceased to be solidly Democratic when the national Democratic Party committed itself to civil rights for blacks. But Republican gains in that region were more than offset by Democratic gains in the Northeast and Midwest. Those two regions had tended to be more Republican than the rest of the country, but Democrats began to gain after their party in 1960 ran the first Catholic candidate for president.

## CHAPTER 22

Reapportionment and Redistricting

REAPPORTIONMENT, THE REDISTRIBUTION of the 435 seats in the House of Representatives among the states to reflect shifts in population, and redistricting, the redrawing of congressional district boundaries for the House within the states, are among the most important and contentious processes in the U.S. political system. They help to determine whether Democrats or Republicans, or liberals or conservatives will dominate the House, and whether districts will be drawn to favor the election of candidates from particular racial or ethnic groups.

Reapportionment and redistricting occur every ten years on the basis of the decennial population census. States where populations grew quickly during the previous ten years typically gain congressional seats, while those that lost population or grew much more slowly than the national average stand to lose seats. The number of House members for the rest of the states remains the same.

The states that gain or lose seats usually must make extensive changes in their congressional maps. Even those states with stable delegations must make modifications to take into account population shifts within their boundaries, in accordance with Supreme Court "one-person, one-vote" rulings.

In most states, the state legislatures are responsible for drafting and enacting the new congressional district map. Thus, the majority party in each state legislature is often in a position to draw a district map that enhances the fortunes of its incumbents and candidates at the expense of the opposing party. "Some members may find their old district no longer recognizable, or their home located in someone else's district. Others will find the music has stopped and they are, quite literally, without a seat. Or they will find themselves thrown together in a single district with another incumbent—often from the same party," wrote one reporter. "The scramble to prevent or minimize such political problems involves some of the most brutal combat in American politics, for the power to draw district lines is the power not only to end one politician's career but often to enfranchise or disenfranchise a neighborhood, a city, a party, a social or economic group or even a race by concentrating or diluting their votes within a given district."[1]

Among the many unique features to emerge in the remarkable nation-creating endeavor of 1787 was a national legislative body whose membership was to be elected by the people and apportioned on the basis of population. In keeping with the nature of the Constitution, however, only fundamental rules and regulations were provided. The interpretation and implementation of the instructions contained in the document were left to future generations.

Within this flexible framework many questions soon arose. How large was the House of Representatives to be? What mathematical formula was to be used in calculating the distribution of seats among the various states? Were the representatives to be elected at large or by districts? If by districts, what standards should be used in fixing their boundaries? Congress and the courts have been wrestling with these questions for more than two hundred years.

Until the mid-twentieth century such questions generally remained in the hands of the legislators. But with the population increasingly concentrated in urban areas, variations in populations among rural and urban districts in a single state grew more and more pronounced. Efforts to persuade Congress and state legislatures to address the issue of heavily populated but underrepresented areas proved unsuccessful. Legislators from rural areas were so intent on preventing power from slipping from their hands that they managed to block reapportionment of the House for a whole decade after the 1920 census.

Not long afterward, litigants began trying to persuade the Supreme Court to order the states to revise congressional district boundaries to reflect population shifts. For years they found the Court unreceptive, but then there was incremental progress, and a breakthrough finally occurred in 1964 in the case of *Wesberry v. Sanders*. In that case, the Court declared that the Constitution required that "as nearly as practicable, one man's vote in a congressional election is to be worth as much as another's."

In the years that followed, the Court repeatedly reaffirmed its one-person, one-vote requirement. Following the 1980 census, several states adopted new maps with districts of nearly equal population that were designed to benefit one party at the expense of the other. These partisan gerrymanders disregarded other traditional tenets of map-drawing, such as making districts compact and respecting the integrity of county and city lines. But as long as the districts in such maps were drawn to be equal in population, these gerrymanders seemed unassailable in the courts. In 1986, in *Davis v. Bandemer*, a slim majority of the Supreme Court held that partisan gerrymanders were subject to constitutional review by federal courts. But the Court offered no opinion on what might constitute an impermissible partisan gerrymander, and maps drawn with a clear partisan slant continued to appear in the 1990s round of redistricting.

Starting in the mid-1980s and continuing through the 1990s, the focus of much redistricting controversy and litigation shifted to the practice of racial gerrymandering—designing constituencies to favor the election of candidates from racial or ethnic groups whose numbers in Congress are lower than their

proportion in the general population. This issue remained the most contentious topic in redistricting as states began drawing new House districts in 2001 following the 2000 census.

In a landmark 1986 ruling (*Thornburg v. Gingles*), the Supreme Court not only said that gerrymandering that deliberately diluted minority voting strength was illegal, but went even further, imposing a requirement that mapmakers do all they can to maximize minority voting strength. The expansion of minority rights sparked by *Gingles* changed redistricting dramatically. After the 1990 census, redistricting in many states was done with an eye toward creating constituencies designed to elect minority candidates. Those new maps resulted in record numbers of blacks and Hispanics winning House seats in 1992.

As if taken aback by the pace of change wrought by *Gingles*, the Supreme Court issued a series of rulings in the 1990s that discouraged states from going to extremes to draw districts for minorities. As a result, mapmakers in the new century found themselves between legal and political pressures to enhance election opportunities for minority group members and court decisions that posed a rigorous examination of the standards and methods to carry out this obligation.

Early History of Reapportionment

Modern legislative bodies are descended from the councils of feudal lords and gentry that medieval kings summoned for the purpose of raising revenues and armies. The councils represented only certain groups of people, such as the nobility, the clergy, the landed gentry, and town merchants; the notion of equal representation for equal numbers of people or even for all groups of people had not yet begun to develop.

Beginning as little more than administrative and advisory arms of the throne, royal councils in time developed into lawmaking bodies and acquired powers that eventually eclipsed those of the monarchs they served. In England the king's council became Parliament, with the higher nobility and clergy making up the House of Lords and representatives of the gentry and merchants making up the House of Commons. The power struggle between king and council climaxed in the mid-1600s, when the king was executed and a "benevolent" dictatorship was set up under Oliver Cromwell. Although the monarchy was soon restored, by 1800 Parliament was clearly the more powerful branch of government.

The growth of the powers of Parliament, as well as the development of English ideas of representation during the seventeenth and eighteenth centuries, had a profound effect on the colonists in America. Representative assemblies were unifying forces behind the breakaway of the colonies from England and the establishment of the newly independent nation.

Colonists in America generally modeled their legislatures after England's, using both population and land units as bases for apportionment. Patterns of early representation varied. "Nowhere did representation bear any uniform relation to the number of electors. Here and there the factor of size had been crudely recognized," Robert Luce noted in his book *Legislative Principles*.[2]

The Continental Congress, with representation from every colony, proclaimed in the Declaration of Independence in 1776 that governments derive "their just powers from the consent of the governed" and that "the right of representation in the legislature" is an "inestimable right" of the people. The Constitutional Convention of 1787 included representatives from all the states. However, in neither of these bodies were the state delegations or voting powers proportional to population.

In New England the town was usually the basis for representation. In the Middle Atlantic region the county frequently was used. Virginia used the county with additional representation for specified cities. In many areas, towns and counties were fairly equal in population, and territorial representation afforded roughly equal representation for equal numbers of people. Delaware's three counties, for example, were of almost equal population and had the same representation in the legislature. But in Virginia the disparity was enormous (from 951 people in one county to 22,015 in another). Thomas Jefferson criticized the state's constitution on the ground that "among those who share the representation, the shares are unequal."[3]

THE FRAMERS' INTENTIONS

What, then, did the Framers of the Constitution have in mind about who would be represented in the House of Representatives and how?

The Constitution declares only that each state is to be allotted a certain number of representatives. It does not state specifically that congressional districts must be equal or nearly equal in population. Nor does it explicitly require that a state create districts at all. However, it seems clear that the first clause of Article I, Section 2, providing that House members should be chosen "by the People of the several States," indicates that the House of Representatives, in contrast to the Senate, was to represent people rather than states. (*See box, Constitutional Provisions, p. 809.*)

The third clause of Article I, Section 2, provided that congressional apportionment among the states must be according to population. "There is little point in giving the states congressmen 'according to their respective numbers' if the states do not redistribute the members of their delegations on the same principle," Andrew Hacker argued in his book *Congressional Districting*. "For representatives are not the property of the states, as are the senators, but rather belong to the people who happen to reside within the boundaries of those states. Thus, each citizen has a claim to be regarded as a political unit equal in value to his neighbors."[4]

Hacker also examined the Constitutional Convention, *The Federalist Papers* (essays written by Alexander Hamilton, John Jay, and James Madison in defense of the Constitution), and the state conventions ratifying the Constitution for evidence of the Framers' intentions with regard to representation. He found that the issue of unequal representation arose only once during debate in the Constitutional Convention. The occasion was Madison's defense of Article I, Section 4, of the proposed Constitution, giving Congress the power to override state regulations on "the times . . . and manner" of holding elections for

Constitutional Provisions

Article I, Section 2

The House of Representatives shall be composed of Members chosen every second Year by the People of the several States, and the Electors in each State shall have the Qualifications requisite for Electors of the most numerous Branch of the State Legislature. . . .

Representatives and direct Taxes shall be apportioned among the several States which may be included within this Union, according to their respective Numbers, which shall be determined by adding to the whole Number of free Persons, including those bound to Service for a Term of Years, and excluding Indians not taxed, three fifths of all other Persons. The actual Enumeration shall be made within three Years after the first Meeting of the Congress of the United States, and within every subsequent Term of ten Years, in such Manner as they shall by Law direct. The Number of Representatives shall not exceed one for every thirty Thousand, but each State shall have at Least one Representative. . . .

Article I, Section 4

The Times, Places and Manner of holding Elections for Senators and Representatives, shall be prescribed in each State by the Legislature thereof; but the Congress may at any time by Law make or alter such Regulations, except as to the Place of Chusing Senators. . . .

Amendment XIV

(Ratified July 28, 1868)

Section 2. Representatives shall be apportioned among the several States according to their respective numbers, counting the whole number of persons in each State, excluding Indians not taxed. But when the right to vote at any election for the choice of electors for President and Vice President of the United States, Representatives in Congress, the Executive and Judicial officers of a State, or the members of the Legislature thereof, is denied to any of the male inhabitants of such State, being twenty-one years of age, and citizens of the United States, or in any way abridged, except for participation in rebellion, or other crime, the basis of representation therein shall be reduced in the proportion which the number of such male citizens shall bear to the whole number of male citizens twenty-one years of age in such State.

members of Congress. Madison's argument related to the fact that many state legislatures of the time were badly malapportioned: "The inequality of the representation in the legislatures of particular states would produce a like inequality in their representation in the national legislature, as it was presumable that the counties having the power in the former case would secure it to themselves in the latter."[5]

The implication was that states would create congressional districts and that unequal districting was undesirable and should be prevented.

Madison made this interpretation even more clear in his contributions to *The Federalist Papers*. Arguing in favor of the relatively small size of the projected House of Representatives, he wrote in No. 56: "Divide the largest state into ten or twelve districts and it will be found that there will be no peculiar local interests . . . which will not be within the knowledge of the Representative of the district."

In the same paper Madison said, "The Representatives of each state will not only bring with them a considerable knowledge of its laws, and a local knowledge of their respective districts, but will probably in all cases have been members, and may even at the very time be members, of the state legislature, where all the local information and interests of the state are assembled, and from whence they may easily be conveyed by a very few hands into the legislature of the United States." And, finally, in the *Federalist* No. 57 Madison stated that "each Representative of the United States will be elected by five or six thousand citizens." In making these arguments, Madison seems to have assumed that all or most representatives would be elected by districts rather than at large.[6]

In the states' ratifying conventions, the grant to Congress by Article I, Section 4, of ultimate jurisdiction over the "Times, Places and Manner of holding Elections" (except the places of choosing senators) held the attention of many delegates. There were differences over the merits of this section, but no justification of unequal districts was prominently used to attack the grant of power. Further evidence that individual districts were the intention of the Founding Fathers was given in the New York ratifying convention, when Alexander Hamilton said, "The natural and proper mode of holding elections will be to divide the state into districts in proportion to the number to be elected. This state will consequently be divided at first into six."[7]

From his study of the sources relating to the question of congressional districting, Hacker concluded,

There is, then, a good deal of evidence that those who framed and ratified the Constitution intended that the House of Representatives have as its constituency a public in which the votes of all citizens were of equal weight. . . . The House of Representatives was designed to be a popular chamber, giving the same electoral power to all who had the vote. And the concern of Madison . . . that districts be equal in size was an institutional step in the direction of securing this democratic principle.[8]

Reapportionment: The Number of Seats

The Constitution made the first apportionment, which was to remain in effect until the first census was taken. No reliable figures on the population were available at the time. The Constitution's apportionment yielded a sixty-five member House. The seats were allotted among the thirteen states as follows: New Hampshire, three; Massachusetts, eight; Rhode Island and Providence Plantations, one; Connecticut, five; New York, six; New Jersey, four; Pennsylvania, eight; Delaware, one; Maryland, six;

Table 22-1
Congressional Apportionment, 1789–2000

	Constitution (1789)[2]	1790	1800	1810	1820	1830	1840	1850	1860	1870	Year of census[1] 1880	1890	1900	1910	1930[3]	1940	1950	1960	1970	1980	1990	2000
Alabama				1[4]	3	5	7	7	6	8	8	9	9	10	9	9	9	8	7	7	7	7
Alaska																	1[4]	1	1	1	1	1
Arizona														1[4]	1	2	2	3	4	5	6	8
Arkansas						1[4]	1	2	3	4	5	6	7	7	7	7	6	4	4	4	4	4
California							2[4]	2	3	4	6	7	8	11	20	23	30	38	43	45	52	53
Colorado										1[4]	1	2	3	4	4	4	4	4	5	6	6	7
Conn.	5	7	7	7	6	6	4	4	4	4	4	4	5	5	6	6	6	6	6	6	6	5
Delaware	1	1	1	2	1	1	1	1	1	1	1	1	1	1	1	1	1	1	1	1	1	1
Florida							1[4]	1	1	2	2	2	3	4	5	6	8	12	15	19	23	25
Georgia	3	2	4	6	7	9	8	8	7	9	10	11	11	12	10	10	10	10	10	10	11	13
Hawaii																	1[4]	2	2	2	2	2
Idaho											1[4]	1	1	2	2	2	2	2	2	2	2	2
Illinois				1[4]	1	3	7	9	14	19	20	22	25	27	27	26	25	24	24	22	20	19
Indiana				1[4]	3	7	10	11	11	13	13	13	13	13	12	11	11	11	11	10	10	9
Iowa							2[4]	2	6	9	11	11	11	11	9	8	8	7	6	6	5	5
Kansas									1	3	7	8	8	8	7	6	6	5	5	5	4	4
Kentucky		2	6	10	12	13	10	10	9	10	11	11	11	11	9	9	8	7	7	7	6	6
Louisiana				1[4]	3	3	4	4	5	6	6	6	7	8	8	8	8	8	8	8	7	7
Maine				7[4]	7	8	7	6	5	5	4	4	4	4	3	3	3	2	2	2	2	2
Maryland	6	8	9	9	9	8	6	6	5	6	6	6	6	6	6	6	7	8	8	8	8	8
Massachusetts	8	14	17	13[5]	13	12	10	11	10	11	12	13	14	16	15	14	14	12	12	11	10	10
Michigan							1[4]	3	4	6	9	11	12	13	17	17	18	19	19	18	16	15
Minnesota								2[4]	2	3	5	7	9	10	9	9	9	8	8	8	8	8
Mississippi				1[4]	1	2	4	5	5	6	7	7	8	8	7	7	6	5	5	5	5	4
Missouri					1	2	5	7	9	13	14	15	16	16	13	13	11	10	10	9	9	9
Montana											1[4]	1	1	2	2	2	2	2	2	2	1	1
Nebraska.									1[4]	1	3	6	6	6	5	4	4	3	3	3	3	3
Nevada									1[4]	1	1	1	1	1	1	1	1	1	1	2	2	3
New Hampshire	3	4	5	6	6	5	4	3	3	3	2	2	2	2	2	2	2	2	2	2	2	2
New Jersey	4	5	6	6	6	6	5	5	5	7	7	8	10	12	14	14	14	15	15	14	13	13
New Mexico														1[4]	1	2	2	2	2	3	3	3
New York	6	10	17	27	34	40	34	33	31	33	34	34	37	43	45	45	43	41	39	34	31	29
North Carolina	5	10	12	13	13	13	9	8	7	8	9	9	10	10	11	12	12	11	11	11	12	13
North Dakota											1[4]	1	2	3	2	2	2	2	1	1	1	1
Ohio			1[4]	6	14	19	21	21	19	20	21	21	21	22	24	23	23	24	23	21	19	18
Oklahoma													5[4]	8	9	8	6	6	6	6	6	5
Oregon				-				1[4]	1	1	1	2	2	3	3	4	4	4	4	5	5	5
Pennsylvania	8	13	18	23	26	28	24	25	24	27	28	30	32	36	34	33	30	27	25	23	21	19
Rhode Island	1	2	2	2	2	2	2	2	2	2	2	2	2	3	2	2	2	2	2	2	2	2
South Carolina	5	6	8	9	9	9	7	6	4	5	7	7	7	7	6	6	6	6	6	6	6	6
South Dakota											2[4]	2	2	3	2	2	2	2	2	1	1	1
Tennessee		1[4]	3	6	9	13	11	10	8	10	10	10	10	10	9	10	9	9	8	9	9	9
Texas							2[4]	2	4	6	11	13	16	18	21	21	22	23	24	27	30	32
Utah												1[4]	1	2	2	2	2	2	2	3	3	3
Vermont		2	4	6	5	5	4	3	3	3	2	2	2	2	1	1	1	1	1	1	1	1
Virginia	10	19	22	23	22	21	15	13	11	9	10	10	10	10	9	9	10	10	10	10	11	11
Washington											1[4]	2	3	5	6	6	7	7	7	8	9	9
West Virginia										3	4	4	5	6	6	6	6	5	4	4	3	3
Wisconsin							2[4]	3	6	8	9	10	11	11	10	10	10	10	9	9	9	8
Wyoming											1[4]	1	1	1	1	1	1	1	1	1	1	1
Total	65	106	142	186	213	242	232	237	243	293	332	357	391	435	435	435	437[6]	435	435	435	435	435

1. Apportionment effective with congressional election two years after census.
2. Original apportionment made in Constitution, pending first census.
3. No apportionment was made in 1920.
4. These figures are not based on any census, but indicate the provisional representation accorded newly admitted states by Congress, pending the next census.
5. Twenty members were assigned to Massachusetts, but seven of these were credited to Maine when that area became a state.
6. Normally 435, but temporarily increased two seats by Congress when Alaska and Hawaii became states.

Sources: Biographical Directory of the American Congress and Bureau of the Census.

A method of reapportionment devised by President Thomas Jefferson resulted in great inequalities among states. This method was in use until 1840.

Virginia, ten; North Carolina, five; South Carolina, five; and Georgia, three. This apportionment remained in effect during the First and Second Congresses (1789–1793).

Apparently realizing that apportionment of the House was likely to become a major bone of contention, the First Congress submitted to the states a proposed constitutional amendment containing a formula to be used in future reapportionments. The amendment provided that following the taking of a decennial census one representative would be allotted for every 30,000 people until the House membership reached 100. Once that level was reached, there would be one representative for every 40,000 people until the House membership reached 200, when there would be one representative for every 50,000 people.

FIRST APPORTIONMENT BY CONGRESS

The states, however, refused to ratify the reapportionment-formula amendment, which forced Congress to enact apportionment legislation after the first census was taken in 1790. The first apportionment bill was sent to the president in March 1792. President George Washington sent the bill back to Congress without his signature—the first presidential veto.

The bill had incorporated the constitutional minimum of 30,000 as the size of each district. But the population of each state was not a simple multiple of 30,000; significant fractions were left over. For example, Vermont was found to be entitled to 2.85 representatives, New Jersey to 5.98, and Virginia to 21.02. A formula had to be found that would deal in the fairest possible manner with unavoidable variations from exact equality.

Accordingly, Congress proposed in the first apportionment bill to distribute the members on a fixed ratio of one representative for each 30,000 inhabitants, and to give an additional member to each state with a fraction exceeding one-half. Washington's veto was based on the belief that eight states would receive more than one representative for each 30,000 people under this formula.

A motion to override the veto was unsuccessful. A new bill meeting the president's objections, approved in April 1792, provided for a ratio of one member for every 33,000 inhabitants and fixed the exact number of representatives to which each state was entitled. The total membership of the House was to be 105. In dividing the population of the various states by 33,000, all remainders were to be disregarded. Thomas Jefferson devised the solution, known as the method of rejected fractions.

JEFFERSON'S METHOD

Jefferson's method of reapportionment resulted in great inequalities among districts. A Vermont district would contain 42,766 inhabitants, a New Jersey district 35,911, and a Virginia district only 33,187. Jefferson's method emphasized what was considered to be the ideal size of a congressional district rather than what the size of the House ought to be.

The reapportionment act based on the census of 1800 continued the ratio of 33,000, which provided a House of 141 members. The third apportionment bill, enacted in 1811, fixed the ratio at 35,000, yielding a House of 181 members. Following the 1820 census Congress set the ratio at 40,000 inhabitants per district, which produced a House of 213 members. The act of May 22, 1832, fixed the ratio at 47,700, resulting in a House of 240 members.

Dissatisfaction with inequalities produced by the method of rejected fractions grew. Launching a vigorous attack against it, Daniel Webster urged adoption of a method that would assign an additional representative to each state with a large fraction. Webster outlined his reasoning in a report he submitted to Congress in 1832:

The Constitution, therefore, must be understood not as enjoining an absolute relative equality—because that would be demanding an impossibility—but as requiring of Congress to make the apportionment of Representatives among the several states according to their respective numbers, *as near as may be*. That which cannot be done perfectly must be done in a manner as near perfection as can be. . . . In such a case approximation becomes a rule.[9]

Following the 1840 census Congress adopted a reapportionment method similar to that advocated by Webster. The method fixed a ratio of one representative for every 70,680 people. This figure was reached by deciding on a fixed size of the House in advance (223), dividing that figure into the total national "representative population," and using the result (70,680) as the fixed ratio. The population of each state was then divided by this ratio to find the number of its representatives and the states were assigned an additional representative for each fraction more than one-half. Under this method the actual size of the House dropped. (*See Table 22-1, p. 810.*)

The modified reapportionment formula adopted by Congress in 1842 was more satisfactory than the previous method, but another change was made following the census of 1850. Proposed by Rep. Samuel F. Vinton of Ohio, the new system became known as the Vinton method.

VINTON APPORTIONMENT FORMULA

Under the Vinton formula Congress first fixed the size of the House and then distributed the seats. The total qualifying population of the country was divided by the desired number of representatives, and the resulting number became the ratio of population to each representative. The population of each state was divided by this ratio, and each state received the number of representatives equal to the whole number in the quotient for that state. Then, to reach the required size of the House, additional representatives were assigned based on the remaining fractions, beginning with the state having the largest fraction. This procedure differed from the 1842 method only in the last step, which assigned one representative to every state having a fraction larger than one-half.

Proponents of the Vinton method pointed out that it had the distinct advantage of fixing the size of the House in advance and taking into account at least the largest fractions. The concern of the House turned from the ideal size of a congressional district to the ideal size of the House itself.

Under the 1842 reapportionment formula, the exact size of the House could not be fixed in advance. If every state with a fraction more than one-half were given an additional representative, the House might wind up with a few more or a few less than the desired number. However, under the Vinton method, only states with the largest fractions were given additional House members and only up to the desired total size of the House.

Vinton Apportionments

Six reapportionments were carried out under the Vinton method. The 1850 census act contained three provisions not included in any previous law. First, it required reapportionment not only after the census of 1850 but also after all the subsequent censuses; second, it purported to fix the size of the House permanently at 233 members; and third, it provided in advance for an automatic apportionment by the secretary of the interior under the method prescribed in the act.

Following the census of 1860 an automatic reapportionment was to be carried out by the Interior Department. However, because the size of the House was to remain at the 1850 level, some states faced loss of representation and others were to gain fewer seats than they expected. To avert that possibility, an act was approved in 1862 increasing the size of the House to 241 and giving an extra representative to eight states—Illinois, Iowa, Kentucky, Minnesota, Ohio, Pennsylvania, Rhode Island, and Vermont.

Apportionment legislation following the 1870 census contained several new provisions. The act fixed the size of the House at 283, with the proviso that the number should be increased if new states were admitted. A supplemental act assigned one additional representative each to Alabama, Florida, Indiana, Louisiana, New Hampshire, New York, Pennsylvania, Tennessee, and Vermont.

With the Reconstruction era at its height in the South, the reapportionment legislation of 1872 reflected the desire of Congress to enforce Section 2 of the new Fourteenth Amendment.

That section attempted to protect the right of blacks to vote by providing for reduction of representation in the House of a state that interfered with the exercise of that right. The number of representatives of such a state was to be reduced in proportion to the number of inhabitants of voting age whose right to go to the polls was denied or abridged. The reapportionment bill repeated the language of Section 2, but the provision never was put into effect because of the difficulty of determining the exact number of people whose right to vote was being abridged.

The reapportionment act of 1882 provided for a House of 325 members, with additional members for any new states admitted to the Union. No new apportionment provisions were added. The acts of 1891 and 1901 were routine as far as apportionment was concerned. The 1891 measure provided for a House of 356 members, and the 1901 statute increased the number to 386.

Problems with Vinton Method

Despite the apparent advantages of the Vinton method, certain difficulties revealed themselves as the formula was applied. Zechariah Chafee Jr., of the Harvard Law School summarized these problems in an article in the *Harvard Law Review* in 1929. The method, he pointed out, suffered from what he called the "Alabama paradox." Under that aberration, an increase in the total size of the House might be accompanied by an actual loss of a seat by some states, even though there had been no corresponding change in population. This phenomenon first appeared in tables prepared for Congress in 1881, which gave Alabama eight members in a House of 299 but only seven members in a House of 300. It could even happen that the state that lost a seat was the one state that had expanded in population, while all the others had fewer people.

Chafee concluded from his study of the Vinton method:

Thus, it is unsatisfactory to fix the ratio of population per Representative before seats are distributed. Either the size of the House comes out haphazard, or, if this be determined in advance, the absurdities of the "Alabama paradox" vitiate the apportionment. Under present conditions, it is essential to determine the size of the House in advance; the problem thereafter is to distribute the required number of seats among the several states as nearly as possible in proportion to their respective populations so that no state is treated unfairly in comparison with any other state.[10]

MAXIMUM MEMBERSHIP OF HOUSE

In 1911 the membership of the House was fixed at 433. Provision was made for the addition of one representative each from Arizona and New Mexico, which were expected to become states in the near future. Thus, the size of the House reached 435, where it has remained with the exception of a brief period, 1959–1963, when the admission of Alaska and Hawaii raised the total temporarily to 437.

Limiting the size of the House amounted to recognition that the body soon would expand to unmanageable proportions if Congress continued the practice of adding new seats every ten years to match population gains without depriving any state of its existing representation. Agreement on a fixed number made the task of reapportionment even more difficult when the pop-

ulation not only increased but also became much more mobile. Population shifts brought Congress up hard against the politically painful necessity of taking seats away from slow-growing states to give the fast-growing states adequate representation.

A new mathematical calculation was adopted for the reapportionment following the 1910 census. Devised by W. F. Willcox of Cornell University, the new system established a priority list that assigned seats progressively, beginning with the first seat above the constitutional minimum of at least one seat for each state. When there were forty-eight states, this method was used to assign the forty-ninth member, the fiftieth member, and so on, until the agreed upon size of the House was reached. The method was called major fractions and was used after the censuses of 1910, 1930, and 1940. There was no reapportionment after the 1920 census.

1920s STRUGGLE

The results of the fourteenth decennial census were announced in December 1920, just after the short session of the Sixty-sixth Congress convened. The 1920 census showed that for the first time in history most Americans were urban residents. This came as a profound shock to people accustomed to emphasizing the nation's rural traditions and the virtues of life on farms and in small towns as Thomas Jefferson had. Jefferson once wrote:

Those who labor in the earth are the chosen people of God, if ever He had a chosen people, whose breasts He had made His peculiar deposit for substantial and genuine virtue. . . . The mobs of great cities add just as much to the support of pure government as sores do to the strength of the human body. . . . I think our governments will remain virtuous for many centuries as long as they are chiefly agricultural: and this shall be as long as there shall be vacant lands in any part of America. When they get piled up upon one another in large cities as in Europe, they will become corrupt as in Europe.[11]

As their power waned throughout the latter part of the nineteenth century and the early part of the twentieth, farmers clung to the Jeffersonian belief that somehow they were more pure and virtuous than the growing number of urban residents. When faced with the fact that they were in the minority, these country residents put up a strong rearguard action to prevent the inevitable shift of congressional districts to the cities. They succeeded in postponing reapportionment legislation for almost a decade.

Rural representatives insisted that, because the 1920 census was taken as of January 1, the farm population had been undercounted. In support of this contention, they argued that many farm laborers were seasonally employed in the cities at that time of year. Furthermore, midwinter road conditions probably had prevented enumerators from visiting many farms, they said, and other farmers were said to have been uncounted because they were absent on winter vacation trips. The change of the census date to January 1 in 1920 had been made to conform to recommendations of the U.S. Department of Agriculture, which had asserted that the census should be taken early in the year if an accurate statistical picture of farming conditions was to be obtained.

Another point raised by rural legislators was that large numbers of unnaturalized aliens were congregated in northern cities, with the result that these cities gained at the expense of constituencies made up mostly of citizens of the United States. Rep. Homer Hoch, R-Kan., submitted a table showing that in a House of 435 representatives, exclusion from the census count of people not naturalized would have altered the allocation of seats in sixteen states. Southern and western farming states would have retained the number of seats allocated to them in 1911 or would have gained, while northern industrial states and California would have lost or at least would have gained fewer seats.

A constitutional amendment to exclude all aliens from the enumeration for purposes of reapportionment was proposed during the Seventieth Congress (1927–1929) by Hoch, Sen. Arthur Capper, R-Kan., and others. But nothing further came of the proposals.

Reapportionment Bills Opposed

The first bill to reapportion the House according to the 1920 census was drafted by the House Census Committee early in 1921. Proceeding on the principle that no state should have its representation reduced, the committee proposed to increase the total number of representatives from 435 to 483. But the House voted 267–76 to keep its membership at 435. The bill then was blocked by a Senate committee, where it died when the Sixty-sixth Congress expired March 4, 1921.

Early in the Sixty-seventh Congress, the House Census Committee again reported a bill, this time fixing the total membership at 460, an increase of 25. Two states—Maine and Massachusetts—would have lost one representative each and sixteen states would have gained. On the House floor an unsuccessful attempt was made to fix the number at the existing 435, and the House sent the bill back to committee.

During the Sixty-eighth Congress (1923–1925), the House Census Committee failed to report any reapportionment bill. In April 1926, midway through the Sixty-ninth Congress (1925–1927), it became apparent that the committee would not produce a reapportionment measure. A motion to discharge a reapportionment bill from the committee failed, however, and the matter once again was put aside.

Coolidge Intervention

President Calvin Coolidge, who previously had made no reference to reapportionment in his communications to Congress, announced in January 1927 that he favored passage of a new apportionment bill during the short session of the Sixty-ninth Congress, which would end in less than two months. The House Census Committee refused to act. Its chairman, Rep. E. Hart Fenn, R-Conn., therefore moved in the House to suspend the rules and pass a bill he had introduced authorizing the secretary of commerce to reapportion the House immediately after the 1930 census. The motion was voted down 183–197.

The Fenn bill was rewritten early in the Seventieth Congress (1927–1929) to give Congress itself a chance to act before the proposed reapportionment by the secretary of commerce should go into effect. The House passed an amended version of

Figure 22–1   2000 Reapportionment: Gainers and Losers

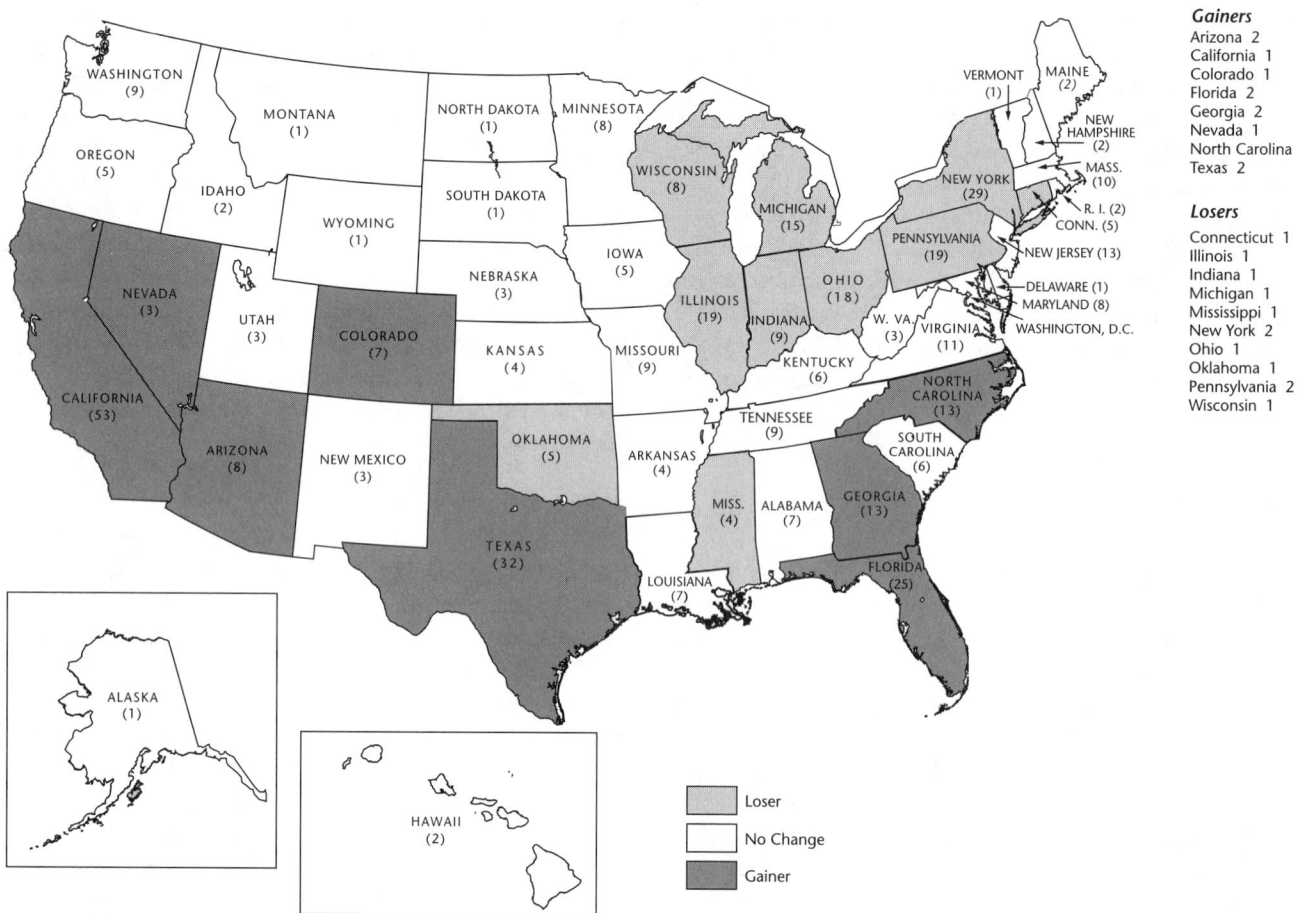

Note: Number in parentheses indicates state's House seats under 2000 reapportionment.

the Fenn bill in January 1929, and it was quickly reported by the Senate Commerce Committee. Repeated efforts to bring it up for floor action ahead of other bills failed. Its supporters gave up the fight when it became evident that senators from states slated to lose representation were ready to carry on a filibuster that would have blocked not only reapportionment but all other measures.

Hoover Intervention

President Herbert Hoover listed provision for the 1930 census and reapportionment as "matters of emergency legislation" that should be acted upon in the special session of the Seventy-first Congress, which was convened on April 15, 1929. In response to this urgent request, the Senate June 13 passed, 48–37, a combined census-reapportionment bill that had been approved by voice vote of the House two days earlier.

The 1929 law established a permanent system of reapportioning the 435 House seats following each census. It provided that immediately after the convening of the Seventy-first Congress for its short session in December 1930, the president was to transmit to Congress a statement showing the population of each state together with an apportionment of representatives to each state based on the existing size of the House. Failing enact-

ment of new apportionment legislation, that apportionment would go into effect without further action and would remain in effect for ensuing elections to the House of Representatives until another census had been taken and another reapportionment made.

Because two decades had passed between reapportionments, a greater shift than usual took place following the 1930 census. California's House delegation was almost doubled, rising from eleven to twenty. Michigan gained four seats, Texas three, and New Jersey, New York, and Ohio two each. Twenty-one states lost a total of twenty-seven seats; Missouri lost three, and Georgia, Iowa, Kentucky, and Pennsylvania each lost two.

To test the fairness of two allocation methods—the familiar major fractions and the new equal proportions system—the 1929 act required the president to report the distribution of seats by both methods. But, pending legislation to the contrary, the method of major fractions was to be used.

The two methods gave an identical distribution of seats based on 1930 census figures. However, in 1940 the two methods gave different results: under major fractions, Michigan would gain a seat lost by Arkansas; under equal proportions, no change would occur in either state. The automatic reapportionment provisions of the 1929 act went into effect in January 1941. But

the House Census Committee moved to reverse the result, favoring the method of equal proportions and the certain Democratic seat in Arkansas over a possible Republican gain if the seat were shifted to Michigan. The Democratic-controlled Congress went along, adopting equal proportions as the method to be used in reapportionment calculations after the 1950 and subsequent censuses, and making this action retroactive to January 1941 to save Arkansas its seat.

While politics doubtless played a part in the timing of the action taken in 1941, the method of equal proportions had come to be accepted as the best available: It had been worked out by Edward V. Huntington of Harvard in 1921. At the request of the Speaker of the House, all known methods of apportionment were considered in 1929 by the National Academy of Sciences Committee on Apportionment. The committee expressed its preference for equal proportions.

METHOD OF EQUAL PROPORTIONS

The method of equal proportions involves complicated mathematical calculations. In brief, each of the fifty states is initially assigned the one seat to which it is entitled by the Constitution. Then "priority numbers" for states to receive second seats, third seats, and so on are calculated by dividing the state's population by the square root of $n(n-1)$, where "n" is the number of seats for that state. The priority numbers are then lined up in order and the seats given to the states with priority numbers until 435 are awarded.

The method is designed to make the proportional difference in the average district size in any two states as small as possible. After the 1990 reapportionment, for example, Montana's single district was the most populous, with 803,655 residents, while Wyoming's single district was the least populous, with 453,588 people. The average population per district nationwide was about 572,500. In 2000 the average population per district increased to 647,000. Montana's single district remained the most populous with 902,195 people; Wyoming's single district remained the least populous with 493,782 residents.

QUESTIONING THE COUNT IN THE 1980S AND 1990S

While the method of equal proportions came to be accepted as the best way to apportion House seats among the states, the 1980s and 1990s brought heated debate over a more fundamental issue: the accuracy of the census itself.

Members of Congress as well as state and local officials have a keen interest in an accurate population count. In addition to being the basis for reapportionment and redistricting, the census also is used to determine the allocation of funding for many federal aid programs.

Concern about the census "undercount" grew after 1980, when the Census Bureau estimated that it counted about 99 percent of the white population but only about 94 percent of the blacks. Democrats, especially those representing inner-city districts where the undercount was comparatively high, argued unsuccessfully for a statistical adjustment to compensate for undercounting.

The controversy over the 1990 count began even before the census was taken, when the Commerce Department, the parent agency to the Census Bureau, announced in 1987 that it would not statistically adjust the 1990 data. New York City, along with other cities, states, and civil rights organizations, pressed a case in court to force the Census Bureau to make a statistical adjustment to account for people who were missed, including sizable numbers of blacks, Hispanics, and Native Americans. In 1996, the Supreme Court rejected adjusting the census.

But by then, the White House had passed from Republican to Democratic hands, and Commerce Department officials were laying plans to have the Census Bureau use statistical sampling techniques that they said would enhance the accuracy of the 2000 census. The Republican majority in Congress gave statistical sampling a cold eye, worrying that it might lead to politically motivated manipulating of the census. (See box, How Should the Census Count the Population, p. 820.)

The same issue arose after the 2000 census. Advocates for minority groups, fearing that many persons of their race or ethnic background were missed in the new count, argued vocally for a statistical adjustment to the actual head count in the census. But by the time the issue was to be resolved in early 2001, the White House and both houses of Congress were under Republican control, making a decision to statistically adjust the count unlikely. Unexpectedly, however, on March 1, 2001, professionals in the Census Bureau said the actual count turned out to be more reliable than expected, and warned that use of the statistical adjustment methods available could make the count less accurate. Their recommendation against adjustment essentially defused the issue politically.

Redistricting: Drawing the Lines

Although the Constitution contained provisions for the apportionment of U.S. House seats among the states, it was silent about how the members should be elected. From the beginning most states divided their territory into geographic districts, permitting only one member of Congress to be elected from each district.

But some states allowed would-be House members to run at large, with voters able to cast as many votes as there were seats to be filled. Still other states created what were known as multimember districts, in which a single geographic unit would elect two or more members of the House. At various times, some states used combinations of these methods. For example, a state might elect ten representatives from ten individual districts and two at large.

In the first few elections to the House, New Hampshire, Pennsylvania, New Jersey, and Georgia elected their representatives at large, as did Rhode Island and Delaware, the two states with only a single representative. Districts were used in Massachusetts, New York, Maryland, Virginia, and South Carolina. In Connecticut a preliminary election was held to nominate three times as many people as the number of representatives to be chosen at large in the subsequent election. In 1840 twenty-two of the thirty-one states elected their representatives by districts. New

Table 22–2
State Population Totals, House Seat Changes after the 2000 Census

State	1990 population[1]	2000 population[1]	Population change	% change	Seats after 2000 census	Seat change in 2000s
Alabama	4,040,587	4,447,100	406,513	10.1	7	0
Alaska	550,043	626,932	76,889	14.0	1	0
Arizona	3,665,228	5,130,632	1,465,404	40.0	8	+2
Arkansas	2,350,725	2,673,400	322,675	13.7	4	0
California	29,760,021	33,871,648	4,111,627	13.8	53	+1
Colorado	3,294,394	4,301,261	1,006,867	30.6	7	+1
Connecticut	3,287,116	3,405,565	118,449	3.6	5	−1
Delaware	666,168	783,600	117,432	17.6	1	0
District of Columbia[2]	606,900	572,059	−34,841	−5.7	—	—
Florida	12,937,926	15,982,378	3,044,452	23.5	25	+2
Georgia	6,478,216	8,186,453	1,708,237	26.4	13	+2
Hawaii	1,108,229	1,211,537	103,308	9.3	2	0
Idaho	1,006,749	1,293,953	287,204	28.5	2	0
Illinois	11,430,602	12,419,293	988,691	8.6	19	−1
Indiana	5,544,159	6,080,485	536,326	9.7	9	−1
Iowa	2,776,755	2,926,324	149,569	5.4	5	0
Kansas	2,477,574	2,688,418	210,844	8.5	4	0
Kentucky	3,685,296	4,041,769	356,473	9.7	6	0
Louisiana	4,219,973	4,468,976	249,003	5.9	7	0
Maine	1,227,928	1,274,923	46,995	3.8	2	0
Maryland	4,781,468	5,296,486	515,018	10.8	8	0
Massachusetts	6,016,425	6,349,097	332,672	5.5	10	0
Michigan	9,295,297	9,938,444	643,147	6.9	15	−1
Minnesota	4,375,099	4,919,479	544,380	12.4	8	0
Mississippi	2,573,216	2,844,658	271,442	10.5	4	−1
Missouri	5,117,073	5,595,211	478,138	9.3	9	0
Montana	799,065	902,195	103,130	12.9	1	0
Nebraska	1,578,385	1,711,263	132,878	8.4	3	0
Nevada	1,201,833	1,998,257	796,424	66.3	3	+1
New Hampshire	1,109,252	1,235,786	126,534	11.4	2	0
New Jersey	7,730,188	8,414,350	684,162	8.9	13	0
New Mexico	1,515,069	1,819,046	303,977	20.1	3	0
New York	17,990,455	18,976,457	986,002	5.5	29	−2
North Carolina	6,628,637	8,049,313	1,420,676	21.4	13	+1
North Dakota	638,800	642,200	3,400	0.5	1	0
Ohio	10,847,115	11,353,140	506,025	4.7	18	−1
Oklahoma	3,145,585	3,450,654	305,069	9.7	5	−1
Oregon	2,842,321	3,421,399	579,078	20.4	5	0
Pennsylvania	11,881,643	12,281,054	399,411	3.4	19	−2
Rhode Island	1,003,464	1,048,319	44,855	4.5	2	0
South Carolina	3,486,703	4,012,012	525,309	15.1	6	0
South Dakota	696,004	754,844	58,840	8.5	1	0
Tennessee	4,877,185	5,689,283	812,098	16.7	9	0
Texas	16,986,510	20,851,820	3,865,310	22.8	32	+2
Utah	1,722,850	2,233,169	510,319	29.6	3	0
Vermont	562,758	608,827	46,069	8.2	1	0
Virginia	6,187,358	7,078,515	891,157	14.4	11	0
Washington	4,866,692	5,894,121	1,027,429	21.1	9	0
West Virginia	1,793,477	1,808,344	14,867	0.8	3	0
Wisconsin	4,891,769	5,363,675	471,906	9.6	8	−1
Wyoming	453,588	493,782	40,194	8.9	1	0
United States[3]	248,709,873	281,421,906	32,712,033	13.2	435	—

1. For comparative purposes, the 1990 and 2000 figures do not include citizens living overseas; nor do these resident population figures reflect the use of statistical sampling.
2. The District of Columbia, which has one nonvoting delegate in the House, is not included in determination of apportionment.
3. Total population in 1990 and 2000 includes the District of Columbia.

Source: U.S. Census Bureau.

Hampshire, New Jersey, Georgia, Alabama, Mississippi, and Missouri, with a combined representation of thirty-three House seats, elected their representatives at large. Three states, Arkansas, Delaware, and Florida, had only one representative each.

Those states that used congressional districts quickly developed what came to be known as the gerrymander. The term refers to the practice of drawing district lines so as to maximize the advantage of a political party or interest group. The name originated from a salamander-shaped congressional district created by the Massachusetts legislature in 1812 when Elbridge Gerry was governor. *(See box, Origins of the Gerrymander, this page.)*

Constant efforts were made during the early 1800s to lay down national rules, by means of a constitutional amendment, for congressional districting. The first resolution proposing a mandatory division of each state into districts was introduced in Congress in 1800. In 1802 the legislatures of Vermont and North Carolina adopted resolutions in support of such action. From 1816 to 1826 twenty-two states adopted resolutions proposing the election of representatives by districts.

In Congress Sen. Mahlon Dickerson, R-N.J., proposed such an amendment regularly almost every year from 1817 to 1826. It was adopted by the Senate three times, in 1819, 1820, and 1822, but each time it failed to reach a vote in the House. Although the constitutional amendment was unsuccessful, a law passed in 1842 required contiguous single-member congressional districts. That law required representatives to be "elected by districts composed of contiguous territory equal in number to the representatives to which said state may be entitled, no one district electing more than one Representative."

The districting provisions of the 1842 act were not repeated in the legislation that followed the 1850 census. But in 1862 an act separate from the reapportionment act revived the provisions of the act of 1842 requiring districts to be composed of contiguous territory.

The 1872 reapportionment act again repeated the districting provisions and went even further by adding that districts should contain "as nearly as practicable an equal number of inhabitants." Similar provisions were included in the acts of 1881 and 1891. In the act of 1901, the words "compact territory" were added, and the clause then read "contiguous and compact territory and containing as nearly as practicable an equal number of inhabitants." This requirement appeared also in the legislation of 1911. The "contiguous and compact" provisions of the act subsequently lapsed, and Congress has never replaced them.

Several unsuccessful attempts were made to enforce redistricting provisions. Despite the districting requirements enacted in 1842, New Hampshire, Georgia, Mississippi, and Missouri elected their representatives at large that autumn. When the new House convened for its first session, on December 4, 1843, objection was made to seating the representatives of the four states.

The House debated the matter in February 1844. With the Democratic Party holding a majority of more than sixty, and with eighteen of the twenty-one challenged members being Democrats, the House decided to seat the members. However, by 1848 all four states had come around to electing their representatives by districts.

Origins of the Gerrymander

The practice of "gerrymandering"—the excessive manipulation of the shape of a legislative district to benefit certain persons or groups—is probably as old as the Republic, but the name originated in 1812.

In that year the Massachusetts Legislature carved out of Essex County a district which historian John Fiske said had a "dragonlike contour." When the painter Gilbert Stuart saw the misshapen district, he penciled in a head, wings, and claws and exclaimed: "That will do for a salamander!"—to which editor Benjamin Russell replied: "Better say a Gerrymander"—after Elbridge Gerry, then governor of Massachusetts.

By the 1990s the term had broadened to include the modern-day practice of drawing maps to benefit racial and ethnic groups. In the past the term was applied largely to districts drawn to benefit incumbents or political parties.

The next challenge a representative encountered over federal districting laws occurred in 1901. A charge was leveled that the existing Kentucky redistricting law did not comply with the reapportionment law of 1901; the charge aimed at preventing the seating of Rep. George G. Gilbert, D, of Kentucky's Eighth District. The committee assigned to investigate the matter turned aside the challenge, asserting that the federal act was not binding on the states. The reasons given were practical and political:

Your committee are therefore of opinion that a proper construction of the Constitution does not warrant the conclusion that by that instrument Congress is clothed with power to determine the boundaries of Congressional districts, or to revise the acts of a State Legislature in fixing such boundaries; and your committee is further of opinion that even if such power is to be implied from the language of the Constitution, it would be in the last degree unwise and intolerable that it should exercise it. To do so would be to put into the hands of Congress

the ability to disfranchise, in effect, a large body of the electors. It would give Congress the power to apply to all the States, in favor of one party, a general system of gerrymandering. It is true that the same method is to a large degree resorted to by the several states, but the division of political power is so general and diverse that notwithstanding the inherent vice of the system of gerrymandering, some kind of equality of distribution results.[12]

In 1908 the Virginia legislature transferred Floyd County from the Fifth District to the Sixth District. As a result, the population of the Fifth was reduced from 175,579 to 160,191 and that of the Sixth was increased from 181,571 to 196,959. The average for the state was 185,418. The newly elected representative from the Fifth District, Edward W. Saunders, D, was challenged by his opponent in the election on the ground that the Virginia law of 1908 was null and void because it did not conform with the federal reapportionment law of 1901, or with the constitution of Virginia. Had the district included the counties that were a part of it before enactment of the 1908 state legislation, Saunders's opponent would have had a majority of the votes.

The majority of the congressional investigating committee upheld the challenge and recommended that Saunders's opponent be seated. For the first time, it appeared that the districting legislation would be enforced, but the House did not take action on the committee's report and Saunders was seated.

COURT ACTION ON REDISTRICTING

After the long and desultory battle over reapportionment in the 1920s, those who were unhappy over the inaction of Congress and the state legislatures began taking their cases to court. At first, the protesters had no luck. But as the population disparities grew in both federal and state legislative districts and the Supreme Court began to show a tendency to intervene, the objectors were more successful.

Finally, in a series of decisions beginning in 1962 with *Baker v. Carr* the Court exerted great influence over the redistricting process, ordering that congressional districts as well as state and local legislative districts be drawn so that their populations would be as nearly equal as possible.[13]

Supreme Court's 1932 Decision

Baker v. Carr essentially reversed the direction the Court had taken in 1932. *Wood v. Broom* was a case challenging the constitutionality of a Mississippi redistricting law because it violated the standards of the 1911 federal redistricting act. The question was whether the federal act was still in effect. That law, which required that districts be separate, compact, contiguous, and equally populated, had been neither specifically repealed nor reaffirmed in the 1929 reapportionment act.

Speaking for the Court, Chief Justice Charles Evans Hughes ruled that the 1911 act, in effect, had expired with the approval of the 1929 apportionment act and that the standards of the 1911 act therefore were no longer applicable. The Court reversed the decision of a lower federal court, which had permanently enjoined elections under the new Mississippi redistricting act.

That the Supreme Court upheld a state law that failed to pro-

vide for districts of equal population was almost less important than the minority opinion that the Court should not have heard the case. Justices Louis D. Brandeis, Harlan F. Stone, Owen J. Roberts, and Benjamin N. Cardozo, while concurring in the majority opinion, said they would have dismissed the *Wood* case for "want of equity." The "want-of-equity" phrase in this context suggested a policy of judicial self-limitation with respect to the entire question of judicial involvement in essentially "political" questions.

"Political Thicket"

Not until 1946, in *Colegrove v. Green*, did the Court again rule in a significant case dealing with congressional redistricting. The case was brought by Kenneth Colegrove, a political science professor at Northwestern University, who alleged that congressional districts in Illinois, which varied between 112,116 and 914,053 in population, were so unequal that they violated the Fourteenth Amendment's guarantee of equal protection of the laws. A seven-member Supreme Court divided 4–3 in dismissing the suit.

Justice Felix Frankfurter gave the opinion of the Court, speaking for himself and Justices Stanley F. Reed and Harold H. Burton. Frankfurter's opinion cited *Wood v. Broom* to indicate that Congress had deliberately removed the standard set by the 1911 act. He also said that he, Reed, and Burton agreed with the minority that the Court should have dismissed the case. The issue, Frankfurter said, was of

a peculiarly political nature and therefore not meant for judicial interpretation. . . . The short of it is that the Constitution has conferred upon Congress exclusive authority to secure fair representation by the states in the popular House and has left to that House determination whether states have fulfilled their responsibility. If Congress failed in exercising its powers, whereby standards of fairness are offended, the remedy lies ultimately with the people. . . . To sustain this action would cut very deep into the very being of Congress. Courts ought not to enter this political thicket. The remedy for unfairness in districting is to secure state legislatures that will apportion properly, or to invoke the ample powers of Congress.

Frankfurter also said that the Court could not affirmatively remap congressional districts and that elections at large would be politically undesirable.

In a dissenting opinion Justice Hugo L. Black, joined by Justices William O. Douglas and Frank Murphy, maintained that the district court did have jurisdiction over congressional redistricting. The three justices cited as evidence a section of the U.S. Code that allowed district courts to redress deprivations of constitutional rights occurring through action of the states. Black's opinion also rested on an earlier case in which the Court had indicated that federal constitutional questions, unless "frivolous," fall under the jurisdiction of the federal courts. Black asserted that the appellants had standing to sue and that the population disparities violated the equal protection clause of the Fourteenth Amendment.

With the Court split 3–3 on whether the judiciary had or should exercise jurisdiction, Justice Wiley B. Rutledge cast the deciding vote in *Colegrove v. Green*. On the question of justicia-

Gerrymandering: The Shape of the House

There are basically three types of gerrymanders. One is the partisan gerrymander, where a single party draws the lines to its advantage. Another is the proincumbent (sometimes called the "bipartisan" or "sweetheart") gerrymander, where the lines are drawn to protect incumbents, with any gains or losses in the number of seats shared between the two parties. In states where control of the state government is divided, proincumbent gerrymanders are common.

A third form of gerrymandering is race-based, where lines are drawn to favor the election of candidates from particular racial or ethnic groups. Initially, racial redistricting referred to the practice of drawing lines to scatter minority voters across several districts, so they would not have a dominant influence in any. But the impact of the 1965 Voting Rights Act and numerous court rulings has resulted in a new version of racial gerrymandering: designing constituencies to concentrate minority voters. These majority-minority districts are more likely to elect a minority candidate.

Sweetheart gerrymandering rarely attracts much attention. But this method of mapping has a powerful effect on the House. "Districts get more Democratic for Democrats and more Republican for Republicans. Competition is minimized," said Bernard Grofman, a political scientist at the University of California at Irvine. Incumbent reelection rates have been high since World War II, in part because a proincumbent spin in much of the line drawing diminishes the prospects for dramatic change in the House's membership.

Still, redistricting at least increases the possibility of turnover because most states must redraw their districts to accommodate population shifts within the state as well as the gain or loss of any seats. Typically, some House members choose to retire rather than stand for election in redesigned districts.

Partisan gerrymanders do not always achieve their goals. Indiana Republicans redrew their map in 1981 with the hope that it would turn the Democrats' congressional majority into a 7–3 Republican edge. Instead, by the end of the decade Democrats held a 7–3 advantage.

But without question, gerrymandering during redistricting is an important determinant of which party controls the House. Many political analysts predicted that the 1980 reapportionment would alter the political makeup of the House because most of the states that lost seats tended to favor liberal Democrats, while the states that gained seats were more likely to favor Republicans or conservative Democrats. But in part because of Democrats' gerrymandering successes in the state redistricting battles, their party remained in control of the House throughout the 1980s.

In the 1990 reapportionment, the shift of House seats to more conservative areas in the South and West continued, but successful gerrymandering by Democrats helped the party hold its House majority in 1992. Finally in 1994 a broad surge of support for Republican candidates helped the GOP take control of the House. Population changes recorded in the 2000 census showed a continuing trend toward states that have voted more Republican than Democratic in recent years. Some of these states received additional House members under the 2000 reapportionment. As a result, the redistricting following the new census—particularly within Republican leaning states—was expected to be a highly contentious exercise beginning in 2001.

---

bility, Rutledge agreed with Black, Douglas, and Murphy that the issue could be considered by the federal courts. Thus a majority of the Court participating in the *Colegrove* case felt that congressional redistricting cases were justiciable.

Yet on the question of granting relief in this specific instance, Rutledge agreed with Frankfurter, Reed, and Burton that the case should be dismissed. He pointed out that four of the nine justices in *Wood v. Broom* had felt that dismissal should be for want of equity. Rutledge saw a "want-of-equity" situation in *Colegrove v. Green* as well. "I think the gravity of the constitutional questions raised [are] so great, together with the possibility of collision [with the political departments of the government], that the admonition [against avoidable constitutional decision] is appropriate to be followed here," Rutledge said. Jurisdiction, he thought, should be exercised "only in the most compelling circumstances." He thought that "the shortness of time remaining [before the forthcoming election] makes it doubtful whether action could or would be taken in time to secure for petitioners the effective relief they seek." Rutledge warned that congressional elections at large would deprive citizens of representation by districts, "which the prevail-

ing policy of Congress demands." In the case of at-large elections, he said, "the cure sought may be worse than the disease." For all these reasons he concluded that the case was "one in which the Court may properly, and should, decline to exercise its jurisdiction."

Changing Views

In the ensuing years, law professors, political scientists, and other commentators increasingly criticized the *Colegrove* doctrine and grew impatient with the Supreme Court's reluctance to intervene in redistricting disputes. At the same time, the membership of the Court was changing, and the new members were more inclined toward judicial action on redistricting.

In the 1950s the Court decided two cases that laid some groundwork for its subsequent reapportionment decisions. The first was *Brown v. Board of Education*, the historic school desegregation case, in which the Court decided that an individual citizen could assert a right to equal protection of the laws under the Fourteenth Amendment, contrary to the "separate but equal" doctrine of public facilities for white and black citizens.

How Should the Census Count the Population?

Counting the number of people in the United States has never been as easy as one, two, three, and that is not just because of logistical problems. When it comes to the decennial census, the political stakes are huge, and so is the interest in how the count is conducted. The constitutionally mandated census not only provides crucial information for reapportioning U.S. House seats among the states, but it also supplies the data for drawing district boundaries for state and local public officials and for determining how billions in federal spending is distributed through dozens of grant programs, including Medicaid, educational assistance to poor children, community development block grants, and job training.

Questions about the accuracy of the census are as old as the Republic. A 1998 report issued by the General Accounting Office (GAO) said, "The census has never counted 100 percent of those it should, in part, because American sensibilities would probably not tolerate more foolproof census-taking methods." For instance, the census could be made more precise if people were required to register with the government. But even proposing such a mandate would stir a huge public fuss.

Disputes over the accuracy of the census have intensified since 1911, when Congress fixed the number of representatives at 435. Since then, a gain of representation in any one state can come only at the loss of representation in another. After the 1920 census showed for the first time that the majority of Americans lived in cities, rural interests objected that the farm population had been undercounted. They pressed their case with such tenacity that legislation reapportioning House seats for the 1920s never passed. In 1941 concerns about the accuracy of the census arose when the number of men turning out for the wartime draft was considerably higher than expectations based on the 1940 census.

In the latter years of the twentieth century, there was intense controversy about the census' undercounting of certain groups, especially minorities. It became more difficult for government census takers to make an accurate population count in crowded inner-city neighborhoods and in some sparsely settled rural areas. The undercount issue became a particular concern for major cities and for the Democrats who tended to represent them. They were in the forefront of an effort to persuade the Census Bureau to use a statistical method to adjust the census for the undercount.

The Census Bureau estimated that it did not count 1.4 percent of the total population in 1980, including roughly 5.9 percent of the nation's blacks. In 1991 Commerce Secretary Robert A. Mosbacher, serving in the administration of Republican president George Bush, said that he would not adjust the 1990 census, even though a postcensus survey found that blacks were undercounted by 4.8 percent, Native Americans by 5 percent, and Hispanics by 5.2 percent. Mosbacher said he was "deeply troubled" by the disproportionate undercount of minorities but decided that sticking with the head count would be "fairest for all Americans."

Several states and cities pursued the matter in court, pressing a suit requesting a statistical adjustment of the census to compensate for the undercount. A 1996 Supreme Court ruling went against them.

By then, though, Democrat Bill Clinton was in the White House, and the Census Bureau was laying the groundwork for a 2000 census that bureau officials said would produce a more accurate count by combining traditional head-tallying methods with large-scale use of statistical sampling techniques. Their plan was to count at least 90 percent of the people in each census tract by tabulating surveys returned in the mail and sending census-takers to interview those who did not respond by mail. Then the remaining population would be estimated by statistically extrapolating the demographics of 750,000 randomly selected homes nationwide.

However, this proposal met with fierce resistance in the Republican-controlled Congress. The GOP majority complained that sampling was unconstitutional and open to political manipulation. "Our Constitution calls for an 'actual enumeration' of citizens, not just an educated guess by Washington bureaucrats," Rep. John A.

Six years later, in *Gomillion v. Lightfoot*, the Court held that the Alabama legislature could not draw the city limits of Tuskegee so as to exclude nearly every black vote. In his opinion Justice Frankfurter drew a clear line between redistricting challenges based on the Fourteenth Amendment, such as *Colegrove*, and challenges to discriminatory redistricting based on the Fifteenth Amendment's voting rights protections, as in *Gomillion*. But Justice Charles E. Whittaker said that the equal protection clause was the proper constitutional basis for the decision. One commentator later remarked that *Gomillion* amounted to a "dragon" in the "political thicket" of *Colegrove*.

By 1962 only three members of the *Colegrove* Court remained: Justices Black and Douglas, dissenters in that case, and Justice Frankfurter, aging spokesperson for restraint in the exercise of judicial power.

By then it was clear that malapportionment within the states no longer could be ignored. By 1960 not a single state legislative body existed in which there was not at least a 2-to-1 population disparity between the most and the least heavily populated districts. For example, the disparity was 242–1 in the Connecticut House, 223–1 in the Nevada Senate, 141–1 in the Rhode Island Senate, and 9–1 in the Georgia Senate. Studies of the effective vote of large and small counties in state legislatures between 1910 and 1960 showed that the effective vote of the most populous counties had slipped while their percentage of the national population had more than doubled. The most lightly populated counties, on the other hand, advanced from a position of slight overrepresentation to one of extreme overrepresentation, holding almost twice as many seats as they would be entitled to by population size alone. Predictably, the rural-dominated state legislatures resisted every move toward reapportioning state legislative districts to reflect new population patterns.

Boehner, R-Ohio, said. Democrats in Congress retorted that conservatives opposed statistical sampling because they feared it would cost the GOP seats in the House. "They believe not counting certain minorities and the poor is to their political advantage," said Rep. Carolyn B. Maloney, D-N.Y.

With the Republican House and the Democratic White House at a standoff on allowing statistical sampling in the 2000 census, the dispute headed to the courts. When the Supreme Court heard arguments on the case in late 1998, justices expressed reluctance to get involved in what looked essentially like a partisan fight.

In January 1999 in *Department of Commerce v. House of Representatives,* the court issued an equivocal 5–4 ruling that seemed likely to spur further litigation. Pleasing Republicans, the court majority said that amendments to the Census Act added in 1976 forbade "the use of sampling in calculating the population for purposes of apportionment." House Speaker Dennis Hastert, R-Ill., declared, "The administration should abandon its illegal and risky polling scheme and start preparing for a true head count."

But Democrats took some solace in the Court majority's position that the Census Act "required" that sampling be used for other purposes (such as establishing the population formulas used to distribute some federal grant monies) if the Census Bureau and the secretary of commerce deem it "feasible."

The ruling led the Clinton administration to plot a course to produce two sets of numbers in the 2000 census—a count based on traditional methods to be used for reapportionment, and an adjusted count to be used for distributing federal money and other purposes, possibly including redistricting within the states. That decision drew a harsh response from Republicans in Congress. Rep. Dan Miller, R-Fla., chairman of the House Census Committee, said, "It will absolutely be a disaster if we have a two-number census. . . . If we try to divide the census, we'll have two failed censuses."

Democrats, and racial and ethnic minority groups, pressed hard for the Census Bureau to adjust the numbers of the 2000 count statistically for purposes of redistricting within states, but were not optimistic that the White House—by then back in the control of Re-

publicans—would do this. But in early March 2001 Census Bureau professionals unexpectedly said they could not guarantee that an adjusted number for redistricting would be any better than the actual head count Republicans favored using. The professionals said unresolved issues in using statistical adjustment could not be solved before the legal deadline of April 1, 2001, to release redistricting data to the states.

Illegal Aliens

Members of Congress and other public officials also have taken a strong interest in the traditional inclusion of illegal aliens in the census. Some complain that the Census Bureau's effort to count all people living in the United States has unfair political ramifications.

The Fourteenth Amendment states that "representatives shall be apportioned among the several states according to their respective numbers, counting the whole number of persons in each state, excluding Indians not taxed." The Census Bureau has never attempted to exclude illegal aliens from the census—a policy troubling to states that fear losing House seats and clout to states with large numbers of illegal aliens.

The Census Bureau does not have a method for excluding illegal aliens, although it has studied some alternatives. Some supporters of the current policy say that any questions used to separate out illegal aliens could discourage others from responding, thus undermining the accuracy of the census.

Overseas Personnel

For the 1990 census the Commerce Department reversed a longstanding policy and counted military personnel and dependents stationed overseas. "Historically we have not included them because the census is based on the concept of usual residence," said Charles Jones, associate director of the Census Bureau. "People overseas have a 'usual residence' overseas." An exception was made once in 1970 during the Vietnam War. This policy was continued in the 2000 census. For the purposes of reapportionment, overseas personnel were assigned to the state each individual considered home.

Population imbalance among congressional districts was substantially lopsided but by no means so gross. In Texas the 1960 census showed the most heavily populated district had four times as many inhabitants as the most lightly populated. Arizona, Maryland, and Ohio each had at least one district with three times as many inhabitants as the least populated. In most cases rural areas benefited from the population imbalance in congressional districts. As a result of the postwar population movement out of central cities to the surrounding areas, the suburbs were the most underrepresented.

Baker v. Carr

Against this background a group of Tennessee city dwellers successfully broke the long-standing precedent against federal court involvement in legislative apportionment problems. For more than half a century, since 1901, the Tennessee legislature

had refused to reapportion itself, even though a decennial reapportionment based on population was specifically required by the state's constitution. In the meantime, Tennessee's population had grown and shifted dramatically to urban areas. By 1960 the House legislative districts ranged from 3,454 to 36,031 in population, while the Senate districts ranged from 39,727 to 108,094. Appeals by urban residents to the rural-controlled Tennessee legislature proved fruitless. A suit brought in the state courts to force reapportionment was rejected on grounds that the courts should stay out of legislative matters.

City dwellers then appealed to the federal courts, stating that they had no redress: the legislature had refused to act for more than half a century, the state courts had refused to intervene, and Tennessee had no referendum or initiative laws. They charged that there was "a debasement of their votes by virtue of the incorrect, obsolete and unconstitutional apportionment" to

such an extent that they were being deprived of their right to equal protection of the laws under the Fourteenth Amendment.

The Supreme Court on March 26, 1962, handed down its historic decision in *Baker v. Carr,* ruling 6–2 in favor of the Tennessee city dwellers. In the majority opinion, Justice William J. Brennan Jr., emphasized that the federal judiciary had the power to review the apportionment of state legislatures under the Fourteenth Amendment's equal protection clause. "The mere fact that a suit seeks protection as a political right," Brennan wrote, "does not mean that it presents a political question" that the courts should avoid.

In a vigorous dissent, Justice Frankfurter said the majority decision constituted "a massive repudiation of the experience of our whole past" and was an assertion of "destructively novel judicial power." He contended that the lack of any clear basis for relief "catapults the lower courts" into a "mathematical quagmire." Frankfurter insisted that "there is not under our Constitution a judicial remedy for every political mischief." Appeal for relief, Frankfurter maintained, should not be made in the courts, but "to an informed civically militant electorate."

The Court had abandoned the view that malapportionment questions were outside its competence. But it stopped there and in *Baker v. Carr* did not address the merits of the challenge to the legislative districts, stating only that federal courts had the power to resolve constitutional challenges to maldistribution of voters among districts.

Gray v. Sanders

The one-person, one-vote rule was set out by the Court almost exactly one year after its decision in *Baker v. Carr.* But the case in which the announcement came did not involve congressional districts.

In *Gray v. Sanders* the Court found that Georgia's county-unit primary system for electing state officials—a system that weighted votes to give advantage to rural districts in statewide primary elections—denied voters equal protection of the laws. All votes in a statewide election must have equal weight, the Court held:

How then can one person be given twice or 10 times the voting power of another person in a statewide election merely because he lives in a rural area or because he lives in the smallest rural county? Once the geographical unit for which a representative is to be chosen is designated, all who participate in the election are to have an equal vote—whatever their race, whatever their sex, whatever their occupation, whatever their income, and wherever their home may be in that geographical unit. This is required by the Equal Protection Clause of the Fourteenth Amendment. The concept of "we the people" under the Constitution visualizes no preferred class of voters but equality among those who meet the basic qualification. The idea that every voter is equal to every other voter in his State, when he casts his ballot in favor of one of several competing candidates, underlies many of our decisions. . . . The conception of political equality from the Declaration of Independence to Lincoln's Gettysburg Address, to the Fifteenth, Seventeenth, and Nineteenth Amendments can mean only one thing—one person, one vote.

The Rule Applied

The Court's rulings in *Baker* and *Gray* concerned the equal weighting and counting of votes cast in state elections. In 1964,

deciding the case of *Wesberry v. Sanders,* the Court applied the one-person, one-vote principle to congressional districts and set equality as the standard for congressional redistricting.

Shortly after the *Baker* decision was handed down, James P. Wesberry Jr., an Atlanta resident and a member of the Georgia Senate, filed suit in federal court in Atlanta claiming that gross disparity in the population of Georgia's congressional districts violated Fourteenth Amendment rights of equal protection of the laws. At the time, Georgia districts ranged in population from 272,154 in the rural Ninth District in the northeastern part of the state to 823,860 in the Fifth District in Atlanta and its suburbs. District lines had not been changed since 1931. The state's number of House seats remained the same in the interim, but Atlanta's district population—already high in 1931 compared with the others—had more than doubled in thirty years, making a Fifth District vote worth about one-third that of a vote in the Ninth.

In June 1962 the three-judge federal court divided 2–1 in dismissing Wesberry's suit. The majority reasoned that the precedent of *Colegrove* still controlled in congressional district cases. The judges cautioned against federal judicial interference with Congress and against "depriving others of the right to vote" if the suit should result in at-large elections. They suggested that the Georgia legislature (under court order to reapportion itself) or the U.S. Congress might better provide relief. Wesberry then appealed to the Supreme Court.

On February 17, 1964, the Supreme Court ruled in *Wesberry v. Sanders* that congressional districts must be substantially equal in population. The Court, which upheld Wesberry's challenge by a 6–3 decision, based its ruling on the history and wording of Article I, Section 2, of the Constitution, which states that representatives shall be apportioned among the states according to their respective numbers and be chosen by the people of the several states. This language, the Court stated, meant that "as nearly as is practicable, one man's vote in a congressional election is to be worth as much as another's."

The majority opinion, written by Justice Black and supported by Chief Justice Earl Warren and Justices Brennan, Douglas, Arthur J. Goldberg, and Byron R. White, said: "While it may not be possible to draw congressional districts with mathematical precision, that is no excuse for ignoring our Constitution's plain objective of making equal representation for equal numbers of people the fundamental goal for the House of Representatives."

In a strongly worded dissent, Justice John M. Harlan asserted that the Constitution did not establish population as the only criterion of congressional districting but left the matter to the discretion of the states, subject only to the supervisory power of Congress. "The constitutional right which the Court creates is manufactured out of whole cloth," Harlan concluded.

The *Wesberry* opinion established no precise standards for districting beyond declaring that districts must be as nearly equal in population "as is practicable." In his dissent Harlan suggested that a disparity of more than 100,000 between a state's largest and smallest districts would "presumably" violate the equality standard enunciated by the majority. On that basis, Harlan estimated, the districts of thirty-seven states with 398

representatives would be unconstitutional, "leaving a constitutional House of 37 members now sitting."

Neither did the Court's decision make any reference to gerrymandering, since it discussed only the population, not the shape of districts. In a separate opinion handed down the same day as *Wesberry,* the Court dismissed a challenge to congressional districts in New York City, which had been brought by voters who charged that Manhattan's "silk-stocking" Seventeenth District had been gerrymandered to exclude blacks and Puerto Ricans.

Strict Equality

Five years elapsed between *Wesberry* and the Court's next application of constitutional standards to congressional districting. In 1967 the Court hinted at the strict stance it would adopt two years later. With two unsigned opinions, the Court sent back to Indiana and Missouri for revision those two states' congressional redistricting plans because they allowed variations of as much as 20 percent from the average district population.

Two years later Missouri's revised plan returned to the Court for full review. By a 6–3 vote, the Court rejected the plan. It was unacceptable, the Court held in *Kirkpatrick v. Preisler,* because it allowed a variation of as much as 3.1 percent from perfectly equal population districts. Thus the Court made clear its stringent application of the one-person, one-vote rule to congressional districts.

There was no "fixed numerical or percentage population variance small enough to be considered *de minimis* and to satisfy without question the 'as nearly as practicable' standard," Justice Brennan wrote for the Court. "Equal representation for equal numbers of people is a principle designed to prevent debasement of voting power and diminution of access to elected Representatives. Toleration of even small deviations detracts from these purposes."

The only permissible variances in population, the Court ruled, were those that were unavoidable despite the effort to achieve absolute equality or those that could be legally justified. The variances in Missouri could have been avoided, the Court said.

None of Missouri's arguments for the plan qualified as "legally acceptable" justifications. The Court rejected the argument that population variance was necessary to allow representation of distinct interest groups. It said that acceptance of such variances to produce districts with specific interests was "antithetical" to the basic purpose of equal representation.

Justice White dissented from the majority opinion, which he characterized as "an unduly rigid and unwarranted application of the Equal Protection Clause which will unnecessarily involve the courts in the abrasive task of drawing district lines." White added that some "acceptably small" population variance could be established. He indicated that considerations of existing political boundaries and geographical compactness could justify to him some variation from "absolute equality" of population.

Justice Harlan, joined by Justice Potter Stewart, dissented, saying that "whatever room remained under this Court's prior decisions for the free play of the political process in matters of reapportionment is now all but eliminated by today's Draconian judgments."

PRACTICAL RESULTS

As a result of the Court's decisions of the 1960s, nearly every state was forced to redraw its congressional district lines—sometimes more than once. By the end of the decade, thirty-nine of the forty-five states with more than one representative had made the necessary adjustments.

However, the effect of the one-person, one-vote standard on congressional districts did not bring about immediate population equality in districts. Most of the new districts were far from equal in population, because the only official population figures came from the 1960 census. Massive population shifts during the decade rendered most post-*Wesberry* efforts to achieve equality useless.

But redistricting based on the 1970 census resulted in districts that differed only slightly in population from the state average. Among House members elected in 1972, 385 of 435 represented districts that varied by less than 1 percent from the state average district population.

By contrast, only nine of the districts in the Eighty-eighth Congress (elected in 1962) deviated less than 1 percent from the state average; eighty-one were between 1 and 5 percent; eighty-seven from 5 to 10 percent; and in 236 districts the deviation was 10 percent or greater. Twenty-two House members were elected at large.

The Supreme Court made only one major ruling concerning congressional districts during the 1970s. In 1973 the Court declared the Texas congressional districts, as redrawn in 1971, unconstitutional because of excessive population variance among districts. The variance between the largest and smallest districts was 4.99 percent. The Court returned the case to a three-judge federal panel, which adopted a new congressional district plan.

Precise Equality

Following the 1980 census, several federal courts accepted or imposed redistricting maps that achieved population equality but were drawn for blatant partisan purposes. In Missouri a federal court accepted the Democrats' remap proposal over the Republican plan because its districts were more nearly equal in population. The Democratic map obtained population equality by dismantling a district in a part of the state where population was growing and preserving a district in inner-city St. Louis that had been losing population. The plan cost one Republican incumbent his seat.

Michigan's map for the 1980s offered an extreme example of fealty to precise population equality. In 1982 a court-imposed redistricting plan created sixteen congressional districts with exactly equal populations—514,560. The state's two other districts each had a population of just one person fewer—514,559. To achieve that equality, however, the line for many districts cut through many small cities and towns, dividing their residents between two or three different districts.

Although maps such as these raised the question whether partisan gerrymandering was also a violation of an individual's voting rights, the Supreme Court in 1983 appeared to make it

even more difficult to challenge a redistricting map on grounds other than population deviation. In a 5–4 decision, the Court ruled in *Karcher v. Daggett* that states must adhere as closely as possible to the one-person, one-vote standard and bear the burden of proving that deviations from precise population equality were made in pursuit of a legitimate goal. The decision overturned New Jersey's congressional map because the variation between the most populated and the least populated districts was 0.69 percent.

Brennan, who wrote the Court's opinion in *Baker* and *Kirkpatrick*, also wrote the opinion in *Karcher*, contending that population differences between districts "could have been avoided or significantly reduced with a good-faith effort to achieve population equality."

"Adopting any standard other than population equality, using the best census data available, would subtly erode the Constitution's ideal of equal representation," Brennan wrote. "In this case, appellants argue that a maximum deviation of approximately 0.7 percent should be considered *de minimis*. If we accept that argument, how are we to regard deviations of 0.8 percent, 0.95 percent, 1.0 percent or 1.1 percent? . . . To accept the legitimacy of unjustified, though small population deviations in this case would mean to reject the basic premise of *Kirkpatrick* and *Wesberry*."

Brennan said that "any number of consistently applied legislative policies might justify" some population variation. These included "making districts compact, respecting municipal boundaries, preserving the cores of prior districts, and avoiding contests between incumbent Representatives." However, he cautioned, the state must show "with some specificity that a particular objective required the specific deviations in its plan, rather than simply relying on general assertions."

In his dissent Justice White criticized the majority for its "unreasonable insistence on an unattainable perfection in the equalizing of congressional districts." He warned that the decision would invite "further litigation of virtually every congressional redistricting plan in the nation."

Partisan Gerrymandering

In *Karcher* the Court did not address the underlying political issue in the New Jersey case, which was that its map had been drawn to serve Democratic interests. As a partisan gerrymander, the map had few peers, boasting some of the most oddly shaped districts in the country. One constituency, known as the "fishhook" by its detractors, twisted through central New Jersey's industrial landscape, picking up Democratic voters along the way. Another stretched from the suburbs of New York to the fringes of Trenton.

In separate dissents Justices Lewis F. Powell Jr., and John Paul Stevens broadly hinted that they were willing to hear constitutional challenges to instances of partisan gerrymandering. "A legislator cannot represent his constituents properly—nor can voters from a fragmented district exercise the ballot intelligently—when a voting district is nothing more than an artificial unit divorced from, and indeed often in conflict with, the various communities established in the State," wrote Powell.

The national census is conducted every ten years to determine, among other things, how many representatives each state will have in Congress. Here a census taker prepares to collect information in person.

The Court's opportunity to address that issue came in *Davis v. Bandemer.* On June 30, 1986, the Court ruled that political gerrymanders are subject to constitutional review by federal courts, even if the disputed districts meet the one-person, one-vote test. The case arose from a challenge by Indiana Democrats who argued that the Republican-drawn map so heavily favored the Republican Party that Democrats were denied appropriate representation. But the Court rejected the Democrats' challenge to the alleged gerrymander, saying that one election was insufficient to prove unconstitutional discrimination. Left unclear were what standards the Court would use to find a partisan gerrymander legally unacceptable.

National Republicans expressed delight with the *Bandemer*

decision. The GOP had long held that Democratic control over most state legislatures had allowed them to draw congressional and legislative districts to their partisan advantage. In particular, Republicans expressed confidence that the *Bandemer* decision lay the groundwork for overturning California's congressional district map, created by Democratic Rep. Phillip Burton in the early 1980s.

Widely recognized as a classic example of a partisan gerrymander, the map featured a number of oddly shaped districts, drawn neither compactly nor with respect to community boundaries, but all with nearly equal populations. As one commentator described it, "Burton carefully stretched districts from one Democratic enclave to another—sometimes joining them with nothing but a bridge, a stretch of harbor, or a spit of land . . .—avoiding Republicans block for block and household for household."[14] Before the 1982 elections, Democrats held twenty-two congressional districts, Republicans twenty-one. With the Burton map in place for the 1982 elections, Democrats held twenty-eight seats, Republicans only seventeen.

Republican Rep. Robert E. Badham filed a lawsuit against the Burton plan in federal district court in 1983. In the wake of the *Bandemer* decision, that court held a hearing on *Badham v. Eu* but dismissed the Republican complaint by a 2–1 vote. The court in essence ruled that a party seeking to overturn a gerrymandered map must show a general pattern of exclusion from the political process, which the California Republican Party, in control of the governorship, a Senate seat, and 40 percent of the House seats, could not do. The Republicans appealed to the Supreme Court, but the Court refused to become involved, voting 6–3 in 1989 to reaffirm the lower court's decision without comment.

MINORITY REPRESENTATION

One form of gerrymandering is expressly forbidden by law: redistricting for the purpose of racial discrimination. The Voting Rights Act of 1965, extended in 1970, 1975, and 1982, banned redistricting that diluted the voting strength of black communities. Other minorities, including Hispanics, Asian-Americans, American Indians, and native Alaskans, subsequently were brought under the protection of the law.

In 1980 the Supreme Court for the first time narrowed the reach of the Voting Rights Act in the case of *Mobile v. Bolden*, a challenge to the at-large system of electing city commissioners used in Mobile, Alabama.[15] By a vote of 6–3, the Court ruled that proof of discriminatory intent by the commissioners was necessary before a violation could be found; the fact that no black had ever been elected under the challenged system was not proof enough.

The *Mobile* decision set off an immediate reaction on Capitol Hill. In extending the Voting Rights Act in 1982, Congress amended it to outlaw any practice that has the effect of discriminating against blacks or other minorities—regardless of the lawmakers' intent.

The Justice Department later adopted a similar "results test" for another part of the act (Section 5), which requires certain states and localities with a history of discrimination to have their electoral plans "precleared" by the department. In 1986 the Supreme Court applied this test in *Thornburg v. Gingles*, ruling that six of North Carolina's multimember legislative districts impermissibly diluted black voting strength. Sharply departing from *Mobile*, the Court held that since very few blacks had been elected from these districts, the system must be in violation of the law.

The Court also used the *Thornburg* decision to develop three criteria that, if met, should lead to the creation of a minority legislative district: the minority group must be large and geographically compact enough to constitute a majority in a single-member electoral district; the group must be politically cohesive; and the white majority must vote as a bloc to the degree that it usually can defeat candidates preferred by the minority.

Thus, within a period of ten years the burden of proof was shifted from minorities, who had been required to show that lines were being drawn to dilute their voting strength, to lawmakers, who had to show that they had done all they could to maximize minority voting strength.

But maps drawn for the 1990s that went to extraordinary lengths to elect minorities came quickly under scrutiny by the Supreme Court. In a 1993 ruling on districts in North Carolina *Shaw v. Reno*, Justice Sandra Day O'Connor wrote for the Court majority that any map that groups people "who may have little in common with one another but the color of their skin bears an uncomfortable resemblance to political apartheid." The ruling reinstated a suit by five white North Carolinians who contended that the state's congressional district map, which created two oddly shaped majority-minority districts, violated their right to "equal protection under law" by diluting their votes.

And in a 1995 case involving districts in Georgia *Miller v. Johnson*, the Court ruled that using race as "the predominant factor" in drawing districts is presumed to be unconstitutional, unless it serves a compelling government interest. The decision struck down a redistricting plan that created three black-majority districts.

Those two rulings represented a speedy swing of the judicial pendulum away from the 1986 Gingles doctrine of maximizing minority voting strength in redistricting. As the 1990s unfolded, the constitutionality of majority-minority districts was widely challenged, and eventually, federal courts ordered a number of states—including North Carolina, Georgia, Florida, Louisiana, New York, Texas, and Virginia—to redraw districts that were adjudged to be unconstitutional racial gerrymanders.

But the Supreme Court did not make sweeping determinations affecting all majority-minority districts. In Illinois, a majority-minority district was allowed to stand after the state argued successfully that it had a "compelling state interest" in giving Chicago's large Hispanic population the opportunity to elect one representative of its own. And in a 1999 North Carolina case *Hunt v. Cromartie*, the Court unanimously ruled that mapmakers could create a district with a "supermajority" of black Democrats as long as the primary reason for doing so was political rather than racial.

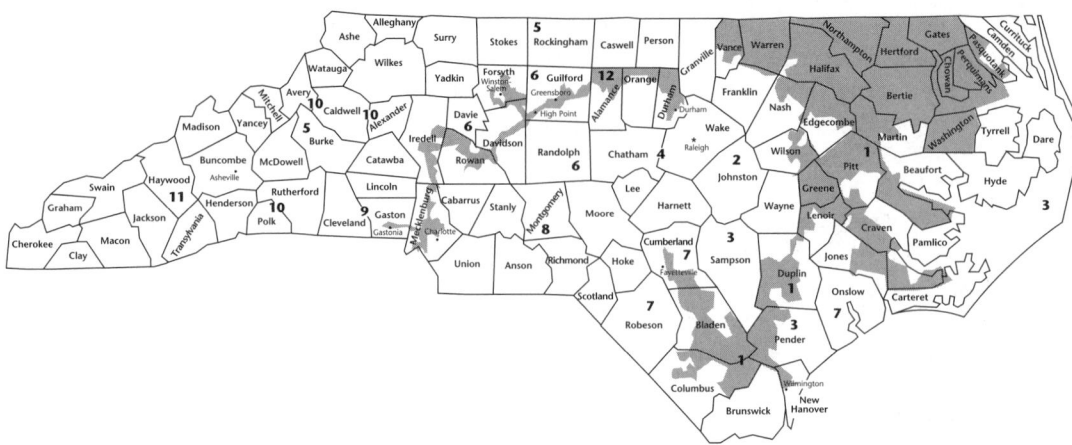

The Supreme Court in 1993 ruled in *Shaw v. Reno* that the bizarrely shaped First and Twelfth Congressional Districts in North Carolina (shaded on map) were unconstitutional because they were too heavily reliant on race.

Even though numerous majority-minority districts were redrawn in the mid- and late-1990s to reduce minority populations, nearly all those districts retained members of minority groups as their representatives by the end of the twentieth century.

CONGRESS AND REDISTRICTING

Congress considered several proposals in the post–World War II period to enact new legislation on redistricting. Only one of these efforts was successful—enactment of a measure barring at-large elections in states with more than one House seat.

In January 1951 President Harry S. Truman asked for a ban on gerrymandering, an end to at-large seats in states having more than one representative, and a sharp reduction in the huge differences in size among congressional districts within most states. On behalf of the administration, Emanuel Celler, D-N.Y., chairman of the House Judiciary Committee, introduced a bill reflecting these requests, but the committee took no action.

Celler regularly introduced his bill throughout the 1950s and early 1960s, but it made no headway until the Supreme Court handed down the *Wesberry* decision in 1964. The House passed a version of the Celler bill in 1965, largely to discourage the Supreme Court from imposing even more rigid criteria. The Senate, however, took no action and the measure died.

In 1967, after defeating a conference report that would have prevented the courts from ordering a state to redistrict or to hold at-large elections until after the 1970 census, Congress approved a measure to ban at-large elections in all states entitled to more than one representative. Exceptions were made for New Mexico and Hawaii, which had a tradition of electing their representatives at large. Both states, however, soon passed dis-

tricting laws, New Mexico for the 1968 elections and Hawaii for 1970.

Bills to increase the size of the House to prevent states from losing seats as a result of population shifts have been introduced after most recent censuses, but Congress has given little consideration to any of them.

Notes

1. Ronald D. Elving, "Redistricting: Drawing Power with a Map," *Editorial Research Reports,* February 15, 1991, 99.

2. Robert Luce, *Legislative Principles* (New York: Houghton Mifflin, 1930; New York: DaCapo Press, 1971), 342.

3. Thomas Jefferson, *The Portable Thomas Jefferson,* ed. Merrill D. Peterson, part 3, *Notes on the State of Virginia* (New York: Viking, 1965), 163.

4. Andrew Hacker, *Congressional Districting: The Issue of Equal Representation,* rev. ed. (Washington, D.C.: Brookings Institution, 1964), 6–7.

5. Max Farrand, ed., *The Records of the Federal Convention of 1787* (New Haven, Conn.: Yale University Press, 1911, 1966), vol. 2, 241.

6. *The Federalist Papers,* with an introduction by Clinton Rossiter (New York: New American Library, 1961), 347–48, 354.

7. Quoted in Laurence F. Schmeckebier, *Congressional Apportionment* (Washington, D.C.: Brookings Institution, 1941), 131.

8. Hacker, *Congressional Districting,* 14.

9. Quoted in Schmeckebier, *Congressional Apportionment,* 113.

10. Zechariah Chafee Jr., "Congressional Reapportionment," *Harvard Law Review* (1929): 1015–1047.

11. Jefferson, *Notes on the State of Virginia,* 217.

12. Schmeckebier, *Congressional Reapportionment,* 137.

13. The following summary is based on *Congressional Quarterly's Guide to the U.S. Supreme Court,* 2nd ed. (Washington, D.C.: Congressional Quarterly, 1990), 483–493.

14. Elving, "Redistricting," 107.

15. The discussion of minority representation is based on Rhodes Cook, "Map-Drawers Must Toe the Line in Upcoming Redistricting," *Congressional Quarterly Weekly Report,* September 1, 1990, 2786–2793.

## CHAPTER 23

House General Election Returns, 1824–2000

GENERAL ELECTION RETURNS for the House of Representatives are presented in this chapter (pages 829–1227). The returns for the years 1824–1973 were obtained from the Inter-University Consortium for Political and Social Research (ICPSR) at the University of Michigan. Major sources for returns for the years 1974–2000 were Congressional Quarterly, which obtained them from the state secretaries of state, and the *America Votes* series, compiled biennially by Congressional Quarterly in Washington, D.C. Richard M. Scammon and Alice V. McGillivray of the Elections Research Center, Washington, D.C., created the series first published in 1956. Since 1996 the series has been compiled by Rhodes Cook.

The symbol # next to returns before 1974 indicates that Congressional Quarterly obtained the returns from a source other than the ICPSR. A complete set of other sources used appears on page 1228. A House Candidates Index is located on pages I-1 to I-111.

While the complete source annotations for the ICPSR collection are too extensive to publish here, information on the sources for specific election returns can be obtained through the ICPSR. *(See box, ICPSR Historical Election Returns File, p. xvi, in Vol. I.)*

PRESENTATION OF RETURNS

The House returns are arranged chronologically by year and alphabetically by state for each year. Within each state, single-member districts are listed first in numerical order. At-large seats appear at the end of the single-member districts with "AL" in the district identification column. Multimember districts, in the few instances in which they appear in the nineteenth century, are listed in numerical order under the separate heading "Multimember Districts."

Special election results appear after all general election returns for each state under a separate "Special Elections" heading. Returns for special off-year elections are listed at the end of the preceding year's general election returns.

MULTIMEMBER DISTRICTS

During part of the nineteenth century, five New England states—Maine, Massachusetts, New Hampshire, Rhode Island, and Vermont—had state laws requiring that candidates win election to the House by a popular vote majority. The specific procedures varied among the five states. The majority vote requirement was last used in 1892 Rhode Island. *(See "Multimember Districts," p. 802.)*

NAMES AND PARTY DESIGNATIONS

Candidate names appear to the right of the district number, with the candidate receiving the highest number of votes listed first. Other candidates who received *at least 5 percent* of the total votes cast are listed in descending order. In multimember districts or at-large districts electing more than one representative, candidates who received fewer than 100 votes were not listed.

In some instances, particularly in the nineteenth century, names in the ICPSR file are incomplete. First names were the element most commonly missing in the original sources consulted by the scholars and archivists who gathered the ICPSR returns. In cases where a vote total is known but there is no name at all, or the name obviously could not be identified, Congressional Quarterly has labeled the votes as being cast for an "Unidentified Candidate."

In the ICPSR returns, the distinct—and in many cases, *multiple*—party designations appearing in the original sources are preserved. In many cases party labels represent combinations of multiparty support received by individual candidates. If, for example, on the ballot and official returns more than one party name was listed next to a candidate's name, then the party designation appearing in the election returns for that candidate will be a unique abbreviation for that combination of parties. *(See "Political Party Abbreviations," p. 1596, in Reference Materials.)*

In the special case of a candidate's name listed separately on the original ballot under more than one party—where returns were reported *separately* for each party—Congressional Quarterly has summed the votes recorded under the several parties and that figure appears as the candidate's total vote. Whenever separate party totals have been summed, a *comma* separates the abbreviations of the parties contributing the largest and second largest share of the total vote.

Most cases of this special situation occurred in New York and Pennsylvania during this century. For example, in the original ICPSR returns for the House election in New York's 10th District in 1938, Emanuel Celler received 31,645 votes as the Democratic Party candidate, 12,181 votes as the American Labor Party candidate and 55 votes as the City Fusion Party candidate, for a total of 43,881 votes. Congressional Quarterly summed all votes received by Celler from these three parties *(see p. 1070)*.

Congressional Quarterly indicated the two parties that contributed the most votes to Celler's total—separated by a comma. Thus, immediately following his name appear the abbreviations (D, AM LAB), indicating that Celler was a candidate of two or more parties and that he received most votes as a Democrat.

VOTE TOTALS AND PERCENTAGES

Each candidate's total vote and percentage of the total vote cast for all candidates appear in columns to the right of the candidate's name and party designation. Percentages have been calculated to two decimal places and rounded to one place. Due to rounding and the scattered votes of minor candidates, percentages in individual House races may not add up to 100.

Only candidates from single-member districts who received *at least 5 percent of the total vote* for that election are included. In multimember districts or at-large districts electing more than one representative, candidates who received fewer than 100 votes were not listed.

If no vote total is shown for a candidate but the percentage listed is 100 percent, in most cases the candidate ran unopposed.

State election officials either did not put the candidate's name on the ballot or simply did not make an effort to record the total number of votes.

No percentages of total vote have been computed for multi-member districts or at-large districts electing more than one representative. Candidates in these types of districts did not run against specific opponents, and in most cases the number of votes cast in any one contest could not be determined.

In some cases, percentages do not appear next to candidates in single-member districts because vote totals for all the candidates who ran in the district were not available even though the names of all candidates may appear. In such cases, the symbol appears in the vote column of the winning candidate.

Explanation of Symbols in House Returns

In the returns for House elections, *symbols* are used to denote special circumstances. Where no symbol is used, the candidate who received the most votes won the election to the House. The following is a key to the symbols used:

✔ Elected to the House. The symbol is used to identify winning candidates in three types of situation: (1) When candidates ran for two or more at-large seats in states that chose all of their at-large representatives in a single election, or ran in a multimember district; (2) when the vote total and percentage of one or more of the candidate are unavailable; and (3) when a candidate who did not receive the highest vote total was seated by the House. *(See "Multimember Districts," p. 802.)*

‡ The symbol is used when an election dispute resulted in the unseating of a representative *after* he or she was sworn in. *(For discussion of specific cases, consult the* Biographical Directory of the American Congress, 1774–1996 (Washington, D.C.: CQ Staff Directories, 1997); hereafter referred to as the *Biographical Directory.)*

* The symbol used for three types of situations: (1) when a representative-elect died or declined a seat before the constitutionally set date for the beginning of his or her term—March 4 until 1935, and January 3 thereafter; (2) when the House refused to seat any candidate claiming election to a seat; and (3) when state law required a candidate to obtain a popular vote majority for election to the House, but the candidate receiving the most votes failed to receive a majority. *(For discussion of specific cases, consult the* Biographical Directory; *See "Majority Elections," p. 801.)*

\# Information for 1824–1973 was obtained from a source other than the Inter-University Consortium for Political and Social Research (ICPSR) *(For a list of the other sources used, see p. 1228.)*

Numbered footnotes are used to explain unusual situations, such as a series of elections in the same year in the same House district, anomalies resulting from reapportionment, and special procedures for conducting House elections in certain states. For elections beginning in 1984, footnotes explain the circumstances surrounding special elections. All footnotes are found at the end of all state returns for a particular year, rather than at the bottom of the page on which the footnote first appears.

1824 House Elections

DELAWARE

	Candidates	Votes	%
AL	Louis McLane (FED)	3,387	51.7
	Arnold Naudain (OLD R)	3,163	48.3

GEORGIA

	Candidates	Votes	%
AL	Wiley Thompson	10,543✓	
	John Forsyth	10,219✓	
	Edward F. Tattnall	10,043✓	
	Alfred Cuthbert	9,950✓	
	George Cary	9,672✓	
	James Meriwether	9,491✓	
	Charles E. Haynes	8,881✓	

Special Election

		Votes	%
AL	Richard H. Wilde	5,002	61.0
	Lyman	3,194	39.0

ILLINOIS

		Votes	%
AL	Daniel P. Cook (NR)	7,425	62.6
	Shadrack Bond	4,409	37.2

INDIANA

		Votes	%
1	Ratliff Boon (JAC D)	4,281	42.1
	Jacob Call	3,222	31.7
	Thomas H. Blake (NR)	2,661	26.2
2	Jonathan Jennings (CLAY R)	4,680	53.2
	Jeremiah Sullivan (NR)	4,119	46.8
3	John Test (NR)	3,434	47.1
	James Brown Ray (CLAY R)	2,471	33.9
	Daniel J. Caswell	1,388	19.0

Special Election

		Votes	%
1	Jacob Call (JAC D)	2,155	50.4
	Thomas H. Blake (NR)	2,087	48.8

KENTUCKY

1	David Trimble (D)	✓
2	Thomas Metcalfe (D)	✓
3	Henry Clay	✓
4	Robert P. Letcher (CD)	✓
5	James Johnson(D)	✓
6	Joseph Lecompte (D)	✓
7	Thomas P. Moore (D)	✓
8	Richard A. Buckner	✓
9	Charles A. Wickliffe (D)	✓
10	Francis Johnson (AD)	✓
11	William S. Young (D)	✓
12	Robert P. Henry (CLAY D)	✓

LOUISIANA

1	Edward Livingston (D)	✓
2	Henry H. Gurley (W)	✓
3	William L. Brent (W)	✓

MAINE

1	William Burleigh (AD)	✓
2	John Anderson (JEFF D)	✓
3	Ebenezer Herrick	✓
4	Peleg Sprague	✓
5	Enoch Lincoln	✓
6	Jeremiah O'Brien (D)	✓
7	David Kidder (W)	✓

MARYLAND

	Candidates	Votes	%
1	Clement Dorsey	1,824	55.3
	Raphael Neale	1,476	44.7
2	Joseph Kent	1,908	52.3
	John C. Weems	1,741	47.7
3	George Peter	1,602	52.5
	George C. Washington	1,448	47.5
4	Thomas Worthington	4,321	55.3
	John Lee	3,491	44.7
6	George Mitchell	2,854	53.9
	Phillip Reed	2,439	46.1
7	John Leeds Kerr	1,950	50.3
	Thomas Emory	1,924	49.7
8	Robert Martin	3,088	51.9
	John Spence	2,858	48.1

Multimember District

		Votes	%
5	Peter Little	9,686✓	
	John Barney	5,515✓	
	Isaac McKim	5,346✓	

MASSACHUSETTS

		Votes	%
1	Daniel Webster (AR)	3,669	99.9
2	Benjamin W. Crowninshield (AR)	1,379	58.1
	Frederick Howes	760	32.0
3	John Varnum	1,736	50.2
	John Merrill	1,659	48.0
4	Edward Everett	1,906	57.2
	Unidentified Candidate	1,357	40.7
5	John Locke (AR)	1,524	60.6
	Joseph G. Kendall	423	16.8
	Tomes	186	7.4
6	Samuel C. Allen (AR)	1,726	55.7
	George Grennell Jr	1,335	43.1
7	Henry W. Dwight (AR)	1,742	54.8
	Nathan Willis	1,375	43.3
8	Tom Lathrop (AR)	1,874	58.2
	James Fowler	1,201	37.3
9	John Bailey	1,669	57.3
	Sher Leland	991	34.0
10	Francis Baylies (JAC R)	1,778	54.8
	James L. Hodges	1,363	42.0
11	John Reed (AR)	1,057	58.2
	Barker Burnell	460	25.3
	Walter Folger	297	16.4
12	Aaron Hobart (AR)	1,606	72.3
	Ebenezer Gay	320	14.4
	William Baylies	263	11.9
13	John Davis (AR)	1,262	51.2
	James Libley	1,195	48.5

MISSOURI

		Votes	%
AL	John Scott (CLAY R)	5,022	47.0
	George F. Strother (JAC D)	4,528	42.4
	Robert Wash	1,125	10.5

NEW HAMPSHIRE[1]

		Votes	%
AL	Ichabod Bartlett	11,603✓	
	Thomas Whipple Jr.	8,690✓	
	James Miller	6,923*	
	Nehemiah Eastman	6,823✓	
	Jonathan Harvey	6,105✓	
	Ezekiel Webster	5,928	
	Joseph Healy	5,479	
	Phinchas Handerson	5,296	
	Titus Brown	5,222	
	Atkinson	4,670	
	Livermore	3,854	
	(Scattering)	801	
	Evans	672	

NEW JERSEY

		Votes	%
AL	George Holcombe (D-R)	17,706✓	
	Samuel Swan (D-R)	17,672✓	
	Lewis Condict (D-R)	17,668✓	
	Daniel Garrison (D-R)	17,595✓	
	George Cassedy (D-R)	17,550✓	
	Ebenezer Tucker (D-R)	17,022✓	

NEW YORK

		Votes	%
1	Silas Wood	2,140	60.5
	James Lent	1,398	39.5
2	Joshua Sands	1,683	53.1
	John T. Bergen	1,484	46.9
4	Aaron Ward	1,586	39.0
	Jonathan Ward	1,297	31.9
	John Hunter	1,188	29.2
5	Bartow White	3,596	52.8
	Peter Livingston	3,210	47.2
6	John Hallock Jr	2,103	47.2
	Hector Craig	1,978	44.4
	Walter Case	374	8.4
7	Abraham Hasbrouck	2,916	51.2
	John Lounsberry	2,781	48.8
8	James Strong	3,129	60.0
	Robert Livingston	2,089	40.0
9	William McManus	3,807	56.6
	George R. Davis	2,925	43.5
10	Stephen Van Rensselaer	3,850	100.0
11	Henry Ashley	3,531	58.4
	William Heermance	2,519	41.6
12	William Deitz	2,810	56.9
	Constant Brown	2,129	43.1
13	William G. Angel	3,379	52.2
	William Campbell	3,094	47.8
14	Henry Storrs	4,146	57.3
	James Lynch	3,094	42.7
15	Michael Hoffman	2,410	52.7
	John Herkimer	2,164	47.3
16	Henry Markell	3,114	54.9
	William Dodge	2,562	45.1
17	John W. Taylor	3,858	100.0
18	Henry C. Martindale	3,448	64.6
	John Gale	1,893	35.4
19	Henry Ross	3,209	52.3
	William Hogan	2,932	47.7
21	Elias Whitmore	3,128	50.4
	Lot Clark	3,073	49.6
22	John Miller	3,857	54.3
	John Lynde	3,243	45.7
23	Luther Badger	3,214	50.8
	Elisha Litchfield	3,116	49.2
24	Charles Kellogg	3,372	53.1
	Rowland Day	2,976	46.9
25	Charles Humphrey	3,144	51.2
	David Woodcook	2,999	48.8
27	Moses Hayden	4,456	59.5
	Charles H. Carroll	3,028	40.5
28	Timothy Porter	2,099	35.3
	William Woods	1,937	32.6
	Daniel Cruger	1,693	28.5
29	Parmenio Adams	4,035	57.6
	Isaac Wilson	2,969	42.4
30	Daniel Garnsey	2,387	35.4
	William Hotchkiss	2,235	33.1
	John G. Camp	2,127	31.5

Multimember Districts

		Votes	%
3	Churchill C. Cambreleng	5,650✓	
	Gulian Verplanck	4,863✓	
	Jeromous Johnson	4,588✓	
	John Rathbone	3,980	
	Charles G. Haines	3,855	
	Peter Sharpe	3,741	
	Henry Wheaton	750	
20	Nicoll Fosdick	5,676✓	
	Egbert Ten Eyck	5,484†	
	Daniel Hugunin Jr.	5,128	
	Horance Allen	5,466	
26	Dudley Marvin	8,366✓	

Candidates	Votes	%
Robert Rose	4,899✓	
John Maynard	4,438	
Aaron Remer	2,732	

OHIO[2]

Candidates	Votes	%
David Jennings	✓	
Mordecai Bartley	✓	
William McLean	✓	
William Wilson	✓	
Philemon Beecher (FED)	✓	
John C. Wright (AD)	✓	
John Sloane (W)	✓	
Elisha Whittlesey (W)	✓	
John Woods (W)	✓	
Samuel F. Vinton (W)	✓	
James Findlay (JAC D)	✓	
John W. Campbell (D)	✓	
John Thomson (D)	✓	
Joseph Vance (D)	✓	

PENNSYLVANIA

	Candidates	Votes	%
1	John Wurts	✓	
2	Joseph Hemphill	✓	
3	Daniel H. Miller	✓	
5	Philip S. Markley	✓	
6	Robert Harris	✓	
	Christian Gleim		
10	James S. Mitchell	✓	

	Candidates	Votes	%
12	John Mitchell	✓	
13	Alexander Thompson	✓	
14	Andrew Stewart	✓	
15	Joseph Lawrence	✓	
16	George Plumer	✓	
	John H. Wise		
18	Patrick Farrelly	✓	

Multimember Districts

	Candidates	Votes	%
4	James Buchanan	✓	
	Charles Miner	✓	
	Samuel Edwards	✓	
	William Anderson		
	Isaac D. Barnard		
	Samuel Houston		
7	William Addams	✓	
	Henry Wilson	✓	
	George Keck		
	Daniel Rose		
8	George Wolf	✓	
	Samuel D. Ingham	✓	
9	Samuel McKean	✓	
	George Kremer	✓	
	Espy Van Horne	✓	
	William Cox Ellis		
11	James Wilson	✓	
	John Findlay	✓	
17	James Allison Jr	✓	
	James S. Stevenson	✓	

SOUTH CAROLINA

	Candidates	Votes	%
1	Joel R. Poinsett (D)	1,474	58.4
	Samuel Warren	1,052	41.7
2	James Hamilton Jr (SR FT)		100.0
3	Thomas R. Mitchell		100.0
4	Andrew R. Govan		100.0
5	Starling Tucker		100.0
6	George McDuffie (D)	✓	
7	Joseph Gist (D)	3,398	54.8
	J. McCreary	1,869	30.2
	F. W. Davie	933	15.1
8	John Wilson	✓	
9	John Carter	1,882	46.3
	Spann	1,132	27.8
	Levy	1,055	25.9

VERMONT

	Candidates	Votes	%
1	William C. Bradley	✓	
2	Rollin C. Mallary	3,284	95.6
3	George E. Wales	✓	
4	Ezra Meech	3,093	54.6
	Benjamin Swift	1,836	32.4
	Stephen Royce	404	7.1
5	John Mattocks	2,434	52.7
	Daniel A. A. Buck	2,099	45.4

1. New Hampshire was entitled to six representatives in the House for the 19th Congress (1825–1827). State law required that to be elected, a candidate had to receive a popular vote majority for any particular House seat. With candidates running at large, as they did in the 1824 election, the determination of what constituted a majority was calculated as follows:

First, the total vote was calculated by summing all votes cast for the House, yielding a figure of 72,066. This figure divided by six, the number of House seats to be filled, equals 12,011. In order to win, a candidate thus needed a majority of the 12,011 votes, that is, one half plus one additional vote. Dividing 12,011 by two equals 6,005.5, which was rounded up to whole votes to 6,006-the vote total needed for election.

Five candidates who were running-Bartlett, Whipple, Miller, Eastman and Harvey-received at least 6,006 votes and thus were elected. Miller did not serve in the House; thus an asterisk appears next to his vote total.

Since none of the other candidates qualified for the sixth seat, it remained vacant until a special election was held in 1825 between Webster and Healy, who finished sixth and seventh in 1824. (See 1825 New Hampshire, p. 831.)

2. No information available as to whether the Ohio representatives ware elected by district or at large.

1825 House Elections

ALABAMA

	Candidates	Votes	%
1	Gabriel Moore (JAC D)	5,098	71.1
	Clement Comer Clay (JAC D)	2,070	28.9
2	Robert E. B. Baylor (JAC D)	1,687	56.8
	John McKee	972✓	31.7
	John D. Terrell (NR)	342	11.5
3	George Owen (JAC D)	543	100.0

CONNECTICUT

	Candidates	Votes	%
AL	Gideon Tomlinson	6,263✓	
	Elisha Phelps	5,934✓	
	Ralph Ingersoll	5,628✓	
	Orange Merwin	5,518✓	
	Noyes Barber	4,401✓	
	John Baldwin	3,653✓	
	Daniel Burrows	1,785	
	Elisha Tracy	1,491	
	Timothy Pitkin	1,293	
	Calvin Willey	911	
	Samual Foot	574	
	Dennis Kimberly	415	
	Asa Barron	407	
	George Learnid	376	
	Samual Church	305	
	Robert Fairchild	220	
	Roger Sherman	186	
	Lyman Law	162	
	Calvin Goddard	160	
	Thomas Williams	149	

MISSISSIPPI

	Candidates	Votes	%
AL	Christopher Rankin (JAC D)	5,671	99.1

NEW HAMPSHIRE[1]

Special Elections

	Candidates	Votes	%
AL	Titus Brown	✓	
AL	Joseph Healy	13,600	56.4
	Ezekiel Webster	10,523	43.6

NORTH CAROLINA

	Candidates	Votes	%
1	Lemuel Sawyer (OPP R)	2,483	59.8
	Alfred M. Gatlin (OLD R)	1,671	40.2
2	Willis Alston (OPP R)	1,321	42.1
	George Outlaw Sr (OLD R)	978	31.2
	James Grant	837	26.7
3	Richard Hines (OPP R)	2,607	52.7
	Thomas H. Hall (OLD R)	2,343	47.3
4	John H. Bryan (OPP R)	2,488	51.0
	Richard D. Spaight (OLD R)	2,392	49.0
5	Gabriel Holmes (OPP R)	3,347	62.8
	Charles Hooks (OLD R)	1,982	37.2
6	Weldon N. Edwards (OLD R)		100.0
7	Archibald McNeill (OLD R)	✓	
	John Culpepper (OPP R)		
8	Willie P. Mangum (FED)	2,301	50.6
	Josiah Crudup	2,243	49.4
9	Romulus M. Saunders (LD R)	✓	
10	John Long Jr	3,252	52.9
	John Giles	2,891	47.1
11	Henry W. Conner (OLD R)	✓	
	T. Hunt (OPP R)	86	
12	Samuel P. Carson (OPP R)	2,081	35.2
	Robert B. Vance (OLD R)	1,924	32.6
	James Graham (OLD R)	1,903	32.2
13	Lewis Williams	✓	

RHODE ISLAND[2]

	Candidates	Votes	%
AL	Tristam Burges	2,932✓	
	Dutee J. Pearce	2,534	
	Job Durfee	2,468	
	Samuel Eddy	2,121	
	William Hunter	364	

Special Election

	Candidates	Votes	%
AL	Dutee J. Pearce	1,960	56.9
	Job Durfee	1,482	43.0

TENNESSEE

	Candidates	Votes	%
1	John Blair	3,613	51.9
	John Tipton	3,348	48.1
2	John Cocke	3,887	56.1
	Thomas Arnold	3,044	43.9
3	James Standifer	4,332	53.3
	James C. Mitchell	3,793✓	46.7
4	Jacob C. Isacks	✓	
6	James K. Polk	3,659	35.3
	Andrew Erwin	2,742	26.5
	Lunsford M. Bramlett	2,347	22.7
	James Sanford	1,508	14.6
7	Samuel Houston	5,684	84.8
	John Bruce	1,014	15.1
8	John H. Marable	2,177	38.7
	James B. Reynolds	1,922	34.1

	Candidates	Votes	%
	Willie Blount	1,533	27.2
9	Adam R. Alexander	2,865	42.0
	David Crockett	2,594	38.1
	James Ferrill	912	13.4
	Thomas H. Persons	447	6.6

VIRGINIA

	Candidates	Votes	%
1	Thomas Newton Jr	✓	
2	James Trezvant	✓	
	Eppes		
3	William S. Archer	✓	
4	Mark Alexander	✓	
5	John Randolph	✓	
6	Thomas Davenport	✓	
	Urquehart		
	Lanier		
	Graves		
7	Nathaniel H. Claiborne	✓	
	J. Leftwich		
8	Burwell Bassett	✓	
	S. Jones		
	James		
9	Robert S. Garnett	✓	
	Upshaw		
10	John Taliaferro	✓	
	Hooe		
11	Andrew Stevenson	✓	
12	William C. Rives	✓	
13	Robert Taylor	✓	
14	Charles F. Mercer	✓	
15	William Armstrong	✓	
	Colston		
16	William McCoy	✓	
	Shetter		
17	John Floyd	✓	
18	Benjamin Estill (AR)	✓	
	Graham		
	Crockett		
19	William Smith	✓	
	Lovell		
20	Alfred H. Powell	✓	
	Smith		
	Steenberger		
	Kercheval		
21	Joseph Johnson	✓	
	Doddridge		
22	John S. Barbour	✓	
	Maxwell		

1. Brown filed a vacancy left when James Miller was elected in 1824 but did not serve. Healy defeated Webster to fill the state's undecided sixth House seat, which no candidate had won in 1824 due to the majority vote requirement.

2. Rhode Island was entitled to two seats in the 19th Congress (1825–1827), but state law required that a candidate receive a popular vote majority for election. Pearce failed to qualify in the general election but won the subsequent special election shown on this page.

1826 House Elections

DELAWARE

	Candidates	Votes	%
AL	Louis McLane (FED)	4,630*	54.1
	Arnold Naudain (OLD R)	3,931	45.9

GEORGIA

		Votes	%
1	Edward F. Tattnall	1,623	100.0
2	John Forsyth	2,717	100.0
3	Wiley Thompson	3,042	60.3
	Cleveland	2,001	39.7
4	Wilson Lumpkin	4,070	50.3
	Colquett	4,026	49.7
5	Charles E. Haynes	2,369	78.7
	Longstreet	640	21.3
6	Tomlinson Fort	2,993	54.0
	Cuthbert	2,552	46.0
7	John Floyd	3,971	51.2
	King	3,786	48.8

ILLINOIS

		Votes	%
AL	Joseph Duncan (JAC D)	6,322	49.3
	Daniel P. Cook (NR)	5,669	44.2
	James Turney	824	6.4

INDIANA

		Votes	%
1	Thomas H. Blake (NR)	5,223	43.0
	Ratliff Boon (JAC D)	5,202	42.8
	Lawrence S. Shuler	1,723	14.2
2	Jonathan Jennings (CLAY R)	7,913	99.5
3	Oliver H. Smith (JAC D)	6,015	54.9
	John Test (NR)	4,946	45.1

KENTUCKY

Special Elections

		Votes	%
5	Robert McHatton (JAC D)	1,479	34.3
	Alfred Sandford	1,167	27.1
	Nicholas D. Coleman	992	23.0
	William Brown	677	15.7
12	John F. Henry (NR)	2,206	51.0
	Chittenden Lyon (JAC D)	2,119	49.0

LOUISIANA

1	Edward Livingston (D)	✓	
2	Henry H. Gurley	✓	
3	William L. Brent	✓	

MAINE

		Votes	%
1	William Burleigh (AD)	2,140	60.5
2	John Anderson (JEFF D)	2,399	57.9
3	Joseph F. Wingate (D)	1,531	55.2
4	Peleg Sprague	1,613	97.2
5	James W. Ripley (D)	1,504	52.7
6	Jeremiah O'Brien (D)	1,716	54.4
7	Samuel Butman	✓	
	W. D. Williamson		

MARYLAND

		Votes	%
1	Clement Dorsey	1,580	91.1
2	John C. Weems	1,687	50.2
	Regin Estep	1,672	49.8
3	George C. Washington	2,100	53.6
	George Peter	1,815	46.4
4	Michael C. Sprigg	3,085	43.5
	John Lee	2,672	37.7
	T. Kennedy	671	9.5
	S. Hughes	668	9.4
6	Levin Gale	1,204	25.2
	I. Demaulsby	1,145	24.0

	Candidates	Votes	%
	J. Williams	1,008	21.1
	William Colliller	763	16.0
	P. Reed	551	11.5
7	John L. Kerr	1,890	52.9
	P. B. Hopper	1,680	47.1
8	Ephraim K. Wilson	3,514	97.7

Multimember District

		Votes	
5	Peter Little	7,017✓	
	John Bailey	6,916✓	
	John Kennedy	3,997	

MASSACHUSETTS

		Votes	%
1	Daniel Webster (AR)	1,545	92.6
2	Benjamin W. Crowninshield (AR)	234	58.9
	Stephen White	39	9.8
3	John Varnum	1,773	61.0
	Caleb Cushing	916	31.5
4	Edward Everett	1,292	96.4
5	John Locke (AR)	886	55.2
	Joseph Kendall	539	33.6
	Luther Lawrence	140	8.7
6	Samuel C. Allen (AR)	1,227	57.6
	George Grennell	826	38.8
7	Henry W. Dwight (AR)	2,597	58.9
	Nathan Willis	1,082	24.5
	Jon Allen	561	12.7
8	Isaac C. Bates	1,833	60.8
	Samuel C. Lathrop	948	31.4
	James Rowler	220	7.3
9	John Bally (AR)	854	60.0
	William Ellis	331	23.2
10	James L. Hodges	1,551	56.1
	Hercules Cushman	717	25.9
	Francis Bayleys (JACS R)	429	15.5
11	John Reed (AR)	998	81.9
	Walter Folger	201	16.5
12	Joseph Richardson	1,188	58.9
	Thomas L. Beats	670	33.2
13	John Davis (AR)	1,316	90.1
	Jonas Tibley	110	7.5

MISSOURI

		Votes	%
AL	Edward Bates (JAC D)	6,636	61.5
	Scott (NR)	4,159	38.5

NEW JERSEY

		Votes	
AL	George Holcombe (JAC&AR)	24,538✓	
	Lewis Condict (AR)	15,615✓	
	Samuel Swan (AR)	14,701✓	
	Isaac Pierson (AR)	14,697✓	
	Hedge Thompson (AR)	14,479✓	
	Ebenezer Tucker (AR)	14,433✓	
	Daniel Garrison (JAC R)	10,166	
	George Cassedy (JAC R)	9,944	
	Isaac G. Farlee (JAC R)	9,752	
	Benjamin B. Cooper (JAC R)	9,512	
	William Kennedy (JAC R)	9,282	
	James Parker	637	
	Ephraim Bateman	297	
	Peter D. Vroom	136	
	Caleb Newbold	110	

NEW YORK

		Votes	%
1	Silas Wood	1,485	97.9
2	John Wood	1,335	54.7
	John Smith	1,104	45.3
4	Aaron Ward	2,566	59.6
	John Haff	1,738	40.4
5	Thomas Oakley	3,266	50.8
	Edmund Pendleton	3,159	49.2

	Candidates	Votes	%
6	John Hallock Jr.	2,393	56.8
	Hector Craig	1,817	43.2
7	George Belden	2,677	50.7
	Lemuel Jenkins	2,608	49.4
8	James Strong	2,984	59.9
	Walter Patterson	2,002	40.2
9	John Dickinson	3,339	51.9
	James Hogeboom	3,098	48.1
10	Stephen Van Rensselaer	3,006	100.0
11	Selah Hobbie	4,076	58.9
	Isaac Burr	2,847	41.1
12	John De Graff	3,309	100.0
13	Samuel Chase	2,618	50.9
	George Morell	2,389	46.4
14	Henry Storrs	4,174	69.8
	Ezekiel Bacon	1,808	30.2
15	Michael Hoffman	2,684	59.5
	Daniel Van Horn	1,829	40.5
16	Henry Markell	2,611	51.6
	Aaron Haring	2,445	48.4
17	John W. Taylor	2,910	57.5
	Alphens Goodrich	2,150	42.5
18	Henry Martindale	2,496	51.1
	John Williard	2,392	48.9
19	Richard Keese	3,328	52.4
	Asa Hascall	3,022	47.6
21	John Clark	3,354	52.6
	Robert Monell	3,024	47.4
22	John G. Stower	3,785	55.6
	John Miller	3,024	44.4
23	Jonas Earll Jr	3,420	51.8
	Luther Badger	3,178	48.2
24	Nathaniel Garrow	3,039	54.1
	Elijah Miller	2,575	45.9
25	David Woodcook	3,366	52.3
	Charles Humphrey	3,076	47.8
27	Daniel Barnard	4,299	52.3
	Enos Pomeroy	3,927	47.7
28	John Magee	3,300	40.8
	Timothy Porter	2,331	28.9
	William Woods	1,246	15.4
	Phillip Church	1,203	14.9
29	David Evans	3,843	54.2
	Simeon Cumings	3,251	45.8
30	Daniel Garnsey	4,801	55.1
	Albert Tracy	3,919	44.9

Multimember Districts

		Votes	
3	Churchill C. Cambreleng	9,108✓	
	Gulian Verplanck	5,705✓	
	Jeromus Johnson	5,376✓	
	King	3,814	
	Vanwych	3,631	
20	Silas Wright	6,579✓	
	Rudolph Bunner	6,558✓	
	Nicolli Fosdick	6,048	
	Elisha Camp	6,039	
26	Dudley Marvin	8,082✓	
	John Maynard	5,554✓	
	Nathaniel Allen	4,153	
	John Knox	2,631	

OHIO

		Votes	%
1	James Findlay (JAC R)	2,954	42.6
	D. Morris (AR)	2,443	35.2
	T. Morris (JAC R)	1,546	22.3
2	John Woods (AR)	✓	
	T. R. Ross (JAC R)		
3	William McLean (AR)	✓	
4	Joseph Vance (AR)	✓	
5	William Russell (JAC R)	2,111	35.5
	Collins (AR)	1,444	24.3
	Morris (AR)	1,249	21.0
	Shephard (AR)	1,140	19.2

	Candidates	Votes	%
6	William Creighton Jr (AR)	3,652	63.5
	John Thompson	2,099	36.5
7	Samuel F. Vinton (AR)	✓	
8	William Wilson (AR)	✓	
9	Philemon Beecher (AR)	3,708	61.3
	Mathews (JAC R)	2,346	38.8
10	John Davenport (AR)	✓	
11	John C. Wright (AR)	2,344	35.5
	Beebe (AR)	2,136	32.4
	John M. Goodenow (JAC R)	2,116	32.1
12	John Sloane (AR)	3,417	50.7
	John Tomson (JAC R)	3,319	49.3
13	Elisha Whittlesey (AR)	✓	
14	Mordecai Bartley (AR)	2,500	59.7
	Cooke	1,688	40.3

Special Election[1]

	Thomas Shannon (D)	✓	

PENNSYLVANIA

	Candidates	Votes	%
1	Joel Sutherland (JAC R)	✓	
	S. Breck (AR)		
	W. Duane		
2	John Sergeant (AR)	✓	
	Horn (JAC R)		
	Thomas Kittera (UNP R)		
3	Daniel H. Miller (JAC R)	✓	
	Harrison		
5	John B. Sterigere	✓	
6	Innis Green	✓	
	John M. Forster		
10	Adam King	✓	

	Candidates	Votes	%
12	John Mitchell	✓	
13	Chauncy Forward	✓	
14	Andrew Stewart	✓	
15	Joseph Lawrence	✓	
16	Richard Coulter (FED)	✓	
18	Stephen Barlow	✓	

Multimember Districts

	Candidates	Votes	%
4	Charles Miner (FED)	✓	
	James Buchanan (FED)	✓	
	Samuel Anderson (FED)	✓	
7	Joseph Fry	✓	
	William Addams	✓	
8	Samuel D. Ingham	✓	
	George Wolf	✓	
9	Samuel McKean	✓	
	Espy Van Horne	✓	
	George Kremer	✓	
11	James Wilson	✓	
	William Ramsey	✓	
17	James S. Stevenson	✓	
	Robert Orr Jr.	✓	

Special Elections

	Candidates	Votes	%
2	Thomas Kittera (FED)	✓	
	Horn (JAC R)		
13	Chauncy Forward	✓	
	William Piper		
18	Thomas H. Sill (FED)	1,812	39.8
	Barlow	1,045	23.0
	Hays	937	20.6
	Herrington	760	16.7

SOUTH CAROLINA

	Candidates	Votes	%
1	William Drayton (UN D)		100.0
2	James Hamilton Jr (SR FT)		100.0
3	Thomas R. Mitchell	✓	
	Robert B. Campbell		
4	William D. Martin (D)	✓	
	Andrew R. Govan		
5	Starling Tucker	✓	
	Caldwell		
6	George McDuffie (D)	✓	
7	William T. Nuckolls	✓	
	Samuel McCreary		
	James McKibbin		
8	Warren R. Davis (SR D)	2,478	50.3
	John Wilson	2,453	49.8
9	John Carter	100.0	

VERMONT[2]

	Candidates	Votes	%
1	Jonathan Hunt (NR)	✓	
2	Rollin C. Mallary	3,050	98.3
3	George E. Wales	2,634	96.2
4	Heman Allen	2,631*	46.5
	Benjamin Swift	2,546	45.0
5	Daniel Azro Ashley Buck (D)	4,400	73.0
	James Bell (NR)	1,542	25.6

VIRGINIA

Special Election

5	George W. Crump (JAC R)		
	Giles	✓	

1. No information available as to whether Shannon was elected in a district or at large.

2. In the 4th district, neither candidate received the majority of the vote required to win. In a later election, for which no returns are available, Swift was elected.

1827 House Elections

ALABAMA

	Candidates	Votes	%
1	Gabriel Moore (JAC D)	846	100.0
2	John McKee	1,140	69.5
	Thomas W. Farrar	500	30.5
3	George Owen (JAC D)		100.0

CONNECTICUT

AL	Ralph Ingersoll	7,838✓	
	Elisha Phelps	6,762✓	
	David Plant	4,890✓	
	Orange Merwin	4,472✓	
	John Baldwin	4,195✓	
	Noyes Barber	3,607✓	
	Alexander Stewart	2,690	
	Ansel Sterling	2,656	
	Andrew Judson	2,509	
	Robert Fairchild	2,451	
	Timothy Pitkin	1,304	
	Lyman Law	1,284	
	Joseph Eaton	1,211	
	Noah Benedict	948	
	Gideon Tomlinson	484	
	Alexander Stewart	474	
	Roger Sherman	448	
	Nathan Pendleton	416	
	Thomas S. Williams	351	

DELAWARE

Special Election

AL	Kensey Johns Jr (FED)	4,148	52.4
	James A. Bayard (OLD R)	3,753	47.4

GEORGIA

Special Elections

AL	Richard H. Wilde	✓	
AL	George R. Gilmer	21,008	63.5
	Charlton	12,094	36.5

KENTUCKY

1	Henry Daniel (JAC D)	4,163	52.2
	David Trimble (JAC D)	3,811	47.8
2	Thomas Metcalfe (JAC D)	2,964	54.9
	Conn	2,436	45.1
3	James Clark (JAC D)	2,914	57.9
	Taylor	2,121	42.1
4	Robert P. Letcher (W)	3,637	53.3
	Rodes	3,182	46.7
5	Robert L. McHatton (JAC D)	3,307	52.5
	Sandford	2,988	47.5
6	Joseph Lecompte (JAC D)	3,546	50.9
	Crittenden	3,183	45.7
7	Thomas P. Moore (JAC D)	3,681	90.5
	Thompson	386	9.5
8	Richard A. Buckner (A-JAC D)	3,527	52.1
	Owens	3,247	47.9
9	Charles A. Wickliffe (JAC D)	3,856	66.1
	White	1,982	34.0
10	Joel Yancey (JAC D)	3,268	50.8
	Johnson	3,169	49.2
11	William S. Young (JAC D)	4,009	56.0
	John Calhoun	3,155	44.0

	Candidates	Votes	%
12	Chittenden Lyon (JAC D)	3,471	52.1
	Henry (NR)	2,070	31.1
	New	1,123	16.9

Special Elections[1]

11	John Calhoon	2,290*	
	Thomas Chilton	1,685	
11	Thomas Chilton	✓	
	John Calhoon		

MAINE

Special Election

1	Rufus McIntire (JAC D)	2,169	54.5
	John Holmes	1,814	45.5

MISSISSIPPI

AL	William Haile (JAC D)	1,914	34.6
	John Norton	1,312	23.7
	Beverly R. Grayson	1,204	21.8
	Adam Benjamin (NR)	1,096	19.8

NEW HAMPSHIRE

AL	Ichabod Bartlett (OLD R)	22,680✓	
	Titus Brown (OLD R)	22,354✓	
	Joseph Healy (OLD R)	21,515✓	
	Jonathan Harvey (OLD R)	20,873✓	
	David Barker Jr (OLD R)	14,456✓	
	Thomas Whipple Jr (OLD R)	12,189✓	
	E. Web (AR)		
	S. C. Web		
	Eastman		
	Cartland		

NORTH CAROLINA

1	Lemuel Sawyer (OLD R)	2,943	65.1
	William B. Shepard (OPP R)	1,579	34.9
2	Willis Alston	✓	
3	Thomas H. Hall (OPP R)	✓	
	Richard Hines (OLD R)		
4	John H. Bryan	✓	
5	Gabriel Holmes	✓	
6	Daniel Turner	1,116	28.5
	Charles A. Hill	1,049	26.8
	Willis Boddie	783	20.0
	William M. Sneed	620	15.8
	Joseph H. Bryan	345	8.8
7	John Culpepper (AR)	2,375	41.2
	John A. Cameron	1,990	34.5
	John Glichrist	1,387	24.1
8	Daniel L. Barringer (OLD R)	2,398	53.3
	Archibald D. Murphey (OPP R)	2,102	46.7
9	Augustine H. Shepperd (OLD R)	4,304	64.6
	Bedford Brown (OPP R)	2,361	35.4
10	John Long (AR)	✓	
	Asa Eubank		
11	Henry W. Conner (OLD R)	3,182	81.9
	Samuel Henderson (OPP R)	702	18.1
12	Samuel P. Carson (OLD R)	4,187	63.4
	Robert B. Vance (OPP R)	2,419	36.6
13	Lewis Williams (AR)	✓	
	John Mushat		

RHODE ISLAND

	Candidates	Votes	%
AL	Tristam Burges (NR)	2,230✓	
	Dutee J. Pearce (NR)	2,126✓	

TENNESSEE

1	John Blair	4,216	55.8
	John Tipton	3,208	42.4
2	Pryor Lea	3,688	39.7
	Thomas D. Arnold	3,316	35.7
	William B. Reese	2,272	24.5
3	James C. Mitchell	5,732	55.7
	James Standifer	4,566	44.3
4	Jacob C. Isacks	6,823	100.0
5	Robert Desha	4,509	61.1
	John Hall	1,581	21.4
	William Trousdale	1,292	17.5
6	James K. Polk	6,351	56.6
	Lunsford M. Bramlett	4,878	43.4
7	John Bell	4,889	55.7
	Felix Grundy	3,887	44.3
8	James B. Reynolds	2,609	51.0
	John H. Marable	2,507✓	49.0
9	David Crockett	5,868	49.1
	Adam R. Alexander	3,646	30.5
	William Arnold	2,427	20.3

VIRGINIA

1	Thomas Newton Jr (AR)	✓
	George Loyall	
2	James Trezvant	✓
3	William S. Archer	✓
4	Mark Alexander	✓
5	John Randolph	✓
6	Thomas Davenport	✓
7	Nathaniel H. Claiborne	✓
	Campbell	
8	Burwell Bassett	✓
9	John Roane	✓
10	John Taliaferro	✓
11	Andrew Stevenson	✓
12	William C. Rives	✓
13	Philip P. Barbour (A-A)	✓
14	Charles F. Mercer	✓
	Thompson	
15	William Armstrong	✓
	Peter	
16	William McCoy	✓
17	John Floyd	✓
18	Alexander Smyth	✓
	Sharp	
19	Lewis Maxwell	✓
	Smith	
	Lovell	
20	Robert Allen	✓
	Samuel Kercheval	
	Alfred H. Powell	
21	Isaac Leffler (AR)	✓
	Haymond	
	Johnson (JAC R)	
22	John S. Barbour	✓
	Hunton	

1. Rep. William S. Young died Sept. 20, 1827, and a special election was held to replace him in November of that year. In initial counting of the returns, Thomas Chilton led John Calhoon 2,704 votes to 2,679. But then returns from Hardin County were thrown out, with Chilton losing 1,019 votes and Calhoon losing only 389 votes, making Calhoon the winner.

The returns minus Hardin County are listed in the ICPSR data above.
Calhoon then resigned, never having formally claimed the House seat, and both candidates then petitioned the governor to call a new election. A second special election was held Dec. 20–22, and was won by Chilton. No returns are available.

1828 House Elections

DELAWARE

	Candidates	Votes	%
AL	Kensey Johns Jr. (FED)	4,769	52.2
	James A. Bayard (OLD R)	4,347	47.5

GEORGIA

	Candidates	
AL	George R. Gilmer	*
	Thomas F. Foster	✓
	Richard H. Wilde	✓
	Wilson Lumpkin	✓
	James M. Wayne	✓
	Charles E. Haynes	✓
	Wiley Thompson	✓

ILLINOIS

	Candidates	Votes	%
AL	Joseph Duncan (JAC D)	10,447	62.9
	George Forquer(NR)	6,158	37.1

INDIANA

	Candidates	Votes	%
1	Ratliff Boon (JAC D)	7,272	52.2
	Thomas H. Blake (NR)	6,671	47.8
2	Jonathan Jennings (CLAY R)	7,659	73.3
	John H. Thompson	2,785	26.7
3	John Test (NR)	6,867	55.8
	Jonathan McCarty (JAC D)	5,433	44.2

LOUISIANA

	Candidates	
1	Edward D. White	✓
2	Henry H. Gurley	✓
3	Walter H. Overton (D)	✓

MAINE[1]

	Candidates	Votes	%
1	Rufus McIntire (JAC D)	2,981	66.0
2	John Anderson (JEFF D)	3,189	76.2
3	Joseph F. Wingate (D)	2,086	73.0
4	Peleg Sprague	2,086*	94.4
5	James W. Ripley (JAC R)	2,394	56.9
	Reuel Washburn (AR)	1,813	43.1
6	Jeremiah O'Brien (D)	1,709*	48.2
	Hathaway	1,119	31.5
7	Samuel Butman	3,336	62.0

MASSACHUSETTS

	Candidates	Votes	%
1	Benjamin Gorham	3,234	78.3
	William Ingalls	819	19.8
2	Benjamin W. Crowninshield (AR)	1,326	54.0
	Leverett Saltonstall	631	25.7
	Ezra Mudge	284	11.6
	Joseph S. Cabot (JACS R)	186	7.6
3	John Varnum	1,663	72.6
	George Savory	379	16.6
	Samuel Phillips	149	6.5
4	Edward Everett	3,004	73.9
	S. M. Parker	470	11.6
	S. Fiske	465	11.4
5	Joseph G. Kendall	1,436	52.7
	John Socke (AR)	1,205	44.2
6	George Grennell Jr	2,023	69.7
	Elihu Hoyt	456	15.7
	Samuel F. Dickinson	277	9.5
7	Henry W. Dwight (AR)	2,237	53.0
	George W. Briggs	1,033	24.5
	Nathan Willis (JACS R)	922	21.8
8	Isaac C. Bates (AR)	2,133	87.7
	John Mills	192	7.9
9	John Bailey (AR)	2,047	77.4
	William Ellis	375	14.2
	Ebenezer Seaver	151	5.7
10	James L. Hodges	1,338	81.5
	Francis Baylies	129	7.9

	Candidates	Votes	%
11	John Reed (AR)	1,027	94.3
12	Joseph Richardson	1,114	50.4
	Thomas P. Beal	1,003	45.4
13	John Davis (AR)	2,293	89.6
	Jonas Sibley (JACS R)	184	7.2

MISSISSIPPI

Special Election

	Candidates	Votes	%
AL	Thomas Hinds (JAC D)	1,844	89.5

MISSOURI

	Candidates	Votes	%
AL	Spencer Pettis (JAC D)	7,108	61.0
	Edward Bates (NR)	4,539	39.0

NEW JERSEY

	Candidates	Votes	
AL	Lewis Condict (NR)	23,783	✓
	Richard M. Cooper (NR)	23,737	✓
	Isaac Pierson (NR)	23,733	✓
	Samuel Swan (NR)	23,709	✓
	James F. Randolph (NR)	23,684	✓
	Thomas H. Hughes (NR)	23,604	✓
	William N. Jeffers (JAC D)	22,014	
	James Parker (JAC D)	22,003	
	Peter D. Vroom Jr (JAC D)	21,994	
	John Clement (JAC D)	21,949	
	George Cassedy (JAC D)	21,921	
	Samuel Fowler (JAC D)	21,902	

Special Elections

	Candidates	Votes	%
AL	Thomas Sinnickson (NR)	23,425	51.8
	James D. Westcott (JAC D)	21,527	47.6
AL	James F. Randolph (NR)	23,388	51.7
	James Parker (JAC D)	21,752	48.1

NEW YORK

	Candidates	Votes	%
1	James Lent	3,105	52.3
	Silas Wood	2,831	47.7
2	Jacob Crocheron	2,885	59.2
	Peter Radcliff	1,988	40.8
4	Henry B. Cowles	3,492	51.0
	Tompkins	3,352	49.0
5	Abraham Bockee	4,640	58.5
	Pendleton	3,293	41.5
6	Hector Craig	3,535	55.7
	Wilkin	2,816	44.3
7	Charles G. De Witt	4,203	61.9
	Bevier	1,857	27.4
	Bogardus	731	10.8
8	James Strong	3,592	50.9
	James Vanderpoel	3,459	49.1
9	John Dickinson	4,588	51.6
	George Davis	4,302	48.4
10	Ambrose Spencer	4,157	51.0
	Charles Dudley	3,889	47.7
11	Perkins King	5,342	61.6
	Jacob Haight	3,335	38.4
12	Peter Borst	3,637	57.5
	Jacob Livingston	2,688	42.5
13	William Angel	4,474	55.7
	Erastus Crafts	3,559	44.3
14	Henry Storrs	5,508	51.1
	Greene C. Bronson	5,274	48.9
15	Michael Hoffman	3,246	100.0
16	Benedict Arnold	4,064	52.9
	William Dodge	3,623	47.1
17	John Taylor	3,533	54.9
	John Cramer	2,900	45.1
18	Henry Martindale	3,902	58.0
	John Willard	2,823	42.0
19	Isaac Finch	4,682	51.8

	Candidates	Votes	%
	William Hogan	4,360	48.2
21	Robert Monell	4,720	63.6
	Tilly Lynde	2,704	36.4
22	Thomas Beekman	4,831	53.4
	John Stower	4,217	46.6
23	Jonas Earll Jr	4,068	44.9
	Daniel Kellogg	3,597	39.7
	Parson Shippman	1,402	15.5
24	Gershom Powers	4,098	61.6
	Charles Kellogg	1,651	24.8
	Moses Dixon	901	13.6
25	Thomas Maxwell	5,462	60.1
	Daniel Woodcook	3,623	39.9
27	Timothy Childs	6,520	54.6
	Addison Gardiner	4,294	36.0
	Daniel Barnard	1,125	9.4
28	John Magee	5,390	55.2
	Timothy Porter	4,382	44.8
29	Phinehas Tracy	6,924	68.9
	Herman Redfield	3,123	31.1
30	Ebenezer Norton	5,226	45.0
	John Birdsall	2,820	24.3
	John Camp	2,003	17.3
	Daniel Garnsey	1,560	13.4

Multimember Districts

	Candidates	Votes	
3	Campbell P. White	18,070	✓
	Gulian C. Verplanck	14,138	✓
	Churchill C. Cambreleng	14,117	✓
	Ogden	11,204	
	Taylor	10,956	
	Lord	6,788	
20	Joseph Hawkins	9,060	✓
	George Fisher	8,939	†
	Silas Wright	8,932	
	Perley Keyes	8,617	
26	Robert Rose	8,444	✓
	Jehiel Halsey	6,833	✓
	Phineas Bates	6,651	
	Dudley Marvin	5,138	
	Isreal Richardson	4,886	

OHIO

	Candidates	
1	James Findlay (JAC R)	✓
2	James Shields (JAC R)	✓
	John Woods (AR)	
3	Joseph H. Crane (AR)	✓
4	Joseph Vance (AR)	✓
5	William Russell (JAC R)	✓
6	William Creighton Jr (AR)	✓
7	Samuel F. Vinton (AR)	✓
8	William Stanbery (JAC D)	✓
9	William W. Irvin (JAC R)	✓
	Philemon Beecher (AR)	
10	William Kennon Sr (JAC R)	✓
	John Davenport (AR)	
11	John M. Goodenow (JAC R)	✓
	John C. Wright (AR)	
12	John Thomson (JAC R)	✓
	John Sloane (AR)	
13	Elisha Whittlesey (AR)	✓

	Candidates	Votes	%
14	Mordecai Bartley (AR)	2,632	50.0
	Hunter	1,432	27.2
	Wood	1,200	22.8

Special Election

	Candidates	
6	Francis S. Muhlenberg (JAC R)	✓

PENNSYLVANIA

	Candidates	
1	Joel B. Sutherland (JAC R)	✓
	Peter A. Browse (AR)	

Candidates	Votes	%
2 Joseph Hemphill (JAC R)	✓	
John Sergeant (AR)		
3 Daniel H. Miller (JAC R)	✓	
Samuel Harvey (AR)		
5 John B. Sterigere (JAC R)	✓	
6 Innis Green (JAC R)	✓	
Valentine Hummel		
10 Adam King (JAC R)	✓	
12 John Scott (JAC R)	✓	
13 Chauncey Forward (JAC R)	✓	
14 Thomas Irwin (JAC R)	✓	
15 William McCreery (JAC R)	✓	
16 Richard Coulter (JAC R)	✓	
18 Thomas H. Sill (AR)	✓	

Multimember Districts

Candidates	Votes	%
4 George C. Leiper (JAC R)	✓	
James Buchanan (JAC R)	✓	
Joshua Evans Jr. (JAC R)	✓	
Anderson		
Hiester		
Haines		

Candidates	Votes	%
7 Henry A. P. Muhlenburg (JAC R)	✓	
Joseph Fry Jr (JAC R)	✓	
Henry King		
William Addams		
8 Samuel Ingham (JAC R)	✓	
George Wolf (JAC R)	✓	
9 James Ford (JAC R)	✓	
Alem Marr (JAC R)	✓	
Philander Stephens (JAC R)	✓	
11 William Ramsey (JAC R)	✓	
Thomas H. Crawford (JAC R)	✓	
17 John Gilmore (JAC R)	✓	
William Wilkins	✓	
James S. Stevenson (JAC R)		
Moore (AR)		

SOUTH CAROLINA

Candidates	Votes	%
1 William Drayton (UN D)		100.0
2 Robert W. Barnwell (D)		100.0
3 John Campbell (SR W)		
Thomas R. Mitchell		
4 William D. Martin (D)		100.0

Candidates	Votes	%
5 Starling Tucker	✓	
6 George McDuffie (D)	✓	
7 William T. Nuckolls	✓	
8 Warren R. Davis (SR D)	✓	
Cobb		
9 James Blair (UN D)	✓	
Richard I. Manning (D)		
Spann		

VERMONT[2]

Candidates	Votes	%
1 Jonathan Hunt (NR)	3,028	86.2
Daniel Kellogg	327	9.3
2 Rollin Carolas Mallary	✓	
3 Horace Everett (W)	✓	
4 Benjamin Swift	4,370	67.5
Ezra Meech (D)	1,936	29.9
5 Daniel Azro Ashley Buck (D)	1,779*	35.1
William Cahoon (A-MASC)	1,427	28.1
Cushman (JAC)	1,303	25.7
James Bell (NR)	564	11.1

1. In the 6th district, no candidate received the majority of the vote required to win. In a later election, for which no returns are available, Leonard Jarvis (D) was the winner.

2. No candidate received the majority of the vote in the 5th district required for election. A series of special elections were held in an attempt to meet the requirement and lilt the seat. In the eighth special election, William Cahoon was elected. No returns are available for these special elections.

1829 House Elections

ALABAMA

	Candidates	Votes	%
1	Clement C. Clay (JAC D)	4,309	52.1
	Nicholas Davis (NR)	3,960	47.9
2	Robert E. B. Baylor (JAC D)	3,845	54.5
	Seth Barton	1,879	26.6
	Henry W. Ellis (JAC D)	1,335	18.9
3	Dixon Hall Lewis (SR D)	4,227	44.1
	Samuel Oliver	2,908	30.3
	Armstrong	2,449	25.6

CONNECTICUT

		Votes	%
AL	Ralph Ingersoll	8,281✓	
	Noyes Barber	7,552✓	
	Ebenezer Young	6,592✓	
	Jabez Huntington	6,285✓	
	William Storrs	5,671✓	
	William Ellsworth	5,588✓	
	David Plant	5,401	
	John Niles	3,189	
	Andrew Judson	3,052	
	Orange Merwin	3,009	
	Elisha Phelps	2,501	
	John Trott	2,278	
	Hinman	2,244	
	Roger Sherman	1,299	
	Daniel Burrows	1,256	
	Joseph Eaton	440	
	Larrd Sherwood	344	
	Timothy Pitkin	290	
	Nathan Smith	241	
	Roger Huntington	204	
	Iriah Isham	144	
	Alex Stewart	130	

GEORGIA

Special Election

		Votes	%
AL	Henry G. Lamar	20,706	57.5
	Charlton	15,296	42.5

KENTUCKY

		Votes	%
1	Henry Daniel (JAC D)	✓	
	Harrison		
2	Nicholas D. Coleman (JAC D)	2,520	45.1
	Adam Beatty (NR)	2,519	45.1
	George M. Bedinger (NR)	461	8.3
3	James Clark	2,605	71.4
	Matthews Flournoy	1,045	28.6
4	Robert P. Letcher (W)	✓	
5	Richard M. Johnson (JAC D)	3,634	55.2
	R. McHatton	2,955	44.9
6	Joseph Lecompte (JAC D)	3,371	51.6
	Thomas P. Wilson	3,167	48.4
7	John Kinkead (D)	3,694	56.3
	William B. Booker	2,872	43.7
8	Nathan Gaither (D)	2,267	34.5
	Martin Beatty	2,168	33.0
	William Owens	988	15.0
	Tunstal Quarles	950	14.5
9	Charles Wickliffe (D)	✓	
10	Joel Yancey (JAC D)	3,235	50.8
	Francis Johnson	3,132	49.2
11	Thomas Chilton	4,185	64.7
	James Crutcher	2,282	35.3
12	Chittenden Lyon		100.0

MARYLAND

		Votes	%
1	Clement Dorsey	1,316	88.0

	Candidates	Votes	%
2	Benedict Semmes (D)	1,947	54.2
	John C. Weems	1,625	45.2
3	George C. Washington (W)	3,116	100.0
4	Michael C. Sprigg (D)	4,190	56.0
	William Price	3,293	44.0
6	George E. Mitchell	2,591	53.5
	James W. Williams	2,253	46.5
7	Richard Spencer (D)	1,711	50.3
	John Leeds Kerr (W)	1,692	49.7
8	Ephraim K. Wilson (D)	4,374	98.0

Multimember District

		Votes	%
5	Benjamin C. Howard (D)	6,297✓	
	Elias Brown (W)	6,153✓	
	P. Little	4,745	
	John Barney	3,763	

MISSISSIPPI

		Votes	%
AL	Thomas Hinds (JAC D)	4,585	42.9
	David Dickson (JAC D)	2,425	22.7
	A. L. Benjamin (NR)	1,920	18.0
	William Haile (JAC D)	1,759	16.5

NEW HAMPSHIRE

AL	John W. Weeks (JAC D)	✓	
	Henry Hubbard (JAC D)	✓	
	Thomas Chandler (JAC D)	✓	
	Jonathan Harvey (JAC D)	✓	
	John Brodhead (JAC D)	✓	
	Joseph Hammons (JAC D)	✓	
	Wallace (NR)		
	Boardman (NR)		
	Webster (NR)		
	Barker (NR)		
	Bell (NR)		
	Lord (NR)		

NORTH CAROLINA

		Votes	%
1	William B. Shepard (D-R)	2,491	54.0
	Lemuel Sawyer (OPP R)	2,121	46.0
2	Willis Alston	✓	
3	Thomas H. Hall (D-R)		100.0
4	Jesse Speight (D-R)	3,137	64.3
	Thomas H. Davies (D-R)	1,282	26.3
	James Manney (OPP R)	459	9.4
5	Gabriel Holmes (D-R)	2,551	52.2
	Edward B. Dudley (D-R)	2,333	47.8
6	Robert Potter (D-R)	2,661	83.9
	Samuel Hillman (OPP R)	396	12.5
7	Edmund Deberry (AR)	3,098	51.9
	John A. Cameron (D-R)	2,869	48.1
8	Daniel L. Barringer (D-R)	2,650	61.7
	James A. Craig (D-R)	1,590	37.0
9	Augustine H. Shepard (D-R)		100.0
10	John Giles (D-R)	3,226*	58.6
	John Long (AR)	2,281	41.4
11	Henry W. Conner	✓	
12	Samuel P. Carson	✓	
13	Lewis Williams (NR)	✓	
	Samuel King (D-R)		

Special Election

		Votes	%
10	Abraham Rencher (NR)	1,972	56.2
	John Long (NR)	1,538	43.8

PENNSYLVANIA

Special Election

17	Harmar Denny (A-MAS)	✓	
	James S. Stevenson (D)		

RHODE ISLAND

	Candidates	Votes	%
AL	Dutee J. Pearce (NR)	4,328✓	
	Tristam Burges (NR)	4,108✓	
	Samuel Eddy (NR)	1,251	
	Job Durfee (NR)	1,126	
	Elisha R. Potter (NR)	518	
	John Dwolf Jr (NR)	208	

TENNESSEE

		Votes	%
1	John Blair	3,899	67.2
	John A. Rogers	1,048	18.1
	William Priestly	856	14.8
2	Pryor Lea	4,813	51.7
	Thomas D. Arnold	4,496	48.3
3	James Standifer	8,383	82.3
	John Lowry	1,802	17.7
4	Jacob C. Isacks	3,869	100.0
5	Robert Desha	4,575	64.2
	William Trousdale	2,547	35.8
6	James K. Polk	9,963	100.0
7	John Bell	5,542	100.0
8	Cave Johnson	3,470	52.9
	John H. Marable	3,085	47.1
9	David Crockett	6,783	64.0
	Adam R. Alexander	3,643	34.4

VIRGINIA

1	Thomas Newton Jr (NR)	‡
	George Loyall (JAC R)	
2	James Trezvant	✓
3	William S. Archer (JAC R)	✓
4	Mark Alexander	✓
5	Thomas T. Bouldin	✓
	Miller	
	George W. Crump	
6	Thomas Davenport	✓
7	Nathaniel H. Claiborne	✓
8	Richard Coke Jr	✓
	Burwell Bassett	
	Braxton	
9	John Roane	✓
10	John Taliaferro (NR)	✓
	Newton	
11	Andrew Stevenson (JAC R)	✓
12	William C. Rives (JAC R)	✓
13	Philip P. Barbour (JAC R)	✓
14	Charles F. Mercer	✓
	Gibson	
15	William Armstrong	✓
16	William McCoy	✓
17	Robert Craig	✓
	Miller	
18	Alexander Smyth	✓
19	Lewis Maxwell	✓
	Lovell	
	Smith	
20	Robert Allen	✓
	Kercheval	
21	Philip Doddridge	✓
	Johnson	
22	John S. Barbour	✓

Special Election

12	William F. Gordon (JAC R)	✓

1830 House Elections

DELAWARE

	Candidates	Votes	%
AL	John J. Milligan (NR)	4,267	52.6
	Henry M. Ridgely (JAC D)	3,833	47.3

GEORGIA

	Candidates	Votes	
AL	Richard H. Wilde	26,313	✓
	Wilson Lumpkin	25,896	✓
	Daniel Newman	24,459	✓
	Henry G. Lamar	22,422	✓
	Thomas F. Foster	21,443	✓
	James M. Wayne	21,210	✓
	Wiley Thompson	20,713	✓
	Charles E. Haynes	17,244	
	T. U. T. Charlton	15,049	
	Roger L. Gamble	14,263	
	Seaton Grantland	13,738	
	Reuben C. Shorter	5,150	

LOUISIANA

1	Edward D. White	✓
2	Philemon Thomas (D)	✓
3	Henry A. Bullard	✓

MAINE

		Votes	%
1	Rufus McIntire (JAC D)	✓	
2	John Anderson (JEFF D)	✓	
3	Edward Kavanagh (D)	2,169	52.4
	Moses Shaw (NR)	1,712	41.4
4	George Evans (NR)	✓	
5	Cornelius Holland (D)	✓	
6	Leonard Jarvis (D)	✓	
7	James Bates (D)	✓	

MASSACHUSETTS

		Votes	%
1	Nathan Appleton (NR)	3,341	56.3
	Henry Lee (A-TARIFF)	2,475	41.7
2	Rufus Choate (NR)	1,740	59.1
	Benjamin Crowninshield	767	26.1
	Cabot (JAC R)	352	12.0
3	Jeremiah Nelson (NR)	2,952	62.3
	Gayton S. Osgood (JACS R)	1,695	35.8
4	Edward Everett (NR)	2,176	82.6
	James Russell	427	16.2
5	Joseph G. Kendall (NR)	1,675	97.0
6	George Grennell Jr (NR)	1,515	72.4
	Isaac Billings	511	24.4
7	George N. Briggs (NR)	1,707	57.5
	Nathan Willis (JACS R)	825	27.8
	Henry W. Dwight	222	7.5
8	Isaac C. Bates (NR)	1,827	77.7
	John Mills (JACS R)	470	20.0
9	Henry A. S. Dearborn (NR)	1,872	55.0
	Moses Thacher (A-MAS)	1,088	32.0
	Abel Cushing	239	7.0
10	James L. Hodges (NR)	3,437	50.5
	Micah B. Ruggles (A-MASDNR)	3,227	47.4
11	John Reed (NR)	949	94.3
12	John Quincy Adams (NR)	1,811	70.7
	Arad Thompson	378	14.8
	William Baylies	327	12.8
13	John Davis (NR)	2,014	72.7
	Dan Thurber (JACS R)	598	21.6
	Unidentified Candidate (A-MAS&SC)	160	5.8

NEW JERSEY

		Votes	
AL	Lewis Condict (NR)	15,268	✓
	Thomas H. Hughes (NR)	15,214	✓
	Richard M. Cooper (NR)	15,150	✓
	Isaac Southard (NR)	15,069	✓
	Silas Condit (NR)	14,823	✓

Candidates	Votes	%
James F. Randolph (NR)	14,513 ✓	
Parker (D)	14,361	
Wurts (D)	14,054	
Mickle (D)	14,011	
Fowler (D)	13,936	
Travers (D)	13,915	
Jeffers (D)	13,086	

NEW YORK

		Votes	%
1	James Lent (JAC D)	2,557	54.5
	John King	2,138	45.5
2	John Bergen (JAC D)	2,147	50.4
	John Wyckoff	2,116	49.6
4	Aaron Ward (JAC D)	2,998	53.6
	John Hunter	1,767	31.6
	Jonathan Ferris	830	14.8
5	Edmund Pendleton (NR)	3,463	52.3
	Stoddard Judd	3,161	47.7
6	Samuel Wilkin (NR)	2,498	50.9
	Isaac Vanduzer	2,414	49.1
7	John Brodhead (JAC D)	3,854	59.7
	Thomas Lockwood	2,602	40.3
8	John King (JAC D)	3,400	56.8
	Robert Leroy Livingston	2,586	43.2
9	Job Pierson (JAC D)	4,453	59.3
	John Dickinson	3,052	40.7
10	Gerrit Lansing (JAC D)	3,684	53.0
	Ambrose Spencer	3,274	47.1
11	Erastus Root (JAC D)	5,004	61.0
	Isaac Ogden	3,201	39.0
12	Joseph Bouck (JAC D)	3,509	64.9
	Peter Mann	1,898	35.1
13	William Angel (JAC D)	4,119	50.9
	Horace Lathrop	3,969	49.1
14	Samuel Beardsley (JAC D)	5,498	57.3
	Simon Dexter	3,850	40.1
15	Michael Hoffman (JAC D)	3,127	60.7
	Hiram Nolton	2,024	39.3
16	Nathan Soule (JAC D)	3,399	52.7
	Daniel Cady	3,049	47.3
17	John Taylor (NR)	2,597	42.0
	Samuel Young	2,350	38.0
	David Garnsey	1,238	20.0
18	Nathaniel Pitcher (JAC D)	3,294	52.5
	Henry Martindale	2,983	47.5
19	William Hogan (JAC D)	3,621	52.5
	Luther Bradish	1,843	26.7
	Thomas Gilson	1,434	20.8
21	John Collier (NR)	4,686	58.9
	Abial Cook	3,267	41.1
22	Edward C. Reed (JAC D)	4,531	51.7
	Eleazar Edgcomb	4,240	48.3
23	Freeborn Jewett (JAC D)	4,539	62.4
	William Jerome	2,739	37.6
24	Ulysses Doubleday (JAC D)	3,643	50.1
	Josiah Hopkins	3,399	46.8
25	Gamaliel Barstow (NR)	3,805	51.2
	Charles Humphrey	3,621	48.8
27	Frederick Whittlesey (NR)	7,410	65.8
	Calvin Bryan	3,846	34.2
28	Grattan Wheeler (NR)	5,950	54.5
	John Magee	4,961	45.5
29	Phineas Tracy (NR)	6,802	68.9
	Isaac Wilson	3,071	31.1
30	Bates Cooke (NR)	6,997	66.7
	Ebenezer Norton	3,093	29.5

Multimember Districts

		Votes	
3	Churchill G. Cambreleng (JAC D)	10,974	✓
	Campbell White (JAC D)	10,801	✓
	Gulian Verplanck (JAC D)	10,791	✓
	Abraham Lawrence	7,614	
	Thomas Smith	7,420	
	Adoniram Chandler	7,331	
	Thomas Hertell	2,246	

Candidates	Votes	%
John Frazce	2,158	
Isaac Pierce	2,126	

		Votes	
20	Daniel Wardwell (JAC D)	9,092	✓
	Charles Dayan (JAC D)	8,982	✓
	Chester Buck	6,172	
	George Fisher	6,044	
26	John Dickson (NR)	9,746	✓
	William Babcock (NR)	9,560	✓
	Jarad Wilson	7,361	
	Jehiel Halsey	7,281	

OHIO

		Votes	%
1	James Findlay (JAC R)	✓	
	Benham (NR)		
2	Thomas Corwin (NR)	✓	
	James Shields (JAC R)		
3	Joseph H. Crane (NR)	✓	
4	Joseph Vance (NR)	✓	
5	William Russell (JAC R)	✓	
6	William Creighton Jr (NR)	✓	
7	Samuel F. Vinton (NR)	✓	
8	William Stanbery (NR)	✓	
	McLean		
9	William W. Irvin (JAC R)	✓	
10	William Kennon Sr (NR)	✓	
11	Humphrey H. Leavitt (JAC R)	✓	
12	John Thomson (JAC R)	✓	
13	Elisha Whittlesey (NR)	4,114	43.6
	Sloane (A-MAS)	3,383	35.9
	Raven (JAC R)	1,938	20.5
14	Leonard Case (NR)	*	

PENNSYLVANIA

1	Joel B. Sutherland (D)	✓
	Simpson (D)	
2	Henry Horn (JAC)	✓
	Coxe (NR)	
3	John G. Watmough (NR)	✓
	Daniel H. Miller (D)	
5	Joel K. Mann	✓
6	John C. Bucher	✓
	Valentine Hummel	
10	Adam King	✓
12	Robert Allison	✓
13	George Burd	✓
14	Andrew Stewart	✓
15	Thomas M. T. McKennan	✓
16	Richard Coulter	✓
18	John Banks	✓

Multimember Districts

4	David Potts Jr	✓
	Joshua Evans Jr	✓
	William Hiester	✓
7	Henry King	✓
	Henry A. P. Muhlenburg	✓
8	Samuel A. Smith	✓
	Peter Ihrie Jr	✓
9	James Ford	✓
	Philander Stephens	✓
	Lewis Dewart	✓
11	Thomas H. Crawford	✓
	William Ramsey	✓
17	Harmar Denny	✓
	John Gilmore	✓

SOUTH CAROLINA

		Votes	%
1	William Drayton (UN D)		100.0
2	Robert W. Barnwell (D)		100.0
3	Thomas R. Mitchell	2,200	53.8
	John Campbell (SR W)	1,893	46.3
5	John K. Griffin (SR W)	✓	
	B. Watts		

	Candidates	Votes	%		Candidates	Votes	%
6	George McDuffie (D)	✓			William Slade	484	11.0
7	William T. Nuckolls	✓		3	Horace Everett	2,876	49.0
8	Warren R. Davis (SR D)	✓			Royal Ransom	2,038	34.7
9	James Blair (D)		100.0		Alden Partridge	790	13.5
				4	Bailey	2,925*	40.5
	VERMONT[1]				Heman Allen	2,613	36.2
					Galusha	842	11.7
1	Jonathan Hunt (NR)	2,735	58.5	5	William Cahoon (A-MAS)	4,128	52.6
	Orsamus C. Merrill (D)	1,483	31.7		Israil P. Dana	3,468	44.2
	Samuel Elliott	286	6.1				
2	Rollin C. Mallary	3,750	84.8				

1. No candidate received a majority of the vote in the 4th district required for election. A series of special elections were held in an attempt to meet the requirement. Herman Allen was finally elected in the eighth special election. No returns are available for these special elections.

1831 House Elections

ALABAMA

	Candidates	Votes	%
1	Clement Comer Clay (D)	2,770	100.0
2	Samuel W. Mardis (D)	5,400	41.6
	Jesse Winston Garth (NR)	4,611	35.5
	Robert E. B. Baylor (D)	2,976	22.9
3	Dixon Hall Lewis (SR D)	6,268	59.5
	John Murphy (D)	4,270	40.5

CONNECTICUT

	Candidates	Votes	%
AL	Ebenezer Young (NR)	15,889✓	
	Noyes Barber (NR)	11,950✓	
	Ralph Ingersoll (NR)	11,938✓	
	Jabez Huntington (NR)	10,946✓	
	William Ellsworth (NR)	10,931✓	
	William Storrs (NR)	10,750✓	
	Simeon Miner (D)	6,022	
	Isaac Touny (D)	5,784	
	Elisha Haley (D)	5,197	
	William Hollabird (D)	4,010	
	Thaddeus Betts (D)	3,242	

ILLINOIS

	Candidates	Votes	%
AL	Joseph Duncan (JAC D)	13,052	54.0
	Sidney Breese	4,659	19.3
	Edward Coles	3,397	14.0
	Alexander P. Field	1,844	7.6

INDIANA

	Candidates	Votes	%
1	Ratliff Boon (JAC D)	11,280	50.9
	John Law (JAC D)	10,868	49.1
2	John Carr (JAC D)	4,854	32.8
	William W. Wick (NR)	4,605	31.1
	James B. Ray (NR)	1,732	11.7
	Jonathan Jennings (NR)	1,680	11.3
	John H. Thompson (NR)	1,486	10.0
3	Jonathan McCarty (JAC D)	6,238	42.6
	Oliver H. Smith (JAC D)	5,297	36.2
	John Test (NR)	3,107	21.2

KENTUCKY[1]

	Candidates		
	Chilton Allen (CLAY D)	✓	
	Henry Daniel (JAC D)	✓	
	Richard M. Johnson (JAC D)	✓	
	Albert G. Hawes (JAC D)	✓	
	Nathan Gaither (D)	✓	
	Chittenden Lyon (D)	✓	
	John Adair (D)	✓	
	Charles A. Wickliffe (D)	✓	
	Joseph Lecompte (D)	✓	
	Robert P. Letcher (W)	✓	
	Christopher Tompkins (W)	✓	
	Thomas A. Marshall (W)	✓	

MARYLAND

	Candidates	Votes	%
1	Daniel Jenifer (NR)	1,717	59.0
	John J. Brooke	1,194	41.0
2	Benedict J. Semmes (D)	1,773	62.3
	Alexander Keech	1,072	37.7
3	George C. Washington (W)	3,145	100.0
4	Francis Thomas (D)	4,452	53.5
	Michael C. Sprigg	3,872	46.5
6	George E. Mitchell	2,770	53.2
	James W. Williams	2,438	46.8
7	John Leeds Kerr (W)	1,794	50.5
	Richard Spencer (D)	1,756	49.5
8	John S. Spence (D)	3,150	92.5

Multimember District

	Candidates	Votes	%
5	Benjamin C. Howard (D)	6,160✓	
	John T. H. Worthington (D)	5,740✓	
	Ebenezer L. Finley	4,973	
	Elias Brown (W)	1,997	

MISSISSIPPI

	Candidates	Votes	%
AL	Franklin E. Plummer (JAC D)	2,922	37.8
	David Dickson (JAC D)	1,981	25.7
	John N. Norton	979	12.7
	James C. Wilkins	958	12.4
	William L. Sharkey (NR)	744	9.6

MISSOURI

	Candidates	Votes	%
AL	Spencer D. Pettis (JAC D)	8,302	63.5
	Barton (NR)	4,775	36.5

Special Election

	Candidates	Votes	%
AL	William H. Ashley (D)	4,897	50.3
	Wells (D)	4,841	49.7

NEW HAMPSHIRE

	Candidates		
AL	Joseph Hammons (JAC D)	✓	
	Thomas Chandler (JAC D)	✓	
	John W. Weeks (JAC D)	✓	
	Henry Hubbard (JAC D)	✓	
	John Brodhead (JAC D)	✓	
	Joseph M. Harper (JAC D)	✓	

NORTH CAROLINA

	Candidates	Votes	%
1	William B. Shepard (D-R)	2,872	61.9
	John H. Wheeler (OPP R)	1,768	38.1
2	John Branch		100.0
3	Thomas H. Hall (D-R)	2,944	55.6
	Joseph R. Lloyd (OPP R)	2,352	44.4
4	Jesse Speight (D-R)		100.0
5	James I. McKay		100.0
6	Robert Potter (D-R)		100.0
7	Lauchlin Bethune (D-R)	3,086	50.3
	Edmund Deberry (OPP R)	3,049	49.7
8	Daniel L. Barringer (D-R)		100.0
9	Augustine H. Shepperd		100.0
10	Abraham Rencher (OPP R)		100.0
11	Henry W. Conner (D-R)	✓	
	Bartlett Shipp (OPP R)		
12	Samuel P. Carson (D-R)	4,422	76.5
	Anthony Casey (OPP R)	1,355	23.5
13	Lewis Williams		100.0

Special Election

	Candidates	Votes	%
6	Micajah T. Hawkins (D-R)	949	35.3
	Mann (D-R)	863	32.1
	James Wyche (OPP R)	533	19.8
	Pope (OPP R)	342	12.7

PENNSYLVANIA

Special Election

	Candidates	Votes	%
11	Robert McCoy (WOLF D)	2,459	44.4
	Mahon (A-WOLF D)	1,931	34.8
	McSherry (A-MAS)	1,154	20.8

RHODE ISLAND

	Candidates	Votes	%
AL	Tristam Burges (NR)	2,931✓	
	Dutee J. Pearce (NR)	2,727✓	

TENNESSEE

	Candidates	Votes	%
1	John Blair (D)	4,120	50.3
	William B. Carter (W)	4,076	49.7
2	Thomas D. Arnold (W)	4,935	51.2
	Pryor Lea (D)	4,702	48.8
3	James Standifer (W)	8,906	99.5
4	Jacob C. Isacks (D)	3,538	45.0
	John B. McCormick	3,068	39.0
	Hopkins L. Turney (D)	1,256	16.0
5	William Hall (D)	4,040	50.7
	Robert H. Burton	3,928	49.3
6	James K. Polk (D)	6,993	99.4
7	John Bell (W)	6,934	100.0
8	Cave Johnson (D)	5,111	99.8
9	William Fitzgerald (D)	8,534	51.8
	David Crockett (W)	7,948	48.2

VERMONT

Special Election

	Candidates	Votes	%
2	William Slade (A-MAS)	4,614	49.0
	Williams (NR)	3,815	40.5
	White (JAC)	838	8.9

VIRGINIA

	Candidates		
1	Thomas Newton Jr (NR)	✓	
	George Loyall (D)		
2	John Y. Mason (D)	✓	
	Eppes		
3	William S. Archer (D)	✓	
4	Mark Alexander	✓	
5	Thomas T. Bouldin (D)	✓	
	George W. Crump		
6	Thomas Davenport	✓	
7	Nathaniel H. Claiborne	✓	
8	Richard Coke Jr	✓	
	Braxton		
9	John J. Roane	✓	
	Upshaw		
	Bernard		
10	Joseph W. Chinn (D)	✓	
	John Taliaferro (NR)		
11	Andrew Stevenson (D)	✓	
12	William F. Gordon (D)	✓	
13	John M. Patton (D)	✓	
	Dade		
14	Charles F. Mercer (NR)	✓	
	Gibson (D)		
15	William Armstrong	✓	
	Lucas		
16	William McCoy	✓	
	Stribling		
17	Robert Craig	✓	
	Miller		
18	Charles C. Johnson	✓	
	Joseph Draper		
19	Lewis Maxwell (NR)	✓	
	Smith (NR)		
	Reynolds		
20	Robert Allen	✓	
	Mason		
21	Philip Doddridge	✓	
22	John S. Barbour	✓	
	Wallace		

1. It is not known whether the Kentucky representatives were elected at large or in districts.

1832 House Elections

DELAWARE

	Candidates	Votes	%
AL	John J. Milligan (W)	4,257	50.7
	Martin W. Bates (D)	4,142	49.3

GEORGIA

	Candidates	Votes	%
AL	James M. Wayne	34,010✓	
	Richard H. Wilde	29,813✓	
	George R. Gilmer	26,061✓	
	Augustin S. Clayton	25,854✓	
	Thomas F. Foster	25,517✓	
	Roger L. Gamble	24,278✓	
	Seaborn Jones	22,640✓	
	William Schley	22,376✓	
	John Coffee	22,284✓	
	Haynes	21,638	
	Owens	21,362	
	Terrell	21,361	
	Watson	20,884	
	Branham	20,535	
	Stewart	20,006	
	Harris	19,288	
	Newman	16,278	
	Lamar	16,136	
	Milton	5,157	

Special Election

		Votes	%
AL	Augustin S. Clayton	12,587	52.2
	William Schley	11,541	47.8

ILLINOIS

	Candidates	Votes	%
1	Charles Slade (D)	2,470	31.3
	Ninian Edwards (NR)	2,078	26.3
	Sidney Breese	1,770	22.4
	Charles Dunn	1,020	12.9
	Henry L. Webb	551	7.0
2	Zadoc Casey (D)	3,208	46.0
	William B. Archer (OPP D)	2,168	31.1
	Wickliff Kitchell	1,593	22.9
3	Joseph Duncan (D)	8,234	76.8
	Jonathan H. Pugh (OPP D)	2,323	21.7

LOUISIANA

	Candidates		
1	Edward D. White (W)	✓	
2	Philemon Thomas (D)	✓	
3	Henry A. Bullard (W)	✓	

MISSOURI[1]

	Candidates	Votes	%
AL	William H. Ashley (A-BANK)	9,498	51.8
	Robert W. Wells (PRO-BANK)	8,836	48.2

NEW JERSEY

	Candidates	Votes	%
AL	William N. Shinn (D)	24,383✓	
	Ferdinand S. Schenck (D&A-MASC)	24,288✓	
	Thomas Lee (D)	24,265✓	
	James Parker (D)	23,903✓	
	Philemon Dickerson (D&A-MASC)	23,860✓	
	Samuel Fowler (D&A-MASC)	23,808✓	
	Condict (NR-A-MAS)	23,784	
	Wright (NR-A-MAS)	23,779	
	Pennington (NR-A-MAS)	23,770	
	Reeves (NR)	23,325	
	Southard (NR)	23,310	
	Budd (NR)	23,257	

NEW YORK

	Candidates	Votes	%
1	Abel Huntington (D)	4,193	59.9
	David Gardiner (NR)	2,806	40.1
2	Isaac Van Houten (D)	3,007	57.5
	John Gurnee (NR)	2,224	42.5
4	Aaron Ward (D)	4,173	57.8
	Henry B. Cowles (NR)	3,051	42.2
5	Abraham Bockee (D)	4,728	52.7
	Edmund Pendleton (NR)	4,241	47.3
6	John Brown (D)	4,200	59.0
	Samuel Wilkin (NR)	2,923	41.0
7	Charles Bodle (D)	5,225	62.3
	Thomas Lockwood (NR)	3,167	37.7
9	Job Pierson (D)	4,849	53.5
	John Dickinson (NR)	4,213	46.5
10	Gerrit Lansing (D)	4,483	51.0
	Ambrose Spencer (NR)	4,302	49.0
11	John Cramer (D)	4,831	51.6
	John Taylor (NR)	4,531	48.4
12	Henry Martindale (NR)	3,037	44.5
	John McIntyre (D)	2,165	31.7
	Samuel Stevens (NR)	1,619	23.7
13	Reuben Whallon (D)	4,251	55.2
	Thomas Gibson (NR)	3,449	44.8
14	Ranson Gillet (D)	3,897	50.5
	Luther Bradish (NR)	3,817	49.5
15	Charles McVean (D)	4,554	56.2
	Howland Fish (NR)	3,546	43.8
16	Abijah Mann Jr (D)	4,964	59.6
	Ela Collins (NR)	3,362	40.4
18	Daniel Wardwell (D)	4,393	50.0
	Daniel Lee (NR)	4,387	50.0
19	Sherman Page (D)	4,914	54.9
	John Morris (NR)	4,039	45.1
20	Noadiah Johnson (D)	4,302	53.8
	John Collier (NR)	3,692	46.2
21	Henry Mitchell (D)	3,719	52.6
	Tilly Lynde (NR)	3,349	47.4
24	Rowland Day (D)	4,456	53.2
	Laban Hoskins (NR)	3,913	46.8
25	Samuel Clark (D)	4,899	52.4
	Joseph Colt (NR)	4,453	47.6
26	John Dickson (NR)	3,903	62.6
	John Price (D)	2,333	37.4
27	Edward Howell (D)	5,748	63.2
	William Woods (NR)	3,349	36.8
28	Frederick Whittlesey (NR)	4,828	58.9
	Isaac Hills (D)	3,374	41.1
29	George Lay (NR)	5,308	70.3
	David Miller (D)	2,248	29.8
30	Philo Fuller (NR)	5,248	57.8
	James Faulkner (D)	3,839	42.3
31	Abner Hazeltine (NR)	5,393	60.7
	Alson Leavenworth (D)	3,494	39.3
32	Millard Fillmore (NR)	4,184	69.6
	Jonathan Hoyt (D)	1,828	30.4
33	Gideon Hard (NR)	3,789	58.6
	Franklin Butterfield (D)	2,678	41.4

Multimember Districts

	Candidates	Votes	%
3	Cornelius Lawrence (D)	18,222✓	
	Campbell White (D)	18,171✓	
	Dudley Selden (D)	18,006✓	
	Churchill C. Cambreleng (D)	17,927✓	
	David Ogden (NR)	12,334	
	Hubert Van Wagenen (NR)	12,326	
	Jonathan Thompson (NR)	12,176	
	George Talman (NR)	12,158	
8	John Adams (D)	9,677✓	
	Aaron Vanderpoel (D)	9,565✓	
	Jedediah Miller (NR)	7,743	
	John Martin (NR)	7,642	
17	Samuel Beardsley (D)	9,121✓	
	Joel Turrill (D)	8,693✓	
	Charles P. Kirkland (NR)	8,487	
	Peter Sken Smith (NR)	8,220	
22	Nicoll Halsey (D)	8,329✓	
	Samuel G. Hathaway (D)	8,300✓	
	Eleazer W. Edgecomb (NR)	7,026	
	Gamaliel H. Barstow (NR)	7,009	
23	William K. Fuller (D)	8,934✓	
	William Taylor (D)	8,933✓	
	Elijah Rhoades (NR)	8,295	
	James B. Eldredge (NR)	8,279	

OHIO

	Candidates	Votes	%
1	Robert T. Lytle (D)	4,458	53.7
	Pendleton	3,847	46.3
2	Taylor Webster (D)	3,635	57.6
	Collins	2,678	42.4
3	Joseph H. Crane	2,821	44.8
	Helfenstein (D)	2,588	41.1
	Young	893	14.2
4	Thomas Corwin	3,756	52.6
	McLean (D)	3,387	47.4
5	Thomas L. Hamer (D)	2,171	32.5
	Fishback	2,069	31.0
	Morris (D)	2,028	30.4
	William Russell	403	6.0
6	Samuel F. Vinton	3,065	66.1
	House	1,569	33.9
7	William Allen (D)	3,739	50.0
	McArthur	3,737	50.0
8	Jeremiah McLene (D)	3,769	45.6
	Olds	3,193	38.7
	Parish	1,296	15.7
9	John Chaney (D)	4,235	54.0
	Irvin	3,609	46.0
10	Joseph Vance	4,854	71.9
	Shelby (D)	1,866	27.6
11	James M. Bell	3,131	50.3
	Shannon (D)	3,091	49.7
12	Robert Mitchell (D)	4,002	52.7
	Stanberry	3,591	47.3
13	David Spangler	3,277	43.8
	Colerick (D)	2,170	29.0
	Rigdon	2,038	27.2
14	William Patterson (D)	2,294	54.1
	Cooke	1,944	45.9
15	Jonathan Sloane	3,117	43.5
	Wood (D)	2,439	34.0
	Humphrey	1,614	22.5
16	Elisha Whittlesey	4,281	46.2
	Rayen (D)	2,980	32.2
	Webb	1,997	21.6
17	John Thomson (D)	2,856	55.5
	Potter	2,286	44.5
18	Benjamin Jones (D)	3,037	56.1
	Quimby	2,379	43.9
19	Humphrey H. Leavitt (D)	3,182	50.8
	Stokely	3,085	49.2

PENNSYLVANIA

	Candidates	Votes	%
1	Joel B. Sutherland (D)	2,366	50.0
	James Gowen (NR)	1,916	40.5
	Samuel B. Davis (UVD)	451	9.5
3	John G. Watnough (NR)	4,041	56.3
	J. R. Burden (D)	2,268	31.6
	Mahon M. Levis (UVD)	869	12.1
5	Joel K. Mann (D)	✓	
6	Robert Ramsey (D)	✓	
7	David D. Wagener (D)	✓	
8	Henry King (D)	✓	
9	Henry A. P. Muhlenburg (D)	✓	
10	William Clark (NR)	✓	
11	Charles A. Barnitz (NR)	✓	
12	George Chambers (NR)	✓	
13	Jesse Miller (D)	✓	
14	Joseph Henderson (D)	✓	
15	Andrew Beaumont (D)	✓	
16	Joseph B. Anthony (D)	✓	

	Candidates	Votes	%
17	John Laporte (D)	✓	
18	George Burd (D)	✓	
19	Richard Coulter (D)	✓	
20	Andrew Stewart (NR)	✓	
21	Thomas M. T. McKennan (NR)	✓	
22	Harmar Denny (A-MAS)	✓	
23	Samuel S. Harrison (D)	✓	
24	John Banks (A-MAS)	✓	
25	John Galbraith (D)	✓	

Multimember Districts

	Candidates	Votes	%
2	Horace Binney (NR)	5,364✓	
	James Harper (NR)	5,104✓	
	B. W. Richards (D)	3,396	
	Henry Horn (D)	3,191	
4	Edward Darlington (A-MAS)	✓	
	William Hiester (A-MAS)	✓	
	David Potts Jr (A-MAS)	✓	

VERMONT

	Candidates	Votes	%
1	Hiland Hall (W)	✓	
2	William Slade (W)	✓	
3	Horace Everett	✓	
4	Heman Allen (W)	✓	
5	Benjamin F. Deming (W)	✓	

1. Missouri's House representation was raised from one seat to two after the 1830 reapportionment, but in the 1832 general election only one seat was filled. The second representative was elected in 1833. See Missouri 1833.

1833 House Elections

ALABAMA

	Candidates	Votes	%
1	Clement C. Clay (D)	1,310	100.0
2	John McKinley (D)	3,724	52.5
	James Davis	3,369	47.5
3	Samuel W. Mardis (D)	5,242	57.2
	Elisha Young (NR)	2,053	22.4
	R. E. B. Baylor (D)	1,867	20.4
4	Dixon H. Lewis (SSR D)		100.0
5	John Murphy (D)	✓	
	James Dellet (W)		

CONNECTICUT

		Votes	%
AL	Noyes Barber (NR)	10,121✓	
	William Ellsworth (NR)	10,064✓	
	Ebenezer Young (NR)	10,045✓	
	Jabez Huntington (NR)	9,449✓	
	Samuel Foot (NR)	8,029✓	
	Samuel Tweedy (NR)	7,815✓	
	Andrew Judson (D&A-MASC)	7,469	
	Epaphias Porter (D&A-MASC)	7,376	
	William Hollabird (D&A-MASC)	7,229	
	Samuel Simons (D&A-MASC)	6,896	
	Gideon Wells (D&A-MASC)	6,842	
	Labern Clarke (D&A-MASC)	6,567	
	Richard Hubbard	2,143	
	Alanson Hamlin	2,021	
	Luther Loomis	446	
	Zalman Wildman	400	

INDIANA

		Votes	%
1	Ratliff Boon (D)	3,973	50.6
	Dennis Pennington	1,120	14.3
	Robert M. Evans	1,069	13.6
	James R. E. Goodlet	788	10.0
	Seth M. Levenworth	611	7.8
2	John Ewing (W)	1,921	20.9
	John W. Davis (D)	1,919	20.9
	John Law	1,668	18.2
	George Boon	1,459	15.9
	William C. Linton	1,183	12.9
	Hugh L. Livingston	1,022	11.1
3	John Carr (D)	4,530	58.2
	Harbin H. Moore	3,257	41.8
4	Amos Lane (D)	4,262	50.8
	John Test (W)	3,455	41.2
	Enoch McCarty	676	8.1
5	Jonathan McCarty (W)	4,590	51.8
	Oliver H. Smith (D)	4,268	48.2
6	George L. Kinnard (D)	5,412	52.8
	William W. Wick (D)	4,818	47.0
7	Edward A. Hannegan (D)	4,794	54.0
	Albert S. White (W)	4,056	45.7

KENTUCKY

		Votes	%
1	Chittenden Lyon	✓	
	Linn Boyd		
2	Albert G. Hawes (D)	2,998	50.8
	Philip Thompson (OPP)	2,902	49.2
3	Christopher Tompkins (W)	4,074	50.4
	Elijah Hise (D)	4,008	49.6
4	Martin Beaty	✓	
	Nathan Gaither		
	Elisha Smith		
5	Thomas P. Moore (D)	2,626*	51.0
	Robert P. Letcher (W)	2,521	49.0
6	Thomas Chilton	✓	
	James Allen		
7	Benjamin Hardin (W)	2,826	52.0
	C. A. Rudd	2,610	48.0
8	Patrick H. Pope	✓	
	Henry Crittenden		
9	James Love (D)	2,445	41.3

	Candidates	Votes	%
	John White (W)	2,189	37.0
	Smith	1,050	17.7
10	Chilton Allen		100.0
11	Amos Davis	2,990✓	
	James Crawford	2,372	
	Henry Daniel		
	Kenaz Farrow		
12	Thomas A. Marshall (W)	2,722	59.2
	Adam Beatty	1,874	40.8
13	Richard M. Johnson (D)	4,737	73.6
	John P. Gaines (W)	1,702	26.4

MAINE

		Votes	%
1	Rufus McIntire (JAC D)	✓	
2	Francis O. J. Smith (D)	✓	
3	Edward Kavanagh (D)	✓	
4	George Evans (NR)	3,542	52.1
	White (D)	2,693	39.6
5	Moses Mason (D)	✓	
6	Joseph Hall (D)	✓	
7	Leonard Jarvis (D)	✓	
8	Gorham Parks (D)	✓	

MARYLAND

		Votes	%
1	Littleton P. Dennis (NR)	3,213	51.7
	James A. Stewart (D)	3,003	48.3
2	Richard B. Carmichael (D)	3,243	51.9
	Hoffer (NR)	3,004	48.1
3	James Turner (NR)	3,049	49.3
	Sewell (D)	1,570	25.4
	Worthington	1,563	25.3
4	James P. Heath (NR)	2,805	52.0
	Howard (D)	2,592	48.0
5	Isaac McKim (D)	3,181	53.3
	Stewart (NR)	2,792	46.7
6	William Cost Johnson (NR)	3,063	55.6
	Dorsey (D)	2,442	44.4
7	Francis Thomas (D)	4,012	54.0
	Dixon (NR)	3,421	46.0
8	John T. Stoddert (D)	2,360	51.3
	David Jenifer (NR)	2,244	48.7

MASSACHUSETTS

		Votes	%
1	Benjamin Gorham (NR)	2,304	56.1
	Theodore Lyman (D)	1,320	32.2
	Amasa Walker (A-MAS)	429	10.5
2	Rufus Choate (NR)	2,216	59.0
	Joseph S. Cabot (D)	1,204	32.1
	William B. Breed	324	8.6
3	Gayton P. Osgood (D&A-MASC)	3,279	51.4
	Caleb Cushing (NR)	2,895	45.4
4	Edward Everett (NR)	2,413	77.7
	John Wade	667	21.5
5	John Davis (NR)	2,848	85.9
	John Spurry	328	9.9
6	George Grennell Jr. (NR)	2,521	71.6
	William Whitaker	599	17.0
	Israel Billings	309	8.8
7	George N. Briggs (NR)	2,705	64.4
	Russell Brown	1,273	30.3
8	Isaac C. Bates (NR)	2,168	72.6
	William W. Thompson	333	11.1
	Samuel Lathrop (A-MAS)	223	7.5
9	William Jackson (A-MAS)	2,869	50.9
	Henry A. S. Dearborn (NR)	1,841	32.7
	Daniel Thurber (D)	652	11.6
10	William Baylies (NR)	2,899	50.9
	Micah B. Ruggles	2,554	44.8
11	John Reed (NR)	1,442	96.9
12	John Quincy Adams (A-MAS)	2,592	75.5
	Frederick Lincoln	714	20.8

MISSISSIPPI

	Candidates	Votes	%
AL	Franklin E. Plummer (W)	7,826✓	
	Harry Cage (D)	7,682✓	
	John L. Guion (W)	4,523	
	Felix H. Walker	2,243	
	Nathan Bouldin	1,223	

MISSOURI[1]

		Votes	%
AL	John Bull (W)	3,671	27.7
	Strother (JAC D)	3,630	27.4
	Shannon (JAC D)	3,430	25.9
	Birch (I)	2,130	16.1

NEW HAMPSHIRE

		Votes	%
AL	Henry Hubbard (D)	✓	
	Franklin Pierce (D)	✓	
	Robert Burns (D)	✓	
	Benning M. Bean (D)	✓	
	Joseph M. Harper (D)	✓	
	Azel Hatch (A-MAS)		
	John Gould (A-MAS)		
	D. C. Atkinson (A-MAS)		
	John Harvey (A-MAS)		
	Caleb Emery (A-MAS)		
	Samuel E. Cones (NR)		
	James Wilson Jr. (NR)		
	John Wingate (NR)		
	Leonard Wilcox (NR)		
	Anthony Colby (NR)		

NORTH CAROLINA

		Votes	%
1	William B. Shepard (W)		100.0
2	Jesse A. Bynum (W)	2,198	59.8
	Andrew Joyner	1,476	40.2
3	Thomas H. Hall	✓	
4	Jesse Speight (D)		100.0
5	James I. McKay (D)	2,570	55.6
	Lewis Dishongh (W)	2,056	44.4
6	Micajah T. Hawkins (D)	1,694	38.9
	Robert P. Gilliam	1,472	33.8
	William P. Williams	1,189	27.3
7	Edmund Deberry (W)	3,268	50.3
	Lauchlin Bethune (D)	3,231	49.7
8	Daniel L. Barringer (W)	2,497	50.6
	John G. A. Williamson (D)	2,436	49.4
9	Augustine H. Shepperd (D)		100.0
10	Abraham Rencher (W)		100.0
11	Henry W. Conner (D)		100.0
12	James Graham (W)	3,272	41.6
	Samuel P. Carson (D)	2,402	30.6
	David Newland	2,183	27.8
13	Lewis Williams		0.0

PENNSYLVANIA[2]

Special Election

		Votes	%
1	Joel B. Sutherland	2,835	57.0
	John Sergeant	2,139	43.0

RHODE ISLAND[3]

		Votes	%
AL	Tristam Burges (W)	3,162✓	
	Dutee J. Pearce (D)	2,078	
	Updike (W)	1,913	
	Sprague (D)	1,499	
	Cranston (W)	376	
	Greene (W)	364	
	Dixon (W)	168	

Candidates	Votes	%
Special Election		
AL Dutee J. Pearce (D)	2,152	55.2
Dixon (W)	1,705	43.7
SOUTH CAROLINA		
1 Henry L. Pinckney (D)	✓	
A. M. S. Harris (UN)		
Joel R. Poinsett (UN)		
2 William J. Grayson (W)	1,282	79.2
Benjamin Allston (UN)	335	20.7
3 Thomas Singleton (SR)	2,089	55.7
Thomas R. Mitchell (UN)	1,665	44.4
4 John M. Felder (D)	✓	
5 John K. Griffin (SR W)	✓	
6 George McDuffie (D)	2,991	70.4
J. Pressley (UN)	1,254	29.5
7 William K. Clowney (SR)	4,514	51.2
Thomas Williams (UN)	4,309	48.8
8 Warren R. Davis (SR D)	✓	
Grisham (UN)		
9 James Blair (D)		100.0
TENNESSEE		
1 John Blair (D)	3,236	42.4
William B. Carter (W)	2,642	34.7
Thomas D. Arnold (W)	1,747	22.9
2 Samuel Bunch (W)	4,319	70.4
John Cocke (D)	1,815	29.6
3 Luke Lea (UN D)	3,558	46.7
Joseph Williams (W)	2,145	28.1
John F. Gillespie	1,921	25.2

Candidates	Votes	%
4 James Standifer (W)	4,172	57.4
James Greene	3,100	42.6
5 John B. Forester	3,862	55.9
Jacob C. Isaacs	3,051	44.1
6 Balie Peyton (W)	4,710	74.4
Archibald W. Overton	1,621	25.6
7 John Bell (W)	5,951	100.0
8 David W. Dickinson (D)	2,452	42.4
William Brady	2,209	38.2
Abraham Maury (W)	1,129	19.5
9 James K. Polk (D)	4,751	68.5
Thomas Porter	1,512	21.8
T. F. Bradford	671	9.7
10 William M. Inge (D)	5,013	61.8
James W. Combs	1,593	19.6
Thomas D. Davenport	1,508	18.6
11 Cave Johnson (D)	3,386	45.1
Richard Cheatham (W)	2,468	32.9
John H. Marable	1,651	22.0
12 David Crockett (W)	3,985	51.1
William Fitzgerald (D)	3,812	48.9
13 Christopher H. Williams (W)	2,374	34.6
William C. Dunlap (D)	2,364✓	34.5
Adam R. Alexander	2,123	30.9
VIRGINIA		
1 George Loyall (D)	1,428	53.1
Miles King (NR)	1,261	46.9
2 John Y. Mason (D)	✓	
3 William S. Archer (D)	✓	
4 James H. Gholson (NR)	✓	
George C. Dromgoole (D)		
Knox		
Goode		

Candidates	Votes	%
5 John Randolph (NR)	✓	
6 Thomas Davenport (NR)	✓	
Cabell		
7 Nathaniel H. Claiborne (D)		
8 Henry A. Wise (D)	✓	
Richard Coke Jr (NR)		
9 William P. Taylor (NR)	✓	
John J. Roane (D)		
Upshaw		
10 Joseph W. Chinn (D)	✓	
John Taliaferro (NR)		
11 Andrew Stevenson (D)	✓	
John Robertson (NR)		
12 William F. Gordon (NR)	✓	
13 John M. Patton (D)	✓	
14 Charles F. Mercer (NR)	✓	
Mason (D)		
15 Edward Lucas (D)	✓	
Archer		
Naylor		
A. Smith		
16 James M. H. Beale (D)	✓	
Meyerhoeffer		
Steele		
17 Samuel McDowell Moore (NR)	✓	
Craig (D)		
18 John H. Fulton (D)	✓	
Byars		
19 William McComas (D)	✓	
Smith		
20 John J. Allen (NR)	✓	
Maxwell		
21 Edgar C. Wilson (NR)	✓	
Morgan		

1. Missouri added a second representative after the 1830 census. See Missouri 1832.

2. Joel B. Sutherland was elected from Pennsylvania's 1st district in 1832. He subsequently resigned to become an associate judge of the court of common pleas in Philadelphia, but then ran for and won back his House seat in an 1833 special election.

3. Rhode Island had two House seats for the 23rd Congress (1833–1835). A majority of the vote was required for election. Dutee J. Pearce failed to qualify in the initial election, but was later elected over Dixon in a special election for which no returns are available.

1834 House Elections

CONNECTICUT

Special Election

	Candidates	Votes	%
AL	Phineas Miner (W)	17,007✓	
	Ebenezer Jackson (W)	16,920✓	
	Joseph Trumbull (W)	16,906✓	
	Luther Loomis (D)	16,696	
	Lancelot Phelps (D)	16,668	
	Samuel Ingham (D)	16,464	
	Richard Hubbard (A-MASC)	1,186	
	Horace Cowles (A-MASC)	1,150	
	Sheldon Leavitt (A-MASC)	1,104	
	Samuel Ingram	230	

DELAWARE

		Votes	%
AL	John J. Milligan (W)	4,779	50.8
	Bayard (D)	4,626	49.2

GEORGIA

		Votes	%
AL	James M. Wayne (D)	32,933*	
	William Schley (D)	32,852✓	
	Charles E. Haynes (D)	32,609✓	
	George W. B. Towns (D)	32,603✓	
	John Coffee (D)	32,581✓	
	George W. Owens (D)	32,530✓	
	James C. Terrell (D)	32,493✓	
	Seaton Grantland (D)	32,445✓	
	John W. A. Sanford (D)	32,412✓	
	Gilmer (W)	28,417	
	Wilde (W)	28,294	
	Foster (W)	28,036	
	Gamble (W)	27,835	
	Chappell (W)	27,673	
	Lamar (W)	27,507	
	Beall (W)	27,500	
	Newman (W)	27,457	
	Daniel (W)	27,447	

ILLINOIS

		Votes	%
1	John Reynolds (D)	4,523	45.9
	Adam W. Snider (D)	3,723	37.8
	Edward Humphrey	1,603	16.3
2	Zadoc Casey (D)	5,647	58.3
	William H. Davidson (D)	4,036	41.7
3	William L. May (D)	6,828	52.8
	Benjamin Mills	6,117	47.3

Special Elections

		Votes	%
1	John Reynolds (D)	1,721	48.0
	Perrie Menard	871	24.3
	William Orr	501	14.0
	H. L. Webb	490	13.7
3	William May (D)	2,705	72.7
	Benjamin Mills	956	25.7

KENTUCKY

Special Election

		Votes	%
5	Robert P. Letcher (W)	3,731	51.9
	Thomas P. Moore (D)	3,461	48.1

LOUISIANA

		Votes	%
1	Henry Johnson (W)	2,417	55.9
	Gayarre	1,384	32.0
	Nicholls	523	12.1
2	Eleazer W. Ripley (D)	1,162	42.2
	Chinn (W)	900	32.7
	J. M. Bradford	434	15.8
	Woodroof	258	9.4

	Candidates	Votes	%
3	Rice Garland (W)	1,989	59.1
	Walker	1,378	40.9

MAINE[1]

		Votes	%
1	Jeremiah Goodwin (D)	3,685*	43.9
	Horace Porter (W)	3,511	41.9
	W. A. Hayes	500	6.0
	J. McDonald	492	5.9
2	Francis O. J. Smith (D)	5,262	51.9
	James C. Churchill (W)	4,827	47.7
3	Jeremiah Bailey (W)	4,240	51.7
	Edward Kavanagh (D)	3,778	46.1
4	George Evans (W)	5,134	59.4
	Amos Nourse (D)	3,301	38.2
5	Moses Mason Jr. (D)	4,791	53.8
	Oliver Herrick (W)	3,736	41.9
6	Joseph Hall (D)	4,251	61.9
	Webster Kelly (W)	2,402	35.0
7	Leonard Jarvis (D)	3,742	50.7
	Elijah Hamlin (W)	3,417	46.3
8	Gorham Parks (D)	6,192	55.4
	Edward Kent (W)	4,831	43.3

MASSACHUSETTS

		Votes	%
1	Abbott Lawrence (W)	5,508	64.9
	William Foster (D)	2,528	29.8
2	Stephen C. Phillips (W)	4,230	59.9
	Joseph S. Cabot (D)	2,784	39.4
3	Caleb Cushing (W)	4,353	58.1
	Gayton P. Osgood (D)	2,683	35.8
4	Samuel Hoar (W)	2,153	54.5
	Herman Lincoln	871	22.1
	James Russell	646	16.4
5	Levi Lincoln (W)	4,777	74.1
	Madison S. Fisher (D)	1,653	25.6
6	George Grennell Jr (W)	3,434	65.5
	Israel Billings (A-MAS)	1,520	29.0
7	George N. Briggs (W)	4,229	59.1
	Theodore Sedgwick (D)	2,902	40.6
8	William B. Calhoun (W)	3,839	61.3
	Oliver Warner (D)	2,409	38.4
9	William Jackson (A-MAS)	3,003	67.5
	Daniel Thurber (D)	1,121	25.2
10	Nathaniel B. Borden (D)	4,306	53.5
	William Baylis (W)	3,697	45.9
11	John Reed (A-MAS)	2,352	79.1
	William J. A. Bradford (D)	607	20.4
12	John Quincy Adams (A-MAS)	3,234	86.8

Special Elections

		Votes	%
2	Stephen C. Phillips (W)	4,245	60.1
	Joseph S. Cabot (D)	2,778	39.3
5	Levi Lincoln (W)	4,226	77.3
	Isaac Davis (D)	1,113	20.4

NEW JERSEY

		Votes	%
AL	William N. Shinn (D)	27,413✓	
	Philemon Dickerson (D)	27,404✓	
	Ferdinand S. Schenck (D)	27,398✓	
	Thomas Lee (D)	27,396✓	
	James Parker (D)	27,390✓	
	Samuel Fowler (D)	27,358✓	
	Condict (W)	26,413	
	Randolph (W)	26,393	
	Pennington (W)	26,384	
	Spencer (W)	26,373	
	Ogden (W)	26,372	
	Brick (W)	26,339	

NEW YORK

	Candidates	Votes	%
1	Abel Huntingdon (D)	4,442	58.5
	Abraham T. Rose (W)	3,152	41.5
2	Samuel Barton (D)	3,943	59.9
	Billop B. Seaman (W)	2,642	40.1
4	Aaron Ward (D)	4,527	57.9
	Horace Bailey (W)	3,290	42.1
5	Abraham Rockee (D)	4,948	55.2
	Edmund H. Pendleton (W)	4,022	44.8
6	John W. Brown (D)	4,337	55.7
	Thomas McKissock (W)	3,445	44.3
7	Nicholas Sickles (D)	5,676	62.6
	Jacob H. Dewitt (W)	3,393	37.4
9	Hiram P. Hunt (W)	4,985	50.1
	Job Pierson (D)	4,961	49.9
10	Gerit Y. Lansing (D)	4,944	52.2
	Daniel D. Barnard (W)	4,521	47.8
11	John Cramer (D)	5,160	50.9
	Anson Brown (W)	4,978	49.1
12	David Russell (W)	3,942	59.5
	John McLean (D)	2,681	40.5
13	Henry H. Ross (W)	4,296	50.3
	Dudley Farlin (D)	4,246	49.7
14	Ransom H. Gillet (D)	4,134	53.5
	Joseph W. Smith (W)	3,589	46.5
15	Matthias J. Bovee (D)	4,695	53.4
	Peter J. Waggoner (W)	4,104	46.6
16	Abijah Mann Jr. (D)	5,246	62.3
	Elisha P. Hurlbut (W)	3,175	37.7
18	Daniel Wardwell (D)	4,512	50.3
	Jesse Smith (W)	4,467	49.8
19	Sherman Page (D)	5,122	57.9
	Don F. Herrick (W)	3,719	42.1
20	William Seymour (D)	4,950	58.4
	Erastus Root (W)	3,532	41.6
21	William Mason (D)	3,930	54.2
	Alvah Hunt (W)	3,320	45.8
24	U. F. Doubleday (D)	4,759	55.0
	Laban Hoskins (W)	3,898	45.0
25	Graham H. Chapin (D)	5,183	52.0
	John M. Holley (W)	4,781	48.0
26	Francis Granger (W)	4,378	59.5
	Oliver Phelps (D)	2,986	40.6
27	Joshua Lee (D)	6,077	60.9
	Aaron Remur (W)	3,907	39.1
28	Timothy Childs (W)	5,076	54.9
	Fletcher M. Haight (D)	4,164	45.1
29	George W. Lay (W)	6,409	62.5
	John B. Skinner (D)	3,844	37.5
30	Philo C. Fuller (W)	5,928	56.0
	James McCall (D)	4,658	44.0
31	Abner Hazeltine (W)	6,250	55.8
	Oliver Lee (D)	4,946	44.2
32	Thomas C. Love (W)	4,783	66.0
	George P. Barker (D)	2,468	34.0
33	Gideon Hard (W)	4,156	51.9
	Nathan Dayton (D)	3,854	48.1

Multimember Districts

		Votes	%
3	Churchill C. Cambreleng (D)	19,019✓	
	Campbell P. White (D)	18,983✓	
	John McKeon (D)	18,871✓	
	Ely Moore (D)	18,552✓	
	Ogden Hoffman (W)	16,822	
	G. C. Verplanck (W)	16,807	
	James G. King (W)	16,642	
	Dudley Selden (W)	16,578	
8	Aaron Vanderpoel (D)	10,287✓	
	Valentine Efner (D)	10,210✓	
	Killian Miller (W)	8,166	
	Benjamin Pond (W)	8,153	
17	Samuel Beardsley (D)	9,597✓	
	Joel Turrill (D)	9,488✓	
	Joshua A. Spencer (W)	8,665	

Candidates	Votes	%
Peter Sken Smith (W)	8,546	
22 Joseph Reynolds (D)	8,870✓	
Stephen B. Leonard (D)	8,859✓	
William A. Ely (W)	7,644	
John James Speed Jr (W)	7,220	
23 William Taylor (D)	9,466✓	
William K. Fuller (D)	9,461✓	
Victory Birdseye (W)	8,045	
J. D. Ledyard (W)	8,034	

OHIO

Candidates	Votes	%
1 Bellamy Storer (W)	4,327	50.6
Lytle (D)	4,231	49.4
2 Taylor Webster (D)	3,328	52.6
McNutt (W)	3,001	47.4
3 Joseph H. Crane (W)	4,165	52.4
Helfenstein (D)	3,781	47.6
4 Thomas Corwin (W)	3,847	58.6
McDowell (D)	2,723	41.5
5 Thomas L. Hamer (D)	3,479	68.7
Jones (W)	1,586	31.3
6 Samuel F. Vinton (W)	3,825	62.6
Jolline (D)	2,283	37.4
7 William K. Bond (W)	4,333	51.8
Allen (D)	4,037	48.2
8 Jeremiah McLene (D)	3,919	51.1
Olds (W)	3,751	48.9
9 John Chaney (D)	4,447	58.5
Irvin (W)	3,158	41.5
10 Samson Mason (W)	4,382	66.2
Ellsbury (D)	1,950	29.5
11 William Kennon Sr (D)	3,496	50.5
Bell (W)	3,427	49.5
12 Elias Howell (W)	4,294	54.3
Mitchell (D)	3,610	45.7
13 David Spangler (W)	3,410	56.3
Colerick (D)	2,644	43.7
14 William Patterson (D)	4,731	52.7
Bartley (W)	4,243	47.3
15 Jonathan Sloane (W)	5,453	51.6
Rice (D)	5,116	48.4
16 Elisha Whittlesey (W)	5,616	60.2
Dart (D)	3,721	39.9
17 John Thompson (D)	2,346	59.8
Richardson (W)	1,327	33.8
McCraig (A-MASC)	253	6.4
18 Benjamin Jones (D)	2,739	51.8
Quinby (W)	2,548	48.2
19 Daniel Kilgore (D)	3,370	51.7
Stokely (W)	3,143	48.3

PENNSYLVANIA

Candidates	Votes	%
1 Joel B. Sutherland (D)	3,782	61.7
Gowen (W)	2,345	38.3
3 Michael W. Ash (D)	5,757	55.6
Watmough (W)	4,598	44.4
5 Jacob Fry Jr (D)	3,766	55.3
Royer (W)	3,047	44.7
6 Mathias Morris (W)	3,341	52.4
Chapman (D)	3,040	47.6
7 David D. Wagener (D)	4,602	72.8
Brown (W)	1,718	27.2
8 Edward B. Hubley (D)	3,648	59.6
Livingston (W)	2,478	40.5
9 Henry A. P. Muhlenburg (D)	4,816	69.3
Kirbey (W)	2,132	30.7
10 William Clark (W)	3,396	54.3
Bucher (D)	2,859	45.7
11 Henry Logan (D)	3,218	55.1
Barnitz (W)	2,619	44.9
12 George Chambers (W)	4,085	59.8
Heck (D)	2,751	40.2
13 Jesse Miller (D)	3,906	51.4
Whitesides (W)	3,696	48.6
14 Joseph Henderson (D)	4,239	52.5
Milliken (W)	3,830	47.5
15 Andrew Beaumont (D)	3,902	56.1
Shoemaker (W)	3,051	43.9
16 Joseph B. Anthony (D)	5,437	62.8
Packer (W)	3,226	37.2
17 John Laporte (D)	4,264	56.8
Williston (W)	3,239	43.2
18 Job Mann (D)	3,535	54.6
Ogle (W)	2,938	45.4
19 John Klingensmith Jr. (D)	4,359	59.7
Coulter (W)	2,939	40.3
20 Andrew Buchanan (D)	3,428	59.0
Stewart (W)	2,387	41.1
21 Thomas M. T. McKennan (W)	2,703	51.3
Ringland (D)	2,569	48.7
22 Harmar Denny (W)	3,428	53.5
Snowden (D)	2,976	46.5
23 Samuel S. Harrison (D)	3,845	69.8
Gilmore (W)	1,664	30.2
24 John Banks (W)	2,748	52.2
Power (D)	2,514	47.8
25 John Galbraith (D)	4,642	60.7
Sill (W)	3,011	39.3

Multimember Districts

Candidates	Votes	%
2 Joseph R. Ingersoll (W)	5,589✓	
James Harper (W)	5,560✓	
Linnard (D)	3,710	
Horn (D)	3,671	
4 David Potts Jr (W)	10,348✓	
William Heister (W)	10,348✓	
Edward Darlington (W)	10,329✓	

Candidates	Votes	%
Archibald T. Dick (D)	8,477	
Benjamin Champneys (D)	8,472	
John Morgan (D)	8,471	

SOUTH CAROLINA

Candidates	Votes	%
1 Henry L. Pinckney (SR)	1,680	52.8
Alfred Huger (UN)	1,503	47.2
2 William J. Grayson (SR)	✓	
Unidentified Candidate (SSR & SC)		
3 Robert B. Campbell (SR)	2,242	53.2
James C. Postell (UN)	1,948	46.3
4 James H. Hammond (SR)	4,025	100.0
5 John K. Griffin (SR)		100.0
6 Francis W. Pickens (SR)	2,836	74.6
John S. Pressly (UN)	968	25.5
7 James Rogers (UN)	4,213	51.1
William K. Clowney (SR)	4,038	48.9
8 Warren R. Davis (SR)	2,925*	50.6
Perry (UN)	2,855	49.4
9 Richard I. Manning (UN)	1,392	64.5
Rees (SR)	765	35.5

Special Elections

Candidates	Votes	%
3 Robert B. Campbell (NULL)	✓	
James C. Postell (UN)		
6 Francis W. Pickens (SR)	✓	
John S. Pressly (UN)		

VERMONT

Candidates	Votes	%
1 Hiland Hall (W)	3,395	50.7
Robinson (D)	1,872	28.0
2 William Slade (A-MAS)	4,012	55.0
Jonas Clark (D)	1,494	20.5
Robert Pierpont (W)	1,491	20.5
3 Horace Everett (W)	3,717	44.6
Sam C. Loveland (A-MAS)	2,774	33.3
Alden Partridge (D)	1,768	21.2
4 Heman Allen (W)	2,574	51.2
Vanness (D)	1,678	33.4
Smith	778	15.5
5 Henry F. Janes (A-MAS)	3,641	51.5
Isaac Fletcher (D)	3,398	48.1

VIRGINIA

Special Elections

Candidates	Votes	%
5 James W. Bouldin (D)	✓	
Beverly Tucker (W)		
11 John Robertson (W)	689	67.6
Roane (D)	331	32.5

1. No candidate in Maine's 1st district received the majority vote required for election. At a later special election, Rufus McIntyre was elected. No returns are available for the special election.

1835 House Elections

ALABAMA

	Candidates	Votes	%
1	Reuben Chapman (D)	4,403	47.8
	Thomas D. Glascock (D)	2,993	32.5
	Scott (D)	1,819	19.7
2	Joshua L. Martin (D)	✓	
	Davis		
	Thatch		
3	Joab Lawler (W)	2,498	40.2
	Shortridge (D)	2,362	38.0
	May	1,356	21.8
4	Dixon H. Lewis (SR D)		100.0
5	Francis S. Lyon (W)	✓	
	Baylor (D)		
	Bates		

CONNECTICUT

	Candidates	Votes	%
AL	Samuel Ingham (D)	21,286✓	
	Isaac Toucey (D)	21,262✓	
	Zalmon Wildman (D)	21,220✓	
	Andrew T. Judson (D)	21,160✓	
	Lancelot Phelps (D)	21,059✓	
	Elisha Haley (D)	21,019✓	
	John Holley (W)	19,170	
	Noyes Barbor (W)	18,931	
	Ebenezer Young (W)	18,888	
	Samuel Tweedy (W)	18,881	
	Ebenezer Jackson (W)	18,809	
	Joseph Trumbull (W)	18,649	
	Horace Cowles	353	
	Sheldon Leavit	328	
	Elisha Stearns	313	
	Richard Hubbard	313	
	William Waterbury	301	

GEORGIA

Special Election

	Candidates	Votes	%
AL	Thomas Glascock (D)	30,540✓	
	Jesse F. Cleveland (D)	30,077✓	
	Jabez Y. Jackson (D)	30,072✓	
	Hopkins Holsey (D)	29,727✓	
	Wilde (W)	27,542	
	Foster (W)	27,525	
	Gamble (W)	27,266	
	Beall (W)	26,871	

INDIANA

	Candidates	Votes	%
1	Ratliff Boon (D)	4,028	51.4
	John G. Clendenin (W)	3,815	48.6
2	John W. Davis (D)	5,499	55.3
	John Ewing (W)	4,440	44.7
3	John Carr (D)	5,048	56.1
	Charles Dewey (W)	3,954	43.9
4	Amos Lane (D)	4,769	50.4
	George H. Dunn (W)	4,667	49.6
5	Jonathan McCarty (W)	4,824	48.9
	James Rariden (W)	2,684	27.2
	John Finley	2,353	23.9
6	George L. Kinnard (D)	7,483	61.6
	Jacob B. Lowe	4,658	38.4
7	Edward A. Hannegan (D)	6,910	66.3
	James Gregory (W)	3,515	33.7

KENTUCKY

	Candidates	Votes	%
1	Linn Boyd (D)	✓	
2	Albert G. Hawes (JAC D)	✓	
3	Joseph R. Underwood (W)	✓	
4	Sherrod Williams (W)	✓	
5	James Harlan (W)	✓	
6	John Calhoon (W)	✓	
7	Benjamin Hardin (W)	✓	

	Candidates	Votes	%
8	William J. Graves (W)	✓	
9	John White (W)	✓	
10	Chilton Allan (CLAY D)	✓	
11	Richard French (D)	✓	
12	John Chambers (W)	✓	
13	Richard M. Johnson (JAC D)	✓	

MARYLAND

	Candidates	Votes	%
1	John N. Steele (W)	1,967	100.0
2	James A. Pearce (W)	3,386	50.2
	Unidentified Candidate (D)	3,363	49.8
3	James Turner (W)	2,866	51.1
	Unidentified Candidate (D)	2,748	49.0
5	George C. Washington (W)	1,058	100.0
6	Francis Thomas (D)	3,838	53.0
	Unidentified Candidate (W)	3,405	47.0
7	Daniel Jenifer (W)	1,919	58.7
	Unidentified Candidate (D)	1,352	41.3

Multimember District

	Candidates	Votes	%
4	Benjamin C. Howard (D)	6,738✓	
	Isaac McKim (D)	6,675✓	
	Unidentified Candidate (W)	6,205	
	Unidentified Candidate (W)	6,111	

MICHIGAN[1]

(Became a state Jan. 26, 1837)

	Candidates	Votes	%
AL	Isaac Crary (D)	7,019	94.9

MISSISSIPPI

	Candidates	Votes	%
AL	David Dickson (D)	9,387✓	
	John F. H. Claiborne (D)	8,836✓	
	James C. Wilkins (W)	7,445	
	Benjamin W. Edwards (D)	7,396	
	Harry Vose	224	

MISSOURI

	Candidates	Votes	%
AL	William H. Ashley (I)	12,825✓	
	Albert G. Harrison (D)	10,856✓	
	Strother (D)	10,677	
	Birch (I)	8,843	

NEW HAMPSHIRE

	Candidates	Votes	%
AL	Robert Burns (D)	✓	
	Samuel Cushman (D)	✓	
	Joseph Weeks (D)	✓	
	Franklin Pierce (D)	✓	
	Benning M. Bean (D)	✓	
	Samuel Hale		
	Samuel W. Carr		
	James Wilson Jr		
	Anthony Colby		
	Joseph Bell		

NORTH CAROLINA

	Candidates	Votes	%
1	William B. Shepard (W)	2,534	85.5
	Isaac Pipkin (D)	429	14.5
2	Jesse A. Bynum (D)	2,228	52.9
	William L. Long (W)	1,986	47.1
3	Ebenezer Pettigrew (W)	3,072	54.9
	Thomas H. Hall (D)	2,529	45.2
4	Jesse Speight (D)	3,017	57.3
	John McLeod (W)	2,250	42.7
5	James I. McKay (D)	2,690	63.4
	Lewis Dishongh (W)	1,553	36.6
6	Micajah T. Hawkins (D)	2,540	62.5
	Josiah Crudup (W)	1,522	37.5
7	Edmund Deberry (W)	3,426	53.8

	Candidates	Votes	%
	Lauchlin Bethune (D)	2,940	46.2
8	William Montgomery (D)	2,695	50.4
	Daniel L. Barringer (D)	2,654	49.6
9	Augustine H. Shepperd (W)	✓	
10	Abraham Rencher (SR W)	3,078	51.4
	Burton Craige (W)	1,619	27.0
	Richard M. Pearson (W)	1,297	21.6
11	Henry W. Conner (D)	3,385	63.2
	Bartlett Shipp (W)	1,974	36.8
12	James Graham (W)	3,733‡	48.6
	David Newland (W)	3,726	48.5
13	Lewis Williams (W)	✓	

RHODE ISLAND

	Candidates	Votes	%
AL	William Sprague (D)	3,924✓	
	Dutee J. Pearce (D)	3,901✓	
	Burges (W)	3,776	
	Cranston (W)	3,659	
	Ruyers	101	

TENNESSEE

	Candidates	Votes	%
1	William B. Carter (W)	3,696	48.6
	Alexander Anderson (D)	2,054	27.0
	Thomas D. Arnold (W)	1,863	24.5
2	Samuel Bunch (W)	4,370	68.3
	David Adams (D)	2,026	31.7
3	Luke Lea (UN D)	4,250	58.7
	Joseph L. Williams (W)	2,992	41.3
4	James Standifer (W)	4,383	60.1
	William T. Senter (D)	2,915	39.9
5	John B. Forester (W)	5,645	83.5
	Peter Buram (D)	1,112	16.5
6	Balie Peyton (W)	3,530	100.0
7	John Bell (W)	4,832	100.0
8	Abram P. Maury (W)	3,006	60.6
	Robert Jetton (D)	1,956	39.4
9	James K. Polk (D)	5,165	100.0
10	Ebenezer J. Shields (W)	3,217	40.5
	Thomas Porter	2,381	30.0
	A. A. Kincannon	2,344	29.5
11	Cave Johnson (D)	2,714	63.7
	William Turner (W)	1,549	36.3
12	Adam Huntsman (D)	4,652	51.4
	David Crockett (W)	4,400	48.6
13	William C. Dunlap (W)	4,903	63.9
	C. H. Williams (W)	2,770	36.1

VIRGINIA

	Candidates	Votes	%
1	George Loyall (D)	1,625	52.5
	Arthur Emmerson (W)	1,471	47.5
2	John Y. Mason (D)	1,193	70.2
	Urquehart (W)	507	29.8
3	John W. Jones (D)	1,566	68.3
	Archer (W)	728	31.7
4	George C. Droomgoole (D)	1,365	55.7
	Gholson (W)	1,088	44.4
5	James W. Bouldin (D)	1,264	59.0
	Boiling (W)	879	41.0
6	Walter Coles (D)	1,728	54.1
	Davenport (W)	1,467	45.9
7	Nathaniel H. Claiborne (W)	1,680	51.3
	Stuart (D)	1,592	48.7
8	Henry A. Wise (D)	1,212	62.9
	Coke (W)	716	37.1
9	John Roane Jr (D)	1,150	50.3
	Taylor (W)	1,138	49.7
10	John Taliaferro (W)	869	50.5
	Chino (W)	852	49.5
11	John Robertson (W)	1,384	53.6
	Roane (D)	1,199	46.4
12	James Garland (D)	1,970	55.6
	Gordon (W)	1,576	44.4
13	John M. Patton (D)	406	100.0

Candidates	Votes	%	Candidates	Votes	%	Candidates	Votes	%
14 Charles F. Mercer (W)	692	83.6	17 Robert Craig (D)	2,592	50.3	20 Joseph Johnson (D)	1,858	46.4
Mason (D)	136	16.4	Moore (W)	2,564	49.7	Allen (W)	1,809	45.1
15 Edward Lucas (D)	1,971	51.6	18 George W. Hopkins (D)	2,518	64.3	Maxwell	342	8.5
Cooke (W)	1,849	48.4	Fulton (W)	1,399	35.7	21 William S. Morgan (D)	2,311	57.5
16 James M. H. Beale (D)	2,112	93.2	19 William McComas (W)	2,121	55.0	Wilson (W)	1,710	42.5
Jones (W)	154	6.8	Smith (D)	1,733	45.0			

1. Crary was elected to the House from Michigan in 1835 in anticipation that admission to the Union would follow soon thereafter. However, Michigan's admission was delayed until Jan. 26, 1837. Crary took his seat the next day. Thus, the 1835 election entitled him to serve just over one month (Jan. 27, 1837–March 3, 1837) in the 24th Congress (1835–1837).

1836 House Elections

ARKANSAS

(Became a state June 15, 1836)

	Candidates	Votes	%
AL	Archibald Yell (D)	5,420	73.4
	William Cummins (W)	1,967	26.6

Special Election

AL	Archibald Yell (VB D)	✓	

CONNECTICUT

Special Election

		Votes	%
AL	Orrin Holt (D)	17,367	51.4
	John Brockway (W)	16,431	48.6

DELAWARE

		Votes	%
AL	John J. Milligan (W)	4,705	52.3
	Unidentified Candidate (D)	4,297	47.7

GEORGIA

		Votes	
AL	Thomas Glascock (D)	48,448	✓
	George W. B. Towns (D)	29,600	✓
	Jesse F. Cleveland (D)	29,580	✓
	Charles E. Haynes (D)	29,490	✓
	Seaton Grantland (D)	29,343	✓
	George W. Owens (D)	29,316	✓
	Hopkins Holsey (D)	29,227	✓
	Jabez Y. Jackson (D)	29,227	✓
	William C. Dawson (W)	29,003	✓
	Julius C. Alford (W)	28,855	
	Colquette (W)	28,677	
	Habersham (W)	28,557	
	John Coffee (D)	28,543	
	King (W)	28,458	
	Nesbit (W)	28,419	
	Black (W)	28,407	
	Joseph Jackson (W)	28,353	

Special Election

		Votes	%
AL	William C. Dawson (W)	24,239	53.0
	John W. A. Sanford (D)	21,472	47.0

ILLINOIS

		Votes	%
1	Adam W. Snyder (VB D)	4,552	40.4
	John Reynolds (D)	4,441	39.4
	William J. Gatewood	2,270	20.2
2	Zadoc Casey (D)	7,142	65.8
	Alexander P. Field	3,568	32.9
3	William L. May (D)	11,764	54.1
	John T. Stewart	10,001	46.0

LOUISIANA

1	Henry Johnson (W)	✓	
2	Eleazar W. Ripley (D)	*	
3	Rice Garland (W)	✓	

MAINE[1]

		Votes	%
1	John Fairfield (D)	✓	
2	Francis O. J. Smith (D)	4,237	52.1
	James Brooks	3,583	44.0
3	Jonathan Cilley (D)	2,153	48.6
	Jeremiah Bailey (W)	2,048	46.2
4	George Evans (W)	✓	
5	Timothy J. Carter (D)	4,165	59.9
	Oliver Herrick (W)	2,397	34.5
6	Alfred Marshall	1,387*	45.9
	Hugh J. Anderson (D)	854	28.2
	Philip Morrill	766	25.3

	Candidates	Votes	%
7	Joseph C. Noyes (W)	✓	
	Timothy Pilsbury	1,848	
	Frederic Hobbs	1,544	
	Anson G. Chandler	895	
8	Thomas Davee (D)	3,498	58.1
	John S. Tenney (W)	2,458	40.8

MASSACHUSETTS

		Votes	%
1	Richard Fletcher (W)	4,702	61.8
	Amasa Walker (D)	2,895	38.0
2	Stephen C. Phillips (W)	3,920	51.1
	Joseph S. Cabot (D)	3,749	48.9
3	Caleb Cushing (W)	3,949	57.2
	Gayton P. Osgood (D)	2,916	42.2
4	William Parmenter (D)	4,034	56.5
	Samuel Hoar (W)	3,097	43.4
5	Levi Lincoln (W)	4,697	65.5
	Jubal Harrington (D)	2,443	34.1
6	George Grennell Jr (W)	3,872	69.9
	Samuel C. Allen (D)	1,645	29.7
7	George A. Briggs (W)	3,567	54.5
	Theodore Sedgwick (D)	2,961	45.2
8	William B. Calhoun (W)	3,798	57.5
	George Bancroft (D)	2,794	42.3
9	William S. Hastings (W)	3,137	55.2
	Alexander H. Everett (D)	2,495	43.9
10	Nathaniel B. Borden (D)	3,093	68.7
	William Baylies (W)	1,399	31.1
11	John Reed (W)	2,628	55.8
	Henry Crocker (D)	2,079	44.2
12	John Quincy Adams (W)	3,125	82.6
	Solomon Lincoln (D)	260	6.9
	John Thomas	222	5.9

MISSOURI

		Votes	
AL	Albert G. Harrison (D)	16,468	✓
	John Miller (D)	15,129	✓
	Birch (WHITE D)	10,007	
	Unidentified Candidate	7,533	

NEW JERSEY

AL	Charles C. Stratton (W)	✓	
	Thomas Jones Yorke (W)	✓	
	John B. Aycrigg (W)	✓	
	John P. B. Maxwell (W)	✓	
	Joseph F. Randolph (W)	✓	
	William Halstead (W)	✓	

NEW YORK

		Votes	%
1	Thomas Jackson (D)	3,731	61.9
	Abraham Rose (W)	2,297	38.1
2	Abraham Vanderveer (D)	3,893	56.3
	John Dikeman (W)	3,019	43.7
4	Gouverneur Kemble (D)	2,738	45.9
	James Turk	1,962	32.9
	Walker Todd	1,265	21.2
5	Obadiah Titus (D)	3,687	63.9
	Bartow White (W)	2,082	36.1
6	Nathaniel Jones (D)	3,479	60.3
	Samuel Eager	2,289	39.7
7	John Brodhead (D)	3,276	41.5
	Benjamin Bevier	2,947	37.3
	Steveryn Bruyn	1,669	21.2
9	Henry Vail (D)	4,935	51.1
	Hiram Hunt (W)	4,729	48.9
10	Albert Gallup (D)	4,882	52.9
	Jonathan Jenkins	4,351	47.1
11	John De Graff (D)	5,322	57.0
	John Taylor	4,014	43.0
12	David Russell (W)	3,543	57.4
	Orville Clark	2,629	42.6
13	John Palmer (D)	4,259	56.8

	Candidates	Votes	%
	Reuben Sandford	3,240	43.2
14	James Spencer (D)	3,843	54.5
	Asa Hascall (W)	3,212	45.5
15	John Edwards (D)	3,740	51.2
	Cornelius Patman	3,571	48.8
16	Arphaxed Loomis (D)	3,410	100.0
18	Isaac Bronson (D)	4,669	56.1
	Elisha Camp	3,653	43.9
19	John Prentiss (D)	3,784	54.0
	Eben Morehouse	3,229	46.0
20	Amasa Parker (D)	4,501	100.0
21	John Clark (D)	3,701	58.7
	Abial Cook	2,602	41.3
24	William Noble (D)	4,303	53.7
	Robert Muir	3,715	46.3
25	Samuel Birdsall (D)	4,915	53.9
	John Maynard (W)	4,213	46.2
26	Mark Sibley (W)	3,410	55.3
	Jared Willson	2,754	44.7
27	John Andrews (D)	5,219	59.3
	George Edwards	3,576	40.7
28	Timothy Childs (W)	4,693	53.6
	Horace Gay	4,067	46.4
29	William Patterson (W)	5,040	60.6
	William Mitchell	3,279	39.4
30	Luther Peck (W)	5,456	53.5
	James Faulkner	4,741	46.5
31	Richard Marvin (W)	5,372	52.9
	Oliver Lee (D)	4,782	47.1
32	Millard Fillmore (W)	4,475	61.4
	Thomas Sherwood	2,810	38.6
33	Charles Mitchell (W)	4,091	50.7
	Washington Hunt	3,980	49.3

Multimember Districts

		Votes	
3	Edward Curtis (W)	17,524	✓
	Ely Moore (D)	16,673	✓
	Churchill Cambreleng (D)	16,447	✓
	J. Ogden Hoffman (W)	16,441	✓
	Gideon Lee (D)	16,198	
	John McKeon (D)	15,943	
	Ira Wheeler (W)	15,920	
	Hubert Wagenen (W)	14,703	
	James Monroe (W)	3,144	
	Stephen Hasbrook	1,334	
8	Zadock Pratt (D)	9,085	✓
	Robert McClellan (D)	8,156	✓
	Colba Reed	6,309	
	Ambrose Jordan	6,293	
17	Abraham Grant (D)	8,249	✓
	Henry Foster (D)	6,878	✓
	Joshua Spencer	5,570	
	John Grant	5,570	
	Israel Stoddard	1,417	
22	Andrew Bruyn (D)	8,151	✓
	Hiram Gray (D)	7,779	✓
	Charles Cook	7,244	
	Benjamin Ferris	6,915	
23	William Taylor (D)	7,665	✓
	Bennet Bicknell (D)	7,635	✓
	B. Davis Noxon	4,676	
	Eliphalet Jackson	4,675	

NORTH CAROLINA

Special Election

		Votes	%
12	James Graham (W)	4,791	60.1
	David Newland (W)	3,177	39.9

OHIO

		Votes	%
1	Alexander Duncan (D)	4,734	52.2
	Bellamy Storer (W)	4,333	47.8

Candidates	Votes	%
2 Taylor Webster (D)	3,891	52.5
Jesse Corwin (W)	3,523	47.5
3 Patrick G. Goode (W)	6,300	55.7
James Brown (D)	5,018	44.3
4 Thomas Corwin (W)	4,770	64.6
Samuel H. Hale (D)	2,614	35.4
5 Thomas L. Hamer (D)	4,375	57.0
Owen T. Fishback (W)	3,305	43.0
6 Calvary Morris (W)	3,780	50.4
Nahum Ward (D)	3,703	49.3
7 William Key Bond (W)	4,844	52.4
William Allen (D)	4,395	47.6
8 Joseph Ridgway (W)	6,499	56.9
Jeremiah M. Lene	4,915	43.1
9 John Chaney (D)	5,838	60.7
Henry Stanberry (W)	3,784	39.3
10 Sampson Mason (W)	6,907	67.8
John Shelby (D)	3,267	32.1
11 James Alexander Jr. (W)	4,305	51.2
William Kennon Sr. (D)	4,102	48.8
12 Alex Harper (W)	5,018	52.1
Jonathan Hamm (D)	4,619	47.9
13 Daniel P. Leadbetter (D)	5,027	56.9
Abraham Shane (W)	3,802	43.1
14 William H. Hunter (D)	6,422	52.7
Jabez Wright (W)	5,766	47.3
15 J. W. Allen (W)	8,206	55.6
Harvey Rice (D)	6,489	44.0
16 Elisha Whittlesey (W)	7,691	62.8
Ashbel Dart (D)	4,550	37.2
17 Andrew W. Loomis (D)	3,382	50.2
George McCook (W)	3,359	49.8
18 Matthias Shepler (D)	4,384	56.9
Samuel Quinby (W)	3,325	43.1
19 Daniel Kilgore (D)	3,570	61.1
John B. Bayliss (W)	2,274	38.9

PENNSYLVANIA

Candidates	Votes	%
1 Lemuel Paynter (D)	2,568	55.3
Unidentified Candidate (W)	2,074	44.7
3 Francis J. Harper (D)	4,432	50.5
Unidentified Candidate (W)	4,339	49.5
5 Jacob Fry Jr (D)	3,194	61.9
Unidentified Candidate (W)	1,963	38.1

Candidates	Votes	%
6 Mathias Morris (W)	3,260	51.4
Unidentified Candidate (D)	3,085	48.6
7 David D. Wagener (D)	✓	
Unidentified Candidate (W)		
8 Edward B. Hubley (D)	2,881	54.3
Unidentified Candidate (W)	2,430	45.8
9 Henry A. P. Muhlenberg (D)	4,276	57.5
Unidentified Candidate (W)	3,160	42.5
10 Luther Reily (D)	2,885	50.8
Unidentified Candidate (W)	2,795	49.2
11 Henry Logan (D)	3,366	58.2
Unidentified Candidate (W)	2,414	41.8
12 Daniel Sheffer (D)	3,108	50.5
Unidentified Candidate (W)	3,047	49.5
13 Charles McClure (D)	3,633	57.8
Unidentified Candidate (W)	2,655	42.2
14 William W. Potter (D)	4,914	61.1
Unidentified Candidate (W)	3,134	38.9
15 Robert H. Hammond (D)	2,881	52.1
Unidentified Candidate (W)	2,646	47.9
16 David Petrikin (D)	4,275	58.6
Unidentified Candidate (W)	3,026	41.5
17 Samuel W. Morris (D)	3,888	60.5
Unidentified Candidate (W)	2,536	39.5
18 Charles Ogle (W)	✓	
Unidentified Candidate (D)		
19 John Klingensmith Jr. (D)	3,694	58.0
Unidentified Candidate (W)	2,674	42.0
20 Andrew Buchanan (D)	3,252	100.0
21 Thomas M. T. McKennan (W)	2,766	52.2
Unidentified Candidate (D)	2,537	47.8
22 Richard Biddle (W)	3,155	51.4
Unidentified Candidate (D)	2,984	48.6
23 William Beatty (D)	✓	
Unidentified Candidate (W)		
24 Thomas Henry (W)	✓	
Unidentified Candidate (D)		
25 Arnold Plummer (D)	4,281	54.4
Unidentified Candidate (W)	3,582	45.6

Multimember Districts

Candidates	Votes	%
2 George W. Toland (W)	✓	
John Sergeant (W)	5,317✓	
Unidentified Candidate (D)	3,072	

Candidates	Votes	%
Unidentified Candidate (D)		
4 David Potts Jr (W)	✓	
Edward Davies (W)	✓	
Edward Darlington (W)	9,916✓	
Unidentified Candidate (D)	8,561	
Unidentified Candidate (D)		
Unidentified Candidate (D)		

Special Elections

Candidates	Votes	%
13 James Black (D)	✓	
Robert Elliot (A-MAS)		
24 John James Pearson (W)	✓	

SOUTH CAROLINA

Candidates	Votes	%
1 Hugh S. Legare (UN D)	✓	
Henry L. Pinckney (D)		
2 Robert Barnwell Smith (D)	✓	
William J. Grayson (SR W)		
3 John Campbell (SR D)	✓	
Thomas Smith		
4 Franklin H. Elmore (SR D)		100.0
5 John K. Griffin (SR W)	✓	
6 Francis W. Pickens (SSR NULL)	✓	
7 William K. Clowney (SR D)	✓	
James Rogers (D)		
8 Waddy Thompson Jr (W)	✓	
9 John P. Richardson (SR D)	✓	
J. G. Bowman		

VERMONT

Candidates	Votes	%
1 Hiland Hall (W)	4,220	57.2
John S. Robinson	3,023	41.0
2 William Slade (W)	3,918	64.5
Jonas Clark	1,536	25.3
E. D. Barber	481	7.9
3 Horace Everett (W)	3,747	47.1
Alden Partridge	3,180	40.0
Martin Flint	961	12.1
4 Heman Allen (W)	3,522	60.2
C. P. Vanness	2,203	37.7
5 Isaac Fletcher (D)	3,765	52.8
Henry F. Janes (W)	3,324	46.6

1. In Maine's 6th district, no candidate received the required majority. A series of special elections were held in an attempt to meet the requirement. In the 5th special election, Anderson was elected. No returns are available for these special elections.

1837 House Elections

ALABAMA

	Candidates	Votes	%
1	Reuben Chapman (D)	7,599	81.4
	Gabriel Moore (W)	1,742	18.7
2	Joshua L. Martin (D)	2,496	46.2
	David Greenhill Lyon (W)	1,461	27.0
	Stone	1,446	26.8
3	Joab Lawler (W)	5,874	52.7
	Henry W. Ellis (D)	5,277	47.3
4	Dixon H. Lewis (SR W)		100.0
5	Francis Lyon (W)	3,651	50.3
	R. E. B. Baylor (NULL-NR)	3,604	49.7

CONNECTICUT

	Candidates	Votes	%
1	Isaac Toucey (D)	4,410	50.4
	Joseph Trumbull (W)	4,334	49.6
2	Samuel Ingham (D)	10,194	54.4
	Henry Flagg (W)	8,558	45.6
3	Elisha Haley (D)	2,367	51.2
	Thomas Williams (W)	2,252	48.8
4	Thomas Whittlesey (D)	3,604	52.7
	Gideon Tomlinson (W)	3,239	47.3
5	Lancelot Phelps (D)	3,493	50.7
	Phineas Miner (W)	3,391	49.3
6	Orrin Holt (D)	5,301	52.3
	John Brockway (W)	4,843	47.7

GEORGIA

Special Election

		Votes	%
AL	Julius C. Alford (W)	17,754	53.4
	Liddell (D)	15,480	46.6

INDIANA

		Votes	%
1	Ratliff Boon (D)	4,534	50.4
	John Pitcher (W)	4,467	49.6
2	John Ewing (W)	5,820	54.4
	John Law (D)	4,887	45.6
3	William Graham (W)	5,717	56.6
	John S. Simonson (D)	4,390	43.4
4	George H. Dunn (W)	6,091	54.6
	Amos Lane (D)	5,057	45.4
5	James Rariden (W)	6,599	57.5
	Johnathan McCarty (W)	4,845	42.2
6	William Herod (W)	9,635	62.1
	James B. Ray (D)	5,888	37.9
7	Albert S. White (W)	10,937	74.2
	Nathan Jackson (W)	3,789	25.7

Special Election

		Votes	%
6	William Herod (W)	3,703	51.5
	William W. Wick (D)	3,493	48.5

KENTUCKY

		Votes	%
1	John L. Murray (D)	2,921	39.7
	Linn Boyd (D)	2,547	34.6
	Campbell (W)	1,888	25.7
2	Edward Rumsey (W)	4,035	89.1
	Jones (D)	496	11.0
3	Joseph R. Underwood (W)	4,589	100.0
4	Sherrod Williams (W)	3,189	47.1
	McHenry (D)	1,819	26.9
	Monroe (W)	1,764	26.1
5	James Harlan (W)		100.0
6	John Calhoon (W)	3,656	55.7
	Vanmetre (D)	2,902	44.2
7	John Pope (I)	3,248	54.4
	Hardin (W)	2,728	45.7
8	William J. Graves (W)	5,021	63.0
	T. F. Marshall (W)	2,950	37.0
9	John White (W)	3,700	60.0

	Candidates	Votes	%
	Garrard (D)	2,464	40.0
10	Richard Hawes (W)		100.0
11	Richard H. Menifee (W)	4,084	51.5
	French (D)	3,850	48.5
12	John Chambers (W)	2,886	74.5
	Leach (D)	989	25.5
13	William W. Southgate (W)	4,457	50.7
	Phelps (D)	4,116	46.8

MARYLAND

		Votes	%
1	John Dennis (W)	2,076	59.6
	Handy (W)	1,409	40.4
2	James A. Pearce (W)	2,714	53.2
	Evans (W)	2,388	46.8
3	John T. H. Worthington (D)	2,413	53.2
	Brown (W)	2,126	46.8
5	William Cost Johnson (I)	1,292	52.8
	Kimmell (W)	1,153	47.2
6	Francis Thomas (D)	3,819	52.0
	Merrick (W)	3,523	48.0
7	Daniel Jenifer (W)		100.0

Multimember District

		Votes	%
4	Benjamin C. Howard (D)	7,184✓	
	Isaac McKim (D)	7,141✓	
	Kennedy (W)	6,950	
	Ridgely (W)	6,873	

MICHIGAN

		Votes	%
AL	Isaac Crary (D)	11,451	52.6
	Hezekiah Wells (W)	10,329	47.4

MISSISSIPPI

		Votes	%
AL	Sergeant S. Prentiss (W)	13,688‡	
	Thomas Word (W)	12,374‡	
	John F. H. Claiborne (D)	6,206	
	Samuel Gholson (D)	5,881	

Special Election

		Votes	%
AL	John F. H. Claiborne (D)	11,198‡	
	Samuel Gholson (D)	9,971‡	
	Prentiss (W)	7,153	
	Acee (W)	6,632	

NEW HAMPSHIRE

AL	Charles G. Atherton (D)	✓
	Jared W. Williams (D)	✓
	James Farrington (D)	✓
	Samuel Cushman (D)	✓
	Joseph Weeks (W)	✓
	Charles B. Goodrich	
	Joseph Bell	
	Richard Bradley	
	Anthony Colby	
	James Wilson Jr.	

NORTH CAROLINA

		Votes	%
1	Samuel T. Sawyer (D)	2,111	55.3
	G. C. Moore (D)	1,706	44.7
2	Jesse Bynum (D)	✓	
	William L. Long (W)		
3	Edward Stanly (W)	2,842	56.6
	Louis D. Wilson (D)	2,176	43.4
4	Charles Shepard (W)	2,392	55.6
	William D. Moseley (D)	1,914	44.5
5	James I. McKay (D)	3,023	81.9
	T. C. Miller (D)	668	18.1
6	Micajah T. Hawkins (D)	1,949	54.1
	Joseph Macklin (D)	894	24.8

	Candidates	Votes	%
	John L. Henderson (W)	762	21.1
7	Edmund Deberry (W)	3,323	57.4
	Lauchlin Bethune (D)	2,465	42.6
8	William Montgomery (D)	2,591	51.9
	William A. Graham (W)	2,400	48.1
9	Augustine H. Shepperd (W)	3,359	50.9
	John Hill (D)	3,239	49.1
10	Abraham Rencher (W)	3,041	90.6
	Micajah Cox (D)	205	6.1
11	Henry W. Conner (D)		100.0
12	James Graham (W)	✓	
13	Lewis Williams (D)	✓	
	Samuel Patterson		

PENNSYLVANIA

Special Election

		Votes	%
3	Charles Naylor (W)	2,356	56.0
	Ingersoll (D)	1,853	44.0

RHODE ISLAND

		Votes	%
AL	Joseph L. Tillinghast (W)	4,282✓	
	Robert B. Cranston (W)	4,221✓	
	Dutee J. Pearce (D)	3,261	
	Howard (D)	3,201	
	Dorr (D)	72	
	King (CONST)	25	

TENNESSEE

		Votes	%
1	William B. Carter (W)	3,994	51.5
	Thomas D. Arnold (W)	3,756	48.5
2	Abraham McClellan (D)	3,612	52.9
	Samuel Bunch (W)	2,357	34.5
	Eliot (W)	865	12.7
3	Joseph L. Williams (W)	6,812	72.0
	R. M. Anderson (W)	2,653	28.0
4	James Standifer (W)	5,110	66.4
	Stone (W)	2,581	33.6
5	Hopkins L. Turney (D)	3,437	49.9
	Coxe (W)	2,984	43.3
	Peter Burum (D)	466	6.8
6	William B. Campbell (W)	4,142	60.0
	William C. Trousdale (D)	2,760	40.0
7	John Bell (W)	4,639	100.0
8	Abram P. Maury (W)	3,043	55.3
	William Crockett (D)	2,458	44.7
9	James K. Polk (D)	4,245	100.0
10	Ebenezer J. Shields (W)	4,432	55.7
	A. A. Kincannon (D)	3,521	44.3
11	Richard Cheatham (W)	3,822	50.6
	Cave Johnson (D)	3,731	49.4
12	John W. Crockett (W)	8,456	85.7
	A. M. Hughes (W)	1,413	14.3
13	Christopher H. Williams (W)	5,360	60.7
	William C. Dunlap (D)	3,478	39.4

VIRGINIA

1	Francis Mallory (W)	✓
	Joel Holleman (D)	
2	Francis E. Rives (D)	✓
	William B. Goodyear (D)	
3	John W. Jones (D)	✓
4	George C. Dromgoole (D)	✓
5	James W. Bouldin (D)	✓
6	Walter Coles (D)	✓
	J. Kerr (W)	
7	Archibald Stuart (D)	✓
	Nathaniel H. Claiborne (D)	
8	Henry A. Wise (W)	✓
9	Robert M. T. Hunter (W)	✓
	Upshaw (D)	
	Harwood (D)	

Candidates	Votes	%	Candidates	Votes	%	Candidates	Votes	%
10 John Talliaferro (W)	✓		J. B. D. Smith (W)			18 George W. Hopkins (D)	✓	
J. Gibson			16 Isaac S. Pennybacker (D)	✓		John N. Humes (D)		
11 John Robertson (W)	✓		David Steele (W)			19 Andrew Beirne (D)	✓	
12 James Garland (D)	✓		17 Robert Craig (D)	✓		Andrew Donnally (W)		
13 John M. Patton (D)	✓		E. Johnston (W)			20 Josep h Johnson (D)	✓	
14 Charles F. Mercer (W)	✓					John J. Jackson (W)		
William T. T. Mason (D)						21 William S. Morgan (D)	✓	
15 James M. Mason (D)	✓							

1838 House Elections

ARKANSAS

	Candidates	Votes	%
AL	Edward Cross (D)	6,771	61.0
	Cummings (W)	4,328	39.0

DELAWARE

	Candidates	Votes	%
AL	Thomas Robinson Jr (D)	4,451	50.3
	John J. Milligan (W)	4,399	49.7

GEORGIA

	Candidates	Votes	%
AL	William C. Dawson (SR W)	33,278✓	
	Julius C. Alford (SR W)	32,320✓	
	Walter T.Colquitt (SR W)	32,299✓	
	Richard W. Habersham (SR W)	32,282✓	
	Thomas Butler King (SR W)	32,213✓	
	Lott Warren (SR W)	31,887✓	
	Eugenius A. Nisbet (SR W)	31,841✓	
	Edward J. Black (SR W)	31,801✓	
	Mark A. Cooper (SR W)	31,723✓	
	David C. Campbell (D)	31,270	
	Alfred Iverson (D)	31,238	
	Josiah S. Patterson (D)	31,187	
	Graves (D)	31,074	
	Robert W. Pooler (D)	31,042	
	Junius Hillyer (D)	30,967	
	Burney (D)	30,932	
	McWhorter (D)	30,796	
	Nelson (D)	30,782	

ILLINOIS

	Candidates	Votes	%
1	John Reynolds (D)	8,029	61.2
	John Hogan (W)	5,100	38.9
2	Zadock Casey (D)	8,367	94.3
	Samuel McRoberts (W)	501	5.6
3	John T. Stuart (W)	18,248	50.0
	Stephen A. Douglas (D)	18,213	49.9

LOUISIANA

	Candidates	Votes	%
1	Edward D. White (W)	3,351	57.4
	Slidell (D)	2,486	42.6
2	Thomas W. Chinn (W)	1,790	55.7
	Lawson (D)	1,423	44.3
3	Rice Garland (W)		100.0

MAINE

	Candidates	Votes	%
1	Nathan Clifford (D)	5,568	54.8
	Nathan D. Appleton (W)	4,560	44.9
2	Albert Smith (D)	5,709	50.1
	Ezekiel Whitman (W)	5,623	49.3
3	John D. McCrate (D)	4,859	50.6
	Benjamin Randall (W)	4,652✓	48.5
4	George Evans (W)	7,143	60.9
	John Hubbard (D)	4,591	39.1
5	Virgil D. Parris (D)	6,765	57.4
	Zadoc Long (W)	4,999	42.4
6	Hugh J. Anderson (D)	5,727	60.9
	William G. Crosby (W)	3,519	37.4
7	Joshua A. Lowell (D)	5,033	51.8
	Joseph C. Noyes (W)	4,666	48.1
8	Thomas Davee (D)	7,839	51.9
	John S. Tenney (W)	7,042	46.6

Special Elections

	Candidates	Votes	%
3	Edward Robinson (W)	✓	
	John D. McCrate (D)		
5	Virgil D. Parris (D)	4,349	57.4
	Zadoc Long (W)	3,690	42.4

MARYLAND

Special Election

	Candidates	Votes	%
4	John P. Kennedy (W)	7,153	53.2
	Marriott (D)	6,291	46.8

MASSACHUSETTS[1]

		Votes	%
1	Richard Fletcher (W)	5,145*	63.1
	Bradford Sumner (D)	2,952	36.2
2	Leverett Saltonstall (W)	3,734	59.1
	Robert Rantoul Jr. (D)	2,031	32.1
	Joseph S. Cabot (D)	536	8.5
3	Caleb Cushing (W)	4,762	61.1
	Gayton P. Osgood (D)	2,730	35.0
4	William Parmenter (D)	4,972	50.1
	Nathan Brooks (W)	4,433	44.7
5	Levi Lincoln (W)	4,251	55.2
	Isaac Davis (D)	2,630	34.1
	Charles Allen	797	10.3
6	James C. Alvord (W)	4,440	61.8
	Thomas Nims (D)	2,054	28.6
	Osmyn Baker (W)	653	9.1
7	George N. Briggs (W)	4,328	54.5
	Henry W. Bishop (D)	3,601	45.3
8	William B. Calhoun (W)	4,363	59.4
	William W. Thompson (D)	2,957	40.3
9	William S. Hastings (W)	4,049	56.6
	Alexander H. Everett (D)	3,090	43.2
10	Henry Williams (D)	3,306	51.7
	Nathaniel B. Borden (W)	2,920	45.7
11	John Reed (W)	3,519	56.4
	Henry Crocker (D)	2,703	43.3
12	John Quincy Adams (W)	4,100	59.0
	William M. Jackson (D)	2,822	40.6

Special Election

		Votes	%
2	Leverett Saltonstall (W)	3,730	58.9
	Robert Rentoul Jr. (D)	2,034	32.1
	Joseph S. Cabot (D)	542	8.6

MICHIGAN

		Votes	%
AL	Isaac E. Crary (D)	16,360	50.4
	Hezekiah E. Wells (W)	16,099	49.6

MISSISSIPPI

Special Election

		Votes	%
AL	Sergeant S. Prentiss (W)	12,721✓	
	Thomas Word (W)	12,077✓	
	J. F. H. Claiborne (D)	11,767	
	Reuben Davis (D)	11,346	

MISSOURI

		Votes	%
AL	Albert G. Harrison (D)	23,410✓	
	John Miller (D)	23,182✓	
	Allen (W)	17,191	
	Wilson (W)	16,706	

NEW JERSEY

		Votes	%
AL	Peter D. Vroom (D)	28,492✓	
	William R. Cooper (D)	28,455✓	
	Philemon Dickerson (D)	28,453✓	
	Daniel B. Ryall (D)	28,441✓	
	Joseph Kille (D)	28,426✓	
	Joseph Randolph (W)	28,426✓	
	Strat (W)	28,395	
	Max (W)	28,386	
	Hal (W)	28,337	
	Yorke (W)	28,321	

Candidates	Votes	%
Force (D)	28,315	
Aigg (W)	28,295	

NEW YORK

		Votes	%
1	Thomas Jackson (D)	4,896	56.5
	Nathaniel Miller (W)	3,776	43.5
2	James De La Montanya (D)	4,405	55.2
	John Gurnee (W)	3,576	44.8
4	Gouverneur Kemble (D)	4,986	54.3
	Joshua Brown (W)	4,203	45.7
5	Charles Johnston (W)	5,262	53.1
	Obadiah Titus (D)	4,645	46.9
6	Nathaniel Jones (D)	4,184	51.3
	Thomas McKissock (W)	3,978	48.7
7	Rufus Palen (W)	5,453	54.2
	Anthony Hasbrouck (D)	4,615	45.8
9	Hiram Hunt (W)	5,483	52.8
	Henry Vail (D)	4,909	47.2
10	Daniel Barnard (W)	5,680	52.5
	Albert Gallup (D)	5,145	47.5
11	Anson Brown (W)	5,401	51.8
	Nicholas Hill (D)	5,028	48.2
12	David Russell (W)	4,346	61.9
	John Williams (D)	2,671	38.1
13	Augustus Hand (D)	4,480	50.3
	Thomas Tomlinson (W)	4,436	49.8
14	John Fine (D)	4,756	50.5
	Henry Van Rensselaer (W)	4,663	49.5
15	Peter Wagner (W)	4,491	50.3
	David Sacia (D)	4,441	49.7
16	Andrew Doig (D)	5,043	56.8
	Seth Miller (W)	3,835	43.2
18	Thomas Chittenden (W)	4,989	53.7
	Isaac Bronson (D)	4,309	46.3
19	John Prentiss (D)	4,724	52.8
	William Averill (W)	4,216	47.2
20	Judson Allen (D)	5,072	54.2
	Erastus Root (W)	4,284	45.8
21	John Clark (W)	3,908	52.3
	John Clapp (D)	3,563	47.7
24	Christopher Morgan (W)	4,631	50.9
	William Noble (D)	4,464	49.1
25	Theron Strong (D)	5,824	50.7
	John Holley (W)	5,670	49.3
26	Francis Granger (W)	4,233	57.9
	Jared Willson (D)	3,083	42.1
27	Meredith Mallory (D)	5,438	51.2
	Thomas Johnson (W)	5,182	48.8
28	Thomas Kempshall (W)	5,476	56.9
	Henry Selden (D)	4,144	43.1
29	Seth Gates (W)	6,033	65.3
	William Mitchell (D)	3,202	34.7
30	Luther Peck (W)	6,521	57.8
	Calvin Chamberlain (D)	4,763	42.2
31	Richard Marvin (W)	7,053	57.6
	Charles Williams (D)	5,198	42.4
32	Millard Fillmore (W)	5,414	65.7
	George Barker (D)	2,831	34.3
33	Charles Mitchell (W)	4,690	55.0
	Henry Curtis (D)	3,840	45.0

Multi-Member Districts

		Votes	%
3	Ogden Hoffman (W)	20,577✓	
	Moses Grinnell (W)	20,563✓	
	Edward Curtis (W)	20,458✓	
	James Monroe (W)	20,454✓	
	John McKeon (D)	19,227	
	Isaac Varian (D)	19,206	
	Churchill Cambreleng (D)	19,205	
	Ely Moore (D)	18,843	
8	John Ely (D)	9,668✓	
	Aaron Vanderpoel (D)	9,628✓	
	Mitchell Sanford (W)	9,499	
	Robert Dorlon (W)	9,469	

Candidates	Votes	%
17 David Brewster (D)	9,395✓	
John Floyd (D)	9,286✓	
Henry Fitzhugh (W)	8,601	
Charles Kirkland (W)	8,362	
22 Amasa Dana (D)	9,157✓	
Stephen Leonard (D)	9,152✓	
William Ely (W)	8,757	
John Miller (W)	8,725	
23 Nehemiah Earll (D)	9,189✓	
Edward Rogers (D)	9,099✓	
A. Lawrence Foster (W)	9,056	
Victory Birdseye (W)	9,015	

OHIO

	Candidates	Votes	%
1	Alexander Duncan (D)	4,572	51.0
	N. G. Pendleton (W)	4,396	49.0
2	John B. Weller (D)	4,877	54.9
	John Beers (W)	4,010	45.1
3	Patrick G. Goode (W)	7,589	50.7
	William Sawyer (D)	7,368	49.3
4	Thomas Corwin (W)	5,866	99.6
5	William Doan (D)	4,543	56.6
	Daniel Fisher (W)	3,479	43.4
6	Calvery Morris (W)	5,321	55.1
	Joseph Morris (D)	4,337	44.9
7	William K. Bond (W)	4,834	50.9
	Allen Latham (D)	4,658	49.1
8	Joseph Ridgway (W)	6,916	51.4
	John McElvain (D)	6,552	48.7
9	William Medill (D)	6,791	64.6
	John M. Creed (W)	3,729	35.5
10	Samson Mason (W)	6,997	58.1
	Rowland Brown (D)	5,040	41.9
11	Isaac Parrish (D)	4,692	52.7
	James Alexander Jr (W)	4,220	47.4
12	Jonathan Taylor (D)	5,668	51.5
	Alexander Harper (W)	5,347	48.5
13	Daniel P. Leadbetter (D)	7,515	57.5
	James S. Irwin (W)	5,555	42.5
14	George Sweeny (D)	8,601	56.4
	Joseph M. Root (W)	6,654	43.6
15	John W. Allen (W)	8,800	53.8
	John W. Willey (D)	7,558	46.2
16	Joshua R. Giddings (W)	7,581	57.7
	Benjamin Bissell (D)	5,556	42.3
17	John Hastings (D)	4,952	53.2
	Charles D. Coffin (W)	4,349	46.8
18	David A. Starkweather (D)	6,154	60.6
	Hiram B. Wellman (W)	4,010	39.5
19	Henry Swearingen (D)	4,036	52.9
	Samuel Stokely (W)	3,589	47.1

PENNSYLVANIA

	Candidates	Votes	%
1	Lemuel Paynter (D)	3,675	55.1
	J. B. Sutherland (W)	2,994	44.9
3	Charles Naylor (W)	6,670	53.1
	C. J. Ingersoll (D)	5,894	46.9
5	Joseph Fornance (D)	4,527	54.9
	Joseph Royer (W)	3,723	45.1
6	John Davis (D)	4,464	51.9
	Matthew Morris (W)	4,138	48.1
7	David D. Wagener (D)	6,189	62.8
	P. S. Michler (W)	3,672	37.2
8	Peter Newhard (D)	4,636	54.5
	W. C. Livingston (W)	3,876	45.5
9	George M. Keim (D)	7,030	68.6
	D. M. Bieber (W)	3,212	31.4
10	William Simonton (W)	5,000	58.7
	William Reily (W)	3,514	41.3
11	James Gerry (D)	4,197	56.6
	C. A. Barnitz (W)	3,220	43.4
12	James Cooper (W)	5,738	56.0
	Daniel Sheffer (D)	4,503	44.0
13	William S. Ramsey (D)	5,569	57.3
	Frederick Watts (W)	4,145	42.7
14	William W. Potter (D)	6,510	50.9
	William Irvin (W)	6,288	49.1
15	Robert Hammond (D)	5,156	56.7
	James Merrill (W)	3,946	43.4
16	David Petrikin (D)	6,225	53.5
	David Hurley (W)	5,411	46.5
17	Samuel W. Morris (D)	5,147	54.2
	William Willard (W)	4,354	45.8
18	Charles Ogle (W)	5,106	55.1
	Job Mann (D)	4,158	44.9
19	Albert G. Marchand (D)	5,800	60.5
	Joseph Markle (W)	3,784	39.5
20	Enos Hook (D)	4,498	63.0
	H. Oliphant (W)	2,643	37.0
21	Isaac Leet (D)	3,508	50.2
	Joseph Lawrence (W)	3,487	49.9
22	Richard Biddle (W)	6,090	58.1
	James Power (D)	4,391	41.9
23	William Beatty (D)	5,694	61.1
	George W. Smith (W)	3,625	38.9
24	Thomas Henry (W)	5,265	54.9
	James D. White (D)	4,330	45.1
25	John Galbraith (D)	6,208	51.2
	David Dick (W)	5,920	48.8

Multimember Districts

	Candidates	Votes	%
2	George W. Toland	✓	

Candidates	Votes	%
John Sergeant (W)	7,132✓	
J. R. Evans (D)	3,152	
J. Brasnears (D)		
4 John Edwards (W)	✓	
Francis James (W)	✓	
Edward Davies (W)	15,192✓	
R. Frazer (D)	11,353	
John Evans (D)		
G. G. Leiper (D)		

Special Election

	Candidates	Votes	%
9	George M. Keim (D)	2,115	89.8

SOUTH CAROLINA[2]

	Candidates	Votes	%
1	Isaac E. Holmes (D)	1,504	63.8
	Hugh S. Legare (UN D)	854	36.2
2	R. Barnwell Rhett (D)		100.0
3	John Campbell (SR D)	1,280	67.4
	Thomas Smith	620	32.6
4	Franklin H. Elmore (SR D)	*	100.0
5	John K. Griffin (SR W)		100.0
6	Francis W. Pickens (NULL)		100.0
7	James Rogers (D)	✓	
	F. W. Davie		
8	Waddy Thompson Jr (W)	3,339	58.9
	J. N. Witner	2,327	41.1
9	John P. Richardson (SR D)	*	100.0

VERMONT

	Candidates	Votes	%
1	Hiland Hall (W)	5,211	53.9
	John Roberts (D)	4,328	44.7
2	William Slade (W)	4,752	68.9
	Charles Linsley (D)	2,095	30.4
3	Horace Everett (W)	5,183	56.8
	Alden Partridge (D)	3,841	42.1
4	John Smith (D)	4,375	49.0
	Heman Allen (W)	4,085	45.8
5	Isaac Fletcher (D)	4,996	52.2
	William Upham (W)	4,515	47.2

VIRGINIA

Special Election

	Candidates	Votes	%
13	Linn Banks (D)	✓	
	Daniel F. Slaughter (W)		

1. Richard Fletcher of the 1st district never served in the 26th Congress (1839–1841). In an 1839 special election, Abbott Lawrence was elected to succeed him.

2. Franklin H. Elmore of the 4th district and John P. Richardson of the 9th district did not serve in the 26th Congress (1839–1841). Sampson Butler and Thomas Sumter were later elected to the seats in special elections for which returns are unavailable.

1839 House Elections

ALABAMA

	Candidates	Votes	%
1	Reuben Chapman (D)	7,384	100.0
2	David Hubbard (D)	3,303	56.3
	Lyon (W)	2,561	43.7
3	George W. Crabb (W)	5,927	50.5
	Ellis (D)	5,816	49.5
4	Dixon H. Lewis (SR W)		100.0
5	James Dellet (W)	4,350	52.6
	Murphey (D)	3,927	47.4

CONNECTICUT

	Candidates	Votes	%
1	Joseph Trumbull (W)	5,180	53.2
	Isaac Toucey (D)	4,108	42.2
2	William L. Storrs (W)	10,525	51.5
	Samuel Ingham (D)	9,924	48.5
3	Thomas Williams (W)	3,066	50.7
	Codington Billings (D)	2,978	49.3
4	Thomas B. Osborne (W)	3,968	52.4
	Thomas Whittlesey (D)	3,604	47.6
5	Truman Smith (W)	3,988	53.5
	Charles Phelps (D)	3,466	46.5
6	John Brockway (W)	3,997	52.5
	Chauncey Cleveland (D)	3,565	46.8

INDIANA

	Candidates	Votes	%
1	George H. Proffit (W)	6,008	53.5
	Robert Dale Owen (D)	5,229	46.5
2	John W. Davis (D)	7,516	54.7
	John Ewing (W)	6,217	45.3
3	John Carr (D)	6,998	57.7
	William Graham (W)	5,121	42.3
4	Thomas Smith (D)	6,541	54.1
	George H. Dunn (W)	5,542	45.9
5	James Rariden (W)	6,257	40.2
	William Thompson (D)	5,333	34.3
	Jonathan McCarty (W)	3,961	25.5
6	William W. Wick (D)	9,505	52.8
	William Herod (W)	8,494	47.2
7	Tilghman A. Howard (D)	9,929	55.3
	Thomas J. Evans (W)	8,036	44.7

KENTUCKY

	Candidates	Votes	%
1	Linn Boyd (D)	✓	
2	Phillip Triplett (W)	✓	
3	Joseph R. Underwood (W)	✓	
4	Sherrod Williams (W)	✓	
5	Simeon H. Anderson (W)	✓	
6	Willis Green (W)	✓	
7	John Pope (D)	✓	
8	William J. Graves (W)	✓	
9	John White (W)	✓	
10	Richard Hawes (W)	✓	
11	Landaff W. Andrews (W)	✓	
12	Garrett Davis (HC W)	✓	
13	William O. Butler (D)	✓	

MARYLAND

	Candidates	Votes	%
1	John Dennis (W)	2,062	52.8
	Stewart (D)	1,817	46.5
2	Philip F. Thomas (D)	3,831	51.3
	Pearce (W)	3,643	48.7
3	John T. H. Worthington (D)	3,924	62.3
	Turner (I)	2,378	37.7
5	William Cost Johnson (W)	3,325	56.7
	Duvall (D)	2,535	43.3
6	Francis Thomas (D)	4,279	53.3
	Price (W)	3,704	46.2
7	Daniel Jenifer (W)	1,984	56.1
	Key (D)	1,553	43.9

Multimember District

	Candidates	Votes	%
4	James Carroll (D)	8,018✓	

Candidates	Votes	%
Solomon Hillen Jr (D)	8,011✓	
Kennedy (W)	7,634	
Pitts (W)	7,629	

MASSACHUSETTS

Special Elections

	Candidates	Votes	%
1	Abbott Lawrence (W)	4,963	57.4
	Bradford Sumner (D)	3,665	42.4
6	Osmyn Baker (W)	2,581	50.8
	Rodolphus Dickinson (D)	2,020	39.8
	Israel Billings (AB-D)	451	8.9

MISSISSIPPI

	Candidates	Votes	%
AL	Albert G. Brown (D)	16,730✓	
	Jacob Thompson (D)	16,501✓	
	A. L. Benjamin (W)	14,094	
	Reuben Davis (W)	13,808	

NEW HAMPSHIRE

	Candidates	Votes	%
AL	Ira A. Eastman (D)	✓	
	Edmund Burke (D)	✓	
	Tristram Shaw (D)	✓	
	Charles G. Atherton (D)	✓	
	Jared W. Williams (D)	✓	
	P. Handerson (FED)		
	J. Smith (FED)		
	Joel Eastman (FED)		
	A. Colby (FED)		
	I. Bartlett (FED)		
	D. Hoit (FEDL AB)		
	P. P. Woodbury (FEDL AB)		
	J. M. Harper (FEDL AB)		
	Southworth (FEDL AB)		

NORTH CAROLINA

	Candidates	Votes	%
1	Kenneth Rayner (W)	2,635	56.7
	Samuel T. Sawyer (D)	2,009	43.3
2	Jesse A. Bynum (D)	✓	
	William L. Long (W)		
3	Edward Stanly (W)	3,098	54.8
	Thomas H. Hall (D)	2,554	45.2
4	Charles Shepard (D)	2,890	57.1
	Samuel J. Biddle (W)	2,175	42.9
5	James I. McKay (D)	2,360	87.9
	Frederick J. Hill (W)	325	12.1
6	Micajah T. Hawkins (D)	1,625	50.1
	Robert C. Hilliard (D)	1,621	49.9
7	Edmund Deberry (W)	3,649	57.0
	William A. Morris (D)	2,753	43.0
8	William Montgomery (D)	2,916	53.3
	G. W. Haywood (W)	2,553	46.7
9	John Hill (D)	3,743	50.3
	Augustine H. Shepperd (W)	3,696	49.7
10	Charles Fisher (D)	3,539	51.4
	Pleasant Henderson (W)	3,348	48.6
11	Henry W. Conner (D)	3,041	54.8
	Edney (W)	2,504	45.2
12	James Graham (W)	✓	
13	Lewis Williams (D)	2,900	51.5
	Roderick Murchison (W)	2,731	48.5

PENNSYLVANIA

Special Election

	Candidates	Votes	%
14	George McCullough (D)	4,094	50.9
	Irvin (W)	3,956	49.1

RHODE ISLAND

	Candidates	Votes	%
AL	Joseph L. Tillinghast (W)	4,050✓	
	Robert B. Cranston (W)	3,912✓	
	Thomas W. Dorr (D)	3,660	

Candidates	Votes	%
Benjamin B. Thurston (D)	3,595	

TENNESSEE

	Candidates	Votes	%
1	William B. Carter (W)	4,787	59.0
	Joseph Powell (D)	3,334	41.1
2	Abraham M. McClellan (D)	3,363	65.3
	John A. McKenny (W)	1,790	34.7
3	Joseph L. Williams (W)	5,173	99.9
4	Julius W. Blackwell (D)	4,448	61.3
	William Stone (W)	2,806	38.7
5	Hopkins L. Turney (D)	4,953	65.6
	Anthony Dibrell (W)	2,603	34.5
6	William B. Campbell (W)	5,126	60.5
	William Trousdale (D)	3,350	39.5
7	John Bell (W)	3,895	59.4
	Robert M. Burton (D)	2,665	40.6
8	Meredith P. Gentry (W)	3,245	54.2
	William G. Childress (D)	2,744	45.8
9	Harvey M. Watterson (D)	4,521	58.9
	Daniel L. Barenger (W)	3,154	41.1
10	Aaron V. Brown (D)	5,017	57.8
	Ebenezer Shields (W)	3,668	42.2
11	Cave Johnson (D)	4,289	57.9
	Richard Cheatham (W)	3,117	42.1
12	John W. Crockett (W)	5,155	58.1
	Stephen C. Pavatt (D)	3,719	41.9
13	Christopher H. Williams (W)	3,447	55.5
	William C. Dunlap (D)	2,767	44.5

VIRGINIA

	Candidates	Votes	%
1	Joel Holleman (D)	1,920	51.9
	Mallory (W)	1,781	48.1
2	Francis E. Rives (D)	1,334	57.6
	Pegram (W)	982	42.4
3	John W. Jones (D)	409	58.5
	Taylor (W)	290	41.5
4	George C. Dromgoole (D)	1,236	57.1
	Gholson (D)	927	42.9
5	John Hill (W)	835	54.1
	Wilson (D)	708	45.9
6	Walter Coles (D)	1,564	51.6
	Witcher (W)	1,465	48.4
7	William L. Goggin (W)	1,498	52.7
	Stuart (D)	1,347	47.4
8	Henry A. Wise (W)	858	88.4
	Shultice (D)	113	11.6
9	Robert M. T. Hunter (W)	1,203	52.0
	Scott (D)	1,109	48.0
10	John Taliaferro (W)	1,331	51.4
	Grayson (D)	1,258	48.6
11	John M. Botts (W)	1,459	53.8
	Selden (D)	1,251	46.2
12	James Garland (W)	1,638	66.3
	Gordon (D)	831	33.7
13	Linn Banks (D)	1,785	56.1
	Slaughter (W)	1,396	43.9
14	Charles F. Mercer (W)	1,355	59.3
	Mason (D)	932	40.8
15	William Lucas (D)	2,074	50.1
	Barton (W)	2,070	50.0
16	Green B. Samuels (D)	1,826	60.3
	Steele (W)	1,201	39.7
17	Robert Craig (D)	2,336	58.8
	Moore (W)	1,635	41.2
18	George W. Hopkins (W)	2,921	55.9
	George (D)	2,308	44.1
19	Andrew Beirne (D)	2,745	61.5
	Wethered (W)	1,721	38.5
20	Joseph Johnson (D)	2,370	47.2
	Camden (W)	1,967	39.2
	Shinn (D)	682	13.6
21	Lewis Steenrod (D)	2,667	55.8
	Hammond (W)	2,112	44.2

1840 House Elections

ARKANSAS

	Candidates	Votes	%
AL	Edward Cross (D)	7,876	57.6
	Fowler (W)	5,788	42.4

DELAWARE

	Candidates	Votes	%
AL	George B. Rodney (W)	5,896	54.2
	Thomas Robinson Jr. (D)	4,974	45.8

GEORGIA

	Candidates	Votes	%
AL	William C. Dawson (W)	39,299✓	
	Richard W. Habersham (W)	39,105✓	
	Eugenius A. Nisbet (W)	39,098✓	
	Thomas F. Foster (W)	39,004✓	
	Lott Warren (W)	39,001✓	
	Julius C. Alford (W)	38,980✓	
	Roger L. Gamble (W)	38,924✓	
	Thomas Butler King (W)	38,895✓	
	James A. Meriwether (W)	38,840✓	
	Mark A. Cooper (D)	35,922	
	Edward J. Black (D)	35,783	
	Lumpkin (D)	35,730	
	Campbell (D)	35,678	
	Hillyer (D)	35,660	
	Pooler (D)	35,657	
	Patterson (D)	35,615	
	Iverson (D)	35,608	

Special Election

	Candidates	Votes	%
AL	Hines Holt (W)	✓	#

INDIANA

Special Election

	Candidates	Votes	%
7	Henry S. Lane (W)	11,726	53.1
	Edward A. Hannegan (D)	10,376	47.0

LOUISIANA

	Candidates	Votes	%
1	Edward D. White (W)	3,802	68.4
	Leonard (D)	1,757	31.6
2	John B. Dawson (D)	1,933	50.2
	Morgan (W)	1,920	49.8
3	John Moore (W)	3,427	50.6
	Winn (D)	3,353	49.5

MAINE

	Candidates	Votes	%
1	Nathan Clifford (D)	5,428	54.6
	Daniel Goodenow (W)	4,516	45.4
2	William Pitt Fessenden (W)	5,794	50.5
	Albert Smith (D)	5,659	49.3
3	Benjamin Randall (W)	5,720	54.3
	Joseph Sewall (D)	4,769	45.3
4	George Evans (W)	7,430*	62.5
	John Hubbard (D)	4,450	37.4
5	Nathaniel S. Littlefield (D)	2,144	47.0
	Zadoc Long (W)	2,123	46.6
6	Alfred Marshall (D)	5,805	58.9
	Stanford A. Kingsbury (W)	3,965	40.2
7	Joshua A. Lowell (D)	5,194	50.0
	Joseph C. Noyes (W)	5,051	48.6
8	Elisha H. Allen (W)	7,738	51.5
	Hannibal Hamlin (D)	7,115	47.4

MASSACHUSETTS

	Candidates	Votes	%
1	Robert C. Winthrop (W)	7,286	63.0
	Bradford Sumner (D)	4,232	36.6
2	Leverett Saltonstall (W)	6,153	58.4
	Robert Rantoul (D)	4,276	40.6
3	Caleb Cushing (W)	6,529	60.9
	Gayton P. Osgood (D)	4,047	37.8
4	William Parmenter (D)	6,156	50.3
	Nathan Brooks (W)	5,912	48.3
5	Levi Lincoln (W)	7,069	62.4
	Isaac Davis (D)	4,126	36.4
6	Osmyn Baker (W)	6,167	62.6
	Rhodelphius Larkenson (D)	3,537	35.9
7	George N. Briggs (W)	5,447	54.1
	Henry W. Bishop (D)	4,561	45.3
8	William B. Calhoun (W)	5,701	56.0
	Chester W. Chapin (D)	4,300	42.2
9	William S. Hastings (W)	5,906	57.8
	Alexander H. Everett (D)	4,197	41.1
10	Nathaniel B. Borden (W)	4,320	52.4
	Henry Williams (D)	3,730	45.2
11	Barker Burnell (W)	5,120	59.5
	Henry Crocker (D)	3,378	39.3
12	John Quincy Adams (W)	5,948	54.2
	William M. Jackson (D)	4,945	45.0

Special Election

	Candidates	Votes	%
1	Robert C. Winthrop (W)	7,280	62.9
	Bradford Sumner (D)	4,239	36.7

MICHIGAN

	Candidates	Votes	%
AL	Jacob M. Howard (W)	22,841	51.2
	Alpheus Felch (D)	21,464	48.1

MISSOURI

	Candidates	Votes	%
AL	John Miller (D)	29,594✓	
	John C. Edwards (D)	29,382✓	
	Samuels (W)	21,492	
	Sibley (W)	21,331	

NEW JERSEY

	Candidates	Votes	%
AL	William Halsted (W)	33,342✓	
	Joseph F. Randolph (W)	33,321✓	
	John B. Aycrigg (W)	33,315✓	
	John P. B. Maxwell (W)	33,315✓	
	Charles C. Stratton (W)	33,313✓	
	Thomas Jones Yorke (W)	33,299✓	
	Peter D. Vroom (D)	31,138	
	William R. Cooper (D)	31,109	
	Joseph Kille (D)	31,106	
	Kennedy (D)	31,103	
	Philemon Dickerson (D)	31,101	
	Daniel B. Ryall (D)	31,098	

NEW YORK

	Candidates	Votes	%
1	Charles Floyd (D)	6,069	55.4
	William Buffett (W)	4,880	44.6
2	Joseph Egbert (D)	5,620	54.0
	Lawrence Hillyer (W)	4,780	46.0
4	Aaron Ward (D)	5,949	54.6
	Nicholas Cruger (W)	4,955	45.4
5	Richard Davis (D)	5,164	51.1
	Charles Johnston (W)	4,947	48.9
6	James Clinton (D)	4,867	52.8
	Thomas McKissock (W)	4,343	47.2
7	John Van Buren (D)	6,007	50.3
	Benjamin Bevier (W)	5,930	49.7
9	Hiram Hunt (W)	5,732	51.0
	Samuel Fowler (D)	5,466	48.7
10	Daniel Barnard (W)	6,351	51.4
	James French (D)	5,973	48.3
11	Archibald Linn (W)	6,074	52.1
	John Cramer (D)	5,579	47.8
12	Bernard Blair (W)	4,996	61.7
	Orville Clark (D)	3,061	37.8
13	Thomas Tomlinson (W)	5,906	53.6
	Augustus Hand (D)	5,107	46.4
14	Henry B. Van Rensselaer (W)	6,258	51.3
	Preston King (D)	5,948	48.7
15	John Sanford (D)	5,341	53.0
	Marcellus Weston (W)	4,732	47.0
16	Andrew Doig (D)	5,981	55.2
	Harvey Doolittle (W)	4,774	44.1
18	Thomas Chittenden (W)	6,212	51.9
	Alpheus Greene (D)	5,750	48.1
19	Samuel Bowne (D)	5,612	53.5
	David Hard (W)	4,831	46.0
20	Samuel Gordon (D)	5,976	52.4
	Herman Gould (W)	5,434	47.6
21	John Clark (W)	4,306	51.3
	John Tacy (D)	4,085	48.7
24	Christopher Morgan (W)	5,148	50.8
	Peter Yawger (D)	4,935	48.7
25	John Maynard (W)	6,749	50.6
	John Demott (D)	6,551	49.2
26	Francis Granger (W)	4,800	57.1
	Jared Willson (D)	3,457	41.1
27	William Oliver (D)	6,949	53.0
	Thomas Johnson (W)	6,170	47.0
28	Timothy Childs (W)	6,052	53.9
	Lyman Langworthy (D)	5,092	45.4
29	Seth Gates (W)	6,970	63.4
	John Skinner (D)	3,881	35.3
30	John Young (W)	7,974	56.7
	Leman Gibbs (D)	6,096	43.3
31	Staley Clarke (W)	8,909	60.2
	Benjamin Chamberlain (D)	5,789	39.2
32	Millard Fillmore (W)	6,682	63.9
	Leader Roberts (D)	3,742	35.8
33	Alfred Babcock (W)	5,524	55.4
	Silas Burroughs (D)	4,309	43.2

Multimember Districts

	Candidates	Votes	%
3	James Roosevelt (D)	22,010✓	
	Charles Ferris (D)	21,975✓	
	John McKeon (D)	21,748✓	
	Fernando Wood (D)	21,730✓	
	Moses Grinnell (W)	20,996	
	James Monroe (W)	20,862	
	Robert Smith (W)	20,862	
	Prescott Hall (W)	20,838	
8	Jacob Houck Jr. (D)	11,210✓	
	Robert McClellan (D)	11,194✓	
	Jededia Miller (W)	10,143	
	Justus McKinstry (W)	10,139	
17	David Brewster (W)	11,837✓	
	John Floyd (D)	11,775✓	
	Fortune White (W)	11,364	
	Thomas Bond (W)	11,328	
	Arba Blair (LIB)	506	
	James Brown (LIB)	505	
22	Samuel Partridge (D)	10,374✓	
	Lewis Riggs (D)	10,363✓	
	Ezra Sweet (W)	10,245	
	James Dunn (W)	10,243	
23	Victory Birdseye (W)	10,854✓	
	A. Lawrence Foster (W)	10,826✓	
	Nehemiah Earll (D)	10,772	
	William Hough (D)	10,747	
	John Pratt (LIB)	274	
	Robert Furman (LIB)	233	

OHIO

	Candidates	Votes	%
1	Nathaniel G. Pendleton (W)	6,119	50.7
	Alexander Duncan (D)	5,959	49.3
2	John B. Weller (D)	5,730	50.3
	Lewis D. Campbell (W)	5,661	49.7
3	Patrick G. Goode (W)	10,438	50.4
	William Sawyer (D)	10,275	49.6
4	Jeremiah Morrow (W)	6,796	60.0
	Benjamin Baldwin (D)	4,529	40.0

	Candidates	Votes	%
5	William Doan (D)	5,671	53.7
	Thomas L. Shields (W)	4,884	46.3
6	Calvary Morris (W)	8,724	55.8
	George House (D)	6,882	44.0
7	William Russell (W)	6,953	56.8
	Allen Latham (D)	5,287	43.2
8	Joseph Ridgway (W)	9,909	57.5
	Henry N. Hedges Sr (D)	7,326	42.5
9	William Medill (D)	8,218	57.1
	George Sanderson (W)	6,163	42.9
10	Sampson Mason (W)	10,055	61.4
	Matthew Bonner (D)	6,317	38.6
11	Benjamin S. Cowan (W)	5,791	53.0
	Isaac Parrish (D)	5,129	47.0
12	Joshua Mathiot (W)	7,540	53.7
	Jonathan Taylor (D)	6,497	46.3
13	James Matthews (D)	8,679	53.6
	Henry B. Curtis (W)	7,508	46.4
14	George Sweeny (D)	11,211	52.3
	James Hedges (W)	10,245	47.8
15	Sherlock J. Andrews (W)	11,874	57.8
	David K. Carter (D)	8,663	42.2
16	Joshua R. Giddings (W)	11,725	66.0
	Thomas J. Mlain (W)	6,033	34.0
17	John Hastings (D)	5,278	50.3
	Charles D. Coffin (W)	5,223	49.7
18	Ezra Dean (D)	6,508	54.7
	Levi Cox (W)	5,399	45.3
19	Samuel Stokely (W)	4,390	51.8
	William C. McAuslen (D)	4,092	48.2

PENNSYLVANIA

	Candidates	Votes	%
1	Charles Brown (D)	✓	
3	Charles J. Ingersoll (D)	✓	
5	Joseph Fornance (D)	4,507	54.9
	Unidentified Candidate (W)	3,704	45.1
6	Robert Ramsey (W)	4,411	50.1
	Unidentified Candidate (D)	4,389	49.9
7	John Westbrook (D)	5,331	64.0
	Unidentified Candidate (W)	3,000	36.0
8	Peter Newhard (D)	4,299	55.7
	Unidentified Candidate (W)	3,415	44.3
9	George M. Keim (D)	4,033	100.0
10	William Simonton (W)	4,525	56.7
	Unidentified Candidate (D)	3,462	43.4
11	James Gerry (D)	3,711	53.3

	Candidates	Votes	%
	Unidentified Candidate (W)	3,248	46.7
12	James Cooper (W)	5,475	55.5
	Unidentified Candidate (D)	4,384	44.5
13	William S. Ramsey (D)	5,311*	56.2
	Unidentified Candidate (W)	4,142	43.8
14	James Irvin (W)	6,762	51.6
	Unidentified Candidate (D)	6,336	48.4
15	Benjamin A. Bidlack (D)	6,040	60.4
	Unidentified Candidate (W)	3,959	39.6
16	John Snyder (D)	5,138	51.6
	Unidentified Candidate (W)	4,813	48.4
17	Davis Dimock Jr (D)	7,054	58.7
	Unidentified Candidate (W)	4,961	41.3
18	Charles Ogle (W)	5,449	56.7
	Unidentified Candidate (D)	4,160	43.3
19	Albert G. Marchand (D)	5,188	59.5
	Unidentified Candidate (W)	3,532	40.5
20	Enos Hook (D)	4,757	56.3
	Unidentified Candidate (W)	3,686	43.7
21	Joseph Lawrence (W)	4,045	52.2
	Unidentified Candidate (D)	3,712	47.9
22	William W. Irwin (W)	6,831	61.4
	Unidentified Candidate (D)	4,287	38.6
23	William Jack (D)	4,414	52.5
	Unidentified Candidate (W)	4,001	47.6
24	Thomas Henry (W)	5,372	56.6
	Unidentified Candidate (D)	4,120	43.4
25	Arnold Plummer (D)	7,906	51.0
	Unidentified Candidate (W)	7,600	49.0

Multimember Districts

	Candidates	Votes	%
2	George W. Toland (W)	✓	
	John Sergeant (W)	✓	
4	John Edwards (W)	✓	
	Francis James (W)	✓	
	Jeremiah Brown (W)	15,779✓	
	Unidentified Candidate (D)		
	Unidentified Candidate (D)		
	Unidentified Candidate (D)		

Special Elections

	Candidates	Votes	%
13	Charles McClure (D)	3,452	94.7
22	Henry M. Brackenridge (W)	6,858	61.5
	Wilkens (D)	4,297	38.5

SOUTH CAROLINA

	Candidates	Votes	%
1	Isaac E. Holmes (D)	1,413	86.9
	Hugh S. Legare	213	13.1
2	R. Barnwell Rhett (D)		100.0
3	John Campbell (SR D)		100.0
4	Sampson H. Butler (D)		100.0
5	Patrick C. Caldwell (D)	2,040	39.3
	James Irby (W)	1,812	34.9
	S. Barkley (D)	1,340	25.8
6	Francis W. Pickens (NULL D)		100.0
7	James Rogers (D)		100.0
8	William Butler (W)	2,718	46.8
	J. W. Norris (D)	2,571	44.2
	J. Powell (D)	523	9.0
9	Thomas D. Sumter (D)	✓	
	Evans (D)		

VERMONT

	Candidates	Votes	%
1	Hiland Hall (W)	6,923	62.7
	Daniel Kellogg (D)	4,084	37.0
2	William Slade (W)	6,728	68.6
	Charles Lindsley (D)	3,034	30.9
3	Horace Everett (W)	6,729	59.1
	Truman B. Ransom (D)	4,497	39.5
4	Augustus Young (W)	6,148	55.9
	John Smith (D)	4,791	43.6
5	John Mattocks (W)	5,479	50.6
	Isaac Fletcher (D)	5,248	48.4

VIRGINIA

Special Election

	Candidates	Votes	%
14	William M. McCarty (W)	1,033	56.6
	Cuthbert Powell (W)	722	39.6

1841 House Elections

ALABAMA

	Candidates	Votes	%
AL	Reuben Chapman (D)	23,376✓	
	Dixon H. Lewis (D)	23,339✓	
	Benjamin Glover Shields (D)	23,092✓	
	William Winter Payne (D)	23,090✓	
	George Houston (D)	23,036✓	
	George Crabb (W)	17,828	
	Henry W. Hilliard (W)	17,429	
	James Taylor Rather (W)	17,290	
	John M. Lewis (W)	17,271	
	J. Burke (W)	16,656	
	William D. Dunn (W)	627	

CONNECTICUT

	Candidates	Votes	%
1	Joseph Trumbull (W)	5,142	57.1
	Thomas Seymour (D)	3,867	42.9
2	William Boardman (W)	6,225	54.3
	Charles Ingersoll (D)	5,234	45.7
3	Thomas Williams (W)	3,230	55.7
	Erastus Coit (D)	2,565	44.3
4	Thomas Osborne (W)	4,089	55.6
	William Pomeroy (D)	3,269	44.4
5	Truman Smith (W)	3,993	55.9
	John Smith (D)	3,157	44.2
6	John Brockway (W)	4,121	57.3
	Chauncey Cleveland (D)	3,076	42.7

ILLINOIS

	Candidates	Votes	%
1	John Reynolds (D)	8,046	59.5
	Henry L. Webb (W)	5,313	39.3
2	Zadok Casey (W)	7,121	50.6
	S. H. Anderson (D)	6,949	49.4
3	John T. Stuart (W)	21,726	52.0
	James H. Ralston (D)	19,562	46.8

INDIANA

	Candidates	Votes	%
1	George H. Proffit (W)	5,311	57.4
	James Lockhart (D)	3,946	42.6
2	Richard W. Thompson (W)	6,323	52.7
	John W. Davis (D)	5,670	47.3
3	Joseph L. White (W)	5,596	51.6
	John Carr (D)	5,250	48.4
4	James H. Cravens (W)	6,056	54.4
	Thomas Smith (D)	5,026	45.2
5	Andrew Kennedy (D)	5,664	39.8
	Jonathan McCarty (W)	4,299	30.2
	Caleb B. Smith (W)	4,048	28.5
6	David Wallace (W)	8,206	53.9
	Nathan B. Palmer (D)	7,009	46.1
7	Henry S. Lane (W)	9,477	59.7
	John Bryce (D)	6,392	40.3

KENTUCKY

	Candidates	Votes	%
1	Linn Boyd (D)	✓	
2	Philip Triplett (W)	✓	
	John H. McHenry (W)		
3	Joseph R. Underwood (W)	3,924	72.7
	J. W. Irwin (W)	1,477	27.4
4	Bryan Y. Owsley (W)	✓	
	Martin Beatty (W)		
	Nathan Gaither (D)		
5	John B. Thompson (W)	2,106	36.6
	Thomas P. Moore (D)	1,939	33.7
	John Kinkead (W)	1,704	29.6
6	Willis Green (W)	2,640	38.2
	John L. Helm (W)	2,298	33.2
	Hough	1,978	28.6
7	John Pope (W)	1,012	87.6
	Gray	58	5.0
8	James C. Sprigg (W)	2,576	66.4
	William H. Field (W)	1,306	33.6

	Candidates	Votes	%
9	John White (W)	1,424	100.0
10	Thomas F. Marshall (W)	✓	
	L. B. Smith (W)		
11	Landaff W. Andrews (W)	✓	
	J. C. Mason (D)		
12	Garrett Davis (W)		100.0
13	William O. Butler (D)	4,840	52.8
	W. W. Southgate (W)	4,334	47.2

MAINE

Special Election

4	David Bronson (W)	✓	

MARYLAND

	Candidates	Votes	%
1	Isaac D. Jones (W)	1,910	50.1
	Cottman (W)	1,904	49.9
2	James Alfred Pearce (W)	1,357	100.0
3	James W. Williams (D)	2,563	68.4
	Orrick (D)	1,187	31.7
5	William Cost Johnson (W)	2,627	68.7
	Kimmell (W)	1,195	31.3
6	John T. Mason (D)	4,130	52.6
	Lynch (W)	3,727	47.4
7	Augustus R. Sollers (W)	✓	
	Somervell (I)		

Multimember District

4	Alexander Randall (W)	7,783✓	
	John P. Kennedy (W)	7,733✓	
	Murray (D)	7,657	
	Gallagher (D)	7,654	

MASSACHUSETTS

Special Election

5	Charles Hudson (W)	3,099	57.8
	Isaac Davis (D)	1,782	33.2
	Cyrus B. Grovesnor	333	6.2

MISSISSIPPI

AL	William L. Gwin (D)	18,988✓	
	Jacob Thompson (D)	18,956✓	
	Adam Benjamin (W)	16,593	
	William Harley (W)	16,333	

NEW HAMPSHIRE

AL	Charles G. Atherton (D)	✓	
	Edmund Burke (D)	✓	
	John R. Reding (D)	✓	
	Tristram Shaw (D)	28,870✓	
	Ira A. Eastman (D)	20,833✓	

NORTH CAROLINA

	Candidates	Votes	%
1	Kenneth Rayner (W)	1,593	93.5
2	John R. J. Daniel (D)	✓	
	William W. Cherry (W)		
3	Edward Stanly (W)	✓	
	H. I. Toole (D)		
4	William H. Washington (W)	✓	
	Joshiah O. Watson (D)		
5	James I. McKay (D)	1,706	85.7
	Baker (W)	284	14.3
6	Archibald H. Arrington (D)	1,569	46.6
	Micajah T. Hawkins (D)	1,450	43.0
	William Russell (D)	351	10.4
7	Edmund Deberry (W)	2,769	70.8
	Edward McCollum (D)	1,145	29.3
8	Romulus M. Saunders (D)	2,576	55.2

	Candidates	Votes	%
	James S. Smith (W)	2,090	44.8
9	Augustine H. Shepperd (W)	3,689	52.6
	David S. Reid (D)	3,321	47.4
10	Abraham Rencher (W)	✓	
	Charles Fisher (W)		
	Jonathan Worth (W)		
11	Greene W. Caldwell (D)	3,063	57.2
	Daniel M. Barringer (W)	2,293	42.8
12	James Graham (W)	3,546	61.8
	Thomas L. Clingman (W)	2,188	38.2
13	Lewis Williams (D)	3,373	65.7
	Roderick Murchison (W)	1,760	34.3

PENNSYLVANIA

Special Elections

2	Joseph R. Ingersoll (W)	5,822	55.4
	Pettit (D)	4,596	43.7
18	Henry Black (W)	3,220	68.1
	Philson (D)	1,507	31.9
20	Henry W. Beeson (D)	3,777	56.5
	Andrew Stewart (W)	2,914	43.6

RHODE ISLAND

AL	Robert B. Cranston (W)	2,516✓	
	Joseph L. Tillinghast (W)	2,487✓	

TENNESSEE

	Candidates	Votes	%
1	Thomas D. Arnold (W)	2,506	88.3
	Robert J. McKinney	157	5.5
2	Abraham McClelland (D)	3,484	53.0
	William T. Senter (W)	3,089	47.0
3	Joseph L. Williams (W)	1,022	99.4
4	Thomas J. Campbell (W)	3,757	49.4
	Julius W. Blackwell (D)	3,699	48.6
5	Hopkins L. Turney (D)	3,974	68.0
	John Goodall (W)	1,872	32.0
6	William B. Campbell (W)	2,207	89.1
	Jesse Skein	271	10.9
7	Robert L. Caruthers (W)	3,211	72.3
	John Hall (D)	1,231	27.7
8	Meredith P. Gentry (W)	2,813	70.1
	Thomas Hogan (D)	1,200	29.9
9	Harvey M. Watterson (D)	3,557	54.8
	Terry H. Cahal (W)	2,933	45.2
10	Aaron V. Brown (D)	3,448	83.7
	Ebenezer J. Shields (W)	670	16.3
11	Cave Johnson (D)	3,264	74.3
	N. H. Allen (W)	1,132	25.8
12	Milton Brown (W)	5,503	63.3
	Stephen C. Davatt (D)	3,195	36.7
13	Christopher H. Williams (W)	4,370	57.9
	Levin H. Coe (D)	3,178	42.1

VIRGINIA

	Candidates	Votes	%
1	Francis Mallory (W)	✓	
	Waltas		
2	George B. Cary (D)	✓	
	Collier		
3	John W. Jones (D)	✓	
	J. Leigh		
4	William O. Goode (D)	✓	
	Baptist		
	Marshall		
5	Edmund W. Hubard (D)	✓	
	John Hill (W)		
6	Walter Coles (D)	✓	
	Witcher (W)		
7	William L. Goggin (W)	✓	
	Stuart (D)		
8	Henry A. Wise (W)	✓	

Candidates	Votes	%	Candidates	Votes	%	Candidates	Votes	%
9 Robert M. T. Hunter (I)	✓		Linn Banks (D)			McDowell		
Corbin (W)			14 Cuthbert Powell (W)	✓		18 George W. Hopkins (D)	✓	
Braxton (D)			Shreve			J. Watson (W)		
10 John Taliaferro (W)	✓		15 Richard W. Barton (W)	✓		19 George W. Summers (W)	✓	
Grayson (D)			William Lucas (D)			Ellis		
11 John M. Botts (W)	✓		16 William A. Harris (D)	✓		Caperton		
12 Thomas W. Gilmer (W)	✓		Samuel C. Williams (D)			20 Samuel L. Hayes (D)	✓	
Garland			M. H. Beale			Augustine J. Smith (W)		
Holladay			G. T. Barbee			21 Lewis Stennrod (D)	✓	
13 William Smith (D)	‡		17 Alexander H. H. Stuart (W)	✓				

1842 House Elections

ARKANSAS

	Candidates	Votes	%
AL	Edward Cross (D)	9,413	57.4
	Cummins (W)	5,315	32.4
	Evans (I)	1,686	10.3

DELAWARE

		Votes	%
AL	George B. Rodney (W)	5,467	50.0
	Jones (D)	5,458	50.0

GEORGIA

		Votes	
AL	Mark A. Cooper (D)	35,451✓	
	John B. Lamar (D)	35,307✓	
	Howell Cobb (D)	35,217✓	
	Edward J. Black (D)	35,181✓	
	William H. Stiles (D)	35,176✓	
	Hugh A. Haralson (D)	35,162✓	
	John H. Lumpkin (D)	35,159✓	
	John Millen (D)	35,026✓	
	Richard W. Habersham (W)	33,474	
	Roger L. Gamble (W)	33,249	
	Augustus R. Wright (W)	33,214	
	Richard H. Wilde (W)	32,997	
	Absalom H. Chappell (W)	32,980	
	Agustus H. Kenan (W)	32,827	
	Thomas B. King (W)	32,822	
	Henry P. Smead (W)	32,560	

LOUISIANA

1	John Slidell (SR D)	✓
2	Alcee La Branche (D)	✓
3	John B. Dawson (D)	✓
4	Pierre E. J. B. Bossier (CALH D)	✓

MASSACHUSETTS

		Votes	%
1	Robert C. Winthrop (W)	5,782	53.7
	William Washburn (D)	4,473	41.5
2	Daniel P. King (W)	3,711	50.6
	J. C. Stickney (D)	2,854	38.9
	Moses P. Hanson	660	9.0
3	Amos Abbott (W)	3,932	50.4
	Gayton P. Osgood (D)	3,064	39.3
	Gardner B. Perry	708	9.1
4	William Parmenter (D)	5,339	52.5
	Samuel Hoar (W)	4,010	39.5
	Thomas W. Ward	783	7.7
5	Charles Hudson (W)	5,010	50.9
	David Henshaw (D)	4,090	41.6
	Phineas Crandall	682	6.9
6	Osmyn Baker (W)	5,150	50.1
	Chester W. Chapin (D)	4,127	40.2

	Candidates	Votes	%
	Lucius Boltwood (LIB)	971	9.5
7	Julius Rockwell (W)	4,680	53.6
	Brown	3,335	38.2
	Joel Hayden	643	7.4
8	John Quincy Adams (W)	5,996	51.8
	Ezra Wilkinson (D)	5,418	46.8
9	Henry Williams (D)	6,575	55.0
	Seth Sprague (W)	4,510	37.7
	Hedges Read	800	6.7
10	Barker Burnell (W)	4,776	52.0
	Julius H. Shaw	4,085	44.5

Special Elections[1]

		Votes	%
1	Nathan Appleton (W)	2,753	67.0
	William Washburn (D)	1,232	30.0
1	Robert Winthrop (W)	5,781	53.8
	William Washburn (D)	4,468	41.6
9	William Jackson (W)	2,775*	48.3
	Ezra Wilkinson (D)	2,773	48.2

MISSOURI

AL	James H. Relfe (D)	✓
	John Jamison (D)	✓
	Gustavus M. Bower (D)	✓
	James B. Bowlin (D)	✓
	James M. Hughes (D)	✓
	John P. Campbell	

NEW YORK

		Votes	%
1	Selah B. Strong (D)	5,463	61.9
	King (W)	3,354	38.0
2	Henry C. Murphy (D)	4,563	51.6
	Silliman (W)	4,214	47.7
3	J. Phillips Phoenix (W)	5,084	54.9
	Nicoll (D)	4,156	44.8
4	William B. Maclay (D)	5,549	53.7
	Williams (W)	4,777	46.2
5	Moses G. Leonard (D)	5,282	54.6
	Scoles (W)	4,389	45.4
6	Hamilton Fish (W)	5,904	50.8
	McKeon (D)	5,699	49.1
7	Joseph H. Anderson (D)	4,811	58.3
	Cruger (W)	3,435	41.7
8	Richard D. Davis (D)	6,069	57.2
	Rankin (W)	4,527	42.6
9	James G. Clinton (D)	5,563	55.6
	Wheeler (W)	4,439	44.4
10	Jeremiah Russell (D)	7,376	57.6
	Elting (W)	5,436	42.4
11	Zadock Pratt (D)	6,967	54.6
	Palen (W)	5,772	45.2
12	David L. Seymour (D)	5,419	50.0
	Stevenson (W)	5,335	49.3

	Candidates	Votes	%
13	Daniel D. Barnard (W)	6,317	51.0
	French (D)	5,980	48.3
14	Charles Rogers (W)	6,143	71.0
	Hunter (D)	2,263	26.2
15	Lemuel Stetson (D)	4,635	52.1
	McDonald (W)	4,092	46.0
16	Chesselden Ellis (D)	7,328	50.4
	Linn (W)	7,110	48.9
17	Charles S. Benton (D)	6,750	57.4
	Frey (W)	4,870	41.4
18	Preston King (D)	6,578	56.2
	Sherman (W)	4,785	40.9
19	Orville Hungerford (D)	5,579	52.3
	Merrick (W)	4,810	45.1
20	Samuel Beardsley (D)	6,404	50.5
	Kirkland (W)	5,619	44.4
	Delong (LIB)	647	5.1
21	Jeremiah Cary (D)	8,085	57.4
	Tuckerman (W)	5,893	41.8
22	Smith M. Purdy (D)	8,560	52.4
	Hunt (W)	7,597	46.5
23	Orville Robinson (D)	7,819	50.9
	Duer (W)	6,598	42.9
	Jackson (LIB)	956	6.2
24	Horace Wheaton (D)	6,558	51.1
	Granger (W)	6,024	46.9
25	George Rathbun (D)	7,177	50.0
	Morgan (W)	6,686	46.6
26	Amasa Dana (D)	7,796	53.0
	Woodwh (W)	6,626	45.0
27	Byram Green (D)	6,446	52.3
	Adams (W)	5,611	45.5
28	Thomas J. Patterson (W)	5,333	48.9
	Sampson (D)	5,298	48.6
29	Charles H. Carroll (W)	6,979	91.8
	Pitts (LIB)	623	8.2
30	William S. Hubbell (D)	7,692	51.9
	Sherman (W)	6,847	46.2
31	Asher Tyler (W)	7,521	56.0
	Tenbrk (D)	5,667	42.2
32	William A. Moseley (W)	4,826	51.9
	Vosbgh (D)	4,113	44.2
33	Albert Smith (W)	4,844	53.3
	Cooley (D)	3,894	42.9
34	Washington Hunt (W)	4,672	50.5
	Piper (D)	4,347	47.0

PENNSYLVANIA

Special Election

		Votes	%
17	Almon H. Read (D)	4,479	60.1
	Kingsbury (W)	2,605	34.9
18	Philson (D)	2,711	50.0
	James M. Russell (W)	2,634✓	48.6

1. In the 9th district, William S. Hastings, who had been elected in 1840, died June 17, 1842. In the special election to succeed him for the remainder of the 27th Congress (1841–1843), no candidate received the requisite majority. A series of special elections were held, all resulting without choice, so the seat remained vacant for the remainder of the term. No returns are available for these special elections.

1843 House Elections

ALABAMA

	Candidates	Votes	%
1	James Dellet (W)	4,843	50.7
	Goldthwaite (D)	4,708	49.3
2	James E. Belser (D)	3,960	52.2
	Pettit (W)	3,633	47.9
3	Dixon H. Lewis (D)	3,509	52.3
	Lea (W)	3,202	47.7
4	William W. Payne (D)	4,298	51.7
	Young (W)	4,021	48.3
5	George S. Houston (D)	2,518	50.3
	Armstrong (D)	2,488	49.7
6	Reuben Chapman (D)		100.0
7	Felix G. McConnell (D)	4,456	52.4
	Chilton (W)	3,860	45.4

CONNECTICUT

	Candidates	Votes	%
1	Thomas H. Seymour (D)	7,005	49.1
	T. K. Brace (W)	6,949	48.7
2	John J. Stewart (D)	6,577	48.9
	S. D. Hubbard (W)	6,500	48.3
3	George S. Catlin (D)	5,582	52.8
	E. Eldredge (W)	4,332	41.0
	I. Wilson (LIB)	534	5.1
4	Samuel Simons (D)	8,061	49.2
	T. B. Osborne (W)	7,948	48.5

GEORGIA

Special Election

	Candidates	Votes	%
AL	Alexander H. Stephens (W)	38,471✓	
	Absalom H. Chappell (W)	37,463✓	
	James H. Stark (W)	34,961	
	Herschel V. Johnson (D)	34,757	

ILLINOIS

	Candidates	Votes	%
1	Robert Smith (D)	7,347	56.1
	J. L. D. Morrison (W)	5,568	42.5
2	John McClernand (D)	6,364	63.7
	Zadok Casey (W)	3,629	36.3
3	Orlando B. Ficklin (D)	6,425	53.8
	Justin Hardin (W)	5,528	46.3
4	John Wentworth (D)	7,552	51.5
	Giles Spring (W)	5,931	40.5
	John H. Henderson (LIB)	1,167	8.0
5	Stephen A. Douglas (D)	8,641	50.6
	Orville H. Browning (W)	8,180	47.9
6	Joseph P. Hoge (D)	7,796	51.0
	Cyrus Walker (W)	7,222	47.3
7	John J. Hardin (W)	6,230	52.9
	James A. McDougall (D)	5,357	45.4

INDIANA

	Candidates	Votes	%
1	Robert Dale Owen (D)	6,679	52.2
	John W. Payne (W)	6,127	47.8
2	Thomas J. Henley (D)	7,020	53.6
	Joseph L. White (W)	6,070	46.4
3	Thomas Smith (D)	7,021	50.9
	John A. Matson (W)	6,766	49.1
4	Caleb B. Smith (W)	4,097	49.1
	Charles H. Test	3,442	41.3
	Hiram P. Bennett	749	9.0
5	William J. Brown (D)	7,399	54.0
	David Wallace (W)	6,314	46.0
6	John W. Davis (D)	7,167	53.6
	George G. Dunn (W)	6,205	46.4
7	Joseph A. Wright (D)	5,441	50.0
	Edward W. McGaughey (W)	5,438	50.0
8	John Pettit (D)	6,403	51.7
	James R. M. Bryant (W)	5,985	48.3
9	Samuel C. Sample (W)	5,693	50.8
	Ebenezer M. Chamberlain (D)	5,379	48.0

	Candidates	Votes	%
10	Andrew Kennedy (D)	5,358	51.2
	Lewis G. Thompson (W)	5,098	48.7

KENTUCKY

	Candidates	Votes	%
1	Linn Boyd (D)	6,097	56.7
	Barbour (W)	4,649	43.3
2	Willis Green (W)	5,236	51.2
	Thomas McCreery (D)	4,984	48.8
3	Henry Grider (W)	4,434	51.6
	Irwin (W)	4,167	48.5
4	George A. Caldwell (D)	4,560	45.0
	Owsley (W)	4,066	40.1
	Stone (W)	1,507	14.9
5	James W. Stone (D)	4,872	44.7
	Grigsby (W)	3,701	33.9
	John Pope (D)	2,338	21.4
6	John White (W)	6,850	90.6
	Daniel Garrard (D)	709	9.4
7	William P. Thomasson (W)	4,900	46.5
	Lecompte (D)	4,497	42.6
	Sprigg (W)	1,152	10.9
8	Garrett Davis (W)	5,788	54.1
	C. A. Wickliffe (D)	4,916	45.9
9	Richard French (D)	5,481	51.9
	L. W. Andrews (W)	5,073	48.1
10	John W. Tibbatts (D)	6,507	51.8
	Wall (W)	6,064	48.2

MAINE

	Candidates	Votes	%
1	Joshua Herrick (D)	4,421	50.6
	Jonathan Tucker	1,142	13.1
	Burleigh Smart	1,114	12.7
	Nathan Clifford	1,063	12.2
2	Robert P. Dunlap (D)	4,837	55.3
	Josiah S. Little	2,790	31.9
	Samuel Fessenden	956	10.9
3	Luther Severance (W)	3,799	53.3
	Samuel Wells (D)	2,700	37.9
	Seth May (LIB)	621	8.7
4	Freeman H. Morse (W)	3,546	50.2
	Charles Andrews (D)	2,701	38.3
5	Benjamin White (D)	6,167	51.2
	William G. Crosby (W)	4,558	37.8
	James Bowen	699	5.8
6	Hannibal Hamlin (D)	4,638	54.5
	Elisha Allen	2,673	31.4
	David Shepherd	1,182	13.9
7	Shepard Cary (D)	5,309	52.9
	Thomas Robinson (W)	4,505	44.9

MARYLAND

	Candidates	Votes	%
1	John M. S. Causin (W)	3,776	57.9
	Bowie (D)	2,741	42.1
2	Francis Brengle (W)	6,116	51.8
	J. T. Mason (D)	5,694	48.2
3	John Wethered (W)	4,448	52.2
	S. Brady (D)	4,074	47.8
4	John P. Kennedy (W)	5,894	52.7
	J. Legrand (D)	5,299	47.3
5	Jacob A. Preston (W)	4,229	50.1
	A. Constable (D)	4,211	49.9
6	Thomas Spence (W)	2,197	91.1

MASSACHUSETTS

Special Election

	Candidates	Votes	%
10	Joseph Grinnell (W)	4,943	53.2
	Sampson Perkins	3,927	42.3

MICHIGAN

	Candidates	Votes	%
1	Robert McClelland (D)	7,862	55.3
	Jacob M. Howard (W)	5,495	38.7
	Arthur S. Porter (LIB)	829	5.8
2	Lucius Lyon (D)	7,171	52.6
	Joseph R. Williams (W)	5,202	38.2
	Rufus B. Bement (LIB)	1,246	9.1
3	James B. Hunt (D)	6,209	56.4
	Thomas J. Drake (W)	4,007	36.4
	William Caufield (LIB)	749	6.8

MISSISSIPPI

	Candidates	Votes	%
AL	Jacob Thompson (A-RPT D)	19,861✓	
	William H. Hammett (A-RPT D)	18,813✓	
	Robert W. Roberts (A-RPT D)	18,518✓	
	Tilghman M. Tucker (A-RPT D)	15,923✓	
	Howard (REDEM D)	15,468	
	Dunbar (REDEM D)	15,185	
	Gilmer (REDEM D)	14,744	
	Kendall (REDEM D)	14,124	

NEW HAMPSHIRE

Candidates		
Edmund Burke (D)	✓	
John R. Reding (D)	✓	
Moses Norris Jr (D)	✓	
John P. Hale (D)	✓	

NEW JERSEY

	Candidates	Votes	%
1	Lucius Q. C. Elmer (D)	5,668	51.3
	Unidentified Candidate (W)	5,374	48.7
2	George Sykes (D)	7,573	52.0
	Unidentified Candidate (W)	6,995	48.0
3	Isaac G. Farlee (D)		100.0
4	Littleton Kirkpatrick (D)	6,207	51.1
	Unidentified Candidate (W)	5,949	48.9
5	William Wright (IRR W)	5,313	52.7
	Unidentified Candidate (W)	4,773	47.3

NORTH CAROLINA

	Candidates	Votes	%
1	Thomas L. Clingman (W)	3,817	56.9
	James Graham (W)	2,888	43.1
2	Daniel M. Barringer (W)	4,136	52.2
	Burton Craige (D)	3,788	47.8
3	David S. Reid (D)	4,195	52.3
	Anderson Mitchell (W)	3,827	47.7
4	Edmund Deberry (W)	2,042	52.5
	George C. Mendenhall (W)	1,850	47.5
5	Romulus M. Saunders (D)	3,142	51.2
	Henry W. Miller (W)	3,001	48.9
6	James I. McKay (D)	1,737	79.0
	Leach (W)	462	21.0
7	John R. J. Daniel (D)	3,644	51.1
	Henry K. Nash (W)	3,486	48.9
8	Archibald H. Arrington (D)	4,803	53.0
	Edward Stanly (W)	4,264	47.0
9	Kenneth Rayner (W)	3,719	56.4
	Moore (D)	2,879	43.6

OHIO

	Candidates	Votes	%
1	Alexander Duncan (D)	6,058	52.3
	Haines (I)	5,044	43.6
2	John B. Weller (D)	5,563	50.7
	Campbell (W)	5,308	48.4
3	Robert C. Schenck (W)	7,870	56.9
	Lowe (D)	5,571	40.2
4	Joseph Vance (W)	7,510	61.1
	Hunt (D)	4,552	37.0
5	Emery D. Potter (D)	4,894	55.9
	Tilden (W)	3,856	44.1
6	Henry St. John (D)	4,367	99.0

Candidates	Votes	%
7 Joseph J. McDowell (D)	5,376	49.9
Thompson (W)	5,052	46.9
8 John I. Vanmeter (W)	5,344	50.5
Lucas (D)	5,142	48.6
9 Elias Florence (W)	5,429	52.7
Medill (D)	4,864	47.3
10 Heman Allen Moore (D)	7,194	49.6
Ridgway (W)	6,939	47.9
11 Jacob Brinckerhoff (D)	5,814	56.3
Irwin (I)	2,520	24.4
Waldan (W)	1,996	19.3
12 Samuel F. Vinton (W)	4,133	54.3
Cleveland (D)	3,269	42.9
13 Perley B. Johnson (W)	4,658	51.0
Barker (D)	4,410	48.3
14 Alexander Harper (W)	5,196	54.7
Jennings (D)	4,002	42.1
15 Joseph Morris (D)	5,321	50.9
Cowen (W)	4,617	44.2
16 James Mathews (D)	4,427	55.7
Douglass (W)	3,524	44.3
17 William C. McCauslin (D)	6,741	51.6
Hanna (W)	5,883	45.1
18 Ezra Dean (D)	3,668	68.5
Wellhouse (W)	1,588	29.7
19 Daniel R. Tilden (W)	6,712	47.9
Luman (D)	6,310	45.1
Hall (LIB)	986	7.0
20 Joshua R. Giddings (W)	6,140	57.4
Ranney (D)	3,757	35.1
Wade (LIB)	797	7.5
21 Henry R. Brinckerhoff (D)	5,949	49.0
Hamlin (W)	5,533	45.6
Parish (LIB)	650	5.4

PENNSYLVANIA

Candidates	Votes	%
1 Edward Joy Morris (W)	2,855	45.3
McCully (D)	2,379	37.7
Croust (D)	1,072	17.0
2 Joseph R. Ingersoll (W)	5,414	63.2
Neal (D)	3,153	36.8
3 John T. Smith (D)	3,997	55.8
Sargent (W)	3,162	44.2
4 Charles J. Ingersoll (D)	3,316	55.5
Conrad (W)	2,664	44.6
5 Jacob S. Yost (D)	4,845	54.6
Huddleson (W)	4,022	45.4
6 Michael H. Jenks (W)	5,750	53.0
Davis (D)	5,101	47.0
7 Abraham R. McIlvaine (W)	4,391	51.7
Allison (D)	4,106	48.3
8 Jeremiah Brown (W)	4,898	47.0
Martin (D)	3,940	37.8
Roberts (A-MAS)	1,582	15.2
9 John Ritter (D)	3,941	69.3
Hehn (W)	1,747	30.7
10 Richard Brodhead (D)	5,049	100.0
11 Benjamin A. Bidlack (D)	5,007	64.8
Willits (W)	2,716	35.2
12 Almon H. Read (D)	4,243	56.5

Candidates	Votes	%
Jones (W)	3,266	43.5
13 Henry Frick (W)	5,430	51.2
Snyder (D)	5,181	48.8
14 Alexander Ramsey (W)	5,893	52.5
Umberger (D)	5,326	47.5
15 Henry Nes (W)	4,016	54.1
Small (D)	3,413	45.9
16 James Black (D)	5,617	52.0
Miller (W)	5,189	48.0
17 James Irvin (W)	5,725	56.6
McCulloh (D)	4,389	43.4
18 Andrew Stewart (W)	5,141	50.7
Clevenger (D)	5,004	49.3
19 Henry D. Foster (D)	6,432	100.0
20 John Dickey (W)	4,962	47.1
Leet (D)	4,903	46.5
Lemoyne (LIB)	681	6.5
21 William Wilkins (D)	4,438	49.7
Craig (W&A-MASC)	2,237	25.0
Breckenridge (W)	1,884	21.1
22 Samuel Hays (D)	5,044	85.0
Doughty (A-MASC)	892	15.0
23 Charles M. Reed (W)	5,073	50.2
Irvine (D)	5,033	49.8
24 Joseph Buffington (W)	5,079	55.4
Lorain (D)	4,082	44.6

RHODE ISLAND

Candidates	Votes	%
1 Henry Y. Cranston (L & O W)	4,078	61.3
John H. Weeden (D)	2,557	38.4
2 Elisha R. Potter (L & O W)	2,917	61.2
Wilmarth N. Aldrich (D)	1,846	38.7

SOUTH CAROLINA

Candidates	Votes	%
1 James A. Black (CALH D)	✓	
William K. Clowney (SR D)		
2 Richard F. Simpson (D)	✓	
William Butler (W)		
Downs (D)		
3 Joseph A. Woodward (D)	✓	
Thomas D. Sumter (W)		
4 John Campbell (SR D)	✓	
5 Armistead Burt (D)	2,198	44.1
Patrick C. Caldwell (SSR D)	1,564	31.4
Brooks	1,225	24.6
6 Isaac E. Holmes (D)	✓	
James S. Rhett		
7 R. Barnwell Rhett (D)	1,883	58.0
S. Trotti	1,363	42.0

TENNESSEE

Candidates	Votes	%
1 Andrew Johnson (D)	5,495	52.9
Aikin (W)	4,892	47.1
2 William T. Senter (W)	6,310	59.6
Wallace (D)	4,280	40.4
3 Julius W. Blackwell (D)	5,793	50.4
Campbell (W)	5,700	49.6
4 Alvan Cullom (D)	5,180	58.7

Candidates	Votes	%
Bransford (W)	3,650	41.3
5 George M. Jones (D)	5,111	63.5
Long (W)	2,943	36.5
6 Aaron V. Brown (D)	5,259	52.3
N. S. Brown (W)	4,798	47.7
7 David W. Dickerson (W)	6,137	100.0
8 Joseph H. Peyton (W)	4,853	55.6
Donnelson (D)	3,874	44.4
9 Cave Johnson (D)	4,904	51.2
Henry (W)	4,676	48.8
10 John B. Ashe (W)	5,457	50.9
Staunton (D)	5,264	49.1
11 Milton Brown (W)	5,852	61.1
Pavatt (D)	3,723	38.9

VERMONT

Candidates	Votes	%
1 Solomon Foot (W)	6,698	54.9
C. B. Harrington (D)	4,926	40.4
2 Jacob Collamer (W)	5,825	48.9
Truman B. Ransom (D)	4,833	40.5
Titus Hutchinson (LIB)	1,003	8.4
3 George Perkins Marsh (W)	6,254	53.5
John Smith (D)	4,595	39.3
W. H. French (LIB)	718	6.1
4 Paul Dillingham Jr (D)	6,317	50.8
George B. Chandler (W)	4,957	39.8
G. Putnam (LIB)	797	6.4

VIRGINIA

Candidates	Votes	%
1 Archibald Atkinson (D)	1,789	50.2
Langhorne (W)	1,778	49.9
2 George C. Dromgoole (D)	762	80.6
3 Walter Coles (D)	2,017	51.4
Gilmer (W)	1,911	48.7
4 Edmund W. Hubard (D)	2,164	51.5
Toler (W)	2,037	48.5
5 Thomas W. Gilmer (D)	2,361	50.2
Goggin (W)	2,341	49.8
6 John W. Jones (D)	2,368	50.4
Botts (W)	2,335	49.7
7 Henry A. Wise (D)	1,470	57.1
Carter (W)	1,105	42.9
8 Willoughby Newton (W)	1,008	55.2
Hunter (D)	818	44.8
9 Samuel Chilton (W)	1,532	57.1
Smith (D)	1,149	42.9
10 William Lucas (D)	2,698	56.2
Faulkner (W)	2,104	43.8
11 William Taylor (D)	1,979	83.5
Stuart (W)	392	16.5
12 Augustus A. Chapman (D)	2,552	64.5
Watts (W)	1,402	35.5
13 George W. Hopkins (D)	761	57.7
Fulton (W)	558	42.3
14 George W. Summers (W)	3,271	52.7
Hays (D)	2,942	47.4
15 Lewis Steenrod (D)		100.0

1844 House Elections

ALABAMA

Special Election

	Candidates	Votes	%
3	William L. Yancey (D)	2,197	50.7
	Daniel Watrous (W)	2,137	49.3

ARKANSAS

		Votes	%
AL	Archibald Yell (D)	11,112	59.1
	Walker (W)	7,576	40.3

DELAWARE

		Votes	%
AL	John W. Houston (W)	6,221	50.7
	Biddle (D)	6,043	49.3

GEORGIA

		Votes	%
1	Thomas Butler King (W)	3,702	55.9
	Spalding (D)	2,918	44.1
2	Seaborn Jones (D)	6,460	51.1
	Crawford (W)	6,182	48.9
3	Washington Poe (W)	4,881*	50.7
	Chappell (D)	4,741	49.3
4	Hugh A. Haralson (D)	5,771	52.5
	Floyd (W)	5,214	47.5
5	John H. Lumpkin (D)	7,720	61.2
	Miller (W)	4,889	38.8
6	Howell Cobb (D)	6,306	59.0
	Underwood (W)	4,379	41.0
7	Alexander H. Stephens (W)	4,199	57.1
	Janes (D)	3,152	42.9
8	Robert Toombs (W)	4,665	58.5
	Black (D)	3,309	41.5

Special Election

		Votes	%
AL	Duncan L. Clinch (W)	33,506	53.4
	Sanford (D)	29,206	46.6

ILLINOIS

		Votes	%
1	Robert Smith (D)	7,966	64.7
	John Reynolds (OPP D)	4,146	33.7
2	John A. McClernand (D)	7,968	99.0
3	Orlando B. Ficklin (D)	7,786	57.6
	Usher F. Linder (W)	5,311	39.3
4	John Wentworth (D)	9,516	54.9
	Buckner S. Morris (W)	5,910	34.1
	John H. Henderson (LIB)	1,875	10.8
5	Stephen A. Douglas (D)	9,799	53.9
	David M. Woodson (W)	8,043	44.2
6	Joseph P. Hoge (D)	8,752	52.0
	Martin P. Sweet (W)	7,563	45.0
7	Edwin D. Baker (W)	6,658	52.4
	John Calhoun (D)	5,948	46.9

LOUISIANA

1	John Slidell (SR D)	✓	
2	Bannon G. Thibodeaux (W)	✓	
3	John H. Harmanson (D)	✓	
4	Isaac E. Morse (D)	✓	

MAINE[1]

		Votes	%
1	William A. Hayes	5,321*	46.5
	John F. Scamman	3,377	29.5
	Joshua Herrick	2,061	18.0
2	Robert P. Dunlap (D)	✓	
3	Luther Severance (W)	✓	
4	John D. McCrate (D)	7,464	52.8
	F. H. Morse	5,948	42.1
5	Cullen Sawtelle (D)	6,377	53.2

	Candidates	Votes	%
	William G. Crosby	4,625	38.6
	Drummond Farnsworth	678	5.7
6	Hannibal Hamlin (D)	✓	
7	Hezekiah Williams (D)	✓	

MASSACHUSETTS

		Votes	%
1	Robert C. Winthrop (W)	8,455	62.7
	Benjamin F. Hallett	4,461	33.1
2	Daniel P. King (W)	4,986	57.6
	George Herod (D)	2,770	32.0
	Henry B. Hanton	886	10.2
3	Amos Abbott (W)	6,315	52.1
	George S. Boutwell (D)	4,770	39.4
	Abner L. Bailey	1,001	8.3
4	Benjamin Thompson (W)	5,269	51.7
	William Parmenter (D)	4,405	43.2
	Thomas W. Ward	516	5.1
5	Charles Hudson (W)	5,463	55.8
	Isaac Davis (D)	3,518	36.0
	Rudolphius B. Hubbard	795	8.1
6	George Ashmun (W)	7,467	51.7
	Chester W. Chapin (D)	5,850	40.5
	Lucius Boltwood (LIB)	1,014	7.0
7	Julius Rockwell (W)	6,769	51.5
	Increase Sumner	5,235	39.8
	Joel Hayden	970	7.4
8	John Quincy Adams (W)	8,089	56.6
	Isaac H. Wright	5,340	37.4
	Appleton Howe	733	5.1
9	Artemas Hale (W)	4,881	50.5
	Foster Hooper	3,599	37.2
	Laban M. Wheaton	998	10.3
10	Joseph Grinnell (W)	5,924	58.5
	Edward W. Greene	3,772	37.3

MICHIGAN

		Votes	%
1	Robert McClelland (D)	10,132	51.2
	Edwin Lawrence (W)	8,677	43.9
2	John J. Chipman (D)	9,435	47.7
	Henry W. Taylor (W)	8,967	45.4
	Edwin A. Atlee (LIB)	1,240	6.3
3	James B. Hunt (D)	8,331	51.3
	George W. Wisner (W)	6,967	42.9
	William Caufield (LIB)	934	5.8

MISSOURI

		Votes	
AL	John S. Phelps (D)	36,023	✓
	James B. Bowlin (D)	35,510	✓
	Sterling Price (D)	35,128	✓
	James H. Relfe (D)	35,007	✓
	Leonard H. Sims (W)	29,225	✓
	Thomas B. Hudson (D)	28,309	
	J. Thornton (W)	27,685	
	Ratliff Boone (W)	27,263	
	A. Jones (W)	27,226	
	D. C. M. Parsons (D)	19,123	

NEW JERSEY

		Votes	%
1	James G. Hampton (W)	7,440	54.7
	Elmer (D)	6,153	45.3
2	Samuel G. Wright (W)	6,910	51.5
	Sykes (D)	6,503	48.5
3	John Runk (W)	8,942	50.0
	Isaac G. Farlee (D)	8,926	50.0
4	Joseph E. Edsall (D)	8,779	60.0
	Robtsn (W)	5,848	40.0
5	William Wright (W)	9,996	100.0

NEW YORK

		Votes	%
1	John W. Lawrence (D)	6,132	55.4
	Cogswell (W)	4,935	44.6

	Candidates	Votes	%
2	Henry I. Seaman (NAM)	6,164	51.8
	Murphy (D)	5,686	47.7
3	William S. Miller (NAM)	6,613	54.7
	Nicoll (D)	5,388	44.6
4	William B. Maclay (D)	6,783	51.0
	Lawrence (NAM)	6,428	48.4
5	Thomas M. Woodruff (NAM)	6,214	49.7
	Leonard (D)	6,009	48.1
6	William W. Campbell (NAM)	7,856	48.8
	Moore (D)	7,750	48.2
7	Joseph H. Anderson (D)	6,098	55.8
	Barretto (W)	4,807	44.0
8	William W. Woodworth (D)	7,340	52.1
	Rankin (W)	6,710	47.6
9	Archibald C. Niven (D)	7,162	52.3
	Hasbrouck (W)	6,474	47.3
10	Samuel Gordon (D)	8,645	51.1
	Gould (W)	8,121	48.0
11	John F. Collin (D)	8,226	53.1
	Sanford (W)	7,254	46.9
12	Richard P. Herrick (W)	6,242	51.6
	Seymour (D)	5,692	47.0
13	Bradford R. Wood (D)	7,058	50.0
	Wheaton (W)	6,967	49.3
14	Erastus D. Culver (W)	7,512	56.6
	Bishop (D)	5,297	39.9
15	Joseph Russell (D)	5,441	50.4
	Moore (W)	4,750	44.0
	Boardn (LIB)	606	5.6
16	Hugh White (W)	8,423	50.1
	Ellis (D)	8,124	48.4
17	Charles S. Benton (D)	7,691	54.7
	Alexander (W)	5,706	40.6
18	Preston King (D)	8,145	54.1
	Hopkins (W)	6,295	41.8
19	Orville Hungerford (D)	6,304	50.0
	Bradley (W)	5,587	44.3
	Porter (LIB)	717	5.7
20	Timothy Jenkins (D)	7,617	48.2
	White (W)	7,094	44.9
	Allen (LIB)	1,086	6.9
21	Charles Goodyear (D)	9,298	52.3
	Danforth (W)	7,966	44.8
22	Stephen Strong (D)	9,608	50.9
	Sweet (W)	8,818	46.7
23	William J. Hough (D)	8,128	45.6
	Ledyd (W)	7,426	41.7
	Brown (LIB)	2,268	12.7
24	Horace Wheaton (D)	6,961	49.2
	Noxon (W)	6,495	45.9
25	George Rathbun (D)	7,511	48.3
	Richardson (W)	7,130	45.8
	Stayles (LIB)	921	5.9
26	Samuel S. Ellsworth (D)	8,763	51.5
	Judd (W)	7,662	45.0
27	John De Mott (D)	6,581	48.4
	Holley (W)	6,387	47.0
28	Elias B. Holmes (W)	6,807	52.7
	Selden (D)	5,722	44.3
29	Charles H. Carroll (W)	8,310	53.9
	Wadsworth (W)	6,465	42.0
30	Martin Grover (D)	9,115	50.6
	Cady (W)	8,893	49.4
31	Abner Lewis (W)	8,299	59.9
	Campbell (D)	3,446	24.9
	Allen (LIB)	2,114	15.3
32	William A. Moseley (W)	6,910	55.7
	Stevens (D)	5,081	41.0
33	Albert Smith (W)	6,366	56.3
	Chand (D)	4,215	37.2
	McKay (LIB)	736	6.5
34	Washington Hunt (W)	5,733	51.0
	Piper (D)	4,948	44.1

OHIO

	Candidates	Votes	%
1	James J. Faran (D)	8,760	54.2
	George P. Torrence (W)	7,071	43.8
2	Francis A. Cunningham (D)	6,381	51.6
	Lewis D. Campbell (W)	5,881	47.5
3	Robert C. Schenck (W)	9,850	55.3
	Edward A. King (D)	7,428	41.7
4	Joseph Vance (W)	10,470	60.9
	John H. Young (D)	6,413	37.3
5	William Sawyer (D)	5,916	54.6
	J. W. Riley (W)	4,901	45.2
6	Henry St. John (D)	6,975	56.8
	Abel Rawson (W)	5,278	43.0
7	Joseph J. McDowell (D)	7,004	52.3
	James H. Thompson (W)	6,044	45.2
8	Allen G. Thurman (D)	7,039	50.6
	John J. Vanmetre (W)	6,707	48.2
9	Augustus L. Perrill (D)	6,475	52.5
	Elias Florence (W)	5,797	47.0
10	Columbus Delano (W)	9,297	49.3
	Caleb H. McNulty (D)	9,285	49.3
11	Jacob Brinkerhoff (D)	8,466	51.9
	William McLaughlin (W)	7,501	46.0
12	Samuel F. Vinton (W)	6,750	58.4
	Elisha Morgan (D)	3,753	32.5
	Francis Cleveland (ID)	738	6.4
13	Isaac Parrish (D)	5,825	50.3
	Perley B. Johnson (W)	5,620	48.5
14	Alexander Harper (W)	6,951	53.0
	George W. Manypenny (D)	5,814	44.3
15	Joseph Morris (D)	6,807	50.3
	Joseph A. Ramage (W)	6,207	45.9
16	John D. Cummins (D)	6,568	54.6
	Christian Deardorff (W)	5,465	45.4
17	George Fries (D)	7,699	50.0
	Samuel Stokely (W)	7,236	47.0
18	David A. Starkweather (D)	6,981	55.4
	John Augustine (D)	5,449	43.3
19	Daniel R. Tilden (W)	8,744	48.8
	William Coolman (D)	7,934	44.3
	Lyman W. Hall (LIB)	1,229	6.9

	Candidates	Votes	%
20	Joshua R. Giddings (F SOIL W)	10,048	60.3
	Samuel Starkweather (D)	5,287	31.7
	Edward Wade (LIB)	1,312	7.9
21	Joseph M. Root (W)	7,641	48.6
	Richard Warner (D)	7,140	45.4
	Joel Tiffany (LIB)	954	6.1

Special Election

		Votes	%
10	Alfred Parish Stone (D)	✓	#
	James R. Stanberry (W)		

PENNSYLVANIA

	Candidates	Votes	%
1	Lewis C. Levin (AM)	✓	
2	Joseph R. Ingersoll (W)	✓	
3	John H. Campbell (AM)	✓	
4	Charles J. Ingersoll (D)	✓	
5	Jacob S. Yost (D)	✓	
6	Jacob Erdman (D)	✓	
7	Abraham R. McIlvaine (W)	✓	
8	John Strohm (W)	✓	
9	John Ritter (D)	✓	
10	Richard Brodhead Jr (D)	✓	
11	Owen D. Leib (D)	✓	
12	David Wilmot (D)	✓	
13	James Pollock (W)	✓	
14	Alexander Ramsey (W)	✓	
15	Moses McLean (D)	✓	
16	James Black (D)	✓	
17	John Blanchard (W)	✓	
18	Andrew Stewart (W)	✓	
19	Henry D. Foster (D)	✓	
20	John H. Ewing (W)	✓	
21	Cornelius Darragh (W)	✓	
22	William S. Garvin (D)	✓	
23	James Thompson (D)	✓	
24	Joseph Buffington (W)	✓	

Special Elections

		Votes	%
12	George Fuller (D)	✓	

	Candidates	Votes	%
13	James Pollock (W)	✓	
21	Cornelius Darragh (W)	✓	

SOUTH CAROLINA

	Candidates	Votes	%
1	James A. Black (CALH D)		100.0
2	Richard F. Simpson (D)	5,162	64.0
	William Butler (W)	2,902	36.0
3	Joseph A. Woodward (D)		100.0
4	Alexander D. Sims (D)	2,706	52.5
	John McQueen (D)	2,448	47.5
5	Armistead Burt (D)		100.0
6	Isaac E. Holmes (D)		100.0
7	R. Barnwell Rhett (D)	✓	

VERMONT

	Candidates	Votes	%
1	Solomon Foot (W)	7,696	56.7
	Charles K. Field (D)	4,681	34.5
	Oscar L. Shafter (LIB)	1,119	8.2
2	Jacob Collamer (W)	7,108	55.4
	Levi B. Vilas (D)	4,527	35.3
	Titus Hutchinson (LIB)	1,189	9.3
3	George P. Marsh (W)	6,331	56.9
	John Smith (D)	3,423	30.8
	William H. French (LIB)	1,357	12.2
4	Paul Dillingham Jr. (D)	6,551	47.9
	George B. Chandler (W)	5,696	41.7
	George Putnam (LIB)	1,369	10.0

VIRGINIA

Special Elections

		Votes	%
5	William L. Goggin (W)	✓	
7	Thomas H. Bayly (D)	✓	
	Carter (W)		

1. In Maine's 1st district, no candidate received the necessary majority. In a special election for which returns are unavailable, John F. Scamman (D) was chosen to fill the vacancy.

1845 House Elections

ALABAMA

	Candidates	Votes	%
1	Edmund S. Dargan (D)	4,962	51.6
	Dunn (W)	4,649	48.4
2	Henry W. Hilliard (W)	5,386	50.6
	Cochran (D)	5,258	49.4
3	William L. Yancey (D)	4,987	100.0
4	William W. Payne (D)	4,935	63.7
	Erwin (W)	2,818	36.4
5	George S. Houston (D)	4,035	81.4
	Nool (D)	922	18.6
6	Reuben Chapman (D)		100.0
7	Felix G. McConnell (D)	3,305	56.9
	Rice (D)	2,504	43.1

CONNECTICUT

	Candidates	Votes	%
1	James Dixon (W)	7,612	50.9
	Seymour (D)	6,941	46.5
2	Samuel Hubbard (W)	7,266	54.2
	Stewart (D)	5,814	43.4
3	John Rockwell (W)	5,734	48.1
	Catlin (D)	5,391	45.3
	Wilson (LIB)	784	6.6
4	Truman Smith (W)	8,957	51.7
	J. C. Smith (D)	7,856	45.3

FLORIDA

(Became a state March 3, 1845)

	Candidates	Votes	%
AL	Edward C. Cabell (W)	2,523‡	50.5
	William H. Brockenbrough (D)	2,472	49.5

INDIANA

	Candidates	Votes	%
1	Robert Dale Owen (D)	7,336	53.7
	George P. R. Wilson (W)	6,331	46.3
2	Thomas J. Henley (D)	7,219	53.1
	Roger Martin (W)	6,376	46.9
3	Thomas Smith (D)	7,246	51.1
	Joseph C. Eggleston (W)	6,706	47.3
4	Caleb B. Smith (W)	4,863	56.4
	John Finley (D)	3,201	37.2
	Matthew R. Hull (LIB)	553	6.4
5	William W. Wick (D)	7,459	54.8
	James P. Foley (W)	5,883	43.2
6	John W. Davis (D)	8,183	60.9
	Eli P. Farmer (W)	5,253	39.1
7	Edward W. McGaughey (W)	6,192	50.7
	Joseph A. Wright (D)	6,023	49.3
8	John Pettit (D)	6,260	51.6
	Albert L. Holmes (W)	5,771	47.6
9	Charles W. Cathcart (D)	6,231	50.0
	Samuel C. Sample (W)	5,959	47.8
10	Andrew Kennedy (D)	5,837	50.0
	Lewis G. Thompson (W)	5,482	47.0

KENTUCKY

	Candidates	Votes	%
1	Linn Boyd (D)	6,377	97.1
2	John H. McHenry (W)	6,070	53.0
	Thomas McCreery (D)	5,385	47.0
3	Henry Grider (W)	5,511	56.0
	S. A. Atchison (D)	4,338	44.1
4	Joshua F. Bell (W)	6,044	50.3
	G. A. Caldwell (D)	5,965	49.7
5	Bryan R. Young (W)	6,126	51.1

	Candidates	Votes	%
	James W. Stone (D)	5,869	48.9
6	John P. Martin (D)	4,074	37.1
	G. Adams (W)	3,658	33.3
	G. R. McKee (W)	3,240	29.5
7	William P. Thomasson (W)	6,023	52.2
	Elijah Nuttall (D)	5,510	47.8
8	Garret Davis (W)	5,819	53.3
	T. F. Marshall (D)	5,109	46.8
9	Andrew Trumbo (W)	5,741	51.6
	Richard French (D)	5,381	48.4
10	John W. Tibbatts (D)	7,107	50.8
	John P. Gaines (W)	6,875	49.2

MARYLAND

	Candidates	Votes	%
1	John G. Chapman (W)	4,238	52.2
	Key (D)	3,884	47.8
2	Thomas J. Perry (D)	6,789	52.7
	Snively (W)	6,095	47.3
3	Thomas W. Ligon (D)	5,924	54.1
	Wethered (W)	5,030	45.9
4	William F. Giles (D)	5,824	48.8
	Kennedy (W)	4,962	41.6
	Duncan (AM)	1,147	9.6
5	Albert Constable (D)	4,631	51.0
	Wright (W)	4,444	49.0
6	Edward H. C. Long (W)	3,735	51.1
	Martin (D)	3,577	48.9

MISSISSIPPI

	Candidates	Votes	%
AL	Jacob Thompson (D)	27,423✓	
	Jefferson Davis (D)	27,193✓	
	Stephen Adams (D)	26,836✓	
	Robert W. Roberts (D)	26,059✓	
	Tompkins (W)	18,194	
	Starke (W)	17,452	
	Brooke (W)	17,094	

NEW HAMPSHIRE[2]

	Candidates	Votes	%
AL	Mace Moulton (D)	24,068✓	
	James H. Johnson (D)	24,011✓	
	Moses Norris Jr (D)	23,765✓	
	Woodbury (D)	21,913	
	Edwards (FEDL)	14,692	
	Nesmith (FEDL)	14,690	
	Goodwin (FEDL)	14,562	
	Sawyer (FEDL)	13,833	
	Hale	7,053	
	Porter (AB)	5,272	
	Moore (AB)	4,968	
	Perkins (AB)	4,554	
	Cilley (AB)	4,503	

NORTH CAROLINA

	Candidates	Votes	%
1	James Graham (W)	5,245	51.6
	Thomas L. Clingman (W)	4,918	48.4
2	Daniel M. Barringer (W)	5,368	50.1
	Charles Fisher (D)	5,342	49.9
3	David S. Reid (D)	5,133	54.0
	Alexander B. McMillan (W)	4,369	46.0
4	Alfred Dockery (W)	4,078	56.5
	Jonathan Worth (W)	3,135	43.5
5	James C. Dobbin (D)	5,242	61.8
	John H. Haughton (W)	3,236	38.2
6	James I. McKay (D)	5,169	66.3

	Candidates	Votes	%
	Thomas D. Meares (W)	2,633	33.8
7	John R. J. Daniel (D)	4,872	64.1
	Robert C. Bond (W)	2,729	35.9
8	Henry S. Clarke (D)	4,654	53.7
	Richard S. Donnell (W)	4,009	46.3
9	Asa Biggs (D)	3,695	51.0
	David Outlaw (W)	3,549	49.0

RHODE ISLAND

	Candidates	Votes	%
1	Henry Cranston (W)	4,900	98.8
2	Lemuel H. Arnold (LIBER W)	3,202	51.1
	Elisha R. Potter (L & O W)	2,995	47.8

TENNESSEE

	Candidates	Votes	%
1	Andrew Johnson (D)	6,068	56.3
	William B. Brownlow (W)	4,715	43.7
2	William M. Cocke (W)	4,884	45.0
	George S. Gilbert (D)	3,864	35.6
	Lewis Reneau (IW)	2,098	19.3
3	John H. Crozier (W)	6,179	51.4
	Julius W. Blackwell (D)	5,841	48.6
4	Alvin Cullom (D)	6,266	93.1
	Isaac Clendenon	467	6.9
5	George W. Jones (D)	6,528	100.0
6	Barclay Martin (D)	4,476	59.8
	William D. Kindrick (W)	3,009	40.2
7	Meredith T. Gentry (W)	5,849	67.9
	Charles L. Nelson (D)	2,760	32.1
8	Edwin Hickman Ewing (W)	✓	#
	Joseph H. Peyton (W)	5,204	55.3
	William Trousdale (D)	4,202	44.7
9	Lucien B. Chase (D)	4,281	57.6
	John J. Mathewson (W)	3,156	42.4
10	Frederick P. Stanton (D)	5,901	52.8
	Phineas T. Scruggs (W)	5,283	47.2
11	Milton Brown (W)	5,166	59.9
	Nelson Hess (D)	3,454	40.1

VIRGINIA

	Candidates	Votes	%
1	Archibald Atkinson (D)	✓	
	Whitfield		
2	George C. Dromgoole (D)	✓	
3	William M. Tredway (D)	✓	
4	Edmund W. Hubard (D)	✓	
5	Shelton F. Leake (D)	✓	
	Irving		
6	James A. Seddon (D)	✓	
	John M. Botts (W)		
7	Thomas H. Bayly (D)	✓	
	Southall		
8	Robert M. T. Hunter (D)	✓	
	Willoughby Newton (W)		
9	John S. Pendleton (W)	✓	
	McCarty		
10	Henry Bedinger (D)	✓	
	Lucas		
11	William Taylor (D)	✓	
12	Augustus A. Chapman (D)	✓	
13	George W. Hopkins (D)	✓	
14	Joseph Johnson (D)	✓	
	Camden		
15	William G. Brown (D)	✓	
	Allen		

1. New Hampshire was entitled to four seats in the 29th Congress (1845–1847), but only elected three representatives. Woodbury did not receive the necessary number of votes to be elected in the 1845 at-large election, and no winner was subsequently chosen in a special election. (See New Hampshire, 1846.) So the fourth seat remained vacant for the entire Congress.

1846 House Elections

ALABAMA

Special Elections

	Candidates	Votes	%
3	James L. F. Cottrell (D)	3,299	50.2
	Samuel S. Beeman (W)	3,269	49.8
7	Franklin W. Bowdon (D)	2,704	45.2
	Benjamin Goodman (W)	1,979	33.1
	T. A. Walker (D)	1,303	21.8

ARKANSAS

AL	Robert W. Johnson (LOCOFOCO)	✓	

Special Election

AL	Thomas W. Newton (W)	1,753	28.6
	Paschal	1,722	28.1
	Albert Rust (D)	1,654	27.0
	Noland (W)	858	14.0

DELAWARE

AL	John W. Houston (W)	6,154	50.6
	Dillw (D)	6,007	49.4

FLORIDA

AL	Edward C. Cabell (W)	✓	

GEORGIA

1	Thomas Butler King (W)	3,274	59.6
	Cohen (D)	2,220	40.4
2	Alfred Iverson (D)	5,599	51.8
	Crawford (W)	5,202	48.2
3	John W. Jones (W)	4,083	51.1
	George W. B. Towns (D)	3,904	48.9
4	Hugh A. Haralson (D)	4,908	50.8
	Mosley (W)	4,756	49.2
5	John H. Lumpkin (D)	5,349	79.4
	Crook (W)	1,263	18.8
6	Howell Cobb (D)	4,368	59.5
	Cleveland (W)	2,968	40.5
7	Alexander H. Stephens (W)	3,507	62.8
	Turner (D)	2,078	37.2
8	Robert Toombs (W)	3,560	65.0
	Unidentified Candidate (D)	1,917	35.0

Special Election

3	George W. B. Towns (D)	4,026	51.6
	Baber (W)	3,773	48.4

ILLINOIS

1	Robert Smith (OPP D)	7,068	58.1
	Lyman Trumbull (D)	5,019	41.3
2	John A. McClernand (D)	7,151	97.3
3	Orlando B. Ficklin (D)	6,707	57.1
	Robert K. McLaughlin (I)	5,014	42.7
4	John Wentworth (D)	12,115	55.8
	John Kerr (W)	6,079	28.0
	Owen Lovejoy (LIB)	3,531	16.3
5	Stephen A. Douglas (D)	9,629*	57.0
	Isaac VanderVenter (W)	6,864	40.6
6	Thomas J. Turner (D)	8,843	48.4
	James Knox (W)	8,456	46.3
	Wade Talcott (LIB)	947	5.2
7	Abraham Lincoln (W)	6,340	55.5
	Peter Cartwright (D)	4,829	42.3

IOWA[1]

(Became a state Dec. 28, 1846)

Candidates	Votes	%
S. Clinton Hastings (D)	✓	
Shepherd Leffler (D)	✓	

MASSACHUSETTS

1	Robert C. Winthrop (W)	5,980	63.9
	Peter F. Homer (D)	1,688	18.1
	Samuel G. Howe (LIB)	1,334	14.3
2	Daniel P. King (W)	3,735	62.6
	George W. Dike (D)	1,621	27.2
	Samuel Gall (LIB)	427	7.2
3	Amos Abbott (W)	4,965	52.5
	George S. Boutwell (D)	3,098	32.7
	Chauncey L. Knapp (LIB)	1,108	11.7
4	John G. Palfrey (W)	4,513	50.6
	Frederick Robinson (D)	3,754	42.1
	James G. Carter (LIB)	544	6.1
5	Charles Hudson (W)	6,068	50.3
	Walter A. Bryant (D)	4,107	34.1
	R. B. Hubbard (LIB)	1,508	12.5
6	George Ashmun (W)	6,628	55.1
	Stephen S. W. Taber (D)	4,245	35.3
	John Dickinson Jr (LIB)	1,021	8.5
7	Julius Rockwell (W)	5,716	53.1
	Heratio Byington (D)	4,138	38.4
	Jasper Bement (LIB)	861	8.0
8	John Quincy Adams (W)	5,765	61.6
	Isaac H. Wright (D)	2,617	28.0
	Appleton Howe (LIB)	882	9.4
9	Artemas Hale (W)	4,937	50.1
	Foster Hooper (D)	3,718	37.7
	Laban M. Wheaton (LIB)	1,023	10.4
10	Joseph Grinnell (W)	3,806	62.8
	Timothy G. Coffin (D)	1,788	29.5

MICHIGAN

1	Robert McClelland (D)	7,877	52.1
	Edwin Lawrence (W)	6,442	42.6
	Charles H. Stewart (LIB)	791	5.2
2	Edward Bradley (D)	9,517	49.1
	James W. Gordon (W)	8,681	44.8
	Erastus Hussey (LIB)	1,156	6.0
3	Kinsley S. Bingham (D)	6,529	48.9
	George W. Wisner (W)	5,811	43.5
	William Caufield (LIB)	981	7.4

MISSOURI

1	James B. Bowlin (D)	7,466	52.2
	Uriel Wright (W)	5,268	36.8
	William Milburn	1,572	11.0
2	John Jamison (D)	8,156	80.3
	Preston P. Brickey (W)	1,814	17.9
3	James S. Green (D)	8,624	55.3
	John G. Miller (W)	6,981	44.7
4	Willard P. Hall (D)	8,884	65.0
	James H. Birch (W)	4,789	35.0
5	John S. Phelps (D)	7,195	53.1
	John P. Campbell (W)	6,348	46.9

Special Election

AL	William McDaniel (D)	9,155	48.6
	William M. Kincaid (W)	8,610	45.7

NEW HAMPSHIRE[2]

Special Election

AL	Woodbury (D)	26,810*	48.8

Candidates	Votes	%
Goodwin (W)	16,567	30.1
Hale (I)	11,475	20.9

NEW JERSEY

1	James G. Hampton (W)	✓	
2	William A. Newell (W)	✓	
3	Joseph E. Edsall (D)	✓	
4	John Van Dyke (W)	✓	
5	Dudley S. Gregory (W)	✓	

NEW YORK

1	Frederick Lord (D)	4,045	54.7
	Abraham Rose (W)	3,353	45.3
2	Henry Murphy (D)	5,267	45.9
	Gerret Van Wagenan (W)	5,070	44.2
	Henry Seaman (AM)	771	6.7
3	Henry Nicoll (D)	4,609	48.6
	Phillip Phoenix (W)	4,560	48.1
4	William Maclay (D)	4,749	46.1
	John Williams (W)	4,057	39.4
	William Picall (AM)	865	8.4
5	Frederick Tallmadge (W)	4,205	42.1
	David Broderick (D)	3,809	38.2
	David Wheeler (AM)	1,493	15.0
6	David S. Jackson (D)	6,071‡	43.3
	James Monroe (W)	5,928	42.3
	William Campbell (AM)	1,841	13.1
7	William Nelson (W)	4,324	51.2
	Edward Suffem (D)	4,099	48.5
8	Cornelius Warren (W)	5,450	45.7
	Henry Delamater (D)	5,221	43.8
	Charles Haight	1,251	10.5
9	Daniel St.John (W)	6,158	56.3
	John Monell (D)	4,719	43.1
10	Eliakim Sherrill (W)	7,967	53.6
	Jeremiah Russell (D)	6,742	45.4
11	Peter Sylvester (W)	6,586	53.3
	Silas Camp (D)	5,770	46.7
12	Gideon Reynold (W)	5,509	52.8
	Nicholas Masters (D)	4,822	46.3
13	John Slingerland (W-A-RENT)	7,155	58.1
	Bradford Wood (D)	5,087	41.3
14	Orlando Kellogg (W)	9,449	67.7
	Winslow Watson (D)	4,020	28.8
15	Sidney Lawrence (D)	5,174	53.4
	William McLean (W)	4,181	43.2
16	Hugh White (W)	7,576	51.3
	Lucio Smith (D)	7,024	47.5
17	George Petrie (ID)	5,532	51.1
	Abraham Van Alstine (D)	4,717	43.6
	John Underwood	576	5.3
18	William Collins (D)	5,878	48.2
	Francis Seger (D-HUNKER)	5,732	47.0
19	Joseph Mullin (W)	4,915	46.6
	Orville Hungerford (D)	4,871	46.2
	Hugh Smith	763	7.2
20	Timothy Jenkins (D)	6,018	47.6
	Orsamus Matteson (W)	5,693	45.0
	James Delong	940	7.4
21	George Starkweather (D)	7,209	50.1
	Ebenezer Blakeley (W)	6,889	47.9
22	Ausburn Birdsall (D)	7,904	51.7
	Gideon Chase (BARN D)	6,995	45.8
23	William Duer (W)	6,431	45.0
	Avery Skinner (D)	6,186	43.3
	Cyrus Hawley	1,597	11.2
24	Daniel Gott (W)	5,561	49.2
	William Fuller (D)	5,157	45.6
	Charles Wheaton	569	5.0
25	Harmon Conger (W)	6,253	47.7
	William Shankland (D)	6,036	46.1
	John Boyd	811	6.2
26	William Lawrence (W)	6,753	48.6
	John Wisner (D)	6,739	48.5

	Candidates	Votes	%
27	John Holley (W)	5,468	48.3
	James Wilson (D)	5,180	45.7
	Levi Gaylord	678	6.0
28	Elias Holmes (W)	6,131	54.0
	Maltby Strong (IW)	4,370	38.5
	Samuel Porter	855	7.5
29	Robert Rose (W)	7,539	55.9
	Peter Mitchel (D)	5,451	40.5
30	David Rumsey Jr (W)	7,034	51.8
	Hugh Magee (D)	6,126	45.1
31	Dudley Marvin (W)	7,022	63.8
	Ebenezer Lester (D)	3,279	29.8
	Constant Allen	711	6.5
32	Nathan Hall (W)	5,660	54.5
	Hiram Barney (D)	4,385	42.2
33	Harvey Putnam (W)	5,628	58.9
	Junius Smith (D)	3,151	33.0
	Ferdinand McKay	559	5.9
34	Washington Hunt (W)	4,992	51.3
	Sanford Church (D)	4,347	44.7

OHIO

1	James J. Faran (D)	7,055	54.1
	Thomas J. Straight (W)	4,301	33.0
	William Green	1,143	8.8
2	David Fisher (W)	7,086	52.7
	Elijah Vance (D)	5,915	44.0
3	Robert C. Schenck (W)	8,863	55.4
	F. A. Cunningham (D)	6,681	41.7
4	Richard S. Canby (W)	7,822	57.5
	William Kershner (D)	5,226	38.4
5	William Sawyer (D)	5,483	53.3
	Morrison R. Waite (W)	4,764	46.3
6	Rodolphus Dickinson (D)	5,802	57.2
	Eli Dresback (W)	4,159	41.0
7	Thomas L. Hamer (D)	6,785*	92.1
	Alex Campbell	384	5.2
8	John L. Taylor (W)	6,127	51.6
	L. Byington (D)	5,465	46.0
9	Thomas O. Edwards (W)	6,030	50.8
	A. L. Perrill (D)	5,779	48.7
10	Daniel Duncan (W)	7,539	49.2
	Samuel Medary (D)	7,239	47.3
11	John K. Miller (D)	7,645	57.8
	W. McLaughlin (W)	2,237	16.9
	J. H. Godman (W)	1,949	14.7
	C. Delano (W)	989	7.5
12	Samuel F. Vinton (W)	3,424	38.8
	Flavius Case (D)	3,245	36.8
	C. Morris	1,240	14.1

	Candidates	Votes	%
	A. Cushing	568	6.4
13	Thomas Ritchey (D)	5,032	48.8
	P. B. Johnson (W)	5,005	48.5
14	Nathan Evans (W)	5,529	52.0
	W. W. Tracy (D)	4,674	44.0
15	William Kennon Jr (D)	5,386	50.1
	B. S. Cowan (W)	4,988	46.4
16	John D. Cummins (D)	5,080	54.0
	John Everhard (W)	4,180	44.4
17	George Fries (D)	5,318	50.4
	Van Brown (W)	4,906	46.5
18	Samuel Lahm (D)	4,651	50.0
	David A. Starkweather (W)	4,530	48.7
19	John Crowell (W)	6,573	48.2
	Rufus P. Ranney (D)	6,041	44.3
	John Hutchins (LIB)	1,016	7.5
20	Joshua R. Giddings (W)	6,548	60.6
	Zenas Blish (D)	2,865	26.5
	Edw. Wade (LIB)	1,398	12.9
21	Joseph M. Root (W)	6,126	48.0
	Josiah Harris (D)	5,160	40.4
	Joel Tiffany (LIB)	1,471	11.5

PENNSYLVANIA

1	Lewis C. Levin (AM)		✓
2	Joseph R. Ingersoll (W)		✓
3	Charles Brown (D)		✓
4	Charles J. Ingersoll (D)		✓
5	John Freedly (W)		✓
6	John W. Hornbeck (W)		✓
7	Abraham R. McIlvaine (W)		✓
8	John Strohm (W)		✓
9	William Strong (D)		✓
10	Richard Brodhead (D)		✓
11	Chester P. Butler (W)		✓
12	David Wilmot (D)		✓
13	James Pollock (W)		✓
14	George N. Eckert (W)		✓
15	Henry Nes (W)		✓
16	Jasper E. Brady (W)		✓
17	John Blanchard (W)		✓
18	Andrew Stewart (W)		✓
19	Job Mann (D)		✓
20	John Dickey (W)		✓
21	Moses Hampton (W)		✓
22	John W. Farrelly (W)		✓
23	James Thompson (D)		✓
24	Alexander Irvin (W)		✓

SOUTH CAROLINA

	Candidates	Votes	%
1	James A. Black (CALH D)	4,364	61.2
	L. P. Herndon	1,665	23.4
	G. A. Alston	1,099	15.4
2	Richard F. Simpson (D)		100.0
3	Joseph A. Woodward (D)	✓	
4	Alexander D. Sims (D)	✓	
5	Armistead Burt (D)		100.0
6	Isaac E. Holmes (D)	✓	
	D. J. Dowling		
7	R. Barnwell Rhett (D)		100.0

TEXAS

(Became a state Dec. 29, 1845)

1	David Kaufman (D)	589	98.7
2	Timothy Pillsbury (CALH D)	1,751	49.9
	William E. Jones	678	19.3
	S. M. Williams	621	17.7
	R. E. B. Baylor	458	13.0

Special Elections

1	David S. Kaufman (D)	1,478	58.9
	William R. Scurry	532	21.2
	William B. Ochiltree	497	19.8
2	Timothy Pillsbury (CALH D)	1,276	30.0
	Samuel M. Williams	1,233	29.0
	William G. Cooke	954	22.5
	N. Lewis	423	10.0
	Joseph C. Megginson	253	6.0

VERMONT

1	William Henry (W)	6,627	54.0
	Bradley (D)	3,071	25.0
	Unidentified Candidate (LIB&SC)	2,580	21.0
2	Jacob Collamer (W)	5,457	49.1
	Hugh H. Henry (D)	3,854	34.7
	Titus Hutchinson (LIB)	1,732	15.6
3	George Perkins Marsh (W)	5,644	53.9
	Homer E. Hubbell (D)	3,207	30.7
	Norris Day (LIB)	1,575	15.1
4	Lucius B. Peck (D)	5,594	44.1
	George B. Chandler (W)	5,059	39.9
	Rowell (LIB)	1,255	9.9

1. Information unavailable as to whether the Iowa elections were at-large or by district.

2. Woodbury did not receive the required majority. (See New Hampshire, 1845.)

1847 House Elections

ALABAMA

	Candidates	Votes	%
1	John Gayle (W)	5,050	52.9
	John Taylor (D)	4,490	47.1
2	Henry W. Hilliard (W)		100.0
3	Sampson W. Harris (D)		100.0
4	Samuel W. Inge (D)	4,528	51.0
	W. M. Murphy (W)	4,360	49.1
5	George S. Houston (D)	4,476	60.1
	D. Hubbard (D)	2,978	40.0
6	Williamson R. W. Cobb (D)	3,321	45.2
	William Acklen (D)	2,747	37.4
	B. F. Pope (D)	1,284	17.5
7	Franklin W. Bowdon (D)	5,419	52.3
	S. F. Rice (D)	4,024	38.9
	Phillips	793	7.7

CONNECTICUT

	Candidates	Votes	%
1	James Dixon (W)	7,676	50.5
	William Hammersley (D)	7,167	47.1
2	Samuel D. Hubbard (W)	7,325	50.9
	Samuel Ingham (D)	6,669	46.4
3	John A. Rockwell (W)	6,112	49.5
	Noyes Billings (D)	5,578	45.2
	Increase Wilson (LIB)	653	5.3
4	Truman Smith (W)	9,082	52.0
	George Taylor (D)	7,980	45.7

ILLINOIS

Special Elections

	Candidates	Votes	%
5	William A. Richardson (D)	11,423	77.5
	Nathaniel G. Wilcox (W)	3,312	22.5
7	John Henry (W)	2,411	56.8
	Issur W. Crosby (D)	1,289	30.3
	Archibald Job (OPP D)	293	6.9

INDIANA

	Candidates	Votes	%
1	Elisha Embree (W)	7,446	51.4
	Robert Dale Owen (D)	7,054	48.7
2	Thomas J. Henley (D)	7,170	50.1
	John S. Davis (W)	7,130	49.9
3	John L. Robinson (D)	7,908	51.5
	Pleasant A. Hackleman (W)	7,422	48.3
4	Caleb B. Smith (W)	4,988	58.5
	Charles H. Test	3,540	41.5
5	William W. Wick (D)	7,087	50.4
	Nicolas McCarty (W)	6,799	48.4
6	George G. Dunn (W)	7,455	50.0
	David M. Dobson (D)	7,454	50.0
7	Richard W. Thompson (W)	6,402	50.7
	Joseph A. Wright (D)	6,224	49.3
8	John Pettit (D)	6,931	51.0
	David Brier (W)	6,511	47.9
9	Charles W. Cathcart (D)	7,555	51.0
	Daniel D. Pratt (W)	7,063	47.7
10	William Rockhill (D)	6,617	50.4
	William G. Ewing (W)	6,441	49.1

IOWA

	Candidates	Votes	%
1	William Thompson (D)	5,530	52.6
	Jesse B. Browne (W)	4,986	47.4
2	Shepherd Leffler (D)	5,160	51.4
	Thomas McKnight (W)	4,873	48.6

KENTUCKY

	Candidates	Votes	%
1	Linn Boyd (D)	7,421	63.9
	Delaney (W)	4,194	36.1
2	Samuel O. Peyton (D)	6,068	50.5
	Waddill (W)	5,958	49.5
3	Beverly L. Clarke (D)	5,291	51.1

	Candidates	Votes	%
	Todd (W)	5,065	48.9
4	Aylett Buckner (W)	6,177	51.6
	James (D)	5,791	48.4
5	John B. Thompson (W)	6,779	53.0
	Wickliffe (D)	6,019	47.0
6	Green Adams (W)	6,303	54.3
	Price (W)	5,307	45.7
7	W. Garnett Duncan (W)	6,760	51.1
	David Meriwether (D)	6,477	48.9
8	Charles S. Morehead (W)	4,348	41.3
	S. F. J. Trabue (AM)	3,143	29.9
	A. K. Marshall (D)	3,037	28.9
9	Richard French (D)	6,473	51.2
	Cox (W)	6,166	48.8
10	John P. Gaines (W)	7,496	50.4
	L. B. Desha (D)	7,372	49.6

LOUISIANA

	Candidates	Votes	%
1	Emile La Sere (D)	2,813	63.6
	Montegut (W)	1,613	36.4
2	Bannon G. Thibodeaux (W)	4,280	55.1
	Landry (D)	3,489	44.9
3	John H. Harmanson (D)	4,118	54.8
	Saunders (W)	3,399	45.2
4	Isaac E. Morse (D)	4,138	53.9
	Waddell (W)	3,534	46.1

MAINE

	Candidates	Votes	%
1	David Hammons (D)	5,430	53.6
	Samuel Hopkins (W)	3,521	34.7
	Theodore Stevens Jr (LIB)	1,101	10.9
2	Asa W. H. Clapp (D)	4,369	52.0
	Josiah S. Little (W)	3,023	36.0
	Unidentified Candidate (LIB & SC)	1,010	12.0
3	Hiram Belcher (W)	5,687	51.8
	Cutter (D)	3,487	31.7
	Unidentified Candidate (LIB & SC)	1,812	16.5
4	Franklin Clark (D)	5,266	49.2
	Freeman H. Morse (W)	4,657	43.5
	Unidentified Candidate (LIB & SC)	775	7.2
5	Ephraim K. Smart (D)	4,548	44.2
	Levi Johnson (W)	3,852	37.4
	Unidentified Candidate (LIB & SC)	1,892	18.4
6	James S. Wiley (D)	4,817	48.2
	Sanford Kingsbury (W)	3,615	36.2
	Unidentified Candidate (LIB & SC)	1,560	15.6
7	Hezekiah Williams (D)	5,033	52.0
	Pike (W)	3,740	38.6
	Unidentified Candidate (LIB & SC)	910	9.4

MARYLAND

	Candidates	Votes	%
1	John G. Chapman (W)		100.0
2	J. Dixon Roman (W)	7,136	51.1
	Shriver (D)	6,820	48.9
3	Thomas W. Ligon (D)	4,202	55.0
	Unidentified Candidate (W)	3,433	45.0
4	Robert M. McLane (D)	10,158	53.8
	Kennedy (W)	8,720	46.2
5	Alexander Evans (W)	4,909	52.5
	Carmichael (D)	4,444	47.5
6	John W. Crisfield (W)	4,497	54.5
	Unidentified Candidate (D)	3,760	45.5

MICHIGAN

Special Election

	Candidates	Votes	%
2	Charles E. Stuart (D)	10,052	52.1
	James W. Gordon (W)	8,455	43.8

MISSISSIPPI

	Candidates	Votes	%
1	Jacob Thompson (D)	7,191	54.4
	Josselyn (W)	6,033	45.6
2	Winfield S. Featherston (D)	6,433	53.5
	McClung (W)	5,587	46.5
3	Patrick W. Tompkins (W)	6,939	52.1
	Roberts (D)	6,390	47.9
4	Albert G. Brown (D)	✓	
	John A. Quitman		

NEW HAMPSHIRE

	Candidates	Votes	%
1	Amos Tuck (I)	5,608	57.7
	Jennes (LOCOFOCO)	4,025	41.4
2	Charles H. Peaslee (D)	8,873	57.2
	Unidentified Candidate	4,275	27.6
	Unidentified Candidate	2,356	15.2
3	James Wilson (W)	5,926	51.2
	Moulton (LOCOFOCO)	5,086	44.0
4	James H. Johnson (LOCOFOCO)	✓	

NORTH CAROLINA

	Candidates	Votes	%
1	Thomas L. Clingman (W)	4,550	57.1
	John Gray Bynum (W)	3,426	43.0
2	Nathaniel Boyden (W)	3,882	51.7
	Joseph M. Bogle (IW)	3,025	40.3
	John N. Vogler (ID)	606	8.1
3	Daniel M. Barringer (W)	3,412	81.2
	Walter F. Leake (D)	792	18.8
4	Augustine H. Shepperd (W)	4,022	60.4
	Junius L. Clemmons (D)	2,634	39.6
5	Abraham W. Venable (D)	4,588	50.9
	John Kerr (W)	4,435	49.2
6	John R. J. Daniel (D)	3,896	51.8
	Archibald H. Arrington (ID)	3,410	45.4
7	James J. McKay (D)	3,894	65.8
	William R. Hall (W)	1,827	30.9
8	Richard S. Donnell (W)	4,293	52.3
	William K. Lane (D)	3,924	47.8
9	David Outlaw (W)	3,795	55.3
	Asa Biggs (D)	3,071	44.7

RHODE ISLAND[1]

	Candidates	Votes	%
1	Robert B. Cranston (W)	3,303	50.4
	Fenner Brown (D)	2,429	37.0
2	Wilkins Updike (W)	2,035*	44.2
	Benjamin B. Thurston (D)	1,928	41.8
	Lemuel H. Arnold (W)	453	9.8

Special Election

	Candidates	Votes	%
2	Benjamin B. Thurston (D)	2,415	50.0
	Wilkins Updike (W)	2,350	48.6

TENNESSEE

	Candidates	Votes	%
1	Andrew Johnson (D)	5,658	51.4
	Oliver P. Temple (W)	5,342	48.6
2	William M. Cocke (W)	7,277	61.0
	Wayne W. Wallace (D)	4,650	39.0
3	John H. Crozier (W)	6,945	51.8
	Samuel S. Smith (D)	6,474	48.3
4	Hugh L. W. Hill (D)	5,604	58.7
	John L. Goodall (W)	3,947	41.3
5	George W. Jones (D)	4,697	98.8
6	James H. Thomas (D)	5,562	55.6
	Boling Gordan (W)	4,443	44.4
7	Meredith P. Gentry (W)	5,989	65.1
	R. G. Ellis (D)	3,207	34.9
8	Washington Barrow (W)	5,544	58.8
	John B. Pittman (D)	3,887	41.2
9	Lucien B. Chase (D)	4,898	53.8
	John T. Swayne (W)	4,205	46.2

Candidates	Votes	%	Candidates	Votes	%	Candidates	Votes	%
10 Frederick P. Stanton (D)	5,564	50.1	Irving (W)	2,138	48.6	Gray (W)	2,135	41.6
John W. Harris (W)	5,539	49.9	5 William L. Goggin (W)	2,980	50.9	12 William B. Preston (W)	3,583	52.4
11 William T. Haskell (W)	6,380	57.2	Leake (D)	2,870	49.1	Chapman (D)	3,257	47.6
John Gardner (D)	4,771	42.8	6 John M. Botts (W)	2,959	54.5	13 Andrew S. Fulton (W)	2,094	38.8
			Leake (D)	2,468	45.5	McMullen (D)	2,078	38.5
VIRGINIA			7 Thomas H. Bayly (D)	1,107	56.1	Goodson	1,230	22.8
			Jones (W)	866	43.9	14 Robert A. Thompson (D)	3,290	50.4
1 Archibald Atkinson (D)	2,238	50.8	8 Richard L. T. Beale (D)	2,016	51.0	McComas (W)	3,235	49.6
Watts (W)	2,166	49.2	Newton (W)	1,934	49.0	15 William G. Brown (D)	✓	
2 George C. Dromgoole (D)	1,641	50.2	9 John S. Pendleton (W)	2,861	58.3			
Bolling (W)	1,625	49.8	Hunter (D)	2,045	41.7	**Special Election**		
3 Thomas S. Flournoy (W)	650	50.0	10 Henry Bedinger (D)	3,053	52.7			
Treadway (D)	649	50.0	Kennedy (W)	2,746	47.4	2 Richard K. Meade (D)	✓	
4 Thomas S. Bocock (D)	2,263	51.4	11 James McDowell (D)	2,995	58.4			

1. In the 1847 general election, no candidate in the 2nd district received the required majority. In a special election for which returns are unavailable, Thurston was the winner.

1848 House Elections

ARKANSAS

	Candidates	Votes	%
AL	Robert W. Johnson (D)	14,456	60.8
	Newton (W)	9,328	39.2

DELAWARE

	Candidates	Votes	%
AL	John W. Houston (W)	6,369	51.4
	Whiteley (D)	6,026	48.6

FLORIDA

	Candidates	Votes	%
AL	Edward Cabell (W)	4,382	53.5
	William P. Duval (D)	3,805	46.5

GEORGIA

	Candidates	Votes	%
1	Thomas Butler King (W)	3,549	57.0
	Joseph W. Jackson (D)	2,680	43.0
2	Marshall J. Wellborn (D)	6,625	50.3
	James S. Calhoun (W)	6,538	49.7
3	Allen F. Owen (W)	4,754	52.7
	John I. Carey (D)	4,260	47.3
4	Hugh A. Haralson (D)	5,532	50.9
	John A. Williamson (W)	5,341	49.1
5	Thomas C. Hackett (D)	8,767	59.8
	James M. Calhoun (W)	5,904	40.2
6	Howell Cobb (D)	5,891	57.7
	James W. Harris (W)	4,314	42.3
7	Alexander H. Stephens (W)	4,019	60.7
	Joseph (D)	2,602	39.3
8	Robert Toombs (W)	4,232	62.4
	Unidentified Candidate (D)	2,551	37.6

ILLINOIS

	Candidates	Votes	%
1	William H. Bissell (D)	9,892	97.1
2	John A. McClernand (D)	6,537	65.0
	Samuel Marshall (W)	3,514	34.9
3	Timothy R. Young (D)	8,207	61.3
	George M. Hanson (W)	5,151	38.5
4	John Wentworth (D)	11,857	50.9
	J. Young Scammon (W)	8,302	35.6
	Owen Lovejoy (F SOIL)	3,138	13.5
5	William A. Richardson (D)	11,463	95.9
6	Edward D. Baker (W)	10,325	50.9
	Joseph B. Wells (D)	9,292	45.8
7	Thomas L. Harris (D)	7,201	49.8
	Stephen V. Logan (W)	7,095	49.1

IOWA

	Candidates	Votes	%
1	William Thompson (D)	6,477	50.3
	Daniel F. Miller (W)	6,091	47.3
2	Shepherd Leffler (D)	5,789	50.9
	Timothy Davis (W)	5,398	47.5

MAINE

	Candidates	Votes	%
1	Elbridge Gerry (D)	5,897	54.4
	John Jameson	3,984	36.8
	David Gerry	840	7.8
2	Nathaniel S. Littlefield (D)	5,160	46.7
	Isaac Lincoln	4,407	39.9
	Samuel Fessenden	1,438	13.0
3	John Otis (W)	5,274	44.2
	Moses Shelburne	4,132	34.6
	Ezekiel Holmes	2,526	21.2
4	Rufus K. Goodenow (W)	6,582	48.6
	John D. McCrate	5,607	41.4
	William H. Vinton	977	7.2
5	Cullen Sawtelle (D)	5,875	50.4
	Abner Coburn	3,589	30.8
	Cyrus Fletcher	2,063	17.7
6	Charles Stetson (D)	5,095	40.8
	Israel Washburn Jr	4,492	36.0

	Candidates	Votes	%
	Jeremiah Curtis	2,043	16.4
	Samuel Veazie	849	6.8
7	Thomas J. D. Fuller (D)	5,807	53.8
	George Downes	4,269	39.6
	Tristram Redman	661	6.1

MASSACHUSETTS[1]

	Candidates	Votes	%
1	Robert C. Winthrop (W)	7,726	66.9
	Charles Sumner (F SOIL)	2,336	20.2
	Benjamin F. Hallett (D)	1,460	12.7
2	Daniel P. King (W)	4,201	54.5
	Benjamin F. Newhall	1,903	24.7
	Robert Rantoul Jr. (D)	1,588	20.6
3	James H. Duncan (W)	6,685	53.0
	Chauncey L. Knapp (F SOIL)	3,038	24.1
	George S. Boutwell (D)	2,868	22.8
4	Benjamin Thompson (W)	3,852*	42.6
	John G. Palfrey (F SOIL)	3,038	33.6
	Richard Frothingham Jr.	2,060	22.8
5	Charles Allen (F SOIL)	5,847	58.7
	Charles Hudson (W)	2,868	28.8
	Isaac Davis (D)	1,217	12.2
6	George Ashmun (W)	7,073	52.2
	Muling Guswold	3,766	27.8
	Daniel W.	2,677	19.8
7	Julius Rockwell (W)	5,865	51.3
	Thomas F. Plunkett	3,220	28.2
	Charles Sedgwick	2,325	20.4
8	Horace Mann (W)	11,087	83.9
	Bradford S. Wales	2,027	15.3
9	Orin Fowler (F SOIL W)	3,726	51.2
	Nathaniel Morton	2,128	29.2
	Foster Hooper	1,414	19.4
10	Joseph Grinnell (W)	4,719	56.2
	A. H. Howland	1,504	17.9
	Charles B. H. Fessenden	1,199	14.3
	Simpson Hart	673	8.0

Special Election

	Candidates	Votes	%
8	Horace Mann (W)	4,357	58.3
	Edgar K. Mutaker	1,952	26.1
	Appleton Howe	944	12.6

MICHIGAN

	Candidates	Votes	%
1	Alexander W. Buel (D)	10,015	46.7
	George C. Bates (W)	8,747	40.8
	Caleb N. Ormsby (F SOIL)	2,665	12.4
2	William Sprague (W FS)	13,559	53.3
	Charles E. Stuart (W)	11,881	46.7
3	Kinsley S. Bingham (D)	9,348	49.1
	George H. Hazelton (W)	7,802	40.9
	John M. Lamb (F SOIL)	1,899	10.0

MISSOURI

	Candidates	Votes	%
1	James B. Bowlin (D)	10,312	60.4
	Cook (W)	6,776	39.7
2	William V. N. Bay (D)	8,394	54.6
	Porter (W)	6,968	45.4
3	James S. Green (D)	9,754	56.8
	Wilson (W)	7,417	43.2
4	Willard P. Hall (D)	10,840	71.0
	Samuel (W)	4,418	29.0
5	John S. Phelps (D)	11,062	65.4
	Winston (W)	5,848	34.6

NEW JERSEY

	Candidates	Votes	%
1	Andrew K. Hay (W)	7,052	51.1
	Unidentified Candidate (D)	6,043	43.8
	Unidentified Candidate (AM)	718	5.2
2	William A. Newell (W)	9,877	54.1
	Unidentified Candidate (D)	8,382	45.9

	Candidates	Votes	%
3	Isaac Wildrick (D)	9,215	76.8
	Unidentified Candidate (W)	2,778	23.2
4	John Van Dyke (W)	7,282	54.5
	Unidentified Candidate (D)	6,023	45.1
5	James G. King (W)	9,679	56.7
	Unidentified Candidate (D)	6,716	39.3

NEW YORK

	Candidates	Votes	%
1	John A. King (W)	4,397	47.9
	Jones (F SOIL)	2,457	26.8
	Brown (D)	2,332	25.4
2	David A. Bokee (W)	8,168	54.2
	Mereac (D)	5,812	38.6
	Crooke (F SOIL)	1,087	7.2
3	J. Phillips Phoenix (W)	5,601	55.0
	Hart (D)	3,788	37.2
	Smith (F SOIL)	793	7.8
4	Walter Underhill (W)	5,649	49.0
	Maclay (D)	3,904	33.9
	Hecker (F SOIL)	1,035	9.0
	Foote (D)	944	8.2
5	George Briggs (W)	5,627	49.1
	Walsh (D)	2,765	24.1
	Hasbrouck (D)	1,602	14.0
	Spencer (F SOIL)	1,476	12.9
6	James Brooks (W)	9,709	51.7
	Law (D)	6,976	37.2
	Field (F SOIL)	2,042	10.9
7	William Nelson (W)	4,948	50.3
	N. C. Blvt (D)	3,133	31.9
	J. C. Blvt (F SOIL)	1,754	17.8
8	Ransom Halloway (W)	6,301	51.2
	Nun (D)	4,333	35.2
	Bailey (F SOIL)	1,681	13.7
9	Thomas McKissock (W)	5,876	47.3
	Woodward (D)	4,667	37.6
	Curtis (F SOIL)	1,874	15.1
10	Herman D. Gould (W)	6,267	40.0
	Edgerton (F SOIL)	4,443	28.3
	Fitch (A-RENT)	3,013	19.2
	Wheeler (D)	1,953	12.5
11	Peter H. Silvester (W)	6,621	47.4
	Olney (D)	3,893	27.9
	Beekman (F SOIL)	3,453	24.7
12	Gideon Reynolds (D&A-RENT)	6,055	53.0
	Warren (D)	5,362	47.0
13	John L. Schoolcraft (W)	7,227	53.9
	Bouton (D)	3,876	28.9
	Wood (F SOIL)	2,315	17.3
14	George R. Andrews (W)	7,088	57.0
	Culver (F SOIL)	3,166	25.5
	Cutting (D)	2,186	17.6
15	John R. Thurman (W)	4,670	42.6
	Heding (D)	3,455	31.5
	Lawrence (F SOIL)	2,828	25.8
16	Hugh White (W)	8,183	52.3
	Campbell (D)	4,059	26.0
	Cowen (F SOIL)	3,392	21.7
17	Henry P. Alexander (W)	6,109	47.2
	Nellis (F SOIL)	5,564	43.0
	Samons (D)	1,264	9.8
18	Preston King (F SOIL)	7,309	53.1
	Squire (W)	5,133	37.3
	Dodge (D)	1,325	9.6
19	Charles E. Clarke (W)	4,636	39.7
	Ives (F SOIL)	4,427	37.9
	Dann (D)	2,624	22.5
20	Orsamus B. Matteson (W)	6,094	42.4
	Mann (F SOIL)	5,069	35.3
	Williams (D)	3,214	22.4
21	Hiram Walden (D)	6,636	42.1
	Smith (W)	6,330	40.2
	Hammond (F SOIL)	2,787	17.7
22	Henry Bennett (W)	8,014	46.5
	Mason (D)	6,394	37.1

Candidates	Votes	%
Smith (F SOIL)	2,839	16.5
23 William Duer (W)	8,107	48.2
Nye (F SOIL)	6,884	41.0
Crouse (D)	1,640	9.8
24 Daniel Gott (W)	5,403	42.2
Sedgwick (F SOIL)	4,906	38.3
Baldwin (D)	2,498	19.5
25 Harmon S. Conger (W)	6,732	46.9
Ballard (F SOIL)	5,747	40.1
Hyde (D)	1,870	13.0
26 William T. Jackson (W)	6,444	40.4
Wisner (F SOIL)	6,396	40.1
Hathaway (D)	3,117	19.5
27 William A. Sackett (W)	5,845	45.2
Bascom (F SOIL)	5,260	40.7
Bigelow (D)	1,802	14.1
28 Abraham M. Schermerhorn (W)	6,611	52.0
Selden (F SOIL)	4,746	37.3
Smith (D)	1,367	10.7
29 Robert L. Rose (W)	7,816	53.4
Garlghse (F SOIL)	4,659	31.8
Parburt (D)	2,166	14.8
30 David Rumsey Jr (W)	7,282	45.0
Grover (F SOIL)	5,938	36.7
Angel (D)	2,982	18.4
31 Elijah Risley (W)	6,946	51.7
Chaffee (D)	3,649	27.2
Colman (F SOIL)	2,832	21.1
32 Elbridge G. Spaulding (W)	7,622	56.9
Clinton (D)	3,408	25.4
Wadsworth (F SOIL)	2,367	17.7
33 Harvey Putnam (W)	5,489	50.6
Smith (F SOIL)	2,780	25.6
Willett (D)	2,575	23.8
34 Lorenzo Burrows (W)	5,372	47.0
Davis (F SOIL)	3,846	33.6
Burroughs (D)	2,214	19.4

Special Elections

Candidates	Votes	%
6 Horace Greeley (W)	9,932	53.9
Bradhst	6,826	37.0
Townsend	1,681	9.1
27 Blackmar (W)	5,921	45.6
Smith (F SOIL)	5,308	40.9
Foster (HUNKER)	1,751	13.5

OHIO

Candidates	Votes	%
1 David T. Disney (D)	9,292	50.9
Thomas J. Strait (W)	6,297	34.5
Samuel Lewis (F SOIL)	2,158	11.8
2 Lewis D. Campbell (F SOIL W)	6,914	51.6
William H. Baldwin (D)	6,479	48.4
3 Robert C. Schenck (W)	9,289	53.5
Joseph W. McCorkle (D)	8,082	46.5
4 Moses B. Corwin (W)	8,761	54.7
John A. Corwin (D)	6,215	38.8
William A. Rogers (F SOIL)	1,030	6.4
5 Emery D. Potter (D)	7,029	62.2
John Fitch (W)	4,240	37.5
6 Rodolphus Dickinson (D)	7,404	58.8
Cooper K. Watson (W)	5,184	41.2
7 Jonathan D. Morris (D)	7,135	59.5
John Joliffe (W)	3,583	29.9
Thomas Gatch (IW)	1,278	10.7
8 John L. Taylor (W)	7,449	52.9
Francis Cleveland (D)	6,624	47.1

Candidates	Votes	%
9 Edson B. Olds (D)	6,984	50.3
Thomas O. Edwards (W)	6,906	49.7
10 Charles Sweetzer (D)	8,454	49.5
Daniel Duncan (W)	8,438	49.4
11 John K. Miller (D)	9,165	62.6
Jacob Brinkerhoff (W)	5,462	37.3
12 Samuel F. Vinton (W)	5,799	53.3
Simeon W. Tucker (D)	4,416	40.6
David Richmond (ID)	670	6.2
13 William A. Whittlesey (D)	6,375	51.4
William P. Cutler (W)	6,037	48.6
14 Nathan Evans (W)	6,606	53.1
Matthew Gaston (D)	5,840	46.9
15 William F. Hunter (W)	6,711	51.4
William Kennon Jr. (D)	6,338	48.5
16 Moses Hoagland (D)	6,104	54.0
Martin Welker (W)	5,144	45.5
17 Joseph Cable (D)	6,987	50.2
James Mason (W)	6,330	45.5
18 David K. Carter (D)	6,682	60.0
Samuel Hemphill (W)	4,448	40.0
19 John Crowell (W)	9,561	56.0
Rufus P. Ranney (D)	7,507	44.0
20 Joshua R. Giddings (F SOIL W)	5,879	62.7
Bushnell White (D)	3,155	33.6
21 Joseph M. Root (F SOIL W)	8,434	57.8
E. M. Stone (D)	6,077	41.6

PENNSYLVANIA

Candidates	Votes	%
1 Lewis C. Levin (AM)	4,897	52.2
Florence (D)	4,228	45.1
2 Joseph R. Chandler (W)	6,656	63.2
Van Dyke (D)	3,874	36.8
3 Henry D. Moore (W)	6,844	52.9
Hallowell (D)	6,098	47.1
4 John Robbins Jr (D)	6,661	51.6
John S. Littell (W)	6,251	48.4
5 John Freedley (W)	6,655	50.7
McKeever (D)	6,474	49.3
6 Thomas Ross (D)	8,036	51.0
Taylor (W)	7,716	49.0
7 Jesse C. Dickey (W)	5,786	52.9
Hemphill (D)	5,160	47.1
8 Thaddeus Stevens (W)	9,565	63.6
Shaffer (D)	5,464	36.4
9 William Strong (D)	8,451	67.8
Adams (W)	4,014	32.2
10 Milo M. Dimmick (D)	7,764	63.6
Wheeler (W)	4,444	36.4
11 Chester P. Butler (W)	5,032	42.4
Wright (D)	4,902	41.3
Collings (ID)	1,938	16.3
12 David Wilmot (F SOIL D)	8,619	60.2
Tracy (W)	4,773	33.3
Brewster (CASS D)	922	6.4
13 Joseph Casey (W)	6,817	51.0
Unidentified Candidate (D)	6,555	49.0
14 Charles W. Pitman (W)	10,203	57.7
Dock (D)	7,472	42.3
15 Henry Nes (W)	6,599	52.4
Joel B. Danner (D)	5,989	47.6
16 James X. McLanahan (D)	8,725	53.9
Brady (W)	7,472	46.1
17 Samuel Calvin (W)	8,712	50.2
Parker (D)	8,648	49.8
18 Andrew Jackson Ogle (W)	6,902	50.9
Dawson (D)	6,649	49.1

Candidates	Votes	%
19 Job Mann (D)	9,110	58.7
Livergood (W)	6,398	41.3
20 Robert R. Reed (W)	6,417	49.5
Hopkins (D)	6,359	49.1
21 Moses Hampton (W)	7,666	50.8
Black (D)	6,613	43.8
22 John W. Howe (F SOIL)	7,509	51.2
McFarland (D)	7,161	48.8
23 James Thompson (D)	7,509	50.9
Campbell (W)	7,026	47.6
24 Alfred Gilmore (D)	7,267	50.2
Smith (W)	7,008	48.4

Special Election

Candidates	Votes	%
6 Samuel A. Bridges (D)	6,526	50.5
Lesher Trexler (W)	6,393	49.5

SOUTH CAROLINA[2]

Candidates	Votes	%
1 Daniel Wallace (W)	3,369	39.8
Thompson	3,044	35.9
Davie	2,061	24.3
2 James L. Orr (D)	✓	
B. F. Perry (D)		
3 Joseph A. Woodward (D)	✓	
J. O'Hanlon		
4 Alexander D. Sims (D)	*	
John McQueen (D)		
5 Armistead Burt (D)	5,991	84.2
Heller	1,121	15.8
6 Isaac E. Holmes (TAYLOR D)	✓	
Samuel G. Barker (CASS D)		
W. C. Clayton		
7 William F. Colcock (D)	✓	

Special Election

Candidates	Votes	%
1 Daniel Wallace (W)	2,139	36.9
Thompson	2,134	36.8
Davis	1,525	26.3

VERMONT

Candidates	Votes	%
1 William P. Henry (W)	✓	
2 William Hebard (W)	✓	
3 George P. Marsh (W)	✓	
4 Lucius B. Peck (D)	✓	

WISCONSIN

(Became a state May 29, 1848)

Candidates	Votes	%
1 Charles Durkee (F SOIL)	5,038	38.5
William P. Lynde (D)	4,436	33.9
Finch (W)	3,615	27.6
2 Orsamus Cole (W)	6,280	45.2
Smith (D)	5,690	41.0
Crabb (F SOIL)	1,916	13.8
3 James Duane Doty (D)	5,746	50.3
Howe (W)	3,338	29.2
Judd (F SOIL)	2,330	20.4

Special Election[3]

Candidates	Votes	%
Mason C. Darling (D)	✓	
William P. Lynde (D)	✓	

1. In the 4th district, no candidate received the necessary majority. Twelve elections were held to try to fill the seat, but all of them resulted without choice. The seat was vacant for the entire 31st Congress (1849–1851).

2. In the South Carolina 4th district, Sims was elected but died Jan. 16, 1848. McQueen was chosen to succeed him in a special election for which no returns are available.

3. This was the first House election held by Wisconsin after it achieved statehood. Information is unavailable as to whether the elections were at-large or by district.

1849 House Elections

ALABAMA

	Candidates	Votes	%
1	William J. Alston (TAYLOR W)	4,922	51.8
	C. C. Sellers (SO RTS D)	4,588	48.2
2	Henry W. Hilliard (W)	6,770	53.1
	J. L. Pugh (IW)	5,975	46.9
3	Sampson W. Harris (D)	5,511	52.6
	John Hunter (W)	4,962	47.4
4	Samuel W. Inge (D)	4,665	52.4
	Joseph Baldwin (W)	4,245	47.6
5	David Hubbard (D)	4,575	49.1
	Wood (W)	3,084	33.1
	O'Neal (D)	1,655	17.8
6	Williamson R. W. Cobb (D)	4,594	53.4
	Jere Clemens (D)	4,005	46.6
7	Franklin W. Bowdon (D)	6,002	55.1
	Bradford (W)	4,895	44.9

CALIFORNIA

(Became a state Sept. 9, 1850)

	Candidates	Votes	
AL	George W. Wright (I)	5,451	✓
	Edward Gilbert (D)	5,300	✓
	R. M. Price	4,040	
	Lewis Dent	2,129	
	D. A. Morse	2,066	
	E. I. Kenon	1,826	
	William M. Shepard	1,773	
	W. E. Shannon	1,327	
	P. O. Halsted	1,271	
	L. W. Hastings	215	

CONNECTICUT

	Candidates	Votes	%
1	Loren P. Waldo (D)	7,444	50.4
	Charles Chapman (W)	7,327	49.6
2	Walter Booth (D)	6,672	50.1
	James F. Babcock (W)	6,532	49.0
3	Chauncey F. Cleveland (D)	6,140	50.6
	John A. Rockwell (W)	5,992	49.4
4	Thomas B. Butler (W)	8,172	51.6
	Nathaniel H. Wildman (D)	7,028	44.4

INDIANA

	Candidates	Votes	%
1	Nathaniel Albertson (D)	8,271	52.1
	Elisha Embree (W)	7,598	47.9
2	Cyrus L. Dunham (D)	7,823	51.6
	William McKee Dunn (W)	7,338	48.4
3	John L. Robinson (D)	8,120	52.5
	Joseph Robinson (W)	7,348	47.5
4	George W. Julian (F SOIL)	4,737	50.8
	Samuel W. Parker (W)	4,583	49.1
5	William J. Brown (D)	8,762	54.7
	William Herod (W)	7,265	45.3
6	Willis A. Gorman (D)	8,466	54.1
	John S. Watts (W)	7,196	45.9
7	Edward W. McGaughey (W)	6,782	58.0
	Grafton F. Cookerly	4,909	42.0
8	Joseph E. McDonald (D)	7,432	51.2
	Henry S. Lane (W)	7,098	48.9
9	Graham N. Fitch (D)	8,800	50.8
	Williamson Wright (W)	8,519	49.2
10	Andrew J. Harlan (D)	7,366	52.1
	David Kilgore (W)	6,777	47.9

KENTUCKY

	Candidates	Votes	%
1	Linn Boyd (D)	5,208	100.0
2	James L. Johnson (W)	8,031	67.4
	Peyton (D)	3,878	32.6
3	Finis E. McLean (W)	5,679	100.0
4	George A. Caldwell (D)	6,719	54.6
	Buckner (W)	5,579	45.4
5	John B. Thompson (W)	6,586	100.0
6	Daniel Breck (W)	6,353	54.7
	Martin (D)	5,271	45.4
7	Humphrey Marshall (W)	6,261	50.3
	Lane (D)	6,197	49.7
8	Charles S. Morehead (W)	5,195	52.7
	Trabue (AM)	4,665	47.3
9	John C. Mason (D)	6,882	52.8
	Houston (W)	6,164	47.3
10	Richard H. Stanton (D)	7,764	51.2
	Gaines (W)	7,400	48.8

LOUISIANA

	Candidates	Votes	%
1	Emile La Sere (D)	3,295	56.3
	Jackson (W)	2,559	43.7
2	Charles M. Conrad (W)	5,092	52.4
	Beatty (D)	4,622	47.6
3	John H. Harmanson (D)	2,464	53.8
	Stewart (W)	2,117	46.2
4	Isaac E. Morse (D)	4,751	51.3
	Ogden (W)	4,516	48.7

MARYLAND

	Candidates	Votes	%
1	Richard J. Bowie (W)	4,283	100.0
2	William T. Hamilton (D)	7,307	50.4
	T. J. McKaig (W)	7,191	49.6
3	Edward Hammond (D)	6,903	60.8
	George W. Gray (W)	4,456	39.2
4	Robert M. McLane (D)	7,277	53.5
	John R. Kenly (W)	6,326	46.5
5	Alexander Evans (W)	4,986	52.6
	S. M. Magraw (D)	4,487	47.4
6	John Bozman Kerr (W)	3,457	100.0

MISSISSIPPI

	Candidates	Votes	%
1	Jacob Thompson (D)	9,109	57.3
	Bradford (W)	6,801	42.8
2	Winfield S. Featherston (D)	7,237	54.0
	Harris (W)	6,170	46.0
3	William McWillie (D)	7,406	52.0
	Gray (W)	6,834	48.0
4	Albert G. Brown (D)	7,980	67.6
	Winans (W)	3,820	32.4

NEW HAMPSHIRE

	Candidates	Votes	%
1	Amos Tuck (F SOIL)	6,971	51.1
	G. W. Kit (D)	6,638	48.6
2	Charles H. Peaslee (D)	8,590	60.6
	Eastman (F SOIL)	3,673	25.9
	Stewart	1,914	13.5
3	James Wilson (F SOIL)	7,766	51.2
	Vose (D)	7,378	48.7
4	Harry Hibbard (D)	7,363	57.8
	J. Kittredge (F SOIL)	3,658	28.7
	Unidentified Candidate	1,712	13.5

NORTH CAROLINA

	Candidates	Votes	%
1	Thomas L. Clingman (W)	7,231	86.3
2	Joseph P. Caldwell (W)	6,353	78.0
	Montford S. Stokes (D)	1,795	22.0
3	Edmund Deberry (W)	4,899	53.3
	Green W. Caldwell (D)	4,299	46.7
4	Augustine H. Shepperd (W)	4,405	58.4
	Thomas J. Keene (D)	3,138	41.6
5	Abraham W. Venable (D)	5,025	53.8
	Henry K. Nash (W)	4,315	46.2
6	John R. J. Daniel (D)	4,413	64.5
	William J. Clarke (D)	2,430	35.5
7	William S. Ashe (D)	5,128	64.6
	David Reid (D)	2,813	35.4
8	Edward Stanly (W)	4,987	50.2
	William K. Lane (D)	4,940	49.8
9	David Outlaw (W)	4,053	53.8
	Thomas Person (D)	3,477	46.2

OHIO

Special Election

	Candidates	Votes	
6	Amos E. Wood (D)		✓

RHODE ISLAND[1]

	Candidates	Votes	%
1	George G. King (W)	3,005	67.3
	Fenner Brown (D)	1,250	28.0
2	Benjamin B. Thurston (D)	2,017*	48.5
	Sylvester G. Sherman (W)	1,959	47.1

Special Election

	Candidates	Votes	%
2	Nathan F. Dixon (W)	2,824	56.1
	Benjamin B. Thurston (FS CLN)	2,209	43.9

TENNESSEE

	Candidates	Votes	%
1	Andrew Johnson (D)	6,068	54.5
	Taylor (W)	5,060	45.5
2	Albert G. Watkins (W)	7,125	58.9
	Cocke (D)	4,968	41.1
3	Josiah M. Anderson (W)	7,269	54.7
	Lyon (D)	6,018	45.3
4	John H. Savage (D)	4,713	79.2
	Rogs (W)	1,239	20.8
5	George W. Jones (D)	6,736	100.0
6	James H. Thomas (D)	6,135	56.1
	Buchanan (W)	4,802	43.9
7	Meredith P. Gentry (W)	5,766	100.0
8	Andrew Ewing (D)	4,894	50.4
	Cullom (W)	4,816	49.6
9	Isham G. Harris (D)	5,433	55.8
	Morris (W)	4,302	44.2
10	Frederick P. Stanton (D)	6,250	51.9
	Harris (W)	5,799	48.1
11	Christopher H. Williams (W)	8,944	100.0

TEXAS

	Candidates	Votes	%
1	David S. Kaufman (D)	8,944	96.0
2	Volney E. Howard (D)	4,120	58.1
	Williamson	2,976	41.9

VERMONT

Special Election

	Candidates	Votes	%
3	James Meacham (W)	6,645	54.5
	Peck (EVA)	4,716	38.7
	Harrington (OPP&SC)	835	6.9

VIRGINIA

	Candidates	Votes	%
1	John S. Millson (D)	2,736	51.7
	Wats (W)	2,559	48.3
2	Richard K. Meade (D)		100.0
3	Thomas H. Averett (D)	2,113	50.8
	Fly (W)	2,048	49.2
4	Thomas S. Bocock (D)	2,694	53.0
	Irving (W)	2,388	47.0
5	Paulus Powell (D)	3,136	50.9
	Goggin (W)	3,029	49.1
6	James A. Seddon (D)	2,844	53.6
	Botts (W)	2,458	46.4
7	Thomas H. Bayly (D)	1,653	64.8
	Mallory (W)	900	35.3
8	Alexander R. Holladay (D)	2,163	51.0
	Forbes (W)	2,078	49.0
9	Jeremiah Morton (D)	2,798	54.0
	Pendleton (W)	2,381	46.0

	Candidates	Votes	%		Candidates	Votes	%
10	Richard Parker (D)	3,429	55.2	14	James M. H. Beale (D)	4,312	51.3
	Far (W)	2,787	44.8		McComas (W)	4,094	48.7
11	James McDowell (D)		100.0	15	Alexander Newman (D)	2,926	53.0
12	Henry A. Edmundson (D)	2,540	54.0		Russell (W)	2,598	47.0
	Anderson (W)	2,161	46.0				
13	Fayette McMullen (D)	4,421	67.2				
	George (W)	2,155	32.8				

Special Election

	Candidates	Votes	%
15	Thomas S. Haymond (W)	2,873	50.6
	Thompson (D)	2,807	49.4

1. In the 2nd District, no candidate received the required majority. In the subsequent special election that year, Nathan F. Dixon defeated Thurston.

1850 House Elections

DELAWARE

	Candidates	Votes	%
AL	George Read Riddle (D)	6,055	48.7
	Rodney (W)	5,926	47.7

FLORIDA

	Candidates	Votes	%
AL	Edward C. Cabell (W)	4,531	52.8
	John Beard (D)	4,050	47.2

ILLINOIS

	Candidates	Votes	%
1	William H. Bissell (D)	12,841	100.0
2	Willis Allen (D)	5,763	54.5
	Thomas G. C. Davis (W)	4,816	45.5
3	Orlando B. Ficklin (D)	7,429	56.3
	E. G. Ryan (W)	5,739	43.5
4	Richard S. Molony (D)	11,231	48.9
	Churchill Coffing (W)	10,587	46.1
5	William A. Richardson (D)	8,099	53.0
	Orville H. Browning (W)	7,197	47.1
6	Thompson Campbell (D)	8,181	50.7
	Martin P. Sweet (W)	7,857	48.7
7	Richard Yates (W)	7,008	52.8
	Thomas L. Harris (D)	6,254	47.1

IOWA

	Candidates	Votes	%
1	Bernhart Henn (D)	7,437	50.5
	George G. Wright (W)	6,985	47.4
2	Lincoln Clark (D)	5,745	54.0
	William H. Henderson (W)	4,725	44.4

Special Election

	Candidates	Votes	%
1	Daniel F. Miller (W)	5,463	51.3
	William Thompson (D)	4,801	45.1

MAINE

	Candidates	Votes	%
1	Moses MacDonald (D)	5,173	49.6
	N. D. Appleton (W)	4,683	44.9
	M. Sweat (F SOIL)	530	5.1
2	John Appleton (D)	5,943	50.1
	William Pitt Fessenden (W FS)	5,903	49.8
3	Robert Goodenow (W)	4,831	44.7
	Lot M. Merrill (D)	4,700	43.5
	Seth May (F SOIL)	1,272	11.8
4	Charles Andrews (D)	6,718	49.6
	Isaac Reed (W)	6,652	49.1
5	Ephraim K. Smart (D)	5,911	52.5
	Theophilus Cushing (W)	5,295	47.0
6	Israel Washburn Jr (W)	5,412	46.3
	Strickland (D)	3,696	31.6
	Stetson (D)	2,554	21.8
7	Thomas J. D. Fuller (D)	4,814	47.0
	James S. Pike (W)	4,629	45.2
	S. C. Foster (F SOIL)	716	7.0

MASSACHUSETTS

	Candidates	Votes	%
1	William Appleton (W)	5,839	65.6
	John T. Heard	1,855	20.9
	Benjamin B. Mufsey (F SOIL)	1,167	13.1
2	Robert Rantoul Jr (D)	7,183	51.4
	Charles W. Upham (W)	6,089	43.6
3	James H. Duncan (W)	4,250	56.8
	Alpheus R. Brown	1,764	23.6
	Thomas W. Higginson (F SOIL)	1,255	16.8
4	Benjamin Thompson (W)	6,380	47.6
	John G. Palfrey (F SOIL)	6,293	47.0
	Richard Frothingham Jr.	717	5.4
5	Charles Allen (F SOIL)	4,819	51.1
	Ira M. Barton (W)	2,620	27.8
	I. S. C. Knowlton	1,990	21.1
6	George T. Davis (W)	4,877	51.8

	Candidates	Votes	%
	Chester W. Chapin	3,031	32.2
	Samuel Williston	1,460	15.5
7	John Z. Goodrich (W)	4,623	52.8
	Henry W. Bishop	4,056	46.3
8	Horace Mann (F SOIL)	6,697	50.3
	Samuel H. Walley (W)	4,301	32.3
	Edgar H. Whittaker	2,262	17.0
9	Orin Fowler (F SOIL W)	6,345	66.1
	Edward P. Little (D)	2,795	29.1
10	Zeno Scudder (W)	2,179	55.3
	Charles B. H. Fessenden	907	23.0
	Simpson Hart (F SOIL)	429	10.9
	Daniel Fisher	239	6.1

Special Election

	Candidates	Votes	%
1	Samuel A. Elliott (W)	2,355	74.9
	Charles Sumner (F SOIL)	473	15.0
	John T. Heard	297	9.4

MICHIGAN

	Candidates	Votes	%
1	Ebenezer J. Penniman (W FS)	10,766	54.7
	Alexander W. Buel (D)	8,914	45.3
2	Charles E. Stuart (D)	11,929	50.8
	Joseph R. Williams (W FS)	11,517	49.0
3	James L. Conger (W FS)	8,646	50.5
	Charles C. Hascall (D)	8,427	49.2

MISSOURI

	Candidates	Votes	%
1	John F. Darby (W)	7,145	39.6
	Rozier (BENTON D)	5,600	31.0
	Bowlin (A-BEN D)	5,317	29.4
2	Gilchrist Porter (W)	6,889	52.9
	Henderson (D)	5,878	45.1
3	John G. Miller (W)	6,578	42.3
	Green (A-BEN D)	6,554	42.2
	J. Miller (BENTON D)	2,411	15.5
4	Willard P. Hall (A-BEN D)	5,606	37.5
	Bowman (D)	5,505	36.9
	Gardenhire (BENTON D)	3,826	25.6
5	John S. Phelps (BENTON D)	8,473	52.4
	Woodson (D)	5,667	35.0
	Shields (A-BEN D)	2,035	12.6

NEW JERSEY

	Candidates	Votes	%
1	Nathan T. Stratton (D)	6,475	52.7
	Whitney (W)	5,824	47.4
2	Charles Skelton (D)	9,259	52.6
	Richards (W)	8,358	47.4
3	Isaac Wildrick (D)	9,097	66.9
	Edsall (W)	4,498	33.1
4	George H. Brown (W)	6,470	50.9
	Vail (D)	6,251	49.1
5	Rodman M. Price (D)	8,286	50.3
	Ryerson (W)	8,149	49.5

NEW YORK

	Candidates	Votes	%
1	John G. Floyd (D)	4,125	53.0
	Rose (W)	3,661	47.0
2	Obadiah Bowne (W)	7,728	52.3
	Bogardus (D)	6,428	43.5
3	Emanuel B. Hart (D)	3,679	48.4
	Rodman (W)	2,164	28.5
	Bowen (D)	1,755	23.1
4	J. H. Hobart Haws (W)	4,155	48.8
	Marsh (D)	3,824	44.9
	McGrath (D)	541	6.4
5	George Briggs (W)	4,444	51.9
	Arculars (D)	4,114	48.1
6	James Brooks (W)	8,357	54.6
	Cochran (D)	6,724	44.0
7	Abraham P. Stevens (D)	4,851	52.6

	Candidates	Votes	%
	Gurnee (W)	4,372	47.4
8	Gilbert Dean (D)	6,218	51.1
	Cruger (W)	5,942	48.9
9	William Murray (D)	5,810	51.1
	McKissock (W)	5,563	48.9
10	Marius Schoonmaker (W)	7,851	52.4
	Allaben (D)	7,135	47.6
11	Josiah Sutherland (D)	6,672	52.9
	Cowles (W)	5,940	47.1
12	David L. Seymour (D)	5,811	51.0
	Sage (W)	5,594	49.1
13	John L. Schoolcraft (W)	7,032	51.0
	Corning (D)	6,746	49.0
14	John H. Boyd (W)	6,286	58.7
	Thompson (D)	4,415	41.3
15	Joseph Russell (D)	5,506	50.8
	Tabor (W)	5,324	49.2
16	John Wells (W)	8,428	53.1
	Marvin (D)	7,460	47.0
17	Alexander H. Buel (D)	6,685	52.5
	Alexander (W)	6,047	47.5
18	Preston King (D)	7,101	59.2
	Grant (W)	4,893	40.8
19	Willard Ives (D)	5,477	52.0
	Clarke (W)	5,058	48.0
20	Timothy Jenkins (D)	7,828	50.4
	Matteson (W)	7,711	49.6
21	William Snow (D)	7,664	50.2
	Chase (W)	7,608	49.8
22	Henry Bennett (W)	9,170	53.0
	Taylor (D)	8,131	47.0
23	Leander Babcock (D)	8,423	54.1
	Williams (W)	7,136	45.9
24	Daniel T. Jones (D)	6,186	51.7
	Smith (W)	5,419	45.3
25	Thomas Y. Howe Jr (D)	7,037	50.1
	Morgan (W)	7,011	49.9
26	Henry S. Walbridge (W)	7,700	50.7
	Halsey (D)	7,497	49.3
27	William A. Sackett (W)	6,305	52.0
	Smith (D)	5,814	48.0
28	Abraham M. Schermerhorn (W)	6,036	51.8
	Buchan (D)	5,623	48.2
29	Jerediah Horsford (W)	7,727	57.9
	Wadsworth (D)	5,609	42.1
30	Reuben Robie (D)	8,368	52.6
	Church (W)	7,538	47.4
31	Frederick S. Martin (W)	7,210	52.4
	Waite (D)	6,549	47.6
32	Soloman G. Haven (W)	6,613	55.2
	Stevens (D)	5,365	44.8
33	Augustus P. Hascall (W)	5,715	60.7
	Sprague (D)	3,699	39.3
34	Lorenzo Burrows (W)	5,753	51.9
	Piper (D)	5,332	48.1

OHIO

	Candidates	Votes	%
1	David T. Disney (D)	16,640	99.3
2	Lewis D. Campbell (W)	5,992	53.2
	Elijah Vance (D)	5,279	46.8
3	Hiram Bell (W)	8,014	53.1
	George B. Holt (D)	7,088	46.9
4	Benjamin Stanton (W)	8,110	60.0
	John A. Corwin (D)	5,181	38.3
5	Alfred P. Edgerton (D)	7,684	59.2
	James W. Riley (W)	5,281	40.7
6	Frederick W. Green (D)	7,224	91.8
	John C. Spink	609	7.7
7	Nelson Barrere (W)	5,515	51.4
	Enoch M. Ellsberry (D)	5,219	48.6
8	John L. Taylor (W)	5,850	51.9
	Joseph McCormick (D)	5,321	47.2
9	Edson B. Olds (D)	6,283	50.7
	P. Van Trump (W)	6,110	49.3
10	Charles Sweetser (D)	8,579	50.4

Candidates	Votes	%
Samuel Galloway (W)	8,442	49.6
11 George H. Busby (D)	7,615	58.6
Thomas H. Ford (W)	5,037	38.8
12 John Welch (W)	5,261	54.9
Hiram G. Daniels (D)	4,037	42.1
13 James M. Gaylord (D)	5,744	49.3
William E. Finck (W)	5,698	48.9
14 Alexander Harper (W)	5,108	50.2
Thomas Maxfield (D)	4,750	46.7
15 William F. Hunter (W)	5,751	51.1
Thomas L. Jewett (D)	5,506	48.9
16 John Johnson (W)	5,458	51.4
Moses Hoagland (D)	5,156	48.6
17 Joseph Cable (D)	6,685	55.8
Matthew Roberts (W)	5,303	44.2
18 David K. Carter (D)	5,754	62.3
John Brown (W)	3,477	37.7
19 Eben Newton (W)	8,277	56.5
Luther Day (D)	6,382	43.5
20 Joshua R. Giddings (F SOIL W)	6,896	77.8
Irad Kelley	1,716	19.4
21 Norton S. Townshend (D)	6,677	47.6
Samuel T. Worcester (W)	6,230	44.4
Joseph Root (F SOIL)	1,120	8.0

PENNSYLVANIA

Candidates	Votes	%
1 Thomas B. Florence (D)	5,352	52.9
Levin (AM)	4,164	41.1
Savery (W)	609	6.0
2 Joseph R. Chandler (W)	5,912	60.7
Martin (D)	3,714	38.1
3 Henry D. Moore (W)	5,604	51.2
Lundy (D)	5,333	48.8
4 John Robbins Jr (D)	6,173	57.6
Littell (W)	4,554	42.5
5 John McNair (D)	5,925	53.3
Freedley (W)	5,199	46.7
6 Thomas Ross (D)	7,568	50.8
Taylor (W)	7,328	49.2

Candidates	Votes	%
7 John A. Morrison (D)	4,671	50.4
Dickey (W)	4,601	49.6
8 Thaddeus Stevens (W)	5,701	58.4
Unidentified Candidate (D)	4,069	41.7
9 J. Glancey Jones (D)	5,377	52.6
Keim (W)	4,847	47.4
10 Milo M. Dimmick (D)	6,400	94.1
11 Henry M. Fuller (W)	6,216	50.2
Wright (D)	6,157	49.8
12 Galusha A. Grow (D)	6,880	54.6
Adams (W)	5,730	45.4
13 James Gamble (D)	6,832	52.5
Armstrong (W)	6,172	47.5
14 Thomas M. Bibighaus (W)	7,048	53.6
Boas (D)	6,095	46.4
15 William H. Kurtz (D)	5,765	51.8
Smyser (W)	5,372	48.2
16 James X. McLanahan (D)	7,276	52.0
Bard (W)	6,705	48.0
17 Andrew Parker (D)	7,270	51.4
McCulloch (W)	6,863	48.6
18 John L. Dawson (D)	6,404	51.1
Ogle (W)	6,135	48.9
19 Joseph H. Kuhns (W)	5,745	42.4
Unidentified Candidate (D)	4,688	34.6
McKinney (D)	1,716	12.7
McDonald (D)	1,391	10.3
20 John Allison (W)	5,596	50.5
Power (D)	5,489	49.5
21 Thomas M. Howe (W)	5,406	51.6
Salisbery (D)	4,247	40.5
Cullen (NAM)	539	5.1
22 John W. Howe (W)	6,284	51.7
Shatk (D)	5,882	48.4
23 Carlton B. Curtis (D)	6,522	50.4
Walker (W)	6,416	49.6
24 Alfred Gilmore (D)	6,513	53.6
Taylor (W)	5,644	46.4

Special Election

Candidates	Votes	%
15 Joel B. Danner (D)	5,970	53.5
W. McIlwain (W)	5,193	46.5

SOUTH CAROLINA

Candidates	Votes	%
1 Daniel Wallace (W)		100.0
2 James L. Orr (D)		100.0
3 Joseph A. Woodward (D)		100.0
4 John McQueen (D)		100.0
5 Armistead Burt (D)		100.0
6 William Aiken (D)	1,928	59.2
Isaac E. Holmes (D)	1,097	33.7
J. Smith Rhett	232	7.1
7 William F. Colcock (D)		100.0

VERMONT

Candidates	Votes	%
1 A. L. Miner (W)	4,369	37.5
A. P. Lyman (W)	4,126	35.4
D. Roberts Jr (D)	2,689	23.1
2 William Hebard (W)	5,652	55.2
Jefferson P. Kidder (D)	4,384	42.8
3 James Meacham (W)	5,945	56.5
Beardsley (D)	2,960	28.1
Harrington (OPP)	1,521	14.5
4 Thomas Bartlett Jr (D)	7,009	54.9
B. N. Davis (W)	5,014	39.2
Willard (OPP)	640	5.0

WISCONSIN

Candidates	Votes	%
1 Charles Durkee (F SOIL)	7,512	57.4
Elme (D)	5,574	42.6
2 Ben C. Eastman (D)	7,262	55.4
Cole (W)	5,852	44.6
3 James Duane Doty (F SOIL)	11,159	67.5
Hobt (D)	5,372	32.5

1851 House Elections

ALABAMA

Candidates	Votes	%
1 John Bragg (SO RTS D)	5,372	58.3
C. C. Langdon (UNT)	3,849	41.7
2 James Abercrombie (UN W)	7,598	56.2
John Cochran (SEC)	5,911	43.8
3 Sampson W. Harris (SEC D)	4,967	53.1
W. S. Mudd (UN W)	4,385	46.9
4 William R. Smith (UNT)	4,173	50.4
John Erwin (SO RTS D)	4,114	49.6
5 George S. Houston (UN D)	✓	
D. Hubbard (SEC D)		
6 Williamson R. W. Cobb (UN D)	3,708	74.0
Robert Murphy (SO RTS D)	1,303	26.0
7 Alexander White (UN W)	5,744	51.7
S. F. Rice (SEC D)	5,371	48.3

ARKANSAS

Candidates	Votes	%
AL Robert W. Johnson (D)	11,970	57.4
Preston (W)	8,877	42.6

CALIFORNIA

Candidates	Votes	%
AL Edward C. Marshall (D)	24,469✓	
Joseph W. McCorkle (D)	24,315✓	
E. J. C. Kewen (W)	21,460	
B. J. Moore (W)	20,224	

CONNECTICUT

Candidates	Votes	%
1 Charles Chapman (W)	7,805	48.8
Loren P. Waldo (D)	7,759	48.5
2 Colin M. Ingersoll (D)	7,331	50.1
Babcock (W)	6,786	46.3
3 Chauncey F. Cleveland (D)	6,261	51.0
Ames (W)	5,810	47.3
4 Origen S. Seymour (D)	8,633	49.3
Butler (W)	8,485	48.4

GEORGIA

Candidates	Votes	%
1 Joseph W. Jackson (SOR W)	4,279	51.6
Hopkins (UN)	4,011	48.4
2 James Johnson (UN)	8,107	53.7
Bening (SOR W)	6,985	46.3
3 David J. Bailey (SOR W)	6,011	50.7
Chappell (UN)	5,853	49.3
4 Charles Murphey (UN)	7,750	58.1
Stell (SOR W)	5,601	42.0
5 Elijah W. Chastain (UN)	13,882	65.0
Stiles (SOR W)	7,481	35.0
6 Junius Hillyer (UN)	6,937	71.1
Jones (SOR W)	2,819	28.9
7 Alexander H. Stephens (UN)	4,744	70.8
Lewis (SOR W)	1,955	29.2
8 Robert Toombs (UN)	4,704	65.0
McMillan (SOR W)	2,538	35.1

INDIANA

Candidates	Votes	%
1 James Lockhart (D)	8,173	51.0
Lemuel Debruler (W)	7,855	49.0
2 Cyrus L. Dunham (D)	8,097	53.2
Roger Martin (W)	7,125	46.8
3 John L. Robinson (D)	8,242	50.2
Johnson Watts (W)	8,173	49.8
4 Samuel W. Parker (W)	5,102	52.9
George W. Julian (F SOIL)	4,540	47.1
5 Thomas A. Hendricks (D)	9,062	62.1
William P. Rush (W)	5,543	38.0
6 Willis A. Gorman (D)	9,474	66.9
Eli P. Farmer (W)	4,693	33.1
7 John G. Davis (D)	6,076	51.1
Edward W. McGaughey (W)	5,814	48.9
8 Daniel Mace (D)	7,552	50.8

Candidates	Votes	%
David Brier (W)	7,294	49.0
9 Graham N. Fitch (D)	9,356	50.6
Schuyler Colfax (W)	9,118	49.4
10 Samuel Brenton (W FS)	8,776	50.9
James W. Borden (D)	8,483	49.2

KENTUCKY

Candidates	Votes	%
1 Linn Boyd (D)	6,638	57.5
H. M. McCarty (W)	3,446	29.9
Hiram McElroy	1,460	12.7
2 Benjamin E. Grey (W)	5,751	63.5
Jeff Jennings	3,301	36.5
3 Presley U. Ewing (W)	5,405	52.1
Beverly L. Clarke (W)	4,978	47.9
4 William T. Ward (W)	4,582	100.0
5 James W. Stone (D)	5,843	51.6
C. S. Hill	5,480	48.4
6 Addison White (W)	5,846	56.6
Theodore T. Garrard	4,130	40.0
7 Humphrey Marshall (W)	6,333	50.5
David Merriwether	6,216	49.5
8 John C. Breckinridge (D)	5,671	52.5
Leslie Combs (W)	5,141	47.6
9 John C. Mason (D)	5,929	72.1
Samuel Montgomery (W)	2,236	27.2
10 Richard Stanton (D)	7,649	53.6
William C. Marshall (W)	6,622	46.4

LOUISIANA

Candidates	Votes	%
1 Louis St. Martin (D)	3,199	53.7
Hagan (W)	2,763	46.3
2 J. Aristide Landry (W)	5,933	56.9
Vanwinder (D)	4,500	43.1
3 Alexander G. Penn (D)	4,740	56.9
Upton (W)	3,590	43.1
4 John Moore (W)	5,852	52.9
Isaac E. Morse (D)	5,214	47.1

MARYLAND

Candidates	Votes	%
1 Richard J. Bowie (W)	✓	
T. F. Bowie (IW)		
2 William T. Hamilton (D)	6,863	50.9
Roman (W)	6,626	49.1
3 Edward Hammond (D)	5,434	64.7
Lynch (I)	2,968	35.3
4 Thomas Yates Walsh (W)	6,683	50.9
William P. Whyte (D)	6,453	49.1
5 Alexander Evans (W)	4,992	52.7
McCullough (D)	4,486	47.3
6 Joseph S. Cottman (IW)	✓	
Henry (W)		

MISSISSIPPI

Candidates	Votes	%
1 Benjamin D. Nabers (UN)	9,659	57.5
Thompson (SR)	7,155	42.6
2 John A. Wilcox (UN)	6,927	52.8
Unidentified Candidate (SR)	6,201	47.2
3 John D. Freeman (UN)	7,774	51.8
Unidentified Candidate (SR)	7,241	48.2
4 Albert G. Brown (SR)	7,010	57.8
Dawson (UN)	5,119	42.2

NEW HAMPSHIRE

Candidates	Votes	%
1 Amos Tuck (W FS)	7,691	51.3
Kittredge (D)	7,304	48.7
2 Charles H. Peaslee (D)	7,170	55.0
Colby (W)	3,803	29.2
Fowler (F SOIL)	2,060	15.8
3 Jared Perkins (W FS)	8,682	52.9
Morrison (D)	7,741	47.1
4 Harry Hibbard (D)	5,125	61.1

Candidates	Votes	%
Kittredge (W)	2,248	26.8
White (F SOIL)	1,018	12.1

NORTH CAROLINA

Candidates	Votes	%
1 Thomas L. Clingman (SEC W)	6,600	70.1
Burgess S. Gaither (W)	2,819	29.9
2 Joseph P. Caldwell (W)	✓	
3 Alfred Dockery (W)	5,344	55.6
Green W. Caldwell (D)	4,260	44.4
4 James T. Morehead (W)	2,512	86.4
5 Abraham W. Venable (SEC D)	4,057	60.0
Calvin Graves (UN D)	2,710	40.1
6 John R. J. Daniel (SEC D)	2,815	72.1
Henry W. Miller (W)	928	23.8
7 William S. Ashe (D)	✓	
8 Edward Stanly (W)	5,236	51.3
Thomas Ruffin (SEC D)	4,966	48.7
9 David Outlaw (W)	2,868	61.6
William F. Martin (D)	1,759	37.8

PENNSYLVANIA

Special Election

Candidates	Votes	%
11 John Brisbin (D)	3,625	52.5
Dana (W)	3,283	47.5

RHODE ISLAND

Candidates	Votes	%
1 George G. King (W)	3,486	51.2
Welcome B. Sayles (D)	3,270	48.0
2 Benjamin B. Thurston (D)	3,335	59.6
Charles Jackson (W)	2,150	38.4

TENNESSEE

Candidates	Votes	%
1 Andrew Johnson (D)	6,538	57.4
Hayns (D)	4,844	42.6
2 Albert G. Watkins (W)	9,592	81.9
Hurley (D)	2,125	18.1
3 William M. Churchwell (D)	6,674	50.1
Anderson (W)	6,658	49.9
4 John H. Savage (D)	5,816	57.2
Goodpasture (W)	4,352	42.8
5 George W. Jones (D)	5,937	100.0
6 William H. Polk (W)	4,228	53.5
James H. Thomas (D)	3,672	46.5
7 Meredith P. Gentry (W)	2,572	100.0
8 William Cullom (W)	5,196	55.6
South (D)	4,145	44.4
9 Isham G. Harris (D)	3,654	56.2
Hornberger (W)	2,852	43.8
10 Frederick P. Stanton (D)	6,495	51.8
Coleman (W)	6,042	48.2
11 Christopher H. Williams (W)	10,693	100.0

TEXAS

Candidates	Votes	%
1 Richardson Scurry (D)	6,758	53.9
William B. Ochiltree (W)	4,009	32.0
B. R. Wallace	1,126	9.0
2 Volney E. Howard (D)	6,724	48.7
G. K. Lewis	2,904	21.0
H. McLeod	2,798	20.3
H. N. Patter	1,200	8.7

VIRGINIA

Candidates	Votes	%
1 John S. Millson (D)	2,271	59.6
Cowper (W)	1,541	40.4
2 Richard K. Meade (D)		100.0
3 Thomas H. Averett (D)	1,365	57.4
Flournoy (W)	1,014	42.6
4 Thomas S. Bocock (D)	1,596	61.2

Candidates	Votes	%		Candidates	Votes	%		Candidates	Votes	%
Bolling (W)	1,014	38.9	8	Alexander R. Holladay (D)		100.0	12	Henry A. Edmundson (D)		100.0
5 Paulus Powell (D)	2,857	51.5	9	James F. Strother (W)	2,367	55.9	13	Fayette McMullen (D)		100.0
Goggin (W)	2,695	48.5		Mton (D)	1,868	44.1	14	James M. H. Beale (D)	4,012	58.8
6 John S. Caskie (D)	2,960	54.5	10	Charles J. Faulkner (W)	2,351	53.7		Smith (W)	2,813	41.2
Botts (W)	2,472	45.5		Bedinger (D)	2,031	46.4	15	George W. Thompson (D)	4,251	52.5
7 Thomas H. Bayly (D)		100.0	11	John Letcher (D)		100.0		Haymond (W)	3,850	47.5

1852 House Elections

ARKANSAS

	Candidates	Votes	%
1	Alfred B. Greenwood (D)	7,939	100.0
2	Edward A. Warren (D)	3,748	53.2
	Unidentified Candidate (W)	3,301	46.8

CALIFORNIA

		Votes	%
AL	Milton S. Latham (D)	39,881✓	
	James A. McDougall (D)	39,387✓	
	P. L. Edwards (W)	34,933	
	G. B. Tingley (W)	34,299	

DELAWARE

		Votes	%
AL	George Read Riddle (D)	6,692	50.2
	John W. Houston (W)	6,630	49.8

FLORIDA

		Votes	%
AL	Augustus E. Maxwell (D)	4,637	50.3
	Cabell (W)	4,587	49.7

ILLINOIS

		Votes	%
1	Elihu B. Washburne (W)	7,392	43.9
	Thompson Campbell (D)	7,106	42.2
	Newman Campbell (F SOIL)	2,245	13.3
2	John Wentworth (D)	7,538	46.7
	Cyrus Aldrich (W)	6,437	39.9
	James H. Collins (F SOIL)	2,149	13.3
3	Jesse O. Norton (W)	8,268	46.0
	William Reddick (D)	8,092	45.0
	J. H. Bryant (F SOIL)	1,603	8.9
4	James Knox (W)	9,871	47.4
	Lewis W. Rop (D)	9,684	46.5
	L. W. Curtis (F SOIL)	1,290	6.2
5	William A. Richardson (D)	9,018	51.6
	O. H. Browning (W)	8,397	48.1
6	Richard Yates (W)	10,105	51.1
	John Calhoun (D)	9,675	48.9
7	James C. Allen (D)	8,283	54.1
	Charles H. Constable (W)	7,005	45.8
8	William H. Bissell (ID)	5,937	39.8
	Joseph Gillespie (W)	4,683	31.4
	T. B. Fouke (D)	4,301	28.8
9	Willis Allen (D)	12,100	98.5

INDIANA

		Votes	%
1	Smith Miller (D)	9,007	59.0
	Kea (W)	6,252	41.0
2	William H. English (D)	8,654	55.0
	Fergason (W)	7,094	45.1
3	Cyrus L. Dunham (D)	8,911	52.8
	Marshall (W)	7,980	47.2
4	James H. Lane (D)	8,783	53.0
	Farquhar (W)	7,789	47.0
5	Samuel W. Parker (W)	7,181	53.9
	Grose (D)	6,153	46.2
6	Thomas A. Hendricks (D)	8,240	53.6
	Bradley (W)	7,135	46.4
7	John G. Davis (D)	8,607	56.3
	Barbour (W)	6,685	43.7
8	Daniel Mace (D)	8,740	54.4
	Gregory (W)	7,337	45.6
9	Norman Eddy (D)	8,038	53.7
	Biddle (W)	6,930	46.3
10	Ebenezer M. Chamberlain (D)	6,875	53.5
	Brenton (W)	5,966	46.5
11	Andrew J. Harlan (D)	7,779	54.1
	Wallace (W)	6,608	45.9

IOWA

	Candidates	Votes	%
1	Bernhart Henn (D)	9,709	55.2
	P. Veile (D)	7,874	44.8
2	John P. Cook (W)	7,777	52.2
	L. Clark (D)	7,114	47.8

KENTUCKY

Special Election

		Votes	%
7	William Preston (W)	6,560	57.5
	Calvin Sanders (D)	4,841	42.5

MAINE

		Votes	%
1	Moses MacDonald (D)	9,218	57.8
	Appleton (W)	5,333	33.4
	Fessenden (F SOIL)	1,358	8.5
2	Samuel Mayall (D)	9,917	52.6
	Gilman (W)	7,932	42.0
3	E. Wilder Farley (W)	5,255	36.4
	Kimball (D)	4,724	32.7
	Smith (D)	3,874	26.8
4	Samuel P. Benson (W)	8,708	54.4
	Porter (D)	5,433	33.9
	May (F SOIL)	1,580	9.9
5	Israel Washburn Jr (W)	8,227	51.1
	Strickland (D)	4,376	27.2
	Waterhouse (D)	3,444	21.4
6	Thomas J. D. Fuller (D)	6,283	52.6
	Robinson (W)	5,280	44.2

MASSACHUSETTS

		Votes	%
1	Zeno Scudder (W)	4,016	61.3
	A. H. Howland	2,368	36.2
2	Samuel L. Crocker (W)	3,599	45.8
	Geishom Weston (F SOIL)	3,455	44.0
	M. Ide (D)	738	9.4
3	J. Wiley Edmands (W)	3,416	48.5
	Charles F. Adams (F SOIL)	2,978	42.3
	Arthur W. Austin (D)	471	6.7
4	Samuel H. Walley (W)	4,290	60.5
	Levi A. Dowley (D)	1,745	24.6
	Charles M. Ellis (F SOIL)	1,028	14.5
5	William Appleton (W)	4,672	55.7
	Adam W. Thasler Jr. (D)	2,081	24.8
	Anson Burlingame (F SOIL)	1,550	18.5
6	Charles W. Upham (W)	4,265	46.6
	George Hood (F SOIL)	4,096	44.8
	Nathaniel J. Lord	532	5.8
7	Nathaniel P. Banks (D)	4,605	50.1
	Luther V. Bell (W)	4,300	46.8
8	Tappan Wentworth (W)	4,411	45.9
	Henry Wilson (F SOIL)	4,319	44.9
	Benjamin F. Butler (D)	481	5.0
9	Alexander De Witt (F SOIL)	4,039	41.3
	Isaac Davis (D)	2,925	29.9
	Ira M. Barton (W)	2,796	28.6
10	Edward Dickinson (W)	4,160	56.9
	Samuel F. Cutler (D)	1,625	22.2
	Eustus Hopkins (F SOIL)	1,507	20.6
11	John Z. Goodrich (W)	5,579	51.9
	Whiting Griswold (D)	4,842	45.1

Special Elections

		Votes	%
2	Francis Fay (W)	4,989	47.2
	George Hood (F SOIL)	4,821	45.6
4	Lorenzo Labine (W)	4,620	50.9
	John A. Bolles (F SOIL)	4,055	44.7
9	Edward P. Little (D)	3,711	50.4
	Jacob H. Loud (W)	3,595	48.8

MICHIGAN

	Candidates	Votes	%
1	David Stuart (D)	10,127	50.4
	William A. Howard (W)	9,370	46.6
2	David A. Noble (D)	10,024	51.7
	Joseph R. Williams (W FS)	9,367	48.3
3	Samuel Clark (D)	10,765	49.2
	Henry R. Williams (W)	9,969	45.6
4	Hestor L. Stevens (D)	10,746	51.8
	George Bradley (W)	8,948	43.1
	Ephraim Calkins (F SOIL)	1,048	5.1

MISSOURI[1]

		Votes	%
1	Thomas H. Benton (BENTON D)	8,437	45.3
	Car (W)	7,595	40.7
	Bogy (A-BEN D)	2,615	14.0
2	Alfred W. Lamb (D)	7,007	53.0
	Gilchrist Poster (W)	6,224	47.0
3	John G. Miller (W)	8,297	51.3
	Green (D)	7,869	48.7
4	Mordecai Oliver (W)	7,612	46.7
	Unidentified Candidate (A-BEN D)	4,452	27.3
	King (BENTON D)	4,243	26.0
5	John S. Phelps (D)	11,392	67.6
	Price (W)	5,458	32.4

NEW JERSEY

		Votes	%
1	Nathan T. Stratton (D)	7,185	51.3
	Boyle (W)	6,816	48.7
2	Charles Skelton (D)	10,229	52.6
	Brown (W)	9,238	47.5
3	Samuel Lilly (D)	10,193	55.1
	Brown (W)	8,315	44.9
4	George Vail (D)	9,247	59.6
	Coursen (W)	6,265	40.4
5	Alexander C. M. Pennington (W)	7,636	50.6
	Price (D)	7,469	49.5

NEW YORK

		Votes	%
1	James Maurice (D)	7,801	53.7
	King (W)	6,136	42.3
2	Thomas W. Cumming (D)	7,228	51.5
	Sanford (W)	6,789	48.4
3	Hiram Walbridge (D)	5,814	54.4
	Bowen (W)	4,797	44.9
4	Mike Walsh (D)	4,802	52.9
	Hawes (W)	2,564	28.2
	Kly (D)	1,712	18.9
5	William M. Tweed (D)	5,394	51.6
	Hoxie (W)	4,243	40.6
	Mor (W)	818	7.8
6	John Wheeler (D)	6,354	54.4
	Varnum (W)	5,243	44.9
7	William A. Walker (D)	5,801	52.1
	Roberts (W)	4,702	42.2
8	Francis B. Cutting (D)	4,414	56.5
	Brooks (W)	3,398	43.5
9	Jared V. Peck (D)	8,533	59.4
	Clark (W)	5,827	40.6
10	William Murray (D)	7,768	54.8
	Farnham (W)	6,407	45.2
11	Theodore R. Westbrook (D)	9,092	53.5
	Smith (W)	7,902	46.5
12	Gilbert Dean (D)	9,937	50.4
	Cruger (W)	9,798	49.7
13	Russell Sage (W)	6,583	51.0
	Seyr (D)	6,185	47.9
14	Rufus W. Peckham (D)	8,363	53.5
	Egberts (W)	7,190	46.0
15	Charles Hughes (D)	9,988	49.5
	Northrup (W)	9,693	48.0

Candidates	Votes	%
16 George A. Simmons (W)	7,093	50.9
Ireland (D)	6,852	49.1
17 Bishop Perkins (D)	10,085	53.2
Vanrenr (W)	7,274	38.4
Reddington (F SOIL)	1,601	8.4
18 Peter Rowe (D)	10,916	52.1
Miller (W)	10,057	48.0
19 George W. Chase (W)	9,550	54.3
Gordon (D)	8,034	45.7
20 Orsamus B. Matteson (W)	8,530	50.2
Mouln (D)	6,600	38.9
Spen (W)	1,542	9.1
21 Henry Bennett (W)	9,876	49.9
Smith (D)	9,534	48.2
22 Gerrit Smith (ULTRA AB)	8,049	40.5
Hoh (D)	6,206	31.2
Tenck (W)	5,620	28.3
23 Caleb Lyon (IW)	8,937	53.1
Mundy (D)	7,891	46.9
24 Daniel T. Jones (D)	6,605	46.6
Gott (W)	6,120	43.2
Ray (F SOIL)	1,458	10.3
25 Edwin B. Morgan (W)	9,150	47.4
How (D)	8,996	46.6
Cuyler (F SOIL)	1,147	6.0
26 Andrew Oliver (D)	8,546	49.2
Woods (W)	8,529	49.1
27 John J. Taylor (D)	9,426	50.4
Cook (W)	8,410	45.0
28 George Hastings (D)	10,681	53.7
Irvine (W)	9,225	46.3
29 Azariah Boody (W)	7,290	50.2
Field (D)	6,578	45.3
30 Benjamin Pringle (W)	9,386	48.7
Sherman (W)	8,903	46.2
Landon (F SOIL)	976	5.1
31 Thomas T. Flagler (W)	5,858	46.0
Woods (D)	5,508	43.3
Murphy (F SOIL)	1,358	10.7
32 Solomon G. Haven (W)	8,037	51.8
Verk (D)	7,054	45.4
33 Reuben E. Fenton (D)	8,717	48.8
Crooker (W)	8,661	48.5

OHIO

Candidates	Votes	%
1 David T. Disney (D)	5,852	57.1
Cassilly (W)	4,317	42.1
2 John Scott Harrison (W)	4,780	54.5
Roll (D)	3,849	43.9
3 Lewis D. Campbell (W)	8,680	50.4
Vallandigham (D)	8,533	49.6
4 Matthias H. Nichols (D)	7,648	53.8
Plunkett (W)	6,378	44.9
5 Alfred P. Edgerton (D)	9,072	66.1
Parker (W)	4,561	33.2
6 Andrew Ellison (D)	7,479	50.6
Barrere (W)	7,208	48.7
7 Aaron Harlan (W)	7,580	54.7
Telfair (D)	5,018	36.2
Nix (F SOIL)	1,252	9.0
8 Moses B. Corwin (W)	8,561	57.9
Young (D)	5,780	39.1
9 Fred W. Green (D)	8,198	74.1
Goodman (W)	2,095	18.9
Sam (F SOIL)	768	6.9
10 John L. Taylor (W)	7,653	53.1
Sherer (D)	6,763	46.9
11 Thomas Ritchey (D)	9,037	56.3
Welch (W)	6,681	41.7
12 Edson B. Olds (D)	8,549	49.2
Galloway (W)	8,480	48.8
13 William D. Lindsley (D)	6,739	44.4
Saddler (W)	6,035	39.8
Jacob Brinkerhoff (F SOIL)	2,390	15.8
14 Harvey H. Johnson (D)	7,591	49.3
Lockwood (W)	4,763	31.0
Norton S. Townshend (F SOIL)	3,030	19.7
15 William R. Sapp (W)	6,140	38.8
William Winnell (D)	6,109	38.6
Rich (F SOIL)	2,650	16.8
Vance	924	5.8
16 Edward Ball (W)	7,161	52.3
Gaylord (D)	6,347	46.3
17 Wilson Shannon (D)	7,142	54.1
Hollister (W)	6,054	45.9
18 George Bliss (D)	6,140	46.7
Lyman (W)	5,307	40.3
Earl (F SOIL)	1,708	13.0
19 Edward Wade (F SOIL)	5,274	40.5
Case (W)	4,046	31.0
Wilson (D)	3,715	28.5
20 Joshua R. Giddings (F SOIL)	5,752	40.1
Woods (D)	4,427	30.8
Newton (W)	4,179	29.1
21 Andrew Stuart (D)	7,423	47.8
Brewer (W)	6,885	44.3
Lee (F SOIL)	1,220	7.9

PENNSYLVANIA

Candidates	Votes	%
1 Thomas B. Florence (D)	4,937	44.5
Price (W)	3,200	28.9
Levin (NAM)	2,953	26.6
2 Joseph R. Chandler (W)	6,594	62.4
Ham (D)	3,556	33.7
3 John Robbins Jr (D)	5,857	51.5
Sanderson (W)	3,300	29.0
Painter (NAM)	2,206	19.4
4 William H. Witte (D)	5,843	46.9
Lambert (W)	4,546	36.5
Cornman (NAM)	2,065	16.6
5 John McNair (D)	7,168	50.9
Hitner (W)	6,336	45.0
6 William Everhart (W)	7,641	54.2
Mur (D)	6,464	45.8
7 Samuel A. Bridges (D)	8,339	52.7
Taylor (W)	7,486	47.3
8 Henry A. Muhlenberg (D)	7,543	68.5
Beiber (W)	3,476	31.6
9 Isaac E. Heister (W)	8,840	57.8
Samp (D)	6,456	42.2
10 Ner Middleswarth (W)	7,921	55.8
Seir (D)	6,278	44.2
11 Christian M. Straub (D)	5,729	51.5
Krebs (W)	5,388	48.5
12 Hendrick B. Wright (D)	7,523	50.6
Fuller (W)	7,350	49.4
13 Asa Packer (D)	8,909	74.6
Foster (W)	3,035	25.4
14 Galusha A. Grow (D)	8,062	94.2
Horton (W)	495	5.8
15 James Gamble (D)	8,742	59.2
Irwin (W)	6,026	40.8
16 William H. Kurtz (D)	9,513	56.6
Biddle (W)	7,306	43.4
17 Samuel L. Russell (W)	9,216	51.0
Danr (D)	8,845	49.0
18 John McCulloch (W)	7,847	56.2
Shaffr (D)	6,112	43.8
19 Augustus Drum (D)	7,968	57.2
Kuhns (W)	5,959	42.8
20 John L. Dawson (D)	9,791	56.8
Gow (W)	7,460	43.2
21 David Ritchie (W)	4,939	52.2
Shan (D)	4,532	47.9
22 Thomas M. Howe (W)	4,620	54.8
Gibn (D)	3,817	45.2
23 Michael C. Trout (D)	5,369	45.6
John Allison (W)	5,340	45.4
Unidentified Candidate (F SOIL)	1,056	9.0
24 Carlton B. Curtis (D)	8,321	65.5
Kerr (W)	4,375	34.5
25 John Dick (W)	6,057	54.8
Cutr (D)	4,049	36.6
Unidentified Candidate (F SOIL)	951	8.6

VERMONT

Candidates	Votes	%
1 James Meacham (W)	7,138	56.5
Pierpoint (F SOIL)	2,801	22.2
Tucke (D)	2,704	21.4
2 Andrew Tracy (W)	9,319	52.2
Daniel Kellogg (D)	3,261	18.3
Isaac Fletcher (F SOIL)	2,928	16.4
Hugh H. Henry (D)	1,675	9.4
3 Alvah Sabin (W)	5,706	48.3
Heyward (D)	3,803	32.2
Kasson (F SOIL)	2,294	19.4

VIRGINIA

Special Election

Candidates	Votes	%
15 Sherrard Clemens (D)	✓	

WISCONSIN

Candidates	Votes	%
1 Daniel Wells Jr (D)	8,342	46.5
Charles Durkee (F SOIL)	5,731	31.9
Henry S. Durand (W)	3,870	21.6
2 Ben C. Eastman (D)	10,893	53.9
Abbott (W)	7,816	38.7
Enos (F SOIL)	1,506	7.5
3 John B. Macy (D)	14,596	55.6
Shafter (W)	9,513	36.2
McKee (F SOIL)	2,168	8.3

1. Missouri's House representation rose from five seats to seven following the 1850 reapportionment, but elections to the two additional seats were not held in time for the regular 1852 election. Instead, they were held in 1853. See Missouri 1853.

1853 House Elections

ALABAMA

	Candidates	Votes	%
1	Philip Phillips (SO RTS D)	4,880	50.5
	E. Lockwood (UN W)	4,777	49.5
2	James Abercrombie (UN W)	7,474	56.1
	D. Clopton (D)	5,838	43.9
3	Sampson W. Harris (SO RTS D)	6,394	79.8
	Moore (UN W)	1,622	20.2
4	William R. Smith (UN D)	3,045	34.7
	Sydenham Moore (SO RTS D)	2,974	33.8
	S. F. Hale (D)	2,769	31.5
5	George S. Houston (D)	4,022	95.0
6	Williamson R. W. Cobb (UN D)	5,221	58.2
	C. C. Clay Jr. (D)	3,744	41.8
7	James F. Dowdell (SO RTS D)	6,098	65.6
	T. G. Garrett (IUN W)	3,200	34.4

CONNECTICUT

	Candidates	Votes	%
1	James T. Pratt (D)	8,225	52.3
	Charles Chapman (W)	6,963	44.2
2	Colin M. Ingersoll (D)	8,551	53.1
	Austin Baldwin (W)	6,773	42.0
3	Nathan Belcher (D)	6,129	51.8
	Daniel P. Tyler (W)	3,906	33.0
	Albert G. Stark (F SOIL)	1,800	15.2
4	Origen S. Seymour (D)	8,700	54.2
	William W. Welch (W)	7,249	45.2

GEORGIA

	Candidates	Votes	%
1	James L. Seward (D)	4,429	51.1
	Barton (W)	4,238	48.9
2	Alfred H. Colquitt (D)	6,795	52.1
	Johnson (W)	6,249	47.9
3	David J. Bailey (D)	5,232	50.0
	Robert P. Trippe (W)	5,227	50.0
4	William B. W. Dent (D)	6,701	51.3
	Calhoun (W)	6,368	48.7
5	Elijah W. Chastain (D)	8,118	50.8
	Tumlin (D)	7,866	49.2
6	Junius Hillyer (D)	5,439	64.8
	Wofld (W)	2,954	35.2
7	David A. Reese (W)	4,997	56.3
	Saffold (D)	3,883	43.7
8	Alexander H. Stephens (W)	5,634	69.7
	Jones (D)	2,444	30.3

KENTUCKY

	Candidates	Votes	%
1	Linn Boyd (D)	7,585	57.6
	Jefferson Brown (ID)	5,590	42.4
2	Ben E. Grey (W)	7,076	52.5
	W. J. Davie (D)	6,408	47.5
3	Presley Ewing (W)	5,318	100.0
4	James S. Crisman (D)	5,657	50.2
	Thomas E. Bramlette (W)	5,622	49.8
5	Clement S. Hill (W)	6,126	50.5
	James W. Stone (D)	5,996	49.5
6	John M. Elliott (D)	6,257	53.8
	Jeremiah S. Pierce (W)	5,376	46.2
7	William Preston (W)	6,609	57.7
	S. S. English (D)	4,847	42.3
8	John C. Breckinridge (D)	6,532	52.1
	Robert P. Letcher (W)	6,006	47.9
9	Leander M. Cox (AM)	6,606	52.5
	James M. Rice (D)	5,974	47.5
10	Richard H. Stanton (D)	7,583	51.8
	George B. Hodge (W)	7,070	48.3

LOUISIANA

	Candidates	Votes	%
1	William Dunbar (D)	4,550	62.8
	Gayarre (W)	2,691	37.2
2	Theodore G. Hunt (W)	6,558	54.6

	Candidates	Votes	%
	Davis (D)	5,445	45.4
3	John Perkins Jr. (D)	4,965	56.7
	Pond (W)	3,787	43.3
4	Roland Jones (D)	7,494	56.8
	Smith (W)	5,695	43.2

MARYLAND

	Candidates	Votes	%
1	John R. Franklin (W)	5,815	53.1
	Stevn (I)	5,127	46.9
2	Jacob Shower (I)	7,246	53.4
	Wethered (W)	6,330	46.6
3	Joshua Vansant (ID)	5,876	53.7
	Preston (W)	5,061	46.3
4	Henry May (ID)	6,792	51.3
	Walsh (W)	6,440	48.7
5	William T. Hamilton (ID)	7,545	54.0
	Thomas (W)	6,429	46.0
6	Augustus R. Sollers (W)	3,815	61.0
	Jenr (I)	2,438	39.0

MISSISSIPPI

	Candidates	Votes	%
1	Daniel B. Wright (D)	8,984	51.6
	Nabers (W)	8,414	48.4
2	William T. S. Barry (D)	7,039	50.7
	Wilcox (W)	6,837	49.3
3	Otho R. Singleton (D)	8,367	55.7
	McLung (W)	6,669	44.4
4	Wiley P. Harris (D)		100.0
AL	William Barksdale (D)	29,702	54.1
	Unidentified Candidate (W)	25,183	45.9

MISSOURI[1]

	Candidates	Votes	%
3	James J. Lindley (W)	6,828	50.6
	Jackson (A-BEN D)	6,674	49.4
7	Samuel Caruthers (W)	4,447	39.8
	Jackson (BENTON D)	2,542	22.8
	English (A-BEN D)	2,424	21.7
	Rosier (BENTON D)	1,750	15.7

NEW HAMPSHIRE

	Candidates	Votes	%
1	George W. Kittredge (D)	10,168	53.2
	Amos Tuck (W)	8,962	46.9
2	George W. Morrison (D)	9,050	67.5
	Hughes (W)	4,353	32.5
3	Harry Hibbard (D)	9,635	56.1
	Perkins (W)	7,556	44.0

NORTH CAROLINA

	Candidates	Votes	%
1	Henry M. Shaw (D)	4,833	50.5
	David Outlaw (W)	4,746	49.6
2	Thomas Ruffin (D)	5,812	68.7
	W. C. Loftin (ID)	2,653	31.3
3	Wlliam S. Ashe (D)	5,520	62.2
	Walter F. Leake (LD D)	3,351	37.8
4	Sion H. Rogers (W)	4,201	38.9
	Abraham W. Venable (LD D)	4,133	38.3
	Augustus M. Lewis (A-LD D)	2,454	22.8
5	John Kerr (W)	6,037	86.2
	Abraham Rencher (ID)	963	13.8
6	Richard C. Puryear (W)	6,173	51.6
	George D. Boyd (W)	5,788	48.4
7	F. Burton Craige (D)	5,965	51.4
	James W. Osborne (W)	5,649	48.6
8	Thomas L. Clingman (D)	7,606	59.3
	Burgess S. Gaither (W)	5,214	40.7

RHODE ISLAND

	Candidates	Votes	%
1	Thomas Davis (D)	5,524	50.8
	George G. King (W)	4,942	45.5

	Candidates	Votes	%
2	Benjamin B. Thurston (D)	4,436	90.5
	Elisha M. Aldrich (W)	450	9.2

SOUTH CAROLINA

	Candidates	Votes	%
1	John McQueen (D)		100.0
2	William Aiken (D)		100.0
3	Laurence M. Keitt (D)		100.0
4	Preston S. Brooks (SSR D)	2,098	32.3
	Sullivan	1,497	23.0
	Francis W. Pickens (NULL D)	1,492	23.0
	Marshall	1,415	21.8
5	James L. Orr (D)		100.0
6	William W. Boyce (SSR D)	2,549	51.0
	Moses	2,270	45.4

TENNESSEE

	Candidates	Votes	%
1	Brookins Campbell (D)	5,525*	37.1
	Nathaniel G. Taylor (W)	5,387	36.2
	Albert G. Watkins (W)	3,988	26.8
2	William M. Churchwell (D)	6,266	56.6
	Maynard (W)	4,797	43.4
3	Samuel A. Smith (D)	7,703	55.5
	Van Dyke (W)	6,180	44.5
4	William Cullom (W)	5,630	50.2
	Gardner (D)	5,593	49.8
5	Charles Ready (W)	6,143	57.3
	Barry (D)	4,577	42.7
6	George W. Jones (D)		100.0
7	Robert M. Bugg (W)	6,421	52.3
	Pavott (D)	5,865	47.7
8	Felix K. Zollicoffer (W)	5,808	53.0
	Allison (D)	5,157	47.0
9	Emerson Etheridge (W)		100.0
10	Frederick P. Stanton (D)	5,126	50.0
	Yerger (W)	5,120	50.0

TEXAS

	Candidates	Votes	%
1	George M. Smyth (D)	12,126	98.8
2	Peter H. Bell (D)	5,918	41.4
	William R. Scurry (D)	2,963	20.7
	G. K. Lewis (D)	2,411	16.9
	B. F. Carothers (W)	2,126	14.9
	F. M. Blake (D)	869	6.1

VIRGINIA

	Candidates	Votes	%
1	Thomas H. Bayly (D)		100.0
2	John S. Millson (D)	3,206	56.7
	Chambliss (W)	2,071	36.6
	Roberts (I)	379	6.7
3	John S. Caskie (D)	4,333	54.9
	Coleman (W)	3,561	45.1
4	William O. Goode (D)		100.0
5	Thomas S. Bocock (D)	4,304	51.7
	Wootton (W)	3,586	43.1
	Arnett (I)	428	5.2
6	Paulus Powell (D)	4,751	54.8
	Mosely (W)	3,912	45.2
7	William Smith (D)	4,223	51.8
	Snowden (W)	3,931	48.2
8	Charles J. Faulkner (D)	6,106	52.3
	Boteler (W)	5,560	47.7
9	John Letcher (D)		100.0
10	Zedekiah Kidwell (D)		100.0
11	John F. Snodgrass (D)	4,707	40.2
	Lewis (D)	4,497	38.4
	Sterrett (W)	2,506	21.4
12	Henry A. Edmonson (D)		100.0
13	Fayette McMullen (D)		100.0

1. Missouri elected two additional House members to raise its total to the seven seats allotted by the 1850 census. The state was redistricted from five seats to seven, with the new districts labeled "3" and "7." The 3rd congressional district of 1853 is not the same 3rd district that elected a representative in 1852. (See Missouri 1852.)

1854 House Elections

ARKANSAS

	Candidates	Votes	%
1	Alfred B. Greenwood (D)	15,374	97.3
2	Albert Rust (D)	8,893	67.0
	E. G. Walker (W)	4,371	32.9

CALIFORNIA

		Votes	
AL	James W. Denver (A-BROD D)	36,819✓	
	Philemon T. Herbert (A-BROD D)	36,542✓	
	G. W. Bowie (W)	34,741	
	Cal Benham (W)	34,411	
	J. Churchman (BROD D)	10,006	
	James A. McDougall (BROD D)	9,968	
	M. S. Latham (BROD D)	1,843	

DELAWARE

		Votes	%
AL	Elisha D. Cullen (AM)	6,820	51.9
	George Read Riddle (D)	6,334	48.2

FLORIDA

		Votes	%
AL	Augustus Maxwell (D)	5,642	55.2
	Thomas Brown (W)	4,583	44.8

ILLINOIS

		Votes	%
1	Elihu B. Washburne (R)	8,372	69.3
	William M. Jackon (D)	2,776	23.0
	E. P. Ferry (A-NEB D)	927	7.7
2	James H. Woodworth (R)	6,927	53.1
	Robert S. Blackwell (W)	2,591	19.8
	John B. Turner (D)	2,544	19.5
	Edward L. Mayo (A-NEB D)	996	7.6
3	Jesse O. Norton (R)	10,474	62.8
	John A. Drake (D)	6,216	37.2
4	James Knox (R)	10,146	57.0
	Unidentified Candidate (D)	7,588	42.6
5	William A. Richardson (D)	8,935	52.4
	Arch Williams (R)	8,122	47.6
6	Thomas L. Harris (D)	10,090	50.5
	Richard Gates (R)	9,890	49.5
7	James C. Allen (D)	8,452‡	50.0
	William B. Archer (R)	8,451	50.0
8	Lyman Trumbull (R)	7,917*	58.1
	Philip B. Fouke (D)	5,306	38.9
9	Samuel S. Marshall (D)	8,497	64.4
	L. Jay S. Turney (R)	2,911	22.0
	Dewitt C. Barber	1,276	9.7

INDIANA

		Votes	%
1	Smith Miller (NEB D)	9,864	52.2
	Hall (R)	9,051	47.9
2	William H. English (NEB D)	8,931	51.7
	Shanter (R)	8,345	48.3
3	George G. Dunn (R)	9,989	54.5
	Dunn (NEB D)	8,329	45.5
4	William Cumback (R)	9,061	51.9
	Holn (NEB D)	8,391	48.1
5	David P. Holloway (R)	9,419	64.3
	Buckles (NEB D)	5,242	35.8
6	Lucien Barbour (R)	9,824	51.4
	Thomas A. Hendricks (NEB D)	9,286	48.6
7	Harvey D. Scott (R)	9,515	52.6
	Davis (NEB D)	8,580	47.4
8	Daniel Mace (R)	10,357	56.9
	Davis (NEB D)	7,838	43.1
9	Schuyler Colfax (R)	9,989	54.9
	Eddy (NEB D)	8,223	45.2
10	Samuel Brenton (R)	7,485	56.0
	Ebenezer M. Chamberlain (NEB D)	5,881	44.0
11	John U. Pettit (R)	9,389	56.6
	Slack (NEB D)	7,201	43.4

IOWA

	Candidates	Votes	%
1	Augustus Hall (D)	11,213	50.3
	R. L. B. Clark (R)	11,042	49.5
2	James Thorington (R)	11,424	53.3
	Stephen Hempstead (D)	9,872	46.1

KENTUCKY

Special Election

		Votes	%
3	Francis M. Bristow (W)	2,533	81.6
	A. J. Harberson (D)	572	18.4

MAINE

		Votes	%
1	John M. Wood (R)	9,227	59.8
	Samuel Wells (D)	6,196	40.2
2	John J. Perry (R)	10,007	57.8
	William Kimball (D)	7,313	42.2
3	Ebenezer Knowlton (R)	5,995	43.9
	J. G. Dickerson (D)	4,072	29.8
	E. W. Farley (W)	3,587	26.3
4	Samuel P. Benson (R)	11,610	77.0
	George Rogers (D)	3,467	23.0
5	Israel Washburn Jr (R)	10,224	63.0
	Samuel H. Blake (D)	6,010	37.0
6	Thomas J. D. Fuller (D)	4,713	42.4
	J. A. Milliken (R)	4,307	38.7
	N. Smith Jr (W)	2,099	18.9

MASSACHUSETTS

		Votes	%
1	Robert B. Hall (AM)	5,353	63.3
	Thomas D. Eliot (W)	2,238	26.5
	Abraham H. Howland	812	9.6
2	James Buffington (AM)	8,074	68.2
	Samuel L. Crocker (W)	1,914	16.2
	Charles R. Vickery	1,064	9.0
	Gersham B. Weston (F SOIL)	774	6.5
3	William S. Damrell (AM)	8,668	74.4
	Nathaniel F. Safford (W)	1,933	16.6
	Edward Avery	624	5.4
4	Linus B. Comins (AM)	4,972	57.4
	Samuel H. Walley (W)	2,770	32.0
	Samuel R. Spinney	913	10.5
5	Anson Burlingame (AM)	5,967	61.5
	William Appleton (W)	3,109	32.1
	William Parmenter (D)	604	6.2
6	Timothy Davis (AM)	7,428	65.3
	Charles W. Upham (W)	3,231	28.4
	Nathaniel J. Lord	633	5.6
7	Nathaniel P. Banks (AM)	8,928	73.3
	Luther V. Bell (W)	2,481	20.4
	Bowen Bualman	724	5.9
8	Chauncy L. Knapp (AM)	7,004	62.7
	Tappan Wentworth (W)	3,556	31.8
	Daniel Needham	593	5.3
9	Alexander De Witt (AM)	8,797	77.0
	Isaac Davis (D)	1,526	13.4
	Ira M. Barton (W)	851	7.5
10	Henry Morris (AM)	7,723*	64.6
	Edward Dickinson (W)	2,757	23.1
	Stephen C. Bemis	1,338	11.2
11	Mark Trafton (AM)	6,640	50.4
	John L. Goodrich (W)	3,998	30.4
	Whiting Griswold	2,505	19.0

Special Election

		Votes	%
1	Thomas D. Eliot (W)	4,059	51.5
	Abraham Howland	3,741	47.4

MICHIGAN

	Candidates	Votes	%
1	William A. Howard (R)	9,877	53.1
	David Stuart (D)	8,723	46.9
2	Henry Waldron (R)	11,055	57.7
	David A. Noble (D)	8,113	42.3
3	David S. Walbridge (R)	12,865	55.8
	Samuel Clark (D)	10,178	44.1
4	George W. Peck (D)	11,233	53.2
	Moses Wisner (R)	9,863	46.7

MISSOURI

		Votes	%
1	Luther M. Kennett (W)	6,259	52.4
	Benton (BENTON D)	5,298	44.4
2	Gilchrist Porter (W)	8,119	54.1
	Corneck	6,877	45.9
3	James J. Lindley (W)	8,150	52.5
	Fournoy (A-BEN D)	7,386	47.5
4	Mordecai Oliver (W)	6,129	44.1
	Leonard (A-BEN D)	4,998	35.9
	Lowe (BENTON D)	2,787	20.0
5	John G. Miller (W)	6,372*	46.2
	Price (BENTON D)	4,904	35.5
	Hough (A-BEN D)	2,530	18.3
6	John S. Phelps (A-BEN D)	8,342	51.1
	Johnson (BENTON D)	7,982	48.9
7	Samuel Caruthers (W)	8,045	58.9
	Jones (BENTON D)	5,625	41.2

NEW JERSEY

		Votes	%
1	Isaiah D. Clawson (W)	6,269	42.9
	Mulford (NEB)	4,383	30.0
	Hazltn (TEMP)	3,949	27.1
2	George R. Robbins (W)	10,539	57.6
	Rue (NEB)	7,769	42.4
3	James Bishop (W)	9,051	54.4
	Lilly (NEB)	7,603	45.7
4	George Vail (NEB)	7,281	51.7
	Osborn (A-NEB)	6,816	48.4
5	Alexander C. M. Pennington (W)	8,137	54.4
	Darey (NEB)	6,816	45.6

NEW YORK

		Votes	%
1	William W. Valk (SOF D & AM)	3,753	28.1
	Allen (HARD D)	2,778	20.8
	Vail (W)	2,676	20.1
	Lord (SOFT D)	2,227	16.7
	Disosway (TEMP)	1,902	14.3
2	James S. T. Stranahan (W)	7,927	50.9
	Taylor (HARD D)	7,623	49.0
3	Guy R. Pelton (W & AM)	4,084	52.6
	Clinton (HARD D)	2,559	33.0
	Miner (SOFT D)	1,123	14.5
4	John Kelly (SOFT D)	3,068	36.0
	Walsh (HARD D)	3,047	35.7
	Bryle (W & AM)	1,594	18.7
	Macomber (W)	821	9.6
5	Thomas R. Whitney (W & AM)	3,321	30.9
	Andrews (W)	2,765	25.7
	Hamilton (HARD D)	2,718	25.3
	Berry (SOFT D)	1,954	18.2
6	John Wheeler (HARD D & AM)	5,101	46.3
	Murphy (SOFT D)	2,533	23.0
	Marshal (W)	2,256	20.5
	Mead (I HARD D)	1,128	10.2
7	Thomas Child Jr (W & AM)	6,557*	56.3
	Kennedy (SOFT D)	5,094	43.7
8	Abram Wakeman (W & AM)	4,895	51.2
	Curtis (HARD D)	2,969	31.1
	Fellows (SOFT D)	1,699	17.8
9	Bayard Clarke (W & AM)	7,764	61.1
	Branth (HARD D)	2,540	20.0
	Whiting (HARD D)	2,038	16.0

Candidates	Votes	%
10 Ambrose S. Murray (W)	5,209	44.0
Woodward (HARD D & AM)	4,574	38.6
Strtn (SOFT D)	2,053	17.4
11 Rufus H. King (W)	8,576	63.0
Strong (HARD D)	5,042	37.0
12 Killian Miller (W)	8,376	51.1
McClellan (SOFT D & AM)	5,540	33.8
Wilson (HARD D)	2,486	15.2
13 Russell Sage (W & AM)	6,954	63.2
Clum (SOFT D)	2,075	18.9
Cook (HARD D)	1,971	17.9
14 Samuel Dickson (W)	4,638	32.2
Harct (SOFT D & AM)	4,270	29.6
Pruyn (SOFT D)	3,244	22.5
Hamilton	2,255	15.7
15 Edward Dodd (W)	6,760	37.7
Clark (HARD D)	6,358	35.4
Hughes (SOFT D)	2,428	13.5
Andrews (TEMP)	2,399	13.4
16 George A. Simmons (W)	5,533	48.7
Bailey (SOFT D & AM)	3,062	26.9
Thomas (SOFT D)	1,752	15.4
Flanders (HARD D)	1,025	9.0
17 Francis E. Spinner (SOFT D)	7,618	46.5
Alexander (W)	5,357	32.7
Benton (HARD D)	3,414	20.8
18 Thomas R. Horton (W)	9,431	51.3
Jackson (HARD D)	8,945	48.7
19 Jonas A. Hughson (W)	6,744	43.3
Palmer (SOFT D)	6,444	41.3
Hawes (F SOIL)	1,339	8.6
Sturges	1,066	6.8
20 Orsamus B. Matteson (W)	6,492	38.2
Johnson (SOFT D)	5,172	30.4
Huntington (W)	4,759	28.0
21 Henry Bennett (W)	9,757	56.0
Tompkins (HARD D)	5,579	32.0
Crocker (SOFT D)	2,077	11.9
22 Andrew Z. McCarty (W)	5,535	32.2
Babcock (SOFT D)	4,728	27.5
Case (F SOIL)	3,652	21.2
Lewis (HARD D)	3,281	19.1
23 William A. Gilbert (W)	6,251	46.4
Ives (SOFT D)	5,645	41.9
Brown (HARD D)	1,513	11.2
24 Amos P. Granger (W)	4,803	37.5
Alvord (SOFT D)	4,109	32.1
Noxon (W & AM)	3,409	26.6
25 Edwin B. Morgan (W)	7,684	48.4
Midton (SOFT D & AM)	6,910	43.5
Aldrich (HARD D)	1,296	8.2
26 Andrew Oliver (SOFT D & AM)	6,880	48.0
Seeley	5,304	37.0
Howell (HARD D)	2,163	15.1
27 John M. Parker (W)	7,915	59.3
McDowell (SOFT D)	3,467	26.0
Cushing (HARD D)	1,964	14.7
28 William H. Kelsey (W & AM)	11,061	70.8
Hastings (SOFT D)	4,450	28.5
29 John Williams (SOFT D & AM)	5,609	47.9
Carpenter (W)	4,227	36.1
Sibley (HARD D)	1,865	15.9
30 Benjamin Pringle (W & AM)	9,510	57.6
Laning (SOFT D)	3,829	23.2
Belden (HARD D)	2,483	15.0
31 Thomas T. Flagler (W & AM)	7,190	76.6
Baker (HARD D)	1,231	13.1
Chase (F SOIL)	962	10.3

Candidates	Votes	%
32 Solomon G. Haven (W & AM)	9,075	62.8
Hatch (SOFT D)	5,388	37.3
33 Francis S. Edwards (W & AM)	8,359	55.6
Fenton (SOFT D)	6,442	42.8

OHIO

Candidates	Votes	%
1 Timothy C. Day (R)	7,716	63.5
George H. Pendleton (D)	4,442	36.5
2 John Scott Harrison (R)	7,562	66.0
Groek (D)	3,891	34.0
3 Lewis D. Campbell (R)	9,058	58.3
Valm (D)	6,493	41.8
4 Matthias H. Nicholas (R)	10,307	70.2
Dorsey (D)	4,377	29.8
5 Richard Mott (R)	8,253	61.6
Commager (D)	5,141	38.4
6 Jonas R. Emrie (R)	9,990	65.0
Ellison (D)	5,370	35.0
7 Aaron Harlan (R)	9,928	81.1
Hinkson (D)	2,307	18.9
8 Benjamin Stanton (R)	11,000	76.7
Dial (D)	3,350	23.3
9 Cooper K. Watson (R)	8,399	59.9
Plants (D)	5,618	40.1
10 Oscar F. Moore (R)	8,865	65.3
Davis (D)	4,706	34.7
11 Valentine B. Horton (R)	9,818	58.7
Smith (D)	6,907	41.3
12 Samuel Galloway (R)	9,698	60.3
Olds (D)	6,390	39.7
13 John Sherman (R)	8,617	59.8
Lindy (D)	5,794	40.2
14 Philemon Bliss (R)	8,788	59.3
Johnson (D)	6,041	40.7
15 William Sapp (R)	9,371	59.0
Dunbar (D)	6,516	41.0
16 Edward Ball (R)	7,265	58.9
Galighr (D)	5,072	41.1
17 Charles J. Albright (R)	8,332	58.1
Wire (D)	6,017	41.9
18 Benjamin F. Leiter (R)	8,738	63.4
Spalding (D)	5,053	36.6
19 Edward Wade (R)	7,699	71.4
Wilder (D)	3,079	28.6
20 Joshua R. Giddings (R)	6,972	64.8
Lee (D)	3,782	35.2
21 John A. Bingham (R)	9,860	65.3
Unidentified Candidate (D)	5,238	34.7

PENNSYLVANIA

Candidates	Votes	%
1 Thomas B. Florence (D)	6,439	51.8
Morris (W)	5,999	48.2
2 Job R. Tyson (W)	5,654	61.8
Haml (D)	3,500	38.2
3 William Millward (W)	5,888	51.6
Landy (D)	5,525	48.4
4 Jacob Broom (NAM)	6,747	53.0
Philps (D)	5,993	47.0
5 John Cadwalader (D)	7,842	50.0
Jones (W)	7,834	50.0
6 John Hickman (D)	8,733	59.0
Brooml (W)	6,077	41.0
7 Samuel C. Bradshaw (W)	8,527	51.0
Samuel A. Bridges (D)	8,182	49.0
8 J. Glancy Jones (D)	8,152	59.8
Myers (W)	5,486	40.2

Candidates	Votes	%
9 Anthony E. Roberts (W)	6,561	40.5
Hiester	5,371	33.2
Leferre	4,266	26.3
10 John C. Kunkel (W)	8,500	58.4
Bougtr (D)	6,049	41.6
11 James H. Campbell (W)	5,384	51.5
Dewart (D)	5,081	48.6
12 Henry M. Fuller (W)	9,115	56.3
Wright (D)	7,087	43.7
13 Asa Packer (D)	9,136	58.7
Stewart (W)	6,433	41.3
14 Galusha A. Grow (F SOIL D)		100.0
15 John J. Pierce (W)	9,588	56.0
White (D)	7,528	44.0
16 Lemuel Todd (W)	10,472	55.7
Booham (D)	8,319	44.3
17 David F. Robison (W)	9,641	51.7
Reilly (D)	9,025	48.4
18 John R. Edie (W)	8,423	72.4
Cresswl (D)	3,218	27.6
19 John Covode (W)	9,342	58.7
Drum (D)	6,585	41.3
20 Jonathan Knight (W)	9,912	56.8
Montgomery (D)	7,552	43.2
21 David Ritchie (W)	5,705	60.6
Shaler (D)	3,714	39.4
22 Samuel A. Purviance (W)	5,926	60.7
Palmer (D)	3,832	39.3
23 John Allison (W)	7,808	60.2
Trout (D)	5,172	39.9
24 David Barclay (D)	10,415	74.7
Arthurs (W)	3,527	25.3
25 John Dick (W)		100.0

Special Election

Candidates	Votes	%
8 J. Glancy Jones (D)	5,078	60.0
Keim (W)	3,382	40.0

SOUTH CAROLINA

Candidates	Votes	%
1 John McQueen (D)	5,154	67.4
Wilson	2,488	32.6
2 William Aiken (D)		100.0
3 Laurence M. Keitt (D)		100.0
4 Preston S. Brooks (SSR D)	6,118	66.7
Garlington	3,051	33.3
5 James L. Orr (D)		100.0
6 William W. Boyce (SSR D)		100.0

VERMONT

Candidates	Votes	%
1 James Meacham (W)	8,626	70.3
S. W. Jewett (D)	3,464	28.3
2 Justin S. Morrill (W)	8,380	50.2
J. W. D. Parker (D)	5,848	35.0
Oscar L. Shafter	2,473	14.8
3 Alvah Sabin (W)	7,862	68.4
W. Heywood (D)	3,608	31.4

WISCONSIN

Candidates	Votes	%
1 Daniel Wells Jr (D)	8,458	54.6
Spooner (R)	7,026	45.4
2 Cadwallader C. Washburn (R)	11,936	60.2
Hoyt (D)	7,894	39.8
3 Charles Billinghurst (R)	13,359	60.9
Macy (D)	8,596	39.2

1855 House Elections

ALABAMA

	Candidates	Votes	%
1	Percy Walker (AM)	5,656	52.4
	James A. Stallworth (D)	5,137	47.6
2	Eli S. Shorter (A-KN D)	6,718	55.0
	J. C. Alford (D)	5,490	45.0
3	James F. Dowdell (D)	6,327	52.2
	T. H. Watts (AM)	5,786	47.8
4	William R. Smith (AM)	4,984	61.1
	Sydenham Moore (D)	3,177	38.9
5	George S. Houston (D)	5,770	100.0
6	Williamson R. W. Cobb (D)	6,260	62.9
	J. M. Adams (A-KN I)	3,697	37.1
7	Sampson W. Harris (D)	6,990	57.3
	W. B. Martin (A-KN ID)	5,220	42.8

CONNECTICUT

	Candidates	Votes	%
1	Ezra Clark Jr (AM)	8,519	52.0
	Pratt (D)	7,852	48.0
2	John Woodruff (AM)	9,876	55.5
	Arld (D)	7,918	44.5
3	Sidney Dean (AM)	8,055	67.5
	White (D)	3,877	32.5
4	William W. Welch (AM)	9,701	55.7
	Noble (D)	7,702	44.3

GEORGIA

	Candidates	Votes	%
1	James L. Seward (D)	6,179	57.6
	Varnadoe (AM)	4,541	42.4
2	Martin J. Crawford (D)	7,746	52.0
	Hawkins (AM)	7,153	48.0
3	Robert P. Trippe (AM)	6,112	54.0
	Smith (D)	5,216	46.1
4	Hiram Warner (D)	6,883	50.3
	Hill (AM)	6,813	49.7
5	John H. Lumpkin (D)	11,290	58.6
	Tumlin (AM)	7,978	41.4
6	Howell Cobb (D)	9,203	63.8
	Franklin (AM)	5,227	36.2
7	Nathaniel G. Foster (AM)	4,792	51.1
	Stephens (D)	4,580	48.9
8	Alexander H. Stephens (D)	5,808	65.4
	Lamar (AM)	3,079	34.7

KENTUCKY

	Candidates	Votes	%
1	Henry C. Burnett (D)	9,323	62.0
	W. G. Hughes (AM)	5,708	38.0
2	John P. Campbell (AM)	7,533	55.3
	Samuel O. Peyton (D)	6,092	44.7
3	Warner L. Underwood (AM)	7,362	56.9
	James P. Bates (D)	5,580	43.1
4	Albert G. Talbott (D)	6,586	50.1
	F. T. Fox (AM)	6,570	49.9
5	Joshua H. Jewett (D)	7,076	51.6
	C. G. Wintersmith (AM)	6,628	48.4
6	John M. Elliott (D)	7,685	54.8
	George W. Dunlap (AM)	6,340	45.2
7	Humphrey Marshall (AM)	6,932	61.3
	William Preston (D)	4,378	38.7
8	Alexander Keith Marshall (AM)	7,039	56.0
	James O. Harrison (D)	5,536	44.0
9	Leander M. Cox (AM)	8,085	55.1
	R. H. Stanton (D)	6,598	44.9
10	Samuel F. Swope (AM)	7,490	51.7
	Henry C. Harris (D)	6,991	48.3

LOUISIANA

	Candidates	Votes	%
1	George Eustis Jr (AM)	2,588	53.4
	Albert Fabre (D)	2,258	46.6
2	Miles Taylor (D)	6,175	51.5
	Hunt (AM)	5,810	48.5
3	Thomas G. Davidson (D)	4,731	50.6
	Pond (AM)	4,616	49.4
4	John M. Sandidge (D)	8,942	58.1
	Lewis (AM)	6,461	42.0

MARYLAND

	Candidates	Votes	%
1	James A. Stewart (D)	6,173	51.3
	Dennis (AM)	5,868	48.7
2	James B. Ricaud (AM)	8,479	56.6
	Jacob Shower (D)	6,506	43.4
3	J. Morrison Harris (AM)	6,538	50.2
	Vansant (D)	6,484	49.8
4	H. Winter Davis (AM)	7,988	51.6
	May (D)	7,493	48.4
5	Henry W. Hoffman (AM)	8,320	52.4
	William T. Hamilton (D)	7,569	47.6
6	Thomas F. Bowie (D)	5,539	53.9
	Watkins (AM)	4,736	46.1

MASSACHUSETTS

Special Elections

	Candidates	Votes	%
10	Calvin C. Chaffee (AM)	4,716	36.0
	John W. Foster	4,349	33.2
	Haynes H. Chilson	3,317	25.3
	Edward Dickenson (W)	725	5.5

MISSISSIPPI

	Candidates	Votes	%
1	Daniel B. Wright (D)	6,547	56.4
	J. H. R. Taylor (AM)	5,055	43.6
2	Hendley S. Bennett (D)	4,229	51.9
	L. E. Housten (AM)	3,922	48.1
3	William Barksdale (D)	6,850	55.3
	Joseph B. Cobb (AM)	5,542	44.7
4	William A. Lake (W)	5,196	52.0
	Otho R. Singleton (D)	4,792	48.0
5	John A. Quitman (D)	5,887	58.5
	Giles M. Hillyer (W)	4,178	41.5

NEW HAMPSHIRE

	Candidates	Votes	%
1	James Pike (AM)	12,806	56.9
	Kittredge (D)	9,697	43.1
2	Mason W. Tappan (AM)	12,202	59.3
	Morrison (D)	8,392	40.8
3	Aaron H. Cragin (AM)	11,715	59.1
	Wheeler (D)	8,099	40.9

NORTH CAROLINA

	Candidates	Votes	%
1	Robert T. Paine (AM)	5,228	51.7
	Henry M. Shaw (D)	4,882	48.3
2	Thomas Ruffin (D)	6,739	66.1
	Thomas J. Latham (AM)	3,464	34.0
3	Warren Winslow (D)	5,929	54.9
	David Reid (AM)	4,863	45.1
4	Lawrence O'B. Branch (D)	6,794	61.7
	James B. Shepard (AM)	4,223	38.3
5	Edwin G. Reade (AM)	7,061	65.3
	John Kerr (W)	3,756	34.7

	Candidates	Votes	%
6	Richard C. Puryear (AM)	6,516	51.4
	Alfred M. Scales (D)	6,150	48.6
7	F. Burton Craige (D)	6,745	62.2
	Samuel N. Stowe (AM)	4,104	37.8
8	Thomas L. Clingman (D)	8,079	55.1
	Leander B. Carmichael (AM)	6,584	44.9

RHODE ISLAND

	Candidates	Votes	%
1	Nathaniel B. Durfee (AM)	5,004	72.9
	Thomas Davis (D)	1,576	23.0
2	Benjamin B. Thurston (AM)	4,359	87.9

TENNESSEE

	Candidates	Votes	%
1	Albert G. Watkins (D)	7,781	50.9
	Taylor (AM)	7,511	49.1
2	William H. Sneed (AM)	6,246	54.0
	Cummins (D)	5,327	46.0
3	Samuel A. Smith (D)	7,872	51.8
	Anderson (AM)	7,331	48.2
4	John H. Savage (D)	6,016	52.0
	Cullom (AM)	5,563	48.0
5	Charles Ready (AM)	7,069	91.8
	Keeble (D)	632	8.2
6	George W. Jones (D)	8,476	65.6
	Gordon (AM)	4,445	34.4
7	John V. Wright (D)	7,927	57.2
	Kendrick (AM)	5,922	42.8
8	Felix K. Zollicoffer (AM)	6,958	58.9
	Torbett (D)	4,857	41.1
9	Emerson Etheridge (AM)	7,952	51.8
	Freeman (D)	7,394	48.2
10	Thomas Rivers (AM)	5,860	53.3
	Currin (D)	5,136	46.7

TEXAS

	Candidates	Votes	%
1	Peter H. Bell (D)	10,342	50.1
	Hancock (AM)	10,311	49.9
2	Lemuel D. Evans (AM)	14,379	60.2
	Ward (D)	9,496	39.8

VIRGINIA

	Candidates	Votes	%
1	Thomas H. Bayly (D)		100.0
2	John S. Millson (D)	4,769	53.3
	Watts (AM)	4,180	46.7
3	John S. Caskie (D)	5,951	52.1
	Scott (AM)	5,466	47.9
4	William O. Goode (D)	1,163	63.8
	Tazewell (AM)	661	36.2
5	Thomas S. Bocock (D)	4,566	52.9
	Claiborne (AM)	4,073	47.2
6	Paulus Powell (D)	3,834	56.3
	Ligon (AM)	2,976	43.7
7	William Smith (D)		100.0
8	Charles J. Faulkner (D)	7,158	50.7
	Boteler (AM)	6,959	49.3
9	John Letcher (D)		100.0
10	Zedekiah Kidwell (D)	6,615	56.7
	Pendleton (AM)	5,059	43.3
11	John S. Carlisle (AM)	8,333	51.2
	Lewis (D)	7,942	48.8
12	Henry A. Edmundson (D)	7,492	54.0
	Staples (AM)	6,385	46.0
13	Fayette McMullen (D)	4,289	60.5
	Trigg (AM)	2,803	39.5

1856 House Elections

ARKANSAS

		Votes	%
1	Alfred B. Greenwood (D)	15,399	71.4
	Thomason (AM)	6,161	28.6
2	Edward A. Warren (D)	11,835	57.6
	Fowler (AM)	8,701	42.4

CALIFORNIA

		Votes	%
AL	Joseph C. McKibbin (D)	50,895✓	
	Charles L. Scott (D)	50,813✓	
	B. C. Whitman (AM)	36,078	
	A. B. Dibble (AM)	35,325	
	L. P. Rankin (R)	21,975	
	J. D. Turner (R)	21,164	

DELAWARE

		Votes	%
AL	William G. Whiteley (D)	8,111	56.1
	Elisha D. Cullen (AM)	6,360	44.0

FLORIDA

		Votes	%
AL	George S. Hawkins (D)	6,392	53.1
	James M. Baker (AM)	5,650	46.9

ILLINOIS

		Votes	%
1	Elihu B. Washburne (R)	18,070	72.6
	Richard S. S. Malony (D)	6,227	25.0
2	John F. Farnsworth (R)	21,518	67.2
	John Van Nortwick (D)	9,814	30.7
3	Owen Lovejoy (R)	19,068	59.4
	Osgood (D)	13,007	40.5
4	William Kellogg (R)	16,175	51.1
	James W. Davidson (D)	14,474	45.7
5	Isaac N. Morris (D)	12,059	53.7
	Jackson Grimshaw (R)	10,294	45.8
6	Thomas L. Harris (D)	14,196	54.0
	John Williams (R)	12,077	46.0
7	Aaron Shaw (D)	12,994	56.8
	Henry P. H. Bromwell (R)	9,878	43.2
8	Robert Smith (D)	11,299	60.1
	I. D. Lansing (R)	7,512	39.9
9	Samuel S. Marshall (D)	15,968	81.5
	Benjamin L. Wiley (R)	3,419	17.4

Special Elections

		Votes	%
5	Jacob C. Davis (D)	12,212	52.6
	Thomas C. Sharp (R)	8,182	35.2
	James B. Kyle	2,826	12.2
7	James C. Allen (D)	13,081	56.3
	William B. Archer (R)	10,136	43.7
8	I. L. D. Morrison (D)	10,756	55.8
	John Thomas (R)	8,231	42.7

INDIANA

		Votes	%
1	James Lockhart (D)	12,747	61.5
	Veach (R)	7,977	38.5
2	William H. English (D)	10,577	57.2
	Wilson (R)	7,927	42.8
3	James Hughes (D)	10,629	53.8
	Hendks (R)	9,113	46.2
4	James B. Foley (D)	10,451	53.7
	Cumback (R)	8,998	46.3
5	David Kilgore (R)	11,132	60.8
	Johnson (D)	7,183	39.2
6	James M. Gregg (D)	11,787	52.1
	Coburn (R)	10,840	47.9
7	John G. Davis (D)	11,137	53.9
	Usher (R)	9,529	46.1
8	James Wilson (R)	11,302	50.5
	Voorhees (D)	11,072	49.5
9	Schuyler Colfax (R)	12,921	52.1
	Stuart (D)	11,890	47.9

Candidates		Votes	%
10	Samuel Brenton (R)	10,699	51.7
	Lowry (D)	9,989	48.3
11	John U. Pettit (R)	11,235	51.8
	Garver (D)	10,443	48.2

IOWA

		Votes	%
1	Samuel R. Curtis (R)	18,065	50.2
	Augustus Hall (D)	17,110	47.5
2	Timothy Davis (R)	21,888	57.9
	Shepherd Leffler (D)	15,868	42.0

MAINE

		Votes	%
1	John M. Wood (R)	11,215	53.4
	Little (COALIT)	9,776	46.6
2	Charles J. Gilman (R)	12,953	57.3
	Pillsbury (COALIT)	9,670	42.7
3	Nehemiah Abbott (R)	10,562	56.1
	Ingalls (COALIT)	8,252	43.9
4	Freeman H. Morse (R)	13,750	65.0
	Bronson (COALIT)	7,378	35.0
5	Israel Washburn Jr (R)	12,517	60.1
	Sanborn (COALIT)	8,312	39.9
6	Stephen C. Foster (R)	8,503	52.9
	Wiswell (COALIT)	7,567	47.1

MASSACHUSETTS

		Votes	%
1	Robert B. Hall (R)	7,904	69.6
	Moses Bates Jr (D)	1,830	16.1
	Daniel Fisher (AM)	1,601	14.1
2	James Buffington (R)	11,658	72.4
	Charles R. Vickery (D)	3,314	20.6
	Danlus Dunbar (AM)	1,132	7.0
3	William L. Damrell (R)	10,433	61.5
	Arthur W. Austin (D)	5,077	29.9
	Alfred B. Ely (AM)	1,435	8.5
4	Linus B. Comins (R)	5,188	45.8
	Charles G. Greene (D)	4,431	39.1
	Benjamin F. Cooke (AM)	1,678	14.8
5	Anson Burlingame (AM)	6,582	50.2
	William Appleton (D & AM)	6,513	49.7
6	Timothy Davis (R)	10,044	69.4
	Ruth J. Lord (D)	3,214	22.2
	Benjamin Parley Poor (AM)	1,121	7.7
7	Nathaniel P. Banks (R)	10,814	61.9
	Isaac H. Wright (D)	4,593	26.3
	Isaac Storey (AM)	2,049	11.7
8	Chauncey L. Knapp (R)	9,616	67.4
	Benjamin F. Butler (D)	3,686	25.9
	Abiel L. Lewis (AM)	864	6.1
9	Eli Thayer (R)	8,920	53.7
	Alex DeWitt (AM)	4,414	26.6
	Nathaniel Wood (D)	2,987	18.0
10	Calvin C. Chaffee (R)	10,845	72.4
	William C. Fowler (D & AM)	4,081	27.2
11	Henry L. Dawes (R)	6,709	43.8
	Josiah D. Weston (D)	4,398	28.7
	Mark Trafton (AM)	4,194	27.4

MICHIGAN

		Votes	%
1	William A. Howard (R)	13,658	51.6
	George Lathrop (D)	12,791	48.4
2	Henry Waldron (R)	16,467	62.1
	John S. Barry (D)	10,064	37.9
3	David S. Walbridge (R)	23,970	59.6
	Flavius Littlejohn (D)	16,268	40.4
4	De Witt C. Leach (R)	18,715	55.2
	George W. Peck (D)	15,186	44.8

MISSOURI

		Votes	%
1	Francis P. Blair Jr (BENTON D)	6,035	43.8
	Kennett (AM)	5,549	40.3

Candidates		Votes	%
	Reynolds (D)	2,181	15.8
2	Thomas L. Anderson (AM)	8,876	52.1
	Richmond (D)	8,149	47.9
3	James S. Green (D)	10,126*	55.3
	Lindley (AM)	8,172	44.7
4	James Craig (D)	8,742	56.8
	Moss (AM)	6,274	40.8
5	Samuel H. Woodson (AM)	6,006	41.6
	Douglas (D)	4,684	32.4
	Price (BENTON D)	3,755	26.0
6	John S. Phelps (D)	9,718	58.1
	Emerson (AM)	6,911	41.3
7	Samuel Caruthers (D)	8,291	52.7
	Perryman (AM)	4,883	31.0
	Stevson (BENTON D)	2,556	16.3

Special Election

		Votes	%
5	Thomas P. Akers (AM)	6,569	55.8
	Jackson (D)	5,211	44.2

NEW JERSEY

		Votes	%
1	Isaiah D. Clawson (FUS)	9,673	56.8
	Hineline (D)	7,351	43.2
2	George R. Robbins (FUS)	11,723	52.3
	Wall (D)	10,692	47.7
3	Garnett B. Adrain (D)	10,781	52.5
	Bishop (FUS)	9,768	47.5
4	John Huyler (D)	9,165	52.7
	Osborne (R)	5,876	33.8
	Inglis (AM)	2,355	13.5
5	Jacob R. Wortendyke (D)	9,099	42.9
	Dodd (R)	6,480	30.5
	Betts (AM)	5,638	26.6

NEW YORK

		Votes	%
1	John A. Searing (D)	8,960	44.1
	Jennings (AM)	5,892	29.0
	Lord (R)	5,449	26.8
2	George Taylor (D)	8,591	40.8
	Stranhan (R)	5,869	27.9
	Wood (AM)	5,476	26.0
	McCue	1,123	5.3
3	Daniel E. Sickles (D)	5,716	53.2
	Duganne (AM)	2,905	27.0
	Guy R. Pelton (R)	2,126	19.8
4	John Kelly (D)	8,319	72.0
	Gould (AM)	1,735	15.0
	Ryckman (R)	1,497	13.0
5	William B. Maclay (D)	5,863	41.6
	Northp (AM)	3,798	26.9
	Andrews (R)	3,274	23.2
	Hamilton (ID)	1,169	8.3
6	John Cochrane (D)	7,531	49.6
	Stillman (R)	3,991	26.3
	Williams (AM)	3,658	24.1
7	Elijah Ward (D)	6,531	41.0
	Briggs (AM)	4,461	28.0
	Nye (R)	4,100	25.7
	Bulloc	854	5.4
8	Horace F. Clark (D)	7,482	50.2
	Abram Wakeman (R)	3,760	25.3
	Knapp (AM)	3,651	24.5
9	John B. Haskin (D)	7,195	39.5
	Strang (R)	5,935	32.6
	Cobb (AM)	5,084	27.9
10	Ambrose S. Murray (R)	6,156	39.3
	Fowler (D)	5,581	35.6
	Trotter (AM)	3,936	25.1
11	William F. Russell (D)	6,878	38.9
	Fream (R)	5,902	33.4
	Brodhd (R)	4,912	27.8
12	John Thompson (R)	9,247	45.5
	Chamberlain (D)	7,972	39.2

Candidates	Votes	%
Teller (AM)	3,116	15.3
13 Abram B. Olin (R)	5,206	37.0
Griswold (D)	4,758	33.8
Fonda (AM)	4,108	29.2
14 Erastus Corning (D)	8,296	46.0
Perry (AM)	5,095	28.3
Van Dyck (R)	4,631	25.7
15 Edward Dodd (R)	11,717	51.6
Cramer (D)	5,633	24.8
Gray (D)	5,373	23.7
16 George W. Palmer (R)	6,799	44.5
Averill (D)	4,363	28.5
Ross (AM)	4,129	27.0
17 Francis E. Spinner (R)	14,722	70.7
Dodge (D & AM)	6,115	29.4
18 Clark B. Cochrane (R)	9,719	44.6
Rossiter (D)	6,123	28.1
Smith (AM)	5,936	27.3
19 Oliver A. Morse (R)	10,724	54.7
Gregory (D & AM)	8,881	45.3
20 Orsamus B. Matteson (R)	10,618	56.2
Johnson (D & AM)	8,275	43.8
21 Henry Bennett (R)	13,357	62.0
Hyde (D & AM)	8,192	38.0
22 Henry C. Goodwin (R)	14,380	65.0
Clark (D)	6,080	27.5
Culver (AM)	1,671	7.6
23 Charles B. Hoard (R)	11,149	64.6
Dorwin (D)	6,070	35.2
24 Amos P. Granger (R)	9,748	61.0
Peck (D)	4,525	28.3
Beach (AM)	1,720	10.8
25 Edwin B. Morgan (R)	12,631	63.3
Richmond (D)	3,685	18.5
Fosgt (AM)	3,644	18.3
26 Emory B. Pottle (R)	9,368	53.0
Andrew Oliver (AM)	4,411	25.0
Ogden (D)	3,897	22.1
27 John M. Parker (R)	12,383	56.3
Hathaway (D)	8,377	38.1
Lawr (AM)	1,229	5.6
28 William H. Kelsey (R)	10,509	53.4
Hallett (AM)	4,895	24.9
Angel (D)	4,266	21.7
29 Samuel G. Andrews (R)	7,786	51.0
Paine (D)	4,337	28.4
Clark (AM)	3,156	20.7
30 Judson W. Sherman (R)	13,867	64.0
Richmond (D)	5,032	23.2
Cooly (AM)	2,758	12.7
31 Silas M. Burroughs (R)	6,885	51.7
Hunt (AM)	4,694	35.3
Church (D)	1,731	13.0
32 Israel T. Hatch (D)	7,399	37.2
Spaulding (R)	6,923	34.8
Haven (AM)	5,548	27.9
33 Reuben E. Fenton (R)	12,046	64.3
Allen (D)	3,436	18.3
Edwds (AM)	3,251	17.4

OHIO

Candidates	Votes	%
1 George H. Pendleton (D)	6,133	47.1
Taft (R)	4,256	32.7
Tornce (AM)	2,642	20.3
2 William S. Groesbeck (D)	5,738	43.1
Gurley (R)	4,343	32.6

Candidates	Votes	%
Harrison (AM)	3,229	24.3
3 Lewis D. Campbell (R)	9,338‡	50.1
Clement I. Vallandigham (D)	9,319	50.0
4 Mathias H. Nichols (R)	9,415	49.7
Dorsey (D)	9,172	48.4
5 Richard Mott (R)	10,018	51.0
Edgerton (D)	9,157	46.6
6 Joseph R. Cockerill (D)	8,603	48.7
Jonas R. Emrie (R)	7,460	42.2
Trimbel (AM)	1,598	9.1
7 Aaron Harlan (R)	9,027	59.7
Ward (D)	5,076	33.6
Elsbury (AM)	1,011	6.7
8 Benjamin Stanton (R)	9,756	56.7
Runkle (D)	6,210	36.1
Glover (AM)	1,239	7.2
9 Lawrence W. Hall (D)	9,561	49.7
Cooper K. Watson (R)	9,382	48.7
10 Joseph Miller (D)	7,403	42.6
Hoffman (R)	5,633	32.4
Oscar F. Moore (AM)	4,326	24.9
11 Valentine B. Horton (R)	10,272	50.9
Medill (D)	9,927	49.2
12 Samuel S. Cox (D)	8,938	48.7
Galloway (R)	8,582	46.7
13 John Sherman (R)	9,926	58.4
Bramback (D)	7,065	41.6
14 Philemon Bliss (R)	10,414	57.8
Firestone (D)	7,617	42.2
15 Joseph Burns (D)	9,194	50.1
Sapp (R)	9,143	49.9
16 Cydnor B. Tompkins (R)	7,248	48.0
Smith (D)	6,462	42.8
Haynes (AM)	1,382	9.2
17 William Lawrence (D)	8,085	47.8
Albright (R)	6,805	40.3
Davenport (AM)	2,013	11.9
18 Benjamin F. Leiter (R)	9,394	58.0
Lahm (D)	6,799	42.0
19 Edward Wade (R)	9,431	67.9
Hilliard (D)	4,467	32.1
20 Joshua R. Giddings (R)	9,567	66.6
Burchard (D)	4,795	33.4
21 John A. Bingham (R)	9,444	57.7
Woods (D)	6,933	42.3

PENNSYLVANIA

Candidates	Votes	%
1 Thomas B. Florence (D)	9,495	56.6
Knight (UN)	7,275	43.4
2 Edward Joy Morris (UN)	6,411	51.6
Marsll (D)	6,018	48.4
3 James Landy (D)	7,933	54.0
William Millward (UN)	6,753	46.0
4 Henry M. Phillips (D)	9,279	50.7
Forst (AM)	6,560	35.9
William D. Kelley (R)	2,457	13.4
5 Owen Jones (D)	9,674	54.9
Mulvany (UN)	7,961	45.1
6 John Hickman (D)	8,024	48.9
Bowen (UN)	7,851	47.9
7 Henry Chapman (D)	10,321	54.0
Bradshaw (UN)	8,789	46.0
8 J. Glancy Jones (D)	9,951	71.6
Yoder (UN)	3,947	28.4
9 Anthony E. Roberts (UN)	10,001	54.6
Heister (D)	8,320	45.4

Candidates	Votes	%
10 John C. Kunkel (UN)	9,227	55.6
Eyer (D)	7,360	44.4
11 William L. Dewart (D)	8,959	58.3
Campbell (UN)	6,418	41.7
12 John G. Montgomery (D)	10,442	57.7
Smith (UN)	7,657	42.3
13 William H. Dimmick (D)	11,235	68.9
E. S. Dimk (UN)	5,065	31.1
14 Galusha A. Grow (R)	13,325	71.3
Sherwd (D)	5,361	28.7
15 Allison White (D)	9,980	51.4
Irwin (UN)	9,450	48.6
16 John A. Ahl (D)	11,191	53.7
Todd (UN)	9,670	46.4
17 Wilson Reilly (D)	10,224	51.3
Pumroy (UN)	9,715	48.7
18 John R. Edie (UN)	8,792	50.8
Pershing (D)	8,508	49.2
19 John Covode (UN)	10,409	54.4
McKinley (D)	8,724	45.6
20 William Montgomery (D)	10,256	52.2
Knight (UN)	9,411	47.9
21 David Ritchie (R)	7,674	54.6
McCans (D)	5,944	42.3
22 Samuel A. Purviance (R)	6,840	57.1
Gibson (D)	4,854	40.5
23 William Stewart (UN)	8,552	61.0
Cunningham (D)	5,467	39.0
24 James L. Gillis (D)	9,785	51.8
Myers (UN)	9,114	48.2
25 John Dick (R)	8,944	68.0
McFadn (D)	4,215	32.0

SOUTH CAROLINA[1]

Candidates	Votes	%
1 John McQueen (D)		100.0
2 W. Porcher Miles (D)	2,323	50.5
James Gadsden	1,684	36.6
John Cunningham	590	12.8
3 Laurence M. Keitt (D)		100.0
4 Preston S. Brooks (SSR D)*		100.0
5 James L. Orr (D)		100.0
6 William W. Boyce (SSR D)		100.0

Special Elections

Candidates	Votes	%
3 Laurence M. Keitt (D)	✓	
4 Preston S. Brooks (SSR D)	7,922	100.0

VERMONT

Candidates	Votes	%
1 Eliakim Persons Walton (R)	10,398	76.2
Needhm (D)	3,242	23.8
2 Justin S. Morrill (R)	13,695	75.9
Chase (D)	4,358	24.1
3 Homer Elihu Royce (R)	9,116	74.4
William H. Bingham (D)	3,134	25.6

WISCONSIN

Candidates	Votes	%
1 John F. Potter (R)	13,111	50.6
Hadley (D)	12,814	49.4
2 Cadwallader C. Washburn (R)	26,004	61.6
Crawford (D)	16,233	38.4
3 Charles Billinghurst (R)	25,808	52.2
Hobart (D)	23,648	47.8

1. Preston S. Brooks of South Carolina's 4th district, who was serving in the 34th Congress (1855–1857) following his election in 1854, resigned July 14, 1856. He was subsequently reelected to the 34th Congress in a special election which appears on this page. He took his seat Aug. 1, 1856 and was reelected in the general election later in 1856 to the 35th Congress (1857–1859). He died Jan. 27, 1857, and thus did not serve in that Congress.

Laurence M. Keitt of the 3rd district was also serving in the 34th Congress when he resigned July 16, 1856. Subsequently reelected to the 34th Congress in the special election shown on this page to fill the vacancy caused by his resignation, he returned to the House Aug. 6, 1856. Later that year he was reelected to the 35th Congress in the general election.

1857 House Elections

ALABAMA

	Candidates	Votes	%
1	James A. Stallworth (D)	7,058	62.0
	J. McCaskill (AM)	4,330	38.0
2	Eli S. Shorter (D)	7,417	62.5
	B. Peterson (AM)	4,454	37.5
3	James F. Dowdell (D)	6,505	50.3
	T. J. Judge (SR W)	6,419	49.7
4	Sydenham Moore (D)	6,432	56.5
	W. R. Smith (AM)	4,952	43.5
5	George S. Houston (D)	4,853	55.1
	D. Hubbard (SO RTS D)	3,956	44.9
6	Williamson R. W. Cobb (D)	5,975	61.0
	Henry Sanford (AM)	3,594	36.7
7	Jabez L. M. Curry (D)	8,311	98.5

CONNECTICUT

	Candidates	Votes	%
1	Ezra Clark Jr (R)	8,410	51.3
	Hubbard (D)	7,973	48.7
2	Samuel Arnold (D)	9,403	51.4
	Woodruff (R)	8,906	48.6
3	Sidney Dean (R)	6,082	54.9
	Hovey (D)	5,006	45.2
4	William D. Bishop (D)	8,403	50.1
	Ferry (R)	8,387	50.0

GEORGIA

	Candidates	Votes	%
1	James L. Seward (D)	5,870	51.2
	Bartow (AM)	5,093	44.4
2	Martin J. Crawford (D)	8,220	56.4
	Elam (AM)	6,365	43.6
3	Robert P. Trippe (AM)	5,803	51.7
	Bailey (D)	5,423	48.3
4	Lucius J. Gartrell (D)	8,008	53.6
	Tidwell (AM)	6,939	46.4
5	Augustus R. Wright (D)	9,669	63.0
	Hooper (ID)	5,690	37.1
6	James Jackson (D)	7,751	56.6
	Simmons (ID)	5,956	43.5
7	Joshua Hill (AM)	4,800	51.5
	L. Stephens (D)	4,525	48.5
8	Alexander H. Stephens (D)	5,151	55.7
	Miller (AM)	4,096	44.3

KENTUCKY

	Candidates	Votes	%
1	Henry C. Burnett (D)	8,989	75.3
	Owen Grimes (AM)	2,945	24.7
2	Samuel O. Peyton (D)	7,212	53.9
	James L. Johnson (AM)	6,173	46.1
3	Warner L. Underwood (AM)	6,359	50.8
	Joseph H. Lewis (D)	6,156	49.2
4	Albert G. Talbott (D)	7,025	50.6
	William C. Anderson (AM)	6,861	49.4
5	Joshua H. Jewett (D)	7,377	59.6
	Bryan R. Young (AM)	4,996	40.4
6	John M. Elliott (D)	7,470	55.7
	John A. Moore (AM)	5,950	44.3
7	Humphrey Marshall (AM)	6,085	55.0
	Thomas H. Holt (D)	4,979	45.0
8	James B. Clay (D)	6,577	50.5
	Roger W. Hanson (AM)	6,451	49.5
9	John C. Mason (D)	8,148	52.0
	Leander M. Cox (AM)	7,534	48.0
10	John W. Stevenson (D)	8,748	67.3
	William Rankin (AM)	4,185	32.2

LOUISIANA

	Candidates	Votes	%
1	George Eustis Jr (AM)	2,336	60.5
	Villiers (D)	1,528	39.5
2	Miles Taylor (D)	4,950	50.3
	Burke (AM)	4,892	49.7
3	Thomas G. Davidson (D)	4,270	54.9
	Watrsn (AM)	3,512	45.1
4	John M. Sandidge (D)	9,060	63.5
	Sparks (AM)	5,205	36.5

MARYLAND

	Candidates	Votes	%
1	James A. Stewart (D)	6,339	50.7
	Townsend (AM)	6,163	49.3
2	James B. Ricaud (AM)	8,701	52.3
	McHenry (D)	7,935	47.7
3	J. Morrison Harris (AM)	8,761	61.6
	William Pinkney Whyte (D)	5,455	38.4
4	H. Winter Davis (AM)	10,515	72.6
	Henry P. Brooks (D)	3,979	27.5
5	Jacob M. Kunkel (D)	8,376	50.5
	Hoffman (AM)	8,208	49.5
6	Thomas F. Bowie (D)	5,735	56.3
	Blackistone (AM)	4,453	43.7

MINNESOTA

(Became a state May 11, 1858)

	Candidates	Votes	%
AL	William W. Phelps (D)	18,218✓	
	James M. Cavanaugh (D)	18,064✓	
	G. L. Becker (D)	18,019	
	C. Aldrich (R)	16,955	
	M. S. Wilkinson (R)	16,938	
	H. A. Swift (R)	16,827	

MISSISSIPPI

	Candidates	Votes	%
1	Lucius Q. C. Lamar (D)	3,705	61.8
	James L. Alcorn (W)	2,288	38.2
2	Reuben Davis (D)	5,026	59.4
	Charles Clark (W)	3,431	40.6
3	William Barksdale (D)	5,129	97.7
4	Otho R. Singleton (D)	5,940	54.3
	William A. Lake (W)	4,997	45.7
5	John A. Quitman (D)	4,017	98.1

NEW HAMPSHIRE

	Candidates	Votes	%
1	James Pike (R)	12,242	52.2
	Kittridge (D)	11,206	47.8
2	Mason W. Tappan (R)	10,685	53.8
	Morrison (D)	9,180	46.2
3	Aaron H. Cragin (R)	10,983	52.7
	Wheeler (D)	9,841	47.3

NORTH CAROLINA

	Candidates	Votes	%
1	Henry M. Shaw (D)	5,293	50.2
	William N. H. Smith (AM)	5,255	49.8
2	Thomas Ruffin (D)	5,940	90.6
3	Warren Winslow (D)	6,337	81.0
	O. P. Meares (AM)	1,488	19.0
4	Lawrence O'B. Branch (D)	7,375	87.0
5	John A. Gilmer (AM)	5,692	54.0
	Stephen W. Williams (D)	4,845	46.0
6	Alfred M. Scales (D)	7,679	52.5
	Richard C. Puryear (AM)	6,950	47.5
7	F. Burton Craige (D)	6,482	92.2
8	Thomas L. Clingman (D)	8,674	69.8

PENNSYLVANIA

Special Election

	Candidates	Votes	%
12	Paul Leidy (D)	9,826	61.0

	Candidates	Votes	%
	Smith Thompson (R)	6,294	39.0

RHODE ISLAND

	Candidates	Votes	%
1	Nathaniel B. Durfee (R)	5,442	73.3
	Ambrose E. Burnside (D)	1,961	26.4
2	William D. Brayton (AM & R)	3,933	54.4
	Charles Jackson (D)	3,209	44.4

SOUTH CAROLINA

Special Elections

	Candidates	Votes	%
4	Milledge L. Bonham (SSR D)	3,646	63.5
	C. P. Sullivan	2,093	36.5

TENNESSEE

	Candidates	Votes	%
1	Albert G. Watkins (D)	7,647	50.6
	Taylor (AM)	7,471	49.4
2	Horace Maynard (AM)	5,565	50.9
	Wallace (D)	5,360	49.1
3	Samuel A. Smith (D)	7,662	53.0
	Heiskell (AM)	6,800	47.0
4	John H. Savage (D)	6,435	55.2
	Pickett (AM)	5,232	44.8
5	Charles Ready (AM)	6,151	51.3
	Guild (D)	5,851	48.8
6	George W. Jones (D)	8,516	100.0
7	John V. Wright (D)	8,620	83.8
	McElrath (AM)	1,665	16.2
8	Felix K. Zollicoffer (AM)	6,088	52.2
	James M. Quarles (D)	5,580	47.8
9	John D. C. Atkins (D)	8,603	50.4
	Etheridge (AM)	8,474	49.6
10	William T. Avery (D)	6,006	51.3
	Stevens (AM)	5,707	48.7

TEXAS

	Candidates	Votes	%
1	John H. Reagan (D)	15,799	61.0
	Evans (AM)	10,085	39.0
2	Guy M. Bryan (D)	21,142	80.8
	Howth (AM)	5,013	19.2

VIRGINIA

	Candidates	Votes	%
1	Muscoe R. H. Garnett (D)	1,881	60.5
	Critcher (AM)	1,226	39.5
2	John S. Millson (D)		100.0
3	John S. Caskie (D)	5,148	63.7
	Crane (AM)	2,931	36.3
4	William O. Goode (D)	3,579	76.0
	Collier (AM)	1,132	24.0
5	Thomas S. Bocock (D)		100.0
6	Paulus Powell (D)		100.0
7	William Smith (D)	5,332	57.5
	Snowdon (AM)	3,941	42.5
8	Charles J. Faulkner (D)	6,631	59.5
	Lucas (AM)	4,516	40.5
9	John Letcher (D)		100.0
10	Sherrard Clemens (D)	7,074	71.5
	Dunngton (AM)	2,821	28.5
11	Albert G. Jenkins (D)	7,758	53.8
	Carlisle (AM)	6,653	46.2
12	Henry A. Edmundson (D)		100.0
13	George W. Hopkins (D)	5,318	50.3
	Martin (AM)	5,249	49.7

1858 House Elections

ARKANSAS

	Candidates	Votes	%
1	Thomas C. Hindman (D)	19,146	87.0
	W. M. Crosby (AM)	2,864	13.0
2	Albert Rust (D)	16,302	70.3
	Thomas S. Drew (ID)	3,780	16.3
	James A. Jones (AM)	3,106	13.4

CALIFORNIA[1]

AL	Joseph C. McKibbin (A-LEC DR)	32,102*	
	W. L. Dudley (A-LEC D)	22,782*	
	L. L. Tracy (R)	9,381	

DELAWARE

AL	William G. Whiteley (D)	7,868	51.4
	Morris	7,452	48.6

FLORIDA

AL	George S. Hawkins (D)	6,465	61.4
	Westcott (ID)	4,070	38.6

ILLINOIS

	Candidates	Votes	%
1	Elihu B. Washburne (R)	15,811	69.8
	Hiram Bright (D)	6,457	28.5
2	John F. Farnsworth (R)	21,797	61.1
	Thomas Dyer (D)	13,198	37.0
3	Owen Lovejoy (R)	22,313	57.7
	George W. Armstrong (D)	14,988	38.8
4	William Kellogg (R)	19,487	52.8
	James W. Davidson (D)	16,860	45.7
5	Isaac N. Morris (D)	13,529	52.7
	Jackson Grimshaw (R)	11,648	45.4
6	Thomas L. Harris (D)	16,193*	57.6
	James N. Mathews (R)	11,646	41.4
7	James C. Robinson (D)	13,588	53.5
	Richard J. Oglesby (R)	11,760	46.3
8	Phillip B. Fouke (D)	11,490	57.2
	John Baker (R)	8,410	41.8
9	John A. Logan (D)	15,878	84.2
	David L. Phillips (R)	2,796	14.8

INDIANA

1	William E. Niblack (D)	10,329	53.6
	Hovey (A-LEC D)	8,946	46.4
2	William H. English (D)	9,293	55.6
	Wilson (R)	7,434	44.4
3	William McKee Dunn (R)	9,363	52.8
	Hughes (D)	8,385	47.2
4	William S. Holman (D)	9,425	54.5
	Hackleman (R)	7,856	45.5
5	David Kilgore (R)	9,383	61.3
	Devlin (D)	5,921	38.7
6	Albert G. Porter (R)	10,776	52.6
	Rar (D)	9,716	47.4
7	John G. Davis (A-LEC D)	10,893	59.0
	Sect (D)	7,584	41.1
8	James Wilson (R)	11,028	51.5
	Blake (D)	10,387	48.5
9	Schuyler Colfax (R)	14,541	53.6
	Walker (D)	12,610	46.4
10	Charles Case (R)	10,780	53.4
	Dawson (D)	9,417	46.6
11	John U. Pettit (R)	10,748	51.7
	Coffroth (D)	10,038	48.3

IOWA

1	Samuel R. Curtis (R)	23,529	50.7
	Henry H. Trimble (D)	22,929	49.4
2	William Vandever (R)	25,503	52.8
	William E. Leffingwell (D)	22,764	47.2

MAINE

	Candidates	Votes	%
1	Daniel E. Somes (R)	10,410	50.6
	Drew (D)	9,955	48.4
2	John J. Perry (R)	12,031	54.5
	Hastings (D)	10,032	45.5
3	Ezra B. French (R)	8,994	50.2
	Johnson (D)	8,931	49.8
4	Freeman H. Morse (R)	10,552	60.1
	Gile (D)	6,990	39.8
5	Israel Washburn Jr (R)	10,300	55.7
	Wiley (D)	8,184	44.3
6	Stephen C. Foster (R)	8,297	51.5
	Bradbury (D)	7,804	48.5

MASSACHUSETTS

1	Thomas D. Eliot (R)	4,854	72.6
	Moses Bates Jr. (D)	1,709	25.6
2	James Buffington (R)	7,385	71.4
	John Wilson (D)	2,941	28.5
3	Charles F. Adams (R)	6,524	54.9
	Authur W. Austin (D)	3,880	32.6
	Moses G. Cobb (AM)	1,462	12.3
4	Alexander H. Rice (R)	4,507	47.7
	Samuel W. Waldron (D)	3,511	37.2
	Newell A. Thompson (AM)	1,396	14.8
5	Anson Burlingame (R)	6,214	51.5
	John F. Heard (D)	5,823	48.2
6	John B. Alley (R)	5,587	52.0
	Otis P. Lord (AM)	3,017	28.1
	George B. Loring (D)	2,116	19.7
7	Daniel W. Gooch (R)	7,129	60.3
	Charles A. Welch (R)	3,868	32.7
	Elihu C. Baker (AM)	810	6.9
8	Charles R. Train (R)	6,196	58.9
	Benjamin F. Butler (D)	3,514	33.4
	Josiah H. Temple (AM)	576	5.5
9	Eli Thayer (R)	7,280	70.9
	Nathaniel Wood (D)	2,962	28.8
10	Charles Delano (R)	6,847	64.1
	Charles Osgood (D)	3,276	30.7
11	Henry L. Dawes (R)	7,631	60.8
	Thomas F. Plunkett (D)	4,911	39.1

Special Election

7	Daniel W. Gooch (R)	4,168	61.5
	George Ashborne	2,162	31.9

MICHIGAN

1	George B. Cooper (D)	13,123‡	50.1
	William A. Howard (R)	13,048	49.8
2	Henry Waldron (R)	14,655	59.1
	Consider A. Stacy (D)	10,138	40.9
3	Francis W. Kellogg (R)	21,952	55.7
	Thomas B. Church (D)	17,438	44.3
4	DeWitt C. Leach (R)	16,193	51.7
	Robert W. Davis (D)	15,120	48.3

MISSOURI

1	John R. Barrett (D)	7,057‡	36.5
	Francis P. Blair Jr. (R)	6,631	34.3
	Buck (AM)	5,668	29.3
2	Thomas L. Anderson (ID)	10,902	64.2
	Hendern (D)	6,089	35.8
3	John B. Clark (D)	16,846	100.0
4	James Craig (D)	12,439	61.4
	Adams	7,824	38.6
5	Samuel H. Woodson (AM)	7,942	53.3
	Reid (D)	6,947	46.7
6	John S. Phelps (D)	13,424	62.5
	Richardson	8,050	37.5
7	John W. Noeli (D)	10,404	64.2

Candidates	Votes	%
Zeigler	5,808	35.8

NEW JERSEY

1	John T. Nixon (R)	8,393	48.0
	Walker (D)	5,342	30.6
	Jones (AM)	3,739	21.4
2	John L. N. Stratton (R)	11,471	56.7
	Wall (D)	8,767	43.3
3	Garnett B. Adrain (R)	9,713	51.2
	Paterson (D)	9,255	48.8
4	Jetur R. Riggs (A-LEC D)	8,837	52.0
	Huyler (D)	8,154	48.0
5	William Pennington (R)	11,641	53.8
	Wortendyke (D)	9,982	46.2

NEW YORK

1	Luther C. Carter (R AM)	8,122	52.5
	John A. Searing (D)	7,339	47.5
2	James Humphrey (R AM)	6,475	36.8
	Litchfield (ID)	5,581	31.7
	Taylor (D)	4,578	26.0
	Backhouse (AM)	974	5.5
3	Daniel E. Sickles (D)	3,177	35.0
	Amor J. Williamson (R AM)	3,015	33.3
	Walbe (ID)	2,874	31.7
4	Thomas J. Barr (ID)	3,949	39.7
	Stephens (D)	2,671	26.8
	Brennau (R)	2,290	23.0
	Farmer (D)	710	7.1
5	William B. Maclay (D)	5,780	49.8
	Hamilton (R AM)	4,982	42.9
	Dean (AM)	821	7.1
6	John Cochrane (D)	7,336	57.1
	McCurdy (R AM)	5,520	42.9
7	George Briggs (R AM)	8,306	55.8
	Ward (D)	6,591	44.2
8	Horace F. Clark (R AM)	9,035	58.8
	Herrick (D)	6,338	41.2
9	John B. Haskin (R AM)	7,637	48.3
	Kemble (D)	7,624	48.2
10	Charles H. Van Wyck (R)	6,681	48.4
	Niven (D)	5,532	40.1
	Friend (ID)	1,587	11.5
11	William S. Kenyon (R AM)	8,166	50.3
	Strong (D)	8,067	49.7
12	Charles L. Beale (R AM)	10,750	56.2
	McClellan (D)	8,385	43.8
13	Abram B. Olin (R AM)	8,267	61.1
	Seymour (D)	5,254	38.9
14	John H. Reynolds (R AM)	9,571	52.0
	Erastus Corning (D)	8,371	46.0
15	James B. McKean (R)	11,428	53.8
	Odell (D)	9,808	46.2
16	George W. Palmer (R)	7,058	47.9
	Waldo (D)	6,079	41.3
	Watson (AM)	1,589	10.8
17	Francis E. Spinner (R)	12,582	68.7
	Goodrich (D)	5,737	31.3
18	Clark B. Cochrane (R AM)	10,581	53.2
	Goodyear (D)	9,320	46.8
19	James H. Graham (R)	9,981	55.1
	Parker (D)	8,142	44.9
20	Roscoe Conkling (R)	11,084	57.3
	Root (D)	8,251	42.7
21	R. Holland Duell (R)	10,951	57.3
	Sands (D)	8,147	42.7
22	M. Lindley Lee (R)	11,450	57.4
	Asher Tyler (D)	7,425	37.2
	Perry (AM)	1,065	5.3
23	Charles B. Hoard (R)	9,162	56.1
	Lyon (D)	7,177	43.9
24	Charles B. Sedgwick (R)	8,478	55.1
	Taylor (D)	6,267	40.7
25	Martin Butterfield (R)	10,855	60.7

Candidates	Votes	%
Griswold (D)	5,389	30.2
Sisson (AM)	1,631	9.1
26 Emory B. Pottle (R)	8,598	54.5
Ogden (D)	7,173	45.5
27 Alfred Wells (R)	10,131	49.2
Arnot (D)	9,788	47.5
28 William Irvine (R)	9,382	53.3
Bradley (D)	6,568	37.3
Denston (AM)	1,651	9.4
29 Alfred Ely (R)	7,276	52.8
Trimmer (D)	5,114	37.1
Angle (AM)	1,393	10.1
30 Augustus Frank (R)	9,917	56.6
Skinner (D)	5,355	30.5
Black (AM)	2,264	12.9
31 Silas M. Burroughs (R)	6,093	52.5
Trott (D)	3,376	29.1
White (AM)	2,132	18.4
32 Elbridge G. Spaulding (R AM)	12,427	62.2
Hatch (D)	7,539	37.8
33 Reuben E. Fenton (R)	10,018	60.3
Jenks (D)	4,711	28.4
Johnn (AM)	1,886	11.4

NORTH CAROLINA

Special Election

8 Zebulon B. Vance (AM)	8,321	57.0
William W. Avery (D)	6,272	43.0

OHIO

1 George H. Pendleton (D)	7,131	51.2
Day (R)	6,785	48.8
2 John A. Gurley (R)	8,054	52.6
Groesbeck (D)	7,263	47.4
3 Clement L. Vallandigham (D)	9,903	50.5
Campbell (R)	9,715	49.5
4 William Allen (D)	9,558	50.5
Nichols (R)	9,371	49.5
5 James M. Ashley (R)	10,532	51.2
Mungen (D)	9,986	48.5
6 William Howard (D)	7,792	51.6
Clark (R)	6,922	45.8
7 Thomas Corwin (R)	8,866	63.9
Blair (D)	5,020	36.2
8 Benjamin Stanton (R)	8,716	59.5
Hubbard (D)	5,928	40.5
9 John Carey (R)	9,304	50.3
Hall (D)	9,197	49.7
10 Carey A. Trimble (R)	10,592	55.1
Joseph Miller (D)	8,643	44.9
11 Charles D. Martin (D)	9,723	50.7
Nelson H. Van Vorhes (R)	9,446	49.3
12 Samuel S. Cox (D)	9,560	51.8
Case (R)	8,913	48.3
13 John Sherman (R)	9,426	57.1

Candidates	Votes	%
Patrick (D)	7,095	43.0
14 Cyrus Spink (R)	9,438	56.3
Jeffries (D)	7,318	43.7
15 William Helmick (R)	8,949	50.7
Burns (D)	8,719	49.4
16 Cydnor B. Tomkins (R)	7,677	52.8
Money (D)	6,855	47.2
17 Thomas C. Theaker (R)	7,311	50.3
Spriggs (D)	7,219	49.7
18 Sidney Edgerton (R)	8,184	53.3
Ranney (D)	7,162	46.7
19 Edward Wade (R)	8,557	65.1
Gray (D)	4,597	35.0
20 John Hutchins (R)	8,321	62.8
Tod (D)	4,541	34.3
21 John A. Bingham (R)	8,883	57.5
Mans (D)	6,577	42.5

OREGON

(Became a state Feb. 14, 1859)

AL La Fayette Grover (D)	5,859	57.9
James K. Kelley (OPP)	4,210	41.6

PENNSYLVANIA

1 Thomas B. Florence (D)	6,823	43.3
Ryan (UN)	6,492	41.2
Nebg (A-LEC D)	2,442	15.5
2 Edward Joy Morris (UN)	5,653	58.4
Martin (D)	4,030	41.6
3 John P. Verree (UN)	6,977	54.2
Landy (D)	5,834	45.4
4 William Millward (UN)	9,749	59.3
Phillips (D)	6,451	39.2
5 John Wood (UN)	9,701	57.4
Jones (D)	7,209	42.6
6 John Hickman (A-LEC D)	6,786	40.8
Manley (D)	5,185	31.2
Broomall (UN)	4,676	28.1
7 Henry C. Longnecker (UN)	8,324	50.8
Roberts (D)	8,076	49.2
8 John Schwartz (UN)	7,321	50.1
Jones (D)	7,302	49.9
9 Thaddeus Stevens (UN)	9,513	60.0
Hopkins (D)	6,341	40.0
10 John W. Killinger (UN)	8,897	61.4
Weidle (D)	5,589	38.6
11 James H. Campbell (UN)	7,153	47.2
Dewart (D)	4,387	29.0
Cake (A-LEC D)	3,614	23.9
12 George W. Scranton (UN)	10,023	61.8
McReynolds (D)	6,186	38.2
13 William H. Dimmick (D)	8,009	55.0
Shoemaker (UN)	6,566	45.1
14 Galusha A. Grow (UN)	11,165	76.9
Parkhurst (D)	3,359	23.1

Candidates	Votes	%
15 James T. Hale (UN)	9,238	55.7
Allison White (D)	7,349	44.3
16 Benjamin F. Junkin (UN)	8,646	50.1
Fisher (D)	8,600	49.9
17 Edward McPherson (UN)	9,348	50.7
Reilly (D)	9,081	49.3
18 Samuel S. Blair (UN)	9,114	57.7
Pershing (D)	6,679	42.3
19 John Covode (UN)	9,257	53.1
Foster (D)	8,165	46.9
20 William Montgomery (D)	9,254	61.5
Knight (UN)	5,798	38.5
21 James K. Moorhead (UN)	6,539	57.3
Burke (D)	4,879	42.7
22 Robert McKnight (UN)	5,438	55.3
Williams (A-TAX)	3,903	39.7
Birmingham (D)	502	5.1
23 William Stewart (UN)	6,721	64.0
McGuffin (D)	3,777	36.0
24 Chapin Hall (UN)	8,905	52.3
Gillis (D)	8,111	47.7
25 Elijah Babbitt (UN)	6,360	60.7
Marshall (D)	4,113	39.3

Special Election

8 William H. Keim (R)	6,156	52.0
Wanner (D)	5,687	48.0

SOUTH CAROLINA

1 John McQueen (D)		100.0
2 William P. Miles (D)		100.0
3 Lawrence M. Keitt (D)		100.0
4 Milledge L. Bonham (SSR D)		100.0
5 John D. Ashmore (D)	7,198	59.4
Thomas O. P. Vernon	4,926	40.6
6 William W. Boyce (SSR D)		100.0

VERMONT

1 Eliakim P. Walton (R)	9,615	72.9
Eastman (D)	3,577	27.1
2 Justin S. Morrill (R)	11,576	70.7
Chase (D)	4,806	29.3
3 Homer E. Royce (R)	7,418	69.3
Bingham (D)	3,280	30.7

WISCONSIN

1 John F. Potter (R)	14,428	56.4
Brown (D)	11,171	43.6
2 Cadwallader C. Washburn (R)	23,917	54.3
Dunn (D)	20,167	45.8
3 Charles H. Larrabee (D)	23,910	51.0
Billinghurst (R)	23,011	49.0

1. The *California Blue Book* reports that the California election to the House of Representatives for the 36th Congress was in 1859, not 1858 as reported here by ICPSR. The vote according to the Blue Book was as follows:

AL John C. Burch (LEC D)	57,665	28.4
Charles L. Scott (LEC D)	56,998	28.1
Joseph C. McKibben (A-LEC D)	43,474	21.4
Edward D. Baker (R)	41,438	20.4

This corresponds to the *Biographical Directory*, which lists Burch and Scott as representing California in the House from 1859–1861.

1859 House Elections

ALABAMA

	Candidates	Votes	%
1	James A. Stallworth (D)	7,352	63.3
	F. B. Shepard (SEC D)	4,258	36.7
2	James L. Pugh (D)	2,643	81.1
	J. E. Sappington (SO RTS)	615	18.9
3	David Clopton (D)	6,879	50.8
	T. J. Judge (SR W)	6,666	49.2
4	Sydenham Moore (D)	1,648	96.9
5	George S. Houston (D)	5,964	58.1
	W. A. Hewlett (D)	4,298	41.9
6	Williamson R. W. Cobb (D)	5,731	55.0
	Alex Snodgrass (D)	2,112	20.3
	Edwin Wallace	1,885	18.1
	H. R. Beaver	695	6.7
7	Jabez L. M. Curry (SO RTS D)	✓	

CONNECTICUT

		Votes	%
1	Dwight Loomis (R)	9,940	49.6
	Alvan P. Hyde (D)	9,875	49.3
2	John Woodruff (R)	10,669	50.6
	Samuel Arnold (D)	10,347	49.0
3	Alfred A. Burnham (R)	7,586	51.7
	Rufus L. Baker (D)	6,883	47.0
4	Orris S. Ferry (R)	11,536	51.3
	William D. Bishop (D)	10,966	48.7

GEORGIA

		Votes	%
1	Peter E. Love (D)	7,253	65.1
	McIntyre (OPP)	3,881	34.9
2	Martin J. Crawford (D)	8,279	56.3
	Douglas (OPP)	6,437	43.7
3	Thomas Hardman (OPP)	5,636	50.7
	Speer (D)	5,483	49.3
4	Lucius J. Gartrell (D)	8,877	59.5
	Wright (OPP)	6,053	40.5
5	John W. H. Underwood (D)	12,339	85.1
	Shackleford (OPP)	2,162	14.9
6	James Jackson (D)	9,644	74.8
	Lytle (OPP)	3,251	25.2
7	Joshua Hill (OPP)	4,492	50.8
	Harper (D)	4,353	49.2
8	John J. Jones (D)	4,912	52.2
	Wright (OPP)	4,507	47.9

ILLINOIS[1]

Special Elections

		Votes	%
6	Charles D. Hodges (D)	11,014	61.1
	James C. Coukling	6,951	38.6
6	John A. McClernand (D)	14,337	58.9
	John M. Palmer	10,001	41.1

KENTUCKY

		Votes	%
1	Henry C. Burnett (D)	11,540	83.7
	William Morrow	2,248	16.3
2	Samuel O. Peyton (D)	7,939	52.4
	James S. Jackson (UNT)	7,199	47.6
3	Francis M. Bristow	7,164	56.2
	W. W. Sale (D)	5,575	43.8
4	William C. Anderson (AM)	7,204	50.0
	James S. Chrisman (D)	7,201	50.0
5	John Young Brown (D)	6,927	57.8
	J. H. Jewett (ID)	5,066	42.2
6	Green Adams (AM)	8,164	53.0
	T. T. Garrard (D)	7,231	47.0
7	Robert Mallory (UN D)	6,416	53.1
	Thomas Holt (D)	5,675	46.9
8	William E. Simms (D)	6,932	50.2
	John M. Harlan	6,865	49.8
9	Laban T. Moore (N AM)	8,505	50.8
	James W. Moore (D)	8,227	49.2

	Candidates	Votes	%
10	John W. Stevenson (D)	9,295	61.4
	Thomas L. Jones	5,839	38.6

LOUISIANA

		Votes	%
1	John E. Bouligny (OPP)	2,215	55.2
	Emile LaSere (D)	1,796	44.8
2	Miles Taylor (D)	5,908	57.0
	Nichols (OPP)	4,459	43.0
3	Thomas G. Davidson (D)	6,288	89.7
	Cannon (OPP)	726	10.4
4	John M. Landrum (D)	8,823	73.3
	Jones (OPP)	3,220	26.7

MARYLAND

		Votes	%
1	James A. Stewart (D)	6,934	52.1
	Cox (AM)	6,384	47.9
2	Edwin H. Webster (AM)	9,237	52.0
	McHenry (D)	8,518	48.0
3	J. Morrison Harris (AM)	9,612	69.5
	William P. Preston (D)	4,224	30.5
4	H. Winter Davis (AM)	10,068	78.3
	William G. Harrison (I)	2,796	21.7
5	Jacob M. Kunkel (D)	8,852	50.4
	Hoffman (AM)	8,719	49.6
6	George W. Hughes (D)	6,337	54.2
	Hagner (I)	5,353	45.8

MINNESOTA

		Votes	%
AL	Cyrus Aldrich (R)	21,360✓	
	William Windom (R)	21,016✓	
	James M. Cavanaugh (D)	17,666	
	Graham (D)	17,514	

MISSISSIPPI

		Votes	%
1	L. Q. C. Lamar (D)	4,140	97.8
2	Reuben Davis (D)	7,555	96.3
3	William Barksdale (D)	6,699	100.0
4	Otho R. Singleton (D)	6,686	74.7
	Frank Smith (UN D)	2,262	25.3
5	John L. McRae (D)	4,567	89.8
	G. W. Wilcox	517	10.2

NEW HAMPSHIRE

		Votes	%
1	Gilman Marston (R)	12,839	51.5
	Marcy (D)	12,082	48.5
2	Mason W. Tappan (R)	11,288	52.5
	George (D)	10,228	47.5
3	Thomas M. Edwards (R)	11,717	52.4
	Burns (D)	10,639	47.6

NORTH CAROLINA

		Votes	%
1	William N. H. Smith (OPP D)	6,045	52.2
	Henry M. Shaw (D)	5,531	47.8
2	Thomas Ruffin (D)	4,382	90.2
3	Warren Winslow (D)	4,774	78.8
	Malcom J. McDuffie (D & AM)	1,284	21.2
4	Lawrence O'B. Branch (D)	5,764	70.2
	Linn B. Sanders (OPP D)	2,446	29.8
5	John A. Gilmer (OPP D)	6,361	58.1
	Stephen E. Williams (D)	4,512	41.2
6	James M. Leach (OPP D)	8,566	52.8
	Alfred M. Scales (D)	7,664	47.2
7	F. Burton Craige (D)	5,495	57.4
	Samuel H. Walkup (OPP D)	4,075	42.6
8	Zebulon B. Vance (OPP D)	8,026	55.9
	David Coleman (D)	6,331	44.1

OREGON

		Votes	%
AL	Lansing Stout (D)	5,646	50.1

	Candidates	Votes	%
	David Logan (R)	5,630	49.9

RHODE ISLAND[2]

		Votes	%
1	Christopher Robinson (AM & R)	3,797	49.0
	Thomas Davis (R)	2,422	31.2
	Olney Arnold (D)	1,532	19.8
2	William D. Brayton (R)	3,101	63.9
	Alfred Anthony (D)	1,746	36.0

Special Election

		Votes	%
1	Christopher Robinson (AM & R)	3,414	56.0
	Thomas Davis (R)	2,648	43.4

TENNESSEE

		Votes	%
1	Thomas A. R. Nelson (OPP)	7,931	50.3
	Haynes (D)	7,827	49.7
2	Horace Maynard (OPP)	6,476	56.8
	Ramsay (D)	4,930	43.2
3	Reese B. Brabson (OPP)	8,372	50.2
	Smith (D)	8,313	49.8
4	William B. Stokes (OPP)	6,633	51.9
	Savage (D)	6,160	48.2
5	Robert H. Hatton (OPP)	6,719	53.5
	Charles Ready (I & D)	5,844	46.5
6	James H. Thomas (D)	9,023	100.0
7	John V. Wright (D)	9,380	77.6
	Gibbs (OPP)	2,711	22.4
8	James M. Quarles (OPP)	6,994	52.9
	Menees (D)	6,236	47.1
9	Emerson Etheridge (OPP)	9,437	50.0
	Atkins (D)	9,430	50.0
10	William T. Avery (D)	5,954	50.3
	Sneed (OPP)	5,648	47.7

TEXAS

		Votes	%
1	John H. Reagan (D)	20,565	85.3
	Ochiltree	3,541	14.7
2	Andrew J. Hamilton (ID)	16,521	50.7
	Waul (D)	16,079	49.3

VIRGINIA

		Votes	%
1	Muscoe H. R. Garnett (D)		100.0
2	John S. Millson (D)		100.0
3	Daniel C. De Jarnette (ID & OPP)	5,581	50.5
	Caskie (D)	5,481	49.6
4	William O. Goode (D)	3,820	63.6
	Flournoy (ID&OPP)	2,185	36.4
5	Thomas S. Bocock (D)		100.0
6	Shelton F. Leake (ID)	5,003	59.2
	Powell (D)	3,453	40.8
7	William Smith (D)	5,147	49.4
	Thomas (OPP)	4,845	46.5
8	Alexander R. Boteler (OPP)	6,616	50.6
	Faulkner (D)	6,449	49.4
9	John T. Harris (ID)	5,345	52.2
	Skinner (D)	4,900	47.8
10	Sherrard Clemens (D)		100.0
11	Albert G. Jenkins (D)	9,038	55.6
	Laidley (OPP)	7,228	44.4
12	Henry A. Edmundson (D)		100.0
13	Elbert S. Martin (ID)	6,382	53.4
	Floyd (D)	5,579	46.6

Special Election

		Votes	%
4	Roger A. Pryor (D)	✓	

1860 House Elections

ARKANSAS

(Seceded May 6, 1861)

	Candidates	Votes	%
1	Thomas C. Hindman (D)	20,051*	67.4
	Cypert (I)	9,699	32.6
2	Gantt (I)	16,569*	56.0
	Mitchell (D)	13,007	44.0

DELAWARE

AL	George P. Fisher (UN)	7,732	48.4
	Briggs (SO D)	7,475	46.8

FLORIDA

(Seceded Jan. 10, 1861)

AL	R. B. Hilton (D)	7,722*	59.9
	B. F. Allen (KST U)	5,172	40.1

ILLINOIS

1	Elihu B. Washburne (R)	21,436	70.6
	Theodore A. C. Beard (D)	8,929	29.4
2	Isaac N. Arnold (R)	30,834	64.4
	Augustus M. Herrington (D)	16,950	35.4
3	Owen Lovejoy (R)	29,600	59.9
	Robert N. Murray (D)	18,843	38.2
4	William Kellogg (R)	25,668	54.6
	Robert G. Ingersoll (D)	21,297	45.3
5	William A. Richardson (D)	16,946	53.5
	Bug Prentiss (R)	14,684	46.4
6	John A. McClernand (D)	21,206	56.6
	Henry Case (R)	16,244	43.4
7	James C. Robinson (D)	19,206	54.1
	James T. Cunningham (R)	16,313	45.9
8	Philip B. Fouke (D)	16,592	55.2
	Joseph Gillespie (R)	13,315	44.3
9	John A. Logan (D)	20,863	79.5
	Unidentified Candidate (R)	5,207	19.9

INDIANA

1	John Law (D)	13,476	55.7
	Debruler (R)	10,731	44.3
2	James A. Cravens (D)	10,811	51.3
	Davis (R)	10,272	48.7
3	William McKee Dunn (R)	11,545	54.5
	Daiy (D)	9,622	45.5
4	William S. Holman (D)	10,299	50.7
	Yatar (R)	10,007	49.3
5	George W. Julian (R)	12,237	62.0
	Bickle (D)	7,501	38.0
6	Albert G. Porter (R)	13,029	52.3
	Walpole (D)	11,887	47.7
7	Daniel W. Voorhees (D)	12,535	52.1
	Nelson (R)	11,516	47.9
8	Albert S. White (R)	13,310	53.7
	Wilson (D)	11,489	46.3
9	Schuyler Colfax (R)	16,860	55.6
	Cathcart (D)	13,458	44.4
10	William Mitchell (R)	14,267	55.6
	Kenkle (D)	11,378	44.4
11	John P. C. Shanks (R)	13,885	54.1
	Steele (D)	11,796	45.9

IOWA

1	Samuel R. Curtis (R)	33,936	52.9
	C. C. Cole (D)	30,240	47.1
2	William Vandever (R)	36,805	57.5
	Ben M. Samuels (D)	27,206	42.5

MAINE

1	John N. Goodwin (R)	12,018	53.0

	Candidates	Votes	%
	Hayes (D)	10,556	46.5
2	Charles W. Walton (R)	12,806	55.6
	Record (D)	10,192	44.3
3	Samuel C. Fessenden (R)	10,065	52.5
	Johnson (D)	9,090	47.4
4	Anson P. Morrill (R)	12,666	61.6
	Fuller (D)	7,262	35.3
5	John H. Rice (R)	12,317	59.8
	Blake (D)	7,965	38.7
6	Frederick A. Pike (R)	9,451	53.9
	Bradbury (D)	7,893	45.1

MASSACHUSETTS

1	Thomas D. Eliot (R)	7,350	72.5
	Daniel Fisher	1,061	10.5
	Moses Bates	878	8.7
	F. C. Sandford	845	8.3
2	James Buffington (R)	10,103	68.4
	Aaron Hobart	4,409	29.9
3	Charles F. Adams (R)	10,530	58.4
	Leverett Saltonstall	7,449	41.3
4	Alexander H. Rice (R)	7,292	52.3
	Erastus B. Bigelow	6,645	47.6
5	William Appleton (R)	8,014	50.8
	Anson Burlingame	7,756	49.2
6	John B. Alley (R)	9,644	63.1
	Otis P. Lord	2,471	16.2
	Jefferson Knight	2,200	14.4
7	Daniel W. Gooch (R)	11,373	60.2
	Charles A. Welch	6,730	35.6
8	Charles R. Train (R)	9,272	64.6
	A. R. Brown	2,390	16.6
	Winthrop E. Faulkner	2,239	15.6
9	Goldsmith F. Bailey (R)	9,745	54.6
	Eli Thayer (I)	7,949	44.6
10	Charles Delano (R)	10,021	75.1
	Josiah Allis	2,528	18.9
	B. Leavitt	744	5.6
11	Henry L. Dawes (R)	10,409	67.6
	Norman T. Leonard	4,396	28.5

MICHIGAN

1	Bradley F. Granger (R)	16,997	52.5
	George V. N. Lathrop (D)	15,216	47.0
2	Fernando C. Beaman (R)	19,162	60.1
	Salathiel C. Coffenberry (D)	12,700	39.8
3	Francis W. Kellogg (R)	28,641	59.0
	Thomas B. Church (D)	19,737	40.6
4	Rowland E. Trowbridge (R)	23,650	55.3
	Edward Thompson (D)	19,099	44.7

MINNESOTA

AL	Cyrus Aldrich (R)	22,333✓	
	William Windom (R)	22,165✓	
	James George (D)	12,172	
	J. M. Gilman (D)	12,168	
	A. J. Edgerton (SO D)	787	
	J. W. Taylor (SO D)	776	

MISSOURI

1	Francis P. Blair Jr. (R)	11,453	44.1
	John H. Barret (D)	9,967	38.4
	Todd (AM)	4,542	17.5
2	James S. Rollins (OPP)	11,161	50.6
	Henderson (D)	10,908	49.4
3	John B. Clark (D)	14,822	59.1
	Hawkins (OPP)	10,276	40.9
4	Elijah H. Norton (D)	13,797	62.3
	Scott (OPP)	8,350	37.7
5	John W. Reid (D)	11,689	52.8
	Mitchell (OPP)	10,432	47.2
6	John S. Phelps (D)	11,363	55.0

	Candidates	Votes	%
	Rains (OPP)	9,301	45.0
7	John W. Noell (D)	11,191	73.6
	Perryman (OPP)	4,007	26.4

Special Election

1	John R. Barret (D)	12,682‡	50.3
	Francis P. Blair Jr (R)	12,538	49.7

NEW JERSEY

1	John T. Nixon (R)	10,843	52.7
	Leaming (D)	9,737	47.3
2	John L. N. Stratton (R)	13,582	52.8
	Green (D)	12,154	47.2
3	William G. Steele (D)	12,843	55.2
	Berthoud (R)	10,438	44.8
4	George T. Cobb (D)	10,789	52.6
	Edsall (R)	9,711	47.4
5	Nehemiah Perry (D)	16,200	50.6
	Pennington (R)	15,802	49.4

NEW YORK

1	Edward H. Smith (FUS)	11,882	52.8
	Carter (R)	10,631	47.2
2	Moses F. Odell (FUS)	13,322	55.1
	Humphrey (R)	10,870	44.9
3	Benjamin Wood (D)	5,892	52.8
	Williamson (R)	4,585	41.1
	Savage (ID)	675	6.1
4	James E. Kerrigan (ID)	5,145	41.3
	Tuomy (D)	3,989	32.0
	Commerford (R)	3,324	26.7
5	William Wall (R)	6,877	41.0
	Taylor (D)	6,811	40.6
	Duffy (ID)	3,085	18.4
6	Frederick A. Conkling (R)	6,536	35.1
	Cochran (ID)	6,360	34.2
	Chanler (D)	5,724	30.7
7	Elijah Ward (D)	10,814	56.2
	Dow (R)	8,417	43.8
8	Isaac C. Delaplaine (D)	13,576	59.0
	Abram Wakeman (R)	9,417	41.0
9	Edward Haight (D)	11,389	53.5
	Nelson (R)	9,882	46.5
10	Charles H. Van Wyck (R)	8,311	50.5
	St. John (FUS)	8,163	49.6
11	John B. Steele (D)	9,938	50.4
	Sylvester (R)	9,789	49.6
12	Stephen Baker (R)	11,795	52.0
	Wager (D)	10,514	46.3
13	Abram B. Olin (R)	8,650	51.1
	McConihe (D)	8,268	48.9
14	Erastus Corning (D)	10,814	51.9
	Olcott (R)	10,043	48.2
15	James B. McKean (R)	14,924	58.8
	Davis (D)	10,474	41.2
16	William A. Wheeler (R)	10,571	58.7
	Hand (D)	7,427	41.3
17	Socrates N. Sherman (R)	16,134	68.4
	Foote (D)	7,456	31.6
18	Chauncey Vibbard (D)	12,019	50.9
	Mix (R)	11,602	49.1
19	Richard Franchot (R)	11,310	57.0
	Walworth (D)	8,542	43.0
20	Roscoe Conkling (R)	12,536	58.3
	Grove (D)	8,973	41.7
21	R. Holland Duell (R)	13,960	62.2
	Hitchcock (D)	4,923	21.9
	Nelson (BRECK D)	3,559	15.9
22	William E. Lansing (R)	15,253	63.7
	Chapman (D)	8,682	36.3
23	Ambrose W. Clark (R)	11,865	59.9
	Starbuck (D)	7,568	38.2
24	Charles B. Sedgwick (R)	11,175	60.4

Candidates	Votes	%
Teft (D)	6,088	32.9
Hay (BRECK D)	1,233	6.7
25 Theodore M. Pomeroy (R)	14,437	64.5
Beardsley (D)	7,961	35.5
26 Jacob P. Chamberlain (R)	11,581	58.3
Lewis (D)	8,153	41.0
27 Alexander S. Diven (R)	13,482	57.2
Dowe (D)	10,088	42.8
28 Robert B. Van Valkenburg (R)	13,167	60.8
Walker (D)	8,507	39.3
29 Alfred Ely (R)	10,704	59.4
Reynolds (D)	7,314	40.6
30 Augustus Frank (R)	15,342	67.5
Robinson (D)	7,389	32.5
31 Burt Van Horn (R)	8,662	58.8
Ely (D)	5,882	39.9
32 Elbridge G. Spaulding (R)	12,256	52.8
Haven (D)	10,947	47.2
33 Reuben E. Fenton (R)	14,303	66.8
Lee (D)	7,111	33.2

Special Election

Candidates	Votes	%
31 Edwin R. Reynolds (R)	8,759	59.4
Peck (D)	5,801	39.4

OHIO

Candidates	Votes	%
1 George H. Pendleton (D)	7,485	48.9
Spencer (R)	6,582	43.0
Jones	1,250	8.2
2 John A. Gurley (R)	8,469	48.1
Long (D)	7,586	43.1
Harrison	1,555	8.8
3 Clement L. Vallandigham (D)	11,052	50.2
Craighead (R)	10,918	49.6
4 William Allen (D)	11,756	51.7
Hart (R)	10,968	48.3
5 James M. Ashley (R)	13,756	52.3
Steedman (D)	12,552	47.7
6 Chilton A. White (D)	10,046	53.2
Murphy (R)	8,828	46.8
7 Thomas Corwin (R)	10,693	70.0
Telfair (D)	3,082	20.2
Stokes	1,512	9.9
8 Samuel Shellabarger (R)	10,931	58.3
Harrison (D)	7,831	41.7
9 Warren P. Noble (D)	12,650	51.1
Carey (R)	12,096	48.9
10 Carey A. Trimble (R)	11,593	51.3
Hutchinson (D)	11,025	48.7
11 Valentine B. Horton (R)	11,965	51.5
Martin (D)	11,275	48.5
12 Samuel S. Cox (D)	11,014	52.1
Galloway (R)	10,131	47.9
13 John Sherman (R)	11,428	57.2
Burns (D)	8,564	42.8

Candidates	Votes	%
14 Harrison G. O. Blake (R)	12,040	57.1
Prentiss (D)	9,053	42.9
15 Robert H. Nugen (D)	10,281	52.1
William Helmick (R)	9,439	47.9
16 William P. Cutler (R)	8,560	50.2
Jewett (D)	8,496	49.8
17 James R. Morris (D)	9,609	51.0
Thomas C. Theaker (R)	8,510	45.2
18 Sidney Edgerton (R)	9,720	58.3
Starkweather (D)	6,956	41.7
19 Albert G. Riddle (R)	11,927	69.1
Williams (D)	5,343	30.9
20 John Hutchins (R)	10,840	72.0
Wilson (D)	4,222	28.0
21 John A. Bingham (R)	9,170	61.2
Wells (D)	5,053	33.7
Blakeley	768	5.1

OREGON

Candidates	Votes	%
AL George K. Sheil (D)	6,632	50.4
D. Logan (R)	6,529	49.6

PENNSYLVANIA

Candidates	Votes	%
1 John M. Butler (R)	8,581	45.1
William E. Lehman (D)	8,383✓	44.1
King (UN)	2,057	10.8
2 Edward Joy Morris (R)	6,259	46.6
Brodhead (D)	5,410	40.3
Fuller (UN)	1,760	13.1
3 John P. Verre (R)	8,931	49.1
Kline (D)	8,909	49.0
4 William D. Kelley (R)	11,568	49.3
Morgan (D)	10,195	43.4
Robinson (UN)	1,715	7.3
5 William Morris Davis (R)	10,020	50.8
Ingersoll (D)	9,724	49.3
6 John Hickman (R)	10,140	56.8
Brinton (D)	7,701	43.2
7 Thomas B. Cooper (D)	10,762	50.3
Longnecker (R)	10,620	49.7
8 Sydenham E. Ancona (D)	9,993	58.4
Smith (R)	7,111	41.6
9 Thaddeus Stevens (R)	12,964	96.5
10 John W. Killinger (R)	12,246	62.1
Worrell (D)	7,488	37.9
11 James H. Campbell (R)	9,867	50.9
Hughes (D)	9,518	49.1
12 George W. Scranton (R)	11,719	51.5
Randall (D)	11,024	48.5
13 Philip Johnson (D)	12,208	57.3
Shoemaker (R)	9,096	42.7
14 Galusha A. Grow (R)	14,922	71.4
Sherwood (D)	5,984	28.6
15 James T. Hale (R)	11,907	53.8
Fleming (D)	10,243	46.2

Candidates	Votes	%
16 Joseph Bailey (D)	12,069	50.8
Junkin (R)	11,712	49.3
17 Edward McPherson (R)	11,945	51.2
Schell (D)	11,372	48.8
18 Samuel S. Blair (R)	11,185	57.6
McAllister (D)	8,220	42.4
19 John Covode (R)	11,769	54.7
Phelps (D)	9,761	45.3
20 Jesse Lazear (D)	10,607	52.9
Stewart (R)	9,443	47.1
21 James K. Morehead (R)	10,507	61.3
Kerr (D)	6,631	38.7
22 Robert McKnight (R)	7,978	72.8
Mitchell (D)	2,979	27.2
23 John W. Wallace (R)	7,636	55.6
Holstein (D)	6,102	44.4
24 John D. Patton (R)	11,745	52.6
Kerr (D)	10,582	47.4
25 Elijah Babbitt (R)	10,705	65.9
Wilson (D)	5,551	34.2

Special Election

Candidates	Votes	%
8 Jacob K. McKenty (D)	9,595	56.2
McKnight (R)	7,482	43.8

SOUTH CAROLINA[1]

(Seceded Dec. 20, 1860)

Candidates	Votes	%
1 John McQueen (D)		
C. W. Miller		
2 William P. Miles (D)		100.0
3 George P. Elliott		
Lewis M. Ayer		
4 Milledge L. Bonham (SSR D)		100.0
5 John D. Ashmore (D)		100.0
6 William W. Boyce (SSR D)		100.0

VERMONT

Candidates	Votes	%
1 Eliakim Persons Walton (R)	10,268	75.2
Wilcox (D)	3,389	24.8
2 Justin S. Morrill (R)	12,555	79.2
Charles N. Davenport (D)	3,295	20.8
3 Portus Baxter (R)	8,326	76.3
Chaffee (D)	2,588	23.7

WISCONSIN

Candidates	Votes	%
1 John F. Potter (R)	16,197	54.5
Arnold (D)	13,508	45.5
2 Luther Hanchett (R)	36,223	61.2
Reynolds (D)	23,008	38.8
3 A. Scott Sloan (R)	34,002	54.0
Charles H. Larrabee (D)	28,986	46.0

1859 Elections

1. Rep. Thomas L. Harris died Nov. 24, 1858, following his reelection to the 36th Congress (1859–1861). In a special election in January 1859 to fill the remaining few months of Harris's term in the 35th Congress (1857–1859), the winner was Charles D. Hodges. John A. McClernand was elected in November 1859 to the unexpired term in the 36th Congress.

2. In the 1st district, no candidate received the majority required by state law for election. In a later special election, Christopher Robinson was finally chosen.

1860 Elections

1. South Carolina's six representatives withdrew from the House before the beginning of the 37th Congress (1861–1863), and thus never assumed the seats they were elected to.

1861 House Elections

ALABAMA

(Seceded Jan. 11, 1861)

CALIFORNIA[1]

	Candidates	Votes	%
AL	Timothy G. Phelps (R)	51,651 ✓	
	Aaron A. Sargent (R)	50,692 ✓	
	H. Edgerton (UN D)	35,449	
	J. C. McKibben (UN D)	35,401	
	D. O. Shattuck (SEC D)	31,712	
	H. P. Barber (SEC D)	31,591	
AL	Frederick F. Low	39,059	45.6
	F. Gunahl	24,036	28.1
	J. R. Gitchell	22,550	26.3

CONNECTICUT

	Candidates	Votes	%
1	Dwight Loomis (R)	10,701	50.3
	Hyde (D)	10,563	49.7
2	James E. English (D)	12,490	52.3
	Wdff (R)	11,396	47.7
3	Alfred A. Burnham (R)	8,701	57.3
	Baker (D)	6,496	42.8
4	George C. Woodruff (D)	11,739	50.2
	Ferry (R)	11,668	49.9

GEORGIA

(Seceded Jan. 28, 1861)

ILLINOIS

Special Election

		Votes	%
6	Anthony L. Knapp (D)	8,283	98.0

IOWA

Special Election

		Votes	%
1	James F. Wilson (R)	28,133	56.7
	Juirus E. Neal (D)	20,328	40.9

KANSAS

(Became a state Jan. 29, 1861)

	Candidates	Votes	%
AL	Martin F. Conway (R)	✓	

KENTUCKY

		Votes	%
1	Henry C. Burnett (SEC D)	8,988	59.1
	Lawrence S. Trimble (UN)	6,225	40.9
2	James S. Jackson (UN)	9,281	73.4
	John T. Bunch (SEC D)	3,364	26.6
3	Henry Grider (UN)	10,392	77.0
	Joseph H. Lewis (SEC D)	3,113	23.1
4	Aaron Harding (UN)	10,339	80.7
	Albert G. Talbott (SEC D)	2,469	19.3
5	Charles A. Wickliffe (UN)	8,217	75.1
	H. E. Read (SEC D)	2,719	24.9
6	George W. Dunlop (UN)	8,101	97.3
7	Robert Mallory (UN)	11,035	79.4
	Horatio W. Bruce (SEC D)	2,862	20.6
8	John J. Crittenden (UN)	8,272	59.2
	William E. Simms (SEC D)	5,706	40.8
9	William H. Wadsworth (UN)	12,130	75.9
	John L. Williams (SEC D)	3,850	24.1
10	John W. Menzies (UN)	8,373	64.9
	Overton P. Hogan (SEC D)	3,774	29.3
	Thomas L. Jones	698	5.4

LOUISIANA

(Seceded Jan. 26, 1861)

MARYLAND

		Votes	%
1	John W. Crisfield (UN R)	7,181	57.4
	Hny (PEACE D)	5,331	42.6
2	Edwin H. Webster (UN R)	7,251	98.3
3	Cornelius L. L. Leary (UN R)	6,702	52.0
	Preston (PEACE D)	6,200	48.1
4	Henry May (PEACE D)	8,424	57.6
	Davis (UN R)	6,214	42.5
5	Francis Thomas (UN R)	10,582	97.1
6	Charles B. Calvert (UN R)	4,467	50.9
	Harris (PEACE D)	4,305	49.1

MISSISSIPPI

(Seceded Jan. 9, 1861)

NEW HAMPSHIRE

	Candidates	Votes	%
1	Gilman Marston (R)	13,055	52.9
	Marcy (D)	11,642	47.1
2	Edward H. Rollins (R)	10,763	52.4
	Bell (D)	9,791	47.6
3	Thomas M. Edwards (R)	11,778	54.2
	Burns (D)	9,940	45.8

NORTH CAROLINA

(Seceded May 21, 1861)

RHODE ISLAND

		Votes	%
1	William P. Sheffield (UN)	6,998	51.2
	Robinson (R)	6,656	48.7
2	George H. Browne (UN)	4,411	53.3
	Brayton (R)	3,856	46.6

TENNESSEE

(Seceded June 8, 1861)

TEXAS

(Seceded Feb. 1, 1861)

VIRGINIA

(Seceded April 17, 1861)

1. California had two seats in the House during the 36th Congress (1859–1861), but following the reapportionment after the census of 1860 it would have been entitled to three in the 38th Congress (1863–1865). Most states held House elections in even-numbered years, so those which were entitled to larger House representation would have had to wait until after the election of 1862 to claim it. But California held its regular House election in 1861, and tried to fill three seats.

Phelps and Sargent were elected to California's two regular seats. The *Biographical Directory* says that Frederick F. Low presented credentials and claimed a third seat Dec. 2, 1861, but the House May 6, 1862, declared him not entitled to a seat. Following passage of an act of June 2, 1862, granting California its third seat before it normally would have received it, he was admitted.

The ballot arrangement for California's 1861 House election was ambiguous. The ICPSR returns suggest that Low, Gunahl and Gitchell were probably listed in a separate column on the ballot as candidates in a separate at-large election for the prospective third seat, and Low's claim to the seat would be based on his having finished first among the three.

A second possibility is that all nine candidates for the House ran against each other in one at-large election. Low would have finished with the third highest number of votes in such a contest, and could conceivably have claimed the House seat on that basis.

1862 House Elections

DELAWARE

	Candidates	Votes	%
AL	William Temple (D)	8,051	50.1
	George P. Fisher (UN)	8,014	49.9

ILLINOIS

	Candidates	Votes	%
1	Isaac N. Arnold (R)	10,025	54.5
	Francis C. Sherman (D)	8,387	45.6
2	John F. Farnsworth (R)	12,612	72.5
	Neil Donnelly (D)	4,785	27.5
3	Elihu B. Washburne (R)	10,496	60.7
	Elias B. Stiles (D)	6,785	39.3
4	Charles M. Harris (D)	11,626	57.2
	Charles B. Lawrence (R)	8,711	42.8
5	Owen Lovejoy (R)	11,683	50.1
	Thomas J. Henderson (D)	11,020	47.3
6	Jesse O. Norton (R)	10,604	55.7
	F. Lyle Dickey (D)	8,419	44.3
7	John R. Eden (D)	11,361	53.2
	Elijah McCarty (R)	10,004	46.8
8	John T. Stuart (D)	12,808	52.8
	Leonard Swett (R)	11,443	47.2
9	Lewis W. Ross (D)	13,391	99.1
10	Anthony L. Knapp (D)	14,259	64.8
	Samuel W. Moulton (R)	7,712	35.0
11	James C. Robinson (D)	13,644	71.2
	Stephen G. Hicks (R)	5,521	28.8
12	William R. Morrison (D)	10,999	61.6
	Robert Smith (R)	6,854	38.4
13	William J. Allen (D)	9,497	68.8
	Milton Bartley (R)	4,290	31.1
AL	James C. Allen (D)	136,257	53.2
	Ebon C. Ingersoll (R)	119,819	46.8

Special Election

	Candidates	Votes	%
9	William J. Allen (D)	4,795	35.7
	Irham W. Hayrin	4,053	30.2
	Samuel S. Marshall	3,983	29.6

INDIANA

	Candidates	Votes	%
1	John Law (D)	11,963	53.1
	Johnson (UN R)	10,583	46.9
2	James A. Cravens (D)	10,911	64.7
	May (UN R)	5,951	35.3
3	Henry W. Harrington (D)	11,524	53.4
	William McKee Dunn (UN R)	10,044	46.6
4	William S. Holman (D)	10,926	57.8
	Gavin (UN R)	7,992	42.3
5	George W. Julian (UN R)	9,272	55.6
	Johnson (D)	7,414	44.4
6	Ebenezer Dumont (UN R)	12,525	53.4
	Contt (D)	10,954	46.7
7	Daniel W. Voorhees (D)	12,457	55.5
	Scott (UN R)	9,976	44.5
8	Godlove S. Orth (UN R)	12,032	51.8
	Pettit (D)	11,181	48.2
9	Schuyler Colfax (UN R)	14,768	50.4
	Turpie (D)	14,546	49.6
10	Joseph K. Edgerton (D)	12,353	50.9
	Mitchell (UN R)	11,917	49.1
11	James F. McDowell (D)	13,142	51.8
	Shanks (UN R)	12,219	48.2

IOWA

	Candidates	Votes	%
1	James F. Wilson (R)	12,705	54.8
	Joseph K. Hornish (D)	10,486	45.2
2	Hiram Price (R)	12,433	58.2
	Edward H. Thayer (D)	8,930	41.8
3	William B. Allison (R)	12,112	58.8
	Dennis A. Mahoney (D)	8,452	41.1
4	Josiah B. Grinnell (R)	12,900	52.8
	Hugh M. Martin (D)	11,529	47.2

	Candidates	Votes	%
5	John A. Kasson (R)	10,306	58.4
	D. O. Finch (D)	7,346	41.6
6	Asahel W. Hubbard (R)	5,386	66.2
	John F. Duncombe (D)	2,755	33.8

KANSAS

	Candidates	Votes	%
AL	A. Carter Wilder (R)	9,671	63.3
	Marcus J. Parrott (UN)	4,666	30.6
	William G. Mathias (D)	930	6.1

KENTUCKY

Special Elections

	Candidates	Votes	%
1	Samuel L. Casey (R)	541	54.1
	L. S. Trimble	442	44.2
2	George H. Yeaman (UN)	2,242	55.7
	Edward R. Weir	1,756	43.6

LOUISIANA[1]

Special Elections

	Candidates	Votes	%
1	Benjamin F. Flanders (UN)	2,330	93.7
	Bolgny (UN)	157	6.3
2	Michael Hahn (UN)	2,581	57.8
	Durell (UN)	1,450	32.5
	Barker (SEC)	436	9.8

MAINE

	Candidates	Votes	%
1	Lorenzo D. M. Sweat (D)	10,452	48.9
	Goodwin (R)	10,205	47.8
2	Sidney Perham (R)	9,976	56.7
	Bates (D)	7,519	42.7
3	James G. Blaine (R)	9,971	54.9
	Gould (D)	7,153	39.4
4	John H. Rice (R)	8,107	60.4
	Boynton (D)	3,806	28.4
5	Frederick A. Pike (R)	8,998	54.3
	White (D)	7,308	44.1

MASSACHUSETTS

	Candidates	Votes	%
1	Thomas D. Eliot (R)	8,399	74.2
	Daniel Fisher (PP)	2,762	24.4
2	Oakes Ames (R)	9,271	61.1
	William D. Swan (PP)	5,907	38.9
3	Alexander H. Rice (R)	5,044	50.1
	John Sleeper (PP)	5,020	49.8
4	Samuel Hooper (R)	5,828	52.1
	Josiah G. Abbott (PP)	5,351	47.8
5	John B. Alley (R)	8,505	61.0
	Benjamin Poole (PP)	5,398	38.7
6	Daniel W. Gooch (R)	8,124	56.9
	Oliver Hazzard Perry (PP)	6,150	43.1
7	George S. Boutwell (R)	7,994	55.2
	Benjamin F. Thomas (PP)	6,496	44.8
8	John D. Baldwin (R)	10,128	66.2
	Paul Whitin (PP)	5,178	33.8
9	William B. Washburne (R)	14,311	99.2
10	Henry L. Dawes (R)	7,449	56.3
	Chester W. Chapin (PP)	5,785	43.7

MICHIGAN

	Candidates	Votes	%
1	Fernando C. Beaman (R)	13,400	50.4
	Ebenezer J. Penniman (D)	13,210	49.6
2	Charles Upson (R)	14,148	55.4
	John W. Turner (D)	11,387	44.6
3	John W. Longyear (R)	12,317	51.7
	Bradley F. Granger (D)	11,488	48.3
4	Francis W. Kellogg (R)	10,013	57.8
	Thomas B. Church (D)	7,308	42.2
5	Augustus C. Baldwin (D)	10,697	50.6

	Candidates	Votes	%
	Rowland E. Trowbridge (R)	10,435	49.4
6	John F. Driggs (R)	8,188	53.7
	John Moore (D)	7,047	46.2

MINNESOTA

	Candidates	Votes	%
1	William Windom (R)	8,663	57.4
	A. G. Chatfield (D)	6,423	42.6
2	Ignatius Donnelly (R)	7,091	58.6
	W. J. Cullen (D)	5,019	41.5

MISSOURI

	Candidates	Votes	%
1	Francis P. Blair Jr (R)	4,743‡	40.0
	Samuel Knox (EMANCIP)	4,590	38.7
	Bogy (D)	2,536	21.4
2	Henry T. Blow (EMANCIP)	7,164	69.6
	Allen (D)	2,984	29.0
3	John W. Noell (EMANCIP)	✓	
	John G. Scott (D)		
	Lawson (I)		
4	Sempronius H. Boyd (EMANCIP)	✓	
	Phelps (D)		
5	Joseph W. McClurg (EMANCIP)	4,930	53.2
	Thomas L. Price (D)	4,333	46.8
6	Austin A. King (D)	4,243	45.3
	Birch (SEC)	2,857	30.5
	Samuel (ID)	1,626	17.4
	Bouton (EMANCIP)	644	6.9
7	Benjamin F. Loan (EMANCIP)	6,580	48.4
	John P. Bruce (D)	4,554	33.5
	Branch (I)	2,465	18.1
8	William A. Hall (D)	6,244	53.0
	Green (EMANCIP)	5,534	47.0
9	James S. Rollins	7,700	73.4
	Krekel (EMANCIP)	2,797	26.7

NEW JERSEY

	Candidates	Votes	%
1	John F. Starr (UN)	9,491	51.4
	Stratton (D)	8,961	48.6
2	George Middleton (D)	12,182	52.9
	Brown (UN)	10,834	47.1
3	William G. Steele (D)	15,708	63.3
	Brwnsn (UN)	9,093	36.7
4	Andrew J. Rogers (D)	12,791	56.1
	Linn (UN)	10,024	43.9
5	Nehemiah Perry (D)	10,779	58.6
	Bradley (UN)	7,622	41.4

NEW YORK

	Candidates	Votes	%
1	Henry G. Stebbins (D)	9,908	56.1
	McCormick (UN)	7,759	43.9
2	Martin Kalbfleisch (D)	10,586	66.3
	Wall (UN)	5,381	33.7
3	Moses F. Odell (D)	8,915	54.3
	Humphrey (UN)	7,506	45.7
4	Benjamin Wood (D)	7,828	63.3
	Walbridge (UN)	4,535	36.7
5	Fernando Wood (D)	8,176	70.1
	Duffy (UN)	3,488	29.9
6	Elijah Ward (D)	6,942	54.3
	Conkling (UN)	4,839	37.9
	Blunt (I)	996	7.8
7	John W. Chanler (D)	9,326	76.1
	Burr (UN)	2,937	24.0
8	James Brooks (D)	9,625	63.3
	Cowdin (UN)	5,570	36.7
9	Anson Herrick (D)	7,323	64.2
	Murphy (UN)	4,085	35.8
10	William Radford (D)	8,878	45.8
	Haight (UN)	7,921	40.9
	Suffn (I)	2,576	13.3
11	Charles H. Winfield (D)	9,326	55.2
	Fullerton (UN)	7,572	44.8

	Candidates	Votes	%
12	Homer A. Nelson (D)	10,712	53.0
	Beale (UN)	9,512	47.0
13	John B. Steele (D)	10,263	54.9
	Cornell (UN)	8,422	45.1
14	Erastus Corning (D)	15,715	59.6
	Smith (UN)	10,665	40.4
15	John A. Griswold (D)	12,226	52.8
	Dodd (UN)	10,939	47.2
16	Orlando Kellogg (UN)	7,654	52.3
	Burhans (D)	6,987	47.7
17	Calvin T. Hulburd (UN)	12,015	67.2
	Judson (D)	5,867	32.8
18	James M. Marvin (UN)	13,096	51.0
	Blood (D)	12,582	49.0
19	Samuel F. Miller (UN)	14,918	52.5
	Parker (D)	13,523	47.6
20	Ambrose W. Clark (UN)	14,826	57.3
	Carryl (D)	11,031	42.7
21	Francis Kernan (D)	9,943	50.3
	Conkling (UN)	9,845	49.8
22	De Witt C. Littlejohn (UN)	12,667	60.0
	Titus (D)	8,453	40.0
23	Thomas T. Davis (UN)	13,032	58.5
	Strong (D)	9,257	41.5
24	Theodore M. Pomeroy (UN)	13,834	55.3
	Hadley (D)	11,196	44.7
25	Daniel Morris (UN)	11,615	58.7
	Lord (D)	8,157	41.3
26	Giles W. Hotchkiss (UN)	13,889	58.7
	Day (D)	9,781	41.3
27	Robert B. Van Valkenburg (UN)	14,887	58.0
	Hathawy (D)	10,774	42.0
28	Freeman Clarke (UN)	11,193	53.2
	Church (D)	9,833	46.8
29	Augustus Frank (UN)	10,470	52.1
	Hunt (D)	9,627	47.9
30	John Ganson (D)	12,400	58.0
	Spaulding (UN)	8,985	42.0
31	Reuben E. Fenton (UN)	11,950	63.1
	Caldwell (D)	6,982	36.9

OHIO

	Candidates	Votes	%
1	George H. Pendleton (D)	7,545	54.0
	Groesbeck (UN R)	6,418	46.0
2	Alexander Long (D)	7,212	50.5
	Gurley (UN R)	7,081	49.5
3	Robert C. Schenck (UN R)	13,027	52.5
	Vallandigham (D)	11,770	47.5
4	John F. McKinney (D)	10,218	52.0
	West (UN R)	9,435	48.0

1. Elected from areas under federal control.

	Candidates	Votes	%
5	Francis C. Le Blond (D)	10,561	63.0
	Gatch (UN R)	6,202	37.0
6	Joseph W. White (D)	10,087	52.0
	Briggs (UN R)	9,320	48.0
7	Samuel S. Cox (D)	10,372	50.7
	Shellabarger (UN R)	10,100	49.3
8	William Johnston (D)	9,012	51.1
	Godman (UN R)	8,642	49.0
9	Warren P. Noble (D)	11,765	52.8
	Worcester (UN R)	10,523	47.2
10	James M. Ashley (UN R)	6,908	38.6
	Waite	5,781	32.3
	Phlpa	5,232	29.2
11	Wells A. Hutchins (D)	8,605	56.2
	Bundy (UN R)	6,702	43.8
12	William E. Finck (D)	13,631	62.8
	Trimble (UN R)	8,087	37.2
13	John O'Neill (D)	12,763	56.8
	Wright (UN R)	9,699	43.2
14	George Bliss (D)	10,490	50.1
	Welker (UN R)	10,454	49.9
15	James R. Morris (D)	10,332	52.9
	Cutler (UN R)	9,183	47.1
16	Chilton A. White (D)	12,299	55.2
	Bingham (UN R)	9,999	44.8
17	Ephraim R. Eckley (UN R)	10,018	52.4
	Belden (D)	9,085	47.6
18	Rufus P. Spalding (UN R)	9,293	68.8
	Paige (D)	4,183	31.0
19	James A. Garfield (UN R)	13,288	66.3
	Wood (D)	6,763	33.7

OREGON

	Candidates	Votes	%
AL	John R. McBride (UN R)	6,809	65.2
	A. E. Wait (D)	3,632	34.8

PENNSYLVANIA

	Candidates	Votes	%
1	Samuel J. Randall (D)	7,720	55.2
	Webb (UN)	6,273	44.8
2	Charles O'Neill (UN)	8,614	58.7
	Biddle (D)	6,068	41.3
3	Leonard Myers (UN)	8,285	50.1
	Kline (D)	8,243	49.9
4	William D. Kelley (UN)	8,946	52.4
	Nichn (D)	8,118	47.6
5	M. Russell Thayer (UN)	9,605	50.2
	Carrin (D)	9,543	49.8
6	John D. Stiles (D)	11,316	58.3
	Krause (UN)	8,092	41.7

	Candidates	Votes	%
7	John M. Broomall (UN)	9,891	60.6
	McCall (D)	6,445	39.5
8	Sydenham E. Ancona (D)	10,022	67.2
	Wanner (UN)	4,898	32.8
9	Thaddeus Stevens (UN)	11,174	62.7
	Steinn (D)	6,650	37.3
10	Myer Strouse (D)	9,239	52.0
	Campbell (UN)	8,518	48.0
11	Philip Johnson (D)	11,676	81.8
	Rouch (UN)	2,592	18.2
12	Charles Denison (D)	11,408	54.2
	Grow (UN)	9,641	45.8
13	Henry W. Tracy (UN)	9,520	55.3
	Clark (D)	7,703	44.7
14	William H. Miller (D)	10,630	51.3
	Patterson (UN)	10,109	48.7
15	Joseph Baily (UN)	11,965	55.1
	Glossbrenner (D)	9,746	44.9
16	Alexander H. Coffroth (D)	10,963	51.3
	Edward McPherson (UN)	10,426	48.7
17	Archibald McAllister (D)	8,328	52.4
	Blair (UN)	7,556	47.6
18	James T. Hale (D)	9,272	49.4
	Armstrong (UN)	8,855	47.2
19	Glenni W. Scofield (UN)	9,954	51.3
	Courtht (D)	9,462	48.7
20	Amos Myers (UN)	12,404	51.7
	Church (D)	11,586	48.3
21	John L. Dawson (D)	10,234	50.6
	Steward (UN)	10,009	49.4
22	James K. Moorhead (UN)	8,037	58.6
	Hamilton (D)	5,678	41.4
23	Thomas Williams (UN)	8,989	54.1
	Ziegler (D)	7,635	45.9
24	Jesse Lazear (D)	9,984	51.1
	Wallace (UN)	9,547	48.9

WISCONSIN

	Candidates	Votes	%
1	James S. Brown (D)	14,291	54.1
	Potter (R)	12,106	45.9
2	Ithamar C. Sloan (R)	13,105	54.4
	Guppy (D)	10,974	45.6
3	Amasa Cobb (D)	11,365	55.3
	Simpson (R)	9,184	44.7
4	Charles A. Eldridge (D)	15,343	61.5
	Bragg (R)	9,613	38.5
5	Ezra Wheeler (D)	11,021	52.4
	Brown (R)	10,005	47.6
6	Luther Hanchett (R)	9,276*	57.5
	Stoddard (D)	6,774	42.0

1863 House Elections

CALIFORNIA

	Candidates	Votes	%
AL	Corneilus Cole (UN R)	65,085✓	
	Thomas B. Shannon (UN R)	64,914✓	
	William Higby (UN R)	64,883✓	
	J. B. Weller (D)	43,567	
	John Bigle (D)	43,520	

CONNECTICUT

		Votes	%
1	Henry C. Deming (R)	10,493	50.8
	Hyde (D)	10,158	49.2
2	James E. English (D)	11,450	52.4
	Warner (R)	10,420	47.7
3	Augustus Brandegee (UN R)	8,878	58.2
	Convse (D)	6,381	41.8
4	John H. Hubbard (R)	11,248	50.8
	Woodruff (D)	10,892	49.2

DELAWARE

Special Election

		Votes	%
AL	Nathaniel B. Smithers (UN)	8,220	99.8

KENTUCKY

		Votes	%
1	Lucien Anderson (UN)	4,323	82.4
	L .S. Trimble (D)	711	13.6
2	George H. Yeaman (UN)	8,311	72.9
	John H. McHenry Jr. (D)	3,087	27.1
3	Henry Grider (UN)	8,654	87.0
	Thomas C. Winfrey (D)	1,293	13.0
4	Aaron Harding (UN)	10,435	80.6
	William J. Heady (D)	2,508	19.4

	Candidates	Votes	%
5	Robert Mallory (UN)	6,257	71.6
	Nathaniel Wolfe (D)	2,477	28.4
6	Green Clay Smith (UN)	6,936	61.9
	J. W. Menzies (D)	2,283	20.4
	J. W. Leathers (D)	1,970	17.6
7	Brutus J. Clay (UN)	4,711	50.4
	J. T. Boyle (D)	2,487	26.6
	R. A. Buckner (D)	2,143	22.9
8	William H. Randall (UN)	8,321	97.2
9	William H. Wadsworth (UN)	6,889	89.0
	Thomas S. Brown (D)	849	11.0

MARYLAND

		Votes	%
1	John A. J. Creswell (UN R)	6,743	55.2
	Crisfield (D)	5,482	44.8
2	Edwin H. Webster (UN R)	7,736	100.0
3	Henry Winter Davis (UN R)	6,200	99.7
4	Francis Thomas (UN R)	13,462	100.0
5	Benjamin G. Harris (D)	4,939	46.9
	Holland (UN R)	3,352	31.8
	Calvert (KST U)	2,237	21.3

MISSOURI

Special Election

		Votes	%
3	John G. Scott (D)	3,559	50.3
	Lindsay (UN)	3,070	43.4
	Bogy (ID)	444	6.3

NEW HAMPSHIRE

		Votes	%
1	Daniel Marcy (D)	12,059	50.2
	Eastman (R)	11,979	49.8

	Candidates	Votes	%
2	Edward H. Rollins (R)	10,365	50.9
	George (D)	9,999	49.1
3	James W. Patterson (R)	10,847	50.6
	Burns (D)	10,571	49.4

RHODE ISLAND

		Votes	%
1	Thomas A. Jenckes (R)	6,532	58.2
	Bradley (D)	4,616	41.1
2	Nathan F. Dixon (R)	4,077	56.4
	Browne (D)	3,121	43.2

VERMONT

		Votes	%
1	Frederick E. Woodbridge (R)	8,565	70.8
	John A. S. White (D)	3,486	28.8
2	Justin S. Morrill (R)	11,358	70.3
	Charles N. Davenport (D)	4,785	29.6
3	Portus Baxter (R)	7,234	71.0
	Giles Harrington (D)	2,673	26.2

WEST VIRGINIA

(Became a state June 19, 1863)

		Votes	%
1	Jacob B. Blair (UN R)	8,066	93.0
	Dehass (UN R)	605	7.0
2	William G. Brown (UN R)	3,576	57.9
	Burdett (UN R)	1,804	29.2
	Zinn (UN R)	800	12.9
3	Kellian V. Whaley (UN R)	2,746	55.7
	Frost (UN R)	2,184	44.3

1864 House Elections

CALIFORNIA

	Candidates	Votes	%
1	Donald C. McRuer (UN R)	20,370	58.9
	J. B. Crocker (D)	14,191	41.1
2	William Higby (UN R)	23,414	61.6
	J. W. Coffroth (D)	14,581	38.4
3	John Bidwell (UN R)	18,255	56.1
	Jack Temple (D)	14,273	43.9

DELAWARE

	Candidates	Votes	%
AL	John A. Nicholson (D)	8,762	51.5
	Nathaniel B. Smithers (UN R)	8,253	48.5

ILLINOIS

	Candidates	Votes	%
1	John Wentworth (UN R)	18,557	56.5
	Cyrus H. McCormick (D)	14,277	43.5
2	John F. Farnsworth (UN R)	18,298	77.8
	M. C. Johnson (D)	5,237	22.3
3	Elihu B. Washburne (UN R)	15,711	67.9
	Elius B. Stiles (D)	7,421	32.1
4	Abner C. Harding (UN R)	13,569	51.6
	Charles M. Harris (D)	12,721	48.4
5	Ebon C. Ingersoll (UN R)	18,152	61.7
	James S. Echels (D)	11,287	38.3
6	Burton C. Cook (UN R)	15,598	61.0
	Samuel K. Casey (D)	9,980	39.0
7	Henry P. H. Bromwell (UN R)	15,373	56.1
	John R. Eden (D)	12,027	43.9
8	Shelby M. Cullom (UN R)	15,812	53.0
	John T. Stuart (D)	14,027	47.0
9	Lewis W. Ross (D)	15,296	55.6
	Hugh Fullerton (UN R)	12,239	44.5
10	Anthony Thornton (UN R)	16,902	58.1
	N. M. Knapp (D)	12,176	41.9
11	Samuel S. Marshall (D)	16,703	61.0
	Ethelbert Callahan (UN R)	10,696	39.0
12	John Baker (UN R)	11,817	50.2
	William R. Morrison (D)	11,741	49.8
13	Andrew J. Kuykendall (UN R)	11,762	52.1
	William J. Allen (D)	10,759	47.7
AL	Samuel W. Moulton (UN R)	190,216	54.5
	J. C. Allen (D)	158,781	45.5

Special Election

5	Ebon C. Ingersoll (R)	12,986	62.8
	H. M. Wead	7,677	37.1

INDIANA

1	William E. Niblack (D)	14,718	53.9
	Cyrus M. Allen (UN R)	12,616	46.2
2	Michael C. Kerr (D)	11,407	54.3
	William W. Curry (UN R)	9,614	45.7
3	Ralph Hill (UN R)	12,017	51.8
	Henry W. Harrington (D)	11,173	48.2
4	John H. Farquhar (UN R)	10,015	50.2
	George Berry (D)	9,949	49.8
5	George W. Julian (UN R)	13,529	68.7
	James Brown (D)	6,161	31.3
6	Ebenezer Dumont (UN R)	18,886	63.4
	John Love (D)	10,905	36.6
7	Daniel W. Voorhees (D)	12,880‡	51.2
	Henry D. Washburn (UN R)	12,296	48.8
8	Godlove S. Orth (UN R)	13,536	52.3
	James F. Harney (D)	12,349	47.7
9	Schuyler Colfax (UN R)	16,658	52.7
	David Turpie (D)	14,942	47.3
10	Joseph D. Defrees (UN R)	14,617	51.0
	Joseph K. Edgerton (D)	14,037	49.0
11	Thomas F. Stillwell (UN R)	15,623	53.9
	James F. McDowell (D)	13,383	46.1

IOWA

	Candidates	Votes	%
1	James F. Wilson (UN R)	16,977	65.2
	J. K. Hornish (D)	9,078	34.8
2	Hiram Price (UN R)	16,571	65.3
	George H. Parker (D)	8,822	34.7
3	William B. Allison (UN R)	16,130	60.4
	B. B. Richards (D)	10,578	39.6
4	Josiah B. Grinnell (UN R)	17,169	61.5
	Ira C. Mitchell (D)	10,619	38.1
5	John A. Kasson (UN R)	13,640	65.8
	M. D. McHenry (D)	7,104	34.3
6	Asahel W. Hubbard (UN R)	8,455	72.8
	Seander Chapman (D)	3,162	27.2

KANSAS

AL	Sidney Clarke (R)	10,820	52.7
	A. L. Lee (R-UNION)	9,708	47.3

MAINE

1	John Lynch (UN)	15,096	54.6
	Sweat (D)	12,568	45.4
2	Sidney Perham (UN)	13,030	61.0
	Andrews (D)	8,344	39.0
3	James G. Blaine (UN)	14,055	59.3
	Gould (D)	9,647	40.7
4	John H. Rice (UN)	11,002	61.2
	Madigan (D)	6,983	38.8
5	Frederick A. Pike (UN)	12,538	58.2
	White (D)	9,016	41.8

MARYLAND

1	Hiram McCullough (D)	9,677	60.5
	J. A. J. Cresswell (UN R)	6,307	39.5
2	Edwin H. Webster (UN R)	9,541	69.9
	William Kimmell (D)	4,102	30.1
3	Charles E. Phelps (UN R)	9,313	84.2
	A. Lewis Knott (D)	1,753	15.8
4	Francis Thomas (UN R)	11,898	61.2
	Syester (D)	7,551	38.8
5	Benjamin G. Harris (D)	8,839	72.3
	John C. Holland (UN R)	3,389	27.7

MASSACHUSETTS

1	Thomas D. Eliot (UNT)	13,687	82.8
	Sylvanus B. Phinney (D)	2,850	17.2
2	Oakes Ames (UNT)	13,591	72.1
	James McGuire (D)	5,266	27.9
3	Alexander H. Rice (UNT)	9,711	62.3
	John S. Sleeper (D)	5,864	37.7
4	Samuel Hooper (UNT)	10,403	65.5
	Josiah G. Abbott (D)	5,485	34.5
5	John B. Alley (UNT)	13,086	75.8
	Joseph B. Morss (D)	4,158	24.1
6	Daniel W. Gooch (UNT)	13,082	71.7
	Thomas J. Greenwood (D)	5,174	28.3
7	George S. Boutwell (UNT)	12,087	69.0
	Theodore H. Sweetser (D)	5,433	31.0
8	John D. Baldwin (UNT)	12,955	74.8
	George Hodges (D)	4,377	25.3
9	William B. Washburn (UNT)	15,721	81.5
	Nathaniel Wood (D)	3,575	18.5
10	Henry L. Dawes (UNT)	11,600	64.7
	Harry Arnold (D)	6,315	35.2

MICHIGAN

1	Fernando C. Beaman (UN)	17,908	53.4
	David A. Noble (D)	15,602	46.5
2	Charles Upson (UN)	19,151	60.4
	Nathaniel A. Balch (D)	12,538	39.6
3	John W. Longyear (UN)	15,432	54.7

	Candidates	Votes	%
	David Johnson (D)	12,758	45.3
4	Thomas W. Ferry (UN)	13,428	59.2
	Frederick Hall (D)	9,256	40.8
5	Rowland E. Trowbridge (UN)	12,651	51.5
	Augustus C. Baldwin (D)	11,937	48.5
6	John F. Driggs (UN)	12,784	53.4
	William Willard (D)	11,166	46.6

MINNESOTA

1	William Windom (UN R)	13,965	60.6
	Henry W. Lamberton (D)	9,092	39.4
2	Ignatius Donnelly (UN R)	10,874	57.0
	John M. Gilman (D)	8,211	43.0

MISSOURI

1	John Hogan (D)	6,026	43.2
	Charles P. Johnson (RAD R)	4,781	34.2
	Samuel Knox (RAD R)	3,157	22.6
2	Henry T. Blow (RAD R)	11,580	90.2
	E. Stafford	1,253	9.8
3	Thomas E. Noell (RAD R)	4,075	61.7
	D. C. Tuttle (D)	1,868	28.3
	W. T. Leeper (I RAD R)	659	10.0
4	John R. Kelso (I RAD R)	3,841	49.3
	Sempronius H. Boyd (RAD R)	3,548	45.6
	M. J. Hubble (D)	400	5.1
5	Joseph W. McClurg (RAD R)	6,976	72.4
	Sample Orr (D)	2,659	27.6
6	Robert T. Van Horn (RAD R)	3,498	47.2
	Elijah H. Norton (D)	3,226	43.5
	Austin A. King (ID)	695	9.4
7	Benjamin F. Loan (RAD R)	10,445	85.9
	H. B. Branch	1,674	13.8
8	John F. Benjamin (RAD R)	8,536	74.1
	John M. Glover (C)	2,978	25.9
9	George W. Anderson (RAD R)	5,329	51.8
	Odon Guitar (D)	4,950	48.2

NEVADA

(Became a state Oct. 31, 1864)

AL	Henry G. Worthington (UN R)	9,776	59.9
	A. C. Bradford (D)	6,552	40.1

NEW JERSEY

1	John F. Starr (UN)	12,091	54.4
	Dickinson (D)	10,126	45.6
2	William A. Newell (UN)	13,953	51.6
	Middleton (D)	13,091	48.4
3	Charles Sitgreaves (D)	16,942	58.4
	Scranton (UN)	12,080	41.6
4	Andrew J. Rogers (D)	14,059	53.6
	Little (UN)	12,173	46.4
5	Edwin R. V. Wright (D)	13,390	53.9
	Wakeman (UN)	11,448	46.1

NEW YORK

1	Stephen Taber (D)	12,232	55.0
	George V. Curtis (UN)	10,023	45.0
2	Teunis G. Bergen (D)	13,610	60.7
	Samuel T. Maddox (UN)	8,829	39.3
3	James Humphrey (UN)	11,752	51.3
	Thomas H. Faron (D)	11,168	48.7
4	Morgan Jones (TAM D)	9,605	57.2
	William Walsh (MOZART D)	5,512	32.8
	Carolan O. Bryant (UN)	1,684	10.0
5	Nelson Taylor (TAM D)	9,272	53.1
	William B. Maclay (MOZART D)	4,286	24.5
	Epes P. Ellery (UN)	3,921	22.4
6	Henry J. Raymond (UN)	7,315	42.4
	Elijah Ward (TAM D)	6,929	40.2

Candidates	Votes	%
Eli P. Norton (MOZART D)	1,647	9.6
Rush C. Hawkins (IRR U)	1,347	7.8
7 John Winthrop Chanler (UN)	11,513	67.1
William Boardman (D)	5,638	32.9
8 James Brooks (D)	8,583‡	39.8
William E. Dodge (R)	8,435	39.1
Thomas J. Barr (TAM D)	4,544	21.1
9 William A. Darling (UN)	5,822	38.9
Fernando Wood (MOZART D)	4,749	31.7
Anson Herrick (TAM D)	4,397	29.4
10 William Radford (D)	13,033	56.1
Francis Larkin (UN)	10,218	44.0
11 Charles H. Winfield (D)	9,975	50.6
Ambrose S. Murray (UN)	9,736	49.4
12 John H. Ketcham (UN)	12,229	51.4
Homer A. Nelson (D)	11,559	48.6
13 Edwin N. Hubbell (D)	11,373	53.1
Theodore B. Gates (UN)	10,028	46.9
14 Charles Goodyear (D)	17,497	57.5
John H. Gardiner (UN)	12,942	42.5
15 John A. Griswold (UN)	15,251	54.1
William A. Van Alstyne (D)	12,928	45.9
16 Orlando Kellogg (UN)	8,988	53.9
Thomas S. Gray (D)	7,675	46.1
17 Calvin T. Hulburd (UN)	13,183	70.0
William J. Averill (D)	5,659	30.0
18 James M. Marvin (UN)	14,453	51.6
Alonzo C. Paige (D)	13,572	48.4
19 Demas Hubbard Jr (UN)	17,067	54.8
Hezekiah Sturges (D)	14,078	45.2
20 Addison H. Laflin (UN)	16,441	56.4
Frederick W. Hubbard (D)	12,704	43.6
21 Roscoe Conkling (UN)	11,966	52.5
Francis Kernan (D)	10,816	47.5
22 Sidney T. Holmes (UN)	14,638	60.0
Albertus Perry (D)	9,781	40.1
23 Thomas T. Davis (UN)	14,800	58.6
William C. Ruger (D)	10,464	41.4
24 Theodore M. Pomeroy (UN)	16,027	57.5
George W. Cuyler (D)	11,832	42.5
25 Daniel Morris (UN)	12,763	58.8
Barzillai Slosson (D)	8,962	41.3
26 Giles W. Hotchkiss (UN)	15,543	59.0
John Magee (D)	10,806	41.0
27 Hamilton Ward (UN)	16,945	60.3
Andrew J. McNett (D)	11,176	39.7
28 Roswell Hart (UN)	13,081	52.5
James L. Angle (D)	11,841	47.5
29 Burt Van Horn (UN)	12,671	57.1
James M. Willett (D)	9,533	42.9
30 James M. Humphrey (D)	13,231	50.7
Samuel J. Holley (UN)	12,861	49.3
31 Henry Van Aernam (UN)	13,996	65.5
Jonas K. Button (D)	7,374	34.5

Special Election

Candidates	Votes	%
1 Dwight Townsend (D)	11,828	55.0
Henry G. Stebbins (UN)	9,697	45.1

OHIO

Candidates	Votes	%
1 Benjamin Eggleston (UN R)	9,893	57.0
George E. Pugh (D)	7,464	43.0
2 Rutherford B. Hays (UN R)	10,425	58.7
J. C. Butler (D)	7,327	41.3
3 Robert C. Schenck (UN R)	14,371	55.3
David A. Houk (D)	11,605	44.7
4 William Lawrence (UN R)	12,242	56.1
John F. McKinney (D)	9,578	43.9
5 Frank C. Le Blond (D)	11,048	55.2
Moses B. Walker (UN R)	8,957	44.8
6 Reader W. Clarke (UN R)	12,615	55.3
Chilton A. White (D)	10,183	44.7
7 Samuel Shellabarger (UN R)	12,756	57.1
Samuel S. Cox (D)	9,587	42.9
8 James R. Hubbell (UN R)	10,903	54.8
William Johnston (D)	8,983	45.2
9 Ralph P. Buckland (UN R)	13,511	53.6
Warren P. Noble (D)	11,717	46.4
10 James M. Ashley (UN R)	11,732	51.8
Americus V. Rice (D)	10,905	48.2
11 Hezekiah S. Bundy (UN R)	11,581	59.8
William A. Hutchins (D)	7,793	40.2
12 William E. Finck (D)	12,965	53.3
Job E. Stevenson (UN R)	11,349	46.7
13 Columbus Delano (UN R)	11,876	50.5
Charles Follet (D)	11,651	49.5
14 Martin Walker (UN R)	12,844	55.5
George Bliss (D)	10,313	44.5
15 Tobias A. Plants (UN R)	12,847	57.3
James M. Morris (D)	9,564	42.7
16 John A. Bingham (UN R)	12,377	52.7
Joseph White (D)	11,119	47.3
17 Ephraim R. Eckley (UN R)	12,758	59.3
J. H. Wallace (D)	8,746	40.7
18 Rufus P. Spalding (UN R)	14,472	68.5
J. H. Wade (D)	6,661	31.5
19 James A. Garfield (UN R)	18,086	74.1
Halsey H. Moses (D)	6,315	25.9

OREGON

Candidates	Votes	%
AL James H. D. Henderson (UN R)	8,759	59.4
James K. Kelly (D)	5,996	40.6

PENNSYLVANIA

Candidates	Votes	%
1 Samuel J. Randall (D)	9,764	55.8
John N. Butler (R)	7,742	44.2
2 Charles O'Neill (UN R)	11,767	61.8
William M. Reilly (D)	7,290	38.3
3 Leonard Myers (UN R)	11,467	53.4
Charles Buckwalter (D)	9,992	46.6
4 William D. Kelley (UN R)	13,088	58.4
Charles Northrop (D)	9,344	41.7
5 M. Russell Thayer (UN R)	11,007	50.6
Henry P. Ross (D)	10,729	49.4
6 Benjamin M. Boyer (D)	12,847	57.1
George Bullock (UN R)	9,661	42.9
7 John M. Broomall (UN R)	10,908	60.1
John C. Beatty (D)	7,231	39.9
8 Sydenham E. Ancona (D)	12,076	66.9
William M. Heister (UN R)	5,971	33.1
9 Thaddeus Stevens (UN R)	11,804	61.7
Henry M. North (D)	7,344	38.4
10 Myer Strouse (D)	11,154	51.2
Howell Fisher (UN R)	10,629	48.8
11 Philip Johnson (D)	13,007	67.1
James L. Selfridge (UN R)	6,384	32.9
12 Charles Dennison (D)	10,573	51.3
Winthrop W. Ketcham (UN R)	10,058	48.8
13 Ulysses Mercur (UN R)	9,727	52.7
Victor E. Piollet (D)	8,723	47.3
14 George F. Miller (UN R)	11,619	51.2
W. H. Miller (D)	11,092	48.8
15 Adam J. Glossbrenner (D)	13,382	55.9
Joseph Baily (UN R)	10,576	44.1
16 William H. Koontz (UN R)	11,242‡	50.2
Alexander H. Coffroth (D)	11,174	49.9
17 Abraham A. Barker (UN R)	9,225	51.4
Robert L. Johnston (D)	8,716	48.6
18 Stephen F. Wilson (UN R)	11,533	51.9
Theo Wright (D)	10,681	48.1
19 Glenni W. Scofield (UN R)	11,631	54.0
William Bigler (D)	9,914	46.0
20 Charles V. Culver (UN R)	13,350	52.8
William L. Corbett (D)	11,942	47.2
21 John L. Dawson (D)	10,855	50.3
Smith Fuller (UN R)	10,730	49.7
22 James K. Moorhead (UN R)	11,233	61.6
James H. Hopkins (D)	7,013	38.4
23 Thomas Williams (UN R)	11,682	59.0
William J. Kountz (D)	8,122	41.0
24 George V. Lawrence (UN R)	11,727	53.7
Jesse Lazear (D)	10,112	46.3

VERMONT

Candidates	Votes	%
1 Frederick E. Woodbridge (UN)	9,133	71.5
Samuel Wells (D)	3,626	28.4
2 Justin S. Morrill (UN)	12,409	72.0
Unidentified Candidate (D)	4,793	27.8
3 Portus Baxter (UN)	9,408	74.1
Giles Harrington (D)	3,281	25.9

WEST VIRGINIA

Candidates	Votes	%
1 Chester D. Hubbard (UN R)	7,198	62.5
Samuel Crane	4,315	37.5
2 George R. Latham (UN R)	5,663	84.4
William B. Zinn	721	10.8
3 Kellian V. Whaley (UN R)	2,446	66.8
John M. Phelps	1,216	33.2

WISCONSIN

Candidates	Votes	%
1 Halbert E. Paine (R)	13,716	50.9
Cary (D)	13,230	49.1
2 Ithamar C. Sloan (R)	15,148	60.3
Smith (D)	9,969	39.7
3 Amasa Cobb (R)	14,342	63.2
Rodolf (D)	8,354	36.8
4 Charles A. Eldridge (D)	15,547	58.9
Sloan (D)	10,835	41.1
5 Philetus Sawyer (R)	12,576	56.8
Bouck (D)	9,550	43.2
6 Walter D. McIndoe (R)	12,962	65.5
Reed (D)	6,836	34.5

1865 House Elections

ALABAMA[1]

	Candidates	Votes	%
1	Charles C. Langdon	2,628*	60.2
	Mathews	918	21.0
	Cleveland	812	18.6
2	George Freeman	6,038*	82.7
	Benjamin Gardner	1,249	17.1
3	Cullen A. Battle	3,914*	44.5
	George Reese	2,031	23.1
	Robert F. Ligon	1,891	21.5
	E. Hamill	671	7.6
4	J. Taylor	5,619*	69.6
	C. W. Lee	2,446	30.3
5	Burwell Pope	3,218	38.9
	James Shield	3,187	38.6
	Morris	1,620	19.6
6	Thomas J. Foster	3,511*	45.1
	Sheats	1,992	25.6
	Skinner	1,471	18.9
	Garth	491	6.3

CONNECTICUT

		Votes	%
1	Henry C. Deming (UN R)	10,619	56.0
	Mitchell (D)	8,033	42.4
2	Samuel L. Warner (UN R)	11,236	54.1
	Russell (D)	9,521	45.9
3	Augustus Brandegee (UNR)	8,566	66.3
	Allen (D)	4,349	33.7
4	John H. Hubbard (UN R)	11,747	56.3
	Taylor (D)	9,112	43.7

KENTUCKY

		Votes	%
1	Lawrence S. Trimble (C)	5,749	61.9
	C. D. Bradley (UN)	3,542	38.1
2	Burwell C. Ritter (C)	6,974	54.7
	George H. Yeaman (UN)	5,786	45.3
3	Henry Grider (C)	6,528	57.3
	J. H. Lowry (UN)	4,871	42.7
4	Aaron Harding (C)	9,437	72.1
	Marion C. Taylor (UN)	3,652	27.9
5	Lovell H. Rousseau (UN)	5,751	54.1
	Robert Mallory (C)	4,704	44.3
6	Green Clay Smith (UN)	7,666	54.4
	A. H. Ward (C)	6,421	45.6
7	George S. Shanklin (C)	7,624	65.9
	Speed S. Fry (UN)	3,943	34.1
8	William H. Randell (UN)	10,634	73.6
	T. T. Garrard (C)	3,824	26.5
9	Samuel McKee (UN)	8,163	56.7
	J. Smith Hurt (C)	6,241	43.3

MARYLAND

Special Election

		Votes	%
2	John L. Thomas Jr (UN R)	4,677	83.1
	Kimmel (D)	950	16.9

MASSACHUSETTS

Special Election

	Candidates	Votes	%
6	Nathaniel P. Banks (UNT)	8,128	80.4
	Thomas Greenwood (D)	1,938	19.2

NEVADA

		Votes	%
AL	Delos R. Ashley (UN)	3,691	62.5
	H. K. Mitchell (D)	2,215	37.5

NEW HAMPSHIRE

		Votes	%
1	Gilman Marston (UN)	12,906	55.9
	Marcy (D)	10,190	44.1
2	Edward H. Rollins (UN)	10,984	55.3
	Clark (D)	8,894	44.7
3	James W. Patterson (UN)	11,687	56.2
	Bingham (D)	9,099	43.8

NEW YORK

Special Election

		Votes	%
16	Robert S. Hale (UN)	7,146	54.5
	Halsey R. Wing (D)	5,979	45.6

NORTH CAROLINA[2]

		Votes	%
1	Jesse R. Stubbs		*
2	Charles C. Clark (N UNION)	4,479*	93.1
3	Thomas C. Fuller (N UNION)	3,094*	52.8
	Alexander Little (N UNION)	2,292	39.2
	Thomas S. Ashe (N UNION)	469	8.0
4	Josiah Turner Jr. (N UNION)	4,179*	54.1
	John P. H. Russ (N UNION)	3,229	41.8
5	Bedford Brown (N UNION)	4,354*	50.6
	Lewis Hawes (N UNION)	4,257	49.4
6	Samuel H. Walkup (N UNION)	3,455*	41.4
	James G. Ramsay (N UNION)	3,397	40.7
	William Sloan (N UNION)	1,503	18.0
7	Alexander H. Jones (N UNION)		*
	Tod R. Caldwell (N UNION)		
	Burgess S. Gaither (N UNION)		
	J. R. Love (N UNION)		

RHODE ISLAND

		Votes	%
1	Thomas A. Jenckes (R)	5,683	99.1
2	Nathan F. Dixon (R)	2,384	64.9
	Bradford (D)	1,286	35.0

TENNESSEE

(Readmitted July 24, 1866)

		Votes	%
1	Nathaniel G. Taylor (UN)	5,056	49.2
	J. R. Miller (C)	3,620	35.2

	Candidates	Votes	%
	Randolph	1,594	15.5
2	Horace Maynard (UN)	5,599	53.0
	J. A. Cooper (C)	2,081	19.7
	Hank	1,650	15.7
	Boyd	1,210	11.5
3	William B. Stokes (UN)	2,599	68.3
	Asa Faulkner (C)	1,024	26.9
	Hood	181	4.8
4	Edmund Cooper (C)	5,318	96.2
5	William B. Campbell (C)	1,311	86.3
	S. J. Carter (UN)	208	13.7
6	Samuel M. Arnell (UN)	1,547	74.8
	Dorsey B. Thomas (C)	521	25.2
7	Isaac R. Hawkins (UN)	2,068	62.7
	Etheridge (C)	704	21.4
	Saunders	525	15.9
8	John W. Leftwich (C)	1,368	44.9
	John Bullock (UN)	597	19.6
	Sands	589	19.3
	Dunlap	493	16.2

VIRGINIA[3]

		Votes	%
1	Curtis	978*	37.8
	Christian	856	33.1
	Doug	756	29.2
2	L. H. Chandler (UN)	1,583*	50.2
	John S. Millson	1,029	32.6
	Kilby	544	17.2
3	B. Johnson Barbour	4,944*	79.4
	Pendleton	906	14.6
	Martin Lipscomb	334	5.4
4	Robert Ridgway	3,369*	76.9
	Alexander Fitzpatrick	1,010	23.1
5	Davis	1,718*	29.3
	Stovall	1,675	28.6
	Mosby	1,187	20.2
	Withers	958	16.3
6	Alexander H. H. Stuart	4,653*	67.3
	John F. Lewis	2,194	31.7
7	Robert Y. Conrad	4,853*	72.1
	Lewis McKenzie	1,722	25.6
8	Hoge	4,897*	64.6
	Miller	1,259	16.6
	Longley	1,118	14.8

1. Alabama held elections for the House but none of the winners was seated. The state was not readmitted until July 13, 1868.

2. North Carolina held elections for the House but none of the winners was seated. The state was not readmitted until July 4, 1868.

3. Virginia held elections for the House but none of the winners was seated. The state was not readmitted until Jan. 26, 1870.

1866 House Elections

ALABAMA[1]

Special Election

	Candidates	Votes	%
2	J. M. Wiley		
	J. L. Pugh		
	Bolling Hall		
	J. Clements		

DELAWARE

	Candidates	Votes	%
AL	John A. Nicholson (D)	9,933	53.7
	John L. McKim (R)	8,553	46.3

ILLINOIS

		Votes	%
1	Norman B. Judd (R)	15,247	72.9
	M. R. M. Wallace (D)	5,667	27.1
2	John F. Farnsworth (R)	16,185	82.9
	E. M. Haines (D)	3,346	17.1
3	Elihu B. Washburne (R)	14,657	70.9
	Thomas J. Turner (D)	5,897	28.5
4	Abner C. Harding (R)	15,952	54.4
	John S. Thompson (D)	13,391	45.6
5	Ebon C. Ingersoll (R)	18,437	65.6
	Silas Ramsey (D)	9,665	34.4
6	Burton C. Cook (R)	15,015	66.0
	S. H. Harris (D)	7,721	34.0
7	Henry P. H. Bromwell (R)	17,410	56.7
	Charles Black (D)	13,272	43.3
8	Shelby M. Cullom (R)	18,623	56.2
	Edwin S. Fowler (D)	14,520	43.8
9	Lewis W. Ross (D)	15,496	51.3
	Charles E. Lippencott (R)	14,721	48.7
10	Albert G. Burr (D)	17,116	53.7
	Henry Case (R)	14,743	46.3
11	Samuel S. Marshall (D)	16,668	53.7
	Edward Kitchell (R)	14,378	46.3
12	Jehu Baker (R)	13,032	52.2
	William R. Morrison (D)	11,956	47.9
13	Green B. Raum (R)	13,459	51.1
	William J. Allen (D)	12,890	48.9
AL	John A. Logan (R)	203,045	57.9
	T. Lyle Dickey (D)	147,435	42.1

INDIANA

		Votes	%
1	William E. Niblack (D)	17,255	52.0
	Debruler (R)	15,905	48.0
2	Michael C. Kerr (D)	13,421	53.5
	Gresham (R)	11,678	46.5
3	Morton C. Hunter (R)	13,848	51.3
	Harrgtn (D)	13,158	48.7
4	William S. Holman (D)	11,921	51.9
	Grover (R)	11,052	48.1
5	George W. Julian (R)	13,416	65.1
	Bundy (D)	7,188	34.9
6	John Coburn (R)	16,719	54.0
	Lord (D)	14,245	46.0
7	Henry D. Washburn (R)	14,871	50.9
	Claypl (D)	14,358	49.1
8	Godlove S. Orth (R)	14,933	50.4
	Purdue (D)	14,728	49.7
9	Schuyler Colfax (R)	20,221	52.8
	David Turpie (D)	18,073	47.2
10	William Williams (R)	17,414	51.9
	Lowry (D)	16,142	48.1
11	John P. C. Shanks (R)	18,145	54.3
	Snow (D)	15,268	45.7

IOWA

		Votes	%
1	James F. Wilson (R)	16,388	60.9
	Fitz Henry Warren (D)	10,515	39.1
2	Hiram Price (R)	16,257	63.8
	John P. Cook (D)	9,220	36.2

	Candidates	Votes	%
3	William B. Allison (R)	15,472	58.7
	Reuben Noble (D)	10,470	39.7
4	William Loughridge (R)	18,529	59.8
	Cyms H. Mackey (D)	12,395	40.0
5	Grenville M. Dodge (R)	14,236	59.0
	James M. Tuttle (D)	9,897	41.0
6	Asahel W. Hubbard (R)	9,970	69.9
	J. D. Thompson (D)	3,938	27.6

KANSAS

		Votes	%
AL	Sidney Clarke (R)	19,200	70.0
	C. W. Blair (N UNION)	8,206	29.9

KENTUCKY

Special Elections

		Votes	%
3	Elijah Hise (D)	6,493	74.3
	P. B. Hawkins (UN)	2,244	25.7
5	Lovell H. Rousseau (R)	2,494	99.0
6	Andrew H. Ward (D)	8,725	88.4
	R. R. Carpenter (UN)	1,068	10.8

MAINE

		Votes	%
1	John Lynch (R)	15,612	57.0
	Sweat (D)	11,753	42.9
2	Sidney Perham (R)	13,883	65.3
	Morrill	7,363	34.7
3	James G. Blaine (R)	14,909	63.8
	Heath (D)	8,338	35.7
4	John A. Peters (R)	11,911	64.4
	Weston (D)	6,565	35.5
5	Frederick A. Pike (R)	12,422	61.0
	Crosby (D)	7,773	38.1

MARYLAND

		Votes	%
1	Hiram McCullough (D)	11,729	74.2
	George Russum (R)	4,052	25.6
2	Stevenson Archer (D)	7,091	58.6
	John Thomas (R)	5,014	41.4
3	Charles E. Phelps (D)	5,545	54.8
	J. J. Stewart (R)	4,568	45.2
4	Francis Thomas (R)	10,252	52.6
	William Omauleby (D)	9,230	47.4
5	Frederick Stone (D)	8,708	81.1
	William Albert (R)	2,032	18.9

MASSACHUSETTS

		Votes	%
1	Thomas D. Eliot (R)	8,184	84.1
	Mathias Ellias (D)	1,539	15.8
2	Oakes Ames (R)	9,581	79.4
	Unidentified Candidate (D)	2,456	20.4
3	Ginery Twichell (R)	6,084	66.5
	William Aspinwall (D)	2,601	28.4
	P. R. Guiney (WM)	463	5.1
4	Samuel Hooper (R)	7,901	71.2
	Joseph Wightman (D)	3,187	28.7
5	Benjamin F. Butler (R)	9,021	75.6
	William D. Northend (D)	2,838	23.8
6	Nathaniel P. Banks (R)	10,075	74.7
	F. O. Prince (D)	3,366	24.9
7	George S. Boutwell (R)	9,847	77.3
	Leverett Saltonstall (D)	2,885	22.7
8	John D. Baldwin (R)	9,039	82.5
	William A. Williams (D)	1,901	17.4
9	William B. Washburn (R)	11,895	87.0
	Levi Haywood (D)	1,768	12.9
10	Henry L. Dawes (R)	8,125	65.7
	Abijah W. Chapin (D)	4,185	33.9

MICHIGAN

	Candidates	Votes	%
1	Fernando C. Beaman (R)	17,319	56.3
	Chipman (D)	13,443	43.7
2	Charles Upson (R)	19,623	63.6
	Severns (D)	11,228	36.4
3	Austin Blair (R)	16,240	56.9
	Granger (D)	12,288	43.1
4	Thomas W. Ferry (R)	15,305	65.2
	Hutchins (D)	8,154	34.8
5	Rowland E. Trowbridge (R)	14,046	54.6
	Bancroft (D)	11,664	45.4
6	John F. Driggs (R)	14,476	57.8
	Rose (D)	10,570	42.2

MINNESOTA

		Votes	%
1	William Windom (R)	14,810	64.2
	Jones (D)	8,245	35.8
2	Ignatius Donnelly (R)	12,022	60.8
	Colvill (D)	7,754	39.2

MISSOURI

		Votes	%
1	William A. Pile (R)	6,728	50.8
	John Hogan	6,510	49.2
2	Carman A. Newcomb (R)	9,568	59.1
	William V. N. Bay	6,636	41.0
3	Thomas E. Noell (RAD R)	✓	
	Albert Jackson		
4	Joseph J. Gravely (R)	✓	
	John S. Waddill		
5	Joseph W. McClurg (RAD R)	✓	
	Thomas L. Price		
6	Robert T. Van Horn (R)	✓	
	James H. Birgh		
	L. S. McCoy		
7	Benjamin F. Loan (RAD R)	✓	
	George A. Hawley		
8	John F. Benjamin (R)	✓	
	John M. Glover		
9	George W. Anderson (RAD R)	✓	
	William F. Switzler (D)		

NEBRASKA

(Became a state March 1, 1867)

		Votes	%
AL	John Taffe (UN R)	4,621	53.0
	A. S. Paddock (D)	4,072	46.7

Special Election

		Votes	%
AL	Turner M. Marquette (R)	4,820	54.2
	J. R. Brooke (D)	4,072	45.8

NEVADA

		Votes	%
AL	Delos R. Ashley (R)	5,047	54.6
	H. K. Mitchell (D)	4,196	45.4

NEW JERSEY

		Votes	%
1	William Moore (R)	12,468	57.8
	Slape (D)	9,108	42.2
2	Charles Haight (D)	13,825	50.6
	Newell (R)	13,476	49.4
3	Charles Sitgreaves (D)	15,768	54.9
	Davidson (R)	12,955	45.1
4	John Hill (R)	13,861	50.5
	Rogers (D)	13,399	48.8
5	George A. Halsey (R)	12,782	51.9
	Gilchrist (D)	11,847	48.1

NEW YORK

	Candidates	Votes	%
1	Stephen Taber (D)	10,458	52.8
	William H. Gleason (R)	9,362	47.2
2	Demas Barnes (D)	15,614	62.5
	James A. Vanbrunt (R)	8,985	36.0
3	William E. Robinson (D)	12,634	53.9
	Simeon B. Chittenden (R)	10,803	46.1
4	John Fox (D)	14,003	78.9
	Horace Greeley (R)	3,743	21.1
5	John Morrissey (ID)	9,162	51.0
	Nelson Taylor (D)	6,503	36.2
	Eneas Elliott (R)	2,293	12.8
6	Thomas E. Stewart (C)	9,452	55.2
	Charles S. Spencer (R)	6,955	40.6
7	John W. Chanler (D)	11,503	63.0
	George F. Steinbrenner (R)	6,743	37.0
8	James Brooks (D)	13,816	62.7
	Legrand B. Cannon (R)	8,210	37.2
9	Fernando Wood (D)	9,605	54.6
	William A. Darling (R)	7,995	45.4
10	William H. Robertson (R)	12,012	54.7
	William Radford (D)	9,957	45.3
11	Charles H. Van Wyck (R)	10,194	50.7
	Isaac Anderson (D)	9,933	49.4
12	John H. Ketcham (R)	12,535	53.6
	Casper P. Collier (D)	10,840	46.4
13	Thomas Cornell (R)	10,521	50.8
	Joseph H. Tuthill (D)	10,179	49.2
14	John V. L. Pruyn (D)	15,620	51.1
	Joseph H. Ramsey (R)	14,972	48.9
15	John A. Griswold (R)	15,689	60.2
	Nathaniel B. Milliman (D)	10,373	39.8
16	Orange Ferriss (R)	9,341	55.8
	George V. Hoyle (D)	7,412	44.2
17	Calvin T. Hulburd (R)	13,449	72.4
	Darius W. Lawrence (D)	5,116	27.6
18	James M. Marvin (R)	15,496	55.7
	Thomas R. Horton (D)	12,342	44.3
19	William C. Fields (R)	17,277	55.9
	Stephen C. Johnson (D)	13,621	44.1
20	Addison H. Laflin (R)	16,498	58.4
	Edward S. Lansing (D)	11,734	41.6
21	Roscoe Conkling (R)	12,470*	53.0
	Palmer V. Kellogg (D)	11,053	47.0
22	John C. Churchill (R)	14,461	62.1
	Albertus Perry (D)	8,827	37.9
23	Dennis McCarthy (R)	15,260	60.5
	William C. Ruger (D)	9,966	39.5
24	Theodore M. Pomeroy (R)	16,189	58.7
	George Humphreys (D)	11,404	41.3
25	William H. Kelsey (R)	12,637	60.3
	Henry O. Chesebro (D)	8,334	39.7
26	William S. Lincoln (R)	16,264	60.0
	Henry McCormick (D)	10,849	40.0
27	Hamilton Ward (R)	17,750	60.8
	John G. Collins (D)	11,435	39.2
28	Lewis Selye (D)	12,791	54.3
	Roswell Hart (R)	10,757	45.7
29	Burt Van Horn (R)	12,204	57.2
	Harlow S. Comstock (D)	9,131	42.8
30	James M. Humphrey (D)	13,402	52.6
	Almon M. Clapp (R)	12,085	47.4
31	Henry Van Aernam (R)	14,405	66.4
	Hanson A. Risley (D)	7,299	33.6

Special Election

	Candidates	Votes	%
3	John W. Hunter (D)	12,774	54.4
	Simeon B. Chittenden (R)	10,715	45.6

OHIO

	Candidates	Votes	%
1	Benjamin Eggleston (UN R)	10,422	52.3
	George H. Pendleton (D)	9,496	47.7
2	Rutherford B. Hayes (UN R)	11,549	56.2
	Theodore Cook (D)	8,991	43.8
3	Robert C. Schenck (UN R)	15,027	51.8
	J. Durbin Ward (D)	13,960	48.2
4	William Lawrence (UN R)	13,313	54.6
	John F. McKinney (D)	11,059	45.4
5	William Mungen (D)	13,524	55.4
	Moses B. Walker (UN R)	10,872	44.6
6	Reader W. Clarke (UN R)	13,846	53.0
	William Howard (D)	12,267	47.0
7	Samuel Shellabarger (UN R)	13,687	54.3
	Thomas Miller (D)	11,516	45.7
8	Cornelius S. Hamilton (UN R)	11,710	54.3
	William P. Reid (D)	9,858	45.7
9	Ralph P. Buckland (UN R)	15,231	52.2
	T. P. Finefrock (D)	13,944	47.8
10	James M. Ashley (UN R)	14,873	53.4
	H. S. Commager (D)	12,956	46.6
11	John T. Wilson (UN R)	12,783	56.2
	Oscar F. Moore (D)	9,945	43.8
12	Philadelph Van Trump (D)	14,546	56.2
	Wells S. Jones (UN R)	11,336	43.8
13	George W. Morgan (D)	13,228‡	50.5
	Columbus Delano (UN R)	12,957	49.5
14	Martin Welker (UN R)	13,494	53.4
	J. B. Young (D)	11,787	46.6
15	Tobias A. Plants (UN R)	12,816	54.4
	M. D. Follett (D)	10,752	45.6
16	John A. Bingham (UN R)	13,369	52.8
	C. H. Mitchner (D)	11,947	47.2
17	Ephraim R. Eckley (UN R)	13,917	60.0
	Louis Schaefer (D)	9,275	40.0
18	Rufus P. Spalding (UN R)	14,479	64.5
	Oliver H. Payne (D)	7,974	35.5
19	James A. Garfield (UN R)	18,362	71.3
	D. C. Coolman (D)	7,376	28.7

OREGON

	Candidates	Votes	%
AL	Rufus Mallory (R)	10,362	51.4
	James D. Fay (D)	9,808	48.6

PENNSYLVANIA

	Candidates	Votes	%
1	Samuel J. Randall (D)	12,192	61.2
	Charles Gibbons (R)	7,728	38.8
2	Charles O'Neill (R)	12,612	57.1
	John Hulme (D)	9,475	42.9
3	Leonard Myers (R)	12,520	52.1
	C. Buckwalter (D)	11,516	47.9
4	William D. Kelley (R)	14,551	54.6
	John Welsh (D)	12,126	45.5
5	Caleb N. Taylor (R)	12,259	51.0
	H. P. Ross (D)	11,800	49.0
6	Benjamin M. Boyer (D)	14,009	55.0
	David Thomas (R)	11,447	45.0
7	John N. Broomall (R)	12,011	58.5
	N. Pratt (D)	8,531	41.5
8	J. Lawrence Getz (D)	13,188	65.3
	D. J. Lincoln (R)	6,999	34.7

	Candidates	Votes	%
9	Thaddeus Stevens (R)	14,298	62.2
	S. H. Reynolds (D)	8,675	37.8
10	Henry L. Cake (R)	13,186	50.4
	C. D. Gloninger (D)	12,971	49.6
11	Daniel M. Van Auken (D)	15,907	63.4
	William Lilly (R)	9,195	36.6
12	Charles Denison (D)	15,280	53.5
	James Archibald (R)	13,274	46.5
13	Ulysses Mercur (R)	11,940	52.9
	William Elwell (D)	10,653	47.2
14	George F. Miller (R)	14,190	52.8
	Bower (D)	12,675	47.2
15	Adam J. Glossbrenner (D)	15,830	55.9
	R. M. Henderson (R)	12,489	44.1
16	William H. Koontz (R)	13,589	51.2
	Sharpe (D)	12,964	48.8
17	Daniel J. Morrell (R)	11,298	52.4
	R. L. Johnston (D)	10,249	47.6
18	Stephen F. Wilson (R)	14,734	53.7
	Theo F. Wright (D)	12,688	46.3
19	Glenni W. Scofield (R)	15,107	54.8
	W. W. L. Scott (D)	12,481	45.2
20	Darwin A. Finney (R)	17,106	52.9
	A. B. McCalmont (D)	15,225	47.1
21	John Covode (R)	13,023	50.7
	Wier (D)	12,669	49.3
22	James K. Moorhead (R)	12,720	56.9
	J. B. Switzer (D)	9,655	43.2
23	Thomas Williams (R)	14,197	58.6
	B. G. Childs (D)	10,012	41.4
24	George V. Lawrence (R)	13,391	53.1
	W. Montgomery (D)	11,853	47.0

VERMONT[2]

	Candidates	Votes	%
1	Frederick E. Woodbridge (R)	10,568	77.5
	Samuel Wells (D)	3,036	22.3
2	Luke P. Poland (R)	10,844	72.2
	Charles M. Chase (D)	3,935	26.2
3	Portus Baxter (R)	7,329*	46.8
	Hogt (D)	4,511	28.8
	Brigham	3,395	21.7

WEST VIRGINIA

	Candidates	Votes	%
1	Chester D. Hubbard (R)	10,001	54.8
	D. D. Johnson (D)	8,239	45.2
2	Bethuel M. Kitchen (R)	8,296	61.5
	E. W. Andrews (D)	5,190	38.5
3	Daniel Polsley (R)	4,927	58.8
	John H. Oley (D)	3,456	41.2

WISCONSIN

	Candidates	Votes	%
1	Halbert E. Paine (R)	14,678	58.8
	Brown (D)	10,298	41.2
2	Benjamin F. Hopkins (R)	14,129	61.5
	Pease (D)	8,833	38.5
3	Amasa Cobb (R)	13,006	63.0
	Virgin (D)	7,655	37.1
4	Charles A. Eldridge (D)	12,839	56.6
	Hatch (R)	9,855	43.4
5	Philetus Sawyer (R)	14,341	60.5
	Martin (D)	9,347	39.5
6	Cadwallader C. Washburn (R)	13,161	66.4
	Park (D)	6,648	33.6

1. The winner of this election is unknown and was not seated by the House.

2. No candidate received a majority of the vote in the 3rd district, which was required for election. Portus Baxter declined to enter a later special election held to determine a winner. Worthington C. Smith (R) was eventually elected; returns are unavailable.

1867 House Elections

CALIFORNIA

	Candidates	Votes	%
1	Samuel B. Axtell (D)	18,793	57.3
	Timothy G. Phelps (R)	13,989	42.7
2	William Higby (R)	16,053	52.1
	J. W. Coffroth (D)	14,786	48.0
3	James A. Johnson (D)	14,767	50.6
	C. Hartson (R)	14,394	49.4

CONNECTICUT

1	Richard D. Hubbard (D)	11,994	51.1
	Henry C. Deming (R)	11,477	48.9
2	Julius Hotchkiss (D)	14,730	53.2
	Cyrus Northrop (R)	12,937	46.8
3	Henry H. Starkweather (R)	9,723	55.4
	Earl Martin (D)	7,827	44.6
4	William H. Barnum (D)	13,083	51.9
	Phineas T. Barnum (R)	12,103	48.0

KENTUCKY

1	Lawrence S. Trimble (D)	9,787	84.6
	George G. Symes (R)	1,780	15.4
2	John Y. Brown (D)	8,922*	69.2
	Samuel E. Smith (R)	2,816	21.8
	B. C. Ritter (C)	1,155	9.0
3	Elijah Hise (D)	7,740	86.6
	George D. Blakey (R)	1,201	13.4
4	J. Proctor Knott (D)	8,199	74.6
	Marion C. Taylor (R)	2,277	20.7
5	Asa P. Grover (D)	7,118	69.3
	R. J. Jacob (C)	2,417	23.5
	William A. Bullitt (R)	742	7.2
6	Thomas L. Jones (D)	9,488	72.4
	W. L. Rankin (R)	3,587	27.4

	Candidates	Votes	%
7	James B. Beck (D)	9,716	76.1
	William Brown (R)	1,664	13.0
	Charles Hanson (C)	1,388	10.9
8	George M. Adams (D)	7,609	51.2
	Milton L. Rice (R)	7,244	48.8
9	John D. Young (D)	9,042	51.8
	Samuel McKee (R)	7,563✓	43.3

Special Election

3	Jacob S. Golladay (D)	6,619	76.2
	J. R. Curd (C)	1,175	13.5
	W. T. Jackman (R)	850	9.8

MISSOURI

Special Election

3	James R. McCormick (D)	✓	
	James H. Chase (R)		

NEW HAMPSHIRE

1	Jacob H. Ela (R)	13,243	51.9
	Daniel Marcy (D)	12,247	48.0
2	Aaron F. Stevens (R)	11,260	52.2
	Edward W. Harrington (D)	10,305	47.8
3	Jacob Benton (R)	11,294	52.2
	Harry Bingham (D)	10,246	47.3

OHIO

Special Election

2	Samuel F. Cary (IR)	10,390	52.1
	Richard Smith (R)	9,431	47.3

PENNSYLVANIA

Special Election

	Candidates	Votes	%
12	George W. Woodward (D)	12,623	51.1
	W. W. Kotcham (R)	12,078	48.9

RHODE ISLAND

1	Thomas A. Jenckes (R)	4,311	97.7
2	Nathan F. Dixon (R)	2,669	64.2
	Carder (D)	1,480	35.6

TENNESSEE

1	Roderick R. Butler (R)	12,472✓	
	J. White (C)	1,746	
	Joseph Powell (R)		
2	Horace Maynard (R)	11,994	79.8
	John Williams (C)	3,039	20.2
3	William B. Stokes (R)	8,030	83.3
	Eli G. Fleming (C)	1,614	16.7
4	James Mullins (R)	9,448	74.6
	Edward Cooper (C)	3,221	25.4
5	John Trimble (R)	9,357✓	
	Bailey Peyton (C)	3,163	
	D. H. Mason (IR)		
6	Samuel M. Arnell (R)	7,596	77.8
	Dorsey B. Thomas (C)	2,170	22.2
7	Isaac R. Hawkins (R)	5,000	83.6
	W. P. Coldwell (C)	981	16.4
8	David A. Nunn (R)	9,057	59.4
	J. F. Leftwick (C)	6,189	40.6

1868 House Elections

ALABAMA[1]

(Readmitted July 13, 1868)

	Candidates	Votes	%
1	Francis W. Kellogg (R)	16,094	100.0
2	Charles W. Buckley (R)	8,440	100.0
3	Benjamin W. Norris (R)	9,451	99.6
4	Charles W. Pierce (R)	19,593	99.8
5	John B. Callis (R)	3,569	54.0
	J. W. Burke	2,458	37.2
	Whitley Thomas Ewing	573	8.7
6	Thomas Haughey	2,678	44.1
	McCauley	1,440	23.7
	Cramer	1,021	16.8
	Snelling (R)	825	13.6

ARKANSAS[2]

(Readmitted June 22, 1868)

	Candidates	Votes	%
1	Logan H. Roots (R)	7,151	50.6
	Charles S. Cameron (D)	6,987	49.4
2	Anthony A. C. Rogers (D)	6,518	55.0
	James T. Elliott (R)	5,332	45.0
3	Thomas Boles (R)	9,547	62.9
	L. B. Nash (D)	5,630	37.1

CALIFORNIA

	Candidates	Votes	%
1	Samuel B. Axtell (D)	23,632	54.1
	F. M. Pixley (R)	20,081	45.9
2	Aaron A. Sargent (R)	18,264	54.7
	J. W. Coffroth (D)	15,124	45.3
3	James A. Johnson (D)	15,792	50.4
	C. Hartson (R)	15,527	49.6

DELAWARE

	Candidates	Votes	%
AL	Benjamin T. Biggs (D)	10,961	58.9
	Torbert (R)	7,636	41.1

FLORIDA[3]

(Readmitted June 25, 1868)

	Candidates	Votes	%
AL	Charles M. Hamilton (R)	✓	
	Friend (D)		
	Liberty Billings		

GEORGIA[4]

	Candidates	Votes	%
1	Joseph W. Clift (R)	11,990	59.6
	Fitch (D)	8,141	40.4
2	Nelson Tift (D)	13,645	53.9
	Richard H. Whitely (R)	11,696	46.2
3	William P. Edwards (R)	12,806	52.5
	Alexander (D)	11,581	47.5
4	Samuel F. Gove (R)	11,078	50.4
	Lochrane (D)	10,917	49.6
5	Charles H. Prince (R)	✓	
	Hilliard (D)		
6	John H. Christy (D)	8,340*	51.3
	John A. Wimpey (R)	7,929	48.7
7	Pierce M. B. Young (D)	11,160	58.1
	James Adkins (R)	8,054	41.9

ILLINOIS

	Candidates	Votes	%
1	Norman B. Judd (R)	27,414	58.8
	M. R. M. Wallace (D)	19,233	41.2
2	John F. Farnsworth (R)	20,725	76.7
	A. M. Herrington (D)	6,307	23.3
3	Elihu B. Washburne (R)	18,584	65.9
	W. J. McKim (D)	9,612	34.1
4	John B. Hawley (R)	17,269	52.6
	James W. Singleton (D)	15,547	47.4

	Candidates	Votes	%
5	Ebon C. Ingersoll (R)	20,991	60.2
	John N. Niglas (D)	13,686	39.2
6	Burton C. Cook (R)	19,607	62.1
	Oliver C. Gray (D)	11,946	37.9
7	Jesse H. Moore (R)	22,321	56.5
	Thomas Brewer (D)	17,171	43.5
8	Shelby M. Cullom (R)	22,193	53.5
	B. S. Edwards (D)	19,309	46.5
9	Thompson W. McNeely (D)	17,877	53.9
	Leonard F. Ross (R)	15,279	46.1
10	Albert G. Burr (D)	21,420	55.2
	Iona B. Turner (R)	17,397	44.8
11	Samuel S. Marshall (D)	20,475	55.2
	James S. Martin (R)	16,642	44.8
12	John B. Hays (R)	14,980	52.9
	William M. Snyder (D)	13,338	47.1
13	John M. Crebs (D)	14,764	50.9
	Green B. Raum (R)	14,261	49.1
AL	John A. Logan (R)	249,422	55.5
	William W. O'Brien (D)	199,861	44.5

INDIANA

	Candidates	Votes	%
1	William E. Niblack (D)	18,116	52.1
	Veatch (R)	16,631	47.9
2	Michael C. Kerr (D)	18,779	60.3
	Gresham (R)	12,343	39.7
3	William S. Holman (D)	15,665	51.3
	Lamb (R)	14,903	48.8
4	George W. Julian (R)	13,413	50.2
	Reid (D)	13,297	49.8
5	John Coburn (R)	15,715	51.7
	Keightly (D)	14,683	48.3
6	Daniel W. Voorhees (D)	16,582	50.2
	Carter (R)	16,455	49.8
7	Godlove S. Orth (R)	16,117	50.7
	Mahlon D. Manson (D)	15,660	49.3
8	Daniel D. Pratt (R)	17,227*	53.5
	Ross (D)	14,946	46.5
9	John P. C. Shanks (R)	15,597	51.6
	Lowry (D)	14,656	48.4
10	William Williams (R)	16,551	53.8
	Ellison (D)	14,228	46.2
11	Jasper Packard (R)	15,489	52.1
	Farrand (D)	14,268	48.0

IOWA

	Candidates	Votes	%
1	George W. McCrary (R)	17,718	58.2
	T. W. Clagett (D)	12,705	41.8
2	William Smyth (R)	18,753	58.6
	William E. Leffingwell (D)	13,227	41.4
3	William B. Allison (R)	20,119	58.5
	William Mills (D)	14,120	41.1
4	William Loughridge (R)	24,057	59.3
	J. P. Irish (D)	16,531	40.7
5	Francis W. Palmer (R)	20,409	60.4
	P. Gad Bryan (D)	13,402	39.6
6	Charles Pomeroy (R)	16,775	72.8
	G. A. L. Roszell (D)	6,257	27.2

KANSAS

	Candidates	Votes	%
AL	Sidney Clarke (R)	29,324	67.7
	C. W. Blair (D)	13,969	32.3

KENTUCKY

	Candidates	Votes	%
1	Lawrence S. Trimble (D)	13,608	87.0
	Charles A. Marshall (R)	1,731	11.1
2	William N. Sweeney (D)	12,786	78.3
	Samuel W. Langley (R)	3,538	21.7
3	Jacob S. Golladay (D)	9,469	80.4
	William E. Hobson (R)	2,303	19.6
4	J. Proctor Knott (D)	13,166	87.9
	William H. Hays (R)	1,811	12.1

	Candidates	Votes	%
5	Boyd Winchester (D)	15,108	90.9
	J. B. English (R)	1,515	9.1
6	Thomas L. Jones (D)	14,082	69.7
	O. W. Root (R)	6,137	30.4
7	James B. Beck (D)	13,019	84.6
	Charles Eginton (R)	2,373	15.4
8	George M. Adams (D)	10,318	51.1
	Sydney M. Barnes (R)	9,861	48.9
9	John M. Rice (D)	10,510	61.2
	J. L. Zeigler (R)	6,652	38.8

LOUISIANA[5]

(Readmitted July 9, 1868)

	Candidates	Votes	%
1	Louis St. Martin (D)	12,377*	85.1
	J. Hale Sypher (R)	2,175	15.0
2	Caleb S. Hunt (D)	14,829	44.8
	Lionel A. Sheldon (R)	9,695✓	29.3
	J. W. Menard (R)	8,615	26.0
3	Adolphe Bailey (D)	17,513	67.1
	Chester B. Darrall (R)	8,593✓	32.9
4	Michael Ryan (D)	13,352	64.4
	Joseph P. Newsham (R)	7,395✓	35.6
5	G. W. McCranie (D)	13,716*	67.9
	Frank Morey (R)	3,423	16.9
	P. J. Kennedy (R)	3,076	15.2

MAINE

	Candidates	Votes	%
1	John Lynch (R)	16,818	53.6
	Charles A. Shaw (D)	14,579	46.4
2	Samuel P. Morrill (R)	14,281	59.6
	Alonzo Garcelon (D)	9,653	40.3
3	James G. Blaine (R)	16,121	57.3
	E. Wilder Farley (D)	11,982	42.6
4	John A. Peters (R)	13,338	61.2
	George W. Ladd (D)	8,304	38.1
5	Eugene Hale (R)	14,363	55.2
	Arno Wiswell (D)	11,680	44.9

MARYLAND

	Candidates	Votes	%
1	Samuel Hambleton (D)	12,703	73.4
	Henry R. Torbert (R)	4,606	26.6
2	Stevenson Archer (D)	12,671	68.6
	John T. Ensor (R)	5,796	31.4
3	Thomas Swann (D)	13,056	69.7
	Adam E. King (R)	5,667	30.3
4	Patrick Hamill (D)	12,289	51.3
	Daniel E. Weisel (R)	11,653	48.7
5	Frederick Stone (D)	9,924	82.0
	William J. Albert (R)	2,176	18.0

MASSACHUSETTS

	Candidates	Votes	%
1	James Buffinton (R)	12,975	78.5
	Philandor Cobb	3,486	21.1
2	Oakes Ames (R)	14,498	71.8
	Edward Arery (D)	5,695	28.2
3	Ginery Twichell (R)	9,074	56.8
	Edwin C. Bailey (D)	6,892	43.1
4	Samuel Hooper (R)	11,328	56.9
	Peter Harvey (D)	8,592	43.1
5	Benjamin F. Butler (R)	13,109	65.5
	Otis P. Lord (D)	5,061	25.3
	Richard A. Dana Jr (IR)	1,811	9.1
6	Nathaniel P. Banks (R)	13,933	65.9
	Frederick O. Prince (D)	7,187	34.0
7	George S. Boutwell (R)	13,214	65.4
	Leverett Saltonstall (D)	6,995	34.6
8	George F. Hoar (R)	14,317	74.1
	Henry H. Stevens (D)	4,974	25.8
9	William B. Washburn (R)	16,985	82.9
	Levi Heywood (D)	1,814	8.9

Candidates	Votes	%
Charles Heywood (D)	1,691	8.3
10 Henry L. Dawes (R)	12,260	62.1
Abijah W. Chapin (D)	7,490	37.9

MICHIGAN

Candidates	Votes	%
1 Fernando C. Beaman (R)	22,197	51.9
Merrill I. Mills (D)	20,595	48.1
2 William L. Stoughton (R)	25,205	59.2
Henry Chamberlain (D)	17,401	40.8
3 Austin Blair (R)	19,268	54.2
Isaac M. Crane (D)	16,268	45.8
4 Thomas W. Ferry (R)	23,043	62.7
Lyman G. Mason (D)	13,714	37.3
5 Omar D. Conger (R)	16,347	52.8
Byron G. Stout (D)	14,622	47.2
6 Randolph Strickland (R)	20,118	54.6
William Newton (D)	16,720	45.4

MINNESOTA

Candidates	Votes	%
1 Morton S. Wilkinson (R)	23,764	61.9
Batchelder (D)	14,646	38.1
2 Eugene M. Wilson (D)	13,506	40.5
Ignatius Donnelly (OPP R)	11,265	33.8
Andrews (R)	8,598	25.8

MISSISSIPPI[6]

(Readmitted Feb. 23, 1870)

Candidates	Votes	%
1 Townsend (D)	11,029	65.5
Wofford (R)	5,823	34.6
2 Martin (D)	11,504	65.5
Railsback (R)	6,068	34.5
3 Turner (D)	11,681	53.4
Sullivan (R)	10,181	46.6
4 George C. McKee (R)	20,444	56.9
Potter (D)	15,510	43.1
5 Martin (D)	12,686	51.6
Pierce (R)	11,886	48.4

MISSOURI

Candidates	Votes	%
1 Erastus Wells (D)	9,734	50.5
William A. Pile (R)	9,553	49.5
2 Gustavus A. Finkelinburg (R)	11,506	58.2
James J. Lindley (D)	8,279	41.8
3 James R. McCormick (D)	5,153	54.9
John F. Bush (R)	4,226	45.1
4 Sempronius H. Boyd (R)	8,919	58.5
Charles B. McAfee (D)	4,949	32.5
John R. Kelso (R)	1,384	9.1
5 Samuel S. Burdett (R)	11,187	58.5
John F. Phillips (D)	7,941	41.5
6 Robert T. Van Horn (R)	5,427	54.3
James Shields (D)	4,560	45.7
7 Joel F. Asper (R)	15,272	65.5
Mordecai Oliver (D)	8,029	34.5
8 John F. Benjamin (R)	8,954	52.1
John F. Williams (D)	8,248	48.0
9 David P. Dyer (R)	5,407	52.1
William F. Switzler (D)	4,981	48.0

Special Election

	Votes	%
5 John H. Stover (R)	11,387	59.5
Ignatius Hazel (D)	7,757	40.5

NEBRASKA

	Votes	%
AL John Taffe (R)	8,715	58.5
Andrew J. Poppleton (D)	6,192	41.5

NEVADA

	Votes	%
AL Thomas Fitch (R)	6,230	53.8
William F. Anderson (D)	5,349	46.2

NEW JERSEY

Candidates	Votes	%
1 William Moore (R)	15,214	56.9
Samuel J. Bayard (D)	11,539	43.1
2 Charles Haight (D)	16,299	51.3
James F. Rusling (R)	15,494	48.7
3 John T. Bird (D)	19,580	55.9
Amos Clark (R)	15,456	44.1
4 John Hill (R)	16,468	50.1
Philip Rafferty (D)	16,389	49.9
5 Orestes Cleveland (D)	19,110	53.1
George A. Halsey (R)	16,862	46.9

NEW YORK

Candidates	Votes	%
1 Henry A. Reeves (D)	13,338	52.8
Alfred M. Wood (R)	11,945	47.3
2 John G. Schumacher (D)	24,418	66.2
Henry S. Bellows (R)	12,492	33.8
3 Henry W. Slocum (D)	16,598	54.7
Samuel Booth (R)	13,734	45.3
4 John Fox (D)	20,074	83.3
Charles V. Lewis (R)	4,024	16.7
5 John Morrissey (D)	16,064	69.4
James M. McCartin (R)	4,494	19.4
George Francis Train (ID)	2,583	11.2
6 Samuel S. Cox (D)	12,362	56.1
George Starr (R)	9,682	43.9
7 Hervey C. Calkin (D)	18,485	75.5
Joseph C. Pinckney (R)	5,987	24.5
8 James Brooks (D)	21,487	68.5
William Laimbeer (R)	9,866	31.5
9 Fernando Wood (D)	14,648	57.5
Francis A. Thomas (R)	9,087	35.6
John Savage (ID)	1,759	6.9
10 Clarkson N. Potter (D)	16,533	56.6
David O. Bradley (R)	12,700	43.4
11 George W. Greene (D)	11,620‡	50.7
Charles H. Van Wyck (R)	11,298	49.3
12 John H. Ketcham (R)	13,568	50.8
Charles Wheaton (D)	13,144	49.2
13 John A. Griswold (D)	12,201	51.1
Thomas Cornell (R)	11,692	48.9
14 Stephen L. Mayham (D)	18,477	54.0
Joseph H. Ramsey (R)	15,734	46.0
15 Adolphus H. Tanner (R)	17,054	53.8
Jason C. Osgood (D)	14,641	46.2
16 Orange Ferriss (R)	10,428	55.9
Robert W. Livingston (D)	8,218	44.1
17 William A. Wheeler (R)	15,262	70.8
William H. Wallace (D)	6,284	29.2
18 Stephen Sanford (R)	16,611	53.4
John H. White (D)	14,508	46.6
19 Charles Knapp (R)	17,949	55.2
Francis R. Gilbert (D)	14,584	44.8
20 Addison H. Laflin (R)	16,856	55.5
Andrew Cornwall (D)	13,508	44.5
21 Alexander H. Bailey (R)	12,543	52.7
J. Thomas Spriggs (D)	11,240	47.3
22 John C. Churchill (R)	15,761	71.9
Charles Stebbins Jr (D)	6,169	28.1
23 Dennis McCarthy (R)	16,470	59.0
William Porter (D)	11,455	41.0
24 George W. Cowles (R)	17,234	57.5
Elmore P. Ross (D)	12,743	42.5
25 William H. Kelsey (R)	13,418	58.3
Lester B. Faulkner (D)	9,610	41.7
26 Giles W. Hotchkiss (R)	17,398	58.6
Alvin Devereaux (D)	12,280	41.4
27 Hamilton Ward (R)	18,647	58.6
Curtiss C. Gardiner (D)	13,180	41.4
28 Noah Davis (R)	15,389	54.8
John McConville (D)	12,699	45.2
29 John Fisher (R)	13,432	56.6
James Jackson Jr (D)	10,294	43.4
30 David S. Bennett (R)	16,004	52.8
Isaac A. Verplanck (D)	14,293	47.2
31 Porter Sheldon (R)	15,416	64.6
John S. Beggs (D)	8,433	35.4

NORTH CAROLINA[7]

(Readmitted July 4, 1868)

Candidates	Votes	%
1 Clinton L. Cobb (R)	15,474	56.5
David A. Barnes (C)	11,893	43.5
2 David Heaton (R)	14,895	54.8
Thomas S. Kenan (C)	12,293	45.2
3 Oliver H. Dockery (R)	15,314	53.4
A. A. McKoy (C)	13,353	46.6
4 John T. Deweese (R)	14,796	52.2
Sion H. Rogers (C)	13,556	47.8
5 Israel G. Lash (R)	14,525	56.6
Livingston Brown (D)	11,123	43.4
6 Francis E. Shober (C)	12,192	52.3
Nathaniel Boyden (R)	11,103	47.7
7 Plato Durham (C)	10,347	50.0
Alexander H. Jones (R)	10,329✓	50.0

Special Elections

	Votes	%
1 John R. French (R)	14,664	58.5
Henry A. Gilliam (C)	10,407	41.5
2 David Heaton (R)	14,693	56.8
Thomas S. Kenan (C)	11,172	43.2
3 Oliver H. Dockery (R)	15,090	56.9
Thomas C. Fuller (C)	11,444	43.1
4 John T. Deweese (R)	14,436	55.4
Samuel T. Williams (C)	11,630	44.6
5 Israel G. Lash (R)	13,020	58.7
David F. Caldwell (C)	9,141	41.2
6 Nathaniel Boyden (C)	11,477	52.8
Calvin I. Cowles (R)	10,251	47.2
7 Alexander H. Jones (R)	10,049	54.2
Burgess S. Gaither (C)	8,467	45.7

OHIO

Candidates	Votes	%
1 Philip W. Strader (D)	10,483	50.5
Benjamin Eggleston (R)	10,272	49.5
2 Job E. Stevenson (R)	11,694	51.1
Samuel F. Cary (D)	11,197	48.9
3 Robert C. Schenck (R)	16,293	50.7
C. L. Vallandigham (D)	15,818	49.3
4 William Lawrence (R)	13,656	51.2
John S. Leedom (D)	13,027	48.8
5 William Mungen (D)	15,435	59.3
Thomas E. Grissell (R)	10,589	40.7
6 John A. Smith (R)	13,463	50.7
Nelson Barrere (D)	13,120	49.4
7 James J. Winans (R)	13,978	50.2
John H. Thomas (D)	13,873	49.8
8 John Beatty (R)	12,198	52.0
J. H. Benson (D)	11,250	48.0
9 Edward F. Dickinson (D)	16,322	52.7
William H. Gibson (R)	14,677	47.4
10 Truman H. Hoag (D)	15,507	51.5
James M. Ashley (R)	14,595	48.5
11 John T. Wilson (R)	13,614	54.2
John Sands (D)	11,503	45.8
12 Philadelph Van Trump (D)	16,287	58.9
Nelson J. Turney (R)	11,374	41.1
13 George W. Morgan (D)	14,614	53.0
Charles Cooper (R)	12,980	47.0
14 Martin Welker (R)	13,575	50.9
L. R. Critchfield (D)	13,113	49.1
15 Eliakim H. Moore (R)	13,773	51.8
Martin D. Follett (D)	12,817	48.2
16 John A. Bingham (R)	13,757	50.8
Josiah M. Estep (D)	13,341	49.2
17 Jacob A. Ambler (R)	14,998	56.4
Daniel T. Lawson (D)	11,602	43.6
18 William H. Upson (R)	18,359	60.5
Franklin T. Backus (D)	11,980	39.5
19 James A. Garfield (R)	20,187	67.4
James McEwen	9,759	32.6

Special Election

	Candidates	Votes	%
8	John Beatty (R)	11,820	51.8
	Burns	10,985	48.2

OREGON

	Candidates	Votes	%
AL	Joseph S. Smith (D)	11,754	52.7
	David Logan (R)	10,555	47.3

PENNSYLVANIA

	Candidates	Votes	%
1	Samuel J. Randall (D)	14,745	63.7
	Benjamin L. Berry (R)	8,408	36.3
2	Charles O'Neill (R)	14,533	55.0
	Thomas B. Florence (D)	11,913	45.1
3	John Moffet (D)	13,856‡	50.2
	Leonard Myers (R)	13,729	49.8
4	William D. Kelley (R)	17,107	52.9
	James B. Nicholson (D)	15,248	47.1
5	John R. Reading (D)	13,199‡	50.1
	Caleb N. Taylor (R)	13,158	49.9
6	John D. Stiles (D)	15,247	54.8
	John R. Breitenbach (R)	12,568	45.2
7	Washington Townsend (R)	12,771	57.4
	Robert C. Monaghan (D)	9,481	42.6
8	J. Lawrence Getz (D)	13,738	64.8
	Henry S. Eckert (R)	7,472	35.2
9	Oliver J. Dickey (R)	14,993	63.4
	Hiram B. Swarr (D)	8,674	36.7
10	Henry L. Cake (R)	12,501	50.5
	James J. Conner (D)	12,276	49.6
11	Daniel M. Van Auken (D)	17,930	63.4
	John Torrey (R)	10,367	36.6
12	George W. Woodward (D)	16,687	52.8
	Theodore Strong (R)	14,898	47.2
13	Ulysses Mercur (R)	12,723	50.6
	Victor E. Piolet (D)	12,412	49.4
14	John B. Packer (R)	15,598	54.7
	Joseph F. Knipe (D)	12,902	45.3
15	Richard J. Haldeman (D)	15,818	55.8
	Samuel Small (R)	12,519	44.2
16	John Cessna (R)	13,653	50.3
	Fran M. Kimmell (D)	13,509	49.7
17	Daniel J. Morrell (R)	12,100	52.4
	John P. Linton (D)	11,006	47.6
18	William H. Armstrong (R)	16,760	53.2
	Levi A. Mackey (D)	14,732	46.8
19	Glenni W. Scofield (R)	16,903	54.1
	Rasselas Brown (D)	14,355	45.9
20	Calvin W. Gilfillan (R)	18,079	52.6
	Robert M. Defrance (D)	16,267	47.4

	Candidates	Votes	%
21	Henry D. Foster (D)	13,807	50.1
	John Covode (R)	13,766✓	49.9
22	James S. Negley (R)	15,175	58.7
	Andrew Burt (D)	10,696	41.3
23	Darwin Phelps (R)	16,095	59.3
	Lewis Z. Mitchell (D)	11,046	40.7
24	Joseph B. Donley (R)	13,860	52.1
	David Crawford (D)	12,737	47.9

Special Elections

		Votes	%
9	Oliver J. Dickey (R)	15,000	63.3
	Robert Crane (D)	8,689	36.7
20	S. Newton Pettus (R)	17,906	52.2
	James B. Knox (D)	16,390	47.8

RHODE ISLAND

		Votes	%
1	Thomas A. Jenckes (R)	7,995	66.4
	Arnold (D)	3,980	33.1
2	Nathan F. Dixon (R)	4,133	60.9
	Waterhouse (D)	2,640	38.9

SOUTH CAROLINA[8]

(Readmitted July 9, 1868)

		Votes	%
1	B. Frank Whittemore (R)	17,467	61.3
	H. J. Covington (D)	11,017	38.7
2	Christopher C. Bowen (R)	25,845	75.7
	R. W. Seymour (D)	8,296	24.3
3	J. P. Reed (D)	11,774	57.3
	Solomon L. Hoge (R)	8,766✓	42.7
4	William D. Simpson (D)	14,098	59.0
	Alexander S. Wallace (R)	9,807✓	41.0
AL	J. P. M. Epping	68,477*	50.2
	E. E. Dickson	67,654	49.6

Special Elections

		Votes	%
1	B. Frank Whittemore (R)	17,512	74.2
	J. N. Frierson (D)	6,075	25.8
2	Christopher C. Bowen (R)	18,000	96.0
	W. Brisbane (R)	5,322	28.4
3	M. Simeon Corley (R)	15,681	71.0
	S. McGowan (D)	6,413	29.0
4	James H. Goss (R)	12,016	57.2
	S. McAllilly (D)	8,993	42.8

TENNESSEE

	Candidates	Votes	%
1	Roderick R. Butler (R)	10,107	98.5
2	Horace Maynard (R)	10,403	79.5
	C. Houk (I)	2,681	20.5
3	William B. Stokes (R)	5,915	74.4
	E. A. Garrett (I)	2,037	25.6
4	C. A. Sheafe (D)	4,476	54.0
	Lewis Tillman (R)	3,810✓	46.0
5	William F. Prosser (R)	5,804	56.5
	Joseph Motley (D)	2,655	25.8
	Samuel C. Mercer (I)	1,817	17.7
6	Samuel M. Arnell (R)	5,143	70.6
	John J. Buck (IR)	2,141	29.4
7	Isaac R. Hawkins (R)	2,825	71.3
	George R. Foote (D)	1,136	28.7
8	John W. Leftwich (D)	6,533	40.6
	William J. Smith (R)	5,543✓	34.4
	David A. Nunn (R)	4,024	25.0

VERMONT

		Votes	%
1	Charles W. Willard (R)	13,999	76.1
	John Cain (D)	4,396	23.9
2	Luke P. Poland (R)	15,407	74.6
	Charles M. Chase (D)	5,252	25.4
3	Worthington C. Smith (R)	11,105	72.4
	Waldo Brigham (D)	4,237	27.6

WEST VIRGINIA

		Votes	%
1	Isaac H. Duval (R)	11,569	51.9
	H. S. Walker (D)	10,729	48.1
2	James C. McGrew (R)	9,147	58.4
	William G. Brown (D)	6,517	41.6
3	John S. Witcher (R)	6,215	56.4
	Charles P. J. Moore (D)	4,806	43.6

WISCONSIN

		Votes	%
1	Halbert E. Paine (R)	17,513	50.6
	Mitchell (D)	17,084	49.4
2	Benjamin F. Hopkins (R)	18,333	59.2
	Winans (D)	12,659	40.9
3	Amasa Cobb (R)	17,903	61.6
	Passmore (D)	11,162	38.4
4	Charles A. Eldridge (D)	17,688	57.3
	Frisby (R)	13,205	42.7
5	Philetus Sawyer (R)	19,622	55.8
	Vilas (D)	15,534	44.2
6	Cadwallader C. Washburn (R)	21,236	64.9
	Ellis (D)	11,481	35.1

1. These were six special elections to fill Alabama's House seats for the remainder of the 40th Congress (1867–1869).

2. These three elections were for a full two-year term in the 41st Congress (1869–1871). Arkansas was readmitted to the Union and had three representatives for part of the 40th Congress (1867–1869), but returns for their election were not available.

3. Florida was readmitted during the 40th Congress (1867–1869) and Charles M. Hamilton served for the remainder of that Congress. He was then reelected to a full term in the 41st Congress (1869–1871). The Florida candidates were running for the full term in the 41st Congress.

4. Figures represent returns in seven special elections held April 20, 1868. All winners listed, except John H. Christy in the 6th district, were seated July 25, 1868 to serve for the remainder of the 40th Congress (1867–1869), even though Georgia had not been formally re-admitted to the Union.

On the convening of the 41st Congress in 1869, the six incumbent Georgia representatives claimed their election of April 20, 1868 also entitled them to seats in the 41st Congress. The House rejected the claim and Georgia then elected representatives to the 41st Congress, but these returns are not available. According to Georgia secretary of state archives, William Wiseham Paine (D) served in the House from the 1st district March 4, 1869, to March 3, 1871; Marion Bethune (R), 3rd district, served Jan.

16, 1871–March 3, 1871; and Stephen Alfestus Corker (D), 5th district, served Jan. 24, 1871–March 3, 1871. No returns on their elections are available. Georgia was readmitted to representation by act of July 15, 1870.

5. Louisiana was readmitted during the 40th Congress (1867–1869) and elected several representatives, but these returns are unavailable. The five elections shown here are for a full two-year term in the 41st Congress (1869–1871).

6. No representatives from Mississippi were seated from this election. Mississippi was not readmitted until Feb. 23, 1870.

7. The special elections were for unexpired terms in the 40th Congress (1867–1869). The general elections were for full two-year terms in the 41st Congress (1869–1871).

8. The "Special Elections" were to fill unexpired terms in the 40th Congress (1867–1869), while the others were for full terms in the 41st Congress (1869–1871). The at-large election in which J. P. M. Epping was the apparent winner was rejected by the House. According to the *Biographical Directory*, a number of southern states upon readmission claimed that since their slaves were emancipated, they were entitled to larger delegations in the House. Epping's election falls in this category. The claims were rejected by the House.

1869 House Elections

ALABAMA

	Candidates	Votes	%
1	Alfred E. Buck (R)	14,191	54.0
	W. D. Mann (D)	12,080	46.0
2	Charles W. Buckley (R)	14,933	58.1
	A. N. Worthy (D)	10,786	41.9
3	Robert S. Heflin (R)	9,895	50.6
	J. C. Parkinson (D)	9,652	49.4
4	Charles Hays (R)	17,243	71.5
	John B. Reed (D)	4,881	20.2
	C. W. Dunstan (I)	2,010	8.3
5	Peter M. Dox (D)	6,047	55.1
	W. J. Haralson (R)	4,933	44.9
6	William C. Sherrod (D)	4,932	57.7
	J. J. Hinds (R)	2,836	33.2
	Thomas Haughey (I)	775	9.1

CONNECTICUT

1	Julius L. Strong (R)	11,617	51.6
	Dixon (D)	10,881	48.4
2	Stephen W. Kellogg (R)	13,102	50.8
	Babk (D)	12,678	49.2
3	Henry H. Starkweather (R)	9,212	57.5
	Conv (D)	6,813	42.5
4	William H. Barnum (D)	13,075	52.3
	William H. Beard (R)	11,915	47.7

ILLINOIS

Special Election

3	Horatio C. Burchard (R)	6,213	76.1
	John V. Eustace	1,843	22.6

MASSACHUSETTS

Special Election

	Candidates	Votes	%
7	George M. Brooks (R)	8,809	67.3
	Leverett Saltonstall (D)	4,284	32.7

MISSISSIPPI

1	George E. Harris (R)	10,215	61.5
	Jefferson L. Wafford (C)	6,389	38.5
2	Joseph L. Morphis (R)	9,089	62.9
	William Kellogg (C)	5,353	37.1
3	Henry W. Barry (R)	12,912	62.9
	Schuyler B. Steers (C)	7,630	37.1
4	George C. McKee (R)	25,082	71.9
	Archie C. Fisk (C)	9,811	28.1
5	Legrand W. Perce (R)	14,450	64.1
	Leroy S. Brown (C)	8,080	35.9

NEW HAMPSHIRE

1	Jacob H. Ela (R)	13,138	53.6
	E. A. Hibbard (D)	11,376	46.4
2	Aaron F. Stevens (R)	11,513	53.9
	Edward W. Harrington (D)	9,866	46.2
3	Jacob Benton (R)	11,254	51.3
	Hosea W. Parker (D)	10,691	48.7

TEXAS

(Readmitted March 30, 1870)

1	George W. Whitmore (R)	8,456	52.0
	James Armstrong (D)	7,406	45.6
2	John C. Conner (D)	6,378	41.9

	Candidates	Votes	%
	B. F. Grafton (R)	4,355	28.6
	J. F. Johnson (ID)	3,540	23.2
	R. H. Taylor (I)	944	6.2
3	William T. Clark (R)	16,582	65.9
	Jacob Elliot (D)	8,564	34.0
4	Edward Degener (R)	9,312	47.7
	J. L. Haynes (D)	9,240	47.3

VIRGINIA[1]

(Readmitted Jan. 26, 1870)

1	Richard S. Ayer (RAD)	8,023	29.7
	Joseph Seger (I)	7,377	27.3
	Norton (I)	6,523	24.2
	Lewis (C)	5,056	18.7
2	James H. Platt Jr (RAD)	16,781	53.4
	D. J. Godwin (C)	11,255	35.8
	Bayne (I)	2,736	8.7
3	Charles H. Porter (RAD)	17,311	55.0
	J. W. Hunnicut (C)	13,101	41.6
4	George W. Booker (C)	13,101	48.0
	George Tucker (RAD)	9,568	35.0
	Stowell (I)	4,639	17.0
5	Robert Ridgway (C)	16,732	55.2
	G. G. Curtis (RAD)	13,571	44.8
6	William Milnes Jr (C)	12,123	56.8
	John T. Harris (I)	6,815	31.9
	Phelps (RAD)	2,425	11.4
7	Lewis McKenzie (C)	15,878	58.9
	Charles Whittlesey (RAD)	11,073	41.1
8	James King Gibson (C)	14,717	69.6
	G. S. Smith (RAD)	6,244	29.5
AL	Joseph Segar (C)	117,499*	53.9
	A. M. Crane (RAD)	100,424	46.1

1. According to the *Biographical Directory* Virginia claimed an extra House seat and elected Joseph Segar at-large to fill it. The House rejected the claim.

1870 House Elections

ALABAMA

	Candidates	Votes	%
1	Benjamin S. Turner (R)	18,226	57.5
	S. J. Cumming (D)	13,466	42.5
2	Charles W. Buckley (R)	19,647	55.4
	M. B. Welbourn (D)	15,831	44.6
3	William A. Handley (D)	12,710	57.1
	B. W. Norris (R)	9,568	43.0
4	Charles Hays (R)	18,373	52.6
	J. G. Harris (D)	16,540	47.4
5	Peter M. Dox (D)	10,689	70.3
	L. J. Standifee (R)	4,523	29.7
6	Joseph H. Sloss (D)	9,221	69.4
	B. O. Masterson (R)	4,068	30.6

ARKANSAS

	Candidates	Votes	%
1	James M. Hanks (D)	5,394	61.4
	Logan H. Roots (R)	3,398	38.7
2	Oliver P. Snyder (R)	8,956	59.1
	A. A. C. Rogers (D)	6,211	41.0
3	John Edwards (D)	6,874‡	53.7
	Thomas Boles (R)	5,919	46.3

DELAWARE

	Candidates	Votes	%
AL	Benjamin T. Biggs (D)	11,446	55.6
	Joshua T. Heald (R)	9,150	44.4

FLORIDA

	Candidates	Votes	%
AL	Josiah T. Walls (R)	12,439‡	51.3
	Silas L. Niblack (D)	11,810	48.7

GEORGIA

(Readmitted July 15, 1870)

	Candidates	Votes	%
1	Archibald T. MacIntyre (D)	15,581	56.9
	Virgil Hillyer (R)	9,662	35.3
	A. A. Bradley (IR)	2,142	7.8
2	Nelson Tift (D)	14,969	51.5
	Richard H. Whiteley (R)	14,088✓	48.5
3	John S. Bigby (R)	14,212	52.9
	William F. Wright (D)	12,649	47.1
4	Thomas J. Speer (R)	11,211	51.1
	Winburn J. Lawton (D)	10,725	48.9
5	Dudley M. DuBose (D)	15,363	62.3
	Isham S. Fannin (R)	9,302	37.7
6	William P. Price (D)	10,358	68.6
	John A. Wimpey (R)	3,911	25.9
	Weir Boyd (ID)	823	5.5
7	Pierce M. B. Young (D)	14,768	73.8
	George P. Burnett (R)	5,257	26.3

ILLINOIS

	Candidates	Votes	%
1	Charles B. Farwell (R)	20,342	57.5
	John Wentworth (D)	15,025	42.4
2	John F. Farnsworth (R)	8,396	48.6
	J. C. Stoughton (P)	6,516	37.8
	Richard Bischop (D)	2,349	13.6
3	Horatio C. Burchard (R)	11,718	65.3
	Charles Betts (D)	6,219	34.6
4	John B. Hawley (R)	12,023	50.1
	P. L. Cable (D)	11,982	49.9
5	Bradford N. Stevens (D)	11,579	51.7
	E. C. Ingersoll (R)	9,963	44.5
6	Burton C. Cook (R)	10,452	56.5
	Julius Avery (D)	7,839	42.4
7	Jesse H. Moore (R)	14,089	51.2
	Andrew J. Hunter (D)	13,418	48.8
8	James C. Robinson (D)	13,702	50.1
	Jonathan Merriam (R)	12,448	45.6
9	Thompson W. McNeely (D)	12,691	55.2
	B. F. Westlake (R)	10,297	44.8

	Candidates	Votes	%
10	Edward Y. Rice (D)	13,963	53.7
	J. W. Kitchell (R)	12,028	46.3
11	Samuel S. Marshall (D)	15,771	57.7
	William H. Robinson (R)	11,546	42.3
12	John B. Hays (D)	10,903	51.8
	William Hartzell (R)	10,126	48.2
13	John M. Crebs (D)	13,947	53.0
	Daniel W. Munn (R)	12,366	47.0
AL	John A. Logan (R)	168,801*	53.2
	William B. Anerson (D)	145,191	45.8

INDIANA

	Candidates	Votes	%
1	William E. Niblack (D)	17,577	53.4
	Hy C. Gooding (R)	15,327	46.6
2	Michael C. Kerr (D)	16,950	60.4
	Carr (R)	11,116	39.6
3	William S. Holman (D)	15,396	54.3
	Pritchard (R)	12,972	45.7
4	Jeremiah M. Wilson (R)	12,561	50.0
	David S. Gooding (D)	12,557	50.0
5	John Coburn (R)	14,123	50.8
	Cottrell (D)	13,707	49.3
6	Daniel W. Voorhees (D)	17,268	52.2
	Dunn (R)	15,843	47.9
7	Mahlon D. Manson (D)	15,539	50.6
	L. Wallace (R)	15,146	49.4
8	James F. Tyner (R)	15,113	53.5
	J. T. Henderson (D)	13,149	46.5
9	John P. C. Shanks (R)	13,790	50.7
	Colerick (D)	13,396	49.3
10	William Williams (R)	14,130	60.8
	M. S. Hascall (IR)	9,112	39.2
11	Jasper Packard (R)	14,459	52.6
	S. I. Anthony (D)	13,052	47.4

IOWA

	Candidates	Votes	%
1	George W. McCrary (R)	13,327	57.2
	Edmund Jaeger (D)	9,961	42.8
2	Aylett R. Cotton (R)	13,586	59.3
	William E. Leffingwell (D)	9,338	40.7
3	William G. Donnan (R)	15,927	59.2
	John T. Stoneman (D)	10,961	40.8
4	Madison M. Walden (R)	19,005	56.0
	William T. Smith (D)	14,883	43.9
5	Frank W. Palmer (R)	19,798	61.2
	B. F. Montgomery (D)	12,516	38.7
6	Jackson Orr (R)	16,993	73.9
	C. C. Smettzer (D)	5,977	26.0

Special Election

	Candidates	Votes	%
2	William P. Wolf (R)	13,858	66.6
	J. M. Preston	4,834	23.2
	R. M. Preston	1,048	5.0

KANSAS

	Candidates	Votes	%
AL	David P. Lowe (R)	40,368	65.8
	R. C. Foster (D)	20,950	34.2

KENTUCKY

	Candidates	Votes	%
1	Edward Crossland (D)	7,930	64.4
	N. R. Black (R)	2,982	24.2
	W. C. Clark (ID)	1,405	11.4
2	Henry D. McHenry (D)	8,214	59.9
	Milton J. Roach (R)	5,490	40.1
3	Joseph H. Lewis (D)	7,314	56.4
	D. R. Carr (R)	5,657	43.6
4	William B. Read (D)	9,314	70.9
	James M. Fidler (R)	3,831	29.1
5	Boyd Winchester (D)	10,599	66.1
	James Speed (R)	5,426	33.9
6	William E. Arthur (D)	9,213	66.7

	Candidates	Votes	%
	Thomas Wrightson (R)	4,578	33.1
7	James B. Beck (D)	14,312	56.7
	William Brown (R)	10,916	43.3
8	George M. Adams (D)	12,226	50.0
	Hugh F. Finley (R)	12,208	50.0
9	John M. Rice (D)	9,823	60.3
	George M. Thomas (R)	6,463	39.7

Special Election

	Candidates	Votes	%
3	Joseph H. Lewis (D)	9,847	65.1
	J. H. Lowry	5,289	34.9

LOUISIANA

	Candidates	Votes	%
1	J. Hale Sypher (R)	13,971	62.0
	A. W. Walker (D)	8,579	38.0
2	Lionel A. Sheldon (R)	17,512	69.6
	John A. Walsh (D)	7,640	30.4
3	Chester B. Darrall (R)	13,202	60.9
	Adolph Bailey (D)	8,483	39.1
4	James McCleery (R)	11,786	62.2
	Michael Ryan (D)	7,171	37.8
5	Frank Morey (R)	9,521	58.7
	J. D. Watkins (D)	6,713	41.4

MAINE

	Candidates	Votes	%
1	John Lynch (R)	12,571	53.2
	Haines (D)	11,075	46.8
2	William P. Frye (R)	10,245	56.3
	Black (D)	7,924	43.6
3	James G. Blaine (R)	11,590	55.0
	Farley (D)	9,279	44.1
4	John A. Peters (R)	9,962	57.6
	Emery (D)	7,322	42.3
5	Eugene Hale (R)	10,086	52.9
	Carlton (D)	8,876	46.5

MARYLAND

	Candidates	Votes	%
1	Samuel Hambleton (D)	17,314	56.5
	Henry R. Torbert (R)	13,348	43.5
2	Stevenson Archer (D)	14,622	64.5
	W. M. Marine (R)	8,062	35.5
3	Thomas Swann (D)	15,137	59.2
	Washington Booth (R)	10,414	40.8
4	John Ritchie (D)	14,304	53.4
	John E. Smith (R)	12,486	46.6
5	William H. Merrick (D)	15,231	53.1
	James A. Gary (R)	13,440	46.9

MASSACHUSETTS

	Candidates	Votes	%
1	James Buffinton (R)	8,281	64.3
	Robert Pitnam (I)	2,667	20.7
	William W. Comstock (D)	1,704	13.2
2	Oakes Ames (R)	9,367	60.0
	Edward Avery (D)	6,013	38.5
3	Ginery Twichell (R)	6,233	50.7
	William Gaiton (D)	5,640	45.9
4	Samuel Hooper (R)	8,025	56.0
	Leopold Morse (D)	5,605	39.1
5	Benjamin F. Butler (R)	8,333	60.4
	William Endicott (D)	4,297	31.1
	Unidentified Candidate (I)	1,076	7.8
6	Nathaniel P. Banks (R)	10,548	64.4
	John K. Tarbox (D)	5,123	31.3
7	George M. Brooks (R)	8,406	57.6
	Seth Adams (D)	4,561	31.3
	J. Chillis Kimball (LAB REF)	1,489	10.2
8	George F. Hoar (R)	8,487	56.2
	Alvin Cook (D)	4,282	28.4
	Moses Johnson (LAB REF)	1,734	11.5
9	William B. Washburn (R)	10,903	70.4
	Lysander B. Jaquith (D)	4,185	27.0

	Candidates	Votes	%
10	Henry L. Dawes (R)	8,419	52.9
	Reuben Noble (D)	7,077	44.5

MICHIGAN

	Candidates	Votes	%
1	Henry Waldron (R)	18,348	50.6
	N. B. Eldridge (D)	17,447	48.2
2	William L. Stoughton (R)	17,502	54.6
	Henry Chamberlain (D)	13,923	43.5
3	Austin Blair (R)	15,236	51.5
	D. D. Hughes (D)	13,768	46.6
4	Thomas W. Ferry (R)	16,854*	60.8
	Myron Rider (D)	10,384	37.4
5	Omar D. Conger (R)	13,782	49.9
	Byron G. Stout (D)	13,593	49.2
6	Jabez G. Sutherland (D)	16,618	52.7
	John F. Driggs (R)	14,879	47.2

MINNESOTA

	Candidates	Votes	%
1	Mark H. Dunnell (R)	19,606	56.8
	Buck (D)	14,904	43.2
2	John T. Averill (R)	17,133	54.2
	Donnelly (D)	14,491	45.8

MISSISSIPPI

	Candidates	Votes	%
1	George E. Harris (R)	✓	
2	Joseph L. Morphis (R)	✓	
3	Henry W. Barry (R)	✓	
4	George C. McKee (R)	✓	
5	Legrand W. Perce (R)	✓	

MISSOURI

	Candidates	Votes	%
1	Erastus Wells (D)	7,629	50.9
	Charles Johnson (LR)	5,444	36.3
	Iron Z. Smith (RAD R)	1,928	12.9
2	Gustavus A. Finkelnburg (LR)	12,708	90.3
	A. Vanwormer (RAD R)	1,359	9.7
3	James R. McCormick (D)	7,572	63.5
	G. J. Vanallen (RAD R)	2,331	19.6
	William M. Nalle (LR)	2,015	16.9
4	Harrison E. Havens (RAD R)	8,830	54.4
	William E. Gilmore (LR)	7,416	45.7
5	Samuel S. Burdett (RAD R)	10,790	47.1
	George R. Smith (LR)	9,066	39.6
	Douglass Dale (D)	3,062	13.4
6	Abraham Comingo (D)	12,511	58.9
	George R. Smith (RAD R)	8,718	41.1
7	Isaac C. Parker (LR)	13,713	56.1
	John H. Ellis (D)	10,723	43.9
8	James G. Blair (LR)	11,710	56.3
	J. T. K. Hayward (RAD R)	9,106	43.7
9	Andrew King (D)	10,393	59.7
	David P. Dyer (LR)	3,803	21.8
	Edward Draper (RAD R)	3,227	18.5

NEBRASKA

	Candidates	Votes	%
AL	John Taffe (R)	12,375	60.8
	George B. Lake (D)	7,967	39.2

NEVADA

	Candidates	Votes	%
AL	Charles W. Kendall (D)	6,821	52.5
	Thomas Fitch (R)	6,161	47.5

NEW JERSEY

	Candidates	Votes	%
1	John W. Hazleton (R)	14,502	53.8
	Benjamin F. Lee (D)	12,469	46.2
2	Samuel C. Forker (D)	15,899	50.7
	William A. Newell (R)	15,452	49.3
3	John T. Bird (D)	18,007	55.7
	Robert Rusling (R)	14,323	44.3
4	John Hill (R)	18,057	54.1
	Philip Rafferty (D)	15,304	45.9
5	George A. Halsey (R)	18,092	54.2
	Orestes Cleveland (D)	14,694	44.0

NEW YORK

	Candidates	Votes	%
1	Dwight Townsend (D)	12,632	52.4
	Caleb C. Norvell (R)	11,466	47.6
2	Thomas Kinsella (D)	20,704	62.4
	Silas B. Dutcher (R)	12,482	37.6
3	Henry W. Slocum (D)	13,799	53.8
	Erastus D. Webster (R)	8,623	33.6
	R. M. Whiting Jr. (IR)	3,248	12.7
4	Robert B. Roosevelt (D)	10,702	63.0
	M. T. McMahon (R&YD)	5,501	32.4
5	William R. Roberts (D)	14,556	86.0
	James A. Briggs (R)	2,215	13.1
6	Samuel S. Cox (D)	9,228	52.9
	Greeley (R)	8,203	47.1
7	Smith Ely Jr (D)	12,514	73.9
	McAlpin (R)	3,503	20.7
	Willis (R)	929	5.5
8	James Brooks (D)	12,845	52.6
	George Wilkes (R)	7,348	30.1
	J. Wadsworth (YD)	4,243	17.4
9	Fernando Wood (D)	15,630	64.8
	W. S. Hillyer (YD&R)	4,789	19.9
	Morris Ellinger (R)	3,708	15.4
10	Clarkson N. Potter (D)	14,249	57.2
	James Westervelt (R)	10,685	42.9
11	Charles St. John (R)	11,247	51.1
	Sherman (D)	10,747	48.9
12	John H. Ketcham (R)	14,432	55.1
	Philip (D)	11,748	44.9
13	Joseph H. Tuthill (D)	11,559	50.7
	Lindsley (R)	11,257	49.3
14	Eli Perry (D)	17,716	54.6
	Harder (R)	14,726	45.4
15	Joseph M. Warren (D)	17,793	60.4
	J. Thomas Davis (R)	11,659	39.6
16	John Rogers (D)	9,444	50.5
	Andrew Williams (R)	9,272	49.5
17	William A. Wheeler (R)	13,020	69.6
	George Mott (D)	5,699	30.4
18	John M. Carroll (D)	14,828	48.6
	James M. Marvin (R)	13,390	43.9
	Samuel McKean (IR)	2,286	7.5
19	Elizur H. Prindle (R)	16,752	53.8
	Juliand (D)	14,389	46.2
20	Clinton L. Merriam (R)	14,863	53.5
	Andrew Cornwall (D)	12,899	46.5
21	Ellis H. Roberts (R)	12,322	53.7
	Weaver (D)	10,606	46.3
22	William E. Lansing (R)	13,450	56.5
	M. J. Shoecraft (D)	9,780	41.1
23	R. Holland Duell (R)	12,954	55.1
	Dennis McCarthy (IR & D)	10,540	44.9
24	John E. Seeley (R)	15,276	55.7
	Daniels (D)	12,134	44.3
25	William H. Lamport (R)	12,115	56.4
	Harlow L. Comstock (D)	9,367	43.6
26	Milo Goodrich (R)	15,471	56.3
	Apgar (D)	12,029	43.7
27	H. Boardman Smith (R)	16,276	54.9
	Lucius Robinson (D)	13,352	45.1
28	Freeman Clarke (R)	13,844	55.3
	J. H. White (D)	11,187	44.7
29	Seth Wakeman (R)	12,134	57.3
	James G. Shepard (D)	9,039	42.7
30	William Williams (R)	15,018	51.0
	Bass (R)	14,415	49.0
31	Walter L. Sessions (R)	10,170	50.9
	Murray (D)	9,793	49.1

Special Election

		Votes	%
28	Charles H. Holmes (R)	✓	
	Alex P. Butts		

NORTH CAROLINA

	Candidates	Votes	%
1	Clinton L. Cobb (R)	10,054	60.7
	Timothy Morgan (IR)	6,520	39.3
2	Charles R. Thomas (R)	15,099	55.0
	Lott W. Humphrey (C)	12,352	45.0
3	Alfred M. Waddell (C)	13,828	50.6
	Oliver H. Dockery (R)	13,477	49.4
4	Sion H. Rogers (C)	14,106	51.7
	James Harris (R)	13,201	48.3
5	James M. Leach (C)	12,541	52.6
	William L. Scoff (R)	11,302	47.4
6	Francis E. Shober (C)	12,474	60.0
	Frederick H. Sprague (R)	8,324	40.0
7	James C. Harper (C)	10,967	56.7
	Alexander H. Jones (R)	8,373	43.3

Special Elections[1]

		Votes	%
2	Joseph Dixon (R)	14,976	54.7
	C. J. O'Hagan (C)	12,396	45.3
4	Robert B. Gilliam (C)	14,014*	50.8
	Madison Hawkins (R)	13,556	49.2
4	John Manning Jr. (C)	11,797	50.7
	Joseph W. Holden (R)	11,472	49.3

OHIO

	Candidates	Votes	%
1	Aaron F. Perry (R)	8,039	52.4
	Milton Sayler (D)	7,294	47.6
2	Job E. Stevenson (R)	9,294	54.6
	Samuel F. Cary (D)	7,745	45.5
3	Lewis D. Campbell (D)	14,838	50.1
	Robert C. Schenck (R)	14,785	49.9
4	John F. McKinney (D)	11,966	50.2
	W. B. McClung (R)	11,741	49.3
5	Charles L. Lamison (D)	11,997	57.4
	Clark (R)	8,894	42.6
6	John A. Smith (R)	12,063	49.8
	J. W. Denver (D)	11,827	48.8
7	Samuel Shellabarger (R)	13,488	52.8
	Hugh J. Jewett (D)	12,060	47.2
8	John Beatty (R)	10,610	52.0
	James R. Hubbell (D)	9,450	46.3
9	Charles Foster (R)	13,274	51.2
	Edward F. Dickinson (D)	12,498	48.2
10	Erasmus D. Peck (R)	11,302	52.2
	William F. Lockwood (D)	10,242	47.3
11	John T. Wilson (R)	11,294	52.6
	Ralph Leete (D)	10,189	47.4
12	Philadelph Van Trump (D)	14,123	57.9
	Charles E. Brown (R)	10,265	42.1
13	George W. Morgan (D)	14,196	54.1
	C. W. Potwin (R)	12,047	45.9
14	James Monroe (R)	12,271	51.3
	L. R. Critchfield (D)	11,545	48.3
15	William P. Sprague (R)	11,263	51.3
	John Cartwright (D)	10,547	48.0
16	John A. Bingham (R)	12,435	51.0
	Robert E. Chambers (D)	11,958	49.0
17	Jacob A. Ambler (R)	11,685	55.1
	John Ball (D)	9,514	44.9
18	William H. Upson (R)	11,053	60.7
	J. M. Coffinberry (D)	6,695	36.8
19	James A. Garfield (R)	13,538	65.1
	Howard (D)	7,263	34.9

OREGON

	Candidates	Votes	%
AL	James H. Slater (D)	11,588	50.8
	Joseph G. Wilson (R)	11,245	49.3

PENNSYLVANIA

	Candidates	Votes	%
1	Samuel J. Randall (D)	10,853	61.8
	Benjamin Huckell (R)	6,705	38.2
2	John V. Creely (D)	11,059	52.2
	Charles O'Neill (R)	10,134	47.8
3	Leonard Myers (R)	9,778	53.6
	John Moffet (D)	8,453	46.4
4	William D. Kelley (R)	14,324	55.2
	William B. Thomas (D)	11,622	44.8
5	Alfred C. Harmer (R)	11,561	50.4
	John R. Reading (D)	11,401	49.7
6	Ephraim L. Acker (D)	12,049	52.1

Candidates	Votes	%
John A. Oliver (R)	11,072	47.9
7 Washington Townsend (R)	10,408	55.8
J. H. Askin (D)	8,231	44.2
8 J. Lawrence Getz (D)	10,411	67.4
Nicholas Hunter (R)	5,045	32.6
9 Oliver J. Dickey (R)	9,722	56.7
A. K. Witmer (D)	7,411	43.3
10 John W. Killinger (R)	11,326	51.4
Cyrus D. Gloninger (D)	10,697	48.6
11 John B. Storm (D)	12,454	70.3
William Davis (R)	5,269	29.7
12 Lazarus D. Shoemaker (R)	13,279	52.4
J. B. McCollum (D)	12,059	47.6
13 Ulysses Mercur (R)	11,117	50.3
Charles B. Brockway (D)	10,993	49.7
14 John B. Packer (R)	13,620	54.7
E. G. Scott (R)	11,266	45.3
15 Richard J. Haldeman (D)	13,866	57.1
William B. Rober (R)	10,416	42.9
16 Benjamin F. Meyers (D)	12,859	50.0
John Cessna (R)	12,844	50.0
17 R. Milton Speer (D)	10,335	50.0
Daniel J. Morrell (R)	10,324	50.0
18 Henry Sherwood (D)	13,205	50.1
William H. Armstrong (R)	13,178	50.0
19 Glenni W. Scofield (R)	13,055	51.2
Selden Marvin (D)	12,451	48.8
20 Samuel Griffith (D)	14,146	51.4
Calvin W. Gilfillan (R)	13,377	48.6
21 Henry D. Foster (D)	12,399	51.5
Andrew Stewart (R)	11,669	48.5
22 James S. Negley (R)	11,230	54.5
James H. Hopkins (D)	8,018	38.9
Frew (IR)	1,372	6.7
23 Ebenezer McJunkin (R)	12,591	58.6
William Sirwell (D)	8,891	41.4
24 William McClelland (D)	12,264	51.6
Joseph B. Donley (R)	11,505	48.4

RHODE ISLAND

Candidates	Votes	%
1 Benjamin T. Eames (R)	4,952	50.9
Thomas A. Jenckes (R)	1,977	20.3
Van Slyck (D)	1,402	14.4
Davis (R)	1,085	11.1
2 James M. Pendleton (R)	1,457	57.7
Rodman (D)	941	37.2

SOUTH CAROLINA[2]

Candidates	Votes	%
1 Joseph H. Rainey (R)	20,221	63.5
C. W. Dudley (D)	11,628	36.5
2 Robert C. De Large (IR)	16,686‡	49.6
Christopher C. Bowen (R)	15,700	46.7
3 Robert B. Elliott (R)	20,664	59.6
John E. Bacon (D)	13,994	40.4
4 Alexander S. Wallace (R)	16,746	55.3
Isaac G. McKissick (D)	13,442	44.4
AL J.P.M. Epping (R)	71,803*	50.0
L. Wimbush (R)	71,742	50.0

Special Election

Candidates	Votes	%
1 Joseph H. Rainey (R)	20,385	86.5
C. W. Dudley (D)	3,192	13.5

TENNESSEE

Candidates	Votes	%
1 Roderick R. Butler (R)	6,584	47.1
James White (D)	5,979	42.7
N. G. Taylor (IR)	1,432	10.2
2 Horace Maynard (R)	8,351	51.7
A. Blizard (D)	7,819	48.4
3 Abraham E. Garrett (D)	9,602	69.7
William B. Stokes (R)	4,168	30.3
4 John M. Bright (D)	11,827	86.5
James Mullins (R)	1,843	13.5
5 Edward J. Golliday (D)	7,991	59.6
William F. Prosser (R)	5,428	40.5
6 Washington C. Whitthorne (D)	9,057	76.3
T. J. Cypert (R)	2,816	23.7
7 Robert P. Caldwell (D)	8,227	81.7
John Norman (R)	1,848	18.3
8 William W. Vaughan (D)	13,990	72.4
W. J. Smith (R)	5,346	27.7

VERMONT

Candidates	Votes	%
1 Charles W. Willard (R)	10,476	74.0
John Cain (D)	3,675	26.0
2 Luke P. Poland (R)	10,479	76.6
L. S. Partridge (D)	3,206	23.4
3 Worthington C. Smith (R)	9,116	75.0
Henry Gillett (D)	3,047	25.1

VIRGINIA[3]

Candidates	Votes	%
1 John Critcher (C)	10,252	46.3
Walter W. Douglas (RAD)	6,618	29.9
Daniel M. Norton (RAD)	5,293	23.9
2 James H. Platt Jr (RAD)	15,880	59.2
Robert B. Bolling (C)	10,902	40.7
3 Charles H. Porter (RAD)	13,555	56.0
Albert Ordway (C)	10,647	44.0
4 William H. H. Stowell (RAD)	13,205	56.9
William L. Owen (C)	9,989	43.1
5 Richard T. W. Duke (C)	12,596	52.4
Alexander Rives (RAD)	11,430	47.6
6 John T. Harris (D)	7,006	49.3
Corbin M. Reynolds	4,591	32.3
C. Douglas Gray	2,626	18.5
7 Elliott M. Braxton (C)	12,719	53.1
Lewis McKenzie (RAD)	11,203	46.8
8 William Terry (C)	9,916	56.9
Fayette McMullen (I)	4,017	23.0
Robert W. Hughes (RAD)	3,508	20.1
AL Raleigh T. Daniel (C)	78,437*	99.6

Special Election

Candidates	Votes	%
5 Richard T. W. Duke (C)	12,469	52.3
Alexander Rives (RAD)	11,378	47.7

WEST VIRGINIA

Candidates	Votes	%
1 John J. Davis (D)	11,630	52.4
Nathan Goff Jr (R)	10,569	47.6
2 James C. McGrew (R)	9,011	52.7
O. P. Downey (D)	8,098	47.3
3 Frank Hereford (D)	8,732	54.9
Witcher (R)	7,189	45.2

WISCONSIN

Candidates	Votes	%
1 Alexander Mitchell (D)	16,558	57.5
Lyon (R)	12,250	42.5
2 Gerry W. Hazelton (R)	11,467	54.5
Cook (D)	9,568	45.5
3 J. Allen Barber (R)	11,503	58.5
Strachan (D)	8,157	41.5
4 Charles A. Eldridge (D)	15,019	62.4
Watrous (R)	9,056	37.6
5 Philetus Sawyer (R)	17,258	59.4
Stringm (D)	11,822	40.7
6 Jeremiah M. Rusk (R)	15,042	61.3
Meggett (D)	9,514	38.7

1. Rep. John T. Deweese of the 4th district resigned Feb. 28, 1870. In the first special election held to fill the remainder of Deweese's term in the 41st Congress (1869–1871), Robert B. Gilliam was elected, but he never claimed the seat. In a second special election, John Manning Jr. was elected and took his seat Dec. 7, 1870.

2. South Carolina claimed an extra seat in the House and J. P. M. Epping was elected at-large to fill it. The House refused to seat him. (See South Carolina 1868.)

3. Virginia claimed an extra seat in the House, and Raleigh T. Daniel was elected at-large to fill it. The House refused to seat him. (See Virginia 1869.)

1871 House Elections

CALIFORNIA

	Candidates	Votes	%
1	Sherman O. Houghton (R)	25,971	51.6
	L. Archer (D)	24,374	48.4
2	Aaron A. Sargent (R)	18,065	54.0
	J. W. Coffroth (D)	15,382	46.0
3	John M. Coghlan (R)	18,503	51.7
	George Pearce (D)	17,309	48.3

CONNECTICUT

		Votes	%
1	Julius L. Strong (R)	11,983	50.5
	Goodrich (D)	11,736	49.5
2	Stephen W. Kellogg (R)	13,784	50.0
	Kendrick (D)	13,761	50.0
3	Henry H. Starkweather (R)	8,937	54.5

	Candidates	Votes	%
	Stedman (D)	7,472	45.5
4	William H. Barnum (D)	13,653	52.1
	Coffing (R)	12,577	48.0

ILLINOIS

Special Elections

		Votes	%
6	Henry Snapp (R)	9,112	57.2
	Lorenzo Leland (D)	6,809	42.8
AL	John L. Beveridge (R)	136,879	53.9
	L. L. Hayes (D)	116,482	45.9

NEW HAMPSHIRE

		Votes	%
1	Ellery A. Hibbard (D)	12,444	50.3

	Candidates	Votes	%
	William B. Small (R)	12,085	48.8
2	Samuel N. Bell (D)	11,484	51.5
	Aaron F. Stevens (R)	10,635	47.7
3	Hosea W. Parker (D)	11,170	49.5
	Simon W. Griffin (R)	11,038	48.9

TEXAS

		Votes	%
1	William S. Herndon (D)	16,172	58.3
	G. W. Whitmore (R)	11,572	41.7
2	John C. Connor (D)	18,285	75.5
	A. M. Bryant (R)	5,948	24.6
3	De Witt C. Giddings (D)	23,374‡	53.4
	William T. Clark (R)	20,406	46.6
4	John Hancock (D)	17,010	57.4
	Edward Degener (R)	12,636	42.6

1872 House Elections

ALABAMA

	Candidates	Votes	%
1	Frederick G. Bromberg (LR)	15,607	54.2
	Benjamin S. Turner (R)	13,174	45.8
2	James T. Rapier (R)	19,397	54.5
	Oates (LR)	16,221	45.5
3	Charles Pelham (R)	14,957	51.0
	William A. Handley (LR)	14,371	49.0
4	Charles Hays (R)	20,333	57.4
	Smith (LR)	15,121	42.7
5	John H. Caldwell (LR)	10,544	62.6
	Campbell (R)	6,293	37.4
6	Joseph H. Sloss (LR)	9,288	66.9
	Parrish (R)	4,593	33.1
AL	Alexander White (R)	89,480✓	
	Charles C. Sheats (R)	89,195✓	
	Baker (D)	81,311	
	Jolly (D)	81,171	

ARKANSAS

	Candidates	Votes	%
1	Lucien C. Gause (D)	11,591	54.1
	Asa Hodges (R)	9,853✓	46.0
2	Marcus L. Bell (D)	13,758	52.8
	Oliver P. Snyder (R)	12,284✓	47.2
3	Thomas M. Gunter (D)	12,298‡	56.6
	William W. Wilshire (R)	9,431	43.4
AL	William J. Hynes (B-T R)	40,023	50.0
	J. M. Bradley (MR)	39,586	49.4

CALIFORNIA

	Candidates	Votes	%
1	Charles Clayton (R)	11,938	52.2
	William A. Piper (LR)	10,883	47.6
2	Horace Frank Page (R)	13,803	51.5
	Pasz Coggins (LR)	12,816	47.8
3	John K. Luttrell (LR)	14,032	51.7
	J. M. Coghlan (R)	13,110	48.3
4	Sherman O. Houghton (R)	10,396	53.2
	E. J. C. Kewen (LR)	9,030	46.2

CONNECTICUT

Special Election

	Candidates	Votes	%
1	Joseph R. Hawley (R)	13,030	51.2
	William W. Eaton (D)	12,397	48.8

DELAWARE

	Candidates	Votes	%
AL	James R. Lofland (R)	11,377	50.8
	Wright (LR)	11,015	49.2

FLORIDA

	Candidates	Votes	%
AL	William J. Purman (R)	17,537✓	
	Josiah T. Walls (R)	17,503✓	
	Silas L. Niblack (LR)	15,881	
	Charles W. Jones (LR)	15,811	

GEORGIA

	Candidates	Votes	%
1	Morgan Rawls (LR)	8,319‡	54.4
	Andrew Sloan (R)	6,979	45.6
2	Richard H. Whiteley (R)	9,616	50.2
	G. J. Wright (LR)	9,530	49.8
3	Philip Cook (LR)	6,147	57.8
	Brown (R)	4,490	42.2
4	Henry R. Harris (LR)	10,319	54.9
	M. Bethune (R)	8,466	45.1
5	James C. Freeman (R)	10,910	50.7
	Glenn (LR)	10,631	49.4
6	James H. Blount (LR)	9,993	61.7
	Anderson (R)	6,196	38.3
7	Pierce M. B. Young (LR)	8,067	64.5
	Dever (R)	4,443	35.5

	Candidates	Votes	%
8	Ambrose R. Wright (LR)	9,697*	56.3
	Clayton (R)	6,230	36.2
	D. M. Dubose	1,293	7.5
9	Hiram P. Bell (LR)	7,437	63.2
	Darrell (R)	4,325	36.8

Special Election

	Candidates	Votes	%
4	Erasmus Williams Beck (D)	✓	#

ILLINOIS

	Candidates	Votes	%
1	John B. Rice (R)	12,870	64.0
	Lusien B. Otis (LR)	7,235	36.0
2	Jasper D. Ward (R)	12,182	57.9
	Carter Henry Harrison (LR)	8,873	42.1
3	Charles B. Farwell (R)	9,202	65.0
	John Valcoulon Lemoyne (LR)	4,962	35.0
4	Stephen A. Hurlbut (R)	15,532	75.2
	Seymour G. Bronson (LR)	5,134	24.8
5	Horatio C. Burchard (R)	14,036	65.1
	James Dinsmoor (LR)	7,538	34.9
6	John B. Hawley (R)	13,123	64.5
	Calvin Truesdale (LR)	7,216	35.5
7	Franklin Corwin (R)	12,404	59.9
	G. D. A. Parks (LR)	8,293	40.1
8	Greenbury L. Fort (R)	13,401	61.7
	George O. Barnes (LR)	8,304	38.3
9	Granville Barrere (R)	12,600	53.9
	N. C. Worthington (LR)	10,799	46.2
10	William H. Ray (R)	12,962	52.1
	William H. Neece (LR)	11,897	47.9
11	Robert M. Knapp (LR)	13,818	55.2
	Asa C. Matthews (R)	10,939	43.7
12	James C. Robinson (LR)	13,234	51.8
	M. N. Chamberlin (R)	12,311	48.2
13	John McNulta (R)	13,490	54.7
	Clifton H. Moore (LR)	10,850	44.0
14	Joseph G. Cannon (R)	15,161	57.1
	William Nelson (LR)	11,405	42.9
15	John R. Eden (LR)	14,653	54.4
	George Hunt (R)	12,298	45.6
16	James S. Martin (R)	12,266	50.5
	Silas L. Bryan (LR)	12,016	49.5
17	William R. Morrison (LR)	13,215	53.9
	John B. Hay (R)	11,316	46.1
18	Isaac Clements (R)	12,999	53.1
	George W. Wall (LR)	11,478	46.9
19	Samuel S. Marshall (LR)	13,297	54.1
	Green B. Raum (R)	11,282	45.9

INDIANA

	Candidates	Votes	%
1	William E. Niblack (LR)	19,259	50.2
	Heilman (R)	19,127	49.8
2	Simeon K. Wolfe (LR)	19,336	58.6
	Voyles (R)	13,652	41.4
3	William S. Holman (LR)	16,367	52.1
	Herod (R)	15,039	47.9
4	Jeremiah M. Wilson (R)	14,499	50.7
	Gooding (LR)	14,119	49.3
5	John Coburn (R)	18,794	51.1
	McNutt (LR)	18,001	48.9
6	Morton C. Hunter (R)	18,792	50.9
	Daniel Wolsey Voorhees (LR)	18,135	49.1
7	Thomas J. Cason (R)	17,927	50.3
	Mahlon Dickerson Manson (LR)	17,730	49.7
8	James M. Tyner (R)	19,737	54.0
	Whiteside (LR)	16,798	46.0
9	John E. Neff (LR)	17,082	50.0
	John Peter Cleaver Shanks (R)	17,058✓	50.0
10	Henry B. Sayler (R)	17,334	53.4
	Long (LR)	15,149	46.6
11	Jaspar Packard (R)	16,813	51.5
	Hendricks (LR)	15,828	48.5

	Candidates	Votes	%
AL	William Williams (R)	188,762✓	
	Godlove S. Orth (R)	188,664✓	
	Michael C. Kerr (LR)	188,502	
	John S. Williams (LR)	188,227	

IOWA

	Candidates	Votes	%
1	George W. McCrary (R)	15,149	58.0
	James M. Shelby (D)	10,961	42.0
2	Aylett R. Cotton (R)	12,521	50.4
	William E. Leffingwell (D)	12,346	49.7
3	William G. Donnan (R)	13,654	53.7
	John T. Stoneman (D)	11,774	46.3
4	Henry O. Pratt (R)	15,615	77.0
	A. T. Lusch (D)	4,574	22.6
5	James Wilson (R)	15,531	67.6
	John P. Irish (D)	7,434	32.4
6	William Loughridge (R)	14,638	55.4
	H. H. Trimble (D)	11,703	44.3
7	John A. Kasson (R)	14,909	65.9
	Q. Palmer (D)	7,702	34.1
8	James W. McDill (R)	12,675	64.4
	W. W. Merritt (D)	6,999	35.6
9	Jackson Orr (R)	12,402	66.8
	John F. Duncomb (D)	6,152	33.1

KANSAS

	Candidates	Votes	%
AL	David P. Lowe (R)	67,400✓	
	William A. Phillips (R)	67,114✓	
	Stephen A. Cobb (R)	66,345✓	
	Samuel A. Riggs (D)	34,450	
	R. B. Mitchell (D)	33,985	
	W. R. Laughlin (D)	33,264	

KENTUCKY

	Candidates	Votes	%
1	Edward Crossland (D)	10,276	64.0
	J. H. Trabue (I)	2,510	15.6
	H. H. Houston	1,796	11.2
	John Martin	1,473	9.2
2	John Y. Brown (D)	10,878	95.3
3	Charles W. Milliken (D)	8,796	64.3
	Jacob S. Golladay	4,853	35.5
4	William B. Read (D)	8,221	92.8
	E. H. Hobson	548	6.2
5	Elisha D. Standiford (D)	11,179	68.9
	W. P. Boone	5,053	31.1
6	William E. Arthur (D)	11,424	63.5
	Harvey Myers	6,564	36.5
7	James B. Beck (D)	13,978	68.9
	S. F. J. Trabue	6,322	31.1
8	Milton J. Durham (D)	10,736	51.6
	W. O. Bradley (R)	10,063	48.4
9	George M. Adams (D)	9,683	54.2
	A. T. Woods (R)	8,199	45.9
10	John D. Young (D)	9,075	50.5
	J. M. Burns (R)	8,885	49.5

LOUISIANA

	Candidates	Votes	%
1	J. Hale Sypher (R)	12,300‡	50.2
	Effingham Lawrence (LR)	12,225	49.9
2	Lionel A. Sheldon (R)	17,068	52.5
	Randall L. Gibson (LR)	15,453	47.5
3	Chester Bidwell Darrall (R)	14,396	53.7
	J. B. Price (D)	7,724	28.8
	Elbert Gantt (LR)	4,701	17.5
4	Samuel Peters (R)	13,787*	64.0
	E. C. Davidson (LR)	7,752	36.0
5	Frank Morey (R)	14,060	62.1
	G. W. McCraney (LR)	8,597	37.9
AL	George Augustus Sheridan (D)	64,975	55.1
	Pinckney B. S. Pinchback (R)	53,011	44.9

LOUISIANA

Special Election

	Candidates	Votes	%
4	Harry Lott (R)	13,790	64.0
	Alexander Boarman (LR)	7,768	36.0

MAINE

	Candidates	Votes	%
1	John H. Burleigh (R)	15,485	53.8
	Clifford (D)	13,216	45.9
2	William P. Frye (R)	13,540	59.1
	Alonzo Garcelon (D)	9,362	40.8
3	James G. Blaine (R)	15,084	56.6
	Lang (D)	11,566	43.4
4	Samuel Hersey (R)	13,804	61.3
	Emery (D)	8,706	38.7
5	Eugene Hale (R)	14,181	55.7
	Frederick Augustus Pike (D)	11,300	44.3

MARYLAND

	Candidates	Votes	%
1	Ephraim K. Wilson (LR)	12,464	51.3
	Spence (R)	11,826	48.7
2	Stevenson Archer (LR)	10,591	50.7
	Hancock (R)	10,303	49.3
3	William J. O'Brien (LR)	9,670	53.7
	Turner (R)	8,346	46.3
4	Thomas Swann (LR)	12,148	52.7
	Griswold (R)	10,886	47.3
5	William J. Albert (R)	11,405	52.6
	Merrick (LR)	10,300	47.5
6	Lloyd Lowndes Jr (R)	14,258	53.2
	Ritchie (LR)	12,545	46.8

MASSACHUSETTS

	Candidates	Votes	%
1	James Buffinton (R)	12,448	82.6
	Joseph M. Day (D)	2,609	17.3
2	Benjamin W. Harris (R)	13,752	73.0
	Edward Avery (LR)	5,090	27.0
3	William Whiting (R)	8,931	63.4
	Samuel C. Cobb (LR)	5,139	36.5
4	Samuel Hooper (R)	8,715	58.1
	Leopold Morse (LR)	6,262	41.8
5	Daniel W. Gooch (R)	12,472	60.8
	Nathaniel P. Banks (LR)	8,039	39.2
6	Benjamin F. Butler (R)	11,881	67.2
	Charles P. Thompson (LR)	5,737	32.5
7	Ebenezer R. Hoar (R)	11,742	64.9
	John K. Tarbox (LR)	5,989	33.1
8	John M. S. Williams (R)	11,929	67.2
	William W. Warren (LR)	5,829	32.8
9	George F. Hoar (R)	12,696	71.0
	George F. Verry (LR)	5,012	28.0
10	Alvah Crocker (R)	14,919	76.4
	D. W. Bond (LR)	4,588	23.5
11	Henry L. Dawes (R)	12,260	63.9
	John F. Arnold (LR)	6,927	36.1

Special Election

7	Constantine C. Esty (R)	13,583	71.4
	George Stevens	5,274	27.7

MICHIGAN

	Candidates	Votes	%
1	Moses W. Field (R)	11,703	53.8
	Bagg (D)	9,843	45.3
2	Henry Waldron (R)	17,427	62.4
	Mahan (D)	10,522	37.6
3	George Willard (R)	17,822	62.6
	Parkhurst (D)	10,275	36.1
4	Julius C. Burrows (R)	16,717	59.3
	Potter (D)	11,451	40.6
5	Wilder Foster (R)	17,353	66.5
	McReynolds (D)	8,744	33.5
6	Josiah W. Begole (R)	19,486	58.0
	Baldwin (D)	13,994	41.6
7	Omar D. Conger (R)	12,037	60.5

	Candidates	Votes	%
	Richardson (D)	7,790	39.2
8	Nathan B. Bradley (R)	11,333	58.0
	Wisner (D)	7,995	40.9
9	Jay A. Hubbell (R)	11,951	68.3
	Ely (D)	5,546	31.7

MINNESOTA

1	Mark H. Dunnell (R)	20,806	65.6
	M. S. Wilkinson (D)	10,901	34.4
2	Horace B. Strait (R)	15,712	57.4
	C. C. Graham (D)	11,668	42.6
3	John T. Averill (R)	19,663	60.7
	G. L. Becker (D)	12,712	39.3

MISSISSIPPI

1	Lucius Q. C. Lamar (LR)	9,679	66.2
	Flournoy (R)	4,954	33.9
2	Albert R. Howe (R)	14,831	64.4
	Alcorn (LR)	8,216	35.7
3	Henry W. Barry (R)	15,047	70.0
	Bolding (LR)	6,440	30.0
4	Jason R. Niles (R)	15,795	69.7
5	George C. McKee (R)	14,817	64.7
	Shelby (LR)	8,073	35.3
6	John R. Lynch (R)	15,101	64.0
	Cassidy (LR)	8,509	36.0

MISSOURI

1	Edwin O. Stanard (R)	5,271	50.7
	Grosvenor (LR)	5,129	49.3
2	Erastus Wells (LR)	8,268	58.7
	Bryton (R)	5,807	41.3
3	William H. Stone (LR)	5,197	51.7
	Hilton (R)	4,859	48.3
4	Robert A. Hatcher (LR)	13,340	74.4
	Ward (R)	4,594	25.6
5	Richard P. Bland (LR)	9,974	53.1
	Seay (R)	8,820	46.9
6	Harrison E. Havens (R)	13,156	51.1
	McAffee (LR)	12,578	48.9
7	Thomas T. Crittenden (LR)	16,341	52.5
	Burdett (R)	14,770	47.5
8	Abram Comingo (LR)	13,235	64.4
	Twichell (R)	7,317	35.6
9	Isaac C. Parker (R)	12,136	50.2
	Pike (LR)	12,053	49.8
10	Ira B. Hyde (R)	13,953	53.1
	Mansur (LR)	12,318	46.9
11	John B. Clark Jr. (LR)	17,341	67.7
	Demotte (R)	8,280	32.3
12	John M. Glover (LR)	13,006	54.9
	Benjamin (R)	10,672	45.1
13	Aylett H. Buckner (LR)	16,249	67.8
	Flagg (R)	7,710	32.2

NEBRASKA

AL	Lorenzo Crounse (R)	17,124	62.2
	Warner (LR)	10,412	37.8

NEVADA

AL	Charles W. Kendall (D)	7,847	52.3
	C. C. Goodwin	7,146	47.7

NEW JERSEY

1	John W. Hazleton (R)	15,312	63.1
	Clute (LR)	8,948	36.9
2	Samuel A. Dobbins (R)	14,192	54.6
	Forker (LR)	11,787	45.4
3	Amos Clark Jr (R)	14,794	54.0
	Patterson (LR)	12,618	46.0
4	Robert Hamilton (LR)	13,458	55.0
	Potts (R)	10,994	45.0
5	William W. Phelps (R)	12,701	56.0
	Woodruff (LR)	9,986	44.0

	Candidates	Votes	%
6	Marcus L. Ward (R)	16,061	60.7
	Randall (LR)	10,403	39.3
7	Isaac W. Scudder (R)	10,377	53.3
	Taylor (LR)	9,108	46.7

NEW YORK

1	Henry J. Scudder (R)	13,877	54.1
	Covert (LR)	11,797	46.0
2	John G. Schumaker (LR)	13,345	58.7
	Perry (R)	8,378	36.8
3	Stewart L. Woodford (R)	15,177	56.9
	Goodrich (LR)	11,506	43.1
4	Philip S. Crooke (R)	11,012	51.9
	Colahan (LR)	10,202	48.1
5	William R. Roberts (LR)	20,281	79.1
	Matthew Stewart (R)	5,356	20.9
6	James Brooks (LR)	16,645	76.9
	Adolph G. Dunn (R)	5,005	23.1
7	Thomas J. Creamer (LR)	10,012	54.7
	Conrad Geib (R)	8,279	45.3
8	John D. Lawson (R)	13,305	58.6
	Charles P. Shaw (LR)	9,395	41.4
9	David B. Mellish (R)	7,841	37.8
	John Hardy (APOLLO)	7,068	34.1
	Michael Connolly (LR)	5,847	28.2
10	Fernando Wood (LR)	10,526	52.2
	William A. Darling (R)	9,641	47.8
11	Clarkson N. Potter (LR)	15,204	51.7
	Flagg (R)	14,179	48.3
12	Charles St. John (R)	11,842	51.1
	Horton (LR)	11,318	48.9
13	John O. Whitehouse (LR)	14,859	51.6
	Ketchim (R)	13,932	48.4
14	David M. De Witt (LR)	12,031	50.0
	Maxwell (R)	12,014	50.0
15	Eli Perry (LR)	18,676	51.6
	Adams (R)	17,538	48.4
16	James S. Smart (R)	17,835	57.2
	Thayer (LR)	13,352	42.8
17	Robert S. Hale (R)	11,025	57.4
	Heaton (LR)	8,174	42.6
18	William A. Wheeler (R)	14,725	69.2
	Cantwell (LR)	6,565	30.8
19	Henry H. Hathorn (R)	17,762	54.6
	Judson (LR)	14,756	45.4
20	David Wilbur (R)	17,368	53.4
	Sturges (LR)	15,171	46.6
21	Clinton L. Merriam (R)	17,337	56.7
	Brockway (LR)	13,220	43.3
22	Ellis H. Roberts (R)	13,284	55.9
	Sherman (LR)	10,481	44.1
23	William E. Lansing (R)	15,410	58.7
	Foster (LR)	10,841	41.3
24	R. Holland Duell (R)	15,457	53.8
	Hiscock (LR)	13,289	46.2
25	Clinton D. MacDougall (R)	16,486	57.2
	Graves (LR)	12,325	42.8
26	William H. Lamport (R)	12,886	57.0
	White (LR)	9,730	43.0
27	Thomas C. Platt (R)	16,603	55.3
	Goodrich (LR)	13,406	44.7
28	Horace Boardman Smith (R)	18,738	56.8
	Hayt (LR)	14,262	43.2
29	Freeman Clarke (R)	16,342	56.7
	Gordon (LR)	12,470	43.3
30	George G. Hoskins (R)	13,233	58.0
	Southworth (LR)	9,599	42.0
31	Lyman K. Bass (R)	17,929	58.3
	Williams (R)	12,813	41.7
32	Walter L. Sessions (R)	12,922	57.4
	Murray (LR)	9,573	42.6
AL	Lyman Tremain (R)	438,396	52.2
	Samuel S. Cox (LR)	400,797	47.8

NORTH CAROLINA

1	Clinton L. Cobb (R)	13,522	52.8
	David M. Carter (D)	12,101	47.2
2	Charles R. Thomas (R)	20,072	63.3

Candidates	Votes	%
William H. Kitchen (D)	11,627	36.7
3 Alfred M. Waddell (D)	14,286	52.7
Neil McKay (R)	12,848	47.4
4 William A. Smith (R)	13,879	51.4
Sion H. Rogers (D)	13,147	48.7
5 James M. Leach (D)	10,755	50.6
Thomas Settle (R)	10,497	49.4
6 Thomas S. Ashe (D)	12,700	54.6
Oliver H. Dockery (R)	10,561	45.4
7 William M. Robbins (D)	10,072	54.4
David M. Furches (R)	8,459	45.7
8 Robert B. Vance (D)	11,038	55.5
William G. Candler (R)	8,853	44.5

OHIO

Candidates	Votes	%
1 Milton Sayler (D)	12,474	58.4
Benjamin Eggleston (R)	8,905	41.7
2 Henry B. Banning (D)	11,034	53.7
Rutherford B. Hayes (R)	9,532	46.4
3 John Q. Smith (R)	14,929	52.1
John W. Sohn (D)	13,700	47.8
4 Lewis B. Gunckel (R)	16,604	52.9
J. J. Winans (D)	14,677	46.8
5 Charles N. Lamison (D)	15,530	60.3
Samuel Lybrand (R)	10,224	39.7
6 Isaac R. Sherwood (R)	13,471	51.9
F. H. Hurd (D)	12,406	47.8
7 Lawrence T. Neal (D)	13,379	52.5
John T. Wilson (R)	12,106	47.5
8 William Lawrence (R)	14,748	57.8
J. J. Musson (D)	10,705	41.9
9 James W. Robinson (R)	13,573	50.4
George W. Morgan (D)	13,146	48.8
10 Charles Foster (R)	14,997	51.0
Rush R. Sloane (D)	14,271	48.6
11 Hezekiah S. Bundy (R)	13,267	56.2
Samuel A. Nash (D)	10,360	43.9
12 Hugh J. Jewett (D)	15,613	58.5
James Taylor (R)	10,936	41.0
13 Milton I. Southard (D)	15,109	54.5
Lucius P. Marsh (R)	12,638	45.6
14 John Berry (D)	13,668	57.8
Thomas E. Douglass (R)	9,925	42.0
15 William P. Sprague (R)	12,987	51.9
Richard R. Hudson (D)	11,996	47.9
16 Lorenzo Danford (R)	14,350	56.3
C. L. Poorman (D)	11,052	43.4
17 Laurin D. Woodworth (R)	15,368	54.0
Richard Brown (D)	13,106	46.0
18 James Monroe (R)	14,662	58.6
N. S. Townshend (D)	10,298	41.2
19 James A. Garfield (R)	19,189	69.4
M. Sutliff (D)	8,254	29.9
20 Richard C. Parsons (R)	13,101	55.4
Selah Chamberlain (D)	10,377	43.9

OREGON

Candidates	Votes	%
AL Joseph G. Wilson (R)	13,168	51.7
John Burnett (D)	12,317	48.3

PENNSYLVANIA

Candidates	Votes	%
1 Samuel J. Randall (LR)	10,133	53.4
Houst (R)	8,845	46.6
2 Charles O'Neill (R)	17,253	63.9
Morris (LR)	9,728	36.1
3 Leonard Meyers (R)	15,429	59.4
Vogelbach (LR)	10,530	40.6
4 William D. Kelley (R)	20,955	61.2
Mitchell (LR)	13,301	38.8
5 Alfred C. Harmer (R)	14,743	55.1
Phillips (LR)	12,040	45.0
6 James S. Biery (R)	13,906	55.0
Witte (LR)	11,400	45.1
7 Washington Townsend (R)	14,011	61.4
Taylor (LR)	8,819	38.6
8 Heister Clymer (LR)	13,854	64.0
Millhol (R)	7,783	36.0

Candidates	Votes	%
9 A. Herr Smith (R)	14,501	63.0
North (LR)	8,526	37.0
10 John W. Killinger (R)	14,419	56.6
Rielly (LR)	11,049	43.4
11 John B. Storm (LR)	16,808	61.4
Howell (R)	10,569	38.6
12 Lazarus D. Shoemaker (R)	17,551	51.1
Woodward (LR)	16,811	48.9
13 James D. Strawbridge (R)	13,079	51.7
Rhodes (LR)	12,243	48.4
14 John B. Packer (R)	17,545	56.5
Rutherford (LR)	13,486	43.5
15 John A. Magee (D)	15,358	53.2
Sponsler (LR)	13,532	46.8
16 John Cessna (R)	14,383	52.4
Meyers (LR)	13,067	47.6
17 R. Milton Speer (LR)	12,011	51.3
Barker (R)	11,422	48.7
18 Sobieski Ross (R)	17,041	53.8
Henry Sherwood (LR)	14,627	46.2
19 Carlton B. Curtis (R)	17,742	52.2
Kane (LR)	16,238	47.8
20 Hiram Richmond (R)	20,704	52.6
Samuel Griffith (LR)	18,627	47.4
21 Alexander W. Taylor (R)	13,980	51.3
Foster (LR)	13,289	48.7
22 James S. Negley (R)	17,248	61.2
King (LR)	10,930	38.8
23 Ebenezer McJunkin (R)	17,431	60.7
Johnston (LR)	11,306	39.3
24 William S. Moore (R)	14,195	51.9
McClelland (LR)	13,169	48.1
AL Glenni W. Scofield (R)	358,013	53.3
E. B. Wright (LR)	314,014	46.7
AL Charles Albright (R)	360,546	53.7
Richard Vaux (LR)	311,036	46.3
AL Lemuel Todd (R)	357,743	53.3
J. H. Hopkins (LR)	313,534	46.7

Special Election

Candidates	Votes	%
13 Frank Charles Bunnell (R)	6,000✓	#
Piolett (D)	5,001	#

SOUTH CAROLINA

Candidates	Votes	%
1 Joseph H. Rainey (R)	19,765	100.0
2 Alonzo J. Ransier (R)	20,061	75.4
William Gurney (D)	6,549	24.6
3 Robert B. Elliott (R)	21,627	92.8
4 Alexander S. Wallace (R)	14,590	53.1
B. F. Perry (D)	12,879	46.9
AL Richard H. Cain (R)	68,825	71.2
L. E. Johnson (ID)	26,394	27.3

TENNESSEE

Candidates	Votes	%
1 Roderick R. Butler (R)	10,289	56.7
Carter (LR)	7,849	43.3
2 Jacob M. Thornburgh (R)	10,015	55.7
Caldwell (LR)	5,403	30.1
Garrett (I)	2,563	14.3
3 William Crutchfield (R)	10,041	52.8
Key (LR)	8,960	47.2
4 John M. Bright (LR)	12,585	69.8
Steele (R)	5,442	30.2
5 Horace H. Harrison (R)	10,033	42.1
Gellad (LR)	8,131	34.1
Brien (I)	5,684	23.8
6 Washington C. Whitthorne (LR)	9,058	53.9
Gibbs (R)	6,849	40.7
Morris (I)	903	5.4
7 John D. C. Atkins (LR)	11,411	55.6
Murray (R)	7,734	37.7
Travis (I)	1,369	6.7
8 David A. Nunn (R)	7,580	37.9
Campbell (LR)	5,967	29.8
Caldw (I)	4,476	22.4
Beel (I)	1,979	9.9
9 Barbour Lewis (R)	13,784	56.7

Candidates	Votes	%
Haynes (LR)	10,541	43.3
AL Horace Maynard (R)	80,825	44.0
Benjamin F. Cheatham (LR)	65,188	35.5
Andrew Johnson (I)	37,900	20.6

TEXAS

Candidates	Votes	%
1 William S. Herndon (D)	13,417	57.1
R. K. Smith	8,780	37.4
William Chambers	1,261	5.4
2 William P. McLean (D)	15,924	73.9
F. W. Minor	5,617	26.1
3 De Witt C. Giddings (D)	20,464	51.5
A. J. Evans	19,287	48.5
4 John Hancock (D)	18,172	61.7
W. O. Hutchinson	11,281	38.3
AL Asa H. Willie (D)	69,085✓	
Roger Q. Mills (D)	68,936✓	
Evans (R)	47,096	
Norton (R)	47,075	

VERMONT

Candidates	Votes	%
1 Charles W. Willard (R)	14,061	79.5
Heaton (LR)	3,618	20.5
2 Luke P. Poland (R)	11,070	65.3
Steele (LR)	2,929	17.3
J. M. Pierce (I)	2,554	15.1
3 George W. Hendee (R)	11,473	78.3
Adams (LR)	3,182	21.7

VIRGINIA

Candidates	Votes	%
1 James B. Sener (R)	10,685	50.9
E. M. Braxton (CD)	10,312	49.1
2 James H. Platt Jr (R)	15,554	59.9
Baker R. Lee (CD)	10,339	39.8
3 J. Ambler Smith (R)	13,082	51.1
George D. Wise (CD)	12,514	48.9
4 William H. H. Stowell (R)	15,393	65.6
P. W. McKinney (CD)	8,068	34.4
5 Alexander M. Davis (R)	9,175‡	50.5
Christopher Y. Thomas (CD)	8,975	49.4
6 Thomas Whitehead (CD)	11,401	51.3
J. Foote Johnson (I)	10,779	48.5
7 John T. Harris (CD)	10,894	61.8
C. T. O. Ferrall (I)	6,738	38.2
8 Eppa Hunton (CD)	11,782	56.2
Edward Daniels (R)	9,178	43.8
9 Rees T. Bowen (CD)	10,352	66.1
Robert W. Hughes (R)	5,304	33.9

WEST VIRGINIA

Candidates	Votes	%
1 Benjamin Wilson (D)	8,054	52.4
John J. Davis (D)	7,317✓	47.6
2 John M. Hagans (R)	3,441	82.3
Alexander R. Boteler (R)	387	9.3
Ward Lamar	255	6.1
3 Frank Hereford (D)	11,417	80.5
J. B. Walker (R)	2,769	19.5

WISCONSIN

Candidates	Votes	%
1 Charles G. Williams (R)	15,666	62.6
Sloan (D)	9,380	37.5
2 Gerry W. Hazelton (R)	13,408	53.2
Smith (D)	11,784	46.8
3 J. Allen Barber (R)	13,745	58.2
Warden (D)	9,880	41.8
4 Alexander Mitchell (D)	13,281	65.1
Winkler (R)	7,120	34.9
5 Charles A. Eldridge (D)	15,587	55.5
Baetz (R)	12,507	44.5
6 Philetus Sawyer (R)	15,803	56.1
Lindsley (D)	12,358	43.9
7 Jeremiah M. Rusk (R)	16,183	65.4
Marston (D)	8,547	34.6
8 Alexander S. McDill (R)	10,711	59.7
Carson (D)	7,238	40.3

1873 House Elections

CONNECTICUT

	Candidates	Votes	%
1	Joseph R. Hawley (R)	12,030	52.8
	Kendall (D)	10,764	47.2
2	Stephen W. Kellogg (R)	12,761	51.2
	English (D)	12,173	48.8
3	Henry H. Starkweather (R)	7,764	56.4
	Bill (D)	6,000	43.6
4	William H. Barnum (D)	12,561	53.8
	Miner (R)	10,797	46.2

LOUISIANA

4	George Luke Smith (D)	✓ #

MICHIGAN

Special Election

	Candidates	Votes	%
5	William B. Williams (R)	6,598	50.4
	Comstock (D)	6,484	49.6

NEW HAMPSHIRE

		Votes	%
1	William B. Small (R)	12,103	49.8
	Hibbard (D)	11,725	48.2
2	Austin F. Pike (R)	10,780	49.3
	Bell (D)	10,773	49.3
3	Hosea W. Parker (D)	10,633	49.9
	Griffin (R)	10,295	48.3

OREGON

Special Election

	Candidates	Votes	%
AL	James W. Nesmith (D)	8,194	57.2
	Smith (R)	6,123	42.8

RHODE ISLAND

	Candidates	Votes	%
1	Benjamin T. Eames (R)	8,977	74.0
	Thomas Davis (D)	3,138	25.9
2	James M. Pendleton (R)	4,310	63.2
	George H. Browne (D)	2,505	36.8

1874 House Elections

ALABAMA

	Candidates	Votes	%
1	Jeremiah Haralson (R)	19,545	53.6
	Frederick G. Bromberg (D)	16,953	46.5
2	Jeremiah N. Williams (D)	20,180	51.3
	James T. Rapier (R)	19,124	48.7
3	Taul Bradford (D)	19,424	58.0
	Betts (R)	14,076	42.0
4	Charles Hays (R)	23,900	56.5
	Jones (D)	18,378	43.5
5	John H. Caldwell (D)	13,011	59.2
	Sheffield (R)	8,969	40.8
6	Goldsmith W. Hewitt (D)	15,048	62.1
	Joseph H. Sloss (R)	9,172	37.9
AL	Burwell B. Lewis (D)	106,023	54.1
	Charles C. Sheets (R)	89,909	46.0
AL	William H. Forney (D)	106,080	54.0
	Alexander White (R)	89,909	46.0

ARKANSAS

1	Lucien C. Gause (C)	9,211	64.0
	Rogers (R)	5,183	36.0
2	William F. Slemmons (C)	12,166	53.7
	Clayton (R)	10,485	46.3
3	William W. Wilshire (C)	11,733	65.0
	Hynes (R)	6,328	35.0
4	Thomas M. Gunter (C)	7,828	90.8
	Lander (R)	791	9.2

DELAWARE

AL	James Williams (D)	12,602	53.3
	James R. Lofland (R)	11,024	46.7

FLORIDA

1	William J. Purman (R)	10,052	51.7
	Henderson (D)	9,377	48.3
2	Josiah T. Walls (R)	8,557‡	51.1
	Jesse J. Finley (D)	8,178	48.9

GEORGIA

1	Julian Hartridge (D)	11,252	59.4
	Bryant (R)	6,714	35.5
	John Wimberley (IR)	974	5.1
2	William E. Smith (D)	12,098	55.3
	Whiteley (R)	9,789	44.7
3	Philip Cook (D)	8,677	67.4
	Brown (R)	4,199	32.6
4	Henry R. Harris (D)	9,230	100.0
5	Milton A. Candler (D)	12,450	66.5
	Mills (R)	6,273	33.5
6	James H. Blount (D)	10,007	78.4
	Gove (R)	2,756	21.6
7	William H. Felton (I)	7,587	49.6
	William H. Dabney (D)	7,505	49.1
8	Alexander H. Stephens (D)	6,822	99.8
9	Garnett McMillan (D)	7,885*	77.3
	O'Neal (R)	2,318	22.7

ILLINOIS

1	Bernard G. Caulfield (D)	10,211	51.0
	Sidney Smith (R)	9,803	49.0
2	Carter H. Harrison (D)	9,189	49.2
	Jasper D. Ward (R)	9,181	49.1
3	Charles B. Farwell (R)	8,177‡	50.1
	John V. Le Moyne (D)	7,991	49.0
4	Stephen A. Hurlbut (R)	9,326	53.3
	John F. Farnsworth (D)	8,167	46.7
5	Horatio C. Burchard (R)	9,232	56.8
	David J. Pinkney (D)	7,008	43.1
6	Thomas J. Henderson (R)	9,390	59.8
	Isaac H. Elliott (D)	6,299	40.1

	Candidates	Votes	%
7	Alexander Campbell (D)	10,308	56.6
	Franklin Corwin (R)	7,905	43.4
8	Greenbury L. Fort (R)	8,753	53.9
	J. G. Bayne (D)	7,463	45.9
9	Richard H. Whiting (R)	9,755	50.7
	Leonard F.Ross (D)	9,495	49.3
10	John C. Bagby (D)	9,784	52.6
	Henderson Richey (R)	8,824	47.4
11	Scott Wike (D)	11,489	59.2
	David Beatty (R)	7,429	38.3
12	William M. Springer (D)	10,623	48.1
	Andrew Simpson (R)	9,027	40.9
	J. B. Turner (IR)	2,417	11.0
13	Adlai E. Stevenson (D)	11,135	52.6
	John McNulta (R)	9,903	46.8
14	Joseph G. Cannon (R)	11,244	51.5
	James H. Pickrell (D)	10,603	48.5
15	John R. Eden (D)	12,084	52.8
	Jacob W. Wilkin (R)	10,789	47.2
16	William A. J. Sparks (D)	8,723	42.2
	James S. Martin (R)	7,932	38.4
	Rolla B. Henry (IR)	4,023	19.5
17	William R. Morrison (D)	13,086	60.8
	John I. Rinaker (R)	8,438	39.2
18	William Hartzell (D)	10,866	53.9
	Isaac Clements (R)	9,280	46.1
19	William B. Anderson (ID)	8,293	38.9
	Samuel S. Marshall (D)	7,556	35.4
	Green B. Rainn (R)	5,486	25.7

INDIANA

1	Benoni S. Fuller (D)	12,864	50.7
	Hellman (R)	12,527	49.3
2	James Douglas Williams (D)	17,404	64.6
	Ferguson (R)	9,088	33.7
3	Michael C. Kerr (D)	13,891	52.3
	Cravens (R)	12,682	47.7
4	Jeptha D. New (D)	13,683	52.5
	Robinson (R)	12,378	47.5
5	William S. Holman (D)	13,302	55.1
	Claypool (R)	10,835	44.9
6	Milton Stapp Robinson (R)	12,471	44.0
	Johnson (D)	12,017	42.4
	A. V. Pendleton (I)	3,888	13.7
7	Franklin Landers (D)	16,977	50.9
	John Coburn (R)	16,411	49.2
8	Morton C. Hunter (R)	14,005	50.4
	Rice (D)	13,798	49.6
9	Thomas J. Cason (D)	13,188	42.3
	McClarg (D)	12,754	40.9
	C. J. Bowles (I)	5,259	16.9
10	William Summerville Haymond (D)	15,088	51.1
	Calkins (R)	14,423	48.9
11	James L. Evans (R)	14,595	52.1
	Cox (D)	13,426	47.9
12	Andrew H. Hamilton (D)	14,318	53.2
	Taylor (R)	12,623	46.9
13	John H. Baker (R)	13,671	50.1
	Kelley (D)	13,613	49.9

IOWA

1	George W. McCrary (R)	11,384	54.5
	Leroy G. Palmer (A-MONOP)	9,521	45.5
2	John Q. Tufts (R)	10,779	51.6
	J. S. Sheean (A-MONOP)	10,122	48.4
3	Lucien Lester Ainsworth (A-MONOP)	11,066	50.1
	Charles F. Granger (R)	11,007	49.8
4	Henry O. Pratt (R)	10,725	60.4
	John Bowman (A-MONOP)	6,975	39.3
5	James Wilson (R)	12,724	63.0
	James Wilkinson (A-MONOP)	7,481	37.0
6	Ezekiel Silas Sampson (R)	12,461	56.1

	Candidates	Votes	%
	E. N. Gates (A-MONOP)	9,737	43.8
7	John A. Kasson (R)	12,274	55.2
	John D. Whitman (A-MONOP)	9,974	44.8
8	James W. McDill (R)	10,808	57.1
	Anson Rood (A-MONOP)	8,115	42.8
9	Samuel Addison Oliver (R)	12,657	64.9
	C. E. Whiting (A-MONOP)	6,825	35.0

KANSAS

1	William A. Phillips (R)	20,087	60.2
	M. J. Parrott (D)	11,223	33.6
	N. Green (G)	2,074	6.2
2	John R. Goodin (I)	14,965	51.2
	S. A. Cobb (R)	14,240	48.7
3	William R. Brown (R)	14,581	59.3
	J. K. Hudson (I)	9,932	40.4

KENTUCKY

1	Andrew R. Boone (D)	5,882	45.5
	Oscar Turner (ID)	5,799	44.8
	T. J. Pickett (IR)	1,255	9.7
2	John Y. Brown (D)	7,381	61.3
	George Smith (I)	3,864	32.1
	E. R. Weir (I)	797	6.6
3	Charles W. Millikin (D)	6,875	72.9
	Franklin Gorin (IR)	2,086	22.1
4	J. Proctor Knott (D)	8,182	64.0
	Clement S. Hill (I)	4,601	36.0
5	Edward Y. Parsons (D)	4,300	78.6
	John T. Gray (I)	859	15.7
	L. O. Wood (I)	313	5.7
6	Thomas L. Jones (D)	7,268	48.9
	Charles Eginton (R)	4,141	27.9
	O. P. Hogan (I)	3,452	23.2
7	Joseph C. S. Blackburn (D)	11,298	69.1
	Edward C. Marshall (I)	5,045	30.9
8	Milton J. Durham (D)	8,195	94.8
	J. L. McMurtry (R)	438	5.1
9	John D. White (R)	8,774	51.3
	Harrison Cockrell (D)	8,145	47.6
10	John B. Clarke (D)	9,324	58.9
	John Means (R)	6,326	40.0

LOUISIANA

1	Randall L. Gibson (D)	✓	
2	E. John Ellis (D)	✓	
3	Chester B. Darrall (R)	✓	
	J. A. Preux (D)		
4	William M. Levy (D)	✓	
5	Frank Morey (R)	‡	
	William B. Spencer (D)		
6	Charles E. Nash (R)	✓	

MAINE

1	John H. Burleigh (R)	12,275	53.2
	Bradbury (D)	10,805	46.8
2	William P. Frye (R)	9,088	57.1
	Clark (D)	6,673	41.9
3	James G. Blaine (R)	11,494	56.8
	E. K. O'Brien (D)	8,693	43.0
4	Samuel F. Hersey (R)	9,648*	58.8
	Boynton (D)	6,705	40.9
5	Eugene Hale (R)	10,695	56.9
	Spofford (D)	8,116	43.1

MARYLAND

1	Philip F. Thomas (D)	12,465	55.1
	Golds (R)	10,147	44.9
2	Charles B. Roberts (D)	10,682	56.5
	Ensor (R)	8,238	43.5
3	William J. O'Brien (D)	9,237	65.7

Candidates	Votes	%
Suter (R)	4,834	34.4
4 Thomas Swann (D)	10,244	60.1
Cox (R)	6,810	39.9
5 Eli J. Henkle (D)	11,856	53.2
Hagner (R)	10,452	46.9
6 William Walsh (D)	12,974	50.2
Lloyd Lowndes (R)	12,896	49.9

MASSACHUSETTS

Candidates	Votes	%
1 James Buffinton (R)	9,927	68.8
Louis Laphani (D & L)	4,171	28.9
2 Benjamin W. Harris (R)	9,651	59.0
Edward Avery (D & L)	6,688	40.9
3 Henry L. Pierce (R)	8,011	61.9
Benjamin Dean (D & L)	4,927	38.1
4 Rufus S. Frost (R)	6,721‡	50.6
Josiah G. Abbott (D & L)	6,511	49.0
5 Nathaniel P. Banks (D & L)	13,438	64.8
Daniel W. Gooch (R)	7,263	35.0
6 Charles P. Thompson (D & L)	8,716	52.9
Benjamin F. Butler (R)	7,747	47.1
7 John K. Tarbox (D & L)	8,979	54.8
James C. Ayer (R)	7,415	45.2
8 William Wirt Warren (D & L)	8,585	52.0
John M. S. Williams (R)	7,861	47.6
9 George F. Hoar (R)	9,423	51.2
Eli Thayer (D & L)	8,961	48.7
10 Julius H. Seelye (D & L)	7,773	41.8
Charles A. Stevens (R)	7,353	39.5
Henry C. Hill	3,474	18.7
11 Chester W. Chapin (D & L)	11,964	65.5
Henry Alexander Jr. (R)	6,227	34.1

MICHIGAN

Candidates	Votes	%
1 Alpheus S. Williams (D)	10,848	54.8
Field (R)	8,892	44.9
2 Henry Waldron (R)	14,611	52.8
Robison (D)	13,075	47.2
3 George Willard (R)	13,372	50.5
Livermore (D)	12,174	45.9
4 Allen Potter (I)	13,317	52.0
Burrows (R)	12,278	48.0
5 William B. Williams (R)	13,370	51.5
Wilber (D)	12,212	47.0
6 George H. Durand (D)	17,758	50.9
Begole (R)	16,122	46.2
7 Omar D. Conger (R)	10,185	54.0
Goodrich (D)	8,203	43.5
8 Nathan B. Bradley (R)	10,258	50.7
Lewis (D)	9,979	49.3
9 Jay A. Hubbell (R)	12,877	78.8
Noble (D)	3,460	21.2

MINNESOTA

Candidates	Votes	%
1 Mark H. Dunnell (R)	16,716	54.9
Waite (D)	13,712	45.1
2 Horace B. Strait (R)	13,742	50.4
Cox (D)	13,521	49.6
3 William S. King (R)	18,179	53.4
Wilson (D)	15,861	46.6

MISSOURI

Candidates	Votes	%
1 Edward C. Kehr (D)	5,921	51.0
Stanard (R)	5,693	49.0
2 Erastus Wells (D)	9,040	71.5
Fisher (R)	3,597	28.5
3 William H. Stone (D)	7,145	56.7
Wingate (R)	5,466	43.3
4 Robert A. Hatcher (D)	19,087	100.0
5 Richard P. Bland (D)	11,350	56.0
Seay (R)	8,929	44.0
6 Charles H. Morgan (D)	12,869	54.7
Thrasher (R)	10,640	45.3
7 John F. Philips (D)	14,446	88.8
Lay (I)	1,831	11.3
8 Benjamin J. Franklin (D)	11,546	63.9

Candidates	Votes	%
Alexander (I)	3,595	19.9
Powell (R)	2,926	16.2
9 David Rea (D)	12,953	55.5
Thompson (R)	10,395	44.5
10 Rezin A. De Bolt (D)	11,727	50.5
Hyde (I)	11,510	49.5
11 John B. Clark Jr. (D)	19,344	100.0
12 John M. Glover (D)	12,206	57.9
Lipscomb (R)	8,867	42.1
13 Aylett H. Buckner (D)	17,516	76.1
Krezel (R)	5,491	23.9

NEBRASKA

Candidates	Votes	%
AL Lorenzo Crounse (R)	22,532	62.7
James W. Savage (D)	8,360	23.3
James W. Davis (I)	4,074	11.3

NEVADA

Candidates	Votes	%
AL William Woodburn (R)	9,317	52.1
Ellis (D)	8,567	47.9

NEW JERSEY

Candidates	Votes	%
1 Clement H. Sinnickson (R)	14,209	52.2
Albtson (D)	13,019	47.8
2 Samuel A. Dobbins (R)	13,977	51.8
Smith (D)	13,011	48.2
3 Miles Ross (D)	15,682	53.5
Clark (R)	13,629	46.5
4 Robert Hamilton (D)	14,585	59.5
Place (R)	9,931	40.5
5 Augustus W. Cutler (D)	11,677	50.0
Phelps (R)	11,670	50.0
6 Frederick H. Teese (D)	13,876	50.2
Marcus L. Ward (R)	13,768	49.8
7 Augustus A. Hardenbergh (D)	13,189	61.5
Isaac W. Scudder (R)	8,272	38.5

NEW YORK

Candidates	Votes	%
1 Henry B. Metcalfe (D)	12,184	52.6
French (R)	11,002	47.5
2 John G. Schumaker(D)	15,123	69.5
Wood (R)	6,652	30.6
3 Simeon B. Chittenden (D)	14,539	61.8
Ostrander (R)	8,996	38.2
4 Archibald M. Bliss (D)	12,439	61.3
Bennett (R)	7,862	38.7
5 Edwin R. Meade (D)	9,199	50.5
Hogan (I)	9,024	49.5
6 Samuel S. Cox (D)	13,762	80.1
Campbell (R)	3,428	19.9
7 Smith Ely Jr. (D)	7,689	54.5
Spencer (R)	6,418	45.5
8 Elijah Ward (D)	10,113	52.3
Lawson (R)	9,232	47.7
9 Fernando Wood (D)	8,763	50.6
Hardy (I)	6,428	37.1
Robert S. Newton	2,131	12.3
10 Abram S. Hewitt (D)	9,503	54.0
O'Brien (I)	8,083	46.0
11 Benjamin A. Willis (D)	10,354	56.3
Bailey (I)	8,036	43.7
12 N. Holmes Odell (D)	12,082	58.2
Wight (R)	8,391	40.4
13 John O. Whitehouse (D)	16,181	57.2
Beale (R)	11,344	40.1
14 George M. Beebe (D)	14,518	56.4
Everett (R)	11,229	43.6
15 John H. Bagley Jr. (D)	16,205	56.1
Stebbins (R)	12,700	43.9
16 Charles H. Adams (R)	12,626	44.1
Terrance J. Quinn (D)	9,903	34.6
Eli Perry (D)	6,108	21.3
17 Martin I. Townsend (R)	15,445	50.9
Hughes (D)	14,931	49.2
18 Andrew Williams (R)	11,251	57.4
Waldo (D)	8,336	42.6

Candidates	Votes	%
19 William A. Wheeler (R)	12,323	68.9
Sawyer (D)	5,553	31.1
20 Henry H. Hathorn (R)	15,933	51.2
Sanders (D)	15,183	48.8
21 Samuel F. Miller (R)	15,574	51.9
Allaben (D)	14,431	48.1
22 George A. Bagley (R)	14,391	52.1
Graves (D)	13,255	48.0
23 Scott Lord (D)	11,922	52.3
Roberts (R)	10,496	46.0
24 William H. Baker (R)	12,123	52.2
Warner (D)	11,109	47.8
25 Elias W. Leavenworth (R)	14,949	57.3
Comstock (D)	11,158	42.7
26 Clinton D. MacDougall (R)	13,433	53.1
Wilson (D)	11,857	46.9
27 Elbridge G. Lapham (R)	10,814	49.7
Pierpont (D)	9,770	44.9
S. B. Ayres (TEMP)	1,163	5.4
28 Thomas C. Platt (R)	13,766	49.6
Jones (D)	13,013	46.9
29 Charles C. B. Walker (D)	17,020	54.6
Hakes (R)	14,148	45.4
30 John M. Davy (R)	12,770	49.2
Angle (D)	12,522	48.2
31 George B. Hoskins (R)	11,323	54.7
Buck (D)	9,398	45.4
32 Lyman K. Bass (R)	15,968	51.6
Nicholls (D)	14,970	48.4
33 Augustus F. Allen (D)	12,302*	54.1
Sessions (R)	10,459	46.0

Special Election

Candidates	Votes	%
9 Richard Schell (D)	12,562	67.9
John Hardy (ID)	5,947	32.1

NORTH CAROLINA

Candidates	Votes	%
1 Jesse J. Yeats (D)	14,071	52.8
Clinton L. Cobb (R)	12,590	47.2
2 John A. Hyman (R)	18,176	62.0
George W. Blount (D)	11,144	38.0
3 Alfred M. Waddell (D)	15,572	52.2
Neil McKay (R)	14,285	47.8
4 Joseph J. Davis (D)	14,924	52.9
James H. Headen (R)	13,312	47.2
5 Alfred M. Scales (D)	10,529	54.2
William F. Henderson (R)	8,909	45.8
6 Thomas S. Ashe (D)	13,579	64.5
E. C. Davidson (I)	7,469	35.5
7 William M. Robbins (D)	11,372	61.9
Columbus L. Cook (R)	6,999	38.1
8 Robert B. Vance (D)	11,126	61.8
Plato Durham (IC)	6,887	38.2

OHIO

Candidates	Votes	%
1 Milton Sayler (D)	11,566	61.5
John K. Green (R)	7,250	38.5
2 Henry B. Banning (D)	10,852	53.8
Job E. Stevenson (R)	9,317	46.2
3 John S. Savage (D)	12,972	52.3
John Q. Smith (R)	11,810	47.6
4 John A. McMahon (D)	15,411	51.5
Lewis B. Gunckle (R)	14,312	47.8
5 Americus V. Rice (D)	13,477	61.9
Reynold K. Lytle (R)	8,279	38.0
6 Frank H. Hurd (D)	13,108	51.9
Albert M. Pratt (R)	11,271	44.6
7 Lawrence T. Neal (D)	11,333	55.4
Thomas W. Gordon (R)	9,108	44.5
8 William Lawrence (R)	10,756	48.6
Joseph E. Pearson (D)	10,378	46.9
9 E. F. Poppleton (D)	11,627	48.7
James W. Robinson (R)	11,199	46.9
10 Charles Foster (R)	13,778	49.8
George E. Seney (D)	13,619	49.2
11 John L. Vance (D)	12,437	53.7
H. S. Bundy (R)	10,496	45.3

	Candidates	Votes	%
12	Ansel T. Walling (D)	13,580	57.5
	David Taylor Jr. (R)	9,667	40.9
13	Milton I. Southard (D)	13,602	57.8
	John H. Barnhill (R)	9,651	41.0
14	Jacob B. Cowan (D)	12,394	62.0
	William W. Armstrong (R)	7,214	36.1
15	Nelson H. Van Vorhes (R)	11,655	51.4
	Wiley H. Oldham (D)	10,656	47.0
16	Lorenzo Danford (R)	12,097	52.6
	Henry Boyles (D)	10,861	47.2
17	Laurin D. Woodworth (R)	11,113	49.6
	David M. Wilson (D)	10,837	48.4
18	James Monroe (R)	12,229	54.5
	John K. McBride (D)	10,095	45.0
19	James A. Garfield (R)	12,591	55.6
	Daniel B. Woods (D)	6,245	27.6
	R. H. Hurlburt (IR)	3,427	15.1
20	Henry B. Payne (D)	13,849	54.2
	Richard C. Parsons (R)	11,330	44.3

Special Election

		Votes	%
12	William E. Finck (D)	14,090	59.3
	David Taylor Jr. (R)	9,301	39.2

OREGON

		Votes	%
AL	George A. La Dow (D)	9,642	38.1
	Richard Williams (R)	9,340	36.9
	T. W. Davenport (I)	6,350	25.1

PENNSYLVANIA

		Votes	%
1	Chapman Freeman (R)	9,637	48.2
	T. B. Florence (D)	7,970	39.9
	David Branson (I)	2,370	11.9
2	Charles O'Neill (R)	11,692	54.8
	Benjamin Rush (D)	9,660	45.2
3	Samuel J. Randall (D)	9,703	57.8
	D. F. Houston (R)	7,060	42.1
4	William D. Kelley (R)	12,436	57.9
	W. V. McGrath (D)	9,049	42.1
5	John Robbins (D)	10,228	38.0
	A. C. Harmer (R)	9,095	33.8
	L. Myers (IR)	7,579	28.2
6	Washington Townsend (R)	9,485	57.8
	J. S. Forwood (D)	6,916	42.2
7	Allan Wood (R)	12,630	52.5
	E. L. Acker (D)	11,432	47.5
8	Heister Clymer (D)	10,553	66.3
	Charles B. McNight (R)	5,358	33.7
9	A. Herr Smith (R)	10,505	62.8
	William Patton (D)	6,220	37.2
10	William Mutchler (D)	13,737	67.2
	S. V. B. Kachline (I)	6,710	32.8
11	Francis D. Collins (D)	12,986	69.0
	A. W. Butler (R)	5,846	31.0
12	Winthrop W. Ketcham (R)	7,932	52.5
	H. B. Wright (D)	7,165	47.5
13	James B. Reilly (D)	8,600	51.2
	Theodore Garrettson (R)	8,056	48.0
14	John B. Packer (R)	12,528	56.4
	William M. Breslin (D)	9,673	43.6
15	Joseph Powell (D)	12,183	50.2
	B. Laporte (R)	12,082	49.8
16	Sobieski Ross (R)	10,660	53.3
	W. W. Early (D)	9,331	46.7
17	John Reilly (D)	11,727	52.6
	S. S. Blair (R)	10,580	47.4
18	William S. Stenger (D)	12,804	52.1
	Langhorne Wister (R)	11,781	47.9
19	Levi Maish (D)	14,534	58.7
	H. G. McNair (R)	7,230	29.2
	William McConky (I)	2,984	12.1

	Candidates	Votes	%
20	Levi A. Mackey (D)	12,050	58.1
	C. T. Alexander (I)	8,677	41.9
21	Jacob Turney (D)	12,065	57.7
	Andrew Stewart (R)	8,854	42.3
22	James H. Hopkins (D)	10,091	55.8
	James S. Negley (R)	7,777	43.0
23	Alexander G. Cochran (D)	5,206	40.0
	Thomas M. Bayne (R)	4,996	38.4
	S. A. Purviance (I)	2,803	21.6
24	John W. Wallace (R)	9,347	52.3
	George W. Miller (D)	8,538	47.7
25	George A. Jenks (D)	11,627	51.1
	Harry White (R)	11,109	48.9
26	James Sheakley (D)	12,810	50.1
	John G. White (R)	12,737	49.9
27	Albert G. Egbert (D)	10,393	50.0
	C. B. Curtis (R)	10,381	50.0

RHODE ISLAND

		Votes	%
1	Benjamin T. Eames (R)	2,292	73.3
	Beach (D)	824	26.4
2	Latimer W. Ballou (R)	2,362	65.0
	Redman (D)	1,235	34.0

SOUTH CAROLINA

		Votes	%
1	Joseph H. Rainey (R)	14,360	51.4
	Samuel Lee (I REF D)	13,563	48.6
2	Edmund W. M. Mackey (I REF D)	16,746‡	54.1
	Charles W. Buttz (R)	14,204	45.9
3	Solomon L. Hoge (R)	16,431	56.1
	Samuel McGowan (D)	12,873	43.9
4	Alexander S. Wallace (R)	16,452	53.2
	J. B. Kershaw (D)	14,455	46.8
5	Robert Smalls (R)	17,752	79.4
	J. P. M. Epping (I)	4,461	20.0

Special Election

		Votes	%
3	Lewis Cass Carpenter (R)	21,248	99.6

TENNESSEE

		Votes	%
1	William McFarland (D)	8,783	55.7
	Butler (R)	6,995	44.3
2	Jacob M. Thornburgh (R)	8,168	52.7
	Mabry (D)	7,338	47.3
3	George G. Dibrell (D)	9,559	65.7
	Nelson (R)	4,597	31.6
4	John W. Head (D)	10,430*	100.0
5	John M. Bright (D)	10,224	72.7
	Wisener (R)	3,831	27.3
6	John F. House (D)	11,992	62.4
	Harrison (R)	7,227	37.6
7	Washington C. Whitthorne (D)	9,672	78.2
	Gibbs (R)	1,773	14.3
	G. W. Blackburn (IR)	928	7.5
8	John D. C. Atkins (D)	9,446	66.4
	Muse (R)	4,789	33.6
9	William P. Caldwell (D)	11,128	72.0
	Nunn (R)	4,336	28.0
10	H. Casey Young (D)	13,825	60.4
	Lewis (R)	9,071	39.6

Special Election

		Votes	%
4	Samuel McClary Fite (CD)	✓	

TEXAS

		Votes	%
1	John H. Reagan (D)	5,793	75.6
	William Chambers	1,855	24.2

	Candidates	Votes	%
2	David B. Culberson (D)	3,804	99.6
3	James W. Throckmorton (D)	4,392	93.0
	J. M. Valentine	262	5.5
4	Roger Q. Mills (D)	9,395	72.2
	Pleasant M. Yell (R)	3,615	27.8
5	John Hancock (D)	3,526	97.3
6	Gustave Schleicher (D)	5,082	69.3
	Jeremiah Galvan	2,234	30.5

VERMONT

		Votes	%
1	Charles H. Joyce (R)	9,638	69.5
	Heaton (D)	2,597	18.7
	Charles W. Willard	1,635	11.8
2	Dudley C. Denison (IR)	7,038	44.7
	Luke P. Poland (R)	5,756	36.6
	C. W. Davenport (D)	1,960	12.5
3	George W. Hendee (R)	9,043	71.3
	Edwards (D)	3,646	28.7

VIRGINIA

		Votes	%
1	Beverly B. Douglas (D)	10,783	50.7
	James B. Sinen (R)	10,488	49.3
2	John Goode Jr. (D)	13,521	49.4
	James H. Platt Jr. (R)	13,390	49.0
3	Gilbert C. Walker (D)	13,325	55.3
	Rush Bargess (R)	10,710	44.5
4	William H. H. Stowell (R)	14,583	63.9
	W. H. Mann (D)	8,201	35.9
5	George C. Cabell (D)	10,291	57.1
	C. Y. Thomas (R)	7,723	42.9
6	John Randolph Tucker (D)	10,708	65.2
	J. F. Johnson (R)	5,707	34.8
7	John T. Harris (D)	9,266	73.6
	John F. Lewis (R)	3,214	25.5
8	Eppa Hunton (D)	9,809	51.4
	James Barbour (R)	9,291	48.6
9	William Terry (D)	8,052	48.4
	Fayette McMullen (ID)	6,760	40.6
	George W. Henderlite (R)	1,821	11.0

WEST VIRGINIA

		Votes	%
1	Benjamin Wilson (D)	12,796	50.3
	Nathan Goff Jr. (R)	12,631	49.7
2	Charles J. Faulkner (D)	11,499	57.5
	Alexander R. Boteler (R)	8,064	40.3
3	Frank Hereford (D)	13,524	63.6
	John D. Witcher (R)	7,745	36.4

WISCONSIN

		Votes	%
1	Charles G. Williams (R)	12,568	56.9
	Fratt (REF)	9,532	43.1
2	Lucien B. Caswell (R)	11,676	50.5
	Cook (REF)	11,459	49.5
3	Henry S. Magoon (R)	11,535	52.6
	Thompson (REF)	10,400	47.4
4	William P. Lynde (REF)	12,046	55.8
	Ludington (R)	9,545	44.2
5	Samuel D. Burchard (REF)	15,784	61.5
	Barber (R)	9,889	38.5
6	Alanson M. Kimball (R)	14,733	50.2
	Bouck (REF)	14,641	49.8
7	Jeremiah M. Rusk (R)	13,637	57.2
	Fulton (REF)	10,196	42.8
8	George W. Cate (REF)	9,546	50.0
	McDill (R)	9,544	50.0

1875 House Elections

CALIFORNIA

	Candidates	Votes	%
1	William A. Piper (D)	12,417	49.0
	Iva P. Rankin (R)	6,791	26.8
	John F. Swift (I)	6,103	24.1
2	Horace F. Page (R)	13,624	43.4
	Hy Larkin (D)	12,329	39.3
	C. R. Tuttle (I)	5,414	17.3
3	John K. Luttrell (D)	18,468	55.1
	C. B. Denio (R)	8,284	24.7
	Charles F. Reed (I)	6,761	20.2
4	Peter D. Wigginton (D)	15,649	48.7
	S. O. Houghton (R)	11,090	34.5
	J. S. Thompson (I)	5,413	16.8

CONNECTICUT

		Votes	%
1	George M. Landers (D)	13,434	50.5
	Joseph R. Hawley (R)	12,946	48.7
2	James Phelps (D)	15,440	51.6
	Stephen Wright Kellogg (R)	13,831	46.3
3	Henry H. Starkweather (R)	9,000	51.1
	Foster (D)	8,054	45.7
4	William H. Barnum (D)	14,273	53.8
	Hubbard (R)	11,648	43.9

ILLINOIS

Special Election

	Candidates	Votes	%
1	Bernard G. Caulfield (D)	3,461	80.7
	Henry Vallettee	454	10.6
	William H. Eddy	308	7.2

MASSACHUSETTS

Special Elections

		Votes	%
1	William W. Crapo (R)	9,553	65.5
	Charles G. Davis	5,017	34.4
10	Charles A. Stevens (R)	2,850	43.7
	Henry M. Burleigh	2,369	36.3
	Lafayette Mattby	727	11.1
	Levi Stockbridge	562	8.6

MISSISSIPPI

1	Lucius Q. C. Lamar (D)	19,233	100.0
2	G. Wiley Wells (I)	19,250	59.4
	Howe (R)	13,149	40.6
3	Hernando D. Money (D)	15,128	68.1
	Powers (R)	7,085	31.9
4	Otho R. Singleton (D)	19,890	66.6
	Niles (R)	9,987	33.4

	Candidates	Votes	%
5	Charles E. Hooker (D)	16,255	59.9
	Hill (R)	10,878	40.1
6	John R. Lynch (R)	13,746	50.5
	Seal (D)	13,460	49.5

NEW HAMPSHIRE

		Votes	%
1	Frank Jones (D)	13,967	50.0
	Withhorn (R)	13,631	48.8
2	Samuel N. Bell (D)	13,084	49.9
	Pike (R)	12,930	49.3
3	Henry W. Blair (R)	12,389	50.1
	Kent (D)	12,180	49.3

NEW YORK

Special Election

		Votes	%
33	Nelson I. Norton (R)	10,770	53.9
	Charles S. Cary	9,139	45.7

OREGON

Special Election

		Votes	%
AL	La Fayette Lane (D)	9,373	47.6
	H. Warren (R)	9,106	46.3

1876 House Elections

ALABAMA

	Candidates	Votes	%
1	James T. Jones (D)	10,582	49.3
	Bromberg (ID)	8,771	40.8
	Turner (R)	2,132	9.9
2	Hilary A. Herbert (D)	11,435	54.9
	Hall (R)	9,393	45.1
3	Jeremiah N. Williams (D)	14,089	78.3
	Betts (R)	3,896	21.7
4	Charles M. Shelley (D)	9,655	37.8
	Haralson (R)	8,670	33.9
	James T. Rapier (COLOR R)	7,236	28.3
5	Robert F. Ligon (R)	13,107	64.8
	Booth (D)	7,120	35.2
6	Goldsmith W. Hewitt (D)	13,634	100.0
7	William H. Forney (D)	14,319	100.0
8	William W. Garth (D)	14,529	62.0
	McClellan (ID)	8,910	38.0

ARKANSAS

1	Lucien C. Gause (D)	15,840	97.5
2	William F. Siemons (D)	15,566	52.4
	Snyder (R)	14,159	47.6
3	Jordan E. Cravens (BOLT D)	8,277	35.9
	McClure (R)	8,016	34.7
	Stuart (D)	5,927	25.7
4	Thomas M. Gunter (D)	12,355	74.7
	Huckleberry (R)	4,176	25.3

CALIFORNIA

1	Horace Davis (R)	22,134	53.3
	William A. Piper (D)	19,363	46.7
2	Horace F. Page (R)	20,815	56.7
	G. J. Carpenter (D)	15,916	43.3
3	John K. Luttrell (D)	19,846	51.1
	Joseph McKenney (R)	18,990	48.9
4	Romualdo Pacheco (R)	19,104‡	50.0
	Peter D. Wigginton (D)	19,083	49.9

COLORADO[1]

(Became a state Aug. 1, 1876)

AL	James B. Belford (LR)	13,532‡	51.9
	Thomas M. Patterson (D)	12,541	48.1

Special Election

AL	James B. Belford (R)	13,302	52.0
	Thomas M. Patterson (D)	12,267	48.0

CONNECTICUT

1	George M. Landers (D)	15,529	50.0
	Hawley (R)	15,390	49.5
2	James Phelps (D)	19,500	53.4
	Stephen Wright Kellogg (R)	16,777	45.9
3	John T. Wait (R)	11,283	53.8
	Waller (D)	9,535	45.4
4	Levi Warner (D)	17,233	52.5
	Robert Hubbard (R)	15,501	47.2

Special Election

4	Levi Warner (D)	17,250	52.7
	Robert Hubbard (R)	15,459	47.3

DELAWARE

AL	James Williams (D)	13,169	55.4
	Bird (R)	10,592	44.6

FLORIDA

	Candidates	Votes	%
1	Robert H. M. Davidson (D)	13,163	51.1
	Purman (R)	12,623	49.0
2	Horatio Bisbee Jr. (R)	11,470‡	50.0
	Jesse J. Finley (D)	11,453	50.0

GEORGIA

1	Julian Hartridge (D)	11,465	65.9
	Bayant (R)	5,922	34.1
2	William E. Smith (D)	13,627	63.0
	Whitley (R)	8,015	37.0
3	Philip Cook (D)	10,684	71.4
	Pierce (R)	4,280	28.6
4	Henry R. Harris (D)	13,797	70.5
	Hilliard (R)	5,785	29.5
5	Milton A. Candler (D)	18,083	67.5
	Markham (R)	8,714	32.5
6	James H. Blount (D)	12,996	74.0
	Gove (R)	4,578	26.1
7	William H. Felton (ID)	13,269	55.1
	Dabney (R)	10,807	44.9
8	Alexander H. Stephens (D)	14,471	91.9
	Tennelle (R)	1,277	8.1
9	Benjamin H. Hill (D)	14,790*	100.0

ILLINOIS

1	William Aldrich (R)	16,578	53.2
	John R. Hoxie (D)	14,101	45.2
2	Carter H. Harrison (D)	14,732	50.9
	George R. Davis (R)	14,090	48.7
3	Lorenzo Brentano (R)	11,722	50.6
	John V. Lemoyne (D)	11,435	49.4
4	William Lathrop (R)	13,241	48.4
	John F. Farnsworth (D)	8,149	29.8
	Stephen A. Hurlbut (IR)	5,991	21.9
5	Horatio C. Burchard (R)	15,793	59.8
	Pattison (D)	10,600	40.2
6	Thomas J. Henderson (R)	15,560	60.6
	Charles Dunham (D)	9,821	38.3
7	Philip C. Hayes (R)	14,849	52.7
	Alexander Campbell (D)	13,313	47.3
8	Greenbury L. Fort (R)	15,011	55.1
	George W. Parker (D)	12,211	44.9
9	Thomas A. Boyd (R)	14,548	49.8
	George A. Wilson (D)	14,001	47.9
10	Benjamin F. Marsh (R)	14,252	51.1
	J. H. Hungate (D)	13,496	48.4
11	Robert M. Knapp (D)	17,949	58.7
	Joseph Robbins (R)	12,618	41.2
12	William M. Springer (D)	17,400	55.8
	David L. Phillips (R)	13,754	44.1
13	Thomas F. Tipton (R)	15,229	50.4
	Adlai E. Stevenson (D)	14,977	49.6
14	Joseph G. Cannon (R)	17,796	52.0
	John C. Black (D)	16,404	48.0
15	John R. Eden (D)	18,714	57.5
	George D. Chape (R)	13,765	42.3
16	William A. J. Sparks (D)	14,591	53.3
	Edwin M. Ashcraft (R)	12,763	46.7
17	William R. Morrison (D)	17,036	56.7
	Henry S. Baker (R)	13,029	43.3
18	William Hartzell (D)	14,691	50.0
	Benjamin L. Wiley (R)	14,671	50.0
19	Richard W. Townshend (D)	12,720	44.3
	Edward Bonham (R)	8,558	29.8
	William B. Anderson (G)	7,463	26.0

INDIANA

1	Benoni S. Fuller (D)	14,727	50.6
	C. A. Debruler (R)	13,158	45.2
2	Thomas R. Cobb (D)	18,918	56.3
	Loveless (R)	13,735	40.9

	Candidates	Votes	%
3	George A. Bicknell (D)	17,225	57.4
	Newsom (R)	11,747	39.2
4	Leonidas Sexton (R)	14,902	49.9
	Woolen (D)	14,570	48.8
5	Thomas M. Browne (R)	15,578	52.5
	Holman (D)	14,069	47.5
6	Milton Stapp Robinson (R)	17,403	49.3
	Chamber (D)	17,118	48.5
7	John Hanna (R)	19,634	49.8
	Franklin Landers (D)	18,236	46.2
8	Morton C. Hunter (R)	14,265	44.4
	McLean (D)	13,155	41.0
	Davis (G)	4,704	14.6
9	Michael D. White (R)	16,990	50.0
	Williams (D)	13,564	39.9
	Leroy Templeton (G)	3,449	10.1
10	William Henry Calkins (R)	17,952	51.8
	William Summerville Haymond (D)	16,693	48.1
11	James L. Evans (R)	18,030	52.2
	Armstrong (D)	16,482	47.8
12	Andrew H. Hamilton (D)	18,842	58.5
	Bonham (R)	12,718	39.5
13	John H. Baker (R)	18,481	52.9
	Kelley (D)	16,273	46.6

Special Elections

2	Andrew Humphreys (D)	18,724	55.7
	W. F. Spicely (R)	14,919	44.4
3	Nathan Tracy Carr (D)	17,214	59.4
	Ara E. S. Long (R)	11,782	40.6

IOWA

1	Joseph C. Stone (R)	17,188	53.4
	Wesley C. Hobbs (D)	14,814	46.1
2	Hiram Price (R)	16,439	52.8
	Jeremiah Henry Murphy (D)	14,683	47.2
3	Theodore W. Burdick (R)	17,423	51.5
	Jeffrey M. Griffith (D)	16,100	47.6
4	Nathaniel C. Deering (R)	20,770	68.9
	Cyrus Foreman (D)	9,379	31.1
5	Rush Clark (R)	19,274	60.4
	Nathan Worley (D)	11,154	35.0
6	Ezekiel Silas Sampson (R)	18,768	54.7
	H. B. Hendershott (D)	14,719	42.9
7	Henry J. B. Cummings (R)	19,496	58.3
	Samuel J. Gilpin (D)	11,688	34.9
	Andrew Hastie (G)	2,160	6.5
8	William F. Sapp (R)	19,358	56.0
	L. R. Bolter (D)	15,236	44.0
9	S. Addison Oliver (R)	19,563	63.5
	Samuel Rees (D)	10,583	34.3

KANSAS

1	William A. Phillips (R)	29,352	64.8
	Thomas Fenion (D)	15,642	34.5
2	Dudley C. Haskell (R)	22,088	55.7
	J. R. Goodin (IG)	17,518	44.2
3	Thomas Ryan (R)	25,171	68.3
	S. J. Crawford (IG)	11,634	31.6

KENTUCKY

1	Andrew R. Boone (D)	10,994	45.1
	Oscar Turner (ID)	7,540	30.9
	H. H. Houston (R)	5,835	23.9
2	James A. McKenzie (D)	17,557	65.2
	J. Z. Moore (R)	9,374	34.8
3	John W. Caldwell (D)	13,285	54.0
	E. L. Mottley (R)	10,590	43.1
4	J. Proctor Knott (D)	15,735	68.9
	J. W. Lewis (R)	7,053	30.9
5	Albert S. Willis (D)	15,046	73.0

Candidates	Votes	%
Walter Evans (R)	5,567	27.0
6 John G. Carlisle (D)	16,404	66.9
John J. Landrum (R)	8,133	33.1
7 Joseph C. S. Blackburn (D)	18,884	62.5
T. O. Shackelford (R)	11,348	37.5
8 Milton J. Durham (D)	15,484	55.0
W. O. Bradley (R)	12,654	44.9
9 Thomas Turner (D)	13,103	50.8
Robert Boyd (R)	12,710	49.2
10 John B. Clarke (D)	14,409	57.7
O. S. Deming (R)	10,561	42.3

Special Election

5 Henry Watterson (D)	11,567	94.5
William J. Heady	677	5.5

LOUISIANA

1 Randall L. Gibson (D)	14,876	55.4
William M. Burwell (R)	11,978	44.6
2 E. John Ellis (D)	14,145	55.1
Henry C. Dibble (R)	11,515	44.9
3 Chester B. Darrall (R)	15,782‡	51.8
Joseph H. Acklen (D)	14,695	48.2
4 Joseph B. Elam (D)	12,136	51.3
George L. Smith (R)	11,540	48.7
5 John Edwards Leonard (R)	14,423	52.6
William W. Farmer (D)	13,016	47.4
6 Edward J. Robertson (D)	15,520	58.2
Charles E. Nash (R)	11,147	41.8

MAINE

1 Thomas B. Reed (R)	16,248	51.4
John M. Goodwin (D)	15,156	47.9
2 William P. Frye (R)	13,681	55.7
S. Clifford Belcher (D)	10,323	42.0
3 Stephen D. Lindsey (R)	15,741	55.2
E. K. O'Brien (D)	12,788	44.8
4 Llewellyn Powers (R)	12,866	53.8
John P. Donworth (D)	10,069	42.1
5 Eugene Hale (R)	15,089	55.1
William H. McClellan (D)	12,278	44.8

Special Election

3 Edwin Flye (R)	15,611	54.8
Isaac Reed (D)	12,848	45.1

MARYLAND

1 Daniel M. Henry (D)	15,287	56.2
Spence (R)	11,905	43.8
2 Charles B. Roberts (D)	15,033	55.6
Morrison J. Harris (R)	11,984	44.4
3 William Kimmell (D)	14,251	62.4
W. E. Goldsborough (R)	8,592	37.6
4 Thomas Swann (D)	15,259	54.5
James H. Butler (R)	12,728	45.5
5 Eli J. Henkle (D)	14,436	55.2
John Henry Sellman (R)	11,705	44.8
6 William Walsh (D)	15,727	50.0
Louis McComas (R)	15,713	50.0

MASSACHUSETTS

1 William W. Crapo (R)	14,153	69.6
Day (D)	6,179	30.4
2 Benjamin W. Harris (R)	15,550	61.4
Avery (D)	9,757	38.5
3 Walbridge A. Field (R)	9,323‡	50.0
Benjamin Dean (D)	9,315	50.0
4 Leopold Morse (D)	10,249	52.6
Frost (R)	9,215	47.3
5 Nathaniel P. Banks (R)	13,325	51.9
Frothingham (D)	12,317	47.9
6 George B. Loring (R)	12,319	52.4
Thompson (D)	11,171	47.5
7 Benjamin F. Butler (R)	12,100	51.6

Candidates	Votes	%
Tarbox (D)	9,379	40.0
Hoar (IR)	1,955	8.3
8 William C. Claflin (R)	14,245	53.2
Warren (D)	12,497	46.7
9 William W. Rice (R)	13,890	57.5
Verry (D)	10,248	42.4
10 Amasa Norcross (R)	15,779	63.9
Lamb (D)	8,928	36.1
11 George D. Robinson (R)	11,922	54.0
Chapin (D)	9,760	44.2

MICHIGAN

1 Alpheus S. Williams (D)	14,471	50.5
Duffield (R)	12,417	43.3
Ruehle (G)	1,736	6.1
2 Edwin Willits (R)	19,211	52.0
Robison (D)	17,024	46.1
3 Jonas H. McGowan (R)	19,878	51.8
Livermore (D)	17,223	44.9
4 Edwin W. Keightley (R)	18,716	53.4
Chamberlain (D & G)	11,330	46.6
5 John W. Stone (R)	21,908	54.1
Harris (D & G)	18,546	45.8
6 Mark S. Brewer (R)	23,356	51.9
Durand (D)	21,615	48.1
7 Omar D. Conger (R)	15,818	54.1
Chadwick (D)	13,177	45.1
8 Charles C. Ellsworth (R)	16,098	50.5
Potter (D)	15,760	49.5
9 Jay A. Hubbell (R)	18,224	59.0
Kilbourne (D & G)	12,656	41.0

MINNESOTA

1 Mark H. Dunnell (R)	26,010	61.8
Stacy (D)	16,064	38.2
2 Horace B. Strait (R)	19,730	52.5
Wilder (D)	14,990	39.9
Donnelly (G)	2,879	7.1
3 Jacob H. Stewart (R)	22,823	52.4
McNair (D)	20,717	47.6

MISSISSIPPI

1 Henry L. Muldrow (D)	20,597	76.2
Lee (R)	6,420	23.8
2 Vannoy H. Manning (D)	20,328	61.0
Watson (R)	12,589	37.8
3 Hernando D. Money (D)	17,983	71.1
Chisholm (R)	7,320	28.9
4 Otho R. Singleton (D)	19,130	80.8
Hancock (R)	4,547	19.2
5 Charles E. Hooker (D)	19,858	69.7
Shaughnessey (R)	8,646	30.3
6 James R. Chalmers (D)	15,788	56.0
John R. Lynch (R)	12,386	44.0

MISSOURI

1 Anthony Ittner (R)	7,043	50.7
E. C. Kerr (D)	6,834	49.2
2 Nathan Cole (R)	7,316	41.3
E. Wells (D)	7,026	39.7
A. W. Slayback (D)	3,229	18.2
3 Lyne S. Metcalfe (R)	8,099	50.1
Richard G. Frost (D)	8,080	49.9
4 Robert A. Hatcher (D)	21,390	79.0
L. Davis	3,953	14.6
W. Ballentine	1,738	6.4
5 Richard P. Bland (D)	14,599	56.1
J. Q. Thompson (R)	11,414	43.9
6 Charles H. Morgan (D)	18,080	49.9
H. E. Havens (R)	17,357	47.9
7 Thomas T. Crittenden (D)	18,700	54.9
J. H. Stover (R)	15,353	45.1
8 Benjamin J. Franklin (D)	15,229	68.0
D. S. Twitchell (R)	7,160	32.0
9 David Rea (D)	15,715	54.1
B. F. Loan (R)	13,343	45.9

Candidates	Votes	%
10 Henry M. Pollard (R)	16,582	51.0
R. A. Debolt (D)	15,802	48.6
11 John B. Clark Jr. (D)	21,671	68.6
M. L. Demotte (R)	9,915	31.4
12 John M. Glover (D)	16,154	57.1
Hayward (R)	11,646	41.1
13 Aylett H. Buckner (D)	21,573	79.2
T. B. Robinson (R)	4,715	17.3

NEBRASKA

AL Frank Welch (R)	30,900	59.7
Joseph Hollman (D)	17,206	33.2
Marvin Warren (G)	3,589	6.9

NEVADA

AL Thomas Wren (R)	10,241	52.3
Ellis (D)	9,330	47.7

NEW JERSEY

1 Clement H. Sinnickson (R)	17,362	52.9
Simrman (D)	15,472	47.1
2 John H. Pugh (R)	16,015	50.8
Smith (D)	15,485	49.2
3 Miles Ross (D)	18,525	54.7
Atherton (R)	15,359	45.3
4 Alvah A. Clark (D)	17,351	59.3
Veghte (ID)	11,900	40.7
5 Augustus W. Cutler (D)	15,034	53.9
Mills (R)	12,882	46.2
6 Thomas B. Peddie (R)	17,565	51.5
Righter (D)	16,041	47.0
7 Augustus A. Hardenbergh (D)	17,260	60.2
Stiastny (R)	11,391	39.8

NEW YORK

1 James W. Covert (D)	20,145	56.7
King (R)	15,222	42.8
2 William D. Veeder (D)	13,406	60.2
Cavanagh (R)	8,331	37.4
3 Simeon B. Chittenden (R)	18,110	50.2
Dakin (D)	17,858	49.5
4 Archibald M. Bliss (D)	18,506	61.5
Spitzer (R)	11,492	38.2
5 Nicholas Muller (D)	15,259	75.2
Kerrigan (I)	4,755	23.4
6 Samuel S. Cox (D)	17,098	95.0
7 Anthony Eickhoff (D)	13,199	68.1
Groom (R)	6,051	31.2
8 Anson G. McCook (R)	13,221	51.3
Ward (D)	12,408	48.1
9 Fernando Wood (D)	14,280	62.1
Ducunha (R)	8,217	35.8
10 Abram S. Hewitt (D)	17,136	69.6
Babcock (R)	6,805	27.6
11 Benjamin A. Willis (D)	12,519	49.7
Morton (R)	12,092	48.0
12 Clarkson N. Potter (D)	16,078	59.0
Brandreth (R)	11,160	41.0
13 John H. Ketcham (R)	18,225	52.7
Davies (D)	16,113	46.6
14 George M. Beebe (D)	17,732	54.7
Sweet (R)	14,667	45.3
15 Stephen L. Mayham (D)	20,494	55.7
Tremper (R)	16,267	44.2
16 Terence J. Quinn (D)	17,497	51.3
Harris (R)	16,596	48.7
17 Martin I. Townsend (R)	19,689	53.0
Parmenter (D)	17,448	47.0
18 Andrew Williams (R)	13,177	56.3
Platt (D)	10,246	43.7
19 Amaziah B. James (R)	17,275	66.4
Magove (D)	8,756	33.6
20 John H. Starin (R)	19,142	51.4
Decker (D)	18,089	48.6
21 Solomon Bundy (R)	18,825	52.5
Matteson (D)	17,056	47.5

	Candidates	Votes	%
22	George A. Bagley (R)	18,668	53.6
	Smith (D)	15,995	45.9
23	William J. Bacon (R)	13,779	51.3
	Lord (D)	13,069	48.7
24	William H. Baker (R)	16,555	57.3
	Bond (D & P)	11,798	40.8
25	Frank Hiscock (R)	18,425	57.1
	Pratt (D)	13,834	42.9
26	John H. Camp (R)	19,036	56.1
	Vanauken (D)	14,879	43.9
27	Elbridge G. Lapham (R)	14,726	55.3
	Comstock (D)	11,852	44.5
28	Jeremiah W. Dwight (R)	18,839	54.3
	Jones (D)	15,662	45.1
29	John N. Hungerford (R)	21,087	54.0
	Loveridge (D)	17,973	46.0
30	E. Kirke Hart (D)	17,797	50.7
	Davy (R)	17,138	48.8
31	Charles B. Benedict (D)	12,250	42.3
	Hoskins (R)	11,866	41.0
	Thomas T. Flagler (IR)	4,837	16.7
32	Daniel N. Lockwood (D)	20,125	50.5
	Spaulding (R)	19,716	49.4
33	George W. Patterson (R)	16,910	61.3
	Unidentified Candidate (D)	10,601	38.4

NORTH CAROLINA

	Candidates	Votes	%
1	Jesse J. Yeates (D)	15,151	51.7
	D. McDonald Lindsey (R)	14,154	48.3
2	Curtis H. Brogden (R)	21,060	64.0
	Wharton J. Green (D)	11,874	36.1
3	Alfred M. Waddell (D)	17,515	52.5
	William P. Canaday (R)	15,826	47.5
4	Joseph J. Davis (D)	16,832	52.5
	Isaac J. Young (R)	15,229	47.5
5	Alfred M. Scales (D)	13,264	54.7
	James E. Boyd (R)	11,001	45.3
6	Walter L. Steele (D)	17,256	62.7
	Allen Jordan (R)	10,283	37.3
7	William M. Robbins (D)	13,724	59.2
	Thomas J. Dula (R)	9,467	40.8
8	Robert B. Vance (D)	15,868	67.9
	Erastus P. Hampton (R)	7,493	32.1

OHIO

	Candidates	Votes	%
1	Milton Sayler (D)	14,144	51.2
	Manning F. Force (R)	13,474	48.8
2	Henry B. Banning (D)	14,133	50.1
	Stanley Matthews (R)	14,058	49.9
3	Mills Gardner (R)	16,594	50.8
	John S. Savage (D)	16,098	49.2
4	John A. McMahon (D)	18,557	50.0
	John Howard (R)	18,461	49.7
5	Americus V. Rice (D)	20,643	62.0
	J. L. H. Long (R)	12,645	38.0
6	Jacob D. Cox (R)	17,276	50.0
	Frank H. Hurd (D)	15,361	44.5
	E. B. Hall (P)	1,887	5.5
7	Henry L. Dickey (D)	14,859	52.3
	A. L. Brown (R)	13,518	47.6
8	J. Warren Keifer (R)	17,728	55.5
	George Arthur (D)	14,012	43.9
9	John S. Jones (R)	15,968	50.7
	L. F. Poppleton (D)	15,175	48.2
10	Charles Foster (R)	17,324	50.3
	John H. Hudson (D)	17,053	49.5
11	Henry S. Neal (R)	15,213	50.9
	John L. Vance (D)	14,639	49.0
12	Thomas Ewing (D)	19,628	57.2
	George K. Nash (R)	14,541	42.4
13	Milton I. Southard (D)	17,706	54.7
	John H. Barnhill (R)	14,642	45.2
14	Ebenezer B. Finley (D)	16,654	60.0
	Peter S. Grosscut (R)	11,067	39.9
15	Nelson H. Van Vorhes (R)	14,620	50.5
	William W. Poston (D)	14,113	48.8
16	Lorenzo Danford (R)	16,089	53.7
	William Lawrence (D)	13,837	46.2

	Candidates	Votes	%
17	William McKinley Jr (R)	16,489	50.2
	Levi L. Lanborn (D)	13,185	40.2
	John B. Powell (G)	2,446	7.5
18	James Monroe (R)	16,906	56.9
	John J. Hall (D)	12,772	43.0
19	James A. Garfield (R)	20,012	63.8
	John S. Casement (D)	11,352	36.2
20	Amos Townsend (R)	17,894	55.0
	Henry B. Payne (D)	14,516	44.6

OREGON

	Candidates	Votes	%
AL	Richard Williams (R)	15,347	51.9
	L. F. Lane (D)	14,239	48.1

PENNSYLVANIA

	Candidates	Votes	%
1	Chapman Freeman (R)	15,021	57.2
	J. S. Thackray (D)	11,231	42.8
2	Charles O'Neill (R)	15,198	56.1
	C. H. Gibson (D)	11,881	43.9
3	Samuel J. Randall (D)	11,651	56.3
	Benjamin L. Berry (R)	9,041	43.7
4	William D. Kelley (R)	18,820	60.2
	J. T. School (D)	12,432	39.8
5	Alfred C. Harmer (R)	17,973	55.0
	Jacob Duvall (D)	14,722	45.0
6	William Ward (R)	15,220	61.0
	W. D. Hartman (D)	9,717	39.0
7	I. Newton Evans (R)	15,765	52.5
	Abel Rambo (D)	14,247	47.5
8	Hiester Clymer (D)	15,239	65.6
	H. D. Markley (R)	6,213	26.7
	C. Shearer (G)	1,780	7.7
9	A. Herr Smith (R)	17,419	64.5
	George Nauman (D)	9,574	35.5
10	Samuel A. Bridges (D)	20,113	62.1
	Howard J. Reeder (R)	12,255	37.9
11	Francis D. Collins (D)	18,548	64.6
	D. J. Waller (R)	10,172	35.4
12	Hendrick B. Wright (D)	13,557	52.7
	H. B. Payne (R)	12,101	47.0
13	James B. Reilly (D)	10,107	50.2
	J. S. Nutting (R)	10,026	49.8
14	John W. Killinger (R)	16,453	53.6
	W. B. Wilson (D)	13,723	44.7
15	Edward Overton Jr. (R)	16,954	53.1
	Joseph Powell (D)	14,952	46.9
16	John I. Mitchell (R)	13,575	50.3
	Henry White (D)	12,097	44.8
17	Jacob M. Campbell (R)	14,668	50.9
	John Reilly (D)	14,148	49.1
18	William S. Stenger (D)	15,301	50.1
	Thad M. Mahon (R)	15,232	49.9
19	Levi Maish (D)	18,932	57.7
	C. H. Bressler (R)	13,898	42.3
20	Levi A. Mackey (D)	16,229	59.2
	R. V. B. Lincoln (R)	11,193	40.8
21	Jacob Turney (D)	16,962	57.1
	Jacob Rush (R)	12,763	42.9
22	Russell Errett (R)	14,551	53.0
	James H. Hopkins (D)	12,913	47.0
23	Thomas M. Bayne (R)	12,506	59.6
	A. G. Cochrane (D)	8,326	39.7
24	William S. Shallenberger (R)	13,151	55.0
	R. B. McComb (D)	10,648	44.5
25	Harry White (R)	15,156	53.1
	George A. Jenks (D)	13,397	46.9
26	John M. Thompson (R)	18,511	52.7
	James Sheakley (D)	16,486	46.9
27	Lewis F. Watson (R)	15,640	55.9
	W. L. Scott (D)	12,093	43.2

Special Election

12	W. H. Stanton (D)	12,703	50.3
	Edward Jones (R)	12,417	49.1

RHODE ISLAND

	Candidates	Votes	%
1	Benjamin T. Eames (R)	8,516	62.5
	Brunsen (D)	5,063	37.2
2	Latimer W. Ballou (R)	7,179	57.3
	Page (D)	5,295	42.3

SOUTH CAROLINA

1	Joseph H. Rainey (R)	18,180	52.2
	John S. Richardson (D)	16,661	47.8
2	Richard H. Cain (R)	21,385	62.1
	Michael P. O'Connor (D)	13,028	37.9
3	D. Wyatt Aiken (R)	21,479	58.0
	L. Cass Carpenter (R)	15,553	42.0
4	John H. Evins (D)	21,875	57.7
	A. S. Wallace (R)	16,071	42.4
5	Robert Smalls (R)	19,954	51.9
	G. D. Tilman (D)	18,516	48.1

Special Election

2	Charles W. Buttz (R)	21,378	62.1
	Michael P. O'Connor (D)	13,030	37.9

TENNESSEE

1	James H. Randolph (R)	12,349	52.4
	McFarland (D)	11,215	47.6
2	Jacob M. Thornburgh (R)	14,328	59.9
	Cullom (D)	9,603	40.1
3	George G. Dibrell (D)	13,132	61.5
	Drake (R)	8,218	38.5
4	Haywood Y. Riddle (D)	11,957	70.6
	Cox (R)	3,545	20.9
	Patton (R)	1,437	8.5
5	John M. Bright (D)	15,094	74.0
	Galbraith (R)	5,309	26.0
6	John F. House (D)	15,719	63.6
	Presser (R)	8,987	36.4
7	Washington C. Whitthorne (D)	12,257	68.7
	Cliffe (R)	3,757	21.0
	G. W. Blackburn (IR)	1,841	10.3
8	John D. C. Atkins (D)	13,412	61.8
	Hawkins (R)	8,296	38.2
9	William P. Caldwell (D)	14,799	69.5
	Folk (R)	6,509	30.6
10	H. Casey Young (D)	13,014	51.8
	Randolph (R)	12,134	48.3

TEXAS

1	John H. Reagan (D)	13,097	67.0
	L. W. Cooper (R)	6,415	32.8
2	David B. Culberson (D)	17,326	65.5
	S. H. Russell (R)	9,130	34.5
3	James W. Throckmorton (D)	24,138	91.4
	J. C. Bigger (R)	2,281	8.6
4	Roger Q. Mills (D)	20,975	73.2
	J. P. Osterhaut (R)	7,655	26.7
5	De Witt C. Giddings (D)	15,886	54.3
	G. W. Jones (R)	13,277	45.4
6	Gustave Schleicher (D)	12,242	81.2
	James P. Newcomb (R)	2,693	17.9

VERMONT

1	Charles H. Joyce (R)	14,496	67.2
	Childs (D)	7,057	32.7
2	Dudley C. Denison (R)	13,630	70.0
	Dickey (D)	5,739	29.5
3	George W. Hendee (R)	11,974	68.5
	Edwards (D)	5,367	30.7

VIRGINIA

1	Beverly B. Douglas (D)	14,228	56.5
	L. C. Boiston (R)	10,940	43.5
2	John Goode Jr. (D)	16,885	53.0
	Joseph Secar (R)	14,989	47.0

	Candidates	Votes	%
3	Gilbert C. Walker (D)	15,536	53.6
	Charles S. Mills (R)	13,430	46.4
4	Joseph Jorgensen (R)	13,896	51.9
	William E. Hunton Jr. (D)	12,492	46.7
5	George C. Cabell (D)	15,146	60.6
	Daniel S. Lewis (R)	9,842	39.4
6	John R. Tucker (D)	16,425	59.6
	George H. Burch (R)	11,127	40.4
7	John T. Harris (D)	17,143	73.1
	Evenett W. Early (R)	6,250	26.7
8	Eppa Hunton (D)	16,660	62.1
	I. C. O'Neal (R)	10,175	37.9
9	Auburn L. Pridemore (D)	15,127	75.8
	George T. Egbert (R)	4,791	24.0

WEST VIRGINIA

	Candidates	Votes	%
1	Benjamin Wilson (D)	17,902	52.7
	G. F. Scott (R)	16,067	47.3
2	Benjamin F. Martin (D)	18,156	56.0
	Ward H. Lamon (R)	14,283	44.0
3	John E. Kenna (D)	20,292	61.5
	Benjamin J. Redmund (R)	12,719	38.5

WISCONSIN

	Candidates	Votes	%
1	Charles G. Williams (R)	18,206	59.3
	Winslow (D)	12,478	40.6
2	Lucien B. Caswell (R)	15,073	50.5

	Candidates	Votes	%
	Orton (D)	14,745	49.4
3	George C. Hazelton (R)	15,582	54.4
	Orton (D)	13,034	45.5
4	William P. Lynde (D)	17,653	59.6
	Smith (R)	11,952	40.4
5	Edward S. Bragg (D)	19,544	58.1
	Carter (R)	14,031	41.7
6	Gabriel Bouck (D)	20,623	53.6
	Kimball (R)	17,847	46.4
7	Herman L. Humphrey (R)	20,702	58.4
	Gage (D)	13,220	37.3
8	Thaddeus C. Pound (R)	14,838	51.7
	Cate (D)	13,860	48.3

1. The special election in Colorado in 1876 was held to elect a representative for the remainder of the 44th Congress (1875–1877). The general election House race was for a full two-year term in the 45th Congress (1877–1879).

1877 House Elections

GEORGIA

Special Election

	Candidates	Votes	%
9	Hiram P. Bell (D)	5,173	49.1
	Speer (I)	3,734	35.5
	Archer (R)	1,619	15.4

NEW HAMPSHIRE

	Candidates	Votes	%
1	Frank Jones (D)	13,925	49.8
	Marston (R)	13,885	49.7
2	James F. Briggs (R)	13,209	52.0
	Sulloway (D)	12,111	47.7
3	Henry W. Blair (R)	12,682	51.6
	Kent (D)	11,832	48.1

NEW YORK

Special Election

	Candidates	Votes	%
7	David Dudley Field (D)	4,884	77.1
	Christian Goetz (R)	1,435	22.7

1878 House Elections

ALABAMA

	Candidates	Votes	%
1	Thomas H. Herndon (D)	6,577	69.1
	Bailey (G)	2,941	30.9
2	Hilary A. Herbert (D)	8,364	56.3
	N. Armstrong (G)	6,505	43.8
3	William J. Samford (D)	6,199	88.4
	Strange (ID)	676	9.6
4	Charles M. Shelley (D)	8,514	55.4
	Haralson (R)	6,545	42.6
5	Thomas Williams (D)	6,537	70.5
	Nunn (G)	2,734	29.5
6	Burwell B. Lewis (D)	7,652	70.5
	Smith (ID)	3,201	29.5
7	William H. Forney (D)	2,653	96.6
8	William M. Lowe (GD)	10,373	55.6
	Garth (D)	8,279	44.4

ARKANSAS

	Candidates	Votes	%
1	Poindexter Dunn (D)	8,863	100.0
2	William F. Slemons (D)	11,226	57.2
	Bradley (G)	8,390	42.8
3	Jordan E. Cravens (D)	7,202	51.2
	Rice (G)	6,868	48.8
4	Thomas M. Gunter (D)	5,361	59.8
	Cunningham (ID)	2,639	29.4
	Smith (G)	969	10.8

COLORADO

	Candidates	Votes	%
AL	James B. Belford (R)	14,294	49.9
	Thomas M. Patterson (D)	12,003	41.9
	Childs (G)	2,329	8.1

CONNECTICUT

	Candidates	Votes	%
1	Joseph R. Hawley (R)	14,187	52.2
	Landers (D)	11,900	43.8
2	James Phelps (D)	16,504	53.2
	Douglas (R)	14,231	45.9
3	John T. Wait (R)	9,236	53.8
	Carter (D)	7,571	44.1
4	Frederick Miles (R)	14,109	48.7
	Bruggerhoff (D)	12,930	44.6
	Taylor (N)	1,848	6.4

DELAWARE

	Candidates	Votes	%
AL	Edward L. Martin (D)	10,576	78.1
	Jackson (NG)	2,966	21.9

FLORIDA

	Candidates	Votes	%
1	Robert H. M. Davidson (D)	11,527	58.1
	Conover (R)	8,302	41.9
2	Noble A. Hull (D)	9,648‡	50.1
	Horatio Bisbee Jr. (R)	9,626	49.9

GEORGIA

	Candidates	Votes	%
1	John C. Nicholls (D)	8,477	62.8
	Corker (G)	5,031	37.2
2	William E. Smith (D)	8,126	69.1
	Wade (R)	3,643	31.0
3	Philip Cook (D)	2,628	99.8
4	Henry Persons (ID)	13,336	56.9
	Harris (D)	10,101	43.1
5	Nathaniel J. Hammond (D)	10,269	55.6
	Arnold (R)	8,196	44.4
6	James H. Blount (D)	3,192	99.4
7	William H. Felton (ID)	14,315	52.5
	Lester (D)	12,971	47.5
8	Alexander H. Stephens (D)	3,673	98.6
9	Emory Speer (ID)	10,897	50.3
	Billups (D)	10,675	49.3

ILLINOIS

	Candidates	Votes	%
1	William Aldrich (R)	12,165	51.8
	James R. Doolittle (D)	7,136	30.4
	John McAscliff (SOC)	2,322	9.9
	William V. Barr (NG)	1,844	7.9
2	George R. Davis (R)	10,347	49.6
	Miles Kehoe (D)	6,111	29.3
	George A. Schilling (SOC)	2,473	11.9
	James Felch (NG)	1,600	7.7
3	Hiram Barber Jr. (R)	9,574	53.1
	Lambert Tree (D)	5,280	29.3
	Benjamin Sebley (I)	2,306	12.8
4	John C. Sherwin (R)	12,753	61.8
	Jonathan C. Staighton (D)	4,438	21.5
	Augustus Adams (NG)	3,448	16.7
5	Robert M. A. Hawk (R)	11,042	53.4
	Mortimer D. Hathaway (D)	4,823	23.3
	John M. King (NG)	4,804	23.2
6	Thomas J. Henderson (R)	10,964	52.5
	James W. Haney (NG)	6,675	31.9
	Charles Dunham (D)	3,257	15.6
7	Philip C. Hayes (R)	10,712	46.5
	Alexander Campbell (NG)	6,512	28.3
	W. S. Brooks (D)	5,795	25.2
8	Greenbury L. Fort (R)	11,271	49.7
	Chris C. Strawn (NG)	6,575	29.0
	Thomas M. Shaw (D)	4,822	21.3
9	Thomas A. Boyd (R)	10,543	43.8
	George A. Wilson (D)	9,802	40.7
	Aloxr H. Keighan (NG)	3,749	15.6
10	Benjamin F. Marsh (R)	11,814	44.5
	Delos P. Phelps (D)	11,238	42.3
	Alson J. Streeter (NG)	3,496	13.2
11	James W. Singleton (D)	11,961	54.5
	James P. Dimmitt (R)	6,956	31.7
	William H. Pogue (P)	3,034	13.8
12	William M. Springer (D)	12,542	47.7
	John Cook (R)	9,146	34.8
	John Mathers (NG)	4,611	17.5
13	Adlai E. Stevenson (D)	13,870	53.2
	Thomas F. Tipton (R)	12,058	46.3
14	Joseph G. Cannon (R)	13,698	46.2
	Maldon Jones (D)	11,527	38.8
	Jesse Harper (NG)	4,451	15.0
15	Albert P. Forsythe (R)	13,106	50.3
	Hiram B. Decias (D)	12,942	49.7
16	William A. J. Sparks (D)	11,493	48.7
	Basil B. Smith (R)	9,946	42.2
	James Creed (NG)	2,139	9.1
17	William R. Morrison (D)	12,436	50.5
	John Baker (R)	10,605	43.0
	William E. Moberly (NG)	1,598	6.5
18	John R. Thomas (R)	12,686	46.6
	N. J. Allen (D)	12,074	44.4
	S. J. Davis (NG)	2,454	9.0
19	Richard W. Townshend (R)	12,603	53.3
	Robert Bell (D)	8,190	34.6
	Seth F. Crews (NG)	2,847	12.0

INDIANA

	Candidates	Votes	%
1	William Hellman (R)	13,928	48.7
	Thomas E. Garvin (D)	13,099	45.8
	Thomas F. Debruler (NG)	1,595	5.6
2	Thomas R. Cobb (D)	17,317	55.1
	Richard M. Welman (R)	12,032	38.3
	William L. Green (NG)	2,103	6.7
3	George A. Bicknell (D)	15,074	57.9
	Ara E. S. Long (R)	9,369	36.0
	John F. Willy (NG)	1,588	6.1
4	Jeptha D. New (D)	15,146	50.5
	Leonidas Sexton (R)	14,655	48.9
5	Thomas M. Browne (R)	13,776	50.1
	William S. Holman (D)	12,936	47.0
6	William R. Myers (D)	16,167	47.9
	William Grose (R)	15,548	46.1

	Candidates	Votes	%
	Reuben A. Riley (NG)	2,044	6.1
7	Gilbert De La Matyr (A-D-FUS)	18,720	51.2
	John Hanna (R)	17,881	48.9
8	Abraham J. Hostetler (D)	13,164	40.9
	Morton C. Hunter (R)	12,124	37.6
	Henry A. White (NG)	6,929	21.5
9	Godlove S. Orth (R)	15,608	43.7
	James McCabe (D)	15,510	43.5
	Leroy Templeton (NG)	4.571	12.8
10	William H. Calkins (R)	15,365	45.2
	Morgan H. Weir (D)	13,408	39.4
	John N. Skinner (NG)	5,252	15.4
11	Calvin Cowgill (R)	15,547	47.8
	David D. Dykeman (D)	13,102	40.3
	David Moss (NG)	3,866	11.9
12	Walpole G. Colerick (D)	17,067	63.7
	John Studebaker (R & NG)	9,712	36.3
13	John B. Baker (R)	15,184	47.2
	John B. Stoll (D)	13,523	42.0
	William C. Williams (NG)	3,462	10.8

IOWA

	Candidates	Votes	%
1	Moses A. McCoid (R)	12,705	48.6
	Wesley C. Hobbs (D)	7,945	30.4
	A. H. Bereman (G)	5,505	21.0
2	Hiram Price (R)	13,337	49.8
	W. F. Brannan (D)	9,509	35.5
	Jacob Geiger (G)	3,960	14.8
3	Thomas Updegraff (R)	12,723	43.9
	Fred O'Donnall (D)	10,886	37.5
	S. T. Spangler (G)	5,406	18.6
4	Nathaniel C. Deering (R)	17,134	60.8
	L. H. Weller (G)	5,742	20.4
	William V. Allen (D)	5,293	18.8
5	Rush Clark (R)	14,205	52.8
	George Carter (G)	12,011	44.6
6	James Baird Weaver (D & G)	16,366	53.3
	Ezekiel Silas Sampson (R)	14,308	46.6
7	Edward Hooker Gillette (D & G)	16,474	51.4
	Henry Johnson Brodhead Cummings (R)	15,546	48.5
8	William F. Sapp (R)	15,343	50.2
	George C. Hieks (G)	7,760	25.4
	John H. Keatley (D)	7,453	24.4
9	Cyrus C. Carpenter (R)	16,489	54.7
	L. Q. Hoggatt (G & D)	12,338	41.0

KANSAS

	Candidates	Votes	%
1	John A. Anderson (R)	30,457	59.6
	J. R. McClure (D)	14,919	29.2
	E. Gale (G)	5,716	11.2
2	Dudley C. Haskell (R)	19,029	45.0
	C. W. Blair (D)	13,327	31.5
	P. P. Elder (G)	9,962	23.5
3	Thomas Ryan (R)	25,228	56.8
	F. Doster (G)	11,055	24.9
	J. B. Fugate (D)	8,109	18.3

KENTUCKY

	Candidates	Votes	%
1	Oscar Turner (ID)	6,878	42.9
	L. S. Trimble (D)	5,611	35.0
	E. W. Bagby (R)	3,554	22.2
2	James A. McKenzie (D)	8,328	61.2
	John W. Feighan (R)	3,189	23.4
	Francis M. English (G)	2,051	15.1
3	John W. Caldwell (D)	9,354	46.3
	W. G. Hunter (R)	8,502	42.1
	George Wright (G)	2,339	11.6
4	J. Proctor Knott (D)	8,969	64.5
	J. D. Belden (R)	4,616	33.2
5	Albert Willis (D)	9,115	40.5
	J. Watts Kearney (D)	7,492	33.3
	Horace Scott (R)	5,508	24.5

Candidates	Votes	%
6 John G. Carlisle (D)	5,901	75.6
Joseph H. Hermes (I)	1,877	24.1
7 Joseph C. S. Blackburn (D)	8,632	69.7
S. T. Drane (G)	3,548	28.7
8 Philip B. Thompson Jr. (D)	12,538	53.8
George Denny (R)	10,766	46.2
9 Thomas Turner (D)	10,784	55.4
John Dills	8,392	43.2
10 Elijah C. Phister (D)	7,293	65.2
B. F. Bennett (R)	2,645	23.7
James Kilgore (G)	1,224	11.0

LOUISIANA

Candidates	Votes	%
1 Randall L. Gibson (D)	12,419	63.6
H. C. Castellanos (R)	7,108	36.4
2 E. John Ellis (D)	10,263	59.0
E. N. Cullom (RG)	6,076	34.9
Michael Hahn (R)	1,065	6.1
3 Joseph Hayes Acklen (D)	10,309	48.8
R. O. Hebert (R)	7,163	33.9
W. B. Merchant (ID)	3,666	17.3
4 Joseph B. Elam (D)	14,432	89.2
J. M. Wells (R)	1,756	10.9
5 J. Floyd King (D)	17,261	77.9
J. T. Ludling (R)	4,905	22.1
6 Edward W. Robertson (D)	13,977	66.1
W. L. Larimore (I)	7,155	33.9

MAINE

Candidates	Votes	%
1 Thomas B. Reed (R)	13,483	46.2
Samuel J. Anderson (D)	9,332	32.0
Edward H. Gove (NG)	6,348	21.8
2 William P. Frye (R)	11,431	49.0
Solon Chase (NG)	8,472	36.3
S. Clifford Belcher (D)	3,407	14.6
3 Stephen D. Lindsey (R)	11,384	44.4
William Philbrick (NG)	8,333	32.5
Franklin Smith (D)	5,895	23.0
4 George W. Ladd (NG)	12,921	56.1
Llewellyn Powers (R)	10,095	43.8
5 Thompson H. Murch (NG)	11,371	47.3
Eugene Hale (R)	10,251	42.7
Joseph H. Martin (D)	2,255	9.4

MARYLAND

Candidates	Votes	%
1 Daniel M. Henry (D)	11,419	52.5
Graham (R)	10,338	47.5
2 J. Fred. C. Talbott (D)	9,826	66.9
Milligan (ID)	3,598	24.5
McCombs (G)	1,268	8.6
3 William Kimmel (D)	11,676	70.4
Thompson (LAB)	4,908	29.6
4 Robert M. McLane (D)	11,064	59.0
Holland	6,671	35.6
5 Eli J. Henkle (D)	11,558	54.4
Crane (R)	9,679	45.6
6 Milton G. Urner (R)	14,148	53.2
Peter (D)	12,437	46.8

MASSACHUSETTS

Candidates	Votes	%
1 William W. Crapo (R)	12,575	62.2
Ellis (D)	7,383	36.5
2 Benjamin W. Harris (R)	14,579	58.4
Dean (N)	5,472	21.9
Avery (D)	4,374	17.5
3 Walbridge A. Field (R)	10,919	50.5
Dean (D)	10,478	48.5
4 Leopold Morse (D)	11,647	60.0
Brimmer (R)	7,654	39.4
5 Selwyn Z. Bowman (R)	15,308	58.2
Clark (D, N)	10,918	41.5
6 George B. Loring (R)	10,339	44.4
E. Moody Boynton (N)	10,226	43.9
Carleton (D)	2,658	11.4
7 William A. Russell (R)	13,169	55.2

Candidates	Votes	%
Tarbox (D)	7,700	32.3
Stevens (N)	2,831	11.9
8 William Claflin (R)	14,300	54.3
Bradford (D)	11,758	44.7
9 William W. Rice (R)	13,295	59.0
Thayer (D)	8,960	39.8
10 Amasa Norcross (R)	13,051	55.5
W. F. Whitney (N)	6,839	29.1
Grinnell (D)	3,609	15.3
11 George D. Robinson (R)	10,927	51.4
Lathrop (BUT D&N)	7,994	37.6
Dunham (D)	2,069	9.7

MICHIGAN

Candidates	Votes	%
1 John S. Newberry (R)	9,894	40.8
Williams (D)	8,567	35.3
Heffron (NG)	5,760	23.7
2 Edwin Willits (R)	14,312	44.5
Card (D)	9,557	29.7
Thomas (NG)	7,742	24.1
3 Jonas H. McGowan (R)	14,381	41.7
Dawson (NG)	12,347	35.8
Upton (D)	6,341	18.4
4 Julius C. Burrows (R)	14,236	47.1
Eldred (D)	8,171	27.1
Sherwood (NG)	7,791	25.8
5 John W. Stone (R)	15,983	45.8
Comstock (NG)	15,273	43.7
Hoyt (D)	3,468	9.9
6 Mark S. Brewer (R)	18,459	45.1
McCurdy (D)	15,549	38.0
Meade (NG)	6,271	15.3
7 Omar D. Conger (R)	11,939	47.4
Mitchell (D)	8,940	35.5
Mallory (NG)	4,316	17.1
8 Roswell G. Horr (R)	11,993	39.7
Thompson (D)	9,571	31.7
Hoyt (NG)	8,500	28.2
9 Jay A. Hubbell (R)	15,264	53.1
Power (D)	7,478	26.0
Parmelee (NG)	6,014	20.9

MINNESOTA

Candidates	Votes	%
1 Mark H. Dunnell (R)	18,613	59.2
Meighen (D)	12,845	40.8
2 Henry Poehler (D)	14,467	51.3
Strait (R)	13,743	48.7
3 William D. Washburn (R)	20,954	53.9
Donnelly (D)	17,938	46.1

MISSISSIPPI

Candidates	Votes	%
1 Henry L. Muldrow (D)	9,632	59.3
Davis (G)	6,533	40.3
2 Vannoy H. Manning (D)	7,339	53.5
Amacker (N)	5,969	43.5
3 Hernando D. Money (D)	4,028	99.7
4 Otho R. Singleton (D)	4,650	99.6
5 Charles E. Hooker (D)	4,816	87.5
Deason (R)	686	12.5
6 James R. Chalmers (D)	6,663	82.7
Castello (R)	1,370	17.0

MISSOURI

Candidates	Votes	%
1 Martin L. Clardy (D)	9,437	48.3
H. Ziegenhein (R)	6,498	33.3
E. Eshbaugh (G)	2,476	12.7
F. Westermeyer (SOC)	1,110	5.7
2 Erastus Wells (D)	7,669	42.7
Nathan Cole (R)	7,403	41.2
John Hogan (G)	2,391	13.3
3 Richard G. Frost (D)	7,237	45.5
L. S. Metcalf (R)	5,319	33.4
H. C. Vandillen (G)	2,213	13.9
Bartholomeus (SOC)	1,140	7.2
4 Lowndes H. Davis (D)	12,052	61.4

Candidates	Votes	%
Sol G. Kitchen (G)	6,834	34.8
5 Richard P. Bland (D)	11,291	56.6
J. J. Ware (G)	8,022	40.2
6 James R. Waddill (D)	17,769	44.0
C. G. Burton (R)	11,622	28.8
M. H. Ritchey (G)	11,004	27.2
7 Alfred M. Lay (D)	16,960	51.5
James Boyd (G)	8,810	26.8
A. Underwood (R)	7,170	21.8
8 Samuel L. Sawyer (D)	9,727	49.0
John T. Crisp (D)	8,917	44.9
L. G. Jeffers (G)	1,227	6.2
9 Nicholas Ford (G)	17,430	51.7
David Rea (D)	16,257	48.2
10 Gideon F. Rothwell (D)	14,793	47.2
H. M. Pollard (R)	10,875	34.7
E. J. Broaddus (G)	5,682	18.1
11 John B. Clark Jr. (D)	16,600	98.9
12 William H. Hatch (D)	12,463	45.1
John M. London (G)	10,597	38.3
Dan M. Draper (R)	4,578	16.6
13 Aylett H. Buckner (D)	15,591	59.2
T. J. C. Fagg (G & R)	8,575	32.6
T. B. Robinson (R)	2,164	8.2

NEBRASKA

Candidates	Votes	%
AL Edward K. Valentine (R)	28,347	56.4
J. W. Davis (D & G)	21,722	43.3

Special Election

Candidates	Votes	%
AL Thomas J. Majors (R)	28,211	57.3
Alex Bear (D)	21,015	42.7

NEVADA

Candidates	Votes	%
AL Rollin M. Daggett (R)	9,727	51.8
Deal (D)	9,047	48.2

NEW HAMPSHIRE

Candidates	Votes	%
1 Joshua G. Hall (R)	13,510	50.3
Norris (D)	11,026	41.1
Chesley (G)	2,284	8.5
2 James F. Briggs (R)	12,981	52.1
A. W. Sulloway (D)	9,860	39.5
C. A. Sulloway (G)	2,077	8.3
3 Evarts W. Farr (R)	11,708	48.8
Kent (D)	10,663	44.5
Johnson (G)	1,496	6.2

NEW JERSEY

Candidates	Votes	%
1 George M. Robeson (R)	14,924	48.1
Grosscup (D)	9,879	31.9
Stratton (D)	6,215	20.0
2 Hezekiah B. Smith (D & G)	14,610	50.6
Pugh (R)	13,699	47.4
3 Miles Ross (D)	13,509	44.2
Clark (R)	13,176	43.1
Hope (G)	3,843	12.6
4 Alvah A. Clark (D)	11,449	45.1
Potts (R)	9,852	38.8
Larrison (G)	4,111	16.2
5 Charles H. Voorhis (R)	10,893	44.9
Demarest (D)	10,089	41.6
Potter (G)	3,268	13.5
6 John L. Blake (R)	14,771	49.7
Allbright (D)	12,832	43.2
Bliss (G)	2,106	7.1
7 Lewis A. Brigham (R)	13,199	50.8
Laverty (D)	11,234	43.3
Winant (G)	1,424	5.5

NEW YORK

	Candidates	Votes	%
1	James W. Covert (D)	13,809	50.8
	Otis (R)	11,798	43.4
	Crooks (G)	1,430	5.3
2	Daniel O'Reilly (R & ID)	13,138	54.8
	Litchfield (D)	9,881	41.2
3	Simeon B. Chittenden (R)	16,667	58.2
	Huntley (D)	10,017	35.0
4	Archibald M. Bliss (D)	13,020	53.8
	Lyon (R)	8,742	36.2
5	Nicholas Muller (TAM)	9,466	52.3
	Bourke (A-TAM)	8,327	46.0
6	Samuel S. Cox (G & TAM)	10,908	62.4
	D'Vries (A-TAM)	6,327	36.2
7	Edwin Einstein (R & A-TAM)	7,617	48.3
	Eickhoff (TAM)	7,162	45.4
	Jahelka (G)	803	5.1
8	Anson G. McCook (R)	12,854	60.4
	Jerome (TAM)	7,512	35.3
9	Fernando Wood (TAM)	7,277	36.7
	Hardy (A-TAM)	6,480	32.7
	Berryman (R)	5,726	28.9
10	James O'Brien (A-TAM)	11,319	53.3
	Potter (TAM)	9,046	42.6
11	Levi P. Morton (R)	14,078	64.7
	Willis (TAM)	7,060	32.4
12	Alexander Smith (R)	11,338*	49.5
	Cobb (D)	9,083	39.7
	N. Smith (G)	2,421	10.6
13	John H. Ketcham (R)	18,240	62.6
	Baker (D)	9,700	33.3
14	John W. Ferdon (R)	11,861	44.4
	Beebe (D)	11,323	42.4
	Voorhis (G)	3,261	12.2
15	William Lounsbery (D)	13,680	47.4
	Nichols (R)	11,442	39.7
	Erkson (G)	3,524	12.2
16	John M. Bailey (R)	12,199	41.0
	Woods (D)	12,004	40.4
	Hilton (G)	5,455	18.3
17	Walter A. Wood (R)	16,771	55.3
	Patterson (D)	9,655	31.8
	Ferguson (G)	3,878	12.8
18	John Hammond (R)	10,650	54.8
	Ross (D)	5,765	29.7
	McDonald (G)	3,005	15.5
19	Amaziah B. James (R)	12,133	70.5
	Hasbrouck (D)	5,056	29.4
20	John H. Starin (R)	17,738	56.7
	Thomson (D)	10,880	34.8
	Wendell (G)	2,588	8.3
21	David Wilber (R)	15,377	48.1
	Scofield (D)	10,180	31.8
	Cone (G)	6,017	18.8
22	Warner Miller (R)	14,855	51.4
	Brown (D)	11,658	40.3
	Lewis (G)	2,102	7.3
23	Cyrus D. Prescott (R)	9,762	42.9
	Spriggs (D)	8,730	38.4
	Mitchell (G)	3,787	16.6
24	Joseph Mason (R)	12,043	50.6
	Sebastian Duffy (G & D)	11,307	47.5
25	Frank Hiscock (R)	14,599	55.9
	Wieting (G & D)	11,174	42.8
26	John H. Camp (R)	14,355	53.0
	Walley (G)	10,979	40.5
	Durston (D)	1,638	6.1
27	Elbridge G. Lapham (R)	12,270	54.5
	Pierpont (G & D)	10,232	45.4
28	Jeremiah W. Dwight (R)	15,569	53.9
	Howe (G)	11,162	38.7
	Mudge (D)	1,883	6.5
29	David P. Richardson (R)	14,330	42.8
	Babcock (D)	10,960	32.7
	Beaumont (G)	8,174	24.4
30	John Van Voorhis (R)	12,008	43.4
	Lamberton (D)	10,367	37.5
	Brown (G)	2,760	10.0
	Alphonso A. Hopkins (P)	2,476	9.0
31	Richard Crowley (R)	12,529	56.7
	Davis (D)	8,713	39.5
32	Ray V. Pierce (R)	18,998	52.3
	Lockwood (D)	16,105	44.3
33	Henry Van Aernam (R)	11,364	49.8
	Morris (D)	6,732	29.5
	Vinton (G)	4,689	20.6

Special Election

	Candidates	Votes	%
16	John M. Balley (R)	12,062	40.5
	Francis H. D. Woods (D)	11,962	40.2
	Philip E. Marshall (G)	5,549	18.7

NORTH CAROLINA

	Candidates	Votes	%
1	Joseph J. Martin (R)	12,135‡	49.2
	Jesse J. Yeates (D)	12,084	49.0
2	William H. Kitchin (D)	10,704	42.9
	James E. O'Hara (IR)	9,682	38.8
	James H. Harris (R)	3,948	15.8
3	Daniel L. Russell (G & R)	11,611	51.9
	Alfred M. Waddell (D)	10,730	48.0
4	Joseph J. Davis (D)	11,864	51.1
	Josiah Turner (IR)	8,353	36.0
	Wiley D. Jones (R)	2,911	12.5
5	Alfred M. Scales (D)	10,326	57.3
	Albion W. Tourgee (R)	7,680	42.6
6	Walter L. Steele (D)	4,908	92.1
7	Robert F. Armfield (D)	4,753	55.7
	John M. Brower (G & R)	3,650	42.8
8	Robert B. Vance (D)	2,894	96.8

OHIO

	Candidates	Votes	%
1	Benjamin Butterworth (R)	12,756	50.5
	Milton Sayler (D)	12,036	47.7
2	Thomas L. Young (R)	12,914	50.9
	Leonard W. Goss (D)	11,940	47.0
3	John A. McMahon (D)	15,437	51.0
	Emanuel Schultz (R)	14,352	47.5
4	J. Warren Keifer (R)	15,895	56.6
	William V. Marquis (D)	10,805	38.5
5	Benjamin Le Fevre (D)	14,676	48.5
	Harrison Wilson (R)	12,843	42.5
	Stephen Johnson (G)	2,392	7.9
6	William D. Hill (D)	16,110	52.4
	James L. Price (R)	12,072	39.3
	William C. Holgate (G)	2,544	8.3
7	Frank H. Hurd (D)	13,182	40.7
	James B. Luckey (R)	11,278	34.9
	Henry Kahlo (G)	7,893	24.4
8	Ebenezer B. Finley (D)	16,237	50.2
	Charles Foster (R)	14,982	46.3
9	George L. Converse (D)	17,786	48.9
	Lorenzo English (R)	16,798	46.2
10	Thomas Ewing (D)	12,679	50.4
	Valentine B. Horton (R)	12,245	48.7
11	Henry L. Dickey (D)	15,355	50.4
	W. W. McKnight (R)	13,986	45.9
12	Henry S. Neal (R)	14,566	52.0
	James Emmitt (D)	12,490	44.6
13	Adoniram J. Warner (D)	11,950	46.2
	Nelson H. Van Voorhees (R)	11,827	46.2
	George E. Geddes (G)	1,487	5.8
14	Gibson Atherton (D)	14,350	49.7
	Isaac Morton (R)	12,063	41.7
	Thomas J. McGinnis (G)	2,491	8.6
15	George W. Geddes (D)	15,597	54.3
	Goshorn A. Jones (R)	11,029	38.4
	George W. Pepper (G)	1,849	6.4
16	William McKinley Jr. (R)	15,489	49.8
	Aquila Wiley (D)	14,255	45.8
17	James Monroe (R)	17,213	54.2
	Lewis Miller (D & G)	14,575	45.9
18	Jonathan T. Updegraff (R)	15,320	50.6
	Daniel T. Lawson (D)	12,593	41.6
	George Smith (G)	2,231	7.4
19	James A. Garfield (R)	17,166	61.4
	John C. Hubbard (D)	7,553	27.0

	Candidates	Votes	%
	Grandison N. Tuttle (G)	3,148	11.3
20	Amos Townsend (R)	13,081	47.8
	Joseph M. Poe (D)	7,271	26.6
	Gilbert O. Shove (P)	4,934	18.0
	William H. Doan (G)	2,085	7.6

OREGON

	Candidates	Votes	%
AL	John Whiteaker (D)	16,744	49.9
	H. K. Hines (R)	15,593	46.5

PENNSYLVANIA

	Candidates	Votes	%
1	Henry H. Bingham (R)	13,751	56.5
	William McCandless (D)	6,324	26.0
	Maxwell Stevenson (G)	4,267	17.5
2	Charles O'Neill (R)	14,063	59.5
	Charles H. Gibson (D)	9,177	38.8
3	Samuel J. Randall (D)	10,717	57.4
	John Shedden (RG)	7,970	42.7
4	William D. Kelley (RG)	17,786	60.3
	Charles H. Barnes (D)	11,697	39.7
5	Alfred C. Harmer (R)	16,784	55.8
	David E. Dallam (D)	11,745	39.1
	U. S. Stephens (G)	1,539	5.1
6	William Ward (R)	13,041	57.8
	Bethel M. Custer (D)	8,285	36.7
7	William Godshalk (R)	15,092	51.3
	Oliver P. James (D)	13,754	46.8
8	Hiester Clymer (D)	12,419	58.6
	H. Maltzberger (R)	6,428	30.4
	Daniel B. Yoder (G)	2,330	11.0
9	A. Herr Smith (R)	15,486	62.8
	W. R. Wilson (D)	8,605	34.9
10	Reuben K. Bachman (D)	16,678	58.7
	A. Brower Longaker (G)	7,329	25.8
	George W. Whittaker (R)	4,429	15.6
11	Robert Klotz (D)	8,211	31.8
	Edwin Albright (R)	8,116	31.4
	E. E. Orvis (G)	5,193	20.1
	C. B. Brockway (D)	4,339	16.8
12	Hendrick B. Wright (D & G)	11,817	55.9
	Henry Roberts (R)	9,124	43.2
13	John W. Ryon (D)	7,320	36.3
	Charles N. Brumm (G)	7,128	35.4
	Howell Fisher (R)	5,698	28.3
14	John W. Killinger (R)	13,660	46.1
	M. J. D. Withington (D)	12,033	40.6
	D. S. Earley (G)	3,962	13.4
15	Edward Overton Jr. (R)	13,160	49.2
	D. C. Dewitt (G)	9,320	34.9
	William H. Dimmick (D)	3,783	14.1
16	John I. Mitchell (R)	11,133	41.0
	J. F. Davis (G)	10,163	37.4
	R. B. Smith (D)	5,849	21.6
17	Alexander H. Coffroth (D)	12,472	46.3
	Jacob M. Campbell (R)	12,167	45.2
	Samuel Adams (G)	2,275	8.5
18	Horatio G. Fisher (R)	14,878	49.1
	William S. Stenger (D)	14,671	48.4
19	Frank E. Beltzhoover (D)	17,819	57.5
	Thomas E. Cochran (R)	12,321	39.8
20	Seth H. Yocum (G & R)	13,454	50.1
	Andrew G. Curtin (D)	13,381	49.9
21	Morgan R. Wise (D)	12,880	49.5
	S. M. Bailey (R)	9,330	35.8
	A. L. McFarlane (G)	3,819	14.7
22	Russell Errett (R)	9,099	38.0
	David Kirk (G)	7,447	31.1
	James K. P. Duff (D)	7,260	30.4
23	Thomas M. Bayne (R)	9,104	51.2
	C. F. Mckenna (D)	5,621	31.6
	Samuel Watson (G)	2,781	15.6
24	William S. Shallenberger (R)	11,261	48.6
	R. W. Clendennin (D)	10,025	43.2
	James E. Emerson (G)	1,911	8.2
25	Harry White (R)	10,715	37.6
	James M. Guffey (D)	8,931	31.3
	James Mosgrove (G)	8,874	31.1
26	Samuel B. Dick (R)	14,010	41.7

Candidates	Votes	%
William C. Plummer (G)	12,716	37.8
John T. Bard (D)	6,558	19.5
27 James H. Osmer (R)	11,205	44.5
George A. Allen (D)	8,551	34.0
Cyrus C. Camp (G)	5,127	20.4

RHODE ISLAND

	Candidates	Votes	%
1	Nelson W. Aldrich (R)	5,969	74.5
	Thomas Davis (D)	1,332	16.6
	Lycurgus Sayles (G)	625	7.8
2	Latimer W. Ballou (R)	5,431	53.3
	Jerothmul B. Barnaby (D)	4,438	43.6

SOUTH CAROLINA

	Candidates	Votes	%
1	John S. Richardson (D)	22,707	61.7
	J. H. Rainey (R)	14,096	38.3
2	Michael P. O'Connor (D)	20,568	60.9
	E. W. M. Mackey (R)	13,182	39.1
3	D. Wyatt Aiken (D)	24,533	79.1
	J. F. Ensor (R)	6,348	20.5
4	John H. Evins (D)	22,702	96.8
5	George D. Tillman (D)	26,409	71.2
	Robert Smalls (R)	10,664	28.8

TENNESSEE

	Candidates	Votes	%
1	Robert L. Taylor (D)	11,698	51.6
	Pettibone (R)	10,960	48.4
2	Leonidas C. Houk (R)	9,548	57.1
	Watkins (ID)	7,167	42.9
3	George G. Dibrell (D)	9,399	69.1
	Wheeler (R)	4,205	30.9
4	Benton McMillin (D)	7,966	65.0
	Golliday (ID)	4,291	35.0
5	John M. Bright (D)	8,385	65.4
	Lillard (D)	2,594	20.2
	Warder (R)	965	7.5
	Isbell (G)	876	6.8
6	John F. House (D)	9,614	57.2
	Akers (G)	4,666	27.8
	Prosser (R)	2,403	14.3
7	Washington C. Whitthorne (D)	6,581	43.2
	Moore (D)	5,533	36.3

	Candidates	Votes	%
	Hughes (R)	3,133	20.6
8	John D. C. Atkins (D)	8,361	61.4
	Warren (G)	5,257	38.6
9	Charles B. Simonton (D)	7,998	63.7
	Black (G)	4,564	36.3
10	H. Casey Young (D)	5,522	54.8
	Randolph (R)	3,199	31.7
	Keller (G)	1,357	13.5

TEXAS

	Candidates	Votes	%
1	John H. Reagan (D)	18,038	98.7
2	David B. Culberson (D)	19,721	63.1
	O'Neill (G)	9,617	30.8
3	Olin Wellborn (D)	40,845	80.5
	Daggett (R)	9,718	19.2
4	Roger Q. Mills (D)	30,535	75.7
	Smith (R)	9,039	22.4
5	George W. Jones (G & D)	21,095	51.6
	Hancock (D)	19,721	48.2
6	Gustave Schleicher (D)	19,699*	56.7
	Ireland (ID)	15,050	43.3

VERMONT

	Candidates	Votes	%
1	Charles H. Joyce (R)	12,599	68.1
	Randall (D)	5,894	31.8
2	James M. Tyler (R)	12,281	71.3
	Dickey (D)	4,890	28.4
3	Bradley Barlow (N)	8,367	60.4
	Grout (R)	4,330	31.3
	Waterman (D)	1,095	7.9

VIRGINIA

	Candidates	Votes	%
1	Richard Lee T. Beale (D)	7,266	48.3
	George C. Round (R)	5,474	36.4
	John Critcher (ID)	2,296	15.3
2	John Goode Jr. (D)	11,547	56.7
	John F. Dezendorf (R)	8,808	43.3
3	Joseph E. Johnston (D)	5,787	58.1
	William W. Newman (G)	4,172	41.9
4	Joseph Jorgensen (R)	12,322	60.7
	William E. Hinton (D)	7,976	39.3
5	George C. Cabell (D)	8,545	66.7

	Candidates	Votes	%
	William A. Witcher (ID)	4,267	33.3
6	John Randolph Tucker (D)	7,893	63.4
	Camm Patterson (ID)	4,520	36.3
7	John T. Harris (D)	7,235	56.4
	John Paul (D)	5,580	43.5
8	Eppa Hunton (D)	5,772	77.9
	John R. Carton (ID)	1,119	15.1
	James Cochran (I)	506	6.8
9	James B. Richmond (D)	5,120	33.7
	Fayette McMullens (ID)	4,827	31.7
	Samuel H. Newberry (ID)	4,640	30.5

WEST VIRGINIA

	Candidates	Votes	%
1	Benjamin Wilson (D)	15,857	49.0
	J. R. Hubbard (R)	12,448	38.4
	James Bassell (N)	4,086	12.6
2	Benjamin F. Martin (D)	15,421	56.6
	F. A. Burr (R)	7,587	27.9
	J. H. Thompson (N)	4,231	15.5
3	John E. Kenna (D)	19,040	54.0
	Henry I. Walker (R)	16,213	46.0

WISCONSIN

	Candidates	Votes	%
1	Charles G. Williams (R)	14,629	59.5
	Parker (D)	9,949	40.5
2	Lucien B. Caswell (R)	12,607	51.5
	Davis (D)	9,502	38.8
	Tenney (G)	2,376	9.7
3	George C. Hazelton (R)	11,695	50.2
	King (D)	11,603	49.8
4	Peter V. Deuster (D)	11,157	47.4
	Frisby (R)	11,022	46.8
	Judd (G)	1,351	5.7
5	Edward S. Bragg (D)	12,392	46.2
	Smith (D)	10,285	38.8
	Giddings (G)	4,157	15.5
6	Gabriel Bouck (D)	14,349	45.9
	Jones (R)	11,748	37.6
	Steele (G)	5,144	16.5
7	Herman L. Humphrey (R)	15,256	54.2
	Parker (D)	12,880	45.8
8	Thaddeus C. Pound (R)	12,795	52.8
	Barrows (D)	11,421	47.2

1879 House Elections

CALIFORNIA

Special Elections

	Candidates	Votes	%
1	Horace Davis (R)	20,074	48.4
	Clitus Barbour (WMP/L)	18,448	44.5
	C. R. Sumner (D)	2,940	7.1
2	Horace F. Page (R)	19,386	51.9

	Candidates	Votes	%
	T. J. Clunie (D)	12,847	34.4
	H. P. Williams (WMP/L)	5,139	13.8
3	Campbell P. Berry (D-WM)	20,019	50.1
	Joseph McKennon (R)	19,800	49.6
4	Romualdo Pacheco (R)	15,391	40.5
	Wallace Leach (D)	12,109	31.8
	J. J. Ayres (WMP/L)	10,527	27.7

NEW YORK

Special Election

	Candidates	Votes	%
12	Waldo Hutchins (D)	13,543	56.9
	N. Smith (R)	10,146	42.7

1880 House Elections

ALABAMA

	Candidates	Votes	%
1	Thomas H. Herndon (D)	10,027	53.8
	J. Gillett (R)	5,595	30.0
	F. H. Threatt (R)	2,303	12.4
2	Hilary A. Herbert (D)	13,271	59.8
	Strobach (R)	8,884	40.0
3	William C. Oates (D)	10,614	64.3
	A. A. Mabson (R)	5,836	35.3
4	Charles M. Shelley (D)	9,301‡	52.7
	James Q. Smith (R)	6,650	37.7
	Stevens (R)	1,693	9.6
5	Thomas Williams (D)	11,219	100.0
6	Goldsmith W. Hewitt (D)	10,043	100.0
7	William H. Forney (D)	13,636	71.4
	Arthur Bingham (R)	5,468	28.6
8	Joseph Wheeler (D)	12,808‡	50.1
	William M. Lowe (GD)	12,765	49.9

Special Election

6	Newton N. Clements	9,973	100.0

ARKANSAS

1	Poindexter Dunn (D)	15,753	60.2
	Johnson (R)	10,407	39.8
2	James K. Jones (D)	16,517	47.3
	Williams (R)	14,513	41.5
	Garland (G)	3,920	11.2
3	Jordan E. Cravens (D)	15,781	57.7
	Boles (R)	11,552	42.3
4	Thomas M. Gunter (D)	7,387	42.8
	Peel (ID)	5,731	33.2
	Murphy (R)	4,125	23.9

CALIFORNIA

1	William S. Rosecrans (D-WM)	21,005	51.0
	Horace Davis (R)	19,496	47.3
2	Horace F. Page (R)	22,038	53.5
	J. R. Glasscock (D-WM)	18,859	45.8
3	Campbell P. Berry (D)	21,743	51.2
	George A. Knight (R)	20,494	48.2
4	Romualdo Pacheco (R)	17,768	45.8
	W. A. Leach (D)	17,577	45.3
	J. F. Godfrey	3,461	8.9

COLORADO

AL	James B. Belford (R)	27,069	50.8
	Robert S. Morrison (D)	24,476	46.0

CONNECTICUT

1	John R. Buck (R)	17,048	52.6
	Beach (D)	15,114	46.7
2	James Phelps (D)	21,632	51.7
	Wallace (R)	20,068	48.0
3	John T. Wait (R)	12,099	56.1
	Sawyer (D)	9,125	42.3
4	Frederick Miles (R)	18,168	50.4
	Peet (D)	17,634	48.9

DELAWARE

AL	Edward L. Martin (D)	14,966	51.1
	Houston (R)	14,336	48.9

FLORIDA

1	Robert H. M. Davidson (D)	14,971	57.5
	Witherspoon (R)	11,082	42.5
2	Jesse J. Finley (D)	13,105‡	52.3
	Horatio Bisbee Jr. (R)	11,953	47.7

GEORGIA

	Candidates	Votes	%
1	George R. Black (D)	11,712	58.6
	Collins (R)	8,265	41.4
2	Henry G. Turner (D)	11,496	64.2
	Brimberry (R)	6,417	35.8
3	Philip Cook (D)	7,122	68.7
	Parker (R)	3,245	31.3
4	Hugh Buchanan (D)	9,998	58.1
	Pou (ID)	7,224	42.0
5	Nathaniel J. Hammond (D)	11,947	62.6
	Clark (R)	7,133	37.4
6	James H. Blount (D)	8,373	100.0
7	Judson C. Clements (D)	11,572	51.9
	Felton (ID)	10,727	48.1
8	Alexander H. Stephens (D)	11,341	99.9
9	Emory Speer (ID)	12,653	59.6
	Bell (D)	8,590	40.4

ILLINOIS

1	William Aldrich (R)	22,307	53.8
	John Mattocks (D)	18,024	43.5
2	George R. Davis (R)	20,603	54.8
	V. F. Farnsworth (D)	16,014	42.6
3	Charles B. Farwell (R)	16,627	57.3
	Perry H. Smith Jr. (D)	11,903	41.0
4	John C. Sherwin (R)	20,381	68.9
	Norman C. Warner (D)	8,055	27.2
5	Robert M. A. Hawk (R)	17,061	59.5
	Larmon G. Johnson (D)	7,468	26.0
	John M. King (G)	4,160	14.5
6	Thomas J. Henderson (R)	16,650	57.6
	Bernard N. Trusdell (D)	9,631	33.3
	P. L. McKinney (G)	2,637	9.1
7	William Cullen (R)	16,628	53.8
	Daniel Evans (D)	12,064	39.0
	Royal E. Barber (G)	2,204	7.1
8	Lewis E. Payson (R)	16,704	54.4
	Robert R. Wallace (D)	13,972	45.5
9	John H. Lewis (R)	14,658	46.5
	John S. Lee (D)	14,294	45.4
	William H. Reynolds (G)	2,548	8.1
10	Benjamin F. Marsh (R)	14,798	50.4
	Robert Holloway (D)	13,877	47.2
11	James W. Singleton (D)	17,842	55.6
	William H. Edgar (R)	12,490	38.9
	A. B. Allen (G)	1,765	5.5
12	William M. Springer (D)	17,376	51.6
	Isaac L. Morrison (R)	14,761	43.8
13	Dietrich Smith (R)	16,433	50.5
	Adlai E. Stevenson (D)	16,115	49.5
14	Joseph G. Cannon (R)	19,710	52.6
	James R. Scott (D)	17,734	47.4
15	Samuel W. Moulton (D)	19,364	53.5
	Albert P. Forsythe (R)	16,810	46.5
16	William A. J. Sparks (D)	15,392	50.2
	P. E. Hosmer (R)	13,921	45.4
17	William R. Morrison (D)	16,950	51.5
	John B. Hay (R)	15,986	48.5
18	John R. Thomas (R)	16,873	51.1
	William Hartzell (D)	15,146	45.9
19	Richard W. Townsend (D)	18,021	52.9
	Charles W. Pavey (R)	14,561	42.8

INDIANA

	Candidates	Votes	%
1	William Heilman (R)	17,719	49.4
	John Kleiner (D)	17,420	48.6
2	Thomas R. Cobb (D)	18,443	54.3
	Braden (R)	14,676	43.2
3	Strother M. Stockslager (D)	18,800	55.2
	Charles (R)	14,493	42.6
4	William S. Holman (D)	17,388	52.0
	J. O. Cravens (R)	15,641	46.7
5	Courtland C. Matson (D)	17,411	49.5
	Treat (R)	16,496	46.9
6	Thomas M. Browne (R)	22,136	62.2
	Miller (D)	12,676	35.6
7	Stanton J. Peelle (R)	17,610	48.3
	Byfield (D)	16,736	45.9
	Gilbert De La Matyr (NG)	2,135	5.9
8	Robert B. F. Peirce (R)	19,291	49.0
	Hanna (D)	16,995	43.1
	Copner (NG)	3,120	7.9
9	Godlove S. Orth (R)	18,287	49.6
	William Ralph Myers (D)	17,475	47.4
10	Mark L. DeMotte (R)	18,024	51.5
	Skinner (D)	17,006	48.5
11	George Washington Steele (R)	20,246	48.1
	Slack (D)	19,713	46.8
	Studebaker (NG)	2,168	5.2
12	Walpole G. Colerick (D)	17,800	51.1
	Taylor (R)	17,030	48.9
13	William Henry Calkins (R)	17,981	49.2
	McDonald (D)	16,817	46.0

IOWA

1	Moses A. McCoid (R)	17,117	53.9
	W. B. Culbertson (D)	12,119	38.2
	D. P. Stubbs (G)	2,497	7.9
2	Sewall S. Farwell (R)	17,465	54.9
	Roderick Rose (D)	13,100	41.2
3	Thomas Updegraff (R)	17,359	51.8
	William G. Stewart (D)	13,969	41.7
	M. H. Moore (G)	2,193	6.5
4	Nathaniel C. Deering (R)	21,940	65.4
	Joseph S. Root (D)	8,731	26.0
	M. B. Doolittle (G)	2,191	6.5
5	William G. Thompson (R)	20,016	59.8
	R. E. Austin (D)	11,315	33.8
	A. F. Palmer (G)	2,114	6.3
6	Marsena E. Cutts (R)	18,017‡	50.1
	John Calhoun Cook (D & G)	17,911	49.8
7	John A. Kasson (R)	19,932	53.8
	Edward Hooker Gillette (D & G)	16,776	45.3
8	William P. Hepburn (R)	24,358	56.3
	Robert Percival (D)	12,984	30.0
	H. C. Ayres (G)	5,920	13.7
9	Cyrus Clay Carpenter (R)	25,533	63.4
	P. M. Guthrie (D)	12,267	30.5
	Daniel Campbell (G)	2,363	5.9

KANSAS

1	John A. Anderson (R)	48,599	61.8
	C. C. Burnes (D)	22,727	28.9
	John Davis (G)	7,318	9.3
2	Dudley C. Haskell (R)	30,758	56.4
	Louis F. Green (G)	23,737	43.5
3	Thomas Ryan (R)	41,094	60.9
	J. Wade McDonald (D)	16,976	25.2
	D. P. Mitchell (G LAB)	9,396	13.9

KENTUCKY

1	Oscar Turner (D)	11,448	53.6
	R. B. Ratliff (R)	6,318	29.6
	W. W. Tice (D)	3,572	16.7
2	James A. McKenzie (D)	14,694	52.0
	John Feland (R)	8,354	29.5
	Charles W. Cook (G)	5,233	18.5
3	John W. Caldwell (D)	13,089	50.7
	M. T. Flippin (R)	10,987	42.6
	George Wright (G)	1,736	6.7
4	J. Proctor Knott (D)	13,778	59.2
	William T. Thurmond (R)	6,603	28.4
	L. E. Green (G)	2,820	12.1
5	Albert S. Willis (D)	11,934	48.5
	Thomas E. Burns (R)	8,445	34.3
	Thomas Hays (D)	3,794	15.4

	Candidates	Votes	%
6	John G. Carlisle (D)	17,291	63.7
	Oliver H. Root (R)	9,862	36.3
7	Joseph C. S. Blackburn (D)	16,799	70.6
	Lycander Hord (R)	5,692	23.9
	W. C. Goodloe (R)	1,207	5.1
8	Philip B. Thompson Jr. (D)	14,249	53.0
	Speed S. Fry (R)	12,004	44.6
9	John D. White (R)	15,317	53.5
	Thomas Turner (D)	13,326	46.5
10	Elijah C. Phister (D)	13,944	51.8
	George M. Thomas (R)	12,955	48.1

LOUISIANA

	Candidates	Votes	%
1	Randall L. Gibson (D)	10,526	66.6
	A. J. Ker (R)	5,291	33.5
2	E. John Ellis (D)	10,032	60.0
	Michael Hahn (R)	6,701	40.1
3	Chester B. Darrall (R)	13,371	63.2
	J. S. Billiu (D)	7,794	36.8
4	Newton C. Blanchard (D)	12,446	88.4
	A. C. Wells (R)	1,638	11.6
5	J. Floyd King (D)	15,305	82.2
	R. H. Lanier (R)	3,318	17.8
6	Edward W. Robertson (D)	9,941	64.9
	Alexander Smith (R)	5,372	35.1

MAINE

	Candidates	Votes	%
1	Thomas B. Reed (R)	16,920	49.8
	Samuel J. Anderson (D & G)	16,803	49.4
2	William P. Frye (R)	14,417	53.6
	Frank M. Fogg (D & G)	12,343	45.9
3	Stephen D. Lindsey (R)	15,131	50.5
	William Philbrick (D & G)	14,824	49.5
4	George W. Ladd (D & G)	14,047	51.5
	Charles A. Boutelle (R)	13,194	48.4
5	Thompson H. Murch (D & G)	14,942	51.6
	Seth L. Milliken (R)	13,977	48.3

MARYLAND

	Candidates	Votes	%
1	George W. Covington (D)	16,025	54.2
	Smith (R)	13,532	45.8
2	J. Fred. C. Talbott (D)	14,988	52.7
	Webster (R)	13,472	47.3
3	Fetter S. Hoblitzell (D)	13,629	57.7
	Horner (R)	9,975	42.3
4	Robert M. McLane (D)	15,702	53.7
	Maund (R)	13,540	46.3
5	Andrew G. Chapman (D)	14,448	53.3
	Wilmer (R)	12,665	46.7
6	Milton G. Urner (R)	17,129	50.5
	Schley (D)	16,339	48.2

MASSACHUSETTS

	Candidates	Votes	%
1	William W. Crapo (R)	16,384	69.7
	Davis (D)	6,669	28.4
2	Benjamin W. Harris (R)	17,047	62.8
	Dean (D)	9,718	35.8
3	Ambrose A. Ranney (R)	13,132	51.9
	Dearborn (D)	12,073	47.7
4	Leopold Morse (D)	10,616	49.4
	Hayes (R)	10,501	48.9
5	Selwyn Z. Bowman (R)	16,688	55.9
	Beebe (D)	11,729	39.3
6	Eben F. Stone (R)	14,124	54.2
	Boynton (D)	11,900	45.7
7	William A. Russell (R)	14,982	58.8
	Aldrich (D)	10,027	39.4
8	John W. Candler (R)	16,644	58.2
	Russell (D)	11,542	40.3
9	William W. Rice (R)	14,935	61.5
	McCafferty (D)	8,925	36.7
10	Amasa Norcross (R)	15,608	62.8
	Ivord (D)	8,627	34.7
11	George D. Robinson (R)	14,235	58.3
	Woodworth (D)	10,007	41.0

MICHIGAN

	Candidates	Votes	%
1	Henry W. Lord (R)	15,962	49.9
	Maybury (D)	15,388	48.1
2	Edwin Willits (R)	18,945	50.7
	Waldby (D)	16,596	44.4
3	Edward S. Lacey (R)	21,267	52.9
	Pringle (D)	9,739	24.2
	Hodge (G)	8,959	22.3
4	Julius C. Burrows (R)	19,096	53.4
	Powers (D)	12,424	34.8
	Yaple (NG)	4,193	11.7
5	George W. Webber (R)	22,824	52.1
	Randall (D)	11,435	26.1
	Blanchard (G)	9,506	21.7
6	Oliver L. Spaulding (R)	23,551	49.5
	Winans (D)	18,235	38.3
	Begole (G)	5,690	12.0
7	Omar D. Conger (R)	17,490*	53.5
	Black (D)	13,806	42.2
8	Roswell G. Horr (R)	21,224	48.3
	Tarsney (D)	18,857	42.9
	Smith (G)	3,829	8.7
9	Jay A. Hubbell (R)	23,437	60.1
	Pratt (D)	14,642	37.5

MINNESOTA

	Candidates	Votes	%
1	Mark H. Dunnell (R)	22,392	51.1
	Wells (D)	13,768	31.4
	Ward (IR)	7,656	17.5
2	Horace B. Strait (R)	24,508	56.7
	Poehler (D)	18,707	43.3
3	William D. Washburn (R)	36,428	60.5
	Sibley (D)	23,804	39.5

MISSISSIPPI

	Candidates	Votes	%
1	Henry L. Muldrow (D)	14,456	74.7
	Morphis (R)	3,828	19.8
	Davidson (G)	1,058	5.5
2	Vannoy H. Manning (D)	15,255	52.9
	George M. Buchanan (R)	9,996	34.7
	Harris (G)	3,585	12.4
3	Hernando D. Money (D)	11,722	80.7
	Gunn (G)	2,790	19.2
4	Otho R. Singleton (D)	13,749	76.7
	Drennan (R)	4,177	23.3
5	Charles E. Hooker (D)	11,771	63.5
	Deason (IR)	5,618	30.3
6	James R. Chalmers (D)	9,172‡	63.0
	John R. Lynch (R)	5,393	37.0

MISSOURI

	Candidates	Votes	%
1	Martin L. Clardy (D)	11,681	51.6
	Fletcher (R)	10,892	48.2
2	Thomas Allen (D)	12,458	55.4
	Rosenblatt (R)	10,022	44.6
3	Richard G. Frost (D)	9,487‡	49.8
	Gustavus Sessinghaus (R)	9,290	48.8
4	Lowndes H. Davis (D)	19,949	94.1
	Simpson (GD)	1,251	5.9
5	Richard P. Bland (D)	12,977	54.5
	Palmer (G)	10,799	45.4
6	Ira S. Hazeltine (G & R)	22,787	50.1
	Waddill (D)	22,680	49.8
7	Theron M. Rice (G & R)	19,744	50.8
	Philips (D)	19,146	49.2
8	Robert T. Van Horn (R)	8,050	33.2
	Allen (D)	7,656	31.6
	Crisp (D)	7,459	30.8
9	Nicholas Ford (G & R)	20,770	50.0
	Craig (D)	20,768	50.0
10	Joseph H. Burrows (G & R)	17,284	50.1
	Mansur (D)	17,219	49.9
11	John B. Clark Jr. (D)	17,021	69.7
	Heberling (GD)	7,370	30.2
12	William H. Hatch (D)	17,401	53.3
	London (G & R)	15,236	46.7

	Candidates	Votes	%
13	Aylett H. Buckner (D)	17,233	69.3
	Haley (GD)	7,394	29.7

NEBRASKA

	Candidates	Votes	%
AL	Edward K. Valentine (R)	52,648	62.5
	James E. North (D)	23,634	28.1

NEVADA

	Candidates	Votes	%
AL	George W. Cassidy (D)	9,815	53.4
	Daggett (R)	8,578	46.6

NEW HAMPSHIRE

	Candidates	Votes	%
1	Joshua G. Hall (R)	16,310	51.5
	Sanborn (D)	15,047	47.5
2	James F. Briggs (R)	14,480	52.4
	Sulloway (D)	13,000	47.1
3	Evarts W. Farr (R)	13,861*	51.3
	Bingham (D)	12,896	47.7

NEW JERSEY

	Candidates	Votes	%
1	George M. Robeson (R)	19,807	53.6
	Carter (D)	16,350	44.2
2	J. Hart Brewer (R)	18,580	52.4
	Smith (D)	16,536	46.6
3	Miles Ross (D)	19,725	53.3
	Robbins (R)	16,953	45.8
4	Henry S. Harris (D)	17,043	56.1
	Kilpatrick (R)	12,870	42.4
5	John Hill (R)	16,766	52.0
	Cutler (D)	15,165	47.0
6	Phineas Jones (R)	20,424	52.5
	Balbach Jr (D)	17,888	46.0
7	Augustus A. Hardenbergh (D)	19,462	56.7
	Brigham (R)	14,714	42.9

NEW YORK

	Candidates	Votes	%
1	Perry Belmont (D)	20,805	53.1
	J. A. King (R)	18,163	46.3
2	William E. Robinson (D)	20,122	60.7
	Daniel O'Reilly (R)	12,166	36.7
3	J. Hyatt Smith (D & G)	22,085	51.3
	S. B. Chittenden (R)	20,626	48.0
4	Archibald M. Bliss (D)	20,030	56.9
	D. W. Talmage (R)	14,614	41.5
5	Benjamin Wood (D)	11,411	47.6
	N. Muller (ID)	9,750	40.6
	C. L. Brockmeier (R)	2,714	11.3
6	Samuel S. Cox (D)	17,025	69.7
	Victor Heimberger (R)	7,162	29.3
7	Philip Henry Dugro (D)	11,723	49.5
	W. W. Astor (R)	11,550	48.8
8	Anson G. McCook (R)	17,392	57.9
	John G. Davis (D)	12,468	41.5
9	Fernando Wood (D)	10,842*	38.0
	J. L. N. Hunt (R)	9,313	32.6
	John Hardy	8,251	28.9
10	Abram S. Hewitt (D)	19,961	65.3
	James Talcott (R)	10,098	33.1
11	Levi P. Morton (R)	18,232	54.7
	James W. Gerard (D)	14,898	44.7
12	Waldo Hutchins (D)	15,852	51.6
	Alex Taylor Jr. (R)	14,803	48.2
13	John H. Ketcham (R)	20,355	56.8
	Edward L. Gaul (D)	15,312	42.7
14	Lewis Beach (D)	16,664	49.8
	Charles T. Pierson (R)	16,134	48.2
15	Thomas Cornell (R)	18,845	50.7
	John S. Pindar (D)	17,991	48.4
16	Michael N. Nolan (D)	19,176	52.7
	S. O. Vanderpool (R)	16,974	46.7
17	Walter A. Wood (R)	21,902	80.8
	R. H. Ferguson (D)	5,163	19.1
18	John Hammond (R)	14,281	58.6
	T. H. Walker (D)	9,360	38.4
19	Abraham X. Parker (R)	17,569	66.7

	Candidates	Votes	%
	A. Andrus (D)	8,385	31.8
20	George West (R)	21,693	56.2
	N. H. Decker (D)	16,490	42.8
21	Ferris Jacobs Jr. (R)	19,078	51.7
	F. R. Gilbert (D)	16,496	44.7
22	Warner Miller (R)	19,792	55.3
	Dennis O'Brien (D)	15,906	44.4
23	Cyrus D. Prescott (R)	14,499	52.8
	R. E. Sutton (D)	12,532	45.6
24	Joseph Mason (R)	17,101	57.9
	Benjamin F. Lewis (D)	11,510	39.0
25	Frank Hiscock (R)	19,828	57.4
	William C. Ruger (D)	14,634	42.4
26	John H. Camp (R)	20,259	56.4
	P. H. Van Auken (D)	14,555	40.5
27	Elbridge G. Lapham (R)	15,673	55.2
	C. W. Bennett (D)	12,263	43.2
28	Jeremiah W. Dwight (R)	19,510	54.7
	F. Davis Jr. (D)	15,082	42.3
29	David P. Richardson (R)	21,211	52.4
	T. K. Beecher (GD)	19,288	47.6
30	John Van Voorhis (R)	21,481	55.4
	A. S. Warner (D)	16,701	43.1
31	Richard Crowley (R)	15,759	54.7
	R. S. Stevens (D)	12,871	44.6
32	Jonathan Scoville (D)	22,702	50.0
	M. P. Bush (R)	22,329	49.2
33	Henry Van Aernam (R)	17,429	58.5
	Van Campen (D)	10,584	35.5

NORTH CAROLINA

	Candidates	Votes	%
1	Louis C. Latham (D)	14,796	50.9
	Cyrus W. Grandy (R)	14,290	49.1
2	Orlando Hubbs (R)	19,259	57.2
	William H. Kitchin (D)	14,305	42.5
3	John W. Shackelford (D)	16,356	51.1
	William P. Canaday (R)	15,017	46.9
4	William R. Cox (D)	17,557	52.0
	Moses A. Bledsoe (R)	16,241	48.1
5	Alfred M. Scales (D)	13,634	52.8
	Thomas B. Keogh (R)	11,623	45.0
6	Clement Dowd (D)	16,401	57.0
	William R. Myers (D)	12,366	43.0
7	Robert F. Armfield (D)	13,331	53.9
	David M. Furches (R)	11,383	46.1
8	Robert B. Vance (D)	14,099	65.0
	Natt Atkinson (I)	6,244	28.8
	Samuel L. Love (I)	1,336	6.2

OHIO

	Candidates	Votes	%
1	Benjamin Butterworth (R)	16,455	52.0
	Samuel F. Hunt (D)	15,157	47.9
2	Thomas L. Young (R)	17,385	51.5
	Henry B. Banning (D)	16,381	48.5
3	Henry L. Morey (R)	17,863	49.7
	Durbin Ward (D)	17,835	49.6
4	Emanuel Schultz (R)	21,572	50.0
	John A. McMahon (D)	21,244	49.3
5	Benjamin Le Fevré (D)	23,598	60.1
	W. K. Boone (R)	15,488	39.5
6	James M. Ritchie (R)	19,773	49.4
	Frank H. Hurd (D)	19,097	47.7
7	John P. Leedom (D)	17,365	52.6
	Alphonso Hart (R)	15,663	47.4
8	J. Warren Keifer (R)	21,182	57.3
	Frank Chance (D)	15,264	41.3
9	James S. Robinson (R)	18,146	51.0
	Caleb H. Norris (D)	17,007	47.8
10	John B. Rice (R)	18,394	50.9
	Morgan D. Shaffer (D)	17,026	47.1
11	Henry S. Neal (R)	17,218	52.9
	William A. Hutchins (D)	15,080	46.3
12	George L. Converse (D)	21,673	54.4
	John Groce (R)	17,484	43.9
13	Gibson Atherton (D)	19,038	53.0
	Appleton B. Clarke (R)	16,565	46.1
14	George W. Geddes (D)	18,520	59.3
	S. Ellis Fink (R)	12,653	40.5
15	Rufus R. Dawes (R)	16,283	50.1
	A. J. Warner (D)	15,781	48.5
16	Jonathan T. Updegraff (R)	17,998	54.2
	James F. Charlesworth (D)	15,150	45.7
17	William McKinley Jr. (R)	20,221	53.5
	Leroy D. Thoman (D)	16,650	44.1
18	Addison S. McClure (R)	18,570	57.0
	David L. Wadsworth (D)	13,474	41.4
19	Ezra B. Taylor (R)	22,794	67.3
	Charles D. Adams (D)	10,116	29.9
20	Amos Townsend (R)	20,333	56.0
	John C. Hutchins (D)	15,106	41.6

OREGON

	Candidates	Votes	%
AL	Melvin C. George (R)	19,578	51.4
	John Whiteaker (D)	18,181	47.8

PENNSYLVANIA

	Candidates	Votes	%
1	Henry H. Bingham (R)	18,914	57.2
	George R. Snowden (D)	14,178	42.8
2	Charles O'Neill (R)	18,924	60.9
	A. S. Hartranft (D)	12,122	39.0
3	Samuel J. Randall (D)	13,639	57.8
	Benjamin L. Berry (R)	9,912	42.0
4	William D. Kelley (R)	25,968	61.2
	George Bull (D)	16,487	38.8
5	Alfred C. Harmer (R)	23,468	57.2
	John K. Folwell (D)	17,332	42.3
6	William Ward (R)	18,368	60.8
	R. J. Monaghan (D)	11,847	39.2
7	William Godshalk (R)	17,944	52.6
	John Slingluff (D)	16,080	47.1
8	Daniel Ermentrout (D)	16,049	63.1
	J. Howard Jacobs (R)	9,152	36.0
9	A. Herr Smith (R)	19,466	64.3
	J. L. Steinmetz (D)	10,655	35.2
10	William Mutchler (D)	21,464	61.3
	Hiram H. Fisher (R)	13,326	38.1
11	Robert Klotz (D)	19,812	62.3
	W. J. Scott (R)	11,465	36.1
12	Joseph A. Scranton (R)	13,455	47.1
	D. W. Connelly (D)	10,948	38.3
	Hendrick B. Wright (NG)	4,174	14.6
13	Charles N. Brumm (G & R)	12,038	52.2
	John W. Ryon (D)	11,007	47.8
14	Samuel F. Barr (R)	18,320	52.7
	Grant Weidman (D)	15,771	45.4
15	Cornelius C. Jadwin (R)	18,223	55.2
	Robert H. Packer (D)	13,602	41.2
16	Robert J. C. Walker (R)	17,850	50.8
	David Kirk (D & G)	17,304	49.2
17	Jacob M. Campbell (R)	17,300	51.6
	A. H. Coffroth (D)	15,864	47.3
18	Horatio G. Fisher (R)	16,847	51.1
	R. Milton Speer (D)	16,130	48.9
19	Frank E. Beltzhoover (D)	20,858	57.5
	Charles J. Little (R)	15,351	42.3
20	Andrew G. Curtin (D)	17,461	54.7
	Thomas H. Murray (D)	14,472	45.3
21	Morgan R. Wise (D)	18,486	53.7
	James E. Sayers (R)	11,879	34.5
	George W. K. Minor (NG)	4,083	11.9
22	Russell Errett (R)	18,241	53.3
	James H. Hopkins (D)	14,084	41.1
	M. J. Sullivan (G)	1,923	5.6
23	Thomas M. Bayne (R)	15,641	63.2
	George T. Miller (D)	8,278	33.5
24	William S. Shallenberger (R)	15,567	56.6
	J. M. Clark (D)	10,986	39.9
25	James Mosgrove (D & G)	16,044	51.2
	Harry White (R)	15,287	48.8
26	Samuel H. Miller (R)	17,630	47.9
	James H. Caldwell (D)	14,976	40.7
	W. C. Plummer (NG)	3,895	10.6
27	Lewis F. Watson (R)	15,740	52.0
	Alf Short (D & G)	14,438	47.7

RHODE ISLAND

	Candidates	Votes	%
1	Nelson W. Aldrich (R)	9,641	67.6
	Isaac Lawrence (D)	4,446	31.2
2	Jonathan Chace (R)	8,515	58.0
	Franklin Treat (D)	6,031	41.1

SOUTH CAROLINA

	Candidates	Votes	%
1	John S. Richardson (D)	20,142	63.3
	Samuel J. Lee (R)	11,674	36.7
2	Michael P. O'Connor (D)	17,569‡	58.8
	Edmund W. M. Mackey (R)	12,297	41.2
3	D. Wyatt Aiken (D)	27,863	74.1
	C. J. Stollbrand (R)	9,758	25.9
4	John H. Evins (D)	27,985	69.7
	A. Blythe (R)	11,780	29.3
5	George D. Tillman (D)	23,325‡	60.4
	Robert Smalls (R)	15,287	39.6

TENNESSEE

	Candidates	Votes	%
1	Augustus H. Pettibone (R)	15,117	52.5
	Taylor (D)	13,693	47.5
2	Leonidas C. Houk (R)	17,479	65.1
	Williams (D)	9,380	34.9
3	George G. Dibrell (D)	12,806	53.6
	Case (R)	9,918	41.5
4	Benton McMillin (D)	12,405	65.0
	Sanders (R)	6,694	35.1
5	Richard Warner (LOWTAX D)	7,777	36.3
	Bright (D)	6,307	29.4
	Holman (R)	5,077	23.7
	Tillman (G)	2,263	10.6
6	John F. House (D)	15,631	60.6
	McClain (R)	9,389	36.4
7	Washington C. Whitthorne (D)	11,118	58.0
	Hughes (R)	8,056	42.0
8	John D. C. Atkins (D)	10,999	46.6
	Hawkins (R)	9,876	41.9
	Travis (D)	2,723	11.5
9	Charles B. Simonton (D)	12,150	52.8
	Shackleford (R)	10,865	47.2
10	William R. Moore (R)	11,844	50.7
	Young (D)	10,998	47.1

TEXAS

	Candidates	Votes	%
1	John H. Reagan (D)	21,227	77.7
	S. R. Withers (G)	6,095	22.3
2	David B. Culberson (D)	26,624	68.6
	H. F. O'Neal (G)	12,194	31.4
3	Olin Wellborn (D)	48,005	78.7
	J. C. Kirby (G)	13,014	21.3
4	Roger Q. Mills (D)	30,087	62.6
	J. T. Brady (G)	17,977	37.4
5	George W. Jones (G)	22,941	50.3
	Seth Shepard (D)	22,708	49.7
6	Christopher C. Upson (D)	27,521	97.3

VERMONT

	Candidates	Votes	%
1	Charles H. Joyce (R)	15,645	68.6
	Randall (D)	6,771	29.7
2	James M. Tyler (R)	15,960	69.0
	Campbell (D)	6,698	29.0
3	William W. Grout (R)	12,253	61.9
	Curree (D)	6,191	31.3
	Tarbell (G)	1,256	6.4

VIRGINIA

	Candidates	Votes	%
1	George T. Garrison (D)	11,595	48.2
	John W. Woltz (R)	10,250	42.6
	John Critcher (READJ)	2,217	9.2
2	John F. Dezendorf (R)	14,775	52.6
	John Goode (D)	9,709	34.6
	B. W. Lacy (READJ)	3,600	12.8
3	George D. Wise (D)	10,931	55.9
	John S. Wise (READJ)	8,566	43.8

	Candidates	Votes	%
4	Joseph Jorgensen (R)	13,825	70.1
	Samuel F. Coleman (D)	5,771	29.2
5	George C. Cabell (D)	11,778	51.9
	John T. Stovall (READJ)	10,919	48.1
6	John Randolph Tucker (D)	13,646	59.5
	James A. Frazier (READJ)	9,265	40.4
7	John Paul (READJ)	10,665	49.3
	Henry C. Allen (D)	9,938	45.9
8	John S. Barbour (D)	15,546	56.6
	Sampson P. Bagley (R)	9,170	33.4
	James H. Williams (READJ)	2,732	10.0
9	Abram Fulkerson (READJ)	8,096	40.7
	Connally F. Trigg (D)	7,621	38.3
	G. G. Goodell (R)	3,660	18.4

WEST VIRGINIA

	Candidates	Votes	%
1	Benjamin Wilson (D)	18,460	46.6
	John H. Hutchinson (R)	18,350	46.3
	James Bassil (G)	2,515	6.3
2	John B. Hogue (D)	17,277	50.5
	J. T. Hoke (R)	14,565	42.6
	D. Farnsworth (G)	2,356	6.9
3	John E. Kenna (D)	21,407	57.0
	H. I. Walker (R)	16,097	42.9

WISCONSIN

	Candidates	Votes	%
1	Charles G. Williams (R)	19,014	61.0
	Babbitt (D)	11,782	37.8

	Candidates	Votes	%
2	Lucien B. Caswell (R)	16,041	52.0
	Gregory (D)	14,390	46.6
3	George C. Hazelton (R)	16,236	55.6
	Cothren (D)	12,941	44.3
4	Peter V. Deuster (D)	17,574	53.7
	Sanger (R)	15,018	45.9
5	Edward S. Bragg (D)	16,984	51.6
	Colman (R)	14,753	44.8
6	Richard W. Guenther (R)	20,168	52.5
	Bouck (D)	16,807	43.7
7	Herman L. Humphrey (R)	23,179	64.7
	Freeman (D)	10,994	30.7
8	Thaddeus C. Pound (R)	19,256	56.8
	Silverthorn (D)	14,590	43.1

1881 House Elections

MAINE

Special Election

	Candidates	Votes	%
2	Nelson Dingley Jr. (R)	10,961	65.3
	Gilbert (G)	5,519	32.9

MICHIGAN

Special Election

11	John T. Rich (R)	15,279	55.7
	Cyrenius P. Black	10,740	39.2

NEW YORK

Special Elections

	Candidates	Votes	%
9	John Hardy (D)	13,013	62.4
	Murphy (R)	7,705	37.0
11	Roswell P. Flower (D)	13,739	56.0
	Astor (R)	10,626	43.3
22	Charles R. Skinner (R)	16,222	54.8
	Lansing (D)	13,065	44.1
27	James W. Wadsworth (R)	12,086	54.2
	Faulkner (D)	9,600	43.0

RHODE ISLAND

Special Election

	Candidates	Votes	%
1	Henry J. Spooner (R)	3,623	66.4
	Henry O. Sisson (D)	1,103	20.2
	C. C. Van Zandt (R)	709	13.0

1882 House Elections

ALABAMA

	Candidates	Votes	%
1	Thomas H. Herndon (D)	9,609	57.4
	Smith (R)	7,130	42.6
2	Hilary A. Herbert (D)	12,823	58.4
	Rice (R)	9,121	41.6
3	William C. Oates (D)	11,238	87.9
	Millen (R)	1,549	12.1
4	Charles M. Shelley (D)	7,119‡	60.8
	George H. Craig (R)	4,435	37.9
5	Thomas Williams (D)	9,629	62.0
	McCoy (ID)	5,880	37.9
6	Goldsmith W. Hewitt (D)	6,402	72.7
	Carpenter (G)	2,406	27.3
7	William H. Forney (D)	7,750	80.7
	Bingham (R)	1,859	19.4
8	Luke Pryor (D)	12,155	51.6
	Shelby (ID)	11,418	48.4

ARKANSAS

	Candidates	Votes	%
1	Poindexter Dunn (D)	12,685	94.4
	J. B. Miles (R)	719	5.4
2	James K. Jones (D)	14,831	55.5
	J. A. Williams (R)	11,525	43.1
3	John H. Rogers (D)	10,522	57.3
	M. W. Benjamin (R)	7,840	42.7
4	Samuel W. Peel (D)	5,668	80.6
	Truman Niman (R)	1,008	14.3
AL	Clifton R. Breckinridge (D)	43,619	66.6
	C. E. Cunningham (G)	21,422	32.7

CALIFORNIA

	Candidates	Votes	%
1	William S. Rosecrans (D)	22,733	59.4
	Paul Neumann (R)	14,847	38.8
2	James H. Budd (D)	20,229	50.5
	H. F. Page (R)	19,246	48.1
3	Barclay Henley (D)	21,807	51.3
	J. J. DeHaven (R)	19,470	45.8
4	Pleasant B. Tully (D)	23,105	54.3
	George L. Woods (R)	18,387	43.2
AL	John R. Glascock (D)	87,259✓	
	Charles A. Sumner (D)	87,233✓	
	W. W. Morrow (R)	73,647	
	Henry Edgerton (R)	73,454	
	J. B. Hotchkiss (P)	2,776	
	J. Yarnell (P)	2,722	
	Warren Chase (G)	1,139	
	S. Maybell (G)	1,090	

COLORADO

	Candidates	Votes	%
AL	James B. Belford (R)	30,847	50.2
	S. S. Wallace (D)	29,380	47.8

CONNECTICUT

	Candidates	Votes	%
1	William W. Eaton (D)	14,740	50.7
	John R. Buck (R)	14,047	48.3
2	Charles L. Mitchell (D)	19,325	51.7
	Merwin (R)	17,530	46.9
3	John T. Wait (R)	9,882	53.4
	Penrose (D)	8,227	44.5
4	Edward W. Seymour (D)	15,703	51.8
	Coe (R)	14,263	47.0

DELAWARE

	Candidates	Votes	%
AL	Charles B. Lore (D)	16,563	53.0
	Washington Hastings (R)	14,640	46.9

FLORIDA

	Candidates	Votes	%
1	Robert H. M. Davidson (D)	11,244	51.5
	Skinner (R)	7,017	32.2
	McKinnon	3,553	16.3
2	Horatio Bisbee Jr. (R)	13,122	50.6
	Finley (D)	12,823	49.4

GEORGIA

	Candidates	Votes	%
1	John C. Nichols (D)	6,055	60.9
	Atkins (R)	3,964	39.1
2	Henry G. Turner (D)	7,794	63.9
	Wessolowsky (R)	4,406	36.1
3	Charles F. Crisp (D)	4,121	92.6
	Harrall (R)	329	7.4
4	Hugh Buchanan (D)	5,583	78.5
	Pou (I)	1,502	21.1
5	Nathaniel J. Hammond (D)	10,788	65.2
	Buck (IR)	5,756	34.8
6	James H. Blount (D)	3,514	99.3
7	Judson C. Clements (D)	12,408	53.6
	Felton (ID)	10,746	46.4
8	Seaborn Reese (D)	4,384	96.0
9	Allen D. Candler (D)	14,521	54.9
	Speer (ID)	11,915	45.1
AL	Thomas Hardeman (D)	79,540	76.3
	Forsyth (R)	24,645	23.7

Special Election

	Candidates	Votes	%
8	Seaborn Reese (D)	4,282	100.0

ILLINOIS

	Candidates	Votes	%
1	Ransom W. Dunham (R)	11,571	50.9
	John W. Downes (D)	10,534	46.3
2	John F. Finerty (ID)	9,360	56.2
	Henry F. Sheridan (D)	6,939	41.6
3	George R. Davis (R)	12,511	53.2
	William T. Black (A-MON D)	10,274	43.7
4	George E. Adams (R)	11,686	53.3
	Lamberd Tree (D)	9,446	43.1
5	Reuben Ellwood (R)	12,994	70.6
	William Price (D)	5,127	27.9
6	Robert R. Hitt (R)	12,726	57.1
	James S. Ticknor (D)	9,045	40.6
7	Thomas J. Henderson (R)	12,751	61.1
	Larmon G. Johnson (D)	6,369	30.5
	M. B. Loyd (P)	1,673	8.0
8	William Cullen (R)	13,851	46.9
	Patrick C. Haley (D)	13,673	46.3
9	Lewis E. Payson (R)	12,619	52.4
	E. B. Buck (D)	9,243	38.4
	O. W. Barnard (G)	2,138	8.9
10	Nicholas E. Worthington (D)	13,571	48.3
	John H. Lewis (R)	13,180	46.9
11	William W. Neece (D)	14,604	45.3
	Benjamin F. Marsh (R)	13,975	43.3
	Richard Haney (P)	3,671	11.4
12	James M. Riggs (D)	15,316	49.0
	James W. Singleton (ID)	11,782	37.7
	Philip N. Minier (P)	4,130	13.2
13	William M. Springer (D)	18,360	54.4
	Dietrich C. Smith (R)	14,042	41.6
14	Jonathan H. Rowell (R)	15,273	48.8
	Adlai E. Stevenson (D)	14,598	46.7
15	Joseph G. Cannon (R)	15,868	51.1
	Andrew J. Hunter (D)	14,651	47.2
16	Aaron Shaw (D)	14,557	50.7
	E. B. Green (R)	13,689	47.7
17	Samuel W. Moulton (D)	14,495	55.9
	William H. Barlow (R)	10,068	38.8
	B. W. F. Corley (R)	1,386	5.3
18	William R. Morrison (D)	14,906	52.2
	W. C. Keuffner (R)	12,561	44.0
19	Richard W. Townshend (D)	15,606	60.7
	George C. Ross (R)	9,930	38.6
20	John R. Thomas (R)	14,504	49.0
	William K. Murphy (D)	14,113	47.6

Special Election

	Candidates	Votes	%
5	Robert R. Hitt (R)	12,430	59.9
	Larmon G. Johnson (D)	8,138	39.2

INDIANA

	Candidates	Votes	%
1	John Kleiner (D)	18,048	51.6
	William Heilman (R)	16,399	46.9
2	Thomas R. Cobb (D)	16,339	55.1
	A. J. Hostetter (R)	13,288	44.8
3	Strother M. Stockslager (D)	17,122	56.2
	Will T. Walker (R)	12,538	41.2
4	William S. Holman (D)	16,640	55.4
	W. J. Johnson (R)	13,146	43.8
5	Courtland C. Matson (D)	16,851	55.9
	Wallingford (R)	13,298	44.1
6	Thomas M. Browne (R)	19,562	60.1
	J. L. Pender (D)	12,249	37.6
7	Stanton J. Peelle (R)	17,451‡	49.4
	William Estin English (D)	17,373	49.1
8	John Edward Lamb (D)	18,110	47.9
	Robert Bruce Frasen Peirce (R)	17,823	47.2
9	Thomas Bayless Ward (D)	17,357	49.7
	Godlove S. Orth (R)	16,481	47.2
10	Thomas J. Wood (D)	17,237	49.5
	Mark Lindsey Demotte (R)	16,223	46.6
11	George Washington Steele (R)	19,863	48.6
	Dailey (D)	19,530	47.8
12	Robert Lowry (D)	16,986	54.4
	Glasgow (R)	13,623	43.6
13	William Henry Calkins (R)	17,478	47.9
	Winterbotham (D)	17,087	46.8
	Shively (NG)	1,942	5.3

Special Election

	Candidates	Votes	%
9	Charles T. Doxey (R)	✓	

IOWA

	Candidates	Votes	%
1	Moses A. McCoid (R)	13,549	48.1
	Benton J. Hall (D)	13,311	47.3
2	Jeremiah Henry Murphy (D)	15,760	54.6
	Sewell S. Farwell (R)	12,561	43.5
3	David B. Henderson (R)	12,907	50.4
	C. M. Durham (D)	11,604	45.3
4	Luman Hamlin Weller (D)	11,473	51.5
	Thomas Updegraff (R)	10,762	48.3
5	James Wilson (R)	11,791‡	47.5
	Benjamin Todd Frederick (D)	11,768	47.4
	David Platner (G)	1,253	5.1
6	Marsena E. Cutts (R)	11,250	40.4
	James Baird Weaver (G)	8,569	30.8
	C. H. Mackey (D)	8,040	28.9
7	John A. Kasson (R)	13,631	50.8
	T. C. Gilpin (D)	7,068	26.3
	E. H. Gillette (G)	6,131	22.9
8	William P. Hepburn (R)	13,792	51.7
	D. M. Clark (G)	7,344	27.5
	Lewis Bonnett (D)	5,533	20.7
9	William H. M. Pusey (D)	14,186	49.0
	Albert Raney Anderson (R)	11,987	41.4
	J. B. Hatton (G)	2,753	9.5
10	Adoniram J. Holmes (R)	14,250	62.2
	John Cliggitt (D)	6,853	29.9
	Josial Doane (G)	1,799	7.9
11	Isaac S. Struble (R)	15,315	58.0
	John P. Allison (D)	9,867	37.3

KANSAS

	Candidates	Votes	%
1	John A. Anderson (R)	41,251	68.3
	Charles H. Moody (G LAB)	17,816	29.5
2	Dudley C. Haskell (R)	23,601	48.7
	N. F. Acers (D)	19,116	39.5

	Candidates	Votes	%
	Alfred Taylor (G LAB)	5,710	11.8
3	Thomas Ryan (R)	36,091	57.1
	John C. Cannon (D)	17,729	28.1
	D. J. Cole (G LAB)	9,356	14.8
AL	Samuel R. Peters (R)	99,866✓	
	Edmund N. Morrill (R)	98,649✓	
	Bishop W. Perkins (R)	98,338✓	
	Lewis Hanback (R)	97,354✓	
	Samuel N. Wood (D)	83,433	
	O'Flanagan (D)	59,872	
	Leland (D)	58,079	
	Davis (G LAB)	26,701	
	Phillips (D)	25,644	
	Williams (G LAB)	22,243	
	Bennett (G LAB)	1,417	
	Cannon (G LAB)	588	

KENTUCKY

	Candidates	Votes	%
1	Oscar Turner (ID)	8,705	39.3
	John R. Grace (D)	7,627	34.5
	Henry Houston (R)	5,803	26.2
2	James F. Clay (D)	5,747	70.7
	W. M. Fuqua (R)	1,979	24.3
3	John E. Halsell (D)	13,546	50.4
	W. G. Hunter (R)	13,356	49.7
4	Thomas A. Robertson (D)	5,878	74.8
	W. H. Parrish (R)	1,974	25.1
5	Albert S. Willis (D)	6,492	62.5
	Silas F. Miller (R)	3,557	34.3
6	John G. Carlisle (D)	4,990	98.2
7	Joseph C. S. Blackburn (D)	11,789	63.8
	John W. Asbury (R)	6,692	36.2
8	P. B. Thompson Jr. (D)	11,202	52.0
	R. L. Ewell (R)	10,338	48.0
9	William W. Culbertson (R)	11,217	53.0
	Z. Smith Hurt (D)	9,948	47.0
10	John D. White (R)	14,240	52.5
	G. M. Adams (D)	12,870	47.5
11	Frank L. Wolford (D)	12,007	54.7
	D. R. Carr (R)	9,934	45.3

LOUISIANA

	Candidates	Votes	%
1	Carleton Hunt (D)	8,498	63.7
	A. C. Janin (R)	4,852	36.3
2	E. John Ellis (D)	7,701	58.4
	Morris Marks (IR)	2,789	21.1
	Henry Demas (R)	2,666	20.2
3	William Pitt Kellogg (R)	7,453	45.7
	Joseph Hayes Acklen (D)	5,564	34.1
	Taylor Beattie (IR)	3,301	20.2
4	Newton C. Blanchard (D)	5,765	99.8
5	J. Floyd King (D)	13,295	76.9
	W. L. McMillen (R)	3,986	23.1
6	Andrew S. Herron (D)	8,004*	66.9
	Louis Trager (R)	3,965	33.1

MAINE

	Candidates	Votes	%
AL	Thomas B. Reed (R)	72,811✓	
	Nelson Dingley Jr. (R)	72,494✓	
	Charles A. Boutelle (R)	72,352✓	
	Seth Llewellyn Milliken (R)	72,310✓	
	Daniel H. Thing (FUS)	63,321	
	Joseph Dane (FUS)	63,304	
	George W. Ladd (FUS)	63,192	
	Thompson H. Murch (FUS)	62,616	
	W. F. Eaton (G)	1,319	
	B. D. Averill (G)	1,290	
	B. K. Kalloch (G)	1,260	
	Eben O. Gerry (G)	1,241	
	James M. Stone (IR&P)	583	
	Henry Tallman (P)	295	
	N. G. Axtell (P)	293	
	Joseph E. Ladd (P)	291	
	Charles E. Nash (IR)	264	
	Daniel Stickney (IR)	198	

MARYLAND

	Candidates	Votes	%
1	George W. Covington (D)	13,170	52.8
	Millikin (R)	11,788	47.2
2	J. Fred C. Talbott (D)	12,728	52.2
	Blair (R)	11,641	47.8
3	Fetter S. Hoblitzell (D)	13,917	56.8
	Lang (R)	9,029	36.8
	Kimmel (ID)	1,576	6.4
4	John V. L. Findlay (D)	14,457	53.1
	Stockbridge (R)	12,793	47.0
5	Hart B. Holton (R)	13,550	53.0
	Chapman (D)	12,011	47.0
6	Louis E. McComas (R)	15,720	51.7
	Blair (D)	14,440	47.5

MASSACHUSETTS

	Candidates	Votes	%
1	Robert T. Davis (R)	11,475	66.0
	Nicholas Hathaway (D)	5,581	32.1
2	John D. Long (R)	12,915	53.9
	Edgar E. Dean (D)	10,152	42.4
3	Ambrose A. Ranney (R)	11,968	57.8
	Horatio E. Swasey (D)	8,540	41.3
4	Patrick A. Collins (D)	12,884	73.1
	Charles T. Gallagher (R)	4,546	25.8
5	Leopold Morse (D)	11,301	56.0
	Selwyn Z. Bowman (R)	8,791	43.6
6	Henry B. Lovering (D & G)	12,840	51.8
	Elisha S. Converse (R)	11,960	48.2
7	Eben F. Stone (R)	10,056	44.3
	Charles P. Thompson (D)	8,764	38.6
	Eben Moody Boynton (G)	3,825	16.9
8	William A. Russell (R)	11,269	51.0
	Charles S. Lilley (D)	10,743	48.6
9	Theodore Lyman (CSR&D)	12,076	54.4
	John W. Candler (R)	9,703	43.7
10	William W. Rice (R)	11,846	55.5
	John Hopkins (D)	9,404	44.1
11	William Whiting (R)	14,485	64.2
	Edward J. Sawyer (D)	7,600	33.7
12	George D. Robinson (R)	11,294	53.3
	Reuben Noble (D)	9,889	46.7

MICHIGAN

	Candidates	Votes	%
1	William C. Maybury (FUS)	16,148	57.4
	Henry W. Lord (R)	11,209	39.8
2	Nathaniel B. Eldredge (D)	15,251	48.2
	John K. Boies (R)	14,709	46.5
3	Edward S. Lacey (R)	18,023	52.0
	Hiram C. Hodge (FUS)	16,329	47.1
4	George L. Yaple (FUS)	16,329	50.4
	Julius C. Burrows (R)	16,077	49.6
5	Julius Houseman (FUS)	16,725	49.5
	William O. Webster (R)	16,609	49.2
6	Edwin B. Winans (FUS)	18,516	49.8
	Oliver L. Spaulding (R)	18,484	49.8
7	Ezra C. Carleton (FUS)	11,540	50.6
	John T. Rich (R)	11,252	49.4
8	Roswell G. Horr (R)	14,872	50.7
	Charles J. Willet (FUS)	13,918	47.5
9	Byron M. Cutcheon (R)	13,529	55.4
	Stephen Bronson (FUS)	10,897	44.6
10	Herschel H. Hatch (R)	11,327	52.6
	Andrew C. Maxwell (FUS)	7,749	36.0
	Jesse M. Miller	2,434	11.3
11	Edward Breitung (R)	11,428	68.5
	Peter White (FUS)	4,840	29.0

MINNESOTA

	Candidates	Votes	%
1	Milo White (R)	12,458	49.1
	A. Bierman (D)	11,789	46.4
2	James B. Wakefield (R)	17,187	63.6
	F. A. Bohrer (D)	6,750	25.0
	J. A. Latimer (P)	3,085	11.4
3	Horace B. Strait (R)	16,583	68.2
	C. P. Adams (D)	7,047	29.0
4	William D. Washburn (R)	17,380	51.5

	Candidates	Votes	%
	A. A. Ames (D)	14,820	43.9
5	Knute Nelson (IR)	16,956	47.8
	C. F. Kindred (R)	12,238	34.5
	E P. Barnum (D)	6,248	17.6

MISSISSIPPI

	Candidates	Votes	%
1	Henry L. Muldrow (D)	6,390	81.9
	Lyon (R)	1,414	18.1
2	James R. Chalmers (I)	9,729‡	52.3
	Vannoy H. Manning (D)	8,749	47.0
3	Elza Jeffords (R)	4,127	69.1
	Clarke (D)	1,321	22.1
	Waddell	521	8.7
4	Hernando D. Money (D)	6,848	68.8
	Griffin (R)	2,644	26.5
5	Otho R. Singleton (D)	6,121	98.9
6	Henry S. Van Eaton (D)	7,615	53.2
	Lynch (R)	6,706	46.8
7	Ethelbert Barksdale (D)	10,933	66.6
	Hill (R)	5,478	33.4

MISSOURI

	Candidates	Votes	%
1	William H. Hatch (D)	16,243	57.4
	Glover (ID)	11,415	40.3
2	Armstead M. Alexander (D)	19,033	57.7
	Dorsey (R)	8,628	26.2
	Quayle (GD)	5,302	16.1
3	Alexander M. Dockery (D)	17,261	52.9
	Thomas (D)	12,887	39.5
	Burrows (G & R)	2,485	7.6
4	James N. Burnes (D)	13,325	51.1
	Reed (R)	10,571	40.5
	Sisson (D)	2,185	8.4
5	Alexander Graves (D)	12,695	58.8
	Crisp (ID)	8,672	40.1
6	John Cosgrove (D)	17,149	60.2
	Alldridge (GD)	11,349	39.8
7	Aylett H. Buckner (D)	14,370	55.2
	Daudt (R)	9,857	37.9
	McNair (GD)	1,786	6.9
8	John J. O'Neill (D)	6,446	47.7
	Sessinghaus (R)	4,795	35.5
	Dailey (R)	1,282	9.5
	Sullivan (GD)	997	7.4
9	James O. Broadhead (D)	6,860	48.7
	McLean (R)	6,758	48.0
10	Martin L. Clardy (D)	13,536	57.2
	Manistre (R)	7,455	31.5
	Jackson (G & R)	2,667	11.3
11	Richard P. Bland (D)	14,259	54.9
	Wallace (R)	10,530	40.5
12	Charles H. Morgan (D)	14,768	53.9
	Terrell (R)	9,061	33.1
	Spring (G)	3,550	13.0
13	Robert W. Fyan (D)	13,904	42.9
	Cloud (R)	12,424	38.3
	Haseltine (G)	6,122	18.9
14	Lowndes H. Davis (D)	14,023	58.1
	Carroll (R)	7,177	29.8
	Kitchen (G)	2,920	12.1

Special Election

	Candidates	Votes	%
9	James O. Broadhead (D)	6,591	49.4
	McLean (R)	6,386	47.9

NEBRASKA

	Candidates	Votes	%
1	Archibald J. Weaver (R)	17,022	50.9
	John I. Reddick (D)	12,690	38.0
	W. S. Gilbert (A-MONOP)	3,707	11.1
2	James Laird (R)	12,983	49.8
	V. S. Moore (A-MONOP)	10,012	38.4
	F. A. Harman (D)	3,070	11.8
3	Edward K. Valentine (R)	11,272	39.5
	W. H. Munger (D)	9,932	34.8
	M. K. Turner (A-MONOP)	7,342	25.7

NEVADA

	Candidates	Votes	%
AL	George W. Cassidy (D)	7,720	54.4
	Powning (R)	6,462	45.6

NEW HAMPSHIRE

	Candidates	Votes	%
1	Martin A. Haynes (R)	19,378	54.4
	Chandler (D)	15,920	44.7
2	Ossian Ray (R)	21,294	52.2
	Hosley (D)	19,139	46.9

NEW JERSEY

	Candidates	Votes	%
1	Thomas M. Ferrell (D)	16,541	50.1
	Robeson (R)	14,825	44.9
2	J. Hart Brewer (R)	15,604	51.3
	Parker Jr. (D)	14,535	47.8
3	John Kean Jr. (R)	15,186	48.2
	Ross (D)	12,891	40.9
	Urner (G)	3,463	11.0
4	Benjamin F. Howey (R)	11,567	49.2
	Harris (D, P)	11,073	47.1
5	William W. Phelps (R)	14,341	50.4
	Ryle (D)	12,703	44.6
6	William H. F. Fiedler (D)	17,200	53.2
	Blake (R)	14,780	45.7
7	William McAdoo (D)	15,147	56.6
	Collins (R)	11,566	43.2

NEW YORK

	Candidates	Votes	%
1	Perry Belmont (D)	18,688	77.6
	Townsend (ID)	4,957	20.6
2	William E. Robinson (D)	19,004	63.1
	Boody (R & ID)	10,778	35.8
3	Darwin R. James (R)	19,260	52.5
	Hester (D)	16,882	46.0
4	Felix Campbell (D)	18,282	61.5
	Godard (R)	10,732	36.1
5	Nicholas Muller (D)	16,148	86.7
6	Samuel S. Cox (D)	16,624	74.6
	Quinn (R)	5,307	23.8
7	William Dorsheimer (D)	11,401	57.7
	Brodsky (R)	6,787	34.4
	McCabe (L)	1,562	7.9
8	John J. Adams (D)	12,089	51.3
	Russell (R)	10,904	46.3
9	John Hardy (D)	16,191	69.2
	O'Beirne (R)	7,217	30.8
10	Abram S. Hewitt (D)	22,144	90.7
11	Orlando B. Potter (D)	15,049	51.9
	Strong (R)	13,947	48.1
12	Waldo Hutchins (D)	15,663	63.7
	Long (R)	8,938	36.3
13	John H. Ketcham (R)	16,217	90.1
	Dorland (D)	916	5.1
14	Lewis Beach (D)	13,454	49.8
	Low (R)	12,821	47.5
15	John H. Bagley Jr. (D)	16,625	55.7
	Bray (R)	13,168	44.1
16	Thomas J. Van Alstyne (D)	17,797	57.0
	Van Heusen (R)	11,404	36.5
	Lemon Thompson (LAB)	2,010	6.4
17	Henry G. Burleigh (R)	17,685	100.0
18	Frederick A. Johnson (R)	10,667	87.8
	Fassett (D)	1,476	12.2
19	Abraham X. Parker (R)	12,578	63.1
	Smith (D)	7,365	36.9
20	Edward Wemple (D)	17,831	50.0
	West (R)	17,742	49.8
21	George W. Ray (R)	15,188	48.0
	Babcock (D)	14,742	46.6
22	Charles R. Skinner (R)	15,236	52.2
	Davenport (D)	13,967	47.8
23	John T. Spriggs (D)	12,299	51.9
	Fox (R)	10,623	44.8
24	Newton W. Nutting (R)	11,516	52.0
	Rhodes (D)	9,905	44.8
25	Frank Hiscock (R)	14,563	48.7

	Candidates	Votes	%
	Davis (D)	13,831	46.2
26	Sereno E. Payne (R)	13,607	48.8
	Hammond (D)	12,651	45.3
27	James W. Wadsworth (R)	12,013	52.3
	Pierpont (D)	10,931	47.6
28	Stephen C. Millard (R)	15,087	51.8
	Davis Jr. (D)	13,378	45.9
29	John Arnot Jr. (D)	17,769	50.0
	Baxter (R)	14,988	42.1
	Baldwin (P)	2,081	5.9
30	Halbert S. Greenleaf (D)	18,042	56.2
	Vanvoorhis (R)	12,308	38.4
31	Robert S. Stevens (D)	12,009	53.6
	Watson (R)	9,379	41.8
32	William F. Rogers (D)	20,531	49.5
	Moulton (R)	19,804	47.7
33	Francis B. Brewer (R)	12,123	51.4
	Lowry (D)	9,591	40.7
AL	Henry Slocum (D)	503,934	56.1
	Unidentified Candidate (R)	394,232	43.9

NORTH CAROLINA

	Candidates	Votes	%
1	Walter F. Pool (L)	14,213	51.0
	Louis C. Latham (D)	13,628	48.9
2	James E. O'Hara (R)	18,531	93.8
	Unidentified Candidate (D)	1,226	6.2
3	Wharton J. Green (D)	16,095	50.8
	William P. Canaday (L)	15,595	49.2
4	William R. Cox (D)	16,586	50.6
	Thomas P. Devereux (L)	16,174	49.4
5	Alfred M. Scales (D)	12,533	55.4
	John R. Winston (L)	9,932	43.9
6	Clement Dowd (D)	15,549	57.2
	William Johnston (L)	11,648	42.8
7	Tyre York (L)	11,415	48.6
	William M. Robbins (D)	11,159	47.5
8	Robert B. Vance (D)	13,000	56.4
	William M. Cooke Jr. (L)	10,038	43.6
AL	Risden T. Bennett (D)	111,763	50.1
	Oliver H. Dockery (L)	111,320	49.9

OHIO

	Candidates	Votes	%
1	John F. Follett (D)	14,540	51.4
	Benjamin Butterworth (R)	13,721	48.5
2	Isaac M. Jordan (D)	15,983	53.0
	Amor Smith (R)	14,166	47.0
3	Robert M. Murray (D)	16,106	49.6
	Emanuel Shultz (R)	15,826	48.8
4	Benjamin Le Fevre (D)	16,596	62.7
	Jacob S. Conklin (R)	9,683	36.6
5	George E. Seney (D)	16,619	59.0
	Lovell B. Harris (R)	11,006	39.1
6	William D. Hill (D)	16,201	49.7
	Joseph H. Brigham (R)	15,480	47.5
7	Henry L. Morey (R)	14,451‡	49.7
	James E. Campbell (D)	14,410	49.6
8	J. Warren Keifer (R)	14,397	50.2
	J. H. Young (D)	13,171	45.9
9	James S. Robinson (R)	15,864	48.8
	Thomas E. Powell (D)	15,458	47.5
10	Frank H. Hurd (D)	14,534	51.2
	Charles A. King (R)	13,430	47.3
11	John W. McCormick (R)	15,228	53.3
	John P. Leedom (D)	13,037	45.6
12	Alphonso Hart (R)	16,898	48.9
	Lawrence T. Neal (D)	16,888	48.9
13	George L. Converse (D)	17,766	54.2
	H. C. Drinkle (R)	14,092	43.0
14	George W. Geddes (D)	14,277	51.2
	Rollin A. Horr (R)	12,604	45.2
15	Adoniram J. Warner (D)	13,739	50.4
	Rufus R. Dawes (R)	13,048	47.9
16	Beriah Wilkins (D)	19,743	57.3
	A. B. Clark (R)	14,422	41.9
17	Jonathan T. Updegraff (R)	14,165*	50.4
	Ross J. Alexander (D)	13,265	47.2
18	William McKinley Jr. (R)	16,906‡	48.2
	Jonathan H. Wallace (D)	16,898	48.2

	Candidates	Votes	%
19	Ezra B. Taylor (R)	15,739	62.7
	David L. Rockwell (D)	7,708	30.7
20	David R. Paige (D)	14,090	47.9
	Addison B. McClure (R)	13,980	47.6
21	Martin A. Foran (D)	15,946	54.3
	Sylvester T. Everett (R)	11,408	38.9
	William H. Doan (P)	1,999	6.8

OREGON

	Candidates	Votes	%
AL	Melvin C. George (R)	22,517	54.0
	W. D. Fenton (D)	19,152	46.0

PENNSYLVANIA

	Candidates	Votes	%
1	Henry H. Bingham (R)	15,709	55.7
	John Cadwalader (D)	11,875	42.1
2	Charles O'Neill (R)	14,984	56.7
	W. Wurt Dundas (D)	11,440	43.3
3	Samuel J. Randall (D)	11,688	61.6
	W. M. Maull (R)	7,302	38.5
4	William D. Kelley (R)	21,896	61.3
	C. M. Swaim (D)	13,824	38.7
5	Alfred C. Harmer (R)	19,049	53.2
	T. J. Martin (D&I)	16,776	46.8
6	James B. Everhart (R)	14,615	59.1
	J. Edward Clyde (D)	9,810	39.7
7	I. Newton Evans (R)	15,732	51.0
	W. W. H. Davis (D)	15,102	49.0
8	Daniel Ermentrout (D)	15,623	64.2
	Isaac McHose (R)	8,466	34.8
9	A. Herr Smith (R)	16,425	62.8
	William B. Given (D)	9,740	37.2
10	William Mutchler (D)	19,867	63.1
	James S. Biery (R)	11,644	37.0
11	John B. Storm (D)	17,810	64.5
	H. C. Smith (R)	9,805	35.5
12	Daniel W. Connelly (D)	11,811	47.9
	Joseph A. Scranton (R)	10,822	43.9
	R. J. Flick (G LAB)	2,016	8.2
13	Charles N. Brumm (G LAB R)	10,773	51.5
	J. M. Wetherill (D)	10,149	48.5
14	Samuel F. Barr (R)	14,184	46.3
	Henry McCormick (D)	14,039	45.9
	John McLeery (IR)	1,870	6.1
15	George A. Post (D)	11,555	42.1
	C. C. Jadwin (IR)	9,101	33.1
	Edward Overton (R)	5,675	20.7
16	William W. Brown (R)	12,876	48.8
	H. W. Earley (D)	11,747	44.5
	J. Stickel (G LAB)	1,756	6.7
17	Jacob M. Campbell (R)	14,961	49.2
	Alex H. Coffroth (D)	14,410	47.4
18	Louis E. Atkinson (R)	14,779	50.6
	F. M. Kimmell (D)	14,049	48.1
19	William A. Duncan (D)	16,780	54.8
	William McSherry (ID)	13,603	44.4
20	Andrew G. Curtin (D)	16,515	59.3
	Samuel H. Orwig (R)	11,288	40.5
21	Charles E. Boyle (D)	16,033	55.6
	Charles S. Seaton (G LAB R)	12,709	44.1
22	James H. Hopkins (D)	12,420	47.5
	Russell Errett (R)	11,191	42.8
	James Campbell (G LAB)	2,345	9.0
23	Thomas M. Bayne (R)	11,734	83.7
	S. G. Barnes (G LAB)	1,882	13.4
24	George V. Lawrence (R)	11,674	50.4
	J. G. McConahy (D)	10,888	47.0
25	John D. Patton (D)	13,990	51.9
	Harry White (R)	12,990	48.2
26	Samuel H. Miller (R)	14,098	47.9
	J. H. Caldwell (D)	13,365	45.4
27	Samuel M. Brainerd (R)	11,170	45.8
	H. B. Plumer (D)	10,247	42.0
	W. T. Everson (G LAB&P)	2,992	12.3
AL	Mortimer Elliott (D)	352,855	47.5
	Marriott Brosius (R)	323,255	43.5
	William McMichael (IR)	40,995	5.5

RHODE ISLAND

	Candidates	Votes	%
1	Henry J. Spooner (R)	3,515	70.0
	Oscar Lapham (D)	1,491	29.7
2	Jonathan Chace (R)	3,349	64.6
	Wheeler (D)	1,831	35.3

SOUTH CAROLINA

	Candidates	Votes	%
1	Samuel Dibble (D)	8,674	56.9
	J. B. Campbell (IG&R)	6,565	43.1
2	George D. Tillman (D)	11,388	67.8
	E. M. Brayton (R)	5,361	31.9
3	D. Wyatt Aiken (D)	9,245	84.7
	T. H. Russell (G & R)	1,677	15.4
4	John H. Evins (D)	11,662	71.8
	D. R. Elkins (G)	4,588	28.2
5	John J. Hemphill (D)	9,518	56.0
	E. B. C. Cash (IG&R)	7,471	44.0
6	George W. Dargan (D)	10,814	64.7
	E. H. Deas (R)	3,628	21.7
	A. H. Bowen (G)	2,263	13.6
7	Edmund W. M. Mackey (R)	18,469	64.8
	Samuel Lee (IR)	10,017	35.2

TENNESSEE

	Candidates	Votes	%
1	Augustus H. Pettibone (R)	14,702	53.9
	Taylor (D)	12,571	46.1
2	Leonidas C. Houck (R)	14,535	62.2
	Rule (IR)	8,821	37.8
3	George G. Dibrell (D)	11,403	53.5
	Trewhitt (R)	9,698	45.5
4	Benton McMillin (D)	14,452	77.9
	Stokes (R)	4,106	22.1
5	Richard Warner (D)	10,911	54.4
	Tillman (STC D)	7,906	39.4
	Duggan (R)	1,247	6.2
6	Andrew J. Caldwell (D)	15,951	61.9
	Dillon (R)	8,856	34.4
7	John G. Ballentine (D)	12,635	63.0
	Perkins (ID)	7,432	37.0
8	John M. Taylor (D)	10,995	51.8
	Hawkins (R)	8,175	38.5
	Warren (G)	1,479	7.0
9	Rice A. Pierce (D)	12,812	61.1
	Lyle (R)	7,885	37.6
10	H. Casey Young (D)	10,696	51.1
	Smith (R)	9,837	47.0

TEXAS

	Candidates	Votes	%
1	Charles Stewart (D)	14,882	62.5
	William Chambers (R)	8,850	37.2
2	John H. Reagan (D)	12,035	82.6
3	James H. Jones (D)	14,045	57.9
	S. H. Russell (R)	9,492	39.1
4	David B. Culberson (D)	13,487	63.4
	E. L. Dehoney (G)	7,785	36.6
5	James W. Throckmorton (D)	16,163	72.0
	J. N. Dixon (G)	6,280	28.0
6	Olin Wellborn (D)	17,510	71.6
	J. C. Kearby (G)	6,949	28.4
7	Thomas P. Ochiltree (I)	12,457	55.8
	George P. Finlay (D)	9,851	44.1
8	James F. Miller (D)	12,297	59.0
	R. Zapp (G)	6,528	31.3
	Joseph O'Connor (I)	1,774	8.5
9	Roger Q. Mills (D)	14,730	63.9
	J. D. Rankin (G)	8,329	36.1
10	John Hancock (D)	16,098	62.2
	E. J. Davis (R)	9,783	37.8
11	Samuel W. T. Lanham (D)	10,493	51.0
	J. W. Barnett (G)	4,744	23.1
	J. H. Davenport (ID)	3,807	18.5
	S. C. Buck (ID)	1,532	7.4

VERMONT

	Candidates	Votes	%
1	John W. Stewart (R)	15,638	69.3
	Syman W. Redington (D)	6,009	26.6
2	Luke P. Poland (R)	12,795	51.8
	George S. Fletcher (D)	6,363	25.8
	William W. Grout (R)	4,598	18.6

VIRGINIA

	Candidates	Votes	%
1	Robert M. Mayo (READJ)	10,505‡	49.6
	George T. Garrison (D)	10,504	49.6
2	Harry Libbey (READJ)	13,226	49.7
	Richard C. Marshall (D)	10,282	38.6
	John F. Dezendorf (R)	3,114	11.7
3	George D. Wise (D)	10,736	57.1
	John Ambler Smith (READJ)	8,060	42.9
4	Benjamin S. Hooper (READ J)	14,764	75.5
	W. A. Reese (D)	4,552	23.3
5	George C. Cabell (D)	12,948	53.0
	William E. Sims (READJ)	11,489	47.0
6	John Randolph Tucker (D)	12,765	55.0
	J. Henry Rives (READ J)	10,362	44.6

	Candidates	Votes	%
7	John Paul (READJ)	12,146‡	50.2
	Charles T. O'Ferrall (D)	11,941	49.4
8	John S. Barbour (D)	14,256	60.6
	Richard R. Farr (READJ)	9,034	38.4
9	Henry Bowen (READJ)	10,073	57.7
	Abram Fulkerson (D)	5,603	32.1
	Samuel H. Newberry (I)	1,467	8.4
AL	John S. Wise (READJ)	99,992	50.4
	John E. Massey (D)	94,184	47.4

WEST VIRGINIA

	Candidates	Votes	%
1	Nathan Goff Jr. (R)	14,154	52.2
	John H. Good (D)	12,335	45.5
2	William L. Wilson (D)	11,406	48.5
	John W. Mason (R)	11,396	48.5
3	John E. Kenna (D)	10,279*	58.3
	E. S. Buttrick (R)	5,814	33.0
	P. B. Reynolds (G)	1,454	8.3
4	Eustace Gibson (D)	11,151	47.9
	George Loomis (R)	9,863	42.3
	A. R. Barber (G)	2,287	9.8

WISCONSIN

	Candidates	Votes	%
1	John Winans (D)	12,307	46.6
	C. G. Williams (R)	11,853	44.9
	C. M. Blackman (P)	2,217	8.4
2	Daniel H. Sumner (D)	10,671	50.4
	J. S. Rowell (R)	8,870	41.9
3	Burr W. Jones (D)	13,035	46.0
	G. C. Hazelton (R)	7,924	28.0
	E. W. Keyes (IR)	3,791	13.4
	S. D. Hastings (P)	3,152	11.1
4	Peter V. Deuster (D)	9,688	48.6
	F. C. Winckler (R)	8,320	41.7
	G. B. Goodwin (LAB)	1,922	9.6
5	Joseph Rankin (D)	12,933	62.7
	L. Howland (R)	6,108	29.6
6	Richard Guenther (R)	10,303	44.1
	A. Haben (D)	9,265	39.7
	T. D. Kanouse (P)	3,275	14.0
7	Gilbert M. Woodward (D)	11,908	48.1
	C. M. Butt (R)	10,604	42.8
	B. F. Parker (P)	1,887	7.6
8	William T. Price (R)	14,059	55.4
	W. F. Bailey (D)	11,315	44.6
9	Isaac Stephenson (R)	12,774	47.4
	G. L. Park (D)	12,518	46.4
	H. H. Woodmansec (P)	1,460	5.4

1883 House Elections

KANSAS

Special Election

	Candidates	Votes	%
2	Edward H. Funston (R)	24,116	57.4
	S. A. Riggs (D)	17,924	42.6

LOUISIANA

Special Election

	Candidates	Votes	%
6	Edward T. Lewis (D)	6,366	91.8
	Louis Trager (R)	568	8.2

OHIO[1]

Special Election

	Candidates	Votes	%
16	Joseph D. Taylor (R)	14,179	53.5
	Ross J. Alexander (D)	12,313	46.5
16	Joseph D. Taylor (R)	14,159	53.5
	Ross J. Alexander (D)	12,322	46.5

1. The first special election in the 16th district was held in January 1883 to fill the remaining two months of the term in the 47th Congress (1881–1883). The second special election was held in February 1883, to fill the House seat for a full term in the 48th Congress (1883–1885). Both elections were necessitated by the death of Rep. Jonathan T. Updegraff Nov. 30, 1882, following his reelection to the 48th Congress.

1884 House Elections

ALABAMA

	Candidates	Votes	%
1	James T. Jones (D)	8,871	58.1
	Thweatt (R)	6,403	41.9
2	Hilary A. Herbert (D)	11,331	55.8
	Whitehead (R)	8,991	44.2
3	William C. Oates (D)	10,965	71.6
	Mabson (R)	4,349	28.4
4	Alexander C. Davidson (D)	14,225	63.7
	Craig (R)	6,749	30.2
5	Thomas W. Sadler (D)	10,775	98.0
6	John M. Martin (D)	10,132	99.3
7	William H. Forney (D)	14,187	63.3
	Ewing (R)	8,217	36.7
8	Joseph Wheeler (D)	12,912	52.8
	Day (IR)	11,559	47.2

ARKANSAS

	Candidates	Votes	%
1	Poindexter Dunn (D)	15,002	61.7
	Remmel (R)	9,322	38.3
2	Clifton R. Breckinridge (D)	13,792	53.0
	Rogers (R)	12,229	47.0
3	James K. Jones (D)	16,193*	54.1
	Mitchell (R)	13,722	45.9
4	John H. Rogers (D)	15,174	57.3
	Sarber (R)	11,307	42.7
5	Samuel W. Peel (D)	11,542	69.1
	Keenor (R)	5,158	30.9

CALIFORNIA

	Candidates	Votes	%
1	Barclay Henley (D)	16,461	49.7
	T. L. Carothers (R)	16,316	49.3
2	James A. Louttit (R)	18,327	49.4
	Charles A. Sumner (D)	18,208	49.1
3	Joseph McKenna (R)	17,435	55.8
	J. A. Glascock (D)	13,197	42.3
4	William W. Morrow (R)	15,083	58.7
	R. P. Hastings (D)	10,422	40.6
5	Charles N. Felton (R)	17,014	51.6
	F. J. Sullivan (D)	15,676	47.6
6	Henry H. Markham (R)	17,397	49.1
	A. F. Devalle (D)	16,988	47.9

COLORADO

	Candidates	Votes	%
AL	George G. Symes (R)	35,446	53.2
	Charles S. Thomas (D)	28,720	43.1

CONNECTICUT

	Candidates	Votes	%
1	John R. Buck (R)	16,589	49.7
	William W. Eaton (D)	16,285	48.8
2	Charles L. Mitchell (D)	22,589	50.8
	Allen (R)	20,573	46.3
3	John T. Wait (R)	11,700	54.4
	Johnson (D)	9,258	43.1
4	Edward W. Seymour (D)	18,526	49.0
	Coe (R)	18,373	48.6

DELAWARE

	Candidates	Votes	%
AL	Charles B. Lore (D)	17,054	56.7
	Anthony Higgins (R)	12,978	43.2

FLORIDA

	Candidates	Votes	%
1	Robert H. M. Davidson (D)	14,619	55.1
	Locke (R)	11,893	44.9
2	Charles Dougherty (D)	17,248	51.8
	Bisbee (R)	15,857	47.6

GEORGIA

	Candidates	Votes	%
1	Thomas M. Norwood (D)	10,857	64.4
	Pleasant (R)	6,012	35.6
2	Henry G. Turner (R)	7,828	100.0
3	Charles F. Crisp (D)	9,963	69.6
	Bell (R)	4,268	29.8
4	Henry R. Harris (D)	10,608	52.4
	Henry Person (ID)	5,473	27.0
	Milner (R)	4,156	20.5
5	Nathaniel J. Hammond (D)	9,008	63.7
	Martin (R)	5,130	36.3
6	James H. Blount (R)	7,922	100.0
7	Judson C. Clements (D)	10,496	71.1
	Kirkwood (R)	3,417	23.1
8	Seaborn Reese (D)	7,834	70.4
	Martin (R)	3,250	29.2
9	Allen D. Candler (D)	8,137	100.0
10	George T. Barnes (D)	9,166	86.2
	Wright (R)	1,277	12.0

ILLINOIS

	Candidates	Votes	%
1	Ransom W. Dunham (R)	20,245	56.7
	William M. Tilden (D)	14,655	41.1
2	Francis Lawler (D)	13,954	54.7
	John F. Finnerty (R&A-MONO)	11,552	45.3
3	James H. Ward (D)	15,601	43.5
	William E. Mason (R)	10,806	30.1
	Charles Fitzsimmons (R)	8,928	24.9
4	George E. Adams (R)	18,333	53.8
	John P. Altgeld (D)	15,291	44.9
5	Reuben Ellwood (R & P)	20,500	68.4
	Richard Bishop (D)	9,424	31.5
6	Robert R. Hitt (R)	18,048	61.5
	E. W. Blaisdell (D)	10,891	37.1
7	Thomas J. Henderson (R)	15,498	57.6
	James S. Eckels (D)	10,689	39.7
8	Ralph Plumb (R)	18,707	51.8
	Pat C. Haley (D)	15,953	44.2
9	Lewis E. Payson (R)	16,481	53.4
	James Kirk (D)	13,716	44.5
10	Nicholas E. Worthington (D)	16,758	50.1
	Julius S. Starr (R)	16,582	49.6
11	William H. Nesce (A-MON D)	18,291	50.1
	Alexander P. Petrie (R)	17,864	48.9
12	James M. Riggs (D)	22,046	57.7
	Thomas G. Black (R)	15,177	39.7
13	William M. Springer (D)	20,808	53.1
	James M. Taylor (R)	16,971	43.3
14	Jonathan H. Rowell (R)	18,052	51.4
	C. C. Clark (D)	15,673	44.6
15	Joseph G. Cannon (R)	17,852	50.2
	John C. Black (D)	17,360	48.8
16	Silas Z. Landes (D)	17,109	50.2
	James McCartney (R)	16,791	49.2
17	John R. Eden (D)	18,402	55.0
	Howland J. Hamlin (G & R)	14,576	43.5
18	William R. Morrison (D)	17,695	53.2
	Thomas B. Needles (R)	15,136	45.5
19	Richard W. Townshend (D)	18,296	56.7
	Thomas S. Ridgway (R)	13,615	42.2
20	John R. Thomas (R)	17,890	52.1
	Fountain E. Albright (D)	15,788	45.9

INDIANA

	Candidates	Votes	%
1	John J. Kleiner (D)	19,930	51.5
	William H. Gudgel (R)	18,493	47.8
2	Thomas R. Cobb (D)	18,832	55.5
	George H. Reilley (R)	15,128	44.6
3	Jonas G. Howard (D)	19,550	56.3
	James Keigwin (R)	14,923	43.0
4	William S. Holman (D)	17,233	52.6
	John O. Cravens (R)	15,494	47.2
5	Courtland C. Matson (D)	17,951	51.3
	George W. Grubbs (R)	16,582	47.4
6	Thomas M. Browne (R)	22,115	61.1
	Nelson G. Smith (D)	13,625	37.7
7	William D. Bynum (D)	20,240	51.0
	Stanton J. Peelle (R)	18,995	47.9
8	James C. Johnston (R)	20,185	50.0
	John Edward Lamb (D)	20,035	49.6
9	Thomas B. Ward (D)	19,241	49.7
	Charles T. Doxey (R)	18,628	48.1
10	William D. Owen (R)	19,262	50.0
	Thomas J. Wood (D)	18,781	48.8
11	George W. Steele (R)	22,679	48.7
	Meredith H. Kidd (D)	22,625	48.6
12	Robert Lowry (D)	19,507	52.5
	T. P. Keator (R)	16,957	45.7
13	George Ford (D)	20,971	52.7
	Henry Thayer (R)	18,792	47.3

Special Election

	Candidates	Votes	%
13	Benjamin Franklin Shively (N)	20,964	52.8
	John Reynolds (R)	18,736	47.2

IOWA

	Candidates	Votes	%
1	Benton Jay Hall (D)	16,734	50.0
	John S. Woolson (R)	16,661	49.7
2	Jeremiah Henry Murphy (D)	19,730	56.4
	William T. Shaw (R)	15,241	43.6
3	David B. Henderson (R)	16,431	52.1
	John J. Linehan (D)	15,105	47.9
4	William Elijah Fuller (R)	15,082	50.4
	Luman Hamlin Weller (G & D)	14,852	49.6
5	Benjamin Todd Frederick (D)	16,679	50.2
	Milo P. Smith (R)	16,541	49.7
6	James Baird Weaver (G & D)	16,684	50.1
	Frank T. Campbell (R)	16,617	49.9
7	Edwin H. Conger (R)	19,274	54.8
	W. H. McHenry (D)	15,924	45.2
8	William P. Hepburn (R)	17,671	53.6
	S. R. Davis (D)	15,294	46.4
9	Joseph H. Lyman (R)	19,071	50.7
	William H. M. Pusey (D)	18,509	49.2
10	Adoniram J. Holmes (R)	20,328	62.7
	H. C. McCoy (D)	12,117	37.3
11	Isaac S. Struble (R)	24,063	58.4
	Thomas F. Barbee (D)	17,107	41.6

Special Election

	Candidates	Votes	%
7	Hiram Ypsilanti Smith (R)	18,905	53.9
	E. H. Kridler (D)	16,151	46.1

KANSAS

	Candidates	Votes	%
1	Edmund N. Morrill (R)	19,535	55.1
	Thomas P. Fenlon (D)	15,934	44.9
2	Edward H. Funston (R)	22,518	60.4
	W. J. Nicholson (D)	14,703	39.4
3	Bishop W. Perkins (R)	23,854	56.3
	G. W. Gabriel (D)	13,341	31.5
	W. A. Tipton (G LAB)	5,163	12.2
4	Thomas Ryan (R)	26,177	61.9
	S. N. Wood (D)	15,799	37.4
5	John A. Anderson (R)	22,548	64.1
	A. A. Carnahan (D)	10,866	30.9
	M.D. Tenney (G LAB)	1,784	5.1
6	Lewis Hanback (R)	14,776	59.5
	L. C. Uhl (D)	10,068	40.5
7	Samuel R. Peters (R)	25,740	61.0
	H. M. Bickel (D)	15,913	37.7

KENTUCKY

	Candidates	Votes	%
1	William J. Stone (D)	10,503	41.8
	Oscar Turner (ID)	7,440	29.6
	H. H. Houston (R)	7,161	28.5
2	Polk Laffoon (D)	12,472	56.8
	T. Z. Moore (R)	9,485	43.2
3	John E. Halsell (D)	12,833	55.3
	J. S. Golladay (R)	10,376	44.7
4	Thomas A. Robertson (D)	12,153	100.0
5	Albert S. Willis (D)	12,152	59.0
	A. E. Wilson (R)	8,373	40.7
6	John G. Carlisle (D)	15,261	60.6
	J. J. Landrum (R)	9,329	37.1
7	William C. P. Breckinridge (D)	16,236	93.2
	D. W. Lindsey (R)	1,173	6.7
8	James B. McCreary (D)	14,924	53.9
	J. M. Sebastian (R)	12,778	46.1
9	William H. Wadsworth (R)	16,189	50.2
	Frank Powers (D)	16,087	49.8
10	William P. Taulbee (D)	14,266	53.7
	A. J. Auxier (R)	12,308	46.3
11	Frank L. Wolford (D)	10,748	52.0
	W. W. Jones (R)	9,932	48.0

LOUISIANA

	Candidates	Votes	%
1	Louis St. Martin (D)	5,685	41.9
	Carleton Hunt (ID)	4,458	32.9
	J. A. Acklin (R)	3,411	25.2
2	Michael Hahn (R)	7,356	54.7
	W. T. Houston (D)	6,103	45.4
3	Edward J. Gay (D)	15,302	51.2
	William Pitt Kellogg (R)	14,603	48.8
4	Newton C. Blanchard (D)	12,269	89.9
	J. B. Slattery (R)	1,377	10.1
5	J. Floyd King (D)	11,692	59.1
	Charles J. Boatner (ID)	5,513	27.9
	Frank Morey (R)	2,565	13.0
6	Alfred B. Irion (D)	9,927	61.6
	C. C. Swayzie (R)	6,197	38.4

MAINE

	Candidates	Votes	%
1	Thomas B. Reed (R)	17,594	51.0
	N. Cleaves (D)	16,669	48.3
2	Nelson Dingley Jr. (R)	20,795	55.1
	D. R. Hastings (D)	15,006	39.8
3	Seth L. Milliken (R)	20,083	57.9
	Daniel H. Thing (D)	13,866	40.0
4	Charles A. Boutelle (R)	19,643	56.1
	John F. Lynch (D)	14,165	40.5

MARYLAND

	Candidates	Votes	%
1	Charles H. Gibson (D)	16,726	53.3
	Russum (R)	14,641	46.7
2	Frank T. Shaw (D)	16,274	53.8
	Blair (R)	14,003	46.3
3	William H. Cole (D)	16,032	58.6
	Pentz (R)	10,756	39.3
4	John V. L. Findlay (D)	15,726	51.2
	Brown (R)	14,324	46.7
5	Barnes Compton (D)	15,612	51.6
	Holton (R)	14,641	48.4
6	Louis E. McComas (R)	17,995	52.3
	Nelson (D)	16,379	47.6

MASSACHUSETTS

	Candidates	Votes	%
1	Robert T. Davis (R)	14,080	66.5
	Weston Howland (D)	5,307	25.1
2	John D. Long (R)	15,039	53.0
	William Everett (D)	9,734	34.3
	Edgar E. Dean (G)	2,630	9.3
3	Ambrose A. Ranney (R)	13,596	53.0
	Horatio Swasey (D)	9,248	36.1
	Eleazar B. Loring (G)	2,412	9.4
4	Patrick A. Collins (D)	13,664	64.8
	Joseph H. O'Neill (R)	7,182	34.1
5	Edward D. Hayden (R)	13,290	52.0
	Robert Trete Paine Jr. (D)	11,018	43.1
6	Henry B. Lovering (D & G)	15,146	49.6
	Henry Cabot Lodge (R)	14,881	48.7
7	Eben F. Stone (R)	12,475	47.8
	Richard S. Spofford (D)	9,623	36.9
	John Baker (G)	3,948	15.1
8	Charles H. Allen (R)	12,643	53.6
	Charles S. Lilley (D)	9,446	40.1
9	Frederick D. Ely (R)	12,265	47.4
	Henry E. Fales (D)	6,301	24.4
	Theodore Lyman (I)	4,265	16.5
	Henry E. Lemon Jr. (G)	2,429	9.4
10	William W. Rice (R)	13,940	58.8
	James E. Esterbrook (D)	6,556	27.6
	Unidentified Candidate (G)	2,637	11.1
11	William Whiting (R)	15,335	59.9
	David Hill (D)	8,693	34.0
12	Francis W. Rockwell (R)	13,012	51.7
	Jarvis N. Dunham (D)	10,856	43.1

MICHIGAN

	Candidates	Votes	%
1	William C. Maybury (D)	21,673	55.8
	John Atkinson (R)	15,549	40.0
2	Nathaniel B. Eldredge (D & G)	17,710	46.9
	Edward P. Allen (R)	17,656	46.7
	Charles Mosher (P)	2,420	6.4
3	James O'Donnell (R)	20,438	48.5
	Henry F. Pennington (D & G)	19,210	45.5
	Michael J. Fanning (P)	2,531	6.0
4	Julius C. Burrows (R)	18,564	48.8
	George L. Yaple (D & G)	18,212	47.9
5	Charles C. Comstock (D & G)	20,406	47.6
	John C. Fitzgerald (R)	20,050	46.7
	Wilson C. Edsell (P)	2,449	5.7
6	Edwin B. Winans (D & G)	19,857	48.8
	James C. Willson (R)	18,377	45.2
	Leander C. Smith (P)	2,445	6.0
7	Ezra C. Carlton (D)	14,535	50.2
	Edgar Weeks (R)	12,316	42.5
8	Timothy E. Tarsney (D)	19,446	50.6
	Roswell G. Horr (R)	17,824	46.4
9	Byron M. Cutcheon (R)	18,963	51.4
	Silas S. Fallas (D & G)	16,207	44.0
10	Spencer O. Fisher (D & G)	15,366	52.4
	Charles F. Gibson (R)	13,081	44.6
11	Seth C. Moffatt (R)	16,464	64.7
	John Powers (D)	8,992	35.3

MINNESOTA

	Candidates	Votes	%
1	Milo White (R)	16,604	53.3
	A. Bierman (D)	13,961	44.8
2	James B. Wakefield (R)	20,813	64.0
	J. J. Thornton (D)	10,639	32.7
3	Horace B. Strait (R)	16,456	51.3
	I. Donnelly (D)	15,038	46.9
4	John B. Gilfillan (R)	28,930	53.2
	O. C. Merriman (D)	24,496	45.0
5	Knute Nelson (R)	25,609	66.0
	L. L. Baxter (D)	13,176	34.0

MISSISSIPPI

	Candidates	Votes	%
1	John M. Allen (D)	11,862	81.7
	Chandler (R)	2,657	18.3
2	James B. Morgan (D)	13,963	57.5
	Chalmers (R)	10,008	41.2
3	Thomas C. Catchings (D)	9,783	69.5
	Pearce (R)	4,297	30.5
4	Frederick G. Barry (D)	13,200	69.8
	Frazee (R)	5,723	30.2
5	Otho R. Singleton (D)	11,934	76.5
	Smith (R)	3,665	23.5
6	Henry S. Van Eaton (D)	10,190	60.8
	Lynch (R)	6,570	39.2
7	Ethelbert Barksdale (D)	10,946	66.6
	Yellowley (R)	5,485	33.4

MISSOURI

	Candidates	Votes	%
1	William H. Hatch (D)	18,932	54.3
	Gray (FUS)	15,955	45.7
2	John B. Hale (D)	20,204	56.2
	Norville (FUS)	15,749	43.8
3	Alexander M. Dockery (D)	19,129	53.4
	Harwood (R)	15,854	44.2
4	James N. Burnes (D)	16,397	55.5
	Kelly (FUS)	13,141	44.5
5	William Warner (FUS)	16,176	52.5
	Graves (R)	14,651	47.5
6	John T. Heard (D)	21,107	56.7
	Shirk (FUS)	16,139	43.3
7	John E. Hutton (D)	16,712	52.8
	Reynolds (FUS)	14,946	47.2
8	John J. O'Neill (D)	9,657	54.7
	Eccles (R)	8,006	45.3
9	John M. Glover (D)	9,830	54.7
	McLean (FU)	8,133	45.3
10	Martin L. Clardy (D)	15,329	52.8
	Morse (FUS)	12,797	44.1
11	Richard P. Bland (D)	16,959	54.3
	Dallmyer (FUS)	14,288	45.7
12	William J. Stone (D)	20,091	55.3
	Warden (FUS)	16,222	44.7
13	William H. Wade (FUS)	20,101	50.3
	Thomas (D)	17,981	45.0
14	William Dawson (D)	17,694	61.6
	Cramer (FUS)	11,020	38.4

NEBRASKA

	Candidates	Votes	%
1	Archibald J. Weaver (R)	22,644	50.0
	Charles H. Brown (D)	21,669	47.8
2	James Laird (R)	21,182	52.9
	J. H. Stickel (D)	17,650	44.1
3	George W. E. Dorsey (R)	25,685	54.7
	William Neville (D)	20,671	44.1

NEVADA

	Candidates	Votes	%
AL	William Woodburn (R)	6,797	53.1
	George W. Cassidy (D)	6,002	46.9

NEW HAMPSHIRE

	Candidates	Votes	%
1	Martin A. Haynes (R)	20,623	51.8
	McKinney (D)	18,383	46.2
2	Jacob H. Gallinger (R)	22,801	51.5
	George (D)	20,426	46.1

NEW JERSEY

	Candidates	Votes	%
1	George Hires (R)	19,745	50.0
	Ferrell (D)	18,003	45.6
2	James Buchanan (R)	19,144	51.5
	Gauntt (D)	16,853	45.4
3	Robert S. Green (D)	19,604	50.8
	John Kean Jr. (R)	17,756	46.0
4	James N. Pidcock (D)	15,225	51.3
	Howey (R)	12,972	43.7
5	William W. Phelps (R)	17,367	51.7
	Stevenson (D)	15,126	45.0
6	Herman Lehlbach (R)	21,162	49.4
	Fiedler (D)	20,818	48.6
7	William McAdoo (D)	21,985	56.7
	Brigham (R)	16,654	43.0

NEW YORK

	Candidates	Votes	%
1	Perry Belmont (D)	22,050	54.9
	Platt (R)	18,104	45.1
2	Felix Campbell (D)	17,503	58.5
	Sheridan (R)	11,771	39.4

Candidates	Votes	%
3 Darwin R. James (R)	20,125	60.5
Smith (D)	13,000	39.1
4 Peter P. Mahoney (D)	18,971	57.8
Mullholland (R)	13,339	40.7
5 Archibald M. Bliss (D)	13,985	50.1
Worth (R)	12,865	46.1
6 Nicholas Muller (D)	13,307	56.9
House (R)	6,796	29.1
Fitzgerald (ID)	2,863	12.2
7 John J. Adams (D)	15,864	65.3
Conkling (R)	8,228	33.9
8 Samuel S. Cox (TAM D)	19,386	80.7
Hall (CO D)	4,483	18.7
9 Joseph Pulitzer (D)	15,518	63.6
Thum (R)	8,497	34.8
10 Abram S. Hewitt (D)	15,254	64.1
Biglin (R)	8,392	35.3
11 Truman A. Merriman (CO D)	19,588	62.4
Hardy (TAM D)	11,563	36.8
12 Abraham Dowdney (D)	18,380	61.3
Perley (R)	11,354	37.8
13 Egbert L. Viele (D)	17,622	60.6
Smith (R)	11,027	37.9
14 William G. Stahlnecker (D)	17,507	51.9
McAlpin (R)	15,745	46.7
15 Lewis Beach (D)	17,728	51.7
Snow (R)	15,794	46.0
16 John H. Ketcham (R)	18,942	54.1
Huntington (D)	15,391	43.9
17 James G. Lindsley (R)	20,557	50.9
Bagley (D)	18,671	46.2
18 Henry G. Burleigh (R)	20,732	88.0
McClellan (P)	2,775	11.8
19 John Swinburne (R)	19,790	53.0
Van Alstyne (D)	17,286	46.3
20 George West (R)	21,174	51.2
Wemple (D)	19,467	47.0
21 Frederick A. Johnson (R)	19,049	58.6
Smith (D)	13,462	41.4
22 Abraham X. Parker (R)	22,541	62.1
Hall (D)	12,920	35.6
23 John T. Spriggs (D)	18,164	49.9
Cookingham (R)	17,327	47.6
24 John S. Pindar (D)	17,884	50.5
Ramsey (R)	16,772	47.4
25 Frank Hiscock (R)	21,148	56.4
W. Porter (D, P)	16,326	43.5
26 Stephen C. Millard (R)	23,773	51.9
Remick (D)	18,783	42.6
27 Sereno E. Payne (R)	26,446	57.1
Beardsley (D)	17,798	38.4
28 John Arnot Jr. (D-R)	28,000	91.0
Beecher (G)	2,044	6.6
29 Ira Davenport (R)	19,987	52.5
Pierpont (D)	16,377	43.0
30 Charles S. Baker (R)	16,733	50.2
Greenleaf (D)	15,496	46.5
31 John G. Sawyer (R)	17,529	51.4
Stevens (D)	14,474	42.4
Richmond (P)	1,869	5.5
32 John M. Farquhar (R)	17,469	50.0
Lockwood (D)	17,302	49.5
33 John B. Weber (R)	14,545	49.1
Payne (D)	13,957	47.2
34 Walter L. Sessions (R)	24,068	54.7
Smith (D)	15,525	35.3
Sill (P)	2,522	5.7

NORTH CAROLINA

Candidates	Votes	%
1 Thomas G. Skinner (D)	16,381	53.8
John B. Respess (R)	14,093	46.3
2 James E. O'Hara (R)	22,309	58.7
Frederick A. Woodward (D)	15,699	41.3
3 Wharton J. Green (D)	16,785	57.8
Curtis H. Brogden (R)	12,156	41.9
4 William R. Cox (D)	18,930	58.5
Josiah Turner (R)	13,448	41.5
5 James W. Reid (D)	15,047	54.6
Leonidas C. Edwards (R)	12,522	45.4

Candidates	Votes	%
6 Risden T. Bennett (D)	19,344	58.0
Oliver H. Dockery (R)	14,010	42.0
7 John S. Henderson (D)	14,262	56.8
James G. Ramsey (R)	10,851	43.2
8 William H. H. Cowles (D)	11,422	58.7
Leander L. Green (R)	8,036	41.3
9 Thomas D. Johnston (D)	13,024	53.2
Hamilton G. Ewart (R)	11,465	46.8

OHIO

Candidates	Votes	%
1 Benjamin Butterworth (R)	17,929	52.1
John F. Follett (D)	16,320	47.4
2 Charles E. Brown (R)	19,718	52.8
Adam A. Kramer (D)	17,513	46.9
3 James E. Campbell (D)	16,398	50.3
Henry L. Morey (R)	15,986	49.0
4 Charles M. Anderson (D)	21,087	50.0
John F. Sinks (R)	20,786	49.3
5 Benjamin Le Fevre (D)	21,968	56.3
William D. Davis (R)	16,852	43.2
6 William D. Hill (D)	20,684	54.1
Hiram C. Glenn (R)	17,154	44.9
7 George E. Seney (D)	20,615	54.5
Daniel Babst Jr. (R)	16,609	43.9
8 John Little (R)	23,019	58.5
James W. Denver (D)	15,381	39.1
9 William C. Cooper (R)	18,415	51.1
E. F. Poppieton (D)	16,634	46.2
10 Jacob Romeis (R)	17,605	50.0
Frank H. Hurd (D)	17,366	49.4
11 William W. Ellsberry (D)	15,251	50.7
Alphonzo Hart (R)	14,841	49.3
12 Albert C. Thompson (R)	15,782	53.8
Leo Ebert (D)	13,384	45.7
13 Joseph H. Outhwaite (D)	23,475	55.2
Allen Miller (R)	18,607	43.8
14 Charles H. Grosvenor (R)	17,008	56.0
John L. Vance (D)	11,281	37.2
Christopher Evans (G)	1,689	5.6
15 Beriah Wilkins (D)	20,717	54.1
Elijah Little (R)	17,421	45.5
16 George W. Geddes (D)	18,528	50.0
Henry C. Hedges (R)	17,835	48.2
17 Adoniram J. Warner (D)	19,173	49.9
Joseph D. Taylor (R)	18,957	49.3
18 Isaac H. Taylor (R)	22,459	56.3
Jonathan H. Wallace (D)	16,309	40.9
19 Ezra B. Taylor (R)	27,039	65.0
Horace Alvord (D)	13,053	31.4
20 William McKinley Jr. (R)	22,672	51.6
David R. Paige (D)	20,643	47.0
21 Martin A. Foran (D & G)	19,154	51.4
Charles C. Burnett (R)	17,884	48.0

OREGON

Candidates	Votes	%
AL Binger Herman (R)	25,699	52.1
John Myers (D)	23,652	47.9

PENNSYLVANIA

Candidates	Votes	%
1 Henry H. Bingham (R)	20,227	60.2
Tipton (D)	13,403	39.9
2 Charles O'Neill (R)	18,336	60.5
Dotts (D)	11,952	39.5
3 Samuel J. Randall (D)	12,340	57.7
Gumper (R)	9,055	42.3
4 William D. Kelley (R)	27,421	63.3
Fahy (D)	15,817	36.5
5 Alfred C. Harmar (R)	26,618	99.9
6 James B. Everhart (R)	18,593	60.5
Heckel (D)	11,551	37.6
7 I. Newton Evans (R)	18,048	52.4
Ross (D)	16,425	47.7
8 Daniel Ermentrout (D)	16,577	63.8
Richards (R)	9,405	36.2
9 John A. Hiestand (R)	19,649	65.6
Haldeman (D)	9,894	33.0
10 William H. Sowden (D)	20,797	59.2

Candidates	Votes	%
Chidsey (D)	14,349	40.8
11 John B. Storm (D)	19,394	60.4
Walter (R)	12,622	39.3
12 Joseph A. Scranton (R)	17,016	51.3
Connolly (D)	15,179	45.7
13 Charles N. Brumm (R)	12,875	52.4
Reilly (D)	11,677	47.6
14 Franklin Bound (R)	20,767	57.7
Foster (D)	15,256	42.4
15 Frank C. Bunnell (R)	17,006	54.4
Post (D)	12,679	40.6
16 William W. Brown (R)	19,400	53.3
Kennedy (D)	16,440	45.2
17 Jacob M. Campbell (R)	19,579	54.3
Enfield (D)	16,005	44.4
18 Louis E. Atkinson (R)	18,367	54.6
Patterson (D)	15,277	45.4
19 William A. Duncan (D)	20,356*	55.9
Seitz (R)	16,094	44.2
20 Andrew G. Curtin (D)	17,656	51.4
Patton (R)	16,419	47.8
21 Charles E. Boyle (D)	19,506	52.8
Ray (R)	17,006	46.0
22 James S. Negley (R)	20,136	56.7
Hopkins (D)	15,113	42.5
23 Thomas M. Bayne (R)	15,854	64.9
Foster (D)	8,073	33.0
24 Oscar L. Jackson (R)	16,436	57.0
Stockdale (D)	11,538	40.0
25 Alexander C. White (R)	16,714	52.8
Reitz (D)	14,929	47.2
26 George W. Fleeger (R)	17,290	47.0
McKinney (D)	15,674	42.6
Roberts (IR)	2,702	7.4
27 William L. Scott (R)	16,002	49.2
Mackey (R)	15,340	47.1
AL Edwin S. Osborne (R)	478,240	53.2
Davis (D)	401,042	44.6

Special Election

	Candidates	Votes	%
19	John Augustus Swope (D)	✓	#

RHODE ISLAND

Candidates	Votes	%
1 Henry J. Spooner (R)	10,140	60.0
Tiba O. Slocum (D)	5,976	35.4
2 William A. Pirce (R)	7,752‡	50.1
Charles H. Page (D)	5,995	38.7
Alfred B. Chadsey (P)	1,501	9.7

SOUTH CAROLINA

Candidates	Votes	%
1 Samuel Dibble (D)	8,612	73.5
W. N. Taft (R)	3,108	26.5
2 George D. Tillman (D)	11,419	85.6
E. J. Dickersin (R)	1,920	14.4
3 D. Wyatt Aiken (D)	10,855	93.5
John R. Tolbert (R)	752	6.5
4 William H. Perry (D)	13,008	100.0
5 John J. Hemphill (D)	9,861	77.4
C. C. Macey (R)	2,881	22.6
6 George W. Dargan (D)	10,465	76.1
Edmund H. Deas (R)	3,289	23.9
7 Robert Smalls (R)	8,419	64.8
William Elliott (D)	4,584	35.3

Special Election

	Candidates	Votes	%
4	John Bratton (D)	3,339✓	#

TENNESSEE

Candidates	Votes	%
1 Augustus H. Pettibone (R)	15,478	54.4
King (D)	12,981	45.6
2 Leonidas C. Houk (R)	19,357	68.3
Ledgerwood (D)	8,975	31.7
3 John R. Neal (D)	14,284	51.2
Evans (R)	13,624	48.8
4 Benton McMillin (D)	12,956	88.0

	Candidates	Votes	%
	Smith (R)	1,771	12.0
5	James D. Richardson (D)	13,285	58.5
	Warder (R)	7,144	31.4
	Martin (ID)	1,882	8.3
6	Andrew J. Caldwell (D)	16,873	58.2
	Baker (R)	12,124	41.8
7	John G. Ballentine (D)	12,157	55.7
	Cliff (R)	9,682	44.3
8	John M. Taylor (D)	12,783	52.6
	Warren (R)	11,529	47.4
9	Presley T. Glass (D)	13,451	55.0
	Etheridge (R)	11,019	45.0
10	Zachary Taylor (R)	14,271	51.0
	Harris (D)	13,713	49.0

TEXAS

	Candidates	Votes	%
1	Charles Stewart (D)	24,150	99.9
2	John H. Reagan (D)	16,840	67.1
	A. T. Monroe (R)	8,276	33.0
3	James H. Jones (D)	23,504	97.2
4	David B. Culberson (D)	23,165	100.0
5	James W. Throckmorton (D)	29,462	98.9
6	Olin Wellborn (D)	27,804	85.5
	J. C. Bigger (R)	4,721	14.5
7	William H. Crain (D)	15,471	59.2
	R. B. Rentfro (R)	9,586	36.7
8	James F. Miller (D)	17,143	66.9
	W. P. Burns (R)	8,473	33.1
9	Roger Q. Mills (D)	22,333	71.2
	J. P. Osterhout (R)	9,049	28.8
10	Joseph D. Sayers (D)	21,523	63.7
	J. B. Rector (IR)	12,253	36.3
11	Samuel W. T. Lanham (D)	29,738	99.4

VERMONT

	Candidates	Votes	%
1	John W. Stewart (R)	18,899	73.5
	George H. Simmons (D)	6,591	25.6
2	William W. Grout (R)	20,026	69.6
	Martin H. Goddard (D)	8,479	29.5

VIRGINIA

		Votes	%
1	Thomas Croxton (D)	14,136	51.0
	R. M. Mayo (R)	13,579	49.0
2	Harry Libby (R)	19,083	58.3
	R. C. Marshall (D)	13,652	41.7
3	George D. Wise (D)	15,741	52.4
	Robert T. Hubard (R)	14,301	47.6
4	James D. Brady (R)	11,408	40.5
	George E. Rives (D)	10,326	36.6
	Joseph P. Evans (IR)	6,451	22.9
5	George C. Cabell (D)	13,588	55.0
	J. W. Hartwell (R)	11,100	45.0
6	John W. Daniel (D)	17,177	55.9
	R. P. W. Morris (R)	13,526	44.1
7	Charles T. O'Ferrall (D)	15,791	56.4
	J. B. Webb (R)	12,221	43.6
8	John S. Barbour (D)	15,792	55.6
	Duff Green (R)	12,598	44.4
9	Connally F. Trigg (D)	13,844	52.2
	Daniel F. Bailey (R)	12,660	47.8
10	John R. Tucker (D)	15,059	52.1
	Jacob Yost (R)	13,872	48.0

WEST VIRGINIA

		Votes	%
1	Nathan Goff Jr. (R)	17,462	50.3
	John Brannon (D)	17,258	49.7

	Candidates	Votes	%
2	William L. Wilson (D)	18,266	52.2
	Francis M. Reynolds (R)	16,737	47.8
3	Charles P. Snyder (D)	15,359	53.7
	James W. Davis (R)	13,240	46.3
4	Eustace Gibson (D)	16,598	50.2
	A. R. Barbee (G & R)	16,445	49.8

WISCONSIN

	Candidates	Votes	%
1	Lucien B. Caswell (R)	19,284	54.6
	Ernst Merton (D)	14,590	41.3
2	Edward S. Bragg (D)	16,865	55.4
	Samuel S. Barney (R)	12,643	41.6
3	Robert M. LaFollette (R)	17,433	48.1
	Burr W. Jones (D)	16,942	46.7
	John M. Olin (P)	1,885	5.2
4	Isaac W. Van Schaick (R)	16,783	49.1
	P. V. Deuster (D)	15,907	46.5
5	Joseph Rankin (D)	17,851	59.3
	Charles Luling (R)	11,610	38.5
6	Richard W. Guenther (R)	16,425	49.9
	A. L. Smith (D)	15,197	46.2
7	Ormsby B. Thomas (R)	18,437	52.6
	G. M. Woodward (D)	15,446	44.1
8	William T. Price (R & P)	24,460	60.2
	L. R. Larson (D)	16,183	39.8
9	Isaac Stephenson (R)	23,414	53.5
	James Meehan (D)	19,885	45.4

1885 House Elections

ILLINOIS

Special Election

	Candidates	Votes	%
5	Albert J. Hopkins (R)	8,977	73.3
	Richard Bishop (D)	3,211	26.2

NORTH CAROLINA

Special Election

	Candidates	Votes	%
5	James W. Reid (D)	4,707	90.5
	Joseph S. Worth (R)	356	6.8

RHODE ISLAND

Special Election

	Candidates	Votes	%
2	Nathan F. Dixon (R)	2,258	69.3
	Philip W. Hawkins (D)	998	30.6

1886 House Elections

ALABAMA

	Candidates	Votes	%
1	James T. Jones (D)	4,220	99.6
2	Hilary A. Herbert (D)	5,659	100.0
3	William C. Oates (D)	4,660	100.0
4	Alexander C. Davidson (D)	14,913	71.2
	McDuffie (R)	3,526	16.8
	Turner (IR)	2,519	12.0
5	James E. Cobb (D)	5,558	87.8
	Edwards (R)	775	12.2
6	John H. Bankhead (D)	7,968	64.6
	Long (R)	4,369	35.4
7	William H. Forney (D)	7,549	62.0
	Hardie (R)	4,608	37.8
8	Joseph Wheeler (D)	11,684	57.5
	Jackson (R)	8,639	42.5

ARKANSAS

	Candidates	Votes	%
1	Poindexter Dunn (D)	6,092	100.0
2	Clifton R. Breckinridge (D)	8,612	54.4
	D. D. Leach (R)	4,380	27.7
	R. B. Carllee (AG WHEEL)	2,846	18.0
3	Thomas C. McRae (D)	8,909	57.8
	J. C. Ray (R)	4,169	27.0
	L. H. Hitt (G)	2,343	15.2
4	John H. Rogers (D)	8,314	62.1
	Isom P. Langley (LAB)	5,077	37.9
5	Samuel W. Peel (D)	4,746	100.0

CALIFORNIA

	Candidates	Votes	%
1	Thomas L. Thompson (D)	16,499	50.0
	C. A. Gartern (R)	15,526	47.1
2	Marion Biggs (D)	17,667	49.8
	J. C. Campbell (R)	16,594	46.8
3	Joseph McKenna (R)	15,801	53.0
	H. C. McPike (D)	13,277	44.5
4	William W. Morrow (R)	11,413	48.4
	F. McCoppin (D)	9,854	41.8
	C. A. Sumner (LAB)	2,184	9.3
5	Charles N. Felton (R)	16,328	48.5
	F. J. Sullivan (D)	16,209	48.2
6	William Vandever (R)	18,259	47.3
	Joe D. Lynch (D)	18,204	47.1
	W. H. Harris (P)	2,159	5.6

COLORADO

	Candidates	Votes	%
AL	George G. Symes (R)	27,732	47.6
	Myron W. Reed (D)	26,929	46.2
	Joseph Murray (P)	3,597	6.2

CONNECTICUT

	Candidates	Votes	%
1	Robert J. Vance (D)	14,898	48.3
	John R. Buck (R)	14,552	47.2
2	Carlos French (D)	18,730	47.9
	Lewis (R)	17,402	44.5
3	Charles A. Russell (R)	9,366	48.9
	Hyde (D)	8,718	45.5
	Rockwell (P)	1,066	5.6
4	Miles T. Granger (D)	16,235	47.8
	Miles (R)	15,914	46.9

DELAWARE

	Candidates	Votes	%
AL	John B. Penington (D)	13,837	62.2
	Cooper (TEMP REF)	8,393	37.8

FLORIDA

	Candidates	Votes	%
1	Robert H. M. Davidson (D)	14,493	66.2
	Pendleton (R)	7,389	33.8
2	Charles Dougherty (D)	18,890	54.1
	Greeley (R)	15,764	45.2

GEORGIA

	Candidates	Votes	%
1	Thomas M. Norwood (D)	2,061	99.2
2	Henry G. Turner (D)	2,411	99.7
3	Charles F. Crisp (D)	1,704	100.0
4	Thomas W. Grimes (D)	2,909	89.8
	Carmical (I)	330	10.2
5	John D. Stewart (D)	2,999	100.0
6	James H. Blount (D)	1,722	99.9
7	Judson C. Clements (D)	5,043	75.5
	Felton (I)	1,537	23.0
8	Henry H. Carlton (D)	2,322	97.7
9	Allen D. Candler (D)	2,355	98.9
10	George T. Barnes (D)	1,944	99.6

ILLINOIS

	Candidates	Votes	%
1	Ransom W. Dunham (R)	12,321	46.9
	Edgar Terhunr (D)	7,258	27.6
	Harvey Sheldon Jr. (UN LAB)	6,358	24.2
2	Frank Lawler (D)	7,369	39.3
	Daniel F. Gluson (UN LAB)	7,353	39.3
	Charles W. Woodman (R)	3,976	21.2
3	William E. Mason (R)	13,721	66.2
	B. W. Goodhur (UN LAB)	6,352	30.7
4	George E. Adams (R)	12,147	48.1
	J. B. Taylor (D)	7,480	29.6
	I. A. Hawkins (UN LAB)	4,997	19.8
5	Albert J. Hopkins (R)	14,224	62.9
	J. F. Glidden (D)	6,258	27.7
	Charles Wheaton (P)	2,121	9.4
6	Robert R. Hitt (R)	13,106	55.5
	James McNamara (D)	8,650	36.6
	Spencer Rising (P)	1,878	8.0
7	Thomas J. Henderson (R)	12,586	58.2
	Sherwood Dixon (D)	7,731	35.8
	David E. Holmes (P)	1,296	6.0
8	Ralph Plumb (R)	16,827	52.1
	Hiram H. Cady (D)	13,893	43.0
9	Lewis E. Payson (R)	13,753	54.2
	Mathews H. Peters (D)	10,633	41.9
10	Philip Sidney Post (R)	15,186	48.7
	Nicholas E. Worthington (D)	15,157	48.6
11	William A. Gest (R)	16,733	48.8
	William H. Neece (D & G)	16,397	47.9
12	George A. Anderson (D & G)	18,718	57.5
	Oruan Pierson (R)	12,755	39.2
13	William M. Springer (D)	17,433	49.5
	James A. Connelly (R)	16,453	46.7
14	Jonathan H. Rowell (R)	15,319	51.0
	William Voorhees (D)	12,917	43.0
	William W. Alder (L)	1,786	6.0
15	Joseph G. Cannon (R)	16,739	50.9
	D. H. Lindsey (D)	15,314	46.6
16	Silas Z. Landes (D)	16,424	50.2
	Charles Churchill (R)	15,564	47.6
17	Edward Lane (D)	14,937	53.9
	Robert McWilliams (R)	11,557	41.7
18	Jehu Baker (R)	15,396	50.8
	William R. Morrison (D)	14,234	46.9
19	Richard W. Townshend (D)	16,316	56.1
	James S. Martin (R)	11,972	41.2
20	John R. Thomas (R)	16,246	50.9
	William Hartzell (D)	15,074	47.3

INDIANA

	Candidates	Votes	%
1	Alvin P. Hovey (R)	18,258	49.0
	J. E. McCullough (D)	16,901	45.4
2	John H. O'Neal (D)	16,075	51.8
	M. S. Ragsdale (R)	14,871	47.9
3	Jonas G. Howard (D)	12,458	46.4
	James K. Marsh (ID)	9,854	36.7
	James Kugwin (IR)	3,714	13.8
4	William S. Holman (D)	15,777	50.8
	Thomas J. Lucas (R)	14,989	48.3

	Candidates	Votes	%
5	Courtland Cushing Matson (D)	16,694	49.9
	Ira J. Chase (R)	16,162	48.3
6	Thomas M. Browne (R)	20,397	60.4
	George S. Jones (D)	12,253	36.3
7	William D. Bynum (D)	22,882	51.3
	Addison C. Harris (R)	21,108	47.3
8	James T. Johnston (R)	20,918	50.6
	John Edward Lamb (D)	19,816	47.9
9	Joseph B. Cheadle (R)	22,437	53.0
	Benjamin F. Ham (D)	19,021	44.9
10	William D. Owen (R)	18,114	52.1
	Hiram D. Hattery (D)	16,041	46.1
11	George Washington Steele (R)	19,649	48.9
	James C. Branyan (D)	19,241	47.9
12	James B. White (R)	17,900	51.8
	Robert Lowry (D)	15,416	44.6
13	Benjamin Franklin Shively (D)	19,105	50.5
	Jasper Packard (R)	18,087	47.8

IOWA

	Candidates	Votes	%
1	John Henry Gear (R)	16,115	51.1
	Benton Jay Hall (FUS)	15,078	47.8
2	Walter I. Hayes (FUS)	15,309	48.0
	Thomas J. O'Meara (LAB)	8,602	27.0
	Samuel Jordan Kirkwood (R)	8,009	25.1
3	David B. Henderson (R)	18,201	54.4
	W. H. Chamberlain (FUS)	15,272	45.6
4	William Elijah Fuller (R)	17,062	53.0
	Wiliard C. Earle (FUS)	15,132	47.0
5	Daniel Kerr (R)	16,696	51.0
	Benjamin Todd Frederick (FUS)	15,963	48.8
6	James Baird Weaver (FUS)	16,572	50.9
	John A. Donnell (R)	15,954	49.0
7	Edwin H. Conger (R)	15,165	51.6
	W. L. Carpenter (FUS)	14,239	48.4
8	Albert Raney Anderson (IR)	17,970	53.2
	William P. Hepburn (R)	15,745	46.7
9	Joseph Lyman (R)	16,953	53.4
	John H. Keatley (FUS)	14,747	46.5
10	Adoniram J. Holmes (R)	16,767	56.6
	George Wilmot (FUS)	12,868	43.4
11	Isaac S. Struble (R)	15,356	58.4
	E. C. Palmer (FUS)	10,919	41.5

KANSAS

	Candidates	Votes	%
1	Edmund N. Morrill (R)	17,347	55.3
	E. Bierer (D)	13,832	44.1
2	Edward H. Funston (R)	18,037	51.9
	Charles Robinson (D)	15,416	44.3
3	Bishop W. Perkins (R)	19,614	53.4
	Frank Bacon (D)	15,875	43.2
4	Thomas Ryan (R)	21,961	56.2
	John Martin (D)	15,706	40.2
5	John A. Anderson (R)	19,240	53.1
	J. G. Lowe (D)	12,751	35.2
	A. S. Wilson (IR)	3,856	10.6
6	Erastus J. Turner (R)	19,624	58.5
	W. S. Gile (D)	11,359	33.9
	C. H. Moody (A-MONOP)	2,098	6.3
7	Samuel R. Peters (R)	34,515	56.2
	Thomas George (D)	25,070	40.8

KENTUCKY

	Candidates	Votes	%
1	William J. Stone (D)	9,730	53.4
	Oscar Turner (ID)	8,476	46.5
2	Polk Laffoon (D)	10,715	58.2
	George W. Jolly (R)	7,695	41.8
3	W. Godfrey Hunter (R)	13,379	51.8
	John S. Rhea (D)	12,372	47.9
4	Alexander B. Montgomery (D)	9,892	56.6
	J. D. Belden (R)	7,572	43.4
5	Asher G. Caruth (D)	9,964	50.4
	A. E. Willson (R)	9,824	49.7

	Candidates	Votes	%
6	John G. Carlisle (D)	6,476	53.3
	George H. Thoebe (LAB)	5,651	46.5
7	William C. P. Breckinridge (D)	4,791	99.7
8	James B. McCreary (D)	10,540	59.8
	Thomas Todd (R)	7,077	40.2
9	George M. Thomas (R)	13,693	50.3
	Garrett S. Wall (D)	13,546	49.7
10	William P. Taulbee (D)	11,940	51.6
	William L. Hurst (R)	11,194	48.4
11	Hugh L. Finley (R)	12,824	53.2
	W. H. Botts (D)	11,278	46.8

LOUISIANA

	Candidates	Votes	%
1	Theodore S. Wilkinson (D)	11,350	87.3
	William M. Burwell (R)	1,649	12.7
2	Matthew D. Lagan (D)	7,930	53.7
	A. Hero Jr. (R)	6,537	44.3
3	Edward J. Gay (D)	14,782	55.1
	Chester B. Darrall (R)	11,692	43.6
4	Newton C. Blanchard (D)	5,747	99.8
5	Cherubusco Newton (D)	13,618	95.6
6	Edward W. Robertson (D)	9,676	95.8

Special Election

	Candidates	Votes	%
2	Nathaniel Dick Wallace (D)	✓	#

MAINE

	Candidates	Votes	%
1	Thomas B. Reed (R)	15,486	49.9
	W. H. Clifford (D)	14,298	46.0
2	Nelson Dingley Jr. (R)	18,137	53.3
	Alonzo Garcelon (D)	11,920	35.1
	William T. Eustis (P-LAB)	3,939	11.6
3	Seth Llewellyn Milliken (R)	17,992	56.5
	Joseph E. Ladd (D)	12,781	40.1
4	Charles A. Boutelle (R)	17,372	54.6
	John F. Lynch (D)	13,655	42.9

MARYLAND

	Candidates	Votes	%
1	Charles H. Gibson (D)	12,791	49.3
	Hodson (R)	11,640	44.8
	Melson (P)	1,529	5.9
2	Frank T. Shaw (D)	12,016	55.5
	Marine (R)	8,362	38.6
	Zouck (P)	1,283	5.9
3	Harry W. Rusk (D)	13,634	72.3
	Bosse (LAB-R)	3,300	17.5
	Glass (P)	1,726	9.2
4	Isidor Rayner (D)	14,750	62.6
	Findlay (I)	7,220	30.6
	Weatherby (R)	1,569	6.7
5	Barnes Compton (D)	13,579	54.8
	Tuck (R)	10,850	43.8
6	Louis E. McComas (R)	16,851	49.7
	Baughman (D)	16,438	48.5

MASSACHUSETTS

	Candidates	Votes	%
1	Robert T. Davis (R)	9,416	58.6
	McLaughlin (D)	5,768	35.9
	Hatfield (P)	847	5.3
2	John D. Long (R)	11,317	52.2
	Morse (D)	9,495	43.8
3	Leopold Morse (D)	11,199	53.7
	Ranney (R)	9,438	45.3
4	Patrick A. Collins (D)	11,201	73.4
	Cutler (R)	3,829	25.1
5	Edward D. Hayden (R)	11,364	57.3
	Randall (D)	8,006	40.3
6	Henry Cabot Lodge (R)	13,495	50.5
	Lovering (D)	12,767	47.8
7	William Cogswell (R)	9,863	46.9
	French (D)	8,489	40.4
	Spaulding (G & P)	2,663	12.7
8	Charles H. Allen (R)	10,216	50.2
	Donovan (D)	9,684	47.6
9	Edward Burnett (D)	10,354	48.7

	Candidates	Votes	%
	Ely (R)	10,143	47.7
10	John E. Russell (D)	9,728	49.7
	Rice (R)	8,977	45.8
11	William Whiting (R)	10,861	53.5
	Currier (D)	8,098	39.9
	Watkins (P)	1,320	6.5
12	Francis W. Rockwell (R)	10,181	49.6
	Joyner (D)	9,366	45.6

MICHIGAN

	Candidates	Votes	%
1	John Logan Chipman (D)	17,367	51.0
	Henry A. Robinson (R)	15,801	46.4
2	Edward P. Allen (R)	16,518	47.9
	Lester H. Salsbury (D)	15,486	45.0
	Alfred O. Crozier (P)	2,448	7.1
3	James O'Donnell (R)	20,215	51.4
	Patrick Hankerd (D)	15,499	39.4
	Hiram D. Allen (P)	3,594	9.1
4	Julius C. Burrows (R)	18,257	50.7
	Harvey C. Sherwood (D)	15,744	43.7
	Jesse S. Boyden (P)	1,999	5.6
5	Melbourne H. Ford (D)	18,567	46.7
	George W. McBride (R)	18,120	45.6
	Edward L. Briggs (P)	3,086	7.8
6	Mark S. Brewer (R)	19,034	48.1
	John H. Fedewa (D)	17,148	43.3
	Azariah S. Partridge (P)	3,427	8.7
7	Justin R. Whiting (D)	13,777	48.6
	John P. Sanborn (R)	12,963	45.8
	William F. Clark (P)	1,593	5.6
8	Timothy E. Tarsney (D)	18,301	48.4
	Roswell G. Horr (R)	17,615	46.5
	George W. Abbey (P)	1,930	5.1
9	Byron M. Cutcheon (R)	17,226	50.9
	Lyman G. Mason (D)	14,198	42.0
	Lathrop S. Ellis (P)	2,393	7.1
10	Spencer O. Fisher (D)	15,047	53.3
	Henry M. Loud (R)	12,900	45.7
11	Seth C. Moffatt (R)	14,485	53.6
	John Power (D)	12,242	45.3

MINNESOTA

	Candidates	Votes	%
1	Thomas Wilson (D)	17,491	52.0
	John A. Lovely (R)	14,663	3.6
2	John Lind (R)	22,908	59.8
	A. H. Bullis (D&F ALNC)	13,260	34.6
	George J. Day (P)	2,114	5.5
3	John L. MacDonald (D)	16,788	50.3
	B. B. Herbert (R)	15,583	46.7
4	Edmund Rice (D)	34,034	52.4
	J. B. Gilfillan (R)	28,909	44.5
5	Knute Nelson (R)	43,937	97.3

MISSISSIPPI

	Candidates	Votes	%
1	John M. Allen (D)	3,140	99.2
2	James B. Morgan (D)	7,857	62.1
	Chalmers (R)	4,791	37.9
3	Thomas C. Catchings (D)	4,518	65.5
	Simrall (R)	2,382	34.5
4	Frederick G. Barry (D)	2,964	96.1
5	Chapman L. Anderson (D)	4,289	99.4
6	Thomas R. Stockdale (D)	8,284	68.4
	Lynch (R)	3,825	31.6
7	Charles E. Hooker (D)	4,507	100.0

MISSOURI

	Candidates	Votes	%
1	William H. Hatch (D)	17,323	54.5
	Harrison (R)	14,455	45.5
2	Charles H. Mansur (D)	17,171	49.2
	Hale (ID)	16,441	47.1
3	Alexander M. Dockery (D)	19,689	56.0
	Harwood (R)	15,327	43.6
4	James N. Burnes (D)	14,051	53.2
	Dunn (R)	11,964	45.3
5	William Warner (R)	16,368	50.9
	Phillips (D)	15,583	48.4

	Candidates	Votes	%
6	John T. Heard (D)	21,558	53.6
	Guitar (R)	18,678	46.4
7	John E. Hutton (D)	15,212	53.7
	Martin (R)	13,135	46.3
8	John J. O'Neill (D)	8,166	47.8
	Cumings (R)	6,802	39.8
	Wind (UN LAB)	2,030	11.9
9	John M. Glover (D)	7,202	44.3
	Nathan Frank (R)	7,102	43.7
	Davisson (UN LAB)	1,792	11.0
10	Martin L. Clardy (D)	13,145	45.1
	Ledergerber (R)	12,097	41.5
	Ratchford (UN LAB)	3,927	13.5
11	Richard P. Bland (D)	16,594	54.3
	Parker (R)	13,996	45.8
12	William J. Stone (D)	21,205	53.9
	Kimball (R)	17,540	44.5
13	William H. Wade (R)	14,631	51.8
	Cravens (D)	12,674	44.9
14	James P. Walker (D)	18,400	63.6
	Davidson (FUS)	10,533	36.4

NEBRASKA

	Candidates	Votes	%
1	John A. McShane (D)	23,396	54.9
	Church Howe (R)	16,373	38.4
	George Bigelow (P)	2,867	6.7
2	James Laird (R)	21,373	51.5
	W. A. McKeighan (D)	16,315	39.3
	C. S. Harrison (P)	3,789	9.1
3	George W. E. Dorsey (R)	28,681	55.2
	A. H. Webster (D)	20,933	40.3

NEVADA

	Candidates	Votes	%
AL	William Woodburn (R)	6,700	54.2
	J. H. Macmillan (D)	5,670	45.8

NEW HAMPSHIRE

	Candidates	Votes	%
1	Luther F. McKinney (D)	18,370	49.1
	Martin A. Haynes (R)	18,165	48.5
2	Jacob H. Gallinger (R)	19,715	49.8
	William W. Bailey (D)	18,549	46.9

NEW JERSEY

	Candidates	Votes	%
1	George Hires (R)	18,347	49.0
	Wescott (D)	15,013	40.1
	Nicholson (P)	4,072	10.9
2	James Buchanan (R)	17,767	50.2
	Reed (D)	15,065	42.6
	Brown (P)	2,547	7.2
3	John Kean Jr. (R)	15,567	46.5
	McMahon (D)	14,930	44.6
	Parker (P)	2,980	8.9
4	James N. Pidcock (D)	11,686	44.9
	Vanblarcom (R)	11,563	44.4
	Morrow (P)	2,772	10.7
5	William W. Phelps (R)	15,297	51.8
	Skinner (D)	12,461	42.2
	Church (P)	1,780	6.0
6	Herman Lehlbach (R)	15,492	40.8
	Haynes (D)	13,719	36.1
	Beckmeyer (LAB)	6,331	16.7
	Anderson (P)	2,429	6.4
7	William McAdoo (D)	15,688	49.7
	Hammerschlag (R)	11,435	36.2
	Kerr (ID)	3,668	11.6

NEW YORK

	Candidates	Votes	%
1	Perry Belmont (D)	16,286	50.0
	McCormick (R)	15,360	47.1
2	Felix Campbell (D)	16,679	70.8
	Donovan (R)	5,580	23.7
3	Stephen V. White (R)	12,740	48.6
	Bell (D)	12,568	48.0
4	Peter P. Mahoney (D)	13,879	53.6
	O'Connor (R)	10,251	39.6

Candidates	Votes	%
5 Archibald M. Bliss (D)	11,583	50.1
Waters (R)	11,111	48.0
6 Amos J. Cummings (D)	13,799	96.4
7 Lloyd S. Bryce (D)	12,895	64.2
Lawson (R)	6,972	34.7
8 Timothy J. Campbell (D)	12,179	50.4
Grady (ID)	11,799	48.8
9 Samuel S. Cox (D)	13,754	62.3
Wagener (R)	8,259	37.4
10 Francis B. Spinola (D)	10,847	50.7
Rice (R)	10,320	48.2
11 Truman A. Merriman (D)	24,502	97.8
12 W. Bourke Cockran (D)	15,886	59.3
Pell (R)	10,680	39.9
13 Ashbel P. Fitch (R)	17,614	55.3
Viele (D)	13,939	43.8
14 William G. Stahlnecker (D)	15,828	52.3
Wood (R)	13,392	44.3
15 Henry Bacon (D)	13,488	48.7
Stivers (R)	13,027	47.0
16 John H. Ketcham (R)	15,585	55.2
Sackett (D)	11,583	41.0
17 Stephen T. Hopkins (R)	17,805	52.3
Lounsbery (D)	14,317	42.1
Howie (P)	1,872	5.5
18 Edward W. Greenman (D)	17,082	49.8
Burleigh (R)	15,819	46.1
19 Nicholas T. Kane (D)	16,552	47.8
Swinburne (R)	16,385	47.3
20 George West (R)	16,339	54.7
Wick (D)	10,035	33.6
French (P)	3,344	11.2
21 John H. Moffitt (R)	15,376	68.4
Winslow (D)	6,049	26.9
22 Abraham X. Parker (R)	14,450	57.5
Corbin (D)	9,120	36.3
Huntington (P)	1,523	6.1
23 James S. Sherman (R)	15,914	49.2
Spriggs (D)	14,430	44.6
Hendee (P)	1,966	6.1
24 David Wilber (R)	16,314	50.3
Smith (D)	14,549	44.9
25 Frank Hiscock (R)	16,087*	58.2
Angel (D)	11,498	41.6
26 Milton De Lano (R)	19,155	55.3
Downs (D)	12,362	35.7
Williams (P)	3,086	8.9
27 Newton W. Nutting (R)	21,465	60.7
Beardsley (D)	11,679	33.0
28 Thomas S. Flood (R)	14,124	52.3
McGuire (D)	11,611	43.0
29 Ira Davenport (R)	17,047	82.8
Ladd (D)	3,009	14.6
30 Charles S. Baker (R)	13,170	53.2
Bacon (D)	10,509	42.5
31 John G. Sawyer (R)	14,611	54.3
Wadsworth (D)	10,022	37.2
Sparrow (P)	2,286	8.5
32 John M. Farquhar (R)	16,785	55.2
Rogers (D)	13,452	44.2
33 John B. Weber (R)	12,215	49.3
Spalding (D)	11,082	44.7
Smith (P)	1,465	5.9
34 William G. Laidlaw (R)	16,966	52.8
Wood (D)	9,305	28.9
Huntington (P)	5,505	17.1

NORTH CAROLINA

Candidates	Votes	%
1 Louis C. Latham (D)	13,390	54.6
Lycurgus J. Barrett (IR)	10,635	43.4
2 Furnifold M. Simmons (D)	15,158	44.8
James E. O'Hara (R)	13,060	38.6
Israel B. Abbott (R)	5,020	14.9
3 Charles W. McClammy (D)	14,538	60.7
F. D. Koonce (D)	8,164	34.1
4 John Nichols (I)	15,861	52.4
John W. Graham (D)	14,423	47.6
5 John M. Brower (R)	13,282	49.7
James W. Reid (D)	11,702	43.8

Candidates	Votes	%
6 Alfred Rowland (D)	14,261	62.5
Charles R. Jones (ID)	7,659	33.6
7 John S. Henderson (D)	10,565	78.6
Joseph A. Blair (R)	1,473	11.0
James E. Walker (P)	1,401	10.4
8 William H. H. Cowles (D)	9,997	65.2
Leander L. Green (R)	5,325	34.7
9 Thomas D. Johnston (D)	11,754	54.2
William H. Malone (ID)	7,014	32.3
Alexander H. Jones (R)	2,934	13.5

OHIO

Candidates	Votes	%
1 Benjamin Butterworth (R)	15,522	53.4
Samuel A. Miller (D)	13,166	45.3
2 Charles E. Brown (R)	17,009	52.3
Hugh Shiels (D)	15,210	46.8
3 Elihu S. Williams (R)	17,235	47.1
Robert M. Murray (D)	16,102	44.0
Jacob W. Nigh (LAB)	2,132	5.8
4 Samuel S. Yoder (D)	16,959	59.2
Theodore W. Brotherton (R)	10,753	37.5
5 George E. Seney (D)	16,996	70.8
David Harpster (R)	5,023	20.9
Rudolph Rock (P)	1,629	6.8
6 Melvin M. Boothman (R)	19,476	50.0
William D. Hill (D)	18,099	46.5
7 James E. Campbell (D)	15,303	48.4
John Little (R)	15,301	48.4
8 Robert P. Kennedy (R)	18,080	49.6
Thomas R. McMillen (D)	16,692	45.8
9 William C. Cooper (R)	17,659	49.8
John C. Levering (D)	15,790	44.6
William H. Elsom (P)	1,900	5.4
10 Jacob Romeis (R)	17,180	51.7
Frank H. Hurd (D)	15,592	46.9
11 Albert C. Thompson (R)	17,550	55.3
Irvin Dungan (D)	13,202	41.6
12 Jacob J. Pugsley (R)	18,283	49.6
James W. Denver (D)	17,025	46.2
13 Joseph H. Outhwaite (D)	20,310	51.7
William Shepard (R)	17,730	45.1
14 Charles P. Wickham (R)	13,835	49.1
Thomas J. Bristor (D)	12,764	45.3
Corydon L. Tambling (P)	1,576	5.6
15 Charles H. Grosvenor (R)	15,794	51.0
Adoniram J. Warner (D)	14,324	46.3
16 Beriah Wilkins (D)	20,258	53.3
Caleb B. Downs (R)	16,284	42.8
17 Joseph D. Taylor (R)	17,623	52.4
David C. Kennon (D)	14,010	41.7
James M. Monroe (P)	1,948	5.8
18 William McKinley Jr. (R)	18,776	49.1
Wallace H. Phelps (D)	16,217	42.4
19 Ezra B. Taylor (R)	17,707	63.2
Thaddeus E. Hoyt (D)	7,831	28.0
Charles E. Holt (P)	2,291	8.2
20 George W. Crouse (R)	15,777	48.5
William Dorsey (D)	14,890	45.8
John J. Ashenhurst (P)	1,805	5.6
21 Martin A. Foran (D)	14,899	51.2
Amos Townsend (R)	13,466	46.3

OREGON

Candidates	Votes	%
AL Binger Hermann (R)	26,918	49.0
N. L. Butler (D)	25,221	46.0
G. M. Miller (P)	2,753	5.0

PENNSYLVANIA

Candidates	Votes	%
1 Henry H. Bingham (R)	18,225	60.0
Ryan (D)	11,826	38.9
2 Charles O'Neill (R)	15,480	59.9
Beasley (D)	9,847	38.1
3 Samuel J. Randall (D)	11,320	98.4
4 William D. Kelley (R)	25,391	62.7
Laverty (D)	13,882	34.3
5 Alfred C. Harmer (R)	23,464	57.4
Smith (D)	12,276	30.1

Candidates	Votes	%
Herwig (LAB)	4,159	10.2
6 Smedley Darlington (R)	11,841	41.4
Dickinson (D)	10,529	36.8
Everhart (IR)	4,966	17.4
7 Robert M. Yardley (R)	17,079	52.0
Satterthwaite (D)	14,944	45.5
8 Daniel Ermentrout (D)	13,978	59.6
Stitzel (R)	9,163	39.0
9 John A. Hiestand (R)	18,683	65.7
McGovern (D)	9,049	31.8
10 William H. Sowden (D)	21,370	96.8
11 Charles R. Buckalew (D)	18,337	95.9
12 John Lynch (D)	14,176	48.3
Joseph A. Scranton (R)	13,526	46.1
Knapp (D)	1,663	5.7
13 Charles N. Brumm (R)	11,293	50.2
Shepherd (D)	10,519	46.8
14 Franklin Bound (R)	17,116	51.9
McDevitt (D)	14,485	43.9
15 Frank C. Bunnell (R)	16,113	56.3
Plolett (D)	10,453	36.5
Dodson (P)	2,041	7.1
16 Henry C. McCormick (R)	17,393	55.3
Keenan (D)	12,567	40.0
17 Edward Scull (R)	16,548	49.7
Tate (D)	15,649	47.0
18 Louis E. Atkinson (R)	17,020	54.2
Jacobs (D)	13,773	43.9
19 Levi Maish (D)	18,174	54.3
Seitz (R)	14,228	42.5
20 John Patton (R)	16,566	48.8
Hall (D)	16,413	48.4
21 Welty McCullogh (R)	15,381	45.2
Donnelly (D)	15,126	44.4
Rafferty (D)	2,581	7.6
22 John Dalzell (R)	16,631	54.3
Parkinson (D)	12,626	41.2
23 Thomas M. Bayne (R)	12,133	58.9
Alcorn (D)	7,094	34.4
Rabe (P)	1,385	6.7
24 Oscar L. Jackson (R)	14,787	55.3
Baird (D)	10,347	38.7
Irish (P)	1,465	5.5
25 James T. Maffett (R)	14,322	51.3
St. Clair (D)	12,700	45.5
26 Norman Hall (D)	14,565	46.3
Roberts (R)	14,034	44.6
Cunningham (P)	2,288	7.3
27 William L. Scott (D)	14,787	48.5
Mackey (R)	13,574	44.5
Andrews (P)	2,140	7.0
AL Edwin S. Osborne (R)	415,166	50.8
Maxwell Stevenson (D)	367,551	45.0

RHODE ISLAND[1]

Candidates	Votes	%
1 Henry J. Spooner (R)	3,457	52.9
Oscar Lapham (D)	2,337	35.7
Howard (P)	746	11.4
2 Charles S. Bradley (D)	5,426*	48.2
Nathan F. Dixon (R)	4,849	43.1
Chace (P)	852	7.6

SOUTH CAROLINA

Candidates	Votes	%
1 Samuel Dibble (D)	3,315	100.0
2 George D. Tillman (D)	5,232	99.6
3 James C. Cothran (D)	4,402	99.8
4 William H. Perry (D)	4,470	100.0
5 John J. Hemphill (D)	4,696	99.9
6 George W. Dargan (D)	4,361	98.7
7 William Elliott (D)	6,493	52.1
Robert Smalls (R)	5,961	47.9

TENNESSEE

Candidates	Votes	%
1 Roderick Butler (R)	16,393	60.0
James White (D)	10,953	40.1
2 Leonidas C. Houk (R)	15,837	67.0
S. G. Heiskell (D)	7,780	32.9

	Candidates	Votes	%
3	John R. Neal (D)	14,115	50.6
	John T. Wilder (R)	13,768	49.4
4	Benton McMillin (D)	12,441	61.5
	J. J. Turner (R)	7,792	38.5
5	James D. Richardson (D)	13,756	68.9
	S. D. Mathew (R)	6,210	31.1
6	Joseph E. Washington (D)	14,919	61.8
	John H. Nye (R)	9,218	38.2
7	Washington C. Whitthorne (D)	12,083	58.8
	G. W. Blackburn (R)	8,459	41.2
8	Benjamin A. Enloe (D)	13,059	53.5
	S. W. Hawkins (R)	11,362	46.5
9	Presley T. Glass (D)	14,272	59.0
	D. A. Nunn (R)	9,934	41.0
10	James Phelan (D)	11,979	60.0
	Zack Taylor (R)	7,983	40.0

TEXAS

	Candidates	Votes	%
1	Charles Stewart (D)	16,844	61.9
	H. D. Johnson (R)	10,344	38.0
2	John H. Reagan (D)	16,413*	95.7
3	Constantine B. Kilgore (D)	16,695	69.3
	W. E. Farmer (I)	7,359	30.6
4	David B. Culberson (D)	17,234	78.5
	James T. Fleming (I)	4,701	21.4
5	Silas Hare (D)	11,774	41.8
	G. B. Pickett (ID)	8,315	29.5
	H. C. Mack (I)	8,065	28.6
6	Jo Abbott (D)	19,185	59.9
	J. C. Kearby (I)	11,756	36.7
7	William H. Crain (D)	18,511	89.1
	J. L. Haynes (R)	1,293	6.2
8	Littleton W. Moore (D)	22,908	92.1
	W. O. Hutchinson (R)	1,912	7.7
9	Roger Q. Mills (D)	17,168	60.2
	J. D. Rankin (P-LAB)	11,337	39.8
10	Joseph D. Sayers (D)	26,809	78.1

	Candidates	Votes	%
	J. P. Newcomb (R)	7,492	21.8
11	Samuel W. T. Lanham (D)	21,980	74.0
	Unidentified Candidate (I)	7,744	26.1

VERMONT

	Candidates	Votes	%
1	John W. Stewart (R)	15,632	72.5
	Waldo Brigham (D)	5,655	26.2
2	William W. Grout (R)	18,685	69.4
	Harley E. Folsom (D)	8,176	30.4

VIRGINIA

	Candidates	Votes	%
1	Thomas H. B. Browne (R)	12,591	54.1
	Thomas Croxton (D)	10,696	45.9
2	George E. Bowden (R)	15,449	60.7
	Marshall Parks (D)	9,993	39.3
3	George D. Wise (D)	14,001	52.7
	Edmond Waddell Jr. (R)	12,549	47.2
4	William E. Gaines (R)	14,708	70.2
	Mann Page (D)	6,233	29.8
5	John R. Brown (R)	12,773	57.1
	George C. Cabell (D)	9,614	42.9
6	Samuel I. Hopkins (LAB)	9,470	50.9
	Samuel Griffin (D)	9,020	48.4
7	Charles T. O'Ferrall (D)	11,580	51.7
	John E. Roller (ID)	10,816	48.3
8	William H. F. Lee (D)	9,836	57.5
	W. C. Elam (I)	7,274	42.5
9	Henry Bowen (R)	13,826	57.6
	R. R. Henry (R)	10,196	42.4
10	Jacob Yost (R)	12,975	53.4
	James Bumgardner Jr. (D)	11,321	46.6

WEST VIRGINIA

	Candidates	Votes	%
1	Nathan Goff Jr. (R)	17,559	50.8
	John Bannon (D)	16,732	48.4

	Candidates	Votes	%
2	William L. Wilson (D)	17,112	49.9
	W. H. H. Flick (R)	17,022	49.6
3	Charles P. Snyder (D)	14,906	50.6
	James H. Brown (R)	14,011	47.6
4	Charles E. Hogg (D)	16,434	50.3
	John H. Hutchinson (R)	15,687	48.0

WISCONSIN

	Candidates	Votes	%
1	Lucien B. Caswell (R)	13,739	46.9
	James R. Doolittle (D)	13,166	44.9
	Edward G. Durand (P)	2,404	8.2
2	Richard Guenther (R)	15,366	55.7
	A. K. Delaney (D)	11,138	40.4
3	Robert M. LaFollette (R)	16,711	50.3
	Hugh J. Gallagher (D)	13,201	39.8
	T. C. Richmond (P)	3,258	9.8
4	Henry Smith (LAB)	13,355	42.5
	Thomas H. Brown (R)	9,645	30.7
	John Black (D)	8,233	26.2
5	Thomas R. Hudd (D)	15,716	60.6
	G. Keusterman (R)	10,168	39.2
6	Charles B. Clark (R)	15,983	54.6
	Andrew Haben (D)	11,526	39.4
	E. D. Kanouse (P)	1,761	6.0
7	Ormsby B. Thomas (R)	16,720	54.2
	S. N. Dickenson (D)	11,917	38.7
	S. B. Loomis (P)	2,175	7.1
8	William T. Price (R)	23,857*	66.7
	James Bracklin (D)	11,850	33.2
9	Isaac Stephenson (R)	22,518	55.8
	John Ringle (D)	17,763	44.0

Special Election

	Candidates	Votes	%
5	Thomas R. Hudd (D)	9,633	62.2
	Charles Luling (R)	5,852	37.8

1. No candidate in the 2nd district secured the majority needed to win in the general election.

1887 House Elections

LOUISIANA

Special Election

	Candidates	Votes	%
6	Samuel M. Robertson (D)	6,706	72.5
	John Yoist (R)	2,550	27.6

MICHIGAN

Special Election

11	Henry W. Seymour (R)	11,014	49.7
	Bartley Breen (FUS)	10,612	47.8

NEW YORK

Special Elections

	Candidates	Votes	%
19	Charles Tracey (D)	17,796	49.9
	Bailey (R)	16,187	45.4
25	James J. Belden (R)	20,144	60.0
	Davis (D)	11,608	34.6
	Sinclair (P)	1,798	5.4

RHODE ISLAND[1]

Special Elections

2	Charles H. Page (D)	5,790	49.3
	William A. Pirce (R)	5,495	46.7

	Candidates	Votes	%
2	Warren O. Arnold (R)	8,086	51.8
	Charles S. Bradley (D)	7,248	46.4

WISCONSIN

Special Elections

8	Hugh H. Price (R)	12,238	69.9
	James Bardon (D)	5,209	29.8
8	Nils P. Haugen (R)	8,159	46.3
	Samuel C. Johnson (D)	6,803	38.6
	Peter Truax (P)	2,620	14.9

1. The first special election, won by Charles H. Page, was to fill a vacancy in the 49th Congress (1885–1887.) A majority of the total vote was apparently not required to win this election.

The second special, won by Warren O. Arnold, was for a full term in the 50th Congress elections (1887–1889). The seat had been left unfilled in the regular 1886 general election because no candidate had the requisite majority. (See Rhode Island 1886.)

1888 House Elections

ALABAMA

	Candidates	Votes	%
1	Richard H. Clarke (D)	11,594	62.0
	Frank H. Threet (R)	7,105	38.0
2	Hilary A. Herbert (D)	14,041	66.1
	Buckley (R)	7,204	33.9
3	William C. Oates (D)	13,287	82.3
	Harvey (R)	2,868	17.8
4	Louis W. Turpin (D)	18,778‡	77.0
	John V. McDuffie (R)	5,625	23.1
5	James E. Cobb (D)	12,597	64.7
	Bingham (R)	6,861	35.3
6	John H. Bankhead (D)	16,491	67.8
	Hanlan (R)	7,849	32.3
7	William H. Forney (D)	17,706	65.7
	Hardy (R)	8,265	30.7
8	Joseph Wheeler (D)	14,091	61.6
	McClellan (R)	8,770	38.4

ARKANSAS

1	William H. Cate (D)	15,576‡	51.9
	Lewis P. Featherston (IR)	14,228	47.4
2	Clifton R. Breckinridge (D)	17,857‡	51.2
	John M. Clayton (R)	17,011	48.8
3	Thomas C. McRae (D)	20,046	59.7
	J. A. Ansley (I)	13,553	40.3
4	John H. Rogers (D)	20,448	57.7
	I. McCracken (I)	14,933	42.2
5	Samuel W. Peel (D)	15,649	68.9
	E. P. Watson (I)	5,000	22.0
	John Gates (R)	2,075	9.1

CALIFORNIA

1	John J. De Haven (R)	19,345	49.9
	T. L. Thompson (D)	19,019	49.0
2	Marion Biggs (D)	19,064	50.7
	John A. Eagon (R)	17,541	46.6
3	Joseph McKenna (R)	19,912	56.0
	Ben Morgan (D)	14,633	41.2
4	William W. Morrow (R)	14,217	50.6
	Robert Ferral (D)	13,624	48.5
5	Thomas J. Clunie (D)	20,276	48.9
	L. G. Phelps (R)	20,225	48.8
6	William Vandever (R)	35,406	52.4
	R. B. Terry (D)	29,453	43.5

COLORADO

AL	Hosea Townsend (R)	50,620	55.0
	Thomas Macon (D)	37,725	41.0

CONNECTICUT

1	William E. Simonds (R)	18,255	49.7
	Vance (D)	17,442	47.5
2	Washington F. Wilcox (D)	24,959	49.6
	Lines (R)	24,161	48.0
3	Charles A. Russell (R)	11,710	49.8
	Hall (D)	10,962	46.6
4	Frederick Miles (R)	21,003	48.7
	Seymour (D)	20,977	48.7

DELAWARE

AL	John B. Penington (D)	16,396	55.2
	Charles H. Treat (R)	12,935	43.5

FLORIDA

1	Robert H. M. Davidson (D)	19,822	67.1
	Benjamin (R)	9,727	32.9
2	Robert Bullock (D)	19,512	52.8
	Goodrich (R)	17,417	47.2

GEORGIA

	Candidates	Votes	%
1	Rufus E. Lester (D)	11,736	69.6
	Floyd Snelson (R)	5,116	30.4
2	Henry G. Turner (D)	11,000	100.0
3	Charles F. Crisp (D)	9,254	72.7
	Peter O. Gibson (R)	3,130	24.6
4	Thomas W. Grimes (D)	9,798	70.4
	Marion Bethune (R)	4,122	29.6
5	John D. Stewart (D)	10,971	68.6
	George S. Thomas (R)	5,032	31.4
6	James H. Blount (D)	8,931	100.0
7	Judson C. Clements (D)	9,051	74.8
	Z. B. Hargraves (R)	3,054	25.2
8	Henry H. Carlton (D)	7,348	76.7
	E. T. Fleming (R)	2,227	23.3
9	Allen D. Candler (D)	11,260	53.0
	Thaddeus Pickett (I)	9,975	47.0
10	George T. Barnes (D)	6,474	89.0
	Judson W. Lyon (R)	797	11.0

ILLINOIS

1	Abner Taylor (R)	26,553	52.7
	James F. Todd (D)	22,697	45.1
2	Frank Lawler (D)	19,051	59.2
	Daniel F. Gleason (R)	12,969	40.3
3	William E. Mason (R)	23,671	50.8
	Milton R. Freshwater (D)	21,295	45.7
4	George E. Adams (R)	22,273	51.3
	Jonathan B. Taylor (D)	19,755	45.5
5	Albert J. Hopkins (R)	20,077	63.0
	James Herrington (D)	10,018	31.4
	John M. Strong (P)	1,765	5.5
6	Robert R. Hitt (R)	18,139	57.2
	Rufus M. Cook (D)	11,903	37.6
	George Richardson (P)	1,659	5.2
7	Thomas J. Henderson (R)	16,380	56.7
	Owen G. Lovejoy (D)	11,341	39.2
8	Charles A. Hill (R)	20,596	51.4
	Lafayette W. Brewer (D)	17,454	43.6
9	Lewis E. Payson (R)	16,871	51.5
	Herman W. Snow (D)	14,490	44.2
10	Philip S. Post (R)	18,824	52.6
	Nicholas E. Worthington (D)	16,166	45.2
11	William H. Gest (R)	19,657	51.3
	William Prentiss (D)	17,580	45.8
12	Scott Wike (D)	21,938	54.1
	William H. Collins (R)	16,628	41.0
13	William M. Springer (D)	21,364	51.4
	Charles Kerr (R)	18,450	44.4
14	Jonathan H. Rowell (R)	18,570	50.1
	Ethelbert Stewart (D)	16,740	45.2
15	Joseph G. Cannon (R)	19,897	51.8
	Robert L. McKinley (D)	17,204	44.8
16	George W. Fithian (D)	17,742	49.6
	Edwin Harlan (R)	17,037	47.6
17	Edward Lane (D)	19,385	54.8
	John J. Brown (R)	14,775	41.7
18	William S. Forman (D)	16,167	47.7
	Jehu Baker (R)	16,151	47.7
19	Richard W. Townshend (D)	18,086	53.0
	W. L. Crim (R)	15,615	45.8
20	George W. Smith (R)	19,005	51.6
	Thomas T. Robinson (D)	17,186	46.6

INDIANA

1	William F. Parrett (D)	20,647	49.3
	Frank B. Posey (R)	20,627	49.3
2	John H. O'Neall (D)	18,537	52.3
	Thomas N. Braxton (R)	16,653	47.0
3	Jason B. Brown (D)	18,274	54.0
	Stephen D. Sayles (R)	15,198	44.9
4	William S. Holman (D)	16,905	50.7
	Manly D. Wilson (R)	16,176	48.5

	Candidates	Votes	%
5	George W. Cooper (D)	18,206	49.6
	Henry C. Duncan (R)	17,506	47.7
6	Thomas M. Browne (R)	23,424	60.3
	Douglas Morris (D)	14,302	36.8
7	William D. Bynum (D)	27,227	50.9
	Thomas E. Chandler (R)	25,500	47.6
8	Elijah V. Brookshire (D)	23,153	49.0
	James F. Johnston (R)	23,084	48.8
9	Joseph B. Cheadle (R)	24,717	53.1
	James McCabe (D)	20,267	43.5
10	William D. Owen (R)	19,546	50.4
	Valentine Zimmerman (D)	18,390	47.5
11	Augustus N. Martin (D)	22,375	48.9
	George W. Steele (R)	21,900	47.8
12	Charles A. O. McClellan (D)	20,139	50.4
	James B. White (R)	18,828	47.1
13	Benjamin F. Shively (D & LAB)	21,561	49.4
	William Hoynes (R)	21,206	48.6

IOWA

1	John H. Gear (R)	18,130	51.0
	John J. Seerley (D)	17,256	48.5
2	Walter I. Hayes (D)	20,874	56.8
	Parker W. McManus (R & LAB)	15,842	43.1
3	David B. Henderson (R)	21,457	56.0
	B. B. Richards (D)	16,872	44.0
4	Joseph H. Sweney (R)	18,852	52.4
	L. S. Reque (D)	16,630	46.2
5	Daniel Kerr (R)	19,453	52.5
	J. H. Preston (D)	16,937	45.7
6	John F. Lacey (R)	18,009	51.0
	James B. Weaver (D & LAB)	17,181	48.6
7	Edwin H. Conger (R)	18,424	55.8
	A. E. Morrison (D)	13,027	39.5
8	James P. Flick (R)	19,207	50.9
	A. R. Anderson (D & LAB)	18,212	48.2
9	Joseph R. Reed (R)	20,380	52.6
	D. M. Harris (D)	16,686	43.0
10	Jonathan P. Dolliver (R)	20,864	56.8
	J. A. Yeoman (D)	15,496	42.2
11	Isaac S. Struble (R)	21,472	57.1
	M. A. Kilso (D)	15,213	40.4

KANSAS

1	Edmund N. Morrill (R)	20,879	56.3
	E. K. Townsend (D)	14,536	39.2
2	Edward H. Funston (R)	24,632	54.6
	J. T. Burris (D)	14,969	33.2
	Delos Walker (UN LAB)	5,517	12.2
3	Bishop W. Perkins (R)	23,315	50.4
	W. H. Utley (UN LAB)	11,775	25.5
	J. A. Eaton (D)	10,556	22.8
4	Thomas Ryan (R)	29,338	59.8
	D. Overmeyer (D)	14,323	29.2
	John Heaton (UN LAB)	4,350	8.9
5	John A. Anderson (R)	22,848	59.6
	N. D. Toby (D)	14,347	37.4
6	Erastus J. Turner (R)	23,428	57.4
	S. W. McElroy (D)	12,282	30.1
	H. A. Hart (UN LAB)	4,550	11.2
7	Samuel R. Peters (R)	37,935	53.2
	C. S. Ebey (D)	22,616	31.7
	S. H. Snyder (UN LAB)	9,489	13.3

KENTUCKY

1	William J. Stone (D)	14,195	60.2
	Edwin Earley (R)	8,850	37.6
2	William T. Ellis (D)	16,459	54.8
	George W. Jolly (R)	13,006	43.3
3	Isaac H. Goodnight (D)	17,365	52.4
	W. Godfrey Hunter (R)	15,630	47.1
4	Alexander B. Montgomery (D)	15,477	57.9

Candidates	Votes	%
C. M. Pendleton (R)	11,019	41.3
5 Asher G. Caruth (D)	16,588	54.9
Augustus E. Willson (R)	13,561	44.9
6 John G. Carlisle (D)	18,907	58.7
Robert Hamilton (R)	12,887	40.0
7 William C. P. Breckinridge (D)	18,920	57.5
Armstead M. Swope (R)	13,265	40.3
8 James B. McCreary (D)	16,209	51.5
R. L. Ewell (R)	14,660	46.6
9 Thomas H. Paynter (D)	18,664	49.9
Drury J. Burchett (R)	18,285	48.9
10 John H. Wilson (R)	15,725	50.6
B. F. Day (D)	15,247	49.1
11 Hugh F. Finley (R)	15,822	52.4
F. L. Wolford (D)	14,006	46.4

LOUISIANA

1	Theodore S. Wilkinson (D)	8,979	64.5
	Charles B. Wilson (R)	4,927	35.4
2	H. Dudley Coleman (R)	9,121	50.5
	Benjamin C. Elliott (D)	8,947	49.5
3	Edward J. Gay (D)	18,854	74.8
	James R. Jolley (R)	6,341	25.2
4	Newton C. Blanchard (D)	16,302	94.4
	W. E. Maples (R)	963	5.6
5	Charles J. Boatner (D)	21,275	93.9
	Frank Morey (R)	1,151	5.1
6	Samuel M. Robertson (D)	12,078	73.7
	W. H. Harrison (R)	4,314	26.3

MAINE

1	Thomas B. Reed (R)	18,288	52.3
	William Emery (D)	15,849	45.3
2	Nelson Dingley Jr. (R)	21,075	55.2
	Charles E. Allen (D)	15,614	40.9
3	Seth L. Milliken (R)	20,558	58.0
	S. S. Brown (D)	14,026	39.5
4	Charles A. Boutelle (R)	19,823	54.6
	T. J. Stewart (D)	15,481	42.7

MARYLAND

1	Charles H. Gibson (D)	15,627	48.3
	Hodson (R)	15,145	46.8
2	Herman Stump (D)	18,470	51.2
	Lang (R)	16,588	46.0
3	Harry W. Rusk (D)	19,578	57.2
	Brinton (R)	14,289	41.7
4	Henry Stockbridge Jr. (R)	19,078	49.5
	Rayner (D)	18,998	49.3
5	Barnes Compton (D)	16,000‡	49.8
	Sydney E. Mudd (R)	15,819	49.2
6	Louis E. McComas (R)	19,056	51.6
	Douglas (D)	17,422	47.2

MASSACHUSETTS

1	Charles S. Randall (R)	14,588	60.8
	Cummings (D)	5,103	21.3
	Delano (D)	3,468	14.5
2	Elijah A. Morse (R)	17,072	54.2
	Quincy (D)	13,388	42.5
3	John F. Andrew (D)	16,338	52.0
	Beard (R)	14,780	47.0
4	Joseph H. O'Neil (D)	14,749	68.0
	Morrison (R)	6,718	31.0
5	Nathaniel P. Banks (R)	14,929	51.8
	Higginson (D)	13,465	46.7
6	Henry Cabot Lodge (R)	19,598	56.3
	Usher (D)	14,304	41.1
7	William Cogswell (R)	16,796	56.8
	Roads (D)	12,224	41.3
8	Frederic T. Greenhalge (R)	14,493	55.3
	Donovan (D)	11,273	43.0
9	John W. Candler (R)	15,714	52.2
	Burnett (D)	13,678	45.4
10	Joseph H. Walker (R)	13,965	52.0

Candidates	Votes	%
Sayles (D)	12,050	44.9
11 Rodney Wallace (R)	16,335	56.4
Skinner (D)	11,519	39.7
12 Francis W. Rockwell (R)	14,853	52.1
Ely (D)	12,826	45.0

MICHIGAN

1	J. Logan Chipman (D)	25,179	52.4
	Hibbard Baker (R)	22,076	45.9
2	Edward P. Allen (R)	19,660	49.3
	Willard Stearns (D & G)	18,096	45.3
	Charles M. Fellows (P)	2,010	5.0
3	James O'Donnell (R)	24,097	53.5
	Eugene Pringle (D)	17,495	38.9
	Almon G. Bruce (P)	2,609	5.8
4	Julius C. Burrows (R)	21,649	52.9
	Charles S. Maynard (D)	17,464	42.7
5	Charles E. Belknap (R)	26,309	50.4
	Melbourne H. Ford (D)	23,642	45.3
6	Mark S. Brewer (R)	21,271	47.6
	Orlando F. Barnes (D)	20,904	46.8
	William W. Root (P)	2,251	5.0
7	Justin R. Whiting (D)	16,894	47.7
	William Hartsuff (R)	16,488	46.6
8	Aaron T. Bliss (R)	23,028	50.4
	Timothy E. Tarsney (D)	20,943	45.9
9	Byron M. Cutcheon (R)	23,025	52.2
	Hiram B. Hudson (D)	18,651	42.2
	Lathrop S. Ellis (P)	2,476	5.6
10	Frank W. Wheeler (R)	18,959	48.3
	Spencer O. Fisher (D)	18,844	48.0
11	Samuel M. Stephenson (R)	20,336	52.8
	John Power (D)	16,978	44.1

MINNESOTA

1	Mark H. Dunnell (R)	18,829	50.4
	Thomas Wilson (D)	16,985	45.4
2	John Lind (R)	25,699	57.0
	M. S. Wilkinson (D)	16,480	36.5
	D. W. Edwards (P)	2,924	6.5
3	Darwin S. Hall (R)	19,259	51.4
	J. L. Macdonald (D)	16,391	43.7
4	Samuel P. Snider (R)	44,329	53.8
	E. Rice (D)	34,323	41.7
5	Solomon G. Comstock (R)	31,350	52.7
	Charles Canning (D)	23,833	40.1
	Z. D. Scott (P)	4,254	7.2

MISSISSIPPI

1	John M. Allen (D)	11,353	86.8
	Joseph M. Bynum (R)	1,732	13.2
2	John B. Morgan (D)	13,978	70.6
	James R. Chalmers (R)	5,817	29.4
3	Thomas C. Catchings (D)	11,624	71.6
	James Hill (R)	4,614	28.4
4	Clarke Lewis (D)	12,855	84.3
	Matthew K. Mister (R)	2,396	15.7
5	Chapman L. Anderson (D)	16,247	80.3
	F. M B. Cook (R)	3,993	19.7
6	Thomas R. Stockdale (D)	10,580	70.3
	Leon C. Duchesne (R)	4,464	29.7
7	Charles E. Hooker (D)	11,977	77.0
	Henry Kernaghan (R)	3,587	23.1

MISSOURI

1	William H. Hatch (D)	20,049	52.9
	Brock (R)	17,349	45.8
2	Charles H. Mansur (D)	21,608	53.8
	Eubanks (R)	16,949	42.2
3	Alexander M. Dockery (D)	20,414	53.4
	Love (R)	16,743	43.8
4	James N. Burnes (D)	16,866*	52.5
	Hartwig (R)	13,729	42.7
5	John C. Tarsney (D)	22,635	52.5
	Bullene (R)	20,499	47.5
6	John T. Heard (D)	25,129	52.0

Candidates	Votes	%
Upton (R)	21,249	44.0
7 Richard H. Norton (D)	18,275	52.8
Edwards (R)	16,312	47.2
8 Frederick G. Niedringhaus (R)	14,210	52.2
O'Neill (D)	12,394	45.5
9 Nathan Frank (R)	13,762	54.7
Castleman (D)	11,312	45.0
10 William M. Kinsey (R)	18,980	50.8
Clardy (D)	16,886	45.2
11 Richard P. Bland (D)	18,095	50.4
Musick (R)	15,836	44.1
Needham (UN LAB)	1,954	5.5
12 William J. Stone (D)	24,054	49.4
Hannah (R)	19,431	39.9
Page (UN LAB)	4,613	9.5
13 William H. Wade (R)	16,480	48.4
Matlock (D)	13,601	40.0
Alter (UN LAB)	3,792	11.1
14 James P. Walker (D)	19,878	58.4
Whybark (R)	14,139	41.6

Special Election

4	Charles F. Booher (D)	12,750	52.3
	R. Posegate (R)	11,632	47.7

NEBRASKA

1	William J. Connell (R)	32,926	49.8
	J. Sterling Morton (D)	29,519	44.7
2	James Laird (R)	30,959	53.4
	W. G. Hastings (D)	21,201	36.6
	George Scott (P)	4,114	7.1
3	George W. E. Dorsey (R)	42,188	54.2
	E. P. Weatherby (D)	31,118	40.0

NEVADA

AL	Horace F. Bartine (R)	6,921	54.9
	G. W. Cassidy (D)	5,682	45.1

NEW HAMPSHIRE

1	Alonzo Nute (R)	21,754	49.6
	McKinney (D)	21,395	48.8
2	Orren C. Moore (R)	23,517	50.2
	Mann (D)	22,540	48.1

NEW JERSEY

1	Christopher A. Bergen (R)	24,906	53.6
	Brindle (D)	19,440	41.9
2	James Buchanan (R)	22,407	52.4
	Beasley (D)	19,104	44.6
3	Jacob A. Geissenhainer (D)	22,961	51.7
	Kean (R)	20,368	45.8
4	Samuel Fowler (D)	12,190	39.4
	Voorhees (R)	12,117	39.2
	Roe (ID)	5,079	16.4
5	Charles D. Beckwith (R)	20,277	50.2
	Hoagland (D)	19,205	47.6
6	Herman Lehlbach (R)	25,536	49.9
	Haynes (D)	24,762	48.4
7	William McAdoo (D)	26,498	56.1
	Collins (R)	20,424	43.3

NEW YORK

1	James W. Covert (D)	24,374	50.8
	Cromwell (R)	22,711	47.3
2	Felix Campbell (D)	23,497	56.3
	T. Seward (R)	17,625	42.2
3	William C. Wallace (R)	21,281	52.9
	Combs (D)	18,410	45.7
4	John M. Clancy (D)	20,987	59.1
	Robinson (R)	14,060	39.6
5	Thomas F. Magner (D)	18,613	52.2
	Hesse (R)	16,469	46.2
6	Frank T. Fitzgerald (TAM D&UL)	13,079	55.8
	Cavanagh (R)	9,833	42.0

	Candidates	Votes	%
7	Edward J. Dunphy (TAM D)	10,257	40.6
	Taintor (R)	8,343	33.0
	Lloyd S. Bryce (CIT&CO D)	6,482	25.7
8	John H. McCarthy (TAM D)	14,827	52.3
	Campbell (CIT&CO D)	9,778	34.5
	Schwartz (R)	3,456	12.2
9	Samuel S. Cox (UN LAB&D)	18,267	68.3
	McMackin (R)	7,320	27.4
10	Francis B. Spinola (UN LAB&D)	13,749	52.1
	Boyhan (R & UL)	12,016	45.5
11	John Quinn (UN LAB&D)	20,073	55.3
	Winch (R & UL)	15,619	43.0
12	Roswell P. Flower (D&UN LAB)	25,546	65.8
	Hildreth (R)	12,273	31.6
13	Ashbel P. Fitch (D)	28,580	58.9
	Hoyt (R)	19,412	40.0
14	William G. Stahlnecker (UN LAB&D)	22,485	53.7
	Wood (R)	18,356	43.9
15	Moses D. Stivers (R)	18,358	48.8
	Bacon (UN LAB&D)	18,284	48.6
16	John H. Ketcham (R)	18,912	74.6
	Downing (P)	6,370	25.1
17	Charles J. Knapp (R)	21,826	50.2
	Gilbert (D)	20,217	46.5
18	John A. Quackenbush (R)	23,639	53.4
	Sanford (D)	19,717	44.6
19	Charles Tracey (D)	21,294	52.3
	Dodge (R)	18,988	46.6
20	John Sanford (R)	23,966	52.2
	Westbrook (D)	20,665	45.0
21	John H. Moffitt (R)	21,361	95.2
22	Frederick Lansing (R)	24,309	62.0
	Sawyer (D)	13,582	34.7
23	James S. Sherman (R)	20,119	50.8
	McMahon (D)	18,387	46.4
24	David Wilber (R)	18,502	50.2
	John S. Pindar (D)	17,273	46.9
25	James J. Belden (R)	24,672	78.0
	Vanderbilt (D)	6,691	21.2
26	Milton De Lano (R)	26,267	55.4
	Maloney (D)	18,955	40.0
27	Newton W. Nutting (R)	28,803	58.6
	Titus (D)	18,327	37.3
28	Thomas S. Flood (R)	16,822	50.3
	Tuttle (D)	15,564	46.5
29	John Raines (R)	21,794	53.6
	Dininny (D)	16,969	41.7
30	Charles S. Baker (R)	21,810	55.4
	Nash (D)	16,106	40.9
31	John G. Sawyer (R)	19,506	54.4
	Stevens (D)	14,082	39.3
	Barnum (P)	2,284	6.4
32	John M. Farquhar (R)	22,468	51.6
	Mackey (D)	20,859	47.9
33	John M. Wiley (D)	15,705	48.8
	Crowley (R)	15,141	47.0
34	William G. Laidlaw (R)	27,453	58.9
	Howe (D)	15,523	33.3
	Corey (P)	3,170	6.8

NORTH CAROLINA

	Candidates	Votes	%
1	Thomas G. Skinner (D)	16,615	51.4
	Elihu A. White (R)	15,457	47.8
2	Henry P. Cheatham (R)	16,704	51.0
	Furnifold M. Simmons (D)	16,051	49.0
3	Charles W. McClammy (D)	16,809	56.7
	William Robinson (R)	12,825	43.3
4	Benjamin H. Bunn (D)	19,926	53.4
	John Nichols (R)	17,368	46.6
5	John M. Brower (R)	15,940	50.4
	James T. Morehead (D)	15,265	48.2
6	Alfred Rowland (D)	20,502	58.1
	Caleb P. Lockey (R)	14,797	41.9
7	John S. Henderson (D)	15,122	54.3
	William J. Ellis (R)	12,125	43.5
8	William H. H. Cowles (D)	13,139	56.7
	Edward W. Ward (R)	10,031	43.3
9	Hamilton G. Ewart (R)	15,433	50.9

	Candidates	Votes	%
	Thomas D. Johnston (D)	14,915	49.2

OHIO

	Candidates	Votes	%
1	Benjamin Butterworth (R)	19,336	51.9
	Otway J. Cosgrave (D)	17,437	46.8
2	John A. Caldwell (R)	21,627	51.0
	Clinton W. Gerard (D)	20,031	47.2
3	Elihu S. Williams (R)	20,912	49.2
	George W. Houk (D)	20,497	48.2
4	Samuel S. Yoder (D)	22,296	58.9
	Robert L. Mattingly (R)	14,500	38.3
5	George E. Seney (D)	22,075	56.1
	Wilson Vance (R)	16,081	40.9
6	Melvin M. Boothman (R)	22,434	48.4
	Gaylard M. Saltzgaber (D)	22,339	48.2
7	Henry L. Morey (R)	17,600	49.9
	John M. Pattison (D)	16,742	47.5
8	Robert P. Kennedy (R)	20,898	51.8
	Andrew R. Bolin (D)	17,628	43.7
9	William C. Cooper (R)	19,491	50.7
	John S. Braddock (D)	17,267	44.9
10	William E. Haynes (D)	19,637	50.7
	Jacob Romeis (R)	18,496	47.8
11	Albert C. Thompson (R)	20,802	55.6
	Joseph W. Shinn (D)	15,817	42.3
12	Jacob J. Pugsley (R)	20,133	49.6
	Lawrence T. Neal (D)	19,453	47.9
13	Joseph H. Outhwaite (D)	24,869	51.4
	John B. Neil (R)	22,298	46.1
14	Charles P. Wickham (R)	16,211	49.5
	David L. Wadsworth (D)	15,254	46.6
15	Charles H. Grosvenor (R)	17,591	51.9
	John P. Spriggs (D)	15,284	45.1
16	James W. Owens (D)	24,444	53.8
	Edwin L. Lybarger (R)	19,819	43.6
17	Joseph D. Taylor (R)	20,584	54.4
	William Lawrence Jr. (D)	15,580	41.2
18	William McKinley Jr. (R)	25,249	52.3
	George P. Ikert (D)	21,160	43.8
19	Ezra B. Taylor (R)	22,991	63.5
	Henry Apthorp (D)	11,091	30.6
	William H. Dana (P)	2,004	5.5
20	Martin L. Smyser (R)	19,381	50.6
	Calvin P. Humphrey (D)	17,283	45.1
21	Theodore E. Burton (R)	20,086	49.8
	Tom L. Johnson (D)	19,470	48.3

OREGON

	Candidates	Votes	%
AL	Binger Hermann (R)	32,820	54.5
	John M. Gearin (D)	25,413	42.2

PENNSYLVANIA

	Candidates	Votes	%
1	Henry H. Bingham (R)	22,523	57.1
	Flanigan (D)	16,838	42.7
2	Charles O'Neill (R)	16,776	57.2
	Dougherty (D)	12,368	42.2
3	Samuel J. Randall (D)	17,642	99.4
4	William D. Kelley (R)	32,841	58.1
	Ayers (D)	23,202	41.1
5	Alfred C. Harmer (R)	29,466	56.2
	Herwig (D)	22,781	43.4
6	Smedley Darlington (R)	19,299	58.1
	Greenwood (D)	12,799	38.5
7	Robert M. Yardley (R)	22,226	50.7
	Ross (D)	21,215	48.4
8	William Mutchler (D)	18,071	59.8
	Reeder (R)	11,731	38.8
9	David B. Brunner (D)	27,032	60.3
	Biery (R)	17,373	38.8
10	Marriott Brosius (R)	21,796	66.4
	Haldeman (D)	10,622	32.4
11	Joseph A. Scranton (R)	10,844	51.1
	Collins (D)	9,158	43.2
	Lathrope (P)	1,212	5.7
12	Edwin S. Osborne (R)	16,117	51.3
	Lynch (D)	14,618	46.5
13	James B. Reilly (D)	13,258	51.0

	Candidates	Votes	%
	Brumm (RG)	12,570	48.4
14	John W. Rife (R)	20,206	58.3
	Bower (D)	13,944	40.3
15	Myron B. Wright (R)	18,833	56.8
	Ham (D)	12,494	37.7
	Brown (P)	1,810	5.5
16	Henry C. McCormick (R)	19,204	54.2
	Steck (D & LAB)	15,550	43.9
17	Charles R. Buckalew (D)	14,012	54.5
	Robinson (R)	11,356	44.2
18	Louis E. Atkinson (R)	20,583	56.2
	McWilliams (D)	15,867	43.3
19	Levi Maish (D)	21,480	55.1
	Young (R)	16,901	43.4
20	Edward Scull (R)	21,739	54.3
	Greevy (D)	17,458	43.6
21	Samuel A. Craig (R)	24,151	54.0
	Donnelly (D)	18,930	42.3
22	John Dalzell (R)	21,970	62.0
	Parkinson (D)	13,065	36.9
23	Thomas M. Bayne (R)	13,999	66.8
	Langfitt (D)	6,711	32.0
24	Joseph W. Ray (R)	26,246	53.2
	Wampler (D)	21,908	44.4
25	Charles C. Townsend (R)	21,636	56.5
	Griffith (D)	14,481	37.8
26	William C. Culbertson (R)	16,924	52.5
	Burns (D)	13,852	43.0
27	Lewis F. Watson (R)	13,582	53.2
	Rankin (D)	9,370	36.7
	Miller (P)	1,670	6.5
28	James Kerr (D)	17,588	53.5
	Rynder (R)	14,899	45.3

RHODE ISLAND

	Candidates	Votes	%
1	Henry J. Spooner (R)	11,092	53.3
	Oscar Lapham (D)	9,002	43.3
2	Warren O. Arnold (R)	10,940	55.9
	Baker (D)	8,049	41.1

SOUTH CAROLINA

	Candidates	Votes	%
1	Samuel Dibble (D)	8,540	86.7
	S. W. McKinlay (R)	1,296	13.2
2	George D. Tillman (D)	10,704	86.8
	Seymour E. Smith (R)	1,405	11.4
3	James S. Cothran (D)	8,758	99.8
4	William H. Perry (D)	11,410	100.0
5	John J. Hemphill (D)	9,559	99.7
6	George W. Dargan (D)	8,586	95.7
7	William Elliott(D)	8,358‡	54.2
	Thomas E. Miller (R)	7,003	45.4

TENNESSEE

	Candidates	Votes	%
1	Alfred A. Taylor (R)	19,465	59.9
	Wilcox (D)	12,324	38.0
2	Leonidas C. Houk (R)	23,368	68.8
	Heiskell (D)	9,844	29.0
3	H. Clay Evans (R)	18,641	50.0
	Bates (D)	18,353	49.2
4	Benton McMillin (D)	16,162	61.6
	Wooten (R)	10,068	38.4
5	James D. Richardson (D)	17,754	67.8
	Shoffner (R)	8,426	32.2
6	Joseph E. Washington (D)	18,956	57.2
	Young (R)	12,677	38.3
7	Washington C. Whitthorne (D)	14,362	57.8
	Hagard (R)	10,507	42.3
8	Benjamin A. Enloe (D)	14,385	54.7
	Smith (R)	11,905	45.3
9	Rice A. Pierce (D)	17,217	63.0
	Brown (R)	10,127	37.0
10	James Phelan (D)	20,149	63.2
	Eaton (R)	11,730	36.8

TEXAS

	Candidates	Votes	%
1	Charles Stewart (D)	16,242	49.8
	Lock McDaniel (R)	12,003	36.8
	Jack Davis (I)	4,271	13.1
2	William H. Martin (D)	16,210	70.9
	R. M. Humphries (UN LAB)	6,656	29.1
3	Constantine B. Kilgore (D)	20,579	68.0
	W. E. Farmer (LAB-R)	9,697	32.0
4	David B. Culberson (D)	26,060	99.9
5	Silas Hare (D)	26,946	85.0
	J. W. Thomas (R)	4,468	14.1
6	Jo Abbott (D)	26,815	68.9
	Sam Evans (LAB)	12,126	31.1
7	William H. Crain (D)	15,610	56.4
	Calvin J. Brewster (R)	12,070	43.6
8	Littleton W. Moore (D)	21,022	69.3
	T. C. Cook (R)	8,460	27.9
9	Roger Q. Mills (D)	20,701	57.5
	E. A. Jones (ID R&P)	15,316	42.5
10	Joseph D. Sayers (D)	24,094	66.3
	A. Belknap (R)	12,251	33.7
11	Samuel W. T. Lanham (D)	28,535	85.9
	D. M. Rumph (R)	3,403	10.2

VERMONT

	Candidates	Votes	%
1	John W. Stewart (R)	23,892	70.2
	Ozro Meacham (D)	9,746	28.6
2	William W. Grout (R)	24,219	70.8
	George W. Smith (D)	9,605	28.1

VIRGINIA

	Candidates	Votes	%
1	Thomas H. B. Browne (R)	14,731	50.7
	G. S. Kendall (D)	14,317	49.3
2	George E. Bowden (R)	19,821	58.7
	R. C. Marshall (D)	13,726	40.6
3	George D. Wise (D)	15,608‡	50.4
	Edmond Waddill Jr. (R)	15,347	49.6
4	Edward C. Venable (D)	13,298‡	45.6
	John M. Langston (R)	12,657	43.4
	R. W. Arnold (R)	3,207	11.0
5	Posey G. Lester (D)	14,417	52.5
	J. D. Blackwell (R)	13,044	47.5
6	Paul C. Edmunds (D)	17,559	55.6
	P. H. M. Caull (R)	13,822	43.8
7	Charles T. O'Ferrall (D)	16,443	54.3
	J. E. Roller (R)	13,623	45.0
8	William H. F. Lee (D)	15,414	51.8
	Park Agnew (R)	14,291	48.0
9	John A. Buchanan (D)	16,520	50.7
	Henry Bowen (R)	16,042	49.3
10	Henry St. George Tucker (D)	14,587	51.0
	Jacob Yost (R)	13,994	49.0

WEST VIRGINIA

	Candidates	Votes	%
1	John O. Pendleton (D)	19,264‡	49.5
	George W. Atkinson (R)	19,242	49.5
2	William L. Wilson (D)	20,468	50.1
	W. H. H. Flick (R)	20,091	49.2
3	John D. Alderson (D)	15,474	50.8

	Candidates	Votes	%
	James H. McGinnis (R)	14,681	48.2
4	James M. Jackson (D)	19,837‡	49.7
	Charles B. Smith (R)	19,834	49.6

WISCONSIN

	Candidates	Votes	%
1	Lucien B. Caswell (R)	19,311	53.4
	Joseph B. Doe Jr. (D)	14,997	41.5
	Stephen Faville (P)	1,809	5.0
2	Charles Barwig (D)	16,813	53.2
	E. C. McFetridge (R)	13,859	43.8
3	Robert M. LaFollette (R)	19,052	50.0
	John B. Parkinson (D)	16,123	42.3
	T. C. Richmond (P)	2,654	7.0
4	Isaac W. Van Schaick (R)	22,212	50.8
	Henry Smith (D & LAB)	20,685	47.3
5	George H. Brickner (D)	17,051	55.2
	Gustav Kustermann (R)	12,825	41.5
6	Charles B. Clark (R)	17,977	52.5
	Charles W. Felger (D)	14,213	41.5
7	Ormsby B. Thomas (R)	19,918	53.5
	Frank P. Coburn (D)	15,433	41.5
	J. H. Mosely (P)	1,871	5.0
8	Nils P. Haugen (R)	26,909	57.0
	S. C. Johnson (D & LAB)	16,476	34.9
	Charles Alexander (P)	3,687	7.8
9	Myron H. McCord (R)	27,538	50.5
	H. W. Early (D)	24,775	45.4

1889 House Elections

ILLINOIS

Special Election

	Candidates	Votes	%
19	James R. Williams (D)	14,858	54.6
	Thomas S. Ridgway (R)	10,462	38.4
	John P. Stelle (F ALNC)	1,645	6.0

KANSAS

Special Election

		Votes	%
4	Harrison Kelley (R)	10,506	85.3
	John Heaston (D)	1,530	12.4

LOUISIANA

Special Election

		Votes	%
3	Edward J. Gay (D)	18,856	74.8
	Jolley (R)	6,351	25.2

MISSOURI

Special Election

	Candidates	Votes	%
4	Robert P. C. Wilson (D)	12,496	51.4
	R. Posegate (R)	11,812	48.6

MONTANA

(Became a state Nov. 8, 1889)

		Votes	%
AL	Thomas H. Carter (R)	19,915	51.9
	Martin Maginnis (D)	18,435	48.1

NEBRASKA

Special Election

		Votes	%
2	Gilbert L. Laws (R)	27,775	54.8
	C. D. Casper (D)	21,123	41.7

NEW YORK

Special Elections

		Votes	%
6	Charles H. Turner (D)	6,811	82.3
	Collier (R)	1,149	13.9
9	Amos J. Cummings (D)	15,508	99.7

	Candidates	Votes	%
27	Sereno E. Payne (R)	20,794	60.1
	Hopkins (D)	13,249	38.3

NORTH DAKOTA

(Became a state Nov. 2, 1889)

		Votes	%
AL	Henry C. Hansbrough (R)	26,077	68.5
	Maratta (D)	12,006	31.5

SOUTH DAKOTA

(Became a state Nov. 2, 1889)

		Votes	%
AL	Oscar S. Gifford (R)	54,983✓	
	John A. Pickler (R)	54,105✓	
	Linneus Q. Jeffries (D)	23,229	
	S. M. Booth (D)	22,541	

WASHINGTON

(Became a state Nov. 11, 1889)

		Votes	%
AL	John L. Wilson (R)	34,039	58.1
	Thomas C. Griffiths (D)	24,492	41.8

1890 House Elections

ALABAMA

	Candidates	Votes	%
1	Richard Henry Clarke (D)	10,071	69.9
	Frank H. Threatt (R)	2,448	17.0
	A. J. Warner	1,890	13.1
2	Hilary A. Herbert (D)	10,611	79.8
	S. A. Pilley	2,681	20.2
3	William C. Oates (D)	10,268	91.7
	Treadwell	930	8.3
4	Louis W. Turpin (D)	9,595	52.1
	John V. McDuffie (R)	4,931	26.8
	G. McCall	3,899	21.2
5	James E. Cobb (D)	5,548	99.8
6	John H. Bankhead (D)	9,182	95.1
7	William H. Forney (D)	10,054	59.2
	Butler	6,060	35.7
	Logan	862	5.1
8	Joseph Wheeler (D)	16,821	58.2
	R. W. Austin	12,076	41.8

ARKANSAS

		Votes	%
1	William H. Cate (D)	15,437	51.0
	L. P. Featherston (POP)	14,834	49.0
2	Clifton R. Breckinridge (D)	20,816	51.1
	I. P. Langley (POP)	19,941	48.9
3	Thomas C. McRae (D)	13,111	96.6
4	William L. Terry (D)	12,670	62.9
	E. M. Harrison (R)	7,488	37.1
5	Samuel W. Peel (D)	7,734	97.4

Special Election

		Votes	%
2	Clifton R. Breckinridge (D)	20,828	51.0
	Isom P. Langley (POP)	20,017	49.0

CALIFORNIA

		Votes	%
1	Thomas J. Geary (D)	19,334	49.3
	J. A. Barham (R)	19,117	48.7
2	Anthony Caminetti (D)	18,644	49.0
	G. G. Blanchard (R)	18,485	48.6
3	Joseph McKenna (R)	20,834	55.0
	J. P. Irish (D)	15,997	42.2
4	John P. Cutting (R)	13,196	49.2
	Robert Ferral (D)	12,091	45.1
	Thomas V. Cator (REF D)	1,492	5.6
5	Eugene F. Loud (R)	22,871	52.7
	T. J. Clunie (D)	19,899	45.8
6	William W. Bowers (R)	33,522	50.4
	W. J. Curtis (D)	28,904	43.5

Special Election

		Votes	%
1	Thomas J. Geary (D)	15,750	49.6
	J. A. Barham (R)	15,397	48.5

COLORADO

		Votes	%
AL	Hosea Townsend (R)	43,118	51.3
	T. J. O'Donnell (D)	34,736	41.3
	J. D. Burr (I)	5,207	12.0

CONNECTICUT

		Votes	%
1	Lewis Sperry (D)	16,195	49.8
	Simonds (R)	15,503	47.7
2	Washington F. Wilcox (D)	23,367	52.9
	Hubbard (R)	19,836	44.9
3	Charles A. Russell (R)	10,541	50.7
	Wells (D)	9,549	45.9
4	Robert E. De Forest (D)	18,777	50.2
	Miles (R)	17,821	47.7

DELAWARE

	Candidates	Votes	%
AL	John W. Causey (D)	17,848	50.6
	Henry P. Carmon (R)	17,150	48.7

FLORIDA

		Votes	%
1	Stephen R. Mallory (D)	11,731	77.7
	Reed (R)	3,362	22.3
2	Robert Bullock (D)	16,735	58.7
	Shipling (R)	11,786	41.3

GEORGIA

		Votes	%
1	Rufus G. Lester (D)	10,905	77.7
	Michael G. Doyle (R)	3,127	22.3
2	Henry G. Turner (D)	7,361	88.6
	C. B. Matteson (R)	948	11.4
3	Charles F. Crisp (D)	8,038	86.6
	Peter O. Gibson (R)	1,248	13.4
4	Charles L. Moses (D)	9,609	73.7
	Walter L. Johnson (R)	3,438	26.4
5	Leonidas F. Livingston (D)	8,688	70.7
	Will Haight (R)	3,608	29.3
6	James H. Blount (D)	2,860	100.0
7	R.W. Everett (D)	11,031	54.8
	W. H. Felton (D)	8,460	42.0
8	Thomas G. Lawson (D)	3,405	100.0
9	Thomas E. Winn (D)	10,315	58.8
	T. Pickett (I)	4,087	23.3
	S. A. Darnell (R)	3,133	17.9
10	Thomas G. Watson (D)	5,456	90.1
	Anthony E. Williams (R)	597	9.9

IDAHO

(Became a state July 3, 1890)

		Votes	%
AL	Willis Sweet (R)	10,171	56.0
	Alex E. Mayhew (D)	7,985	44.0

Special Election

		Votes	%
AL	Willis Sweet (R)	10,130	55.8
	Alex E. Mayhew (D)	8,026	44.2

ILLINOIS

		Votes	%
1	Abner Taylor (R)	22,235	50.0
	William G. Ewing (D)	21,796	49.0
2	Lawrence E. McGann (D)	17,383	60.4
	John G. Schaar (R)	10,633	36.9
3	Allan C. Durborow Jr. (D)	21,069	53.7
	William E. Mason (R)	17,933	45.7
4	Walter C. Newberry (D)	19,835	50.1
	George E. Adams (R)	19,173	48.4
5	Albert J. Hopkins (R)	15,845	59.7
	Jacob Haish (D)	9,664	36.4
6	Robert R. Hitt (R)	14,028	50.9
	Andrew Ashton (D)	13,517	49.1
7	Thomas J. Henderson (R)	12,946	53.8
	John W. Blee (D)	10,374	43.1
8	Lewis Steward (D)	17,496	49.4
	Charles A. Hill (R)	16,794	47.4
9	Herman W. Snow (D)	15,427	50.1
	Lewis E. Payson (R)	14,480	47.0
10	Philip S. Post (R)	16,194	50.1
	George A. Wilson (D)	15,576	48.2
11	Benjamin T. Cable (D)	19,334	51.2
	William H. Gest (R)	17,461	46.3
12	Scott Wike (D)	20,805	58.1
	Milton McClure (R)	13,336	37.2
13	William M. Springer (D)	20,951	54.3
	Jesse Hanon (R)	15,946	41.4
14	Owen Scott (D)	16,670	49.5

	Candidates	Votes	%
	Jonathan H. Rowell (R)	15,448	45.9
15	Samuel T. Busey (D)	19,010	49.7
	Joseph G. Cannon (R)	18,428	48.2
16	George W. Fithian (D)	16,473	50.3
	John D. Reeder (R)	15,957	48.7
17	Edward Lane (D)	16,700	51.7
	Fletcher H. Chapman (R)	9,761	30.2
	Edward Roessler (F ALNC)	4,845	15.0
18	William S. Forman (D)	16,279	51.7
	Cicero J. Lindley (R)	14,529	46.2
19	James R. Williams (D)	17,410	56.4
	George W. Pillow (R)	12,613	40.9
20	George H. Smith (R)	17,580	49.5
	William S. Morris (D)	16,273	45.9

INDIANA

		Votes	%
1	William F. Parrett (D)	17,730	50.4
	James S. Wright (R)	16,875	48.0
2	John L. Bretz (D)	14,697	43.6
	William N. Darnell (R)	11,996	35.6
	Sampson Cox (PP)	6,649	19.7
3	Jason B. Brown (D)	16,369	56.2
	William J. Durham (R)	12,430	42.7
4	William S. Holman (D)	15,639	52.4
	John T. Rankin (R)	13,867	46.4
5	George W. Cooper (D)	17,070	51.5
	John G. Dunbar (R)	15,355	46.3
6	Henry U. Johnson (R)	18,786	57.3
	David S. Trowbridge (D)	12,807	39.1
7	William D. Bynum (D)	27,401	54.2
	John J. W. Billingsly (R)	22,086	43.7
8	Elijah V. Brookshire (D)	21,389	52.8
	James A. Mount (R)	18,333	45.2
9	Daniel Waugh (R)	20,752	50.2
	Leroy Templeton (D)	19,453	47.1
10	David H. Patton (D)	17,262	50.3
	William D. Owen (R)	16,100	46.9
11	Augustus N. Martin (D)	20,813	51.5
	Cyrus Y. Bryant (R)	18,000	44.5
12	Charles A. O. McClellan (D)	17,970	54.7
	Jaques N. Babcock (R)	13,920	42.4
13	Benjamin F. Shively (D)	20,311	52.2
	H. B. Wilson (R)	17,614	45.2

IOWA

		Votes	%
1	John J. Seerley (D)	17,459	51.4
	John H. Gier (R)	16,388	48.2
2	Walter I. Hayes (D)	20,748	63.8
	Bruce T. Seaman (R)	11,740	36.1
3	David B. Henderson (R)	19,689	50.2
	C. F. Couch (D)	19,491	49.7
4	Walter H. Butler (D)	17,972	52.7
	J. H. Swaney (R)	16,023	47.0
5	John T. Hamilton (D)	18,153	50.1
	George R. Struble (R)	17,860	49.2
6	Frederick E. White (D)	17,092	49.0
	John F. Lacey (R)	16,572	47.5
7	John A. T. Hull (R)	16,821	53.9
	H. C. Hargis (D)	14,276	45.8
8	James P. Flick (R)	19,003	49.6
	Allen R. Anderson (D)	18,887	49.3
9	Thomas Bowman (D)	18,685	50.1
	Joseph R. Reed (R)	17,322	46.4
10	Jonathan P. Dolliver (R)	18,395	51.7
	I. L. Woode (D)	17,084	48.0
11	George D. Perkins (R)	15,972	44.6
	John Pallison (D)	15,065	42.1
	A. J. Westfall (PP)	4,658	13.0

Special Election

		Votes	%
7	Edward R. Hayes (R)	16,702	54.1
	J. H. Barnett	14,142	45.8

KANSAS

	Candidates	Votes	%
1	Case Broderick (R)	14,630	41.7
	Thomas Moonlight (D)	13,250	37.7
	L. C. Clark (ALNC D)	7,176	20.4
2	Edward H. Funston (R)	17,713	43.9
	A. F. Allen (ALNC D)	12,273	30.4
	J. B. Chapman (D)	10,130	25.1
3	Benjamin H. Clover (ALNC D)	23,492	55.2
	Bishop W. Perkins (R)	19,061	44.8
4	John G. Otis (ALNC D)	24,993	55.6
	Harrison Kelley (R)	19,984	44.4
5	John Davis (ALNC D)	19,482	52.9
	William A. Phillips (R)	13,998	38.0
	Park S. Warren (D)	3,337	9.1
6	William Baker (ALNC D)	20,749	62.6
	Webb McNall (R)	12,105	36.5
7	Jerry Simpson (ALNC D)	32,603	56.4
	James R. Hallowell (R)	25,181	43.6

KENTUCKY

1	William J. Stone (D)	9,749	66.9
	E. F. Franks (R)	3,743	25.7
	William Curd (P)	1,086	7.5
2	William T. Ellis (D)	13,983	56.9
	H. R. Bourland (R&F ALNC)	10,592	43.1
3	Isaac H. Goodnight (D)	11,649	61.1
	Addison D. James (R)	7,426	38.9
4	Alexander B. Montgomery (D)	11,036	61.2
	G. W. Long (R)	6,990	38.8
5	Asher G. Caruth (D)	14,395	60.8
	St. John Boyle (R)	9,291	39.2
6	William W. Dickerson (D)	11,310	62.3
	Weden O'Neal (R)	6,801	37.4
7	William C. P. Breckinridge (D)	7,146	92.9
	Hiram Ford (P)	442	5.7
8	James B. McCreary (D)	7,430	94.8
	J. C. Gilliam (R)	394	5.0
9	Thomas H. Paynter (D)	15,276	60.0
	Alexander Bruce (R)	10,053	39.5
10	John W. Kendall (D)	10,746	53.8
	R. C. Hill (R)	9,218	46.1
11	John H. Wilson (R)	9,612	60.5
	E. J. Howard (D)	5,964	37.5

Special Election

6	William W. Dickerson (D)	8,412	63.7
	Wesley M. Rardin (R)	4,742	35.9

LOUISIANA

1	Adolph Meyer (D)	10,824	63.2
	H. C. Warmoth (R)	6,155	36.0
2	Matthew D. Lagan (D)	10,948	61.6
	H. D. Coleman (R)	6,412	36.1
3	Andrew Price (D)	11,318	99.4
4	Newton C. Blanchard (D)	8,307	96.3
5	Charles J. Boatner (D)	11,793	92.7
6	Samuel M. Robertson (D)	6,611	99.9

MAINE

1	Thomas B. Reed (R)	16,797	57.2
	M.P. Frank (D)	11,971	40.7
2	Nelson Dingley Jr. (R)	16,499	58.0
	E. Allen (D)	11,187	39.3
3	Seth L. Milliken (R)	14,477	54.5
	Charles Baker (D)	11,011	41.5
4	Charles A. Boutelle (R)	15,713	56.2
	Josiah Crosby (D)	11,144	39.9

MARYLAND

1	Henry Page (D)	14,817	52.4
	George M. Russum (R)	12,437	44.0
2	Herman Stump (D)	17,740	57.1
	John E. Wilson (R)	12,130	39.0
3	Harry Wells Rusk (D)	16,914	59.1

	Candidates	Votes	%
	Royal H. Pullman (R)	11,273	39.4
4	Isidor Rayner (D)	18,740	59.7
	Henry H. Goldsborough (R)	12,106	38.6
5	Barnes Compton (D)	14,697	54.0
	Sidney E. Mudd (R)	12,479	45.8
6	William M. McKaig (D)	16,940	49.3
	Louis E. McComas (R)	16,775	48.8

MASSACHUSETTS

1	Charles S. Randall (R)	8,728	53.8
	Charles R. Codman (D)	6,518	40.2
	John D. Flint (P)	984	6.1
2	Elijah A. Morse (R)	12,339	52.3
	Bushrod Morse (D)	10,489	44.4
3	John F. Andrew (D)	14,992	56.2
	Edward L. Pierce (R)	11,184	41.9
4	Joseph H. O'Neil (D)	11,780	72.4
	Thomas Copeland (R)	4,170	25.6
5	Sherman Hoar (D)	13,081	53.0
	James A. Fox (R)	10,807	43.8
6	Henry Cabot Lodge (R)	14,579	50.0
	William Everett (D)	13,539	46.4
7	William Cogswell (R)	12,496	51.5
	Jonas H. French (D)	10,910	45.0
8	Moses T. Stevens (D)	11,726	49.9
	Frederic T. Greenhalge (R)	11,272	47.9
9	George Fred Williams (D)	12,207	48.5
	John W. Candler (R)	12,076	48.0
10	Joseph H. Walker (R)	11,130	49.4
	Charles B. Pratt (R)	10,431	46.3
11	Frederick S. Coolidge (D)	9,304	40.0
	Timothy G. Spaulding (R)	9,145	39.3
	Myron P. Walker (IR)	3,533	15.2
	Henry C. Smith (P)	1,260	5.4
12	John C. Crosby (D)	12,106	49.0
	Francis W. Rockwell (R)	11,724	47.5

MICHIGAN

1	J. Logan Chipman (D)	21,791	56.5
	Hibbard Baker (R)	15,861	41.1
2	James S. Gorman (D)	16,471	49.1
	Edward P. Allen (R)	14,568	43.4
	Thomas F. Moore (P)	2,522	7.5
3	James O'Donnell (R)	16,679	44.5
	John W. Fletcher (D)	14,216	37.9
	Robert Fraser (P)	3,423	9.1
	Samuel Dickie (INDUST)	3,187	8.5
4	Julius C. Burrows (R)	16,067	45.3
	George L. Yaple (D)	15,673	44.1
	George F. Cunningham (P)	2,843	8.0
5	Melbourne Ford (D)	22,451	49.6
	Charles W. Watkins (R)	20,153	44.5
	Edward L. Briggs (P)	2,587	5.7
6	Byron G. Stout (D)	17,140	44.5
	William Ball (R)	16,457	42.7
	Jay Sessions (P)	3,004	7.8
	George W. Caswell (INDUST)	1,940	5.0
7	Justin R. Whiting (D)	14,553	50.7
	James S. Ayres (R)	12,566	43.8
8	Henry M. Youmans (D)	17,230	47.2
	Aaron T. Bliss (R)	17,154	47.0
	William M. Smith (P)	2,106	5.8
9	Harrison H. Wheeler (D)	15,854	45.7
	Byron M. Cutcheon (R)	15,794	45.6
	Oscar M. Brownson (P)	2,778	8.0
10	Thomas A. E. Weadock (D)	16,721	50.6
	Watts S. Humphrey (R)	15,055	45.6
11	Samuel M. Stephenson (R)	16,667	50.4
	John Semer (D)	14,549	44.0
	William H. Simmons (P)	1,759	5.3

MINNESOTA

1	William H. Harries (D)	17,198	53.6
	Dunnell (R)	14,875	46.4
2	John Lind (R)	20,789	49.2
	Baker (ALNC D)	20,306	48.1
3	Osee M. Hall (D)	17,639	50.5

	Candidates	Votes	%
	D. S. Hall (R)	13,106	37.5
	Gamble (ALNC D)	3,054	8.8
4	James N. Castle (D)	35,903	51.8
	R. Snider (R)	30,175	43.5
5	Kittel Halvorson (ALNC D)	21,514	37.7
	Comstock (R)	19,372	33.9
	Whiteman (D)	16,203	28.4

MISSISSIPPI

1	John M. Allen (D)	3,501	100.0
2	John C. Kyle (D)	8,282	70.5
	G. M. Buchanan (R)	3,468	29.5
3	Thomas C. Catchings (D)	8,689	76.2
	James Hill (R)	2,717	23.8
4	Clarke Lewis (D)	6,753	81.1
	W. D. Frazer (R)	1,572	18.9
5	Joseph H. Beeman (D)	6,305	100.0
6	Thomas R. Stockdale (D)	9,340	71.3
	H. C. Griffin (R)	3,768	28.8
7	Charles E. Hooker (D)	6,284	75.6
	J. M. Matthews (R)	2,028	24.4

MISSOURI

1	William H. Hatch (D)	20,234	56.7
	Harrington (R)	15,080	42.3
2	Charles H. Mansur (D)	20,527	57.2
	Pettyjohn (R)	13,147	36.7
	Donovan (UN LAB)	2,188	6.1
3	Alexander M. Dockery (D)	20,594	55.0
	Kinney (R)	13,139	35.1
	Hillis (UN LAB)	3,681	9.8
4	Robert P. C. Wilson (D)	15,753	51.4
	Ford (R)	12,444	40.6
	Whipple (UN LAB)	2,191	7.2
5	John C. Tarsney (D)	19,387	57.7
	Twitchell (R)	13,505	40.2
6	John T. Heard (D)	24,027	54.6
	Redman (R)	16,365	37.2
	Alldredge (UN LAB)	3,625	8.2
7	Richard H. Norton (D)	17,926	58.1
	Barnett (R)	12,946	41.9
8	John J. O'Neill (D)	11,621	54.9
	Joy (R)	9,563	45.1
9	Seth W. Cobb (D)	10,576	58.8
	Prosser (R)	6,962	38.7
10	Samuel Byrns (D)	16,744	52.5
	Kinsey (R)	15,095	47.3
11	Richard P. Bland (D)	18,991	56.1
	Erwin (R)	14,885	43.9
12	David A. De Armond (D)	21,556	48.2
	Lewis (R)	14,441	32.3
	Wykoff (UN LAB)	8,537	19.1
13	Robert W. Fyan (D)	16,488	49.9
	Wade (R)	13,728	41.6
	Vertrees (UN LAB)	2,803	8.5
14	Marshall Arnold (D)	19,312	59.7
	Rogers (R)	13,037	40.3

Special Election

14	Robert H. Whitelaw (D)	19,329	60.8
	Farnsworth (R)	12,481	39.2

MONTANA

AL	William W. Dixon (D)	15,411	49.6
	Thomas H. Carter (R)	15,128	48.7

NEBRASKA

1	William Jennings Bryan (D)	32,376	44.5
	W. J. Connell (R)	25,663	35.3
	Allen Root (I)	13,066	18.0
2	William A. McKeighan (I & D)	36,104	61.1
	N. V. Harlan (R)	21,776	36.9
3	Omer M. Kem (I)	31,731	39.4
	George W. E. Dorsey (R)	25,440	31.6
	W. H. Thompson (D)	22,353	27.8

NEVADA

Candidates	Votes	%
AL Horace F. Bartine (R)	6,610	53.4
George W. Cassidy (D)	5,736	46.3

NEW HAMPSHIRE

Candidates	Votes	%
1 Luther F. McKinney (D)	21,432	50.7
David A. Taggart (R)	20,296	48.0
2 Warren F. Daniell (D)	21,438	49.7
Orren C. Moore (R)	21,079	48.8

NEW JERSEY

Candidates	Votes	%
1 Christopher A. Bergen (R)	19,082	50.9
Newell (D)	16,372	43.7
Nicholson (P)	2,007	5.4
2 James Buchanan (R)	17,515	50.0
Haven (D)	16,352	46.6
3 Jacob A. Geissenhainer (D)	20,266	54.6
Clark Jr. (R)	15,748	42.4
4 Samuel Fowler (D)	13,459	56.5
Goodman (R)	8,775	36.8
Schenk (P)	1,583	6.7
5 Cornelius A. Cadmus (D)	16,815	50.4
Beckwith (R)	15,459	46.4
6 Thomas D. English (D)	23,278	50.9
Condit (R)	21,468	46.9
7 Edward F. McDonald (D)	21,875	56.0
McEwan Jr. (R)	16,761	42.9

NEW YORK

Candidates	Votes	%
1 James W. Covert (D)	18,999	56.0
John Lewis Childs (R)	14,085	41.5
2 David A. Boody (D)	21,609	57.7
James Gresham (R)	15,028	40.1
3 William J. Coombs (D)	15,670	48.9
William Wallace (R)	15,652	48.8
4 John M. Clancy (D)	18,216	67.6
Andrew J. Perry (R)	8,454	31.4
5 Thomas F. Magner (D)	16,470	58.4
John R. Smith (R)	10,814	38.4
6 John R. Fellows (D)	10,170	57.2
Cornelius Donovan (R)	5,574	31.3
Edwin L. Abbett (CO D)	1,928	10.8
7 Edward J. Dunphy (D)	10,855	60.0
William Morgan (R)	4,351	24.1
William T. Croasdale (CO D)	2,787	15.4
8 Timothy J. Campbell (D)	15,958	77.9
Samuel Rinaldo (R)	3,840	18.7
9 Amos J. Cummings (D)	14,252	71.8
John Weiss (R)	4,462	22.5
Christian Ensminger (CO D)	1,072	5.4
10 Francis B. Spinola (D)	13,884	70.5
Cortlandt S. Van Rensselaer (R)	5,288	26.9
11 John De Witt Warner (D)	17,033	64.2
Charles A. Flammer (R)	8,850	33.3
12 Roswell P. Flower (D)	19,160	69.4
Charles H. Blair (R)	7,187	26.0
13 Ashbel P. Fitch (D)	28,268	68.9
Percy D. Adams (R)	11,820	28.8
14 William G. Stahlnecker (D)	18,391	53.4
J. Thomas Stearns (R)	12,211	35.5
Alexander Taylor Jr. (IR)	2,561	7.4
15 Henry Bacon (D)	14,640	50.9
Clarence Lexow (R)	13,061	45.4
16 John H. Ketcham (R)	13,474	75.3
William W. Smith (P)	4,428	24.7
17 Isaac N. Cox (D)	15,439	53.5
Theodore C. Teale (R)	13,429	46.5
18 John A. Quackenbush (R)	17,185	50.2
Michael F. Collins (D)	15,939	46.6
19 Charles Tracey (D)	18,021	56.9
Angus McDuffie Shoemaker (R)	12,942	40.9
20 John Sanford (R)	18,369	50.4
Alexander B. Baucus (D)	16,788	46.1
21 John M. Wever (R)	13,314	55.6
Anthony J. B. Ross (D)	9,820	41.0
22 Leslie W. Russell (R)	13,893	56.3

Candidates	Votes	%
Smith T. Woolworth (D)	9,116	36.9
Henry P. Forbes (P)	1,679	6.8
23 Henry W. Bentley (D)	15,449	50.4
James S. Sherman (R)	14,933	48.7
24 George Van Horn (D)	14,127	48.3
Frank B. Arnold (R)	13,929	47.6
25 James J. Belden (R)	17,283	57.1
William Stitt (D)	11,455	37.8
Andrew N. Vanderbilt (P)	1,547	5.1
26 George W. Ray (R)	17,804	51.7
Thomas H. Beal (D)	14,402	41.9
Mott C. Dixon (P)	2,208	6.4
27 Sereno E. Payne (R)	17,970	50.6
Edwin K. Burnham (D)	15,978	45.0
28 Hosea H. Rockwell (D)	12,440	47.9
Henry T. Noyes (R)	12,351	47.6
29 John Raines (R)	14,722	49.7
Demerville Page (D)	13,369	45.1
Daniel J. Chittenden (P)	1,540	5.2
30 Halbert S. Greenleaf (D)	15,047	48.5
John Van Voorhis (R)	14,796	47.7
31 James W. Wadsworth (R)	13,716	82.2
Alva Carpenter (P)	2,275	13.6
32 Daniel N. Lockwood (D)	21,213	55.7
Benjamin H. Williams (R)	16,240	42.6
33 Thomas L. Bunting (D)	12,585	51.6
George A. Davis (R)	10,793	44.2
34 Warren B. Hooker (R)	15,843	54.7
Hiram Smith (D)	10,117	35.0
Jesse D. Rogers (P)	2,981	10.3

Special Election

Candidates	Votes	%
24 John S. Pindar (D)	14,030	48.1
Frank B. Arnold (R)	13,916	47.7

NORTH CAROLINA

Candidates	Votes	%
1 William A. B. Branch (D)	16,436	56.3
Claude M. Bernard (R)	12,683	43.4
2 Henry P. Cheatham (R)	16,942	51.7
James M. Mewboorne (D)	15,713	47.9
3 Benjamin F. Grady (D)	17,348	67.0
George C. Scurlock (R)	8,541	33.0
4 Benjamin H. Bunn (D)	18,995	59.8
Alexander McIver (R&F ALNC)	12,417	39.1
5 Archibald H. A. Williams (D)	16,143	52.6
John M. Brower (R)	14,204	46.2
6 Sydenham B. Alexander (D)	16,820	66.6
Richard M. Norment (R)	8,424	33.4
7 John S. Henderson (D)	13,246	57.4
Pleasant C. Thomas (R)	9,280	40.2
8 William H. H. Cowles (D)	8,586	53.7
Edward W. Faucette (R)	7,256	45.4
9 William T. Crawford (D)	15,979	51.8
Hamilton G. Ewart (R)	14,851	48.2

NORTH DAKOTA

Candidates	Votes	%
AL Martin N. Johnson (R)	21,365	59.0
Benton (D)	14,830	41.0

OHIO

Candidates	Votes	%
1 Bellamy Storer (R)	16,661	53.3
O. J. Cosgrave (D)	14,373	46.0
2 John A. Caldwell (R)	22,021	59.9
Oliver Brown (D)	14,291	38.9
3 George W. Houk (D)	21,270	51.5
H. L. Morey (R)	18,639	45.1
4 Martin K. Gantz (D)	20,705	49.5
William P. Orr (R)	19,295	46.2
5 Fernando C. Layton (D)	20,179	52.7
L. K. Stroup (R)	15,973	41.7
6 Dennis D. Donovan (D)	18,741	51.0
J. H. Brigham (R)	17,029	46.3
7 William E. Haynes (D)	18,126	52.4
J. M. Ashley (R)	16,070	46.4
8 Darius D. Hare (D)	17,414	48.3
Charles Foster (R)	17,220	47.7

Candidates	Votes	%
9 Joseph H. Outhwaite (D)	18,550	51.8
T. B. Wilson (R)	16,418	45.8
10 Robert E. Doan (R)	19,353	52.5
J. Q. Smith (D)	15,569	42.2
R. Rathburn (P)	1,954	5.3
11 John M. Pattison (D)	16,110	51.9
D. W. C. Loudon (R)	13,157	42.4
12 W. H. Enochs (R)	16,851	61.1
Ezra V. Dean (D)	9,814	35.6
13 Irvine Dungan (D)	16,225	50.7
William T. Lewis (R)	14,759	46.1
14 James W. Owens (D)	19,193	53.2
Samuel Slade (R)	15,773	43.8
15 Michael D. Harter (D)	19,832	52.5
G. L. Sackett (R)	16,084	42.6
16 John G. Warwick (D)	20,059	49.3
William McKinley Jr. (R)	19,757	48.6
17 Albert J. Pearson (D)	14,928	49.8
C. L. Poorman (R)	14,224	47.5
18 Joseph D. Taylor (R)	16,993	56.0
H. H. McFadden (D)	11,783	38.8
S. W. Wilkins (P)	1,568	5.2
19 Ezra B. Taylor (R)	19,419	58.5
T. E. Hoyt (D)	11,972	36.1
Richard Brown (P)	1,753	5.3
20 Vincent A. Taylor (R)	22,672	58.1
H. L. Stewart (D)	14,748	37.8
21 Tom L. Johnson (D)	17,646	54.6
T. E. Burton (R)	14,256	44.1

OREGON

Candidates	Votes	%
AL Binger Herman (R)	40,176	54.8
Robert A. Miller (D)	30,263	41.3

PENNSYLVANIA

Candidates	Votes	%
1 Henry H. Bingham (R)	22,166	60.3
Edwin G. Flanagan (D)	14,497	39.5
2 Charles O'Neill (R)	16,324	62.2
Edwin F. Lott (D)	9,785	37.3
3 William McAleer (D)	13,121	56.6
Richard Vaux (ID)	10,037	43.3
4 John E. Reyburn (R)	33,253	60.9
William M. Ayrres (D)	20,988	38.4
5 Alfred C. Harmer (R)	30,616	61.2
J. Henry Taylor (D)	19,213	38.4
6 John B. Robinson (R)	17,447	55.0
Thomas W. Pierce (D)	13,342	42.1
7 Edwin Hallowell (D)	20,810	49.5
Irving P. Wauger (R)	20,623	49.1
8 William Mutchler (D)	17,424	62.3
George M. Davies (R)	10,549	37.7
9 David B. Brunner (D)	26,627	62.8
Daniel H. Wingerd (R)	15,434	36.4
10 Marriott Brosius (R)	19,126	66.4
D. F. Magee (D)	9,358	32.5
11 Lemuel Amerman (D)	9,336	48.6
Joseph A. Scranton (R)	9,033	47.0
12 George W. Shonk (R)	14,558	51.3
John B. Reynolds (D)	13,074	46.0
13 James B. Reilly (D)	13,308	52.9
John T. Shoener (R)	11,828	47.1
14 John W. Rife (R)	17,795	54.8
William L. Gorgas (D)	14,308	44.0
15 Myron B. Wright (R)	16,076	51.8
Clar W. Canfield (D)	13,854	44.7
16 Albert C. Hopkins (R)	15,824	48.5
Mortimer F. Elliott (D)	15,773	48.3
17 Simon P. Wolverton (D)	15,178	60.2
W. C. Farnsworth (R)	9,234	36.6
18 Louis E. Atkinson (R)	17,443	50.9
George W. Skinner (D)	16,834	49.1
19 Frank E. Beltzhoover (D)	21,969	58.7
D. K. Trimmer (R)	14,860	39.7
20 Edward Scull (R)	17,434	49.5
Thomas H. Greevy (D)	16,908	48.0
21 George F. Huff (R)	21,212	51.8
Jacob Creps (D)	19,714	48.2
22 John Dalzell (R)	21,464	60.9

Candidates	Votes	%
William J. Brennan (D)	13,559	38.4
23 William A. Stone (R)	13,904	66.8
Morrison Foster (D)	6,788	32.6
24 Andrew J. Stewart (R)	21,708‡	49.0
Alexander K. Craig (D)	21,585	48.7
25 Eugene P. Gillespie (D)	13,797	38.3
Thomas W. Phillips (R)	10,636	29.5
Alex McDowell (R)	10,531	29.2
26 Matthew Griswold (R)	13,779	49.8
A. L. Tilden (D)	12,891	46.6
27 Charles W. Stone (R)	12,718	54.5
Robert W. Dunn (D)	9,405	40.3
D. H. Boulton (P)	1,212	5.2
28 George F. Kribbs (D)	17,636	56.4
Daniel C. Oyster (R)	12,944	41.4

Special Elections

Candidates	Votes	%
3 Richard Vaux (D)	7,977	92.1
4 John E. Reyburn (R)	25,152	59.9
William M. Ayres (D)	16,573	39.5
27 Charles W. Stone (R)	11,825	72.0
Robert W. Dunn (D)	4,499	27.4

RHODE ISLAND[1]

Candidates	Votes	%
1 Oscar Lapham (D)	10,382	52.6
Henry J. Spooner (R)	8,616	43.6
2 Charles H. Page (D)	8,341*	47.8
Warren O. Arnold (R)	8,325	47.7

SOUTH CAROLINA

Candidates	Votes	%
1 William H. Brawley (D)	7,249	84.2
William D. Crum (R)	1,349	15.7
2 George D. Tillman (D)	9,996	85.6
S. E. Smith (R)	1,671	14.3
3 George Johnstone (D)	8,942	91.4
John R. Tolbert (R)	803	8.2
4 George W. Shell (D)	10,372	81.9
J. F. Ensor (R)	2,258	17.8
5 John J. Hemphill (D)	9,432	87.1
G. G. Alexander (R)	1,321	12.2
6 Eli T. Stackhouse (D)	9,022	78.8
Edmund H. Deas (R)	2,352	20.5
7 William Elliott (D)	3,792	44.4
Thomas E. Miller (R)	3,315	38.8
E. W. Brayton (IR)	1,410	16.5

SOUTH DAKOTA

Candidates	Votes	%
AL John A. Pickler (R)	34,856✓	
John R. Gamble (R)	34,553✓	
F. A. Leavitt (I)	24,907	
Fred Zipp (I)	24,808	
F. A. Clark (D)	17,527	
W. Y. Quigley (D)	17,267	

TENNESSEE

Candidates	Votes	%
1 Alfred A. Taylor (R)	11,466	49.0
R. R. Butler (IR)	10,717	45.8
2 Leonidas C. Houk (R)	12,765	60.1
J. C. J. Williams (D)	7,378	34.8
3 Henry C. Snodgrass (D)	13,773	50.3

Candidates	Votes	%
H. Clay Evans (R)	13,250	48.4
4 Benton McMillin (D)	14,514	64.0
C. W. Garratt (R)	7,630	33.7
5 James D. Richardson (D)	12,890	68.4
P. C. Smithson (R)	4,340	23.0
H. R. Moore (P)	1,474	7.8
6 Joseph E. Washington (D)	11,656	74.4
L. M. Watson (R)	2,708	17.3
W. D. Turnley (P)	1,302	8.3
7 Nicholas N. Cox (D)	10,362	60.7
A.M. Hughes Jr. (R)	5,364	31.4
John Graham (P)	1,289	7.6
8 Benjamin A. Enloe (D)	12,444	62.7
J. R. McKinney (R)	4,469	22.5
George T. McCall (R)	1,339	6.7
John T. Warren (P)	1,070	5.4
9 Rice A. Pierce (D)	12,191	70.6
W. F. Poston (R)	3,959	22.9
J. B. Cummings (P)	1,109	6.4
10 Josiah Patterson (D)	9,108	74.5
L. B. Eaton (R)	3,033	24.8

TEXAS

Candidates	Votes	%
1 Charles Stewart (D)	19,356	63.1
E. L. Angier (R)	11,292	36.8
2 John B. Long (D)	12,973	99.6
3 Constantine B. Kilgore (D)	19,038	71.3
L. B. Fish (R)	7,340	27.5
4 David B. Culberson (D)	17,290	74.8
J. C. Gibbons (R)	5,279	22.8
5 Joseph W. Bailey (D)	26,791	81.9
A. W. Achison (R)	4,252	13.0
W. R. Lamb (I)	1,683	5.1
6 Jo Abbott (D)	29,982	85.7
Darter Isaac (R)	4,430	12.7
7 William H. Crain (D)	18,550	67.2
J. V. Spohn (R)	9,069	32.8
8 Littleton W. Moore (D)	20,739	71.2
William Greene (R)	8,368	28.8
9 Roger Q. Mills (D)	21,847	79.6
D. W. Roberts (R)	5,600	20.4
10 Joseph D. Sayers (D)	32,479	92.4
W. G. Robinson (R)	2,537	7.2
11 Samuel W. T. Lanham (D)	38,348	97.8

VERMONT

Candidates	Votes	%
1 H. Henry Powers (R)	17,136	66.5
Thomas W. Moloney (D)	8,605	33.4
2 William W. Grout (R)	18,092	66.8
Stephen C. Shurtleff (D)	8,960	33.1

VIRGINIA

Candidates	Votes	%
1 William A. Jones (D)	14,613	54.3
I. H. Bayly Browne (R)	12,150	45.2
2 John W. Lawson (D)	13,484	50.7
George E. Bowden (R)	12,317	46.3
3 George D. Wise (D)	13,937	99.9
4 James F. Epes (D)	13,325	57.1
J. M. Langston (R)	9,991	42.8
5 Posey G. Lester (D)	10,569	82.0
S. C. Adams (I)	1,360	10.6
J. Ring (I)	959	7.4

Candidates	Votes	%
6 Paul C. Edmunds (D)	11,615	92.6
William J. Shelburne (P)	901	7.2
7 Charles T. O'Ferrall (D)	10,167	89.0
I. M. Underwood (P)	1,225	10.7
8 William H. F. Lee (D)	13,499	57.0
Frank Hume (ID)	10,181	43.0
9 John A. Buchanan (D)	15,324	56.1
George T. Mills (R)	11,977	43.9
10 Henry St. George Tucker (D)	9,721	94.6
A. J. Taylor (I)	531	5.2

WASHINGTON

Candidates	Votes	%
AL John L. Wilson (R)	29,133	56.0
Carroll (D)	22,861	44.0

WEST VIRGINIA

Candidates	Votes	%
1 John O. Pendleton (D)	18,470	50.2
William P. Hubbard (R)	17,831	48.5
2 William L. Wilson (D)	20,439	52.5
George Hourian (R)	18,374	47.2
3 John D. Alderson (D)	20,433	56.1
Theophilus Gaines (R)	15,778	43.3
4 Jones Capehart (D)	19,576	52.3
C. B. Smith (R)	17,648	47.2

WISCONSIN

Candidates	Votes	%
1 Clinton Babbitt (D)	14,532	48.3
Cooper (R)	14,209	47.3
2 Charles Barwig (D)	17,826	65.8
D. C. Van Brunt (R)	9,266	34.2
3 Allen R. Bushnell (D)	16,432	49.2
Robert M. LaFollette (R)	15,430	46.2
4 John L. Mitchell (D)	24,679	56.1
R.C. Spencer (R)	17,605	40.0
5 George H. Brickner (D)	17,708	67.2
Blackstock (R)	8,093	30.7
6 Lucas M. Miller (D)	15,573	51.7
Clark (R)	13,409	44.5
7 Frank P. Coburn (D)	15,399	50.8
Thomas (R)	13,397	44.2
8 Nils P. Haugen (R)	17,609	49.2
Bailey (R)	15,261	42.7
Jones (P)	2,911	8.1
9 Thomas Lynch (D)	24,491	54.4
Myron H. McCord (R)	19,161	42.6

WYOMING

(Became a state July 10, 1890)

Candidates	Votes	%
AL Clarence D. Clark (R)	9,087	58.2
George T. Beck (D)	6,520	41.8

1. No candidate in the 2nd district received the majority of the vote required for election.

1891 House Elections

MICHIGAN

Special Election

	Candidates	Votes	%
5	Charles E. Belknap (R)	14,652	44.5
	John S. Lawrence (D)	13,150	40.0
	Edward Hutchins (PP)	3,687	11.2

NEW YORK

Special Elections

	Candidates	Votes	%
2	Alfred C. Chapin (D)	24,018	52.7
	Bristow (R)	21,522	47.3
10	W. Bourke Cockran (TAM&NY D)	13,234	63.5
	Townsend (R)	7,160	34.4
12	Joseph J. Little (TAM&NY D)	19,306	58.1

	Candidates	Votes	%
	McMichael (R)	11,465	34.5
22	Newton M. Curtis (R)	19,096	54.8
	Porter (D)	14,423	41.4

RHODE ISLAND[1]

Special Election

	Candidates	Votes	%
2	Charles H. Page (D)	6,899	85.4
	Warren O. Arnold (R)	721	8.9
	Tripp (P)	461	5.7

SOUTH DAKOTA

Special Election

	Candidates	Votes	%
AL	John L. Jolley (R)	17,614	44.5
	Henry W. Smith (I)	14,687	37.1
	James M. Wood (D)	7,299	18.4

TENNESSEE

Special Election

	Candidates	Votes	%
2	John C. Houk (R)	14,095	63.7
	J. C. J. Williams (D)	7,829	35.4

VIRGINIA

Special Election

		Votes	%
8	Elisha E. Meredith (R)	8,891	67.8
	John Ambler Brooks	4,218	32.2

1. Since no candidate running for the House in Rhode Island's 2nd district in 1890 received the majority needed for election (see Rhode Island 1890), a special election in 1891 was ordered by the legislature. According to the *Biographical Directory*, incumbent Warren O. Arnold, who had run for reelection in 1890, but failed to win a majority, refused to participate actively in the special election. Without serious opposition, Charles H. Page won easily.

1892 House Elections

ALABAMA

	Candidates	Votes	%
1	Richard H. Clarke (D)	12,514	60.5
	William Mason (K POP)	7,156	34.6
2	Jesse F. Stallings (D)	16,781	58.6
	Frank Baltzell (K POP)	10,331	36.1
	John O. Bibb (R)	1,506	5.3
3	William Oates (D)	16,885	62.4
	J. F. Tate (K POP)	9,931	36.7
4	Gaston A. Robbins (D)	16,159	60.7
	Adolphus P. Longshore (K POP)	8,534	32.1
	George H. Craig (R)	1,848	6.9
5	James E. Cobb (D)	13,456	49.4
	M. W. Whatley (K POP)	11,468	42.1
	John McDuffie (R)	2,306	8.5
6	John Bankhead (D)	14,342	62.8
	T. M. Barbour (K POP)	6,453	28.2
	Ignatius Green (R)	2,054	9.0
7	William H. Denson (D)	10,911	54.3
	William Wood (K POP)	9,091	45.2
8	Joseph Wheeler (D)	15,607	52.4
	R. W. Austin (POP)	11,868	39.9
	R. T. Blackwell (R)	2,279	7.7
9	L. W. Turpin (D)	19,848	67.4
	Joseph H. Parsons (POP)	8,954	30.4

ARKANSAS

	Candidates	Votes	%
1	Philip D. McCulloch Jr. (D)	16,680	63.6
	Jacob Trieber (R)	9,541	36.4
2	Clifton R. Breckinridge (D)	16,508	70.8
	W. B. W. Heartsill (PP)	6,808	29.2
3	Thomas C. McRae (D)	17,493	68.1
	J. O. A. Bush (PP)	8,197	31.9
4	William L. Terry (D)	13,630	69.7
	T. M. C. Birmingham (PP)	5,910	30.2
5	Hugh A. Dinsmore (D)	13,698	57.2
	J. E. Bryan (PP)	10,267	42.8
6	Robert Neill (D)	16,594	87.6
	George Martin (I)	1,926	10.2

CALIFORNIA

	Candidates	Votes	%
1	Thomas J. Geary (D)	19,308	56.8
	Edw. W. Davis (R)	13,123	38.6
2	Anthony Caminetti (D)	20,741	53.2
	John F. Davis (R)	16,781	43.1
3	Samuel G. Hilborn (R)	13,163‡	43.2
	Warren B. English (D)	13,138	43.1
	J. L. Lyon (PP)	3,495	11.5
4	James G. Maguire (D)	14,997	49.2
	C. O. Alexander (R)	13,226	43.4
	E. P. Burman (PP)	1,980	6.5
5	Eugene F. Loud (R)	14,660	46.4
	J. W. Ryland (D)	13,694	43.3
	J. J. Morrison (PP)	2,484	7.9
6	Marion Cannon (D, PP)	20,680	56.3
	Hervey Lindley (R)	14,271	38.8
7	William W. Bowers (R)	15,856	41.6
	Olin Welborn (D)	14,869	39.0
	Hiram Hamilton (PP)	5,578	14.6

Special Election

	Candidates	Votes	%
3	Samuel G. Hilborn (R)	16,911	47.3
	Warren B. English (D)	14,493	40.5
	J. L. Lyon (PP)	4,326	12.1

COLORADO

	Candidates	Votes	%
1	Lafayette Pence (D & POP)	20,004	49.1
	Earl B. Coe (R)	17,609	43.2
	John G. Taylor (D)	2,240	5.5
2	John C. Bell (D & POP)	31,587	61.0
	Henderson H. Eddy (R)	19,572	37.8

CONNECTICUT

	Candidates	Votes	%
1	Lewis Sperry (D)	19,068	49.0
	Henry (R)	18,506	47.5
2	James P. Pigott (D)	27,624	50.9
	Kellogg (R)	24,772	45.7
3	Charles A. Russell (R)	11,928	49.5
	Thayer (D)	11,277	46.8
4	Robert E. DeForest (D)	24,035	51.3
	Frederick Miles (R)	21,825	46.6

DELAWARE

	Candidates	Votes	%
AL	John W. Causey (D)	18,554	49.9
	Jonathan S. Willis (R)	18,080	48.6

FLORIDA

	Candidates	Votes	%
1	Stephen R. Mallory (PP & D)	16,114	99.2
2	Charles M. Cooper (D)	14,668	75.8
	Austin S. Mann (PP)	4,636	24.0

GEORGIA

	Candidates	Votes	%
1	Rufus E. Lester (D)	12,337	62.6
	Louis M. Pleasant (R)	4,414	22.4
	W. R. Kemp (PP)	2,944	15.0
2	Benjamin E. Russell (D)	11,517	65.2
	I. H. Hand (PP)	6,060	34.3
3	Charles F. Crisp (D)	11,574	69.9
	F. D. Wimberly (PP & R)	4,982	30.1
4	Charles L. Moses (D)	12,779	64.1
	J. H. Turner (PP & R)	7,145	35.9
5	Leonidas F. Livingston (D)	9,732	60.2
	Samuel Small (PP & R)	6,447	39.9
6	Thomas B. Cabaniss (D)	11,628	64.6
	C. F. Turner (PP & R)	6,387	35.5
7	John W. Maddox (D)	13,572	65.9
	John A. Sibley (PP & R)	7,037	34.2
8	Thomas G. Lawson (D)	11,133	66.7
	James B. Robins (PP & R)	5,550	33.3
9	Farish C. Tate (D)	13,952	59.5
	Thaddeus K. Pickett (PP & R)	9,481	40.5
10	James C. C. Black (D)	17,772	59.0
	Thomas E. Watson (PP & R)	12,330	41.0
11	Henry G. Turner (D)	11,091	65.3
	Lucius C. Mattox (PP & R)	5,882	34.7

IDAHO

	Candidates	Votes	%
AL	Willis Sweet (R)	8,549	44.1
	Edward B. True (D)	6,029	31.1
	James Gunn (PP)	4,567	23.6

ILLINOIS

	Candidates	Votes	%
1	J. Frank Aldrich (R)	39,726	49.7
	Edwin B. Smith (D)	37,904	47.4
2	Lawrence E. McGann (D)	32,609	68.9
	Edward D. Connor (R)	14,168	29.9
3	Allan C. Durborow Jr. (D)	38,652	57.4
	Thomas C. Macmillan (R)	27,392	40.7
4	Julius Goldzier (D)	34,454	52.2
	William Vocke (R)	29,851	45.2
5	Albert J. Hopkins (R)	19,864	58.1
	Samuel Alschuler (D)	12,486	36.5
	Henry Wood (PP)	1,861	5.4
6	Robert R. Hitt (R)	18,307	54.9
	Henry D. Dennis (D)	12,794	38.4
7	Thomas J. Henderson (R)	15,849	52.1
	James E. McPherran (D)	11,350	37.3
	Horace M. Gilbert (PP)	1,965	6.5
8	Robert A. Childs (R)	20,852	48.2
	Lewis Steward (D)	20,835	48.2
9	Hamilton K. Wheeler (R)	16,921	48.2
	Herman W. Snow (D)	16,403	46.7

	Candidates	Votes	%
10	Philip Sidney Post (R)	19,215	49.7
	James W. Hunter (D)	17,246	44.6
11	Benjamin F. Marsh (R)	19,652	48.0
	Truman Plantz (D)	18,594	45.4
12	John J. McDannold (D)	22,207	53.1
	T. M. Rogers (R)	15,940	38.1
	William Hess (PP)	2,489	6.0
13	William M. Springer (D)	22,954	52.1
	Charles P. Kane (R)	18,238	41.4
14	Benjamin F. Funk (R)	18,578	48.0
	Owen Scott (D)	18,264	47.2
15	Joseph G. Cannon (R)	20,596	49.6
	Samuel T. Busey (D)	19,098	46.0
16	George W. Fithian (D)	17,320	46.0
	J. O. Burton (R)	16,540	43.9
	Thomas Ratcliff (PP)	2,794	7.4
17	Edward Lane (D)	19,107	51.9
	John N. Gwin (R)	13,710	37.2
	Presley G. Donaldson (PP)	2,554	6.9
18	William S. Forman (D)	17,696	49.2
	W. A. Northcott (R)	16,552	46.0
19	James R. Williams (D)	18,411	49.8
	Norman H. Moss (R)	14,972	40.5
	Joseph H. Crasno (PP)	2,599	7.0
20	George W. Smith (R)	19,944	51.7
	Benjamin W. Pope (D)	17,446	45.2
AL	John C. Black (D)	425,336✓	
	Andrew J. Hunter (D)	423,868✓	
	Richard Yates (R)	399,321	
	George S. Willits (R)	399,096	
	Frances E. Andrews (P)	25,596	
	James S. Felter (P)	25,428	
	Jesse Harper (PP)	21,707	
	Michael McDonough (PP)	21,541	

INDIANA

	Candidates	Votes	%
1	Arthur H. Taylor (D)	19,720	47.4
	A. P. Twineham (R)	19,266	46.3
	Moses Smith (PP)	2,110	5.1
2	John L. Bretz (D)	17,700	47.9
	Ben L. Willoughby (R)	15,731	42.6
	Merrick W. Ackerty (PP)	3,010	8.2
3	Jason B. Brown (D)	20,928	51.6
	William W. Borden (R)	17,957	44.3
4	William S. Holman (D)	19,008	52.5
	Samuel M. Jones (R)	15,927	44.0
5	George W. Cooper (D)	17,698	48.3
	John Worrell (R)	16,640	45.4
6	Henry U. Johnson (R)	20,444	56.7
	Luther M. Mering (D)	11,820	32.8
	Nathan T. Butts (PP)	2,581	7.2
7	William D. Bynum (D)	28,267	49.5
	Charles L. Henry (R)	26,951	47.2
8	Elijah V. Brookshire (D)	22,949	48.4
	Winfield S. Carpenter (R)	21,327	45.0
9	Daniel Waugh (R)	23,416	50.1
	Eli W. Brown (D)	19,291	41.3
	George W. Swan (PP)	2,517	5.4
10	Thomas Hammond (D)	18,298	46.1
	William Johnston (R)	18,256	46.0
11	Augustus N. Martin (D)	21,893	45.9
	William T. Daley (R)	21,060	44.1
	Joshua Strange (PP)	3,026	6.3
12	William F. McNagny (D)	19,991	50.0
	Adolph J. You (R)	16,926	42.3
	Calvin Husselman (PP)	2,027	5.1
13	Charles G. Conn (D)	21,627	50.4
	James S. Dodge (R)	19,687	45.9

IOWA

	Candidates	Votes	%
1	John H. Gear (R)	18,416	49.4
	John J. Surley (D)	17,787	47.7
2	Walter I. Hayes (D)	23,129	58.9
	John H. Munroe (R)	15,357	39.1

Candidates	Votes	%
3 David B. Henderson (R)	22,045	51.3
James H. Shields (D)	20,586	47.9
4 Thomas Updegraff (R)	19,681	51.5
W. H. Butler (D)	18,091	47.4
5 Robert G. Cousins (R)	20,033	49.9
John T. Hamilton (D)	18,935	47.2
6 John F. Lacey (R)	17,747	47.1
F. E. White (D)	16,572	44.0
E. S. Owens (PP)	2,889	7.7
7 John A. T. Hull (R)	19,963	54.0
Joseph A. Dyer (D)	13,883	37.5
Ed A. Ott (PP)	2,562	6.9
8 William P. Hepburn (R)	20,299	49.8
Thomas L. Maxwell (D)	15,968	39.2
Walter S. Scott (PP)	3,687	9.0
9 Alva L. Hager (R)	20,287	49.3
John E. F. McGee (D)	17,809	43.3
F. W. Myers (PP)	2,610	6.4
10 Jonathan P. Dolliver (R)	23,402	53.7
J. J. Ryan (D)	18,458	42.4
11 George D. Perkins (R)	21,984	50.6
Daniel Campbell (D-PP)	20,707	47.6

KANSAS

Candidates	Votes	%
1 Case Broderick (R)	19,401	54.5
Fred J. Close (PP)	15,782	44.3
2 Edward H. Funston (R)	22,900‡	49.4
Horace L. Moore (D-PP)	22,817	49.2
3 Thomas J. Hudson (D-PP)	23,998	52.2
L. U. Humphrey (R)	21,594	47.0
4 Charles Curtis (R)	25,327	52.0
E. V. Wharton (D-PP)	22,603	46.4
5 John Davis (PP)	20,162	50.3
Joseph R. Burton (R)	18,842	47.0
6 William Baker (PP)	19,398	49.9
H. L. Pestana (R)	17,887	46.0
7 Jeremiah Simpson (D-PP)	33,812	50.8
Chester I. Long (R)	32,053	48.2
AL William A. Harris (PP & D)	164,624	50.7
George T. Anthony (R)	155,791	48.0

KENTUCKY

Candidates	Votes	%
1 William J. Stone (D)	15,295	53.0
W. J. Deboe (R)	8,438	29.2
B. C. Key (POP)	4,686	16.2
2 William T. Ellis (D)	15,053	47.4
J. T. Kimbly (R)	9,781	30.8
Thomas S. Pettit (POP)	6,903	21.8
3 Isaac H. Goodnight (D)	14,986	47.2
W. G. Hunter (R)	14,056	44.2
C. W. Biggers (POP)	2,742	8.6
4 Alexander B. Montgomery (D)	16,043	48.1
C. M. Barnett (R)	11,385	34.1
M. R. Gardner (POP)	5,954	17.8
5 Asher G. Caruth (D)	20,445	58.7
Augustus E. Willson (R)	13,767	39.6
6 Albert S. Berry (D)	18,564	60.7
Weden O'Neal (R)	10,731	35.1
7 William C. P. Breckinridge (D)	16,588	62.0
T. J. Hardin (R)	9,433	35.3
8 James B. McCreary (D)	14,092	100.0
9 Thomas H. Paynter (D)	18,295	53.3
John P. McCartney (R)	15,339	44.7
10 Marcus C. Lisle (D)	14,515	54.9
Charles W. Russell (R)	11,943	45.1
11 Silas R. Adams (R)	17,087	59.5
James R. Hindman (D)	10,483	36.5

Special Elections

Candidates	Votes	%
10 Joseph M. Kendall (D)	5,846	91.2
C. F. Ward	544	8.5

LOUISIANA

Candidates	Votes	%
1 Adolph Meyer (D)	10,878	69.2
James Wilkinson (ID)	4,787	30.5
2 Robert C. Davey (D)	12,588	67.4
Morris Marks (POP & R)	6,102	32.7

Candidates	Votes	%
3 Andrew Price (D)	14,033	81.8
I. J. Willis (POP & R)	3,123	18.2
4 Newton C. Blanchard (D)	16,432	76.1
T. J. Guice (POP & R)	5,167	23.9
5 Charles J. Boatner (D)	19,371	72.3
R. P. Welch (POP & R)	4,301	16.0
A. A. Gundy (ID)	3,119	11.6
6 Samuel M. Robertson (D)	11,758	85.2
J. Kleinpeter (POP & R)	2,043	14.8

MAINE

Candidates	Votes	%
1 Thomas B. Reed (R)	16,312	51.5
D. H. Ingraham (D)	14,635	46.2
2 Nelson Dingley Jr. (R)	17,194	52.4
D. J. McGillicuddy (D)	13,546	41.3
3 Seth L. Milliken (R)	15,582	50.3
W. P. Thompson (D)	13,700	44.2
4 Charles A. Boutelle (R)	16,549	51.3
D. A. H. Powers (D)	12,261	38.0
S. D. Leavitt (ID)	1,616	5.0

MARYLAND

Candidates	Votes	%
1 Robert F. Brattan (D)	15,608	49.7
George M. Russum (R)	13,714	43.6
D. Miles (P)	1,778	5.7
2 J. Fred C. Talbott (D)	22,772	54.0
George Baker (R)	17,926	42.5
3 Harry Wells Rusk (D)	19,806	58.4
Charles Herzog (R)	13,679	40.3
4 Isidor Rayner (D)	21,455	58.4
Alburtus Spates (R)	14,646	39.8
5 Barnes Compton (D)	15,391	52.3
Thomas Parrau (R)	13,505	45.9
6 William M. McKaig (D)	18,899	49.8
George Willington (R)	18,292	48.2

Special Elections

Candidates	Votes	%
1 John Brown (D)	15,502	52.3
George M. Russum (R)	13,787	46.5

MASSACHUSETTS

Candidates	Votes	%
1 Ashley B. Wright (R)	14,198	48.8
John C. Crosby (D)	13,995	48.1
2 Frederick H. Gillett (R)	15,131	52.4
Edward Howard (D)	12,718	44.1
3 Joseph H. Walker (R)	14,139	50.1
John R. Thayer (D)	13,262	47.0
4 Lewis D. Apsley (R)	16,209	53.7
Frederic S. Coolidge (D)	13,058	43.3
5 Moses T. Stevens (D)	14,423	52.3
William S. Knox (R)	12,645	45.8
6 William Cogswell (R)	16,385	58.4
Henry B. Little (D)	10,228	36.5
7 Henry Cabot Lodge (R)	17,002*	52.7
William Everett (D)	14,391	44.6
8 Samuel W. McCall (R)	15,671	51.6
John F. Andrew (D)	14,679	48.4
9 Joseph H. O'Neil (D)	14,354	61.1
Benjamin C. Lane (R)	8,622	36.7
10 Michael J. McEttrick (D & CIT)	9,507	33.4
Harrison H. Atwood (R)	8,822	31.0
William S. McNary (D)	7,591	26.7
Richard C. Humphreys (I)	2,235	7.9
11 William F. Draper (R)	16,961	53.1
George Fred Williams (D)	14,404	45.1
12 Elijah A. Morse (R)	17,316	56.0
Elbridge Cushman (D)	12,673	41.0
13 Charles S. Randall (R)	13,945	60.7
Henry C. Thacher (D)	9,006	39.2

MICHIGAN

Candidates	Votes	%
1 John Logan Chipman (D)	20,239	52.4
Frank J. Hecker (R)	17,533	45.4
2 James S. Gorman (D)	22,007	47.0
James O'Donnell (R)	21,443	45.8
3 Julius C. Burrows (R)	21,287	50.1
Daniel Strange (D)	15,802	37.2
Leroy E. Lockwood (POP)	2,898	6.8

Candidates	Votes	%
Paul T. Butler (P)	2,510	5.9
4 Henry F. Thomas (R)	21,352	49.1
George L. Yaple (D & POP)	20,246	46.5
5 Charles E. Belknap (R)	20,139	47.8
George F. Richardson (D & POP)	20,120✓	47.8
6 David D. Aitken (R)	21,046	46.5
Byron G. Stout (D)	19,669	43.5
Arthur E. Cole (POP)	2,289	5.1
7 Justin R. Whiting (D)	16,125	46.3
Philip L. Wixson (R)	15,602	44.8
Alfred Pagett (POP)	1,837	5.3
8 William S. Linton (R)	17,411	49.2
Henry M. Youmins (D & POP)	15,886	44.9
9 John W. Moon (R)	13,969	47.0
Harrison H. Wheeler (D)	13,053	43.9
Charles A. Sessions (P)	1,673	5.6
10 Thomas A. E. Weadock (D)	14,858	47.7
James Van Kleeck (R)	14,599	46.8
11 John Avery (R)	18,359	50.6
Woodbridge N. Ferris (D & POP)	16,038	44.2
George R. Catton (P)	1,886	5.2
12 Samuel M. Stephenson (R)	20,097	50.7
J. Maurice Finn (D & POP)	16,674	42.1

MINNESOTA

Candidates	Votes	%
1 James A. Tawney (R)	18,146	49.0
William H. Harries (D)	14,995	40.5
James I. Vermilya (PP)	2,342	6.3
2 James T. McCleary (R)	18,207	48.4
Winfield S. Hammond (D)	11,298	30.0
S. C. Long (PP)	6,268	16.7
3 Osee M. Hall (D)	15,890	44.8
Joel P. Heatwole (R)	14,727	41.5
Ferdinand Borchert (PP)	3,464	9.8
4 Andrew R. Kiefer (R)	16,624	48.6
James N. Castle (D)	13,435	39.2
James G. Dougherty (PP)	2,213	6.5
David Morgan (P)	1,963	5.7
5 Loren Fletcher (R)	18,463	46.1
James W. Lawrence (D)	15,960	39.9
Thomas H. Lucas (PP)	3,151	7.9
J. T. Caton (P)	2,458	6.1
6 Melvin R. Baldwin (D)	17,317	43.4
Dolson B. Searle (R)	16,941	42.4
A. C. Parsons (PP)	3,973	10.0
7 Haldor E. Boen (PP)	12,614	35.6
Henry Feig (R)	12,529	35.4
W. F. Kelso (D)	7,526	21.3
L. F. Hampson (P)	2,731	7.7

MISSISSIPPI

Candidates	Votes	%
1 John M. Allen (D)	5,605	79.8
James Burkitt (PP)	1,272	18.1
2 John C. Kyle (D)	6,113	77.8
J. H. Simpson (PP)	1,740	22.2
3 Thomas C. Catchings (D)	2,750	93.4
George W. Gayles (R)	194	6.6
4 Hernando D. Money (D)	6,223	61.4
Frank Burkitt (PP)	3,905	38.6
5 John S. Williams (D)	7,541	71.4
W. P. Ratliff (PP)	3,028	28.7
6 Thomas R. Stockdale (D)	4,984	82.5
T. N. Jackson (PP)	1,054	17.5
7 Charles E. Hooker (D)	4,984	72.4
S. W. Robinson (PP)	1,695	24.6

MISSOURI

Candidates	Votes	%
1 William H. Hatch (D)	19,263	50.0
Cramer (R)	15,919	41.3
Bronson (PP)	3,316	8.6
2 Uriel S. Hall (D)	21,928	53.7
Burkholder (R)	16,626	40.7
Jackson (PP)	2,317	5.7
3 Alexander M. Dockery (D)	18,749	48.8
Birch (R)	15,288	39.8
Reece (PP)	4,365	11.4
4 Daniel D. Burnes (D)	15,859	46.7

Candidates	Votes	%
Crowther (R)	14,600	43.0
Wilcox (PP)	3,221	9.5
5 John C. Tarsney (D)	19,407	55.0
Davis (R)	14,240	40.4
6 David A. De Armond (D)	16,545	46.3
Cundiff (R)	13,151	36.8
Donnohue (PP)	5,587	15.6
7 John T. Heard (D)	21,549	48.7
Hastain (R)	17,843	40.3
Pinkham (PP)	4,847	11.0
8 Richard P. Bland (D)	18,927	53.3
Murphy (R)	16,453	46.4
9 James Beauchamp Clark (D)	17,536	53.0
Morsey (R)	14,944	45.2
10 Richard Bartholdt (R)	15,628	54.6
Kehr (D)	12,465	43.5
11 Charles F. Joy (R)	14,969‡	49.5
John J. O'Neill (D)	14,902	49.3
12 Seth W. Cobb (D)	12,813	52.0
Rodgers (R)	11,481	46.6
13 Robert W. Fyan (D)	19,993	57.1
Whitledge (R)	15,006	42.8
14 Marshall Arnold (D)	19,440	49.8
Clarke (R)	15,737	40.3
Taber (PP)	3,864	9.9
15 Charles H. Morgan (D)	17,489	44.2
Purdy (R)	15,767	39.8
Withers (PP)	5,815	14.7

MONTANA

Candidates	Votes	%
AL Charles S. Hartman (R)	17,934	41.4
William W. Dixon (D)	17,762	41.0
Caldwell Edwards (PP)	7,027	16.2

NEBRASKA

Candidates	Votes	%
1 William Jennings Bryan (D)	13,784	44.9
Allen W. Field (R)	13,644	44.4
Jerome Shamp (POP)	2,409	7.9
2 David H. Mercer (R)	11,488	45.3
George W. Doane (D)	10,388	40.9
Robert L. Wheeler (POP)	3,152	12.4
3 George Meiklejohn (R)	13,635	39.2
George F. Keiper (D)	10,630	30.6
W. A. Poynter (POP)	9,636	27.7
4 Eugene J. Hainer (R)	15,648	41.8
William H. Dech (POP)	11,486	30.7
Victor Vifquain (D)	8,988	24.0
5 William A. McKeighan (D & POP)	17,490	53.7
W. E. Andrews (R)	14,230	43.7
6 Omer M. Kem (POP)	16,328	46.1
James Whitehead (R)	14,197	40.1
A. T. Gatewood (D)	4,202	11.9

NEVADA

Candidates	Votes	%
AL Francis G. Newlands (POP SIL)	7,171	72.5
William Woodburn (R)	2,295	23.2

NEW HAMPSHIRE

Candidates	Votes	%
1 Henry W. Blair (R)	21,031	49.9
Charles F. Stone (D)	20,412	48.4
2 Henry M. Baker (R)	21,425	49.3
Hosea W. Parker (D)	20,996	48.3

NEW JERSEY

Candidates	Votes	%
1 Henry C. Loudenslager (R)	25,099	50.7
Porch (D)	22,511	45.4
2 John J. Gardner (R)	22,716	50.7
Wetherill (D)	20,592	45.9
3 Jacob A. Geissenhainer (D)	20,407	53.0
Hoffman (R)	17,080	44.4
4 Johnston Cornish (D)	21,765	48.0
Howey (R)	20,726	45.7
Johnston (P)	2,307	5.1
5 Cornelius A. Cadmus (D)	20,693	50.7
Doherty (R)	19,231	47.1

Candidates	Votes	%
6 Thomas D. English (D)	21,651	51.0
Richard W. Parker (R)	20,284	47.8
7 George B. Fielder (D)	22,416	49.9
Cole (R)	19,585	43.6
Edward F. McDonald (D)	2,368	5.3
8 John T. Dunn (D)	14,393	50.4
Chamberlin (R)	13,470	47.1

NEW YORK

Candidates	Votes	%
1 James W. Covert (D)	21,550	52.1
John Lewis Childs (R)	18,749	45.3
2 John M. Clancy (D)	20,697	59.1
William H. Grace (R)	13,593	38.8
3 Joseph C. Hendrix (D)	21,607	55.9
Michael J. Dady (R)	15,907	41.1
4 William J. Coombs (D)	22,818	58.5
Charles B. Hobbs (R)	14,885	38.1
5 John H. Graham (D)	16,675	50.8
Charles G. Bennett (R)	14,488	44.2
6 Thomas F. Magner (D)	17,151	56.1
John Greaney (R)	12,131	39.7
7 Franklin Bartlett (D)	14,905	66.3
Samuel A. Brown (R)	7,122	31.7
8 Edward J. Dunphy (D)	15,287	66.3
Austin E. Ford (R)	7,132	30.9
9 Timothy J. Campbell (D)	16,897	66.2
John Phelan (R)	7,175	28.1
10 Daniel E. Sickles (D)	18,452	58.0
Charles E. Coon (R)	12,224	38.5
11 Amos J. Cummings (D)	16,780	63.0
Abraham H. Sarasohn (R)	8,355	31.4
12 William Bourke Cockran (D)	16,575	65.6
Daniel Butterfield (R)	7,766	30.7
13 J. DeWitt Warner (D)	18,979	60.8
James J. Flick (R)	11,181	35.8
14 John R. Fellows (D)	26,267	57.8
H. Charles Ullman (R)	17,442	38.4
15 Ashbel P. Fitch (D)	27,741	61.2
Henry C. Robinson (R)	15,872	35.0
16 William Ryan (D)	25,795	55.0
George A. Brandreth (R)	19,312	41.2
17 Francis Marvin (R)	17,806	48.5
Henry Bacon (D)	17,659	48.1
18 Jacob Le Fever (R)	21,034	49.3
Isaac N. Cox (D)	20,114	47.1
19 Charles D. Haines (D)	20,757	50.7
John A. Quackenbush (R)	19,104	46.6
20 Charles Tracey (D)	19,509	50.3
John G. Ward (R)	17,883	46.1
21 Simon J. Schermerhorn (D)	24,508	49.5
Erastus F. Beadle (R)	23,181	46.8
22 Newton Martin Curtis (R)	26,207	57.4
Warren Curtis (D)	16,707	36.6
23 John M. Wever (R)	25,690	57.7
George S. Weed (D)	16,947	38.1
24 Charles A. Chickering (R)	23,858	55.8
William A. Kelley (D)	17,283	40.4
25 James S. Sherman (R)	20,443	49.7
Henry W. Bentley (D)	19,299	46.9
26 George W. Ray (R)	28,979	85.9
George F. Hand (P)	3,871	11.5
27 James J. Belden (R)	25,737	55.5
Riley V. Miller (D)	18,412	39.7
28 Sereno E. Payne (R)	28,723	55.3
Hull Greenfield (D)	20,601	39.7
29 Charles W. Gillet (R)	21,443	50.4
Franz S. Wolf (D)	17,646	41.5
Albert C. Hill (P)	2,242	5.3
30 James W. Wadsworth (R)	24,205	51.2
John F. McDonald (D)	19,679	41.6
Albert J. Rumsey (P)	2,494	5.3
31 John Van Voorhis (R)	19,762	47.8
Donald McNaughton (D)	19,255	46.6
32 Daniel N. Lockwood (D)	16,440	52.9
Rowland B. Mahany (R)	12,966	41.8
33 Charles Daniels (R)	19,701	53.0
John S. Hertel (D)	15,548	41.8
34 Warren B. Hooker (R)	24,951	55.0
Andrew J. McNett (D)	15,098	33.3

Candidates	Votes	%
Benjamin W. Taylor (P)	2,905	6.4
F. Eugene Hammond (POP)	2,395	5.3

NORTH CAROLINA

Candidates	Votes	%
1 William A. B. Branch (D)	14,263	55.1
Reddick Gatling (PP)	11,579	44.7
2 Frederick A. Woodard (D)	13,925	44.4
Henry P. Cheatham (R)	11,896	37.9
Edward A. Thorne (PP)	5,457	17.4
3 Benjamin F. Grady (D)	12,457	45.0
Frank D. Koonce (PP)	9,869	35.6
Asoph M. Clark (R)	5,271	19.0
4 Benjamin H. Bunn (D)	14,630	48.4
William F. Strowd (PP)	13,125	43.4
John H. Williamson (R)	2,106	7.0
5 Thomas Settle (R)	14,148	43.3
Archibald H. A. Williams (D)	13,746	42.1
William R. Lindsay (PP)	4,358	13.3
6 Sydenham B. Alexander (D)	16,624	57.8
Atlas A. Maynard (PP)	12,127	42.1
7 John S. Henderson (D)	14,303	49.2
Alfred E. Holton (R)	9,136	31.4
Alonzo C. Shuford (PP)	5,399	18.6
8 William H. Bower (D)	16,886	50.1
Joseph B. Wilcox (R)	13,215	39.2
Robert L. Patton (PP)	3,564	10.6
9 William T. Crawford (D)	16,010	50.9
Jeter C. Pritchard (R)	14,560	46.3

NORTH DAKOTA

Candidates	Votes	%
AL Martin N. Johnson (R)	17,715	49.0
O'Brien (D)	11,021	30.5
Foss (I)	7,439	20.6

OHIO

Candidates	Votes	%
1 Bellamy Storer (R)	19,269	50.6
Robert B. Bowler (D)	18,014	47.3
2 John A. Caldwell (R)	22,240	51.5
Charles T. Greve (D)	20,074	46.5
3 George W. Houk (D)	24,686	53.0
Charles C. Donley (R)	20,370	43.7
4 Fernando C. Layton (D)	20,417	56.7
C. S. Mauk (R)	12,823	35.6
5 Dennis D. Donovan (D)	19,873	53.4
George L. Griffeth (R)	15,269	41.0
6 George W. Hulick (R)	21,341	51.4
John M. Pattison (D)	18,091	43.6
7 George W. Wilson (R)	19,434	49.6
Martin K. Gantz (D)	17,608	45.0
8 Luther M. Strong (R)	21,742	51.7
Fremont Arford (D)	18,384	43.7
9 Byron F. Ritchie (D)	20,041	48.0
James M. Ashley (R)	20,027	48.0
10 William H. Enochs (R)	19,847	55.2
Irvine Dungan (D)	15,486	43.0
11 Charles H. Grosvenor (R)	19,905	51.4
Charles E. Peoples (D)	17,254	44.6
12 Joseph H. Outhwaite (D)	20,298	52.6
Edward N. Huggins (R)	17,045	44.2
13 Darius D. Hare (D)	24,186	54.8
Lewis W. Hull (R)	17,937	40.7
14 Michael D. Harter (D)	22,285	49.8
Elizur G. Johnson (R)	20,396	45.6
15 Henry C. Van Voorhis (R)	18,718	49.4
Milton Turner (D)	17,550	46.4
16 Albert J. Pearson (D)	17,314	47.5
Christian L. Poorman (R)	17,273	47.3
17 James A. D. Richards (D)	23,077	55.8
Arthur H. Walkey (R)	16,723	40.5
18 George B. Ikirt (D)	22,600	48.2
Thomas R. Morgan Sr. (R)	21,389	45.6
19 Stephen A. Northway (R)	23,870	55.2
A. H. Tidball (D)	16,069	37.2
Bailey S. Dean (P)	2,185	5.1
20 William White (R)	17,417	49.1
John S. Ellen (D)	16,460	46.4
21 Tom L. Johnson (D)	17,389	53.4

Candidates	Votes	%
Orlando J. Hodge (R)	14,165	43.5

Special Elections

	Candidates	Votes	%
16	Lewis P. Ohliger (D)	20,220	52.5
	George Adams (R)	16,958	44.0

OREGON

	Candidates	Votes	%
1	Binger Hermann (R)	18,929	46.5
	R. M. Veatch (D)	13,019	32.0
	M. V. Rork (POP)	7,518	18.5
2	William R. Ellis (R)	15,657	44.9
	James H. Slater (D)	12,120	34.7
	John C. Luce (POP)	5,940	17.0

PENNSYLVANIA

	Candidates	Votes	%
1	Henry H. Bingham (R)	22,908	62.6
	Edwin G. Flanigen (D)	13,693	37.4
2	Charles O'Neill (R)	16,107	64.0
	John J. Malony (D)	9,056	36.0
3	William McAleer (ID)	15,516	73.8
	William W. Kerr (D)	5,500	26.2
4	John E. Reyburn (R)	37,200	61.4
	Elbridge E. Nock (D)	22,950	37.9
5	Alfred C. Harmer (R)	32,638	60.4
	Frederick A. Herwig (D)	21,426	39.6
6	John B. Robinson (R)	19,129	55.3
	Garrett C. Smedley (D)	13,938	40.3
7	Irving P. Wanger (R)	21,985	49.5
	Edwin Hallowell (D)	21,805	49.0
8	William Mutchler (D)	17,837	60.6
	Thomas C. Walton (R)	11,593	39.4
9	Constantine J. Erdman (D)	28,175	62.1
	H. A. Muhlenberg (R)	17,217	37.9
10	Marriott Brosius (R)	20,052	64.7
	John E. Malone (D)	10,266	33.1
11	Joseph A. Scranton (R)	10,814	49.0
	Lemuel Amerman (D)	10,225	46.3
12	William H. Hines (D)	15,554	50.1
	Charles D. Foster (R)	14,092	45.4
13	James B. Reilly (D)	13,440	53.2
	Charles W. Brumm (R)	11,539	45.7
14	Ephraim M. Woomer (R)	19,058	56.0
	William M. Breslin (D)	13,993	41.1
15	Myron B. Wright (R)	17,241	55.1
	Roger S. Searle (D)	12,655	40.4
16	Albert C. Hopkins (R)	17,966	52.6
	Frederick K. Wright (D)	14,724	43.1
17	Simon P. Wolverton (D)	15,333	58.4
	Chandlee Eves (R)	10,030	38.2
18	Thaddeus M. Mahon (R)	19,247	54.1
	William W. Trout (D)	15,631	44.0
19	Frank E. Beltzhoover (D)	21,963	56.6
	Nesbit S. Ross (R)	16,198	41.7
20	Josiah D. Hicks (R)	22,601	56.0
	Lucian D. Woodruff (D)	17,420	43.2
21	Daniel B. Heiner (R)	23,942	52.6
	John B. Keenan (D)	20,245	44.5
22	John Dalzell (R)	22,674	58.3
	James W. Breen (D)	15,939	41.0
23	William A. Stone (R)	14,628	63.6
	Frank C. Osburn (D)	8,177	35.6
24	William A. Sipe (D)	25,224	48.2
	Ernest F. Acheson (R)	23,971	45.8
25	Thomas W. Phillips (R)	19,658	51.8
	Eugene P. Gillespie (D)	15,559	41.0
	Judson W. Vandeventer (P)	1,930	5.1
26	Joseph C. Sibley (D)	17,887	54.9
	Theodore L. Flood (R)	14,500	44.5
27	Charles W. Stone (R)	12,479	51.9
	James D. Hancock (D)	9,523	39.6
	Charles Lott (P)	1,486	6.2
28	George F. Kribbs (D)	17,285	54.3
	Charles E. Andrews (R)	13,284	41.7
AL	William Lilly (R)	512,557✓	
	Alexander McDowell (R)	511,433✓	
	George A. Allen (D)	448,714	
	Thomas Polk Merritt (D)	447,456	
	Simeon B. Chase (P)	23,677	
	James T. McCrory (P)	22,930	

Candidates	Votes	%
S. P. Chase (PP)	7,466	
G. W. Dawson (PP)	7,313	
J. Mahlon Barnes (SOC LAB)	674	
Thomas Grundy (SOC LAB)	625	

Special Elections

	Candidates	Votes	%
24	William A. Sipe (D)	25,181	49.1
	Andrew Stewart (R)	24,635	48.1

RHODE ISLAND[1]

	Candidates	Votes	%
1	Melville Bull (R)	13,645*	49.3
	Oscar Lapham (D)	13,051	47.2
2	Adin B. Capron (R)	11,523*	49.5
	Charles H. Page (D)	10,591	45.5

SOUTH CAROLINA

	Candidates	Votes	%
1	William H. Brawley (D)	6,318	99.8
2	W. Jasper Talbert (D)	8,001	99.6
3	Asbury C. Latimer (D)	8,330	89.7
	John R. Tolbert (R)	787	8.5
4	George W. Shell (D)	10,401	85.7
	Joshua A. T. Ensor (R)	1,730	14.3
5	Thomas J. Strait (D)	8,791	80.7
	E. Brooks Sligh (R)	2,099	19.3
6	John L. McLaurin (D)	10,133	84.6
	E. J. Sawyer (R)	1,832	15.3
7	George W. Murray (R)	4,995	50.0
	E. M. Moise (D)	4,955	49.6

Special Elections

	Candidates	Votes	%
6	John L. McLaurin (D)	8,572	90.2
	Sawyer (R)	934	9.8

SOUTH DAKOTA

	Candidates	Votes	%
AL	John A. Pickler (R)	33,769✓	
	William V. Lucas (R)	33,350✓	
	J. E. Kelley (PP)	25,444	
	William Lardner (PP)	24,539	
	L. E. Whitcher (D)	14,218	
	Chauncey L. Wood (D)	736	

TENNESSEE

	Candidates	Votes	%
1	Alfred A. Taylor (R)	17,890	56.2
	W. J. McSween (D)	13,207	41.5
2	John C. Houk (R)	18,952	67.2
	W. L. Welcker (D)	7,815	27.7
3	Henry C. Snodgrass (D)	15,984	47.5
	H. Clay Evans (R)	15,035	44.6
	Frank P. Dickey (POP)	2,171	6.5
4	Benton McMillin (D)	14,010	55.5
	W. D. Gold (R & ID)	11,225	44.5
5	James D. Richardson (D)	13,709	61.1
	Thomas J. Ogilvie (R)	8,062	36.0
6	Joseph E. Washington (D)	15,645	62.0
	John B. Allen (R)	9,002	35.7
7	Nicholas N. Cox (D)	12,113	57.5
	W. A. Witherspoon (POP)	8,480	40.3
8	Benjamin A. Enloe (D)	13,038	50.2
	P. H. Threasher (R)	12,920	49.7
9	James C. McDearmon (D)	14,334	56.1
	Rice A. Pearce (ID)	10,883	42.6
10	Josiah Patterson (D)	12,164	71.8
	T. V. Neal (R)	4,785	28.2

TEXAS

	Candidates	Votes	%
1	Joseph C. Hutcheson (D)	14,489	59.7
	J. B. Stephenson (PP)	6,081	25.1
	Daniel Taylor (R)	3,703	15.3
2	Samuel B. Cooper (D)	19,894	61.4
	T. A. Wilson (PP)	10,275	31.7
3	Constantine B. Kligore (D)	16,335	57.3
	J. M. Perdue (PP)	12,177	42.7
4	David B. Culberson (D)	16,521	52.3
	Pat B. Clark (PP)	10,371	32.8
	J. A. Hurley (R)	4,709	14.9

	Candidates	Votes	%
5	Joseph W. Bailey (D)	24,983	66.2
	R. B. Bell (LW R)	8,170	21.7
	John Grant (R)	4,563	12.1
6	Jo Abbott (D)	24,913	59.3
	J. C. Kearby (PP & R)	17,078	40.6
7	George C. Pendleton (D)	19,937	56.1
	I. N. Barber (PP)	15,587	43.8
8	Charles K. Bell (D)	17,997	54.5
	Evan Jones (PP)	12,937	39.2
	C. C. Drake (R)	2,009	6.1
9	Joseph D. Sayers (D)	19,763	61.5
	J. M. Horner (PP & R)	12,384	38.5
10	Walter Gresham (D)	13,017	48.6
	A. J. Rosenthal (R)	9,452	35.3
	E. O. Meitzn (PP)	4,297	16.1
11	William H. Crain (D)	15,257	52.4
	C. G. Brewster (R)	8,075	27.7
	Ben Terrell (PP)	5,770	19.8
12	Thomas M. Paschal (D)	13,930	50.1
	Henry Terrell (R)	7,290	26.2
	T. J. McMinn (PP)	6,574	23.6
13	Jeremiah V. Cockrell (D)	21,922	65.5
	W. J. Maltby (PP)	9,825	29.4

Special Elections

	Candidates	Votes	%
9	Edwin LeRoy Antony (D)	✓	#

VERMONT

	Candidates	Votes	%
1	H. Henry Powers (R)	19,427	65.9
	Felix W. McGettrick (D)	9,396	31.9
2	William W. Grout (R)	18,568	66.7
	George W. Smith (D)	8,649	31.1

VIRGINIA

	Candidates	Votes	%
1	William A. Jones (D)	15,004	56.2
	Orres A. Browne (R)	11,543	43.2
2	D. Gardiner Tyler (D)	17,432	55.6
	P. C. Garrigan (IR)	8,594	27.4
	John F. Deyendorf (R)	3,870	12.3
3	George D. Wise (D)	18,595	63.9
	Walter E. Grant (R)	10,489	36.1
4	James F. Epes (D)	10,330	52.1
	J. Thomas Goodes (POP)	9,462	47.8
5	Claude A. Swanson (D)	14,112	53.9
	Benjamin T. Jones (POP)	12,066	46.1
6	Paul C. Edmunds (D)	18,265	58.6
	Thomas E. Cobbs (POP)	12,924	41.4
7	Charles T. O'Ferrall (R)	18,558	64.0
	J. R. C. Lewis (POP)	10,441	36.0
8	Elisha E. Meredith (D)	17,124	63.0
	B. B. Turner (POP)	10,066	37.0
9	James M. Marshall (D)	18,431	55.9
	Henry C. Wood (R)	12,699	38.5
	George R. Cowan (POP)	1,709	5.2
10	Henry St. George Tucker (D)	17,779	57.7
	D. Mott Robertson (POP)	13,027	42.3

WASHINGTON

	Candidates	Votes	%
AL	William H. Doolittle (R)	35,434✓	
	John L. Wilson (R)	35,407✓	
	Thomas Carroll (D)	30,659	
	James A. Munday (D)	27,014	
	M. F. Knox (PP)	20,083	
	J. C. Van Patton (PP)	19,891	
	D. E. Newberry (P)	2,412	
	A. C. Dickinson (P)	2,357	

WEST VIRGINIA

	Candidates	Votes	%
1	John O. Pendleton (D)	19,314	47.6
	B. B. Dovener (R)	19,108	47.1
2	William L. Wilson (D)	21,807	50.2
	J. Nelson Wisner (R)	20,702	47.7
3	John D. Alderson (D)	22,696	51.3
	Edgar P. Rucker (R)	20,750	46.9

	Candidates	Votes	%		Candidates	Votes	%		Candidates	Votes	%
4	James Capehart (D)	22,006	52.4		A. H. Krauskop (D)	16,419	42.4		H. A. Frambach (R)	15,173	44.1
	Charles T. Caldwell (R)	19,924	47.4	4	John L. Mitchell (D)	19,616*	50.2	9	Thomas Lynch (D)	19,608	52.2
					Theobald Otjen (R)	18,294	46.8		Myron H. McCord (R)	16,519	44.0
	WISCONSIN			5	George H. Brickner (D)	17,929	51.7	10	Nils P. Haugen (R)	17,674	50.6
					Julius Wechselberg (R)	15,960	46.0		Daniel Buchanan Jr. (D)	13,044	37.4
1	Henry Allen Cooper (R)	20,222	52.3	6	Owen A. Wells (D)	20,212	51.1		Peter L. Scritsmier (PP)	4,186	12.0
	Babbitt (D)	16,449	42.5		Emil Baensch (R)	17,847	45.1				
	Murdock (P)	2,021	5.2	7	George B. Shaw (R)	15,344	48.5		**WYOMING**		
2	Charles Barwig (D)	21,303	55.9		Frank P. Coburn (D)	13,074	41.3				
	L. B. Caswell (R)	15,003	39.4		Ole B. Oleson (P)	1,635	5.2	AL	Henry A. Coffeen (D)	8,855	51.3
3	Joseph W. Babcock (R)	19,506	50.4	8	Lyman E. Barnes (D)	18,187	52.9		Clarence D. Clark (R)	8,394	48.6

1. *In both congressional districts, no candidate received the majority of the votes necessary to win in the 1892 general election. (See Rhode Island 1893.)*

1893 House Elections

MASSACHUSETTS

Special Election

	Candidates	Votes	%
7	William Everett (D)	9,733	46.3
	William E. Barrett (R)	9,699	46.1

MICHIGAN

Special Elections

1	Levi T. Griffin (D)	18,854	50.3
	James H. Stone (R)	17,587	46.9

OHIO

Special Elections

	Candidates	Votes	%
10	Hezekiah S. Bundy (R)	✓	

PENNSYLVANIA

Special Elections

2	Robert Adams Jr (R)	10,487	97.0
8	Howard Mutchler (D)	10,143	64.0
	Frank Reeder (R)	5,663	35.8

RHODE ISLAND[1]

Special Elections

	Candidates	Votes	%
1	Oscar Lapham (D)	11,298	47.7
	Melville Bull (R)	10,816	45.7
2	Charles H. Page (D)	10,670	47.6
	Adin B. Capron (R)	10,021	44.7
	Lewis (P)	1,571	7.0

WISCONSIN

Special Elections

4	Peter J. Somers (D)	13,567	51.3
	Theobald Otgen (R)	12,125	45.8

1. No candidate in either congressional district had received a majority of the vote in the November 1892 general election for the House, so a special election was necessary in April 1893. Under the usual practice, the state kept holding elections until a majority was received, but in 1893 it was agreed that whoever received the most votes in the special election would be considered as elected, regardless of whether a majority was achieved. So Lapham and Page were elected and took their seats in the 53rd Congress (1893–1895) even though neither won a majority and would not have qualified under the usual practices of Rhode Island law. The majority requirement—which caused problems in elections for other offices as well as the House—was repealed in a referendum in November 1893.

1894 House Elections

ALABAMA

	Candidates	Votes	%
1	Richard H. Clarke (D)	6,314	76.9
	Sibley (POP)	1,898	23.1
2	Jesse F. Stallings (D)	9,728	64.6
	Gardner (POP)	5,324	35.4
3	George P. Harrison (D)	10,719	65.2
	Robinson (POP)	5,713	34.8
4	Gaston A. Robbins (D)	10,494‡	58.6
	William F. Aldrich (R)	7,406	41.4
5	James E. Cobb (D)	10,651‡	51.8
	Albert T. Goodwyn (POP)	9,903	48.2
6	John H. Bankhead (D)	5,721	55.8
	Sanford (POP)	2,622	25.6
	Long (R)	1,914	18.7
7	Milford W. Howard (POP)	6,838	66.5
	William H. Denson (D)	3,452	33.6
8	Joseph Wheeler (D)	8,901	57.9
	Crandall (POP)	6,474	42.1
9	Oscar W. Underwood (D)	7,319‡	54.3
	Truman H. Aldrich (R)	6,153	45.7

Special Elections

		Votes	%
3	George P. Harrison (D)	10,822	65.3
	W. C. Robinson (POP)	5,743	34.7

ARKANSAS

		Votes	%
1	Philip D. McCulloch Jr. (D)	6,025	81.8
	Russ Coffman (POP)	1,299	17.6
2	John S. Little (D)	5,097	94.5
3	Thomas C. McRae (D)	6,193	97.1
4	William L. Terry (D)	6,299	62.2
	P. Raleigh (R)	2,260	22.3
	J. H. Cherry (POP)	1,557	15.4
5	Hugh A. Dinsmore (D)	7,531	56.8
	T. J. Hunt (D)	4,976	37.5
	W. M. Peel (POP)	759	5.7
6	Robert Neill (D)	6,439	65.0
	H. H. Myers (R)	3,153	31.8

CALIFORNIA

		Votes	%
1	John A. Barham (R)	15,101	41.1
	Thomas J. Geary (D)	13,570	37.0
	Robert F. Grigsby (PP)	7,246	19.7
2	Grove L. Johnson (R)	19,302	43.0
	Anthony Caminetti (D)	15,732	35.1
	Burdett Cornell (PP)	8,946	20.0
3	Samuel G. Hilborn (R)	15,795	45.5
	Warren B. English (D)	13,103	37.8
	W. A. Vann (PP)	5,162	14.9
4	James G. Maguire (D)	14,748	48.3
	Thomas B. Shannon (R)	9,785	32.0
	B. K. Collier (PP)	5,627	18.4
5	Eugene F. Loud (R)	13,379	35.9
	Joseph P. Kelly (D)	8,384	22.5
	James T. Rogers (PP)	7,820	21.0
	James Denman (I DEMOC)	6,811	18.3
6	James McLachlan (R)	18,746	44.3
	George S. Patton (D)	11,693	27.6
	W. C. Bowman (PP)	9,769	23.1
	J. E. McComas (R)	2,120	5.0
7	William W. Bowers (R)	18,434	42.9
	W. H. Alford (D)	12,111	28.2
	J. L. Gilbert (PP)	10,719	25.0

COLORADO

		Votes	%
1	John F. Shafroth (R)	47,710	55.3
	La Fayette Pence (POP)	34,223	39.7
2	John C. Bell (POP & D)	47,703	51.7
	T. M. Bowen (R)	42,369	45.9

CONNECTICUT

	Candidates	Votes	%
1	E. Stevens Henry (R)	20,322	55.4
	Lewis Sperry (D)	15,115	41.2
2	Nehemiah D. Sperry (R)	28,749	54.9
	Pigott (D)	21,821	41.7
3	Charles A. Russell (R)	12,095	55.5
	Beckwith (D)	9,047	41.6
4	Ebenezer J. Hill (R)	24,012	55.2
	Deforest (D)	18,559	42.7

DELAWARE

		Votes	%
AL	Jonathan S. Willis (R)	19,699	50.7
	S. H. Bancroft Jr. (D)	18,492	47.6

FLORIDA

		Votes	%
1	Stephen M. Sparkman (D)	12,397	85.1
	D. L. McKinnon (POP)	2,135	14.7
2	Charles M. Cooper (D)	9,229	79.6
	M. Atkinson (POP)	2,334	20.1

GEORGIA

		Votes	%
1	Rufus E. Lester (D)	14,024	72.0
	J. F. Brown (PP)	5,453	28.0
2	Benjamin E. Russell (D)	10,073	62.4
	William E. Smith (PP)	6,064	37.6
3	Charles F. Crisp (D)	9,037	74.7
	Andrew White (PP)	3,062	25.3
4	Charles L. Moses (D)	10,293	57.4
	Carey Thornton (PP)	7,637	42.6
5	Leonidas F. Livingston (D)	7,781	59.7
	Robert Todd (PP)	5,264	40.4
6	Charles L. Bartlett (D)	11,671	65.5
	W. T. Whitaker (PP)	6,147	34.5
7	John W. Maddox (D)	11,500	54.4
	William H. Felton (PP)	9,646	45.6
8	Thomas G. Lawson (D)	11,066	59.5
	W. T. Carter (PP)	7,527	40.5
9	Farish C. Tate (D)	13,059	56.1
	J. N. Twitty (PP)	10,201	43.9
10	James C. C. Black (D)	20,942	60.8
	Thomas E. Watson (PP)	13,498	39.2
11	Henry G. Turner (D)	9,085	60.2
	W. S. Johnson (PP)	6,015	39.8

IDAHO

		Votes	%
AL	Edgar Wilson (R)	10,383	43.4
	James Gunn (PP)	7,547	31.5
	James M. Ballentine (D)	5,834	24.4

ILLINOIS

		Votes	%
1	J. Frank Aldrich (R)	33,902	63.2
	Max Dembufsky (D)	12,854	23.9
	Howard S. Taylor (POP)	5,996	11.2
2	William Lorimer (R)	21,194	45.6
	John J. Hanahan (D)	16,852	36.2
	John Z. White (POP)	8,484	18.2
3	Lawrence E. McGann (D)	15,356‡	44.4
	Hugh R. Belknap (R)	15,325	44.3
	John B. Clarke (POP)	3,945	11.4
4	Charles W. Woodman (R)	14,017	38.2
	Frank Lawler (I)	10,638	29.0
	T. E. Ryan (D)	8,801	24.0
	Patrick J. Miniter (POP)	2,812	7.7
5	George E. White (R)	18,732	49.5
	Edward T. Noonan (D)	14,875	39.3
	Charles G. Dixon (POP)	4,143	10.9
6	Edward D. Cooke (R)	17,602	47.3
	Julius Goldzier (D)	15,433	41.5
	Louis W. Rogers (POP)	4,159	11.2
7	George Edmund Foss (R)	25,546	59.3

	Candidates	Votes	%
	Philip Jackson (D)	11,450	26.6
	Henry D. Lloyd (POP)	6,109	14.2
8	Albert J. Hopkins (R)	22,631	66.0
	Lewis Steward (D)	9,104	26.6
9	Robert R. Hitt (R)	24,177	63.9
	David F. Thompson (D)	11,301	29.9
10	Philip S. Post (R)	22,949*	63.7
	Jones W. Olson (D)	9,770	27.1
	William W. Mathews (POP)	2,143	6.0
11	Walter Reeves (R)	19,372	52.3
	Robert R. Gibbons (D)	14,390	38.8
	William M. Hirschy (POP)	2,216	6.0
12	Joseph G. Cannon (R)	21,122	59.4
	Thomas F. Donovan (D)	11,925	33.5
13	Vespasian Warner (R)	20,896	57.8
	A. J. Barr (D)	12,725	35.2
14	Joseph R. Graff (R)	20,579	51.2
	George O. Barnes (D)	17,224	42.8
15	Benjamin F. Marsh (R)	20,550	48.4
	Truman Plantz (D)	19,115	45.0
16	Finis E. Downing (D)	17,816‡	46.5
	John I. Rinaker (R)	17,776	46.4
	Peter D. Stout (POP)	1,929	5.0
17	James A. Connolly (R)	20,441	50.3
	William M. Springer (D)	17,503	43.0
18	Frederick Remann (R)	16,669	49.4
	Edward Lane (D)	14,069	41.7
	Joseph S. Barnes (POP)	2,020	6.0
19	Benson Wood (R)	20,028	48.2
	George W. Fithian (D)	18,758	45.1
20	Orlando Burrell (R)	17,429	47.6
	James R. Williams (D)	15,775	43.1
	Harvey G. Jones (POP)	2,769	7.6
21	Everett J. Murphy (R)	18,958	48.0
	John J. Higgins (D)	17,159	43.4
	Henry C. McDill (POP)	2,764	7.0
22	George W. Smith (R)	18,180	57.4
	Francis M. Youngblood (D)	10,585	33.4
	John J. Hall (POP)	2,509	7.9

INDIANA

		Votes	%
1	James A. Hemenway (R)	20,535	47.8
	Arthur H. Taylor (D)	18,245	42.5
	James A. Boyce (POP)	3,820	8.9
2	Alexander M. Hardy (R)	17,624	47.6
	John L. Bretz (D)	15,896	42.9
	Elisha J. Riggins (POP)	3,217	8.7
3	Robert J. Tracewell (R)	19,709	49.0
	Strother M. Stockslager (D)	19,153	47.6
4	James E. Watson (R)	17,905	48.9
	William S. Holman (D)	17,471	47.7
5	Jesse Overstreet (R)	18,286	49.5
	George W. Cooper (D)	16,416	44.4
6	Henry U. Johnson (R)	22,724	63.1
	Nimrod R. Elliott (D)	10,707	29.7
7	Charles L. Henry (R)	29,900	51.1
	William D. Bynum (D)	25,557	43.7
8	George W. Faris (R)	23,238	48.0
	Elijah V. Brookshire (D)	20,669	42.7
	Morton C. Rankin (POP)	3,658	7.6
9	J. Frank Hanly (R)	25,479	54.1
	A. G. Burkhart (D)	20,237	43.0
10	Jethro A. Hatch (R)	20,858	51.0
	Valentine Zimmerman (D)	16,923	41.4
	Samuel M. Hathorn (POP)	2,296	5.6
11	George W. Steele (R)	25,008	50.1
	Augustus N. Martin (D)	21,079	42.2
12	Jacob D. Leighty (R)	19,658	49.9
	William F. McNagny (D)	17,145	43.5
	Freeman Kelly (POP)	2,195	5.6
13	Lemuel W. Royse (R)	23,523	52.3
	Lewellyn Wanner (D)	19,376	43.1

IOWA

	Candidates	Votes	%
1	Samuel M. Clark (R)	17,583	51.9
	W. A. Buckworth (D)	13,747	40.6
	J. O. Bube (PP)	2,065	6.1
2	George M. Curtis (R)	18,710	48.4
	Walter I. Hayes (D)	18,274	47.2
3	David B. Henderson (R)	22,892	57.1
	Stephen H. Bashor (D-PP)	17,200	42.9
4	Thomas Updegraff (R)	20,457	57.4
	James F. Babcock (D)	13,267	37.2
5	Robert G. Cousins (R)	21,261	55.2
	William P. Daniels (D)	15,487	40.2
6	John F. Lacey (R)	18,418	50.9
	W. H. Taylor (D)	11,587	32.0
	Allen Clark (PP)	5,663	15.7
7	John A. T. Hull (R)	20,167	60.9
	J. R. Barcoft (D-PP)	12,942	39.1
8	William P. Hepburn (R)	21,672	55.3
	Frank G. Stuart (D-PP)	17,538	44.7
9	Alva L. Hager (R)	21,874	53.3
	James B. Weaver (D-PP)	18,817	45.8
10	Jonathan P. Dolliver (R)	25,262	59.9
	J. C. Baker (D-PP)	16,905	40.1
11	George D. Perkins (R)	22,406	54.7
	Bernard Graiser (D)	12,425	30.3
	J. L. Bartholomew (PP)	5,265	12.8

KANSAS

	Candidates	Votes	%
1	Case Broderick (R)	19,202	54.2
	H. C. Solomon (FUS)	15,844	44.7
2	Orrin L. Miller (R)	22,763	53.9
	F. A. Willard (PP)	13,811	32.7
	H. L. Moore (D)	4,780	11.3
3	Snyder S. Kirkpatrick (R)	20,631	49.3
	Jeremiah D. Botkin (PP)	18,505	44.2
	William F. Sapp (D)	2,695	6.4
4	Charles Curtis (R)	25,154	53.3
	S. M. Scott (PP)	18,790	39.8
	Thomas J. O'Neil (D)	2,546	5.4
5	William A. Calderhead (R)	18,428	49.1
	John Davis (PP)	15,831	42.1
	C. W. Brandenburg (D)	2,788	7.4
6	William Baker (PP)	16,585	45.7
	Abram H. Ellis (R)	16,391	45.1
	Roscoe G. Heard (D)	2,934	8.1
7	Chester I. Long (R)	27,444	50.9
	Jerry Simpson (D-PP)	25,459	47.2
AL	Richard W. Blue (R)	147,858	50.4
	W. A. Harris (PP)	114,429	39.0
	Joseph G. Lowe (D)	26,093	8.9

KENTUCKY

	Candidates	Votes	%
1	John K. Hendrick (D)	13,912	49.8
	Ben C. Keys (POP)	10,794	38.7
	W. J. Chitwood (R)	2,701	9.7
2	John D. Clardy (D)	13,363	46.8
	Elijah G. Sebree Jr. (R)	10,381	36.3
	Henry Turner (POP)	4,385	15.3
3	W. Godfrey Hunter (R)	16,545	49.7
	C. McElroy (D)	15,644	47.0
4	John W. Lewis (R)	16,826	51.0
	Alexander B. Montgomery (D)	15,636	47.4
5	Walter Evans (R)	20,592	55.6
	E. J. McDermott (D)	16,462	44.4
6	Albert S. Berry (D)	14,008	52.1
	Thomas B. Mathews (R)	11,968	44.5
7	William C. Owens (D)	13,677	48.7
	George Denny Jr. (R)	13,576	48.4
8	James B. McCreary (D)	13,532	50.6
	Phil Roberts (R)	12,155	45.4
9	Samuel J. Pugh (R)	19,058	50.2
	Rawleigh K. Hart (D)	18,396	48.4
10	Joseph M. Kendall (D)	14,845‡	50.4
	Nathan T. Hopkins (R)	14,592	49.6
11	David G. Colson (R)	14,628	47.7
	George E. Stone (D)	10,932	35.6
	Silas Adams (IR)	4,975	16.2

	Candidates	Votes	%
	Special Elections		
10	William M. Beckner (D)	14,231	52.3
	John L. Bosley (R)	12,970	47.7

LOUISIANA

	Candidates	Votes	%
1	Adolph Meyer (D)	13,405	65.5
	H. P. Kernochan (R)	6,676	32.6
2	Charles F. Buck (D)	14,864	66.8
	H. D. Coleman (R)	7,211	32.4
3	Andrew Price (D)	14,388	60.8
	Taylor Beattle (R)	8,620	36.5
4	Henry W. Ogden (D)	12,257	67.4
	B. W. Bailey (POP)	5,932	32.6
5	Charles J. Boatner (D)	14,755‡	76.4
	Alexis Benoit (POP)	4,549	23.6
6	Samuel M. Robertson (D)	7,981	78.2
	M. R. Wilson (POP)	2,230	21.8

	Candidates	Votes	%
	Special Elections		
4	Henry W. Ogden (D)	8,261	71.2
	C. D. Hicks (POP & R)	3,333	28.7

MAINE

	Candidates	Votes	%
1	Thomas B. Reed (R)	17,086	63.5
	J. W. Deering (D)	8,901	33.1
2	Nelson Dingley Jr. (R)	18,097	63.7
	D. J. McGillicuddy (D)	8,059	28.4
	Elbert Y. Turner (PP)	1,693	6.0
3	Seth L. Milliken (R)	16,891	64.7
	M. R. Leighton (D)	6,663	25.5
	G. C. Sheldon (PP)	1,986	7.6
4	Charles A. Boutelle (R)	17,383	65.5
	A. L. Simpson (D)	6,879	25.9

MARYLAND

	Candidates	Votes	%
1	Joshua W. Miles (D)	13,953	43.2
	A. L. Dryden (R)	12,914	40.0
	B. P. Miles (P)	2,728	8.4
	B. Morris (PP)	2,728	8.4
2	William B. Baker (R)	19,291	48.0
	J. F. Talbott (D)	19,100	47.5
3	Harry W. Rusk (D)	16,228	49.8
	William Booze (R)	15,709	48.2
4	John K. Cowen (D)	17,184	50.5
	Robert Smith (R)	16,178	47.5
5	Charles E. Coffin (R)	15,443	52.0
	John Rogers (D)	13,421	45.2
6	George L. Wellington (R)	19,709	52.1
	Frederick Williams (D)	16,742	44.2

	Candidates	Votes	%
	Special Elections		
1	W. L. Henry (D)	13,858	46.3
	Joseph Mallalieu (R)	12,955	43.2
	James Anthony (P)	2,763	9.2
5	Charles E. Coffin (R)	15,492	52.0
	George Welles (D)	13,495	45.3

MASSACHUSETTS

	Candidates	Votes	%
1	Ashley B. Wright (R)	14,018	55.2
	Addison L. Green (D)	9,961	39.2
2	Frederick H. Gillett (R)	15,480	61.4
	Edward A. Hall (D)	7,924	31.4
3	Joseph H. Walker (R)	13,788	59.4
	Charles Haggerty (D)	8,251	35.6
4	Lewis D. Apsley (R)	16,992	64.8
	John J. Desmond (D)	8,432	32.2
5	William S. Knox (R)	14,372	51.7
	George W. Fifield (D)	12,341	44.4
6	William Cogswell (R)	16,206	68.3
	Henry B. Little (D)	5,747	24.2
	Joseph K. Harris (PP)	1,772	7.5
7	William E. Barrett (R)	16,453	57.7
	Samuel K. Hamilton (D)	9,601	33.7
8	Samuel W. McCall (R)	15,188	61.5
	Charles A. Conant (D)	8,747	35.4
9	John F. Fitzgerald (D)	11,459	53.3
	Jesse M. Gove (R)	9,545	44.4
10	Harrison H. Atwood (R)	9,833	35.9
	Michael J. McEttrick (D & CIT)	8,868	32.4
	William S. McNary (D)	7,113	26.0
11	William F. Draper (R)	16,905	62.0
	Bentley Wirt Warren (D)	9,456	34.7
12	Elijah A. Morse (R)	15,865	65.3
	William H. Jordan (D)	6,359	26.2
	Elbridge Gerry Brown (PP)	2,065	8.5
13	John Simpkins (R)	13,497	61.1
	Robert Howard (D)	8,548	38.7

MICHIGAN

	Candidates	Votes	%
1	John B. Corliss (R)	18,605	55.0
	Levi T. Griffin (D)	13,441	39.7
2	George Spalding (R)	23,708	54.7
	Thomas E. Barkworth (PP & D)	17,596	40.6
3	Julius Burrows (R)	20,115*	58.7
	Nathaniel H. Stewart (D)	8,075	23.6
	Frederick Lackore (PP)	3,888	11.3
	Lucian U. Underwood (P)	2,217	6.5
4	Henry F. Thomas (R)	21,722	58.8
	Leroy F. Weaver (D)	9,874	26.7
	Sullivan Cook (PP)	3,744	10.1
5	William Alden Smith (R)	19,973	58.5
	Gideon L. Rutherford (D)	10,405	30.5
	Josiah Tibbitts (PP)	2,168	6.4
6	David D. Aitken (R)	22,894	57.3
	Elliott R. Wilcox (D)	13,831	34.6
	Thomas C. Williams (P)	2,394	6.0
7	Horace G. Snover (R)	18,172	54.6
	Ezra C. Carleton (D)	12,334	37.1
8	William S. Linton (R)	16,565	54.1
	Rowland Connor (D)	10,118	33.0
	Emery L. Brewer (P)	1,572	5.1
	Poe R. Crosby (PP)	1,778	5.8
9	Roswell P. Bishop (R)	15,761	58.4
	William T. Evans (D)	7,142	26.5
	Norman B. Farnsworth (PP)	2,768	10.3
10	Rousseau O. Crump (R)	16,304	52.6
	Worthy L. Churchill (D)	12,456	40.2
	Alexander Forsyth (PP)	2,130	6.9
11	John Avery (R)	19,575	62.2
	Hiram B. Hudson (D)	6,503	20.7
	William T. Pitt (PP)	3,660	11.6
	Austin Barber (P)	1,728	5.5
12	Samuel M. Stephenson (R)	20,935	64.0
	Rush Culver (D)	8,714	27.0
	Andrew E. Anderson (PP)	3,053	9.3

MINNESOTA

	Candidates	Votes	%
1	James A. Tawney (R)	22,651	58.0
	John Moonan (D)	10,479	26.8
	Thomas G. Meighen (PP)	4,675	12.0
2	James T. McCleary (R)	23,136	53.9
	L. C. Long (PP)	10,362	24.2
	James H. Baker (D)	7,912	18.5
3	Joel P. Heatwole (R)	19,461	49.2
	Osee M. Hall (D)	14,193	35.9
	J. M. Bowler (PP)	4,988	12.6
4	Andrew R. Keifer (R)	20,573	56.5
	Edw. J. Darragh (D)	10,168	28.0
	Francis H. Clark (PP)	5,055	13.9
5	Loren Fletcher (R)	20,465	51.1
	Oliver T. Erickson (D)	11,506	28.7
	Ernest F. Clark (PP)	7,043	17.6
6	Charles A. Towne (R)	25,487	53.3
	M. R. Baldwin (D)	15,846	33.2
	Kittel Halvorson (PP)	6,475	13.5
7	Frank M. Eddy (R)	18,200	43.5
	Haldor E. Boen (PP)	17,408	41.6
	Thomas N. McLean (D)	3,486	8.3
	Ole Kron (P)	2,726	6.5

MISSISSIPPI

	Candidates	Votes	%
1	John M. Allen (D)	3,177	76.3
	J. A. Brown (PP)	985	23.7

	Candidates	Votes	%
2	John C. Kyle (D)	3,845	75.3
	R. J. Lyle (PP)	1,067	20.9
3	Thomas C. Catchings (D)	1,696	87.1
	Thomas Monuh (P)	207	10.6
4	Hernando D. Money (D)	5,213	57.9
	J. H. Jamison (PP)	3,751	41.7
5	John Sharp Williams (D)	5,319	69.1
	W. P. Ratiff (POP)	2,380	30.9
6	Walter McK. Denny (D)	3,889	64.6
	A. C. Hathorn (POP)	2,127	35.4
7	James G. Spencer (D)	3,597	70.5
	A. M. Newman (PP)	1,329	26.1

MISSOURI

	Candidates	Votes	%
1	Charles N. Clark (R)	15,786	44.3
	Hatch (D)	15,367	43.1
	London (PP)	4,270	12.0
2	Uriel S. Hall (D)	18,039	48.8
	Loomis (R)	16,178	43.8
	Goodson (PP)	2,761	7.5
3	Alexander M. Dockery (D)	16,230	44.5
	Orton (R)	15,890	43.6
	Penny (PP)	4,053	11.1
4	George C. Crowther (R)	15,695	47.8
	Ellison (D)	14,034	42.7
	Missemer (PP)	2,910	8.9
5	John C. Tarsney (D)	16,538‡	47.3
	Robert T. Van Horn (R)	5,798	45.2
	Crosby (PP)	2,541	7.3
6	David A. De Armond (D)	13,735	40.7
	Lewis (R)	13,643	40.4
	Francisco (PP)	6,391	18.9
7	John P. Tracey (R)	17,775	45.5
	Heard (D)	17,490	44.7
	Tippin (PP)	3,567	9.1
8	Joel D. Hubbard (R)	16,885	45.4
	Richard P. Bland (D)	16,815	45.2
	Alldredge (PP)	3,528	9.5
9	William M. Trelcar (R)	15,082	49.2
	Clark (D)	14,950	48.8
10	Richard Bartholdt (R)	16,654	62.2
	Coppinger (D)	8,887	33.2
11	Charles F. Joy (R)	15,175	52.5
	Espenschled (D)	12,893	44.6
12	Seth W. Cobb (D)	10,095	53.4
	Sterrett (R)	7,469	39.5
	Nelson (I)	1,094	5.8
13	John H. Raney (R)	16,849	51.3
	Fox (D)	16,021	48.7
14	Norman A. Mozley (R)	16,184	43.9
	Arnold (D)	15,097	40.9
	Livingston (PP)	5,591	15.2
15	Charles G. Burton (R)	16,630	45.2
	Morgan (D)	14,036	38.2
	Bigbee (PP)	5,741	15.6

MONTANA

	Candidates	Votes	%
AL	Charles S. Hartman (R)	23,140	47.0
	Robert B. Smith (PP)	15,240	30.9
	Hal S. Corbett (D)	10,369	21.1

NEBRASKA

	Candidates	Votes	%
1	Jesse B. Strode (R)	18,185	56.8
	Austin H. Weir (D-POP I)	12,730	39.8
2	David Mercer (R)	12,946	50.8
	James E. Boyd (D)	8,165	32.0
	D. Clem Deaver (POP I)	4,007	15.7
3	George D. Meiklejohn (R)	16,531	45.2
	John M. Devine (POP I)	11,138	30.5
	W. A. Hensley (D)	8,018	21.9
4	Eugene J. Hainer (R)	19,493	50.4
	William L. Stark (D-POP I)	15,542	40.2
	Shannon S. Alley (D)	2,763	7.1
5	William E. Andrews (R)	16,270	48.9
	W. A. McKeighan (D-POP I)	15,460	46.5
6	O. M. Kern (D-POP I)	17,077	52.3
	Matt A. Daugherty (R)	14,676	45.0

NEVADA

	Candidates	Votes	%
AL	Francis G. Newlands (D SIL)	4,581	44.4
	Bartine (R)	2,774	26.9
	J. C. Doughty (POP)	2,751	26.7

NEW HAMPSHIRE

	Candidates	Votes	%
1	Cyrus A. Sulloway (R)	22,730	56.3
	John B. Nash (D)	16,507	40.9
2	Henry M. Baker (R)	23,416	56.3
	Charles McDaniel (D)	17,122	41.2

NEW JERSEY

	Candidates	Votes	%
1	Henry C. Loudenslager (R)	24,462	61.0
	Ferrell (D)	12,082	30.1
2	John J. Gardner (R)	22,641	60.5
	Haines (D)	12,900	34.5
3	Benjamin F. Howell (R)	18,403	53.7
	Geisenhainer (D)	14,427	42.1
4	Mahlon Pitney (R)	16,116	49.0
	Cornish (D)	14,709	44.7
5	James F. Stewart (R)	16,441	54.9
	Demarest (D)	10,469	34.9
	Ball (SOC LAB)	2,511	8.4
6	Richard W. Parker (R)	23,219	57.9
	English (D)	14,746	36.8
7	Thomas McEwan Jr. (R)	23,500	44.8
	Stevens (D)	2,207	48.2
8	Charles N. Fowler (R)	19,041	57.4
	Dunn (D)	12,805	38.6

NEW YORK

	Candidates	Votes	%
1	Richard C. McCormick (R)	20,864	56.9
	Joseph Fitch (D)	14,961	40.8
2	Denis M. Hurley (R)	14,507	45.1
	James O. Cleveland (D)	13,194	41.0
	Daniel Bradley (D-REF)	3,924	12.2
3	Francis H. Willis (R)	18,568	49.8
	James A. Murtha Jr. (D)	14,215	38.2
	Stephen Perry Sturges (D-REF)	3,741	10.0
4	Israel T. Fischer (R)	19,802	51.5
	William J. Coombs (D)	17,514	45.6
5	Charles G. Bennett (R)	19,372	58.8
	Anton Vigelius (D)	11,885	36.1
6	James R. Howe (R)	14,427	51.5
	Arthur Somers (D)	12,525	44.7
7	Franklin Bartlett (D)	9,138	47.0
	Austin E. Ford (R)	7,676	39.5
	John Murphy (STATED)	2,159	11.1
8	James J. Walsh (D)	9,466‡	50.3
	John M. Mitchell (R)	9,099	48.3
9	Henry C. Miner (D)	8,038	35.1
	Timothy J. Campbell (SOCIAL D)	7,084	31.0
	John Simpson (R)	5,214	22.8
	Daniel Deleon (SOC LAB)	2,358	10.3
10	Andrew J. Campbell (R)	13,845*	46.5
	Daniel E. Sickles (D)	12,982	43.6
	George Karsch (STATE D)	2,331	7.8
11	William Sulzer (D)	11,208	47.9
	Ferdinand Eidmann (R)	10,524	45.0
	Francis H. Koenig (SOC WB)	1,448	6.2
12	George B. McClellan (D)	10,933	47.4
	Robert A. Chesebrough (R)	9,592	41.6
	George Walton Green (STATE D)	2,042	8.9
13	Richard C. Shannon (R)	13,555	46.3
	Amos J. Cummings (D)	13,089	44.7
	Edward C. Baker (STATE D)	1,943	6.6
14	Lemuel E. Quigg (R)	24,332	55.4
	John Connelly (D)	18,355	41.8
15	Philip B. Low (R)	21,562	48.0
	Jacob A. Cantor (D)	17,028	37.9
	Robert G. Monroe (STATE D)	4,827	10.7
16	Benjamin L. Fairchild (R)	24,853	54.1
	William Ryan (D)	19,294	42.0
17	Benjamin B. Odell Jr. (R)	19,327	57.5
	Eugene S. Ives (D)	13,520	40.2
18	Jacob Le Fever (R)	22,169	55.8

	Candidates	Votes	%
	William M. Ketcham (D)	16,640	41.9
19	Frank S. Black (R)	20,954	53.4
	Charles D. Haines (D)	17,514	44.6
20	George N. Southwick (R)	19,199	51.1
	Charles Tracey (D)	17,549	46.7
21	David Forrest Wilber (R)	24,472	53.1
	George Vanhorn (D)	20,395	44.2
22	Newton M. Curtis (R)	22,383	61.0
	Thomas R. Hossie (D)	12,785	34.8
23	Wallace T. Foote Jr. (R)	25,526	69.0
	Winslow C. Watson (D)	11,143	30.1
24	Charles A. Chickering (R)	23,320	61.3
	Washington T. Henderson (D)	13,473	35.4
25	James S. Sherman (R)	22,371	56.2
	John D. Henderson (D)	16,130	40.5
26	George W. Ray (R)	29,149	63.8
	Sherrill E. Smith (D)	15,877	34.8
27	Theodore L. Poole (R)	24,647	57.3
	Walter E. Northrup (D)	16,307	37.9
28	Sereno E. Payne (R)	29,528	61.4
	Eli McConnell (D)	15,926	33.1
29	Charles W. Gillet (R)	22,051	54.1
	George Henry Roberts (D)	16,510	40.5
30	James W. Wadsworth (R)	24,541	59.8
	Francis Murphy (D)	13,950	34.0
31	Henry C. Brewster (R)	21,488	55.6
	John D. Lynn (D)	15,530	40.2
32	Rowland B. Mahany (R)	15,548	51.3
	Joseph E. Garvin (D)	13,893	45.8
33	Charles Daniels (R)	23,595	65.5
	J. Morgenstein (D)	11,095	30.8
34	Warren B. Hooker (R)	25,964	64.2
	Staley N. Wood (D)	10,674	26.4
	Andrew Yates Freeman (P)	2,181	5.4

Special Elections

	Candidates	Votes	%
14	Lemuel E. Quigg (R)	13,535	50.1
	Brown (D)	12,586	46.6
15	Isidor Straus (D)	15,364	55.5
	Sigrist (R)	10,653	38.5

NORTH CAROLINA

	Candidates	Votes	%
1	Harry Skinner (PP)	16,510	54.9
	William A. B. Branch (D)	13,546	45.1
2	Frederick A. Woodard (D)	14,721	50.0
	Henry P. Cheatham (R)	9,413	31.9
	Howard F. Freeman	5,314	18.0
3	John G. Shaw (D)	10,699	39.1
	Cyrus Thompson (PP)	9,705	35.5
	Oscar J. Spear (R)	6,966	25.5
4	William F. Strowd (PP & R)	18,667	56.5
	Charles M. Cooke (D)	14,335	43.4
5	Thomas Settle (R)	16,934	50.8
	Augustus W. Graham (D)	14,046	42.2
	William Merritt (POP)	2,104	6.3
6	James H. Lockhart (D)	13,996‡	50.8
	Charles H. Martin (PP)	13,505	49.0
7	Alonzo C. Shuford (PP)	15,383	53.9
	John S. Henderson (D)	13,124	46.0
8	Romulus Z. Linney (PP & R)	18,775	54.6
	William H. Bower (D)	15,491	45.1
9	Richmond Pearson (R)	16,869	50.2
	William T. Crawford (D)	16,734	49.8

NORTH DAKOTA

	Candidates	Votes	%
AL	Martin N. Johnson (R)	21,615	57.3
	Muir (POP)	15,660	41.5

OHIO

	Candidates	Votes	%
1	Charles P. Taft (R)	19,315	61.0
	Hiram D. Peck (D)	10,378	32.8
	Thomas John Donnelly (PP)	1,679	5.3
2	Jacob H. Bromwell (R)	22,221	62.5
	James B. Matson (D)	10,667	30.0
	Robert H. H. Wheeler (PP)	2,456	6.9
3	Paul J. Sorg (D)	22,529	48.0
	Andrew L. Harris (R)	22,327	47.6
4	Fernando C. Layton (D)	15,388	47.2

Candidates	Votes	%
William D. Davies (R)	13,910	42.6
Joseph White (PP)	2,323	7.1
5 Francis B. De Witt (R)	16,546	49.4
John S. Snook (D)	14,899	44.5
Henry L. Goll (PP)	2,015	6.0
6 George W. Hulick (R)	20,283	57.3
Joseph L. Stephens (D)	12,505	35.3
7 George W. Wilson (R)	18,021	54.9
Charles E. Gain (D)	11,731	35.8
8 Luther M. Strong (R)	21,730	58.5
Elijah T. Dunn (D)	11,740	31.6
George Riddle (PP)	2,045	5.5
9 James Harding Southard (R)	20,715	54.8
Byron F. Ritchie (D)	14,109	37.3
George Candee (PP, P)	2,964	7.8
10 Lucien J. Fenton (R)	19,768	62.5
John O. Yates (D)	9,465	30.0
11 Charles H. Grosvenor (R)	20,731	56.9
Eli Reynolds Lash (D)	11,601	31.8
William H. Crawford (PP)	3,115	8.6
12 David K. Watson (R)	18,953	49.4
Joseph H. Outhwaite (D)	17,362	45.3
George F. Ebner (PP)	2,015	5.3
13 Stephen R. Harris (R)	19,131	46.0
Boston G. Young (D)	18,453	44.4
Amos Kellar (PP)	2,983	7.2
14 Winfield S. Kerr (R)	21,302	54.6
James C. Laser (D)	14,262	36.6
15 Henry C. Van Voorhis (R)	19,291	56.7
Charles Richardson (D)	12,010	35.3
16 Lorenzo Danford (R)	17,481	55.9
Albert O. Barnes (D)	10,300	33.0
James Brettelle (PP)	1,977	6.3
17 Addison S. McClure (R)	19,061	48.8
James A. D. Richards (D)	17,403	44.5
William F. Lloyd (PP)	2,268	5.8
18 Robert W. Tayler (R)	20,803	49.0
Edward S. Raff (D)	11,051	26.0
Jacob S. Coxey (PP)	8,912	21.0
19 Stephen A. Northway (R)	22,361	62.9
Henry Apthorp (D)	7,164	20.2
George A. Wise (PP)	4,492	12.6
20 Clifton B. Beach (R)	17,327	59.1
H. B. Harrington (D)	8,351	28.5
Luther S. Copper (PP)	2,456	8.4
21 Theodore E. Burton (R)	17,968	53.4
Tom L. Johnson (D)	13,260	39.4
George A. Groot (PP)	1,805	5.4

Special Elections

Candidates	Votes	%
2 Jacob H. Bromwell (R)	22,247	62.4
James B. Matson (D)	10,709	30.1
William R. Fox (PP)	2,448	6.9

OREGON

Candidates	Votes	%
1 Binger Hermann (R)	22,264	47.6
Charles Miller (POP)	12,620	27.0
J. K. Weatherford (D)	10,790	23.1
2 William R. Ellis (R)	18,875	47.9
Joseph Waldrop (POP)	10,749	27.3
James H. Raley (D)	9,013	22.9

PENNSYLVANIA

Candidates	Votes	%
1 Henry H. Bingham (R)	26,957	70.7
Denis J. Callaghan (D)	10,995	28.8
2 Robert Adams Jr. (R)	17,550	75.7
Max Herzberg (D)	5,488	23.7
3 Frederick Halterman (R)	13,443	65.8
Joseph P. McCullen (D)	6,980	34.2
4 John E. Reyburn (R)	42,461	71.8
Gustav A. Muller (D)	16,056	27.2
5 Alfred C. Harmer (R)	38,986	74.8
David Moffet (D)	12,530	24.1
6 John B. Robinson (R)	20,717	64.7
Thomas E. Parke (D)	9,803	30.6
7 Irving P. Wanger (R)	22,913	54.8
John Todd (D)	18,087	43.3
8 Joseph J. Hart (D)	14,762	49.2

Candidates	Votes	%
William S. Kirkpatrick (R)	14,565	48.5
9 Constantine J. Erdman (D)	21,273	51.7
Jeremiah S. Trexler (R)	19,325	47.0
10 Marriott Brosius (R)	19,266	70.9
John A. Coyle (D)	7,181	26.4
11 Joseph A. Scranton (R)	14,104	51.1
Edward Merrifield (D)	12,027	43.5
12 John Leisenring (R)	18,114	56.1
William H. Hines (D)	12,644	39.2
13 Charles N. Brumm (R)	13,947	54.3
James B. Reilly (D)	11,718	45.7
14 Ephraim M. Woomer (R)	19,139	64.1
William H. Minick (D)	9,177	30.7
15 Myron B. Wright (R)	15,651*	64.3
Rhamanthus M. Stocker (D)	7,501	30.8
16 Fred C. Leonard (R)	16,791	53.8
James B. Benson (D)	11,687	37.5
Andrew Sherwood (P)	1,676	5.4
17 Monroe H. Kulp (R)	12,677	49.3
Charles R. Buckalew (D)	11,783	45.8
18 Thaddeus M. Mahon (R)	19,597	61.1
D. G. Smith (D)	12,456	38.9
19 James A. Stable (R)	21,138	52.1
Peter H. Strubinger (D)	18,754	46.2
20 Josiah D. Hicks (R)	23,969	62.9
Thomas J. Burke (D)	12,592	33.1
21 Daniel B. Heiner (R)	24,754	56.7
William M. Fairman (D)	14,107	32.3
22 John Dalzell (R)	29,136	76.6
James A. Wakefield (D)	7,430	19.5
23 William A. Stone (R)	13,771	77.6
James Semple (D)	3,420	19.3
24 Ernest F. Acheson (R)	27,538	57.2
William A. Sipe (D)	17,304	35.9
25 Thomas W. Phillips (R)	22,156	61.6
Joseph C. Vanderlin (D)	10,435	29.0
William J. Kirker (PP)	1,919	5.3
26 Matthew Griswold (R)	15,729	52.9
Joseph C. Sibley (D)	13,265	44.6
27 Charles W. Stone (R)	11,717	61.1
John F. Parsons (D)	4,845	25.2
S. P. McCalmont (D)	1,724	9.0
28 William C. Arnold (R)	16,994	50.6
Aaron Williams (D)	15,197	45.2
AL Galusha A. Grow (R, IR)	571,124✓	
George F. Huff (R, IR)	566,290✓	
Henry Meyer (D)	328,677	
Thomas Collins (D)	324,623	
Elisha Kent Kane (P)	23,481	
Lewis G. Jordan (P)	22,980	
Victor A. Lotier (PP)	17,820	
B. F. Greenman (D)	17,299	
Ernest Kreft (SOC LAB)	1,524	
Gottfried Metzler (SOC LAB)	1,466	

Special Elections

Candidates	Votes	%
AL Galusha A. Grow (R)	485,804	60.4
James Denton Hancock (D)	297,966	37.0

RHODE ISLAND

Candidates	Votes	%
1 Melville Bull (R)	11,422	57.2
Oscar Lapham (D)	7,311	36.6
2 Warren O. Arnold (R)	11,259	59.8
Garvin (D)	6,555	34.8

SOUTH CAROLINA

Candidates	Votes	%
1 William Elliott (D)	5,650‡	59.1
George W. Murray (R)	3,913	40.9
2 W. Jasper Talbert (D)	5,942	99.5
3 Asbury C. Latimer (D)	5,778	81.3
Robert Moorman (R)	985	13.9
4 Stanyarne Wilson (D)	8,425	75.1
L. D. Metton (D)	2,771	24.7
5 Thomas J. Straight (D)	6,141	67.6
G. G. Alexander (R)	1,545	17.0
W. R. Davie (ID)	1,163	12.8
6 John L. McLaurin (D)	8,171	76.9
J. E. Wilson (R)	2,452	23.1

Candidates	Votes	%
7 J. William Stokes (D)	7,358‡	73.0
James B. Johnston (R)	2,656	26.3

SOUTH DAKOTA

Candidates	Votes	%
AL Robert J. Gamble (R)	40,683✓	
John A. Pickler (R)	40,623✓	
John E. Kelley (I)	27,379	
Freeman Knowles (I)	27,348	
William A. Lynch (D)	8,102	
Roger F. Connor (D)	8,041	
George A. Ragan (P)	872	
A. Jamieson (P)	833	

TENNESSEE

Candidates	Votes	%
1 William C. Anderson (R)	18,017	61.7
Thad A. Cox (D)	8,542	29.2
R. S. Cheves (P)	2,662	9.1
2 Henry R. Gibson (R)	16,215	53.2
John C. Hauk (R-D)	13,191	43.3
3 Foster V. Brown (R)	17,019	52.2
Henry C. Snodgrass (D)	13,947	42.7
F. B. Dickey (POP)	1,669	5.1
4 Benton McMillin (D)	11,958	54.2
J. A. Denton (R)	10,115	45.8
5 James D. Richardson (D)	11,440	53.7
W. W. Erwin (POP)	9,543	44.8
6 James E. Washington (D)	11,234	54.0
Tip Gamble (R)	4,798	23.1
T. N. Lewis (POP)	4,783	23.0
7 Nicholas N. Cox (D)	9,098	52.6
H. F. Farris (R)	6,366	36.8
J. K. P. Blackburn (POP)	1,844	10.7
8 John E. McCall (R)	13,064	51.6
B. A. Enloe (D)	12,243	48.4
9 James C. McDearmon (D)	10,634	57.1
Atwood Pierson (POP)	7,983	42.9
10 Josiah Patterson (D)	6,654	66.1
J. N. Brown (R)	1,955	19.4
R. J. Rawlings (POP)	1,454	14.5

TEXAS

Candidates	Votes	%
1 Joseph C. Hutcheson (D)	14,920	55.0
J. J. Burroughs (POP)	10,037	37.0
L. E. Dunn (R)	2,164	8.0
2 Samuel B. Cooper (D)	23,323	59.3
B. A. Calhoun (POP)	16,025	40.7
3 Charles H. Yoakum (D)	15,461	55.5
J. M. Perdue (POP)	12,411	44.5
4 David B. Culberson (D)	15,872	49.2
J. H. Davis (POP)	14,604	45.3
H. S. Sanderson (R)	1,728	5.4
5 Joseph W. Bailey (D)	19,722	56.7
N. M. Browder (POP)	13,540	38.9
6 Jo Abbott (D)	19,965	49.2
J. C. Kearby (POP)	19,621	48.4
7 George C. Pendleton (D)	18,822	52.4
I. N. Barber (POP)	17,092	47.6
8 Charles K. Bell (D)	16,480	50.6
C. H. Jenkins (POP)	16,104	49.4
9 Joseph D. Sayers (D)	18,460	52.7
W. O. Hutchison (POP)	16,591	47.3
10 Miles Crowley (D)	12,177	39.4
A. J. Rosenthal (POP)	10,874	35.2
J. C. McBride (POP)	7,847	25.4
11 William H. Crain (D)	17,946	52.7
V. Weldon (POP)	16,089	47.3
12 George H. Noonan (R)	11,958	43.4
A. W. Houston (D)	11,045	40.1
A. V. Gates (POP)	4,545	16.5
13 Jeremiah V. Cockrell (D)	13,687	39.8
D. B. Gilliland (POP)	13,321	38.8
J. M. Dean (ID)	5,780	16.8

VERMONT

Candidates	Votes	%
1 H. Henry Powers (R)	21,546	75.5
Vernon A. Rutlard (D)	6,987	24.5
2 William W. Grout (R)	20,337	75.2
George S. Fletcher (D)	6,658	24.6

VIRGINIA

	Candidates	Votes	%
1	William A. Jones (D)	11,598	60.1
	James J. McDonald (R)	6,944	36.0
2	D. Gardiner Tyler (D)	12,375	56.3
	T. R. Borland (R)	8,868	40.3
3	Tazewell Ellett (D)	11,745	63.3
	J. W. Southward (R)	4,653	25.1
	James M. Gregory (POP)	1,788	9.6
4	William R. McKenney (D)	8,773‡	48.1
	Robert T. Thorp (R)	7,909	43.3
	J. Haskins Hobson (POP)	1,107	6.1
5	Claude A. Swanson (D)	10,750	52.3
	George W. Cornett (R)	8,417	41.0
	G. W. B. Hale (POP)	1,121	5.5
6	Peter J. Otey (D)	10,602	47.1
	John Hampton Hoge (R)	8,288	36.9
	O. C. Rucker (POP)	3,550	15.8
7	Smith S. Turner (D)	11,041	52.1
	Robert J. Walker (R)	9,500	44.9
8	Elisha E. Meredith (D)	10,801	54.3
	P. H. McCaull (R)	8,450	42.5
9	James Alexander Walker (R)	14,287	51.2
	H. S. K. Morison (D)	13,332	47.8
10	Henry St. George Tucker (D)	12,422	50.3
	J. Yost (R)	11,530	46.7

Special Elections

		Votes	%
7	Smith S. Turner (D)	7,882	65.0
	E. D. Root	4,189	34.5

WASHINGTON

	Candidates	Votes	%
AL	William H. Doolittle (R)	35,981✓	
	Samuel C. Hyde (R)	35,075✓	
	W. P. C. Adams (PP, SPP)	26,285	
	J. C. Van Patten (PP, SPP)	25,643	
	B. F. Heuston (D)	14,602	
	N. T. Caton (D)	14,503	
	W. W. Van Dusen (P)	210	
	B. F. Brown (P)	203	
	W. P. C. Adams (SPP)	157	
	Lawrence E. Doyle (I)	110	

WEST VIRGINIA

	Candidates	Votes	%
1	Blackburn B. Dovener (R)	21,821	53.4
	John A. Howard (D)	17,375	42.5
2	Alston G. Dayton (R)	23,444	51.8
	William S. Wilson (D)	21,397	47.3
3	James H. Huling (R)	23,457	53.5
	John D. Alderson (D)	19,538	44.5
4	Warren Miller (R)	20,795	52.0
	Thomas H. Harvey (D)	17,767	44.4

WISCONSIN

	Candidates	Votes	%
1	Henry Allen Cooper (R)	21,972	56.7
	Andrew Kull (D)	12,334	31.8
	Hamilton Utley (PP)	2,828	7.3
2	Edward Sauerhering (R)	18,197	47.9
	Charles Barwig (D)	17,932	47.2
3	Joseph W. Babcock (R)	22,262	58.2

	Candidates	Votes	%
	Cyrus M. Butt (D & POP)	14,608	38.2
4	Theobald Otjen (R)	17,719	47.9
	David S. Rose (D)	12,214	33.0
	Henry Smith (PP)	7,092	19.2
5	Samuel S. Barney (R)	18,681	52.6
	Henry Blank (D)	13,057	36.7
	Fred C. Runge (PP)	3,794	10.7
6	Samuel A. Cook (R)	21,718	55.8
	Owen A. Wells (D)	14,919	38.3
7	Michael Griffin (R)	17,489	57.4
	George W. Levis (D)	9,996	32.8
	Clements H. Van Worner (PP)	1,626	5.3
8	Edward S. Minor (R)	19,902	54.2
	Lyman E. Barnes (D)	15,522	42.3
9	Alexander Stewart (R)	22,741	56.0
	Thomas Lynch (D)	14,910	36.7
	John F. Miles (PP)	2,187	5.4
10	John J. Jenkins (R)	19,836	57.9
	E. C. Kennedy (D)	9,054	26.4
	William Munro (PP)	3,855	11.3

Special Elections

		Votes	%
7	Michael Griffin (R)	17,766	57.8
	George W. Levis (D)	9,992	32.5
	Clement H. Van Worner (PP)	1,619	5.3

WYOMING

	Candidates	Votes	%
AL	Frank W. Mondell (R)	10,068	52.6
	Henry A. Coffeen (D)	6,152	32.2
	Shakespeare E. Sealey (POP)	2,906	15.2

1895 House Elections

ILLINOIS

Special Elections

	Candidates	Votes	%
10	George W. Prince (R)	21,829	66.0
	Fred K. Bastian (D)	8,392	25.4
	E. K. Kempster	2,877	8.7
18	William F. L. Hadley (R)	15,291	51.8
	Edward Lane (D)	12,040	40.8

MASSACHUSETTS

Special Election

		Votes	%
6	William H. Moody (R)	15,064	66.3
	Harvey N. Shepard (D)	5,819	25.6
	Wilbert Ormand Dwinell (PP)	1,299	5.7

MICHIGAN

Special Elections

	Candidates	Votes	%
3	Alfred Milnes (R)	16,167	51.7
	Albert M. Todd (DPOP PFS)	14,851	47.5

NEW YORK

Special Elections

		Votes	%
10	Amos J. Cummin (TAM)	15,295	56.4
	R. A. Greacen (R)	10,223	37.7

PENNSYLVANIA[1]

Special Elections

	Candidates	Votes	%
15	Edwin J. Jorden (R)	13,445	64.1
	Rhamanthus M. Stocker (D)	6,690	31.9
15	James H. Codding (R)	14,356	66.0
	Rhamanthus M. Stocker (D)	6,575	30.2

1. Edwin J. Jorden was elected to fill an unexpired term in the 53rd Congress (1893–1895) following the death of incumbent Myron B. Wright. Wright had previously been reelected to the 54th Congress (1895– 1897). James H. Codding was elected to a full two-year term to replace Wright. (See Pennsylvania's 15th district for 1892 and 1894.)

1896 House Elections

ALABAMA

	Candidates	Votes	%
1	George W. Taylor (D SIL)	11,890	70.5
	Frank H. Threatt (R)	4,281	25.4
2	Jesse Stallings (D SIL)	11,703	55.9
	Thomas H. Clarke (D SM)	5,361	25.6
	John C. Fonville (POP)	3,856	18.4
3	Henry Clayton (D SIL)	11,671	52.6
	George L. Comer (D SM)	5,754	25.9
	Emmett C. Jackson (POP)	759	21.5
4	Thomas S. Plowman (D SIL)	10,312‡	56.3
	William F. Aldrich (POP & R)	7,345	40.1
5	Willis Brewer (D SIL)	13,587	60.9
	A. T. Goodwyn (POP & R)	8,742	39.2
6	John H. Bankhead (D)	10,148	55.1
	A. S. Van de Graaf (D SM)	4,985	27.1
	George S. Youngblood (POP)	3,295	17.9
7	Milford W. Howard (POP)	6,168	35.8
	William I. Bullock (D SIL)	5,628	32.7
	Curtis (R)	4,982	28.9
8	Joseph Wheeler (D)	15,640	56.7
	Oscar H. Hundley (R)	11,630	42.1
9	Oscar Underwood (D SIL)	13,499	63.0
	Grattan B. Crowe (POP)	5,618	26.2
	Lawson (D SM)	2,316	10.8

ARKANSAS

	Candidates	Votes	%
1	Philip D. McCulloch Jr. (D)	20,419	76.8
	F. W. Tucker (R)	6,178	23.2
2	John S. Little (D)	19,099	74.7
	C. D. Greaves (R)	6,483	25.3
3	Thomas C. McRae (D)	19,321	70.0
	J. B. Freidheim (R)	8,273	30.0
4	William L. Terry (D)	16,133	70.6
	C. C. Waters (R)	6,714	29.4
5	Hugh A. Dinsmore (D)	17,566	65.9
	W. H. Neal (R)	9,087	34.1
6	Stephen Brundidge Jr. (D)	17,106	77.4
	B. F. Bodenhammer (R)	5,010	22.7

CALIFORNIA

	Candidates	Votes	%
1	John A. Barham (R)	17,826	49.7
	Fletcher A. Cutler (D)	16,328	45.5
2	Marion De Vries (D&I POP)	24,434	55.5
	Grove L. Johnson (R)	18,613	42.3
3	Samuel G. Hilborn (R)	19,778	54.0
	Warren B. English (D-PP)	16,119	44.0
4	James G. Maguire (D-PP)	19,074	61.0
	Thomas B. O'Brien (R)	10,940	35.0
5	Eugene F. Loud (R)	19,351	48.6
	Joseph P. Kelly (D)	10,494	26.4
	A. B. Kinne (PP)	8,825	22.2
6	Charles A. Barlow (D-PP)	24,157	48.9
	James McLachlan (R)	23,494	47.6
7	Curtis H. Castle (D-PP)	19,183	46.7
	William W. Bowers (R)	18,939	46.1
	William H. Carlson (I)	2,139	5.2

COLORADO

	Candidates	Votes	%
1	John F. Shafroth (FUS)	67,821	84.9
	T. E. McClelland (R)	9,625	12.1
2	John C. Bell (FUS)	84,018	84.5
	T. F. Hoffmire (R)	14,385	14.5

CONNECTICUT

	Candidates	Votes	%
1	E. Stevens Henry (R)	27,623	66.7
	Tuttle (D)	10,859	26.2
	Hyde (ND)	2,114	5.1
2	Nehemiah D. Sperry (R)	35,944	59.3
	Fuller (D)	22,317	36.8
3	Charles A. Russell (R)	15,269	64.0
	Fanning (D)	7,665	32.1

	Candidates	Votes	%
4	Ebenezer J. Hill (R)	30,658	63.3
	Houlihan (D)	15,723	32.5

DELAWARE

	Candidates	Votes	%
AL	Levin Irving Handy (D)	15,407	44.0
	Jonathan S. Willis (AK R)	11,159	31.8
	Robert G. Houston (HIG R)	7,123	20.3

FLORIDA

	Candidates	Votes	%
1	Stephen M. Sparkman (D)	14,822	77.5
	E. K. Nichols (R)	2,797	14.6
	J. Asakiah Williams (POP)	1,308	6.8
2	Robert W. Davis (D)	14,375	61.9
	Joseph N. Stripling (R)	6,633	28.6

GEORGIA

	Candidates	Votes	%
1	Rufus E. Lester (D)	8,063	53.8
	Joseph F. Doyle (R)	4,095	27.3
	George H. Miller (POP)	2,826	18.9
2	James M. Griggs (D)	7,104	53.2
	J. E. Peterson (R)	3,780	28.3
	John A. Sibley (POP)	2,483	18.6
3	Elijah B. Lewis (D)	7,459	70.7
	Seaborn S. Montgomery (POP)	3,096	29.3
4	William C. Adamson (D)	8,519	65.2
	A. H. Freeman (R)	4,304	32.9
5	Leonidas F. Livingston (D)	9,258	58.0
	J. C. Hendrix (R)	6,715	42.0
6	Charles L. Bartlett (D)	8,236	63.7
	A. A. Murphy (POP)	4,696	36.3
7	John W. Maddox (D)	10,719	53.4
	W. L. Massey (R)	5,087	25.4
	J. W. McGarrity (POP)	4,256	21.2
8	William M. Howard (D)	9,088	61.6
	G. L. Anderson (POP)	2,962	20.1
	W. Patrick Henry (R)	2,701	18.3
9	Farish C. Tate (D)	11,037	54.2
	H. P. Farrow (R)	5,421	26.6
	Thomas C. Winn (POP)	3,926	19.3
10	William H. Fleming (D)	10,119	58.8
	John T. West (POP)	7,105	41.3
11	William G. Brantley (D)	9,141	60.3
	Benjamin Milliken (POP)	6,019	39.7

IDAHO

	Candidates	Votes	%
AL	James T. Gunn (POP & D)	13,187	46.6
	William E. Borah (SIL R)	9,034	32.0
	John T. Morrison	6,054	21.4

ILLINOIS

	Candidates	Votes	%
1	James R. Mann (R)	51,582	67.6
	James H. Teller (D)	23,123	30.3
2	William Lorimer (R)	35,045	54.3
	John Z. White (D & POP)	28,309	43.9
3	Hugh R. Belknap (R)	22,075	50.0
	Clarence S. Darrow (D&SILVER)	21,485	48.7
4	Daniel W. Mills (R)	22,364	50.9
	James McAndrews (D&SILVER)	20,454	46.5
5	George E. White (R)	23,053	50.9
	Edward T. Noonan (D & POP)	19,975	44.1
6	Edward D. Cooke (R)	25,723	56.3
	Joseph L. Martin (D & POP)	19,144	41.9
7	George Edmund Foss (R)	41,510	65.1
	Olaf E. Ray (D & POP)	21,213	33.3
8	Albert J. Hopkins(R)	32,073	70.1
	Simeon N. Hoover (D)	12,861	28.1
9	Robert R. Hitt (R)	32,949	67.2
	Charles O. Knudson (D)	15,241	31.1
10	George W. Prince (R)	31,459	64.0
	William R. Moore (D)	15,741	32.0

	Candidates	Votes	%
11	Walter Reeves (R)	24,765	56.5
	Charles M. Golden (D)	18,514	42.2
12	Joseph G. Cannon (R)	28,566	59.9
	George L. Vance (D & POP)	18,613	39.1
13	Vespasian Warner (R)	27,324	58.2
	Frank M. Palmer (D & POP)	18,811	40.1
14	Joseph V. Graff (R)	25,144	50.9
	Nicholas E. Worthington (D)	23,413	47.4
15	Benjamin F. Marsh (R)	24,605	49.7
	William H. Neece (D)	24,296	49.1
16	William H. Hinrichsen (D & POP)	26,615	56.0
	John I. Rinaker (R)	20,472	43.1
17	James A. Connolly (R)	23,813	49.4
	Benjamin F. Caldwell (D)	23,714	49.2
18	Thomas M. Jett (D)	22,358	51.5
	William F. L. Hadley (R)	20,599	47.4
19	Andrew J. Hunter (D & POP)	23,960	50.0
	Benson Wood (R)	22,793	47.6
20	James R. Campbell (D & POP)	22,359	53.3
	Orlando Burrel (R)	19,508	46.5
21	Jehu Baker (D)	23,581	50.4
	Everett J. Murphy (R)	23,179	49.6
22	George W. Smith (R)	22,066	55.3
	John J. Hale (D & POP)	17,811	44.7

INDIANA

	Candidates	Votes	%
1	James A. Hemenway (R)	21,807	49.6
	Thomas Duncan (D)	20,856	47.4
2	Robert W. Miers (D)	21,757	48.2
	Alexander M. Hardy (R)	20,759	46.0
	Newel H. Motsinger (POP)	2,625	5.8
3	William J. Zenor (D)	22,418	52.6
	Robert J. Tracewell (R)	19,984	46.9
4	William S. Holman (D)	23,594	50.8
	Marcus R. Sulzer (R)	22,769	49.0
5	George W. Faris (R)	25,290	50.4
	John Clark Ridpath (D & POP)	24,925	49.6
6	Henry U. Johnson (R)	24,083	52.4
	Charles A. Robinson (D & POP)	21,867	47.6
7	Jesse Overstreet (R)	29,075	53.8
	Charles M. Cooper (D & POP)	24,187	44.8
8	Charles L. Henry (R)	30,045	52.3
	John R. Brunt (D & POP)	27,413	47.7
9	Charles B. Landis (R)	23,616	50.3
	Joseph B. Cheadle (D & POP)	23,367	49.7
10	Edgar D. Crumpacker (R)	28,259	55.0
	Martin L. Kruger (D & POP)	23,120	45.0
11	George W. Steele (R)	27,853	53.5
	Joseph H. Larimer (D)	23,584	45.3
12	James N. Robinson (D & POP)	22,752	50.6
	Jacob D. Leighty (R)	22,196	49.4
13	Lemuel W. Royse (R)	25,514	51.6
	Charles Kellison (D & POP)	23,928	48.4

IOWA

	Candidates	Votes	%
1	Samuel M. Clark (R)	21,944	53.7
	Sabut M. Casey (D-PP)	18,649	45.6
2	George M. Curtis (R)	23,202	52.8
	Alfred Hurst (D)	19,882	45.2
3	David B. Henderson (R)	29,654	60.7
	George Stachl (D)	19,231	39.3
4	Thomas Updegraff (R)	26,659	59.6
	F. D. Bayless (D-PP)	17,791	39.8
5	Robert G. Cousins (R)	26,133	57.7
	John R. Caldwell (D-PP)	18,765	41.5
6	John F. Lacey (R)	21,970	51.1
	F. E. White (D-PP)	20,769	48.3
7	John A. T. Hull (R)	25,578	56.9
	Frank W. Evans (D-PP)	19,352	43.1
8	William P. Hepburn (R)	24,783	50.9
	W. H. Robb (D-PP)	23,956	49.2
9	Alva L. Hager (R)	24,904	52.4
	L. T. Genning (D-PP)	22,522	47.4
10	Jonathan P. Dolliver (R)	33,523	59.4

Candidates	Votes	%
John B. Romans (D-PP)	22,555	40.0
11 George D. Perkins (R)	29,601	56.1
H. Vanwagener (D-PP)	22,773	43.2

KANSAS

	Candidates	Votes	%
1	Case Broderick (R)	22,115	53.1
	H. E. Ballou (D-PP)	19,513	46.9
2	Mason S. Peters (D-PP)	26,307	50.4
	John P. Harris (R)	25,919	49.6
3	Edwin R. Ridgely (D-PP)	27,034	54.2
	S. S. Kirkpatrick (R)	22,849	45.8
4	Charles Curtis (R)	26,643	50.7
	John Madden (D-PP)	25,889	49.3
5	William D. Vincent (D-PP)	19,735	50.8
	W. A. Calderhead (R)	19,101	49.2
6	Nelson B. McCormick (PP)	18,257	50.8
	A. H. Ellis (R)	16,106	44.9
7	Jeremiah Simpson (D-PP)	29,789	52.5
	Chester I. Long (R)	26,966	47.5
AL	Jeremiah D. Botkin (PP & D)	168,420	51.3
	R. W. Blue (R)	158,147	48.2

KENTUCKY

	Candidates	Votes	%
1	Charles K. Wheeler (D)	14,808	37.4
	G. P. Thomas (R)	12,842	32.4
	B. F. Keys (POP)	11,991	30.3
2	John D. Clardy (D)	23,535	57.0
	E. T. Franks (R)	17,276	41.8
3	John S. Rhea (D)	19,670	49.6
	W. G. Hunter (R)	19,324	48.7
4	David H. Smith (D)	21,655	49.1
	John W. Lewis (R)	20,222	45.8
5	Walter Evans (R)	27,780	59.7
	John Y. Brown (D)	17,150	36.8
6	Albert S. Berry (D)	16,660	58.9
	Richard P. Ernst (R)	11,638	41.1
7	Evan E. Settle (D)	18,826	52.5
	W. C. P. Breckinridge (R-GOLD D)	17,019	47.5
8	George M. Davison (R)	18,110	53.7
	John B. Thompson (D)	15,629	46.3
9	Samuel J. Pugh (R)	22,014	50.5
	W. Larue Thomas (D)	21,591	49.5
10	Thomas Y. Fitzpatrick (D)	17,453	51.9
	John W. Langley (R)	16,196	48.1
11	David G. Colson (R)	22,391	56.2
	James D. Black (D)	12,878	32.3
	J. D. White (I)	4,547	11.4

LOUISIANA

	Candidates	Votes	%
1	Adolph Meyer (D)	10,776	70.5
	Armand Romain (IR)	3,982	26.1
2	Robert C. Davey (D)	10,269	60.8
	James Legendre (NR)	5,235	31.0
	Fred N. Wicker (R)	1,344	8.0
3	Robert F. Broussard (D)	9,323	57.7
	Taylor Beattie (NR)	6,490	40.2
4	Henry W. Ogden (D)	10,775	66.7
	B. W. Balley (POP)	4,726	29.3
5	Samuel T. Baird (D)	11,494	70.2
	Alexis Benoit (POP)	4,870	29.8
6	Samuel M. Robertson (D)	11,872	72.0
	C. C. Duson (NR)	3,686	22.4
	William M. Thompson (POP)	924	5.6

MAINE

	Candidates	Votes	%
1	Thomas B. Reed (R)	19,329	66.9
	E. W. Staples (D)	8,790	30.4
2	Nelson Dingley Jr. (R)	22,418	69.2
	A. Levensaler (D)	8,424	26.0
3	Seth L. Milliken (R)	20,900	68.2
	M. S. Holway (D)	8,024	26.2
4	Charles A. Boutelle (R)	21,300	65.9
	A. J. Chase (D)	9,166	28.4

MARYLAND

	Candidates	Votes	%
1	Isaac A. Barber (R)	17,969	48.5
	John Miles (D SIL)	17,389	46.9
2	William B. Baker (R)	28,530	53.6
	George Jewett (D SIL)	23,163	43.5
3	William S. Booze (R)	22,671	57.2
	Thomas Weeks (D)	15,977	40.3
4	William W. McIntire (R)	24,899	59.3
	William Ogden (D)	16,424	39.1
5	Sydney E. Mudd (R)	18,954	54.3
	Robert Mass (D)	15,442	44.3
6	John McDonald (R)	22,400	53.3
	Blair Lee (D)	18,837	44.8

MASSACHUSETTS

	Candidates	Votes	%
1	Ashley B. Wright (R)	18,075	65.4
	Patrick H. Sheehan (D)	8,579	31.0
2	Frederick H. Gillett (R)	19,793	71.8
	Thomas A. Fitzgibbon (D)	7,778	28.2
3	Joseph H. Walker (R)	18,993	72.5
	John O'Gara (D)	7,185	27.4
4	George W. Weymouth (R)	20,062	69.3
	I. Porter Morse (D)	8,847	30.6
5	William S. Knox (R)	17,835	60.7
	John H. Harrington (D)	11,531	39.3
6	William H. Moody (R)	19,947	72.8
	Eben Moody Boynton (D)	7,460	27.2
7	William E. Barrett (R)	22,759	68.2
	Philip J. Doherty (D)	10,609	31.8
8	Samuel W. McCall (R)	22,054	74.4
	Frederick H. Jackson (D)	7,590	25.6
9	John F. Fitzgerald (D)	13,979	54.7
	Walter Lincoln Sears (R)	7,819	30.6
	John A. Ryan (D SIL)	3,238	12.7
10	Samuel J. Barrows (R)	17,147	50.4
	Bordman Hall (D)	14,259	41.9
	William L. Chase (R CIT)	2,612	7.7
11	Charles F. Sprague (R)	22,993	69.3
	William H. Baker (D)	10,154	30.6
12	William C. Lovering (R)	21,107	76.8
	Elbridge Gerry Brown (PPL DRS)	6,354	23.1
13	John Simpkins (R)	17,685	74.7
	James Francis Morris (D)	5,993	25.3

MICHIGAN

	Candidates	Votes	%
1	John B. Corliss (R)	24,021	55.5
	Edwin Henderson (DPUS)	19,291	44.5
2	George Spalding (R)	26,557	50.5
	Thomas B. Barkworth (DPUS)	25,061	47.7
3	Albert M. Todd (DPUS)	24,466	49.4
	Alfred Milnes (R)	24,041	48.5
4	Edward L. Hamilton (R)	26,518	53.6
	Roman I. Jarvis (DPUS)	22,994	46.4
5	William Alden Smith (R)	26,819	54.8
	George P. Hummer (DPUS)	22,155	45.2
6	Samuel W. Smith (R)	26,889	53.4
	Quincy A. Smith (DPUS)	23,474	46.6
7	Horace G. Snover (R)	22,761	55.5
	O'Brien J. Atkinson (DPUS)	18,267	44.5
8	Ferdinand Brucker (DPUS)	20,992	51.0
	William S. Linton (R)	20,158	49.0
9	Roswell P. Bishop (R)	20,418	58.3
	Armond F. Tibbitts (DPUS)	14,243	40.6
10	Rousseau O. Crump (R)	19,535	52.7
	Charles S. Hampton (DPUS)	17,536	47.3
11	William S. Mesick (R)	24,368	54.9
	Jonathan G. Ramsdell (DPUS)	19,605	44.1
12	Carlos D. Shelden (R)	29,612	70.4
	Henry W. Seymour (DPUS)	12,479	29.7

MINNESOTA

	Candidates	Votes	%
1	James A. Tawney (R)	27,920	60.7
	P. Fitzpatrick (PP & D)	17,219	37.4
2	James T. McCleary (R)	29,481	57.1
	Frank A. Day (PP & D)	21,142	40.9

	Candidates	Votes	%
3	Joel P. Heatwole (R)	24,483	55.9
	H. J. Peck (PP & D)	18,532	42.3
4	Frederick C. Stevens (R)	24,854	62.2
	Francis H. Clark (PP & D)	14,640	36.7
5	Loren Fletcher (R)	24,508	53.2
	S. M. Owen (PP & D)	21,521	46.8
6	R. Page W. Morris (R)	30,317	50.6
	Charles A. Towne (PP & D)	29,598	49.4
7	Frank M. Eddy (R)	26,003	50.9
	Edwin E. Lommen (PP & D)	23,932	46.8

MISSISSIPPI

	Candidates	Votes	%
1	John M. Allen (D)	7,221	86.9
	A. W. Kearley (POP)	752	9.1
2	William V. Sullivan (D)	6,941	70.2
	F. E. Ray (POP)	1,472	14.9
	W. D. Miller (GOLD D)	779	7.9
	M. A. Montgomery (R)	692	7.0
3	Thomas C. Catchings (D)	3,069	75.8
	J. R. Chalmers (F SIL R)	532	13.1
	C. J. Jones (R)	369	9.1
4	Andrew F. Fox (D)	8,343	70.0
	R. K. Prewitt (POP)	3,086	25.9
5	John Sharp Williams (D)	10,475	80.1
	W. H. Stinson (POP)	2,248	17.2
6	William F. Love (D)	6,718	64.3
	N. C. Hathorn (POP)	2,683	25.7
	H. C. Griffin (R)	1,055	10.1
7	Patrick Henry (D)	7,327	84.7
	G. M. Cain (POP)	897	10.4

MISSOURI

	Candidates	Votes	%
1	Richard P. Giles (D)	24,044*	53.3
	Clark (R)	19,320	42.8
2	Robert N. Bodine (D)	25,862	55.7
	Loomis (R)	19,367	41.7
3	Alexander M. Dockery (D)	23,952	53.5
	Orton (R)	18,634	41.6
4	Charles F. Cochran (D)	21,512	54.7
	Crowther (R)	17,683	45.0
5	William S. Cowherd (D)	25,966	54.9
	Neff (R)	21,306	45.1
6	David A. De Armond (D)	22,524	53.5
	Hamilton (R)	16,722	39.7
	Linton (PP)	2,606	6.2
7	James Cooney (D)	27,846	53.5
	Tracy (R)	21,772	41.8
8	Richard P. Bland (D)	24,605	53.7
	Hubbard (R)	19,754	43.1
9	James Beauchamp Clark (D)	19,970	53.0
	Treloar (R)	17,475	46.4
10	Richard Bartholdt (R)	25,513	73.2
	Lemp (D)	9,060	26.0
11	Charles F. Joy (R)	28,341	53.3
	Hunt (D-PP)	24,676	46.4
12	Charles E. Pearce (R)	21,483	54.9
	Kern (D)	17,568	44.9
13	Edward Robb (D)	22,310	51.9
	Steel (R)	19,062	44.4
14	Willard D. Vandiver (D)	25,089	49.6
	Snider (R)	20,659	40.8
	Livingston (PP)	4,860	9.6
15	Maecenas E. Benton (D)	24,155	55.7
	Burton (R)	17,010	39.2

MONTANA

	Candidates	Votes	%
AL	Charles S. Hartman (SIL R)	33,932	78.1
	O. F. Goddard (R)	9,492	21.9

NEBRASKA

	Candidates	Votes	%
1	Jesse B. Strode (R)	17,356	49.4
	Jefferson H. Broady (D-POP I)	17,137	48.8
2	David H. Mercer (R)	14,861	52.3
	Edward R. Duffie (D-POP I)	13,286	46.8
3	Samuel Maxwell (D-POP I)	23,487	54.8
	R. L. Hammond (R)	18,633	43.4

	Candidates	Votes	%
4	William L. Stark (D-POP I)	20,515	50.5
	E. J. Hainer (R)	18,844	46.4
5	Roderick D. Sutherland (D-POP I)	18,332	52.8
	William E. Andrews (R)	15,541	44.8
6	William L. Greene (D-POP I)	19,378	55.7
	Addison E. Cady (R)	14,841	42.7

NEVADA

	Candidates	Votes	%
AL	Francis G. Newlands (D SIL)	6,429	66.3
	James C. Doughty (PP)	1,948	20.1
	M. J. Davis (R)	1,319	13.6

NEW HAMPSHIRE

	Candidates	Votes	%
1	Cyrus A. Sulloway (R)	25,661	63.0
	John B. Nash (D)	13,928	34.2
2	Frank G. Clarke (R)	26,689	64.3
	Daniel M. White (D)	13,877	33.4

NEW JERSEY

	Candidates	Votes	%
1	Henry C. Loudenslager (R)	33,659	64.2
	John T. Wright (D & N S)	17,118	32.6
2	John J. Gardner (R)	31,418	66.0
	Abraham E. Conrow (D & N S)	13,969	29.3
3	Benjamin F. Howell (R)	24,308	57.8
	John A. Wells (D)	16,087	38.3
4	Mahlon Pitney (R & ND)	20,494	52.5
	Augustus W. Cutler (D)	17,517	44.8
5	James F. Stewart (R)	23,845	59.9
	Addison Ely (D)	13,667	34.3
6	Richard Wayne Parker (R)	31,059	64.2
	Joseph A. Beecher (D)	15,393	31.8
7	Thomas McEwan Jr. (R)	30,557	51.8
	Alexander C. Young (D)	26,080	44.2
8	Charles N. Fowler (R)	25,131	61.7
	Freeman O. Willey (D)	13,487	33.1

NEW YORK

	Candidates	Votes	%
1	Joseph M. Belford (R)	27,191	59.4
	William D. Marvel (D)	15,923	34.8
2	Denis M. Hurley (R)	18,268	50.8
	John M. Clancy (D)	15,901	44.2
3	Francis H. Wilson (R)	23,813	56.3
	Charles F. Brandt (D)	16,260	38.5
4	Israel F. Fischer (R)	25,810	56.2
	Thomas F. Larkin (D)	18,381	40.0
5	Charles G. Bennett (R)	22,605	57.4
	Thomas S. Delaney (D)	14,186	36.1
6	James R. Howe (R)	15,314	49.1
	William Fickermann (D)	14,287	45.8
7	John H. G. Vehslage (D)	11,032	51.9
	Franklin Bartlett (R & ND)	9,848	46.4
8	John Murray Mitchell (R & ND)	10,488	52.6
	James J. Walsh (D)	9,219	46.3
9	Thomas J. Bradley (D)	11,002	46.3
	Timothy J. Campbell (R & ND)	8,379	35.2
	Daniel Deleon (SOC LAB)	4,371	18.4
10	Amos J. Cummings (D)	17,446	53.3
	Clarence W. Meade (R)	14,245	43.5
11	William Sulzer (D)	12,195	48.8
	Ferdinand Eldmann (R)	10,435	41.8
	Herman Miller (SOC LAB)	2,011	8.1
12	George B. McClellan (D)	12,815	50.9
	Charles A. Hess (R)	11,038	43.9
13	Richard C. Shannon (R)	15,413	48.0
	Thomas Smith (D)	14,067	43.8
14	Lemuel E. Quigg (R)	27,875	55.5
	John Quincy Adams (D)	18,553	37.0
15	Philip B. Low (R & ND)	29,602	54.5
	William H. Burke (D)	22,520	41.5
16	William L. Ward (R)	30,709	52.6
	Eugene B. Travis (D)	23,456	40.2
17	Benjamin B. Odell Jr. (R)	22,622	58.5
	David A. Morrison (D)	15,500	40.1
18	John H. Ketcham (R)	25,531	60.9
	Richard E. Connell (D)	15,956	38.0
19	Aaron V. S. Cochrane (R)	23,509	55.7

	Candidates	Votes	%
	George G. Miller (D)	17,735	42.0
20	George N. Southwick (R)	22,342	54.7
	Thomas F. Wilkinson (D)	17,637	43.2
21	David Forrest Wilber (R)	28,567	55.7
	John H. Bagley (D)	22,267	43.4
22	Lucius N. Littauer (R)	32,269	93.3
23	Wallace T. Foote Jr. (R)	30,475	97.0
24	Charles A. Chickering (R)	27,242	61.4
	Oscar M. Wood (D)	16,248	36.6
25	James S. Sherman (R)	26,996	60.8
	Cornelius Haley (D)	16,512	37.2
26	George W. Ray (R)	34,686	60.8
	Alexander D. Wales (D)	20,383	35.7
27	James J. Belden (R)	27,427	53.2
	Theodore L. Poole (D)	22,657	44.0
28	Sereno E. Payne (R)	33,628	62.4
	Robert L. Drummond (D)	19,822	36.8
29	Charles W. Gillet (R)	27,192	59.7
	Henry W. Bowes (D)	17,994	39.5
30	James W. Wadsworth (R)	28,478	57.3
	Frank P. Hulette (D)	19,066	38.4
31	Henry C. Brewster (R)	25,399	56.9
	William E. Ryan (D)	17,109	38.3
32	Rowland B. Mahany (R)	18,623	54.7
	Charles Rung (D)	14,765	43.4
33	De Alva S. Alexander (R)	27,573	63.0
	Harvey W. Richardson (D)	14,636	33.4
34	Warren B. Hooker (R)	30,696	86.0
	David F. Allen (POP & R)	3,298	9.2

NORTH CAROLINA

	Candidates	Votes	%
1	Harry Skinner (POP & R)	20,724	58.3
	Wilson H. Lucas (D)	14,849	41.7
2	George H. White (R)	19,332	51.6
	Frederick A. Woodard (D)	15,378	41.1
	D. S. Moss (POP)	2,738	7.3
3	John E. Fowler (POP & R)	17,989	58.9
	Frank Thompson (D)	12,536	41.1
4	William F. Strowd (POP)	20,977	55.6
	Edward W. Pou (D)	16,405	43.5
5	William W. Kitchin (D)	19,082	49.9
	Thomas Settle (R)	18,639	48.8
6	Charles H. Martin (POP & R)	22,051	56.1
	James A. Lockhart (D)	17,235	43.9
7	Alonzo C. Shuford (POP & R)	17,669	55.3
	Samuel J. Pemberton (D)	14,289	44.7
8	Romulus Z. Linney (POP & R)	19,419	51.8
	Rufus A. Doughton (D)	18,007	48.0
9	Richmond Pearson (POP & R)	20,495	51.6
	Joseph S. Adams (D)	19,189	48.3

NORTH DAKOTA

	Candidates	Votes	%
AL	Martin N. Johnson (R)	25,233	54.0
	Burke (FUS)	21,172	45.3

OHIO

	Candidates	Votes	%
1	William B. Shattuc (R)	27,093	60.8
	Thomas J. Donnelly (D)	17,466	39.2
2	Jacob H. Bromwell (R)	30,075	59.0
	David S. Oliver (D)	20,878	41.0
3	John L. Brenner (D)	27,435	49.7
	Robert M. Nevin (R)	27,334	49.5
4	George A. Marshall (D)	25,688	59.5
	John P. MacLean (R)	16,671	38.6
5	David Meekison (D)	24,383	56.1
	Francis B. DeWitt (R)	18,478	42.5
6	Seth W. Brown (R)	25,360	53.9
	Harry W. Paxton (D)	21,358	45.4
7	Walter L. Weaver (R)	22,745	51.4
	Francis M. Hunt (D)	21,171	47.8
8	Archibald Lybrand (R)	26,211	53.8
	McEldin Dun (D)	22,519	46.2
9	James H. Southard (R)	29,603	53.5
	Stephen Brophy (D)	25,698	46.5
10	Lucien J. Fenton (R)	24,809	57.9
	T. S. Hogan (D)	18,029	42.1
11	Charles H. Grosvenor (R)	24,333	54.8

	Candidates	Votes	%
	William E. Finck Jr. (D)	19,850	44.7
12	John J. Lentz (D)	23,673	49.7
	David K. Watson (R)	23,624	49.6
13	James A. Norton (D)	28,878	54.4
	Stephen R. Harris (R)	23,506	44.3
14	Winfield S. Kerr (R)	26,850	52.0
	John B. Coffinberry (D)	24,574	47.6
15	Henry Clay Van Voorhis (R)	22,560	52.6
	James B. Tannehill (D)	19,837	46.2
16	Lorenzo Danford (R)	21,690	53.8
	Henry H. McFadden (D)	18,635	46.2
17	John A. McDowell (D)	26,109	54.7
	Addison S. McClure (R)	21,169	44.3
18	Robert W. Tayler (R)	29,814	54.2
	Isaac R. Sherwood (D)	24,770	45.0
19	Stephen A. Northway (R)	31,789	60.3
	William T. Sawyer (D)	20,626	39.1
20	Clifton B. Beach (R)	24,531	52.8
	A. T. Vantassel (D)	21,384	46.0
21	Theodore E. Burton (R)	25,527	55.2
	L. A. Russell (D)	20,025	43.3

OREGON

	Candidates	Votes	%
1	Thomas H. Tongue (R)	19,355	40.4
	W. S. Vanderburg (POP)	19,292	40.3
	Jefferson Myers (D)	7,914	16.5
2	William R. Ellis (R)	12,617	30.4
	Martin Quinn (POP)	12,239	29.5
	H. H. Northup (SM D)	8,807	21.2
	A. S. Bennett (D)	7,099	17.1

PENNSYLVANIA

	Candidates	Votes	%
1	Henry H. Bingham (R)	32,466	69.7
	Horace E. James (D)	13,962	30.0
2	Robert Adams Jr (R)	22,205	78.0
	Fenton P. F. Mullins (D)	6,100	21.4
3	William McAleer (D)	11,655	49.7
	Frederick Halterman (R)	9,556	40.7
	Samuel E. Hudson (F SIL)	2,064	8.8
4	James Rankin Young (R)	59,147	77.6
	Mark D. Cunningham (D)	16,536	21.7
5	Alfred C. Harmer (R)	47,953	76.1
	Frank D. Wright (D)	14,484	23.0
6	Thomas S. Butler (BUT R)	15,016	39.4
	John B. Robinson (ROB R)	13,369	35.1
	William H. Berry (DN&FS)	9,288	24.4
7	Irving P. Wanger (R)	26,725	60.7
	Charles S. Van de Grift (D)	16,740	38.1
8	William S. Kirkpatrick (R)	17,072	50.5
	Laird H. Barber (D)	16,743	49.5
9	Daniel Ermentrout (D)	26,123	51.1
	Oliver Williams (R)	23,022	45.0
10	Marriott Brosius (R)	24,122	73.3
	Edward D. Reilly (D)	8,252	25.1
11	William Connell (R)	18,598	61.6
	Edward Merrifield (D)	10,741	35.6
12	Morgan B. Williams (R)	20,920	52.4
	John M. Garman (D)	17,976	45.0
13	Charles N. Brumm (R)	16,613	53.0
	Watson F. Shepherd (D)	14,512	46.3
14	Marlin E. Olmsted (R)	25,014	87.6
	Abraham Mattis (PP)	1,948	6.8
15	James H. Codding (R)	20,210	61.6
	Charles Percival Shaw (D)	11,444	34.9
16	Horace B. Packer (R)	21,543	56.2
	Luther B. Seibert (D)	15,152	39.5
17	Monroe H. Kulp (R)	15,195	50.1
	Alphonsus Walsh (D)	14,073	46.4
18	Thaddeus M. Mahon (R)	22,455	61.2
	Willis F. Kearns (D)	14,222	38.8
19	George J. Benner (D)	22,160	49.7
	Frank E. Hollar (R)	21,382	48.0
20	Josiah D. Hicks (MCK SM)	19,974	43.8
	Robert C. McNamara (D)	17,297	37.9
	Joseph E. Thropp (PT)	7,468	16.4
21	Edward E. Robbins (R)	32,149	59.9
	Samuel S. Blyholder (D)	19,464	36.3
22	John Dalzell (R)	28,860	69.0

	Candidates	Votes	%
	John F. Miller (D)	12,788	30.6
23	William A. Stone (R)	21,379	77.2
	Morrison Foster (D)	6,191	22.3
24	Ernest F. Acheson (R)	36,554	57.1
	John Purman (D)	26,538	41.5
25	James J. Davidson (R)	26,529*	59.5
	John G. McConahy (D)	17,050	38.2
26	John C. Sturtevant (R)	18,840	50.4
	Joseph C. Sibley (D)	18,114	48.5
27	Charles W. Stone (R)	15,777	58.3
	William J. Breene (D)	10,058	37.2
28	William C. Arnold (R)	19,295	50.2
	Jackson L. Spangler (D)	18,090	47.1
AL	Galusha A. Grow (R, MCK CIT)	711,346✓	
	Samuel A. Davenport (R, MCK CIT)	708,633✓	
	Jerome T. Ailman (D, PP)	418,218	
	DeWitt C. DeWitt (D, F SIL)	413,802	
	Abraham A. Barker (P)	18,336	
	George Alcorn (P)	18,091	
	John P. Correll (PP)	7,482	
	Hay Walker Jr. (JEFFS)	7,255	
	Benjamin C. Potts (JEFFS)	7,237	
	Emil Guwang (SOC LAB)	1,455	
	Fred W. Long (SOC LAB)	1,432	
	Henry S. Kent (N)	671	
	Isaac G. Pollard (N)	663	

RHODE ISLAND

	Candidates	Votes	%
1	Melville Bull (R)	17,378	63.7
	Brown (D)	8,542	31.3
2	Adin B. Capron (R)	16,612	63.5
	Garvin (D)	8,088	30.9

SOUTH CAROLINA

	Candidates	Votes	%
1	William Elliott (D)	4,648	63.7
	George W. Murray (LW R)	2,478	34.0
2	W. Jasper Talbert (D)	7,999	92.4
	B. P. Chatfield (R)	635	7.3
3	Asbury C. Latimer (D)	9,746	92.0
	A. C. Merrick (B&T R)	659	6.2
4	Stanyarne Wilson (D)	11,230	92.2
5	Thomas J. Strait (D)	8,511	91.0
	John F. Jones (R)	838	9.0
6	John L. McLaurin (D)	9,731	87.7
	J. E. Wilson (B&T R)	878	7.9
7	J. William Stokes (D)	8,065	85.5
	T. B. Johnson (B&T R)	1,342	14.2

Special Election

7	J. William Stokes (D)	8,223	88.3
	T. B. Johnson (B&T R)	1,068	11.5

SOUTH DAKOTA

	Candidates	Votes	%
AL	Freeman Knowles (PP)	41,216✓	
	John E. Kelley (PP)	41,122✓	
	Robert J. Gamble (R)	40,943	
	Coe I. Crawford (R)	40,575	
	K. Lewis (P)	723	
	M. H. Alexander (P)	683	

TENNESSEE

	Candidates	Votes	%
1	Walter P. Brownlow (R)	25,075	62.4
	L. L. Lawrence (D)	13,956	34.7
2	Henry R. Gibson (R)	28,112	74.3
	W. L. Ledgerwood (D)	9,448	25.0
3	John A. Moon (D)	19,498	51.9
	W. J. Clift (R)	17,716	47.2

	Candidates	Votes	%
4	Benton McMillin (D)	18,070	59.6
	C. H. Whitney (R)	12,269	40.4
5	James D. Richardson (D)	16,089	58.6
	Syd Houston (R)	9,000	32.8
	W. W. Erwin (POP)	2,384	8.7
6	John W. Gaines (D SIL)	17,646	57.5
	J. C. McReynold (GOLD D)	12,135	39.5
7	Nicholas N. Cox (D)	15,434	55.2
	A. M. Hughes Jr. (R)	10,744	38.4
	J. K, P. Blackburn (POP)	1,794	6.4
8	Thetus W. Sims (D)	16,568	53.4
	J. E. McCall (D)	13,219	42.6
9	Rice A. Pierce (D SIL)	19,138	64.1
	J. H. McDowell (POP)	10,714	35.9
10	Edward W. Carmack (D SIL)	10,924	48.8
	Josiah Patterson (GOLD D)	10,556	47.1

TEXAS

	Candidates	Votes	%
1	Thomas H. Ball (D)	19,161	55.5
	Joe H. Eagle (POP & R)	15,189	44.0
2	Samuel B. Cooper (D)	25,158	57.0
	B. A. Calhoun (POP)	12,822	29.0
	J. M. Claiborne (R)	6,188	14.0
3	Reese C. De Graffenreid (D)	21,208	56.5
	W. E. Farmer (POP)	16,351	43.5
4	John W. Cranford (D)	20,187	54.0
	J. H. Davis (POP)	13,703	36.7
	M. W. Johnson (R)	3,468	9.3
5	Joseph W. Bailey (D)	28,416	61.2
	W. D. Gordon (R)	13,242	28.5
	R. C. Foster (POP)	4,747	10.2
6	Robert E. Burke (D)	33,144	56.8
	Barnett Gibbs (POP)	25,230	43.2
7	Robert L. Henry (D)	26,151	55.2
	T. A. Pope (R)	11,632	24.5
	W. F. Douthitt (POP)	9,634	20.3
8	Samuel W. T. Lanham (D)	20,935	53.4
	C. H. Jenkins (POP)	17,510	44.7
9	Joseph D. Sayers (D)	20,381	51.4
	W. K. Makemson (R)	11,495	29.0
	Reddin Andrews (POP)	6,787	17.1
10	Robert B. Hawley (R)	17,936	45.7
	J. H. Shelburne (D)	15,757	40.2
	Noah Allen (POP)	5,476	14.0
11	Rudolph Kleburg (D)	19,059	45.6
	H. Gras (R)	18,449	44.1
	J. M. Smith (POP)	4,074	9.8
12	James L. Slayden (D)	14,744	46.0
	G. H. Noonan (R)	13,558	42.3
	Taylor McRae (POP)	3,730	11.6
13	John H. Stephens (D)	22,988	61.0
	H. L. Bentley (R)	14,219	37.8

UTAH

(Became a state Jan. 4, 1896)

AL	William H. King (D)	47,456	61.2
	Holbrook (SIL R)	27,813	35.9

Special Election

AL	C. E. Allen (R)	20,563	49.7
	B. H. Roberts (D)	19,666	47.5

VERMONT

1	H. Henry Powers (R)	26,145	76.4
	Peter F. McManus (D)	7,693	22.5
2	William W. Grout (R)	26,319	80.4
	Henry E. Fitzgerald (D)	6,202	18.9

VIRGINIA

	Candidates	Votes	%
1	William A. Jones (D)	15,525	58.4
	Walter B. Tyler (R)	10,752	40.5
2	William A. Young (D)	15,789‡	50.5
	Richard A. Wise (R)	13,390	42.8
	W. M. Whaley (SM D)	1,895	6.1
3	John Lamb (D)	16,634	55.5
	L. L. Lewis (R)	12,716	42.5
4	Sydney P. Epes (D)	12,894‡	54.4
	Robert T. Thorp (R)	10,273	43.4
5	Claude A. Swanson (D)	14,333	51.0
	John R. Brown (R)	13,782	49.0
6	Peter J. Otey (D)	17,187	57.0
	Duval Radford (SM D)	11,682	38.7
7	James Hay (D)	17,447	55.8
	Robert J. Walker (R)	13,250	42.4
8	John F. Rixey (D)	17,030	56.1
	Patrick H. McCauli (R)	13,114	43.2
9	James Alexander Walker (R)	20,024	52.7
	Samuel Walker Williams (D)	17,944	47.3
10	Jacob Yost (R)	16,095	49.8
	Henry D. Flood (D)	16,047	49.6

WASHINGTON

AL	James Hamilton Lewis (PP)	51,554✓	
	William C. Jones (PP)	51,158✓	
	W. H. Doolittle (R)	38,196	
	S. C. Hyde (R)	37,939	
	C. A. Salyer (P)	1,011	
	Martin Olsen (P)	887	
	C. E. Mix (N)	154	

WEST VIRGINIA

1	Blackburn B. Dovener (R)	25,232	53.5
	W. W. Arnett (D)	21,687	46.0
2	Alston G. Dayton (R)	25,500	52.3
	William G. Brown (D)	23,249	47.7
3	Charles P. Dorr (R)	29,277	52.9
	E. W. Wilson (D)	26,029	47.1
4	Warren Miller (R)	24,942	51.2
	Walter Pendleton (D)	23,774	48.8

WISCONSIN

1	Henry Allen Cooper (R)	28,235	64.1
	Jeremiah L. Mahoney (D)	14,723	33.4
2	Edward Sauerherring (R)	24,011	56.5
	William H. Rogers (D)	17,480	41.1
3	Joseph W. Babcock (R)	26,691	63.8
	Alfred J. Davis (D)	15,168	36.2
4	Theobald Otjen (R)	25,896	54.2
	Robert Schilling (D)	21,429	44.9
5	Samuel S. Barney (R)	26,613	61.0
	George W. Winans (D)	16,492	37.8
6	James H. Davidson (R)	26,649	57.7
	William F. Gruenewald (D)	18,944	41.0
7	Michael Griffin (R)	24,073	65.8
	Caleb M. Hilliard (D)	11,718	32.0
8	Edward S. Minor (R)	26,471	60.3
	George W. Cate (D)	16,845	38.4
9	Alexander Stewart (R)	30,438	63.2
	William W. O'Keefe (D)	17,705	36.8
10	John J. Jenkins (R)	28,149	65.5
	Frederick H. Remington (D)	14,823	34.5

WYOMING

AL	John E. Osborne (D)	10,310	49.1
	F. W. Mondell (R)	10,044	47.9

1897 House Elections

ILLINOIS

Special Election

Candidates	Votes	%
6 Henry Sherman Boutell (R)	10,211	51.4
Vincent H. Perkins (D)	9,349	47.0

MAINE

Special Election

3 E. C. Burleigh (R)	9,699	73.9
Frederick W. Plaisted (D)	3,128	23.8

MASSACHUSETTS

Special Election

Candidates	Votes	%
1 George P. Lawrence (R)	11,889	58.6
Roger P. Donoghue (D)	7,573	37.3

MISSOURI

Special Election

1 James T. Lloyd (D)	18,809	56.9
Clark (R)	13,158	39.8

NEW YORK

Special Election

Candidates	Votes	%
3 Edmund H. Driggs (D)	16,753	47.6
William A. Prendergast (R)	14,557	41.4
Horatio C. King (ND)	3,390	9.6

PENNSYLVANIA

Special Election

25 Joseph B. Showalter (R)	12,221	66.2
Salem Heilman (D)	6,222	33.7

1898 House Elections

ALABAMA

	Candidates	Votes	%
1	George W. Taylor (D)	5,886	84.7
	Johnson (COLOR R)	1,061	15.3
2	Jesse Stallings (D)	9,145	83.3
	Simmons (R)	1,620	14.8
3	Henry Clayton (D)	8,287	96.6
4	Gaston A. Robbins (D)	6,915‡	54.9
	William F. Aldrich (R)	5,685	45.1
5	Willis Brewer (D)	8,842	77.8
	Smith (R)	2,504	22.0
6	John H. Bankhead (D)	7,009	69.8
	Daniel N. Cooper (R)	2,942	29.3
7	John L. Burnett (D)	6,949	44.4
	Oliver Day Street (R)	5,032	32.2
	Lathrop (R)	3,592	23.0
8	Joseph Wheeler (D)	6,368	99.9
9	Oscar W. Underwood (D)	7,155	83.0
	McEniry (R)	1,051	12.2

ARKANSAS

1	Philip D. McCulloch (D)	4,103	99.3
2	John S. Little (D)	3,615	99.8
3	Thomas C. McRae (D)	4,066	100.0
4	William T. Terry (D)	3,665	99.0
5	Hugh A. Dinsmore (D)	6,633	71.0
	J. T. Hopper (R)	2,706	29.0
6	Stephen Brundidge Jr. (D)	2,732	99.9

CALIFORNIA

1	John A. Barham (R)	19,598	51.8
	Emmet Seawell (D & POP)	18,244	48.2
2	Marion De Vries (D & POP)	25,196	55.2
	Frank D. Ryan (R)	20,400	44. 7
3	Victor H. Metcalf (R)	20,592	57.3
	John Aubrey Jones (D & POP)	14,051	39.1
4	Julius Kahn (R)	13,695	50.0
	James H. Barry (D & POP)	12,084	44.1
5	Eugene F. Loud (R)	20,254	51.8
	William Craig (D & POP)	17,352	44.3
6	Russell J. Waters (R)	24,050	52.6
	Charles A. Barlow (D & POP)	20,499	44.9
7	James C. Needham (R)	20,793	50.1
	Curtis H. Castle (D & POP)	20,680	49.8

COLORADO

1	John F. Shafroth (FUS)	43,111	67.6
	Charles Hartsell (R)	18,580	29.1
2	John C. Bell (FUS)	52,372	64.9
	B. Clark Wheeler (R)	27,583	34.2

CONNECTICUT

1	E. Stevens Henry (R)	18,818	55.5
	Vance (D)	13,520	39.9
2	Nehemiah D. Sperry (R)	27,004	51.9
	Webb (D)	23,556	45.2
3	Charles A. Russell (R)	12,218	58.1
	Thayer (D)	8,507	40.4
4	Ebenezer J. Hill (R)	23,707	56.1
	Lyman (D)	17,754	42.0

DELAWARE

AL	John H. Hoffecker (R)	17,566	53.1
	L. Irving Handy (D)	15,053	45.5

FLORIDA

1	Stephen M. Sparkman (D)	13,506	84.1
	E. R. Gunby (R)	2,543	15.8
2	Robert W. Davis (D)	12,150	71.8
	H. L. Anderson (R)	4,773	28.2

GEORGIA

	Candidates	Votes	%
1	Rufus E. Lester (D)	5,344	86.0
	John E. Myrick (R)	873	14.0
2	James M. Griggs (D)	8,298	80.0
	J. H. Smith (R)	2,071	20.0
3	Elijah B. Lewis (D)	3,539	96.2
4	William C. Adamson (D)	3,218	99.1
5	Leonidas F. Livingston (D)	3,027	97.6
6	Charles L. Bartlett (D)	3,008	99.9
7	John W. Maddox (D)	5,296	80.7
	A. B. Austin (POP)	1,252	19.1
8	William M. Howard (D)	4,379	83.5
	John A. Neese (POP)	861	16.4
9	Farish C. Tate (D)	9,277	72.3
	J. P. Brooke (POP)	3,557	27.7
10	William H. Fleming (D)	2,290	97.6
11	William G. Brantley (D)	9,256	69.2
	J. M. Wilkinson (R)	4,112	30.8

IDAHO

AL	Edgar Wilson (SIL-R-D)	17,694	45.3
	Weldon B. Heyburn (R)	13,056	33.4
	James Gunn (PP)	7,428	19.0

ILLINOIS

1	James R. Mann (R)	37,506	63.2
	Rollin B. Organ (D)	20,424	34.4
2	William Lorimer (R)	27,151	52.1
	C. Porter Johnson (D)	23,354	44.8
3	George P. Foster (D)	18,463	53.3
	Hugh R. Belknap (R)	15,659	45.2
4	Thomas Cusack (D)	18,876	52.6
	Daniel W. Mills (R)	16,656	46.4
5	Edward T. Noonan (D)	19,186	53.3
	George E. White (R)	16,018	44.5
6	Henry Sherman Boutell (R)	18,283	50.7
	Emil Hoechster (D)	17,167	47.6
7	George Edmund Foss (R)	30,903	60.8
	Frank O. Rogers (D)	18,572	36.5
8	Albert J. Hopkins (R)	19,592	68.2
	John W. Leonard (D)	8,000	27.8
9	Robert R. Hitt (R)	22,165	64.9
	William H. Wagner (D)	11,020	32.3
10	George W. Prince (R)	24,469	66.1
	Francis E. Andrews (D)	12,042	32.5
11	Walter Reeves (R)	20,060	53.5
	Maurice T. Moloney (D)	16,564	44.1
12	Joseph G. Cannon (R)	21,484	59.1
	John M. Thompson (D)	14,178	39.0
13	Vespasian Warner (R)	20,635	56.6
	Jerome G. Quisenbery (D)	14,977	41.1
14	Joseph V. Graff (R)	21,417	51.6
	Charles N. Barnes (D)	19,431	46.8
15	Benjamin F. Marsh (R)	21,143	49.1
	Joseph A. Roy (D)	20,901	48.6
16	William Elza Williams (D)	21,682	54.6
	James H. Danskin (R)	17,021	42.9
17	Ben F. Caldwell (D)	23,293	51.9
	Isaac R. Mills (R)	21,053	46.9
18	Thomas M. Jett (D)	18,829	49.5
	Benjamin F. Johnston (R)	18,109	47.6
19	Joseph B. Crowley (D)	21,520	50.5
	William W. Jacobs (R)	20,006	47.0
20	James R. Williams (D)	18,321	51.5
	Theodore G. Risley (R)	16,307	45.9
21	William A. Rodenberg (R)	20,461	49.1
	Frederick J. Kern (D)	19,956	47.9
22	George W. Smith (R)	17,200	54.5
	A. B. Garrett (D)	14,131	44.8

INDIANA

	Candidates	Votes	%
1	James A. Hemenway (R)	20,383	50.7
	Thomas Duncan (D)	19,337	48.1
2	Robert W. Miers (D)	20,245	50.3
	William R. Gardiner (R)	18,656	46.4
3	William T. Zenor (D)	21,111	55.2
	Isaac F. Whiteside (R)	16,791	43.9
4	Francis M. Griffith (D)	21,751	52.2
	Charles W. Lee (R)	19,733	47.3
5	George W. Faris (R)	22,557	49.4
	Samuel R. Hamill (D)	22,305	48.8
6	James E. Watson (R)	21,048	52.6
	Charles A. Robinson (D)	18,844	47.1
7	Jesse Overstreet (R)	25,868	51.8
	Leon O. Bailey (D)	23,269	46.6
8	George W. Cromer (R)	25,388	50.1
	Orlando J. Lotz (R)	24,021	47.4
9	Charles B. Landis (R)	22,447	50.2
	Joseph B. Cheadle (D)	21,357	47.7
10	Edgar D. Crumpacker (R)	24,656	55.0
	John Ross (D)	20,206	45.0
11	George W. Steele (R)	24,367	52.7
	George W. Michael (D)	20,281	43.9
12	James M. Robinson (D)	19,484	51.3
	Christian B. Stevens (R)	18,044	47.5
13	Abraham L. Brick (R)	23,368	51.4
	Medary M. Hathaway (D)	20,886	46.0

IOWA

1	Thomas Hedge (R)	17,817	54.3
	D. J. O'Connell (D)	14,568	44.4
2	Joseph P. Lane (R)	18,790	50.6
	John J. Ney (D)	17,508	47.1
3	David B. Henderson (R)	22,512	59.1
	John H. Howell (D)	15,493	40.7
4	Gilbert N. Haugen (R)	21,468	59.8
	T. T. Blaise (D)	13,849	38.6
5	Robert G. Cousins (R)	21,335	55.9
	L. J. Rowell (D)	15,970	41.9
6	John F. Lacey (R)	19,738	50.9
	James B. Weaver (D)	18,267	47.1
7	John A. T. Hull (R)	19,913	59.3
	Charles O. Holly (D)	12,261	36.5
8	William P. Hepburn (R)	22,327	53.1
	George L. Finn (D)	18,503	44.0
9	Smith McPherson (R)	21,976	54.8
	J. A. Lyons (D)	17,484	43.6
10	Jonathan P. Dolliver (R)	25,180	57.6
	Edwin Anderson (D)	17,777	40.7
11	Lot Thomas (R)	22,400	56.6
	Arthur S. Garretson (D)	16,117	40.7

KANSAS

1	Charles Curtis (R)	23,899	59.6
	W. W. Price (D-PP)	16,187	40.4
2	Justin D. Bowersock (R)	21,029	52.5
	M. S. Peters (D-PP)	19,024	47.5
3	Edwin R. Ridgely (D-PP)	21,739	51.4
	S. S. Kirkpatrick (R)	20,589	48.6
4	James M. Miller (R)	20,312	53.9
	Henderson S. Martin (D-PP)	17,410	46.2
5	William A. Calderhead (R)	18,991	53.5
	W. D. Vincent (D-PP)	16,508	46.5
6	William A. Reeder (R)	16,833	49.7
	N. B. McCormick (PP)	14,732	43.5
	William G. Hoffer (D)	2,334	6.9
7	Chester I. Long (R)	26,622	51.7
	Jerry Simpson (D-PP)	24,834	48.3
AL	Willis J. Bailey (R)	147,691	52.5
	J. D. Botkin (D-PP)	130,801	46.5

KENTUCKY

	Candidates	Votes	%
1	Charles K. Wheeler (D)	10,580	67.7
	G. W. Reeves (R)	5,036	32.2
2	Henry D. Allen (D)	8,939	57.3
	W. T. Fowler (R)	4,463	28.6
	G. W. Jolly (I)	1,641	10.5
3	John S. Rhea (D)	14,771	54.9
	M. P. Creel (R)	11,748	43.7
4	David H. Smith (D)	16,696	55.3
	Charles Biford (R)	12,826	42.5
5	Oscar Turner (D)	14,770	49.6
	Walter Evans (R)	14,202	47.7
6	Albert S. Berry (D)	13,130	59.4
	W. M. Donson (R)	8,962	40.6
7	Evan E. Settle (D)	12,904	67.7
	T. J. Hardin (R)	6,168	32.3
8	George G. Gilbert (D)	13,047	50.8
	G. M. Davson (R)	12,206	47.5
9	Samuel J. Pugh (R)	✓	
	Mordecai Williams (D)		
10	Thomas Y. Fitzpatrick (D)	13,456	54.1
	W. J. Seitz (R)	11,402	45.9
11	Vincent Boreing (R)	15,706	51.5
	J. D. White (IR)	11,324	37.2
	H. H. Tye (D)	3,319	10.9

LOUISIANA

		Votes	%
1	Adolph Meyer (D)	5,422	85.8
	C. W. Keeting (R)	896	14.2
2	Robert C. Davey (D)	6,802	86.6
	Frank N. Wicker (R)	1,054	13.4
3	Robert F. Broussard (D)	4,928	84.9
	Charles Fontelleu (R)	874	15.1
4	Phanor Breazeale (D)	4,524	75.3
	Hardy L. Brian (POP)	1,476	24.6
5	Samuel T. Baird (D)	3,558	74.0
	J. G. Taliaferro (R)	1,096	22.8
6	Samuel M. Robertson (D)	2,494	99.6

MAINE

		Votes	%
1	Thomas B. Reed (R)	14,598	59.8
	L. F. McKinney (D)	9,072	37.2
2	Nelson Dingley Jr. (R)	15,149*	63.7
	John Scott (D)	8,126	34.2
3	Edwin C. Burleigh (R)	12,854	64.3
	F. W. Plaisted (D)	6,634	33.2
4	Charles A. Boutelle (R)	12,380	66.5
	A. J. Chase (D)	5,534	29.7

Special Election

		Votes	%
1	Amos L. Allen (R)	12,337	61.6
	L. F. McKinney (D)	7,705	38.4

MARYLAND

		Votes	%
1	John W. Smith (D)	16,748	47.9
	W. F. Jackson (R)	15,823	45.3
	J. Swann (P)	1,823	5.2
2	William B. Baker (R)	20,806	48.4
	Richard Tippett (D)	20,436	47.5
3	Frank C. Wachter (R)	17,508	49.1
	J. Schwatka (D)	17,386	48.8
4	James W. Denny (D)	17,260	48.8
	William McIntire (R)	16,664	47.1
5	Sydney E. Mudd (R)	17,248	52.1
	J. S. Cummings (D)	14,672	44.3
6	George Alexander Pearre (R)	18,878	54.8
	T. A. Poffenberger (D)	14,372	41.8

MASSACHUSETTS

		Votes	%
1	George P. Lawrence (R)	14,315	58.0
	Charles P. Davis (D)	8,760	35.5
	Edward A. Buckland (SOC LAB)	1,602	6.5
2	Frederick H. Gillett (R)	13,327	60.3
	Robert E. Bisbee (D)	8,054	36.5

	Candidates	Votes	%
3	John R. Thayer (D)	11,167	50.4
	Joseph H. Walker (R)	11,008	49.6
4	George W. Weymouth (R)	14,411	62.9
	I. Porter Morse (D)	8,485	37.1
5	William S. Knox (R)	14,737	51.8
	Joseph J. Flynn (D)	13,716	48.2
6	William H. Moody (R)	13,494	64.5
	E. Moody Boynton (D)	6,035	28.9
	Albert L. Gillen (D SOCIAL)	1,390	6.6
7	Ernest W. Roberts (R)	16,559	55.8
	Walter L. Ramsdell (D)	12,338	41.6
8	Samuel W. McCall (R)	14,935	69.9
	George A. Perkins (D)	5,846	27.4
9	John F. Fitzgerald (D)	10,303	48.7
	Franz H. Krebs (R)	5,450	25.8
	James A. Gallvan (DI)	5,000	23.6
10	Henry F. Naphen (D)	17,149	55.2
	Samuel J. Barrows (R)	13,909	44.8
11	Charles F. Sprague (R)	17,001	61.3
	William H. Baker (D)	10,709	38.6
12	William C. Lovering (R)	13,653	65.9
	Philip E. Brady (D)	6,210	30.0
13	William S. Greene (R)	13,463	68.6
	Charles T. Luce (D)	4,868	24.8
	Thomas Stevenson (SOC LAB)	1,287	6.6

MICHIGAN

		Votes	%
1	John B. Corliss (R)	16,659	51.2
	James H. Pound (DPUS)	15,401	47.3
2	Henry C. Smith (R)	21,912	51.2
	Orrin R. Pierce (DPUS)	19,999	46.7
3	Washington Gardner (R)	21,182	51.6
	Albert M. Todd (DPUS)	19,864	48.4
4	Edward L. Hamilton (R)	21,740	54.8
	Roman I. Jarvis (DPUS)	17,146	43.2
5	William Alden Smith (R)	22,021	56.8
	George R. Perry (DPUS)	16,064	41.4
6	Samuel W. Smith (R)	22,981	55.8
	Charles Fishbeck (DPUS)	17,171	41.7
7	Edgar Weeks (R)	18,623	58.6
	Fred E. Burton (DPUS)	12,888	40.5
8	Joseph W. Fordney (R)	16,798	52.7
	Ferdinand Brucker (DPUS)	15,089	47.3
9	Roswell P. Bishop (R)	15,687	61.3
	Chauncey J. Chaddock (DPUS)	9,291	36.3
10	Rousseau O. Crump (R)	16,482	55.3
	Robert J. Kelly (DPUS)	13,230	44.4
11	William S. Mesick (R)	18,545	59.9
	Alva W. Nichols (DPUS)	11,799	38.1
12	Carlos D. Shelden (R)	19,895	66.9
	Solomon S. Curry (DPUS)	8,921	30.0

MINNESOTA

		Votes	%
1	James A. Tawney (R)	18,939	59.3
	White (PP & D)	11,931	37.3
2	James T. McCleary (R)	21,296	57.0
	Evans (PP & D)	14,784	39.6
3	Joel P. Heatwole (R)	19,271	56.9
	Hinds (D)	13,183	38.9
4	Frederick C. Stevens (R)	15,952	54.1
	Willis (D)	11,602	39.3
5	Loren Fletcher (R)	18,736	55.4
	Caton (PP & D)	2,896	38.1
6	R. Page W. Morris (R)	22,194	50.1
	Towne (PP & D)	21,731	49.0
7	Frank M. Eddy (R)	20,409	52.6
	Ringdal (PP & D)	16,715	43.1

MISSISSIPPI

		Votes	%
1	John M. Allen (D)	2,469	100.0
2	Thomas Spight (D)	2,949	92.9
	C. M. Haynie (POP)	167	5.3
3	Thomas C. Catchings (D)	2,068	85.1
	C. T. Jones (COLOR R)	363	14.9
4	Andrew F. Fox (D)	3,431	77.1
	Raleigh Brewer (POP)	1,020	22.9

	Candidates	Votes	%
5	John Sharp Williams (D)	4,941	97.0
6	Frank A. McLain (D)	3,276	53.7
	M. M. Evans (ID)	1,390	22.8
	N. C. Hathorn (POP)	998	16.4
	H. C. Turley (R)	427	7.0
7	Patrick Henry (D)	3,278	91.0

Special Election

		Votes	%
2	Thomas Spight (D)	2,722	46.6
	Z. M. Stephens	2,461	42.2
	L. L. Pearson	653	11.2

MISSOURI

		Votes	%
1	James T. Lloyd (D)	20,068	55.3
	Seaber (R)	15,460	42.6
2	William W. Rucker (D)	20,768	56.3
	Irwin (R)	15,627	42.4
3	John Dougherty (D)	19,560	53.1
	Goodrich (R)	16,440	44.6
4	Charles F. Cochran (D)	18,294	52.9
	Brewster (R)	16,261	47.1
5	William S. Cowherd (D)	20,487	53.6
	Welborn (R)	17,144	44.8
6	David A. De Armond (D)	16,645	52.0
	Jurden (R)	13,595	42.4
7	James Cooney (D)	22,586	55.2
	Robertson (R)	17,642	43.1
8	Richard P. Bland (D)	21,674	53.1
	Vosholl (R)	18,831	46.2
9	James Beauchamp Clark (D)	17,463	54.4
	Shackelford (R)	14,449	45.0
10	Richard Bartholdt (R)	19,850	59.3
	Gill (D)	13,254	39.6
11	Charles F. Joy (R)	21,315	52.3
	Noonan (D)	18,657	45.7
12	Charles E. Pearce (R)	15,300	52.6
	Kern (D)	12,989	44.7
13	Edward Robb (D)	20,601	52.0
	Reppy (R)	18,314	46.2
14	Willard D. Vandiver (D)	21,771	51.3
	Miley (R)	18,650	43.9
15	Maecenas E. Benton (D)	20,202	54.3
	Williams (R)	16,918	45.5

MONTANA

		Votes	%
AL	Albert J. Campbell (D)	23,351	46.9
	Thomas C. Marshall (R)	14,829	29.8
	Thomas S. Hogan (PP&SIL R)	11,607	23.3

NEBRASKA

		Votes	%
1	Elmer J. Burkett (R)	16,960	53.9
	James Manahan (D & POP)	14,466	46.0
2	David H. Mercer (R)	11,951	52.0
	G. M. Hitchcock (D & POP)	11,023	48.0
3	John S. Robinson (D & POP)	18,722	51.9
	W. F. Norris (R)	17,333	48.1
4	William L. Stark (D & POP)	18,904	50.7
	E. H. Hinshaw (R)	18,377	49.3
5	Roderick D. Sutherland (D & POP)	16,354	51.4
	C. E. Adams (R)	15,487	48.6
6	William L. Greene (D & POP)	15,415	53.5
	Norris Brown (R)	13,401	46.5

NEVADA

		Votes	%
AL	Francis G. Newlands (D SIL)	5,766	65.0
	Thomas Wren (PP)	3,111	35.1

NEW HAMPSHIRE

		Votes	%
1	Cyrus A. Sulloway (R)	21,373	52.2
	Edgar J. Knowlton (D)	18,518	45.2
2	Frank G. Clarke (R)	22,395	55.5
	Warren F. Daniell (D)	17,266	42.8

NEW JERSEY

	Candidates	Votes	%
1	Henry C. Loudenslager (R)	23,864	54.3
	Samuel Iredell (D)	18,102	41.2
2	John J. Gardner (R)	24,035	56.1
	John F. Hall (D)	17,367	40.5
3	Benjamin F. Howell (R)	19,412	49.8
	Patrick Convery (D)	18,683	48.0
4	Joshua S. Salmon (D)	17,866	51.5
	John I. Blair Reilly (R)	15,207	43.8
5	James F. Stewart (R)	18,367	50.6
	Francis J. Marley (D)	16,342	45.0
6	Richard Wayne Parker (R)	23,843	52.5
	Henry G. Atwater (D)	20,150	44.4
7	William D. Daly (D)	30,270	57.8
	Zebina K. Pangborn (R)	20,162	38.5
8	Charles N. Fowler (R)	20,230	54.1
	Edward H. Snyder (D)	15,878	42.4

NEW YORK

	Candidates	Votes	%
1	Townsend Scudder (D)	22,893	49.8
	Joseph M. Belford (R)	22,483	48.9
2	John J. Fitzgerald (D)	18,431	55.6
	Denis M. Hurley (R)	14,323	43.2
3	Edmund H. Driggs (D)	20,995	50.7
	William A. Prendergast (R)	19,872	48.0
4	Bertram T. Clayton (D)	24,581	52.8
	Israel T. Fischer (R)	20,893	44.9
5	Frank E. Wilson (D)	19,579	51.4
	Charles E. Bennett (R)	16,669	43.8
6	Mitchell May (D)	16,215	55.4
	Henry C. Fischer (R)	11,899	40.6
7	Nicholas Muller (D)	14,122	66.5
	Charles Wilmot Townsend (R)	6,639	31.3
8	Daniel J. Riordan (D)	10,716	58.6
	John Murray Mitchell (R)	7,347	40.2
9	Thomas J. Bradley (D)	11,694	56.8
	John Stiebling (R)	6,447	31.3
	Lucien Sanial (SOC LAB)	2,396	11.7
10	Amos J. Cummings (D)	18,859	62.8
	Elijah M. Fisher (R)	10,620	35.4
11	William Sulzer (D)	14,364	62.8
	William Volkel (R)	6,178	27.0
	Howard Balkam (SOC LAB)	2,310	10.1
12	George B. McClellan (D)	15,108	64.5
	Howard Conkling (R)	7,710	32.9
13	Jefferson M. Levy (D)	17,985	59.8
	James W. Perry (R)	11,393	37.9
14	William Astor Chanler (D)	31,604	54.3
	Lemuel E. Quigg (R)	25,209	43.3
15	Jacob Ruppert Jr. (D)	31,292	57.8
	Philip B. Low (R)	20,848	38.5
16	John Q. Underhill (D)	32,578	54.6
	James Irving Burns (R)	26,130	43.8
17	Arthur S. Tompkins (R)	19,195	54.2
	Samuel D. Roberson (D)	15,564	43.9
18	John H. Ketcham (R)	23,276	55.1
	Thomas E. Benedict (D)	18,348	43.4
19	Aaron V. S. Cochrane (R)	19,593	49.1
	John Henry Livingston (D)	19,565	49.1
20	Martin H. Glynn (D)	20,026	50.1
	George N. Southwick (R)	19,475	48.7
21	John K. Stewart (R)	25,561	50.9
	Stephen L. Mayham (D)	23,347	46.5
22	Lucius N. Littauer (R)	27,083	61.3
	Dennis B. Lucy (D)	15,448	35.0
23	Louis W. Emerson (R)	25,662	96.3
24	Charles A. Chickering (R)	23,991	58.9
	Eber T. Strickland (D)	15,724	38.6
25	James S. Sherman (R)	22,368	52.8
	Walter Ballou (D)	19,160	45.2
26	George W. Ray (R)	30,007	58.6
	Edward E. Pease (D)	19,199	37.5
27	Michael E. Driscoll (R)	26,025	56.5
	George H. Gilbert (D)	14,207	30.9
	Thomas Crimmins	2,434	5.3
	John McCarthy	2,433	5.3
28	Sereno E. Payne (R)	29,536	59.4
	John H. Young (D)	18,831	37.9
29	Charles W. Gillet (R)	22,348	52.7
	Albert L. Childs (D)	18,311	43.2
30	James W. Wadsworth (R)	25,799	55.8
	James T. Gordon (D)	18,911	40.9
31	James M. E. O'Grady (R)	20,717	51.8
	John R. Fanning (D)	17,227	43.1
32	William H. Ryan (D)	15,546	49.5
	Rowland B. Mahany (R)	14,858	47.4
33	De Alva S. Alexander (R)	22,924	55.8
	Harvey W. Richardson (D)	17,233	41.9
34	Warren B. Hooker (R)	25,856*	62.8
	William J. Sanbury (D)	13,666	33.2

NORTH CAROLINA

	Candidates	Votes	%
1	John H. Small (D)	19,732	51.8
	Harry Skinner (POP & R)	18,263	47.9
2	George H. White (R)	17,560	49.5
	William E. Fountain (D)	14,947	42.1
	James B. Lloyd (POP)	2,447	6.9
3	Charles R. Thomas (D)	16,008	50.3
	John E. Fowler (POP & R)	15,819	49.7
4	John M. Atwater (POP & D)	19,416	51.1
	Joseph J. Jenkins (POP & R)	18,577	48.9
5	William W. Kitchin (D)	20,869	52.9
	Spencer B. Adams (POP & R)	18,607	47.1
6	John D. Bellamy (D)	23,213	57.2
	Oliver H. Dockery (POP & R)	17,359	42.8
7	Theodore F. Kluttz (D)	20,733	58.5
	Morrison H. Caldwell (POP)	14,651	41.3
8	Romulus Z. Linney (POP & R)	17,414	51.7
	Edward F. Lovell (D)	16,137	47.9
9	William T. Crawford (D)	19,606‡	50.2
	Richmond Pearson (POP)	19,368	49.6

NORTH DAKOTA

	Candidates	Votes	%
AL	Burleigh F. Spalding (R)	27,776	60.9
	Creel (FUS)	17,844	39.1

OHIO

	Candidates	Votes	%
1	William B. Shattuc (R)	20,132	58.5
	John F. Follett (D)	13,980	40.6
2	Jacob H. Bromwell (R)	22,506	58.0
	Charles L. Swain (D)	15,998	41.3
3	John L. Brenner (D)	21,449	50.1
	William J. White (R)	21,327	49.9
4	Robert B. Gordon (D)	18,020	57.7
	Philip Sheets (R)	12,276	39.3
5	David Meekison (D)	19,264	54.1
	Alfred N. Wilcox (R)	15,612	43.9
6	Seth W. Brown (R)	19,896	54.0
	Lewis H. Whiteman (D)	16,206	44.0
7	Walter L. Weaver (R)	17,565	49.5
	John L. Zimmerman (D)	17,159	48.4
8	Archibald Lybrand (R)	21,560	51.6
	Harvey Walter Doty (D)	19,156	45.8
9	James H. Southard (R)	21,913	54.8
	Samuel E. Niece (D)	18,081	45.2
10	Stephen Morgan (R)	19,297	58.4
	Alva Crabtree (D)	13,769	41.6
11	Charles H. Grosvenor (R)	19,806	54.6
	Charles E. Peoples (D)	16,434	45.3
12	John J. Lentz (D)	21,232	50.2
	Edward N. Huggins (R)	20,530	48.6
13	James A. Norton (D)	21,410	54.1
	Henry L. Wenner (R)	17,606	44.5
14	Winfield Kerr (R)	22,464	54.0
	Thomas A. Gruber (D)	19,134	46.0
15	Henry Clay Van Voorhis (R)	19,404	54.0
	Henry R. Stanbery (D)	16,509	46.0
16	Lorenzo Danford (R)	16,263	54.9
	Elliott D. Moore (D)	13,377	45.1
17	John A. McDowell (D)	19,989	55.5
	George E. Broome (R)	16,016	44.5
18	Robert W. Tayler (R)	22,635	51.8
	Charles C. Weybrecht (D)	19,575	44.8
19	Charles Dick (R)	23,358	64.9
	Isaac H. Phelps (D)	12,612	35.1
20	Fremont O. Phillips (R)	16,894	56.5
	William J. Hart (D)	11,992	40.1
21	Theodore E. Burton (R)	17,599	59.2
	Lemuel A. Russell (D)	10,823	36.4

Special Election

	Candidates	Votes	%
19	Charles Dick (R)	23,359	65.0
	Unidentified Candidate (D)	12,574	35.0

OREGON

	Candidates	Votes	%
1	Thomas H. Tongue (R)	21,324	49.0
	R. M. Veatch (FUS)	19,287	44.3
2	Malcolm A. Moody (R)	21,291	54.2
	C. M. Donaldson (FUS)	14,634	37.2
	H. E. Courtney (POP)	2,273	5.8

PENNSYLVANIA

	Candidates	Votes	%
1	Henry H. Bingham (R)	25,665	72.1
	Michael Francis Doyle (D)	8,213	23.1
2	Robert Adams Jr. (R)	19,547	83.5
	Herman V. Hetzel (D)	3,850	16.5
3	William McAleer (R, D)	18,321	98.3
4	James Rankin Young (R)	41,627	72.7
	Gideon Sibley (D)	12,250	21.4
	Clinton C. Hancock (P)	3,372	5.9
5	Alfred C. Harmer (R)	39,239	79.8
	Frank D. Wright (D)	9,942	20.2
6	Thomas S. Butler (BC)	15,169	53.7
	John B. Robinson (ROBINSON, HG)	6,537	23.6
	William H. Berry (D, L)	6,514	23.1
7	Irving P. Wanger (R)	21,567	53.1
	Clinton Rorer (D)	17,872	44.0
8	Laird H. Barber (D)	16,400	54.8
	William S. Kirkpatrick (R)	13,516	45.2
9	Daniel Ermentrout (D)	24,137	57.3
	Jeremiah S. Parvin (R)	16,613	39.4
10	Marriott Brosius (R)	17,482	67.9
	A. J. Steinman (D)	7,083	27.5
11	William Connell (R)	11,404	46.1
	M. F. Sando (D)	9,861	39.8
	Freeman Leach (P, HG)	3,164	12.8
12	Stanley W. Davenport (D)	17,220	49.9
	Morgan B. Williams (R)	15,772	45.7
13	James W. Ryan (D)	15,042	54.2
	Charles N. Brumm (R)	12,542	45.2
14	Marlin E. Olmsted (R)	19,352	60.8
	Wilson W. Gray (D)	9,926	31.2
	Lee L. Grumbine (P)	2,564	8.1
15	Charles Frederick Wright (R)	14,541	55.3
	Archibald B. Gammell (D)	9,331	35.5
	Chauncey S. Russell (P)	2,416	9.2
16	Horace B. Packer (R)	15,839	49.4
	Jonathan F. Strieby (D)	12,858	40.1
	Lewis P. Thurston (P)	3,378	10.5
17	Rufus K. Polk (D)	14,792	51.8
	William Hartman Woodin (R)	12,487	43.8
18	Thaddeus M. Mahon (R)	17,722	57.8
	Robert McMeen (D)	12,921	42.2
19	Edward D. Ziegler (D)	20,126	51.4
	Robert J. Lewis (R)	19,016	48.6
20	Joseph E. Thropp (R)	19,358	48.9
	James M. Walters (D)	17,858	45.2
	John J. Irwin (D)	2,091	5.3
21	Summers M. Jack (R)	23,277	55.7
	Jacob R. Spiegel (D)	16,191	38.7
	Thomas J. Baldridge (P)	2,360	5.6
22	John Dalzell (R)	25,693	66.6
	George W. Acklin (D)	11,049	28.6
23	William H. Graham (R)	14,008	68.1
	John H. Stevenson (D)	5,608	27.3
24	Ernest F. Acheson (R)	25,524	54.5
	Mark M. Cochran (D)	21,290	45.5
25	Joseph B. Showalter (R)	18,220	51.3
	M. L. Lockwood (D)	15,271	43.0
	John A. Bailey (P)	2,006	5.7
26	Athelston Gaston (D)	13,516	47.8

Candidates	Votes	%
George H. Higgins (R)	13,482	47.6
27 Joseph C. Sibley (D)	14,138	52.1
Charles W. Stone (R)	11,757	43.3
28 James K. P. Hall (D)	17,550	52.1
William C. Arnold (R)	14,209	42.2
George W. Rheem (P)	1,898	5.6
AL Galusha A. Grow (R)	532,890✓	
Samuel A. Davenport (R)	520,774✓	
Jerry N. Weiler (D, PP)	357,500	
Franklin P. Iams (D)	350,214	
George H. Garber (P)	48,600	
Pennock E. Sharpless (P)	47,543	
John R. Root (SOC LAB)	4,495	
Donald L. Munro (SOC LAB)	4,300	
Dennis E. Johnston (PP)	3,995	
J. Acker Guss (L)	839	
Charles P. Shaw (L)	837	

RHODE ISLAND

Candidates	Votes	%
1 Melville Bull (R)	12,081	60.4
Hogan (D)	6,392	31.9
Theinert (SOC LAB)	1,081	5.4
2 Adin B. Capron (R)	9,095	52.0
Garvin (D)	6,435	36.8
Dana (SOC LAB)	1,473	8.4

SOUTH CAROLINA

Candidates	Votes	%
1 William Elliott (D)	3,030	66.5
G. W. Murray (R)	1,529	33.5
2 W. Jasper Talbert (D)	4,013	97.0
3 Asbury C. Latimer (D)	4,029	92.1
R. R. Tolbert (R)	332	7.6
4 Stanyarne Wilson (D)	4,467	96.4
5 David E. Finley (D)	4,230	100.0
6 James Norton (D)	4,765	96.9
7 J. William Stokes (D)	4,433	89.8
James Weston (R)	505	10.2

SOUTH DAKOTA

Candidates	Votes	%
AL Robert J. Gamble (R)	38,780✓	
Charles H. Burke (R)	36,295✓	
J. E. Kelley (FUS)	32,314	
F. Knowles (FUS)	32,240	
A. Jamieson (P)	882	
M. D. Alexander (P)	849	

TENNESSEE

Candidates	Votes	%
1 Walter P. Brownlow (R)	14,616	55.0
Gouchenaur (D)	11,732	44.1
2 Henry R. Gibson (R)	13,848	66.3
Davis (D)	6,904	33.1
3 John A. Moon (D)	13,347	58.9
Cate (R)	9,209	40.6
4 Charles E. Snodgrass (D)	13,413	62.3
Morgan (R)	8,122	37.7
5 James D. Richardson (D)	11,087	69.8
Elliott (R)	4,800	30.2
6 John W. Gaines (D)	11,539	78.8
Napier (R)	2,088	14.3
Gill (P)	1,021	7.0
7 Nicholas N. Cox (D)	9,590	70.3
Cunningham (R)	4,055	29.7

Candidates	Votes	%
8 Thetus W. Sims (D)	10,747	60.3
Hinkle (R)	6,549	36.8
9 Rice A. Pierce (D)	9,860	76.8
Reville (R)	2,728	21.3
10 Edward W. Carmack (D)	8,419	81.8
Vernon (R)	1,873	18.2

TEXAS

Candidates	Votes	%
1 Thomas H. Ball (D)	18,544	67.2
O. A. Blackwell (R)	5,276	19.1
Joe Eagle (POP)	3,764	13.6
2 Samuel B. Cooper (D)	22,086	68.9
T. J. Russell (POP)	7,853	24.5
J. A. McAyeal (R)	2,021	6.3
3 Reese C. De Graffenreid (D)	17,996	66.3
H. D. Wood (POP)	9,169	33.8
4 John L. Sheppard (D)	18,190	63.6
J. L. Whittle (POP)	10,409	36.4
5 Joseph W. Bailey (D)	16,978	74.1
W. S. Holt (POP)	4,345	19.0
A. W. Acheson (R)	1,487	6.5
6 Robert E. Burke (D)	25,116	65.8
T. B. Goren (POP)	9,677	25.4
A. J. Houston (R)	3,375	8.8
7 Robert L. Henry (D)	22,203	68.7
A. W. Cunningham (POP)	7,927	24.5
Russell Kingsbury (R)	2,197	6.8
8 Samuel W. T. Lanham (D)	18,580	58.1
W. J. Shands (POP)	11,138	34.9
Arthur Springer (R)	2,239	7.0
9 Albert S. Burleson (D)	20,378	61.7
G. W. Jones (POP)	12,628	38.3
10 Robert B. Hawley (R)	17,759	48.0
W. S. Robson (D)	16,462	44.5
J. W. Baird (POP)	2,604	7.0
11 Rudolph Kleberg (D)	18,319	55.5
B. L. Crouch (R)	14,687	44.5
12 James L. Slayden (D)	16,363	56.1
G. H. Nooran (R)	10,472	35.9
A. B. Surber	2,114	7.3
13 John H. Stephens (D)	25,000	73.5
J. J. Eager (POP)	8,995	26.5

UTAH

Candidates	Votes	%
AL Brigham H. Roberts (D)	35,646*	54.6
Eldridge (R)	29,603	45.4

VERMONT

Candidates	Votes	%
1 H. Henry Powers (R)	20,350	71.7
Herbert F. Brigham (D)	8,026	28.3
2 William W. Grout (R)	17,728	74.6
C. A. G. Jackson (D)	5,967	25.1

VIRGINIA

Candidates	Votes	%
1 William A. Jones (D)	8,934	66.5
Joseph A. Bristow (R)	4,270	31.8
2 William A. Young (D)	12,183‡	55.8
Richard A. Wise (R)	6,204	28.4
William S. Holland (IR)	3,445	15.8
3 John Lamb (D)	7,058	69.1
Otis H. Russell (R)	1,914	18.8
Benjamin B. Weisiger (R)	1,138	11.1

Candidates	Votes	%
4 Sydney P. Epes (D)	8,633	57.5
R. T. Thorp (R)	5,889	39.2
5 Claude A. Swanson (D)	13,459	57.0
E. Parr (R)	9,858	41.8
6 Peter J. Otey (D)	10,759	66.9
Daniel Butler (R)	2,535	15.8
Charles A. Heermans (R)	2,310	14.4
7 James Hay (D)	9,841	77.1
D. C. O'Flaherty (D SIL)	2,931	23.0
8 John F. Rixey (D)	6,469	88.6
Edward Hughes (I)	616	8.4
9 William F. Rhea (D)	17,344	51.0
James A. Walker (R)	16,595	48.8
10 Julian M. Quarles (D)	10,784	56.1
Robert T. Hubard (R)	8,377	43.6

WASHINGTON

Candidates	Votes	%
AL Wesley L. Jones (R)	39,809✓	
Francis W. Cushman (R)	38,983✓	
James Hamilton Lewis (PP)	36,385	
William C. Jones (PP)	32,903	
A. C. Dickenson (P)	1,169	
C. L. Haggard (P)	1,037	
M. A. Hamilton (SOC LAB)	929	
Walter Walker (SOC LAB)	897	

WEST VIRGINIA

Candidates	Votes	%
1 Blackburn B. Dovener (R)	20,891	51.9
J. V. Blair (D)	19,031	47.3
2 Alston G. Dayton (R)	23,364	50.3
John T. McGraw (D)	22,720	49.0
3 David Johnston (D)	22,802	50.6
William S. Edwards (R)	22,037	48.9
4 Romeo H. Freer (R)	21,727	50.8
George I. Neal (D)	20,896	48.8

WISCONSIN

Candidates	Votes	%
1 Henry Allen Cooper (R)	19,887	61.5
Clinton Babbitt (D)	11,447	35.4
2 Herman B. Dahle (R)	16,892	50.4
James E. Jones (D)	15,768	47.0
3 Joseph W. Babcock (R)	19,195	59.5
Thomas L. Cleary (D)	12,037	37.3
4 Theobald Otjen (R)	15,903	47.3
Joseph G. Donnelly (D)	14,022	41.7
Robert Schilling (PP)	2,227	6.6
5 Samuel S. Barney (R)	17,056	51.8
Charles E. Armin (D)	13,233	40.2
6 James H. Davidson (R)	20,107	53.6
Frank C. Stewart (D)	1,680	44.5
7 John J. Esch (R)	16,136	64.7
John F. Doherty (D)	8,128	32.6
8 Edward S. Minor (R)	16,910	54.2
Philip Sheridan (D)	13,668	43.8
9 Alexander Stewart (R)	20,825	58.1
Wells M. Ruggles (D)	14,373	40.1
10 John J. Jenkins (R)	17,601	63.2
John R. Mathews (D)	8,435	30.3

WYOMING

Candidates	Votes	%
AL Frank W. Mondell (R)	10,762	54.7
Constantine P. Arnold (D)	8,466	43.0

1899 House Elections

MAINE

Special Election

	Candidates	Votes	%
2	Charles E. Littlefield (R)	11,624	81.0
	John Scott (D)	2,736	19.1

NEBRASKA

Special Election

	Candidates	Votes	%
6	William Neville (FUS)	18,759	53.4
	Moses P. Kinkaid (R)	16,399	46.6

OHIO

Special Election

	Candidates	Votes	%
16	Joseph J. Gill (R)	19,368	55.5
	Lavosier Spence (D)	15,302	43.8

MISSOURI

Special Election

		Votes	%
8	Dorsey W. Shackleford (D)	19,331	53.6
	W. J. Vosholl (R)	15,858	44.0

NEW YORK

Special Election

		Votes	%
34	Edward B. Vreeland (R)	21,773	63.7
	S. E. Lewis (D)	12,406	36.3

PENNSYLVANIA

Special Election

		Votes	%
9	Henry D. Green (D)	17,736	59.9
	Jeremiah S. Parvin	11,878	40.1

1900 House Elections

ALABAMA

	Candidates	Votes	%
1	George Taylor (D)	9,804	82.7
	John W. Schell (R)	2,046	17.3
2	Ariosto A. Wiley (D)	12,496	98.3
3	Henry Clayton (D)	13,420	80.2
	W. O. Mulkey (POP & R)	3,179	19.0
4	Sidney J. Bowie (D)	10,733	97.3
5	Charles W. Thompson (D)	15,767	66.9
	Andrew J. Milstead (R)	7,782	33.0
6	John Bankhead (D)	8,073	65.7
	Thomas B. Morton (R)	4,218	34.3
7	John L. Burnett (D)	10,549	51.8
	N. B. Spears (R)	9,802	48.2
8	William Richardson (D)	13,193	59.7
	A. N. Holland (R)	8,900	40.3
9	Oscar Underwood (D)	10,591	99.9

Special Election

	Candidates	Votes	%
8	William Richardson (D)	14,632	84.8
	Cutler Smith (R)	2,631	15.2

ARKANSAS

	Candidates	Votes	%
1	Philip D. McCulloch (D)	17,066	72.4
	T. O. Fitzpatrick (R)	6,496	27.6
2	John S. Little (D)	13,792	67.9
	E. H. Vance Jr. (R)	6,522	32.1
3	Thomas C. McRae (D)	14,945	63.3
	B. M. Foreman (R)	8,664	36.7
4	Charles C. Reid (D)	12,336	65.3
	Sam Davis (R)	6,556	34.7
5	Hugh A. Dinsmore (D)	13,924	61.1
	U. S. Bratton (R)	8,885	39.0
6	Stephen Brundidge Jr. (D)	12,256	68.9
	C. F. Cole (R)	5,527	31.1

CALIFORNIA

	Candidates	Votes	%
1	Frank L. Coombs (R)	21,227	55.3
	James F. Farraher (D)	16,270	42.4
2	Samuel D. Woods (R)	23,019	50.4
	J. D. Sproul (D)	21,851	47.9
3	Victor H. Metcalf (R)	22,109	58.3
	Frank Freeman (D)	14,408	38.0
4	Julius Kahn (R)	18,904	56.8
	R. Porter Ashe (D)	12,336	37.1
5	Eugene F. Loud (R)	21,651	54.4
	J. H. Henry (D)	16,781	42.1
6	James McLachlan (R)	27,081	51.8
	William Graves (D)	19,793	37.9
	Unidentified Candidate (SOC LAB)	3,674	7.0
7	James Carson Needham (R)	23,450	52.4
	W. D. Crichton (D)	18,981	42.4

Special Election

	Candidates	Votes	%
2	Samuel D. Woods (R)	22,799	51.0
	J. D. Sproul (D)	21,917	49.0

COLORADO

	Candidates	Votes	%
1	John F. Shafroth (FUS)	54,591	55.3
	Robert W. Bonynge (R)	41,518	42.1
2	John C. Bell (FUS)	66,361	56.0
	Herschel M. Hogg (R)	51,287	43.3

CONNECTICUT

	Candidates	Votes	%
1	E. Stevens Henry (R)	25,048	58.2
	Tuttle (D)	16,836	39.1
2	Nehemiah D. Sperry (R)	33,205	52.9
	Gildersleeve (D)	28,349	45.2
3	Charles A. Russell (R)	14,727	60.4

	Candidates	Votes	%
	Potter (D)	9,284	38.1
4	Ebenezer J. Hill (R)	29,579	58.2
	Lyman (D)	20,520	40.3

DELAWARE

	Candidates	Votes	%
AL	Lewis Heisler Ball (R)	22,353	53.1
	Alexander M. Daly (D)	19,157	45.5

Special Election

	Candidates	Votes	%
AL	Walter O. Hoffecker (R)	22,389	53.5
	Edward Fowler (D)	19,012	45.4

FLORIDA

	Candidates	Votes	%
1	Stephen M. Sparkman (D)	13,440	87.0
	G. Brown Patterson (R)	2,005	13.0
2	Robert W. Davis (D)	13,011	80.0
	John M. Cheney (R)	3,259	20.0

GEORGIA

	Candidates	Votes	%
1	Rufus E. Lester (D)	7,272	64.0
	W. R. Leaken (R)	4,098	36.0
2	James M. Griggs (D)	7,299	99.7
3	Elijah B. Lewis (D)	6,119	99.9
4	William C. Adamson (D)	7,234	76.0
	A. H. Freeman (R)	2,238	23.5
5	Leonidas F. Livingston (D)	8,828	76.6
	Charles I. Brannan (I)	2,685	23.3
6	Charles L. Bartlett (D)	7,375	94.1
	J. T. Dickey (POP)	449	5.7
7	John W. Maddox (D)	9,113	62.0
	S. J. McKnight (POP)	4,574	31.1
	J. J. Hamilton (R)	1,006	6.9
8	William M. Howard (D)	6,952	92.0
	S. P. Bond (POP)	597	7.9
9	Farish C. Tate (D)	9,140	83.6
	H. L. Peeples (POP)	1,690	15.5
10	William H. Fleming (D)	5,585	92.2
11	W. G. Brantley (D)	8,587	66.8
	W. H. Marston (R)	4,263	33.2

IDAHO

	Candidates	Votes	%
AL	Thomas L. Glenn (POP & D)	28,079	51.1
	J. T. Morrison (R)	26,860	48.9

ILLINOIS

	Candidates	Votes	%
1	James R. Mann (R)	52,775	63.0
	Leon Hornstein (D)	28,858	34.5
2	John J. Feely (D)	34,946	50.1
	William Lorimer (R)	32,921	47.2
3	George P. Foster (D)	23,142	55.4
	William E. O'Neill (R)	17,920	42.9
4	James McAndrews (D)	24,435	54.4
	Daniel W. Mills (R)	19,346	43.1
5	William F. Mahoney (D)	23,648	53.8
	Charles C. Carnahan (R)	19,254	43.8
6	Henry Sherman Boutell (R)	22,655	49.5
	Emil Hoechster (D)	22,125	48.3
7	George Edmund Foss (R)	41,841	57.5
	William Peacock (D)	28,581	39.3
8	Albert J. Hopkins (R)	32,452	68.5
	John W. Leonard (D)	13,683	28.9
9	Robert R. Hitt (R)	32,616	65.7
	Hiram A. Brooks (D)	15,692	31.6
10	George W. Prince (R)	33,454	65.2
	Lavergne B. DeForest (D)	16,699	32.6
11	Walter Reeves (R)	25,367	56.1
	Edgar P. Holley (D)	18,835	41.6
12	Joseph G. Cannon (R)	30,633	60.2
	C. M. Briggs (D)	19,226	37.8
13	Vespasian Warner (R)	26,865	56.2

	Candidates	Votes	%
	John Eddy (D)	19,397	40.6
14	Joseph V. Graff (R)	25,169	49.5
	Jesse Black Jr (D)	24,775	48.7
15	J. Ross Mickey (D)	24,491	49.5
	Benjamin F. Marsh (R)	24,175	48.8
16	Thomas J. Selby (D)	25,795	55.7
	Thomas Worthington (R)	19,618	42.3
17	Ben F. Caldwell (D)	25,673	51.2
	David Ross (R)	23,648	47.2
18	Thomas M. Jett (D)	22,847	50.8
	John Jacob Brenholt (R)	21,245	47.2
19	Joseph B. Crowley (D)	24,536	50.7
	Horace S. Clark (R)	23,057	47.6
20	James R. Williams (D)	21,976	51.8
	Alexander M. Funkhouser (R)	19,716	46.4
21	Frederick J. Kern (D)	25,299	49.8
	William A. Rodenberg (R)	24,810	48.8
22	George W. Smith (R)	22,349	55.5
	Lindorf O. Whitnel (D)	17,528	43.6

INDIANA

	Candidates	Votes	%
1	James H. Hemenway (R)	22,262	49.7
	Alfred Dale Owen (D)	22,060	49.3
2	Robert W. Miers (D)	24,420	51.8
	Peter R. Wadsworth (R)	21,799	46.3
3	William T. Zenor (D)	24,049	54.9
	Hugh T. O'Conner (R)	19,440	44.4
4	Francis M. Griffith (D)	24,249	51.2
	Nathan Powell (R)	22,641	47.8
5	Elias S. Holliday (R)	25,932	50.6
	Frank A. Horner (D)	24,244	47.3
6	James E. Watson (R)	24,203	52.0
	David W. McKee (D)	21,320	45.8
7	Jesse Overstreet (R)	31,021	52.4
	Frank B. Burke (D)	27,012	45.7
8	George W. Cromer (R)	31,949	51.7
	Joseph T. Day (D)	28,180	45.6
9	Charles B. Landis (R)	24,138	50.3
	David F. Allen (D)	22,621	47.1
10	Edgar D. Crumpacker (R)	29,537	55.5
	John Ross (D)	23,045	43.3
11	George W. Steele (R)	29,177	53.3
	William J. Houck (D)	23,688	43.2
12	James M. Robinson (D)	22,750	49.7
	Robert B. Hanna (R)	22,122	48.4
13	Abraham L. Brick (R)	26,592	51.1
	Charles C. Bower (D)	24,376	46.8

IOWA

	Candidates	Votes	%
1	Thomas Hedge (R)	21,419	53.1
	D. J. O'Connell (D)	18,051	44.8
2	John N. W. Rumple (R)	23,202	50.4
	Henry Vollmer (D)	21,737	47.2
3	David B. Henderson (R)	30,181	61.4
	Willis N. Birdsall (D)	18,856	38.3
4	Gilbert N. Haugen (R)	27,659	61.2
	John Foley (D)	16,796	37.1
5	Robert G. Cousins (R)	27,124	59.5
	Daniel Kerr (D)	18,266	40.1
6	John F. Lacey (R)	22,956	53.2
	A. C. Steck (D)	19,812	45.9
7	John A. T. Hull (R)	28,508	61.6
	George C. Crozier (D)	16,365	35.4
8	William P. Hepburn (R)	26,798	54.7
	V. R. McGinnis (D)	21,347	43.6
9	Walter I. Smith (R)	27,155	56.8
	S. B. Wadsworth (D)	20,207	42.3
10	James P. Conner (R)	36,584	62.9
	Robert F. Dale (D)	20,648	35.5
11	Lot Thomas (R)	32,716	60.2
	William Muloaney (D)	20,564	37.8

Special Elections

	Candidates	Votes	%
9	Walter I. Smith (R)	27,154	57.3
	S. B. Wadsworth (D)	20,229	42.7
10	James P. Conner (R)	35,009	63.8
	Robert F. Dale (D)	19,830	36.2

KANSAS

	Candidates	Votes	%
1	Charles Curtis (R)	28,733	59.1
	George W. Glick (D-PP)	19,915	40.9
2	Justin D. Bowersock (R)	28,083	52.3
	M. S. Peters (D-PP)	25,623	47.7
3	Alfred M. Jackson (D-PP)	26,760	50.0
	George W. Wheatley (R)	26,492	49.5
4	James M. Miller (R)	24,106	53.8
	Thomas H. Grisham (D-PP)	20,670	46.2
5	William A. Calderhead (R)	22,436	53.9
	W. D. Vincent (D-PP)	19,211	46.1
6	William A. Reeder (R)	19,660	48.9
	John B. Dykes (PP)	15,083	37.6
	Tully Scott (D)	5,430	13.5
7	Chester I. Long (R)	31,479	51.2
	Claud Duval (D-PP)	29,960	48.8
AL	Charles F. Scott (R)	180,162	52.3
	J. D. Botkin (D-PP)	160,980	46.7

KENTUCKY

	Candidates	Votes	%
1	Charles K. Wheeler (D)	25,264	59.6
	Keys (R)	16,809	39.7
2	Henry D. Allen (D)	23,410	53.9
	Lynch (R)	19,788	45.6
3	John S. Rhea (D)	19,505‡	50.0
	J. McKenzie Moss (R)	19,344	49.6
4	David H. Smith (D)	24,920	53.2
	Jolly (R)	21,944	46.8
5	Harvey S. Irwin (R)	25,085	53.7
	Gregory (D)	21,374	45.8
6	Daniel L. Gooch (D)	22,572	56.7
	Shaw (R)	16,857	42.3
7	South Trimble (D)	20,325	54.7
	Stoll (R)	16,810	45.3
8	George G. Gilbert (D)	17,646	51.2
	Willms (R)	16,602	48.1
9	James N. Kehoe (D)	23,197	50.3
	Pugh (R)	22,961	49.7
10	James B. White (D)	19,443	51.8
	Hopkins (R)	18,070	48.2
11	Vincent Boreing (R)	34,406	69.2
	Smith (D)	15,281	30.8

LOUISIANA

	Candidates	Votes	%
1	Adolph Meyer (D)	9,727	81.0
	William Brophy (R)	2,274	18.9
2	Robert C. Davey (D)	11,420	77.8
	Samuel C. Heaslip (R)	3,234	22.0
3	Robert F. Broussard (D)	9,382	62.3
	Frank B. Williams (R)	5,673	37.7
4	Phanor Breazeale (D)	8,592	86.9
	F. M. Welch (R)	1,290	13.1
5	Joseph E. Ransdell (D)	6,172	90.8
	Henry E. Hardtner (R)	628	9.2
6	Samuel M. Robertson (D)	7,432	83.6
	James H. Ducote (R)	1,455	16.4

MAINE

	Candidates	Votes	%
1	Amos L. Allen (R)	17,803	60.3
	John J. Lynch (D)	10,040	34.0
	D. P. Parker (P)	1,533	5.2
2	Charles E. Littlefield (R)	19,215	61.0
	H. H. Monroe (D)	11,439	36.3
3	Edwin C. Burleigh (R)	17,057	60.7
	A. F. Gerald (D)	10,241	36.4
4	Charles A. Boutelle (R)	18,826*	66.3
	Thomas White (D)	8,765	30.9

MARYLAND

	Candidates	Votes	%
1	William H. Jackson (R)	19,714	50.2
	John P. Moore (D)	18,173	46.3
2	Albert A. Blakeney (R)	27,710	48.7
	J. F. C. Talbott (D)	27,420	48.2
3	Frank C. Wachter (R)	21,641	51.8
	Robert Fulton Leach Jr. (D)	19,570	46.8
4	Charles R. Schirm (R)	21,932	51.4
	James W. Denny (D)	20,149	47.2
5	Sydney E. Mudd (R)	20,936	54.2
	Benjamin H. Camalier (D)	17,305	44.8
6	George A. Pearre (R)	23,541	53.0
	Charles A. Little (D)	20,161	45.4

Special Election

	Candidates	Votes	%
1	Josiah L. Kerr (R)	19,320	50.9
	Edwin H. Brown (D)	18,650	49.1

MASSACHUSETTS

	Candidates	Votes	%
1	George P. Lawrence (R)	16,520	58.0
	James H. Bryan (D)	10,924	38.4
2	Frederick H. Gillett (R)	17,604	60.6
	Thomas W. Kenefick (D)	10,766	37.1
3	John R. Thayer (D)	16,039	50.2
	Charles G. Washburn (R)	15,909	49.8
4	Charles Q. Tirrell (R)	19,718	65.3
	Charles D. Lewis (D)	10,493	34.7
5	William S. Knox (R)	15,887	49.4
	Joseph J. Flynn (D)	15,466	48.1
6	William H. Moody (R)	18,328	64.6
	Daniel N. Crowley (D)	6,534	23.0
	Albert L. Gillen (D SOCIAL)	2,725	9.6
7	Ernest W. Roberts (R)	19,595	60.3
	Henry Winn (D)	10,815	33.3
8	Samuel W. McCall (R)	19,901	69.4
	Philip T. Nickerson (D)	7,970	27.8
9	Joseph A. Conry (D)	14,701	66.7
	Charles T. Witt (R)	6,633	30.1
10	Henry F. Naphen (D)	23,507	59.0
	George B. Pierce (R)	16,318	41.0
11	Samuel L. Powers (R)	21,761	60.0
	William H. Baker (D)	10,885	30.0
	Moorfield Storey (I)	2,858	7.9
12	William C. Lovering (R)	17,788	61.4
	Charles F. King (D)	7,434	25.7
	Charles E. Lowell (D SOCIAL)	2,404	8.3
13	William S. Greene (R)	16,337	69.1
	Charles T. Luce (D)	5,954	25.2

MICHIGAN

	Candidates	Votes	%
1	John B. Corliss (R)	24,785	54.0
	Rufus W. Jacklin (D)	20,295	44.2
2	Henry C. Smith (R)	26,945	52.4
	Martin G. Loennecker (D)	23,368	45.5
3	Washington Gardner (R)	25,998	53.3
	Stephen D. Williams (D)	21,306	43.6
4	Edward L. Hamilton (R)	26,883	55.6
	Roman I. Jarvis (D)	20,498	42.4
5	William Alden Smith (R)	27,898	55.6
	William F. McKnight (D)	21,497	42.8
6	Samuel W. Smith (R)	27,941	53.9
	Everett L. Bray (D)	22,532	43.4
7	Edgar Weeks (R)	22,924	57.7
	Justin R. Whiting (D)	15,938	40.1
8	Joseph W. Fordney (R)	21,522	53.5
	Wellington R. Burt (D)	17,212	42.8
9	Roswell P. Bishop (R)	21,408	62.4
	Frank L. Fowler (D)	12,197	35.5
10	Rousseau O. Crump (R)	23,308	59.3
	Lee E. Joslyn (D)	15,241	38.8
11	Archibald B. Darragh (R)	29,540	66.1
	George Killeen (D)	15,064	33.7
12	Carlos D. Shelden (R)	33,759	72.7
	Edward F. Legendre (D)	11,516	24.8

MINNESOTA

	Candidates	Votes	%
1	James A. Tawney (R)	23,112	56.0
	Brown (PP & D)	18,130	44.0
2	James T. McCleary (R)	30,558	59.8
	Mathews (PP & D)	18,933	37.1
3	Joel P. Heatwole (R)	23,110	57.7
	Schaller (PP & D)	16,498	41.2
4	Frederick C. Stevens (R)	21,322	57.7
	Stone (PP & D)	14,886	40.3
5	Loren Fletcher (R)	24,724	59.4
	Stockwell (PP)	14,269	34.3
6	R. Page W. Morris (R)	31,792	55.5
	Truelson (PP & D)	24,219	42.3
7	Frank M. Eddy (R)	25,738	51.8
	Daly (PP & D)	21,012	42.3
	Aaker (P)	2,483	5.0

MISSISSIPPI

	Candidates	Votes	%
1	Ezekiel S. Candler Jr. (D)	6,749	95.4
2	Thomas Spight (D)	7,548	93.8
	John S. Burton (R)	500	6.2
3	Patrick Henry (D)	3,202	100.0
4	Andrew F. Fox (D)	8,211	86.0
	W. D. Frazee (R)	686	7.2
	Raleigh Brewer (POP)	653	6.8
5	John Sharp Williams (D)	9,385	99.9
6	Frank A. McLain (D)	7,032	87.0
	H. C. Turley (R)	1,048	13.0
7	Charles E. Hooker (D)	5,722	92.6
	N. M. Hollingsmith (MID ROAD)	457	7.4

MISSOURI

	Candidates	Votes	%
1	James T. Lloyd (D)	23,920	55.4
	Pickler (R)	19,189	44.5
2	William W. Rucker (D)	25,046	57.4
	Irwin (R)	18,485	42.4
3	John Dougherty (D)	22,993	54.5
	Leeper (R)	19,131	45.3
4	Charles F. Cochran (D)	22,211	53.1
	Kennish (R)	19,595	46.9
5	William S. Cowherd (D)	27,644	52.7
	Brown (R)	24,367	46.4
6	David A. De Armond (D)	20,017	53.9
	Jurden (R)	16,366	44.0
7	James Cooney (D)	26,834	55.4
	Parsons (R)	21,601	44.6
8	Dorsey W. Shackleford (D)	23,718	53.4
	Moore (R)	20,634	46.5
9	James Beauchamp Clark (D)	19,202	53.9
	Flagg (R)	16,451	46.1
10	Richard Bartholdt (R)	24,252	55.2
	Bolte (R)	17,848	40.7
11	Charles F. Joy (R)	28,375	51.7
	O'Malley (D)	25,607	46.6
12	James J. Butler (D)	22,104‡	53.2
	William M. Horton (R)	18,551	44.7
13	Edward Robb (D)	23,798	53.7
	Reppy (R)	20,524	46.3
14	Willard D. Vandiver (D)	26,434	53.0
	Mozley (R)	23,364	46.8
15	Maecenas E. Benton (D)	26,804	53.5
	Holmes (R)	22,678	45.3

MONTANA

	Candidates	Votes	%
AL	Caldwell Edwards (D)	28,130	45.8
	Samuel G. Murray (R)	23,207	37.8
	Cornielius F. Kelley (ID)	9,443	15.4

NEBRASKA

	Candidates	Votes	%
1	Elmer J. Burkett (R)	19,449	53.1
	George W. Berge (FUS)	16,548	45.2
2	David H. Mercer (R)	16,277	51.8
	Edgar Howard (FUS)	14,807	47.1
3	John S. Robinson (FUS)	22,425	49.4
	John R. Hays (R)	22,250	49.0

Candidates	Votes	%
4 William L. Stark (FUS)	21,032	49.9
John D. Pope (R)	20,435	48.5
5 Ashton C. Shallenberger (FUS)	17,688	49.4
Webster L. Morlan (R)	17,279	48.2
6 William Neville (FUS)	17,699	48.7
M. P. Kinkaid (R)	17,501	48.2

NEVADA

Candidates	Votes	%
AL Francis G. Newlands		
(D & SILVER)	5,975	58.8
E. S. Farrington (R)	4,190	41.2

NEW HAMPSHIRE

Candidates	Votes	%
1 Cyrus A. Sulloway (R)	26,072	58.6
Timothy J. Howard (D)	17,401	39.1
2 Frank D. Currier (R)	27,440	60.0
Henry F. Hollis (D)	17,517	38.3

NEW JERSEY

Candidates	Votes	%
1 Henry C. Loudenslager (R)	31,942	59.7
George Pfeiffer Jr. (D)	19,169	35.8
2 John J. Gardner (R)	31,359	62.0
Thomas J. Prickett (D)	17,351	34.3
3 Benjamin F. Howell (R)	24,286	55.0
James J. Bergen (D)	18,781	42.6
4 Joshua S. Salmon (D)	19,661	50.1
H. Burdett Herr (R)	18,017	45.9
5 James F. Stewart (R)	24,323	53.6
John Johnson (D)	19,708	43.4
6 Richard Wayne Parker (R)	32,830	60.7
George H. Lambert (D)	19,477	36.0
7 Allan L. McDermott (D)	33,713	50.8
Marshall Vanwinkle (R)	30,472	46.0
8 Charles N. Fowler (R)	27,121	58.8
Edward A. S. Man (D)	17,510	38.0

Special Election

Candidates	Votes	%
7 Allan L. McDermott (D)	33,898	52.6
Marshall Vanwinkle (R)	30,472	47.3

NEW YORK

Candidates	Votes	%
1 Frederick Storm (R)	28,046	51.2
Rowland Miles (D)	25,715	46.9
2 John J. Fitzgerald (D)	18,387	50.1
Henry B. Ketcham (R)	18,066	49.2
3 Henry Bristow (R)	24,660	51.4
Edmund H. Driggs (D)	22,904	47.7
4 Harry A. Hanbury (R)	28,596	50.8
Bertram T. Clayton (D)	26,955	47.9
5 Frank E. Wilson (D)	22,041	49.1
Jacob Worth (R)	21,164	47.1
6 George H. Lindsay (D)	18,073	54.7
Bert Reiss (R)	14,460	43.8
7 Nicholas Muller (D)	13,654	58.5
James R. O'Beirne (R)	9,323	39.9
8 Thomas J. Creamer (D)	10,330	50.1
Richard Vancott (R)	10,157	49.3
9 Henry M. Goldfogle (D)	13,570	57.6
Theodore Cox (R)	7,438	31.6
Rudolph Katz (SOC LAB)	1,261	5.4
Alexander Jones (SOCIAL D)	1,190	5.1
10 Amos J. Cummings (D)	20,585	60.9
John Glass Jr. (R)	12,886	38.1
11 William Sulzer (D)	14,055	55.7
Charles Schwick (R)	8,976	35.6
12 George B. McClellan (D)	15,177	57.9
Herbert Parsons (R)	10,736	41.0
13 Oliver H. P. Belmont (D)	18,021	53.7
William R. Wilcox (R)	14,781	44.0
14 William H. Douglas (R)	36,904	52.1
John Sprunt Hill (D)	32,167	45.5
15 Jacob Ruppert Jr. (D)	31,592	49.6
Elias Goodman (R)	29,837	46.8
16 Cornelius A. Pugsley (D)	37,665	48.8
Norton P. Otis (R)	36,954	47.9

Candidates	Votes	%
17 Arthur S. Tompkins (R)	22,663	54.9
John D. Blauvelt (D)	17,953	43.5
18 John H. Ketcham (R)	25,618	96.4
19 William H. Draper (R)	24,104	56.3
Edward F. McCormick (D)	17,936	41.9
20 George N. Southwick (R)	22,360	52.3
Martin H. Glynn (D)	19,904	46.5
21 John K. Stewart (R)	30,027	53.2
Joseph B. Handy (D)	24,965	44.3
22 Lucius N. Littauer (R)	32,436	64.5
William L. Pert (D)	16,085	32.0
23 Louis W. Emerson (R)	30,604	65.7
Charles A. Burke (D)	14,977	32.1
24 Albert D. Shaw (R)	27,272*	60.8
James S. Boyer (D)	16,385	36.5
25 James S. Sherman (R)	26,782	57.5
Henry Martin (D)	18,831	40.5
26 George W. Ray (R)	34,184	58.0
Myron B. Ferris (D)	22,542	38.2
27 Michael E. Driscoll (R)	31,409	62.2
Luke McHenry (D)	17,993	35.6
28 Sereno E. Payne (R)	33,998	59.2
Robert L. Drummond (D)	21,789	37.9
29 Charles W. Gillet (R)	25,330	52.4
Frank J. Nelson (D)	21,358	44.2
30 James W. Wadsworth (R)	29,368	56.1
Charles Ward (D)	21,196	40.5
31 James Breck Perkins (R)	26,187	53.6
Martin S. Mindnich (D)	20,064	41.1
32 William H. Ryan (D)	18,088	49.6
Rowland B. Mahany (R)	17,772	48.7
33 De Alva S. Alexander (R)	29,120	59.5
Harvey W. Richardson (D)	19,529	39.9
34 Edward B. Vreeland (R)	32,357	63.7
Stillman E. Lewis (D)	16,547	32.6

NORTH CAROLINA

Candidates	Votes	%
1 John H. Small (D)	18,709	57.4
Abner Alexander (R)	9,493	29.1
Isaac M. Meekins (IR)	4,355	13.4
2 Claude Kitchin (D)	22,901	64.6
Joseph J. Martin (R)	12,521	35.3
3 Charles R. Thomas (D)	13,541	53.8
John E. Fowler (POP)	11,632	46.2
4 Edward W. Pou (D)	18,929	57.1
Jesse A. Giles (R)	13,057	39.4
5 William W. Kitchin (D)	18,538	52.5
John R. Joyce (R)	16,687	47.3
6 John D. Bellamy (D)	18,902	72.5
Oliver H. Dockery (R)	7,146	27.4
7 Theodore F. Kluttz (D)	15,712	52.3
John Q. Holton (R)	13,380	44.5
8 E. Spencer Blackburn (R)	19,629	52.3
John C. Buxton (D)	17,778	47.4
9 James M. Moody (R)	19,334	52.8
William T. Crawford (D)	17,250	47.1

NORTH DAKOTA

Candidates	Votes	%
AL Thomas F. Marshall (R)	34,887	61.0
Hildreth (D&I)	21,175	37.0

OHIO

Candidates	Votes	%
1 William B. Shattuc (R)	26,434	58.2
John B. Peaslee (D)	18,430	40.6
2 Jacob H. Bromwell (R)	28,029	54.3
Henry Ketter (D)	22,859	44.3
3 Robert M. Nevin (R)	28,882	49.5
Ulysses F. Bickley (D)	28,728	49.2
4 Robert B. Gordon (D)	25,870	59.9
Edwin C. Wright (R)	17,327	40.1
5 John S. Snook (D)	22,884	54.4
Frederick L. Hay (R)	19,176	45.6
6 Charles Q. Hildebrant (R)	24,610	54.2
Adam Bridge (D)	20,407	45.0
7 Thomas B. Kyle (R)	24,818	54.7
Stewart L. Tatum (D)	20,326	44.8
8 William R. Warnock (R)	26,287	54.4

Candidates	Votes	%
William J. Frey (D)	21,748	45.0
9 James H. Southard (R)	29,544	51.6
Negley D. Cochran (D)	26,697	46.6
10 Stephen Morgan (R)	26,244	60.2
James K. McClung (D)	17,369	39.8
11 Charles H. Grosvenor (R)	25,154	57.8
Thomas H. Craig (D)	18,174	41.7
12 Emmett Tompkins (R)	25,705	49.5
John J. Lentz (D)	25,687	49.5
13 James A. Norton (D)	29,672	56.1
Daniel W. Locke (R)	23,062	43.6
14 William Woodburn Skiles (R)	28,021	52.6
William G. Sharp (D)	25,247	47.4
15 Henry C. Van Voorhis (R)	22,623	51.3
L. W. Ellenwood (D)	21,458	48.6
16 Joseph J. Gill (R)	22,838	56.0
Marion Huffman (D)	17,926	44.0
17 John W. Cassingham (D)	26,275	55.0
George Adams (R)	21,283	44.5
18 Robert W. Tayler (R)	31,479	54.6
John H. Morris (D)	25,026	43.4
19 Charles Dick (R)	34,129	62.4
Charles E. Chadman (D)	20,351	37.2
20 Jacob A. Beidler (R)	22,776	45.8
H. B. Harrington (D)	22,087	44.4
Fremont O. Phillips (I.R.)	3,973	8.0
21 Theodore E. Burton (R)	28,605	55.1
Sylvester V. McMahon (D)	21,947	42.3

OREGON

Candidates	Votes	%
1 Thomas H. Tongue (R)	21,212	49.5
Bernard Daly (FUS-D-PO)	18,193	42.4
2 Malcolm Moody (R)	22,088	55.1
William Smith (FUS-D-PO)	12,708	31.7
J. E. Simmons (MID ROAD)	3,384	8.4

PENNSYLVANIA

Candidates	Votes	%
1 Henry H. Bingham (R)	29,973	71.5
Michael Francis Doyle (D)	11,765	28.1
2 Robert Adams Jr (R)	19,657	79.7
William E. Hooper (D)	4,998	20.3
3 Henry Burk (R)	11,095	52.7
William McAleer (D, MLP)	9,839	46.7
4 James Rankin Young (R)	55,648	75.5
Peter J. Hughes (D)	17,330	23.5
5 Edward de V. Morrell (R)	45,089	75.7
Samuel R. Carter (D)	13,898	23.3
6 Thomas S. Butler (R)	26,379	70.2
Nathaniel M. Ellis (D)	10,098	26.9
7 Irving P. Wanger (R)	25,422	57.1
Christopher Vanartsdalen (D)	18,542	41.7
8 Howard Mutchler (D)	18,448	51.3
Russel C. Stewart (R)	16,753	46.6
9 Henry D. Green (R)	29,160	55.9
William Kerper Stevens (R)	22,758	43.6
10 Marriott Brosius (R)	23,143	71.8
Louis N. Spencer (D)	8,502	26.4
11 William Connell (R)	15,536	49.5
Michael F. Conry (D)	13,598	43.3
12 Henry W. Palmer (R)	18,931	54.3
S. W. Davenport (A-TRUST)	13,698	39.3
13 George R. Patterson (R)	15,519	52.4
James W. Ryan (D)	13,895	46.9
14 Marlin E. Olmsted (R)	23,726	89.5
Edwin H. Molly (P)	1,451	5.5
Benjamin L. Forster (D)	1,335	5.0
15 Charles F. Wright (R)	18,261	56.7
William B. Packard (D)	12,396	38.5
16 Elias Deemer (R)	19,844	52.6
Otto G. Kaupp (D)	16,509	43.8
17 Rufus K. Polk (D)	16,615	54.3
Clarence F. Huth (R)	13,071	42.7
18 Thaddeus M. Mahon (R)	20,756	58.9
James G. Heading (D)	14,464	41.1
19 Robert J. Lewis (R)	22,266	50.3
Harry N. Gitt (D)	21,280	48.1
20 Alvin Evans (R)	30,777	62.5
James M. Walters (D)	17,450	35.4

	Candidates	Votes	%
21	Summers M. Jack (R)	32,909	61.6
	Curtis H. Gregg (D)	19,156	35.9
22	John Dalzell (R)	36,409	69.7
	John F. Miller (D)	14,343	27.5
23	William H. Graham (R)	19,957	74.6
	John Huckenstine (D)	6,142	23.0
24	Ernest F. Acheson (R)	35,939	58.7
	Wooda N. Carr (D)	23,568	38.5
25	Joseph B. Showalter (R)	24,472	55.5
	M. L. Lockwood (D)	19,641	44.5
26	Arthur L. Bates (R)	18,723	53.6
	Athelston Gaston (D)	14,918	42.7
27	Joseph C. Sibley (R)	15,804	50.8
	Lewis Emery Jr. (D, LIN)	13,906	44.7
28	J. K. P. Hall (D)	19,132	49.5
	A. A. Clearwater (R)	18,511	47.9
AL	Galusha A. Grow (R)	683,941 ✓	
	Robert H. Foerderer (R)	675,099 ✓	
	Harry E. Grim (D)	411,552	
	Nicholas M. Edwards (D)	409,918	
	William W. Hague (P)	24,531	
	Lee L. Grumbine (P)	24,412	
	John W. Slayton (SOC)	4,026	
	Edward Kuppinger (SOC)	3,995	
	John R. Root (SOC LAB)	2,660	
	Donald L. Monro (SOC LAB)	2,657	
	Robert Bringham (PP)	795	
	George Main (PP)	775	
	Benjamin A. Bubbett	278	

Special Election

5	Edward de V. Morrell (R)	34,789	100.0

RHODE ISLAND

1	Melville Bull (R)	16,591	59.5
	Gorman (D)	9,498	34.0
2	Adin B. Capron (R)	13,975	57.8
	Garvin (D)	8,870	36.7

SOUTH CAROLINA

1	William Elliott (D)	3,666	72.7
	W. W. Beckett (R)	1,378	27.3
2	William J. Talbert (D)	6,713	97.7
3	Asbury C. Latimer (D)	7,834	97.5
4	Joseph T. Johnston (D)	8,189	97.1
5	David E. Finley (D)	5,634	96.8
6	Robert B. Scarborough (D)	7,608	94.2
	R. A. Stuart (R)	473	5.9
7	J. William Stokes (D)	7,285	93.2
	Alexander D. Dantzler (R)	534	6.8

SOUTH DAKOTA

AL	Charles H. Burke (R)	53,583 ✓	
	Eben W. Martin (R)	53,549 ✓	
	Andrew E. Lee (FUS)	40,560	
	Joseph B. Moore (FUS)	40,151	
	O. A. Harpel (P)	1,323	
	M. Rogers (P)	1,188	
	Edm. F. English (POP)	305	
	John M. Pease (POP)	304	

TENNESSEE

1	Walter P. Brownlow (R)	22,374	62.8
	Reaves (D)	13,107	36.8
2	Henry R. Gibson (R)	22,062	68.7
	Park (D)	9,913	30.9
3	John A. Moon (D)	18,363	52.1
	Sharp (R)	16,591	47.1
4	Charles E. Snodgrass (D)	15,659	59.8
	Gore (R)	10,515	40.1
5	James D. Richardson (D)	14,653	68.0
	McClain (R)	6,895	32.0
6	John W. Gaines (D)	17,192	71.9
	Brock (R)	6,256	26.2
7	Lemuel P. Padgett (D)	12,636	54.4
	Fuzzell (I)	10,610	45.6
8	Thetus W. Sims (D)	14,509	53.1
	Hawkins (R)	12,258	44.8
9	Rice A. Pierce (D)	16,680	71.8
	Austin (R)	6,050	26.0
10	Malcolm R. Patterson (D)	10,218	62.1
	Taylor (R)	6,247	37.9

TEXAS

1	Thomas H. Ball (D)	11,887	65.7
	S. E. Tracy (R)	5,391	29.8
2	Samuel B. Cooper (D)	31,774	98.5
3	Reese C. De Graffenreid (D)	19,091	61.0
	C. G. White (R)	12,230	39.1
4	John L. Sheppard (D)	17,647	57.6
	J. C. Gibbons (R)	9,818	32.1
	J. L. Darwin (POP)	3,154	10.3
5	Choice B. Randell (D)	28,074	90.4
	J. W. Thomas (R)	1,790	5.8
6	Robert E. Burke (D)	33,220	77.7
	S. H. Lumpkin (POP)	7,432	17.4
7	Robert L. Henry (D)	27,243	92.1
8	Samuel W. T. Lanham (D)	24,093	68.2
	J. S. Daley (POP)	6,465	18.3
	N. A. Dodge (R)	4,760	13.5
9	Albert S. Burleson (D)	25,494	91.3
	Nat Q. Henderson (R)	2,419	8.7
10	George F. Burgess (D)	18,203	59.5
	Walter C. Jones (R)	12,255	40.1
11	Rudolph Kleberg (D)	21,329	59.2
	B. L. Crouch (R)	14,706	40.8
12	James L. Slayden (D)	18,421	60.8
	C. C. Drake (R)	11,530	38.1
13	John H. Stephens (D)	30,726	85.1
	C. W. Johnson (R)	5,354	14.8

UTAH

AL	George Sutherland (R)	46,180	50.1
	W. H. King (D)	45,939	49.9

VERMONT

1	David J. Foster (R)	22,845	68.5
	Ozro Meacham (D)	9,441	28.3
2	Kittredge Haskins (R)	23,273	75.5
	George T. Swasey (D)	7,291	23.7

VIRGINIA

1	William A. Jones (D)	16,076	64.1
	James Monroe Stubbs (R)	8,737	34.9
2	Harry L. Maynard (D)	20,113	62.2
	R. A. Wise (R)	10,203	31.6
3	John Lamb (D)	15,274	65.6
	Edgar Allan (R)	7,793	33.5
4	Francis R. Lassiter (D)	12,796	61.4
	C. E. Wilson (R)	8,058	38.6
5	Claude A. Swanson (D)	14,293	58.1
	John R. Whitehead (R)	10,292	41.9
6	Peter J. Otey (D)	15,948	77.5

	J. B. Stovall (R)	2,467	12.0
	A. E. Fairweather (I)	2,152	10.5
7	James Hay (D)	17,276	63.4
	C. M. Gibbens (R)	9,995	36.7
8	John F. Rixey (D)	17,071	63.2
	William J. Rogers (R)	9,858	36.5
9	William F. Rhea (D)	20,164	52.3
	James A. Walker (R)	18,412	47.7
10	Henry D. Flood (D)	16,064	54.3
	Robert T. Hubard (R)	12,913	43.7

Special Election

4	Francis R. Lassiter (D)	3,217	98.7

WASHINGTON

AL	Wesley L. Jones (R)	55,393 ✓	
	Francis W. Cushman (R)	55,268 ✓	
	J. T. Ronald (D)	45,448	
	F. C. Robertson (D)	44,882	
	Guy Posson (P)	2,239	
	J. A. Adams (P)	2,059	
	William Hogan (SOCIAL D)	1,954	
	Herman F. Titus (SOCIAL D)	1,916	
	Walter Walker (SOC LAB)	922	
	Christian F. Larsen (SOC LAB)	878	

WEST VIRGINIA

1	Blackburn B. Dovener (R)	27,767	54.2
	William E. Haymond (D)	22,778	44.5
2	Alston G. Dayton (R)	27,735	51.9
	Thomas B. Davis (D)	25,347	47.4
3	Joseph Holt Gaines (R)	34,243	55.1
	David E. Johnson (D)	27,667	44.5
4	James H. Hughes (R)	28,476	53.2
	Creed Collins (D)	24,748	46.2

WISCONSIN

1	Henry A. Cooper (R)	28,256	64.1
	Gilbert T. Hodges (D)	14,556	33.0
2	Herman B. Dahle (R)	22,175	52.8
	John A. Aylward (D)	18,819	44.8
3	Joseph W. Babcock (R)	26,593	63.5
	Edward L. Luckow (D)	14,017	33.5
4	Theobald Otjen (R)	24,637	49.5
	George W. Peck (D)	21,691	43.5
	Robert Meister (SOCIAL D)	2,991	6.0
5	Samuel S. Barney (R)	23,089	52.4
	Charles H. Weisse (D)	18,066	41.0
	Henry C. Berger (SOC LAB)	2,284	5.2
6	James H. Davidson (R)	26,326	55.8
	James W. Watson (D)	19,758	41.9
7	John J. Esch (R)	22,715	65.2
	John P. Rice (D)	11,254	32.3
8	Edward S. Minor (R)	25,263	60.2
	Nathan E. Morgan (D)	16,740	39.9
9	Webster E. Brown (R)	33,329	64.7
	Ernest Schwepke (D)	16,988	33.0
10	John J. Jenkins (R)	29,144	68.7
	Frank A. Partlow (D)	11,930	28.1

WYOMING

AL	Frank W. Mondell (R)	14,539	59.2
	John Charles Thompson (D)	10,017	40.8

1901 House Elections

PENNSYLVANIA

Special Election

	Candidates	Votes	%
10	Henry B. Cassel (R)	12,465	73.9
	Daniel R. McCormick (D)	4,410	26.1

TEXAS

Special Election

	Candidates	Votes	%
6	Dudley G. Wooten (D)	11,174	84.1
	Philip Lindsey	2,063	15.5

1902 House Elections

ALABAMA

	Candidates	Votes	%
1	George W. Taylor (D)	5,364	89.8
	E. B. Hubbard (R)	545	9.1
2	Ariosto A. Wiley (D)	7,696	89.9
	Julius Sternfeld (R)	861	10.1
3	Henry D. Clayton (D)	7,595	84.1
	M. W. Carden (R)	905	10.0
	J.P. Pelham (R)	535	5.9
4	Sydney J. Bowie (D)	6,880	69.3
	J. A. Edwards (R)	3,048	30.7
5	Charles W. Thompson (D)	9,043	78.4
	R. S. Nolen (R)	2,495	21.6
6	John H. Bankhead (D)	7,481	72.8
	William B. Ford (R)	2,798	27.2
7	John L. Burnett (D)	9,298	52.9
	O. D. Street (R)	8,044	45.8
8	William Richardson (D)	7,935	80.8
	James Jackson (R)	1,889	19.2
9	Oscar W. Underwood (D)	6,782	77.3
	J. Clyde Miller (R)	1,793	20.4

ARKANSAS

	Candidates	Votes	%
1	Robert B. Macon (D)	4,796	99.8
2	Stephen Brundidge Jr. (D)	4,549	84.1
	R. S. Coffman (R)	858	15.9
3	Hugh A. Dinsmore (D)	4,808	72.4
	W. L. McPherson (R)	1,833	27.6
4	John S. Little (D)	4,213	78.7
	F. A. Youmans (R)	1,142	21.3
5	Charles C. Reid (D)	4,530	79.6
	Henry M. Sugg (R)	1,161	20.4
6	Joseph T. Robinson (D)	5,195	89.3
	W. H. Carpenter (R)	622	10.7
7	Robert Minor Wallace (D)	4,730	83.0
	R. L. Floyd (R)	971	17.0

CALIFORNIA

	Candidates	Votes	%
1	James N. Gillett (R)	21,268	50.5
	Thomas S. Ford (D)	19,696	46.7
2	Theodore A. Bell (D)	21,536	49.2
	Frank L. Coombs (R)	21,181	48.3
3	Victor H. Metcalf (R)	20,532	66.2
	Calvin B. White (D)	8,574	27.7
	M. W. Wilkins (SOC)	1,556	5.0
4	Edward J. Livernash (D & UN LAB)	16,146	49.2
	Julius Kahn (R)	16,005	48.7
5	William J. Wynn (D&UN LAB)	22,712	56.5
	E. F. Loud (R)	16,577	41.2
6	James C. Needham (R)	17,268	53.5
	Gaston M. Ashe (D)	13,732	42.6
7	James McLachlan (R)	19,407	64.8
	Carl A. Johnson (D)	8,075	27.0
8	Milton J. Daniels (R)	20,135	51.9
	William E. Smythe (D)	15,819	40.8
	N. A. Richardson (SOC)	2,091	5.4

COLORADO

	Candidates	Votes	%
1	John F. Shafroth (D)	41,440‡	49.0
	Robert W. Bonynge (R)	38,648	45.7
2	Herschel M. Hogg (R)	47,546	47.6
	John C. Bell (FUS)	45,234	45.3
AL	Franklin E. Brooks (R)	85,217	46.1
	Alva Adams (D)	84,367	45.6

CONNECTICUT

	Candidates	Votes	%
1	E. Stevens Henry (R)	20,289	52.4
	O'Neil (D)	17,211	44.4
2	Nehemiah D. Sperry (R)	29,658	54.7
	Morse (D)	22,283	41.1

	Candidates	Votes	%
3	Frank B. Brandegee (R)	12,547	58.7
	Potter (D)	8,364	39.1
4	Ebenezer J. Hill (R)	24,333	54.0
	Bishop (D)	19,888	44.2
AL	George L. Lilley (R)	83,666	52.6
	Cummings (D)	70,590	44.3
	Special Election		
3	Frank B. Brandegee (R)	5,208	94.2

DELAWARE

	Candidates	Votes	%
AL	Henry A. Houston (D)	16,396	42.9
	William Michael Byrne (UN R)	12,998	34.0
	Lewis Heisler Ball (R)	8,028	21.0

FLORIDA

	Candidates	Votes	%
1	Stephen M. Sparkman (D)	5,597	100.0
2	Robert W. Davis (D)	6,488	100.0
3	William B. Lamar (D)	4,249	100.0

GEORGIA

	Candidates	Votes	%
1	Rufus E. Lester (D)	4,349	100.0
2	James M. Griggs (D)	3,797	100.0
3	Elijah B. Lewis (D)	2,957	100.0
4	William C. Adamson (D)	2,883	100.0
5	Leonidas F. Livingston (D)	2,485	100.0
6	Charles L. Bartlett (D)	4,522	100.0
7	John W. Maddox (D)	5,305	93.2
	S. J. McKnight (POP)	389	6.8
8	William M. Howard (D)	3,139	100.0
9	F. Carter Tate (D)	4,749	99.6
10	Thomas W. Hardwick (D)	2,675	100.0
11	William G. Brantley (D)	3,606	100.0

IDAHO

	Candidates	Votes	%
AL	Burton L. French (R)	32,384	54.3
	Joseph Henry Hutchinson (D)	24,878	41.7

ILLINOIS

	Candidates	Votes	%
1	Martin Emerich (D)	16,591	51.3
	Martin B. Madden (R)	15,339	47.4
2	James R. Mann (R)	18,697	60.1
	Frank Brust (D)	9,532	30.6
	Bernard Berlyn (SOC)	2,332	7.5
3	William Warfield Wilson (R)	13,977	53.5
	Dan Morgan Smith Jr. (D)	10,517	40.3
4	George P. Foster (D)	14,698	92.6
	F. Finsterbach (SOC)	850	5.4
5	James McAndrews (D)	12,346	88.7
	Jacob Winnen (SOC)	1,263	9.1
6	William Lorimer (R)	16,540	49.7
	Allan C. Durborow (D)	15,555	46.7
7	Philip Knopf (R)	18,167	51.1
	John M. Hess (D)	13,443	37.8
	James H. Bard (SOC)	3,471	9.8
8	William F. Mahoney (D)	19,688	90.6
	George D. Evans (SOC)	1,546	7.1
9	Henry Sherman Boutell (R)	15,857	50.8
	Lockwood Honore (D)	13,774	44.1
10	George Edmund Foss (R)	15,318	57.5
	John J. Philbin (D)	9,733	36.6
11	Howard M. Snapp (R)	20,549	64.1
	James O. Monroe (D)	9,968	31.1
12	Charles E. Fuller (R)	19,812	62.5
	Julian R. Steward (D)	9,356	29.5
	Frank S. Regan (P)	2,558	8.1
13	Robert R. Hitt (R)	19,229	65.5
	Louis Dickes (D)	9,401	32.0
14	Benjamin F. Marsh (R)	19,404	55.9
	John W. Lusk (D)	13,195	38.0
15	George W. Prince (R)	21,899	55.5
	Jonas W. Olson (D)	16,045	40.7

	Candidates	Votes	%
16	Joseph V. Graff (R)	19,360	54.5
	John M. Niehaus (D)	15,623	43.9
17	John A. Sterling (R)	18,331	54.4
	Z. F. Yost (D)	14,040	41.6
18	Joseph G. Cannon (R)	22,941	58.3
	Henry C. Bell (D)	15,254	38.8
19	Vespasian Warner (R)	24,155	53.3
	W. B. Hinds (D)	19,895	43.9
20	Henry T. Rainey (D)	20,165	56.5
	James H. Danskin (R)	14,889	41.7
21	Ben F. Caldwell (D)	20,774	54.0
	Leroy Anderson (R)	16,998	44.2
22	William A. Rodenberg (R)	21,101	52.6
	Fred J. Kern (D)	18,747	46.7
23	Joseph B. Crowley (D)	20,735	52.4
	Hiram Gilmore Vansandt (R)	17,557	44.4
24	James R. Williams (D)	17,971	49.5
	Pleasant T. Chapman (R)	17,719	48.8
25	George W. Smith (R)	18,743	51.9
	James Lingle (D)	16,444	45.5

INDIANA

	Candidates	Votes	%
1	James A. Hemenway (R)	21,524	52.0
	John W. Spencer (D)	17,833	43.1
2	Robert W. Miers (D)	21,162	49.5
	John C. Chaney (R)	20,423	47.7
3	William T. Zenor (D)	20,740	54.6
	Edmund A. Maginness (R)	16,784	44.2
4	Francis M. Griffith (D)	21,751	52.0
	Joshua M. Spencer (R)	18,894	45.2
5	Elias S. Holliday (R)	23,795	50.3
	John A. Wiltermood (D)	21,562	45.6
6	James E. Watson (R)	23,641	52.9
	James T. Arbuckle (D)	19,535	43.7
7	Jesse Overstreet (R)	25,191	52.0
	Jacob P. Dunn (D)	20,933	43.2
8	George W. Cromer (R)	25,842	52.0
	James Edward Truesdale (D)	21,474	43.2
9	Charles B. Landis (R)	25,824	51.0
	Lex J. Kirkpatrick (D)	23,317	46.0
10	Edgar D. Crumpacker (R)	26,016	56.4
	William Guthrie (D)	19,428	42.1
11	Frederick K. Landis (R)	24,390	52.6
	John C. Nelson (D)	19,596	42.3
	Bennet L. Shugart (P)	2,344	5.1
12	James M. Robinson (D)	19,320	48.1
	Clarence C. Gilhams (R)	19,035	47.4
13	Abraham L. Brick (R)	24,206	50.3
	Frank E. Hering (D)	22,289	46.3

IOWA

	Candidates	Votes	%
1	Thomas Hedge (R)	15,266	51.7
	John E. Craig (D)	13,343	45.2
2	Martin J. Wade (D)	19,825	49.6
	William Hoffman (R)	18,667	46.7
3	Benjamin P. Birdsall (R)	22,300	54.5
	Horace Boise (D)	16,761	40.9
4	Gilbert N. Haugen (R)	19,303	56.1
	A. L. Sortor Jr. (D)	14,280	41.5
5	Robert G. Cousins (R)	19,516	56.5
	Anthony P. Daly (D)	13,733	39.8
6	John F. Lacey (R)	18,828	51.2
	John P. Reese (D)	17,015	46.2
7	John A. T. Hull (R)	19,037	61.6
	Parley Sheldon (D)	9,914	32.1
8	William P. Hepburn (R)	21,657	59.4
	F. M. Stuart (D)	14,796	40.6
9	Walter I. Smith (R)	20,997	59.6
	George W. Cullison (D)	13,639	38.7
10	James P. Connor (R)	25,596	64.1
	Kasper Faltison (D)	12,822	32.1
11	Lot Thomas (R)	21,854	62.4
	James M. Parsons (D)	12,721	36.3

KANSAS

	Candidates	Votes	%
1	Charles Curtis (R)	23,954	62.8
	John E. Wagner (D)	13,774	36.1
2	Justin D. Bowersock (R)	23,608	54.2
	Noah Bowman (D)	19,250	44.2
3	Philip P. Campbell (R)	22,753	53.7
	Alfred M. Jackson (D)	18,690	44.1
4	James M. Miller (R)	20,799	58.7
	Thomas H. Grisham (D)	14,361	40.5
5	William A. Calderhead (R)	18,921	56.5
	Andrew Sherer (D)	13,930	41.6
6	William A. Reeder (R)	18,307	53.2
	C. M. Cole (D)	15,832	46.0
7	Chester I. Long (R)	30,123*	56.8
	Vernon J. Rose (D)	22,300	42.1
AL	Charles F. Scott (R)	158,307	56.1
	J. D. Botkin (D)	115,342	40.9

KENTUCKY

	Candidates	Votes	%
1	Ollie M. James (D)	12,731	66.4
	C. H. Linn (R)	5,469	28.5
2	Augustus O. Stanley (D)	15,522	52.3
	R. W. Slack (R)	13,675	46.1
3	John S. Rhea (D)	16,820	50.7
	J. McKenzie Moss (R)	16,056	48.4
4	David H. Smith (D)	14,054	93.1
	J. A. Barret (P)	881	5.8
5	J. Swagar Sherley (D)	17,896	50.0
	Harvey S. Irwin (R)	15,892	44.4
6	Daniel Linn Gooch (D)	12,978	50.8
	Applegate (R)	10,370	40.6
	Breill (SOC)	1,683	6.6
7	South Trimble (D)	12,093	59.9
	W. L. Cannon (R)	7,639	37.8
8	George G. Gilbert (D)	13,531	53.2
	Lawson Sumrall (R)	11,458	45.1
9	James N. Kehoe (D)	20,823	52.4
	W. H. Castner (R)	18,493	46.6
10	Frank A. Hopkins (D)	15,947	55.7
	John G. White (R)	12,458	43.5
11	Vincent Boreing (R)	13,443	69.2
	J.P. Harrison (D)	5,076	26.1

LOUISIANA

	Candidates	Votes	%
1	Adolph Meyer (D)	3,910	81.9
	Oliver S. Livaudais (R)	866	18.1
2	Robert C. Davey (D)	5,014	85.2
	Robert E. Lee (R)	868	14.8
3	Robert F. Broussard (D)	2,725	79.4
	William E. Howell (R)	707	20.6
4	Phanor Breazeale (D)	2,567	94.3
	S. M. Thomas (R)	156	5.7
5	Joseph E. Ransdell (D)	2,645	91.9
	Henry B. Taliaferro (R)	232	8.1
6	Samuel M. Robertson (D)	2,124	75.9
	Clarence S. Hebert (R)	673	24.1
7	Arsene P. Pujo (D)	3,233	85.6
	Gilbert L. Dupre (R)	545	14.4

MAINE

	Candidates	Votes	%
1	Amos L. Allen (R)	16,232	58.2
	Seth C. Gordon (D)	11,097	39.8
2	Charles E. Littlefield (R)	17,297	58.1
	Horatio G. Foss (D)	11,739	39.5
3	Edwin C. Burleigh (R)	15,613	64.3
	E. N. Benson (D)	8,032	33.1
4	Llewellyn Powers (R)	16,349	64.6
	Thomas White (D)	7,763	30.7

MARYLAND

	Candidates	Votes	%
1	William H. Jackson (R)	17,968	50.6
	James E. Ellegood (D)	16,179	45.5
2	J. Fred. C. Talbott (D)	16,971	50.8
	William T. Page (R)	15,422	46.2
3	Frank C. Wachter (R)	15,214	48.8

	Candidates	Votes	%
	Lee S. Meyer (D)	15,031	48.2
4	James W. Denny (D)	16,105	50.0
	Charles R. Schirm (R)	15,519	48.1
5	Sydney E. Mudd (R)	17,621	56.9
	B. H. Camalier (D)	12,781	41.3
6	George A. Pearre (R)	18,310	54.1
	C. F. Kenneweg (D)	14,479	42.8

MASSACHUSETTS

	Candidates	Votes	%
1	George P. Lawrence (R)	14,093	54.0
	Henry M. Fern (D)	9,949	38.1
2	Frederick H. Gillett (R)	14,067	58.1
	Arthur F. Nutting (D)	6,998	28.9
	George H. Wrenn (SOC)	2,779	11.5
3	John R. Thayer (D)	14,382	49.1
	Rufus B. Dodge (R)	13,602	46.4
4	Charles Q. Tirrell (R)	15,660	53.4
	Marcus A. Coolidge (D)	10,564	36.0
	John F. Mullen (SOC)	2,739	9.3
5	Butler Ames (R)	13,648	48.4
	John T. Sparks (D)	12,765	45.3
6	Augustus P. Gardner (R)	16,164	51.4
	Samuel Roads Jr. (D)	12,246	39.0
	George E. Littlefield (SOC)	2,679	8.5
7	Ernest W. Roberts (R)	15,728	54.3
	Arthur Lyman (D)	9,034	31.2
	William B. Turner (SOC)	2,811	9.7
8	Samuel W. McCall (R)	15,077	57.6
	Grenville S. MacFarland (D)	8,872	33.9
	Charles W. White (SOC)	1,634	6.2
9	John A. Keliher (D CIT)	10,352	38.1
	Joseph A. Conry (DN)	10,099	37.2
	Charles T. Witt (R)	5,108	18.8
	James J. McVey (SOC)	1,581	5.8
10	William S. McNary (D)	17,569	54.1
	William W. Towle (R)	11,374	35.1
	John Weaver Sherman (SOC)	3,506	10.8
11	John A. Sullivan (D)	16,333	49.4
	Eugene N. Foss (R)	14,467	43.8
	George G. Cutting (SOC)	2,230	6.8
12	Samuel L. Powers (R)	14,807	52.6
	Frederic J. Stimson (D)	10,303	36.6
	J. Frank Hayward (SOC)	2,683	9.5
13	William S. Greene (R)	13,565	67.9
	Charles T. Luce (D)	5,241	26.2
	Elijah Humphries (P)	1,178	5.9
14	William C. Lovering (R)	14,410	57.3
	Charles A. Gilday (D)	5,447	21.7
	Isaac W. Skinner (SOC)	4,300	17.1

Special Elections

	Candidates	Votes	%
6	Augustus P. Gardner (R)	15,561	52.1
	Samuel Roads Jr. (D)	11,348	38.0
	George E. Littlefield (SOC)	2,606	8.7

MICHIGAN

	Candidates	Votes	%
1	Alfred Lucking (D)	20,009	53.6
	John B. Corliss (R)	16,743	44.9
2	Charles E. Townsend (R)	22,198	53.3
	Frederick B. Wood (D)	18,390	44.2
3	Washington Gardner (R)	19,741	56.7
	Warner J. Sampson (D)	13,900	40.0
4	Edward L. Hamilton (R)	20,617	57.1
	Thomas O'Hara (D)	15,368	42.5
5	William Alden Smith (R)	19,040	60.2
	Myron H. Walker (D)	11,525	36.5
6	Samuel W. Smith (R)	23,869	56.3
	William H. S. Wood (D)	18,300	43.2
7	Henry McMorran (R)	17,830	57.3
	Martin Crocker (D)	12,481	40.1
8	Joseph W. Fordney (R)	17,392	56.7
	Henry M. Youmans (D)	11,389	37.1
9	Roswell P. Bishop (R)	14,502	66.0
	Daniel W. Goodenough (D)	6,166	28.1
10	George A. Loud (R)	17,069	57.9
	Michael O'Brien (D)	11,846	40.2

	Candidates	Votes	%
11	Archibald B. Darragh (R)	18,174	69.7
	David J. Erwin (D)	7,891	30.3
12	H. Olin Young (R)	21,224	71.5
	John Power (D)	8,467	28.5

MINNESOTA

	Candidates	Votes	%
1	James A. Tawney (R)	19,561	60.9
	McGovern (D)	12,545	39.1
2	James T. McCleary (R)	16,100	63.4
	Andrews (D)	9,316	36.7
3	Charles R. Davis (R)	16,700	58.9
	Kolars (D)	10,996	38.8
4	Frederick C. Stevens (R)	17,404	60.4
	Gieske (D)	11,412	39.6
5	John Lind (D)	19,863	51.3
	Fletcher (R)	17,809	46.0
6	Clarence B. Buckman (R)	17,894	56.6
	Dubois (D)	13,705	43.4
7	Andrew J. Volstead (R)	20,826	78.6
	Forsberg (PP)	5,397	20.4
8	J. Adam Bede (R)	14,613	60.8
	Fay (D)	8,882	37.0
9	Halvor Steenerson (R)	18,055	61.4
	Moen (PP)	6,784	23.1
	McKinnon (D)	4,572	15.6

MISSISSIPPI

	Candidates	Votes	%
1	Ezekiel S. Candler Jr. (D)	3,245	100.0
2	Thomas Spight (D)	2,523	100.0
3	Benjamin G. Humphreys (D)	1,146	100.0
4	Wilson S. Hill (D)	2,834	100.0
5	Adam M. Byrd (D)	3,081	100.0
6	Eaton J. Bowers (D)	1,774	100.0
7	Frank A. McLain (D)	2,022	100.0
8	John Sharp Williams (D)	1,433	100.0

MISSOURI

	Candidates	Votes	%
1	James T. Lloyd (D)	16,972	56.2
	Robison (R)	13,179	43.6
2	William W. Rucker (D)	18,045	57.6
	Schmitz (R)	13,293	42.4
3	John Dougherty (D)	17,270	54.2
	Ward (R)	14,618	45.8
4	Charles F. Cochran (D)	18,392	55.9
	Gilmer (R)	14,510	44.1
5	William S. Cowherd (D)	20,628	58.1
	Vanhorn (R)	14,393	40.6
6	David A. De Armond (D)	15,639	54.3
	Shafer (R)	13,124	45.6
7	Courtney W. Hamlin (D)	19,277	52.7
	Peale (R)	17,250	47.7
8	Dorsey W. Shackleford (D)	14,465	52.4
	Enloe (R)	13,133	47.6
9	James Beauchamp Clark (D)	18,591	55.7
	Tubbs (R)	14,770	44.3
10	Richard Bartholdt (R)	21,516	55.1
	Blow (D)	15,262	39.1
11	John T. Hunt (D)	14,913	57.5
	Charles F. Joy (R)	10,077	38.9
12	James J. Butler (D)	15,316	62.5
	Reynolds (R)	8,698	35.5
13	Edward Robb (D)	15,442	52.8
	Raney (R)	13,793	47.2
14	Willard D. Vandiver (D)	19,868	54.1
	Kinsalving (R)	16,788	45.7
15	Maecenas E. Benton (D)	20,038	51.0
	Lacaff (R)	18,511	47.1
16	J. Robert Lamar (D)	14,102	52.0
	Russell (R)	12,996	47.9

MONTANA

	Candidates	Votes	%
AL	Joseph M. Dixon (R)	24,626	46.2
	John M. Evans (D)	19,560	36.7
	Martin Dee (LAB&POP)	6,005	11.3
	George B. Sproule (SOC)	3,131	5.9

NEBRASKA

	Candidates	Votes	%
1	Elmer J. Burkett (R)	16,534	56.9
	Howard H. Hanks (FUS)	11,603	39.9
2	Gilbert M. Hitchcock (FUS)	13,509	50.9
	David H. Mercer (R)	11,669	43.9
	Bernard McCaffery (SOC)	1,379	5.2
3	John J. McCarthy (R)	19,201	50.0
	John S. Robinson (FUS)	18,541	48.3
4	Edmund H. Hinshaw (R)	19,337	52.4
	William L. Stark (FUS)	16,838	45.6
5	George W. Norris (R)	14,927	49.5
	A. C. Shallenberger (FUS)	14,746	48.9
6	Moses P. Kinkaid (R)	16,699	52.5
	Patrick H. Barry (FUS)	13,997	44.0

NEVADA

	Candidates	Votes	%
AL	Clarence D. Van Duzer (D SIL)	5,848	53.6
	E. S. Farrington (R)	5,073	46.5

NEW HAMPSHIRE

	Candidates	Votes	%
1	Cyrus A. Sulloway (R)	22,491	58.0
	Albert S. Langley (D)	15,218	39.2
2	Frank D. Currier (R)	22,138	58.0
	George E. Bales (D)	14,986	39.2

NEW JERSEY

	Candidates	Votes	%
1	Henry C. Loudenslager (R)	20,371	55.4
	Richard T. Miller (D)	15,279	41.6
2	John J. Gardner (R)	19,966	62.5
	Thomas A. Gash (D)	9,465	29.6
	Marion R. Owen (P)	2,323	7.3
3	Benjamin F. Howell (R)	20,014	51.4
	Jacob A. Geisenhainer (D)	18,345	47.2
4	William M. Lanning (R)	18,972	51.4
	Lewis Perrine (D)	16,966	46.0
5	Charles N. Fowler (R)	21,030	49.6
	Dewitt C. Flanagan (D)	19,881	46.8
6	William Hughes (D)	24,084	52.4
	William Barbour (R)	20,236	44.0
7	Richard Wayne Parker (R)	19,878	56.6
	George A. Miller (D)	14,371	40.9
8	William H. Wiley (R)	18,814	59.3
	Henry G. Atwater (D)	12,005	37.8
9	Allan Benny (D)	14,492	49.1
	Robert Carey (R)	13,700	46.4
10	Allan L. McDermott (D)	19,311	61.6
	James D. Manning (R)	10,595	33.8

NEW YORK

	Candidates	Votes	%
1	Townsend Scudder (D)	17,788	49.8
	Frederic Storm (R)	17,681	49.5
2	George H. Lindsay (D)	18,728	61.9
	James R. Howe (R)	9,593	31.7
3	Charles T. Dunwell (R)	17,457	48.3
	Hugh E. Rogers (D)	17,043	47.2
4	Frank E. Wilson (D)	16,415	50.9
	William Schnitzpan (R)	13,695	42.5
5	Edward M. Bassett (D)	16,149	48.8
	Harry A. Hanbury (R)	15,216	46.0
6	Robert Baker (D)	17,886	49.5
	Henry Bristow (R)	17,420	48.2
7	John J. Fitzgerald (D)	23,112	67.5
	James T. Williamson (R)	10,432	30.5
8	Timothy D. Sullivan (D)	26,101	69.4
	Montague Lessler (R)	10,386	27.6
9	Henry M. Goldfogle (D)	7,739	55.6
	Charles S. Adler (R)	4,235	30.5
	Alexander Jonas (SOCIAL D)	1,355	9.7
10	William Sulzer (D)	15,451	62.2
	William Blau (R)	6,088	24.5
	H. G. Wilshire (SOCIAL D)	1,873	7.5
	James T. Hunter (SOC LAB)	1,391	5.6
11	William Randolph Hearst (D)	26,953	69.1

	Candidates	Votes	%
	Henry Birrell (R)	10,841	27.8
12	George B. McClellan (D)	21,275	71.1
	Charles Thongood (R)	7,039	23.5
13	Francis Burton Harrison (D)	15,524	51.7
	James W. Perry (R)	13,987	46.5
14	Ira Edgar Rider (D)	20,402	63.7
	Andrew J. Anderson (R)	8,492	26.5
	William Ehret (SOCIAL D)	2,348	7.3
15	William H. Douglass (R)	12,575	49.8
	Henry B. Martin (D)	12,161	48.2
16	Jacob Ruppert Jr (D)	15,657	62.5
	William R. Spooner (R)	7,485	29.9
17	Frank E. Shober (D)	19,248	50.6
	Harvey T. Andrews (R)	17,731	46.6
18	Joseph A. Goulden (D)	28,411	61.8
	Frank C. Schaeffler (R)	14,844	32.3
19	Norton P. Otis (R)	17,878	48.7
	Cornelius A. Pugsley (D)	17,338	47.2
20	Thomas W. Bradley (R)	19,747	55.5
	Theodore H. Babcock (D)	14,874	41.8
21	John H. Ketcham (R)	22,363	57.3
	Curtis F. Hoag (D)	15,777	40.4
22	William H. Draper (R)	21,689	57.5
	John H. Morrison (D)	15,698	41.6
23	George N. Southwick (R)	28,858	55.2
	B. Cleveland Sloan (D)	22,459	42.9
24	George J. Smith (R)	26,842	55.8
	Clifford Champion (D)	20,045	41.7
25	Lucius N. Littauer (R)	23,018	55.1
	Frank Beebe (D)	18,132	43.4
26	William H. Flack (R)	27,816	70.8
	Henry Holland (D)	10,392	26.4
27	James S. Sherman (R)	21,743	52.4
	Edward Lewis (D)	18,497	44.5
28	Charles L. Knapp (R)	23,196	58.9
	C. Frank Smith (D)	14,883	37.8
29	Michael E. Driscoll (R)	27,023	60.1
	Martin F. Dillon (D)	16,330	36.3
30	John W. Dwight (R)	28,211	62.2
	Charles D. Pratt (D)	17,176	37.8
31	Sereno E. Payne (R)	24,130	60.1
	Harry B. Harpending (D)	14,833	37.0
32	James Breck Perkins (R)	22,119	52.5
	William Degraff (D)	15,933	37.8
	Charles R. Bach (SOCIAL D)	2,249	5.3
33	Charles W. Gillet (R)	21,587	54.5
	Frank P. Frost (D)	16,494	41.7
34	James W. Wadsworth (R)	26,007	56.2
	Dean F. Currie (D)	18,787	40.6
35	William H. Ryan (D)	19,884	55.3
	John M. Farquhar (R)	14,715	40.9
36	De Alva S. Alexander (R)	21,525	55.9
	Ole L. Snyder (D)	16,016	41.6
37	Edward B. Vreeland (R)	27,579	67.8
	George J. Ball (D)	11,470	28.2

NORTH CAROLINA

	Candidates	Votes	%
1	John H. Small (D)	14,086	88.5
	H. E. Hodges (R)	1,834	11.5
2	Claude Kitchin (D)	12,705	99.0
3	Charles R. Thomas (D)	11,198	71.0
	G. E. Butler (R)	4,567	29.0
4	Edward W. Pou (D)	13,799	82.7
	John W. Atwater	2,105	12.6
5	William W. Kitchin (D)	17,900	65.3
	J. L. Patterson (R)	9,511	34.7
6	Gilbert B. Patterson (D)	9,901	69.1
	Albert H. Slocumb (R)	4,430	30.9
7	Robert N. Page (D)	13,269	83.5
	E. H. Morris (R)	2,482	15.6
8	Theodore F. Kluttz (D)	15,632	52.4
	E. S. Blackburn (R)	14,158	47.4
9	Edwin Y. Webb (D)	14,087	61.6
	G. B. Hiss (R)	8,778	38.4
10	James M. Gudger Jr. (D)	12,700	50.4
	James M. Moody (R)	12,517	49.6

NORTH DAKOTA

	Candidates	Votes	%
AL	Thomas F. Marshall (R)	32,976✓	
	Burleigh F. Spalding (R)	32,854✓	
	Ueland (D)	14,775	
	Lovell (D)	14,392	
	King (SOC)	1,195	

OHIO

	Candidates	Votes	%
1	Nicholas Longworth (R)	24,082	67.9
	Thomas Bentham (D)	9,471	26.7
2	Herman P. Goebel (R)	24,274	61.8
	Harry C. Busch (D)	12,095	30.8
	William R. Fox (SOC)	2,681	6.8
3	Robert M. Nevin (R)	25,406	52.8
	Thomas A. Selz (D)	19,551	40.6
4	Harvey C. Garber (D)	18,342	54.5
	Lewis H. Rogers (R)	14,879	44.2
5	John S. Snook (D)	19,086	53.6
	George Russell (R)	16,548	46.4
6	Charles Q. Hildebrant (R)	19,609	55.1
	William G. Thompson (D)	15,188	42.6
7	Thomas B. Kyle (R)	18,381	55.0
	Chester Bryan (D)	13,994	41.9
8	William R. Warnock (R)	22,177	55.9
	William R. Niven (D)	16,643	42.0
9	James H. Southard (R)	23,815	56.6
	Charles I. York (D)	15,873	37.7
10	Stephen Morgan (R)	21,593	59.6
	C. E. Belcher (D)	14,118	39.0
11	Charles H. Grosvenor (R)	23,124	53.7
	Edward I. Lawrence (D)	19,487	45.3
12	De Witt C. Badger (D)	18,569	50.4
	Cyrus Huling (R)	17,793	48.3
13	Amos H. Jackson (R)	22,496	49.4
	James A. Norton (D)	22,169	48.7
14	William W. Skiles (R)	22,365	54.9
	George B. Neal (D)	17,615	43.2
15	Henry C. Van Voorhis (R)	17,462	49.3
	Ernest B. Schneider (D)	16,850	47.6
16	Joseph J. Gill (R)	16,129	56.9
	Joseph V. Lawler (D)	11,501	40.6
17	John W. Cassingham (D)	19,753	52.9
	W. B. Stevens (R)	17,563	47.1
18	James Kennedy (R)	22,461	53.8
	William J. Foley (D)	10,502	25.1
	Thomas J. Duffy (LAB)	7,923	19.0
19	Charles Dick (R)	24,732	62.0
	Oliver D. Everhard (D)	13,261	33.3
20	Jacob A. Beidler (R)	20,523	52.4
	Charles A. Kohl (D)	16,885	43.1
21	Theodore E. Burton (R)	24,353	57.0
	Edmund G. Vail (D)	16,805	39.3

OREGON

	Candidates	Votes	%
1	Thomas H. Tongue (R)	23,585*	52.9
	J. K. Weatherford (D)	16,213	36.4
	B. F. Ramp (SOC)	2,576	5.8
2	John N. Williamson (R)	23,397	53.5
	W. F. Butcher (D)	15,598	35.7
	Diedrich T. Gerdes (SOC)	2,753	6.3

PENNSYLVANIA

	Candidates	Votes	%
1	Henry H. Bingham (R, UN)	32,119	100.0
2	Robert Adams Jr. (R, UN)	35,274	99.4
3	Henry Burk (R, UN)	36,911	98.8
4	Robert H. Foerderer (R, UN)	21,094	98.3
5	Edward de V. Morrell (R, UN)	25,358	98.9
6	George D. McCreary (R, BALLOT)	30,626	98.4
7	Thomas S. Butler (R)	20,062	65.4
	Frank B. Rhodes (D)	9,751	31.8
8	Irving P. Wanger (R, BALLOT)	22,689	52.0
	Charles E. Ingersoll (D)	20,080	46.1
9	Henry B. Cassel (R)	18,287	69.7
	James F. McCoy (D)	7,036	26.8

Candidates	Votes	%
10 George Howell (A-MACH)	13,600‡	48.4
William Connell (R, BALLOT)	13,139	46.8
11 Henry W. Palmer (R, P)	16,787	48.3
T. R. Martin (D, WMP/L)	14,091	40.5
C. F. Quinn (SOC)	3,911	11.2
12 George R. Patterson (R)	14,151	49.2
James W. Ryan (D)	12,402	43.1
Thomas J. Lannon (SOC)	1,928	6.7
13 Marcus C. L. Kline (D)	24,771	54.1
William H. Sowden (R)	19,772	43.2
14 Charles F. Wright (R)	14,401	54.9
James West (D)	10,727	40.9
15 Elias Deemer (R)	17,518	52.4
James Mansel (D, P)	15,012	44.9
16 Charles H. Dickerman (D)	14,019	50.3
Fred A. Godcharles (R)	13,171	47.2
17 Thaddeus M. Mahon (R)	21,197	55.9
Harry I. Huber (D)	16,740	44.1
18 Marlin E. Olmsted (R)	22,193	59.7
Benjamin L. Forster (D)	13,715	36.9
19 Alvin Evans (R)	20,814	56.8
Robert E. Creswell (D)	15,690	42.8
20 Daniel F. Lafean (R)	15,553	50.5
William McClean (D)	14,962	48.5
21 Solomon R. Dresser (R)	16,722	53.5
Delos Eugene Hibner (D)	13,243	42.4
22 George F. Huff (R)	18,827	57.7
Charles M. Heineman (D)	13,014	39.9
23 Allen F. Cooper (R)	15,546	51.1
Orram W. Kennedy (D)	13,791	45.3
24 E. F. Acheson (REG)	15,147	55.1
Charles R. Eckert (D)	9,974	36.3
25 A. L. Bates (R)	15,538	52.4
A. B. Osborne (D)	11,311	38.1
Faye B. Ocamb (SOC)	1,639	5.5
26 Joseph H. Shull (D)	15,765	53.3
Fred Nesbit (R)	11,599	39.2
James Hughes (SOC)	1,671	5.7
27 William O. Smith (R)	16,018	57.9
Alfred W. Smiley (D)	10,618	38.4
28 Joseph C. Sibley (R)	17,616	52.5
James B. Watson (D)	12,889	38.4
Richard A. Buzza (P)	3,042	9.1
29 George Shiras III (D & CIT)	14,553	49.4
William H. Graham (R)	14,535	49.4
30 John Dalzell (R)	19,085	95.1
31 H. Kirke Porter (D & CIT)	16,241	52.6
James F. Burke (R)	14,532	47.1
32 James W. Brown (D & CIT)	14,517	50.8
A. J. Barchfeld (R)	13,471	47.1

Special Elections

17 Alexander Billmeyer (D)	14,658	54.7
William K. Lord (R)	12,143	45.3

RHODE ISLAND

1 Daniel L. D. Granger (D)	15,198	49.0
Melville Bull (R)	14,535	46.9
2 Adin B. Capron (R)	13,680	50.2
Unidentified Candidate (D)	12,657	46.5

SOUTH CAROLINA

1 George S. Legare (D)	3,749	95.5
2 George W. Croft (D)	5,134	95.3
3 Wyatt Aiken (D)	5,082	98.9
4 Joseph T. Johnson (D)	4,642	98.7
5 David E. Finley (D)	4,535	99.3
6 Robert B. Scarborough (D)	3,981	100.0
7 Asbury F. Lever (D)	4,220	96.2

SOUTH DAKOTA

AL Eben W. Martin (R)	48,454✓	
Charles H. Burke (R)	48,310✓	
Wilson (D)	21,113	
Robinson (D)	20,814	
Knowles (SOC)	2,738	
Price (SOC)	2,578	

Candidates	Votes	%
Kelley (P)	2,319	
Smith (P)	2,252	

TENNESSEE

1 Walter P. Brownlow (R)	15,373	61.2
Lyle (D)	9,751	38.8
2 Henry R. Gibson (R)	11,993	55.5
Hannah (D)	9,636	44.6
3 John A. Moon (D)	14,152	97.6
4 Morgan C. Fitzpatrick (D)	11,509	64.9
West (R)	6,228	35.1
5 James D. Richardson (D)	10,314	76.8
Parker (R)	3,113	23.2
6 John W. Gaines (D)	9,422	82.3
Tillman (R)	2,025	17.7
7 Lemuel P. Padgett (D)	9,470	75.3
Gregory (R)	3,106	24.7
8 Thetus W. Sims (D)	9,293	52.8
Davis (R)	8,317	47.2
9 Rice A. Pierce (D)	7,371	82.5
Kellar (R)	1,567	17.5
10 Malcolm R. Patterson (D)	7,869	83.2
Phelan (R)	1,500	15.9

TEXAS

1 Morris Sheppard (D)	19,214	83.2
John Hurley (R)	3,875	16.8
2 Samuel B. Cooper (D)	17,165	86.7
Warren McDaniel (R)	2,632	13.3
3 Gordon J. Russell (D)	16,628	95.0
4 Choice B. Randell (D)	17,464	85.1
C. A. Gray (R)	3,063	14.9
5 Jack Beall (D)	16,310	88.4
S. H. Lumpkin (R)	1,633	8.9
6 Scott Field (D)	16,753	100.0
7 Alexander W. Gregg (D)	13,162	100.0
8 Thomas H. Ball (D)	14,301	68.0
Lock McDaniel (R)	6,431	30.6
9 George F. Burgess (D)	18,316	61.3
B. R. Burow (R)	11,574	38.7
10 Albert S. Burleson (D)	20,539	87.2
Charles Schenken (R)	2,990	12.7
11 Robert L. Henry (D)	14,548	94.2
12 Oscar W. Gillespie (D)	16,220	82.6
S. A. Greenwell (R)	3,424	17.4
13 John A. Stephens (D)	24,027	91.8
R. O. Rector (R)	2,034	7.8
14 James L. Slayden (D)	19,889	78.4
D. H. Meek (R)	4,915	19.4
15 John N. Garner (D)	16,542	60.6
John C. Scott (R)	10,707	39.2
16 William R. Smith (D)	22,118	88.0
D. G. Hunt (R)	2,911	11.6

Special Elections

1 Morris Sheppard (D)	8,972	86.1
Frank Lee	1,426	13.7
14 Gordon Russell (D)	13,710	100.0

UTAH

AL Joseph Howell (R)	43,710	51.5
William H. King (D)	38,196	45.0

VERMONT

1 David J. Foster (R)	16,007	75.2
J. Walter Lyons (D)	4,394	20.6
2 Kittredge Haskins (R)	17,532	76.8
Harris Miller (D)	4,150	18.2

VIRGINIA

1 William A. Jones (D)	7,381	72.8
Malcolm A. Coles (R)	2,762	27.2
2 Harry L. Maynard (D)	9,746	75.9
Robert M. Hughes (R)	2,917	22.7
3 John Lamb (D)	5,300	81.1
B. W. Edwards (R)	969	14.8

Candidates	Votes	%
4 Robert G. Southall (D)	5,717	90.0
R. T. Vaughan	507	8.0
5 Claude A. Swanson (D)	10,363	60.8
Beverly A. Davis (R)	6,414	37.6
6 Carter Glass (D)	6,345	79.4
Aaron Graham (P)	1,418	17.8
7 James Hay (D)	8,461	64.7
S. J. Hoffman (R)	4,620	35.3
8 John F. Rixey (D)	6,618	76.7
W. K. Skinker (R)	2,011	23.3
9 Campbell Slemp (R)	13,694	50.4
William F. Rhea (D)	13,476	49.6
10 Henry D. Flood (D)	9,119	68.3
James Lyons	4,235	31.7

Special Elections

6 Carter Glass (D)	6,556	95.4

WASHINGTON

AL Francis W. Cushman (R)	58,453✓	
Wesley L. Jones (R)	58,193✓	
William L. Humphrey (R)	57,435✓	
George F. Cotterill (D)	33,435	
Frank B. Cole (D)	32,406	
O. R. Holcomb (D)	31,497	
George W. Scott (SOC)	4,612	
D. Burgess (SOC)	4,585	
J. H. C. Scurlock (SOC)	4,546	
O. L. Fowler (P)	1,732	
W. J. McKean (P)	1,725	
A. H. Sherwood (P)	1,708	
William McCormick (SOC LAB)	817	
Jense C. Martin (SOC LAB)	808	
Hans P. Jorgensen (SOC LAB)	801	

WEST VIRGINIA

1 Blackburn B. Dovener (R)	19,962	52.1
Owen S. McKinney (D)	16,922	44.1
2 Alston G. Dayton (R)	20,968	50.9
John T. McGraw (D)	19,628	47.6
3 Joseph Holt Gaines (R)	19,014	51.7
James H. Miller (D)	17,215	46.8
4 Harry C. Woodyard (R)	19,158	52.0
W. N. Chancellor (D)	16,968	46.1
5 James A. Hughes (R)	20,164	53.3
David E. Johnson (D)	17,617	46.6

WISCONSIN

1 Henry Allen Cooper (R)	20,437	60.7
Lewis C. Baker (D)	12,122	36.0
2 Henry C. Adams (R)	17,519	52.8
John J. Wood Jr (D)	14,483	43.6
3 Joseph W. Babcock (R)	19,405	60.8
Jackson Silbaugh (D)	11,155	35.0
4 Theobald Otjen (R)	15,101	44.1
John F. Donovan (D)	13,468	39.3
Herman W. Bisborins (SOCIAL D)	5,167	15.1
5 William H. Stafford (R)	14,971	45.8
Henry Smith (D)	10,971	33.6
H. C. Berger (SOCIAL D)	6,060	18.6
6 Charles H. Weisse (D)	17,991	52.2
William H. Froehlich (R)	14,575	42.3
7 John J. Esch (R)	18,694	64.6
William Cernahan (D)	9,343	32.3
8 James H. Davidson (R)	19,553	57.8
T. H. Patterson (D)	12,651	37.4
9 Edward S. Minor (R)	15,958	57.1
Edward Decker (D)	11,479	41.1
10 Webster E. Brown (R)	19,554	55.6
Burt Williams (D)	14,935	42.5
11 John J. Jenkins (R)	19,329	67.4
Joseph A. Rene (D)	8,261	28.8

WYOMING

AL Frank W. Mondell (R)	15,808	64.0
Charles P. Clemmons (D)	8,892	36.0

1904 House Elections

ALABAMA

	Candidates	Votes	%
1	George W. Taylor (D)	7,686	100.0
2	Ariosto A. Wiley (D)	10,177	100.0
3	Henry D. Clayton (D)	9,566	98.3
4	Sydney J. Bowie (D)	7,087	76.3
	J. W. Kitchens (R)	2,201	23.7
5	J. Thomas Heflin (D)	10,105	76.3
	B. W. Walker (R)	3,095	23.4
6	John H. Bankhead (D)	8,873	76.6
	S. R. Crumpton (R)	2,718	23.5
7	John L. Burnett (D)	9,819	55.9
	T. W. Powell (R)	7,756	44.1
8	William Richardson (D)	9,898	84.3
	J. W. Roberts (R)	1,846	15.7
9	Oscar W. Underwood (D)	9,615	81.7
	J. T. Blakemore (R)	1,775	15.1

Special Election

5	J. Thomas Heflin (D)	4,065	99.7

ARKANSAS

1	Robert B. Macon (D)	14,391	99.3
2	Stephen Brundidge Jr. (D)	9,065	62.7
	F. W. Tucker (R)	5,388	37.3
3	John C. Floyd (D)	9,719	56.3
	J. F. Mayes (R)	7,547	43.7
4	John S. Little (D)	9,308	59.4
	James Brizzolara (R)	6,352	40.6
5	Charles C. Reid (D)	11,371	60.9
	A. S. Fowler (R)	7,288	39.1
6	Joseph T. Robinson (D)	9,459	62.0
	R. C. Thompson (R)	5,810	38.1
7	Robert Minor Wallace (D)	14,147	99.1

CALIFORNIA

1	James N. Gillett (R)	21,602	54.1
	A. Caminetti (D)	15,706	39.3
	A. J. Gaylord (SOC)	2,197	5.5
2	Duncan E. McKinlay (R)	22,873	49.2
	Theodore A. Bell (D)	21,640	46.6
3	Joseph R. Knowland (R)	24,637	68.6
	Henry C. McPike (D)	7,210	20.1
	M. Lesser (SOC)	3,617	10.1
4	Julius Kahn (R)	20,012	56.8
	Edward J. Livernash (D&UN LAB)	12,812	36.4
	William Costley (SOC)	2,267	6.4
5	E. A. Hayes (R)	23,701	52.3
	William J. Wynn (D)	18,025	39.8
6	James C. Needham (R)	18,828	55.1
	William M. Conley (D)	13,074	38.3
7	James McLachlan (R)	31,091	64.2
	W. O. Morton (D)	11,259	23.3
	F. I. Wheat (SOC)	3,594	7.4
	John Sobieski (P)	2,467	5.1
8	S. C. Smith (R)	23,683	55.6
	William T. Lucas (D)	12,861	30.2
	N. A. Richardson (SOC)	4,636	10.9

Special Election

3	Joseph R. Knowland (R)	24,564	77.5
	Henry C. McPike (D)	7,123	22.5

COLORADO

1	Robert W. Bonynge (R)	55,940	51.0
	Clay B. Whitford (D)	50,022	45.6
2	Herschel M. Hogg (R)	68,101	52.0
	Joseph H. Maupin (D)	58,554	44.7
AL	Franklin E. Brooks (R)	121,236	50.2
	John F. Shafroth (D)	112,373	46.5

CONNECTICUT

	Candidates	Votes	%
1	E. Stevens Henry (R)	26,363	56.9
	Morse (D)	18,218	39.3
2	Nehemiah D. Sperry (R)	36,832	56.9
	Fisk (D)	24,679	38.1
3	Frank B. Brandegee (R)	15,541	60.2
	Tanner (D)	9,718	37.7
4	Ebenezer J. Hill (R)	31,822	59.1
	Hallen (D)	20,760	38.6
AL	George L. Lilley (R)	108,918	57.1
	Kennedy (D)	75,212	39.4

DELAWARE

AL	Hiram R. Burton (R)	23,512	53.7
	Edward D. Hearne (D)	19,552	44.6

FLORIDA

1	Stephen M. Sparkman (D)	8,418	75.1
	E. R. Gunby (R)	2,257	20.1
2	Frank Clark (D)	10,711	77.2
	J. M. Cheney (R)	2,767	19.9
3	William B. Lamar (D)	6,463	84.3
	L. M. Ware (R)	986	12.9

GEORGIA

1	Rufus E. Lester (D)	7,246	94.9
2	James M. Griggs (D)	8,034	99.9
3	Elijah B. Lewis (D)	6,908	99.0
4	William C. Adamson (D)	7,850	91.6
	J. F. Jones (R)	722	8.4
5	Leonidas F. Livingston (D)	9,387	71.4
	C. P. Goree (R)	3,760	28.6
6	Charles L. Bartlett (D)	7,197	96.4
7	Gordon Lee (D)	10,350	69.2
	T. Pickett (D)	4,606	30.8
8	William M. Howard (D)	7,616	88.9
	W. M. Hairston (POP)	877	10.2
9	Thomas M. Bell (D)	12,813	68.1
	James Finley (R)	6,000	31.9
10	Thomas W. Hardwick (D)	8,606	91.6
	H. M. Porter (POP)	788	8.4
11	William G. Brantley (D)	9,970	77.3
	A. B. Finley (R)	2,921	22.7

IDAHO

AL	Burton L. French (R)	44,813	63.7
	Benjamin F. Clay (D)	20,146	28.6
	John H. Morrison (SOC)	4,209	6.0

ILLINOIS

1	Martin B. Madden (R)	24,097	58.0
	John S. Oehmen (D)	9,166	22.1
	David S. Geer (IR)	5,175	12.5
	Edward Loewenthal (SOC)	2,334	5.6
2	James R. Mann (R)	29,010	66.3
	Charles B. Stafford (D)	9,221	21.1
	H. Van Middlesworth (SOC)	4,817	11.0
3	William W. Wilson (R)	22,709	61.7
	Willis C. Stone (D)	8,749	23.8
	Edward Dierkes (SOC)	4,476	12.2
4	Charles S. Wharton (R)	13,481	45.2
	George P. Foster (D)	9,947	33.4
	James W. Johnson (SOC)	5,944	20.0
5	Anthony Michalek (R)	12,904	44.9
	Charles J. Vopicka (D)	12,019	41.9
	Robert W. Schoening (SOC)	3,480	12.1
6	William Lorimer (R)	21,824	50.8
	George P. Gubbins (D)	12,309	28.7
	Arthur Gourley (P)	6,112	14.2

	Candidates	Votes	%
	A. S. Edwards (SOC)	2,690	6.3
7	Philip Knopf (R)	29,100	59.4
	George S. Foster (D)	12,490	25.5
	George Koop (SOC)	6,540	13.4
8	Charles McGavin (R)	20,107	51.7
	William Preston Harrison (D)	13,025	33.5
	Marcus H. Taft (SOC)	4,223	10.9
9	Henry S. Boutell (R)	22,442	57.2
	Quin O'Brien (D)	13,525	34.5
	Adolph Harrick (SOC)	2,801	7.1
10	George Edmund Foss (R)	27,096	66.2
	James L. Turnock (D)	10,243	25.0
	Robert Knox (SOC)	2,917	7.1
11	Howard M. Snapp (R)	31,019	70.7
	James O. Monroe (D)	9,324	21.2
12	Charles E. Fuller (R)	33,898	70.2
	Alex Vaughey (D)	9,718	20.1
	David A. Syme (P)	2,481	5.1
13	Robert R. Hitt (R)	26,454	67.7
	John Erwin (D)	10,049	25.7
14	Benjamin F. Marsh (R)	24,004	58.4
	David W. Matthews (D)	12,256	29.8
	John Higgins (SOC)	2,852	6.9
15	George W. Prince (R)	29,792	60.7
	Meredith Walker (D)	15,159	30.9
16	Joseph V. Graff (R)	25,803	60.5
	Thomas Cooper (D)	13,780	32.3
17	John A. Sterling (R)	23,414	58.8
	Z. F. Yost (D)	12,978	32.6
	William W. Houser (P)	2,285	5.7
18	Joseph G. Cannon (R)	30,520	62.0
	Coulson V. McClenathan (D)	15,168	30.8
19	William B. McKinley (R)	30,574	56.9
	Adolph Sumerlin (D)	19,931	37.1
20	Henry T. Rainey (D)	19,881	48.9
	Cornelius J. Doyle (R)	18,329	45.1
21	Zeno J. Rives (R)	21,330	47.7
	Ben F. Caldwell (D)	20,238	45.2
22	William A. Rodenberg (R)	25,770	53.5
	J. Nick Perrin (D)	19,494	40.5
23	Frank L. Dickson (R)	21,931	47.7
	M. D. Foster (D)	21,123	45.9
	William P. Habberton (P)	2,404	5.2
24	Pleasant T. Chapman (R)	20,556	50.7
	J. R. Williams (D)	18,664	46.1
25	George W. Smith (R)	22,527	55.6
	Charles L. Otrich (D)	14,668	36.2
	Charles F. Kiest (P)	2,306	5.7

INDIANA

1	James A. Hemenway (R)	23,158*	51.1
	Albert G. Holcomb (D)	19,399	42.8
2	John C. Chaney (R)	25,143	49.7
	Robert W. Miers (D)	23,670	46.8
3	William T. Zenor (D)	22,708	53.1
	John E. Dillon (R)	19,119	44.7
4	Lincoln Dixon (D)	23,451	50.8
	Anderson Percifield (R)	21,516	46.6
5	Elias S. Holliday (R)	28,192	52.0
	Claude G. Bowers (D)	23,101	42.6
6	James E. Watson (R)	29,089	56.3
	Uriah S. Jackson (D)	22,046	42.7
7	Jesse Overstreet (R)	34,178	57.1
	Levi P. Harlan (D)	23,334	39.0
8	George W. Cromer (R)	29,462	52.2
	Edward C. Dehority (D)	22,097	39.1
	Aaron Worth (P)	3,675	6.5
9	Charles B. Landis (R)	29,492	52.9
	Clyde H. Jones (D)	23,267	41.8
10	Edgar D. Crumpacker (R)	31,583	58.5
	Worth W. Pepple (D)	21,451	39.7
11	Frederick Landis (R)	29,591	53.6
	Clement M. Holderman (D)	21,406	38.8
	Edward H. Kennedy (P)	3,364	6.1
12	Newton W. Gilbert (R)	23,203	50.5

Candidates	Votes	%
James M. Robinson (D)	21,322	46.4
13 Abraham L. Brick (R)	29,361	55.1
Frank E. Hering (D)	21,454	40.3

IOWA

Candidates	Votes	%
1 Thomas Hedge (R)	19,929	54.7
John E. Craig (D)	14,886	40.9
2 Albert F. Dawson (R)	22,116	48.1
Martin J. Wade (D)	21,930	47.7
3 Benjamin P. Birdsall (R)	29,297	65.3
J. W. Mallon (D)	14,200	31.6
4 Gilbert N. Haugen (R)	26,399	64.5
W. O. Holman (D)	13,403	32.8
5 Robert G. Cousins (R)	25,313	59.7
John A. Green (D)	15,019	35.4
6 John F. Lacey (R)	23,213	58.4
S. A. Brewster (D)	13,840	34.9
7 John A. T. Hull (R)	27,637	64.3
John T. Mulvaney (D)	12,046	28.0
8 William P. Hepburn (R)	26,603	63.0
John V. Bennett (D)	14,518	34.4
9 Walter I. Smith (R)	27,214	63.9
H. Wilcox (D)	13,907	32.7
10 James P. Conner (R)	34,977	67.3
W. J. Branagan (D)	14,531	28.0
11 Elbert H. Hubbard (R)	32,560	69.1
P. D. Vanoosterhaut (D)	13,521	28.7

KANSAS

Candidates	Votes	%
AL Charles F. Scott (R)	187,983	60.3
Francis M. Brady (D)	105,479	33.9
1 Charles Curtis (R)	25,376	57.8
A. M. Harvey (D)	17,808	40.6
2 Justin D. Bowersock (R)	26,443	54.8
C. F. Hutchings (D)	20,308	42.1
3 Philip P. Campbell (R)	29,998	59.5
William H. Ryan (D)	15,762	31.2
T. C. Davis (SOC)	4,696	9.3
4 James M. Miller (R)	24,185	62.8
Frank B. Lowrance (D-PP)	14,326	37.2
5 William A. Calderhead (R)	22,076	65.1
John A. Flack (D-PP)	11,825	34.9
6 William A. Reeder (R)	21,808	60.5
H. O. Caster (D)	13,274	36.8
7 Victor Murdock (R)	35,598	60.4
M. Belisle (D)	19,548	33.2

KENTUCKY

Candidates	Votes	%
1 Ollie M. James (D)	25,558	62.3
J. C. Spaight (R)	13,755	33.5
2 Augustus O. Stanley (D)	20,732	55.7
W. A. Overby (R)	16,517	44.3
3 James M. Richardson (D)	18,432	50.1
W. H. Jones (R)	18,332	49.9
4 David H. Smith (D)	21,979	53.1
Ben L. Bruner (R)	19,419	46.9
5 J. Swagar Sherley (D)	23,712	51.0
William C. Owens (R)	22,229	47.8
6 Joseph L. Rhinock (D)	18,854	50.7
Leslie T. Applegate (R)	16,089	43.3
7 South Trimble (D)	20,356	60.0
Joseph W. Calvert (R)	13,187	38.9
8 George G. Gilbert (D)	16,481	52.4
N. D. Miles (R)	14,536	46.2
9 Joseph B. Bennett (R)	21,335	50.1
James N. Kehoe (D)	21,291	50.0
10 Frank A. Hopkins (D)	19,154	51.9
Theodore D. Blakey (R)	17,736	48.1
11 Don C. Edwards (R)	31,349	70.3
George E. Stone (D)	13,200	29.6

LOUISIANA

Candidates	Votes	%
1 Adolph Meyer (D)	9,157	89.8
Hugh S. Suthon (R)	791	7.8

Candidates	Votes	%
2 Robert C. Davey (D)	9,786	91.0
George H. Vennard (R)	798	7.4
3 Robert F. Broussard (D)	5,649	84.5
Henry N. Pharr (R)	1,038	15.5
4 John T. Watkins (D)	6,266	99.1
5 Joseph E. Ransdell (D)	5,747	95.4
6 Samuel M. Robertson (D)	5,351	88.1
L. E. Bentley (R)	721	11.9
7 Arsene P. Pujo (D)	5,432	84.2
Joseph Lassalle (R)	1,007	15.6

MAINE

Candidates	Votes	%
1 Amos L. Allen (R)	18,301	57.2
L. R. Moore (D)	13,320	41.6
2 Charles E. Littlefield (R)	19,176	57.2
Horatio G. Foss (D)	13,785	41.2
3 Edwin C. Burleigh (R)	18,541	60.3
E. N. Benson (D)	11,678	38.0
4 Llewellyn Powers (R)	20,501	62.4
William R. Pattangall (D)	11,600	35.3

MARYLAND

Candidates	Votes	%
1 Thomas A. Smith (D)	17,582	49.4
William H. Jackson (R)	17,072	48.0
2 J. Fred. C. Talbott (D)	18,922	52.2
Robert Garrett (R)	16,734	46.2
3 Frank C. Wachter (R)	17,405	51.8
Lee S. Meyer (D)	15,373	45.8
4 John Gill Jr. (D)	18,464	51.8
William C. Smith (R)	16,754	47.0
5 Sydney E. Mudd (R)	16,896	53.6
Richard S. Hill (D)	13,762	43.6
6 George A. Pearre (R)	19,131	53.9
Walter A. Johnston (D)	15,077	42.5

MASSACHUSETTS

Candidates	Votes	%
1 George P. Lawrence (R)	17,217	58.0
Charles Giddings (D)	11,117	37.4
2 Frederick H. Gillett (R)	17,611	63.5
George W. Wheelwright (D)	7,992	28.8
George H. Wrenn (SOC)	1,744	6.3
3 Rockwood Hoar (R)	17,796	61.1
John B. Ratigan (D)	10,617	36.4
4 Charles Q. Tirrell (R)	18,982	61.4
Marcus A. Coolidge (D)	10,478	33.9
5 Butler Ames (R)	16,287	54.6
Alexander B. Bruce (D)	12,657	42.5
6 Augustus P. Gardner (R)	18,157	61.0
Daniel N. Crowley (D)	8,880	29.8
James F. Carey (SOC)	2,716	9.1
7 Ernest W. Roberts (R)	20,821	62.9
Willam A. Kelley (D)	10,165	30.7
8 Samuel W. McCall (R)	21,511	89.1
Thomas A. Scott (SOC)	2,623	10.9
9 John A. Kellher (D)	17,003	67.7
Walter L. Sears (R)	6,895	27.5
10 William S. McNary (D)	19,211	57.3
Jay B. Crawford (R)	12,740	38.0
11 John A. Sullivan (D)	18,045	51.6
Eugene N. Foss (R)	15,990	45.7
12 John W. Weeks (R)	19,312	61.3
Augustus Hemenway (D)	10,813	34.3
13 William S. Greene (R)	13,631	62.8
Francis M. Kennedy (D)	8,064	37.2
14 William C. Lovering (R)	18,415	60.4
Thomas H. Buttimer (D)	7,100	23.3
Charles H. Coulter (SOC)	4,279	14.0

MICHIGAN

Candidates	Votes	%
1 Edwin Denby (R)	28,874	58.0
Alfred Lucking (D)	20,490	41.2
2 Charles E. Townsend (R)	28,797	59.2
John P. Kirk (D)	18,874	38.8

Candidates	Votes	%
3 Washington Gardner (R)	28,089	63.4
Lloyd C. Feighner (D)	13,535	30.6
4 Edward L. Hamilton (R)	28,066	66.5
Theodore G. Beaver (D)	14,143	33.5
5 William Alden Smith (R)	30,869	70.3
Vernon H. Smith (D)	12,253	27.9
6 Samuel W. Smith (R)	31,403	61.4
Charles A. Durand (D)	18,224	35.6
7 Henry McMorran (R)	25,562	66.4
Charles Wellman (D)	12,619	32.8
8 Joseph W. Fordney (R)	24,417	65.2
Henry J. Patterson (D)	11,898	31.8
9 Roswell P. Bishop (R)	22,463	71.7
George S. Stanley (D)	7,076	22.6
10 George A. Loud (R)	27,187	70.4
Stephen P. Flynn (D)	10,527	27.3
11 Archibald B. Darragh (R)	31,661	73.0
William A. Bahlke (D)	10,639	24.5
12 H. Olin Young (R)	36,655	80.3
John W. Black (D)	7,915	17.3

MINNESOTA

Candidates	Votes	%
1 James A. Tawney (R)	23,188	64.5
Nelson (D)	12,770	35.5
2 James T. McCleary (R)	19,246	64.1
Jones (D)	10,784	35.9
3 Charles R. Davis (R)	20,116	66.0
Craven (D)	10,386	34.1
4 Frederick C. Stevens (R)	25,631	100.0
5 Loren Fletcher (R)	21,933	51.3
Kohler (D)	15,923	37.2
Hirshfield (LAB)	3,184	7.4
6 Clarence B. Buckman (R)	19,309	54.0
Vandyke (D)	16,430	46.0
7 Andrew J. Volstead (R)	27,060	100.0
8 J. Adam Bede (R)	22,095	76.9
Hughes (D)	6,626	23.1
9 Halvor Steenerson (R)	27,061	100.0

MISSISSIPPI

Candidates	Votes	%
1 Ezekiel S. Candler Jr. (D)	8,049	100.0
2 Thomas Spight (D)	7,279	100.0
3 Benjamin G. Humphreys (D)	3,744	100.0
4 Wilson S. Hill (D)	7,135	100.0
5 Adam Byrd (D)	9,362	99.0
6 Eaton J. Bowers (D)	6,563	93.6
C. W. Baylis (SOC)	449	6.4
7 Frank McLain (D)	5,730	100.0
8 John S. Williams (D)	4,934	100.0

MISSOURI

Candidates	Votes	%
1 James T. Lloyd (D)	20,216	51.4
Higbee (R)	19,131	48.6
2 William W. Rucker (D)	21,639	53.8
Hudson (R)	18,596	46.2
3 Frank B. Klepper (R)	19,088	50.4
D. Sullinger (D)	18,791	49.6
4 Frank B. Fulkerson (R)	19,831	51.7
Wilson (D)	18,531	48.3
5 Edgar C. Ellis (R)	23,873	49.2
Cowherd (D)	22,912	47.2
6 David A. De Armond (D)	17,678	51.5
Rhodes (R)	16,637	48.5
7 John Welborn (R)	23,682	51.6
Hamlin (D)	22,204	48.4
8 Dorsey W. Shackleford (D)	16,059	51.6
Chalfant (R)	15,091	48.5
9 James Beauchamp Clark (D)	21,508	51.6
Garber (R)	19,937	48.1
10 Richard Bartholdt (R)	34,254	58.5
Tichacek (D)	21,271	36.3
11 John T. Hunt (D)	17,018	49.1
Caulfield (R)	16,326	47.1
12 Ernest E. Wood (D)	15,134‡	50.3
Harry M. Coudrey (R)	14,177	47.1
13 Marion E. Rhodes (R)	16,166	50.6

Candidates	Votes	%
Edward Robb (D)	15,788	49.4
14 William T. Tyndall (R)	23,401	52.8
Russell (D)	20,873	47.1
15 Cassius M. Shartel (R)	21,654	49.0
Benton (D)	19,646	44.4
16 Arthur P. Murphy (R)	15,159	50.1
J. Robert Lamar (D)	15,123	49.9

MONTANA

	Candidates	Votes	%
AL	Joseph M. Dixon (R)	32,957	51.7
	Austin C. Gormley (D-LAB-PP)	26,729	42.0
	John H. Walsh (SOC)	4,025	6.3

NEBRASKA

	Candidates	Votes	%
1	Elmer J. Burkett (R)	19,786*	59.7
	Hugh Lamaster (FUS)	11,863	35.8
2	John L. Kennedy (R)	14,417	46.4
	Gilbert M. Hitchcock (FUS)	13,628	44.2
	Clark W. Adair (SOC)	2,534	8.2
3	John J. McCarthy (R)	24,151	51.9
	Patrick E. McKillip (FUS)	21,210	45.6
4	Edmond H. Hinshaw (R)	23,407	57.9
	Charles F. Gilbert (FUS)	15,702	38.8
5	George W. Norris (R)	19,645	56.1
	Harry H. Mauck (FUS)	13,831	39.5
6	Moses P. Kinkaid (R)	22,580	58.8
	Walter B. McNeel (FUS)	13,725	35.8

NEVADA

	Candidates	Votes	%
AL	Clarence D. Van Duzer (D & SILVER)	5,525	48.5
	J. A. Yerington (R)	5,301	46.5
	Reinhold Sadler (STAL SIL)	572	5.0

NEW HAMPSHIRE

	Candidates	Votes	%
1	Cyrus A. Sulloway (R)	25,364	58.9
	Napoleon J. Dyer (D)	16,866	39.1
2	Frank D. Currier (R)	26,748	60.7
	Harry W. Daniell (D)	16,462	37.4

NEW JERSEY

	Candidates	Votes	%
1	Henry C. Loudenslager (R)	26,169	60.3
	Swackhamer (D)	15,365	35.4
2	John J. Gardner (R)	26,296	63.7
	Perry (D)	13,035	31.6
3	Benjamin F. Howell (R)	24,565	56.1
	Otis (D)	17,862	40.8
4	Ira W. Wood (R)	22,579	54.7
	Stevens (D)	16,953	41.1
5	Charles N. Fowler (R)	24,488	52.3
	Martine (D)	19,254	41.1
6	Henry C. Allen (R)	26,612	47.8
	William Hughes (D)	26,102	46.9
7	Richard W. Parker (R)	25,578	61.4
	Jackson (D)	14,347	34.5
8	William H. Wiley (R)	24,148	63.2
	Seymour (D)	11,607	30.4
9	Marshall Van Winkle (R)	19,824	50.7
	Benny (D)	17,399	44.5
10	Allan L. McDermott (D)	21,293	53.8
	Walker (R)	15,959	40.3

NEW YORK

	Candidates	Votes	%
1	William W. Cocks (R)	25,481	55.7
	William Willett Jr. (D)	19,362	42.3
2	George H. Lindsay (D)	18,506	55.8
	Herbert J. Knapp (R)	12,899	38.9
3	Charles T. Dunwell (R)	21,208	52.6
	Ephraim Byk (D)	17,571	43.5
4	Charles P. Law (R)	19,418	49.4
	Frank E. Wilson (D)	17,684	45.0
5	George E. Waldo (R)	21,299	51.8
	John J. Roach (D)	18,889	45.9
6	William M. Calder (R)	22,109	52.4

	Candidates	Votes	%
	Robert Baker (D)	19,430	46.0
7	John J. Fitzgerald (D)	23,463	62.6
	Robert H. Haskell (R)	13,282	35.4
8	Timothy D. Sullivan (D)	24,532	61.5
	Frank L. Frugone (R)	14,262	35.7
9	Henry M. Goldfogle (D)	5,982	39.7
	Joseph Levenson (R)	5,667	37.7
	Joseph Barondess (SOCIAL D)	3,167	21.0
10	William Sulzer (D)	13,381	51.0
	William Byrnes (R)	9,383	35.8
	Isidor Phillips (SOCIAL D)	2,789	10.6
11	William Randolph Hearst (D)	26,255	59.3
	Henry Clay Piercy (R)	16,594	37.5
12	William Bourke Cochran (D)	20,972	63.1
	Henry Carey (R)	10,500	31.6
13	Herbert Parsons (R)	18,700	52.9
	Edward Swann (D)	16,038	45.4
14	Charles A. Towne (D)	21,627	57.1
	Lucian Knapp (R)	12,664	33.4
	William F. Ehret (SOCIAL D)	2,973	7.8
15	Jacob Van Vechten Olcott (R)	16,924	51.7
	M. Francis Loughman (D)	15,199	46.4
16	Jacob Ruppert Jr. (D)	15,049	52.7
	Theodore Prince (R)	11,212	39.3
	Adolph Groelinger (SOCIAL D)	1,882	6.6
17	William S. Bennett (R)	25,655	51.3
	Franklin Leonard Jr (D)	23,029	46.0
18	Joseph A. Goulden (D)	32,266	57.2
	William W. Niles (R)	20,606	36.5
19	John E. Andrus (R)	24,199	54.1
	J. Harvey Bell (D)	19,079	42.7
20	Thomas W. Bradley (R)	23,224	55.5
	Charles C. Dill (D)	17,562	42.0
21	John H. Ketcham (R)	24,791	95.9
22	William H. Draper (R)	25,755	59.4
	Isaac C. Blandy (D)	16,261	37.5
23	George N. Southwick (R)	33,763	55.7
	Daniel C. McElwain (D)	25,618	42.3
24	Frank J. Lefevre (R)	30,980	95.5
25	Lucius N. Littauer (R)	27,290	54.8
	Joseph A. Kellogg (D)	20,491	41.1
26	William H. Flack (R)	33,564	67.5
	Henry Holland (D)	14,801	29.8
27	James S. Sherman (R)	26,657	54.5
	William H. Squires (D)	20,892	42.7
28	Charles L. Knapp (R)	27,357	60.2
	Henry Purcell (D)	15,808	34.8
29	Michael E. Driscoll (R)	33,738	62.6
	Harrison W. Coley (D)	18,324	34.0
30	John W. Dwight (R)	32,272	59.8
	George L. Church (D)	19,846	36.8
31	Sereno E. Payne (R)	29,760	61.5
	D. J. Vanauken (D)	17,576	36.4
32	James Breck Perkins (R)	30,091	58.9
	Henry Selden Bacon (D)	17,382	34.1
33	Jacob Sloat Fassett (R)	26,276	57.5
	Frank P. Frost (D)	18,055	39.5
34	James W. Wadsworth (R)	32,364	60.5
	James E. Crisfield (D)	19,328	36.2
35	William H. Ryan (D)	20,840	49.4
	Warren P. Bender (R)	19,943	47.2
36	De Alva S. Alexander (R)	27,958	59.8
	Edwin Gaw Flanigen (D)	17,569	37.6
37	Edward B. Vreeland (R)	33,573	67.7
	S. B. McClure (D)	13,229	26.7

NORTH CAROLINA

	Candidates	Votes	%
1	John H. Small (D)	13,065	80.5
	D. O. Newberry (R)	3,167	19.5
2	Claude Kitchin (D)	12,064	86.3
	P. C. Jenkins (R)	1,919	13.7
3	Charles R. Thomas (D)	10,645	66.0
	W. S. Robinson (R)	5,496	34.1
4	Edward W. Pou (D)	12,658	70.9
	Claude Pearson (R)	5,197	29.1
5	William W. Kitchin (D)	16,497	58.7
	C. A. Reynolds (R)	11,546	41.1
6	Gilbert B. Patterson (D)	9,770	70.0
	O. J. Spears (R)	4,193	30.0

	Candidates	Votes	%
7	Robert N. Page (D)	12,642	58.5
	L. D. Mendenhall (R)	8,986	41.6
8	E. Spencer Blackburn (R)	15,566	50.3
	W. C. Newland (D)	15,321	49.5
9	Edwin Y. Webb (D)	13,822	58.1
	J. F. Newell (R)	9,957	41.9
10	James M. Gudger Jr. (D)	13,554	51.7
	H. G. Ewart (R)	12,666	48.3

NORTH DAKOTA

	Candidates	Votes	%
AL	Thomas F. Marshall (R)	49,111✓	
	Asle J. Gronna (R)	47,648✓	
	N. P. Rasmussen (D)	15,622	
	A. G. Burr (D)	15,398	
	L. F. Dow (SOC)	1,734	
	E. D. Herring (SOC)	1,697	
	B. H. Tibbets (P)	971	
	N. A. Colby (P)	967	

OHIO

	Candidates	Votes	%
1	Nicholas Longworth (R)	32,105	68.7
	Braxton W. Campbell (D)	11,631	24.9
	Bishop W. Mason (SOC)	2,737	5.9
2	Herman P. Goebel (R)	31,873	62.8
	Charles A. Miller (D)	14,215	28.0
	John F. Ditchen (SOC)	4,487	8.8
3	Robert M. Nevin (R)	31,626	53.0
	Charles Conley (D)	25,594	42.9
4	Harvey C. Garber (D)	20,653	50.8
	R. D. Kahle (R)	18,858	46.4
5	William W. Campbell (R)	19,707	49.4
	Timothy T. Ansberry (D)	19,383	48.6
6	Thomas E. Scroggy (R)	21,485	51.4
	James Runyan (D)	19,148	45.8
7	J. Warren Keifer (R)	25,245	60.0
	P. E. Montanus (D)	15,966	37.9
8	Ralph D. Cole (R)	27,523	60.5
	Henry H. MacCracken (D)	16,257	35.8
9	James H. Southard (R)	35,128	63.7
	William H. Althof (D)	16,488	29.9
10	Henry Bannon (R)	25,097	62.6
	Matthew S. Merriman (D)	13,316	33.2
11	Charles H. Grosvenor (R)	29,415	58.9
	John T. Bridwell (D)	19,501	39.1
12	Edward L. Taylor Jr. (R)	25,178	56.6
	Dewitt C. Badger (D)	17,999	40.5
13	Grant E. Mouser (R)	25,054	49.5
	D. R. Crissinger (D)	24,004	47.4
14	Amos R. Webber (R)	29,187	57.4
	Benjamin F. Long (D)	19,318	38.0
15	Beman G. Dawes (R)	20,763	48.4
	Ernest B. Schneider (D)	20,231	47.2
16	Capell L. Weems (R)	23,265	59.1
	H. W. Hermann (D)	13,676	34.8
17	Martin L. Smyser (R)	23,847	50.7
	J. E. Hurst (D)	21,571	45.8
18	James Kennedy (R)	36,939	63.9
	W. J. Foley (D)	16,472	28.5
19	W. Aubrey Thomas (R)	35,676	68.9
	Charles J. McCormick (D)	11,942	23.1
	F. N. Prevey (SOC)	2,927	5.7
20	Jacob A. Beidler (R)	29,475	59.8
	Charles W. Lapp (D)	17,106	34.7
21	Theodore E. Burton (R)	33,930	86.6
	Max S. Hayes (SOC)	4,144	10.6

Special Elections

	Candidates	Votes	%
14	Amos R. Webber (R)	29,148	57.3
	Benjamin F. Long (D)	19,350	38.0
19	W. Aubrey Thomas (R)	35,802	83.5
	Charles J. McCormick (D)	5,467	12.8

OREGON

	Candidates	Votes	%
1	Binger Hermann (R)	23,970	51.2
	R. M. Veatch (D)	17,157	36.7
	H. Gould (P)	2,867	6.1
	B. F. Ramp (SOC)	2,800	6.0
2	John N. Williamson (R)	27,126	57.6
	J. E. Simmons (D)	12,773	27.1
	George R. Cook (SOC)	3,678	7.8
	H. W. Stone (P)	3,535	7.5

PENNSYLVANIA

	Candidates	Votes	%
1	Henry H. Bingham (R)	42,228	84.7
	Joseph L. Galen (D)	7,623	15.3
2	Robert Adams Jr. (R)	41,637	84.9
	John Cadwalader Jr. (D)	7,010	14.3
3	George A. Castor (R)	39,982	83.3
	John H. Fow (D, I)	7,873	16.4
4	Reuben O. Moon (R)	25,610	81.1
	Charles F. Stilz (D)	5,253	16.6
5	Edward de V. Morrell (R)	28,146	78.8
	David Moffet (D)	6,524	18.3
6	George D. McCreary (R)	34,984	76.7
	William A. Carr (D)	8,709	19.1
7	Thomas S. Butler (R)	26,145	77.5
	Archibald M. Holding (D)	6,470	19.2
8	Irving P. Wanger (R)	26,099	60.9
	Joseph J. Broadhurst (D)	15,847	37.0
9	Henry B. Cassel (R)	17,685	54.7
	Milton J. Brecht (CI/IC)	11,526	35.6
	Hugh M. North Jr (D)	2,894	8.9
10	Thomas H. Dale (R)	15,003	53.2
	George Howell (D)	12,683	44.9
11	Henry W. Palmer (R)	23,324	60.8
	William L. Raeder (D)	14,224	37.1
12	George R. Patterson (R)	17,419	57.4
	Harry O. Haag (D)	12,005	39.6
13	Marcus C. L. Kline (D)	25,711	50.1
	William H. Sowden (R)	23,781	46.4
14	Mial E. Lilly (R)	15,568	58.4
	John Kuhbach (D)	8,696	32.6
	William S. H. Heermans (P)	2,393	9.0
15	Elias Deemer (R)	19,807	58.3
	George B. McMetzger (D)	11,959	35.2
16	E. W. Samuel (R)	14,969	51.6
	Henry E. Davis (D)	13,191	45.5
17	Thaddeus M. Mahon (R)	22,860	61.4
	O. C. Bowers (D)	13,337	35.8
18	Marlin E. Olmsted (R)	26,996	67.6
	John L. Saylor (D)	11,663	29.2
19	John M. Reynolds (R)	23,164	54.9
	Joseph E. Thropp (D, P)	19,066	45.1
20	Daniel F. Lafean (R)	19,088	55.8
	William McSherry (D)	14,782	43.2
21	Solomon R. Dresser (R)	18,281	59.6
	Charles W. Shaffer (D)	9,559	31.2
	Samuel C. Watts (P)	2,407	7.9
22	George F. Huff (R)	21,547	65.5
	Charles M. Heineman (D)	9,824	29.9
23	Allen F. Cooper (R)	18,206	58.7
	Charles F. Uhl Jr. (D)	10,597	34.2
	George H. Hocking (P)	2,226	7.2
24	Ernest F. Acheson (R)	23,131	69.4
	William J. Mellon (D)	8,420	25.3
	John J. Ashenhurst (P)	1,798	5.4
25	Arthur L. Bates (R)	17,271	61.9
	E. W. McArthur (D)	8,082	28.9
	R. C. Loupe (P)	1,644	5.9
26	G. A. Schneebeli (R)	14,763	45.3
	J. Davis Brodhead (D, CIT)	12,895	39.6
	Joseph H. Shull (PURE POL)	3,759	11.5
27	William O. Smith (R)	18,697	71.8
	A. C. Smith (D)	7,353	28.2
28	George C. Sibley (R)	19,861	55.2
	Salem Heilman (D)	10,651	29.6
	John E. Gill (P)	4,640	12.9
29	William H. Graham (R)	18,400	80.1
	W. H. S. Thomson (D)	3,437	15.0
30	John Dalzell (R)	17,322	79.0

	Candidates	Votes	%
	M. L. Thompson (D)	3,330	15.2
31	James Francis Burke (R)	18,403	75.2
	John F. McGrath (D)	5,289	21.6
32	A. J. Barchfeld (R)	19,383	75.9
	John Pierce (D)	4,690	18.4

RHODE ISLAND

	Candidates	Votes	%
1	Daniel L. D. Granger (D)	15,583	49.5
	Stiness (R)	15,450	49.0
2	Adin B. Capron (R)	18,212	56.8
	Owen (D)	13,278	41.4

SOUTH CAROLINA

	Candidates	Votes	%
1	George S. Legare (D)	6,068	91.3
	J. A. Noland (R)	346	5.2
2	James O'H. Patterson (D)	7,421	94.6
	Isaac Myers (R)	423	5.4
3	Wyatt Aiken (D)	7,659	98.1
4	Joseph T. Johnson (D)	8,516	97.5
5	David E. Finley (D)	7,928	97.9
6	J. Edwin Ellerbe (D)	8,348	95.7
7	Asbury F. Lever (D)	8,726	93.8
	Charles C. Jocobs (R)	563	6.1

SOUTH DAKOTA

	Candidates	Votes	%
AL	Eben W. Martin (R)	70,002✓	
	Charles H. Burke (R)	69,936✓	
	Wesley A. Stuart (D)	22,692	
	W. A. Lynch (D)	22,640	
	H. W. Smith (SOC)	3,115	
	S. A. Cochrane (SOC)	3,064	
	A. Jamison (P)	3,012	
	C. K. Thompson (P)	2,961	
	A. J. McCain (POP)	1,216	
	G. W. Lattin (POP)	1,175	

TENNESSEE

	Candidates	Votes	%
1	Walter P. Brownlow (R)	19,657	68.9
	R. E. Styll (D)	8,879	31.1
2	Nathan W. Hale (R)	14,963	70.9
	Staples (D)	6,013	28.5
3	John A. Moon (D)	16,541	53.2
	Sharp (R)	14,285	46.0
4	Mounce G. Butler (D)	13,359	53.3
	Pickering (R)	11,596	46.2
5	William C. Houston (D)	13,581	68.7
	Brown (R)	6,192	31.3
6	John W. Gaines (D)	13,777	79.0
	Maxwell (R)	3,517	20.2
7	Lemuel P. Padgett (D)	13,090	61.9
	Hughes (R)	8,027	38.0
8	Thetus W. Sims (D)	13,395	53.9
	Davis (R)	11,452	46.1
9	Finis J. Garrett (D)	16,222	74.9
	Walker (R)	5,443	25.1
10	Malcolm R. Patterson (D)	13,595	75.9
	Matthews (R)	4,307	24.1

TEXAS

	Candidates	Votes	%
1	Morris Sheppard (D)	12,473	72.1
	J. A. Armistead (R)	4,838	28.0
2	Moses L. Broocks (D)	13,119	76.2
	A. J. Houston (R)	4,099	23.8
3	Gordon J. Russell (D)	12,473	73.7
	C. T. White (R)	4,441	26.3
4	Choice B. Randell (D)	14,435	90.4
	R. E. Martin (R)	1,537	9.6
5	Jack Beall (D)	14,292	86.0
	J. J. Cypert (R)	2,327	14.0
6	Scott Field (D)	9,438	100.0
7	Alexander W. Gregg (D)	8,040	100.0
8	John M. Pinckney (D)	9,804	69.1
	H. F. McGregor (R)	4,384	30.9
9	George F. Burgess (D)	14,316	72.3
	B. L. Osgood (R)	5,484	27.7

	Candidates	Votes	%
10	Albert S. Burleson (D)	11,761	100.0
11	Robert L. Henry (D)	10,305	84.4
	Joe E. Williams (R)	1,912	15.7
12	Oscar W. Gillespie (D)	12,480	74.4
	Frank B. Stanley	2,357	14.1
	J. M. Mallett (R)	1,933	11.5
13	John H. Stephens (D)	18,604	89.6
	James M. Kindred (R)	2,157	10.4
14	James L. Slayden (D)	15,097	98.3
15	John N. Garner (D)	10,647	64.9
	J. S. Morin (R)	5,767	35.1
16	William R. Smith (D)	17,488	83.1
	Logan McPherson (R)	3,562	16.9

UTAH

	Candidates	Votes	%
AL	Joseph Howell (R)	52,675	51.8
	Orlando W. Powers (D)	37,445	36.8
	Ogden Hiles (AM)	6,796	6.7

VERMONT

	Candidates	Votes	%
1	David J. Foster (R)	23,208	70.4
	Frank L. Graves (D)	8,868	26.9
2	Kittredge Haskins (R)	23,781	74.8
	Harland B. Howe (D)	7,066	22.2

VIRGINIA

	Candidates	Votes	%
1	William A. Jones (D)	7,826	77.1
	Trader (R)	2,331	23.0
2	Harry L. Maynard (D)	10,762	78.3
	Robert M. Hughes (R)	2,800	20.4
3	John Lamb (D)	7,121	78.0
	Edgar Allan Jr. (R)	1,020	11.2
	George A. Harrison (IR)	773	8.5
4	Robert G. Southall (D)	6,031	82.8
	Charles Alexander (R)	1,248	17.1
5	Claude A. Swanson (D)	8,893	65.0
	J. B. Stovall (R)	4,793	35.0
6	Carter Glass (D)	7,798	69.1
	Samuel H. Hoge (R)	3,429	30.4
7	James Hay (D)	9,051	64.7
	Charles M. Kelzel (R)	4,949	35.4
8	John F. Rixey (D)	7,986	76.6
	Ernest Lincoln Howard (R)	2,443	23.4
9	Campbell Slemp (R)	15,627	57.2
	J. C. Wysor (D)	11,710	42.8
10	Henry D. Flood (D)	9,183	61.3
	George A. Revercomb (R)	5,460	36.5

WASHINGTON

	Candidates	Votes	%
AL	Francis W. Cushman (R)	93,328✓	
	Wesley L. Jones (R)	92,743✓	
	William E. Humphrey (R)	92,436✓	
	James J. Anderson (D)	35,698	
	Howard Hathaway (D)	35,636	
	W. T. Beck (D)	35,193	
	T. C. Wiswell (SOC)	9,005	
	George Croston (SOC)	8,940	
	H. D. Jory (SOC)	8,940	
	Ferdinand B. Hawes (P)	3,059	
	Henry Brown (P)	3,052	
	William Bonstein (SOC LAB)	1,320	
	R. McDonald (SOC LAB)	1,308	
	G. Norling (SOC LAB)	1,306	

WEST VIRGINIA

	Candidates	Votes	%
1	Blackburn B. Dovener (R)	27,459	54.3
	J. W. Barnes (D)	21,100	41.7
2	Alston G. Dayton (R)	24,225	51.6
	Stuart W. Walker (D)	21,888	46.6
3	Joseph Holt Gaines (R)	26,236	52.8
	H. B. Davenport (D)	22,125	44.5
4	Harry C. Woodyard (R)	22,942	53.6
	Allen C. Murdock (D)	18,912	44.2
5	James A. Hughes (R)	27,593	55.8
	S. S. Altezer (D)	21,276	43.0

WISCONSIN

	Candidates	Votes	%
1	Henry Allen Cooper (R)	25,125	59.5
	Calvin Stewart (D)	13,379	31.7
	J. W. Born (SOCIAL D)	2,461	5.8
2	Henry C. Adams (R)	22,773	57.7
	John J. Wood (D)	15,265	38.7
3	Joseph W. Babcock (R)	19,047	48.8
	Herman Grotophorst (D)	18,662	47.8
4	Theobald Otjen (R)	17,582	43.8
	Peter J. Sommers (D)	12,385	30.8

	Candidates	Votes	%
	W. R. Gaylord (SOCIAL D)	9,625	24.0
5	William H. Stafford (R)	17,231	44.8
	Victor L. Berger (SOCIAL D)	10,626	27.6
	Arthur Dopp (D)	9,978	26.0
6	Charles H. Weisse (D)	20,665	53.4
	Roy L. Morse (R)	17,687	45.7
7	John J. Esch (R)	25,505	66.8
	N. C. Basheller (D)	11,271	29.5
8	James H. Davidson (R)	25,233	63.1
	C. F. Crane (D)	12,889	32.2
9	Edward S. Minor (R)	19,764	58.1

	Candidates	Votes	%
	R. J. McGrehan (D)	13,124	38.6
10	Webster E. Brown (R)	29,392	65.4
	Wells M. Ruggles (D)	14,121	31.4
11	John J. Jenkins (R)	31,270	74.8
	George C. Cooper (D)	8,637	20.7

WYOMING

	Candidates	Votes	%
AL	Frank W. Mondell (R)	19,862	64.6
	T. S. Taliaferro Jr (D)	9,903	32.2

1905 House Election

ILLINOIS

Special Election

	Candidates	Votes	%
14	James McKinney (R)	12,356	57.2
	James Howard Pattee	7,316	33.9
	Homer L. Darby	1,176	5.4

1906 House Elections

ALABAMA

	Candidates	Votes	%
1	George W. Taylor (D)	3,592	100.0
2	Ariosto A. Wiley (D)	6,001	88.9
	J. C. Fonville (R)	751	11.1
3	Henry D. Clayton (D)	6,922	100.0
4	William B. Craig (D)	5,783	100.0
5	J. Thomas Heflin (D)	6,940	100.0
6	Richmond P. Hobson (D)	8,308	100.0
7	John L. Burnett (D)	8,265	62.7
	C. B. Kennamer (R)	4,914	37.3
8	William Richardson (D)	5,873	94.9
	John T. Masterson (R)	317	5.1
9	Oscar W. Underwood (D)	7,864	100.0

ARKANSAS

	Candidates	Votes	%
1	Robert B. Macon (D)	5,635	82.2
	D. F. Taylor (R)	1,223	17.8
2	Stephen Brundidge Jr (D)	5,137	80.9
	E. J. Mason (R)	1,216	19.1
3	John C. Floyd (D)	5,715	63.8
	W. N. Ivie (R)	3,246	36.2
4	William Ben Cravens (D)	7,290	65.5
	George Tilles (R)	3,840	34.5
5	Charles C. Reid (D)	5,967	75.1
	Alonzo Hedges (R)	1,976	24.9
6	Joseph T. Robinson (D)	5,473	84.4
	R. C. Thompson (R)	1,010	15.6
7	Robert M. Wallace (D)	3,255	99.1

CALIFORNIA

	Candidates	Votes	%
1	William F. Englebright (R)	18,954	54.1
	F. W. Taft (D)	13,984	39.9
2	Duncan E. McKinlay (R)	23,411	51.8
	W. A. Beard (D)	20,262	44.8
3	Joseph R. Knowland (R)	21,510	60.0
	Hugh W. Brunk (D)	7,716	21.5
	Charles C. Boynton (I LEAGUE)	3,614	10.1
	William McDevitt (SOC)	2,514	7.0
4	Julius Kahn (R)	5,678	62.4
	David S. Hirshberg (D)	3,016	33.2
5	Everis A. Hayes (R)	22,530	52.6
	Hiram G. Davis (D)	17,925	41.9
	Joseph Lawrence (SOC)	2,343	5.5
6	James C. Needham (R)	18,928	55.6
	Harry A. Greene (D)	12,868	37.8
7	James McLachlan (R)	22,338	56.7
	Robert G. Laucks (D)	11,197	28.4
	Claude Riddle (SOC)	3,641	9.3
	Levi D. Johnson (P)	2,189	5.6
8	Sylvester C. Smith (R)	22,548	55.6
	C. A. Barlow (D)	13,992	34.5
	N. A. Richardson (SOC)	4,001	9.9

Special Election

		Votes	%
1	William F. Englebright (R)	18,125	95.2

COLORADO

	Candidates	Votes	%
1	Robert William Bonynge (R)	47,549	55.5
	Charles F. Tew (D)	31,133	36.3
	Luella Twining (SOC)	4,989	5.8
2	Warren A. Haggott (R)	54,869	49.3
	William W. Rowan (D)	46,783	42.1
	Flavius E. Ashburn (SOC)	7,666	6.9
AL	George W. Cook (R)	102,426	52.2
	Samuel W. Belford (D)	76,792	39.1
	Guy E. Miller (SOC)	12,668	6.5

CONNECTICUT

	Candidates	Votes	%
1	E. Stevens Henry (R)	21,605	56.8
	Holden (D)	15,039	39.6
2	Nehemiah D. Sperry (R)	29,058	53.1
	Wallace (D)	23,757	43.4
3	Edwin W. Higgins (R)	12,391	57.3
	Larue (D)	8,833	40.8
4	Ebenezer J. Hill (R)	26,484	56.9
	Beers (D)	18,969	40.8
AL	George L. Lilley (R)	88,115	54.8
	Donahue (D)	67,747	42.1

DELAWARE

	Candidates	Votes	%
AL	Hiram R. Burton (R)	20,210	52.8
	David T. Marvel (D)	17,118	44.8

FLORIDA

	Candidates	Votes	%
1	Stephen M. Sparkman (D)	6,212	86.5
	C. C. Allen (SOC)	967	13.5
2	Frank Clark (D)	8,792	88.1
	J. F. McClelland (SOC)	1,179	11.8
3	William B. Lamar (D)	5,415	93.4
	T. B. Meeker (SOC)	384	6.6

GEORGIA

	Candidates	Votes	%
1	Charles G. Edwards (D)	4,964	92.1
	D. B. Rigdon (R)	429	8.0
2	James M. Griggs (D)	3,425	100.0
3	Elijah B. Lewis (D)	2,386	100.0
4	William C. Adamson (D)	2,705	100.0
5	Leonidas F. Livingston (D)	3,030	100.0
6	Charles L. Bartlett (D)	3,374	100.0
7	Gordon Lee (D)	3,132	100.0
8	William M. Howard (D)	2,246	100.0
9	Thomas M. Bell (D)	3,159	100.0
10	Thomas W. Hardwick (D)	1,743	99.8
11	William G. Brantley (D)	2,748	100.0

IDAHO

	Candidates	Votes	%
AL	Burton L. French (R)	42,134	58.6
	Murray R. Hattabaugh (D)	23,818	33.1
	Edward L. Rigg (SOC)	4,834	6.7

ILLINOIS

	Candidates	Votes	%
1	Martin B. Madden (R)	17,015	59.3
	Martin Emerich (D)	10,015	34.9
2	James R. Mann (R)	20,660	63.4
	Herbert J. Friedman (D)	8,565	26.3
	Bernard Berlyn (SOC)	3,032	9.3
3	William W. Wilson (R)	14,130	49.7
	Paul A. Dratz (D)	6,569	23.1
	Willis C. Stone (I LG)	4,775	16.8
	James A. Prout (SOC)	2,457	8.6
4	James T. McDermott (D)	9,997	46.7
	Charles S. Wharton (R)	8,377	39.1
	James McCarthy (SOC)	2,859	13.3
5	Adolph J. Sabath (D)	9,545	46.1
	Anthony Michalek (R)	8,634	41.7
	Joseph Kral (SOC)	2,373	11.5
6	William Lorimer (R)	18,153	55.4
	Edmund J. Stack (D)	10,734	32.8
	Walter F. Huggins (SOC)	2,082	6.4
	Edward E. Blake (P)	1,794	5.5
7	Philip Knopf (R)	18,595	51.3
	Frank Buchanan (D)	11,383	31.4
	George Koop (SOC)	5,587	15.4
8	Charles McGavin (R)	11,421	40.0
	Stanley H. Kunz (D)	11,336	39.7
	Abraham Priess (I LG)	3,128	11.0
	James B. Smiley (SOC)	2,664	9.3
9	Henry S. Boutell (R)	15,316	50.6
	Arthur J. Donoghue (D)	8,504	28.1
	John M. Vail (I LG)	3,607	11.9
	Charles L. Breckon (SOC)	2,592	8.6
10	George Edmund Foss (R)	18,886	62.7
	Charles L. Young (D)	7,598	25.2
	Lewis W. Hardy (SOC)	2,777	9.2
11	Howard M. Snapp (R)	18,569	60.7
	Benjamin P. Alschuler (D)	9,104	29.8
	George McGinnis (P)	2,201	7.2
12	Charles E. Fuller (R)	19,463	86.9
	Victor Irving Clark (P)	1,712	7.6
	A. A. Patterson (SOC)	1,224	5.5
13	Frank O. Lowden (R)	16,590	51.2
	James P. Wilson (D)	14,747	45.5
14	James McKinney (R)	18,583	54.7
	David W. Matthews (D)	12,978	38.2
15	George W. Prince (R)	19,975	54.2
	Hiram N. Wheeler (D)	14,191	38.5
16	Joseph V. Graff (R)	16,983	50.3
	Louis F. Meek (D)	13,876	41.1
	C. E. Stebbins (P)	1,966	5.8
17	John A. Sterling (R)	16,804	55.8
	L. W. MacNeil (D)	11,377	37.8
	James H. Burrows (P)	1,927	6.4
18	Joseph G. Cannon (R)	22,804	58.4
	Charles G. Taylor (D)	12,777	32.7
19	William B. McKinley (R)	23,662	52.7
	John W. Yantis (D)	19,247	42.9
20	Henry T. Rainey (D)	19,578	54.9
	Jacob G. Pope (R)	14,645	41.1
21	Benjamin F. Caldwell (D)	22,429	53.5
	Zeno J. Rives (R)	17,396	41.5
22	William A. Rodenberg (R)	23,138	56.2
	James J. McInerney (D)	15,371	37.3
23	Martin D. Foster (D)	21,680	49.5
	Frank S. Dickson (R)	20,361	46.5
24	Pleasant T. Chapman (R)	17,990	51.1
	James R. Williams (D)	16,241	46.2
25	George W. Smith (R)	17,835	52.6
	James M. Joplin (D)	14,240	42.0

Special Election

		Votes	%
13	Frank O. Lowden (R)	17,003	96.9

INDIANA

	Candidates	Votes	%
1	John H. Foster (R)	20,278	50.0
	Gustavus V. Menzies (D)	18,959	46.7
2	John C. Chaney (R)	22,299	48.7
	Cyrus E. Davis (D)	21,889	47.8
3	William E. Cox (D)	18,606	49.3
	George H. Hester (R)	18,151	48.1
4	Lincoln Dixon (D)	20,049	51.0
	John H. Kamman (R)	18,181	46.2
5	Elias S. Holliday (R)	22,532	48.8
	Claud G. Bowers (D)	21,579	46.8
6	James E. Watson (R)	22,135	49.5
	Thomas H. Kuhn (D)	20,629	46.2
7	Jesse Overstreet (R)	28,020	52.8
	Frank E. Gavin (D)	23,234	43.8
8	John A. M. Adair (D)	24,027	51.4
	George W. Cromer (R)	19,783	42.3
9	Charles B. Landis (R)	23,865	49.5
	Marion E. Clodfelter (D)	21,633	44.9
10	Edgar D. Crumpacker (R)	24,695	54.0
	William Darroch (D)	20,072	43.9
11	George W. Rauch (D)	22,988	50.2
	Frederick Landis (R)	19,833	43.3
	Levi T. Pennington (P)	2,367	5.2
12	Clarence C. Gilhams (R)	19,695	48.6
	John W. Morr (D)	19,345	47.7
13	Abraham L. Brick (R)	23,360	48.0
	Benjamin F. Shively (D)	23,153	47.5

Special Election

		Votes	%
12	Clarence C. Gilhams (R)	19,249	50.5
	John W. Morr (D)	18,870	49.5

IOWA

	Candidates	Votes	%
1	Charles A. Kennedy (R)	16,145	49.1
	George S. Tracy (D)	15,875	48.3
2	Albert F. Dawson (R)	20,112	50.2
	George W. Ball (D)	18,520	46.2
3	Benjamin P. Birdsall (R)	22,315	57.7
	J. C. Murtagh (D)	15,113	39.0
4	Gilbert N. Haugen (R)	20,731	60.6
	M. J. Carter (D)	12,739	37.2
5	Robert G. Cousins (R)	19,076	54.3
	Robert C. Stinton (D)	14,612	41.6
6	Daniel W. Hamilton (D)	18,987	51.8
	John F. Lacey (R)	16,713	45.6
7	John A. T. Hull (R)	19,617	59.2
	John Nathan Smith (D)	11,464	34.6
8	William Peter Hepburn (R)	19,516	53.0
	Joel S. Estes (D)	16,074	43.7
9	Walter I. Smith (R)	21,863	60.7
	William C. Campbell (D)	13,250	36.8
10	James Perry Conner (R)	26,017	60.9
	John B. Butler (D)	15,317	35.9
11	Elbert H. Hubbard (R)	22,236	55.9
	Charles A. Dickson (D)	16,893	42.5

KANSAS

	Candidates	Votes	%
1	Charles Curtis (R)	22,790*	57.5
	W. D. Webb (D)	16,215	40.9
2	Charles F. Scott (R)	23,521	53.1
	Mason S. Peters (D)	19,653	44.4
3	Philip P. Campbell (R)	25,669	52.5
	Francis M. Brady (D)	19,807	40.5
	Fred D. Warren (SOC)	2,908	5.9
4	James Monroe Miller (R)	17,393	53.5
	J. W. Moore (D)	14,313	44.0
5	William A. Calderhead (R)	18,183	54.1
	Hugh Alexander (D)	14,561	43.3
6	William A. Reeder (R)	21,212	51.9
	John B. Rea (D)	17,116	41.9
7	Edmond H. Madison (R)	21,580	55.0
	O. H. Truman (D)	15,623	39.8
8	Victor Murdock (R)	14,862	56.5
	Frank B. Lawrence (D)	10,427	39.6

KENTUCKY

	Candidates	Votes	%
1	Ollie M. James (D)	12,870	85.9
	J. D. Smith (P)	2,118	14.1
2	Augustus O. Stanley (D)	13,282	61.9
	Paul M. Moore (R)	7,406	34.5
3	Addison D. James (R)	14,987	50.2
	James M. Richardson (D)	14,288	47.8
4	Ben Johnson (D)	15,128	59.1
	M. L. Heavrin (R)	9,819	38.4
5	J. Swagar Sherley (D)	15,698	54.8
	William C. Owens (R)	12,210	42.6
6	Joseph L. Rhinock (D)	13,358	48.3
	William F. Schuerman (R)	12,973	46.9
7	William P. Kimball (D)	15,658	74.0
	Joseph W. Calvert (R)	5,066	23.9
8	Harvey Helm (D)	13,182	55.1
	L. W. Bethurum (R)	10,164	42.4
9	Joseph B. Bennett (R)	18,430	51.4
	James N. Kehoe (D)	17,314	48.2
10	John W. Langley (R)	17,254	50.7
	Frank A. Hopkins (D)	16,343	48.0
11	Don C. Edwards (R)	15,645	61.9
	Ancil Gatliff (D)	8,714	34.5

LOUISIANA

	Candidates	Votes	%
1	Adolph Meyer (D)	8,667	90.0
	Henry Seiner (R)	681	7.1
2	Robert C. Davey (D)	6,349	91.9
	A. L. Redden (R)	409	5.9
3	Robert F. Broussard (D)	4,267	85.0
	S. P. Watts (R)	753	15.0
4	John T. Watkins (D)	3,210	97.3
5	Joseph E. Ransdell (D)	3,177	100.0

	Candidates	Votes	%
6	George K. Favrot (D)	3,270	92.4
	John Deblieux (R)	269	7.6
7	Arsene P. Pujo (D)	3,761	66.1
	C. C. Duson (R)	1,762	31.0

MAINE

	Candidates	Votes	%
1	Amos L. Allen (R)	16,903	51.9
	James C. Hamlen (D)	15,254	46.8
2	Charles E. Littlefield (R)	18,708	50.9
	Daniel J. McGillicuddy (D)	17,346	47.2
3	Edwin C. Burleigh (R)	16,682	51.7
	E. J. Lawrence (D)	14,891	46.2
4	Llewellyn Powers (R)	17,279	54.9
	George M. Hanson (D)	13,705	43.6

MARYLAND

	Candidates	Votes	%
1	William H. Jackson (R)	18,567	51.5
	Thomas A. Smith (D)	16,124	44.8
2	J. Fred C. Talbott (D)	17,870	50.3
	Robert Garrett (R)	16,618	46.7
3	Harry B. Wolf (D)	15,725	49.8
	William W. Johnson (R)	14,841	47.0
4	John Gill Jr. (D)	18,010	50.7
	John V. L. Findlay Jr. (R)	16,306	45.9
5	Sydney E. Mudd (R)	16,798	53.7
	George M. Smith (D)	13,405	42.8
6	George A. Pearre (R)	16,136	55.3
	Harvey R. Spessard (D)	11,232	38.5

MASSACHUSETTS

	Candidates	Votes	%
1	George P. Lawrence (R)	15,622	59.7
	Frank J. Lawler (D)	9,528	36.4
2	Frederick H. Gillett (R)	15,873	61.3
	Edward A. Hall (D)	8,412	32.5
	George H. Wrenn (SOC)	1,622	6.3
3	Charles G. Washburn (R)	15,686	58.6
	William I. McLoughlin (D)	10,415	38.9
4	Charles Q. Tirrell (R)	20,750	79.0
	Timothy Richardson (SOC)	5,501	20.9
5	Butler Ames (R)	15,778	54.2
	Joseph J. Flynn (D)	12,881	44.2
6	Augustus P. Gardner (R)	18,390	54.8
	George A. Schofield (D)	14,055	41.9
7	Ernest W. Roberts (R)	21,752	66.4
	John A. O'Keefe (D)	9,816	30.0
8	Samuel W. McCall (R)	17,952	59.4
	Frederick S. Deitrick (D)	11,690	38.7
9	John A. Keliher (D)	15,997	68.1
	Edward C. Webb (R)	6,256	26.6
	George W. Galvin (SOC)	1,242	5.3
10	Joseph F. O'Connell (D)	18,979	54.9
	Edward B. Callender (R)	14,621	42.3
11	Andrew J. Peters (D)	18,099	53.9
	Daniel W. Lane (R)	14,670	43.7
12	John W. Weeks (R)	18,948	61.5
	David W. Murray (D)	10,591	34.4
13	William S. Greene (R)	14,236	68.3
	Francis M. Kennedy (D)	6,603	31.7
14	William C. Lovering (R)	18,002	61.8
	Thomas F. Loorem (D)	6,815	23.4
	Daniel A. White (SOC)	4,301	14.8

MICHIGAN

	Candidates	Votes	%
1	Edwin Denby (R)	23,741	57.5
	Frederick F. Ingram (D)	16,975	41.1
2	Charles E. Townsend (R)	23,397	96.2
3	Washington Gardner (R)	16,821	58.4
	John B. Shipman (D)	10,388	36.1
4	Edward L. Hamilton (R)	18,553	60.6
	George R. Herkimer (D)	11,561	37.8
5	William Alden Smith (R)	18,487*	88.9
	John E. Nicles (SOC)	1,302	6.3
6	Samuel W. Smith (R)	24,001	60.4
	Peter B. Delisle (D)	14,360	36.1
7	Henry McMorran (R)	17,100	59.6
	William Springer (D)	11,028	38.4

	Candidates	Votes	%
8	Joseph W. Fordney (R)	16,849	92.4
9	James C. McLaughlin (R)	14,374	69.8
	Charles G. Wing (D)	5,288	25.7
10	George A. Loud (R)	18,958	97.2
11	Archibald B. Darragh (R)	18,110	70.7
	Arthur J. Lacy (D)	7,517	29.3
12	H. Olin Young (R)	22,271	75.6
	John F. Ryan (D)	6,315	21.4

MINNESOTA

	Candidates	Votes	%
1	James A. Tawney (R)	17,352	57.8
	French (D)	12,676	42.2
2	Winfield S. Hammond (D)	13,526	50.5
	McCleary (R)	12,466	46.5
3	Charles R. Davis (R)	19,461	100.0
4	Frederick C. Stevens (R)	19,300	64.3
	Scholle (D)	9,179	30.6
	Lando (PUB OWN)	1,544	5.1
5	Frank M. Nye (R)	23,742	55.6
	Larrabee (D)	16,448	38.5
6	Charles A. Lindbergh (R)	16,752	56.1
	Tift (D)	13,115	43.9
7	Andrew G. Volstead (R)	21,491	100.0
8	J. Adam Bede (R)	18,640	75.6
	Peterson (PUB OWN)	6,025	24.4
9	Halvor Steenerson (R)	22,145	80.1
	Boen (PUB OWN)	5,490	19.9

MISSISSIPPI

	Candidates	Votes	%
1	Ezekiel S. Candler Jr. (D)	2,566	100.0
2	Thomas Spight (D)	2,567	100.0
3	Benjamin G. Humphreys (D)	1,540	100.0
4	Wilson S. Hill (D)	2,536	100.0
5	Adam Byrd (D)	2,782	100.0
6	Eaton J. Bowers (D)	4,077	95.9
7	F. A. McLain (D)	1,933	100.0
8	John S. Williams (D)	2,091	100.0

MISSOURI

	Candidates	Votes	%
1	James T. Lloyd (D)	19,796	54.3
	Clements (R)	16,655	45.7
2	William W. Rucker (D)	20,732	56.7
	Beazell (R)	15,814	43.2
3	Joshua W. Alexander (D)	18,669	52.9
	Unidentified Candidate (R)	16,616	47.1
4	Charles F. Booher (D)	18,631	51.3
	Fulkerson (D)	17,458	48.1
5	Edgar C. Ellis (R)	21,496	52.2
	Wallace (D)	19,710	47.8
6	David A. De Armond (D)	17,574	53.0
	Atkeson (R)	15,579	47.0
7	Courtney W. Hamlin (D)	22,248	51.3
	Welborn (R)	20,497	47.3
8	Dorsey W. Shackleford (D)	16,245	53.4
	Quigley (R)	14,186	46.6
9	James Beauchamp Clark (D)	21,364	54.3
	Garber (R)	17,972	45.7
10	Richard Bartholdt (R)	31,639	61.9
	Coale (D)	16,336	32.0
	Hoehn (SOC)	3,102	6.1
11	Henry S. Caulfield (R)	13,171	47.8
	Neville (D)	13,133	47.6
12	Harry M. Coudrey (R)	11,281	50.1
	Selph (D)	10,451	46.4
13	Madison R. Smith (D)	16,056	50.7
	Rhodes (R)	15,628	49.3
14	Joseph J. Russell (D)	24,288	51.4
	Tyndall (R)	22,799	48.3
15	Thomas Hackney (D)	20,677	48.3
	Caulkins (R)	20,402	47.6
16	J. Robert Lamar (D)	15,366	50.7
	Murphy (R)	14,939	49.3

MONTANA

	Candidates	Votes	%
AL	Charles N. Pray (R&A-T R)	28,368	50.5
	Thomas J. Walsh (D & LAB)	22,894	40.8

Candidates	Votes	%
John Hudson (SOC)	4,638	8.3

NEBRASKA

	Candidates	Votes	%
1	Ernest M. Pollard (R)	14,771	52.8
	T. J. Doyle (D & PPI)	11,870	42.4
2	Gilbert M. Hitchcock (D)	11,644	51.0
	John L. Kennedy (R)	11,136	48.8
3	John F. Boyd (R)	18,837	49.0
	Guy T. Graves (D & PPI)	18,546	48.2
4	Edmund H. Hinshaw (R)	19,032	55.0
	J. J. Thomas (D & PPI)	15,211	44.0
5	George W. Norris (R)	16,450	53.1
	Roderick D. Sutherland (D & PPI)	14,031	45.3
6	Moses P. Kinkaid (R)	18,677	57.1
	G. L. Shumway (D & PPI)	13,147	40.2

NEVADA

	Candidates	Votes	%
AL	George A. Bartlett (D&SILVER)	7,320	51.4
	Oscar J. Smith (R)	5,665	39.8
	H. T. Jardine (SOC)	1,251	8.8

NEW HAMPSHIRE

	Candidates	Votes	%
1	Cyrus A. Sulloway (R)	22,701	57.8
	Charles A. Morse (D)	15,601	39.7
2	Frank D. Currier (R)	23,073	58.0
	Henri T. Ledoux (D)	15,669	39.4

NEW JERSEY

	Candidates	Votes	%
1	Henry C. Loudenslager (R)	20,674	65.8
	Summerill (D)	9,308	29.6
2	John J. Gardner (R)	19,637	63.0
	Perry (D)	8,921	28.6
3	Benjamin F. Howell (R)	20,472	54.3
	Harvey (D)	16,638	44.1
4	Ira W. Wood (R)	17,497	52.9
	Southwick (D)	13,989	42.3
5	Charles N. Fowler (R)	19,760	48.8
	Martine (D & ID)	19,208	47.5
6	William Hughes (D)	25,438	50.2
	Burke (R)	23,335	46.1
7	Richard W. Parker (R)	16,493	49.5
	Kaemer (D)	15,983	48.0
8	Le Gage Pratt (D)	18,334	56.9
	Gottlob (R)	12,460	38.7
9	Eugene W. Leake (D)	18,367	55.4
	Pickett (R)	12,628	38.1
10	James A. Hamill (D)	22,882	65.2
	Cruse (R)	9,305	26.5

NEW YORK

	Candidates	Votes	%
1	William W. Cocks (R)	22,569	60.3
	Monson Morris (D)	14,418	38.5
2	George H. Lindsay (D)	11,420	39.2
	John J. McManus (I LEAGUE)	9,069	31.2
	Ernest C. Wagner (R)	7,591	26.1
3	Charles T. Dunwell (R)	16,546	45.5
	Walter B. Raymond (D)	10,707	29.5
	Henry Clay Peters (I LEAGUE)	8,089	22.3
4	Charles B. Law (R)	17,079	41.3
	Herman H. Torborg (D)	12,114	29.3
	Edson Lawrence (I LEAGUE)	10,590	25.6
5	George E. Waldo (R)	19,832	46.1
	John J. Roach (D)	11,995	27.9
	Michael A. Fitzgerald (I LEAGUE)	10,575	24.6
6	William M. Calder (R)	21,195	54.9
	Robert Baker (D & IL)	17,102	44.3
7	John J. Fitzgerald (D)	15,055	47.1
	Charles R. Banks (R)	8,433	26.4
	John T. Moran (I LEAGUE)	8,220	25.7
8	Daniel J. Riordan (D)	21,340	65.6
	Frank L. Frugone (R)	10,632	32.7
9	Henry M. Goldfogle (D)	7,276	53.3
	Morris Hillquit (SOC)	3,586	26.3

	Candidates	Votes	%
	Charles S. Adler (R)	2,734	20.0
10	William Sulzer (D & IL)	15,962	71.3
	Frederick J. Etzel (R)	4,843	21.6
	Alexander Jonas (SOC)	1,560	7.0
11	Charles V. Fornes (D & IL)	26,511	70.3
	Charles W. Lefler (R)	10,640	28.2
12	William Bourke Cockran (D & IL)	20,481	71.4
	Henry Carey (R)	7,410	25.8
13	Herbert Persons (R)	16,381	55.0
	William H. Jackson (D)	9,881	33.2
	Frank Hendrick (I LEAGUE)	3,172	10.7
14	William Willett Jr. (D)	17,675	46.3
	Frank E. Losee (R)	10,006	26.2
	Charles E. Shober (I LEAGUE)	8,110	21.3
	Richard Morton (SOC)	2,328	6.1
15	Jacob Van Vechten Olcott (R)	16,210	54.8
	John J. Halligan (D & IL)	13,123	44.4
16	Francis Burton Harrison (D & IL)	16,954	66.3
	Jacob R. Schiff (R)	7,062	27.6
17	William S. Bennet (R)	27,159	53.1
	Francis E. Shober (D & IL)	23,284	45.5
18	Joseph A. Goulden (D)	28,339	46.9
	James L. Wells (R)	17,943	29.7
	James T. Farrelly (I LEAGUE)	12,109	20.1
19	John E. Andrus (R)	23,356	53.8
	Timothy Healy (D)	19,218	44.3
20	Thomas W. Bradley (R)	21,191	55.9
	Victor A. Wilder (D, I LEAGUE)	16,111	42.5
21	Samuel McMillan (R)	20,717	51.0
	Percy W. Decker (D, I LEAGUE)	19,745	48.6
22	William H. Draper (R)	22,344	55.3
	Thomas A. Paterson (D, I LEAGUE)	17,188	42.5
23	George N. Southwick (R)	29,099	50.7
	George C. Hisgen (D, I LEAGUE)	27,344	47.7
24	George W. Fairchild (R)	24,474	51.3
	Walter Scott (D, I LEAGUE)	23,215	48.7
25	Cyrus Durey (R)	25,041	55.4
	Frank Beebe (D)	18,385	40.7
26	George R. Malby (R)	26,209	70.2
	Andrew B. Cooney (D)	10,931	29.3
27	James S. Sherman (R)	24,027	53.3
	James K. O'Connor (D, U LAB)	19,757	43.8
28	Charles L. Knapp (R)	23,451	60.7
	Jay C. Bardo (D)	12,573	32.5
	Frank H. Lewis (P)	2,197	5.7
29	Michael E. Driscoll (R)	30,350	61.4
	William W. Vanbrocklin (D)	17,385	35.2
30	John W. Dwight (R)	27,069	59.9
	Amasa G. Genung (D)	16,269	36.0
31	Sereno E. Payne (R)	25,475	62.6
	Dudley M. Warner (D)	14,150	34.8
32	James Breck Perkins (R)	25,343	52.4
	William L. Manning (D)	21,393	44.2
33	Jacob Sloat Fassett (R)	21,235	55.0
	Frank P. Frost (D)	15,883	41.1
34	Peter A. Porter (D, IND CONG)	25,837	55.6
	James W. Wadsworth (R)	19,935	42.9
35	William H. Ryan (D)	22,140	56.5
	Frank X. Bernhardt (R)	16,494	42.1
36	De Alva S. Alexander (R)	24,457	58.0
	John W. Williams (D)	16,209	38.5
37	Edward B. Vreeland (R)	25,468	65.2
	Mark Graves (D)	11,562	29.6

NORTH CAROLINA

	Candidates	Votes	%
1	John H. Small (D)	11,401	75.8
	J. Q. A. Wood (R)	3,610	24.0
2	Claude Kitchin (D)	10,057	84.6
	J. R. Gaskill (R)	1,816	15.3
3	Charles R. Thomas (D)	10,382	66.3
	W. R. Dixon (R)	5,280	33.7
4	Edward W. Pou (D)	12,161	69.8
	Berry Godwin (R)	5,270	30.2
5	William W. Kitchin (D)	16,503	59.6
	C. A. Reynolds (R)	11,089	40.0
6	Hannibal L. Godwin (D)	9,729	67.7
	James B. Schulken (R)	4,645	32.3

	Candidates	Votes	%
7	Robert N. Page (D)	11,780	56.7
	G. D. B. Reynolds (R)	9,008	43.3
8	Richard N. Hackett (D)	16,907	51.6
	E. S. Blackburn (R)	15,841	48.4
9	Edwin Y. Webb (D)	12,727	58.6
	F. Roberts (R)	8,988	41.4
10	William T. Crawford (D)	13,049	51.6
	James J. Britt (R)	12,200	48.2

NORTH DAKOTA

	Candidates	Votes	%
AL	Thomas F. Marshall (R)	38,923✓	
	Asle J. Gronna (R)	36,772✓	
	A. G. Burr (D)	21,350	
	John D. Benton (D)	21,050	
	H. Halvorson (SOC)	1,151	
	W. J. Bailey (SOC)	1,129	

OHIO

	Candidates	Votes	%
1	Nicholas Longworth (R)	25,161	56.9
	Thomas H. Bentham (D)	18,004	40.7
2	Herman P. Goebel (R)	23,219	59.1
	John H. Meyer (D)	12,258	31.2
	Harry R. Probasco (I)	2,259	5.8
3	J. Eugene Harding (R)	24,567	49.5
	James E. Campbell (D)	22,837	46.0
4	William E. Tou Velle (D)	17,582	55.6
	J. C. Rosser (R)	12,934	40.9
5	Timothy T. Ansberry (D)	17,256	50.7
	William W. Campbell (R)	16,241	47.7
6	Matthew R. Denver (D)	17,471	50.6
	Charles Q. Hildebrant (R)	16,291	47.2
7	J. Warren Keifer (R)	15,975	53.8
	William B. Rodgers (D)	12,387	41.8
8	Ralph D. Cole (R)	21,524	54.9
	Homer Southard (D)	16,396	41.9
9	Isaac R. Sherwood (D, I)	18,411	47.8
	E. G. McClelland (R)	18,370	47.7
10	Henry Bannon (R)	17,979	53.3
	Thomas H. B. Jones (D)	14,686	43.5
11	Albert Douglas (R)	21,247	50.4
	Oliver W. H. Wright (D)	19,914	47.2
12	Edward L. Taylor Jr. (R)	19,629	56.9
	William A. Taylor (D)	13,351	38.7
13	Grant E. Mouser (R)	20,736	49.2
	Daniel R. Crissinger (D)	20,463	48.5
14	J. Ford Laning (R)	20,962	51.7
	William H. Budd (D)	18,443	45.5
15	Beman G. Dawes (R)	18,364	49.6
	George White (D)	16,945	45.8
16	Capell L. Weems (R)	14,712	53.9
	Frank A. Summers (D)	11,347	41.6
17	William A. Ashbrook (D)	19,982	49.3
	Martin L. Suyser (R)	19,497	48.1
18	James Kennedy (R)	19,684	49.5
	John C. Welty (D)	17,840	44.9
19	W. Aubrey Thomas (R)	20,341	61.3
	Thaddeus E. Hoyt (D)	10,926	32.9
20	Paul Howland (R)	19,439	51.8
	Charles W. Lapp (D)	16,966	45.3
21	Theodore E. Burton (R)	20,826	92.9
	Robert Bandlow (SOC)	1,376	6.1

OREGON

	Candidates	Votes	%
1	Willis C. Hawley (R)	23,120	49.1
	Charles V. Galloway (D)	19,340	41.1
	W. W. Myers (SOC)	2,794	5.9
2	William R. Ellis (R)	28,315	61.0
	James Harvey Graham (D)	12,151	26.2
	A. M. Paul (SOC)	3,532	7.6
	H. W. Stone (P)	2,408	5.2

PENNSYLVANIA

	Candidates	Votes	%
1	Henry H. Bingham (R, JEFF)	24,280	63.7
	E. Spencer Miller (LINCOLN)	8,718	22.9
	Joseph L. Galen (D)	4,738	12.4
2	John E. Reyburn (R, LINCOLN)	28,140	85.7

Candidates	Votes	%
G. Frank Stephens (D)	4,262	13.0
3 J. Hampton Moore (R, JEFF)	20,337	63.6
William J. O'Brien (LINCOLN, D)	11,240	35.1
4 Reuben O. Moon (R, LINCOLN)	26,289	85.6
Horace S. Fogel (D)	3,993	13.0
5 William W. Foulkrod (R, LINCOLN)	29,390	86.1
Thomas P. Dolan (D)	3,987	11.7
6 George D. McCreary (R, LINCOLN)	38,269	84.6
Francis X. Ward (D)	6,425	14.2
7 Thomas S. Butler (R, BC)	19,676	70.0
John J. Buckley (D, P)	8,249	29.3
8 Irving P. Wanger (R, CP)	22,416	54.6
Walter F. Leedom (D, LINCOLN)	18,231	44.4
9 Henry B. Cassel (R)	18,903	67.7
J. Harold Wickersham (LINCOLN)	9,007	32.3
10 T. D. Nichols (D)	18,037	60.3
Thomas H. Dale (R, LINCOLN)	11,796	39.4
11 John T. Lenahan (D)	16,176	50.6
Bennett J. Cobleigh (RO SOC D)	9,627	30.1
William H. Dettry (SOC)	5,197	16.3
12 Charles N. Brumm (R)	15,652	58.5
Watson F. Shepperd (D)	10,247	38.3
13 John H. Rothermel (D)	21,885	54.2
J. Wilmer Fisher (R)	16,488	40.8
Morris E. Gibson (SOC)	2,044	5.1
14 George W. Kipp (D)	12,091	49.2
Mial E. Lilly (R)	11,288	46.0
15 William B. Wilson (D)	14,582	48.2
Elias Deemer (R)	14,201	47.0
16 John G. McHenry (D)	14,707	53.8
Edmund W. Samuel (R, P)	12,131	44.4
17 Benjamin K. Focht (R)	17,130	52.2
William Alexander (D)	14,036	42.8
18 Marlin E. Olmsted (R)	22,447	58.9
John Lindner (D)	14,457	37.9
19 John M. Reynolds (R)	17,521	50.6
Joseph E. Thropp (D, LINCOLN)	13,649	39.4
Warren W. Bailey (BRYAN)	2,140	6.2
20 Daniel F. Lafean (R)	15,653	50.7
Horace Keesey (D)	15,204	49.3
21 Charles F. Barclay (R, P)	15,210	57.5
Hugh S. Taylor (D)	10,572	40.0
22 George F. Huff (R)	15,924	59.0
Silas A. Kline (D, LINCOLN)	10,490	38.9
23 Allen F. Cooper (R)	15,008	54.7
Ernest O. Kooser (D, LINCOLN)	10,309	37.6
John O. Stoner (P)	1,789	6.5
24 Ernest F. Acheson (R)	15,490	49.2
Robert K. Aiken (D, LINCOLN)	14,163	45.0
25 Arthur L. Bates (R)	13,564	60.6
Andrew J. Palm (D, P)	8,109	36.2
26 J. Davis Brodhead (D, LINCOLN)	15,371	54.3
Gustav A. Schneebeli (R)	12,427	43.9
27 Joseph G. Beale (R)	14,646	58.3
S. C. Hepler (D)	9,101	36.2
Enoch McGary (P)	1,392	5.5
28 Nelson P. Wheeler (R)	16,550	52.7
Earl H. Beshlin (D)	10,433	33.2
H. E. Horne (P)	3,750	11.9
29 William H. Graham (R, CIT)	17,688	91.8
30 John Dalzell (R, CIT)	13,984	65.1
Robert J. Black (D, UN LAB)	6,452	30.0
31 James Francis Burke (R, CIT)	13,364	67.5
Frank Lackner (D)	5,740	29.0
32 A. J. Barchfeld (R)	14,525	68.1
M. C. O'Donovan (D)	4,811	22.6

RHODE ISLAND

	Candidates	Votes	%
1	Daniel L. D. Granger (D)	16,846	50.4
	Dyer (R)	16,030	48.0

	Candidates	Votes	%
2	Adin B. Capron (R)	16,979	53.0
	Garvin (D)	14,593	45.5

SOUTH CAROLINA

1	George S. Legare (D)	3,965	99.3
2	James O'H. Patterson (D)	4,588	95.3
3	Wyatt Aiken (D)	2,938	100.0
4	Joseph T. Johnson (D)	5,124	98.7
5	David E. Finley (D)	3,585	100.0
6	J. Edwin Ellerbe (D)	3,483	100.0
7	Asbury F. Lever (D)	5,191	97.5

SOUTH DAKOTA

AL	Philo Hall (R)	48,096✓	
	William H. Parker (R)	48,010✓	
	William S. Elder (D)	19,976	
	Samuel A. Ramsey (D)	19,791	
	C. V. Templeton (P)	3,392	
	R. J. Day (P)	3,313	
	James Kirwan (SOC)	2,439	
	Henry A. Berge (SOC)	2,322	

TENNESSEE

1	Walter P. Brownlow (R)	17,249	52.1
	John H. Coldwell (D)	9,145	27.6
	A. A. Taylor (IR)	6,700	20.2
2	Nathan W. Hale (R)	13,817	71.5
	E. L. Foster (D)	5,125	26.5
3	John A. Moon (D)	15,388	56.9
	T. W. Peace (R)	11,409	42.2
4	Cordell Hull (D)	11,951	53.6
	John E. Oliver (R)	10,312	46.3
5	William C. Houston (D)	11,450	71.5
	T. W. Wade (R)	4,446	27.8
6	John W. Gaines (D)	12,546	79.8
	J. W. Johnson (R)	2,981	19.0
7	Lemuel P. Padgett (D)	12,750	68.7
	Joe P. Kidd (R)	5,818	31.3
8	Thetus W. Sims (D)	11,209	50.7
	J. C. R. McCall (R)	10,874	49.2
9	Finis J. Garrett (D)	11,538	76.9
	Yandell Hann (R)	3,437	22.9
10	George W. Gordon (D)	10,378	95.4

TEXAS

1	Morris Sheppard (D)	9,479	90.6
	Phil E. Baer (R)	886	8.5
2	Samuel B. Cooper (D)	9,593	93.0
	J. H. Kurth (R)	622	6.0
3	Gordon J. Russell (D)	8,522	89.3
	G. W. L. Smith (R)	753	7.9
4	Choice B. Randell (D)	11,508	87.3
	W. G. McGinnis (R)	1,678	12.7
5	Jack Beall (D)	9,060	91.9
	A. M. Cochran (R)	525	5.3
6	Rufus Hardy (D)	5,536	92.1
7	Alexander W. Gregg (D)	6,590	100.0
8	John M. Moore (D)	8,536	84.3
	W. A. Matthai (R)	1,593	15.7
9	George F. Burgess (D)	10,257	75.6
	A. M. Waugh (R)	3,043	22.4
10	Albert S. Burleson (D)	8,103	88.6
	Carl Beck (R)	1,041	11.4
11	Robert L. Henry (D)	7,183	100.0
12	Oscar W. Gillespie (D)	9,790	95.6
13	John H. Stephens (D)	14,120	90.0
	E. E. Diggs (R)	1,295	8.3
14	James L. Slayden (D)	10,811	80.1
	D. Doole (R)	2,692	19.9
15	John N. Garner (D)	9,284	63.7
	T. W. Moore (R)	5,281	36.3
16	William R. Smith (D)	13,030	92.0
	Ben Vantuys (R)	744	5.3

UTAH

	Candidates	Votes	%
AL	Joseph Howell (R)	42,620	50.1
	Orlando W. Powers (D)	28,031	33.0
	Thomas Weir (AM)	11,411	13.4

VERMONT

1	David J. Foster (R)	20,660	69.0
	Edwin B. Clift (D)	8,957	29.9
2	Kittredge Haskins (R)	20,738	70.1
	John H. Fenter (D)	8,157	27.6

VIRGINIA

1	William A. Jones (D)	5,773	81.7
	Bristow (R)	1,294	18.3
2	Harry L. Maynard (D)	4,358	74.5
	Hughes (R)	1,489	25.5
3	John Lamb (D)	3,908	82.2
	Hanson (R)	639	13.4
4	Francis R. Lassiter (D)	2,615	100.0
5	Edward W. Saunders (D)	6,194	50.9
	Simmons (R)	5,972	49.1
6	Carter Glass (D)	4,060	74.8
	Heermans (R)	1,336	24.6
7	James Hay (D)	5,573	70.1
	Beecher (R)	2,372	29.9
8	John F. Rixey (D)	5,059*	84.0
	Henderson (R)	962	16.0
9	Campbell Slemp (R)	13,798	54.0
	Bruce (D)	11,757	46.0
10	Henry D. Flood (D)	5,962	68.9
	Gregory (R)	2,696	31.1

WASHINGTON

AL	Francis W. Cushman (R)	71,921✓	
	Wesley L. Jones (R)	71,656✓	
	William E. Humphrey (R)	71,353✓	
	William Blackman (D)	31,811	
	Patrick S. Byrne (D)	30,689	
	Dudley Eshleman (D)	30,369	
	Emil Herman (SOC)	8,431	
	J. H. Barkley (SOC)	8,420	
	A. Wagenknecht (SOC)	8,367	
	J. M. Wilkin (P)	2,584	
	A. S. Caton (P)	2,582	
	William Everett (P)	2,571	

WEST VIRGINIA

1	William P. Hubbard (R)	19,362	52.5
	T. S. Riley (D)	15,315	41.5
2	George C. Sturgiss (R)	20,384	53.7
	M. H. Dent (D)	16,712	44.0
3	Joseph Holt Gaines (R)	19,888	52.8
	George Byrne (D)	15,482	41.1
4	Harry C. Woodyard (R)	16,310	52.3
	George W. Hardman (D)	13,637	43.8
5	James A. Hughes (R)	22,395	57.4
	Joseph S. Miller (D)	15,971	40.9

WISCONSIN

1	Henry Allen Cooper (R)	16,226	61.1
	John J. Cunningham (D)	8,818	33.2
	Moses Hull (SOCIAL D)	1,504	5.7
2	John M. Nelson (R)	14,806	51.5
	George W. Levis (D)	12,881	44.8
3	James W. Murphy (D)	14,701	50.1
	Joseph W. Babcock (R)	13,690	46.6
4	William J. Cary (R)	12,231	41.3
	Edmund T. Melms (SOCIAL D)	8,759	29.6
	Thomas J. Fleming (D)	8,656	29.2
5	William H. Stafford (R)	13,948	44.3
	Albert J. Welch (SOCIAL D)	8,870	28.1
	Joseph G. Donnelly (D)	8,192	26.0
6	Charles H. Weisse (D)	19,446	63.3
	Alvin Dreger (R)	10,512	34.2

	Candidates	Votes	%
7	John J. Esch (R)	18,042	72.7
	Charles F. Hulle (D)	6,779	27.3
8	James H. Davidson (R)	16,966	59.7
	John E. McMuller (D)	9,594	33.8
9	Gustav Kustermann (R)	14,180	60.5
	Phillip A. Badour (D)	8,689	37.1
10	Elmer A. Morse (R)	20,225	63.6
	Dennis D. Conway (D)	10,669	33.5

	Candidates	Votes	%
11	John J. Jenkins (R)	19,002	74.9
	Francis J. Maguire (D)	5,147	20.3

Special Election

	Candidates	Votes	%
2	John M. Nelson (R)	10,098	71.2
	Grant Thomas (PRI R)	3,703	26.1

WYOMING

	Candidates	Votes	%
AL	Frank W. Mondell (R)	16,813	62.2
	John C. Hamm (D)	8,944	33.1

1907 House Elections

MICHIGAN

Special Election

	Candidates	Votes	%
5	Gerrit John Diekema (R)	11,898	51.8
	George P. Hummer (D)	10,508	45.7

OKLAHOMA

(Became a state Nov. 16, 1907)

	Candidates	Votes	%
1	Bird S. McGuire (R)	22,362	50.3
	William L. Eagleton (D)	21,003	47.3
2	Elmer L. Fulton (D)	26,006	51.0
	Thompson B. Ferguson (R)	25,028	49.0

	Candidates	Votes	%
3	James S. Davenport (D)	26,370	52.8
	Henry D. Hubbard (R)	23,623	47.3
4	Charles D. Carter (D)	29,782	62.6
	Frank C. Disney (R)	15,752	33.1
5	Scott Ferris (D)	32,935	66.2
	Loren G. McKnight (R)	14,883	29.9

1908 House Elections

ALABAMA

	Candidates	Votes	%
1	George W. Taylor (D)	7,457	100.0
2	S. Hubert Dent Jr. (D)	10,754	100.0
3	Henry D. Clayton (D)	9,993	100.0
4	William B. Craig (D)	6,239	65.1
	J. Osmond Middleton (R)	3,341	34.9
5	J. Thomas Heflin (D)	8,024	83.9
	W. W. Wadsworth	1,543	16.1
6	Richmond P. Hobson (D)	9,211	78.0
	Henry T. Nations	2,593	22.0
7	John L. Burnett (D)	8,972	56.0
	N.H. Freeman (R)	7,046	44.0
8	William Richardson (D)	9,691	82.7
	Jeremiah Murphy (R)	2,028	17.3
9	Oscar W. Underwood (D)	11,288	79.4
	J. B. Sloan	2,567	18.1

Special Election

		Votes	%
2	Oliver C. Wiley (D)	7,710	100.0

ARKANSAS

		Votes	%
1	Robert B. Macon (D)	12,957	66.5
	C. T. Bloodworth (R)	6,534	33.5
2	William A. Oldfield (D)	13,056	63.8
	H. H. Myers (R)	7,421	36.2
3	John C. Floyd (D)	13,710	59.9
	W. T. Mills (R)	9,186	40.1
4	William B. Cravens (D)	13,064	59.8
	Edwin Mechem (R)	8,779	40.2
5	Charles C. Reid (D)	15,331	66.1
	Guy W. Caron (R)	7,849	33.9
6	Joseph T. Robinson (D)	24,389	100.0
7	Robert M. Wallace (D)	12,354	59.8
	S. R. Young (R)	8,312	40.2

CALIFORNIA

		Votes	%
1	William F. Englebright (R)	20,624	54.1
	E. W. Holland (D)	14,031	36.8
	D. N. Cunningham (SOC)	2,898	7.6
2	Duncan E. McKinlay (R)	28,627	57.4
	W. K. Hays (D)	19,193	38.5
3	Joseph R. Knowland (R)	27,857	64.1
	George W. Peckham (D)	9,889	22.8
	O. H. Philbrick (SOC)	4,052	9.3
4	Julius Kahn (R)	9,202	52.7
	James G. Maguire (D)	7,497	42.9
5	Everis A. Hayes (R)	28,127	49.1
	George A. Tracy (D)	24,531	42.8
	E. H. Misner (SOC)	3,640	6.4
6	James C. Needham (R)	21,323	52.0
	Fred P. Feliz (D)	15,868	38.7
	W. M. Pattison (SOC)	2,288	5.6
7	James McLachlan (R)	37,244	51.9
	Jud R. Rush (D)	25,445	35.4
	A. R. Holston (SOC)	4,432	6.2
	M. W. Atwood (P)	3,899	5.4
8	Sylvester C. Smith (R)	29,305	55.7
	W. E. Shepherd (D)	18,245	34.7
	N. A. Richardson (SOC)	5,025	9.6

COLORADO

		Votes	%
1	Atterson W. Rucker (D)	60,643	49.9
	Robert William Bonynge (R)	57,597	47.4
2	John A. Martin (D)	65,814	48.7
	Warren A. Haggott (R)	64,553	47.8
AL	Edward T. Taylor (D)	126,934	48.4
	James C. Burger (R)	121,265	46.2

CONNECTICUT

		Votes	%
1	E. Stevens Henry (R)	26,829	59.5

	Candidates	Votes	%
	Gerth (D)	15,595	34.6
2	Nehemiah D. Sperry (R)	36,083	55.0
	Reilly (D)	26,832	40.9
3	Edwin W. Higgins (R)	14,935	60.3
	Hunter (D)	9,190	37.1
4	Ebenezer J. Hill (R)	32,843	60.7
	Wilson (D)	19,423	35.9
AL	John Q. Tilson (R)	111,557	58.6
	Avery (D)	70,029	36.8

DELAWARE

		Votes	%
AL	William H. Heald (R)	24,314	50.7
	Levin Irving Handy (D)	22,515	46.9

FLORIDA

		Votes	%
1	Stephen M. Sparkman (D)	9,971	75.2
	George W. Allen (R)	1,990	15.0
	C. C. Allen (SOC)	1,297	9.8
2	Frank Clark (D)	10,726	75.9
	William R. O'Neal (R)	2,552	18.1
	A. N. Jackson (SOC)	862	6.1
3	Dannitte H. Mays (D)	9,314	80.2
	William H. Northup (R)	1,712	14.7

GEORGIA

		Votes	%
1	Charles G. Edwards (D)	9,845	95.7
2	James M. Griggs (D)	9,273	100.0
3	Dudley M. Hughes (D)	7,627	99.7
4	William C. Adamson (D)	7,242	100.0
5	Leonidas F. Livingston (D)	8,909	100.0
6	Charles L. Bartlett (D)	6,575	100.0
7	Gordon Lee (D)	11,396	100.0
8	William M. Howard (D)	7,112	100.0
9	Thomas M. Bell (D)	11,653	100.0
10	Thomas W. Hardwick (D)	6,853	100.0
11	William G. Brantley (D)	9,741	100.0

IDAHO

		Votes	%
AL	Thomas R. Hamer (R)	49,983	52.0
	James L. McClear (D)	37,605	39.2
	Halbert Barton (SOC)	6,248	6.5

ILLINOIS

		Votes	%
1	Martin B. Madden (R)	23,370	60.9
	Matthew J. Mandable (D)	13,692	35.7
2	James R. Mann (R)	32,024	64.8
	John T. Donahoe (D)	14,351	29.0
3	William Warfield Wilson (R)	24,979	56.0
	Fred J. Crowley (D)	15,995	35.8
4	James T. McDermott (D)	16,606	54.7
	Charles S. Wharton (R)	12,196	40.2
5	Adolph J. Sabath (D)	12,997	53.3
	Anthony Michalek (R)	9,876	40.5
	Morris Siskind (SOC)	1,285	5.3
6	William Lorimer (R)	32,540	61.1
	Frank C. Wood (D)	17,093	32.1
7	Fred Lundin (R)	31,513	54.1
	Frank Buchanan (D)	20,088	34.5
	George Koop (SOC)	4,183	7.2
8	Thomas Gallagher (D)	15,963	49.2
	Philip M. Ksycki (R)	14,660	45.2
9	Henry Sherman Boutell (R)	21,110	56.2
	Charles C. Stilwell (D)	13,544	36.1
10	George Edmund Foss (R)	31,130	62.0
	Western Starr (D)	14,840	29.6
11	Howard M. Snapp (R)	29,821	61.2
	Coll McNaughton (D)	15,875	32.6
12	Charles E. Fuller (R)	33,340	65.4
	M. N. Armstrong (D)	13,795	27.1
13	Frank O. Lowden (R)	24,797	61.4
	William C. Green (D)	13,273	32.9

	Candidates	Votes	%
14	James McKinney (R)	23,394	54.3
	Matt J. McEniry (D)	16,745	38.9
15	George W. Prince (R)	26,770	50.9
	W. Emery Lancaster (D)	22,410	42.6
16	Joseph V. Graff (R)	23,880	53.2
	James W. Hill (D)	18,557	41.3
17	John A. Sterling (R)	22,014	53.2
	C. S. Schneider (D)	16,737	40.5
	William P. Allin (P)	2,228	5.4
18	Joseph G. Cannon (R)	29,170	54.9
	Henry C. Bell (D)	21,795	41.0
19	William B. McKinley (R)	30,588	52.9
	Fred B. Hamill (D)	24,913	43.1
20	Henry T. Rainey (D)	24,023	55.3
	James H. Danskin (R)	17,726	40.8
21	James M. Graham (D)	23,433	47.9
	H. Clay Wilson (R)	21,716	44.4
22	William A. Rodenberg (R)	27,858	50.2
	Charles A. Karch (D)	24,341	43.9
23	Martin D. Foster (D)	28,181	53.6
	Frank S. Dickson (R)	23,772	45.2
24	Pleasant T. Chapman (R)	21,833	52.4
	John Q. A. Ledbetter (D)	18,333	44.0
25	Napoleon B. Thistlewood (R)	24,319	51.6
	I. R. Spilman (D)	20,537	43.6

Special Election

		Votes	%
25	Napoleon B. Thistlewood (R)	12,263	47.2
	William H. Warder (D)	8,620	33.2
	Sam T. Brush	3,987	15.3

INDIANA

		Votes	%
1	John W. Boehne (D)	23,054	48.3
	John H. Foster (R)	22,965	48.1
2	William A. Cullop (D)	27,172	50.0
	John C. Chaney (R)	24,609	45.3
3	William E. Cox (D)	24,139	54.9
	John W. Lewis (R)	18,966	43.1
4	Lincoln Dixon (D)	25,231	53.6
	James A. Cox (R)	20,726	44.0
5	Ralph W. Moss (D)	28,844	48.9
	Howard Maxwell (R)	27,361	46.4
6	William O. Barnard (R)	27,053	49.2
	Thomas H. Kuhn (D)	25,905	47.2
7	Charles A. Korbly (D)	34,686	49.2
	Jesse Overstreet (R)	34,003	48.2
8	John A.M. Adair (D)	29,259	52.5
	Nathan B. Hawkins (R)	23,890	42.9
9	Martin A. Morrison (D)	27,540	48.9
	Charles B. Landis (R)	26,449	47.0
10	Edgar D. Crumpacker (R)	32,954	54.4
	William Darroch (D)	26,742	44.1
11	George W. Rauch (D)	25,526	48.3
	Charles H. Good (R)	24,313	46.0
12	Cyrus Cline (D)	25,051	50.6
	Clarence L. Gilhams (R)	22,706	45.8
13	Henry A. Barnhart (D)	28,509	48.2
	Charles W. Miller (R)	28,229	47.7

Special Election

		Votes	%
13	Henry A. Barnhart (D)	28,131	48.4
	Charles W. Miller (R)	27,708	47.7

IOWA

		Votes	%
1	Charles A. Kennedy (R)	18,318	51.2
	George S. Tracy (D)	16,695	46.7
2	Albert F. Dawson (R)	22,915	51.0
	Mark A. Walsh (D)	21,050	46.9
3	Charles E. Pickett (R)	25,530	57.6
	Charles Elliott (D)	17,362	39.2
4	Gilbert N. Haugen (R)	20,929	55.3
	M. E. Geiser (D)	16,296	43.1

	Candidates	Votes	%
5	James W. Good (R)	22,773	57.3
	Samuel K. Tracy (D)	15,994	40.2
6	Nathan E. Kendall (R)	18,909	48.3
	Daniel W. Hamilton (D)	18,628	47.6
7	John A. T. Hull (R)	24,931	55.7
	Charles O. Holley (D)	17,620	39.4
8	William D. Jamieson (D)	20,436	49.2
	William P. Hepburn (R)	20,126	48.4
9	Walter I. Smith (R)	23,215	55.8
	R. C. Spencer (D)	17,661	42.4
10	Frank P. Woods (R)	29,608	61.4
	Montague Hakes (D)	17,256	35.8
11	Elbert H. Hubbard (R)	26,572	57.1
	W. G. Sears (D)	19,033	40.9

KANSAS

	Candidates	Votes	%
1	Daniel R. Anthony Jr. (R)	27,792	57.6
	F. M. Pearl (D)	19,842	41.1
2	Charles F. Scott (R)	28,499	50.5
	B. J. Sheridan (D)	26,242	46.5
3	Philip P. Campbell (R)	29,207	49.8
	T. J. Hudson (D)	23,377	39.8
	Ben F. Wilson (SOC)	5,776	9.8
4	James M. Miller (R)	20,978	55.3
	Thomas H. Grisham (D)	16,024	42.2
5	William A. Calderhead (R)	21,093	51.6
	R. A. Lovitt (D)	18,555	45.4
6	William A. Reeder (R)	22,200	48.6
	John R. Connelly (D)	21,923	48.0
7	Edmond H. Madison (R)	26,315	52.5
	Samuel I. Hale (D)	21,460	42.9
8	Victor Murdock (R)	19,029	56.4
	Frank B. Lawrence (D)	13,477	39.9

KENTUCKY

	Candidates	Votes	%
1	Ollie M. James (D)	27,435	64.1
	Porter (R)	15,163	35.4
2	Augustus O. Stanley (D)	23,320	54.3
	Worsham (R)	19,302	45.0
3	Robert Y. Thomas Jr. (D)	20,079	49.8
	James (R)	19,583	48.6
4	Ben Johnson (D)	24,344	53.2
	Gaddle (R)	21,246	46.4
5	J. Swagar Sherley (D)	27,953	51.7
	Kinkead (R)	25,513	47.1
6	Joseph L. Rhinock (D)	23,945	55.4
	Inglis (R)	18,057	41.8
7	James C. Cantrill (D)	21,157	59.0
	Bristow (R)	14,697	41.0
8	Harvey Helm (D)	17,725	51.8
	Benthrum (R)	16,049	46.9
9	Joseph B. Bennett (R)	22,832	50.0
	Kehoe (D)	22,107	48.4
10	John W. Langley (R)	20,092	52.0
	Davis (D)	18,570	48.0
11	Don C. Edwards (R)	36,073	69.8
	Patterson (D)	14,729	28.5

LOUISIANA

	Candidates	Votes	%
1	Albert Estopinal (D)	13,923	87.9
	Henry C. Warmoth (R)	1,916	12.1
2	Robert C. Davey (D)	14,447*	95.7
3	Robert F. Broussard (D)	5,845	75.9
	Carlton R. Beattie (R)	1,696	22.0
4	John T. Watkins (D)	7,188	88.2
	W. S. Emmons (SOC)	513	6.3
	John F. Slattery (R)	449	5.5
5	Joseph E. Ransdell (D)	7,110	96.5
6	Robert C. Wickliffe (D)	7,108	91.8
	George J. Reiley (R)	632	8.2
7	Arsene P. Pujo (D)	8,270	93.4
	Alex Hymes (SOC)	585	6.6

MAINE

	Candidates	Votes	%
1	Amos L. Allen (R)	18,887	53.5
	John C. Scates (D)	15,615	44.2
2	John P. Swasey (R)	18,479	50.7
	Daniel J. McGillicuddy (D)	17,115	46.9
3	Edwin C. Burleigh (R)	18,282	53.1
	Samuel W. Gould (D)	15,611	45.3
4	Frank E. Guernsey (R)	19,659	54.1
	George M. Hanson (D)	16,152	44.4

MARYLAND

	Candidates	Votes	%
1	James Harry Covington (D)	19,381	52.7
	William H. Jackson (R)	16,547	45.0
2	J. Fred C. Talbott (D)	21,526	52.2
	Robert Garrett (R)	19,040	46.1
3	John Kronmiller (R)	14,772	49.1
	Harry B. Wolf (D)	14,510	48.2
4	John Gill Jr. (D)	18,562	52.1
	John P. Hill (R)	16,626	46.7
5	Sydney E. Mudd (R)	15,057	49.2
	George M. Smith (D)	14,740	48.2
6	George A. Pearre (R)	18,619	49.1
	David J. Lewis (D)	18,073	47.6

MASSACHUSETTS

	Candidates	Votes	%
1	George P. Lawrence (R)	17,990	60.2
	David T. Clark (D)	10,765	36.0
2	Frederick H. Gillett (R)	17,515	62.0
	John L. Rice (D)	7,839	27.8
	George W. Curtis (I LEAGUE)	1,623	5.8
3	Charles G. Washburn (R)	18,265	62.2
	William I. McLoughlin (D)	9,654	32.9
4	Charles Q. Tirrell (R)	18,842	55.0
	John J. Mitchell (D)	15,431	45.0
5	Butler Ames (R)	16,251	56.0
	Joseph J. Flynn (DI)	11,910	41.1
6	Augustus P. Gardner (R)	22,093	69.4
	Arthur Withington (D)	7,334	23.0
	Franklin H. Wentworth (SOC)	2,418	7.6
7	Ernest W. Roberts (R)	22,179	68.9
	George Brickett (D)	7,958	24.7
	Clarence L. McIver (I LEAGUE)	2,078	6.5
8	Samuel W. McCall (R)	19,147	63.6
	Frederick S. Deltrick (D)	9,638	32.0
9	John A. Kellher (D)	14,060	62.3
	John A. Campbell (R)	6,002	26.6
	Junlus T. Auerbach (I LEAGUE)	2,492	11.1
10	Joseph F. O'Connell (D)	16,553	46.4
	J. Mitchell Galvin (R)	16,549	46.4
11	Andrew J. Peters (D)	15,881	48.7
	Daniel W. Lane (R)	15,447	47.4
12	John W. Weeks (R)	21,097	66.0
	Jesse C. Ivy (D)	9,069	28.4
	Albert E. George (I LEAGUE)	1,779	5.6
13	William S. Greene (R)	16,870	72.5
	John F. McGuinness (D)	4,977	21.4
	Charles W. Copeland (I LEAGUE)	1,436	6.2
14	William C. Lovering (R)	20,959	66.8
	Eliot L. Packard (D)	6,709	21.4
	Charles B. Drew (I LEAGUE)	1,855	5.9
	George J. Alcott (SOC)	1,851	5.9

MICHIGAN

	Candidates	Votes	%
1	Edwin Denby (R)	30,696	56.4
	William D. Mahon (D)	21,695	39.9
2	Charles E. Townsend (R)	28,442	58.0
	James C. Henderson (D)	19,306	39.4
3	Washington Gardner (R)	24,078	53.7
	Hiram C. Blackman (D)	18,907	42.1
4	Edward L. Hamilton (R)	27,074	59.4
	Charles H. Kimmerle (D)	16,731	36.7
5	Gerrit J. Diekema (R)	25,030	54.1
	Edwin F. Sweet (D)	19,437	42.0
6	Samuel W. Smith (R)	32,043	56.8
	Frank L. Dodge (D)	21,304	37.8
7	Henry McMorran (R)	22,879	59.4
	William Springer (D)	13,843	36.0
8	Joseph W. Fordney (R)	21,210	59.7
	Jenner E. Morse (D)	13,948	39.3
9	James C. McLaughlin (R)	22,459	72.1

	Candidates	Votes	%
	Cornellus Gerber (D)	8,688	27.9
10	George A. Loud (R)	24,780	64.6
	Lewis P. Coumans (D)	12,677	33.1
11	Francis H. Dodds (R)	29,402	70.5
	Leavitt S. Griswold (D)	12,315	29.5
12	H. Olin Young (R)	35,310	72.2
	Patrick H. Obrien (D)	13,586	27.8

MINNESOTA

	Candidates	Votes	%
1	James A. Tawney (R)	20,464	53.6
	French (D)	17,708	46.4
2	Winfield S. Hammond (D)	17,716	55.7
	McCleary (R)	14,091	44.3
3	Charles R. Davis (R)	19,896	59.7
4	Frederick C. Stevens (R)	21,818	60.8
	Peebles (D)	12,395	34.5
5	Frank M. Nye (R)	24,542	61.7
	Thomas P. Dwyer (D)	13,429	33.8
6	Charles A. Lindbergh (R)	22,574	63.2
	Gilkinson (D)	13,174	36.9
7	Andrew J. Volstead (R)	26,597	100.0
8	Clarence B. Miller (R)	27,873	81.6
	Halliday (PUB OWN)	6,298	18.4
9	Halvor Steenerson (R)	17,957	50.0
	Sageng (I)	15,010	41.8
	Braaten (PUB OWN)	2,985	8.3

MISSISSIPPI

	Candidates	Votes	%
1	Ezekiel S. Candler Jr. (D)	8,043	100.0
2	Thomas Spight (D)	7,511	100.0
3	Benjamin G. Humphreys (D)	4,808	100.0
4	Thomas U. Sisson (D)	8,039	100.0
5	Adam M. Byrd (D)	9,750	100.0
6	Eaton J. Bowers (D)	8,702	100.0
7	William A. Dickson (D)	6,807	94.7
	H. C. Turley (R)	384	5.3
8	James W. Collier (D)	5,657	100.0

MISSOURI

	Candidates	Votes	%
1	James T. Lloyd (D)	22,133	52.4
	Chamberlain (R)	19,122	45.2
2	William W. Rucker (D)	23,263	55.6
	Haley (R)	18,266	43.6
3	Joshua W. Alexander (D)	20,387	52.6
	Eads (R)	18,341	47.3
4	Charles F. Booher (D)	21,671	53.1
	Reed (R)	18,908	46.4
5	William P. Borland (D)	31,635	52.7
	Ellis (R)	27,289	45.5
6	David A. De Armond (D)	18,532	52.7
	Atkeson (R)	16,372	46.6
7	Courtney W. Hamlin (D)	24,731	49.8
	Whitaker (R)	23,927	48.2
8	Dorsey W. Shackleford (D)	17,230	52.3
	Irwin (R)	15,691	47.7
9	James Beauchamp Clark (D)	23,090	51.5
	Roy (R)	21,702	48.4
10	Richard Bartholdt (R)	49,127	60.4
	Thompson (D)	28,634	35.2
11	Patrick F. Gill (D)	21,001	50.9
	Findly (R)	19,195	46.5
12	Harry M. Coudrey (R)	16,471	49.7
	Selph (D)	15,930	48.1
13	Politte Elvins (R)	17,125	50.3
	Smith (D)	16,918	49.7
14	Charles A. Crow (R)	25,951	48.3
	Russell (D)	25,187	46.8
15	Charles H. Morgan (R)	23,040	47.9
	Hackney (D)	22,410	46.6
16	Arthur P. Murphy (R)	16,835	50.8
	J. Robert Lamar (D)	16,295	49.2

MONTANA

	Candidates	Votes	%
AL	Charles N. Pray (R)	32,819	48.9
	Thomas D. Long (D)	29,032	43.2
	Lewis J. Duncan (SOC)	5,318	7.9

NEBRASKA

	Candidates	Votes	%
1	John A. Maguire (D & PPI)	19,651	51.2
	E. M. Pollard (R)	18,716	48.8
2	Gilbert M. Hitchcock (D)	18,781	52.6
	A. W. Jefferies (R)	16,206	45.4
3	James P. Latta (D & PPI)	26,832	51.6
	J. F. Boyd (R)	24,865	47.8
4	Edmund H. Hinshaw (R)	22,674	50.0
	C. F. Gilbert (D & PPI)	21,819	48.1
5	George W. Norris (R)	20,649#	49.4
	F. W. Ashton (D & PPI)	20,627	49.4
6	Moses P. Kinkaid (R)	25,786	50.7
	W. H. Westover (D & PPI)	23,317	45.8

NEVADA

	Candidates	Votes	%
AL	George A. Bartlett (D)	11,253	47.3
	H. B. Maxson (R)	7,552	31.7
	A. L. Fitzgerald (INDEP)	3,031	12.7
	J. Critchfield (SOC)	1,965	8.3

NEW HAMPSHIRE

	Candidates	Votes	%
1	Cyrus A. Sulloway (R)	24,413	56.9
	Michael J. White (D)	17,400	40.5
2	Frank D. Currier (R)	26,007	59.3
	Frederick M. Colby (D)	16,666	38.0

NEW JERSEY

	Candidates	Votes	%
1	Henry C. Loudenslager (R)	27,443	58.4
	Grosscup (D)	17,640	37.5
2	John J. Gardner (D)	23,906	52.2
	Grubb (D)	20,506	44.8
3	Benjamin F. Howell (R)	26,302	56.6
	Clark (D)	19,766	42.5
4	Ira W. Wood (R)	23,919	56.5
	Steele (D)	17,210	40.7
5	Charles N. Fowler (R)	27,948	55.5
	Barber (D)	20,485	40.7
6	William Hughes (D)	29,516	49.5
	Foxhall (R)	27,989	46.9
7	Richard W. Parker (R)	24,863	56.6
	Townsend (D)	18,104	41.2
8	William H. Wiley (R)	24,536	57.9
	Le Gage Pratt (D)	16,276	38.4
9	Eugene F. Kinkead (D)	23,485	54.5
	Critchfield (R)	18,608	43.2
10	James A. Hamill (D)	23,820	57.7
	Dwyer (R)	16,105	39.0

NEW YORK

	Candidates	Votes	%
1	William W. Cocks (R)	29,459	56.6
	Monson Morris (D)	19,519	37.5
	Edward Walsh (I LEAGUE)	1,886	6.6
2	George H. Lindsay (D)	15,455	53.9
	William Liebermann (R)	9,999	34.9
3	Otto Godfrey Foelker (R)	18,614	50.3
	James P. Maher (D)	15,395	41.6
4	Charles B. Law (R)	23,944	49.7
	Edward R. Gilman (D)	18,910	39.2
	Otto Wegener (SOC)	2,707	5.6
	Arthur S. Colborne (I LEAGUE)	2,542	5.3
5	Richard Young (R)	28,075	54.2
	J. Harry Snook (D)	19,897	38.4
6	William M. Calder (R)	22,050	55.4
7	John J. Fitzgerald (D)	17,773	58.5
	William R. A. Koehl (R)	10,296	33.9
	William T. Smith (I LEAGUE)	1,841	6.1
8	Daniel J. Riordan (D)	22,329	62.5
	James E. Winterbottom (R)	11,484	32.2
9	Henry M. Goldfogle (D)	6,194	53.8
	Morris Hillquit (SOC)	2,483	21.6
	Louis I. Cherey (R)	2,312	20.1
10	William Sulzer (D)	10,602	54.4
	Gustave Hartman (R)	6,511	33.4
	Morris Brown (SOC)	1,754	9.0
11	Charles V. Fornes (D)	20,637	58.9

	Candidates	Votes	%
	Laurence L. Driggs (R)	11,700	33.4
	Alexander Porter (I LEAGUE)	1,853	5.3
12	Michael F. Conroy (D)	16,757	60.9
	Victor H. Duras (R)	8,090	29.4
	James D. Bush (I LEAGUE)	1,482	5.4
13	Herbert Parsons (R)	15,108	51.4
	Gerald Hull Gray (D)	12,380	42.2
14	William Willett Jr. (D)	21,643	52.2
	Emanuel Castka (R)	14,189	34.2
	Philip H. Schmitt (SOC)	3,055	7.4
	Herbert Wade (I LEAGUE)	2,485	6.0
15	Jacob Van Vechten Olcott (R)	16,921	56.5
	Rhinelander Waldo (D)	12,531	41.8
16	Francis Burton Harrison (D)	12,555	50.8
	Francis A. Adams (R)	8,822	35.7
	John Parr (SOC)	1,966	8.0
	Edwin D. Ackerman (I LEAGUE)	1,334	5.4
17	William S. Bennet (R)	32,764	53.5
	William Madoo (D)	24,736	40.4
18	Joseph A. Goulden (D)	35,569	51.5
	Joel Elias Spingarn (R)	25,590	37.1
	Frank McGarry (I LEAGUE)	4,144	6.0
	George B. Staring (SOC)	3,649	5.3
19	John E. Andrus (R)	27,966	55.6
	William H. Lynn (D)	19,851	39.4
20	Thomas W. Bradley (R)	23,927	55.9
	Richard E. King (D)	17,979	42.0
21	Hamilton Fish (R)	22,832	52.0
	Andrew C. Zabriskie (D)	19,725	44.9
22	William H. Draper (R)	22,980	52.7
	Winfield A. Huppuch (D)	19,074	43.7
23	George N. Southwick (R)	30,593	48.5
	William H. Keeler (D)	30,008	47.6
24	George W. Fairchild (R)	28,496	53.8
	G. Hyde Clark (D)	23,059	43.5
25	Cyrus Durey (R)	27,152	54.4
	Joseph D. Baucus (D)	19,927	39.9
26	George R. Malby (R)	30,615	66.4
	Ellis Woodworth (D)	14,914	32.3
27	Charles S. Millington (R)	26,962	54.0
	Curtis F. Alliaume (D)	21,365	42.8
28	Charles L. Knapp (R)	25,948	57.9
	Andrew C. Cornwall (D)	15,756	35.1
	Sylvanus V. Barker (P)	2,372	5.3
29	Michael E. Driscoll (R)	33,664	59.1
	Alphonso E. Fitch (D)	20,527	36.0
30	John W. Dwight (R)	30,622	57.4
	Alexander D. Wales (D)	19,818	37.2
31	Sereno E. Payne (R)	28,990	59.7
	John A. Curtis (D)	17,891	36.8
32	James B. Perkins (R)	33,025	56.4
	Herman S. Searle (D)	22,858	39.0
33	Jacob Sloat Fassett (R)	24,580	52.2
	James A. Parsons (D)	20,319	43.1
34	James S. Simmons (R)	30,298	54.7
	Frank W. Brown (D)	23,298	42.1
35	Daniel A. Driscoll (D)	25,866	55.2
	L. Bradley Dorr (R)	20,093	42.9
36	De Alva S. Alexander (R)	30,621	58.2
	William H. Follette (D)	20,790	39.5
37	Edward Butterfield		
	Vreeland (R)	32,327	62.4
	Sanford H. Thorne (D)	15,718	30.4

NORTH CAROLINA

	Candidates	Votes	%
1	John H. Small (D)	13,119	71.1
	I. M. Meekins (R)	5,342	28.9
2	Claude Kitchin (D)	12,275	78.2
	M. Ferguson (R)	3,361	21.4
3	Charles R. Thomas (D)	11,544	59.4
	Eli W. Hill (R)	7,896	40.6
4	Edward W. Pou (D)	13,463	60.0
	Willis G. Briggs (R)	8,966	40.0
5	John M. Morehead (R)	19,288	50.1
	A. L. Brooks (D)	18,938	49.2
6	Hannibal L. Godwin (D)	12,542	66.3
	Albert H. Slocumb (R)	6,385	33.7
7	Robert N. Page (D)	15,057	56.2
	Z. V. Walser (R)	11,732	43.8

	Candidates	Votes	%
8	Charles H. Cowles (R)	16,863	52.1
	R. N. Hackett (D)	15,488	47.8
9	Edwin Y. Webb (D)	16,530	55.0
	John A. Smith (R)	13,514	45.0
10	John G. Grant (R)	15,245	50.5
	William T. Crawford (D)	14,884	49.3

NORTH DAKOTA

	Candidates	Votes	%
AL	Asle J. Gronna (R)	57,357✓	
	Louis B. Hanna (R)	55,610✓	
	T. D. Casey (D)	29,426	
	O. G. Major (D)	28,448	
	Francis Cooper (I)	591	
	E. D. Herring (I)	533	

OHIO

	Candidates	Votes	%
1	Nicholas Longworth (R)	30,444	55.2
	Thomas P. Hart (D)	23,224	42.1
2	Herman P. Goebel (R)	28,008	48.6
	Charles N. Danenhower (D)	27,904	48.4
3	James M. Cox (D)	32,524	48.1
	John Eugene Harding (I)	19,306	28.5
	William G. Frizell (R)	12,593	18.6
4	William E. Tou Velle (D)	26,896	58.2
	Thomas J. Mulligan (R)	18,305	39.6
5	Timothy T. Ansberry (D)	23,712	57.7
	William W. Campbell (R)	16,745	40.7
6	Matthew R. Denver (D)	23,192	51.6
	Jesse Taylor (R)	21,592	48.0
7	J. Warren Keifer (R)	24,323	51.2
	O. E. Duff (D)	21,503	45.2
8	Ralph D. Cole (R)	24,476	50.0
	William R. Niven (D)	23,271	47.5
9	Isaac R. Sherwood (D)	29,171	47.8
	James H. Southard (R)	27,523	45.1
	Charles H. Miller (SOC)	3,285	5.4
10	Adna R. Johnson (R)	23,687	53.8
	Thomas H. B. Jones (D)	18,918	43.0
11	Albert Douglas (R)	27,796	49.9
	L. A. Sears (D)	26,650	47.8
12	Edward L. Taylor Jr. (R)	29,483	54.5
	Benjamin F. Gayman (D)	22,813	42.2
13	Carl C. Anderson (D)	29,736	53.2
	Grant E. Mouser (R)	25,019	44.7
14	William G. Sharp (D)	28,525	50.0
	Frank V. Owen (R)	26,799	47.0
15	James Joyce (R)	22,186	48.8
	George White (D)	22,129	48.7
16	David A. Hollingsworth (R)	23,318	51.7
	N. A. McCombs (D)	19,914	44.2
17	William A. Ashbrook (D)	28,712	55.3
	John F. Harrison (R)	21,341	41.1
18	James Kennedy (R)	32,287	48.3
	John J. Whitacre (D)	29,040	43.4
19	W. Aubrey Thomas (R)	32,182	55.3
	Stephen A. Robinson (D)	22,529	38.7
20	Paul Howland (R)	32,839	55.9
	Charles Lapp (D)	23,592	40.1
21	Theodore E. Burton (R)	31,968*	59.3
	James E. Wertman (D)	19,451	36.1

OKLAHOMA

	Candidates	Votes	%
1	Bird S. McGuire (R)	23,312	50.6
	Henry S. Johnston (D)	20,501	44.5
2	Dick T. Morgan (R)	26,273	46.9
	Elmer L. Fulton (D)	25,349	45.2
	Charles P. Randall (SOC)	4,443	7.9
3	Charles E. Creager (R)	24,952	48.3
	James S. Davenport (D)	23,881	46.2
	Winston T. Banks (SOC)	2,827	5.5
4	Charles D. Carter (D)	22,047	50.6
	Benjamin F. Hackett (R)	15,727	36.1
	M. C. Carter (SOC)	5,769	13.3
5	Scott Ferris (D)	31,026	55.7
	Thompson (R)	19,149	34.4
	Davis (SOC)	5,478	9.8

OREGON

	Candidates	Votes	%
1	Willis C. Hawley (R)	31,889	58.8
	J. J. Whitney (D)	14,841	27.4
	W. S. Richards (SOC)	4,349	8.0
	Daniel Staver (P)	3,189	5.9
2	William R. Ellis (R)	35,579	63.6
	John A. Jeffrey (D)	13,865	24.8
	G. E. Sanders (SOC)	3,855	6.9

PENNSYLVANIA

	Candidates	Votes	%
1	Henry H. Bingham (R, CITY)	27,507	76.2
	Michael J. Geraghty (D)	7,773	21.5
2	Joel Cook (R, CITY)	24,579	77.4
	William Schlipf Jr. (D)	6,381	20.1
3	J. Hampton Moore (R, CITY)	23,877	76.6
	William Beerli (D)	6,608	21.2
4	Reuben O. Moon (R)	17,518	66.2
	Haines D. Albright (D, CITY)	7,613	28.8
5	William W. Foulkrod (R, CITY)	21,756	66.7
	Michael Donohue	8,488	26.0
6	George D. McCreary (R, CITY)	31,129	72.5
	Frederick J. Bailey (D)	10,205	23.8
7	Thomas S. Butler (R)	26,684	69.3
	D. P. Hibberd (D)	10,364	26.9
8	Irving P. Wanger (R)	26,384	59.9
	Wynne James (D)	17,684	40.1
9	William W. Griest (R)	22,022	74.8
	George B. Willson (D)	7,428	25.2
10	Thomas D. Nichols (D)	16,855	51.1
	John R. Farr (R)	16,138	48.9
11	Henry W. Palmer (R, P)	21,033	51.9
	John H. Bigelow (D)	18,569	45.8
12	Alfred B. Garner (R)	17,446	51.9
	Robert E. Lee (D)	15,339	45.6
13	John H. Rothermel (D)	27,655	53.3
	Alex N. Ulrich (R)	21,416	41.3
14	Charles C. Pratt (R)	15,024	51.2
	George W. Kipp (D)	12,980	44.3
15	William B. Wilson (D)	18,592	50.4
	Elias Deemer (R)	16,577	44.9
16	John G. McHenry (D)	18,412	57.1
	Edmund W. Samuel (R)	12,866	39.9
17	Benjamin K. Focht (R, P)	23,761	62.8
	George C. Bentz (D)	14,044	37.2
18	Marlin E. Olmsted (R)	27,717	62.8
	John L. Whisler (D)	13,876	31.5
19	John M. Reynolds (R)	26,157	62.2
	Humphrey D. Tate (D)	15,906	37.8
20	Daniel F. Lafean (R)	19,176	52.0
	Edward D. Ziegler (D)	16,928	45.9
21	Charles F. Barclay (R)	15,631	50.3
	W. Harrison Walker (D)	12,848	41.4
	B. W. McCoy (P)	1,888	6.1
22	George F. Huff (R)	19,339	51.0
	Silas W. Kline (D)	16,234	42.8
	R. A. Dornon (P)	2,338	6.2
23	Allen F. Cooper (R)	16,769	50.7
	Milton R. Travis (D)	12,125	36.7
	William M. Likins (P)	3,366	10.2
24	John K. Tener (R)	20,538	52.2
	Charles H. Akens (D)	10,985	27.9
	Frank Fish (P)	5,982	15.2
25	Arthur L. Bates (R)	16,457	52.6
	John B. Brooks (D)	11,995	38.4
	N. J. MacIntyre (P)	1,849	5.9
26	A. Mitchell Palmer (D)	18,865	52.8
	Gustav A. Schneebeli (R)	15,123	42.3
27	Jonathan N. Langham (R)	19,010	59.7
	John Smith Shirley (D)	10,088	31.7
	J. T. Pender (P)	2,739	8.6
28	Nelson P. Wheeler (R)	18,728	55.1
	Till Reiss (D)	11,256	33.1
	J. M. Brown (P)	4,018	11.8
29	William H. Graham (R)	15,616	65.5
	John G. Schirmer (D)	5,401	22.6
	J. W. Slayton (SOC)	1,500	6.3
	John A. McConnell (P)	1,337	5.6
30	John Dalzell (R)	15,574	58.2

	Candidates	Votes	%
	Edward F. Duffy (D)	7,512	28.1
	William Adams (SOC)	2,001	7.5
	Joseph Fidler (P)	1,674	6.3
31	James Francis Burke (R)	13,380	66.6
	Thomas B. Alcorn (D)	5,320	26.5
32	Andrew J. Barchfeld (R,UN LAB)	17,015	58.1
	John Murphy (D)	8,769	29.9
	Thomas F. Kennedy (SOC)	1,871	6.4
	H. S. Gleiss (P)	1,648	5.6

RHODE ISLAND

	Candidates	Votes	%
1	William P. Sheffield (R)	18,222	48.6
	Granger (D)	18,141	48.4
2	Adin B. Capron (R)	21,374	60.9
	Cooney (D)	12,634	36.0

SOUTH CAROLINA

	Candidates	Votes	%
1	George S. Legare (D)	5,759	90.1
	A. R. Prioleau (R)	631	9.9
2	James O'H. Patterson (D)	8,440	99.3
3	Wyatt Aiken (D)	10,274	100.0
4	Joseph T. Johnston (D)	10,806	100.0
5	David E. Finley (D)	9,468	100.0
6	J. Edwin Ellerbe (D)	9,035	100.0
7	Asbury F. Lever (D)	9,950	90.9
	R. H. Richardson (R)	998	9.1

SOUTH DAKOTA

	Candidates	Votes	%
AL	Eben W. Martin (R)	67,582✓	
	Charles H. Burke (R)	67,400✓	
	Robert E. Dowdell (D)	38,758	
	Andrew H. Olson (D)	38,624	
	E. S. Chappell (P)	3,785	
	L. R. Erskine (P)	3,733	
	T. G. Deffebach (SOC)	2,676	
	S. H. Goodfellow (SOC)	2,660	
	L. V. Schneider (SOJ)	55	
	W. S. Bray (SOJ)	55	

Special Election

	Candidates	Votes	%
AL	Eben W. Martin (R)	65,962	62.3
	W. W. Soule (D)	39,865	37.7

TENNESSEE

	Candidates	Votes	%
1	Walter P. Brownlow (R)	21,998	79.5
	J. T. Fugate (D)	5,686	20.5
2	Richard W. Austin (R)	15,337	50.9
	N. W. Hale (D)	14,528	48.2
3	John A. Moon (D)	18,403	60.2
	John T. Raulston (R)	12,174	39.8
4	Cordell Hull (D)	15,193	54.9
	R. Q. Lillard (R)	12,419	44.9
5	William C. Houston (D)	13,123	69.7
	Z. T. Cason (R)	5,697	30.2
6	Joseph W. Byrns (D)	18,192	97.3
7	Lemuel P. Padgett (D)	14,499	64.2
	J. S. Beasley (R)	8,087	35.8
8	Thetus W. Sims (D)	12,874	57.5
	R. H. Thrasher (R)	9,446	42.2
9	Finis J. Garrett (D)	14,312	73.3
	W. L. Terrell (R)	5,205	26.7
10	George W. Gordon (D)	13,672	96.1

TEXAS

	Candidates	Votes	%
1	Morris Sheppard (D)	14,775	84.7
	H. L. McQuiston (R)	2,304	13.2
2	Martin Dies (D)	14,559	81.9
	C. E. Smith (R)	2,719	15.3
3	Gordon J. Russell (D)	11,651	74.3
	J. A. Harper (R)	3,289	21.0
4	Choice B. Randell (D)	16,017	80.6
	R. H. Crabb (R)	3,205	16.1
5	Jack Beall (D)	17,840	84.4
	Marion T. Connor (R)	3,177	15.0

	Candidates	Votes	%
6	Rufus Hardy (D)	10,350	84.4
	C. L. McCoy (R)	1,919	15.6
7	Alexander W. Gregg (D)	8,625	97.6
8	John M. Moore (D)	12,285	77.6
	T. M. Kennerly (R)	3,482	22.0
9	George F. Burgess (D)	13,191	67.6
	O. S. York (R)	5,897	30.2
10	Albert S. Burleson (D)	13,314	80.7
	Joseph W. Burke (R)	3,185	19.3
11	Robert L. Henry (D)	10,114	100.0
12	Oscar W. Gillespie (D)	17,778	81.6
	W. A. Dodge (R)	3,095	14.2
13	John H. Stephens (D)	24,705	84.3
	Jasper W. Haney (R)	3,715	12.7
14	James L. Slayden (D)	16,801	99.5
15	John N. Garner (D)	11,682	61.7
	W. T. Moore (R)	7,179	37.9
16	William R. Smith (D)	22,159	88.7
	G. W. Boynton (R)	2,544	10.2

UTAH

	Candidates	Votes	%
AL	Joseph Howell (R)	57,544	51.6
	L. R. Martineau (D)	35,981	32.3
	Charles I. Douglas (AM)	13,484	12.1

VERMONT

	Candidates	Votes	%
1	David J. Foster (R)	22,190	71.8
	Emile Blais (D)	8,028	26.0
2	Frank Plumley (R)	22,868	75.0
	Andrew J. Sibley (D)	6,914	22.7

VIRGINIA

	Candidates	Votes	%
1	William A. Jones (D)	9,733	74.2
	George N. Wise (R)	3,287	25.1
2	Harry L. Maynard (D)	7,358	70.7
	D. L. Groner (R)	3,026	29.1
3	John Lamb (D)	8,105	77.2
	J. G. Luce (R)	2,339	22.3
4	Francis R. Lassiter (D)	7,200	99.9
5	Edward W. Saunders (D)	7,079	50.3
	J. M. Parsons (R)	6,988	49.6
6	Carter Glass (D)	8,807	65.9
	M. Hartman (R)	3,421	25.6
	J. M. Parsons	994	7.4
7	James Hay (D)	9,560	62.9
	L. Pritchard (R)	5,652	37.2
8	Charles C. Carlin (D)	10,182	79.7
	J. W. Gregg (R)	2,597	20.3
9	C. Bascom Slemp (R)	15,693	56.3
	J. C. Byars (D)	12,192	43.7
10	Henry D. Flood (D)	10,140	65.8
	W. C. Franklin (R)	5,281	34.3

WASHINGTON

	Candidates	Votes	%
1	William E. Humphrey (R)	39,643	63.7
	Charles H. Miller (D)	21,089	33.9
2	Francis W. Cushman (R)	29,850	69.8
	Browder D. Brown (D)	12,006	28.1
3	Miles Pointdexter (R)	38,369	61.0
	William Goodyear (D)	23,227	36.9

WEST VIRGINIA

	Candidates	Votes	%
1	William P. Hubbard (R)	27,351	51.3
	E. L. Robinson (D)	23,580	44.2
2	George C. Sturgiss (R)	25,322	51.1
	B. H. Hines (D)	22,771	45.9
3	Joseph Holt Gaines (R)	29,266	53.2
	Andrew Price (D)	23,355	42.5
4	Harry C. Woodyard (R)	21,777	51.9
	W. O. Parsons (D)	19,095	45.5
5	James A. Hughes (R)	31,958	55.6
	L. H. Clarke (D)	24,778	43.1

WISCONSIN

	Candidates	Votes	%
1	Henry Allen Cooper (R)	26,728	60.6
	H. A. Moehlenpah (D)	14,018	31.8
2	John M. Nelson (R)	20,925	53.6
	J. E. Jones (D)	17,748	45.5
3	Arthur W. Kopp (R)	21,409	55.8
	J. W. Murphy (D)	16,010	41.7
4	William J. Cary (R)	15,509	39.1
	William J. Kershaw (D)	14,370	36.2
	Ed T. Melms (SOCIAL D)	9,788	24.7

	Candidates	Votes	%
5	William H. Stafford (R)	16,394	40.4
	G. Holmes Daubner (D)	12,871	31.8
	Albert J. Welch (SOCIAL D)	11,279	27.8
6	Charles H. Weisse (D)	23,317	57.8
	George Spratt (R)	16,184	40.1
7	John J. Esch (R)	25,202	68.0
	B. F. Keeler (D)	11,466	31.0
8	James H. Davidson (R)	23,097	57.3
	Lyman J. Nash (D)	14,984	37.2
9	Gustav Kustermann (R)	18,562	53.6
	L. Lindauer (D)	15,249	44.1

	Candidates	Votes	%
10	Elmer A. Morse (R)	26,081	60.9
	Wells M. Ruggles (D)	16,777	39.1
11	Irvine L. Lenroot (R)	30,104	71.7
	J. S. Konkel (D)	10,467	24.9

WYOMING

	Candidates	Votes	%
AL	Frank W. Mondell (R)	21,431	57.1
	Hayden M. White (D)	13,643	36.3
	James Morgan (SOC)	2,486	6.6

1909 House Elections

ILLINOIS

Special Election

	Candidates	Votes	%
6	William J. Moxley (R)	14,623	48.4
	Carl L. Barnes	8,342	27.6
	Frank S. Ryan	6,435	21.3

LOUISIANA

Special Election

		Votes	%
2	Samuel L. Gilmore (D)	5,535	100.0

1910 House Elections

ALABAMA

	Candidates	Votes	%
1	George W. Taylor (D)	7,071	97.0
2	S. Hubert Dent Jr. (D)	9,593	100.0
3	Henry D. Clayton (D)	9,573	100.0
4	Fred L. Blackmon (D)	8,286	69.9
	J. M. Atkins (R)	3,572	30.1
5	J. Thomas Heflin (D)	10,058	100.0
6	Richmond P. Hobson (D)	9,296	81.5
	Andrew D. Mitchell (R)	2,114	18.5
7	John L. Burnett (D)	9,496	51.4
	M. W. Howard (R)	8,977	48.6
8	William Richardson (D)	8,785	98.1
9	Oscar W. Underwood (D)	10,114	100.0

ARKANSAS

	Candidates	Votes	%
1	Robert B. Macon (D)	2,803	100.0
2	William A. Oldfield (D)	5,053	81.7
	J. T. Hall (R)	1,131	18.3
3	John C. Floyd (D)	5,131	55.6
	B. S. Granger (R)	4,197	45.5
4	William B. Cravens (D)	3,369	100.0
5	Henderson M. Jacoway (D)	5,505	76.4
	A. C. Remmel (R)	1,702	23.6
6	Joseph T. Robinson (D)	4,701	81.6
	B. C. Thompson (R)	1,062	18.4
7	William S. Goodwin (D)	5,266	82.2
	A. L. Wilson (R)	1,143	17.8

CALIFORNIA

	Candidates	Votes	%
1	John E. Raker (D)	16,704	45.4
	William F. Englebright (R)	16,570	45.1
	W. M. Morgan (SOC)	3,231	8.8
2	William Kent (R)	25,346	50.1
	I. G. Zumwalt (D)	22,229	44.0
	W. H. Ferber (SOC)	2,647	5.2
3	Joseph R. Knowland (R-D)	34,291	81.9
	S. Miller (SOC)	6,653	15.9
4	Julius Kahn (R)	10,188	56.2
	Walter Macarthur (D)	6,636	36.6
	Austin Lewis (SOC)	1,178	6.5
5	Everis Anson Hayes (R)	33,265	59.4
	Thomas E. Hayden (D)	15,345	27.4
	E. L. Reguin (SOC)	7,052	12.6
6	James C. Needham (R)	19,717	47.3
	A. L. Cowell (D)	18,408	44.1
	Richard Kirk (SOC)	2,568	6.2
7	William D. Stephens (R)	36,435	58.7
	Lorin A. Handley (D)	13,340	21.5
	T. W. Williams (SOC)	10,305	16.6
8	Sylvester C. Smith (R)	28,202	50.5
	William G. Irving (D)	18,958	34.0
	George A. Garrett (SOC)	7,302	13.1

COLORADO

	Candidates	Votes	%
1	Atterson W. Rucker (D)	40,458	40.8
	James C. Burger (R)	37,966	38.3
	George J. Kindel (P)	17,144	17.3
2	John A. Martin (D)	60,201	48.6
	James A. Orr (R)	57,006	46.0
AL	Edward T. Taylor (D)	105,700	47.9
	Isaac H. Stevens (R)	101,722	46.1

CONNECTICUT

	Candidates	Votes	%
1	E. Stevens Henry (R)	19,367	48.1
	Augustine Lonergan (D)	18,132	45.0
2	Thomas L. Reilly (D)	27,492	48.7
	Shepard (R)	24,480	43.3
	Paecht (SOC)	3,708	6.6
3	Edwin W. Higgins (R)	10,011	47.8
	Raymond J. Jodoin (D)	9,933	47.4
4	Ebenezer J. Hill (R)	23,479	48.4

	Candidates	Votes	%
	Wilson (D)	20,636	42.5
	Peach (SOC)	3,606	7.4
AL	John Q. Tilson (R)	79,585	47.9
	Ingersoll (D)	73,221	44.1
	Beardsley (SOC)	10,304	6.2

DELAWARE

	Candidates	Votes	%
AL	William H. Heald (R)	22,410	50.9
	Robert C. White (D)	20,281	46.1

FLORIDA

	Candidates	Votes	%
1	Stephen M. Sparkman (D)	10,525	81.8
	C. C. Allen (SOC)	2,346	18.2
2	Frank Clark (D)	11,626	78.5
	Thomas W. Cox (SOC)	1,804	12.2
	Thomas C. Buddington (R)	1,372	9.3
3	Dannitte H. Mays (D)	8,844	89.6
	Eric Vonaxelson (SOC)	1,032	10.5

GEORGIA

	Candidates	Votes	%
1	Charles Edwards (D)	2,019	100.0
2	Seaborn A. Roddenberry (D)	3,179	100.0
3	Dudley Hughes (D)	2,855	100.0
4	William C. Adamson (D)	2,815	100.0
5	William S. Howard (D)	4,091	100.0
6	Charles L. Bartlett (D)	3,351	100.0
7	Gordon Lee (D)	7,146	75.8
	Walter Akerman (R)	2,285	24.2
8	Samuel J. Tribble (ID)	8,635	58.1
	William Howard (D)	6,222	41.9
9	Thomas M. Bell (D)	4,285	100.0
10	Thomas Hardwick (D)	4,331	75.3
	C. E. McGregor (ID)	1,418	24.7
11	William Brantley (D)	3,160	100.0

IDAHO

	Candidates	Votes	%
AL	Burton L. French (R)	46,401	55.4
	A. M. Bowen (D)	31,832	38.0
	Rolla Myer (SOC)	5,463	6.5

ILLINOIS

	Candidates	Votes	%
1	Martin B. Madden (R)	14,920	50.0
	Michael E. Maher (D)	13,466	45.1
2	James R. Mann (R)	20,128	48.4
	John Charles Vaughan (D)	18,717	45.0
	J. O. Bentall (SOC)	2,711	6.5
3	William Warfield Wilson (R)	16,661	44.9
	Fred J. Crowley (D)	16,604	44.8
	J. Clifford Cox (SOC)	2,920	7.9
4	James T. McDermott (D)	15,764	62.9
	Michael G. Walsh (R)	7,028	28.1
	Peter Bulthouse (SOC)	1,994	8.0
5	Adolph J. Sabath (D)	13,936	71.7
	Louis H. Clusmann (R)	3,533	18.2
	Joseph J. Kral (SOC)	1,775	9.1
6	Edmund J. Stack (D)	22,951	51.1
	William J. Moxley (R)	17,178	38.2
	George Chant (SOC)	3,551	7.9
7	Frank Buchanan (D)	22,520	43.6
	Frederick Lundin (R)	21,096	40.8
	John Collins (SOC)	7,016	13.6
8	Thomas Gallagher (D)	14,281	58.7
	Daniel D. Coffey (R)	7,975	32.8
	John Drexler (SOC)	1,903	7.8
9	Lynden Evans (D)	13,501	45.7
	Frederick H. Gansbergen (R)	12,991	44.0
	Frank Shiflersmith (SOC)	2,650	9.0
10	George Edmund Foss (R)	20,130	47.7
	Richard J. Finnegan (D)	17,541	41.5
	Robert C. Magisen (SOC)	3,370	8.0
11	Ira C. Copley (R)	17,899	57.1

	Candidates	Votes	%
	Frank O. Hawley (D)	11,276	36.0
12	Charles E. Fuller (R)	20,665	62.3
	J. W. Rausch (D)	9,185	27.7
	Thomas Johnson (SOC)	2,277	6.9
13	John C. McKenzie (R)	17,249	61.3
	O. H. Wright (D)	9,752	34.7
14	James McKinney (R)	17,004	52.3
	Clyde H. Tavenner (D)	12,980	40.0
	Milton L. Morrill (SOC)	1,658	5.1
15	George W. Prince (R)	16,753	47.0
	Albert E. Bergland (D)	16,487	46.3
16	Claudius U. Stone (D)	17,633	51.2
	Joseph V. Graff (R)	15,024	43.6
17	John A. Sterling (R)	16,601	52.0
	Louis Fitzhenry (D)	14,215	44.5
18	Joseph G. Cannon (R)	20,943	53.0
	William L. Cundiff (D)	16,186	41.0
19	William B. McKinley (R)	23,107	52.6
	I. J. Martin (D)	19,259	43.9
20	Henry T. Rainey (D)	20,194	59.3
	James H. Danskin (R)	12,961	38.0
21	James M. Graham (D)	19,886	50.1
	H. Clay Wilson (R)	17,318	43.6
22	William A. Rodenberg (R)	23,024	49.7
	Bruce A. Campbell (D)	18,787	40.6
	Henry Groeteka (SOC)	3,826	8.3
23	Martin D. Foster (D)	23,535	53.7
	J. H. Loy (R)	18,230	41.6
24	H. Robert Fowler (D)	17,235	48.8
	Pleasant T. Chapman (R)	16,918	47.9
25	Napoleon B. Thistlewood (R)	18,233	49.1
	William D. Lyerle (D)	16,442	44.2

INDIANA

	Candidates	Votes	%
1	John W. Boehne (D)	22,420	52.3
	Francis B. Posey (R)	18,606	43.4
2	William A. Cullop (D)	22,960	48.4
	Oscar E. Bland (R)	21,419	45.2
3	William E. Cox (D)	21,670	58.4
	Harry C. Poindexter (R)	14,969	40.3
4	Lincoln Dixon (D)	22,001	53.8
	John H. Kemman (R)	17,921	43.8
5	Ralph W. Moss (D)	25,917	51.6
	Frank Tilley (R)	21,267	42.4
6	Finley P. Gray (D)	23,740	49.0
	William O. Barnard (R)	22,242	45.9
7	Charles A. Korbly (D)	30,330	50.3
	Linton A. Cox (R)	26,968	44.7
8	John A. M. Adair (D)	25,454	51.8
	Rollin Warner (R)	19,309	39.3
	Orville G. Overcarsh (SOC)	2,910	5.9
9	Martin A. Morrison (D)	24,434	48.0
	Everett E. Neal (R)	23,841	46.8
10	Edgar D. Crumpacker (R)	27,722	50.3
	John B. Peterson (D)	25,692	46.6
11	George W. Rauch (D)	22,528	47.8
	John L. Thompson (R)	21,282	45.2
12	Cyrus Cline (D)	19,754	49.9
	Owen N. Heaton (R)	17,937	45.3
13	Henry A. Barnhart (D)	25,253	48.2
	John L. Moorman (D)	24,153	46.1

IOWA

	Candidates	Votes	%
1	Charles A. Kennedy (R)	15,602	51.9
	J. A. S. Pollard (D)	13,427	44.7
2	Irvin S. Pepper (D)	19,815	51.5
	Charles Grilk (R)	16,971	44.1
3	Charles E. Pickett (R)	19,324	54.3
	John D. Denison Jr (D)	15,572	43.7
4	Gilbert N. Haugen (R)	16,928	49.9
	Daniel D. Murphy (D)	16,708	49.3
5	James W. Good (R)	16,953	51.8
	S. C. Huber (D)	14,676	44.8
6	Nathan E. Kendall (R)	16,335	48.2

Candidates	Votes	%
Daniel W. Hamilton (D)	15,914	47.0
7 Solomon F. Prouty (R)	17,722	53.1
Clint L. Price (D)	14,534	43.5
8 Horace M. Towner (R)	19,548	54.9
Frank Q. Stewart (D)	15,565	43.7
9 Walter I. Smith (R)	18,763	52.0
W. F. Cleeland (D)	16,916	46.9
10 Frank P. Woods (R)	26,927	97.0
11 Elbert H. Hubbard (R)	22,199	59.9
M. M. White (D)	14,377	38.8

KANSAS

Candidates	Votes	%
1 Daniel R. Anthony Jr. (R)	21,852	72.3
J. B. Chapman (D)	7,486	24.8
2 Alexander C. Mitchell (R)	23,282	50.9
John Caldwell (D)	19,852	43.4
3 Phillip P. Campbell (R)	20,771	44.5
Jeremiah D. Botkin (D)	19,943	42.7
C. S. Bendure (SOC)	5,748	12.3
4 Fred S. Jackson (R)	17,111	54.9
Henderson S. Martin (D)	14,051	45.1
5 Rollin R. Rees (R)	17,680	51.3
G. T. Helvering (D)	15,775	45.8
6 Isaac D. Young (R)	21,020	50.9
Frank S. Rockefeller (D)	18,985	46.0
7 Edmond H. Madison (R)	24,925	53.1
George A. Neeley (D)	20,133	42.9
8 Victor Murdock (R)	16,239	87.3
George Burnett (SOC)	2,354	12.7

KENTUCKY

Candidates	Votes	%
1 Ollie M. James (D)	11,574	89.3
C. L. Harney (SOC)	1,389	10.7
2 Augustus O. Stanley (D)	12,040	62.2
R. J. Salmon (R)	6,902	35.7
3 Robert Y. Thomas Jr. (D)	16,063	51.3
W. H. Jones (R)	14,850	47.5
4 Ben Johnson (D)	18,263	59.2
D. W. Gaddie (R)	11,952	38.8
5 J. Swagar Sherley (D)	21,437	53.2
J. Wheeler McGee (R)	17,376	43.1
6 Arthur B. Rouse (D)	15,454	55.6
Charles W. Nagel (R)	11,007	39.6
7 James C. Cantrill (D)	13,858	56.0
M. C. Rankin (R)	10,877	44.0
8 Harvey Helm (D)	12,412	56.9
Hugh Miller (R)	9,385	43.1
9 William J. Fields (D)	19,350	50.8
Joseph B. Bennett (R)	18,737	49.2
10 John W. Langley (R)	20,664	52.4
A. Floyd Byrd (D)	18,766	47.6
11 Caleb Powers (R)	25,622	60.5
Elza Bertrand (D)	16,357	38.6

LOUISIANA

Candidates	Votes	%
1 Albert Estopinal (D)	11,932	89.5
John A. Wogan (R)	1,408	10.6
2 H. Garland Dupre (D)	10,218	83.2
Victor Loisel (R)	2,071	16.9
3 Robert F. Broussard (D)	4,011	91.0
Jules Dreyfus (R)	395	9.0
4 John T. Watkins (D)	4,244	95.9
5 Joseph E. Ransdell (D)	4,469	99.0
6 Robert C. Wickliffe (D)	4,016	100.0
7 Arsene P. Pujo (D)	7,393	91.3
J. R. Jones (SOC)	706	8.7

Special Election

Candidates	Votes	%
2 H. Garland Dupre (D)	10,333	82.7
Victor Loisel (R)	2,160	17.3

MAINE

Candidates	Votes	%
1 Asher C. Hinds (R)	17,521	49.8
W. M. Pennell (D)	16,901	48.0
2 Daniel J. McGillicuddy (D)	18,938	52.6

Candidates	Votes	%
John P. Swasey (R)	16,227	45.1
3 Samuel W. Gould (D)	17,187	51.1
Edwin C. Burleigh (R)	15,798	46.9
4 Frank E. Guernsey (R)	18,017	50.3
George M. Hanson (D)	17,516	48.9

MARYLAND

Candidates	Votes	%
1 James Harry Covington (D)	18,341	51.6
A. Lincoln Dryden (R)	16,066	45.2
2 Joshua Frederick C. Talbott (D)	19,352	51.8
William B. Baker (R)	17,124	45.8
3 George Konig (D)	15,028	48.4
Charles W. Main (R)	14,740	47.5
4 John Charles Linthicum (D)	17,478	50.8
Addison E. Mullikin (R)	15,698	45.7
5 Thomas Parran (R)	15,706	49.5
J. Enos Ray Jr. (D)	14,879	46.9
6 David J. Lewis (D)	16,585	48.1
Brainard Henry Warner Jr. (R)	15,896	46.1

MASSACHUSETTS

Candidates	Votes	%
1 George P. Lawrence (R)	14,109	48.9
Edward Morgan (D)	13,244	45.9
Louis B. Clark (SOC)	1,476	5.1
2 Frederick H. Gillett (R)	14,242	48.8
William G. McKechnie (D)	13,774	47.2
3 John A. Thayer (D)	15,243	51.2
Charles G. Washburn (R)	14,544	48.8
4 William H. Wilder (R)	16,965	49.1
John J. Mitchell (D)	16,835	48.7
5 Butler Ames (R)	13,760	51.1
James H. Carmichael (D)	13,163	48.9
6 Augustus P. Gardner (R)	17,272	54.0
William H. O'Brien (D)	12,038	37.6
James F. Carey (SOC)	2,667	8.3
7 Ernest W. Roberts (R)	16,624	50.7
Walter H. Creamer (D)	14,337	43.7
W. Lathrop Meaker (DPPC)	1,837	5.6
8 Samuel W. McCall (R)	15,854	53.4
Frederick S. Deitrick (D)	13,842	46.6
9 William F. Murray (D)	11,652	49.0
John A. Keliher (DI)	10,037	42.2
William H. Oakes (R)	2,081	8.8
10 James M. Curley (D)	20,345	56.3
J. Mitchel Galvin (R)	15,783	43.7
11 Andrew J. Peters (D)	18,933	59.2
William Dudley (R)	13,033	40.8
12 John W. Weeks (R)	19,037	56.4
Daniel J. Daley (D)	14,696	43.6
13 William S. Greene (R)	14,079	58.9
James F. Morris (D)	9,831	41.1
14 Robert O. Harris (R)	15,753	47.9
Thomas C. Thacher (D)	15,686	47.6

Special Election

Candidates	Votes	%
4 John J. Mitchell (D)	16,688	50.0
William H. Wilder (R)	16,664	50.0

MICHIGAN

Candidates	Votes	%
1 Frank E. Doremus (D)	20,843	52.0
Edwin Denby (R)	17,676	44.1
2 William W. Wedemeyer (R)	21,485	57.0
John V. Sheehan (D)	15,125	40.1
3 John M. C. Smith (R)	18,606	57.7
Nathaniel H. Stewart (D)	11,935	37.0
4 Edward L. Hamilton (R)	17,282	56.2
John E. Barnes (D)	12,185	39.6
5 Edwin F. Sweet (D)	15,219	48.4
Gerrit J. Diekema (R)	14,589	46.4
6 Samuel W. Smith (R)	23,321	52.9
Alva M. Cummins (D)	18,403	41.7
7 Henry McMorran (R)	15,897	55.6
Thomas Wellman (D)	11,595	40.5
8 Joseph W. Fordney (R)	14,878	56.5
James P. Devereaux (D)	10,571	40.2

Candidates	Votes	%
9 James C. McLaughlin (R)	13,029	65.7
Emery D. Weimer (D)	6,171	31.1
10 George A. Loud (R)	15,060	59.8
Albert Miller (D)	8,746	34.7
11 Francis H. Dodds (R)	16,179	64.8
Hubbard Head (D)	7,157	28.7
12 H. Olin Young (R)	24,661	73.6
Gideon T. Werline (D)	8,751	26.1

MINNESOTA

Candidates	Votes	%
1 Sydney Anderson (R)	18,315	55.3
Buck (D)	14,816	44.7
2 Winfield S. Hammond (D)	14,745	53.2
Ellsworth (R)	12,426	44.8
3 Charles R. Davis (R)	21,863	100.0
4 Frederick C. Stevens (R)	18,830	56.6
Gieske (D)	12,495	37.6
Stratton (PUB OWN)	1,953	5.9
5 Frank M. Nye (R)	17,433	50.0
Thomas P. Dwyer (D)	15,113	43.3
Lindsay (PUB OWN)	2,323	6.7
6 Charles A. Lindbergh (R)	25,272	100.0
7 Andrew J. Volstead (R)	24,395	100.0
8 Clarence B. Miller (R)	17,018	53.7
Jaques (D)	10,305	32.5
Watkins (PUB OWN)	4,354	13.7
9 Halvor Steenerson (R)	24,572	74.5
Sanders (PUB OWN)	8,421	25.5

MISSISSIPPI

Candidates	Votes	%
1 Ezekiel S. Candler Jr. (D)	2,904	100.0
2 Hubert D. Stephens (D)	3,304	100.0
3 Benjamin G. Humphreys (D)	1,799	100.0
4 Thomas U. Sisson (D)	3,719	100.0
5 Samuel A. Witherspoon (D)	3,921	100.0
6 Pat Harrison (D)	4,011	99.4
7 William A. Dickson (D)	2,468	100.0
8 James W. Collier (D)	1,739	100.0

MISSOURI

Candidates	Votes	%
1 James T. Lloyd (D)	19,953	54.2
Higbee	15,572	42.3
2 William W. Rucker (D)	21,090	55.6
Haley (R)	16,122	42.5
3 Joshua W. Alexander (D)	19,213	56.3
Davisson (R)	14,900	43.7
4 Charles F. Booher (D)	20,231	55.1
Amick (R)	15,825	43.1
5 William P. Borland (D)	31,026	54.6
Lea (R)	23,982	42.2
6 Clement C. Dickinson (D)	17,504	53.2
Devol (R)	14,374	43.7
7 Courtney W. Hamlin (D)	22,433	49.1
Hall (R)	21,951	48.0
8 Dorsey W. Shackleford (D)	16,642	53.3
Norfleet (R)	14,349	45.9
9 James Beauchamp Clark (D)	23,124	54.5
Roy (R)	19,105	45.0
10 Richard Bartholdt (R)	53,298	60.8
Charles J. Maurer (D)	28,054	32.0
Hoehn (SOC)	5,865	6.7
11 Theron E. Catlin (R)	20,089‡	49.7
Patrick F. Gill (D)	18,695	46.3
12 Leonidas Dyer (R)	15,965	53.1
Thomas E. Kinney (D)	13,121	43.7
13 Walter L. Hensley (D)	16,020	49.3
Elvins (R)	15,386	47.4
14 Joseph J. Russell (D)	23,612	47.8
Crow (R)	22,463	45.5
Hafner (SOC)	2,973	6.0
15 James A. Daugherty (D)	21,259	47.4
Morgan (R)	20,443	45.6
16 Thomas L. Rubey (D)	16,239	52.1
Murphy (R)	14,763	47.4

MONTANA

	Candidates	Votes	%
AL	Charles N. Pray (R)	32,519	49.4
	Charles S. Hartman (D)	28,071	42.7
	J. Frank Mabie (SOC)	5,184	7.9

NEBRASKA

	Candidates	Votes	%
1	John A. Maguire (D & PPI)	16,501	50.4
	William Hayward (R)	15,763	48.2
2	C. O. Lobeck (D)	15,912	48.9
	Abraham L. Sutton (R)	15,673	48.1
3	James P. Latta (D & PPI)	25,945	57.7
	J. F. Boyd (R)	18,566	41.3
4	Charles H. Sloan (R)	20,807	50.8
	Benjamin F. Good (D & PPI)	19,540	47.8
5	George W. Norris (R)	19,929	53.7
	Roderick D. Sutherland (D & PPI)	15,925	42.9
6	Moses P. Kinkaid (R)	24,327	52.8
	William J. Taylor (D & PPI)	19,682	42.7

NEVADA

	Candidates	Votes	%
AL	Edwin E. Roberts (R)	10,066	49.9
	Charles S. Sprague (D)	7,688	38.1
	Ashley Grant Miller (SOC)	2,409	12.0

NEW HAMPSHIRE

	Candidates	Votes	%
1	Cyrus A. Sulloway (R)	20,941	50.5
	Eugene E. Reed (D)	20,093	48.5
2	Frank D. Currier (R)	21,639	55.1
	Henry H. Metcalf (D)	16,913	43.0

NEW JERSEY

	Candidates	Votes	%
1	Henry C. Loudenslager (R)	21,394	48.6
	Nowrey (D)	20,554	46.7
2	John J. Gardner (R)	22,861	51.6
	Hampton (D)	16,915	38.2
	Riddle (I)	3,508	7.9
3	Thomas J. Scully (D)	24,657	54.8
	Howell (R)	20,160	44.8
4	Ira W. Wood (R)	19,354	49.1
	Libbey (D)	19,089	48.4
5	William E. Tuttle Jr. (D)	23,768	51.0
	Runyon (R)	20,675	44.4
6	William Hughes (D)	29,458	51.6
	McClave (R)	25,301	44.3
7	Edward W. Townsend (D)	21,962	54.0
	Parker (R)	17,756	43.7
8	Walter I. McCoy (D)	19,364	51.2
	William H. Wiley (R)	16,847	44.6
9	Eugene F. Kinkead (D)	23,784	62.3
	Record (R)	13,390	35.1
10	James A. Hamill (D)	26,266	70.2
	Seibel (R)	10,104	27.0

NEW YORK

	Candidates	Votes	%
1	Martin W. Littleton (D & IL)	26,974	54.0
	William W. Cocks (R)	21,826	43.7
2	George H. Lindsay (D)	14,248	59.2
	Ladislaus W. Schwenk (R & IL)	8,304	34.5
	Paul Muller Jr. (SOC)	1,428	5.9
3	James P. Maher (D)	15,432	48.3
	Alfred T. Hobley (R & IL)	14,570	45.6
	John J. Jennings (SOC)	1,806	5.7
4	Frank E. Wilson (D & IL)	20,676	46.6
	Charles B. Law (R)	20,295	45.8
	Barnet Wolff (SOC)	3,257	7.4
5	William C. Redfield (D & IL)	26,220	51.7
	Warren I. Lee (R)	22,576	44.5
6	William M. Calder (R)	17,249	48.6
	Michael E. Butler (D)	16,805	47.3
7	John J. Fitzgerald (D)	16,847	67.3

	Candidates	Votes	%
	William R. A. Koehl (R & IL)	7,748	31.0
8	Daniel J. Riordan (D)	20,683	66.2
	George S. Husch (R)	8,311	26.6
9	Henry M. Goldfogle (D)	4,606	46.8
	Meyer London (SOC)	3,322	33.8
	Jacob W. Block (R & IL)	1,850	18.8
10	William Sulzer (D & IL)	9,850	60.2
	Anthony M. McCabe (R)	4,807	29.4
	John Mullen (SOC)	1,694	10.4
11	Charles V. Fornes (D)	17,384	61.2
	Henry H. Curran (R & IL)	10,171	35.8
12	Michael Conry (D)	14,376	62.7
	Peter R. Gatens (R & IL)	7,467	32.6
13	Jefferson M. Levy (D)	11,539	50.4
	Herbert Parsons (R)	9,951	43.5
14	John Joseph Kindred (D)	20,875	54.3
	Victor Hugo Duras (R & IL)	14,018	36.5
	William F. Ehret (SOC)	3,481	9.1
15	Thomas G. Patten (D & IL)	13,838	54.4
	William M. Bennett (R)	11,152	43.8
16	Francis Burton Harrison (D)	10,450	55.0
	Samuel Bell Thomas (CIV A)	6,518	34.3
	George F. Miner (SOC)	2,012	10.6
17	Henry George Jr. (D & IL)	28,306	50.7
	William S. Bennet (R)	26,010	46.6
18	Steven B. Ayres (D)	33,600	51.2
	Gottlieb Haneke (R & IL)	27,607	42.0
	Joshua Wauhope (SOC)	4,354	6.6
19	John E. Andrus (R)	23,140	49.7
	Cornelius A. Pugsley (D)	22,247	47.7
20	Thomas W. Bradley (R)	19,363	51.6
	John Bigelow Jr. (D)	17,307	46.2
21	Richard E. Connell (D)	18,832	49.8
	Hamilton Fish (R)	18,315	48.4
22	William H. Draper (R)	20,424	51.8
	Elisha C. Tower (D)	17,277	43.8
23	Henry S. De Forest (R)	28,218	48.1
	Curtis N. Douglas (D)	26,228	44.7
	Harvey A. Simmons (SOC)	2,978	5.1
24	George W. Fairchild (R)	23,636	49.9
	George M. Palmer (D)	22,416	47.3
25	Theron Akin (D, I LEAGUE)	21,754	48.9
	Cyrus Durey (R)	21,442	48.2
26	George R. Malby (R)	21,980	55.7
	Thomas Cantwell (D)	15,584	39.5
27	Charles A. Talcott (D & IL)	22,458	50.8
	Charles S. Millington (R)	20,242	45.8
28	Luther W. Mott (R, I LEAGUE)	18,844	50.1
	George W. Reeves (D)	15,629	41.5
	Charles F. Simpson (P)	2,514	6.7
29	Michael E. Driscoll (R)	26,589	52.5
	Henry E. Wilson (D & IL)	20,281	40.0
30	John W. Dwight (R)	21,789	49.2
	Ira A. Hix (D, I LEAGUE)	18,346	41.4
	Frank Dewitt Reese (P)	3,521	8.0
31	Sereno E. Payne (R)	21,121	51.8
	John Colmey (D)	17,728	43.5
32	Henry G. Danforth (R)	26,375	52.7
	George P. Decker (D)	21,176	42.3
33	Edwin S. Underhill (D)	19,517	49.5
	Jacob Sloat Fassett (R)	17,556	44.5
34	James S. Simmons (R)	25,051	54.0
	Elliot W. Horton (D)	19,307	41.6
35	Daniel A. Driscoll (D & IL)	21,727	56.9
	Patrick J. Keeler (R)	14,605	38.3
36	Charles Bennett Smith (D & IL)	20,685	48.9
	De Alva S. Alexander (R)	20,684	48.8
37	Edward Butterfield Vreeland (R)	20,530	53.1
	J. William Sanbury (D, I LEAGUE)	14,314	37.0
	Arthur A. Amidon (P)	2,099	5.4

NORTH CAROLINA

	Candidates	Votes	%
1	John H. Small (D)	11,544	75.3
	Henry T. King (R)	3,721	24.3
2	Claude Kitchin (D)	10,749	85.1
	R. H. Norfleet (R)	1,867	14.8
3	John M. Faison (D)	10,428	58.1
	George E. Butler (R)	7,505	41.8

	Candidates	Votes	%
4	Edward W. Pou (D)	13,728	65.8
	R. A. P. Cooley (R)	7,110	34.1
5	Charles M. Stedman (D)	20,392	54.2
	David H. Blair (R)	17,060	45.3
6	Hannibal L. Godwin (D)	10,806	71.7
	Iredell Meares (R)	4,257	28.3
7	Robert N. Page (D)	14,367	56.5
	John J. Parker (R)	11,006	43.3
8	Robert L. Doughton (D)	16,560	51.1
	Charles H. Cowles (R)	15,801	48.8
9	Edwin Y. Webb (D)	16,574	59.3
	S.S. McNinch (R)	11,332	40.6
10	James M. Gudger Jr. (D)	15,901	51.8
	John G. Grant (R)	14,771	48.1

NORTH DAKOTA

	Candidates	Votes	%
AL	Louis B. Hanna (R)	51,556 ✓	
	Henry T. Helgesen (R)	50,600 ✓	
	Tobias D. Casey (D)	25,880	
	M. A. Hildreth (D)	25,322	
	Arthur Hagendorf (SOC)	3,225	
	N. H. Bjornstead (SOC)	3,179	

OHIO

	Candidates	Votes	%
1	Nicholas Longworth (R)	24,453	51.1
	Thomas P. Hart (D)	21,497	44.9
2	Alfred G. Allen (R)	24,323	47.9
	Herman P. Goebel (D)	23,834	47.0
3	James M. Cox (D)	31,539	55.5
	George R. Young (R)	18,730	33.0
	Harmon Evans (SOC)	6,275	11.0
4	J. Henry Goeke (D)	20,865	58.4
	C. E. Johnston (R)	13,482	37.7
5	Timothy T. Ansberry (D)	21,201	60.1
	C. S. Roe (R)	13,309	37.7
6	Matthew R. Denver (D)	20,056	54.0
	Jesse Taylor (R)	17,105	46.0
7	James D. Post (D)	20,776	52.8
	J. Warren Keifer (R)	17,569	44.6
8	Frank B. Willis (R)	21,030	50.0
	Thomas C. Mahon (D)	19,519	46.4
9	Isaac R. Sherwood (D)	21,908	48.0
	J. Kent Hamilton (R)	19,593	43.0
	W. F. Ries (SOC)	3,917	8.6
10	Robert M. Switzer (R)	18,548	51.3
	Edmond H. Willis (D)	16,250	45.0
11	Horatio C. Claypool (D)	22,894	49.9
	Albert Douglas (R)	20,168	44.0
	Austin B. Shinn (SOC)	2,397	5.2
12	Edward L. Taylor Jr. (R)	17,696	39.9
	Frank S. Monnett (D)	15,151	34.2
	Jacob L. Bachman (SOC)	11,142	25.1
13	Carl C. Anderson (D)	30,196	63.7
	Miles H. McLaughlin (R)	15,486	32.7
14	William G. Sharp (D)	25,287	54.6
	George H. Chamberlain (R)	18,459	39.8
15	George White (D)	19,723	49.3
	James Joyce (R)	17,674	44.2
	Frank Martin (SOC)	2,218	5.6
16	William B. Francis (D)	15,731	46.6
	David A. Hollingsworth (R)	15,323	45.4
	Robert J. Murray (SOC)	2,325	6.9
17	William A. Ashbrook (D)	25,875	59.3
	A. B. Critchfield (R)	14,964	34.3
	Edward Schmidt (SOC)	2,508	5.8
18	John J. Whitacre (D)	23,568	46.6
	James Kennedy (R)	20,617	40.8
	Thomas Williams (SOC)	4,907	9.7
19	Ellsworth R. Bathrick (D)	19,255	46.0
	W. Aubrey Thomas (R)	18,290	43.7
	Paul G. Miller (SOC)	3,720	8.9
20	Paul Howland (R)	20,699	46.8
	William Gordon (D)	20,519	46.4
	John G. Willert (SOC)	2,847	6.4
21	Robert J. Bulkley (D)	18,091	48.1
	James H. Cassidy (R)	16,716	44.5
	Karl A. Cheyney (SOC)	2,649	7.1

OKLAHOMA

Candidates	Votes	%
1 Bird S. McGuire (R)	20,301	49.2
Neil E. McNeill (D)	18,415	44.7
W. L. Reynolds (SOC)	2,522	6.1
2 Dick T. Morgan (R)	25,134	46.1
Elmer L. Fulton (D)	24,062	44.1
H. I. Bryant (SOC)	5,382	9.9
3 James S. Davenport (D)	25,312	50.0
Charles E. Creager (R)	22,367	44.2
G. M. Snyder (SOC)	2,923	5.8
4 Charles D. Carter (D)	21,959	55.6
Charles M. Campbell (R)	11,979	30.4
J. N. Gilmore (SOC)	5,534	14.0
5 Scott Ferris (D)	28,600	58.9
J. H. Franklin (R)	13,425	27.6
H. H. Stallard (SOC)	6,539	13.5

OREGON

Candidates	Votes	%
1 Willis C. Hawley (R)	26,256	48.6
R. G. Smith (D)	18,232	33.7
C. W. Sherman (SOC)	4,971	9.2
W. P. Elmore (P)	4,585	8.5
2 Abraham W. Lafferty (R)	30,642	51.8
John Manning (D)	19,477	32.9
William A. Crawford (SOC)	5,583	9.4
George B. Pratt (P)	3,464	5.9

PENNSYLVANIA

Candidates	Votes	%
1 Henry H. Bingham (R, P)	28,054	69.9
Henry V. Garrett (KEY, WM PENN)	8,827	22.0
Michael J. Geraghty (D)	2,657	6.6
2 Joel Cook (R, WMP/L)	24,888*	69.4
Daniel W. Simpkins (KEY, WM PENN)	7,665	21.4
Edward B. Seiberlich (D)	2,542	7.1
3 J. Hampton Moore (R, WMP/L)	23,994	69.2
James G. Ramsdell (KEY)	7,030	20.3
William A. Hayes (D)	2,712	7.8
4 Reuben O. Moon (R, WMP/L)	16,309	72.6
William C. Mitchell (D)	2,459	10.9
Albert W. Sanson (WM PENN, CITY)	2,526	11.2
5 Michael Donohoe (KEY, D)	19,209	48.4
William W. Foulkrod (R, WMP/L)	18,016	45.4
Martin McCue (SOC)	2,328	5.9
6 George D. McCreary (R, WMP/L)	25,747	46.2
Frank H. Hawkins (KEY, WM PENN)	23,672	42.5
William A. Carr (D)	4,319	7.8
7 Thomas S. Butler (R)	16,490	51.7
Eugene C. Bonniwell (KEY, D)	14,498	45.5
8 Robert E. Difenderfer (D, KEY)	19,683	49.6
Irving P. Wanger (R)	19,016	48.1
9 William W. Griest (R)	14,718	79.1
James G. McSparran (D)	3,120	16.8
10 John R. Farr (R)	13,457	50.4
P. F. Calpin (D)	11,240	42.1
11 Charles C. Bowman (R, P)	14,384‡	47.5
George R. McLean (D)	13,834	45.7
Charles F. Quinn (SOC, FEDR LAB)	2,079	6.9
12 Robert E. Lee (D)	9,492	40.1
Robert D. Heaton (R)	9,441	39.9
C. F. Foley (SOC)	4,739	20.0
13 John H. Rothermel (D)	19,680	49.8
John K. Hahn (R)	12,939	32.7
Caleb Harrison (SOC)	6,209	15.7
14 George W. Kipp (KEY, D)	10,276	49.0
Charles C. Pratt (R)	9,481	45.2
15 William B. Wilson (D)	13,624	49.7
Clarence L. Peaslee (R)	10,588	38.6
Clarence C. Ricker (SOC)	2,004	7.3
16 John G. McHenry (D, R)	12,578	53.0
Theodore C. Harter (KEY)	6,366	26.8

Candidates	Votes	%
Jacob W. Renn (SOC)	3,818	16.1
17 Benjamin K. Focht (R)	14,473	50.8
J. Murray Africa (D)	11,681	41.0
18 Marlin E. Olmsted (R)	21,221	59.7
W. Jonathan Kiefer (D)	11,686	32.9
19 Jesse L. Hartman (R)	18,133	60.4
Isaiah Scheenline (D)	7,669	25.5
Stewart C. Cowan (P)	2,173	7.2
Anslem B. Kirsch (SOC)	2,048	6.8
20 Daniel F. Lafean (R)	15,713	50.9
Andrew R. Brodbeck (D)	13,786	44.7
21 Charles E. Patton (R)	10,493	49.6
William C. Heinle (D)	6,903	32.6
George W. Fox (SOC)	2,389	11.3
Charles E. Patton (P)	1,363	6.4
22 Curtis H. Gregg (D, KEY)	12,988	42.3
J. David McJunkin (R)	12,490	40.7
Robert Dudley (SOC)	3,242	10.6
E. S. Littell (P)	1,981	6.5
23 S. Crago Thomas (R)	13,665	52.9
Jesse H. Wise (D, KEY)	8,894	34.4
Washington Herd (SOC)	2,036	7.9
24 Charles Matthews (R)	15,177	44.1
Henry H. Wilson (KEY, D)	14,372	41.8
Charles A. Collins (SOC)	3,332	9.7
25 Arthur L. Bates (R)	10,668	46.4
John B. Brooks (D, KEY)	9,632	41.9
George B. Allen (SOC)	1,377	6.0
Richard A. Buzza (P)	1,313	5.7
26 A. Mitchell Palmer (D)	16,284	61.3
Robert Brown (R)	8,867	33.4
27 J. N. Langham (R)	13,073	58.8
John Smith Shirler (D)	5,451	24.5
John Houk (D)	2,479	11.1
M. A. Vanhorn (SOC)	1,245	5.6
28 Peter M. Speer (R)	10,932	41.7
William J. Breene (D)	9,492	36.2
John E. Gill (D)	3,047	11.6
John R. McKeown (SOC)	2,163	8.3
29 Stephen G. Porter (R)	14,785	74.2
George T. McConnell (SOC)	2,468	12.4
Fleming Jamieson (D)	2,110	10.6
30 John Dalzell (R)	13,261	46.5
Robert J. Black (P, UN LAB)	7,807	27.4
W. J. Wright (SOC)	2,942	10.3
James A. Wakefield (KEY, D)	4,208	14.8
31 James Francis Burke (R)	12,996	64.5
John J. Thorpe (KEY, D)	5,798	28.8
John Connor (SOC)	1,164	5.8
32 A. J. Barchfeld (R)	13,483	49.7
Hermann L. Hegner (KEY, D)	9,933	36.6
Valentine Remmel (SOC)	3,152	11.6

RHODE ISLAND

Candidates	Votes	%
1 George F. O'Shaunessy (D)	17,532	51.3
William P. Sheffield (R)	15,681	45.9
2 George H. Utter (R)	18,983	57.2
Cooney (D)	13,704	41.3

SOUTH CAROLINA

Candidates	Votes	%
1 George S. Legare (D)	3,432	97.4
2 James F. Byrnes (D)	4,392	100.0
3 Wyatt Aiken (D)	3,381	99.9
4 Joseph T. Johnston (D)	7,616	98.9
5 David E. Finley (D)	3,470	100.0
6 J. Edwin Ellerbe (D)	3,734	100.0
7 Asbury F. Lever (D)	4,762	95.6

SOUTH DAKOTA

Candidates	Votes	%
AL Charles H. Burke (R)	64,777✓	
Eben W. Martin (R)	64,495✓	
W. W. Soule (D)	32,655	
J. E. Kelley (D)	32,329	
Knute Lewis (P)	4,139	
W. J. Edgar (P)	4,124	
Isaac M. Burnside (I)	1,641	

TENNESSEE

Candidates	Votes	%
1 Sam R. Sells (R)	20,955	74.0
Cy H. Lyle (D)	7,380	26.1
2 Richard W. Austin (R)	15,761	57.3
N. W. Hale (R)	11,755	42.7
3 John A. Moon (D)	17,654	56.9
Charles R. Evans (R)	12,953	41.7
4 Cordell Hull (D)	19,298	78.9
J. T. Odum (ID)	5,169	21.1
5 William C. Houston (D)	16,697	98.9
6 Joseph W. Byrns (D)	16,764	87.0
W. H. Jackson (SOC)	2,502	13.0
7 Lemuel P. Padgett (D)	21,299	96.8
8 Thetus W. Sims (D)	13,764	57.9
S. E. Murrey (R)	9,860	41.5
9 Finis J. Garrett (D)	15,000	85.8
J. W. Brown (R)	1,416	8.1
W. R. Landrum (IR)	940	5.4
10 George W. Gordon (D)	14,862	94.8
T. H. Haines (SOC)	824	5.3

Special Election

Candidates	Votes	%
1 Zachary D. Massey (R)	19,181	77.4
Cy H. Lyle (D)	5,618	22.7

TEXAS

Candidates	Votes	%
1 Morris Sheppard (D)	10,707	87.4
Velmar Antle (R)	1,148	9.4
2 Martin Dies (D)	10,898	94.4
3 James Young (D)	9,450	98.9
4 Choice B. Randell (D)	9,719	88.9
C. A. Gray (R)	1,208	11.1
5 Jack Beall (D)	10,939	95.0
6 Rufus Hardy (D)	7,826	97.9
7 Alexander W. Gregg (D)	6,566	88.2
Willis Kendall (R)	843	11.3
8 John M. Moore (D)	11,654	90.4
A.M. Lawson (R)	1,112	8.6
9 George F. Burgess (D)	10,244	78.0
E. C. Webster (R)	2,108	16.1
10 Albert S. Burleson (D)	10,118	100.0
11 Robert L. Henry (D)	7,384	98.6
12 Oscar Callaway (D)	10,525	82.0
Robert G. Martin (SOC)	1,270	9.9
C. C. Littleton (R)	836	6.5
13 John H. Stephens (D)	19,543	83.4
T. S. Bugbee (R)	2,039	8.7
John I. Green (SOC)	1,488	6.4
14 James L. Slayden (D)	14,251	94.8
15 John N. Garner (D)	14,300	71.7
Noah Allen (R)	5,287	26.5
16 William R. Smith (D)	18,258	85.4
W. H. Harvey (SOC)	1,749	8.2
Robert A. Webb (R)	1,384	6.5

UTAH

Candidates	Votes	%
AL Joseph Howell (R)	50,614	49.5
Ferdinand Erickson (D)	32,730	32.0
Allen T. Sanford (AM)	14,042	13.7

VERMONT

Candidates	Votes	%
1 David J. Foster (R)	18,951	68.6
P. M. Meldon (D)	8,215	29.7
2 Frank Plumley (R)	18,185	73.4
Alexander Cochran (D)	6,226	25.1

VIRGINIA

Candidates	Votes	%
1 William A. Jones (D)	5,908	80.5
George N. Wise (R)	1,431	19.5
2 Edward E. Holland (D)	6,649	79.6
H. H. Rumble (R)	1,703	20.4
3 John Lamb (D)	5,408	86.9
W. R. Vawter (R)	813	13.1
4 Robert Turnbull (D)	3,769	100.0

Candidates	Votes	%
5 Edward W. Saunders (D)	7,537	50.5
John M. Parsons (R)	7,382	49.5
6 Carter Glass (D)	5,203	87.6
W. Allison (R)	734	12.4
7 James Hay (D)	5,818	58.0
John Paul (R)	2,589	25.8
S. Lupton (I)	1,631	16.3
8 Charles C. Carlin (D)	4,669	100.0
9 Campbell Bascom Slemp (R)	16,958	50.3
Henry C. Stuart (D)	16,731	49.7
10 Henry D. Flood (D)	5,878	100.0

WASHINGTON

Candidates	Votes	%
1 William E. Humphrey (R)	27,717	51.2
W. W. Black (D)	20,116	37.2
W. W. Smith (SOC)	5,088	9.4
2 Stanton Warburton (R)	20,448	57.5
Maurice Langhorne (D)	10,288	28.9
Leslie E. Aller (SOC)	3,978	11.2
3 William L. LaFollette (R)	30,126	62.1
Harry D. Merritt (D)	14,423	29.7
David C. Coates (SOC)	3,998	8.2

WEST VIRGINIA

Candidates	Votes	%
1 John W. Davis (D)	20,370	48.9
Charles E. Carrigan (R)	16,962	40.7

Candidates	Votes	%
A. L. Bauer (SOC)	3,243	7.8
2 William G. Brown Jr. (D)	21,276	53.3
George C. Sturgiss (R)	16,791	42.1
3 Adam B. Littlepage (D)	21,311	47.3
Joseph H. Gaines (R)	20,105	44.6
L. C. Rogers (SOC)	2,799	6.2
4 John M. Hamilton (D)	17,822	51.9
Harry C. Woodyard (R)	15,592	45.4
5 James A. Hughes (R)	25,007	51.8
Rankin Wiley (D)	22,154	45.9

WISCONSIN

Candidates	Votes	%
1 Henry Allen Cooper (R)	15,096	57.2
Calvin Stewart (D)	8,606	32.6
Michael Yabs (SOCIAL D)	1,869	7.1
2 John M. Nelson (R)	14,009	51.5
Albert C. Schmedeman (D)	12,090	44.4
3 Arthur W. Kopp (R)	13,360	56.0
William Coffland (D)	9,042	37.9
4 William J. Cary (R)	12,261	38.0
William R. Gaylord (SOCIAL D)	11,814	36.7
William J. Kershaw (D)	8,081	25.1
5 Victor L. Berger (SOCIAL D)	13,497	38.3
Henry F. Cochems (R)	13,147	37.3
Joseph P. Carney (D)	8,433	23.9
6 Michael E. Burke (D)	15,749	51.0
William H. Froelich (R)	13,278	43.0

Candidates	Votes	%
John C. Boll (SOCIAL D)	1,705	5.5
7 John J. Esch (R)	15,365	63.1
Paul W. Mahoney (D)	7,365	30.2
8 James H. Davidson (R)	15,934	55.2
Fred B. Rawson (D)	10,654	36.9
Richard W. Burke (SOCIAL D)	2,005	7.0
9 Thomas F. Konop (D)	12,140	45.6
Gustav Kustermann (R)	12,135	45.6
Thomas J. Oliver (SOCIAL D)	1,777	6.7
10 Elmer A. Morse (R)	17,360	54.2
John F. Lamont (D)	11,798	36.8
Lynn Thompson (SOCIAL D)	2,882	9.0
11 Irvine L. Lenroot (R)	19,224	88.5
Henry M. Parks (SOCIAL D)	2,473	11.4

WYOMING

Candidates	Votes	%
AL Frank W. Mondell (R)	20,312	54.7
W. B. Ross (D)	14,659	39.5
J. B. Morgan (SOC)	2,155	5.8

1911 House Elections

ARIZONA

(Became a state Feb. 14, 1912)

Candidates	Votes	%
AL Carl Hayden (D)	11,556	54.1
John S. Williams (R)	8,485	39.7
John Halberg (SOC)	1,252	5.9

NEW MEXICO

(Became a state Jan. 6, 1912)

Candidates	Votes	%
AL George Curry (R)✓	30,162	
Harvey B. Fergusson (D)✓	29,999	

Candidates	Votes	%
Elfego Baca (R)	28,836	
Paz Valverde (D)	28,353	
J. W. Hansen (SOC)	1,845	
C. Cutting (SOC)	1,745	

PENNSYLVANIA

Candidates	Votes	%
2 William Stuart Rayburn (R)	15,470	76.3
Henry Baur (D)	4,373	21.6
14 W. D. B. Ainey (R)	13,860	55.6
Oscar H. Rockwell (D, KEY)	11,062	44.4

TENNESSEE

Special Election

Candidates	Votes	%
10 Kenneth D. McKellar (D)	11,573	85.0
W. A. Weatherall (SOC)	2,040	15.0

1912 House Elections

ALABAMA

	Candidates	Votes	%
1	George W. Taylor (D)	7,414	97.2
2	S. Hubert Dent Jr. (D)	11,197	100.0
3	Henry D. Clayton (D)	11,225	100.0
4	Fred L. Blackmon (D)	7,740	67.4
	A. P. Longshore (PROG)	3,060	26.6
	W. H. Sturdivant (R)	693	6.0
5	J. Thomas Heflin (D)	10,210	100.0
6	Richmond P. Hobson (D)	10,065	82.0
	Charles P. Lunsford (R)	2,210	18.0
7	John L. Burnett (D)	9,770	54.5
	Sumter Cogswell (PROG)	5,462	30.4
	John J. Stephens (R)	2,711	15.1
8	William Richardson (D)	10,753	88.4
	William E. Hotchkiss (R)	1,160	9.5
9	Oscar W. Underwood (D)	12,584	88.7
	Frederick B. Parker (R)	1,598	11.3
AL	John W. Abercrombie (D)	87,519	87.8
	Asa E. Stratton (R)	9,589	9.6

ARIZONA

	Candidates	Votes	%
AL	Carl Hayden (D)	11,389	48.4
	Robert S. Fisher (PROG)	5,819	24.7
	Thomas E. Campbell (R)	3,110	13.2
	A. Charles Smith (SOC)	3,034	12.9

ARKANSAS

	Candidates	Votes	%
1	Thaddeus H. Caraway (D)	15,036	100.0
2	William A. Oldfield (D)	11,880	73.0
	G. W. Wells (R)	4,394	27.0
3	John C. Floyd (D)	10,849	64.6
	J. F. Carlton (R)	5,954	35.4
4	Otis T. Wingo (D)	11,680	67.6
	J. O. Livesay (R)	5,601	32.4
5	Henderson M. Jacoway (D)	13,438	70.3
	A. C. Remmel (R)	5,680	29.7
6	Samuel M. Taylor (D)	15,879	100.0
7	William S. Goodwin (D)	10,956	69.4
	Pat McNalley (R)	4,824	30.6

CALIFORNIA

	Candidates	Votes	%
1	William Kent (PROG)	20,341	37.3
	I. G. Zumwalt (D)	18,756	34.4
	Edward H. Hart (R)	10,585	19.4
	Joseph Bredsteen (SOC)	4,892	9.0
2	John E. Raker (D)	23,467	62.6
	Frank M. Rutherford (R)	10,178	27.2
	J. C. Williams (SOC)	3,818	10.2
3	Charles F. Curry (R)	31,060	58.8
	Gilbert McMillan Ross (D)	15,197	28.8
	William L. Wilson (SOC)	6,522	12.4
4	Julius Kahn (R)	25,515	56.1
	Bert Schlesinger (D)	14,884	32.7
	Norman W. Pendleton (SOC)	5,090	11.2
5	John I. Nolan (R)	27,902	52.3
	Stephen V. Costello (D)	18,516	34.7
	E. L. Reguin (SOC)	6,962	13.0
6	Joseph R. Knowland (R)	35,219	53.7
	J. Stitt Wilson (SOC)	26,234	40.0
	Hiram A. Luttrell (D)	4,135	6.3
7	Denver S. Church (D)	23,752	44.1
	James C. Needham (R)	22,994	42.6
	J. S. Cato (SOC)	7,171	13.3
8	Everis A. Hayes (R)	29,861	50.9
	James B. Holohan (D)	20,620	35.2
	Robert Whitaker (SOC)	8,125	13.9
9	Charles W. Bell (R)	28,845	47.2
	Thomas H. Kirk (D)	14,571	23.8
	Ralph L. Criswell (SOC)	11,123	18.2
	George S. Yarnall (P)	6,510	10.7
10	William D. Stephens (R)	43,637	53.4
	George Ringo (D)	17,890	21.9

	Candidates	Votes	%
	Fred C. Wheeler (SOC)	17,126	21.0
11	William Kettner (D)	24,822	42.7
	Samuel C. Evans (R)	21,426	36.9
	Noble Asa Richardson (SOC)	7,059	12.1
	Helen M. Stoddard (P)	4,842	8.3

COLORADO

	Candidates	Votes	%
1	George J. Kindel (D)	54,504	45.8
	W. J. L. Crank (PROG-BMR)	30,121	25.3
	Rice W. Means (R)	24,887	20.9
	J. W. Martin (SOC)	6,755	5.7
2	Harry H. Seldomridge (D)	63,271	44.5
	Charles A. Ballreich (R)	40,990	28.8
	Neil N. McLean (RO PROG)	27,975	19.7
	S. A. Van Buskirk (SOC)	9,993	7.0
AL	Edward T. Taylor (D)	115,143✓	
	Edward Keating (D)	110,516✓	
	Clarence P. Dodge (PROG-BMR)	64,835	
	Samuel H. Kinsley (R)	63,714	
	Jesse J. Laton (R)	62,085	
	Charles E. Fisher (PROG-BMR)	58,764	
	Robert Knight (SOC)	16,108	
	F. W. Brainard (SOC)	15,808	
	Samuel S. Stutzman (P)	5,853	

CONNECTICUT

	Candidates	Votes	%
1	Augustine Lonergan (D)	17,256	40.0
	Bissell (R)	16,726	38.7
	Alsop (PROG)	6,445	14.9
2	Bryan F. Mahan (D)	14,936	41.8
	King (R)	14,421	40.3
	Davis (PROG)	4,742	13.3
3	Thomas L. Reilly (D)	16,267	42.7
	Tilson (R)	12,989	34.1
	Henderson (PROG)	5,480	14.4
	Applegate (SOC)	2,658	7.0
4	Jeremiah Donovan (D)	15,616	37.6
	Hill (R)	14,188	34.1
	Vincent (PROG)	8,263	19.9
	Hunter (SOC)	2,849	6.9
5	William Kennedy (D)	12,073	39.2
	Bradstreet (R)	11,724	38.0
	Hoadley (PROG)	4,807	15.6
	Hull (SOC)	1,923	6.2

DELAWARE

	Candidates	Votes	%
AL	Franklin Brockson (D)	22,485	46.2
	George H. Hall (R)	16,740	34.4
	Hiram R. Burton (N PROG)	5,497	11.3
	Louis A. Drexler (PROG)	2,825	5.8

FLORIDA

	Candidates	Votes	%
1	Stephen M. Sparkman (D)	12,400	78.5
	C. C. Allen (SOC)	1,901	12.0
2	Frank Clark (D)	14,035	80.5
	J. J. Collins (SOC)	1,318	7.6
	John W. Howell (R)	1,210	6.9
	C. E. Speir (PROG)	875	5.0
3	Emmett Wilson (D)	9,057	86.4
	W. N. Lamberry (SOC)	659	6.3
AL	Claude L'Engle (D)	34,324	77.4
	A. N. Jackson (SOC)	3,636	8.2
	George W. Allen (R)	2,942	6.6
	E. R. Gunby (PROG)	2,680	6.0

GEORGIA

	Candidates	Votes	%
1	Charles G. Edwards (D)	7,944	95.7
2	Seaborn A. Roddenberry (D)	7,957	100.0
3	Charles R. Crisp (D)	7,321	100.0
4	William C. Adamson (D)	8,904	100.0
5	William Schley Howard (D)	12,000	100.0

	Candidates	Votes	%
6	Charles L. Bartlett (D)	13,171	100.0
7	Gordon Lee (D)	14,099	100.0
8	Samuel J. Tribble (D)	10,013	100.0
9	Thomas M. Bell (D)	12,496	100.0
10	Thomas W. Hardwick (D)	6,474	100.0
11	John R. Walker (D)	7,922	100.0
12	Dudley M. Hughes (D)	7,791	100.0

IDAHO

	Candidates	Votes	%
AL	Burton L. French (R)	53,542✓	
	Addison T. Smith (R)	43,571✓	
	Perry W. Mitchell (D)	30,172	
	Edward M. Pugmire (D)	30,053	
	P. Monroe Smock (PROG)	12,066	
	G. W. Belloit (SOC)	11,393	
	E. L. Riggs (SOC)	11,389	
	John Tucker (P)	1,176	
	Johathan G. Carrick (P)	1,169	

ILLINOIS

	Candidates	Votes	%
1	Martin B. Madden (R)	13,608	52.2
	Andrew Donovan (D)	9,967	38.2
	William F. Barnard (SOC)	2,217	8.5
2	James R. Mann (R)	21,374	37.4
	John Charles Vaughan (D)	15,827	27.7
	Thomas D. Knight (PROG)	15,042	26.3
	John C. Flora (SOC)	4,637	8.1
3	George E. Gorman (D)	16,285	33.2
	William W. Wilson (R)	14,133	28.8
	Franklin P. Simons (PROG)	13,039	26.6
	George H. Gibson (SOC)	5,123	10.4
4	James T. McDermott (D)	14,225	57.3
	Charles J. Tomkiewicz (R)	6,097	24.6
	Carl F. Gauger (SOC)	4,503	18.1
5	Adolph J. Sabath (D)	11,150	51.8
	Jacob Gartenstein (R)	4,192	19.5
	Charles Toepper (SOC)	3,359	15.6
	L. H. Clusman (PROG)	2,825	13.1
6	James McAndrews (D)	22,520	45.3
	Arthur W. Fulton (R)	18,974	38.2
	John Will (SOC)	7,776	15.6
7	Frank Buchanan (D)	19,452	28.2
	Elton C. Armitage (PROG)	18,816	27.3
	Niels Juul (R)	15,265	22.1
	Otto C. Christensen (SOC)	15,043	21.8
8	Thomas Gallagher (D)	10,922	52.4
	William G. Herrmann (R)	6,030	29.0
	N. F. Holm (SOC)	3,674	17.6
9	Fred A. Britten (R)	11,650	34.6
	Lynden Evans (D)	10,210	30.3
	C. O. Ludlow (PROG)	7,566	22.5
	Frank Schiflersmith (SOC)	3,964	11.8
10	Charles M. Thomson (PROG)	21,028	35.2
	George Edmund Foss (R)	17,325	29.0
	Frank L. Fowler (D)	15,515	26.0
	Charles A. Larson (SOC)	5,311	8.9
11	Ira C. Copley (R)	25,750	61.1
	Thomas H. Riley (D)	14,330	34.0
12	William H. Hinebaugh (PROG)	18,334	36.4
	Charles E. Fuller (R)	16,905	33.6
	J. W. Rausch (D)	12,234	24.3
13	John C. McKenzie (R)	14,398	36.5
	I. F. Edwards (PROG)	11,875	30.1
	Ray Rariden (D)	11,704	29.7
14	Clyde H. Tavenner (D)	17,024	47.3
	Charles J. Searle (R)	15,816	44.0
	Charles Block (SOC)	2,466	6.9
15	Stephen A. Hoxworth (D)	17,156	35.8
	Charles F. Kincheloe (PROG)	15,173	31.7
	George W. Prince (R)	12,008	25.1
	John C. Sjodin (SOC)	2,642	5.5
16	Claudius U. Stone (D)	20,956	45.7
	William E. Cadmus (PROG)	12,659	27.6
	Frederick H. Smith (R)	9,295	20.3

Candidates	Votes	%
Rudolf Pfeiffer (SOC)	2,474	5.4
17 Louis FitzHenry (D)	14,966	38.0
John A. Sterling (R)	13,572	34.5
George E. Stump (PROG)	9,266	23.6
18 Frank T. O'Hair (D)	19,485	38.9
Joseph G. Cannon (R)	18,707	37.3
E. F. Royse (PROG)	9,511	19.0
19 Charles M. Borchers (D)	22,166	40.2
William B. McKinley (R)	20,643	37.4
John H. Chadwick (PROG)	10,755	19.5
20 Henry T. Rainey (D)	21,203	54.1
E. E. Brass (R)	9,478	24.2
B. O. Aylesworth (PROG)	7,007	17.9
21 James M. Graham (D)	21,361	46.8
H. Clay Wilson (R)	13,556	29.7
Robert Johns (PROG)	7,286	16.0
Herman Rahm (SOC)	2,554	5.6
22 William N. Baltz (D)	23,112	43.5
William A. Rodenberg (R)	19,438	36.6
Utten S. Nixon (PROG)	5,608	10.6
William C. Pierce (SOC)	4,276	8.1
23 Martin D. Foster (D)	26,938	52.4
Robert B. Clark (R)	12,837	25.0
George W. Jones (PROG)	9,116	17.7
24 H. Robert Fowler (D)	19,811	47.7
James B. Blackman (R)	15,004	36.1
A. J. Gibbons (PROG)	5,129	12.3
25 Robert P. Hill (D)	19,992	43.3
Napoleon B. Thistlewood (R)	16,706	36.2
Robert T. Cook (PROG)	6,545	14.2
AL Lawrence B. Stringer (D)	415,386✓	
William Elza Williams (D)	401,497✓	
William E. Mason (R)	313,608	
Lawrence P. Boyle (PROG)	311,311	
B. M. Maxey (PROG)	304,072	
Burnett M. Chiperfield (R)	299,940	
Walter Huggins (SOC)	84,352	
D. L. Thomas (SOC)	84,027	
Walter H. Harris (P)	15,721	
James H. Shaw (P)	15,590	
George Martin (SOC LAB)	4,118	
Joseph Fenyves (SOC LAB)	4,012	

INDIANA

Candidates	Votes	%
1 Charles Lieb (D)	20,014	45.7
D. H. Ortmeyer (R)	13,158	30.0
Humphrey C. Heldt (PROG)	6,022	13.7
William H. Rainey (SOC)	3,737	8.5
2 William A. Cullop (D)	22,082	45.3
Oscar E. Bland (R)	15,858	32.6
John N. Dyer (PROG)	6,001	12.3
John L. B. Shepherd (SOC)	3,888	8.0
3 William E. Cox (D)	23,150	51.5
William D. Barnes (R)	10,049	22.4
S. G. Wilkinson (PROG)	10,005	22.3
4 Lincoln Dixon (D)	24,250	52.4
Rollin A. Turner (R)	12,436	26.9
Charles Zoller Jr. (PROG)	7,540	16.3
5 Ralph W. Moss (D)	20,634	45.2
F. W. Blankenlaker (R)	11,995	26.3
Joseph W. Amis (SOC)	8,268	18.1
William Houston (PROG)	3,351	7.3
6 Finly H. Gray (D)	19,987	43.9
William L. Risk (R)	11,242	24.7
Gierluf Jansen (PROG)	10,797	23.7
7 Charles A. Korbly (D)	28,901	42.8
Joseph V. Zartman (PROG)	18,402	27.3
Thomas R. Shipp (R)	13,320	19.7
Frank J. Hays (SOC)	5,501	8.2
8 John A. M. Adair (D)	23,530	46.5
E. C. Toner (PROG)	13,157	26.0
I. P. Watts (R)	8,298	16.4
Hunter McDonald (SOC)	3,611	7.1
9 Martin A. Morrison (D)	23,574	45.1
William Robinson (R)	15,901	30.4
John F. Nell (PROG)	9,205	17.6
10 John B. Peterson (D)	18,401	38.8
E. D. Crumpacker (R)	17,294	36.5
John O. Bowers (PROG)	9,793	20.6

Candidates	Votes	%
11 George W. Rauch (D)	21,894	43.8
John W. G. Stewart (R)	12,213	24.4
Edgar M. Baldwin (PROG)	10,830	21.7
Ernest Malott (SOC)	2,813	5.6
12 Cyrus Cline (D)	19,903	48.3
Charles R. Lane (R)	11,147	27.1
Louis N. Littman (PROG)	8,114	19.7
13 Henry A. Barnhart (D)	24,968	43.9
R. Clarence Stephens (PROG)	13,822	24.3
Charles A. Carlisle (R)	13,787	24.3
Ervin H. Cady (SOC)	2,937	5.2

IOWA

Candidates	Votes	%
1 Charles A. Kennedy (R)	14,167	42.1
Joshua F. Elder (D)	12,114	36.0
Joe S. Crail (PROG)	6,457	19.2
2 Irvin S. Pepper (D)	24,769	85.7
Michael T. Kennedy (SOC)	3,176	11.0
3 Maurice Connolly (D)	19,445	42.3
Charles E. Picket (R)	18,166	39.6
Robert E. Leach (PROG)	6,640	14.5
4 Gilbert N. Haugen (R)	19,829	52.6
G. A. Meyer (D)	16,764	44.5
5 James W. Good (R)	19,030	47.7
S. C. Huber (D)	17,631	44.2
6 Sanford Kirkpatrick (D)	14,915	42.5
M. A. McCord (R)	13,796	39.3
John H. Patton (PROG)	4,350	12.4
Andrew Engle (SOC)	2,060	5.9
7 Solomon F. Prouty (R)	17,465	43.2
Clint L. Price (D)	14,075	34.8
George C. White (PROG)	5,944	14.7
8 Horace M. Towner (R)	18,462	49.2
V. R. McGinnis (D)	15,477	41.3
L. W. Laughlin (PROG)	2,704	7.2
9 William R. Green (R)	20,030	53.3
Orris Mosher (D)	16,369	43.5
10 Frank P. Woods (R)	25,263	53.9
Nelson L. Rood (D)	15,242	32.5
S. B. Philpot (PROG)	5,251	11.2
11 George C. Scott (R)	18,568	40.1
A. Vanwagenen (D)	16,168	34.9
J. W. Hallam (PROG)	10,405	22.5

Special Election

Candidates	Votes	%
11 George C. Scott (R)	18,041	41.1
A. Vanwagenen (D)	15,910	36.2
J. W. Hallam (PROG)	10,003	22.8

KANSAS

Candidates	Votes	%
1 Daniel R. Anthony Jr. (R)	22,978	51.8
J. B. Chapman (D)	20,646	46.5
2 Joseph Taggart (D)	25,830	50.1
J. L. Brady (R)	21,995	42.7
Unidentified Candidate (SOC)	3,705	7.2
3 Philip P. Campbell (R)	20,973	39.0
Francis M. Brady (D)	20,142	37.4
George D. Brewer (SOC)	12,732	23.6
4 Dudley Doolittle (D)	16,997	48.6
Fred S. Jackson (R)	16,479	47.1
5 Guy T. Helvering (D)	19,618	49.8
Rollin N. Rees (R)	18,098	45.9
6 John R. Connelly (D)	20,065	48.0
I. D. Young (R)	19,077	45.6
Daniel W. Stoner (SOC)	2,102	5.0
7 George A. Neeley (D)	26,140	51.3
Gordon L. Finley (R)	21,690	42.5
M. L. Amos (SOC)	2,828	5.6
8 Victor Murdock (R)	17,958	53.4
John I. Saunders (D)	14,488	43.1

KENTUCKY

Candidates	Votes	%
1 Alben W. Barkley (D)	22,591	64.5
Charles Furgeson (R)	10,664	30.4
I. O. Ford (SOC)	1,787	5.1
2 Augustus O. Stanley (D)	19,739	71.3
L. R. Fox (PROG)	6,500	23.5

Candidates	Votes	%
Carr Hawkins (SOC)	1,462	5.3
3 Robert Y. Thomas Jr. (D)	18,220	47.9
T. B. Dixon (R)	11,181	29.4
J. D. Duncan (PROG)	7,456	19.6
4 Ben Johnson (D)	22,168	53.2
E. R. Bassett (PROG)	11,907	28.6
John C. Thompson (R)	6,713	16.1
5 J. Swagar Sherley (D)	24,795	46.2
Henry I. Fox (PROG)	23,115	43.0
E. J. Ashcraft (R)	3,823	7.1
6 Arthur B. Rouse (D)	20,690	57.3
D. B. Wallace (R)	7,255	20.1
J. G. Blackburn (PROG)	5,701	15.8
M. A. Brinkman (SOC)	2,489	6.9
7 James C. Cantrill (D)	24,617	80.8
J. E. Jones (PROG)	5,841	19.2
8 Harvey Helm (D)	18,690	71.0
J. W. Dinsmore (PROG)	7,631	29.0
9 William J. Fields (D)	27,415	50.7
Harry Bailey (R)	16,608	30.7
E. S. Hutchins (PROG)	8,903	16.5
10 John W. Langley (R)	12,200	69.8
W. T. Stafford (PROG)	5,286	30.2
11 Caleb Powers (R)	18,531	46.4
Ben V. Smith (D)	11,760	29.5
H. H. Seavey (PROG)	9,044	22.7

LOUISIANA

Candidates	Votes	%
1 Albert Estopinal (D)	14,770	100.0
2 H. Garland Dupre (D)	14,406	100.0
3 Robert F. Broussard (D)	5,035	100.0
4 John T. Watkins (D)	5,693	93.5
Lee Norris (SOC)	394	6.5
5 Walter Elder (D)	5,795	100.0
6 Lewis L. Morgan (D)	6,101	100.0
7 Ladislas Lazaro (D)	4,943	87.4
Otis Putnam (SOC)	713	12.6
8 James B. Aswell (D)	6,033	77.7
J. R. Jones (SOC)	1,734	22.3

MAINE

Candidates	Votes	%
1 Asher C. Hinds (R)	17,635	51.7
M. T. O'Brien (D)	15,580	45.7
2 Daniel J. McGillicuddy (D)	18,077	50.4
W. B. Skelton (R)	16,796	46.8
3 Forrest Goodwin (R)	17,221	49.9
Samuel W. Gould (D)	16,512	47.8
4 Frank E. Guernsey (R)	20,198	54.4
C. N. Mullen (D)	16,725	45.0

MARYLAND

Candidates	Votes	%
1 James Harry Covington (D)	17,606	85.2
Robert D. Grier (PROG)	2,303	11.2
2 Joshua Frederick C. Talbott (D)	22,087	59.9
Labin Sparks (R)	13,732	37.2
3 George Konig (D)	15,189	54.7
Albert M. Sproesser (R)	11,078	39.9
4 J. Charles Linthicum (D)	19,075	60.9
Jacob F. Murback (R)	11,257	35.9
5 Frank O. Smith (D)	13,085	49.0
Thomas Parran (R)	12,168	45.5
6 David J. Lewis (D)	20,434	56.0
Charles D. Wagaman (R)	14,147	38.8

MASSACHUSETTS

Candidates	Votes	%
1 Allen T. Treadway (R)	12,920	42.8
Richard J. Morrissey (D)	12,075	40.0
Samuel P. Blagden (PROG)	3,883	12.9
2 Frederick H. Gillett (R)	12,301	42.8
William G. McKechnie (D)	10,940	38.1
Thomas L. Hisgen (PROG)	5,442	18.9
3 William Henry Wilder (R)	12,945	45.0
M. Fred O'Connell (D)	9,742	33.8
Stephen M. Marshall (PROG)	5,287	18.4
4 Samuel E. Winslow (R)	15,153	49.6
John A. Thayer (D)	11,216	36.7

Candidates	Votes	%
Burton W. Potter (PROG)	3,626	11.9
5 John Jacob Rogers (R)	12,827	44.8
Humphrey O'Sullivan (D)	11,037	38.5
William N. Osgood (PROG)	4,200	14.7
6 Augustus P. Gardner (R)	16,918	49.8
George A. Schofield (D)	9,704	28.6
Arthur L. Nason (PROG)	7,326	21.6
7 Michael F. Phelan (D)	12,964	45.9
Frank P. Bennett Jr. (R)	8,952	31.7
Lynn M. Ranger (PROG)	5,086	18.0
8 Frederick S. Deitrick (D)	12,484	40.5
Frederick W. Dallinger (R)	11,209	36.4
Henry C. Long (PROG)	6,665	21.6
9 Ernest W. Roberts (R)	14,021	45.1
Henry C. Rowland (D)	8,732	28.1
John Herbert (PROG)	7,364	23.7
10 William F. Murray (D)	12,031	64.0
Daniel T. Callahan (PROG)	3,711	19.7
Loyal L. Jenkins (R)	2,418	12.9
11 Andrew J. Peters (D)	17,875	64.0
Sherwin L. Cook (R)	8,786	31.5
12 James M. Curley (D)	14,875	48.8
James B. Connolly (PROG)	9,001	29.5
Charles H. S. Robinson (R)	5,812	19.1
13 John W. Weeks (R)	15,934*	45.1
John J. Mitchell (D)	13,583	38.4
George A. Fiel (PROG)	5,853	16.6
14 Edward Gilmore (D)	11,939	33.9
Henry L. Kincaide (PROG)	11,341	32.2
Robert O. Harris (R)	9,968	28.3
John McCarty (SOC)	2,005	5.7
15 William S. Greene (R)	11,207	45.1
John W. Coughlin (D)	8,975	36.1
Alvin G. Weeks (PROG)	4,172	16.8
16 Thomas C. Thacher (D)	10,461	40.2
William J. Bullock (R)	8,186	31.5
Thomas Thompson (PROG)	6,540	25.1

MICHIGAN

Candidates	Votes	%
1 Frank E. Doremus (D)	22,573	38.3
James H. Pound (N PROG)	16,801	28.5
Ezra P. Beechler (R)	16,687	28.3
2 Samuel W. Beakes (D)	16,761	35.0
William W. Wedemeyer (R)	16,650	34.8
Hubert F. Probert (N PROG)	13,660	28.5
3 John M. C. Smith (R)	14,609	32.7
Claude S. Carney (D)	14,482	32.4
Edward N. Dingley (N PROG)	12,907	28.9
Levant L. Rogers (SOC)	2,746	6.1
4 Edward L. Hamilton (R)	14,788	34.2
Albert E. Beebe (D)	14,382	33.2
George M. Valentine (N PROG)	12,712	29.4
5 Carl E. Mapes (R)	16,749	35.3
Edwin F. Sweet (D)	16,148	34.0
Suel A. Sheldon (N PROG)	11,747	24.7
6 Samuel W. Smith (R)	21,686	36.9
Alva M. Cummins (D)	18,412	31.3
William S. Kellogg (N PROG)	18,157	30.9
7 Louis C. Cramton (R)	15,089	37.0
Loren A. Sherman (N PROG)	12,588	30.8
John J. Bell (D)	11,998	29.4
8 Joseph W. Fordney (R)	13,215	34.4
Albert L. Chandler (N PROG)	11,593	30.1
Miles J. Purcell (D)	11,527	30.0
9 James C. McLaughlin (R)	11,966	39.1
William H. Sears (N PROG)	10,619	34.7
Herman R. O'Connor (D)	8,020	26.2
10 Roy O. Woodruff (N PROG)	12,882	35.1
George A. Loud (R)	12,141	33.1
Lewis P. Coumans (D)	10,129	27.6
11 Francis O. Lindquist (R)	19,303	48.2
Archie McCall (D)	9,361	23.4
John W. Patchin (N PROG)	9,231	23.1
12 William J. MacDonald (N PROG)	18,433‡	38.4
H. Olin Young (R)	18,190	37.9
John Power (D)	10,322	21.5
AL Patrick H. Kelley (R)	185,657	34.3
William H. Hill (N PROG)	174,451	32.2
Edward Frensdorf (D)	152,188	28.1

MINNESOTA

Candidates	Votes	%
1 Sydney Anderson (R)	24,681	69.6
Clinton Robinson (D)	10,786	30.4
2 Winfield S. Hammond (D)	14,718	50.3
Franklin F. Ellsworth (R)	13,093	44.7
John R. Hollister (PUB OWN)	1,479	5.1
3 Charles R. Davis (R)	18,536	61.3
Frank L. Glotzbach (D)	9,763	32.3
Frank F. Marzahn (P)	1,919	6.4
4 Frederick C. Stevens (R)	15,479	36.8
James J. Regan (D)	11,333	27.0
H. T. Halbert (PROG)	9,220	21.9
Albert Rosenquist (PUB OWN)	6,021	14.3
5 George R. Smith (R)	17,861	44.3
Thomas D. Schall (PROG)	8,574	21.3
Thomas P. Dwyer (D)	6,987	17.3
Thomas E. Latimer (PUB OWN)	6,929	17.2
6 Charles A. Lindbergh (R)	21,286	62.5
Andrew J. Gilkinson (D)	9,920	29.1
A. W. Uhl (PUB OWN)	2,839	8.3
7 A. J. Volstead (D)	25,053	100.0
8 Clarence B. Miller (R)	20,523	50.8
John Jenswold Jr. (D)	12,494	30.9
Morris Kaplan (PUB OWN)	7,398	18.3
9 Halvor Steenerson (R)	22,481	66.8
M. A. Brattland (PUB OWN)	11,190	33.2
AL James Manahan (R)	154,308	55.1
Carl Johnson Buell (D)	69,652	24.9
J. S. Ingalls (PUB OWN)	30,042	10.7
William G. Calderwood (P)	25,863	9.2

MISSISSIPPI

Candidates	Votes	%
1 Ezekiel S. Candler Jr. (D)	7,951	100.0
2 Hubert D. Stephens (D)	5,801	100.0
3 Benjamin G. Humphreys (D)	3,154	100.0
4 Thomas U. Sisson (D)	7,402	100.0
5 Samuel A. Witherspoon (D)	7,996	100.0
6 Pat Harrison (D)	7,347	96.1
7 Percy E. Quin (D)	4,486	100.0
8 James W. Collier (D)	4,660	100.0

MISSOURI

Candidates	Votes	%
1 James T. Lloyd (D)	20,874	53.9
Bonfoey (R)	12,144	31.4
Warner (PROG)	5,686	14.7
2 William W. Rucker (D)	22,786	57.3
Haley (R)	10,132	25.5
Williams (PROG)	6,776	17.1
3 Joshua W. Alexander (D)	20,179	52.8
Morroway (R)	11,192	29.3
Wightman (PROG)	6,812	17.8
4 Charles F. Booher (D)	20,232	53.8
Hickman (R)	11,284	30.0
Robinson (PROG)	5,347	14.2
5 William P. Borland (D)	33,397	52.9
Sumner (PROG)	21,863	34.6
Kimbrell (R)	5,759	9.1
6 Clement C. Dickinson (D)	17,858	52.2
Dunaway (R)	9,093	26.6
Theilmann (PROG)	6,788	19.9
7 Courtney W. Hamlin (D)	23,178	48.9
Owen (R)	15,685	33.1
Blain (PROG)	7,305	15.4
8 Dorsey W. Shackleford (D)	16,219	53.0
Peters (R)	11,965	39.1
Pemberton (PROG)	2,391	7.8
9 James Beauchamp Clark (D)	21,782	56.5
Cole (R)	16,283	42.2
10 Richard Bartholdt (R)	33,242	37.6
O'Connor (D)	31,227	35.3
Siebert (PROG)	16,417	18.6
Hoehn (SOC)	7,154	8.1
11 William L. Igoe (D)	19,653	50.4
Catlin (R)	12,448	31.9
Ward (PROG)	4,812	12.3
12 Leonidas C. Dyer (R)	11,981‡	43.6
Michael J. Gill (D)	11,249	41.0

Candidates	Votes	%
Cotton (PROG)	3,041	11.1
13 Walter L. Hensley (D)	16,079	52.1
Nipper (R)	13,406	43.4
14 Joseph J. Russell (D)	26,081	46.5
Curry (R & PROG)	25,066	44.7
Bumpas (SOC)	4,957	8.8
15 Perl D. Decker (D)	21,000	46.0
McPherson (R)	12,850	28.2
Gregg (PROG)	7,797	17.1
Bedingfield (SOC)	3,203	7.0
16 Thomas L. Rubey (D)	15,908	52.3
O'Bannon (R)	10,811	35.6
Bradford (PROG)	3,678	12.1

MONTANA

Candidates	Votes	%
AL Thomas Stout (D)	25,891✓	
John M. Evans (D)	24,492✓	
Charles N. Pray (R)	23,505	
William R. Allen (R)	19,633	
Thomas M. Everett (PROG)	16,644	
George A. Horkan (PROG)	15,336	
Henri Labeau (SOC)	10,271	
J. Frank Mabie (SOC)	10,056	

NEBRASKA

Candidates	Votes	%
1 John A. Maguire (D & PPI)	17,410	50.5
Paul F. Clark (R & PROG)	15,706	45.6
2 Charles O. Lobeck (D & PPI)	16,075	47.4
Howard H. Baldridge (R & PROG)	15,662	46.2
J. N. Carter (SOC)	2,146	6.3
3 Daniel V. Stephens (D)	26,229	53.1
Joseph C. Cook (R & PROG)	21,677	43.9
4 Charles H. Sloan (R & PROG)	22,293	53.0
Charles M. Skiles (D & PPI)	18,279	43.4
5 Silas R. Barton (R & PROG)	18,818	49.0
Roderick D. Sutherland (D & PPI)	17,522	45.7
6 Moses P. Kinkaid (R)	24,766	47.5
W. J. Taylor (D & PPI)	18,529	35.5
Florence Armstrong (P)	4,997	9.6
Fred J. Warren (SOC)	3,758	7.2

NEVADA

Candidates	Votes	%
AL Edwin E. Roberts (R)	7,380	37.3
Clay Tallman (D)	7,311	37.0
John E. Worden (SOC)	3,011	15.2
George Springmeyer (PROG)	2,072	10.5

NEW HAMPSHIRE

Candidates	Votes	%
1 Eugene E. Reed (D)	18,888	45.4
Cyrus A. Sulloway (R)	17,363	41.7
Samuel O. Titus (PROG)	4,307	10.4
2 Raymond B. Stevens (D)	21,794	53.6
Frank D. Currier (R)	17,961	44.2

NEW JERSEY

Candidates	Votes	%
1 William J. Browning (R)	14,512	39.3
Craven (D)	13,170	35.6
Jess (RO PROG)	5,891	15.9
2 J. Thompson Baker (D)	16,130	43.1
Gardner (R)	12,330	33.0
Potter (PROG)	7,384	19.7
3 Thomas J. Scully (D)	20,596	56.9
Brown (R)	14,363	39.7
4 Allan B. Walsh (D)	13,222	45.0
Blackman (R)	8,607	29.3
Gill (PROG)	6,685	22.7
5 William E. Tuttle Jr. (D)	13,920	41.0
Runyon (R)	10,085	29.7
Ennis (PROG)	7,393	21.8
Matthews (SOC)	2,066	6.1
6 Lewis J. Martin (D)	15,216	46.5
McClave (R)	8,373	25.6
Sage (PROG)	7,007	21.4
7 Robert G. Bremner (D)	9,990	42.2
Smith (R)	6,666	28.2

Candidates	Votes	%
Marelli (PROG)	4,746	20.0
Luthringer (SOC)	1,649	7.0
8 Eugene F. Kinkead (D)	14,058	52.3
Bouton (R & PROG)	9,527	35.4
Tew (TAFT)	2,269	8.4
9 Walter I. McCoy (D)	10,196	42.4
Walker (PROG)	6,403	26.6
Parker (R)	5,818	24.2
Bohm	1,454	6.1
10 Edward W. Townsend (D)	10,854	39.6
Morgan (PROG)	7,847	28.6
Adams (R)	7,111	25.9
Cairns	1,514	5.5
11 John J. Eagan (D)	14,208	62.3
Besson (R)	7,018	30.8
Reilly	1,429	6.3
12 James A. Hamill (D)	17,980	67.5
Record (R & PROG)	8,089	30.4

Special Election

Candidates	Votes	%
6 Archibald C. Hart (D)	17,197	38.8
Smith (R)	15,325	34.6
Shay (PROG)	11,287	25.5
David J. Haney (D)	3,369	7.6

NEW MEXICO

Candidates	Votes	%
AL Harvey B. Fergusson (D)	22,139	45.6
Nathan Jaffa (R)	17,892	36.9
Andrew Eggum (SOC)	5,882	12.1
Marcos C. DeBaca (PROG)	2,644	5.5

NEW YORK

Candidates	Votes	%
1 Lathrop Brown (D)	16,505	40.7
Frederick C. Hicks (R)	11,753	29.0
W. Bourke Cockran (N PROG)	11,306	27.9
2 Denis O'Leary (D)	23,090	57.0
Felix Fritsche (N PROG)	7,175	17.7
Frank E. Hopkins (R)	6,941	17.1
William Danmar (SOC)	2,918	7.2
3 Frank E. Wilson (D)	12,658	48.0
Frank F. Schulz (R)	6,633	25.1
Westervelt Prentice (N PROG)	4,918	18.6
John H. Jennings (SOC)	1,801	6.8
4 Harry Howard Dale (D)	9,059	47.1
Samuel Greenblatt (N PROG)	5,139	26.7
William Liebermann (R & IL)	3,574	18.6
Robert J. Nolan (SOC)	1,441	7.5
5 James P. Maher (D)	12,504	46.0
John S. Gaynor (R)	7,677	28.2
Charles J. Ryan (N PROG)	5,794	21.3
6 William M. Calder (R)	21,691	47.9
Robert H. Roy (D)	13,290	29.4
Jesse Fuller Jr. (IL & NPR)	9,310	20.6
7 John J. Fitzgerald (D)	16,082	59.1
Michael A. Fitzgerald (I LEAGUE)	5,513	20.3
John E. Brady (R)	5,021	18.5
8 Daniel J. Griffin (D)	17,403	52.0
Albert H. T. Banzhaf (IL & NPR)	8,867	26.5
Ernest P. Seelman (R)	6,027	18.0
9 James H. O'Brien (D)	15,903	41.0
John F. Kennedy (N PROG)	10,362	26.7
Oscar W. Swift (R)	10,122	26.1
William Koenig (SOC)	2,027	5.2
10 Herman A. Metz (D)	7,459	36.6
Jacob L. Holtzmann (N PROG)	5,889	28.9
Reuben L. Haskell (R & IL)	5,174	25.4
Barnet Wolff (SOC)	1,785	8.8
11 Daniel J. Riordan (D)	15,417	60.1
William Wirt Mills (IL & NPR)	5,570	21.7
William G. Rose (R)	4,078	15.9
12 Henry M. Goldfogle (D & IL)	4,592	39.3
Meyer London (SOC)	3,646	31.2
Henry Moskowitz (N PROG)	2,602	22.3
Alexander Wolf (R)	839	7.2
13 Timothy D. Sullivan (D)	5,697	50.6
Sigmund S. Rotter (N PROG)	3,615	32.1
John B. G. Rinehart (R & IL)	1,151	10.2
Joshua Wauhope (SOC)	790	7.0
14 Jefferson M. Levy (D)	8,950	49.4

Candidates	Votes	%
Abraham H. Goodman (N PROG)	4,457	24.6
E. Crosby Kindleberger (R)	3,468	19.1
Marie Macdonald (SOC)	958	5.3
15 Michael F. Conry (D)	16,791	61.7
James H. Hickey (N PROG)	4,791	17.6
Francis A. O'Neill (R)	4,721	17.4
16 Peter J. Dooling (D)	15,036	56.3
Francis C. Dale (R & IL)	5,929	22.2
Timothy Healy (N PROG)	5,019	18.8
17 John F. Carew (D)	12,350	51.8
Lindon Bates Jr. (IL & NPR)	5,516	23.1
Ogden L. Mills (R)	4,891	20.5
18 Thomas G. Patten (D)	13,704	50.0
Amos R. E. Pinchot (N PROG)	6,644	24.3
S. Walter Kaufman (R & IL)	4,943	18.0
Algernon Lee (SOC)	2,085	7.6
19 Walter M. Chandler (IL & NPR)	13,987	39.2
Franklin Leonard Jr. (D)	13,684	38.3
Alexander Brough (R)	7,104	19.9
20 Francis Burton Harrison (D)	5,221	41.7
Julius H. Reiter (N PROG)	4,694	37.5
Abram Goodman (R & IL)	1,596	12.8
Nicholas Aleinikoff (SOC)	996	8.0
21 Henry George Jr. (D & IL)	13,189	47.0
Jerome F. Reilly (N PROG)	8,384	29.9
Martin C. Ansorge (R)	5,265	18.8
22 Henry Bruckner (D)	15,886	47.7
Irving M. Crane (N PROG)	9,462	28.4
Rufus P. Johnston (R)	6,098	18.3
Charles Gall (SOC)	1,835	5.5
23 Joseph A. Goulden (D)	19,320	44.3
Edward J. L. Raldiris (N PROG)	13,150	30.1
Peter Wynne (R & IL)	8,779	20.1
Fred Paulitsch (SOC)	2,351	5.4
24 Woodson R. Oglesby (D, I LEAGUE)	17,804	44.1
Alfred E. Smith (N PROG)	12,496	30.9
Barton E. Kingman (R)	8,219	20.3
25 Benjamin Irving Taylor (D, I LEAGUE)	16,168	42.2
James H. Husted (R)	12,522	32.7
John C. Bucher (N PROG)	8,559	22.3
26 Edmund Platt (R)	20,618	44.5
John K. Sague (D)	20,191	43.6
Augustus B. Gray (N PROG)	4,418	9.5
27 George McClellan (D)	23,743	48.3
Charles B. Ward (R)	19,125	38.9
Horatio Seymour Manning (N PROG)	4,779	9.7
28 Peter G. Ten Eyck (D)	23,193	44.1
Daniel H. Prior (R)	23,076	43.9
Joseph F. McLaughlin (N PROG)	4,918	9.4
29 James S. Parker (R)	22,348	44.0
Milton K. Huppuch (D)	18,180	35.8
Frederick E. Draper Jr. (N PROG)	8,163	16.1
30 Samuel Wallin (R)	14,194	33.1
R. E. Lee Reynolds (D)	13,881	32.4
George R. Lunn (SOC)	9,468	22.1
Edward Everett Hale (N PROG)	4,721	11.0
31 Edwin A. Merritt Jr. (R)	18,458	46.8
Dennis B. Lucey (D)	12,995	33.0
John B. Burnham (N PROG)	7,971	20.2
32 Luther W. Mott (R, P)	21,607	45.6
Robert E. Gregg (D)	15,848	33.4
William W. Kelley (N PROG)	8,926	18.8
33 Charles A. Talcott (D)	17,855	38.0
Homer P. Snyder (R)	16,703	35.6
Benjamin Thorne Gilbert (N PROG)	9,914	21.1
34 George W. Fairchild (R)	22,072	43.8
James J. Byard Jr (D, I LEAGUE)	20,322	40.3
Jared C. Estelow (N PROG)	5,572	11.1
35 John R. Clancy (D)	18,009	35.4
Michael E. Driscoll (R)	17,874	35.1
Giles H. Stilwell (N PROG)	11,626	22.8
36 Sereno E. Payne (R)	20,604	42.2
Richard C. S. Drummond (D)	17,900	36.7
Wilson M. Gould (N PROG)	8,151	16.7
37 Edwin S. Underhill (D)	19,526	39.9
Thomas F. Fennell (R)	18,335	37.5

Candidates	Votes	%
Wiley W. Capron (N PROG)	7,891	16.1
38 Thomas B. Dunn (R)	15,776	35.4
George P. Decker (D)	14,440	32.4
A. Emerson Babcock (N PROG)	11,202	25.2
Kendrick P. Shedd (SOC)	2,657	6.0
39 Henry G. Danforth (R)	17,881	39.1
Charles Ward (D)	15,529	33.9
Silas L. Strivings (N PROG)	10,413	22.8
40 Robert H. Gittins (D)	16,065	37.5
James S. Simmons (R)	14,450	33.7
Frank C. Ferguson (N PROG)	9,889	23.1
41 Charles B. Smith (D)	14,866	40.5
George A. Davis (R)	9,578	26.1
Henry Kobler (N PROG)	9,471	25.8
Edward Simon Jr. (SOC)	2,528	6.9
42 Daniel A. Driscoll (D)	14,851	45.7
Willard H. Ticknor (R)	8,613	26.5
L. Bradley Dorr (N PROG)	7,161	22.0
43 Charles M. Hamilton (R)	17,346	37.9
Manton M. Wyvell (D)	12,479	27.3
Samuel A. Carlson (N PROG)	11,709	25.6

Special Election

Candidates	Votes	%
13 George W. Loft (D & IL)	5,945	51.2
Samuel M. Hyman (R)	2,409	20.7
Victor Tozzi (N PROG)	2,132	18.4
Joshua Wanhope (SOC)	828	7.1
20 Jacob A. Cantor (D & IL)	5,337	41.9
Isaac A. Hourwich (N PROG)	3,206	25.2
Louis H. Guterman (R)	2,991	23.5
Edward F. Cassidy (SOC)	1,210	9.5

NORTH CAROLINA

Candidates	Votes	%
1 John H. Small (D)	12,537	98.4
2 Claude Kitchin (D)	11,091	91.9
Thomas B. Brown (R)	982	8.1
3 John M. Faison (D)	11,624	65.8
James T. Kennedy (R)	6,042	34.2
4 Edward W. Pou (D)	13,906	79.5
John F. Mitchell (R)	3,586	20.5
5 Charles M. Stedman (D)	21,075	56.1
C. W. Curry (R)	15,995	42.6
6 Hannibal L. Godwin (D)	13,028	98.6
7 Robert N. Page (D)	17,873	58.9
R. Don Laws (R)	12,449	41.1
8 Robert L. Doughton (D)	15,180	55.6
George D. B. Reynolds (R)	12,078	44.2
9 Edwin Y. Webb (D)	17,072	62.7
J. A. Smith (PROG)	7,869	28.9
D. B. Paul (R)	2,228	8.2
10 James M. Gudger Jr. (D)	16,183	53.1
R. Hilliard Staton (R)	14,237	46.7

NORTH DAKOTA

Candidates	Votes	%
1 Henry T. Helgesen (R)	17,156	61.1
V. R. Lovell (D)	9,609	34.2
2 George M. Young (R)	16,912	64.3
J. A. Minckler (D)	7,426	28.2
John A. Yoder (SOC)	1,922	7.3
3 Patrick D. Norton (R)	12,935	50.7
Hal Halvorsen (D)	7,306	28.7
Arthur Leseuer (SOC)	5,254	20.6

OHIO

Candidates	Votes	%
1 Stanley E. Bowdle (D)	22,330	42.0
Nicholas Longworth (R)	22,229	41.8
Millard F. Andrew (PROG)	5,771	10.9
Lawrence A. Zitt (SOC)	2,853	5.4
2 Alfred G. Allen (D)	26,066	46.6
Otto J. Renner (R)	21,113	37.7
William H. Hay (PROG)	4,940	8.8
R. S. Moore (SOC)	3,820	6.8
3 Warren Gard (D)	26,711	42.9
Bert B. Buckley (R)	15,339	24.7
Frederick Guy Strickland (SOC)	12,774	20.5
Edward G. Pease (PROG)	6,976	11.2
4 J. Henry Goeke (D)	21,512	53.8

Candidates	Votes	%
John L. Cable (R)	10,267	25.7
William E. Rudy (PROG)	4,993	12.5
Scott Wilkins (SOC)	2,132	5.3
5 Timothy T. Ansberry (D)	20,091	64.0
Edward Staley (R)	10,177	32.4
6 Simeon D. Fess (R)	18,090	49.2
D. K. Hempstead (D)	17,300	47.0
7 James D. Post (D)	19,301	46.7
R. M. Hughey (R)	18,595	45.0
Winfield S. Tibbetts (SOC)	3,002	7.3
8 Frank B. Willis (R)	19,379	43.8
W. W. Durbin (D)	17,965	40.6
Lemuel G. Herbert (PROG)	5,429	12.3
9 Isaac R. Sherwood (D)	26,528	53.3
Holland C. Webster (PROG)	17,490	35.1
Thomas C. Devine (SOC)	5,769	11.6
10 Robert M. Switzer (R)	13,606	37.1
Charles M. Caldwell (D)	13,424	36.6
William E. Pricer (PROG)	7,091	19.3
William Miller (SOC)	2,581	7.0
11 Horatio C. Claypool (D)	21,469	49.1
Albert Douglas (R)	18,729	42.8
Albert Smith (SOC)	3,519	8.1
12 Clement L. Brumbaugh (D)	24,340	52.3
Edward L. Taylor Jr. (R)	14,682	31.5
Jacob L. Bachman (SOC)	7,095	15.2
13 John A. Key (D)	26,395	53.4
Miles H. McLaughlin (R)	13,021	26.3
Benjamin F. Sheidler (PROG)	6,779	13.7
George P. Maxwell (SOC)	3,272	6.6
14 William G. Sharp (D)	25,523	59.0
W. S. Kerr (R)	14,142	32.7
George A. Storck (SOC)	3,569	8.3
15 George White (D)	18,169	43.9
James Joyce (R)	14,678	35.5
Howard E. Buker (PROG)	4,968	12.0
F. L. Martin (SOC)	3,033	7.3
16 William B. Francis (D)	16,568	45.6
David A. Hollingsworth (R)	15,781	43.5
Robert Carson (SOC)	3,953	10.9
17 William A. Ashbrook (D)	25,453	72.1
Albert R. Milner (PROG)	5,895	16.7
Dan McCarton (SOC)	3,958	11.2
18 John J. Whitacre (D)	23,936	43.6
Roscoe C. McCullough (R)	23,350	42.5
George F. Lelansky (SOC)	7,617	13.9
19 Ellsworth R. Bathrick (D)	20,251	35.9
W. S. Harris (PROG)	16,035	28.4
Hiram E. Starkey (R)	11,574	20.5
C. E. Sheplin (SOC)	7,805	13.8
20 William Gordon (D)	24,385	40.3
Frank W. Woods (PROG)	18,194	30.1
Paul Howland (R)	12,733	21.0
John G. Willert (SOC)	5,240	8.7
21 Robert J. Bulkley (D)	20,742	42.9
Augustus R. Hatton (PROG)	13,760	28.5
Frederick L. Taft (R)	8,811	18.2
Fred C. Ruppel (SOC)	5,059	10.5
AL Robert M. Crosser (D)	423,301	41.6
Lawrence K. Langdon (R)	297,355	29.3
Randolph W. Walton (PROG)	192,809	19.0
Harry D. Thomas (SOC)	91,201	9.0

OKLAHOMA

Candidates	Votes	%
1 Bird S. McGuire (R)	19,035	45.0
John J. Davis (D)	18,456	43.7
A. W. Renshaw (SOC)	4,447	10.5
2 Dick T. Morgan (R)	24,349	43.8
J. J. Carney (D)	23,773	42.8
P. D. McKenzie (SOC)	7,486	13.5
3 James S. Davenport (D)	27,184	49.5
R. T. Daniel (R)	20,884	38.0
Lewis B. Irvin (SOC)	6,429	11.7
4 Charles D. Carter (D)	23,987	51.3
F. W. Holt (SOC)	11,513	24.6
E. N. Wright (R)	11,239	24.1
5 Scott Ferris (D)	29,574	56.2
C. O. Clark (R)	11,987	22.8
H. H. Stallard (SOC)	11,033	21.0

Candidates	Votes	%
AL William H. Murray (D)	121,411✓	
Claude Weaver (D)	120,753✓	
Joseph B. Thompson (D)	120,371✓	
Alvin D. Allen (R)	87,468	
James L. Brown (R)	87,262	
Emory D. Brownlee (R)	86,883	
Oscar T. Ameringer (SOC)	41,235	
J. T. Cumbie (SOC)	41,073	
J. Luther Langston (SOC)	41,022	

OREGON

Candidates	Votes	%
1 Willis C. Hawley (R)	26,925	43.1
R. G. Smith (D)	15,410	24.6
John W. Campbell (PROG)	8,679	13.9
W. S. Richards (SOC)	7,181	11.5
O. A. Stillman (P)	4,335	6.9
2 Nicholas J. Sinnott (R)	15,121	53.5
James H. Graham (D)	8,322	29.4
C. H. Abercrombie (SOC)	3,037	10.7
George L. Cleaver (P)	1,800	6.4
3 Abraham W. Lafferty (R & PROG)	16,783	42.9
M. G. Munly (D)	11,553	29.6
Thomas McCusker (I)	6,280	16.1
Lee Campbell (SOC)	3,065	7.8

PENNSYLVANIA

Candidates	Votes	%
1 William S. Vare (R, WASH)	25,205	68.7
John H. Hall (D, KEY)	10,492	28.6
2 George S. Graham (R, LINCOLN)	14,803	50.7
William Schlipf Jr (D, KEY)	7,604	26.0
Harry W. Lambirth (WASH)	5,796	19.9
3 J. Hampton Moore (R, LINCOLN)	15,492	54.1
John H. Fow (D)	6,212	21.7
Harry E. Walter (WASH, KEY)	5,920	20.7
4 George W. Edmonds (WASH, R)	21,728	68.5
Thomas T. Nelson (D)	8,482	26.7
5 Michael Donohoe (D, WASH)	22,001	55.2
Henry S. Borneman (R, LINCOLN)	15,181	38.1
John Whitehead (SOC)	2,604	6.5
6 J. Washington Logue (D, KEY)	22,091	43.5
Frederick S. Drake (WASH)	19,642	31.0
Harry A. Mackey (R, RO PROG)	19,291	30.5
7 Thomas S. Butler (R)	18,276	46.7
Eugene C. Bonniwell (D & KEY)	12,225	31.2
Frederick A. Howard (WASH)	7,647	19.5
8 Robert E. Difenderfer (D & KEY)	18,230	38.2
Oscar O. Bean (R)	15,840	33.2
Thomas K. Ober Jr. (WASH)	12,205	25.6
9 William W. Griest (R & WASH)	14,112	42.7
John N. Hetrick (B MOOSE)	9,947	30.1
Richard M. Reilly (D)	8,043	24.3
10 John R. Farr (R & WASH)	14,939	49.6
Michael A. McGinley (D & KEY)	12,777	42.5
11 John J. Casey (D & KEY)	15,343	40.5
Clarence D. Coughlin (WASH)	10,597	27.9
Charles C. Bowman (R P & PROG)	9,864	26.0
C. F. Quinn (SOC)	2,119	5.6
12 Robert E. Lee (D K & PROG)	14,902	50.4
Alfred B. Garner (R & WASH)	10,463	35.4
Cornelius F. Foley (SOC)	3,464	11.7
13 John H. Rothermel (D)	26,369	50.6
Claude T. Reno (R & WASH)	20,403	39.2
Clarence T. Wixson (SOC)	4,938	9.5
14 William D. B. Ainey (R K & WASH)	14,747	61.1
Joel G. Hill (D)	8,384	34.7
15 Edgar R. Kiess (R & WASH)	14,211	45.9
William B. Wilson (D & KEY)	13,643	44.1
Aaron Noll (SOC)	2,282	7.4
16 John V. Lesher (D)	14,209	47.1
I. Clinton Kline (R & WASH)	12,783	42.4
George W. Dornbach (SOC)	2,737	9.1
17 Frank L. Dershem (D & KEY)	14,073	38.9
Benjamin K. Focht (R & PROG)	10,978	30.3

Candidates	Votes	%
Frank B. Clayton (WASH)	9,442	26.1
18 Aaron S. Kreider (R BM & PR)	14,485	32.3
David L. Kaufman (D & KEY)	14,082	31.4
Henry C. Demming (WASH)	13,504	30.1
19 Warren Worth Bailey (D)	13,626	31.8
Lynn A. Brua (WASH)	12,688	29.6
Jesse L. Hartman (R & PROG)	12,633	29.5
D. W. B. Murphy (SOC)	2,879	6.7
20 Andrew R. Brodbeck (D)	16,514	46.0
Daniel F. Lafean (R & BM)	14,283	39.8
Robert C. Bair (WASH)	3,186	8.9
21 Charles E. Patton (R K & WASH)	13,732	50.3
James A. Gleason (D)	10,588	38.8
George Fox (SOC)	2,041	7.5
22 Abraham L. Keister (R & WASH)	15,560	41.6
Curtis H. Gregg (D & PROG)	14,943	39.9
Charles Cunningham (SOC)	4,735	12.7
Daniel K. Albright (P)	2,206	5.9
23 Wooda N. Carr (D)	12,211	38.8
Thomas S. Crago (R)	7,836	24.9
Harvey L. Berkeley (WASH)	7,588	24.1
Charles L. Gans (SOC)	2,928	9.3
24 Henry W. Temple (WASH)	11,495	30.8
Charles Matthews (R)	10,797	28.9
S. A. Lacock (D)	8,585	23.0
George C. Frethy (SOC)	5,082	13.6
25 Milton W. Shreve (R & WASH)	13,078	47.6
Turner B. Shacklett (D)	10,446	38.0
Sidney A. Schwartz (SOC)	2,727	9.9
26 A. Mitchell Palmer (D)	18,201	53.4
Francis A. March Jr. (R & WASH)	14,451	42.4
27 J. N. Langham (R & WASH)	17,138	56.7
Foster M. Mohney (R)	9,472	31.4
Thomas Jackson Fredericks (SOC)	1,858	6.2
John Houk (P)	1,743	5.8
28 Willis J. Hulings (WASH)	10,363	31.4
John P. Hines (D)	9,741	29.5
Peter M. Speer (R)	7,136	21.6
John R. McKeown (SOC)	4,097	12.4
J. W. Neilly (P)	1,692	5.1
29 Stephen G. Porter (R & WASH)	15,925	61.3
Joseph Gallagher (D)	5,509	21.2
George T. McConnell (SOC)	3,899	15.0
30 M. Clyde Kelly (RKW & ROPR)	17,230	54.5
Fred H. Merrick (SOC)	7,570	24.0
Delmont K. Ferree (D & PROG)	6,708	21.2
31 James Francis Burke (R & WASH)	10,679	51.1
William A. Prosser (SOC)	5,101	24.4
Joseph F. Joyce (D)	4,894	23.4
32 Andrew J. Barchfeld (R & WASH)	12,265	40.8
Herman L. Hegner (D & PROG)	7,987	26.5
Thomas F. Kennedy (SOC)	5,672	18.9
William McClintock Shrodes (KEY)	4,169	13.9
AL John M. Morin (WASH, R)	618,537✓	
Anderson H. Walters (WASH, R)	608,709✓	
Frederick E. Lewis (WASH, R)	607,702✓	
Arthur R. Rupley (WASH, R)	606,709✓	
George Benton Shaw (D)	357,562	
George R. McLean (D)	352,396	
Joseph Howley (D)	346,814	
E. E. Greenawalt (D)	343,163	
John W. Slayton (SOC)	81,785	
William Parker (SOC)	81,125	
Charles W. Erwin (SOC)	80,808	
E. S. Musser (SOC)	80,247	
Howard R. Sheppard (KEY)	21,553	
E. L. McKee (P)	21,074	
Henry S. Gill (P)	20,465	
Howard J. Force (P)	20,284	
Thomas H. Hamilton (P)	20,213	
Albin Garrett (KEY)	20,088	
Charles A. Hawkins (KEY)	19,701	
Daniel W. Simkins (KEY)	18,961	
William H. Thomas (INDL)	1,081	

Special Election

	Candidates	Votes	%
1	William S. Vare (R)	20,461	87.8
	Henry V. Garrett (KEY)	2,762	11.9

RHODE ISLAND

	Candidates	Votes	%
1	George F. O'Shaunessy (D)	13,057	50.3
	Sheffield (R)	9,663	37.2
	Bolan (PROG)	3,044	11.7
2	Peter G. Gerry (D)	10,728	42.9
	Bliss (R)	10,335	41.4
	Ball (PROG)	3,642	14.6
3	Ambrose Kennedy (R)	11,718	49.0
	Rattey (D)	9,841	41.2
	Tuttie (PROG)	2,158	9.0

SOUTH CAROLINA

	Candidates	Votes	%
1	George S. Legare (D)	4,550*	97.2
2	James F. Byrnes (D)	6,133	100.0
3	Wyatt Aiken (D)	7,458	100.0
4	Joseph T. Johnson (D)	10,144	100.0
5	David E. Finley (D)	7,901	100.0
6	J. Willard Ragsdale (D)	6,446	100.0
7	Asbury F. Lever (D)	6,660	98.5

SOUTH DAKOTA

	Candidates	Votes	%
1	Charles H. Dillon (R)	25,498	55.9
	Robert E. Dowdell (D)	18,050	39.6
2	Charles H. Burke (R)	23,170	57.1
	C. Boyd Barrett Sr. (D)	14,283	35.2
3	Eben W. Martin (R)	15,141	52.5
	Harry L. Gandy (D)	12,154	42.1
	J. E. Ballinger (SOC)	1,564	5.4

TENNESSEE

	Candidates	Votes	%
1	Sam R. Sells (R)	16,660	50.9
	Z. D. Massey (PROG R)	16,053	49.0
2	Richard W. Austin (R)	12,712	47.6
	W. H. Buttram (PROG R)	7,025	26.3
	J. C. J. Williams (D)	6,681	25.0
3	John A. Moon (D)	18,240	67.4
	C. S. Stewart (R)	6,380	23.6
	J. W. Eastman (PROG)	2,168	8.0
4	Cordell Hull (D)	17,077	64.9
	I. J. Human (R)	9,166	34.8
5	William C. Houston (D)	12,055	54.3
	J. C. Beasley (D)	8,437	38.0
	Doak Aydelott (D)	1,685	7.6
6	Joseph W. Byrns (D)	15,341	82.0
	J. A. Althauser (R)	2,862	15.3
7	Lemuel P. Padgett (D)	12,751	55.1
	C. W. Turner (D)	10,380	44.8
8	Thetus W. Sims (D)	12,451	54.2
	J. W. Ross (R)	8,368	36.4
	C. Grissam (PROG)	2,017	8.8
9	Finis J. Garrett (D)	13,392	79.0
	B.C. Cochran (R)	3,500	20.7
10	Kenneth D. McKellar (D)	12,910	94.3
	George Pardue (SOC)	777	5.7

TEXAS

	Candidates	Votes	%
1	Horace W. Vaughan (D)	13,288	85.9
	S. L. Willyard	1,646	10.6
2	Martin Dies(D)	14,116	80.3
	J. A. Freeland	2,415	13.7
3	James Young (D)	12,158	96.6
4	Sam Rayburn (D)	13,900	89.6
	C. E. Obsuchain	1,340	8.6
5	Jack Beall (D)	16,915	96.6
6	Rufus Hardy (D)	9,743	96.0
7	Alexander W. Gregg (D)	9,132	100.0
8	Joe H. Eagle (D)	13,762	83.3
	Jeff N. Miller (R)	1,658	10.0
	J.E. Curd	1,111	6.7
9	George F. Burgess (D)	13,738	99.7
10	Albert S. Burleson (D)	12,383	100.0
11	Robert L. Henry (D)	11,429	98.1
12	Oscar Calloway (D)	17,283	97.6
13	John H. Stephens (D)	25,630	89.0
	L. B. Lindsey	1,656	5.8
	H. H. Cooper (R)	1,465	5.1
14	James L. Slayden (D)	17,675	97.5
15	John N. Garner (D)	17,231	99.9
16	William R. Smith (D)	23,763	99.9
AL	Daniel E. Garrett (D)	235,065✓	
	Hatton W. Sumners (D)	234,591✓	
	D. D. Richardson (SOC)	24,466	
	J. M. Haggard (SOC)	24,398	
	R. B. Harrison (R)	22,795	
	J. E. Elgin (R)	22,656	
	Z. T. White (PROG)	16,422	
	F. M. Etheridge (PROG)	16,408	
	E. H. Coniber (P)	1,195	

UTAH

	Candidates	Votes	%
AL	Joseph Howell (R)	43,133✓	
	Jacob Johnson (R)	42,047✓	
	Mathonihah Thomas (D)	37,192	
	T. D. Johnson (D)	36,640	
	Stephen H. Love (PROG)	22,358	
	Lewis Larson (PROG)	21,934	
	Murray E. King (SOC)	8,971	
	William M. Knerr (SOC)	8,953	
	Elias Anderson (SOC LAB)	505	
	Harry S. Joseph (NON PART)	187	

VERMONT

	Candidates	Votes	%
1	Frank L. Greene (R)	15,469	59.8
	Patrick M. Meldon (D)	9,154	35.4
2	Frank Plumley (R)	13,316	58.0
	O. C. Sawyer (D)	8,268	36.0

VIRGINIA

	Candidates	Votes	%
1	William A. Jones (D)	10,361	91.0
	T. E. Coleman (SOC)	753	6.6
2	Edward E. Holland (D)	10,061	89.1
	Nathaniel T. Green (PROG)	1,121	9.9
3	Andrew Jackson Montague (D)	10,541	97.6
4	Walter A. Watson (D)	7,847	96.4
5	Edward W. Saunders (D)	9,479	62.1
	A. B. Hamner (R)	5,449	35.7
6	Carter Glass (D)	8,194	72.8
	James S. Browning (PROG)	2,312	20.6
7	James Hay (D)	10,015	71.5
	George N. Earman (R)	3,539	25.3
8	Charles C. Carlin (D)	9,083	90.7
	F. T. Evans (SOC)	628	6.3
9	C. Bascom Slemp (R)	14,868	50.0
	R. A. Ayers (D)	13,857	46.6
10	Henry D. Flood (D)	9,615	74.5
	E. J. McCulloch (PROG)	2,458	19.0
	Nathan Parkins (SOC)	842	6.5

WASHINGTON

	Candidates	Votes	%
1	William E. Humphrey (R)	35,252	31.0
	Daniel Landon (PROG)	34,562	30.4
	Charles G. Heifner (D)	26,973	23.7
	Joseph Gilbert (SOC)	16,987	14.9
2	Albert Johnson (R)	25,497	32.5
	Stanton Warburton (PROG)	24,214	30.9
	James A. Munday (D)	16,790	21.4
	Leslie E. Aller (SOC)	11,999	15.3
3	William L. LaFollette (R)	35,049	33.1
	Roscoe M. Drumheller (D)	31,148	29.4
	F. M. Goodwin (PROG)	29,666	28.0
	Robert Burnes Martin (SOC)	10,138	9.6
AL	Jacob A. Falconer (PROG)	95,049✓	
	James W. Bryan (PROG)	90,348✓	
	Henry B. Dewey (R)	87,613	
	J. E. Frost (R)	86,300	
	E. O. Connor (D)	73,133	
	Henry M. White (D)	72,184	
	M. E. Giles (SOC)	39,772	
	Alfred Wagenknecht (SOC)	39,134	
	N. A. Thompson (P)	8,185	

WEST VIRGINIA

	Candidates	Votes	%
1	John W. Davis (D)	24,777	45.0
	G. A. Laughlin (R)	24,613	44.7
	D. M. S. Holt (SOC)	4,230	7.7
2	William G. Brown Jr. (D)	23,669	47.5
	W. C. Conley (R)	23,455	47.0
3	Samuel B. Avis (R)	26,041	46.1
	A. B. Littlepage (D)	24,573	43.5
	L. C. Rogers (SOC)	5,213	9.2
4	Hunter H. Moss Jr. (R)	20,445	50.2
	J. M. Hamilton (D)	19,346	47.5
5	James A. Hughes (R)	33,128	51.9
	J. F. Beaver (D)	27,697	43.4
AL	Howard Sutherland (R)	128,467	49.2
	Ben H. Hiner (D)	114,485	43.9
	William A. Peter (SOC)	13,944	5.3

WISCONSIN

	Candidates	Votes	%
1	Henry Allen Cooper (R)	18,914	53.2
	Calvin Stewart (D)	13,816	38.8
2	Michael E. Burke (D)	20,665	55.2
	Henry J. Grell (R)	14,698	39.3
3	John M. Nelson (R)	22,388	52.9
	Albert Long (D)	18,219	43.1
4	William J. Cary (D)	14,906	44.9
	Winfield R. Gaylord (SOCIAL D)	10,840	32.6
	John M. Beffel (R)	6,945	20.9
5	William H. Stafford (R)	15,933	41.3
	Victor L. Berger (SOCIAL D)	14,025	36.3
	James F. Trottman (D)	8,251	21.4
6	Michael K. Reily (D)	16,742	48.7
	James H. Davidson (R)	15,505	45.1
7	John J. Esch (R)	20,065	61.0
	William N. Coffland (D)	10,795	32.8
8	Edward E. Browne (R)	17,099	54.6
	Arthur J. Plowman (D)	12,266	39.2
9	Thomas F. Konop (D)	16,843	48.5
	Elmer A. Morse (R)	16,139	46.4
10	James A. Frear (R)	19,915	65.1
	Charles Donohue (D)	8,794	28.7
11	Irvine L. Lenroot (R)	17,466	59.6
	Henry A. Johnson (D)	7,998	27.3
	Ellis B. Harris (SOCIAL D)	3,122	10.7

WYOMING

	Candidates	Votes	%
AL	Frank W. Mondell (R)	19,130	46.4
	Thomas P. Fahey (D)	14,720	35.7
	Charles E. Winter (PROG)	4,828	11.7
	Anthony Carlson (SOC)	2,230	5.4

1914 House Elections

ALABAMA

	Candidates	Votes	%
1	Oscar L. Gray (D)	4,609	98.5
2	S. Hubert Dent Jr. (D)	7,470	100.0
3	Henry B. Steagall (D)	8,220	100.0
4	Fred L. Blackmon (D)	5,441	99.9
5	J. Thomas Heflin (D)	8,100	100.0
6	William B. Oliver (D)	8,539	79.7
	Samuel L. Studdard (R)	2,178	20.3
7	John L. Burnett (D)	8,905	53.1
	Thomas H. Stephens (R)	6,922	41.3
8	Edward B. Almon (D)	6,101	96.6
9	George Huddleston (D)	6,756	83.7
	Robert Fullenweider (R)	1,316	16.3
AL	John W. Abercrombie (D)	62,830	78.0
	James F. Abercrombie (R)	12,832	15.9

Special Election

		Votes	%
3	William O. Mulkey (D)	6,225	53.7
	J. J. Speight	5,367	46.3

ARIZONA

		Votes	%
AL	Carl Hayden (D)	33,306	74.6
	Henry L. Eads (R)	7,586	17.0
	Ulrich Grill (SOC)	3,773	8.5

ARKANSAS

		Votes	%
1	Thaddeus H. Caraway (D)	4,806	100.0
2	William A. Oldfield (D)	5,253	100.0
3	John N. Tillman (D)	7,588	61.8
	W. N. Ivie (R)	4,087	33.3
4	Otis T. Wingo (D)	5,166	82.0
	L. C. Packard (PROG)	1,135	18.0
5	Henderson M. Jacoway (D)	5,586	100.0
6	Samuel K. Taylor (D)	4,110	100.0
7	William S. Goodwin (D)	4,757	100.0

CALIFORNIA

		Votes	%
1	William Kent (I-PR-SOC)	35,403	47.6
	Edward H. Hart (R)	28,166	37.8
	O. F. Meldon (D)	7,987	10.7
2	John E. Raker (D SOC)	32,575	64.6
	James T. Matlock (R & PROG)	15,716	31.2
3	Charles F. Curry (R-D-PROG)	66,034	85.0
	David T. Ross (SOC)	6,752	8.7
	Edwin F. Vanvlear (P)	4,911	6.3
4	Julius Kahn (R & PROG)	41,044	69.1
	Henry Colombat (D)	13,550	22.8
	A. K. Gifford (SOC)	3,928	6.6
5	John I. Nolan (R-D-PROG)	53,875	83.3
	Mads P. Christensen (SOC)	7,366	11.4
	Frederick Head (P)	3,410	5.3
6	John A. Elston (PROG)	36,164	44.4
	George H. Derrick (R)	30,704	37.7
	Howard H. Caldwell (SOC)	11,355	13.9
7	Denver S. Church (D)	39,389	49.9
	A. M. Drew (R)	25,106	31.8
	Harry M. McKee (SOC)	7,797	9.9
	Don A. Allen (P)	6,573	8.3
8	Everis A. Hayes (R)	36,499	49.1
	L. D. Bohnett (PROG D)	33,706	45.3
	Joseph Merritt Horton (P)	4,157	5.6
9	Charles H. Randall (P & D)	28,097	30.9
	Charles W. Bell (PROG)	27,560	30.3
	Frank C. Roberts (R)	25,176	27.7
	Henry A. Hart (SOC)	10,084	11.1
10	William D. Stephens (PROG)	44,141	38.4
	H. Z. Osborne (R)	33,172	28.9
	Nathan Newby (D)	17,810	15.5
	Ralph L. Criswell (SOC)	14,900	13.0
11	William Kettner (D & PROG)	47,165	52.7
	James Carson Needham (R)	25,001	27.9

Candidates	Votes	%
James S. Edwards (P)	11,278	12.6
Kaspar Bauer (SOC)	6,033	6.7

COLORADO

		Votes	%
1	Benjamin C. Hilliard (D)	26,169	44.7
	Horace Phelps (R)	21,569	36.9
	A. W. Rucker (WILSON I)	5,445	9.3
2	Charles R. Timberlake (R)	30,749	45.7
	Harry H. Seldomridge (D)	28,290	42.0
	Charles E. Fisher (PROG)	8,256	12.3
3	Edward Keating (D)	37,191	53.3
	Neil H. McLean (R & PROG)	32,567	46.7
4	Edward T. Taylor (D)	26,562	57.8
	H. J. Baird (R & PROG)	15,015	32.7
	George Kunkle (SOC)	4,353	9.5

CONNECTICUT

		Votes	%
1	P. Davis Oakey (R)	19,899	46.7
	Augustine Lonergan (D)	19,043	44.7
2	Richard P. Freeman (R)	18,255	52.5
	Mahan (D)	14,270	41.0
3	John Q. Tilson (R)	16,072	46.5
	Reilly (D)	15,310	44.3
4	Ebenezer J. Hill (R)	20,231	51.0
	Jeremiah Donovan (D)	16,610	41.8
5	James P. Glynn (R)	14,543	48.9
	Kennedy (D)	12,877	43.3

DELAWARE

		Votes	%
AL	Thomas W. Miller (R)	22,922	50.1
	Franklin Brockson (D)	20,681	45.2

FLORIDA

		Votes	%
1	Stephen M. Sparkman (D)	5,956	99.2
2	Frank Clark (D)	4,577	100.0
3	Emmett Wilson (D)	5,484	98.8
4	William J. Sears (D)	7,934	99.8

GEORGIA

		Votes	%
1	Charles G. Edwards (D)	5,600	100.0
2	Frank Park (D)	5,633	100.0
3	Charles R. Crisp (D)	4,357	100.0
4	William C. Adamson (D)	4,754	100.0
5	William S. Howard (D)	4,780	88.2
	Dewar (PROG)	640	11.8
6	James W. Wise (D)	7,100	100.0
7	Gordon Lee (D)	10,364	100.0
8	Samuel J. Tribble (D)	7,673	100.0
9	Thomas M. Bell (D)	12,943	100.0
10	Carl Vinson (D)	5,833	100.0
11	John R. Walker (D)	4,959	100.0
12	Dudley M. Hughes (D)	6,836	100.0

IDAHO

		Votes	%
AL	Addison T. Smith (R)	45,365✓	
	Robert M. McCracken (R)	43,918✓	
	James H. Forney (D)	39,736	
	Bert H. Miller (D)	37,000	
	Charles W. Luck (EP)	8,295	
	A. B. Clark (SOC)	8,093	
	G. W. Beloit (SOC)	8,061	
	E. H. Rettig (EP)	7,399	
	R. P. Logan (P)	1,329	
	J. J. Pugh (P)	1,276	

ILLINOIS

		Votes	%
1	Martin B. Madden (R)	13,063	53.2
	James M. Quinlan (D)	9,060	36.9
	Henry M. Ashton (PROG)	1,758	7.2

	Candidates	Votes	%
2	James R. Mann (R)	21,612	48.5
	Mark B. O'Leary (D)	11,940	26.8
	John C. Vaughan (PROG)	8,506	19.1
	Thomas P. Costello (SOC)	2,532	5.7
3	William W. Wilson (R)	18,511	44.9
	Joseph E. Pendergast (D)	16,614	40.3
	William C. Lewis (PROG)	4,001	9.7
	George W. Stone (SOC)	2,093	5.1
4	James T. McDermott (D)	13,313	58.2
	William W. Wilcox (R)	7,019	30.7
	Harry P. Turner (SOC)	1,422	6.2
5	Adolph J. Sabath (D)	9,921	54.2
	Abram J. Harris (R)	4,390	24.0
	E. F. Napieralski (PROG)	2,623	14.3
	Jacob Danhoff (SOC)	1,364	7.5
6	James McAndrews (D)	23,103	45.5
	Frederick E. Coyne (R)	17,328	34.1
	Robert F. Kolb (PROG)	6,161	12.1
	Frank L. Wood (SOC)	4,162	8.2
7	Frank Buchanan (D)	22,377	39.3
	Niels Juul (R)	20,143	35.4
	Carl D. Thompson (SOC)	7,663	13.5
	Charles S. Stewart (PROG)	6,724	11.8
8	Thomas Gallagher (D)	12,524	69.5
	Edward I. Williams (R)	3,558	19.7
	Henry Anielewski (SOC)	1,159	6.4
9	Fred A. Britten (R)	11,358	43.2
	Oscar F. Nelson (D)	8,242	31.4
	R. T. Crane (PROG)	5,365	20.4
	Frank Schiflersmith (SOC)	1,315	5.0
10	George Edmund Foss (R)	18,038	38.8
	John F. Waters (D)	13,096	28.2
	Charles M. Thomson (PROG)	13,039	28.0
	John M. Work (SOC)	2,343	5.0
11	Ira C. Copley (PROG)	18,371	40.5
	Frank W. Shepherd (R)	17,197	37.9
	John A. Logan (D)	9,098	20.1
12	Charles E. Fuller (R)	20,811	50.8
	William H. Hinebaugh (PROG)	9,700	23.7
	George V. B. Weeks (D)	8,726	21.3
13	John C. McKenzie (R)	18,143	57.9
	Frank M. Goodwin (D)	8,735	27.9
	Isaac N. Evans (PROG)	4,054	12.9
14	Clyde H. Tavenner (D)	17,221	44.1
	Frank E. Abbey (R)	16,132	41.3
	Henry E. Burgess (PROG)	4,272	10.9
15	Edward J. King (R)	16,217	41.3
	Edward P. Allen (D)	14,537	37.0
	Julius Kespohl (PROG)	7,122	18.1
16	Claude U. Stone (D)	18,399	48.8
	George A. Zeller (R)	16,462	43.7
17	John A. Sterling (R)	16,720	48.1
	Louis Fitzhenry (D)	14,842	42.7
	George E. Stump (PROG)	2,757	7.9
18	Joseph G. Cannon (R)	22,035	47.1
	Frank T. O'Hair (D)	20,005	42.8
	Wendell P. Kay (PROG)	4,112	8.8
19	William B. McKinley (R)	25,576	51.0
	Charles M. Borchers (D)	19,931	39.7
	Frank B. Thomas (PROG)	4,083	8.1
20	Henry T. Rainey (D)	20,340	58.0
	Jarvis F. Dubois (R)	12,885	36.8
21	Loren E. Wheeler (R)	20,800	47.8
	James M. Graham (D)	18,361	42.2
	Porter Paddock (PROG)	2,417	5.6
22	William A. Rodenberg (R)	23,362	46.5
	William N. Baltz (D)	21,364	42.5
	Charles F. Stelzel (PROG)	2,799	5.6
	M. E. Kirkpatrick (SOC)	2,772	5.5
23	Martin D. Foster (D)	24,414	53.1
	John J. Bundy (R)	18,036	39.3
	Logan B. Skipper (PROG)	2,659	5.8
24	Thomas S. Williams (R)	18,311	49.9
	H. Robert Fowler (D)	17,369	47.3
25	Edward E. Denison (R)	20,271	48.5
	Robert P. Hill (D)	17,922	42.8

Candidates	Votes	%
George W. Dowell (PROG)	2,468	5.9
AL Burnett M. Chiperfield (R)	388,896✓	
William Elza Williams (D)	375,465✓	
J. McLean Davis (R)	373,682	
Thomas P. Sullivan (D)	356,678	
Harry L. Heer (PROG)	113,510	
George N. Kreider (PROG)	105,088	
Dan R. Thomas (SOC)	42,841	
Carl Strover (SOC)	41,949	
Frank E. Herrick (P)	7,644	
John A. Shields (P)	7,275	
Harry (SOC LAB)	2,060	

INDIANA

Candidates	Votes	%
1 Charles Lieb (D)	20,488	46.6
S. Wallace Cook (R)	17,661	40.1
U. H. Seider (PROG)	3,519	8.0
2 William A. Cullop (D)	21,451	44.3
O. E. Bland (R)	19,145	39.5
J. B. Wilson (PROG)	5,087	10.5
3 William E. Cox (D)	23,679	56.4
Edgar D. Bush (R)	12,260	29.2
Lawson Mace (PROG)	5,344	12.7
4 Lincoln Dixon (D)	22,795	50.3
M. D. Wilson (R)	16,856	37.2
Roy W. Ewing (PROG)	4,609	10.2
5 Ralph W. Moss (D)	21,785	45.9
R. L. Shattuck (R)	17,552	37.0
Otis E. Gulley (PROG)	5,254	11.1
6 Finly H. Gray (D)	18,371	41.4
P. J. Lynch (R)	14,880	33.6
Elbert Russell (PROG)	9,449	21.3
7 Merrill Moores (R)	26,451	42.0
Charles S. Korbly (D)	21,343	33.9
Paxton Hibben (PROG)	10,530	16.7
W. H. Henry (SOC)	4,002	6.4
8 John A. M. Adair (D)	21,840	44.5
A. H. Vestal (R)	13,160	26.8
H. L. Kitselman (PROG)	10,785	22.0
9 Martin A. Morrison (D)	21,992	42.8
F. S. Purnell (R)	21,035	40.9
C. A. Ford (PROG)	6,198	12.1
10 William R. Wood (R)	22,318	45.4
John B. Peterson (D)	17,735	36.0
William H. Ade (PROG)	8,637	17.6
11 George W. Rauch (D)	20,666	41.6
S. L. Strickler (R)	16,999	34.3
B. B. Shively (PROG)	8,106	16.3
12 Cyrus Cline (D)	18,612	46.9
Charles R. Lane (R)	15,052	37.9
H. M. Widney (P)	3,976	10.0
13 Henry A. Barnhart (D)	25,134	44.4
A. J. Hickney (R)	19,771	34.9
R. S. Stephens (PROG)	8,542	15.1

IOWA

Candidates	Votes	%
1 Charles A. Kennedy (R)	14,866	49.2
F. B. Whittaker (D)	12,381	41.0
Daniel B. Heller (PROG)	1,600	5.3
2 Harry E. Hull (R)	20,145	50.8
W. J. McDonald (D)	16,940	42.8
3 Burton E. Sweet (R)	22,386	56.5
James C. Murtagh (D)	15,427	39.0
4 Gilbert N. Haugen (R)	20,001	56.6
G. A. Meyer (D)	13,653	38.6
5 James W. Good (R)	20,752	56.2
Joseph Mekota (D)	14,497	39.2
6 C. William Ramseyer (R)	16,616	48.1
W. H. Hamilton (D)	14,552	42.1
7 Cassius C. Dowell (R)	17,225	53.8
John T. Mulvaney (D)	10,871	33.9
John E. Holmes (PROG)	2,193	6.9
8 Horace M. Towner (R)	19,817	54.1
H. E. Valentine (D)	14,324	39.1
9 William R. Green (R)	19,265	53.9
H. S. Mosher (D)	14,677	41.1
10 Frank P. Woods (R)	24,192	54.5
D. M. Kelleher (D)	14,401	32.5

Candidates	Votes	%
William B. Quarton (PROG)	4,656	10.5
11 Thomas J. Steele (D)	21,259	48.9
George C. Scott (R)	17,600	40.5
Edward H. Crane (PROG)	3,724	8.6

Special Election

Candidates	Votes	%
2 Henry Vollmer (D)	12,625	44.5
Harry E. Hull (R)	10,809	38.1
Charles P. Hanley (PROG)	3,709	13.1

KANSAS

Candidates	Votes	%
1 Daniel R. Anthony Jr. (R)	31,539	51.6
J. B. Chapman (D)	20,279	33.2
Sheffield Ingalls (PROG)	9,259	15.2
2 Joseph Taggart (D)	28,412	41.7
John H. Crider (R)	24,732	36.3
J. L. Brady (PROG)	12,271	18.0
3 Philip P. Campbell (R)	30,644	41.2
P. J. McGinley (D)	21,492	28.9
L. F. Fuller (SOC)	11,370	15.3
G. E. Bertch (PROG)	7,871	10.6
4 Dudley Doolittle (D)	23,894	47.0
Howard F. Martindale (R)	19,331	38.0
N. D. Welty (PROG)	6,626	13.0
5 Guy T. Helvering (D)	25,142	45.7
W. A. Calderhead (R)	22,756	41.4
Loring Trott (PROG)	7,083	12.9
6 John R. Connelly (D)	27,359	47.0
John B. Dykes (R)	21,353	36.7
Eva Morley Murphy (PROG)	6,847	11.8
7 Jouett Shouse (D)	27,740	39.7
John S. Simmons (R)	26,181	37.5
O. W. Dawson (PROG)	12,537	18.0
8 William A. Ayres (D)	21,512	46.6
Charles L. Davidson (PROG)	11,907	25.8
Ezra Branine (R)	11,520	24.9

KENTUCKY

Candidates	Votes	%
1 Alben W. Barkley (D)	18,407	65.9
Edwin Farley (R)	8,522	30.5
2 David H. Kincheloe (D)	15,019	57.0
Alvin H. Clark (R)	10,593	40.2
3 Robert Y. Thomas Jr. (D)	16,020	49.7
J. F. Taylor (R)	14,414	44.7
4 Ben Johnson (D)	17,218	56.9
W. Sherman Ball (R)	11,496	38.0
5 J. Swagar Sherley (D)	23,765	60.6
Charles T. Gardiner (PROG)	8,106	20.7
Roy Wilhoit (R)	6,611	16.9
6 Arthur B. Rouse (D)	18,018	87.9
Emmett Orr (PROG)	1,689	8.2
7 James Campbell Cantrill (D)	20,040	61.2
Louis L. Bristow (R)	12,295	37.5
8 Harvey Helm (D)	14,393	55.0
James P. Spilman (R)	10,460	40.0
9 William J. Fields (D)	22,739	53.0
H. Glenn Ireland (R)	19,291	45.0
10 John W. Langley (R)	13,150	61.5
F. Tom Hatcher (D)	7,755	36.3
11 Caleb Powers (R)	16,686	70.8
John H. Wilson (I)	6,893	29.2

LOUISIANA

Candidates	Votes	%
1 Albert Estopinal (D)	9,657	91.4
Louis Henry Burns (PROG)	903	8.6
2 H. Garland Dupre (D)	8,641	81.7
Louis Lebourgeois (PROG)	1,939	18.3
3 Whitmell P. Martin (PROG)	6,030	56.6
Henri Gueydan (D)	4,604	43.2
4 John Thomas Watkins (D)	3,330	96.4
5 Riley J. Wilson (D)	2,865	95.1
6 Lewis L. Morgan (D)	3,190	99.4
7 Ladislas Lazaro (D)	3,792	86.0
Walter F. Dietz (SOC)	615	14.0
8 James B. Aswell (D)	4,466	85.9
J. R. Jones (SOC)	729	14.0

MAINE

Candidates	Votes	%
1 Asher C. Hinds (R)	16,622	47.0
John C. Scates (D)	16,035	45.4
W. C. Emerson (PROG)	2,276	6.4
2 Daniel J. McGillicuddy (D)	16,508	46.9
H. M. Sewall (R)	11,335	32.2
A. C. Wheeler (PROG)	6,539	18.6
3 John A. Peters (R)	19,600	46.5
W. R. Pattangall (D)	18,085	42.9
E. M. Thompson (PROG)	3,697	8.8
4 Frank E. Guernsey (R)	12,707	45.0
C. W. Mullen (D)	10,021	35.5
Del Merrill (PROG)	5,371	19.0

MARYLAND

Candidates	Votes	%
1 Jesse D. Price (D)	17,543	49.0
Robert F. Duer (R)	17,146	47.9
2 Joshua Frederick C. Talbott (D)	23,124	53.5
William J. Heaps (R)	17,956	41.5
3 Charles P. Coady (D)	16,279	52.9
John A. Janetzke (R)	12,901	41.9
4 J. Charles Linthicum (D)	19,791	58.2
Thomas T. Hammond (R)	12,595	37.0
5 Sydney E. Mudd (R)	16,236	48.6
Richard A. Johnson (D)	15,179	45.5
6 David J. Lewis (D)	19,494	49.1
Frederick N. Zihlman (R)	18,752	47.2

Special Election

Candidates	Votes	%
1 Jesse D. Price (D)	17,858	74.7
Thomas S. Hodson (PROG)	6,053	25.3

MASSACHUSETTS

Candidates	Votes	%
1 Allen T. Treadway (R)	15,556	55.0
Morton H. Burdick (D)	10,695	37.8
2 Frederick H. Gillett (R)	15,635	56.3
Edward M. Lewis (D & PROG)	11,252	40.5
3 Calvin D. Paige (R)	15,838	56.0
Owen A. Hoban (D)	10,539	37.2
Jonas Bemis (PROG)	1,925	6.8
4 Samuel E. Winslow (R)	16,972	57.8
Hugh O'Rourke (D)	12,373	42.2
5 John Jacob Rogers (R)	17,249	62.1
J. Joseph O'Connor (D)	9,136	32.9
William N. Osgood (PROG)	1,404	5.1
6 Augustus P. Gardner (R)	19,960	69.2
George A. Schofield (D)	7,692	26.7
7 Michael F. Phelan (D)	13,962	50.4
Charles Cabot Johnson (R)	11,530	41.6
8 Frederick W. Dallinger (R & PROG)	15,227	49.7
Frederick S. Deitrick (D)	14,359	46.9
9 Ernest W. Roberts (R)	16,087	54.8
Peter W. Collins (D)	9,773	33.3
H. Huestis Newton (PROG)	3,482	11.9
10 Peter F. Tague (D)	12,409	73.7
James A. Cochran (R)	3,018	17.9
Daniel T. Callahan (PROG)	1,407	8.4
11 George Holden Tinkham (R)	13,510	49.8
Francis J. Horgan (D)	11,863	43.7
Henry Clay Peters (PROG)	1,765	6.5
12 James A. Gallivan (D)	18,315	66.2
Charles H. S. Robinson (R)	7,673	27.7
Chester R. Lawrence (PROG)	1,678	6.1
13 William H. Carter (R)	17,988	50.5
John J. Mitchell (D)	15,935	44.7
14 Richard Olney (D)	13,246	36.5
Harry C. Howard (R)	12,556	34.6
Henry L. Kincaide (PROG)	9,147	25.2
15 William S. Greene (R)	12,729	57.9
James F. Morris (D)	7,495	34.1
Alvin G. Weeks (PROG)	1,746	8.0
16 Joseph Walsh (R)	11,322	46.9
Thomas C. Thacher (D)	10,153	42.0
Thomas Thompson (PROG)	2,669	11.1

MICHIGAN

	Candidates	Votes	%
1	Frank E. Doremus (D)	19,197	62.5
	Charles E. McCarty (R)	9,483	30.9
2	Samuel W. Beakes (D)	18,085	45.2
	Mark R. Bacon (R)	17,876	44.7
	Hubert F. Probert (N PROG)	3,345	8.4
3	John M. C. Smith (R)	15,644	45.6
	Orville J. Cornell (D)	13,245	38.6
	Edward N. Dingley (N PROG)	3,846	11.2
4	Edward L. Hamilton (R)	18,577	53.2
	Albert E. Beebe (D)	13,452	38.5
	J. Mark Harvey (N PROG)	1,826	5.2
5	Carl E. Mapes (R)	17,223	58.7
	Thaddeus B. Taylor (D)	9,031	30.8
	Alvin E. Ewing (N PROG)	1,823	6.2
6	Patrick H. Kelley (R)	19,154	49.3
	Frank L. Dodge (D)	15,013	38.7
	William S. Kellogg (N PROG)	3,696	9.5
7	Louis C. Cramton (R)	20,294	60.0
	John F. Murphy (D)	9,488	28.0
	Jefferson G. Brown (N PROG)	3,342	9.9
8	Joseph W. Fordney (R)	20,249	52.7
	Laurence W. Smith (D)	15,729	40.9
9	James C. McLaughlin (R)	16,148	55.3
	Amos O. White (D)	6,602	22.6
	William H. Sears (N PROG)	4,913	16.8
10	George A. Loud (R)	13,854	45.5
	Roy O. Woodruff (N PROG)	8,167	26.8
	Charles W. Hitchcock (D)	7,564	24.8
11	Frank D. Scott (R)	18,290	55.5
	Francis T. McDonald (D)	9,977	30.3
	Herbert F. Baker (N PROG)	3,246	9.9
12	W. Frank James (R)	14,562	49.3
	William J. Macdonald (N PROG)	9,205	31.1
	Frederic J. Bawden (D)	4,962	16.8
13	Charles A. Nichols (R)	17,091	62.6
	Antonio Entenza (D)	7,417	27.2
	Ralph Hall Ferris (N PROG)	2,001	7.3

MINNESOTA

	Candidates	Votes	%
1	Sydney Anderson (R)	23,939	65.6
	Witherstine (D)	12,540	34.4
2	Franklin F. Ellsworth (R)	18,888	55.3
	Flittie (D)	10,760	31.5
	Dehual (PROG)	3,206	9.4
3	Charles R. Davis (R)	21,151	57.4
	Avery (D)	13,791	37.4
	Mackintosh (PROG)	1,899	5.2
4	Carl C. Van Dyke (D)	16,988	55.2
	Stevens (R)	11,058	35.9
	Mahoney (SOC)	2,221	7.2
5	George R. Smith (R)	12,576	40.7
	Van Lear (SOC)	10,312	33.3
	Long (D)	4,423	14.3
	Powers (PROG)	3,618	11.7
6	Charles A. Lindbergh (R)	15,364	47.5
	Dubois (D)	11,409	35.2
	Thomason (SOC)	3,769	11.6
	Sharkey (PROG)	1,836	5.7
7	Andrew J. Volstead (R)	28,815	100.0
8	Clarence B. Miller (R)	14,135	50.4
	Nelson (D)	8,872	31.6
	Towne (SOC)	4,179	14.9
9	Halvor Steenerson (R)	24,173	76.4
	Brattland (PUB OWN)	7,489	23.7
10	Thomas D. Schall (PROG)	12,786	39.1
	Jepson (R)	11,383	34.8
	Swenson (D)	8,522	26.1

MISSISSIPPI

	Candidates	Votes	%
1	Ezekiel S. Candler Jr. (D)	5,251	100.0
2	Hubert D. Stephens (D)	5,159	100.0
3	Benjamin G. Humphreys (D)	2,125	98.0
4	Thomas U. Sisson (D)	4,684	95.6
5	Samuel A. Witherspoon (D)	6,451	92.8
	C. W. Smith (SOC)	500	7.2
6	Pat Harrison (D)	6,225	95.5

	Candidates	Votes	%
7	Percy E. Quin (D)	3,702	100.0
8	James W. Collier (D)	2,233	96.9

MISSOURI

	Candidates	Votes	%
1	James T. Lloyd (D)	18,712	56.2
	Brown (R)	12,783	38.4
2	William W. Rucker (D)	22,243	98.7
3	Joshua W. Alexander (D)	18,072	55.6
	Morroway (R)	11,933	36.7
	Courtney (PROG)	2,045	6.3
4	Charles F. Booher (D)	17,293	53.5
	Otis (R)	13,907	43.1
5	William P. Borland (D)	36,966	70.5
	Brown (PROG)	9,309	17.8
	Orr (R)	5,387	10.3
6	Clement C. Dickinson (D)	15,402	56.4
	Young (R)	9,474	34.7
	Theilmann (PROG)	1,989	7.3
7	Courtney W. Hamlin (D)	21,953	52.0
	Lovan (R)	18,025	42.7
8	Dorsey W. Shackleford (D)	15,546	52.2
	Gentry (R)	13,918	46.8
9	James Beauchamp Clark (D)	20,058	55.8
	Brown (R)	14,733	41.0
10	Jacob E. Meeker (R)	44,912	54.2
	Curlee (D)	30,153	36.4
	Brandt (SOC)	5,162	6.2
11	William L. Igoe (D)	17,163	51.1
	Hamilton (R)	15,152	45.1
12	Leonidas C. Dyer (R)	12,047	53.2
	Collins (D)	9,768	43.1
13	Walter L. Hensley (D)	15,796	50.2
	Reppy (R)	14,832	47.1
14	Joseph J. Russell (D)	23,295	47.0
	Brown (R)	22,266	44.9
	Knecht (SOC)	3,150	6.4
15	Perl D. Decker (D)	19,827	48.1
	Manlove (R)	18,471	44.8
16	Thomas L. Rubey (D)	16,340	53.0
	Diffenderffer (R)	13,057	42.4

MONTANA

	Candidates	Votes	%
AL	John M. Evans (D)	37,011✓	
	Thomas Stout (D)	35,156✓	
	Wash J. McCormick (R)	26,161	
	Fletcher Maddox (R)	26,046	
	Lewis J. Duncan (SOC)	12,282	
	W. E. Kent (SOC)	9,424	
	Wellington D. Rankin (PROG)	6,654	
	James M. Brinson (PROG)	6,166	

NEBRASKA

	Candidates	Votes	%
1	C. F. Reavis (R)	15,462	48.1
	John A. Maguire (D & PPI)	15,138	47.1
2	Charles O. Lobeck (D)	16,773	58.1
	Thomas W. Blackburn (R)	8,979	31.1
	Nathan Merriam (PROG)	1,616	5.6
3	Daniel V. Stephens (D & PPI)	26,488	57.7
	O. S. Spillman (R & PROG)	18,007	39.2
4	Charles H. Sloan (R & PROG)	22,948	54.8
	Walter H. Rhodes (D & PPI)	18,177	43.4
5	Ashton C. Shallenberger (D & PPI)	16,387	48.7
	Silas R. Barton (R & PROG)	16,217	48.2
6	Moses P. Kinkaid (R & PROG)	29,226	57.1
	Frank J. Taylor (D & PPI)	19,346	37.8

NEVADA

	Candidates	Votes	%
AL	Edwin E. Roberts (R)	8,915	42.0
	Leonard B. Fowler (D)	8,031	37.8
	Martin J. Scanlan (SOC)	4,294	20.2

NEW HAMPSHIRE

	Candidates	Votes	%
1	Cyrus A. Sulloway (R)	20,657	50.0

	Candidates	Votes	%
	Eugene E. Reed (D)	19,140	46.3
2	Edward H. Wason (R)	21,793	54.8
	Charles J. French (D)	16,101	40.5

NEW JERSEY

	Candidates	Votes	%
1	William J. Browning (R)	24,142	58.5
	Nowrey (D)	13,271	32.1
2	Isaac Bacharach (R)	21,448	54.3
	Baker (D)	14,352	36.3
	Bright (RO PROG)	2,276	5.8
3	Thomas J. Scully (D)	21,338	50.7
	Havens (R)	19,303	45.8
4	Elijah C. Hutchinson (R)	17,078	50.9
	Walsh (D)	13,766	41.0
	Thorn (RO PROG)	1,711	5.1
5	John H. Capstick (R)	16,951	45.7
	William E. Tuttle Jr. (D)	15,718	42.4
	May (RO PROG)	2,218	6.0
	Seeholzor (SOC)	1,854	5.0
6	Archibald C. Hart (D)	16,286	45.4
	Prince (R)	15,880	44.3
7	Dow H. Drukker (R)	12,664	54.7
	Cabell (D)	6,944	30.0
	Demarest (SOC)	3,370	14.6
8	Edward W. Gray (R)	13,438	44.9
	McDonald (D)	11,678	39.1
	Archibald (PROG R)	2,232	7.5
9	Richard W. Parker (R)	9,482	37.3
	Gregory (D)	8,069	31.7
	Seymour (D)	5,672	22.3
	Bohn (SOC)	1,342	5.3
10	Frederick R. Lehlbach (R)	13,765	47.5
	Edward W. Townsend (D)	12,278	42.4
11	John J. Eagan (D)	17,551	64.9
	Straus (R)	8,400	31.1
12	James A. Hamill (D)	16,260	62.6
	Higginbotham Jr. (R)	7,379	28.4
	Anderson (PROG R)	1,313	5.1

Special Elections

	Candidates	Votes	%
7	Dow H. Drukker (R)	10,613	49.0
	O'Byrne (D)	5,240	24.2
	Demarest (SOC)	5,064	23.4
9	Richard W. Parker (R)	4,675	50.1
	Seymour (D)	4,178	44.8
	Bohn (SOC)	475	5.1

NEW MEXICO

	Candidates	Votes	%
AL	Benigno C. Hernandez (R)	23,812	51.3
	H. B. Fergusson (D)	19,805	42.7

NEW YORK

	Candidates	Votes	%
1	Frederick C. Hicks (R)	17,726	47.6
	Lathrop Brown (D)	17,722	47.5
2	Charles Pope Caldwell (D)	21,330	54.5
	Frank E. Hopkins (R)	10,552	27.0
	Lawrence T. Gresser (I)	3,672	9.4
	Benjamin Katz (SOC)	2,352	6.0
3	Joseph V. Flynn (D)	11,298	50.1
	George B. Serenbetz (R)	8,368	37.1
	Joseph E. Kleinn (SOC)	1,559	6.9
4	Harry Howard Dale (D)	7,860	47.0
	John Kissel (R & IL)	5,496	32.9
	J. Chante Lipes (SOC)	1,870	11.2
	Max Schaffer (PROG)`	1,404	8.4
5	James P. Maher (D)	11,754	49.5
	Alfred T. Hobley (R)	8,327	35.1
	John S. Gaynor (PROG&IL)	2,512	10.6
6	Frederick W. Rowe (R & IL)	22,262	53.8
	Leroy W. Ross (D)	16,180	39.1
7	John J. Fitzgerald (D & IL)	15,065	65.9
	C. G. Finney Wilcox (R)	6,659	29.1
8	Daniel J. Griffin (D & IL)	20,213	62.0

Candidates	Votes	%
Thomas E. Clark (R)	9,935	30.5
9 Oscar W. Swift (R & IL)	18,547	48.7
James H. O'Brien (D)	15,224	40.0
Anna C. Wright (SOC)	2,371	6.2
10 Reuben L. Haskell (R PR IL)	8,213	40.5
Phillip A. Riley (D)	6,240	30.8
Alex S. Drescher (A-BOSS)	2,884	14.2
Harry D. Smith (SOC)	2,732	13.5
11 Daniel J. Riordan (D)	13,200	59.0
George S. Schofield (R)	7,680	34.3
12 Meyer London (SOC)	5,969	49.5
Henry M. Goldfogle (D AM IL)	4,947	41.1
Benjamin Borowsky (R & PROG)	1,133	9.4
13 George W. Loft (D AM IL)	5,934	58.2
James E. March (R & PROG)	3,081	30.2
Bouck White (SOC)	1,177	11.6
14 Michael F. Farley (D & IL)	7,310	46.5
Fiorello H. LaGuardia (R)	5,331	33.9
Henry L. Slobodin (SOC)	1,534	9.8
John B. Golden (PROG)	1,456	9.3
15 Michael F. Conry (D & IL)	13,846	65.1
Oscar W. Ehrhorn (R & PROG)	6,698	31.5
16 Peter J. Dooling (D & IL)	12,874	62.5
Harry B. Stowell (R)	6,012	29.2
William J. Moran (PROG)	1,156	5.6
17 John F. Carew (D)	10,243	53.7
Lindon Bates Jr. (R PR IL)	7,851	41.2
18 Thomas G. Patten (D & IL)	12,434	53.2
George B. Francis (R & PROG)	8,804	37.7
Ernest Ramn (SOC)	2,047	8.8
19 Walter M. Chandler (PROG&IL)	10,682	34.1
Joseph L. Buttenweiser (D)	10,150	32.4
Albert Ottinger (R)	9,588	30.6
20 Isaac Siegel (R PR IL)	4,923	44.1
Jacob A. Cantor (D)	4,843	43.3
Ludwig Schmidt (SOC)	1,356	12.1
21 Murray Hulbert (D & IL)	11,575	51.2
Martin Ansorge (R AM&PR)	9,826	43.5
22 Henry Bruckner (D)	17,886	62.4
Francis J. Kuerzi (R IL PR)	8,900	31.0
Maxie McDonald (SOC)	1,770	6.2
23 Joseph A. Goulden (D)	18,822	44.1
Robert L. Niles (R & IL)	12,060	28.3
Steven B. Ayres (PROG&BUS)	8,228	19.3
M. Rubinow (SOC)	3,378	7.9
24 Woodson R. Oglesby (D)	17,605	43.8
William Foster (R)	16,554	41.2
Alfred E. Smith (PROG)	3,143	7.8
Allen L. Benson (SOC)	2,238	5.6
25 James W. Husted (R)	17,888	51.7
Benjamin Irving Taylor (D)	14,369	41.5
26 Edmund Platt (R)	21,634	58.0
Alonzo F. Albott (D)	14,412	38.6
27 Charles B. Ward (R)	22,505	53.0
George McClellan (D)	18,074	42.6
28 Rollin B. Sanford (R)	27,158	51.9
Peter G. Ten Eyck (D PR&IL)	24,405	46.6
29 James S. Parker (R)	29,454	63.7
James Farrell (D & PROG)	15,171	32.8
30 William B. Charles (R)	16,521	42.4
William C. D. Willson (D)	9,950	25.5
Philip H. Callery (SOC)	5,705	14.6
Theron Akin (PROG)	5,105	13.1
31 Edwin A. Merritt Jr. (R)	17,720*	54.6
Andrew B. Cooney (D)	7,850	24.2
Howard D. Hadley (PROG)	5,351	16.5
32 Luther W. Mott (R & PROG)	24,684	63.6
John Fitzgibbons (D)	11,544	29.7
33 Homer P. Snyder (R)	21,144	52.6
Charles A. Talcott (D)	15,035	37.4
George H. Spitzli (PROG)	2,582	6.4
34 George W. Fairchild (R)	22,786	56.2
George J. West (D)	12,564	31.0
Albert S. Barnes (PROG, P)	4,610	11.4
35 Walter W. Magee (R)	23,075	52.8
John R. Clancy (D)	15,131	34.6
Hugh M. Tilroe (PROG)	3,211	7.3
36 Sereno E. Payne (R)	22,523*	58.9

Candidates	Votes	%
Herman L. Kelly (D)	10,970	28.7
Amasa J. Parker (PROG)	2,278	6.0
Wallace E. Brown (P)	1,995	5.2
37 Harry H. Pratt (R)	16,081	38.9
John Seeley (D)	14,056	34.0
Milo Shanks (P)	8,438	20.4
Jonas S. Vanduzer (PROG)	2,075	5.0
38 Thomas B. Dunn (R)	21,250	57.7
George P. Decker (D)	8,832	24.0
Oscar M. Arnold (SOC)	5,324	14.5
39 Henry G. Danforth (R)	23,694	63.8
M. A. Bowen (D)	9,776	26.3
Daniel M. Anthony (PROG)	2,027	5.5
40 S. Wallace Dempsey (R)	22,324	57.4
Robert H. Gittins (D)	12,857	33.1
Frank C. Ferguson (PROG)	2,395	6.2
41 Charles B. Smith (D)	11,915	38.0
Frank J. Eberle (R)	11,324	36.1
Conrad J. Meyer (PROG)	6,488	20.7
42 Daniel A. Driscoll (D)	13,081	46.9
Willard H. Ticknor (R)	12,633	45.3
43 Charles M. Hamilton (R)	20,726	60.6
Manton H. Wyvell (D)	7,619	22.3
Ernest H. Woodruff (P)	2,159	6.3
Walter N. Renwick (PROG)	2,119	6.2

NORTH CAROLINA

	Candidates	Votes	%
1	John H. Small (D)	8,940	99.8
2	Claude Kitchin (D)	6,964	88.6
	W. O. Dixon (R)	879	11.2
3	George E. Hood (D)	8,620	57.7
	Buck H. Crumpler (R)	6,305	42.2
4	Edward W. Pou (D)	11,141	99.9
5	Charles M. Stedman (D)	18,592	55.9
	John T. Benbow (R)	13,990	42.0
6	Hannibal L. Godwin (D)	8,392	65.0
	Robert W. Davis (R)	4,521	35.0
7	Robert N. Page (D)	14,789	53.5
	Theo E. McCrary (R)	12,863	46.5
8	Robert L. Doughton (D)	14,976	53.2
	Frank A. Linney (R)	13,160	46.8
9	Edwin Y. Webb (D)	15,136	54.2
	Jacob F. Newell (R)	12,777	45.8
10	James J. Britt (R)	15,347	51.3
	James M. Gudger Jr. (D)	14,579	48.7

NORTH DAKOTA

	Candidates	Votes	%
1	Henry T. Helgesen (R)	16,565	56.0
	F. Bartholomew (D)	12,217	41.3
2	George M. Young (R)	18,680	68.4
	James J. Weeks (D)	7,073	25.9
	N. H. Bjornstad (SOC)	1,553	5.7
3	Patrick D. Norton (R)	15,547	57.1
	Halvor Halvorson (D)	7,394	27.2
	S. Griffith (SOC)	3,791	13.9

OHIO

	Candidates	Votes	%
1	Nicholas Longworth (R)	29,822	52.9
	Stanley E. Bowdle (D)	24,054	42.7
2	Alfred G. Allen (D)	27,811	48.6
	Stanley Struble (R)	26,656	46.6
3	Warren Gard (D)	29,707	45.9
	Frank I. Brown (R)	23,535	36.3
	Fred Guy Strickland (SOC)	8,859	13.7
4	J. E. Russell (R)	25,096	47.9
	N. W. Cunningham (D)	24,114	46.1
5	Nelson E. Matthews (R)	19,859	47.8
	T. T. Ansberry (D)	19,281	46.4
	Curtis A. Baxter (PROG)	2,409	5.8
6	Charles C. Kearns (R)	19,456	50.6
	William A. Inman (D)	17,766	46.2
7	Simeon D. Fess (R)	37,847	58.7
	Charles E. Buroker (D)	22,544	35.0
8	John A. Key (D)	22,490	51.0
	John H. Clark (R)	20,453	46.4
9	Isaac R. Sherwood (D)	29,399	53.8

	Candidates	Votes	%
	William E. Cordill (R)	16,152	29.5
	Herbert P. Whitney (PROG)	5,949	10.9
	Edward Hoskins (SOC)	3,200	5.9
10	Robert M. Switzer (R)	18,001	54.0
	C. L. Martzolff (D)	12,375	37.1
	Edgar Ervin (PROG)	2,981	8.9
11	Edwin D. Ricketts (R)	17,708	47.0
	Horatio C. Claypool (D)	17,598	46.7
12	Clement L. Brumbaugh (D)	25,608	46.9
	Ralph E. Westfall (R)	22,499	41.2
	Frank E. Hayden (PROG)	3,278	6.0
	Fred P. Zimpfer (SOC)	3,178	5.8
13	Arthur W. Overmeyer (D)	22,085	46.8
	Charles S. Hatfield (R)	22,011	46.7
14	Seward H. Williams (R)	21,717	41.6
	E. R. Bathrick (D)	20,339	39.0
	Henry M. Hagelbarger (PROG)	5,602	10.7
	C. E Sheplin (SOC)	4,079	7.8
15	William C. Mooney (R)	21,145	45.8
	George White (D)	21,046	45.5
16	Roscoe C. McCulloch (R)	28,609	52.5
	Ed J. Meyer (D)	20,658	37.9
	G. A. Kohr (SOC)	3,933	7.2
17	William A. Ashbrook (D)	29,504	56.3
	Walter A. Irvine (R)	21,375	40.8
18	David A. Hollingsworth (R)	23,650	45.9
	William B. Francis (D)	22,476	43.7
	Fred White (SOC)	2,936	5.7
19	John G. Cooper (R)	24,471	52.4
	William S. King (D)	16,897	36.2
	G. L. Arner (SOC)	2,971	6.4
	W. S. Harris (PROG)	2,363	5.1
20	William Gordon (D)	23,541	55.7
	James E. Mathews (R)	14,215	33.6
	C. E. Ruthenberg (SOC)	2,418	5.7
	Frank G. Carpenter (PROG)	2,127	5.0
21	Robert Crosser (D)	18,962	61.1
	Harry L. Vail (R)	9,039	29.1
	Tom Clifford (SOC)	1,979	6.4
22	Henry I. Emerson (R)	17,166	39.1
	Roy A. Tuttle (D)	16,093	36.7
	J.R. McQuigg (PROG)	9,023	20.6

OKLAHOMA

	Candidates	Votes	%
1	James S. Davenport (D)	15,489	46.4
	Gill (R)	14,251	42.7
	Lafayette (SOC)	3,318	9.9
2	William W. Hastings (D)	12,719	49.1
	Cook (R)	8,569	33.1
	Crain (SOC)	4,420	17.1
3	Charles D. Carter (D)	17,474	50.3
	Norman (SOC)	10,588	30.5
	Elting (R)	6,479	18.7
4	William H. Murray (D)	13,758	42.2
	Flynn (R)	9,395	28.8
	Hughes (SOC)	9,198	28.2
5	Joseph B. Thompson (D)	14,040	47.6
	Pope (R)	9,286	31.5
	Lurry (SOC)	5,391	18.3
6	Scott Ferris (D)	14,578	48.1
	Campbell (R)	8,291	27.4
	J. T. Cumbie (SOC)	6,671	22.0
7	James V. McClintic (D)	11,861	43.3
	Stallard (SOC)	9,021	32.9
	Mills (R)	6,179	22.6
8	Dick T. Morgan (R)	13,294	41.7
	Johnston (D)	12,529	39.3
	Green (SOC)	4,231	13.3
	Alexander (PROG)	1,645	5.2

OREGON

	Candidates	Votes	%
1	Willis C. Hawley (R)	51,295	46.4
	Frederick Holister (D)	32,639	29.5
	Curtis P. Coe (P)	16,465	14.9
	W. S. Richards (SOC)	7,415	6.7
2	Nicholas J. Sinnott (R & PROG)	24,176	47.5
	George L. Cleaver (P)	15,685	30.8
	Sam Evans (D)	11,013	21.7

Candidates	Votes	%
3 Clifton N. McArthur (R)	26,636	35.6
A. F. Flegel (D)	23,697	31.6
A. W. Lafferty (I-PO)	16,649	22.2
Arthur L. Moulton (PROG-P)	5,770	7.7

PENNSYLVANIA

Candidates	Votes	%
1 William S. Vare (R, RO PROG)	31,800	77.6
Lawrence E. McCrossin (D)	4,220	10.3
John Burt (WASH, P)	4,491	11.0
2 George S. Graham (R, KEY)	24,371	77.4
Patrick P. Conway (D, WASH)	6,582	20.9
3 J. Hampton Moore (R, KEY)	24,468	79.2
John H. Fow (D)	3,303	10.7
Abraham L. Weinstock (WASH, RO PROG)	2,642	8.6
4 George W. Edmonds (R, WASH)	28,460	83.2
Patrick H. Lynch (D)	4,853	14.2
5 Peter E. Costello (R)	26,352	60.8
Michael Donohoe (D, WASH)	15,113	34.9
6 George P. Darrow (R, B MOOSE)	38,068	56.1
Frederick S. Drake (WASH)	13,884	20.4
J. Washington Logue (D, KEY)	14,656	21.6
7 Thomas S. Butler (R)	23,239	63.6
Norris B. Slack (D)	8,340	22.8
Arthur H. Tomlinson (WASH)	4,096	11.2
8 Henry W. Watson (R)	22,691	50.9
Harry E. Grim (D)	15,706	35.2
Harold G. Knight (WASH)	4,941	11.1
9 William W. Griest (R)	17,410	61.0
John N. Hetrick (D, WASH)	10,439	36.6
10 John R. Farr (R, WASH)	16,474	54.7
John J. Loftus (D, KEY)	12,044	40.0
11 John J. Casey (D, B MOOSE)	22,762	57.1
Lewis P. Kniffen (R, WASH)	16,011	40.2
12 Robert D. Heaton (R)	17,213	53.7
Robert E. Lee (D)	12,416	38.7
William W. Thorn (WASH)	1,619	5.1
13 Arthur Granville Dewalt (D)	19,887	45.5
John K. Stauffer (R)	14,850	33.9
John L. Stewart (WASH)	4,516	10.3
L. Birch Wilson Jr. (SOC)	4,138	9.5
14 Louis T. McFadden (R)	9,153	40.3
Fred W. Dean (D)	6,219	27.4
Dana R. Stephens (WASH)	6,196	27.3
15 Edgar R. Kiess (R)	11,525	41.8
John J. Reardon (D)	8,118	29.5
Montfort T. Stokes (WASH, P)	6,447	23.4
Peter J. Homler (SOC)	1,472	5.3
16 John V. Lesher (D)	12,982	44.3
Charles H. Robbins (R)	9,129	31.2
W. W. Heffner (WASH)	4,719	16.1
17 Benjamin K. Focht (R)	14,176	41.4
Frank L. Dershem (D)	12,597	36.8
Charles L. Johnson (WASH)	5,894	17.2
18 Aaron S. Kreider (R)	23,789	52.3
David L. Kaufman (D)	13,159	28.9
John H. Kreider (WASH)	6,378	14.0
19 Warren Worth Bailey (D, UN)	14,993	35.8
Jesse L. Hartman (R)	14,503	34.6
Lynn A. Brua (WASH, P)	10,246	24.5
20 C. William Beales (R)	14,225	45.3
Andrew R. Brodbeck (D)	13,483	43.0
Robert C. Bair (WASH)	2,419	7.7
21 Charles H. Rowland (R)	10,403	39.3
William E. Tobias (D)	9,339	35.3
Guy B. Mayo (WASH)	4,574	17.3
22 Abraham L. Keister (R, PERS LIB)	15,214	43.7
James B. Hammond (D, WASH)	14,802	42.5
Joseph B. Slack (SOC)	2,867	8.2
A. P. Hutchison (P)	1,961	5.6
23 Robert F. Hopwood (R)	14,308	44.7
Wooda N. Carr (D)	11,801	36.9
Charles F. Hood (WASH)	3,565	11.1
24 William M. Brown (R)	14,694*	41.0
Henry W. Temple (WASH)	10,771	30.1
Samuel A. Barnum (D)	7,051	19.7

Candidates	Votes	%
H. R. Norman (SOC)	2,370	6.6
25 Michael Liebel Jr. (D)	10,025	36.6
Milton W. Shreve (R)	9,222	33.6
Frank C. Lockwood (WASH, P)	6,449	23.5
F. J. Weaver (SOC)	1,735	6.3
26 Henry J. Steele (D, PERS LIB)	15,118	51.3
John D. Hoffman (D)	8,306	28.2
Edward Hart (WASH)	4,671	15.8
27 S. Taylor North (R)	10,560	36.5
R. M. Matson (D)	8,822	30.5
Charles P. Wolfe (WASH)	6,744	23.3
Samuel Dible (P)	1,673	5.8
28 S. H. Miller (R)	9,379	30.8
William McIntyre (D)	8,043	26.4
Willis J. Hulings (WASH)	6,825	22.4
William P. F. Ferguson (P)	4,420	14.5
William McKay (SOC)	1,806	5.9
29 Stephen Geyer Porter (R, WASH)	20,543	76.1
John M. Henry (D)	3,972	14.7
Henry Peter (SOC)	1,879	7.0
30 William H. Coleman (R, PERS LIB)	16,620	48.6
M. Clyde Kelly (WASH, D)	15,268	44.9
Andrew Hunter (SOC)	2,232	6.5
31 John M. Morin (R, D)	17,659	78.2
William A. Prosser (SOC, P)	4,333	19.2
32 Andrew J. Barchfeld (R, PERS LIB)	15,109	47.0
W. McClintock (WASH, RO PROG)	7,938	24.7
Guy E. Campbell (D)	6,626	20.6
John W. Slayton (SOC)	2,464	7.7
AL Thomas S. Crago (R, PERS LIB)	514,270✓	
John R. K. Scott (R, PERS LIB)	513,676✓	
Mahlon M. Garland (R, PERS LIB)	507,626✓	
Daniel F. Lafean (R, PERS LIB)	501,804✓	
Robert S. Bright (D)	281,154	
Arthur B. Clark (D)	272,829	
Martin Jennings Caton (D)	265,474	
Charles N. Crosby (D)	263,280	
Lex N. Mitchell (WASH, B MOOSE)	193,106	
Arthur R. Rupley (WASH, B MOOSE)	185,553	
Anderson H. Walters (WASH, B MOOSE)	185,028	
Harry Watson (WASH, B MOOSE)	180,744	
Edward W. Hayden (SOC)	43,932	
W. S. Greely King (SOC)	43,188	
Dennis O'Brien Coughlin (SOC)	43,148	
Charles Sehl (SOC)	42,048	
George Hart (P)	27,561	
James J. Patton (P)	27,038	
S. Harper Smith (P)	26,075	
B. R. Pike (P)	24,709	
Joseph B. Holtz (KEY)	1,462	
Howard S. Welker (KEY)	1,387	
Albert W. Binz (KEY)	1,343	
A. M. Fisher (INDL)	1,124	
John Lipsett (KEY)	1,080	
James Erwin (INDL)	759	
H. G. Meinel (INDL)	558	

RHODE ISLAND

Candidates	Votes	%
1 George F. O'Shaunessy (D)	12,983	49.8
Burchard (R)	12,080	46.3
2 Walter R. Stiness (R)	13,072	49.0
Gerry (D)	12,097	45.4
3 Ambrose Kennedy (R)	13,849	55.3
Haven (D)	10,110	40.4

SOUTH CAROLINA

Candidates	Votes	%
1 Richard S. Whaley (D)	3,018	98.5
2 James F. Byrnes (D)	4,688	100.0
3 Wyatt Aiken (D)	4,521	100.0
4 Joseph T. Johnson (D)	6,175	99.5
5 David E. Finley (D)	5,180	100.0
6 J. Willard Ragsdale (D)	4,263	100.0
7 Asbury F. Lever (D)	5,231	95.2

SOUTH DAKOTA

Candidates	Votes	%
1 Charles H. Dillon (R)	22,058	57.9
Theodore Bailey (D)	13,678	35.9
2 Royal C. Johnson (R)	20,054	57.9
John M. King (D)	11,810	34.1
3 Harry L. Gandy (D)	12,454	51.8
William G. Rice (R)	10,732	44.6

TENNESSEE

Candidates	Votes	%
1 Sam R. Sells (R)	15,959	61.3
James B. Cox (PROG)	7,753	29.8
Cy H. Lyle (D)	2,337	9.0
2 Richard W. Austin (R)	14,870	67.0
H. H. Hannah (D)	6,949	31.3
3 John A. Moon (D)	19,407	90.2
G. W. James (R)	2,111	9.8
4 Cordell Hull (D)	19,152	98.2
5 William C. Houston (D)	14,694	71.7
H. C. Watts (ID)	5,810	28.3
6 Joseph W. Byrns (D)	19,319	94.4
7 Lemuel P. Padgett (D)	18,227	97.3
8 Thetus W. Sims (D)	14,421	54.4
J. E. Deford (R)	11,930	45.0
9 Finis J. Garrett (D)	15,582	83.2
R. C. Cochran (R)	3,062	16.4
10 Kenneth D. McKellar (D)	19,160	93.0
J. O. Davison (SOC)	1,447	7.0

TEXAS

Candidates	Votes	%
1 Eugene Black (D)	10,711	87.7
J. C. Thompson (SOC)	1,498	12.3
2 Martin Dies (D)	11,425	84.0
A. Lingan (SOC)	2,132	15.7
3 James Young (D)	11,584	75.2
E. T. Bryant (SOC)	3,818	24.8
4 Sam Rayburn (D)	9,762	85.0
C. E. Obenchain (SOC)	1,449	12.6
5 Hatton W. Sumners (D)	10,430	94.9
6 Rufus Hardy (D)	7,772	86.4
W. H. Wilson (R)	1,229	13.7
7 Alexander W. Gregg (D)	7,001	100.0
8 Joe H. Eagle (D)	10,078	84.7
E. B. Miller (SOC)	1,090	9.2
S. L. Hain (R)	725	6.1
9 George F. Burgess (D)	11,083	88.5
B. F. Wright (SOC)	1,169	9.3
10 James P. Buchanan (D)	8,351	100.0
11 Robert L. Henry (D)	6,677	92.9
Duncan Carrick (R)	484	6.7
12 Oscar Calloway (D)	11,997	85.4
S. J. Browson (R)	2,043	14.5
13 John H. Stephens (D)	15,680	87.0
C. T. Griffin (R)	2,335	13.0
14 James L. Slayden (D)	13,896	90.7
John A. Currie (SOC)	921	6.0
15 John N. Garner (D)	15,678	100.0
16 William R. Smith (D)	15,181	99.9
AL James H. Davis (D)	173,803✓	
Atkins Jeff. McLemore (D)	173,177✓	
Nat B. Hunt (D)	24,557	
Reddin Andrews (SOC)	24,276	
Charles A. Warnken (R)	10,538	
E. E. Diggs (R)	10,489	
J. E. Williams (PROG)	1,542	
H. L. McCuiston (PROG)	1,541	

UTAH

	Candidates	Votes	%
1	Joseph Howell (R)	29,481	49.4
	Larson (D & PROG)	27,440	45.9
2	James H. Mays (D & PROG)	25,617	47.5
	Leatherwood (R)	25,459	47.2
	Kempton (SOC)	2,861	5.3

VERMONT

	Candidates	Votes	%
1	Frank L. Greene (R)	19,237	62.9
	Daniel E. O'Sullivan (D)	6,817	22.3
	Raymond McFarland (PROG, P)	4,064	13.3
2	Porter H. Dale (R, P)	17,743	57.5
	John Reardon (D)	6,868	22.2
	Fraser Metzger (PROG)	5,481	17.8

VIRGINIA

	Candidates	Votes	%
1	William A. Jones (D)	4,742	94.3
2	Edward E. Holland (D)	4,039	87.9
	E. B. Everton (SOC)	406	8.8
3	Andrew J. Montague (D)	5,054	95.8
4	Walter A. Watson (D)	2,887	96.2
5	Edward W. Saunders (D)	6,534	65.5
	Charles A. Hermans (R)	2,771	27.8
6	Carter Glass (D)	3,823	90.7
	B. F. Ginther (SOC)	391	9.3
7	James Hay (D)	4,569	87.0
	E. C. Garrison (R)	685	13.0
8	Charles C. Carlin (D)	5,864	75.4
	Joseph L. Crupper (R)	1,753	22.5
9	C. Bascom Slemp (R)	15,321	51.4
	R. Tate Irvine (D)	14,153	47.5
10	Henry D. Flood (D)	7,105	68.4
	George A. Revercomb (R)	3,124	30.1

WASHINGTON

	Candidates	Votes	%
1	William E. Humphrey (R)	25,320	36.9
	William Hickman Moore (D)	18,336	26.7
	Austin E. Griffith (PROG)	18,134	26.4
	Glenn E. Hoover (SOC)	5,827	8.5
2	Lindley H. Hadley (R)	23,551	35.8
	Earl W. Husted (D)	15,032	22.9
	J. E. Campbell (PROG)	14,394	21.9
	George E. Boomer (SOC)	10,099	15.4
3	Albert Johnson (R)	33,556	42.6
	Charles Drury (D)	21,978	27.9
	S. Warburton (PROG)	11,677	14.8
	Leslie E. Aller (SOC)	8,775	11.1
4	William L. LaFollette (R)	25,541	46.2
	Roscoe M. Drumheller (D)	16,896	30.6
	M. A. Peacock (PROG)	6,952	12.6
	John Storland (SOC)	3,309	6.0
5	Clarence C. Dill (D)	24,410	36.6
	Harry Rosenhaupt (R)	20,033	30.0
	Thomas Corkery (PROG)	15,509	23.2
	J. C. Harkness (SOC)	4,502	6.8

WEST VIRGINIA

	Candidates	Votes	%
1	Matthew M. Neely (D)	21,115	44.4
	George E. White (R)	20,654	43.5
	M. S. Holt (SOC)	3,054	6.4
2	William G. Brown Jr. (D)	20,666	47.5
	George M. Bowers (R)	19,305	44.4
3	Adam B. Littlepage (D)	21,890	43.4
	S. B. Avis (R)	21,457	42.5
	H. F. Link (SOC)	4,769	9.5
4	Hunter H. Moss Jr. (R)	18,356	48.9
	J. M. Hamilton (D)	17,532	46.7
5	Edward Cooper (R)	27,975	49.4
	George S. Neal (D)	24,839	43.9

	Candidates	Votes	%
AL	Howard Sutherland (R)	110,520	47.0
	Hodges (D)	102,223	43.4
	Kintzer (SOC)	11,944	5.1

WISCONSIN

	Candidates	Votes	%
1	Henry Allen Cooper (R)	16,547	58.2
	Calvin Stewart (D)	9,911	34.9
2	Michael E. Burke (D)	16,809	52.2
	Edward Voigt (R)	14,071	43.7
3	John M. Nelson (R)	17,511	54.8
	W. F. Pierstorff (D)	13,216	41.4
4	William G. Cary (R)	9,911	36.5
	Winfield Gaylord (SOCIAL D)	9,546	35.1
	Francis A. Cannon (D)	7,490	27.6
5	William H. Stafford (R)	15,620	46.7
	Victor L. Berger (SOCIAL D)	11,674	34.9
	Lawrence McGreal (D)	5,988	17.9
6	Michael K. Reilly (D)	15,115	49.5
	James H. Davidson (R)	13,998	45.9
7	John J. Esch (R)	15,113	63.5
	Virgil W. Cady (D)	7,558	31.8
8	Edward E. Browne (R)	13,863	55.5
	Albert C. Schmidt (D)	9,880	39.6
9	Thomas F. Konop (D)	15,462	51.3
	John W. Reynolds (R)	13,525	44.9
10	James A. Frear (R)	13,377	60.9
	Andrew Sutherland (D)	7,326	33.4
11	Irvine L. Lenroot (R)	15,834	65.3
	John L. Molone (D)	6,746	27.8
	Otto F. Eick (SOCIAL D)	1,580	6.5

WYOMING

	Candidates	Votes	%
AL	Frank W. Mondell (R)	21,362	51.3
	Douglas A. Preston (D)	17,246	41.5

1915 House Elections

PENNSYLVANIA

Special Election

	Candidates	Votes	%
24	Henry W. Temple (R)	27,307	65.6
	Carl E. Gibson (D)	9,295	22.3
	W. K. Ramsey (SOC)	3,362	8.1

1916 House Elections

ALABAMA

	Candidates	Votes	%
1	Oscar L. Gray (D)	8,538	100.0
2	S. Hubert Dent Jr. (D)	12,524	97.6
3	Henry B. Steagall (D)	11,761	100.0
4	Fred L. Blackmon (D)	8,443	67.6
	J. B. Atkinson (R)	4,055	32.5
5	J. Thomas Heflin (D)	8,908	81.4
	W. D. Harwell (R)	2,039	18.6
6	William B. Oliver (D)	6,620	100.0
7	John L. Burnett (D)	10,894	60.1
	T. H. Davidson (R)	7,231	39.9
8	Edward B. Almon (D)	11,862	85.2
	W. R. Hutchens (R)	1,812	13.0
9	George Huddleston (D)	11,139	86.1
	Francis Latady (R)	1,565	12.1
10	William B. Bankhead (D)	8,091	54.3
	Newman H. Freeman (R)	6,813	45.7

ARIZONA

	Candidates	Votes	%
AL	Carl Hayden (D)	34,377	65.7
	Henry L. Eads (R)	14,907	28.5
	J. R. Barnette (SOC)	3,060	5.9

ARKANSAS

	Candidates	Votes	%
1	Thaddeus H. Caraway (D)	21,440	100.0
2	William A. Oldfield (D)	17,256	73.6
	G. W. Wells (R)	6,205	26.5
3	John N. Tillman (D)	16,438	62.4
	A. J. Russell (R)	9,918	37.6
4	Otis T. Wingo (D)	25,457	100.0
5	Henderson M. Jacoway (D)	19,973	74.2
	G. A. McConnell (R)	6,930	25.8
6	Samuel M. Taylor (D)	25,901	100.0
7	William S. Goodwin (D)	16,823	71.9
	J. G. Brown (R)	6,573	28.1

CALIFORNIA

	Candidates	Votes	%
1	Clarence F. Lea (D)	32,797	48.8
	Edward H. Hart (R)	28,769	42.8
	Mary M. Morgan (SOC)	3,730	5.6
2	John E. Raker (D SOC)	30,042	71.0
	James T. Matlock (R)	12,282	29.0
3	Charles F. Curry (R)	48,193	66.7
	O. W. Kennedy (D)	16,900	23.4
	Ben Cooper (SOC)	4,455	6.2
4	Julius Kahn (R)	51,968	77.2
	J. M. Fernald (D)	10,579	15.7
	A. K. Gifford (SOC)	3,775	5.6
5	John I. Nolan (R-D)	59,333	84.6
	Charles A. Preston (SOC)	6,708	9.6
	Frederick Head (P)	4,046	5.8
6	John A. Elston (R & PROG)	56,520	64.6
	H. Avery Whitney (D)	19,787	22.6
	Luella Twining (SOC)	7,588	8.7
7	Denver S. Church (D)	38,787	51.0
	W. W. Phillips (R)	27,676	36.4
	Harry M. McKee (SOC)	5,492	7.2
	J. F. Butler (P)	4,042	5.3
8	Everis A. Hayes (R-D)	50,659	68.6
	George S. Walker (PROG-P)	17,576	23.8
	Cora Pattleton Wilson (SOC)	5,564	7.5
9	Charles H. Randall (P D-R&PR)	58,826	57.8
	Charles W. Bell (I)	33,270	32.7
	Ralph L. Criswell (SOC)	9,661	9.5
10	Henry Z. Osborne (R)	63,913	49.3
	Rufus V. Bowden (D)	33,225	25.6
	Henry Stanley Benedict (PROG)	14,305	11.0
	James H. Ryckman (SOC)	9,000	6.9
	Henry Clay Needham (P)	8,781	6.8
11	William Kettner (D)	42,051	44.5
	Robert C. Harbison (R)	33,765	35.7
	James S. Edwards (P)	14,759	15.6

Special Election

	Candidates	Votes	%
10	Henry Stanley Benedict (PROG)	19,032	56.4
	Joy Clark	7,147	21.2

COLORADO

	Candidates	Votes	%
1	Benjamin C. Hilliard (D)	30,146	48.5
	William N. Vaile (R)	26,121	42.1
	George J. Kindel (L)	3,306	5.3
2	Charles B. Timberlake (R)	42,665	55.9
	R. E. Jones (D)	29,334	38.4
	J. Edward Johnson (SOC)	3,884	5.1
3	Edward Keating (D)	40,183	53.8
	George E. McClelland (R)	31,137	41.7
4	Edward T. Taylor (D)	30,926	65.8
	Henry J. Baird (R)	13,397	28.5
	Emery D. Cox (SOC)	2,695	5.7

CONNECTICUT

	Candidates	Votes	%
1	Augustine Lonergan (D)	24,565	49.6
	Oakey (R)	22,876	46.2
2	Richard P. Freeman (R)	20,406	52.7
	Dunn (D)	17,233	44.5
3	John Q. Tilson (R)	20,859	48.5
	Reilly (D)	20,272	47.2
4	Ebenezer J. Hill (R)	25,917	53.8
	Donovan (D)	20,700	43.0
5	James P. Glynn (R)	16,872	49.8
	Kennedy (D)	15,882	46.9

DELAWARE

	Candidates	Votes	%
AL	Albert F. Polk (D)	24,395	47.6
	Thomas W. Miller (R)	24,202	47.3

FLORIDA

	Candidates	Votes	%
1	Herbert J. Drane (D)	15,353	82.2
	H. W. Bishop (R)	2,164	11.6
	Frank L. Sullivan (SOC)	1,158	6.2
2	Frank Clark (D)	10,047	79.9
	W. H. Gober (R)	1,367	10.9
	F. P. Coffin (P)	1,156	9.2
3	Walter Kehoe (D)	12,241	83.7
	Peter H. Miller (R)	2,393	16.4
4	William J. Sears (D)	14,748	68.9
	D. T. Gerow (R)	5,071	23.7
	A. N. Jackson (SOC)	1,592	7.4

GEORGIA

	Candidates	Votes	%
1	James W. Overstreet (D)	9,203	99.9
2	Frank Park (D)	9,462	100.0
3	Charles R. Crisp (D)	8,040	100.0
4	William C. Adamson (D)	9,871	100.0
5	William S. Howard (D)	13,174	88.8
	Moore	1,656	11.2
6	James W. Wise (D)	7,370	100.0
7	Gordon Lee (D)	12,831	77.9
	Walter Akerman	3,382	20.5
8	Samuel J. Tribble (D)	13,891*	99.9
9	Thomas M. Bell (D)	15,369	88.9
	Adams	1,926	11.1
10	Carl Vinson (D)	5,702	100.0
11	John R. Walker (D)	11,826	100.0
12	William W. Larsen (D)	9,816	95.8

IDAHO

	Candidates	Votes	%
AL	Burton L. French (R)	64,648✓	
	Addison T. Smith (R)	63,790✓	
	Marion J. Kerr (D)	55,807	
	John V. Stanley (D)	54,339	

Candidates	Votes	%
Albert B. Clark (SOC)	8,079	
Sam G. Gilleland (SOC)	8,033	

ILLINOIS

	Candidates	Votes	%
1	Martin B. Madden (R)	20,380	59.1
	William J. Hennessey (D)	13,380	38.8
2	James R. Mann (R)	44,159	63.0
	Philip H. Treacy (D)	22,722	32.4
3	William W. Wilson (R)	35,885	55.7
	Bernard McMahon (D)	25,954	40.3
4	Charles Martin (D)	18,722	58.5
	John Golombiewski (R)	11,793	36.8
5	Adolph J. Sabath (D)	12,884	60.7
	David T. Alexander (R)	6,850	32.3
	Charles Toepper (SOC)	1,500	7.1
6	James McAndrews (D)	39,749	48.5
	Arthur W. Fulton (R)	37,347	45.6
	Charles H. Hair (SOC)	4,586	5.6
7	Niels Juul (R)	47,514	50.9
	Frank Buchanan (D)	37,460	40.1
	Carl D. Thompson (SOC)	8,372	9.0
8	Thomas Gallagher (D)	14,970	63.4
	Frank Sullivan (D)	8,636	36.6
9	Fred A. Britten (R)	20,609	59.2
	Eugene L. McGarry (D)	12,295	35.3
	Andrew Lafin (SOC)	1,891	5.4
10	George Edmund Foss (R)	44,749	59.3
	Samuel C. Herren (D)	22,398	29.7
	Carl Hjalmar Lundquist (I)	4,622	6.1
11	Ira C. Copley (R)	38,418	69.0
	William C. Mooney (D)	15,715	28.2
12	Charles E. Fuller (R)	35,741	66.0
	Walter Panneck (D)	16,033	29.6
13	John C. McKenzie (R)	28,123	68.1
	F. P. Dudley (D)	12,436	30.1
14	William J. Graham (R)	23,099	48.5
	Clyde H. Tavenner (D)	22,591	47.4
15	Edward J. King (R)	28,143	54.5
	Edward P. Allen (D)	21,604	41.9
16	Clifford Ireland (R)	25,091	49.9
	Claude U. Stone (D)	24,073	47.9
17	John A. Sterling (R)	23,956	56.6
	S. A. Rathbun	17,571	41.5
18	Joseph G. Cannon (R)	29,318	54.2
	Armand E. Smith (D)	23,668	43.7
19	William B. McKinley (R)	33,162	52.7
	F. R. Dove (D)	28,870	45.8
20	Henry T. Rainey (D)	24,364	55.6
	Walter B. Sayler (R)	19,019	43.4
21	Loren E. Wheeler (R)	26,367	50.0
	Thomas Rees (D)	23,936	45.4
22	William A. Rodenberg (R)	31,958	50.4
	D. H. Mudge (D)	29,451	46.5
23	Martin D. Foster (D)	28,805	52.9
	Harry C. Ferriman (R)	24,328	44.7
24	Thomas S. Williams (R)	23,768	55.0
	Louis W. Goetzman (D)	18,540	42.9
25	Edward E. Denison (R)	27,905	52.2
	Andrew J. Rendleman (D)	24,034	44.9
AL	Medill McCormick (R)	707,958✓	
	William E. Mason (R)	687,198✓	
	William Elza Williams (D)	546,471	
	Joseph O. Kosture (D)	538,756	
	J. Louis Engdahl (SOC)	49,842	
	Walter Huggins (SOC)	48,842	
	Charles W. Williams (P)	9,569	
	Unidentified Candidate (P)	9,366	
	Frank Hosking (SOC LAB)	1,790	
	John Kowatzrk (SOC LAB)	1,739	

INDIANA

	Candidates	Votes	%
1	George F. Denton (D)	23,278	48.1
	S. Wallace Cook (R)	22,955	47.4
2	Oscar E. Bland (R)	24,764	47.3

Candidates	Votes	%
William A. Cullop (D)	23,759	45.4
Z. M. Garten (SOC)	2,860	5.5
3 William E. Cox (D)	24,738	52.1
John H. Edwards (R)	21,831	46.0
4 Lincoln Dixon (D)	24,925	51.5
Mauley D. Wilson (R)	22,730	47.0
5 Everett Sanders (R)	20,977	40.6
Ralph W. Moss (D)	20,270	39.3
E. V. Debs (SOC)	8,866	17.2
6 Daniel W. Comstock (R)	23,831	48.6
Finley H. Gray (D)	22,853	46.6
7 Merrill Moores (R)	40,862	51.8
Chalmer Schlosser (D)	34,732	44.1
8 Albert H. Vestal (R)	26,135	48.0
Jacob F. Danny (D)	23,854	43.8
9 Fred S. Purnell (R)	27,712	50.4
David F. Maish (D)	24,547	44.6
10 William R. Wood (R)	31,895	56.9
George E. Hershman (D)	23,077	41.1
11 Milton Kraus (R)	25,005	46.3
George W. Rauch (D)	24,578	45.5
12 Louis William Fairfield (R)	23,863	51.2
Cyrus Cline (D)	20,603	44.2
13 Harry A. Barnhart (D)	30,537	47.7
Andrew J. Hickey (R)	30,246	47.2

IOWA

Candidates	Votes	%
1 Charles A. Kennedy (R)	20,421	58.6
F. B. Whitaker (D)	14,276	41.0
2 Harry E. Hull (R)	25,548	55.3
M. F. Cronin (D)	18,591	40.3
3 Burton E. Sweet (R)	31,567	67.0
James C. Murtagh (D)	14,825	31.4
4 Gilbert N. Haugen (R)	23,416	57.9
Earl Evans (D)	16,490	40.8
5 James W. Good (R)	27,438	64.1
Robert Melvin Peet (D)	14,654	34.2
6 C. William Ramseyer (R)	21,757	57.3
S. Kirkpatrick (D)	14,927	39.3
7 Cassius C. Dowell (R)	25,993	61.7
H. C. Evans (D)	14,677	34.8
8 Horace M. Towner (R)	24,195	59.0
H. B. Bracewell (D)	15,940	38.9
9 William R. Green (R)	23,446	55.4
John C. Pryor (D)	18,743	44.3
10 Frank P. Woods (R)	32,332	63.6
J. R. Files (D)	17,300	34.1
11 George C. Scott (R)	26,066	49.6
Thomas J. Steele (D)	25,935	49.4

KANSAS

Candidates	Votes	%
1 Daniel R. Anthony Jr. (R)	37,705	55.8
Herbert J. Corwine (D)	23,272	34.4
Eva Harding (I)	5,144	7.6
2 Edward C. Little (R)	42,780	50.4
Joseph Taggart (D)	38,815	45.7
3 Phillip P. Campbell (R)	40,272	47.8
William S. Hyatt (D)	32,837	39.0
T. P. Laughlin (SOC)	9,177	10.9
4 Dudley Doolittle (D)	29,370	51.5
Clyde W. Miller (R)	26,831	47.0
5 Guy T. Helvering (D)	32,198	50.4
Charles M. Harger (R)	29,861	46.8
6 John R. Connelly (D)	40,005	56.4
Otis L. Benton (R)	28,332	40.0
7 Jouett Shouse (D)	38,099	43.9
J. S. Simmons (R)	31,621	36.4
Howard E. Kershner (P)	13,566	15.6
8 William A. Ayres (D)	26,993	51.0
Thomas C. Wilson (R)	24,220	45.8

KENTUCKY

Candidates	Votes	%
1 Alben W. Barkley (D)	30,029	63.7
Thomas (R)	16,128	34.2
2 David H. Kincheloe (D)	24,138	54.2
Fowler (R)	19,953	44.8
3 Robert Y. Thomas Jr. (D)	22,194	49.6

Candidates	Votes	%
Taylor (R)	22,180	49.6
4 Ben Johnson (D)	25,012	52.7
Haswell (R)	21,958	46.3
5 J. Swagar Sherley (D)	29,204	50.1
Owens (R)	27,861	47.8
6 Arthur B. Rouse (D)	27,001	62.5
Sheppard (R)	14,959	34.7
7 James C. Cantrill (D)	28,734	59.8
Manby (R)	19,304	40.2
8 Harvey Helm (D)	21,187	53.7
Neat (R)	18,036	45.7
9 William J. Fields (D)	32,957	54.3
Pennington (R)	27,119	44.7
10 John W. Langley (R)	19,113	60.9
Stanton (D)	11,981	38.2
11 Caleb Powers (R)	33,867	70.0
Dishman (D)	14,280	29.5

LOUISIANA

Candidates	Votes	%
1 Albert Estopinal (D)	17,939	100.0
2 H. Garland Dupre (D)	16,328	100.0
3 Whitmell P. Martin (PROG)	6,481	49.0
Wade O. Martin (D)	6,382	48.3
4 John T. Watkins (D)	8,306	100.0
5 Riley J. Wilson (D)	7,650	97.6
6 Jared Y. Sanders (D)	7,377	100.0
7 Ladislas Lazaro (D)	7,307	94.9
M. McManus (SOC)	394	5.1
8 James B. Aswell (D)	7,318	94.2
H. O. Bower (SOC)	449	5.8

MAINE

Candidates	Votes	%
1 Louis B. Goodall (R)	20,357	54.2
Stevens (D)	16,807	44.8
2 Wallace H. White Jr. (R)	19,338	50.1
McGillicuddy (D)	18,791	48.7
3 John A. Peters (R)	23,656	53.5
Bunker (D)	20,002	45.3
4 Ira G. Hersey (R)	17,647	57.4
Pierce (D)	12,969	42.2

MARYLAND

Candidates	Votes	%
1 Jesse D. Price (D)	17,047	48.6
Robert F. Duer (R)	16,981	48.4
2 Joshua Frederick C. Talbott (D)	24,648	50.3
William H. Lawrence (R)	20,420	41.7
John S. Green (P)	3,513	7.2
3 Charles P. Coady (D)	16,546	52.5
Charles W. Main (R)	13,857	44.0
4 J. Charles Linthicum (D)	19,774	52.5
J. Frank Fox (R)	17,030	45.2
5 Sydney E. Mudd (R)	17,407	53.9
Jackson H. Ralston (D)	13,909	43.0
6 Frederick N. Zihlman (R)	19,932	51.1
Henry Dorsey Etchison (D)	17,214	44.1

MASSACHUSETTS

Candidates	Votes	%
1 Allen T. Treadway (R)	19,667	60.2
Timothy C. Collins (D)	11,795	36.1
2 Frederick H. Gillett (R)	20,064	60.3
Theobald M. Connor (D)	11,895	35.7
3 Calvin D. Paige (R)	19,371	66.2
Michael A. Scanlon (D)	9,905	33.8
4 Samuel E. Winslow (R)	17,647	55.6
John H. Hunt (D)	13,315	41.9
5 John Jacob Rogers (R)	20,345	64.7
Roger Sherman Hoar (D)	11,097	35.3
6 Augustus P. Gardner (R)	21,916	67.3
Arthur Howard (D)	8,578	26.4
Charles W. Fitzgerald (SOC)	2,049	6.3
7 Michael F. Phelan (D)	16,597	51.2
Charles Neal Barney (R)	14,350	44.3
8 Frederick W. Dallinger (R)	21,178	59.7
Frederick S. Deitrick (D)	14,308	40.3
9 Alvan T. Fuller (I)	17,079	50.5
Ernest W. Roberts (R)	16,765	49.5

Candidates	Votes	%
10 Peter F. Tague (D)	13,646	78.7
James L. Hourihan (R)	3,684	21.3
11 George Holden Tinkham (R)	18,424	60.1
Francis J. Horgan (D)	12,244	39.9
12 James A. Gallivan (D)	22,105	67.6
Charles H. S. Robinson (R)	10,613	32.4
13 William H. Carter (R)	25,527	66.3
William H. Murphy (D)	12,985	33.7
14 Richard Olney (D)	21,707	53.2
Henry L. Kincaide (R)	17,702	43.4
15 William S. Greene (R)	15,788	63.2
Arthur J. B. Cartier (D)	9,203	36.8
16 Joseph Walsh (R)	18,505	68.8
Ralph W. Crosby (D)	8,392	31.2

MICHIGAN

Candidates	Votes	%
1 Frank E. Doremus (D)	29,571	51.2
Hugh Shepherd (R)	26,679	46.2
2 Mark R. Bacon (R)	27,182‡	49.0
Samuel W. Beakes (D)	27,133	48.9
3 John M. C. Smith (R)	24,897	49.4
James W. Marsh (D)	23,117	45.8
4 Edward L. Hamilton (R)	26,764	55.5
Roy J. Wade (D)	20,445	42.4
5 Carl E. Mapes (R)	24,258	51.1
Peter J. Danhof (D)	21,639	45.6
6 Patrick H. Kelley (R)	38,110	54.0
William S. Kellogg (D)	30,664	43.5
7 Louis C. Cramton (R)	30,101	66.9
Varnum J. Bowers (D)	14,020	31.1
8 Joseph W. Fordney (R)	28,288	53.6
William A. Seegmiller (D)	23,692	44.9
9 James C. McLaughlin (R)	24,624	58.3
Curtis D. Alway (D)	15,726	37.3
10 Gilbert A. Currie (R)	24,240	58.1
Henry C. Haller (D)	16,056	38.5
11 Frank D. Scott (R)	24,840	60.6
John J. Reycraft (D)	14,499	35.4
12 W. Frank James (R)	22,998	64.1
William J. Macdonald (D & PROG)	12,882	35.9
13 Charles A. Nichols (R)	32,317	59.3
Eugene P. Berry (D)	20,921	38.4

MINNESOTA

Candidates	Votes	%
1 Sydney Anderson (R)	25,278	65.5
Lamberton (D)	13,290	34.5
2 Franklin F. Ellsworth (R)	29,392	100.0
3 Charles R. Davis (R)	25,527	71.1
Kelly Jr. (D)	10,354	28.9
4 Carl C. Van Dyke (D)	23,516	61.2
Reese (R)	11,737	30.6
5 Ernest Lundeen (R)	19,131	42.4
Bowler (D)	11,849	26.3
Latimer (SOC)	7,526	16.7
Markve (P)	6,599	14.6
6 Harold Knutson (R)	20,889	56.8
Donohue (D)	13,107	35.7
Knutsen (P)	2,766	7.5
7 Andrew J. Volstead (R)	21,300	53.6
Lobeck (D)	11,961	30.1
Townsend (D)	6,518	16.4
8 Clarence B. Miller (R)	17,758	51.6
Anderson (SOC)	9,034	26.3
Wheeler (P)	7,621	22.2
9 Halvor Steenerson (R)	25,429	66.8
Swanson (D)	8,313	21.8
Thompson (SOC)	4,347	11.4
10 Thomas D. Schall (PROG)	19,696	45.0
Jepson (R)	13,170	30.1
Cronin (D)	7,148	16.3
Soltis (SOC)	3,782	8.6

MISSISSIPPI

Candidates	Votes	%
1 Ezekiel S. Candler Jr. (D)	✓	
2 Hubert D. Stephens (D)	10,192	97.6

Candidates	Votes	%
3 Benjamin G. Humphreys (D)	✓	
4 Thomas U. Sisson (D)	✓	
5 William A. Venable (D)	11,966	94.5
Charles Evans (SOC)	692	5.5
6 Pat Harrison (D)	12,492	94.6
F. T. Maxwell (SOC)	716	5.4
7 Percy E. Quin (D)	✓	
8 James W. Collier (D)	6,147	97.6

MISSOURI

Candidates	Votes	%
1 Milton A. Romjue (D)	22,840	54.4
Brown (R)	18,566	44.2
2 William W. Rucker (D)	24,964	57.7
Pickett (R)	17,936	41.5
3 Joshua W. Alexander (D)	21,658	54.2
Moulton (R)	17,769	44.5
4 Charles F. Booher (D)	22,155	53.6
Geiger (R)	18,632	45.1
5 William P. Borland (D)	46,065	58.7
Kimbrell (R)	31,292	39.9
6 Clement C. Dickinson (D)	18,869	54.2
Crawford (R)	15,948	45.8
7 Courtney W. Hamlin (D)	26,766	50.5
Houston (R)	25,953	48.9
8 Dorsey W. Shackleford (D)	17,599	52.0
Gentry (R)	16,255	48.0
9 James Beauchamp Clark (D)	23,755	51.9
Cole (R)	21,704	47.5
10 Jacob E. Meeker (R)	63,663	57.7
Brennan (D)	43,271	39.3
11 William L. Igoe (D)	23,928	56.8
Barto (R)	17,434	41.4
12 Leonidas C. Dyer (R)	16,345	55.9
Gill (D)	12,465	42.6
13 Walter L. Hensley (D)	17,850	49.7
Rhodes (R)	17,537	48.8
14 Joseph J. Russell (D)	30,889	49.3
Hill (R)	29,727	47.4
15 Perl D. Decker (D)	26,240	49.8
Manlove (R)	24,013	45.6
16 Thomas L. Rubey (D)	17,303	51.0
Harrison (R)	16,058	47.3

MONTANA

Candidates	Votes	%
AL John M. Evans (D)	84,499 ✓	
Jeanette Rankin (R)	76,932 ✓	
Harry B. Mitchell (D)	70,578	
George W. Farr (R)	66,974	
John H. McGuffey (SOC)	9,002	
Albert F. Meissener (SOC)	8,479	

NEBRASKA

Candidates	Votes	%
1 C. Frank Reavis (R & PROG)	21,021	54.5
John A. Maguire (D & PPI)	16,894	43.8
2 Charles O. Lobeck (D & PPI)	25,617	55.6
Benjamin S. Baker (R)	17,578	38.1
G. C. Porter (SOC)	2,922	6.3
3 Daniel V. Stephens (D & PPI)	28,055	51.6
William P. Warner (R & PROG)	25,541	47.0
4 Charles H. Sloan (R & PROG)	24,054	55.3
William L. Stark (D & PPI)	18,798	43.2
5 Ashton C. Shallenberger (D PPI&PR)	22,686	54.0
Silas R. Barton (R)	18,293	43.5
6 Moses P. Kinkaid (R & PROG)	33,559	57.4
Ed B. McDermott (D & PPI)	22,317	38.1

NEVADA

Candidates	Votes	%
AL Edwin E. Roberts (R)	14,106	43.6
Edwin E. Caine (D)	13,100	40.5
M. J. Scanlan (SOC)	5,125	15.9

NEW HAMPSHIRE

Candidates	Votes	%
1 Cyrus A. Sulloway (R)	21,826	51.5
Woodbury (D)	19,806	46.8
2 Edward H. Wason (R)	22,296	51.7
Stevens (D)	20,145	46.7

NEW JERSEY

Candidates	Votes	%
1 William J. Browning (R)	26,589	58.8
Cattell (D)	15,329	33.9
2 Isaac Bacharach (R)	24,865	59.7
Myers (D)	14,220	34.2
3 Thomas J. Scully (D)	21,896	48.6
Carson (R)	21,694	48.1
4 Elijah C. Hutchinson (R)	18,131	50.0
Beekman (D)	16,926	46.6
5 John H. Capstick (R)	20,951	51.8
Tuttle Jr. (D)	17,176	42.5
6 John R. Ramsey (R)	21,464	50.8
Heath (D)	18,770	44.4
7 Dow H. Drukker (R)	15,931	53.0
Beardmore (D)	7,980	26.6
Kershot (SOC)	3,326	11.1
Schweikert (NP)	2,617	8.7
8 Edward W. Gray (R)	18,663	52.7
Kinkead (D)	15,395	43.5
9 Richard W. Parker (R)	14,641	47.9
Matthews (D)	13,625	44.6
Wherett (SOC)	1,923	6.3
10 Frederick R. Lehlbach (R)	21,822	60.7
Flanagan (D)	12,341	34.3
11 John J. Eagan (D)	15,769	59.2
Brennan (R)	9,049	34.0
12 James A. Hamill (D)	17,365	57.0
Dear (R)	12,058	39.6

NEW MEXICO

Candidates	Votes	%
AL William B. Walton (D)	32,731	49.0
B. C. Hernandez (R)	32,056	48.0

NEW YORK

Candidates	Votes	%
1 Frederick C. Hicks (R IL&NPR)	29,041	63.2
Lathrop Brown (D & AM)	16,302	35.5
2 Charles Pope Caldwell (D IL)	24,110	51.8
Theron H. Burden (R AM)	19,504	41.9
Benjamin Katz (SOC)	2,611	5.6
3 Joseph V. Flynn (D & IL)	11,670	49.3
Jared J. Chambers (R NPR AM)	10,381	43.9
William A. Ross (SOC)	1,552	6.6
4 Harry Howard Dale (D & IL)	8,861	48.2
Michael Stein (R NPR AM)	7,044	38.3
Richard Haffner (SOC)	2,451	13.3
5 James P. Maher (D & IL)	12,658	49.9
Charles W. Philipbar (R NPR AM)	11,264	44.4
Hans A. Hansen (SOC)	1,357	5.4
6 Frederick R. Rowe (R NPR)	29,107	60.7
Charles I. Stengle (D & IL)	17,436	36.4
7 John J. Fitzgerald (D IL NPR)	15,454	63.5
Ralph Waldo Bowman (R)	8,330	34.2
8 Daniel J. Griffin (D IL NPR)	22,850	60.7
Wilmot L. Morehouse (R)	13,387	35.6
9 Oscar W. Swift (R & P)	25,701	57.0
Herman H. Torborg (DIL A NP)	16,575	36.8
Ludwig Lore (SOC)	2,815	6.2
10 Reuben L. Haskell (R IL&NPR)	11,057	45.0
Frank Wasserman (D & AM)	8,853	36.1
William M. Feigenbaum (SOC)	4,567	18.6
11 Daniel J. Riordan (D IL)	13,047	56.2
Montague Lessler (R NPR)	9,535	41.1
12 Meyer London (SOC)	6,103	47.4
Leon Sanders (D IL)	5,763	44.8
Louis M. Block (R)	968	7.5
13 Christopher D. Sullivan (D & IL)	5,114	48.0
Frank Dostel (R NPR AM)	3,886	36.5
Hilda G. Claessens (SOC)	1,644	15.4
14 Fiorello H. LaGuardia (R NPR AM)	7,272	43.3
Michael F. Farley (D & IL)	6,915	41.2
William I. Sockheim (SOC)	2,536	15.1
15 Michael F. Conry (D & IL)	13,362*	59.9
William Henkel Jr. (R)	7,996	35.8
16 Peter J. Dooling (D & IL)	12,115	51.6
Walbridge S. Taft (R NPR)	10,761	45.9
17 John F. Carew (D & IL)	11,213	51.2
Lindell T. Bates (R NPR)	9,764	44.6
18 George B. Francis (R IL&NPR)	12,196	46.1
Thomas G. Patten (D)	11,826	44.7
Irving Ottenberg (SOC)	2,407	9.1
19 Walter M. Chandler (R IL&NPR)	19,922	54.8
Michael Schaap (D)	14,817	40.8
20 Isaac Siegel (R IL&NPR)	4,542	36.0
Morris Hillquit (SOC)	4,129	32.7
Bernard R. Rosenblatt (D)	3,907	31.0
21 Murray Hulbert (D & IL)	14,107	53.1
Martin Ansorge (R NPR)	10,953	41.3
Alexander Braunstein (SOC)	1,434	5.4
22 Henry Bruckner (D IL NPR)	21,284	63.5
James A. Francis (R)	9,878	29.5
Max B. Gollin (SOC)	2,244	6.7
23 Daniel C. Oliver (D)	25,535	46.9
William S. Bennett (RIL A NP)	22,856	42.0
J. George Gobsevage (SOC)	5,810	10.7
24 Benjamin L. Fairchild (RIL P NP)	25,713	53.7
Woodson R. Oglesby (D & AM)	18,439	38.5
Mary G. Schonberg (SOC)	3,710	7.8
25 James W. Husted (R)	23,363	59.5
Chester D. Pugsley (D IL NPR)	14,816	37.7
26 Edmund Platt (R IL&NPR)	23,314	54.2
Rosslyn M. Cox (D)	18,825	43.8
27 Charles B. Ward (RIL A NP)	24,634	56.4
James O. Woodward (D)	17,674	40.5
28 Rollin B. Sanford (R NPR)	27,722	55.5
Michael F. Collins (D IL)	21,436	42.9
29 James S. Parker (R NPR)	31,888	89.2
Charles E. Robbins (P)	2,134	6.0
30 George R. Lunn (DIL ANPI)	19,818	47.1
Henry S. Deforest (R)	19,199	45.6
Herbert M. Merrill (SOC)	2,126	5.1
31 Bertrand H. Snell (R)	24,938	67.2
Louis F. Roberts (D)	10,934	29.5
32 Luther W. Mott (R IL&NPR)	28,744	62.7
Otto Pfaff (D)	14,323	31.2
33 Homer P. Snyder (R NPR AM)	25,299	55.6
Charles A. Talcott (D)	18,944	41.6
34 George W. Fairchild (R IL&NPR)	27,075	58.7
Cortland A. Wilber (D)	15,895	34.5
Levi Hoag (P)	2,537	5.5
35 Walter W. Magee (R IL&NPR)	31,429	60.9
Arlington H. Mallery (D)	16,059	31.1
36 Norman J. Gould (R NPR)	28,325	62.3
Hiram O. Hotchkiss (D)	15,293	33.6
37 Harry H. Pratt (R IL&NPR)	23,029	49.9
Frederick W. Palmer (D & AM)	20,291	44.0
38 Thomas B. Dunn (R)	29,894	65.1
Jacob Gerling (D)	13,867	30.2
39 Archie D. Sanders (R)	28,393	65.1
David A. White (D)	13,424	30.8
40 S. Wallace Dempsey (R)	27,652	61.9
Andrew B. Gilfillan (D NPR)	15,011	33.6
41 Charles B. Smith (D & AM)	21,265	56.2
William H. Crosby (R P NPR)	15,508	41.0
42 William F. Waldow (R NPR)	16,623	51.0
Daniel A. Driscoll (D)	15,411	47.3
43 Charles M. Hamilton (R NPR)	27,186	64.7
A. F. French (D)	11,414	27.2

NORTH CAROLINA

Candidates	Votes	%
1 John H. Small (D)	13,211	72.2
Leslie E. Jones (R)	5,098	27.8
2 Claude Kitchin (D)	13,255	86.9
W. O. Dixon (R)	1,999	13.1
3 George E. Hood (D)	12,269	58.0
George E. Butler (R)	8,889	42.0
4 Edward W. Pou (D)	15,305	64.3
Joseph J. Jenkins (R)	8,483	35.7
5 Charles M. Stedman (D)	23,932	52.5
Gilliam Grissom (R)	21,429	47.0
6 Hannibal L. Godwin (D)	13,337	63.9
Alex L. McCaskill (R)	7,521	36.1
7 Leonidas D. Robinson (D)	20,518	54.7
Presley E. Brown (R)	17,021	45.3

Candidates	Votes	%
8 Robert L. Doughton (D)	17,249	52.8
H. Sinclair Williams (R)	15,411	47.2
9 Edwin Y. Webb (D)	18,855	53.5
Charles E. Greene (R)	16,381	46.5
10 Zebulon Weaver (D)	18,023‡	50.0
James J. Britt (R)	18,014	50.0

NORTH DAKOTA

Candidates	Votes	%
1 Henry T. Helgesen (R)	20,709	59.9
George A. Bangs (D)	13,236	38.3
2 George M. Young (R)	22,227	71.7
Hugh McDonald (D)	7,638	24.6
3 Patrick D. Norton (R)	20,393	65.2
Charles Simon (D)	8,293	26.5
Anton Klemmens (SOC)	2,586	8.3

OHIO

Candidates	Votes	%
1 Nicholas Longworth (R)	33,903	56.7
Edward H. Brink (D)	24,290	40.6
2 Victor Heintz (R)	29,612	49.4
Stanley E. Bowdle (D)	28,156	47.0
3 Warren Gard (D)	37,982	53.3
Charles W. Dustin (R)	26,571	40.1
Jeremiah F. Mincker (SOC)	4,699	6.6
4 Benjamin F. Welty (D)	29,486	53.7
J. E. Russell (R)	25,378	46.3
5 John S. Snook (D)	22,852	52.8
Nelson E. Matthews (R)	20,424	47.2
6 Charles C. Kearns (R)	21,315	49.6
A. G. Turnipseed (D)	20,811	48.5
7 Simeon D. Fess (R)	39,975	94.8
8 John A. Key (R)	25,164	53.9
John H. Clark (R)	21,525	46.1
9 Isaac R. Sherwood (D)	31,921	58.2
Frank L. Mulholland (R)	19,882	36.2
Thomas C. Devine (SOC)	3,091	5.6
10 Robert M. Switzer (R)	21,185	58.0
Charles W. Haslett (D)	15,375	42.1
11 Horatio C. Claypool (D)	20,144	50.5
Edwin D. Ricketts (R)	19,022	47.7
12 Clement L. Brumbaugh (D)	31,362	52.8
Hugh Huntington (R)	26,415	44.5
13 Arthur W. Overmeyer (D)	26,882	54.4
Franklin P. Riegle (R)	21,523	43.6
14 Ellsworth R. Bathrick (D)	32,301	53.4
S. H. Williams (R)	26,010	43.0
15 George White (D)	23,221	48.8
W. C. Mooney (R)	22,934	48.2
16 Roscoe C. McCulloch (R)	31,945	56.2
John J. Whitacre (D)	24,948	43.9
17 William A. Ashbrook (D)	31,749	56.2
E. Lee Porterfield (R)	23,705	42.0
18 David A. Hollingsworth (R)	26,991	49.8
William B. Francis (D)	24,538	45.3
19 John G. Cooper (R)	26,983	55.3
William S. King (D)	21,828	44.7
20 William Gordon (D)	26,950	58.2
Eugene Quigley (R)	17,235	37.2
21 Robert Crosser (D)	22,263	65.0
R. S. Taylor (R)	10,138	29.6
Moses Benjamin (SOC)	1,845	5.4
22 Henry I. Emerson (R)	29,270	55.4
Stephen M. Young (D)	23,611	44.7

OKLAHOMA

Candidates	Votes	%
1 Thomas A. Chandler (R)	18,218	45.6
James S. Davenport (D)	17,949	44.9
Reese (SOC)	3,671	9.2
2 William W. Hastings (D)	15,158	52.5
Henry Ward (R)	10,224	35.4
J. A. Lewis (SOC)	3,511	12.2
3 Charles D. Carter (D)	21,182	55.1
Gratton C. McVay (R)	10,386	27.0
H. M. Shelton (SOC)	6,862	17.9
4 Thomas D. McKeown (D)	19,076	48.3
James E. Gresham (R)	12,399	31.4
Allen C. Adams (SOC)	8,026	20.3

Candidates	Votes	%
5 Joseph B. Thompson (D)	17,828	49.5
George H. Dodson (R)	12,716	35.3
Robert A. Allen (SOC)	5,294	14.7
6 Scott Ferris (D)	18,212	50.8
H.H.Hinkle (R)	10,930	30.5
O.M.Morris (SOC)	6,727	18.8
7 James V. McClintic (D)	17,810	53.8
H.H. Stellard (SOC)	8,140	24.6
T.W. Jones Jr. (R)	7,030	21.2
8 Dick T. Morgan (R)	16,691	45.1
Zach A. Harris (D)	14,816	40.0
Joseph Otil (SOC)	5,158	13.9

OREGON

Candidates	Votes	%
1 Willis C. Hawley (R & PROG)	60,530	56.6
Mark V. Weatherford (D & P)	39,101	36.6
W. S. Richards (SOC)	7,243	6.8
2 Nicholas J. Sinnott (R-D-PROG)	36,059	84.6
James Hickman Barkley (SOC)	6,028	14.1
3 Clifton N. McArthur (R)	35,832	47.6
A. W. Lafferty (I PROG)	27,649	36.7
John A. Jeffrey (D)	9,824	13.0

PENNSYLVANIA

Candidates	Votes	%
1 William S. Vare (R)	33,330	71.7
Lawrence E. McCrossin (D)	12,243	26.3
2 George S. Graham (R, WASH)	23,921	76.0
Thomas E. Shea (D)	7,117	22.6
3 J. Hampton Moore (R, KEY)	23,753	73.6
Joseph Hagerty (D)	7,611	23.6
4 George W. Edmonds (R, WASH)	26,122	68.2
Patrick H. Lynch (D)	11,101	29.0
5 Peter E. Costello (R, PERS LIB)	29,689	59.3
Michael Donohoe (D, KEY)	17,074	34.1
6 George P. Darrow (R, WASH)	56,207	67.6
J. Washington Logue (D, KEY)	25,665	30.9
7 Thomas S. Butler (R)	27,879	63.0
Edward B. Cassatt (D, WASH)	15,102	34.1
8 Henry Winfield Watson (R)	28,852	57.0
Joseph Heacock (D)	20,232	40.0
9 William W. Griest (R)	20,058	64.2
Henry F. Myers (D)	9,506	30.4
10 John R. Farr (R, B MOOSE)	17,823	53.1
Victor Burschel (D)	14,694	43.7
11 T. W. Templeton (R)	24,123	53.2
John J. Casey (D, KEY)	19,185	42.3
12 Robert D. Heaton (R, WASH)	19,172	61.1
Robert E. Lee (D)	11,340	36.1
13 Arthur G. Dewalt (D)	28,296	49.9
Horace W. Schantz (R, WASH)	23,412	41.3
Elwood W. Leffier (SOC)	4,507	7.9
14 Louis T. McFadden (R)	13,638	55.6
John D. Brennan (D)	8,881	36.2
William S. H. Heermans (P)	1,279	5.2
15 Edgar R. Kiess (R, P)	18,478	59.5
Chester H. Ashton (D)	10,766	34.7
P. A. McGowan (SOC)	1,789	5.8
16 John V. Lesher (D)	16,490	51.8
I. Clinton Kline (R, P)	14,154	44.5
17 Benjamin K. Focht (R, P)	18,673	50.4
George A. Harris (D)	17,420	47.0
18 Aaron S. Kreider (R)	24,630	51.6
Harry B. Saussaman (D)	20,343	42.7
19 John M. Rose (R)	22,652	50.4
Warren Worth Bailey (D, UN)	21,007	46.8
20 Andrew R. Brodbeck (D)	18,490	50.2
Samuel K. McCall (R, WASH)	16,327	44.3
21 Charles H. Rowland (R)	14,150	47.6
William E. Tobias (D, P)	13,938	46.9
George Fox (SOC)	1,605	5.4
22 Edward E. Robbins (R, WASH)	19,978	48.4
Silas A. Kline (D)	16,165	39.2
Charles Cunningham (SOC)	2,945	7.1
R. S. Irwin (P)	2,153	5.2
23 Bruce F. Sterling (D)	17,348	48.4
Robert F. Hopwood (R, WASH)	16,453	45.7
24 Henry W. Temple (R, WASH)	22,839	54.3
William J. Mellon (D)	14,679	34.9

Candidates	Votes	%
W. K. Ramsey (SOC)	2,839	6.8
25 Henry A. Clark (R)	13,441	43.1
Charles N. Crosby (D)	13,068	41.9
William W. Kincaid (P, WASH)	3,038	9.7
Ralph W. Tillotson (SOC)	1,612	5.2
26 Henry J. Steele (D, SOC)	18,374	53.5
Winfred D. Lewis (R, WASH)	14,857	43.2
27 Nathan L. Strong (R, WASH)	17,702	55.9
Harry C. Golden (D)	10,751	34.0
John B. Desantis (P)	1,793	5.7
28 Orrin D. Bleakley (R)	16,514	47.9
E. H. Beshlin (D)	12,406	36.0
A. R. Rich (P)	3,470	10.1
William E. Ashe (SOC)	2,102	6.1
29 Stephen Geyer Porter (R, WASH)	21,123	67.8
A. M. Thompson (D)	7,518	24.1
Karl C. Jursek (SOC)	1,869	6.0
30 M. Clyde Kelly (D, P)	18,637	47.6
William H. Coleman (R, B MOOSE)	18,386	46.9
William Adams (SOC)	2,147	5.5
31 John M. Morin (R, D)	20,497	87.2
F. C. Brittain (P)	1,504	6.4
James Devlin (SOC)	1,504	6.4
32 Guy E. Campbell (D, B MOOSE)	17,134	45.8
Andrew J. Barcheld (R)	17,088	45.7
William W. Nooning (SOC)	2,422	6.5
AL Thomas S. Crago (R, RO PROG)	668,581✓	
John R. K. Scott (R, RO PROG)	661,930✓	
Mahlon M. Garland (R, PERS LIB)	654,945✓	
Joseph McLaughlin (R)	605,657✓	
Thomas Ross (D)	471,308	
John J. Moore (D)	439,881	
Joseph T. Kinsley (D)	439,846	
Jacob B. Waidelich (D)	427,923	
William A. Prosser (SOC)	46,896	
Elizabeth N. Baer (SOC)	45,441	
John W. Slayton (SOC)	45,330	
Fred Willard Whiteside (SOC)	43,314	
Fred Groff (P)	29,937	
Frank L. Morton (P)	26,483	
B. C. McGrew (P)	26,116	
J. C. Rummel (P)	24,952	
Robert C. Bair (WASH)	24,529	
Arthur G. Graham (WASH)	24,219	
J. C. Buchanan (KEY)	3,703	
Michael Donohoe (KEY)	3,517	
M. J. Lewis (KEY)	3,382	
Robert C. Bair (B MOOSE)	3,356	
Arthur G. Graham (B MOOSE)	3,245	
Oliver Knight (SINGLE T)	931	
Royd E. Morrison (SINGLE T)	833	
Jerome C. Reis (SINGLE T)	769	
Alfred Guerrero (SINGLE T)	729	
Richard Love (INDL)	616	
B. H. Brenner (INDL)	591	
H. G. Meinel (INDL)	458	
G. W. Ohls (INDL)	455	

RHODE ISLAND

Candidates	Votes	%
1 George F. O'Shaunessy (D)	15,996	53.9
Dixon (R)	13,099	44.2
2 Walter R. Stiness (R)	15,784	54.9
Mowry (D)	12,207	42.5
3 Ambrose Kennedy (R)	14,376	50.4
McDonald (D)	13,427	47.1

SOUTH CAROLINA

Candidates	Votes	%
1 Richard S. Whaley (D)	4,999	95.4
2 James F. Byrnes (D)	7,681	98.5
3 Fred H. Dominick (D)	9,447	100.0
4 Samuel J. Nichols (D)	11,312	99.4
5 David E. Finley (D)	8,846*	100.0
6 J. Willard Ragsdale (D)	9,767	99.1
7 Asbury F. Lever (D)	9,817	93.5
I. S. Leevy (R)	683	6.5

SOUTH DAKOTA

	Candidates	Votes	%
1	Charles H. Dillon (R)	28,674	58.1
	Anderson (D)	19,846	40.2
2	Royal C. Johnson (R)	28,366	60.2
	Batterton (D)	16,342	34.7
3	Harry L. Gandy (D)	16,581	55.6
	Bartine (R)	12,203	41.0

TENNESSEE

		Votes	%
1	Sam R. Sells (R)	23,651	96.9
2	Richard W. Austin (R)	19,835	90.0
	Fitsgerald (D)	1,195	5.4
3	John A. Moon (D)	19,018	53.9
	Jessie M. Littleton (R)	16,004	45.3
4	Cordell Hull (D)	17,170	60.2
	J. F. Benson (R)	11,287	39.6
5	William C. Houston (D)	14,656	86.5
	Sid Houston (R)	2,287	13.5
6	Joseph W. Byrns (D)	17,190	83.7
	C. E. Tippens (R)	2,919	14.2
7	Lemuel P. Padgett (D)	15,313	63.0
	G. A. Yost (R)	8,955	36.8
8	Thetus W. Sims (D)	13,474	50.3
	L. M. Rhodes (R)	13,255	49.5
9	Finis J. Garrett (D)	17,826	75.4
	W. N. Beasley (R)	5,817	24.6
10	Hubert F. Fisher (D)	14,926	72.8
	W. Wilkerson (COLORED)	2,677	13.1
	John W. Farley (R)	2,089	10.2

TEXAS

		Votes	%
1	Eugene Black (D)	16,525	83.3
	David H. Morris (R)	2,182	11.0
	J. C. Thompson (SOC)	1,122	5.7
2	Martin Dies (D)	16,956	86.1
	J. B. Truitt (SOC)	1,462	7.4
	A. E. Sweatland (R)	1,266	6.4
3	James Young (D)	15,168	88.3
	J. L. Scoggin (SOC)	2,014	11.7
4	Sam Rayburn (D)	17,785	83.5
	G. J. Barlow (R)	2,043	9.6
	W. J. Lennon (SOC)	1,460	6.9
5	Hatton W. Sumners (D)	24,949	88.2
	B. F. Crews (R)	2,879	10.2
6	Rufus Hardy (D)	12,046	95.3
7	Alexander W. Gregg (D)	10,921	79.5
	Theo F. Heiger (R)	1,541	11.2
8	J. H. Eagle (D)	18,980	82.2
	Ira P. Jones (R)	3,276	14.2
9	Joseph J. Mansfield (D)	16,453	76.2
	C. M. Hughes (R)	4,149	19.2
10	James P. Buchanan (D)	15,634	86.7
	Robert A. Brooks (R)	2,405	13.3
11	Tom Connally (D)	14,695	87.7
	John L. Vaughn (R)	1,443	8.6
12	James C. Wilson (D)	20,175	85.7
	Henry Zweifel (R)	1,843	7.8
	Leland G. Baker (SOC)	1,517	6.5
13	Marion Jones (D)	33,942	85.8

	Candidates	Votes	%
	J. L. Vannatto (R)	3,125	7.9
	J. A. Pressly (SOC)	2,489	6.3
14	James L. Slayden (D)	22,435	79.4
	D. F. Johnson (R)	5,815	20.6
15	John N. Garner (D)	16,906	73.4
	H. M. Wingback (R)	5,551	24.1
16	Thomas L. Blanton (D)	30,650	85.2
	T. B. Holiday (SOC)	2,826	7.9
	C. O. Harris (R)	2,503	7.0
AL	Atkins Jeff. McLemore (D)	300,302✓	
	Daniel E. Garrett (D)	298,966✓	
	Charles A. Warnken (R)	46,914	
	M. A. Taylor (R)	46,467	
	Arch Lingan (SOC)	18,583	
	W. D. Simpson (SOC)	18,192	
	I. E. Teague (P)	1,525	
	E. G. Cook (P)	1,457	

UTAH

		Votes	%
1	Milton H. Welling (D, PROG)	40,035	55.5
	Timothy C. Hoyt (R)	29,902	41.5
2	James H. Mays (D, PROG)	39,847	56.9
	Charles R. Mabey (R)	27,778	39.7

VERMONT

		Votes	%
1	Frank L. Greene (R)	22,030	71.1
	Emmett B. Daley (D)	7,972	25.7
2	Porter H. Dale (R, P)	22,692	72.2
	G. Herbert Pape (D)	7,983	25.4

VIRGINIA

		Votes	%
1	William A. Jones (D)	9,772	76.5
	William W. Butzner (R)	2,823	22.1
2	Edward E. Holland (D)	10,123	82.4
	Luther B. Way (R)	1,939	15.8
3	Andrew Jackson Montague (D)	10,967	93.6
	F. E. Maxey (SOC)	751	6.4
4	Walter A. Watson (D)	8,119	90.8
5	Edward W. Saunders (D)	10,614	57.8
	Beverly A. Davis (R)	7,601	41.4
6	Carter Glass (D)	9,119	73.6
	George W. Wilson (R)	2,920	23.6
7	Thomas W. Harrison (D)	10,052	61.8
	John Paul (R)	6,064	37.3
8	Charles C. Carlin (D)	9,168	71.8
	Joseph L. Crupper (R)	3,450	27.0
9	C. Bascom Slemp (R)	17,848	51.9
	E. Lee Trinkle (D)	16,430	47.8
10	Henry D. Flood (D)	11,282	69.9
	C. P. Nair (R)	4,583	28.4

Special Election

		Votes	%
7	Thomas W. Harrison (D)	9,918	61.3
	John Paul (R)	6,110	37.8

WASHINGTON

		Votes	%
1	John F. Miller (R)	38,769	50.3

	Candidates	Votes	%
	George F. Cotterill (D)	35,718	46.3
2	Lindley H. Hadley (R)	31,655	47.1
	Frances C. Axtell (D)	28,075	41.7
	R. J. Olinger (SOC)	7,537	11.2
3	Albert Johnson (R)	47,415	57.1
	George P. Fishburne (D)	29,949	36.1
	W. F. Ferguson (SOC)	5,662	6.8
4	William L. LaFollette (R)	33,980	58.8
	Charles W. Masterson (D)	21,189	36.7
5	Clarence C. Dill (D)	37,479	51.5
	Tom Corkery (R)	32,298	44.4

WEST VIRGINIA

		Votes	%
1	Matthew M. Neely (D)	22,138	50.7
	T. W. Fleming (R)	21,574	49.4
2	George M. Bowers (R)	24,055	50.9
	Samuel V. Woods (D)	23,194	49.1
3	Stuart F. Reed (R)	23,442	50.7
	Fleming N. Alderson (D)	22,762	49.3
4	Harry C. Woodyard (R)	23,139	50.3
	T. A. Null (D)	22,855	49.7
5	Edward Cooper (R)	25,563	51.7
	G. R. C. Wiles (D)	23,857	48.3
6	Adam B. Littlepage (D)	25,963	51.5
	M. V. Godbey (R)	24,415	48.5

WISCONSIN

		Votes	%
1	Henry Allen Cooper (R)	24,851	61.6
	Jay W. Page (D)	12,587	31.2
2	Edward Voigt (R)	20,718	51.3
	Michael E. Burke (D)	18,546	45.9
3	John M. Nelson (R)	26,785	61.8
	M. J. Briggs (D)	15,198	35.1
4	William J. Cary (R)	12,361	35.5
	Winfield R. Gaylord (SOCIAL D)	11,380	32.7
	Anthony Szczerbinski (D)	10,757	30.9
5	William H. Stafford (R)	19,585	45.4
	Victor L. Berger (SOCIAL D)	15,936	36.9
	Lyman H. Browne (R)	7,420	17.2
6	James H. Davidson (R)	20,317	52.3
	Michael K. Reilly (D)	17,080	44.0
7	John Jacob Esch (R)	24,157	68.2
	Herman Grotophorst (D)	9,549	27.0
8	Edward E. Browne (R)	23,089	67.5
	John Kalmes (D)	10,083	29.5
9	David G. Classon (R)	20,614	52.5
	Thomas F. Konop (D)	18,078	46.0
10	James A. Frear (R)	23,320	69.6
	Andrew J. Sutherland (D)	9,367	28.0
11	Irvine L. Lenroot (R)	22,740	67.4
	George C. Cooper (D)	8,726	25.9
	Henry M. Parks (SOCIAL D)	2,252	6.7

WYOMING

		Votes	%
AL	Frank W. Mondell (R)	24,693	49.0
	John D. Clark (D)	24,156	48.0

1917 House Election

PENNSYLVANIA

Special Election

	Candidates	Votes	%
28	Earl H. Beshlin (D, P)	12,878	47.6
	U. G. Lyons (R)	11,100	41.0
	Willis J. Hulings (WASH)	1,622	6.0
	Richard Crawshaw (SOC)	1,452	5.4

1918 House Elections

ALABAMA

	Candidates	Votes	%
1	John McDuffie (D)	3,721	100.0
2	S. Hubert Dent Jr. (D)	5,717	100.0
3	Henry B. Steagall (D)	5,868	100.0
4	Fred L. Blackmon (D)	4,266	66.2
	J. A. Bingham (R)	2,183	33.9
5	J. Thomas Heflin (D)	6,254	100.0
6	William B. Oliver (D)	2,741	100.0
7	John L. Burnett (D)	7,221	56.2
	O. D. Street (R)	5,622	43.8
8	Edward B. Almon (D)	5,598	100.0
9	George Huddleston (D)	6,338	85.8
	J. O. Thompson (R)	1,051	14.2
10	William B. Bankhead (D)	5,765	100.0

ARIZONA

	Candidates	Votes	%
AL	Carl Hayden (D)	26,805	60.4
	Thomas Maddock (R)	16,822	37.9

ARKANSAS

	Candidates	Votes	%
1	Thaddeus H. Caraway (D)	10,343	100.0
2	William A. Oldfield (D)	10,775	100.0
3	John N. Tillman (D)	14,995	100.0
4	Otis Wingo (D)	12,279	100.0
5	Henderson M. Jacoway (D)	11,045	100.0
6	Samuel M. Taylor (D)	10,444	100.0
7	William S. Goodwin (D)	8,692	100.0

CALIFORNIA

	Candidates	Votes	%
1	Clarence F. Lea (DR)	42,063	99.7
2	John E. Raker (DR SOC P)	28,249	99.9
3	Charles F. Curry (R-D)	51,690	91.6
	A. K. Gifford (SOC)	4,746	8.4
4	Julius Kahn (R-D-PROG)	38,278	86.6
	William Short (SOC)	5,913	13.4
5	John I. Nolan (R-D)	40,375	87.0
	Thomas F. Feeley (SOC)	6,032	13.0
6	John A. Elston (R-D)	59,082	88.4
	Luella Twining (SOC)	7,721	11.6
7	Henry E. Barbour (R)	33,476	52.1
	Henry Hawson (D)	30,745	47.9
8	Hugh S. Hersman (D)	31,167	53.0
	Everis A. Hayes (R)	27,641	47.0
9	Charles H. Randall (P & D)	38,782	53.0
	Montaville Flowers (R-D-P)	31,689	43.3
10	Henry Z. Osborne (R-D-P)	72,773	88.0
	James H. Ryckman (SOC)	9,725	11.8
11	William Kettner (D R&SOC)	45,915	72.2
	Stella B. Irvine (P)	17,642	27.8

COLORADO

	Candidates	Votes	%
1	William N. Vaile (R)	27,815	54.2
	Stack (D)	16,364	31.9
	Hilliard (I)	6,112	11.9
2	Charles B. Timberlake (R)	41,562	61.5
	Jones (D)	26,044	38.5
3	Guy U. Hardy (R)	31,715	51.0
	Keating (D)	29,075	46.7
4	Edward T. Taylor (D)	22,423	65.7
	Logan (R)	11,695	34.3

CONNECTICUT

	Candidates	Votes	%
1	Augustine Lonergan (D)	21,169	53.5
	Quigley (R)	16,868	42.6
2	Richard P. Freeman (R)	16,251	53.1
	Fenton (D)	13,467	44.0
3	John Q. Tilson (R)	17,401	50.5
	O'Keefe (D)	15,711	45.6
4	Schuyler Merritt (R)	19,008	53.6
	Peck (D)	15,386	43.4

	Candidates	Votes	%
5	James P. Glynn (R)	13,455	50.1
	Seery (D)	12,640	47.1

DELAWARE

	Candidates	Votes	%
AL	Caleb R. Layton (R)	21,226	51.4
	Albert F. Polk (D)	19,652	47.6

FLORIDA

	Candidates	Votes	%
1	Herbert J. Drane (D)	8,446	100.0
2	Frank Clark (D)	6,322	100.0
3	John H. Smithwick (D)	6,644	100.0
4	William J. Sears (D)	10,401	100.0

GEORGIA

	Candidates	Votes	%
1	James W. Overstreet (D)	4,253	100.0
2	Frank Park (D)	3,953	100.0
3	Charles R. Crisp (D)	3,244	100.0
4	William C. Wright (D)	4,991	100.0
5	William D. Upshaw (D)	5,251	100.0
6	James W. Wise (D)	4,707	100.0
7	Gordon Lee (D)	5,960	82.5
	T. R. Glenn (R)	1,261	17.5
8	Charles H. Brand (D)	5,797	100.0
9	Thomas M. Bell (D)	6,911	81.5
	John M. Johnson (R)	1,570	18.5
10	Carl Vinson (D)	3,440	100.0
11	William C. Lankford (D)	4,959	100.0
12	William W. Larsen (D)	3,808	100.0

IDAHO

	Candidates	Votes	%
1	Burton L. French (R)	27,084	63.4
	L. I. Purcell (D)	15,672	36.7
2	Addison T. Smith (R)	32,274	63.2
	C. R. Jeppesen (D)	18,827	36.8

ILLINOIS

	Candidates	Votes	%
1	Martin B. Madden (R)	12,580	55.3
	George Mayer (D)	9,776	43.0
2	James R. Mann (R)	29,099	59.5
	Leo S. Lebosky (D)	17,895	36.6
3	William W. Wilson (R)	24,011	52.9
	Fred J. Crowley (D)	19,372	42.7
4	John W. Rainey (D)	15,514	94.6
	Carl G. Hoffman (SOC)	886	5.4
5	Adolph J. Sabath (D)	10,517	69.1
	Louis C. Mau (R)	3,789	24.9
	Emil Jaeger (SOC)	919	6.0
6	James McAndrews (D)	32,638	55.9
	Hervey C. Foster (R)	22,692	38.8
	William F. Kruse (SOC)	3,101	5.3
7	Niels Juul (R)	35,428	51.3
	Frank M. Padden (D)	26,261	38.0
	J. Louis Engdahl (SOC)	7,387	10.7
8	Thomas Gallagher (D)	11,472	78.2
	Dan Parrillo (R)	3,201	21.8
9	Fred A. Britten (R)	12,654	53.0
	James H. Poage (D)	10,074	42.2
10	Carl R. Chindblom (R)	33,097	62.1
	Philip J. Finnegan (D)	16,933	31.8
	Irving St. John Tucker (SOC)	3,284	6.2
11	Ira C. Copley (R)	25,744	92.9
	Carl F. Schutz (SOC)	1,954	7.1
12	Charles E. Fuller (R)	25,623	93.1
	Oscar Ogren (SOC)	1,895	6.9
13	John C. McKenzie (R)	20,861	96.2
14	William J. Graham (R)	20,635	90.6
	Edmond B. Passmore (SOC)	1,791	7.9
15	Edward J. King (R)	21,334	60.2
	Edward P. Allen (D)	13,148	37.1
16	Clifford Ireland (R)	20,617	57.3
	Leander O. Eagleton (D)	14,759	41.0

	Candidates	Votes	%
17	Frank L. Smith (R)	19,123	69.7
	C. S. Schneider (D)	8,321	30.3
18	Joseph G. Cannon (R)	22,427	60.3
	Frank M. Crangle (D)	14,402	38.7
19	William B. McKinley (R)	26,259	60.8
	Thomas B. Jack (D)	16,474	38.1
20	Henry T. Rainey (D)	17,355	55.0
	Frank E. Blane (R)	14,184	45.0
21	Loren E. Wheeler (R)	20,380	50.4
	James M. Graham (D)	19,064	47.2
22	William A. Rodenberg (R)	21,925	51.3
	J. Nick Perrin (D)	18,592	43.5
	Marshal E. Kirkpatrick (SOC)	2,240	5.2
23	Edwin B. Brooks (R)	20,619	49.9
	Martin D. Foster (D)	19,397	46.9
24	Thomas S. Williams (R)	18,689	59.4
	James R. Campbell (D)	12,412	39.4
25	Edward E. Denison (R)	22,886	60.4
	D. T. Woodard (D)	15,000	39.6
AL	Richard Yates (R)	501,974✓	
	William E. Mason (R)	479,533✓	
	William Elza Williams (D)	361,505	
	Michael H. Cleary (D)	356,168	
	Clarence C. Brooks (SOC)	33,835	
	Frank Watts (SOC)	32,065	
	Edward E. Blake (P)	3,189	
	Charles P. Corson (P)	3,110	
	William Hartness (SOC LAB)	2,956	
	Joseph Hamrie (SOC LAB)	2,790	

Special Election

	Candidates	Votes	%
4	John W. Rainey (D)	13,094	65.5
	O. W. Christopher (R)	4,366	21.8
	Kasimer P. Gugis (SOC)	2,530	12.7

INDIANA

	Candidates	Votes	%
1	Oscar R. Luhring (R)	20,440	52.0
	George K. Denton (D)	18,837	48.0
2	Oscar E. Bland (R)	23,943	53.6
	Fred F. Bays (D)	19,731	44.2
3	James W. Dunbar (R)	20,556	50.3
	William E. Cox (D)	19,989	48.9
4	John S. Benham (R)	20,745	50.4
	Lincoln Dixon (D)	20,428	49.6
5	Everett Sanders (R)	20,271	50.5
	Ralph W. Moss (D)	19,213	47.9
6	Richard N. Elliott (R)	21,266	54.2
	Harry G. Strickland (D)	17,755	45.3
7	Merrill Moores (R)	29,714	58.3
	Chalmer Schlosser (D)	20,284	39.8
8	Albert H. Vestal (R)	24,124	53.5
	William H. Eichorn (D)	19,421	43.1
9	Fred S. Purnell (R)	25,486	55.9
	Charles F. Howard (D)	18,948	41.6
10	William R. Wood (R)	26,384	61.4
	George R. Kirschman (D)	16,064	37.4
11	Milton W. Krauss (R)	24,358	54.0
	George W. Rauch (D)	19,849	44.0
12	Louis W. Fairfield (R)	22,251	54.7
	Harry H. Hilgeman (D)	17,538	43.1
13	Andrew J. Hickey (R)	27,269	52.8
	Henry A. Barnhart (D)	23,274	45.1

IOWA

	Candidates	Votes	%
1	Charles A. Kennedy (R)	15,921	60.6
	Edward L. Hirsch (D)	10,358	39.4
2	Harry E. Hull (R)	19,958	54.7
	Nathan D. Ely (D)	14,395	39.5
	William E. McIntosh (SOC)	2,140	5.9
3	Burton E. Sweet (R)	22,997	64.7
	Harry B. Clark (D)	12,527	35.3
4	Gilbert N. Haugen (R)	20,643	64.7
	Joseph C. Campbell (D)	11,283	35.3

	Candidates	Votes	%
5	James W. Good (R)	20,655	65.1
	Sherman W. Dewolf (D)	11,078	34.9
6	C. William Ramseyer (R)	17,082	56.1
	Buell McCash (D)	12,988	42.6
7	Cassius C. Dowell (R)	18,182	66.8
	H. C. Evans (D)	8,493	31.2
8	Horace M. Towner (R)	20,409	64.5
	D. Fulton Rice (D)	11,258	35.6
9	William R. Green (R)	22,234	99.8
10	Lester J. Dickinson (R)	23,635	64.3
	J. R. Files (D)	13,153	35.8
11	William D. Boies (R)	21,665	56.4
	Thomas J. Steele (D)	16,461	42.8

KANSAS

	Candidates	Votes	%
1	Daniel R. Anthony Jr. (R)	33,720	65.0
	Frank E. Whitney (D)	17,100	33.0
2	Edward C. Little (R)	32,653	57.2
	Henderson S. Martin (D)	23,262	40.8
3	Phillip P. Campbell (R)	32,837	54.8
	C. E. Pile (D)	22,849	38.1
4	Homer Hoch (R)	26,880	58.8
	Dudley Doolittle (D)	17,787	38.9
5	James G. Strong (R)	29,703	60.8
	Guy T. Helvering (D)	18,112	37.1
6	Hays B. White (R)	30,427	55.4
	John R. Connelly (D)	22,898	41.7
7	Jasper N. Tincher (R)	37,875	56.2
	Jouett Shouse (D)	27,722	41.1
8	William A. Ayres (D)	22,167	51.2
	Charles C. Mack (R)	20,279	46.9

KENTUCKY

	Candidates	Votes	%
1	Alben W. Barkley (D)	19,998	66.8
	W. G. Howard (R)	9,947	33.2
2	David H. Kincheloe (D)	18,749	57.7
	Ben T. Robinson (R)	13,740	42.3
3	Robert Y. Thomas Jr. (D)	18,032	52.3
	Bishop S. Huntsman (R)	16,443	47.7
4	Ben Johnson (D)	18,834	52.5
	John P. Haswell Jr. (R)	17,075	47.6
5	Charles F. Ogden (R)	21,788	51.3
	J. Swager Sherley (D)	20,703	48.7
6	Arthur B. Rouse (D)	19,039	68.3
	Virgil Weaver (R)	8,842	31.7
7	James C. Cantrill (D)	19,612	60.9
	A. B. Hammond (R)	12,590	39.1
8	Harvey Helm (D)	15,270*	52.8
	Robert L. Davidson (R)	13,673	47.2
9	William J. Fields (D)	21,810	54.6
	Trumbo Sindegas (R)	18,106	45.4
10	John W. Langley (R)	13,284	67.1
	David Hays (D)	6,511	32.9
11	John M. Robsion (R)	24,730	76.4
	Nat W. Elliott (D)	7,656	23.6

LOUISIANA

	Candidates	Votes	%
1	Albert Estopinal (D)	11,060	100.0
2	H. Garland Dupre (D)	10,391	100.0
3	Whitmell P. Martin (D)	2,888	100.0
4	John T. Watkins (D)	5,299	100.0
5	Riley J. Wilson (D)	3,831	100.0
6	Jared Y. Sanders (D)	3,659	100.0
7	Ladislas Lazaro (D)	3,584	100.0
8	James B. Aswell (D)	4,082	100.0

MAINE

	Candidates	Votes	%
1	Louis B. Goodall (R)	15,565	53.8
	L. B. Swett (D)	13,388	46.2
2	Wallace H. White Jr. (R)	17,928	54.2
	D. J. McGillicuddy (D)	15,144	45.8
3	John A. Peters (R)	20,293	57.6
	Chase (D)	14,930	42.4
4	Ira G. Hersey (R)	14,275	58.1
	L. G. C. Brown (D)	10,313	41.9

MARYLAND

	Candidates	Votes	%
1	William N. Andrews (R)	14,199	50.5
	Jesse D. Price (D)	13,913	49.5
2	Carville D. Benson (D)	17,985	54.3
	Charles J. Hull (R)	14,758	44.6
3	Charles P. Coady (D)	12,422	58.4
	Charles A. Jording (R)	8,244	38.8
4	J. Charles Linthicum (D)	14,689	57.0
	Walter E. Knickman (R)	10,718	41.6
5	Sydney E. Mudd (R)	13,266	53.7
	Frank M. Duvall (D)	10,987	44.5
6	Frederick N. Zihlman (R)	14,872	54.9
	Henry Dorsey Etchison (D)	11,489	42.4

Special Election

	Candidates	Votes	%
2	Carville D. Benson (D)	17,748	54.7
	Herbert R. Wooden (R)	14,674	45.3

MASSACHUSETTS

	Candidates	Votes	%
1	Allen T. Treadway (R)	15,933	58.3
	Thomas F. Cassidy (D)	11,394	41.7
2	Frederick H. Gillett (R)	20,277	99.9
3	Calvin D. Paige (R)	15,267	60.5
	Eaton D. Sargent (D)	9,982	39.5
4	Samuel E. Winslow (R)	14,141	52.5
	John F. McGrath (D)	12,792	47.5
5	John Jacob Rogers (R)	20,496	99.2
6	Willfred W. Lufkin (R)	21,147	88.9
	Estus E. Eames (SOC)	2,648	11.1
7	Michael F. Phelan (D)	14,437	57.3
	Charles Cabot Johnson (R)	10,754	42.7
8	Frederick W. Dallinger (R)	16,858	60.3
	James F. Aylward (D)	11,093	39.7
9	Alvan T. Fuller (R)	17,597	68.7
	Henry C. Rowland (D)	8,022	31.3
10	John F. Fitzgerald (D)	7,241‡	47.3
	Peter F. Tague (R)	7,003	45.7
	Hammond T. Fletcher (R)	1,071	7.0
11	George Holden Tinkham (R)	13,644	56.4
	Francis J. Horgan (D)	10,529	43.6
12	James A. Gallivan (D)	18,349	70.4
	Harrison H. Atwood (R)	7,709	29.6
13	Robert Luce (R)	18,257	59.3
	Aloysius J. Doon (D)	12,538	40.7
14	Richard Olney (D)	18,009	56.6
	Louis F. R. Langelier (R)	13,832	43.4
15	William S. Greene (R)	12,952	61.7
	Arthur J. B. Cartier (D)	8,031	38.3
16	Joseph Walsh (R)	13,874	62.4
	Frederic Tudor (D)	8,357	37.6

MICHIGAN

	Candidates	Votes	%
1	Frank E. Doremus (D)	22,549	60.4
	James W. Hanley (R)	14,063	37.6
2	Earl C. Michener (R)	20,831	55.7
	Samuel W. Beakes (D)	16,276	43.5
3	John M. C. Smith (R)	20,385	61.8
	Howard W. Cavanagh (D)	12,119	36.8
4	Edward L. Hamilton (R)	20,904	65.9
	James O'Hara (D)	10,842	34.2
5	Carl E. Mapes (R)	22,917	66.8
	Peter J. Danhof (D)	10,783	31.5
6	Patrick H. Kelley (R)	29,183	97.3
7	Louis C. Cramton (R)	20,573	73.3
	John W. Scully (D)	7,155	25.5
8	Joseph W. Fordney (R)	22,240	62.8
	Miles J. Purcell (D)	13,153	37.2
9	James C. McLaughlin (R)	17,624	66.4
	Charles M. Black (D)	8,317	31.3
10	Gilbert A. Currie (R)	18,409	68.0
	Henry C. Haller (D)	8,312	30.7
11	Frank D. Scott (R)	16,365	66.7
	Michael J. Doyle (D)	8,183	33.3
12	W. Frank James (R)	17,315	69.8
	Albert S. Ley (D)	6,681	26.9

	Candidates	Votes	%
13	Charles A. Nichols (R)	24,525	66.9
	Louis W. McClear (D)	11,617	31.7

MINNESOTA

	Candidates	Votes	%
1	Sydney Anderson (R)	29,337	100.0
2	Franklin F. Ellsworth (R)	24,888	69.0
	Simon (D)	11,161	31.0
3	Charles R. Davis (R)	20,092	53.4
	Farrell (D)	17,530	46.6
4	Carl C. Van Dyke (D)	18,736	62.0
	Mallory (R)	11,498	38.0
5	Walter H. Newton (R)	21,607	57.6
	Robertson (D)	15,912	42.4
6	Harold Knutson (R)	22,633	72.3
	Russell (D)	8,660	27.7
7	Andrew J. Volstead (R)	21,406	56.3
	Lobeck (N)	16,587	43.7
8	William L. Carss (UN LAB)	17,266	57.1
	Miller (D)	12,964	42.9
9	Halvor Steenerson (R)	26,303	100.0
10	Thomas D. Schall (R)	25,866	71.1
	Finlayson (D)	10,534	28.9

MISSISSIPPI

	Candidates	Votes	%
1	Ezekiel S. Candler Jr. (D)	4,240	100.0
2	Hubert D. Stephens (D)	4,270	100.0
3	Benjamin G. Humphreys (D)	2,339	100.0
4	Thomas U. Sisson (D)	4,135	96.3
5	William W. Venable (D)	6,174	100.0
6	Paul B. Johnson (D)	4,972	94.3
	F. T. Maxwell (SOC)	303	5.7
7	Percy E. Quin (D)	3,093	93.4
	J. B. Sternberger (SOC)	220	6.6
8	James W. Collier (D)	2,376	98.8

MISSOURI

	Candidates	Votes	%
1	Milton A. Romjue (D)	17,184	54.2
	Frank C. Millspaugh (R)	14,255	45.0
2	William W. Rucker (D)	19,769	98.7
3	Joshua W. Alexander (D)	15,910	52.9
	Frost (R)	14,117	46.9
4	Charles F. Booher (D)	15,707	51.7
	McNeeley (R)	14,597	48.0
5	William T. Bland (D)	31,561	62.7
	Reeves (R)	18,540	36.8
6	Clement C. Dickinson (D)	14,898	52.7
	Atkeson (R)	13,188	46.7
7	Samuel C. Major (D)	20,300	49.8
	Salts (R)	20,222	49.6
8	William L. Nelson (D)	13,326	50.4
	Gentry (R)	13,133	49.6
9	James Beauchamp Clark (D)	18,248	51.7
	Dyer (R)	16,719	47.4
10	Cleveland A. Newton (R)	50,390	60.2
	Read (D)	30,080	35.9
11	William L. Igoe (D)	16,229	96.8
12	Leonidas C. Dyer (R)	12,612	58.9
	Rosenfeld (D)	8,538	39.9
13	Marion E. Rhodes (R)	14,776	51.4
	Brewster (D)	13,773	47.9
14	Edward D. Hayes (R)	21,472	50.5
	Russell (D)	21,001	49.4
15	Isaac V. McPherson (R)	19,133	51.0
	Decker (D)	17,826	47.5
16	Thomas L. Rubey (D)	13,490	49.9
	Shelton (R)	13,320	49.2

Special Election

	Candidates	Votes	%
10	Frederick Essen (R)	49,416	59.6
	Read (D)	30,536	36.8

MONTANA

	Candidates	Votes	%
1	John M. Evans (D)	25,530	47.9
	Frank B. Linderman (R)	22,398	42.1

Candidates	Votes	%
Tom Kane (N)	5,335	10.0
2 Carl W. Riddick (R)	24,960	49.4
Harry B. Mitchell (D)	22,826	45.1
Joseph Pope (N)	2,786	5.5

NEBRASKA

	Candidates	Votes	%
1	C. Frank Reavis (R)	18,097	62.3
	Frank A. Peterson (D)	10,945	37.7
2	Albert W. Jefferis (R)	13,302	50.9
	Charles Lobeck (D)	12,839	49.1
3	Robert E. Evans (R)	22,654	52.0
	Daniel V. Stephens (D)	20,903	48.0
4	Melvin O. McLaughlin (R)	21,041	58.1
	W. H. Smith (D)	14,763	40.8
5	William E. Andrews (R)	17,819	50.8
	A. C. Shallenberger (D)	17,268	49.2
6	Moses P. Kinkaid (R)	28,563	60.8
	Charles W. Pool (D)	17,820	37.9

NEVADA

	Candidates	Votes	%
AL	Charles R. Evans (D)	12,670	51.3
	Sylvester S. Downer (R)	10,660	43.2
	H. H. Cordill (SOC)	1,377	5.6

NEW HAMPSHIRE

	Candidates	Votes	%
1	Sherman E. Burroughs (R)	18,658	52.2
	William N. Rogers (D)	17,122	47.9
2	Edward H. Wason (R)	19,343	56.5
	Harry F. Lake (D)	14,923	43.6

NEW JERSEY

	Candidates	Votes	%
1	William J. Browning (R)	23,785	63.8
	Dickerson (D)	10,627	28.5
2	Isaac Bacharach (R)	20,744	67.9
	French (D)	8,610	28.2
3	Thomas J. Scully (D)	19,965	53.1
	Carson (R)	17,068	45.4
4	Elijah C. Hutchinson (R)	17,875	55.1
	Vanderbilt (D)	14,556	44.9
5	Ernest R. Ackerman (R)	17,510	52.7
	Clement (D)	13,545	40.7
	Furber (SOC)	1,755	5.3
6	John R. Ramsey (R)	18,663	53.3
	Sibbald (D)	15,542	44.4
7	Amos H. Radcliffe (R)	12,515	53.6
	Delaney (D)	8,581	36.8
	Derrick (SOC)	1,657	7.1
8	Cornelius A. McGlennon (D)	12,436	48.7
	Ross (R)	12,137	47.6
9	Daniel F. Minahan (D)	10,996	50.4
	Parker (R)	9,338	42.8
	Bircher (SOC)	1,303	6.0
10	Frederick R. Lehlbach (R)	12,566	48.3
	Flannagan (D)	11,979	46.1
	Poole (SOC)	1,450	5.6
11	John J. Eagan (D)	14,281	67.5
	Brennan (D)	4,979	23.5
	Reilly (SOC)	1,894	9.0
12	James A. Hamill (D)	17,781	70.8
	Bierch (R)	6,048	24.1
	Bausch (SOC)	1,277	5.1

Special Election

	Candidates	Votes	%
5	William F. Birch (R)	17,481	53.0
	Clement (D)	13,771	41.7
	Furber (SOC)	1,760	5.3

NEW MEXICO

	Candidates	Votes	%
AL	Bendigno C. Hernandez (R)	23,862	50.7
	G. A. Richardson (D)	22,627	48.1

NEW YORK

	Candidates	Votes	%
1	Frederick C. Hicks (R-D-P)	53,579	96.6
2	Charles Pope Caldwell (R, D)	54,394	85.9
	William Burkle (SOC)	8,946	14.1
3	John MacCrate (R, D)	14,720	48.9
	Michael Fogarty (BUSINESS)	10,249	34.1
	Joseph A. Whitehorn (SOC)	5,107	17.0
4	Thomas H. Cullen (D)	23,146	75.2
	Ralph Waldo Bowman (R & P)	6,599	21.4
5	John B. Johnston (D)	32,090	55.8
	George A. Green (R)	23,844	41.5
6	Frederick W. Rowe (R & P)	26,806	46.6
	Franklin Taylor (D)	26,476	46.0
	Bernard J. Riley (SOC)	4,287	7.5
7	James P. Maher (D)	19,834	58.9
	John Hill Morgan (R & P)	9,309	27.7
	James O'Neal (SOC)	4,513	13.4
8	William E. Cleary (D)	24,069	54.5
	Allison L. Adams (R)	14,778	33.5
	Abraham H. Shulman (SOC)	5,114	11.6
9	David J. O'Connell (D)	28,882	45.8
	Oscar W. Swift (R & P)	27,393	43.5
	Wilhemus B. Robinson (SOC)	6,751	10.7
10	Reuben L. Haskell (R)	17,441	40.2
	George W. Martin (D)	15,911	36.7
	Abraham I. Shiplacoff (SOC)	9,987	23.0
11	Daniel J. Riordan (D)	21,525	71.2
	William H. Michales (R)	7,080	23.4
12	Henry M. Goldfogle (R, D)	7,452	52.9
	Meyer London (SOC)	6,625	47.0
13	Christopher D. Sullivan (R, D)	6,962	66.4
	Algernon Lee (SOC)	3,502	33.4
14	Fiorello H. LaGuardia (R, D)	14,523	69.7
	Scott Nearing (SOC)	6,214	29.8
15	Peter J. Dooling (D)	23,492	78.4
	Jacob I. Wiener (R)	5,373	17.9
16	Thomas F. Smith (D)	21,289	71.9
	Thomas Rock (R)	6,188	20.9
	Samuel E. Beardsley (SOC)	2,057	6.9
17	Herbert C. Pell Jr. (D)	19,593	50.2
	Frederick C. Tanner (R)	17,839	45.7
18	John F. Carew (D)	23,806	71.2
	Julius M. Leder (R)	4,797	14.4
	Pauline Newman (SOC)	4,741	14.2
19	Joseph Rowan (D)	24,961	48.3
	Walter M. Chandler (R)	23,125	44.8
	Theresa Malkiel (SOC)	3,319	6.4
20	Isaac Siegel (R-D)	9,417	60.9
	Morris Hillquit (SOC)	6,005	38.9
21	Jerome F. Donovan (D)	33,233	53.4
	John A. Bolles (R)	25,677	41.2
	George Fraser Miller (SOC)	3,156	5.1
22	Anthony J. Griffin (D)	22,713	69.9
	Sadie Kost (R)	5,269	16.2
	Patrick J. Murphy (SOC)	4,323	13.3
23	Richard F. McKiniry (D)	39,573	55.2
	Owen A. Haley (R)	17,975	25.1
	Max Geisler (SOC)	14,146	19.7
24	James V. Ganly (D)	28,636	44.3
	Benjamin L. Fairchild (R & P)	27,037	41.8
	Irvin E. Klein (SOC)	8,968	13.9
25	James W. Husted (R)	22,562	56.2
	Arthur O. Sherman (D)	16,248	40.5
26	Edmund Platt (R)	30,010	57.1
	George A. Coleman (D)	20,727	39.4
27	Charles B. Ward (R)	30,839	53.9
	John K. Evans (D & P)	25,620	44.7
28	Rollin B. Sanford (R & P)	41,981	54.5
	Joseph A. Lawson (D)	33,712	43.8
29	James S. Parker (R)	42,035	62.3
	Gustavus A. Rogers (D)	23,139	34.3
30	Frank Crowther (R)	24,443	47.9
	George R. Lunn (D & P)	23,820	46.7
	Herbert M. Merrill (SOC)	2,786	5.5
31	Bertrand H. Snell (R)	30,701	71.6
	Elizabeth Arthur (D)	10,459	24.4
32	Luther W. Mott (R)	37,068	63.2
	Charles A. Hitchcock (D)	17,742	30.2
	Stephen R. Lockwood (P)	3,263	5.6

	Candidates	Votes	%
33	Homer P. Snyder (R)	31,120	54.0
	Clarence E. Williams (D)	23,340	40.5
34	William H. Hill (R)	38,597	57.4
	Lavern P. Butts (D)	21,748	32.4
	Julius E. Rogers (P)	6,373	9.5
35	Walter W. Magee (R)	42,769	59.3
	Ben Wiles (D)	23,378	32.4
36	Norman J. Gould (R & P)	40,991	70.9
	Everett E. Calman (D)	16,857	29.1
37	Alanson B. Houghton (R & P)	38,310	62.9
	Frederick W. Palmer (D)	21,800	35.8
38	Thomas B. Dunn (R)	37,029	62.1
	Jacob Gerling (D)	16,563	27.8
	John W. Dennis (SOC)	4,098	6.9
39	Archie D. Sanders (R & P)	35,481	68.9
	Clara B. Mann (D)	14,816	28.8
40	S. Wallace Dempsey (R)	35,710	63.0
	Matthew P. Young (D)	17,962	31.7
	Lee P. Smith (SOC)	3,045	5.4
41	Clarence MacGregor (R)	16,492	41.2
	Charles B. Smith (D & P)	16,458	41.2
	Franklin P. Brill (SOC)	7,038	17.6
42	James M. Mead (D)	16,453	46.2
	William F. Waldow (R)	15,390	43.2
	Hattie Kreuger (SOC)	3,099	8.7
43	Daniel A. Reed (R & P)	35,693	73.4
	Frank H. Mott (D)	11,351	23.3

NORTH CAROLINA

	Candidates	Votes	%
1	John H. Small (D)	10,427	75.4
	C. R. Pugh (R)	3,401	24.6
2	Claude Kitchin (D)	9,986	100.0
3	Samuel L. Brinson (D)	10,205	59.3
	Claude R. Wheatley (R)	7,000	40.7
4	Edward W. Pou (D)	12,853	68.1
	Robert H. Dixon (R)	6,028	31.9
5	Charles M. Stedman (D)	21,076	55.9
	John W. Kurfees (R)	16,635	44.1
6	Hannibal L. Godwin (D)	9,575	72.1
	Alexander L. McCaskill (R)	3,702	27.9
7	Leonidas D. Robinson (D)	18,275	59.3
	James D. Gregg (R)	12,552	40.7
8	Robert L. Doughton (D)	16,105	53.8
	Frank A. Linney (R)	13,826	46.2
9	Edwin Y. Webb (D)	16,982	57.0
	Charles A. Jonas (R)	12,830	43.0
10	Zebulon Weaver (D)	16,323	51.7
	James J. Britt (R)	15,271	48.3

NORTH DAKOTA

	Candidates	Votes	%
1	John M. Baer (R)	16,428	55.1
	Fred Bartholomew (D)	13,416	45.0
2	George M. Young (R)	20,516	74.5
	L. N. Torson (D)	7,038	25.5
3	James H. Sinclair (R)	17,564	66.2
	Halvor Halvorson (D)	8,951	33.8

OHIO

	Candidates	Votes	%
1	Nicholas Longworth (R)	27,030	56.5
	Sidney G. Stricker (D)	20,826	43.5
2	Ambrose E. B. Stephens (R)	25,406	52.1
	Richard A. Powell (R)	21,867	44.8
3	Warren Gard (D)	29,653	49.2
	Charles W. Dustin (R)	26,625	44.2
	John M. Cahalane (SOC)	3,978	6.6
4	Benjamin F. Welty (R)	22,580	50.5
	J. E. Russell (R)	22,136	49.5
5	Charles J. Thompson (R)	19,071	52.6
	John S. Snook (D)	17,162	47.4
6	Charles C. Kearns (R)	18,592	52.8
	A. G. Turnipseed (D)	16,591	47.2
7	Simeon D. Fess (R)	34,554	61.6
	George H. Thorne (D)	21,043	37.5
8	R. Clint Cole (R)	20,688	52.9
	John A. Key (D)	18,441	47.1
9	Isaac R. Sherwood (D)	25,122	55.1

Candidates	Votes	%
James M. Ashley (R)	18,398	40.3
10 Israel M. Foster (R)	18,438	100.0
11 Edwin D. Ricketts (R)	17,608	53.5
H. C. Claypool (D)	15,287	46.5
12 Clement L. Brumbaugh (D)	23,444	50.5
John C. Speaks (R)	22,216	47.8
13 James T. Begg (R)	21,552	53.0
Arthur W. Overmeyer (D)	18,775	46.1
14 Martin L. Davey (D)	25,932	50.3
Charles Dick (R)	24,170	46.9
15 C. Ellis Moore (R)	20,063	52.5
George White (D)	18,169	47.5
16 Roscoe C. McCulloch (R)	29,893	61.3
Joseph C. Breitenstein (D)	17,694	36.3
17 William A. Ashbrook (D)	24,436	52.1
William M. Morgan (R)	22,499	47.9
18 Frank Murphy (R)	22,899	53.0
William B. Francis (D)	20,272	47.0
19 John G. Cooper (R)	26,857	95.6
20 Charles A. Mooney (D)	19,776	55.0
Jerry R. Zmunt (R)	13,759	38.3
C. E. Ruthenberg (SOC)	2,429	6.8
21 John J. Babka (D)	15,511	55.9
Harry L. Vail (R)	10,417	37.5
Tom Clifford (SOC)	1,829	6.6
22 Henry I. Emerson (R)	32,745	100.0

OKLAHOMA

Candidates	Votes	%
1 Everette B. Howard (D)	15,394	50.6
T. A. Chandler (R)	14,506	47.6
2 William W. Hastings (D)	11,601	58.9
Gus H. Tinch (R)	7,670	39.0
3 Charles D. Carter (D)	15,635	66.8
H. J. Fowler (R)	6,982	29.8
4 Thomas D. McKeown (D)	13,861	57.0
E. R. Waite (R)	9,706	39.9
5 Joseph B. Thompson (D)	13,303	57.4
B. A. McAleer (R)	9,180	39.6
6 Scott Ferris (D)	12,085	54.8
L. A. Holmes (R)	8,925	40.5
7 James V. McClintic (D)	11,190	59.7
C. B. Leedy (R)	6,014	32.1
Orville E. Enfield (SOC)	1,526	8.2
8 Dick T. Morgan (R)	15,261	56.3
C. H. Hyde (D)	10,633	39.2

OREGON

Candidates	Votes	%
1 Willis C. Hawley (R-D-P)	57,245	89.6
Harlin Talbert (SOC)	6,624	10.4
2 Nicholas J. Sinnott (R)	18,312	61.3
James Harvey Graham (D)	10,461	35.0
3 Clinton N. McArthur (R)	23,277	48.4
John S. Smith (D)	15,728	32.7
A. W. Lafferty (I-N)	7,661	15.9

PENNSYLVANIA

Candidates	Votes	%
1 William S. Vare (R, WASH)	26,120	76.4
Paul B. Cassidy (D)	7,146	20.9
2 George S. Graham (R, WASH)	20,578	81.5
John H. Berkley (D)	4,295	17.0
3 J. Hampton Moore (R, P)	20,099	78.8
William A. Hayes (D)	5,046	19.8
4 George W. Edmonds (R, WASH)	19,187	68.8
Joseph E. Fabian (D)	7,874	28.2
5 Peter E. Costello (R, SOC)	25,169	69.6
Emanuel R. Clinton (D)	10,987	30.4
6 George P. Darrow (R, P)	42,376	72.1
John K. Laughlin (D)	15,722	26.8
7 Thomas S. Butler (R)	23,882	76.1
James G. Milbourn (D)	6,702	21.3
8 Henry Winfield Watson (R)	23,127	63.4
Harry E. Grim (D, F PLAY)	12,213	33.5
9 William W. Griest (R)	17,398	77.1
Austin E. McCullough (D)	4,537	20.1
10 Patrick McLane (D, F PLAY)	11,765‡	50.0
John R. Farr (R, P)	11,564	49.1
11 John J. Casey (D, SOC)	16,547	50.1

Candidates	Votes	%
Edmund N. Carpenter (R, P)	16,505	49.9
12 John Reber (R)	13,500	57.3
James J. Moran (D, F PLAY)	9,712	41.2
13 Arthur G. Dewalt (D, F PLAY)	19,776	51.9
J. Wilmer Fisher (R, WASH)	15,608	40.9
L. Birch Wilson Jr (SOC)	2,397	6.3
14 Louis T. McFadden (R)	11,267	66.0
A. M. Cornell (D)	4,873	28.6
15 Edgar R. Kiess (R, P)	14,153	63.8
Charles E. Spotts (D)	7,372	33.2
16 John V. Lesher (D)	11,782	48.7
Albert W. Duy (R)	11,509	47.6
17 Benjamin K. Focht (R)	16,762	59.0
Scott S. Leiby (D, P)	11,348	39.9
18 Aaron S. Kreider (R)	24,981	86.2
John A. Sprenkle (P)	2,905	10.0
19 John M. Rose (R, P)	20,036	61.4
Bernard J. Clark (D)	11,857	36.4
20 Edward S. Brooks (R, WASH)	15,362	52.5
Andrew R. Brodbeck (D, P)	13,525	46.2
21 Evan J. Jones (R, SOC)	12,673	56.5
William E. Tobias (D)	8,958	39.9
22 Edward E. Robbins (R, P)	17,160*	61.1
George H. McWherter (D, F PLAY)	9,904	35.3
23 Samuel A. Kendall (R)	14,550	50.1
Bruce F. Sterling (D, P)	14,029	48.3
24 Henry W. Temple (R, P)	18,851	69.1
William M. Hartman (D)	7,398	27.1
25 Milton W. Shreve (R, WASH)	11,164	51.0
Charles N. Crosby (D)	8,766	40.0
26 Henry J. Steele (D, F PLAY)	11,872	49.4
Francis A. March Jr. (R, WASH)	9,781	40.7
Delbert Strader Bachman (P, I PROG)	2,035	8.5
27 Nathan L. Strong (R, P)	14,804	70.7
Don C. Corbett (D)	5,686	27.2
28 Willis J. Hulings (R, WASH)	13,751	55.5
Earl H. Beshlin (D, P)	10,367	41.9
29 Stephen G. Porter (R, D)	19,045	89.0
C. G. Porter (P)	1,222	5.7
Henry Peter (SOC)	1,138	5.3
30 M. Clyde Kelly (R, D)	21,559	90.5
H. J. Lohr (SOC)	2,262	9.5
31 John M. Morin (R, D)	14,081	91.4
William A. Prosser (SOC)	773	5.0
32 Guy E. Campbell (R, D)	20,567	87.2
John W. Slayton (SOC)	1,553	6.6
William C. Wallace (P)	1,458	6.2
AL William J. Burke (R)	546,373✓	
Mahlon M. Garland (R)	529,510✓	
Thomas S. Crago (R, WASH)	527,961✓	
Anderson H. Walters (R, WASH)	525,615✓	
Joseph F. Gorman (D)	276,836	
J. Calvin Strayer (D, F PLAY)	268,533	
Samuel R. Tarner (D, F PLAY)	264,971	
Fred Ikeler (D, F PLAY)	264,065	
O. D. Brubaker (P)	29,309	
Elisha Kent Kane (P)	26,473	
Albert Gaddis (P)	25,347	
E. L McKee (P)	23,793	
Cora M. Bixler (SOC)	23,273	
Henry W. Schlegel (SOC)	21,831	
John C. Euler (SOC)	21,477	
Harry T. Vaughn (SOC)	21,143	
John W. Dix (SINGLE T)	2,211	
Lewis Ryan (SINGLE T)	2,129	
Oliver McKnight (SINGLE T)	2,006	
Calvin B. Power (SINGLE T)	1,631	

RHODE ISLAND

Candidates	Votes	%
1 Clark Burdick (R)	14,478	54.3
Green (D)	11,556	43.4
2 Walter R. Stiness (R)	14,710	56.0
Casey (D)	10,914	41.6
3 Ambrose Kennedy (R)	14,037	52.6
Troy (D)	12,176	45.6

SOUTH CAROLINA

Candidates	Votes	%
1 Richard S. Whaley (D)	2,328	100.0
2 James F. Byrnes (D)	3,155	100.0
3 Fred H. Dominick (D)	3,701	100.0
4 Samuel J. Nichols (D)	4,069	100.0
5 William F. Stevenson (D)	3,640	100.0
6 J. Willard Ragsdale (D)	3,626	100.0
7 Asbury F. Lever (D)	4,761	96.4

SOUTH DAKOTA

Candidates	Votes	%
1 Charles A. Christopherson (R)	19,443	54.1
Dowdell (D)	14,899	41.5
2 Royal C. Johnson (R)	21,657	72.1
McArthur (D)	8,401	28.0
3 Harry L. Gandy (D)	10,865	50.7
Atwater (R)	7,805	36.4
Ayers (I)	2,526	11.8

TENNESSEE

Candidates	Votes	%
1 Sam R. Sells (R)	13,752	100.0
2 J. Will Taylor (R)	13,868	73.3
Sam Johnson (D)	4,879	25.8
3 John A. Moon (D)	12,566	100.0
4 Cordell Hull (D)	11,646	100.0
5 Ewen L. Davis (D)	11,089	100.0
6 Joseph W. Byrns (D)	10,794	100.0
7 Lemuel P. Padgett (D)	10,178	100.0
8 Thetus W. Sims (D)	9,010	100.0
9 Finis J. Garrett (D)	11,122	100.0
10 Hubert F. Fisher (D)	11,606	100.0

TEXAS

Candidates	Votes	%
1 Eugene Black (D)	9,640	100.0
2 John C. Box (D)	10,474	100.0
3 James Young (D)	10,183	100.0
4 Sam Rayburn (D)	9,755	100.0
5 Hatton W. Sumners (D)	6,946	100.0
6 Rufus Hardy (D)	10,496	86.9
Charles W. Beck (R)	1,577	13.1
7 Clay S. Briggs (D)	6,671	100.0
8 Joe H. Eagle (D)	7,554	96.1
9 Joseph J. Mansfield (D)	7,672	100.0
10 James P. Buchanan (D)	8,576	100.0
11 Tom T. Connally (D)	9,304	100.0
12 James C. Wilson (D)	9,307	100.0
13 Lucian W. Parrish (D)	9,700	100.0
14 Carlos Bee (D)	8,038	68.4
John D. Hartman (R)	3,717	31.6
15 John N. Garner (D)	6,814	100.0
16 Claude Hudspeth (D)	6,211	100.0
17 Thomas L. Blanton (D)	11,194	100.0
18 Marvin Jones (D)	10,497	95.3

UTAH

Candidates	Votes	%
1 Milton H. Welling (D)	25,327	54.9
William H. Wattis (R)	20,478	44.4
2 James H. Mays (D & PROG)	23,931	58.7
William Spry (R)	16,134	39.6

VERMONT

Candidates	Votes	%
1 Frank L. Greene (R)	16,301	75.9
John Higgins (D)	5,179	24.1
2 Porter H. Dale (R, P)	16,145	74.5
John B. Reardon (D)	5,518	25.5

VIRGINIA

Candidates	Votes	%
1 S. Otis Bland (D)	4,835	99.9
2 Edward E. Holland (D)	3,420	100.0
3 Andrew Jackson Montague (D)	3,074	100.0
4 Walter A. Watson (D)	2,506	99.9
5 Edward W. Saunders (D)	3,880	100.0
6 Carter Glass (D)	2,705*	99.6
7 Thomas W. Harrison (D)	3,767	88.8

	Candidates	Votes	%
	John Paul (R)	466	11.0
8	Charles C. Carlin (D)	4,501*	100.0
9	C. Bascom Slemp (R)	8,089	93.9
	D. B. Dale (D)	515	6.0
10	Henry D. Flood (D)	4,699	99.7

WASHINGTON

	Candidates	Votes	%
1	John F. Miller (R)	23,326	50.6
	J. M. Hawthorne (D)	20,488	44.4
	Hulet M. Wells (SOC)	2,333	5.1
2	Lindley H. Hadley (R)	19,797	53.7
	Joseph A. Sloan (D)	15,059	40.8
	James M. Salter (SOC)	2,045	5.5
3	Albert Johnson (R)	29,178	66.6
	Theodore Hoss (D)	12,407	28.3
	O. T. Clark (SOC)	2,243	5.1
4	John W. Summers (R)	17,439	55.3
	William E. McCroskey (D)	13,335	42.3
5	J. Stanley Webster (R)	22,426	52.2
	C. C. Dill (D)	20,061	46.7

WEST VIRGINIA

	Candidates	Votes	%
1	Matthew M. Neely (D)	17,428	52.8
	Charles J. Schuck (R)	15,330	46.4

	Candidates	Votes	%
2	George M. Bowers (R)	18,444	52.7
	B. H. Hiner (D)	16,084	46.0
3	Stuart F. Reed (R)	19,414	53.9
	Ernest Randolph (D)	16,254	45.1
4	Harry C. Woodyard (R)	19,679	55.2
	Stuart H. Bowman (D)	15,799	44.3
5	Wells Goodykoontz (R)	19,304	54.2
	W. W. McNeal (D)	16,332	45.8
6	Leonard S. Echols (R)	19,851	51.5
	Adam B. Littlepage (D)	18,020	46.8

WISCONSIN

	Candidates	Votes	%
1	Clifford E. Randall (R)	13,177	42.3
	Cooper (I)	9,018	28.9
	Stewart (D)	7,718	24.8
2	Edward Voigt (R)	15,289	44.0
	Clifford (D)	12,532	36.1
	Ameringer (SOC)	6,936	20.0
3	James G. Monahan (R)	18,398	73.4
	Warner (I)	4,397	17.5
	Reynolds (I)	2,232	8.9
4	John C. Kleczka (R)	16,524	58.1
	Melms (SOC)	11,890	41.8
5	Victor L. Berger (SOC)	17,920*	43.7
	Joseph P. Carney (D)	12,450	30.3

	Candidates	Votes	%
	Stafford (R)	10,678	26.0
6	Florian Lampert (R)	12,728	41.5
	Husting (D)	10,856	35.4
	Thompson (SOC)	6,737	22.0
7	John J. Esch (R)	16,140	70.9
	Bentley (D)	6,109	26.8
8	Edward E. Browne (R)	13,755	51.8
	Brown (D)	6,862	25.9
	Krzycki (SOC)	5,904	22.3
9	David G. Classon (R)	16,352	60.4
	McDonald (D)	10,702	39.6
10	James A. Frear (R)	16,900	90.2
	Frawley (I)	1,814	9.7
11	Adolphus P. Nelson (R)	16,413	84.3
	Jensen (SOC)	2,976	15.3

WYOMING

	Candidates	Votes	%
AL	Frank W. Mondell (R)	26,244	64.2
	Hayden M. White (D)	14,639	35.8

1919 House Elections

OKLAHOMA

Special Election

	Candidates	Votes	%
5	J. W. Harreld (R)	11,782	51.3
	Claude Weaver (D)	11,076	48.2

PENNSYLVANIA

Special Election

	Candidates	Votes	%
22	John H. Wilson (D)	10,148	51.1
	John M. Jamison (R)	9,721	48.9

WISCONSIN

Special Election

	Candidates	Votes	%
5	Victor L. Berger (SOC)	24,367	55.5
	Henry H. Bodenstab (R-D)	19,561	44.5

1920 House Elections

ALABAMA

	Candidates	Votes	%
1	John McDuffie (D)	12,978	98.7
2	John R. Tyson (D)	18,469	99.6
3	Henry B. Steagall (D)	11,959	82.5
	Dallas B. Smith (R)	2,532	17.5
4	Fred L. Blackmon (D)	12,236*	59.6
	A. P. Longshore (R)	8,305	40.4
5	William B. Bowling (D)	13,290	73.5
	W. M. Russell (R)	4,793	26.5
6	William B. Oliver (D)	8,721	100.0
7	Lilius B. Rainey (D)	23,709	50.5
	Charles B. Kennamer (R)	22,970	49.0
8	Edward B. Almon (D)	17,640	76.4
	W. E. Hotchkiss (R)	5,306	23.0
9	George Huddleston (D)	26,776	85.4
	Alex Birch (R)	4,452	14.2
10	William B. Bankhead (D)	15,465	52.6
	W. L. Chenault (R)	13,737	46.7

ARIZONA

	Candidates	Votes	%
AL	Carl Hayden (D)	35,397	57.8
	James A. Dunseath (R)	25,841	42.2

ARKANSAS

	Candidates	Votes	%
1	William J. Driver (D)	19,843	73.6
	T. H. Mayes (R)	7,110	26.4
2	William A. Oldfield (D)	16,080	66.4
	Thad Rowden (R)	8,137	33.6
3	John N. Tillman (D)	14,341	53.3
	John I. Worthington (R)	12,587	46.7
4	Otis Wingo (D)	19,722	64.1
	W. H. Dunblazier (R)	11,031	35.9
5	Henderson M. Jacoway (D)	21,948	73.2
	G. A. McConnell (R)	8,039	26.8
6	Samuel M. Taylor (D)	18,028	69.4
	W. R. Day (R)	7,956	30.6
7	Tilman B. Parks (D)	18,303	72.2
	J. C. Russell (R)	7,064	27.9

CALIFORNIA

	Candidates	Votes	%
1	Clarence F. Lea (D-R)	34,427	61.7
	Charles A. Bodwell Jr. (I)	18,569	33.3
2	John E. Raker (D R&SOC)	26,172	99.9
3	Charles F. Curry (R)	54,984	74.7
	J. W. Struckenbruck (D)	14,964	20.3
4	Julius Kahn (R-D)	50,841	84.6
	Milton Harlan (SOC)	9,289	15.5
5	John I. Nolan (R-D)	50,274	82.1
	Thomas Conway (SOC)	10,952	17.9
6	John A. Elston (R)	75,610	83.3
	Maynard Shipley (SOC)	15,151	16.7
7	Henry E. Barbour (R-D)	57,647	87.2
	Harry M. McKee (SOC)	8,449	12.8
8	Arthur M. Free (R)	46,823	64.0
	Hugh S. Hersman (D SOC)	26,311	36.0
9	Charles F. Van de Water (R)	62,952*	59.7
	Charles H. Randall (P & D)	36,675	34.8
	Mary E. Garbutt (SOC)	5,819	5.5
10	Henry Z. Osborne (R-D-P)	97,469	82.6
	Upton Sinclair (SOC)	20,439	17.3
11	Philip D. Swing (R)	59,425	72.8
	Hugh L. Dickson (D)	22,144	27.1

COLORADO

	Candidates	Votes	%
1	William N. Vaile (R)	45,658	66.9
	Benjamin C. Hilliard (D)	22,557	33.1
2	Charles B. Timberlake (R)	57,512	66.4
	A. F. Browns (D)	29,158	33.6
3	Guy U. Hardy (R)	43,426	57.7
	Samuel J. Burris (D)	31,896	42.4
4	Edward T. Taylor (D)	25,994	55.3

Candidates	Votes	%
Merle D. Vincent (R)	20,991	44.7

CONNECTICUT

	Candidates	Votes	%
1	E. Hart Fenn (R)	53,461	60.5
	Joseph F. Dutton (D)	30,757	34.8
2	Richard P. Freeman (R)	39,432	63.7
	Thomas R. Murray (D)	20,868	33.7
3	John Q. Tilson (R)	45,406	63.7
	William F. Alcorn (D)	22,357	31.4
4	Schuyler Merritt (R)	54,715	66.3
	Harry J. Platt (D)	25,087	30.4
5	James P. Glynn (R)	34,621	58.7
	Michael L. Caine (D)	22,950	38.9

DELAWARE

	Candidates	Votes	%
AL	Caleb R. Layton (R)	52,145	55.7
	James R. Clements (D)	40,206	43.0

FLORIDA

	Candidates	Votes	%
1	Herbert J. Drane (D)	26,385	78.1
	H. B. Jeffries (R)	4,729	14.0
2	Frank Clark (D)	15,143	84.9
	Fred Cubberly (R)	2,383	13.4
3	J. H. Smithwick (D)	17,199	86.2
	Millard M. Owens (R)	2,753	13.8
4	William J. Sears (D)	38,355	74.4
	C. D. Bowen (R)	11,159	21.7

GEORGIA

	Candidates	Votes	%
1	James W. Overstreet (D)	10,156	82.5
	E. S. Fuller (R)	2,161	17.5
2	Frank Park (D)	2,217	100.0
3	Charles R. Crisp (D)	7,001	92.6
	H. E. Locket (R)	563	7.4
4	William C. Wright (D)	10,040	100.0
5	William D. Upshaw (D)	10,649	70.1
	John W. Martin (R)	4,544	29.9
6	James W. Wise (D)	9,325	97.7
7	Gordon Lee (D)	18,385	99.6
8	Charles H. Brand (D)	11,708	100.0
9	Thomas M. Bell (D)	13,265	62.2
	O. L. Barnwell (R)	8,053	37.8
10	Carl Vinson (D)	8,685	100.0
11	William C. Lankford (D)	9,012	100.0
12	William W. Larsen (D)	8,461	100.0

IDAHO

	Candidates	Votes	%
1	Burton L. French (R)	34,654	59.3
	Nell K. Irion (D)	15,218	26.0
	Riley Rice (I)	8,605	14.7
2	Addison T. Smith (R)	49,642	63.0
	William P. Whitaker (D)	29,130	37.0

ILLINOIS

	Candidates	Votes	%
1	Martin B. Madden (R)	41,907	75.9
	James A. Gorman (D)	12,398	22.5
2	James R. Mann (R)	92,217	72.9
	James J. Leddy (D)	29,754	23.5
3	Elliott W. Sproul (R)	73,547	67.4
	Thomas M. Crane (D)	30,631	28.1
4	John W. Rainey (D)	23,230	48.9
	John Golombiewski (R)	21,546	45.3
	Charles Beranek (SOC)	2,750	5.8
5	Adolph J. Sabath (D)	14,374	45.3
	Jacob Gartenstein (R)	14,076	44.4
	William Neumann (SOC)	3,290	10.4
6	John J. Gorman (R)	88,975	63.8
	James McAndrews (D)	40,576	29.1
	William F. Kruse (SOC)	9,937	7.1
7	M. A. Michaelson (R)	110,758	70.0

Candidates	Votes	%
William J. Cullerton (D)	34,202	21.6
Samuel Holland (SOC)	12,097	7.7
8 Stanley Henry Kunz (D)	15,432	49.2
Dan Parrillo (R)	14,627	46.6
9 Fred A. Britten (R)	40,548	72.5
Eugene L. McGarry (D)	13,257	23.7
10 Carl R. Chindblom (R)	101,361	74.4
John Haderlin (D)	30,924	22.7
11 Ira C. Copley (R)	68,691	80.4
Anton Nemanich Jr. (D)	14,885	17.4
12 Charles E. Fuller (R)	67,391	95.8
13 John C. McKenzie (R)	48,453	80.5
J. L. Dickson (D)	10,821	18.0
14 William J. Graham (R)	49,329	67.1
Andrew Olson (D)	21,822	29.7
15 Edward J. King (R)	49,852	69.0
William F. Gilroy (D)	20,771	28.7
16 Clifford Ireland (R)	47,936	67.4
Jefferson Earle Houston (D)	21,438	30.1
17 Frank H. Funk (R)	42,790	70.5
Frank Gillespie (D)	17,912	29.5
18 Joseph G. Cannon (R)	53,772	64.1
Armand E. Smith (D)	27,295	32.5
19 Allen F. Moore (R)	63,124	63.7
Edward F. Poorman (D)	35,210	35.5
20 Guy L. Shaw (R)	33,375	53.1
Henry T. Rainey (D)	29,466	46.9
21 Loren E. Wheeler (R)	43,223	52.0
J. Earl Major (D)	29,054	34.9
Duncan McDonald (F-LAB)	8,970	10.8
22 William A. Rodenberg (R)	49,802	54.8
Guy R. McCasland (D)	26,866	29.6
Cornelius J. Hayes (F-LAB)	11,929	13.1
23 Edwin B. Brooks (R)	44,950	54.4
Albert H. Gravenhorst (D)	34,740	42.1
24 Thomas S. Williams (R)	38,472	60.9
Asher R. Cox (D)	22,019	34.9
25 Edward E. Denison (R)	49,145	58.2
J. Herman Clayton (D)	28,444	33.7
John H. Reed (F-LAB)	5,690	6.7
AL Richard Yates (R)	1,369,673✓	
William E. Mason (R)	1,355,392✓	
William Murphy (D)	579,799	
C. S. Schneider (D)	565,792	
Frank H. Hall (SOC)	66,385	
John Hubert (SOC)	65,150	
Gifford Ernest (F-LAB)	49,432	
Robert Weber (F-LAB)	49,191	
Margaret Wintringer (P)	19,123	
W. W. Jones (P)	9,136	
Henry Schilling (SOC LAB)	3,429	
Frank K. Kuchenbecker (SOC LAB)	2,985	
Henry Neil (I)	627	

INDIANA

	Candidates	Votes	%
1	Oscar R. Luhring (R)	44,694	51.7
	William E. Wilson (D)	36,834	42.6
2	Oscar E. Bland (R)	47,896	52.1
	William A. Cullop (D)	39,349	42.8
3	James W. Dunbar (R)	44,743	51.0
	John W. Ewing (D)	42,569	48.5
4	John S. Benham (R)	46,360	53.0
	Harry C. Canfield (D)	41,163	47.0
5	Everett Sanders (R)	46,464	52.1
	Charles S. Batt (D)	36,403	40.8
6	Richard N. Elliott (R)	48,752	55.3
	William A. Yarling (D)	38,721	43.9
7	Merrill Moores (R)	79,782	54.9
	Henry N. Spaan (D)	61,893	42.6
8	Albert H. Vestal (R)	54,416	56.8
	Charles A. Paddock (D)	38,725	40.4
9	Fred S. Purnell (R)	56,465	55.9
	Ben M. Scifres (D)	42,766	42.4
10	William R. Wood (R)	62,438	65.5

Candidates	Votes	%
Fred Barnett (D)	26,139	27.4
James H. McGill (F-LAB)	5,086	5.3
11 Milton Kraus (R)	51,106	54.7
Samuel E. Cook (D)	40,088	42.9
12 Louis W. Fairfield (R)	49,709	58.6
Joseph R. Harrison (D)	31,182	36.8
13 Andrew J. Hickey (R)	62,206	59.8
George Y. Hepler (D)	39,253	37.7

IOWA

	Candidates	Votes	%
1	William F. Kopp (R)	38,100	64.5
	E. W. McManus (D)	20,977	35.5
2	Harry E. Hull (R)	50,160	89.0
	F. B. Althouse (F-LAB)	6,058	10.8
3	Burton E. Sweet (R)	67,859	97.1
4	Gilbert N. Haugen (R)	53,083	74.6
	Carl Evans (D)	18,104	25.4
5	James W. Good (R)	58,197	99.9
6	C. William Ramseyer (R)	41,644	65.9
	O. P. Meyers (D)	21,538	34.1
7	Cassius C. Dowell (R)	66,367	98.1
8	Horace M. Towner (R)	49,522	99.6
9	William R. Green (R)	48,558	82.1
	Hattie T. Harl (I)	10,607	17.9
10	Lester J. Dickinson (R)	67,700	96.0
11	William D. Boles (R)	64,342	69.7
	E. H. Birmingham (D)	27,953	30.3

KANSAS

	Candidates	Votes	%
1	Daniel R. Anthony Jr. (R)	42,471	67.2
	J. B. Billard (D)	20,730	32.8
2	Edward C. Little (R)	48,307	58.9
	C. A. Bowman (D)	31,862	38.9
3	Philip P. Campbell (R)	47,220	60.4
	J. D. Turkington (D)	30,932	39.6
4	Homer Hoch (R)	32,619	67.0
	Walter W. Austin (D)	14,944	30.7
5	James G. Strong (R)	38,992	68.6
	Thomas F. Johnson (D)	16,303	28.7
6	Hays B. White (R)	36,400	61.9
	J. C. Ruppenthal (D)	20,600	35.0
7	Jasper N. Tincher (R)	49,601	62.9
	J. R. Beeching (D)	26,992	34.2
8	Richard E. Bird (R)	30,076	49.4
	W. A. Ayres (D)	29,899	49.1

KENTUCKY

	Candidates	Votes	%
1	Alben W. Barkley (D)	50,635	64.3
	Miller Hughes (R)	28,070	35.7
2	David H. Kincheloe (D)	45,741	55.8
	Erskine B. Bassett (R)	36,280	44.2
3	Robert Y. Thomas Jr. (D)	36,430	50.4
	John H. Gilliam (R)	35,873	49.6
4	Ben Johnson (D)	41,620	52.5
	John P. Haswell (R)	37,702	47.5
5	Charles F. Ogden (R)	67,436	53.7
	James H. Richmond (D)	55,037	43.9
6	Arthur B. Rouse (D)	39,833	53.7
	Rodney G. Bryson (R)	26,099	35.2
	Harry V. Dill (I)	8,231	11.1
7	James C. Cantrill (D)	52,780	100.0
8	Ralph Gilbert (D)	37,381	52.0
	King Swope (R)	34,525	48.0
9	William J. Fields (D)	51,530	52.9
	W. G. Blair (R)	45,897	47.1
10	John W. Langley (R)	33,035	100.0
11	John M. Robsion (R)	64,248	75.4
	J. E. Sampson (D)	20,926	24.6

LOUISIANA

	Candidates	Votes	%
1	James O'Connor (D)	19,716	99.9
2	H. Garland Dupre (D)	19,777	100.0
3	Whitmell P. Martin (D)	4,201	100.0
4	John N. Sandlin (D)	10,507	100.0
5	Riley J. Wilson (D)	9,502	100.0
6	George K. Favrot (D)	9,426	100.0

	Candidates	Votes	%
7	Ladislas Lazaro (D)	8,551	100.0
8	James B. Aswell (D)	10,357	100.0

MAINE

	Candidates	Votes	%
1	Carroll L. Beedy (R)	30,810	66.6
	F. H. Haskell (D)	15,456	33.4
2	Wallace H. White Jr. (R)	35,015	62.5
	W. N. Price (D)	20,978	37.5
3	John A. Peters (R)	38,533	66.7
	A. C. Towle (D)	19,276	33.3
4	Ira G. Hersey (R)	30,872	72.3
	L. G. C. Brown (D)	11,805	27.7

MARYLAND

	Candidates	Votes	%
1	Thomas Alan Goldsborough (D)	29,969	52.5
	William N. Andrews (R)	27,090	47.5
2	Albert A. Blakeney (R)	41,608	49.7
	Carville D. Benson (D)	34,151	40.8
	Samuel C. Appleby (I)	5,679	6.8
3	John Philip Hill (R)	24,617	49.4
	Charles P. Coady (D)	23,104	46.4
4	J. Charles Linthicum (D)	32,135	42.4
	William O. Atwood (I)	30,891	40.8
	Walter E. Knickman (I)	8,417	11.1
5	Sydney E. Mudd (R)	29,867	58.9
	Thomas S. Klinger (D)	18,569	36.6
6	Frederick N. Zihlman (R)	35,864	56.3
	Frank W. Mish (D)	25,992	40.8

MASSACHUSETTS

	Candidates	Votes	%
1	Allen T. Treadway (R)	36,105	61.5
	Thomas F. Cassidy (D)	22,577	38.5
2	Frederick H. Gillett (R)	47,658	99.9
3	Calvin D. Paige (R)	38,313	71.5
	Nixon Campbell (D)	15,311	28.6
4	Samuel E. Winslow (R)	37,323	56.8
	John F. McGrath (D)	28,438	43.2
5	John Jacob Rogers (R)	41,861	70.1
	Jackson Palmer (D)	17,861	29.9
6	Willfred W. Lufkin (R)	47,231	75.3
	John P. O'Connell (L-LAB D)	15,523	24.7
7	Robert S. Maloney (R)	28,009	47.6
	Michael F. Phelan (D)	25,691	43.7
	George F. Hogan (P)	5,121	8.7
8	Frederick W. Dallinger (R)	54,246	72.9
	Whitfield L. Tuck (D)	12,754	17.1
	John D. Lynch (I)	7,407	10.0
9	Charles L. Underhill (R)	43,111	71.1
	Maurice F. Ahearn (D)	17,542	28.9
10	Peter F. Tague (D)	14,535	51.0
	James E. Maguire (R)	13,995	49.1
11	George Holden Tinkham (R)	40,278	68.5
	Alfred J. Moore (D)	18,553	31.5
12	James A. Gallivan (D)	32,622	58.6
	Harrison H. Atwood (R)	18,259	32.8
	William H. O'Brien (PP CAND)	4,813	8.6
13	Robert Luce (R)	56,451	70.9
	Charles F. McCarthy (D)	23,122	29.1
14	Louis A. Frothingham (R)	46,894	60.4
	Richard Olney (D)	28,596	36.8
15	William S. Greene (R)	28,095	60.2
	Arthur J. B. Cartier (D)	18,615	39.9
16	Joseph Walsh (R)	40,303	84.8
	George Richards (LAB)	7,239	15.2

MICHIGAN

	Candidates	Votes	%
1	George P. Codd (R)	89,171	80.3
	Frank Murphy (D)	19,803	17.8
2	Earl C. Michener (R)	61,857	70.9
	William H. Moore (D)	25,281	29.0
3	William H. Frankhauser (R)	50,778	71.4
	Gordon L. Stewart (D)	19,652	27.6
4	John C. Ketcham (R)	47,671	75.1
	Roman I. Jarvis Sr. (D)	15,199	23.9
5	Carl E. Mapes (R)	53,379	75.0
	Frank C. Jarvis (D)	15,963	22.4

	Candidates	Votes	%
6	Patrick H. Kelley (R)	102,627	72.7
	Frank L. Dodge (D)	33,319	23.6
7	Louis C. Cramton (R)	53,416	80.1
	John Hooker (D)	12,755	19.1
8	Joseph W. Fordney (R)	54,337	72.2
	Austin M. Brown (D)	20,766	27.6
9	James C. McLaughlin (R)	42,992	76.3
	Michael B. Danaher (D)	12,095	21.5
10	Roy O. Woodruff (R)	43,678	75.5
	David J. Lynch (D)	13,935	24.1
11	Frank D. Scott (R)	41,529	100.0
12	W. Frank James (R)	41,783	80.4
	Edward C. Anthony (D)	8,446	16.3
13	Vincent M. Brennan (R)	78,116	68.1
	James H. Lee (D)	31,369	27.3

Special Election

	Candidates	Votes	%
13	Clarence J. McLeod (R)	77,975	72.8
	James H. Lee (D)	29,110	27.2

MINNESOTA

	Candidates	Votes	%
1	Sydney Anderson (R)	50,387	70.4
	Julius I. Reiter (F-LAB)	21,158	29.6
2	Frank Clague (R)	49,181	65.2
	H. A. Fuller (I)	19,274	25.6
	Frank Simon (I)	6,934	9.2
3	Charles R. Davis (R)	41,678	58.8
	James M. Millett (D)	15,146	21.4
	R. A. Pomadt (I)	14,034	19.8
4	Oscar E. Keller (R)	38,792	58.7
	Thomas J. Brady (D)	22,610	34.2
	Carl W. Cummins (I)	4,702	7.1
5	Walter H. Newton (R)	54,962	57.6
	Lynn Thompson (F-LAB)	22,584	23.7
	Ernest Lundeen (I)	9,573	10.0
	T. O. Dahl (D)	8,357	8.8
6	Harold Knutson (R)	47,954	69.0
	Charles A. Lindbergh (I)	21,587	31.0
7	Andrew J. Volstead (R)	36,822	47.5
	Ole J. Kvale (I)	35,370	45.6
	James C. Mitchell (D)	5,358	6.9
8	Oscar J. Larson (R)	33,428	50.8
	William L. Carss (D)	32,395	49.2
9	Halvor Steenerson (R)	39,122	52.7
	N. E. Thormodson (I)	28,443	38.3
	Frank Jeffers (D)	6,741	9.1
10	Thomas D. Schall (R)	54,971	68.3
	John G. Soltis (F-LAB)	18,590	23.1
	H. A. Finlayson (D)	6,917	8.6

MISSISSIPPI

	Candidates	Votes	%
1	John E. Rankin (D)	10,400	100.0
2	Bill G. Lowrey (D)	6,960	100.0
3	Benjamin G. Humphreys (D)	6,338	100.0
4	Thomas U. Sisson (D)	8,979	93.8
	J. A. Washington (SOC)	598	6.2
5	Ross A. Collins (D)	11,507	94.1
6	Paul B. Johnson (D)	9,483	86.2
	L. B. Collins (R)	906	8.2
	T. J. Lyon (SOC)	610	5.6
7	Percy E. Quin (D)	6,695	92.7
8	James W. Collier (D)	5,944	95.4

MISSOURI

	Candidates	Votes	%
1	Frank C. Millspaugh (R)	34,259	50.5
	Milton A. Romjue (D)	32,952	48.6
2	William W. Rucker (D)	38,771	52.7
	B. F. Beazell (R)	34,645	47.1
3	Henry F. Lawrence (R)	33,949	51.9
	Jacob L. Milligan (D)	31,475	48.1
4	Charles L. Faust (R)	38,047	54.1
	L. C. Gabbert (D)	32,098	45.7
5	Edgar C. Ellis (R)	79,075	50.1
	William T. Bland (D)	77,793	49.3
6	William O. Atkeson (R)	29,802	52.2
	Clement C. Dickinson (D)	26,995	47.3

Candidates	Votes	%
7 Roscoe C. Patterson (R)	50,213	54.9
Sam C. Major (D)	40,541	44.3
8 Sidney C. Roach (R)	30,158	53.8
William L. Nelson (D)	25,733	45.9
9 Theodore W. Hukriede (R)	39,213	52.2
Champ Clark (D)	35,626	47.5
10 Cleveland A. Newton (R)	122,100	61.1
Hughes (D)	65,472	32.8
11 Harry B. Hawes (D)	35,726	49.8
Bernard P. Bogy (R)	33,592	46.8
12 Leonidas C. Dyer (R)	28,400	60.6
Samuel Rosenfeld (D)	16,901	36.1
13 Marion E. Rhodes (R)	30,610	55.2
A. T. Brewster (D)	24,394	44.0
14 Edward D. Hays (R)	56,525	56.8
Robert L. Ward (D)	41,547	41.8
15 Isaac V. McPherson (R)	44,176	55.7
E. M. Roseberry (D)	33,844	42.7
16 Samuel A. Shelton (R)	28,500	54.5
Thomas L. Rubey (D)	23,510	45.0

MONTANA

Candidates	Votes	%
1 Washington J. McCormick (R)	39,729	57.2
Burton Watson (D)	29,688	42.8
2 Carl W. Riddick (R)	68,486	64.9
M. McCusker (D)	37,104	35.1

NEBRASKA

Candidates	Votes	%
1 C. Frank Reavis (R)	35,293	67.6
Frank A. Peterson (D)	16,880	32.4
2 Albert W. Jefferis (R)	33,196	64.4
James O'Hara (D)	18,346	35.6
3 Robert E. Evans (R)	38,370	54.0
Webb Rice (D)	17,171	24.2
Marie Weekes (I)	15,516	21.8
4 Melvin O. McLaughlin (R)	34,384	62.5
Albert P. Sprague (D)	20,662	37.5
5 William E. Andrews (R)	31,695	58.3
Harry S. Dungan (D)	22,663	41.7
6 Moses P. Kinkaid (R)	49,122	64.5
Thomas C. Grimes (D)	20,790	27.3
Lucien Stebbins (I)	6,222	8.2

NEVADA

Candidates	Votes	%
AL Samuel S. Arentz (R)	13,149	48.9
Charles R. Evans (D)	9,167	34.1
Paul Jones (I)	3,349	12.5

NEW HAMPSHIRE

Candidates	Votes	%
1 Sherman E. Burroughs (R)	46,606	59.3
Rosecrans W. Pillsbury (D)	31,354	39.9
2 Edward H. Wason (R)	46,720	61.4
Charles J. French (D)	29,376	38.6

NEW JERSEY

Candidates	Votes	%
1 Francis F. Patterson Jr. (R)	55,885	65.3
W. P. Kramer (D)	23,711	27.7
2 Isaac Bacharach (R)	51,006	70.0
William E. Jonah (D)	21,511	29.5
3 T. Frank Appleby (R)	55,098	64.4
W. E. Ramsay (D)	29,796	34.8
4 Elijah C. Hutchinson (R)	39,582	55.0
Charles Browne (D)	31,695	44.0
5 Ernest R. Ackerman (R)	53,681	68.8
R. E. Clement (D)	21,949	28.1
6 Randolph Perkins (R)	54,334	66.4
Thomas A. Shields (D)	25,764	31.5
7 Amos H. Radcliff (R)	33,844	64.5
Nicholas Hughes (D)	15,291	29.2
Frank Hubschmitt (SOC)	2,939	5.6
8 Herbert W. Taylor (R)	41,898	59.3
C. A. McGlennon (D)	27,822	39.4
9 Richard W. Parker (R)	32,240	59.3
Daniel F. Minahan (D)	20,244	37.3
10 Frederick R. Lehlbach (R)	40,965	63.6

Candidates	Votes	%
Dallas Flannagan (D)	19,548	30.4
11 Archibald E. Olpp (R)	30,046	55.2
John J. Eagan (D)	23,402	43.0
12 Charles F. X. O'Brien (D)	34,527	53.1
Walter Williams (R)	29,080	44.8

Special Election

1 Francis F. Patterson Jr. (R)	54,971	67.2
W. P. Kramer (D)	23,279	28.5

NEW MEXICO

Candidates	Votes	%
AL Nestor Montoya (R)	54,672	51.9
Antonio Lucero (D)	49,426	46.9

NEW YORK

Candidates	Votes	%
1 Frederick C. Hicks (R & P)	61,502	69.5
Alfred J. Kennedy (D)	24,868	28.1
2 John J. Kindred (D)	42,530	47.7
Rudolph Hantusch (R)	40,201	45.1
William Burkle Sr. (SOC)	5,872	6.6
3 John Kissel (R)	16,576	44.6
Christian J. McWilliams (D)	15,224	40.9
Harry W. Laidler (SOC)	5,257	14.1
4 Thomas H. Cullen (D)	21,070	56.2
James J. Astorita (R)	14,686	39.2
5 Ardolph L. Kline (R)	42,129	58.2
Edward Cassin (D)	27,650	38.2
6 Warren I. Lee (R)	44,527	59.4
William F. X. Geoghan (D)	22,476	30.0
W. W. Passage (SOC)	6,867	9.2
7 Michael J. Hogan (R)	20,489	46.5
James P. Maher (D)	16,554	37.6
Jean Jacques Coronel (SOC)	6,561	14.9
8 Charles G. Bond (R)	30,916	49.1
William E. Cleary (D)	22,586	35.8
Victor H. Lawn (SOC)	9,124	14.5
9 Andrew N. Petersen (R)	41,399	52.1
David J. O'Connell (D)	30,212	38.1
Wilhemus B. Robinson (SOC)	7,420	9.3
10 Lester D. Volk (R)	25,808	50.0
Gilbert H. Rhoades (D)	14,071	27.3
James O'Neal (SOC)	11,529	22.4
11 Daniel J. Riordan (D)	19,097	50.7
Wilbur F. Wakeman (R)	17,358	46.1
12 Meyer London (SOC)	10,212	54.1
Henry M. Goldfogle (D, R)	8,654	45.9
13 Christopher D. Sullivan (D, R)	8,979	64.6
Charles W. Irwin (SOC)	4,925	35.4
14 Nathan S. Perlman (R, D)	18,042	67.9
Algernon Lee (SOC)	8,515	32.1
15 Thomas J. Ryan (R)	18,936	51.6
Peter J. Dooling (D)	14,971	40.8
16 W. Bourke Cockran (D)	19,275	53.0
Warren S. Fisher (R & P)	14,336	39.4
Bertha H. Mailly (SOC)	2,748	7.6
17 Ogden L. Mills (R)	33,659	62.0
Herbert J. Pell Jr. (D)	18,345	33.8
18 John F. Carew (D)	12,169	31.2
Henry J. O'Connor (R)	11,148	28.6
Jeremiah A. O'Leary (F-LAB)	9,998	25.7
Marie MacDonald (SOC)	5,668	14.5
19 Walter M. Chandler (R)	41,832	59.2
William Kennelly (D)	23,126	32.7
Esther Friedman (SOC)	5,667	8.0
20 Isaac Siegel (R, D)	12,605	57.2
Morris Hillquit (SOC)	9,442	42.8
21 Martin C. Ansorge (R)	48,959	58.7
Jerome F. Donovan (D)	28,535	34.2
22 Anthony J. Griffin (D)	20,389	45.7
Wilbur J. Murphy (R)	17,657	39.6
Patrick J. Murphy (SOC)	6,580	14.7
23 Albert B. Rossdale (R)	38,915	39.4
Richard F. McKiniry (D)	36,835	37.3
Abraham Josephson (SOC)	22,949	23.3
24 Benjamin L. Fairchild (R)	50,409	53.7
James V. Ganly (D)	28,006	29.8
George Orr (SOC)	15,550	16.6

Candidates	Votes	%
25 James W. Husted (R & P)	49,829	67.4
A. Outram Sherman (D)	20,632	27.9
26 Hamilton Fish Jr. (R & P)	43,916	63.7
Rosslyn M. Cox (D)	22,772	33.0
27 Charles B. Ward (R)	42,504	60.8
John R. Green (D)	23,115	33.1
28 Peter G. Ten Eyck (D)	51,210	53.8
Edward J. Halter (R)	42,214	44.4
29 James S. Parker (R & P)	54,313	67.9
J. Ward Russell (D)	23,663	29.6
30 Frank Crowther (R & P)	41,413	61.9
John E. Kelly (D)	18,687	27.9
Harry Christian (SOC)	6,242	9.3
31 Bertrand H. Snell (R & P)	45,059	74.7
John C. Russell (D)	14,772	24.5
32 Luther W. Mott (R & P)	53,249	72.6
Newton S. Beebe (D)	20,085	27.4
33 Homer P. Snyder (R)	47,251	64.6
Roger W. Huntington (D)	21,732	29.7
34 John Davenport Clarke (R)	52,809	69.8
Charles R. Seymour (D)	21,496	28.4
35 Walter W. Magee (R)	60,018	65.0
John F. Nash (D)	25,699	27.8
36 Norman J. Gould (R & P)	49,160	67.6
George K. Shuler (D)	23,534	32.4
37 Alanson B. Houghton (R & P)	51,512	68.0
Charles L. Durham (D)	21,762	28.7
38 Thomas B. Dunn (R & P)	56,796	66.0
Hiram H. Wood (D)	20,281	23.6
Charles Messinger (SOC)	8,369	9.7
39 Archie D. Sanders (R & P)	53,079	71.1
David A. White (D)	17,602	23.6
George Weber (SOC)	3,943	5.3
40 S. Wallace Dempsey (R & P)	56,129	69.5
Frank S. Nicholson (D)	19,253	23.8
Augustus Meas (SOC)	5,389	6.7
41 Clarence MacGregor (R & P)	30,560	54.5
Al J. Egloff (D)	20,692	36.9
Martin B. Heisler (SOC)	4,836	8.6
42 James M. Mead (D)	22,869	48.3
C. Hamilton Cook (R & P)	21,224	44.9
John H. Gibbons (SOC)	3,218	6.8
43 Daniel A. Reed (R & P)	52,343	74.4
Fred H. Sylvester (D)	13,720	19.5
Gust C. Peterson (SOC)	4,273	6.1

NORTH CAROLINA

Candidates	Votes	%
1 Hallett S. Ward (D)	21,414	74.1
Wheeler Martin (R)	7,495	25.9
2 Claude Kitchin (D)	20,890	86.1
W. O. Dixon (R)	3,367	13.9
3 Samuel L. Brinson (D)	21,547	56.9
Richard L. Herring (R)	16,347	43.1
4 Edward W. Pou (D)	26,470	65.3
James D. Parker (R)	14,084	34.7
5 Charles M. Stedman (D)	45,301	54.1
William D. Merritt (R)	38,484	45.9
6 Homer L. Lyon (D)	24,174	68.7
R. S. White (R)	11,040	31.4
7 William C. Hammer (D)	37,071	53.1
William H. Cox (R)	32,784	46.9
8 Robert L. Doughton (D)	32,934	51.2
J. Ike Campbell (R)	31,456	48.9
9 Alfred L. Bulwinkle (D)	40,195	53.0
Jake F. Newell (R)	35,686	47.0
10 Zebulon Weaver (D)	36,923	51.6
L. L. Jenkins (R)	34,625	48.4

NORTH DAKOTA

Candidates	Votes	%
1 Olger B. Burtness (R)	43,530	57.6
John M. Baer (I N-PART)	32,072	42.4
2 George M. Young (R)	34,849	51.7
Ole H. Olson (I N-PART)	32,618	48.4
3 James H. Sinclair (R)	41,409	62.9
R. H. Johnson (D&I)	24,460	37.1

OHIO

	Candidates	Votes	%
1	Nicholas Longworth (R)	57,328	57.6
	John H. Allen (D)	40,195	40.4
2	Ambrose E. B. Stephens (R)	47,797	52.6
	Thomas H. Morrow (D)	41,781	46.0
3	Roy G. Fitzgerald (R)	66,259	50.2
	William G. Pickrel (D)	59,214	44.9
4	John S. Cable (R)	50,478	52.6
	B. F. Welty (D)	45,489	47.4
5	Charles J. Thompson (R)	40,384	61.4
	Newt Bronson (D)	25,395	38.6
6	Charles C. Kearns (R)	38,044	55.2
	Cleona Searles (D)	30,903	44.8
7	Simeon D. Fess (R)	73,794	61.0
	Paul F. Dye (D)	47,196	39.0
8	R. Clint Cole (R)	43,473	54.3
	Fred E. Guthery (D)	36,665	45.8
9	William W. Chalmers (R)	49,732	56.5
	Isaac R. Sherwood (D)	38,292	43.5
10	Israel M. Foster (R)	38,436	64.2
	Benjamin F. Reynolds (D)	21,429	35.8
11	Edwin D. Ricketts (R)	33,524	51.7
	Mell G. Underwood (D)	31,359	48.3
12	John C. Speaks (R)	62,247	57.9
	Arthur P. Lamneck (D)	43,845	40.8
13	James T. Begg (R)	48,416	64.5
	Alfred Waggoner (D)	26,646	35.5
14	Charles L. Knight (R)	63,010	52.6
	Martin L. Davey (D)	56,507	47.2
15	C. Ellis Moore (R)	42,419	58.3
	John Sherman Talbott (D)	30,326	41.7
16	Joseph H. Himes (R)	56,584	56.9
	John McSweeney Jr. (D)	42,799	43.1
17	William M. Morgan (R)	46,968	50.2
	William A. Ashbrook (D)	46,675	49.8
18	Frank Murphy (R)	52,862	61.7
	Albert O. Barnes (D)	32,802	38.3
19	John G. Cooper (R)	60,147	70.4
	James Kennedy (D)	25,250	29.6
20	Miner G. Norton (R)	35,483	56.0
	Charles A. Mooney (D)	27,223	42.9
21	Harry C. Gahn (R)	27,127	59.1
	John J. Babka (D)	18,252	39.7
22	Theodore E. Burton (R)	91,062	74.3
	Mathew B. Excell (D)	30,738	25.1

OKLAHOMA

	Candidates	Votes	%
1	Thomas A. Chandler (R)	42,782	53.3
	E. B. Howard (D)	35,201	43.8
2	Alice M. Robertson (R)	24,188	48.8
	W. W. Hastings (D)	23,979	48.4
3	Charles D. Carter (D)	33,347	51.3
	James L. Shinaberger (R)	27,465	42.2
	Robert L. Allen (SOC)	4,227	6.5
4	Joseph C. Pringey (R)	31,458	48.6
	Tom D. McKeown (D)	29,832	46.1
	J. E. Bartos (SOC)	3,438	5.3
5	Fletcher B. Swank (D)	35,067	50.6
	B. T. Hainer (R)	31,304	45.2
6	Lorraine M. Gensman (R)	26,076	47.7
	Elmer Thomas (D)	25,304	46.3
	J. V. Kolachny (SOC)	3,202	5.9
7	James V. McClintic (D)	21,422	49.4
	D. Montgomery (R)	17,664	40.8
	O. E. Enfield (SOC)	4,251	9.8
8	Manuel Herrick (R)	31,265	53.9
	Zach A. Harris (D)	23,405	40.4
	H. C. Geist (SOC)	3,304	5.7

Special Election

		Votes	%
8	Charles Swindall (R)	32,420	55.3
	Zach A. Harris (D)	22,389	38.2
	H. C. Geist (SOC)	3,835	6.5

OREGON

	Candidates	Votes	%
1	Willis C. Hawley (R-D-P)	75,597	90.2
	Harlin Talbert (SOC)	8,258	9.9
2	Nicholas J. Sinnott (R)	29,655	69.4
	James Harvey Graham (D)	13,049	30.6
3	Clifton N. McArthur (R)	37,884	51.9
	Esther Lovejoy (P)	31,853	43.6

PENNSYLVANIA

	Candidates	Votes	%
1	William S. Vare (R)	43,108	73.9
	Lawrence E. McCrossin (D)	11,682	20.0
	H. J. Nelson (SOC)	3,509	6.0
2	George S. Graham (R)	34,848	78.7
	Herman Becker (D)	7,877	17.8
3	Harry C. Ransley (R, LAB)	29,075	77.2
	Joseph Hagerty (D)	6,991	18.6
4	George W. Edmonds (R)	41,102	72.3
	Harry J. Ruesscamp (D)	12,003	21.1
	L. L. Klein (SOC)	2,969	5.2
5	James J. Connolly (R)	48,455	69.1
	Henry J. Burns (D)	15,671	22.4
6	George P. Darrow (R, P)	104,576	73.5
	Harry S. Jeffery (D)	33,363	23.5
7	Thomas S. Butler (R, P)	52,863	75.6
	Freeland S. Brown (D)	15,942	22.8
8	Henry W. Watson (R)	44,032	67.5
	Harvey S. Plummer (D)	18,605	28.5
9	William W. Griest (R)	29,252	74.2
	David F. Magee (D)	9,504	24.1
10	Charles R. Connell (R)	35,181	52.1
	Patrick McLane (D)	30,411	45.0
11	Clarence D. Coughlin (R, P)	45,092	59.7
	John J. Casey (D, SOC)	30,412	40.3
12	John Reber (R)	26,816	55.2
	Thomas J. Butler (D)	21,787	44.8
13	Fred B. Gernerd (R)	38,026	50.6
	Harry J. Dunn (D, LAB)	29,922	39.8
	Charles E. Yeager (SOC)	6,245	8.3
14	Louis T. McFadden (R, P)	27,782	76.0
	Thomas A. Doherty (D)	8,248	22.6
15	Edgar R. Kiess (R, P)	30,182	71.6
	C. Edmund Gilmore (D)	10,802	25.6
16	I. Clinton Kline (R, P)	25,980	52.1
	John V. Lesher (D)	22,417	45.0
17	Benjamin K. Focht (R, P)	29,874	62.6
	John C. Dunkle (D)	17,234	36.1
18	Aaron S. Kreider (R, P)	42,745	64.1
	Milton H. Plank (D)	18,951	28.4
	George A. Herring (LAB)	4,110	6.2
19	John M. Rose (R)	35,068	53.5
	Warren Worth Bailey (D)	18,865	28.8
	William T. Welsh (LAB, SOC)	9,842	15.0
20	Edward S. Brooks (R)	22,989	51.7
	Charles A. Hawkins (D, P)	20,701	46.5
21	Evan J. Jones (R, P)	27,780	63.4
	J. D. Connelly (D, LAB)	15,000	34.2
22	Adam M. Wyant (R)	30,540	51.6
	John H. Wilson (D)	22,533	38.1
	S. E. Miller (SOC)	3,234	5.5
23	Samuel A. Kendall (R, P)	36,152	59.0
	Bruce F. Sterling (D)	23,517	38.4
24	Henry W. Temple (R, P)	42,402	73.3
	Samuel Amspoker (D)	15,405	26.7
25	Milton W. Shreve (P, I)	19,706	43.0
	Robert J. Firman (R)	18,785	41.0
	Max B. Haibach (D)	5,442	11.9
26	William H. Kirkpatrick (R)	25,446	56.0
	George W. Geiser Jr. (D)	19,219	42.3
27	Nathan L. Strong (R, P)	31,209	71.4
	Lafayette F. Sutter (D, P)	10,814	24.7
28	Harris J. Bixler (R, D)	28,718	56.4
	Willis J. Hulings (P, CIT)	20,676	40.6
29	Stephen G. Porter (R, P)	32,766	69.5
	George J. Shaffer (D)	10,749	22.8
	James J. Marshall (SOC)	3,604	7.7
30	M. Clyde Kelly (R, D)	51,850	91.5
	Charles A. Fike (SOC)	4,847	8.6
31	John M. Morin (R, D)	29,399	89.8

	Candidates	Votes	%
	Albert R. Jerling (SOC)	2,280	7.0
32	Guy E. Campbell (R, D)	44,307	83.9
	Earl O. Gunther (SOC)	4,552	8.6
	George E. Briggs (P)	3,953	7.5
AL	Anderson H. Walters (R)	1,140,836✓	
	William J. Burke (R)	1,134,013✓	
	Mahlon M. Garland (R)	1,126,406*	
	Joseph McLaughlin (R)	1,108,538✓	
	John P. Bracken (D)	466,564	
	M. J. Hanlan (D)	463,866	
	Charles M. Bowman (D)	459,552	
	John B. McDonough (D)	444,306	
	Flora J. Diefenderfer (P)	89,683	
	George Hart (P)	85,771	
	Luther S. Kauffman (P)	85,375	
	Charles J. Bauer (SOC)	67,596	
	A. M. Buckwalter (SOC)	66,628	
	Edward W. Hayden (SOC)	65,928	
	Henry W. Schlegel (SOC)	65,058	
	F. E. Whittlesey (P)	60,278	
	Frieda S. Miller (LAB)	25,265	
	Howard Cessna (LAB)	24,062	
	William A. Hagan (SINGLE T)	1,795	
	William R. Kline (SINGLE T)	1,790	
	Thomas A. Kavanagh (SINGLE T)	1,766	
	Joseph E. Robinson (SINGLE T)	1,727	
	Joseph P. Smith (INDL)	1,197	
	Frank Kalcec (INDL)	977	
	Herman Spittal (INDL)	810	
	Joseph Rack (INDL)	794	

Special Election

		Votes	%
3	Harry C. Ransley (R, LAB)	29,097	76.6
	Joseph Hagerty (D)	7,041	18.6

RHODE ISLAND

		Votes	%
1	Clark Burdick (R)	37,116	67.9
	Patrick J. Boyle (D)	17,537	32.1
2	Walter R. Stiness (R)	33,801	62.5
	Luigi De Pasquale (D)	19,004	35.1
3	Ambrose Kennedy (R)	34,775	59.7
	Herve J. Legace (D)	22,386	38.4

SOUTH CAROLINA

		Votes	%
1	W. Turner Logan (D)	6,301	92.6
	Saspartas (R)	502	7.4
2	James F. Byrnes (D)	6,685	100.0
3	Fred H. Dominick (D)	9,699	100.0
4	John J. McSwain (D)	13,436	100.0
5	William F. Stevenson (D)	10,186	100.0
6	Philip H. Stoll (D)	8,681	100.0
7	Hampton P. Fulmer (D)	9,412	91.9
	Hawkins (R)	834	8.1

SOUTH DAKOTA

		Votes	%
1	Charles A. Christopherson (R)	39,231	56.2
	Engebret J. Holter (NON PART)	15,810	22.6
	Ralph E. Johnson (D)	14,815	21.2
2	Royal C. Johnson (R)	44,759	62.3
	Frank Wahlen (NON PART)	18,357	25.5
	Lewis W. Bicknell (D)	8,770	12.2
3	William Williamson (R)	19,335	48.0
	Harry L. Gandy (D)	16,214	40.2
	O. E. Farnam (NON PART)	4,765	11.8

TENNESSEE

		Votes	%
1	B. Carroll Reece (R)	46,010	98.3
2	J. Will Taylor (R)	37,722	74.8
	Curtis Gentry (D)	12,436	24.7
3	Joseph Brown (R)	29,366	51.6
	John A. Moon (D)	27,149	47.7
4	Wynne F. Clouse (R)	22,440	50.3
	Cordell Hull (D)	22,109	49.5
5	Ewin L. Davis (D)	14,845	61.9
	Jesse Davenport (R)	9,102	38.0

	Candidates	Votes	%
6	Joseph W. Byrns (D)	24,422	82.9
	W. T. Perry (R)	4,679	15.9
7	Lemuel P. Padgett (D)	17,517	55.7
	A. M. Hughes (R)	13,813	43.9
8	Lon A. Scott (R)	22,938	50.6
	Gordon Browning (D)	22,279	49.1
9	Finis J. Garrett (D)	25,409	68.3
	John R. Walker Jr (R)	11,671	31.4
10	Hubert F. Fisher (D)	23,987	80.8
	Wayman Wilkerson (I, R)	4,927	16.6

TEXAS

	Candidates	Votes	%
1	Eugene Black (D)	17,814	92.3
	G. T. Bartlett (R)	1,497	7.8
2	John C. Box (D)	21,692	92.8
	G. E. H. Meyer (AM)	1,671	7.2
3	Morgan G. Sanders (D)	15,575	83.2
	J. A. Butler (R)	3,149	16.8
4	Sam Rayburn (D)	17,795	77.6
	A. W. Acheson (R)	5,124	22.4
5	Hatton W. Sumners (D)	19,785	80.2
	J. O. Burleson (R)	4,883	19.8
6	Rufus Hardy (D)	17,555	72.5
	Clyde Essex (AM)	3,668	15.2
	D. H. Merrill (R)	2,512	10.4
7	Clay Stone Briggs (D)	12,656	96.6
8	Daniel E. Garrett (D)	18,474	55.7
	E. B. Barden (R)	7,001	21.1
	M. H. Broyles (B&T R)	5,750	17.4
	J. M. Gibson (AM)	1,918	5.8
9	Joseph J. Mansfield (D)	12,311	58.7
	James W. Rugeley (R)	8,667	41.3
10	James P. Buchanan (D)	14,411	65.5
	B. G. Neighbors (AM)	7,597	34.5
11	Tom T. Connally (D)	15,621	79.1
	W. D. Lewis (AM)	4,124	20.9
12	Fritz G. Lanham (D)	20,925	80.5
	Sam Davidson (R)	4,203	16.2
13	Lucian W. Parish (D)	18,951	88.4
	C. W. Johnson (R)	2,483	11.6
14	Harry M. Wurzbach (R)	17,265	55.6
	Carlos Bee (D)	13,771	44.4
15	John N. Garner (D)	10,265	99.9
16	Claude B. Hudspeth (D)	15,658	69.7
	William S. Easterling (R)	6,796	30.3
17	Thomas L. Blanton (D)	22,311	83.8
	W. D. Cowan (AM)	4,298	16.2
18	Marvin Jones (D)	25,996	97.0

UTAH

	Candidates	Votes	%
1	Don B. Colton (R)	41,749	57.3
	James W. Funk (D)	27,974	38.4
2	Elmer O. Leatherwood (R)	39,235	54.8
	Mathonihah Thomas (D)	28,201	39.4

VERMONT

		Votes	%
1	Frank L. Greene (R)	33,670	74.7
	Jeremiah C. Durick (D)	11,398	25.3
2	Porter H. Dale (R, P)	34,221	78.7
	Harry W. Witters (D)	9,189	21.1

VIRGINIA

		Votes	%
1	Schuyler Otis Bland (D)	14,646	79.8
	S. P. Powell (R)	3,562	19.4
2	Joseph T. Deal (D)	15,318	73.6
	Menalcus Lankford (R)	5,389	25.9
3	Andrew J. Montague (D)	20,069	72.5
	Walker G. Decourcy (R)	4,146	15.0
	H. H. Price	2,682	9.7
4	Patrick Henry Drewry (D)	11,427	92.6
	F. L. Mason (R)	909	7.4
5	Rorer A. James (D)	15,567	58.4
	S. Floyd Landreth (R)	11,109	41.6
6	James P. Woods (D)	13,101	59.0
	W. M. Doah (R)	9,114	41.0
7	Thomas W. Harrison (D)	13,221‡	50.9
	John Paul (R)	12,773	49.1
8	R. Walton Moore (D)	13,142	71.7
	F. M. Broyles (R)	5,200	28.4
9	C. Bascom Slemp (R)	28,057	54.8
	Bolling H. Handy (D)	23,100	45.2
10	Henry D. Flood (D)	14,811	64.8
	James H. C. Grasty (R)	8,027	35.1

WASHINGTON

		Votes	%
1	John F. Miller (R)	51,459	56.7
	James A. Duncan (F-LAB)	28,154	31.0
	Hugh C. Todd (D)	11,184	12.3
2	Lindley H. Hadley (R)	39,315	59.8
	William Bouck (F-LAB)	26,398	40.2
3	Albert Johnson (R)	50,667	55.7
	Homer T. Bone (F-LAB)	27,824	30.6
	George P. Fishburne (D)	12,553	13.8
4	John W. Summers (R)	37,986	63.2
	Fred Miller (D)	11,353	18.9
	Knute Hill (F-LAB)	10,735	17.9

	Candidates	Votes	%
5	J. Stanley Webster (R)	39,228	58.1
	Charles A. Fleming (D)	28,300	41.9

WEST VIRGINIA

		Votes	%
1	Benjamin L. Rosenbloom (R)	40,818	50.3
	Matthew M. Neely (D)	40,393	49.7
2	George M. Bowers (R)	43,238	56.8
	Forrest W. Brown (D)	32,896	43.2
3	Stuart F. Reed (R)	45,146	57.7
	Robert F. Kidd (D)	33,056	42.3
4	Harry C. Woodyard (R)	47,146	55.4
	John L. Conner (D)	37,951	44.6
5	Wells Goodykoontz (R)	45,193	54.1
	W. W. McNeal (D)	38,394	45.9
6	Leonard Sidney Echols (R)	51,747	54.4
	William Edwin Wilson (D)	43,327	45.6

WISCONSIN

		Votes	%
1	Henry Allen Cooper (R)	51,144	75.9
	Andrew F. Stahl (D)	13,661	20.3
2	Edward Voigt (R)	39,563	67.3
	Harry W. Bolens (D)	14,291	24.3
	Jacob F. Miller (SOC)	4,969	8.5
3	John M. Nelson (R)	44,359	69.1
	James W. Murphy (D)	19,794	30.8
4	John C. Kleczka (R)	28,854	50.2
	Robert Buech (SOC)	22,137	38.6
	Gerald P. Hayes (D)	6,436	11.2
5	William H. Stafford (R)	40,777	54.5
	Victor L. Berger (SOC)	34,004	45.5
6	Florian Lampert (R)	38,034	68.7
	Leo P. Fox (D)	11,606	21.0
	Edward C. Damrow (SOC)	5,714	10.3
7	Joseph D. Beck (R)	37,137	78.4
	Robert H. Clarke (D)	8,929	18.8
8	Edward E. Browne (R)	34,215	61.8
	George W. Lippert (SOC)	14,661	26.5
	Leo P. Pasternacki (D)	6,425	11.6
9	David G. Classon (R)	32,027	59.2
	Andrew R. McDonald (D)	20,108	37.2
10	James A. Frear (R)	44,658	99.4
11	Adolphus P. Nelson (R)	38,057	85.3
	John P. Jensen (D)	6,524	14.6

WYOMING

		Votes	%
AL	Frank W. Mondell (R)	34,689	61.5
	Wade H. Fowler (D)	14,952	26.5
	James Morgan (F-LAB)	6,021	10.7

1921 House Election

PENNSYLVANIA

Special Election

AL	Thomas S. Crago (R)	705,876	68.2
	John P. Bracken (D)	225,268	21.8
	B. E. P. Prugh (P)	74,837	7.2

1922 House Elections

ALABAMA

	Candidates	Votes	%
1	John McDuffie (D)	13,960	100.0
2	John R. Tyson (D)	9,255	100.0
3	Henry B. Steagall (D)	9,141	90.3
	Charles E. Roberts	987	9.8
4	Lamar Jeffers (D)	9,976	81.5
	J. C. Harper	2,265	18.5
5	William B. Bowling (D)	10,411	80.4
	W. M. Russell	2,539	19.6
6	William B. Oliver (D)	4,864	100.0
7	Miles C. Allgood (D)	18,597	62.6
	B. L. Noogin	11,130	37.4
8	Edward B. Almon (D)	12,303	96.3
9	George Huddleston (D)	11,300	94.7
	G. L. Lemon	630	5.3
10	William B. Bankhead (D)	14,803	63.2
	W. A. McMurray	8,631	36.8

ARIZONA

	Candidates	Votes	%
AL	Carl Hayden (D)	37,262	71.9
	Emma M. Guild (R)	14,601	28.2

ARKANSAS

	Candidates	Votes	%
1	William J. Driver (D)	1,454	100.0
2	William A. Oldfield (D)	5,220	86.7
	J. N. Hout	798	13.3
3	John N. Tillman (D)	5,327	98.2
4	Otis Wingo (D)	7,330	79.5
	George Tillis	1,896	20.6
5	Heartsill Ragon (D)	5,944	79.7
	John W. White	1,513	20.3
6	Lewis E. Sawyer (D)	3,232	100.0
7	Tilman B. Parks (D)	2,167	100.0

CALIFORNIA

	Candidates	Votes	%
1	Clarence F. Lea (DR)	53,129	100.0
2	John E. Raker (DR)	32,981	100.0
3	Charles F. Curry (R-D)	71,316	91.5
	Marcus H. Steely (SOC)	6,561	8.4
4	Julius Kahn (R-D)	46,527	82.9
	Hugo Ernst (SOC)	9,547	17.0
5	John I. Nolan (R-D)	49,414*	99.8
6	James H. MacLafferty (R)	59,858	66.4
	Hugh W. Brunk (D)	22,711	25.2
	Elvina S. Beals (SOC)	7,616	8.4
7	Henry E. Barbour (R-D)	67,000	99.9
8	Arthur Monroe Free (R-D)	57,926	99.8
9	Walter F. Lineberger (R)	66,265	59.1
	Charles H. Randall (P & D)	45,794	40.9
10	Henry Z. Osborne (R-D-P)	98,739*	99.9
11	Philip D. Swing (R-D)	79,039	91.3
	George Bauer (SOC)	7,466	8.6

Special Election

		Votes	%
6	James H. MacLafferty (I)	53,285	68.4
	Hugh W. Brunk (I)	24,626	31.6

COLORADO

	Candidates	Votes	%
1	William N. Vaile (R)	32,939	55.5
	Benjamin C. Hilliard (D)	25,477	42.9
2	Charles B. Timberlake (R)	43,601	57.3
	Charles M. Worth (D)	32,443	42.7
3	Guy U. Hardy (R)	43,508	52.4
	Chester B. Horn (D)	39,500	47.6
4	Edward T. Taylor (D)	30,331	64.3
	Merle D. Vincent (R)	16,878	35.8

CONNECTICUT

	Candidates	Votes	%
1	E. Hart Fenn (R)	40,124	52.2
	Joseph F. Dutton (D)	35,003	45.6
2	Richard P. Freeman (R)	31,484	55.4
	Raymond J. Jodoin (D)	24,732	43.5
3	John Q. Tilson (R)	36,247	52.3
	Stephen Whitney (D)	31,674	45.7
4	Schuyler Merritt (R)	35,274	53.9
	Archibald McNeil (D)	28,992	44.3
5	Patrick B. O'Sullivan (D)	27,359	49.7
	James P. Glynn (R)	27,065	49.1

DELAWARE

	Candidates	Votes	%
AL	William H. Boyce (D)	39,126	53.9
	Caleb R. Layton (R)	32,577	44.9

FLORIDA

	Candidates	Votes	%
1	Herbert J. Drane (D)	14,371	82.9
	William M. Gober (R)	2,961	17.1
2	Frank Clark (D)	6,931	100.0
3	John H. Smithwick (D)	7,564	100.0
4	William J. Sears (D)	15,678	82.3
	Howard W. McCay (R)	3,362	17.6

GEORGIA

	Candidates	Votes	%
1	R. Lee Moore (D)	5,579	90.0
	D. H. Clarke (R)	426	6.9
2	Frank Park (D)	5,449	100.0
3	Charles R. Crisp (D)	7,298	100.0
4	William C. Wright (D)	4,777	100.0
5	William D. Upshaw (D)	4,646	93.1
	Max H. Wilensky	347	7.0
6	James W. Wise (D)	6,961	100.0
7	Gordon Lee (D)	7,278	100.0
8	Charles H. Brand (D)	5,148	100.0
9	Thomas M. Bell (D)	11,088	94.6
10	Carl Vinson (D)	4,639	100.0
11	William C. Lankford (D)	6,879	100.0
12	William W. Larsen (D)	5,020	100.0

IDAHO

	Candidates	Votes	%
1	Burton L. French (R)	24,167	46.8
	George Waters (D)	13,772	26.7
	W. W. Deal (PROG)	13,673	26.5
2	Addison T. Smith (R)	33,206	47.8
	W. P. Whitaker (D)	19,875	28.6
	Dow Dunning (PROG)	16,450	23.7

ILLINOIS

	Candidates	Votes	%
1	Martin B. Madden (R)	23,895	59.1
	George Mayer (D)	15,999	39.6
2	James R. Mann (R)	58,694*	58.2
	Adam F. Bloch (D)	38,487	38.2
3	Elliott W. Sproul (R)	48,486	48.8
	Thomas M. Crane (D)	47,335	47.7
4	John W. Rainey (D)	32,403	69.2
	Henry G. Dobler (R)	13,328	28.5
5	Adolph J. Sabath (D)	20,377	66.5
	Jacob Gartenstein (R)	9,007	29.4
6	James R. Buckley (D)	58,928	48.2
	John J. Gorman (R)	58,886	48.2
7	M. Alfred Michaelson (R)	69,367	49.8
	Frank M. Padden (D)	61,035	43.8
	John M. Collins (SOC)	7,276	5.2
8	Stanley Henry Kunz (D)	18,749	65.3
	Fred S. DeCola (R)	9,311	32.5
9	Fred A. Britten (R)	26,143	60.0
	James A. Prendergast (D)	16,223	37.3
10	Carl R. Chindblom (R)	62,324	61.6
	Bernard Moulton Wiedinger (D)	35,535	35.1
11	Frank R. Reid (R)	43,581	68.8
	Edward J. O'Beirne (D)	18,816	29.7
12	Charles E. Fuller (R)	46,893	77.6
	John A. Dowdall (D)	11,733	19.4
13	John C. McKenzie (R)	30,064	70.0
	William G. Curtiss (D)	12,319	28.7
14	William J. Graham (R)	34,946	59.9
	L. S. Mayer (D)	21,541	36.9
15	Edward J. King (R)	36,547	60.1
	Charles C. Craig (D)	23,298	38.3
16	William E. Hull (R)	39,372	55.2
	Jesse Black Jr. (D)	30,395	42.6
17	Frank H. Funk (R)	28,466	55.7
	Frank Gillespie (D)	22,233	43.5
18	William P. Holaday (R)	35,880	52.8
	Andrew B. Dennis (D)	30,123	44.4
19	Allen F. Moore (R)	39,636	54.4
	Raymond D. Meeker (D)	32,529	44.6
20	Henry T. Rainey (D)	31,430	54.2
	Guy L. Shaw (R)	26,541	45.8
21	J. Earl Major (D)	37,661	49.3
	Loren E. Wheeler (R)	33,086	43.3
	Duncan McDonald (F-LAB)	4,438	5.8
22	Edward E. Miller (R)	34,224	47.6
	Edward E. Campbell (D)	31,539	43.9
	Daniel L. Thomas (F-LAB)	4,980	6.9
23	William W. Arnold (D)	38,908	52.5
	Edwin B. Brooks (R)	34,610	46.7
24	Thomas S. Williams (R)	29,141	50.8
	Dempsey T. Woodard (D)	28,252	49.2
25	Edward E. Denison (R)	37,907	54.4
	A. S. Caldwell (D)	28,697	41.2
AL	Richard Yates (R)	943,684✓	
	Henry R. Rathborne (R)	911,599✓	
	Simon J. Gorman (D)	666,583	
	William Murphy (D)	662,059	
	Fred W. Wenschoff (SOC)	36,311	
	Andrew Lafin (SOC)	35,655	
	Edward Ellis Carr (F-LAB)	32,595	
	Henry W. Olinger (F-LAB)	30,756	

Special Election

		Votes	%
AL	Winnifred Mason Huck (R)	865,971	52.6
	Allen D. Albert (D)	710,716	43.2

INDIANA

	Candidates	Votes	%
1	William E. Wilson (D)	42,797	53.6
	Oscar R. Luhring (R)	35,835	44.9
2	Arthur H. Greenwood (D)	43,632	49.5
	Oscar E. Bland (R)	42,752	48.5
3	Frank Gardner (D)	43,344	53.5
	Samuel A. Lambdin (R)	37,202	46.0
4	Harry C. Canfield (D)	43,749	51.1
	John S. Benham (R)	41,825	48.9
5	Everett Sanders (R)	38,759	49.5
	Charles H. Bidaman (D)	37,748	48.2
6	Richard N. Elliott (R)	39,281	51.6
	James A. Clifton (D)	36,818	48.4
7	Merrill Moores (R)	49,629	53.9
	Joseph P. Turk (D)	41,118	44.6
8	Albert H. Vestal (R)	43,470	52.2
	John W. Tyndall (D)	39,169	47.0
9	Fred S. Purnell (R)	46,919	51.5
	George Lee Moffett (D)	42,074	46.2
10	William R. Wood (R)	45,590	59.2
	William F. Spencer (D)	30,835	40.0
11	Samuel E. Cook (R)	45,389	52.8
	Milton Kraus (R)	39,285	45.7
12	Louis W. Fairfield (R)	36,045	51.1
	Charles W. Branstrator (D)	34,457	48.9
13	Andrew J. Hickey (R)	50,003	53.7
	Esther Kathleen O'Keefe (D)	43,053	46.3

IOWA

	Candidates	Votes	%
1	William F. Kopp (R)	26,651	65.0
	John M. Lindley (D)	14,056	34.3

Candidates	Votes	%
2 Harry E. Hull (R)	27,450	51.4
Wayne G. Cook (D)	25,620	47.9
3 Thomas J. B. Robinson (R)	34,518	57.6
Fred P. Hageman (D)	24,304	40.6
4 Gilbert N. Haugen (R)	32,586	57.1
A. M. Schanke (D)	24,532	43.0
5 Cyrenus Cole (R)	33,607	68.0
G. A. Smith (D)	15,825	32.0
6 C. William Ramseyer (R)	28,702	61.9
James E. Craven (D)	17,489	37.7
7 Cassius C. Dowell (R)	34,012	62.3
Winfred E. Robb (D)	19,987	36.6
8 Horace M. Towner (R)	30,551	56.6
J. P. Daughton (D)	23,478	43.5
9 William R. Green (R)	31,757	61.7
Paul W. Richards (D)	19,722	38.3
10 Lester J. Dickinson (R)	41,290	71.1
Mrs. Jett W. Douglas (D)	16,781	28.9
11 William D. Boies (R)	36,050	60.0
Guy M. Gillette (D)	24,027	40.0

KANSAS

Candidates	Votes	%
1 Daniel R. Anthony Jr. (R)	39,463	63.7
Frank Gragg (D)	22,480	36.3
2 Edward C. Little (R)	41,482	54.4
William H. Thompson (D)	34,816	45.6
3 William H. Sproul (R)	38,321	49.0
Charles Stephens (D)	37,829	48.4
4 Homer Hoch (R)	29,657	62.0
Walter W. Austin (D)	17,294	36.2
5 James G. Strong (R)	32,064	56.3
Clarence E. Hatfield (D)	24,881	43.7
6 Hays B. White (R)	33,464	54.1
F. W. Boyd (D)	26,666	43.1
7 Jasper N. Tincher (R)	47,515	58.3
A. S. Allphin (D)	32,159	39.5
8 William A. Ayres (R)	37,581	62.3
Richard E. Bird (R)	22,721	37.7

KENTUCKY

Candidates	Votes	%
1 Alben W. Barkley (D)	9,492	70.0
F. M. McClain (R)	4,075	30.0
2 David H. Kincheloe (D)	14,837	63.5
George W. Jolly (R)	8,541	36.5
3 Robert Y. Thomas Jr. (D)	21,189	60.9
W. O. Moats (R)	13,613	39.1
4 Ben Johnson (D)	19,142	93.1
P. N. Woodruff (F-LAB)	1,429	7.0
5 Maurice H. Thatcher (R)	38,806	49.1
Kendrick R. Lewis (D)	35,124	44.4
Herman F. Young (F-LAB)	5,154	6.5
6 Arthur B. Rouse (D)	18,131	63.9
Leo E. Keller (NON PL)	9,197	32.4
7 James C. Cantrill (D)	9,389	100.0
8 Ralph Gilbert (D)	21,296	57.4
D. H. Kincaid (R)	15,802	42.6
9 William J. Fields (D)	22,816	65.1
J. H. Stricklin (R)	12,249	34.9
10 John N. Langley (R)	17,067	55.5
F. T. Hatcher (D)	13,668	44.5
11 John M. Robsion (R)	28,086	66.6
C. J. Sipple (D)	11,396	27.0
H. H. Seavy (F-LAB)	2,670	6.3

LOUISIANA

Candidates	Votes	%
1 James O'Connor (D)	14,760	100.0
2 H. Garland Dupre (D)	12,287	100.0
3 Whitmell P. Martin (D)	1,954	99.7
4 John N. Sandlin (D)	3,618	100.0
5 Riley J. Wilson (D)	2,345	100.0
6 George K. Favrot (D)	3,317	99.5
7 Ladislas Lazaro (D)	3,069	99.5
8 James B. Aswell (D)	2,987	100.0

MAINE

Candidates	Votes	%
1 Carroll L. Beedy (R)	26,050	58.7
Louis A. Donahue (D)	18,312	41.3
2 Wallace H. White Jr. (R)	25,719	53.7
B. G. McIntire (D)	22,150	46.3
3 John E. Nelson (R)	30,654	58.4
Leon O. Tebbetts (D)	21,828	41.6
4 Ira G. Hersey (R)	18,641	60.8
James W. Sewall (D)	11,997	39.2

MARYLAND

Candidates	Votes	%
1 T. Alan Goldsborough (D)	27,117	55.8
Charles J. Butler (R)	21,524	44.3
2 Millard E. Tydings (D)	36,565	52.8
Albert Alex Blakeney (R)	31,053	44.8
3 John Philip Hill (R)	27,740	67.3
Antony Dimarco (D)	12,454	30.2
4 J. Charles Linthicum (D)	33,322	61.7
L. Edward Wolf (R)	18,972	35.1
5 Sydney E. Mudd (R)	23,764	50.8
Clarence M. Roberts (D)	21,112	45.1
6 Frederick N. Zihlman (R)	22,261	50.7
Frank W. Mish (D)	20,838	47.5

MASSACHUSETTS

Candidates	Votes	%
1 Allen T. Treadway (R)	26,229	50.7
Thomas F. Cassidy (D)	25,529	49.3
2 Frederick H. Gillett (R)	28,639	59.6
Joseph E. Kerigan (D)	19,376	40.4
3 Calvin D. Paige (R)	26,944	56.4
M. Fred O'Connell (D)	19,311	40.4
4 Samuel E. Winslow (R)	32,942	52.8
William H. Dyer (D)	29,399	47.2
5 John Jacob Rogers (R)	33,673	64.0
Andrew E. Barrett (D)	18,936	36.0
6 A. Piatt Andrew (R)	36,426	77.0
Charles I. Pettingell (D)	10,895	23.0
7 William P. Connery Jr. (D)	30,493	56.0
Frederick Butler (R)	23,978	44.0
8 Frederick W. Dallinger (R)	42,248	65.9
John F. Daly (D)	21,893	34.1
9 Charles L. Underhill (R)	31,229	57.7
Arthur D. Healey (D)	22,867	42.3
10 Peter F. Tague (D)	21,029	79.5
Loyal L. Jenkins (R)	5,422	20.5
11 George Holden Tinkham (R)	33,396	60.3
David J. Brickley (D)	21,999	39.7
12 James A. Gallivan (D)	42,779	75.9
Alexander H. Rice (R)	13,575	24.1
13 Robert Luce (R)	50,710	100.0
14 Louis A. Frothingham (R)	41,490	63.3
David W. Murray (D)	24,014	36.7
15 William S. Greene (R)	25,179	57.4
Arthur J. B. Cartier (D)	18,662	42.6
16 Charles L. Gifford (R)	23,862	54.4
James P. Doran (D)	20,021	45.6

MICHIGAN

Candidates	Votes	%
1 Robert H. Clancy (D)	22,996	55.4
Hugh Shepherd (R)	17,722	42.7
2 Earl C. Michener (R)	31,509	57.4
James W. Helme (D)	23,393	42.6
3 John M. C. Smith (R)	23,869	61.1
George Burr Smith (R)	15,226	39.0
4 John C. Ketcham (R)	26,050	65.4
Homer S. Carr (D)	13,772	34.6
5 Carl E. Mapes (R)	25,853	71.1
Claude O. Taylor (D)	10,501	28.9
6 Grant M. Hudson (R)	46,691	61.4
Charles R. Adair (D)	29,241	38.3
7 Louis C. Cramton (R)	35,328	72.3
Patrick H. Kane (D)	13,431	27.5
8 Bird J. Vincent (R)	33,864	63.4
De Witt Vought (D)	19,538	36.6
9 James C. McLaughlin (R)	21,703	95.6
10 Roy O. Woodruff (R)	23,792	100.0
11 Frank D. Scott (R)	24,390	69.3
Robert H. Rayburn (D)	10,823	30.7
12 W. Frank James (R)	26,228	79.4

Candidates	Votes	%
Frederick Kappler (D)	6,784	20.6
13 Clarence J. McLeod (R)	28,871	69.8
Ferris H. Fitch (D)	11,948	28.9

MINNESOTA

Candidates	Votes	%
1 Sydney Anderson (R)	36,698	57.3
J. F. Lynn (D)	27,316	42.7
2 Frank Clague (R)	47,591	100.0
3 Charles R. Davis (R)	42,708	69.8
Lillien Cox Gault (D)	18,462	30.2
4 Oscar E. Keller (R)	33,259	58.7
Paul E. Doty (D)	20,187	35.6
O. J. McCartney (I)	3,243	5.7
5 Walter H. Newton (R)	45,221	53.9
John R. Coan (D)	38,760	46.2
6 Harold Knutson (R)	37,201	60.9
Peter J. Seberger (F-LAB)	19,365	31.7
John Knutsen (I)	4,550	7.4
7 Ole J. Kvale (F-LAB)	42,832	59.7
Andrew J. Volstead (R)	28,918	40.3
8 Oscar J. Larson (R)	32,420	53.0
William L. Carss (D)	28,757	47.0
9 Knud Wefald (F-LAB)	35,551	56.3
Halvor Steenerson (R)	27,590	43.7
10 Thomas D. Schall (R)	53,424	80.6
Henry B. Rutledge (D)	12,843	19.4

MISSISSIPPI

Candidates	Votes	%
1 John E. Rankin (D)	9,407	99.8
2 Bill G. Lowrey (D)	7,985	94.7
William McDonough (R)	450	5.3
3 Benjamin G. Humphreys (D)	4,403	97.0
4 T. Jeff Busby (D)	9,260	98.2
5 Ross A. Collins (D)	11,336	96.3
6 T. Webber Wilson (D)	12,640	98.2
7 Percy E. Quin (D)	5,842	97.4
8 James W. Collier (D)	5,609	99.0

MISSOURI

Candidates	Votes	%
1 Milton A. Romjue (D)	30,102	55.8
Frank C. Millspaugh (R)	23,577	43.7
2 Ralph F. Lozier (D)	34,041	61.7
E. Y. Keiter (R)	21,016	38.1
3 Jacob L. Milligan (D)	25,997	52.1
Henry F. Lawrence (R)	23,919	47.9
4 Charles L. Faust (R)	28,110	51.5
William E. Spratt (D)	26,394	48.4
5 Henry L. Jost (D)	62,702	53.0
Edgar C. Ellis (R)	55,262	46.7
6 Clement C. Dickinson (D)	27,038	53.3
William O. Atkeson (R)	23,492	46.3
7 Samuel C. Major (D)	36,950	50.7
Roscoe C. Patterson (R)	35,627	48.9
8 Sidney C. Roach (R)	25,927	54.6
Mrs. St. Clair Moss (D)	21,559	45.4
9 Clarence Cannon (D)	30,063	56.6
Theodore W. Hukriede (R)	23,058	43.4
10 Cleveland A. Newton (R)	71,827	59.4
A. A. Alexander (D)	46,704	38.7
11 Harry B. Hawes (D)	24,839	58.4
Bernard P. Bogy (R)	17,188	40.4
12 Leonidas C. Dyer (R)	15,667	56.7
David D. Israel (D)	11,679	42.3
13 J. Scott Wolff (D)	23,622	51.6
Marion E. Rhodes (R)	21,870	47.8
14 James F. Fullbright (D)	37,896	52.0
Edward D. Hays (R)	34,573	47.4
15 Joe J. Manlove (R)	32,843	52.8
Frank H. Lee (D)	28,801	46.3
16 Thomas L. Rubey (D)	25,989	53.7
Phil A. Bennett (R)	22,153	45.8

MONTANA

Candidates	Votes	%
1 John M. Evans (D)	36,589	57.0
Washington J. McCormick (R)	26,684	41.6
2 Scott Leavitt (R)	46,499	54.3

Candidates	Votes	%
Preston B. Moss (D)	39,147	45.7

NEBRASKA

	Candidates	Votes	%
1	John H. Morehead (D)	25,079	49.2
	Walter L. Anderson (R)	23,075	45.3
2	Willis G. Sears (R)	26,308	48.2
	James H. Hanley (D)	25,251	46.2
	Roy M. Harrop (PROG)	3,048	5.6
3	Edgar Howard (D)	34,843	48.4
	Robert E. Evans (R)	32,930	45.7
	John Havekost (PROG)	4,252	5.9
4	Melvin O. McLaughlin (R)	29,743	51.0
	H. B. Cummins (D)	25,504	43.8
	John O. Schmidt (PROG)	3,034	5.2
5	Ashton C. Shallenberger (D)	26,923	45.9
	William E. Andrews (R)	25,456	43.4
	S. J. Franklin (PROG)	6,250	10.7
6	Robert G. Simmons (R)	41,558	51.3
	Charles W. Beal (D)	35,784	44.2

NEVADA

	Candidates	Votes	%
AL	Charles L. Richards (D)	15,991	57.0
	A. Grant Miller (R)	12,084	43.0

NEW HAMPSHIRE

	Candidates	Votes	%
1	William N. Rogers (D)	36,793	54.5
	John Scammon (R)	30,694	45.5
2	Edward H. Wason (R)	31,570	53.0
	William H. Barry (D)	27,980	47.0

NEW JERSEY

	Candidates	Votes	%
1	Francis F. Patterson Jr. (R)	46,505	60.5
	Ethan P. Wescott (D)	29,381	38.2
2	Isaac Bacharach (R)	50,925	69.8
	Charles S. Stevens (D)	22,001	30.2
3	Elmer H. Geran (D)	44,337	50.3
	T. Frank Appleby (R)	43,809	49.7
4	Charles Browne (D)	32,422	52.8
	Elijah C. Hutchinson (R)	28,934	47.2
5	Ernest R. Ackerman (R)	43,460	56.7
	Monell Sayre (D)	32,039	41.8
6	Randolph Perkins (R)	41,564	52.5
	Thomas A. Shields (D)	37,561	47.5
7	George N. Seger (R)	26,613	54.6
	Wilmer A. Cadmus (D)	21,190	43.5
8	Frank J. McNulty (D)	40,379#	58.5
	Warren P. Coon (R)	27,936	40.5
9	Daniel F. Minahan (D)	21,276	52.6
	Richard W. Parker (R)	19,182	47.4
10	Frederick R. Lehlbach (R)	28,570	57.4
	John F. Cahill (D)	21,211	42.6
11	John J. Eagan (D)	39,957	66.8
	Archibald E. Olpp (R)	18,399	30.8
12	Charles F. X. O'Brien (D)	51,596	74.3
	William A. O'Brien (R)	17,372	25.0

NEW MEXICO

	Candidates	Votes	%
AL	John Morrow (D)	59,254	54.0
	Adelina Otero-Warren (R)	49,698	45.3

NEW YORK

	Candidates	Votes	%
1	Robert L. Bacon (R)	47,191	57.6
	S. A. Warner Baltazzi (DFL)	32,224	39.3
2	John J. Kindred (D)	60,306	72.1
	Frank E. Hopkins (R)	19,560	23.4
3	George W. Lindsay (D)	21,513	65.4
	John Kissel (R)	8,587	26.1
	William W. Passage (SOC &F-L)	2,716	8.3
4	Thomas H. Cullen (D)	27,100	76.5
	Dominic E. Picone (R)	7,104	20.1
5	Loring M. Black Jr. (D)	33,840	54.9
	Ardolph L. Kline (R)	25,917	42.1
6	Charles I. Stengle (D)	31,363	48.3

	Candidates	Votes	%
	Warren I. Lee (R)	28,240	43.5
	Mina Eskenazi (SOC &F-L)	4,713	7.3
7	John F. Quayle (D)	21,688	53.4
	Michael J. Hogan (R)	14,772	36.4
	Henry Fruchter (SOC &F-L)	3,807	9.4
8	William E. Cleary (D)	34,622	56.4
	Charles G. Bond (R)	19,745	32.1
	David P. Berenberg (SOC &F-L)	6,804	11.1
9	David J. O'Connell (D)	38,833	58.1
	Andrew N. Petersen (R)	23,251	34.8
	Wilhelmus B. Robinson (SOC &F-L)	4,528	6.8
10	Emanuel Celler (D)	20,210	45.6
	Lester D. Volk (R)	17,099	38.6
	Jerome T. Dehunt (SOC &F-L)	6,522	14.7
11	Daniel J. Riordan (D)	29,134	67.6
	Joseph B. Handy (R)	12,889	29.9
12	Samuel Dickstein (D)	11,027	60.9
	Meyer London (SOC &F-L)	5,900	32.6
	Louis Zeltner (R)	1,183	6.5
13	Christopher D. Sullivan (D)	11,424	66.7
	Murray D. Firstman (R)	3,041	17.8
	Abraham Lefkowitz (SOC&F-L)	2,659	15.5
14	Nathan D. Perlman (R)	8,782	37.4
	David H. Knott (D)	8,173	34.8
	Jacob Panken (SOC &F-L)	6,459	27.5
15	John J. Boylan (D)	20,382	60.8
	Thomas Jefferson Ryan (R)	12,205	36.4
16	W. Bourke Cockran (D)	23,370*	70.0
	John C. O'Connor (R)	8,277	24.8
17	Ogden L. Mills (R)	21,274	50.5
	Herman A. Metz (D)	19,355	46.0
18	John F. Carew (D)	24,248	66.8
	Albert E. Schwartz (R)	8,398	23.1
	Ben Howe (SOC &F-L)	3,535	9.7
19	Samuel Marx (D)	29,798*	50.3
	Walter M. Chandler (R)	26,172	44.2
20	Fiorello H. LaGuardia (P)	8,492	38.3
	Henry Frank (D)	8,324	37.5
	William Karlin (SOC &F-L)	5,260	23.7
21	Royal H. Weller (D)	32,393	48.2
	Martin C. Ansorge (R)	32,053	47.6
22	Anthony J. Griffin (D)	29,544	72.8
	Charles Francis Connolly (R)	7,188	17.7
	Ernest Bohm (SOC &F-L)	3,752	9.2
23	Frank Oliver (D)	50,382	56.5
	Albert B. Rossdale (R)	25,154	28.2
	Salvatore Ninfo (SOC&F-L)	12,411	13.9
24	James V. Ganly (D)	40,058	47.4
	Benjamin L. Fairchild (R)	35,656	42.2
	Philip Umstadter (SOC&F-L)	8,873	10.5
25	J. Mayhew Wainwright (R & P)	33,674	53.3
	Robert A. Osborn (D)	27,412	43.4
26	Hamilton Fish Jr. (R F-L-P)	34,633	61.1
	Thomas Pendell (D)	20,831	36.7
27	Charles B. Ward (R)	30,154	46.5
	John J. Burns (DFL)	27,937	43.1
	H. Westlake Coons (P)	5,830	9.0
28	Parker Corning (D)	54,570	55.3
	Charles M. Winchester (R)	42,531	43.1
29	James S. Parker (R & P)	45,895	60.5
	William H. Faxon (D)	28,726	37.9
30	Frank Crowther (R & P)	32,225	53.3
	George H. Derry (D)	25,261	41.8
31	Bertrand H. Snell (R F-L-P)	38,205	68.3
	J. Franklin Sharp (D)	17,257	30.9
32	Luther W. Mott (R)	44,091	65.1
	M. J. Daley (D)	22,279	32.9
33	Homer P. Snyder (R)	31,978	49.6
	Fred J. Sisson (D)	30,118	46.7
34	John D. Clarke (R & P)	40,902	62.7
	Clayton L. Wheeler (D)	23,323	35.8
35	Walter W. Magee (R)	47,119	54.1
	Frederick W. Thomson (D)	37,785	43.4
36	John Taber (R & P)	43,633	65.5
	David J. Sims (D)	22,980	34.5
37	Gale H. Stalker (R & P)	42,144	59.2
	Charles P. Smith (DFL)	28,290	39.7
38	Meyer Jacobstein (D)	35,319	47.7
	Frederick T. Pierson (R)	33,690	45.5

	Candidates	Votes	%
	Joel Moses (SOC)	5,101	6.9
39	Archie D. Sanders (R)	37,852	60.5
	David A. White (DFL)	22,585	36.1
40	S. Wallace Dempsey (R-F-LAB)	41,754	63.4
	Philip Clancy (D)	21,590	32.8
41	Clarence MacGregor (R)	25,342	55.4
	William P. Greiner (D)	16,301	35.7
	Frank Ehrenfried (SOC)	4,067	8.9
42	James M. Mead (DFL)	25,070	61.9
	Louis J. Schwendler (R)	12,494	30.9
	Jacob F. Griesinger (SOC)	2,913	7.2
43	Daniel A. Reed (R & P)	40,374	70.5
	Frederick Garfield (D)	15,261	26.7

NORTH CAROLINA

	Candidates	Votes	%
1	Hallett S. Ward (D)	10,201	80.8
	C. E. Kramer (R)	2,421	19.2
2	Claude Kitchin (D)	8,533	100.0
3	Charles L. Abernethy (D)	14,101	67.1
	Thomas J. Hood (R)	6,924	32.9
4	Edward W. Pou (D)	17,205	68.0
	F. Eugene Hester (R)	8,086	32.0
5	Charles M. Stedman (D)	33,694	62.3
	Lucy B. Patterson (R)	20,380	37.7
6	Homer L. Lyon (D)	14,996	74.0
	William J. McDonald (R)	5,266	26.0
7	William C. Hammer (D)	30,629	56.5
	W. B. Love (R)	23,592	43.5
8	Robert L. Doughton (D)	31,340	56.1
	J. Ike Campbell (R)	24,493	43.9
9	Alfred L. Bulwinkle (D)	28,596	59.9
	R. H. Shuford (R)	19,168	40.1
10	Zebulon Weaver (D)	37,626	57.2
	Ralph A. Fisher (R)	28,192	42.8

NORTH DAKOTA

	Candidates	Votes	%
1	Olger B. Burtness (R)	45,959	100.0
2	George M. Young (R)	36,528	69.8
	J. W. Deemey (PROG)	15,834	30.2
3	James H. Sinclair (R)	33,499	64.2
	E. J. Hughes (IR)	18,672	35.8

OHIO

	Candidates	Votes	%
1	Nicholas Longworth (R)	45,253	57.1
	Sidney G. Stricker (D)	30,945	39.0
2	Ambrose E. B. Stephens (R)	39,898	54.0
	John R. Quane (D)	30,051	40.6
	Charles A. Herbst (F-LAB)	4,001	5.4
3	Roy G. Fitzgerald (R)	52,111	51.8
	Warren Gard (D)	46,127	45.9
4	John C. Cable (R)	43,251	54.6
	J. Henry Goeke (D)	35,916	45.4
5	Charles J. Thompson (R)	31,700	53.0
	Frank C. Kniffin (D)	28,067	47.0
6	Charles C. Kearns (R)	32,416	51.2
	William N. Gableman (D)	30,939	48.8
7	Charles Brand (R)	54,180	58.5
	Charles B. Zimmerman (D)	38,522	41.6
8	R. Clint Cole (R)	37,065	52.1
	H. H. Hartman (D)	34,105	47.9
9	Isaac R. Sherwood (D)	45,059	51.3
	William W. Chalmers (R)	42,712	48.7
10	Israel M. Foster (R)	30,341	63.0
	James Sharp (D)	17,811	37.0
11	Mell G. Underwood (D)	29,058	51.7
	Edwin D. Ricketts (R)	27,162	48.3
12	John C. Speaks (R)	47,265	55.1
	H. Sage Valentine (D)	37,875	44.2
13	James T. Begg (R)	38,994	56.4
	Arthur W. Overmeyer (D)	30,199	43.6
14	Martin L. Davey (D)	49,935	52.0
	Frank E. Whittemore (R)	46,087	48.0
15	C. Ellis Moore (R)	32,894	51.4
	James R. Alexander (D)	30,120	47.1
16	John McSweeney Jr. (D)	43,590	51.8
	J. H. Himes (R)	39,881	47.3

Candidates	Votes	%
17 William M. Morgan (R)	42,331	50.4
William A. Ashbrook (D)	41,745	49.7
18 Frank Murphy (R)	41,572	57.0
Marion Huffman (D)	25,449	34.9
Jacob S. Carey Sr. (I)	5,907	8.1
19 John G. Cooper (R)	40,492	59.3
W. B. Kilpatrick (D)	27,836	40.7
20 Charles A. Mooney (D)	23,469	54.4
Minor G. Morton (R)	17,968	41.7
21 Robert Crosser (D)	18,645	55.1
Harry C. Gahn (R)	14,024	41.4
22 Theodore E. Burton (R)	57,781	73.4
William J. Zoul (D)	20,511	26.1

OKLAHOMA

1 Everette B. Howard (D)	39,135	54.7
T. A. Chandler (R)	32,478	45.4
2 William H. Hastings (D)	30,418	57.7
Alice M. Robertson (R)	21,973	41.7
3 Charles D. Carter (D)	39,464	71.6
Philas S. Jones (R)	15,022	27.3
4 Thomas D. McKeown (D)	39,247	65.2
Joseph C. Pringey (R)	20,568	34.2
5 Fletcher B. Swank (D)	46,120	62.7
U.S. Stone (R)	26,893	36.6
6 Elmer Thomas (D)	30,532	56.6
L. M. Gensman (R)	22,757	42.2
7 James V. McClintic (D)	28,956	70.2
W. G. Roe (R)	11,444	27.8
8 Milton C. Garber (R)	29,068	52.0
Zach A. Harris (D)	26,111	46.7

OREGON

1 Willis C. Hawley (R)	64,567	100.0
2 Nicholas J. Sinnott (R)	22,861	59.2
James Harvey Graham (D)	15,789	40.9
3 Elton Watkins (D)	36,690	47.6
Clifton N. McArthur (R)	35,696	46.3

PENNSYLVANIA

1 William S. Vare (R)	46,946	83.6
Stephen Flanagan (D)	8,227	14.7
2 George S. Graham (R, P)	31,470	85.4
Ellen Duane Davis (D)	4,739	12.9
3 Harry C. Ransley (R)	33,058	84.4
Edward P. Carroll (D)	5,507	14.1
4 George W. Edmonds (R, P)	28,757	74.1
Joseph K. Willing (D)	8,954	23.1
5 James J. Connolly (R, WELFARE)	31,357	76.6
James J. Sweeney (D)	7,717	18.9
6 George A. Welsh (R)	44,159	73.4
Robert J. Sterrett (D)	13,629	22.7
7 George P. Darrow (R, P)	31,580	74.2
John W. Graham (D, VL)	9,694	22.8
8 Thomas S. Butler (R)	30,349	61.1
William T. Ellis (D, INDL)	18,306	36.9
9 Henry Winfield Watson (R)	32,052	61.8
C. William Freed (D)	18,083	34.9
10 William W. Griest (R)	33,545	52.8
Frank C. Musser (D, LANCAST)	30,017	47.2
11 Laurence H. Watres (R, P)	23,266	50.1
Patrick McLane (D)	22,540	48.5
12 John J. Casey (D, SOC)	35,953	54.1
Clarence D. Coughlin (R, P)	30,532	45.9
13 George Franklin Brumm (R, P)	23,218	52.9
Charles F. Ditchey (D)	19,305	44.0
14 William M. Croll (D)	31,592	48.2
Fred B. Gernerd (R)	29,617	45.2
George W. Snyder (SOC)	4,294	6.6
15 Louis T. McFadden (R, P)	20,399	64.0
T. Francis Carroll (D)	11,498	36.1
16 Edgar R. Kiess (R, P)	17,499	57.2
James M. Rook (D)	12,014	39.2
17 Herbert W. Cummings (D, SOC)	22,588	57.4
I. Clinton Kline (R, P)	16,796	42.6
18 Edward M. Beers (R, P)	24,675	54.6
King Alexander (D)	20,069	44.4

Candidates	Votes	%
19 Frank C. Sites (D)	33,570	53.6
Aaron S. Kreider (R, P)	28,115	44.9
20 George M. Wertz (R, P)	12,276	41.9
Warren Worth Bailey (D, SOC)	11,969	40.9
Robert M. Palmer (RO)	2,671	9.1
Faber V. McCloskey (LAB)	2,337	8.0
21 J. Banks Kurtz (R, P)	13,106	47.5
Daniel S. Brumbaugh (D)	11,425	41.4
Earl W. Rothrock (LAB, SOC)	3,050	11.1
22 Samuel F. Glatfelter (D)	22,181	53.0
Mahlon N. Haines (R, P)	17,694	42.3
23 William Irvin Swoope (R, SOC)	16,928	48.0
J. Frank Snyder (D)	14,292	40.5
Elisha Kent Kane (P)	4,041	11.5
24 Samuel A. Kendall (R, P)	18,261	54.0
Harrison N. Boyd (D)	12,937	38.3
Herman G. Lepley (SOC)	1,985	5.9
25 Henry W. Temple (R, SOC)	14,098	53.5
Charles I. Faddis (D)	12,242	46.5
26 Thomas W. Phillips Jr (R)	17,730	51.5
John G. Cobler (D, P)	15,533	45.1
27 Nathan L. Strong (R)	18,682	53.6
Jane E. Leonard (D)	12,927	37.1
28 Harry J. Bixler (R)	22,631	64.4
Charles E. Bordwell (D)	11,604	33.0
29 Milton W. Shreve (R, P)	19,043	58.9
Charles N. Crosby (D)	11,917	36.9
30 Everett Kent (D)	25,644	58.2
William H. Kirkpatrick (R)	17,844	40.5
31 Adam M. Wyant (R, P)	17,421	53.4
James M. Cramer (D)	13,081	40.1
Harry Eckard (SOC)	2,146	6.6
32 Stephen Geyer Porter (R)	19,942	70.0
P.M. O'Donnell (D)	5,938	20.9
33 M. Clyde Kelly (R, D)	21,899	87.4
William Adams (SOC)	3,106	12.4
34 John M. Morin (R)	15,499	72.7
William N. McNair (D, P)	5,134	24.1
35 James M. Magee (R)	16,227	53.9
Louis K. Manley (D, P)	12,838	42.6
36 Guy E. Campbell (R, D)	20,783	91.7
William W. Nooning (SOC)	1,880	8.3

RHODE ISLAND

1 Clark Burdick (R)	25,860	54.1
George F. O'Shaunessy (D)	21,935	45.9
2 Richard S. Aldrich (R)	26,247	52.6
Percy J. Cantwell (D)	23,680	47.4
3 Jeremiah E. O'Connell (D)	36,147	62.6
Isaac Gill (R)	21,581	37.4

SOUTH CAROLINA

1 W. Turner Logan (D)	5,992	94.0
S. L. Blomgren (D)	383	6.0
2 James F. Byrnes (D)	4,163	100.0
3 Fred H. Dominick (D)	3,822	100.0
4 John J. McSwain (D)	8,346	97.3
5 William F. Stevenson (D)	4,015	100.0
6 Allard H. Gasque (D)	3,642	100.0
7 Hampton P. Fulmer (D)	4,411	98.5

SOUTH DAKOTA

1 Charles A. Christopherson (R)	31,250	48.9
John Stredronsky (D)	16,372	25.6
G. L. Hasvold (NON PART)	16,230	25.4
2 Royal C. Johnson (R)	37,208	64.5
Andrew Francis Lockhart (NON PART)	18,968	32.9
3 William Williamson (R)	18,819	49.2
George Philip (D)	14,857	38.8
George H. Smith (NON PART)	4,581	12.0

TENNESSEE

1 B. Carroll Reece (R)	17,050	77.0
J. T. Fugate (D)	5,085	23.0
2 J. Will Taylor (R)	14,988	64.3

Candidates	Votes	%
J. Rupert Reynolds (D)	8,330	35.7
3 Sam D. McReynolds (D)	20,603	61.3
R. L. Burnett (R)	13,027	38.7
4 Cordell Hull (D)	20,323	62.6
W. F. Clouse (R)	12,125	37.4
5 Ewin L. Davis (D)	11,634	100.0
6 Joseph W. Byrns (D)	19,596	100.0
7 William C. Salmon (D)	13,662	78.2
S. A. Vest (R)	3,818	21.8
8 Gordon Browning (D)	16,571	57.3
Lon A. Scott (R)	12,328	42.7
9 Finis J. Garrett (D)	15,822	84.8
Homer S. Tatum (R)	2,846	15.3
10 Hubert F. Fisher (D)	10,407	89.1
Thomas C. Phelen (I)	1,279	10.9

Special Election

7 Clarence W. Turner (D)	12,914	86.3
S. W. Williams (R)	2,053	13.7

TEXAS

1 Eugene Black (D)	15,697	93.5
G. T. Bartlett (R)	1,087	6.5
2 John C. Box (D)	21,216	94.8
C. A. Lord (R)	1,171	5.2
3 Morgan G. Sanders (D)	16,323	91.7
L. B. Crawford (R)	1,478	8.3
4 Sam Rayburn (D)	21,327	91.1
C. A. Gray (R)	2,079	8.9
5 Hatton W. Sumners (D)	23,051	88.3
Heber Page (R)	3,046	11.7
6 Luther A. Johnson (D)	18,938	94.0
D. H. Merrill (R)	1,208	6.0
7 Clay Stone Briggs (D)	12,171	93.3
Frank Sneed Camper (R)	880	6.7
8 Daniel E. Garrett (D)	20,058	85.3
E. B. Barden (R)	3,454	14.7
9 Joseph J. Mansfield (D)	17,479	64.7
Willett Wilson (R)	9,554	35.3
10 James P. Buchanan (D)	18,590	81.0
W. J. Kveton (R)	4,374	19.1
11 Tom T. Connally (D)	16,092	90.8
R. A. Hanrick (R)	1,630	9.2
12 Fritz G. Lanham (D)	20,014	91.9
Joe Kingsberry Jr. (R)	1,772	8.1
13 Guinn Williams (D)	21,187	93.2
J. B. Schmitz (R)	1,538	6.8
14 Harry M. Wurzbach (R)	19,083	54.8
Harry Hertzberg (D)	15,760	45.2
15 John N. Garner (D)	14,319	100.0
16 Claude B. Hudspeth (D)	18,164	81.0
J. A. Simpson (R)	4,257	19.0
17 Thomas L. Blanton (D)	24,576	91.6
W. D. Girand (R)	2,266	8.4
18 Marvin Jones (D)	24,515	93.7
H. O. Ward (R)	1,649	6.3

UTAH

1 Don B. Colton (R)	33,188	52.7
Milton H. Welling (D)	27,801	44.2
2 Elmer O. Leatherwood (R)	28,591	50.5
David C. Dunbar (D)	26,145	46.1

VERMONT

1 Frederick G. Fleetwood (R, P)	19,359	52.1
James E. Kennedy (D)	17,821	47.9
2 Porter H. Dale (R, P)	25,981	78.4
John J. Wilson (D)	7,170	21.6

VIRGINIA

1 Schuyler Otis Bland (D)	8,639	83.5
George N. Wise (R)	1,492	14.4
2 Joseph T. Deal (D)	7,367	86.5
Percy S. Stephenson (R)	1,045	12.3
3 Andrew Jackson Montague (D)	7,746	90.1

Candidates	Votes	%
Channing M. Ward (R)	847	9.9
4 Patrick Henry Drewry (D)	5,737	86.2
Herbert Rogers (R)	822	12.4
5 James M. Hooker (D)	11,458	70.9
Charles P. Smith (R)	4,699	29.1
6 Clifton A. Woodrum (D)	9,505	77.9
J. W. McWane (R)	2,688	22.0
7 Thomas W. Harrison (D)	12,954	62.3
John Paul (R)	7,841	37.7
8 R. Walton Moore (D)	8,702	83.3
John Sidney Wiley (R)	1,741	16.7
9 George C. Peery (D)	32,163	52.4
John H. Hassinger (R)	29,227	47.6
10 Henry St. George Tucker (D)	8,635	77.4
John Martin (R)	2,521	22.6

WASHINGTON

Candidates	Votes	%
1 John F. Miller (R)	29,579	57.4
Edgar C. Snyder (D)	13,127	25.5
Fred N. Nelson (F-LAB)	8,862	17.2
2 Lindley H. Hadley (R)	29,906	59.0
Fred A. Clise (D)	10,608	20.9
P. B. Tyler (F-LAB)	10,150	20.0
3 Albert Johnson (R)	45,482	76.3
J. M. Phillips (F-LAB)	14,158	23.7

Candidates	Votes	%
4 John W. Summers (R)	29,697	68.5
Charles R. Hill (D)	10,337	23.9
Elihu Bowles (F-LAB)	3,292	7.6
5 J. Stanley Webster (R)	26,982	49.2
Sam B. Hill (D)	24,810	45.2
Harry J. Vaughan (F-LAB)	3,095	5.6

WEST VIRGINIA

Candidates	Votes	%
1 Benjamin L. Rosenbloom (R)	28,644	52.6
Raymond Kenny (D)	25,794	47.3
2 Robert E. L. Allen (D)	27,320	51.5
George M. Bowers (R)	24,764	46.6
3 Stuart F. Reed (R)	32,066	50.5
Eskridge H. Morton (D)	31,382	49.5
4 George W. Johnson (D)	32,355	50.7
Harry C. Woodyard (R)	31,448	49.3
5 Thomas J. Lilly (D)	35,354	51.5
Wells Goodykoontz (R)	33,267	48.5
6 J. Alfred Taylor (D)	42,320	54.2
Leonard S. Echols (R)	34,901	44.7

WISCONSIN

Candidates	Votes	%
1 Henry Allen Cooper (R)	37,958	94.4
Niels P. Nielsen (SOC)	2,179	5.4

Candidates	Votes	%
2 Edward Voigt (R)	32,494	80.9
William F. Schanen (D)	7,667	19.1
3 John M. Nelson (R)	33,002	79.7
Martha Riley (ID)	8,379	20.2
4 John C. Schafer (R)	19,179	46.0
Edmund T. Melms (SOC)	18,548	44.5
Joseph F. Drezdzon (D)	3,918	9.4
5 Victor L. Berger (SOC)	30,045	53.3
William H. Stafford (R)	26,274	46.6
6 Florian Lampert (R)	34,365	86.0
William E. Cavanaugh (ID)	5,572	14.0
7 Joseph D. Beck (R)	27,371	87.4
Bert A. Jolivette (ID)	3,923	12.5
8 Edward E. Browne (R)	33,860	91.8
Herman A. Marth (I SOC)	2,946	8.0
9 George J. Schneider (R)	35,117	61.5
Henry Graass (IR)	22,015	38.5
10 James A. Frear (R)	29,781	98.3
11 Hubert H. Peavey (R)	36,635	99.0

WYOMING

	Candidates	Votes	%
AL	Charles E. Winter (R)	30,885	53.3
	Robert R. Rose (D)	27,017	46.7

1923 House Elections

ALABAMA

Special Election

	Candidates	Votes	%
2	Lister Hill (D)	4,483	100.0

ARKANSAS

Special Election

	Candidates	Votes	%
6	James B. Reed (D)	1,793	100.0

ILLINOIS

Special Elections

	Candidates	Votes	%
2	Morton D. Hull (R)	56,355	53.9
	Barratt O'Hara (D)	42,427	40.6
	Seymorse Stedman (SOC)	5,759	5.5
4	Thomas A. Doyle (D)	17,624	95.0

IOWA

Special Election

	Candidates	Votes	%
8	Hiram K. Evans (R)	14,334	52.6
	J. P. Daughton (D)	12,901	47.4

NEW YORK

Special Elections

	Candidates	Votes	%
11	Anning S. Prall (D)	28,215	72.9
	Guy O. Walser (R)	9,972	25.8
16	John J. O'Connor (D, R)	27,746	96.7
19	Sol Bloom (D)	17,909	49.8
	Walter M. Chandler (R)	17,718	49.3
24	Benjamin L. Fairchild (R)	43,475	49.0
	Edward R. Koch (D)	38,435	43.3
	Alexander Braunstein (SOC)	6,913	7.8
32	Thaddeus C. Sweet (R)	41,775	65.1
	Daniel C. Burke (D)	21,391	33.4

1924 House Elections

ALABAMA

	Candidates	Votes	%
1	John McDuffie (D)	9,932	86.1
	Frank J. Thompson (R)	1,604	13.9
2	Lister Hill (D)	15,066	100.0
3	Henry B. Steagall (D)	10,425	87.7
	Carlos E. Roberts (R)	1,457	12.3
4	Lamar Jeffers (D)	9,945	75.6
	J. O. Middleton (R)	3,208	24.4
5	William B. Bowling (D)	8,492	78.3
	John C. Walker (R)	2,355	21.7
6	William B. Oliver (D)	6,672	100.0
7	Miles C. Allgood (D)	15,984	57.1
	B. S. Cooley (R)	11,987	42.9
8	Edward B. Almon (D)	13,353	81.5
	G. M. Huckaba (R)	3,040	18.5
9	George Huddleston (D)	18,958	99.9
10	William B. Bankhead (D)	11,394	59.7
	W. A. McMurray (R)	7,706	40.4

ARIZONA

	Candidates	Votes	%
AL	Carl Hayden (D)	40,329	82.4
	W. J. Galbraith (R)	8,628	17.6

ARKANSAS

	Candidates	Votes	%
1	William J. Driver (D)	15,514	77.2
	Virgil Greene (R)	4,580	22.8
2	William A. Oldfield (D)	11,412	73.8
	M. D. Bowers (R)	4,057	26.2
3	John N. Tillman (D)	13,202	60.0
	J. S. Thompson (R)	8,789	40.0
4	Otis T. Wingo (D)	15,935	72.5
	Charles A. Darling (R)	6,060	27.6
5	Heartsill Ragon (D)	16,287	76.8
	Powell Clayton (R)	4,922	23.2
6	James B. Reed (D)	13,101	75.6
	Martin A. Eisele (R)	4,219	24.4
7	Tilman B. Parks (D)	13,975	76.5
	J. K. Prescott (R)	4,302	23.5

CALIFORNIA

	Candidates	Votes	%
1	Clarence F. Lea (D-R)	47,250	99.9
2	John E. Raker (D-R)	30,590	100.0
3	Charles F. Curry (R-D)	61,512	80.7
	James H. Barkley (SOC)	14,665	19.3
4	Julius Kahn (R-D)	44,048*	81.0
	William McDevitt (SOC)	10,360	19.0
5	Lawrence J. Flaherty (R-D)	38,893	76.2
	Isabel C. King (SOC)	12,175	23.8
6	Albert E. Carter (R)	68,547	57.5
	John L. Davie (I)	42,873	35.9
	Herbert L. Coggins (SOC)	7,858	6.6
7	Henry E. Barbour (R-D)	65,740	99.9
8	Arthur Monroe Free (R-D)	55,713	97.9
9	Walter F. Lineberger (R)	119,993	63.9
	Charles H. Randall (P D SOC)	67,735	36.1
10	John D. Fredericks (R)	133,780	62.3
	Robert W. Richardson (D)	80,870	37.7
11	Philip D. Swing (DR SOC P)	93,811	100.0

COLORADO

	Candidates	Votes	%
1	William N. Vaile (R)	47,155	54.2
	James G. Edgeworth (D)	36,519	42.0
2	Charles B. Timberlake (R)	51,028	56.9
	James M. Taylor (D)	31,378	35.0
	James A. Ownbey (LAF)	6,630	7.4
3	Guy U. Hardy (R)	53,877	58.7
	Charles B. Hughes (D)	37,976	41.3
4	Edward T. Taylor (D)	33,262	65.5
	Webster S. Whinnery (R)	17,486	34.5

CONNECTICUT

	Candidates	Votes	%
1	E. Hart Fenn (R)	61,451	66.8
	Johnstone Vance (D)	29,381	31.9
2	Richard P. Freeman (R)	42,161	65.0
	Fenton (D)	22,258	34.3
3	John Q. Tilson (R)	48,963	67.9
	William T. Hoyt (D)	21,858	30.3
4	Schuyler Merritt (R)	57,966	71.1
	Walling (D)	22,031	27.0
5	James P. Glynn (R)	34,548	55.0
	Patrick B. O'Sullivan (D, PROG)	28,248	45.0

DELAWARE

	Candidates	Votes	%
AL	Robert G. Houston (R)	51,536	58.6
	William H. Boyce (D)	35,943	40.9

FLORIDA

	Candidates	Votes	%
1	Herbert J. Drane (D)	23,244	80.0
	A. W. Gage (R)	5,816	20.0
2	Robert A. Green (D)	11,021	90.7
	H. O. Brown (R)	1,137	9.4
3	John H. Smithwick (D)	12,660	84.1
	J. H. Drummond (R)	2,389	15.9
4	William J. Sears (D)	25,318	62.5
	G. W. Bingham (R)	12,183	30.1
	Billy Parker (AM)	2,993	7.4

GEORGIA

	Candidates	Votes	%
1	Charles G. Edwards (D)	14,694	93.2
2	E. E. Cox (D)	10,667	100.0
3	Charles R. Crisp (D)	8,138	100.0
4	William C. Wright (D)	10,420	100.0
5	William D. Upshaw (D)	16,608	100.0
6	Samuel Rutherford (D)	12,488	100.0
7	Gordon Lee (D)	20,008	99.9
8	Charles H. Brand (D)	12,261	100.0
9	Thomas M. Bell (D)	17,007	87.5
	J. M. Johnson (R)	2,425#	12.5
10	Carl Vinson (D)	9,280	100.0
11	William C. Lankford (D)	11,590	100.0
12	William W. Larsen (D)	11,754	100.0

IDAHO

	Candidates	Votes	%
1	Burton L. French (R)	33,347	61.8
	Perry Mitchell (D)	20,234	37.5
2	Addison T. Smith (R)	44,365	54.6
	William A. Shuldberg (PROG)	23,257	28.6
	Asher B. Wilson (D)	13,470	16.6

ILLINOIS

	Candidates	Votes	%
1	Martin B. Madden (R)	43,661	73.1
	James F. Doyle (D)	13,623	22.8
2	Morton D. Hull (R)	113,349	74.5
	Frank A. Wright (D)	37,482	24.6
3	Elliott W. Sproul (R)	87,563	67.0
	Joseph F. Timmis (D)	42,278	32.3
4	Thomas A. Doyle (D)	30,955	56.0
	Stanley Jankowski (R)	23,947	43.3
5	Adolph J. Sabath (D)	20,588	57.8
	Bernard A. Weaver (R)	14,730	41.4
6	John J. Gorman (R)	116,066	67.8
	James R. Buckley (D)	53,463	31.2
7	M. Alfred Michaelson (R)	133,563	67.7
	Hynek M. Howell (D)	46,253	23.5
	Edward A. Russell	13,040	6.6
8	Stanley Henry Kunz (D)	17,799	53.1
	Ernest D. Potts (R)	13,853	41.3
	Gerard Kasmarek	1,675	5.0
9	Fred A. Britten (R)	42,829	76.6
	Urban A. Lavery (D)	12,541	22.4

	Candidates	Votes	%
10	Carl R. Chindblom (R)	126,383	80.0
	John P. Reed (D)	30,474	19.3
11	Frank R. Reid (R)	83,696	84.2
	Charles L. Schwartz (D)	15,246	15.3
12	Charles E. Fuller (R)	68,696	84.5
	Marvin C. Parsons (PROG)	12,105	14.9
13	William R. Johnson (R)	49,717	77.8
	William G. Curtiss (D)	13,887	21.7
14	John C. Allen (R)	48,920	64.7
	William A. Schaeffer (D)	26,680	35.3
15	Edward J. King (R)	53,123	69.2
	Henry E. Schmiedeskamp (D)	23,051	30.0
16	William E. Hull (R)	43,098	55.4
	Charles C. Hatcher (D)	34,185	44.0
17	Frank H. Funk (R)	40,226	60.1
	Frank Gillespie (D)	26,497	39.6
18	William P. Holaday (R)	52,992	64.4
	Andrew B. Dennis (D)	29,034	35.3
19	Charles Adkins (R)	55,605	56.5
	Edward F. Poorman (D)	42,490	43.1
20	Henry T. Rainey (D)	36,669	53.0
	Guy L. Shaw (R)	32,569	47.0
21	Loren E. Wheeler (R)	45,588	50.0
	J. Earl Major (D)	44,414	48.7
22	Edward M. Irwin (R)	56,525	57.7
	Edward E. Campbell (D)	40,604	41.5
23	William W. Arnold (D)	45,644	53.9
	Charles J. Metzger (R)	38,670	45.7
24	Thomas S. Williams (R)	35,356	54.1
	H. Robert Fowler (D)	29,954	45.9
25	Edward E. Denison (R)	47,080	58.1
	Philip N. Lewis (D)	33,638	41.5
AL	Richard Yates (R)	1,519,021✔	
	Henry R. Rathbone (R)	1,513,708✔	
	Mary Ward Hart (D)	669,555	
	Allen D. Albert (D)	658,265	
	Gus C. Sandberg (SOC)	17,580	
	John C. Flora (SOC)	17,438	
	J. E. Procum (SOC LAB)	2,437	
	C. E. Clouse (SOC LAB)	2,368	
	Robert Minor (WP AM)	2,235	
	E. B. Hewlett (WP AM)	2,160	
	Patrick H. Morrissey (IR)	752	
	Dora Welty (CLP)	396	
	James W. Hill (CLP)	363	

INDIANA

	Candidates	Votes	%
1	Harry E. Rowbottom (R)	48,203	52.1
	William E. Wilson (D)	44,335	47.9
2	Arthur H. Greenwood (D)	43,690	49.8
	John E. Sedwick (R)	43,073	49.1
3	Frank Gardner (D)	44,376	52.8
	Lindley M. Barlow (R)	39,446	46.9
4	Harry C. Canfield (D)	48,803	58.2
	James W. Hill (R)	35,007	41.8
5	Noble J. Johnson (R)	46,264	55.5
	J. R. Shannon (D)	28,573	34.3
	Jesse Rice Burks (P)	7,476	9.0
6	Richard N. Elliott (R)	46,094	55.3
	Lawrence A. Handley (D)	37,309	44.7
7	Ralph E. Updike (R)	94,751	60.0
	Joseph P. Turk (D)	62,279	39.4
8	Albert H. Vestal (R)	51,864	55.8
	John A. M. Adair (D)	41,119	44.2
9	Fred S. Purnell (R)	51,280	54.5
	James P. Davis (D)	41,973	44.6
10	William R. Wood (R)	67,143	66.8
	Harry O. Rhodes (D)	33,344	33.2
11	Albert R. Hall (R)	47,978	54.0
	Samuel E. Cook (D)	39,998	45.0
12	David Hogg (R)	49,921	58.4
	Charles W. Branstrator (D)	35,565	41.6
13	Andrew J. Hickey (R)	69,042	61.7
	James L. Harmon (D)	42,895	38.3

IOWA

	Candidates	Votes	%
1	William F. Kopp (R)	42,711	71.4
	James M. Bell (D)	17,100	28.6
2	F. Dickinson Letts (R)	49,416	60.1
	W. Thompson (D)	32,842	39.9
3	Thomas J. B. Robinson (R)	54,921	68.5
	Willis N. Birdsall (D)	25,213	31.5
4	Gilbert N. Haugen (R)	50,811	71.1
	J. M. Berry (D)	20,646	28.9
5	Cyrenus Cole (R)	52,180	70.2
	W. N. Townsend (D)	22,175	29.8
6	C. William Ramseyer (R)	42,848	69.3
	James V. Curran (D)	18,976	30.7
7	Cassius C. Dowell (R)	66,550	78.3
	William M. Wade (D)	18,454	21.7
8	Lloyd Thurston (R)	42,222	62.5
	Le Roy Munyon (D)	25,321	37.5
9	William R. Green (R)	49,153	68.4
	Charles F. Paschel (D)	22,741	31.6
10	Lester J. Dickinson (R)	59,954	75.4
	R. F. Mitchell (D)	19,571	24.6
11	William D. Boies (R)	56,152	61.5
	A. Sykes (D)	35,086	38.5

KANSAS

	Candidates	Votes	%
1	Daniel R. Anthony Jr. (R)	49,676	70.8
	Lee Eppinger (D)	20,474	29.2
2	Chauncey B. Little (D)	43,285	48.8
	Russell Dyer (R)	39,523	44.6
	Arthur L. McKenney (I)	5,895	6.7
3	William H. Sproul (R)	49,482	57.3
	Charles Stephens (D)	36,876	42.7
4	Homer Hoch (R)	34,731	65.0
	R. W. Woodside (D)	18,728	35.0
5	James G. Strong (R)	38,754	60.0
	C. E. Hatfield (D)	25,842	40.0
6	Hays B. White (R)	35,690	52.5
	John R. Connelly (D)	32,285	47.5
7	Jasper N. Tincher (R)	48,826	54.6
	Nellie Cline (D)	40,583	45.4
8	William A. Ayres (D)	44,312	60.6
	Chester I. Long (R)	28,868	39.5

Special Election

2	U.S. Guyer (R)	55,765	62.0
	Mrs. James A. Cable (D)	34,170	38.0

KENTUCKY

1	Alben W. Barkley (D)	41,861	67.0
	R. L. Myre (R)	20,669	33.1
2	David H. Kincheloe (D)	35,717	100.0
3	Robert Y. Thomas Jr (D)	33,084	52.7
	George Baker (R)	29,753	47.4
4	Ben Johnson (D)	34,954	53.5
	Z. T. Proctor (R)	29,865	45.7
5	Maurice Thatcher (R)	60,403	54.5
	Sam H. McMeekin (D)	50,508	45.5
6	Arthur B. Rouse (D)	36,400	49.5
	B. S. Landram (R)	21,951	29.8
	William H. Bornhorst (PROG)	15,219	20.7
7	Virgil Chapman (D)	40,654	100.0
8	Ralph Gilbert (D)	29,888	100.0
9	Fred M. Vinson (D)	45,899	54.5
	George Osborne (R)	38,295	45.5
10	John W. Langley (R)	31,057	59.7
	Alex L. Ratliff (D)	20,577	39.6
11	John M. Robsion (R)	57,130	74.4
	Nat B. Sewell (D)	19,626	25.6

Special Election

9	Fred M. Vinson (D)	15,681	72.9
	W. S. Yazell (R)	5,822	27.1

LOUISIANA

	Candidates	Votes	%
1	James O'Connor (D)	20,027	100.0
2	J. Zach Spearing (D)	19,503	100.0
3	Whitmell P. Martin (D)	6,209	100.0
4	John N. Sandlin (D)	9,893	100.0
5	Riley J. Wilson (D)	8,523	100.0
6	Bolivar E. Kemp (D)	10,216	100.0
7	Ladislas Lazaro (D)	10,054	100.0
8	James B. Aswell (D)	8,886	100.0

MAINE

1	Carroll L. Beedy (R)	39,269	59.2
	William M. Ingraham (D)	27,058	40.8
2	Wallace H. White Jr. (R)	34,335	57.8
	Bertrand G. McIntire (D)	25,086	42.2
3	John E. Nelson (R)	40,730	62.1
	Leon O. Tebbetts (D)	24,860	37.9
4	Ira G. Hersey (R)	34,011	62.0
	Clinton C. Stevens (D)	20,851	38.0

MARYLAND

1	Thomas Alan Goldsborough (D)	27,963	57.0
	Harry T. Phoebus (R)	21,060	43.0
2	Millard E. Tydings (D)	35,051	53.2
	Edward Ridgely Simpson (R)	29,421	44.7
3	John Philip Hill (R)	23,760	61.5
	George Heller (D)	14,217	36.8
4	J. Charles Linthicum (D)	28,054	59.9
	John R. M. Staum (R)	17,773	38.0
5	Stephen W. Gambrill (D)	24,971	51.6
	Thomas B. R. Mudd (R)	23,412	48.4
6	Frederick N. Zihlman (R)	33,800	53.8
	David C. Winebranner (D)	28,016	44.6

Special Election

5	Stephen W. Gambrill (D)	23,474	50.3
	Thomas B. R. Mudd (R)	23,204	49.7

MASSACHUSETTS

1	Allen T. Treadway (R)	38,359	58.5
	Thomas F. Cassidy (D)	27,246	41.5
2	George B. Churchill (R)	41,126	57.3
	Joseph E. Kerigan (D)	30,703	42.7
3	Frank H. Foss (R)	38,626	64.4
	Wilfrid J. Lamoureux (D)	21,368	35.6
4	George R. Stobbs (R)	43,221	57.3
	William H. Dyer (D)	31,022	41.2
5	John Jacob Rogers (R)	46,841	67.4
	Humphrey O'Sullivan (D)	22,691	32.6
6	A. Platt Andrew (R)	55,023	100.0
7	William P. Connery Jr (D)	34,710	55.7
	Charles A. Littlefield (R)	27,600	44.3
8	Harry I. Thayer (R)	52,051	62.0
	Daniel P. Leahy (D)	31,844	38.0
9	Charles L. Underhill (R)	42,212	59.0
	Arthur D. Healey (D)	29,398	41.1
10	John J. Douglass (D)	19,558	58.9
	Peter F. Tague	8,694	26.2
	James E. Maguire (R)	4,168	12.6
11	George Holden Tinkham (R)	46,865	66.0
	Timothy J. Driscoll (D)	24,111	34.0
12	James A. Gallivan (D)	51,108	73.4
	Howard A. Morton (R)	18,573	26.7
13	Robert Luce (R)	61,851	69.3
	Edwin F. Tuttle (D)	27,450	30.7
14	Louis A. Frothingham (R)	59,746	69.1
	David W. Murray (D)	26,686	30.9
15	Joseph W. Martin Jr. (R)	33,360	58.4
	Arthur J. B. Cartier (D)	23,764	41.6
16	Charles L. Gifford (R)	37,913	69.5
	John H. Backus Jr. (D)	14,051	25.8

MICHIGAN

	Candidates	Votes	%
1	John B. Sosnowski (R)	76,566	67.5
	Robert H. Clancy (D)	36,516	32.2
2	Earl C. Michener (R)	69,680	73.8
	James W. Helme (D)	24,742	26.2
3	Arthur B. Williams (R)	50,375	65.1
	Claude S. Carney (D)	27,044	34.9
4	John C. Ketcham (R)	49,060	70.3
	Fremont Evans (D)	20,631	29.6
5	Carl E. Mapes (R)	58,682	81.3
	Harry C. White (D)	13,497	18.7
6	Grant M. Hudson (R)	173,705	85.6
	Willis M. Brewer (D)	29,191	14.4
7	Louis C. Cramton (R)	60,404	80.8
	Varnum J. Bowers (D)	14,291	19.1
8	Bird J. Vincent (R)	64,749	77.5
	William A. Seegmiller (D)	18,795	22.5
9	James C. McLaughlin (R)	47,386	84.1
	Charles M. Black (D)	8,781	15.6
10	Roy O. Woodruff (R)	47,555	81.3
	Judson E. Richardson (D)	10,944	18.7
11	Frank D. Scott (R)	41,686	73.3
	Prentiss M. Brown (D)	15,222	26.8
12	W. Frank James (R)	47,114	100.0
13	Clarence J. McLeod (R)	95,747	88.4
	Joel R. Moore (D)	12,526	11.6

MINNESOTA

1	Allen J. Furlow (R)	41,484	53.4
	Julius J. Reiter (F-LAB)	28,558	36.8
	L. B. Hanna (D)	7,659	9.9
2	Frank Clague (R)	45,730	60.5
	O. F. Swanjord (F-LAB)	29,901	39.5
3	August H. Andresen (R)	40,398	57.3
	A. C. Welch (F-LAB)	30,093	42.7
4	Oscar E. Keller (R)	39,217	47.8
	Dan W. Lawler (D)	30,277	36.9
	Julius F. Emme (F-LAB)	12,629	15.4
5	Walter H. Newton (R)	68,333	58.9
	A. G. Bastis (F-LAB)	36,804	31.7
	John S. Crosby (D)	10,967	9.5
6	Harold Knutson (R)	39,800	54.1
	S. C. Shipstead (F-LAB)	33,831	46.0
7	Ole J. Kvale (F-LAB)	43,555	58.5
	Gunnar B. Bjornson (R)	30,871	41.5
8	William L. Carss (F-LAB)	46,926	54.3
	Victor L. Power (D)	39,505	45.7
9	Knud Wefald (F-LAB)	38,248	56.8
	F. H. Peterson (D)	29,095	43.2
10	Godfrey G. Goodwin (R)	47,749	53.8
	George D. Brewer (F-LAB)	36,490	41.1
	Frank Hicks (D)	4,485	5.1

MISSISSIPPI

1	John E. Rankin (D)	13,971	100.0
2	Bill G. Lowery (D)	10,534	100.0
3	William M. Whittington (D)	9,282	100.0
4	T. Jeff Busby (D)	12,861	95.7
5	Ross A. Collins (D)	14,738	100.0
6	T. Webber Wilson (D)	17,337	100.0
7	Percy E. Quin (D)	9,547	100.0
8	James W. Collier (D)	10,278	100.0

MISSOURI

1	Milton A. Romjue (D)	37,831	57.3
	Frank Millspaugh (R)	28,175	42.7
2	Ralph F. Lozier (D)	41,643	62.8
	Sweeney	24,195	36.5
3	Jacob L. Milligan (D)	33,285	52.8
	Henry F. Lawrence (R)	29,773	47.2
4	Charles L. Faust (R)	35,752	51.3
	John McDaniel (D)	33,948	48.7
5	Edgar C. Ellis (R)	87,124	49.8
	George H. Combs Jr. (D)	85,581	48.9
6	Clement C. Dickinson (D)	28,911	53.8
	William O. Atkeson (R)	24,815	46.2

Candidates	Votes	%
7 Samuel C. Major (D)	46,264	52.0
O. B. Whitaker (R)	42,686	48.0
8 William L. Nelson (D)	28,895	50.8
Sidney C. Roach (R)	27,955	49.2
9 Clarence Cannon (D)	38,228	56.1
George E. Hackmann (R)	29,509	43.3
10 Cleveland A. Newton (R)	123,199	61.2
Henry J. Schleper (D)	70,976	35.3
11 Harry B. Hawes (D)	31,940	50.6
Michael J. Hart (R)	29,972	47.5
12 Leonidas C. Dyer (R)	25,749	63.2
Jerome F. Duggan (D)	14,022	34.4
13 Charles E. Kiefner (R)	27,743	53.0
J. Scott Wolff (D)	24,598	47.0
14 Ralph E. Bailey (R)	46,541	50.3
James F. Fulbright (D)	46,020	49.7
15 Joe J. Manlove (R)	39,148	56.4
William G. Warner (D)	30,051	43.3
16 Thomas L. Rubey (D)	28,353	55.8
William P. Elmer (R)	22,426	44.2

MONTANA

Candidates	Votes	%
1 John M. Evans (D)	44,139	63.9
John O. Davies (R)	24,012	34.8
2 Scott Leavitt (R)	55,190	61.4
Joseph Kirschwing (D)	28,708	32.0
Charles E. Taylor (F-LAB)	5,938	6.6

NEBRASKA

Candidates	Votes	%
1 John H. Morehead (D & PROG)	33,584	51.8
Roy H. Thorpe (R)	29,755	45.9
2 Willis G. Sears (R)	38,382	55.5
William V. Jamieson (D)	24,756	35.8
Roy M. Harrop (PROG)	6,059	8.8
3 Edgar Howard (D & PROG)	46,631	57.5
E. C. Houston (R)	34,541	42.6
4 Melvin O. McLaughlin (R)	32,235	49.0
E. E. Placek (D)	28,962	44.0
John O. Schmidt (PROG)	4,563	6.9
5 Ashton C. Shallenberger (D & PROG)	34,766	53.8
William E. Andrews (R)	29,871	46.2
6 Robert G. Simmons (R)	54,686	59.2
Charles W. Beal (D)	32,275	34.9
Jesse Gandy (P)	5,467	5.9

NEVADA

Candidates	Votes	%
AL Samuel S. Arentz (R)	13,107	50.4
Charles L. Richards (D)	12,880	49.6

NEW HAMPSHIRE

Candidates	Votes	%
1 Fletcher Hale (R)	44,758	55.2
William N. Rogers (D)	36,306	44.8
2 Edward H. Wason (R)	47,588	61.4
William H. Barry (D)	29,880	38.6

NEW JERSEY

Candidates	Votes	%
1 Francis F. Patterson Jr. (R)	64,592	69.1
Robert A. Irving (D)	25,232	27.0
2 Isaac Bacharach (R)	67,668	76.2
Charles S. Stevens (D)	21,185	23.8
3 T. Frank Appleby (R)	67,445*	60.3
Elmer H. Geran (D)	44,361	39.7
4 Charles A. Eaton (R)	41,734	53.8
Charles Browne (D)	35,840	46.2
5 Ernest R. Ackerman (R)	69,423	72.3
Monell Sayre (D)	26,662	27.8
6 Randolph Perkins (R)	66,555	66.3
Alfred T. Holley (D)	30,954	30.8
7 George N. Seger (R)	44,932	73.0
Andrew J. Callahan (D)	13,441	21.8
8 Herbert W. Taylor (R)	45,744	57.0
Frank J. McNulty (D)	34,463	43.0
9 Franklin W. Fort (R)	32,916	59.3
Daniel F. Minahan (D)	20,356	36.7

Candidates	Votes	%
10 Frederick R. Lehlbach (R)	50,890	70.1
Moses Greenwood (D)	18,578	25.6
11 Oscar L. Auf der Heide (D)	37,813	60.5
John F. Gardner (R)	22,085	35.3
12 Mary T. Norton (D)	44,815	61.7
Douglas D. T. Story (R)	26,368	36.3

NEW MEXICO

Candidates	Votes	%
AL John Morrow (D)	57,802	51.2
J. Felipe Hubbell (R)	53,960	47.8

NEW YORK

Candidates	Votes	%
1 Robert L. Bacon (R)	87,370	67.1
Ira L. Terry (D)	39,765	30.5
2 John J. Kindred (D)	73,757	62.6
Frank E. Hopkins (R)	40,507	34.4
3 George W. Lindsay (D)	22,621	64.8
Herman E. Sprigade (R)	9,804	28.1
Joseph A. Weil (SOC)	2,488	7.1
4 Thomas H. Cullen (D)	27,008	73.9
Joseph Rosenbaum (R)	8,780	24.0
5 Loring M. Black Jr. (D)	37,200	51.1
William T. Simpson (R)	33,938	46.6
6 Andrew L. Somers (D)	42,894	47.8
Warren I. Lee (R)	41,110	45.8
W. W. Passage (SOC)	5,779	6.4
7 John F. Quayle (D)	24,048	56.7
Otis S. Carroll (R)	14,650	34.5
Jacob Axelrad (SOC)	3,730	8.8
8 William E. Cleary (D)	49,479	51.3
Max Perlman (R)	38,638	40.1
William M. Feigenbaum (SOC)	8,333	8.6
9 David J. O'Connell (D)	43,655	50.2
Andrew N. Petersen (R)	38,708	44.5
Wilhelmus B. Robinson (SOC)	4,620	5.3
10 Emanuel Celler (D)	25,251	50.0
James N. Little (R)	19,444	38.5
Joseph A. Whitehorn (SOC)	5,449	10.8
11 Anning S. Prall (D)	34,265	68.7
Frederick W. Lahr (R)	14,990	30.0
12 Samuel Dickstein (D)	14,994	75.8
Harry Schlissel (R)	2,464	12.5
Israel Feinberg (SOC)	2,164	10.9
13 Christopher D. Sullivan (D)	13,708	71.1
Murray D. Firstman (R)	3,960	20.6
Julius Hochman (SOC)	1,600	8.3
14 Nathan D. Perlman (R)	12,046	44.1
William Irving Sirovich (D)	11,920	43.6
William Karlin (SOC)	3,165	11.6
15 John J. Boylan (D)	28,132	77.0
Warren Bigelow (R)	7,732	21.2
16 John J. O'Connor (D)	27,585	72.3
L. Wilfred Nidt (R)	9,329	24.4
17 Ogden L. Mills (R)	31,553	57.0
Charles E. Gehring (D)	22,526	40.7
18 John F. Carew (D)	25,975	66.1
Charles W. Ferry (R)	10,777	27.4
Samuel E. Beardsley (SOC)	2,519	6.4
19 Sol Bloom (D)	39,760	54.5
Walter M. Chandler (R)	31,008	42.5
20 Fiorello H. LaGuardia (SOC)	10,756	42.7
Henry Frank (D)	7,141	28.4
Isaac Siegel (R)	7,099	28.2
21 Royal H. Weller (D)	43,793	52.5
Charles H. Roberts (R)	35,881	43.1
22 Anthony J. Griffin (D)	30,469	69.7
William E. Devlin (R)	10,169	23.3
Joseph B. Hagerty (SOC)	3,081	7.1
23 Frank Oliver (D)	67,650	56.3
Albert B. Rossdale (R)	35,721	29.7
August Claessens (SOC)	15,771	13.1
24 Benjamin L. Fairchild (R)	50,745	45.5
John J. Kinney (D)	49,948	44.7
Philip Umstadter (SOC&PROG)	10,937	9.8
25 J. Mayhew Wainwright (R)	57,539	64.8
A. Outram Sherman (D)	26,909	30.3
26 Hamilton Fish Jr. (R)	55,386	69.7
Rosslyn M. Cox (D)	21,621	27.2

Candidates	Votes	%
27 Harcourt J. Pratt (R)	45,764	58.6
William C. DeWitt (D)	30,805	39.4
28 Parker Corning (D)	57,194	52.7
Charles H. Johnson (R)	50,108	46.2
29 James S. Parker (R)	60,730	67.2
James E. Dwyer (D)	28,079	31.1
30 Frank Crowther (R)	47,073	62.9
James P. Boyle (D & PROG)	24,840	33.2
31 Bertrand H. Snell (R)	45,372	70.5
John M. Cantwell (D)	19,018	29.5
32 Thaddeus C. Sweet (R)	52,506	68.9
Charles R. Lee (D)	23,715	31.1
33 Frederick M. Davenport (R)	48,591	58.1
Albert R. Kessinger (D)	33,068	39.5
34 Harold S. Tolley (R)	61,547	69.7
Charles R. Seymour (D)	24,800	28.1
35 Walter W. Magee (R)	70,268	64.7
John J. Kesel (D)	35,008	32.2
36 John Taber (R)	57,865	71.7
Michael J. Maney (D)	22,890	28.3
37 Gale H. Stalker (R)	59,498	66.9
Charles L. Durham (D)	27,763	31.2
38 Meyer Jacobstein (D&SOC)	63,997	65.4
John J. McInerney (R)	33,895	34.6
39 Archie D. Sanders (R)	58,165	67.9
Michael L. Coleman (D)	23,689	27.7
40 S. Wallace Dempsey (R)	66,939	67.8
Thurman W. Stoner (D)	26,382	26.7
Eustace Reynolds (SOC)	5,478	5.5
41 Clarence MacGregor (R)	40,449	68.1
Edward C. Dethloff (D)	13,754	23.1
Frank Ehrenfried (SOC)	5,237	8.8
42 James M. Mead (D)	28,152	50.1
Richard S. Persons (R)	25,256	45.0
43 Daniel A. Reed (R & SOC)	61,769	91.0
J. Samuel Fowler (PROG)	6,141	9.0

NORTH CAROLINA

Candidates	Votes	%
1 Lindsay C. Warren (D)	16,387	78.5
Peter D. Burgess (R)	4,478	21.5
2 John H. Kerr (D)	16,312	93.3
M. R. Vick (R)	1,169	6.7
3 Charles L. Abernethy (D)	17,685	67.7
William H. Fisher (R)	8,431	32.3
4 Edward W. Pou (D)	24,057	69.6
Young Z. Parker (R)	10,505	30.4
5 Charles M. Stedman (D)	44,048	59.3
Thomas C. Carter (R)	30,255	40.7
6 Homer L. Lyon (D)	21,682	72.7
William J. McDonald (R)	8,153	27.3
7 William C. Hammer (D)	36,491	55.2
S. Carter Williams (R)	29,652	44.8
8 Robert L. Doughton (D)	34,692	56.5
James D. Dorsett (R)	26,666	43.5
9 Alfred L. Bulwinkle (D)	37,370	57.7
John A. Hendricks (R)	27,427	42.3
10 Zebulon Weaver (D)	41,030	55.5
Lewis P. Hamlin (R)	32,871	44.5

NORTH DAKOTA

Candidates	Votes	%
1 Olger B. Burtness (R)	44,573	75.4
Walter Welford (D)	14,511	24.6
2 Thomas Hall (R)	31,212	52.1
Gerald P. Nye (PROG)	28,193	47.0
3 James H. Sinclair (R)	37,925	73.4
R. A. Johnson (D)	13,730	26.6

Special Election

Candidates	Votes	%
2 Thomas Hall (R)	33,460	51.0
Gerald P. Nye (PROG)	32,205	49.0

OHIO

Candidates	Votes	%
1 Nicholas Longworth (R)	58,185	61.7
Thomas B. Paxton (D)	36,065	38.3
2 Ambrose E. B. Stephens (R)	47,331	58.1
Robert J. O'Donnell (D)	34,118	41.9

Candidates	Votes	%
3 Roy Fitzgerald (R)	73,513	62.3
John P. Rogers (D)	43,426	36.8
4 W. T. Fitzgerald (R)	43,984	50.8
Hugh T. Mathers (D)	42,652	49.2
5 Charles J. Thompson (R)	31,046	51.5
Frank C. Kniffin (D)	29,245	48.5
6 Charles C. Kearns (R)	33,064	53.0
Ed. N. Kennedy (D)	29,283	47.0
7 Charles Brand (R)	61,557	63.9
C. K. Wolf (D)	34,709	36.1
8 Brooks Fletcher (D)	38,439	53.2
R. Clint Cole (R)	33,258	46.0
9 William W. Chalmers (R)	54,792	51.6
Isaac R. Sherwood (D)	48,442	45.6
10 Thomas A. Jenkins (R)	32,617	64.5
W. F. Rutherford (D)	17,923	35.5
11 Mell G. Underwood (D)	35,696	59.5
Edwin D. Ricketts (R)	24,272	40.5
12 John C. Speaks (R)	58,705	58.7
Lowry F. Sater (D)	41,291	41.3
13 James T. Begg (R)	45,307	62.1
John Dreitzler (D)	27,623	37.9
14 Martin L. Davey (D)	62,314	50.8
Arthur W. Doyle (R)	60,251	49.2
15 C. Ellis Moore (R)	39,155	56.1
James R. Alexander (D)	30,608	43.9
16 John McSweeney (D)	51,491	51.5
Thomas C. Hunsicker (R)	45,559	45.6
17 William M. Morgan (R)	50,226	57.9
J. Freer Bittinger (D)	36,532	42.1
18 Frank Murphy (R)	56,206	66.3
James M. Barton (D)	26,656	31.4
19 John G. Cooper (R)	67,581	75.5
Phebe T. Sutliff (D)	21,926	24.5
20 Charles A. Mooney (D)	34,173	59.7
Harvey Drucker (R)	22,507	39.3
21 Robert Crosser (D)	24,889	53.2
Harry C. Gahn (R)	21,629	46.2
22 Theodore E. Burton (R)	95,174#	61.8
Samuel B. Fitzsimmons (D)	32,970#	21.4
Alfred F. Coyle (I)	25,489#	16.6

OKLAHOMA

Candidates	Votes	%
1 Samuel J. Montgomery (R)	45,949	49.3
Wayne W. Bayless (D)	45,806	49.2
2 William W. Hastings (D)	30,352	54.9
P. E. Reed (R)	24,413	44.2
3 Charles D. Carter (D)	38,674	68.1
Don Welch (R)	15,433	27.2
4 Thomas D. McKeown (D)	36,437	58.8
Charles E. Wells (R)	23,313	37.6
5 Fletcher B. Swank (D)	44,683	59.4
John Golobie (R)	28,510	37.9
6 Elmer Thomas (D)	31,188	56.4
Lorraine M. Gensman (R)	21,915	39.6
7 James V. McClintic (D)	26,582	66.6
Walter S. Mills (R)	10,316	25.8
M. Shadid (F-LAB)	3,041	7.6
8 Milton C. Garber (R)	34,020	51.0
V. P. Crowe (D)	29,710	44.5

OREGON

Candidates	Votes	%
1 Willis C. Hawley (R)	72,910	63.5
Harvey L. Clark (D)	25,293	22.0
W. J. Butler (I)	13,494	11.8
2 Nicholas J. Sinnott (R)	29,937	61.6
James H. Graham (D)	18,652	38.4
3 Maurice E. Crumpacker (R)	50,834	54.7
Elton Watkins (D & PROG)	39,731	42.7

PENNSYLVANIA

Candidates	Votes	%
1 William S. Vare (R)	59,287	84.4
Joseph A. Robbins (D, PROG)	7,631	10.9
2 George S. Graham (R)	37,645	82.7
Jessie L. Collet (D, LAB)	6,355	14.0
3 Harry C. Ransley (R)	39,171	83.9
Edward P. Carroll (D)	4,092	8.8

Candidates	Votes	%
Jennie Dorriblum (SOC, LAB)	3,301	7.1
4 Benjamin M. Golder (R)	40,783	77.8
Adolph Class (D)	8,365	16.0
Henry P. Thomas (SOC)	3,237	6.2
5 James J. Connolly (R)	47,033	81.0
Daniel J. C. O'Donnell (D)	7,525	13.0
Harry Calse (SOC)	3,118	5.4
6 George A. Welsh (R)	66,340	74.6
Francis I. J. Coyle (D, LAB)	17,457	19.6
7 George P. Darrow (R, P)	55,990	80.7
Thomas A. O'Hara (D)	9,999	14.4
8 Thomas S. Butler (R)	63,480	80.7
Gordon H. Cilley (D, PROG)	12,816	16.3
9 Henry W. Watson (R)	60,316	72.5
C. William Freed (D)	18,843	22.7
10 William W. Griest (R)	35,257	60.4
Frank C. Musser (D, INDL)	22,503	38.6
11 Laurence H. Watres (R)	35,461	56.7
David Fowler (D, LAB)	25,471	40.7
12 Edmund N. Carpenter (R, P)	44,483	55.6
John J. Casey (D, SOC)	35,562	44.4
13 George Franklin Brumm (R, P)	35,737	69.5
Thomas J. Butler (D)	14,637	28.5
14 Charles J. Esterly (R)	43,335	50.5
William M. Croll (D)	36,582	42.6
Raymond S. Hofses (SOC)	5,884	6.9
15 Louis T. McFadden (R, P)	27,565	68.8
Charles M. Driggs (D, LAB)	11,854	29.6
16 Edgar R. Kless (R, P)	26,865	55.5
Thomas Wood (D)	18,246	37.7
P. A. McGowan (LAB, SOC)	3,317	6.8
17 Frederick W. Magrady (R, P)	27,969	53.5
Herbert W. Cummings (D, LAB)	24,321	46.5
18 Edward M. Beers (R, P)	35,743	66.4
Meredith Meyers (D, LAB)	18,048	33.6
19 Joshua W. Swartz (R)	39,465	53.9
Frank C. Sites (D, P)	33,038	45.1
20 Anderson H. Walters (R, P)	23,519	50.1
Warren Worth Bailey (D, LAB)	23,456	49.9
21 J. Banks Kurtz (R, SOC)	27,335	69.4
Harry K. Filler (D)	7,290	18.5
J. E. Miller (LAB)	4,748	12.1
22 Franklin Menges (R)	26,924	53.4
Samuel F. Glatfelter (D, P)	22,784	45.2
23 William Irvin Swoope (R, P)	31,205	64.7
Edward R. Benson (D, LAB)	17,008	35.3
24 Samuel A. Kendall (R, P)	31,443	68.5
Harrison N. Boyd (D)	11,810	25.7
25 Henry W. Temple (R, SOC)	27,192	62.5
Grant Furlong (D)	15,641	36.0
26 Thomas W. Phillips Jr. (R)	38,723	68.8
John G. Cobler (D, P)	15,307	27.2
27 Nathan L. Strong (R)	33,267	58.9
John H. Murray (P)	11,208	19.8
Harry W. Fee (D)	10,119	17.9
28 Harris J. Bixler (R, P)	43,247	79.1
William G. Barker (D)	11,409	20.9
29 Milton W. Shreve (R)	27,502	57.7
Edward M. Murphy (D)	10,304	21.6
Elizabeth R. Culbertson (P, LAB)	8,261	17.3
30 William R. Coyle (R)	31,036	50.9
Everett Kent (D, LAB)	28,723	47.1
31 Adam M. Wyant (R, SOC)	36,314	60.4
Chester D. Sensenich (D, LAB)	23,790	39.6
32 Stephen Geyer Porter (R, P)	31,102	79.5
P. M. O'Donnell (D)	5,055	12.9
33 M. Clyde Kelly (R, P)	37,314	81.1
Gilbert F. Myer (D)	6,017	13.1
34 John M. Morin (R, LAB)	22,669	82.5
William N. McNair (D)	3,289	12.0
35 James M. Magee (R, PROG)	28,381	59.9
John W. Slayton (LAB, SOC)	9,039	19.1
John Murphy (D)	5,755	12.1
Thomas P. Moran (INDL)	2,544	5.4
36 Guy E. Campbell (R, D)	34,266	87.2
William H. Bright (P)	5,048	12.8

RHODE ISLAND

Candidates	Votes	%
1 Clark Burdick (R)	44,952	65.2
Alfred H. Jones (D)	23,958	34.8
2 Richard S. Aldrich (R)	44,870	63.9
Charles M. Hall (D)	25,361	36.1
3 Jeremiah E. O'Connell (D)	35,224	51.7
Louis Monast (R)	32,953	48.3

SOUTH CAROLINA

Candidates	Votes	%
1 Thomas S. McMillan (D)	5,278	95.4
2 Butler B. Hare (D)	6,695	100.0
3 Fred H. Dominick (D)	8,331	100.0
4 John J. McSwain (D)	7,718	100.0
5 William F. Stevenson (D)	7,689	100.0
6 Allard H. Gasque (D)	6,278	100.0
7 Hampton P. Fulmer (D)	7,249	100.0

SOUTH DAKOTA

Candidates	Votes	%
1 Charles A. Christopherson (R)	39,138	53.5
Warren E. Beck (D)	19,904	27.2
William Bartling (I)	7,206	9.9
William T. Jones (F-LAB)	6,901	9.4
2 Royal C. Johnson (R)	44,869	60.3
Walter P. Wohlheter (F-LAB)	11,468	15.4
Fred H. Hildebrandt (I)	10,067	13.5
Jack P. Reinhard (I)	8,043	10.8
3 William Williamson (R)	28,150	58.3
John R. Russell (D)	10,026	20.8
Arthur W. Watwood (F-LAB)	6,950	14.4

TENNESSEE

Candidates	Votes	%
1 B. Carroll Reece (R)	23,445	62.6
R. M. Barry (D)	11,362	30.3
F. P. Robinson	1,970	5.3
2 J. Will Taylor (R)	28,975	96.3
3 Sam D. McReynolds (D)	22,857	56.9
May Giles Howard (R)	17,341	43.1
4 Cordell Hull (D)	16,908	100.0
5 Ewin L. Davis (D)	11,373	81.7
A. L. Davidson (R)	2,551	18.3
6 Joseph W. Byrns (D)	19,756	100.0
7 Edward E. Eslick (D)	13,547	100.0
8 Gordon Browning (D)	12,940	100.0
9 Finis J. Garrett (D)	18,367	100.0
10 Hubert F. Fisher (D)	16,306	74.0
George H. Poole	2,923	13.3
Harry Speers (R)	2,801	12.7

TEXAS

Candidates	Votes	%
1 Eugene Black (D)	28,218	90.9
R. B. Johnson (R)	2,826	9.1
2 John C. Box (D)	41,188	89.9
A. E. Sweatland (R)	4,625	10.1
3 Morgan G. Sanders (D)	30,618	100.0
4 Sam Rayburn (D)	31,825	91.1
C. A. Gray (R)	3,111	8.9
5 Hatton W. Sumners (D)	43,781	87.6
George G. Atkinson (R)	6,193	12.4
6 Luther A. Johnson (D)	33,169	93.2
Tyler Haswell (R)	2,440	6.9
7 Clay Stone Briggs (D)	23,947	89.1
John T. Wheeler (R)	2,941	10.9
8 Daniel E. Garrett (D)	35,189	86.0
Clarence A. Miller (R)	5,712	14.0
9 Joseph J. Mansfield (D)	31,444	82.3
Ed. Franz (R)	6,742	17.7
10 James P. Buchanan (D)	36,681	90.5
Otto Stolley (R)	3,850	9.5
11 Tom T. Connally (D)	29,247	88.2
C. C. Baker (R)	3,918	11.8
12 Fritz G. Lanham (D)	33,186	100.0
13 Guinn Williams (D)	32,721	88.6
C. W. Johnson Jr. (R)	4,197	11.4
14 Harry M. Wurzbach (R)	31,784	62.4
D. S. Davenport (D)	19,165	37.6

Candidates	Votes	%
15 John N. Garner (D)	22,776	99.9
16 Claude B. Hudspeth (D)	27,506	82.6
Vernon L. Sullivan (R)	5,800	17.4
17 Thomas L. Blanton (D)	44,377	100.0
18 Marvin Jones (D)	42,399	89.7
A. B. Spencer (R)	4,887	10.3

UTAH

Candidates	Votes	%
1 Don B. Colton (R)	40,883	54.9
Frank Francis (D)	33,644	45.1
2 Elmer O. Leatherwood (R)	41,888	56.7
James H. Waters (D)	32,045	43.3

VERMONT

Candidates	Votes	%
1 Elbert S. Brigham (R, P)	36,278	76.0
Allan T. Calhoun (D)	11,457	24.0
2 Ernest Willard Gibson (R, P)	41,099	82.8
Harry C. Shurtleff (D)	8,479	17.1

VIRGINIA

Candidates	Votes	%
1 Schuyler Otis Bland (D)	16,958	99.9
2 Joseph T. Deal (D)	11,795	65.8
Menalcus Lankford (R)	6,145	34.3
3 Andrew Jackson Montague (D)	20,864	100.0
4 Patrick Henry Drewry (D)	12,106	100.0
5 Joseph Whitehead (D)	16,371	76.0
G. A. De Hart (R)	5,181	24.0
6 Clifton A. Woodrum (D)	13,917	69.0
F. W. McWane (R)	6,251	31.0
7 Thomas W. Harrison (D)	13,013	59.2
J. H. Ruebush (R)	7,294	33.2

Candidates	Votes	%
Dabney C. Harrison (I)	1,692	7.7
8 R. Walton Moore (D)	14,113	79.9
John G. Dudley (R)	3,551	20.1
9 George C. Peery (D)	31,407	52.6
C. Henry Harman (R)	28,341	47.4
10 Henry St. George Tucker (D)	14,472	69.7
Henry S. Reid (R)	6,288	30.3

WASHINGTON

Candidates	Votes	%
1 John F. Miller (R)	53,152	78.8
David J. Williams (D)	13,922	20.6
2 Lindley H. Hadley (R)	37,636	57.4
Lloyd L. Black (D)	27,154	41.4
3 Albert Johnson (R)	60,272	70.5
O. M. Nelson (PROG)	25,146	29.4
4 John W. Summers (R)	36,918	65.3
H. C. Bohlke (D)	12,254	21.7
Knute Hill (F-LAB)	7,380	13.1
5 Sam B. Hill (D)	36,844	50.7
J. Edward Ferguson (R)	35,815	49.3

WEST VIRGINIA

Candidates	Votes	%
1 Carl G. Bachmann (R)	47,318	55.2
George W. Oldham (D)	38,417	44.8
2 Frank L. Bowman (R)	41,825	50.1
Robert E. Lee Allen (D)	40,474	48.5
3 John M. Wolverton (R)	45,995	51.9
Robert H. Kidd (D)	42,626	48.1
4 Harry C. Woodyard (R)	47,136	51.2
George W. Johnson (D)	44,877	48.8
5 James French Strother (R)	50,629	51.5
Thomas Jefferson Lilly (D)	47,719	48.5

Candidates	Votes	%
6 J. Alfred Taylor (D)	56,570	49.8
Leonard S. Echols (R)	55,089	48.5

WISCONSIN

Candidates	Votes	%
1 Henry Allen Cooper (R)	60,770	72.0
Calvin Stewart (D)	23,612	28.0
2 Edward Voigt (R)	44,617	70.5
Ernest C. Wrucke (D)	18,696	29.5
3 John M. Nelson (R)	56,868	77.0
William Victora (D)	16,968	23.0
4 John C. Schafer (R)	30,837	49.6
Leo Krzycki (SOC)	19,770	31.8
Thomas H. Dorr (D)	11,524	18.6
5 Victor L. Berger (SOC)	32,211	41.6
Ernst A. Braun (R)	31,702	41.0
Raymond Moore (D)	13,441	17.4
6 Florian Lampert (R)	45,982	70.6
Michael K. Reilly (D)	19,128	29.4
7 Joseph D. Beck (R)	47,075	80.0
W. D. Martin (D)	10,228	17.4
8 Edward E. Browne (R)	47,423	99.9
9 George J. Schneider (R)	45,159	71.0
T. J. Reinert (D)	18,449	29.0
10 James A. Frear (R)	46,563	78.7
Thomas A. Ryan (D)	10,481	17.7
11 Hubert H. Peavey (R)	48,234	78.1
John Cadigan (D)	13,455	21.8

WYOMING

Candidates	Votes	%
AL Charles E. Winter (R)	43,026	60.1
Theodore Wanerus (D)	28,537	39.9

1925 House Election

NEW JERSEY

Special Election

Candidates	Votes	%
3 Stewart H. Appleby (R)	53,925	53.3
J. Lyle Kinmonth (D)	47,271	46.7

1926 House Elections

ALABAMA

	Candidates	Votes	%
1	John McDuffie (D)	8,297	84.0
	Aubrey Boyles (R)	1,578	16.0
2	Lister Hill (D)	10,170	100.0
3	Henry B. Steagall (D)	7,619	94.6
	C. E. Roberts (R)	437	5.4
4	Lamar Jeffers (D)	8,392	68.1
	Omar H. Reynolds (R)	3,933	31.9
5	William B. Bowling (D)	9,012	88.4
	John A. Alexander (R)	1,183	11.6
6	William B. Oliver (D)	3,984	99.0
7	Miles C. Allgood (D)	14,937	64.7
	John J. Stephens (R)	8,162	35.3
8	Edward B. Almon (D)	8,800	90.1
	Robert M. Sims (R)	964	9.9
9	George Huddleston (D)	7,260	94.4
	Frank H. Lathrop (R)	430	5.6
10	William B. Bankhead (D)	11,895	100.0

ARIZONA

	Candidates	Votes	%
AL	Lewis W. Douglas (D)	43,725	64.1
	Otis J. Baughn (R)	24,502	35.9

ARKANSAS

	Candidates	Votes	%
1	William J. Driver (D)	3,680	100.0
2	William A. Oldfield (D)	4,013	78.8
	J. L. McKamey (R)	1,081	21.2
3	John N. Tillman (D)	5,696	64.4
	Hardy Kuykendall (R)	3,146	35.6
4	Otis T. Wingo (D)	4,729	100.0
5	Heartsill Ragon (D)	4,282	88.2
	Harry M. Williams (R)	574	11.8
6	James B. Reed (D)	3,013	100.0
7	Tilman B. Parks (D)	3,498	100.0

CALIFORNIA

	Candidates	Votes	%
1	Clarence F. Lea (D-R)	60,207	100.0
2	Harry L. Englebright (R)	32,264	99.8
3	Charles F. Curry (R-D)	72,912	100.0
4	Florence P. Kahn (R)	37,353	63.8
	Chauncey F. Tramutolo (D)	18,210	31.1
	William McDevitt (SOC)	2,960	5.1
5	Richard J. Welch (R-D)	47,694	100.0
6	Albert E. Carter (R)	91,995	100.0
7	Henry E. Barbour (R-D)	73,271	100.0
8	Arthur Monroe Free (R)	60,384	67.7
	Philip G. Sheehy (D)	28,836	32.3
9	William E. Evans (R)	102,270	59.5
	Charles H. Randall (P & D)	61,719	35.9
10	Joe Crail (R-D-P)	144,677	86.8
	N. Jackson Wright (SOC)	21,997	13.2
11	Philip D. Swing (R-D)	89,726	100.0

COLORADO

	Candidates	Votes	%
1	William N. Vaile (R)	39,909	54.9
	Benjamin C. Hilliard (D)	30,337	41.7
2	Charles B. Timberlake (R)	55,581	66.6
	William B. Washburn (D)	27,939	33.5
3	Guy U. Hardy (R)	46,916	54.0
	Edmond I. Crockett (D)	40,009	46.0
4	Edward T. Taylor (D)	32,092	66.7
	Webster S. Whinnery (R)	15,990	33.3

CONNECTICUT

	Candidates	Votes	%
1	E. Hart Fenn (R)	45,054	63.0
	Henry J. Calnen (D)	25,777	36.0
2	Richard P. Freeman (R)	33,809	61.7
	Hermon J. Gibbs (D)	20,538	37.5
3	John Q. Tilson (R)	40,055	65.6
	John E. Doughan (D)	20,281	33.2
4	Schuyler Merritt (R)	44,477	68.4
	John Held Jr. (D)	19,623	30.2
5	James P. Glynn (R)	28,687	58.5
	Arthur F. O'Leary (D)	20,352	41.5

DELAWARE

	Candidates	Votes	%
AL	Robert G. Houston (R)	38,909	56.9
	Merrill H. Tilghman (D)	29,424	43.1

FLORIDA

	Candidates	Votes	%
1	Herbert J. Drane (D)	16,034	72.8
	Ora E. Chapin (RP & DC)	6,007	27.3
2	Robert A. Green (D)	6,727	86.2
	A. F. Knotts (R)	1,080	13.8
3	Tom A. Yon (D)	7,156	86.8
	J. H. Drummond (R)	1,084	13.2
4	William J. Sears (D)	19,578	73.6
	W. C. Lawson (RDC)	4,235	15.9
	E. D. Housholder (R)	2,783	10.5

GEORGIA

	Candidates	Votes	%
1	Charles G. Edwards (D)	7,641	100.0
2	E. E. Cox (D)	2,384	100.0
3	Charles R. Crisp (D)	3,422	100.0
4	William C. Wright (D)	2,583	100.0
5	Leslie J. Steele (D)	2,919	99.9
6	Samuel Rutherford (D)	2,365	100.0
7	Malcolm C. Tarver (D)	5,902	94.1
	George A. Coffee	373	5.9
8	Charles H. Brand (D)	3,124	100.0
9	Thomas M. Bell (D)	7,788	100.0
10	Carl Vinson (D)	3,015	100.0
11	William C. Lankford (D)	3,461	100.0
12	William W. Larsen (D)	2,388	100.0

IDAHO

	Candidates	Votes	%
1	Burton L. French (R)	31,250	66.3
	L. L. Burtenshaw (D, PROG)	15,903	33.7
2	Addison T. Smith (R)	40,960	60.6
	H. F. Fait (PROG)	15,368	22.7
	Mary George Gray (D)	11,259	16.7

ILLINOIS

	Candidates	Votes	%
1	Martin B. Madden (R)	26,559	68.2
	James F. Doyle (D)	12,283	31.5
2	Morton D. Hull (R)	71,750	65.5
	Michael C. Walsh (D)	37,518	34.3
3	Elliott W. Sproul (R)	57,692	52.7
	Edward J. Glackin (D)	51,590	47.1
4	Thomas A. Doyle (D)	30,817	62.9
	John J. Dever (R)	18,184	37.1
5	Adolph J. Sabath (D)	18,027	58.8
	Matt J. Vogel (R)	12,643	41.2
6	James T. Igoe (D)	74,817	52.6
	John J. Gorman (R)	67,419	47.4
7	M. Alfred Michaelson (R)	86,405	57.8
	John S. Hall (D)	62,469	41.8
8	Stanley Henry Kunz (D)	15,321	55.3
	Wencil F. Hetman (R)	12,388	44.7
9	Fred A. Britten (R)	26,530	97.8
10	Carl R. Chindblom (R)	68,137	66.0
	William X. Meyer (D)	35,123	34.0
11	Frank R. Reid (R)	44,574	69.5
	Edward J. O'Beirne (D)	19,600	30.5
12	John T. Buckbee (R)	36,597	57.8
	John A. Logan Warren (D)	26,727	42.2
13	William R. Johnson (R)	30,197	74.8
	John Ascher (D)	10,190	25.2
14	John C. Allen (R)	33,089	68.0
	John W. Casto (D)	15,572	32.0
15	Edward J. King (R)	35,396	62.6

	Candidates	Votes	%
	F. William Heckenkamp Jr. (D)	21,157	37.4
16	William E. Hull (R)	37,170	63.3
	Carl M. Behrman (D)	21,530	36.7
17	Homer W. Hall (R)	31,874	64.9
	Frank Gillespie (D)	17,220	35.1
18	William P. Holaday (R)	44,112	65.2
	Wilbur Hickman (D)	23,569	34.8
19	Charles Adkins (R)	40,456	62.3
	Joel T. Davis (D)	24,507	37.7
20	Henry T. Rainey (D)	29,935	57.8
	Horace H. Bancroft (R)	21,875	42.2
21	J. Earl Major (D)	39,365	52.8
	Loren E. Wheeler (R)	35,191	47.2
22	Edward M. Irwin (R)	38,714	58.5
	William N. Baltz (D)	27,428	41.5
23	William W. Arnold (D)	38,575	55.9
	Erastus D. Telford (R)	29,896	43.3
24	Thomas S. Williams (R)	26,295	56.1
	John Marshall Karns (D)	20,612	43.9
25	Edward E. Denison (R)	36,644	59.6
	A. F. Gourley (D)	24,849	40.4
AL	Henry R. Rathbone (R)	987,968✓	
	Richard Yates (R)	986,090✓	
	Frank J. Wise (D)	631,708	
	Charles A. Karch (D)	616,713	
	Mrs. P. J. Carlson (PROG)	5,413	
	Charles Pogoreles (SOC)	2,662	
	George Koop (SOC)	2,476	
	James S. O'Rourke (SOC LAB)	1,977	
	A. H. Otto Beneze (SOC LAB)	1,746	
	Charles D. Harrison (HL)	451	
	Andrew A. Gour (CLP)	431	
	Mary C. Connor (CLP)	428	

INDIANA

	Candidates	Votes	%
1	Harry E. Rowbottom (R)	37,503	52.4
	William E. Wilson (D)	34,061	47.6
2	Arthur H. Greenwood (D)	44,690	55.4
	John E. Sedwick (R)	35,964	44.6
3	Frank Gardner (D)	42,422	54.6
	W. Clyde Martin (R)	35,229	45.4
4	Harry C. Canfield (D)	42,882	53.9
	John W. Holcomb (R)	36,655	46.1
5	Noble J. Johnson (R)	43,458	57.8
	Henry W. Moore (D)	31,693	42.2
6	Richard N. Elliott (R)	38,347	55.2
	William H. Myers (D)	31,107	44.8
7	Ralph E. Updike (R)	48,313	52.1
	William O. Headrick (D)	44,142	47.6
8	Albert H. Vestal (R)	40,963	53.8
	Claude C. Ball (D)	35,205	46.2
9	Fred S. Purnell (R)	43,891	52.6
	Roy W. Adney (D)	39,597	47.4
10	William R. Wood (R)	52,286	68.2
	Harry O. Rhodes (D)	24,349	31.8
11	Albert R. Hall (R)	42,519	54.2
	Samuel E. Cook (D)	35,870	45.8
12	David Hogg (R)	38,936	55.3
	Waldemar E. Eickhoff (D)	31,442	44.7
13	Andrew J. Hickey (R)	52,541	54.9
	Charles Weldler (D)	43,119	45.1

IOWA

	Candidates	Votes	%
1	William F. Kopp (R)	27,358	70.6
	James M. Bell (D)	11,408	29.4
2	F. Dickinson Letts (R)	29,200	59.1
	J. P. Gallagher (D)	19,612	39.7
3	Thomas J. B. Robinson (R)	32,180	70.2
	Ellis E. Wilson (D)	13,696	29.9
4	Gilbert N. Haugen (R)	30,611	60.4
	Frank E. Howard (D)	20,076	39.6
5	Cyrenus Cole (R)	31,253	71.8
	C. E. Watters (D)	12,263	28.2
6	C. William Ramseyer (R)	27,967	66.3

Candidates	Votes	%
W. L. Etter (D)	14,193	33.7
7 Cassius C. Dowell (R)	34,159	76.9
William M. Wade (D)	10,255	23.1
8 Lloyd Thurston (R)	30,568	61.9
W. S. Bradley (D)	18,743	37.9
9 William R. Green (R)	30,373	67.2
Charles F. Paschel (D)	14,837	32.8
10 Lester J. Dickinson (R)	39,677	97.7
11 William D. Boies (R)	35,381	64.4
R. J. Koehler (D)	19,542	35.6

KANSAS

Candidates	Votes	%
1 Daniel R. Anthony Jr. (R)	46,232	100.0
2 Ulysses S. Guyer (R)	37,465	51.6
Chauncey B. Little (D)	35,108	48.3
3 William H. Sproul (R)	35,510	50.5
Thurman Hill (D)	34,765	49.5
4 Homer Hoch (R)	29,285	65.2
Edwin F. Hammond (D)	15,643	34.8
5 James G. Strong (R)	33,817	62.8
Rex Montgomery (D)	20,033	37.2
6 Hays B. White (R)	31,159	50.1
W. H. Clark (D)	31,065	49.9
7 Clifford R. Hope (R)	49,072	64.1
Harry F. Brown (D)	27,374	35.8
8 William A. Ayres (D)	32,096	60.1
Fred L. Bell (R)	21,350	40.0

KENTUCKY

Candidates	Votes	%
1 William V. Gregory (D)	28,306	67.8
Mrs. William H. Mason (R)	13,460	32.2
2 David H. Kincheloe (D)	23,445	56.2
Ernest Rowe (R)	18,279	43.8
3 John W. Moore (D)	24,303	56.2
Charles E. Whittle (R)	18,941	43.8
4 Henry D. Moorman (D)	24,348	55.3
Pal Garner (R)	19,658	44.7
5 Maurice H. Thatcher (R)	51,328	54.8
S. M. Russell (D)	42,339	45.2
6 Orie S. Ware (D)	26,063	57.2
E. H. Daugherty (R)	19,487	42.8
7 Virgil Chapman (D)	26,924	100.0
8 Ralph Gilbert (D)	21,938	54.5
E. W. Draffen (R)	18,321	45.5
9 Fred M. Vinson (D)	31,063	59.1
Trumbo Snedegar (R)	21,498	40.9
10 Katherine Langley (R)	20,463	58.4
Doug Hays (D)	14,578	41.6
11 John M. Robsion (R)	38,474	100.0

Special Elections

Candidates	Votes	%
3 John W. Moore (D)	27,640	52.9
Thurman B. Dixon (R)	24,580	47.1
10 Andrew J. Kirk (R)	10,540	60.7
J. C. Cantrell (D)	6,838	39.4

LOUISIANA

Candidates	Votes	%
1 James O'Connor (D)	14,486	94.3
Gus Oertling (R)	869	5.7
2 J. Zach Spearing (D)	15,110	100.0
3 Whitmell P. Martin (D)	3,488	100.0
4 John N. Sandlin (D)	5,490	100.0
5 Riley J. Wilson (D)	2,778	100.0
6 Bolivar E. Kemp (D)	4,055	100.0
7 Ladislas Lazaro (D)	3,721	100.0
8 James B. Aswell (D)	4,192	100.0

MAINE

Candidates	Votes	%
1 Carroll L. Beedy (R)	27,040	62.8
Richard E. Hersom (D)	16,032	37.2
2 Wallace H. White Jr. (R)	26,593	56.6
Charles M. Starbird (D)	20,422	43.4
3 John E. Nelson (R)	30,216	64.8
Edward Chase (D)	16,421	35.2

Candidates	Votes	%
4 Ira G. Hersey (R)	22,858	62.9
Frank A. Peabody (D)	13,457	37.1

MARYLAND

Candidates	Votes	%
1 T. Alan Goldsborough (D)	30,845	59.1
Lawrence B. Towers (R)	21,359	40.9
2 William P. Cole Jr. (D)	50,305	58.9
Linwood L. Clark (R)	34,327	40.2
3 Vincent L. Palmisano (D)	21,466	58.7
John J. McGinity (D)	14,284	39.1
4 J. Charles Linthicum (D)	32,620	62.0
Julius F. Diehl (R)	19,531	37.1
5 Stephen W. Gambrill (D)	26,905	55.1
Thomas Brackett Reed Mudd (R)	21,911	44.9
6 Frederick N. Zihlman (R)	35,247	58.3
Frank W. Mish (D)	24,749	40.9

MASSACHUSETTS

Candidates	Votes	%
1 Allen T. Treadway (R)	37,878	58.8
Eugene A. Lynch (D)	26,592	41.3
2 Henry L. Bowles (R)	36,333	64.0
John Hall (D)	20,450	36.0
3 Frank H. Foss (R)	35,887	62.8
Joseph E. Casey (D)	21,257	37.2
4 George R. Stobbs (R)	37,744	57.7
Peter F. Sullivan (D)	27,706	42.3
5 Edith Nourse Rogers (R)	46,464	71.1
James M. Hurley (D)	18,846	28.9
6 A. Piatt Andrew (R)	39,918	76.9
James McPherson (D)	11,975	23.1
7 William P. Connery Jr. (D)	32,130	64.0
George F. Hogan (R)	18,045	36.0
8 Frederick W. Dallinger (R)	46,642	63.7
John P. Brennan (D)	26,601	36.3
9 Charles L. Underhill (R)	34,468	57.8
Francis X. Tyrrell (D)	25,211	42.2
10 John J. Douglass (D)	29,443	100.0
11 George Holden Tinkham (R, D)	48,948	100.0
12 James A. Gallivan (D)	49,865	100.0
13 Robert Luce (R)	50,463	64.0
John P. Tierney (D)	28,346	36.0
14 Louis A. Frothingham (R)	51,920	66.2
Frank A. Manning (D)	26,469	33.8
15 Joseph W. Martin Jr. (R)	33,687	65.2
Minerva D. Kepple (D)	17,963	34.8
16 Charles L. Gifford (R)	35,235	68.0
George Fox Tucker (D)	16,570	32.0

Special Election

Candidates	Votes	%
8 Frederick W. Dallinger (R)	44,761#	64.3
John P. Brennan (D)	24,800#	35.7

MICHIGAN

Candidates	Votes	%
1 Robert H. Clancy (R)	27,004	74.1
William M. Donnelly (D)	9,119	25.0
2 Earl C. Michener (R)	38,182	66.7
Boyez Dansard (D)	19,034	33.3
3 Joseph L. Hooper (R)	30,704	70.2
Frank L. Willison (D)	13,034	29.8
4 John C. Ketcham (R)	31,881	72.3
Earl B. Sill (D)	12,223	27.7
5 Carl E. Mapes (R)	29,653	80.2
Frank C. Jarvis (D)	7,339	19.8
6 Grant M. Hudson (R)	67,796	68.0
Frank L. Dodge (D)	31,945	32.0
7 Louis C. Cramton (R)	35,967	78.1
Frank W. Merrick (D)	10,081	21.9
8 Bird J. Vincent (R)	39,541	100.0
9 James C. McLaughlin (R)	24,927	99.3
10 Roy O. Woodruff (R)	23,875	100.0
11 Frank P. Bohn (R)	25,816	77.6
Robert H. Wright (D)	7,468	22.4
12 W. Frank James (R)	37,117	100.0
13 Clarence J. McLeod (R)	26,190	68.0
Henry A. Behrendt (D)	12,152	31.6

MINNESOTA

Candidates	Votes	%
1 Allen J. Furlow (R)	46,956	74.5
L. B. Hanna (D)	16,070	25.5
2 Frank Clague (R)	56,679	100.0
3 August H. Andresen (R)	40,484	63.3
August M. Gagen (F-LAB)	13,636	21.3
Charles C. Kolars (D)	9,825	15.4
4 Melvin J. Maas (R)	22,976#	54.3
Thomas V. Sullivan (F-LAB)	17,355#	41.0
5 Walter H. Newton (R)	47,162	64.8
Albert G. Bastis (F-LAB)	19,647	27.0
Fred Jensen (R)	5,942	8.2
6 Harold Knutson (R)	39,570	59.4
Joseph B. Himsel (F-LAB)	27,076	40.6
7 Ole J. Kvale (F-LAB)	41,151	59.0
E. E. Howard (R)	28,641	41.0
8 William L. Carss (F-LAB)	41,766	55.4
Oscar J. Larson (R)	33,606	44.6
9 Conrad G. Selvig (R)	33,477	50.7
Knud Wefald (F-LAB)	32,505	49.3
10 Godfrey G. Goodwin (R)	36,897	59.1
Ernest Lundeen (F-LAB)	21,552	34.5
Henry A. Finlayson (D)	4,013	6.4

MISSISSIPPI

Candidates	Votes	%
1 John E. Rankin (D)	3,423	100.0
2 Bill G. Lowrey (D)	3,167	100.0
3 William M. Whittington (D)	2,949	100.0
4 T. Jeff Busby (D)	3,945	100.0
5 Ross A. Collins (D)	4,832	100.0
6 T. Webber Wilson (D)	4,792	100.0
7 Percy E. Quin (D)	1,781	100.0
8 James W. Collier (D)	2,028	100.0

MISSOURI

Candidates	Votes	%
1 Milton A. Romjue (D)	29,629	60.4
J. Frank Culler (R)	19,384	39.5
2 Ralph F. Lozier (D)	31,999	62.4
Sam A. Clark (R)	19,243	37.5
3 Jacob L. Milligan (D)	26,596	56.3
Charles T. McLaughlin (R)	20,611	43.7
4 Charles L. Faust (R)	30,320	56.3
J. C. Whitsell (D)	23,573	43.7
5 George H. Combs Jr. (D)	78,700	56.2
Edgar C. Ellis (R)	61,189	43.7
6 Clement C. Dickinson (D)	24,161	55.2
Millard E. Lane (R)	19,524	44.6
7 Samuel C. Major (D)	37,392	52.1
Harold T. Lincoln (R)	34,339	47.8
8 William L. Nelson (D)	26,156	56.2
C. W. Thomas (R)	20,422	43.8
9 Clarence Cannon (D)	28,720	61.2
Osmund Haenssler (R)	18,163	38.7
10 Henry F. Niedringhaus (R)	91,419	66.1
Irvin Sale (D)	46,880	33.9
11 John J. Cochran (D)	22,854	52.6
Henri Chouteau (R)	20,554	47.3
12 Leonidas C. Dyer (R)	14,494	61.3
David D. Israel (D)	9,120	38.6
13 Clyde Williams (D)	23,338	50.6
Charles E. Kiefner (R)	22,764	49.3
14 James F. Fullbright (D)	40,871	51.5
James F. Adams (R)	38,501	48.5
15 Joe J. Manlove (R)	36,995	59.7
Robert W. Moore (D)	24,786	40.0
16 Thomas L. Rubey (D)	25,032	56.5
Anna Covert (R)	19,251	43.5

Special Election

Candidates	Votes	%
11 John J. Cochran (D)	22,971	52.8
Henri Chouteau (R)	20,521	47.2

MONTANA

Candidates	Votes	%
1 John M. Evans (D)	38,527	59.4
Ronald Higgins (R)	25,898	39.9

Candidates	Votes	%
2 Scott Leavitt (R)	48,617	54.9
Harry B. Mitchell (D)	37,306	42.1

NEBRASKA

Candidates	Votes	%
1 John H. Morehead (D)	30,840	55.3
George W. Marsh (R)	24,169	43.4
2 Willis G. Sears (R)	33,211	59.5
Grenville P. North (D)	22,641	40.5
3 Edgar Howard (D)	43,915	60.7
John F. Nesbit (R)	21,075	29.1
Willis E. Reed (LAF I)	7,383	10.2
4 John N. Norton (D)	31,107	50.6
Melvin O. McLaughlin (R)	30,397	49.4
5 Ashton C. Shallenberger (D-LAF I)	36,058	60.3
W. E. Andrews (R)	23,781	39.7
6 Robert G. Simmons (R)	55,330	65.8
Thomas C. Osborne (D)	28,746	34.2

NEVADA

Candidates	Votes	%
AL Samuel S. Arentz (R)	17,598	57.7
Maurice J. Sullivan (D)	12,910	42.3

NEW HAMPSHIRE

Candidates	Votes	%
1 Fletcher Hale (R)	40,566	61.4
F. Clyde Keefe (D)	25,555	38.7
2 Edward H. Wason (R)	36,598	63.2
George H. Duncan (D)	21,312	36.8

NEW JERSEY

Candidates	Votes	%
1 Charles A. Wolverton (R)	57,522	69.7
Edward J. Kelleher (D)	24,990	30.3
2 Isaac Bacharach (R)	53,147	80.6
Frank Melville (D)	12,775	19.4
3 Harold Hoffman (R)	61,484	60.7
Fred W. DeVoe (D)	39,074	38.6
4 Charles A. Eaton (R)	35,948	62.0
William M. Williams (D)	22,059	38.0
5 Ernest R. Ackerman (R)	50,209	63.7
Frank K. Sauer (D)	28,644	36.3
6 Randolph Perkins (R)	58,244	62.9
Francis C. Koehler (D)	33,132	35.8
7 George N. Seger (R)	29,383	70.6
Susan A. McNair (D)	11,083	26.6
8 Paul J. Moore (D)	39,436	58.1
Herbert W. Taylor (R)	28,273	41.6
9 Franklin W. Fort (R)	19,751	60.2
James J. Whalen (D)	13,058	39.8
10 Frederick R. Lehlbach (R)	28,960	64.8
Edward W. Townsend (D)	15,727	35.2
11 Oscar L. Auf der Helde (D)	45,877	76.1
George M. Eichler (R)	14,083	23.4
12 Mary T. Norton (D)	54,082	83.1
Philip W. Grece (R)	11,034	17.0

NEW MEXICO

Candidates	Votes	%
AL John Morrow (D)	55,433	51.4
Juan A. A. Sedillo (R)	52,075	48.3

NEW YORK

Candidates	Votes	%
1 Robert L. Bacon (R)	82,090	63.4
W. Irving Vanderpoel (D)	45,699	35.3
2 John J. Kindred (D)	89,062	69.4
Louis C. Gosdorfer (R)	37,163	29.0
3 George W. Lindsay (D)	21,713	75.1
Walter H. Kreiner (R)	5,984	20.7
4 Thomas H. Cullen (D)	24,734	78.1
George H. Teommey Sr. (R)	6,624	20.9
5 Loring M. Black Jr. (D)	34,488	56.0
Robert C. Lee (R)	26,295	42.7
6 Andrew L. Somers (D)	47,407	57.0
William F. Heissenbuttel (R)	30,906	37.2
William W. Passage (SOC)	4,799	5.8
7 John F. Quayle (D)	22,551	65.0

Candidates	Votes	%
Harland B. Tibbetts (R)	9,747	28.1
Mendel Bromberg (SOC)	2,394	6.9
8 Patrick J. Carley (D)	62,091	61.4
George W. Criss (R)	30,548	30.2
W. M. Feigenbaum (SOC)	8,526	8.4
9 David J. O'Connell (D)	45,191	57.1
Edward W. Patterson (R)	31,131	39.3
10 Emanuel Celler (D)	24,102	58.3
Samuel Rubin (R)	13,428	32.5
Abraham I. Shiplacoff (SOC)	3,576	8.6
11 Anning S. Prall (D)	34,584	72.2
Esli L. Sutton (R)	12,929	27.0
12 Samuel Dickstein (D)	13,135	79.7
Joseph D. Tarlowe (R)	2,142	13.0
Harry Rogoff (SOC)	1,201	7.3
13 Christopher D. Sullivan (D)	12,307	75.7
John Fanelle (R)	3,067	18.9
Algernon Lee (SOC)	846	5.2
14 William Irving Sirovich (D)	11,809	49.4
Nathan D. Perlman (R)	10,688	44.8
Samuel E. Beardsley (SOC)	1,277	5.4
15 John J. Boylan (D)	24,083	80.8
John J. Curry (R)	5,312	17.8
16 John J. O'Connor (D)	24,476	76.7
Fred W. Meyer (R)	6,918	21.7
17 William W. Cohen (D)	22,401	50.4
Louis W. Stotesbury (R)	21,251	47.8
18 John F. Carew (D)	25,832	77.7
Bernard Katzen (R)	6,076	18.3
19 Sol Bloom (D)	36,274	64.6
Harold Korn (R)	18,810	33.5
20 Fiorello H. LaGuardia (R & PROG)	9,122	47.1
H. Warren Hubbard (D)	9,067	46.8
George Dobsevage (SOC)	1,058	5.5
21 Royal H. Weller (D)	38,111	55.4
Emanuel Hertz (R)	29,359	42.7
22 Anthony J. Griffin (D)	26,372	73.2
R. Fred Talento (R)	8,037	22.3
23 Frank Oliver (D)	78,582	65.7
Morris S. Schector (R)	29,247	24.5
Samuel Orr (SOC)	10,689	8.9
24 James M. Fitzpatrick (D)	54,153	50.6
Benjamin L. Fairchild (R)	47,439	44.3
Patrick J. Murphy (SOC)	5,509	5.1
25 J. Mayhew Wainwright (R)	50,080	62.3
David L. Frank (D)	28,853	35.9
26 Hamilton Fish Jr. (R)	43,173	63.1
Walter G. Russell (D)	23,232	34.0
27 Harcourt J. Pratt (R)	44,557	61.3
Ransom H. Gillett (D)	28,112	38.7
28 Parker Corning (D)	63,919	58.6
George W. Greene (R)	43,342	39.7
29 James S. Parker (R, D)	81,798	97.9
30 Frank Crowther (R)	38,043	57.3
E. Watson Gardiner (D)	26,510	39.9
31 Bertrand H. Snell (R)	40,474	70.1
Abner D. Whitney (D)	17,237	29.9
32 Thaddeus C. Sweet (R)	46,232	67.9
John M. Reynolds (D)	21,007	30.8
33 Frederick M. Davenport (R)	40,845	56.2
Isaac C. Flint (D)	30,265	41.6
34 John D. Clarke (R)	52,363	71.6
Bernard J. McGuire (D)	20,792	28.4
35 Walter W. Magee (R)	62,889	62.0
Wilber M. Jones (D)	38,581	38.0
36 John Taber (R)	48,783	70.0
J. Seldon Brandt (D)	20,886	30.0
37 Gale H. Stalker (R)	46,757	58.2
Edwin S. Underhill (D)	32,618	40.6
38 Meyer Jacobstein (D)	42,803	48.9
James E. Cuff (R)	41,191	47.1
39 Archie D. Sanders (R)	48,623	67.7
David A. White (D)	20,449	28.5
40 S. Wallace Dempsey (R)	60,310	65.7
William F. Sheehan (D)	27,751	30.3
41 Clarence MacGregor (R)	35,739	65.1
Robert M. Smyth (D)	16,913	30.8
42 James M. Mead (D)	28,873	58.1
John Buno McGrath (R)	19,362	38.9

Candidates	Votes	%
43 Daniel A. Reed (R & SOC)	44,073	73.9
John B. Leach (D)	15,555	26.1

NORTH CAROLINA

Candidates	Votes	%
1 Lindsay C. Warren (D)	9,501	100.0
2 John H. Kerr (D)	7,484	100.0
3 Charles L. Abernethy (D)	14,520	72.5
Roscoe Butler (R)	5,498	27.5
4 Edward W. Pou (D)	18,000	69.6
Hobart Brantley (R)	7,881	30.5
5 Charles M. Stedman (D)	32,727	59.8
O.C. Durland (R)	22,016	40.2
6 Homer L. Lyon (D)	12,888	62.3
Leaman Baggett (R)	7,810	37.7
7 William C. Hammer (D)	31,332	55.9
S. Carter Williams (R)	24,769	44.2
8 Robert L. Doughton (D)	30,520	58.6
O. F. Pool (R)	21,543	41.4
9 Alfred L. Bulwinkle (D)	26,354	56.8
Garrett D. Bailey (R)	20,045	43.2
10 Zebulon Weaver (D)	36,829	55.8
R. Kenneth Smathers (R)	29,200	44.2

NORTH DAKOTA

Candidates	Votes	%
1 Olger B. Burtness (R)	37,326	79.9
R. E. Smith (D)	6,136	13.1
Donald McDonald (F-LAB)	3,246	7.0
2 Thomas Hall (R)	33,607	66.3
J. L. Page (D)	13,735	27.1
C. W. Reichert (F-LAB)	3,350	6.6
3 James H. Sinclair (R)	42,923	87.8
Reuben H. Leavitt (D)	5,960	12.2

OHIO

Candidates	Votes	%
1 Nicholas Longworth (R)	45,317	62.9
John C. Rogers (D)	26,511	36.8
2 Ambrose E. B. Stephens (R)	36,608*	58.2
R. J. O'Donnell (D)	26,322	41.8
3 Roy Fitzgerald (R)	50,639	60.4
T. A. McCann (D)	33,253	39.6
4 W.T. Fitzgerald (R)	32,236	50.7
B. F. Welty (D)	31,293	49.3
5 Charles J. Thompson (R)	23,638	50.7
Frank Kniffin (D)	23,022	49.3
6 Charles Kearns (R)	27,688	52.9
B. F. Kennedy (D)	24,630	47.1
7 Charles Brand (R)	45,699	67.2
H. E. Rice (D)	22,314	32.8
8 Thomas Brooks Fletcher (D)	30,167	56.5
James R. Hopley (R)	23,247	43.5
9 William W. Chalmers (R)	47,331	64.5
C. W. Davis (D)	23,947	32.6
10 Thomas A. Jenkins (R)	25,571	63.9
Guy Stevenson (D)	14,460	36.1
11 Mell Underwood (D)	29,950	62.1
Walter S. Barrett (R)	18,300	37.9
12 John C. Speaks (R)	41,119	56.5
H. S. Atkinson (D)	31,724	43.6
13 James T. Begg (R)	36,444	65.1
G. C. Steineman (D)	19,571	34.9
14 Martin L. Davey (D)	53,659	65.4
Arthur Sweeney (R)	28,446	34.7
15 C. Ellis Moore (R)	28,519	54.6
E. B. Schneider (D)	23,703	45.4
16 John McSweeney (D)	40,283	59.8
C. D. McClintock (R)	27,116	40.2
17 William M. Morgan (R)	36,249	55.0
J. F. Bittinger (D)	29,674	45.0
18 Frank Murphy (D)	36,599	65.4
John F. Nolan (D)	19,341	34.6
19 John G. Cooper (R)	45,788	72.3
James Kennedy (D)	17,513	27.7
20 Charles Mooney (D)	22,050	100.0
21 Robert Crosser (D)	17,819	62.4
Harry C. Gahn (R)	10,733	37.6
22 Theodore E. Burton (R)	55,589	100.0

OKLAHOMA

	Candidates	Votes	%
1	Everette B. Howard (D)	33,475	50.6
	Samuel J. Montgomery (R)	32,692	49.4
2	William W. Hastings (D)	24,024	56.9
	H. L. Wineland (R)	18,220	43.1
3	Wilburn Cartwright (D)	28,883	67.1
	George W. Strawn (R)	13,964	32.5
4	Thomas D. McKeown (D)	29,208	59.4
	Charles E. Wells (R)	19,997	40.6
5	Fletcher B. Swank (D)	29,988	60.6
	Barritt Galloway (R)	19,491	39.4
6	Jed Johnson (D)	21,838	54.2
	Fred W. Lankard (R)	18,188	45.1
7	James V. McClintic (D)	17,962	70.4
	Walter S. Mills (R)	7,416	29.1
8	Milton C. Garber (R)	27,377	58.8
	C. H. Hyde (D)	18,957	40.7

OREGON

		Votes	%
1	Willis C. Hawley (R)	67,020	71.1
	Newton W. Borden (D)	27,273	28.9
2	Nicholas J. Sinnott (R)	29,357	70.4
	John S. Hodgin (D)	12,348	29.6
3	Maurice E. Crumpacker (R)	51,889	71.8
	Joseph K. Carson Jr. (D & PROG)	20,372	28.2

PENNSYLVANIA

		Votes	%
1	James M. Hazlett (R)	64,781	92.8
	William L. Rooney (D)	4,799	6.9
2	George S. Graham (R)	37,470	91.3
	John Joseph Shanahan (D)	3,223	7.9
3	Harry C. Ransley (R)	42,661	93.2
	Frank J. McDonnell (D)	2,827	6.2
4	Benjamin M. Golder (R)	34,904	82.9
	David Louis Ullman (D)	5,977	14.2
5	James J. Connolly (R, P)	46,997	85.9
	Daniel J. C. O'Donnell (D)	6,507	11.9
6	George A. Welsh (R)	51,844	79.4
	Thomas A. Logue (D)	10,344	15.8
7	George P. Darrow (R)	44,411	80.5
	Harry J. Conway (D)	9,440	17.1
8	Thomas S. Butler (R, SOC)	44,664	82.2
	Frank B. Rhodes (D)	8,802	16.2
9	Henry W. Watson (R)	38,350	71.3
	Richard J. Hamilton (D, LAB)	14,337	26.7
10	William W. Griest (R, LAB)	28,664	66.8
	W. W. Heidelbaugh (D, I)	14,272	33.2
11	Laurence H. Watres (R, P)	32,091	70.1
	Joseph J. Walsh (D)	13,662	29.9
12	John J. Casey (R, D)	49,467	76.5
	Edmund N. Carpenter (P)	15,166	23.5
13	Cyrus M. Palmer (R)	22,850	54.3
	Neal J. Ferry (D)	18,480	43.9
14	Robert Grey Bushong (R)	30,240	50.2
	Arthur G. Dewalt (D)	26,930	44.7
	Raymond S. Hofses (SOC, LAB)	3,050	5.1
15	Louis T. McFadden (R, P)	19,864	69.4
	C. M. Driggs (D)	8,763	30.6
16	Edgar R. Kiess (R, D)	26,047	99.9
17	Frederick W. Magrady (R, P)	19,717	52.7
	Herbert W. Cummings (D, SOC)	17,695	47.3
18	Edward M. Beers (R, P)	26,067	67.8
	Frederick A. Rupp (D)	12,349	32.1
19	Isaac H. Doutrich (R, LAB)	32,833	60.1
	Frank C. Sites (D)	21,563	39.5
20	J. Russell Leech (R)	16,254	54.8
	Warren Worth Bailey (D, LAB)	11,182	37.7
	Harry Crichton (P)	2,217	7.5
21	J. Banks Kurtz (R, P)	18,094	74.7
	Harry K. Filler (D)	4,799	19.8
	Charles Kutz (LAB)	1,215	5.0
22	Franklin Menges (R, P)	20,485	57.0
	Samuel F. Glatfelter (D)	15,268	42.5
23	J. Mitchell Chase (R, P)	22,337	69.8
	Clarence R. Kramer (D)	9,664	30.2

	Candidates	Votes	%
24	Samuel Austin Kendall (R, SOC)	20,097	75.7
	Clark W. Martin (D)	6,464	24.3
25	Henry W. Temple (R, P)	17,004	58.8
	James S. Pates (D, LAB)	11,890	41.2
26	J. Howard Swick (R, LAB)	22,062	62.0
	James P. Leaf (D, P)	13,516	38.0
27	Nathan L. Strong (R, LAB)	27,757	74.5
	D. A. Dorn (D)	9,038	24.3
28	Thomas C. Cochran (R, D)	30,520	99.7
29	Milton W. Shreve (R)	17,870	82.6
	William H. Kerschner (P)	3,758	17.4
30	Everett Kent (D, LAB)	24,392	50.9
	William R. Coyle (R)	22,981	47.9
31	Adam M. Wyant (R)	24,911	65.7
	Albert H. Bell (D, P)	12,175	32.1
32	Stephen G. Porter (R, LAB)	28,290	82.3
	Walter P. Berner (D)	4,680	13.6
33	M. Clyde Kelly (R, D)	31,886	96.1
34	John M. Morin (R, D)	28,783	98.8
35	Harry A. Estep (R)	23,881	77.5
	John Murphy (D)	4,242	13.8
	James M. Magee (LAB, P)	2,191	7.1
36	Guy C. Campbell (R, D)	25,474	84.2
	Ellsworth C. Trott (P)	3,264	10.8

RHODE ISLAND

		Votes	%
1	Clark Burdick (R)	32,459	63.0
	Arthur L. Conaty (D)	19,066	37.0
2	Richard S. Aldrich (R)	33,542	61.8
	Clarence E. Palmer (D)	20,738	38.2
3	Louis Monast (R)	29,366	50.4
	Jeremiah E. O'Connell (D)	28,909	49.6

SOUTH CAROLINA

		Votes	%
1	Thomas S. McMillan (D)	2,244	100.0
2	Butler B. Hare (D)	1,766	100.0
3	Fred H. Dominick (D)	2,374	100.0
4	John J. McSwain (D)	2,057	100.0
5	William F. Stevenson (D)	2,416	100.0
6	Allard H. Gasque (D)	1,532	100.0
7	Hampton P. Fulmer (D)	1,933	100.0

SOUTH DAKOTA

		Votes	%
1	Charles A. Christopherson (R)	37,185	56.3
	J. E. House (D)	26,103	39.5
2	Royal C. Johnson (R)	38,928	64.3
	Fred H. Hildebrandt (D)	21,585	35.7
3	William Williamson (R)	22,932	52.3
	Arthur W. Watwood (D)	20,902	47.7

TENNESSEE

		Votes	%
1	B. Carroll Reece (R)	10,553	88.0
	W. I. Giles (D)	1,439	12.0
2	J. Will Taylor (R)	11,789	99.8
3	Sam D. McReynolds (D)	13,012	75.6
	L. D. Copeland (R)	4,194	24.4
4	Cordell Hull (D)	10,726	71.4
	Mrs. Wilson Thompson (R)	4,292	28.6
5	Ewin L. Davis (D)	5,481	100.0
6	Joseph W. Byrns (D)	10,271	100.0
7	Edward E. Eslick (D)	8,049	100.0
8	Gordon Browning (D)	9,456	100.0
9	Finis J. Garrett (D)	9,180	100.0
10	Hubert F. Fisher (D)	4,217	100.0

TEXAS

		Votes	%
1	Eugene Black (D)	9,828	94.4
	D. F. Wimmer (R)	579	5.6
2	John C. Box (D)	11,955	95.6
3	Morgan G. Sanders (D)	11,336	91.2
	Enoch G. Fletcher (R)	1,098	8.8
4	Sam Rayburn (D)	13,499	89.9
	Henry C. Barlow (R)	1,524	10.1
5	Hatton W. Sumners (D)	29,687	96.5
6	Luther A. Johnson (D)	10,162	96.1

	Candidates	Votes	%
7	Clay Stone Briggs (D)	7,678	94.1
	S. R. Halstead (R)	478	5.9
8	Daniel E. Garrett (D)	8,459	91.0
	J. M. Gibson (R)	842	9.1
9	Joseph J. Mansfield (D)	10,577	82.6
	E. F. Glaze (R)	2,228	17.4
10	James P. Buchanan (D)	12,051	93.2
	W. H. Matthaei (R)	886	6.9
11	Tom T. Connally (D)	8,481	94.2
	W. H. Black (R)	526	5.8
12	Fritz G. Lanham (D)	10,466	94.4
	David Sutton (R)	620	5.6
13	Guinn Williams (D)	12,406	94.0
	Mel E. Peters (R)	797	6.0
14	Harry M. Wurzbach (R)	14,224	57.2
	A.D. Rogers (D)	10,633	42.8
15	John N. Garner (D)	13,551	82.8
	Hardie H. Jeffries (R)	2,825	17.3
16	Claude B. Hudspeth (D)	15,732	86.1
	A. W. Norcop (R)	2,542	13.9
17	Thomas L. Blanton (D)	15,935	93.7
	H. B. Tanner (R)	1,065	6.3
18	Marvin Jones (D)	18,027	93.6
	S. E. Fish (R)	1,237	6.4

UTAH

		Votes	%
1	Don B. Colton (R)	44,007	61.4
	Ephraim Bergeson (D)	27,198	38.0
2	Elmer O. Leatherwood (R)	42,073	60.2
	William R. Wallace Jr. (D)	27,006	38.6

VERMONT

		Votes	%
1	Elbert S. Brigham (R)	27,419	72.3
	Allan T. Calhoun (D)	10,529	27.7
2	Ernest Willard Gibson (R)	27,711	80.4
	George F. Root (D)	6,753	19.6

VIRGINIA

		Votes	%
1	Schuyler Otis Bland (D)	3,847	99.9
2	Joseph T. Deal (D)	7,741	65.4
	L. S. Parsons (R)	4,093	34.6
3	Andrew Jackson Montague (D)	3,738	99.8
4	Patrick Henry Drewry (D)	2,694	99.3
5	Joseph Whitehead (D)	6,491	100.0
6	Clifton A. Woodrum (D)	2,936	99.8
7	Thomas W. Harrison (D)	8,302	64.9
	Walter R. Talbot (R)	3,758	29.4
	Dabney C. Harrison (I)	727	5.7
8	R. Walton Moore (D)	5,655	95.4
9	George C. Peery (D)	28,304	53.4
	S. R. Hurley (R)	24,685	46.6
10	Henry St. George Tucker (D)	4,657	99.8

WASHINGTON

		Votes	%
1	John F. Miller (R)	35,944	51.1
	Stephen F. Chadwick (D)	34,401	48.9
2	Lindley H. Hadley (R)	35,510	68.5
	Frances C. Axtell (D)	15,876	30.6
3	Albert Johnson (R)	58,361	100.0
4	John W. Summers (R)	34,199	99.8
5	Sam B. Hill (D)	29,157	52.1
	Jack T. Fancher (R)	26,783	47.9

WEST VIRGINIA

		Votes	%
1	Carl G. Bachmann (R)	31,839	52.2
	George W. Oldham (D)	29,117	47.8
2	Frank L. Bowman (R)	32,803	54.0
	Robert E. Lee Allen (D)	27,744	45.7
3	William S. O'Brien (D)	31,954	51.7
	John M. Wolverton (R)	29,819	48.3
4	James A. Hughes (R)	36,394	52.4
	John D. Sweeney (D)	33,065	47.6
5	James F. Strother (R)	44,263	53.3
	Emmet F. Scaggs (D)	38,723	46.7

	Candidates	Votes	%
6	Edward T. England (R)	45,898	50.1
	J. Alfred Taylor (D)	45,681	49.9

WISCONSIN

	Candidates	Votes	%
1	Henry Allen Cooper (R)	50,531	100.0
2	Charles A. Kading (R)	29,785	69.5
	Ernest C. Wrucke (D)	8,285	19.3
	John H. Kaiser (I-PROG-R)	4,817	11.2
3	John Mandt Nelson (R)	41,666	99.9
4	John C. Schafer (R)	20,324	48.0

	Candidates	Votes	%
	Edmund T. Melms (SOC)	14,911	35.2
	William J. Kershaw (D)	7,099	16.8
5	Victor L. Berger (SOC)	26,377	48.8
	William H. Stafford (R)	24,297	44.9
	Rose Horwitz (D)	3,394	6.3
6	Florian Lampert (R)	34,445	75.9
	B. F. Sheridan (D)	10,895	24.0
7	Joseph D. Beck (R)	32,479	86.1
	A. H. Schubert (ID)	3,628	9.6
8	Edward E. Browne (R)	35,472	91.8
	R. J. Walsh (ID)	3,130	8.1

	Candidates	Votes	%
9	George J. Schneider (R)	41,498	99.9
10	James A. Frear (R)	40,888	97.4
11	Hubert H. Peavey (R)	31,105	70.1
	Theodore M. Thomas (I-PROG-R)	11,860	26.7

WYOMING

	Candidates	Votes	%
AL	Charles E. Winter (R)	39,392	60.8
	Thomas M. Fagan (D)	25,082	38.7

1927 House Elections

LOUISIANA

Special Election

	Candidates	Votes	%
7	Rene L. DeRouen (D)	3,699	98.5

NEW YORK

Special Election

	Candidates	Votes	%
35	Clarence E. Hancock (R)	68,502	69.0
	Henry B. Brewster (D)	29,302	29.5

1928 House Elections

ALABAMA

	Candidates	Votes	%
1	John McDuffie (D)	16,712	100.0
2	Lister Hill (D)	20,945	100.0
3	Henry B. Steagall (D)	14,611	100.0
4	Lamar Jeffers (D)	13,271	63.1
	A. B. Baxley (R)	7,768	36.9
5	Lafayette L. Patterson (D)	13,067	100.0
6	William B. Oliver (D)	9,539	100.0
7	Miles C. Allgood (D)	18,186	51.7
	Wallace M. Sloan (R)	16,983	48.3
8	Edward B. Almon (D)	20,006	100.0
9	George Huddleston (D)	23,553	100.0
10	William B. Bankhead (D)	15,133	58.2
	John A. Posey (R)	10,862	41.8

Special Election

		Votes	%
5	Lafayette L. Patterson (D)	7,683	99.9

ARIZONA

		Votes	%
AL	Lewis W. Douglas (D)	50,231	61.6
	Guy Axline (R)	31,382	38.5

ARKANSAS

		Votes	%
1	William J. Driver (D)	24,844	83.9
	S. E. Simonson (R)	4,770	16.1
2	William A. Oldfield (D)	18,772*	77.4
	J. L. McKamey (R)	5,471	22.6
3	Claude A. Fuller (D)	18,160	57.7
	Sam B. Cecil (R)	13,129	41.7
4	Otis Wingo (D)	21,494	71.9
	G. W. Johnston (R)	8,397	28.1
5	Heartsill Ragon (D)	25,583	78.2
	Alonzo A. Ross (R)	7,144	21.8
6	David D. Glover (D)	28,101	100.0
7	Tilman B. Parks (D)	20,954	81.5
	Pat McNally (R)	4,759	18.5

CALIFORNIA

		Votes	%
1	Clarence F. Lea (D-R)	56,381	100.0
2	Harry L. Englebright (R-D)	32,455	100.0
3	Charles F. Curry (R-D)	77,750	100.0
4	Florence P. Kahn (R)	50,206	74.9
	Harry W. Hutton (I)	16,838	25.1
5	Richard J. Welch (R-D)	51,708	100.0
6	Albert E. Carter (R-D)	113,579	99.9
7	Henry E. Barbour (R-D)	71,195	99.9
8	Arthur Monroe Free (R)	80,613	68.0
	Cecelia C. Casserly (D)	37,947	32.0
9	William E. Evans (R)	222,261	77.0
	James B. Ogg (D)	58,263	20.2
10	Joe Crail (R-D)	301,028	93.5
	Harry Sherr (SOC)	19,659	6.1
11	Philip D. Swing (R-D)	127,115	100.0

COLORADO

		Votes	%
1	William R. Eaton (R)	63,258	58.1
	S. Harrison White (D)	44,713	41.1
2	Charles B. Timberlake (R)	62,375	66.5
	Earl E. House (D)	31,480	33.5
3	Guy U. Hardy (R)	64,116	64.9
	Harry A. McIntyre (D)	34,670	35.1
4	Edward T. Taylor (D)	30,142	58.8
	William P. Dale (R)	21,089	41.2

CONNECTICUT

		Votes	%
1	E. Hart Fenn (R)	75,743	53.1
	Herman P. Kopplemann (D)	65,922	46.2
2	Richard P. Freeman (R)	48,590	56.0
	William M. Citron (D)	37,786	43.5
3	John Q. Tilson (R)	58,337	52.3
	Nicholas Moseley (D)	52,358	46.9
4	Schuyler Merritt (R)	71,649	56.1
	Anthony Sunderland (D)	55,106	43.2
5	James P. Glynn (R)	43,332	52.4
	Edward Mascolo (D)	39,354	47.6

DELAWARE

		Votes	%
AL	Robert G. Houston (R)	66,361	63.6
	John M. Richardson (D)	38,045	36.4

FLORIDA

		Votes	%
1	Herbert J. Drane (D)	42,003	58.4
	Abner B. Brown (R)	29,871	41.6
2	Robert A. Green (D)	17,228	83.9
	Thomas Peter Chaires (R)	3,310	16.1
3	Tom A. Yon (D)	22,167	100.0
4	Ruth Bryan Owen (D)	67,130	64.9
	William C. Lawson (R)	36,288	35.1

GEORGIA

		Votes	%
1	Charles G. Edwards (D)	16,438	100.0
2	E. E. Cox (D)	15,235	100.0
3	Charles R. Crisp (D)	11,183	100.0
4	William C. Wright (D)	16,037	100.0
5	Leslie J. Steele (D)	19,328	100.0
6	Samuel Rutherford (D)	15,310	100.0
7	Malcolm C. Tarver (D)	23,251	100.0
8	Charles H. Brand (D)	15,940	100.0
9	Thomas M. Bell (D)	22,916	100.0
10	Carl Vinson (D)	12,644	100.0
11	William C. Lankford (D)	18,044	100.0
12	William W. Larsen (D)	13,862	100.0

IDAHO

		Votes	%
1	Burton L. French (R)	43,770	68.9
	Joe Tyler (D)	19,064	30.0
2	Addison T. Smith (R)	53,236	64.1
	Ralph W. Harding (D)	29,422	35.4

ILLINOIS

		Votes	%
1	Oscar De Priest (R)	24,479	47.8
	Harry Baker (D)	20,664	40.3
	William Harrison	5,861	11.4
2	Morton D. Hull (R)	126,005	62.1
	Michael C. Walsh (D)	76,909	37.9
3	Elliott W. Sproul (R)	101,384	51.4
	Henry P. Bergen (D)	95,999	48.6
4	Thomas A. Doyle (D)	40,940	64.3
	Frank George Zelezinskl (R)	22,741	35.7
5	Adolph J. Sabath (D)	25,225	69.8
	Edward J. Gates (R)	10,799	29.9
6	James T. Igoe (D)	143,989	60.3
	Samuel L. Golan (R)	94,941	39.7
7	M. Alfred Michaelson (R)	164,447	57.8
	Emil Selten (D)	119,933	42.2
8	Stanley Henry Kunz (D)	24,517	70.8
	Edward Walz (R)	10,110	29.2
9	Fred A. Britten (R)	43,394	62.0
	James T. McDermott (D)	26,450	37.8
10	Carl R. Chindblom (R)	138,386	62.6
	Joseph A. Weber (D)	82,598	37.4
11	Frank R. Reid (R)	97,938	68.9
	Edwin L. Wilson (D)	44,306	31.2
12	John T. Buckbee (R)	82,938	73.8
	Jules Vallatt (D)	29,385	26.2
13	William R. Johnson (R)	53,985	73.7
	William G. Curtis (D)	19,209	26.2
14	John C. Allen (R)	53,680	64.3
	William H. Hartzell (D)	29,768	35.7
15	Edward J. King (R)	57,284*	64.2

	Candidates	Votes	%
	James H. Andrews (D)	31,944	35.8
16	William E. Hull (R)	59,190	61.1
	George H. Rinkenberger (D)	37,662	38.9
17	Homer W. Hall (R)	47,266	65.0
	Frank Gillespie (D)	25,480	35.0
18	William P. Holaday (R)	57,373	62.0
	James H. Elliott (D)	35,213	38.0
19	Charles Adkins (R)	73,243	66.2
	W. W. Reeves (D)	37,358	33.8
20	Henry T. Rainey (D)	38,409	56.0
	E. T. Hunter (R)	30,100	43.9
21	Frank M. Ramey (R)	52,320	50.1
	J. Earl Major (D)	52,183	49.9
22	Edward M. Irwin (R)	72,448	56.0
	Eugene W. Kreitner (D)	56,825	44.0
23	William W. Arnold (D)	49,378	53.9
	C. T. Wade (R)	42,263	46.1
24	Thomas S. Williams (R)	36,239	58.4
	Val B. Campbell (D)	25,773	41.6
25	Edward E. Denison (R)	51,025	54.4
	A. F. Gourley (D)	42,799	45.6
AL	Ruth Hanna McCormick (R)	1,711,651✔	
	Richard Yates (R)	1,673,962✔	
	Charles F. Brown (D)	1,171,520	
	C. D. Joplin (D)	1,111,253	
	Florence Kirkpatrick (SOC)	11,958	
	John E. Mahoney (SOC)	11,538	
	Elizabeth G. Doty (WCP AM)	2,887	
	Frank Gushes (WCP AM)	2,802	
	James S. O'Rourke (SOC LAB)	1,384	
	Thomas Buckley (SOC LAB)	1,340	

INDIANA

		Votes	%
1	Harry E. Rowbottom (R)	49,013	50.8
	John W. Boehne Jr. (D)	47,404	49.2
2	Arthur H. Greenwood (D)	45,901	50.2
	Orville T. Stout (R)	44,941	49.1
3	James W. Dunbar (R)	47,768	51.1
	Frank Gardner (D)	45,718	48.9
4	Harry C. Canfield (D)	44,671	52.5
	Charles S. Hisey (R)	40,345	47.5
5	Noble J. Johnson (R)	51,138	56.1
	Henry W. Moore (D)	39,538	43.3
6	Richard N. Elliott (R)	50,795	57.0
	William H. Larrabee (D)	38,326	43.0
7	Louis Ludlow (D)	94,643	51.5
	Ralph E. Updike (R)	88,263	48.0
8	Albert H. Vestal (R)	59,704	58.3
	Don C. Ward (D)	42,645	41.7
9	Fred S. Purnell (R)	53,998	57.2
	George L. Mackintosh (D)	40,357	42.8
10	William R. Wood (R)	87,972	62.0
	John W. Sobraske (D)	53,874	38.0
11	Albert R. Hall (R)	49,326	54.1
	M. Clifford Townsend (D)	41,836	45.9
12	David Hogg (R)	56,436	55.3
	Samuel D. Jackson (D)	45,592	44.7
13	Andrew J. Hickey (R)	90,618	59.8
	Chester A. Perkins (D)	60,993	40.2

IOWA

		Votes	%
1	William F. Kopp (R)	45,806	100.0
2	F. Dickinson Letts (R)	49,691	57.0
	Frank C. Titzell (D)	37,442	43.0
3	Thomas J. B. Robinson (R)	60,025	60.9
	Leo F. Tierney (D)	38,469	39.1
4	Gilbert N. Haugen (R)	50,938	61.4
	Erwin Larson (D)	31,968	38.6
5	Cyrenus Cole (R)	54,603	66.3
	Maurice Cahill (D)	27,793	33.7
6	C. William Ramseyer (R)	43,259	65.2
	C. Ver Ploeg (D)	23,065	34.8
7	Cassius C. Dowell (R)	72,404	100.0
8	Lloyd Thurston (R)	43,050	60.0

#	Candidates	Votes	%
	James Pearson (D)	28,686	40.0
9	Charles E. Swanson (R)	47,632	63.2
	W. J. Burke (D)	27,760	36.8
10	Lester J. Dickinson (R)	59,374	100.0
11	Ed H. Campbell (R)	49,279	70.9
	George Finch (D)	20,244	29.1

KANSAS

#	Candidates	Votes	%
1	William P. Lambertson (R)	48,543	68.3
	Maurice P. O'Keefe (D)	22,492	31.7
2	Ulysses S. Guyer (R)	66,044	70.2
	Lee R. Hettick (D)	28,106	29.9
3	William H. Sproul (R)	45,121	53.4
	Joe E. Gaitskill (D)	39,323	46.6
4	Homer Hoch (R)	38,664	74.2
	C. T. Neihart (D)	13,450	25.8
5	James G. Strong (R)	45,053	69.9
	John F. Corder (D)	19,425	30.1
6	Charles I. Sparks (R)	41,272	63.4
	William H. Clark (D)	23,836	36.6
7	Clifford R. Hope (R)	58,001	69.5
	W. C. Dickey (D)	25,433	30.5
8	William A. Ayres (D)	46,117	58.4
	Richard E. Bird (R)	32,802	41.6

KENTUCKY

#	Candidates	Votes	%
1	William V. Gregory (D)	36,325	56.8
	Miller Hughes (R)	27,581	43.2
2	David H. Kincheloe (D)	38,093	52.7
	Clark M. Donald (R)	34,194	47.3
3	Charles W. Roark (R)	37,216	52.8
	John W. Moore (D)	33,210	47.2
4	John D. Craddock (R)	39,244	53.1
	Henry D. Moorman (D)	34,639	46.9
5	Maurice H. Thatcher (R)	96,926	60.2
	Arthur Yager (D)	64,201	39.8
6	J. Lincoln Newhall (R)	48,009	53.1
	Brent Spence (D)	42,309	46.8
7	Robert E. Lee Blackburn (R)	43,604	53.5
	Virgil Chapman (D)	37,936	46.5
8	Lewis L. Walker (R)	33,931	52.7
	Ralph Gilbert (D)	30,424	47.3
9	Elva R. Kendall (R)	51,019	52.9
	Fred M. Vinson (D)	45,426	47.1
10	Katherine Langley (R)	39,541	56.1
	A. J. May (D)	30,919	43.9
11	John M. Robsion (R)	74,929	79.8
	H. F. Reed (D)	18,939	20.2

LOUISIANA

#	Candidates	Votes	%
1	James O'Connor (D)	28,066	100.0
2	J. Zach Spearing (D)	33,176	69.4
	Peter I. J. Fletchinger (R)	14,661	30.7
3	Whitmell P. Martin (D)	15,219	100.0
4	John N. Sandlin (D)	14,949	100.0
5	Riley J. Wilson (D)	11,827	100.0
6	Bolivar E. Kemp (D)	18,379	100.0
7	Rene L. DeRouen (D)	16,582	100.0
8	James B. Aswell (D)	14,618	100.0

MAINE

#	Candidates	Votes	%
1	Carroll L. Beedy (R)	40,255	67.7
	Elvington P. Spinney (D)	19,219	32.3
2	Wallace H. White Jr. (R)	36,791	65.5
	Albert Beliveau (D)	19,420	34.6
3	John E. Nelson (R)	36,686	74.6
	S. Curtis C. Ward (D)	12,498	25.4
4	Donald F. Snow (R)	32,223	75.0
	Clinton C. Stevens (D)	10,753	25.0

MARYLAND

#	Candidates	Votes	%
1	T. Alan Goldsborough (D)	28,795	50.7
	A. Stengle Marine (R)	28,059	49.4
2	Linwood L. Clark (R)	69,267	53.3
	William P. Cole Jr. (D)	59,912	46.1
3	Vincent L. Palmisano (D)	27,377	49.8
	John Philip Hill (R)	27,047	49.2
4	J. Charles Linthicum (D)	41,432	54.5
	John P. Brandau (R)	34,112	44.8
5	Stephen W. Gambrill (D)	31,403	51.9
	Oliver Metzerott (R)	28,574	47.2
6	Frederick N. Zihlman (R)	47,789	56.2
	David J. Lewis (D)	37,197	43.8

MASSACHUSETTS

#	Candidates	Votes	%
1	Allen T. Treadway (R)	51,791	55.7
	Daniel A. Martin (D)	41,216	44.3
2	William Kirk Kaynor (R)	52,344	54.4
	John D. O'Connor (D)	43,856	45.6
3	Frank H. Foss (R)	46,204	57.1
	Joseph E. Casey (D)	34,776	42.9
4	George R. Stobbs (R)	51,145	54.8
	Freeman M. Saltus (D)	42,115	45.2
5	Edith Nourse Rogers (R)	56,004	61.1
	Cornelius F. Cronin (D)	35,713	38.9
6	A. Piatt Andrew (R)	58,293	68.2
	George J. Ferguson (D)	27,130	31.8
7	William P. Connery Jr. (R-D)	61,697	100.0
8	Frederick W. Dallinger (R)	71,850	57.2
	James P. Brennan (D)	53,721	42.8
9	Charles L. Underhill (R)	48,947	50.3
	Arthur D. Healey (D)	48,290	49.7
10	John J. Douglass (D)	42,594	85.0
	Edward L. Donnelly (R)	7,498	15.0
11	George Holden Tinkham (R)	52,576	58.4
	Maurice J. Tobin (D)	37,514	41.6
12	John W. McCormack (D)	64,351	76.4
	Herbert W. Burr (R)	19,937	23.7
13	Robert Luce (R)	74,097	58.2
	Thomas D. Lavelle (D)	53,266	41.8
14	Richard B. Wigglesworth (R)	73,598	61.3
	Christopher M. Clifford (D)	46,498	38.7
15	Joseph W. Martin Jr. (R)	39,905	56.8
	John F. Trainor (D)	30,373	43.2
16	Charles L. Gifford (R)	49,202	63.1
	Willard E. Boyden (D)	23,590	30.3
	Frank J. Manning (SOC)	5,115	6.6

MICHIGAN

#	Candidates	Votes	%
1	Robert H. Clancy (R)	64,606	61.5
	William M. Donnelly (D)	39,870	38.0
2	Earl C. Michener (R)	86,804	73.6
	Grover L. Morden (D)	31,223	26.5
3	Joseph Hooper (R)	71,650	79.5
	William Fitzgerald (D)	18,535	20.6
4	John C. Ketcham (R)	60,334	75.4
	Roman I. Jarvis Sr. (D)	19,708	24.6
5	Carl E. Mapes (R)	73,241	78.8
	Frank C. Jarvis (D)	19,627	21.1
6	Grant M. Hudson (R)	238,223	72.5
	A. Bruce Atwell (D)	89,085	27.1
7	Louis C. Cramton (R)	61,439	73.9
	Varnum J. Bowers (D)	21,659	26.1
8	Bird J. Vincent (R)	65,600	75.4
	Burnett J. Abbott (D)	21,387	24.6
9	James C. McLaughlin (R)	51,246	99.8
10	Roy O. Woodruff (R)	43,800	73.7
	Judson E. Richardson (D)	15,598	26.3
11	Frank P. Bohn (R)	44,546	67.2
	Carl R. Henry (D)	21,760	32.8
12	W. Frank James (R)	47,069	69.1
	L. A. Barry (D)	21,039	30.9
13	Clarence J. McLeod (R)	70,513	64.9
	John S. Hall (D)	37,574	34.6

MINNESOTA

#	Candidates	Votes	%
1	Victor Christgau (R)	59,628	64.8
	James F. Lynn (D)	32,398	35.2
2	Frank Clague (R)	60,259	69.4
	J. A. Cashel (D)	26,606	30.6
3	August H. Andresen (R)	52,526	58.8
	Charles C. Kolars (D)	19,844	22.2
	Henry Arens (F-LAB)	15,749	17.6
4	Melvin Joseph Maas (R)	39,648	36.0
	John P. J. Dolan (D)	31,521	28.6
	Howard Y. Williams (F-LAB)	23,068	21.0
	Fred A. Snyder (I)	15,365	14.0
5	Walter H. Newton (R)	80,856	58.6
	James Robertson (D)	31,528	22.9
	Ferdinand Johnson (F-LAB)	24,869	18.0
6	Harold Knutson (R)	55,663	66.3
	John Knutsen (F-LAB)	28,276	33.7
7	Ole J. Kvale (F-LAB)	56,029	66.9
	Lawrence M. Carlson (R)	27,735	33.1
8	William A. Pittenger (R)	43,777	44.2
	William L. Carss (F-LAB)	42,508	42.9
	Dana C. Reed (D)	9,784	9.9
9	Conrad G. Selvig (R)	45,319	55.2
	Knud Wefald (F-LAB)	36,853	44.9
10	Godfrey G. Goodwin (R)	60,100	56.4
	C. R. Hedlund (F-LAB)	23,774	22.3
	Ernest W. Erickson (D)	22,702	21.3

MISSISSIPPI

#	Candidates	Votes	%
1	John E. Rankin (D)	13,816	100.0
2	Wall Doxey (D)	12,276	100.0
3	William M. Whittington (D)	13,039	100.0
4	T. Jeff Busby (D)	13,456	100.0
5	Ross A. Collins (D)	17,967	100.0
6	Robert S. Hall (D)	18,212	100.0
7	Percy E. Quin (D)	12,338	100.0
8	James W. Collier (D)	11,442	100.0

MISSOURI

#	Candidates	Votes	%
1	Milton A. Romjue (D)	35,702	52.9
	J. Frank Culler (R)	31,751	47.1
2	Ralph Lozier (D)	37,829	53.2
	Lloyd V. Harmon (R)	33,273	46.8
3	Jacob L. Milligan (D)	32,665	50.0
	H. F. Lawrence (R)	32,626	50.0
4	Charles L. Faust (R)	43,733*	57.1
	Richard M. Duncan (D)	32,892	42.9
5	Edgar C. Ellis (R)	113,043	50.5
	Floyd E. Jacobs (D)	110,529	49.4
6	Thomas J. Halsey (R)	30,557	53.2
	C. C. Dickinson (D)	26,838	46.8
7	John W. Palmer (R)	52,317	53.3
	Samuel C. Major (D)	45,832	46.7
8	William L. Nelson (D)	32,877	55.3
	David W. Peters (R)	26,619	44.7
9	Clarence Cannon (D)	41,036	54.5
	A. H. Steinbeck (R)	34,248	45.5
10	Henry F. Niedringhaus (R)	164,083	55.0
	John R. Green (D)	134,324	45.0
11	John J. Cochran (D)	44,130	57.4
	William Gray (R)	32,706	42.6
12	Leonidas C. Dyer (R)	24,701	58.4
	Joseph L. McLemore (D)	17,609	41.6
13	Charles E. Kiefner (R)	30,535	50.6
	Clyde Williams (D)	29,842	49.4
14	Dewey Short (R)	57,880	53.9
	James F. Fulbright (D)	49,495	46.1
15	Joe J. Manlove (R)	52,142	64.6
	George B. Lang (D)	28,551	35.4
16	Rowland L. Johnston (R)	29,848	53.5
	S. A. Cunningham (D)	25,899	46.5

MONTANA

#	Candidates	Votes	%
1	John M. Evans (D)	44,618	57.3
	Mark D. Fitzgerald (R)	32,796	42.1
2	Scott Leavitt (R)	70,682	67.9
	B. A. Taylor (D)	33,033	31.7

NEBRASKA

#	Candidates	Votes	%
1	John H. Morehead (D)	39,202	50.4
	Elmer J. Burkett (R)	38,583	49.6
2	Willis G. Sears (R)	52,801	56.0
	Harry B. Fleharty (D)	41,424	44.0

	Candidates	Votes	%
3	Edgar Howard (D)	50,974	54.9
	James Nichols (R)	41,967	45.2
4	Charles H. Sloan (R)	37,114	50.2
	J. N. Norton (D)	36,896	49.9
5	Fred G. Johnson (R)	37,853	51.0
	Ashton C. Shallenberger (D)	36,383	49.0
6	Robert G. Simmons (R)	81,581	74.3
	John McCoy (D)	28,215	25.7

NEVADA

	Candidates	Votes	%
AL	Samuel S. Arentz (R)	18,815	58.6
	Charles Lee Horsey (D)	13,287	41.4

NEW HAMPSHIRE

	Candidates	Votes	%
1	Fletcher Hale (R)	53,642	57.5
	Francis C. Keefe (D)	39,568	42.4
2	Edward H. Wason (R)	54,642	60.0
	Alfred W. Levensaler (D)	36,275	39.9

NEW JERSEY

	Candidates	Votes	%
1	Charles A. Wolverton (R)	109,510	74.9
	Alfred R. White (D)	36,778	25.1
2	Isaac Bacharach (R)	99,109	76.3
	George R. Greis (D)	30,856	23.7
3	Harold G. Hoffman (R)	95,669	63.0
	John R. Phillips Jr. (D)	56,290	37.0
4	Charles A. Eaton (R)	65,149	63.6
	Orren Jack Turner (D)	37,341	36.4
5	Ernest R. Ackerman (R)	95,458	67.4
	Roswell S. Nichols (D)	46,211	32.6
6	Randolph Perkins (R)	98,859	61.7
	Frank L. Sample (D)	60,988	38.1
7	George N. Seger (R)	54,896	57.0
	Abram Klenert (D)	41,012	42.6
8	Fred A. Hartley Jr. (R)	64,915#	50.1
	Paul J. Moore (D)	64,594#	49.9
9	Franklin W. Fort (R)	46,685	56.5
	Francis X. Purcell (D)	35,730	43.3
10	Frederick R. Lehlbach (R)	74,154	62.1
	Eugene J. O'Mara (D)	45,287	37.9
11	Oscar L. Auf der Heide (D)	51,982	62.1
	George M. Eichler (R)	31,728	37.9
12	Mary T. Norton (D)	56,748	62.0
	Philip W. Grece (R)	34,817	38.0

NEW MEXICO

	Candidates	Votes	%
AL	Albert Gallatin Simms (R)	61,208	52.2
	John Morrow (D)	56,045	47.8

NEW YORK

	Candidates	Votes	%
1	Robert L. Bacon (R)	143,230	62.0
	Thomas J. Cuff (D)	83,535	36.2
2	William F. Brunner (D)	137,214	62.4
	Jacob A. Visel (R)	78,536	35.7
3	George W. Lindsay (D)	26,626	72.2
	Francis J. Nicosia (R)	9,139	24.8
4	Thomas H. Cullen (D)	34,496	75.0
	Charles O. Winnie (R)	10,696	23.2
5	Loring M. Black Jr. (D)	50,158	56.7
	Robert C. Lee (R)	35,935	40.6
6	Andrew L. Somers (D)	70,953	53.9
	John L. Lotsch (R)	53,700	40.8
	Bernard J. Riley (SOC)	7,026	5.3
7	John F. Quayle (D)	30,897	67.2
	Peter S. Gehris (R)	13,211	28.7
8	Patrick J. Carley (D)	108,028	58.5
	William A. Blank (R)	66,180	35.8
	William M. Feigenbaum (SOC)	10,551	5.7
9	David J. O'Connell (D)	60,097	51.1
	Ernest C. Wagner (R)	53,552	45.5
10	Emanuel Celler (D)	31,152	58.0
	William G. Bushell (R)	18,411	34.3
	Abraham I. Shiplacoff (SOC)	3,645	6.8
11	Anning S. Prall (D)	44,820	66.4
	James A. Simonson (R)	22,099	32.7

	Candidates	Votes	%
12	Samuel Dickstein (D)	15,093	78.7
	Samuel K. Beier (R)	3,321	17.3
13	Christopher D. Sullivan (D)	16,062	77.3
	Jacob Rosenberg (R)	4,076	19.6
14	William I. Sirovich (D)	16,602	54.4
	Sol Ullman (R)	11,974	39.2
	August Claessens (SOC)	1,648	5.4
15	John J. Boylan (D)	30,849	77.6
	Gabriel L. Kaplan (R)	8,294	20.9
16	John J. O'Connor (D)	29,351	68.7
	Michael G. Panzer (R)	12,600	29.5
17	Ruth Baker Pratt (R)	36,655	51.8
	Philip Berolzheimer (D)	32,466	45.9
18	John F. Carew (D)	30,030	74.0
	Bernard Katzen (R)	9,562	23.6
19	Sol Bloom (D)	48,054	59.4
	David Steinhardt (R)	30,617	37.8
20	Fiorello H. LaGuardia (R)	11,956	50.1
	Saul J. Dickheiser (D)	10,856	45.5
21	Royal H. Weller (D)	56,992*	53.3
	Edward A. Johnson (R)	45,610	42.7
22	Anthony J. Griffin (D)	35,711	71.5
	Thomas J. Burke (R)	12,868	25.7
23	Frank Oliver (D)	128,372	66.6
	Henry H. Spitz (R)	52,588	27.3
24	James M. Fitzpatrick (D)	96,556	54.2
	Benjamin L. Fairchild (R)	72,408	40.6
	Louis Painken (SOC)	9,347	5.2
25	J. Mayhew Wainwright (R)	79,228	59.9
	Herbert McKennis (D)	50,589	38.3
26	Hamilton Fish Jr. (R)	69,445	63.6
	George C. Rogers (D)	36,591	33.5
27	Harcourt J. Pratt (R)	59,183	62.8
	Robert R. Livingston (D)	34,993	37.2
28	Parker Corning (D)	77,365	58.2
	Franklin D. Sargent (R)	53,383	40.1
29	James S. Parker (R)	71,326	62.8
	Theodore A. Knapp (D)	40,541	35.7
30	Frank Crowther (R)	58,022	59.8
	E. Watson Gardiner (D)	36,956	38.1
31	Bertrand H. Snell (R)	52,702	63.3
	John C. Howard (D)	30,602	36.7
32	Francis D. Culkin (R)	65,009	67.5
	Frank Bowman (D)	30,201	31.3
33	Frederick M. Davenport (R)	62,746	56.5
34	John D. Clarke (R)	80,531	71.0
	William W. Lampman (D)	32,925	29.0
35	Clarence E. Hancock (R)	90,370	61.8
	Augustus C. Stevens (D)	52,926	36.2
36	John Taber (R)	68,095	69.1
	Joseph P. Craugh (D)	30,503	30.9
37	Gale H. Stalker (R & SOC)	78,789	70.4
	Paul Smith (D)	33,212	29.7
38	James L. Whitley (R)	47,298	36.0
	Charles Stanton (D)	43,009	32.7
	William MacFarlane (I)	38,324	29.2
39	Archie D. Sanders (R)	69,615	65.0
	Frank L. Morris (D)	34,175	31.9
40	S. Wallace Dempsey (R)	99,896	65.4
	John M. Powers (D)	46,860	30.7
41	Edmund F. Cooke (R)	44,641	52.7
	Fred C. Fornes (D)	37,057	43.7
42	James M. Mead (D)	44,373	56.1
	C. Hamilton Cook (R)	31,785	40.2
43	Daniel A. Reed (R)	73,571	76.0
	Arthur E. Towne (D)	23,176	24.0

NORTH CAROLINA

	Candidates	Votes	%
1	Lindsay C. Warren (D)	23,140	76.3
	Marion B. Prescott (R)	7,209	23.8
2	John H. Kerr (D)	24,129	88.9
	J. L. Johnston (R)	3,005	11.1
3	Charles L. Abernethy (D)	21,740	55.7
	William G. Mebane (R)	17,307	44.3
4	Edward W. Pou (D)	31,288	65.6
	Lossing L. Wrenn (R)	16,434	34.4
5	Charles M. Stedman (D)	54,980	50.1
	Junius H. Harden (R)	54,813	49.9
6	J. Bayard Clark (D)	26,061	61.4

	Candidates	Votes	%
	W. C. Downing (R)	16,364	38.6
7	William C. Hammer (D)	41,124	51.3
	A. I. Ferree (R)	39,106	48.7
8	Robert L. Doughton (D)	37,535	50.9
	W. S. Bogle (R)	36,251	49.1
9	Charles A. Jonas (R)	49,799	51.6
	Alfred L. Bulwinkle (D)	46,756	48.4
10	George M. Pritchard (R)	49,045	50.2
	Zebulon Weaver (D)	48,607	49.8

NORTH DAKOTA

	Candidates	Votes	%
1	Olger B. Burtness (R)	53,941	77.5
	W. S. Hooper (D)	15,646	22.5
2	Thomas Hall (R)	42,844	61.7
	J. L. Page (D)	26,566	38.3
3	James H. Sinclair (R)	52,220	84.8
	Reuben H. Leavitt (D)	9,335	15.2

OHIO

	Candidates	Votes	%
1	Nicholas Longworth (R)	80,812	61.8
	Arthur Espy (D)	49,880	38.2
2	William E. Hess (R)	63,605	53.0
	James H. Cleveland (D)	54,332	46.1
3	Roy Fitzgerald (R)	101,050	64.4
	Frank L. Humphrey (D)	55,767	35.6
4	John L. Cable (R)	56,291	57.5
	William Klinger (D)	41,677	42.5
5	Charles J. Thompson (R)	36,096	53.5
	Frank C. Kniffin (D)	31,385	46.5
6	Charles C. Kearns (R)	43,519	56.9
	George D. Nye (D)	33,020	43.1
7	Charles Brand (R)	75,753	68.8
	Harry E. Rice (D)	34,323	31.2
8	Grant E. Mouser Jr. (R)	42,199	52.2
	Brooks Fletcher (D)	38,651	47.8
9	William W. Chalmers (R)	82,560	61.9
	William P. Clarke (D)	50,601	38.0
10	Thomas A. Jenkins (R)	38,347	69.9
	Charles E. Poston (D)	16,551	30.2
11	Mell G. Underwood (D)	34,257	52.8
	Edwin D. Ricketts (R)	30,574	47.2
12	John C. Speaks (R)	82,574	62.2
	Carl H. Valentine (D)	50,216	37.8
13	Joe E. Baird (R)	54,174	61.4
	William C. Martin (D)	34,015	38.6
14	Francis Seiberling (R)	106,253	64.4
	A. F. O'Nell (D)	58,848	35.6
15	C. Ellis Moore (R)	50,941	65.8
	Frank H. Ward (D)	26,441	34.2
16	C. B. McClintock (R)	73,966	56.4
	John McSweeney (D)	55,778	42.5
17	William M. Morgan (R)	56,823	58.2
	Charles West (D)	40,846	41.8
18	B. Frank Murphy (R)	71,378	69.2
	John J. Whitacre (D)	31,422	30.5
19	John G. Cooper (R)	89,731	68.7
	Locke Miller (D)	40,948	31.3
20	Charles A. Mooney (D)	47,313	62.3
	Oscar V. Hensley (R)	28,381	37.4
21	Robert Crosser (D)	39,090	59.8
	Joseph F. Lange (R)	26,267	40.2
22	Chester C. Bolton (R)	151,565	69.8
	Simon B. Fitzsimmons (D)	65,742	30.3

OKLAHOMA

	Candidates	Votes	%
1	Charles O'Connor (R)	63,641	52.2
	Everette B. Howard (D)	58,148	47.7
2	William W. Hastings (D)	31,287	51.9
	E. L. Kirby (R)	28,959	48.0
3	Wilburn Cartwright (D)	39,467	64.1
	Robert N. Allen (R)	21,804	35.4
4	Thomas D. McKeown (D)	37,191	50.5
	Fred L. Patrick (R)	36,151	49.1
5	Ulysses S. Stone (R)	44,814	50.9
	Fletcher B. Swank (D)	42,856	48.7
6	Jed Johnson (D)	32,820	53.4
	Walter C. Stephens (R)	28,304	46.0

Candidates	Votes	%
7 James V. McClintic (D)	27,670	55.6
Walter S. Mills (R)	21,758	43.7
8 Milton C. Garber (R)	48,445	63.8
J. P. Battenberg (D)	27,135	35.7

OREGON

Candidates	Votes	%
1 Willis C. Hawley (R)	91,839	70.9
Harvey G. Starkweather (D)	33,772	26.1
2 Robert R. Butler (R)	28,865	55.7
Walter M. Pierce (D)	22,108	42.6
3 Franklin F. Korell (R)	75,835	67.6
William C. Culbertson (D)	29,673#	26.5

PENNSYLVANIA

Candidates	Votes	%
1 James M. Beck (R)	45,070	49.8
William L. Rooney (D)	44,956	49.7
2 George S. Graham (R)	34,432	64.6
John J. Shanahan (D)	18,697	35.1
3 Harry C. Ransley (R)	30,458	57.4
James J. Hayes (D)	22,559	42.5
4 Benjamin M. Golder (R)	49,877	61.2
Thomas J. Carroll (D, LAB)	31,082	38.1
5 James J. Connolly (R, D)	110,648	99.4
6 George A. Welsh (R)	89,362	59.8
Bruce A. Metzger (D)	59,410	39.7
7 George P. Darrow (R)	91,305	68.0
Thomas A. O'Hara (D)	42,217	31.5
8 James Wolfenden (R)	116,266	76.2
Henry W. Davis (D)	34,607	22.7
9 Henry W. Watson (R)	102,019	76.3
Richard Vaux (D)	31,389	23.5
10 William W. Griest (R, LAB)	55,623	82.5
John A. McSparran (D)	11,395	16.9
11 Laurence H. Watres (R, P)	48,626	50.3
Frank M. Walsh (D)	48,017	49.7
12 John J. Casey (D, LAB)	70,943	51.6
Henry W. Merritt (R, P)	66,661	48.4
13 George Franklin Brumm (R)	46,486	55.5
Bernard V. O'Hare (D)	37,243	44.5
14 Charles J. Esterly (R)	76,670	61.9
Abraham H. Rothermel (D)	36,176	29.2
Howard McDonough (SOC, LAB)	10,950	8.8
15 Louis T. McFadden (R, D)	50,770	93.8
Cornelia Bryce Pinchot (P)	3,348	6.2
16 Edgar R. Kiess (R, P)	48,041	74.0
Thomas Wood (D)	16,693	25.7
17 Frederick W. Magrady (R)	45,437	60.0
Samuel M. Shipman (D, P)	30,290	40.0
18 Edward M. Beers (R, LAB)	55,736	81.0
Frederick A. Rupp (D)	13,070	19.0
19 Isaac H. Doutrich (R, LAB)	80,291	80.3
John E. Blair (D)	19,032	19.1
20 J. Russell Leech (R)	29,383	53.3
George E. Wolfe (D, LAB)	25,737	46.7
21 J. Banks Kurtz (R, LAB)	42,965	76.2
Harry K. Filler (D)	13,420	23.8
22 Franklin Menges (R, P)	44,198	63.3
John H. Myers (D)	25,622	36.7
23 J. Mitchell Chase (R, LAB)	43,294	74.0
T. E. Costello (D)	15,219	26.0
24 Samuel A. Kendall (R, P)	42,118	64.3
J. Calvin Core (D)	23,176	35.4
25 Henry W. Temple (R, P)	34,806	59.6
James S. Pates (D)	23,260	39.9
26 J. Howard Swick (R, P)	64,160	72.2
C. Hale Sipe (D)	24,352	27.4
27 Nathan L. Strong (R, P)	52,868	75.2
Harry W. Fee (D)	17,433	24.8
28 Thomas C. Cochran (R, P)	59,143	74.3
Harry B. Mitchell (D)	20,443	25.7
29 Milton W. Shreve (R, P)	42,747	60.4
Albert L. Thomas (D)	28,004	39.6
30 William R. Coyle (R)	48,421	56.9
Everett Kent (D, LAB)	36,612	43.1
31 Adam M. Wyant (R, P)	50,981	95.8
32 Stephen G. Porter (R)	48,837	64.6
Edward S. Michalowski (D)	26,145	34.6
33 M. Clyde Kelly (R, D)	81,328	99.0

Candidates	Votes	%
34 Patrick J. Sullivan (R, D)	48,638	97.4
35 Harry A. Estep (R)	42,450	57.3
John J. Murray (D)	30,619	41.4
36 Guy E. Campbell (R, P)	48,190	60.3
William E. Madden Jr. (D)	31,151	39.0

Special Election

	Votes	%
8 James Wolfenden (R)	116,504	97.8

RHODE ISLAND

Candidates	Votes	%
1 Clark Burdick (R)	42,366	55.6
John J. Cooney (D)	33,902	44.5
2 Richard S. Aldrich (R)	43,772	55.6
Sumner Mowry (D)	34,947	44.4
3 Jeremiah E. O'Connell (D)	45,605	57.1
Louis Monast (R)	34,223	42.9

SOUTH CAROLINA

Candidates	Votes	%
1 Thomas S. McMillan (D)	8,469	100.0
2 Butler B. Hare (D)	7,648	100.0
3 Fred H. Dominick (D)	10,917	100.0
4 John J. McSwain (D)	8,873	100.0
5 William F. Stevenson (D)	8,911	100.0
6 Allard H. Gasque (D)	7,757	100.0
7 Hampton P. Fulmer (D)	8,772	100.0

SOUTH DAKOTA

Candidates	Votes	%
1 Charles A. Christopherson (R)	54,573	58.4
A. O. Steensland (D)	38,055	40.7
2 Royal C. Johnson (R)	54,846	57.2
Fred Hildebrandt (D)	39,970	41.7
3 William Williamson (R)	33,245	55.7
Arthur W. Watwood (D)	26,412	44.3

TENNESSEE

Candidates	Votes	%
1 B. Carroll Reece (R)	28,142	78.6
W. I. Giles (D)	7,646	21.4
2 J. Will Taylor (R)	30,917	68.9
Leon Jourolmon (D)	13,968	31.1
3 Sam D. McReynolds (D)	25,667	53.4
Silas Williams (R)	22,405	46.6
4 Cordell Hull (D)	17,141	68.2
S. H. Justice (R)	7,999	31.8
5 Ewin L. Davis (D)	12,847	80.4
John F. Aplinger (D)	3,126#	19.6
6 Joseph W. Byrns (D)	24,738	79.9
E. L. Bradbury (R)	6,220	20.1
7 Edward E. Eslick (D)	16,893	93.0
S. E. Stephens (R)	1,268	7.0
8 Gordon Browning (D)	17,868	66.1
Harvey E. Cantrell (R)	9,184	34.0
9 Jere Cooper (D)	20,184	90.1
Carmack Murchison (R)	2,222	9.9
10 Hubert F. Fisher (D)	21,524	81.3
R. L. Harper (R)	4,964	18.7

TEXAS

Candidates	Votes	%
1 Wright Patman (D)	24,267	87.9
Richard E. Stephens (R)	3,349	12.1
2 John C. Box (D)	38,901	100.0
3 Morgan G. Sanders (D)	22,221	100.0
4 Sam Rayburn (D)	23,847	84.2
Floyd Harry (R)	4,488	15.8
5 Hatton W. Sumners (D)	42,482	100.0
6 Luther A. Johnson (D)	26,412	90.7
H. Lee Monroe (R)	2,714	9.3
7 Clay Stone Briggs (D)	21,461	88.4
A. J. Long (R)	2,827	11.6
8 Daniel E. Garrett (D)	43,891	81.8
George E. Kepple (R)	9,739	18.2
9 Joseph J. Mansfield (D)	24,742	86.9
Louis B. Allen (R)	3,718	13.1
10 James P. Buchanan (D)	27,890	91.9
David H. Morris (R)	2,457	8.1

Candidates	Votes	%
11 Oliver H. Crass (D)	21,484	90.9
R. C. Bush (R)	2,141	9.1
12 Fritz G. Lanham (D)	30,905	79.6
David Sutter (R)	7,921	20.4
13 Guinn Williams (D)	30,926	88.5
Mrs. P. A. Welty (R)	4,026	11.5
14 Augustus McCloskey (D)	29,085‡	50.3
Harry M. Wurzbach (R)	28,766	49.7
15 John N. Garner (D)	28,417	100.0
16 Claude B. Hudspeth (D)	31,132	100.0
17 Robert Q. Lee (D)	41,727	100.0
18 Marvin Jones (D)	58,667	86.5
V. C. Nelson (R)	9,137	13.5

UTAH

Candidates	Votes	%
1 Don B. Colton (R)	50,274	60.9
Knox Patterson (D)	31,889	38.6
2 Elmer O. Leatherwood (R)	46,866	50.2
Joshua H. Paul (D)	46,025	49.3

VERMONT

Candidates	Votes	%
1 Elbert S. Brigham (R)	44,082	63.0
Jeremiah C. Durick (D)	25,095	35.9
2 Ernest Willard Gibson (R)	47,141	79.3
Harry W. Witters (D)	11,356	19.1

VIRGINIA

Candidates	Votes	%
1 Schuyler Otis Bland (D)	23,912	99.7
2 Menalcus Lankford (R)	18,614	55.9
Joseph T. Deal (D)	14,668	44.1
3 Andrew J. Montague (D)	23,350	75.9
J. D. Peake (I)	5,854	19.0
James E. Maynard (I)	1,561	5.1
4 Patrick Henry Drewry (D)	16,904	99.7
5 Joseph Whitehead (D)	16,672	54.3
Taylor G. Vaughan (R)	14,049	45.7
6 Clifton A. Woodrum (D)	25,091	99.7
7 Jacob A. Garber (R)	15,243	50.4
Thomas W. Harrison (D)	15,009	49.6
8 R. Walton Moore (D)	24,368	99.1
9 Joseph C. Shaffer (R)	32,696	50.8
William H. Rouse (D)	31,722	49.2
10 Henry St. George Tucker (D)	14,817	56.9
M. J. Putnam (R)	11,230	43.1

WASHINGTON

Candidates	Votes	%
1 John F. Miller (R)	70,703	65.5
Hugh Todd (D)	36,858	34.1
2 Lindley H. Hadley (R)	59,534	99.3
3 Albert Johnson (R)	77,314	70.0
O. M. Nelson (D)	33,217	30.1
4 John W. Summers (R)	48,766	77.1
H. C. Bohlke (D)	14,512	22.9
5 Sam B. Hill (D)	50,323	58.5
Thomas Corkery (R)	35,660	41.5

WEST VIRGINIA

Candidates	Votes	%
1 Carl G. Bachmann (R)	62,646	60.6
Paul R. Wellman (D)	40,666	39.4
2 Frank L. Bowman (R)	52,424	55.7
Ben H. Hiner (D)	41,640	44.2
3 John M. Wolverton (R)	45,167	50.4
William S. O'Brien (D)	44,477	49.6
4 James A. Hughes (R)	55,672	57.0
Harry H. Darnall (D)	42,057	43.0
5 Hugh Ike Shott (R)	63,559	53.4
John Kee (D)	55,376	46.6
6 Joe L. Smith (D)	67,845	50.1
Edward T. England (R)	67,617	49.9

WISCONSIN

Candidates	Votes	%
1 Henry Allen Cooper (R)	83,069	80.2
William C. Kiernan (D)	20,534	19.8
2 Charles A. Kading (R)	53,530	69.9

Candidates	Votes	%		Candidates	Votes	%		Candidates	Votes	%
	Eugene A. Clifford (D)	23,101	30.1	6	Florian Lampert (R)	53,952	69.2		Miles H. McNally (D)	13,590	18.6
3	John Mandt Nelson (R)	62,938	74.7		Morley G. Kelly (D)	24,009	30.8	11	Hubert H. Peavey (R)	56,586	80.8
	William Victora (D)	20,262	24.1	7	Merlin Hull (R)	49,590	72.4		Frank P. Kennedy (D)	11,962	17.1
4	John C. Schafer (R)	37,685	44.1		A. H. Schubert (D)	18,530	27.0				
	William J. Kershaw (D)	28,956	33.9	8	Edward E. Browne (R)	47,848	74.0		**WYOMING**		
	Walter Polakowski (SOC)	18,885	22.1		R. J. Walsh (D)	16,316	25.2	AL	Vincent M. Carter (R)	38,935	51.8
5	William H. Stafford (R)	41,265	38.9	9	George J. Schneider (R)	52,300	60.4		W. S. Kimball (D)	35,972	47.8
	Victor L. Berger (SOC)	40,536	38.2		James H. McGillan (D)	33,302	38.5				
	Thomas O'Malley (D)	24,037	22.7	10	James A. Frear (R)	59,314	81.4				

1929 House Elections

KENTUCKY

Special Election

	Candidates	Votes	%
3	John W. Moore (D)	19,669	51.3
	Homer Beliles (R)	18,644	48.7

LOUISIANA

Special Election

	Candidates	Votes	%
3	Numa F. Montet (D)	11,460	57.7
	M. E. Norman (R)	8,399	42.3

MISSOURI

Special Election

	Candidates	Votes	%
4	David Hopkins (R)	23,898	53.0
	Louis V. Stigall (D)	21,179	47.0

NEW YORK

Special Election

	Candidates	Votes	%
21	Joseph A. Gavagan (D)	39,893	56.7
	Hubert T. Delany (R&SQDEAL)	26,666	37.9
	Frank Crosswaith (SOC)	3,561	5.1

1930 House Elections

ALABAMA

	Candidates	Votes	%
1	John McDuffie (D)	16,839	100.0
2	Lister Hill (D)	22,630	100.0
3	Henry B. Steagall (D)	13,398	100.0
4	Lamar Jeffers (D)	13,502	65.2
	E. D. Banks (I)	7,209	34.8
5	Lafayette L. Patterson (D)	13,221	100.0
6	William B. Oliver (D)	9,439	100.0
7	Miles C. Allgood (D)	18,932	61.1
	John B. Isbell (R)	12,062	38.9
8	Edward B. Almon (D)	18,570	100.0
9	George Huddleston (D)	24,484	81.0
	Hollis B. Parris (I)	5,750	19.0
10	William B. Bankhead (D)	14,388	64.2
	Charles P. G. Lunsford (R)	8,009	35.8

ARIZONA

	Candidates	Votes	%
AL	Lewis W. Douglas (D)	52,342	100.0

ARKANSAS

	Candidates	Votes	%
1	William J. Driver (D)	19,103	100.0
2	John E. Miller (D)	18,623	100.0
3	Claude A. Fuller (D)	28,809	100.0
4	Effiegene Wingo (D)	21,753	100.0
5	Heartsill Ragon (D)	21,896	100.0
6	David D. Glover (D)	18,127	100.0
7	Tilman B. Parks (D)	15,860	100.0

CALIFORNIA

	Candidates	Votes	%
1	Clarence F. Lea (D-R)	66,703	100.0
2	Harry L. Englebright (R-D)	35,941	99.9
3	Charles F. Curry	43,336	53.4
	J. M. Inman (R)	26,785#	33.0
	Frank H. Buck (D)	9,172#	11.3
4	Florence P. Kahn (R-D)	47,397	100.0
5	Richard J. Welch (R-D)	59,853	100.0
6	Albert E. Carter (R-D)	110,190	100.0
7	Henry E. Barbour (R-D)	79,041	100.0
8	Arthur Monroe Free (R-D)	93,377	99.9
9	William E. Evans (R)	182,176	99.9
10	Joe Crail (R)	162,502	75.0
	John F. Dockweiler (D)	54,231	25.0
11	Philip D. Swing (R-D)	124,092	100.0

COLORADO

	Candidates	Votes	%
1	William R. Eaton (R)	39,907	50.3
	Lawrence Lewis (D)	38,152	48.1
2	Charles B. Timberlake (R)	55,099	59.3
	O. E. Webb (D)	37,760	40.7
3	Guy U. Hardy (R)	55,170	60.7
	Guy M. Weybright (D)	35,744	39.3
4	Edward T. Taylor (D)	34,536	67.0
	Webster S. Whinnery (R)	17,051	33.1

CONNECTICUT

	Candidates	Votes	%
1	Augustine Lonergan (D)	51,551	50.3
	Clarence W. Seymour (R)	50,877	49.7
2	Richard P. Freeman (R)	37,801	53.1
	William C. Fox (D)	33,329	46.9
3	John Q. Tilson (R)	45,329	52.1
	James A. Shanley (D)	40,269	46.3
4	William L. Tierney (D)	50,769	49.7
	Schuyler Merritt (R)	49,209	48.2
5	Edward W. Goss (R)	33,302	50.5
	Martin E. Gormley (D)	32,584	49.5

Special Election

	Candidates	Votes	%
5	Edward W. Goss (R)	33,284	50.6
	Martin E. Gormley (D)	32,479	49.4

DELAWARE

	Candidates	Votes	%
AL	Robert G. Houston (R)	48,493	55.4
	John P. Le Fevre (D)	38,891	44.4

FLORIDA

	Candidates	Votes	%
1	Herbert J. Drane (D)	24,792	67.7
	L. E. Womack (R)	11,819	32.3
2	Robert A. Green (D)	7,060	100.0
3	Tom A. Yon (D)	11,796	99.8
4	Ruth Bryan Owen (D)	40,422	99.9

GEORGIA

	Candidates	Votes	%
1	Charles G. Edwards (D)	2,465	100.0
2	E. E. Cox (D)	2,518	100.0
3	Charles R. Crisp (D)	2,440	100.0
4	William C. Wright (D)	2,721	100.0
5	Robert Ramspeck (D)	10,752	100.0
6	Samuel Rutherford (D)	4,333	100.0
7	Malcolm C. Tarver (D)	5,590	100.0
8	Charles H. Brand (D)	5,058	93.2
	W. N. Phillips (I)	369#	6.8
9	John S. Wood (D)	7,089	100.0
10	Carl Vinson (D)	2,691	100.0
11	William C. Lankford (D)	6,462	80.9
	H. J. Carswell (R)	1,526#	19.1
12	William W. Larsen (D)	2,444	100.0

IDAHO

	Candidates	Votes	%
1	Burton L. French (R)	34,527	64.9
	Compton I. White (D)	18,657	35.1
2	Addison T. Smith (R)	46,342	63.2
	W. F. Alworth (D)	27,002	36.8

ILLINOIS

	Candidates	Votes	%
1	Oscar De Priest (R)	23,719	58.4
	Harry Baker (D)	16,747	41.2
2	Morton D. Hull (R)	76,665	54.4
	Michael C. Walsh (D)	63,341	44.9
3	Edward A. Kelly (D)	83,028	58.1
	Elliott W. Sproul (R)	59,644	41.8
4	Harry P. Beam (D)	36,736	69.3
	Frank George Zelezinski (R)	16,192	30.5
5	Adolph J. Sabath (D)	21,460	66.2
	Frank V. Kara (R)	10,816	33.3
6	James T. Igoe (D)	120,408	66.7
	Henry R. Lundblad (R)	59,052	32.7
7	Leonard W. Schuetz (D)	111,525	55.0
	James C. Moreland (R)	90,844	44.8
8	Peter C. Granata (R)	16,565	51.8
	Stanley H. Kunz (D)	15,394	48.1
9	Fred A. Britten (R)	24,028	99.4
10	Carl R. Chindblom (R)	72,938	50.8
	John E. Hesse (D)	70,621	49.2
11	Frank R. Reid (R)	56,957	63.1
	Elmer P. Schaefer (D)	33,169	36.8
12	John T. Buckbee (R)	55,754	76.1
	Richard J. O'Halloran (D)	17,497	23.9
13	William R. Johnson (R)	28,113	70.2
	John A. Ascher (D)	11,937	29.8
14	John C. Allen (R)	36,370	56.9
	William H. Hartzell (D)	27,592	43.1
15	Burnett M. Chiperfield (R)	35,114	56.5
	J. Hays Paxton (D)	27,031	43.5
16	William E. Hull (R)	36,572	52.8
	Edwin S. Carr (D)	32,692	47.2
17	Homer W. Hall (R)	27,696	58.4
	C. S. Schneider (D)	19,711	41.6
18	William P. Holaday (R)	38,102	56.8
	Charles R. Hill (D)	29,012	43.2
19	Charles Adkins (R)	43,794	55.4
	Charles M. Borchers (D)	35,310	44.6

	Candidates	Votes	%
20	Henry T. Rainey (D)	37,537	64.9
	William J. Thornton (R)	20,262	35.1
21	J. Earl Major (D)	46,058	57.1
	Roger E. Chapin (R)	34,521	42.8
22	Charles A. Karch (D)	48,281	50.3
	Ed. M. Irwin (R)	47,715	49.7
23	William W. Arnold (D)	49,111	62.6
	Joe Frank Allen (R)	29,291	37.4
24	Claude V. Parsons (D)	27,325	50.0
	James V. Heidinger (R)	27,296	50.0
25	Kent E. Keller (D)	38,796	52.6
	Edward E. Denison (R)	34,927	47.4
AL	William H. Dieterich (D)	1,062,606✓	
	Richard Yates (R)	991,083✓	
	Walter Nesbit (D)	975,422	
	Frank L. Smith (R)	890,327	
	Emil Z. Levitin (SOC)	9,526	
	Morris A. Gold (SOC)	9,207	
	William S. Feinberg (AM NAT)	1,337	
	John W. McLain (AM NAT)	1,228	
	I. J. Brown (LIB)	884	
	Charles A. Reinhart (LIB)	824	

Special Elections

	Candidates	Votes	%
15	Burnett M. Chiperfield (R)	34,063	56.2
	J. Hays Paxton (D)	26,467	43.7
24	Claude V. Parsons (D)	26,929	50.2
	James V. Heidinger (R)	26,732	49.8

INDIANA

	Candidates	Votes	%
1	John W. Boehne Jr. (D)	46,836	53.9
	Harry E. Rowbottom (R)	40,015	46.1
2	Arthur H. Greenwood (D)	52,452	59.5
	Ray S. Sisson (R)	35,689	40.5
3	Eugene B. Crowe (D)	45,070	50.2
	James W. Dunbar (R)	44,808	49.9
4	Harry C. Canfield (D)	46,396	57.1
	Scott Thompson (R)	34,856	42.9
5	Courtland C. Gillen (D)	43,355	51.5
	Noble J. Johnson (R)	40,919	48.6
6	William H. Larrabee (D)	40,803	51.8
	Richard N. Elliott (R)	37,969	48.2
7	Louis Ludlow (D)	87,777	61.6
	Archibald M. Hall (R)	53,822	37.8
8	Albert H. Vestal (R)	44,203	50.0
	Claude C. Ball (D)	44,194	50.0
9	Fred S. Purnell (R)	43,681	50.2
	Harry L. Matlock (D)	43,346	49.8
10	William R. Wood (R)	53,702	53.3
	Charles J. Murphy (D)	47,057	46.7
11	Glenn Griswold (D)	41,823	51.3
	Albert R. Hall (R)	39,771	48.7
12	David R. Hogg (R)	43,286	52.3
	Thomas P. Riddle (D)	39,488	47.7
13	Samuel B. Pettengill (D)	62,609	51.3
	Andrew J. Hickey (R)	59,361	48.7

IOWA

	Candidates	Votes	%
1	William F. Kopp (R)	27,053	63.3
	Max A. Conrad (D)	15,538	36.4
2	Bernhard M. Jacobsen (D)	30,006	55.4
	F. D. Letts (R)	24,113	44.6
3	Thomas J. B. Robinson (R)	27,098	63.0
	W. L. Beecher (D)	15,908	37.0
4	Gilbert N. Haugen (R)	29,224	59.1
	Wilbur L. Peck (D)	20,236	40.9
5	Cyrenus Cole (R)	23,221	53.8
	H. M. Cooper (D)	19,931	46.2
6	C. William Ramseyer (R)	25,875	60.6
	S. F. McConnell (D)	16,811	39.4
7	Cassius C. Dowell (R)	36,715	76.5
	Carl Evans (D)	11,272	23.5
8	Lloyd Thurston (R)	27,960	51.5

Candidates	Votes	%
James Pearson (D)	26,373	48.5
9 Charles E. Swanson (R)	27,873	57.1
June M. Fickel (D)	20,587	42.2
10 Fred C. Gilchrist (R)	34,915	66.1
Paul Anderson (D)	17,540	33.2
11 Ed H. Campbell (R)	37,659	73.8
Fordyce W. Bisbee (D)	13,382	26.2

KANSAS

Candidates	Votes	%
1 William P. Lambertson (R)	53,799	100.0
2 Ulysses S. Guyer (R)	49,844	56.8
Chauncey B. Little (D)	37,991	43.3
3 Harold McGugin (R)	42,106	52.7
Earl Knight (D)	37,807	47.3
4 Homer Hoch (R)	30,840	58.4
James E. Hilkey (D)	21,933	41.6
5 James G. Strong (R)	33,871	53.9
Clyde Short (D)	28,971	46.1
6 Charles I. Sparks (R)	40,132	61.6
Robert Good (D)	24,975	38.4
7 Clifford R. Hope (R)	52,858	61.1
A. S. Allphin (D)	33,627	38.9
8 William A. Ayres (D)	57,173	74.7
Stella B. Haines (R)	19,325	25.3

KENTUCKY

Candidates	Votes	%
1 William V. Gregory (D)	24,622	100.0
2 Glover H. Cary (D)	21,685	100.0
3 John W. Moore (D)	25,981	99.7
4 Cap R. Carden (D)	30,910	52.3
John Craddock (R)	28,220	47.7
5 Maurice H. Thatcher (R)	61,832	97.9
6 Brent Spence (D)	31,520	56.9
J. Lincoln Newhall (R)	18,891	34.1
Blaine McLaughlin (I)	4,746	8.6
7 Virgil Chapman (D)	33,402	57.8
Robert Blackburn (R)	24,380	42.2
8 Ralph Gilbert (D)	25,688	57.5
Patrick H. Taylor (R)	19,023	42.6
9 Fred M. Vinson (D)	42,671	59.7
Elva R. Kendall (R)	28,850	40.3
10 Andrew J. May (D)	27,159	52.9
Katherine Langley (R)	24,172	47.1
11 Charles Finley (R)	48,535	66.3
Will Ward Duffield (D)	24,716	33.7

Special Elections

Candidates	Votes	%
2 John L. Dorsey Jr. (D)	21,406#	100.0
11 Charles Finley (R)	14,148	76.0
M. B. Sewell (D)	4,471	24.0

LOUISIANA

Candidates	Votes	%
1 Joachim O. Fernandez (D)	30,629	95.8
2 Paul H. Maloney (D)	30,739	97.2
3 Numa F. Montet (D)	8,517	100.0
4 John N. Sandlin (D)	11,833	100.0
5 Riley J. Wilson (D)	11,168	100.0
6 Bolivar E. Kemp (D)	15,524	100.0
7 Rene L. DeRouen (D)	9,293	100.0
8 James B. Aswell (D)	12,383	100.0

MAINE

Candidates	Votes	%
1 Carroll L. Beedy (R)	23,434	61.4
Thomas F. Locke (D)	14,741	38.6
2 Donald B. Partridge (R)	24,338	56.2
Albert Beliveau (D)	18,943	43.8
3 John E. Nelson (R)	25,099	64.3
Leo D. Lamond (D)	13,948	35.7
4 Donald F. Snow (R)	15,199	66.0
Clinton C. Stevens (D)	7,839	34.0

MARYLAND

Candidates	Votes	%
1 T. Alan Goldsborough (D)	34,553	57.3
A. Stengle Marine (R)	25,792	42.7
2 William P. Cole Jr. (D)	79,963	59.3
Linwood L. Clark (R)	54,914	40.7
3 Vincent L. Palmisano (D)	28,633	53.4
John Philip Hill (R)	24,170	45.1
4 J. Charles Linthicum (D)	49,471	65.0
W. O. Atwood (R)	26,661	35.0
5 Stephen Warfield Gambrill (D)	40,315	65.3
A. Kingsley Love (R)	21,463	34.7
6 David J. Lewis (D)	42,526	53.6
Frederick N. Zihlman (R)	36,815	46.4

MASSACHUSETTS

Candidates	Votes	%
1 Allen T. Treadway (R)	41,334	54.9
Hugh McLean (D)	33,934	45.1
2 William J. Granfield (D)	46,432	55.5
Joshua L. Brooks (R)	37,247	44.5
3 Frank H. Foss (R)	36,620	57.1
Frank W. Barr (D)	27,568	43.0
4 Pehr G. Holmes (R)	42,996	54.7
David Goldstein (D)	35,661	45.3
5 Edith Nourse Rogers (R)	50,541	66.3
Joseph M. Halloran (D)	25,742	33.8
6 A. Piatt Andrew (R)	50,814	76.4
Charles D. Smith (D)	15,683	23.6
7 William P. Connery Jr. (D)	45,521	67.6
Charles W. Lovett (R)	21,821	32.4
8 Frederick W. Dallinger (R)	57,428	56.6
John P. Brennan (D)	44,041	43.4
9 Charles L. Underhill (R)	41,040	50.7
Joseph J. Borgatti (D)	39,948	49.3
10 John J. Douglass (D)	33,218	87.3
Edward L. Donnelly (R)	4,815	12.7
11 George Holden Tinkham (R)	40,417	63.0
John Joseph Kelleher (D)	23,739	37.0
12 John W. McCormack (D)	50,894	76.7
Samuel Abrams (R)	15,422	23.3
13 Robert Luce (R)	55,470	55.9
Donald M. Hill (D)	43,800	44.1
14 Richard B. Wigglesworth (R)	56,803	57.3
Edward G. Morris (D)	42,307	42.7
15 Joseph W. Martin Jr. (R)	37,100	64.1
William J. Murphy (D)	20,780	35.9
16 Charles L. Gifford (R)	39,953	69.6
John D. W. Bodfish (I)	17,467	30.4

MICHIGAN

Candidates	Votes	%
1 Robert H. Clancy (R)	44,021	82.2
William M. Donnelly (D)	8,758	16.4
2 Earl C. Michener (R)	41,478	58.0
Edward Frensdorf (D)	29,979	41.9
3 Joseph L Hooper (R)	36,190	71.1
Rosslyn L. Sowers (D)	14,737	28.9
4 John C. Ketcham (R)	34,980	66.1
Roman I. Jarvis Sr. (D)	17,953	33.9
5 Carl E. Mapes (R)	31,297	98.7
6 Seymour H. Person (R)	124,797	70.2
Patrick H. O'Brien (D)	50,221	28.2
7 Jesse P. Wolcott (R)	42,256	94.3
Emerald B. Dixon (D)	2,534	5.7
8 Bird J. Vincent (R)	38,891	67.4
Michael J. Hart (D)	18,838	32.6
9 James C. McLaughlin (R)	31,318	75.0
Loren N. O'Brien (D)	10,462	25.0
10 Roy O. Woodruff (R)	31,033	78.8
Henry C. Haller (D)	8,345	21.2
11 Frank P. Bohn (R)	34,971	100.0
12 W. Frank James (R)	36,909	98.1
13 Clarence J. McLeod (R)	39,064	78.8
Walter I. McKenzie (D)	9,575	19.3

MINNESOTA

Candidates	Votes	%
1 Victor Christgau (R)	45,330	65.1
Matt Fitzpatrick (F-LAB)	24,357	35.0
2 Frank Clague (R)	38,431	53.7
L. A. Fritsche (F-LAB)	33,092	46.3
3 August H. Andresen (R)	35,704	48.1
Francis H. Shoemaker (F-LAB)	21,118	28.4
Joseph J. Moriarity (D)	17,485	23.5
4 Melvin J. Maas (R)	48,633	66.5
Claus V. Hammerstrom (F-LAB)	16,180	22.1
Frank Munger Sr. (D)	6,593	9.0
5 W. I. Nolan (R)	55,502	61.3
Silas M. Bryan (D)	32,215	35.6
6 Harold Knutson (R)	44,058	60.6
John Knutsen (F-LAB)	19,461	26.8
P. J. Russell (D)	9,197	12.7
7 Paul John Kvale (F-LAB)	58,334	81.2
Frank Hopkins (R)	13,506	18.8
8 William A. Pittenger (R)	55,802	63.3
William L. Carss (F-LAB)	29,001	32.9
9 Conrad G. Selvig (R)	37,531	53.3
Knud Wefald (F-LAB)	32,874	46.7
10 Godfrey G. Goodwin (R)	38,391	49.5
Erling Swenson (F-LAB)	37,182	48.0

MISSISSIPPI

Candidates	Votes	%
1 John E. Rankin (D)	5,378	100.0
2 Wall Doxey (D)	4,202	100.0
3 William M. Whittington (D)	4,282	100.0
4 Jeff Busby (D)	4,017	100.0
5 Ross A. Collins (D)	5,107	100.0
6 Robert S. Hall (D)	5,995	100.0
7 Percy L. Quin (D)	3,356	100.0
8 James W. Collier (D)	2,560	100.0

MISSOURI

Candidates	Votes	%
1 Milton A. Romjue (D)	28,974	61.8
J. F. Culler (R)	17,898	38.2
2 Ralph F. Lozier (D)	30,020	62.8
Pearl Gehrig (R)	17,746	37.1
3 Jacob L. Milligan (D)	25,853	58.9
H. F. Lawrence (R)	18,074	41.2
4 David Hopkins (R)	33,284	50.8
Romulus E. Culver (D)	32,208	49.2
5 Joseph B. Shannon (D)	102,569	64.3
Edgar C. Ellis (R)	56,918	35.7
6 Clement C. Dickinson (D)	24,713	54.9
Thomas J. Halsey (R)	20,249	45.0
7 Samuel C. Major (D)	36,543	51.8
John W. Palmer (R)	33,964	48.2
8 William L. Nelson (D)	27,321	57.9
E. J. Melton (R)	19,850	42.1
9 Clarence Cannon (D)	25,796	62.4
Frank H. Hollmann (R)	15,472	37.5
10 Henry F. Niedringhaus (R)	93,433	99.8
11 John J. Cochran (D)	17,726	99.9
12 Leonidas C. Dyer (R)	14,195	99.8
13 Clyde Williams (D)	27,633	53.1
Charles E. Kiefner (R)	24,378	46.9
14 James F. Fulbright (D)	45,332	51.6
Dewey Short (R)	42,579	48.4
15 Joe J. Manlove (R)	37,788	57.8
Frank H. Lee (D)	27,387	41.9
16 William E. Barton (D)	25,392	52.4
Rowland L. Johnston (R)	23,025	47.6

MONTANA

Candidates	Votes	%
1 John M. Evans (D)	39,166	56.1
Mark D. Fitzgerald (R)	29,793	42.7
2 Scott Leavitt (R)	52,943	52.8
Tom Stout (D)	45,438	45.3

NEBRASKA

Candidates	Votes	%
1 John H. Morehead (D)	34,662	63.9
Ralph S. Moseley (R)	19,589	36.1
2 Malcolm Baldrige (R)	34,114	50.6
Edward R. Burke (D)	33,276	49.4
3 Edgar Howard (D)	53,221	69.3
H. Halderson (R)	23,599	30.7
4 John N. Norton (D)	35,812	56.0
Charles H. Sloan (R)	28,196	44.1
5 Ashton C. Shallenberger (D)	34,915	55.6
Fred G. Johnson (R)	27,932	44.4

	Candidates	Votes	%
6	Robert G. Simmons (R)	65,766	72.8
	John McCoy (D)	24,519	27.2

NEVADA

	Candidates	Votes	%
AL	Samuel S. Arentz (R)	18,279	54.4
	Maurice J. Sullivan (D)	15,343	45.6

NEW HAMPSHIRE

	Candidates	Votes	%
1	Fletcher Hale (R)	37,570	56.3
	Napoleon J. Dyer (D)	29,166	43.7
2	Edward H. Wason (R)	34,253	59.7
	Eaton D. Sargent (D)	23,157	40.3

NEW JERSEY

	Candidates	Votes	%
1	Charles A. Wolverton (R)	78,019	79.1
	Francis G. Homan (D)	19,486	19.8
2	Isaac Bacharach (R)	67,729	79.7
	Hans Froelicher Jr. (D)	17,125	20.1
3	William H. Sutphin (D)	57,911	51.1
	Thomas M. Gopsill (R)	54,889	48.5
4	Charles A. Eaton (R)	39,019	57.6
	Charles Browne (D)	28,330	41.9
5	Ernest R. Ackerman (R)	65,178	65.3
	Warren N. Gaffney (D)	33,851	33.9
6	Randolph Perkins (R)	72,868	56.5
	Archibald C. Hart (D)	55,283	42.8
7	George N. Seger (R)	35,636	53.7
	Harry Joelson (D)	29,879	45.0
8	Fred A. Hartley Jr. (R)	44,038	50.4
	Paul J. Moore (D)	43,195	49.4
9	Peter A. Cavicchia (R)	24,312	53.8
	Daniel F. Minahan (D)	20,497	45.4
10	Frederick R. Lehlbach (R)	44,435	66.6
	Edward W. Simms (D)	21,539	32.3
11	Oscar L. Auf der Heide (D)	44,691	73.0
	Irving W. Taft (R)	16,087	26.3
12	Mary T. Norton (D)	53,565	75.9
	Douglas D. T. Story (R)	16,715	23.7

NEW MEXICO

	Candidates	Votes	%
AL	Dennis Chavez (D)	65,228	57.5
	Albert G. Simms (R)	47,955	42.3

NEW YORK

	Candidates	Votes	%
1	Robert L. Bacon (R)	96,390	58.4
	James S. Shevlin (D)	64,172	38.9
2	William F. Brunner (D)	110,081	67.5
	James C. MacDevitt (R)	45,651	28.0
3	George W. Lindsay (D)	20,525	75.1
	James A. Campbell (R)	5,159	18.9
	Joseph A. Weil (SOC)	1,443	5.3
4	Thomas H. Cullen (D)	25,935	79.8
	Charles A. Walter (R)	5,713	17.6
5	Loring M. Black Jr. (D)	35,580	63.4
	Henry C. Reiners (R)	18,150	32.3
6	Andrew L. Somers (D)	46,681	47.0
	Joseph G. Myerson (R)	29,862	30.1
	Norman Thomas (SOC)	21,938	22.1
7	John F. Quayle (D)	22,387*	65.0
	Louis W. Arnold Jr. (R)	8,884	25.8
	Benjamin Jackson (SOC)	2,749	8.0
8	Patrick J. Carley (D)	80,119	57.2
	Benjamin Ammerman (R)	36,421	26.0
	Baruch C. Vladeck (SOC)	23,662	16.9
9	David J. O'Connell (D)	48,065*	58.9
	William Koch (R)	27,698	34.0
	Wilhelmus B. Robinson (SOC)	5,783	7.1
10	Emanuel Celler (D)	23,711	58.0
	George J. Beldock (R)	11,532	28.2
	Abraham I. Shiplacoff (SOC)	5,050	12.4
11	Anning S. Prall (D)	37,148	71.1
	Wilbur F. Wakeman (R)	13,856	26.5
12	Samuel Dickstein (D)	14,327	79.1
	Gustave J. Landau (R)	2,663	14.7
	Marx Lewis (SOC)	941	5.2

	Candidates	Votes	%
13	Christopher D. Sullivan (D)	13,034	76.6
	Michael R. Matteo (R)	3,192	18.8
14	William I. Sirovich (D)	12,431	47.3
	Jacob Panken (SOC)	6,793	25.9
	Edward E. Spafford (R)	6,658	25.4
15	John J. Boylan (D)	21,758	81.3
	Alexander Todd (R)	4,377	16.4
16	John J. O'Connor (D)	20,707	72.1
	Irwin Ira Rackoff (R)	7,081	24.7
17	Ruth Baker Pratt (R)	19,913	43.3
	Louis B. Brodsky (D)	19,218	41.8
	Heywood Broun (SOC)	6,841	14.9
18	Martin J. Kennedy (D)	22,131	77.0
	Patrick S. Hickey (R)	5,288	18.4
19	Sol Bloom (D)	35,322	66.9
	Julius D. Tobias (R)	14,919	28.3
20	Fiorello H. LaGuardia (R)	10,606	52.1
	Vincent H. Auleta (D)	8,709	42.8
21	Joseph A. Gavagan (D)	42,468	60.2
	Mortimer Kraus (R)	24,202	34.3
	Frank R. Crosswaith (SOC)	3,699	5.2
22	Anthony J. Griffin (D)	25,198	73.9
	William E. Devlin (R)	7,060	20.7
	Andrew A. MacLean (SOC)	1,832	5.4
23	Frank Oliver (D)	93,426	67.1
	George M. Fayles (R)	27,456	19.7
	Samuel Orr (SOC)	16,539	11.9
24	James M. Fitzpatrick (D)	79,917	57.0
	Benjamin L. Fairchild (R)	48,154	34.3
	Louis Weil (SOC)	12,224	8.7
25	Charles D. Millard (R)	51,332	50.3
	Thomas George Barnes (D)	34,940	34.2
	John M. Holzworth (REPEAL L)	14,086	13.8
26	Hamilton Fish Jr. (R)	46,082	61.1
	John K. Sague (D)	26,545	35.2
27	Harcourt J. Pratt (R)	41,423	52.9
	Guernsey T. Cross (D)	35,574	45.4
28	Parker Corning (D)	74,386	63.5
	Laura B. Treadwell (R)	40,628	34.7
29	James S. Parker (R)	51,341	58.5
	Theodore A. Knapp (D)	35,316	40.2
30	Frank Crowther (R)	36,190	52.1
	Izetta Jewel Miller (D)	31,567	45.4
31	Bertrand H. Snell (R)	36,308	61.8
	Rufus A. Prescott (D)	21,811	37.1
32	Francis D. Culkin (R)	43,625	66.6
	Walter W. Wilcox (D)	20,905	31.9
33	Frederick M. Davenport (R)	39,810	50.3
	James J. Loftis (D&SOC)	39,340	49.7
34	John D. Clarke (R)	51,460	68.2
	James F. Byrne (D)	23,968	31.8
35	Clarence E. Hancock (R)	63,955	57.6
	Frederick B. Northrup (D)	44,336	40.0
36	John Taber (R)	43,132	63.3
	Joseph P. Craugh (D)	23,763	34.9
37	Gale H. Stalker (R)	44,374	59.4
	Julian P. Bretz (D)	28,723	38.4
38	James L. Whitley (R)	50,083	55.3
	Nelson E. Spencer (D)	37,500	41.4
39	Archie D. Sanders (R)	40,069	55.8
	James M. Dwyer (D)	29,610	41.2
40	Walter Gresham Andrews (R)	61,333	63.1
	Roland Crangle (D)	27,268	28.0
	Frank C. Perkins (I CIT AL)	5,126	5.3
41	Edmund F. Cooke (R)	26,995	48.9
	Henry F. Jerge (D)	25,861	46.9
42	James M. Mead (D)	33,195	65.6
	Frank A. Dorn (R)	16,072	31.8
43	Daniel A. Reed (R)	38,913	70.6
	Mattie C. Dellone (D)	14,755	26.8

Special Election

	Candidates	Votes	%
18	Martin J. Kennedy (D)	8,716	80.5
	Bernard Katzen (R)	1,898	17.5

NORTH CAROLINA

	Candidates	Votes	%
1	Lindsay C. Warren (D)	17,985	100.0
2	John H. Kerr (D)	15,987	93.4

	Candidates	Votes	%
	E. Dana Dickens (R)	1,124	6.6
3	Charles L. Abernethy (D)	20,197	66.4
	W. G. Mebane (R)	10,215	33.6
4	Edward W. Pou (D)	25,724	73.4
	John C. Matthews (R)	9,339	26.6
5	Franklin W. Hancock Jr. (D)	54,277	61.3
	John F. Reynolds (R)	34,259	38.7
6	J. Bayard Clark (D)	20,786	71.4
	C. Ed Taylor (R)	8,348	28.7
7	J. Walter Lambeth (D)	38,229	59.0
	Colin G. Spencer (R)	26,583	41.0
8	Robert L. Doughton (D)	44,068	60.1
	E. F. Wakefield (R)	29,307	39.9
9	Alfred L. Bulwinkle (D)	44,699	54.1
	Charles A. Jonas (R)	37,911	45.9
10	Zebulon Weaver (D)	52,964	56.2
	Brownlow Jackson (R)	41,224	43.8

NORTH DAKOTA

	Candidates	Votes	%
1	Olger B. Burtness (R)	42,598	75.0
	J. E. Garvey (D)	14,208	25.0
2	Thomas Hall (R)	33,863	55.6
	P. W. Lanier (D)	25,780	42.3
3	James H. Sinclair (R)	50,917	77.8
	R. H. Leavitt (D)	12,296	18.8

OHIO

	Candidates	Votes	%
1	Nicholas Longworth (R)	50,481	51.8
	John W. Pattison (D)	46,974	48.2
2	William E. Hess (R)	46,347	50.3
	Charles Sawyer (D)	45,761	49.7
3	Byron B. Harlan (D)	62,107	50.8
	Roy G. Fitzgerald (R)	60,249	49.2
4	John L. Cable (R)	43,104	53.4
	Gainor Jennings (D)	37,673	46.6
5	Frank C. Kniffin (D)	29,117	51.4
	Charles J. Thompson (R)	27,497	48.6
6	James G. Polk (D)	37,158	52.7
	Charles C. Kearns (R)	33,300	47.3
7	Charles Brand (R)	50,595	56.4
	John L. Zimmerman Jr. (D)	39,142	43.6
8	Grant E. Mouser Jr. (R)	35,663	51.3
	Carl W. Smith (D)	33,906	48.7
9	Wilbur M. White (R)	49,498	57.6
	Scott Stahl (D)	36,375	42.4
10	Thomas A. Jenkins (R)	31,836	62.4
	H. L. Crary (D)	19,157	37.6
11	Mell G. Underwood (D)	37,887	64.0
	Ned Thacher (R)	21,339	36.0
12	Arthur T. Lamneck (D)	59,330	57.5
	John C. Speaks (R)	43,840	42.5
13	William L. Fiesinger (D)	38,067	52.0
	Joe E. Baird (R)	35,199	48.0
14	Francis Seiberling (R)	61,628	50.3
	Dow W. Harter (D)	60,951	49.7
15	C. Ellis Moore (R)	35,611	51.2
	H. R. McClintock (D)	33,968	48.8
16	C. B. McClintock (R)	51,113	52.0
	William R. Thom (D)	47,237	48.0
17	Charles West (D)	45,633	51.4
	William M. Morgan (R)	43,197	48.6
18	B. Frank Murphy (R)	47,096	60.5
	Emerson Campbell (D)	30,815	39.6
19	John G. Cooper (R)	53,966	56.9
	W. B. Kilpatrick (D)	40,960	43.2
20	Charles A. Mooney (D)	42,123	75.3
	Max D. Gustin (R)	13,824	24.7
21	Robert Crosser (D)	30,722	51.3
	George H. Bender (R)	29,081	48.6
22	Chester C. Bolton (R)	91,222	56.9
	Edw. F. Carran (D)	55,868	34.8
	Helen Green (I)	13,372	8.3

OKLAHOMA

	Candidates	Votes	%
1	Wesley E. Disney (D)	41,902	50.2
	Charles O'Connor (R)	41,642	49.8
2	William W. Hastings (D)	31,093	61.5

	Candidates	Votes	%
	E. L. Kirby (R)	19,464	38.5
3	Wilburn Cartwright (D)	39,943	80.4
	Palestine Brice (R)	9,721	19.6
4	Thomas D. McKeown (D)	42,885	69.7
	M. L. Matson (R)	18,616	30.3
5	Fletcher B. Swank (D)	38,215	58.7
	U. S. Stone (R)	26,943	41.4
6	Jed Johnson (D)	35,969	71.7
	Ann W. Dillard (R)	14,233	28.4
7	James V. McClintic (D)	29,829	78.2
	R. C. Holt (R)	8,298	21.8
8	Milton C. Garber (R)	35,027	60.4
	H. B. King (D)	22,784	39.3

OREGON

	Candidates	Votes	%
1	Willis C. Hawley (R)	55,855	55.5
	William A. Delzell (D)	44,810	44.5
2	Robert R. Butler (R)	25,304	66.0
	Robert E. Bradford (D)	13,061	34.0
3	Charles H. Martin (D)	49,316	55.1
	F. F. Korell (R)	35,483	39.7
	Peter Streiff Jr. (I SOC)	4,690	5.2

PENNSYLVANIA

	Candidates	Votes	%
1	James M. Beck (R)	57,382	78.9
	John P. Mulrenan (D)	14,918	20.5
2	George S. Graham (R)	34,387	84.6
	Charles S. Hill (D)	6,084	15.0
3	Harry C. Ransley (R)	38,346	84.4
	Edward P. Carroll (D)	6,921	15.2
4	Benjamin M. Golder (R)	41,549	78.0
	Thomas J. Carroll (D)	11,084	20.8
5	James J. Connolly (R)	57,501	76.6
	Frank W. Dougherty (D)	17,182	22.9
6	George A. Welsh (R)	66,799	76.1
	John P. Boylan (D)	21,004	23.9
7	George P. Darrow (R)	61,573	77.5
	Robert V. Bolger (D)	17,860	22.5
8	James Wolfenden (R)	84,521	80.5
	Harry D. Wescott (D)	20,443	19.5
9	Henry W. Watson (R)	63,286	73.0
	John F. Headly (D)	23,375	27.0
10	J. Roland Kinzer (R)	32,455	77.3
	William A. Brinkman (D)	9,547	22.7
11	Patrick J. Boland (D, R)	62,994	100.0
12	C. Murray Turpin (R)	53,336	57.8
	John T. Kmetz (D, LAB)	38,938	42.2
13	George Franklin Brumm (R, D)	47,344	92.3
	William Wilhelm (U)	3,968	7.7
14	Norton L. Lichtenwalner (D)	44,546	52.4
	Robert Grey Bushong (R)	29,164	34.3
	Andrew P. Bower (SOC)	11,309	13.3
15	Louis T. McFadden (R, P)	29,150	72.6
	Frank J. Price (D)	10,998	27.4
16	Robert F. Rich (R)	32,964	75.5
	J. Drew Fague (D)	10,719	24.5
17	Frederick W. Magrady (R)	31,247	60.5
	Samuel M. Shipman (D, L)	20,413	39.5
18	Edward M. Beers (R)	39,116	68.0
	T. Z. Minehart (D)	18,389	32.0
19	Isaac H. Doutrich (R)	64,345	79.4
	Harold V. McNair (D)	16,685	20.6
20	J. Russell Leech (R, P)	20,361	54.9
	George E. Wolfe (D, LAB)	16,740	45.1
21	J. Banks Kurtz (R)	25,619	71.8
	Bernard J. Clark (D)	10,045	28.2
22	Harry L. Haines (D)	27,943	54.4
	Franklin Menges (R)	22,716	44.2
23	J. Mitchell Chase (R)	28,916	70.8
	Maxwell J. Moore (D)	11,954	29.3
24	Samuel A. Kendall (R)	28,279	67.6
	Milton M. Brooke (D)	13,581	32.4
25	Henry W. Temple (R, LAB)	27,561	69.8
	James S. Pates (D)	11,910	30.2
26	J. Howard Swick (R, D)	50,858	100.0
27	Nathan L. Strong (R)	42,569	79.2
	D. R. Tomb (D)	11,200	20.8

	Candidates	Votes	%
28	Thomas C. Cochran (R)	36,367	70.9
	Guy Thorne (D)	14,953	29.1
29	Milton W. Shreve (R)	24,511	54.5
	Charles N. Crosby (D)	20,470	45.5
30	William R. Coyle (R)	28,503	50.8
	Everett Kent (D)	27,621	49.2
31	Adam M. Wyant (R, P)	38,990	70.5
	James M. Cramer (D)	15,022	27.2
32	Edmund F. Erk (R)	36,355	82.6
	Edward S. Michalowski (D)	7,294	16.6
33	M. Clyde Kelly (D)	47,187	96.4
34	Patrick J. Sullivan (R,D)	29,074	97.6
35	Harry A. Estep (R)	31,172	81.6
	John Murphy (D)	7,005	18.3
36	Guy E. Campbell (R, D)	46,172	99.9

Special Elections

16	Robert F. Rich (R)	32,393	99.5
32	Edmund F. Erk (R)	35,176	99.9

RHODE ISLAND

1	Clark Burdick (R)	39,712	57.5
	Samuel W. Smith Jr. (D)	29,341	42.5
2	Richard S. Aldrich (R)	40,037	54.7
	Arthur L. Conaty (D)	33,164	45.3
3	Francis B. Condon (D)	43,463	56.4
	William R. Fortin (R)	33,605	43.6

Special Election

3	Francis Condon (D)	43,429	56.5
	William R. Fortin (R)	33,387	43.5

SOUTH CAROLINA

1	Thomas S. McMillan (D)	2,536	100.0
2	Butler B. Hare (D)	2,149	100.0
3	Fred H. Dominick (D)	2,221	100.0
4	John J. McSwain (D)	3,685	100.0
5	William F. Stevenson (D)	2,319	100.0
6	Allard H. Gasque (D)	1,881	100.0
7	Hampton P. Fulmer (D)	1,372	100.0

SOUTH DAKOTA

1	Charles A. Christopherson (R)	41,151	84.7
	Henry Borman (I)	7,451	15.3
2	Royal C. Johnson (R)	38,195	52.4
	Fred H. Hildebrandt (D)	34,245	47.0
3	William Williamson (R)	27,083	55.8
	Theodore B. Werner (D)	21,473	44.2

TENNESSEE

1	Oscar B. Lovette (IR)	20,893	53.4
	B. Carroll Reece (R)	18,241	46.6
2	J. Will Taylor (R)	17,831	55.5
	E. E. Patton (IR)	13,355	41.6
3	Sam D. McReynolds (D)	21,401	100.0
4	John R. Mitchell (D)	15,269	100.0
5	Ewin L. Davis (D)	11,792	92.0
	George Motlow (R)	1,032	8.1
6	Joseph W. Byrns (D)	13,879	93.3
	E. L. Bradbury (I)	990	6.7
7	Edward E. Eslick (D)	13,927	100.0
8	Gordon Browning (D)	14,024	100.0
9	Jere Cooper (D)	17,979	100.0
10	Edward H. Crump (D)	23,746	93.7

TEXAS

1	Wright Patman (D)	9,160	94.7
	Thomas A. Clark (R)	515	5.3
2	Martin Dies (D)	14,236	100.0
3	Morgan G. Sanders (D)	8,162	100.0
4	Sam Rayburn (D)	9,385	88.8
	Floyd Harry (R)	1,189	11.2
5	Hatton W. Sumners (D)	9,924	88.1

	Candidates	Votes	%
	Clinton S. Bailey (R)	1,344	11.9
6	Luther A. Johnson (D)	12,396	100.0
7	Clay Stone Briggs (D)	9,357	100.0
8	Daniel E. Garrett (D)	12,877	100.0
9	Joseph J. Mansfield (D)	14,855	86.9
	George Seydler Sr. (R)	2,239	13.1
10	James P. Buchanan (D)	12,780	100.0
11	Oliver H. Cross (D)	10,381	100.0
12	Fritz G. Lanham (D)	9,846	100.0
13	Guinn Williams (D)	12,840	91.1
	W. C. Witcher (R)	1,257	8.9
14	Harry M. Wurzbach (R)	27,206	59.3
	Henry B. Dielmann (D)	18,707	40.7
15	John N. Garner (D)	20,733	77.5
	Carlos G. Watson (R)	6,016	22.5
16	R. Ewing Thomason (D)	18,915	84.1
	Mitchell Waldrop (R)	3,581	15.9
17	Thomas L. Blanton (D)	17,199	100.0
18	Marvin Jones (D)	26,697	93.3
	S. E. Fish (R)	1,934	6.8

Special Election

17	Thomas L. Blanton (D)	10,225	56.1
	Mrs. R. Q. Lee	8,012	43.9

UTAH

1	Don B. Colton (R)	45,875	60.8
	Joseph Ririe (D)	29,210	38.7
2	Frederick C. Loofbourow (R)	35,106	44.3
	Joshua H. Paul (D)	33,618	42.4
	George N. Lawrence (LIB)	10,303	13.0

Special Election

2	Frederick C. Loofbourow (R)	35,349	44.1
	Joshua H. Paul (D)	33,915	42.3
	George N. Lawrence (LIB)	10,591	13.2

VERMONT

1	John D. Weeks (R)	25,170	58.0
	Joseph A. McNamara (D)	18,205	42.0
2	Ernest W. Gibson (R)	23,904	81.2
	James Cosgrove (D)	5,536	18.8

VIRGINIA

1	Schuyler Otis Bland (D)	7,324	91.0
	W. A. Rowe	705	8.8
2	Menalcus Lankford (R)	14,678	54.4
	Joseph T. Deal (D)	12,297	45.6
3	Andrew Jackson Montague (D)	6,134	87.4
	R. Houston Brett (IR)	853	12.2
4	Patrick Henry Drewry (D)	4,296	99.9
5	Thomas G. Burch (D)	7,095	99.9
6	Clifton A. Woodrum (D)	5,979	99.7
7	John W. Fishburne (D)	13,951	58.4
	Jacob A. Garber (R)	9,934	41.6
8	Howard W. Smith (D)	11,201	79.3
	F. M. Brooks (R)	2,742	19.4
9	John W. Flannagan Jr. (D)	32,802	55.6
	Joseph C. Shaffer (R)	26,244	44.5
10	Henry St. George Tucker (D)	7,229	85.9
	Carney Kelly Rosser (IR)	620	7.4
	M. J. Putman (R)	563	6.7

WASHINGTON

1	Ralph A. Horr (R)	43,998	55.8
	Charles G. Heifner (D)	32,365	41.0
2	Lindley H. Hadley (R)	47,679	89.7
	William M. Bouck (F-LAB)	3,428	6.5
3	Albert Johnson (R)	63,451	100.0
4	John W. Summers (R)	35,917	100.0
5	Sam B. Hill (D)	43,059	74.3
	T. W. Symons Jr. (R)	14,892	25.7

WEST VIRGINIA

	Candidates	Votes	%
1	Carl G. Bachmann (R)	43,919	56.1
	Robert L. Ramsay (D)	34,368	43.9
2	Frank L. Bowman (R)	36,079	50.8
	Jennings Randolph (D)	34,968	49.2
3	Lynn S. Hornor (D)	37,970	51.4
	John M. Wolverton (R)	35,853	48.6
4	Robert L. Hogg (R)	43,152	50.3
	Mary M. Johnson (D)	42,677	49.7
5	Hugh Ike Shott (R)	44,978	52.2
	T. J. Lilly (D)	41,162	47.8
6	Joe L. Smith (D)	80,648	56.6
	Fred O. Blue (R)	61,876	43.4

Special Election

		Votes	%
4	Robert L. Hogg (R)	41,455	53.8
	Mary M. Johnson (D)	35,649	46.2

WISCONSIN

	Candidates	Votes	%
1	Henry Allen Cooper (R)	46,272*	95.7
2	Charles A. Kading (R)	37,071	71.5
	A. A. Nowak (D)	14,780	28.5
3	John M. Nelson (R)	43,184	95.1
4	John C. Schafer (R)	26,763	46.6
	William F. Quick Sr. (SOC)	20,789	36.2
	William J. Kershaw (D)	8,871	15.5
5	William H. Stafford (R)	27,533	42.2
	James P. Sheehan (SOC)	26,357#	40.4
	Thomas O'Malley (D)	10,947	16.8
6	Michael K. Reilly (D)	25,605	50.2
	Philip Lehner (R)	24,986	49.0
7	Gardner R. Withrow (R)	31,530	82.3
	Merlin Hull (R)	5,606	14.6
8	Gerald J. Boileau (R)	30,045	79.1
	William F. Collins (D)	7,927	20.9
9	George J. Schneider (R)	43,080	100.0

	Candidates	Votes	%
10	James A. Frear (R)	36,804	97.5
11	Hubert H. Peavey (R)	43,004	100.0

Special Election

		Votes	%
6	Michael K. Reilly (D)	25,400	50.6
	Philip Lehner (R)	24,825	49.4

WYOMING

		Votes	%
AL	Vincent M. Carter (R)	44,890	65.5
	John P. Rusk (D)	23,519	34.4

1931 House Elections

LOUISIANA

Special Election

	Candidates	Votes	%
8	John H. Overton (D)	4,674	99.9

NEW YORK[1]

Special Elections

		Votes	%
7	Matthew V. O'Malley (D)	9,969	70.0
	Leonard Greenstone (R)	4,014	28.2
7	John J. Delaney (D)	24,587	69.3
	William L. Padgett (R)	7,840	22.1
	Abraham Zucker (SOC)	2,724	7.7
9	Stephen A. Rudd (D)	15,342	71.5
	William Koch (R)	5,605	26.1

TEXAS

Special Election

	Candidates	Votes	%
14	Richard M. Kleberg (D)	19,038	46.9
	C. W. Johnson	13,945	34.4
	C. W. Anderson	5,759	14.2

WISCONSIN

Special Election

		Votes	%
1	Thomas R. Amlie (R)	14,447	54.4
	O. J. Bouma (SOC)	7,282	27.4
	G. H. Herzog (ID)	3,440	13.0

1. Rep. John F. Quayle died Nov. 27, 1930, following his re-election to the 72nd Congress (1931–1933). According to the Biographical Directory, Matthew V. O'Malley was elected Feb. 17, 1931 to fill Quayle's seat for the term beginning March 4, 1931. O'Malley died May 26, 1931. In a second special election, John J. Delaney was elected to fill the seat for the remainder of the term.

1932 House Elections

ALABAMA

	Candidates	Votes	%
1	John D. McDuffie (D)	20,675	100.0
2	Lister Hill (D)	28,250	95.7
3	Henry B. Steagall (D)	20,959	100.0
4	Lamar Jeffers (D)	20,960	83.9
	Hogan D. Stewart (R)	4,016	16.1
5	Miles C. Allgood (D)	24,783	80.2
	Joe Brown (R)	6,135	19.8
6	William B. Oliver (D)	15,296	100.0
7	William B. Bankhead (D)	21,322	73.5
	James B. Sloan (R)	7,699	26.5
8	Edward B. Almon (D)	23,705	100.0
9	George Huddleston (D)	31,539	86.2
	Paul G. Parsons (R)	3,701	10.1

ARIZONA

	Candidates	Votes	%
AL	Lewis W. Douglas (D)	75,469*	70.8
	H. B. Wilkinson (R)	29,710	27.9

ARKANSAS

	Candidates	Votes	%
1	William J. Driver (D)	35,975	100.0
2	John E. Miller (D)	23,351	92.1
	Ira J. Mock (R)	1,995	7.9
3	Claude A. Fuller (D)	30,337	100.0
4	William B. Cravens (D)	30,443	100.0
5	Heartsill Ragon (D)	29,240	90.7
	A. L. Barber (R)	3,001	9.3
6	David D. Glover (D)	33,503	100.0
7	Tilman B. Parks (D)	30,340	100.0

CALIFORNIA

	Candidates	Votes	%
1	Clarence F. Lea (D-R)	73,400	99.9
2	Harry L. Englebright (R-D)	43,146	100.0
3	Frank H. Buck (D)	61,694	56.8
	Charles F. Curry (R)	46,887	43.1
4	Florence P. Kahn (R-D)	67,425	85.3
	Milen C. Dempster (SOC)	11,603	14.7
5	Richard J. Welch (R-D)	67,349	100.0
6	Albert E. Carter (R-D)	75,528	99.9
7	Ralph R. Eltse (R)	45,944	45.5
	Frank V. Cornish (D)	32,365	32.0
	J. Stitt Wilson (SOC)	22,767	22.5
8	John J. McGrath (D)	65,455	56.9
	Arthur M. Free (R)	49,487	43.1
9	Denver S. Church (D)	50,125	61.6
	Henry E. Barbour (R)	31,209	38.4
10	Henry E. Stubbs (D)	50,390	55.3
	Arthur S. Crites (R)	40,794	44.7
11	William E. Evans (R)	57,739	51.8
	Albert D. Hadley (D)	38,240	34.3
	Marshall V. Hartranft (LIB)	15,520	13.9
12	John H. Hoeppel (D)	43,122	45.8
	Frederick F. Houser (R)	40,674	43.2
	Richard M. Cannon (P)	10,308	11.0
13	Charles Kramer (D)	65,261	52.6
	Charles H. Randall (R)	53,449	43.1
14	Thomas F. Ford (D)	47,368	57.1
	William D. Campbell (R)	35,598	42.9
15	William L. Traeger (R)	67,390	52.8
	John M. Costello (D)	57,518	45.1
16	John F. Dockweiler (D)	70,333	54.9
	Clyde Woodworth (R)	57,718	45.1
17	Charles J. Colden (D)	50,720	62.2
	A. E. Henning (R)	26,868	32.9
18	John H. Burke (D)	48,179	53.2
	Robert Henderson (R)	33,817	37.4
	William E. Hinshaw (I)	8,399	9.3
19	Sam L. Collins (R)	56,889	51.0
	B. Z. McKinney (D)	51,796	46.4
20	George Burnham (R)	43,757	50.3
	Claude Chandler (D)	43,304	49.7

COLORADO

	Candidates	Votes	%
1	Lawrence Lewis (D)	70,826	54.4
	William R. Eaton (R)	56,601	43.5
2	Fred Cummings (D)	63,399	52.9
	George H. Bradfield (R)	56,516	47.1
3	John A. Martin (D)	59,882	50.9
	Guy U. Hardy (R)	57,793	49.1
4	Edward T. Taylor (D)	40,736	66.0
	Richard C. Callen (R)	20,993	34.0

CONNECTICUT

	Candidates	Votes	%
1	Herman P. Kopplemann (D)	72,807	48.8
	Clarence W. Seymour (R)	70,920	47.5
2	William L. Higgins (R)	45,232	49.4
	William C. Fox (D)	45,011	49.2
3	Francis T. Maloney (D)	57,881	48.4
	T. A. D. Jones (R)	55,254	46.2
4	Schuyler Merritt (R)	71,670	49.7
	William L. Tierney (D)	64,268	44.5
	Arnold E. Freese (SOC)	7,237	5.0
5	Edward W. Goss (R)	42,132	49.3
	Martin E. Gormley (D)	42,054	49.2
AL	Charles M. Bakewell (R)	284,438	48.5
	William M. Citron (D)	282,557	48.2

DELAWARE

	Candidates	Votes	%
AL	Wilbur L. Adams (D)	51,698	46.1
	Reuben Satterthwaite Jr (R)	48,841	43.6
	Francis Burgette Short (P)	10,560	9.4

FLORIDA

	Candidates	Votes	%
1	J. Hardin Peterson (D)	61,381	76.4
	Arthur R. Thompson (R)	19,010	23.7
2	Robert A. Green (D)	22,213	100.0
3	Millard F. Caldwell (D)	28,208	100.0
4	J. Mark Wilcox (D)	86,101	99.6
AL	William J. Sears (D)	186,284	75.2
	Glenn S. Skipper (R)	61,300	24.8

GEORGIA

	Candidates	Votes	%
1	Homer C. Parker (D)	24,429	93.4
	E. K. Overstreet Jr. (R)	1,726	6.6
2	E. E. Cox (D)	22,446	100.0
3	B. T. Castellow (D)	22,691	100.0
	Emmett M. Owen (D)	24,783	99.9
5	Robert Ramspeck (D)	26,657	100.0
6	Carl Vinson (D)	19,615	99.9
7	M. C. Tarver (D)	24,689	85.2
	Regina Rambo Benson (I)	4,295	14.8
8	Braswell Deen (D)	20,021	95.6
9	John S. Wood (D)	24,673	80.6
	J. M. Johnson (R)	5,898	19.3
10	Charles H. Brand (D)	23,911	100.0

IDAHO

	Candidates	Votes	%
1	Compton I. White (D)	42,784	54.9
	Burton L. French (R)	32,545	41.8
2	Thomas C. Coffin (D)	58,138	55.0
	Addison T. Smith (R)	46,293	43.8

ILLINOIS

	Candidates	Votes	%
1	Oscar De Priest (R)	33,672	54.8
	Harry Baker (D)	26,959	43.9
2	P. H. Moynihan (R)	113,447	50.8
	Victor L. Schlaeger (D)	102,099	45.7
3	Edward A. Kelly (D)	120,093	55.8
	Elliott W. Sproul (R)	95,282	44.2
4	Harry P. Beam (D)	53,722	74.2
	Casimir T. Janowski (R)	18,659	25.8
5	Adolph J. Sabath (D)	30,747	70.9
	Samuel S. Epstein (R)	12,254	28.3
6	Thomas J. O'Brien (D)	164,187	63.2
	Alfred F. Rueben (R)	95,637	36.8
7	Leonard W. Schuetz (D)	190,446	58.1
	M. A. Michaelson (R)	134,801	41.1
8	Leo Kocialkowski (D)	30,147	72.2
	Peter C. Granata (R)	11,625	27.8
9	Fred A. Britten (R)	40,253	52.0
	James McAndrews (D)	36,596	47.3
10	James Simpson Jr. (R)	101,671	41.1
	Charles H. Weber (D)	100,449	40.6
	Ralph E. Church (I)	45,067	18.2
11	Frank R. Reid (R)	82,195	50.4
	James A. Howell (D)	80,862	49.6
12	John T. Buckbee (R)	65,122	53.1
	Charles H. Linscott (D)	57,578	46.9
13	Leo E. Allen (R)	44,655	56.1
	Orestes H. Wright (D)	34,917	43.9
14	Chester Thompson (D)	50,277	53.9
	John C. Allen (R)	43,082	46.2
15	J. Leroy Adair (D)	55,739	56.9
	Burnett M. Chiperfield (R)	42,255	43.1
16	Everett M. Dirksen (R)	67,949	60.3
	Edwin S. Carr (D)	44,802	39.7
17	Frank Gillespie (D)	43,198	53.5
	Homer W. Hall (R)	37,594	46.5
18	James A. Meeks (D)	58,483	56.6
	William P. Holaday (R)	44,787	43.4
19	D. C. Dobbins (D)	72,366	57.7
	Charles Adkins (R)	53,151	42.4
20	Henry T. Rainey (D)	48,612	63.8
	William J. Thornton (R)	27,540	36.2
21	J. Earl Major (D)	66,213	59.8
	Roy M. Seeley (R)	44,430	40.1
22	Edwin M. Schaefer (D)	88,151	63.8
	Stewart Campbell (R)	49,965	36.2
23	William W. Arnold (D)	64,551	64.3
	T. Edward Austin (R)	35,885	35.7
24	Claude V. Parsons (D)	43,107	58.8
	Arthur A. Miles (R)	30,175	41.2
25	Kent E. Keller (D)	64,286	59.6
	Edward E. Denison (R)	43,580	40.4
AL	Martin A. Brennan (D)	1,676,274✓	
	Walter Nesbit (D)	1,655,147✓	
	Richard Yates (R)	1,421,221	
	Julius Klein (R)	1,406,771	
	Hyman Schneid (SOC)	38,486	
	George Koop (SOC)	36,324	
	Anthony Pszczolkowski (COM)	11,243	
	Leslie Raymond Hurt (COM)	11,019	
	W. F. Alexander (SOC LAB)	2,837	
	Clifton Crawford (SOC LAB)	2,684	
	Pasquale Iovino (I)	1,067	

INDIANA

	Candidates	Votes	%
1	William T. Schulte (D)	45,473	50.0
	Oscar A. Ahlgren (R)	42,575	46.8
2	George R. Durgan (D)	73,357	54.0
	William R. Wood (R)	61,897	45.6
3	Samuel B. Pettengill (D)	67,686	55.1
	Andrew J. Hickey (R)	52,965	43.2
4	James I. Farley (D)	73,258	56.1
	David Hogg (R)	56,602	43.3
5	Glenn Griswold (D)	70,698	53.5
	J. Raymond Schutz (R)	59,904	45.3
6	Virginia E. Jenckes (D)	74,827	53.6
	Fred S. Purnell (R)	64,081	45.9
7	Arthur H. Greenwood (D)	78,356	56.7
	George W. Henley (R)	59,949	43.4
8	John W. Boehne Jr. (D)	83,396	63.5
	French Clements (R)	48,031	36.6
9	Eugene B. Crowe (D)	76,157	57.5
	Chester A. Davis (R)	55,868	42.2
10	Finly H. Gray (D)	68,974	52.0

	Candidates	Votes	%
	Ephriam F. Bowen (R)	63,398	47.8
11	William H. Larrabee (D)	67,871	54.2
	Dale B. Spencer (R)	57,006	45.5
12	Louis Ludlow (D)	70,128	52.1
	William H. Harrison (R)	61,241	45.5

IOWA

	Candidates	Votes	%
1	Edward C. Eicher (D)	55,378	54.2
	W. F. Kopp (R)	46,738	45.8
2	Bernhard M. Jacobsen (D)	71,914	58.7
	Frank Elliott (R)	50,636	41.3
3	Albert C. Willford (D)	48,939	50.6
	T. J. B. Robinson (R)	47,776	49.4
4	Fred Biermann (D)	62,598	59.7
	Gilbert N. Haugen (R)	42,217	40.3
5	Lloyd Thurston (R)	51,909	50.1
	Lloyd Ellis (D)	51,732	49.9
6	Cassius C. Dowell (R)	56,962	56.5
	Charles S. Cooter (D)	43,891	43.5
7	Otha D. Wearin (D)	57,803	56.3
	Charles E. Swanson (R)	44,925	43.7
8	Fred C. Gilchrist (R)	47,834	53.4
	William T. Branagan (D)	41,772	46.6
9	Guy M. Gillette (D)	61,755	54.9
	Ed. H. Campbell (R)	50,796	45.1

KANSAS

	Candidates	Votes	%
1	William P. Lambertson (R)	59,241	57.8
	M. R. Howard (D)	34,244	33.4
	George C. Hall (I)	9,019	8.8
2	Ulysses S. Guyer (R)	60,902	51.7
	B. J. Sheridan (D)	56,805	48.3
3	Harold McGugin (R)	52,881	52.9
	E. W. Patterson (D)	44,910	44.9
4	William Randolph Carpenter (D)	45,246	50.2
	Homer Hoch (R)	44,621	49.5
5	William A. Ayres (D)	65,713	73.9
	W. L. Farquharson (R)	23,176	26.1
6	Kathryn E. O'Loughlin (D)	62,818	55.6
	Charles I. Sparks (R)	50,242	44.4
7	Clifford R. Hope (R)	59,269	55.6
	Aaron Coleman (D)	47,418	44.5

KENTUCKY

	Candidates	Votes	%
AL	Fred M. Vinson (D)	575,289 ✓	
	John Young Brown (D)	574,278 ✓	
	Brent Spence (D)	574,035 ✓	
	Andrew J. May (D)	573,966 ✓	
	Virgil Chapman (D)	573,719 ✓	
	Glover H. Cary (D)	573,504 ✓	
	William V. Gregory (D)	573,233 ✓	
	Cap R. Carden (D)	573,219 ✓	
	Finley Hamilton (D)	573,061 ✓	
	Hillard H. Smith (R)	391,878	
	Robert Blackburn (R)	391,673	
	William Lewis (R)	390,977	
	George P. Ellison (R)	390,839	
	D. E. McClure (R)	390,474	
	J. C. Speight (R)	390,370	
	Hugh H. Asher (R)	390,148	
	B. T. Rountree (R)	390,141	
	Frank B. Russell (R)	389,950	
	J. T. Scopes (SOC)	3,273	
	W. G. Haag (SOC)	3,261	
	C. E. Trimble (SOC)	3,260	
	E. L. Nance (SOC)	3,256	
	E. C. Schulz (SOC)	3,256	
	J. J. Thobe (SOC)	3,246	
	J. M. Woodward (SOC)	3,237	
	H. L. Harwood (SOC)	3,236	
	D. S. Bennett (SOC)	3,234	
	Frank Reynolds (COM)	241	
	George N. Conway (COM)	236	

LOUISIANA

	Candidates	Votes	%
1	Joachim O. Fernandez (D)	48,784	100.0
2	Paul H. Maloney (D)	50,327	100.0
3	Numa F. Montet (D)	18,340	100.0
4	John N. Sandlin (D)	26,262	100.0
5	Riley J. Wilson (D)	25,853	100.0
6	Bolivar E. Kemp (D)	25,238	100.0
7	Rene L. DeRouen (D)	24,233	100.0
8	Cleveland Dear (D)	25,644	100.0

MAINE

	Candidates	Votes	%
1	Carroll L. Beedy (R)	41,034	51.0
	Joseph E. F. Connolly (D)	39,381	49.0
2	Edward C. Moran (D)	44,490	51.8
	John E. Nelson (R)	40,703	47.4
3	John G. Utterback (D)	34,520	50.1
	Ralph O. Brewster (R)	34,226	49.6

MARYLAND

	Candidates	Votes	%
1	T. Alan Goldsborough (D)	39,471	64.9
	Harry T. Phoebus (R)	21,387	35.1
2	William P. Cole Jr. (D)	87,841	67.3
	David L. Elliott (R)	42,740	32.7
3	Vincent L. Palmisano (D)	34,724	72.8
	R. Palmer Ingram (R)	11,370	23.8
4	Ambrose J. Kennedy (D)	46,463	66.0
	Claude B. Sweezey (R)	22,231	31.6
5	Stephen W. Gambrill (D)	42,329	70.4
	A. Kingsley Love (R)	17,835	29.6
6	David J. Lewis (D)	49,126	58.4
	Harold C. Smith (R)	34,989	41.6

Special Election

	Candidates	Votes	%
4	Ambrose J. Kennedy (D)	46,781	100.0

MASSACHUSETTS

	Candidates	Votes	%
1	Allen T. Treadway (R)	56,767	54.7
	Thomas F. Cassidy (D)	44,211	42.6
2	William J. Granfield (D)	52,346	49.9
	Joshua L. Brooks (R)	47,920	45.7
3	Frank H. Foss (R)	50,617	51.5
	M. Fred O'Connell (D)	47,632	48.5
4	Pehr G. Holmes (R)	56,408	55.0
	John Walsh (D)	46,081	45.0
5	Edith Nourse Rogers (R)	74,459	59.9
	James J. Bruin (D)	49,788	40.1
6	A. Piatt Andrew (R)	65,728	67.7
	James D. Burns (D)	31,416	32.3
7	William P. Connery Jr. (D)	61,591	56.6
	Charles W. Lovett (R)	44,331	40.7
8	Arthur D. Healey (D)	50,266	51.1
	George H. Norton (R)	48,070	48.9
9	Robert Luce (R)	61,178	51.4
	Frederick S. Deitrick (D)	56,425	47.4
10	George Holden Tinkham (R)	60,926	60.3
	John Crehan (D)	40,099	39.7
11	John J. Douglass (D)	45,343	85.7
	William F. McDonald (R)	7,583	14.3
12	John W. McCormack (D)	69,994	72.9
	Bernard Ginsburg (R)	25,995	27.1
13	Richard B. Wigglesworth (R)	64,589	58.4
	Edward G. Morris (D)	45,964	41.6
14	Joseph William Martin Jr. (R)	51,680	56.8
	Andrew J. McGraw (D)	39,259	43.2
15	Charles L. Gifford (R)	53,066	57.5
	Thomas H. Buckley (D)	36,556	39.6

MICHIGAN

	Candidates	Votes	%
1	George G. Sadowski (D)	51,620	68.1
	Charles H. Mahoney (R)	21,764	28.7
2	John C. Lehr (D)	51,592	50.6
	Earl C. Michener (R)	49,257	48.3
3	Joseph L. Hooper (R)	49,383	50.2
	Charles E. Gauss (D)	46,093	46.9
4	George Foulkes (D)	46,927	51.6
	John C. Ketcham (R)	42,922	47.2
5	Carl E. Mapes (R)	52,870	51.3
	Winfield H. Caslow (D)	48,686	47.3
6	Claude E. Cady (D)	55,478	47.8
	Seymour H. Person (R)	45,818	39.5
	Grant M. Hudson (R)	14,541	12.5
7	Jesse P. Wolcott (R)	51,974	56.1
	James G. Tucker (D)	38,738	41.8
8	Michael J. Hart (D)	53,959	53.5
	William M. Smith (R)	45,263	44.9
9	Harry W. Musselwhite (D)	40,200	52.2
	James C. McLaughlin (R)	36,434	47.3
10	Roy O. Woodruff (R)	38,937	54.0
	William J. Kelly (D)	32,376	44.9
11	Prentiss M. Brown (D)	39,261	50.1
	Frank P. Bohn (R)	37,311	47.6
12	W. Frank James (R)	48,014	62.5
	Levi S. Rice (D)	26,925	35.0
13	Clarence J. McLeod (R)	50,437	52.4
	Clarence E. Seebaldt (D)	43,374	45.1
14	Carl M. Weideman (D)	53,789	50.4
	Robert H. Clancy (R)	50,491	47.3
15	John D. Dingell (D)	52,376	48.3
	Charles Bowles (R)	49,801	46.0
16	John Lesinski (D)	43,369	53.0
	Frank P. Darin (R)	36,174	44.2
17	George A. Dondero (R)	51,918	52.6
	Harry Mitchell (D)	44,325	44.9

MINNESOTA

	Candidates	Votes	%
AL	Magnus Johnson (F-LAB)	388,616 ✓	
	Paul John Kvale (F-LAB)	380,444 ✓	
	Henry Arens (F-LAB)	361,724 ✓	
	Ernest Lundeen (F-LAB)	350,455 ✓	
	Theodore Christianson (R)	337,110 ✓	
	Einar Hoidale (D)	321,949 ✓	
	Ray P. Chase (R)	321,102 ✓	
	Francis H. Shoemaker (F-LAB)	317,109 ✓	
	Harold Knutson (R)	313,221 ✓	
	August H. Andresen (R)	312,198	
	W. I. Nolan (R)	306,266	
	Conrad G. Selvig (R)	304,846	
	J. A. A. Burnquist (R)	302,356	
	J. L. Peterson (F-LAB)	298,331	
	Henry G. Teigan (F-LAB)	291,837	
	C. F. Gaarenstroom (F-LAB)	291,687	
	William A. Pittenger (R)	291,478	
	N. J. Holmberg (R)	287,381	
	A. C. Townley (F-LAB)	261,120	
	Robert C. Bell (D)	237,881	
	John P. Coughlin (D)	214,462	
	Silas M. Bryan (D)	207,419	
	Emil E. Holmes (D)	205,673	
	James R. Bennett (D)	198,421	
	Donald A. Chapman (D)	190,530	
	Hugh T. Kennedy (D)	186,466	
	John Bowe (D)	184,587	
	Victor Christgau (STICKER)	82,826	
	J. W. Anderson (COM)	16,299	
	M. Karson (COM)	9,573	
	Fred Lequier (COM)	8,927	
	Melvin Maas (STICKER)	784	

MISSISSIPPI

	Candidates	Votes	%
1	John E. Rankin (D)	19,549	97.0
2	Wall Doxey (D)	15,092	98.5
3	Will M. Whittington (D)	13,562	95.8
4	Jeff Busby (D)	14,072	97.8
5	Ross A. Collins (D)	19,123	97.1
6	William M. Colmer (D)	22,831	94.5
7	Russell Ellzey (D)	25,725	95.6

MISSOURI

	Candidates	Votes	%
AL	John J. Cochran (D)	1,013,824 ✓	
	James R. Claiborne (D)	1,004,170 ✓	
	Joseph B. Shannon (D)	1,002,545 ✓	
	Clyde Williams (D)	1,000,218 ✓	

Candidates	Votes	%
Clarence Cannon (D)	997,642✓	
Frank H. Lee (D)	997,148✓	
James E. Ruffin (D)	996,969✓	
Ralph F. Lozier (D)	995,676✓	
Jacob L. Milligan (D)	995,002✓	
Reuben T. Wood (D)	994,487✓	
Milton A. Romjue (D)	994,123✓	
Richard M. Duncan (D)	988,200✓	
Clement C. Dickinson (D)	981,847✓	
Leonidas C. Dyer (R)	609,268	
Henry F. Niedringhaus (R)	603,345	
James Stewart (R)	589,615	
John M. Hadley (R)	589,205	
Carl Otto (R)	588,647	
Louis E. Miller (R)	588,246	
Phil A. Bennett (R)	586,272	
Sam A. Clark (R)	586,215	
Joe J. Manlove (R)	585,840	
Rowland L. Johnston (R)	584,256	
David Hopkins (R)	582,662	
John W. Palmer (R)	582,324	
Manvel H. Davis (R)	578,995	
Phillips (SOC)	11,658	
Morrison (SOC)	11,637	
Langley (SOC)	11,625	
Becker (SOC)	11,606	
Elliff (SOC)	11,598	
Anderson (SOC)	11,573	
Henschel (SOC)	11,571	
Davidson (SOC)	11,543	
Turner (SOC)	11,493	
Hill (SOC)	11,459	
Harrison (SOC)	11,417	
Shumaker (SOC)	11,356	
Thayer (SOC)	11,324	
Benz (COM)	627	

MONTANA

	Candidates	Votes	%
1	Joseph P. Monaghan (D)	51,159	59.0
	Mark D. Fitzgerald (R)	33,333	38.4
2	Roy E. Ayers (D)	64,103	52.5
	Scott Leavitt (R)	53,890	44.1

NEBRASKA

	Candidates	Votes	%
1	John H. Morehead (D)	63,022	58.0
	Marcus L. Poteet (R)	43,653	40.2
2	Edward R. Burke (D)	51,728	51.3
	Malcolm Baldrige (R)	44,209	43.8
3	Edgar Howard (D)	74,207	66.0
	H. Halderson (R)	32,954	29.3
4	Ashton C. Shallenberger (D)	53,713	44.8
	Fred G. Johnson (R)	38,938	32.5
	Charles G. Binderup (R)	21,100	17.6
5	Terry Carpenter (D)	53,586	51.3
	Robert G. Simmons (R)	49,200	47.1

NEVADA

	Candidates	Votes	%
AL	James G. Scrugham (D)	24,979	60.8
	Samuel S. Arentz (R)	16,133	39.2

NEW HAMPSHIRE

	Candidates	Votes	%
1	William N. Rogers (D)	50,306	51.3
	William P. Straw (R)	47,646	48.6
2	Charles W. Tobey (R)	50,156	52.8
	Jeremiah J. Doyle (D)	44,459	46.8

NEW JERSEY

	Candidates	Votes	%
1	Charles A. Wolverton (R)	89,816	60.2
	Samuel T. French (D)	54,701	36.7
2	Isaac Bacharach (R)	60,963	62.9
	Harry R. Coulomb (D)	35,257	36.4
3	William H. Sutphin (D)	61,253	50.9
	Stanley Washburn (R)	58,217	48.4
4	D. Lane Powers (R)	51,794	55.0
	Monell Sayre (D)	40,705	43.2
5	Charles A. Eaton (R)	60,713	53.2
	Frederick M. P. Pearse (D)	51,964	45.6
6	Donald H. McLean (R)	65,653	57.4
	Fred C. Hyer (D)	47,938	41.9
7	Randolph Perkins (R)	52,003	51.6
	Hamilton Cross (D)	47,688	47.3
8	George N. Seger (R)	50,997	49.2
	Harry Joelson (D)	50,759	48.9
9	Edward A. Kenney (D)	53,822	47.6
	Joseph W. Marini (R)	52,968	46.8
10	Fred A. Hartley Jr. (R)	53,316	55.2
	William W. Harrison (D)	41,901	43.4
11	Peter A. Cavicchia (R)	47,495	49.8
	John J. McCloskey (D)	46,540	48.8
12	Frederick R. Lehlbach (R)	54,783	56.1
	Joseph M. Degnan (D)	40,746	41.7
13	Mary T. Norton (D)	73,779	72.1
	Mortimer Neuman (R)	27,964	27.3
14	Oscar L. Auf der Heide (D)	77,519	75.1
	Vincent P. McGann (R)	24,448	23.7

NEW MEXICO

	Candidates	Votes	%
AL	Dennis Chavez (D)	95,363	63.5
	Jose E. Armijo (R)	52,905	35.2

NEW YORK

	Candidates	Votes	%
1	Robert L. Bacon (R)	153,435	54.0
	Cornelius V. Whitney (D)	121,909	42.9
2	William F. Brunner (D)	172,512	68.6
	Horace A. Demarest (R)	68,525	27.3
3	George W. Lindsay (D)	33,750	80.8
	Edgar H. Hazelwood (R)	5,799	13.9
4	Thomas H. Cullen (D)	39,562	82.1
	Conrad F. Printzlien (R)	7,429	15.4
5	Loring M. Black Jr. (D)	51,932	64.8
	Irving C. Maltz (R)	24,814	31.0
6	Andrew L. Somers (D)	81,011	57.0
	Joseph P. Byrne (R)	42,221	29.7
	Harry W. Laidler (SOC)	15,568	11.0
7	John J. Delaney (D)	36,088	72.5
	Richard W. Thomas (R)	9,696	19.5
	David M. Cory (SOC)	3,181	6.4
8	Patrick J. Carley (D)	140,853	62.1
	Daniel Adelman (R)	49,471	21.8
	Baruch C. Vladeck (SOC)	31,930	14.1
9	Stephen A. Rudd (D)	69,634	59.9
	James Virdone (R)	38,047	32.7
	Abraham I. Shiplacoff (SOC)	7,496	6.5
10	Emanuel Celler (D)	36,460	63.9
	William A. Ronalds (R)	14,167	24.8
	Louis Sadoff (SOC)	5,334	9.3
11	Anning S. Prall (D)	50,418	69.2
	Frank Homer Fay (R)	20,323	27.9
12	Samuel Dickstein (D)	21,248	86.5
	Henry Steinberg (R)	2,068	8.4
13	Christopher D. Sullivan (D)	21,939	86.5
	John Rosenberg (R)	2,513	9.9
14	William I. Sirovich (D)	20,668	60.7
	Henry A. Lowenberg (R)	9,651	28.3
	August Claessens (SOC)	2,735	8.0
15	John J. Boylan (D)	30,112	80.9
	Charles Coudert Nast (R)	5,987	16.1
16	John J. O'Connor (D)	29,485	67.1
	Eugene S. Taliaferro (R)	12,449	28.3
17	Theodore A. Peyser (D)	36,397	52.9
	Ruth Pratt (R)	29,776	43.3
18	Martin J. Kennedy (D)	30,245	75.1
	Patrick S. Hickey (R)	7,997	19.9
19	Sol Bloom (D)	57,400	69.0
	William L. Carns (R)	21,758	26.2
20	James J. Lanzetta (D)	16,447	50.7
	Fiorello H. LaGuardia (R)	15,227	47.0
21	Joseph A. Gavagan (D)	67,583	64.6
	Oscar J. Smith (R)	28,955	27.7
	Frank R. Crosswaith (SOC)	7,390	7.1
22	Anthony J. Griffin (D)	38,172	76.7
	Wilbur J. Murphy (R)	8,768	17.6
23	Frank Oliver (D)	131,852	69.5
	Samuel J. Krinn (R)	31,753	16.7
	Samuel Orr (SOC)	21,349	11.3
24	James M. Fitzpatrick (D)	128,881	60.1
	Benjamin L. Fairchild (R & LP)	65,189	30.4
	Esther Friedman (SOC)	15,389	7.2
25	Charles D. Millard (R)	80,909	54.3
	Jesse B. Perlman (D)	63,345	42.5
26	Hamilton Fish Jr. (R)	61,687	58.3
	Roslyn M. Cox (D)	43,174	40.8
27	Philip A. Goodwin (R & LP)	52,099	52.5
	Clifford L. Miller (D)	46,154	46.5
28	Parker Corning (D)	89,096	64.7
	Isaac G. Braman (R)	47,706	34.7
29	James S. Parker (R & LP)	65,359	57.8
	John J. Nyhoff (D)	46,935	41.5
30	Frank Crowther (R & LP)	55,981	55.5
	George D. Lamberton (D)	42,632	42.3
31	Bertrand H. Snell (R)	47,937	57.5
	Kenneth Gardner (D)	35,153	42.1
32	Francis D. Culkin (R & LP)	56,654	61.9
	John C. Purcell (D)	34,199	37.3
33	Fred J. Sisson (D)	53,427	50.0
	Frederick M. Davenport (R & LP)	52,398	49.0
34	John D. Clarke (R)	58,735	53.3
	Charles R. Seymour (D)	44,174	40.1
	Leon Ray Steenburg (LAW PRES)	6,676	6.1
35	Clarence E. Hancock (R)	79,345	55.6
	Edmund L. Weston (D)	60,376	42.3
36	John Taber (R & LP)	58,484	60.9
	Lithgow Osborne (D)	36,648	38.2
37	Gale H. Stalker (R & LP)	55,305	52.5
	Julian P. Bretz (D)	48,048	45.6
38	James L. Whitley (R)	64,003	46.2
	Charles Stanton (D)	58,775	42.4
	Arthur Rathjen (LAW PRES)	12,097	8.7
39	James W. Wadsworth (R)	50,855	47.1
	David A. White (D)	35,367	32.8
	Ernest R. Clark (LAW PRES)	20,209	18.7
40	Walter Gresham Andrews (R)	92,929	61.8
	Ralph W. Nolan (D)	54,363	36.1
41	Alfred F. Beiter (D)	45,120	50.1
	Edmund F. Cooke (R)	42,743	47.4
42	James M. Mead (D)	51,516	62.0
	Henry Adsit Bull (R)	30,230	36.4
43	Daniel A. Reed (R & LP)	55,988	60.1
	Gerald A. Herrick (D)	34,561	37.1
AL	Elmer E. Studley (D)	2,363,627✓	
	John Fitzgibbons (D)	2,333,787✓	
	Nicholas Howard Pinto (R)	1,756,343	
	Sherman J. Lowell (R)	1,740,325	
	G. August Gerber (SOC)	166,781	
	Fred Sander (SOC)	163,648	
	Elizabeth Smart (LAW PRES)	74,436	
	J. Elmer Cates (LAW PRES)	68,622	
	Jacob Berlin (SOC LAB)	12,546	
	O. Martin Olson (SOC LAB)	11,623	

NORTH CAROLINA

	Candidates	Votes	%
1	Lindsay C. Warren (D)	32,790	90.8
	John B. Respass (R)	3,313	9.2
2	John H. Kerr (D)	34,325	96.0
3	Charles L. Abernethy (D)	30,395	73.2
	H. B. Ivey (R)	11,146	26.8
4	Edward W. Pou (D)	51,103	76.0
	L. P. Dixon (R)	16,129	24.0
5	Franklin W. Hancock Jr. (D)	40,825	70.2
	L. L. Wall (R)	17,326	29.8
6	William B. Umstead (D)	38,074	67.8
	William I. Ward (R)	18,093	32.2
7	J. Bayard Clark (D)	35,416	80.4
	J. M. Byrd (R)	8,657	19.6
8	J. Walter Lambeth (D)	49,584	65.4
	A. H. Ragan (R)	26,260	34.6
9	Robert L. Doughton (D)	51,145	63.5
	P. P. Dulin (R)	29,421	36.5
10	Alfred L. Bulwinkle (D)	63,776	59.7
	Charles A. Jonas (R)	43,067	40.3

	Candidates	Votes	%
11	Zebulon Weaver (D)	64,667	62.3
	Crawford F. James (R)	39,180	37.7

NORTH DAKOTA

	Candidates	Votes	%
AL	James H. Sinclair (R)	144,339✓	
	William Lemke (R)	135,339✓	
	W. D. Lynch (D)	72,659	
	R. B. Murphy (D)	71,695	
	Pat J. Barrett (I)	690	
	Ella Reeve Bloor (I)	678	

OHIO

	Candidates	Votes	%
1	John B. Hollister (R)	66,018	54.4
	Edward H. Brink (D)	55,416	45.6
2	William E. Hess (R)	58,971	50.7
	Ed. F. Alexander (D)	57,258	49.3
3	Byron B. Harlan (D)	85,069	54.8
	Edith McClure Patterson (R)	66,107	42.6
4	Frank L. Kloeb (D)	59,003	54.6
	John L. Cable (R)	49,100	45.4
5	Frank C. Kniffin (D)	44,433	60.0
	William L. Manahan (R)	29,605	40.0
6	James G. Polk (D)	50,913	56.2
	Mack Sauer (R)	39,668	43.8
7	L. T. Marshall (R)	65,064	53.0
	Aaron J. Halloran (D)	57,715	47.0
8	Brooks Fletcher (D)	45,930	52.7
	Grant E. Mouser Jr. (R)	41,234	47.3
9	Warren J. Duffey (D)	56,755	47.7
	Wilbur M. White (R)	54,078	45.4
10	Thomas A. Jenkins (R)	41,654	58.9
	Charles M. Hogan (D)	29,027	41.1
11	Mell G. Underwood (D)	44,380	63.0
	David J. Lewis (R)	26,075	37.0
12	Arthur P. Lamneck (D)	63,135	50.2
	John C. Speaks (R)	62,704	49.8
13	William L. Fiesinger (D)	56,070	58.9
	Walter E. Kruger (R)	39,122	41.1
14	Dow W. Harter (D)	93,057	53.9
	Francis Seiberling (R)	78,852	45.7
15	Robert T. Secrest (D)	50,313	56.6
	C. Ellis Moore (R)	38,113	42.9
16	William R. Thom (D)	67,670	51.6
	C. B. McClintock (R)	63,609	48.5
17	Charles West (D)	55,396	51.8
	William M. Morgan (R)	51,611	48.2
18	Lawrence E. Imhoff (D)	56,576	50.3
	Frank Murphy (R)	56,013	49.8
19	John G. Cooper (R)	74,534	53.3
	D. F. Dunlavy (D)	65,024	46.5
20	Martin L. Sweeney (D)	52,933	98.8
21	Robert Crosser (D)	49,436	65.2
	Gerard Pilliod (R)	25,527	33.7
22	Chester C. Bolton (R)	141,296	58.7
	Florence E. Allen (D)	98,427	40.9
AL	Charles V. Truax (D)	1,206,631✓	
	Stephen M. Young (D)	1,200,946✓	
	George H. Bender (R)	1,109,562	
	L. T. Palmer (R)	1,102,567	
	Edward R. Stafford (P)	24,625	
	Alfred H. Stratton (P)	18,844	
	John Rehms (COM)	7,053	
	William Hughey (COM)	6,010	

OKLAHOMA

	Candidates	Votes	%
1	Wesley E. Disney (D)	81,080	63.3
	Frank Frantz (R)	46,472	36.3
2	William W. Hastings (D)	46,710	70.5
	William F. Head (R)	19,567	29.5
3	Wilburn Cartwright (D)	59,090	85.3
	Walter Colbert (R)	10,225	14.8
4	Thomas D. McKeown (D)	61,867	75.5
	E. W. Kemp (R)	20,069	24.5
5	Fletcher B. Swank (D)	64,303	64.3
	Paul Huston (R)	35,785	35.8
6	Jed Johnson (D)	53,869	79.3
	George E. Young (R)	14,048	20.7

	Candidates	Votes	%
7	James V. McClintic (D)	43,809	77.9
	W. G. Roe (R)	8,756	15.6
	T. H. McLemore (I)	3,651	6.5
8	E. W. Marland (D)	51,404	61.3
	M. C. Garber (R)	31,677	37.8
AL	Will Rogers (D)	467,644	72.8
	R. A. Howard (R)	171,415	26.7

OREGON

	Candidates	Votes	%
1	James W. Mott (R)	82,443	51.2
	Harvey G. Starkweather (D)	60,066	37.3
	W. J. Butler (I)	12,417	7.7
2	Walter M. Pierce (D)	30,219	48.2
	Robert R. Butler (R)	25,169	40.1
	Hugh E. Brady (I)	5,133	8.2
3	Charles H. Martin (D)	74,397	59.0
	Homer D. Angell (R)	40,650	32.2

PENNSYLVANIA

	Candidates	Votes	%
1	Harry C. Ransley (R, D)	65,508	91.5
	Harry T. Glenn (F PLAY)	4,933	6.9
2	James M. Beck (R, R&P)	42,233	59.2
	John J. Shanahan (D, LAB)	27,571	38.7
3	Alfred M. Waldron (R, R&P)	53,044	57.4
	Frank M. O'Brien (D)	37,487	40.6
4	George W. Edmonds (R)	43,086	52.9
	William J. O'Rourke (D)	36,198	44.4
5	James J. Connolly (R, L)	49,516	55.3
	Carroll J. Agnew (D, A-CB)	36,240	40.5
6	Edward Lowber Stokes (R, L)	44,884	51.0
	Harry V. Dougherty (D, R&P)	40,440	45.9
7	George P. Darrow (R)	62,031	62.2
	James C. Crumlish (D)	35,096	35.2
8	James Wolfenden (R, L)	70,177	65.8
	Matthew Randall (D)	32,139	30.1
9	Henry W. Watson (R)	40,726	50.3
	Norton L. Lichtenwalner (D)	37,490	46.3
10	J. Roland Kinzer (R, P)	62,682	61.5
	Richard P. McGrann (D, REPEAL)	36,841	36.2
11	Patrick J. Boland (D, R)	69,684	95.9
12	C. Murray Turpin (R)	57,377	50.8
	John J. Casey (D, SOC)	55,650	49.2
13	George Franklin Brumm (R, D)	97,120	90.8
14	William E. Richardson (D)	29,386	41.0
	Thomas L. Rhodes (R)	22,898	31.9
	Raymond S. Hofses (SOC)	19,319	27.0
15	Louis T. McFadden (R, D)	71,345	95.9
16	Robert F. Rich (R, P)	46,044	63.5
	Paul A. Rothfuss (D)	24,671	34.0
17	J. William Ditter (R, L)	59,693	59.9
	Phillip Childs Pendleton (D, R&P)	32,706	32.8
18	Benjamin K. Focht (R)	28,749	48.3
	J. G. Harry Rippman (D)	19,230	32.3
	Omer B. Poulson (CIT)	11,568	19.4
19	Isaac H. Doutrich (R)	59,120	58.1
	Carl K. Deen (D)	37,752	37.1
20	Thomas C. Cochran (R, P)	44,754	53.6
	D. J. Driscoll (D)	38,798	46.4
21	Francis E. Walter (D)	39,996	52.7
	William R. Coyle (R)	34,189	45.1
22	Harry L. Haines (D, P)	51,894	57.2
	Leighton C. Taylor (R)	37,434	41.3
23	J. Banks Kurtz (R, P)	35,342	49.2
	Frederick B. Kerr (D)	33,948	47.2
24	J. Buell Snyder (D)	33,633	53.0
	Samuel A. Kendall (R, P)	28,498	44.9
25	Charles I. Faddis (D)	36,781	56.1
	Henry W. Temple (R, P)	27,351	41.7
26	J. Howard Swick (R, P)	45,029	54.0
	Sam B. Wilson (D)	38,402	46.0
27	Nathan L. Strong (R, P)	52,884	50.7
	D. A. Dorn (D)	42,763	41.0
28	William M. Berlin (D, JOBLESS)	43,619	55.2
	Adam M. Wyant (R, P)	32,177	40.8
29	Charles N. Crosby (D, I)	30,106	50.1
	Milton W. Shreve (R, P)	27,949	46.5

	Candidates	Votes	%
30	Twing Brooks (D)	35,186	47.2
	Edward F. Erk (R, I)	35,045	47.0
31	Clyde Kelly (R, D)	68,944	85.5
	Leo O. Guthrie (REPEAL)	6,031	7.5
	William B. Kane (SOC)	5,620	7.0
32	Michael J. Muldowney (R, JOBLESS)	24,785	53.3
	Anne E. Felix (D)	18,986	40.9
33	Henry Ellenbogen (D, JOBLESS)	35,612	52.0
	Harry A. Estep (R)	30,076	43.9
34	Matthew A. Dunn (D, JOBLESS)	40,651	49.9
	Guy E. Campbell (R, L)	36,101	44.3

Special Election

	Candidates	Votes	%
6	Robert L. Davis (R)	63,929	54.1
	Leo J. Horton (D)	54,178	45.9
18	Joseph F. Biddle (R)	38,584	59.3
	Meredith Meyers (D)	26,370	40.6

RHODE ISLAND

	Candidates	Votes	%
1	Francis B. Condon (D)	70,566	55.6
	Clark Burdick (R)	56,153	44.2
2	John M. O'Connell (D)	73,086	54.7
	Thomas P. Hazard (R)	60,153	45.0

SOUTH CAROLINA

	Candidates	Votes	%
1	Thomas S. McMillan (D)	14,415	95.9
2	Hampton P. Fulmer (D)	18,699	97.9
3	John C. Taylor (D)	19,286	99.2
4	John J. McSwain (D)	23,041	98.4
5	James P. Richards (D)	15,046	98.5
6	Allard H. Gasque (D)	14,159	98.7

SOUTH DAKOTA

	Candidates	Votes	%
1	Fred H. Hildebrandt (D)	110,047	53.1
	C. A. Christopherson (R)	92,062	44.4
2	Theodore B. Werner (D)	36,839	55.7
	William Williamson (R)	29,066	43.9

TENNESSEE

	Candidates	Votes	%
1	B. Carroll Reece (R)	30,336	45.7
	O. B. Lovette (I)	27,888	42.0
	Albert C. Tipton (D)	7,950	12.0
2	J. Will Taylor (R)	32,460	57.7
	Hamilton S. Burnett (D)	22,818	40.5
3	Sam D. McReynolds (D)	28,758	91.6
4	John R. Mitchell (D)	30,580	82.6
	W. H. Crowell (R)	5,882	15.9
5	Joseph W. Byrns (D)	33,833	87.6
	J. Y. Freeman (R)	4,066	10.5
6	Clarence W. Turner (D)	15,779	79.1
	G. C. Stephenson (R)	3,915	19.6
7	Gordon Browning (D)	20,315	77.8
	Willoughy Stewart (R)	5,485	21.0
8	Jere Cooper (D)	19,871	88.2
	Mary Burnett (R)	2,307	10.2
9	Edward H. Crump (D)	38,001	90.1
	S. A. Godsey (R)	2,953	7.0

TEXAS

	Candidates	Votes	%
1	Wright Patman (D)	30,854	98.0
2	Martin Dies (D)	51,999	95.4
3	M.G. Sanders (D)	36,507	100.0
4	Sam Rayburn (D)	23,404	95.2
5	Hatton W. Sumners (D)	52,598	92.1
	G. J. McManus (R)	4,539	7.9
6	Luther A. Johnson (D)	32,966	100.0
7	Clay S. Briggs (D)	28,490	95.3
8	Daniel E. Garrett (D)	57,882*	92.0
	W. E. Long (R)	5,015	8.0
9	J. J. Mansfield (D)	33,366	97.5
10	J. P. Buchanan (D)	33,232	100.0
11	O. H. Cross (D)	35,186	96.6
12	Fritz G. Lanham (D)	41,151	93.3
	George Calvert (R)	2,968	6.7

Candidates	Votes	%
13 W. D. McFarlane (D)	33,023	100.0
14 Richard M. Kleberg (D)	69,471	91.5
Frank B. Vaughn (R)	6,456	8.5
15 John N. Garner (D)	44,300*	88.4
C. G. Watson (R)	5,785	11.6
16 R. E. Thomason (D)	49,068	99.7
17 Thomas L. Blanton (D)	43,959	100.0
18 Marvin Jones (D)	76,918	96.1
AL George B. Terrell (D)	794,521✓	
Sterling P. Strong (D)	794,333✓	
Joseph W. Bailey Jr. (D)	790,024✓	
Enoch J. Fletcher (R)	62,957	
F. A. Blankenbeckler (R)	60,360	
J. A. Simpson (R)	59,390	
H. M. Shelton (SOC)	2,534	
P. L. Petersen (SOC)	2,530	
Ben O. Miller (SOC)	2,424	
P. A. Spain (LIB)	188	
H. G. Eastridge (LIB)	172	

UTAH

1 Abe Murdock (D)	47,776	50.7
Don B. Colton (R)	44,827	47.6
2 J. W. Robinson (D)	62,400	56.0
Frederick C. Loofbourow (R)	46,919	42.1

VERMONT

AL Ernest Willard Gibson (R)	86,194	64.4
Joseph A. McNamara (D)	47,591	35.6

VIRGINIA

AL Clifton A. Woodrum (D)	206,631✓	
Andrew J. Montague (D)	205,133✓	
Schuyler Otis Bland (D)	204,372✓	
Thomas G. Burch (D)	204,069✓	
A. Willis Robertson (D)	203,727✓	
Howard W. Smith (D)	203,023✓	
Patrick Henry Drewry (D)	202,800✓	
Colgate W. Darden Jr. (D)	202,759✓	
John W. Flannagan Jr. (D)	201,474✓	

Candidates	Votes	%
Menalcus Lankford (R)	92,586	
J. A. Garber (R)	84,464	
Fred W. McWane (R)	82,480	
Roland E. Chase (R)	81,909	
George Cole Scott (R)	81,025	
Henry A. Wise (R)	78,622	
W. M. Brown (I)	43,936	
C. C. Berkeley (I)	43,202	
R. Lindsay Gordon Jr. (I)	16,504	
A. J. Dunning Jr. (P)	16,392	
Albon James Royal (SOC)	4,782	
Winston F. Dawson (SOC)	4,629	
Herman R. Ansell (SOC)	4,603	
David G. George (SOC)	4,165	
Angie M. Norris (SOC)	3,956	
J. F. Spaulding (R)	3,601	
Frank Lyon	207	

Special Election

10 Joel W. Flood (D)	23,129	99.9

WASHINGTON

1 Marion A. Zioncheck (D)	80,665	55.6
John F. Miller (R)	62,283	42.9
2 Monrad C. Wallgren (D)	49,002	56.1
Lindley H. Hadley (R)	30,780	35.2
Floyd Hatfield (LIB)	6,687	7.7
3 Martin F. Smith (D)	38,713	46.9
Albert Johnson (R)	28,388	34.4
J. T. Sullivan (LIB)	15,427	18.7
4 Knute Hill (D)	41,708	56.3
John W. Summers (R)	32,360	43.7
5 Sam B. Hill (D)	73,041	96.8
6 Wesley Lloyd (D)	44,573	50.1
John T. McCutcheon (R)	32,760	36.8
Tom Martin (LIB)	11,554	13.0

WEST VIRGINIA

1 Robert L. Ramsay (D)	58,060	50.9
Carl G. Bachmann (R)	55,023	48.3

Candidates	Votes	%
2 Jennings Randolph (D)	55,556	53.4
Frank L. Bowman (R)	48,055	46.2
3 Lynn S. Hornor (D)	52,287	53.6
John M. Wolverton (R)	45,274	46.4
4 George W. Johnson (D)	62,848	52.3
Robert L. Hogg (R)	56,993	47.4
5 John Kee (D)	61,277	52.1
Hugh Ike Shott (R)	56,355	47.9
6 Joe L. Smith (D)	102,896	56.4
James O. Lakin (R)	79,470	43.6

WISCONSIN

1 George W. Blanchard (R)	50,874	48.5
William D. Thompson (D)	48,093	45.8
2 Charles W. Henney (D)	63,091	56.2
John B. Gay (R)	47,193	42.0
3 Gardner R. Withrow (R)	59,535	61.1
John J. Boyle (D)	37,846	38.9
4 Raymond J. Cannon (D)	61,058	51.0
John C. Schafer (R)	33,609	28.1
Walter Polakowski (SOC)	24,377	20.4
5 Thomas O'Malley (D)	57,294	43.8
Joseph A. Padway (D)	32,559	24.9
Herman O. Kent (SOC)	30,534	23.3
6 Michael K. Reilly (D)	59,055	59.1
Louis J. Fellenz (R)	38,708	38.7
7 Gerald J. Boileau (R)	49,322	51.4
Frank D. Chapman (D)	46,737	48.7
8 James Hughes (D)	53,414	50.7
George J. Schneider (R)	51,932	49.3
9 James A. Frear (R)	52,680	56.9
Miles H. McNally (D)	39,874	43.1
10 Hubert H. Peavey (R)	49,764	59.2
Peter B. Cadigan (D)	33,448	39.8

WYOMING

AL Vincent M. Carter (R)	44,816	49.7
Paul R. Greever (D)	43,056	47.7

1933 House Elections

ARIZONA

Special Election

	Candidates	Votes	%
AL	Isabella S. Greenway (D)	24,163	73.6
	D. E. Sumpter (SOC)	5,556	16.9
	H. B. Wilkinson (R)	3,123	9.5

LOUISIANA

Special Election

	Candidates	Votes	%
6	Mrs. Bolivar E. Kemp (D)	5,029*	99.8

NEW YORK

Special Election

	Candidates	Votes	%
34	Marian W. Clarke (R)	16,806	59.3
	John J. Burns (D)	11,559	40.8

1934 House Elections

ALABAMA

	Candidates	Votes	%
1	John McDuffie (D)	13,076	99.7
2	Lister Hill (D)	18,592	100.0
3	Henry B. Steagall (D)	13,191	100.0
4	Sam Hobbs (D)	14,728	87.6
	Charles R. Robinson (R)	2,086	12.4
5	Joe Starnes (D)	22,040	75.2
	J. C. Swann (R)	7,282	24.8
6	William B. Oliver (D)	12,342	100.0
7	William B. Bankhead (D)	22,001	80.4
	J. W. Dodd (I)	5,361	19.6
8	Archibald H. Carmichael (D)	13,817	100.0
9	George Huddleston (D)	19,317	95.0

ARIZONA

		Votes	%
AL	Isabella S. Greenway (D)	65,914	68.6
	H. A. Smith (R)	28,283	29.5

ARKANSAS

		Votes	%
1	William J. Driver (D)	20,136	100.0
2	John E. Miller (D)	18,629	100.0
3	Claude A. Fuller (D)	17,363	66.3
	Pat W. Murphy (R)	8,823	33.7
4	William B. Cravens (D)	21,157	100.0
5	David D. Terry (D)	20,209	100.0
6	John L. McClellan (D)	19,078	100.0
7	Tilman B. Parks (D)	13,887	95.8

CALIFORNIA

		Votes	%
1	Clarence F. Lea (D-R)	98,661	93.6
	Allen K. Gifford (SOC)	6,698	6.4
2	Harry L. Englebright (R-D-PROG)	66,370	100.0
3	Frank H. Buck (D)	65,566	53.3
	J. M. Inman (R & PROG)	56,222	45.7
4	Florence P. Kahn (R)	50,491	48.0
	Chauncey Tramutolo (D)	46,871	44.5
5	Richard J. Welch (R-D-PROG)	89,751	93.8
	Alexander Noral (COM)	5,933	6.2
6	Albert E. Carter (R-D-PROG)	48,180	99.8
7	John H. Tolan (D)	51,962	52.3
	Ralph R. Eltse (R)	47,414	47.7
8	John J. McGrath (R-D-PROG)	107,325	99.9
9	B.W. Gearhart (R-D)	77,650	100.0
10	Henry E. Stubbs (D)	68,475	64.4
	George R. Bliss (R)	37,860	35.6
11	John Steven McGroarty (D)	66,999	53.5
	William E. Evans (R)	56,350	45.0
12	John Henry Hoeppel (D)	52,595	50.6
	Frederick F. Houser (R)	51,216	49.3
13	Charles Kramer (D)	83,384	62.4
	Thomas K. Case (R)	27,993	21.0
	Charles H. Randall (PROG)	18,760	14.0
14	Thomas F. Ford (D)	52,761	57.7
	William D. Campbell (R)	33,945	37.1
15	John M. Costello (D)	67,247	50.5
	William I. Traeger (R)	65,858	49.5
16	John F. Dockweiler (D-R)	119,332	98.8
17	Charles J. Colden (D)	60,045	70.3
	C. P. Wright (R)	20,508	24.0
	Richard Pomeroy (SOC)	4,721	5.5
18	Byron N. Scott (D)	52,377	56.3
	William Brayton (R)	40,179	43.2
19	Sam L. Collins (R-D)	97,119	88.6
	A. B. Hillabold	12,301	11.2
20	George Burnham (R)	51,682	52.4
	Ed V. Izac (D & PROG)	46,957	47.6

COLORADO

		Votes	%
1	Lawrence Lewis (D)	59,744	56.0
	William R. Eaton (R)	34,073	32.0

		Votes	%
	Charles W. Varnum (OLD AGE)	9,511	8.9
2	Fred Cummings (D)	64,719	55.9
	George H. Bradfield (R)	49,142	42.4
3	John A. Martin (D)	73,281	64.2
	W. O. Peterson (R)	39,753	34.8
4	Edward T. Taylor (D)	39,747	67.3
	Harry McDevitt (R)	17,234	29.2

CONNECTICUT

		Votes	%
1	Herman P. Kopplemann (D)	74,533	54.3
	Anson T. McCook (R)	59,240	43.2
2	William L. Higgins (R)	44,899	49.6
	John M. Dowe (D)	43,816	48.4
3	James A. Shanley (D)	55,894	48.8
	Joseph F. Morrissey (R)	52,832	46.1
4	Schuyler Merritt (R)	54,178	44.1
	Edward T. Buckingham (D)	45,835	37.3
	Arnold L. Freese (SOC)	21,021	17.1
5	J. Joseph Smith (D)	42,594	51.4
	Edward W. Goss (R)	38,547	46.5
AL	William M. Citron (D)	263,794	51.4
	Charles M. Bakewell (R)	249,146	48.6

DELAWARE

		Votes	%
AL	John George Stewart (R)	52,468	53.1
	John C. Hazzard (D)	45,927	46.5

FLORIDA

		Votes	%
1	J. Hardin Peterson (D)	42,051	100.0
2	Robert A. Green (D)	13,740	100.0
3	Millard F. Caldwell (D)	16,740	100.0
4	J. Mark Wilcox (D)	59,286	100.0
AL	William J. Sears (D)	125,263	100.0

GEORGIA

		Votes	%
1	Hugh Peterson Jr. (D)	5,392	100.0
2	E. E. Cox (D)	3,369	100.0
3	Bryant T. Castellow (D)	4,078	100.0
4	E. M. Owen (D)	5,131	95.5
5	Robert Ramspeck (D)	5,206	100.0
6	Carl Vinson (D)	3,067	100.0
7	Malcolm C. Tarver (D)	5,179	100.0
8	Braswell Deen (D)	4,501	100.0
9	B. Frank Whelchel (D)	8,391	100.0
10	Paul Brown (D)	8,129	100.0

IDAHO

		Votes	%
1	Compton I. White (D)	42,223	61.9
	Burton L. French (R)	25,969	38.1
2	D. Worth Clark (D)	57,547	60.5
	Heber Q. Hale (R)	37,200	39.1

ILLINOIS

		Votes	%
1	Arthur W. Mitchell (D)	27,963	53.0
	Oscar De Priest (R)	24,829	47.0
2	Raymond S. McKeough (D)	104,479	56.3
	P. H. Moynihan (R)	81,034	43.7
3	Edward A. Kelly (D)	122,109	63.5
	Frank M. Fulton (R)	70,329	36.6
4	Harry P. Beam (D)	53,448	78.8
	Frank George Zelezinski (R)	14,401	21.2
5	Adolph J. Sabath (D)	29,107	72.5
	John A. Stanek (R)	10,923	27.2
6	Thomas J. O'Brien (D)	148,645	65.7
	Arnold L. Lund (R)	77,462	34.3
7	Leonard W. Schuetz (D)	185,658	64.0
	Raymond J. Peacock (R)	104,079	35.9
8	Leo Kocialkowski (D)	27,682	74.1
	Edward Richard Piszatowski (R)	9,671	25.9
9	James McAndrews (D)	36,949	56.3
	Fred A. Britten (R)	28,663	43.7

		Votes	%
10	Ralph E. Church (R)	100,161	51.3
	David B. Maloney (D)	94,993	48.7
11	Chauncey W. Reed (R)	69,469	50.3
	James A. Howell (D)	68,748	49.7
12	John T. Buckbee (R)	57,126	55.3
	C. H. Smith (D)	46,111	44.7
13	Leo S. Allen (R)	40,423	60.5
	Edward S. Nicholas (D)	26,427	39.5
14	Chester Thompson (D)	44,965	53.3
	John C. Allen (R)	39,330	46.7
15	J. Leroy Adair (D)	48,682	54.9
	Burnett M. Chiperfield (R)	40,035	45.1
16	Everett M. Dirksen (R)	58,716	65.4
	Rayburn L. Russell (D)	31,044	34.6
17	Leslie C. Arends (R)	36,552	52.1
	Frank Gillespie (D)	33,621	47.9
18	James A. Meeks (D)	48,791	52.0
	Elmer A. Taylor (R)	44,617	47.6
19	Donald C. Dobbins (D)	59,179	53.9
	Charles H. Fletcher (R)	50,571	46.1
20	Scott W. Lucas (D)	39,761	56.9
	Warren W. Wright (R)	30,085	43.1
21	Harry H. Mason (D)	49,825	51.0
	Frank M. Ramey (R)	47,330	48.4
22	Edwin M. Schaefer (D)	62,161	56.3
	Jesse R. Brown (R)	48,285	43.7
23	William W. Arnold (D)	51,712	55.5
	Ben O. Sumner (R)	41,520	44.5
24	Claude V. Parsons (D)	39,442	51.7
	James V. Heidinger (R)	36,891	48.3
25	Kent E. Keller (D)	55,824	54.8
	J. Lester Buford (R)	45,955	45.2
AL	Michael L. Igoe (D)	1,507,714✓	
	Martin A. Brennan (D)	1,459,890✓	
	C. Wayland Brooks (R)	1,201,373	
	Milton E. Jones (R)	1,112,802	
	Walter Nesbit (N PROG)	19,329	
	Arthur McDowell (SOC)	13,586	
	Harold O. Hatcher (SOC)	13,580	
	Martin Powroznik (N PROG)	7,778	
	Frank Earl Herrick (P)	4,863	
	Clay F. Gaumer (P)	4,659	
	John L. Lindsey (SOC LAB)	3,396	
	Frank Schnur (SOC LAB)	3,195	

INDIANA

		Votes	%
1	William T. Schulte (D)	44,983	53.5
	E. Miles Norton (R)	38,531	45.9
2	Frederick Landis (R)	72,552*	53.9
	George R. Durgan (D)	61,610	45.8
3	Samuel B. Pettengill (D)	55,283	50.7
	Andrew J. Hickey (R)	52,410	48.1
4	James I. Farley (D)	58,625	51.7
	David Hogg (R)	54,510	48.1
5	Glenn Griswold (D)	68,079	54.1
	Albert R. Hall (R)	56,420	44.8
6	Virginia E. Jenckes (D)	67,521	49.8
	Fred S. Purnell (R)	67,138	49.6
7	Arthur H. Greenwood (D)	73,324	51.5
	Gerald W. Landis (R)	67,987	47.7
8	John W. Boehne Jr. (D)	75,268	56.9
	Charles F. Werner (R)	56,470	42.7
9	Eugene B. Crowe (D)	68,329	52.1
	Chester A. Davis (R)	62,403	47.6
10	Finly H. Gray (D)	64,939	51.5
	Robert F. Murray (R)	60,693	48.1
11	William H. Larrabee (D)	61,476	54.4
	Ralph A. Scott (R)	50,350	44.5
12	Louis Ludlow (D)	60,358	55.6
	Delbert O. Wilmeth (R)	47,134	43.4

IOWA

Candidates	Votes	%
1 Edward C. Eicher (D)	48,544	55.4
E. R. Hicklin (R)	39,047	44.6
2 Bernhard M. Jacobsen (D)	60,654	64.0
M. B. Andelfinger (R)	34,153	36.0
3 John W. Gwynne (R)	42,063	54.5
Albert C. Willford (D)	35,159	45.5
4 Fred Biermann (D)	49,504	53.1
C. A. Benson (R)	43,794	46.9
5 Lloyd Thurston (R)	54,699	53.0
Ernest H. Fabritz (D)	48,449	47.0
6 Hubert Utterback (D)	50,828	52.5
Cassius C. Dowell (R)	46,084	47.6
7 Otha D. Wearin (D)	51,395	52.0
Charles E. Swanson (R)	47,508	48.0
8 Fred C. Gilchrist (R)	45,875	53.2
Joseph J. Meyers (D)	40,434	46.9
9 Guy M. Gillette (D)	58,598	64.2
Thomas H. McBride (R)	32,639	35.8

KANSAS

Candidates	Votes	%
1 William P. Lambertson (R)	66,293	60.5
John H. Arnett (D)	43,205	39.5
2 Ulysses S. Guyer (R)	60,401	49.7
Howard E. Payne (D)	59,698	49.1
3 Edward W. Patterson (D)	51,793	50.0
Harold McGugin (R)	49,710	48.0
4 William Randolph Carpenter (D)	50,309	52.6
Hal E. Harlan (R)	45,346	47.4
5 John M. Houston (D)	49,610	57.0
Ira C. Watson (R)	31,511	36.2
C. F. Whitson	4,661	5.4
6 Frank Carlson (R)	62,824	51.1
Kathryn O'Loughlin McCarthy (D)	60,028	48.8
7 Clifford R. Hope (R)	63,952	54.6
L. E. Webb (D)	53,104	45.4

KENTUCKY

Candidates	Votes	%
1 William V. Gregory (D)	18,868	61.1
John W. Taylor (R)	12,008	38.9
2 Glover H. Cary (D)	18,410	75.1
William M. Likins (P)	5,188	21.2
3 Emmet O'Neal (D)	48,664	56.2
Frank M. Drake (R)	36,922	42.6
4 Cap R. Carden (D)	25,669	52.1
James Tudor (R)	23,644	48.0
5 Brent Spence (D)	24,666	65.1
J. L. Newhall (R)	11,576	30.6
6 Virgil Chapman (D)	34,641	60.0
W. D. Rogers (R)	23,070	40.0
7 Andrew J. May (D)	35,642	52.9
Harry H. Ramey (R)	31,799	47.2
8 Fred M. Vinson (D)	35,288	59.2
George R. Ellison (R)	24,358	40.8
9 John M. Robsion (R)	42,741	77.0
L. L. Terrell (D)	12,736	23.0

LOUISIANA

Candidates	Votes	%
1 Joachim O. Fernandez (D)	45,678	99.9
2 Paul H. Maloney (D)	45,793	100.0
3 Numa F. Montet (D)	12,636	100.0
4 John N. Sandlin (D)	14,680	100.0
5 Riley J. Wilson (D)	14,158	100.0
6 Jared Y. Sanders Jr. (D)	19,377	100.0
7 Rene L. DeRouen (D)	16,528	100.0
8 Cleveland Dear (D)	17,213	100.0

Special Election

6 Jared Y. Sanders Jr. (D)	9,649	99.6

MAINE

Candidates	Votes	%
1 Simon M. Hamlin (D)	48,235	50.8
Carroll L. Beedy (R)	46,635	49.2
2 Edward C. Moran Jr. (D)	52,491	53.2
Zelma M. Dwinal (R)	46,200	46.8
3 Ralph O. Brewster (R)	44,024	51.4
J. G. Utterback (D)	41,710	48.7

MARYLAND

Candidates	Votes	%
1 T. Alan Goldsborough (D)	41,627	64.0
H. Burdett Messenger (R)	23,378	36.0
2 William P. Cole (D)	75,244	57.7
Theodore F. Brown (R)	51,303	39.3
3 Vincent L. Palmisano (D)	27,988	66.4
F. Stanley Porter (R)	13,042	30.9
4 Ambrose J. Kennedy (D)	37,006	59.1
William J. Stocksdale (R)	24,162	38.6
5 Stephen W. Gambrill (D)	39,734	61.4
Joseph Allison Wilmer (R)	24,364	37.7
6 David J. Lewis (D)	45,605	50.3
Frederick N. Zihlman (R)	44,244	48.8

MASSACHUSETTS

Candidates	Votes	%
1 Allen T. Treadway (R)	51,046	57.6
George E. Haggerty (D)	35,061	39.6
2 William J. Granfield (D)	47,894	51.2
Charles R. Clason (R)	42,495	45.5
3 Joseph E. Casey (D)	46,830	50.1
Frank H. Foss (R)	46,572	49.9
4 Pehr G. Holmes (R)	54,601	57.5
James H. Ferguson (D)	38,984	41.0
5 Edith Nourse Rogers (R)	75,754	62.2
Jeremiah J. O'Sullivan (D)	46,124	37.8
6 A. Piatt Andrew (R)	64,610	100.0
7 William P. Connery Jr. (D)	62,666	59.1
C. F. Nelson Pratt (R)	40,988	38.6
8 Arthur D. Healey (D)	53,581	58.6
William S. Howe (R)	37,873	41.4
9 Richard M. Russell (D)	60,141	52.6
Robert Luce (R)	54,198	47.4
10 George Holden Tinkham (R, D)	84,244	100.0
11 John P. Higgins (D)	46,383	100.0
12 John W. McCormack (D)	78,783	82.8
Francis A. Pentoney (R)	16,370	17.2
13 Richard B. Wigglesworth (R)	58,653	54.9
Francis H. Foy (D)	48,241	45.1
14 Joseph W. Martin Jr. (R)	46,411	54.8
Arthur E. Seagrave (D)	38,325	45.2
15 Charles L. Gifford (R)	46,446	53.4
John D. W. Bodfish (D)	38,336	44.0

MICHIGAN

Candidates	Votes	%
1 George G. Sadowski (D)	40,054	65.8
Charles A. Roxborough (R)	19,194	31.5
2 Earl C. Michener (R)	40,119	50.2
John C. Lehr (D)	38,972	48.7
3 Henry M. Kimball (R)	41,587	55.0
Paul H. Todd (D)	32,928	43.6
4 Clare E. Hoffman (R)	45,224	58.2
George Foulkes (D)	31,646	40.7
5 Carl E. Mapes (R)	39,682	50.5
Thomas F. McAllister (D)	37,847	48.2
6 William W. Blackney (R)	42,424	50.6
Claude E. Cady (D)	41,100	49.0
7 Jesse P. Wolcott (R)	42,857	59.9
Frank J. Wiegand (D)	27,690	38.7
8 Fred L. Crawford (R)	40,333	51.5
Michael J. Hart (D)	35,945	45.9
9 Albert J. Engel (R)	33,222	52.0
Harry W. Musselwhite (D)	30,513	47.7
10 Roy O. Woodruff (R)	36,719	59.5
Hubert J. Gaffney (D)	24,526	39.8
11 Prentiss M. Brown (D)	39,293	54.8
John J. O'Hara (R)	32,460	45.2
12 Frank E. Hook (D)	37,298	52.1
W. Frank James (R)	34,281	47.9
13 Clarence J. McLeod (R)	35,879	56.7
John H. Slevin (D)	25,869	40.9
14 Louis C. Rabaut (D)	45,301	62.2

MICHIGAN (cont.)

Candidates	Votes	%
John H. McPherson (R)	26,006	35.7
15 John D. Dingell (D)	40,119	54.4
Charles Bowles (R)	32,011	43.4
16 John Lesinski (D)	32,269	52.7
Clyde M. Ford (R)	27,487	44.9
17 George A. Dondero (R)	35,562	53.8
Charles P. Webster (D)	29,250	44.2

MINNESOTA

Candidates	Votes	%
1 August H. Andresen (R)	51,099	46.6
John W. Feller (D)	29,581	27.0
Otto Baudler (F-LAB)	29,038	26.5
2 Elmer J. Ryan (D)	43,677	37.2
Henry Arens (F-LAB)	37,663	32.1
L. P. Johnson (R)	35,968	30.7
3 Ernest Lundeen (F-LAB)	59,097	53.3
Josiah H. Chase (R)	28,637	25.8
John W. Schmidt (D)	22,556	20.3
4 Melvin J. Maas (R)	37,933	36.8
A. E. Smith (F-LAB)	30,354	29.5
John J. McDonough (D)	24,122	23.4
Charles J. Andre (I)	10,180	9.9
5 Theodore Christianson (R)	45,875	39.3
Dewey W. Johnson (F-LAB)	42,322	36.2
Sidney Benson	27,814	23.8
6 Harold Knutson (R)	56,642	46.2
Magnus Johnson (F-LAB)	46,346	37.8
Frank R. Weber (D)	19,572	16.0
7 Paul John Kvale (F-LAB)	65,261	59.3
Richard T. Daly (R)	44,762	40.7
8 William A. Pittenger (R)	39,513	35.7
F. H. Shoemaker (I)	25,386	23.0
A. L. Winterquist (F-LAB)	25,024	22.6
Jerry A. Harri (D)	18,707	16.9
9 Richard T. Buckler (F-LAB)	41,822	44.2
Ole O. Sageng (R)	27,522	29.1
Martin Oscar Brandon (D)	25,210	26.7

MISSISSIPPI

Candidates	Votes	%
1 John E. Rankin (D)	6,825	100.0
2 Wall Doxey (D)	5,721	100.0
3 William M. Whittington (D)	3,586	100.0
4 Aaron Lane Ford (D)	8,051	100.0
5 Aubert C. Dunn (D)	9,412	100.0
6 William M. Colmer (D)	9,002	100.0
7 Dan R. McGehee (D)	14,730	100.0

MISSOURI

Candidates	Votes	%
1 Milton A. Romjue (D)	52,273	54.8
J. Grover Morgan (R)	42,513	44.5
2 William L. Nelson (D)	59,557	58.6
Logan (R)	41,916	41.2
3 Richard M. Duncan (D)	61,548	60.6
William A. Black (R)	39,953	39.3
4 C. Jasper Bell (D)	82,995	81.7
Horace Guffin (R)	18,368	18.1
5 Joseph B. Shannon (D)	96,798	84.3
Claude E. Sowers (R)	17,889	15.6
6 Reuben T. Wood (D)	58,902	55.1
Oliver J. Page (R)	47,769	44.7
7 Dewey Short (R)	65,211	52.9
Frank H. Lee (D)	57,446	46.6
8 Clyde Williams (D)	54,006	54.4
Breuer (R)	45,354	45.7
9 Clarence Cannon (D)	41,514	62.4
Voelkerding (R)	24,380	36.7
10 Orville Zimmerman (D)	42,865	58.2
McAnally (R)	29,949	40.7
11 Thomas C. Hennings (D)	59,119	56.4
Leonidas C. Dyer (R)	44,693	42.6
12 James R. Claiborne (D)	70,754	51.0
Cleveland A. Newton (R)	66,108	47.7
13 John J. Cochran (D)	60,198	65.5
George W. Strodtman (R)	31,165	33.9

MONTANA

	Candidates	Votes	%
1	Joseph P. Monaghan (D)	55,877	67.8
	D. D. Evans (R)	25,567	31.0
2	Roy E. Ayers (D)	79,856	69.8
	Stanley E. Felt (R)	33,703	29.5

NEBRASKA

	Candidates	Votes	%
1	Henry C. Luckey (D)	55,897	52.8
	Marcus L. Poteet (R)	45,258	42.8
2	Charles F. McLaughlin (D)	46,790	54.2
	Herbert Rhoades (R)	36,743	42.5
3	Karl Stefan (R)	69,363	57.8
	Edgar Howard (D)	50,707	42.2
4	C. G. Binderup (D)	69,275	58.4
	James W. Hammond (R)	49,357	41.6
5	Harry B. Coffee (D)	55,709	52.1
	Albert N. Mathers (R)	49,161	45.9

NEVADA

	Candidates	Votes	%
AL	James G. Scrugham (D)	29,691	71.2
	George B. Russell (R)	11,992	28.8

NEW HAMPSHIRE

	Candidates	Votes	%
1	William N. Rogers (D)	48,568	53.9
	Arthur B. Jenks (R)	41,425	46.0
2	Charles W. Tobey (R)	42,706	53.3
	Harry B. Metcalf (D)	37,122	46.3

NEW JERSEY

	Candidates	Votes	%
1	Charles A. Wolverton (R)	81,634	61.2
	Willis Tullis Porch (D)	48,770	36.6
2	Isaac Bacharach (R)	49,824	50.4
	Charles W. Ackley (D)	48,743	49.3
3	William H. Sutphin (D)	58,670	52.2
	Oliver F. Van Camp (R)	53,170	47.3
4	D. Lane Powers (R)	48,760	56.7
	Walter Lincoln Whittlesey (D)	36,326	42.2
5	Charles A. Eaton (R)	54,938	51.7
	Charles S. MacKenzie (D)	50,395	47.4
6	Donald H. McLean (R)	51,528	52.5
	Richard U. Strong (D)	45,581	46.4
7	Randolph Perkins (R)	47,083	51.4
	Hamilton Cross (D)	43,771	47.7
8	George N. Seger (R)	45,123	53.6
	Frank J. Van Noort (D)	37,119	44.1
9	Edward A. Kenney (D)	54,941	54.6
	John Pollock (R)	44,704	44.4
10	Fred A. Hartley Jr. (R)	40,205	52.9
	William Herda Smith (D)	35,261	46.4
11	Peter A. Cavicchia (R)	34,110	50.0
	Edward L. O'Neill (D)	33,531	49.1
12	Frederick R. Lehlbach (R)	39,817	54.3
	Charles P. McCann (D)	32,546	44.4
13	Mary T. Norton (D)	73,342	73.2
	Anthony L. Montelli (R)	26,447	26.4
14	Edward J. Hart (D)	77,020	77.7
	Fred G. Tauber (R)	21,081	21.3

NEW MEXICO

	Candidates	Votes	%
AL	John J. Dempsey (D)	76,833	51.8
	M. F. Miera (R)	70,659	47.7

NEW YORK

	Candidates	Votes	%
1	Robert L. Bacon (RCF & LP)	127,082	56.0
	Gerald Morrell (D)	93,794	41.4
2	William F. Brunner (D)	140,520	69.6
	Thomas J. Styles (R & VIC)	48,306	23.9
3	Joseph L. Pfeifer (D)	26,738	72.8
	Alex Pisciotta (R CF&REC)	8,179	22.3
4	Thomas H. Cullen (D & REC)	29,858	74.5
	Charles E. Miller (R VIC&CF)	8,935	22.3
5	Marcellus H. Evans (D & REC)	41,154	64.7
	Frank E. Davis (RCF & LP)	19,010	29.9

	Candidates	Votes	%
6	Andrew L. Somers (D & LP)	70,164	60.9
	Donald C. Strachan (R & CF)	30,671	26.6
	Jacob Axelrad (SOC)	10,327	9.0
7	John J. Delaney (D)	28,945	67.9
	Joseph M. Aimee (RCF & LP)	9,897	23.2
	Alexander Kahn (SOC & LP)	2,503	5.9
8	Richard J. Tonry (D & REC)	111,247	59.2
	Sigurd J. Arnesen (R & CF)	44,423	23.6
	Baruch C. Vladeck (SOC)	22,149	11.8
9	Stephen A. Rudd (D)	56,617	60.6
	Murray Rosof (R & CF)	30,462	32.6
	Theodore Shapiro (SOC)	4,738	5.1
10	Emanuel Celler (D LP & L)	31,193	60.9
	Michael C. Antonelli (R CF&REC)	14,770	28.8
	Samuel H. Friedman (SOC)	3,470	6.8
11	James A. O'Leary (D)	36,393	59.9
	Arthur L. Willshaw (R)	15,595	25.7
	Vernon B. Hampton (RC I)	6,666	11.0
12	Samuel Dickstein (D)	14,895	76.8
	Solomon Siss (R & CF)	3,029	15.6
13	Christopher D. Sullivan (D)	13,090	72.3
	John Rosenberg (R)	3,828	21.1
14	William I. Sirovich (D)	15,437	52.8
	Frederick J. Groehl (R)	9,744	33.4
	Rachel Panken (SOC)	2,259	7.7
	Peter E. Cacchione (COM)	1,612	5.5
15	John J. Boylan (D)	23,482	80.2
	Frank J. McCoy (R)	4,726	16.1
16	John J. O'Connor (D)	22,528	66.3
	J. Homer Cudmore (R)	9,735	28.6
17	Theodore A. Peyser (D)	29,338	53.9
	George A. Spiegelberg (R CST&CF)	22,688	41.7
18	Martin J. Kennedy (D)	23,480	69.0
	Charles W. Ferry (R)	8,832	26.0
19	Sol Bloom (D & LP)	42,614	65.3
	Harold Goldman (R & CF)	18,612	28.5
20	Vito Marcantonio (R & CF)	13,083	46.6
	James J. Lanzetta (LAW PRES)	12,836	45.8
21	Joseph A. Gavagan (D)	62,042	68.2
	Kenneth Cameron (R & CF)	23,534	25.9
22	Anthony J. Griffin (D)	28,535	69.3
	John J. Sochurek (R & IV)	9,162	22.3
23	Charles A. Buckley (D)	109,319	64.2
	Isaac F. Becker (R)	31,028	18.2
	Samuel Orr (SOC)	14,333	8.4
24	James M. Fitzpatrick (D)	104,652	60.1
	John H. Nichols (R)	51,535	29.6
	Solomon Perrin (SOC)	11,256	6.5
25	Charles D. Millard (R)	63,782	54.8
	Homer A. Stebbins (D)	49,469	42.5
26	Hamilton Fish Jr. (R SOC&LP)	50,849	61.9
	Thomas Pendell (D)	31,292	38.1
27	Philip A. Goodwin (R & SOC)	46,924	55.7
	Willis G. Nash (D & LP)	37,295	44.3
28	Parker Corning (D)	89,511	70.1
	Frank R. Lanagan (R)	36,117	28.3
29	William D. Thomas (R & LP)	56,401	58.4
	Buell G. Brayton (D)	38,054	39.4
30	Frank Crowther (R & LP)	42,740	50.8
	Carroll A. Gardner (D)	39,048	46.4
31	Bertrand H. Snell (R)	43,942	62.0
	Kenneth Gardner (D)	26,308	37.1
32	Francis D. Culkin (R & LP)	49,055	67.0
	Annie D. Mills (D)	22,959	31.3
33	Fred J. Sisson (D)	45,831	49.1
	Frederick M. Davenport (R)	45,579	48.9
34	Bert Lord (R)	50,528	60.2
	Charles C. Flaesch (D)	32,075	38.2
35	Clarence E. Hancock (R)	65,732	54.7
	Richard P. Byrne (D)	50,599	42.1
36	John Taber (R)	45,431	61.0
	Dennis F. Sullivan (D)	27,129	36.4
37	W. Sterling Cole (R)	48,964	59.8
	Julian P. Bretz (D)	28,979	35.4
38	James P. B. Duffy (D)	64,434	54.2
	James L. Whitley (R & LP)	50,066	42.1
39	James W. Wadsworth Jr. (R & LP)	49,915	56.2

	Candidates	Votes	%
	David A. White (D)	36,658	41.3
40	Walter G. Andrews (R)	69,353	55.7
	Frank S. Anderson (D)	50,532	40.6
41	Alfred F. Beiter (D)	45,830	55.7
	Carlton A. Fisher (R)	33,793	41.1
42	James M. Mead (D)	49,251	63.8
	Walter J. Lohr (R & LP)	26,036	33.7
43	Daniel A. Reed (R & LP)	42,513	63.3
	Peter B. Hogan (D)	21,856	32.6
AL	Caroline O'Day (D)	1,978,670✓	
	Matthew J. Merritt (D)	1,952,039✓	
	Natalie F. Couch (R)	1,417,271	
	William B. Groat Jr (R)	1,387,460	
	Charles W. Noonan (SOC)	141,799	
	August Claessens (SOC)	138,778	
	Henry Sheppard (COM)	48,851	
	Emanuel Levin (COM)	47,812	
	Dorothy Frooks (LAW PRES)	19,853	
	William E. Barron (LAW PRES)	16,770	
	Jeremiah D. Crowley (SOC LAB)	7,529	
	Jacob Berlin (SOC LAB)	6,701	

Special Election

		Votes	%
29	William D. Thomas (R)	25,048	60.1
	John J. Nyhoff (D)	16,030	38.5

NORTH CAROLINA

	Candidates	Votes	%
1	Lindsay C. Warren (D)	11,786	87.8
	R. C. Dozier (R)	1,637	12.2
2	John H. Kerr (D)	11,329	100.0
3	Graham A. Barden (D)	20,218	67.1
	W. B. Rouse (R)	9,922	32.9
4	Harold D. Cooley (D)	29,431	68.5
	Hobart Brantley (R)	13,507	31.5
5	Franklin W. Hancock Jr. (D)	28,221	100.0
6	William B. Umstead (D)	21,241	69.0
	B.C. Campbell (R)	9,543	31.0
7	J. Bayard Clark (D)	17,774	78.9
	Louis Goodman (R)	4,747	21.1
8	J. Walter Lambeth (D)	35,794	58.0
	Avalon E. Hall (R)	25,974	42.1
9	Robert L. Doughton (D)	44,780	58.2
	J. M. Prevette (R)	32,171	41.8
10	Alfred L. Bulwinkle (D)	43,483	53.5
	Calvin R. Edney (R)	37,820	46.5
11	Zebulon Weaver (D)	56,199	59.6
	Halsey B. Leavitt (R)	38,126	40.4

Special Election

		Votes	%
4	Harold D. Cooley (D)	16,881	93.8
	Hobart Brantley (R)	1,110	6.2

NORTH DAKOTA

	Candidates	Votes	%
AL	William Lemke (R)	144,705✓	
	Usher L. Burdick (R)	114,841✓	
	William D. Lynch (D)	85,771	
	G. F. Lamb (D)	79,338	
	J. H. Sinclair (I)	46,304	
	Jasper Haaland (I)	1,299	
	Effie Kjorstad (I)	1,090	

OHIO

	Candidates	Votes	%
1	John B. Hollister (R)	53,985	55.8
	Edwin G. Becker (D)	42,723	44.2
2	William E. Hess (R)	51,171	55.1
	Charles E. Miller (D)	41,701	44.9
3	Byron B. Harlan (D)	67,695	53.6
	Howard F. Heald (R)	56,480	44.8
4	Frank L. Kloeb (D)	48,613	53.9
	Guy D. Hawley (R)	41,504	46.1
5	Frank C. Kniffin (D)	34,249	55.5
	Davis B. Johnson (R)	27,423	44.5
6	James G. Polk (D)	42,340	52.2
	Albert L. Daniels (R)	38,538	47.5
7	Leroy T. Marshall (R)	56,453	56.6
	C. W. Rich (D)	43,226	43.4
8	Brooks Fletcher (D)	39,466	52.2

Candidates	Votes	%
Gertrude Jones (R)	36,112	47.8
9 Warren J. Duffey (D)	61,037	62.3
Frank L. Mulholland (R)	35,732	36.5
10 Thomas A. Jenkins (R)	36,824	58.4
W. F. Marting (D)	26,278	41.6
11 Mell G. Underwood (D)	36,020	57.4
Renick W. Dunlap (R)	26,723	42.6
12 Arthur P. Lamneck (D)	63,396	55.7
John C. Speaks (R)	50,386	44.3
13 William L. Fiesinger (D)	43,617	54.3
Walter E. Kruger (R)	35,889	44.7
14 Dow W. Harter (D)	65,152	49.1
Carl D. Sheppard (R)	63,274	47.7
15 Robert T. Secrest (D)	42,722	55.7
Kenneth C. Ray (R)	33,950	44.3
16 William R. Thom (D)	59,354	56.7
C. B. McClintock (R)	45,390	43.3
17 William A. Ashbrook (D)	49,211	54.0
James A. Glenn (R)	41,954	46.0
18 Lawrence E. Imhoff (D)	49,160	55.4
Frank Murphy (R)	39,642	44.6
19 John G. Cooper (R)	56,200	51.2
Locke Miller (D)	52,023	47.4
20 Martin L. Sweeney (D)	50,611	67.9
Joseph E. Cassidy (R)	21,952	29.4
21 Robert W. Crosser (D)	47,540	63.8
Frank W. Sotak (R)	25,253	33.9
22 Chester C. Bolton (R)	99,535	52.1
William C. Dixon (D)	88,551	46.3
AL Charles V. Truax (D)	1,061,857✔	
Stephen M. Young (D)	1,050,089✔	
George H. Bender (R)	905,233	
L. L. Marshall (R)	871,432	
Ben Atkins (COM)	13,972	
John Marshall (COM)	13,808	

OKLAHOMA

Candidates	Votes	%
1 Wesley E. Disney (D)	61,470	60.1
Robert W. Kellough (R)	39,085	38.2
2 Jack Nichols (D)	40,210	62.2
C. E. Creager (R)	24,001	37.1
3 Wilburn Cartwright (D)	50,435	76.9
John D. Morrison (R)	14,202	21.7
4 P. L. Gassaway (D)	47,140	67.5
James S. Davidson (R)	19,875	28.5
5 Josh Lee (D)	58,322	74.6
Paul Huston (R)	18,640	23.9
6 Jed Johnson (D)	37,567	67.2
George E. Young (R)	15,567	27.8
7 Sam C. Massingale (D)	35,210	76.0
Fred Langley (R)	8,214	17.7
Orville E. Enfield (SOC)	2,891	6.2
8 Phil Ferguson (D)	40,248	56.8
T. J. Sargent (R)	30,019	42.4
AL Will Rogers (D)	354,542	66.9
U.S. Stone (R)	162,991	30.7

OREGON

Candidates	Votes	%
1 James W. Mott (R)	67,286	49.9
R. R. Turner (D)	51,443	38.1
Emmett W. Gulley (I)	12,963	9.6
2 Walter M. Pierce (D)	29,221	56.7
Jay H. Upton (R)	21,255	41.3
3 William A. Ekwall (R)	43,900	41.1
Walter B. Gleason (D)	41,152	38.5
Andrew C. Smith (I)	9,968	9.3

PENNSYLVANIA

Candidates	Votes	%
1 Harry C. Ransley (R)	46,039	52.1
Joseph Marinelli (D)	41,733	47.2
2 William H. Wilson (R)	44,478	54.7
James P. McGranery (D)	36,212	44.6
3 Ciare Gerald Fenerty (R)	53,152	52.0
Michael Joseph Bradley (D)	48,141	46.8
4 J. Burrwood Daly (D)	45,901	49.7
George W. Edmonds (R)	45,526	49.2
5 Frank J. G. Dorsey (D)	50,650	52.2

Candidates	Votes	%
James J. Connolly (R)	45,287	46.7
6 Michael J. Stack (D)	50,977	50.8
Robert L. Davis (R)	48,308	48.2
7 George P. Darrow (R)	56,990	52.7
James C. Crumlich (D)	50,207	46.4
8 James Wolfenden (R)	60,139	57.2
John E. McDonough (D)	43,426	41.3
9 Oliver W. Frey (D)	40,494	50.2
Theodore R. Gardner (R)	38,427	47.6
10 J. Roland Kinzer (R, P)	58,773	57.6
Charles T. Carpenter (D)	42,540	41.7
11 Patrick J. Boland (R, D)	76,568	98.1
12 C. Murray Turpin (R)	60,608	51.4
John J. Casey (D, SOC)	56,554	48.0
13 James H. Gildea (D)	54,309	50.1
David W. Bechtel (R)	49,584	45.7
14 William E. Richardson (D, R)	39,134	63.3
Raymond S. Hofses (SOC)	19,871	32.2
15 C. Elmer Dietrich (D)	39,566	50.1
Louis T. McFadden (R, P)	38,905	49.3
16 Robert F. Rich (R, P)	38,761	53.0
Paul A. Rothfuss (D, SOC)	32,436	44.4
17 J. William Ditter (R)	50,149	56.2
Howard J. Dager (D)	37,541	42.1
18 Benjamin K. Focht (R, P)	37,992	55.6
B. Stiles Duncan (D)	30,320	44.4
19 Isaac H. Doutrich (R)	62,576	55.1
Forrest Mercer (D)	48,743	42.9
20 D. J. Driscoll (D)	48,245	52.7
Leon H. Gavin (R)	40,050	43.7
21 Francis E. Walter (D, P)	41,789	58.6
T. Fred Woodley (R)	28,520	40.0
22 Harry L. Haines (D)	49,629	54.6
Emanuel C. Beck (R)	39,719	43.7
23 Don Gingery (D)	41,088	52.4
J. Banks Kurtz (R, P)	34,631	44.2
24 J. Buell Snyder (D)	43,530	57.3
Paul H. Griffith (R, P)	31,904	42.0
25 Charles I. Faddis (D, SOC)	39,122	59.4
Albert S. Sickman (R)	25,435	38.6
26 Charles R. Eckert (D)	52,243	59.1
J. Howard Swick (R, P)	35,302	40.0
27 Joseph Gray (D)	59,891	54.4
Nathan L. Strong (R, P)	49,005	44.5
28 William M. Berlin (D, R)	63,262	92.5
29 Charles N. Crosby (D)	32,530	52.5
Will Rose (R)	28,292	45.6
30 J. Twing Brooks (D)	40,864	53.4
Edmund F. Erk (R, RO)	34,412	45.0
31 James L. Quinn (D)	44,711	52.3
Clyde Kelly (R, P)	38,984	45.6
32 Theodore L. Moritz (D)	24,275	43.3
Michael J. Muldowney (R)	19,134	34.1
Alexander H. Schullman (I)	8,441	15.0
Anne E. Felix (HE)	2,865	5.1
33 Henry Ellenbogen (D, R)	72,584	95.2
34 Matthew A. Dunn (D, R)	72,215	89.2
Guy E. Campbell (LFD)	5,474	6.8

RHODE ISLAND

Candidates	Votes	%
1 Francis Bernard Condon (D)	70,516	59.0
John C. Cosseboom (R)	49,087	41.0
2 John Matthew O'Connell (D)	69,765	55.8
George C. Clark (R)	55,191	44.2

SOUTH CAROLINA

Candidates	Votes	%
1 Thomas S. McMillan (D)	4,264	97.7
2 Hampton P. Fulmer (D)	3,518	99.2
3 John C. Taylor (D)	3,830	99.4
4 John J. McSwain (D)	4,681	99.4
5 James P. Richards (D)	2,645	98.7
6 Allard H. Gasque (D)	2,983	99.3

SOUTH DAKOTA

Candidates	Votes	%
1 Fred H. Hildebrandt (D)	122,932	58.5
C. A. Christopherson (R)	84,830	40.4
2 Theodore B. Werner (D)	35,467	52.5
Francis H. Case (R)	32,105	47.5

TENNESSEE

	Candidates	Votes	%
1	B. Carroll Reece (R)	22,156	56.8
	W. A. S. Furlow (D)	13,708	35.2
2	J. Will Taylor (R)	25,729	58.7
	T. C. Drinnon (D)	9,740	22.2
	E. E. Patton (I)	7,081	16.2
3	Sam D. McReynolds (D)	21,559	60.0
	Pat H. Thach (R)	14,387	40.0
4	J. Ridley Mitchell (D)	26,064	78.4
	H. E. McLean (R)	7,182	21.6
5	Joseph W. Byrns (D)	26,856	100.0
6	Clarence W. Turner (D)	16,102	100.0
7	Herron Pearson (D)	15,808	100.0
8	Jere Cooper (D)	18,112	100.0
9	Walter Chandler (D)	46,363	100.0

TEXAS

	Candidates	Votes	%
1	Wright Patman (D)	18,608	98.5
2	Martin Dies (D)	16,628	100.0
3	Morgan G. Sanders (D)	14,790	100.0
4	Sam Rayburn (D)	16,684	96.8
5	Hatton Sumners (D)	27,302	96.9
6	Luther Johnson (D)	16,294	100.0
7	Nat Patton (D)	18,063	99.1
8	Joe H. Eagle (D)	40,400	99.5
9	Joseph J. Mansfield (D)	23,257	100.0
10	James P. Buchanan (D)	19,306	100.0
11	Oliver H. Cross (D)	20,383	100.0
12	Fritz G. Lanham (D)	24,984	98.4
13	W. D. McFarlane (D)	21,005	100.0
14	Richard M. Kleberg (D)	26,276	100.0
15	Milton H. West (D)	20,102	88.0
	G. C. Mann (R)	2,739	12.0
16	R. Ewing Thomason (D)	11,063	100.0
17	Thomas L. Blanton (D)	17,266	100.0
18	Marvin Jones (D)	23,202	96.9
19	George Mahon (D)	20,169	100.0
20	Maury Maverick (D)	17,810	98.6
21	Charles L. South (D)	26,093	100.0

UTAH

	Candidates	Votes	%
1	Abe Murdock (D)	55,800	64.4
	Arthur Woolley (R)	29,878	34.5
2	J. Will Robinson (D)	58,175	62.3
	Frederick Loofbourow (R)	34,007	36.4

VERMONT

	Candidates	Votes	%
AL	Charles A. Plumley (R)	73,809	56.9
	Carroll E. Jenkins (D)	54,967	42.4

VIRGINIA

	Candidates	Votes	%
1	Schuyler Otis Bland (D)	7,637	91.4
2	Colgate W. Darden Jr. (D)	11,102	76.1
	Gerould M. Rumble (R)	3,321	22.8
3	Andrew Jackson Montague (D)	9,738	80.5
	Roy C. Parks (R)	2,129	17.6
4	Patrick Henry Drewry (D)	7,850	93.4
5	Thomas G. Burch (D)	11,964	88.2
	Henry P. Wilder	1,168	8.6
6	Clifton A. Woodrum (D)	10,738	67.1
	Thomas J. Wilson Jr. (R)	5,060	31.6
7	A. Willis Robertson (D)	14,903	68.3
	J. Everett Will (R)	6,562	30.1
8	Howard W. Smith (D)	14,191	78.8
	John Locke Green (R)	3,583	19.9
9	John W. Flannagan Jr. (D)	20,532	58.1
	Fred C. Parks (R)	12,355	35.0
	Bruce Crawford (I)	2,402	6.8

WASHINGTON

	Candidates	Votes	%
1	Marion A. Zioncheck (D)	68,395	57.7
	Bert C. Ross (R)	38,350	32.4
	Cecil R. Fuller (CNM)	8,500	7.2
2	Mon C. Wallgren (D)	50,486	67.0

	Payson Peterson (R)	23,638	31.4
3	Martin F. Smith (D)	48,887	69.2
	Russell V. Mack (R)	21,750	30.8
4	Knute Hill (D)	35,702	56.4
	John W. Summers (R)	27,637	43.6
5	Sam B. Hill (D)	58,901	76.2
	Mansfield E. Mack (R)	18,397	23.8
6	Wesley Lloyd (D)	52,314	70.5
	Emery Asbury (R)	21,883	29.5

WEST VIRGINIA

1	Robert L. Ramsay (D)	52,714	53.3
	Carl G. Bachmann (R)	45,442	45.9
2	Jennings Randolph (D)	54,531	57.6
	Herbert E. Hannis (R)	39,832	42.1
3	Andrew Edmiston (D)	54,885	53.6
	James A. Rusmisell (R)	46,978	45.9
4	George W. Johnson (D)	60,684	50.4
	Robert B. McDougle (R)	59,013	49.1
5	John Kee (D)	54,659	58.5
	C. M. (Casey) Jones (R)	38,599	41.3

6	Joe L. Smith (D)	67,671	61.4
	Frank C. Burdette (R)	42,147	38.3

WISCONSIN

1	Thomas R. Amlie (PROG)	32,397	37.4
	Judson W. Staplekamp (R)	28,459	32.9
	Ralph V. Brown (D)	23,532	27.2
2	Harry Sauthoff (PROG)	41,458	41.8
	Charles W. Henney (D)	33,347	33.6
	John B. Gay (R)	22,995	23.2
3	Gardner R. Withrow (PROG)	47,311	52.1
	Levi H. Bancroft (R)	25,851	28.5
	Bart E. McGonigle (D)	17,222	19.0
4	Raymond J. Cannon (D)	33,886	38.6
	John C. Schafer (R)	19,840	22.6
	Marvin V. Baxter (SOC)	18,166	20.7
	Laurence C. Gram (PROG)	15,364	17.5
5	Thomas O'Malley (D)	32,931	34.7
	Otto Hauser (SOC)	23,334	24.6
	Arthur T. Spence (R)	21,533	22.7
	Carl J. Ludwig (PROG)	16,693	17.6

6	Michael K. Reilly (D)	34,664	42.3
	Walter D. Corrigan (PROG)	28,477	34.7
	William J. Campbell (R)	18,825	23.0
7	Gerald J. Boileau (PROG)	41,321	48.5
	Frank D. Chapman (D)	24,871	29.2
	Caspar Wallrich (R)	17,461	20.5
8	George J. Schneider (PROG)	39,505	43.8
	Gerald F. Clifford (D)	34,397	38.2
	L. Herman Waite (R)	15,748	17.5
9	Merlin Hull (PROG)	42,422	49.6
	Willis E. Donley (D)	20,828	24.3
	Knute Anderson (R)	20,043	23.4
10	Bernard J. Gehrmann (PROG)	29,397	35.4
	Hubert H. Peavey (R)	24,850	29.9
	Charles P. Cadigan (D)	24,689	29.7

WYOMING

AL	Paul R. Greever (D)	53,288	58.3
	Charles E. Winter (R)	37,492	41.0

1935 House Election

INDIANA

Special Election

	Candidates	Votes	%
2	Charles A. Halleck (R)	50,324	52.7
	George R. Durgan (D)	45,089	47.3

1936 House Elections

ALABAMA

	Candidates	Votes	%
1	Frank W. Boykin (D)	23,421	100.0
2	Lister Hill (D)	32,452	99.1
3	Henry B. Steagall (D)	22,535	100.0
4	Sam Hobbs (D)	22,615	86.4
	Charles R. Robinson (R)	3,556	13.6
5	Joe Starnes (D)	29,891	100.0
6	Pete Jarman (D)	18,325	100.0
7	William B. Bankhead (D)	25,126	73.0
	J. B. Weaver (R)	9,311	27.0
8	John J. Sparkman (D)	27,788	99.7
9	Luther Patrick (D)	36,405	91.8
	J. G. Bass (R)	3,177	8.0

ARIZONA

	Candidates	Votes	%
AL	John R. Murdock (D)	84,403	77.6
	G. L. Burgess (R)	20,383	18.7

ARKANSAS

	Candidates	Votes	%
1	William J. Driver (D)	32,066	100.0
2	John E. Miller (D)	19,146	85.6
	J. N. Hout Jr. (R)	3,224	14.4
3	Claude A. Fuller (D)	18,417	65.3
	J. S. Thompson (R)	9,796	34.7
4	William B. Cravens (D)	25,902	100.0
5	David D. Terry (D)	26,102	100.0
6	John L. McClellan (D)	25,411	100.0
7	Wade Kitchens (D)	20,117	95.4

CALIFORNIA

	Candidates	Votes	%
1	Clarence F. Lea (D)	58,073	53.8
	Nelson B. Van Matre (R)	48,647	45.1
2	Harry L. Englebright (R-D-PROG)	51,416	100.0
3	Frank H. Buck (D-R)	93,110	90.4
	Walter Schaefer	5,310	5.2
4	Franck R. Havenner (D & PROG)	64,063	58.5
	Florence P. Kahn (R)	43,805	40.0
5	Richard J. Welch (R-D-PROG)	82,910	94.8
	Lawrence Ross (COM)	4,545	5.2
6	Albert E. Carter (R-D)	103,712	91.0
	Clarence E. Rust (SOC)	8,247	7.2
7	John H. Tolan (D)	69,463	59.8
	Charles W. Fisher (R)	46,647	40.2
8	John Joseph McGrath (D & PROG)	78,557	57.6
	Alonzo L. Baker (R)	57,808	42.4
9	Bertrand W. Gearhart (R-D)	82,360	97.0
10	Henry E. Stubbs (D)	72,367	69.5
	George R. Bliss (R)	31,700	30.4
11	John Steven McGroarty (D)	69,679	50.5
	Carl Hinshaw (R)	54,914	39.8
	Robert S. Funk (PROG)	12,340	8.9
12	H. Jerry Voorhis (D)	62,034	53.7
	Frederick F. Houser (R)	53,445	46.3
13	Charles Kramer (D-R)	119,251	89.4
	Floyd Seaman	6,946	5.2
14	Thomas F. Ford (D)	63,365	61.0
	William D. Campbell (R)	25,497	24.6
	Albert L. Johnson (PROG)	12,874	12.4
15	John M. Costello (D & PROG)	99,107	69.0
	Ernest Walker Sawyer (R)	44,559	31.0
16	John F. Dockweiler (D)	90,986	57.7
	Raymond V. Darby (R)	66,583	42.2
17	Charles J. Colden (D)	68,189	71.9
	Leonard Roach (R)	24,981	26.3
18	Byron N. Scott (D)	61,415	58.9
	James F. Collins (R)	42,748	41.0
19	Harry R. Sheppard (D)	70,339	53.8
	Sam L. Collins (R)	59,071	45.2

	Candidates	Votes	%
20	Edouard V. M. Izac (D)	59,208	56.4
	Ed P. Sample (R)	44,925	42.8

COLORADO

	Candidates	Votes	%
1	Lawrence Lewis (D)	100,704	69.0
	Harry Zimmerhackel (R)	41,574	28.5
2	Fred Cummings (D)	66,420	53.3
	George H. Bradfield (R)	57,145	45.8
3	John A. Martin (D)	74,013	60.2
	J. Arthur Phelps (R)	48,871	39.8
4	Edward T. Taylor (D)	42,010	65.5
	John S. Woody (R)	22,175	34.6

CONNECTICUT

	Candidates	Votes	%
1	Herman P. Kopplemann (D)	101,766	57.9
	Walter E. Batterson (R)	66,005	37.6
2	William J. Fitzgerald (D)	55,369	50.9
	William L. Higgins (R)	50,369	46.3
3	James A. Shanley (D)	77,295	54.6
	John F. Lynch (R)	57,243	40.4
4	Alfred N. Phillips Jr. (D)	80,875	50.0
	Schuyler Merritt (R)	67,768	41.9
5	J. Joseph Smith (D)	55,897	58.6
	J. Warren Upson (R)	39,230	41.1
AL	William M. Citron (D)	371,572	53.9
	Francis Pallotti (R)	282,618	41.0

DELAWARE

	Candidates	Votes	%
AL	William F. Allen (D)	65,485	51.7
	John George Stewart (R)	55,664	44.0

FLORIDA

	Candidates	Votes	%
1	J. Hardin Peterson (D)	61,855	74.5
	B. L. Hamner (R)	21,215	25.5
2	R. A. Green (D)	47,520	100.0
3	Millard Caldwell (D)	34,239	100.0
4	J. Mark Wilcox (D)	46,854	70.6
	Thomas E. Swanson (R)	19,515	29.4
5	Joe Hendricks (D)	42,937	79.9
	C. F. Batchelder (R)	10,802	20.1

GEORGIA

	Candidates	Votes	%
1	Hugh Peterson Jr. (D)	25,846	100.0
2	E. E. Cox (D)	21,405	100.0
3	Stephen Pace (D)	25,613	100.0
4	E. M. Owen (D)	24,643	100.0
5	Robert Ramspeck (D)	35,540	89.4
	H. H. Alexander (R)	4,213	10.6
6	Carl Vinson (D)	20,595	100.0
7	Malcolm C. Tarver (D)	31,343	92.6
	L. Mitchell Johnson (R)	2,493	7.4
8	Braswell Deen (D)	24,695	94.9
	Ben J. Ford (R)	1,320	5.1
9	B. Frank Whelchel (D)	23,682	75.4
	John M. Johnson (R)	7,739	24.6
10	Paul Brown (D)	27,147	100.0

IDAHO

	Candidates	Votes	%
1	Compton I. White (D)	58,941	70.3
	John S. Heckathorn (R)	24,959	29.8
2	D. Worth Clark (D)	67,238	60.5
	Henry C. Dworshak (R)	43,834	39.5

ILLINOIS

	Candidates	Votes	%
1	Arthur W. Mitchell (D)	35,376	55.1
	Oscar De Priest (R)	28,640	44.6
2	Raymond S. McKeough (D)	163,198	55.6
	P. H. Moynihan (R)	130,197	44.4
3	Edward A. Kelly (D)	156,425	59.3

	Candidates	Votes	%
	Frank M. Fulton (R)	106,300	40.3
4	Harry P. Beam (D)	69,931	80.8
	Irene A. Tomas (R)	16,591	19.2
5	Adolph J. Sabath (D)	35,019	77.4
	Max Price (R)	10,252	22.6
6	Thomas J. O'Brien (D)	204,548	65.5
	Frederick A. Virkus (R)	107,649	34.5
7	Leonard W. Schuetz (D)	248,835	59.2
	James C. Moreland (R)	158,755	37.7
8	Leo Kocialkowski (D)	34,452	78.6
	Edw. Richard Piszatowski (R)	8,945	20.4
9	James McAndrews (D)	60,307	59.2
	Bertha Baur (R)	41,587	40.8
10	Ralph E. Church (R)	158,497	51.4
	Charles J. Wightman (D)	140,225	45.5
11	Chauncey W. Reed (R)	99,027	56.0
	John R. Barber (D)	77,938	44.0
12	Noah M. Mason (R)	69,721	51.6
	D. O. Thompson (D)	58,263	43.1
	D. S. Gishwiller (TOWN OAP)	7,203	5.3
13	Leo E. Allen (R)	52,495	58.4
	David L. Trunck (D)	37,346	41.6
14	Chester Thompson (D)	58,890	54.4
	Clinton Searle (R)	49,250	45.6
15	Lewis L. Boyer (D)	54,703	49.4
	Joe E. Anderson (R)	53,531	48.3
16	Everett M. Dirksen (R)	68,964	53.2
	Charles C. Dickman (D)	60,559	46.8
17	Leslie C. Arends (R)	46,646	52.6
	Frank Gillespie (D)	42,071	47.4
18	James A. Meeks (D)	61,286	53.8
	Hugh M. Luckey (R)	52,730	46.3
19	Hugh M. Rigney (D)	77,446	55.7
	William H. Wheat (R)	61,535	44.3
20	Scott W. Lucas (D)	48,128	56.7
	Harry C. Montgomery (R)	36,732	43.3
21	Frank W. Fries (D)	62,769	51.7
	Frank M. Ramey (R)	58,573	48.2
22	Edwin M. Schaefer (D)	96,589	59.1
	Jesse R. Brown (R)	66,960	40.9
23	Laurence F. Arnold (D)	62,044	55.2
	Ben O. Sumner (R)	50,354	44.8
24	Claude V. Parsons (D)	45,740	51.7
	W. A. Spence (R)	42,764	48.3
25	Kent E. Keller (D)	68,995	53.9
	J. Lester Buford (R)	59,101	46.1
AL	Lewis M. Long (D)	2,062,886✓	
	Edwin V. Champion (D)	2,032,432✓	
	Rodney H. Brandon (R)	1,568,552	
	John T. Dempsey (R)	1,564,889	
	Severin H. Hanson (UN PROG)	83,886	
	Rad Burnett (UN PROG)	81,551	
	Ina M. White (SOC)	7,817	
	Nate Egnor (SOC)	7,651	
	Mary Morgan Williams (P)	3,269	
	Frank Earl Herrick (P)	3,262	
	Edward K. Schooley (SOC LAB)	2,374	
	Mathilda M. Deavers (SOC LAB)	2,235	

INDIANA

	Candidates	Votes	%
1	William T. Schulte (D)	68,210	66.4
	Fred F. Schultz (R)	34,259	33.3
2	Charles A. Halleck (R)	73,072	51.5
	Hugh A. Barnhart (D)	68,318	48.2
3	Samuel B. Pettingill (D)	71,315	56.2
	Andrew J. Hickey (R)	52,462	41.4
4	James I. Farley (D)	72,210	55.2
	David Hogg (R)	58,519	44.8
5	Glenn Griswold (D)	70,854	52.6
	Benjamin J. Brown (R)	63,517	47.2
6	Virginia A. Jenckes (D)	82,096	54.9
	Noble J. Johnson (R)	66,942	44.8

Candidates	Votes	%
7 Arthur Greenwood (D)	81,901	53.8
Gerald W. Landis (R)	69,928	45.9
8 John W. Boehne Jr. (D)	89,548	62.6
Charles F. Werner (R)	50,590	35.4
9 Eugene B. Crowe (D)	74,486	54.2
Chester A. Davis (R)	62,714	45.7
10 Finly H. Gray (D)	73,547	52.6
Clarence M. Brown (R)	66,299	47.4
11 William H. Larrabee (D)	80,856	59.4
Don Roberts (R)	53,801	39.5
12 Louis Ludlow (D)	77,510	57.7
Homer Elliott (R)	54,885	40.9

IOWA

Candidates	Votes	%
1 Edward C. Eicher (D)	55,721	51.0
John N. Calhoun (R)	53,474	49.0
2 William S. Jacobsen (D)	70,923	54.6
Charles Penningroth (R)	55,255	42.5
3 John W. Gwynne (R)	53,928	53.2
A. C. Willford (D)	47,391	46.8
4 Fred Biermann (D)	56,308	50.6
Henry O. Talle (R)	51,805	46.6
5 Lloyd Thurston (R)	63,802	51.5
Kenneth F. Baldridge (R)	58,971	47.6
6 Cassius C. Dowell (R)	63,026	52.4
Harry B. Dunlap (D)	55,975	46.5
7 Otha D. Wearin (D)	61,398	50.4
Henry K. Peterson (R)	59,834	49.2
8 Fred C. Gilchrist (R)	56,076	52.5
Ray Murray (D)	48,403	45.3
9 Vincent F. Harrington (D)	63,995	53.5
Fred B. Wolf (R)	53,675	44.9

KANSAS

Candidates	Votes	%
1 William P. Lambertson (R)	66,158	58.3
Howard S. Miller (D)	47,303	41.7
2 Ulysses S. Guyer (R)	72,038	53.3
David C. Doten (D)	60,049	44.5
3 Edward W. Patterson (D)	55,541	48.4
Harold McGugin (R)	52,235	45.5
L. P. Beard (I)	6,921	6.0
4 Edward H. Rees (R)	51,732	54.5
C. D. Hill (D)	42,818	45.1
5 John M. Houston (D)	62,501	60.0
J. B. Patterson (R)	41,656	40.0
6 Frank Carlson (R)	61,669	52.0
Arthur Connelly (D)	56,850	48.0
7 Clifford R. Hope (R)	66,553	56.0
Thomas A. Ralston (D)	52,370	44.0

KENTUCKY

Candidates	Votes	%
1 Noble J. Gregory (D)	58,265	71.9
R. N. Brumfield (R)	22,757	28.1
2 Glover H. Cary (D)	70,949*	64.0
Claude E. Smith (R)	39,887	36.0
3 Emmet O'Neal (D)	85,034	60.3
W. A. Armstrong (R)	52,600	37.3
4 Edward W. Creal (D)	54,616	59.0
Stanley Jaggers (R)	37,979	41.0
5 Brent Spence (D)	57,842	66.7
Ervin L. Bramlage (R)	25,011	28.8
6 Virgil Chapman (D)	70,094	57.9
A. R. Anderson (R)	48,771	40.3
7 Andrew J. May (D)	40,366	55.9
John B. Mollette (R)	31,865	44.1
8 Fred M. Vinson (D)	60,474	58.7
W. Hoffman Wood (R)	42,507	41.3
9 John M. Robsion (R)	67,199	61.6
George L. Tye (D)	41,958	38.4

LOUISIANA

Candidates	Votes	%
1 Joachim O. Fernandez (D)	61,142	100.0
2 Paul H. Maloney (D)	65,345	100.0
3 Robert L. Mouton (D)	20,605	100.0
4 Overton Brooks (D)	26,152	99.9
5 Newton V. Mills (D)	29,144	100.0

Candidates	Votes	%
6 John K. Griffith (D)	34,908	100.0
7 Rene L. DeRouen (D)	27,563	100.0
8 A. Leonard Allen (D)	27,071	100.0

MAINE

Candidates	Votes	%
1 James C. Oliver (R)	60,565	57.9
Simon M. Hamlin (D)	44,106	42.1
2 Clyde H. Smith (R)	53,822	51.6
Ernest L. McLean (D)	38,986	37.4
J. C. Leckemby (IR)	8,197	7.9
3 Ralph O. Brewster (R)	56,044	60.8
Wallace F. Mabee (D)	36,103	39.2

MARYLAND

Candidates	Votes	%
1 T. Alan Goldsborough (D)	38,705	60.0
O. Straughn Lloyd (R)	25,780	40.0
2 William P. Cole Jr. (D)	98,515	61.7
Henry C. Whiteford (R)	60,003	37.6
3 Vincent L. Palmisano (D)	37,446	60.5
John Philip Hill (R)	23,941	38.7
4 Ambrose J. Kennedy (D)	46,132	51.5
Daniel Ellison (R)	39,653	44.3
5 Stephen Warfield Gambrill (D)	47,145	64.7
Roscoe C. Rowe (R)	25,036	34.4
6 David J. Lewis (D)	53,504	56.4
Harry W. Le Gore (R)	40,823	43.0

MASSACHUSETTS

Candidates	Votes	%
1 Allen T. Treadway (R)	60,043	50.5
Owen Johnson (D)	52,342	44.0
2 Charles R. Clason (R)	57,618	49.0
Agnes C. Reavey (D)	52,197	44.3
3 Joseph E. Casey (D)	64,960	54.1
Bernard W. Doyle (R)	54,154	45.1
4 Pehr G. Holmes (R)	61,624	51.5
Edward A. Ryan (D)	56,770	47.4
5 Edith Nourse Rogers (R)	90,845	62.8
Daniel J. Coughlin (D)	48,701	33.7
6 George J. Bates (R)	79,145	68.6
John E. Taffe (TOWN-SJD)	36,171	31.4
7 William P. Connery Jr. (D)	76,521	59.1
C. F. Nelson Pratt (R)	51,009	39.4
8 Arthur D. Healey (D)	60,211	52.6
William S. Howe (R)	46,446	40.5
Nelson F. Wright (UN)	6,010	5.3
9 Robert Luce (R)	70,852	50.6
Richard M. Russell (D)	61,582	44.0
10 George Holden Tinkham (R)	74,251	59.5
William F. Madden (D)	39,112	31.4
John McLaren (TOWN-C-L)	11,349	9.1
11 John P. Higgins (D)	53,129	81.3
Joseph M. De Napoli (R)	8,523	13.1
12 John W. McCormack (D)	78,711	68.7
Albert P. McCulloch (FACP R)	35,827	31.3
13 Richard B. Wigglesworth (R)	76,793	58.5
Harry J. Dowd (D)	54,576	41.5
14 Joseph W. Martin Jr. (R)	58,758	53.3
Arthur E. Seagrave (D)	38,609	35.0
Lawrence O. Witter (UN)	12,872	11.7
15 Charles L. Gifford (R)	58,355	50.1
John D. W. Bodfish (D)	42,538	36.5
John Henry McNeece (TOWN SJ)	12,419	10.7

MICHIGAN

Candidates	Votes	%
1 George G. Sadowski (D)	72,713	80.4
Charles A. Roxborough (R)	17,265	19.1
2 Earl C. Michener (R)	53,845	51.7
Charles E. Downing (D)	50,238	48.3
3 Paul W. Shafer (R)	54,767	51.8
Rosslyn L. Sowers (D)	50,956	48.2
4 Clare E. Hoffman (R)	49,641	50.5
Guy M. Tyler (D)	44,365	45.1
5 Carl E. Mapes (R)	49,860	48.2
Thomas F. McAllister (D)	48,998	47.4
6 Andrew J. Transue (D)	72,556	57.7

Candidates	Votes	%
William W. Blackney (R)	53,140	42.3
7 Jesse P. Wolcott (R)	54,693	59.9
Albert A. Wagner (D)	36,462	39.9
8 Fred L. Crawford (R)	45,379	46.8
Michael J. Hart (D)	44,309	45.7
Clarence J. Brainerd (UN)	7,249	7.6
9 Albert J. Engel (R)	40,675	50.2
Jack Hay (D)	40,095	49.5
10 Roy O. Woodruff (R)	41,997	57.6
William J. Kelly (D)	30,784	42.3
11 John Luecke (D)	44,528	52.8
Herbert J. Rushton (R)	39,602	46.9
12 Frank E. Hook (D)	46,284	54.7
W. Frank James (R)	37,714	44.6
13 George D. O'Brien (D)	63,479	55.1
Clarence J. McLeod (R)	49,910	43.3
14 Louis C. Rabaut (D)	66,791	55.9
Frederick M. Alger Jr. (R)	41,130	34.4
Edgar J. Auclair (THIRD)	10,660	8.9
15 John D. Dingell (D)	68,264	57.5
Nathaniel H. Goldstick (R)	49,443	41.6
16 John Lesinski (D)	56,589	58.3
Clyde M. Ford (R)	35,223	36.3
17 George A. Dondero (R)	51,603	47.7
Draper Allen (D)	50,463	46.6
Maynard Seibert (UN)	5,593	5.2

MINNESOTA

Candidates	Votes	%
1 August H. Andresen (R)	60,980	50.7
Chester Watson (F-LAB)	27,753	23.1
Richard W. Morin (D)	26,058	21.7
2 Elmer J. Ryan (D)	47,567	39.2
Henry Arens (F-LAB)	39,489	32.6
Christian J. Laurisch (R)	34,268	28.3
3 Henry G. Teigan (F-LAB)	58,023	46.3
Milton Lindbloom (R)	40,775	32.5
Martin A. Hogan (D)	15,170	12.1
Mrs. Frank McConville (I)	11,476	9.2
4 Melvin J. Maas (R)	48,399	38.3
Howard Y. Williams (F-LAB)	48,039	38.0
A. B. C. Doherty (D)	28,957	22.9
5 Dewey W. Johnson (F-LAB)	67,349	47.8
Walter H. Newton (R)	58,110	41.3
M. J. Dillon (D)	15,337	10.9
6 Harold Knutson (R)	55,504	46.1
C. A. Ryan (F-LAB)	47,707	39.6
Joseph H. Kowalkowski (D)	17,235	14.3
7 Paul John Kvale (F-LAB)	56,310	49.7
H. Carl Andersen (R)	37,190	32.8
C. L. Cole (D)	19,878	17.5
8 John T. Bernard (F-LAB)	69,788	56.4
William A. Pittenger (R)	53,914	43.6
9 Richard Thompson Buckler (F-LAB)	48,256	48.5
Elmer A. Haugen (R)	31,181	31.3
Martin O. Brandon (D)	20,165	20.3

MISSISSIPPI

Candidates	Votes	%
1 John E. Rankin (D)	19,208	98.0
2 Wall Doxey (D)	13,632	98.9
3 William M. Whittington (D)	15,688	97.5
4 A. L. Ford (D)	14,444	100.0
5 Ross A. Collins (D)	26,150	99.4
6 William M. Colmer (D)	25,385	100.0
7 Daniel R. McGehee (D)	32,004	97.5

MISSOURI

Candidates	Votes	%
1 Milton A. Romjue (D)	68,447	55.4
James G. Morgan (R)	55,032	44.5
2 William L. Nelson (D)	81,293	58.1
O. B. Whitaker (R)	58,610	41.9
3 Richard M. Duncan (D)	86,199	58.8
Miles Elliott (R)	60,411	41.2
4 C. Jasper Bell (D)	103,492	74.6
Paul R. Byrum (R)	35,081	25.3
5 Joseph B. Shannon (D)	113,946	73.7
Lowell R. Johnson (R)	40,546	26.2

Candidates	Votes	%
6 Reuben T. Wood (D)	74,202	53.0
Thomas H. Douglas (R)	65,679	46.9
7 Dewey Short (R)	73,861	52.5
Gene Frost (D)	66,695	47.4
8 Clyde Williams (D)	65,780	56.6
C. M. Becker (R)	50,216	43.2
9 Clarence Cannon (D)	62,623	61.8
Herschel Schooley (R)	38,706	38.2
10 Orville Zimmerman (D)	65,168	61.4
Linder Deimund (R)	40,860	38.5
11 Thomas C. Hennings (D)	94,330	61.1
L. C. Dyer (R)	59,536	38.6
12 C. Arthur Anderson (D)	125,333	56.2
Harry P. Rosecan (R)	97,151	43.5
13 John J. Cochran (D)	85,630	68.2
Harry E. Wiehe (R)	39,714	31.6

MONTANA

1 Jerry J. O'Connell (D)	54,816	63.4
H. L. Hart (R)	31,231	36.1
2 James F. O'Connor (D)	79,190	64.9
T. S. Stockdal (R)	42,454	34.8

NEBRASKA

1 Henry C. Luckey (D)	61,104	53.3
Ernest B. Perry (R)	52,137	45.5
2 Charles F. McLaughlin (D)	66,833	62.0
Jackson B. Chase (R)	38,511	35.7
3 Karl Stefan (R)	83,587	70.5
John Havekost (D)	31,967	27.0
4 Charles Binderup (D)	66,763	55.3
Arthur J. Denney (R)	51,524	42.7
5 Harry B. Coffee (D)	62,714	58.3
Cullen N. Wright (R)	36,396	33.8
Frank Brown (UN)	7,912	7.4

NEVADA

AL James G. Scrugham (D)	25,575	58.4
Ed C. Peterson (R)	11,785	26.9
Harry H. Austin (I)	6,444	14.7

NEW HAMPSHIRE

1 Arthur B. Jenks (R)	51,920‡	50.0
Alphonse Roy (D)	51,370	49.5
2 Charles W. Tobey (R)	53,706	53.7
Daniel J. Hagerty (D)	45,437	45.4

NEW JERSEY

1 Charles A. Wolverton (R)	84,980	51.8
Guy Lee Jr. (D)	75,631	46.1
2 Elmer H. Wene (D)	55,580	50.0
Isaac Bacharach (R)	50,958	45.8
3 William H. Sutphin (D)	68,189	50.6
Albert B. Hermann (R)	64,237	47.7
4 D. Lane Powers (R)	58,258	52.3
Joseph A. Daly (D)	52,735	47.4
5 Charles A. Eaton (R)	65,459	50.9
Charles S. Mackenzie (D)	62,904	48.9
6 Donald H. McLean (R)	62,525	50.2
Frank Moore (D)	61,351	49.3
7 J. Parnell Thomas (R)	58,021	51.6
H. P. J. Hoffmann (D)	54,163	48.2
8 George N. Seger (R)	57,778	50.8
Leo V. Becker (D)	52,430	46.1
9 Edward A. Kenney (D)	67,874	53.9
Lawrence A. Cavinato (R)	57,547	45.7
10 Fred A. Hartley Jr. (R)	52,197	50.2
Lindsay H. Rudd (D)	51,532	49.6
11 Edward L. O'Neill (D)	54,402	52.6
Peter A. Cavicchia (R)	48,672	47.1
12 Frank W. Towey Jr. (D)	54,688	49.9
Frederick R. Lehlbach (R)	54,363	49.6
13 Mary T. Norton (D)	93,702	75.8
John J. Grossi (R)	27,615	22.3
14 Edward J. Hart (D)	96,053	79.3

Candidates	Votes	%
Fred G. Tauber (R)	23,985	19.8

NEW MEXICO

Candidates	Votes	%
AL John J. Dempsey (D)	106,951	63.1
M. Ralph Brown (R)	62,375	36.8

NEW YORK

1 Robert L. Bacon (R)	185,891	55.2
Gerald Morrell (D, UN)	144,562	42.9
2 William B. Barry (D)	222,217	69.2
Allen E. R. Craig (R)	90,437	28.2
3 Joseph L. Pfeifer (D)	40,640	80.3
Jerome G. Licari (R)	8,680	17.2
4 Thomas H. Cullen (D)	43,917	77.7
William G. Nolan (R)	11,594	20.5
5 Marcellus H. Evans (D)	63,661	64.9
Frank A. Dalton (R)	30,995	31.6
6 Andrew L. Somers (D)	126,024	69.1
Donald C. Strachan (R)	43,862	24.1
7 John J. Delaney (D)	46,154	75.5
Joseph M. Aimee (R)	12,085	19.8
8 Donald L. O'Toole (D)	217,568	72.2
Nathan Greenbaum (R)	64,002	21.2
9 Eugene J. Keogh (D)	91,803	65.6
Robert E. Hower (R)	42,456	30.4
10 Emanuel Celler (D)	47,872	68.8
Mortimer H. Michaels (R)	17,643	25.4
11 James A. O'Leary (D)	56,307	66.7
Archibald Cooper (R)	25,553	30.3
12 Samuel Dickstein (D)	19,280	86.5
Joseph Levine (R)	2,136	9.6
13 Christopher D. Sullivan (D)	20,456	79.7
Vincent A. Marsicano (R)	4,254	16.6
14 William I. Sirovich (D)	25,528	61.5
Emanuel A. Manginelli (R)	13,059	31.4
15 John J. Boylan (D)	32,435	77.5
Arthur Wyler (R)	7,953	19.0
16 John J. O'Connor (D)	33,082	60.0
J. Homer Cudmore (R)	17,832	32.3
17 Theodore A. Peyser (D)	48,611	52.1
Frederick F. Greenman (R)	41,430	44.4
18 Martin J. Kennedy (D)	36,317	72.9
William I. Cohen (R)	11,851	23.8
19 Sol Bloom (D)	74,160	69.5
William S. Bennet (R)	24,835	23.3
20 James J. Lanzetta (D)	18,772	51.2
Vito Marcantonio (R, ALL PP)	17,212	46.9
21 Joseph A. Gavagan (D)	114,626	73.7
Melinda Alexander (R)	31,504	20.3
22 Edwin W. Curley (D)	49,495	77.6
Victor Santini (R)	12,220	19.2
23 Charles A. Buckley (D)	202,730	74.3
Isaac F. Becker (R)	51,623	18.9
24 James M. Fitzpatrick (D)	183,823	65.2
Oliver C. Carpenter (R)	82,759	29.4
25 Charles D. Millard (R)	97,953	56.3
Homer A. Stebbins (D)	73,132	42.0
26 Hamilton Fish (R)	72,302	58.5
Alpha R. Whiton (D, AM LAB)	49,137	39.7
27 Philip A. Goodwin (R)	61,748	57.2
D. Roy Shafer (D)	44,220	40.9
28 William T. Byrne (D)	85,004	58.4
Colin D. Macrae (R)	52,498	36.1
29 E. Harold Cluett (R)	74,644	61.3
John J. Nyhoff (D)	44,567	36.6
30 Frank Crowther (R)	57,482	51.6
Earl E. Cummins (D, AM LAB)	51,590	46.3
31 Bertrand H. Snell (R)	54,160	58.8
George C. Owens (D)	31,752	34.5
Jesse W. Williams (TOWN)	6,185	6.7
32 Francis D. Culkin (R)	65,761	66.1
Paul J. Woodard (D)	32,318	32.5
33 Fred J. Douglas (R)	63,281	53.1
Fred J. Sisson (D, AM LAB)	45,969	38.6
William D. Arquint	8,479	7.1
34 Bert Lord (R)	75,580	60.6
John T. Buckley (D)	47,857	38.4

Candidates	Votes	%
35 Clarence E. Hancock (R)	85,702	54.3
Arthur R. Perrin (D)	59,540	37.8
Robert H. Anderson (YP)	9,798	6.2
36 John Taber (R)	61,271	59.2
William A. Aiken (D)	32,318	31.2
John E. DuBois (TOWN)	8,003	7.7
37 W. Sterling Cole (R)	73,018	64.5
Paul Smith (D)	38,560	34.1
38 George B. Kelly (D)	82,708	51.6
Joseph Fritsch Jr (R)	72,910	45.5
39 James W. Wadsworth (R)	66,869	58.5
Donald J. Corbett (D)	41,699	36.5
40 Walter Gresham Andrews (R)	94,682	52.5
John L. Beyer (D)	68,241	37.8
Melvin L. Payne (UN&SQD)	13,593	7.5
41 Alfred F. Belter (D, AM LAB)	55,508	50.4
Fred Kohler (R)	45,113	41.0
42 James M. Mead (D, AM LAB)	57,132	56.4
Eugene D. Crooker (R)	32,395	32.0
Anthony Fitzgibbons (UN)	6,840	6.8
43 Daniel A. Reed (R)	56,129	54.9
Clare Barnes (D)	44,585	43.6
AL Matthew J. Merritt (D)	3,013,931✓	
Caroline O'Day (D)	2,992,057✓	
Natalie F. Couch (R)	2,078,803	
Anthony J. Contiguglia (R)	2,028,865	
Edna Mitchell Blue (SOC)	102,133	
Frank R. Crosswaith (SOC)	101,184	
Roy Hudson (COM)	69,336	
Simon W. Gerson (COM)	68,868	

NORTH CAROLINA

1 Lindsay C. Warren (D)	35,333	90.2
John Wilkinson (R)	3,833	9.8
2 John H. Kerr (D)	37,771	95.2
3 Graham A. Barden (D)	34,524	74.3
Julian T. Gaskill (R)	11,967	25.7
4 Harold D. Cooley (D)	56,703	76.8
A. I. Ferree (R)	17,179	23.3
5 Frank W. Hancock Jr. (D)	48,500	73.3
Edward F. Butler (R)	17,671	26.7
6 William B. Umstead (D)	46,329	69.8
Willis H. Slane (R)	20,092	30.3
7 J. Bayard Clark (D)	41,549	83.2
W. C. Downing (R)	8,396	16.8
8 J. Walter Lambeth (D)	54,846	64.1
Kyle Hayes (R)	30,699	35.9
9 Robert L. Doughton (D)	60,223	64.8
Watt Gragg (R)	32,659	35.2
10 Alfred L. Bulwinkle (D)	79,059	65.0
Calvin R. Edney (R)	42,650	35.0
11 Zebulon Weaver (D)	73,645	63.0
Clyde H. Jarrett (R)	43,346	37.1

NORTH DAKOTA

AL William Lemke (R)	131,117✓	
Usher L. Burdick (R)	115,913✓	
Henry Holt (D)	100,609	
J. J. Nygaard (D)	89,713	
I. J. Moe (I)	3,310	
P. H. Miller (I)	3,273	
E. A. Johansson (I)	2,697	
Jasper Haaland (I)	540	
W. D. Webster (I)	461	

OHIO

1 Joseph A. Dixon (D)	71,935	52.1
John B. Hollister (R)	66,082	47.9
2 Herbert S. Bigelow (D)	67,213	51.8
William E. Hess (R)	62,546	48.2
3 Byron B. Harlan (D)	101,115	55.9
Robert N. Brumbaugh (R)	70,023	38.7
Leonidas E. Speer (I)	9,886	5.5
4 Frank L. Kloeb (D)	61,927	53.7
Robert W. Turner (R)	53,352	46.3
5 Frank C. Kniffin (D)	41,693	53.1
Stephen S. Beard (R)	33,212	42.3

	Candidates	Votes	%
6	James G. Polk (D)	54,904	54.6
	Emory F. Smith (R)	45,733	45.4
7	Arthur W. Aleshire (D)	68,456	50.4
	L. T. Marshall (R)	67,454	49.6
8	Brooks Fletcher (D)	49,668	53.9
	Grant E. Mouser Jr. (R)	42,565	46.2
9	John F. Hunter (D)	75,737	56.3
	Raymond E. Hilderbrand (R)	55,043	40.9
10	Thomas A. Jenkins (R)	46,965	57.7
	O. J. Kleffner (D)	34,477	42.3
11	Harold K. Claypool (D)	41,773	53.4
	L. P. Mooney (R)	33,249	42.5
12	Arthur P. Lamneck (D)	88,222	57.7
	Grant P. Ward (R)	64,766	42.3
13	Dudley A. White (R)	46,623	47.3
	Forrest R. Black (D)	39,042	39.6
	Merrell E. Martin (I)	12,959	13.1
14	Dow W. Harter (D)	118,659	58.1
	Carl D. Sheppard (R)	77,039	37.7
15	Robert T. Secrest (D)	53,263	55.7
	Kenneth C. Ray (R)	42,053	44.0
16	William R. Thom (D)	89,911	59.2
	H. Ross Ake (R)	54,979	36.2
17	William A. Ashbrook (D)	69,446	57.7
	James A. Glenn (R)	48,270	40.1
18	Lawrence E. Imhoff (D)	83,052	60.6
	Earl R. Lewis (R)	54,119	39.5
19	Michael J. Kirwan (D)	93,636	58.4
	John G. Cooper (R)	65,926	41.1
20	Martin L. Sweeney (D)	54,295	54.4
	Blase A. Buonpane (R)	23,367	23.4
	John L. Mihelich (I)	22,158	22.2
21	Robert Crosser (D)	70,596	74.8
	Harry C. Gahn (R)	23,811	25.2
22	Anthony A. Fleger (D)	131,250	51.3
	Chester C. Bolton (R)	124,446	48.7
AL	John McSweeney (D)	1,553,059✓	
	Harold G. Mosier (D)	1,493,053✓	
	George H. Bender (R)	1,226,247	
	L. L. Marshall (R)	1,121,370	
	William C. Sandberg (COM)	8,945	

Special Elections

	Candidates	Votes	%
11	Peter F. Hammond (D)	41,310	56.5
	John L. Moriarty (R)	31,864	43.6
AL	Daniel S. Earhart (D)	1,479,284	58.3
	Benson Ogier (R)	1,057,473	41.7

OKLAHOMA

	Candidates	Votes	%
1	Wesley E. Disney (D)	81,286	57.7
	Jo O. Ferguson (R)	58,983	41.9
2	Jack Nichols (D)	45,724	63.5
	V. S. Cannon (R)	26,310	36.5
3	Wilburn Cartwright (D)	58,261	79.9
	John D. Morrison (R)	14,672	20.1
4	Lyle H. Boren (D)	63,306	72.7
	Fred L. Patrick (R)	23,615	27.1
5	Robert P. Hill (D)	78,873	70.2
	John William Mee (R)	33,071	29.4
6	Jed Johnson (D)	52,373	72.8
	L. M. Gensman (R)	19,495	27.1
7	Sam C. Massingale (D)	46,940	83.3
	Clyde J. Matherly (R)	9,396	16.7
8	Phil Ferguson (D)	47,497	58.9
	T. J. Sargent (R)	32,858	40.7
AL	Will Rogers (D)	475,567	70.7
	John C. Burns (R)	193,487	28.8

OREGON

	Candidates	Votes	%
1	James W. Mott (R)	114,073	65.6
	E. W. Kirkpatrick (D)	59,788	34.4
2	Walter M. Pierce (D)	46,412	68.0
	Roy W. Ritner (R)	21,813	32.0
3	Nan Wood Honeyman (D)	78,624	53.2
	William A. Ekwall (R)	45,872	31.0
	John A. Jeffrey (I)	21,848	14.8

PENNSYLVANIA

	Candidates	Votes	%
1	Leon Sacks (D, D-OP)	67,276	64.6
	Harry C. Ransley (R, R-OP)	34,813	33.4
2	James P. McGranery (D, D-OP)	65,779	59.8
	William H. Wilson (R, R-OP)	41,267	37.5
3	Michael J. Bradley (D)	75,445	60.8
	Clare Gerald Fenerty (R, R-OP)	48,035	38.7
4	J. Burrwood Daly (D, D-OP)	77,406	62.8
	Boies Penrose Jr. (R, R-OP)	41,545	33.7
5	Frank J. G. Dorsey (D, D-OP)	72,210	56.6
	James J. Connolly (R, R-OP)	46,238	36.2
6	Michael J. Stack (D, D-OP)	84,487	61.1
	George F. Holmes (R, R-OP)	51,892	37.5
7	Ira Walton Drew (D, D-OP)	77,949	51.8
	George P. Darrow (R)	71,749	47.7
8	James Wolfenden (R)	73,335	52.2
	Howard Kirk (D, D-OP)	66,119	47.1
9	Oliver W. Frey (D)	56,108	51.0
	Theodore R. Gardner (R)	50,361	45.8
10	J. Roland Kinzer (R)	72,181	52.7
	H. Clay Burkholder (D)	62,768	45.8
11	Patrick J. Boland (D)	75,905	57.5
	John J. Owens (R)	50,123	38.0
12	J. Harold Flannery (D)	99,161	53.7
	C. Murray Turpin (R)	84,902	46.0
13	James H. Gildea (D, D-OP)	83,662	54.6
	James H. Kirchner (R)	68,772	44.9
14	Guy L. Moser (D, D-OP)	46,192	53.2
	Charles E. Roth (R)	28,001	32.3
15	Albert G. Rutherford (R)	55,268	54.3
	C. Elmer Dietrich (D)	45,808	45.0
16	Robert F. Rich (R)	54,040	51.8
	Paul A. Rothfuss (D, D-OP)	49,249	47.2
17	J. William Ditter (R)	67,850	53.9
	George H. Bartholomew (D)	55,083	43.8
18	Benjamin K. Focht (R)	49,243	54.0
	John M. Keichline (D)	41,881	46.0
19	Guy J. Swope (D)	73,374	51.4
	Isaac H. Doutrich (R, R-OP)	67,884	47.5
20	Benjamin Jarrett (R)	58,738	48.4
	D. J. Driscoll (D)	56,941	46.9
21	Francis E. Walter (D)	56,566	56.8
	William R. Coyle (R)	39,537	39.7
22	Harry L. Haines (D)	66,306	54.7
	Frank S. Magill (R, R-OP)	49,273	40.6
23	Don Gingery (D)	53,629	48.9
	Benjamin C. Jones (R)	46,726	42.6
24	J. Buell Snyder (D)	62,009	60.5
	Davis W. Henderson (R)	40,067	39.1
25	Charles I. Faddis (D)	61,988	65.5
	John C. Judson (R)	30,208	31.9
26	Charles R. Eckert (D)	71,332	56.0
	Orville Brown (R)	52,925	41.5
27	Joseph Gray (D)	83,908	54.1
	Walter E. Morris (R)	67,809	43.7
28	Robert G. Allen (D)	67,169	60.2
	James B. Weaver (R, R-OP)	42,259	37.9
29	Charles N. Crosby (D, D-OP)	48,993	53.7
	Will Rose (R)	40,687	44.6
30	Peter J. Demuth (D, D-OP)	65,465	59.4
	James A. Geltz (R, R-OP)	43,878	39.8
31	James L. Quinn (D, D-OP)	81,544	63.0
	James H. McClure (R)	45,742	35.3
32	Herman P. Eberharter (D, D-OP)	49,722	66.2
	Jacob E. Kalson (R, R-OP)	21,067	28.0
33	Henry Ellenbogen (D, D-OP)	70,601	64.5
	Edward O. Tabor (R)	38,383	35.1
34	Matthew A. Dunn (D, D-OP)	80,194	64.4
	Elmer A. Barchfeld (R, R-OP)	43,827	35.2

RHODE ISLAND

	Candidates	Votes	%
1	Aime J. Forand (D)	74,058	50.5
	Charles F. Risk (R)	62,199	42.4
	Dunn (UN)	9,973	6.8
2	John M. O'Connell (D)	75,899	47.8
	Harry Sandager (R)	71,981	45.3
	Dougherty (UN)	10,689	6.7

SOUTH CAROLINA

	Candidates	Votes	%
1	Thomas S. McMillan (D)	15,772	96.9
2	H. P. Fulmer (D)	21,653	98.3
3	John C. Taylor (D)	18,983	99.0
4	G. Hayward Mahon Jr. (D)	25,468	98.9
5	James P. Richards (D)	15,748	99.2
6	Allard H. Gasque (D)	16,027	99.3

Special Election

		Votes	%
4	G. Heyward Mahon Jr. (D)	24,715	100.0

SOUTH DAKOTA

		Votes	%
1	Fred H. Hildebrandt (D)	110,829	50.6
	Karl Mundt (R)	108,259	49.4
2	Francis H. Case (R)	34,812	51.7
	Theodore B. Werner (D)	32,549	48.3

TENNESSEE

		Votes	%
1	B. Carroll Reece (R)	33,501	60.4
	William M. Crawford (D)	17,289	31.2
	Charles W. Clark	4,684	8.4
2	J. Will Taylor (R)	40,595	50.8
	John T. O'Connor (D)	38,991	48.8
3	Sam D. McReynolds (D)	32,065	68.0
	William Hillery (R)	15,096	32.0
4	J. Ridley Mitchell (D)	33,154	81.8
	H. E. McLean (R)	7,382	18.2
5	Richard M. Atkinson (D)	34,277	94.1
	E. L. Bradbury (R)	2,163	5.9
6	Clarence W. Turner (D)	20,390	80.9
	M. C. Ridings (R)	4,819	19.1
7	Herron Pearson (D)	20,432	100.0
8	Jere Cooper (D)	27,032	93.8
	Allen J. Strawbridge (R)	1,780	6.2
9	Walter Chandler (D)	58,034	99.2

TEXAS

		Votes	%
1	Wright Patman (D)	29,351	97.6
2	Martin Dies (D)	39,484	100.0
3	Morgan G. Sanders (D)	29,482	96.3
4	Sam Rayburn (D)	33,355	97.5
5	Hatton W. Sumners (D)	43,954	88.5
	D. C. Humphrey (R)	5,579	11.2
6	Luther A. Johnson (D)	29,574	97.3
7	Nat Patton (D)	29,011	97.6
8	Albert Thomas (D)	61,616	91.8
	R. B. Nichols (R)	5,456	8.1
9	Joseph J. Mansfield (D)	36,968	93.2
	F. W. Dusek (R)	2,700	6.8
10	James P. Buchanan (D)	33,631	99.5
11	W.R. Poage (D)	31,227	100.0
12	Fritz Lanham (D)	39,708	93.3
	Arnold Davis (R)	2,845	6.7
13	William D. McFarlane (D)	40,935	95.2
14	Richard M. Kleberg (D)	39,576	92.1
	Howell Ward (R)	3,408	7.9
15	Milton H. West (D)	29,598	82.6
	J. A. Simpson (R)	6,244	17.4
16	R. Ewing Thomason (D)	26,353	100.0
17	Clyde L. Garrett (D)	35,386	100.0
18	Marvin Jones (D)	44,652	94.1
	S. E. Fish (R)	2,526	5.3
19	George H. Mahon (D)	39,059	100.0
20	Maury Maverick (D)	34,478	71.6
	E. W. Clements (R)	12,056	25.0
21	Charles L. South (D)	37,964	88.6
	M. J. Bierschwale (R)	4,891	11.4

UTAH

		Votes	%
1	Abe Murdock (D)	68,877	69.2
	Charles W. Dunn (R)	30,415	30.6
2	J. Will Robinson (D)	81,119	69.8
	A. V. Watkins (R)	34,855	30.0

VERMONT

	Candidates	Votes	%
AL	Charles A. Plumley (R)	83,091	59.2
	John B. Candon (D)	56,334	40.1

VIRGINIA

	Candidates	Votes	%
1	S. Otis Bland (D)	20,012	80.9
	William A. Dickinson (R)	4,592	18.6
2	Norman R. Hamilton (D)	29,269	88.7
	G. M. Rumble (R)	3,287	10.0
3	Andrew Jackson Montague (D)	28,803	84.4
	Charles G. Wilson (R)	4,936	14.5
4	Patrick Henry Drewry (D)	19,539	90.4
	John Martin (R)	1,832	8.5
5	Thomas G. Burch (D)	25,752	64.9
	Taylor G. Vaughan (R)	13,890	35.0
6	Clifton A. Woodrum (D)	25,327	60.7
	T. X. Parsons (R)	16,404	39.3
7	A. Willis Robertson (D)	24,790	63.9
	J. Everett Will (R)	13,814	35.6
8	Howard W. Smith (D)	28,052	75.4
	John Locke Green (R)	8,685	23.3
9	John W. Flannagan Jr. (D)	31,918	62.2
	Luther E. Fuller (R)	19,400	37.8

WASHINGTON

	Candidates	Votes	%
1	Warren G. Magnuson (D)	103,967	63.7
	Frederick J. Wettrick (R)	58,794	36.0
2	Mon C. Wallgren (D)	64,214	63.6

	Candidates	Votes	%
	Payson Peterson (R)	36,508	36.2
3	Martin F. Smith (D)	67,159	72.0
	Herbert H. Sieler (R)	25,717	27.6
4	Knute Hill (D)	48,264	57.9
	John W. Summers (R)	35,063	42.0
5	Charles H. Leavy (D)	76,048	70.8
	Warren O. Dow (R)	31,218	29.1
6	John M. Coffee (D)	66,333	67.3
	Paul A. Preus (R)	31,724	32.2

WEST VIRGINIA

	Candidates	Votes	%
1	Robert L. Ramsay (D)	75,859	59.9
	Charles J. Shuck (R)	50,885	40.2
2	Jennings Randolph (D)	78,856	59.9
	C. S. Musser (R)	52,847	40.1
3	Andrew Edmiston (D)	82,059	59.3
	John M. Wolverton (R)	56,251	40.7
4	George W. Johnson (D)	80,856	53.5
	Raymond V. Humphreys (R)	70,304	46.5
5	John Kee (D)	79,855	64.5
	C. M. Jones (R)	44,010	35.5
6	Joe L. Smith (D)	98,148	63.9
	M. F. Matheny (R)	55,536	36.1

WISCONSIN

	Candidates	Votes	%
1	Thomas R. Amlie (PROG)	49,402	43.1
	Paul E. Jorgensen (R)	44,687	39.0
	Wolf (D)	20,597	18.0
2	Harry Sauthoff (PROG)	57,874	47.9

	Candidates	Votes	%
	Frank R. Bentley (R)	34,565	28.6
	Dempsey (D)	28,326	23.5
3	Gardner R. Withrow (PROG)	56,141	51.2
	J. Charles Pile (R)	38,698	35.3
	McGonigle (D)	14,920	13.6
4	Raymond J. Cannon (D)	63,565	47.3
	Paul Gauer (PROG)	42,029	31.2
	Schafer (R)	28,930	21.5
5	Thomas O'Malley (D)	60,716	41.5
	Carl P. Dietz (PROG)	50,466	34.5
	Spence (R)	35,121	24.0
6	Michael K. Reilly (D)	41,688	39.3
	Frank B. Keefe (R)	38,904	36.7
	Poltl (PROG)	25,395	24.0
7	Gerald J. Boileau (PROG)	48,637	47.0
	Arthur W. Prehn (R)	30,555	29.5
	Coleman (D)	24,315	23.5
8	George J. Schneider (PROG)	38,721	33.5
	John E. Cashman (D)	38,138	33.0
	Farrell (R)	33,459	28.9
9	Merlin Hull (PROG)	61,593	80.7
	Edwin J. Larkin (D)	14,702	19.3
10	Bernard J. Gehrmann (PROG)	49,005	51.5
	Philip E. Nelson (R)	30,121	31.7
	Bostrom (D)	15,956	16.8

WYOMING

	Candidates	Votes	%
AL	Paul R. Greever (D)	56,204	57.2
	Frank A. Barrett (R)	41,362	42.1

1937 House Elections

NEW YORK

Special Election

	Candidates	Votes	%
17	Bruce Barton (R)	35,314#	47.6
	Stanley Osserman (D)	21,599#	29.1
	George Backer (AM LAB)	9,325#	12.6

OKLAHOMA

Special Election

	Candidates	Votes	%
5	Gomer Smith (D)	21,131	74.5
	Harlan Deupree (R)	7,132	25.2

PENNSYLVANIA

Special Election

	Candidates	Votes	%
18	Richard M. Simpson (R)	34,104	58.0
	Lowell H. Alexander (D)	24,735	42.0

TEXAS

Special Election

	Candidates	Votes	%
10	Lyndon B. Johnson (D)	8,280	27.7
	Morton Harris	5,111	17.1
	Polk Shelton	4,420	14.8
	Sam V. Stone	4,048	13.5
	C. N. Avery	3,951	13.2
	Houghton Brownell	3,019	10.1

1938 House Elections

ALABAMA

	Candidates	Votes	%
1	Frank W. Boykin (D)	9,853	100.0
2	George Grant (D)	15,569	100.0
3	Henry B. Steagall (D)	10,089	100.0
4	Sam Hobbs (D)	11,113	88.2
	C. W. McKay (R)	1,488	11.8
5	Joe Starnes (D)	16,587	99.7
6	Pete Jarman (D)	10,246	100.0
7	William B. Bankhead (D)	17,903	71.3
	E. M. Reed (R)	7,207	28.7
8	John J. Sparkman (D)	10,266	100.0
9	Luther Patrick (D)	12,627	93.5
	J. G. Bass (R)	878	6.5

ARIZONA

	Candidates	Votes	%
AL	John R. Murdock (D)	83,556	80.3
	M. E. Cassidy (R)	20,502	19.7

ARKANSAS

	Candidates	Votes	%
1	Ezekiel C. Gathings (D)	23,274	100.0
2	Wilbur D. Mills (D)	18,913	100.0
3	Clyde T. Ellis (D)	22,141	100.0
4	William B. Cravens (D)	22,272	100.0
5	David D. Terry (D)	23,949	100.0
6	William F. Norrell (D)	17,662	100.0
7	Wade Kitchens (D)	16,145	100.0

CALIFORNIA

	Candidates	Votes	%
1	Clarence F. Lea (D-R)	73,636	62.9
	Ernest S. Mitchell (TOWN)	43,320	37.0
2	Harry L. Englebright (R D P T)	71,496	99.9
3	Frank H. Buck (D-R)	119,236	92.7
	Nora Conklin (COM)	8,271	6.4
4	Franck R. Havenner (D & PROG)	64,452	61.2
	Kennett B. Dawson (R)	40,842	38.8
5	Richard J. Welch (R-D-PROG)	91,868	100.0
6	Albert E. Carter (R D P T)	118,632	94.1
	Dave L. Saunders (COM)	7,015	5.6
7	John H. Tolan (D)	62,599	55.3
	Charles Wade Snook (R)	50,504	44.6
8	John Z. Anderson (R)	84,084	55.0
	John J. McGrath (D)	68,681	45.0
9	Bertrand W. Gearhart (R-D)	91,128	96.2
10	Alfred J. Elliott (D)	84,791	67.2
	F. Fred Hoelscher (R)	41,194	32.7
11	Carl Hinshaw (R)	68,712	47.0
	Carl Stuart Hamblen (D)	59,993	41.0
	Ralph D. Horton (TOWN)	12,713	8.7
12	H. Jerry Voorhis (D)	75,003	60.7
	Eugene W. Nixon (R)	40,457	32.8
	Russell R. Hand (TOWN)	7,903	6.4
13	Charles Kramer (D & PROG)	96,258	65.6
	K. L. Stockton (R T)	44,808	30.6
14	Thomas F. Ford (D)	67,588	67.8
	William D. Campbell (R)	31,375	31.5
15	John M. Costello (D)	83,086	60.2
	O. D. Thomas (R)	51,483	37.3
16	Leland M. Ford (R-D)	97,407	62.8
	John F. Dockweiler (D)	32,863	21.2
	Ted E. Felt (TOWN)	16,045	10.3
17	Lee E. Geyer (D)	56,513	58.6
	Clifton A. Hix (R)	26,891	27.9
	Fred C. Wagner (TOWN)	8,870	9.2
18	Thomas M. Eaton (R)	52,216	48.5
	Byron N. Scott (D)	51,874	48.2
19	Harry R. Sheppard (D)	75,819	53.3
	C. T. Johnson (R T)	66,402	46.7
20	Edouard V. M. Izac (D)	65,243	60.4
	John L. Bacon (R)	42,710	39.5

COLORADO

	Candidates	Votes	%
1	Lawrence Lewis (D)	83,517	65.3
	William I. Reilly (R)	42,758	33.4
2	Fred Cummings (D)	65,448	51.7
	William S. Hill (R)	60,259	47.6
3	John A. Martin (D)	72,736	57.4
	Henry Leonard (R)	54,007	42.6
4	Edward T. Taylor (D)	43,596	63.7
	John S. Woody (R)	24,805	36.3

CONNECTICUT

	Candidates	Votes	%
1	William J. Miller (R)	68,229	43.2
	Herman P. Kopplemann (D)	64,483	40.8
	Edward C. Roffler (SOC)	24,718	15.7
2	Thomas R. Ball (R)	48,180	48.3
	William J. Fitzgerald (D)	45,056	45.2
	Thomas E. Bowman (SOC)	6,333	6.4
3	James A. Shanley (D)	55,893	43.4
	Ranulf Compton (R)	55,501	43.1
	Harry Watstein (SOC)	17,111	13.3
4	Albert E. Austin (R)	61,161	43.1
	Alfred N. Phillips Jr. (D)	44,626	31.4
	Charles H. McLevy (SOC)	35,328	24.9
5	J. Joseph Smith (D)	39,824	42.0
	Roy E. Rice (R)	39,652	41.8
	John W. Ring (SOC)	15,369	16.2
AL	Boleslaus J. Monkiewicz (R)	271,329	43.1
	William M. Citron (D)	250,013	39.7
	Arthur F. King (SOC)	99,717	15.8

DELAWARE

	Candidates	Votes	%
AL	George S. Williams (R)	60,661	55.9
	William F. Allen (D)	46,989	43.3

FLORIDA

	Candidates	Votes	%
1	J. Hardin Peterson (D)	43,837	100.0
2	Robert A. Green (D)	24,830	100.0
3	Millard Caldwell (D)	20,174	100.0
4	Arthur P. Cannon (D)	29,621	81.5
	J. S. G. Gallagher (R)	6,705	18.5
5	Joe Hendricks (D)	27,894	100.0

GEORGIA

	Candidates	Votes	%
1	Hugh Peterson (D)	10,920	99.3
2	E. E. Cox (D)	5,137	100.0
3	Stephen Pace (D)	5,987	100.0
4	E. M. Owen (D)	5,413	100.0
5	Robert Ramspeck (D)	6,906	97.2
6	Carl Vinson (D)	4,360	100.0
7	Malcolm Tarver (D)	5,622	100.0
8	W. Benjamin Gibbs (D)	4,929	100.0
9	B. Frank Whelchel (D)	8,934	100.0
10	Paul Brown (D)	9,044	94.4

IDAHO

	Candidates	Votes	%
1	Compton I. White (D)	48,318	62.8
	Rex T. Henson (R)	28,640	37.2
2	Henry C. Dworshak (R)	54,527	53.6
	Bert H. Miller (D)	47,199	46.4

ILLINOIS

	Candidates	Votes	%
1	Arthur W. Mitchell (D)	30,207	53.4
	William L. Dawson (R)	26,396	46.6
2	Raymond S. McKeough (D)	129,620	54.4
	Noble W. Lee (R)	108,483	45.6
3	Edward A. Kelly (D)	127,597	56.0
	Goodwin L. Dosland (R)	100,357	44.0
4	Harry P. Beam (D)	61,504	76.4
	Dominic M. Janec Jr. (R)	18,962	23.6
5	Adolph J. Sabath (D)	32,104	74.8
	Max Price (R)	10,842	25.3
6	A. F. Maciejewski (D)	154,818	58.7
	Robert Isham Randolph (R)	109,031	41.3
7	Leonard W. Schuetz (D)	192,750	54.3
	James C. Moreland (R)	162,069	45.7
8	Leo Kocialkowski (D)	31,823	75.3
	Rena E. Pikiel (R)	10,440	24.7
9	James McAndrews (D)	44,064	52.7
	Charles S. Dewey (R)	39,512	47.3
10	Ralph E. Church (R)	141,685	58.1
	Joseph F. Elward (D)	102,234	41.9
11	Chauncey W. Reed (R)	94,565	65.9
	William J. Bossingham (D)	48,876	34.1
12	Noah M. Mason (R)	67,326	60.7
	Edward C. Hunter (D)	43,631	39.3
13	Leo E. Allen (R)	45,177	65.6
	Theodore A. Secker (D)	23,708	34.4
14	Anton J. Johnson (R)	44,243	51.5
	Chester Thompson (D)	41,682	48.5
15	Robert B. Chiperfield (R)	47,703	54.5
	Lewis L. Boyer (D)	39,779	45.5
16	Everett M. Dirksen (R)	61,012	63.5
	James C. Dillon (D)	35,081	36.5
17	Leslie C. Arends (R)	45,235	60.9
	Thomas V. Watson (D)	29,023	39.1
18	Jessie Sumner (R)	56,587	55.3
	James A. Meeks (D)	45,691	44.7
19	William H. Wheat (R)	59,446	51.5
	Hugh M. Rigney (D)	55,956	48.5
20	James M. Barnes (D)	37,184	55.4
	Stuart E. Pierson (R)	29,907	44.6
21	Frank W. Fries (D)	52,173	50.3
	Frank M. Ramey (R)	51,651	49.8
22	Edwin M. Schaefer (D)	66,743	52.5
	Jesse R. Brown (R)	60,518	47.6
23	Laurence F. Arnold (D)	49,537	53.8
	O. A. James (R)	42,572	46.2
24	Claude V. Parsons (D)	40,633	51.1
	R. R. Randolph (R)	38,889	48.9
25	Kent E. Keller (D)	59,203	52.3
	R. G. Crisenberry (R)	53,999	47.7
AL	Thomas V. Smith (D)	1,572,870✔	
	John C. Martin (D)	1,560,283✔	
	Stephen A. Day (R)	1,472,638	
	Simon E. Lantz (R)	1,456,535	
	Harmon W. Reed (P)	9,337	
	A. G. Carnine (P)	8,808	

INDIANA

	Candidates	Votes	%
1	William T. Schulte (D)	56,630	54.9
	M. Elliott Belshaw (R)	46,370	45.0
2	Charles A. Halleck (R)	79,304	57.8
	Homer Stonebraker (D)	57,860	42.2
3	Robert A. Grant (R)	61,836	51.0
	George N. Beamer (D)	59,359	49.0
4	George W. Gillie (R)	72,567	58.1
	James I. Farley (D)	52,293	41.9
5	Forest A. Harness (R)	73,102	54.7
	Glenn Griswold (D)	60,643	45.3
6	Noble J. Johnson (R)	71,883	50.6
	Virginia E. Jenckes (D)	70,128	49.4
7	Gerald W. Landis (R)	78,870	51.6
	Arthur H. Greenwood (D)	74,001	48.4
8	John W. Boehne Jr. (D)	76,780	56.4
	Charles F. Werner (R)	59,254	43.6
9	Eugene B. Crowe (D)	70,237	52.1
	Clifford H. Long (R)	64,541	47.9
10	Raymond S. Springer (R)	73,782	53.5
	Finly H. Gray (D)	64,176	46.5
11	William H. Larrabee (D)	65,646	51.6
	William O. Nelson (R)	61,627	48.4
12	Louis Ludlow (D)	65,368	53.7
	Charles Jewett (R)	56,319	46.3

IOWA

	Candidates	Votes	%
1	Thomas E. Martin (R)	46,636	57.7
	James P. Gaffney (D)	33,765	41.8
2	William S. Jacobsen (D)	48,155	50.3
	Alfred C. Mueller (R)	47,535	49.7
3	John W. Gwynne (R)	45,541	59.7
	W. F. Hayes (D)	30,158	39.5
4	Henry O. Talle (R)	48,640	51.9
	Fred Biermann (D)	44,601	47.6
5	Karl M. LeCompte (R)	50,860	53.9
	Ruth F. Hollingshead (D)	43,452	46.1
6	Cassius C. Dowell (R)	53,505	58.5
	Hubert Utterback (D)	37,056	40.5
7	Ben F. Jensen (R)	54,922	59.0
	Roger F. Warin (D)	37,992	40.8
8	Fred C. Gilchrist (R)	51,934	62.5
	H. Lloyd Eveland (D)	30,632	36.9
9	Vincent F. Herrington (D)	46,705	49.7
	Albert F. Swanson (R)	46,366	49.3

KANSAS

	Candidates	Votes	%
1	William P. Lambertson (R)	65,945	60.3
	H. N. Hensley (D)	43,374	39.7
2	Ulysses S. Guyer (R)	70,605	56.4
	W. F. Jackson (D)	54,582	43.6
3	Thomas D. Winter (R)	56,361	53.4
	Edward W. Patterson (D)	49,117	46.6
4	Edward H. Rees (R)	55,419	63.1
	J. Donald Coffin (D)	32,443	36.9
5	John M. Houston (D)	43,990	50.3
	Stanley Taylor (R)	43,480	49.7
6	Frank Carlson (R)	69,989	63.4
	Roy L. Hamilton (D)	40,466	36.6
7	Clifford R. Hope (R)	72,893	65.5
	Claude E. Main (D)	38,357	34.5

KENTUCKY

	Candidates	Votes	%
1	Noble J. Gregory (D)	35,332	76.0
	Alvin Schutz (R)	11,153	24.0
2	Beverly M. Vincent (D)	36,170	63.8
	Richard Slack (R)	20,566	36.3
3	Emmet O'Neal (D)	57,227	61.2
	Frank A. Ropke (R)	36,361	38.9
4	Edward W. Creal (D)	32,179	59.2
	Harry H. Wilson (R)	22,139	40.8
5	Brent Spence (D)	28,383	68.4
	Joseph A. Kreke (R)	13,095	31.6
6	Virgil Chapman (D)	38,148	64.9
	Chester D. Silvers (R)	20,471	34.8
7	Andrew J. May (D)	27,655	53.2
	Hillard H. Smith (R)	24,337	46.8
8	Joe B. Bates (D)	39,006	58.8
	H. Clell Hayes (R)	27,308	41.2
9	John M. Robsion (R)	42,901	66.8
	Bert Rowland (D)	21,327	33.2

Special Election

		Votes	%
8	Joe B. Bates (D)	21,318	52.9
	James C. Sparks (R)	18,972	47.1

LOUISIANA

	Candidates	Votes	%
1	Joachim O. Fernandez (D)	50,453	100.0
2	Paul H. Maloney (D)	47,746	100.0
3	Robert L. Mouton (D)	5,236	100.0
4	Overton Brooks (D)	10,661	99.6
5	Newt V. Mills (D)	11,644	100.0
6	John K. Griffith (D)	12,225	100.0
7	Rene L. DeRouen (D)	5,313	100.0
8	A. Leonard Allen (D)	9,088	100.0

MAINE

	Candidates	Votes	%
1	James C. Oliver (R)	57,642	59.0
	H. B. Emery (D)	40,103	41.0
2	Clyde H. Smith (R)	55,718	48.9
	F. H. Dubord (D)	46,900	41.1
	J. C. Leckemby (R)	8,197	7.2
3	Ralph O. Brewster (R)	51,485	63.4
	Melvin P. Roberts (D)	29,771	36.6

MARYLAND

	Candidates	Votes	%
1	T. Alan Goldsborough (D)	38,926	62.8
	Charles H. Gibson (R)	23,096	37.2
2	William P. Cole Jr. (D)	91,231	66.3
	Irving H. Mezger (R)	44,699	32.5
3	Thomas D'Alesandro Jr. (D)	29,891	56.6
	John A. Janetzke Jr. (R)	22,909	43.4
4	Ambrose J. Kennedy (D)	37,416	50.2
	Daniel Ellison (R)	37,126	49.8
5	Stephen W. Gambrill (D)	46,678*	68.0
	A. Kingsley Love (R)	19,604	28.6
6	William D. Byron (D)	46,200	50.8
	A. Charles Stewart (R)	44,734	49.2

MASSACHUSETTS

	Candidates	Votes	%
1	Allen T. Treadway (R)	64,886	58.8
	Owen Johnson (D)	45,397	41.2
2	Charles R. Clason (R)	68,106	61.9
	James F. Egan (D)	41,935	38.1
3	Joseph E. Casey (D)	58,600	51.8
	J. Walton Tuttle (R)	54,557	48.2
4	Pehr G. Holmes (R)	62,874	54.1
	Edward A. Ryan (D)	53,266	45.9
5	Edith Nourse Rogers (R)	104,912	74.8
	Francis J. Roane (D)	35,323	25.2
6	George J. Bates (R)	82,434	74.7
	James D. Burns (D)	27,967	25.3
7	Lawrence J. Connery (D)	83,618	63.7
	George W. Eastman (R)	47,533	36.2
8	Arthur D. Healey (D)	62,152	55.1
	Rufus H. Bond (R)	50,711	44.9
9	Robert Luce (R)	70,059	50.7
	Thomas H. Eliot (D)	68,258	49.4
10	George Holden Tinkham (R)	78,052	64.4
	Martin J. Kelly (D)	43,093	35.6
11	Thomas A. Flaherty (D)	56,939	100.0
12	John W. McCormack (D)	86,618	77.1
	Henry J. Allen (R)	25,678	22.9
13	Richard B. Wigglesworth (R)	86,389	68.4
	Andrew T. Clancy (D)	39,939	31.6
14	Joseph W. Martin Jr. (R)	63,608	58.7
	Lawrence J. Bresnahan (D)	43,876	40.5
15	Charles L. Gifford (R)	66,054	59.0
	John D. W. Bodfish (D)	45,867	41.0

MICHIGAN

	Candidates	Votes	%
1	Rudolph G. Tenerowicz (D)	71,533	80.4
	Charles A. Roxborough (R)	16,752	18.8
2	Earl C. Michener (R)	58,921	64.4
	Walter C. Averill Jr. (D)	32,468	35.5
3	Paul W. Shafer (R)	58,128	66.1
	Gordon L. Stewart (D)	29,832	33.9
4	Clare E. Hoffman (R)	49,279	59.2
	Felix A. Racette (D)	33,912	40.8
5	Carl E. Mapes (R)	50,473	59.1
	Tunis Johnson (D)	34,991	40.9
6	William W. Blackney (R)	66,612	55.0
	Andrew J. Transue (D)	54,491	45.0
7	Jesse P. Wolcott (R)	62,910	69.0
	Charles F. Mann (D)	28,259	31.0
8	Fred L. Crawford (R)	52,250	58.7
	Louis C. Schwinger (D)	36,758	41.3
9	Albert J. Engel (R)	40,849	58.2
	Noel P. Fox (D)	29,397	41.9
10	Roy O. Woodruff (R)	44,818	66.4
	Harold C. Bellows (D)	22,615	33.5
11	Fred Bradley (R)	40,904	51.4
	John Luecke (D)	38,707	48.6
12	Frank E. Hook (D)	43,453	51.7
	John B. Bennett (R)	40,587	48.3
13	Clarence J. McLeod (R)	50,123	50.6
	George D. O'Brien (D)	48,443	48.9
14	Louis C. Rabaut (D)	62,872	57.6
	O. Z. Ide (R)	45,967	42.1
15	John D. Dingell (D)	57,401	54.0
	Archie C. Fraser (R)	48,429	45.6
16	John Lesinski (D)	49,101	55.1
	John L. Carey (R)	39,623	44.5
17	George A. Dondero (R)	63,769	61.4
	Samuel G. Backus (D)	39,784	38.3

MINNESOTA

	Candidates	Votes	%
1	August H. Andresen (R)	74,493	64.9
	Ray G. Moonan (D)	40,340	35.1
2	Elmer J. Ryan (D)	53,258	43.6
	Joseph P. O'Hara (R)	43,919	35.9
	C. F. Gaarenstroom (F-LAB)	25,060	20.5
3	John G. Alexander (R)	53,442	45.3
	Henry G. Teigan (F-LAB)	50,505	42.8
	Martin A. Hogan (D)	14,073	11.9
4	Melvin J. Maas (R)	60,252	53.1
	Howard Y. Williams (F-LAB)	40,558	35.8
	A. B. C. Doherty (D)	12,619	11.1
5	Oscar Youngdahl (R)	67,722	54.7
	Dewey W. Johnson (F-LAB)	45,568	36.8
	John L. Gleason (D)	10,598	8.6
6	Harold Knutson (R)	79,900	63.2
	Harry W. Christenson (F-LAB)	36,023	28.5
	Harold F. Deering (D)	10,448	8.3
7	H. Carl Andersen (R)	49,394	42.6
	Paul John Kvale (F-LAB)	42,572	36.7
	J. L. O'Connor (D)	19,330	16.7
8	William A. Pittenger (R)	67,960	51.8
	John T. Bernard (F-LAB)	54,381	41.4
	Merle J. McKeon (D)	8,945	6.8
9	Richard Thompson Buckler (F-LAB)	44,017	42.0
	Ole O. Sageng (R)	40,383	38.5
	Martin O. Brandon (D)	20,425	19.5

MISSISSIPPI

	Candidates	Votes	%
1	John E. Rankin (D)	4,384	100.0
2	Wall Doxey (D)	4,134	100.0
3	William M. Whittington (D)	2,172	100.0
4	Aaron Lane Ford (D)	3,502	100.0
5	Ross A. Collins (D)	11,540	100.0
6	William M. Colmer (D)	4,873	100.0
7	Dan R. McGehee (D)	4,834	100.0

MISSOURI

	Candidates	Votes	%
1	Milton A. Romjue (D)	43,607	54.7
	J. G. Morgan (R)	36,064	45.2
2	William L. Nelson (D)	51,451	57.9
	Mrs. George B. Simmons (R)	37,294	42.0
3	Richard M. Duncan (D)	50,501	55.3
	Fred Maughmer (R)	40,801	44.7
4	C. Jasper Bell (D)	71,940	80.4
	George E. Kimball (R)	17,560	19.6
5	Joseph B. Shannon (D)	75,810	81.0
	Leslie J. Lyons (R)	17,809	19.0
6	Reuben T. Wood (D)	52,774	50.3
	Phil A. Bennett (R)	52,159	49.7
7	Dewey Short (R)	63,758	56.3
	Frank H. Lee (D)	49,396	43.6
8	Clyde Williams (D)	56,489	55.3
	Homer S. Cotton (R)	45,673	44.7
9	Clarence Cannon (D)	40,686	60.5
	F. B. Meyer (R)	26,510	39.4
10	Orville Zimmerman (D)	44,182	58.9
	Ralph Hutchison (R)	30,804	41.1
11	Thomas C. Hennings (D)	63,332	61.8
	William H. Buder (R)	38,866	37.9
12	C. Arthur Anderson (D)	78,481	52.0
	Russell J. Horsefield (R)	71,831	47.6
13	John J. Cochran (D)	59,202	69.0
	William Gray (R)	26,476	30.9

MONTANA

	Candidates	Votes	%
1	Jacob Thorkelson (R)	49,253	54.4
	Jerry J. O'Connell (D)	41,319	45.6
2	James F. O'Connor (D)	63,506	53.8
	W. C. Husband (R)	54,632	46.2

NEBRASKA

	Candidates	Votes	%
1	George H. Heinke (R)	45,527	47.0
	Henry C. Luckey (D)	45,178	46.6
	Catherine F. McGerr	6,153	6.4
2	Charles F. McLaughlin (D)	46,927	57.3
	M. F. Mulvaney (R)	32,685	39.9
3	Karl Stefan (R)	78,765	75.3
	Edgar Howard (D)	25,862	24.7
4	Carl T. Curtis (R)	59,794	58.2
	Charles G. Binderup (D)	42,957	41.8
5	Harry B. Coffee (D)	57,192	62.4
	William E. Shuman (R)	31,225	34.1

NEVADA

	Candidates	Votes	%
AL	James G. Scrugham (D)	30,156	66.4
	Harry E. Stewart (R)	15,285	33.6

NEW HAMPSHIRE

	Candidates	Votes	%
1	Arthur B. Jenks (R)	52,444	54.0
	Alphonse Roy (D)	44,681	46.0
2	Foster Stearns (R)	49,696	59.1
	Alvin A. Lucier (D)	34,452	40.9

NEW JERSEY

	Candidates	Votes	%
1	Charles A. Wolverton (R)	96,518	62.0
	Thomas M. Madden (D)	58,450	37.5
2	Walter Sooy Jeffries (R)	57,090	50.6
	Elmer H. Wene (D)	55,344	49.1
3	Walter H. Sutphin (D)	64,621	50.5
	James K. Allardice (R)	63,345	49.5
4	D. Lane Powers (R)	62,123	61.3
	Richard J. Hughes (D)	38,921	38.4
5	Charles A. Eaton (R)	71,661	56.7
	Franklin W. Rice (D)	54,690	43.2
6	Donald H. McLean (R)	63,583	61.4
	Richard F. Green (D)	38,667	37.4
7	J. Parnell Thomas (R)	64,147	64.0
	Edward W. Wildrick (D)	35,628	35.6
8	George N. Seger (R)	61,988	59.2
	Fred Hoelscher (D)	42,030	40.2
9	Frank C. Osmers Jr. (R)	64,903	59.3
	Vincent Clausen (D)	43,641	39.9
10	Fred A. Hartley Jr. (R)	51,025	55.6
	Lindsay H. Rudd (D)	36,273	39.5
11	Albert L. Vreeland (R)	43,747	50.4
	Edward L. O'Neill (D)	38,885	44.8
12	Robert W. Kean (R)	48,854	55.0
	Frank W. Towey Jr (D)	36,736	41.3
13	Mary T. Norton (D)	89,287	79.8
	T. Burton Coyle (R)	22,459	20.1
14	Edward J. Hart (D)	86,128	78.6
	Henry T. Stuhr (R)	23,166	21.1

NEW MEXICO

	Candidates	Votes	%
AL	John J. Dempsey (D)	90,608	58.4
	Pearce Rodey (R)	64,281	41.4

NEW YORK

	Candidates	Votes	%
1	Leonard W. Hall (R)	184,539	63.0
	John F. Kiernan (D)	99,521	34.0
2	William B. Barry (D, AM LAB)	175,009	67.6
	George Archinal (R, C)	81,534	31.5
3	Joseph L. Pfeifer (D)	28,317	64.8
	Philip Tirone (R)	10,174	23.3
	Bernard Kleban (AM LAB)	4,898	11.2
4	Thomas H. Cullen (D, AM LAB)	31,881	74.5
	Edwin R. Kaprat (R)	10,620	24.8
5	Marcellus H. Evans (D)	45,387	58.3
	Francis H. Warland (R, CITY FUS)	23,410	30.1
	Joseph Dermody (AM LAB)	8,352	10.7
6	Andrew L. Somers (D, PROG)	78,530	52.0
	Gustav Drews (R, AM LAB)	69,793	46.2
7	John J. Delaney (D)	29,823	59.6
	John J. Blust (R)	9,930	19.8
	Bernard Reswick (AM LAB)	9,734	19.5
8	Donald L. O'Toole (D)	134,461	54.1
	Dorothy J. Bellanca (AM LAB, R)	111,252	44.7
9	Eugene J. Keogh (D, CITY FUS)	60,164	54.1
	Nelson S. Kirk II (R)	37,740	34.0
	Spencer K. Binyon (AM LAB)	12,199	11.0
10	Emanuel Celler (D, AM LAB)	43,881	73.5
	Arthur H. J. MacMullen (R)	14,852	24.9
11	James A. O'Leary (D)	40,407	58.9
	Percy C. Ryder (R)	23,220	33.9
	John V. Murphy (AM LAB)	4,527	6.6
12	Samuel Dickstein (D, AM LAB)	17,295	89.0
	Hyman Hecht (R)	1,865	9.6
13	Christopher D. Sullivan (D)	13,313	63.8
	John Rosenberg (R)	3,809	18.3
	Eugene P. Connolly (AM LAB)	3,541	17.0
14	William I. Sirovich (D, AM LAB)	23,722	68.4
	Maurice Wahl (R)	10,392	30.0
15	Michael J. Kennedy (D)	22,237	67.3
	John Kane Jr. (R)	7,477	22.6
	Daniel L. McDonough (AM LAB)	3,103	9.4
16	James H. Fay (D, AM LAB)	24,500	52.1
	John J. O'Connor (R, AJAC)	22,037	46.9
17	Bruce Barton (R, I PROG)	40,421	55.0
	Walter H. Liebman (D)	26,581	36.2
	George Backer (AM LAB)	6,120	8.3
18	Martin J. Kennedy (D)	25,817	60.8
	Raymond S. Fanning (R)	12,952	30.5
	Martin C. Kyne (AM LAB)	3,440	8.1
19	Sol Bloom (D)	43,134	53.3
	Robert P. Levis (R, I PROG)	22,741	28.1
	Joseph Schlossberg (AM LAB, SOC)	15,033	18.6
20	Vito Marcantonio (R, AM LAB)	18,960	59.7
	James J. Lanzetta (D)	12,376	39.0
21	Joseph A. Gavagan (D, AM LAB)	84,629	69.5
	Lorenzo H. King (R)	36,034	29.6
22	Edward W. Curley (D, CITY FUS)	34,094	64.5
	Arthur D. Fisher (R)	12,177	23.0
	Thomas C. O'Leary (AM LAB)	6,141	11.6
23	Charles A. Buckley (D, L)	120,474	50.8
	Isidore Nagler (AM LAB, SOC)	67,273	28.4
	Robert H. Brennen (R, I PROG)	49,235	20.8
24	James M. Fitzpatrick (D, CITY FUS)	116,733	48.7
	Louis Goldrich (R)	79,537	33.2
	Bartholomew F. Murphy (AM LAB)	40,931	17.1
25	Ralph A. Gamble (R)	94,865	64.9
	Homer A. Stebbins (D)	46,730	32.0
26	Hamilton Fish (R)	67,837	64.3
	Ben Martin (D, AM LAB)	36,937	35.0
27	Lewis K. Rockefeller (R, SOC)	58,565	61.0
	George W. Markey (D, AM LAB)	37,452	39.0
28	William T. Byrne (D)	88,037	60.5
	William B. Cornell (R)	54,610	37.5
29	E. Harold Cluett (R)	74,888	65.0
	Harry M. Brooks (D, AM LAB)	40,004	34.7
30	Frank Crowther (R)	58,691	60.1
	C. Dorothea Greene (D)	38,535	39.4
31	Wallace E. Pierce (R)	49,240	64.1
	George C. Owens (D)	19,784	25.7
	Jesse W. Williams (TOWN)	7,638	9.9
32	Francis D. Culkin (R)	60,947	75.5
	Virginia A. Spencer (D)	19,631	24.3
33	Fred J. Douglas (R)	63,857	61.2
	Ralph A. Peters (D)	37,195	35.7
34	Bert Lord (R)	67,330	65.3
	John V. Johnson (D, AM LAB)	35,456	34.4
35	Clarence E. Hancock (R)	90,078	64.1
	Caleb Candee Brown Jr. (D, AM LAB)	50,083	35.6
36	John Taber (R)	48,344	54.7
	George F. Davie (D)	20,636	23.3
	Charles P. Russell (AM LAB, TOWN)	19,020	21.5
37	W. Sterling Cole (R)	57,648	60.5
	David Moses (D, AM LAB)	37,216	39.1
38	Joseph J. O'Brien (R)	80,963	55.8
	George B. Kelly (D, AM LAB)	63,325	43.7
39	James W. Wadsworth (R)	65,489	65.8
	J. Frank Gilligan (D)	28,292	28.4
	Edward J. Wagner (AM LAB)	5,460	5.5
40	Walter G. Andrews (R)	92,271	62.6
	John L. Beyer (D)	50,705	34.4
41	J. Francis Harter (R)	46,784	50.5
	Alfred F. Beiter (D, AM LAB)	45,516	49.1
42	Pius L. Schwert (D, AM LAB)	39,287	45.8
	John C. Butler (R)	36,326	42.3
	John A. Ulinski (OB)	9,537	11.1
43	Daniel A. Reed (R)	53,261	65.3
	Samuel A. Carlson (D, AM LAB)	28,289	34.7
AL	Caroline O'Day (D, AM LAB)	2,363,463✓	
	Matthew J. Merritt (D, AM LAB)	2,352,159✓	
	Helen Z. M. Rodgers (R, I PROG)	2,011,507	
	Richard B. Scandrett Jr. (R, I PROG)	1,990,455	
	Israel Amter (COM)	105,681	
	Edna Mitchell Blue (SOC)	25,214	
	Brendan Sexton (SOC)	24,990	
	Jeremiah D. Crowley (IND GOVT)	5,080	
	William Herlet (IND GOVT)	4,291	

NORTH CAROLINA

	Candidates	Votes	%
1	Lindsay C. Warren (D)	12,083	100.0
2	John H. Kerr (D)	9,955	100.0
3	Graham A. Barden (D)	17,507	100.0
4	Harold D. Cooley (D)	26,932	63.9
	Willis G. Briggs (R)	15,209	36.1
5	Alonzo D. Folger (D)	25,472	69.7
	John W. Kurfees Jr. (R)	11,087	30.3
6	Carl T. Durham (D)	15,730	75.2
	Oscar G. Barker (D)	5,188	24.8
7	J. Bayard Clark (D)	17,175	75.7
	Edgar C. Geddie (R)	5,501	24.3
8	William O. Burgin (D)	34,757	55.2
	John R. Jones (R)	28,187	44.8
9	Robert L. Doughton (D)	43,912	60.9
	Monroe Adams (R)	28,202	39.1
10	Alfred L. Bulwinkle (D)	48,590	56.5
	Frank C. Patton (R)	37,360	43.5
11	Zebulon Weaver (D)	61,508	63.8
	Vonno L. Gudger (R)	34,912	36.2

NORTH DAKOTA

	Candidates	Votes	%
AL	William Lemke (R)	153,288✓	
	Usher L. Burdick (R)	149,047✓	
	Howard I. Henry (D)	55,125	
	Alfred S. Dale (D)	44,691	
	J. B. Field (I)	8,109	

OHIO

	Candidates	Votes	%
1	Charles H. Elston (R)	63,285	58.2
	Joseph A. Dixon (D)	45,536	41.8
2	William E. Hess (R)	61,480	59.0
	Herbert S. Bigelow (D)	42,773	41.0
3	Harry N. Routzohn (R)	73,534	55.9
	Byron B. Harlan (D)	58,139	44.2
4	Robert F. Jones (R)	56,399	59.8
	William B. Swonger (D)	33,284	35.3
5	Cliff Clevenger (R)	37,027	56.9
	Frank C. Kniffin (D)	28,109	43.2

Candidates	Votes	%
6 James G. Polk (D)	43,646	50.5
Emory F. Smith (R)	42,847	49.5
7 Clarence J. Brown (R)	68,185	57.6
Arthur W. Aleshire (D)	50,163	42.4
8 Frederick C. Smith (R)	40,772	54.6
Brooks Fletcher (D)	33,972	45.5
9 John F. Hunter (D)	56,306	50.4
Homer A. Ramey (R)	55,441	49.6
10 Thomas A. Jenkins (R)	47,036	66.0
Elsie Stanton (D)	24,198	34.0
11 Harold K. Claypool (D)	33,764	52.1
Tom P. White (R)	31,004	47.9
12 John M. Vorys (R)	64,409	50.9
Arthur P. Lamneck (D)	62,026	49.1
13 Dudley A. White (R)	56,204	69.4
William L. Fiesinger (D)	24,749	30.6
14 Dow W. Harter (D)	87,303	53.4
Edward S. Sheck (R)	76,346	46.7
15 Robert T. Secrest (D)	42,573	52.3
P. W. Griffiths (R)	38,903	47.8
16 Jim Seccombe (R)	62,176	50.7
William R. Thom (D)	60,382	49.3
17 William A. Ashbrook (D)	51,305	52.6
Walter B. Woodward (R)	46,300	47.4
18 Earl R. Lewis (R)	56,468	50.3
Lawrence E. Imhoff (D)	55,809	49.7
19 Michael J. Kirwan (D)	76,268	52.4
William P. Barnum (R)	69,214	47.6
20 Martin L. Sweeney (D)	54,185	70.4
Thomas F. McCafferty (R)	22,775	29.6
21 Robert Crosser (D)	53,180	68.7
J. E. Chizek (R)	24,240	31.3
22 Chester C. Bolton (R)	109,494	55.5
Anthony A. Fleger (D)	87,635	44.5
AL George H. Bender (R)	1,177,982✓	
Lycurgus L. Marshall (R)	1,101,194✓	
John McSweeney (D)	1,068,916	
Stephen M. Young (D)	1,015,035	

Special Election

	Candidates	Votes	%
4	Walter H. Albaugh (R)	47,631	54.9
	Roy E. Layton (D)	39,112	45.1

OKLAHOMA

	Candidates	Votes	%
1	Wesley E. Disney (D)	55,253	63.2
	A.M. Armstrong (R)	31,755	36.3
2	Jack Nichols (D)	38,058	71.3
	Bruce L. Keenan (R)	15,335	28.7
3	Wilburn Cartwright (D)	42,616	85.4
	Frank D. McSherry (R)	7,286	14.6
4	Lyle H. Boren (D)	44,233	71.7
	Ed Ball (R)	17,506	28.4
5	A. S. Mike Monroney (D)	47,692	71.9
	Harlan Deupree (R)	18,271	27.6
6	Jed Johnson (D)	33,808	69.5
	James F. Rowell (R)	14,617	30.1
7	Sam C. Massingale (D)	24,986	76.1
	A. L. Smith (R)	7,862	23.9
8	Phil Ferguson (D)	34,113	50.2
	Charles E. Knox (R)	33,438	49.2
AL	Will Rogers (D)	306,241	68.7
	R. R. Wilson (R)	137,733	30.9

OREGON

	Candidates	Votes	%
1	James W. Mott (R)	119,965	70.7
	Andrew C. Burk (D)	49,666	29.3
2	Walter M. Pierce (D)	35,200	57.9
	U. S. Balentine (R)	25,557	42.1
3	Homer D. Angell (R)	69,049	50.9
	Nan Wood Honeyman (D)	66,498	49.1

PENNSYLVANIA

	Candidates	Votes	%
1	Leon Sachs (D, D-OP)	54,819	53.5
	John Alessandroni (R)	47,692	46.5
2	James P. McGranery (D)	51,565	52.4
	Edward W. Henry (R)	46,248	47.0
3	Michael J. Bradley (D)	61,686	52.0
	William T. Connor (R, R-OP)	56,958	48.0
4	J. Burrwood Daly (D)	60,514	53.8
	Edward F. Roberts (R)	51,343	45.7
5	Fred C. Gartner (R)	63,877	52.5
	Frank J. G. Dorsey (D)	56,492	46.5
6	Francis J. Myers (D)	62,524	49.9
	J. Howard Berry Jr. (R)	59,548	47.5
7	George P. Darrow (R)	84,077	59.3
	Ira W. Drew (D)	57,046	40.2
8	James Wolfenden (R)	84,103	67.6
	C. Fenno Hoffman (D)	40,324	32.4
9	Charles L. Gerlach (R)	56,589	56.7
	Oliver W. Frey (D)	43,055	43.1
10	J. Roland Kinzer (R)	78,986	64.1
	Thomas Jefferson McClelland (D)	43,928	35.7
11	Patrick J. Boland (D)	66,626	52.5
	William F. Hallstead (R, R-OP)	60,307	47.5
12	J. Harold Flannery (D)	98,715	51.2
	Michael A. Yeosock (R)	94,108	48.8
13	Ivor D. Fenton (R, R-OP)	79,468	53.2
	James H. Gildea (D)	69,817	46.8
14	Guy L. Moser (D)	34,678	52.7
	John C. Evans (R)	31,068	47.3
15	Albert G. Rutherford (R)	58,571	61.6
	Harry M. Turrell (D, D-OP)	36,096	37.9
16	Robert F. Rich (R, R-OP)	63,241	61.5
	Paul A. Rothfuss (D)	38,908	37.8
17	J. William Ditter (R)	72,225	68.5
	Carroll L. Rutter (D)	32,921	31.2
18	Richard M. Simpson (R)	53,067	60.5
	Richard L. Schroyer (D)	34,578	39.5
19	John C. Kunkel (R, R-OP)	77,354	55.0
	Guy J. Swope (D)	63,180	45.0
20	Benjamin Jarrett (R)	65,547	61.8
	Earl H. Beshlin (D, D-OP)	40,511	38.2
21	Francis E. Walter (D)	43,276	50.2
	Alonzo L. Reinhard (R)	41,665	48.4
22	Chester H. Gross (R)	55,565	50.3
	Harry L. Haines (D, D-OP)	54,880	49.7
23	James E. Van Zandt (R)	61,372	57.1
	Don Gingery (D, D-OP)	45,694	42.5
24	J. Buell Snyder (D)	47,045	51.2
	J. C. Glassburn (R)	44,604	48.5
25	Charles I. Faddis (D, D-OP)	43,604	53.1
	Warren S. Burchinal (R)	38,549	46.9
26	Louis E. Graham (R)	59,754	52.4
	Charles R. Eckert (D, D-OP)	53,434	46.8
27	Harve Tibbott (R, R-OP)	81,690	55.8
	Joseph H. Gray (D, D-OP)	63,790	43.5
28	Robert G. Allen (D, D-OP)	52,034	53.9
	Roy C. McKenna (R)	44,196	45.8
29	Robert L. Rodgers (R)	46,856	53.8
	Norbert James Fitzgerald (D)	39,762	45.6
30	Robert J. Corbett (R)	53,541	51.2
	Peter J. DeMuth (D, D-OP)	51,028	48.8
31	John McDowell (R, R-OP)	57,392	50.7
	James J. Quinn (D)	55,211	48.8
32	Herman P. Eberharter (D)	48,025	63.3
	Jacob E. Kalson (R)	27,440	36.2
33	Joseph A. McArdle (D, D-OP)	54,888	51.6
	James I. Marsh (R)	51,427	48.4
34	Matthew A. Dunn (D, D-OP)	55,502	50.0
	Robert B. McKinley (R)	55,055	49.6

RHODE ISLAND

	Candidates	Votes	%
1	Charles F. Risk (R)	73,394	50.3
	Aime J. Forand (D)	72,484	49.7
2	Harry Sandager (R, GOOD GOV)	87,932	57.0
	Edward J. Fenelon Jr. (D)	66,408	43.0

SOUTH CAROLINA

	Candidates	Votes	%
1	Thomas S. McMillan (D)	7,649	98.2
2	Hampton P. Fulmer (D)	7,236	98.8
3	Butler B. Hare (D)	10,028	99.6
4	Joseph R. Bryson (D)	8,995	99.4
5	James P. Richards (D)	6,191	99.8
6	John L. McMillan (D)	5,707	99.2

SOUTH DAKOTA

	Candidates	Votes	%
1	Karl E. Mundt (R)	111,805	54.0
	Emil Loriks (D)	95,353	46.0
2	Francis H. Case (R)	41,335	61.5
	Theodore B. Werner (D)	25,932	38.6

TENNESSEE

	Candidates	Votes	%
1	B. Carroll Reece (R)	23,251	58.0
	John A. Armstrong (D)	10,609	26.5
	James P. Kinett	4,382	10.9
2	J. Will Taylor (R)	32,312	64.1
	Judd Acuff (I)	16,079	31.9
3	Sam D. McReynolds (D)	21,804	73.9
	Joe F. Benson (R)	7,708	26.1
4	Albert Gore (D)	25,220	100.0
5	Joseph Byrns (D)	16,819	90.6
	William I. Love (I)	1,749	9.4
6	Clarence W. Turner (D)	14,318	82.2
	John U. McDonough (I)	1,957	11.2
	Maurice C. Riding	1,146	6.6
7	Herron Pearson (D)	19,554	100.0
8	Jere Cooper (D)	18,173	95.4
9	Walter Chandler (D)	43,976	98.4

TEXAS

	Candidates	Votes	%
1	Wright Patman (D)	14,833	98.8
2	Martin Dies (D)	12,816	100.0
3	Lindley Beckworth (D)	17,115	100.0
4	Sam Rayburn (D)	16,523	97.9
5	Hatton W. Sumners (D)	10,344	95.3
6	Luther A. Johnson (D)	15,619	100.0
7	Nat Patton (D)	16,467	100.0
8	Albert Thomas (D)	36,989	98.3
9	Joseph J. Mansfield (D)	16,680	100.0
10	Lyndon B. Johnson (D)	14,476	100.0
11	W. R. Poage (D)	14,664	100.0
12	Fritz G. Lanham (D)	12,972	100.0
13	Ed Gossett (D)	20,620	100.0
14	Richard M. Kleberg (D)	23,438	100.0
15	Milton H. West (D)	18,995	100.0
16	R. Ewing Thomason (D)	9,237	100.0
17	Clyde L. Garrett (D)	17,107	100.0
18	Marvin Jones (D)	18,048	100.0
19	George H. Mahon (D)	16,372	100.0
20	Paul J. Kilday (D)	16,703	100.0
21	Charles L. South (D)	21,671	93.0
	M. J. Bierschwale (R)	1,621	7.0

UTAH

	Candidates	Votes	%
1	Abe Murdock (D)	52,927	59.7
	LeRoy B. Young (R)	35,790	40.3
2	J. W. Robinson (D)	58,456	62.3
	Dean F. Brayton (R)	35,359	37.7

VERMONT

	Candidates	Votes	%
AL	Charles A. Plumley (R)	71,901	64.0
	James P. Leamy (D)	40,483	36.0

VIRGINIA

	Candidates	Votes	%
1	Schuyler Otis Bland (D)	7,191	99.7
2	Colgate W. Darden Jr. (D)	15,276	87.2
	Carl P. Spaeth	2,142	12.2
3	David E. Satterfield Jr. (D)	5,560	99.7
4	Patrick Henry Drewry (D)	5,805	99.9
5	Thomas G. Burch (D)	5,761	99.6
6	Clifton A. Woodrum (D)	11,509	55.9
	Fred W. McWane (R)	9,083	44.1
7	A. Willis Robertson (D)	11,398	63.9
	Charles C. Leap (R)	6,449	36.1
8	Howard W. Smith (D)	13,796	99.6
9	John W. Flannagan Jr. (D)	21,235	66.7
	L. E. Gulliford (R)	10,612	33.3

WASHINGTON

	Candidates	Votes	%
1	Warren G. Magnuson (D)	90,768	61.7
	Matthew W. Hill (R)	56,293	38.3
2	Mon C. Wallgren (D)	58,313	61.5
	Charles A. Sather (R)	36,442	38.5
3	Martin F. Smith (D)	52,305	60.3
	Walter S. Talbott (R)	34,394	39.7
4	Knute Hill (D)	38,647	50.4
	Frank Miller (R)	37,969	49.6
5	Charles H. Leavy (D)	52,782	57.1
	Norman A. Ericson (R)	38,858	42.0
6	John M. Coffee (D)	64,871	73.0
	Willard V. Young (R)	24,002	27.0

WEST VIRGINIA

	Candidates	Votes	%
1	Andrew C. Schiffler (R)	57,043	54.8
	Robert L. Ramsay (D)	47,051	45.2
2	Jennings Randolph (D)	53,277	54.6
	Melvin C. Snyder (R)	44,334	45.4
3	Andrew Edmiston (D)	53,722	55.3
	H. Roy Waugh (R)	43,407	44.7

	Candidates	Votes	%
4	George W. Johnson (D)	65,965	52.9
	Raymond V. Humphreys (R)	58,749	47.1
5	John Kee (D)	55,501	61.3
	Hartley Sanders (R)	34,989	38.7
6	Joe L. Smith (D)	67,818	62.3
	R. E. O'Connor (R)	40,965	37.7

WISCONSIN

	Candidates	Votes	%
1	Stephen Bolles (R)	45,247	49.1
	Francis H. Wendt (PROG)	29,478	32.0
	Calvin Stewart (D)	14,573	15.8
2	Charles Hawks Jr. (R)	42,154	44.9
	Harry Sauthoff (PROG)	40,656	43.3
	Reinhold A. Gerth (D)	11,185	11.9
3	Harry W. Griswold (R)	43,495	50.1
	Gardner R. Withrow (PROG)	36,509	42.0
	Bart E. McGonigle (D)	6,887	7.9
4	John C. Schafer (R)	34,196	32.0
	Thaddeus F. B. Wasielewski (D)	33,559	31.4
	Paul Gauer (PROG)	30,817	28.8
	Raymond J. Cannon (I)	7,498	7.0
5	Lewis D. Thill (R)	47,032	43.1

	Candidates	Votes	%
	Thomas O'Malley (D)	31,154	28.6
	Alfred Benson (PROG)	29,874	27.4
6	Frank B. Keefe (R)	46,082	53.6
	Michael K. Reilly (D)	25,842	30.1
	Adam F. Poltl (PROG)	13,258	15.4
7	Reid F. Murray (R)	41,662	48.9
	Gerald J. Boileau (PROG)	32,442	38.0
	James J. Cavanaugh (D)	9,727	11.4
8	Joshua L. Johns (R)	33,354	36.2
	George J. Schneider (PROG)	29,035	31.5
	John E. Cashman (D)	28,221	30.6
9	Merlin Hull (PROG)	42,880	53.4
	Hugh M. Jones (R)	32,375	40.3
	William F. Crane (D)	5,066	6.3
10	Bernard J. Gehrmann (PROG)	45,874	57.5
	James H. Carroll (R)	33,854	42.5

WYOMING

	Candidates	Votes	%
AL	Frank O. Horton (R)	49,975	52.9
	Paul R. Greever (D)	44,525	47.1

1939 House Election

PENNSYLVANIA

Special Election

	Candidates	Votes	%
4	John Edward Sheridan (D)	52,250	51.8
	Boies Penrose (R)	48,648	48.2

1940 House Elections

ALABAMA

	Candidates	Votes	%
1	Frank W. Boykin (D)	25,993	100.0
2	George Grant (D)	33,433	100.0
3	Henry B. Steagall (D)	22,906	100.0
4	Sam Hobbs (D)	24,870	87.9
	Thomas G. McNaron (R)	3,428	12.1
5	Joe Starnes (D)	31,966	100.0
6	Pete Jarman (D)	18,881	100.0
7	Walter Will Bankhead (D)	27,696	70.9
	A. W. Hargett (R)	11,368	29.1
8	John J. Sparkman (D)	29,020	100.0
9	Luther Patrick (D)	39,660	99.2

ARIZONA

	Candidates	Votes	%
AL	John R. Murdock (D)	99,424	71.1
	K. T. Palmer (R)	40,360	28.9

ARKANSAS

	Candidates	Votes	%
1	Ezekiel C. Gathings (D)	33,127	100.0
2	Wilbur D. Mills (D)	25,718	100.0
3	Clyde E. Ellis (D)	21,060	71.1
	Clyde M. Williams (R)	8,566	28.9
4	Fadjo Cravens (D)	28,999	100.0
5	David D. Terry (D)	36,067	100.0
6	William F. Norrell (D)	27,972	100.0
7	Oren Harris (D)	26,994	100.0

CALIFORNIA

	Candidates	Votes	%
1	Clarence F. Lea (D-R)	103,547	93.0
	Albert J. Lima (COM)	5,647	5.1
2	Harry L. Englebright (R D P T)	71,033	100.0
3	Frank H. Buck (D-R)	135,461	91.0
	C. H. Farman (P)	10,539	7.1
4	Thomas Rolph (R)	75,369	54.6
	Franck R. Havenner (D & PROG)	61,341	44.4
5	Richard J. Welch (R-D)	119,122	95.8
6	Albert E. Carter (R D P T)	131,584	96.0
7	John H. Tolan (D)	72,838	55.5
	Ralph R. Eltse (R)	56,808	43.3
8	John Z. Anderson (R-D)	148,180	96.5
9	Bertrand W. Gearhart (R-D)	99,708	99.9
10	Alfred J. Elliott (D-R)	125,845	96.8
11	Carl Hinshaw (R-D-PROG)	170,504	96.2
12	H. Jerry Voorhis (D)	99,494	64.0
	Irwin W. Minger (R)	54,731	35.2
13	Charles Kramer (D-R)	127,167	75.6
	Charles H. Randall (PROG-P)	36,406	21.7
14	Thomas F. Ford (D)	73,137	64.2
	Herbert L. Herberts (R)	37,939	33.3
15	John M. Costello (D)	94,435	56.2
	Norris J. Nelson (R & PROG)	71,667	42.6
16	Leland Merritt Ford (R-D)	188,049	96.2
17	Lee E. Geyer (D)	75,109	65.5
	Clifton A. Hix (R)	32,862	28.6
18	Ward Johnson (R)	73,932	54.3
	Byron N. Scott (D)	60,764	44.6
19	Harry R. Sheppard (D)	84,931	52.9
	Lotus H. Loudon (R)	75,495	47.0
20	Edouard V. M. Izac (D)	69,874	51.1
	Ed Fletcher (R)	66,132	48.3

COLORADO

	Candidates	Votes	%
1	Lawrence Lewis (D)	110,078	64.6
	James D. Parriott (R)	59,427	34.9
2	William S. Hill (R)	76,859	53.3
	Fred Cummings (D)	66,662	46.2
3	J. Edgar Chenoweth (R)	70,842	52.1
	Byron G. Rogers (D)	65,269	48.0
4	Edward T. Taylor (D)	44,095	59.4
	Paul W. Crawford (R)	30,126	40.6

Special Election

	Candidates	Votes	%
3	William E. Burney (D)	68,225	51.0
	Henry Leonard (R)	65,675	49.1

CONNECTICUT

	Candidates	Votes	%
1	Herman P. Kopplemann (D)	109,880	54.2
	William J. Miller (R, SOC)	92,980	45.8
2	William J. Fitzgerald (D)	63,021	52.4
	Thomas R. Ball (R)	56,825	47.3
3	James A. Shanley (D)	84,439	53.6
	Ranulf Compton (R, UN)	73,078	46.4
4	Le Roy D. Downs (D)	90,942	49.0
	Albert E. Austin (R)	90,239	48.6
5	J. Joseph Smith (D)	62,783	54.9
	Frank T. Johnson (R)	51,049	44.7
AL	Lucien J. Maciora (D)	407,868	52.1
	Boleslaus J. Monkiewicz (R)	365,851	46.8

DELAWARE

	Candidates	Votes	%
AL	Philip A. Traynor (D)	68,205	50.6
	George S. Williams (R)	64,384	47.8

FLORIDA

	Candidates	Votes	%
1	J. Hardin Peterson (D)	88,158	100.0
2	Robert A. Green (D)	68,797	89.1
	Francis McHale (R)	8,382	10.9
3	Robert L. F. Sikes (D)	36,573	100.0
4	Arthur P. Cannon (D)	84,594	75.3
	Bert L. Acker (R)	27,815	24.7
5	Joe Hendricks (D)	49,715	75.4
	Emory Akerman (R)	16,214	24.6

GEORGIA

	Candidates	Votes	%
1	Hugh Peterson (D)	28,601	99.5
2	E. E. Cox (D)	19,443	96.8
3	Stephen Pace (D)	22,882	100.0
4	A. Sidney Camp (D)	25,609	100.0
5	Robert Ramspeck (D, I)	41,677	99.9
6	Carl Vinson (D)	21,966	99.9
7	Malcolm C. Tarver (D)	32,280	86.4
	Lewis H. Crawford (R)	5,062	13.6
8	John S. Gibson (D, R)	24,454	100.0
9	B. Frank Whelchel (D)	25,461	84.4
	William C. Horton (R)	4,025	13.3
10	Paul Brown (D)	18,291	98.7

IDAHO

	Candidates	Votes	%
1	Compton I. White (D)	62,107	62.0
	Edward Gaffney (R)	37,999	38.0
2	Henry C. Dworshak (R)	69,804	53.1
	Ira H. Masters (D)	61,726	46.9

ILLINOIS

	Candidates	Votes	%
1	Arthur W. Mitchell (D)	34,641	53.0
	William E. King (R)	30,698	47.0
2	Raymond S. McKeough (D)	155,698	51.5
	P. H. Moynihan (R)	146,927	48.6
3	Edward A. Kelly (D)	148,382	51.1
	Waldemar J. Roehler (R)	141,768	48.9
4	Harry P. Beam (D)	74,977	77.4
	Henry F. Schmudde (R)	21,858	22.6
5	Adolph J. Sabath (D)	35,637	71.0
	Martin Dykema (R)	14,540	29.0
6	A. F. Maciejewski (D)	187,393	56.2
	Joseph Wagner (R)	146,253	43.8
7	Leonard W. Schuetz (D)	229,161	50.9
	James C. Moreland (R)	220,793	49.1
8	Leo Kocialkowski (D)	40,074	78.1
	Anthony V. Champagne (R)	11,232	21.9
9	Charles S. Dewey (R)	56,806	53.3
	James McAndrews (D)	49,816	46.7
10	George A. Paddock (R)	199,418	61.3
	John Haderlein (D)	125,827	38.7
11	Chauncey W. Reed (R)	128,645	64.6
	Edgar O. Eakin (D)	70,581	35.4
12	Noah M. Mason (R)	90,744	60.6
	August C. Engh (D)	58,945	39.4
13	Leo E. Allen (R)	65,698	67.6
	John B. Hayes (D)	31,502	32.4
14	Anton J. Johnson (R)	60,909	52.4
	Forest Dizotell (D)	55,451	47.7
15	Robert B. Chiperfield (R)	65,639	56.4
	Russell M. Gunn (D)	50,820	43.6
16	Everett M. Dirksen (R)	79,780	58.1
	M. R. Clark (D)	57,567	41.9
17	Leslie C. Arends (R)	56,712	61.1
	J. Joseph Pitts (D)	36,102	38.9
18	Jessie Sumner (R)	64,409	53.2
	James A. Meeks (D)	56,744	46.8
19	William H. Wheat (R)	75,933	50.6
	Alfred D. Huston (D)	74,091	49.4
20	James M. Barnes (D)	44,824	51.7
	Hardin E. Hanks (R)	41,806	48.3
21	Evan Howell (R)	67,896	51.6
	Frank W. Fries (D)	63,740	48.4
22	Edwin M. Schaefer (D)	98,162	53.8
	Calvin D. Johnson (R)	84,381	46.2
23	Laurence F. Arnold (D)	65,062	51.4
	Ben O. Sumner (R)	61,521	48.6
24	James V. Heidinger (R)	49,731	53.6
	Claude V. Parsons (D)	43,050	46.4
25	Cecil W. Bishop (R)	69,165	50.5
	Kent E. Keller (D)	67,891	49.5
AL	William G. Stratton (R)	2,050,493✓	
	Stephen A. Day (R)	2,020,008✓	
	Thomas V. Smith (D)	1,968,143	
	Walter J. Orlikoski (D)	1,913,950	
	Harry Fleischman (SOC)	7,377	
	Lee S. Gregory (SOC)	7,191	
	Willis Ray Wilson (P)	6,786	
	Lena Duell Vincent (P)	6,621	

INDIANA

	Candidates	Votes	%
1	William T. Schulte (D)	71,606	60.8
	Elliot Belshaw (R)	45,947	39.0
2	Charles A. Halleck (R)	87,652	58.1
	James O. Cox (D)	63,290	41.9
3	Robert A. Grant (R)	73,914	51.3
	George Sands (D)	70,208	48.7
4	George W. Gillie (R)	80,259	58.0
	Frank E. Corbett (D)	58,157	42.0
5	Forest A. Harness (R)	78,691	54.7
	George W. Wolf (D)	65,200	45.3
6	Noble J. Johnson (R)	80,595	52.3
	Lenhardt E. Bauer (D)	73,449	47.7
7	Gerald W. Landis (R)	81,632	52.2
	Charles H. Bedwell (D)	74,746	47.8
8	John W. Boehne Jr. (D)	87,141	55.5
	Charles F. Werner (R)	69,761	44.5
9	Earl Wilson (R)	71,624	50.9
	Eugene B. Crowe (D)	69,227	49.2
10	Raymond S. Springer (R)	80,725	53.0
	Don C. Ward (D)	71,478	47.0
11	William H. Larrabee (D)	79,070	51.7
	Maurice G. Robinson (R)	73,867	48.3
12	Louis Ludlow (D)	80,954	52.9
	James A. Collins (R)	72,174	47.1

IOWA

	Candidates	Votes	%
1	Thomas E. Martin (R)	70,120	60.4
	Zoe S. Nabers (D)	46,040	39.6
2	William S. Jacobsen (D)	75,774	52.2
	W. A. McCullough (R)	69,298	47.8

	Candidates	Votes	%
3	John W. Gwynne (R)	65,425	60.0
	Ernest J. Seemann (D)	43,709	40.1
4	Henry O. Talle (R)	66,691	56.4
	Morgan J. McEnaney (D)	51,558	43.6
5	Karl M. LeCompte (R)	66,940	53.3
	Roy E. Stevens (D)	58,718	46.7
6	Paul Cunningham (R)	70,707	52.3
	E. Frank Fox (D)	64,314	47.6
7	Ben F. Jensen (R)	71,633	58.6
	Ernest M. Miller (D)	50,644	41.4
8	Fred C. Gilchrist (R)	64,687	58.1
	Frank J. Lund (D)	46,597	41.9
9	Vincent F. Harrington (D)	67,017	50.8
	Albert F. Swanson (R)	64,877	49.2

KANSAS

	Candidates	Votes	%
1	William P. Lambertson (R)	64,766	61.0
	Clive R. Lane (D)	41,375	39.0
2	Ulysses S. Guyer (R)	73,659	54.0
	Harold H. Harding (D)	62,787	46.0
3	Thomas D. Winter (R)	60,381	55.2
	W. E. Ledbetter (D)	48,971	44.8
4	Edward H. Rees (R)	58,183	62.5
	Dudley Doolittle (D)	34,957	37.5
5	John M. Houston (D)	58,486	52.5
	Stanley Taylor (R)	52,901	47.5
6	Frank Carlson (R)	69,627	60.9
	Max Jones (D)	44,702	39.1
7	Clifford R. Hope (R)	75,349	63.9
	Claude E. Main (D)	42,518	36.1

KENTUCKY

	Candidates	Votes	%
1	Noble J. Gregory (D)	60,777	100.0
2	Beverly M. Vincent (D)	69,905	100.0
3	Emmet O'Neal (D)	96,253	60.0
	Ben J. Brumleve (R)	64,053	40.0
4	Edward W. Creal (D)	55,561	58.5
	Lewis H. Mather (R)	39,447	41.5
5	Brent Spence (D)	51,954	61.2
	Henry J. Cook (R)	32,981	38.8
6	Virgil Chapman (D)	74,463	60.5
	William D. Rogers (R)	48,700	39.5
7	Andrew J. May (D)	44,185	56.8
	James W. Turner (R)	33,574	43.2
8	Joe B. Bates (D)	61,881	58.0
	H. Clell Hayes (R)	44,736	42.0
9	John M. Robsion (R)	71,750	62.5
	Bert Rowland (D)	43,013	37.5

LOUISIANA

	Candidates	Votes	%
1	F. Edward Hebert (D)	58,234	100.0
2	Hale Boggs (D)	56,026	100.0
3	James Domengeaux (D)	27,081	66.0
	David W. Pipes Jr. (R)	13,933	34.0
4	Overton Brooks (D)	33,704	100.0
5	Newt V. Mills (D)	33,462	100.0
6	Jared Y. Sanders Jr. (D)	41,173	100.0
7	Vance Plauche (D)	28,518	100.0
8	A. Leonard Allen (D)	28,904	100.0

MAINE

	Candidates	Votes	%
1	James C. Oliver (R)	55,503	63.4
	Peter M. McDonald (D)	32,018	36.6
2	Margaret Chase Smith (R)	57,152	64.6
	Edward J. Beauchamp (D)	31,334	35.4
3	Frank Fellows (R)	46,732	66.1
	Thomas N. Curran (D)	23,934	33.9

MARYLAND

	Candidates	Votes	%
1	David J. Ward (D)	36,057	53.9
	Robert F. Duer (R)	30,810	46.1
2	William P. Cole Jr. (D)	113,495	65.7
	Theodore F. Brown (R)	59,223	34.3
3	Thomas D'Alesandro Jr. (D)	38,540	61.5
	John A. Janetzke (R)	24,153	38.5
4	John A. Meyer (D)	50,120	56.6
	Daniel Ellison (R)	38,444	43.4
5	Lansdale Sasscer (D)	58,418	71.0
	John N. Torvestad (R)	23,857	29.0
6	William D. Byron (D)	60,037	53.5
	Walter P. Johnson (R)	52,258	46.5

MASSACHUSETTS

	Candidates	Votes	%
1	Allen T. Treadway (R)	72,750	57.1
	Clifford J. Akey (D)	54,634	42.9
2	Charles R. Clason (R)	76,373	58.4
	Patrick A. Doyle (D)	54,428	41.6
3	Joseph E. Casey (D)	72,839	54.6
	Edward T. Simoneau (R)	60,676	45.4
4	Pehr G. Holmes (R)	70,542	53.2
	Frank J. McGrail (D)	60,988	46.0
5	Edith Nourse Rogers (R)	120,435	76.2
	Francis J. Roane (D)	37,593	23.8
6	George J. Bates (R)	88,834	71.6
	James D. Burns (D)	35,214	28.4
7	Lawrence J. Connery (D)	89,966	62.1
	William Henry Haskell (R)	52,701	36.4
8	Arthur D. Healey (D)	71,127	55.4
	John J. Irwin (R)	57,217	44.6
9	Thomas H. Eliot (D)	81,523	52.1
	Robert Luce (R)	74,922	47.9
10	George Holden Tinkham (R)	78,029	59.1
	David M. Owens (D)	54,093	40.9
11	Thomas A. Flaherty (D)	58,041	81.5
	Benjamin J. Green (R)	13,176	18.5
12	John W. McCormack (D)	97,588	78.1
	Henry J. Allen (R)	27,302	21.9
13	Richard B. Wigglesworth (R)	92,651	65.0
	Francis G. O'Neill (D)	48,606	34.1
14	Joseph W. Martin Jr. (R)	65,780	54.4
	Harold E. Cole (D)	55,241	45.7
15	Charles L. Gifford (R)	73,358	57.8
	George F. Backus (D)	53,581	42.2

MICHIGAN

	Candidates	Votes	%
1	Rudolph G. Tenerowicz (D)	87,451	79.9
	Donald J. Marshall (R)	21,399	19.5
2	Earl C. Michener (R)	72,235	62.3
	Redmond M. Burr (D)	43,733	37.7
3	Paul W. Shafer (R)	74,614	62.1
	Charles T. McSherry (D)	45,138	37.6
4	Clare E. Hoffman (R)	65,666	61.8
	Harvey Hope Jarvis (D)	40,443	38.1
5	Bartel J. Jonkman (R)	65,240	53.7
	Garrett Heyns (D)	56,172	46.3
6	William W. Blackney (R)	77,340	51.1
	Charles R. Adair (D)	73,629	48.6
7	Jesse P. Wolcott (R)	73,926	65.2
	Albert A. Wagner (D)	39,416	34.8
8	Fred L. Crawford (R)	68,265	61.2
	Louis C. Schwinger (D)	43,297	38.8
9	Albert J. Engel (R)	52,343	56.9
	Noel P. Fox (D)	39,667	43.1
10	Roy O. Woodruff (R)	52,685	61.9
	William J. Kelly (D)	32,289	37.9
11	Fred Bradley (R)	48,087	51.1
	Wendell L. Lund (D)	45,826	48.7
12	Frank E. Hook (D)	47,429	51.3
	John B. Bennett (R)	44,733	48.4
13	George D. O'Brien (D)	66,985	54.6
	Clarence J. McLeod (R)	55,115	44.9
14	Louis C. Rabaut (D)	80,463	59.0
	George B. Shaeffer (R)	55,910	41.0
15	John D. Dingell (D)	85,239	61.9
	Archie C. Fraser (R)	52,131	37.9
16	John Lesinski (D)	73,956	58.8
	Robert Ford (R)	51,276	40.8
17	George A. Dondero (R)	82,809	54.7
	Draper Allen (D)	68,195	45.1

MINNESOTA

	Candidates	Votes	%
1	August H. Andresen (R)	88,814	64.8
	Francis L. Murphy (D)	27,479	20.1
	Endre B. Anderson (F-LAB)	20,700	15.1
2	Joseph P. O'Hara (R)	66,610	49.0
	Elmer J. Ryan (D)	57,673	42.5
	C. E. McNaught (F-LAB)	11,534	8.5
3	Richard P. Gale (R)	63,854	43.5
	Henry G. Teigan (F-LAB)	50,222	34.2
	Martin A. Hogan (D)	28,321	19.3
4	Melvin J. Maas (R)	68,525	58.8
	George L. Siegel (F-LAB)	32,898	28.3
	Willard J. Moran (D)	15,050	12.9
5	Oscar Youngdahl (R)	79,491	52.1
	Dewey W. Johnson (F-LAB)	52,289	34.3
	Lamoine Montgomery Dowling (D)	20,720	13.6
6	Harold Knutson (R)	84,023	61.5
	E. Thomas O'Brien (D)	52,504	38.5
7	H. Carl Andersen (R)	65,958	50.7
	Harold L. Peterson (F-LAB)	42,356	32.6
	J. L. O'Connor (D)	21,796	16.8
8	William A. Pittenger (R)	74,521	54.2
	John T. Bernard (F-LAB)	39,252	28.5
	M. W. Raihala (D)	23,845	17.3
9	Richard Thompson Buckler (F-LAB)	48,999	43.4
	Colvin G. Butler (R)	48,324	42.8
	Frank H. Timm (D)	15,507	13.7

MISSISSIPPI

	Candidates	Votes	%
1	John E. Rankin (D)	19,390	100.0
2	Wall Doxey (D)	16,939	100.0
3	William M. Whittington (D)	16,597	100.0
4	Aaron Lane Ford (D)	15,329	100.0
5	Ross A. Collins (D)	24,079	100.0
6	William M. Colmer (D)	26,679	100.0
7	Dan R. McGehee (D)	29,799	100.0

MISSOURI

	Candidates	Votes	%
1	Milton A. Romjue (D)	62,461	50.5
	Henry S. Beardsley (R)	61,123	49.5
2	William L. Nelson (D)	77,922	53.8
	Roy O. Miller (R)	66,794	46.2
3	Richard M. Duncan (D)	77,424	53.3
	Fred Maughmer (R)	67,757	46.7
4	C. Jasper Bell (D)	72,331	60.0
	John W. Mitchell (R)	48,181	40.0
5	Joseph B. Shannon (D)	63,202	54.2
	Forest W. Hanna (R)	53,390	45.8
6	Philip A. Bennett (R)	78,746	53.7
	Reuben T. Wood (D)	67,902	46.3
7	Dewey Short (R)	86,547	59.3
	Vernon Sigars (D)	59,344	40.7
8	Clyde Williams (D)	64,263	51.1
	Parke M. Banta (R)	61,567	48.9
9	Clarence Cannon (D)	60,204	55.3
	F. B. Meyer (R)	48,704	44.7
10	Orville Zimmerman (D)	69,859	57.4
	C. E. Davenport (R)	51,755	42.6
11	John B. Sullivan (D)	85,722	55.7
	Charles J. Riley (R)	68,088	44.3
12	Walter C. Ploeser (R)	127,005	53.9
	C. Arthur Anderson (D)	108,605	46.1
13	John J. Cochran (D)	82,417	64.5
	W. S. Sanford (R)	45,262	35.5

MONTANA

	Candidates	Votes	%
1	Jeanette Rankin (R)	56,616	54.5
	Jerry J. O'Connell (D)	47,352	45.5
2	James F. O'Connor (D)	83,101	62.0
	Melvin N. Hoiness (R)	49,710	37.1

NEBRASKA

	Candidates	Votes	%
1	Oren S. Copeland (R)	64,431	55.6
	Henry C. Luckey (D)	51,524	44.4
2	Charles F. McLaughlin (D)	68,760	56.6

Candidates	Votes	%
Theodore W. Metcalfe (R)	52,669	43.4
3 Karl Stefan (R)	90,561	80.0
Victor J. McGonigle (D)	19,253	17.0
4 Carl T. Curtis (R)	66,966	57.7
R. O. Canaday (D)	29,311	25.3
Charles G. Binderup	19,807	17.1
5 Harry B. Coffee (D)	63,025	58.1
Bert Howard (R)	45,548	42.0

NEVADA

Candidates	Votes	%
AL James G. Scrugham (D)	32,714	64.5
Ralph W. Lattin (R)	18,032	35.5

NEW HAMPSHIRE

Candidates	Votes	%
1 Arthur B. Jenks (R)	57,982	51.1
Alphonse Roy (D)	55,434	48.9
2 Foster Stearns (R)	55,530	53.0
Daniel J. Moriarty (D)	49,260	47.0

NEW JERSEY

Candidates	Votes	%
1 Charles A. Wolverton (R)	97,547	55.5
Harry Roye (D)	77,931	44.3
2 Elmer H. Wene (D)	60,392	52.2
Walter Sooy Jeffries (R)	55,382	47.8
3 William H. Sutphin (D)	76,048	51.7
Joseph C. Irwin (R)	70,890	48.2
4 D. Lane Powers (R)	69,834	55.9
Thomas S. Dignan (D)	54,909	44.0
5 Charles A. Eaton (R)	82,840	55.9
Charles R. M. Tuttle (D)	65,200	44.0
6 Donald H. McLean (R)	78,361	54.9
James E. Downes (D)	62,888	44.1
7 J. Parnell Thomas (R)	82,287	64.6
Mort L. O'Connell (D)	44,527	35.0
8 Gordon Canfield (R)	72,197	58.6
Addison P. Rosenkrans (D)	50,622	41.1
9 Frank C. Osmers Jr. (R)	91,352	62.7
Abram A. Lebson (D)	54,254	37.2
10 Fred A. Hartley Jr. (R)	64,699	56.8
William E. Holmwood (D)	46,934	41.2
11 Albert L. Vreeland (R)	61,606	55.8
Mary C. Duffy (D)	46,130	41.8
12 Robert Winthrop Kean (R)	67,996	53.7
Thomas J. Halleran (D)	53,677	42.4
13 Mary T. Norton (D)	92,356	70.2
Raymond J. Cuddy (R)	39,274	29.8
14 Edward J. Hart (D)	84,538	65.3
Otto Trankler (R)	44,893	34.7

NEW MEXICO

Candidates	Votes	%
AL Clinton P. Anderson (D)	106,972	58.8
Herman R. Crile (R)	75,085	41.2

NEW YORK

Candidates	Votes	%
1 Leonard W. Hall (R)	267,873	63.7
Frederic S. Farah (D)	141,774	33.7
2 William B. Barry (D)	216,309	52.8
Thomas J. Styles (R)	170,004	41.5
Matthew Napear (AM LAB)	20,827	5.1
3 Joseph L. Pfeifer (D, AM LAB)	42,884	70.6
Samuel Rosenthal (R)	17,839	29.4
4 Thomas H. Cullen (D)	36,995	56.2
Alfred A. Larossa (R)	25,207	38.3
Michael Giaratano (AM LAB)	3,636	5.5
5 James J. Heffernan (D, AM LAB)	63,295	55.2
Marcellus H. Evans (R)	51,428	44.8
6 Andrew L. Somers (D)	130,391	57.7
Alfred E. Buck (R)	58,507	25.9
Irving B. Altman (AM LAB)	31,945	14.1
7 John J. Delaney (D, AM LAB)	50,189	72.8
Julius Reinlieb (R)	18,765	27.2
8 Donald L. O'Toole (D)	217,599	56.8
Jacob M. Offenhender (R)	103,753	27.1
Benjamin Brenner (AM LAB)	52,972	13.8

Candidates	Votes	%
9 Eugene J. Keogh (D, AM LAB)	92,559	57.7
William J. McGahie (R)	67,901	42.3
10 Emanuel Celler (D, AM LAB)	57,286	71.4
Edward H. Wilson (R)	21,358	26.6
11 James A. O'Leary (D)	46,616	49.4
Thomas Garrett (R)	42,631	45.1
Wellington Roe (AM LAB)	5,193	5.5
12 Samuel Dickstein (D)	17,176	72.1
Bernard Harkavy (AM LAB)	3,664	15.4
Joseph Levine (R)	2,976	12.5
13 Louis J. Capozzoli (D)	18,334	62.7
John Rosenberg (R)	8,367	28.6
Gino Bardi (AM LAB)	2,534	8.7
14 M. Michael Edelstein (D)	26,455	56.9
Peter J. Bakanatch (R)	13,940	30.0
Samuel Burt (AM LAB)	6,103	13.1
15 Michael J. Kennedy (D)	26,314	59.7
Arthur A. Wyler (R)	13,158	29.8
Joseph Curran (AM LAB)	4,623	10.5
16 William T. Pheiffer (R)	31,020	48.7
James H. Fay (D)	28,837	45.3
Thomas Darcy (AM LAB)	3,874	6.1
17 Kenneth F. Simpson (R)	54,636	50.8
Samuel Kramer (D)	47,155	43.8
Morris Watson (AM LAB)	5,845	5.4
18 Martin J. Kennedy (D)	31,151	52.7
James B. Walker Jr. (R)	24,312	41.2
Shaemas O'Sheal (AM LAB)	3,612	6.1
19 Sol Bloom (D)	71,018	62.8
Daniel J. Riesner (R)	32,821	29.0
Benjamin M. Zelman (AM LAB)	9,209	8.2
20 Vito Marcantonio (R, AM LAB)	25,254	62.5
James J. Lanzetta (D)	15,160	37.5
21 Joseph A. Gavagan (D)	108,139	63.2
Charles H. Roberts (R)	46,324	27.1
Alfred K. Stern (AM LAB)	16,529	9.7
22 Walter A. Lynch (D)	44,296	60.1
F. Shepard Cornell (R)	23,532	31.9
Frank R. Crosswaith (AM LAB)	5,931	8.0
23 Charles A. Buckley (D)	190,396	56.5
Lowell H. Brown (R)	88,083	26.1
Jack Altman (AM LAB)	50,293	14.9
24 James M. Fitzpatrick (D)	161,577	47.7
Ralph W. Gwinn (R)	136,835	40.4
George Thomas (AM LAB)	35,233	10.4
25 Ralph A. Gamble (R)	125,412	64.0
Homer A. Stebbins (D)	64,889	33.1
26 Hamilton Fish (R)	68,715	51.9
Hardy Steeholm (D)	59,739	45.1
27 Lewis K. Rockefeller (R)	65,618	58.0
George J. Mutari (D, AM LAB)	47,610	42.1
28 William T. Byrne (D)	89,592	57.8
William V. A. Waterman (R)	59,344	38.3
29 E. Harold Cluett (R)	82,328	63.7
Salvatore J. Leombruno (D)	43,588	33.7
30 Frank Crowther (R)	66,159	54.8
Burlin G. McKillip (D)	51,270	42.5
31 Clarence E. Kilburn (R)	58,727	62.5
Horatio W. Thomas (D, AM LAB)	35,307	37.5
32 Francis D. Culkin (R)	71,782	68.8
Frank M. McCormack (D)	30,105	28.8
33 Fred J. Douglas (R)	72,412	56.5
Samuel H. Miller (D)	52,469	40.9
34 Edwin Arthur Hall (R)	93,990	68.3
Donald W. Kramer (D)	41,027	29.8
35 Clarence E. Hancock (R)	97,688	56.8
Flora D. Johnson (D)	69,730	40.6
36 John Taber (R)	64,507	59.6
John W. Kennelly (D)	40,929	37.8
37 W. Sterling Cole (R)	76,630	64.9
David Moses (D)	38,878	32.9
38 Joseph J. O'Brien (R)	92,866	51.9
George B. Kelly (D, AM LAB)	86,197	48.1
39 James W. Wadsworth (R)	73,316	60.4
J. Frederick Colson (D, AM LAB)	48,133	39.6
40 Walter Gresham Andrews (R)	119,972	61.1

Candidates	Votes	%
Robert A. Hoffman (D, AM LAB)	76,468	38.9
41 Alfred F. Beiter (D, AM LAB)	62,843	52.3
J. Francis Harter (R)	57,335	47.7
42 Pius L. Schwert (D, AM LAB)	64,250	58.8
Edward F. Moss (R)	44,866	41.0
43 Daniel A. Reed (R)	67,520	62.2
Milton A. Bissell (D, AM LAB)	40,980	37.8
AL Caroline O'Day (D, AM LAB)	3,199,019✓	
Matthew J. Merritt (D, AM LAB)	3,182,936✓	
Mary Donlon (R)	2,830,517	
Messmore Kendall (R)	2,812,066	
Helen G. H. Estella (P)	5,679	
Neil Dow Cranmer (P)	5,212	

NORTH CAROLINA

Candidates	Votes	%
1 Herbert C. Bonner (D)	36,722	92.8
John A. Wilkinson (R)	2,851	7.2
2 John H. Kerr (D)	41,217	100.0
3 Graham A. Barden (D)	33,760	75.0
Julian T. Gaskill (R)	11,248	25.0
4 Harold D. Cooley (D)	57,610	79.4
Ezra Parker (R)	14,926	20.6
5 Alonzo D. Folger (D)	53,778	77.2
Ottis James Reynolds (R)	15,872	22.8
6 Carl T. Durham (D)	55,549	78.5
Gilliam Grissom (R)	15,259	21.6
7 J. Bayard Clark (D)	41,663	85.3
Fred R. Keith (R)	7,168	14.7
8 William O. Burgin (D)	57,879	67.2
F. D. B. Harding (R)	28,232	32.8
9 Robert L. Doughton (D)	60,875	68.3
Monroe Adams (R)	28,287	31.7
10 Alfred L. Bulwinkle (D)	87,156	69.8
Ernest M. Morgan (R)	37,736	30.2
11 Zebulon Weaver (D)	75,763	69.0
Robert Frank Jarrett (R)	34,104	31.0

NORTH DAKOTA

Candidates	Votes	%
AL Usher L. Burdick (R)	148,227✓	
Charles R. Robertson (R)	111,125✓	
R. J. Downey (D)	63,662	
Adolph Michelson (D)	63,028	
Thomas Hall (I)	23,399	
John Omdahl (I)	20,845	

OHIO

Candidates	Votes	%
1 Charles H. Elston (R)	84,622	58.0
Joseph A. Dixon (D)	61,382	42.0
2 William E. Hess (R)	77,769	56.3
James E. O'Connell (D)	60,410	43.7
3 Greg Holbrock (D)	103,291	52.6
Harry N. Routzohn (R)	93,002	47.4
4 Robert F. Jones (R)	65,603	57.8
Clarence C. Miller (D)	47,820	42.2
5 Cliff Clevenger (R)	48,040	60.7
C. H. Armbruster (D)	31,063	39.3
6 Jacob E. Davis (D)	52,769	52.2
Chester P. Fitch (R)	48,257	47.8
7 Clarence J. Brown (R)	83,415	58.3
J. Fuller Trump (D)	59,667	41.7
8 Frederick C. Smith (R)	49,218	52.5
Kenneth M. Petri (D)	44,605	47.5
9 John F. Hunter (D)	86,956	54.7
Wilbur M. White (R)	71,927	45.3
10 Thomas A. Jenkins (R)	48,217	58.9
John P. Kelso (D)	33,698	41.1
11 Harold K. Claypool (D)	43,548	53.8
Ray W. Davis (R)	37,398	46.2
12 John M. Vorys (R)	91,767	51.3
A. P. Lammeck (D)	87,115	48.7
13 A.D. Baumhart Jr. (R)	62,442	60.8
Werner S. Haslinger (D)	40,274	39.2
14 Dow W. Harter (D)	121,037	52.3
Walter B. Wanamaker (R)	108,016	46.6

	Candidates	Votes	%
15	Robert T. Secrest (D)	57,359	58.8
	Clair A. Young (R)	40,233	41.2
16	William R. Thom (D)	92,469	56.4
	Jim Seccombe (R)	71,629	43.7
17	J. Harry McGregor (R)	69,102	55.1
	Ralph C. Lutz (D)	56,343	44.9
18	Lawrence E. Imhoff (D)	79,718	54.5
	Earl R. Lewis (R)	66,666	45.5
19	Michael J. Kirwan (D)	122,075	61.9
	Charles H. Anderson (R)	75,016	38.1
20	Martin L. Sweeney (D)	72,385	67.7
	George Pillersdorf (R)	34,609	32.4
21	Robert Crosser (D)	79,602	77.1
	J. E. Chizek (R)	23,658	22.9
22	Frances P. Bolton (R)	165,322	56.7
	Anthony A. Fleger (D)	126,273	43.3
AL	George H. Bender (R)	1,519,628✓	
	Stephen M. Young (D)	1,483,934✓	
	L. L. Marshall (R)	1,386,696	
	Francis W. Durbin (D)	1,384,800	

OKLAHOMA

	Candidates	Votes	%
1	Wesley E. Disney (D)	93,366	62.2
	W. R. Boyd (R)	56,112	37.4
2	Jack Nichols (D)	50,351	62.2
	E. O. Clark (R)	30,630	37.8
3	Wilburn Cartwright (D)	68,344	79.0
	Frank D. McSherry (R)	18,145	21.0
4	Lyle H. Boren (D)	69,040	71.1
	Clyde T. Patrick (R)	28,046	28.9
5	A. S. Mike Monroney (D)	93,457	72.4
	U. S. Stone (R)	34,942	27.1
6	Jed Johnson (D)	52,338	70.1
	Walter Hubbell (R)	22,343	29.9
7	Sam C. Massingale (D)	39,884	70.0
	Place Montgomery (R)	16,246	28.5
8	Ross Rizley (R)	48,737	53.8
	Phil Ferguson (D)	41,417	45.7
AL	Will Rogers (D)	479,433	65.7
	John W. Harreld (R)	245,384	33.6

OREGON

	Candidates	Votes	%
1	James W. Mott (R)	145,675	68.4
	Charles A. Robertson (D)	63,940	30.0
2	Walter M. Pierce (D)	44,832	56.3
	Rex Ellis (R)	33,529	42.1
3	Homer D. Angell (R)	84,275	49.9
	Nan Wood Honeyman (D)	80,930	47.9

PENNSYLVANIA

	Candidates	Votes	%
1	Leon Sacks (D)	64,599	61.7
	Emanuel W. Beloff (R)	39,770	38.0
2	James P. McGranery (D)	62,844	60.9
	Augustus Trask Ashton (R)	39,489	38.3
3	Michael J. Bradley (D)	77,436	63.1
	Frank J. Kownacki (R)	44,757	36.5
4	John Edward Sheridan (D)	74,458	63.0
	Benjamin M. Golder (R)	42,578	36.1
5	Francis R. Smith (D)	76,724	55.8
	Fred C. Gartner (R)	60,109	43.7
6	Francis J. Myers (D)	82,550	61.1
	Frank F. Truscott (R)	51,313	38.0
7	Hugh Scott (R)	79,416	50.9
	Gilbert Cassidy (D)	76,054	48.8
8	James Wolfenden (R)	69,649	59.6
	E. Adele Scott Saul (D)	46,960	40.2
9	Charles L. Gerlach (R)	55,919	52.4
	Henry V. Scheirer (D)	50,632	47.4
10	J. Roland Kinzer (R)	72,843	57.7
	George M. May (D)	53,333	42.2
11	Patrick J. Boland (D)	65,368	52.6
	Joseph F. Gunster (R)	58,831	47.4
12	J. Harold Flannery (D)	101,854	57.8
	J. Henry Pool (R)	74,305	42.2
13	Ivor D. Fenton (R)	70,647	50.5
	James H. Gildea (D)	68,501	48.9
14	Guy L. Moser (D)	48,140	56.0

	Candidates	Votes	%
	Joseph C. Evans (R)	31,839	37.1
	Raymond S. Hofses (SOC)	4,980	5.8
15	Albert G. Rutherford (R)	46,740	59.3
	F. R. Clark (D)	31,675	40.2
16	Robert F. Rich (R)	61,167	60.5
	Hugh Gilmore (D)	39,988	39.5
17	J. William Ditter (R)	75,006	62.2
	Victor Eppstein (D)	45,616	37.8
18	Richard M. Simpson (R)	46,595	57.6
	John W. Keichline (D)	34,328	42.4
19	John C. Kunkel (R)	74,420	54.4
	John A. Smith (D)	62,298	45.6
20	Benjamin Jarrett (R)	64,189	58.2
	John R. Boland Jr. (D)	44,919	40.8
21	Francis E. Walter (D)	52,530	56.2
	T. Fred Woodley (R)	40,863	43.7
22	Harry L. Haines (D)	60,848	54.8
	Chester H. Gross (R)	49,532	44.6
23	James E. Van Zandt (R)	57,027	56.3
	William M. Aukerman (D)	44,263	43.7
24	J. Buell Snyder (D)	54,631	56.6
	J. Clark Glassburn (R)	41,641	43.2
25	Charles I. Faddis (D)	58,442	61.0
	Lucius McK. Crumrine (R)	37,357	39.0
26	Louis E. Graham (R)	64,669	50.9
	Peter P. Reising (D)	62,273	49.1
27	Harve Tibbott (R)	75,243	51.6
	Joseph Gray (D)	69,736	47.9
28	Augustine B. Kelley (D)	58,772	55.5
	James M. Underwood (R)	44,528	42.0
29	Robert L. Rodgers (R)	50,147	54.3
	James F. Lavery (D)	41,924	45.4
30	Thomas E. Scanlon (D)	62,450	50.1
	Robert J. Corbett (R)	62,097	49.9
31	Samuel A. Weiss (D)	76,819	55.7
	John McDowell (R)	59,960	43.5
32	Herman P. Eberharter (D)	62,121	68.6
	Samuel M. Jackson (R)	28,196	31.1
33	Joseph A. McArdle (D)	70,824	55.0
	James I. Marsh (R)	57,737	44.9
34	James A. Wright (D)	75,004	53.8
	Robert B. McKinley (R)	64,336	46.2

RHODE ISLAND

	Candidates	Votes	%
1	Aime J. Forand (D)	87,530	57.6
	Charles F. Risk (R)	64,539	42.4
2	John E. Fogarty (D)	87,332	53.8
	Harry Sandager (R)	74,987	46.2

SOUTH CAROLINA

	Candidates	Votes	%
1	L. Mendel Rivers (D)	16,626	98.4
2	Hampton P. Fulmer (D)	14,920	98.6
3	Butler B. Hare (D)	15,977	98.9
4	Joseph R. Bryson (D)	23,825	97.3
5	James P. Richards (D)	14,754	99.2
6	John L. McMillan (D)	12,074	99.0

SOUTH DAKOTA

	Candidates	Votes	%
1	Karl E. Mundt (R)	135,406	59.6
	Oscar Fosheim (D)	91,967	40.5
2	Francis H. Case (R)	47,051	66.1
	Arthur W. Watwood (D)	24,177	33.9

TENNESSEE

	Candidates	Votes	%
1	B. Carroll Reece (R)	39,577	68.7
	R. E. Walker (D)	18,051	31.3
2	John Jennings Jr. (R)	41,274	56.6
	Clay Jones (D)	31,663	43.4
3	Estes Kefauver (D)	35,332	68.7
	Jerome Taylor (R)	16,099	31.3
4	Albert Gore (D)	38,278	88.9
	H. E. McLean (R)	4,777	11.1
5	J. Percy Priest (I)	24,565	50.2
	Joseph W. Byrns Jr. (D)	20,933	42.8
	Julian H. Campbell (R)	3,459	7.1
6	Wirt Courtney (D)	24,536	100.0

	Candidates	Votes	%
7	Herron Pearson (D)	25,590	100.0
8	Jere Cooper (D)	32,002	92.1
	Julian Palmer	2,760	7.9
9	Clifford Davis (D)	55,952	96.0

TEXAS

	Candidates	Votes	%
1	Wright Patman (D)	27,030	100.0
2	Martin Dies (D)	43,597	100.0
3	Lindley Beckworth (D)	47,292	100.0
4	Sam Rayburn (D)	46,333	100.0
5	Hatton W. Sumners (D)	57,789	87.5
	Floyd E. Royer (R)	8,273	12.5
6	Luther A. Johnson (D)	33,546	100.0
7	Nat Patton (D)	30,384	98.2
8	Albert Thomas (D)	89,796	95.2
9	Joseph J. Mansfield (D)	52,754	100.0
10	Lyndon B. Johnson (D)	48,442	100.0
11	W. R. Poage (D)	41,432	99.9
12	Fritz G. Lanham (D)	54,108	100.0
13	Ed Gossett (D)	50,076	96.5
14	Richard M. Kleberg (D)	59,016	100.0
15	Milton H. West (D)	32,300	92.5
	J. A. Simpson (R)	2,628	7.5
16	R. Ewing Thomason (D)	34,515	99.9
17	Sam Russell (D)	45,456	100.0
18	Eugene Worley (D)	51,660	96.5
19	George H. Mahon (D)	56,343	100.0
20	Paul J. Kilday (D)	47,075	83.4
	Harry Hotchkin (R)	9,296	16.5
21	Charles L. South (D)	49,468	92.8
	Ray Ridenhower (R)	3,832	7.2

UTAH

	Candidates	Votes	%
1	Walter K. Granger (D)	62,654	57.1
	LeRoy B. Young (R)	47,021	42.9
2	J. W. Robinson (D)	84,874	62.8
	A. Sherman Christensen (R)	50,332	37.2

VERMONT

	Candidates	Votes	%
AL	Charles A. Plumley (R)	89,637	63.8
	Michael J. Rock (D)	50,804	36.2

VIRGINIA

	Candidates	Votes	%
1	Schuyler Otis Bland (D)	22,493	99.9
2	Colgate W. Darden Jr. (D)	29,788	100.0
3	Dave E. Satterfield Jr. (D)	34,885	96.8
4	Patrick Henry Drewry (D)	19,043	96.0
5	Thomas G. Burch (D)	25,631	100.0
6	Clifton A. Woodrum (D)	30,046	68.1
	Fred W. McWane (R)	13,864	31.4
7	A. Willis Robertson (D)	26,233	65.1
	J. A. Garber (R)	13,964	34.7
8	Howard W. Smith (D)	33,031	79.0
	Henry B. Goodloe (R)	8,794	21.0
9	John W. Flannagan Jr. (D)	32,412	57.3
	Fred C. Parks (R)	24,109	42.7

WASHINGTON

	Candidates	Votes	%
1	Warren G. Magnuson (D)	113,988	61.6
	Fred J. Wettrick (R)	71,110	38.4
2	Henry M. Jackson (R)	66,314	57.4
	Payson Peterson (R)	49,209	42.6
3	Martin F. Smith (D)	60,529	55.3
	Russell V. Mack (R)	48,700	44.5
4	Knute Hill (D)	50,493	51.3
	Frank Miller (R)	48,003	48.7
5	Charles H. Leavy (D)	67,582	55.5
	Walt Horan (R)	54,258	44.5
6	John M. Coffee (D)	71,536	62.8
	Paul A. Preus (R)	42,334	37.2

WEST VIRGINIA

	Candidates	Votes	%
1	Robert L. Ramsay (D)	72,717	53.2
	A. C. Schiffler (R)	63,906	46.8

	Candidates	Votes	%
2	Jennings Randolph (D)	77,045	57.5
	Summers H. Sharp (R)	56,911	42.5
3	Andrew Edmiston (D)	79,441	56.6
	H. Roy Waugh (R)	60,810	43.4
4	George W. Johnson (D)	82,979	52.7
	Harry O. Hiteshew (R)	74,491	47.3
5	John Kee (D)	81,903	62.9
	Hartley Sanders (R)	48,223	37.1
6	Joe L. Smith (D)	105,927	61.7
	R. E. O'Connor (R)	65,762	38.3

WISCONSIN

	Candidates	Votes	%
1	Stephen Bolles (R)	69,276	55.8
	Stanley W. Slagg (PROG)	28,308	22.8
	Jacob M. Weisman (D)	26,520	21.4

	Candidates	Votes	%
2	Harry Sauthoff (PROG)	60,481	44.2
	Charles Hawks Jr. (R)	58,121	42.5
	Thomas R. Brooks (D)	18,237	13.3
3	William H. Stevenson (R)	54,457	46.0
	Gardner R. Withrow (PROG)	52,131	44.0
	George T. Doherty (D)	11,806	10.0
4	Thaddeus F. B. Wasielewski (D)	57,381	35.6
	Leonard C. Fons (PROG)	52,907	32.8
	John C. Schafer (R)	50,796	31.5
5	Lewis D. Thill (R)	73,728	44.4
	James M. Pasch (PROG)	54,501	32.8
	Francis T. Murphy (D)	37,872	22.8
6	Frank B. Keefe (R)	66,821	57.4
	Jacob A. Fessler (D)	30,162	25.9
	Walter D. Corrigan (PROG)	19,387	16.7
7	Reid F. Murray (R)	58,696	51.6

	Candidates	Votes	%
	Gerald J. Boileau (PROG)	40,558	35.7
	Wallace A. Bloedorn (D)	14,495	12.7
8	Joshua L. Johns (R)	61,987	55.9
	Michael F. Kresky (PROG)	49,005	44.2
9	Merlin Hull (PROG)	61,009	52.8
	John R. Nygaard (R)	47,825	41.4
	James E. Hughes (D)	6,763	5.9
10	Bernard J. Gehrmann (PROG)	50,776	48.0
	Peter Van Nostrand (R)	37,819	35.7
	John G. Green (D)	17,284	16.3

WYOMING

	Candidates	Votes	%
AL	John J. McIntyre (D)	57,030	53.4
	Frank O. Horton (R)	49,701	46.5

1941 House Elections

MISSISSIPPI

Special Election

	Candidates	Votes	%
2	Jamie L. Whitten (D)	8,703	69.3
	L. A. Plye	3,865	30.8

NEW YORK

Special Elections

	Candidates	Votes	%
14	Arthur G. Klein (D, LIB)	8,615	68.0
	George A. Hastings (R)	3,337	26.3
	Leonard H. Wacker (AM LAB)	714	5.6

	Candidates	Votes	%
17	Joseph Clark Baldwin (R)	23,254	52.9
	Dean Alfange (D)	16,690	38.0
	Eugene P. Connolly (AM LAB)	3,985	9.1
42	John C. Butler (R)	15,065	40.6
	Hattie E. Schwert (D, AM LAB)	13,554	36.5
	Edmund P. Radwan (NEW DEAL)	7,787	21.0

OKLAHOMA

Special Election

	Candidates	Votes	%
7	Victor Wickersham (D)	19,884	82.5
	George Davidson (R)	4,004	16.6

WISCONSIN

Special Election

	Candidates	Votes	%
1	Lawrence H. Smith (R)	29,638	63.6
	Thomas R. Amlie (D)	16,949	36.4

1942 House Elections

ALABAMA

	Candidates	Votes	%
1	Frank W. Boykin (D)	5,600	100.0
2	George Grant (D)	6,672	100.0
3	Henry B. Steagall (D)	5,043	100.0
4	Sam Hobbs (D)	7,468	100.0
5	Joe Starnes (D)	11,841	100.0
6	Pete Jarman (D)	7,556	100.0
7	Carter Manasco (D)	9,788	100.0
8	John J. Sparkman (D)	5,954	100.0
9	John P. Newsome (D)	8,802	95.6

ARIZONA

	Candidates	Votes	%
AL	Richard F. Harless (D)	56,357✓	
	John R. Murdock (D)	55,825✓	
	George R. Darnell (R)	23,015	
	Joseph S. Jenckes Jr. (R)	18,205	
	Morris Graham (COM)	375	

ARKANSAS

	Candidates	Votes	%
1	Ezekiel C. Gathings (D)	13,998	100.0
2	Wilbur D. Mills (D)	11,380	100.0
3	J. William Fulbright (D)	16,111	100.0
4	Fadjo Cravens (D)	14,733	100.0
5	Brooks Hays (D)	16,850	100.0
6	William F. Norrell (D)	13,166	100.0
7	Oren Harris (D)	12,108	100.0

CALIFORNIA

	Candidates	Votes	%
1	Clarence F. Lea (D-R)	78,281	93.2
	Albert Jason Lima (COM)	5,703	6.8
2	Harry L. Englebright (R D T)	50,094	99.8
3	J. Leroy Johnson (R)	63,982	54.5
	Joseph B. O'Neil (D)	53,521	45.6
4	Thomas Rolph (R-D)	62,735	98.2
5	Richard J. Welch (R-D)	85,747	92.7
	Walter Raymond Lambert (COM)	6,749	7.3
6	Albert E. Carter (R-D)	108,585	92.4
	Clarence Paton (COM)	8,532	7.3
7	John H. Tolan (D-R)	77,292	99.4
8	John Z. Anderson (R-D)	91,536	99.6
9	Bertrand W. Gearhart (R-D)	65,791	99.9
10	Alfred J. Elliott (D-R)	43,864	99.8
11	George E. Outland (D)	31,611	50.7
	A. J. Dingeman (R)	30,781	49.3
12	H. Jerry Voorhis (D)	53,705	56.8
	Robert P. Shuler (R & P)	40,780	43.2
13	Norris Poulson (R)	38,577	49.2
	Charles Kramer (D)	33,060	42.2
	Calvert S. Wilson (TOWN)	6,306	8.0
14	Thomas F. Ford (D)	49,326	66.9
	Herbert L. Herberts (R)	24,349	33.0
15	John M. Costello (D-R)	88,798	86.1
	B. Tarkington Dowden (PRC TOWN)	10,185	9.9
16	Will Rogers Jr. (D)	61,437	53.7
	Leland Merritt Ford (R)	52,023	45.4
17	Cecil R. King (D-R)	92,260	99.8
18	Ward Johnson (R)	53,136	56.8
	Francis H. Gentry (D)	40,339	43.1
19	Chet Holifield (D)	34,918	63.1
	Carlton H. Casjens (R)	20,446	36.9
20	Carl Hinshaw (R)	62,628	48.4
	Joseph O. Donovan (D)	55,479	42.9
	Virgil G. Hinshaw (P)	6,864	5.3
21	Harry R. Sheppard (D-R)	38,419	96.4
22	John Phillips (R)	42,765	57.6
	N. E. West (D)	31,440	42.4
23	Edouard V. M. Izac (D)	42,864	50.5
	James B. Abbey (R)	42,087	49.5

COLORADO

	Candidates	Votes	%
1	Lawrence Lewis (D)	58,143	53.4
	Olaf H. Jacobson (R)	50,083	46.0
2	William S. Hill (R)	64,984	67.7
	Julian E. Hall (D)	30,485	31.7
3	J. Edgar Chenoweth (R)	55,838	62.7
	J. C. Jarrett (D)	33,154	37.3
4	Robert F. Rockwell (R)	28,460	58.8
	Elizabeth E. Pellet (D)	19,979	41.3

CONNECTICUT

	Candidates	Votes	%
1	William J. Miller (R)	72,306	51.4
	Herman P. Kopplemann (D)	68,435	48.6
2	John D. McWilliams (R)	46,426	51.3
	William J. Fitzgerald (D)	43,934	48.6
3	Ranulf Compton (R)	57,612	51.7
	James A. Shanley (D)	53,825	48.3
4	Clare Boothe Luce (R)	63,719	46.5
	LeRoy D. Downs (D)	56,861	41.5
	David Mansell (SOC)	15,573	11.4
5	Joseph E. Talbot (R)	42,602	53.6
	William A. Patten (D)	36,327	45.7
AL	Boleslaus J. Monkiewicz (R)	283,280	49.8
	Lucien J. Maciora (D)	257,941	45.3

DELAWARE

	Candidates	Votes	%
AL	Earle D. Willey (R)	45,376	53.6
	Philip A. Traynor (D)	38,791	45.8

FLORIDA

	Candidates	Votes	%
1	J. Hardin Peterson (D)	25,037	100.0
2	Emory H. Price (D)	15,777	100.0
3	Robert L. F. Sikes (D)	11,739	100.0
4	Arthur P. Cannon (D)	25,056	81.4
	Bert Leigh Acker (R)	5,725	18.6
5	Joe Hendricks (D)	16,850	70.9
	Emory Akerman (R)	6,906	29.1
AL	Robert A. Green (D)	91,120	100.0

GEORGIA

	Candidates	Votes	%
1	Hugh Peterson (D)	6,980	98.2
2	E. E. Cox (D)	3,793	100.0
3	Stephen Pace (D)	4,818	100.0
4	A. Sidney Camp (D)	5,106	100.0
5	Robert Ramspeck (D)	9,176	96.0
6	Carl Vinson (D)	5,725	100.0
7	Malcolm Tarver (D)	5,172	100.0
8	John Gibson (D)	4,785	100.0
9	B. Frank Whelchel (D)	7,404	71.1
	Roscoe Pickett (I)	3,013	28.9
10	Paul Brown (D)	5,393	100.0

IDAHO

	Candidates	Votes	%
1	Compton I. White (D)	30,105	54.1
	H. C. Baldridge (R)	25,562	45.9
2	Henry C. Dworshak (R)	45,805	54.8
	Ira H. Masters (D)	37,815	45.2

ILLINOIS

	Candidates	Votes	%
1	William L. Dawson (D)	26,280	52.8
	William E. King (R)	23,537	47.3
2	William A. Rowan (D)	110,069	50.8
	Thomas J. Downs (R)	106,552	49.2
3	Fred E. Busbey (R)	115,390	51.3
	Edward A. Kelly (D)	109,409	48.7
4	Martin Gorski (D)	60,623	78.7
	Arthur Joseph Rutshaw (R)	16,396	21.3
5	Adolph J. Sabath (D)	29,167	72.2
	Clem Graver (R)	11,255	27.8
6	Thomas J. O'Brien (D)	149,342	57.4
	Raymond E. Trafelet (R)	110,823	42.6
7	Leonard W. Schuetz (D)	179,906	50.3
	James C. Moreland (R)	177,931	49.7
8	Thomas S. Gordon (D)	33,425	78.8
	Rena E. Pikiel (R)	8,995	21.2
9	Charles S. Dewey (R)	40,803	51.3
	Irwin N. Walker (D)	38,679	48.7
10	Ralph E. Church (R)	150,558	63.0
	Jack Bairstow (D)	88,266	37.0
11	Chauncey W. Reed (R)	97,316	71.0
	Joseph S. Perry (D)	39,829	29.0
12	Noah M. Mason (R)	68,426	71.4
	Tony R. Berrettini (D)	27,405	28.6
13	Leo E. Allen (R)	48,500	79.4
	Michael M. Kinney (D)	12,596	20.6
14	Anton J. Johnson (R)	47,294	59.3
	Robert M. Harper (D)	32,450	40.7
15	Robert B. Chiperfield (R)	48,677	62.1
	Montgomery B. Carrott (D)	29,741	37.9
16	Everett M. Dirksen (R)	55,135	68.8
	James D. Carrigan (D)	24,969	31.2
17	Leslie C. Arends (R)	44,563	72.4
	Frank Gillespie (D)	17,023	27.6
18	Jessie Sumner (R)	51,281	62.4
	Fred E. Butcher (D)	30,852	37.6
19	William H. Wheat (R)	56,657	57.3
	Alfred D. Huston (D)	42,171	42.7
20	Sid Simpson (R)	31,360	51.0
	James M. Barnes (D)	30,131	49.0
21	Evan Howell (R)	54,585	58.1
	William P. Roberts (D)	39,318	41.9
22	Calvin D. Johnson (R)	67,313	55.7
	Harry C. Odum (D)	53,470	44.3
23	Charles W. Vursell (R)	47,526	52.7
	Laurence F. Arnold (D)	42,736	47.4
24	James V. Heidinger (R)	37,008	58.4
	Leroy Barham (D)	26,377	41.6
25	C. W. Bishop (R)	49,965	55.1
	Kent E. Keller (D)	40,762	44.9
AL	Stephen A. Day (R)	1,481,419	51.3
	Benjamin S. Adamowski (D)	1,395,053	48.3

INDIANA

	Candidates	Votes	%
1	Ray J. Madden (D)	44,334	53.6
	Samuel W. Cullison (R)	38,450	46.5
2	Charles A. Halleck (R)	63,120	61.2
	Emmett Ferguson (D)	39,943	38.8
3	Robert A. Grant (R)	66,434	55.2
	Lewis J. Murphy (D)	53,992	44.8
4	George W. Gillie (R)	61,032	61.0
	Samuel C. Cleland (D)	39,032	39.0
5	Forest A. Harness (R)	80,464	55.7
	Edward C. Hays (D)	63,994	44.3
6	Noble J. Johnson (R)	65,764	58.1
	Floyd I. McMurray (D)	47,363	41.9
7	Gerald W. Landis (R)	69,044	56.9
	O. A. Noland (D)	52,386	43.1
8	Charles M. LaFollette (R)	67,237	53.7
	John W. Boehne Jr. (D)	57,868	46.3
9	Earl Wilson (R)	55,949	55.9
	Roy Huckleberry (D)	44,096	44.1
10	Raymond S. Springer (R)	67,201	57.4
	William H. Larrabee (D)	49,963	42.6
11	Louis Ludlow (D)	79,932	50.3
	Howard M. Meyer (R)	79,136	49.8

IOWA

	Candidates	Votes	%
1	Thomas E. Martin (R)	55,139	61.5
	Vern W. Nall (D)	32,893	36.7
2	Henry O. Talle (R)	62,290	57.4
	William S. Jacobsen (D)	46,310	42.6
3	John W. Gwynne (R)	54,124	60.7
	William D. Kearney (D)	35,065	39.3

Candidates	Votes	%
4 Karl M. LeCompte (R)	52,258	64.5
Thomas L. Curran (D)	28,745	35.5
5 Paul Cunningham (R)	48,578	63.2
E. Frank Fox (D)	28,287	36.8
6 Fred C. Gilchrist (R)	46,843	60.3
Edward Breen (D)	30,802	39.7
7 Ben F. Jensen (R)	49,086	64.2
Jess Alton (D)	27,409	35.8
8 Charles B. Hoeven (R)	42,154	64.6
Walter T. Mahoney (D)	23,059	35.4

KANSAS

Candidates	Votes	%
1 William P. Lambertson (R)	49,962	59.2
John E. Barrett (D)	34,404	40.8
2 Ulysses S. Guyer (R)	48,594	59.1
Herbert L. Drake (D)	33,625	40.9
3 Thomas D. Winter (R)	40,789	59.9
William E. Murphy (D)	27,364	40.2
4 Edward H. Rees (R)	55,612	55.7
John M. Houston (D)	44,313	44.4
5 Clifford R. Hope (R)	54,655	66.6
S. S. Alexander (D)	27,381	33.4
6 Frank Carlson (R)	49,403	64.2
Lud W. Strnad (D)	27,590	35.8

KENTUCKY

Candidates	Votes	%
1 Noble J. Gregory (D)	17,027	67.5
Walter L. Prince (R)	8,195	32.5
2 Beverly M. Vincent (D)	21,866	100.0
3 Emmet O'Neal (D)	39,866	55.2
J. R. Todd (R)	32,404	44.8
4 Edward W. Creal (D)	23,871	55.7
Don Victor Drye (R)	19,015	44.3
5 Brent Spence (D)	18,510	53.5
Lewis R. Kimberly (R)	12,073	34.9
Ed Wimmer (I)	3,806	11.0
6 Virgil Chapman (D)	27,382	100.0
7 Andrew J. May (D)	22,160	50.6
Elmer E. Gabbard (R)	21,620	49.4
8 Joe B. Bates (D)	22,499	56.0
F. A. Easterling (R)	17,644	44.0
9 John M. Robsion (R)	34,440	100.0

LOUISIANA

Candidates	Votes	%
1 F. Edward Hebert (D)	20,973	100.0
2 Paul H. Maloney (D)	19,007	100.0
3 James Domengeaux (D)	6,260	100.0
4 Overton Brooks (D)	7,184	100.0
5 Charles E. McKenzie (D)	7,949	100.0
6 James H. Morrison (D)	9,313	100.0
7 Henry D. Larcade Jr. (D)	6,201	100.0
8 A. Leonard Allen (D)	8,100	100.0

MAINE

Candidates	Votes	%
1 Robert Hale (R)	38,128	57.0
Louis J. Brann (D)	28,759	43.0
2 Margaret Chase Smith (R)	42,062	67.6
Bradford C. Redonnett (D)	20,164	32.4
3 Frank Fellows (R)	31,728	100.0

MARYLAND

Candidates	Votes	%
1 David Jenkins Ward (D)	25,270	55.9
William H. Lloyd (R)	19,938	44.1
2 Harry Streett Baldwin (D)	57,865	62.2
George R. Norris (R)	35,228	37.8
3 Thomas D'Alesandro Jr. (D)	20,450	73.3
Edward S. Panetti (R)	7,469	26.8
4 Daniel Ellison (R)	22,673	50.9
John M. Wyatt (D)	21,845	49.1
5 Lansdale G. Sasscer (D)	33,191	66.7
John Torvestad (R)	16,596	33.3
6 J. Glenn Beall (R)	45,724	59.5
E. Brooke Lee (D)	31,187	40.6

MASSACHUSETTS

Candidates	Votes	%
1 Allen T. Treadway (R)	50,302	56.7
Frank Hurley (D)	36,257	40.9
2 Charles R. Clason (R)	58,781	61.6
John J. Granfield (D)	36,675	38.4
3 Philip J. Philbin (D)	46,412	50.4
Alfred Woollacott (R)	45,689	49.6
4 Pehr G. Holmes (R)	57,323	57.2
John S. Sullivan (D)	42,895	42.8
5 Edith Nourse Rogers (R)	95,231	100.0
6 George J. Bates (R)	68,739	75.3
James D. Burns (D)	22,523	24.7
7 Thomas J. Lane (D)	68,073	100.0
8 Angier L. Goodwin (R)	57,016	56.2
Frederick McDermott (D)	44,401	43.8
9 Charles L. Gifford (R)	50,902	58.8
George F. Backus (D)	35,633	41.2
10 Christian A. Herter (R)	64,247	51.2
William A. Carey (D)	61,359	48.9
11 James M. Curley (D)	60,850	69.3
Vincent Mottola (R)	27,008	30.7
12 John W. McCormack (D)	76,043	78.7
Francis P. O'Neill (R)	20,600	21.3
13 Richard B. Wigglesworth (R)	62,608	59.3
Francis H. Foy (D)	42,995	40.7
14 Joseph W. Martin Jr. (R)	54,977	59.4
Terrance J. Lomax Jr. (D)	37,598	40.6

MICHIGAN

Candidates	Votes	%
1 George G. Sadowski (D)	48,620	78.0
John B. Sosnowski (R)	13,691	22.0
2 Earl C. Michener (R)	40,439	63.1
Redmond M. Burr (D)	23,277	36.3
3 Paul Shafer (R)	41,002	65.7
Harold E. Steinbacher (D)	20,334	32.6
4 Clare E. Hoffman (R)	42,653	68.6
Dean Morley (D)	19,065	30.7
5 Bartel J. Jonkman (R)	37,020	54.0
Herman J. Wierenga (D)	30,840	45.0
6 William W. Blackney (R)	48,364	57.6
David M. Martin (D)	34,893	41.6
7 Jesse P. Wolcott (R)	46,946	67.3
Leroy S. Wilson (D)	22,775	32.7
8 Fred L. Crawford (R)	45,182	66.9
Michael J. Hart (D)	21,689	32.1
9 Albert J. Engel (R)	34,548	65.4
Arnold B. Coxhill (D)	17,954	34.0
10 Roy O. Woodruff (R)	31,895	60.1
John E. Morrison (D)	20,852	39.3
11 Fred Bradley (R)	32,579	58.0
Paul L. Adams (D)	23,555	42.0
12 John B. Bennett (R)	31,643	51.5
Frank E. Hook (D)	27,983	45.6
13 George D. O'Brien (D)	33,807	51.1
Clarence J. McLeod (R)	32,298	48.9
14 Louis C. Rabaut (D)	50,707	58.7
Claude G. McDonald (R)	35,638	41.3
15 John D. Dingell (D)	52,384	64.6
Ivan L. Bowman (R)	28,694	35.4
16 John Lesinski (D)	42,911	58.5
Robert W. Ford (R)	30,480	41.5
17 George A. Dondero (R)	56,607	56.8
Dorothy K. Roosevelt (D)	43,036	43.2

MINNESOTA

Candidates	Votes	%
1 August H. Andresen (R)	58,387	66.2
Harold R. Atwood (D)	29,771	33.8
2 Joseph P. O'Hara (R)	60,028	70.0
R. J. Neunsinger (D)	13,866	16.2
Charles D. Peterson (F-LAB)	11,819	13.8
3 Richard P. Gale (R)	44,662	49.0
Charles Munn (F-LAB)	29,936	32.9
William J. Gallagher (D)	16,505	18.1
4 Melvin J. Maas (R)	45,903	65.1
William Mahoney (F-LAB)	17,071	24.2
Edward K. Delaney (D)	6,938	9.8
5 Walter H. Judd (R)	60,883	63.8

Candidates	Votes	%
Joseph Gilbert (F-LAB)	18,566	19.5
Thomas P. Ryan (D)	15,976	16.7
6 Harold Knutson (R)	49,295	57.1
E. Thomas O'Brien (D)	37,070	43.0
7 H. Carl Andersen (R)	46,570	54.8
Theodor S. Slen (D)	21,192	24.9
Francis H. Shoemaker (F-LAB)	17,241	20.3
8 William A. Pittenger (R)	51,803	58.2
Rudolph Rautio (F-LAB)	21,786	24.5
E. J. Larsen (D)	10,284	11.6
S. B. Ruohoniemi (D)	5,148	5.8
9 Harold C. Hagen (F-LAB)	35,265	50.4
John W. Padden (R)	34,661	49.6

MISSISSIPPI

Candidates	Votes	%
1 John E. Rankin (D)	7,079	100.0
2 Jamie L. Whitten (D)	5,698	100.0
3 William M. Whittington (D)	5,552	100.0
4 Thomas G. Abernethy (D)	5,660	100.0
5 W. Arthur Winstead (D)	10,548	100.0
6 William M. Colmer (D)	7,462	100.0
7 Dan R. McGehee (D)	9,699	100.0

MISSOURI

Candidates	Votes	%
1 Samuel W. Arnold (R)	41,809	55.5
Milton A. Romjue (D)	33,465	44.5
2 Max Schwabe (R)	37,635	50.4
William L. Nelson (D)	37,069	49.6
3 William C. Cole (R)	40,227	56.4
Richard M. Duncan (D)	31,108	43.6
4 C. Jasper Bell (D)	30,227	60.5
John W. Mitchell (R)	19,709	39.5
5 Roger C. Slaughter (D)	27,243	50.9
Ralph B. Innis (R)	26,163	48.9
6 Philip A. Bennett (R)	46,735*	54.6
Sam M. Wear (D)	38,946	45.5
7 Dewey Short (R)	49,595	63.5
Ralph C. Max (D)	28,542	36.5
8 William P. Elmer (R)	39,422	51.5
Clyde Williams (D)	37,072	48.5
9 Clarence Cannon (D)	30,082	54.6
Carl E. Starkloff (R)	24,912	45.2
10 Orville Zimmerman (D)	29,514	56.7
Merrill Spitler (R)	22,555	43.3
11 Louis E. Miller (R)	36,133	50.4
John B. Sullivan (D)	35,510	49.6
12 Walter C. Ploeser (R)	68,329	57.0
Martin N. Neaf (D)	51,649	43.1
13 John J. Cochran (D)	37,651	61.3
D. E. Horn (R)	23,770	38.7

MONTANA

Candidates	Votes	%
1 Mike Mansfield (D)	42,754	59.0
H. K. Hazelbaker (R)	28,603	39.5
2 James F. O'Connor (D)	50,489	52.0
F. F. Haynes (R)	45,051	46.4

NEBRASKA

Candidates	Votes	%
1 Carl T. Curtis (R)	69,651	66.6
Ralph G. Brooks (D)	31,422	30.0
2 Howard Buffett (R)	40,646	53.2
Charles F. McLaughlin (D)	35,743	46.8
3 Karl Stefan (R)	61,813	66.3
George Hally (D)	27,708	29.7
4 Arthur L. Miller (R)	55,914	67.1
Tom Lanigan (D)	27,406	32.9

NEVADA

Candidates	Votes	%
AL Maurice J. Sullivan (D)	21,100	53.6
Ernest Brooks (R)	18,269	46.4

NEW HAMPSHIRE

Candidates	Votes	%
1 Chester E. Merrow (R)	43,281	52.1
Thomas A. Murray (D)	39,743	47.9

Candidates	Votes	%
2 Foster Stearns (R)	42,718	58.4
Henry J. Prouix (D)	30,473	41.6

NEW JERSEY

Candidates	Votes	%
1 Charles A. Wolverton (R)	74,867	61.4
Ralph W. Wescott (D)	46,445	38.1
2 Elmer H. Wene (D)	40,478	53.0
Benjamin D. Foulois (R)	35,930	47.0
3 James C. Auchincloss (R)	51,573	53.4
William H. Sutphin (D)	45,037	46.6
4 D. Lane Powers (R)	51,498	63.8
William H. Thompson Jr. (D)	29,088	36.0
5 Charles A. Eaton (R)	61,896	64.7
J. Ellis Kirkham (D)	32,999	34.5
6 Donald H. McLean (R)	52,211	57.8
George R. Walsh (D)	36,425	40.4
7 J. Parnell Thomas (R)	55,424	68.8
Emil M. Wulster (D)	25,171	31.2
8 Gordon Canfield (R)	56,582	66.6
Irving Abramson (D)	28,060	33.0
9 Harry L. Towe (R)	51,692	61.8
Frank H. Hennessy (D)	32,021	38.3
10 Fred A. Hartley Jr. (R)	37,189	53.0
Frederic Bigelow (D)	31,504	44.9
11 Frank L. Sundstrom (R)	36,500	58.9
William Freiday (D)	23,630	38.2
12 Robert W. Kean (R)	43,942	60.8
Joseph Siegler (D)	26,188	36.3
13 Mary T. Norton (D)	73,766	79.6
Raymond J. Cuddy (R)	18,894	20.4
14 Edward J. Hart (D)	75,322	78.9
Otto A. Trankler (R)	20,161	21.1

NEW MEXICO

Candidates	Votes	%
AL Clinton P. Anderson (D)	62,320✓	
Antonio M. Fernandez (D)	57,474✓	
William A. Sutherland (R)	43,627	
Reese P. Fullerton (R)	43,071	

NEW YORK

Candidates	Votes	%
1 Leonard W. Hall (R)	197,473	68.1
Rene A. Carreau (D)	83,453	28.8
2 William B. Barry (D)	125,090	50.3
William D. Rawlins (R)	95,240	38.3
William F. Brunner (AM LAB)	26,224	11.4
3 Joseph L. Pfeifer (D)	18,700	59.6
Samuel Rosenthal (R)	8,979	28.6
Joseph A. Weil (AM LAB)	3,693	11.8
4 Thomas H. Cullen (D)	21,456	63.3
Frederick H. Gutkes (R)	10,070	29.7
Matthew P. Coleman (AM LAB)	2,370	7.0
5 James J. Heffernan (D, AM LAB)	44,522	65.7
Charles G. Jochum (R)	23,285	34.3
6 Andrew L. Somers (D, AM LAB)	96,990	72.2
Theodore R. Studwell (R)	37,427	27.8
7 John J. Delaney (D, AM LAB)	27,688	72.8
Harry Boyarsky (R)	10,353	27.2
8 Donald L. O'Toole (D, AM LAB)	158,685	72.8
George F. Picken (R)	59,408	27.2
9 Eugene J. Keogh (D)	44,064	45.7
William J. Drake (R)	41,491	43.0
Albert Slade (AM LAB)	10,957	11.4
10 Emanuel Celler (D, AM LAB)	32,026	68.5
Jerome Lewis (R)	14,693	31.5
11 James A. O'Leary (D, AM LAB)	31,723	57.9
Robert S. Woodward (R)	23,029	42.1
12 Samuel Dickstein (D, AM LAB)	13,584	87.0
Hyman Hecht (R)	2,031	13.0
13 Louis J. Capozzoli (D, AM LAB)	11,245	74.0
John Rosenberg (R)	3,947	26.0
14 Arthur G. Klein (D, AM LAB)	17,652	63.7
Stuart Scheftel (R)	10,037	36.3
15 Thomas F. Burchill (D)	14,746	58.7
Walter A. Lockwood (R)	7,566	30.1
John Rogan (AM LAB)	2,798	11.1
16 James H. Fay (D, AM LAB)	18,710	50.1
William T. Pheiffer (R)	18,630	49.9
17 Joseph Clark Baldwin (R, AM LAB)	38,079	61.0
Carl Sherman (D)	24,365	39.0
18 Martin J. Kennedy (D)	18,636	52.8
Garrow T. Gear Jr. (R, AM LAB)	16,665	47.2
19 Sol Bloom (D, AM LAB)	41,566	67.5
Clarence McMillan (R)	20,000	32.5
20 Vito Marcantonio (R, D)	18,924	100.0
21 Joseph A. Gavagan (D, AM LAB)	60,588	66.3
Herbert Malkin (R)	30,796	33.7
22 Walter A. Lynch (D, AM LAB)	25,933	67.1
Richard C. Califano (R)	12,714	32.9
23 Charles A. Buckley (D, AM LAB)	142,395	74.0
William J. Waterman (R)	50,063	26.0
24 James M. Fitzpatrick (D, AM LAB)	117,198	57.5
Ralph W. Gwinn (R)	86,506	42.5
25 Ralph A. Gamble (R)	85,024	69.7
James J. Butterly (D)	33,040	27.1
26 Hamilton Fish (R)	48,793	52.2
Ferdinand A. Hoyt (D, AM LAB)	44,751	47.8
27 Jay LeFevre (R)	53,626	63.1
Sharon J. Mauhs (D, AM LAB)	31,426	36.9
28 William T. Byrne (D, AM LAB)	86,767	62.9
Ernest B. Morris (R)	51,190	37.1
29 Dean P. Taylor (R, AM LAB)	69,794	68.8
John T. Degnan (D)	31,616	31.2
30 Bernard W. Kearney (R)	53,147	62.6
Burlin G. McKillip (D)	29,414	34.6
31 Clarence E. Kilburn (R)	43,197	69.0
Thomas Q. Ryan (D, AM LAB)	19,448	31.0
32 Francis D. Culkin (R)	50,970	73.2
Vanche F. Milligan (D)	17,631	25.3
33 Fred J. Douglas (R)	53,030	60.3
Stanard Dow Butler (D, AM LAB)	34,965	39.7
34 Edwin Arthur Hall (R)	53,762	60.8
Arthur J. Ruland (D)	33,276	37.6
35 Clarence E. Hancock (R)	82,021	64.5
Arthur B. McGuire (D)	42,270	33.2
36 John Taber (R)	47,620	62.6
Charles Osborne (D, AM LAB)	28,502	37.4
37 W. Sterling Cole (R)	54,700	70.9
Daniel Crowley (D, AM LAB)	22,452	29.1
38 Joseph J. O'Brien (R)	77,970	59.1
Walden Moore (D, AM LAB)	53,889	40.9
39 James W. Wadsworth (R, D)	83,195	100.0
40 Walter Gresham Andrews (R)	91,222	68.8
Julian Park (D, AM LAB)	41,459	31.2
41 Joseph Mruk (R)	49,239	57.4
Alfred F. Beiter (D, AM LAB)	36,589	42.6
42 John C. Butler (R)	39,650	53.7
Frank J. Caffery (D, AM LAB)	34,248	46.3
43 Daniel Reed (R)	43,730	64.3
Clare Barnes (D)	20,867	30.7
Nelson M. Fuller (AM LAB)	3,466	5.1
AL Winifred C. Stanley (R)	1,965,794✓	
Matthew J. Merritt (D, AM LAB)	1,909,706✓	
Charles Muzzicato (R)	1,887,688	
Flora D. Johnson (D, AM LAB)	1,872,321	
Benjamin J. Davis Jr. (COM)	52,002	
Elizabeth Gurley Flynn (COM)	50,305	
Layle Lane (SOC)	22,361	
Amicus Most (SOC)	19,249	

NORTH CAROLINA

Candidates	Votes	%
1 Herbert C. Bonner (D)	8,444	92.6
J. C. Meekins Jr. (R)	671	7.4
2 John H. Kerr (D)	7,124	100.0
3 Graham A. Barden (D)	9,596	100.0
4 Harold D. Cooley (D)	20,703	65.2
Wiley L. Ward (R)	11,064	34.8
5 John Hamlin Folger (D)	20,601	67.5
S. Evan Hall (R)	9,899	32.5
6 Carl T. Durham (D)	16,548	74.5
Hobart M. Patterson (R)	5,660	25.5
7 J. Bayard Clark (D)	12,112	100.0
8 William O. Burgin (D)	27,146	56.5
A. D. Barber (R)	20,868	43.5
9 Robert L. Doughton (D)	29,213	100.0
10 Cameron Morrison (D)	26,785	55.4
Charles A. Jonas (R)	21,535	44.6
11 Alfred L. Bulwinkle (D)	20,270	100.0
12 Zebulon Weaver (D)	30,438	65.3
Gola P. Ferguson (R)	16,150	34.7

NORTH DAKOTA

Candidates	Votes	%
AL Usher L. Burdick (R)	85,936✓	
William Lemke (R)	65,905✓	
Charles R. Robertson (IR)	48,472	
Halvor L. Halvorson (IR)	47,972	
E. A. Johanson (D)	31,547	

OHIO

Candidates	Votes	%
1 Charles H. Elston (R)	54,120	61.5
William H. Hessler (D)	33,884	38.5
2 William E. Hess (R)	53,083	64.0
Nicholas Bauer (D)	29,823	36.0
3 Harry P. Jeffrey (R)	51,477	51.6
Greg Holbrock (D)	48,338	48.4
4 Robert F. Jones (R)	39,275	63.5
Clarence C. Miller (D)	22,567	36.5
5 Cliff Clevenger (R)	30,667	63.7
Ferdinand E. Warren (D)	17,514	36.4
6 Edward O. McCowen (R)	33,171	51.1
Jacob E. Davis (D)	31,793	48.9
7 Clarence J. Brown (R)	52,270	69.1
George H. Smith (D)	23,384	30.9
8 Frederick C. Smith (R)	33,797	59.8
Brooks Fletcher (D)	22,753	40.2
9 Homer A. Ramey (R)	47,377	51.8
John F. Hunter (D)	44,027	48.2
10 Thomas A. Jenkins (R)	29,691	64.2
Oral Daugherty (D)	16,582	35.8
11 Walter E. Brehm (R)	31,385	61.3
Harold K. Claypool (D)	19,817	38.7
12 John M. Vorys (R)	56,558	58.4
A. P. Lamneck (D)	40,290	41.6
13 Alvin Weichel (R)	37,923	61.6
E. C. Alexander (D)	23,618	38.4
14 Ed Rowe (R)	60,868	51.3
Dow W. Harter (D)	57,759	48.7
15 P. W. Griffiths (R)	35,137	60.2
Charles W. Lynch (D)	23,213	39.8
16 Henderson H. Carson (R)	50,657	52.7
William R. Thom (D)	45,531	47.3
17 J. Harry McGregor (R)	47,565	62.8
Samuel A. Anderson (D)	28,235	37.3
18 Earl R. Lewis (R)	43,279	53.3
Lawrence E. Imhoff (D)	37,951	46.7
19 Michael J. Kirwan (D)	60,248	56.4
James T. Begg (R)	46,567	43.6
20 Michael A. Feighan (D)	34,462	61.8
Harry T. Marshall (R)	14,001	25.1
Marie R. Sweeney (I)	7,289	13.1
21 Robert Crosser (D)	35,109	63.9
William J. Rogers (R)	19,137	34.8
22 Frances P. Bolton (R)	92,644	57.1
James Metzenbaum (D)	69,601	42.9
AL George H. Bender (R)	945,995	56.9
Stephen M. Young (D)	717,692	43.1

OKLAHOMA

Candidates	Votes	%
1 Wesley E. Disney (D)	42,907	54.2
W. R. Boyd (R)	35,174	44.4
2 Jack Nichols (D)	21,651	50.5
E. O. Clark (R)	21,266	49.6
3 Paul Stewart (D)	23,317	78.6

Candidates	Votes	%
Frank D. McSherry (R)	6,346	21.4
4 Lyle H. Boren (D)	23,921	56.8
Charles E. Wells (R)	18,177	43.2
5 A. S. Mike Monroney (D)	36,736	69.7
George Wesley Colvert (R)	15,738	29.9
6 Jed Johnson (D)	19,945	57.9
J. L Hart Jr. (R)	14,532	42.2
7 Victor Wickersham (D)	14,042	70.0
Roscoe C. Holt (R)	6,009	30.0
8 Ross Rizley (R)	30,522	60.3
Julius W. Cox (D)	19,765	39.1

OREGON

	Candidates	Votes	%
1	James W. Mott (R)	49,021	64.3
	Earl A. Nott (D)	27,208	35.7
2	Lowell Stockman (R)	26,723	61.4
	Walter M. Pierce (D)	16,809	38.6
3	Homer D. Angell (R)	55,775	51.8
	Thomas R. Mahoney (D)	51,870	48.2
4	Harris Ellsworth (R)	29,385	60.0
	Edward C. Kelly (D)	19,632	40.0

PENNSYLVANIA

	Candidates	Votes	%
1	James Gallagher (R)	44,519	53.5
	Leon Sacks (D)	38,768	46.6
2	James P. McGranery (D)	36,258	50.5
	Augustus Trask Ashton (R)	35,545	49.5
3	Michael J. Bradley (D)	47,515	51.4
	John R. K. Scott (R)	45,014	48.7
4	John Edward Sheridan (D)	43,284	53.2
	Howard T. Scott (R)	36,689	45.1
5	C. Frederick Pracht (R)	48,781	51.1
	Francis R. Smith (D)	46,691	48.9
6	Francis J. Myers (D)	53,284	55.3
	William H. Sylk (R)	42,995	44.7
7	Hugh Scott (R)	60,836	55.7
	Thomas Z. Minehart (D)	48,373	44.3
8	James Wolfenden (R)	48,210	58.5
	Vernon A. O'Rourke (D)	34,164	41.5
9	Charles L. Gerlach (R)	41,282	62.0
	Francis L. Collum (D)	25,284	38.0
10	J. Roland Kinzer (R)	52,380	68.8
	Daniel J. C. O'Donnell (D)	23,784	31.2
11	John W. Murphy (D)	43,585	55.8
	James K. Peck (R)	34,527	44.2
12	Thomas Byron Miller (R)	55,679	54.5
	Daniel J. Flood (D)	46,550	45.5
13	Ivor D. Fenton (R)	50,721	58.2
	J. Noble Hirsch (D)	36,466	41.8
14	Daniel K. Hoch (D)	23,247	51.0
	John C. Griesemer (R)	19,498	42.8
	Raymond Hofses (SOC)	2,783	6.1
15	Wilson D. Gillette (R)	63,077	65.7
	Michael E. Yurkovsky (D)	32,953	34.3
16	Thomas E. Scanlon (D)	47,920	51.3
	Robert Van Der Voort (R)	45,472	48.7
17	J. William Ditter (R)	52,661	69.2
	Charles W. Moyer (D)	23,492	30.9
18	Richard M. Simpson (R)	33,147	62.0
	John W. Mann (D, I)	20,340	38.0
19	John C. Kunkel (R)	62,119	66.0
	A. S. Beshore (D)	31,969	34.0
20	Leon H. Gavin (R)	37,738	64.5
	John C. Brecht (D)	20,171	34.5
21	Francis E. Walter (D)	32,498	53.5
	William Radford Coyle (R)	28,272	46.5
22	Chester H. Gross (R)	34,202	50.0
	Harry L. Haines (D)	34,131	49.9
23	James E. Van Zandt (R)	38,235	61.0
	Harry E. Diehl (D)	24,432	39.0
24	J. Buell Snyder (D)	33,480	51.1
	Carl H. Hoffman (R)	32,014	48.9
25	Grant Furlong (D)	38,316	50.3
	M. B. Armstrong (R)	37,903	49.7
26	Louis E. Graham (R)	41,730	58.5
	Peter P. Reising (D)	29,652	41.5
27	Harve Tibbott (R)	50,153	55.6
	Eddie McCloskey (D)	40,096	44.4

	Candidates	Votes	%
28	Augustine B. Kelley (D)	32,886	53.5
	Edward R. Stirling (R)	28,543	46.5
29	Robert L. Rodgers (R)	40,243	59.3
	James F. Lavery (D)	27,573	40.7
30	Samuel A. Weiss (D)	43,482	56.4
	John McDowell (R)	33,568	43.6
31	Herman P. Eberharter (D)	50,316	58.1
	Robert Garland (R)	36,239	41.9
32	James A. Wright (D)	41,798	51.6
	James Grove Fulton (R)	39,262	48.4
AL	William I. Troutman (R)	1,360,664	54.7
	Inez B. Peel (D)	1,105,992	44.4

RHODE ISLAND

	Candidates	Votes	%
1	Aime J. Forand (D)	68,242	59.0
	Charles H. Eden (R)	47,480	41.0
2	John E. Fogarty (D)	69,411	57.4
	Harry Sandager (R)	51,471	42.6

SOUTH CAROLINA

	Candidates	Votes	%
1	L. Mendel Rivers (D)	5,452	100.0
2	Hampton P. Fulmer (D)	4,448	100.0
3	Butler B. Hare (D)	3,201	100.0
4	Joseph R. Bryson (D)	4,228	100.0
5	James P. Richards (D)	3,122	100.0
6	John L. McMillan (D)	2,905	100.0

SOUTH DAKOTA

	Candidates	Votes	%
1	Karl E. Mundt (R)	81,373	59.9
	Fred Hildebrandt (D)	54,457	40.1
2	Francis H. Case (R)	30,389	71.9
	George M, Bailey (D)	11,892	28.1

TENNESSEE

	Candidates	Votes	%
1	B. Carroll Reece (R)	19,777	96.1
2	John Jennings Jr. (R)	18,613	53.6
	John T. O'Connor (D)	16,132	46.4
3	Estes Kefauver (D)	14,704	75.7
	Walter M. Higgins (R)	3,831	19.7
4	Albert Gore (D)	7,667	68.9
	H. E. McLean (R)	3,463	31.1
5	Jim Nance McCord (D)	9,841	100.0
6	J. Percy Priest (D)	4,945	100.0
7	Wirt Courtney (D)	8,689	100.0
8	Thomas J. Murray (D)	9,151	61.2
	P. W. Maddox (R)	5,801	38.8
9	Jere Cooper (D)	7,354	89.3
	S. Homer Tatum (R)	882	10.7
10	Clifford Davis (D)	23,660	100.0

TEXAS

	Candidates	Votes	%
1	Wright Patman (D)	9,502	100.0
2	Martin Dies (D)	10,128	100.0
3	Lindley Beckworth (D)	10,929	100.0
4	Sam Rayburn (D)	11,768	100.0
5	Hatton W. Sumners (D)	10,568	100.0
6	Luther A. Johnson (D)	10,726	100.0
7	Nat Patton (D)	11,043	99.1
8	Albert Thomas (D)	31,038	96.9
9	Joseph J. Mansfield (D)	13,852	100.0
10	Lyndon B. Johnson (D)	12,799	100.0
11	W. R. Poage (D)	7,554	100.0
12	Fritz Lanham (D)	25,894	100.0
13	Ed Gossett (D)	12,677	98.1
14	Richard M. Kleberg (D)	16,212	100.0
15	Milton H. West (D)	12,169	100.0
16	R. Ewing Thomason (D)	6,612	100.0
17	Sam Russell (D)	13,261	100.0
18	Eugene Worley (D)	10,739	100.0
19	George Mahon (D)	12,216	100.0
20	Paul J. Kilday (D)	8,860	81.7
	W. H. Turner (R)	1,980	18.3
21	O. Clark Fisher (D)	16,554	100.0

UTAH

	Candidates	Votes	%
1	Walter K. Granger (D)	36,297	50.2
	J. Bracken Lee (R)	36,028	49.8
2	J. W. Robinson (D)	43,582	55.8
	Reed E. Vetterli (R)	34,586	44.3

VERMONT

		Votes	%
AL	Charles A. Plumley (R)	40,751	70.2
	John B. Candon (D)	17,304	29.8

VIRGINIA

		Votes	%
1	Schuyler Otis Bland (D)	5,207	100.0
2	Winder R. Harris (D)	5,369	100.0
3	David E. Satterfield Jr. (D)	5,822	99.9
4	Patrick Henry Drewry (D)	4,457	99.9
5	Thomas G. Burch (D)	8,166	93.1
	Howard H. Carwile (SOC)	601	6.9
6	Clifton A. Woodrum (D)	10,510	93.4
	Stephen A. Moore (SOC)	724	6.4
7	A. Willis Robertson (D)	7,521	99.7
8	Howard W. Smith (D)	13,380	86.6
	Harrie Byrd Conlin (R)	1,757	11.4
9	John W. Flannagan Jr. (D)	16,655	63.6
	Cary Ingram Crockett (R)	9,534	36.4

WASHINGTON

		Votes	%
1	Warren G. Magnuson (D)	69,010	65.5
	Harold H. Stewart (R)	35,910	34.1
2	Henry M. Jackson (D)	39,628	59.9
	Payson Peterson (R)	26,573	40.1
3	Fred Norman (R)	34,462	57.1
	Martin F. Smith (D)	25,894	42.9
4	Hal Holmes (R)	34,495	63.6
	Knute Hill (D)	19,751	36.4
5	Walt Horan (R)	47,242	62.7
	C. C. Dill (D)	28,076	37.3
6	John M. Coffee (D)	42,666	64.0
	Ralph Woods (R)	23,650	35.5

WEST VIRGINIA

		Votes	%
1	Andrew C. Schiffler (R)	42,787	54.7
	Robert L. Ramsay (D)	35,498	45.3
2	Jennings Randolph (D)	32,935	50.2
	Charles G. Baker (R)	32,676	49.8
3	Edward G. Rohrbough (R)	37,135	53.2
	Andrew Edmiston (D)	32,682	46.8
4	Hubert S. Ellis (R)	48,697	52.2
	George W. Johnson (D)	44,528	47.8
5	John Kee (D)	36,625	57.2
	B. F. Howard (R)	27,400	42.8
6	Joe L. Smith (D)	46,281	51.8
	Houston G. Young (R)	43,043	48.2

WISCONSIN

		Votes	%
1	Lawrence H. Smith (R)	46,453	71.9
	Bernard F. Magruder (D)	16,848	26.1
2	Harry Sauthoff (PROG)	43,412	50.2
	Charles Hawks Jr. (R)	34,272	39.6
	Thomas R. Brooks (D)	8,315	9.6
3	William H. Stevenson (R)	34,177	46.9
	Gardner R. Withrow (PROG)	31,092	42.6
	William D. Carroll (D)	7,385	10.1
4	Thaddeus F. B. Wasielewski (D)	46,819	48.8
	John C. Schafer (R)	29,104	30.3
	John C. Brophy (PROG)	17,468	18.2
5	Howard J. McMurray (D)	44,337	43.2
	Lewis D. Thill (R)	38,345	37.4
	Roy A. Roush (PROG)	16,409	16.0
6	Frank B. Keefe (R)	41,385	62.2
	Eugene Schallern (D)	13,364	20.1
	Adam F. Poltl (PROG)	10,645	16.0
7	Reid F. Murray (R)	40,520	71.9
	John A. Kennedy (D)	15,821	28.1
8	LaVern R. Dilweg (D)	40,002	54.5

Candidates	Votes	%
Joshua L. Johns (R)	33,441	45.5
9 Merlin Hull (PROG)	37,919	61.8
George H. Hipke (R)	19,972	32.6
Jack E. Joyce (D)	3,448	5.6
10 Alvin E. O'Konski (R)	33,143	48.4
Bernard J. Gehrmann (PROG)	28,169	41.1
John G. Green (D)	7,198	10.5

WYOMING

Candidates	Votes	%
AL Frank A. Barrett (R)	37,965	50.7
John J. McIntyre (D)	36,892	49.3

1943 House Elections

KANSAS

Special Election

Candidates	Votes	%
2 Errett P. Scrivner (R)	19,798	69.1
Herbert L. Drake (D)	8,859	30.9

KENTUCKY

Special Election

Candidates	Votes	%
4 Chester O. Carrier (R)	29,855	63.4
J. Dan Talbott (D)	17,218	36.6

MISSOURI

Special Election

Candidates	Votes	%
6 Marion T. Bennett (R)	36,448	62.9
Sam M. Wear (D)	21,496	37.1

1944 House Elections

ALABAMA

	Candidates	Votes	%
1	Frank W. Boykin (D)	19,082	100.0
2	George M. Grant (D)	24,180	100.0
3	George W. Andrews (D)	20,470	100.0
4	Sam Hobbs (D)	19,391	84.5
	O. D. Beard (R)	3,554	15.5
5	Albert Rains (D)	25,317	100.0
6	Pete Jarman (D)	14,561	100.0
7	Carter Manasco (D)	21,671	34.1
	I. B. Burdick (R)	11,202	34.1
8	John J. Sparkman (D)	24,023	100.0
9	Luther Patrick (D)	31,767	81.7
	H. H. Grooms (R)	7,120	18.3

ARIZONA

	Candidates	Votes	%
AL	John R. Murdock (D)	88,532✓	
	Richard F. Harless (D)	86,691✓	
	Margaret Adams Rockwell (R)	39,035	
	A. M. Ward (R)	36,352	
	A. Walter Gehres (P)	469	

ARKANSAS

	Candidates	Votes	%
1	Ezekiel C. Gathings (D)	32,501	100.0
2	Wilbur D. Mills (D)	24,977	100.0
3	James W. Trimble (D)	20,061	63.3
	Lonzo A. Ross (R)	11,613	36.7
4	Fadjo Cravens (D)	30,310	100.0
5	Brooks Hays (D)	33,215	87.1
	Ross (R)	4,902	12.9
6	William F. Norrell (D)	31,785	100.0
7	Oren Harris (D)	27,851	100.0

CALIFORNIA

	Candidates	Votes	%
1	Clarence F. Lea (D-R)	92,706	99.9
2	Clair Engle (D)	48,201	63.8
	Jesse M. Mayo (R)	27,312	36.2
3	J. Leroy Johnson (R-D)	131,705	99.9
4	Franck R. Havenner (D)	73,582	50.1
	Thomas Rolph (R)	73,367	49.9
5	Richard J. Welch (R-D)	112,151	100.0
6	George P. Miller (D)	104,441	52.0
	Albert E. Carter (R)	96,395	48.0
7	John H. Tolan (D-R)	81,762	57.9
	Chesley M. Walter (R)	59,360	42.0
8	John Z. Anderson (R)	94,218	56.5
	Arthur L. Johnson (D)	72,420	43.5
9	Bertrand W. Gearhart (R-D)	66,845	99.5
10	Alfred J. Elliott (D-R)	60,001	99.9
11	George E. Outland (D)	52,218	56.0
	Fred J. Hart (R)	41,005	44.0
12	H. Jerry Voorhis (D)	77,385	55.3
	Roy P. McLaughlin (R)	62,524	44.7
13	Ned R. Healy (D)	66,854	54.9
	Norris Poulson (R)	54,792	45.0
14	Helen Gahagan Douglas (D)	65,729	51.5
	William D. Campbell (R)	61,767	48.4
15	Gordon L. McDonough (R)	100,305	56.6
	Hal Styles (D)	73,655	41.6
16	Ellis E. Patterson (D)	105,835	54.1
	Jesse Randolph Kellems (R)	89,700	45.9
17	Cecil R. King (D-R)	147,217	99.8
18	Clyde G. Doyle (D)	95,090	55.6
	Ward Johnson (R)	75,749	44.3
19	Chet Holifield (D)	65,758	71.7
	Carlton H. Casjens (R)	25,852	28.2
20	Carl Hinshaw (R)	112,663	51.8
	Archibald B. Young (D)	101,090	46.5
21	Harry R. Sheppard (D)	48,539	58.5
	Earl S. Webb (R)	34,409	41.5
22	John Phillips (R-D)	88,537	99.8
23	Edouard V. M. Izac (D)	86,707	55.1
	James B. Abbey (R)	70,787	45.0

COLORADO

	Candidates	Votes	%
1	Dean M. Gillespie (R)	90,151	51.8
	Charles A. Graham (D)	83,253	47.8
2	William S. Hill (R)	83,264	62.3
	David J. Miller (D)	49,079	36.8
3	J. Edgar Chenoweth (R)	69,492	56.3
	Arthur M. Wimmel (D)	53,904	43.7
4	Robert F. Rockwell (R)	38,671	61.7
	John L. Heuschkel (D)	24,039	38.3

CONNECTICUT

	Candidates	Votes	%
1	Herman P. Kopplemann (D)	120,100	54.0
	William J. Miller (R)	102,257	46.0
2	Chase Going Woodhouse (D)	63,013	51.2
	John D. McWilliams (R)	59,973	48.8
3	James P. Geelan (D)	82,472	51.5
	Ranulf Compton (R)	77,753	48.5
4	Clare Boothe Luce (R)	102,043	49.9
	Margaret Connor (D)	100,035	48.9
5	Joseph E. Talbot (R)	60,137	52.2
	Peter M. Higgins (D)	54,885	47.7
AL	Joseph F. Ryter (D)	424,146	51.2
	Boleslaus J. Monkiewicz (R)	397,725	48.1

DELAWARE

	Candidates	Votes	%
AL	Philip A. Traynor (D)	63,649	50.3
	Earle D. Willey (R)	62,378	49.3

FLORIDA

	Candidates	Votes	%
1	J. Hardin Peterson (D)	84,280	100.0
2	Emory H. Price (D)	66,604	100.0
3	Robert L. F. Sikes (D)	51,693	100.0
4	Pat Cannon (D)	65,900	72.0
	Edith Shaffer Stearn (R)	25,643	28.0
5	Joe Hendricks (D)	48,602	67.5
	Emory Akerman (R)	23,406	32.5
6	Dwight L. Rogers (D)	32,491	69.7
	Edward W. Greb (R)	14,134	30.3

GEORGIA

	Candidates	Votes	%
1	Hugh Peterson (D)	24,468	100.0
2	E. E. Cox (D)	21,791	100.0
3	Stephen Pace (D)	25,276	100.0
4	A. Sidney Camp (D)	27,375	100.0
5	Robert Ramspeck (D)	50,257	94.5
	H. A. Alexander (I)	2,929	5.5
6	Carl Vinson (D)	18,989	100.0
7	Malcolm Tarver (D)	31,400	100.0
8	John S. Gibson (D)	21,916	100.0
9	John S. Wood (D)	25,880	100.0
10	Paul Brown (D)	25,102	100.0

IDAHO

	Candidates	Votes	%
1	Compton I. White (D)	49,581	56.6
	Robert L. Brainard (R)	37,998	43.4
2	Henry C. Dworshak (R)	61,751	52.3
	Phil J. Evans (D)	56,249	47.7

ILLINOIS

	Candidates	Votes	%
1	William L. Dawson (D)	42,713	62.0
	William E. King (R)	26,204	38.0
2	William A. Rowan (D)	186,089	57.3
	Thomas J. Downs (R)	138,579	42.7
3	Edward A. Kelly (D)	158,944	52.0
	Fred E. Busbey (R)	146,961	48.0
4	Martin Gorski (D)	79,243	80.4
	Leo J. Kozicki (R)	19,346	19.6
5	Adolph J. Sabath (D)	38,370	76.3
	Max Price (R)	11,929	23.7

	Candidates	Votes	%
6	Thomas J. O'Brien (D)	211,056	59.9
	Charles J. Anderson Jr. (R)	140,069	39.7
7	William W. Link (D)	261,473	54.6
	Charles H. Garland (R)	217,207	45.4
8	Thomas S. Gordon (D)	39,866	79.2
	John F. Uczciwek (R)	10,474	20.8
9	Alexander J. Resa (D)	61,168	52.8
	Charles S. Dewey (R)	54,698	47.2
10	Ralph E. Church (R)	193,948	55.8
	Curtis D. MacDougall (D)	153,644	44.2
11	Chauncey W. Reed (R)	128,064	66.2
	Otto Joseph Hruby Jr. (D)	65,296	33.8
12	Noah M. Mason (R)	86,228	61.0
	Herbert J. Max (D)	55,236	39.1
13	Leo E. Allen (R)	59,372	70.0
	Garret J. Schutt (D)	25,482	30.0
14	Anton J. Johnson (R)	55,812	54.4
	Carl M. Seaberg (D)	46,759	45.6
15	Robert B. Chiperfield (R)	58,358	59.3
	Ray Simpkins (D)	40,093	40.7
16	Everett M. Dirksen (R)	70,301	59.0
	M. R. Clark (D)	48,779	41.0
17	Leslie C. Arends (R)	52,706	66.4
	Ruth G. Fillingham (D)	26,732	33.7
18	Jessie Sumner (R)	58,617	56.9
	Carl B. Jewell (D)	44,340	43.1
19	Rolla C. McMillen (R)	70,942	55.8
	George M. Brown (D)	56,247	44.2
20	Sid Simpson (R)	38,922	55.6
	Don Irving (D)	31,092	44.4
21	Evan Howell (R)	62,879	55.7
	Thomas L. Jarrett (D)	50,050	44.3
22	Melvin Price (D)	83,311	50.8
	Calvin D. Johnson (R)	80,616	49.2
23	Charles W. Vursell (R)	56,712	54.7
	J. E. McMackin (D)	46,957	45.3
24	James V. Heidinger (R)	42,927	58.2
	Early C. Phelps (D)	30,808	41.8
25	C. W. Bishop (R)	57,672	53.5
	Kent E. Keller (D)	50,140	46.5
AL	Emily Taft Douglas (D)	2,030,755	52.3
	Stephen A. Day (R)	1,839,518	47.4

Special Election

	Candidates	Votes	%
19	Rolla McMillen (R)	4,722	98.7

INDIANA

	Candidates	Votes	%
1	Ray J. Madden (D)	75,635	61.3
	Otto G. Fifield (R)	46,969	38.7
2	Charles A. Halleck (R)	78,061	61.6
	James O. Cox (D)	48,103	37.9
3	Robert A. Grant (R)	85,362	51.8
	Marshall A. Kizer (D)	78,621	47.7
4	George W. Gillie (R)	81,110	59.9
	Robert W. Bushee (D)	53,636	39.6
5	Forest A. Harness (R)	94,274	53.1
	Bennett H. Rockey (D)	80,208	45.1
6	Noble J. Johnson (R)	75,517	55.2
	Otis G. Jamison (D)	60,758	44.5
7	Gerald W. Landis (R)	73,417	53.9
	Arthur H. Greenwood (D)	62,136	45.6
8	Charles M. LaFollette (R)	84,095	52.0
	Charles J. Eichel (D)	76,905	47.6
9	Earl Wilson (R)	62,831	55.6
	George W. Elliott (D)	49,380	43.7
10	Raymond S. Springer (R)	82,582	54.3
	Sidney E. Baker (D)	67,724	44.5
11	Louis Ludlow (D)	114,051	51.1
	Judson L. Stark (R)	108,503	48.6

IOWA

	Candidates	Votes	%
1	Thomas E. Martin (R)	78,729	56.7
	Clair A. Williams (D)	60,048	43.3

	Candidates	Votes	%
2	Henry O. Talle (R)	86,903	55.9
	George C. Classen (D)	68,489	44.1
3	John W. Gwynne (R)	74,901	56.8
	William D. Kearney (D)	56,985	43.2
4	Karl M. LeCompte (R)	59,658	54.9
	Harold J. Fleck (D)	49,098	45.2
5	Paul Cunningham (R)	66,260	54.1
	Ralph N. Lynch (D)	56,138	45.8
6	James I. Dolliver (R)	60,153	58.8
	Charles Hanna (D)	42,098	41.1
7	Ben F. Jensen (R)	66,905	61.5
	Albert McGinn (D)	41,802	38.4
8	Charles B. Hoeven (R)	58,537	56.2
	Lester S. Gillette (D)	45,682	43.8

KANSAS

1	Albert M. Cole (R)	71,565	67.3
	Ralph Ulm (D)	34,731	32.7
2	Errett P. Scrivner (R)	68,815	59.1
	Albert Baker (D)	47,676	40.9
3	Thomas D. Winter (R)	52,361	60.2
	Herman L. Gees (D)	34,645	39.8
4	Edward H. Rees (R)	90,186	58.6
	William J. Kropp (D)	63,843	41.5
5	Clifford R. Hope (R)	72,370	69.0
	A. E. Hawes (D)	32,557	31.0
6	Frank Carlson (R)	63,035	66.0
	Dan M. McCarthy (D)	32,408	34.0

KENTUCKY

1	Noble J. Gregory (D)	51,369	69.3
	A. R. Anderson (R)	22,196	29.9
2	Earle C. Clements (D)	57,948	57.3
	Otis White (R)	42,802	42.4
3	Emmet O'Neal (D)	79,922	57.3
	Garland R. Hubbard (R)	59,190	42.5
4	Frank L. Chelf (D)	48,671	54.5
	Chester O. Carrier (R)	40,317	45.2
5	Brent Spence (D)	45,228	58.0
	Olin W. Davis (R)	32,606	41.8
6	Virgil Chapman (D)	63,404	58.8
	George W. Boner (R)	44,214	41.0
7	Andrew J. May (D)	33,406	52.5
	Elmer Gabbard (R)	30,165	47.4
8	Joe B. Bates (D)	48,969	54.3
	Thomas S. Yates (R)	41,154	45.6
9	John M. Robsion (R)	68,908	68.8
	H. F. Reed (D)	31,019	31.0

LOUISIANA

1	F. Edward Hebert (D)	55,887	100.0
2	Paul H. Maloney (D)	56,636	100.0
3	James Domengeaux (D)	28,123	100.0
4	Overton Brooks (D)	27,886	100.0
5	Charles E. McKenzie (D)	25,462	100.0
6	James H. Morrison (D)	38,561	100.0
7	Henry D. Larcade Jr. (D)	26,931	100.0
8	A. Leonard Allen (D)	23,083	100.0

Special Election

3	James Domengeaux (D)	26,093	100.0

MAINE

1	Robert Hale (R)	47,721	68.8
	Andrew A. Pettis (D)	21,620	31.2
2	Margaret Chase Smith (R)	46,545	67.8
	David H. Staples (D)	22,139	32.2
3	Frank Fellows (R)	35,644	77.9
	Ralph E. Graham (D)	10,102	22.1

MARYLAND

1	Dudley G. Roe (D)	30,257	50.8
	Wilmer F. Davis (R)	29,298	49.2
2	H.S. Baldwin (D)	97,239	57.0

	Candidates	Votes	%
	Wilfred T. McQuaid (R)	73,469	43.0
3	Thomas D'Alesandro Jr. (D)	39,032	73.5
	John W. Benson (R)	14,046	26.5
4	George Fallon (D)	47,088	59.2
	Daniel Ellison (R)	32,416	40.8
5	Lansdale Sasscer (D)	51,318	64.9
	C. Maurice Weidemeyer (R)	27,821	35.2
6	J. Glenn Beall (R)	63,079	57.9
	Daniel F. McMullen (D)	45,877	42.1

MASSACHUSETTS

1	John W. Heselton (R)	63,693	50.5
	James P. McAndrews (D)	62,525	49.5
2	Charles R. Clason (R)	75,571	55.7
	Michael W. Albano (D)	60,195	44.3
3	Philip J. Philbin (D)	78,848	61.5
	Wilfred P. Bazinet (R)	49,300	38.5
4	Pehr G. Holmes (R)	76,097	55.5
	Frank J. McGrail (D)	60,967	44.5
5	Edith Nourse Rogers (R)	109,242	73.2
	Milton A. Wesson (D)	39,911	26.8
6	George J. Bates (R)	87,211	67.0
	John M. Bresnahan (D)	42,937	33.0
7	Thomas J. Lane (D)	78,008	67.9
	Ernest Bentley (R)	36,877	32.1
8	Angier L. Goodwin (R)	79,912	57.5
	Frederick J. McDermott (D)	59,058	42.5
9	Charles L. Gifford (R)	75,803	58.5
	William McAuliffe (D)	53,820	41.5
10	Christian A. Herter (R)	100,334	55.8
	William A. Carey (D)	79,380	44.2
11	James M. Curley (D)	75,469	65.6
	Lester W. Bowen (R)	39,523	34.4
12	John W. McCormack (D)	97,469	75.8
	Henry J. Allen (R)	31,178	24.2
13	Richard B. Wigglesworth (R)	97,013	65.8
	Andrew T. Clancy (D)	50,377	34.2
14	Joseph W. Martin Jr. (R)	79,928	62.0
	Edmond P. Talbot (D)	48,993	38.0

MICHIGAN

1	George G. Sadowski (D)	103,782	80.6
	John B. Sosnowski (R)	24,542	19.1
2	Earl C. Michener (R)	80,594	64.8
	Redmond M. Burr (D)	43,536	35.0
3	Paul W. Shafer (R)	73,134	62.5
	Charles V. Hampton (D)	42,902	36.7
4	Clare E. Hoffman (R)	68,233	64.1
	Bernard T. Foley (D)	37,754	35.5
5	Bartel J. Jonkman (R)	73,034	57.8
	J. Neal Lamoreaux (D)	53,437	42.3
6	William W. Blackney (R)	87,105	55.2
	Robert B. McLaughlin (D)	70,104	44.5
7	Jesse P. Wolcott (R)	79,455	65.9
	Charles F. Mann (D)	40,298	33.4
8	Fred L. Crawford (R)	75,700	67.5
	William A. Hemmer (D)	35,982	32.1
9	Albert J. Engel (R)	56,308	62.6
	Arnold B. Coxhill (D)	33,705	37.4
10	Roy O. Woodruff (R)	54,066	64.8
	William J. Kelly (D)	29,108	34.9
11	Fred Bradley (R)	46,985	59.0
	Cecil W. Bailey (D)	32,400	40.7
12	Frank E. Hook (D)	41,481	50.6
	John B. Bennett (R)	40,573	49.5
13	George D. O'Brien (D)	80,565	57.9
	Clarence J. McLeod (R)	58,101	41.8
14	Louis C. Rabaut (D)	98,988	56.4
	Claude G. McDonald (R)	76,358	43.5
15	John D. Dingell (D)	100,879	63.7
	Harry Henderson (R)	57,070	36.1
16	John Lesinski (D)	95,483	61.4
	Albert A. Riddering (R)	59,456	38.2
17	George A. Dondero (R)	116,242	56.4
	John W. L. Hicks (D)	87,767	42.6

MINNESOTA

	Candidates	Votes	%
1	August H. Andresen (R)	77,798	61.7
	Andrew Meldahl (DFL)	48,301	38.3
2	Joseph P. O'Hara (R)	91,867	75.7
	L. J. Kilbride (DFL)	29,548	24.3
3	William J. Gallagher (DFL)	71,856	50.9
	Richard P. Gale (R)	69,277	49.1
4	Frank T. Starkey (DFL)	64,434	51.8
	Melvin J. Maas (R)	59,994	48.2
5	Walter H. Judd (R)	81,798	56.6
	Edgar T. Buckley (DFL)	62,761	43.4
6	Harold Knutson (R)	76,421	64.6
	Harry J. O'Brien (DFL)	38,947	32.9
7	H. Carl Andersen (R)	75,315	65.9
	Arthur F. Nellermoe (DFL)	38,949	34.1
8	William A. Pittenger (R)	62,600	51.9
	William McKinnon (DFL)	58,131	48.2
9	Harold C. Hagen (R)	58,080	59.2
	Halvor Langslet (DFL)	40,018	40.8

MISSISSIPPI

1	John E. Rankin (D)	17,793	96.9
2	Jamie L. Whitten (D)	16,251	98.7
3	William M. Whittington (D)	16,222	96.4
4	Thomas G. Abernethy (D)	13,343	100.0
5	W. Arthur Winstead (D)	22,924	100.0
6	William M. Colmer (D)	31,742	95.7
7	Dan R. McGehee (D)	29,594	92.8
	L. R. Collins (R)	2,313	7.3

MISSOURI

1	Samuel W. Arnold (R)	52,561	50.8
	Edward M. Jayne (D)	50,910	49.2
2	Max Schwabe (R)	60,857	50.1
	Lue C. Lozier (D)	60,587	49.9
3	William C. Cole (R)	61,720	50.6
	Maurice Hoffman (D)	60,273	49.4
4	C. Jasper Bell (D)	60,594	57.2
	John W. Mitchell (R)	45,381	42.8
5	Roger C. Slaughter (D)	53,320	52.6
	Ralph B. Innis (R)	48,127	47.4
6	Marion T. Bennett (R)	71,705	57.0
	George A. Clason (D)	54,095	43.0
7	Dewey Short (R)	76,180	64.0
	A. L. McCawley (D)	42,929	36.0
8	Albert S. J. Carnahan (D)	54,010	50.5
	William P. Elmer (R)	52,924	49.5
9	Clarence Cannon (D)	50,594	53.2
	William Barton (R)	44,476	46.8
10	Orville Zimmerman (D)	55,243	56.7
	Ralph Hutchison (R)	42,129	43.3
11	John B. Sullivan (D)	69,351	58.9
	Louis E. Miller (R)	48,435	41.1
12	Walter C. Ploeser (R)	118,394	51.8
	Phelim O'Toole (D)	110,060	48.2
13	John J. Cochran (D)	76,408	100.0

MONTANA

1	Mike Mansfield (D)	57,008	67.9
	M. S. Galasso (R)	26,141	31.1
2	James F. O'Connor (D)	61,123	54.0
	F. F. Haynes (R)	51,372	45.4

NEBRASKA

1	Carl T. Curtis (R)	100,816	69.9
	Charles A. Chappell (D)	43,341	30.1
2	Howard Buffett (R)	78,686	59.5
	Mabel Gillespie (D)	53,637	40.5
3	Karl Stefan (R)	84,251	68.4
	George Hally (D)	34,317	27.8
4	Arthur L. Miller (R)	72,647	63.1
	Tom Lanigan (D)	34,394	29.9
	Willis B. Furman	8,102	7.0

NEVADA

	Candidates	Votes	%
AL	Berkeley L. Bunker (D)	32,648	63.1
	Rex Bell (R)	19,096	36.9

NEW HAMPSHIRE

1	Chester E. Merrow (R)	57,537	50.9
	Fortunat E. Normandin (D)	55,492	49.1
2	Sherman Adams (R)	55,911	54.4
	Harry Carlson (D)	46,872	45.6

NEW JERSEY

1	Charles A. Wolverton (R)	87,950	50.4
	John F. Gorman (D)	86,178	49.4
2	T. Millet Hand (R)	51,194	54.4
	Edison Hedges (D)	42,862	45.6
3	James C. Auchincloss (R)	80,438	57.0
	Arnold E. Ascherfeld (D)	60,769	43.0
4	D. Lane Powers (R)	68,647	55.6
	Don Guinness (D)	54,680	44.3
5	Charles A. Eaton (R)	87,129	58.4
	Andrew D. Desmond (D)	61,153	41.0
6	Clifford P. Case (R)	84,143	55.5
	Walter H. Van Hoesen (D)	65,344	43.1
7	J. Parnell Thomas (R)	86,759	66.0
	James J. Cannon (D)	44,423	33.8
8	Gordon Canfield (R)	75,479	58.5
	Harry Smith (D)	53,136	41.2
9	Harry L. Towe (R)	93,687	63.5
	Elmer I. Zabriskie (D)	53,847	36.5
10	Fred A. Hartley Jr. (R)	62,004	53.0
	Luke A. Kiernan Jr. (D)	53,577	45.8
11	Frank L. Sundstrom (R)	58,586	51.7
	John J. Francis (D)	52,376	46.3
12	Robert W. Kean (R)	67,680	50.6
	John W. Suling (D)	63,087	47.2
13	Mary T. Norton (D)	89,736	69.9
	Frank J. V. Gimino (R)	38,336	29.9
14	Edward J. Hart (D)	79,158	63.2
	Otto Trankler (R)	46,076	36.8

NEW MEXICO

AL	Clinton P. Anderson (D)	85,244✓	
	Antonio M. Fernandez (D)	80,752✓	
	Manuel Lujan (R)	66,644	
	Ben F. Meyer (R)	66,309	

NEW YORK

1	Edgar A. Sharp (R)	92,044	69.6
	Edward Hudson (D, AM LAB)	40,294	30.4
2	Leonard W. Hall (R)	131,906	67.9
	John S. Thorp (D, AM LAB)	62,242	32.1
3	Henry J. Latham (R)	108,118	60.6
	George H. Bruns (D, AM LAB)	70,163	39.4
4	William B. Barry (D, AM LAB)	73,098	52.8
	Alfred J. Phillips (R)	65,390	47.2
5	James A. Roe (D, AM LAB)	90,338	54.3
	Raymond S. Richmond (R)	76,014	45.7
6	James J. Delaney (D, AM LAB)	81,228	55.2
	Otto Schuler (R)	65,821	44.8
7	John J. Delaney (D, AM LAB)	73,868	63.4
	Roy M. D. Richardson (R)	42,716	36.6
8	Joseph L. Pfeifer (D, AM LAB)	55,565	59.5
	Frank W. Porcaro (R)	37,816	40.5
9	Eugene J. Keogh (D, L)	63,400	55.4
	Harry Chiert (R)	34,517	30.2
	Jacob A. Salzman (AM LAB)	16,521	14.4
10	Andrew L. Somers (D, AM LAB)	78,753	57.8
	Philip Kahaner (R)	36,854	27.0
	Louis P. Goldberg (L)	20,719	15.2
11	James J. Heffernan (D, AM LAB)	95,213	65.8
	John Patrick Devery (R)	49,442	34.2
12	John J. Rooney (D, AM LAB)	51,411	55.0
	William G. Nolan (R)	42,007	45.0

	Candidates	Votes	%
13	Donald L. O'Toole (D, AM LAB)	81,640	60.3
	Clarence W. Archibald (R)	53,854	39.8
14	Leo F. Rayfiel (D, L)	85,534	58.3
	Bernard P. Levy (R)	32,393	22.1
	James V. King (AM LAB)	28,766	19.6
15	Emanuel Celler (D, AM LAB)	105,943	81.1
	Nathan J. Paulson (R)	24,650	18.9
16	Ellsworth B. Buck (R)	55,647	53.5
	Rae L. Egbert (D, AM LAB)	48,411	46.5
17	Joseph Clark Baldwin (R)	77,196	52.4
	Max Waterman (D)	57,769	39.2
	Seon Felshin (AM LAB)	12,278	8.3
18	Vito Marcantonio (D, R)	82,316	100.0
19	Samuel Dickstein (D, AM LAB)	69,973	73.3
	William I. Lehrfeld (R)	25,494	26.7
20	Sol Bloom (D, AM LAB)	87,724	70.8
	Lawrence S. Mayers (R)	36,197	29.2
21	James H. Torrens (D, AM LAB)	91,747	69.3
	Herbert Malkin (R)	40,718	30.7
22	Adam C. Powell Jr. (D, R)	83,140	100.0
23	Walter A. Lynch (D, AM LAB)	126,245	79.5
	William J. Waterman (R)	32,594	20.5
24	Benjamin J. Rabin (D, AM LAB)	102,684	84.8
	Morris Schaeffer (R)	18,461	15.2
25	Charles A. Buckley (D, AM LAB)	114,248	62.1
	Roderick Stephens (R)	50,274	27.3
	John A. Devany Jr (CST)	19,561	10.6
26	Peter A. Quinn (D, AM LAB)	91,665	56.4
	Samuel T. Shay (R)	70,746	43.6
27	Ralph W. Gwinn (R)	90,699	61.9
	Joseph E. Venuti (D, AM LAB)	55,756	38.1
28	Ralph A. Gamble (R)	90,623	65.5
	John H. Jackson (D, AM LAB)	47,646	34.5
29	Augustus W. Bennet (D, AM LAB)	70,630	53.0
	Hamilton Fish (R, JEFF)	62,583	47.0
30	Jay LeFevre (R)	88,067	63.0
	Sharon J. Mauhs (D, AM LAB)	51,725	37.0
31	Bernard W. Kearney (R)	85,178	60.0
	Alexander Grasso (D, AM LAB)	56,706	40.0
32	William T. Byrne (D, AM LAB)	85,147	57.2
	Miles A. McGrane Jr. (R)	63,603	42.8
33	Dean P. Taylor (R)	95,299	62.6
	Thomas P. McLoughlin (D)	52,354	34.4
34	Clarence E. Kilburn (R)	75,532	62.9
	John D. Van Kennen (D)	44,557	37.1
35	Hadwen C. Fuller (R)	65,857	52.3
	Samuel H. Miller Jr. (D, AM LAB)	60,025	47.7
36	Clarence E. Hancock (R)	79,535	53.2
	George M. Haight (D, AM LAB)	70,012	46.8
37	Edwin Arthur Hall (R)	75,246	69.2
	James S. Byrne (D, AM LAB)	33,465	30.8
38	John Taber (R)	75,432	65.6
	Frank J. Erwin (D)	36,327	31.6
39	W. Sterling Cole (R)	75,740	68.1
	Charlotte D. Curren (D)	31,152	28.0
40	George F. Rogers (D, AM LAB)	90,369	50.4
	Joseph J. O'Brien (R)	88,782	49.6
41	James W. Wadsworth (R)	71,988	63.2
	Jean Walrath (D, AM LAB)	41,991	36.8
42	Walter Gresham Andrews (R)	83,781	57.2
	William Haeseler Jr. (D, AM LAB)	62,590	42.8
43	Edward J. Elsaesser (R)	74,366	51.1
	Raymond J. Barnes (D, AM LAB)	71,216	48.9
44	John C. Butler (R)	72,402	50.1
	Leon A. Dombrowski (D, AM LAB)	72,164	49.9
45	Daniel A. Reed (R)	64,456	64.1
	Orrin H. Parker (D, AM LAB)	36,050	35.9

NORTH CAROLINA

	Candidates	Votes	%
1	Herbert C. Bonner (D)	30,149	90.6
	R. Clarence Dozier (R)	3,139	9.4
2	John H. Kerr (D)	34,949	95.9
3	Graham A. Barden (D)	30,447	71.6
	H. B. Kornegay (R)	12,055	28.4
4	Harold D. Cooley (D)	53,340	74.7
	J. Ira Lee (R)	18,046	25.3
5	John H. Folger (D)	42,982	66.5
	John J. Ingle (R)	21,669	33.5
6	Carl T. Durham (D)	50,003	73.3
	Worth Henderson (R)	18,195	26.7
7	J. Bayard Clark (D)	39,342	79.3
	Josiah A. Maultsby (R)	10,260	20.7
8	William O. Burgin (D)	48,244	59.8
	B.C. Brock (R)	32,450	40.2
9	Robert L. Doughton (D)	50,595	58.8
	Emory C. McCall (R)	35,506	41.2
10	Joe W. Ervin (D)	50,605	65.4
	Loomis F. Klutz (R)	26,757	34.6
11	Alfred L. Bulwinkle (D)	41,576	65.6
	C. V. Moss (R)	21,829	34.4
12	Zebulon Weaver (D)	52,042	64.2
	Lewis P. Hamlin (R)	28,965	35.8

NORTH DAKOTA

AL	William Lemke (R)	101,007✓	
	Charles R. Robertson (R)	91,419✓	
	Halvor L. Halvorson (D)	56,699	
	J. R. Kennedy (D)	44,708	
	Usher L. Burdick (IR)	39,888	
	George McClellan (R)	3,135	
	A. C. Townley	2,307	

OHIO

1	Charles H. Elston (R)	82,373	56.8
	Frank J. Richter (D)	62,617	43.2
2	William E. Hess (R)	78,185	56.0
	J. Harry Moore (D)	61,473	44.0
3	Edward J. Gardner (D)	104,247	52.6
	Harry P. Jeffrey (R)	94,064	47.4
4	Robert F. Jones (R)	67,829	61.2
	Earl Ludwig (D)	42,983	38.8
5	Cliff Clevenger (R)	48,490	68.1
	T. Walter Williams (D)	22,740	31.9
6	Edward O. McCowen (R)	45,284	51.8
	John W. Bush (D)	42,167	48.2
7	Clarence J. Brown (R)	84,770	61.7
	John L. Cashin (D)	52,403	38.1
8	Frederick C. Smith (R)	51,253	59.8
	Roy Warren Roof (D)	34,494	40.2
9	Homer A. Ramey (R)	82,735	51.6
	John F. Hunter (D)	77,693	48.4
10	Thomas A. Jenkins (R)	43,388	64.4
	Elsie Stanton (D)	23,986	35.6
11	Walter E. Brehm (R)	38,263	53.6
	Mell G. Underwood Jr. (D)	33,098	46.4
12	John M. Vorys (R)	97,856	54.3
	Forrest F. Smith (D)	82,503	45.7
13	Alvin F. Weichel (R)	67,298	100.0
14	Walter B. Huber (D)	117,770	50.6
	Ed Rowe (R)	115,145	49.4
15	P. W. Griffiths (R)	47,710	60.0
	Olney R. Gillogly (D)	31,756	40.0
16	William R. Thom (D)	85,755	52.7
	Henderson H. Carson (R)	75,948	46.6
17	J. Harry McGregor (R)	73,206	62.9
	Thomas A. Wilson (D)	43,271	37.2
18	Earl R. Lewis (R)	65,847	51.1
	Ross Michener (D)	63,098	48.9
19	Michael J. Kirwan (D)	120,191	63.4
	Herschel Hunt (R)	69,403	36.6
20	Michael A. Feighan (D)	75,218	75.9
	A. R. McNamara (R)	23,945	24.2
21	Robert Crosser (D)	77,525	77.7
	Harry C. Gahn (R)	22,288	22.3
22	Frances P. Bolton (R)	185,187	57.4

Candidates	Votes	%
Don O. Cameron (D)	137,546	42.6
AL George H. Bender (R)	1,542,422	53.1
William Glass (D)	1,362,843	46.9

OKLAHOMA

	Candidates	Votes	%
1	George B. Schwabe (R)	71,545	51.1
	Dennis Bushyhead (D)	68,561	48.9
2	William G. Stigler (D)	39,052	58.0
	E.O. Clark (R)	28,282	42.0
3	Paul Stewart (D)	51,135	76.2
	Russell Overstreet (R)	16,016	23.9
4	Lyle H. Boren (D)	47,733	61.7
	Ralph R. Kirchner (R)	29,582	38.3
5	A.S. Mike Monroney (D)	85,132	62.7
	Howard B. Hopps (R)	50,207	37.0
6	Jed Johnson (D)	41.987	60.0
	Ted R. Fisher (R)	27,979	40.0
7	Victor Wickersham (D)	35,895	70.8
	J. Warren White (R)	14,790	29.2
8	Ross Rizley (R)	43,878	57.6
	Philip C. Ferguson (D)	31,737	41.6

Special Election

	Candidates	Votes	%
2	William G. Stigler (D)	22,036	54.4
	Ralph R. Kirchner (R)	18,502	45.6

OREGON

	Candidates	Votes	%
1	James W. Mott (R)	80,106	66.7
	O. Henry Oleen (D)	39,928	33.3
2	Lowell Stockman (R)	43,145	65.7
	C. J. Shorb (D)	22,498	34.3
3	Homer D. Angell (R)	95,605	55.1
	Lester Sheeley (D)	77,814	44.9
4	Harris Ellsworth (R)	53,356	64.0
	Floyd K. Dover (D)	30,024	36.0

PENNSYLVANIA

	Candidates	Votes	%
1	William A. Barrett (D)	73,289	58.4
	James Gallagher (R)	52,159	41.6
2	William T. Granahan (D)	97,351	62.7
	Charles M. Mosser (R)	57,849	37.3
3	Michael J. Bradley (D)	80,920	58.3
	Joseph M. Pratt (R)	57,856	41.7
4	John Edward Sheridan (D)	80,367	66.2
	Franklin J. Maloney (R)	41,018	33.8
5	William J. Green Jr. (D)	74,744	54.2
	C. Frederick Pracht (R)	63,085	45.8
6	Herbert J. McGlinchey (D)	78,123	50.7
	Hugh Scott (R)	75,794	49.2
7	James Wolfenden (R)	72,289	51.5
	Vernon A. O'Rourke (D)	68,161	48.5
8	Charles J. Gerlach (R)	59,497	58.0
	Marie M. Bickert (D)	43,073	42.0
9	J. Roland Kinzer (R)	71,129	61.3
	H. Clay Burkholder (D)	44,952	38.7
10	John W. Murphy (D)	59,047	56.4
	Walter W. Kohler (R)	45,593	43.6
11	Daniel J. Flood (D)	71,843	52.2
	Thomas Byron Miller (R)	65,922	47.9
12	Ivor D. Fenton (R)	65,960	56.8
	Charles E. Klinger (D)	50,153	43.2
13	Daniel K. Hoch (D)	43,233	54.1
	Randolph Stauffer (R)	33,240	41.6
14	Wilson D. Gillette (R)	51,333	65.0
	Clement J. Reap (D)	27,653	35.0
15	Robert F. Rich (R)	52,826	61.0
	Richard F. Hartzell (D)	33,750	39.0
16	Samuel K. McConnell Jr. (R)	79,555	63.7
	Marvin B. Brunner (D)	45,392	36.3
17	Richard M. Simpson (R)	45,198	64.5
	John W. Mann (D, I)	24,875	35.5
18	John C. Kunkel (R)	81,814	62.5
	Howard K. Beard (D)	49,080	37.5
19	Leon H. Gavin (R)	49,670	63.3
	John C. Brecht (D)	27,655	35.2
20	Francis E. Walter (D)	51,594	57.3
	Charles A. P. Bartlett (R)	38,460	42.7
21	Chester H. Gross (R)	55,984	52.6
	Josiah W. Gitt (D)	50,548	47.5
22	D. Emmett Brumbaugh (R)	50,000	57.8
	Bernard J. D. Clark (D)	36,476	42.2
23	J. Buell Snyder (D)	44,585	54.6
	Carl H. Hoffman (R)	37,062	45.4
24	Thomas E. Morgan (D)	52,500	62.2
	Gilbert E. Koedel (R)	31,940	37.8
25	Louis E. Graham (R)	61,544	50.4
	Samuel G. Neff (D)	60,473	49.6
26	Harve Tibbott (R)	58,743	52.6
	Eddie McCloskey (D)	52,994	47.4
27	Augustine B. Kelley (D)	61,263	59.7
	Edward J. Howard (R)	41,289	40.3
28	Robert L. Rodgers (R)	68,675	54.6
	James F. Lavery (D)	57,044	45.4
29	Howard E. Campbell (R)	63,086	50.2
	John F. Lowers (D)	62,592	49.8
30	Robert J. Corbett (R)	60,391	51.7
	Thomas E. Scanlon (D)	56,423	48.3
31	James G. Fulton (R)	71,222	53.8
	James A. Wright (D)	61,104	46.2
32	Herman P. Eberharter (D)	83,724	71.6
	Gregory Zatkovich (R)	33,221	28.4
33	Samuel A. Weiss (D)	75,796	69.3
	Ray A. Liddle (R)	33,651	30.8

RHODE ISLAND

	Candidates	Votes	%
1	Aime J. Forand (D)	88,179	61.9
	Charles A. Curran (R)	54,233	38.1
2	John E. Fogarty (D)	87,189	57.8
	Charles T. Algren (R)	63,778	42.3

SOUTH CAROLINA

	Candidates	Votes	%
1	L. Mendel Rivers (D)	15,326	92.8
	O. H. Wilcox (R)	1,190	7.2
2	John J. Riley (D)	19,342	98.0
3	Butler B. Hare (D)	13,105	97.0
4	Joseph R. Bryson (D)	20,988	95.7
5	James P. Richards (D)	14,435	98.1
6	John L. McMillan (D)	14,164	98.0

SOUTH DAKOTA

	Candidates	Votes	%
1	Karl E. Mundt (R)	113,769	64.0
	Grover Lothrop (D)	63,981	36.0
2	Francis H. Case (R)	33,119	69.0
	H. W. Clarkson (D)	14,869	31.0

TENNESSEE

	Candidates	Votes	%
1	B. Carroll Reece (R)	45,498	100.0
2	John Jennings Jr. (R)	45,416	55.5
	Lowell Blanchard (D)	36,441	44.5
3	Estes Kefauver (D)	32,497	67.8
	Foster Johnson (R)	11,541	24.1
	Ernest W. Forstner (I)	3,894	8.1
4	Albert Gore (D)	20,684	65.1
	E. M. Shelley (R)	9,642	30.4
5	Harold H. Earthman (D)	27,087	85.5
	W. H. Crowell (R)	4,598	14.5
6	J. Percy Priest (D)	28,752	97.0
7	Wirt Courtney (D)	22,592	100.0
8	Thomas J. Murray (D)	19,822	63.3
	A. Bradley Frazier (R)	11,509	36.7
9	Jere Cooper (D)	25,250	87.8
	Homer Tatum (R)	3,510	12.2
10	Clifford Davis (D)	47,569	100.0

TEXAS

	Candidates	Votes	%
1	Wright Patman (D)	39,404	100.0
2	Jesse M. Combs (D)	54,258	94.0
	Lanar Cecil (R)	3,442	6.0
3	Lindley Beckworth (D)	36,954	93.3
	O. P. Stephens (R)	2,668	6.7
4	Sam Rayburn (D)	40,039	100.0
5	Hatton W. Sumners (D)	62,459	71.4
	C. D. Turner (R)	25,027	28.6
6	Luther A. Johnson (D)	36,884	100.0
7	Tom Pickett (D)	32,850	96.1
8	Albert Thomas (D)	90,963	92.3
	L. B. Robinson (R)	7,555	7.7
9	Joseph J. Mansfield (D)	56,194	93.4
	Lewis Allen (R)	3,967	6.6
10	Lyndon B. Johnson (D)	44,602	92.9
	A. H. Bartelt (R)	3,423	7.1
11	W.R. Poage (D)	39,866	95.3
12	Fritz Lanham (D)	59,119	100.0
13	Ed Gossett (D)	53,503	95.4
14	John E. Lyle (D)	53,756	100.0
15	Milton H. West (D)	35,862	100.0
16	R. Ewing Thomason (D)	31,658	100.0
17	Sam Russell (D)	43,785	96.8
18	Eugene Worley (D)	47,588	93.3
	M. C. P. Bybee (R)	3,435	6.7
19	George H. Mahon (D)	53,326	100.0
20	Paul J. Kilday (D)	39,394	100.0
21	O. Clark Fisher (D)	47,796	88.1
	M. J. Lehman (R)	6,474	11.9

UTAH

	Candidates	Votes	%
1	Walter K. Granger (D)	59,755	57.8
	B. H. Stringham (R)	43,642	42.2
2	J. Will Robinson (D)	89,844	62.3
	Quayle Cannon Jr. (R)	54,440	37.7

VERMONT

	Candidates	Votes	%
AL	Charles A. Plumley (R)	76,800	62.4
	Robert W. Ready (D)	46,230	37.6

VIRGINIA

	Candidates	Votes	%
1	S. Otis Bland (D)	23,284	81.2
	Walter Johnson (R)	5,391	18.8
2	Ralph H. Daughton (D)	21,268	57.7
	Thomas L. Woodward (R)	9,304	25.2
	W. B. Shafer Jr. (I)	6,302	17.1
3	David E. Satterfield Jr. (D)	32,918	100.0
4	Patrick Henry Drewry (D)	15,724	100.0
5	Thomas G. Burch (D)	24,781	84.6
	Howard H. Carwile (I)	4,509	15.4
6	Clifton A. Woodrum (D)	30,844	68.7
	John Strickler (R)	13,798	30.8
7	A. Willis Robertson (D)	24,967	59.9
	D. Wampler Earman (R)	16,738	40.1
8	Howard W. Smith (D)	31,618	60.1
	Elizabeth Chilton Murray (ID)	11,019	21.0
	Lawrence Michael (IR)	9,019	17.2
9	John W. Flannagan Jr. (D)	33,943	56.3
	Ralph L. Lincoln (R)	26,373	43.7

WASHINGTON

	Candidates	Votes	%
1	Hugh De Lacy (D)	118,354	53.1
	Robert H. Harlin (R)	103,099	46.2
2	Henry M. Jackson (D)	74,676	60.4
	Payson Peterson (R)	48,974	39.6
3	Charles Savage (D)	57,942	52.0
	Fred Norman (R)	53,503	48.0
4	Hal Holmes (R)	56,211	60.2
	Al McCoy (D)	37,150	39.8
5	Walt Horan (R)	62,648	52.3
	Edward J. Reilly (D)	57,235	47.7
6	John M. Coffee (D)	80,679	61.2
	Thor C. Tollefson (R)	51,119	38.8

WEST VIRGINIA

	Candidates	Votes	%
1	Matthew M. Neely (D)	58,313	50.4
	A. C. Schiffler (R)	57,363	49.6
2	Jennings Randolph (D)	58,695	54.1
	Melvin C. Muntzing (R)	49,722	45.9
3	Cleveland M. Bailey (D)	57,912	52.5
	Edward G. Rohrbough (R)	52,457	47.5

Candidates	Votes	%
4 Hubert S. Ellis (R)	68,204	51.2
E. B. Pennybacker (D)	64,986	48.8
5 John Kee (D)	65,463	61.7
Hartley Sanders (R)	40,568	38.3
6 E. H. Hedrick (D)	84,369	58.3
J. W. Maxwell (R)	60,457	41.7

WISCONSIN

Candidates	Votes	%
1 Lawrence H. Smith (R)	74,223	74.8
John K. Kyle (PROG)	24,013	24.2
2 Robert K. Henry (R)	74,937	56.8

Candidates	Votes	%
John W. Nash (D)	34,145	25.9
Herbert C. Schenk (PROG)	22,095	16.7
3 William H. Stevenson (R)	74,092	69.9
William D. Carroll (D)	26,978	25.4
4 Thaddeus F.B. Wasielewski (D)	103,583	63.5
Robert Blackwood (R)	55,375	34.0
5 Andrew J. Biemiller (D)	88,606	50.8
Lewis D. Thill (R)	78,834	45.2
6 Frank B. Keefe (R)	74,487	66.5
Henry Danes (D)	36,180	32.3
7 Reid F. Murray (R)	73,531	69.3
William H. Ludwig (D)	31,991	30.1

Candidates	Votes	%
8 John W. Byrnes (R)	64,623#	51.1
La Vern R. Dilweg (R)	57,458#	45.5
9 Merlin Hull (PROG)	48,064	98.5
10 Alvin E. O'Konski (R)	54,731	57.8
Elizabeth Hawkes (D)	29,773	31.4
Harry P. Van Guilder (PROG)	9,567	10.1

WYOMING

Candidates	Votes	%
AL Frank A. Barrett (R)	53,533	55.7
Charles E. Norris (D)	42,569	44.3

1945 House Elections

ILLINOIS

Special Election

Candidates	Votes	%
24 Roy Clippinger (R)	5,617	98.9

MONTANA

Special Election

Candidates	Votes	%
2 Wesley A. D'Ewart (R)	26,158	50.4
Leo C. Graybill (D)	22,126	42.6
Robert Yellowtail (I)	3,417	6.6

1946 House Elections

ALABAMA

	Candidates	Votes	%
1	Frank W. Boykin (D)	12,448	100.0
2	George M. Grant (D)	17,711	100.0
3	George W. Andrews (D)	13,397	100.0
4	Sam Hobbs (D)	16,299	88.1
	Roger S. Bingham (R)	2,207	11.9
5	Albert Rains (D)	21,560	100.0
6	Pete Jarman (D)	13,551	100.0
7	Carter Manasco (D)	22,853	72.7
	M. H. Woodward (R)	8,565	27.3
8	John J. Sparkman (D)	17,624*	92.4
	Arthur South (R)	1,453	7.6
9	Laurie C. Battle (D)	29,940	94.1
	J. G. Bass (R)	1,880	5.9

ARIZONA

	Candidates	Votes	%
AL	John R. Murdock (D)	74,948✓	
	Richard F. Harless (D)	71,836✓	
	Denver C. Henson (R)	37,033	
	John H. Curnutte (R)	36,185	
	Karl M. Wilson (COM)	831	

ARKANSAS

	Candidates	Votes	%
1	Ezekiel C. Gathings (D)	20,250	100.0
2	Wilbur D. Mills (D)	22,955	100.0
3	James W. Trimble (D)	24,950	100.0
4	Fadjo Cravens (D)	13,844	100.0
5	Brooks Hays (D)	21,777	85.2
	James R. Harris (R)	2,881	11.3
6	William F. Norrell (D)	23,892	84.7
	M. O. Evans (I)	4,305	15.3
7	Oren Harris (D)	15,584	100.0

CALIFORNIA

	Candidates	Votes	%
1	Clarence F. Lea (D-R)	77,653	99.8
2	Clair Engle (D-R)	57,895	100.0
3	Leroy Johnson (R-D)	116,792	100.0
4	Franck R. Havenner (D)	60,655	52.9
	Truman R. Young (R)	54,113	47.2
5	Richard J. Welch (R-D)	94,293	100.0
6	George P. Miller (D-R)	118,548	99.9
7	John J. Allen Jr. (R)	61,508	56.2
	Patrick W. McDonough (D)	47,988	43.8
8	John Z. Anderson (R-D)	113,325	99.9
9	Bertrand W. Gearhart (R)	50,171	53.7
	Hubert Phillips (D)	43,244	46.3
10	Alfred J. Elliott (D-R)	51,843	99.8
11	Ernest K. Bramblett (R)	41,902	53.1
	George E. Outland (D)	36,996	46.9
12	Richard M. Nixon (R)	65,586	56.0
	H. Jerry Voorhis (D)	49,994	42.7
13	Norris Poulson (R)	48,071	51.8
	Ned R. Healy (D)	44,712	48.2
14	Helen Gahagan Douglas (D)	53,536	54.3
	Frederick M. Roberts (R)	44,914	45.6
15	Gordon L. McDonough (R-D)	106,020	99.4
16	Donald L. Jackson (R)	78,264	53.9
	Harold Harby (D)	45,951	31.6
	Ellis E. Patterson	20,945	14.4
17	Cecil R. King (D-R)	110,654	99.4
18	Willis W. Bradley (R)	67,363	52.8
	Clyde Doyle (D)	60,218	47.2
19	Chet Holifield (D-R)	50,666	97.2
20	Carl Hinshaw (R)	98,283	59.3
	Everett G. Burkhalter (D)	67,317	40.6
21	Harry R. Sheppard (D)	37,229	52.7
	Lowell E. Lathrop (R)	33,395	47.3
22	John Phillips (R)	59,935	62.1
	Ray Adkinson (D)	36,649	37.9
23	Charles K. Fletcher (R)	69,411	56.3
	Ed V. Izac (D)	53,898	43.7

COLORADO

	Candidates	Votes	%
1	John A. Carroll (D)	60,513	51.8
	Dean M. Gillespie (R)	55,724	47.7
2	William S. Hill (R)	54,768	65.7
	Frank A. Safranek (D)	27,393	32.9
3	J. Edgar Chenoweth (R)	45,043	54.6
	Walter W. Johnson (D)	37,496	45.4
4	Robert F. Rockwell (R)	28,894	58.8
	Thomas Matthews (D)	20,290	41.3

CONNECTICUT

	Candidates	Votes	%
1	William J. Miller (R)	93,006	53.1
	Herman P. Kopplemann (D)	82,231	46.9
2	Horace Seely-Brown Jr. (R)	59,828	55.3
	Chase Going Woodhouse (D)	48,376	44.7
3	Ellsworth B. Foote (R)	76,408	58.9
	James P. Geelan (D)	53,404	41.1
4	John Davis Lodge (R)	93,513	57.1
	Henry A. Mucci (D)	57,913	35.4
	Stanley W. Mayhew (SOC)	9,427	5.8
5	James T. Patterson (R)	51,790	53.1
	Thomas Radzevich (D)	39,785	40.8
	John C. Cluney (SOC, CLUNEY)	5,984	6.1
AL	Antoni N. Sadlak (R)	377,972	55.6
	Joseph F. Ryter (D)	277,872	40.9

DELAWARE

	Candidates	Votes	%
AL	J. Caleb Boggs (R)	63,516	56.4
	Philip A. Traynor (D)	49,105	43.6

FLORIDA

	Candidates	Votes	%
1	J. Hardin Peterson (D)	31,145	100.0
2	Emory H. Price (D)	26,093	100.0
3	Robert L. F. Sikes (D)	18,455	100.0
4	George A. Smathers (D)	37,002	71.9
	Norman N. Curtis (R)	14,458	28.1
5	Joe Hendricks (D)	24,695	61.3
	M. J. Moss Jr. (R)	15,591	38.7
6	Dwight L. Rogers (D)	13,733	71.1
	Joseph P. Moe (R)	5,591	28.9

GEORGIA

	Candidates	Votes	%
1	Prince H. Preston (D)	20,937	99.8
2	E. E. Cox (D)	10,805	100.0
3	Stephen Pace (D)	8,961	100.0
4	A. Sidney Camp (D)	8,476	100.0
5	James C. Davis (D)	31,444	61.6
	Helen Douglas Mankin (I)	19,527#	38.3
6	Carl Vinson (D)	13,566	100.0
7	Henderson Lanham (D)	7,573	100.0
8	W. M. Wheeler (D)	8,986	100.0
9	John Wood (D)	14,815	100.0
10	Paul Brown (D)	16,398	100.0

Special Election

	Candidates	Votes	%
5	Helen Douglas Mankin (D)	11,067	36.5
	Thomas L. Camp	10,275	33.9
	Ben T. Huiet	2,724	9.0
	J. E. B. Stewart	2,363	7.8

IDAHO

	Candidates	Votes	%
1	Abe McGregor Goff (R)	37,326	50.6
	Compton I. White (D)	36,509	49.5
2	John Sanborn (R)	63,692	60.7
	Pete Leguineche (D)	41,231	39.3

ILLINOIS

	Candidates	Votes	%
1	William L. Dawson (D)	38,040	56.8
	William E. King (R)	28,945	43.2
2	Richard B. Vail (R)	156,697	51.3
	William A. Rowan (D)	148,995	48.7
3	Fred E. Busbey (R)	169,543	57.2
	Edward A. Kelly (D)	126,638	42.8
4	Martin Gorski (D)	68,113	70.7
	John T. Parsons (R)	28,251	29.3
5	Adolph J. Sabath (D)	34,904	71.6
	Michael A. Francisco (R)	13,859	28.4
6	Thomas J. O'Brien (D)	171,778	52.0
	Harold C. Woodward (R)	158,702	48.0
7	Thomas L. Owens (R)	252,981	55.0
	William W. Link (D)	206,963	45.0
8	Thomas S. Gordon (D)	38,317	77.3
	Scott John Vitell (R)	11,266	22.7
9	Robert J. Twyman (R)	54,615	51.3
	Alexander J. Resa (D)	51,788	48.7
10	Ralph E. Church (R)	201,010	64.7
	Harold H. Kolbe (D)	109,712	35.3
11	Chauncey W. Reed (R)	120,640	74.9
	Louis William Oswald (D)	40,355	25.1
12	Noah M. Mason (R)	73,431	69.1
	Richard G. Myrland (D)	32,816	30.9
13	Leo E. Allen (R)	48,238	77.8
	Michael M. Kinney (D)	13,767	22.2
14	Anton J. Johnson (R)	45,723	62.1
	Carl E. Wright Jr. (D)	27,877	37.9
15	Robert B. Chiperfield (R)	49,895	64.3
	Henry D. Sullivan (D)	27,667	35.7
16	Everett M. Dirksen (R)	64,534	67.5
	Hans A. Spading (D)	31,091	32.5
17	Leslie C. Arends (R)	45,969	71.2
	Carl Vrooman (D)	18,617	28.8
18	Edward H. Jenison (R)	56,537	65.1
	C. E. Spang (D)	30,305	34.9
19	Rolla C. McMillen (R)	64,063	62.5
	Olive Remington Goldman (D)	38,485	37.5
20	Sidney E. Simpson (R)	34,923	58.8
	Don Irving (D)	24,508	41.2
21	Evan Howell (R)	55,609	55.1
	Roscoe Bonjean (D)	45,293	44.9
22	Melvin Price (D)	69,669	50.7
	Calvin D. Johnson (R)	67,665	49.3
23	Charles W. Vursell (R)	51,440	54.9
	Homer Kasserman (D)	42,237	45.1
24	Roy Clippinger (R)	37,909	58.9
	Edward Hines (D)	26,483	41.1
25	C. W. Bishop (R)	53,831	59.8
	Sherman S. Carr (D)	36,217	40.2
AL	William G. Stratton (R)	1,906,717	55.1
	Emily Taft Douglas (D)	1,539,248	44.5

INDIANA

	Candidates	Votes	%
1	Ray J. Madden (D)	51,809	51.9
	Charles W. Gannon (R)	46,677	46.8
2	Charles A. Halleck (R)	66,423	61.3
	Margaret A. Afflis (D)	40,847	37.7
3	Robert A. Grant (R)	73,239	55.6
	John S. Gonas (D)	57,425	43.6
4	George W. Gillie (R)	59,790	59.4
	Walter E. Frederick (D)	39,766	39.5
5	Forest A. Harness (R)	79,752	55.0
	William W. Welsh (D)	61,364	42.3
6	Noble J. Johnson (R)	65,926	57.4
	Thomas A. Sigler (D)	47,972	41.7
7	Gerald W. Landis (R)	63,667	50.7
	James E. Noland (D)	59,908	47.7
8	Edward A. Mitchell (R)	66,050	51.8
	Winfield K. Denton (D)	60,385	47.3
9	Earl Wilson (R)	58,384	55.8
	Oliver O. Dixon (D)	45,316	43.3

	Candidates	Votes	%
10	Raymond S. Springer (R)	70,969	59.3
	Frank C. Unger (D)	44,807	37.4
11	Louis Ludlow (D)	79,040	51.1
	Albert J. Beveridge (R)	74,745	48.3

IOWA

1	Thomas E. Martin (R)	52,488	61.5
	Clair A. Williams (D)	32,849	38.5
2	Henry O. Talle (R)	60,111	59.1
	Richard V. Bernhart (D)	41,544	40.9
3	John W. Gwynne (R)	48,346	62.0
	Dan J. P. Ryan (D)	29,661	38.0
4	Karl M. LeCompte (R)	43,753	58.4
	A. E. Augustine (D)	31,203	41.6
5	Paul Cunningham (R)	41,679	59.4
	Vince L. Browner (D)	28,490	40.6
6	James I. Dolliver (R)	40,595	63.4
	Oscar E. Johnson (D)	23,422	36.6
7	Ben F. Jensen (R)	40,152	63.0
	Philip A. Allen (D)	23,567	37.0
8	Charles B. Hoeven (R)	37,868	68.6
	George A. Heikens (D)	17,303	31.4

KANSAS

1	Albert M. Cole (R)	63,076	64.3
	James W. Lowry (D)	35,045	35.7
2	Errett P. Scrivner (R)	56,363	58.8
	Murray H. Hodges (D)	39,484	41.2
3	Herbert A. Meyer (R)	41,624	55.4
	Jo E. Gaitskill (D)	33,578	44.7
4	Edward H. Rees (R)	68,658	56.2
	William P. Warren (D)	53,617	43.9
5	Clifford R. Hope (R)	54,578	62.7
	Arthur L. Sparks (D)	32,538	37.4
6	Wint Smith (R)	44,343	58.1
	G. E. Bengtson (D)	28,911	37.9

KENTUCKY

1	Noble J. Gregory (D)	32,121	66.2
	William E. Porter (R)	16,064	33.1
2	Earle C. Clements (D)	38,020	56.6
	Thomas W. Hines (R)	29,124	43.4
3	Thruston B. Morton (R)	61,899	58.1
	Emmet O'Neal (D)	44,599	41.9
4	Frank L. Chelf (D)	33,116	53.1
	Don Victor Drye Sr. (R)	29,304	47.0
5	Brent Spence (D)	26,444	51.2
	Marion W. Moore (R)	25,240	48.8
6	Virgil Chapman (D)	43,176	55.0
	W. D. Rogers (R)	35,368	45.0
7	W. Howes Meade (D)	30,070	59.4
	A. J. May (D)	20,596	40.7
8	Joe B. Bates (D)	33,408	52.6
	Ray Schmauch (R)	30,127	47.4
9	John M. Robsion (R)	54,306	100.0

LOUISIANA

1	F. Edward Hebert (D)	29,329	91.8
	Dennison Suarez (R)	2,614	8.2
2	Hale Boggs (D)	29,457	90.7
	Harold M. Herbst (R)	3,037	9.4
3	James Domengeaux (D)	4,595	100.0
4	Overton Brooks (D)	8,499	100.0
5	Otto E. Passman (D)	6,049	100.0
6	James H. Morrison (D)	8,781	100.0
7	Henry D. Larcade Jr. (D)	5,907	100.0
8	A. Leonard Allen (D)	7,740	100.0

MAINE

1	Robert Hale (R)	38,975	59.6
	John C. Fitzgerald (D)	26,378	40.4
2	Margaret Chase Smith (R)	39,791	60.7
	Edward J. Beauchamp (D)	25,739	39.3
3	Frank Fellows (R)	31,622	72.9
	John M. Coghill (D)	11,743	27.1

MARYLAND

	Candidates	Votes	%
1	Edward T. Miller (R)	27,364	50.9
	Dudley George Roe (D)	26,360	49.1
2	Hugh A. Meade (D)	69,211	52.4
	David G. Harry (R)	62,760	47.6
3	Thomas D'Alesandro Jr. (D)	24,347	63.9
	Edward N. Kowzan (R)	13,761	36.1
4	George H. Fallon (D)	31,453	57.2
	Paul Robertson (R)	23,499	42.8
5	Lansdale G. Sasscer (D)	40,929	58.2
	Edwin A. Glenn (R)	29,406	41.8
6	J. Glenn Beall (R)	55,667	58.1
	Arch McDonald (D)	40,198	41.9

MASSACHUSETTS

1	John W. Heselton (R)	59,222	58.0
	John J. Falvey (D)	40,549	39.7
2	Charles R. Clason (R)	59,754	51.4
	Foster Furcolo (D)	56,459	48.6
3	Philip J. Philbin (D)	69,038	62.2
	Carroll H. Balcom (R)	42,033	37.8
4	Harold D. Donohue (D)	59,847	49.5
	Pehr G. Holmes (R)	58,663	48.5
5	Edith Nourse Rogers (R)	98,488	71.6
	Oliver S. Allen (D)	38,575	28.0
6	George J. Bates (R)	79,709	70.2
	Richard B. O'Keefe (D)	33,823	29.8
7	Thomas J. Lane (D)	59,871	60.8
	Ernest Bentley (R)	37,250	37.8
8	Angier L. Goodwin (R)	76,305	63.5
	Anthony M. Roche (D)	43,827	36.5
9	Charles L. Gifford (R)	69,831	60.8
	William McAuliffe (D)	43,367	37.8
10	Christian A. Herter (R)	96,607	64.0
	Paul J. McCarty (D)	54,421	36.0
11	John F. Kennedy (D)	69,093	71.9
	Lester W. Bowen (R)	26,007	27.1
12	John W. McCormack (D)	92,622	100.0
13	Richard B. Wigglesworth (R)	87,839	67.5
	James J. Goode Jr. (D)	42,274	32.5
14	Joseph W. Martin Jr. (R)	71,566	63.6
	Martha Sharp (D)	40,999	36.4

MICHIGAN

1	George G. Sadowski (D)	57,753	65.9
	John B. Sosnowski (R)	29,293	33.4
2	Earl C. Michener (R)	66,486	71.2
	William R. Kelley (D)	26,141	28.0
3	Paul W. Shafer (R)	59,823	68.9
	Herschel W. Carney (D)	25,914	29.9
4	Clare E. Hoffman (R)	58,798	72.5
	Harvey Hope Jarvis (D)	21,514	26.5
5	Bartel J. Jonkman (R)	63,093	71.6
	Earle W. Reynolds (D)	25,022	28.4
6	William W. Blackney (R)	69,203	57.3
	Arthur Elliott (D)	50,684	42.0
7	Jesse P. Wolcott (R)	64,404	74.2
	Earl J. Tallman (D)	21,708	25.0
8	Fred L. Crawford (R)	58,725	72.6
	J. Charles Mottashed (D)	21,375	26.4
9	Albert J. Engel (R)	49,017	71.8
	J. Willard Krause (D)	18,828	27.6
10	Roy O. Woodruff (R)	44,853	71.1
	Herman N. Butler (D)	17,737	28.1
11	Fred Bradley (R)	41,436	65.9
	Cecil W. Bailey (D)	21,340	33.9
12	John B. Bennett (R)	40,717	54.4
	Frank E. Hook (D)	33,799	45.2
13	Howard A. Coffin (R)	50,539	52.8
	George D. O'Brien (D)	44,883	46.9
14	Harold F. Youngblood (R)	69,968	53.3
	Louis C. Rabaut (D)	60,808	46.3
15	John D. Dingell (D)	59,111	51.9
	Harry Henderson (R)	54,296	47.7
16	John Lesinski (D)	57,773	51.9
	Albert A. Riddering (R)	52,376	47.1

	Candidates	Votes	%
17	George A. Dondero (R)	102,336	64.7
	John W. L. Hicks (D)	54,928	34.7

MINNESOTA

1	August H. Andresen (R)	65,906	68.4
	Karl F. Rolvaag (DFL)	30,439	31.6
2	Joseph P. O'Hara (R)	69,487	76.0
	L. J. Kilbride (DFL)	21,947	24.0
3	George MacKinnon (R)	57,397	51.5
	Roy W. Wier (DFL)	52,797	47.3
4	Edward J. Devitt (R)	45,667	51.5
	Frank T. Starkey (DFL)	41,897	47.2
5	Walter H. Judd (R)	66,837	58.3
	Douglas Hall (DFL)	47,777	41.7
6	Harold Knutson (R)	55,401	57.4
	J. Edward Anderson (DFL)	41,147	42.6
7	H. Carl Andersen (R)	57,869	65.4
	Donald M. Lawson (DFL)	30,667	34.6
8	John A. Blatnik (DFL)	62,876	57.7
	William A. Pittenger (R)	46,189	42.4
9	Harold C. Hagen (R)	50,031	63.9
	Verner Nelson (DFL)	28,211	36.1

MISSISSIPPI

1	John E. Rankin (D)	5,429	100.0
2	Jamie L. Whitten (D)	6,411	100.0
3	William M. Whittington (D)	4,265	100.0
4	Thomas G. Abernethy (D)	10,017	100.0
5	W. Arthur Winstead (D)	7,122	100.0
6	William M. Colmer (D)	6,448	100.0
7	John Bell Williams (D)	10,345	100.0

MISSOURI

1	Samuel W. Arnold (R)	37,584	50.3
	Walter G. Stillwell (D)	37,105	49.7
2	Max Schwabe (R)	44,292	51.1
	Will L. Nelson Jr. (D)	42,437	48.9
3	William C. Cole (R)	38,828	52.8
	William Orr Sawyers (D)	34,730	47.2
4	C. Jasper Bell (D)	41,843	55.1
	Vernon D. Fulcrut (R)	34,066	44.9
5	Albert L. Reeves Jr. (R)	42,065	53.7
	Enos A. Axtell (D)	36,324	46.3
6	Marion T. Bennett (R)	54,034	58.6
	Tom B. Hembree (D)	38,113	41.4
7	Dewey Short (R)	50,588	65.4
	Don Ervin (D)	26,712	34.6
8	Parke M. Banta (R)	42,076	51.1
	A. S. J. Carnahan (D)	40,241	48.9
9	Clarence Cannon (D)	35,253	53.9
	William Barton (R)	30,199	46.1
10	Orville Zimmerman (D)	37,236	60.6
	Walter K. Dillon (R)	24,164	39.4
11	Claude I. Bakewell (R)	41,202	50.8
	John B. Sullivan (D)	39,879	49.2
12	Walter C. Ploeser (R)	93,136	58.2
	Henry W. Simpson (D)	66,878	41.8
13	Frank M. Karsten (D)	41,229	54.8
	Alfred L. Grattendick (R)	34,062	45.2

MONTANA

1	Mike Mansfield (D)	47,418	57.6
	W. R. Rankin (R)	34,958	42.4
2	Wesley A. D'Ewart (R)	58,307	54.1
	John J. Holmes (D)	48,564	45.1

NEBRASKA

1	Carl T. Curtis (R)	73,602	66.4
	William H. Meier (D)	37,280	33.6
2	Howard Buffett (R)	53,398	58.3
	Frank A. Jelen (D)	38,125	41.7
3	Karl Stefan (R)	64,016	72.2
	Hans O. Jensen (D)	20,161	22.7
	Paul Burke (I)	4,516#	5.1

	Candidates	Votes	%
4	Arthur L. Miller (R)	57,708	71.3
	Stanley D. Long (D)	23,234	28.7

NEVADA

	Candidates	Votes	%
AL	Charles H. Russell (R)	28,859	58.8
	Malcolm McEachin (D)	20,187	41.2

NEW HAMPSHIRE

	Candidates	Votes	%
1	Chester E. Merrow (R)	53,909	59.8
	Josaphet T. Benoit (D)	36,316	40.3
2	Norris Cotton (R)	45,963	64.9
	Patrick J. Hinchey (D)	24,904	35.1

NEW JERSEY

	Candidates	Votes	%
1	Charles A. Wolverton (R)	82,919	63.5
	George F. Neutze (D)	47,631	36.5
2	T. Millet Hand (R)	54,511	67.1
	Edward T. Keeley (D)	26,740	32.9
3	James C. Auchincloss (R)	70,302	64.9
	John W. Zimmermann (D)	36,177	33.4
4	Frank A. Mathews Jr. (R)	50,221	52.6
	Charles R. Howell (D)	45,225	47.4
5	Charles A. Eaton (R)	69,338	61.3
	John J. George (D)	43,593	38.6
6	Clifford P. Case (R)	69,395	64.7
	Walter H. Van Hoesen (D)	35,378	33.0
7	J. Parnell Thomas (R)	65,426	69.0
	Robert B. Meyner (D)	29,418	31.0
8	Gordon Canfield (R)	57,616	70.5
	John V. Breslin (D)	23,007	28.2
9	Harry L. Towe (R)	74,870	69.1
	John M. Mehler (D)	33,553	31.0
10	Fred A. Hartley Jr. (R)	44,619	52.5
	Peter W. Rodino Jr. (D)	38,889	45.7
11	Frank L. Sundstrom (R)	46,034	60.4
	Robert F. J. McGarry (D)	28,545	37.5
12	Robert W. Kean (R)	55,732	63.6
	Raymond C. Connell (D)	30,389	34.7
13	Mary T. Norton (D)	69,440	64.4
	John A. Jones (R)	36,270	33.7
14	Edward J. Hart (D)	65,979	63.2
	Edward P. Nicolay (R)	38,008	36.4

NEW MEXICO

	Candidates	Votes	%
AL	Georgia L. Lusk (D)	66,420✓	
	Antonio M. Fernandez (D)	65,242✓	
	Earl Douglas (R)	60,519	
	Herman G. Baca (R)	58,937	

NEW YORK

	Candidates	Votes	%
1	W. Kingsland Macy (R)	83,877	77.3
	Eugene T. O'Neill (D)	22,855	21.1
2	Leonard W. Hall (R)	123,873	78.4
	Josephine U. Mayes (D, AM LAB)	34,217	21.6
3	Henry J. Latham (R)	98,722	69.7
	Aloysius J. Maickel (D)	32,002	22.6
4	Gregory McMahon (R)	57,176	53.3
	Emily B. Barry (D)	38,227	35.6
	George H. Rooney (AM LAB)	7,439	6.9
5	Robert Tripp Ross (R)	66,754	53.0
	James A. Phillips (D, AM LAB)	59,092	47.0
6	Robert J. Nodar Jr. (R)	59,438	53.9
	James J. Delaney (D, AM LAB)	50,944	46.1
7	John J. Delaney (D, AM LAB)	49,449	57.5
	Roy M. D. Richardson (R)	36,510	42.5
8	Joseph L. Pfeifer (D, AM LAB)	34,876	53.9
	Paul W. Williams (R)	29,851	46.1
9	Eugene J. Keogh (D, L)	41,304	48.6
	Samuel R. Scialabba (R)	27,289	32.1
	Anthony Scimeca (AM LAB)	16,359	19.3
10	Andrew L. Somers (D, AM LAB)	57,658	57.9
	Victor Wichum (R)	33,642	33.8
	August Claessens (L)	8,314	8.4
11	James J. Heffernan (D, AM LAB)	69,089	60.4
	Alfred C. McKenzie (R)	45,279	39.6
12	John J. Rooney (D)	36,399	54.0
	Vincent J. Longhi (R, AM LAB)	31,052	46.0
13	Donald L. O'Toole (D, AM LAB)	51,406	53.5
	Charles H. Weadon (R)	44,674	46.5
14	Leo F. Rayfiel (D, AM LAB)	79,336	75.0
	Robert H. Thayer (R)	26,450	25.0
15	Emanuel Celler (D, AM LAB)	78,543	78.7
	Lauri T. Laisi (D)	21,094	21.1
16	Ellsworth B. Buck (R, VETS V)	49,758	61.2
	John Burry (D, AM LAB)	31,583	38.8
17	Frederic R. Coudert Jr. (R)	66,063	57.5
	Myron Sulzberger (D)	39,216	34.2
	Joseph Clark Baldwin (AM LAB)	9,527	8.3
18	Vito Marcantonio (D, AM LAB)	42,229	54.2
	Frederick V. P. Bryan (R)	35,693	45.8
19	Arthur G. Klein (D, AM LAB)	48,437	71.4
	William I. Lehrfeld (R)	19,410	28.6
20	Sol Bloom (D, AM LAB)	57,208	61.1
	Jules J. Justin (R)	36,450	38.9
21	Jacob K. Javits (R, L)	46,897	46.0
	Daniel Flynn (D)	40,652	39.9
	Eugene P. Connolly (AM LAB)	14,359	14.1
22	Adam Clayton Powell Jr. (D, AM LAB)	32,573	62.5
	Grant Reynolds (R)	19,514	37.5
23	Walter A. Lynch (D)	52,616	43.4
	Peter Wynne (R)	30,534	25.2
	David A. Schlossberg (AM LAB)	25,229	20.8
	William Wacks (L)	12,803	10.6
24	Benjamin J. Rabin (D)	39,316	44.2
	Roy Soden (AM LAB)	24,249	27.3
	David Scher (R)	16,931	19.0
	Bernice Benedick (L)	8,504	9.6
25	Charles A. Buckley (D)	47,142	32.5
	Charles Garside (R)	46,853	32.3
	Edward V. Morand (AM LAB)	25,353	17.5
	Ira J. Palestine (L)	15,814	10.9
	John A. Devany (VETS V)	9,791	6.8
26	David Potts (R)	58,061	44.1
	Peter A. Quinn (D)	49,067	37.3
	Gerald O'Reilly (AM LAB)	17,379	13.2
	Augustus Batten (L)	7,140	5.4
27	Ralph W. Gwinn (R)	84,882	68.6
	Francis X. Nulty (D, AM LAB)	38,950	31.5
28	Ralph A. Gamble (R)	83,533	75.4
	Morris Karnes, (D, AM LAB)	27,236	24.6
29	Katharine St. George (R)	60,769	58.2
	James K. Welsh (D, VETS F)	40,174	38.4
30	Jay LeFevre (R)	80,469	69.5
	John F. Killgrew (D, AM LAB)	35,240	30.5
31	Bernard W. Kearney (R)	66,395	59.2
	Carroll A. Gardner (D, AM LAB)	45,777	40.8
32	William T. Byrne (D, AM LAB)	79,042	55.1
	William K. Sanford (R)	64,325	44.9
33	Dean P. Taylor (R)	89,778	69.9
	David J. Fitzgerald (D, AM LAB)	38,666	30.1
34	Clarence E. Kilburn (R)	64,217	73.0
	William G. Houk (D)	22,368	25.4
35	Hadwen C. Fuller (R)	58,040	54.3
	Frank A. Emma (D, AM LAB)	48,854	45.7
36	R. Walter Riehlman (R)	76,372	63.3
	Lawson Barnes (D, AM LAB)	44,371	36.7
37	Edwin Arthur Hall (R)	59,920	71.7
	Charles R. Wilson (D, AM LAB)	23,687	28.3
38	John Taber (R)	63,382	72.1
	George T. Franklin (D)	24,576	27.9
39	W. Sterling Cole (R)	61,330	72.6
	William Heidt Jr. (D, AM LAB)	23,205	27.4
40	Kenneth B. Keating (R)	84,852	60.5
	George F. Rogers (D, AM LAB)	55,321	39.5
41	James W. Wadsworth (R)	65,975	71.5
	Charles J. Reap (D, AM LAB)	26,332	28.5
42	Walter Gresham Andrews (R)	71,862	62.6
	William R. Lupton (D, AM LAB)	43,028	37.4
43	Edward J. Elsaesser (R)	71,758	62.6
	Charles P. McCabe (D)	38,108	33.2
44	John C. Butler (R)	67,495	57.5
	James B. Downey (D, AM LAB)	49,798	42.5
45	Daniel A. Reed (R)	53,327	70.4
	Joseph E. Proudman (D, AM LAB)	20,205	26.7

Special Election

	Candidates	Votes	%
19	Arthur G. Klein (D)	17,360	49.5
	Johannes Stell (AM LAB)	13,415	38.2
	William S. Shea (R)	4,314	12.3

NORTH CAROLINA

	Candidates	Votes	%
1	Herbert C. Bonner (D)	9,993	89.2
	Zeno O. Ratcliff (R)	1,208	10.8
2	John H. Kerr (D)	9,426	100.0
3	Graham A. Barden (D)	14,798	66.7
	H. B. Kornegay (R)	7,385	33.3
4	Harold D. Cooley (D)	22,977	65.7
	Ben L. Spence (R)	12,005	34.3
5	John H. Folger (D)	26,316	62.9
	S. Evan Hall (R)	15,521	37.1
6	Carl T. Durham (D)	18,564	63.4
	A. A. McDonald (R)	10,721	36.6
7	J. Bayard Clark (D)	15,428	73.9
	H. Edmund Rodgers (R)	5,445	26.1
8	Charles B. Deane (D)	29,920	54.2
	Joseph H. Whicker Sr. (R)	25,305	45.8
9	Robert L. Doughton (D)	36,007	54.9
	Clyde R. Greene (R)	29,585	45.1
10	Hamilton C. Jones (D)	24,614	53.9
	P. C. Burkholder (R)	21,096	46.2
11	Alfred L. Bulwinkle (D)	25,544	58.5
	C. Y. Nanney Jr. (R)	18,143	41.5
12	Monroe M. Redden (D)	43,690	60.5
	Guy Weaver (R)	28,531	39.5

Special Elections

	Candidates	Votes	%
8	Jane Pratt (D)	31,058	79.5
	H. Frank Hulin (R)	8,017	20.5
10	Sam J. Ervin Jr. (D)	2,303	99.7

NORTH DAKOTA

	Candidates	Votes	%
AL	William Lemke (R)	103,205✓	
	Charles R. Robertson (R)	102,087✓	
	James M. Hanley (D)	41,189	
	Edwin Cooper (D)	29,865	

OHIO

	Candidates	Votes	%
1	Charles H. Elston (R)	72,909	64.2
	G. Andrews Espy (D)	40,594	35.8
2	William E. Hess (R)	67,067	63.2
	Francis G. Davis (D)	39,112	36.8
3	Raymond H. Burke (R)	71,171	52.0
	Edward J. Gardner (D)	65,749	48.0
4	Robert F. Jones (R)	46,718	59.2
	Merl J. Bragg (D)	32,160	40.8
5	Cliff Clevenger (R)	30,623	60.3
	Willard Thomas (D)	20,163	39.7
6	Edward O. McCowen (R)	39,992	54.8
	Franklin E. Smith (D)	33,013	45.2
7	Clarence J. Brown (R)	63,390	68.0
	Carl H. Ehl (D)	29,824	32.0
8	Frederick C. Smith (R)	40,755	64.0
	John T. Siemon (D)	22,945	36.0
9	Homer A. Ramey (R)	59,394	50.1
	Michael V. DiSalle (D)	59,057	49.9
10	Thomas A. Jenkins (R)	35,406	66.7
	H. A. McCown (D)	17,719	33.4
11	Walter E. Brehm (R)	31,576	60.6
	Lester S. Reid (D)	20,543	39.4
12	John M. Vorys (R)	74,691	62.0
	Arthur P. Lamneck (D)	45,779	38.0
13	Alvin F. Weichel (R)	49,725	72.1
	Frank W. Thomas (D)	19,237	27.9
14	Walter B. Huber (D)	88,178	52.6
	Fred W. Danner (R)	77,674	46.4

	Candidates	Votes	%
15	Percy W. Griffiths (R)	36,564	53.2
	Robert T. Secrest (D)	32,159	46.8
16	Henderson H. Carson (R)	65,639	55.8
	William R. Thom (D)	51,931	44.2
17	J. Harry McGregor (R)	57,167	65.3
	Wesley W. Purdy (D)	30,406	34.7
18	Earl R. Lewis (R)	55,140	58.8
	Eugene A. Blum (D)	38,606	41.2
19	Michael J. Kirwan (D)	88,872	59.9
	Norman W. Adams (R)	59,607	40.2
20	Michael A. Feighan (D)	49,670	67.0
	Walter E. Obert (R)	24,476	33.0
21	Robert Crosser (D)	49,111	64.0
	James S. Hudec (R)	27,657	36.0
22	Frances P. Bolton (R)	174,823	69.1
	Earl Heffley (D)	69,050	27.3
AL	George H. Bender (R)	1,281,864	59.5
	William M. Boyd (D)	871,660	40.5

OKLAHOMA

	Candidates	Votes	%
1	George B. Schwabe (R)	61,205	54.5
	Oras A. Shaw (D)	51,041	45.5
2	William G. Stigler (D)	32,559	63.1
	Ferd P. Snider (R)	19,029	36.9
3	Carl Albert (D)	38,699	85.0
	Eleanor L. Watson (R)	6,835	15.0
4	Glen D. Johnson (D)	36,559	64.4
	Pliney S. Frye (R)	20,230	35.6
5	A. S. Mike Monroney (D)	47,173	52.0
	Carmon C. Harris (R)	43,508	48.0
6	Toby Morris (D)	30,408	65.7
	Joe Hart Jr. (R)	15,912	34.4
7	Preston E. Peden (D)	26,585	78.7
	J. Warren White (R)	7,204	21.3
8	Ross Rizley (R)	30,240	54.8
	Tom Hieronymus (D)	24,954	45.2

OREGON

	Candidates	Votes	%
1	Walter Norblad (R)	67,535	72.0
	Lyman Ross (D)	26,278	28.0
2	Lowell Stockman (R)	32,541	67.4
	Lamar Townsend (D)	15,744	32.6
3	Homer D. Angell (R)	74,061	56.7
	Lew Wallace (D)	56,525	43.3
4	Harris Ellsworth (R)	42,868	69.2
	Louis A. Wood (D)	19,118	30.8

PENNSYLVANIA

	Candidates	Votes	%
1	James Gallagher (R)	70,680	57.3
	William Barrett (D)	52,593	42.7
2	Robert N. McGarvey (R)	70,474	51.4
	William T. Granahan (D)	66,674	48.6
3	Hardie Scott (R)	83,618	62.1
	Albert S. Townsend (D)	50,962	37.9
4	Franklin J. Maloney (R)	55,239	50.2
	John Edward Sheridan (D)	49,025	44.6
	John K. Rice (U CIT)	5,688	5.2
5	George W. Sarbacher Jr. (R)	73,946	56.9
	William J. Green Jr. (D)	56,086	43.1
6	Hugh Scott (R)	82,671	58.5
	Herbert J. McGlinchey (D)	58,557	41.5
7	E. Wallace Chadwick (R)	76,021	66.5
	Vernon A. O'Rourke (D)	38,253	33.5
8	Charles L. Gerlach (R)	49,196	59.0
	Henry Chapin (D)	34,260	41.1
9	Paul B. Dague (R)	64,311	72.7
	Edgar Campbell (D)	24,175	27.3
10	James P. Scoblick (R)	47,704	51.0
	Frank X. Murray (D)	45,843	49.0
11	Mitchell Jenkins (R)	58,413	50.8
	Daniel J. Flood (D)	56,570	49.2
12	Ivor D. Fenton (R)	62,151	62.7
	Ralph M. Bashore (D)	36,954	37.3
13	Frederick A. Muhlenberg (R)	33,409	54.6
	Daniel K. Hoch (D)	25,073	41.0
14	Wilson D. Gillette (R)	43,142	67.4
	James S. Fields (D)	20,842	32.6

	Candidates	Votes	%
15	Robert F. Rich (R)	44,264	68.5
	Richard F. Hartzell (D)	20,376	31.5
16	Samuel K. McConnell Jr. (R)	76,314	74.4
	William L. Batt Jr. (D)	26,305	25.6
17	Richard M. Simpson (R)	37,194	66.2
	Lowell H. Alexander (D)	18,972	33.8
18	John C. Kunkel (R)	77,349	69.0
	William B. Freeland (D)	34,708	31.0
19	Leon H. Gavin (R)	41,500	68.0
	Lloyd N. Huth (D)	18,199	29.8
20	Francis E. Walter (D)	39,751	52.5
	Norman A. Peil (R)	36,008	47.5
21	Chester H. Gross (R)	45,559	52.0
	John W. Brehm (D)	42,118	48.0
22	James E. Van Zandt (R)	42,217	65.9
	John A. Shartle (D)	21,853	34.1
23	William J. Crow (R)	34,194	52.9
	John W. Rankin (D)	30,493	47.1
24	Thomas E. Morgan (D)	39,749	56.8
	Roy A. Purviance (R)	30,231	43.2
25	Louis E. Graham (R)	53,932	58.8
	Samuel G. Neff (D)	37,723	41.2
26	Harve Tibbott (R)	49,573	54.6
	Thomas A. Owens (D)	41,224	45.4
27	Augustine B. Kelley (D)	46,137	52.9
	Roy C. McKenna (R)	41,030	47.1
28	Carroll D. Kearns (R)	56,835	63.9
	Charles W. Webb (D)	32,166	36.1
29	John McDowell (R)	55,329	53.5
	Harry J. Davenport (D)	48,091	46.5
30	Robert J. Corbett (R)	57,827	60.1
	James W. Knox (D)	38,362	39.9
31	James G. Fulton (R)	70,419	63.8
	Edward A. Schultz (D)	40,010	36.2
32	Herman P. Eberharter (D)	62,963	62.8
	Ignatius J. Pillart (R)	37,247	37.2
33	Frank Buchanan (D)	51,656	57.9
	John Robert Brown Jr. (R)	37,555	42.1

RHODE ISLAND

	Candidates	Votes	%
1	Aime J. Forand (D)	74,324	56.7
	Raymond A. Mailloux (R)	55,900	42.6
2	John E. Fogarty (D)	74,349	52.6
	John J. Kelly Jr. (R)	66,987	47.4

SOUTH CAROLINA

	Candidates	Votes	%
1	L. Mendel Rivers (D)	5,354	99.5
2	John J. Riley (D)	4,795	98.6
3	W. J. Bryan Dorn (D)	3,527	99.9
4	Joseph R. Bryson (D)	3,363	99.6
5	James P. Richards (D)	3,357	100.0
6	John L. McMillan (D)	5,671	96.9

SOUTH DAKOTA

	Candidates	Votes	%
1	Karl E. Mundt (R)	76,720	61.5
	Merton B. Tice (D)	48,065	38.5
2	Francis H. Case (R)	28,011	73.7
	John B. Reinhard (D)	10,008	26.3

TENNESSEE

	Candidates	Votes	%
1	Dayton E. Phillips (R)	24,144	100.0
2	John Jennings Jr. (R)	28,752	84.0
	James Douglas Wyrick (I)	5,485	16.0
3	Estes Kefauver (D)	26,779	90.8
	George Bagwell (I)	2,725	9.2
4	Albert A. Gore (D)	7,624	67.5
	H. E. McLean (R)	3,673	32.5
5	Joe L. Evins (D)	11,646	100.0
6	J. Percy Priest (D)	7,178	77.1
	Will T. Perry (R)	2,135	22.9
7	Wirt Courtney (D)	11,658	100.0
8	Thomas J. Murray (D)	11,891	100.0
9	Jere Cooper (D)	12,685	100.0
10	Clifford Davis (D)	37,069	100.0

TEXAS

	Candidates	Votes	%
1	Wright Patman (D)	11,929	100.0
2	Jesse M. Combs (D)	19,909	96.2
3	Lindley Beckworth (D)	10,686	100.0
4	Sam Rayburn (D)	11,957	93.7
	Floyd Harry (R)	800	6.3
5	J. Frank Wilson (D)	12,267	75.8
	L. W. Stayart (R)	3,921	24.2
6	Olin E. Teague (D)	11,421	100.0
7	Tom Pickett (D)	14,810	100.0
8	Albert Thomas (D)	42,163	90.8
	R. F. Burns (R)	4,253	9.2
9	Joseph J. Mansfield (D)	16,712	100.0
10	Lyndon B. Johnson (D)	16,947	100.0
11	W.R. Poage (D)	9,178	100.0
12	Wingate H. Lucas (D)	15,266	87.7
	E. M. Hyder (R)	2,146	12.3
13	Ed Gossett (D)	17,714	100.0
14	John E. Lyle (D)	30,064	100.0
15	Milton H. West (D)	16,674	100.0
16	R. Ewing Thomason (D)	8,114	100.0
17	Omar Burleson (D)	14,874	100.0
18	Eugene Worley (D)	12,475	74.1
	F. T. O'Brien (R)	4,357	25.9
19	George H. Mahon (D)	15,791	94.6
	M. D. Temple (R)	905	5.4
20	Paul J. Kilday (D)	10,543	100.0
21	O. Clark Fisher (D)	15,943	100.0

UTAH

	Candidates	Votes	%
1	Walter K. Granger (D)	44,888	50.1
	David J. Wilson (R)	44,784	49.9
2	William A. Dawson (R)	56,402	52.7
	J. Will Robinson (D)	50,598	47.3

VERMONT

	Candidates	Votes	%
AL	Charles A. Plumley (R)	46,985	64.3
	Matthew J. Caldbeck (D)	26,056	35.7

VIRGINIA

	Candidates	Votes	%
1	S. Otis Bland (D)	13,863	75.0
	Walter Johnson (R)	4,628	25.0
2	Porter Hardy Jr. (D)	19,267	65.7
	Sidney H. Kelsey (R)	10,078	34.3
3	J. Vaughan Gary (D)	21,947	73.3
	Earle Lutz (R)	7,974	26.7
4	Patrick Henry Drewry (D)	13,636	87.1
	Andrew S. Condrey (P)	2,012	12.9
5	Thomas B. Stanley (D)	17,741	73.5
	William L. Creasy (R)	6,390	26.5
6	J. Lindsay Almond Jr. (D)	20,068	64.8
	Frank R. Angell (R)	10,641	34.4
7	Burr P. Harrison (D)	19,535	62.3
	Karl Jenkins (R)	11,813	37.7
8	Howard Worth Smith (D)	21,252	62.1
	Lawrence Michael (R)	12,950	37.9
9	John W. Flannagan Jr. (D)	20,610	51.8
	S. H. Sutherland (R)	17,152	43.1
	John Albert Goodpasture Jr. (I)	2,026	5.1

Special Election

	Candidates	Votes	%
5	Thomas B. Stanley (D)	17,862	75.4
	William L. Creasy (R)	5,829	24.6
7	Burr P. Harrison (D)	19,711	62.5
	Karl Jenkins (R)	11,809	37.5

WASHINGTON

	Candidates	Votes	%
1	Homer R. Jones (R)	113,289	63.8
	Hugh De Lacy (D)	64,155	36.2
2	Henry M. Jackson (D)	54,089	53.1
	Payson Peterson (R)	47,838	46.9
3	Fred Norman (R)	47,875	53.9
	Charles R. Savage (D)	40,980	46.1
4	Hal Holmes (R)	51,476	67.6
	Earl S. Coe (D)	24,662	32.4
5	Walt Horan (R)	58,535	61.3

Candidates	Votes	%
John T. Little (D)	34,870	36.5
6 Thor C. Tollefson (R)	56,702	53.9
John M. Coffee (D)	48,431	46.1

WEST VIRGINIA

	Candidates	Votes	%
1	Francis J. Love (R)	45,691	53.1
	Matthew M. Neely (D)	40,370	46.9
2	Melvin C. Snyder (R)	41,224	51.4
	Jennings Randolph (D)	39,041	48.6
3	Edward G. Rohrbough (R)	42,386	51.5
	Cleveland M. Bailey (D)	39,872	48.5
4	Hubert S. Ellis (R)	54,932	52.7
	M. G. Burnside (D)	49,408	47.4
5	John Kee (D)	43,154	56.9

	Candidates	Votes	%
	Hartley Sanders (R)	32,754	43.2
6	Erland H. Hedrick (D)	57,461	53.0
	Harold H. Neff (R)	51,064	47.1

WISCONSIN

	Candidates	Votes	%
1	Lawrence H. Smith (R)	58,344	56.5
	John R. Redstrom (D)	44,188	42.8
2	Robert K. Henry (R)	68,794*	62.9
	William G. Rice (D)	39,657	36.3
3	William H. Stevenson (R)	65,177	96.1
4	John C. Brophy (R)	49,144	36.5
	Edmund V. Bobrowicz (D)	44,398	33.0
	Thaddeus F. B. Wasielewski (I)	38,502	28.6
5	Charles J. Kersten (R)	76,364	54.1

	Candidates	Votes	%
	Andrew J. Biemiller (D)	59,764	42.3
6	Frank B. Keefe (R)	58,444	64.2
	Edwin W. Webster (D)	31,550	34.7
7	Reid F. Murray (R)	60,390	71.6
	Elmer E. Fraley (D)	23,481	27.8
8	John W. Byrnes (R)	67,840	64.7
	Martin J. Young (D)	37,013	35.3
9	Merlin Hull (R)	70,527	99.0
10	Alvin E. O'Konski (R)	40,263	53.0
	Henry J. Berquist (D)	32,238	42.4

WYOMING

	Candidates	Votes	%
AL	Frank A. Barrett (R)	44,512	56.0
	John J. McIntyre (D)	34,946	44.0

1947 House Elections

NEW YORK

Special Election

	Candidates	Votes	%
14	Abraham J. Multer (D, L)	47,849	58.2
	Victor J. Rabinowitz (AM LAB)	20,800	25.3
	Jacob P. Fefkowitz (R)	13,597	16.5

WISCONSIN

Special Election

		Votes	%
2	Glenn R. Davis (R)	24,023	50.6
	Thompson (D)	23,181	48.8

1948 House Elections

ALABAMA

	Candidates	Votes	%
1	Frank W. Boykin (D)	19,778	100.0
2	George M. Grant (D)	21,271	100.0
3	George W. Andrews (D)	16,279	100.0
4	Sam Hobbs (D)	17,282	85.0
	B. Hogan Stewart (R)	3,054	15.0
5	Albert Rains (D)	20,548	100.0
6	Edward deGraffenried (D)	13,968	82.4
	W. P. Ivey (R)	2,994	17.7
7	Carl A. Elliott (D)	21,552	100.0
8	Robert E. Jones Jr. (D)	19,060	88.4
	Harry J. Frahn (R)	2,510	11.6
9	Laurie C. Battle (D)	33,781	87.1
	Hiram Dodd (R)	5,006	12.9

ARIZONA

	Candidates	Votes	%
1	John R. Murdock (D)	42,565	58.4
	John H. Udall (R)	29,864	41.0
2	Harold A. Patten (D)	54,066	62.8
	Albert R. Buehman (R)	30,140	35.0

ARKANSAS

	Candidates	Votes	%
1	Ezekiel C. Gathings (D)	34,676	100.0
2	Wilbur D. Mills (D)	29,922	100.0
3	James W. Trimble (D)	27,278	68.6
	Dalton Dotson (R)	12,462	31.4
4	Boyd Tackett (D)	29,338	87.8
	C. R. Starbird (R)	4,094	12.3
5	Brooks Hays (D)	36,440	87.0
	Thad Tisdale (R)	5,471	13.1
6	William F. Norrell (D)	40,291	100.0
7	Oren Harris (D)	32,982	100.0

CALIFORNIA

	Candidates	Votes	%
1	Hubert B. Scudder (R)	82,947	54.5
	Sterling J. Norgard (D-IP)	68,951	45.3
2	Clair Engle (D-R)	78,555	100.0
3	Leroy Johnson (R-D)	166,571	84.4
	James B. Willard (I PROG)	30,878	15.6
4	Franck R. Havenner (D)	73,704	51.0
	William S. Mailliard (R)	68,875	47.7
5	Richard J. Welch (R-D)	116,347	100.0
6	George P. Miller (D-R)	194,985	99.9
7	John J. Allen Jr. (R)	78,534	51.4
	Buel G. Gallagher (D-IP)	74,318	48.6
8	Jack Z. Anderson (R-D)	161,743	79.9
	Paul Taylor (I PROG)	40,670	20.1
9	Cecil F. White (D)	72,826	51.3
	Bertrand W. Gearhart (R)	66,563	46.9
10	Thomas H. Werdel (R-D)	67,448	71.3
	Sam James Miller (I PROG)	27,168	28.7
11	Ernest K. Bramblett (R-D)	87,143	80.7
	Cole Weston (I PROG)	14,582	13.5
	George E. Outland	6,157	5.7
12	Richard M. Nixon (R-D)	141,509	86.9
	Una W. Rice (I PROG)	19,631	12.1
13	Norris Poulson (R)	62,951	52.6
	Ned R. Healy (D-IP)	56,624	47.3
14	Helen Gahagan Douglas (D)	89,581	65.3
	W. Wallace Braden (R)	44,611	32.5
15	Gordon L. McDonough (R-D)	131,933	83.0
	Maynard J. Omerberg (I PROG)	27,007	17.0
16	Donald L. Jackson (R)	121,198	57.0
	Ellis E. Patterson (D-IP)	91,268	42.9
17	Cecil R. King (D-R)	194,782	99.9
18	Clyde Doyle (D)	105,687	51.1
	Willis W. Bradley (R)	92,721	44.9
19	Chet Holifield (D)	72,900	69.7
	Joseph Francis Quigley (R)	28,698	27.5
20	Carl Hinshaw (R-D)	204,710	81.5

	Candidates	Votes	%
	William B. Esterman (I PROG)	46,232	18.4
21	Harry R. Sheppard (D)	61,383	55.2
	Lowell E. Lathrop (R)	47,411	42.6
22	John Phillips (R-D)	115,697	99.9
23	Clinton D. McKinnon (D)	112,534	55.8
	Charles K. Fletcher (R)	87,138	43.2

COLORADO

	Candidates	Votes	%
1	John A. Carroll (D)	106,096	64.8
	Christopher F. Cusack (R)	57,541	35.2
2	William S. Hill (R)	71,868	51.9
	George L. Bickel (D)	66,579	48.1
3	John H. Marsalis (D)	65,114	50.7
	J. Edgar Chenoweth (R)	63,312	49.3
4	Wayne N. Aspinall (D)	34,695	51.9
	Robert F. Rockwell (R)	32,206	48.1

CONNECTICUT

	Candidates	Votes	%
1	Abraham A. Ribicoff (D)	127,802	54.7
	William J. Miller (R)	103,294	44.2
2	Chase Going Woodhouse (D)	69,339	51.7
	Horace Seely-Brown Jr. (R)	64,916	48.4
3	John A. McGuire (D)	84,449	49.7
	Ellsworth B. Foote (R)	83,310	49.0
4	John Davis Lodge (R)	117,727	55.2
	William Gaston (D)	92,618	43.4
5	James T. Patterson (R)	62,804	51.1
	Vincent P. Kiernan (D)	58,300	47.4
AL	Antoni N. Sadlak (R)	433,311	49.3
	Fred Trotta (D)	429,348	48.8

DELAWARE

	Candidates	Votes	%
AL	J. Caleb Boggs (R)	71,127	50.6
	J. Carl McGuigan (D)	68,909	49.0

FLORIDA

	Candidates	Votes	%
1	J. Hardin Peterson (D)	66,348	100.0
2	Charles E. Bennett (D)	55,715	91.1
	Camille Geneau (R)	5,413	8.9
3	Robert L. F. Sikes (D)	30,730	100.0
4	George A. Smathers (D)	63,665	81.0
	J. L. Wambaugh (R)	14,912	19.0
5	A. S. Herlong Jr. (D)	46,939	70.7
	M. J. Moss Jr. (R)	19,501	29.4
6	Dwight L. Rogers (D)	31,933	66.7
	Rolf Kaltenborn (R)	15,977	33.4

GEORGIA

	Candidates	Votes	%
1	Prince H. Preston (D)	42,677	100.0
2	E. E. Cox (D)	26,815	100.0
3	Stephen Pace (D)	32,098	100.0
4	A. Sidney Camp (D)	33,522	100.0
5	James C. Davis (D)	54,637	99.6
6	Carl Vinson (D)	29,446	100.0
7	Henderson Lanham (D)	45,195	100.0
8	W. M. Wheeler (D)	35,608	100.0
9	John S. Wood (D)	29,699	100.0
10	Paul Brown (D)	35,479	100.0

IDAHO

	Candidates	Votes	%
1	Compton I. White (D)	46,846	51.8
	Abe McGregor Goff (R)	41,404	45.7
2	John C. Sanborn (R)	61,690	50.7
	Asael Lyman (D)	59,006	48.5

ILLINOIS

	Candidates	Votes	%
1	William L. Dawson (D)	98,690	67.0
	William E. King (R)	43,034	29.2
2	Barratt O'Hara (D)	91,648	50.5
	Richard B. Vail (R)	85,119	46.9
3	Neil J. Linehan (D)	91,204	52.9
	Fred E. Busbey (R)	81,175	47.1
4	James V. Buckley (D)	89,557	52.1
	Leslie E. Salter (R)	82,310	47.9
5	Martin Gorski (D)	114,660	72.5
	John L. Waner (R)	43,610	27.6
6	Thomas J. O'Brien (D)	127,918	68.4
	John M. Coan (R)	53,548	28.6
7	Adolph J. Sabath (D)	133,199	73.7
	Francis C. Sperry (R)	47,602	26.3
8	Thomas S. Gordon (D)	101,098	65.1
	Herbert F. Geisler (R)	54,316	35.0
9	Sidney R. Yates (D)	91,271	54.5
	Robert J. Twyman (R)	73,301	43.8
10	Richard W. Hoffman (R)	109,031	58.1
	Marvin J. Peters (D)	78,533	41.9
11	Chester A. Chesney (D)	80,750	50.8
	James C. Moreland (R)	78,269	49.2
12	Edgar A. Jonas (R)	98,956	51.4
	Blair L. Varnes (D)	88,795	46.1
13	Ralph E. Church (R)	123,978	68.0
	Willard C. Walters (D)	58,340	32.0
14	Chauncey W. Reed (R)	94,962	68.3
	Richard Plum (D)	44,050	31.7
15	Noah M. Mason (R)	74,213	56.4
	G. M. Wells (D)	57,296	43.6
16	Leo E. Allen (R)	76,840	58.5
	Albert H. Manus Jr. (D)	54,481	41.5
17	Leslie C. Arends (R)	71,220	62.8
	Carl Vrooman (D)	42,226	37.2
18	Harold H. Velde (R)	61,652	52.1
	Dale E. Sutton (D)	56,688	47.9
19	Robert B. Chiperfield (R)	69,733	54.0
	Fred J. Brown (D)	59,397	46.0
20	Sid Simpson (R)	59,067	53.1
	Henry D. Sullivan (D)	52,235	46.9
21	Peter F. Mack Jr. (D)	69,619	53.1
	Joseph L. Moore (R)	61,452	46.9
22	Rolla C. McMillen (R)	64,625	53.2
	Olive Remington Goldman (D)	56,893	46.8
23	Edward H. Jenison (R)	57,800	51.8
	Wayne R. Cook (D)	53,885	48.3
24	Charles W. Vursell (R)	57,732	50.6
	John David Upchurch (D)	56,262	49.4
25	Melvin Price (D)	101,927	69.5
	Russell H. Classen (R)	44,728	30.5
26	C. W. Bishop (R)	54,993	51.9
	Kent E. Keller (D)	51,028	48.1

INDIANA

	Candidates	Votes	%
1	Ray J. Madden (D)	78,898	60.7
	Theodore L. Sendak (R)	50,194	38.6
2	Charles A. Halleck (R)	71,907	55.2
	Theodore J. Smith (D)	57,245	44.0
3	Thurman C. Crook (D)	86,382	51.9
	Robert A. Grant (R)	78,935	47.5
4	Edward H. Kruse Jr. (D)	66,689	50.8
	George W. Gillie (R)	63,403	48.3
5	John R. Walsh (D)	91,861	51.9
	Forest A. Harness (R)	82,730	46.8
6	Cecil M. Harden (R)	66,414	49.9
	Jack J. O'Grady (D)	65,931	49.5
7	James E. Noland (D)	74,396	53.7
	Gerald W. Landis (R)	62,855	45.4
8	Winfield K. Denton (D)	89,990	55.4
	Edward A. Mitchell (R)	71,634	44.1
9	Earl Wilson (R)	59,787	51.6
	Christopher D. Moritz (D)	55,333	47.7
10	Ralph Harvey (R)	76,036	52.5
	Robert C. Oliver (D)	67,081	46.3
11	Andrew Jacobs Sr. (D)	103,046	50.6
	George L. Denny (R)	98,451	48.4

IOWA

	Candidates	Votes	%
1	Thomas E. Martin (R)	70,959	53.6
	James D. France (D)	60,860	45.9
2	Henry O. Talle (R)	82,139	53.6
	T. W. Mullaney (D)	70,272	45.9
3	H. R. Gross (R)	78,838	58.3
	Dan J. P. Ryan (D)	56,002	41.4
4	Karl LeCompte (R)	53,384	51.5
	Steven V. Carter (D)	49,894	48.2
5	Paul Cunningham (R)	60,103	50.8
	Vincent L. Browner (D)	57,370	48.5
6	James I. Dolliver (R)	55,641	55.8
	James E. Irwin (D)	43,997	44.2
7	Ben F. Jensen (R)	59,173	56.9
	W. A. Byers (D)	44,857	43.1
8	Charles B. Hoeven (R)	56,970	55.2
	L. J. McGivern (D)	45,796	44.4

KANSAS

	Candidates	Votes	%
1	Albert M. Cole (R)	68,395	60.5
	James L. Quinn (D)	44,711	39.5
2	Errett P. Scrivner (R)	68,324	51.9
	Philip A. Dergance (D)	63,431	48.1
3	Herbert A. Meyer (R)	46,935	55.0
	Marcus C. Black (D)	38,391	45.0
4	Edward H. Rees (R)	88,605	55.6
	William J. Kropp (D)	70,778	44.4
5	Clifford R. Hope (R)	77,160	65.0
	Henry D. Parkinson (D)	41,614	35.0
6	Wint Smith (R)	55,013	57.6
	Leslie E. Davis (D)	40,553	42.4

KENTUCKY

	Candidates	Votes	%
1	Noble J. Gregory (D)	50,720	100.0
2	John Whitaker (D)	54,586	63.4
	Mallam Lake (R)	31,527	36.6
3	Thruston B. Morton (R)	74,168	53.0
	Ralph H. Logan (D)	64,877	46.3
4	Frank L. Chelf (D)	45,538	59.5
	Stanley Jaggers (R)	31,062	40.6
5	Brent Spence (D)	47,518	66.2
	George T. Smith (R)	24,240	33.8
6	Thomas R. Underwood (D)	60,659	60.7
	John N. Menefee (R)	39,251	39.3
7	Carl D. Perkins (D)	39,788	60.5
	W. Howes Meade (R)	26,007	39.5
8	Joe B. Bates (D)	52,328	58.6
	Hubert Counts (R)	34,127	38.2
9	James S. Golden (R)	60,309	100.0

LOUISIANA

	Candidates	Votes	%
1	F. Edward Hebert (D)	36,748	100.0
2	Hale Boggs (D)	61,316	100.0
3	Edwin E. Willis (D)	26,587	66.4
	J. Paulin Duhe (R)	13,437	33.6
4	Overton Brooks (D)	32,045	100.0
5	Otto E. Passman (D)	34,362	100.0
6	James H. Morrison (D)	47,515	100.0
7	Henry D. Larcade Jr. (D)	36,053	100.0
8	A. Leonard Allen (D)	33,613	100.0

MAINE

	Candidates	Votes	%
1	Robert Hale (R)	52,536	62.5
	James A. McVicar (D)	31,528	37.5
2	Charles P. Nelson (R)	50,552	67.2
	Benjamin J. Arena (D)	24,698	32.8
3	Frank Fellows (R)	38,692	70.9
	F. Davis Clark (D)	15,888	29.1

MARYLAND

	Candidates	Votes	%
1	Edward T. Miller (R)	29,700	52.4
	S. Scott Beck Jr. (D)	27,024	47.6
2	William P. Bolton (D)	99,157	55.2
	A. Earl Shipley (R)	76,235	42.5
3	Edward A. Garmatz (D)	32,138	68.8
	John A. Janetzke Jr. (R)	13,131	28.1
4	George H. Fallon (D)	38,486	58.2
	James W. Miller (R)	21,084	31.9
	John E. T. Camper (PROG)	6,552	9.9
5	Lansdale G. Sasscer (D)	45,902	59.7
	C. Maurice Weidemeyer (R)	30,997	40.3
6	J. Glenn Beall (R)	59,856	55.3
	F. Byrne Austin (D)	48,304	44.7

MASSACHUSETTS

	Candidates	Votes	%
1	John W. Heselton (R)	75,582	57.2
	Patrick J. O'Malley (D)	56,604	42.8
2	Foster Furcolo (D)	81,775	54.9
	Charles R. Clason (R)	67,267	45.1
3	Philip J. Philbin (D)	104,601	73.9
	Carroll H. Balcom (R)	36,855	26.1
4	Harold D. Donohue (D)	89,064	59.2
	John J. Maginnis (R)	61,448	40.8
5	Edith Nourse Rogers (R)	139,288	100.0
6	George J. Bates (R)	108,179	100.0
7	Thomas J. Lane (D)	100,333	79.2
	A. Prescott Barker (R)	26,339	20.8
8	Angier L. Goodwin (R)	75,844	51.0
	Anthony M. Roche (D)	72,767	49.0
9	Donald W. Nicholson (R)	82,750	56.7
	Jacinto F. Diniz (D)	63,275	43.3
10	Christian A. Herter (R)	118,741	69.5
	Walter A. O'Brien Jr. (D)	52,022	30.5
11	John F. Kennedy (D)	106,366	100.0
12	John W. McCormack (D)	125,015	100.0
13	Richard B. Wigglesworth (R)	89,913	56.6
	David J. Concannon (D)	69,050	43.4
14	Joseph W. Martin Jr. (R)	87,973	61.4
	Joseph M. Mendonca (D)	55,369	38.6

MICHIGAN

	Candidates	Votes	%
1	George G. Sadowski (D)	101,954	83.5
	Rudolph G. Tenerowicz (R)	19,609	16.1
2	Earl C. Michener (R)	65,006	55.8
	Preston W. Slosson (D)	50,148	43.0
3	Paul W. Shafer (R)	64,637	59.4
	Leeman J. McCarty (D)	42,146	38.7
4	Clare E. Hoffman (R)	61,059	64.9
	Tom Surprise (D)	31,429	33.4
5	Gerald R. Ford Jr. (R)	74,191	60.5
	Fred J. Barr Jr. (D)	46,972	38.3
6	William W. Blackney (R)	73,465	49.8
	George D. Stevens (D)	72,681	49.3
7	Jesse P. Wolcott (R)	68,903	59.0
	Harvey C. Whetzel (D)	47,040	40.3
8	Fred L. Crawford (R)	61,394	61.3
	Louis C. Schwinger (D)	37,125	37.1
9	Albert J. Engel (R)	51,771	58.5
	John George Hosko (D)	35,805	40.5
10	Roy O. Woodruff (R)	49,206	63.3
	Edward J. Daugherty (D)	27,742	35.7
11	Charles E. Potter (R)	48,633	63.6
	Violet L. Patterson (D)	27,265	35.6
12	John B. Bennett (R)	42,955	56.6
	Gene A. Saari (D)	32,485	42.8
13	George D. O'Brien (D)	76,947	62.5
	Howard A. Coffin (R)	45,761	37.1
14	Louis C. Rabaut (D)	99,227	57.0
	Harold F. Youngblood (R)	74,474	42.7
15	John D. Dingell (R)	92,579	65.0
	Charles G. Burns (R)	49,286	34.6
16	John Lesinski (D)	97,826	62.5
	Kirby L. Wilson Jr. (R)	57,730	36.9
17	George A. Dondero (R)	116,427	52.7
	John J. Brown (D)	103,390	46.8

MINNESOTA

	Candidates	Votes	%
1	August H. Andresen (R)	80,345	61.4
	Karl F. Rolvaag (DFL)	50,533	38.6
2	Joseph P. O'Hara (R)	82,886	63.9
	Milton F. Maxwell (DFL)	46,894	36.1
3	Roy W. Wier (DFL)	87,171	54.6
	George MacKinnon (R)	72,402	45.4
4	Eugene J. McCarthy (DFL)	78,476	59.4
	Edward J. Devitt (R)	53,574	40.6
5	Walter H. Judd (R)	76,313	54.0
	Marcella F. Killen (DFL)	65,113	46.0
6	Fred Marshall (DFL)	66,601	51.7
	Harold Knutson (R)	62,194	48.3
7	H. Carl Andersen (R)	63,879	52.5
	James M. Youngdale (DFL)	57,863	47.5
8	John A. Blatnik (DFL)	88,501	66.6
	William A. Berlin (R)	44,306	33.4
9	Harold C. Hagen (R)	57,189	54.6
	Oscar A. Johnson (DFL)	47,476	45.4

MISSISSIPPI

	Candidates	Votes	%
1	John E. Rankin (D)	16,800	100.0
2	Jamie L. Whitten (D)	13,771	100.0
3	William M. Whittington (D)	17,369	100.0
4	Thomas G. Abernethy (D)	15,290	98.4
5	W. Arthur Winstead (D)	22,641	100.0
6	William M. Colmer (D)	29,751	100.0
7	John Bell Williams (D)	36,663	100.0

MISSOURI

	Candidates	Votes	%
1	Clare Magee (D)	56,226	57.6
	Wat Arnold (R)	41,365	42.4
2	Morgan M. Moulder (D)	66,062	56.7
	Max Schwabe (R)	50,372	43.2
3	Philip J. Welch (D)	69,599	57.1
	William C. Cole (R)	52,290	42.9
4	Theodore Leonard Irving (D)	74,752	64.1
	Richard A. Erickson (R)	41,576	35.7
5	Richard W. Bolling (D)	59,961	55.9
	Albert L. Reeves Jr. (R)	47,371	44.1
6	George H. Christopher (D)	63,390	51.4
	Marion T. Bennett (R)	59,959	48.6
7	Dewey Short (R)	61,242	54.0
	Thomas A. Johnson (D)	52,255	46.0
8	Albert S. J. Carnahan (D)	60,081	57.2
	Parke M. Banta (R)	44,887	42.8
9	Clarence Cannon (D)	56,669	61.7
	Robert V. Niedner (R)	35,232	38.3
10	Paul C. Jones (D)	67,564	71.6
	W. K. Dillon (R)	26,760	28.4
11	John B. Sullivan (D)	78,162	64.7
	Claude I. Bakewell (R)	40,719	33.7
12	Raymond W. Karst (D)	132,920	55.0
	Walter C. Ploeser (R)	107,861	44.6
13	Frank M. Karsten (D)	77,245	70.6
	Charles P. McBride (R)	32,217	29.4

MONTANA

	Candidates	Votes	%
1	Mike Mansfield (D)	64,276	67.9
	Albert H. Angstman (R)	29,937	31.6
2	Wesley A. D'Ewart (R)	61,124	51.0
	Willard E. Fraser (D)	58,711	49.0

NEBRASKA

	Candidates	Votes	%
1	Carl T. Curtis (R)	76,359	57.2
	Frank B. Morrison (D)	57,031	42.8
2	Eugene D. O'Sullivan (D)	58,443	51.4
	Howard Buffett (R)	55,199	48.6
3	Karl Stefan (R)	71,513	64.8
	Duane K. Peterson (D)	38,846	35.2
4	Arthur L. Miller (R)	65,549	63.6
	C. Edgar Leafdale (D)	37,511	36.4

NEVADA

	Candidates	Votes	%
AL	Walter S. Baring (D)	29,733	50.7
	Charles H. Russell (R)	28,972	49.4

NEW HAMPSHIRE

	Candidates	Votes	%
1	Chester E. Merrow (R)	64,794	55.5
	Peter R. Poirier (D)	51,262	43.9
2	Norris Cotton (R)	59,505	57.4
	Richard W. Leonard (D)	43,289	41.8

NEW JERSEY

1	Charles A. Wolverton (R)	89,211	53.0
	John W. Donges (D)	77,012	45.8
2	T. Millet Hand (R)	62,804	61.7
	William E. Stringer (D)	38,194	37.5
3	James C. Auchincloss (R)	87,538	58.5
	Charles F. Sullivan (D)	59,810	40.0
4	Charles R. Howell (D)	77,018	61.5
	Albert C. Jones (R)	48,204	38.5
5	Charles A. Eaton (R)	92,286	57.4
	George C. Miller (D)	66,387	41.3
6	Clifford P. Case (R)	83,285	55.3
	H. Frank Pettit (D)	61,465	40.8
7	J. Parnell Thomas (R)	72,873	56.2
	John J. Carlin (D)	56,095	43.2
8	Gordon Canfield (R)	59,191	47.5
	Charles S. Joelson (D)	59,043	47.4
9	Harry L. Towe (R)	90,153	62.3
	James S. Brown (D)	54,682	37.8
10	Peter W. Rodino Jr. (D)	58,668	50.7
	Anthony Giuliano (R)	52,898	45.7
11	Hugh J. Addonizio (D)	52,644	47.7
	Frank L. Sundstrom (R)	50,920	46.2
12	Robert W. Kean (R)	63,232	48.6
	Harry Dudkin (D)	58,495	44.9
13	Mary T. Norton (D)	84,487	68.1
	Leon Banach (R)	39,661	32.0
14	Edward J. Hart (D)	76,881	62.8
	Michael Bongiovanni (R)	45,564	37.2

NEW MEXICO

AL	John E. Miles (D)	108,529✓	
	Antonio M. Fernandez (D)	105,300✓	
	Ben F. Meyer (R)	76,695	
	Herman G. Baca (R)	73,661	
	Clinton E. Jencks (PROG)	805	

NEW YORK

1	W. Kingsland Macy (R)	101,924	66.0
	Harold W. Worzel (D)	48,816	31.6
2	Leonard W. Hall (R)	144,052	68.1
	Richard T. Mayes (D, L)	62,142	29.4
3	Henry J. Latham (R)	104,476	56.5
	George J. Gross (D)	65,247	35.3
4	L. Gary Clemente (D)	62,190	46.9
	Gregory McMahon (R)	58,192	43.8
	Thomas J. McCabe (AM LAB)	7,681	5.8
5	T. Vincent Quinn (D, L)	83,213	49.8
	Robert Tripp Ross (R)	72,012	43.1
	Morris Pottish (AM LAB)	11,994	7.2
6	James J. Delaney (D, L)	76,828	54.2
	Robert Nodar Jr. (R)	55,844	39.4
	Irma Lindheim (AM LAB)	9,092	6.4
7	John J. Delaney (D, AM LAB)	65,162*	60.0
	Francis E. Dorn (R, L)	43,483	40.0
8	Joseph L. Pfeifer (D, AM LAB)	61,037	67.7
	Benjamin F. Westervelt Jr (R)	25,773	28.6
9	Eugene J. Keogh (D, L)	59,711	56.2
	Philip Hodes (R)	26,700	25.1
	Murray Rosof (AM LAB)	19,803	18.6
10	Andrew L. Somers (D, L)	69,502	56.1
	Arthur S. Hirsch (R)	32,290	26.1
	Ada B. Jackson (AM LAB)	22,067	17.8
11	James J. Heffernan (D, L)	74,974	54.9
	Alfred C. McKenzie (R)	41,289	30.2
	Frank Serri (AM LAB)	20,340	14.9
12	John J. Rooney (D, L)	55,021	60.4
	John J. Miller (R)	29,061	31.9
	Vincent J. Longhi (AM LAB)	6,968	7.7
13	Donald L. O'Toole (D, L)	66,111	52.8
	Charles A. Fisher (R)	44,718	35.7
	James Griesi (AM LAB)	14,440	11.5
14	Abraham J. Multer (D, R)	103,676	77.8
	Lee Pressman (AM LAB)	29,502	22.2
15	Emanuel Celler (D, AM LAB)	94,828	81.4
	Henry D. Dorfman (R)	21,703	18.6
16	James J. Murphy (D, L)	51,185	49.3
	Frank A. Pavis (R)	45,623	44.0
	Frank Cremonesi (AM LAB)	6,991	6.7
17	Frederic R. Coudert Jr. (R)	74,581	53.2
	Arthur T. Sawyer (D, L)	52,101	37.2
	Alvin Udell (AM LAB)	13,401	9.6
18	Vito Marcantonio (AM LAB)	36,278	36.9
	John P. Morrissey (D)	31,211	31.7
	John Ellis (R, L)	30,899	31.4
19	Arthur G. Klein (D, AM LAB)	77,426	74.4
	Herbert Lasky (R)	20,697	19.9
	Stephen C. Vladeck (L)	5,886	5.7
20	Sol Bloom (D, L)	73,866	59.4
	Jules J. Justin (R)	34,819	28.0
	Eugene P. Connolly (AM LAB)	15,727	12.6
21	Jacob K. Javits (R, L)	66,527	50.7
	Paul O'Dwyer (D, AM LAB)	64,654	49.3
22	Adam Clayton Powell Jr. (D, AM LAB)	63,523	76.4
	Harold C. Burton (R)	14,012	16.9
	Edna D. Moseley (L)	5,583	6.7
23	Walter A. Lynch (D, R)	121,523	83.0
	Leon Straus (AM LAB)	24,903	17.0
24	Isidore Dollinger (D, R)	74,971	63.1
	Leo Isacson (AM LAB)	43,933	37.0
25	Charles A. Buckley (D, R)	138,706	82.2
	Albert E. Kahn (AM LAB)	30,112	17.8
26	Christopher C. McGrath (D, L)	91,456	54.8
	David M. Potts (R)	57,061	34.2
	Nicholas Carnes (AM LAB)	18,379	11.0
27	Ralph W. Gwinn (R)	81,144	52.1
	Richard W. McSpedon (D, L)	67,541	43.4
28	Ralph A. Gamble (R)	88,822	62.7
	Charles J. Nager (D, L)	46,335	32.7
29	Katharine St. George (R)	79,229	60.1
	William G. Pendergast (D, L)	48,063	36.5
30	Jay LeFevre (R)	91,649	64.8
	Robert R. Decormier (D, AM LAB)	49,691	35.2
31	Bernard W. Kearney (R)	77,725	55.3
	William M. Murphy (D, L)	58,215	41.4
32	William T. Byrne (D, L)	88,476	55.6
	Lawrence J. Collins (R)	65,341	41.1
33	Dean P. Taylor (R)	98,618	63.7
	Joseph T. Hammer (D, L)	52,059	33.6
34	Clarence E. Kilburn (R)	70,715	60.7
	Francis K. Purcell (D)	43,777	37.6
35	John C. Davies (D, L)	62,855	48.9
	Hadwen C. Fuller (R)	62,717	48.8
36	R. Walter Riehlman (R)	78,409	50.5
	Richard T. Mosher (D, L)	71,847	46.3
37	Edwin Arthur Hall (R)	65,848	63.4
	Myron C. Sloat (D)	35,503	34.2
38	John Taber (R)	66,695	58.0
	Francis J. Souhan (D)	48,222	42.0
39	W. Sterling Cole (R)	70,659	64.3
	Donald J. O'Connor (D, L)	37,272	33.9
40	Kenneth B. Keating (R)	90,305	51.4
	George F. Rogers (D, AM LAB)	85,505	48.6
41	James W. Wadsworth Jr. (R)	67,882	59.1
	Bernard E. Hart (D)	45,155	39.3
42	William L. Pfeiffer (R)	75,842	51.1
	Mary Louise Nice (D, L)	69,290	46.6
43	Anthony F. Tauriello (D, L)	72,388	50.8
	Edward J. Elsaesser (R)	66,729	46.9
44	Chester C. Gorski (D, L)	79,795	51.8
	John C. Butler (R)	71,275	46.2
45	Daniel A. Reed (R)	58,340	60.1
	Hubert D. Bliss (D)	35,406	36.5

Special Election

	Candidates	Votes	%
24	Leo Isacson (AM LAB)	22,697	55.9
	Karl Propper (D)	12,598	31.0
	Dean Alfange (L)	3,843	9.5

NORTH CAROLINA

1	Herbert C. Bonner (D)	31,850	92.7
	Zeno O. Ratcliff (R)	2,507	7.3
2	John H. Kerr (D)	36,227	96.0
3	Graham A. Barden (D)	34,997	78.8
	Perry G. Crumpler (R)	9,407	21.2
4	Harold D. Cooley (D)	57,658	78.1
	Joel A. Johnson (R)	15,866	21.5
5	Richard Thurmond Chatham (D)	47,575	72.7
	John Tucker Day (R)	17,041	26.1
6	Carl T. Durham (D)	50,659	72.1
	Ralph O. Smith (R)	17,906	25.5
7	F. Ertel Carlyle (D)	43,292	84.3
	J. O. West (R)	7,839	15.3
8	Charles B. Deane (D)	46,941	62.7
	Lafayette Williams (R)	27,924	37.3
9	Robert L. Doughton (D)	51,586	59.6
	Clyde R. Greene (R)	35,008	40.4
10	Hamilton C. Jones (D)	48,043	59.6
	Roy A. Harmon (R)	32,321	40.1
11	Alfred L. Bulwinkle (D)	40,009	64.9
	Calvin R. Edney (R)	21,614	35.1
12	Monroe M. Redden (D)	52,036	63.1
	W. W. Candler (R)	30,456	36.9

NORTH DAKOTA

AL	William Lemke (R)	132,343✓	
	Usher L. Burdick (R)	128,454✓	
	Alfred Dale (D)	56,702	
	John M. Weiler	1,758	

OHIO

1	Charles H. Elston (R)	73,952	51.7
	Morse Johnson (D)	69,240	48.4
2	Earl T. Wagner (D)	75,062	52.9
	William E. Hess (R)	66,968	47.2
3	Edward Breen (D)	110,204	58.2
	Raymond H. Burke (R)	79,162	41.8
4	William M. McCulloch (R)	57,321	55.7
	Earl Ludwig (D)	45,534	44.3
5	Cliff Clevenger (R)	34,950	52.1
	Dan Batt (D)	32,076	47.9
6	James G. Polk (D)	46,944	53.1
	Edward O. McCowen (R)	41,492	46.9
7	Clarence J. Brown (R)	71,737	100.0
8	Frederick C. Smith (R)	43,929	54.5
	Andrew T. Durbin (D)	36,685	45.5
9	Thomas H. Burke (D)	85,409	53.8
	Homer A. Ramey (R)	73,394	46.2
10	Thomas A. Jenkins (R)	38,330	57.9
	Delmar A. Canaday (D)	27,913	42.1
11	Walter E. Brehm (R)	33,796	50.9
	Joseph C. Allen (D)	32,667	49.2
12	John M. Vorys (R)	95,575	52.1
	Robert M. Draper (D)	87,770	47.9
13	Alvin F. Weichel (R)	55,408	59.2
	Dwight A. Blackmore (D)	38,264	40.9
14	Walter B. Huber (D)	125,346	57.2
	Ed Rowe (R)	92,535	42.2
15	Robert T. Secrest (D)	45,575	56.4
	P. W. Griffiths (R)	35,294	43.6
16	John McSweeney (D)	79,859	52.6
	Henderson H. Carson (R)	71,871	47.4
17	J. Harry McGregor (R)	60,234	52.9
	Robert W. Levering (D)	53,651	47.1
18	Wayne L. Hays (D)	65,475	54.1
	Earl R. Lewis (R)	55,455	45.9
19	Michael J. Kirwan (D)	134,448	68.1
	William Bacon (R)	63,079	31.9

	Candidates	Votes	%
20	Michael A. Feighan (D)	64,241	100.0
21	Robert Crosser (D)	72,417	76.0
	Harry W. Mitchell (R)	22,932	24.1
22	Frances P. Bolton (R)	170,085	54.7
	Jack G. Day (D)	141,018	45.3
AL	Stephen M. Young (D)	1,455,972	52.0
	George H. Bender (R)	1,342,409	48.0

OKLAHOMA

1	William Franklin Gilmer (D)	77,949	53.3
	George B. Schwabe (R)	68,423	46.8
2	William G. Stigler (D)	43,801	70.6
	George T. Balch (R)	18,236	29.4
3	Carl Albert (D)	57,300	83.9
	Russell Overstreet (R)	11,007	16.1
4	Tom Steed (D)	53,419	72.1
	Clyde T. Patrick (R)	20,716	27.9
5	A. S. Mike Monroney (D)	95,248	67.4
	Carmon C. Harris (R)	45,985	32.6
6	Toby Morris (D)	47,857	73.7
	George E. Young (R)	17,100	26.3
7	Victor E. Wickersham (D)	39,380	79.4
	J. Warren White (R)	10,236	20.6
8	George H. Wilson (D)	42,417	58.0
	Martin Garber (R)	30,687	42.0

OREGON

1	Walter Norblad (R)	88,587	63.3
	Edward E. Gideon (D)	45,904	32.8
2	Lowell Stockman (R)	42,730	58.2
	C. J. Shorb (D)	30,743	41.8
3	Homer D. Angell (R)	99,464	55.5
	Roland C. Bartlett (D)	66,436	37.1
	Peggy T. Carlson (PROG)	13,171	7.4
4	Harris Ellsworth (R)	65,606	66.6
	William F. Tanton (D & PROG)	32,931	33.4

PENNSYLVANIA

1	William A. Barrett (D)	70,165	53.4
	John De Nero (R)	61,165	46.6
2	William T. Granahan (D)	82,863	54.4
	Robert N. McGarvey (R)	69,604	45.7
3	Hardie Scott (R)	76,009	52.0
	Maurice S. Osser (D)	70,075	48.0
4	Earl Chudoff (D)	70,129	55.7
	Franklin J. Maloney (R)	50,236	39.9
5	William J. Green Jr. (D)	77,221	50.7
	George W. Sarbacher Jr. (R)	75,007	49.3
6	Hugh Scott (R)	86,755	57.0
	Herbert J. McGlinchey (D)	65,535	43.0
7	Benjamin F. James (R)	91,394	61.3
	Arnold M. Snyder (D)	56,263	37.8
8	Franklin H. Lichtenwalter (R)	62,229	59.2
	Wynne James Jr. (D)	42,878	40.8
9	Paul B. Dague (R)	74,726	67.1
	W. Roger Simpson (D)	36,677	32.9
10	Harry P. O'Neill (D)	64,289	58.5
	Nelson Nichols (R)	45,587	41.5
11	Daniel J. Flood (D)	68,628	51.8
	Robert H. Stroh (R)	63,797	48.2
12	Ivor D. Fenton (R)	68,089	60.6
	John Oshinskie (D)	44,345	39.4
13	George M. Rhodes (D)	40,415	50.3
	Frederick A. Muhlenberg (R)	37,261	46.4
14	Wilson D. Gillette (R)	47,715	65.2
	David Burchell (D)	25,484	34.8
15	Robert F. Rich (R, P)	48,760	61.6
	Patrick A. McGowan (D)	30,457	38.5
16	Samuel K. McConnell Jr. (R)	84,997	66.9
	Harry Hellar Kelly (D)	42,118	33.1
17	Richard M. Simpson (R)	38,735	64.5
	Ira Garman (D)	21,339	35.5
18	John C. Kunkel (R)	81,704	63.7
	Theodore C. Frederick Jr. (D)	46,586	36.3
19	Leon H. Gavin (R)	43,520	63.7
	Francis J. Manno (D)	24,800	36.3

20	Francis E. Walter (D)	54,041	58.8
	Roy E. James (R)	37,904	41.2
21	James F. Lind (D)	54,152	53.7
	Chester H. Gross (R)	46,701	46.3
22	James E. Van Zandt (R)	46,451	60.4
	Julia Luigia Maietta (D)	30,454	39.6
23	Anthony Cavalcante (D)	42,084	54.3
	William J. Crow (R)	35,384	45.7
24	Thomas E. Morgan (D)	56,282	65.4
	Roy A. Purviance (R)	29,768	34.6
25	Louis E. Graham (R)	56,966	52.6
	Andrew J. Katcher (D)	51,391	47.4
26	Robert L. Coffey Jr. (D)	62,061	55.4
	Harve Tibbott (R)	50,005	44.6
27	Augustine B. Kelley (D)	64,943	62.2
	W. Urban Gillespie (R)	39,517	37.8
28	Carroll D. Kearns (R)	65,276	54.5
	James A. Kennedy (D)	54,402	45.5
29	Harry J. Davenport (D)	63,454	54.2
	John McDowell (R)	53,609	45.8
30	Robert J. Corbett (R)	56,932	50.3
	J. R. Montgomery (D)	56,233	49.7
31	James G. Fulton (R)	75,147	56.4
	John J. Kane Jr. (D)	58,113	43.6
32	Herman P. Eberharter (D)	80,600	72.7
	Albert J. Weilersbacher (R)	30,328	27.3
33	Frank Buchanan (D)	74,508	69.2
	Albert G. Brown (R)	33,107	30.8

RHODE ISLAND

1	Aime J. Forand (D)	95,045	62.0
	Oscar J. V. Hurteau (R)	58,209	38.0
2	John E. Fogarty (D)	98,586	59.7
	Thomas J. Paolino (R)	66,672	40.3

SOUTH CAROLINA

1	L. Mendel Rivers (D)	24,529	89.1
	W. T. Baggott (R)	2,989	10.9
2	Hugo S. Sims Jr. (D)	27,677	96.5
3	James B. Hare (D)	19,181	97.8
4	Joseph R. Bryson (D)	26,098	94.9
	James B. Gaston (R)	1,410	5.1
5	James P. Richards (D)	14,544	97.1
6	John L. McMillan (D)	21,703	97.1

SOUTH DAKOTA

1	Harold O. Lovre (R)	99,062	53.5
	Merton B. Tice (D)	85,957	46.5
2	Francis H. Case (R)	36,713	65.9
	Jessie E. Sanders (D)	18,988	34.1

TENNESSEE

1	Dayton E. Phillips (R)	54,439	84.7
	Arthur W. Bright (D)	9,806	15.3
2	John Jennings Jr. (R)	43,849	58.0
	Thomas P. Fowler (IR)	31,743	42.0
3	James B. Frazier Jr. (D)	44,683	67.3
	W. E. Michael (R)	20,740	31.3
4	Albert Gore (D)	21,445	64.3
	Tom T. Tucker Jr. (R)	11,910	35.7
5	Joe L. Evins (D)	27,777	100.0
6	J. Percy Priest (D)	28,951	81.4
	Jesse L. Perry (R)	6,056	17.0
7	James P. Sutton (D)	28,058	100.0
8	Thomas J. Murray (D)	25,170	69.2
	J. Sam Johnson Jr. (R)	11,229	30.9
9	Jere Cooper (D)	26,033	91.1
	S. Homer Tatum (R)	2,555	8.9
10	Clifford Davis (D)	49,371	93.1
	Dwight V. Kyle (R)	3,670	6.9

TEXAS

1	Wright Patman (D)	40,162	100.0
2	Jesse M. Combs (D)	55,072	93.3
	Don Parker (R)	3,978	6.7

3	Lindley Beckworth (D)	36,361	88.7
	R. E. Kennedy (R)	4,642	11.3
4	Sam Rayburn (D)	38,211	100.0
5	J. Frank Wilson (D)	66,484	98.4
6	Olin E. Teague (D)	18,731	99.8
7	Tom Pickett (D)	27,945	100.0
8	Albert Thomas (D)	100,721	85.5
	Joe Ingraham (R)	17,124	14.5
9	Clark W. Thompson (D)	55,606	100.0
10	Homer Thornberry (D)	45,007	100.0
11	W. R. Poage (D)	39,795	96.2
12	Wingate H. Lucas (D)	61,206	89.1
	Elton M. Hyder (R)	7,480	10.9
13	Ed Gossett (D)	44,274	100.0
14	John E. Lyle Jr. (D)	59,163	88.9
	J. M. Swafford (R)	7,202	10.8
15	Lloyd M. Bentsen Jr. (D)	27,402	100.0
16	Ken Regan (D)	37,173	99.5
17	Omar Burleson (D)	34,078	100.0
18	Eugene Worley (D)	48,985	88.7
	J. Evetts Haley (R)	6,266	11.3
19	George Mahon (D)	58,585	95.6
20	Paul J. Kilday (D)	43,709	75.3
	J. P. Ledvina (R)	14,376	24.8
21	O. Clark Fisher (D)	45,274	100.0

UTAH

1	Walter K. Granger (D)	66,641	59.0
	David J. Wilson (R)	46,229	41.0
2	Reva Beck Bosone (D)	92,770	57.5
	William A. Dawson (R)	68,693	42.5

VERMONT

AL	Charles A. Plumley (R)	74,076	60.7
	Robert W. Ready (D)	47,767	39.2

VIRGINIA

1	S. Otis Bland (D)	24,746	80.0
	Stanley G. Adams (R)	5,753	18.6
2	Porter Hardy Jr. (D)	28,071	61.2
	Walter E. Hoffman (R)	15,800	34.4
3	J. Vaughan Gary (D)	33,950	72.9
	Richard C. Poage (R)	11,291	24.3
4	Watkins M. Abbitt (D)	22,029	100.0
5	Thomas B. Stanley (D)	23,879	99.5
6	Clarence G. Burton (D)	29,589	64.7
	John Strickler (R)	15,854	34.7
7	Burr P. Harrison (D)	25,799	60.4
	Stephen D. Timberlake (R)	16,890	39.6
8	Howard W. Smith (D)	33,563	54.8
	Tyrrell Krum (R)	25,420	41.5
9	Thomas B. Fugate (D)	33,550	52.4
	T. Eugene Worrell (R)	30,466	47.6

Special Election

6	Clarence G. Burton (D)	30,841	65.2
	John Strickler (R)	16,435	34.8

WASHINGTON

1	Hugh B. Mitchell (D)	100,030	50.8
	Homer R. Jones (R)	92,215	46.8
2	Henry M. Jackson (D)	83,824	61.6
	Payson Peterson (R)	48,413	35.6
3	Russell V. Mack (R)	61,856	52.1
	Charles R. Savage (D)	56,947	47.9
4	Hal Holmes (R)	58,105	53.2
	John F. Eubank (D)	51,195	46.8
5	Walt Horan (R)	67,757	54.6
	John F. McKay (D)	56,343	45.4
6	Thor C. Tollefson (R)	72,988	55.1
	Jack E. Knudsen (D)	54,166	40.9

WEST VIRGINIA

	Candidates	Votes	%
1	Robert L. Ramsay (D)	68,829	57.3
	Francis J. Love (R)	51,381	42.7
2	Harley O. Staggers (D)	61,786	54.7
	Melvin C. Snyder (R)	51,226	45.3
3	Cleveland M. Bailey (D)	68,055	57.1
	Edward G. Rohrbough (R)	51,123	42.9
4	Maurice G. Burnside (D)	72,378	53.1
	Hubert S. Ellis (R)	64,001	46.9
5	John Kee (D)	71,664	65.1
	Hartley Sanders (R)	38,446	34.9
6	Erland H. Hedrick (D)	99,842	62.5
	D. L. Salisbury (R)	59,900	37.5

WISCONSIN

	Candidates	Votes	%
1	Lawrence H. Smith (R)	67,387	51.9
	Jack Harvey (D)	61,791	47.6
2	Glenn R. Davis (R)	74,306	53.9
	Horace W. Wilkie (D)	62,953	45.6
3	Gardner R. Withrow (R)	69,727	69.2
	Frank J. Antoine (D)	30,650	30.4
4	Clement J. Zablocki (D)	89,391	55.9
	John C. Brophy (R)	63,161	39.5
5	Andrew J. Biemiller (D)	91,072	53.1
	Charles J. Kersten (R)	76,782	44.8
6	Frank B. Keefe (R)	60,675	55.5
	Kenneth Kunde (D)	47,844	43.8

	Candidates	Votes	%
7	Reid F. Murray (R)	64,531	62.5
	Ralph E. Kronenwetter (D)	37,307	36.1
8	John W. Byrnes (R)	70,905	56.7
	Martin J. Young (D)	53,287	42.6
9	Merlin Hull (R)	76,903	98.1
10	Alvin E. O'Konski (R)	52,124	54.8
	Daniel W. Hoan (D)	39,523	41.6

WYOMING

	Candidates	Votes	%
AL	Frank A. Barrett (R)	50,218	51.5
	L. G. Flannery (D)	47,246	48.5

1949 House Elections

NEW YORK

Special Elections

	Candidates	Votes	%
7	Louis B. Heller (D, L)	22,939	54.8
	Francis E. Dorn (R)	16,179	38.7
	Minneola Ingersoll (AM LAB)	2,712	6.5
10	Edna F. Kelly (D)	48,945	55.1
	Jules Cohen (L)	24,419	27.5
	George H. Fankuchen (R)	15,514	17.5
20	Franklin D. Roosevelt Jr (L, FF)	40,822	50.7
	Benjamin Shalleck (D)	24,352	30.2
	William H. McIntyre (R)	10,026	12.5
	Annette T. Rubinstein (AM LAB)	5,348	6.6

1950 House Elections

ALABAMA

	Candidates	Votes	%
1	Frank W. Boykin (D)	14,206	100.0
2	George M. Grant (D)	17,441	100.0
3	George W. Andrews (D)	10,914	100.0
4	Kenneth A. Roberts (D)	14,608	93.7
	J. P. Carter (R)	980	6.3
5	Albert Rains (D)	17,269	100.0
6	Edward deGraffenried (D)	11,709	100.0
7	Carl A. Elliott (D)	20,580	100.0
8	Robert E. Jones Jr. (D)	13,742	100.0
9	Laurie C. Battle (D)	30,743	100.0

ARIZONA

	Candidates	Votes	%
1	John R. Murdock (D)	51,526	60.6
	Carl W. Divelbiss (R)	33,528	39.4
2	Harold A. Patten (D)	63,991	69.1
	John H. Curnutte (R)	28,622	30.9

ARKANSAS

	Candidates	Votes	%
1	Ezekiel C. Gathings (D)	47,238	100.0
2	Wilbur D. Mills (D)	31,048	100.0
3	James W. Trimble (D)	34,434	100.0
4	Boyd Tackett (D)	43,156	100.0
5	Brooks Hays (D)	54,338	100.0
6	William F. Norrell (D)	46,467	100.0
7	Oren Harris (D)	39,121	100.0

CALIFORNIA

	Candidates	Votes	%
1	Hubert B. Scudder (R)	85,122	54.0
	Roger Kent (D)	72,584	46.0
2	Clair Engle (D-R)	85,103	100.0
3	Leroy Johnson (R-D)	177,269	100.0
4	Franck R. Havenner (D)	83,078	67.2
	Raymond D. Smith (R)	40,569	32.8
5	John F. Shelley (D-R)	117,888	100.0
6	George P. Miller (D-R)	192,342	100.0
7	John J. Allen Jr. (R)	74,069	55.3
	Lyle E. Cook (D)	59,976	44.7
8	Jack Z. Anderson (R-D)	168,510	83.1
	John A. Peterson (I PROG)	34,176	16.9
9	Allan Oakley Hunter (R)	76,015	52.0
	Cecil F. White (D)	70,201	48.0
10	Thomas H. Werdel (R)	59,313	53.6
	Ardis M. Walker (D)	51,409	46.4
11	Ernest K. Bramblett (R)	59,780	52.1
	Marion R. Walker (D)	55,020	47.9
12	Patrick J. Hillings (R)	107,933	60.1
	Steve Zetterberg (D)	71,682	39.9
13	Norris Poulson (R-D)	83,296	84.8
	Ellen P. Davidson (I PROG)	14,789	15.1
14	Samuel William Yorty (D)	47,653	49.4
	Jack W. Hardy (R)	35,543	36.8
	Charlotta A. Bass (I PROG)	13,364	13.8
15	Gordon L. McDonough (R-D)	112,704	87.1
	Jeanne Cole (I PROG)	16,559	12.8
16	Donald L. Jackson (R)	115,970	59.2
	Esther Murray (D)	79,744	40.7
17	Cecil R. King (D-R)	166,334	99.9
18	Clyde Doyle (D)	97,177	50.5
	Craig Hosmer (R)	95,308	49.5
19	Chet Holifield (D-R)	73,317	90.9
	Myra Tanner Weiss (I)	7,329	9.1
20	Carl Hinshaw (R-D)	211,012	85.1
	William B. Esterman (I PROG)	26,508	10.7
21	Harry R. Sheppard (D)	62,994	57.4
	R. E. Reynolds (R)	46,693	42.6
22	John Phillips (R-D)	114,497	99.9
23	Clinton D. McKinnon (D)	94,137	51.0
	Leslie E. Gehres (R)	90,398	49.0

COLORADO

	Candidates	Votes	%
1	Byron Rogers (D)	70,165	50.3
	Richard Luxford (R)	67,436	48.4
2	William S. Hill (R)	73,045	57.5
	George L. Bickel (D)	53,313	42.0
3	J. Edgar Chenoweth (R)	58,831	51.6
	John H. Marsalis (D)	55,110	48.4
4	Wayne N. Aspinall (D)	35,797	57.3
	Jack Evans (R)	26,674	42.7

CONNECTICUT

	Candidates	Votes	%
1	Abraham A. Ribicoff (D)	134,258	58.1
	Harry Schwolsky (R)	96,251	41.7
2	Horace Seely-Brown Jr. (R)	68,747	50.8
	Chase Going Woodhouse (D)	66,523	49.2
3	John A. McGuire (D)	89,391	51.9
	Ellsworth B. Foote (R)	82,304	47.8
4	Albert P. Morano (R)	111,939	53.1
	Dennis M. Carroll (D)	88,682	42.1
5	James T. Patterson (R)	65,915	53.0
	J. Gregory Lynch (D)	56,752	45.7
AL	Antoni N. Sadlak (R)	433,912	49.4
	Joseph W. Bogdanski (D)	426,485	48.6

DELAWARE

	Candidates	Votes	%
AL	J. Caleb Boggs (R)	73,313	56.7
	Henry M. Winchester (D)	56,091	43.4

FLORIDA

	Candidates	Votes	%
1	Chester B. McMullen (D)	40,466	100.0
2	Charles E. Bennett (D)	34,334	100.0
3	Robert L. F. Sikes (D)	24,548	100.0
4	Bill Lantaff (D)	65,758	82.1
	Joseph Edward Worton (R)	14,305	17.9
5	A. S. Herlong Jr. (D)	32,475	76.5
	Carl K. Landes (R)	9,958	23.5
6	Dwight L. Rogers (D)	31,205	100.0

GEORGIA

	Candidates	Votes	%
1	Prince H. Preston (D)	29,716	100.0
2	E. E. Cox (D)	18,920	100.0
3	E. L. Forrester (D)	24,221	100.0
4	A. Sidney Camp (D)	21,900	100.0
5	James C. Davis (D)	49,317	100.0
6	Carl Vinson (D)	22,402	100.0
7	Henderson Lanham (D)	23,595	100.0
8	W. M. Wheeler (D)	21,573	100.0
9	John S. Wood (D)	20,943	100.0
10	Paul Brown (D)	27,568	100.0

IDAHO

	Candidates	Votes	%
1	John T. Wood (R)	41,823	50.5
	Gracie Pfost (D)	41,040	49.5
2	Hamer Budge (R)	66,966	57.1
	James H. Hawley Jr. (D)	50,255	42.9

ILLINOIS

	Candidates	Votes	%
1	William L. Dawson (D)	69,056	61.6
	Archibald James Carey Jr. (R)	41,944	37.4
2	Richard B. Vail (R)	83,023	53.6
	Barratt O'Hara (D)	71,945	46.4
3	Fred E. Busbey (R)	87,241	54.5
	Neil J. Linehan (D)	72,676	45.4
4	William E. McVey (R)	73,542	55.8
	James V. Buckley (D)	58,190	44.2
5	John C. Kluczynski (D)	91,589	65.6
	Edward M. Gaynor (R)	48,052	34.4
6	Thomas J. O'Brien (D)	106,701	64.5
	John M. Fay (R)	58,534	35.4
7	Adolph J. Sabath (D)	109,841	71.8
	Henry E. Hayes (R)	43,211	28.2
8	Thomas S. Gordon (D)	77,736	59.3
	Philip Grontkowski (R)	53,305	40.7
9	Sidney R. Yates (D)	74,699	51.8
	Maxwell A. Goodwin (R)	69,552	48.2
10	Richard W. Hoffman (R)	117,498	66.5
	Charles J. Michal (D)	59,127	33.5
11	Timothy P. Sheehan (R)	81,358	56.7
	Chester A. Chesney (D)	62,050	43.3
12	Edgar A. Jonas (R)	96,489	56.2
	Charles J. Komaiko (D)	75,226	43.8
13	Marguerite Stitt Church (R)	140,750	74.1
	Thomas F. Dolan (D)	49,187	25.9
14	Chauncey W. Reed (R)	103,312	74.2
	Homer R. McElroy (D)	35,856	25.8
15	Noah M. Mason (R)	82,155	63.3
	Wayne F. Caskey (D)	47,633	36.7
16	Leo E. Allen (R)	82,190	67.3
	Russell J. Goldman (D)	39,944	32.7
17	Leslie C. Arends (R)	74,643	66.8
	Joe W. Russell (D)	37,096	33.2
18	Harold H. Velde (R)	72,499	61.6
	Walter Durley Boyle (D)	45,214	38.4
19	Robert B. Chiperfield (R)	69,379	59.0
	John Michael Kerwin Jr. (D)	48,286	41.0
20	Sid Simpson (R)	62,138	59.3
	Howard Manning (D)	42,647	40.7
21	Peter F. Mack Jr. (D)	67,704	52.8
	Benjamin S. Deboice (R)	60,530	47.2
22	William L. Springer (R)	67,668	60.7
	Robert B. Borchers (D)	43,795	39.3
23	Edward H. Jenison (R)	63,669	55.9
	Laurence F. Arnold (D)	50,143	44.1
24	Charles W. Vursell (R)	62,692	55.3
	John David Upchurch (D)	50,638	44.7
25	Melvin Price (D)	78,812	64.9
	Rogers D. Jones (R)	42,696	35.1
26	C. W. Bishop (R)	53,207	51.2
	Kent E. Keller (D)	50,759	48.8

INDIANA

	Candidates	Votes	%
1	Ray J. Madden (D)	62,666	52.6
	Paul Cyr (R)	56,063	47.0
2	Charles A. Halleck (R)	74,872	57.2
	Dale E. Beck (D)	55,153	42.2
3	Shepard J. Crumpacker Jr. (R)	83,816	52.8
	Thurman C. Crook (D)	73,646	46.4
4	E. Ross Adair (R)	69,741	56.2
	Edward H. Kruse Jr. (D)	53,550	43.1
5	John V. Beamer (R)	91,929	54.1
	John R. Walsh (D)	76,878	45.3
6	Cecil M. Harden (R)	69,789	52.4
	Jack H. Mankin (D)	62,915	47.2
7	William G. Bray (R)	68,885	50.0
	James E. Noland (D)	67,992	49.3
8	Winfield K. Denton (D)	78,750	51.1
	Herman L. McCray (R)	74,573	48.3
9	Earl Wilson (R)	63,229	54.9
	Charles W. Long (D)	51,350	44.6
10	Ralph Harvey (R)	81,392	58.7
	Vernon J. Dwyer (D)	56,149	40.5
11	Charles B. Brownson (R)	116,068	56.5
	Andrew Jacobs Sr. (D)	88,418	43.0

IOWA

	Candidates	Votes	%
1	Thomas E. Martin (R)	70,058	61.7
	James D. France (D)	43,140	38.0
2	Henry O. Talle (R)	79,066	58.8
	Eugene E. Kean (D)	55,359	41.2
3	Harold R. Gross (R)	73,490	64.0
	James O. Babcock (D)	40,786	35.5
4	Karl M. LeCompte (R)	51,168	56.7
	Steven V. Carter (D)	38,649	42.8

	Candidates	Votes	%
5	Paul Cunningham (R)	57,429	56.9
	Gibson C. Holliday (D)	43,105	42.7
6	James I. Dolliver (R)	56,982	64.6
	Maurice O'Reilly (D)	30,877	35.0
7	Ben F. Jensen (R)	55,291	62.1
	James A. Hart (D)	33,617	37.7
8	Charles B. Hoeven (R)	56,942	64.1
	L. J. McGivern (D)	31,689	35.7

KANSAS

1	Albert M. Cole (R)	66,607	66.5
	Ewell Steward (D)	33,562	33.5
2	Errett P. Scrivner (R)	56,862	52.2
	Milton Sullivant (D)	52,015	47.8
3	Myron V. George (R)	42,263	54.7
	Barnes Griffith (D)	35,028	45.3
4	Edward H. Rees (R)	77,856	58.9
	Louis A. Donnell (D)	54,438	41.2
5	Clifford R. Hope (R)	60,608	61.0
	Robert L. Bock (D)	38,767	39.0
6	Wint Smith (R)	51,653	59.6
	F. F. Wasinger (D)	35,087	40.5

Special Election

3	Myron V. George (R)	41,676	54.5
	Barnes Griffith (D)	34,845	45.5

KENTUCKY

1	Noble J. Gregory (D)	34,970	100.0
2	John A. Whitaker (D)	41,226	100.0
3	Thruston B. Morton (R)	62,363	55.5
	Alex P. Humphrey (D)	49,935	44.5
4	Frank L. Chelf (D)	35,529	100.0
5	Brent Spence (D)	33,920	63.3
	Thomas W. Hardesty (R)	19,670	36.7
6	Thomas R. Underwood (D)	39,762	100.0
7	Carl D. Perkins (D)	34,767	56.1
	O. W. Thompson (R)	27,190	43.9
8	Joe B. Bates (D)	37,727	60.5
	Elmer C. Roberts (R)	24,627	39.5
9	James S. Golden (R)	46,928	100.0

LOUISIANA

1	F. Edward Hebert (D)	35,456	100.0
2	Hale Boggs (D)	39,232	100.0
3	Edwin E. Willis (D)	21,591	100.0
4	Overton Brooks (D)	25,529	100.0
5	Otto E. Passman (D)	22,478	100.0
6	James H. Morrison (D)	34,718	100.0
7	Henry D. Larcade Jr. (D)	22,931	100.0
8	A. Leonard Allen (D)	25,140	100.0

MAINE

1	Robert Hale (R)	48,869	54.0
	Lucia M. Cormier (D)	41,620	46.0
2	Charles P. Nelson (R)	49,743	57.7
	John J. Maloney Jr. (D)	36,506	42.3
3	Frank Fellows (R)	38,289	62.9
	John V. Keenan (D)	22,605	37.1

MARYLAND

1	Edward T. Miller (R)	36,005	57.0
	Thomas F. Johnson (D)	27,122	43.0
2	James P. S. Devereux (R)	99,497	50.2
	William P. Bolton (D)	96,498	48.7
3	Edward A. Garmatz (D)	27,646	65.7
	Louis R. Milio (R)	14,430	34.3
4	George H. Fallon (D)	34,769	56.8
	James W. Miller (R)	25,287	41.3
5	Lansdale G. Sasscer (D)	54,152	57.5
	Thomas S. Carr (D)	40,031	42.5
6	J. Glenn Beall (R)	70,707	61.9
	Russell Peter Hartie (D)	43,540	38.1

MASSACHUSETTS

	Candidates	Votes	%
1	John W. Heselton (R)	88,018	68.9
	Anna Sullivan (D)	39,717	31.1
2	Foster Furcolo(D)	76,497	54.6
	Chester T. Skibinski (R)	63,493	45.4
3	Philip J.Philbin (D)	93,591	71.5
	John F. Fuller (R)	37,258	28.5
4	Harold D. Donohue (D)	76,881	56.9
	John Winslow (R)	57,483	42.6
5	Edith Nourse Rogers (R)	116,474	76.1
	Clement Gregory		
	McDonough (D)	36,530	23.9
6	William H. Bates (R)	94,162	73.7
	Richard M. Russell (D)	33,578	26.3
7	Thomas J. Lane (D)	91,854	78.5
	Laurence A. Doyle (R)	24,307	20.8
8	Angier L. Goodwin (R)	71,938	53.9
	John B. Carr (D)	61,559	46.1
9	Donald W. Nicholson (R)	78,655	58.1
	August J. Cormier (D)	55,949	41.3
10	Christian A. Herter (R)	88,549	57.8
	Francis X. Hurley (D)	63,618	41.5
11	John F. Kennedy (D)	87,699	82.3
	Vincent J. Celeste (R)	18,302	17.2
12	John W. McCormack (D)	102,940	84.0
	John J. Biggins (R)	16,746	13.7
13	Richard B. Wigglesworth (R)	90,387	62.2
	David J. Concannon (D)	54,243	37.3
14	Joseph W. Martin Jr. (R)	84,508	64.3
	Edward P. Grace (D)	46,332	35.3

MICHIGAN

1	Thaddeus M. Machrowicz (D)	75,478	82.2
	Rudolph G. Tenerowicz (R)	14,619	15.9
2	George Meader (R)	61,574	60.4
	John P. Dawson (D)	39,771	39.0
3	Paul W. Shafer (R)	58,489	61.4
	Thomas B. Woodworth (D)	35,877	37.6
4	Clare E. Hoffman (R)	58,625	68.6
	Forest A. Schoonard (D)	26,301	30.8
5	Gerald R. Ford Jr. (R)	72,829	66.7
	James H. McLaughlin (D)	35,927	32.9
6	William W. Blackney (R)	70,100	52.8
	Herbert W. Devine (D)	61,435	46.3
7	Jesse P. Wolcott (R)	66,951	63.0
	Roy E. Visnaw (D)	38,953	36.6
8	Fred L. Crawford (R)	55,001	60.5
	Leland S. Jennings (D)	35,164	38.7
9	Ruth Thompson (R)	43,910	54.5
	Noel P. Fox (D)	36,222	45.0
10	Roy O. Woodruff (R)	47,489	66.2
	William J. Kelly (D)	24,198	33.8
11	Charles E. Potter (R)	50,523	66.5
	Fred L. Hanscom (D)	25,254	33.2
12	John B. Bennett (R)	43,010	61.7
	John Sabol (D)	26,667	38.3
13	George D. O'Brien (D)	56,388	61.4
	Clarence J. McLeod (R)	35,178	38.3
14	Louis C. Rabaut (D)	76,938	51.5
	Richard Durant (R)	72,137	48.3
15	John D. Dingell (D)	73,238	64.1
	Robert L. Berry (R)	40,865	35.7
16	John Lesinski Jr. (D)	80,229	60.7
	Kirby L. Wilson Jr. (R)	50,873	38.5
17	George A. Dondero (R)	114,274	55.6
	Eugene G. Donohoe (D)	90,712	44.1

MINNESOTA

1	August H. Andresen (R)	75,016	67.1
	Burton Chambers (DFL)	36,839	32.9
2	Joseph P. O'Hara (R)	69,304	59.9
	Harry Sieben (DFL)	46,452	40.1
3	Roy W. Wier (DFL)	73,786	51.7
	Alfred O. Lindley (R)	68,947	48.3
4	Eugene J. McCarthy (DFL)	59,930	60.4
	Ward Fleming (R)	39,307	39.6
5	Walter H. Judd (R)	71,243	58.7

	Candidates	Votes	%
	Marcella F. Killen (DFL)	48,759	40.2
6	Fred Marshall (DFL)	63,911	56.2
	Robert F. Lee (R)	49,879	43.8
7	H. Carl Andersen (R)	65,644	61.7
	Carl J. Eastvold (DFL)	40,785	38.3
8	John A. Blatnik (DFL)	72,440	62.9
	William A. Pittenger (R)	42,705	37.1
9	Harold C. Hagen (R)	56,928	61.9
	Curtiss Olson (DFL)	30,808	33.5

MISSISSIPPI

1	John E. Rankin (D)	8,994	92.5
	Glenn Haynes (R)	730	7.5
2	Jamie L. Whitten (D)	5,891	100.0
3	Frank E. Smith (D)	6,529	92.5
	Nelson E. Taylor (R)	529	7.5
4	Thomas G. Abernethy (D)	12,602	95.8
5	W. Arthur Winstead (D)	13,395	97.6
6	William M.Colmer (D)	15,964	87.9
	Frank H. Harper (I)	2,199	12.1
7	John Bell Williams (D)	19,321	96.4

MISSOURI

1	Clare Magee (D)	43,384	54.4
	Wat Arnold (R)	36,403	45.6
2	Morgan M. Moulder (D)	49,408	53.0
	Max Schwabe (R)	43,816	47.0
3	Philip J. Welch (D)	48,244	51.1
	William C. Cole (R)	46,154	48.9
4	Theodore Leonard Irving (D)	53,424	61.6
	Vernon D. Fulcrut (R)	33,367	38.5
5	Richard W. Bolling (D)	45,762	54.5
	Richard C. Jensen (R)	38,276	45.6
6	Orland K. Armstrong (R)	55,176	50.7
	George H. Christopher (D)	53,593	49.3
7	Dewey Short (R)	60,557	58.7
	Daniel J. Leary (D)	42,629	41.3
8	Albert S. J. Carnahan (D)	49,894	54.7
	Parke M. Banta (R)	41,406	45.4
9	Clarence Cannon (D)	43,950	61.5
	John H. Fahien (R)	27,573	38.6
10	Paul C. Jones (D)	44,469	100.0
11	John B. Sullivan (D)	57,225	64.5
	Sidney J. Redman (R)	31,163	35.2
12	Thomas B. Curtis (R)	110,757	50.9
	Raymond W. Karst (D)	106,728	49.0
13	Frank M. Karsten (D)	58,832	68.2
	Hal A. Hamilton (R)	27,366	31.7

MONTANA

1	Mike Mansfield (D)	54,394	60.3
	Ralph Y. McGinnis (R)	34,945	38.7
2	Wesley A. D'Ewart (R)	65,003	54.1
	John J. Holmes (D)	53,854	44.8

NEBRASKA

1	Carl T. Curtis (R)	67,164	54.5
	Clarence G. Miles (D)	55,972	45.5
2	Howard Buffett (R)	71,126	63.5
	Eugene D. O'Sullivan (D)	40,939	36.5
3	Karl Stefan (R)	68,889	66.9
	Duane K. Peterson (D)	34,017	33.1
4	Arthur L. Miller (R)	64,661	65.8
	Hans J. Holtorf Jr. (D)	33,562	34.2

NEVADA

AL	Walter S. Baring (D)	31,843	52.8
	A. E. MacKenzie (R)	28,485	47.2

NEW HAMPSHIRE

1	Chester E. Merrow (R)	57,371	57.5
	Frank L. Sullivan (D)	42,371	42.5
2	Norris Cotton (R)	55,116	64.5
	George Brummer (D)	30,389	35.5

NEW JERSEY

	Candidates	Votes	%
1	Charles A. Wolverton (R)	85,100	56.8
	John J. Crean (D)	64,868	43.3
2	T. Millet Hand (R)	54,897	54.3
	Elmer H. Wene (D)	46,121	45.7
3	James C. Auchincloss (R)	79,374	62.4
	John C. Applegate (D)	47,055	37.0
4	Charles R. Howell (D)	60,364	52.2
	Gill Robb Wilson (R)	55,364	47.8
5	Charles A. Eaton (R)	80,678	61.6
	Thomas Chabrak (D)	50,220	38.4
6	Clifford P. Case (R)	74,739	62.2
	Harry Mopsick (D)	45,376	37.8
7	William B. Widnall (R)	79,421	69.7
	Emil M. Wulster (D)	34,578	30.3
8	Gordon Canfield (R)	60,420	63.6
	Charles H. Roemer (D)	34,194	36.0
9	Harry L. Towe (R)	67,712	57.8
	Karl D. Van Wagner (D)	38,421	32.8
	Carl E. Ring (I)	10,932	9.3
10	Peter W. Rodino Jr. (D)	60,432	61.0
	William H. Rawson (R)	38,613	39.0
11	Hugh J. Addonizio (D)	46,242	51.6
	Albert L. Vreeland (R)	42,581	47.5
12	Robert Winthrop Kean (R)	54,123	53.1
	Harry Dudkin (D)	45,525	44.7
13	Alfred D. Sieminski (D)	55,008	51.9
	Edward S. Binkowski (R)	43,851	41.4
	Michael A. Fiore (IPP CH)	7,072	6.7
14	Edward J. Hart (D)	61,410	59.2
	Michael Bongiovanni (R)	42,272	40.8

NEW MEXICO

		Votes	%
AL	John J. Dempsey (D)	97,187✓	
	Antonio M. Fernandez (D)	96,291✓	
	Steiner Mason (R)	75,447	
	Jose E. Armijo (R)	68,762	

NEW YORK

	Candidates	Votes	%
1	Ernest Greenwood (D, L)	76,375	49.2
	W. Kingsland Macy (R)	76,240	49.1
2	Leonard W. Hall (R)	129,291	67.1
	Lawrence W. McKeown (D, L)	60,152	31.2
3	Henry J. Latham (R)	92,466	56.3
	James Pasta (D)	55,285	33.6
	Mark Starr (L)	11,122	6.8
4	L. Gary Clemente (D, L)	55,793	54.2
	Gregory McMahon (R)	43,055	41.8
5	T. Vincent Quinn (D)	63,620	48.4
	Robert Tripp Ross (R)	54,061	41.1
	Bernard Brown (L)	7,857	6.0
6	James J. Delaney (D, L)	60,725	56.8
	Herbert Suppan (R)	41,615	38.9
7	Louis B. Heller (D, L)	47,466	57.0
	Francis E. Dorn (R)	30,379	36.5
	Lester Zirin (AM LAB)	5,454	6.6
8	Victor L. Anfuso (D)	42,305	61.9
	Joseph R. Fontanetta (R)	18,551	27.2
	Antonio Iandiorio (AM LAB)	4,119	6.0
9	Eugene J. Keogh (D, R)	73,280	91.0
	Helen Wishnofsky (AM LAB)	7,267	9.0
10	Edna F. Kelly (D, L)	66,847	67.1
	David L. Samuels (R)	25,485	25.6
	Gerald Root (AM LAB)	7,327	7.4
11	James J. Heffernan (D, L)	67,560	62.9
	Alfred C. McKenzie (R)	31,558	29.4
	Blanche Katz (AM LAB)	8,270	7.7
12	John J. Rooney (D, L)	42,396	61.6
	Joseph J. Petito (R)	22,796	33.1
	Vincent J. Longhi (AM LAB)	3,628	5.3
13	Donald L. O'Toole (D, L)	54,919	59.6
	James F. O'Hara (R)	35,418	36.7
	Ralph Shapiro (AM LAB)	6,247	6.5
14	Abraham J. Multer (D, L)	75,020	70.6
	P. Vincent Landi (R)	21,350	20.1
	Helen Phillips (AM LAB)	9,859	9.3
15	Emanuel Celler (D, L)	72,396	72.8

	Candidates	Votes	%
	Louis H. Heiger (R)	17,144	17.2
	William Podell (AM LAB)	9,916	10.0
16	James J. Murphy (D, L)	42,516	50.5
	Edward J. McCormick (R)	37,363	44.4
	Frank Cremonesi (AM LAB)	4,340	5.2
17	Frederic R. Coudert Jr. (R)	57,247	53.4
	Irving M. Engel (D, L)	44,502	41.5
	Robert T. Leicester (AM LAB)	5,492	5.1
18	James G. Donovan (D, R)	49,448	57.8
	Vito Marcantonio (AM LAB)	36,095	42.2
19	Arthur G. Klein (D, L)	58,616	66.4
	Edward I. Goldberg (R)	21,034	23.8
	Bernard Harkavy (AM LAB)	8,597	9.7
20	Franklin D. Roosevelt Jr. (D, L)	57,432	62.1
	Henry V. Poor (R)	29,305	31.7
	John W. Darr Jr. (AM LAB)	5,717	6.2
21	Jacob K. Javits (R, L)	62,604	61.7
	Bennett I. Schlessel (D)	33,349	32.9
	William M. Mandel (AM LAB)	5,419	5.4
22	Adam Clayton Powell Jr. (D)	35,233	63.5
	Elmer A. Carter (R, L)	15,208	27.4
	John Quillian (AM LAB)	5,050	9.1
23	Sidney A. Fine (D)	64,270	56.3
	William J. Waterman (R)	22,103	19.4
	Harold Bauman (L)	17,882	15.7
	Robert Diamond (AM LAB)	9,847	8.6
24	Isidore Dollinger (D)	54,628	62.5
	Barnett Levy (R)	11,303	12.9
	Herman Woskow (L)	10,774	12.3
	Stephen J. White (AM LAB)	10,755	12.3
25	Charles A. Buckley (D)	64,353	46.8
	Solon S. Kane (R)	40,552	29.5
	Max Bloom (L)	20,929	15.2
	Charles J. Hendley (AM LAB)	11,707	8.5
26	Christopher C. McGrath (D)	69,152	51.4
	Fred E. Schiemann (R)	44,598	33.1
	Ernest Doerfler (L)	11,518	8.6
	August Buhr (AM LAB)	9,333	6.9
27	Ralph W. Gwinn (R)	78,221	55.9
	George A. Brenner (D, L)	59,759	42.7
28	Ralph A. Gamble (R)	79,490	67.5
	Morris E. Lasker (D)	35,059	29.8
29	Katharine St. George (R)	72,721	61.8
	Harry O. Prince (D, L)	43,315	36.8
30	James Ernest Wharton (R)	86,053	65.8
	James R. Bourne (D)	41,833	32.0
31	Bernard W. Kearney (R)	79,007	64.1
	John H. Peterson (D)	41,680	33.8
32	William T. Byrne (D)	90,420	58.8
	John T. Casey (R)	60,087	39.1
33	Dean P. Taylor (R)	100,425	69.0
	Joseph T. Hammer (D)	42,680	29.3
34	Clarence E. Kilburn (R)	67,739	66.4
	Mildred McGill (D)	32,446	31.8
35	William R. Williams (R)	60,657	51.6
	John C. Davies (D, L)	54,284	46.2
36	R. Walter Riehlman (R)	81,508	61.9
	Alfred W. Haight (L)	50,107	38.9
37	Edwin Arthur Hall (R)	60,278	64.6
	John J. Burns (D, L)	33,018	35.4
38	John Taber (R)	68,474	68.8
	Robert G. Gordon (D, L)	31,115	31.2
39	W. Sterling Cole (R)	64,377	66.3
	Donald J. O'Connor (D, L)	31,639	32.6
40	Kenneth B. Keating (R)	103,710	65.8
	A. Roger Clarke (D, L)	52,363	33.2
41	Harold C. Ostertag (R)	64,801	64.1
	Bernard E. Hart (D, L)	35,370	35.0
42	William E. Miller (R)	75,377	58.6
	Mary Louise Nice (D, L)	53,310	41.4
43	Edmund P. Radwan (R)	61,781	50.8
	Anthony F. Tauriello (D, L)	58,327	48.0
44	John C. Butler (R)	69,260	50.3
	Chester C. Gorski (D, L)	66,541	48.3
45	Daniel A. Reed (R)	54,490	66.0
	Frederick S. Buck (D)	27,317	33.1

NORTH CAROLINA

	Candidates	Votes	%
1	Herbert C. Bonner (D)	14,698	92.8
	Zeno O. Ratcliff (R)	1,147	7.2
2	John H. Kerr (D)	15,602	100.0
3	Graham A. Barden (D)	21,287	100.0
4	Harold D. Cooley (D)	34,580	72.8
	Ray F. Swain (R)	12,945	27.2
5	Richard Thurmond Chatham (D)	29,598	100.0
6	Carl T. Durham (D)	27,751	75.4
	A. A. McDonald (R)	9,075	24.6
7	F. Ertel Carlyle (D)	21,911	84.0
	Irvin B. Tucker Jr. (R)	4,171	16.0
8	Charles B. Deane (D)	40,834	59.6
	T. E. Story (R)	27,688	40.4
9	Robert L. Doughton (D)	47,183	61.2
	Fate J. Beal (R)	29,982	38.9
10	Hamilton C. Jones (D)	33,591	52.3
	Louis G. Rogers (R)	30,591	47.7
11	Woodrow W. Jones (D)	31,712	68.9
	A. W. Whitehurst (R)	14,293	31.1
12	Monroe M. Redden (D)	46,851	63.7
	John A. Wagner (R)	26,710	36.3

Special Election

		Votes	%
11	Woodrow W. Jones (D)	31,460	67.3
	A. W. Whitehurst (R)	15,295	32.7

NORTH DAKOTA

		Votes	%
AL	Fred G. Aandahl (R)	119,047✓	
	Usher L. Burdick (R)	110,534✓	
	Ervin Schumacher (D)	62,322	
	E. A. Johansson (D)	32,946	

OHIO

		Votes	%
1	Charles H. Elston (R)	77,507	59.1
	Rollin H. Everett (D)	53,760	41.0
2	William E. Hess (R)	69,543	52.7
	Earl T. Wagner (D)	62,542	47.4
3	Edward Breen (D)	92,840	54.5
	Paul F. Schenck (R)	77,634	45.5
4	William M. McCulloch (R)	65,640	66.8
	Carleton Carl Reiser (D)	32,686	33.2
5	Cliff Clevenger (R)	36,096	57.5
	Dan Batt (D)	26,689	42.5
6	James G. Polk (D)	40,335	50.8
	Edward O. McCowen (R)	38,996	49.2
7	Clarence J. Brown (R)	77,660	68.4
	Ben J. Goldman (D)	35,818	31.6
8	Jackson E. Betts (R)	47,761	62.7
	W. Dexter Hazen (D)	28,379	37.3
9	Frazier Reams (I)	51,024	36.6
	Thomas H. Burke (D)	45,268	32.4
	Homer A. Ramey (R)	43,301	31.0
10	Thomas A. Jenkins (R)	39,584	65.2
	William J. Curry (D)	21,117	34.8
11	Walter E. Brehm (R)	33,648	53.1
	Mell G. Underwood Jr. (D)	29,687	46.9
12	John M. Vorys (R)	117,396	64.1
	John W. Guy (D)	65,860	35.9
13	Alvin F. Weichel (R)	58,484	70.9
	Dwight A. Blackmore (D)	24,042	29.1
14	William H. Ayres (R)	102,868	48.7
	Walter B. Huber (D)	100,947	47.8
15	Robert T. Secrest (D)	47,448	61.6
	Holland M. Gary (R)	29,573	38.4
16	Frank T. Bow (R)	77,306	50.7
	John McSweeney (D)	75,255	49.3
17	J. Harry McGregor (R)	71,382	64.3
	Robert W. Levering (D)	39,726	35.8
18	Wayne L. Hays (D)	58,295	50.8
	Robert L. Quinn (R)	56,508	49.2
19	Michael J. Kirwan (D)	119,245	63.8
	Henry P. Kosling (R)	67,661	36.2
20	Michael A. Feighan (D)	60,565	74.2
	Paul W. Cassidy (R)	21,044	25.8

Candidates	Votes	%
Alan A. Dusatko (D)	35,213	28.2
4 Arthur L. Miller (R)	98,032	73.3
Francis D. Lee (D)	35,628	26.7

NEVADA

Candidates	Votes	%
AL Clifton Young (R)	40,683	50.5
Walter S. Baring (D)	39,912	49.5

NEW HAMPSHIRE

Candidates	Votes	%
1 Chester E. Merrow (R)	82,689	60.2
Peter R. Poirier (D)	54,746	39.8
2 Norris Cotton (R)	80,061	66.5
John Guay (D)	40,373	33.5

NEW JERSEY

Candidates	Votes	%
1 Charles A. Wolverton (R)	118,367	55.0
Alfred R. Pierce (D)	96,162	44.7
2 T. Millet Hand (R)	79,955	63.4
Charles Edward Rupp (D)	46,174	36.6
3 James C. Auchincloss (R)	124,292	64.4
John W. Zimmermann (D)	67,642	35.0
4 Charles R. Howell (D)	84,733	54.7
John J. Inglesby (R)	70,076	45.3
5 Peter H. B. Frelinghuysen Jr. (R)	133,276	62.2
Aldona L. Appleton (D)	80,922	37.8
6 Clifford P. Case (R)	121,252	63.9
H. Frank Pettit (D)	67,159	35.4
7 William B. Widnall (R)	130,603	68.3
Vito A. Concilio (D)	60,553	31.7
8 Gordon Canfield (R)	97,338	62.6
John J. Winberry (D)	54,367	35.0
9 Frank C. Osmers Jr. (R)	125,402	66.2
William H. McNulty (D)	63,175	33.4
10 Peter W. Rodino Jr. (D)	78,612	56.9
Alexander J. Matturri (R)	57,740	41.8
11 Hugh J. Addonizio (D)	68,273	52.2
William O. Barnes Jr. (R)	60,461	46.3
12 Robert Winthrop Kean (R)	84,949	54.8
Martin S. Fox (D)	70,046	45.2
13 Alfred D. Sieminski (D)	72,987	55.2
Julius D. Canter (R)	54,581	41.2
14 Edward J. Hart (D)	67,109	51.5
William J. Bozzuffi (R)	59,112	45.4

NEW MEXICO

Candidates	Votes	%
AL John J. Dempsey (D)	121,477✓	
Antonio M. Fernandez (D)	119,925✓	
Homer J. Berkshire (R)	112,297	
Ed Guthmann (R)	109,595	

NEW YORK

Candidates	Votes	%
1 Stuyvesant Wainwright (R)	114,135	60.4
Ernest Greenwood (D, L)	74,174	39.3
2 Steven B. Derounian (R)	132,512	68.8
Joseph Liff (D)	54,725	28.4
3 Frank J. Becker (R)	128,007	65.4
Richard A. O'Leary (D)	60,800	31.0
4 Henry J. Latham (R)	123,132	62.6
Joseph J. Perrini (D, L)	70,755	36.0
5 Albert H. Bosch (R)	86,168	53.5
L. Gary Clemente (D, L)	73,083	45.3
6 Lester Holtzman (D, L)	105,261	49.2
Robert Tripp Ross (R)	104,720	48.9
7 James J. Delaney (D, L)	87,204	51.0
William Adam Schulz (R)	80,896	47.3
8 Louis B. Heller (D, L)	75,772	65.3
Benjamin F. Westervelt Jr. (R)	37,884	32.6
9 Eugene J. Keogh (D, L)	83,841	61.1
Joseph M. Soviero (R)	48,994	35.7
10 Edna F. Kelly (D, L)	105,302	71.2
George W. Thomas (R)	42,498	28.8
11 Emanuel Celler (D, L)	127,091	73.8
Henry D. Dorfman (R)	37,244	21.6
12 Francis E. Dorn (R)	75,895	52.7

Candidates	Votes	%
Donald L. O'Toole (D, L)	65,650	45.6
13 Abraham J. Multer (D, L)	112,152	68.3
P. Vincent Landi (R)	45,664	27.8
14 John J. Rooney (D, L)	86,952	64.2
Jacob P. Lefkowitz (R)	45,004	33.2
15 John H. Ray (R)	97,023	57.9
James J. Murphy (D, L)	69,538	41.5
16 Adam Clayton Powell Jr. (D)	72,562	73.9
Richard L. Baltimore Jr. (R)	15,937	16.2
Clarence Francis (L)	7,125	7.3
17 Frederic R. Coudert Jr. (R)	84,821	57.0
Harry Grossman (D, L)	60,624	40.7
18 James G. Donovan (D, R)	88,629	92.6
Vito Magli (AM LAB)	7,047	7.4
19 Arthur G. Klein (D, L)	77,267	66.0
Edward I. Goldberg (R)	34,795	29.7
20 Franklin D. Roosevelt Jr. (D, L)	81,591	60.2
Clarence C. Vambell (R)	49,905	36.8
21 Jacob K. Javits (R, L)	89,866	63.4
John C. Hart (D)	47,637	33.6
22 Sidney A. Fine (D)	90,474	58.0
Martin Greene (R)	38,681	24.8
David Wells (L)	21,606	13.9
23 Isidore Dollinger (D)	78,350	63.8
Sidney S. Flaum (R)	23,238	18.9
Harry Kavesh (L)	14,393	11.7
Howard Fast (AM LAB)	6,834	5.6
24 Charles A. Buckley (D)	82,343	46.5
Solon S. Kane (R)	58,096	32.8
Herman Woskow (L)	29,425	16.6
25 Paul A. Fino (R)	85,308	50.1
Bernard J. O'Connell (D)	68,862	40.4
Louis Schifrin (L)	13,325	7.8
26 Ralph A. Gamble (R)	116,091	67.3
Flora Chudson (D, L)	55,184	32.0
27 Ralph W. Gwinn (R)	108,575	58.5
George A. Brenner (D, L)	75,781	40.9
28 Katharine St. George (R)	102,476	65.6
Marion K. Sanders (D, L)	52,994	33.9
29 J. Ernest Wharton (R)	115,502	69.8
Walter Donnaruma (D)	46,727	28.2
30 Leo W. O'Brien (D, L)	101,178	53.7
John F. Forner Jr. (R)	86,651	46.0
31 Dean P. Taylor (R)	114,656	70.6
Helen Nolan Neil (D)	44,367	27.3
32 Bernard W. Kearney (R)	111,025	67.4
33 Clarence E. Kilburn (R)	98,653	69.0
Maurice N. McGrath (D)	41,803	29.2
34 William R. Williams (R)	97,488	58.8
Charles Ray Wilson (D)	65,080	39.3
35 R. Walter Riehlman (R)	113,778	63.2
Arthur B. McGuire (D, L)	65,763	36.5
36 John Taber (R)	110,304	69.9
Donald J. O'Connor (D, L)	47,189	29.9
37 W. Sterling Cole (R)	131,172	69.4
Jean Ivory (D, L)	57,474	30.4
38 Kenneth B. Keating (R)	128,566	69.3
Victor Kruppenbacher (D, L)	56,177	30.3
39 Harold C. Ostertag (R)	107,501	65.8
O. Richard Judson (D, L)	55,483	34.0
40 William E. Miller (R)	102,565	59.6
E. Dent Lackey (D, L)	69,087	40.2
41 Edmund P. Radwan (R)	95,755	55.9
Anthony F. Tauriello (D, L)	75,552	44.1
42 John R. Pillion (R)	100,434	55.2
Chester C. Gorski (D, L)	81,201	44.6
43 Daniel A. Reed (R)	91,534	66.2
Harry D. Johnson (D)	44,276	32.0

Special Election

Candidates	Votes	%
30 Leo W. O'Brien (D, L)	66,849	70.8
John F. Forner Jr. (R)	27,276	28.9

NORTH CAROLINA

Candidates	Votes	%
1 Herbert C. Bonner (D)	43,104	100.0
2 L. H. Fountain (D)	51,213	94.8
W. B. White (R)	2,822	5.2

Candidates	Votes	%
3 Graham A. Barden (D)	45,458	76.2
Everette L. Peterson (R)	14,239	23.9
4 Harold D. Cooley (D)	79,520	75.3
Paul C. West (R)	26,039	24.7
5 Thurmond Chatham (D)	74,884	98.2
6 Carl T. Durham (D)	84,203	69.5
Louis F. Ferree (R)	36,912	30.5
7 F. Ertel Carlyle (D)	62,884	98.5
8 Charles B. Deane (D)	67,764	59.9
Walter B. Love (R)	45,451	40.2
9 Hugh Q. Alexander (D)	68,624	51.5
Walter P. Johnson (R)	64,662	48.5
10 Charles Raper Jonas (R)	82,428	57.4
Hamilton C. Jones (D)	61,149	42.6
11 Woodrow W. Jones (D)	61,540	63.0
George M. Pritchard (R)	36,157	37.0
12 George A. Shuford (D)	63,045	56.9
Hugh Montieth (R)	47,752	43.1

NORTH DAKOTA

Candidates	Votes	%
AL Usher L. Burdick (R)	181,218✓	
Otto Krueger (R)	156,829✓	
Edward Nesemeier (D)	49,829	

OHIO

Candidates	Votes	%
1 Gordon H. Scherer (R)	96,385	61.6
Walter A. Kelly (D)	60,015	38.4
2 William E. Hess (R)	90,417	56.6
Earl T. Wagner (D)	69,341	43.4
3 Paul F. Schenck (R)	112,325	51.1
Thomas B. Talbot (D)	107,551	48.9
4 William M. McCulloch (R)	93,442	68.3
Carleton Carl Reiser (D)	43,426	31.7
5 Cliff Clevenger (R)	72,168	63.2
Dan Batt (D)	42,104	36.9
6 James G. Polk (D)	67,220	50.1
Leo Blackburn (R)	66,896	49.9
7 Clarence J. Brown (R)	98,354	100.0
8 Jackson E. Betts (R)	75,768	68.7
Henry P. Drake (D)	34,474	31.3
9 Frazier Reams (I)	74,821	40.9
Thomas H. Burke (D)	61,047	33.4
Gilmore Flues (R)	46,989	25.7
10 Thomas A. Jenkins (R)	63,339	64.0
Delmar A. Canaday (D)	35,666	36.0
11 Oliver P. Bolton (R)	91,204	58.8
Robert J. Kilpatrick (D)	63,930	41.2
12 John M. Vorys (R)	134,693	62.3
George T. Tarbutton (D)	81,665	37.8
13 Alvin F. Weichel (R)	63,344	58.8
George C. Steinemann (D)	44,467	41.3
14 William H. Ayres (R)	117,475	58.5
Walter B. Huber (D)	83,463	41.5
15 Robert T. Secrest (D)	62,913	64.3
P. W. Griffiths (R)	34,966	35.7
16 Frank T. Bow (R)	98,447	54.4
John McSweeney (D)	82,522	45.6
17 J. Harry McGregor (R)	94,624	68.2
James J. Mayer (D)	44,117	31.8
18 Wayne L. Hays (D)	78,277	55.8
Clarence L. Wetzel (R)	62,081	44.2
19 Michael J. Kirwan (D)	91,074	66.3
Allen Russell (R)	46,202	33.7
20 Michael A. Feighan (D)	109,211	65.2
John H. Ferguson (R)	58,271	34.8
21 Robert Crosser (D)	100,340	68.6
Lawrence O. Payne (R)	45,896	31.4
22 Frances P. Bolton (R)	87,316	58.8
Chat Paterson (D)	61,197	41.2
23 George H. Bender (R)	85,752	64.6
Michael P. O'Brien (D)	47,090	35.5

OKLAHOMA

Candidates	Votes	%
1 Page Belcher (R)	121,442	58.6
H. G. Dickey (D)	85,647	41.4
2 Ed Edmondson (D)	92,407	59.2
Edward E. Easton (R)	60,550	38.8

	Candidates	Votes	%
3	Carl Albert (D)	73,185	77.9
	Frank D. McSherry (R)	20,735	22.1
4	Tom Steed (D)	67,024	58.7
	John L. Goode (R)	46,446	40.7
5	John Jarman (D)	128,627	62.4
	Edwin Whitney Burch (R)	77,425	37.6
6	Victor E. Wickersham (D)	98,823	63.3
	K. B. Cornell (R)	57,261	36.7

OREGON

1	Walter Norblad (R)	124,720	68.0
	Robert B. Jones (D)	58,796	32.0
2	Sam Coon (R)	57,155	58.5
	John G. Jones (D)	40,550	41.5
3	Homer D. Angell (R)	125,504	54.0
	Alfred H. Corbett (D)	107,099	46.0
4	Harris Ellsworth (R)	100,970	66.3
	Walter A. Swanson (D)	51,298	33.7

PENNSYLVANIA

1	William A. Barrett (D)	89,879	68.2
	James Iannucci (R)	41,948	31.8
2	William T. Granahan (D)	105,553	61.8
	Daniel J. McCauley Jr. (R)	65,159	38.2
3	James A. Byrne (D)	81,837	58.4
	Morton Witkin (R)	58,191	41.6
4	Earl Chudoff (D)	90,077	69.9
	Joseph R. Burns (R)	38,228	29.7
5	William J. Green Jr (D)	104,112	54.2
	Philip Richman (R)	88,040	45.8
6	Hugh Scott (R)	93,368	51.7
	Harrington Herr (D)	87,124	48.2
7	Benjamin F. James (R)	127,918	61.7
	Murray P. Zealor (D)	79,423	38.3
8	Karl C. King (R)	83,966	59.3
	Wilson H. Stephenson (D)	57,723	40.7
9	Paul B. Dague (R)	100,578	66.2
	Philip E. Ragan (D)	51,268	33.8
10	Joseph L. Carrigg (R)	89,820	53.6
	Harry P. O'Neill (D)	77,758	46.4
11	Edward J. Bonin (R)	80,310	50.2
	Daniel J. Flood (D)	79,722	49.8
12	Ivor D. Fenton (R)	79,859	60.7
	Peter Krehel (D)	51,736	39.3
13	Samuel K. McConnell Jr. (R)	114,672	66.4
	Frank A. Keegan (D)	57,974	33.6
14	George M. Rhodes (D)	48,427	49.7
	James W. Bertolet (R)	48,019	49.2
15	Francis E. Walter (D)	61,566	54.8
	John Russell Craig (R)	50,871	45.2
16	Walter M. Mumma (R)	83,493	61.7
	David V. Randall (D)	51,825	38.3
17	Alvin R. Bush (R)	82,058	64.2
	Patrick A. McGowan (D)	44,376	34.7
18	Richard M. Simpson (R)	75,723	63.5
	Philip R. Shoemaker (D)	43,555	36.5
19	S. Walter Stauffer (R)	72,466	52.3
	James F. Lind (D)	66,165	47.7
20	James E. Van Zandt (R)	62,804	62.8
	Joseph A. Moran (D)	37,152	37.2
21	Augustine B. Kelley (D)	73,223	52.9
	J. Cleveland McKenna (R)	65,252	47.1
22	John P. Saylor (R)	77,391	52.4
	William D. Shettig (D)	70,218	47.6
23	Leon H. Gavin (R)	73,001	67.8
	Fred C. Barr (D)	34,633	32.2
24	Carroll D. Kearns (R)	90,276	57.1
	Clinton J. Bebell (D)	67,790	42.9
25	Louis E. Graham (R)	77,577	50.4
	Frank M. Clark (D)	76,214	49.6
26	Thomas E. Morgan (D)	105,581	59.1
	Edward J. Sittler Jr. (R)	72,981	40.9
27	James C. Fulton (R)	118,915	62.6
	Thomas J. O'Toole (D)	71,039	37.4
28	Herman P. Eberharter (D)	98,432	58.7
	Harmar D. Denny (R)	69,288	41.3
29	Robert J. Corbett (R)	115,069	61.7
	Lee T. Sellars (D)	71,573	38.4

	Candidates	Votes	%
30	Vera Buchanan (D)	115,292	63.6
	Peter F. Bender (R)	65,926	36.4

RHODE ISLAND

1	Aime J. Forand (D)	105,404	54.9
	Berthelot Leclaire (R)	86,523	45.1
2	John E. Fogarty (D)	115,057	53.4
	James O. Watts (R)	100,305	46.6

SOUTH CAROLINA

1	L. Mendel Rivers (D)	30,483	100.0
2	John J. Riley (D)	42,201	100.0
3	W. J. Bryan Dorn (D)	44,237	93.8
	David Dows (R)	2,849	6.0
4	Joseph R. Bryson (D)	77,850	100.0
5	James P. Richards (D)	42,081	93.9
	Herbert L. Crosland (R)	2,722	6.1
6	John L. McMillan (D)	41,328	100.0

SOUTH DAKOTA

1	Harold O. Lovre (R)	151,449	68.5
	Goldie Wells (D)	69,777	31.5
2	E. Y. Berry (R)	45,688	69.0
	George A. Bangs (D)	20,561	31.0

TENNESSEE

1	B. Carroll Reece (R)	70,556	65.9
	Arthur W. Bright (D)	36,477	34.1
2	Howard H. Baker (R)	84,977	69.0
	Boyd W. Cox (D)	38,268	31.1
3	James B. Frazier Jr. (D)	56,473	70.0
	Joseph M. Parker (R)	24,177	30.0
4	Joe L. Evins (D)	65,787	100.0
5	J. Percy Priest (D)	49,925	67.5
	Homer P. Wall (R)	24,056	32.5
6	Pat Sutton (D)	56,878	100.0
7	Tom Murray (D)	39,529	100.0
8	Jere Cooper (D)	34,877	100.0
9	Clifford Davis (D)	101,427	85.7
	William P. Chenault (I)	16,972	14.3

TEXAS

1	Wright Patman (D)	56,491	100.0
2	Jack Brooks (D)	83,267	79.0
	R. C. Reed (R)	22,108	21.0
3	Brady Gentry (D)	57,033	100.0
4	Sam Rayburn (D)	47,888	100.0
5	J. Frank Wilson (D)	172,539	100.0
6	Olin E. Teague (D)	49,461	100.0
7	John Dowdy (D)	52,420	100.0
8	Albert Thomas (D)	200,608	100.0
9	Clark W. Thompson (D)	96,214	100.0
10	Homer Thornberry (D)	65,924	100.0
11	W. R. Poage (D)	59,088	100.0
12	Wingate Lucas (D)	101,964	100.0
13	Frank Ikard (D)	72,373	100.0
14	John E. Lyle Jr. (D)	94,866	100.0
15	Lloyd M. Bentsen Jr. (D)	63,753	99.9
16	Ken Regan (D)	67,782	100.0
17	Omar Burleson (D)	59,386	100.0
18	Walter Rogers (D)	77,661	100.0
19	George Mahon (D)	87,894	100.0
20	Paul J. Kilday (D)	64,841	100.0
21	O. C. Fisher (D)	65,762	100.0
AL	Martin Dies (D, R)	1,979,811	100.0

UTAH

1	Douglas R. Stringfellow (R)	76,545	60.5
	Ernest R. McKay (D)	49,898	39.5
2	William A. Dawson (R)	105,296	52.6
	Reva Beck Bosone (D)	95,084	47.5

VERMONT

	Candidates	Votes	%
AL	Winston L. Prouty (R)	109,871	71.8
	Herbert B. Comings (D)	43,187	28.2

VIRGINIA

1	Edward J. Robeson Jr. (D)	24,836	99.6
2	Porter Hardy Jr. (D)	28,948	99.9
3	J. Vaughan Gary (D)	36,085	57.5
	Walter R. Gambill (R)	26,488	42.2
4	Watkins M. Abbitt (D)	23,806	99.8
5	Thomas B. Stanley (D)	19,971	99.9
6	Richard H. Poff (R)	34,041	51.5
	Clarence G. Burton (D)	31,997	48.4
7	Burr P. Harrison (D)	37,360	79.1
	Glenn W. Ruebush (R)	9,876	20.9
8	Howard W. Smith (D)	29,670	75.7
	Homer G. Richey (I)	9,495	24.2
9	William C. Wampler (R)	35,047	51.7
	M. M. Long (D)	32,735	48.3
10	Joel T. Broyhill (R)	33,152	50.2
	Edmund D. Campbell (D)	32,830	49.7

WASHINGTON

1	Thomas M. Pelly (R)	121,926	51.4
	Stimson Bullitt (D)	114,617	48.3
2	Jack Westland (R)	91,853	54.2
	Harry F. Henson (D)	77,179	45.6
3	Russell V. Mack (R)	75,165	53.3
	Gordon M. Quarnstrom (D)	65,715	46.6
4	Hal Holmes (R)	92,551	67.6
	William Bryan (D)	44,464	32.5
5	Walter F. Horan (R)	82,530	56.0
	Robert D. Dellwo (D)	64,820	44.0
6	Thor C. Tollefson (R)	110,169	59.8
	John J. O'Connell (D)	74,143	40.2
AL	Don Magnuson (D)	515,213	50.5
	Al Canwell (R)	504,783	49.5

WEST VIRGINIA

1	Robert H. Mollohan (D)	72,218	52.9
	Francis J. Love (R)	64,216	47.1
2	Harley O. Staggers (D)	67,172	51.5
	Kermit R. Mason (R)	63,320	48.5
3	Cleveland M. Bailey (D)	71,926	53.4
	Frank Love (R)	62,839	46.6
4	Will E. Neal (R)	82,104	53.3
	M. G. Burnside (D)	71,819	46.7
5	Elizabeth Kee (D)	83,653	63.8
	Cyrus H. Gadd (R)	47,519	36.2
6	Robert C. Byrd (D)	104,387	55.6
	Latelle M. LaFollette (R)	83,429	44.4

WISCONSIN

1	Lawrence H. Smith (R)	99,742	59.4
	Arnie W. Agnew (D)	68,269	40.6
2	Glenn R. Davis (R)	116,542	62.9
	Horace W. Wilkie (D)	68,665	37.1
3	Gardner R. Withrow (R)	96,908	75.1
	Edna Bowen (D)	32,165	24.9
4	Clement J. Zablocki (D)	131,098	64.3
	John C. Schafer (R)	72,869	35.7
5	Charles J. Kersten (R)	112,048	51.6
	Andrew J. Biemiller (D)	105,013	48.4
6	William K. Van Pelt (R)	103,464	71.7
	Ralph A. Norem (D)	40,910	28.3
7	Melvin R. Laird (R)	95,049	72.3
	Ernest Kluck (D)	36,387	27.7
8	John W. Byrnes (R)	114,183	73.6
	Robert C. Schultz (D)	40,980	26.4
9	Merlin Hull (R)	81,258	65.2
	Kent L. Pillsbury (D)	43,437	34.8
10	Alvin E. O'Konski (R)	73,527	67.4
	Roland Kannenberg (D)	35,597	32.6

WYOMING

Candidates	Votes	%
AL William Henry Harrison (R)	76,161	60.1
Robert R. Ross Jr. (D)	50,559	39.9

1953 House Elections

GEORGIA

Special Election

Candidates	Votes	%
2 J. L. Pilcher (D)	10,936	35.5
H. Grady Rawls	9,764	31.7
H. L. Wingate Jr.	6,073	19.7
John E. Sheffield Jr.	3,130	10.2

ILLINOIS

Special Election

Candidates	Votes	%
7 James B. Bowler (D)	31,600	83.5
Philip J. Boffa (R)	6,239	16.5

NEW JERSEY

Special Election

Candidates	Votes	%
6 Harrison A. Williams Jr. (D)	68,871	50.8
George F. Hetfield (R)	66,796	49.2

VIRGINIA

Special Election

Candidates	Votes	%
5 William M. Tuck (D)	16,693	57.8
Lorne R. Campbell	12,182	42.2

WISCONSIN

Special Election

Candidates	Votes	%
9 Lester R. Johnson (D)	27,852	56.9
Arthur L. Padrutt (R)	21,127	43.1

1954 House Elections

ALABAMA

	Candidates	Votes	%
1	Frank W. Boykin (D)	27,462	100.0
2	George Grant (D)	30,661	100.0
3	George Andrews (D)	22,371	100.0
4	Kenneth A. Roberts (D)	28,660	100.0
5	Albert Rains (D)	38,257	100.0
6	Armistead I. Selden Jr. (D)	18,753	100.0
7	Carl Elliott (D)	31,988	78.9
	W. B. Engle (R)	8,547	21.1
8	Robert E. Jones Jr. (D)	29,414	91.6
	Adin Batson (R)	2,689	8.4
9	George Huddleston Jr. (D)	40,986	100.0

ARIZONA

		Votes	%
1	John J. Rhodes (R)	60,423	53.1
	L. S. Adams (D)	53,307	46.9
2	Stewart L. Udall (D)	68,085	62.1
	Henry Zipf (R)	41,587	37.9

ARKANSAS

		Votes	%
1	Ezekiel C. Gathings (D)	38,951	100.0
2	Wilbur D. Mills (D)	33,038	100.0
3	James W. Trimble (D)	60,035	100.0
4	Oren Harris (D)	51,579	100.0
5	Brooks Hays (D)	51,828	100.0
6	William F. Norrell (D)	44,833	100.0

CALIFORNIA

		Votes	%
1	Hubert B. Scudder (R)	83,762	59.1
	Max Kortum (D)	58,004	40.9
2	Clair Engle (D-R)	113,104	100.0
3	John E. Moss Jr. (D)	96,238	65.3
	James H. Phillips (R)	51,111	34.7
4	William S. Mailliard (R)	88,439	61.2
	Philip A. O'Rourke (D)	52,980	36.7
5	John F. Shelley (D-R)	86,428	100.0
6	John F. Baldwin Jr. (R)	72,336	50.9
	Robert L. Condon (D)	69,776	49.1
7	John J. Allen Jr. (R)	64,083	53.0
	Stanley K. Crook (D)	56,807	47.0
8	George P. Miller (D)	101,803	65.4
	Jess M. Ritchie (R)	53,869	34.6
9	J. Arthur Younger (R)	60,648	54.5
	Harold F. Taggart (D)	50,619	45.5
10	Charles S. Gubser (R)	94,418	61.2
	Paul V. Birmingham (D)	59,843	38.8
11	Leroy Johnson (R)	54,716	52.6
	Carl Sugar (D)	49,388	47.4
12	B. F. Sisk (D)	63,911	53.8
	Oakley Hunter (R)	54,903	46.2
13	Charles M. Teague (R)	69,287	52.5
	Timothy I. O'Reilly (D)	62,786	47.5
14	Harlan Hagen (D)	75,194	65.1
	Al Blain (R)	40,270	34.9
15	Gordon L. McDonough (R)	77,651	56.9
	Frank P. O'Sullivan (D)	58,785	43.1
16	Donald L. Jackson (R)	63,124	60.8
	S. Mark Hogue (D)	40,659	39.2
17	Cecil R. King (D)	97,828	60.1
	Robert H. Finch (R)	64,967	39.9
18	Craig Hosmer (R)	71,731	55.0
	Joseph M. Kennick (D)	58,647	45.0
19	Chet Holifield (D)	90,269	74.8
	Raymond R. Pritchard (R)	30,404	25.2
20	Carl Hinshaw (R)	71,213	71.2
	Eugene Radding (D)	28,838	28.8
21	Edgar W. Hiestand (R)	100,258	58.7
	William E. Roskam (D)	70,486	41.3
22	Joe Holt (R)	65,165	58.2
	William M. Costley (D)	46,875	41.8
23	Clyde Doyle (D)	90,729	70.9
	Frank G. Bussing (R)	34,911	27.3
24	Glenard P. Lipscomb (R)	65,431	56.9
	George Arnold (D)	49,592	43.1
25	Patrick J. Hillings (R)	113,027	65.2
	John G. Sobieski (D)	60,370	34.8
26	James Roosevelt (D)	94,261	60.1
	Theodore R. Owings (R)	62,585	39.9
27	Harry R. Sheppard (D)	65,389	64.8
	Martin K. Barrett (R)	35,594	35.3
28	James B. Utt (R)	95,680	66.2
	Harriet Enderle (D)	48,785	33.8
29	John Phillips (R)	42,420	57.9
	Bruce Shangle (D)	30,781	42.1
30	Bob Wilson (R)	94,623	60.4
	Ross T. McIntire (D)	61,994	39.6

COLORADO

		Votes	%
1	Byron G. Rogers (D)	84,745	55.6
	Ellen G. Harris (R)	67,210	44.1
2	William S. Hill (R)	80,162	55.3
	Lacy L. Wilkinson (D)	64,776	44.7
3	J. Edgar Chenoweth (R)	62,884	53.0
	Alva B. Adams (D)	55,750	47.0
4	Wayne N. Aspinall (D)	34,294	53.5
	Charles E. Wilson (R)	29,818	46.5

CONNECTICUT

		Votes	%
1	Thomas J. Dodd (D)	148,935	57.0
	Wallace Barnes (R)	112,526	43.0
2	Horace Seely-Brown Jr. (R)	72,833	50.7
	Henry H. Pierce Jr. (D)	70,853	49.3
3	Albert W. Cretella (R)	94,977	52.7
	James F. Gartland (D)	85,369	47.3
4	Albert P. Morano (R)	123,890	56.2
	Edward R. Fay Jr. (D)	91,184	41.4
5	James T. Patterson (R)	68,451	52.8
	David Brady (D)	61,313	47.3
AL	Antoni N. Sadlak (R)	474,585	51.0
	Joseph P. Lyford (D)	455,887	49.0

DELAWARE

		Votes	%
AL	Harris B. McDowell Jr. (D)	79,201	54.9
	Lillian I. Martin (R)	65,035	45.1

FLORIDA

		Votes	%
1	William C. Cramer (R)	52,287	50.8
	Courtney Campbell (D)	50,744	49.3
2	Charles E. Bennett (D)	14,376	100.0
3	Robert L. F. Sikes (D)	27,013	100.0
4	Dante B. Fascell (D)	47,697	100.0
5	A. S. Herlong Jr. (D)	35,971	100.0
6	Dwight L. Rogers (D)	39,148	100.0
7	James A. Haley (D)	23,469	55.5
	E. B. Sutton (R)	18,850	44.5
8	D. R. Matthews (D)	16,732	100.0

GEORGIA

		Votes	%
1	Prince H. Preston (D)	26,205	83.7
	Frank Downing	5,100	16.3
2	J. L. Pilcher (D)	26,705	99.9
3	E. L. Forrester (D)	34,973	100.0
4	John J. Flynt Jr. (D)	32,400	100.0
5	James C. Davis (D)	54,069	64.4
	Charles A. Moye Jr. (R)	29,911	35.6
6	Carl Vinson (D)	26,250	100.0
7	Henderson L. Lanham (D)	35,147	100.0
8	Iris Faircloth Blitch (D)	27,037	100.0
9	Phil M. Landrum (D)	26,849	100.0
10	Paul Brown (D)	28,068	100.0

IDAHO

	Candidates	Votes	%
1	Gracie B. Pfost (D)	50,214	54.9
	Erwin H. Schwiebert (R)	41,293	45.1
2	Hamer H. Budge (R)	81,824	60.8
	William P. Whitaker (D)	52,681	39.2

ILLINOIS

		Votes	%
1	William L. Dawson (D)	71,472	75.3
	Genoa S. Washington (R)	23,470	24.7
2	Barratt O'Hara (D)	80,016	61.6
	Richard B. Vail (R)	49,970	38.4
3	James C. Murray (D)	77,675	53.8
	Fred E. Busbey (R)	66,767	46.2
4	William E. McVey (R)	94,125	52.2
	William A. Rowan (D)	86,372	47.9
5	John C. Kluczynski (D)	92,780	73.2
	S. Charles Bubacz (R)	33,987	26.8
6	Thomas J. O'Brien (D)	99,590	71.7
	Orville F. Corbin (R)	39,289	28.3
7	James B. Bowler (D)	97,398	78.4
	Charles M. Barrett (R)	26,763	21.6
8	Thomas S. Gordon (D)	74,837	68.4
	James L. Doherty (R)	34,535	31.6
9	Sidney R. Yates (D)	73,187	60.3
	Ralph Lee Goodman (R)	48,130	39.7
10	Richard W. Hoffman (R)	90,961	57.3
	Helen J. Kelleher (D)	67,903	42.7
11	Timothy P. Sheehan (R)	67,141	50.9
	Harry H. Semrow (D)	64,788	49.1
12	Charles A. Boyle (D)	82,518	54.1
	Edgar A. Jonas (R)	69,999	45.9
13	Marguerite Stitt Church (R)	146,184	69.6
	Richard A. Griffin (D)	63,852	30.4
14	Chauncey W. Reed (R)	100,024	72.4
	Richard Plum (D)	38,161	27.6
15	Noah M. Mason (R)	72,576	62.8
	Richard A. Mohan (D)	42,934	37.2
16	Leo E. Allen (R)	77,557	100.0
17	Leslie C. Arends (R)	79,044	65.0
	Branson Wright (D)	42,600	35.0
18	Harold H. Velde (R)	59,963	57.5
	Howard S. Beeney (D)	44,408	42.6
19	Robert B. Chiperfield (R)	64,772	56.5
	John M. Kerwin Jr. (D)	49,876	43.5
20	Sidney E. Simpson (R)	68,104	62.9
	James A. Barry (D)	40,165	37.1
21	Peter F. Mack Jr. (D)	83,501	54.8
	Edward H. Jenison (R)	68,924	45.2
22	William L. Springer (R)	66,797	62.0
	Robert W. Martin (D)	40,873	38.0
23	Charles W. Vursell (R)	69,179	52.9
	Albert R. Imle (D)	61,493	47.1
24	Melvin Price (D)	90,482	69.2
	John T. Thomas (R)	40,358	30.9
25	Kenneth J. Gray (D)	69,562	52.6
	C. W. Bishop (R)	62,659	47.4

INDIANA

		Votes	%
1	Ray J. Madden (D)	81,217	61.4
	Robert H. Moore (R)	50,439	38.2
2	Charles A. Halleck (R)	73,717	59.6
	James H. Berg (D)	49,996	40.4
3	Shepard J. Crumpacker Jr. (R)	85,884	50.4
	John Brademas (D)	83,851	49.2
4	E. Ross Adair (R)	71,436	59.8
	Fred W. Greene (D)	47,384	39.7
5	John V. Beamer (R)	88,428	53.1
	John R. Walsh (D)	76,972	46.2
6	Cecil M. Harden (R)	67,371	52.5
	John W. King (D)	60,896	47.5
7	William G. Bray (R)	75,608	55.4
	George D. Gettinger (D)	60,594	44.4

	Candidates	Votes	%
8	Winfield K. Denton (D)	82,264	52.1
	D. Bailey Merrill (R)	74,960	47.5
9	Earl Wilson (R)	61,285	51.7
	Wilfrid J. Ullrich (D)	57,350	48.3
10	Ralph Harvey (R)	76,132	55.9
	Inez M. Scholl (D)	59,103	43.4
11	Charles B. Brownson (R)	108,044	54.9
	Charles H. Boswell (D)	88,173	44.8

IOWA

	Candidates	Votes	%
1	Fred Schwengel (R)	67,128	57.0
	John O'Connor (D)	50,577	43.0
2	Henry O. Talle (R)	72,231	55.4
	Ruben V. Austin (D)	58,092	44.6
3	H. R. Gross (R)	68,307	62.1
	George R. Laub (D)	41,622	37.9
4	Karl M. LeCompte (R)	49,608	55.6
	Herschel C. Loveless (D)	39,652	44.4
5	Paul Cunningham (R)	61,355	55.6
	James A. McLaughlin (D)	49,063	44.4
6	James I. Dolliver (R)	53,457	60.3
	Lumund F. Wilcox (D)	35,137	39.7
7	Ben F. Jensen (R)	51,022	60.4
	Elmer G. Carlson (D)	33,492	39.6
8	Charles B. Hoeven (R)	55,214	63.8
	Roy B. Holland (D)	31,296	36.2

KANSAS

	Candidates	Votes	%
1	William H. Avery (R)	56,079	54.3
	Howard S. Miller (D)	47,165	45.7
2	Errett P. Scrivner (R)	64,263	54.7
	Newell A. George (D)	53,302	45.3
3	Myron V. George (R)	41,342	55.4
	William W. Monypeny (D)	33,307	44.6
4	Ed H. Rees (R)	77,920	56.2
	Robert M. Green (D)	60,697	43.8
5	Clifford R. Hope (R)	64,023	64.9
	Robert L. Bock (D)	34,691	35.1
6	Wint Smith (R)	43,831	53.3
	Elmo J. Mahoney (D)	38,369	46.7

KENTUCKY

	Candidates	Votes	%
1	Noble J. Gregory (D)	62,210	100.0
2	William H. Natcher (D)	49,231	100.0
3	John M. Robsion Jr. (R)	72,073	50.2
	Harrison M. Robertson (D)	71,500	49.8
4	Frank Chelf (D)	49,496	100.0
5	Brent Spence (D)	63,640	61.0
	M. J. See (R)	40,679	39.0
6	John C. Watts (D)	59,434	60.9
	Robert L. Milby (R)	38,145	39.1
7	Carl D. Perkins (D)	44,353	60.4
	Curtis Clark (R)	29,115	39.6
8	Eugene T. Siler (R)	56,182	63.4
	Mitchel S. Fannin (D)	32,128	36.3

LOUISIANA

	Candidates	Votes	%
1	F. Edward Hebert (D)	38,213	82.3
	George W. Reese Jr. (R)	8,212	17.7
2	Hale Boggs (D)	37,583	100.0
3	Edwin E. Willis (D)	15,808	100.0
4	Overton Brooks (D)	24,587	100.0
5	Otto E. Passman (D)	21,831	100.0
6	James H. Morrison (D)	30,082	100.0
7	T. Ashton Thompson (D)	21,525	100.0
8	George S. Long (D)	18,482	100.0

MAINE

	Candidates	Votes	%
1	Robert Hale (R)	47,327	52.1
	James C. Oliver (D)	43,561	47.9
2	Charles P. Nelson (R)	45,819	54.0
	Thomas E. Delahanty (D)	39,075	46.0
3	Clifford G. McIntire (R)	39,749	60.5
	Kenneth B. Colbath (D)	25,912	39.5

MARYLAND

	Candidates	Votes	%
1	Edward T. Miller (R)	35,221	55.6
	Edward Turner (D)	28,184	44.5
2	James P. S. Devereux (R)	67,179	56.1
	William P. Bolton (D)	52,540	43.9
3	Edward A. Garmatz (D)	45,531	97.2
4	George H. Fallon (D)	40,029	57.2
	Arthur W. Sherwood (R)	29,921	42.8
5	Richard E. Lankford (D)	60,850	53.7
	Frank Small Jr. (R)	52,420	46.3
6	DeWitt S. Hyde (R)	69,658	51.4
	Edward J. Ryan (D)	65,760	48.6
7	Samuel N. Friedel (D)	49,221	54.5
	Edward C. Dukehart (R)	41,027	45.5

MASSACHUSETTS

	Candidates	Votes	%
1	John W. Heselton (R)	68,420	55.6
	John J. Dwyer (D)	54,675	44.4
2	Edward P. Boland (D)	77,899	59.6
	Vernon E. Bradley (R)	52,725	40.4
3	Philip J. Philbin (D)	110,013	100.0
4	Harold D. Donohue (D)	83,053	57.1
	Andrew B. Holmstrom (R)	62,318	42.9
5	Edith Nourse Rogers (R)	139,989	100.0
6	William H. Bates (R)	91,916	71.2
	Andrew J. Gillis (D)	37,216	28.8
7	Thomas J. Lane (D, R)	102,659	100.0
8	Torbert H. Macdonald (D)	74,568	53.2
	Angier L. Goodwin (R)	65,614	46.8
9	Donald W. Nicholson (R)	81,378	56.6
	James F. O'Neill (D)	62,445	43.4
10	Laurence Curtis (R)	72,502	50.7
	Jackson J. Holtz (D)	70,608	49.3
11	Thomas P. O'Neill Jr. (D)	75,613	78.2
	Charles S. Bolster (R)	21,039	21.8
12	John W. McCormack (D)	79,073	100.0
13	Richard B. Wigglesworth (R)	90,924	58.0
	James F. Gardner (D)	65,854	42.0
14	Joseph W. Martin Jr. (R)	87,840	62.0
	Edward F. Doolan (D)	53,818	38.0

MICHIGAN

	Candidates	Votes	%
1	Thaddeus M. Machrowicz (D)	91,435	88.3
	Rudolph G. Tenerowicz (R)	11,731	11.3
2	George Meader (R)	69,825	59.8
	J. Henry Owens (D)	46,817	40.1
3	August E. Johansen (R)	65,942	59.4
	Charles C. Wickett (D)	44,574	40.2
4	Clare E. Hoffman (R)	62,025	62.3
	Gordon A. Elferdink (D)	37,500	37.7
5	Gerald R. Ford Jr. (R)	81,702	63.3
	Robert S. McAllister (D)	47,453	36.7
6	Don Hayworth (D)	80,325	51.1
	Kit Clardy (R)	76,335	48.6
7	Jesse P. Wolcott (R)	71,651	52.8
	Ira D. McCoy (D)	63,797	47.0
8	Alvin M. Bentley (R)	65,813	62.7
	Clarence V. Smazel (D)	38,828	37.0
9	Ruth Thompson (R)	50,659	55.7
	Theodore E. A. Engstrom (D)	39,966	44.0
10	Elford A. Cederberg (R)	50,570	61.4
	William J. Kelly (D)	31,794	38.6
11	Victor A. Knox (R)	41,665	54.9
	Harold Beaton (D)	34,204	45.1
12	John B. Bennett (R)	39,531	55.9
	Frank E. Hook (D)	31,187	44.1
13	Charles C. Diggs Jr. (D)	64,716	65.8
	Landon Knight (R)	33,127	33.7
14	Louis C. Rabaut (D)	97,297	58.2
	Joseph A. Moynihan Jr. (R)	69,503	41.6
15	John D. Dingell (D)	85,100	72.7
	Gregory M. Pillon (R)	31,815	27.2
16	John Lesinski (D)	121,557	67.9
	Stanley A. Grendel (R)	56,815	31.7
17	Martha W. Griffiths (D)	75,258	52.2
	Charles G. Oakman (R)	68,613	47.6
18	George A. Dondero (R)	80,771	53.9
	Paul Sutton (D)	89,131	46.1

MINNESOTA

	Candidates	Votes	%
1	August H. Andresen (R)	72,686	60.9
	Robert C. Olson (DFL)	46,678	39.1
2	Joseph P. O'Hara (R)	71,592	57.9
	Harry Sieben (DFL)	52,089	42.1
3	Roy W. Wier (DFL)	98,407	54.4
	Edward Willow (R)	82,389	45.6
4	Eugene J. McCarthy (DFL)	81,651	63.0
	Richard C. Hansen (R)	47,933	37.0
5	Walter H. Judd (R)	69,901	55.8
	Anders Thompson (DFL)	55,452	44.2
6	Fred Marshall (DFL)	72,922	61.9
	Oscar J. Jerde (R)	44,850	38.1
7	H. Carl Andersen (R)	60,120	52.6
	Douglas P. Hunt (DFL)	54,140	47.4
8	John A. Blatnik (DFL)	89,778	71.8
	Ernie Orchard (R)	35,241	28.2
9	Coya Knutson (DFL)	48,999	51.2
	Harold C. Hagen (R)	46,664	48.8

MISSISSIPPI

	Candidates	Votes	%
1	Thomas G. Abernethy (D)	15,944	100.0
2	Jamie L. Whitten (D)	13,516	100.0
3	Frank E. Smith (D)	13,468	100.0
4	John Bell Williams (D)	19,164	100.0
5	Arthur Winstead (D)	17,400	100.0
6	William M. Colmer (D)	21,806	100.0

MISSOURI

	Candidates	Votes	%
1	Frank M. Karsten (D)	89,649	66.3
	Bill Bangert (R)	45,653	33.7
2	Thomas B. Curtis (R)	83,861	54.7
	Eugene H. Buder (D)	69,450	45.3
3	Leonor K. Sullivan (D)	67,715	71.0
	George W. Curran (R)	27,598	29.0
4	George H. Christopher (D)	62,012	51.6
	Jeffrey P. Hillelson (R)	58,152	48.4
5	Richard Bolling (D)	50,874	58.9
	Samuel Lee Chaney (R)	35,477	41.1
6	W. R. Hull Jr. (D)	60,380	53.6
	William C. Cole (R)	52,203	46.4
7	Dewey Short (R)	67,918	53.6
	J. M. Lowry (D)	58,729	46.4
8	A. S. J. Carnahan (D)	52,658	57.3
	Dorman L. Steelman (R)	39,326	42.8
9	Clarence Cannon (D)	65,862	59.0
	Noel Carpenter (R)	45,765	41.0
10	Paul C. Jones (D)	34,009	63.9
	Clyde Whaley (R)	19,179	36.1
11	Morgan M. Moulder (D)	54,384	55.3
	L. C. Davis (R)	43,959	44.7

MONTANA

	Candidates	Votes	%
1	Lee Metcalf (D)	52,614	56.0
	Winfield E. Page (R)	41,375	44.0
2	Orvin B. Fjare (R)	66,103	50.6
	LeRoy H. Anderson (D)	64,495	49.4

NEBRASKA

	Candidates	Votes	%
1	Phil Weaver (R)	68,563	58.6
	Frank B. Morrison (D)	48,457	41.4
2	Jackson B. Chase (R)	52,471	53.0
	James A. Hart (D)	46,629	47.1
3	Robert D. Harrison (R)	61,124	65.2
	Ernest M. Luther (D)	32,562	34.8
4	Arthur L. Miller (R)	68,189	70.4
	Carlton W. Laird (D)	28,695	29.6

NEVADA

	Candidates	Votes	%
AL	Clifton Young (R)	42,321	54.5
	Walter S. Baring (D)	35,318	45.5

NEW HAMPSHIRE

	Candidates	Votes	%
1	Chester E. Merrow (R)	54,052	50.2
	Thomas J. McIntyre (D)	53,584	49.8
2	Perkins Bass (R)	51,010	60.4
	George F. Brown (D)	33,415	39.6

NEW JERSEY

	Candidates	Votes	%
1	Charles A. Wolverton (R)	92,070	54.4
	J. Frank Crawford (D)	77,100	45.5
2	T. Millet Hand (R)	65,551	63.6
	Clayton E. Burdick (D)	37,541	36.4
3	James C. Auchincloss (R)	89,085	57.6
	Charles F. Sullivan (D)	65,685	42.4
4	Frank Thompson Jr. (D)	72,884	58.4
	William G. Freeman (R)	51,998	41.6
5	Peter H. B. Frelinghuysen (R)	99,946	59.3
	Luther H. Martin (D)	68,702	40.7
6	Harrison A. Williams Jr. (D)	85,784	56.1
	Fred E. Shepard (R)	64,164	41.9
7	William B. Widnall (R)	99,977	63.2
	Eugene E. Demarest (D)	58,211	36.8
8	Gordon Canfield (R)	65,359	54.8
	Charles S. Joelson (D)	53,844	45.1
9	Frank C. Osmers Jr. (R)	87,008	60.2
	Walter J. O'Connell (D)	57,445	39.8
10	Peter W. Rodino Jr. (D)	62,384	63.4
	William E. McGlynn (R)	36,056	36.6
11	Hugh J. Addonizio (D)	52,311	56.3
	Philip Insabella (R)	38,351	41.2
12	Robert Winthrop Kean (R)	59,151	53.1
	Martin S. Fox (D)	52,314	46.9
13	Alfred D. Sieminski (D)	60,108	60.8
	Norman Roth (R)	26,638	26.9
	Jeremiah J. O'Callaghan (I)	12,174	12.3
14	T. James Tumulty (D)	58,069	62.4
	Vincent J. Dellay (R)	32,485	34.9

NEW MEXICO

	Candidates	Votes	%
AL	John J. Dempsey (D)	111,713✓	
	Antonio M. Fernandez (D)	109,837✓	
	Thomas H. Childers (R)	77,151	
	Warren R. Cobean (R)	76,528	

NEW YORK

	Candidates	Votes	%
1	Stuyvesant Wainwright (R)	108,130	63.1
	Ernest Greenwood (D, L)	62,853	36.7
2	Steven B. Derounian (R)	98,610	63.7
	William R. Brennan Jr. (D, L)	55,477	35.8
3	Frank J. Becker (R)	93,396	58.3
	John T. Cogley (D, L)	66,703	41.7
4	Henry J. Latham (R)	74,621	54.2
	Thomas A. Dent (D)	55,479	40.3
	Robert A. Rose (L)	7,526	5.5
5	Albert H. Bosch (R)	50,778	51.7
	William Kerwick (D)	43,086	43.9
6	Lester Holtzman (D, L)	81,033	54.4
	Seymour Halpern (R)	67,681	45.5
7	James J. Delaney (D, L)	62,541	59.0
	Joseph Stockinger (R)	43,525	41.0
8	Victor L. Anfuso (D, L)	51,993	77.7
	Eugene J. Renne (R)	14,948	22.3
9	Eugene J. Keogh (D, L)	59,392	71.1
	Harry Keller (R)	22,808	27.3
10	Edna F. Kelly (D, L)	80,541	76.8
	Abraham Sher (R)	22,479	21.4
11	Emanuel Celler (D, L)	103,788	83.5
	Henry D. Dorfman (R)	20,452	16.5
12	Francis E. Dorn (R)	49,449	51.3
	Donald L. O'Toole (D, L)	46,926	48.7
13	Abraham J. Multer (D, L)	89,907	78.8
	Joseph Moriber (R)	21,881	19.2
14	John J. Rooney (D, L)	61,879	73.1
	Alfred A. Manti (R)	21,598	25.5
15	John H. Ray (R)	56,020	51.6
	Vincent R. Fitzpatrick (D, L)	52,292	48.1
16	Adam Clayton Powell Jr. (D)	43,545	77.6
	Harold C. Burton (R)	8,904	15.9
	Formington Taylor (L)	3,701	6.6
17	Frederic R. Coudert Jr. (R)	48,999	50.2
	Anthony B. Akers (D, L)	48,685	49.8
18	James G. Donovan (D, R)	49,850	86.8
	Amos Basel (L)	6,219	10.8
19	Arthur G. Klein (D, L)	56,634	74.6
	Henry E. Delrosso (R)	19,310	25.4
20	Irwin D. Davidson (D, L)	58,030	67.2
	Warren L. Schnur (R)	26,462	30.7
21	Herbert Zelenko (D, L)	63,284	67.8
	Floyd Cramer (R)	29,995	32.2
22	Sidney A. Fine (D)	72,091	67.9
	Henry Rose (R)	18,952	17.8
	Louis Schifrin (L)	13,249	12.5
23	Isidore Dollinger (D)	58,490	75.6
	Philip Myer (R)	9,976	12.9
	Bernice Benedick (L)	8,869	11.5
24	Charles A. Buckley (D)	69,552	58.3
	Charles V. Scanlan (R)	31,670	26.6
	Elias Rosenblatt (L)	18,067	15.2
25	Paul A. Fino (R)	59,409	50.4
	Salvatore J. Milano (D)	50,818	43.1
	Ernest Doerfler (L)	7,624	6.5
26	Ralph A. Gamble (R)	81,608	64.0
	Julia L. Crews (D, L)	45,892	36.0
27	Ralph W. Gwinn (R)	83,866	57.2
	John H. Harold (D, L)	62,797	42.8
28	Katharine St. George (R)	79,587	64.9
	Paul G. Reilly (D)	40,109	32.7
29	J. Ernest Wharton (R)	88,227	66.5
	Robert D. Byron (D)	42,084	31.7
30	Leo W. O'Brien (D, L)	104,585	61.2
	James W. Smith (R)	66,319	38.8
31	Dean P. Taylor (R)	86,768	66.3
	Joseph R. MacLaren (D, L)	44,212	33.8
32	Bernard W. Kearney (R)	77,891	61.5
	David C. Prince (D, L)	48,808	38.5
33	Clarence E. Kilburn (R)	70,708	68.1
	Harold Blake (D)	31,279	30.1
34	William R. Williams (R)	77,659	59.3
	Vernon E. Olin (D, L)	53,112	40.6
35	R. Walter Riehlman (R)	90,002	63.5
	James H. O'Connor (D, L)	51,358	36.3
36	John Taber (R)	79,850	68.4
	Daniel J. Carey (D, L)	36,910	31.6
37	W. Sterling Cole (R)	94,840	71.7
	John E. Bloomer (D, L)	37,525	28.3
38	Kenneth B. Keating (R)	103,293	71.9
	Rubin Brodsky (L)	40,400	28.1
39	Harold C. Ostertag (R)	82,769	64.8
	George W. Cooke (D, L)	45,000	35.2
40	William E. Miller (R)	77,016	60.9
	Mariano A. Lucca (D)	46,956	37.1
41	Edmund P. Radwan (R)	77,259	63.1
	Bernard J. Wojtkowiak (D, L)	45,144	36.9
42	John R. Pillion (R)	82,707	57.6
	John J. Zablotny (D, L)	60,880	42.4
43	Daniel A. Reed (R)	66,852	64.8
	James F. Crowley (D)	34,590	33.5

NORTH CAROLINA

	Candidates	Votes	%
1	Herbert C. Bonner (D)	20,650	92.5
	W. T. Love (R)	1,685	7.5
2	L. H. Fountain (D)	14,471	100.0
3	Graham A. Barden (D)	24,837	77.3
	Christine P. Odom (R)	7,301	22.7
4	Harold D. Cooley (D)	34,406	100.0
5	Thurmond Chatham (D)	31,781	66.2
	Joe New (R)	16,194	33.8
6	Carl T. Durham (D)	30,118	74.3
	Rufus K. Haworth Jr. (R)	10,446	25.8
7	F. Ertel Carlyle (D)	21,669	81.3
	J. O. West (R)	5,001	18.8
8	Charles B. Deane (D)	39,028	59.1
	Harold W. Gavin (R)	26,966	40.9
9	Hugh Q. Alexander (D)	54,103	52.2
	William E. Stevens Jr. (R)	49,555	47.8
10	Charles Raper Jonas (R)	51,492	57.5
	J. C. Sedberry (D)	38,080	42.5
11	Woodrow W. Jones (D)	36,766	67.5
	R. R. Ramsey (R)	17,721	32.5
12	George A. Shuford (D)	44,258	61.6
	Charles Cunningham (R)	27,651	38.5

NORTH DAKOTA

	Candidates	Votes	%
AL	Usher L. Burdick (R)	124,845✓	
	Otto Krueger (R)	106,341✓	
	P. W. Lanier (D)	64,089	
	Raymond G. Vendsel (D)	49,183	

OHIO

	Candidates	Votes	%
1	Gordon H. Scherer (R)	71,042	64.3
	Mrs. Warwick B. Hobart (D)	39,421	35.7
2	William E. Hess (R)	69,695	58.4
	Earl T. Wagner (D)	49,690	41.6
3	Paul F. Schenck (R)	82,701	52.6
	Thomas B. Talbot (D)	74,585	47.4
4	William M. McCulloch (R)	67,762	67.6
	Forrest L. Blankenship (D)	32,474	32.4
5	Cliff Clevenger (R)	49,265	59.5
	Martin W. Feigert (D)	33,483	40.5
6	James G. Polk (D)	54,044	52.2
	Leo Blackburn (R)	49,531	47.8
7	Clarence J. Brown (R)	62,821	63.9
	G. Louie Wren (D)	35,504	36.1
8	Jackson E. Betts (R)	52,196	63.1
	Thomas M. Dowd (D)	30,592	37.0
9	Thomas L. Ashley (D)	48,471	36.4
	Frazier Reams (I)	44,656	33.6
	Irving C. Reynolds (R)	39,933	30.0
10	Thomas A. Jenkins (R)	45,277	61.7
	Truman A. Morris (D)	28,150	38.3
11	Oliver P. Bolton (R)	74,065	65.3
	Edward C. Kaley (D)	39,404	34.7
12	John M. Vorys (R)	94,585	61.5
	Jacob F. Myers (D)	59,210	38.5
13	A. D. Baumhart Jr. (R)	46,524	59.1
	George C. Steinemann (D)	32,177	40.9
14	William H. Ayres (R)	82,086	54.6
	John L. Smith (D)	68,204	45.4
15	John E. Henderson (R)	38,524	54.0
	Max Lewis Underwood (D)	32,795	46.0
16	Frank T. Bow (R)	79,371	58.3
	Thomas H. Nichols (D)	56,787	41.7
17	J. Harry McGregor (R)	63,301	64.6
	Robert W. Levering (D)	34,638	35.4
18	Wayne L. Hays (D)	59,165	57.3
	Walter J. Hunston (R)	44,143	42.7
19	Michael J. Kirwan (D)	69,324	67.5
	David S. Edwards (R)	33,352	32.5
20	Michael A. Feighan (D)	81,304	67.7
	John H. Ferguson (R)	38,865	32.3
21	Charles A. Vanik (D)	76,201	76.0
	Francis E. Young (R)	24,076	24.0
22	Frances P. Bolton (R)	61,738	58.4
	Chat Paterson (D)	44,072	41.7
23	William E. Minshall Jr. (R)	69,994	67.5
	Bernice S. Pyke (D)	33,639	32.5

OKLAHOMA

	Candidates	Votes	%
1	Page Belcher (R)	79,151	58.8
	Ben Crowley (D)	55,391	41.2
2	Ed Edmondson (D)	67,872	64.7
	Percy Butler (R)	37,030	35.3
3	Carl Albert (D)	52,662	83.3
	Jasper N. Butler (R)	10,554	16.7
4	Tom Steed (D)	43,915	100.0
5	John Jarman (D)	72,380	66.0
	George E. Young (R)	37,223	34.0
6	Victor E. Wickersham (D)	62,119	69.3
	Reece L. Russell (R)	27,492	30.7

OREGON

	Candidates	Votes	%
1	Walter Norblad (R)	98,592	63.0
	Donnell Mitchell (D)	57,882	37.0
2	Sam Coon (R)	43,731	52.6
	Al Ullman (D)	39,475	47.4
3	Edith Green (D)	103,976	52.4
	Tom McCall (R)	94,368	47.6
4	Harris Ellsworth (R)	70,695	55.9
	Charles O. Porter (D)	55,775	44.1

PENNSYLVANIA

	Candidates	Votes	%
1	William A. Barrett (D)	68,531	61.5
	Joseph A. Graham Jr. (R)	42,893	38.5
2	William T. Granahan (D)	80,377	61.3
	Albert A. Ciardi (R)	50,857	38.8
3	James A. Byrne (D)	61,639	55.4
	Charles H. Sporkin (R)	49,702	44.6
4	Earl Chudoff (D)	60,564	65.7
	W. Beverly Carter Jr. (R)	31,551	34.2
5	William J. Green Jr. (D)	87,435	55.0
	Francis P. McCusker (R)	71,462	45.0
6	Hugh Scott (R)	74,328	50.6
	Alexander Hemphill (D)	72,587	49.4
7	Benjamin F. James (R)	101,282	60.9
	O. Arthur Cappiello (D)	65,086	39.1
8	Karl C. King (R)	62,897	51.2
	John P. Fullam (D)	59,848	48.8
9	Paul B. Dague (R)	76,163	62.7
	Edward G. Wilson (D)	45,402	37.4
10	Joseph L. Carrigg (R)	74,515	50.5
	Robert H. Jones (D)	73,046	49.5
11	Daniel J. Flood (D)	70,254	50.9
	Edward J. Bonin (R)	67,682	49.1
12	Ivor D. Fenton (R)	62,779	55.5
	Charles E. Lotz (D)	50,373	44.5
13	Samuel K. McConnell Jr. (R)	91,639	64.3
	Joseph C. Mansfield (D)	50,796	35.7
14	George M. Rhodes (D)	50,765	62.0
	Donald F. Spang (R)	31,136	38.0
15	Francis E. Walter (D)	56,871	61.6
	LeRoy Mikels (R)	35,464	38.4
16	Walter M. Mumma (R)	69,240	59.8
	Richard A. Swank (D)	46,619	40.2
17	Alvin R. Bush (R)	57,928	56.5
	William T. Longe (D)	44,543	43.5
18	Richard M. Simpson (R)	58,959	55.9
	Robert M. Meyers (D)	46,463	44.1
19	James M. Quigley (D)	62,108	51.0
	S. Walter Stauffer (R)	59,594	49.0
20	James E. Van Zandt (R)	48,561	56.3
	John R. Stewart (D)	37,725	43.7
21	Augustine B. Kelley (D)	70,224	61.1
	Herbert O. Morrison (R)	44,789	38.9
22	John P. Saylor (R)	66,270	51.9
	Robert S. Glass (D)	61,474	48.1
23	Leon H. Gavin (R)	53,616	61.9
	Fred C. Barr (D)	33,044	38.1
24	Carroll D. Kearns (R)	66,005	52.0
	Edmund T. Rogers (D)	60,842	48.0
25	Frank M. Clark (D)	66,223	53.5
	Louis E. Graham (R)	57,657	46.5
26	Thomas E. Morgan (D)	95,531	65.3
	Branko Stupar (R)	50,768	34.7
27	James G. Fulton (R)	92,533	62.8
	Charles J. Chamberlin (D)	54,876	37.2
28	Herman P. Eberharter (D)	85,550	65.1
	Guy C. Read (R)	45,913	34.9
29	Robert J. Corbett (R)	83,846	60.6
	William G. Foley (D)	54,511	39.4
30	Vera D. Buchanan (D)	98,318	69.0
	David J. Smith (R)	44,157	31.0

RHODE ISLAND

	Candidates	Votes	%
1	Aime J. Forand (D)	89,678	59.1
	Arthur Carrelas (R)	61,990	40.9
2	John E. Fogarty (D)	105,522	60.5
	James O. Watts (R)	68,869	39.5

SOUTH CAROLINA

	Candidates	Votes	%
1	L. Mendel Rivers (D)	33,402	97.8
2	John J. Riley (D)	44,484	97.7
3	W. J. Bryan Dorn (D)	30,790	99.3
4	Robert T. Ashmore (D)	43,857	99.2
5	James P. Richards (D)	26,950	100.0
6	John L. McMillan (D)	31,141	98.9

SOUTH DAKOTA

		Votes	%
1	Harold O. Lovre (R)	102,797	58.0
	Francis G. Dunn (D)	74,450	42.0
2	E. Y. Berry (R)	34,476	63.9
	Ray Satterlee (D)	19,444	36.1

TENNESSEE

		Votes	%
1	B. Carroll Reece (R)	32,991	62.5
	Arthur Bright (D)	19,828	37.5
2	Howard H. Baker (R)	47,989	58.0
	C. Howard Bozeman (D)	34,688	42.0
3	James B. Frazier Jr. (D)	30,558	59.2
	O. M. Spence (R)	21,081	40.8
4	Joe L. Evins (D)	27,613	100.0
5	J. Percy Priest (D)	20,849	90.8
	Robert M. Donihi (R)	2,123	9.2
6	Ross Bass (D)	26,081	99.4
7	Tom Murray (D)	17,708	100.0
8	Jere Cooper (D)	15,078	100.0
9	Clifford Davis (D)	40,121	83.5
	W. A. Danielson (R)	7,926	16.5

TEXAS

		Votes	%
1	Wright Patman (D)	18,104	100.0
2	Jack Brooks (D)	25,008	100.0
3	Brady Gentry (D)	20,767	100.0
4	Sam Rayburn (D)	15,177	100.0
5	Bruce Alger (R)	27,982	52.9
	Wallace Savage (D)	24,904	47.1
6	Olin E. Teague (D)	15,161	100.0
7	John Dowdy (D)	18,361	100.0
8	Albert Thomas (D)	60,374	62.1
	W. B. Butler (R)	36,405	37.4
9	Clark W. Thompson (D)	29,972	100.0
10	Homer Thornberry (D)	23,752	100.0
11	W. R. Poage (D)	17,739	100.0
12	Jim Wright (D)	35,611	98.8
13	Frank Ikard (D)	25,085	100.0
14	John J. Bell (D)	36,284	93.8
	D. C. DeWitt (R)	2,384	6.2
15	Joe M. Kilgore (D)	29,113	100.0
16	J. T. Rutherford (D)	25,122	100.0
17	Omar Burleson (D)	18,484	100.0
18	Walter Rogers (D)	25,430	64.9
	Leroy LaMaster (R)	13,756	35.1
19	George Mahon (D)	26,829	100.0
20	Paul J. Kilday (D)	23,533	100.0
21	O. C. Fisher (D)	25,381	100.0
AL	Martin Dies (D)	555,446	88.0
	Tom Nolan (R)	75,472	12.0

UTAH

		Votes	%
1	Henry Aldous Dixon (R)	55,542	53.4
	Walter K. Granger (D)	48,535	46.6
2	William A. Dawson (R)	90,864	57.2
	Reva Beck Bosone (D)	68,090	42.8

VERMONT

		Votes	%
AL	Winston L. Prouty (R)	70,143	61.4
	John J. Boylan Jr. (D)	44,141	38.6

VIRGINIA

		Votes	%
1	Edward J. Robeson Jr. (D)	16,029	99.8
2	Porter Hardy Jr. (D)	18,190	74.4
	George V. Credle Jr. (R)	6,243	25.6
3	J. Vaughan Gary (D)	19,466	58.0
	J. Calvitt Clarke Jr. (R)	14,088	42.0
4	Watkins M. Abbitt (D)	14,728	99.9
5	William M. Tuck (D)	13,042	99.9
6	Richard H. Poff (R)	32,855	62.3
	Ernest Robertson (D)	19,727	37.4
7	Burr P. Harrison (D)	22,025	74.2
	John Paul Ruddick (R)	7,669	25.8
8	Howard W. Smith (D)	17,321	66.6
	C. S. Lenhart (I)	8,679	33.4
9	W. Pat Jennings (D)	39,238	50.5
	William C. Wampler (R)	38,239	49.2
10	Joel T. Broyhill (R)	29,221	53.8
	John C. Webb (D)	24,667	45.4

WASHINGTON

		Votes	%
1	Thomas M. Pelly (R)	101,913	52.6
	Hugh B. Mitchell (D)	91,721	47.4
2	Jack Westland (R)	73,264	52.2
	Harry F. Henson (D)	67,232	47.9
3	Russell V. Mack (R)	70,844	64.9
	Clyde V. Tisdale (D)	38,344	35.1
4	Hal Holmes (R)	67,171	61.0
	Fred Yoder (D)	42,911	39.0
5	Walt Horan (R)	68,628	58.6
	Art Garton (D)	48,542	41.4
6	Thor C. Tollefson (R)	80,241	55.2
	John T. McCutcheon (D)	65,011	44.8
AL	Don Magnuson (D)	464,045	57.3
	Al Canwell (R)	342,089	42.2

WEST VIRGINIA

		Votes	%
1	Robert H. Mollohan (D)	52,609	52.7
	Arch A. Moore Jr. (R)	47,199	47.3
2	Harley O. Staggers (D)	50,283	55.0
	Albert M. Morgan (R)	41,171	45.0
3	Cleveland M. Bailey (D)	54,684	58.9
	Joseph B. Lightburn (R)	38,218	41.1
4	M. G. Burnside (D)	56,498	50.2
	Will E. Neal (R)	55,994	49.8
5	Elizabeth Kee (D)	52,349	67.5
	Fred O. Blue (R)	25,267	32.6
6	Robert C. Byrd (D)	73,535	62.7
	Pat B. Withrow Jr. (R)	43,685	37.3

WISCONSIN

		Votes	%
1	Lawrence H. Smith (R)	65,562	54.4
	Edward A. Krenzke (D)	54,864	45.6
2	Glenn R. Davis (R)	74,460	54.0
	Gaylord A. Nelson (D)	63,449	46.0
3	Gardner R. Withrow (R)	56,228	62.1
	Joseph A. Seep (D)	34,375	37.9
4	Clement J. Zablocki (D)	100,120	71.1
	John C. Schafer (R)	40,723	28.9
5	Henry S. Reuss (D)	77,208	52.3
	Charles J. Kersten (R)	70,565	47.8
6	William K. Van Pelt (R)	68,653	62.5
	Russell S. Johnson (D)	41,191	37.5
7	Melvin R. Laird (R)	57,581	59.1
	Kenneth E. Anderson (D)	39,828	40.9
8	John W. Byrnes (R)	73,588	62.0
	Jerome J. Reinke (D)	45,037	38.0
9	Lester R. Johnson (D)	52,485	55.4
	William E. Owen (R)	42,234	44.6
10	Alvin E. O'Konski (R)	49,325	59.8
	Basil G. Kennedy (D)	33,219	40.2

WYOMING

		Votes	%
AL	E. Keith Thomson (R)	61,111	56.2
	Sam Tully (D)	47,660	43.8

1956 House Elections

ALABAMA

	Candidates	Votes	%
1	Frank W. Boykin (D)	31,469	100.0
2	George Grant (D)	36,613	100.0
3	George W. Andrews (D)	29,547	100.0
4	Kenneth A. Roberts (D)	33,591	73.4
	Roy Banks (R)	12,166	26.6
5	Albert Rains (D)	45,281	100.0
6	Armistead I. Selden Jr. (D)	22,513	100.0
7	Carl Elliott (D)	31,988	100.0
8	Robert E. Jones Jr. (D)	46,730	80.1
	Mrs. James G. Fortney (R)	11,634	19.9
9	George Huddleston Jr. (D)	56,414	65.9
	W. L. Longshore Jr. (R)	29,222	34.1

ARIZONA

	Candidates	Votes	%
1	John J. Rhodes (R)	78,998	54.9
	William P. Mahoney Jr. (D)	64,805	45.1
2	Stewart L. Udall (D)	82,110	60.1
	John G. Speiden (R)	54,596	39.9

ARKANSAS

	Candidates	Votes	%
1	Ezekiel C. Gathings (D)	25,622	100.0
2	Wilbur D. Mills (D)	19,540	100.0
3	James W. Trimble (D)	54,481	61.4
	William S. Spicer (R)	34,318	38.7
4	Oren Harris (D)	37,284	100.0
5	Brooks Hays (D)	56,271	100.0
6	William F. Norrell (D)	42,447	100.0

CALIFORNIA

	Candidates	Votes	%
1	Hubert B. Scudder (R)	102,604	53.6
	Clement W. Miller (D)	88,962	46.4
2	Clair Engle (D-R)	136,544	100.0
3	John E. Moss Jr. (D)	132,930	68.6
	Noel C. Stevenson (R)	60,889	31.4
4	William S. Mailliard (R)	109,188	61.9
	James L. Quigley (D)	67,132	38.1
5	John F. Shelley (D-R)	104,358	100.0
6	John F. Baldwin Jr. (R)	98,683	53.7
	H. Roberts Quinney (D)	84,965	46.3
7	John J. Allen Jr. (R)	75,932	52.8
	Laurence L. Cross (D)	67,931	47.2
8	George P. Miller (D)	136,720	65.6
	Robert Lee Watkins (R)	71,700	34.4
9	J. Arthur Younger (R)	96,388	60.3
	James T. McKay (D)	63,504	39.7
10	Charles S. Gubser (R)	128,891	60.7
	William H. Vatcher Jr. (D)	83,586	39.3
11	John J. McFall (D)	70,630	53.1
	Leroy Johnson (R)	62,448	46.9
12	B. F. Sisk (D)	109,920	73.0
	Robert B. Moore (R)	40,663	27.0
13	Charles M. Teague (R)	104,009	59.6
	William Kirk Stewart (D)	70,567	40.4
14	Harlan Hagan (D)	94,461	63.0
	Myron D. Tisdel (R)	55,509	37.0
15	Gordon L. McDonough (R)	97,182	57.9
	Emery S. Petty (D)	70,681	42.1
16	Donald L. Jackson (R)	83,050	60.8
	G. Robert Fleming (D)	53,624	39.2
17	Cecil R. King (D)	157,270	64.9
	Charles A. Franklin (R)	84,900	35.1
18	Craig Hosmer (R)	103,108	59.3
	Raymond C. Simpson (D)	70,911	40.8
19	Chet Holifield (D)	116,287	73.8
	Roy E. Reynolds (R)	41,269	26.2
20	H. Allen Smith (R)	85,459	70.8
	Eugene Radding (D)	35,249	29.2
21	Edgar W. Hiestand (R)	153,679	62.6
	W. C. Stethem (D)	91,683	37.4
22	Joe Holt (R)	97,317	59.8
	Irving Glasband (D)	65,314	40.2

	Candidates	Votes	%
23	Clyde Doyle (D & P)	120,109	70.9
	E. Elgie Calvin (R)	49,198	29.1
24	Glenard P. Lipscomb (R)	84,120	61.9
	Fay Porter (D)	51,692	38.1
25	Patrick J. Hillings (R)	166,305	63.8
	John G. Sobieski (D)	94,180	36.2
26	James Roosevelt (D)	133,036	68.8
	Edward H. Gibbons (R)	60,230	31.2
27	Harry R. Sheppard (D-R)	124,662	99.8
28	James B. Utt (R)	159,456	64.5
	Gordon T. Shepard (D)	87,691	35.5
29	Dalip S. Saund (D)	54,989	51.5
	Jacqueline Cochran Odlum (R)	51,690	48.4
30	Bob Wilson (R)	142,753	66.8
	George A. Cheney (D)	71,112	33.3

COLORADO

	Candidates	Votes	%
1	Byron G. Rogers (D)	116,487	57.8
	Robert S. McCollum (R)	85,127	42.2
2	William S. Hill (R)	107,153	53.4
	Byron L. Johnson (D)	93,572	46.6
3	J. Edgar Chenoweth (R)	74,196	50.2
	Alva B. Adams (D)	73,503	49.8
4	Wayne N. Aspinall (D)	48,489	61.8
	Hugh L. Caldwell (R)	30,026	38.2

CONNECTICUT

	Candidates	Votes	%
1	Edwin H. May Jr. (R)	161,360	53.5
	Patrick J. Ward (D)	139,147	46.1
2	Horace Seely-Brown Jr. (R)	99,274	59.1
	Douglas J. Bennet (D)	68,847	41.0
3	Albert W. Cretella (R)	126,850	60.0
	Robert N. Giaimo (D)	84,568	40.0
4	Albert P. Morano (R)	194,333	68.4
	Jack Stock (D)	88,487	31.1
5	James T. Patterson (R)	91,690	61.9
	Luke F. Martin (D)	56,375	38.1
AL	Antoni N. Sadlak (R)	683,387	61.5
	Matthew P. Kuta (D)	428,709	38.6

DELAWARE

	Candidates	Votes	%
AL	Harry G. Haskell Jr. (R)	91,538	52.0
	Harris B. McDowell Jr. (D)	84,644	48.0

FLORIDA

	Candidates	Votes	%
1	William C. Cramer (R)	105,958	56.4
	Winton H. King (D)	82,075	43.7
2	Charles E. Bennett (D)	66,614	100.0
3	Robert L. F. Sikes (D)	86,272	89.6
	Arthur Barker Sr. (R)	10,042	10.4
4	Dante B. Fascell (D)	120,509	60.9
	Leland Hyzer (R)	77,301	39.1
5	A. S. Herlong Jr. (D)	73,498	51.4
	Arnold L. Lund (R)	69,378	48.6
6	Paul G. Rogers (D)	73,259	54.7
	Dorothy A. Smith (R)	60,570	45.3
7	James A. Haley (D)	47,985	62.4
	G. M. Nelson (R)	28,900	37.6
8	Donald R. Matthews (D)	39,362	100.0

GEORGIA

	Candidates	Votes	%
1	Prince H. Preston (D)	40,360	78.3
	Harry P. Anestos (I)	10,931	21.2
2	J. L. Pilcher (D)	41,270	100.0
3	E. L. Forrester (D)	51,703	100.0
4	John J. Flynt Jr. (D)	51,568	100.0
5	James C. Davis (D)	85,292	59.2
	Randolph W. Thrower (R)	58,777	40.8
6	Carl Vinson (D)	42,766	100.0
7	Henderson Lanham (D)	69,873	99.5

	Candidates	Votes	%
8	Iris Faircloth Blitch (D)	50,068	100.0
9	Phil M. Landrum (D)	47,360	100.0
10	Paul Brown (D)	41,812	99.8

IDAHO

	Candidates	Votes	%
1	Gracie B. Pfost (D)	60,170	55.1
	Louise Shadduck (R)	48,974	44.9
2	Hamer H. Budge (R)	90,738	60.0
	J. W. Reynolds (D)	60,552	40.0

ILLINOIS

	Candidates	Votes	%
1	William L. Dawson (D)	66,704	64.4
	George W. Lawrence (R)	36,847	35.6
2	Barratt O'Hara (D)	86,386	55.3
	George B. McKibbin (R)	69,892	44.7
3	Emmet F. Byrne (R)	92,907	51.5
	James C. Murray (D)	87,677	48.6
4	William E. McVey (R)	155,447	60.0
	Michael Hinko (D)	103,494	40.0
5	John C. Kluczynski (D)	96,399	61.8
	Lawrence Welnowski (R)	59,608	38.2
6	Thomas J. O'Brien (D)	94,281	62.0
	John J. Dillon (R)	57,750	38.0
7	James B. Bowler (D)	93,732	71.7
	Gabriel L. Grimaldi (R)	37,068	28.3
8	Thomas S. Gordon (D)	73,628	59.5
	Victor O. Wright (R)	50,055	40.5
9	Sidney R. Yates (D)	75,511	54.0
	Johann S. Ackerman (R)	64,237	46.0
10	Harold R. Collier (R)	132,928	64.5
	Marvin E. Lore (D)	73,331	35.6
11	Timothy P. Sheehan (R)	95,140	55.5
	Roman C. Pucinski (D)	76,400	44.5
12	Charles A. Boyle (D)	100,273	53.2
	Edgar A. Jonas (R)	88,315	46.8
13	Marguerite Stitt Church (R)	229,358	71.6
	Helen Benson Leys (D)	91,059	28.4
14	Russell W. Keeney (R)	151,236	70.6
	Harold J. Spelman (D)	63,067	29.4
15	Noah M. Mason (R)	103,557	64.6
	Stanley Hubbs (D)	56,802	35.4
16	Leo E. Allen (R)	106,734	63.7
	Glen F. Kunkle (D)	60,748	36.3
17	Leslie C. Arends (R)	106,463	64.9
	C. E. Spang (D)	57,467	35.1
18	Robert H. Michel (R)	87,187	58.8
	Fred Allen (D)	61,099	41.2
19	Robert B. Chiperfield (R)	85,497	55.8
	Martin P. Sutor (D)	67,691	44.2
20	Sidney E. Simpson (R)	79,641	59.7
	Henry W. Pollock (D)	53,882	40.4
21	Peter F. Mack Jr. (D)	94,565	53.5
	Frederic S. O'Hara (R)	82,251	46.5
22	William L. Springer (R)	93,399	62.3
	E. H. Winegarner (D)	56,612	37.7
23	Charles W. Vursell (R)	79,862	52.6
	Albert R. Imle (D)	72,070	47.4
24	Melvin Price (D)	121,381	68.2
	Waldo E. Schellenger (R)	56,568	31.8
25	Kenneth J. Gray (D)	82,845	53.8
	Samuel J. Scott (R)	71,048	46.2

INDIANA

	Candidates	Votes	%
1	Ray J. Madden (D)	93,658	52.6
	Donald K. Stimson Jr. (R)	84,125	47.2
2	Charles A. Halleck (R)	94,852	62.2
	Thurman C. Crook (D)	57,049	37.4
3	F. Jay Nimtz (R)	109,907	53.1
	John Brademas (D)	97,196	46.9
4	E. Ross Adair (R)	96,531	63.5
	F. Dean Bechtol (D)	55,284	36.3
5	John V. Beamer (R)	113,586	56.4
	William C. Whitehead (D)	86,797	43.1

	Candidates	Votes	%
6	Cecil M. Harden (R)	86,020	55.0
	John W. King (D)	70,035	44.8
7	William G. Bray (R)	87,635	57.2
	Vernon R. Hill (D)	65,482	42.8
8	Winfield K. Denton (D)	95,699	50.1
	D. Bailey Merrill (R)	95,003	49.7
9	Earl Wilson (R)	70,926	53.4
	Wilfrid J. Ullrich (D)	61,465	46.3
10	Ralph Harvey (R)	98,301	56.3
	Gerald C. Carmony (D)	75,665	43.3
11	Charles B. Brownson (R)	155,541	59.4
	John C. Carvey (D)	106,021	40.5

IOWA

1	Fred D. Schwengel (R)	94,223	58.0
	Ronald O. Bramhall (D)	68,287	42.0
2	Henry O. Talle (R)	95,999	51.4
	Leonard G. Wolf (D)	90,843	48.6
3	H. R. Gross (R)	97,590	58.6
	Michael Micich (D)	69,076	41.5
4	Karl M. LeCompte (R)	58,024	50.7
	Steven V. Carter (D)	56,406	49.3
5	Paul Cunningham (R)	85,178	51.1
	William F. Denman (D)	81,418	48.9
6	Merwin Coad (D)	64,625	50.1
	James I. Dolliver (R)	64,427	49.9
7	Ben F. Jensen (R)	64,967	55.4
	John L. Jensen (D)	52,389	44.6
8	Charles B. Hoeven (R)	76,165	60.1
	Robert J. Salem (D)	50,597	39.9

KANSAS

1	William H. Avery (R)	69,841	53.1
	Howard S. Miller (D)	60,313	45.8
2	Errett P. Scrivner (R)	93,609	54.9
	Newell A. George (D)	77,049	45.2
3	Myron V. George (R)	48,246	55.0
	Denver D. Hargis (D)	39,407	45.0
4	Edward H. Rees (R)	111,970	53.8
	John D. Montgomery (D)	96,002	46.2
5	J. Floyd Breeding (D)	64,392	50.5
	John W. Crutcher (R)	63,057	49.5
6	Wint Smith (R)	52,145	51.1
	Elmo J. Mahoney (D)	49,933	48.9

KENTUCKY

1	Noble J. Gregory (D)	75,726	100.0
2	William H. Natcher (D)	55,103	52.3
	R. B. Blankenship (R)	50,266	47.7
3	John M. Robsion Jr. (R)	111,598	56.8
	Philip Ardery (D)	84,912	43.2
4	Frank Chelf (D)	51,675	56.3
	John B. Preston (R)	40,129	43.7
5	Brent Spence (D)	59,402	55.9
	Jule Appel (R)	46,821	44.1
6	John C. Watts (D)	69,468	52.7
	Wallace Jones (R)	62,313	47.3
7	Carl D. Perkins (D)	77,564	52.4
	Scott Craft (R)	70,450	47.6
8	Eugene Siler (R)	80,067	71.7
	W. D. Scalf (D)	31,632	28.3

LOUISIANA

1	F. Edward Hebert (D)	69,500	100.0
2	Hale Boggs (D)	69,715	64.5
	George R. Blue (R)	38,344	35.5
3	Edwin E. Willis (D)	19,075	100.0
4	Overton Brooks (D)	40,583	68.1
	Calhoun Allen Jr. (R)	19,041	31.9
5	Otto E. Passman (D)	18,210	100.0
6	James H. Morrison (D)	58,414	100.0
7	T. A. Thompson (D)	36,432	100.0
8	George S. Long (D)	18,341	100.0

MAINE

	Candidates	Votes	%
1	Robert Hale (R)	58,028	50.0
	James C. Oliver (D)	57,999	50.0
2	Frank M. Coffin (D)	55,430	53.4
	James L. Reid (R)	48,292	46.6
3	Clifford G. McIntire (R)	44,095	60.7
	Kenneth B. Colbath (D)	28,612	39.4

MARYLAND

1	Edward T. Miller (R)	42,731	55.7
	Hamilton P. Fox (D)	33,961	44.3
2	James P. S. Devereux (R)	103,103	58.1
	A. Gordon Boone (D)	74,224	41.9
3	Edward A. Garmatz (D)	48,397	69.8
	Harry Kemper (R)	20,990	30.3
4	George H. Fallon (D)	44,260	53.8
	George Denys Hubbard (R)	37,957	46.2
5	Richard E. Lankford (D)	88,227	56.8
	William B. Prendergast (R)	67,072	43.2
6	DeWitt S. Hyde (R)	100,580	54.3
	John R. Foley (D)	84,837	45.8
7	Samuel N. Friedel (D)	70,512	59.0
	David A. Halley (R)	48,949	41.0

MASSACHUSETTS

1	John W. Heselton (R)	92,269	63.6
	Howard W. Shea (D)	52,213	36.0
2	Edward P. Boland (D)	103,563	61.2
	Foster W. Doty (R)	65,598	38.8
3	Philip J. Philbin (D)	114,848	70.9
	Robert A. Parker (R)	47,041	29.1
4	Harold D. Donohue (D)	104,653	59.4
	Mary R. Wheeler (R)	71,437	40.6
5	Edith Nourse Rogers (R)	150,957	73.3
	Lawrence E. Corcoran (D)	55,038	26.7
6	William H. Bates (R)	131,310	100.0
7	Thomas J. Lane (D)	87,415	64.5
	Robert T. Breed (R)	48,173	35.5
8	Torbert H. Macdonald (D)	92,463	54.8
	C. Eugene Farnam (R)	76,312	45.2
9	Donald W. Nicholson (R)	111,860	61.1
	William McAuliffe (D)	71,245	38.9
10	Laurence Curtis (R)	93,327	53.0
	Jackson J. Holtz (D)	82,882	47.0
11	Thomas P. O'Neill Jr. (D)	83,532	75.3
	Rudolph E. Mottola (R)	27,384	24.7
12	John W. McCormack (D)	89,943	82.5
	James S. Tremblay (R)	19,099	17.5
13	Richard B. Wigglesworth (R)	109,950	55.6
	Richard E. McCormack (D)	87,719	44.4
14	Joseph W. Martin Jr. (R)	111,420	62.4
	Edward F. Doolan (D)	67,183	37.6

MICHIGAN

1	Thaddeus M. Machrowicz (D)	112,290	86.1
	Walter Czarnecki (R)	18,137	13.9
2	George Meader (R)	105,940	63.1
	Franklin J. Shepherd (D)	61,456	36.6
3	August E. Johansen (R)	100,056	63.8
	Truman Barkhuff (D)	56,119	35.8
4	Clare E. Hoffman (R)	83,876	62.0
	Samuel I. Clark (D)	51,491	38.0
5	Gerald R. Ford Jr. (R)	120,349	67.1
	George E. Clay (D)	58,899	32.9
6	Charles E. Chamberlain (R)	116,570	50.8
	Don Hayworth (D)	112,603	49.0
7	Robert J. McIntosh (R)	114,674	53.7
	Ira D. McCoy (D)	98,928	46.3
8	Alvin M. Bentley (R)	93,357	64.1
	William R. Hart (D)	51,897	35.6
9	Robert P. Griffin (R)	68,166	56.0
	William E. Baker (D)	53,609	44.0
10	Elford A. Cederberg (R)	72,781	65.6
	William J. Kelly (D)	38,166	34.4
11	Victor A. Knox (R)	53,117	56.1
	Prentiss M. Brown Jr. (D)	41,600	43.9

	Candidates	Votes	%
12	John B. Bennett (R)	45,721	58.3
	Joseph S. Mack (D)	35,434	43.7
13	Charles C. Diggs Jr. (D)	87,353	69.8
	Willis F. Ward (R)	37,860	30.2
14	Louis C. Rabaut (D)	122,079	56.8
	Harold F. Youngblood (R)	92,933	43.2
15	John D. Dingell (D)	111,827	74.1
	Larry Middleton (R)	38,973	25.8
16	John Lesinski (D)	176,663	64.1
	Arthur Kurtz (R)	98,172	35.6
17	Martha W. Griffiths (D)	112,811	53.3
	George E. Smith (R)	98,432	46.5
18	William S. Broomfield (R)	141,058	56.7
	Paul Sutton (D)	107,609	43.3

MINNESOTA

1	August H. Andresen (R)	92,092	61.5
	Arnold L. Fredriksen (DFL)	57,747	38.5
2	Joseph P. O'Hara (R)	97,520	63.8
	Harold Zupp (DFL)	55,336	36.2
3	Roy W. Wier (DFL)	127,356	52.0
	George Mikan (R)	117,716	48.0
4	Eugene J. McCarthy (DFL)	103,320	64.1
	Edward C. Slettedahl (R)	57,947	35.9
5	Walter H. Judd (R)	82,258	56.0
	Joseph Robbie (DFL)	64,602	44.0
6	Fred Marshall (DFL)	76,396	56.2
	Joseph L. Kaczmarek (R)	59,568	43.8
7	H. Carl Andersen (R)	76,271	55.9
	Clint Haroldson (DFL)	60,168	44.1
8	John A. Blatnik (DFL)	108,565	73.2
	Alfred J. Weinberg (R)	39,795	26.8
9	Coya Knutson (DFL)	58,916	52.7
	Harold C. Hagen (R)	52,937	47.3

MISSISSIPPI

1	Thomas G. Abernethy (D)	38,021	100.0
2	Jamie L. Whitten (D)	23,513	100.0
3	Frank E. Smith (D)	19,369	100.0
4	John Bell Williams (D)	42,085	100.0
5	Arthur Winstead (D)	35,461	100.0
6	William M. Colmer (D)	47,083	100.0

MISSOURI

1	Frank M. Karsten (D)	136,873	66.3
	Bill Bangert (R)	69,661	33.7
2	Thomas B. Curtis (R)	123,596	51.8
	James L. Sullivan (D)	114,837	48.2
3	Leonor K. Sullivan (D)	96,416	69.7
	Sidney R. Redmond (R)	42,023	30.4
4	George H. Christopher (D)	98,106	51.8
	Jeffrey P. Hillelson (R)	91,392	48.2
5	Richard Bolling (D)	77,287	57.2
	Lemot Jones Jr. (R)	57,778	42.8
6	W. R. Hull Jr. (D)	85,021	52.0
	Stanley I. Dale (R)	78,637	48.1
7	Charles H. Brown (D)	90,986	50.3
	Dewey Short (R)	89,926	49.7
8	A. S. J. Carnahan (D)	69,336	54.3
	Frank W. May (R)	58,425	45.7
9	Clarence Cannon (D)	100,065	100.0
10	Paul C. Jones (D)	69,536	100.0
11	Morgan M. Moulder (D)	72,594	50.8
	George H. Miller (R)	70,286	49.2

MONTANA

1	Lee Metcalf (D)	69,644	62.1
	W. D. McDonald (R)	42,591	38.0
2	Leroy H. Anderson (D)	76,805	50.9
	Orvin B. Fjare (R)	74,164	49.1

NEBRASKA

1	Phil Weaver (R)	102,012	67.0
	Samuel Freeman (D)	50,351	33.1
2	Glenn Cunningham (R)	77,253	53.4

Candidates	Votes	%
Joseph V. Benesch (D)	65,039	45.0
3 Robert D. Harrison (R)	62,645	50.1
Lawrence Brock (D)	62,399	49.9
4 Arthur L. Miller (R)	81,731	65.8
Carlton W. Laird (D)	42,583	34.3

NEVADA

AL Walter S. Baring (D)	51,100	54.2
Richard W. Horton (R)	43,154	45.8

NEW HAMPSHIRE

1 Chester E. Merrow (R)	78,296	57.4
James B. Sullivan (D)	58,104	42.6
2 Perkins Bass (R)	77,019	66.0
George F. Brown (D)	39,726	34.0

NEW JERSEY

1 Charles A. Wolverton (R)	133,153	58.3
J. Frank Crawford (D)	94,758	41.5
2 T. Millet Hand (R)	83,433*	67.9
Thomas C. Stewart (D)	39,383	32.0
3 James C. Auchincloss (R)	136,780	65.3
Sidney Shiff (D)	72,617	34.7
4 Frank Thompson Jr. (D)	89,646	54.5
William H. Wells (R)	74,737	45.5
5 Peter H. B. Frelinghuysen Jr. (R)	153,829	64.5
Francis C. Foley Jr. (D)	84,374	35.4
6 Florence P. Dwyer (R)	106,414	50.6
Harrison A. Williams Jr. (D)	102,015	48.5
7 William B. Widnall (R)	151,573	70.7
Daniel Amster (D)	62,924	29.3
8 Gordon Canfield (R)	96,494	60.8
Walter H. Gardner (D)	61,464	38.7
9 Frank C. Osmers Jr. (R)	135,498	67.8
Robert D. Gruen (D)	63,728	31.9
10 Peter W. Rodino Jr. (D)	71,311	56.1
G. George Addonizio (R)	55,761	43.9
11 Hugh J. Addonizio (D)	63,482	51.7
Chester K. Ligham (R)	57,447	46.8
12 Robert Winthrop Kean (R)	90,032	59.7
Irving L. Hodes (D)	58,364	38.7
13 Alfred D. Sieminski (D)	54,841	45.0
Norman H. Roth (R)	54,784	44.9
14 Vincent J. Dellay (R)	61,600	52.3
T. James Tumulty (D)	53,713	45.6

NEW MEXICO

AL John J. Dempsey (D)	129,625✓	
Antonio M. Fernandez (D)	128,330*	
Dudley Cornell (R)	114,719	
Forrest Atchley (R)	112,531	

NEW YORK

1 Stuyvesant Wainwright (R)	191,356	65.8
T. Bronson O'Reilly (D, L)	99,304	34.2
2 Steven B. Derounian (R)	148,098	67.5
Julius J. Damato (D, L)	71,422	32.5
3 Frank J. Becker (R)	143,559	61.9
Francis X. Hardiman (D, L)	88,245	38.1
4 Henry J. Latham (R)	116,470	55.8
Joseph J. Perrini (D, L)	92,217	44.2
5 Albert H. Bosch (R)	87,154	58.6
John J. Quinn (D, L)	61,678	41.4
6 Lester Holtzman (D, L)	128,545	56.9
Albert H. Buschmann (R)	97,558	43.2
7 James J. Delaney (D)	78,030	50.0
Joseph Stockinger (R)	77,928	50.0
8 Victor L. Anfuso (D, L)	59,998	65.6
Julius Reinlieb (R)	31,399	34.4
9 Eugene J. Keogh (D, L)	75,814	62.8
Benjamin W. Feldman (R)	44,916	37.2
10 Edna F. Kelly (D, L)	100,808	73.2
Abraham Sher (R)	36,878	26.8

Candidates	Votes	%
11 Emanuel Celler (D, L)	131,508	77.7
Henry D. Dorfman (R)	37,651	22.3
12 Francis E. Dorn (R)	76,137	57.6
Donald L. O'Toole (D, L)	56,035	42.4
13 Abraham J. Multer (D, L)	110,469	71.2
Joseph Moriber (R)	44,771	28.8
14 John J. Rooney (D, L)	77,706	64.2
Jacob P. Lefkowitz (R)	43,343	35.8
15 John H. Ray (R)	98,093	61.4
Ralph Di Iorio (D, L)	60,989	38.2
16 Adam Clayton Powell Jr. (D)	59,339	69.7
Joseph A. Bailey (R)	16,960	19.9
Formington Taylor (L)	8,801	10.3
17 Frederic R. Coudert Jr. (R)	68,874	50.9
Anthony B. Akers (D, L)	66,396	49.1
18 Alfred E. Santangelo (D, L)	47,953	58.0
James G. Donovan (R)	34,748	42.0
19 Leonard Farbstein (D, L)	68,411	68.4
Maurice G. Henry Jr. (R)	31,546	31.6
20 Ludwig Teller (D, L)	70,726	63.8
Milton H. Adler (R)	40,191	36.2
21 Herbert Zelenko (D, L)	81,464	66.5
Dalton J. Shapo (R)	41,070	33.5
22 James C. Healey (D)	88,441	64.1
Henry Rose (R)	34,084	24.7
David I. Wells (L)	15,524	11.3
23 Isidore Dollinger (D)	70,238	68.5
Philip Myer (R)	22,414	21.9
Hyman Fromowitz (L)	9,880	9.6
24 Charles A. Buckley (D)	90,076	54.7
Harold Grosberg (R)	53,172	32.3
Elias Rosenblatt (L)	21,444	13.0
25 Paul A. Fino (R)	104,771	59.4
Edward A. Cunningham (D)	62,729	35.5
Bernard Tobacman (L)	8,989	5.1
26 Edwin B. Dooley (R)	123,996	67.5
Julia L. Crews (D, L)	59,842	32.6
27 Ralph W. Gwinn (R)	117,100	58.1
William D. Carlebach (D, L)	84,568	41.9
28 Katharine St. George (R)	103,114	62.2
William H. Mauldin (D, L)	62,770	37.8
29 J. Ernest Wharton (R)	124,211	71.4
Vincent di Gennaro (D, L)	49,725	28.6
30 Leo W. O'Brien (D, L)	104,022	55.8
Robert E. Gray (R)	82,429	44.2
31 Dean P. Taylor (R)	116,682	71.8
Theodore A. Knapp (D, L)	45,767	28.2
32 Bernard W. Kearney (R)	107,959	67.5
R. Joseph Giblin (D, L)	52,064	32.5
33 Clarence E. Kilburn (R)	103,419	72.7
Louis C. Britton (D, L)	38,793	27.3
34 William R. Williams (R)	95,681	57.5
Edwin L. Slusarczyk (D, L)	70,837	42.5
35 R. Walter Riehlman (R)	124,108	67.1
Thomas J. Lowery (D)	59,534	32.2
36 John Taber (R)	109,101	69.6
Lewis S. Bell (D, L)	47,764	30.4
37 Sterling Cole (R)	136,044	71.7
Francis P. Hogan (D, L)	53,830	28.4
38 Kenneth B. Keating (R)	135,572	71.7
Reed Harding (D, L)	53,477	28.3
39 Harold C. Ostertag (R)	116,043	70.5
William H. Mostyn (D, L)	48,634	29.5
40 William E. Miller (R)	117,051	64.3
A. Thorne Hills (D, L)	64,872	35.7
41 Edmund P. Radwan (R)	99,151	64.4
Edward P. Jehle (D, L)	54,776	35.6
42 John R. Pillion (R)	117,178	58.7
James Kane Jr. (D)	80,568	40.3
43 Daniel A. Reed (R)	93,079	68.7
T. Joseph Lynch (D, L)	42,476	31.3

Special Election

22 James C. Healey (D)	9,473	72.3
Sidney Burnstein (L)	1,943	14.8
Barnett Davis (R)	1,691	12.9

NORTH CAROLINA

Candidates	Votes	%
1 Herbert C. Bonner (D)	44,271	88.6
Zeno O. Ratcliff (R)	5,693	11.4
2 L. H. Fountain (D)	49,812	100.0
3 Graham A. Barden (D)	47,251	78.8
Joe Reynolds (R)	12,698	21.2
4 Harold D. Cooley (D)	76,560	100.0
5 Ralph J. Scott (D)	58,552	59.7
Joe New (R)	39,561	40.3
6 Carl T. Durham (D)	73,111	100.0
7 Alton Lennon (D)	65,424	84.0
C. Dana Malpass (R)	12,477	16.0
8 A. Paul Kitchin (D)	64,220	59.5
Fred Myers (R)	43,732	40.5
9 Hugh Q. Alexander (D)	68,181	53.9
A. M. Miller (R)	58,407	46.1
10 Charles Raper Jonas (R)	89,743	62.7
Ben E. Douglas (D)	53,475	37.3
11 Basil L. Whitener (D)	59,417	100.0
12 George A. Shuford (D)	55,927	54.5
Richard C. Clarke Jr. (R)	46,760	45.5

NORTH DAKOTA

AL Usher L. Burdick (R)	143,514✓	
Otto Krueger (R)	136,003✓	
Agnes Geelan (D)	85,743	
S. B. Hocking (D)	83,284	

OHIO

1 Gordon H. Scherer (R)	91,181	64.7
Leonard D. Slutz (D)	49,701	35.3
2 William E. Hess (R)	109,099	65.5
James T. Dewan (D)	57,554	34.5
3 Paul F. Schenck (R)	135,152	59.0
R. William Patterson (D)	93,782	41.0
4 William M. McCulloch (R)	93,607	68.8
Ortha O. Barr Jr. (R)	42,416	31.2
5 Cliff Clevenger (R)	69,774	62.3
George E. Rafferty (D)	42,181	37.7
6 James G. Polk (D)	72,229	54.5
Albert L. Daniels (R)	60,300	45.5
7 Clarence J. Brown (R)	91,439	66.0
Joseph A. Sullivan (D)	47,220	34.1
8 Jackson E. Betts (R)	70,690	63.5
Robert M. Corry (D)	40,716	36.6
9 Thomas L. Ashley (D)	100,696	55.3
Harvey G. Straub (R)	81,562	44.8
10 Thomas A. Jenkins (R)	71,295	100.0
11 David S. Dennison Jr. (R)	96,707	58.4
James P. Bennett (D)	68,831	41.6
12 John M. Vorys (R)	128,682	61.8
Walter J. Shapter Jr. (D)	79,597	38.2
13 A. D. Baumhart Jr. (R)	79,324	70.7
J. P. Henderson (D)	32,900	29.3
14 William H. Ayres (R)	123,105	58.9
Bernard Rosen (D)	85,946	41.1
15 John E. Henderson (R)	55,126	60.5
Herbert U. Smith (D)	35,954	39.5
16 Frank T. Bow (R)	101,324	55.2
John McSweeney (D)	82,206	44.8
17 J. Harry McGregor (R)	88,931	66.5
Robert W. Levering (D)	44,806	33.5
18 Wayne L. Hays (D)	78,962	59.6
Joseph Miller (R)	53,627	40.5
19 Michael J. Kirwan (D)	92,924	68.7
Ralph E. Turner (R)	42,293	31.3
20 Michael A. Feighan (D)	105,562	65.3
John H. Ferguson (R)	56,209	34.8
21 Charles A. Vanik (D)	96,106	71.6
Charles H. Loeb (R)	38,060	28.4
22 Frances P. Bolton (R)	96,468	66.7
Harry A. Blachman (D)	48,169	33.3
23 William E. Minshall Jr. (R)	102,707	69.0
George A. Hurley (D)	46,247	31.1

OKLAHOMA

	Candidates	Votes	%
1	Page Belcher (R)	114,896	57.2
	Harry B. Moreland (D)	86,123	42.8
2	Ed Edmondson (D)	83,976	60.2
	Percy Butler (R)	55,416	39.8
3	Carl Albert (D)	60,620	76.5
	Chapin Wallace (R)	18,182	23.0
4	Tom Steed (D)	57,416	61.1
	Harold H. Potter (R)	36,534	38.9
5	John Jarman (D)	110,416	63.7
	Hobart H. Hobbs (R)	62,812	36.3
6	Toby Morris (D)	86,770	68.9
	Fred L. Coogan (R)	39,153	31.1

OREGON

	Candidates	Votes	%
1	Walter Norblad (R)	109,360	54.7
	Jason Lee (D)	90,567	45.3
2	Al Ullman (D)	53,219	50.7
	Sam Coon (R)	51,844	49.4
3	Edith Green (D)	146,250	61.6
	Phil J. Roth (R)	91,239	38.4
4	Charles O. Porter (D)	90,355	51.3
	Harris Ellsworth (R)	85,860	48.7

PENNSYLVANIA

	Candidates	Votes	%
1	William A. Barrett (D)	74,511	62.7
	A. J. Cammarota (R)	44,333	37.3
2	Kathryn E. Granahan (D)	95,567	62.3
	Robert F. Frankenfield (R)	57,773	37.7
3	James A. Byrne (D)	71,161	59.9
	Charles H. Sporkin (R)	47,550	40.1
4	Earl Chudoff (D)	75,374	69.1
	Horace C. Scott (R)	33,672	30.9
5	William J. Green Jr. (D)	107,021	53.3
	James J. Schissler (R)	93,612	46.7
6	Hugh Scott (R)	90,966	51.5
	Herbert J. McGlinchey (D)	85,541	48.5
7	Benjamin F. James (R)	137,764	61.9
	William A. Welsh (D)	84,764	38.1
8	Willard S. Curtin (R)	98,023	55.9
	John P. Fullam (D)	77,229	44.1
9	Paul B. Dague (R)	110,230	68.4
	Edward G. Wilson (D)	50,947	31.6
10	Joseph L. Carrigg (R)	91,103	55.8
	Jerome P. Casey (D)	72,178	44.2
11	Daniel J. Flood (D)	83,178	53.1
	Enoch H. Thomas Jr. (R)	73,606	47.0
12	Ivor D. Fenton (R)	72,125	56.5
	George G. Lindsay (D)	55,642	43.6
13	Samuel K. McConnell Jr. (R)	127,627	66.7
	Alfred M. Klein (D)	63,610	33.3
14	George M. Rhodes (D)	51,088	51.3
	Thomas K. Leinbach (R)	48,129	48.4
15	Francis E. Walter (D)	63,204	55.6
	George M. Berg (R)	50,491	44.4
16	Walter M. Mumma (R)	84,617	60.5
	Guy J. Swope (D)	55,260	39.5
17	Alvin R. Bush (R)	74,748	58.6
	Dean R. Fisher (D)	52,900	41.4
18	Richard M. Simpson (R)	77,833	59.9
	Ross E. Hershberger (D)	52,180	40.1
19	S. Walter Stauffer (R)	79,448	53.8
	James M. Quigley (D)	68,171	46.2
20	James E. Van Zandt (R)	65,457	63.0
	John R. Stewart (D)	38,483	37.0
21	Augustine B. Kelley (D)	78,744	56.8
	Herbert O. Morrison (R)	59,786	43.2
22	John P. Saylor (R)	85,540	56.9
	Joseph C. Dolan (D)	64,689	43.1
23	Leon H. Gavin (R)	72,365	66.1
	Grace M. Sloan (D)	37,122	33.9
24	Carroll D. Kearns (R)	93,824	57.8
	William D. Thomas (D)	68,625	42.2
25	Frank M. Clark (D)	81,339	51.3
	Sidney L. Lockley (R)	77,150	48.7
26	Thomas E. Morgan (D)	104,049	61.9
	I. Willits McCaskey (R)	64,129	38.1
27	James G. Fulton (R)	126,247	66.0
	Kenneth L. Stilley (D)	64,917	34.0
28	Herman P. Eberharter (D)	88,725	57.8
	Richard C. Witt (R)	64,905	42.3
29	Robert J. Corbett (R)	114,109	64.7
	Joseph A. Guerrier (D)	62,225	35.3
30	Elmer J. Holland (D)	103,389	59.8
	Ross V. Walker (R)	69,495	40.2

RHODE ISLAND

	Candidates	Votes	%
1	Aime J. Forand (D)	96,732	55.8
	Samuel H. Ramsay (R)	76,714	44.2
2	John E. Fogerty (D)	105,496	52.2
	Thomas H. Needham (R)	96,568	47.8

SOUTH CAROLINA

	Candidates	Votes	%
1	L. Mendel Rivers (D)	31,112	100.0
2	John J. Riley (D)	49,284	100.0
3	W. J. Bryan Dorn (D)	39,270	92.9
	Mrs. Maka Knox (R)	2,885	6.8
4	Robert T. Ashmore (D)	53,722	85.1
	Dan H. Wallace Jr (R)	9,393	14.9
5	Robert Hemphill (D)	36,454	100.0
6	John L. McMillan (D)	39,749	100.0

SOUTH DAKOTA

	Candidates	Votes	%
1	George McGovern (D)	116,516	52.4
	Harold O. Lovre (R)	105,835	47.6
2	E. Y. Berry (R)	36,681	55.9
	Tom Eastman Jr. (D)	28,984	44.1

TENNESSEE

	Candidates	Votes	%
1	B. Carroll Reece (R)	86,531	72.1
	Arthur Bright (D)	33,403	27.9
2	Howard H. Baker (R)	90,127	100.0
3	James B. Frazier Jr. (D)	55,715	53.7
	P. H. Wood (R)	47,954	46.3
4	Joe L. Evins (D)	56,191	98.4
5	J. Carlton Loser (D)	54,318	74.5
	George S. Spence (R)	18,585	25.5
6	Ross Bass (D)	47,098	100.0
7	Tom Murray (D)	36,301	100.0
8	Jere Cooper (D)	27,485	100.0
9	Clifford Davis (D)	90,874	71.8
	Herbert Harper (R)	35,783	28.3

TEXAS

	Candidates	Votes	%
1	Wright Patman (D)	54,837	100.0
2	Jack Brooks (D)	81,343	100.0
3	Lindley Beckworth (D)	47,570	83.5
	R. E. Kennedy (R)	9,402	16.5
4	Sam Rayburn (D)	41,867	100.0
5	Bruce Alger (R)	102,380	55.6
	Henry Wade (D)	81,705	44.4
6	Olin Teague (D)	42,383	100.0
7	John Dowdy (D)	44,456	100.0
8	Albert Thomas (D)	137,950	60.5
	C. A. Friloux Jr. (R)	86,640	38.0
9	Clark W. Thompson (D)	88,487	100.0
10	Homer Thornberry (D)	68,697	100.0
11	W. R. Poage (D)	56,990	100.0
12	Jim Wright (D)	110,196	100.0
13	Frank Ikard (D)	66,108	100.0
14	John Young (D)	85,922	87.3
	Olive B. Stichter (R)	12,517	12.7
15	Joe M. Kilgore (D)	64,011	100.0
16	J. T. Rutherford (D)	50,704	64.6
	Charles H. Gibson (R)	27,821	35.4
17	Omar Burleson (D)	53,003	100.0
18	Walter Rogers (D)	75,243	100.0
19	George Mahon (D)	85,566	100.0
20	Paul J. Kilday (D)	67,707	100.0
21	O. C. Fisher (D)	60,344	100.0
AL	Martin Dies (D)	1,436,831	98.5

UTAH

	Candidates	Votes	%
1	Henry Aldous Dixon (R)	74,107	60.9
	Carlyle F. Gronning (D)	47,533	39.1
2	William A. Dawson (R)	119,683	57.6
	Oscar W. McConkie Jr. (D)	87,970	42.4

VERMONT

		Votes	%
AL	Winston L. Prouty (R)	103,736	67.1
	Camille E. St. Amour (D)	50,797	32.9

VIRGINIA

	Candidates	Votes	%
1	Edward J. Robeson Jr. (D)	31,839	50.8
	Horace E. Henderson (R)	30,799	49.2
2	Porter Hardy Jr. (D)	46,958	76.4
	William R. Burns (R)	14,483	23.6
3	J. Vaughan Gary (D)	46,109	59.1
	Roy E. Cabell Jr. (R)	31,947	40.9
4	Watkins M. Abbitt (D)	51,434	99.9
5	William M. Tuck (D)	39,771	67.4
	Jackson L. Kiser (R)	19,263	32.6
6	Richard H. Poff (R)	51,279	62.1
	John L. Whitehead (D)	31,043	37.6
7	Burr P. Harrison (D)	40,069	69.0
	A. R. Dunning (R)	17,970	31.0
8	Howard W. Smith (D)	38,648	67.3
	Horace B. Clay (R)	18,813	32.7
9	W. Pat Jennings (D)	49,448	54.1
	William C. Wampler (R)	41,957	45.9
10	Joel T. Broyhill (R)	53,149	56.2
	Warren D. Quenstedt (D)	40,553	42.9

WASHINGTON

	Candidates	Votes	%
1	Thomas M. Pelly (R)	129,768	58.1
	James B. Wilson (D)	93,492	41.9
2	Jack Westland (R)	105,975	56.0
	Payson Peterson (D)	83,195	44.0
3	Russell V. Mack (R)	80,520	56.5
	Al McCoy (D)	61,962	43.5
4	Hal Holmes (R)	76,769	50.4
	Frank LeRoux (D)	75,519	49.6
5	Walt Horan (R)	83,230	53.8
	Tom Delaney (D)	71,571	46.2
6	Thor C. Tollefson (R)	108,014	54.0
	John T. McCutcheon (D)	91,878	46.0
AL	Don Magnuson (D)	621,118	58.5
	Philip Evans (R)	439,896	41.5

WEST VIRGINIA

	Candidates	Votes	%
1	Arch A. Moore Jr. (R)	65,096	50.3
	C. Lee Spillers (D)	64,334	49.7
2	Harley O. Staggers (D)	63,327	52.4
	Mary Elkins (R)	57,597	47.6
3	Cleveland M. Bailey (D)	62,240	51.5
	Daniel L. Louchery (R)	58,623	48.5
4	Will E. Neal (R)	78,225	52.8
	M. G. Burnside (D)	69,871	47.2
5	Elizabeth Kee (D)	68,638	60.7
	William H. Sanders (R)	44,479	39.3
6	Robert C. Byrd (D)	99,854	57.4
	Cleo S. Jones (R)	74,110	42.6

WISCONSIN

	Candidates	Votes	%
1	Lawrence H. Smith (R)	94,882	57.1
	Gerald T. Flynn (D)	71,379	42.9
2	Donald E. Tewes (R)	101,444	55.3
	Robert W. Kastenmeier (D)	81,922	44.7
3	Gardner R. Withrow (R)	74,000	61.2
	Norman M. Clapp (D)	46,911	38.8
4	Clement J. Zablocki (D)	128,213	65.7
	William J. Burke (R)	67,063	34.3
5	Henry S. Reuss (D)	118,603	57.8
	Russell Wirth Jr. (R)	86,764	42.3
6	William K. Van Pelt (R)	96,783	67.2
	Rudolph J. Ploetz (D)	47,277	32.8

	Candidates	Votes	%
7	Melvin R. Laird (R)	80,143	61.9
	Margaret Anderson (D)	49,442	38.2
8	John W. Byrnes (R)	97,952	64.7
	Milo Singler (D)	53,567	35.4
9	Lester R. Johnson (D)	62,476	51.4
	Arthur L. Peterson (R)	59,024	48.6
10	Alvin E. O'Konski (R)	67,250	64.5
	Carl E. Lauri (D)	36,941	35.5

WYOMING

	Candidates	Votes	%
AL	Keith Thomson (R)	69,903	58.2
	Jerry A. O'Callaghan (D)	50,225	41.8

1957 House Elections

ILLINOIS

Special Election

	Candidates	Votes	%
7	Roland V. Libonati (D)	32,221	88.1
	Anthony C. Catena (R)	4,353	11.9

NEW JERSEY

Special Election

		Votes	%
2	Milton W. Glenn (R)	58,129	54.8
	Joseph G. Hancock (D)	47,647	44.9

1958 House Elections

ALABAMA

	Candidates	Votes	%
1	Frank W. Boykin (D)	19,499	100.0
2	George Grant (D)	27,972	100.0
3	George W. Andrews (D)	17,389	100.0
4	Kenneth A. Roberts (D)	25,133	100.0
5	Albert Rains (D)	31,687	100.0
6	Armistead I. Selden Jr. (D)	18,557	100.0
7	Carl Elliott (D)	29,936	100.0
8	Robert E. Jones (D)	22,710	100.0
9	George Huddleston Jr. (D)	38,229	86.3
	Frank L. Mason (R)	6,050	13.7

ALASKA

(Became a state Jan. 3, 1959)

	Candidates	Votes	%
AL	Ralph J. Rivers (D)	27,945	57.5
	Henry A. Benson (R)	20,699	42.6

ARIZONA

	Candidates	Votes	%
1	John J. Rhodes (R)	86,959	59.3
	Joe Haldiman Jr. (D)	59,816	40.8
2	Stewart L. Udall (D)	79,651	60.9
	John G. Speiden (R)	51,140	39.1

ARKANSAS

	Candidates	Votes	%
1	Ezekiel C. Gathings (D)		100.0
2	Wilbur D. Mills (D)		100.0
3	James W. Trimble (D)		100.0
4	Oran Harris (D)		100.0
5	Dale Alford (WRITE IN)	30,739	51.0
	Brooks Hays (D)	29,483	49.0
6	William F. Norrell (D)		100.0

CALIFORNIA

	Candidates	Votes	%
1	Clem W. Miller (D)	102,096	54.9
	Frederick G. Dupuis (R)	83,807	45.1
2	Harold T. Johnson (D)	90,850	61.0
	Curtis W. Tarr (R)	58,199	39.1
3	John E. Moss Jr. (D-R)	169,727	100.0
4	William S. Mailliard (R)	98,574	60.0
	George D. Collins Jr. (D)	65,798	40.0
5	John F. Shelley (D-R)	99,171	100.0
6	John F. Baldwin Jr. (R)	92,669	51.0
	Howard H. Jewel (D)	89,192	49.0
7	Jeffery Cohelan (D)	65,699	50.9
	John J. Allen Jr. (R)	63,270	49.1
8	George P. Miller (D-R)	181,437	100.0
9	J. Arthur Younger (R)	90,735	58.8
	Elma D. Oddstad (D)	63,597	41.2
10	Charles S. Gubser (R)	118,715	54.6
	Russell B. Bryan (D)	98,894	45.4
11	John J. McFall (D)	86,924	69.3
	Frederick S. Van Dyke (R)	38,427	30.7
12	B. F. Sisk (D)	112,702	81.1
	Daniel K. Halpin (R)	26,228	18.9
13	Charles M. Teague (R)	98,381	57.0
	William Kirk Stewart (D)	74,160	43.0
14	Harlan Hagen (D-R)	120,347	99.9
15	Gordon L. McDonough (R)	77,267	52.0
	Emery S. Petty (D)	71,192	48.0
16	Donald L. Jackson (R)	70,724	57.8
	Melvin Lennard (D)	51,616	42.2
17	Cecil R. King (D)	182,965	75.3
	Leonard Di Miceli (R)	59,973	24.7
18	Craig Hosmer (R)	95,682	60.0
	Harry S. May (D)	63,684	40.0
19	Chet Holifield (D)	131,421	83.4
	Harry Vincent Leppek (R)	26,092	16.6
20	H. Allen Smith (R)	72,311	66.0
	Raymond Robert Farrell (D)	37,331	34.1
21	Edgar W. Hiestand (R)	127,238	51.9

	Candidates	Votes	%
	Mrs. Rudd Brown (D)	118,141	48.1
22	Joe Holt (R)	87,785	55.4
	Irving Glasband (D)	70,777	44.6
23	Clyde Doyle (D-R)	140,817	100.0
24	Glenard P. Lipscomb (R)	68,184	56.4
	William H. Ware Jr. (D)	52,804	43.6
25	George A. Kasem (D)	135,009	50.1
	Prescott O. Lieberg (R)	134,406	49.9
26	James Roosevelt (D)	125,495	72.2
	Crispus Wright (R)	48,248	27.8
27	Harry R. Sheppard (D)	105,062	72.3
	Robert M. Castle (R)	40,317	27.7
28	James B. Utt (R)	152,855	58.2
	T. R. Boyett (D)	109,794	41.8
29	Dalip S. Saund (D)	64,518	62.4
	John Babbage (R)	38,899	37.6
30	Bob Wilson (R)	112,290	55.3
	Lionel Van Deerlin (D)	90,641	44.7

COLORADO

	Candidates	Votes	%
1	Byron G. Rogers (D)	107,567	66.7
	John L. Harpel (R)	53,801	33.3
2	Byron L. Johnson (D)	95,409	53.9
	John G. Mackle (R)	80,467	45.5
3	J. Edgar Chenoweth (R)	63,655	50.2
	Fred M. Betz (D)	63,112	49.8
4	Wayne N. Aspinall (D)	43,785	63.6
	J. R. (Dick) Wells (R)	25,048	36.4

CONNECTICUT

	Candidates	Votes	%
1	Emilio Q. Daddario (D)	146,115	54.3
	Edwin H. May Jr. (R)	122,770	45.7
2	Chester Bowles (D)	79,672	53.3
	Horace Seely-Brown Jr. (R)	69,837	46.7
3	Robert N. Giaimo (D)	101,028	56.2
	Albert W. Cretella (R)	78,665	43.8
4	Donald J. Irwin (D)	119,766	50.9
	Albert P. Morano (R)	115,505	49.1
5	John S. Monagan (D)	72,604	53.8
	James T. Patterson (R)	62,353	46.2
AL	Frank Kowalski (D)	542,315	56.0
	Antoni N. Sadlak (R)	425,452	44.0

DELAWARE

	Candidates	Votes	%
AL	Harris B. McDowell Jr. (D)	76,797	50.2
	Harry G. Haskell Jr. (R)	76,099	49.8

FLORIDA

	Candidates	Votes	%
1	William C. Cramer (R)	79,876	58.8
	Winton H. King (D)	56,005	41.2
2	Charles E. Bennett (D)	32,975	100.0
3	Robert L. F. Sikes (D)	27,855	100.0
4	Dante B. Fascell (D)	56,051	100.0
5	A. Sydney Herlong Jr. (D)	63,245	67.0
	William C. Coleman (R)	31,188	33.0
6	Paul G. Rogers (D)	71,189	71.5
	Charles P. Ware (R)	28,355	28.5
7	James A. Haley (D)	28,953	100.0
8	D. R. Matthews (D)	18,669	100.0

GEORGIA

	Candidates	Votes	%
1	Prince H. Preston (D)	13,488	100.0
2	John L. Pilcher (D)	8,712	100.0
3	E. L. Forrester (D)	16,703	100.0
4	John J. Flynt Jr. (D)	17,054	100.0
5	James C. Davis (D)	32,135	100.0
6	Carl Vinson (D)	15,569	100.0
7	Harlan Erwin Mitchell (D)	13,913	100.0
8	Iris Faircloth Blitch (D)	12,940	100.0
9	Phil M. Landrum (D)	14,019	100.0
10	Paul Brown (D)	14,103	100.0

Special Election

	Candidates	Votes	%
7	Harlan Erwin Mitchell (D)	16,426	95.5

IDAHO

	Candidates	Votes	%
1	Gracie B. Pfost (D)	60,083	62.4
	A. B. Curtis (R)	36,178	37.6
2	Hamer H. Budge (R)	78,553	55.0
	Tim Brennan (D)	64,214	45.0

ILLINOIS

	Candidates	Votes	%
1	William L. Dawson (D)	60,778	72.2
	Theodore R. M. Howard (R)	23,384	27.8
2	Barratt O'Hara (D)	75,691	68.3
	Harold E. Marks (R)	34,203	30.9
3	William T. Murphy (D)	79,886	56.5
	Emmet F. Byrne (R)	55,513	39.2
4	Edward J. Derwinski (R)	106,691	52.0
	Leland H. Rayson (D)	98,657	48.0
5	John C. Kluczynski (D)	96,591	76.1
	Theodore Wozniak (R)	30,374	23.9
6	Thomas J. O'Brien (D)	90,796	73.1
	Frank S. Estes (R)	33,392	26.9
7	Roland V. Libonati (D)	90,974	83.0
	Anthony C. Catena (R)	18,595	17.0
8	Daniel D. Rostenkowski (D)	73,413	74.6
	William F. H. Schmidt (R)	25,011	25.4
9	Sidney R. Yates (D)	70,989	67.0
	Homer P. Hargraves Jr. (R)	34,909	33.0
10	Harold R. Collier (R)	84,045	54.3
	William J. McGah Jr. (D)	70,621	45.7
11	Roman C. Pucinski (D)	79,167	56.7
	Timothy P. Sheehan (R)	60,347	43.3
12	Charles A. Boyle (D)	85,129	60.8
	Allen A. Freeman (R)	54,967	39.2
13	Marguerite Stitt Church (R)	165,910	67.1
	Laurence A. Kusek (D)	81,326	32.9
14	Elmer J. Hoffman (R)	96,381	64.3
	Peter J. Fiefer (D)	53,449	35.7
15	Noah M. Mason (R)	58,829	52.5
	Dorothy G. O'Brien (D)	53,196	47.5
16	Leo E. Allen (R)	71,049	61.4
	Milton A. Lundstrom (D)	44,723	38.6
17	Leslie C. Arends (R)	70,125	61.0
	William T. Larkin (D)	44,821	39.0
18	Robert H. Michel (R)	57,929	59.5
	James W. McGee (D)	39,464	40.5
19	Robert B. Chiperfield (R)	52,049	50.5
	John C. Watson (D)	51,104	49.5
20	Edna Simpson (R)	57,412	55.3
	Henry W. Pollock (D)	46,076	44.4
21	Peter F. Mack Jr. (D)	87,134	58.8
	Norma Eaton (R)	61,137	41.2
22	William L. Springer (R)	65,080	60.5
	Carlton H. Myers (D)	42,533	39.5
23	George E. Shipley (D)	65,114	50.1
	Charles W. Vursell (R)	64,927	49.9
24	Melvin Price (D)	94,231	76.1
	Alex Chouinard (R)	29,670	24.0
25	Kenneth J. Gray (D)	78,385	58.2
	Carl D. Sneed (R)	56,257	41.8

INDIANA

	Candidates	Votes	%
1	Ray J. Madden (D)	95,801	66.4
	Edward P. Keck (R)	47,588	33.0
2	Charles A. Halleck (R)	71,933	52.2
	George H. Bowers (D)	65,792	47.8
3	John Brademas (D)	101,802	56.9
	F. Jay Nimtz (R)	77,014	43.1
4	E. Ross Adair (R)	69,745	50.1
	W. Robert Fleming (D)	69,478	49.9
5	J. Edward Roush (D)	97,184	53.7
	John V. Beamer (R)	83,852	46.3

Candidates	Votes	%
6 Fred Wampler (D)	71,669	51.5
Cecil M. Harden (R)	67,549	48.5
7 William G. Bray (R)	77,045	53.8
Thomas L. Lemon (D)	66,217	46.2
8 Winfield K. Denton (D)	100,611	61.5
Franklin E. Katterjohn (R)	63,005	38.5
9 Earl Hogan (D)	62,810	50.3
Earl Wilson (R)	62,064	49.7
10 Randall S. Harmon (D)	76,757	50.8
Ralph Harvey (R)	74,500	49.3
11 Joseph W. Barr (D)	113,674	52.1
Charles B. Brownson (R)	104,555	47.9

IOWA

Candidates	Votes	%
1 Fred Schwengel (R)	59,577	53.4
Thomas J. Dailey (D)	51,996	46.6
2 Leonard G. Wolf (D)	67,022	51.1
Henry O. Talle (R)	64,073	48.9
3 H. R. Gross (R)	61,920	53.7
Michael Micich (D)	53,467	46.3
4 Steven V. Carter (D)	42,479	52.0
John Kyl (R)	39,233	48.0
5 Neal Smith (D)	61,693	52.3
Paul Cunningham (R)	56,320	47.7
6 Merwin Coad (D)	57,491	58.3
Robert E. Waggoner (R)	41,204	41.8
7 Ben F. Jensen (R)	41,053	51.5
Ellsworth O. Hays (D)	38,660	48.5
8 Charles B. Hoeven (R)	49,418	52.7
Donald E. O'Brien (D)	44,310	47.3

KANSAS

Candidates	Votes	%
1 William H. Avery (R)	60,198	51.2
Robert W. Domme (D)	55,749	47.4
2 Newell A. George (D)	69,954	50.8
Errett P. Scrivner (R)	67,882	49.3
3 Denver D. Hargis (D)	42,718	51.7
Myron V. George (R)	39,872	48.3
4 Edward H. Rees (R)	89,611	50.7
Warner Moore (D)	87,244	49.3
5 J. Floyd Breeding (D)	60,549	53.1
Clifford R. Hope Jr. (R)	53,387	46.9
6 Wint Smith (R)	43,782	49.2
Elmo J. Mahoney (D)	43,549	49.0

KENTUCKY

Candidates	Votes	%
1 Frank Stubblefield (D)	41,214	85.0
James G. Bondy (R)	7,263	15.0
2 William H. Natcher (D)	38,941	76.1
Wayland Render (R)	12,239	23.9
3 Frank W. Burke (D)	73,121	52.2
John M. Robsion Jr. (R)	67,059	47.8
4 Frank Chelf (D)	19,310	100.0
5 Brent Spence (D)	34,919	71.9
Jule Appel (R)	13,631	28.1
6 John C. Watts (D)	29,199	94.7
Wallace Jones (I)	1,622	5.3
7 Carl D. Perkins (D)	56,756	65.8
E. L. Raybourn (R)	29,505	34.2
8 Eugene Siler (R)	34,728	68.0
W. D. Scalf (D)	16,311	32.0

LOUISIANA

Candidates	Votes	%
1 F. Edward Hebert (D)	41,861	100.0
2 Hale Boggs (D)	46,614	91.8
John Patrick Conway (R)	4,160	8.2
3 Edwin E. Willis (D)	8,692	100.0
4 Overton Brooks (D)	23,844	100.0
5 Otto E. Passman (D)	14,900	100.0
6 James H. Morrison (D)	20,599	100.0
7 T. A. Thompson (D)	10,328	100.0
8 Harold B. McSween (D)	11,125	100.0

MAINE

Candidates	Votes	%
1 James C. Oliver (D)	55,686	52.1
Robert Hale (R)	51,231	47.9
2 Frank M. Coffin (D)	59,054	61.3
Neil Bishop (R)	37,219	38.7
3 Clifford G. McIntire (R)	40,156	56.0
Gerald J. Grady (D)	31,616	44.1

MARYLAND

Candidates	Votes	%
1 Thomas F. Johnson (D)	32,328	50.6
Edward T. Miller (R)	31,610	49.4
2 Daniel B. Brewster (D)	87,667	61.0
Fife Symington (R)	56,165	39.1
3 Edward A. Garmatz (D)	49,649	84.0
Harry Kemper (R)	9,470	16.0
4 George H. Fallon (D)	45,646	71.6
Louis W. Collier (R)	18,094	28.4
5 Richard E. Lankford (D)	96,919	75.1
Robert E. Ennis (R)	32,072	24.9
6 John R. Foley (D)	78,987	51.4
DeWitt S. Hyde (R)	74,683	48.6
7 Samuel N. Friedel (D)	72,692	73.6
Elizabeth P. Brown (R)	26,144	26.5

MASSACHUSETTS

Candidates	Votes	%
1 Silvio O. Conte (R)	66,067	55.3
James M. Burns (D)	52,853	44.2
2 Edward P. Boland (D)	103,079	100.0
3 Phillip J. Philbin (D)	114,483	100.0
4 Harold D. Donohue (D)	93,993	63.8
Charles D. Briggs Jr. (R)	53,359	36.2
5 Edith Nourse Rogers (R)	116,072	66.0
William H. Sullivan (D)	59,746	34.0
6 William H. Bates (R)	106,807	100.0
7 Thomas J. Lane (D)	84,243	75.6
Robert T. Breed (R)	27,215	24.4
8 Torbert H. Macdonald (D)	91,263	66.4
Gordon F. Hughes (R)	46,274	33.6
9 Hastings Keith (R)	82,659	54.7
John Almeida Jr. (D)	68,486	45.3
10 Laurence Curtis (R)	71,100	52.2
John L. Saltonstall Jr. (D)	65,159	47.8
11 Thomas P. O'Neill Jr. (D)	68,353	80.4
Elliott H. Stone (R)	16,669	19.6
12 John W. McCormack (D)	72,523	100.0
13 James A. Burke (D)	89,073	53.5
William W. Jenness (R)	77,400	46.5
14 Joseph W. Martin Jr. (R)	90,751	61.0
Edward F. Doolan (D)	57,920	39.0

MICHIGAN

Candidates	Votes	%
1 Thaddeus M. Machrowicz (D)	82,288	90.4
Walter Czarnecki (R)	8,502	9.3
2 George Meader (R)	73,954	58.8
Robert G. Hall (D)	51,323	40.8
3 August E. Johansen (R)	68,144	60.4
John R. O'Meara (D)	44,189	39.2
4 Clare E. Hoffman (R)	59,780	59.9
Gordon A. Elferdink (D)	39,765	39.8
5 Gerald R. Ford Jr. (R)	88,156	63.6
Richard F. Vander Veen (D)	50,203	36.2
6 Charles E. Chamberlain (R)	92,313	52.1
Don Hayworth (D)	84,418	47.7
7 James G. O'Hara (D)	87,299	50.7
Robert J. McIntosh (R)	84,531	49.1
8 Alvin M. Bentley (R)	69,858	62.2
James O. Pino (D)	42,467	37.8
9 Robert P. Griffin (R)	56,780	56.7
Jan B. Vanderploeg (D)	43,196	43.1
10 Elford A. Cederberg (R)	54,316	61.1
Daniel E. Reed (D)	34,390	38.7
11 Victor A. Knox (R)	41,689	52.3
Prentiss M. Brown Jr. (D)	37,995	47.6
12 John B. Bennett (R)	39,239	57.0
Joseph S. Mack (D)	29,506	42.9
13 Charles C. Diggs Jr. (D)	57,354	72.7

Candidates	Votes	%
Charles P. White (R)	21,280	27.0
14 Louis C. Rabaut (D)	97,236	64.2
Lois V. Nair (R)	53,987	35.7
15 John D. Dingell (D)	79,216	78.5
Austin W. Curtis Jr. (R)	21,414	21.2
16 John Lesinski (D)	145,665	71.8
Ralph B. Guy (R)	56,488	27.8
17 Martha W. Griffiths (D)	96,660	60.3
Lucas S. Miel (R)	63,323	39.5
18 William S. Broomfield (R)	101,100	52.6
Leslie H. Hudson (D)	90,526	47.1

MINNESOTA

Candidates	Votes	%
1 Albert H. Quie (R)	73,345	57.0
Eugene P. Foley (DFL)	55,445	43.1
2 Ancher Nelsen (R)	71,623	57.1
Conrad H. Hammar (DFL)	53,869	42.9
3 Roy W. Wier (DFL)	98,449	51.6
Leonard E. Lindquist (R)	92,190	48.4
4 Joseph E. Karth (DFL)	72,952	56.4
Frank S. Farrell (R)	56,484	43.6
5 Walter H. Judd (R)	59,739	57.3
Joseph Robbie (DFL)	44,453	42.7
6 Fred Marshall (DFL)	73,881	64.3
Hugo Holmstrom (R)	41,018	35.7
7 H. Carl Andersen (R)	61,265	53.3
A. I. Johnson (DFL)	53,689	46.7
8 John A. Blatnik (DFL)	97,046	75.6
Roy W. Ranum (R)	31,343	24.4
9 Odin Langen (R)	47,863	50.7
Coya Knutson (DFL)	46,473	49.3

Special Election

Candidates	Votes	%
1 Albert H. Quie (R)	44,276	50.3
Eugene P. Foley (DFL)	43,674	49.7

MISSISSIPPI

Candidates	Votes	%
1 Thomas G. Abernethy (D)	12,413	100.0
2 Jamie L. Whitten (D)	7,982	100.0
3 Frank E. Smith (D)	4,644	100.0
4 John Bell Williams (D)	8,665	100.0
5 Arthur Winstead (D)	14,517	100.0
6 William M. Colmer (D)	13,243	100.0

MISSOURI

Candidates	Votes	%
1 Frank M. Karsten (D)	99,368	75.8
Paul E. Corning Jr. (R)	31,804	24.3
2 Thomas B. Curtis (R)	88,321	51.9
James L. Sullivan (D)	81,811	48.1
3 Leonor K. Sullivan (D)	63,679	79.2
Josiah C. Thomas (R)	16,753	20.8
4 George H. Christopher (D)	72,792	64.0
James A. Rahm (R)	40,912	36.0
5 Richard Bolling (D)	53,622	70.0
Richard W. Byrne (R)	22,953	30.0
6 W. R. Hull Jr. (D)	64,277	64.9
Clyde M. Kirk (R)	34,758	35.1
7 Charles H. Brown (D)	76,239	53.7
Noel Cox (R)	65,666	46.3
8 A. S. J. Carnahan (D)	58,628	64.3
Francis Howard (R)	32,543	35.7
9 Clarence Cannon (D)	67,555	64.8
Anthony Schroeder (R)	36,758	35.2
10 Paul C. Jones (D)	44,892	70.7
Gilbert Degenhardt (R)	18,633	29.3
11 Morgan M. Moulder (D)	54,014	56.9
Don W. Owensby (R)	40,839	43.1

MONTANA

Candidates	Votes	%
1 Lee Metcalf (D)	68,586	69.5
Jean Walterskirschen (R)	30,111	30.5
2 LeRoy H. Anderson (D)	79,140	61.0
Ashton Jones (R)	50,633	39.0

NEBRASKA

	Candidates	Votes	%
1	Phil Weaver (R)	62,770	53.4
	Clair A. Callan (D)	54,705	46.6
2	Glenn Cunningham (R)	67,660	64.8
	Francis M. Casey (D)	36,842	35.3
3	Lawrence Brock (D)	53,033	55.1
	Robert D. Harrison (R)	43,236	44.9
4	Donald F. McGinley (D)	50,870	52.3
	Arthur L. Miller (R)	46,474	47.7

NEVADA

		Votes	%
AL	Walter S. Baring (D)	55,053	66.9
	Robert C. Horton (R)	27,275	33.1

NEW HAMPSHIRE

		Votes	%
1	Chester E. Merrow (R)	62,734	58.5
	Alphonse Roy (D)	44,051	41.0
2	Perkins Bass (R)	52,636	58.4
	Stuart V. Nims (D)	37,212	41.3

NEW JERSEY

		Votes	%
1	William T. Cahill (R)	96,619	50.3
	Alexander Feinberg (D)	94,790	49.3
2	Milton W. Glenn (R)	58,621	53.4
	Joseph G. Hancock (D)	50,558	46.1
3	James C. Auchincloss (R)	98,826	56.1
	Thomas F. Guthrie Jr. (D)	77,423	43.9
4	Frank Thompson Jr. (D)	83,388	63.0
	A. Jerome Moore (R)	48,990	37.0
5	Peter H. B. Frelinghuysen Jr. (R)	111,250	55.7
	David S. North (D)	87,966	44.0
6	Florence P. Dwyer (R)	88,084	51.1
	Jack B. Dunn (D)	80,779	46.9
7	William B. Widnall (R)	103,169	59.6
	J. Emmet Cassidy (D)	69,250	40.0
8	Gordon Canfield (R)	68,385	58.1
	Joseph R. Brumale (D)	48,481	41.2
9	Frank C. Osmers Jr. (R)	92,513	57.4
	Daniel W. Allen (D)	67,633	42.0
10	Peter W. Rodino Jr. (D)	60,482	63.9
	G. George Addonizio (R)	32,946	34.8
11	Hugh J. Addonizio (D)	50,821	59.3
	John P. Langan (R)	34,821	40.7
12	George M. Wallhauser (R)	57,510	52.7
	Thomas J. Holleran (D)	49,463	45.3
13	Cornelius E. Gallagher (D)	61,094	66.1
	Samuel F. Kanis (R)	23,001	24.9
14	Dominick V. Danieis (D)	56,475	62.9
	Frank A. Musto (R)	29,614	33.0

NEW MEXICO

		Votes	%
AL	Joseph M. Montoya (D)	124,924✓	
	Thomas G. Morris (D)	115,928✓	
	William A. Thompson (R)	72,922	
	George W. McKim (R)	70,925	

NEW YORK

		Votes	%
1	Stuyvesant Wainwright (R)	155,387	57.5
	Otis G. Pike (D, L)	115,019	42.5
2	Steven B. Derounian (R)	113,820	60.5
	Walter A. Lynch Jr. (D, L)	74,194	39.5
3	Frank J. Becker (R)	109,245	54.4
	A. William Larson (D, L)	91,514	45.6
4	Seymour Halpern (R)	78,054	52.6
	Joseph J. Perrini (D, L)	70,437	47.4
5	Albert A. Bosch (R)	56,839	52.1
	William Kerwick (D)	47,661	43.7
6	Lester Holtzman (D, L)	106,762	63.6
	George T. Reilly (R)	61,204	36.4
7	James J. Delaney (D, L)	71,007	61.1
	Edward V. Lisoski (R)	45,135	38.9
8	Victor L. Anfuso (D, L)	43,656	71.7
	Leon F. Nadrowski (R)	17,271	28.4

	Candidates	Votes	%
9	Eugene J. Keogh (D, L)	61,816	72.1
	Anton Eyring (R)	23,957	27.9
10	Edna F. Kelly (D, L)	77,351	76.1
	Jerome P. Schneider (R)	24,286	23.9
11	Emanuel Celler (D, L)	105,011	81.4
	Jesse M. Browser (R)	24,034	18.6
12	Francis E. Dorn (R)	51,861	52.7
	Thomas J. Cuite (D)	39,275	39.9
	Leroy Bowman (L)	7,322	7.4
13	Abraham J. Multer (D, L)	88,406	76.1
	Hyman D. Siegel (R)	27,701	23.9
14	John J. Rooney (D, L)	60,703	70.6
	Anthony D'Allessandro (R)	25,319	29.4
15	John H. Ray (R, U TAX)	65,318	52.8
	Vincent R. Fitzpatrick (D, L)	58,351	47.2
16	Adam Clayton Powell Jr. (D, R)	56,383	90.8
	Earl Brown (L)	5,705	9.2
17	John V. Lindsay (R)	54,459	53.9
	Anthony B. Akers (D, L)	46,570	46.1
18	Alfred E. Santangelo (D)	36,601	59.4
	George A. Eyer Jr. (R)	20,848	33.8
	Manuel Velazquez (L)	4,201	6.8
19	Leonard Farbstein (D, L)	55,069	73.1
	Gonzales Suarez (R)	20,232	26.9
20	Ludwig Teller (D, L)	50,735	67.0
	Milton H. Adler (R)	24,933	33.0
21	Herbert Zelenko (D, L)	67,743	72.5
	Carl Medonick (R)	25,699	27.5
22	James C. Healey (D)	65,996	65.2
	Alex J. Soled (R)	20,777	20.5
	David I. Wells (L)	14,391	14.2
23	Isidore Dollinger (D)	49,452	71.5
	Simon M. Koenig (R)	12,278	17.7
	Hector Mathew (L)	7,469	10.8
24	Charles A. Buckley (D)	71,616	56.2
	Charles V. Scanlan (R)	35,993	28.3
	Murray Koenig (L)	19,759	15.5
25	Paul A. Fino (R)	79,857	57.8
	Neal P. Bottiglieri (D, L)	58,396	42.2
26	Edwin B. Dooley (R)	98,677	63.2
	Phil E. Gilbert Jr. (D, L)	57,465	36.8
27	Robert R. Barry (R)	104,240	58.2
	Richard W. McSpedon (D, L)	74,883	41.8
28	Katharine St. George (R)	84,536	59.7
	David Sive (D)	53,981	38.1
29	J. Ernest Wharton (R)	93,647	63.4
	Christopher D. Morris (D, L)	54,153	36.6
30	Leo W. O'Brien (D, L)	109,744	64.7
	George H. Witbeck Jr. (R)	59,958	35.3
31	Dean P. Taylor (R)	87,704	63.8
	John R. Cummins (D, L)	49,777	36.2
32	Samuel S. Stratton (D, L)	73,384	54.0
	Walter C. Shaw (R)	62,443	46.0
33	Clarence E. Kilburn (R)	73,698	64.8
	Robert P. McDonald (D, L)	40,010	35.2
34	Alexander Pirnie (R)	70,482	50.8
	Edwin L. Slusarczyk (D, L)	68,271	49.2
35	R. Walter Riehlman (R)	90,285	53.8
	Caryl M. Kline (D, L)	77,449	46.2
36	John Taber (R)	84,019	64.7
	Frank B. Lent (D, L)	45,822	35.3
37	Howard W. Robison (R)	101,279	65.8
	Francis P. Hogan (D, L)	52,636	34.2
38	Jessica McC. Weis (R)	92,944	58.2
	Alphonse L. Cassetti (D, L)	66,806	41.8
39	Harold C. Ostertag (R)	90,004	65.2
	Harold L. Rakov (D, L)	48,144	34.8
40	William E. Miller (R)	90,066	60.8
	Mariano A. Lucca (D)	54,728	36.9
41	Thaddeus J. Dulski (D, L)	60,360	50.3
	James O. Moore Jr. (R)	59,634	49.7
42	John R. Pillion (R)	99,799	58.9
	Joseph R. Stiglmeier (D, L)	69,747	41.1
43	Daniel A. Reed (R)	68,896	63.8
	T. Joseph Lynch (D)	36,799	34.1

Special Election

		Votes	%
37	Howard W. Robison (R)	45,920	59.8
	Francis P. Hogan (D, L)	30,891	40.2

NORTH CAROLINA

	Candidates	Votes	%
1	Herbert C. Bonner (D)	12,743	100.0
2	L. H. Fountain (D)	17,061	100.0
3	Graham A. Barden (D)	22,426	79.1
	Joe A. Dunn (R)	5,927	20.9
4	Harold D. Cooley (D)	30,505	75.6
	L. T. Dark Jr. (R)	9,863	24.4
5	Ralph J. Scott (D)	40,544	71.6
	William E. Morrow (R)	16,048	28.4
6	Carl T. Durham (D)	35,715	100.0
7	Alton Lennon (D)	27,902	89.0
	C. Dana Malpass (R)	3,461	11.0
8	A. Paul Kitchin (D)	43,793	63.4
	F. D. B. Harding (R)	25,276	36.6
9	Hugh Q. Alexander (D)	57,672	66.5
	William White (R)	29,065	33.5
10	Charles Raper Jonas (R)	56,487	51.9
	David Clark (D)	52,306	48.1
11	Basil L. Whitener (D)	37,926	100.0
12	David M. Hall (D)	52,609	62.5
	W. Harold Sams (R)	31,524	37.5

NORTH DAKOTA

		Votes	%
AL	Quentin N. Burdick (D)	99,562✓	
	Don L. Short (R)	97,862✓	
	Orris G. Nordhougen (R)	92,124	
	S. B. Hocking (D)	78,889	

OHIO

		Votes	%
1	Gordon H. Scherer (R)	70,686	56.6
	W. Ted Osborne (D)	54,119	43.4
2	William E. Hess (R)	86,656	54.7
	James O. Bradley (D)	71,674	45.3
3	Paul F. Schenck (R)	102,806	52.4
	Thomas B. Talbot (D)	93,401	47.6
4	William M. McCulloch (R)	73,448	61.0
	Marjorie Conrad Struna (D)	46,933	39.0
5	Delbert L. Latta (R)	52,612	53.9
	George Rafferty (D)	44,971	46.1
6	James G. Polk (D)	76,566	62.0
	Elmer S. Barrett (R)	46,924	38.0
7	Clarence J. Brown (R)	75,085	60.5
	Joseph A. Sullivan (D)	48,994	39.5
8	Jackson E. Betts (R)	62,232	61.3
	Virgil M. Gase (D)	39,343	38.7
9	Thomas L. Ashley (D)	102,115	61.6
	William K. Gernheuser (R)	63,660	38.4
10	Walter H. Moeller (D)	47,939	52.9
	Homer E. Abele (R)	42,607	47.1
11	Robert E. Cook (D)	79,468	50.3
	David Dennison Jr. (R)	78,501	49.7
12	Samuel L. Devine (R)	100,684	54.4
	Walter J. Shapter Jr. (D)	84,470	45.6
13	Albert D. Baumhart Jr. (R)	65,169	58.9
	J. William McCray (D)	45,390	41.1
14	William H. Ayres (R)	114,827	60.1
	Jack B. Arnold (D)	76,138	39.9
15	John E. Henderson (R)	48,316	57.3
	Herbert U. Smith (D)	36,062	42.7
16	Frank T. Bow (R)	100,678	57.4
	John G. Freedom (D)	74,660	42.6
17	Robert W. Levering (D)	63,650	51.7
	Lawrence Burns (R)	59,490	48.3
18	Wayne L. Hays (D)	88,813	71.6
	Francis Wallace (R)	35,322	28.5
19	Michael J. Kirwan (D)	93,660	75.0
	Loren E. Van Brocklin (R)	31,192	25.0
20	Michael A. Feighan (D)	113,200	79.4
	Malvern E. Schultz (R)	29,308	20.6
21	Charles A. Vanik (D)	93,987	80.4
	Ermer L. Watson (R)	22,956	19.6
22	Frances P. Bolton (R)	71,139	55.3
	Chat Paterson (D)	57,508	44.7
23	William E. Minshall Jr. (R)	95,267	66.5
	Daniel Winston (D)	47,953	33.5

OKLAHOMA

	Candidates	Votes	%
1	Page H. Belcher (R)	74,853	50.8
	Herbert William Wright Jr. (D)	71,190	48.3
2	Ed Edmondson (D)	75,492	79.1
	Milo Ritter (R)	19,996	20.9
3	Carl Albert (D)	43,868	90.9
	Chapin Wallace (R)	4,398	9.1
4	Tom Steed (D)	43,837	74.1
	Rolla C. Calkins (R)	15,359	26.0
5	John Jarman (D)	79,917	82.3
	Hobart H. Hobbs (R)	17,137	17.7
6	Toby Morris (D)	54,967	66.7
	Fred L. Coogan (R)	27,425	33.3

OREGON

	Candidates	Votes	%
1	Walter Norblad (R)	95,420	54.9
	Robert Y. Thornton (D)	78,362	45.1
2	Al Ullman (D)	50,166	61.1
	Marion T. Weatherford (R)	31,987	38.9
3	Edith Green (D)	131,164	65.8
	John Johnston (R)	68,235	34.2
4	Charles O. Porter (D)	79,166	56.3
	Paul Geddes (R)	61,386	43.7

PENNSYLVANIA

	Candidates	Votes	%
1	William A. Barrett (D)	67,531	64.7
	Gerard Iannelli (R)	36,854	35.3
2	Kathryn E. Granahan (D)	84,058	66.3
	Maurice M. Green (R)	42,759	33.7
3	James A. Byrne (D)	65,201	63.5
	James Thomas McDermott (R)	37,420	36.5
4	Robert N. C. Nix (D)	63,031	72.6
	Cecil B. Moore (R)	23,845	27.5
5	William J. Green Jr. (D)	100,680	55.3
	D. Donald Jamieson (R)	81,530	44.8
6	Herman Toll (D)	83,491	55.4
	Fred C. Gartner (R)	67,205	44.6
7	William H. Milliken Jr. (R)	114,275	59.2
	Hubert P. Earle (D)	78,747	40.8
8	Willard S. Curtin (R)	85,010	54.3
	Harold Lefcourt (D)	71,583	45.7
9	Paul B. Dague (R)	88,193	61.9
	James C. N. Paul (D)	54,220	38.1
10	Stanley A. Prokop (D)	74,890	50.4
	Joseph L. Carrigg (R)	73,601	49.6
11	Daniel J. Flood (D)	89,167	61.7
	Herman C. Kersteen (R)	55,349	38.3
12	Ivor D. Fenton (R)	64,960	54.9
	Charles E. Lotz (D)	53,402	45.1
13	John A. Lafore Jr. (R)	104,156	62.9
	John T. Synnestvedt (D)	61,475	37.1
14	George M. Rhodes (D)	51,281	58.3
	Thomas C. Anthony Jr. (R)	36,170	41.1
15	Francis E. Walter (D)	60,742	61.1
	Luther H. Ackerman (R)	38,726	38.9
16	Walter M. Mumma (R)	70,810	56.6
	John H. Bream (D)	54,245	43.4
17	Alvin Bush (R)	65,071	56.0
	C. Max Hess (D)	51,053	44.0
18	Richard M. Simpson (R)	67,719	56.3
	Ross E. Hershberger (D)	52,514	43.7
19	James M. Quigley (D)	67,603	51.5
	S. Walter Stauffer (R)	63,749	48.5
20	James E. Van Zandt (R)	61,010	64.9
	Julia L. Maietta (D)	33,060	35.1
21	John H. Dent (D)	70,828	59.2
	Edward S. Stiteler (R)	48,925	40.9
22	John P. Saylor (R)	77,407	57.0
	Robert S. Glass (D)	58,434	43.0
23	Leon H. Gavin (R)	60,080	61.1
	Thomas P. Kennedy (D)	38,179	38.9
24	Carroll D. Kearns (R)	76,870	53.8
	James P. O'Brien (D)	65,937	46.2
25	Frank M. Clark (D)	80,704	58.9
	Thomas W. King Jr. (R)	56,375	41.1
26	Thomas E. Morgan (D)	92,755	64.8
	Harry T. Zimmer Jr. (R)	50,403	35.2
27	James G. Fulton (R)	105,998	64.1
	Emery F. Bacon (D)	59,283	35.9
28	William S. Moorhead (D)	82,081	67.3
	Harry L. Verbofsky (R)	39,900	32.7
29	Robert J. Corbett (R)	97,203	63.6
	Lee T. Sellars (D)	55,575	36.4
30	Elmer J. Holland (D)	98,244	66.7
	Harold E. Morgan (R)	49,093	33.3

RHODE ISLAND

	Candidates	Votes	%
1	Aime J. Forand (D)	97,425	62.9
	Francis E. Martineau (R)	57,581	37.2
2	John E. Fogarty (D)	117,506	63.3
	Robert L. Gammell (R)	67,942	36.6

SOUTH CAROLINA

	Candidates	Votes	%
1	L. Mendel Rivers (D)	13,538	100.0
2	John J. Riley (D)	13,677	100.0
3	W. J. Bryan Dorn (D)	9,528	99.9
4	Robert T. Ashmore (D)	17,247	100.0
5	Robert W. Hemphill (D)	9,780	100.0
6	John L. McMillan (D)	12,862	100.0

SOUTH DAKOTA

	Candidates	Votes	%
1	George McGovern (D)	107,202	53.4
	Joe Foss (R)	93,388	46.6
2	E. Y. Berry (R)	31,908	55.6
	J. T. McCullen (D)	25,491	44.4

TENNESSEE

	Candidates	Votes	%
1	B. Carroll Reece (R)	42,615	58.7
	Mayne W. Miller (D)	29,999	41.3
2	Howard H. Baker (R)	49,420	67.7
	John Grady O'Hara Sr. (D)	23,470	32.2
3	James B. Frazier Jr. (D)	31,267	100.0
4	Joe L. Evins (D)	38,062	100.0
5	J. Carlton Loser (D)	30,879	94.4
	Porter Freeman (R)	1,824#	5.6
6	Ross Bass (D)	33,445	97.2
7	Tom Murray (D)	24,053	100.0
8	Robert A. Everett (D)	19,145	100.0
9	Clifford Davis (D)	46,550	100.0

TEXAS

	Candidates	Votes	%
1	Wright Patman (D)	19,203	100.0
2	Jack Brooks (D)	47,092	100.0
3	Lindley Beckworth (D)	22,751	100.0
4	Sam Rayburn (D)	15,942	100.0
5	Bruce Alger (R)	62,722	52.6
	Barefoot Sanders (D)	56,566	47.4
6	Olin Teague (D)	25,827	100.0
7	John Dowdy (D)	22,733	96.7
8	Albert Thomas (D)	33,393	88.2
	R. E. Nesmith (R)	4,477	11.8
9	Clark W. Thompson (D)	36,012	100.0
10	Homer Thornberry (D)	28,990	100.0
11	W. R. Poage (D)	21,900	100.0
12	Jim Wright (D)	38,180	100.0
13	Frank Ikard (D)	27,671	100.0
14	John Young (D)	37,861	100.0
15	Joe M. Kilgore (D)	28,404	100.0
16	J. T. Rutherford (D)	28,744	100.0
17	Omar Burleson (D)	25,123	100.0
18	Walter Rogers (D)	34,617	100.0
19	George Mahon (D)	29,068	100.0
20	Paul J. Kilday (D)	23,539	100.0
21	O. C. Fisher (D)	26,497	100.0
22	Bob Casey (D)	43,660	61.7
	T. Everton Kennerly (R)	23,317	33.0
	Jack Gardner	3,789	5.4

UTAH

	Candidates	Votes	%
1	Henry Aldous Dixon (R)	58,141	53.9
	M. Blaine Peterson (D)	49,735	46.1
2	David S. King (D)	91,213	51.1
	William A. Dawson (R)	87,234	48.9

VERMONT

	Candidates	Votes	%
AL	William H. Meyer (D)	63,131	51.5
	Harold J. Arthur (R)	59,536	48.5

VIRGINIA

	Candidates	Votes	%
1	Thomas N. Downing (D)	31,765	99.9
2	Porter Hardy Jr. (D)	32,758	100.0
3	J. Vaughan Gary (D)	34,040	76.1
	Richard R. Ryder (R)	10,668	23.9
4	Watkins M. Abbitt (D)	37,679	87.1
	Frank M. McCann (I)	5,556	12.9
5	William M. Tuck (D)	26,322	100.0
6	Richard H. Poff (R)	37,779	56.7
	Richard F. Pence (D)	28,530	42.9
7	Burr P. Harrison (D)	30,486	76.6
	Henry A. Oder Jr. (I)	9,294	23.4
8	Howard W. Smith (D)	28,815	99.7
9	W. Pat Jennings (D)	34,685	76.6
	T. L. Maness (I)	10,615	23.4
10	Joel T. Broyhill (R)	37,764	52.3
	Joseph H. Freehill (D)	33,553	46.5

WASHINGTON

	Candidates	Votes	%
1	Thomas M. Pelly (R)	98,897	70.1
	Robert Odman (D)	42,128	29.9
2	Jack Westland (R)	62,152	53.6
	Hugh B. Mitchell (D)	53,436	46.1
3	Russell V. Mack (R)	69,745	60.9
	Victor A. Meyers (D)	44,515	38.9
4	Catherine May (R)	66,544	54.0
	Frank LeRoux (D)	56,308	45.7
5	Walt Horan (R)	67,072	53.2
	Tom Delaney (D)	58,431	46.3
6	Thor C. Tollefson (R)	63,560	53.5
	John M. Coffee (D)	54,536	45.9
7	Don Magnuson (D)	96,841	70.9
	Bob Jones (R)	39,708	29.1

WEST VIRGINIA

	Candidates	Votes	%
1	Arch A. Moore Jr. (R)	55,613	54.6
	Robert H. Mollohan (D)	46,262	45.4
2	Harley O. Staggers (D)	57,761	62.7
	Ward W. Keesecker (R)	34,436	37.4
3	Cleveland M. Bailey (D)	59,084	59.9
	Rex Keith Bumgardner (R)	39,507	40.1
4	Ken Hechler (D)	60,794	51.5
	Will E. Neal (R)	57,291	48.5
5	Elizabeth Kee (D)	63,873	99.8
6	John M. Slack Jr. (D)	93,209	66.1
	F. O'Dair Duff (R)	47,852	33.9

WISCONSIN

	Candidates	Votes	%
1	Gerald T. Flynn (D)	63,065	50.6
	Eleanor J. Smith (R)	61,615	49.4
2	Robert W. Kastenmeier (D)	78,009	52.1
	Donald E. Tewes (R)	71,748	47.9
3	Gardner R. Withrow (R)	47,858	51.2
	Norman M. Clapp (D)	45,608	48.8
4	Clement J. Zablocki (D)	112,226	74.1
	James J. Arnold (R)	39,167	25.9
5	Henry S. Reuss (D)	104,374	69.5
	Otto R. Werkmeister (R)	45,901	30.5
6	William K. Van Pelt (R)	61,490	52.8
	James Megellas (D)	55,031	47.2
7	Melvin R. Laird (R)	59,186	60.5
	Kenneth Traeger (D)	38,702	39.5
8	John W. Byrnes (R)	69,682	57.3
	Milo Singler (D)	51,887	42.7
9	Lester R. Johnson (D)	55,420	63.1
	Charles A. Hornbeck (R)	32,425	36.9
10	Alvin E. O'Konski (R)	56,801	67.1
	Basil G. Kennedy (D)	28,830	32.9

WYOMING

	Candidates	Votes	%
AL	Keith Thomson (R)	59,894	53.6
	Ray Whitaker (D)	51,886	46.4

1959 House Elections

HAWAII

(Became a state Aug. 21, 1959)

	Candidates	Votes	%
AL	Daniel K. Inouye (D)	111,727	68.2
	Charles H. Silva (R)	51,058	31.2

IOWA

Special Election

	Candidates	Votes	%
4	John Henry Kyt (R)#	28,326	52.3
	C. Edwin Gilmour (D)	25,809	47.7

NEW YORK

Special Election

	Candidates	Votes	%
43	Charles E. Goodell (R)	27,454	65.0
	Robert E. McCaffery (D)	14,250	33.8

1960 House Elections

ALABAMA

	Candidates	Votes	%
1	Frank W. Boykin (D)	45,225	100.0
2	George Grant (D)	44,487	100.0
3	George Andrews (D)	33,881	100.0
4	Kenneth A. Roberts (D)	34,855	99.9
5	Albert Rains (D)	48,772	100.0
6	Armistead I. Selden Jr. (D)	23,245	100.0
7	Carl Elliott (D)	36,124	100.0
8	Robert E. Jones (D)	52,411	79.2
	H. G. Williams (R)	13,800	20.8
9	George Huddleston Jr. (D)	70,567	67.3
	William P. Ivey (R)	34,317	32.7

ALASKA

		Votes	%
AL	Ralph J. Rivers (D)	33,546	56.8
	R. L. (Ron) Rettig (R)	25,517	43.2

ARIZONA

		Votes	%
1	John J. Rhodes (R)	121,563	59.2
	Richard F. Harless (D)	83,676	40.8
2	Stewart L. Udall (D)	95,512	55.8
	Mac C. Matheson (R)	75,811	44.3

ARKANSAS

		Votes	%
1	Ezekiel C. Gathings (D)		100.0
2	Wilbur D. Mills (D)		100.0
3	James W. Trimble (D)		100.0
4	Oren Harris (D)		100.0
5	Dale Alford (D)	57,617	82.7
	L. J. Churchill (R)	12,054	17.3
6	William F. Norrell (D)		100.0

CALIFORNIA

		Votes	%
1	Clem Miller (D)	115,829	51.6
	Fred G. Dupuis (R)	108,505	48.4
2	Harold T. Johnson (D)	109,565	62.7
	Fredric H. Nagel Jr. (R)	65,198	37.3
3	John E. Moss Jr. (D)	200,439	100.0
4	William S. Mailliard (R)	118,249	65.3
	Phillips S. Davies (D)	62,814	34.7
5	John F. Shelley (D)	104,507	83.7
	Nick Verreos (R)	20,305	16.3
6	John F. Baldwin (R)	128,418	58.7
	Douglas R. Page (D)	90,260	41.3
7	Jeffery Cohelan (D)	79,776	57.0
	Lewis F. Sherman (R)	60,065	43.0
8	George P. Miller (D)	152,476	62.0
	Robert E. Hannon (R)	93,403	38.0
9	J. Arthur Younger (R)	116,589	59.2
	John D. Kaster (D)	80,227	40.8
10	Charles S. Gubser (R)	170,063	58.9
	Russell B. Bryan (D)	118,520	41.1
11	John J. McFall (D)	97,368	65.4
	Clifford B. Bull (R)	51,473	34.6
12	B. F. Sisk (D-R)	141,974	99.9
13	Charles M. Teague (R)	146,072	65.0
	L. Boyd Finch (D)	78,597	35.0
14	Harlen Hagen (D)	97,026	56.5
	G. Ray Arnett (R)	74,800	43.5
15	Gordon L. McDonough (R)	89,234	51.3
	Norman H. Martell (D)	84,650	48.6
16	Alphonzo Bell (R)	83,601	55.4
	Jerry Pacht (D)	67,318	44.6
17	Cecil R. King (D)	206,620	67.7
	Tom Coffee (R)	98,510	32.3
18	Craig Hosmer (R)	129,851	70.0
	D. Patrick Ahern (D)	55,735	30.0
19	Chet Holifield (D)	145,479	78.2
	Gordon S. McWilliams (R)	40,491	21.8
20	H. Allen Smith (R)	90,214	70.1
	Gareth W. Sadler (D)	38,497	29.9

	Candidates	Votes	%
21	Edgar W. Hiestand (R)	179,376	58.4
	Mrs. Rudd Brown (D)	127,591	41.6
22	James C. Corman (D)	104,919	51.1
	Lemoine Blanchard (R)	100,321	48.9
23	Clyde Doyle (D)	148,415	74.2
	Emmett A. Schwartz (R)	51,548	25.8
24	Glenard P. Lipscomb (R)	82,497	59.7
	Norman Hass (D)	55,613	40.3
25	John H. Rousselot (R)	182,545	53.6
	George A. Kasem (D)	158,289	46.4
26	James Roosevelt (D)	150,318	73.4
	William E. McIntyre (R)	54,540	26.6
27	Harry R. Sheppard (D)	123,645	66.8
	Robert M. Castle (R)	61,484	33.2
28	James B. Utt (R)	241,765	60.9
	Max E. Woods (D)	155,221	39.1
29	D. S. Saund (D)	76,139	57.1
	Charles H. Jameson (R)	57,319	43.0
30	Bob Wilson (R)	158,679	59.3
	Walter Wencke (D)	108,882	40.7

COLORADO

		Votes	%
1	Byron G. Rogers (D)	121,610	60.0
	Robert D. Rolander (R)	81,042	40.0
2	Peter H. Dominick (R)	150,964	57.6
	Byron L. Johnson (D)	111,077	42.4
3	J. Edgar Chenoweth (R)	85,825	52.1
	Franklin R. Stewart (D)	79,069	48.0
4	Wayne N. Aspinall (D)	58,731	68.5
	Charles P. Casteel (R)	26,961	31.5

CONNECTICUT

		Votes	%
1	Emilio Q. Daddario (D)	193,330	58.5
	Thomas F. Brennan (R)	137,386	41.5
2	Horace Seely-Brown Jr. (R)	93,971	50.1
	William L. St. Onge (D)	93,515	49.9
3	Robert N. Giaimo (D)	124,547	54.9
	Albert W. Cretella (R)	102,271	45.1
4	Abner W. Sibal (R)	160,654	51.3
	Donald J. Irwin (D)	150,205	48.0
5	John S. Monagan (D)	88,310	55.1
	James T. Patterson (R)	71,964	44.9
AL	Frank Kowalski (D)	657,680	54.0
	Antoni N. Sadlak (R)	560,803	46.0

DELAWARE

		Votes	%
AL	Harris B. McDowell Jr. (D)	98,227	50.5
	James T. McKinstry (R)	96,337	49.5

FLORIDA

		Votes	%
1	William C. Cramer (R)	159,515	58.4
	James M. McEwen (D)	113,504	41.6
2	Charles E. Bennett (D)	94,570	82.5
	J. Edward Musser (R)	20,090	17.5
3	Robert L. F. Sikes (D)	95,062	100.0
4	Dante B. Fascell (D)	194,023	70.5
	Hugh M. Tartagila (R)	81,209	29.5
5	A. Sydney Herlong Jr. (D)	113,938	100.0
6	Paul G. Rogers (D)	138,226	62.0
	John D. Kruse (R)	84,776	38.0
7	James A. Haley (D)	65,144	61.4
	Henry S. Bartholomew (R)	40,923	38.6
8	D. R. Matthews (D)	46,794	100.0

GEORGIA

		Votes	%
1	G. Elliott Hagan (D)	53,749	100.0
2	J. L. Pilcher (D)	43,596	100.0
3	E. L. Forrester (D)	55,005	99.7
4	John J. Flynt Jr. (D)	53,394	100.0
5	James C. Davis (D)	80,023	99.7
6	Carl Vinson (D)	44,237	100.0

	Candidates	Votes	%
7	John W. Davis (D)	69,717	74.2
	E. Ralph Ivey (R)	24,285	25.8
8	Iris Faircloth Blitch (D)	50,456	99.8
9	Phil M. Landrum (D)	57,549	100.0
10	Robert G. Stephens Jr. (D)	41,679	99.9

HAWAII

		Votes	%
AL	Daniel K. Inouye (D)	135,827	74.4
	Fred Titcomb (R)	46,812	25.6

IDAHO

		Votes	%
1	Gracie B. Pfost (D)	68,863	60.4
	Thomas A. Leupp (R)	45,166	39.6
2	Ralph R. Harding (D)	90,161	51.2
	Hamer H. Budge (R)	86,100	48.9

ILLINOIS

		Votes	%
1	William L. Dawson (D)	75,938	77.8
	Genoa S. Washington (R)	21,660	22.2
2	Barratt O'Hara (D)	103,535	66.6
	Bernard A. Epton (R)	52,028	33.4
3	William T. Murphy (D)	114,523	59.1
	Emmet F. Byrne (R)	79,307	40.9
4	Edward J. Derwinski (R)	179,480	55.7
	Frank G. Sulewski (D)	142,772	44.3
5	John C. Kluczynski (D)	121,240	71.2
	Edward J. Tomek (R)	49,030	28.8
6	Thomas J. O'Brien (D)	107,474	71.7
	Frank Estes (R)	42,361	28.3
7	Roland Victor Libonati (D)	28,494	54.5
	Lawrence J. Blasi (R)	23,840	45.6
8	Dan Rostenkowski (D)	81,092	67.2
	Henry Klinger Jr. (R)	39,651	32.8
9	Sidney R. Yates (D)	80,681	60.1
	Chester E. Emanuelson (R)	53,686	40.0
10	Harold R. Collier (R)	126,671	57.1
	Edward V. Hanrahan (D)	95,214	42.9
11	Roman C. Pucinski (D)	101,224	54.0
	Timothy P. Sheehan (R)	86,305	46.0
12	Edward R. Finnegan (D)	94,907	50.8
	Theodore P. Fields (R)	91,978	49.2
13	Marguerite Stitt Church (R)	268,647	66.0
	Tyler Thompson (D)	138,348	34.0
14	Elmer J. Hoffman (R)	167,128	63.8
	Hayes Beall (D)	94,945	36.2
15	Noah M. Mason (R)	93,986	50.5
	Dorothy G. O'Brien (D)	92,301	49.6
16	John B. Anderson (R)	115,693	62.3
	Edwin M. Nelson (D)	69,944	37.7
17	Leslie C. Arends (R)	107,896	61.3
	William T. Larkin (D)	68,020	38.7
18	Robert H. Michel (R)	94,388	59.3
	Richard A. Estep (D)	64,885	40.7
19	Robert B. Chiperfield (R)	82,622	50.6
	John C. Watson (D)	80,700	49.4
20	Paul Findley (R)	77,286	55.6
	Montgomery B. Carrott (D)	61,790	44.4
21	Peter F. Mack Jr. (D)	102,154	54.7
	J. Waldo Ackerman Jr. (R)	84,471	45.3
22	William L. Springer (R)	98,438	61.4
	James T. Nally (D)	61,837	38.6
23	George E. Shipley (D)	80,718	51.6
	Frank H. Walker (R)	75,809	48.4
24	Melvin Price (D)	144,560	72.2
	Phyllis Schlafly (R)	55,620	27.8
25	Kenneth J. Gray (D)	92,227	57.9
	Gordon E. Kerr (R)	67,067	42.1

INDIANA

		Votes	%
1	Ray J. Madden (D)	136,443	64.7
	Philip P. Parker (R)	73,984	35.1
2	Charles A. Halleck (R)	95,920	57.5

	Candidates	Votes	%
	George H. Bowers (D)	70,464	42.2
3	John Brademas (D)	115,070	52.4
	F. Jay Nimtz (R)	104,430	47.6
4	E. Ross Adair (R)	100,419	58.2
	Byron McCammon (D)	72,251	41.8
5	J. Edward Roush (D)	107,357#	50.0
	George O. Chambers (R)	107,258#	50.0
6	Richard L. Roudebush (R)	84,662	52.0
	Fred Wampler (D)	78,247	48.0
7	William G. Bray (R)	95,998	60.1
	Thomas C. Cravens (D)	63,646	39.9
8	Winfield K. Denton (D)	108,058	53.2
	Alvan V. Burch (R)	94,694	46.6
9	Earl Wilson (R)	71,402	50.6
	Earl Hogan (D)	69,761	49.4
10	Ralph Harvey (R)	104,885	57.1
	Randall S. Harmon (D)	78,716	42.9
11	Donald Cogley Bruce (R)	154,676	53.7
	Joseph W. Barr (D)	133,153	46.2

IOWA

	Candidates	Votes	%
1	Fred Schwengel (R)	104,737	60.9
	Walter J. Guenther (D)	67,287	39.1
2	James E. Bromwell (R)	108,137	52.6
	Leonard G. Wolf (D)	97,608	47.4
3	H. R. Gross (R)	99,046	56.3
	Edward J. Gallagher Jr. (D)	76,837	43.7
4	John Kyl (R)	65,016	56.6
	C. Edwin Gilmour (D)	49,918	43.4
5	Neal Smith (D)	91,808	53.0
	Floyd M. Burgeson (R)	81,474	47.0
6	Merwin Coad (D)	70,353	53.6
	Curtis G. Riehm (R)	60,834	46.4
7	Ben F. Jensen (R)	66,037	55.8
	Duane Orton (D)	52,214	44.2
8	Charles B. Hoeven (R)	77,583	57.5
	Donald E. O'Brien (D)	57,333	42.5

KANSAS

	Candidates	Votes	%
1	William H. Avery (R)	84,816	63.1
	Marshall G. Gardiner (D)	49,598	36.9
2	Robert F. Ellsworth (R)	95,346	52.3
	Newell A. George (D)	86,905	47.7
3	Walter L. McVey (R)	49,429	51.2
	Denver D. Hargis (D)	47,127	48.8
4	Garner E. Shriver (R)	119,275	55.2
	William I. Robinson (D)	96,706	44.8
5	J. Floyd Breeding (D)	75,687	55.5
	Joe W. Hunter (R)	60,794	44.5
6	Bob Dole (R)	62,335	59.3
	William A. Davis (D)	42,869	40.8

KENTUCKY

	Candidates	Votes	%
1	Frank A. Stubblefield (D)	66,248	100.0
2	William H. Natcher (D)	55,877	100.0
3	Frank W. Burke (D)	115,421	50.3
	Henry R. Heyburn (R)	114,263	49.8
4	Frank Chelf (D)	48,743	100.0
5	Brent Spence (D)	63,555	55.4
	Jule Appel (R)	51,125	44.6
	John C. Watts (D)	74,500	54.7
	Howard A. Dickey (R)	61,795	45.3
7	Carl D. Perkins (D)	82,746	56.1
	Herbert Rowland (R)	64,687	43.9
8	Eugene Slier (R)	81,903	71.8
	Donald R. Shepherd (D)	32,163	28.2

LOUISIANA

	Candidates	Votes	%
1	F. Edward Hebert (D)	70,465	82.2
	Norman W. Prendergast (R)	15,314	17.9
2	Hale Boggs (D)	81,034	78.0
	Elliot Ross Buckley (R)	22,818	22.0
3	Edwin E. Willis (D)	52,428	83.6
	Floyd J. Duplantis (R)	10,286	16.4
4	Overton Brooks (D)	48,286	74.2
	Fred C. McClanahan (R)	16,827	25.8
5	Otto E. Passman (D)	22,181	100.0
6	James H. Morrison (D)	78,640	85.6
	Charles H. Dillemuth (R)	13,233	14.4
7	T. A. Thompson (D)	60,007	100.0
8	Harold B. McSween (D)	28,492	100.0

MAINE

	Candidates	Votes	%
1	Peter Garland (R)	85,821	53.8
	James C. Oliver (D)	73,826	46.2
2	Stanley R. Tupper (R)	71,271	53.2
	John C. Donovan (D)	62,309	46.5
3	Clifford G. McIntire (R)	73,742	64.1
	David G. Roberts (D)	41,307	35.9

MARYLAND

	Candidates	Votes	%
1	Thomas F. Johnson (D)	42,219	53.6
	Edward T. Miller (R)	36,508	46.4
2	Daniel B. Brewster (D)	126,452	58.6
	Fife Symington (R)	89,262	41.4
3	Edward A. Garmatz (D)	57,154	80.3
	Robert J. Gerstung (R)	14,026	19.7
4	George H. Fallon (D)	48,145	65.5
	Melvin R. Kenney (R)	25,394	34.5
5	Richard E. Lankford (D)	120,773	62.2
	Carlyle J. Lancaster (R)	73,433	37.8
6	Charles McC. Mathias Jr. (R)	115,088	52.0
	John R. Foley (D)	106,098	48.0
7	Samuel N. Friedel (D)	81,474	64.5
	David M. Blum (R)	44,779	35.5

MASSACHUSETTS

	Candidates	Votes	%
1	Silvio O. Conte (R)	102,921	68.5
	William H. Burns (D)	46,863	31.2
2	Edward P. Boland (D)	135,815	100.0
3	Philip J. Philbin (D)	145,237	100.0
4	Harold D. Donohue (D)	122,364	64.5
	Robert N. Scola (R)	67,270	35.5
5	F. Bradford Morse (R)	123,161	54.5
	William C. Madden (D)	102,765	45.5
6	William H. Bates (R)	112,835	65.9
	Mary Kennedy (D)	58,312	34.1
7	Thomas J. Lane (D)	117,237	100.0
8	Torbert H. Macdonald (D)	114,333	65.8
	Ward Collins Cramer (R)	59,550	34.3
9	Hastings Keith (R)	110,955	55.7
	Edward F. Harrington (D)	88,222	44.3
10	Laurence Curtis (R)	98,257	58.2
	Joseph J. Mulhern (D)	70,510	41.8
11	Thomas P. O'Neill Jr. (D)	87,866	100.0
12	John W. McCormack (D)	86,057	100.0
13	James A. Burke (D)	126,936	58.5
	Charles J. Gabriel (R)	89,921	41.5
14	Joseph W. Martin Jr. (R)	115,209	60.3
	Edward F. Doolan (D)	75,815	39.7

MICHIGAN

	Candidates	Votes	%
1	Thaddeus M. Machrowicz (D)	102,948	88.4
	Walter Czarnecki (R)	13,157	11.3
2	George Meader (R)	110,124	59.6
	Thomas P. Payne (D)	74,276	40.2
3	August E. Johansen (R)	100,918	60.6
	Samuel I. Clark (D)	65,402	39.2
4	Clare E. Hoffman (R)	90,831	62.3
	Edward Burns (D)	54,655	37.5
5	Gerald R. Ford Jr. (R)	131,461	66.8
	William S. Reamon (D)	65,064	33.1
6	Charles E. Chamberlain (R)	138,355	56.6
	Jerome F. O'Rourke (D)	105,864	43.3
7	James G. O'Hara (D)	142,795	53.3
	Robert J. McIntosh (R)	124,750	46.6
8	James Harvey (R)	94,405	62.2
	Mary M. Harden (D)	57,126	37.6
9	Robert P. Griffin (R)	77,541	59.6
	Donald G. Jennings (D)	52,375	40.3
10	Elford A. Cederberg (R)	75,846	62.1
	Daniel E. Reed (D)	46,140	37.8
11	Victor A. Knox (R)	54,300	54.9
	Prentiss M. Brown Jr. (D)	44,650	45.1
12	John B. Bennett (R)	48,422	60.8
	Robert C. McCarthy (D)	31,137	39.1
13	Charles C. Diggs Jr. (D)	76,812	71.4
	Robert B. Blackwell (R)	30,369	28.2
14	Louis C. Rabaut (D)	132,602	62.7
	Lois V. Nair (R)	78,548	37.1
15	John D. Dingell (D)	111,671	79.4
	Robert J. Robbins (R)	28,532	20.3
16	John Lesinski (D)	211,733	66.0
	Lee H. Clark (R)	108,332	33.8
17	Martha W. Griffiths (D)	134,660	57.6
	Richard E. Morell (R)	98,721	42.2
18	William S. Broomfield (R)	163,233	55.9
	James Kellis (D)	128,678	44.0

MINNESOTA

	Candidates	Votes	%
1	Albert H. Quie (R)	100,381	60.5
	George Shepherd (DFL)	65,422	39.5
2	Ancher Nelsen (R)	96,471	57.2
	Russel Schwandt (DFL)	72,239	42.8
3	Clark MacGregor (R)	154,847	51.6
	Roy W. Wier (DFL)	139,908	46.6
4	Joseph E. Karth (DFL)	108,738	61.0
	Joseph J. Mitchell (R)	69,635	39.0
5	Walter H. Judd (R)	86,223	60.9
	George W. Matthews (DFL)	55,377	39.1
6	Fred Marshall (DFL)	87,332	59.6
	Frank L. King (R)	59,305	40.4
7	H. Carl Andersen (R)	73,487	52.5
	Gordon E. Duenow (DFL)	66,609	47.6
8	John A. Blatnik (DFL)	107,154	69.5
	Jerry H. Ketola (R)	47,099	30.5
9	Odin Langen (R)	62,322	52.2
	Coya Knutson (DFL)	57,114	47.8

MISSISSIPPI

	Candidates	Votes	%
1	Thomas G. Abernethy (D)	44,381	93.6
	Edward W. Scott (R)	3,018	6.4
2	Jamie L. Whitten (D)	23,942	100.0
3	Frank E. Smith (D)	25,592	92.7
	W. A. Clark (R)	2,018	7.3
4	John Bell Williams (D)	58,974	100.0
5	Arthur Winstead (D)	40,480	100.0
6	William M. Colmer (D)	59,372	100.0

MISSOURI

	Candidates	Votes	%
1	Frank M. Karsten (D)	161,394	70.8
	Sam J. Kallaos (R)	66,640	29.2
2	Thomas B. Curtis (R)	150,327	56.7
	Richard L. Carp (D)	114,803	43.3
3	Leonor K. Sullivan (D)	87,637	73.3
	Morton L. Schwartz (R)	31,902	26.7
4	William J. Randall (D)	111,557	54.0
	Kenneth K. Lowe (R)	95,070	46.0
5	Richard Bolling (D)	74,834	61.0
	Clinton H. Gates (R)	47,810	39.0
6	W. R. Hull Jr. (D)	93,285	54.6
	Ethan H. Campbell (R)	77,638	45.4
7	Durward G. Hall (R)	107,208	54.9
	Charles H. Brown (D)	88,162	45.1
8	Richard Ichord (D)	79,020	58.0
	Curtis J. Tindel (R)	57,234	42.0
9	Clarence Cannon (D)	107,384	59.8
	Anthony C. Schroeder (R)	72,098	40.2
10	Paul C. Jones (D)	69,997	100.0
11	Morgan M. Moulder (D)	74,866	50.1
	Robert A. Bartel (R)	74,505	49.9

MONTANA

	Candidates	Votes	%
1	Arnold Olsen (D)	63,081	53.3
	George P. Sarsfield (R)	55,347	46.7
2	James F. Battin (R)	78,277	50.9
	Leo Graybill Jr. (D)	75,507	49.1

NEBRASKA

	Candidates	Votes	%
1	Phil Weaver (R)	89,016	55.8
	Gerald T. Whelan (D)	70,626	44.2
2	Glenn Cunningham (R)	101,347	66.6
	Joseph V. Benesch (D)	50,768	33.4
3	Ralph F. Beermann (R)	67,129	51.3
	Lawrence Brock (D)	63,838	48.7
4	Dave Martin (R)	69,754	51.1
	Donald F. McGinley (D)	66,699	48.9

NEVADA

	Candidates	Votes	%
AL	Walter S. Baring (D)	59,616	57.5
	George W. Malone (R)	43,986	42.5

NEW HAMPSHIRE

	Candidates	Votes	%
1	Chester E. Merrow (R)	88,118	56.6
	Romeo J. Champagne (D)	67,717	43.5
2	Perkins Bass (R)	77,701	60.3
	Stuart V. Nims (D)	51,145	39.7

NEW JERSEY

	Candidates	Votes	%
1	William T. Cahill (R)	153,817	57.6
	John A. Healey (D)	112,802	42.2
2	Milton W. Glenn (R)	77,894	56.6
	John A. Miller (D)	59,520	43.2
3	James C. Auchincloss (R)	139,590	53.1
	Katharine E. White (D)	123,280	46.9
4	Frank Thompson Jr. (D)	115,761	60.2
	A. Jerome Moore (R)	76,067	39.6
5	Peter H. B. Frelinghuysen Jr. (R)	170,859	58.6
	Jerome H. Taub (D)	120,302	41.3
6	Florence P. Dwyer (R)	136,723	57.7
	Jack B. Dunn (D)	98,043	41.4
7	William B. Widnall (R)	156,758	63.7
	James Dobbins (D)	88,649	36.0
8	Charles S. Joelson (D)	88,100	52.0
	Walter P. Kennedy (R)	74,165	43.8
9	Frank C. Osmers Jr. (R)	127,088	58.1
	Vincent T. McKenna (D)	91,065	41.6
10	Peter W. Rodino Jr. (D)	84,859	65.3
	Alphonse A. Miele (R)	43,238	33.3
11	Hugh J. Addonizio (D)	75,533	61.4
	Frank A. Palmieri (R)	44,580	36.2
12	George M. Wallhauser (R)	76,945	50.2
	Robert R. Peacock (D)	73,119	47.7
13	Cornelius E. Gallagher (D)	80,490	68.3
	Samuel F. Kanis (R)	37,350	31.7
14	Dominick V. Daniels (D)	64,359	57.4
	Frank A. Musto (R)	46,770	41.7

NEW MEXICO

	Candidates	Votes	%
AL	Thomas C. Morris (D)	172,577	58.0
	John D. Robb (R)	124,101	41.7
AL	Joseph M. Montoya (D)	176,514	58.6
	Edward W. Balcomb (R)	123,683	41.1

NEW YORK

	Candidates	Votes	%
1	Otis G. Pike (D, L)	187,286	50.4
	Stuyvesant Wainwright (R)	184,549	49.6
2	Steven B. Derounian (R)	139,423	61.0
	John J. Drury (D, L)	89,176	39.0
3	Frank J. Becker (R)	133,416	54.1
	Julius J. Rosen (D, L)	113,143	45.9
4	Seymour Halpern (R)	115,736	55.1
	Bernard A. Helfat (D, L)	94,390	44.9
5	Joseph P. Addabbo (D, L)	60,453	54.2
	George Archinal (R)	51,129	45.8
6	Lester Holtzman (D, L)	155,904	65.6
	Vincent L. Pitaro (R)	81,694	34.4
7	James J. Delaney (D, L)	92,424	60.7
	Edward V. Lisoski (R)	59,882	39.3
8	Victor L. Anfuso (D, L)	60,030	72.9
	Leon F. Nadrowski (R)	22,318	27.1
9	Eugene J. Keogh (D, L)	84,941	72.3
	Herman Sanders (R)	32,538	27.7
10	Edna F. Kelly (D, L)	98,938	76.6
	Jerome P. Schneider (R)	30,243	23.4
11	Emanuel Celler (D, L)	139,397	81.6
	Seymour Besunder (R)	31,378	18.4
12	Hugh L. Carey (D, L)	65,996	50.4
	Francis E. Dorn (R)	64,899	49.6
13	Abraham J. Multer (D, L)	117,087	75.4
	Joseph A. DeMarco (R)	38,189	24.6
14	John J. Rooney (D, L)	80,972	70.6
	Carlo G. Colavito (R)	33,769	29.4
15	John H. Ray (R)	80,218	48.7
	John M. Murphy (D)	77,812	47.2
16	Adam Clayton Powell Jr. (D)	59,957	71.6
	Joseph A. Bailey (R)	14,706	17.6
	Arthur O. Boyer (L)	9,093	10.9
17	John V. Lindsay (R)	81,006	60.2
	William J. Vanden Heuvel (D, L)	53,574	39.8
18	Alfred E. Santangelo (D)	47,749	58.3
	Charles Muzzicato (R)	27,419	33.5
	Faustino Louis Garcia (L)	6,680	8.2
19	Leonard Farbstein (D, L)	68,445	72.4
	Thomas P. O'Callaghan (R)	26,054	27.6
20	William F. Ryan (D)	55,272	55.7
	Morris Aarons (R)	30,046	30.3
	Ludwig Teller (L)	13,884	14.0
21	Herbert Zelenko (D, L)	87,775	74.6
	Thomas H. Bartzos (R)	29,835	25.4
22	James C. Healey (D)	78,717	65.0
	Dominick A. Fusco (R)	24,958	20.6
	David I. Wells (L)	17,438	14.4
23	Jacob H. Gilbert (D)	61,474	70.6
	Benjamin Thornley (R)	15,208	17.5
	Nicholas B. Gyory (L)	10,420	12.0
24	Charles A. Buckley (D)	89,140	56.6
	Michael R. Cappelli (R)	43,110	27.4
	Murray Koenig (L)	25,283	16.1
25	Paul A. Fino (R)	112,187	59.8
	Eugene L. Sugarman (D)	66,539	35.5
26	Edwin B. Dooley (R)	98,506	52.6
	Phil E. Gilbert Jr. (D, L)	88,879	47.4
27	Robert R. Barry (R)	121,533	56.3
	John R. Harold (D)	86,997	40.3
28	Katharine St. George (R)	107,179	58.7
	James E. Truex (D, L)	75,448	41.3
29	J. Ernest Wharton (R)	103,966	56.7
	Gore Vidal (D, L)	79,252	43.3
30	Leo W. O'Brien (D, L)	117,692	62.9
	Irving I. Waxman (R)	69,549	37.1
31	Carleton J. King (R)	99,604	60.4
	Louis E. Wolfe (D, L)	65,305	39.6
32	Samuel S. Stratton (D, L)	98,990	62.3
	W. Clyde Wright (R)	59,890	37.7
33	Clarence E. Kilburn (R)	91,710	61.9
	Edward J. Gosier (D)	53,130	35.9
34	Alexander Pirnie (R)	98,063	55.3
	Edwin L. Slusarczyk (D, L)	79,153	44.7
35	R. Walter Riehlman (R)	105,241	53.8
	Jerome M. Wilson (D)	87,347	44.6
36	John Taber (R)	84,441	52.6
	Francis J. Souhan (D, L)	76,120	47.4
37	Howard W. Robison (R)	123,782	63.4
	Joseph V. Julian (D, L)	71,354	36.6
38	Jessica McC. Weis (R)	114,871	57.6
	Arthur B. Curran Jr. (D, L)	84,716	42.4
39	Harold C. Ostertag (R)	103,162	59.7
	Henry R. Dutcher Jr. (D, L)	69,704	40.3
40	William E. Miller (R)	104,752	53.6
	Mariano A. Lucca (D)	85,005	43.5
41	Thaddeus J. Dulski (D, L)	82,114	56.2
	Ralph J. Radwan (R)	63,889	43.8
42	John R. Pillion (R)	122,073	55.4
	Charles J. McCabe (D)	93,492	42.4
43	Charles E. Goodell (R)	87,585	62.8
	T. Joseph Lynch (D)	48,423	34.7

Special Election

	Candidates	Votes	%
23	Jacob H. Gilbert (D)	4,594	82.3
	Simon M. Koenig (R)	574	10.3
	Hector Mathew (L)	411	7.4

NORTH CAROLINA

	Candidates	Votes	%
1	Herbert C. Bonner (D)	48,809	86.6
	Zeno O. Ratcliff (R)	7,587	13.5
2	L. H. Fountain (D)	51,156	87.8
	L. Paul Gooding (R)	7,135	12.2
3	David N. Henderson (D)	51,193	71.2
	Jack D. Brinson (R)	20,674	28.8
4	Harold D. Cooley (D)	75,464	66.6
	Elam Reamuel Temple Jr. (R)	37,821	33.4
5	Ralph J. Scott (D)	66,079	57.6
	Russell F. Biggam (R)	48,572	42.4
6	Horace R. Kornegay (D)	79,809	59.6
	Holland L. Robb (R)	54,028	40.4
7	Alton Lennon (D)	71,726	76.5
	Joel C. Clifton (R)	21,997	23.5
8	A. Paul Kitchin (D)	71,429	56.3
	A.M. Snipes (R)	55,372	43.7
9	Hugh Q. Alexander (D)	75,909	53.1
	W. S. Bogle (R)	67,033	46.9
10	Charles Raper Jonas (R)	97,138	58.6
	David Clark (D)	68,761	41.5
11	Basil L. Whitener (D)	65,478	61.1
	Kelly Dixon (R)	41,763	38.9
12	Roy A. Taylor (D)	61,170	52.0
	Heinz Rollman (R)	56,368	48.0

Special Election

	Candidates	Votes	%
12	Roy A. Taylor (D)	28,744	98.6

NORTH DAKOTA

	Candidates	Votes	%
AL	Don L. Short (R)	135,579✓	
	Hjalmar Nygaard (R)	127,118✓	
	Raymond Vendsel (D)	120,773	
	Anson J. Anderson (D)	109,207	

OHIO

	Candidates	Votes	%
1	Gordon H. Scherer (R)	88,899	58.9
	W. Ted Osborne (D)	62,043	41.1
2	Donald D. Clancy (R)	118,046	57.4
	H. A. Sand (D)	87,531	42.6
3	Paul F. Schenck (R)	167,117	62.0
	R. William Patterson (D)	102,237	38.0
4	William M. McCulloch (R)	99,683	65.4
	Joseph J. Murphy (D)	52,797	34.6
5	Delbert L. Latta (R)	85,175	67.3
	Tom P. McRitchie (D)	41,375	32.7
6	William H. Harsha Jr. (R)	80,124	55.2
	Franklin E. Smith (D)	65,045	44.8
7	Clarence J. Brown (R)	105,026	65.5
	Joseph A. Sullivan (D)	55,451	34.6
8	Jackson E. Betts (R)	81,373	67.7
	Virgil M. Gase (D)	38,871	32.3
9	Thomas Ludlow Ashley (D)	108,688	56.9
	Howard C. Cook (R)	82,433	43.1
10	Walter H. Moeller (D)	58,085	52.5
	Oakley C. Collins (R)	52,479	47.5
11	Robert E. Cook (D)	104,183	51.0
	David S. Dennison Jr. (R)	99,991	49.0
12	Samuel L. Devine (R)	140,236	60.7
	Richard E. Liming (D)	90,894	39.3
13	Charles A. Mosher (R)	73,110	51.4
	J. William McCray (D)	69,033	48.6
14	William H. Ayres (R)	145,526	61.5
	John H. Mihaly (D)	91,103	38.5
15	Tom V. Moorehead (R)	49,742	51.2
	Herbert U. Smith (D)	47,366	48.8
16	Frank T. Bow (R)	130,542	62.5
	John G. Freedom (D)	78,257	37.5
17	John M. Ashbrook (R)	79,609	53.0
	Robert W. Levering (D)	70,470	47.0

Candidates	Votes	%
18 Wayne L. Hays (D)	96,474	65.6
Walter Jay Hunston (R)	50,698	34.5
19 Michael J. Kirwan (D)	102,874	68.9
Paul E. Stevens (R)	46,537	31.2
20 Michael A. Feighan (D)	113,302	67.8
Leonard G. Richter (R)	53,845	32.2
21 Charles A. Vanik (D)	103,460	73.0
William O. Walker (R)	38,326	27.0
22 Frances P. Bolton (R)	88,389	56.9
Chat Paterson (D)	68,930	43.1
23 William E. Minshall (R)	123,364	67.3
Daniel Winston (D)	59,893	32.7

Special Election

6 Ward M. Miller (R)	76,520	55.4
Gladys E. Davis (D)	61,713	44.6

OKLAHOMA

1 Page Belcher (R)	133,964	63.8
Yates Land (D)	75,934	36.2
2 Ed Edmondson (D)	79,732	57.0
Bill Sharp (R)	60,253	43.0
3 Carl Albert (D)	56,138	74.9
George B. Sherritt (R)	18,799	25.1
4 Tom Steed (D)	54,181	60.7
Don H. Crall (R)	35,028	39.3
5 John Jarman (D)	125,286	66.6
Hobart H. Hobbs (R)	62,971	33.5
6[1] Victor Wickersham (D)	68,192	50.4
Clyde Wheeler Jr. (R)	67,116	49.6

OREGON

1 Walter Norblad (R)	144,743	65.1
Mary Owens (D)	77,689	34.9
2 Al Ullman (D)	62,690	59.6
Ronald E. Phair (R)	42,516	40.4
3 Edith Green (D)	157,243	63.9
Wallace L. Lee (R)	88,906	36.1
4 Edwin R. Durno (R)	96,022	51.1
Charles O. Porter (D)	91,947	48.9

PENNSYLVANIA

1 William A. Barrett (D)	88,805	77.0
Michael Grasso Jr. (R)	26,601	23.1
2 Kathryn E. Granahan (D)	109,452	72.3
Joseph C. Bruno (R)	42,019	27.7
3 James A. Byrne (D)	80,258	69.7
Joseph Patrick Gorham (R)	34,956	30.3
4 Robert N. C. Nix (D)	84,053	78.4
Clarence M. Smith (R)	23,146	21.6
5 William J. Green Jr. (D)	140,658	61.0
James W. Gilmour (R)	90,087	39.0
6 Herman Toll (D)	109,275	59.6
David O. Maxwell (R)	74,132	40.4
7 William H. Milliken Jr. (R)	136,021	53.0
Henry Gouley (D)	120,839	47.0
8 Willard S. Curtin (R)	121,564	56.1
Donald V. Hock (D)	95,140	43.9
9 Paul B. Dague (R)	128,917	66.6
Howard H. Halsey (D)	64,659	33.4
10 William W. Scranton (R)	97,012	54.8
Stanley A. Prokop (D)	80,097	45.2
11 Daniel J. Flood (D)	115,042	67.1
Donald B. Ayers (R)	56,428	32.9
12 Ivor D. Fenton (R)	72,061	52.4
William H. Deitman (D)	65,585	47.7
13 Richard S. Schweiker (R)	142,966	61.8
Warren M. Ballard (D)	88,486	38.2
14 George M. Rhodes (D)	60,211	53.8
James H. Mantis (R)	51,746	46.2
15 Francis E. Walter (D)	67,830	55.2
Woodrow A. Horn (R)	55,125	44.8
16 Walter M. Mumma (R)	93,831	62.5
Miles Albright (D)	56,267	37.5
17 Herman T. Schneebeli (R)	82,040	56.7

Candidates	Votes	%
Dean R. Fisher (D)	62,695	43.3
18 J. Irving Whalley	88,397	62.3
Robert M. Meyers (D)	53,453	37.7
19 George A. Goodling (R)	88,776	53.2
James M. Quigley (D)	78,043	46.8
20 James E. Van Zandt (R)	77,776	67.8
Robert N. Hendershot (D)	36,997	32.2
21 John H. Dent (D)	85,853	56.0
William L. Batten (R)	65,551	42.8
22 John P. Saylor (R)	89,261	57.4
William D. Patton (D)	66,383	42.7
23 Leon H. Gavin (R)	74,542	62.4
John H. Cartwright (D)	43,927	36.8
24 Carroll D. Kearns (R)	95,149	51.0
Chester C. Hampton (D)	91,498	49.0
25 Frank M. Clark (D)	102,750	58.1
Fred A. Obley (R)	74,217	41.9
26 Thomas E. Morgan (D)	111,362	63.6
Bartley P. Osborne (R)	63,702	36.4
27 James G. Fulton (R)	127,995	59.1
Margaret Lee Walgren (D)	88,660	40.9
28 William S. Moorhead (D)	99,491	67.8
Arthur O. Sharron (R)	47,232	32.2
29 Robert J. Corbett (R)	117,009	59.2
Russell M. Douthett (D)	80,497	40.8
30 Elmer J. Holland (D)	126,619	68.6
Jerome M. Meyers (R)	58,063	31.4

Special Election

18 J. Irving Whalley (R)	86,527	62.3
Robert M. Meyers (D)	52,324	37.7

RHODE ISLAND

1 Fernard J. St. Germain (D)	117,162	66.2
Theophile Martin (R)	59,737	33.8
2 John E. Fogarty (D)	151,544	70.4
Robert L. Gammell (R)	63,795	29.6

SOUTH CAROLINA

1 L. Mendel Rivers (D)	47,153	100.0
2 John J. Riley (D)	63,207	100.0
3 William J. Bryan Dorn (D)	52,398	100.0
4 Robert T. Ashmore (D)	68,973	100.0
5 Robert W. Hemphill (D)	46,815	99.8
6 John L. McMillan (D)	49,780	100.0

SOUTH DAKOTA

1 Ben Reifel (R)	126,033	54.9
Ray Fitzgerald (D)	103,755	45.2
2 E.Y. Berry (R)	42,550	59.8
W. H. Raff (D)	28,666	40.3

TENNESSEE

1 B. Carroll Reece (R)	103,872	75.4
Arthur Bright (D)	33,873	24.6
2 Howard H. Baker (R)	98,839	100.0
3 James B. Frazier Jr. (D)	62,827	100.0
4 Joe L. Evins (D)	60,730	100.0
5 J. Carlton Loser (D)	42,524	100.0
6 Ross Bass (D)	55,736	100.0
7 Tom Murray (D)	34,130	100.0
8 Robert A. Everett (D)	30,124	100.0
9 Clifford Davis (D)	120,159	100.0

TEXAS

1 Wright Patman (D)	58,674	100.0
2 Jack Brooks (D)	75,657	69.7
F. S. Newmann (R)	32,473	29.9
3 Lindley Beckworth (D)	59,386	100.0
Sam Rayburn (D)	44,902	100.0
5 Bruce Alger (R)	129,886	57.3
Joe Pool (D)	96,709	42.7
6 Olin Teague (D)	56,603	100.0

Candidates	Votes	%
7 John Dowdy (D)	61,586	100.0
8 Albert Thomas (D)	76,767	68.6
Anthony J. P. Farris (R)	24,486	21.9
Robert Nesmith (CST)	10,684	9.5
9 Clark Thompson (D)	98,586	94.3
P. D. Rogers (CST)	5,981	5.7
10 Homer Thornberry (D)	75,165	98.1
11 W. R. Poage (D)	64,351	100.0
12 Jim Wright (D)	115,797	100.0
13 Frank Ikard (D)	75,972	100.0
14 John Young (D)	105,792	100.0
15 Joe Kilgore (D)	76,421	100.0
16 J. T. Rutherford (D)	63,634	58.9
Dorothy Wynell (CST)	24,996	23.1
Ford Chapman (R)	19,491	18.0
17 Omar Burleson (D)	60,401	77.6
Max Mossholder (CST)	17,400	22.4
18 Walter Rogers (D)	79,675	100.0
19 George Mahon (D)	77,415	85.7
J. R. Anderson (CST)	12,953	14.3
20 Paul J. Kilday (D)	84,487	100.0
21 O. C. Fisher (D)	63,277	100.0
22 Bob Casey (D)	109,418	58.3
J. C. Noonan (R)	73,503	39.2

UTAH

1 M. Blaine Peterson (D)	65,939	50.0
A. Walter Stevenson (R)	65,871	50.0
2 David S. King (D)	120,771	50.8
Sherman P. Lloyd (R)	116,881	49.2

VERMONT

AL Robert T. Stafford (R)	94,905	57.2
William H. Meyer (D)	71,111	42.8

VIRGINIA

1 Thomas N. Downing (D)	53,768	82.4
Richard A. May (R)	11,429	17.5
2 Porter Hardy Jr. (D)	49,750	75.8
Louis B. Fine (R)	15,758	24.0
3 J. Vaughan Gary (D)	52,908	77.8
T. Coleman Andrews	14,907	21.9
4 Watkins M. Abbitt (D)	39,408	99.5
5 William M. Tuck (D)	30,154	98.9
6 Richard H. Poff (R)	60,371	82.4
J. B. Brayman (SOCIAL D)	12,700	17.3
7 Burr P. Harrison (D)	42,199	99.6
8 Howard W. Smith (D)	42,809	75.7
Lawrence M. Traylor (R)	13,410	23.7
9 W. Pat Jennings (D)	47,372	58.0
E. Summers Sheffey (R)	34,280	42.0
10 Joel T. Broyhill (R)	64,408	55.0
Ralph Kaul (D)	52,647	45.0

WASHINGTON

1 Thomas M. Pelly (R)	124,721	70.2
Carl Viking Holman (D)	53,009	29.8
2 Jack Westland (R)	87,802	60.2
Payson Peterson (D)	58,154	39.8
3 Julia Butler Hansen (D)	76,930	53.4
Dale M. Nordquist (R)	67,060	46.6
4 Catherine May (R)	94,210	58.8
Roy Mundy (D)	65,964	41.2
5 Walt Horan (R)	94,042	59.4
Bernard J. Gallagher (D)	64,321	40.6
6 Thor C. Tollefson (R)	83,158	56.5
John G. McCutcheon (D)	64,167	43.6
7 Don Magnuson (D)	95,663	50.0
John Stender (R)	95,524	50.0

Special Election

3 Julia Butler Hansen (D)	71,416	53.1
Dale M. Nordquist (R)	63,058	46.9

WEST VIRGINIA

	Candidates	Votes	%
1	Arch A. Moore Jr. (R)	81,018	60.3
	Steven D. Narick (D)	53,318	39.7
2	Harley O. Staggers (D)	74,184	60.3
	Charles J. Whiston (R)	48,903	39.7
3	Cleveland M. Bailey (D)	71,718	59.8
	James M. Knowles Jr. (R)	48,258	40.2
4	Ken Hechler (D)	82,931	53.2
	Clyde Pinson (R)	73,052	46.8
5	Elizabeth Kee (D)	77,524	69.5
	L. M. LaFollette (R)	34,052	30.5
6	John M. Slack Jr. (D)	108,452	61.8
	George W. King (R)	67,070	38.2

1. Figures are for December recount. Election was contested after initial vote tally had Wheeler winning by 188 votes.

WISCONSIN

	Candidates	Votes	%
1	Henry C. Schadeberg (R)	97,662	52.7
	Gerald T. Flynn (D)	87,646	47.3
2	Robert W. Kastenmeier (D)	119,885	53.4
	Donald E. Tewes (R)	104,744	46.6
3	Vernon W. Thomson (R)	71,677	54.6
	Norman M. Clapp (D)	59,527	45.4
4	Clement J. Zablocki (D)	155,789	71.7
	Samuel P. Murray (R)	61,468	28.3
5	Henry S. Reuss (D)	126,314	57.7
	Kirby Hendee (R)	92,526	42.3
6	William K. Van Pelt (R)	91,450	55.8
	James Megellas (D)	72,442	44.2

	Candidates	Votes	%
7	Melvin R. Laird (R)	95,152	67.1
	Kenneth Traeger (D)	46,606	32.9
8	John W. Byrnes (R)	101,132	58.8
	Milo Singler (D)	70,740	41.2
9	Lester R. Johnson (D)	74,268	56.6
	Perry M. Hull (R)	57,069	43.5
10	Alvin E. O'Konski (R)	73,114	95.0

WYOMING

	Candidates	Votes	%
AL	William Henry Harrison (R)	70,241	52.3
	Hepburn T. Armstrong (D)	64,090	47.7

1961 House Elections

ARIZONA

Special Election

	Candidates	Votes	%
2	Morris K. Udall (D)#	51,304	51.0
	Mac C. Matheson (R)#	49,297	49.0

ARKANSAS

Special Election

	Candidates	Votes	%
6	Catherine D. Norrell (D)#	10,209	43.1
	John Harris Jones (D)#	5,955	25.1
	M. C. Lewis Jr. (D)#	5,499	23.2
	James F. Cross (D)#	1,727	7.3

LOUISIANA

Special Election

	Candidates	Votes	%
4	Joe D. Waggonner Jr. (D)	33,892	54.5
	Charlton H. Lyons (R)	28,250	45.5

MICHIGAN[1]

Special Election

	Candidates	Votes	%
1	Lucien N. Nedzi (D)#	33,690	85.5
	Walter Czarnecki (R)#	5,729	14.5

PENNSYLVANIA

Special Election

	Candidates	Votes	%
16	John C. Kunkel (R)	43,220	65.6
	Kathryn Z. Vanderslice (D)	22,698	34.4

TENNESSEE

Special Election

	Candidates	Votes	%
1	Louise G. Reece (R)#	29,819	62.9
	William W. Faw (D)#	15,718	33.2

TEXAS[1]

Special Elections

	Candidates	Votes	%
4	Ray Roberts (D)	8,154	36.9
	R. C. Slagle (D)	5,945	26.9
	David Brown (D)	2,393	10.8
	Conner Harrington (R)	2,353	10.6
	Jack Finney (D)	2,211	10.0
13	Graham B. Purcell Jr. (D)	8,960	33.6
	Joe Meissner (R)	6,740	25.3
	Jack Hightower (D)	6,157	23.1
	Vernon Stewart (D)	2,706	10.2
	Jimmy P. Horany (D)	2,076	7.8
20	Henry B. Gonzalez (D)	52,696	54.6
	John Goode	42,511	44.0

1. In Texas special elections for the House held prior to 1961, all candidates ran against each other in one election regardless of party; the candidate receiving the most votes was the winner. Thus Lyndon B. Johnson won a 1937 special election with 27.7 percent of the vote. (See Texas 1937.)

The Texas law was changed in 1961 to require that in a special election, if no candidate received a majority, a special election runoff would be held between the top two candidates.

Thus, in the three House special elections held in Texas in 1961, only the election in the 20th district produced a majority vote winner. In the 4th and 13th districts, no candidate received a majority. Runoff special elections between the top two candidates in each district were held in 1962. (See Texas 1962.)

1962 House Elections

ALABAMA

	Candidates	Votes	%
AL	George Huddleston Jr. (D)	304,210✓	
	Armistead I. Selden Jr. (D)	295,882✓	
	George Andrews (D)	293,182✓	
	George Grant (D)	288,074✓	
	Albert Rains (D)	271,075✓	
	Kenneth A. Roberts (D)	269,410✓	
	Robert E. Jones (D)	258,674✓	
	Carl Elliott (D)	257,299✓	
	John H. Buchanan Jr. (R)	141,202	
	Tom Abernethy (R)	138,963	
	Evan Foreman Jr. (R)	136,339	
	J. Chester Robinson (N SR)	32,446	

ALASKA

	Candidates	Votes	%
AL	Ralph J. Rivers (D)	31,953	54.5
	Lowell Thomas Jr. (R)	26,638	45.5

ARIZONA

	Candidates	Votes	%
1	John J. Rhodes (R)	113,240	58.7
	Howard V. Peterson (D)	79,763	41.3
2	Morris K. Udall (D)	64,510	58.3
	Richard K. Burke (R)	46,219	41.7
3	George F. Senner Jr. (D)	25,359	56.0
	John P. Clark (R)	19,933	44.0

ARKANSAS

	Candidates	Votes	%
1	Ezekiel C. Gathings (D)		100.0
2	Wilbur D. Mills (D)		100.0
3	James W. Trimble (D)	58,786	69.4
	Cy Carney Jr. (R)	25,987	30.7
4	Oren Harris (D)	74,972	77.4
	Warren Lieblong (R)	21,818	22.5

CALIFORNIA

	Candidates	Votes	%
1	Clem Miller (D)	100,962*	50.8
	Don H. Clausen (R)	97,949	49.2
2	Harold T. Johnson (D)	106,239	64.6
	Fredric H. Nagel Jr. (R)	58,150	35.4
3	John E. Moss Jr. (D)	138,257	74.8
	George W. G. Smith (R)	46,510	25.2
4	Robert L. Leggett (D)	55,563	56.5
	L. V. Honsinger (R)	42,762	43.5
5	John F. Shelley (D)	64,493	80.4
	Roland S. Charles (R)	15,670	19.5
6	William S. Mailliard (R)	105,762	58.7
	John A. O'Connell (D)	74,429	41.3
7	Jeffery Cohelan (D)	86,215	64.5
	Leonard L. Cantando (R)	47,409	35.5
8	George P. Miller (D)	97,014	72.5
	Harold Petersen (R)	36,810	27.5
9	Don Edwards (D)	79,616	65.9
	Joseph Francis Donovan (R)	41,104	34.0
10	Charles S. Gubser (R)	106,419	60.7
	James P. Thurber Jr. (D)	68,885	39.3
11	J. Arthur Younger (R)	101,963	62.3
	William J. Keller (D)	61,623	37.7
12	Burt L. Talcott (R)	75,424	61.3
	William K. Stewart (D)	47,576	38.7
13	Charles M. Teague (R)	84,743	64.9
	George J. Holgate (D)	45,746	35.1
14	John F. Baldwin (R)	99,040	62.9
	Charles R. Weidner (D)	58,369	37.1
15	John J. McFall (D)	97,322	70.0
	Arthur L. Young (R)	41,726	30.0
16	B. F. Sisk (D)	108,339	71.9
	Arthur L. Selland (R)	42,401	28.1
17	Cecil R. King (D)	74,964	67.2
	Ted Bruinsma (R)	36,663	32.8
18	Harlan Hagen (D)	91,684	58.9
	Ray Arnett (R)	64,037	41.1
19	Chet Holifield (D)	78,436	61.6
	Robert T. Ramsay (R)	48,976	38.4
20	H. Allen Smith (R)	119,938	70.6
	Leon Mayer (D)	49,850	29.4
21	Augustus F. Hawkins (D)	73,465	84.5
	Herman Smith (R)	13,371	15.4
22	James C. Corman (D)	75,294	53.6
	Charles S. Foote (R)	65,087	46.4
23	Clyde Doyle (D)	83,269	64.2
	Del Clawson (R)	46,488	35.8
24	Glenard P. Lipscomb (R)	120,884	70.3
	Knox Mellon (D)	50,970	29.7
25	Ronald Brooks Cameron (D)	62,371	53.1
	John H. Rousselot (R)	53,961	45.9
26	James Roosevelt (D)	112,162	68.3
	Daniel Beltz (R)	52,063	31.7
27	Everett G. Burkhalter (D)	66,979	52.1
	Edgar W. Hiestand (R)	61,538	47.9
28	Alphonzo Bell (R)	162,233	64.0
	Robert J. Felixson (D)	91,305	36.0
29	George E. Brown Jr. (D)	73,740	55.6
	H. L. Richardson (R)	58,760	44.3
30	Edward R. Roybal (D)	69,008	56.5
	Gordon L. McDonough (R)	53,104	43.5
31	Charles H. Wilson (D)	76,631	52.2
	Gordon Hahn (R)	70,154	47.8
32	Craig Hosmer (R)	115,915	70.7
	J. J. Johovich (D)	47,917	29.2
33	Harry R. Sheppard (D)	96,192	59.0
	William R. Thomas (R)	66,764	41.0
34	Richard T. Hanna (D)	90,758	55.9
	Robert A. Geier (R)	71,478	44.1
35	James B. Utt (R)	133,737	68.5
	Burton Shamsky (D)	61,395	31.5
36	Bob Wilson (R)	91,626	61.8
	William C. Godfrey (D)	56,637	38.2
37	Lionel Van Deerlin (D)	63,821	51.3
	Dick Wilson (R)	60,460	48.6
38	Patrick Minor Martin (R)	68,583	55.9
	Dalip S. Saund (D)	54,022	44.1

COLORADO

	Candidates	Votes	%
1	Byron G. Rogers (D)	94,680	56.0
	William B. Chenoweth (R)	74,392	44.0
2	Donald G. Brotzman (R)	134,939	61.9
	Conrad L. McBride (D)	83,235	38.2
3	J. Edgar Chenoweth (R)	74,848	54.7
	Albert J. Tomsic (D)	62,097	45.3
4	Wayne N. Aspinall (D)	42,462	58.7
	Leo R. Sommerville (R)	29,943	41.4

CONNECTICUT

	Candidates	Votes	%
1	Emilio Q. Daddario (D)	162,844	57.5
	James F. Collins (R)	118,767	41.9
2	William L. St. Onge (D)	83,652	50.8
	Moses A. Savin (R)	81,010	49.2
3	Robert Giaimo (D)	104,728	56.0
	Daniel Reinhardsen Jr. (R)	82,215	44.0
4	Abner W. Sibal (R)	132,595	52.0
	Francis X. Lennon Jr. (D)	122,362	48.0
5	John B. Monagan (D)	83,321	58.5
	John A. Rand (R)	59,072	41.5
AL	Bernard F. Grabowski (D)	543,424	52.7
	John M. Lupton (R)	487,575	47.3

DELAWARE

	Candidates	Votes	%
AL	Harris B. McDowell Jr. (D)	81,166	52.9
	Wilmer F. Williams (R)	71,934	46.9

FLORIDA

	Candidates	Votes	%
1	Robert L. F. Sikes (D)	35,781	81.9
	M. M. Woolley (R)	7,902	18.1
2	Charles E. Bennett (D)	41,378	99.7
3	Claude Pepper (D)	59,985	57.6
	Bob Peterson (R)	44,164	42.4
4	Dante B. Fascell (D)	67,136	64.5
	J. C. McGlon Jr. (R)	36,981	35.5
5	A. Sydney Herlong Jr. (D)	54,383	65.2
	Hubert H. Hevey Jr. (R)	29,008	34.8
6	Paul G. Rogers (D)	102,396	64.2
	Frederick A. Kibbe (R)	57,112	35.8
7	James A. Haley (D)	52,417	66.8
	F. Onell Rogells (R)	26,042	33.2
8	D. R. Matthews (D)	23,387	100.0
9	Don Fuqua (D)	23,651	75.3
	Wilfred C. Varn (R)	7,735	24.6
10	Sam M. Gibbons (D)	41,426	70.6
	Victor A. Rule (R)	17,214	29.4
11	Edward J. Gurney (R)	46,814	51.9
	John A. Sutton (D)	43,348	48.1
12	William C. Cramer (R)	78,982	64.5
	Grover C. Criswell Jr. (D)	43,431	35.5

GEORGIA

	Candidates	Votes	%
1	G. Elliott Hagan (D)	25,229	97.6
2	John L. Pilcher (D)	18,967	96.3
3	E. L. Forrester (D)	25,001	100.0
4	John J. Flynt Jr. (D)	21,214	100.0
5	Charles L. Weltner (D)	60,583	55.6
	L. J. O'Callaghan (R)	48,466	44.4
6	Carl Vinson (D)	19,701	100.0
7	John W. Davis (D)	28,994	72.4
	Ralph Ivey (R)	11,048	27.6
8	J. Russell Tuten (D)	19,694	100.0
9	Phil M. Landrum (D)	25,942	100.0
10	Robert G. Stephens Jr. (D)	27,169	100.0

HAWAII

	Candidates	Votes	%
AL	Thomas P. Gill (D)	123,649✓	
	Spark M. Matsunaga (D)	123,599✓	
	Albert W. Evensen (R)	70,880	
	Richard Ike Sutton (R)	46,292	

IDAHO

	Candidates	Votes	%
1	Compton I. White Jr. (D)	51,422	53.0
	Erwin H. Schwiebert (R)	45,552	47.0
2	Ralph R. Harding (D)	83,152	52.8
	Orval Hansen (R)	74,203	47.2

ILLINOIS

	Candidates	Votes	%
1	William L. Dawson (D)	98,305	74.1
	Benjamin C. Duster (R)	34,379	25.9
2	Barratt O'Hara (D)	78,119	62.3
	Philip G. Bixler (R)	47,336	37.7
3	William T. Murphy (D)	82,866	51.6
	Ernest E. Michaels (R)	77,814	48.4
4	Edward J. Derwinski (R)	114,954	64.9
	Richard E. Friedman (D)	62,189	35.1
5	John C. Kluczynski (D)	84,455	63.4
	Joseph Potempa (R)	48,825	36.6
6	Thomas J. O'Brien (D)	72,183	77.7
	Adolph Herda (R)	20,690	22.3
7	Roland Victor Libonati (D)	86,677	78.8
	Joseph D. Day (R)	23,285	21.2
8	Dan Rostenkowski (D)	112,778	60.8
	Irvin R. Techon (R)	72,726	39.2
9	Edward R. Finnegan (D)	80,378	54.8
	Thomas E. Ward (R)	66,196	45.2
10	Harold R. Collier (R)	149,761	66.6
	Joseph A. Salerno (R)	74,986	33.4
11	Roman C. Pucinski (D)	103,677	52.7
	Henry J. Hyde (R)	92,910	47.3
12	Robert McClory (R)	76,335	63.9
	John Clark Kimball (D)	43,200	36.1

	Candidates	Votes	%
13	Donald Rumsfeld (R)	139,230	63.5
	John A. Kennedy (D)	79,419	36.2
14	Elmer J. Hoffman (R)	107,285	59.7
	Jerome M. Ziegler (D)	72,390	40.3
15	Charlotte T. Reid (R)	77,718	60.3
	Stanley H. Cowan (D)	49,444	38.3
16	John B. Anderson (R)	78,594	66.9
	Walter S. Busky (D)	38,853	33.1
17	Leslie C. Arends (R)	87,612	62.5
	Donald M. Laughlin (D)	52,592	37.5
18	Robert H. Michel (R)	75,957	61.2
	Francis D. Nash (D)	48,177	38.8
19	Robert T. McLoskey (R)	66,547	55.9
	David Dedoncker (D)	52,482	44.1
20	Paul Findley (R)	100,558	52.9
	Peter F. Mack Jr. (D)	89,522	47.1
21	Kenneth J. Gray (D)	96,971	60.0
	Frank H. Walker (R)	64,687	40.0
22	William L. Springer (R)	70,870	59.8
	Bob Wilson (D)	47,745	40.3
23	George E. Shipley (D)	99,133	51.7
	Edward H. Jenison (R)	92,562	48.3
24	Melvin Price (D)	95,522	73.8
	Kurt Glaser (R)	33,993	26.3

INDIANA

1	Ray J. Madden (D)	104,212	60.5
	Harold Moody (R)	67,230	39.0
2	Charles A. Halleck (R)	82,971	57.6
	John J. Murray (D)	61,076	42.4
3	John Brademas (D)	92,609	51.9
	Charles W. Ainlay (R)	85,845	48.1
4	E. Ross Adair (R)	80,693	55.6
	Ronald R. Ross (D)	64,553	44.4
5	J. Edward Roush (D)	92,264	51.6
	George O. Chambers (R)	86,403	48.4
6	Richard L. Roudebush (R)	* 76,506	52.7
	Fred Wampler (D)	68,777	47.3
7	William G. Bray (R)	82,160	57.8
	Elden C. Tipton (D)	59,953	42.2
8	Winfield K. Denton (D)	95,126	55.7
	Earl J. Heseman (R)	75,731	44.3
9	Earl Wilson (R)	65,287	52.1
	John Pritchard (O)	59,985	47.9
10	Ralph Harvey (R)	81,007	52.9
	John E. Mitchell (D)	72,009	47.1
11	Donald Cogley Bruce (R)	127,763	54.3
	Andrew Jacobs Jr. (D)	107,747	45.8

IOWA

1	Fred Schwengel (R)	65,975	61.1
	Harold Stephens (D)	42,000	38.9
2	James E. Bromwell (R)	67,475	52.8
	Frank W. Less (D)	60,296	47.2
3	H. R. Gross (R)	66,337	56.7
	Neel F. Hill (D)	50,580	43.3
4	John Kyl (R)	65,538	55.9
	Gene W. Glenn (D)	51,810	44.2
5	Neal Smith (D)	73,963	62.8
	Sonja C. Egenes (R)	43,877	37.2
6	Charles B. Hoeven (R)	66,940	58.5
	Donald W. Murray (D)	47,542	41.5
7	Ben F. Jensen (R)	56,341	56.1
	Edward J. Peters (D)	44,171	44.0

KANSAS

1	Bob Dole (R)	102,499	55.8
	J. Floyd Breeding (D)	81,092	44.2
2	William H. Avery (R)	72,945	65.2
	Harry F. Kehoe (D)	38,923	34.8
3	Robert F. Ellsworth (R)	60,865	63.4
	Bill Sparks (D)	35,166	36.6
4	Garner E. Shriver (R)	72,712	66.9
	Lawrence J. Wetzel (D)	35,922	33.1
5	Joe Skubitz (R)	66,705	53.3
	Wade A. Myers (D)	58,453	46.7

KENTUCKY

	Candidates	Votes	%
1	Frank A. Stubblefield (D)	53,240	100.0
2	William H. Natcher (D)	45,999	100.0
3	M. G. (Gene) Snyder (R)	94,579	50.8
	Frank W. Burke (D)	91,544	49.2
4	Frank Chelf (D)	57,956	52.9
	Clyde Middleton (R)	51,637	47.1
5	Eugene Siler (R)	59,326	100.0
6	John C. Watts (D)	53,454	100.0
7	Carl D. Perkins (D)	70,195	56.8
	C. Alex Parker Jr. (R)	52,640	42.6

LOUISIANA

1	F. Edward Hebert (D)	57,326	100.0
2	Hale Boggs (D)	57,395	67.2
	David C. Treen (R)	27,971	32.8
3	Edwin E. Willis (D)	26,170	100.0
4	Joe D. Waggonner Jr. (D)	29,754	100.0
5	Otto E. Passman (D)	24,609	100.0
6	James H. Morrison (D)	48,894	100.0
7	T. Ashton Thompson (D)	33,983	100.0
8	Gillis W. Long (D)	25,682	64.0
	John W. Lewis Jr. (R)	14,448	36.0

MAINE

1	Stanley R. Tupper (R)	85,864	59.6
	Ronald Kellam (D)	58,129	40.4
2	Clifford G. McIntire (R)	72,349	51.1
	William D. Hathaway (D)	69,159	48.9

MARYLAND

1	Rogers C. B. Morton (R)	33,674	53.2
	Thomas F. Johnson (D)	29,653	46.8
2	Clarence D. Long (D)	85,383	51.9
	Fife Symington (R)	79,075	48.1
3	Edward A. Garmatz (D)	41,446	100.0
4	George H. Fallon (D)	35,077	72.3
	John E. Brondau (R)	13,425	27.7
5	Richard E. Lankford (D)	85,612	59.5
	Joseph M. Baker Jr. (R)	58,332	40.5
6	Charles McC. Mathias Jr. (R)	106,212	60.9
	John Foley (D)	68,116	39.1
7	Samuel N. Friedel (D)	57,958	70.0
	Caroline R. Ramsay (R)	24,825	30.0
AL	Carlton R. Sickles (D)	388,107	55.7
	Newton Steers (R)	308,792	44.3

MASSACHUSETTS

1	Silvio O. Conte (R)	106,498	74.4
	William K. Hefner (D)	36,711	25.6
2	Edward P. Boland (D)	92,340	67.8
	Samuel S. Rodman (R)	43,873	32.2
3	Philip J. Philbin (D)	129,326	72.4
	Frank Anthony (R)	49,418	27.7
4	Harold D. Donohue (D)	145,166	90.4
	Stanley Shogren (P)	15,310	9.5
5	F. Bradford Morse (R)	112,455	57.4
	Thomas J. Lane (D)	83,504	42.6
6	William H. Bates (R)	113,104	56.2
	George J. O'Shea (D)	88,187	43.8
7	Torbert H. Macdonald (D)	119,117	71.6
	Gordon F. Hughes (R)	47,289	28.4
8	Thomas P. O'Neill Jr. (D)	100,814	73.0
	Howard Greyber (R)	37,374	27.1
9	John W. McCormack (D)	105,565	100.0
10	Joseph W. Martin Jr. (R)	124,091	65.5
	Edward F. Doolan (D)	65,443	34.5
11	James A. Burke (D)	121,030	64.3
	Harry F. Stimpson (R)	67,138	35.7
12	Hastings Keith (R)	107,000	64.2
	Alexander Byron (D)	59,681	35.8

MICHIGAN

	Candidates	Votes	%
1	Lucien N. Nedzi (D)	82,321	89.3
	Walter Czarnecki (R)	9,916	10.8
2	George Meader (R)	88,427	58.4
	Thomas P. Payne (D)	63,036	41.6
3	August E. Johansen (R)	77,316	59.5
	Paul H. Todd Jr. (D)	52,667	40.5
4	Edward Hutchinson (R)	73,308	63.8
	Leland D. Mitchell (D)	41,620	36.2
5	Gerald R. Ford Jr. (R)	110,043	67.0
	William G. Reamon (D)	54,112	33.0
6	Charles E. Chamberlain (R)	112,861	54.5
	Don Hayworth (D)	94,157	45.5
7	James G. O'Hara (D)	127,067	56.3
	H. Charles Knill (R)	98,742	43.7
8	James Harvey (R)	77,022	60.5
	Jerome T. Hart (D)	50,376	39.5
9	Robert P. Griffin (R)	66,645	59.4
	Donald G. Jennings (D)	45,536	40.6
10	Elford A. Cederberg (R)	63,452	61.5
	Hubert C. Evans (D)	39,771	38.5
11	Victor A. Knox (R)	48,244	56.7
	Warren P. Cleary (D)	36,886	43.3
12	John B. Bennett (R)	41,784	63.3
	William J. Bolognesi (D)	24,240	36.7
13	Charles C. Diggs Jr. (D)	59,688	71.2
	Robert B. Blackwell (R)	24,134	28.8
14	Harold M. Ryan (D)	108,025	61.8
	Lois V. Nair (R)	66,889	38.2
15	John D. Dingell (D)	94,197	83.0
	Ernest Richards (R)	19,258	17.0
16	John Lesinski Jr. (D)	180,626	67.9
	Laverne O. Elliott (R)	85,485	32.1
17	Martha W. Griffiths (D)	122,021	59.3
	James F. O'Neil (R)	83,870	40.7
18	William S. Broomfield (R)	149,863	59.6
	George J. Fulkerson (D)	101,468	40.4
AL	Neil Staebler (D)	1,392,221	52.0
	Alvin M. Bentley (R)	1,282,082	47.9

Special Election

14	Harold M. Ryan (D)	30,367#	50.5
	Robert E. Waldron (R)	29,600#	49.2

MINNESOTA

1	Albert H. Quie (R)	90,632	57.5
	David L. Graven (DFL)	66,956	42.5
2	Ancher Nelsen (R)	81,557	62.2
	Conrad H. Hammar (DFL)	49,543	37.8
3	Clark MacGregor (R)	87,730	60.2
	Irving R. Keldsen (DFL)	58,066	39.8
4	Joseph E. Karth (DFL)	93,519	59.5
	Harry Strong (R)	63,766	40.5
5	Donald M. Fraser (DFL)	87,002	51.8
	Walter H. Judd (R)	80,865	48.2
6	Alec G. Olson (DFL)	77,310	50.1
	Robert J. Odegard (R)	76,962	49.9
7	Odin Langen (R)	70,546	52.0
	Harding C. Noblitt (DFL)	65,161	48.0
8	John A. Blatnik (DFL)	101,567	65.7
	Jerry H. Ketola (R)	52,996	34.3

MISSISSIPPI

1	Thomas G. Abernethy (D)	26,251	100.0
2	Jamie L. Whitten (D)	31,344	100.0
3	John Bell Williams (D)	38,093	100.0
4	Arthur Winstead (D)	21,730	83.0
	Sterling P. Davis (I)	4,461	17.0
5	William M. Colmer (D)	39,735	100.0

MISSOURI

1	Frank M. Karsten (D)	82,216	70.7
	Charles F. Cherry (R)	34,089	29.3
2	Thomas B. Curtis (R)	102,861	56.3
	Philip V. Maher (D)	79,732	43.7

	Candidates	Votes	%
3	Leonor K. Sullivan (D)	81,346	70.5
	J. Marvin Krause (R)	34,031	29.5
4	William J. Randall (D)	59,599	53.9
	John D. Fox (R)	50,945	46.1
5	Richard Bolling (D)	54,166	58.9
	Walter McCarty (R)	37,835	41.1
6	W. R. Hull Jr. (D)	62,366	55.3
	Ethan H. Campbell (R)	50,339	44.7
7	Durward G. Hall (R)	84,631	57.7
	Jim Thomas (D)	62,082	42.3
8	Richard Ichord (D)	77,535	59.0
	David W. Bernhardt (R)	53,862	41.0
9	Clarence Cannon (D)	74,254	61.2
	Anthony C. Schroeder (R)	47,026	38.8
10	Paul C. Jones (D)	50,581	60.6
	Truman Farrow (R)	32,828	39.4

MONTANA

	Candidates	Votes	%
1	Arnold Olsen (D)	55,611	52.8
	Wayne Montgomery (R)	49,760	47.2
2	James F. Battin (R)	79,315	55.4
	Leo Graybill Jr. (D)	63,755	44.6

NEBRASKA

	Candidates	Votes	%
1	Ralph F. Beermann (R)	85,559	50.9
	Clair A. Callan (D)	73,768	43.9
	George C. Menkens	8,794	5.2
2	Glenn Cunningham (R)	83,139	69.5
	Thomas N. Bonner (D)	36,577	30.6
3	Dave Martin (R)	103,079	65.6
	John A. Hoffman (D)	54,058	34.4

NEVADA

	Candidates	Votes	%
AL	Walter S. Baring (D)	66,866	71.7
	J. Carlton Adair (R)	26,458	28.4

NEW HAMPSHIRE

	Candidates	Votes	%
1	Louis C. Wyman (R)	65,651	53.1
	J. Oliva Huot (D)	57,910	46.9
2	James C. Cleveland (R)	56,152	57.5
	Eugene S. Daniell (D)	41,539	42.5

NEW JERSEY

	Candidates	Votes	%
1	William T. Cahill (R)	119,633	58.8
	Neil F. Deighan Jr. (D)	83,405	41.0
2	Milton W. Glenn (R)	61,285	52.7
	Paul R. Porreca (D)	54,317	46.7
3	James C. Auchincloss (R)	82,220	56.9
	Peter J. Gannon (D)	62,258	43.1
4	Frank Thompson Jr. (D)	88,668	63.8
	Ephraim Tomlinson (R)	49,952	35.9
5	Peter H. B. Frelinghuysen Jr. (R)	86,133	66.0
	Eugene M. Friedman (D)	43,347	33.2
6	Florence P. Dwyer (R)	110,143	59.6
	Lillian Walsh Egolf (D)	73,436	39.8
7	William B. Widnall (R)	110,926	61.4
	J. Emmet Cassidy (D)	68,330	37.8
8	Charles S. Joelson (D)	75,820	65.0
	Walter W. Porter Jr. (R)	39,903	34.2
9	Frank C. Osmers Jr. (R)	89,345	56.9
	Donald R. Sorkow (D)	66,140	42.2
10	Peter W. Rodino Jr. (D)	62,616	72.8
	Charles Allan Baretski (R)	22,819	26.5
11	Joseph G. Minish (D)	48,102	59.5
	Frank A. Palmieri (R)	30,244	37.4
12	George M. Wallhauser (R)	57,169	52.5
	Robert R. Peacock (D)	50,783	46.6
13	Cornelius E. Gallagher (D)	62,636	77.1
	Eugene P. Kenny (R)	17,063	21.0
14	Dominick V. Daniels (D)	54,000	70.6
	Michael J. Bell (R)	21,303	27.9
15	Edward J. Patten (D)	86,651	56.7
	Bernard F. Rodgers (R)	66,142	43.3

NEW MEXICO

	Candidates	Votes	%
AL	Thomas G. Morris (D)	152,684	64.4
	Junio Lopez (R)	84,457	35.6
AL	Joseph M. Montoya (D)	128,651	52.5
	Jack C. Redman (R)	116,262	47.5

NEW YORK

	Candidates	Votes	%
1	Otis G. Pike (D, L)	85,619	61.7
	Walter M. Ormsby (R)	53,133	38.3
2	James R. Grover Jr. (R)	70,352	55.7
	Robert J. Flynn (D, L)	55,964	44.3
3	Steven B. Derounian (R)	86,430	59.2
	George Soll (D, L)	59,635	40.8
4	John W. Wydler (R)	74,508	56.4
	Joseph A. Daley (D, L)	56,438	42.7
5	Frank J. Becker (R)	89,964	57.5
	Franklin Bear (D, L)	66,502	42.5
6	Seymour Halpern (R)	96,475	63.3
	Leonard L. Finz (D, L)	55,883	36.7
7	Joseph P. Addabbo (D, L)	80,983	59.3
	George Archinal (R)	55,654	40.7
8	Benjamin S. Rosenthal (D, L)	104,895	66.4
	Arthur McCrossen (R)	53,122	33.6
9	James J. Delaney (D)	85,987	58.8
	Charles H. Cohen (R)	51,325	35.1
	Mark Starr (L)	9,051	6.2
10	Emanuel Celler (D, L)	90,216	80.0
	Seymour Besunder (R)	21,210	19.0
11	Eugene J. Keogh (D, L)	60,082	71.6
	Abraham L. Banner (R)	23,844	28.4
12	Edna F. Kelly (D, L)	106,375	70.0
	Louis London Goldberg (R)	45,492	30.0
13	Abraham J. Multer (D, L)	116,753	74.6
	Melvyn M. Rothman (R)	39,765	25.4
14	John J. Rooney (D, L)	54,298	70.9
	Leon F. Nadrowski (R)	22,287	29.1
15	Hugh L. Carey (D, L)	55,602	50.2
	Francis E. Dorn (R)	55,219	49.8
16	John M. Murphy (D)	57,666	47.5
	Robert T. Connor (R)	55,821	45.9
	George B. Murphy (L)	8,043	6.6
17	John V. Lindsay (R)	98,024	68.7
	Martin B. Dworkis (D, L)	44,728	31.3
18	Adam Clayton Powell Jr. (D)	59,125	69.6
	Ramon A. Martinez (R)	18,313	21.6
	Mae P. Watts (L)	7,457	8.8
19	Leonard Farbstein (D)	59,880	58.5
	Richard S. Aldrich (R, OP)	31,244	30.5
	Bentley Kassal (L)	11,233	11.0
20	William F. Ryan (D, L)	94,425	72.6
	Gilbert A. Robinson (R)	35,664	27.4
21	James C. Healey (D)	65,242	67.4
	Stanley L. Slater (R)	20,354	21.0
	Lillian Gulker (L)	11,187	11.6
22	Jacob H. Gilbert (D)	51,241	70.4
	Oscar Gonzalez-Suarez (R)	14,901	20.5
	David Grand (L)	6,629	9.1
23	Charles A. Buckley (D)	69,836	54.4
	John J. Parker (R)	39,692	30.9
	John P. Hagan (L)	18,749	14.6
24	Paul A. Fino (R)	77,785	60.1
	Alfred E. Santangelo (D)	46,455	35.9
25	Robert Barry (R)	109,989	61.5
	A. Frank Reel (D, L)	68,859	38.5
26	Ogden R. Reid (R)	93,064	60.9
	Stanley W. Church (D, L)	59,725	39.1
27	Katharine St. George (R)	86,958	57.9
	William F. Ward Jr. (D, L)	63,306	42.1
28	J. Ernest Wharton (R)	94,531	64.1
	Morton E. Gilday (D, L)	52,994	35.9
29	Leo W. O'Brien (D, L)	126,313	60.1
	Wolfgang J. Riemer (R)	83,719	39.9
30	Carleton J. King (R)	108,860	63.8
	William W. Egan (D)	57,822	33.9
31	Clarence E. Kilburn (R)	66,283	60.0
	Francis G. Healey (D, L)	44,171	40.0
32	Alexander Pirnie (R)	77,875	57.6
	Virgil C. Crisafulli (D, L)	57,414	42.4

	Candidates	Votes	%
33	Howard W. Robison (R)	92,460	66.8
	Theodore W. Maurer (D)	41,412	29.9
34	R. Walter Riehlman (R)	84,780	54.8
	Lee Alexander (D)	67,149	43.4
35	Samuel S. Stratton (D, L)	78,560	54.5
	Janet Hill Gordon (R)	65,697	45.5
36	Frank J. Horton (R)	96,581	59.3
	Robert R. Bickal (D, L)	66,371	40.7
37	Harold C. Ostertag (R)	101,821	64.3
	Norman C. Katner (D, L)	56,428	35.7
38	Charles E. Goodell (R)	83,361	68.4
	T. Joseph Lynch (D)	36,992	30.3
39	John R. Pillion (R)	99,527	62.6
	Angelo S. Deloia (D)	55,774	35.1
40	William E. Miller (R)	72,706	52.0
	E. Dent Lackey (D, L)	67,004	48.0
41	Thaddeus J. Dulski (D, L)	93,982	71.5
	Daniel J. Kij (R)	37,544	28.5

Special Election

	Candidates	Votes	%
6	Benjamin S. Rosenthal (D, L)	16,115#	44.5
	Thomas F. Galvin (R)	15,851#	43.8
	Emil Levin (I)	4,245#	11.7

NORTH CAROLINA

	Candidates	Votes	%
1	Herbert C. Bonner (D)	17,898	100.0
2	L. H. Fountain (D)	21,050	100.0
3	David N. Henderson (D)	34,056	100.0
4	Harold D. Cooley (D)	45,249	58.1
	George E. Ward (R)	32,593	41.9
5	Ralph J. Scott (D)	47,009	59.2
	A. M. Snipes (R)	32,427	40.8
6	Horace R. Kornegay (D)	43,021	59.9
	Blackwell P. Robinson (R)	28,827	40.1
7	Alton Lennon (D)	33,173	77.0
	James E. Walsh Jr. (R)	9,895	23.0
8	Charles R. Jonas (R)	64,703	56.0
	A. Paul Kitchin (D)	50,926	44.0
9	James T. Broyhill (R)	67,608	50.5
	Hugh Q. Alexander (D)	66,332	49.5
10	Basil L. Whitener (D)	52,641	55.1
	Carrol M. Barringer (R)	42,908	44.9
11	Roy A. Taylor (D)	70,791	55.2
	Robert Brown (R)	57,422	44.8

NORTH DAKOTA

	Candidates	Votes	%
1	Hjalmar C. Nygaard (R)	61,330	54.6
	Scott Anderson (D)	50,924	45.4
2	Don L. Short (R)	56,203	54.0
	Robert Vogel (D)	47,825	46.0

OHIO

	Candidates	Votes	%
1	Carl W. Rich (R)	74,320	62.7
	Monica Nolan (D)	44,264	37.3
2	Donald D. Clancy (R)	105,750	62.8
	H. A. Sand (D)	62,733	37.2
3	Paul F. Schenck (R)	113,584	57.0
	Martin A. Evers (D)	85,573	43.0
4	William M. McCulloch (R)	77,790	70.3
	Marjorie Conrad Struna (D)	32,866	29.7
5	Delbert L. Latta (R)	69,272	70.4
	William T. Hunt (D)	29,114	29.6
6	William H. Harsha (R)	72,743	60.4
	Jerry C. Rasor (D)	47,737	39.6
7	Clarence J. Brown (R)	83,680	67.7
	Robert A. Riley (D)	39,908	32.3
8	Jackson E. Betts (R)	66,458	70.1
	Morris Laderman (D)	28,400	29.9
9	Thomas L. Ashley (D)	86,443	57.4
	Martin A. Janis (R)	64,279	42.7
10	Homer E. Abele (R)	46,158	52.3
	Walter H. Moeller (D)	42,131	47.7
11	Oliver P. Bolton (R)	74,573	50.6
	Robert E. Cook (D)	72,936	49.5
12	Samuel L. Devine (R)	130,316	68.3
	Paul D. Cassidy (D)	60,563	31.7

Candidates	Votes	%
13 Charles A. Mosher (R)	63,858	55.1
J. Grant Keys (D)	52,030	44.9
14 William H. Ayres (R)	100,909	53.7
Oliver Ocasek (D)	86,947	46.3
15 Robert T. Secrest (D)	41,856	52.4
Tom V. Moorehead (R)	38,095	47.7
16 Frank T. Bow (R)	96,512	60.1
Ed Witmer (D)	64,213	40.0
17 John M. Ashbrook (R)	69,976	58.6
Robert W. Levering (D)	49,415	41.4
18 Wayne L. Hays (D)	66,327	61.0
John J. Carrigg (R)	42,336	39.0
19 Michael J. Kirwan (D)	75,967	62.2
William Vincent Williams (R)	46,200	37.8
20 Michael A. Feighan (D)	91,544	71.0
Leonard G. Richter (R)	37,325	29.0
21 Charles A. Vanik (D)	79,514	79.9
Leodis Harris (R)	20,027	20.1
22 Frances P. Bolton (R)	74,603	64.6
Edward Corrigan (D)	35,353	30.6
23 William E. Minshall (R)	107,510	71.5
Emil C. Weber (D)	42,907	28.5
AL Robert Taft Jr. (R)	1,786,018	60.5
Richard D. Kennedy (D)	1,164,776	39.5

OKLAHOMA

Candidates	Votes	%
1 Page Belcher (R)	102,585	68.6
Herbert W. Wright Jr. (D)	46,949	31.4
2 Ed Edmondson (D)	65,968	56.7
Bill Sharp (R)	50,481	43.4
3 Carl Albert (D)	56,010	100.0
4 Tom Steed (D)	66,000	100.0
5 John Jarman (D)	90,392	68.9
William P. Pointon Jr. (R)	40,825	31.1
6 Victor Wickersham (D)	56,508	53.6
Glenn L. Gibson (R)	48,985	46.4

OREGON

Candidates	Votes	%
1 Walter Norblad (R)	119,263	61.8
R. Blaine Whipple (D)	73,641	38.2
2 Al Ullman (D)	53,335	64.0
Robert W. Chandler (R)	29,995	36.0
3 Edith Green (D)	131,573	66.0
Stanley E. Hartman (R)	67,830	34.0
4 Robert B. Duncan (D)	83,660	53.9
Carl Fisher (R)	71,483	46.1

PENNSYLVANIA

Candidates	Votes	%
1 William A. Barrett (D)	102,722	63.5
Winifred H. Malinowsky (R)	58,953	36.5
2 Robert N. C. Nix (D)	86,812	67.1
Arthur C. Thomas (R)	42,607	32.9
3 James A. Byrne (D)	81,405	59.3
Joseph R. Burns (R)	55,827	40.7
4 Herman Toll (D)	104,300	56.0
Frank J. Barbera (R)	82,014	44.0
5 William J. Green Jr. (D)	94,501	55.9
Michael J. Bednarek (R)	74,557	44.1
6 George M. Rhodes (D)	112,959	51.2
Ivor D. Fenton (R)	107,724	48.8
7 William H. Milliken (R)	136,955	60.8
John A. Reilly (D)	88,482	39.3
8 Willard S. Curtin (R)	101,853	54.8
James A. Michener (D)	84,043	45.2
9 Paul B. Dague (R)	113,880	67.2
Richard C. Keller (D)	55,565	32.8
10 Joseph M. McDade (R)	95,754	52.5
William D. Combar (D)	86,680	47.5
11 Daniel J. Flood (D)	101,754	66.5
Donald B. Ayers (R)	51,263	33.5
12 J. Irving Whalley (R)	98,190	60.5
A. Reed Hayes (D)	64,227	39.5
13 Richard S. Schweiker (R)	135,847	66.6
Lee F. Driscoll Jr. (D)	68,234	33.4
14 William S. Moorhead (D)	93,130	65.7
Joseph M. Beatty (R)	48,726	34.4
15 Francis E. Walter (D)	63,574	57.5

Candidates	Votes	%
Woodrow A. Horn (R)	46,928	42.5
16 John C. Kunkel (R)	90,113	66.7
John A. Walter (D)	44,932	33.3
17 Herman T. Schneebeli (R)	96,088	62.9
William W. Litke (D)	56,692	37.1
18 Robert J. Corbett (R)	108,433	64.3
Edward F. Cook (D)	60,260	35.7
19 George A. Goodling (R)	82,924	56.8
Earl D. Warner (D)	62,995	43.2
20 Elmer J. Holland (D)	106,971	67.4
Budd Edward Sheppard (R)	51,688	32.6
21 John H. Dent (D)	80,410	59.6
Charles E. Scalf (R)	54,543	40.4
22 John P. Saylor (R)	82,584	57.5
Donald J. Perry (D)	61,054	42.5
23 Leon H. Gavin (R)	79,158	58.6
Frank M. O'Neil (D)	54,798	40.6
24 James D. Weaver (R)	82,213	51.4
Peter J. Joyce (D)	77,749	48.6
25 Frank M. Clark (D)	87,552	56.4
Harvey R. Robinson (R)	67,630	43.6
26 Thomas E. Morgan (D)	94,932	61.7
Jerome Hahn (R)	58,945	38.3
27 James G. Fulton (R)	112,034	65.5
Margaret Lee Walgren (D)	58,984	34.5

RHODE ISLAND

Candidates	Votes	%
1 Fernand J. St. Germain (D)	80,333	56.8
R. Gordon Butler (R)	61,186	43.2
2 John E. Fogarty (D)	127,184	71.8
John F. Kennedy (R)	49,955	28.2

SOUTH CAROLINA

Candidates	Votes	%
1 L. Mendel Rivers (D)	39,176	100.0
2 Albert W. Watson (D)	39,149	52.8
Floyd D. Spence (R)	34,947	47.2
3 W. J. Bryan Dorn (D)	34,545	100.0
4 Robert T. Ashmore (D)	47,044	100.0
5 Robert W. Hemphill (D)	28,989	93.9
Robert M. Doster (R)	1,861	6.0
6 John L. McMillan (D)	36,811	100.0

Special Election

Candidates	Votes	%
2 Corinne B. Riley (D)	3,626#	100.0

SOUTH DAKOTA

Candidates	Votes	%
1 Ben Reifel (R)	113,975	59.2
Ralph A. Nauman (D)	78,421	40.8
2 E.Y. Berry (R)	37,092	61.5
M. W. Morrie Clarkson (D)	23,243	38.5

TENNESSEE[1]

Candidates	Votes	%
1 James Quillen (R)	49,320	53.9
Herbert Silvers (D)	40,113	43.8
2 Howard H. Baker (R)	61,306	70.6
Tally R. Livingston (D)	25,579	29.4
3 Bill Brock (R)	47,604	51.1
Wilkes T. Thrasher Jr. (D)	45,597	48.9
4 Joe L. Evins (D)	46,005	87.9
Arch M. Eaton Sr. (I)	6,310	12.1
5 Richard Fulton (D)	47,756	60.4
J. Carleton Loser (D)	30,182	38.2
6 Ross Bass (D)	36,404	81.8
J. J. Underwood Jr. (I)	8,120	18.2
7 Tom Murray (D)	24,746	100.0
8 Robert A. Everett (D)	23,521	97.3
9 Clifford Davis (D)	55,345	50.6
Robert B. James (R)	54,132	49.5

TEXAS

Candidates	Votes	%
1 Wright Patman (D)	26,669	67.3
James Timberlake (R)	12,938	32.7
2 Jack Brooks (D)	47,137	68.8
Roy James Jr. (R)	21,385	31.2

Candidates	Votes	%
3 Lindley Beckworth (D)	26,915	52.0
William Steger (R)	24,803	48.0
4 Ray Roberts (D)	23,573	72.0
Conner Harrington (R)	9,165	28.0
5 Bruce Alger (R)	89,938	56.3
Bill Jones (D)	69,813	43.7
6 Olin E. Teague (D)	33,617	100.0
7 John Dowdy (D)	37,756	88.2
Raymond Ramage (R)	5,045	11.8
8 Albert Thomas (D)	51,285	71.5
Anthony Farris (R)	20,475	28.5
9 Clark W. Thompson (D)	56,179	66.3
Dave Oaks (R)	28,594	33.7
10 Homer Thornberry (D)	43,396	63.3
Jim Dobbs (R)	25,165	36.7
11 W. R. Poage (D)	41,698	100.0
12 Jim Wright (D)	53,705	60.6
Del Barron (R)	34,879	39.4
13 Graham B. Purcell (D)	37,941	67.1
Joe Meissner (R)	18,578	32.9
14 John Young (D)	60,803	70.4
Lawrence E. Hoover (R)	25,623	29.7
15 Joe Kilgore (D)	53,552	100.0
16 Ed Foreman (R)	44,095	53.8
J. T. Rutherford (D)	37,821	46.2
17 Omar Burleson (D)	46,895	100.0
18 Walter Rogers (D)	43,389	58.8
Jack Seale (R)	30,393	41.2
19 George Mahon (D)	46,925	67.1
Dennis Taylor (R)	23,022	32.9
20 Henry B. Gonzalez (D)	62,776	100.0
21 O. C. Fisher (D)	39,261	76.1
E. S. Mayer Jr. (R)	12,310	23.9
22 Bob Casey (D)	73,141	53.6
Ross Baker (R)	63,452	46.5
AL Joe Pool (D)	870,860	56.1
Desmond A. Barry (R)	680,569	43.9

Special Runoff Elections[2]

Candidates	Votes	%
4 Ray Roberts (D)	16,109	54.3
R. C. Slagle Jr. (D)	13,572	45.7
13 Graham B. Purcell Jr. (D)	23,905	62.9
Joe Meissner (R)	14,098	37.1

UTAH

Candidates	Votes	%
1 Laurence J. Burton (R)	59,032	50.9
Morris Blaine Peterson (D)	56,989	49.1
2 Sherman P. Lloyd (R)	108,355	53.9
Bruce S. Jenkins (D)	92,631	46.1

VERMONT

Candidates	Votes	%
AL Robert T. Stafford (R)	68,822	56.7
Harold Reynolds (D)	52,535	43.3

VIRGINIA

Candidates	Votes	%
1 Thomas N. Downing (D)	21,664	99.7
2 Porter Hardy Jr. (D)	30,306	75.0
Louis B. Fine (R)	10,121	25.0
3 J. Vaughan Gary (D)	28,914	49.8
Louis H. Williams (R)	28,566	49.2
4 Watkins M. Abbitt (D)	30,642	99.5
5 William M. Tuck (D)	13,827	99.8
6 Richard H. Poff (R)	44,060	65.2
John P. Wheeler (D)	23,280	34.5
7 John O. Marsh Jr. (D)	26,302	50.6
J. Kenneth Robinson (R)	25,704	49.4
8 Howard W. Smith (D)	20,931	98.7
9 W. Pat Jennings (D)	32,893	61.2
Leon Owens (R)	20,851	38.8
10 Joel T. Broyhill (R)	49,611	55.4
Augustus C. Johnson (D)	39,940	44.6

WASHINGTON

Candidates	Votes	%
1 Thomas M. Pelly (R)	108,561	73.7
Alice Franklin Bryant (D)	38,669	26.3

	Candidates	Votes	%
2	Jack Westland (R)	70,498	59.8
	Milo Moore (D)	47,333	40.2
3	Julia Butler Hansen (D)	69,045	65.3
	Edwin J. Alexander (R)	36,629	34.7
4	Catherine May (R)	83,182	67.0
	David A. Gallant (D)	40,887	33.0
5	Walt Horan (R)	78,504	64.4
	Bernard J. Gallagher (D)	43,333	35.6
6	Thor C. Tollefson (R)	79,838	71.1
	Dawn Olson (D)	32,513	28.9
7	K.W. Stinson (R)	86,106	56.6
	Don Magnuson (D)	66,052	43.4

WEST VIRGINIA

	Candidates	Votes	%
1	Arch A. Moore Jr. (R)	97,556	59.9
	Cleveland M. Bailey (D)	65,328	40.1
2	Harley O. Staggers (D)	62,291	58.7

	Candidates	Votes	%
	Cooper P. Benedict (R)	43,769	41.3
3	John M. Slack Jr. (D)	74,743	61.7
	M. G. Guthrie (R)	46,344	38.3
4	Ken Hechler (D)	83,507	57.8
	Clyde B. Pinson (R)	60,931	42.2
5	Elizabeth Kee (D)	57,405	73.1
	James Strother Crockett (R)	21,144	26.9

WISCONSIN

	Candidates	Votes	%
1	Henry C. Schadeberg (R)	71,657	53.3
	Gerald T. Flynn (D)	62,800	46.7
2	Robert W. Kastenmeier (D)	89,740	52.5
	Ivan H. Kindschi (R)	81,274	47.5
3	Vernon W. Thomson (R)	54,237	61.3
	Walter P. Thoresen (D)	34,240	38.7
4	Clement J. Zablocki (D)	117,029	72.5
	David F. Tillotson (R)	44,368	27.5

	Candidates	Votes	%
5	Henry S. Reuss (D)	103,705	63.6
	Thomas F. Nelson (R)	59,441	36.4
6	William K. Van Pelt (R)	71,298	59.2
	John A. Race (D)	49,238	40.9
7	Melvin R. Laird (R)	68,418	66.1
	John E. Evans (D)	35,151	33.9
8	John W. Byrnes (R)	80,808	62.8
	Owen F. Monfils (D)	47,833	37.2
9	Lester R. Johnson (D)	50,025	55.6
	Dennis B. Danielson (R)	39,955	44.4
10	Alvin E. O'Konski (R)	52,451	63.2
	J. Louis Hanson (D)	30,556	36.8

WYOMING

	Candidates	Votes	%
AL	William Henry Harrison (R)	71,489	61.4
	Louis A. Mankus (D)	44,985	38.6

1. The race in Tennessee's 5th district was held without party affiliation. It was an outgrowth of a disputed Democratic primary between Fulton and Loser. Neither was given the Democratic nomination and the general election was conducted on a non-partisan basis.

2. These elections were runoffs between the two candidates who finished with the most votes in special primaries held in 1961, but failed to win a majority. (See Texas 1961.)

1963 House Elections

CALIFORNIA

Special Elections

	Candidates	Votes	%
1	Don Clausen (R)	79,292	54.2
	William F. Grader (D)	65,339	44.7
23	Del Clawson (R)	33,042	53.2
	Carley V. Porter (D)	21,969	35.4

NORTH DAKOTA

Special Election

	Candidates	Votes	%
1	Mark Andrews (R)	47,062#	49.1
	John Hove (D)	42,470#	44.3
	John W. Scott (CR)	5,995#	6.3

PENNSYLVANIA

Special Elections

	Candidates	Votes	%
15	Fred B. Rooney (D)	48,846#	53.5
	Robert G. Bartlett (R)	42,374#	46.5
23	Albert W. Johnson (R)	64,137#	58.4
	William T. Hagerty (D)	45,677#	41.6

TEXAS[1]

Special Election

	Candidates	Votes	%
10	J. J. Pickle (D)	14,389#	35.0
	Jim Dobbs (R)	13,702#	33.3
	Jack Ritter (D)	13,027#	31.7

Special Runoff Election

	Candidates	Votes	%
10	J. J. Pickle (D)	27,228#	62.9
	Jim Dobbs (R)	16,052#	37.1

1. Under Texas's special election law, a majority was required to win the House seat. Since no candidate had a majority in the initial special election, a runoff special election was held between the top two finishers. (See Texas 1961 for explanation of Texas special election law, p. 1126.)

1964 House Elections

ALABAMA

	Candidates	Votes	%
1	Jack Edwards (R)	54,522	59.9
	John Tyson (D)	36,482	40.1
2	William L. Dickinson (R)	49,936	61.7
	George M. Grant (D)	29,628	36.6
3	George Andrews (D)	27,939	100.0
4	Glenn Andrews (R)	40,143	58.6
	Kenneth A. Roberts (D)	27,800	40.6
5	Armistead I. Selden Jr. (D)	42,784	53.0
	Robert French (R)	37,960	47.0
6	John Buchanan (R)	69,246	60.6
	George Huddleston Jr. (D)	45,090	39.4
7	James D. Martin (R)	65,353	59.6
	George C. Hawkins (D)	44,386	40.5
8	Robert E. Jones (D)	43,842	100.0

ALASKA

		Votes	%
AL	Ralph J. Rivers (D)	34,605	51.5
	Lowell Thomas Jr. (R)	32,566	48.5

ARIZONA

		Votes	%
1	John J. Rhodes (R)	140,507	55.3
	John Ahearn (D)	113,669	44.7
2	Morris K. Udall (D)	86,499	58.7
	William E. Kimble (R)	60,782	41.3
3	George F. Senner Jr. (D)	30,565	51.5
	Sam Steiger (R)	28,802	48.5

ARKANSAS

		Votes	%
1	E. C. Gathings (D)		100.0
2	Wilbur D. Mills (D)		100.0
3	James W. Trimble (D)	71,228	54.7
	J. E. Hinshaw (R)	58,884	45.3
4	Oren Harris (D)		100.0

CALIFORNIA

		Votes	%
1	Don H. Clausen (R)	141,018	59.1
	George McCabe (D)	97,651	40.9
2	Harold T. Johnson (D)	125,774	64.6
	Chester C. Merriam (R)	68,835	35.4
3	John E. Moss (D)	166,688	74.3
	Einar B. Gjelsteen (R)	57,630	25.7
4	Robert L. Leggett (D)	84,949	71.9
	Ivan Norris (R)	33,160	28.1
5	Phillip Burton (D)	71,638	100.0
6	William S. Mailliard (R)	125,869	63.7
	Thomas P. O'Toole (D)	71,894	36.4
7	Jeffery Cohelan (D)	100,901	66.1
	Lawrence E. McNutt (R)	51,675	33.9
8	George P. Miller (D)	108,771	70.3
	Donald E. Mckay (R)	46,063	29.8
9	Don Edwards (D)	115,954	69.8
	William P. Hyde (R)	50,261	30.2
10	Charles S. Gubser (R)	151,027	63.1
	E. Day Carman (D)	88,240	36.9
11	J. Arthur Younger (R)	116,022	54.8
	W. Mark Sullivan (D)	95,747	45.2
12	Burt L. Talcott (R)	93,112	61.9
	Sanford Bolz (D)	57,243	38.1
13	Charles M. Teague (R)	104,744	57.4
	George E. Taylor (D)	77,763	42. 6
14	John F. Baldwin (R)	117,272	64.9
	Russell M. Koch (D)	63,469	35.1
15	John J. McFall (D)	109,560	70.9
	Kenneth B. Gibson (R)	44,977	29.1
16	B. F. Sisk (D)	117,727	66.8
	David T. Harris (R)	58,604	33.2
17	Cecil R. King (D)	95,640	67.7
	Robert Muncaster (R)	45,688	32.3
18	Harlan Hagen (D)	121,304	66.7

	Candidates	Votes	%
	James E. Williams Jr. (R)	60,523	33.3
19	Chet Holifield (D)	97,934	65.4
	C. Everett Hunt (R)	51,747	34.6
20	H. Allen Smith (R)	132,402	67.9
	C. Bernard Kaufman (D)	62,645	32.1
21	Augustus F. Hawkins (D)	106,231	90.3
	Rayfield Lundy (R)	11,374	9.7
22	James C. Corman (D)	94,141	50.5
	Robert C. Cline (R)	92,133	49.5
23	Del Clawson (R)	90,721	55.4
	H. O. Van Petten (D)	72,903	44.5
24	Glenard P. Lipscomb (R)	139,784	67.9
	Bryan W. Stevens (D)	65,967	32.1
25	Ronald Brooks Cameron (D)	81,320	55.4
	Frank J. Walton (R)	65,344	44.6
26	James Roosevelt (D)	136,025	70.4
	Gil Seton (R)	57,209	29.6
27	Ed Reinecke (R)	83,141	51.7
	Tom Bane (D)	77,587	48.3
28	Alphonzo Bell (R)	205,473	65.6
	Gerald H. Gottlieb (D)	107,852	34.4
29	George E. Brown Jr. (D)	90,208	58.6
	Charles J. Farrington Jr. (R)	63,836	41.4
30	Edward R. Roybal (D)	90,329	66.3
	Alfred J. Feder (R)	45,912	33.7
31	Charles H. Wilson (D)	114,246	64.0
	Norman G. Shanahan (R)	64,256	36.0
32	Craig Hosmer (R)	132,603	68.9
	Michael Cullen (D)	59,765	31.1
33	Kenneth W. Dyal (D)	109,047	51.7
	Jerry L. Pettis (R)	101,742	48.3
34	Richard T. Hanna (D)	137,588	58.3
	Robert A. Geier (R)	98,606	41.8
35	James B. Utt (R)	167,791	65.0
	Paul B. Carpenter (D)	90,295	35.0
36	Bob Wilson (R)	105,346	59.1
	Quinton Whelan (D)	73,034	40.9
37	Lionel Van Deerlin (D)	85,624	58.2
	Dick Wilson (R)	61,373	41.8
38	John V. Tunney (D)	85,661	52.8
	Patrick Minor Martin (R)	76,525	47.2

Special Election

		Votes	%
5	Phillip Burton (D)	26,698	53.6
	Nick A. Verreos (R)	12,777	25.7
	Tom Flowers (R)	3,841	7.7
	Joe Bortin (D)	3,327	6.7

COLORADO

		Votes	%
1	Byron G. Rogers (D)	138,475	67.5
	Glenn R. Jones (R)	65,423	31.9
2	Roy H. McVicker (D)	109,526	50.6
	Donald G. Brotzman (R)	106,738	49.4
3	Frank E. Evans (D)	85,404	51.2
	J. Edgar Chenoweth (R)	81,544	48.8
4	Wayne N. Aspinall (D)	106,685	63.0
	Edwin S. Lamm (R)	62,617	37.0

CONNECTICUT

		Votes	%
1	Emilio Q. Daddario (D)	141,310	70.0
	James F. Collins (R)	60,654	30.0
2	William L. St.Onge (D)	119,530	63.3
	Belton A. Copp (R)	69,403	36.7
3	Robert N. Giaimo (D)	126,353	63.9
	Bernard J. Burns (R)	71,393	36.1
4	Donald J. Irwin (D)	117,220	51.8
	Abner W. Sibal (R)	109,027	48.2
5	John S. Monagan (D)	133,072	67.3
	Charles W. Terrell Jr. (R)	64,651	32.7
6	Bernard F. Grabowski (D)	115,498	58.7
	Thomas J. Meskill Jr. (R)	81,105	41.2

DELAWARE

	Candidates	Votes	%
AL	Harris B. McDowell Jr. (D)	112,361	56.6
	James H. Snowden (R)	86,254	43.4

FLORIDA

		Votes	%
1	Robert L. F. Sikes (D)	74,615	98.0
2	Charles E. Bennett (D)	99,191	72.7
	William T. Stockton Jr. (R)	37,283	27.3
3	Claude Pepper (D)	101,162	65.7
	Paul J. O'Neil (R)	52,758	34.3
4	Dante B. Fascell (D)	94,726	63.9
	Jay McGlon (R)	53,468	36.1
5	A. Sydney Herlong Jr. (D)	85,851	100.0
6	Paul G. Rogers (D)	168,573	66.1
	John D. Steele (R)	86,657	34.0
7	James A. Haley (D)	79,504	100.0
8	D. R. Matthews (D)	49,374	99.9
9	Don Fuqua (D)	44,917	98.8
10	Sam M. Gibbons (D)	69,860	99.6
11	Edward J. Gurney (R)	91,731	60.6
	Thomas S. Kenney (D)	59,746	39.4
12	William C. Cramer (R)	98,959	60.6
	F. Marion Harrelson (D)	64,378	39.4

GEORGIA

		Votes	%
1	G. Elliott Hagan (D)	65,146	72.3
	J. Milton Lent (I)	25,006	27.7
2	Maston O'Neal (D)	37,634	99.9
3	Howard H. Callaway (R)	45,545	57.4
	Garland T. Byrd (D)	33,733	42.5
4	James A. Mackay (D)	66,488	56.9
	Roscoe Pickett (R)	50,326	43.1
5	Charles L. Weltner (D)	65,803	54.0
	L. J. O'Callaghan (R)	55,983	46.0
6	John J. Flynt Jr. (D)	69,712	100.0
7	John W. Davis (D)	69,575	54.7
	Ed Chapin (R)	57,562	45.3
8	J. Russell Tuten (D)	49,727	100.0
9	Phil M. Landrum (D)	59,186	60.5
	Jack Prince (R)	38,608	39.5
10	Robert G. Stephens Jr. (D)	45,418	100.0

HAWAII

		Votes	
AL	Spark M. Matsunaga (D)	140,224	✓
	Patsy Takemoto Mink (D)	106,909	✓
	John E. Milligan (R)	89,425	
	Richard Ike Sutton (R)	56,147	

IDAHO

		Votes	%
1	Compton I. White Jr. (D)	56,203	51.7
	John N. Mattmiller (R)	52,468	48.3
2	George V. Hansen (R)	91,838	52.2
	Ralph R. Harding (D)	84,022	47.8

ILLINOIS

		Votes	%
1	William L. Dawson (D)	150,953	84.9
	Wilbur N. Daniel (R)	26,823	15.1
2	Barratt O'Hara (D)	107,795	67.3
	William F. Scannell (R)	52,416	32.7
3	William T. Murphy (D)	120,711	59.1
	Emmet F. Byrne (R)	83,404	40.9
4	Edward J. Derwinski (R)	144,762	58.9
	Ray J. Rybacki (D)	100,895	41.1
5	John C. Kluczynski (D)	101,626	63.7
	Robert V. Kotowski (R)	57,871	36.3
6	Daniel J. Ronan (D)	89,850	83.4
	Joseph W. Halac (R)	17,918	16.6
7	Frank Annunzio (D)	106,708	85.9
	Ray Wolfram (R)	17,471	14.1

	Candidates	Votes	%
8	Dan Rostenkowski (D)	137,715	66.1
	Eugene L. Ebrom (R)	70,624	33.9
9	Sidney R. Yates (D)	113,851	63.9
	Robert S. Decker (R)	64,428	36.1
10	Harold R. Collier (R)	172,499	60.8
	Thomas E. Gause (D)	111,029	39.2
11	Roman C. Pucinski (D)	129,337	56.9
	Chester T. Podgorski (R)	98,132	43.1
12	Robert McClory (R)	97,003	58.6
	John Clark Kimball (D)	68,555	41.4
13	Donald Rumsfeld (R)	165,129	57.8
	Lynn A. Williams (D)	120,449	42.2
14	John N. Erlenborn (R)	145,830	59.0
	Jerome M. Ziegler (D)	101,432	41.0
15	Charlotte T. Reid (R)	103,709	58.4
	Poppy X. Mitchell (D)	73,741	41.6
16	John B. Anderson (R)	93,051	56.4
	Robert E. Brinkmeier (D)	71,992	43.6
17	Leslie C. Arends (R)	96,209	56.4
	Bernard J. Hughes (D)	74,261	43.6
18	Robert H. Michel (R)	91,173	54.0
	Edward P. Kohlbacher (D)	77,711	46.0
19	Gale Schisler (D)	81,800	52.4
	Robert T. McLoskey (R)	74,290	47.6
20	Paul Findley (R)	119,184	54.8
	Lester E. Collins (D)	98,256	45.2
21	Kenneth J. Gray (D)	117,701	65.0
	Mrs. Stillman J. Stanard (R)	63,431	35.0
22	William L. Springer (R)	80,895	53.0
	John J. Desmond (D)	71,875	47.1
23	George E. Shipley (D)	119,447	54.6
	Wayne S. Jones (R)	99,496	45.4
24	Melvin Price (D)	144,743	75.7
	G. S. Mirza (R)	46,419	24.3

INDIANA

	Candidates	Votes	%
1	Ray J. Madden (D)	133,089	63.7
	Arthur F. Endres (R)	75,226	36.0
2	Charles A. Halleck (R)	88,204	52.9
	John C. Raber (D)	78,566	47.1
3	John Brademas (D)	121,209	60.7
	Robert Lowell Miller (R)	78,642	39.4
4	E. Ross Adair (R)	89,437	52.1
	Max E. Hobbs (D)	82,284	47.9
5	J. Edward Roush (D)	114,252	55.2
	John R. Feighner (R)	92,802	44.8
6	Richard L. Roudebush (R)	86,168	54.1
	Karl O'Lessker (D)	73,002	45.9
7	William G. Bray (R)	84,427	54.2
	Elden C. Tipton (D)	71,461	45.8
8	Winfield K. Denton (D)	109,134	56.5
	Roger H. Zion (R)	84,135	43.5
9	Lee H. Hamilton (D)	74,939	54.4
	Earl Wilson (R)	62,780	45.6
10	Ralph Harvey (R)	89,303	50.5
	Russell E. Davis (D)	87,721	49.6
11	Andrew Jacobs Jr. (D)	149,342	50.5
	Don A. Tabbert (R)	146,424	49.5

IOWA

	Candidates	Votes	%
1	John R. Schmidhauser (D)	84,042	51.0
	Fred Schwengel (R)	80,697	48.9
2	John C. Culver (D)	97,470	52.2
	James E. Bromwell (R)	89,299	47.8
3	H. R. Gross (R)	83,455	50.1
	Stephen M. Peterson (D)	83,036	49.9
4	Bert Bandstra (D)	85,518	53.6
	John Kyl (R)	73,898	46.4
5	Neal Smith (D)	108,212	69.6
	Benjamin J. Gibson Jr. (R).	46,160	29.7
6	Stanley L. Greigg (D)	86,323	53.2
	Howard N. Sokol (R)	75,478	46.5
7	John R. Hansen (D)	78,243	53.5
	Ben F. Jensen (R)	67,942	46.5

KANSAS

	Candidates	Votes	%
1	Bob Dole (R)	113,212	51.2
	Bill Bork (D)	108,086	48.8
2	Chester L. Mize (R)	80,806	51.1
	John Montgomery (D)	77,189	48.9
3	Robert F. Ellsworth (R)	89,588	62.2
	A. Clayton Dial (D)	54,522	37.8
4	Garner Shriver (R)	84,800	59.4
	Jack Glaves (D)	58,057	40.6
5	Joe Skubitz (R)	83,120	56.4
	Reb Russell (D)	64,308	43.6

KENTUCKY

	Candidates	Votes	%
1	Frank Stubblefield (D)	84,574	100.0
2	William H. Natcher (D)	79,519	68.4
	Rhodes Bratcher (R)	36,664	31.6
3	Charles P. Farnsley (D)	117,892	53.8
	M. G. (Gene) Snyder (R)	101,168	46.2
4	Frank Chelf (D)	88,337	61.7
	Clyde Middleton (R)	54,937	38.3
5	Tim Lee Carter (R)	61,137	53.1
	Francis Jones Mills (D)	53,916	46.9
6	John C. Watts (D)	93,322	70.6
	John W. Swope (R)	38,869	29.4
7	Carl D. Perkins (D)	100,929	69.7
	Walter Clay Van Hoose (R)	43,921	30.3

LOUISIANA

	Candidates	Votes	%
1	F. Edward Hebert (D)	76,455	100.0
2	Hale Boggs (D)	77,009	55.1
	David C. Treen (R)	62,881	45.0
3	Edwin E. Willis (D)	52,532	62.3
	Robert J. Angers Jr. (R)	31,806	37.7
4	Joe D. Waggonner Jr. (D)	44,599	100.0
5	Otto E. Passman (D)	24,544	100.0
6	James H. Morrison (D)	82,686	62.9
	Floyd O. Crawford (R)	48,715	37.1
7	T. A. Thompson (D)	38,492	100.0
8	Speedy O. Long (D)	33,250	54.5
	William S. Walker (R)	27,735	45.5

MAINE

	Candidates	Votes	%
1	Stanley R. Tupper (R)	95,398	50.1
	Kenneth M. Curtis (D)	95,195	50.0
2	William D. Hathaway (D)	110,931	62.0
	Kenneth P. MacLeod (R)	67,978	38.0

MARYLAND

	Candidates	Votes	%
1	Rogers C. B. Morton (R)	40,762	53.1
	Harry R. Hughes (D)	36,013	46.9
2	Clarence D. Long (D)	143,132	65.9
	George A. Price (R)	74,067	34.1
3	Edward A. Garmatz (D)	56,295	100.0
4	George H. Fallon (D)	57,229	77.8
	Charles O'Donovan (R)	16,372	22.2
5	Hervey G. Machen (D)	131,712	61.0
	Edward A. Potts (R)	84,318	39.0
6	Charles McC. Mathias Jr. (R)	134,521	54.5
	Royce Hanson (D)	112,410	45.5
7	Samuel N. Friedel (D)	99,654	79.5
	Thomas C. Hofstetter (R)	25,706	20.5
AL	Carlton R. Sickles (D)	683,143	69.4
	David Scull (R)	301,250	30.6

MASSACHUSETTS

	Candidates	Votes	%
1	Silvio O. Conte (R)	139,503	100.0
2	Edward P. Boland (D)	125,894	100.0
3	Philip J. Philbin (D)	177,917	100.0
4	Harold D. Donohue (D)	142,339	71.8
	Dudley B. Dumaine (R)	56,034	28.3
5	F. Bradford Morse (R)	137,735	65.0
	George W. Arvanitis (D)	74,133	35.0
6	William H. Bates (R)	141,733	64.6

	Candidates	Votes	%
	James G. Zafris Jr. (D)	77,646	35.4
7	Torbert H. Macdonald (D)	139,095	77.0
	Gordon F. Hughes (R)	41,671	23.1
8	Thomas P. O'Neill Jr. (D)	122,050	100.0
9	John W. McCormack (D)	118,385	80.3
	Jack A. Molesworth (R)	21,557	14.6
	Noel A. Day (I)	7,440	5.1
10	Joseph W. Martin Jr. (R)	133,403	63.0
	Edward F. Doolan (D)	78,415	37.0
11	James A. Burke (D)	179,261	100.0
12	Hastings Keith (R)	115,656	59.6
	Alexander Byron (D)	78,313	40.4

MICHIGAN

	Candidates	Votes	%
1	John Conyers Jr. (D)	138,589	83.6
	Robert B. Blackwell (R)	25,735	15.5
2	Weston E. Vivian (D)	77,806	50.4
	George Meader (R)	76,280	49.4
3	Paul H. Todd (D)	85,001	52.7
	August E. Johansen (R)	76,350	47.3
4	Edward Hutchinson (R)	83,391	54.3
	Russell W. Holcomb (D)	70,212	45.7
5	Gerald R. Ford (R)	101,810	61.2
	William G. Reamon (D)	64,488	38.8
6	Charles E. Chamberlain (R)	88,882	56.6
	Boyd K. Benedict (D)	68,265	43.4
7	John C. Mackie (D)	104,115	65.7
	Claude E. Sadler (R)	54,307	34.3
8	James Harvey (R)	84,588	54.7
	Sanford A. Brown (D)	69,931	45.3
9	Robert P. Griffin (R)	95,376	57.4
	Daniel Griffen (D)	70,693	42.6
10	Elford A. Cederberg (R)	87,232	56.6
	Hubert C. Evans (D)	66,835	43.4
11	Raymond F. Clevenger (D)	86,557	53.3
	Victor A. Knox (R)	75,955	46.7
12	James G. O'Hara (D)	126,769	74.8
	Robert G. Powell (R)	42,615	25.2
13	Charles C. Diggs Jr. (D)	102,413	85.8
	Bruce Watson (R)	16,585	13.9
14	Lucien N. Nedzi (D)	120,308	66.9
	George Bashara (R)	59,487	33.1
15	William D. Ford (D)	103,724	71.0
	John F. Fellrath Jr. (R)	42,464	29.1
16	John D. Dingell (D)	112,763	73.4
	Raymond B. Leonard (R)	40,673	26.5
17	Martha W. Griffiths (D)	136,230	72.8
	William P. Harrington (R)	50,580	27.0
18	William S. Broomfield (R)	109,777	59.5
	Frank J. Sierawski (D)	74,576	40.4
19	Billie S. Farnum (D)	88,441	53.4
	Richard D. Kuhn (R)	77,204	46.6

MINNESOTA

	Candidates	Votes	%
1	Albert H. Quie (R)	108,639	55.3
	George Daley (DFL)	87,789	44.7
2	Ancher Nelsen (R)	97,804	58.4
	Charles V. Simpson (DFL)	69,801	41.7
3	Clark MacGregor (R)	125,464	57.0
	Richard J. Parish (DFL)	94,682	43.0
4	Joseph E. Karth (DFL)	144,801	73.0
	John M. Drexler (R)	52,221	26.3
5	Donald M. Fraser (DFL)	127,963	61.9
	John W. Johnson (R)	78,767	38.1
6	Alec G. Olson (DFL)	95,848	51.8
	Robert J. Odegard (R)	89,228	48.2
7	Odin Langen (R)	84,304	50.8
	Ben M. Wichterman (DFL)	81,718	49.2
8	John A. Blatnik (DFL)	124,277	69.4
	David W. Glossbrenner (R)	54,691	30.6

MISSISSIPPI

	Candidates	Votes	%
1	Thomas G. Abernethy (D)	60,052	100.0
2	Jamie L. Whitten (D)	70,218	100.0
3	John Bell Williams (D)	84,503	100.0
4	Prentiss Walker (R)	35,277	55.7

Candidates	Votes	%
Arthur Winstead (D)	28,057	44.3
5 William M. Colmer (D)	83,120	100.0

MISSOURI

	Candidates	Votes	%
1	Frank M. Karsten (D)	140,848	76.9
	Theodore J. Fischer (R)	42,351	23.1
2	Thomas B. Curtis (R)	130,894	53.1
	Sidney B. McClanahan (D)	115,446	46.9
3	Leonor K. Sullivan (D)	123,193	71.7
	Howard C. Ohlendorf (R)	48,709	28.3
4	William J. Randall (D)	109,375	63.9
	James M. Taylor (R)	61,854	36.1
5	Richard Bolling (D)	91,721	67.9
	Robert B. Langworthy (R)	43,314	32.1
6	W. R. Hull Jr. (D)	110,532	64.7
	Henry E. Wurst (R)	60,356	35.3
7	Durward G. Hall (R)	102,926	51.7
	Jim Thomas (D)	96,120	48.3
8	Richard Ichord (D)	117,672	65.2
	Ben A. Rogers (R)	62,823	34.8
9	William L. Hungate (D)	112,907	62.3
	Anthony C. Schroeder (R)	68,032	37.6
10	Paul C. Jones (D)	89,698	67.4
	Carl F. Painter (R)	43,304	32.6

Special Election

	Candidates	Votes	%
9	William L. Hungate (D)	102,422	62.5
	Anthony C. Schroeder (R)	61,439	37.5

MONTANA

	Candidates	Votes	%
1	Arnold Olsen (D)	64,847	53.6
	Wayne Montgomery (R)	55,417	45.8
2	James F. Battin (R)	84,241	54.1
	Jack C. Toole (D)	71,461	45.9

NEBRASKA

	Candidates	Votes	%
1	Clair A. Callan (D)	107,683	51.3
	Ralph F. Beermann (R)	102,113	48.7
2	Glenn Cunningham (R)	81,660	53.1
	John Richard Swenson (D)	72,003	46.9
3	Dave Martin (R)	104,380	52.8
	William E. Colwell (D)	93,236	47.2

NEVADA

	Candidates	Votes	%
AL	Walter S. Baring (D)	82,748	63.3
	George Von Tobel (R)	47,989	36.7

NEW HAMPSHIRE

	Candidates	Votes	%
1	J. Oliva Huot (D)	79,097	51.4
	Louis C. Wyman (R)	74,939	48.7
2	James C. Cleveland (R)	62,680	50.1
	Charles B. Officer (D)	62,382	49.9

NEW JERSEY

	Candidates	Votes	%
1	William T. Cahill (R)	150,805	56.2
	William J. Procacci (D)	117,227	43.7
2	Thomas C. McGrath Jr. (D)	73,264	50.8
	Milton W. Glenn (R)	70,997	49.2
3	James J. Howard (D)	105,803	50.4
	Marcus Daly (R)	104,063	49.6
4	Frank Thompson Jr. (D)	134,747	67.5
	Ephraim Tomlinson (R)	64,447	32.3
5	Peter H. B. Frelinghuysen (R)	122,168	63.6
	Eugene M. Friedman (D)	70,001	36.4
6	Florence P. Dwyer (R)	140,999	59.7
	Richard J. Traynor (D)	95,021	40.3
7	William B. Widnall (R)	144,585	56.5
	Edward H. Ihnen (D)	110,328	43.1
8	Charles S. Joelson (D)	112,483	67.5
	J. Palmer Murphy (R)	53,732	32.3
9	Henry Helstoski (D)	111,741	50.1
	Frank C. Osmers Jr. (R)	109,313	49.0
10	Peter W. Rodino Jr. (D)	92,488	74.0

	Candidates	Votes	%
	Raymond W. Schroeder (R)	31,306	25.1
11	Joseph G. Minish (D)	82,457	69.6
	William L. Stubbs (R)	35,956	30.4
12	Paul J. Krebs (D)	82,726	52.4
	David H. Wiener (R)	72,601	46.0
13	Cornelius E. Gallagher (D)	89,360	77.1
	Cresenzi W. Castaldo (R)	24,874	21.5
14	Dominick V. Daniels (D)	73,635	74.6
	Cecil T. Woolsey (R)	25,068	25.4
15	Edward J. Patten (D)	131,393	63.2
	Bernard F. Rodgers (R)	76,686	36.9

NEW MEXICO

	Candidates	Votes	%
AL	Thomas G. Morris (D)	194,407	61.8
	Mike Sims (R)	120,349	38.2
AL	E. S. Johnny Walker (D)	164,863	51.6
	Jack C. Redman (R)	154,780	48.4

NEW YORK

	Candidates	Votes	%
1	Otis G. Pike (D, L)	126,529	64.9
	John J. Hart Jr. (R)	68,362	35.1
2	James R. Grover Jr. (R)	88,390	51.7
	Edwyn Silberling (D, L)	82,757	48.4
3	Lester L. Wolff (D, L)	96,503	50.7
	Steven B. Derounian (R)	93,883	49.3
4	John W. Wydler (R)	89,971	53.2
	Joseph L. Marino (D)	73,148	43.2
5	Herbert Tenzer (D, L)	112,899	55.8
	Ralph J. Edsell Jr. (R)	89,455	44.2
6	Seymour Halpern (R)	100,069	57.1
	Emil Levin (D)	75,327	43.0
7	Joseph P. Addabbo (D, L)	121,091	69.8
	Robert L. Nelson (R)	49,151	28.3
8	Benjamin S. Rosenthal (D, L)	148,696	75.0
	Vincent P. Brevetti (R)	44,398	22.4
9	James J. Delaney (D)	109,973	65.9
	Charles H. Cohen (R)	48,878	29.3
10	Emanuel Celler (D, L)	118,941	87.5
	Samuel W. Held (R)	16,941	12.5
11	Eugene J. Keogh (D, L)	75,073	78.8
	Herman Sanders (R)	17,732	18.6
12	Edna F. Kelly (D, L)	141,570	81.7
	Carlo G. Colavito (R)	31,737	18.3
13	Abraham J. Multer (D)	129,414	69.1
	Gerald S. Held (R)	34,809	18.6
	Gerald M. Weisberg (L)	23,148	12.4
14	John J. Rooney (D, L)	68,165	77.4
	Victor J. Tirabasso Jr. (R)	19,861	22.6
15	Hugh L. Carey (D, L)	66,567	53.6
	Luigi R. Marano (R, C)	57,626	46.4
16	John M. Murphy (D, L)	89,438	61.4
	David D. Smith (R, C)	56,238	38.6
17	John V. Lindsay (R)	135,807	71.5
	Eleanor C. French (D, L)	44,533	23.5
	Kieran O'Doherty (C)	9,491	5.0
18	Adam Clayton Powell Jr. (D)	94,222	84.6
	Joseph A. Bailey (R)	11,621	10.4
19	Leonard Farbstein (D)	84,781	68.9
	Henry E. Delrosso (R)	24,829	20.2
	Edward A. Morrison (L)	12,129	9.9
20	William F. Ryan (D, L)	124,128	82.5
	Ronald N. Gottlieb (R)	23,409	15.6
21	James H. Scheuer (D, L)	91,898	84.3
	Henry Rose (R)	15,380	14.1
22	Jacob H. Gilbert (D)	70,147	81.6
	Manuel R. Roque (R)	10,134	11.8
	Joseph A. Mazar (L)	5,026	5.8
23	Jonathan B. Bingham (D)	108,205	71.3
	Patrick J. Foley (R)	30,476	20.1
	John P. Hagan (L)	10,602	7.0
24	Paul A. Fino (R)	89,814	61.2
	Robert J. Malang (D)	51,740	35.3
25	Richard Ottinger (D, L)	122,260	56.2
	Robert R. Barry (R)	95,214	43.8
26	Ogden R. Reid (R)	102,064	54.9
	Frank Conniff (D, L)	78,546	42.2
27	John G. Dow (D, L)	97,337	51.6
	Katherine St. George (R)	91,172	48.4

	Candidates	Votes	%
28	Joseph Y. Resnick (D)	95,820	51.7
	J. Ernest Wharton (R, C)	84,008	45.3
29	Leo W. O'Brien (D, L)	158,797	69.2
	John D. Meader (R, C)	70,518	30.8
30	Carleton J. King (R)	100,950	50.3
	Joseph J. Martin (D, L)	99,841	49.7
31	Robert C. McEwen (R, C)	74,380	54.6
	Raymond E. Bishop (D, L)	61,726	45.4
32	Alexander Pirnie (R)	86,717	53.4
	Robert Castle (D)	75,660	46.6
33	Howard W. Robison (R)	97,213	58.4
	John L. Joy (D, L)	69,277	41.6
34	James M. Hanley (D, L)	96,219	51.2
	R. Walter Riehlman (R, C)	91,697	48.8
35	Samuel S. Stratton (D, L)	110,948	64.0
	Robert M. Quigley (R, C)	62,463	36.0
36	Frank J. Horton (R)	107,406	56.0
	John C. Williams (D)	81,509	42.5
37	Barber B. Conable Jr. (R)	98,923	54.2
	Neil F. Bubel (D)	80,411	44.0
38	Charles E. Goodell (R)	90,201	58.4
	Robert V. Kelley (D, L)	64,179	41.6
39	Richard D. McCarthy (D, L)	108,235	52.8
	John R. Pillion (R)	96,934	47.3
40	Henry P. Smith III (R)	90,745	51.5
	Wesley J. Hilts (D)	81,531	46.3
41	Thaddeus J. Dulski (D, L)	130,961	82.1
	Joseph A. Klawon (R)	28,578	17.9

NORTH CAROLINA

	Candidates	Votes	%
1	Herbert C. Bonner (D)	52,567	82.6
	Zeno O. Ratcliff (R)	11,108	17.4
2	L. H. Fountain (D)	62,406	100.0
3	David N. Henderson (D)	63,235	67.4
	Sherman T. Rock (R)	30,557	32.6
4	Harold D. Cooley (D)	73,470	51.8
	James C. Gardner (R)	68,387	48.2
5	Ralph J. Scott (D)	72,254	51.6
	W. A. Armfield (R)	67,781	48.4
6	Horace R. Kornegay (D)	84,151	61.4
	Walter G. Green (R)	52,964	38.6
7	Alton Lennon (D)	71,357	100.0
8	Charles R. Jonas (R)	85,869	54.3
	W. D. James (D)	72,269	45.7
9	James T. Broyhill (R)	88,195	55.2
	Robert M. Davis (D)	71,629	44.8
10	Basil L. Whitener (D)	78,684	58.7
	W. Hall Young (R)	55,483	41.4
11	Roy A. Taylor (D)	85,880	60.5
	Clyde M. Roberts (R)	55,996	39.5

NORTH DAKOTA

	Candidates	Votes	%
1	Mark Andrews (R)	69,575	52.1
	George A. Sinner (D)	63,208	47.4
2	Rolland Redlin (D)	60,751	52.5
	Don L. Short (R)	54,878	47.5

OHIO

	Candidates	Votes	%
1	John J. Gilligan (D)	74,525	51.9
	Carl W. Rich (R)	69,114	48.1
2	Donald D. Clancy (R)	122,487	60.5
	H. A. Sand (D)	79,824	39.5
3	Rodney M. Love (D)	129,469	52.0
	Paul F. Schenck (R)	119,400	48.0
4	William M. McCulloch (R)	81,204	55.7
	Robert H. Mihlbaugh (D)	64,667	44.3
5	Delbert L. Latta (R)	80,394	65.9
	Milford Landis (D)	41,621	34.1
6	William H. Harsha (R)	86,015	60.1
	Frank E. Smith (D)	57,223	40.0
7	Clarence J. Brown (R)	93,022	56.8
	Jerry R. Graham (D)	70,857	43.2
8	Jackson E. Betts (R)	73,395	61.8
	Frank Bennett (D)	45,445	38.2
9	Thomas L. Ashley (D)	109,167	62.9
	John O. Celusta (R)	64,401	37.1
10	Walter H. Moeller (D)	54,729	52.4

Candidates	Votes	%
Homer E. Abele (R)	49,744	47.6
11 J. William Stanton (R)	102,619	55.4
C. D. Lambros (D)	82,728	44.6
12 Samuel L. Devine (R)	146,971	55.4
Robert L. Van Heyde (D)	118,299	44.6
13 Charles A. Mosher (R)	75,945	54.7
Louis G. Frey (D)	62,780	45.3
14 William H. Ayres (R)	126,088	54.7
Frances McGovern (D)	104,547	45.3
15 Robert T. Secrest (D)	62,438	66.1
Randall Metcalf (R)	31,983	33.9
16 Frank T. Bow (R)	101,802	52.2
Robert D. Freeman (D)	93,255	47.8
17 John M. Ashbrook (R)	75,674	51.5
Robert W. Levering (D)	71,291	48.5
18 Wayne L. Hays (D)	94,768	68.8
Allen J. Dalrymple (R)	42,960	31.2
19 Michael J. Kirwan (D)	111,682	76.3
Albert H. James (R)	34,654	23.7
20 Michael A. Feighan (D)	115,675	74.4
Joseph A. Cipollone (R)	39,747	25.6
21 Charles A. Vanik (D)	113,157	90.1
Eugene E. Smith (R)	12,416	9.9
22 Frances P. Bolton (R)	84,183	56.6
Chat Paterson (D)	64,454	43.4
23 William E. Minshall (R)	131,554	67.2
Norbert G. Dennerll Jr. (D)	64,162	32.8
AL Robert E. Sweeney (D)	1,872,351	52.2
Oliver P. Bolton (R)	1,716,480	47.8

OKLAHOMA

Candidates	Votes	%
1 Page Belcher (R)	125,377	63.5
Doug Martin (D)	71,998	36.5
2 Ed Edmondson (D)	90,466	61.4
George L. Lange (R)	56,843	38.6
3 Carl Albert (D)	62,952	79.0
Frank D. McSherry (R)	16,706	21.0
4 Tom Steed (D)	98,419	100.0
5 John Jarman (D)	130,014	70.8
Homer Cowan (R)	53,596	29.2
6 Jed Johnson Jr. (D)	75,879	56.7
Bayard C. Auchincloss (R)	58,041	43.3

OREGON

Candidates	Votes	%
1 Wendell Wyatt (R)	122,010	53.1
R. Blaine Whipple (D)	107,920	46.9
2 Al Ullman (D)	70,136	68.1
Everett J. Thoren (R)	32,916	31.9
3 Edith Green (D)	157,882	65.6
Lyle Dean (R)	82,468	34.3
4 Robert B. Duncan (D)	125,752	64.8
Paul Jaffarian (R)	68,288	35.2

Special Election

Candidates	Votes	%
1 Wendell Wyatt (R)	125,473	52.8
R. Blaine Whipple (D)	112,112	47.2

PENNSYLVANIA

Candidates	Votes	%
1 William A. Barrett (D)	129,471	71.8
Alvin J. Bello (R)	50,780	28.2
2 Robert N. C. Nix (D)	125,100	80.2
Melvin C. Howell (R)	30,801	19.8
3 James A. Byrne (D)	111,885	72.0
John J. Poserina Jr. (R)	43,471	28.0
4 Herman Toll (D)	135,681	64.1
James R. Cavanaugh (R)	75,901	35.9
5 William J. Green III (D)	117,049	65.2
Edward H. Rovner (R)	62,446	34.8
6 George M. Rhodes (D)	144,697#	62.1
James B. Bamford (R)	88,495#	37.9
7 G. Robert Watkins (R)	129,572	51.2
Leonard Bachman (D)	123,750	48.9
8 Willard S. Curtin (R)	112,472	51.1
Ralph O. Samuel (D)	107,670	48.9
9 Paul B. Dague (R)	111,545	57.7
John A. O'Brien (D)	81,823	42.3
10 Joseph M. McDade (R)	90,903	50.8
James J. Haggerty (D)	88,082	49.2
11 Daniel J. Flood (D)	116,875	77.4
Charles R. Thomas (R)	34,057	22.6
12 J. Irving Whalley (R)	97,114	58.6
Paul A. Stephens (D)	68,703	41.4
13 Richard S. Schweiker (R)	139,817	59.1
William D. Searle (D)	96,849	40.9
14 William S. Moorhead (D)	117,525	74.8
Alvin D. Capozzi (R)	39,513	25.2
15 Fred B. Rooney (D)	81,062	66.1
Leo W. McCormick (R)	41,656	33.9
16 John C. Kunkel (R)	90,331	64.1
William F. Stefanic (D)	50,509	35.9
17 Herman T. Schneebeli (R)	91,504	58.0
William F. Plankenhorn (D)	66,266	42.0
18 Robert J. Corbett (R)	119,938	62.6
Frank J. Reed (D)	71,621	37.4
19 N. Neiman Craley Jr. (D)	82,498	50.8
George A. Goodling (R)	79,809	49.2
20 Elmer J. Holland (D)	126,846	74.4
Ronald Bryan (R)	43,591	25.6
21 John H. Dent (D)	97,379	65.8
Thomas M. Schooley Jr. (R)	50,513	34.2
22 John P. Saylor (R)	81,400	57.0
James E. McCaffery (D)	61,482	43.0
23 Albert W. Johnson (R)	76,575	54.9
John Still (D)	62,932	45.1
24 Joseph P. Vigorito (D)	92,612	50.8
James D. Weaver (R)	89,828	49.2
25 Frank M. Clark (D)	121,140	70.3
John Loth (R)	51,071	29.7
26 Thomas E. Morgan (D)	109,532	68.1
Paul B. Riggle (R)	51,219	31.9
27 James G. Futton (R)	120,395	62.7
John A. Young (D)	71,519	37.3

Special Election

Candidates	Votes	%
5 William J. Green III (D)	30,904#	58.6
Edward H. Rovner (R)	21,832#	41.4

RHODE ISLAND

Candidates	Votes	%
1 Fernard J. St. Germain (D)	110,056	66.3
Roland H. Blanchette (R)	56,056	33.8
2 John E. Fogarty (D)	168,374	81.4
Guy J. Wells (R)	38,601	18.7

SOUTH CAROLINA

Candidates	Votes	%
1 L. Mendel Rivers (D)	64,804	99.6
2 Albert W. Watson (D)	88,682	97.6
3 W. J. Bryan Dorn (D)	65,920	99.9
4 Robert T. Ashmore (D)	81,727	100.0
5 Tom S. Gettys (D)	44,859	66.7
Robert M. Doster (R)	22,384	33.3
6 John L. McMillan (D)	49,398	65.0
E. R. Kirkland (R)	26,586	35.0

Special Election

Candidates	Votes	%
5 Tom S. Gettys (D)	44,241	66.8
Robert M. Doster (R)	22,031	33.2

SOUTH DAKOTA

Candidates	Votes	%
1 Ben Reifel (R)	124,791	57.6
George May (D)	92,057	42.5
2 E. Y. Berry (R)	39,657	56.0
Byron T. Brown (D)	31,208	44.0

TENNESSEE

Candidates	Votes	%
1 James H. Quillen (R)	94,535	71.7
Arthur Bright (D)	37,252	28.3
2 John J. Duncan (R)	84,868	53.8
Willard V. Yarbrough (D)	70,119	44.5
3 Bill Brock (R)	71,005	54.6
Robert M. Summitt (D)	59,027	45.4
4 Joe L. Evins (D)	85,286	100.0
5 Richard Fulton (D)	74,597	59.8
William R. Wills (R)	50,210	40.2
6 William R. Anderson (D)	66,817	78.2
Cecil R. Hill (R)	18,595	21.8
7 Tom Murray (D)	35,612	53.6
Julius Hurst (IR)	24,496	36.8
Earl Maclin (I)	6,382	9.6
8 Robert A. Everett (D)	43,876	93.9
Sarah Flannary (I)	2,865	6.1
9 George W. Grider (D)	108,425	52.5
Robert James (R)	97,537	47.2

Special Election

Candidates	Votes	%
2 Irene Baker (R)	40,708#	55.5
Willard V. Yarbrough (D)	31,763#	43.3

TEXAS

Candidates	Votes	%
1 Wright Patman (D)	52,698	74.6
Mrs. William E. Jones (R)	17,967	25.4
2 Jack Brooks (D)	75,226	62.7
John Greco (R)	44,772	37.3
3 Lindley Beckworth (D)	53,331	59.3
James Warren (R)	36,566	40.7
4 Ray Roberts (D)	46,782	81.4
Fred Banfield (R)	10,707	18.6
5 Earle Cabell (D)	172,287	57.5
Bruce Alger (R)	127,568	42.5
6 Olin Teague (D)	55,155	82.2
William Van Winkle (R)	11,967	17.8
7 John Dowdy (D)	64,456	83.6
James W. Orr (R)	12,606	16.4
8 Albert Thomas (D)	103,595	76.8
Bob Gilbert (R)	31,351	23.2
9 Clark Thompson (D)	105,631	75.3
Dave Oakes (R)	34,692	24.7
10 Jake Pickle (D)	80,045	75.8
Billie Pratt (R)	25,594	24.2
11 W. R. Poage (D)	62,175	81.5
Charles M. Isenhower (R)	14,094	18.5
12 Jim Wright (D)	107,896	68.5
Fred Dielman (R)	49,633	31.5
13 Graham Purcell (D)	67,947	75.2
George Corse (R)	22,429	24.8
14 John Young (D)	105,352	77.5
Billy Patton (R)	30,522	22.5
15 Eligio de la Garza (D)	66,897	69.4
Joe Coulter (R)	29,551	30.6
16 Richard C. White (D)	70,262	55.7
Ed Foreman (R)	55,951	44.3
17 Omar Burleson (D)	59,769	76.4
Phil M. Bridges (R)	18,440	23.6
18 Walter Rogers (D)	58,701	55.0
Robert Price (R)	48,054	45.0
19 George Mahon (D)	87,555	77.6
Joe B. Phillips (R)	25,243	22.4
20 Henry B. Gonzalez (D)	103,464	64.6
John M. O'Connell (R)	56,601	35.4
21 O. C. Fisher (D)	61,785	78.1
Harry Claypool (R)	17,295	21.9
22 Bob Casey (D)	136,289	58.1
Desmond Barry (R)	98,287	41.9
AL Joe Pool (D)	1,690,674	66.9
Bill Hayes (R)	826,991	32.7

UTAH

Candidates	Votes	%
1 Laurence J. Burton (R)	75,986	56.0
William G. Bruhn (D)	59,768	44.0
2 David S. King (D)	149,754	57.5
Thomas G. Judd (R)	110,512	42.5

VERMONT

Candidates	Votes	%
AL Robert T. Stafford (R, I)	92,252	56.4
Bernard G. O'Shea (D)	71,193	43.6

VIRGINIA

	Candidates	Votes	%
1	Thomas N. Downing (D)	72,819	78.7
	Wayne C. Thiessen (R)	19,698	21.3
2	Porter Hardy Jr. (D)	54,315	68.7
	Wayne Lustig (R)	17,082	21.6
	H. W. Grady Speers Jr. (I)	7,635	9.7
3	David E. Satterfield III (D)	43,880	34.5
	Richard D. Obenshain (R)	43,226	34.0
	Edward E. Haddock (I)	39,223	30.8
4	Watkins M. Abbitt (D)	53,857	69.5
	S. W. Tucker (R)	23,682	30.5
5	William M. Tuck (D)	39,867	63.5
	Robert L. Gilliam (R)	22,946	36.5
6	Richard H. Poff (R)	57,987	56.2
	William B. Hopkins (D)	45,113	43.8
7	John O. Marsh Jr. (D)	47,888	69.6
	Roy Erickson (R)	20,911	30.4
8	Howard W. Smith (D)	49,440	69.4
	Floyd Caldwell Bagley (I)	21,813	30.6
9	W. Pat Jennings (D)	51,106	58.2
	Glen M. Williams (R)	36,668	41.8
10	Joel T. Broyhill (R)	80,370	50.7
	Augustus C. Johnson (D)	78,242	49.3

WASHINGTON

		Votes	%
1	Thomas M. Pelly (R)	117,851	59.9
	Edward Palmason (D)	78,876	40.1
2	Lloyd Meeds (D)	88,551	54.9

	Candidates	Votes	%
	Jack Westland (R)	72,830	45.1
3	Julia Butler Hansen (D)	102,080	70.2
	Harold L. Anderson (R)	43,415	29.8
4	Catherine May (R)	102,964	65.3
	Stephen H. Huza (D)	54,819	34.7
5	Thomas S. Foley (D)	84,830	53.5
	Walt Horan (R)	73,884	46.6
6	Floyd V. Hicks (D)	79,042	52.1
	Thor C. Tollefson (R)	72,702	47.9
7	Brock Adams (D)	125,222	55.5
	William Stinson (R)	100,119	44.4

WEST VIRGINIA

		Votes	%
1	Arch A. Moore Jr. (R)	115,799	61.4
	John L. Bailey (D)	72,714	38.6
2	Harley O. Staggers (D)	87,928	65.0
	Stanley R. Cox Jr. (R)	47,457	35.1
3	John M. Slack Jr. (D)	103,117	65.4
	Jim Comstock (R)	54,566	34.6
4	Ken Hechler (D)	109,287	61.2
	Jack L. Miller (R)	69,253	38.8
5	James Kee (D)	77,156	70.0
	Wade Hampton Ballard III (R)	33,108	30.0

WISCONSIN

		Votes	%
1	Lynn E. Stalbaum (D)	90,450	51.5
	Henry C. Schadeberg (R)	85,117	48.5
2	Robert W. Kastenmeier (D)	108,148	63.6

	Candidates	Votes	%
	Carl V. Kolata (R)	61,865	36.4
3	Vernon W. Thomson (R)	91,092	60.6
	Harold C. Ristow (D)	59,173	39.4
4	Clement J. Zablocki (D)	125,683	74.2
	Edward E. Estkowski (R)	43,773	25.8
5	Henry S. Reuss (D)	107,610	75.9
	Robert Taylor (R)	34,059	24.0
6	John A. Race (D)	84,690	50.8
	William K. Van Pelt (R)	82,103	49.2
7	Melvin R. Laird (R)	98,110	61.8
	Thomas E. Martin (D)	60,758	38.2
8	John W. Byrnes (R)	96,160	59.6
	Cletus J. Johnson (D)	65,292	40.4
9	Glenn R. Davis (R)	105,332	55.3
	James P. Buckley (D)	85,071	44.7
10	Alvin E. O'Konski (R)	92,198	56.2
	Edmund A. Nix (D)	71,983	43.8

WYOMING

		Votes	%
AL	Teno Roncalio (D)	70,693	50.8
	William Henry Harrison (R)	68,482	49.2

1965 House Elections

CALIFORNIA

Special Election

	Candidates	Votes	%
26	Thomas M. Rees (D)	40,430	59.4
	Edward M. Marshall (R)	27,579	40.5

LOUISIANA

Special Election

	Candidates	Votes	%
7	Edwin W. Edwards (D)	✓	

OHIO

Special Election

		Votes	%
7	Clarence J. Brown Jr. (R)	70,573	59.6
	James A. Berry (D)	47,830	40.4

SOUTH CAROLINA

Special Election

	Candidates	Votes	%
2	Albert W. Watson (R)	55,977#	69.3
	Preston H. Callison (D)	24,761#	30.7

1966 House Elections

ALABAMA

	Candidates	Votes	%
1	Jack Edwards (R)	58,515	65.8
	Warren L. Finch (D)	30,474	34.2
2	William L. Dickinson (R)	49,203	54.7
	Robert F. Whaley (D)	40,832	45.4
3	George Andrews (D)	61,015	100.0
4	Bill Nichols (D)	54,515	58.7
	Glenn Andrews (R)	38,402	41.3
5	Armistead I. Selden Jr. (D)	68,486	100.0
6	John Buchanan (R)	64,435	63.4
	Walter Emmett Perry (D)	37,131	36.6
7	Tom Bevill (D)	73,987	64.4
	Wayman Sherrer (R)	40,972	35.6
8	Robert E. Jones (D)	65,982	71.3
	Don Mayhall (R)	26,561	28.7

ALASKA

	Candidates	Votes	%
AL	Howard W. Pollock (R)	34,040	51.7
	Ralph J. Rivers (D)	31,867	48.4

ARIZONA

	Candidates	Votes	%
1	John J. Rhodes (R)	102,007	67.2
	L. Alton Riggs (D)	49,913	32.9
2	Morris K. Udall (D)	66,813	59.6
	G. Alfred McGinnis (R)	45,326	40.4
3	Sam Steiger (R)	57,145	56.9
	George F. Senner Jr. (D)	43,219	43.1

ARKANSAS

	Candidates	Votes	%
1	E. C. Gathings (D)		100.0
2	Wilbur Mills (D)		100.0
3	John P. Hammerschmidt (R)	83,938	53.1
	James W. Trimble (D)	74,009	46.9
4	David Pryor (D)	86,887	65.0
	Lynn Lowe (R)	46,804	35.0

Special Election

		Votes	%
4	David Pryor (D)	85,125	64.5
	Lynn Lowe (R)	46,764	35.0

CALIFORNIA

	Candidates	Votes	%
1	Don H. Clausen (R)	143,755	64.9
	Thomas T. Storer (D)	77,000	34.7
2	Harold T. Johnson (D)	131,145	70.9
	William H. Romack (R)	53,753	29.1
3	John E. Moss Jr. (D)	143,177	67.5
	Terry G. Fell (R)	69,057	32.5
4	Robert L. Leggett (D)	67,942	59.5
	Tom McHatton (R)	46,337	40.5
5	Phillip Burton (D)	56,476	71.3
	Terry R. Macken (R)	22,778	28.7
6	William S. Mailliard (R)	132,506	76.6
	Lerue Grim (D)	40,514	23.4
7	Jeffery Cohelan (D)	84,644	63.9
	Malcolm M. Champlin (R)	46,763	35.3
8	George P. Miller (D)	92,263	65.4
	Raymond P. Britton (R)	48,727	34.6
9	Don Edwards (D)	97,311	63.1
	Wilbur G. Durkee (R)	56,784	36.9
10	Charles S. Gubser (R)	156,549	69.1
	George Leppert (D)	70,013	30.9
11	J. Arthur Younger (R)	113,679	59.4
	Mark Sullivan (D)	77,605	40.6
12	Burt L. Talcott (R)	108,070	77.2
	Gerald V. Barron (D)	31,787	22.7
13	Charles M. Teague (R)	116,701	67.5
	Charles A. Storke (D)	56,240	32.5
14	Jerome R. Waldie (D)	108,668	56.4
	Frank J. Newman (R)	83,878	43.5
15	John J. McFall (D)	81,733	57.0

	Candidates	Votes	%
	Sam Van Dyken (R)	61,550	43.0
16	B. F. Sisk (D)	118,063	71.3
	Cecil F. White (R)	47,329	28.6
17	Cecil R. King (D)	76,962	60.8
	Don Cortum (R)	49,615	39.2
18	Robert B. Mathias (R)	96,699	55.9
	Harlan Hagen (D)	76,346	44.1
19	Chat Holifield (D)	82,592	62.2
	William R. Sutton (R)	50,068	37.7
20	H. Allen Smith (R)	128,896	73.4
	Raymond Freschi (D)	46,730	26.6
21	Augustus F. Hawkins (D)	74,216	84.8
	Norman A. Hodges (R)	13,294	15.2
22	James C. Corman (D)	94,420	53.5
	Robert C. Cline (R)	82,207	46.5
23	Del Clawson (R)	93,320	67.4
	Ed O'Connor (D)	45,141	32.6
24	Glenard P. Lipscomb (R)	148,190	76.2
	Earl G. McNall (D)	46,115	23.7
25	Charles E. Wiggins (R)	70,154	52.6
	Ronald Brooks Cameron (D)	63,345	47.5
26	Thomas M. Rees (D)	103,289	62.3
	Irving Teichner (R)	62,441	37.7
27	Ed Reinecke (R)	93,890	65.3
	John A. Howard (D)	49,785	34.6
28	Alphonzo Bell (R)	211,404	72.3
	Lawrence Sherman (D)	81,007	27.7
29	George E. Brown Jr. (D)	69,115	51.1
	Bill Orozco (R)	66,079	48.9
30	Edward R. Roybal (D)	72,173	66.4
	Henri O'Bryant Jr. (R)	36,506	33.6
31	Charles H. Wilson (D)	92,875	63.4
	Theodore Smith (R)	53,708	36.6
32	Craig Hosmer (R)	139,328	80.1
	Tracy Odell (D)	34,609	19.9
33	Jerry L. Pettis (R)	102,401	53.5
	Kenneth W. Dyal (D)	89,071	46.5
34	Richard T. Hanna (D)	127,976	55.8
	Frank La Magna (R)	101,410	44.2
35	James B. Utt (R)	189,582	73.1
	Thomas B. Lenhart (D)	69,873	26.9
36	Bob Wilson (R)	119,274	72.7
	William C. Godfrey (D)	44,365	27.1
37	Lionel Van Deerlin (D)	80,060	61.1
	Samuel S. Vener (R)	50,817	38. 8
38	John V. Tunney (D)	83,216	54.5
	Robert R. Barry (R)	69,444	45.5

Special Election

		Votes	%
14	Jerome R. Waldie (D)	71,501#	51.2
	Frank J. Newman (R)	43,539#	31.2
	John A. Richardson (R)	14,693#	10.5

COLORADO

	Candidates	Votes	%
1	Byron G. Rogers (D)	92,688	56.0
	Greg Pearson (R)	72,732	44.0
2	Donald G. Brotzman (R)	95,123	51.7
	Roy H. McVicker (D)	86,685	47.1
3	Frank E. Evans (D)	76,270	51.7
	David W. Enoch (R)	71,213	48.3
4	Wayne N. Aspinall (D)	84,107	58.6
	James P. Johnson (R)	59,404	41.4

CONNECTICUT

	Candidates	Votes	%
1	Emilio Q. Daddario (D)	100,447	58.0
	John L. Bonee (R)	71,353	41.2
2	William L. St. Onge (D)	90,298	56.2
	Joseph H. Goldberg (R)	69,402	43.2
3	Robert Giaimo (D)	86,029	53.1
	Stello Salmona (R)	67,226	41.5
	Robert M. Cook (AM I)	8,730	5.4
4	Donald J. Irwin (D)	89,709	50.9
	Abner W. Sibal (R)	86,337	49.0

	Candidates	Votes	%
5	John S. Monagan (D)	96,801	59.1
	Romeo G. Petroni (R)	67,094	40.9
6	Thomas J. Meskill Jr. (R)	81,907	48.9
	Bernard F. Grabowski (D)	79,865	47.7

DELAWARE

	Candidates	Votes	%
AL	William V. Roth (R)	90,961	55.8
	Harris B. McDowell Jr. (D)	72,132	44.2

FLORIDA

	Candidates	Votes	%
1	Robert L. F. Sikes (D)	55,547	95.1
2	Don Fuqua (D)	71,565	76.3
	Harold Hill (R)	22,281	23.7
3	Charles E. Bennett (D)	72,038	99.9
4	A. Sydney Herlong Jr. (D)	70,155	100.0
5	Edward J. Gurney (R)	75,875	99.7
6	Sam M. Gibbons (D)	50,772	99.8
7	James A. Haley (D)	64,498	63.2
	Joe Z. Lovingood (R)	37,586	36.8
8	William C. Cramer (R)	105,019	70.8
	Roy L. Reynolds (D)	43,275	29.2
9	Paul G. Rogers (D)	76,328	100.0
10	J. Herbert Burke (R)	80,989	60.6
	Joe Varon (D)	51,636	38.7
11	Claude Pepper (D)	62,195	99.9
12	Dante B. Fascell (D)	62,457	56.9
	Mike Thompson (R)	47,226	43.1

GEORGIA

	Candidates	Votes	%
1	G. Elliott Hagan (D)	53,413	58.0
	Porter W. Carswell (R)	38,619	41.9
2	Maston O'Neal (D)	54,487	100.0
3	Jack Brinkley (D)	42,424	61.2
	Billy Mixon (R)	26,255	37.9
4	Ben B. Blackburn (R)	55,249	50.2
	James A. Mackay (D)	54,889	49.8
5	Fletcher Thompson (R)	55,423	60.1
	Archie Lindsey (D)	36,751	39.9
6	John J. Flynt Jr. (D)	74,175	67.9
	G. Paul Jones Jr. (R)	35,048	32.1
7	John W. Davis (D)	65,614	65.0
	E. Y. Chapin III (R)	35,383	35.0
8	W. S. Stuckey Jr. (D)	60,059	77.0
	Mack F. Mattingly (R)	17,926	23.0
9	Phil M. Landrum (D)	61,930	100.0
10	Robert G. Stephens Jr. (D)	54,141	65.7
	Leroy H. Simkins Jr. (R)	28,247	34.3

HAWAII

	Candidates	Votes	%
AL	Patsy T. Mink (D)	140,880✓	
	Spark M. Matsunaga (D)	140,110✓	
	John S. Carroll	67,281	
	James K. Kealoha (R)	62,473	

IDAHO

	Candidates	Votes	%
1	James A. McClure (R)	70,410	51.8
	Compton I. White Jr. (D)	65,446	48.2
2	George V. Hansen (R)	79,024	70.3
	A. W. Brunt (D)	33,348	29.7

ILLINOIS

	Candidates	Votes	%
1	William L. Dawson (D)	91,119	72.6
	David R. Reed (R)	34,421	27.4
2	Barratt O'Hara (D)	83,471	59.2
	Philip G. Bixler (R)	57,629	40.8
3	William T. Murphy (D)	83,857	52.0
	Albert F. Manion (R)	77,442	48.0
4	Edward J. Derwinski (R)	125,365	72.0
	Ray J. Rybacki (D)	48,673	28.0
5	John C. Kluczynski (D)	85,770	56.2

Candidates	Votes	%
Walter K. Kiltz (R)	66,735	43.8
6 Daniel J. Ronan (D)	84,126	57.0
Samuel A. Decaro (R)	63,374	43.0
7 Frank Annunzio (D)	82,962	80.9
Joseph D. Day (R)	19,650	19.2
8 Daniel D. Rostenkowski (D)	94,631	59.9
John H. Leszynski (R)	63,377	40.1
9 Sydney R. Yates (D)	96,746	59.9
Richard C. Storey Jr. (R)	64,875	40.1
10 Harold R. Collier (R)	132,650	69.4
Frank J. Jirka Jr. (D)	58,376	30.6
11 Roman C. Pucinski (D)	105,996	50.9
John J. Hoellen (R)	102,244	49.1
12 Robert McClory (R)	90,483	69.1
Herbert L. Stern (D)	40,502	30.9
13 Donald Rumsfeld (R)	158,769	76.0
James L. McCabe (D)	50,107	24.0
14 John N. Erlenborn (R)	130,442	71.7
Kenneth McCleary (D)	51,385	28.3
15 Charlotte T. Reid (R)	102,018	72.3
Selwyn L. Boyer (D)	39,123	27.7
16 John B. Anderson (R)	89,990	73.0
Robert M. Whiteford (D)	33,274	27.0
17 Leslie C. Arends (R)	104,240	67.4
Bernard J. Hughes (D)	50,350	32.6
18 Robert H. Michel (R)	80,293	58.4
Thomas V. Cassidy (D)	57,100	41.6
19 Tom Railsback (R)	77,895	52.3
Gale Schisler (D)	71,050	47.7
20 Paul Findley (R)	102,609	62.2
Richard R. Wolfe (D)	62,343	37.8
21 Kenneth J. Gray (D)	103,128	56.2
Bob Beckmeyer (R)	80,382	43.8
22 William L. Springer (R)	96,453	63.3
Cameron B. Satterthwaite (D)	55,818	36.7
23 George E. Shipley (D)	95,156	56.4
Leslie N. Jones (R)	73,463	43.6
24 Melvin Price (D)	82,513	71.5
John S. Guthrie (R)	32,915	28.5

INDIANA

1 Ray J. Madden (D)	71,040	58.3
Albert F. Harrigan (R)	50,804	41.7
2 Charles A. Halleck (R)	97,161	57.5
Ralph G. McFadden (D)	71,825	42.5
3 John Brademas (D)	75,321	55.8
Robert A. Ehlers (R)	59,731	44.2
4 E. Ross Adair (R)	94,457	63.5
J. Byron Hayes (D)	54,331	36.5
5 J. Edward Roush (D)	76,176	51.1
Kenneth Bowman (R)	72,873	48.9
6 William G. Bray (R)	124,087	65.7
James M. Nicholson (D)	63,342	33.6
7 John T. Myers (R)	79,864	54.3
Elden C. Tipton (D)	67,135	45.7
8 Roger H. Zion (R)	94,924	51.1
Winfield K. Denton (D)	90,887	48.9
9 Lee H. Hamilton (D)	89,392	53.8
John W. Lewis (R)	76,661	46.2
10 Richard L. Roudebush (R)	94,428	63.4
Robert H. Staton (D)	54,515	36.6
11 Andrew Jacobs Jr. (D)	65,624	55.8
Paul R. Oakes (R)	52,096	44.3

IOWA

1 Fred Schwengel (R)	64,795	51.3
John R. Schmidhauser (D)	60,534	47.9
2 John C. Culver (D)	76,281	54.0
Robert M. L. Johnson (R)	65,079	46.0
3 H. R. Gross (R)	79,343	62.1
L. A. Touchae (D)	48,530	38.0
4 John Kyl (R)	65,259	51.7
Bert Bandstra (D)	61,074	48.3
5 Neal Smith (D)	72,875	60.4
Don Mahon (R)	46,981	39.0
6 Wiley Mayne (R)	73,274	57.4
Stanley L. Greigg (D)	53,917	42.3

Candidates	Votes	%
7 William J. Scherle (R)	64,217	59.0
John R. Hansen (D)	44,529	40.9

KANSAS

1 Bob Dole (R)	97,487	68.6
Berniece Henkle (D)	44,569	31.4
2 Chester L. Mize (R)	85,128	62.8
Harry Wiles (D)	50,336	37.2
3 Larry Winn Jr. (R)	60,107	52.9
Marvin E. Rainey (D)	51,108	45.0
4 Garner E. Shriver (R)	86,944	68.7
Paul H. Gerling (D)	39,625	31.3
5 Joe Skubitz (R)	86,944	60.9
Delno E. Bass (D)	55,933	39.2

KENTUCKY

1 Frank A. Stubblefield (D)	57,736	70.6
Richard Nicholson (R)	24,085	29.4
2 William H. Natcher (D)	51,311	58.9
R. Douglas Ford (R)	35,770	41.1
3 William O. Cowger (R)	66,577	59.0
Norbert Blume (D)	46,240	41.0
4 M. G. (Gene) Snyder (R)	66,801	53.9
Frank Chelf (D)	56,902	46.0
5 Tim Lee Carter (R)	65,596	75.4
Eugene C. Harter (D)	21,452	24.6
6 John C. Watts (D)	58,182	65.1
William McKinley Hendren (R)	31,266	35.0
7 Carl D. Perkins (D)	65,522	68.9
C. F. See (R)	29,541	31.1

LOUISIANA

1 F. Edward Hebert (D)	68,523	100.0
2 Hale Boggs (D)	90,149	68.6
Leonard L. Limes (R)	41,209	31.4
3 Edwin E. Willis (D)	46,533	59.7
Hall M. Lyons (R)	31,444	40.3
4 Joe D. Waggonner Jr. (D)	48,345	100.0
5 Otto E. Passman (D)	38,660	100.0
6 John R. Rarick (D)	86,958	76.6
Crayton G. Hall (R)	26,599	23.4
7 Edwin W. Edwards (D)	34,655	100.0
8 Speedy O. Long (D)	33,183	100.0

MAINE

1 Peter N. Kyros (D)	81,302	50.4
Peter A. Garland (R)	72,984	45.2
2 William D. Hathaway (D)	85,956	56.8
Howard M. Foley (R)	65,476	43.2

MARYLAND

1 Rogers C. B. Morton (R)	69,940	71.4
H. C. Byrd (D)	28,025	28.6
2 Clarence D. Long (D)	79,963	69.3
Paul T. McHenry Jr. (R)	35,476	30.7
3 Edward A. Garmatz (D)	56,980	100.0
4 George H. Fallon (D)	57,572	74.3
G. Neilson Sigler (R)	19,930	25.7
5 Hervey G. Machen (D)	55,676	53.9
Lawrence J. Hogan (R)	47,703	46.1
6 Charles McC. Mathias Jr. (R)	72,360	70.9
Walter G. Finch (D)	29,637	29.1
7 Samuel N. Friedel (D)	61,959	76.0
Stephen L. Rosenstein (R)	19,584	24.0
8 Gilbert Gude (R)	71,050	54.4
Royce Hanson (D)	59,568	45.6

MASSACHUSETTS

1 Silvio O. Conte (R)	109,370	100.0
2 Edward P. Boland (D)	95,985	100.0
3 Philip J. Philbin (D)	126,664	71.0
Howard A. Miller (R)	51,646	29.0
4 Harold D. Donohue (D)	137,681	100.0

Candidates	Votes	%
5 F. Bradford Morse (R)	140,702	74.8
Charles N. Tsapatsaris (D)	47,377	25.2
6 William H. Bates (R)	127,744	65.7
Daniel L. Parent (D)	66,675	34.3
7 Torbert H. Macdonald (D)	119,543	74.5
Gordon F. Hughes (R)	40,930	25.5
8 Thomas P. O'Neill Jr. (D)	102,104	100.0
9 John W. McCormack (D)	87,879	100.0
10 Margaret M. Heckler (R)	96,675	51.1
Patrick H. Harrington Jr. (D)	92,516	48.9
11 James A. Burke (D)	141,465	74.8
James L. Hofford (R)	47,705	25.2
12 Hastings Keith (R)	98,372	55.0
Edward F. Harrington (D)	80,473	45.0

MICHIGAN

1 John Conyers (D)	89,908	84.2
Rhecha R. Ross (R)	16,853	15.8
2 Marvin L. Esch (R)	65,205	51.0
Weston E. Vivian (D)	62,536	49.0
3 Garry Brown (R)	68,912	52.3
Paul H. Todd Jr. (D)	62,984	47.8
4 Edward Hutchinson (R)	78,190	67.8
John V. Martin (D)	37,177	32.2
5 Gerald R. Ford (R)	88,108	68.5
James Mathew Catchick (D)	40,435	31.5
6 Charles E. Chamberlain (R)	85,669	67.3
Lee H. Wenke (D)	41,695	32.7
7 Donald W. Riegle Jr. (R)	71,166	54.1
John C. Mackie (D)	60,408	45.9
8 James Harvey (R)	85,657	69.9
Wager F. Clunis (D)	36,967	30.2
9 Guy Vander Jagt (R)	92,710	66.7
Henry J. Dongvillo (D)	46,266	33.3
10 Elford A. Cederberg (R)	85,754	67.4
Hubert C. Evans (D)	41,410	32.6
11 Phillip E. Ruppe (R)	70,820	51.8
Raymond F. Clevenger (D)	65,875	48.2
12 James G. O'Hara (D)	84,379	65.1
Patrick J. Driscoll (R)	45,199	34.9
13 Charles C. Diggs Jr. (D)	60,660	83.0
Frank Daniels (R)	12,393	17.0
14 Lucien N. Nedzi (D)	77,851	59.7
William J. Kennedy (R)	52,490	40.3
15 William D. Ford (D)	72,987	67.8
Arpo Yemen (R)	34,619	32.2
16 John D. Dingell Jr. (D)	71,787	62.7
John T. Dempsey (R)	42,738	37.3
17 Martha W. Griffiths (D)	90,541	69.2
William P. Harrington (R)	40,334	30.8
18 William S. Broomfield (R)	102,501	67.8
William H. Merrill (D)	48,627	32.2
19 Jack H. McDonald (R)	76,884	57.0
Billie S. Farnum (D)	57,907	43.0

Special Election

9 Guy Vander Jagt (R)	91,056	66.6
Henry J. Dongvillo (D)	45,699	33.4

MINNESOTA

1 Albert H. Quie (R)	109,312	65.9
George Daley (DFL)	56,547	34.1
2 Ancher Nelsen (R)	93,855	66.2
Charles M. Christensen (DFL)	47,899	33.8
3 Clark MacGregor (R)	122,775	65.4
Elva D. Walker (DFL)	64,861	34.6
4 Joseph Karth (DFL)	91,271	53.4
Stephan Maxwell (R)	79,667	46.6
5 Donald M. Fraser (DFL)	86,953	59.7
William Hathaway (R)	58,816	40.4
6 John M. Zwach (R)	80,710	51.4
Alec G. Olson (DFL)	76,439	48.6
7 Odin Langen (R)	84,914	63.2
Keith C. Davison (DFL)	49,388	36.8
8 John A. Blatnik (DFL)	116,969	100.0

MISSISSIPPI

	Candidates	Votes	%
1	Thomas G. Abernethy (D)	47,359	68.8
	W. B. Alexander (I)	14,700	21.4
	Dock Drummond (I)	6,805	9.9
2	Jamie L. Whitten (D)	53,620	83.5
	S. B. Wise (R)	10,622	16.5
3	John Bell Williams (D)	71,377	82.4
	Emma Sanders (I)	15,218	17.6
4	G. V. (Sonny) Montgomery (D)	52,138	65.3
	L. L. McAllister Jr. (R)	26,027	32.6
5	William M. Colmer (D)	58,080	70.0
	James M. Moye (R)	24,865	30.0

MISSOURI

	Candidates	Votes	%
1	Frank M. Karsten (D)	62,143	63.9
	Robert L. Sharp (R)	35,053	36.1
2	Thomas B. Curtis (R)	102,985	66.2
	William B. Milius (D)	52,527	33.8
3	Leonor K. Sullivan (D)	59,014	71.1
	Homer McCracken (R)	23,953	28.9
4	William J. Randall (D)	54,330	60.9
	Forest Nave Jr. (R)	34,952	39.2
5	Richard Bolling (D)	46,674	61.2
	Willis Earl Salyers (R)	29,641	38.8
6	W. R. Hull Jr. (D)	55,418	58.0
	John L. Leims (R)	40,185	42.0
7	Durward G. Hall (R)	86,626	62.3
	Arch M. Skelton (D)	52,421	37.7
8	Richard Ichord (D)	61,128	58.1
	Ben Rogers (R)	44,035	41.9
9	William L. Hungate (D)	68,472	55.3
	Anthony C. Schroeder (R)	55,405	44.7
10	Paul C. Jones (D)	48,985	61.0
	William Bruckerhoff (R)	31,263	39.0

MONTANA

	Candidates	Votes	%
1	Arnold Olsen (D)	67,123	50.8
	Richard Smiley (R)	64,925	49.2
2	James F. Battin (R)	76,015	60.2
	John Melcher (D)	50,308	39.8

NEBRASKA

	Candidates	Votes	%
1	Robert V. Denney (R)	93,628	51.2
	Clair A. Callan (D)	89,363	48.8
2	Glenn Cunningham (R)	83,082	64.3
	Richard Fellman (D)	46,235	35.8
3	David Martin (R)	115,893	73.0
	John Homan (D)	42,920	27.0

NEVADA

	Candidates	Votes	%
AL	Walter S. Baring (D)	86,467	67.6
	Ralph L. Kraemer (R)	41,383	32.4

NEW HAMPSHIRE

	Candidates	Votes	%
1	Louis C. Wyman (R)	72,909	56.2
	J. Oliva Huot (D)	56,750	43.8
2	James C. Cleveland (R)	66,176	66.7
	William H. Barry Jr. (D)	32,838	33.1

NEW JERSEY

	Candidates	Votes	%
1	John E. Hunt (R)	68,248	51.4
	Michael J. Piarulli (D)	61,469	46.3
2	Charles W. Sandman Jr. (R)	72,014	51.5
	Thomas C. McGrath Jr. (D)	65,494	46.9
3	James J. Howard (D)	81,382	52.7
	James M. Coleman (R)	72,043	46.6
4	Frank Thompson Jr. (D)	82,271	56.2
	Ralph Clark Chandler (R)	63,730	43.5
5	Peter H. B. Frelinghuysen (R)	108,375	70.8
	Carter Jefferson (D)	41,476	27.1
6	William T. Cahill (R)	106,406	66.9
	Walter Dubrow (D)	48,738	30.7

	Candidates	Votes	%
7	William B. Widnall (R)	101,253	66.4
	Robert E. Hamer (D)	51,204	33.6
8	Charles S. Joelson (D)	80,725	59.6
	Richard M. DeMarco (R)	51,784	38.2
9	Henry Helstoski (D)	74,320	50.9
	Frank C. Osmers Jr. (R)	71,756	49.1
10	Peter W. Rodino Jr. (D)	71,699	64.3
	Earl Harris (R)	36,508	32.7
11	Joseph G. Minish (D)	64,023	58.3
	Leonard J. Felzenberg (R)	44,803	40.8
12	Florence P. Dwyer (R)	116,701	73.9
	Robert F. Allen (D)	37,790	23.9
13	Cornelius E. Gallagher (D)	90,488	71.8
	Ruth Swayze (R)	35,486	28.2
14	Dominick V. Daniels (D)	87,741	68.0
	Thomas R. McSherry (R)	36,828	28.5
15	Edward J. Patten (D)	81,959	57.0
	C. John Stroumtsos (R)	59,706	41.5

NEW MEXICO

	Candidates	Votes	%
AL	Thomas G. Morris (D)	140,057	55.9
	Schuble C. Cook (R)	110,441	44.1
AL	E. S. Johnny Walker (D)	126,984	50.5
	Robert C. Davidson (R)	124,536	49.5

NEW YORK

	Candidates	Votes	%
1	Otis G. Pike (D, L)	101,963	58.9
	James M. Catterson Jr. (R)	58,296	33.7
	Domenico Crachi Jr. (C)	12,731	7.4
2	James R. Grover Jr. (R)	79,649	54.7
	Frank M. Corso (D, L)	49,743	34.1
	Edward Campbell (C)	14,820	10.2
3	Lester L. Wolff (D, L)	81,959	50.3
	Steven B. Derounian (R)	81,122	49.7
4	John W. Wydler (R)	86,677	59.7
	Martin J. Steadman (D, L)	46,555	32.0
	Donald H. Serrell (C)	10,035	6.9
5	Herbert Tenzer (D, L)	88,602	49.9
	Thomas M. Brennan (R, C)	86,356	48.6
6	Seymour Halpern (R, L)	91,526	59.0
	Gilbert T. Redleaf (D)	45,621	29.4
	Ronald E. Weiss (C)	17,863	11.5
7	Joseph P. Addabbo (D, L)	93,758	64.9
	Louis R. Mercogliano (R)	34,644	24.0
	Raymond G. Carpenter (C)	16,070	11.1
8	Benjamin S. Rosenthal (D, L)	115,310	69.6
	Thomas C. Gowlan (R)	36,573	22.1
	Cyrus S. Jullen (C)	13,726	8.3
9	James J. Delaney (D)	75,915	53.5
	John F. Haggerty (R, C)	56,754	40.0
	David Green (L)	9,182	6.5
10	Emanuel Celler (D, L)	76,439	82.1
	Irwin A. Rosenberg (R)	16,702	17.9
11	Frank J. Brasco (D)	39,386	70.6
	Benjamin W. Feldman (R)	12,200	21.9
	Edward L. Johnson (L)	4,174	7.5
12	Edna F. Kelley (D, L)	87,651	72.7
	Alfred Grant Walton (R)	29,390	24.4
13	Abraham J. Multer (D)	95,511	61.9
	Mary Gravina (R)	28,750	18.6
	Herschell Chanin (L)	20,557	13.3
	Michael J. Spadaro (C)	9,463	6.1
14	John J. Rooney (D, L)	43,142	76.2
	Leon F. Nadrowski (R)	13,482	23.8
15	Hugh L. Carey (D, U TAX)	52,919	56.8
	Herbert F. Ryan (R, C)	40,181	43.2
16	John M. Murphy (D, L)	71,889	57.4
	Frank J. Biondollilo (R, C)	53,346	42.6
17	Theodore R. Kupferman (R)	69,492	47.7
	Jerome H. Wilson (D, L)	67,334	46.2
	Richard J. Callahan (C)	8,818	6.1
18	Adam C. Powell (D)	45,308*	74.1
	Lassen L. Walsh (R)	10,711	17.5
	Richard Prideaux (L)	3,954	6.5
19	Leonard Farbstein (D)	53,581	57.8
	Henry E. Del Rosso (R, C)	24,340	26.2
	Elaine M. Morrison (L)	11,349	12.2

	Candidates	Votes	%
20	William F. Ryan (D, L)	74,215	74.8
	Norman C. Harlowe (R)	20,560	20.7
21	James H. Scheuer (D, L)	63,173	83.6
	Burton Siegel (R)	12,414	16.4
22	Jacob H. Gilbert (D)	40,787	74.2
	Pedro Luis Rodriguez (R, ALL PP)	10,603	19.3
	Carlos Rosario (L)	3,552	6.5
23	Jonathan B. Bingham (D, L)	84,540	73.4
	Harold Grosberg (R)	21,735	18.9
	Walter A. Quinn Jr. (C)	8,949	7.8
24	Paul A. Fino (R, C)	80,882	63.9
	Aileen B. Ryan (D)	42,291	33.4
25	Richard L. Ottinger (D, L)	106,952	54.6
	Frederick J. Martin Jr. (R)	88,769	45.4
26	Ogden R. Reid (R)	107,031	69.3
	Joseph L. Hutner (D)	39,203	25.4
	Albert M. Gants (C)	8,159	5.3
27	John G. Dow (D, L)	79,424	47.2
	Louis V. Mills (R)	74,816	44.5
	Frederick P. Roland (C)	13,946	8.3
28	Joseph Y. Resnick (D, L)	84,940	50.3
	Hamilton Fish Jr. (R)	78,258	46.3
29	Daniel E. Button (R, L)	107,651	53.3
	Richard J. Conners (D)	91,174	45.1
30	Carleton J. King (R)	113,759	65.0
	John S. Hall (D, L)	61,216	35.0
31	Robert C. McEwen (R)	75,680	67.6
	Raymond E. Bishop (D, L)	36,723	32.4
32	Alexander Pirnie (R, L)	94,331	72.3
	Robert Castle (D)	36,195	27.7
33	Howard W. Robison (R)	88,378	65.7
	Blair G. Ewing (D, L)	45,761	34.0
34	James M. Hanley (D)	90,044	55.1
	Stewart F. Hancock Jr. (R)	62,559	38.3
35	Samuel S. Stratton (D, L)	93,746	65.8
	Frederick D. Dugan (R)	48,668	34.2
36	Frank J. Horton (R)	110,514	67.3
	Milo Thomas (D)	37,129	22.6
	Robert H. Detig (C)	10,493	6.4
37	Barber B. Conable Jr. (R)	104,342	67.7
	Kenneth Hed (D)	46,201	30.0
38	Charles E. Goodell (R)	82,137	67.2
	Edison Leroy Jr. (D)	35,785	29.3
39	Richard D. McCarthy (D, L)	95,671	52.3
	John R. Pillion (R, C)	87,230	47.7
40	Henry P. Smith III (R)	85,801	61.2
	William Levitt (D, L)	54,303	38.8
41	Thaddeus J. Dulski (D, L)	92,222	76.4
	Frank X. Schwab (R, C)	28,491	23.6

Special Election

	Candidates	Votes	%
17	Theodore R. Kupferman (R)	44,125	46.4
	Orin Lehman (D)	43,206	45.4
	Jeffrey St. John (C)	7,796	8.2

NORTH CAROLINA

	Candidates	Votes	%
1	Walter B. Jones (D)	43,539	61.4
	John P. East (R)	27,434	38.7
2	L. H. Fountain (D)	36,849	65.0
	Reece B. Gardiner (R)	19,888	35.1
3	David N. Henderson (D)	33,809	100.0
4	James C. Gardner (R)	60,686	56.5
	Harold D. Cooley (D)	46,673	43.5
5	Nick Galifianakis (D)	46,035	53.1
	G. Fred Steele Jr. (R)	40,729	46.9
6	Horace R. Kornegay (D)	42,677	51.6
	Richard B. Barnwell (R)	40,000	48.4
7	Alton Lennon (D)	40,512	100.0
8	Charles Raper Jonas (R)	56,382	71.5
	John G. Plumides (D)	22,465	28.5
9	James T. Broyhill (R)	80,989	63.3
	Robert Bingham (D)	46,882	36.7
10	Basil L. Whitener (D)	52,111	56.1
	W. Hall Young (R)	40,741	43.9
11	Roy A. Taylor (D)	72,855	52.8
	W. Scott Harvey (R)	65,187	47.2

Special Election

	Candidates	Votes	%
1	Walter B. Jones (D)	21,773	60.3
	John P. East (R)	14,308	39.7

NORTH DAKOTA

	Candidates	Votes	%
1	Mark Andrews (R)	66,011	66.2
	S. F. (Buckshot) Hoffner (D)	33,694	33.8
2	Thomas S. Kleppe (R)	50,801	52.0
	Rolland Redlin (D)	46,993	48.1

OHIO

	Candidates	Votes	%
1	Robert Taft Jr. (R)	70,366	52.9
	John J. Gilligan (D)	62,580	47.1
2	Donald D. Clancy (R)	102,313	70.7
	Thomas E. Anderson (D)	42,367	29.3
3	Charles W. Whalen Jr. (R)	62,471	53.8
	Rodney M. Love (D)	53,658	46.2
4	William M. McCulloch (R)	66,142	63.6
	Robert H. Mihlbaugh (D)	37,855	36.4
5	Delbert L. Latta (R)	80,906	75.3
	John H. Shock (D)	26,503	24.7
6	William H. Harsha (R)	74,847	67.9
	Ottie W. Reno (D)	35,345	32.1
7	Clarence J. Brown Jr. (R)	81,225	100.0
8	Jackson E. Betts (R)	78,933	67.1
	Frank B. Bennett (D)	38,787	33.0
9	Thomas L. Ashley (D)	83,261	60.8
	Jane M. Kuebbeler (R)	53,777	39.2
10	Clarence E. Miller (R)	56,659	52.0
	Walter H. Moeller (D)	52,258	48.0
11	J. William Stanton (R)	86,273	69.3
	James F. Henderson (D)	38,206	30.7
12	Samuel L. Devine (R)	70,102	64.2
	Robert N. Shamansky (D)	39,140	35.8
13	Charles A. Mosher (R)	69,862	65.5
	Thomas E. Wolfe (D)	36,751	34.5
14	William H. Ayres (R)	77,819	59.7
	Charles F. Madden Jr. (D)	52,646	40.4
15	Chalmers P. Wylie (R)	57,993	59.9
	Robert L. Van Heyde (D)	38,805	40.1
16	Frank T. Bow (R)	87,597	61.1
	Robert D. Freeman (D)	55,775	38.9
17	John M. Ashbrook (R)	73,132	55.3
	Robert T. Secrest (D)	59,031	44.7
18	Wayne L. Hays (D)	73,657	64.2
	William H. Weir (R)	41,165	35.9
19	Michael J. Kirwan (D)	86,975	71.9
	Donald J. Lewis (R)	34,037	28.1
20	Michael A. Feighan (D)	63,629	76.1
	Clarence E. McLeod (R)	20,034	24.0
21	Charles A. Vanik (D)	81,210	81.7
	Frederick M. Coleman (R)	18,205	18.3
22	Frances P. Bolton (R)	71,927	55.9
	Anthony O. Calabrese Jr. (D)	56,803	44.1
23	William E. Minshall (R)	102,513	73.2
	Sheldon D. Clark (D)	37,489	26.8
24	Donald E. Lukens (R)	61,194	58.5
	James H. Pelley (D)	43,418	41.5

OKLAHOMA

	Candidates	Votes	%
1	Page Belcher (R)	106,259	69.7
	Ed Cadenhead (D)	46,286	30.3
2	Ed Edmondson (D)	62,324	53.6
	Denzil D. Garrison (R)	53,919	46.4
3	Carl Albert (D)	43,049	77.2
	Whit Pate (R)	12,697	22.8
4	Tom Steed (D)	36,719	50.3
	Truman T. Branscum (R)	36,355	49.8
5	John Jarman (D)	96,464	69.6
	Melvin H. Gragg (R)	42,088	30.4
6	James V. Smith (R)	51,474	51.4
	Jed Johnson Jr. (D)	48,755	48.6

OREGON

	Candidates	Votes	%
1	Wendell Wyatt (R)	144,361	74.3
	Malcolm H. Cross (D)	49,841	25.7
2	Al Ullman (D)	94,346	63.3
	Everett J. Thoren (R)	54,789	36.7
3	Edith Green (D)	114,687	66.9
	Lyle Dean (R)	56,598	33.0
4	John R. Dellenback (R)	94,154	62.7
	Charles O. Porter (D)	56,007	37.3

PENNSYLVANIA

	Candidates	Votes	%
1	William A. Barrett (D)	90,100	66.1
	Beatrice K. Chernock (R)	46,280	33.9
2	Robert N. C. Nix (D)	76,372	59.9
	Herbert R. Cain Jr. (R)	51,079	40.1
3	James A. Byrne (D)	64,575	56.6
	Walter T. Darmopray (R)	49,434	43.4
4	Joshua Eilberg (D)	98,793	51.9
	Robert Baer Cohen (R)	91,620	48.1
5	William J. Green III (D)	86,128	59.1
	Michael J. Bednarek (R)	59,515	40.9
6	George M. Rhodes (D)	91,538	56.1
	Daniel B. Boyer Jr. (R)	71,508	43.9
7	Lawrence G. Williams (R)	101,042	63.2
	John J. Logue (D)	58,766	36.8
8	Edward G. Biester Jr. (R)	70,435	59.6
	Walter S. Farley Jr. (D)	47,845	40.5
9	G. Robert Watkins (R)	81,516	62.6
	Louis F. Waldmann (D)	48,656	37.4
10	Joseph M. McDade (R)	115,765	66.8
	Neil Trama (D)	57,615	33.2
11	Daniel J. Flood (D)	110,877	67.2
	Gerald C. Broadt (R)	54,032	32.8
12	J. Irving Whalley (R)	107,374	66.9
	J. Robert Rohm (D)	53,044	33.1
13	Richard S. Schweiker (R)	134,414	72.5
	William D. Searle (D)	51,024	27.5
14	William S. Moorhead (D)	83,967	68.3
	Richard L. Thornburgh (R)	39,024	31.7
15	Fred B. Rooney (D)	80,407	52.3
	George J. Joseph (R)	73,404	47.7
16	Edwin D. Eshleman (R)	82,527	69.2
	Richard F. Charles (D)	36,721	30.8
17	Herman T. Schneebeli (R)	109,169	66.2
	William Conrad Reuter (D)	55,761	33.8
18	Robert J. Corbett (R)	107,677	67.1
	John R. Wohlfarth (D)	52,714	32.9
19	George A. Goodling (R)	70,445	51.7
	N. Neiman Craley Jr. (D)	65,907	48.3
20	Elmer J. Holland (D)	93,068	65.9
	Joseph Sabol Jr. (R)	48,229	34.1
21	John H. Dent (D)	80,472	64.2
	Edward B. Byrne (R)	44,800	35.8
22	John P. Saylor (R)	103,868	67.5
	Frank H. Buck (D)	50,017	32.5
23	Albert W. Johnson (R)	81,658	62.8
	Robert W. Mitchell (D)	48,373	37.2
24	Joseph P. Vigorito (D)	85,193	55.3
	James D. Weaver (R)	68,955	44.7
25	Frank M. Clark (D)	92,073	64.5
	John F. Heath (R)	50,639	35.5
26	Thomas E. Morgan (D)	83,687	64.1
	Paul P. Riggle (R)	46,957	35.9
27	James G. Fulton (R)	108,731	67.7
	Stephen J. Arnold (D)	51,928	32.3

RHODE ISLAND

	Candidates	Votes	%
1	Fernand J. St. Germain (D)	79,046	56.6
	Raymond W. Houghton (R)	60,093	43.0
2	John E. Fogarty (D)	117,911	64.7
	Everett C. Sammartino (R)	64,438	35.3

SOUTH CAROLINA

	Candidates	Votes	%
1	L. Mendel Rivers (D)	59,055	100.0
2	Albert W. Watson (R)	48,742	64.3

	Candidates	Votes	%
	Fred Leclercq (D)	27,013	35.7
3	William J. Bryan Dorn (D)	42,834	57.8
	John Grisso (R)	31,331	42.2
4	Robert T. Ashmore (D)	43,611	100.0
5	Thomas S. Gettys (D)	41,550	99.2
6	John L. McMillan (D)	43,090	61.7
	Archie C. Odom (R)	26,702	38.3

SOUTH DAKOTA

	Candidates	Votes	%
1	Ben Reifel (R)	80,592	66.7
	Francis C. Richter (D)	40,236	33.3
2	E. Y. Berry (R)	63,063	60.5
	Jack Allmon (D)	41,155	39.5

TENNESSEE

	Candidates	Votes	%
1	James A. Quillen (R)	86,421	87.1
	Temus Bright (I)	12,819	12.9
2	John J. Duncan (R)	87,777	78.9
	Jake Armstrong (D)	23,538	21.2
3	Bill Brock (R)	67,705	64.2
	Franklin Haney (D)	37,720	35.8
4	Joe L. Evins (D)	72,621	90.0
	William Bean (I)	8,061	10.0
5	Richard H. Fulton (D)	55,685	63.0
	George Kelly (R)	32,706	37.0
6	William R. Anderson (D)	50,758	79.6
	Cecil Hill (I)	12,987	20.4
7	Ray Blanton (D)	45,083	50.6
	Julius Hurst (R)	43,118	48.4
8	Robert A. Everett (D)	53,338	75.2
	Jim Boyd (R)	17,608	24.8
9	Dan H. Kuykendall (R)	47,489	52.2
	George W. Grider (D)	43,553	47.8

TEXAS

	Candidates	Votes	%
1	Wright Patman (D)	50,072	100.0
2	John Dowdy (D)	55,134	99.9
3	Joe Pool (D)	35,081	53.4
	James M. Collins (R)	30,588	46.6
4	Ray Roberts (D)	51,895	100.0
5	Earle Cabell (D)	39,977	61.0
	Duke Burgess (R)	25,563	39.0
6	Olin Teague (D)	42,017	100.0
7	George Bush (R)	53,756	57.1
	Frank Briscoe (D)	39,958	42.4
8	Bob Eckhardt (D)	38,497	92.3
	W. D. Spayne (CONST)	3,207	7.7
9	Jack Brooks (D)	47,604	100.0
10	J. J. Pickle (D)	55,424	74.3
	Jane Sumner (R)	18,343	24.6
11	W. R. Poage (D)	39,140	94.9
	Laurel N. Dunn (C)	2,102	5.1
12	Jim Wright (D)	27,010	100.0
13	Graham Purcell (D)	43,820	57.1
	D. C. Norwood (R)	32,960	42.9
14	John Young (D)	52,861	100.0
15	Eligio de la Garza (D)	33,129	100.0
16	Richard C. White (D)	33,179	100.0
17	Omar Burleson (D)	52,169	100.0
18	Bob Price (R)	45,209	59.5
	Dee D. Miller (D)	30,822	40.5
19	George Mahon (D)	56,792	100.0
20	Henry Gonzalez (D)	41,067	87.1
	Robert C. Moore (C)	3,671	7.8
	Bert Ellis (CONST)	2,390	5.1
21	O. C. Fisher (D)	60,497	100.0
22	Bob Casey (D)	60,817	100.0
23	Abraham Kazen (D)	50,322	96.4

Special Election

		Votes	%
8	Lera M. Thomas (D)	6,120#	74.0
	Louis Leman (R)	2,147#	26.0

UTAH

	Candidates	Votes	%
1	Laurence J. Burton (R)	99,750	66.5
	J. Keith Melville (D)	50,260	33.5
2	Sherman P. Lloyd (R)	96,426	61.3
	David S. King (D)	61,001	38.8

VERMONT

	Candidates	Votes	%
AL	Robert T. Stafford (R)	89,097	65.6
	William J. Ryan (D)	46,643	34.4

VIRGINIA

	Candidates	Votes	%
1	Thomas N. Downing (D)	51,016	99.8
2	Porter Hardy Jr. (D)	33,761	100.0
3	David E. Satterfield III (D)	51,576	99.6
4	Watkins M. Abbitt (D)	45,226	66.6
	Edward J. Silverman (C)	14,827	21.8
5	William M. Tuck (D)	32,312	56.2
	Robert L. Gilliam (R)	25,203	43.8
6	Richard H. Poff (R)	55,342	80.8
	Murray A. Stoller (D)	13,113	19.2
7	John O. Marsh Jr. (D)	42,532	59.2
	Edward O. McCue (R)	29,249	40.7
8	William Lloyd Scott (R)	50,782	57.2
	George C. Rawlings Jr. (D)	37,929	42.8
9	William C. Wampler (R)	49,413	53.7
	W. Pat Jennings (D)	42,571	46.3
10	Joel T. Broyhill (R)	58,105	58.3
	Clive L. Duval II (D)	41,502	41.7

WASHINGTON

	Candidates	Votes	%
1	Thomas M. Pelly (R)	120,747	80.3
	Alice Franklin Bryant (D)	29,686	19.7
2	Lloyd Meeds (D)	75,357	60.7
	Eugene M. Smith (R)	44,727	36.0
3	Julia Butler Hansen (D)	78,601	65.8
	Keith Kisor (R)	40,946	34.3
4	Catherine May (R)	77,929	62.1
	Gustav Bansmer (D)	38,029	30.3
	Floyd Paxton (C)	9,585	7.6
5	Thomas S. Foley (D)	74,571	56.5
	Dorothy R. Powers (R)	57,310	43.5
6	Floyd V. Hicks (D)	73,164	60.4
	George Mahler (R)	48,041	39.6
7	Brock Adams (D)	104,613	62.8
	James Munn (R)	60,065	36.0

WEST VIRGINIA

	Candidates	Votes	%
1	Arch A. Moore Jr. (R)	88,364	70.9
	William M. Kidd (D)	36,242	29.1
2	Harley O. Staggers (D)	51,235	60.3
	George L. Strader (R)	33,676	39.7
3	John M. Slack (D)	60,073	61.6
	Mal Guthrie (R)	37,416	38.4
4	Ken Hechler (D)	71,751	59.7
	Harry D. Humphreys (R)	48,396	40.3
5	James Kee (D)	42,722	63.6
	Elizabeth Ann Bowen (R)	24,470	36.4

WISCONSIN

	Candidates	Votes	%
1	Henry C. Schadeberg (R)	65,041	51.0
	Lynn E. Stalbaum (D)	62,398	49.0
2	Robert W. Kastenmeier (D)	70,311	58.0
	William B. Smith (R)	50,850	42.0
3	Vernon W. Thomson (R)	72,586	68.8
	John D. Rice (D)	32,849	31.2
4	Clement J. Zablocki (D)	77,690	74.3
	James E. Laessig (R)	26,863	25.7
5	Henry S. Reuss (D)	52,332	70.0
	Curtis T. Pechtel (R)	22,167	29.7
6	William A. Steiger (R)	67,941	52.4
	John A. Race (D)	61,761	47.6
7	Melvin R. Laird (R)	74,942	65.2
	Norman L. Myhra (D)	40,093	34.9
8	John W. Byrnes (R)	75,817	61.3
	Marvin S. Kagen (D)	47,926	38.7
9	Glenn R. Davis (R)	85,297	64.1
	James P. Buckley (D)	47,674	35.9
10	Alvin E. O'Konski (R)	79,282	66.5
	Carl E. Lauri (D)	39,863	33.5

WYOMING

	Candidates	Votes	%
AL	William Henry Harrison (R)	62,984	52.3
	Al Christian (D)	57,442	47.7

1967 House Elections

CALIFORNIA

Special Primary Election[1]

	Candidates	Votes	%
11	Paul N. McCloskey Jr. (R)	52,882	34.3
	Shirley Temple Black (R)	34,521	22.4
	William H. Draper III (R)	19,566	12.7
	Roy Archibald (D)	15,069	9.8
	Earl B. Whitmore (R)	12,823	8.3
	Edward M. Keating (D)	8,813	5.7

Special Election

	Candidates	Votes	%
11	Paul N. McCloskey Jr. (R)	66,385#	57.8
	Roy Archibald (D)	44,319#	38.6

NEW YORK

Special Election[2]

	Candidates	Votes	%
18	Adam C. Powell (D)	27,963#	86.3
	Lucille P. Williams (R)	3,999#	12.3

RHODE ISLAND

Special Election

	Candidates	Votes	%
2	Robert O. Tiernan (D)	56,051#	48.8
	James DiPrete (R)	55,748#	48.5

1. Under California's special election law, a majority of the total vote cast was required for election. If no candidate achieved it, another election would be held with the top candidates from each party competing. In the 11th district, McCloskey had more votes than any other Republican, but not a majority of the total vote, so he became the Republican nominee against Archibald, the top Democrat, in the special election.

2. Following his reelection to the 90th Congress (1967–1969) In 1966, Powell was not allowed to take the oath of office in January 1967 and was subsequently excluded by vote of the House March 1, 1967. A special election was held April 11, 1967, to fill the vacancy. Powell was again a candidate and won easily, but he never attempted to claim the seat and it remained vacant for the remainder of the Congress.

1968 House Elections

ALABAMA

	Candidates	Votes	%
1	Jack Edwards (R)	60,318	57.1
	Arnold Debrow (D)	40,593	38.4
2	William L. Dickinson (R)	60,743	55.4
	Robert Whaley (D)	37,533	34.2
	Richard Boone (NDPA)	11,446	10.4
3	George Andrews (D)	86,796	90.8
	Wilbur Johnston (NDPA)	8,031	8.4
4	Bill Nichols (D)	94,726	81.4
	Robert Kerr (R)	12,427	10.7
	T. Clemons (NDPA)	9,248	7.9
5	Walter Flowers (D)	69,110	56.2
	William McKinley Branch (NDPA)	28,040	22.8
	Frank Donaldson (R)	14,582	11.9
	Mike Simpson (I)	9,429	7.7
6	John Buchanan (R)	69,445	59.3
	Quinton Bowers (D)	34,608	29.6
	Thomas Wrenn (NDPA)	12,976	11.1
7	Tom Bevill (D)	106,132	76.1
	Jodie Connell (R)	29,923	21.5
8	Robert E. Jones (D)	85,528	76.1
	Ken Hearn (C)	16,900	15.0
	Charlie Burgess (NDPA)	7,140	6.4

ALASKA

	Candidates	Votes	%
AL	Howard W. Pollock (R)	43,577	54.2
	Nick Begich (D)	36,785	45.8

ARIZONA

	Candidates	Votes	%
1	John J. Rhodes (R)	137,761	71.6
	Robert E. Miller (D)	54,594	28.4
2	Morris K. Udall (D)	102,301	70.3
	G. Alfred McGinnis (R)	43,235	29.7
3	Sam Steiger (R)	79,667	63.4
	Ralph Watkins Jr. (D)	46,072	36.6

ARKANSAS

	Candidates	Votes	%
1	Bill Alexander (D)	80,293	68.9
	Guy Newcomb (R)	36,284	31.1
2	Wilbur D. Mills (D)		100.0
3	John Paul Hammerschmidt (R)	121,771	67.1
	Hardy Croxton (D)	59,642	32.9
4	David Pryor (D)		100.0

CALIFORNIA

	Candidates	Votes	%
1	Don H. Clausen (R)	133,597	75.2
	Donald W. Graham (D)	37,756	21.3
2	Harold T. Johnson (D)	127,744	60.7
	Osmer E. Dunaway (R)	78,986	37.6
3	John E. Moss (D)	107,446	56.0
	Elmore J. Duffy (R)	80,193	41.8
4	Robert L. Leggett (D)	90,126	55.6
	James M. Shumway (R)	67,225	41.5
5	Phillip Burton (D)	95,630	72.8
	Waldo Velasquez (R)	31,157	23.7
6	William S. Mailliard (R)	151,336	73.4
	Phillip Drath (D)	54,928	26.6
7	Jeffery Cohelan (D)	102,689	62.9
	Barney E. Hilburn (R)	48,397	29.6
	Huey P. Newton (PFP)	12,279	7.5
8	George P. Miller (D)	104,768	64.0
	Raymond P. Britton (R)	58,887	36.0
9	Don Edwards (D)	101,329	56.6
	Larry Fargher (R)	77,847	43.5
10	Charles S. Gubser (R)	160,563	67.3
	Grayson S. Taketa (D)	73,720	30.9
11	Paul N. McCloskey Jr. (R)	166,252	79.4
	Urban G. Whitaker (D)	40,957	19.6
12	Burt L. Talcott (R)	143,222	92.6
13	Charles M. Teague (R)	151,608	65.9
	Stanley K. Sheinbaum (D)	78,628	34.2
14	Jerome R. Waldie (D)	152,847	71.6
	David W. Schuh (R)	56,730	26.6
15	John J. McFall (D)	86,386	53.8
	Sam Van Dyken (R)	74,058	46.2
16	B. F. Sisk (D)	97,476	62.5
	Dave Harris (R)	55,188	35.4
17	Glenn M. Anderson (D)	77,250	50.7
	Joe Blatchford (R)	73,351	48.1
18	Robert B. Mathias (R)	100,115	65.2
	Harlan Hagen (D)	51,373	33.5
19	Chet Holifield (D)	99,069	63.1
	Bill Jones (R)	53,842	34.3
20	H. Allen Smith (R)	136,238	69.4
	Don White (D)	57,064	29.1
21	Augustus F. Hawkins (D)	89,536	91.6
	Rayfield Lundy (R)	8,244	8.4
22	James C. Corman (D)	103,695	56.9
	Joe Holt (R)	75,457	41.4
23	Del Clawson (R)	97,232	65.1
	Jim Sperrazzo (D)	52,202	34.9
24	Glenard P. Lipscomb (R)	155,443	72.8
	Fred W. Neal (D)	57,972	27.2
25	Charles E. Wiggins (R)	145,245	68.7
	Keith F. Shirey (D)	66,263	31.3
26	Thomas M. Rees (D)	134,642	65.4
	Irving Teichner (R)	64,505	31.4
27	Ed Reinecke (R)	162,854	72.2
	John T. Butchko (D)	62,824	27.8
28	Alphonzo Bell (R)	173,680	71.3
	John M. Pratt (D)	65,233	26.8
29	George E. Brown Jr. (D)	76,091	52.3
	Bill Orozco (R)	69,485	47.7
30	Edward R. Roybal (D)	76,967	67.4
	Samuel M. Cavnar (R)	37,234	32.6
31	Charles H. Wilson (D)	97,855	58.9
	James R. Dunn (R)	65,004	39.1
32	Craig Hosmer (R)	142,401	73.9
	Arthur J. Gottlieb (D)	46,404	24.1
33	Jerry L. Pettis (R)	123,507	66.3
	Al C. Ballard (D)	59,649	32.0
34	Richard T. Hanna (D)	107,113	50.9
	William J. Teague (R)	103,470	49.1
35	James B. Utt (R)	216,093	72.5
	Thomas B. Lenhart (D)	74,798	25.1
36	Bob Wilson (R)	148,854	71.6
	Don Lindgren (D)	59,011	28.4
37	Lionel Van Deerlin (D)	96,130	64.7
	Mike Schaefer (R)	52,547	35.3
38	John V. Tunney (D)	121,749	62.7
	Robert O. Hunter (R)	68,887	35.5

COLORADO

	Candidates	Votes	%
1	Byron G. Rogers (D)	91,199	45.7
	Frank A. Kemp (R)	82,677	41.5
	Gordon G. Barnewall (DENVER I)	25,499	12.8
2	Donald G. Brotzman (R)	152,153	62.9
	Roy H. McVicker (D)	89,917	37.2
3	Frank E. Evans (D)	88,368	52.1
	Paul Bradley (R)	81,173	47.9
4	Wayne N. Aspinall (D)	92,680	54.7
	Fred E. Anderson (R)	76,776	45.3

CONNECTICUT

	Candidates	Votes	%
1	Emilio Q. Daddario (D)	124,966	62.4
	Roger B. Ladd (R)	74,615	37.3
2	William L. St. Onge (D)	106,203	54.1
	Peter P. Mariani (R)	89,098	45.4
3	Robert Giaimo (D)	102,636	54.0
	Stelio Salmona (R)	80,696	42.5
4	Lowell P. Weicker Jr. (R)	113,749	51.4
	Donald J. Irwin (D)	104,723	47.3
5	John S. Monagan (D)	110,337	56.3
	Gaetano A. Russo Jr. (R)	85,591	43.7
6	Thomas J. Meskill (R)	126,208	62.3
	Robert M. Sharaf (D)	76,413	37.7

DELAWARE

	Candidates	Votes	%
AL	William V. Roth (R)	117,827	58.7
	Harris B. McDowell Jr. (D)	82,993	41.3

FLORIDA

	Candidates	Votes	%
1	Robert L. F. Sikes (D)	116,215	84.7
	John Drzazga (R)	21,063	15.3
2	Don Fuqua (D)	87,313	100.0
3	Charles E. Bennett (D)	103,540	78.9
	Bill Parsons (R)	27,696	21.1
4	Bill Chappell Jr. (D)	86,251	52.8
	William F. Herlong Jr. (R)	76,974	47.2
5	Louis Frey (R)	108,620	61.7
	James C. Robinson (D)	67,505	38.3
6	Sam M. Gibbons (D)	84,193	62.0
	Paul A. Saad (R)	51,637	38.0
7	James A. Haley (D)	91,539	55.0
	Joe Z. Lovingood (R)	74,896	45.0
8	William C. Cramer (R)	117,747	100.0
9	Paul G. Rogers (D)	111,539	56.2
	Robert W. Rust (R)	87,074	43.8
10	J. Herbert Burke (R)	99,844	54.9
	Elton J. Glssendanner (D)	82,138	45.1
11	Claude Pepper (D)	99,154	76.6
	Ronald I. Strauss (R)	30,324	23.4
12	Dante B. Fascell (D)	82,362	57.0
	Mike Thompson (R)	62,032	43.0

GEORGIA

	Candidates	Votes	%
1	G. Elliott Hagan (D)	77,403	68.2
	Joseph J. Tribble (R)	36,118	31.8
2	Maston O'Neal (D)	72,830	100.0
3	Jack Brinkley (D)	55,759	100.0
4	Ben B. Blackburn (R)	78,753	57.5
	James A. Mackay (D)	58,154	42.5
5	Fletcher Thompson (R)	79,258	55.6
	Charles L. Weltner (D)	63,183	44.4
6	John J. Flynt Jr. (D)	97,289	100.0
7	John W. Davis (D)	96,505	99.8
8	W. S. Stuckey Jr. (D)	64,912	100.0
9	Phil M. Landrum (D)	83,829	100.0
10	Robert G. Stephens (D)	80,674	100.0

HAWAII

	Candidates	Votes	%
AL	Spark M. Matsunaga (D)	161,954✓	
	Patsy T. Mink (D)	149,207✓	
	Neal S. Blaisdell (R)	78,733	
	George Dubois (R)	39,233	
	Jon D. Olsen (PFP)	2,432	
	Peter O. Lombardi (PFP)	2,026	

IDAHO

	Candidates	Votes	%
1	James A. McClure (R)	90,870	59.4
	Compton I. White (D)	62,002	40.6
2	Orval Hansen (R)	65,029	52.6
	Darrell Manning (D)	54,256	43.9

ILLINOIS

	Candidates	Votes	%
1	William L. Dawson (D)	119,207	84.6
	Janet Roberts Jenning (R)	21,758	15.4
2	Abner J. Mikva (D)	106,642	65.4
	Thomas R. Ireland (R)	56,513	34.6
3	William T. Murphy (D)	101,729	54.0
	Robert A. Podesta (R)	86,535	46.0
4	Edward J. Derwinski (R)	151,216	68.3
	Robert E. Creighton (D)	70,145	31.7

Candidates	Votes	%
5 John C. Kluczynski (D)	96,584	55.4
Joseph J. Krasowski (R)	77,887	44.6
6 Daniel J. Ronan (D)	94,779	59.7
Gerald Dolezal (R)	63,999	40.3
7 Frank Annunzio (D)	86,769	83.1
Thomas J. Lento (R)	17,594	16.9
8 Daniel Rostenkowski (D)	105,003	62.8
Henry S. Kaplinski (R)	62,254	37.2
9 Sidney R. Yates (D)	119,032	64.4
Edward V. Notz (R)	65,687	35.6
10 Harold R. Collier (R)	148,398	66.8
Seymour C. Axelrood (D)	73,766	33.2
11 Roman C. Pucinski (D)	128,152	55.8
John J. Hoellen (R)	101,665	44.2
12 Robert McClory (R)	120,370	70.4
Albert S. Salvi (D)	50,525	29.6
13 Donald Rumsfeld (R)	186,714	72.7
David C. Baylor (D)	69,987	27.3
14 John N. Erlenborn (R)	163,332	71.1
Marc Karson (D)	66,293	28.9
15 Charlotte T. Reid (R)	121,432	68.7
Benjamin P. Alschuler (D)	55,291	31.3
16 John B. Anderson (R)	111,037	67.4
Stan Major (D)	53,838	32.7
17 Leslie C. Arends (R)	122,513	65.3
Lester A. Hawthorne (D)	65,192	34.7
18 Robert H. Michel (R)	106,122	60.9
James G. Hatcher (D)	68,173	39.1
19 Tom Railsback (R)	114,948	63.5
Craig Lovitt (D)	66,135	36.5
20 Paul Findley (R)	124,121	66.2
Donald L. Schilson (D)	63,412	33.8
21 Kenneth J. Gray (D)	111,425	54.2
Val Oshel (R)	94,363	45.9
22 William L. Springer (R)	115,258	64.3
Carl F. Firley (D)	63,957	35.7
23 George E. Shipley (D)	104,349	54.0
Bert Hopper (R)	88,945	46.0
24 Melvin Price (D)	113,507	71.3
John S. Guthrie (R)	45,649	28.7

INDIANA

Candidates	Votes	%
1 Ray J. Madden (D)	90,055	56.7
Donald E. Taylor (R)	68,318	43.0
2 Earl F. Landgrebe (R)	104,238	55.1
Edward F. Kelly (D)	85,084	44.9
3 John Brademas (D)	94,452	52.2
William W. Erwin (R)	86,354	47.8
4 E. Ross Adair (R)	98,977	51.4
J. Edward Roush (D)	93,515	48.6
5 Richard L. Roudebush (R)	114,537	63.0
Robert C. Ford (D)	67,370	37.0
6 William G. Bray (R)	142,207	64.9
Phillip L. Bayt (D)	76,940	35.1
7 JohnT. Myers (R)	115,921	59.8
Elden C. Tipton (D)	78,045	40.2
8 Roger H. Zion (R)	109,585	54.5
K. Wayne Kent (D)	91,642	45.5
9 Lee H. Hamilton (D)	102,707	54.4
Robert D. Garton (R)	86,012	45.6
10 David W. Dennis (R)	98,090	53.9
William J. Norton (D)	83,981	46.1
11 Andrew Jacobs Jr. (D)	80,015	53.1
W. W. Hill Jr. (R)	70,725	46.9

IOWA

Candidates	Votes	%
1 Fred Schwengel (R)	91,419	53.0
John R. Schmidhauser (D)	81,049	47.0
2 John C. Culver (D)	103,651	55.1
Tom Riley (R)	84,634	45.0
3 H. R. Gross (R)	101,839	64.1
John E. Van Eschen (D)	57,164	36.0
4 John Kyl (R)	83,259	53.9
Bert Bandstra (D)	71,134	46.1
5 Neal Smith (D)	99,586	62.1
Don Mahon (D)	60,710	37.9
6 Wiley Mayne (R)	100,802	65.0
Jerry O'Sullivan (D)	54,171	35.0

Candidates	Votes	%
7 William Scherle (R)	86,212	64.8
Richard Oshlo (D)	46,774	35.2

KANSAS

Candidates	Votes	%
1 Keith G. Sebelius (R)	87,012	51.5
George W. Meeker (D)	82,102	48.6
2 Chester L. Mize (R)	110,768	67.6
Robert A. Swan (D)	53,151	32.4
3 Larry Winn (R)	100,877	62.8
Newell A. George (D)	59,672	37.2
4 Garner E. Shriver (R)	101,991	64.7
Patrick F. Kelly (D)	55,621	35.3
5 Joe Skubitz (R)	107,085	64.5
A. F. Bramble (D)	59,005	35.5

KENTUCKY

Candidates	Votes	%
1 Frank A. Stubblefield (D)	72,072	100.0
2 William H. Natcher (D)	65,860	56.4
Robert D. Simmons (R)	50,904	43.6
3 William O. Cowger (R)	70,318	56.0
Tom Ray (D)	55,366	44.1
4 M. G. (Gene) Snyder (R)	103,793	65.0
Gus Sheehan (D)	55,971	35.0
5 Tim Lee Carter (R)	86,391	72.8
Thomas J. Roberts (D)	30,575	25.8
6 John C. Watts (D)	78,536	56.5
Russell G. Mobley (R)	58,950	42.4
7 Carl D. Perkins (D)	82,594	62.0
James D. Nickell (R)	50,699	38.0

LOUISIANA

Candidates	Votes	%
1 F. Edward Hebert (D)	70,658	100.0
2 Hale Boggs (D)	81,537	51.2
David C. Treen (R)	77,633	48.8
3 Patrick T. Caffery (D)	39,215	100.0
4 Joe D. Waggonner Jr. (D)	63,788	100.0
5 Otto E. Passman (D)	34,901	100.0
6 John R. Rarick (D)	100,461	79.5
Loyd J. Rockhold (R)	25,867	20.5
7 Edwin W. Edwards (D)	79,709	85.0
Vance W. Plauche (R)	14,126	15.1
8 Speedy O. Long (D)	41,086	100.0

MAINE

Candidates	Votes	%
1 Peter N. Kyros (D)	113,501	56.6
Horace A. Hildreth Jr. (R)	86,949	43.4
2 William D. Hathaway (D)	102,369	55.7
Elden H. Shute (R)	81,398	44.3

MARYLAND

Candidates	Votes	%
1 Rogers C. B. Morton (R)	87,078	73.6
E. Homer White Jr. (D)	31,250	26.4
2 Clarence D. Long (D)	86,025	59.1
John E. Mudd (R)	59,635	40.9
3 Edward A. Garmatz (D)	63,269	81.3
James E. Chew (R)	14,604	18.8
4 George H. Fallon (D)	60,651	65.6
Thomas Paul Raimondi (R)	31,813	34.4
5 Lawrence J. Hogan (R)	89,073	52.7
Hervey G. Machen (D)	79,870	47.3
6 J. Glenn Beall Jr. (R)	71,174	53.0
Goodloe E. Byron (D)	63,597	47.0
7 Samuel N. Friedel (D)	81,048	79.6
Arthur W. Downs (R)	20,745	20.4
8 Gilbert Gude (R)	109,167	60.9
Margaret C. Schweinhaut (D)	70,109	39.1

MASSACHUSETTS

Candidates	Votes	%
1 Silvio O. Conte (R)	140,419	99.8
2 Edward P. Boland (D)	126,485	73.7
Frederick M. Whitney Jr. (R)	45,262	26.4
3 Philip J. Philbin (D)	91,587	47.8
Chandler Harrison Stevens (I)	53,047	27.7
Laurence Curtis (R)	46,860	24.5

Candidates	Votes	%
4 Harold D. Donohue (D)	121,211	61.0
Howard A. Miller Jr. (R)	77,658	39.1
5 F. Bradford Morse (R)	124,930	60.4
Robert C. Maguire (D)	81,875	39.6
6 William H. Bates (R)	136,951	66.1
Deirdre Henderson (D)	70,304	33.9
7 Torbert H. Macdonald (D)	119,562	62.5
William S. Abbot (R)	71,689	34.8
8 Thomas P. O'Neill Jr. (D)	107,645	100.0
9 John W. McCormack (D)	77,347	89.2
Allan C. Freeman (R)	15,906	17.1
10 Margaret M. Heckler (R)	138,220	67.4
Edmund Dinis (D)	66,949	32.6
11 James A. Burke (D)	169,766	100.0
12 Hastings Keith (R)	173,295	99.9

MICHIGAN

Candidates	Votes	%
1 John Conyers Jr. (D)	127,847	100.0
2 Marvin L. Esch (R)	90,804	54.4
Weston E. Vivian (D)	75,009	44.9
3 Garry Brown (R)	109,754	65.2
Thomas L. Keenan (D)	58,692	34.8
4 Edward Hutchinson (R)	100,128	65.6
John V. Martin (D)	52,441	34.4
5 Gerald R. Ford (R)	105,085	62.8
Laurence E. Howard (D)	62,219	37.2
6 Charles E. Chamberlain (R)	103,423	64.1
James A. Harrison (D)	57,839	35.9
7 Donald W. Riegle Jr. (R)	104,502	60.7
William R. Blue (D)	67,779	39.3
8 James Harvey (R)	105,238	68.8
Richard E. Davies (D)	47,639	31.2
9 Guy Vander Jagt (R)	111,774	67.5
Jay A. Wabeke (D)	53,886	32.5
10 Elford A. Cederberg (R)	104,791	65.9
Wayne Miller (D)	54,152	34.1
11 Philip E. Ruppe (R)	94,513	58.8
Raymond F. Clevenger (D)	66,251	41.2
12 James G. O'Hara (D)	131,517	70.3
Max B. Harris Jr. (R)	54,760	29.3
13 Charles C. Diggs Jr. (D)	81,951	86.4
Eugene Beauregard (R)	12,873	13.6
14 Lucien N. Nedzi (D)	101,961	63.1
Peter O'Rourke (R)	59,757	37.0
15 William D. Ford (D)	106,960	71.1
John F. Boyle (R)	43,582	29.0
16 John D. Dingell Jr. (D)	105,690	73.9
Monte R. Bona (R)	37,000	25.9
17 Martha W. Griffths (D)	123,376	74.8
John M. Siviter (R)	40,906	24.8
18 William S. Broomfield (R)	124,025	59.9
Allen Zemmol (D)	82,234	39.7
19 Jack McDonald (R)	104,057	58.0
Garry F. Frink (D)	75,250	42.0

MINNESOTA

Candidates	Votes	%
1 Albert H. Quie (R)	138,400	68.8
George Daley (DFL)	62,916	31.3
2 Ancher Nelsen (R)	100,623	59.5
Jon Wefald (DFL)	68,528	40.5
3 Clark MacGregor (R)	158,989	64.8
Eugene E. Stokowski (DFL)	86,434	35.2
4 Joseph E. Karth (DFL)	129,082	61.3
Emery Barrette (R)	81,392	38.7
5 Donald M. Fraser (DFL)	108,588	57.5
Harmon T. Ogdahl (R)	78,819	41.8
6 John M. Zwach (R)	104,664	56.2
J. Buford Johnson (DFL)	81,578	43.8
7 Odin Langen (R)	83,113	51.3
Bob Bergland (DFL)	79,067	48.8
8 John A. Blatnik (DFL)	115,343	67.6
James A. Hennen (R)	55,209	32.4

MISSISSIPPI

Candidates	Votes	%
1 Thomas G. Abernethy (D)	73,800	100.0
2 Jamie L. Whitten (D)	71,260	100.0
3 Charles H. Griffin (D)	82,896	100.0

Candidates	Votes	%
4 G. V. (Sonny) Montgomery (D)	78,768	70.1
Prentiss Walker (R)	33,683	30.0
5 William M. Colmer (D)	108,297	100.0

Special Runoff Election[1]

Candidates	Votes	%
3 Charles H. Griffin (D)	87,713#	66.9
Charles Evers (D)	43,303#	33.1

MISSOURI

Candidates	Votes	%
1 William Clay (D)	79,295	64.2
Curtis C. Crawford (R)	44,316	35.9
2 James W. Symington (D)	115,476	53.2
Hugh Scott (R)	101,500	46.8
3 Leonor K. Sullivan (D)	106,150	73.4
Homer McCracken (R)	38,439	26.6
4 William B. Randall (D)	104,056	57.9
Leslie O. Olson (R)	75,790	42.1
5 Richard Bolling (D)	86,681	65.4
Harold Masters (R)	45,951	34.7
6 W. R. Hull Jr. (D)	102,315	54.6
James E. Austin (R)	85,237	45.5
7 Durward G. Hall (R)	123,958	63.8
Edward J. Bonitt (D)	70,455	36.2
8 Richard Ichord (D)	108,416	57.5
Eugene E. Northern (R)	79,179	42.0
9 William L. Hungate (D)	108,184	52.2
Christopher S. Bond (R)	98,923	47.8
10 Bill D. Burlison (D)	78,326	54.0
Vernon H. Landgraf (R)	66,830	46.0

MONTANA

Candidates	Votes	%
1 Arnold Olsen (D)	74,974	53.6
Richard Smiley (R)	64,862	46.4
2 James F. Battin (R)	83,888	67.9
Robert L. Kelleher (D)	39,752	32.2

NEBRASKA

Candidates	Votes	%
1 Robert V. Denney (R)	97,697	54.1
Clair A. Callan (D)	78,374	43.4
2 Glenn Cunningham (R)	87,683	55.2
Mrs. Frank B. Morrison (D)	71,254	44.8
3 Dave Martin (R)	123,838	67.8
J. B. Dean (D)	58,728	32.2

NEVADA

Candidates	Votes	%
AL Walter S. Baring (D)	104,136	72.1
James Michael Slattery (R)	40,209	27.9

NEW HAMPSHIRE

Candidates	Votes	%
1 Louis C. Wyman (R)	100,269	63.4
James T. Keefe (D)	57,959	36.6
2 James C. Cleveland (R)	88,609	71.1
David C. Hoeh (D)	35,942	28.9

NEW JERSEY

Candidates	Votes	%
1 John E. Hunt (R)	105,856	58.0
Thomas S. Higgins (D)	74,703	41.0
2 Charles W. Sandman Jr. (R)	91,218	55.3
David Dichter (D)	73,361	44.4
3 James J. Howard (D)	113,587	57.8
Richard R. Stout (R)	82,441	41.9
4 Frank Thompson Jr. (R)	106,504	53.4
Sydney S. Souter (D)	92,710	46.4
5 Peter H. B. Frelinghuysen Jr. (R)	143,963	68.2
Robert F. Allen (D)	63,208	29.9
6 William T. Cahill (R)	138,060	65.7
Robert A. Gasser (D)	71,338	34.0
7 William B. Widnall (R)	120,523	62.2
Charles S. Gregg (D)	71,123	36.7
8 Charles S. Joelson (D)	100,653	61.4
Richard M. DeMarco (R)	62,661	38.2
9 Henry Helstoski (D)	97,599	49.8
Peter Moraites (R)	95,267	48.7
10 Peter W. Rodino Jr. (D)	89,109	63.8
Celestino Clemente (R)	47,989	34.4
11 Joseph G. Minish (D)	91,496	65.5
George M. Wallhauser Jr. (R)	46,426	33.2
12 Florence P. Dwyer (R)	146,264	71.6
John B. Duff (D)	58,112	28.4
13 Cornelius E. Gallagher (D)	83,151	55.5
Marion D. Dwyer (R)	52,159	34.8
Jeremiah J. O'Callaghan (VI)	9,399	6.3
14 Dominick V. Daniels (D)	87,187	58.5
Joseph Bartletta (R)	50,829	34.1
Mervin Murray (C)	7,634	5.1
15 Edward J. Patten (D)	107,316	54.6
George W. Luke (R)	88,043	44.8

NEW MEXICO

Candidates	Votes	%
1 Manuel Lujan Jr. (R)	88,517	52.9
Thomas G. Morris (D)	78,117	46.6
2 Ed Foreman (R)	71,857	50.5
E. S. Johnny Walker (D)	69,858	49.1

NEW YORK

Candidates	Votes	%
1 Otis G. Pike (D)	118,913	53.9
James M. Catterson Jr. (R)	79,208	35.9
Harold Haar (C)	19,470	8.8
2 James R. Grover Jr. (R, C)	129,731	69.0
Charles A. Heeg (D)	53,552	28.5
3 Lester L. Wolff (D, L)	98,226	52.1
Abe Seldin (R)	75,910	40.2
Daniel L. Rice (C)	14,556	7.7
4 John W. Wydler (R, C)	116,190	70.1
Michael J. Delguidice (D)	45,130	27.2
5 Allard K. Lowenstein (D, L)	99,193	50.7
Mason L. Hampton Jr. (R, C)	96,427	49.3
6 Seymour Halpern (R, L)	95,016	57.5
Franklin Miller (D)	49,676	30.1
Thomas J. Adams (C)	20,511	12.4
7 Joseph P. Addabbo (D, L)	90,204#	66.3
Louis R. Mercogliano (R, C)	45,813#	33.7
8 Benjamin S. Rosenthal (D, L)	120,257	69.8
Jack M. Weinstein (R)	37,314	21.7
Charles Witteck Jr. (C)	14,714	8.5
9 James J. Delaney (D)	69,462	49.7
John F. Haggerty (R, C)	59,690	42.7
Rose L. Rubin (L)	8,935	6.4
10 Emanuel Celler (D, L)	106,622	70.5
Frank L. Martano (R, C)	44,551	29.5
11 Frank J. Brasco (D)	40,460	69.7
Robert J. Hower (R)	10,708	18.4
Basil E. Reynolds (C)	3,807	6.6
Edward L. Johnson (L)	3,101	5.3
12 Shirley Chisholm (D)	34,885	66.5
James Farmer (R, L)	13,777	26.3
Ralph J. Carrano (C)	3,771	7.2
13 Bertram L. Podell (D)	107,960	68.2
Jack Sterngass (R)	25,499	16.1
Kenneth Haber (L)	15,392	9.7
Robert C. Laborde (C)	9,504	6.0
14 John J. Rooney (D, L)	42,149	63.9
Victor J. Tirabasso (R)	18,396	27.9
Alice A. Capatosto (C)	5,422	8.2
15 Hugh L. Carey (D)	59,707	57.6
Frank C. Spinner (R)	31,802	30.7
Stephen P. Marion (C)	7,920	7.6
16 John M. Murphy (D)	73,253	48.8
Frank J. Biondolillo (R, C)	69,126	46.0
Joseph Kottler (L)	7,883	5.3
17 Edward I. Koch (D, L)	84,627	51.7
Whitney North Seymour Jr. (R)	70,086	42.8
Richard J. Callahan (C)	9,030	5.5
18 Adam Clayton Powell Jr. (D)	37,146	80.8
Henry L. Hall (R)	7,215	15.7
19 Leonard Farbstein (D)	44,843	53.3
Donald E. Weeden (R)	27,959	33.2
20 William F. Ryan (D, L)	66,192	78.8
John G. Proudfit (R)	13,968	16.6
21 James H. Scheuer (D, L)	55,129	82.6
Stanley L. Shapiro (R)	8,778	13.2
22 Jacob H. Gilbert (D)	45,144	76.2
James N. Harris (R)	7,087	12.0
Sergio S. Pena (L)	4,402	7.4
23 Jonathan B. Bingham (D, L)	94,108	71.9
Alexander Sacks (R, C)	36,823	28.1
24 Mario Biaggi (D, C)	83,234	60.5
Andrew Mantovani (R)	46,510	33.8
John Patrick Hagan (L)	7,758	5.6
25 Richard L. Ottinger (D, L)	125,415	58.6
Samuel Nakasian (R)	74,275	34.7
Anthony J. DeVito (C)	14,463	6.8
26 Ogden R. Reid (R, L)	130,229	68.1
Paul Davidoff (D)	44,084	23.1
A. Lining Burnet (C)	16,877	8.8
27 Martin B. McKneally (R)	94,689	47.9
John G. Dow (D, L)	88,894	44.9
Frederick P. Roland (C)	14,239	7.2
28 Hamilton Fish Jr. (R)	91,590	48.2
John S. Dyson (D)	86,827	45.6
29 Daniel E. Button (R, CIT)	119,039	56.9
Jacob H. Herzog (D, C)	87,896	42.0
30 Carleton J. King (R, C)	124,995	66.5
Orlando D. Potter (D, L)	62,897	33.5
31 Robert C. McEwen (R, C)	88,562	58.4
K. Daniel Haley (D)	61,947	40.9
32 Alexander Pirnie (R, L)	95,793	64.1
Anthony J. Montoya (D)	43,254	28.9
Albert J. Bushong (C)	10,393	7.0
33 Howard W. Robison (R)	110,080	68.5
Benjamin Nichols (D, L)	50,549	31.5
34 James M. Hanley (D)	96,520	51.3
David V. O'Brien (R)	82,333	43.8
35 Samuel S. Stratton (D)	112,640	69.4
George R. Metcalf (R)	47,849	29.5
36 Frank J. Horton (R)	138,400	70.4
Augustine J. Marvin (D)	46,008	23.4
Leo J. Kesselring (C)	9,916	5.0
37 Barber B. Conable Jr. (R)	129,697	71.1
Norman M. Gerhard (D)	50,930	27.9
38 James F. Hastings (R)	90,281	63.4
Wilbur White Jr. (D)	47,093	33.1
39 Richard D. McCarthy (D)	120,509	54.6
Daniel E. Weber (R, L)	92,589	42.0
40 Henry P. Smith III (R, C)	106,984	64.8
Eugene O'Connor (D)	56,201	34.0
41 Thaddeus J. Dulski (D, L)	96,703	77.6
Edward P. Matter (R)	27,920	22.4

Special Election

Candidates	Votes	%
13 Bertram L. Podell (D)	36,093#	49.7
Melvin Dubin (NEW LEAD)	27,856#	38.4
Gerald S. Held (R)	4,848#	6.7
Michael V. Ajello (C)	3,806#	5.2

NORTH CAROLINA

Candidates	Votes	%
1 Walter B. Jones (D)	75,796	66.2
Reece B. Gardner (R)	38,660	33.8
2 L. H. Fountain (D)	92,542	100.0
3 David N. Henderson (D)	57,244	54.0
Herbert H. Howell (R)	48,815	46.0
4 Nick Galifianakis (D)	77,871	51.5
G. Fred Steele Jr. (R)	73,471	48.6
5 Wilmer Mizell (R)	84,905	52.4
Smith Bagley (D)	77,112	47.6
6 Richardson Preyer (D)	76,028	53.6
William L. Osteen (R)	65,703	46.4
7 Alton A. Lennon (D)	77,419	100.0
8 Earl B. Ruth (R)	70,480	51.2
Voit Gilmore (D)	67,281	48.8
9 Charles Raper Jonas (R)	94,510	100.0
10 James T. Broyhill (R)	87,811	54.9
Basil L. Whitener (D)	72,295	45.2
11 Roy A. Taylor (D)	91,477	56.3
W. Scott Harvey (R)	71,041	43.7

NORTH DAKOTA

	Candidates	Votes	%
1	Mark Andrews (R)	84,114	66.8
	Bruce Hagen (D)	39,692	31.5
2	Thomas S. Kleppe (R)	55,962	49.9
	Rolland Redlin (D)	54,655	48.7

OHIO

	Candidates	Votes	%
1	Robert Taft Jr. (R)	102,219	67.2
	Karl F. Heiser (D)	49,830	32.8
2	Donald D. Clancy (R)	108,157	67.4
	Don Driehaus (D)	52,327	32.6
3	Charles W. Whalen Jr. (R)	114,549	78.2
	Paul Tipps (D)	32,012	21.6
4	William M. McCulloch (R)	129,435	99.9
5	Delbert L. Latta (R)	113,381	71.2
	Louis Richard Batzler (D)	45,884	28.8
6	William H. Harsha (R)	107,289	72.4
	Kenneth L. Kirby (D)	40,964	27.6
7	Clarence J. Brown Jr. (R)	97,581	63.8
	Robert E. Cecile (D)	55,386	36.2
8	Jackson E. Betts (R)	101,974	71.4
	Marie Baker (D)	40,898	28.6
9	Thomas L. Ashley (D)	85,280	57.4
	Ben Marsh (R)	63,290	42.6
10	Clarence E. Miller (R)	102,890	69.3
	Harry B. Crewson (D)	45,686	30.8
11	J. William Stanton (R)	116,323	75.4
	Alan D. Wright (D)	38,063	24.7
12	Samuel L. Devine (R)	106,664	67.6
	Herbert J. Pfeifer (D)	51,202	32.4
13	Charles A. Mosher (R)	97,158	61.9
	Adrian F. Betleski (D)	59,864	38.1
14	William H. Ayres (R)	84,561	55.1
	Oliver Ocasek (D)	68,889	44.9
15	Chalmers P. Wylie (R)	98,499	73.1
	Russell H. Volkema (D)	35,861	26.6
16	Frank T. Bow (R)	101,495	59.6
	Virgil L. Musser (D)	68,916	40.4
17	John M. Ashbrook (R)	100,148	64.9
	Robert W. Levering (D)	54,127	35.1
18	Wayne L. Hays (D)	96,711	60.3
	James F. Sutherland (R)	63,747	39.7
19	Michael J. Kirwan (D)	101,813	69.7
	Donald J. Lewis (R)	44,363	30.4
20	Michael A. Feighan (D)	72,918	72.4
	J. William Petro (R)	27,827	27.6
21	Louis Stokes (D)	85,509	74.7
	Charles P. Lucas (R)	28,931	25.3
22	Charles A. Vanik (D)	102,656	54.7
	Frances P. Bolton (R)	84,975	45.3
23	William E. Minshall (R)	106,852	52.0
	James V. Stanton (D)	98,825	48.1
24	Donald E. Lukens (R)	105,350	70.4
	Lloyd D. Miller (D)	44,400	29.7

OKLAHOMA

	Candidates	Votes	%
1	Page Belcher (R)	92,513	59.3
	John B. Jarboe (D)	63,451	40.7
2	Ed Edmondson (D)	77,192	54.9
	Robert G. Smith (R)	63,437	45.1
3	Carl Albert (D)	85,981	68.4
	Gerald L. Beasley Jr. (R)	39,740	31.6
4	Tom Steed (D)	67,352	53.6
	James V. Smith (R)	58,253	46.4
5	John Jarman (D)	86,420	73.6
	Bob Leeper (R)	30,931	26.4
6	John N. Happy Camp (R)	79,992	55.3
	John W. Goodwin (D)	64,599	44.7

OREGON

	Candidates	Votes	%
1	Wendell Wyatt (R)	189,023	80.6
	Thomas M. Baggs (D)	45,479	19.4
2	Al Ullman (D)	114,232	63.9
	Marv Root (R)	64,478	36.1
3	Edith Green (D)	137,746	69.8
	Douglas S. Warren (R)	59,447	30.1

	Candidates	Votes	%
4	John Dellenback (R)	104,159	58.9
	Edward N. Fadely (D)	72,579	41.1

PENNSYLVANIA

	Candidates	Votes	%
1	William A. Barrett (D)	113,696	74.7
	Leslie J. Carson Jr. (R)	38,432	25.3
2	Robert N. C. Nix (D)	102,869	70.0
	Herbert R. McMaster (R)	44,041	30.0
3	James A. Byrne (D)	75,728	61.3
	Richard R. Block (R)	47,813	38.7
4	Joshua Eilberg (D)	131,810	59.3
	Alexander Kaptik Jr. (R)	88,229	39.7
5	William J. Green III (D)	108,243	69.1
	Gregory J. Meade (R)	48,455	30.9
6	Gus Yatron (D)	94,247	51.4
	Peter Yonavick (R)	87,090	47.5
7	Lawrence G. Williams (R)	105,699	56.5
	Edward J. O'Halloran (D)	79,782	42.7
8	Edward G. Biester Jr. (R)	94,254	58.0
	Richard M. Hepburn (D)	60,324	37.1
9	G. Robert Watkins (R)	100,399	62.9
	Philip L. Harding (D)	56,532	35.4
10	Joseph M. McDade (R)	125,916	66.6
	Robert J. Landy (D)	61,960	32.8
11	Daniel J. Flood (D)	128,794	70.0
	Stanley Bunn (R)	52,475	28.5
12	J. Irving Whalley (R)	119,522	67.5
	H. Richard Hostetler (D)	55,838	31.5
13	R. Lawrence Coughlin (R)	141,764	62.0
	Robert D. Gates (D)	84,137	36.8
14	William S. Moorhead (D)	96,117	69.4
	Algia Gary (R)	39,671	28.7
15	Fred B. Rooney (D)	106,877	58.8
	Paul E. Henderson (R)	70,333	38.7
16	Edwin D. Eshleman (R)	98,877	68.9
	Robert M. Going (D)	39,507	27.5
17	Herman T. Schneebeli (R, YOUNGMAN)	119,003	66.2
	Donald J. Rippon (D)	57,093	31.7
18	Robert J. Corbett (R)	121,664	62.7
	William T. Sherman (D)	68,434	35.3
19	George A. Goodling (R)	93,352	57.7
	Robert L. Myers (D)	65,903	40.8
20	Joseph M. Gaydos (D)	109,236	70.2
	Joseph Sabol Jr. (R)	44,037	28.3
21	John H. Dent (D)	93,033	62.8
	Thomas H. Young (R, CONST)	55,099	37.2
22	John P. Saylor (R)	98,576	58.0
	John P. Murtha (D)	71,297	42.0
23	Albert W. Johnson (R)	87,968	61.5
	Alan R. Cleeton (D)	54,453	38.0
24	Joseph P. Vigorito (D)	106,869	61.1
	John V. Edwards (R)	66,429	38.0
25	Frank M. Clark (D)	105,048	63.1
	Richard L. Doolittle (R)	59,576	35.8
26	Thomas E. Morgan (D)	95,898	63.6
	Paul P. Riggle (R)	50,594	33.6
27	James G. Fulton (R)	130,784	66.7
	Joseph L. Cosetti (D)	62,638	31.9

RHODE ISLAND

	Candidates	Votes	%
1	Fernand J. St. Germain (D)	97,945	60.4
	Lincoln C. Almond (R)	62,394	38.5
2	Robert O. Tiernan (D)	124,044	61.2
	Howard E. Russell Jr. (R)	78,502	38.8

SOUTH CAROLINA

	Candidates	Votes	%
1	L. Mendel Rivers (D)	95,428	100.0
2	Albert W. Watson (R)	63,877	57.6
	Frank K. Sloan (D)	47,053	42.4
3	William J. Bryan Dorn (D)	74,104	66.1
	John K. Grisso (R)	35,463	31.7
4	James R. Mann (D)	68,437	61.2
	Charles Bradshaw (R)	43,440	38.8
5	Thomas S. Gettys (D)	72,805	74.7
	Hugh J. Boyd (R)	21,246	21.8

	Candidates	Votes	%
6	John L. McMillan (D)	58,304	58.3
	Ray Harris (R)	39,876	39.9

SOUTH DAKOTA

	Candidates	Votes	%
1	Ben Reifel (R)	85,232	58.0
	Frank E. Denholm (D)	61,738	42.0
2	E. Y. Berry (R)	73,987	59.4
	David Garner (D)	50,683	40.7

TENNESSEE

	Candidates	Votes	%
1	James H. Quillen (R)	100,712	85.2
	Arthur Bright (D)	17,441	14.8
2	John J. Duncan (R)	97,832	82.4
	Jake Armstrong (D)	17,547	14.8
3	Bill Brock (R)	76,390	57.0
	J. William Pope Jr. (D)	57,565	43.0
4	Joe L. Evins (D)	74,041	75.9
	J. D. Boles (R)	23,553	24.1
5	Richard Fulton (D)	61,045	48.7
	George Kelley (R)	52,836	42.2
	William F. Burton Jr. (I)	11,412	9.1
6	William Anderson (D)	61,223	59.4
	Ronnie Page (R)	41,923	40.6
7	Ray Blanton (D)	80,893	66.1
	John T. Williams (R)	41,457	33.9
8	Robert A. Everett (D)	70,644	100.0
9	Dan Kuykendall (R)	73,293	59.4
	James E. Irwin (D)	45,434	36.8

TEXAS

	Candidates	Votes	%
1	Wright Patman (D)	87,038	100.0
2	John Dowdy (D)	87,565	100.0
3	James M. Collins (R)	81,696	59.4
	Robert H. Hughes (D)	55,939	46.0
4	Ray Roberts (D)	95,413	100.0
5	Earle Cabell (D)	79,317	61.4
	Roy Wagoner (R)	49,821	38.6
6	Olin E. Teague (D)	90,889	100.0
7	George Bush (R)	110,455	100.0
8	Bob Eckhardt (D)	63,256	70.6
	Joe Stevens (R)	26,402	29.5
9	Jack Brooks (D)	71,937	60.6
	Henry Pressler (R)	46,829	39.4
10	J. J. (Jake) Pickle (D)	85,037	62.1
	Ray Gabler (R)	51,933	37.9
11	W. R. Poage (D)	78,127	96.5
12	Jim Wright (D)	86,069	100.0
13	Graham Purcell (D)	83,839	55.8
	Frank Crowley (R)	66,477	44.2
14	John Young (D)	89,868	100.0
15	Eligio de la Garza (D)	57,618	100.0
16	Richard C. White (D)	62,491	73.5
	Donald Slaughter (R)	22,510	26.5
17	Omar Burleson (D)	90,856	100.0
18	Bob Price (R)	81,715	65.2
	J. R. Burton (D)	43,568	34.8
19	George Mahon (D)	79,161	100.0
20	Henry B. Gonzalez (D)	64,112	81.5
	Robert Schneider (R)	14,569	18.5
21	O. C. Fisher (D)	91,784	60.8
	W. J. Alexander (R)	59,082	39.2
22	Bob Casey (D)	101,498	62.4
	Walter Blaney (R)	61,278	37.7
23	Abraham Kazen Jr. (D)	75,026	100.0

Special Election

	Candidates	Votes	%
3	James M. Collins (R)	13,828#	60.0
	Mrs. Joe Pool (D)	9,209#	40.0

UTAH

	Candidates	Votes	%
1	Laurence J. Burton (R)	139,456	68.1
	Richard J. Maughan (D)	65,265	31.9
2	Sherman P. Lloyd (R)	130,127	61.7
	Galen J. Ross (D)	80,948	38.4

VERMONT

	Candidates	Votes	%
AL	Robert T. Stafford (R, D)	156,956	99.9

VIRGINIA

	Candidates	Votes	%
1	Thomas N. Downing (D)	96,265	72..9
	J. Cornelius Fauntleroy Jr. (I)	19,229	14.6
	James S. Stafford (R)	16,456	12.5
2	G. William Whitehurst (R)	51,184	54.2
	Frederick T. Stant Jr. (D)	43,229	45.8
3	David E. Satterfield III (D)	94,118	60.3
	John S. Hansen (R)	62,082	39.7
4	Watkins M. Abbitt (D)	81,723	71.5
	S. W. Tucker (R)	32,548	28.5
5	W. C. (Dan) Daniel (D)	70,681	54.6
	Weldon W. Tuck (R)	34,608	26.7
	Ruth L. Harvey (I)	24,196	18.7
6	Richard H. Poff (R)	91,549	92.2
	Tom Hufford (D)	7,221	7.3
7	John O. Marsh Jr. (D)	64,717	54.4
	A. R. (Pete) Giesen Jr. (R)	51,349	43.2
8	William L. Scott (R)	92,121	64.9
	Andrew H. McCutcheon (D)	49,731	35.1
9	William C. Wampler (R)	71,531	59.9
	Joseph P. Johnson Jr. (D)	47,906	40.1
10	Joel T. Broyhill (R)	97,465	59.8
	David Kinney (D)	65,474	40.2

WASHINGTON

	Candidates	Votes	%
1	Thomas M. Pelly (R)	124,513	61.4
	Don Cole (D)	76,456	37.7
2	Lloyd Meeds (D)	102,522	56.2
	Wally Turner (R)	79,800	43.8
3	Julia Butler Hansen (D)	89,777	56.8
	Wayne N. Adams (R)	68,387	43.2
4	Catherine May (R)	99,840	66.8
	Lee Lukson (D)	49,601	33.2
5	Thomas S. Foley (D)	88,446	56.8
	Richard M. Bond (R)	67,304	43.2
6	Floyd V. Hicks (D)	93,399	55.8
	Anthony Chase (R)	72,177	43.1
7	Brock Adams (D)	123,429	65.6
	Robert Eberle (R)	64,051	34.0

WEST VIRGINIA

	Candidates	Votes	%
1	Robert H. Mollohan (D)	85,436	53.9
	Tom Sweeney (R)	73,176	46.1
2	Harley O. Staggers (D)	91,022	61.5
	George L. Strader (R)	56,911	38.5
3	John Slack (D)	82,911	60.5
	Neal A. Kinsolving (R)	54,164	39.5
4	Ken Hechler (D)	94,507	64.2
	Ralph Lewis Shannon (R)	52,636	35.8
5	James Kee (D)	80,204	66.2
	J. Donald Clark (R)	41,038	33.9

WISCONSIN

	Candidates	Votes	%
1	Henry C. Schadeberg (R)	89,182	50.9
	Lynn E. Stalbaum (D)	86,067	49.1
2	Robert W. Kastenmeier (D)	107,804	59.9
	Richard D. Murray (R)	72,229	40.1
3	Vernon W. Thomson (R)	95,606	63.7
	Gunnar A. Gundersen (D)	54,517	36.3
4	Clement J. Zablocki (D)	118,203	72.6
	Walter McCullough (R)	44,558	27.4
5	Henry S. Reuss (D)	76,607	67.8
	Robert J. Dwyer (R)	35,536	31.4
6	William A. Steiger (R)	111,934	64.0
	John A. Race (D)	60,059	34.3
7	Melvin R. Laird (R)	101,808	64.1
	Lawrence Dahl (D)	56,964	35.9
8	John W. Byrnes (R)	111,859	68.0
	John E. Nixon (D)	52,660	32.0
9	Glenn R. Davis (R)	126,392	63.1
	Carol E. Baumann (D)	73,891	36.9
10	Alvin E. O'Konski (R)	106,266	65.9
	Timothy J. Hirsch (D)	54,889	34.1

WYOMING

	Candidates	Votes	%
AL	John Wold (R)	77,363	62.7
	Velma Linford (D)	45,950	37.3

1. The election returns shown from Mississippi's 3rd district were from a special runoff between Griffin and Evers, who had finished with the highest number of votes in an earlier special election. Both elections were held under a provision of Mississippi law requiring that all candidates in a special election for the House run against each other, regardless of party affiliations, with a majority required for election. Since neither Evers nor Griffin had a majority, the runoff was required.

The returns from the first special election were as follows: Charles Evers (D), 33, 706, 29.3%; Charles H. Griffin (D), 28,927, 25.2; Ellis Bodron (D), 22,842, 19.9; Troy Watkins (D), 10,476, 9.1; Joe Pigott (D), 8,314, 7.2; Hagan Thompson (R), 7,978, 6.9. Source: Mississippi secretary of state.

1969 House Elections

CALIFORNIA[1]

Special Primary

	Candidates	Votes	%
27	Barry Goldwater Jr. (R)	39,580#	31.3
	John K. Van de Kamp (D)	17,356#	13.7
	James B. Potter Jr. (R)	16,908#	13.4
	Jack B. Lindsey (R)	13,818#	10.9
	Gary Schlessinger (D)	12,278#	9.7
	Patrick D. McGee (R)	8,532#	6.7

Special Election

27	Barry M. Goldwater Jr. (R)	64,734	56.9
	John K. Van de Kamp (D)	48,983	43.1

ILLINOIS

Special Election

13	Philip M. Crane (R)	68,418	58.4
	Edward A. Warman (D)	48,759	41.6

MASSACHUSETTS

Special Election

	Candidates	Votes	%
6	Michael J. Harrington (D)	72,092#	52.4
	William Saltonstall (R)	65,452#	47.6

MONTANA

Special Election

2	John Melcher (D)	45,473#	50.8
	W. S. Mather (R)	43,441#	48.6

NEW JERSEY

Special Election

8	Robert A. Roe (D)	67,188	49.2
	Eugene Boyle Jr. (R)	66,228	48.5

TENNESSEE

Special Election

	Candidates	Votes	%
8	Ed Jones (D)	33,028#	47.6
	W. J. Davis (AM)	16,375#	23.6
	Leonard Dunavant (R)	15,773#	22.7

WISCONSIN

Special Election

7	David R. Obey (D)	63,567	51.6
	Walter J. Chilsen (R)	59,512	48.4

1. No candidate received a majority of the vote, which was required to win in the first special election. Under California's special election law, the highest vote recipients from the first election from each party then faced each other in another election. In this case, Goldwater became the Republican nominee against Van de Kamp, the Democratic nominee.

1970 House Elections

ALABAMA

	Candidates	Votes	%
1	Jack Edwards (R)	63,457	60.6
	John Tyson (D)	27,457	26.2
	Noble Beasley (NDPA)	13,798	13.2
2	William L. Dickinson (R)	62,316	61.4
	Jack Winfield (D)	25,966	25.6
	Percy Smith Jr. (NDPA)	13,281	13.1
3	George Andrews (D)	70,015	89.1
	Detroit Lee (NDPA)	8,537	10.9
4	Bill Nichols (D)	77,701	83.7
	Glenn Andrews (R)	13,217	14.2
5	Walter Flowers (D)	78,368	75.9
	T. Y. Rogers (NDPA)	24,863	24.1
6	John Buchanan (R)	50,060	60.1
	John C. Schmarkey (D)	31,378	37.7
7	Tom Bevill (D)	87,797	100.0
8	Robert E. Jones (D)	76,413	84.9
	Ken Hearn (C)	7,599	8.4
	Thornton Stanley (NDPA)	4,846	5.4

ALASKA

	Candidates	Votes	%
AL	Nick Begich (D)	44,137	55.1
	Frank H. Murkowski (R)	35,947	44.9

ARIZONA

	Candidates	Votes	%
1	John J. Rhodes (R)	99,706	68.5
	Gerald A. Pollock (D)	45,870	31.5
2	Morris K. Udall (D)	86,760	69.0
	Morris Herring (R)	37,561	29.9
3	Sam Steiger (R)	81,239	62.1
	Orren Beaty (D)	49,626	37.9

ARKANSAS

	Candidates	Votes	%
1	Bill Alexander (D)		100.0
2	Wilbur D. Mills (D)		100.0
3	John Paul Hammerschmidt (R)	115,532	66.7
	Donald Poe (D)	57,679	33.3
4	David Pryor (D)		100.0

CALIFORNIA

	Candidates	Votes	%
1	Don H. Clausen (R)	108,358	63.4
	William M. Kortum (D)	62,688	36.7
2	Harold T. Johnson (D)	151,070	77.9
	Lloyd E. Gilbert (R)	37,223	19.2
3	John E. Moss (D)	117,496	61.6
	Elmore J. Duffy (R)	69,811	36.6
4	Robert L. Leggett (D)	103,485	68.0
	Andrew Gyorke (R)	48,783	32.0
5	Phillip Burton (D)	76,567	70.8
	John E. Parks (R)	31,570	29.2
6	William S. Mailliard (R)	96,393	53.4
	Russell R. Miller (D)	84,255	46.6
7	Ronald V. Dellums (D)	89,784	57.3
	John E. Healy (R)	64,691	41.3
8	George P. Miller (D)	104,311	69.0
	Michael A. Crane (R)	46,872	31.0
9	Don Edwards (D)	120,041	69.2
	Mark Guerra (R)	49,556	28.6
10	Charles S. Gubser (R)	135,864	62.0
	Stuart D. McLean (D)	80,530	36.8
11	Paul N. McCloskey Jr. (R)	144,500	77.5
	Robert E. Gomperts (D)	39,188	21.0
12	Burt L. Talcott (R)	95,549	63.6
	O'Brien Riordan (D)	50,942	33.9
13	Charles M. Teague (R)	127,507	59.1
	Gary K. Hart (D)	87,980	40.8
14	Jerome R. Waldie (D)	148,655	74.6
	Byron D. Athan (R)	50,750	25.5
15	John J. McFall (D)	98,442	63.1
	Sam Van Dyken (R)	55,546	35.6
16	B. F. Sisk (D)	95,118	66.4

	Candidates	Votes	%
	Phillip V. Sanchez (R)	43,843	30.6
17	Glenn M. Anderson (D)	83,739	62.2
	Michael C. Donaldson (R)	47,778	35.5
18	Robert B. Mathias (R)	86,071	63.2
	Milton S. Miller (D)	48,415	35.6
19	Chet Holifield (D)	98,578	70.4
	Bill Jones (R)	41,462	29.6
20	H. Allen Smith (R)	116,437	69.1
	Michael M. Stolzberg (D)	50,033	29.7
21	Augustus F. Hawkins (D)	75,127	94.5
	Southey M. Johnson (R)	4,349	5.5
22	James C. Corman (D)	95,256	59.4
	Tom Hayden (R)	63,297	39.5
23	Del Clawson (R)	77,346	63.3
	G. L. Chapman (D)	44,767	36.7
24	John H. Rousselot (R)	124,071	65.1
	Myrlie B. Evers (D)	61,777	32.4
25	Charles E. Wiggins (R)	116,169	63.3
	Leslie W. Craven (D)	64,386	35.1
26	Thomas M. Rees (D)	130,499	71.3
	Nathaniel Jay Friedman (R)	47,260	25.8
27	Barry M. Goldwater Jr. (R)	139,326	66.7
	N. (Toni) Kimmel (D)	63,652	30.5
28	Alphonzo Bell (R)	154,691	69.3
	Don McLaughlin (D)	57,882	25.9
29	George E. Danielson (D)	71,308	62.6
	Tom McMann (R)	42,620	37.4
30	Edward R. Roybal (D)	63,903	68.3
	Samuel M. Cavnar (R)	28,038	30.0
31	Charles H. Wilson (D)	102,071	73.2
	Fred L. Casmir (R)	37,416	26.8
32	Craig Hosmer (R)	119,340	71.5
	Walter L. Mallonee (D)	44,278	26.5
33	Jerry L. Pettis (R)	116,093	72.2
	Chester M. Wright (D)	44,764	27.8
34	Richard T. Hanna (D)	101,664	54.5
	William J. Teague (R)	82,167	44.0
35	John G. Schmitz (R)	192,765	67.0
	Thomas B. Lenhart (D)	87,019	30.3
36	Bob Wilson (R)	132,446	71.5
	Daniel K. Hostetter (D)	44,841	24.2
37	Lionel Van Deerlin (D)	93,952	72.1
	James B. Kuhn (R)	31,968	24.5
38	Victor V. Veysey (R)	87,479	49.8
	David A. Tunno (D)	85,684	48.8

Special Elections[1]

	Candidates	Votes	%
24	John H. Rousselot (R)	62,749	68.2
	Myrlie B. Evers (D)	29,248	31.8
35	John G. Schmitz (R)	67,209	72.4
	David N. Hartman (D)	25,655	27.6

COLORADO

	Candidates	Votes	%
1	James D. McKevitt (R)	84,843	51.6
	Craig S. Barnes (D)	74,444	45.3
2	Donald G. Brotzman (R)	125,274	63.4
	Richard G. Gebhardt (D)	72,339	36.6
3	Frank E. Evans (D)	87,090	63.7
	John C. Mitchell Jr. (R)	45,610	33.4
4	Wayne N. Aspinall (D)	76,244	55.1
	Bill Gossard (R)	62,169	44.9

CONNECTICUT

	Candidates	Votes	%
1	William R. Cotter (D)	88,374	48.7
	Antonina P. Uccello (R)	87,209	48.1
2	Robert H. Steele (R)	92,846	53.3
	John F. Pickett (D)	81,492	46.7
3	Robert Giaimo (D)	89,042	52.9
	Robert J. Dunn (R)	69,084	41.1
4	Stewart B. McKinney (R)	104,494	56.6
	T. F. Gilroy Daly (D)	78,699	42.6
5	John S. Monagan (D)	96,947	54.8
	James T. Patterson (R)	78,414	44.3

	Candidates	Votes	%
6	Ella T. Grasso (D)	96,969	51.1
	Richard C. Kilbourne (R)	92,906	48.9

Special Election

		Votes	%
2	Robert H. Steele (R)	92,816	53.3
	John F. Pickett (D)	81,333	46.7

DELAWARE

		Votes	%
AL	Pierre S. duPont IV (R)	86,125	53.7
	John Daniello (D)	71,429	44.6

FLORIDA

		Votes	%
1	Robert L. F. Sikes (D)	88,744	80.2
	H. D. Shuemake (R)	21,951	19.8
2	Don Fuqua (D)		100.0
3	Charles E. Bennett (D)		100.0
4	Bill Chappell (D)	75,673	57.8
	Leonard V. Wood (R)	55,311	42.2
5	Louis Frey Jr. (R)	110,841	75.8
	Roy Girod (D)	35,398	24.2
6	Sam M. Gibbons (D)	78,832	72.3
	Robert A. Carter (R)	30,252	27.7
7	James A. Haley (D)	78,535	53.4
	Joe Z. Lovingood (R)	68,646	46.6
8	C. W. Bill Young (R)	120,466	67.2
	Ted A. Bailey (D)	58,904	32.8
9	Paul G. Rogers (D)	120,565	70.6
	Emil F. Danciu (R)	50,146	29.4
10	J. Herbert Burke (R)	81,170	54.1
	James J. Ward Jr. (D)	68,847	45.9
11	Claude Pepper (D)		100.0
12	Dante B. Fascell (D)	75,895	71.7
	Robert A. Zinzell (R)	29,935	28.3

GEORGIA

		Votes	%
1	G. Elliot Hagan (D)	70,856	100.0
2	Dawson Mathis (D)	59,994	91.8
	Thomas Ragsdale (R)	5,376	8.2
3	Jack Brinkley (D)	54,588	99.5
4	Ben B. Blackburn (R)	85,848	65.2
	Franklin Shumake (D)	45,908	34.8
5	Fletcher Thompson (R)	78,540	57.4
	Andrew Young (D)	58,394	42.6
6	John J. Flynt Jr. (D)	92,500	100.0
7	John W. Davis (D)	80,149	72.5
	Dick Fullerton (R)	30,392	27.5
8	W. S. Stuckey Jr. (D)	52,446	100.0
9	Phil M. Landrum (D)	64,603	71.7
	Bob Cooper (R)	25,476	28.3
10	Robert G. Stephens Jr. (D)	74,075	100.0

HAWAII

		Votes	%
1	Spark M. Matsunaga (D)	85,411	72.9
	Richard K. Cockey (R)	31,764	27.1
2	Patsy T. Mink (D)	91,038	100.0

IDAHO

		Votes	%
1	James A. McClure (R)	77,515	58.2
	William J. Brauner (D)	55,743	41.8
2	Orval Hansen (R)	66,428	65.7
	Marden E. Wells (D)	31,872	31.5

ILLINOIS

		Votes	%
1	Ralph H. Metcalfe (D)	93,272	91.0
	Janet Roberts Jennings (R)	9,267	9.0
2	Abner J. Mikva (D)	88,252	74.7
	Harold E. Marks (R)	29,853	25.3
3	Morgan F. Murphy (D)	97,693	68.9
	Robert P. Rowan (R)	44,013	31.1

	Candidates	Votes	%
4	Edward J. Derwinski (R)	117,590	68.0
	Melvin W. Morgan (D)	55,328	32.0
5	John C. Kluczynski (D)	97,278	68.8
	Edmund W. Ochenkowski (R)	44,049	31.2
6	George W. Collins (D)	68,182	56.2
	Alex J. Zabrosky (R)	53,240	43.9
7	Frank Annunzio (D)	70,112	87.3
	Thomas J. Lento (R)	10,235	12.7
8	Dan Rostenkowski (D)	98,453	73.9
	Henry S. Kaplinski (R)	34,841	26.1
9	Sidney R. Yates (D)	111,955	75.8
	Edward Wolbank (R)	35,795	24.2
10	Harold R. Collier (R)	107,416	62.2
	R. G. Logan (D)	65,170	37.8
11	Roman C. Pucinski (D)	137,090	71.9
	James R. Mason (R)	53,461	28.1
12	Robert McClory (R)	84,356	62.1
	James J. Cone (D)	51,499	37.9
13	Philip M. Crane (R)	124,649	58.0
	Edward A. Warman (D)	90,364	42.0
14	John N. Erlenborn (R)	122,115	65.5
	William J. Adelman (D)	64,231	34.5
15	Charlotte T. Reid (R)	95,222	68.9
	James E. Todd (D)	43,014	31.1
16	John B. Anderson (R)	83,296	66.8
	John E. Devine Jr. (D)	41,459	33.2
17	Leslie C. Arends (R)	92,917	62.3
	Lester A. Hawthorne (D)	56,340	37.8
18	Robert H. Michel (R)	84,864	66.1
	Rosa Lee Fox (D)	43,601	33.9
19	Tom Railsback (R)	92,247	68.2
	James L. Shaw (D)	43,094	31.8
20	Paul Findley (R)	103,485	67.5
	Billie M. Cox (D)	49,727	32.5
21	Kenneth J. Gray (D)	110,374	62.5
	Fred Evans (R)	66,273	37.5
22	William L. Springer (R)	83,131	59.0
	Robert C. Miller (D)	57,781	41.0
23	George E. Shipley (D)	91,158	54.0
	Phyllis Schlafly (R)	77,762	46.0
24	Melvin Price (D)	88,637	74.2
	Scott R. Randolph (R)	30,784	25.8

Special Election

	Candidates	Votes	%
6	George W. Collins (D)	68,949	55.7
	Alex J. Zabrosky (R)	54,746	44.3

INDIANA

	Candidates	Votes	%
1	Ray J. Madden (D)	73,145	65.6
	Eugene M. Kirtland (R)	38,294	34.4
2	Earl F. Landgrebe (R)	79,163	50.4
	Philip A. Sprague (D)	77,959	49.6
3	John Brademas (D)	87,064	57.5
	Don M. Newman (R)	64,249	42.5
4	J. Edward Roush (D)	86,582	51.9
	E. Ross Adair (R)	80,326	48.1
5	Elwood H. Hillis (R)	86,199	56.0
	Kathleen Z. Williams (D)	67,740	44.0
6	William G. Bray (R)	115,113	60.7
	Terrence D. Straub (D)	74,599	39.3
7	John T. Myers (R)	97,152	57.1
	William D. Roach (D)	73,042	42.9
8	Roger H. Zion (R)	93,088	52.6
	J. David Huber (D)	83,911	47.4
9	Lee H. Hamilton (D)	104,599	62.5
	Richard B. Wathen (R)	62,772	37.5
10	David W. Dennis (R)	81,439	50.8
	Philip R. Sharp (D)	78,871	49.2
11	Andrew Jacobs Jr. (D)	71,329	58.3
	Danny L. Burton (R)	50,990	41.7

IOWA

	Candidates	Votes	%
1	Fred Schwengel (R)	60,270	49.8
	Edward Mezvinsky (D)	59,505	49.2
2	John C. Culver (D)	84,049	60.5
··	Cole McMartin (R)	54,932	39.5
3	H. R. Gross (R)	66,087	59.0
	Lyle D. Taylor (D)	45,958	41.0
4	John Kyl (R)	59,396	54.6
	Roger Blobaum (D)	49,369	45.4
5	Neal Smith (D)	73,820	64.9
	Don Mahon (R)	37,374	32.9
6	Wiley Mayne (R)	57,285	57.0
	Fred H. Moore (D)	43,257	43.0
7	William J. Scherle (R)	53,084	62.7
	Lou Galetich (D)	31,552	37.3

KANSAS

	Candidates	Votes	%
1	Keith G. Sebelius (R)	83,923	56.8
	Billy D. Jellison (D)	63,791	43.2
2	William R. Roy (D)	80,161	52.3
	Chester L. Mize (R)	68,843	45.0
3	Larry Winn Jr. (R)	74,603	53.0
	James H. DeCoursey Jr. (D)	64,344	45.7
4	Garner E. Shriver (R)	85,058	63.2
	James C. Junhke (D)	47,004	34.9
5	Joe Skubitz (R)	94,837	66.1
	T. D. Saar Jr. (D)	48,688	33.9

KENTUCKY

	Candidates	Votes	%
1	Frank A. Stubblefield (D)	27,829	100.0
2	William H. Natcher (D)	21,024	100.0
3	Romano L. Mazzoli (D)	50,102	48.5
	William O. Cowger (R)	49,891	48.3
4	M. G. (Gene) Snyder (R)	83,037	66.6
	Charles W. Webster (D)	41,659	33.4
5	Tim Lee Carter (R)	49,266	80.4
	Lyle Leonard Willis (D)	11,977	19.6
6	John C. Watts (D)	44,322	64.9
	Gerald G. Gregory (R)	23,971	35.1
7	Carl D. Perkins (D)	50,672	75.3
	Herbert E. Myers (R)	16,648	24.7

LOUISIANA

	Candidates	Votes	%
1	F. Edward Hebert (D)	66,284	87.4
	Luke J. Fontana (I)	9,602	12.7
2	Hale Boggs (D)	51,812	69.3
	Robert E. Lee (R)	19,703	26.3
3	Patrick T. Caffery (D)	48,677	100.0
4	Joe D. Waggonner Jr. (D)	44,848	100.0
5	Otto E. Passman (D)	31,087	100.0
6	John R. Rarick (D)	36,632	100.0
7	Edwin W. Edwards (D)	24,517	100.0
8	Speedy O. Long (D)	26,607	100.0

MAINE

	Candidates	Votes	%
1	Peter N. Kyros (D)	99,483	59.2
	Ronald T. Speers (R)	68,671	40.8
2	William D. Hathaway (D)	96,235	64.2
	Maynard G. Conners (R)	53,642	35.8

MARYLAND

	Candidates	Votes	%
1	Rogers C. B. Morton (R)	79,594	75.6
	David S. Aland (D)	24,923	23.7
2	Clarence D. Long (D)	87,224	68.5
	Ross Z. Pierpont (R)	40,171	31.5
3	Edward A. Garmatz (D)	52,374	100.0
4	Paul S. Sarbanes (D)	54,936	70.1
	David Fentress (R)	23,491	30.0
5	Lawrence J. Hogan (R)	84,314	61.4
	Royal Hart (D)	52,979	38.6
6	Goodloe E. Byron (D)	59,267	50.8
	George R. Hughes Jr. (R)	55,511	47.6
7	Parren J. Mitchell (D)	60,390	58.7
	Peter Parker (R)	42,566	41.3
8	Gilbert Gude (R)	104,647	63.4
	Thomas Hale Boggs Jr. (D)	60,453	36.6

MASSACHUSETTS

	Candidates	Votes	%
1	Silvio O. Conte (R)	117,045	100.0
2	Edward P. Boland (D)	111,430	100.0
3	Robert F. Drinan (D)	63,942	37.7
	John McGlennon (R)	60,575	35.7
	Philip J. Philbin (WRITE IN)	45,278	26.7
4	Harold D. Donohue (D)	95,016	54.3
	Howard A. Miller Jr. (R)	79,870	45.7
5	F. Bradford Morse (R)	116,666	63.3
	Richard Williams (D)	67,646	36.7
6	Michael J. Harrington (D)	114,276	61.7
	Howard Phillips (R)	70,955	38.3
7	Torbert H. Macdonald (D)	115,597	72.2
	Gordon F. Hughes (R)	44,463	27.8
8	Thomas P. O'Neill Jr. (D)	89,875	100.0
9	Louise Day Hicks (D)	50,269	59.2
	Daniel J. Houton (I)	17,395	20.5
	Laurence Curtis (R)	17,324	20.4
10	Margaret M. Heckler (R)	102,895	57.0
	Bertram A. Yaffe (D)	77,497	43.0
11	James A. Burke (D)	143,026	100.0
12	Hastings Keith (R)	100,432	50.4
	Gerry E. Studds (D)	98,910	49.6

MICHIGAN

	Candidates	Votes	%
1	John Conyers Jr. (D)	93,075	88.2
	Howard L. Johnson (R)	11,876	11.3
2	Marvin L. Esch (R)	88,071	62.5
	R. Michael Stillwagon (D)	52,782	37.5
3	Garry Brown (R)	80,447	56.3
	Richard A. Enslen (D)	62,530	43.7
4	Edward Hutchinson (R)	74,471	61.9
	David R. McCormack (D)	45,838	38.1
5	Gerald R. Ford Jr (R)	88,208	61.4
	Jean McKee (D)	55,337	38.5
6	Charles E. Chamberlain (R)	84,276	60.3
	John A. Cihon (D)	55,591	39.8
7	Donald W. Riegle Jr. (R)	97,683	69.2
	Richard J. Ruhala (D)	41,235	29.2
8	James Harvey (R)	85,634	65.9
	Richard E. Davies (D)	44,400	34.1
9	Guy A. Vander Jagt (R)	94,027	64.4
	Charles Arthur Rogers (D)	51,223	35.1
10	Elford A. Cederberg (R)	82,528	59.1
	Gerald J. Parent (D)	57,031	40.9
11	Philip E. Ruppe (R)	85,323	61.6
	Nino Green (D)	53,146	38.4
12	James G. O'Hara (D)	129,287	76.1
	Patrick Driscoll (R)	38,946	22.9
13	Charles C. Diggs Jr. (D)	56,872	86.2
	Fred Engel (R)	9,141	13.9
14	Lucien N. Nedzi (D)	91,111	70.1
	John L. Owen (R)	38,956	30.0
15	William D. Ford (D)	101,018	80.0
	Ernest C. Fackler (R)	25,340	20.1
16	John D. Dingell (D)	90,540	79.1
	William E. Rostron (R)	23,867	20.9
17	Martha W. Griffiths (D)	108,176	79.7
	Thomas E. Klunzinger (R)	27,608	20.3
18	William S. Broomfield (R)	113,309	64.6
	August Scholle (D)	62,081	35.4
19	Jack McDonald (R)	91,763	58.9
	Fred L. Harris (D)	63,175	40.5

MINNESOTA

	Candidates	Votes	%
1	Albert H. Quie (R)	121,802	69.3
	B. A. Lundeen (DFL)	53,995	30.7
2	Ancher Nelsen (R)	94,080	63.3
	Clifford R. Adams (DFL)	54,498	36.7
3	Bill Frenzel (R)	110,921	50.6
	George Rice (DFL)	108,141	49.4
4	Joseph E. Karth (DFL)	131,263	74.2
	Frank L. Loss (R)	45,680	25.8
5	Donald M. Fraser (DFL)	83,207	57.1
	Dick Enroth (R)	61,682	42.3
6	John M. Zwach (R)	88,753	51.8
	Terry Montgomery (DFL)	81,004	47.3
7	Bob Bergland (DFL)	79,378	54.1
	Odin Langen (R)	67,296	45.9
8	John A. Blatnik (DFL)	118,149	78.0
	Paul Reed (R)	38,369	25.3

MISSISSIPPI

	Candidates	Votes	%
1	Thomas G. Abernethy (D)	42,367	100.0
2	Jamie L. Whitten (D)	51,689	86.5
	Eugene Carter (I)	8,092	13.5
3	Charles H. Griffin (D)	50,527	63.7
	Ray Lee (R)	28,847	36.3
4	G. V. (Sonny) Montgomery (D)	66,064	100.0
5	William M. Colmer (D)	58,546	90.4
	Earnest J. Creel (I)	6,225	9.6

MISSOURI

	Candidates	Votes	%
1	William Clay (D)	58,082	90.5
	Gerald G. Frischer (AM MO)	6,078	9.5
2	James W. Symington (D)	93,294	57.6
	Philip R. Hoffman (R)	66,503	41.1
3	Leonor K. Sullivan (D)	73,021	74.8
	Dale F. Troske (R)	24,651	25.2
4	William J. Randall (D)	80,153	60.1
	Leslie O. Olsen (R)	53,204	39.9
5	Richard Bolling (D)	51,668	61.3
	Randall Vanet (R)	31,806	37.8
6	W. R. Hull Jr. (D)	74,496	53.6
	Hugh A. Sprague (R)	63,789	45.9
7	Durward G. Hall (R)	92,965	100.0
8	Richard Ichord (D)	97,560	64.4
	John L. Caskanett (R)	53,181	35.1
9	William L. Hungate (D)	100,988	63.0
	Anthony C. Schroeder (R)	58,103	36.3
10	Bill D. Burlison (D)	62,764	56.0
	Gary Rust (R)	49,355	44.0

MONTANA

	Candidates	Votes	%
1	Richard G. Shoup (R)	64,388	50.5
	Arnold Olsen (D)	63,175	49.5
2	John Melcher (D)	78,082	64.1
	Jack Rehberg (R)	43,752	35.9

NEBRASKA

	Candidates	Votes	%
1	Charles Thone (R)	79,131	50.6
	Clair A. Callan (I)	40,919	26.2
	George Burrows (D)	36,240	23.2
2	John Y. McCollister (R)	69,671	51.8
	John Hlavacek (D)	64,520	48.0
3	Dave Martin (R)	93,705	59.5
	Donald Searcy (D)	63,698	40.5

NEVADA

	Candidates	Votes	%
AL	Walter S. Baring (D)	113,496	82.5
	J. Robert Charles (R)	24,147	17.5

NEW HAMPSHIRE

	Candidates	Votes	%
1	Louis C. Wyman (R)	72,170	67.4
	Chester E. Merrow (D)	34,882	32.6
2	James C. Cleveland (R)	74,219	69.6
	Eugene S. Daniell Jr. (D)	32,374	30.4

NEW JERSEY

	Candidates	Votes	%
1	John E. Hunt (R)	83,726	61.2
	Salvatore T. Mansi (D)	52,567	38.4
2	Charles W. Sandman Jr. (R)	69,392	51.7
	William J. Hughes (D)	64,882	48.3
3	James J. Howard (D)	87,973	55.2
	William F. Dowd (R)	68,675	43.1
4	Frank Thompson Jr. (D)	91,670	58.4
	Edward A. Costigan (R)	65,030	41.4
5	Peter H. B. Frelinghuysen (R)	111,553	66.4
	Ronald C. Eisele (D)	53,436	31.8
6	Edwin B. Forsythe (R)	88,051	53.6
	Charles B. Yates (D)	72,347	44.1
7	William B. Widnall (R)	90,410	58.6
	Arthur J. Lesemann (D)	63,928	41.4
8	Robert A. Roe (D)	75,056	61.0
	Alfred E. Fontanella (R)	48,011	39.0

	Candidates	Votes	%
9	Henry Helstoski (D)	91,589	56.6
	Henry L. Hoebel (R)	68,974	42.6
10	Peter W. Rodino Jr. (D)	71,003	70.0
	Griffith H. Jones (R)	30,460	30.0
11	Joseph G. Minish (D)	68,075	68.5
	James W. Shue (R)	31,369	31.5
12	Florence P. Dwyer (R)	109,537	66.2
	Daniel F. Lundy (D)	55,930	33.8
13	Cornelius E. Gallagher (D)	77,789	71.1
	Raul E. L. Comesanas (R)	27,929	25.5
14	Dominick V. Daniels (D)	77,771	69.7
	Carlo N. DeGennaro (R)	31,161	27.9
15	Edward J. Patten (D)	94,772	61.1
	Peter P. Garibaldi (R)	60,450	38.9

Special Election

	Candidates	Votes	%
6	Edwin B. Forsythe (R)	89,565	54.8
	Charles B. Yates (D)	73,821	45.2

NEW MEXICO

	Candidates	Votes	%
1	Manuel Lujan Jr. (R)	91,187	57.6
	Fabian Chavez Jr. (D)	64,598	40.8
2	Harold Runnels (D)	64,518	50.8
	Ed Foreman (R)	61,074	48.1

NEW YORK

	Candidates	Votes	%
1	Otis G. Pike (D, L)	108,746	52.2
	Malcolm E. Smith Jr. (R, C)	99,503	47.8
2	James R. Grover Jr. (R, C)	107,443	66.1
	Harvey W. Sherman (D)	54,996	33.9
3	Lester L. Wolff (D, L)	94,414	54.4
	Raymond J. Rice (R, ENVIRON)	66,196	38.1
	Lola Camardi (C)	12,925	7.5
4	John W. Wydler (R)	91,787	57.1
	Karen S. Burstein (D, L)	56,411	35.1
	Donald A. Derham (C)	12,701	7.9
5	Norman F. Lent (R, C)	93,824	51.0
	Allard K. Lowenstein (D, L)	84,738	46.1
6	Seymour Halpern (R, L)	89,250	77.3
	John J. Flynn (C)	26,244	22.7
7	Joseph P. Addabbo (D, R)	112,983	90.8
	Christopher T. Acer (C)	11,515	9.3
8	Benjamin S. Rosenthal (D, L)	93,666	62.8
	Cosmo J. DiTucci (R, C)	55,406	37.2
9	James J. Delaney (D, R)	102,205	91.9
	Rose L. Rubin (L)	9,025	8.1
10	Emanuel Celler (D, L)	78,324	73.0
	Frank J. Occhiogrosso (R, C)	29,012	27.0
11	Frank J. Brasco (D)	60,919	78.6
	William Sampol (C)	9,462	12.2
	Paul Myrowitz (L)	7,156	9.2
12	Shirley Chisholm (D, L)	31,500	81.8
	John Coleman (R)	5,816	15.1
13	Bertram L. Podell (D)	102,247	77.0
	George W. McKenzie (R)	20,550	15.5
	Herbert Dicker (L)	9,925	7.5
14	John J. Rooney (D)	31,586	55.2
	John F. Jacobs (R, C)	15,222	26.6
	Peter E. Eikenberry (L)	10,452	18.3
15	Hugh L. Carey (D)	50,767	64.7
	Frank C. Spinner (R)	17,931	22.8
	Stephen P. Marion (C)	5,307	6.8
	Carl Saks (L)	4,506	5.7
16	John M. Murphy (D, CSI)	71,553	51.6
	David D. Smith (R, C)	62,597	45.2
17	Edward I. Koch (D, L)	98,300	62.0
	Peter J. Sprague (R)	50,647	32.0
	Richard J. Callahan (C)	9,586	6.1
18	Charles B. Rangel (D, R)	52,651	86.8
	Charles Taylor (L)	6,385	10.5
19	Bella S. Abzug (D)	46,947	52.3
	Barry Farber (R, L)	38,460	42.8
20	William F. Ryan (D, L)	73,509	78.7
	William Goldstein (R)	13,527	14.5
	Francis C. Saunders (C)	6,315	6.8
21	Herman Badillo (D, L)	38,866	83.7
	George B. Smaragdas (C)	7,561	16.3

	Candidates	Votes	%
22	James H. Scheuer (D, L)	50,372	71.6
	Robert M. Schneck (R, C)	19,994	28.4
23	Jonathan B. Bingham (D, L)	78,723	76.2
	George E. Sweeney (R)	16,172	15.7
	Nora M. Kardian (C)	8,456	8.2
24	Mario Biaggi (D, C)	106,942	69.9
	Joseph F. Periconi (R, SILENT)	38,173	24.9
	John Patrick Hagan (L)	7,970	5.2
25	Peter A. Peyser (R)	76,611	42.5
	William Dretzin (D)	66,688	37.0
	Anthony J. De Vito (C)	31,250	17.3
26	Ogden R. Reid (R, L)	109,783	66.4
	Michael A. Coffey (C)	29,702	18.0
	G. Russell James (D)	25,909	15.7
27	John G. Dow (D, L)	89,787	52.2
	Martin B. McKneally (R, C)	82,191	47.8
28	Hamilton Fish Jr. (R)	119,954	70.8
	John J. Greaney (D)	41,908	24.7
29	Samuel S. Stratton (D)	128,017	66.2
	Daniel E. Button (R, L)	65,339	33.8
30	Carleton J. King (R, C)	95,470	57.1
	Edward W. Pattison (D, L)	71,832	42.9
31	Robert C. McEwen (R, C)	90,585	72.4
	Erwin L. Bornstein (D)	34,568	27.6
32	Alexander Pirnie (R, L)	90,884	65.8
	Joseph Simmons (D)	47,306	34.2
33	Howard W. Robison (R)	90,196	66.5
	David Bernstein (D, L)	45,373	33.5
34	John H. Terry (R, C)	88,786	59.5
	Neal P. McCurn (D)	60,452	40.5
35	James M. Hanley (D)	82,425	51.9
	John F. O'Connor (R, C)	76,381	48.1
36	Frank J. Horton (R)	123,209	70.5
	Jordan E. Pappas (D)	38,898	22.3
	David F. Hampson (C)	10,442	6.0
37	Barber B. Conable Jr. (R)	107,677	65.9
	Richard N. Anderson (D, L)	48,061	29.4
38	James F. Hastings (R, C)	94,906	71.4
	James G. Cretekos (D)	37,961	28.6
39	Jack F. Kemp (R, C)	96,989	51.6
	Thomas P. Flaherty (D, L)	90,949	48.4
40	Henry P. Smith III (R, C)	87,183	63.4
	Edward Cuddy (D, L)	50,418	36.6
41	Thaddeus J. Dulski (D, L)	79,151	79.7
	William M. Johns (R, C)	20,108	20.3

NORTH CAROLINA

	Candidates	Votes	%
1	Walter B. Jones (D)	41,674	70.2
	R. Frank Everett (R)	16,217	27.3
2	L. H. Fountain (D)	38,891	100.0
3	David N. Henderson (D)	41,065	60.1
	Herbert H. Howell (R)	27,224	39.9
4	Nick Galifianakis (D)	49,866	52.4
	R. Jack Hawke (R)	45,386	47.7
5	Wilmer D. Mizell (R)	68,937	58.1
	James G. White (D)	49,663	41.9
6	Richardson Preyer (D)	47,693	66.0
	Clifton B. Barham Jr. (R)	20,739	28.7
	Lynwood Bullock (AM)	3,849	5.3
7	Alton A. Lennon (D)	37,377	72.0
	Frederick R. Weber (R)	14,529	28.0
8	Earl B. Ruth (R)	51,873	56.1
	H. Clifton Blue (D)	40,563	43.9
9	Charles Raper Jonas (R)	57,525	66.6
	Cy N. Bahakel (D)	28,801	33.4
10	James T. Broyhill (R)	63,936	57.1
	Basil L. Whitener (D)	48,113	42.9
11	Roy A. Taylor (D)	90,199	67.0
	Luke Atkinson (R)	44,376	33.0

NORTH DAKOTA

	Candidates	Votes	%
1	Mark Andrews (R)	72,168	65.7
	James E. Brooks (D)	37,688	34.3
2	Arthur A. Link (D)	50,416	50.3
	Robert P. McCarney (R)	49,888	49.7

OHIO

	Candidates	Votes	%
1	William J. Keating (R)	89,169	69.1
	Bailey W. Turner (D)	39,820	30.9
2	Donald D. Clancy (R)	77,071	55.9
	Gerald N. Springer (D)	60,860	44.1
3	Charles W. Whalen Jr. (R)	86,973	74.2
	Dempsey A. Kerr (D)	26,735	22.8
4	William M. McCulloch (R)	82,521	64.4
	Donald B. Laws (D)	45,619	35.6
5	Delbert L. Latta (R)	92,577	71.2
	Carl G. Sherer (D)	37,545	28.9
6	William H. Harsha (R)	82,772	67.8
	Raymond H. Stevens (D)	39,265	32.2
7	Clarence J. Brown Jr. (R)	84,448	69.4
	Joseph D. Lewis (D)	37,294	30.6
8	Jackson E. Betts (R)	90,916	100.0
9	Thomas L. Ashley (D)	82,777	70.9
	Allen H. Shapiro (R)	33,947	29.1
10	Clarence E. Miller (R)	80,838	66.5
	Doug Arnett (D)	40,669	33.5
11	J. William Stanton (R)	91,437	68.3
	Ralph Rudd (D)	42,542	31.8
12	Samuel L. Devine (R)	82,486	57.7
	James W. Goodrich (D)	60,538	42.3
13	Charles A. Mosher (R)	85,858	61.7
	Joseph J. Bartolomeo (D)	53,271	38.3
14	John F. Seiberling Jr. (D)	71,282	56.4
	William H. Ayres (R)	55,038	43.6
15	Chalmers P. Wylie (R)	81,536	70.6
	Manley L. McGee (D)	34,018	29.4
16	Frank T. Bow (R)	81,208	56.2
	Virgil L. Musser (D)	63,187	43.8
17	John M. Ashbrook (R)	79,472	62.2
	James C. Hood (D)	44,066	34.5
18	Wayne L. Hays (D)	82,071	68.3
	Robert Stewart (R)	38,104	31.7
19	Charles J. Carney (D)	73,222	58.5
	Margaret Dennison (R)	52,057	41.6
20	James V. Stanton (D)	70,140	81.3
	J. William Petro (R)	16,118	18.7
21	Louis Stokes (D)	74,340	77.6
	Bill Mack (R)	21,440	22.4
22	Charles A. Vanik (D)	114,790	71.5
	Adrian Fink (R)	45,657	28.5
23	William E. Minshall (R)	111,218	60.0
	Ronald M. Motti (D)	73,765	39.8
24	Walter E. Powell (R)	63,344	51.5
	James D. Ruppert (D)	55,455	45.1

Special Election

		Votes	%
19	Charles J. Carney (D)	70,161	58.4
	Margaret Dennison (R)	50,005	41.6

OKLAHOMA

		Votes	%
1	Page Belcher (R)	67,386	55.7
	James R. Jones (D)	53,598	44.3
2	Ed Edmondson (D)	87,131	70.8
	Gene Humphries (R)	35,989	29.2
3	Carl Albert (D)	112,458	100.0
4	Tom Steed (D)	67,743	63.7
	Jay G. Wilkinson (R)	37,081	34.9
5	John Jarman (D)	62,034	73.1
	Terry L. Campbell (R)	22,801	26.9
6	John N. Happy Camp (R)	81,959	64.2
	R. O. Cassity Jr. (D)	45,742	35.8

OREGON

		Votes	%
1	Wendell Wyatt (R)	147,239	71.8
	Vern Cook (D)	57,837	28.2
2	Al Ullman (D)	100,943	71.2
	Everett Thoren (R)	40,620	28.7
3	Edith Green (D)	118,919	73.7
	Robert E. Dugdale (R)	42,391	26.3
4	John Dellenback (R)	84,474	58.3
	James Weaver (D)	60,299	41.7

PENNSYLVANIA

	Candidates	Votes	%
1	William A. Barrett (D)	79,425	69.2
	Joseph S. Ziccardi (R)	34,649	30.2
2	Robert N. C. Nix (D)	70,530	68.2
	Edward L. Taylor (R)	32,858	31.8
3	James A. Byrne (D)	54,755	56.4
	Gustine D. Pelagatti (R)	42,393	43.6
4	Joshua Eilberg (D)	113,920	59.4
	Charles F. Dougherty (R)	77,817	40.6
5	William J. Green III (D)	80,142	66.9
	James H. Ring (R)	38,955	32.5
6	Gus Yatron (D)	96,453	65.0
	Michael Kitsock (R)	48,397	32.6
7	Lawrence G. Williams (R)	91,042	59.2
	Joseph R. Breslin (D)	62,722	40.8
8	Edward G. Biester Jr. (R)	73,041	56.4
	Arthur Leo Hennessy Jr. (D)	51,464	39.7
9	John H. Ware III (R)	76,535	59.2
	Louis F. Waldman (D)	52,852	40.9
10	Joseph M. McDade (R)	102,716	65.4
	Edward J. Smith (D)	51,506	32.8
11	Daniel J. Flood (D)	146,789	96.6
12	J. Irving Whalley (R)	93,385	64.0
	Victor J. Karycki Jr. (D)	48,738	33.4
13	R. Lawrence Coughlin (R)	101,953	58.3
	Frank R. Romano (D)	68,743	39.3
14	William S. Moorhead (D)	72,509	76.5
	Barry Levine (R)	21,572	22.8
15	Fred B. Rooney (D)	93,169	66.9
	Charles H. Roberts (R)	44,103	31.7
16	Edwin D. Eshleman (R)	74,006	66.5
	John E. Pflum (D)	33,986	30.5
17	Herman T. Schneebeli (R)	88,173	57.9
	William P. Zurick (D)	60,714	39.9
18	Robert J. Corbett (R)	87,246	60.2
	Ronald E. Leslie (D)	54,639	37.7
19	George A. Goodling (R)	71,497	53.9
	Arthur L. Berger (D)	58,399	44.0
20	Joseph M. Gaydos (D)	84,911	77.0
	Joseph Honeygosky (R)	22,553	20.5
21	John H. Dent (D)	76,915	68.5
	Glenn G. Anderson (R)	33,396	29.7
22	John P. Saylor (R)	81,675	57.7
	Joseph F. O'Kicki (D)	58,720	41.5
23	Albert W. Johnson (R)	70,074	57.9
	Cecil E. Harrington (D)	50,908	42.1
24	Joseph P. Vigorito (D)	94,029	66.8
	Wayne R. Merrick (R)	44,395	31.5
25	Frank M. Clark (D)	92,638	69.7
	John Loth (R)	37,355	28.1
26	Thomas E. Morgan (D)	80,734	68.4
	Domenick A. Cupelli (R)	35,083	29.7
27	James G. Fulton (R)	86,932	60.5
	Douglas Walgren (D)	55,050	38.3

Special Election

		Votes	%
9	John H. Ware III (R)	44,077	57.0
	Louis F. Waldman (D)	31,353	40.5

RHODE ISLAND

		Votes	%
1	Fernand J. St. Germain (D)	86,283	61.0
	Walter J. Miska (R)	52,962	37.4
2	Robert O. Tiernan (D)	121,704	67.2
	William A. Dimitri Jr. (R)	61,819	34.2

SOUTH CAROLINA

		Votes	%
1	L. Mendel Rivers (D)	63,891*	100.0
2	Floyd Spence (R)	48,093	53.1
	Heyward McDonald (D)	42,005	46.4
3	William Jennings Bryan Dorn (D)	60,708	75.2
	H. Grady Ballard (R)	19,981	24.8
4	James R. Mann (D)	52,175	100.0
5	Thomas S. Gettys (D)	43,742	65.9
	B. Leonard Phillips (R)	21,911	33.0

	Candidates	Votes	%
6	John L. McMillan (D)	46,966	64.1
	Edward B. Baskin (R)	25,546	34.9

SOUTH DAKOTA

		Votes	%
1	Frank E. Denholm (D)	71,636	56.0
	Dexter H. Gunderson (R)	56,330	44.0
2	James Abourezk (D)	55,925	52.3
	Fred D. Brady (R)	51,092	47.7

TENNESSEE

		Votes	%
1	James H. Quillen (R)	78,896	67.9
	David Bruce Shine (D)	37,348	32.1
2	John J. Duncan (R)	85,849	73.3
	Roger Cowan (D)	30,146	25.7
3	LaMar Baker (R)	61,527	51.3
	Richard Winningham (D)	54,662	45.6
4	Joe L. Evins (D)	86,437	82.6
	J. Durelle Boles (R)	18,180	17.4
5	Richard Fulton (D)	89,900	70.6
	George Kelly (R)	37,522	29.5
6	William R. Anderson (D)	87,517	81.7
	Elmer Davies Jr. (R)	19,622	18.3
7	Ray Blanton (D)	83,904	74.2
	W. G. Doss (R)	29,139	25.8
8	Ed Jones (D)	66,590	100.0
9	Dan Kuykendall (R)	72,498	62.6
	Michael Osborn (D)	43,279	37.4

TEXAS

		Votes	%
1	Wright Patman (D)	67,883	78.9
	James Hogan (R)	18,614	21.6
2	John Dowdy (D)	52,634	73.6
	Eugene Hoyt (WRITE IN)	11,987#	17.2
	Joe Runnels (WRITE IN)	4,693#	6.8
3	James M. Collins (R)	63,690	60.6
	John Mead (D)	41,425	39.4
4	Ray Roberts (D)	70,103	100.0
5	Earle Cabell (D)	57,058	59.7
	Frank Crowley (R)	38,481	40.3
6	Olin E. Teague (D)	74,038	100.0
7	Bill Archer (R)	93,457	64.8
	Jim Greenwood (D)	50,750	35.2
8	Bob Eckhardt (D)	26,294	100.0
9	Jack Brooks (D)	57,180	64.5
	Henry Pressler (R)	31,483	35.5
10	J. J. Pickle (D)	78,872	100.0
11	W. R. Poage (D)	59,641	99.9
12	Jim Wright (D)	62,057	100.0
13	Graham B. Purcell (D)	80,070	64.9
	Joe Staley (R)	43,319	35.1
14	John Young (D)	62,560	100.0
15	Eligio de la Garza (D)	54,498	76.2
	Ben A. Martinez (R)	17,049	23.8
16	Richard C. White (D)	54,617	82.7
	J. R. Provencio (R)	11,420	17.3
17	Omar Burleson (D)	70,040	100.0
18	Bob Price (R)	52,845	99.9
19	George Mahon (D)	59,996	100.0
20	Henry B. Gonzalez (D)	48,710	100.0
21	O. C. Fisher (D)	76,004	61.4
	Richardson B. Gill (R)	47,868	38.6
22	Bob Casey (D)	73,514	55.7
	A. W. Busch (R)	58,598	44.4
23	Abraham Kazen Jr. (D)	61,068	100.0

UTAH

		Votes	%
1	K. Gunn McKay (D)	95,499	51.3
	Richard Richards (R)	89,269	47.9
2	Sherman P. Lloyd (R)	97,549	52.3
	A. H. (Bob) Nance (D)	87,000	46.6

VERMONT

		Votes	%
AL	Robert T. Stafford (R)	103,806	68.0
	Bernard O'Shea (D)	44,415	29.1

VIRGINIA

	Candidates	Votes	%
1	Thomas N. Downing (D)	71,465	100.0
2	G. William Whitehurst (R)	44,108	61.7
	Joseph T. Fitzpatrick (D)	27,367	38.3
3	David E. Satterfield III (D)	73,123	65.2
	J. Harvie Wilkinson III (R)	35,258	31.5
4	Watkins M. Abbitt (D)	55,246	61.0
	Ben Ragsdale (I)	25,403	28.1
	James M. Helms (R)	9,883	10.9
5	W. C. "Dan" Daniel (D)	54,274	73.0
	Allen T. St. Clair Jr. (R)	20,039	27.0
6	Richard H. Poff (R)	62,350	74.6
	Roy R. White (D)	21,241	25.4
7	J. Kenneth Robinson (R)	52,716	61.8
	Murat Williams (D)	32,642	38.2
8	William L. Scott (R)	68,311	63.7
	Darrel H. Stearns (D)	38,848	36.3
9	William C. Wampler (R)	53,960	60.9
	Tate C. Buchanan (D)	34,609	39.1
10	Joel T. Broyhill (R)	67,650	54.5
	Harold O. Miller (D)	56,603	45.6

WASHINGTON

	Candidates	Votes	%
1	Thomas M. Pelly (R)	107,072	64.4
	David A. Hughes (D)	53,156	32.0
2	Lloyd Meeds (D)	117,562	72.7
	Edward A. McBride (R)	44,049	27.3
3	Julia Butler Hansen (D)	81,892	59.2
	R. C. (Skip) McConkey (R)	56,566	40.9
4	Mike McCormack (D)	70,119	52.6
	Catherine May (R)	63,244	47.4
5	Thomas S. Foley (D)	88,189	67.0
	George Gamble (R)	43,376	33.0
6	Floyd V. Hicks (D)	98,282	69.4
	John Jarstad (R)	42,213	29.8
7	Brock Adams (D)	99,308	66.6
	Brian Lewis (R)	47,426	31.8

WEST VIRGINIA

	Candidates	Votes	%
1	Robert H. Mollohan (D)	61,296	61.5
	Ken Doll (R)	38,327	38.5
2	Harvey O. Staggers (D)	56,263	62.7
	Richard M. Reddecliff (R)	33,509	37.3
3	John Slack (D)	57,630	65.4
	Neal A. Kinsolving (R)	30,525	34.6
4	Ken Hechler (D)	62,531	67.4
	Ralph Shannon (R)	30,255	32.6
5	James Kee (D)	48,286	70.4
	Marian McQuade (R)	20,261	29.6

WISCONSIN

	Candidates	Votes	%
1	Les Aspin (D)	87,428	60.9
	Henry C. Schadeberg (R)	56,067	39.1
2	Robert W. Kastenmeier (D)	102,879	68.5
	Norman Anderson (R)	46,620	31.0
3	Vernon W. Thomson (R)	64,891	55.5
	Ray Short (D)	52,085	44.5
4	Clement J. Zablocki (D)	102,464	81.6
	Phillip D. Mrozinski (R)	23,081	18.4
5	Henry S. Reuss (D)	60,630	75.9
	Robert J. Dwyer (R)	18,360	23.0
6	William A. Steiger (R)	98,587	67.7
	Franklin R. Utech (D)	44,794	30.8
7	David R. Obey (D)	88,746	67.6
	Andre E. Le Tendre (R)	41,330	31.5
8	John W. Byrnes (R)	76,893	55.5
	Robert J. Cornell (D)	60,345	43.6
9	Glenn R. Davis (R)	84,732	52.0
	Fred N. Tabak (D)	78,123	48.0
10	Alvin E. O'Konski (R)	66,014	50.9
	Walter Thoresen (D)	62,991	48.6

WYOMING

	Candidates	Votes	%
AL	Teno Roncalio (D)	58,456	50.3
	Harry Roberts (R)	57,848	49.7

1. These two California special elections were held to fill unexpired terms in the 91st Congress (1969–1971).

The returns for special House elections in the 24th and 35th districts are from elections held after no candidate received a majority of the vote in the initial special primary elections. (California special primary law, see p. 1141.)

Special primary election returns, 24th district: John H. Rousselot (R), 37,348, 29.0%; Bill McColl (R), 35,682, 27.7; Myrlie B. Evers (D), 23,688, 18.4; Patrick J. Hillings (R), 22,394, 17.4; Jack Alex (R), 8,230, 6.4. Rousselot, the top Republican, and Evers, the top Democrat, thus qualified to meet in the special election. Source: California secretary of state.

Special primary election returns, 35th district: Congressional Quarterly was unable to obtain complete official returns. Seven candidates competed for the seat, five Republicans and two Democrats. Schmitz, the Republican receiving the highest number of votes, and Hartman, the top Democrat, qualified to meet in the special election.

1971 House Elections

KENTUCKY

Special Election

	Candidates	Votes	%
6	William P. Curlin (D)	29,778#	52.6
	Raymond Nutter (R)	21,584#	38.1
	Edgar A. Wallace	4,070#	7.2

MARYLAND

Special Election

	Candidates	Votes	%
1	William O. Mills (R)	31,165	53.4
	Elroy G. Boyer (D)	27,234	46.6

PENNSYLVANIA

Special Election

	Candidates	Votes	%
18	H. John Heinz III (R)	103,543	66.6
	John E. Connelly (D)	49,269	31.7

SOUTH CAROLINA

Special Election

	Candidates	Votes	%
1	Mendel J. Davis (D)	38,012	48.6
	James B. Edwards (R)	32,227	41.2
	Victoria DeLee (I)	7,965	10.2

1972 House Elections

ALABAMA

	Candidates	Votes	%
1	Jack Edwards (R)	104,606	76.5
	O. W. McCrory (D)	24,357	17.8
	Thomas McAboy Jr. (NDPA)	7,747	5.7
2	William L. Dickinson (R)	80,362	54.9
	Ben C. Reeves (D)	60,769	41.5
3	Bill Nichols (D)	100,045	75.6
	Robert M. Kerr (R)	27,253	20.6
4	Tom Bevill (D)	108,039	69.6
	Ed Nelson (R)	46,551	30.0
5	Robert E. Jones (D)	101,303	74.2
	Digter J. Schrader (R)	33,352	24.4
6	John H. Buchanan Jr. (R)	91,499	59.8
	Ben Erdreich (D)	54,497	35.6
7	Walter Flowers (D)	95,060	84.8
	Lewis Black (NDPA)	15,703	14.0

Special Election

3	Elizabeth Andrews (D)	✓

ALASKA

		Votes	%
AL	Nick Begich (D)	53,651*	56.2
	Don Young (R)	41,750	43.8

ARIZONA

		Votes	%
1	John J. Rhodes (R)	80,453	57.3
	Gerald A. Pollock (D)	59,900	42.7
2	Morris K. Udall (D)	97,616	63.5
	Gene Savoie (R)	56,188	36.5
3	Sam Steiger (R)	90,710	63.0
	Ted Wyckoff (D)	53,220	37.0
4	John B. Conlan (R)	82,511	53.0
	Jack E. Brown (D)	73,309	47.1

ARKANSAS

		Votes	%
1	Bill Alexander (D)	✓	
2	Wilbur D. Mills (D)	✓	
3	John Paul Hammerschmidt (R)	144,571	77.3
	Guy W. Hatfield (D)	42,481	22.7
4	Ray Thornton (D)	✓	

CALIFORNIA

		Votes	%
1	Don H. Clausen (R)	141,226	62.3
	William A. Nighswonger (D)	77,610	34.2
2	Harold T. Johnson (D)	149,590	68.4
	Frances X. Callahan (R)	62,727	28.7
3	John E. Moss (D)	151,706	69.9
	John Rakus (R)	65,298	30.1
4	Robert L. Leggett (D)	115,038	67.4
	Benjamin Chang (R)	55,540	32.6
5	Phillip Burton (D)	124,164	81.8
	Edlo E. Powell (R)	27,474	18.1
6	William S. Mailliard (R)	119,704	52.1
	Roger Boas (D)	110,144	47.9
7	Ronald V. Dellums (D)	126,913	55.9
	Peter Hannaford (R)	86,587	38.1
	Frank V. Cortese (AM I)	13,550	6.0
8	Fortney H. (Pete) Stark Jr. (D)	102,153	52.9
	Lew M. Warden Jr. (R)	90,970	47.1
9	Don Edwards (D)	123,994	72.3
	Herb Smith (R)	43,140	25.2
10	Charles S. Gubser (R)	140,342	64.6
	B. Frank Gillette (D)	76,839	35.4
11	Leo J. Ryan (D)	114,134	60.5
	Charles E. Chase (R)	69,632	36.9
12	Burt L. Talcott (R)	105,556	51.4
	Julian Camacho (D)	84,174	41.0
13	Charles M. Teague (R)	153,877	73.9
	Lester D. Cleveland (D)	54,299	26.1

	Candidates	Votes	%
14	Jerome R. Waldie (D)	159,335	77.6
	Floyd E. Sims (R)	46,082	22.4
15	John J. McFall (D)	146,358	100.0
16	B. F. Sisk (D)	134,132	79.1
	Carol O. Harner (R)	35,385	20.9
17	Paul N. McCloskey Jr. (R)	110,988	54.5
	James Stewart (D)	73,123	35.9
	James Gordon Knapp (WRITE IN)	19,377	9.5
18	Bob Mathias (R)	110,153	66.4
	Vincent J. Lavery (D)	55,829	33.6
19	Chet Holifield (D)	105,699	67.2
	Kenneth M. Fisher (R)	43,792	27.9
20	Carlos J. Moorhead (R)	122,309	57.4
	John Binkley (D)	90,842	42.6
21	Augustus F. Hawkins (D)	95,050	82.9
	Rayfield Lundy (R)	19,569	17.1
22	James C. Corman (D)	123,863	67.6
	Bruce P. Wolfe (R)	53,603	29.3
23	Del Clawson (R)	120,313	61.4
	Conrad G. Tuohey (D)	75,546	38.6
24	John H. Rousselot (R)	144,057	70.1
	Luther Mandell (D)	61,326	29.9
25	Charles E. Wiggins (R)	118,631	65.0
	Leslie W. Craven (D)	58,323	31.9
26	Thomas M. Rees (D)	164,351	68.7
	Philip Robert Rutta (R)	66,731	27.9
27	Barry Goldwater Jr. (R)	119,475	57.4
	Mark S. Novak (D)	88,548	42.6
28	Alphonzo Bell (R)	144,815	60.7
	Michael Shapiro (D)	89,517	37.5
29	George E. Danielson (D)	92,856	62.7
	Richard E. Ferraro (R)	49,590	33.5
30	Edward R. Roybal (D)	78,193	68.4
	Bill Brophy (R)	32,717	28.6
31	Charles H. Wilson (D)	87,975	52.3
	Ben Valentine (R)	71,395	42.5
	Roberta Lynn Wood (PFP)	8,788	5.2
32	Craig Hosmer (R)	149,514	65.9
	Dennis Murray (D)	72,481	32.0
33	Jerry L. Pettis (R)	140,868	75.0
	Ken Thompson (D)	46,911	25.0
34	Richard T. Hanna (D)	115,880	67.1
	John D. Ratterree (R)	49,971	29.0
35	Glenn M. Anderson (D)	105,667	74.8
	Vernon E. Brown (R)	35,614	25.2
36	William M. Ketchum (R)	88,071	52.7
	Timothy Lemucchi (D)	72,623	43.5
37	Yvonne Brathwaite Burke (D)	123,468	60.2
	Gregg Tria (R)	41,562	20.3
38	George E. Brown Jr. (D)	77,922	55.9
	Howard J. Snider (R)	60,459	43.4
39	Andrew J. Hinshaw (R)	149,081	65.7
	John W. Black (D)	77,817	34.3
40	Bob Wilson (R)	155,269	67.8
	Frank Caprio (D)	69,377	30.3
41	Lionel Van Deerlin (D)	116,980	74.1
	D. Richard Kau (R)	40,997	26.0
42	Clair W. Burgener (R)	158,475	67.5
	Bob Lowe (D)	68,381	29.1
43	Victor V. Veysey (R)	118,536	62.7
	Ernest Z. Robles (D)	70,455	37.3

COLORADO

		Votes	%
1	Patricia Schroeder (D)	101,832	52.0
	James D. McKevitt (R)	93,733	47.9
2	Donald G. Brotzman (R)	132,562	66.3
	Francis W. Brush (D)	66,817	33.4
3	Frank E. Evans (D)	107,511	66.3
	Chuck Brady (R)	54,556	33.7
4	James P. Johnson (R)	94,994	51.0
	Alan Merson (D)	91,151	49.0
5	William L. Armstrong (R)	104,214	62.3
	Byron L. Johnson (D)	60,948	36.5

CONNECTICUT

	Candidates	Votes	%
1	William R. Cotter (D)	130,701	56.9
	Richard M. Rittenband (R)	96,188	41.9
2	Robert H. Steele (R)	142,094	65.9
	Roger Hilsman (D)	73,400	34.1
3	Robert N. Giaimo (D)	121,217	53.3
	Henry A. Povinelli (R)	106,313	46.7
4	Stewart B. McKinney (R)	135,883	63.1
	James P. McLoughlin (D)	79,515	36.9
5	Ronald A. Sarasin (R)	117,578	51.2
	John S. Monagan (D)	112,142	48.8
6	Ella T. Grasso (D)	140,290	60.2
	John F. Walsh (R)	92,783	39.8

DELAWARE

		Votes	%
AL	Pierre S. duPont IV (R)	141,237	62.5
	Norma Handloff (D)	83,230	36.9

FLORIDA

		Votes	%
1	Robert L. F. Sikes (D)	✓	
2	Don Fuqua (D)	✓	
3	Charles E. Bennett (D)	101,441	82.0
	John F. Bowen (R)	22,219	18.0
4	Bill Chappell (D)	92,541	55.9
	P. T. Fleuchaus (R)	72,960	44.1
5	William D. Gunter Jr. (D)	97,902	55.5
	Jack P. Insco (R)	78,463	44.5
6	C. W. Bill Young (R)	156,150	76.0
	Michael O. Plunkett (D)	49,399	24.0
7	Sam Gibbons (D)	91,931	68.0
	Robert A. Carter (R)	43,343	32.0
8	James A. Haley (D)	89,068	57.8
	Roy Thompson Jr. (R)	64,920	42.2
9	Louis Frey Jr. (R)	✓	
10	L. A. (Skip) Bafalis (R)	113,461	62.0
	Bill Sikes (D)	69,502	38.0
11	Paul G. Rogers (D)	116,157	60.2
	Joel Karl Gustafson (R)	76,739	39.8
12	J. Herbert Burke (R)	110,750	62.8
	James T. Stephanis (D)	65,526	37.2
13	William Lehman (D)	92,258	61.6
	Paul D. Bethel (R)	57,418	38.4
14	Claude Pepper (D)	75,131	67.7
	Evelio S. Estrella (R)	35,935	32.4
15	Dante B. Fascell (D)	89,961	56.8
	Ellis S. Rubin (R)	68,320	43.2

GEORGIA

		Votes	%
1	Ronald B. (Bo) Ginn (D)	55,256	100.0
2	Dawson Mathis (D)	65,997	100.0
3	Jack Brinkley (D)	71,756	100.0
4	Ben B. Blackburn (R)	103,155	75.9
	F. Odell Welborn (D)	32,731	24.1
5	Andrew Young (D)	72,289	52.8
	Rodney M. Cook (R)	64,495	47.1
6	John J. Flynt Jr. (D)	70,586	100.0
7	John W. Davis (D)	59,031	58.3
	Charles B. Sherrill (R)	42,265	41.7
8	W. S. Stuckey Jr. (D)	71,283	62.4
	Ronnie Thompson (R)	42,986	37.6
9	Phil M. Landrum (D)	71,801	100.0
10	Robert G. Stephens Jr. (D)	68,096	100.0

HAWAII

		Votes	%
1	Spark M. Matsunaga (D)	73,826	54.7
	Fred W. Rohlfing (R)	61,138	45.3
2	Patsy T. Mink (D)	79,856	57.1
	Diana Hansen (R)	60,043	42.9

IDAHO

	Candidates	Votes	%
1	Steven D. Symms (R)	85,270	55.6
	Edward Williams (D)	68,106	44.4
2	Orval Hansen (R)	102,537	69.2
	Willis H. Ludlow (D)	40,081	27.1

ILLINOIS

	Candidates	Votes	%
1	Ralph H. Metcalfe (D)	136,755	91.4
	Louis H. Coggs (R)	12,877	8.6
2	Morgan F. Murphy (D)	115,306	75.0
	James E. Doyle (R)	38,391	25.0
3	Robert P. Hanrahan (R)	128,329	62.3
	Daniel P. Coman (D)	77,814	37.8
4	Edward J. Derwinski (R)	141,402	70.5
	C. F. Dore (D)	59,057	29.5
5	John C. Kluczynski (D)	121,278	72.8
	Leonard C. Jarzab (R)	45,264	27.2
6	Harold R. Collier (R)	124,486	61.2
	Michael R. Galasso (D)	79,002	38.8
7	George W. Collins (D)	95,018*	82.8
	Thomas J. Lento (R)	19,758	17.2
8	Daniel D. Rostenkowski (D)	110,457	74.0
	Edward L. Stepnowski (R)	38,758	26.0
9	Sidney R. Yates (D)	131,777	68.3
	Clark W. Fetridge (R)	61,083	31.7
10	Samuel H. Young (R)	120,681	51.6
	Abner J. Mlkva (D)	113,222	48.4
11	Frank Annunzio (D)	118,637	53.3
	John J. Hoellen (R)	103,773	46.7
12	Philip M. Crane (R)	152,938	74.2
	E. L. Frank (D)	53,055	25.8
13	Robert McClory (R)	98,201	61.5
	Stanley W. Beetham (D)	61,537	38.5
14	John N. Erlenborn (R)	154,794	72.8
	James M. Wall (D)	57,874	27.2
15	Leslie C. Arends (R)	111,022	57.2
	Tim L. Hall (D)	82,925	42.8
16	John B. Anderson (R)	129,640	71.9
	John E. Devine Jr. (D)	50,649	28.1
17	George M. O'Brien (R)	100,175	55.7
	John J. Houlihan (D)	79,840	44.4
18	Robert H. Michel (R)	124,407	64.8
	Stephen L. Nordvall (D)	67,514	35.2
19	Thomas F. Railsback (R)	138,123	100.0
20	Paul Findley (R)	148,419	68.8
	Robert S. O'Shea (D)	67,445	31.2
21	Edward R. Madigan (R)	99,966	54.8
	Lawrence E. Johnson (D)	82,523	45.2
22	George E. Shipley (D)	124,589	56.5
	Robert B. Lamkin (R)	90,390	41.0
23	Melvin Price (D)	121,682	75.1
	Robert Mays (R)	40,428	24.9
24	Kenneth J. Gray (D)	138,867	93.7
	Hugh Muldoon (I)	9,398	6.3

Special Election

		Votes	%
15	Cliffard D. Carlson (R)	31,543	54.8
	Tim L. Hall (D)	26,030	45.2

INDIANA

		Votes	%
1	Ray J. Madden (D)	95,873	56.9
	Bruce R. Haller (R)	72,662	43.1
2	Earl F. Landgrebe (R)	110,406	54.7
	Floyd Fithian (D)	91,533	45.3
3	John Brademas (D)	103,949	55.2
	Don M. Newman (R)	81,369	43.2
4	J. Edward Roush (D)	100,327	51.5
	Allan Bloom (R)	94,492	48.5
5	Elwood Hillis (R)	124,692	64.1
	Kathleen Z. Williams (D)	69,746	35.9
6	William G. Bray (R)	112,525	64.8
	David W. Evans (D)	61,070	35.2
7	John T. Myers (R)	128,688	61.6
	Warren Henegar (D)	80,145	38.4
8	Roger H. Zion (R)	133,850	63.3

	Candidates	Votes	%
	Richard L. Deen (D)	77,371	36.6
9	Lee Hamilton (D)	122,698	62.9
	William A. Johnson (R)	72,325	37.1
10	David W. Dennis (R)	106,798	57.3
	Philip R. Sharp (D)	79,756	42.8
11	William H. Hudnut III (R)	95,839	51.2
	Andrew Jacobs Jr. (D)	91,238	48.8

IOWA

		Votes	%
1	Edward Mezvinsky (D)	107,099	53.4
	Fred Schwengel (R)	91,609	45.7
2	John C. Culver (D)	115,491	59.2
	Theodore R. Ellsworth (R)	79,667	40.8
3	H. R. Gross (R)	109,113	55.7
	Lyle Taylor (D)	86,848	44.3
4	Neal Smith (D)	125,431	59.6
	John Kyl (R)	85,156	40.4
5	William J. Scherle (R)	108,596	55.3
	Tom Harkin (D)	87,937	44.7
6	Wiley Mayne (R)	103,284	52.5
	Berkley Bedell (D)	93,574	47.5

KANSAS

		Votes	%
1	Keith G. Sebelius (R)	145,712	77.2
	Morris Coover (D)	40,678	21.6
2	William R. Roy (D)	106,276	60.6
	Charles D. McAtee (R)	65,071	37.1
3	Larry Winn Jr. (R)	122,358	71.0
	Charles Barsotti (D)	43,777	25.4
4	Garner E. Shriver (R)	120,120	73.2
	John S. Stevens (D)	40,753	24.8
5	Joe Skubitz (R)	128,639	72.3
	Lloyd L. Kitch (R)	49,169	27.7

KENTUCKY

		Votes	%
1	Frank A. Stubblefield (D)	81,456	64.8
	Charles T. Banken (R)	42,286	33.7
2	William H. Natcher (D)	75,871	61.5
	J. C. Carter (R)	47,436	38.5
3	Romano L. Mazzoli (D)	86,810	62.2
	Phil Kaelin Jr. (R)	51,634	37.0
4	M. G. (Gene) Snyder (R)	110,902	73.8
	James W. Rogers (D)	39,332	26.2
5	Tim Lee Carter (R)	109,264	73.6
	Lyle L. Willis (D)	39,301	26.5
6	John Breckinridge (D)	76,185	52.4
	Laban P. Jackson (R)	68,012	46.8
7	Carl D. Perkins (D)	94,840	61.9
	Robert Holcomb (R)	58,286	38.1

LOUISIANA

		Votes	%
1	F. Edward Hebert (D)	78,156	100.0
2	Hale Boggs (D)	68,093*	100.0
3	David C. Treen (R)	71,090	54.0
	J. Louis Watkins Jr. (D)	60,521	46.0
4	Joe D. Waggonner Jr. (D)	74,397	100.0
5	Otto E. Passman (D)	64,027	100.0
6	John R. Rarick (D)	84,275	100.0
7	John B. Breaux (D)	71,901	100.0
8	Gillis W. Long (D)	72,607	68.5
	R. S. Abramson (AM)	17,844	16.8
	Roy C. Strickland (R)	15,517	14.6

Special Election

7	John B. Breaux (D)	✓	

MAINE

		Votes	%
1	Peter N. Kyros (D)	129,408	59.4
	L. Robert Porteous Jr. (R)	88,588	40.6
2	William S. Cohen (R)	106,280	54.4
	Elmer H. Violette (D)	89,135	45.6

MARYLAND

	Candidates	Votes	%
1	William O. Mills (R)	86,326	70.5
	John R. Hargreaves (D)	36,139	29.5
2	Clarence D. Long (D)	123,346	65.8
	John J. Bishop Jr. (R)	64,119	34.2
3	Paul S. Sarbanes (D)	93,093	69.7
	Robert D. Morrow (R)	40,442	30.3
4	Marjorie S. Holt (R)	87,534	59.4
	Werner Fornos (D)	59,877	40.6
5	Lawrence J. Hogan (R)	90,016	62.9
	Edward T. Conroy (D)	53,049	37.1
6	Goodloe E. Byron (D)	107,283	64.8
	Edward J. Mason (R)	58,259	35.2
7	Parren J. Mitchell (D)	83,749	80.1
	Verdell Adair (R)	20,876	20.0
8	Gilbert Gude (R)	137,287	63.9
	Joseph G. Anastasi (D)	77,551	36.1

MASSACHUSETTS

		Votes	%
1	Silvio O. Conte (R)	159,282	99.9
2	Edward P. Boland (D)	137,616	100.0
3	Harold D. Donohue (D)	156,703	99.9
4	Robert F. Drinan (D)	101,714	49.5
	Martin A. Linsky (R)	92,250	44.9
	John T. Collins (IC)	11,141	5.4
5	Paul W. Cronin (R)	110,970	53.5
	John F. Kerry (D)	92,847	44.7
6	Michael J. Harrington (D)	139,697	64.1
	James Brady Moseley (R)	78,381	35.9
7	Torbert H. Macdonald (D)	135,193	67.7
	Joan M. Aliberti (R)	64,357	32.3
8	Thomas P. O'Neill Jr. (D)	142,470	88.7
	John E. Powers Jr. (SOC WORK)	18,169	11.3
9	John Joseph Moakley (I)	70,571	43.2
	Louise Day Hicks (D)	67,143	41.1
	Howard M. Miller (R)	23,177	14.2
10	Margaret M. Heckler (R)	161,708	100.0
11	James A. Burke (D)	154,397	100.0
12	Gerry E. Studds (D)	117,710	50.2
	William D. Weeks (R)	116,592	49.8

MICHIGAN

		Votes	%
1	John Conyers Jr. (D)	131,353	88.4
	Walter F. Girardot (R)	16,096	10.8
2	Marvin L. Esch (R)	103,321	56.0
	Marvin R. Stempien (D)	79,762	43.3
3	Garry Brown (R)	110,082	59.2
	James T. Brignall (D)	74,114	39.9
4	Edward Hutchinson (R)	111,185	67.3
	Charles W. Jameson (D)	54,141	32.8
5	Gerald Ford (R)	118,027	61.1
	Jean McKee (D)	72,782	37.7
6	Charles E. Chamberlain (R)	97,666	50.6
	Bob Carr (D)	95,209	49.4
7	Donald W. Riegle Jr. (R)	114,656	71.4
	Eugene L. Mattison (D)	48,883	30.5
8	James Harvey (R)	100,597	59.3
	Jerome Hart (D)	66,873	39.4
9	Guy A. Vander Jagt (R)	132,268	69.4
	Larry H. Olson (D)	56,236	29.5
10	Elford A. Cederberg (R)	121,368	66.7
	Bennie D. Graves (D)	56,149	30.9
11	Philip E. Ruppe (R)	135,786	69.4
	James Edward McNamara (D)	58,334	29.8
12	James G. O'Hara (D)	83,351	50.7
	David M. Serotkin (R)	80,667	49.0
13	Charles C. Diggs Jr. (D)	97,562	85.6
	Leonard T. Edwards (R)	15,180	13.3
14	Lucien N. Nedzi (D)	93,923	54.9
	Robert V. McGrath (R)	77,273	45.1
15	William D. Ford (D)	97,054	65.8
	Ernest D. Fackler (R)	48,504	32.9
16	John D. Dingell Jr. (D)	110,715	68.1
	William E. Rostron (R)	48,414	29.8
17	Martha W. Griffiths (D)	123,331	66.4
	Ralph E. Judd (R)	60,337	32.5

	Candidates	Votes	%
18	Robert J. Huber (R)	95,053	52.6
	Daniel S. Cooper (D)	85,580	47.4
19	William S. Broomfield (R)	123,697	70.4
	George F. Montgomery (D)	50,355	28.6

MINNESOTA

1	Albert H. Quie (R)	142,698	70.7
	Charles S. Thompson (DFL)	59,106	29.3
2	Ancher Nelsen (R)	124,350	57.1
	Charles V. Turnbull (DFL)	93,433	42.9
3	Bill Frenzel (R)	132,638	62.9
	Jim Bell (DFL)	66,070	31.3
	Donald Wright (MINN TAX)	12,234	5.8
4	Joseph E. Karth (DFL)	138,292	72.4
	Steve Thompson (R)	52,786	27.6
5	Donald M. Fraser (DFL)	135,108	65.8
	Allan Davisson (R)	50,014	24.4
	Norm Selby (MINN TAX)	15,845	7.7
6	John M. Zwach (R)	114,537	51.0
	Richard M. Nolan (DFL)	109,955	49.0
7	Bob Bergland (DFL)	133,067	59.1
	Jon O. Haaven (R)	92,283	41.0
8	John A. Blatnik (DFL)	161,823	75.9
	Edward Johnson (R)	51,314	24.1

MISSISSIPPI

1	Jamie L. Whitten (D)	87,526	100.0
2	David R. Bowen (D)	69,892	61.9
	Carl Butler (R)	39,117	34.7
3	G. V. (Sonny) Montgomery (D)	105,722	100.0
4	Thad Cochran (R)	67,655	47.9
	Ellis B. Bodron (D)	62,148	44.0
	Eddie L. McBride (I)	11,571	8.2
5	Trent Lott (R)	77,826	55.4
	Ben Stone (D)	62,101	44.2

MISSOURI

1	William Clay (D)	95,098	64.0
	Richard O. Funsch (R)	53,596	36.0
2	James W. Symington (D)	134,332	63.5
	John W. Cooper Jr. (R)	77,192	36.5
3	Leonor K. Sullivan (D)	124,365	69.3
	Albert Holst (R)	54,523	30.4
4	William J. Randall (D)	108,131	57.4
	Raymond E. Barrows (R)	80,228	42.6
5	Richard Bolling (D)	93,812	62.8
	Vernon E. Rice (R)	53,257	35.6
6	Jerry Litton (D)	110,047	52.2
	Russell Sloan (R)	91,610	43.5
7	Gene Taylor (R)	132,780	63.7
	William Thomas (D)	75,613	36.3
8	Richard Ichord (D)	112,556	62.1
	David R. Countie (R)	68,580	37.9
9	William L. Hungate (D)	132,150	66.5
	Robert L. Prange (R)	66,528	33.5
10	Bill D. Burlison (D)	106,301	64.3
	M. Francis Svendrowski (R)	59,083	35.7

MONTANA

1	Richard G. Shoup (R)	88,373	53.7
	Arnold Olsen (D)	76,073	46.3
2	John Melcher (D)	114,524	76.1
	Richard L. Forester (R)	36,063	24.0

NEBRASKA

1	Charles Thone (R)	126,789	64.2
	Darrel E. Berg (D)	70,570	35.8
2	John Y. McCollister (R)	114,669	63.9
	Patrick L. Cooney (D)	64,696	36.1
3	Dave Martin (R)	133,607	69.6
	Warren Fitzgerald (D)	58,378	30.4

NEVADA

	Candidates	Votes	%
AL	David Towell (R)	94,113	52.2
	James H. Bilbray (D)	86,349	47.9

NEW HAMPSHIRE

1	Louis C. Wyman (R)	115,732	72.9
	Chester E. Merrow (D)	42,996	27.1
2	James C. Cleveland (R)	107,021	67.6
	Charles B. Officer (D)	51,259	32.4

NEW JERSEY

1	John E. Hunt (R)	97,650	52.5
	James J. Florio (D)	87,492	47.0
2	Charles W. Sandman Jr. (R)	133,096	65.7
	John D. Rose (D)	69,374	34.3
3	James J. Howard (D)	103,893	53.0
	William F. Dowd (R)	92,285	47.0
4	Frank Thompson Jr. (D)	98,206	58.0
	Peter P. Garibaldi (R)	71,030	42.0
5	Peter H. B. Frelinghuysen Jr. (R)	127,310	62.0
	Frederick M. Bohen (D)	78,076	38.0
6	Edwin B. Forsythe (R)	123,610	62.8
	Francis P. Brennen (D)	71,113	36.1
7	William B. Widnall (R)	124,365	57.9
	Arthur J. Lesemann (D)	85,712	39.9
8	Robert A. Roe (D)	104,381	63.1
	Walter E. Johnson (R)	61,073	36.9
9	Henry Helstoski (D)	119,543	55.8
	Alfred D. Schiaffo (R)	94,747	44.2
10	Peter W. Rodino Jr. (D)	94,308	79.8
	Kenneth C. Miller (R)	23,949	20.3
11	Joseph G. Minish (D)	120,227	57.5
	Milton A. Waldor (R)	82,957	39.7
12	Matthew J. Rinaldo (R)	127,690	63.5
	Jerry Fitzgerald English (D)	72,758	36.2
13	Joseph J. Maraziti (R)	109,640	55.7
	Helen S. Meyner (D)	84,492	42.9
14	Dominick V. Daniels (D)	103,089	61.2
	Richard T. Bozzone (R)	57,683	34.3
15	Edward J. Patten (D)	98,155	52.3
	Fuller H. Brooks (R)	89,400	47.7

NEW MEXICO

1	Manuel Lujan Jr. (R)	118,403	55.7
	Eugene Gallegos (D)	94,239	44.3
2	Harold Runnels (D)	116,152	72.2
	George E. Presson (R)	44,784	27.8

NEW YORK

1	Otis G. Pike (D)	102,628	52.5
	Joseph H. Boyd (R)	72,133	36.9
	Robert D. L. Gardiner (C)	18,627	9.5
2	James R. Grover Jr. (R)	99,348	65.8
	Fern Coste Dennison (D)	49,454	32.8
3	Angelo D. Roncallo (R)	103,620	57.0
	Carter F. Bales (D)	73,429	40.4
	Lawrence P. Russo (C)	14,768	8.1
4	Norman F. Lent (R)	125,422	62.4
	Elaine B. Horowitz (D)	72,280	36.0
5	John W. Wydler (R)	133,332	62.4
	Ferne M. Steckler (D)	67,709	31.7
6	Lester L. Wolff (D, L)	109,620	51.5
	John T. Gallagher (R, C)	103,038	48.5
7	Joseph P. Addabbo (D, L)	103,110	75.0
	John E. Hall (R)	28,296	20.6
8	Benjamin S. Rosenthal (D, L)	110,293	64.7
	Frank A. La Pina (R, C)	60,166	35.3
9	James J. Delaney (D, R)	141,323	93.4
	Loretta E. Gressey (L)	9,965	6.6
10	Mario Biaggi (D, R)	130,200	93.9
	Michael S. Bank (L)	8,397	6.1
11	Frank J. Brasco (D)	87,869	63.9
	Melvin Solomon (R, C)	43,105	31.3
12	Shirley Chisholm (D, L)	57,821	87.9
	John M. Coleman (R)	6,373	9.7

13	Bertram L. Podell (D)	113,294	65.2
	Joseph F. Marcucci (R)	44,293	25.5
	Leonard M. Simon (L)	9,173	5.3
14	John J. Rooney (D, C)	45,515	53.9
	Allard K. Lowenstein (L)	23,732	28.1
	Francis J. Voyticky (R)	14,813	17.5
15	Hugh L. Carey (D)	77,019	52.2
	John F. Gangemi (R)	63,446	43.0
16	Elizabeth Holtzman (D)	96,984	65.6
	Nicholas R. Macchio (R)	33,828	22.9
	Emanuel Cellar (L)	10,337	7.0
17	John M. Murphy (D)	92,252	60.3
	Mario D. Belardino (R, C)	60,812	39.7
18	Edward I. Koch (D, L)	125,117	69.9
	Jane P. Langley (R, C)	52,379	29.3
19	Charles Rangel (D, R)	104,427	96.0
20	Bella S. Abzug (D)	85,558	55.7
	Priscilla M. Ryan (L)	43,045	28.0
	Annette Flatto Levy (R)	18,024	11.7
21	Herman Badillo (D, L)	48,441	86.9
	Manuel A. Ramos (R)	6,366	11.4
22	Jonathan B. Bingham (D, L)	107,448	76.5
	Charles A. Avarello (R, C)	33,045	23.5
23	Peter A. Peyser (R, C)	99,737	50.4
	Richard L. Ottinger (D, L)	98,335	49.6
24	Ogden R. Reid (D, L)	107,979	52.2
	Carl A. Vergari (R, C)	98,818	47.8
25	Hamilton Fish Jr. (R, C)	144,386	71.6
	John M. Burns III (D)	54,271	26.9
26	Benjamin A. Gilman (R)	90,922	47.8
	John G. Dow (D)	74,906	39.3
	Yale Rapkin (C, NEW I)	24,569	12.9
27	Howard W. Robison (R)	114,902	62.2
	David H. Blazer (D)	55,076	29.8
	Patrick M. O'Neil (C)	9,521	5.2
28	Samuel S. Stratton (D)	182,395	80.0
	John F. Ryan Jr. (R, C)	45,623	20.0
29	Carleton J. King (R, C)	148,170	69.9
	Harold B. Gordon (D, L)	63,920	30.1
30	Robert C. McEwen (R, C)	114,193	66.0
	Ernest J. Labaff (D, L)	58,788	34.0
31	Donald J. Mitchell (R, C)	98,454	51.0
	Robert Castle (D)	75,513	39.1
	Franklin Nichols (AP)	12,075	6.3
32	James M. Hanley (D)	111,481	57.2
	Leonard C. Koldin (R, C)	83,451	42.8
33	William F. Walsh (R, C)	132,139	71.4
	Clarence Kadys (D)	53,039	28.6
34	Frank Horton (R)	142,803	72.1
	Jack Rubens (D)	46,509	23.5
35	Barber B. Conable (R)	127,298	67.9
	Terence J. Spencer (D)	53,321	28.4
36	Henry P. Smith III (R, C)	110,238	57.3
	Richard D. (Max) McCarthy (D, L)	82,095	42.7
37	Thaddeus J. Dulski (D, L)	114,603	72.2
	William F. McLaughlin (R, C)	44,103	27.8
38	Jack F. Kemp (R, C)	156,967	73.2
	Anthony P. Lo Russo (D, L)	57,585	26.8
39	James F. Hastings (R, C)	126,147	71.9
	Wilbur White Jr. (D)	49,253	28.1

NORTH CAROLINA

1	Walter B. Jones (D)	77,438	68.8
	J. Jordan Bonner (R)	35,063	31.2
2	L. H. Fountain (D)	88,798	71.6
	Erick P. Little (R)	35,193	28.4
3	David N. Henderson (D)	56,968	100.0
4	Ike F. Andrews (D)	72,972	50.3
	R. Jack Hawke (R)	71,972	49.7
5	Wilmer D. Mizell (R)	101,375	64.8
	Brooks Hays (D)	54,986	35.2
6	L. Richardson Preyer (D)	82,158	93.9
	Lynwood Bullock (AM)	5,331	6.1
7	Charles Rose (D)	57,348	60.4
	Jerry C. Scott (R)	36,726	38.7
8	Earl B. Ruth (R)	82,060	60.2
	Richard Clark (D)	54,198	39.8
9	James G. Martin (R)	80,356	58.9

Candidates	Votes	%
James Beatty (D)	56,171	41.1
10 James T. Broyhill (R)	103,119	72.6
Paul L. Beck (D)	39,025	27.5
11 Roy A. Taylor (D)	94,465	59.6
Jesse I. Ledbetter (R)	64,062	40.4

NORTH DAKOTA

Candidates	Votes	%
AL Mark Andrews (R)	195,360	72.7
Richard Ista (D)	72,850	27.1

OHIO

Candidates	Votes	%
1 William J. Keating (R)	119,469	70.3
Karl F. Heiser (D)	50,575	29.7
2 Donald D. Clancy (R)	109,961	62.8
Penny Manes (D)	65,237	37.2
3 Charles W. Whalen Jr. (R)	111,253	76.2
John W. Lelack Jr. (D)	34,819	23.8
4 Tennyson Guyer (R)	109,612	62.7
Dimitri Nicholas (D)	65,216	37.3
5 Delbert L. Latta (R)	132,032	72.8
Bruce Edwards (D)	49,465	27.3
6 William H. Harsha (R)	128,394	100.0
7 Clarence J. Brown (R)	112,350	73.3
Dorothy Franke (I)	40,945	26.7
8 Walter E. Powell (R)	80,050	52.2
James D. Ruppert (D)	73,344	47.8
9 Thomas L. Ashley (D)	110,450	69.1
Joseph C. Richards (R)	49,388	30.9
10 Clarence E. Miller (R)	129,683	73.2
Robert H. Wheatley (D)	47,456	26.8
11 J. William Stanton (R)	106,841	68.2
Dennis M. Callahan (D)	49,891	31.8
12 Samuel L. Devine (R)	103,655	56.1
James W. Goodrich (D)	81,074	43.9
13 Charles A. Mosher (R)	111,242	68.2
John Michael Ryan (D)	51,991	31.9
14 John F. Seiberling (D)	135,068	74.4
Norman W. Holt (R)	46,490	25.6
15 Chalmers P. Wylie (R)	115,779	65.8
M. L. McGee (D)	55,314	31.4
16 Ralph S. Regula (R)	102,013	57.3
Virgil L. Musser (D)	75,929	42.7
17 John M. Ashbrook (R)	92,666	57.4
Raymond C. Beck (D)	62,512	38.7
18 Wayne L. Hays (D)	128,663	70.2
Robert Stewart (R)	54,572	29.8
19 Charles J. Carney (D)	109,979	64.0
Norman M. Parr (R)	61,934	36.0
20 James V. Stanton (D)	117,302	84.3
Thomas E. Vilt (R)	16,624	11.9
21 Louis Stokes (D)	99,190	81.1
James D. Johnson (R)	13,861	11.3
22 Charles A. Vanik (D)	126,462	63.9
Donald W. Gropp (R)	64,577	32.6
23 William E. Minshall (R)	98,594	49.4
Dennis J. Kucinich (D)	94,366	47.3

OKLAHOMA

Candidates	Votes	%
1 James R. Jones (D)	91,684	54.4
J. M. Hewgley (R)	73,786	43.8
2 Clem Rogers McSpadden (D)	105,110	71.1
Emery H. Toliver (R)	42,632	28.9
3 Carl Albert (D)	101,732	93.4
Harold J. Marshall (I)	7,242	6.7
4 Tom Steed (D)	85,578	71.3
William E. Crozier (R)	34,484	28.7
5 John Jarman (D)	69,710	60.4
Llewllyn L. Keller (R)	45,711	39.6
6 John N. Happy Camp (R)	113,567	72.7
William Patrick Schmitt (D)	42,663	27.3

OREGON

Candidates	Votes	%
1 Wendell Wyatt (R)	166,476	68.6
Ralph E. Bunch (D)	76,307	31.4
2 Al Ullman (D)	178,537	99.9
3 Edith Green (D)	141,086	62.4
Mike Walsh (R)	84,697	37.5
4 John Dellenback (R)	138,965	62.0
Charles O. Porter (D)	83,134	37.1

PENNSYLVANIA

Candidates	Votes	%
1 William A. Barrett (D)	118,953	66.1
Gus A. Pedicone (R)	59,807	33.2
2 Robert N. C. Nix (D)	107,509	70.2
Frederick D. Bryant (R)	45,753	29.9
3 William J. Green III (D)	101,144	63.3
Alfred Marroletti (R)	57,787	36.2
4 Joshua Eilberg (D)	129,105	55.9
William Pfender (R)	102,013	44.1
5 John H. Ware III (R)	121,346	64.7
Brower B. Yerger (D)	66,329	35.3
6 Gus Yatron (D)	119,557	64.5
Eugene W. Hubler (R)	64,076	34.6
7 Lawrence G. Williams (R)	122,622	60.6
Stuart S. Bowie (D)	79,578	39.4
8 Edward G. Biester (R)	115,799	64.4
Alan Williams (D)	64,069	35.6
9 E. G. Shuster (R)	95,913	61.7
Earl D. Collins (D)	59,386	38.2
10 Joseph M. McDade (R)	143,670	73.6
Stanley R. Coveleskie (D)	51,550	26.4
11 Daniel J. Flood (D)	124,336	68.3
Donald B. Ayers (R)	57,809	31.7
12 John P. Saylor (R)	122,628	68.2
Joseph Murphy (D)	57,314	31.9
13 R. Lawrence Coughlin (R)	139,085	66.6
Katherine L. Camp (D)	69,728	33.4
14 William S. Moorhead (D)	106,158	59.3
Roland S. Catarinella (R)	72,275	40.4
15 Fred B. Rooney (D)	99,937	60.8
Wardell F. Steigerwalt (R)	64,560	39.3
16 Edwin D. Eshleman (R)	112,292	73.5
Shirley S. Garrett (O)	40,534	26.5
17 Herman T. Schneebeli (R)	120,214	72.2
Donald J. Rippon (D)	44,202	26.6
18 H. John Heinz III (R)	144,521	72.8
Douglas Walgren (D)	53,929	27.2
19 George A. Goodling (R)	93,536	57.5
Richard P. Noll (D)	67,018	41.2
20 Joseph M. Gaydos (D)	117,933	61.5
William R. Hunt (R)	73,817	38.5
21 John H. Dent (D)	104,203	62.0
Thomas H. Young (R)	63,812	38.0
22 Thomas E. Morgan (D)	100,918	60.8
James R. Montgomery (R)	65,005	39.2
23 Albert W. Johnson (R)	90,615	56.5
Ernest A. Kassab (D)	69,813	43.5
24 Joseph P. Vigorito (D)	122,092	68.8
Alvin W. Levenhagen (R)	55,406	31.2
25 Frank M. Clark (D)	97,549	55.8
Gary A. Myers (R)	77,123	44.2

Special Election[1]

Candidates	Votes	%
27 William S. Conover (R)	28,647#	51.1
Douglas Walgren (D)	25,956#	46.3

RHODE ISLAND

Candidates	Votes	%
1 Fernand J. St.Germain (D)	120,705	62.4
John M. Feeley (R)	67,125	34.7
2 Robert O. Tiernan (D)	122,739	63.1
Donald P. Ryan (R)	77,661	40.0

SOUTH CAROLINA

Candidates	Votes	%
1 Mendel J. Davis (D)	61,625	54.5
J. Sidi Limehouse (R)	51,469	45.5
2 Floyd Spence (R)	83,543	99.9
3 William Jennings Bryan Dorn (D)	82,579	75.2
Roy Ethridge (R)	27,173	24.8
4 James R. Mann (D)	64,989	66.1
Wayne N. Whatley (R)	33,363	33.9
5 Tom S. Getlye (D)	66,343	60.9
B. Leonard Phillips (R)	42,620	39.1
6 Edward L. Young (R)	63,527	54.4
John W. Jenrette Jr. (D)	53,324	45.6

SOUTH DAKOTA

Candidates	Votes	%
1 Frank E. Denholm (D)	94,442	60.5
John Vickerman (R)	61,589	39.5
2 James Abdnor (R)	79,546	54.9
Pat McKeever (D)	65,415	45.1

TENNESSEE

Candidates	Votes	%
1 James H. Quillen (R)	110,868	79.4
Bernard Cantor (D)	28,736	20.6
2 John J. Duncan (R)	109,925	100.0
3 LaMar Baker (R)	82,561	55.3
Howard Sompayrac (D)	62,536	41.9
4 Joe L. Evins (D)	93,042	81.1
Billy Joe Finney (R)	21,689	18.9
5 Richard Fulton (D)	93,555	62.6
Alfred Adams (R)	55,067	36.8
6 Robin L. Beard (R)	77,263	55.3
William R. Anderson (D)	60,264	43.1
7 Ed Jones (D)	92,419	70.5
Stockton Adkins (R)	38,726	29.5
8 Dan Kuykendall (R)	93,173	55.4
J. O. Patterson Jr. (D)	74,240	44.1

TEXAS

Candidates	Votes	%
1 Wright Patman (D)	93,891	100.0
2 Charles Wilson (D)	100,345	73.8
Charles O. Brightwell (R)	35,600	26.2
3 James Collins (R)	122,984	73.3
George A. Hughes (D)	44,708	26.7
4 Ray Roberts (D)	95,674	70.2
James Russell (R)	40,548	29.8
5 Alan Steelman (R)	74,932	55.7
Earle Cabell (D)	59,601	44.3
6 Olin E. Teague (D)	100,917	72.6
Carl Nigliazzo (R)	38,086	27.4
7 Bill Archer (R)	171,127	82.3
Jim Brady (D)	36,899	17.7
8 Bob Eckhardt (D)	73,909	64.6
Lewis Emerich (R)	39,686	34.7
9 Jack Brooks (D)	89,113	66.2
Randolph Reed (R)	45,462	33.8
10 J. J. Pickle (D)	130,973	91.2
Melissa Singler (SOC WORK)	12,682	8.8
11 W. R. Poage (D)	88,861	100.0
12 Jim Wright (D)	84,356	100.0
13 Bob Price (R)	87,084	54.8
Graham Purcell (D)	71,730	45.2
14 John Young (D)	89,725	100.0
15 Eligio de la Garza (D)	73,994	100.0
16 Richard C. White (D)	81,347	100.0
17 Omar Burleson (D)	95,122	100.0
18 Barbara C. Jordan (D)	85,672	80.6
Paul Merritt (R)	19,355	18.2
19 George Mahon (D)	97,084	100.0
20 Henry B. Gonzalez (D)	81,443	96.9
21 O. C. Fisher (D)	91,180	56.8
Douglas S. Harlan (R)	69,374	43.2
22 Bob Casey (D)	101,786	70.2
James Griffin (R)	42,094	29.0
23 Abraham Kazen (D)	72,799	100.0
24 Dale Milford (D)	91,054	65.1
Courtney Roberts (R)	48,853	34.9

UTAH

Candidates	Votes	%
1 K. Gunn McKay (D)	127,027	55.4
Robert K. Wolthuis (R)	96,296	42.0
2 Wayne Owens (D)	132,832	54.5
Sherman P. Lloyd (R)	107,185	44.0

VERMONT

	Candidates	Votes	%
AL	Richard W. Mallary (R)	120,924	65.0
	William H. Meyer (D)	65,062	35.0

Special Election

	Candidates	Votes	%
AL	Richard W. Mallary (R)	39,903#	55.8
	J. William O'Brien (D)	26,889#	37.6

VIRGINIA

	Candidates	Votes	%
1	Thomas N. Downing (D)	100,901	78.1
	Kenneth D. Wells (R)	28,310	21.9
2	G. William Whitehurst (R)	79,672	73.4
	L. Charles Burlage (D)	28,803	26.6
3	David E. Satterfield III (D)	102,523	99.9
4	Robert W. Daniel Jr. (R)	57,520	47.1
	Robert E. Gibson (D)	45,776	37.5
	Robert R. Hardy (I)	8,668	7.1
	William E. Ward	6,172	5.1
5	W. C. (Dan) Daniel (D)	83,772	99.9
6	M. Caldwell Butler (R)	75,189	54.6
	Willis N. Anderson (D)	53,928	39.2
	Roy R. White (I)	8,531	6.2
7	J. Kenneth Robinson (R)	89,120	66.2
	Murat Wills Williams (D)	45,513	33.8
8	Stanford E. Parris (R)	60,446	44.4
	Robert F. Horan (D)	51,444	37.8
	William R. Durland (I)	18,654	13.7
9	William C. Wampler (R)	98,178	71.9
	Zane Dale Christian (D)	36,000	26.4

	Candidates	Votes	%
10	Joel T. Broyhill (R)	101,138	56.3
	Harold O. Miller (D)	78,638	43.7

Special Election

	Candidates	Votes	%
6	M. Caldwell Butler (R)	61,898	51.8
	Willis M. Anderson (D)	47,588	39.8
	Roy R. White (I)	10,098	8.4

WASHINGTON

	Candidates	Votes	%
1	Joel Pritchard (R)	107,581	50.9
	John Hempelmann (D)	104,959	49.7
2	Lloyd Meeds (D)	114,900	60.5
	Bill Reams (R)	75,181	39.6
3	Julia Butler Hansen (D)	122,933	66.3
	R. C. (Skip) McConkey (R)	62,564	33.7
4	Mike McCormack (D)	97,593	52.1
	Stewart Bledsoe (R)	89,812	47.9
5	Thomas Foley (D)	150,580	81.3
	Clarice L. R. Privette (R)	34,742	18.8
6	Floyd V. Hicks (D)	126,349	72.1
	Thomas C. Lowry (R)	48,914	27.9
7	Brock Adams (D)	140,307	85.4
	J. J. (Tiny) Freeman (R)	19,889	12.1

WEST VIRGINIA

	Candidates	Votes	%
1	Robert H. Mollohan (D)	130,062	69.4
	George E. Kapnicky (R)	57,724	30.8
2	Harley O. Staggers (D)	128,286	70.0
	David Dix (R)	54,949	30.0

	Candidates	Votes	%
3	John M. Slack (D)	118,346	63.7
	T. David Higgins (R)	67,441	36.3
4	Ken Hechler (D)	100,600	61.0
	Joe Neal (R)	64,242	39.0

WISCONSIN

	Candidates	Votes	%
1	Les Aspin (D)	122,973	64.4
	Merrill E. Stalbaum (R)	66,665	34.9
2	Robert W. Kastenmeier (D)	148,136	68.2
	J. Michael Kelly (R)	68,167	31.4
3	Vernon W. Thomson (R)	112,905	54.7
	Walter Thoresen (D)	91,953	44.6
4	Clement J. Zablocki (D)	149,078	75.7
	Phillip D. Mrozinski (R)	45,003	22.8
5	Henry S. Reuss (D)	127,273	77.3
	Frederick Van Hecke (R)	33,627	20.4
6	William A. Steiger (R)	130,701	65.8
	James A Adams (D)	63,643	32.0
7	David R. Obey (D)	135,385	62.8
	Alvin E. O'Konski (R)	80,207	37.2
8	Harold V. Froehlich (R)	101,634	50.4
	Robert J. Cornell (D)	97,795	48.5
9	Glenn R. Davis (R)	128,230	61.4
	Ralph A. Fine (D)	76,585	36.7

WYOMING

	Candidates	Votes	%
AL	Teno Roncalio (D)	75,632	51.7
	Bill Kidd (R)	70,667	48.3

1. Pennsylvania lost two House seats between the 1970 and 1972 general elections due to redistricting. The special election in the 27th district, held April 25, 1972, was for a partial term expiring Jan. 3, 1973, after which the district ceased to exist.

1973 House Elections

ALASKA

Special Election

	Candidates	Vote	%
AL	Don Young (R)	35,044	51.4
	Emil Notti (D)	33,123	48.6

ILLINOIS

Special Election

	Candidates	Votes	%
7	Cardiss Collins (D)	33,875#	92.5

LOUISIANA

Special Election

	Candidates	Votes	%
2	Corinne (Lindy) Boggs (D)	42,583	80.4
	Robert E. Lee (R)	10,352	19.6

MARYLAND

Special Election

	Candidates	Votes	%
1	Robert E. Bauman (R)	27,248	51.2
	Frederick C. Malkus (D)	26,001	48.8

1974 House Elections

ALABAMA

	Candidates	Votes	%
1	Jack Edwards (R)	60,710	59.5
	Augusta E. Wilson (D)	37,718	37.0
2	William L. Dickinson (R)	54,089	66.1
	Clair Chisler (D)	27,729	33.9
3	Bill Nichols (D)	63,582	95.9
4	Tom Bevill (D)	77,925	99.8
5	Robert E. Jones (D)	56,375	100.0
6	John Buchanan (R)	54,505	56.6
	Nina Miglionico (D)	39,444	41.0
7	Walter Flowers (D)	73,203	91.0
	Frank P. Walls (C)	5,175	6.4

ALASKA

		Votes	%
AL	Donald E. Young (R)	51,641	53.8
	William L. Hensley (D)	44,280	46.2

ARIZONA[1]

		Votes	%
1	John J. Rhodes (R)	63,847	51.1
	Patricia M. Fullinwider (D)	52,897	42.3
	J. M. Sanders (LLJ)	8,199	6.6
2	Morris K. Udall (D)	84,491	62.0
	Keith Dolgaard (R)	51,886	38.0
3	Sam Steiger (R)	71,497	51.1
	Pat Bosch (D)	68,424	48.9
4	John B. Conlan (R)	78,887	55.3
	Byron T. Brown (D)	63,677	44.7

ARKANSAS

		Votes	%
1	Bill Alexander (D)	104,247	90.6
	James Lawrence Dauer (R)	10,821	9.4
2	Wilbur D. Mills (D)	80,296	58.9
	Judy Petty (R)	56,038	41.1
3	John Paul Hammerschmidt (R)	89,324	51.8
	Bill Clinton (D)	83,030	48.2
4	Ray Thornton (D)		100.0

CALIFORNIA

		Votes	%
1	Harold T. Johnson (D)	138,082	85.8
	Dorothy D. Paradis (AIP)	22,881	14.2
2	Don H. Clausen (R)	95,929	53.0
	Oscar H. Klee (D)	77,232	42.7
3	John E. Moss (D)	122,134	72.3
	Ivaldo Lenci (R)	46,712	27.7
4	Robert L. Leggett (D)	101,152	100.0
5	John L. Burton (D)	88,909	59.6
	Thomas Caylor (R)	56,274	37.7
6	Phillip Burton (D)	85,712	71.3
	Tom Spinosa (R)	26,260	21.8
7	George Miller (D)	83,054	55.6
	Gary Fernandez (R)	66,325	44.4
8	Ronald V. Dellums (D)	95,041	56.6
	Jack Redden (R)	66,386	39.6
9	Fortney H. (Pete) Stark Jr. (D)	92,436	70.6
	Edson Adams (R)	38,521	29.4
10	Don Edwards (D)	87,978	77.0
	John M. Enright (R)	26,288	23.0
11	Leo J. Ryan (D)	106,429	75.8
	Brainard G. Merdinger (R)	29,861	21.3
12	Paul N. McCloskey Jr. (R)	103,692	69.1
	Gary G. Gillmor (D)	46,383	30.9
13	Norman Y. Mineta (D)	78,858	52.6
	George W. Milias (R)	63,573	42.4
14	John J. McFall (D)	102,180	70.9
	Charles M. Gibson (R)	34,775	24.1
15	B. F. Sisk (D)	80,897	72.0
	Carol O. Harner (R)	31,439	28.0
16	Burt L. Talcott (R)	76,356	49.2
	Julian Camacho (D)	74,168	47.8
17	John Krebs (D)	66,675	51.9
	Robert B. Mathias (R)	61,812	48.1

	Candidates	Votes	%
18	William M. Ketchum (R)	67,650	52.7
	George A. Seielstad (D)	60,733	47.3
19	Robert J. Lagomarsino (R)	84,249	56.3
	James D. Loebl (D)	65,469	43.7
20	Barry M. Goldwater Jr. (R)	98,410	61.2
	Arline Mathews (D)	62,326	38.8
21	James C. Corman (D)	88,915	73.5
	Mel Nadell (R)	32,038	26.5
22	Carlos J. Moorhead (R)	81,641	55.8
	Richard Hallin (D)	64,691	44.2
23	Thomas M. Rees (D)	122,076	71.4
	Jack E. Roberts (R)	48,826	28.6
24	Henry A. Waxman (D)	87,521	64.0
	Elliott Stone Graham (R)	45,128	33.0
25	Edward R. Roybal (D)	45,059	100.0
26	John H. Rousselot (R)	82,735	58.9
	Paul A. Conforti (D)	57,685	41.1
27	Alphonzo Bell (R)	102,663	63.9
	John Delessio (D)	52,236	32.5
28	Yvonne Burke (D)	88,655	80.1
	Tom Neddy (R)	21,957	19.9
29	Augustus F. Hawkins (D)	47,204	100.0
30	George E. Danielson (D)	67,328	74.2
	John J. Perez (D)	23,383	25.8
31	Charles H. Wilson (D)	61,322	70.4
	Norman A. Hodges (R)	23,359	26.8
32	Glenn M. Anderson (D)	84,428	87.7
	Virgil V. Badalich (AIP)	8,874	9.2
33	Del Clawson (R)	72,471	53.4
	Robert E. White (D)	58,492	43.1
34	Mark W. Hannaford (D)	81,151	49.8
	Bill Bond (R)	75,426	46.3
35	Jim Lloyd (D)	61,903	50.3
	Victor V. Veysey (R)	61,168	49.7
36	George E. Brown Jr. (D)	69,766	62.6
	Jim Osgood (R)	35,938	32.3
	William E. Pasley (AIP)	5,711	5.1
37	Jerry L. Pettis (R)	89,849	63.2
	Bobby Ray Vincent (D)	46,783	32.9
38	Jerry M. Patterson (D)	68,335	54.0
	David Rehmann (R)	52,207	41.3
39	Charles E. Wiggins (R)	89,220	55.3
	William E. Farris (D)	65,170	40.4
40	Andrew J. Hinshaw (R)	116,449	63.4
	Roderick J. Wilson (D)	56,850	30.9
	Grayson L. Watkins (AIP)	10,498	5.7
41	Bob Wilson (R)	94,709	54.5
	Colleen M. O'Connor (D)	74,823	43.0
42	Lionel Van Deerlin (D)	70,579	69.9
	Wes Marden (R)	30,435	30.1
43	Clair W. Burgener (R)	115,275	60.4
	Bill Bandes (D)	75,629	39.6

Special Elections[2]

		Votes	%
6	John L. Burton (D)	73,114	50.0
	Thomas Caylor (R)	30,908	21.2
	Terence McGuire (D)	12,777	8.7
	Jean Wall (R)	8,501	5.8
	Sean McCarthy (R)	7,783	5.3
13	Robert J. Lagomarsino (R)	52,140	53.6
	James D. Loebl (D)	18,223	18.8
	James A. Browning (D)	7,536	7.8
	Roger I. Ikola (D)	6,155	6.3
	E.T. Jolicoeur (D)	5,786	6.0

COLORADO

		Votes	%
1	Patricia Schroeder (D)	94,583	58.5
	Frank K. Southworth (R)	66,046	40.8
2	Timothy W. Wirth (D)	93,728	51.9
	Donald G. Brotzman (R)	86,720	48.0
3	Frank E. Evans (D)	91,783	67.9
	E. Keith Records (R)	43,298	32.1
4	James P. Johnson (R)	82,982	52.0
	John S. Carroll (D)	76,452	48.0

	Candidates	Votes	%
5	William L. Armstrong (R)	85,326	57.7
	Ben Galloway (D)	56,888	38.5

CONNECTICUT

		Votes	%
1	William R. Cotter (D)	117,038	62.7
	F. Mac Buckley (R)	67,080	35.9
2	Christopher J. Dodd (D)	104,436	59.0
	Samuel B. Hellier (R)	69,380	39.2
3	Robert N. Giaimo (D)	114,316	65.1
	James F. Altham Jr. (R)	55,177	31.4
4	Stewart B. McKinney (R)	83,630	53.2
	James G. Kellis (D)	71,047	45.2
5	Ronald A. Sarasin (R)	94,998	50.4
	William R. Ratchford (D)	90,407	48.0
6	Anthony J. Moffett (D)	122,785	63.4
	Patsy J. Piscopo (R)	69,942	36.1

DELAWARE

		Votes	%
AL	Pierre S. duPont IV (R)	93,826	58.5
	James R. Soles (D)	63,490	39.6

FLORIDA

		Votes	%
1	Robert L. F. Sikes (D)		100.0
2	Don Fuqua (D)		100.0
3	Charles E. Bennett (D)		100.0
4	Bill Chappell Jr. (D)	74,720	68.2
	Warren A. Hauser (R)	34,867	31.8
5	Richard Kelly (R)	74,954	52.8
	JoAnn Saunders (D)	63,610	44.8
6	C. W. Bill Young (R)	109,302	75.8
	Herbert M. Monrose (D)	34,886	24.2
7	Sam Gibbons (D)		100.0
8	James A. Haley (D)	63,283	56.7
	Joe Z. Lovingood (R)	48,240	43.3
9	Louis Frey Jr. (R)	86,226	76.7
	William D. Rowland (D)	26,255	23.3
10	L. A. (Skip) Befalis (R)	117,368	73.7
	Evelyn Tucker (D)	41,925	26.3
11	Paul G. Rogers (D)		100.0
12	J. Herbert Burke (R)	61,191	51.0
	Charles Friedman (D)	58,899	49.0
13	William Lehman (D)		100.0
14	Claude Pepper (D)	45,479	69.1
	Michael A. Carricarte (R)	20,383	30.9
15	Dante B. Fascell (D)	68,064	70.5
	S. Peter Capua (R)	28,444	29.5

GEORGIA

		Votes	%
1	Ronald B. (Bo) Ginn (D)	64,958	86.1
	Bill Gowan (R)	10,485	13.9
2	Dawson Mathis (D)	59,514	100.0
3	Jack Brinkley (D)	67,438	87.7
	Carl Savage (R)	9,453	12.3
4	Elliott H. Levitas (D)	61,211	55.1
	Ben B. Blackburn (R)	49,922	44.9
5	Andrew Young (D)	69,221	71.6
	Wyman C. Lowe (R)	27,397	28.3
6	John J. Flynt Jr. (D)	49,082	51.5
	Newt Gingrich (R)	46,308	48.5
7	Lawrence P. McDonald (D)	47,993	50.3
	Quincy Collins (R)	47,450	49.7
8	W. S. (Bill) Stuckey Jr. (D)	59,182	100.0
9	Phil M. Landrum (D)	64,096	74.8
	Ronald D. Reeves (R)	21,540	25.2
10	Robert G. Stephens Jr. (D)	45,843	68.4
	Gary Pleger (R)	21,214	31.6

HAWAII

		Votes	%
1	Spark M. Matsunaga (D)	71,552	59.3
	William S. Paul (R)	49,065	40.7

Candidates	Votes	%
2 Patsy T. Mink (D)	86,916	62.6
Carla W. Coray (R)	51,894	37.4

IDAHO

Candidates	Votes	%
1 Steven D. Symms (R)	75,414	58.3
J. Ray Cox (D)	54,001	41.7
2 George V. Hansen (R)	67,274	55.7
Max Hanson (D)	53,599	44.3

ILLINOIS

Candidates	Votes	%
1 Ralph H. Metcalfe (D)	75,206	93.7
Oscar H. Haynes (R)	4,399	5.5
2 Morgan F. Murphy (D)	65,812	87.5
James Ginderske (R)	9,386	12.5
3 Martin A. Russo (D)	65,336	52.6
Robert P. Hanrahan (R)	58,891	47.4
4 Edward J. Derwinski (R)	68,428	59.2
Ronald A. Rodger (D)	47,096	40.8
5 John C. Kluczynski (D)	93,069	86.0
William H. G. Toms (R)	15,108	14.0
6 Henry J. Hyde (R)	66,027	53.4
Edward V. Hanrahan (D)	57,654	46.6
7 Cardiss Collins (D)	63,962	87.9
Donald L. Metzger (R)	8,800	12.1
8 Dan Rostenkowski (D)	75,011	86.5
Salvatore E. Oddo (R)	11,664	13.5
9 Sidney R. Yates (D)	93,864	100.0
10 Abner J. Mikva (D)	83,457	50.9
Samuel H. Young (R)	80,597	49.1
11 Frank Annunzio (D)	102,541	72.4
Mitchell G. Zadrozny (R)	39,182	27.6
12 Philip M. Crane (R)	70,731	61.1
Betty C. Spence (D)	45,049	38.9
13 Robert McClory (R)	51,405	54.5
Stanley W. Beetham (D)	42,903	45.5
14 John N. Erlenborn (R)	77,718	66.6
Robert H. Renshaw (D)	38,981	33.4
15 Tim L. Hall (D)	61,912	52.0
Clifford D. Carlson (R)	54,278	45.6
16 John B. Anderson (R)	65,175	55.5
Marshall Hungness (R)	33,724	28.7
W. John Schade Jr. (IND)	18,580	15.8
17 George M. O'Brien (R)	59,984	51.5
John J. Houlihan (D)	56,541	48.5
18 Robert H. Michel (R)	71,681	54.8
Stephen L. Nordvall (D)	59,225	45.2
19 Tom Railsback (R)	84,049	65.3
Jim Gende (D)	44,677	34.7
20 Paul Findley (R)	84,426	54.8
Peter F. Mack (D)	69,551	45.2
21 Edward R. Madigan (R)	78,640	65.8
Richard N. Small (D)	40,896	34.2
22 George E. Shipley (D)	97,921	59.8
William A. Young (R)	65,731	40.2
23 Melvin Price (D)	78,347	80.5
Scott R. Randolph (R)	18,987	19.5
24 Paul Simon (D)	108,417	59.6
Val Oshel (R)	73,634	40.4

INDIANA

Candidates	Votes	%
1 Ray J. Madden (D)	71,759	68.6
Joseph D. Harkin (R)	32,793	31.4
2 Floyd J. Fithian (D)	101,856	61.1
Earl F. Landgrebe (R)	64,950	38.9
3 John Brademas (D)	89,306	64.1
Virginia R. Black (R)	50,116	35.9
4 J. Edward Roush (D)	83,604	51.9
Walter P. Helmke (R)	75,031	46.5
5 Elwood Hillis (R)	95,331	56.6
William T. Sebree (D)	73,239	43.4
6 David W. Evans (D)	78,414	52.4
William G. Bray (R)	71,134	47.6
7 John T. Myers (R)	100,128	57.1
Elden C. Tipton (D)	73,802	42.1
8 Philip H. Hayes (D)	100,121	53.4
Roger H. Zion (R)	87,296	46.6
9 Lee H. Hamilton (D)	117,648	71.1

Candidates	Votes	%
Delson Cox Jr. (R)	47,881	28.9
10 Philip R. Sharp (D)	85,418	54.4
David W. Dennis (R)	71,701	45.6
11 Andrew Jacobs Jr. (D)	81,508	52.5
William H. Hudnut III (R)	73,793	47.5

IOWA

Candidates	Votes	%
1 Edward Mezvinsky (D)	75,687	54.4
James A. S. Leach (R)	63,540	45.6
2 Michael T. Blouin (D)	73,416	51.1
Tom Riley (R)	69,088	48.1
3 Charles E. Grassley (R)	77,468	50.8
Stephen J. Rapp (D)	74,895	49.2
4 Neal Smith (D)	96,755	63.9
Chuck Dick (R)	53,756	35.5
5 Tom Harkin (D)	81,186	51.1
William J. Scherle (R)	77,683	48.9
6 Berkley Bedell (D)	86,315	54.6
Wiley Mayne (R)	71,695	45.4

KANSAS

Candidates	Votes	%
1 Keith G. Sebelius (R)	101,565	58.4
Donald C. Smith (D)	57,326	33.0
Thelma Morgan (A)	13,009	7.5
2 Martha E. Keys (D)	84,864	55.0
John C. Peterson (R)	67,650	43.9
3 Larry Winn Jr. (R)	89,694	62.9
Samuel J. Wells (D)	49,976	35.0
4 Garner E. Shriver (R)	70,401	48.8
Bert Chaney (D)	61,210	42.5
John S. Stevens (A)	12,520	8.7
5 Joe Skubitz (R)	88,646	55.2
Franklin D. Gaines (D)	72,024	44.8

KENTUCKY

Candidates	Votes	%
1 Carroll Hubbard Jr. (D)	70,723	78.2
Charles T. Banken Jr. (R)	16,937	18.7
2 William H. Natcher (D)	56,502	73.0
Art Eddleman (R)	18,312	23.7
3 Romano L. Mazzoli (D)	75,571	69.7
Vincent N. Barclay (R)	28,813	26.6
4 M. G. (Gene) Snyder (R)	63,845	51.7
Kyle Hubbard (D)	59,539	48.3
5 Tim Lee Carter (R)	66,709	68.2
Lyle L. Willis (D)	28,706	29.3
6 John B. Breckinridge (D)	63,010	72.1
Thomas F. Rogers III (R)	21,039	24.1
7 Carl D. Perkins (D)	71,221	75.6
Granville Thomas (R)	22,982	24.4

LOUISIANA[3]

Candidates	Votes	%
1 F. Edward Hebert (D)	48,452	100.0
2 Corinne C. Boggs (D)	58,802	81.8
Diane Morphos (R)	9,632	14.6
3 David C. Treen (R)	55,574	58.5
Charles Grisbaum Jr. (D)	39,412	41.5
4 Joe D. Waggonner Jr. (D)	47,371	100.0
5 Otto E. Passman (D)	43,068	100.0
6 W. Henson Moore (R)		
Jeff LaCaze (D)		
7 John B. Breaux (D)	59,406	89.3
Jeremy J. Millett (IND)	7,131	10.7
8 Gillis W. Long (D)	41,704	100.0

MAINE[4]

Candidates	Votes	%
1 David F. Emery (R)	94,203	50.2
Peter N. Kyros (D)	93,524	49.8
2 William S. Cohen (R)	118,154	71.4
Markham L. Gartley (D)	47,399	28.6

MARYLAND

Candidates	Votes	%
1 Robert E. Bauman (R)	59,570	53.0
Thomas J. Hatem (D)	52,853	47.0
2 Clarence D. Long (D)	103,222	77.1

Candidates	Votes	%
John M. Seney (R)	30,639	22.9
3 Paul S. Sarbanes (D)	93,218	83.8
William H. Mathews (R)	17,967	16.2
4 Marjorie S. Holt (R)	61,208	58.1
Fred L. Wineland (D)	44,059	41.9
5 Gladys N. Spellman (D)	45,211	52.6
John B. Burcham Jr. (R)	40,805	47.4
6 Goodloe E. Byron (D)	90,882	73.7
Elton R. Wampler (R)	32,416	26.3
7 Parren J. Mitchell (D)	43,252	100.0
8 Gilbert Gude (R)	104,675	65.9
Sidney Kramer (D)	54,112	34.1

MASSACHUSETTS

Candidates	Votes	%
1 Silvio O. Conte (R)	107,285	71.1
Thomas R. Manning (D)	43,524	28.9
2 Edward P. Boland (D)	105,763	100.0
3 Joseph D. Early (D)	78,244	49.5
David J. Lionett (R)	60,717	38.4
Douglas J. Rowe (IND)	19,018	12.0
4 Robert F. Drinan (D)	77,286	50.8
Jon Rotenberg (IND)	52,785	34.7
Alvin Mandell (R)	21,922	14.4
5 Paul E. Tsongas (D)	99,518	60.6
Paul W. Cronin (R)	64,596	39.4
6 Michael J. Harrington (D)	119,278	100.0
7 Torbert H. Macdonald (D)	122,165	79.8
James J. Murphy (IND)	30,959	20.2
8 Thomas P. O'Neill Jr. (D)	107,042	87.9
James Kiggin (USLP)	8,363	6.9
Laura Ross (COM)	6,421	5.3
9 John Joseph Moakley (D)	94,804	89.3
L. R. Sherman (USLP)	11,344	10.7
10 Margaret M. Heckler (R)	99,993	64.2
Barry F. Monahan (D)	55,871	35.8
11 James A. Burke (D)	125,978	100.0
12 Gerry E. Studds (D)	138,779	74.8
J. Alan MacKay (R)	46,787	25.2

MICHIGAN

Candidates	Votes	%
1 John Conyers Jr. (D)	97,620	90.7
Walter F. Girardot (R)	9,358	8.7
2 Marvin L. Esch (R)	72,245	52.3
John S. Reuther (D)	62,755	45.4
3 Garry Brown (R)	70,157	51.2
Paul H. Todd Jr. (D)	65,212	47.6
4 Edward Hutchinson (R)	64,731	53.1
Richard E. Daugherty (D)	55,469	45.5
5 Richard F. Vander Veen (D)	80,778	52.6
Paul G. Goebel Jr. (R)	66,659	43.4
6 Bob Carr (D)	73,956	49.3
Clifford W. Taylor (R)	73,309	48.9
7 Donald W. Riegle Jr. (D)	81,014	64.7
Robert E. Eastman (R)	41,603	33.2
8 Bob Traxler (D)	77,795	54.8
James M. Sparling Jr. (R)	61,578	43.4
9 Guy A. Vander Jagt (R)	87,551	56.6
Norman C. Halbower (D)	65,235	42.1
10 Elford A. Cederberg (R)	78,897	53.7
Samuel D. Marble (D)	67,467	45.9
11 Philip E. Ruppe (R)	83,293	50.9
Francis D. Brouillette (D)	79,793	48.8
12 James G. O'Hara (D)	89,822	72.2
Eugene J. Tyza (R)	34,293	27.6
13 Charles C. Diggs Jr. (D)	63,246	87.4
George E. McCall (R)	8,036	11.1
14 Lucien N. Nedzi (D)	93,973	71.2
Herbert J. Steiger (R)	35,723	27.1
15 William D. Ford (D)	86,601	78.1
Jack A. Underwood (R)	23,028	20.8
16 John D. Dingell (D)	95,834	77.7
Wallace D. English (R)	25,248	20.5
17 William M. Brodhead (D)	94,242	69.5
Kenneth C. Gallagher (R)	39,856	29.4
18 James J. Blanchard (D)	83,523	58.7
Robert J. Huber (R)	57,133	40.2
19 William S. Broomfield (R)	86,846	62.9
George F. Montgomery (D)	50,924	36.9

Special Elections

	Candidates	Votes	%
5	Richard F. Vander Veen (D)	53,083	50.9
	Robert Vander Laan (R)	46,160	44.3
8	Bob Traxler (D)	59,993	51.5
	James M. Sparling Jr. (R)	56,548	48.5

MINNESOTA

1	Albert H. Quie (R)	95,138	62.6
	Uric Scott (D)	56,868	37.4
2	Tom Hagedorn (R)	88,071	53.1
	Steve Babcock (D)	77,780	46.9
3	Bill Frenzel (R)	83,325	60.4
	Bob Riggs (D)	54,630	39.6
4	Joseph E. Karth (D)	95,437	76.0
	Joseph A. Rheinberger (R)	30,083	24.0
5	Donald M. Fraser (D)	90,012	73.8
	Phil Ratte (R)	30,146	24.7
6	Richard Nolan (D)	96,465	55.4
	Jon Grunseth (R)	77,797	44.6
7	Bob Bergland (D)	129,207	75.0
	Dan Reber (R)	43,045	25.0
8	James L. Oberstar (D)	104,740	62.0
	Jerome Arnold (R)	44,298	26.2
	William R. Ojala (EJ)	16,932	10.0

MISSISSIPPI

1	Jamie L. Whitten (D)	39,158	88.2
	Jack Benney (IND)	5,250	11.8
2	David R. Bowen (D)	37,909	66.1
	Ben F. Hilbun Jr. (R)	15,876	27.7
	H. B. Wells (IND)	3,573	6.2
3	G. V. (Sonny) Montgomery (D)	43,020	100.0
4	Thad Cochran (R)	62,634	70.2
	Kenneth L. Dean (D)	25,699	28.8
5	Trent Lott (R)	52,489	73.0
	Walter W. Murphey (D)	10,333	14.4
	Claudia Mertz (IND)	6,404	8.9

MISSOURI

1	William (Bill) Clay (D)	61,933	68.3
	Arthur O. Martin (R)	28,707	31.7
2	James W. Symington (D)	85,977	61.0
	Howard C. Ohlendorf (R)	55,026	39.0
3	Leonor K. Sullivan (D)	96,201	74.3
	Jo Ann P. Raisch (R)	31,489	24.3
4	William J. Randall (D)	82,447	67.9
	Claude Patterson (R)	39,055	32.1
5	Richard Bolling (D)	57,081	69.1
	John J. McDonough (R)	24,669	29.9
6	Jerry Litton (D)	101,609	78.9
	Grover H. Speers (R)	27,147	21.1
7	Gene Taylor (R)	79,787	52.3
	Richard L. Franks (D)	72,653	47.7
8	Richard H. Ichord (D)	86,595	69.9
	James A. Noland Jr. (R)	37,369	30.1
9	William L. Hungate (D)	87,546	66.4
	Milton Bischof Jr. (R)	44,318	33.6
10	Bill D. Burlison (D)	77,677	72.8
	Truman Farrow (R)	29,050	27.2

MONTANA

1	Max S. Baucus (D)	74,304	54.8
	Richard G. Shoup (R)	61,309	45.2
2	John Melcher (D)	74,680	63.0
	John K. McDonald (R)	43,853	37.0

NEBRASKA

1	Charles Thone (R)	82,353	53.3
	Hess Dyas (D)	72,099	46.7
2	John Y. McCollister (R)	72,731	55.2
	Daniel C. Lynch (D)	59,142	44.8
3	Virginia Smith (R)	80,992	50.2
	Wayne W. Ziebarth (D)	80,255	49.8

NEVADA

	Candidates	Votes	%
AL	James Santini (D)	93,665	55.8
	David Towell (R)	61,182	36.4
	Joel F. Hansen (IA)	13,119	7.8

NEW HAMPSHIRE

1	Norman E. D'Amours (D)	58,388	52.1
	David A. Banks (R)	53,610	47.9
2	James C. Cleveland (R)	69,068	64.2
	Helen L. Bliss (D)	38,463	35.8

NEW JERSEY

1	James J. Florio (D)	80,768	57.5
	John E. Hunt (R)	54,069	38.5
2	William J. Hughes (D)	109,763	57.3
	Charles W. Sandman Jr. (R)	79,064	41.3
3	James J. Howard (D)	105,979	68.9
	Kenneth W. Clark (R)	45,932	29.8
4	Frank Thompson Jr. (D)	82,195	66.8
	Henry J. Keller (R)	40,797	33.2
5	Millicent Fenwick (R)	81,498	53.4
	Frederick M. Bohen (D)	66,380	43.5
6	Edwin B. Forsythe (R)	81,190	52.5
	Charles B. Yates (D)	70,353	45.5
7	Andrew Maguire (D)	79,808	49.7
	William B. Widnall (R)	71,377	44.4
	Milton Gralla (IND)	9,520	5.9
8	Robert A. Roe (D)	83,724	73.9
	Herman Schmidt (R)	27,839	24.6
9	Henry Helstoski (D)	99,592	64.5
	Harold A. Pareti (R)	50,859	32.9
10	Peter W. Rodino Jr. (D)	53,094	81.0
	John R. Taliaferro (R)	9,936	15.2
11	Joseph G. Minish (D)	98,957	69.2
	William B. Grant (R)	42,036	29.4
12	Matthew J. Rinaldo (R)	92,829	65.0
	Adam K. Levin (D)	46,246	32.4
13	Helen S. Meyner (D)	86,043	57.3
	Joseph J. Maraziti (R)	64,166	42.7
14	Dominick V. Daniels (D)	85,438	79.9
	Claire J. Sheridan (R)	17,231	16.1
15	Edward J. Patten (D)	92,593	71.0
	E. J. Hammesfahr (R)	35,875	27.5

NEW MEXICO

1	Manuel Lujan Jr. (R)	106,268	58.6
	Robert A. Mondragon (D)	71,968	39.7
2	Harold Runnels (D)	90,127	66.7
	Donald W. Trubey (R)	43,045	31.9

NEW YORK

1	Otis G. Pike (D-L)	101,130	65.0
	Donald R. Sallah (R)	44,513	28.6
	Seth C. Morgan (C)	10,038	6.4
2	Thomas J. Downey (D)	58,289	48.8
	James R. Grover Jr. (R)	53,344	44.7
	Neil Greene (C)	7,818	6.5
3	Jerome A. Ambro Jr. (D)	76,383	51.8
	Angelo D. Roncalio (R-C)	67,986	46.1
4	Norman F. Lent (R-C)	85,382	53.6
	Franklin Ornstein (D-L)	73,822	46.4
5	John W. Wydler (R-C)	91,677	54.2
	Allard K. Lowenstein (D-L)	77,356	45.8
6	Lester L. Wolff (D-L)	101,237	66.7
	Edythe Layne (R-C)	50,528	33.3
7	Joseph P. Addabbo (D-R-L)	83,972	100.0
8	Benjamin S. Rosenthal (D-L)	90,200	79.0
	Albert Lemishow (R-C)	23,980	21.0
9	James J. Delaney (D-R-C)	92,231	93.0
	Theodore E. Garrison (L)	6,924	7.0
10	Mario Biaggi (D-R)	75,375	82.4
	Francis L. McHugh (C)	10,250	11.2
	John P. Hagan (L)	5,797	6.3
11	James H. Scheuer (D)	62,388	72.2
	E. G. Desborough (R)	12,297	14.2

	Candidates	Votes	%
	Christopher Acer (C)	7,181	8.3
	Tibby Blum (L)	4,485	5.2
12	Shirley Chisholm (D-L)	26,468	80.2
	Francis J. Voyticky (R)	4,577	13.9
13	Stephen J. Solarz (D-L)	91,008	81.8
	Jack N. Dobosh (R-C)	20,229	18.2
14	Frederick W. Richmond (D)	33,195	71.3
	Michael Carbajal Jr. (R)	5,360	11.5
	Donald H. Elliott (L)	6,186	13.3
15	Leo C. Zeferetti (D-C)	53,733	58.4
	Austen D. Canade (R)	34,814	37.9
16	Elizabeth Holtzman (D-L)	74,010	78.9
	Joseph L. Gentili (R-C)	19,806	21.1
17	John M. Murphy (D)	63,805	57.7
	Frank J. Biondolillo (R)	28,269	25.6
	Jerome Kretchmer (L)	10,622	9.6
	Michael Ajello (C)	7,808	7.1
18	Edward I. Koch (D-L)	91,985	76.7
	John Boogaerts Jr. (R)	22,560	18.8
19	Charles B. Rangel (D-R-L)	63,146	96.9
20	Bella S. Abzug (D-L)	76,074	78.7
	Stephen Posner (R)	15,053	15.6
21	Herman Badillo (D-L)	28,025	96.7
22	Jonathan B. Bingham (D-L)	77,157	85.1
	Robert Black (R)	8,142	9.0
	John DiGiovanni (C)	5,333	5.9
23	Peter A. Peyser (R-C)	80,361	57.6
	W. S. Greenawalt (D-L)	59,108	42.4
24	Richard L. Ottinger (D)	82,542	57.8
	Charles J. Stephens (R-C)	60,180	42.2
25	Hamilton Fish Jr. (R-C)	103,799	65.3
	Nicholas B. Angell (D)	53,357	33.6
26	Benjamin A. Gilman (R)	81,562	54.0
	John G. Dow (D-L)	58,161	38.5
	Thomas Moore (C)	11,345	7.5
27	Matthew F. McHugh (D-L)	83,562	52.8
	Alfred J. Libous (R)	68,273	43.1
28	Samuel S. Stratton (D-L)	156,439	80.6
	Wayne E. Wagner (R)	33,493	17.3
29	Edward W. Pattison (D-L)	100,324	54.5
	Carleton J. King (R-C)	83,768	45.5
30	Robert C. McEwen (R-C)	78,117	55.0
	Roger W. Tubby (D-L)	63,893	45.0
31	Donald J. Mitchell (R-C)	94,319	59.6
	Donald J. Reile (D)	59,639	37.7
32	James M. Hanley (D)	88,660	59.1
	William E. Bush (R-C)	61,379	40.9
33	William F. Walsh (R)	97,380	65.3
	Robert H. Bockman (D)	45,043	30.2
34	Frank Horton (R)	105,585	67.5
	Irene Gossin (D)	45,408	29.0
35	Barber B. Conable Jr. (R)	90,269	56.8
	Margaret Costanza (D)	63,012	39.6
36	John J. LaFalce (D-L)	90,498	59.6
	Russell A. Rourke (R-C)	61,442	40.4
37	Henry J. Nowak (D-L)	84,064	75.0
	Joseph R. Bala (R-C)	27,531	24.6
38	Jack F. Kemp (R-C)	126,687	72.1
	Barbara C. Wicks (D-L)	48,929	27.9
39	James F. Hastings (R)	87,321	60.2
	W. L. Parment (D-L)	53,866	37.1

NORTH CAROLINA

1	Walter B. Jones (D)	55,323	77.5
	Harry McMullan (R)	16,097	22.5
2	L. H. Fountain (D)	52,786	100.0
3	David N. Henderson (D)	50,931	100.0
4	Ike F. Andrews (D)	62,600	64.7
	Ward Purrington (R)	33,521	34.6
5	Stephen L. Neal (D)	64,634	52.0
	Wilmer Mizell (R)	59,182	47.6
6	Richardson Preyer (D)	56,507	63.7
	R. S. Ritchie (R)	31,906	35.9
7	Charles G. Rose III (D)	49,780	100.0
8	W. G. (Bill) Hefner (D)	61,591	57.0
	Earl B. Ruth (R)	46,500	43.0
9	James G. Martin (R)	51,032	54.4
	Milton Short (D)	41,387	44.1
10	James T. Broyhill (R)	63,382	54.4

Candidates	Votes	%
Jack L. Rhyne (D)	53,131	45.6
11 Roy A. Taylor (D)	89,163	66.0
Albert F. Gilman (R)	45,983	34.0

NORTH DAKOTA

	Candidates	Votes	%
AL	Mark Andrews (R)	130,184	55.7
	Byron Dorgan (D)	103,504	44.3

OHIO

	Candidates	Votes	%
1	Willis D. Gradison Jr. (R)	70,284	50.9
	Thomas A. Luken (D)	67,685	49.1
2	Donald D. Clancy (R)	71,512	53.4
	Edward W. Wolterman (D)	62,530	46.6
3	Charles W. Whalen Jr. (R)	82,159	100.0
4	Tennyson Guyer (R)	81,674	61.5
	James L. Gehrlich (D)	51,065	38.5
5	Delbert L. Latta (R)	89,161	62.5
	Bruce Edwards (D)	53,391	37.5
6	William H. Harsha (R)	93,400	68.2
	Lloyd Allen Wood (D)	42,316	31.2
7	Clarence J. Brown (R)	73,503	60.5
	Patrick L. Nelson (D)	34,828	28.7
	Dorothy Franke (IND)	13,088	10.8
8	Thomas N. Kindness (R)	51,097	42.4
	T. Edward Strinko (D)	45,701	38.0
	Don Gingerich (IND)	23,616	19.6
9	Thomas L. Ashley (D)	64,831	52.8
	C. S. Finkbeiner Jr. (R)	57,892	47.2
10	Clarence E. Miller (R)	100,521	70.4
	H. Kent Bumpass (D)	42,333	29.6
11	J. William Stanton (R)	79,756	60.5
	Michael D. Coffey (D)	52,017	39.5
12	Samuel L. Devine (R)	73,303	50.9
	Fran Ryan (D)	70,818	49.1
13	Charles A. Mosher (R)	72,881	57.5
	Fred M. Ritenauer (D)	53,766	42.5
14	John F. Seiberling (D)	93,931	75.4
	Mark Figetakis (R)	30,603	24.6
15	Chalmers P. Wylie (R)	79,376	61.5
	Mike McGee (D)	49,683	38.5
16	Ralph S. Regula (R)	92,986	65.6
	John G. Freedom (D)	48,754	34.4
17	John M. Ashbrook (R)	70,708	52.7
	David D. Noble (D)	63,342	47.3
18	Wayne L. Hays (D)	90,447	65.6
	Ralph H. Romig (R)	47,385	34.4
19	Charles J. Carney (D)	97,709	72.7
	James L. Ripple (R)	36,649	27.3
20	James V. Stanton (D)	86,405	86.9
	Robert A. Frantz (R)	12,991	13.1
21	Louis Stokes (D)	58,969	82.0
	Bill Mack (R)	12,986	18.0
22	Charles A. Vanik (D)	112,671	78.7
	William J. Franz (R)	30,585	21.3
23	Ronald M. Mottl (D)	53,338	34.8
	George E. Mastics (R)	46,810	30.5
	Dennis J. Kucinich (IND)	45,186	29.4

Special Election

		Votes	%
1	Thomas A. Luken (D)	55,134	51.9
	Willis D. Gradison Jr. (R)	51,063	48.1

OKLAHOMA

		Votes	%
1	James R. Jones (D)	88,159	67.9
	George Alfred Mizer Jr. (R)	41,697	32.1
2	Theodore Risenhoover (D)	78,046	59.1
	Ralph F. Keen (R)	54,110	40.9
3	Carl Albert (D)		100.0
4	Tom Steed (D)		100.0
5	John Jarman (D)	52,107	51.7
	M. H. Edwards (R)	48,705	48.3
6	Glenn English (D)	76,392	53.2
	John N. Happy Camp (R)	63,731	44.4

OREGON

	Candidates	Votes	%
1	Les AuCoin (D)	114,629	56.0
	Diarmuid O'Scannlain (R)	89,848	43.9
2	Al Ullman (D)	140,963	78.1
	Kenneth Brown (R)	39,441	21.9
3	Robert Duncan (D)	129,290	70.4
	John Piacentini (R)	54,080	29.5
4	James Weaver (D)	97,580	52.9
	John Dellenback (R)	86,950	47.1

PENNSYLVANIA

		Votes	%
1	William A. Barrett (D)	96,988	75.8
	Russell M. Nigro (R)	29,772	23.3
2	Robert N. C. Nix (D)	75,033	74.0
	Jesse W. Woods Jr. (R)	26,353	26.0
3	William J. Green III (D)	84,675	75.4
	Richard P. Colbert (R)	27,692	24.6
4	Joshua Eilberg (D)	123,952	71.0
	Isadore Einhorn (R)	50,688	29.0
5	Richard T. Schulze (R)	83,526	59.6
	Leo D. McDermott (D)	56,626	40.4
6	Gus Yatron (D)	111,127	74.6
	Stephen Postupack (R)	35,805	24.0
7	Robert W. Edgar (D)	89,680	55.3
	Stephen J. McEwen Jr. (R)	70,894	43.7
8	Edward G. Biester Jr. (R)	75,313	56.3
	William B. Moyer (D)	54,815	40.9
9	E. G. Shuster (R)	73,881	56.5
	Robert D. Ford (D)	56,844	43.5
10	Joseph M. McDade (R)	100,793	64.9
	Thomas J. Hanlon (D)	54,401	35.1
11	Daniel J. Flood (D)	111,572	74.5
	Richard A. Muzyka (R)	38,106	25.5
12	John P. Murtha (D)	89,193	58.1
	Harry M. Fox (R)	64,416	41.9
13	R. Lawrence Coughlin (R)	98,985	62.5
	Lawrence H. Curry (D)	59,433	37.5
14	William S. Moorhead (D)	93,169	77.4
	Zachary Taylor Davis (R)	27,116	22.5
15	Fred B. Rooney (D)	85,905	100.0
16	Edwin D. Eshleman (R)	73,130	63.5
	Michael J. Minney (D)	40,273	35.0
17	Herman T. Schneebeli (R)	70,274	52.1
	Peter C. Wambach (D)	64,576	47.9
18	H. John Heinz III (R)	107,723	72.1
	Francis J. McArdle (D)	41,706	27.9
19	William F. Goodling (R)	66,417	51.4
	Arthur L. Berger (D)	61,414	47.6
20	Joseph M. Gaydos (D)	112,237	81.7
	Joseph J. Anderko (R)	25,129	18.3
21	John H. Dent (D)	88,701	69.9
	C. L. Sconing (R)	38,111	30.1
22	Thomas E. Morgan (D)	83,654	63.6
	J. R. Montgomery (R)	41,706	31.7
23	Albert W. Johnson (R)	67,192	52.7
	Yates Mast (D)	60,211	47.3
24	Joseph P. Vigorito (D)	76,920	58.6
	Clement R. Scalzitti (R)	54,277	41.4
25	Gary A. Myers (R)	74,645	53.8
	Frank M. Clark (D)	64,049	46.2

Special Election

		Votes	%
12	John P. Murtha (D)	60,538	49.9
	Harry M. Fox (R)	60,416	49.8

RHODE ISLAND

		Votes	%
1	Fernand J. St. Germain (D)	105,288	72.9
	Ernest Barone (R)	39,096	27.1
2	Edward P. Beard (D)	124,759	78.2
	Vincent J. Rotondo (R)	34,728	21.8

SOUTH CAROLINA

		Votes	%
1	Mendel J. Davis (D)	63,111	72.7
	George B. Rast (R)	22,450	25.9
2	Floyd Spence (R)	58,936	56.1

	Candidates	Votes	%
	Matthew J. Perry (D)	45,205	43.0
3	Butler C. Derrick Jr. (D)	55,120	61.8
	Marshall J. Parker (R)	34,046	38.2
4	James R. Mann (D)	45,070	63.3
	Robert L. Watkins (R)	26,185	36.7
5	Kenneth L. Holland (D)	47,614	61.4
	Len Phillips (R)	29,294	37.8
6	John W. Jenrette Jr. (D)	45,396	52.0
	Edward L. Young (R)	41,982	48.0

SOUTH DAKOTA

		Votes	%
1	Larry Pressler (R)	78,266	55.3
	Frank E. Denholm (D)	63,339	44.7
2	James Abdnor (R)	88,746	67.8
	Jack M. Weiland (D)	42,119	32.2

TENNESSEE

		Votes	%
1	James H. Quillen (R)	76,394	64.2
	Lloyd Blevins (D)	42,523	35.8
2	John J. Duncan (R)	87,419	70.9
	Jesse James Brown (D)	35,920	29.1
3	Marilyn Lloyd (D)	61,926	51.1
	LaMar Baker (R)	55,580	45.9
4	Joe L. Evins (D)	94,847	99.9
5	Richard Fulton (D)	88,206	99.8
6	Robin L. Beard Jr. (R)	76,928	56.7
	Tim Schaeffer (D)	58,824	43.3
7	Ed Jones (D)	83,231	100.0
8	Harold E. Ford (D)	67,925	49.9
	Dan Kuykendall (R)	67,181	49.4

TEXAS

		Votes	%
1	Wright Patman (D)	49,426	68.6
	James W. Farris (R)	22,619	31.4
2	Charles Wilson (D)	57,096	100.0
3	James M. Collins (R)	63,489	64.7
	Harold Collum (D)	34,623	35.3
4	Ray Roberts (D)	48,209	74.9
	Dick LeTourneau (R)	16,113	25.1
5	Alan Steelman (R)	28,446	52.1
	Mike McKool (D)	26,190	47.9
6	Olin E. Teague (D)	53,345	83.0
	Carl A. Nigliazzo (R)	10,908	17.0
7	Bill Archer (R)	70,363	79.2
	Jim Brady (D)	18,524	20.8
8	Bob Eckhardt (D)	30,158	72.2
	Donald D. Whitefield (R)	11,605	27.8
9	Jack Brooks (D)	37,275	61.9
	Coleman R. Ferguson (R)	22,935	38.1
10	J. J. Pickle (D)	76,240	80.4
	Paul A. Weiss (R)	18,560	19.6
11	W. R. Poage (D)	46,828	81.6
	Don Clements (R)	9,883	17.2
12	Jim Wright (D)	42,632	78.7
	James S. Garvey (R)	11,543	21.3
13	Jack Hightower (D)	53,094	57.6
	Robert Price (R)	39,087	42.4
14	John Young (D)	41,066	100.0
15	Eligio de la Garza (D)	42,567	100.0
16	Richard C. White (D)	42,880	100.0
17	Omar Burleson (D)	64,595	100.0
18	Barbara C. Jordan (D)	36,597	84.8
	Robbins Mitchell (R)	6,053	14.0
19	George Mahon (D)	49,610	100.0
20	Henry B. Gonzalez (D)	39,358	100.0
21	Robert Krueger (D)	53,543	52.6
	Douglas S. Harlan (R)	45,959	45.2
22	Bob Casey (D)	47,783	69.5
	Ron Paul (R)	19,483	28.4
23	Abraham Kazen Jr. (D)	47,249	100.0
24	Dale Milford (D)	36,085	76.1
	Joseph Beaman Jr. (R)	9,698	20.4

UTAH

		Votes	%
1	K. Gunn McKay (D)	124,793	62.6
	Ronald W. Inkley (R)	62,807	31.5

Candidates	Votes	%
L. S. Brown (A)	11,664	5.9
2 Allan T. Howe (D)	105,739	49.5
Stephen M. Harmsen (R)	100,259	46.9

VERMONT

	Candidates	Votes	%
AL	James M. Jeffords (R)	74,561	52.9
	Francis J. Cain (D I VT)	56,342	40.0
	Michael Parenti (LU)	9,961	7.1

VIRGINIA

	Candidates	Votes	%
1	Thomas N. Downing (D)	58,338	99.8
2	G. William Whitehurst (R)	49,369	60.0
	Robert R. Richards (D)	32,923	40.0
3	David E. Satterfield III (D)	64,627	88.5
	A. R. Ogden (IND)	7,574	10.4
4	Robert W. Daniel Jr. (R)	48,032	47.2
	Lester E. Schlitz (D)	36,489	35.9
	Curtis W. Harris (IND)	17,224	16.9
5	W. C. (Dan) Daniel (D)	52,459	99.4
6	M. Caldwell Butler (R)	45,805	45.1
	Paul J. Puckett (D)	27,350	27.0
	Warren D. Saunders (IND)	26,466	26.1
7	J. Kenneth Robinson (R)	54,267	52.6
	George H. Gilliam (D)	48,611	47.1
8	Herbert E. Harris (D)	53,074	57.6
	Stanford E. Parris (R)	38,997	42.4
9	William C. Wampier (R)	68,183	50.9
	Charles J. Horne (D)	65,783	49.1

	Candidates	Votes	%
10	Joseph L. Fisher (D)	67,184	53.6
	Joel T. Broyhill (R)	56,649	45.2

WASHINGTON

	Candidates	Votes	%
1	Joel Pritchard (R)	108,391	69.5
	W. R. Knedlik (D)	44,655	28.6
2	Lloyd Meeds (D)	81,565	59.7
	Ronald C. Reed (R)	53,157	38.9
3	Don Bonker (D)	93,980	60.9
	A. Ludlow Kramer (R)	58,774	38.1
4	Mike McCormack (D)	84,949	58.9
	Floyd Paxton (R)	59,249	41.1
5	Thomas S. Foley (D)	87,959	64.3
	Gary G. Gage (R)	48,739	35.7
6	Floyd V. Hicks (D)	95,354	71.8
	George M. Nalley (R)	37,400	28.2
7	Brock Adams (D)	85,593	71.1
	Raymond Pritchard (R)	34,847	28.9

WEST VIRGINIA

	Candidates	Votes	%
1	Robert H. Mollohan (D)	72,457	59.7
	Joe Laurita Jr. (R)	48,966	40.3
2	Harley O. Staggers (D)	73,683	64.4
	William H. Loy (R)	40,779	35.6
3	John M. Slack (D)	77,586	68.5
	William L. Larcamp (R)	35,623	31.5
4	Ken Hechler (D)	66,420	100.0

WISCONSIN

	Candidates	Votes	%
1	Les Aspin (D)	81,902	70.5
	Leonard W. Smith (R)	34,288	29.5
2	Robert W. Kastenmeier (D)	93,561	64.8
	Elizabeth T. Miller (R)	50,890	35.2
3	Alvin J. Baldus (D)	76,668	51.1
	Vernon W. Thomson (R)	71,171	47.4
4	Clement J. Zablocki (D)	84,768	72.5
	Lewis H. Collison (R)	27,818	23.8
5	Henry S. Reuss (D)	65,060	80.0
	Mildred A. Morries (R)	16,293	20.0
6	William A. Steiger (R)	86,652	59.5
	Nancy J. Simenz (D)	51,571	35.4
	Harvey C. LeRoy (A)	7,432	5.1
7	David R. Obey (D)	104,468	70.5
	Josef Burger (R)	43,558	29.4
8	Robert J. Cornell (D)	79,923	54.4
	Howard V. Froehlich (R)	66,889	45.6
9	Robert W. Kasten Jr. (R)	77,733	52.9
	Lynn S. Adelman (D)	66,071	45.0

WYOMING

	Candidates	Votes	%
AL	Teno Roncalio (D)	69,434	54.7
	Tom Stroock (R)	57,499	45.3

1. LLJ, the party affiliation of the 1st district candidate, J. M. Sanders, stands for "Life, Liberty, Justice."

2. In the 6th district special election, 146,147 votes were were cast. To win outright without a second election, a candidate needed 73,074 votes. John L. Burton received 73,114 votes, 40 more than needed.

California was redistricted in 1974 for the November general election, changing the numbers of many of the districts. Burton was reelected to the 94th Congress (1975–1977) from the 5th district and Robert J. Lagomarsino from the 19th.

3. There are no reliable final returns for the House race in the 6th district. Postelection results showed Moore leading LaCaze by a handful of votes, but the outcome could not be determined because one voting ma-

chine had malfunctioned and did not record votes for LaCaze.

The case went to the Louisiana courts for resolution. LaCaze asked that persons who voted on the malfunctioning machine be polled again in court under oath and their votes added to the total, but the Louisiana Supreme Court rejected this plan and ordered a new election. Moore won easily. (See Louisiana 1975.)

4. The returns from the 1st district House race are not final. Kyros challenged Emary's election before the House Administration Committee, which conducted a partial recount of the returns until Kyros conceded defeat. The recount changed the total votes received by each candidate. but not the result.

1975 House Elections

CALIFORNIA

Special Election

	Candidates	Votes	%
37	Shirley N. Pettis (R)	53,165	60.5
	Ron Pettis (D)	12,940	14.7
	James L. Mayfield (D)	11,140	12.7
	Frank M. Bogert (R)	4,773	5.4

ILLINOIS

Special Election

	Candidates	Votes	%
5	John G. Fary (D)	55,036	71.9
	Francis X. Lawlor (R)	21,491	28.1

LOUISIANA

Special Election[1]

	Candidates	Votes	%
6	W. Henson Moore (R)	74,802	54.1
	Jeff LaCaze (D)	63,366	45.9

TENNESSEE

Special Election

	Candidates	Votes	%
5	Clifford Allen (D)	46,593	64.6
	Bob Olsen (R)	24,901	34.5

1. This election, Jan. 7, 1975, was a court-ordered rerun held after it was found impossible to determine who won the November 1974 House race between the same two candidates. (See Louisiana 1974.)

1976 House Elections

ALABAMA

	Candidates	Votes	%
1	Jack Edwards (R)	98,257	62.5
	Bill Davenport (D)	58,906	37.5
2	William L. Dickinson (R)	90,069	57.6
	J. Carole Keahey (D)	66,288	42.4
3	Bill Nichols (D)	106,935	99.0
4	Tom Bevill (D)	141,490	80.4
	Leonard Wilson (R)	34,531	19.6
5	Ronnie G. Flippo (D)	113,553	100.0
6	John Buchanan (R)	92,113	56.7
	Mel Bailey (D)	69,384	42.7
7	Walter Flowers (D)	110,496	100.0

ALASKA

		Votes	%
AL	Donald E. Young (R)	83,722	70.8
	Eben Hopson (D)	34,194	28.9

ARIZONA

		Votes	%
1	John J. Rhodes (R)	96,397	57.3
	Patricia Fullinwider (D)	68,404	40.7
2	Morris K. Udall (D)	106,054	58.2
	Laird Guttersen (D)	71,765	39.4
3	Bob Stump (R)	88,854	47.5
	Fred Koory Jr. (R)	79,162	42.3
	Bill McCune (NON PART I)	19,149	10.2
4	Eldon Rudd (R)	93,154	48.6
	Tony Mason (D)	92,435	48.2

ARKANSAS

		Votes	%
1	Bill Alexander (D)	116,217	68.9
	Harlan (Bo) Holleman (R)	52,565	31.1
2	Jim Guy Tucker (D)	144,780	86.4
	James J. Kelly (R)	22,819	13.6
3	John Paul Hammerschmidt (R)[1]		100.0
4	Ray Thornton (D)[1]		100.0

CALIFORNIA

		Votes	%
1	Harold T. (Bizz) Johnson (D)	160,477	73.9
	James E. Taylor (R)	56,539	26.1
2	Don H. Clausen (R)	121,290	56.0
	Oscar H. Klee (D)	88,829	41.0
3	John E. Moss (D)	139,779	72.9
	George R. Marsh Jr. (R)	52,075	27.1
4	Robert L. Leggett (D)	75,844	46.7
	Albert Dehr (R)	75,193	46.3
	Joseph E. (Ted) Sheedy (WRITE IN)	11,279	6.9
5	John L. Burton (D)	103,746	61.8
	Branwell Fanning (R)	64,008	38.2
6	Phillip Burton (D)	86,493	66.1
	Tom Spinosa (R)	35,359	27.0
	Emily Siegel (PFP)	6,570	5.0
7	George Miller (D)	147,064	74.7
	Robert L. Vickers (R)	45,863	23.3
8	Ronald V. Dellums (D)	122,342	62.1
	Philip S. Breck Jr. (R)	68,374	34.7
9	Fortney H. Stark Jr. (D)	116,398	70.8
	James K. Mills (R)	44,607	27.1
10	Don Edwards (D)	111,992	72.0
	Herb Smith (R)	38,088	24.5
11	Leo J. Ryan (D)	107,618	61.1
	Bob Jones (R)	62,435	35.4
12	Paul N. McCloskey Jr. (R)	130,332	66.2
	David Harris (D)	61,526	31.3
13	Norman Y. Mineta (D)	135,291	66.8
	Ernest L. Konnyu (R)	63,130	31.2
14	John J. McFall (D)	123,285	72.5
	Roger A. Blain (R)	46,674	27.5
15	B. F. Sisk (D)	92,735	72.2
	Carol O. Harner (R)	35,700	27.8

	Candidates	Votes	%
16	Leon E. Panetta (D)	104,545	53.4
	Burt L. Talcott (R)	91,160	46.6
17	John Krebs (D)	103,898	65.7
	Henry J. Andreas (R)	54,270	34.3
18	William M. Ketchum (R)	101,658	64.2
	Dean Close (D)	56,683	35.8
19	Robert J. Lagomarsino (R)	124,201	64.4
	Dan Sisson (D)	68,722	35.6
20	Barry M. Goldwater Jr. (R)	146,158	67.2
	Patti Lear Corman (D)	71,193	32.8
21	James C. Corman (D)	101,837	66.5
	Erwin G. (Ed) Hogan (R)	44,094	28.8
22	Carlos J. Moorhead (R)	114,769	62.6
	Robert L. Salley (D)	68,543	37.4
23	Anthony C. (Tony) Beilenson (D)	130,619	60.2
	Thomas F. Bartman (R)	86,434	39.8
24	Henry A. Waxman (D)	108,296	67.8
	David I. Simmons (R)	51,478	32.2
25	Edward R. Roybal (D)	57,966	71.9
	Jim Madrid (R)	17,737	22.0
	Marilyn Seals (PFP)	4,922	6.1
26	John H. Rousselot (R)	112,619	65.6
	Bruce Latta (D)	59,093	34.4
27	Robert K. Dornan (R)	114,623	54.7
	Gary Familian (D)	94,988	45.3
28	Yvonne Brathwaite Burke (D)	114,612	80.2
	Edward S. Skinner (R)	28,303	19.8
29	Augustus F. Hawkins (D)	82,515	85.4
	Michael D. Germonprez (R)	10,852	11.2
30	George E. Danielson (D)	82,767	74.4
	Harry Couch (R)	28,503	25.6
31	Charles H. Wilson (D)	83,155	100.0
32	Glenn M. Anderson (D)	92,034	72.2
	Clifford O. Young (R)	35,394	27.8
33	Del Clawson (R)	95,398	55.1
	Ted Snyder (D)	77,807	44.9
34	Mark W. Hannaford (D)	100,988	50.7
	Daniel E. Lungren (R)	98,147	49.3
35	Jim Lloyd (D)	87,472	53.3
	Louis Brutocao (R)	76,765	46.7
36	George E. Brown Jr. (D)	90,830	61.6
	Grant C. Carner (R)	49,368	33.5
	William E. Pasley (AMI)	7,358	5.0
37	Shirley N. Pettis (R)	133,634	71.1
	Douglas C. Nilson Jr. (D)	49,021	26.1
38	Jerry M. Patterson (D)	103,317	63.6
	James Combs (R)	59,092	36.4
39	Charles E. Wiggins (R)	122,657	58.6
	William E. Farris (D)	86,745	41.4
40	Robert E. Badham (R)	148,512	59.3
	Vivian Hall (D)	102,132	40.7
41	Bob Wilson (R)	128,784	57.7
	King Golden Jr. (D)	94,590	42.3
42	Lionel Van Deerlin (D)	103,062	76.0
	Wes Marden (R)	32,565	24.0
43	Clair W. Burgener (R)	173,576	65.0
	Pat Kelly (D)	93,475	35.0

COLORADO

		Votes	%
1	Patricia Schroeder (D)	103,037	53.2
	Don Friedman (R)	89,384	46.2
2	Timothy E. Wirth (D)	121,336	50.5
	Ed Scott (R)	118,936	49.5
3	Frank E. Evans (D)	89,308	51.0
	Melvin H. Takaki (R)	82,269	47.0
4	James P. Johnson (R)	119,408	53.7
	Dan Ogden (D)	78,355	35.2
	Dick Davis (I)	20,398	9.2
5	William L. Armstrong (R)	126,784	66.4
	Dorothy Hores (D)	64,067	33.6

CONNECTICUT

	Candidates	Votes	%
1	William R. Cotter (D)	128,479	57.1
	Lucien P. DiFazio Jr. (R)	94,106	41.8
2	Christopher J. Dodd (D)	142,684	65.1
	Richard M. Jackson (R)	74,743	34.1
3	Robert N. Giaimo (D)	121,623	54.6
	John G. Pucciano (R)	96,714	43.4
4	Stewart B. McKinney (R)	126,314	61.0
	Geoffrey G. Peterson (D)	76,722	37.1
5	Ronald A. Sarasin (R)	157,009	66.5
	Michael J. Adanti (D)	77,308	32.7
6	Anthony J. Moffett (D)	134,914	56.6
	Thomas F. Upson (R)	102,364	43.0

DELAWARE

		Votes	%
AL	Thomas B. Evans Jr. (R)	110,677	51.5
	Samuel L. Shipley (D)	102,431	47.7

FLORIDA

		Votes	%
1	Robert L. F. Sikes (D)[1]		100.0
2	Don Fuqua (D)[1]		100.0
3	Charles E. Bennett (D)[1]		100.0
4	Bill Chappell Jr. (D)[1]		100.0
5	Richard Kelly (R)	138,371	59.0
	Jo Ann Saunders (D)	96,260	41.0
6	C. W. Bill Young (R)	151,371	65.2
	Gabriel Cazares (D)	80,821	34.8
7	Sam M. Gibbons (D)	102,739	65.7
	Dusty Owens (R)	53,599	34.3
8	Andy Ireland (D)	103,360	58.0
	Robert Johnson (R)	74,794	42.0
9	Louis Frey Jr. (R)	130,509	78.1
	Joseph A. Rosier (D)	36,630	21.9
10	L. A. (Skip) Bafalis (R)	164,273	66.3
	Bill Sikes (D)	83,413	33.7
11	Paul G. Rogers (D)	199,051	91.1
	Clyde Adams (AM)	19,406	8.9
12	J. Herbert Burke (R)	107,268	53.9
	Charles Friedman (D)	91,749	46.1
13	William Lehman (D)	127,822	78.3
	Lee Arnold Spiegelman (R)	35,357	21.7
14	Claude Pepper (D)	82,665	72.9
	Evelio S. Estrella (R)	30,774	27.1
15	Dante B. Fascell (D)	121,292	70.4
	Paul R. Cobb (R)	50,941	29.6

GEORGIA

		Votes	%
1	Ronald B. Ginn (D)	73,826	99.9
2	Dawson Mathis (D)	95,807	99.8
3	Jack Brinkley (D)	93,174	88.7
	Steve Dugan (R)	11,829	11.3
4	Elliott H. Levitas (D)	110,261	68.3
	George Warren (R)	51,140	31.7
5	Andrew Young (D)	96,056	66.7
	Ed Gadrix (R)	47,998	33.3
6	John J. Flynt Jr. (D)	77,532	51.7
	Newt Gingrich (R)	72,400	48.3
7	Lawrence P. McDonald (D)	84,587	55.1
	Quincy Collins (R)	68,947	44.9
8	Billy Lee Evans (D)	91,351	69.7
	Billy Adams (R)	39,623	30.3
9	Ed Jenkins (D)	113,245	79.0
	Louise Wofford (R)	29,954	20.9
10	Doug Barnard (D)	94,782	99.9

HAWAII

		Votes	%
1	Cecil (Cec) Heftel (D)	60,050	43.6
	Fred W. Rohlfing (R)	53,745	39.1
	Kathy Hoshijo (I GOD GOV)	23,807	17.3
2	Daniel K. Akaka (D)	124,116	79.5
	Hank Inouye (R)	23,917	15.3

IDAHO

	Candidates	Votes	%
1	Steven D. Symms (R)	95,833	54.6
	Ken Pursley (D)	79,662	45.4
2	George V. Hansen (R)	84,175	50.6
	Stan Kress (D)	82,237	49.4

ILLINOIS

	Candidates	Votes	%
1	Ralph H. Metcalfe (D)	126,632	92.3
	A. A. Rayner (R)	10,147	7.4
2	Morgan F. Murphy (D)	127,297	84.7
	Spencer Leak (R)	23,037	15.3
3	Martin A. Russo (D)	115,591	58.9
	Ronald Buikema (R)	79,434	40.5
4	Edward J. Derwinski (R)	124,847	65.8
	Ronald A. Rodger (D)	64,924	34.2
5	John G. Fary (D)	119,336	76.9
	Vincent Krok (R)	35,756	23.1
6	Henry J. Hyde (R)	106,667	60.6
	Marilyn D. Clancy (D)	69,359	39.4
7	Cardiss Collins (D)	88,239	84.8
	Newell Ward (R)	15,854	15.2
8	Dan Rostenkowski (D)	105,595	80.5
	John F. Urbaszewski (R)	25,512	19.5
9	Sidney R. Yates (D)	121,915	72.1
	Thomas J. Wajerski (R)	47,054	27.8
10	Abner J. Mikva (D)	106,804	50.0
	Samuel H. Young (R)	106,603	50.0
11	Frank Annunzio (D)	135,755	67.4
	Daniel C. Reber (R)	65,680	32.6
12	Philip M. Crane (R)	151,899	72.8
	E. L. Frank (D)	56,644	27.2
13	Robert McClory (R)	109,726	66.8
	James J. Cummings (D)	49,777	30.3
14	John N. Erlenborn (R)	176,076	74.4
	Marie Agnes Fese (D)	60,505	25.6
15	Tom Corcoran (R)	102,555	53.9
	Tim L. Hall (D)	87,676	46.1
16	John B. Anderson (R)	114,324	67.9
	Stephen Eytalis (D)	54,002	32.1
17	George M. O'Brien (R)	113,145	58.2
	Merlin E. Karlock (D)	81,220	41.8
18	Robert H. Michel (R)	108,028	57.7
	Matthew Ryan (D)	79,102	42.3
19	Thomas F. Railsback (R)	132,571	68.5
	John Craver (D)	60,967	31.5
20	Paul Findley (R)	137,223	63.6
	Peter F. Mack Jr. (D)	78,634	36.4
21	Edward R. Madigan (R)	137,037	74.5
	Anna Wall Scott (D)	46,996	25.5
22	George E. Shipley (D)	129,187	61.4
	Ralph Y. McGinnis (R)	81,102	38.6
23	Melvin Price (D)	128,113	78.6
	Sam P. Drenovac (R)	34,825	21.4
24	Paul Simon (D)	152,344	67.4
	Peter G. Prineas (R)	73,766	32.6

INDIANA

	Candidates	Votes	%
1	Adam Benjamin Jr. (D)	121,155	71.3
	Robert J. Billings (R)	48,756	28.7
2	Floyd Fithian (D)	117,617	54.8
	William W. Erwin (R)	95,505	44.5
3	John Brademas (D)	101,777	56.9
	Thomas L. Thorson (R)	77,094	43.1
4	Dan Quayle (R)	107,762	54.4
	J. Edward Roush (D)	88,361	44.6
5	Elwood H. Hillis (R)	127,194	61.7
	William C. Stout (D)	78,807	38.3
6	David W. Evans (D)	105,773	54.9
	David G. Crane (R)	86,854	45.1
7	John T. Myers (R)	130,005	62.7
	John Elden Tipton (D)	77,355	37.3
8	David L. Cornwell (D)	109,013	50.5
	Belden Bell (R)	107,013	49.5
9	Lee H. Hamilton (D)	136,056	100.0
10	Philip R. Sharp (D)	114,559	59.8
	William G. Frazier (R)	76,890	40.2

	Candidates	Votes	%
11	Andrew Jacobs Jr. (D)	115,895	60.4
	Lawrence L. Buell (R)	74,829	39.0

IOWA

	Candidates	Votes	%
1	James A. S. Leach (R)	109,694	51.9
	Edward Mezvinsky (D)	101,024	47.8
2	Michael T. Blouin (D)	102,980	50.3
	Tom Riley (R)	100,344	49.1
3	Charles E. Grassley (R)	117,957	56.5
	Stephen J. Rapp (D)	90,981	43.5
4	Neal Smith (D)	145,343	69.1
	Charles E. Minor (R)	65,013	30.9
5	Tom Harkin (D)	135,600	64.9
	Kenneth R. Fulk (R)	71,377	34.1
6	Berkley Bedell (D)	133,507	67.4
	Joanne D. Soper (R)	62,292	31.5

KANSAS

	Candidates	Votes	%
1	Keith G. Sebelius (R)	142,311	73.1
	Randy D. Yowell (D)	52,459	26.9
2	Martha E. Keys (D)	88,645	50.7
	Ross R. Freeman (R)	82,946	47.4
3	Larry Winn Jr. (R)	123,578	68.7
	Philip S. Rhoads (D)	52,110	29.0
4	Dan Glickman (D)	90,067	50.3
	Garner E. Shriver (R)	86,832	48.5
5	Joe Skubitz (R)	109,573	60.7
	Virgil L. Olson (D)	65,340	36.2

KENTUCKY

	Candidates	Votes	%
1	Carroll Hubbard Jr. (D)	118,886	82.0
	Bob Bersky (R)	26,089	18.0
2	William H. Natcher (D)	79,016	60.4
	Walter A. Baker (R)	51,900	39.6
3	Romano L. Mazzoli (D)	80,496	57.2
	Denzil J. Ramsey (R)	58,019	41.2
4	M. G. (Gene) Snyder (R)	97,493	55.9
	Edward J. Winterberg (D)	77,009	44.1
5	Tim Lee Carter (R)	100,204	66.6
	Charles C. Smith (D)	49,128	32.6
6	John Breckinridge (D)	90,695	94.0
	Anthony A. McCord (AM)	5,795	6.0
7	Carl D. Perkins (D)	110,450	73.2
	Granville Thomas (R)	40,381	26.8

LOUISIANA

	Candidates	Votes	%
1	Richard A. Tonry (D)	61,652	47.2
	Bob Livingston (R)	56,679	43.4
	John R. Rarick (I)	12,227	9.4
2	Corinne (Lindy) (Mrs. Hale) Boggs (D)	85,923	92.6
	Jules W. Hillery (I)	6,904	7.4
3	David C. Treen (R)	109,135	73.3
	David H. Scheuermann Sr. (D)	39,728	26.7
4	Joe D. Waggonner Jr. (D)	76,406	100.0
5	Jerry Huckaby (D)	83,696	52.5
	Frank Spooner (R)	75,574	47.5
6	W. Henson Moore III (R)	99,780	65.2
	J. D. DeBlieux (D)	53,212	34.8
7	John B. Breaux (D)	117,196	83.3
	Charles F. Huff (R)	23,414	16.7
8	Gillis W. Long (D)	106,285	94.2
	Kent Courtney (I)	6,526	5.8

MAINE

	Candidates	Votes	%
1	David F. Emery (R)	145,523	57.4
	Frederick D. Barton (D)	108,105	42.6
2	William S. Cohen (R)	169,292	77.1
	Leighton Cooney (D)	43,150	19.7

MARYLAND

	Candidates	Votes	%
1	Robert E. Bauman (R)	85,919	54.1
	Roy Dyson (D)	72,993	45.9
2	Clarence D. Long (D)	139,196	70.9

	Candidates	Votes	%
	John M. Seney (R)	35,258	18.0
	Ronald A. Meroney (I)	21,849	11.1
3	Barbara Mikulski (D)	107,014	74.6
	Samuel A. Culotta (R)	36,447	25.4
4	Marjorie S. Holt (R)	95,158	57.7
	Werner Fornos (D)	69,855	42.3
5	Gladys N. Spellman (D)	77,836	57.7
	John B. Burcham Jr. (R)	57,057	42.3
6	Goodloe E. Bryon (D)	126,801	70.8
	Arthur T. Bond (R)	52,203	29.2
7	Parren J. Mitchell (D)	94,991	94.4
	William Salisbury (I)	5,642	5.6
8	Newton Steers (R)	111,274	46.8
	Lanny Davis (D)	100,343	42.2
	Robin Ficker (I)	26,035	11.0

MASSACHUSETTS

	Candidates	Votes	%
1	Silvio O. Conte (R)	137,652	63.8
	Edward A. McColgan (D)	78,181	36.2
2	Edward P. Boland (D)	134,408	72.4
	Thomas P. Swank (R)	41,563	22.4
	John D. McCarthy (USLP)	9,776	5.3
3	Joseph D. Early (D)	168,520	100.0
4	Robert F. Drinan (D)	109,268	52.1
	Arthur D. Mason (R)	100,562	47.9
5	Paul E. Tsongas (D)	144,217	67.3
	Roger P. Durkin (R)	70,036	32.7
6	Michael J. Harrington (D)	121,562	54.8
	William E. Bronson (R)	91,655	41.3
7	Edward J. Markey (D)	162,126	76.9
	Richard W. Daly (R)	37,063	17.6
8	Thomas P. O'Neill Jr. (D)	133,131	74.4
	William A. Barnstead (R)	33,437	18.7
9	John Joseph Moakley (D)	103,901	69.6
	Robert G. Cunningham (R)	34,547	23.1
	Joseph M. O'Loughlin (I)	7,862	5.3
10	Margaret M. Heckler (R)	176,604	100.0
11	James A. Burke (D)	131,789	69.0
	Danielle DeBenedictis (I)	59,240	31.0
12	Gerry E. Studds (D)	222,418	100.0

MICHIGAN

	Candidates	Votes	%
1	John Conyers Jr. (D)	126,161	92.4
	Isaac Hood (R)	8,927	6.5
2	Carl D. Pursell (R)	95,397	49.8
	Edward C. Pierce (D)	95,053	49.6
3	Garry Brown (R)	99,231	50.6
	Howard Wolpe (D)	95,261	48.6
4	Dave Stockman (R)	107,881	60.0
	Richard E. Daugherty (D)	69,655	38.8
5	Harold S. Sawyer (R)	109,589	53.3
	Richard F. Vander Veen (D)	94,973	46.2
6	Bob Carr (D)	108,909	52.7
	Clifford W. Taylor (R)	96,008	46.5
7	Dale E. Kildee (D)	124,260	70.0
	Robin Widgery (R)	50,301	28.3
8	Bob Traxler (D)	110,127	59.0
	E. Brady Denton (R)	75,323	40.4
9	Guy A. Vander Jagt (R)	146,712	70.0
	Stephen Fawley (D)	61,641	29.4
10	Elford A. Cederberg (R)	118,726	56.5
	Donald J. Albosta (D)	89,980	42.8
11	Philip E. Ruppe (R)	118,871	54.7
	Francis D. Brouillette (D)	97,325	44.8
12	David E. Bonior (D)	94,815	52.4
	David M. Serotkin (R)	85,326	47.2
13	Charles C. Diggs Jr. (D)	83,387	89.0
	Richard A. Golden (R)	9,002	9.6
14	Lucien N. Nedzi (D)	107,503	66.5
	John Edward Getz (R)	52,995	32.8
15	William D. Ford (D)	117,313	74.0
	James D. Walaskay (R)	39,177	24.7
16	John D. Dingell Jr. (D)	121,682	75.9
	William E. Rostron (R)	36,378	22.7
17	William M. Brodhead (D)	112,746	64.3
	James W. Burdick (R)	60,476	34.5
18	James J. Blanchard (D)	123,113	66.1
	John E. Olsen (R)	60,995	32.8

Candidates	Votes	%
19 William S. Broomfield (R)	131,799	66.7
Dorothea Becker (D)	64,337	32.6

MINNESOTA

Candidates	Votes	%
1 Albert H. Quie (I-R)	158,177	68.2
Robert C. Olson Jr. (DFL)	70,630	30.5
2 Tom Hagedorn (I-R)	148,322	60.3
Gloria Griffin (DFL)	97,488	39.7
3 Bill Frenzel (I-R)	149,013	66.1
Jerome W. Coughlin (DFL)	72,044	32.0
4 Bruce F. Vento (DFL)	133,282	66.4
Andrew Engebretson (I-R)	59,767	29.8
5 Donald M. Fraser (DFL)	138,213	70.7
Richard M. Erdall (I-R)	50,764	26.0
6 Richard M. Nolan (DFL)	147,507	59.8
James Anderson (I-R)	99,201	40.2
7 Bob Bergland (DFL)	174,080	72.0
Bob Leiseth (I-R)	64,333	26.6
8 James L. Oberstar (DFL)	206,755	100.0

MISSISSIPPI

Candidates	Votes	%
1 Jamie L. Whitten (D)	93,687	100.0
2 David R. Bowen (D)	75,092	63.0
Roland Byrd (R)	42,601	35.7
3 G. V. (Sonny) Montgomery (D)	129,088	93.9
Dorothy Colby Cleveland (R)	8,321	6.1
4 Thad Cochran (R)	101,132	76.0
Sterling P. Davis (D)	28,737	21.6
5 Trent Lott (R)	104,554	68.2
Gerald Blessey (D)	48,724	31.8

MISSOURI

Candidates	Votes	%
1 William Clay (D)	87,310	65.5
Robert L. Witherspoon (R)	45,874	34.4
2 Robert A. Young (D)	111,568	51.1
Robert O. Snyder (R)	106,811	48.9
3 Richard A. Gephardt (D)	115,109	63.7
Joseph L. Badaracco (R)	65,623	36.3
4 Ike Skelton (D)	115,955	55.9
Richard A. King (R)	91,605	44.1
5 Richard Bolling (D)	100,876	68.0
Joanne M. Collins (R)	41,681	28.1
6 E. Thomas Coleman (R)	120,969	58.5
Morgan Maxfield (D)	83,755	40.5
7 Gene Taylor (R)	133,656	62.0
Dolan G. Hawkins (D)	81,848	38.0
8 Richard Ichord (D)	132,386	67.3
Charles R. Leick (R)	60,179	30.6
9 Harold L. Volkmer (D)	120,325	55.9
J. H. Frappier (R)	94,816	44.1
10 Bill D. Burlison (D)	131,675	72.1
Joe Carron (R)	51,024	27.9

MONTANA

Candidates	Votes	%
1 Max S. Baucus (D)	111,487	66.4
W. D. (Bill) Diehl (R)	56,297	33.6
2 Ron Marlenee (R)	84,149	55.0
Thomas E. Towe (D)	68,972	45.0

NEBRASKA

Candidates	Votes	%
1 Charles Thone (R)	146,558	73.2
Pauline F. Anderson (D)	53,703	26.8
2 John J. Cavanaugh (D)	106,296	54.6
Lee Terry (R)	88,352	45.4
3 Virginia Smith (R)	150,720	72.9
James T. Hansen (D)	51,012	24.7

NEVADA

Candidates	Votes	%
AL James Santini (D)	153,996	77.1
Walden Charles Earhart (R)	24,124	12.1
Janine M. Hansen (IA)	12,038	6.0

NEW HAMPSHIRE

Candidates	Votes	%
1 Norman E. D'Amours (D)	107,806	68.0
John Adams (R)	48,087	30.3
2 James C. Cleveland (R)	100,911	60.5
J. Joseph Grandmaison (D)	65,792	39.5

NEW JERSEY

Candidates	Votes	%
1 James J. Florio (D)	136,624	70.1
Joseph I. McCullough Jr. (R)	56,363	28.9
2 William J. Hughes (D)	141,753	61.7
James R. Hurley (R)	87,915	38.3
3 James J. Howard (D)	127,164	62.1
Ralph A. Siciliano (R)	75,934	37.1
4 Frank Thompson Jr. (D)	113,281	66.3
Joseph S. Indyk (R)	54,789	32.1
5 Millicent Fenwick (R)	137,803	66.9
Frank R. Nero (D)	64,598	31.3
6 Edwin B. Forsythe (R)	125,920	58.8
Catherine A. Costa (D)	85,053	39.7
7 Andrew Maguire (D)	120,526	56.5
James J. Sheehan (R)	92,624	43.5
8 Robert A. Roe (D)	108,841	70.6
Bessie Doty (R)	44,775	29.0
9 Harold C. Hollenbeck (R)	107,454	53.1
Henry Helstoski (D)	89,723	44.3
10 Peter W. Rodino Jr. (D)	88,245	82.6
Tony Grandison (R)	17,129	16.0
11 Joseph G. Minish (D)	129,026	67.6
Charles A. Poekel Jr. (R)	59,397	31.1
12 Matthew J. Rinaldo (R)	136,973	73.1
Richard A. Buggelli (D)	49,189	26.3
13 Helen S. Meyner (D)	105,291	50.4
William E. Schluter (R)	100,050	47.9
14 Joseph A. LeFante (D)	73,174	49.9
Anthony L. Campenni (R)	66,319	45.2
15 Edward J. Patten (D)	106,170	59.0
Charles W. Wiley (R)	54,487	30.3
Dennis Adams Sr. (I)	14,543	8.1

NEW MEXICO

Candidates	Votes	%
1 Manuel Lujan Jr. (R)	162,587	72.1
Raymond Garcia (D)	61,800	27.4
2 Harold Runnels (D)	123,563	70.3
Donald W. Trubey (R)	52,131	29.7

NEW YORK

Candidates	Votes	%
1 Otis G. Pike (D,L)	135,528	65.3
Salvatore Nicosia (R)	61,671	29.7
2 Thomas J. Downey (D,I)	91,241	57.1
Peter Cohalan (R,C)	67,755	42.4
3 Jerome A. Ambro Jr. (D)	94,265	52.0
Howard T. Hogan Jr. (R,C)	84,824	46.8
4 Norman F. Lent (R,C)	106,058	55.8
Gerald P. Halpern (D,L)	83,971	44.2
5 John W. Wydler (R,C)	110,366	55.7
Allard K. Lowenstein (D,L)	87,868	44.3
6 Lester L. Wolff (D,L)	112,422	61.8
Vincent R. Balletta Jr. (R)	60,567	33.3
7 Joseph P. Addabbo (D,R,L)	107,312	94.7
8 Benjamin S. Rosenthal (D,L)	107,295	77.8
Albert Lemishow (R,C)	30,191	21.9
9 James J. Delaney (D,R,C)	109,552	95.1
10 Mario Biaggi (D,R)	106,222	91.6
Joanne S. Fuchs (C)	5,868	5.1
11 James H. Scheuer (D)	84,770	74.1
Arthur Cuccia (R)	19,203	16.8
Bryan F. Levinson (C)	6,316	5.5
12 Shirley Chisholm (D,L)	43,203	87.0
Horace Morancie (R)	5,336	10.8
13 Stephen J. Solarz (D,L)	110,624	83.7
Jack N. Dobosh (R,C)	21,600	16.3
14 Frederick W. Richmond (D,L)	55,723	85.0
Frank X. Gargiulo (R,C)	8,977	13.7
15 Leo C. Zeferetti (D,C)	69,242	63.2
Ronald J. D'Angelo (R)	33,641	30.7
Arthur J. Paone (L)	6,604	6.0
16 Elizabeth Holtzman (D,L)	93,995	82.9
Gladys Pemberton (R,C)	19,423	17.1
17 John M. Murphy (D)	89,126	65.6
Kenneth J. Grossberger (R)	27,734	20.4
John M. Peters (C)	10,399	7.7
Ned Schneir (L)	8,656	6.4
18 Edward I. Koch (D,L)	112,187	75.1
Sonia Landau (R)	29,728	19.9
19 Charles B. Rangel (D,R,L)	91,672	97.0
20 Theodore S. Weiss (D,L)	91,977	83.2
Denise Weiseman (R)	14,114	12.8
21 Herman Badillo (D,R,L)	41,285	98.6
22 Jonathan B. Bingham (D,L)	92,044	86.4
Paul Slotkin (R)	11,130	10.4
23 Bruce F. Caputo (R,C)	93,006	53.6
J. Edward Meyer (D,L)	80,424	46.4
24 Richard L. Ottinger (D)	99,761	54.5
David V. Hicks (R,C)	81,111	44.3
25 Hamilton Fish Jr. (R,C)	139,434	70.5
Minna Post Peyser (D)	58,216	29.5
26 Benjamin A. Gilman (R)	120,049	65.3
John R. Maloney (D)	60,511	32.9
27 Matthew F. McHugh (D,L)	127,048	66.6
William H. Harter (R,C)	63,626	33.4
28 Samuel S. Stratton (D)	170,034	79.0
Mary A. Bradt (R,C)	44,053	20.5
29 Edward W. Pattison (D,L)	100,663	47.0
Joseph A. Martino (R)	96,476	45.0
James E. DeYoung (C)	15,337	7.2
30 Robert C. McEwen (R,C)	95,564	55.7
Norma A. Bartle (D)	75,951	44.3
31 Donald J. Mitchell (R,C)	123,143	66.5
Anita Maxwell (D)	62,032	33.5
32 James M. Hanley (D)	101,419	54.8
George C. Wortley (R,C)	81,597	44.1
33 William F. Walsh (R)	125,163	68.5
Charles R. Welch (D)	48,855	26.7
34 Frank J. Horton (R)	126,566	65.9
William C. Larsen (D)	58,247	30.3
35 Barber S. Conable Jr. (R)	120,738	64.3
Michael Macaluso (D,C)	67,177	35.7
36 John J. LaFalce (D,L)	123,246	66.6
Ralph J. Argen (R,C)	61,701	33.4
37 Henry J. Nowak (D,L)	100,042	78.2
Calvin Kimbrough (R)	23,660	18.5
38 Jack F. Kemp (R,C)	165,702	78.2
Peter J. Geraci (D,L)	46,307	21.8
39 Stanley N. Lundine (D)	109,986	61.8
Richard A. Snowden (R,C)	68,018	38.2

Special Election

Candidates	Votes	%
39 Stanley N. Lundine (D)	55,402	61.2
John T. Calkins (R)	35,107	38.8

NORTH CAROLINA

Candidates	Votes	%
1 Walter B. Jones (D)	98,611	75.9
Joseph M. Ward (R)	29,295	22.5
2 L. H. Fountain (D)	113,368	99.8
3 Charlie Whitley (D)	77,193	68.7
Willard J. Blanchard (R)	35,089	31.2
4 Ike F. Andrews (D)	92,165	60.6
Johnnie L. Gallemore Jr. (R)	59,917	39.4
5 Stephen L. Neal (D)	98,789	54.2
Wilmer D. Mizell (R)	83,129	45.6
6 Richardson Preyer (D)	103,851	96.3
7 Charles Rose (D)	95,463	81.3
M. H. (Mike) Vaughan (R)	21,955	18.7
8 W. G. (Bill) Hefner (D)	99,296	65.7
Carl Eagle (R)	49,094	32.5
9 James G. Martin (R)	82,297	53.5
Arthur Goodman Jr. (D)	70,847	46.1
10 James T. Broyhill (R)	99,882	59.8
John J. Hunt (D)	67,190	40.2
11 Lamar Gudger (D)	93,857	50.9
Bruce B. Briggs (R)	88,752	48.1

NORTH DAKOTA

Candidates	Votes	%
AL Mark Andrews (R)	181,018	62.4
Lloyd Omdahl (D)	104,263	36.0

OHIO

	Candidates	Votes	%
1	Willis D. Gradison Jr. (R)	109,789	64.8
	William F. Bowen (D)	56,995	33.6
2	Thomas A. Luken (D)	88,178	51.4
	Donald D. Clancy (R)	83,459	48.6
3	Charles W. Whalen Jr. (R)	100,871	69.4
	Leonard Stubbs (D)	33,873	23.3
4	Tennyson Guyer (R)	121,173	70.1
	Clinton G. Dorsey (D)	51,784	29.9
5	Delbert L. Latta (R)	124,910	67.4
	Bruce Edwards (D)	60,304	32.6
6	William H. Harsha (R)	107,064	61.5
	Ted Strickland (D)	67,067	38.5
7	Clarence J. Brown Jr. (R)	101,027	64.9
	Dorothy Franke (D)	54,755	35.1
8	Thomas N. Kindness (R)	110,775	68.7
	John W. Griffin (D)	46,424	28.8
9	Thomas L. Ashley (D)	91,040	54.2
	C. S. Finkbeiner (R)	73,919	44.0
10	Clarence E. Miller (R)	127,147	68.8
	James A. Plummer (D)	57,757	31.2
11	J. William Stanton (R)	120,716	71.7
	Thomas R. West Jr. (D)	47,548	28.3
12	Samuel L. Devine (R)	90,987	46.5
	Fran Ryan (D)	89,424	45.7
	William R. Moss (I)	15,429	7.9
13	Don J. Pease (D)	108,061	66.0
	Woodrow W. Mathna (R)	49,828	30.4
14	John F. Seiberling Jr. (D)	121,652	74.1
	James E. Houston (R)	39,917	24.3
15	Chalmers P. Wylie (R)	109,630	65.5
	Mike McGee (D)	57,741	34.5
16	Ralph S. Regula (R)	116,374	66.8
	John G. Freedom (D)	55,671	32.0
17	John M. Ashbrook (R)	94,874	56.8
	John C. McDonald (D)	72,168	43.2
18	Douglas Applegate (D)	116,901	62.9
	Ralph R. McCoy (R)	45,735	24.6
	William Crabbe (I)	21,537	11.6
19	Charles J. Carney (D)	90,386	50.2
	Jack C. Hunter (R)	86,162	47.9
20	Mary Rose Oakar (D)	98,785	81.0
	Raymond J. Grabow (I)	20,553	16.9
21	Louis Stokes (D)	91,903	83.8
	Barbara Sparks (R)	12,434	11.3
22	Charles A. Vanlk (D)	128,535	72.7
	Harry A. Hanna (R)	42,727	24.2
23	Ronald M. Mottl (D)	130,576	73.2
	Michael T. Scanlon (R)	47,804	26.8

OKLAHOMA

		Votes	%
1	James R. Jones (D)	100,945	54.0
	James M. Inhofe (R)	84,374	45.1
2	Theodore Risenhoover (D)	102,402	54.0
	E. L. (Bud) Stewart (R)	87,341	46.0
3	Wes Watkins (D)	151,271	82.0
	Gerald L. Beasley Jr. (R)	31,732	17.2
4	Tom Steed (D)	116,425	74.9
	M. C. Stanley (R)	34,170	22.0
5	M. H. Edwards (R)	78,651	49.9
	Tom Dunlap (D)	74,752	47.4
6	Glenn English (D)	137,498	71.1
	Carol McCurley (R)	55,953	28.9

OREGON

		Votes	%
1	Les AuCoin (D)	154,844	58.7
	Philip N. Bladine (R)	109,140	41.3
2	Al Ullman (D)	173,313	72.0
	Thomas H. Mercer (R)	67,431	28.0
3	Robert Duncan (D)	148,503	83.9
	Martin Simon (I)	28,245	16.0
4	James Weaver (D)	122,475	50.0
	Jerry Lausmann (R)	85,943	35.1
	Jim Howard (I)	22,104	9.0
	Theodora Nathan (I)	14,307	5.8

PENNSYLVANIA

	Candidates	Votes	%
1	Michael (Ozzie) Myers (D)	117,087	73.5
	Samuel N. Fanelli (R)	40,191	25.2
2	Robert N. C. Nix (D)	109,855	73.5
	Jesse W. Woods Jr. (R)	37,907	25.4
3	Raymond F. Lederer (D)	98,627	73.2
	Terrence J. Schade (R)	35,491	26.3
4	Joshua Eilberg (D)	144,890	67.5
	James E. Mugford (R)	69,700	32.5
5	Richard T. Schulze (R)	119,682	59.5
	Anthony Campolo (D)	81,299	40.5
6	Gus Yatron (D)	133,624	73.8
	Stephen Postupack (R)	46,103	25.5
7	Robert W. Edgar (D)	109,436	54.1
	John N. Kenney (R)	92,788	45.9
8	Peter H. Kostmayer (D)	93,855	49.5
	John S. Renninger (R)	92,543	48.8
9	E. G. Shuster (R,D)	154,359	100.0
10	Joseph M. McDade (R)	125,218	62.6
	Edward Mitchell (D)	74,925	37.4
11	Daniel J. Flood (D)	130,175	70.8
	Howard G. Williams (R)	53,621	29.2
12	John P. Murtha (D)	122,504	67.7
	Ted Humes (R)	58,489	32.3
13	R. Lawrence Coughlin (R)	130,705	63.4
	Gertrude Strick (D)	75,435	36.6
14	William S. Moorhead (D)	114,472	71.7
	John F. Bradley (R)	43,308	27.1
15	Fred B. Rooney (D)	108,844	65.2
	Alice Sivulich (R)	57,616	34.5
16	Robert S. Walker (R)	97,527	62.3
	Michael J. Minney (D)	57,836	37.0
17	Allen E. Ertel (D)	86,158	50.7
	H. Joseph Hepford (R)	82,370	48.5
18	Douglas Walgren (D)	113,787	59.5
	Robert J. Casey (R)	77,594	40.5
19	William F. Goodling (R)	124,098	70.6
	Richard P. Noll (D)	51,686	29.4
20	Joseph M. Gaydos (D)	134,961	75.0
	John P. Kostelac (R)	44,432	24.7
21	John H. Dent (D)	99,160	59.4
	Robert H. Miller (R)	67,763	40.6
22	Austin J. Murphy (D)	97,036	55.3
	Roger Fischer (R)	77,030	43.9
23	Joseph S. Ammerman (D)	95,821	56.5
	Albert W. Johnson (R)	73,641	43.5
24	Marc L. Marks (R)	101,048	55.4
	Joseph P. Vigorito (D)	79,937	43.8
25	Gary A. Myers (R)	103,632	56.8
	Eugene V. Atkinson (D)	78,857	43.2

RHODE ISLAND

		Votes	%
1	Fernand J. St. Germain (D)	116,674	62.4
	John J. Slocum Jr. (R)	68,080	36.4
2	Edward P. Beard (D)	154,453	76.5
	Thomas V. Iannitti (R)	45,438	22.5

SOUTH CAROLINA

		Votes	%
1	Mendel J. Davis (D)	89,891	68.9
	Lonnie Rowell (R)	40,598	31.1
2	Floyd D. Spence (R)	83,426	57.5
	Clyde B. Livingston (D)	60,602	41.8
3	Butler C. Derrick (D)	117,740	99.9
4	James R. Mann (D)	91,721	73.5
	Robert L. Watkins (R)	32,983	26.4
5	Kenneth L. Holland (D)	66,073	51.4
	Bobby Richardson (R)	62,095	48.3
6	John W. Jenrette Jr. (D)	75,916	55.5
	Edward L. Young (R)	60,288	44.0

SOUTH DAKOTA

		Votes	%
1	Larry Pressler (R)	121,587	79.8
	James V. Guffey (D)	29,533	19.4
2	James Abdnor (R)	99,601	69.9
	Grace Mickelson (D)	42,968	30.1

TENNESSEE

	Candidates	Votes	%
1	James H. (Jimmy) Quillen (R)	97,781	57.9
	Lloyd Blevins (D)	69,507	41.2
2	John J. Duncan (R)	117,256	62.8
	Mike Rowland (D)	69,449	37.2
3	Marilyn Lloyd (D)	123,872	67.5
	LaMar Baker (R)	57,116	31.1
4	Albert Gore Jr. (D)	115,392	94.0
	William H. McGlamery (I)	7,320	6.0
5	Clifford R. Allen (D)	125,830	92.4
	Roger E. Bissell (I)	10,292	7.6
6	Robin L. Beard (R)	116,905	64.5
	Ross Bass (D)	64,462	35.5
7	Ed Jones (D)	105,832	100.0
8	Harold E. Ford (D)	100,683	60.7
	A. D. Alissandratos (R)	63,819	38.5

TEXAS

		Votes	%
1	Sam B. Hall Jr. (D)	135,384	83.7
	James Hogan (R)	26,334	16.3
2	Charles Wilson (D)	133,910	95.0
	James William Doyle III (AM)	6,992	5.0
3	James M. Collins (R)	171,343	74.0
	Lee E. Shackelford Jr. (D)	60,070	26.0
4	Ray Roberts (D)	105,394	62.7
	Frank S. Glenn (R)	62,641	37.3
5	Jim Mattox (D)	67,871	54.0
	Nancy Judy (R)	56,056	44.6
6	Olin E. Teague (D)	119,025	65.9
	Wes Mowery (R)	60,316	33.4
7	Bill Archer (R)	193,127	100.0
8	Bob Eckhardt (D)	84,404	60.7
	Nick Gearhart (R)	54,566	39.2
9	Jack Brooks (D)	112,945	99.9
10	J. J. (Jake) Pickle (D)	160,683	76.8
	Paul McClure (R)	48,482	23.2
11	W. R. Poage (D)	92,142	57.4
	Jack Burgess (R)	68,373	42.6
12	Jim Wright (D)	101,814	75.8
	W. R. Durham (R)	31,941	23.8
13	Jack Hightower (D)	101,798	59.3
	Bob Price (R)	69,328	40.4
14	John Young (D)	93,589	61.4
	L. Dean Holford (R)	58,788	38.6
15	Eligio de la Garza (D)	102,837	74.4
	R. L. (Lendy) McDonald (R)	35,446	25.6
16	Richard C. White (D)	71,876	57.8
	Vic Shackelford (R)	52,499	42.2
17	Omar Burleson (D)	127,613	99.9
18	Barbara C. Jordan (D)	93,953	85.5
	Sam H. Wright (R)	15,381	14.0
19	George Mahon (D)	87,908	54.6
	Jim Reese (R)	72,991	45.4
20	Henry B. Gonzalez (D)	90,173	100.0
21	Robert Krueger (D)	149,395	71.0
	Bobby A. Locke (R)	56,211	26.7
22	Bob Gammage (D)	96,535	50.1
	Ron Paul (R)	96,267	49.9
23	Abraham Kazen Jr. (D)	96,481	100.0
24	Dale Milford (D)	82,743	63.4
	Leo Berman (R)	47,075	36.1

Special Elections[2]

		Votes	%
1	Sam B. Hall Jr. (D)	20,556	72.0
	Glen Jones (D)	6,327	22.2
22	Bob Gammage (D)	15,287	42.1
	Ron Paul (R)	14,386	39.6
	John S. Brunson (D)	3,670	10.1

Special Runoff Election

		Votes	%
22	Ron Paul (R)	39,041	56.2
	Bob Gammage (D)	30,483	43.8

UTAH

		Votes	%
1	K. Gunn McKay (D)	155,631	58.2
	Joe H. Ferguson (R)	106,542	39.8
2	Dan Marriott (R)	144,861	52.4
	Allan T. Howe (D)	110,931	40.1
	D. J. McCarty (WRITE IN)	20,508	7.4

VERMONT

	Candidates	Votes	%
AL	James M. Jeffords (R)	124,458	67.4
	John A. Burgess (D,I VT)	60,202	32.6

VIRGINIA

	Candidates	Votes	%
1	Paul S. Trible Jr. (R)	71,789	48.6
	Robert E. Quinn (D)	70,159	47.5
2	G. William Whitehurst (R)	79,381	65.7
	Robert E. Washington (D)	41,464	34.3
3	David E. Satterfield III (D)	129,066	87.9
	A. R. Ogden (I)	17,503	11.9
4	Robert W. Daniel Jr. (R)	74,495	53.0
	J. W. (Billy) O'Brien (D)	65,982	47.0
5	W. C. (Dan) Daniel (D)	101,038	100.0
6	M. Caldwell Butler (R)	90,830	62.2
	Warren D. Saunders (I)	55,115	37.8
7	J. Kenneth Robinson (R)	115,508	81.6
	James B. Hutt Jr. (I)	25,731	18.2
8	Herbert E. Harris (D)	83,245	51.6
	James R. Tate (R)	68,729	42.6
	Michael D. Cannon (I)	9,292	5.8
9	William C. Wampler (R)	96,052	57.3
	Charles J. Horne (D)	71,439	42.6
10	Joseph L. Fisher (D)	103,689	54.7
	Vincent F. Callahan Jr. (R)	73,616	38.8
	E. Stanley Rittenhouse (I)	12,124	6.4

WASHINGTON

	Candidates	Votes	%
1	Joel Pritchard (R)	161,354	71.9
	Dave Wood (D)	58,006	25.8
2	Lloyd Meeds (D)	107,328	49.3
	John Nance Garner (R)	106,786	49.0
3	Don Bonker (D)	145,198	70.8
	Chuck Elhart (R)	57,517	28.0
4	Mike McCormack (D)	115,364	57.8
	Dick Granger (R)	81,813	41.0
5	Thomas S. Foley (D)	120,415	58.0
	Duane Alton (R)	84,262	40.6
6	Norman D. Dicks (D)	137,964	73.5
	Robert M. Reynolds (R)	47,539	25.3
7	Brock Adams (D)	133,673	73.0
	Raymond Pritchard (R)	46,448	25.4

WEST VIRGINIA

	Candidates	Votes	%
1	Robert H. Mollohan (D)	108,103	58.0
	John F. McCuskey (R)	78,159	42.0
2	Harley O. Staggers (D)	136,749	73.2
	Jim Sloan (R)	50,079	26.8
3	John M. Slack (D)	128,086	99.7
4	Nick J. Rahall (D)	73,626	45.6
	Ken Hechler (WRITE IN)	59,067	36.6
	E. S. (Steve) Goodman (R)	28,825	17.8

WISCONSIN

	Candidates	Votes	%
1	Les Aspin (D)	136,162	64.9
	William W. Petrie (R)	71,427	34.0
2	Robert W. Kastenmeier (D)	155,158	65.6
	Elizabeth T. Miller (R)	81,350	34.4
3	Alvin J. Baldus (D)	139,083	58.1
	Adolf L. Gundersen (R)	100,218	41.9
4	Clement J. Zablocki (D)	172,166	100.0
5	Henry S. Reuss (D)	134,935	77.8
	Robert L. Hicks (R)	36,413	21.0
6	William A. Steiger (R)	139,541	63.3
	Joseph C. Smith (D)	80,715	36.6
7	David R. Obey (D)	171,366	73.3
	Frank A. Savino (R)	60,952	26.1
8	Robert J. Cornell (D)	115,996	50.9
	Harold V. Froehlich (R)	107,048	46.9
9	Robert W. Kasten Jr. (R)	163,791	65.9
	Lynn M. McDonald (D)	84,706	34.1

WYOMING

	Candidates	Votes	%
AL	Teno Roncalio (D)	85,721	56.4
	Larry Joe Hart (R)	66,147	43.6

1. Arkansas and Florida did not record the votes for unopposed candidates.
2. Texas election law required all candidates in special elections to run against each other, regardless of party. If no candidate received a majority, a special election runoff was held between the two candidates receiving the most votes in the special election.

1977 House Elections

GEORGIA

Special Election[1]

	Candidates	Votes	%
5	Wyche Fowler Jr. (D)	29,898	39.6
	John Lewis (D)	21,531	28.6
	Paul D. Coverdell (R)	16,509	21.9

Special Runoff Election

	Candidates	Votes	%
5	Wyche Fowler Jr. (D)	54,378	62.4
	John Lewis (D)	32,732	37.6

LOUISIANA

Special Election

	Candidates	Votes	%
1	Robert L. Livingston (R)	56,121	51.2
	Ron Faucheux (D)	40,802	37.2
	Sanford Krasnoff (I)	12,665	11.6

MINNESOTA

Special Election

	Candidates	Votes	%
7	Arian Stangeland (I-R)	71,340	57.6
	Michael J. Sullivan (DFL)	45,490	36.7

WASHINGTON

Special Election

	Candidates	Votes	%
7	John E. Cunningham (R)	42,650	54.0
	Marvin Durning (D)	35,525	45.0

1. Georgia election law required all candidates in special elections to run against each other, regardless of party. If no candidate received a majority, a special election runoff was held between the two candidates receiving the most votes in the special election.

1978 House Elections

ALABAMA

	Candidates	Votes	%
1	Jack Edwards (R)	71,711	63.9
	L. W. (Red) Noonan (D)	40,450	36.1
2	William L. Dickinson (R)	57,924	54.0
	Wendell Mitchell (D)	49,341	46.0
3	Bill Nichols (D)	74,895	100.0
4	Tom Bevill (D)	87,380	100.0
5	Ronnie G. Flippo (D)	68,985	96.8
6	John Buchanan (R)	65,700	61.7
	Don Hawkins (D)	40,771	38.3
7	Richard C. Shelby (D)	77,742	93.8

ALASKA

	Candidates	Votes	%
AL	Don Young (R)	68,811	55.4
	Patrick Rodey (D)	55,176	44.4

ARIZONA

	Candidates	Votes	%
1	John J. Rhodes (R)	81,108	71.0
	Ken Graves (D)	33,178	29.0
2	Morris K. Udall (D)	67,878	52.5
	Tom Richey (R)	58,697	45.4
3	Bob Stump (D)	111,850	85.0
	Kathleen Cooke (LIBERT)	19,813	15.0
4	Eldon Rudd (R)	90,768	63.1
	Michael L. McCormick (D)	48,661	33.8

ARKANSAS

	Candidates	Votes	%
1	Bill Alexander (D)		100.0
2	Ed Bethune (R)	65,285	51.2
	Doug Brandon (D)	62,140	48.8
3	John Paul Hammerschmidt (R)	130,086	78.4
	William C. Mears (D)	35,748	21.6
4	Beryl F. Anthony Jr. (D)		100.0

CALIFORNIA

	Candidates	Votes	%
1	Harold T. Johnson (D)	125,122	59.4
	James E. Taylor (R)	85,690	40.6
2	Don H. Clausen (R)	114,451	52.0
	Norma Bork (D)	99,712	45.3
3	Robert T. Matsui (D)	105,537	53.4
	Sandy Smoley (R)	91,966	46.6
4	Vic Fazio (D)	87,764	55.4
	Rex Hime (R)	70,733	44.6
5	John L. Burton (D)	106,046	66.8
	Dolores Skore (R)	52,603	33.2
6	Phillip Burton (D)	81,801	68.3
	Tom Spinosa (R)	33,515	27.9
7	George Miller (D)	109,676	63.4
	Paula Gordon (R)	58,332	33.7
8	Ronald V. Dellums (D)	94,824	57.4
	Charles V. Hughes (R)	70,481	42.6
9	Fortney H. (Pete) Stark (D)	88,179	65.4
	Robert S. Allen (R)	41,138	30.5
10	Don Edwards (D)	84,488	67.1
	Rudy Hansen (R)	41,374	32.9
11	Leo J. Ryan (D)	92,882	60.5
	David Welch (R)	54,621	35.6
12	Paul N. McCloskey Jr. (R)	116,982	73.1
	Kirsten Olsen (D)	34,472	21.5
13	Norman Y. Mineta (D)	100,809	57.5
	Dan O'Keefe (R)	69,306	39.5
14	Norman D. Shumway (R)	95,962	53.4
	John J. McFall (D)	76,602	42.6
15	Tony Coelho (D)	75,212	60.1
	Chris Patterakis (R)	49,914	39.9
16	Leon E. Panetta (D)	104,550	61.4
	Eric Seastrand (R)	65,808	38.6
17	Charles (Chip) Pashayan Jr. (R)	81,296	54.5
	John Krebs (D)	67,885	45.5
18	William Thomas (R)	85,663	59.2
	Bob Sogge (D)	58,900	40.7

	Candidates	Votes	%
19	Robert J. Lagomarsino (R)	123,192	71.7
	Jerome Zamos (D)	41,672	24.3
20	Barry M. Goldwater Jr. (R)	129,714	66.4
	Pat Lear (D)	65,695	33.6
21	James C. Corman (D)	73,869	59.5
	G. (Rod) Walsh (R)	44,519	35.9
22	Carlos J. Moorehead (R)	99,502	64.6
	Robert S. Henry (D)	54,442	35.4
23	Anthony C. (Tony) Beilenson (D)	117,498	65.6
	Joseph Barbara (R)	61,496	34.4
24	Henry A. Waxman (D)	85,075	62.7
	Howard G. Schaefer (R)	44,243	32.6
25	Edward R. Roybal (D)	45,881	67.4
	Robert K. Watson (R)	22,205	32.6
26	John H. Rousselot (R)	113,059	100.0
27	Robert K. Dornan (R)	89,392	51.0
	Carey Peck (D)	85,880	49.0
28	Julian C. Dixon (D)	97,592	100.0
29	Augustus F. Hawkins (D)	65,214	85.0
	Uriah J. Fields (R)	11,512	15.0
30	George E. Danielson (D)	66,241	71.4
	Henry Ares (R)	26,511	28.6
31	Charles H. Wilson (D)	55,667	67.7
	Don Grimshaw (R)	26,490	32.2
32	Glenn M. Anderson (D)	74,004	71.4
	Sonya (Sonny) Mathison (R)	23,242	22.4
	Ida Bader (AM I)	6,363	6.1
33	Wayne Grisham (R)	79,533	56.0
	Dennis S. Kazarian (D)	62,540	44.0
34	Daniel E. Lungren (R)	90,554	53.7
	Mark W. Hannaford (D)	73,608	43.7
35	Jim Lloyd (D)	80,388	54.0
	David Dreier (R)	68,442	46.0
36	George E. Brown Jr. (D)	80,448	62.9
	Dana Warren Carmody (R)	47,417	37.1
37	Jerry Lewis (R)	106,581	61.4
	Dan Corcoran (D)	60,463	34.8
38	Jerry M. Patterson (D)	75,471	58.6
	Don Goedeke (R)	53,298	41.4
39	William E. Dannemeyer (R)	112,160	63.7
	William E. Farris (D)	63,891	36.3
40	Robert E. Badham (R)	147,882	65.9
	Jim McGuy (D)	76,358	34.1
41	Bob Wilson (R)	107,685	58.1
	King Golden Jr. (D)	77,540	41.9
42	Lionel Van Deerlin (D)	85,126	73.7
	Lawrence C. Mattera (R)	30,319	26.3
43	Clair W. Burgener (R)	167,150	68.7
	Ruben B. Brooks (D)	76,308	31.3

COLORADO

	Candidates	Votes	%
1	Patricia Schroeder (D)	82,742	61.5
	Gene Hutcheson (R)	49,845	37.0
2	Timothy E. Wirth (D)	98,889	52.9
	Ed Scott (R)	88,072	47.1
3	Ray Kogovsek (D)	69,669	49.3
	Harold L. McCormick (R)	69,303	49.0
4	James P. (Jim) Johnson (R)	103,121	61.2
	Morgan Smith (D)	65,241	38.8
5	Ken Kramer (R)	91,933	59.8
	Gerry Frank (D)	52,914	34.4
	L. W. Dan Bridges (I)	8,933	5.8

CONNECTICUT

	Candidates	Votes	%
1	William R. Cotter (D)	102,749	59.5
	Ben F. Andrews Jr. (R)	67,828	39.3
2	Christopher J. Dodd (D)	116,624	69.9
	Thomas H. Connell (R)	50,167	30.1
3	Robert N. Giaimo (D)	96,830	58.1
	John G. Pucciano (R)	66,663	40.0
4	Stewart B. McKinney (R)	83,990	58.4
	Michael G. Morgan (D)	59,918	41.6

	Candidates	Votes	%
5	William R. Ratchford (D)	96,738	52.3
	George C. Guidera (R)	88,162	47.7
6	Toby Moffett (D)	119,537	64.2
	Daniel F. MacKinnon (R)	66,664	35.8

DELAWARE

	Candidates	Votes	%
AL	Thomas B. Evans Jr. (R)	91,689	58.2
	Gary E. Hindes (D)	64,863	41.2

FLORIDA

	Candidates	Votes	%
1	Earl D. Hutto (D)	85,608	63.3
	Warren Briggs (R)	49,715	36.7
2	Don Fuqua (D)	112,649	81.7
	Peter L. W. Brathwaite (R)	25,148	18.3
3	Charles E. Bennett (D)		100.0
4	Bill Chappell Jr. (D)	113,302	73.1
	Tom Boney (R)	41,647	26.9
5	Richard Kelly (R)	106,319	51.1
	David R. Best (D)	101,867	48.9
6	C. W. Bill Young (R)	150,694	78.8
	James A. Christison (D)	40,654	21.2
7	Sam Gibbons (D)		100.0
8	Andy Ireland (D)		100.0
9	Bill Nelson (D)	89,543	61.5
	Edward J. Gurney (R)	56,074	38.5
10	L. A. (Skip) Bafalis (R)		100.0
11	Dan Mica (D)	123,346	55.3
	Bill James (R)	99,757	44.7
12	Edward J. Stack (D)	107,037	61.6
	J. Herbert Burke (R)	66,610	38.4
13	William Lehman (D)		100.0
14	Claude Pepper (D)	65,202	63.1
	Al Cardenas (R)	38,081	36.9
15	Dante B. Fascell (D)	108,837	74.2
	Herbert J. Hoodwin (R)	37,897	25.8

GEORGIA

	Candidates	Votes	%
1	Bo Ginn (D)	36,961	100.0
2	Dawson Mathis (D)	42,234	100.0
3	Jack Brinkley (D)	54,881	100.0
4	Elliott H. Levitas (D)	60,284	80.9
	Homer Cheung (R)	14,221	19.1
5	Wyche Fowler Jr. (D)	52,739	75.5
	Thomas P. Bowles Jr. (R)	17,132	24.5
6	Newt Gingrich (R)	47,078	54.4
	Virginia Shapard (D)	39,451	45.6
7	Larry P. McDonald (D)	47,090	66.5
	Ernie Norsworthy (R)	23,698	33.5
8	Billy Lee Evans (D)	41,184	100.0
9	Ed Jenkins (D)	47,264	76.9
	David G. Ashworth (R)	14,172	23.1
10	Doug Barnard (D)	50,122	100.0

HAWAII

	Candidates	Votes	%
1	Cecil (Cec) Heftel (D)	84,552	73.3
	William D. Spillane (R)	24,470	21.2
2	Daniel K. Akaka (D)	118,272	85.7
	Charles Isaak (R)	15,697	11.4

IDAHO

	Candidates	Votes	%
1	Steven D. Symms (R)	86,680	59.9
	Roy Truby (D)	57,972	40.1
2	George Hansen (R)	80,591	57.3
	Stan Kress (D)	60,040	42.7

ILLINOIS

	Candidates	Votes	%
1	Bennett Stewart (D)	47,581	58.5
	A. A. Rayner (R)	33,540	41.3
2	Morgan F. Murphy (D)	80,906	86.0
	James Wognum (R)	11,104	11.8

Candidates	Votes	%
3 Marty Russo (D)	95,701	65.2
Robert L. Dunne (R)	51,098	34.8
4 Edward J. Derwinski (R)	94,435	66.9
Andrew D. Thomas (D)	46,788	33.1
5 John G. Fary (D)	98,702	84.0
Joseph A. Barracca (R)	18,802	16.0
6 Henry J. Hyde (R)	87,193	66.2
Jeanne P. Quinn (D)	44,543	33.8
7 Cardiss Collins (D)	64,716	86.3
James C. Holt (R)	10,273	13.7
8 Dan Rostenkowski (D)	81,457	86.0
Carl C. LoDico (R)	13,302	14.0
9 Sidney R. Yates (D)	87,543	75.3
John M. Collins (R)	28,673	24.7
10 Abner J. Mikva (D)	89,479	50.2
John E. Porter (R)	88,829	49.8
11 Frank Annunzio (D)	112,365	73.7
John Hoeger (R)	40,044	26.3
12 Philip M. Crane (R)	110,503	79.5
Gilbert Bogen (D)	28,424	20.5
13 Robert McClory (R)	64,060	61.2
Frederick J. Steffen (D)	40,675	38.8
14 John N. Erlenborn (R)	118,741	75.1
James A. Romanyak (D)	39,438	24.9
15 Tom Corcoran (R)	80,856	62.4
Tim L. Hall (D)	48,756	37.6
16 John B. Anderson (R)	76,752	65.4
Ernest W. Dahlin (D)	40,471	34.5
17 George M. O'Brien (R)	94,375	70.6
Clifford J. Sinclair (D)	39,260	29.4
18 Robert H. Michel (R)	85,973	65.9
Virgil R. Grunkemeyer (D)	44,527	34.1
19 Tom Railsback (R)	89,770	100.0
20 Paul Findley (R)	111,054	69.6
Victor W. Roberts (D)	48,426	30.4
21 Edward R. Madigan (R)	97,473	78.3
Kenneth E. Baughman (D)	27,054	21.7
22 Daniel B. Crane (R)	86,051	54.0
Terry L. Bruce (D)	73,331	46.0
23 Melvin Price (D)	74,247	74.2
Daniel J. Stack (R)	25,858	25.8
24 Paul Simon (D)	110,298	65.6
John T. Anderson (R)	57,763	34.4

INDIANA

Candidates	Votes	%
1 Adam Benjamin Jr. (D)	72,367	80.3
Owen W. Crumpacker (R)	17,419	19.3
2 Floyd Fithian (D)	82,402	56.5
J. Philip Oppenheim (R)	52,842	36.2
William Costas (I)	9,368	6.4
3 John Brademas (D)	64,336	55.5
Thomas L. Thorson (R)	50,145	43.3
4 Dan Quayle (R)	80,527	64.4
John D. Walda (D)	42,238	33.8
5 Elwood Hillis (R)	94,950	67.6
Max E. Heiss (D)	45,479	32.4
6 David W. Evans (D)	66,421	52.2
David G. Crane (R)	60,630	47.6
7 John T. Myers (R)	86,955	56.3
Charlotte Zietlow (D)	67,469	43.7
8 H. Joel Deckard (R)	83,019	52.0
David L. Cornwell (D)	76,654	48.0
9 Lee H. Hamilton Jr. (D)	99,727	65.6
Frank I. Hamilton Jr. (R)	52,218	34.4
10 Phil Sharp (D)	73,343	56.1
William G. Frazier (R)	55,999	42.8
11 Andy Jacobs Jr. (D)	61,504	57.2
Charles F. Bosma (R)	45,809	42.6

IOWA

Candidates	Votes	%
1 Jim Leach (R)	79,940	63.5
Dick Myers (D)	45,037	35.8
2 Tom Tauke (R)	72,644	52.3
Michael T. Blouin (D)	63,450	47.1
3 Charles E. Grassley (R)	103,659	74.8
John Knudson (D)	34,880	25.2
4 Neal Smith (D)	88,526	64.7
Charles E. Minor (R)	48,308	35.3

Candidates	Votes	%
5 Tom Harkin (D)	82,333	58.9
Julian B. Garrett (R)	57,377	41.1
6 Berkley Bedell (D)	87,139	66.3
Willis E. Junker (R)	44,320	33.7

KANSAS

Candidates	Votes	%
1 Keith G. Sebelius (R)	131,037	100.0
2 Jim Jeffries (R)	76,419	52.0
Martha Keys (D)	70,460	48.0
3 Larry Winn Jr. (R)	103,265	100.0
4 Dan Glickman (D)	100,139	69.5
James P. Litsey (R)	43,854	30.5
5 Robert Whittaker (R)	86,011	57.0
Donald L. Allegrucci (D)	62,402	41.4

KENTUCKY

Candidates	Votes	%
1 Carroll Hubbard Jr. (D)	44,090	100.0
2 William H. Natcher (D)	36,441	100.0
3 Romano L. Mazoli (D)	37,346	65.7
Norbert D. Leveronne (R)	17,785	31.3
4 Gene Snyder (R)	62,087	65.8
George C. Martin (D)	32,212	34.2
5 Tim Lee Carter (R)	59,743	79.2
Jesse M. Ramey (D)	15,714	20.8
6 Larry J. Hopkins (R)	52,092	50.6
Tom Easterly (D)	47,436	46.1
7 Carl D. Perkins (D)	51,559	76.5
Granville Thomas (R)	15,861	23.5

LOUISIANA[1]

Candidates	Votes	%
1 Robert L. Livingston (R)		100.0
2 Lindy Boggs (D)		100.0
3 David C. Treen (R)		100.0
4 Claude (Buddy) Leach (D)	65,583	50.1
Jimmy Wilson (R)	65,317	49.9
5 Jerry Huckaby (D)		100.0
6 W. Henson Moore (R)		100.0
7 John B. Breaux (D)		100.0
8 Gillis W. Long (D)		100.0

MAINE

Candidates	Votes	%
1 David F. Emery (R)	120,791	61.5
John Quinn (D)	70,348	35.8
2 Olympia J. Snowe (R)	87,939	50.8
Markham L. Gartley (D)	70,691	40.8

MARYLAND

Candidates	Votes	%
1 Robert E. Bauman (R)	80,202	63.5
Joseph D. Quinn (D)	46,093	36.5
2 Clarence D. Long (D)	98,601	66.4
Malcolm M. McKnight (R)	49,886	33.6
3 Barbara A. Mikulski (D)	91,189	100.0
4 Marjorie S. Holt (R)	71,374	62.0
Sue F. Ward (D)	43,663	38.0
5 Gladys Noon Spellman (D)	64,868	77.2
Saul J. Harris (R)	19,160	22.8
6 Beverly Byron (D)	126,196	89.7
Melvin Perkins (R)	14,545	10.3
7 Parren J. Mitchell (D)	51,996	88.7
Debra Hanania Freeman (I)	6,626	11.3
8 Michael D. Barnes (D)	81,851	51.3
Newton I. Steers Jr. (R)	77,807	48.7

MASSACHUSETTS

Candidates	Votes	%
1 Silvio O. Conte (R)	131,773	100.0
2 Edward P. Boland (D)	101,570	72.8
Thomas P. Swank (R)	37,881	27.2
3 Joseph D. Early (D)	119,337	75.2
Charles Kevin MacLeod (R)	39,259	24.7
4 Robert F. Drinan (D)	111,353	100.0
5 James M. Shannon (D)	90,156	52.2
John J. Buckley (R)	48,685	28.2
James J. Gaffney III (I)	33,835	19.6
6 Nicholas Mavroules (D)	97,099	53.8

Candidates	Votes	%
William E. Bronson (R)	83,511	46.2
7 Edward J. Markey (D)	145,615	84.8
James J. Murphy (I)	26,017	15.2
8 Thomas P. O'Neill Jr. (D)	102,160	74.6
William A. Barnstead (R)	28,566	20.9
9 Joe Moakley (D)	106,805	91.8
Brenda Lee Franklin (SOC WORK)	6,794	5.8
10 Margaret M. Heckler (R)	102,080	61.1
John J. Marino (D)	64,868	38.9
11 Brian J. Donnelly (D)	133,644	91.7
H. Graham Lowry (USLP)	12,044	8.3
12 Gerry E. Studds (D)	176,704	99.9

MICHIGAN

Candidates	Votes	%
1 John Conyers Jr. (D)	89,646	92.9
Robert S. Arnold (R)	6,878	7.1
2 Carl D. Pursell (R)	97,503	67.6
Earl Greene (D)	45,631	31.6
3 Howard Wolpe (D)	83,932	51.3
Garry Brown (R)	79,572	48.7
4 Dave Stockman (R)	95,440	70.6
Morgan L. Hager Jr. (D)	38,204	28.3
5 Harold S. Sawyer (R)	81,794	49.4
Dale R. Sprik (D)	80,622	48.7
6 Bob Carr (D)	97,971	56.7
Mike Conlin (R)	74,718	43.3
7 Dale E. Kildee (D)	105,402	76.6
Gale M. Cronk (R)	29,958	21.8
8 Bob Traxler (D)	103,346	66.6
Norman R. Hughes (R)	51,900	33.4
9 Guy Vander Jagt (R)	122,363	69.6
Howard M. Leroux (D)	53,450	30.4
10 Donald J. Albosta (D)	94,913	51.5
Elford A. Cederberg (R)	89,451	48.5
11 Robert W. Davis (R)	96,351	54.9
Keith McLeod (D)	79,081	45.1
12 David E. Bonior (D)	82,892	54.9
Kirby Holmes (R)	68,063	45.1
13 Charles C. Diggs Jr. (D)	44,771	79.2
Dovie T. Pickett (R)	11,749	20.8
14 Lucien N. Nedzi (D)	84,032	67.4
John Edward Getz (R)	40,716	32.6
15 William D. Ford (D)	95,137	79.6
Edgar Nieten (R)	23,177	19.4
16 John D. Dingell (D)	93,387	76.5
Melvin E. Heuer (R)	26,827	22.0
17 William M. Brodhead (D)	106,303	95.2
18 James J. Blanchard (D)	113,037	74.5
Robert J. Salloum (R)	36,913	24.3
19 William S. Broomfield (R)	117,122	71.3
Betty F. Collier (D)	47,165	28.7

MINNESOTA

Candidates	Votes	%
1 Arlen Erdahl (I-R)	110,090	56.2
Gerry Sikorski (DFL)	83,271	42.5
2 Tom Hagedorn (I-R)	145,415	70.4
John F. Considine (DFL)	61,173	29.6
3 Bill Frenzel (I-R)	128,759	65.7
Michael O. Freeman (DFL)	67,120	34.3
4 Bruce F. Vento (DFL)	95,989	58.0
John R. Berg (I-R)	69,396	42.0
5 Martin Olav Sabo (DFL)	91,673	62.3
Michael Till (I-R)	55,412	37.7
6 Richard Nolan (DFL)	115,880	55.3
Russ Bjorhus (I-R)	93,742	44.7
7 Arlan Stangeland (I-R)	109,456	52.4
Gene R. Wenstrom (DFL)	93,055	44.5
8 James L. Oberstar (DFL)	171,125	87.2
John W. Hull (AM)	25,015	12.7

MISSISSIPPI

Candidates	Votes	%
1 Jamie L. Whitten (D)	57,358	66.6
T. K. Moffett (R)	26,734	31.0
2 David R. Bowen (D)	57,678	61.7
Roland Byrd (R)	35,730	38.2

Candidates	Votes	%
3 G. V. (Sonny) Montgomery (D)	101,685	92.3
Dorothy Cleveland (R)	8,408	7.6
4 Jon C. Hinson (R)	68,225	51.6
John Hampton Stennis (D)	34,837	26.4
Evan Doss (I)	25,134	19.0
5 Trent Lott (R)	97,177	100.0

MISSOURI

Candidates	Votes	%
1 William (Bill) Clay (D)	65,950	66.6
William E. White (R)	30,995	31.3
2 Robert A. Young (D)	102,911	56.4
Robert C. Chase (R)	79,495	43.6
3 Richard A. Gephardt (D)	121,565	81.9
Lee Buchschacher (R)	26,881	18.1
4 Ike Skelton (D)	120,748	72.8
William D. Baker (R)	45,116	27.2
5 Richard Bolling (D)	82,140	72.0
Steven L Walter (R)	30,360	26.6
6 E. Thomas Coleman (R)	96,574	55.9
Phil Snowden (D)	76,061	44.1
7 Gene Taylor (R)	104,566	61.2
Jim Thomas (D)	66,351	38.8
8 Richard H. Ichord (D)	96,509	60.5
Donald D. Meyer (R)	63,109	39.5
9 Harold L. Volkmer (D)	135,170	74.7
Jerry A. Dent (R)	45,795	25.3
10 Bill D. Burlison (D)	99,148	65.3
James A. Weir (R)	52,687	34.7

MONTANA

Candidates	Votes	%
1 Pat Williams (D)	86,016	57.3
Jim Waltermire (R)	64,093	42.7
2 Ron Marlenee (R)	75,766	56.9
Thomas G. Monahan (D)	57,480	43.1

NEBRASKA

Candidates	Votes	%
1 Douglas K. Bereuter (R)	99,013	58.1
Hess Dyas (D)	71,311	41.9
2 John J. Cavanaugh (D)	77,135	52.3
Harold J. Daub Jr. (R)	70,309	47.7
3 Virginia Smith (R)	141,597	80.0
Marilyn Fowler (D)	35,371	20.0

NEVADA

Candidates	Votes	%
AL Jim Santini (D)	132,513	69.5
Bill O'Mara (R)	44,425	23.3

NEW HAMPSHIRE

Candidates	Votes	%
1 Norman E. D'Amours (D)	82,697	61.6
Daniel M. Hughes (R)	49,131	36.6
2 James C. Cleveland (R)	84,535	68.1
Edgar J. Helms (D)	39,546	31.9

NEW JERSEY

Candidates	Votes	%
1 James J. Florio (D)	106,096	79.4
Robert M. Deitch (R)	26,853	20.1
2 William J. Hughes (D)	112,768	66.4
James H. Biggs (R)	56,997	33.6
3 James J. Howard (D)	83,349	56.0
Bruce G. Coe (R)	64,730	43.5
4 Frank Thompson Jr. (D)	69,259	61.1
Christopher H. Smith (R)	41,833	36.9
5 Millicent Fenwick (R)	100,739	72.6
John T. Fahy (D)	38,108	27.4
6 Edwin B. Forsythe (R)	89,446	60.4
W. Thomas McGann (D)	56,874	38.4
7 Andrew Maguire (D)	78,358	52.5
Margaret S. Roukema (R)	69,543	46.6
8 Robert A. Roe (D)	69,496	74.5
Thomas Melani (R)	23,842	25.5
9 Harold C. Hollenback (R)	73,478	48.9
Nicholas S. Mastorelli (D)	56,888	37.9
Henry Helstoski (I)	19,126	12.7

Candidates	Votes	%
10 Peter W. Rodino Jr. (D)	55,074	86.4
John L. Pelt (R)	8,066	12.6
11 Joseph G. Minish (D)	88,294	70.5
Julius George Feld (R)	35,642	28.5
12 Matthew J. Rinaldo (R)	94,850	73.4
Richard McCormack (D)	34,423	26.6
13 James A. Courter (R)	77,301	51.8
Helen Meyner (D)	71,808	48.2
14 Frank J. Guarini (D)	67,008	63.6
Henry J. Hill (R)	21,355	20.3
Thomas E. McDonough (I)	15,015	14.3
15 Edward J. Patten (D)	55,944	48.3
Charles W. Wiley (R)	53,108	45.8

NEW MEXICO

Candidates	Votes	%
1 Manuel Lujan Jr. (R)	118,075	62.5
Robert Hawk (D)	70,761	37.5
2 Harold Runnels (D)	95,710	100.0

NEW YORK

Candidates	Votes	%
1 William Carney (R, C)	90,115	56.3
John F. Randolph (D)	67,180	41.9
2 Thomas J. Downey (D)	64,807	54.9
Harold J. Withers Jr. (R, C)	53,322	45.1
3 Jerome A. Ambro (D)	70,526	50.9
Gregory W. Carman (R, C)	66,458	47.9
4 Norman F. Lent (R, C)	94,711	66.1
Everett A. Rosenblum (D)	46,508	32.5
5 John W. Wydler (R, C)	84,864	58.4
John W. Matthews (D, L)	60,519	41.6
6 Lester L. Wolff (D, L)	80,799	60.0
Stuart L. Ain (R)	44,304	32.9
Howard Horowitz (C)	9,503	7.1
7 Joseph P. Addabbo (D, R, L)	73,066	94.9
Mark Elliott Scott (C)	3,935	5.1
8 Benjamin S. Rosenthal (D, L)	74,872	78.6
Albert Lemishow (R)	15,165	15.9
Paul C. Ruebenacker (C)	5,165	5.4
9 Geraldine A. Ferraro (D)	51,350	54.2
Alfred A. DelliBovi (R, C)	42,108	44.4
10 Mario Biaggi (D, R, L)	77,979	95.0
Carmen Ricciardi (C)	4,082	5.0
11 James H. Scheuer (D, L)	58,997	78.5
Kenneth Huhn (R, C)	16,206	21.5
12 Shirley Chisholm (D, L)	25,697	87.8
Charles Gibb (R)	3,580	12.2
13 Stephen J. Solarz (D, L)	68,837	81.1
Max Carasso (R, C)	16,002	18.9
14 Frederick Richmond (D, L)	31,339	76.9
Arthur Bramwell (R)	7,516	18.4
15 Leo C. Zeferetti (D, C)	49,272	68.1
Robert P. Whelan (R)	20,508	28.4
16 Elizabeth Holtzman (D, L)	59,703	81.9
Larry Penner (R, UT)	9,405	12.9
John H. Fox (C)	3,782	5.2
17 John M. Murphy (D)	54,228	54.2
John Michael Peters (R, C)	33,071	33.1
Thomas H. Stokes (L)	12,662	12.7
18 S. William Green (R)	60,867	53.3
Carter Burden (D, L)	53,434	46.7
19 Charles B. Rangel (D, R, L)	59,731	96.4
20 Ted Weiss (D, L)	64,275	84.6
Harry Torczyner (R)	11,661	15.4
21 Robert Garcia (D, R, L)	23,950	98.0
22 Jonathan B. Bingham (D, L)	58,727	84.1
Anthony J. Geidel Jr. (R, C)	11,110	15.9
23 Peter A. Peyser (D)	66,354	51.6
Angelo R. Martinelli (R, C)	59,455	46.2
24 Richard L. Ottinger (D)	75,397	56.1
Michael R. Edelman (R, C)	57,451	42.7
25 Hamilton Fish Jr. (R)	114,641	78.2
Gunars M. Ozols (D)	31,213	21.3
26 Benjamin A. Gilman (R)	87,059	62.3
Charles E. Holbrook (D, L)	41,870	30.0
William R. Schaeffer Jr. (C)	10,708	7.7
27 Matthew F. McHugh (D)	83,413	55.8
Nell Tyler Wallace (R, C)	66,177	44.2
28 Samuel S. Stratton (D)	139,575	76.3

Candidates	Votes	%
Paul H. Tocker (R, C)	36,017	19.7
29 Gerald B. Solomon (R, C)	99,518	54.0
Edward W. Pattison (D, L)	84,705	46.0
30 Robert C. McEwen (R. C)	85,478	60.5
Norma A. Bartle (D, L)	55,785	39.5
31 Donald J. Mitchell (R, C)	107,791	100.0
32 James M. Hanley (D)	76,251	52.4
Peter J. Del Giorno (R, C)	67,071	46.1
33 Gary A. Lee (R)	82,501	56.0
Roy A. Bernardi (D)	58,286	39.5
34 Frank Horton (R, D)	122,785	87.1
Leo J. Kesselring (C)	18,127	12.9
35 Barber B. Conable Jr. (R)	96,119	69.4
Francis C. Repicci (D)	36,428	26.3
36 John J. LaFalce (D, L)	99,497	74.1
Francina J. Cartonia (R)	31,527	23.5
37 Henry J. Nowak (D, L)	70,911	78.6
Charles Roth III (R)	17,585	19.5
38 Jack F. Kemp (R, C)	113,928	94.8
James A. Peck (L)	6,204	5.2
39 Stanley N. Lundine (D)	79,385	58.5
Crispin M. Maguire (R, C)	56,431	41.5

Special Elections

Candidates	Votes	%
18 S. William Green (R)	30,332	50.5
Bella S. Abzug (D, L)	29,189	48.5
21 Robert Garcia (R, L)	7,959	55.4
Louis Nine (D, C)	3,514	24.5
Ramon S. Valez (I)	2,280	15.9

NORTH CAROLINA

Candidates	Votes	%
1 Walter B. Jones (D)	67,716	80.1
James Newcomb (R)	16,814	19.9
2 L. H. Fountain (D)	61,851	78.2
Barry L. Gardner (R)	15,988	20.2
3 Charlie Whitley (D)	54,452	71.1
Willard J. Blanchard (R)	22,150	28.9
4 Ike F. Andrews (D)	74,249	94.4
Naudeen Beek (LIBERT)	4,436	5.6
5 Stephen L. Neal (D)	68,778	54.2
Hamilton C. Horton Jr. (R)	58,161	45.8
6 Richardson Preyer (D)	58,193	68.4
George Bemus (R)	26,882	31.6
7 Charlie Rose (D)	53,696	69.9
Raymond C. Schrump (R)	23,146	30.1
8 W. G. (Bill) Hefner (D)	63,168	59.0
Roger Austin (R)	43,942	41.0
9 James G. Martin (R)	66,157	68.3
Charles Maxwell (D)	29,761	30.7
10 James T. Broyhill (R)	67,004	100.0
11 Lamar Gudger (D)	75,460	53.4
R. Curtis Ratcliff (R)	65,832	46.6

NORTH DAKOTA

Candidates	Votes	%
AL Mark Andrews (R)	147,746	67.1
Bruce Hagen (D)	68,016	30.9

OHIO

Candidates	Votes	%
1 Bill Gradison (R)	73,593	64.5
Timothy M. Burke (D)	38,669	33.9
2 Thomas A. Luken (D)	64,522	52.4
Stanley J. Aronoff (R)	58,716	47.6
3 Tony P. Hall (D)	62,849	53.8
Dudley P. Kircher (R)	51,833	44.4
4 Tennyson Guyer (R)	85,575	68.5
John W. Griffin (D)	39,360	31.5
5 Delbert L. Latta (R)	85,547	62.6
James R. Sherck (D)	51,071	37.4
6 William H. Harsha (R)	85,592	64.9
Ted Strickland (D)	46,318	35.1
7 Clarence J. Brown (R)	92,507	100.0
8 Thomas N. Kindness (R)	81,156	71.4
Lou Schroeder (D)	32,493	28.6
9 Thomas L. Ashley (D)	71,709	63.4
John C. Hoyt (R)	34,326	30.3
10 Clarence E. Miller (R)	99,329	73.9

Candidates	Votes	%
James A. Plummer (D)	35,039	26.1
11 J. William Stanton (R)	89,327	68.1
Patrick J. Donlin (D)	37,131	28.3
12 Samuel L. Devine (R)	81,573	56.9
James L. Baumann (D)	61,698	43.1
13 Don J. Pease (D)	80,875	65.1
Mark W. Whitfield (R)	43,269	34.9
14 John F. Seiberling (D)	82,356	72.5
Walter J. Vogel (R)	31,311	27.5
15 Chalmers P. Wylie (R)	91,023	71.1
Henry W. Eckhart (D)	37,000	28.9
16 Ralph S. Regula (R)	105,152	78.0
Owen S. Hand Jr. (D)	29,640	22.0
17 John M. Ashbrook (R)	87,010	67.4
Kenneth R. Grier (D)	42,117	32.6
18 Douglas Applegate (D)	71,894	59.5
Bill Ress (R)	48,931	40.5
19 Lyle Williams (R)	71,890	50.7
Charles J. Carney (D)	69,977	49.3
20 Mary Rose Oakar (D)	76,973	100.0
21 Louis Stokes (D)	58,934	86.1
Bill Mack (R)	9,533	13.9
22 Charles A. Vanik (D)	87,551	66.0
Richard W. Sander (R)	30,935	23.3
Jamas F. Sexton (I)	7,126	5.4
Robert E. Lehman (I)	6,960	5.2
23 Ronald M. Mottl (D)	99,975	74.8
Homes S. Taft (R)	33,732	25.2

OKLAHOMA

Candidates	Votes	%
1 James R. Jones (D)	73,886	59.9
Paula Unruh (R)	49,404	40.1
2 Mike Synar (D)	72,583	54.8
Gary L. Richardson (R)	59,853	45.2
3 Wes Watkins (D)		100.0
4 Tom Steed (D)	62,993	60.3
Scotty Robb (R)	41,421	39.7
5 Mickey Edwards (R)	71,451	79.9
Jesse D. Knipp (D)	17,978	20.1
6 Glenn English (D)	103,512	74.2
Harold Hunter (R)	36,031	25.8

OREGON

Candidates	Votes	%
1 Les AuCoin (D)	158,706	62.9
Nick Bunick (R)	93,640	37.1
2 Al Ullman (D)	152,099	69.1
Terry L. Hicks (R)	67,547	30.7
3 Robert Duncan (D)	151,895	84.6
Martin Simon (USLP)	27,120	15.1
4 James Weaver (D)	124,745	56.3
Jerry L. Lausmann (R)	96,953	43.7

PENNSYLVANIA

Candidates	Votes	%
1 Michael (Ozzie) Myers (D)	104,412	71.9
Samuel N. Fanelli (R)	37,913	26.1
2 William H. Gray III (D)	132,594	82.0
Roland J. Atkins (R)	25,785	15.9
3 Raymond F. Lederer (D)	86,915	71.8
Raymond S. Kauffman (R)	33,750	28.2
4 Charles F. Dougherty (R)	119,445	55.8
Joshua Eilberg (D)	87,555	44.2
5 Richard T. Schulze (R)	119,565	75.1
Murray P. Zealor (D)	36,704	24.9
6 Gus Yatron (D)	196,432	73.8
Stephen Mazur (R)	37,746	26.2
7 Robert W. Edgar (D)	79,771	50.3
Eugene D. Kane (R)	78,403	49.4
8 Peter H. Kostmayer (D)	89,276	61.1
G. Roger Bowers (R)	56,776	38.9
9 Bud Shuster (R)	101,151	74.9
Blaine L. Havice Jr. (D)	33,882	25.1
10 Joseph M. McDade (R)	116,003	76.5
Gene Basalyga (D)	35,721	23.5
11 Daniel J. Flood (D)	61,433	57.5
Robert P. Hudock (R)	45,335	42.5
12 John P. Murtha (D)	194,216	68.7
Luther V. Elkins (R)	47,442	31.3

Candidates	Votes	%
13 Lawrence Coughlin (R)	112,711	70.5
Alan B. Rubenstein (D)	47,151	29.5
14 William S. Moorhead (D)	68,004	57.0
Stan Thomas (R)	49,992	41.9
15 Donald L. Ritter (R)	65,986	53.2
Fred B. Rooney (D)	58,077	46.8
16 Robert S. Walker (R)	91,910	77.0
Charles W. Boohar (D)	27,386	23.0
17 Allen E. Ertel (D)	79,234	59.6
Thomas R. Rippon (R)	53,613	40.4
18 Doug Walgren (D)	88,299	57.1
Ted Jacob (R)	65,088	42.1
19 Bill Goodling (R)	105,424	78.7
Rajeshwar Kumar (D)	28,577	21.3
20 Joseph M. Gaydos (D)	97,745	72.1
Kathleen M. Meyer (R)	37,745	27.9
21 Don Bailey (D)	73,712	52.9
Robert H. Miller (R)	65,622	47.1
22 Austin J. Murphy (D)	99,559	71.6
Marilyn C. Ecoff (R)	39,518	28.4
23 William F. Clinger Jr. (R)	73,194	54.3
Joseph S. Ammerman (D)	61,657	45.7
24 Marc L. Marks (R)	87,041	64.0
Joseph F. Vigorito (D)	48,894	36.0
25 Eugene V. Atkinson (D)	68,293	46.5
Tim Shaffer (R)	62,160	42.3
Robert Morris (I)	10,588	7.2

RHODE ISLAND

Candidates	Votes	%
1 Fernand J. St Germain (D)	86,768	61.2
John J. Slocum Jr. (R)	54,912	38.8
2 Edward P. Beard (D)	87,397	52.6
Claudine Schneider (R)	78,725	47.4

SOUTH CAROLINA

Candidates	Votes	%
1 Mendel J. Davis (D)	65,835	60.6
C. C. Wannamaker (R)	42,811	39.4
2 Floyd Spence (R)	71,208	57.3
Jack Bass (D)	53,021	42.7
3 Butler Derrick (D)	81,638	82.0
Anthony Panuccio (R)	17,973	18.0
4 Carroll A. Campbell Jr. (R)	51,377	52.1
Max M. Heller (D)	45,484	46.2
5 Ken Holland (D)	63,538	82.7
Harold Hough (I)	13,251	17.3
6 John W. Jenrette Jr. (D)	69,372	100.0

SOUTH DAKOTA

Candidates	Votes	%
1 Thomas A. Daschle (D)	64,683	50.1
Leo K. Thorsness (R)	64,544	49.9
2 James Abdnor (R)	70,780	56.0
Bob Samuelson (D)	55,516	44.0

TENNESSEE

Candidates	Votes	%
1 James H. (Jimmy) Quillen (R)	92,143	64.5
Gordon Ball (D)	50,694	35.5
2 John J. Duncan (R)	125,082	81.8
Margaret Francis (D)	27,745	18.2
3 Marilyn Lloyd (D)	108,282	88.9
Dan East (I)	13,535	11.1
4 Albert Gore Jr. (D)	108,695	100.0
5 Bill Boner (D)	68,608	51.4
Bill Goodwin (R)	47,288	35.4
Henry Haile (I)	17,674	13.2
6 Robin L. Beard Jr. (R)	114,630	74.6
Ron Arline (D)	38,954	25.4
7 Ed Jones (D)	96,863	72.9
Ross Cook (R)	36,003	27.1
8 Harold E. Ford (D)	80,776	69.7
Duncan Ragsdale (R)	33,679	29.1

TEXAS

Candidates	Votes	%
1 Sam B. Hall Jr. (D)	73,708	78.1
Fred Hudson (R)	20,700	21.9
2 Charles Wilson (D)	66,986	70.1

Candidates	Votes	%
Jim (Matt) Dillon (R)	28,584	29.9
3 James M. Collins (R)	96,406	100.0
4 Ray Roberts (D)	58,336	61.5
Frank S. Glenn (R)	36,582	38.5
5 Jim Mattox (D)	35,524	50.3
Tom Pauken (R)	34,672	49.1
6 Phil Gramm (D)	66,025	65.1
Wesley H. Mowrey (R)	35,393	34.9
7 Bill Archer (R)	128,214	85.1
Robert L. Hutchings (D)	22,415	14.9
8 Bob Eckhardt (D)	39,429	61.5
Nick Gearhart (R)	24,673	38.5
9 Jack Brooks (D)	50,792	63.3
Randy Evans (R)	29,473	36.7
10 J. J. Pickle (D)	94,529	76.3
Emmett L. Hudspeth (R)	29,328	23.7
11 J. Marvin Leath (D)	53,354	51.6
Jack Burgess (R)	49,965	48.4
12 Jim Wright (D)	46,456	68.5
Claude K. Brown (R)	21,364	31.5
13 Jack Hightower (D)	75,271	74.9
Clifford A. Jones (D)	25,275	25.1
14 Joe Wyatt (D)	63,953	72.4
Joy Yates (R)	24,325	27.6
15 E. (Kika) de la Garza (D)	54,560	66.2
Robert L. McDonald (R)	27,853	33.8
16 Richard C. White (D)	53,090	70.0
Michael Giare (R)	22,743	30.0
17 Charles W. Stenholm (D)	69,030	68.1
Billy Lee Fisher (R)	32,302	31.9
18 Mickey Leland (D)	36,783	96.8
19 Kent Hance (D)	54,729	53.2
George W. Bush (R)	48,070	46.8
20 Henry B. Gonzalez (D)	51,584	100.0
21 Tom Loeffler (R)	84,336	57.0
Nelson W. Wolff (R)	63,501	43.0
22 Ron Paul (R)	54,643	50.6
Bob Gammage (D)	53,443	49.4
23 Abraham Kazen Jr. (D)	62,649	89.7
Augustin Mata (LRU)	7,185	10.3
24 Martin Frost (D)	39,201	54.1
Leo Berman (R)	33,314	45.9

UTAH

Candidates	Votes	%
1 Gunn McKay (D)	93,892	51.0
Jed J. Richardson (R)	85,028	46.2
2 Dan Marriott (R)	121,492	62.3
Edwin B. Firmage (D)	68,899	35.3

VERMONT

Candidates	Votes	%
AL James M. Jeffords (R)	90,688	75.3
S. Marie Dietz (D)	23,228	19.3
Peter Diamondstone (LU)	6,505	5.4

VIRGINIA

Candidates	Votes	%
1 Paul S. Trible Jr. (R)	89,158	72.1
Lew Puller (D)	34,578	27.9
2 G. William Whitehurst (R)	63,512	100.0
3 David E. Satterfield III (D)	104,550	87.7
Alan R. Ogden (I)	14,453	12.1
4 Robert W. Daniel Jr. (R)	77,827	99.9
5 Dan Daniel (D)	83,575	99.9
6 M. Caldwell Butler (R)	88,647	99.8
7 J. Kenneth Robinson (R)	84,517	64.3
Lewis Fickett (D)	46,950	35.7
8 Herbert E. Harris II (D)	56,137	50.5
John F. Herrity (R)	52,396	47.1
9 William C. Wampler (R)	76,877	61.9
Champ Clark (D)	47,367	38.1
10 Joseph L. Fisher (D)	70,892	53.3
Frank Wolf (R)	61,981	46.6

WASHINGTON

Candidates	Votes	%
1 Joel Pritchard (R)	99,942	64.0
Janice Niemi (D)	52,706	33.7
2 Al Swift (D)	70,620	51.4

Candidates	Votes	%
John Nance Garner (R)	66,793	48.6
3 Don Bonker (D)	82,616	58.6
Rick Bennett (R)	58,270	41.4
4 Mike McCormack (D)	85,602	61.1
Susan Roylance (R)	54,389	38.9
5 Thomas S. Foley (D)	77,201	48.0
Duane Alton (R)	68,761	42.7
Mel Tonasket (I)	14,887	9.3
6 Norman D. Dicks (D)	71,057	60.9
James E. Beaver (R)	43,640	37.4
7 Mike Lowry (D)	67,450	53.3
John E. Cunningham (R)	59,052	46.7

WEST VIRGINIA

Candidates	Votes	%
1 Robert H. Mollohan (D)	76,372	63.4
Gene A. Haynes (R)	44,062	36.6

Candidates	Votes	%
2 Harley O. Staggers (D)	69,683	55.3
Cleveland K. Benedict (R)	56,272	44.7
3 John M. Slack (D)	74,837	59.2
David M. Staton (R)	51,584	40.8
4 Nick J. Rahall (D)	70,035	100.0

WISCONSIN

Candidates	Votes	%
1 Les Aspin (D)	77,146	54.5
William W. Petrie (R)	64,437	45.5
2 Robert W. Kastenmeier (D)	99,631	57.7
James A. Wright (R)	71,412	41.3
3 Alvin Baldus (D)	96,326	62.8
Michael S. Ellis (R)	57,060	37.2
4 Clement J. Zablocki (D)	101,575	66.1
Elroy G. Honadel (R)	52,125	33.9
5 Henry S. Reuss (D)	85,067	73.1

Candidates	Votes	%
James R. Medina (R)	30,185	25.9
6 William A. Steiger (R)	114,742	69.6
Robert J. Steffes (D)	48,785	29.6
7 David R. Obey (D)	110,874	62.2
Vinton A. Vesta (R)	65,750	36.9
8 Tobias A. Roth (R)	101,856	57.9
Robert J. Cornell (D)	73,925	42.1
9 F. James Sensenbrenner Jr. (R)	118,386	61.1
Matthew J. Flynn (D)	75,207	38.8

WYOMING

Candidates	Votes	%
AL Richard Cheney (R)	75,855	58.6
Bill Bagley (D)	53,522	41.4

1. For the 1978 House elections in Louisiana, an open primary was held with candidates from all parties running on the same ballot. Any candidate who received a majority was elected unopposed without any further appearance on the general election ballot. Where no candidate received 50 percent, there was a general election runoff between the top two finishers regardless of party.

1979 House Elections

CALIFORNIA

Special Election

Candidates	Votes	%
11 Bill Royer (R)	52,585	57.3
G. W. Holsinger (D)	37,685	41.1

WISCONSIN

Special Election

Candidates	Votes	%
6 Thomas E. Petri (R)	71,715	50.0
Gary R. Goyke (D)	70,492	49.5

1980 House Elections

ALABAMA

	Candidates	Votes	%
1	Jack Edwards (R)	111,089	94.8
	Steve Smith (LIBERT)	6,130	5.2
2	William L. Dickinson (R)	104,796	60.6
	Cecil Wyatt (D)	63,447	36.7
3	Bill Nichols (D)	107,654	100.0
4	Tom Bevill (D)	129,365	97.9
5	Ronnie G. Flippo (D)	117,626	94.1
	Betty T. Benson (LIBERT)	7,341	5.9
6	Albert Lee Smith Jr. (R)	95,019	50.5
	W. B. (Pete) Clifford (D)	87,536	46.6
7	Richard C. Shelby (D)	122,505	72.6
	James E. Bacon (R)	43,320	25.7

ALASKA

		Votes	%
AL	Don Young (R)	114,089	73.8
	Kevin (Pat) Parnell (D)	39,922	25.8

ARIZONA

		Votes	%
1	John J. Rhodes (R)	136,961	73.3
	Steve Jancek (D)	40,045	21.4
2	Morris K. Udall (D)	127,736	58.1
	Richard H. Huff (R)	88,653	40.4
3	Bob Stump (D)	141,448	64.3
	Bob Croft (R)	65,845	30.0
	Sharon Hayse (LIBERT)	12,529	5.7
4	Eldon Rudd (R)	142,565	62.6
	Les Miller (D)	85,046	37.4

ARKANSAS

		Votes	%
1	Bill Alexander (D)		100.0
2	Ed Bethune (R)	159,148	78.9
	James G. Reid (D)	42,278	21.0
3	John Paul Hammerschmidt (R)		100.0
4	Beryl Anthony Jr. (D)		100.0

CALIFORNIA

		Votes	%
1	Eugene A. Chappie (R)	145,585	53.7
	Harold T. Johnson (D)	107,993	39.8
	Jim McClarin (LIBERT)	17,497	6.5
2	Don H. Clausen (R)	141,698	54.2
	Norma K. Bork (D)	109,789	42.0
3	Robert T. Matsui (D)	170,670	70.6
	Joseph Murphy (R)	64,215	26.5
4	Vic Fazio (D)	133,853	65.1
	Albert Dehr (R)	60,935	29.6
	Robert J. Burnside (LIBERT)	10,267	5.0
5	John L. Burton (D)	101,105	51.1
	Dennis McQuaid (R)	89,624	45.3
6	Phillip Burton (D)	93,400	69.4
	Tom Spinosa (R)	34,500	25.6
	Roy Childs (LIBERT)	6,750	5.0
7	George Miller (D)	142,044	63.3
	Giles St. Clair (R)	70,479	31.4
8	Ronald V. Dellums (D)	108,380	55.5
	Charles V. Hughes (R)	76,580	39.2
	Tom Mikuriya (LIBERT)	10,465	5.3
9	Fortney H. (Pete) Stark (D)	90,504	55.3
	William J. Kennedy (R)	67,265	41.1
10	Don Edwards (D)	102,231	62.1
	John M. Lutton (R)	45,987	27.9
	Joseph Fuhrig (LIBERT)	11,904	7.2
11	Tom Lantos (D)	85,823	46.4
	Bill Royer (R)	80,100	43.3
	Wilson Branch (PFP)	13,723	7.4
12	Paul N. McCloskey Jr. (R)	143,817	72.2
	Kirsten Olsen (D)	37,009	18.6
	Bill Evers (LIBERT)	15,073	7.6
13	Norman Y. Mineta (D)	132,246	58.9
	W. E. (Ted) Gagne (R)	79,766	35.5

	Candidates	Votes	%
14	Norman D. Shumway (R)	133,979	60.7
	Ann Cerney (D)	79,883	36.2
15	Tony Coelho (D)	108,072	71.8
	Ron Schwartz (R)	37,895	25.2
16	Leon E. Panetta (D)	158,360	71.0
	W. A. (Jack) Roth (R)	54,675	24.5
17	Charles Pashayan Jr. (R)	129,159	70.6
	Willard H. Johnson (D)	53,780	29.4
18	William M. Thomas (R)	126,046	71.0
	Mary (Pat) Timmermans (D)	51,415	29.0
19	Robert J. Lagomarsino (R)	162,854	77.7
	Carmen Lodise (D)	36,990	17.6
20	Barry Goldwater Jr. (R)	199,681	78.8
	Matt Miller (D)	43,025	17.0
21	Bobbi Fiedler (R)	74,843	48.7
	James C. Corman (D)	74,091	48.2
22	Carlos J. Moorhead (R)	115,241	63.9
	Pierce O'Donnell (D)	57,477	31.9
23	Anthony C. Beilenson (D)	126,020	63.2
	Robert Winckler (R)	62,742	31.5
	Jeffrey P. Lieb (LIBERT)	10,623	5.3
24	Henry A. Waxman (D)	93,569	63.8
	Roland Cayard (R)	39,744	27.1
25	Edward R. Roybal (D)	49,080	66.0
	Richard L. Ferraro Jr. (R)	21,116	28.4
	William D. Mitchell (LIBERT)	4,169	5.6
26	Joseph L. Lisoni (D)	40,099	24.4
	John H. Rousselot (R)	116,715	70.9
27	Robert K. Dornan (R)	109,807	51.0
	Carey Peck (D)	100,061	46.5
28	Julian C. Dixon (D)	108,725	79.2
	Robert Reid (R)	23,179	16.9
29	Augustus F. Hawkins (D)	80,095	86.1
	Michael A. Hirt (R)	10,282	11.1
30	George E. Danielson (D)	74,119	72.1
	J. Arthur Platten (R)	24,136	23.5
31	Mervyn M. Dymally (D)	69,146	64.4
	Don Grimshaw (R)	38,203	35.6
32	Glenn M. Anderson (D)	84,057	65.9
	John R. Adler (R)	39,260	30.8
33	Wayne Grisham (R)	122,439	70.9
	Fred L. Anderson (D)	50,365	29.1
34	Dan Lungren (R)	138,024	71.8
	Simone (D)	46,351	24.1
35	David Dreier (R)	100,743	51.8
	Jim Lloyd (D)	88,279	45.4
36	George E. Brown Jr. (D)	88,634	52.5
	John Paul Stark (R)	73,252	43.4
37	Jerry Lewis (R)	166,640	71.6
	Donald M. Rusk (D)	58,462	25.1
38	Jerry M. Patterson (D)	91,880	55.5
	Art Jacobson (R)	66,256	40.0
39	William Dannemeyer (R)	175,228	76.3
	Leonard L. Lahtinen (D)	54,504	23.7
40	Robert E. Badham (R)	213,999	70.2
	Michael F. Dow (D)	66,512	21.8
	Dan Mahaffey (LIBERT)	24,486	8.0
41	Bill Lowery (R)	123,187	52.7
	Bob Wilson (D)	101,101	43.2
42	Duncan L. Hunter (R)	79,713	53.3
	Lionel Van Deerlin (D)	69,936	46.7
43	Clair W. Burgener (R)	299,037	86.5
	Tom Metzger (D)	46,383	13.4

COLORADO

		Votes	%
1	Patricia Schroeder (D)	107,364	59.8
	Naomi Bradford (R)	67,804	37.7
2	Timothy E. Wirth (D)	153,618	56.4
	John McElderry (R)	111,825	41.1
3	Ray Kogovsek (D)	105,820	54.9
	Harold McCormick (R)	84,292	43.7
4	Hank Brown (R)	178,221	68.4
	Polly Baca Barragan (D)	76,849	29.5
5	Ken Kramer (R)	177,319	72.4
	Ed Schreiber (D)	62,003	25.3

CONNECTICUT

	Candidates	Votes	%
1	William R. Cotter (D)	137,849	63.0
	Marjorie D. Anderson (R)	80,816	37.0
2	Samuel Gejdenson (D)	119,176	53.4
	Tony Guglielmo (R)	104,107	46.6
3	Lawrence J. DeNardis (R)	117,024	52.3
	Joseph I. Lieberman (D)	103,903	46.5
4	Stewart B. McKinney (R)	124,285	62.6
	John A. Phillips (D)	74,326	37.4
5	William R. Ratchford (D)	117,316	50.4
	Edward M. Donahue (R)	115,614	49.6
6	Toby Moffett (D)	142,685	59.0
	Nicholas Schaus (R)	98,331	40.6

DELAWARE

		Votes	%
AL	Thomas B. Evans Jr. (R)	133,842	61.8
	Robert L. Maxwell (D)	81,227	37.5

FLORIDA

		Votes	%
1	Earl Hutto (D)	119,829	61.2
	Warren Briggs (R)	75,939	38.8
2	Don Fuqua (D)	138,252	70.6
	John R. LaCapra (R)	57,588	29.4
3	Charles E. Bennett (D)	104,672	77.0
	Harry Radcliffe (R)	31,208	23.0
4	Bill Chappell Jr. (D)	147,775	65.8
	Barney E. Dillard Jr. (R)	76,924	34.2
5	Bill McCollum (R)	177,603	55.8
	David Best (D)	140,903	44.2
6	C. W. Bill Young (R)		100.0
7	Sam Gibbons (D)	132,529	71.8
	Charles P. Jones (R)	52,138	28.2
8	Andy Ireland (D)	151,613	69.3
	Scott Nicholson (R)	61,820	28.2
9	Bill Nelson (D)	139,468	70.4
	Stan Dowiat (R)	58,734	29.6
10	L. A. (Skip) Bafalis (R)	272,393	78.9
	Richard D. Sparkman (D)	72,646	21.1
11	Dan Mica (D)	201,713	59.5
	Al Coogler (R)	137,520	40.5
12	Clay Shaw (R)	128,561	54.5
	Alan S. Becker (D)	107,164	45.5
13	William Lehman (D)	127,828	74.9
	Alvin E. Entin (R)	42,830	25.1
14	Claude Pepper (D)	95,820	74.9
	Evelio S. Estrella (R)	32,027	25.1
15	Dante B. Fascell (D)	132,952	65.4
	Herbert J. Hoodwin (R)	70,433	34.6

GEORGIA

		Votes	%
1	Bo Ginn (D)	82,145	100.0
2	Charles F. Hatcher (D)	92,264	73.6
	Jack E. Harrell Jr. (R)	33,107	26.4
3	Jack Brinkley (D)	89,040	100.0
4	Elliott H. Levitas (D)	117,091	69.4
	Barry E. Billington (R)	51,546	30.6
5	Wyche Fowler Jr. (D)	101,646	74.0
	F. William Dowda (R)	35,640	26.0
6	Newt Gingrich (R)	96,071	59.1
	Dock H. Davis (D)	66,606	40.9
7	Larry P. McDonald (D)	115,892	68.1
	Richard L. Castellucis (R)	54,242	31.9
8	Billy Lee Evans (D)	91,103	74.6
	Darwin Carter (R)	31,033	25.4
9	Ed Jenkins (D)	115,576	68.0
	David G. Ashworth (R)	54,341	32.0
10	Doug Barnard (D)	102,177	80.2
	Bruce J. Neubauer (R)	25,194	19.8

HAWAII

	Candidates	Votes	%
1	Cecil Heftel (D)	98,256	79.8
	Aloma Keen Noble (R)	19,819	16.1
2	Daniel K. Akaka (D)	141,477	89.9
	Don G. Smith (LIBERT)	15,903	10.1

IDAHO

	Candidates	Votes	%
1	Larry Craig (R)	116,845	53.7
	Glenn W. Nichols (D)	100,697	46.3
2	George Hansen (R)	116,196	58.8
	Diane Bilyeu (D)	81,364	41.2

ILLINOIS

	Candidates	Votes	%
1	Harold Washington (D)	119,562	95.5
2	Gus Savage (D)	129,771	88.1
	Marsha A. Harris (R)	17,428	11.8
3	Marty Russo (D)	137,283	68.9
	Lawrence C. Sarsoun (R)	61,955	31.1
4	Edward J. Derwinski (R)	152,377	68.0
	Richard S. Jalovec (D)	71,814	32.0
5	John G. Fary (D)	106,142	79.6
	Robert V. Kotowski (R)	27,136	20.4
6	Henry J. Hyde (R)	123,593	67.0
	Mario Raymond Reda (D)	60,951	33.0
7	Cardiss Collins (D)	80,056	85.1
	Ruth R. Hooper (R)	14,041	14.9
8	Dan Rostenkowski (D)	98,524	84.7
	Walter F. Zilke (R)	17,845	15.3
9	Sidney R. Yates (D)	106,543	73.1
	John D. Andrica (R)	39,244	26.9
10	John E. Porter (R)	137,707	60.7
	Robert A. Weinberger (D)	89,008	39.3
11	Frank Annunzio (D)	121,166	69.8
	Michael R. Zanillo (R)	52,417	30.2
12	Philip M. Crane (R)	185,080	74.1
	David McCartney (D)	64,729	25.9
13	Robert McClory (R)	131,448	71.7
	Michael Reese (D)	52,000	28.3
14	John N. Erlenborn (R)	202,583	76.8
	LeRoy E. Kennel (D)	61,224	23.2
15	Tom Corcoran (R)	150,898	76.7
	John P. Quillin (D)	45,721	23.3
16	Lynn M. Martin (R)	132,905	67.4
	Douglas R. Aurand (D)	64,224	32.6
17	George M. O'Brien (R)	125,806	65.8
	Michael A. Murer (D)	65,305	34.2
18	Robert H. Michel (R)	125,561	62.1
	John L. Knuppel (D)	76,471	37.9
19	Tom Railsback (R)	142,616	73.4
	Thomas J. Hand (D)	51,753	26.6
20	Paul Findley (R)	123,427	56.0
	David L. Robinson (D)	96,950	44.0
21	Edward R. Madigan (R)	132,186	67.6
	Penny L. Severns (D)	63,476	32.4
22	Daniel B. Crane (R)	146,014	68.8
	Peter M. Voelz (D)	66,065	31.2
23	Melvin Price (D)	107,786	64.4
	Ronald L. Davinroy (R)	59,644	35.6
24	Paul Simon (D)	112,134	49.1
	John T. Anderson (R)	110,176	48.3

Special Election

		Votes	%
10	John E. Porter (R)	36,981	54.0
	Robert Weinberger (D)	30,929	46.0

INDIANA

	Candidates	Votes	%
1	Adam Benjamin Jr. (D)	112,016	72.0
	Joseph D. Harkin (R)	43,537	28.0
2	Floyd Fithian (D)	122,326	54.1
	Ernest Niemeyer (R)	103,957	45.9
3	John P. Hiler (R)	103,972	55.0
	John Brademas (D)	85,136	45.0
4	Daniel R. Coats (R)	120,055	60.5
	John D. Walda (D)	77,542	39.1
5	Elwood Hillis (R)	129,474	61.7

	Candidates	Votes	%
	Nels J. Ackerson (D)	80,378	38.3
6	David W. Evans (D)	98,482	50.2
	David G. Crane (R)	97,582	49.8
7	John T. Myers (R)	137,604	66.1
	Patrick D. Carroll (D)	69,051	33.2
8	H. Joel Deckard (R)	119,415	55.2
	Kenneth C. Snider (D)	97,059	44.8
9	Lee H. Hamilton (D)	136,574	64.4
	George Meyers Jr. (R)	75,601	35.6
10	Phil Sharp (D)	103,083	53.4
	William G. Frazier (R)	90,051	46.6
11	Andy Jacobs Jr. (D)	105,468	57.3
	Sheila Suess (R)	78,743	42.7

IOWA

	Candidates	Votes	%
1	Jim Leach (R)	133,349	64.1
	Jim Larew (D)	72,602	34.9
2	Tom Tauke (R)	111,587	54.0
	Steve Sovern (D)	93,175	45.1
3	Cooper Evans (R)	107,869	51.4
	Lynn G. Cutler (D)	101,735	48.4
4	Neal Smith (D)	117,896	53.9
	Donald C. Young (R)	100,335	45.9
5	Tom Harkin (D)	127,895	60.2
	Cal Hultman (R)	84,472	39.8
6	Berkley Bedell (D)	129,460	64.3
	Clarence S. Carney (R)	71,866	35.7

KANSAS

	Candidates	Votes	%
1	Pat Roberts (R)	121,545	62.3
	Phil Martin (D)	73,586	37.7
2	Jim Jeffries (R)	92,107	53.9
	Sam Keys (D)	78,859	46.1
3	Larry Winn Jr. (R)	109,294	55.5
	Dan Watkins (D)	82,414	41.8
4	Dan Glickman (D)	124,014	68.9
	Clay Hunter (R)	55,899	31.1
5	Bob Whittaker (R)	141,029	74.2
	David L. Miller (D)	45,676	24.0

KENTUCKY

	Candidates	Votes	%
1	Carroll Hubbard Jr. (D)	118,565	100.0
2	William H. Natcher (D)	99,670	65.7
	Mark T. Watson (R)	52,110	34.3
3	Romano L. Mazzoli (D)	85,873	63.7
	Richard Cesler (R)	46,681	34.6
4	Gene Snyder (R)	126,049	67.0
	Phil M. McGary (D)	62,138	33.0
5	Harold Rogers (R)	112,093	67.5
	Ted R. Marcum (D)	54,027	32.5
6	Larry J. Hopkins (R)	105,376	58.9
	Tom Easterly (D)	72,473	40.5
7	Carl D. Perkins (D)	117,665	100.0

LOUISIANA[1]

	Candidates	Votes	%
1	Robert L. Livingston (R)		100.0
2	Lindy Boggs (D)		100.0
3	W. J. (Billy) Tauzin (D)		100.0
4	Buddy Roemer (D)	103,625	63.8
	Claude (Buddy) Leach (D)	58,705	36.2
5	Jerry Huckaby (D)		100.0
6	W. Henson Moore (R)		100.0
7	John B. Breaux (D)		100.0
8	Gillis W. Long (D)		100.0

Special Election

		Votes	%
3.	W. J. (Billy) Tauzin (D)	62,108	53.0
	James Donelon (R)	54,815	47.0

MAINE

	Candidates	Votes	%
1	David F. Emery (R)	188,667	68.5
	Harold C. Pachios (D)	86,819	31.5
2	Olympia J. Snowe (R)	186,406	78.5
	Harold L. Silverman (D)	51,026	21.5

MARYLAND

	Candidates	Votes	%
1	Roy Dyson (D)	97,743	51.7
	Robert E. Bauman (R)	91,143	48.3
2	Clarence D. Long (D)	121,017	57.4
	Helen D. Bentley (R)	89,961	42.6
3	Barbara A. Mikulski (D)	102,293	76.1
	Russell T. Schaffer (R)	32,074	23.9
4	Marjorie S. Holt (R)	120,985	71.9
	James J. Riley (D)	47,375	28.1
5	Gladys Noon Spellman (D)	106,035	80.5
	Kevin R. Igoe (R)	25,693	19.5
6	Beverly B. Byron (D)	146,101	69.9
	Raymond E. Beck (R)	62,913	30.1
7	Parren J. Mitchell (D)	97,104	88.5
	Victor Clark Jr. (R)	12,650	11.5
8	Michael D. Barnes (D)	148,301	59.3
	Newton I. Steers Jr. (R)	101,659	40.7

MASSACHUSETTS

	Candidates	Votes	%
1	Silvio O. Conte (R)	156,415	74.9
	Helen Poppy Doyle (D)	52,457	25.1
2	Edward P. Boland (D)	120,711	67.2
	Thomas P. Swank (R)	38,672	21.5
	John B. Aubuchon (I)	20,247	11.3
3	Joseph D. Early (D)	141,560	72.3
	David G. Skehan (R)	54,123	27.7
4	Barney Frank (D)	103,466	51.9
	Richard A. Jones (R)	95,898	48.1
5	James M. Shannon (D)	136,758	66.0
	William C. Sawyer (R)	70,547	34.0
6	Nicholas Mavroules (D)	111,393	50.8
	Thomas H. Trimarco (R)	103,192	47.1
7	Edward J. Markey (D)	155,759	100.0
8	Thomas P. O'Neill Jr. (D)	128,689	78.4
	William A. Barnstead (R)	35,477	21.6
9	Joe Moakley (D)	104,010	100.0
10	Margaret M. Heckler (R)	131,794	60.6
	Robert E. McCarthy (D)	85,629	39.4
11	Brian J. Donnelly (D)	137,066	100.0
12	Gerry E. Studds (D)	195,791	73.2
	Paul V. Doane (R)	71,620	26.8

MICHIGAN

	Candidates	Votes	%
1	John Conyers Jr. (D)	123,286	94.7
2	Carl D. Pursell (R)	115,562	57.3
	Kathleen F. O'Reilly (D)	83,550	41.4
3	Howard Wolpe (D)	113,080	52.0
	James S. Gilmore (R)	102,591	47.2
4	Dave Stockman (R)	148,950	74.7
	Lyndon G. Furst (D)	47,777	24.0
5	Harold S. Sawyer (R)	118,061	53.1
	Dale R. Sprik (D)	101,737	45.8
6	Jim Dunn (R)	111,272	50.6
	Bob Carr (D)	108,548	49.4
7	Dale E. Kildee (D)	147,280	92.7
	Dennis L. Berry (LIBERT)	11,507	7.2
8	Bob Traxler (D)	124,155	60.7
	Norman R. Hughes (R)	77,009	37.7
9	Guy Vander Jagt (R)	168,713	96.5
10	Don Albosta (D)	126,962	52.4
	Richard J. Allen (R)	111,496	46.0
11	Robert W. Davis (R)	146,205	65.5
	Dan Dorrity (D)	75,515	33.8
12	David E. Bonior (D)	112,698	55.3
	Kirk Walsh (R)	90,931	44.7
13	George W. Crockett Jr. (D)	79,719	91.5
	M. Michael Hurd (R)	6,473	7.4
14	Dennis M. Hertel (D)	90,362	53.3
	Vic Caputo (R)	78,395	46.2
15	William D. Ford (D)	113,492	67.6
	Gerald R. Carlson (R)	53,046	31.6
16	John D. Dingell (D)	105,844	69.9
	Pamella A. Seay (R)	42,735	28.2
17	William M. Brodhead (D)	127,525	73.1
	Alfred L. Patterson (R)	44,313	25.4
18	James J. Blanchard (D)	135,705	65.3
	Betty J. Suida (R)	68,575	33.0

	Candidates	Votes	%
19	William S. Broomfield (R)	168,530	72.7
	Wayne E. Daniels (D)	60,100	25.9

MINNESOTA[2]

	Candidates	Votes	%
1	Arlen Erdahl (I-R)	171,099	71.8
	Russell V. Smith (DFL)	67,279	28.2
2	Tom Hagedorn (I-R)	158,082	60.6
	Harold J. Bergquist (DFL)	102,586	39.4
3	Bill Frenzel (I-R)	179,393	75.6
	Joel Alexander Saliterman (DFL)	57,868	24.4
4	Bruce F. Vento (DFL)	119,182	58.5
	John Berg (I-R)	82,537	40.5
5	Martin Olav Sabo (DFL)	126,451	70.1
	John Doherty (I-R)	48,200	26.7
6	Vin Weber (I-R)	140,402	52.7
	Archie Baumann (DFL)	126,173	47.3
7	Arlan Stangeland (I-R)	135,084	52.1
	Gene Wenstrom (DFL)	124,026	47.9
8	James L. Oberstar (DFL)	182,228	70.4
	Edward Fiore (I-R)	72,350	28.0

MISSISSIPPI

	Candidates	Votes	%
1	Jamie L. Whitten (D)	104,269	63.0
	T.K. Moffett (R)	61,292	37.0
2	David R. Bowen (D)	96,750	69.6
	Frank Drake (R)	42,300	30.4
3	G.V. Montgomery (D)	128,035	100.0
4	Jon C. Hinson (R)	69,321	39.0
	Leslie Burl McLemore (I)	52,959	29.8
	Britt R. Singletary (D)	52,303	29.4
5	Trent Lott (R)	131,559	73.9
	Jimmy McVeay (D)	46,416	26.1

MISSOURI

	Candidates	Votes	%
1	William Clay (D)	91,272	70.2
	Bill White (R)	38,667	29.8
2	Robert A. Young (D)	148,227	64.4
	John O. Shields (R)	81,762	35.6
3	Richard A. Gephardt (D)	143,132	77.6
	Robert A. Cedarburg (R)	41,277	22.4
4	Ike Skelton (D)	151,459	67.8
	Bill Baker (R)	71,869	32.2
5	Richard Bolling (D)	110,957	70.1
	Vincent E. Baker (R)	47,309	29.9
6	E. Thomas Coleman (R)	149,281	70.6
	Vernon King (D)	62,048	29.4
7	Gene Taylor (R)	161,668	67.8
	Ken Young (D)	76,844	32.2
8	Wendell Bailey (R)	127,675	57.1
	Steve Gardner (D)	95,751	42.9
9	Harold L. Volkmer (D)	135,905	56.5
	John W. Turner (R)	104,835	43.5
10	Bill Emerson (R)	116,167	55.2
	Bill D. Burlison (D)	94,465	44.8

MONTANA

	Candidates	Votes	%
1	Pat Williams (D)	112,866	61.4
	John K. McDonald (R)	70,874	38.6
2	Ron Marlenee (R)	91,431	59.1
	Tom Monahan (D)	63,370	40.9

NEBRASKA

	Candidates	Votes	%
1	Douglas K. Bereuter (R)	160,705	78.6
	Rex S. Story (D)	43,605	21.3
2	Hal Daub (R)	107,736	53.1
	Richard M. Fellman (D)	88,843	43.8
3	Virginia Smith (R)	182,887	83.9
	Stan Ditus (D)	34,967	16.0

NEVADA

	Candidates	Votes	%
AL	Jim Santini (D)	165,107	67.5
	Vince Saunders (R)	63,163	25.8

NEW HAMPSHIRE

	Candidates	Votes	%
1	Norman E. D'Amours (D)	114,061	60.8
	Marshall W. Cobleigh (R)	73,565	39.2
2	Judd Gregg (R)	113,304	64.1
	Maurice L. Arel (D)	63,350	35.9

NEW JERSEY

	Candidates	Votes	%
1	James J. Florio (D)	147,352	76.7
	Scott L. Sibert (R)	42,154	21.9
2	William J. Hughes (D)	135,437	57.5
	Beech N. Fox (R)	97,072	41.2
3	James J. Howard (D)	106,269	49.9
	Marie Sheehan Muhler (R)	104,184	49.0
4	Christopher H. Smith (R)	95,447	56.6
	Frank Thompson Jr. (D)	68,480	40.6
5	Millicent Fenwick (R)	156,016	77.5
	Kieran E. Pillion Jr. (D)	41,269	20.5
6	Edwin B. Forsythe (R)	125,792	56.3
	Lewis M. Weinstein (D)	92,227	41.3
7	Marge Roukema (R)	108,760	50.7
	Andrew Maguire (D)	99,737	46.5
8	Robert A. Roe (D)	95,493	67.2
	William R. Cleveland (R)	44,625	31.4
9	Harold C. Hollenbeck (R)	116,128	59.1
	Gabriel Ambrosio (D)	75,321	38.3
10	Peter W. Rodino Jr. (D)	76,154	85.3
	Everett J. Jennings (R)	11,778	13.2
11	Joseph G. Minish (D)	106,155	63.0
	Robert A. Davis (R)	57,772	34.3
12	Matthew J. Rinaldo (R)	134,973	77.1
	Rose Zeidwerg Monyek (D)	36,577	20.9
13	Jim Courter (R)	152,862	71.6
	Dave Stickle (D)	56,251	26.4
14	Frank J. Guarini (D)	86,921	64.2
	Dennis E. Teti (R)	45,606	33.7
15	Bernard J. Dwyer (D)	92,457	53.4
	William O'Sullivan Jr. (R)	75,812	43.8

NEW MEXICO

	Candidates	Votes	%
1	Manuel Lujan Jr. (R)	125,910	51.0
	Bill Richardson (D)	120,903	49.0
2	Joe Skeen (WRITE IN)	61,564	38.0
	David King (D)	55,085	34.0
	Dorothy Runnels (WRITE IN)	45,343	28.0

NEW YORK

	Candidates	Votes	%
1	William Carney (R,C,RTL)	115,213	56.3
	Thomas A. Twomey (D)	85,629	41.9
2	Thomas J. Downey (D)	84,035	56.3
	Louis J. Modica (R,RTL)	65,106	43.7
3	Gregory W. Carman (R,C)	87,952	50.1
	Jerome A. Ambro (D,RTL)	83,389	47.5
4	Norman F. Lent (R,C,RTL)	117,455	66.8
	Charles F. Brennan (D,L)	58,270	33.2
5	Raymond McGrath (R,C, RTL)	105,140	57.7
	Karen S. Burstein (D,L)	77,228	42.3
6	John LeBoutillier (R,C,RTL)	89,762	52.8
	Lester L. Wolff (D,L)	80,209	47.2
7	Joseph Addabbo (D,R,L)	96,137	95.3
8	Benjamin Rosenthal (D,L)	84,273	75.6
	Albert Lemishow (R,C,RTL)	27,156	24.4
9	Geraldine A. Ferraro (D)	63,796	58.3
	Vito P. Battista (R,C,RTL)	44,473	40.7
10	Mario Biaggi (D,R,L)	95,322	94.5
11	James H. Scheuer (D,L)	72,798	74.1
	Andrew E. Carlan (R,C,RTL)	25,424	25.9
12	Shirley Chisholm (D,L)	35,446	87.1
	Charles Gibbs (R)	3,372	8.3
13	Stephen J. Solarz (D,L)	81,954	79.4
	Harry DeMell (R,C)	19,536	18.9
14	Fred Richmond (D,L)	45,029	76.1
	Christopher Lovell (R,C)	8,257	14.0
	Moses S. Harris (I)	4,151	7.0
15	Leo C. Zeferetti (D)	49,684	50.2
	Paul M. Atanasio (R,C,RTL)	46,467	46.9
16	Charles E. Schumer (D,L)	67,343	77.5

	Candidates	Votes	%
	Theodore Silverman (R,C)	17,050	19.6
17	Guy V. Molinari (R,C)	69,573	47.8
	John M. Murphy (D,RTL)	50,954	35.0
	Mary T. Codd (L)	25,118	17.2
18	S. William Green (R)	91,341	56.7
	Mark J. Green (D,L)	68,786	42.7
19	Charles B. Rangel (D,R,L)	84,062	96.2
20	Ted Weiss (D,L)	86,454	82.4
	James E. Greene (R)	15,350	14.6
21	Robert Garcia (D,R,L)	32,173	98.2
22	Jonathan B. Bingham (D,L)	66,301	83.9
	Robert S. Black (R)	9,943	12.6
23	Peter A. Peyser (D)	85,749	56.2
	Andrew Albanese (R,C)	66,771	43.8
24	Richard L. Ottinger (D)	100,182	59.4
	Joseph Christiana (R,C,RTL)	66,689	39.6
25	Hamilton Fish Jr. (R,C)	158,936	81.0
	Gunars Ozols (D)	37,369	19.0
26	Benjamin A. Gilman (R)	137,159	74.3
	Eugene Victor (D,L)	37,475	20.3
27	Matthew F. McHugh (D)	103,863	55.0
	Neil T. Wallace (R,C)	83,096	44.0
28	Samuel S. Stratton (D)	164,088	77.9
	Frank Wicks (R)	37,504	17.8
29	Gerald Solomon (R,C,RTL)	141,631	66.7
	Rodger L. Hurley (D,L)	70,697	33.3
30	David O'B. Martin (R,C)	111,008	63.8
	Mary Anne Krupsak (D,L)	54,896	31.6
31	Donald J. Mitchell (R,RTL)	135,976	77.5
	Irving A. Schwartz (D,L)	39,589	22.5
32	George Wortley (R,C)	108,128	60.4
	Jeffery S. Brooks (D, L)	56,535	31.6
	Peter J. Del Giorno (RTL)	11,978	6.7
33	Gary A. Lee (R,C)	132,831	75.8
	Dolores M. Reed (D,L)	39,542	22.6
34	Frank Horton (R)	133,278	72.9
	James Toole (D)	37,883	20.7
35	Barber B. Conable Jr. (R)	127,623	72.2
	John M. Owens (D,C)	44,754	25.3
36	John J. LaFalce (D,L)	122,929	71.7
	H. William Feder (R,C,RTL)	48,428	28.3
37	Henry J. Nowak (D,L)	94,890	83.0
	Roger Heymanowski (R,C)	16,560	14.5
38	Jack F. Kemp (R,C,RTL)	167,434	81.6
	Gale A. Denn (D,L)	37,875	18.4
39	Stanley N. Lundine (D)	93,839	54.7
	James Abdella (R,C)	75,039	43.8

NORTH CAROLINA

	Candidates	Votes	%
1	Walter B. Jones (D)	108,738	100.0
2	L. H. Fountain (D)	99,297	73.4
	Barry L. Gardner (R)	35,946	26.6
3	Charles Whitley (D)	84,862	68.3
	Larry J. Parker (R)	39,393	31.7
4	Ike F. Andrews (D)	97,167	52.6
	Thurman Hogan (R)	84,631	45.8
5	Stephen L. Neal (D)	99,117	51.0
	Anne Bagnal (R)	94,894	48.8
6	Eugene Johnston (R)	80,275	51.1
	Richardson Preyer (D)	76,957	48.9
7	Charlie Rose (D)	88,564	68.7
	Vivian S. Wright (R)	40,270	31.3
8	W. G. (Bill) Hefner (D)	95,013	58.5
	L. E. (Larry) Harris (R)	67,317	41.5
9	James G. Martin (R)	101,156	58.6
	Randall R. Kincaid (D)	71,504	41.4
10	James T. Broyhill (R)	120,777	69.7
	James O. Icenhour (D)	52,485	30.3
11	William M. Hendon (R)	104,485	53.5
	Lamar Gudger (D)	90,789	46.5

NORTH DAKOTA

	Candidates	Votes	%
AL	Byron L. Dorgan (D)	166,437	56.8
	Jim Smykowski (R)	124,707	42.6

OHIO

#	Candidates	Votes	%
1	Bill Gradison (R)	124,080	74.7
	Donald J. Zwick (D)	38,529	23.2
2	Thomas A. Luken (D)	103,423	58.7
	Tom Atkins (R)	72,693	41.3
3	Tony P. Hall (D)	95,558	57.3
	Albert H. Sealy (R)	66,698	40.0
4	Tennyson Guyer (R)	133,795	72.3
	Geraldine Tebben (D)	51,150	27.7
5	Delbert L. Latta (R)	137,003	70.4
	James R. Sherck (D)	57,704	29.6
6	Bob McEwen (R)	101,288	54.6
	Ted Strickland (D)	84,235	45.4
7	Clarence J. Brown (R)	124,137	76.1
	Donald Hollister (D)	38,952	23.9
8	Thomas N. Kindness (R)	139,590	76.0
	John W. Griffin (D)	44,162	24.0
9	Ed Weber (R)	96,927	56.2
	Thomas L Ashley (D)	68,728	39.9
10	Clarence E. Miller (R)	143,403	74.4
	Jack E. Stecher (D)	49,433	25.6
11	J. William Stanton (R)	128,507	69.3
	Patrick J. Donlin (D)	51,224	27.6
12	Robert N. Shamansky (D)	108,690	52.6
	Samuel L. Devine (R)	98,110	47.4
13	Don J. Pease (D)	113,439	63.8
	David E. Armstrong (R)	64,296	36.2
14	John F. Seiberling (D)	103,336	64.9
	Louis A. Mangels (R)	55,962	35.1
15	Chalmers P. Wylie (R)	129,025	72.6
	Terry Freeman (D)	48,708	27.4
16	Ralph S. Regula (R)	149,960	79.3
	Larry V. Slagle (D)	39,219	20.7
17	John M. Ashbrook (R)	128,870	72.9
	Donald E. Yunker (D)	47,900	27.1
18	Douglas Applegate (D)	134,835	76.1
	Gary L. Hammersley (R)	42,354	23.9
19	Lyle Williams (R)	107,032	58.1
	Harry Meshel (D)	77,272	41.9
20	Mary Rose Oakar (D)	96,217	100.0
21	Louis Stokes (D)	83,188	88.2
	Robert L. Woodall (R)	11,103	11.8
22	Dennis E. Eckart (D)	108,137	55.2
	Joseph J. Nahra (R)	80,836	41.3
23	Ronald M. Mottl (D)	144,317	100.0

OKLAHOMA

#	Candidates	Votes	%
1	James R. Jones (D)	115,381	58.4
	Richard C. Freeman (R)	82,293	41.6
2	Mike Synar (D)	101,516	54.0
	Gary Richardson (R)	86,544	46.0
3	Wes Watkins (D)		100.0
4	Dave McCurdy (D)	74,245	51.0
	Howard Rutledge (R)	71,339	49.0
5	Mickey Edwards (R)	90,053	68.4
	David C. Hood (D)	36,815	28.0
6	Glenn English (D)	111,694	64.7
	Carol McCurley (R)	60,980	35.3

OREGON

#	Candidates	Votes	%
1	Les AuCoin (D)	203,532	65.9
	Lynn Engdahl (R)	105,083	34.0
2	Denny Smith (R)	141,854	48.8
	Al Ullman (D)	138,089	47.5
3	Ron Wyden (D)	156,371	71.9
	Darrell R. Conger (R)	60,940	28.0
4	James Weaver (D)	158,745	54.8
	Michael Fitzgerald (R)	130,861	45.2

PENNSYLVANIA

#	Candidates	Votes	%
1	Thomas M. Foglietta (I)	58,737	37.8
	Michael (Ozzie) Myers (D)	52,956	34.1
	Robert R. Burke (R)	37,893	24.4
2	William H. Gray III (D)	127,106	96.4
3	Raymond F. Lederer (D)	67,942	54.5
	William J. Phillips (R)	40,866	32.8
	Max Weiner (CONSU)	11,849	9.5
4	Charles F. Dougherty (R)	127,475	63.3
	Thomas J. Magrann (D)	73,895	36.7
5	Richard T. Schulze (R)	148,898	75.1
	Grady G. Brickhouse (D)	47,092	23.8
6	Gus Yatron (D)	117,965	67.1
	George Hulshart (R)	57,844	32.9
7	Robert W. Edgar (D)	99,381	53.1
	Dennis J. Rochford (R)	87,643	46.9
8	James K. Coyne (R)	103,585	50.7
	Peter H. Kostmayer (D)	99,593	48.7
9	Bud Shuster (R, D)	157,241	100.0
10	Joseph M. McDade (R)	145,703	76.6
	Gene Basalyga (D)	43,152	22.7
11	James L. Nelligan (R)	93,621	51.9
	Raphael Musto (D)	86,703	48.1
12	John P. Murtha (D)	106,750	59.4
	Charles A. Getty (R)	72,999	40.6
13	Lawrence Coughlin (R)	138,212	70.0
	Pete Slawek (D)	57,745	29.2
14	William J. Coyne (D)	102,545	68.5
	Stan Thomas (R)	44,071	29.5
15	Don Ritter (R)	99,874	59.6
	Jeanette Reibman (D)	66,626	39.7
16	James A. Woodcock (D)	38,891	23.1
	Robert S. Walker (R)	129,765	76.9
17	Allen E. Ertel (D)	97,995	60.6
	Daniel S. Seiverling (R)	63,790	39.4
18	Doug Walgren (D)	127,641	68.5
	Steven R. Snyder (R)	58,821	31.5
19	Bill Goodling (R)	136,873	76.0
	Richard P. Noll (D)	41,584	23.1
20	Joseph M. Gaydos (D)	122,100	72.5
	Kathleen M. Meyer (R)	46,313	27.5
21	Don Bailey (D)	112,427	68.4
	Dirk Matson (R)	51,821	31.6
22	Austin J. Murphy (D)	118,084	69.5
	Marilyn C. Ecoff (R)	50,020	29.5
23	William F. Clinger Jr. (R)	122,855	73.5
	Peter Atigan (D)	41,033	24.6
24	Marc L. Marks (R)	86,687	49.7
	David C. DiCarlo (D)	86,567	49.6
25	Eugene V. Atkinson (D)	119,817	67.1
	Robert H. Morris (R)	58,768	32.9

Special Election

#	Candidates	Votes	%
11	Raphael Musto (D)	32,073	27.3
	James Nelligan (R)	27,496	23.4
	Frank Harrison (I)	20,475	17.4
	Paul Kanjorski (I)	18,241	15.5
	Ted Mitchell (I)	12,009	10.2

RHODE ISLAND

#	Candidates	Votes	%
1	Fernand J. St Germain (D)	120,756	67.6
	William P. Montgomery (R)	57,844	32.4
2	Claudine Schneider (R)	115,057	55.3
	Edward P. Beard (D)	92,970	44.7

SOUTH CAROLINA

#	Candidates	Votes	%
1	Thomas F. Hartnett (R)	81,988	51.6
	Charles D. Ravenel (D)	76,743	48.3
2	Floyd Spence (R)	92,306	55.7
	Tom Turnipseed (D)	73,353	44.3
3	Butler Derrick (D)	87,680	59.8
	Marshall Parker (R)	57,840	39.4
4	Carroll Campbell Jr. (R)	90,941	92.6
	Thomas Waldenfels (LIBERT)	6,984	7.1
5	Ken Holland (D)	99,773	87.5
	Thomas Campbell (LIBERT)	14,252	12.5
6	John L Napier (R)	75,964	51.7
	John W. Jenrette Jr. (D)	70,747	48.2

SOUTH DAKOTA

#	Candidates	Votes	%
1	Thomas A. Daschle (D)	109,910	65.8
	Bart Kull (R)	57,155	34.2
2	Clint Roberts (R)	88,991	58.4
	Kenneth D. Stofferahn (D)	63,447	41.6

TENNESSEE

#	Candidates	Votes	%
1	James H. Quillen (R)	130,296	86.2
	John Curtis (I)	20,816	13.8
2	John J. Duncan (R)	147,947	76.1
	Dave Dunaway (D)	46,578	23.9
3	Marilyn Lloyd Bouquard (D)	117,355	61.1
	Glen M. Byers (R)	74,761	38.9
4	Albert Gore Jr. (D)	137,612	79.3
	James Beau Seigneur (R)	35,954	20.7
5	Bill Boner (D)	118,506	65.4
	Mike Adams (R)	62,746	34.6
6	Robin L. Beard Jr. (R)	127,945	99.6
7	Ed Jones (D)	133,606	77.3
	Daniel Campbell (R)	39,227	22.7
8	Harold E. Ford (D)	110,139	99.9

TEXAS

#	Candidates	Votes	%
1	Sam B. Hall Jr. (D)	137,665	100.0
2	Charles Wilson (D)	142,496	69.3
	F. H. Pannill Sr. (R)	60,742	29.5
3	James M. Collins (R)	218,228	79.3
	Earle S. Porter (D)	49,667	18.0
4	Ralph M. Hall (D)	102,787	52.3
	John H. Wright (R)	93,915	47.7
5	Jim Mattox (D)	70,892	51.0
	Tom Pauken (R)	67,848	48.8
6	Phil Gramm (D)	144,816	70.9
	Dave (Buster) Haskins (R)	59,503	29.1
7	Bill Archer (R)	242,810	82.1
	Robert L. Hutchings (D)	48,594	16.4
8	Jack Fields (R)	72,856	51.8
	Bob Eckhardt (D)	67,921	48.2
9	Jack Brooks (D)	103,225	99.7
10	J. J. Pickle (D)	135,618	59.1
	John Biggar (R)	88,940	38.8
11	Marvin Leath (D)	128,520	100.0
12	Jim Wright (D)	99,104	59.9
	Jim Bradshaw (R)	65,005	39.3
13	Jack Hightower (D)	98,779	55.0
	Ron Slover (R)	80,819	45.0
14	William N. Patman (D)	93,884	56.8
	Charles L. Concklin (R)	71,495	43.2
15	E. (Kika) de la Garza (D)	105,325	70.0
	Lendy McDonald (R)	45,090	30.0
16	Richard C. White (D)	104,734	84.6
	Catherine McDivitt (LIBERT)	19,010	15.4
17	Charles W. Stenholm (D)	130,465	100.0
18	Mickey Leland (D)	71,985	79.9
	C. L. Kennedy (R)	16,128	17.9
19	Kent Hance (D)	126,632	93.5
	J. D. Webster (LIBERT)	8,792	6.5
20	Henry B. Gonzalez (D)	84,113	81.9
	Merle W. Nash (R)	17,725	17.3
21	Tom Loeffler (R)	196,424	76.5
	Joe Sullivan (D)	58,425	22.8
22	Ron Paul (R)	106,797	51.0
	Mike Andrews (D)	101,094	48.3
23	Abraham Kazen Jr. (D)	104,595	69.8
	Bobby Locke (R)	45,139	30.1
24	Martin Frost (D)	93,690	61.3
	Clay Smothers (R)	59,172	38.7

UTAH

#	Candidates	Votes	%
1	James V. Hansen (R)	157,111	52.1
	Gunn McKay (D)	144,459	47.9
2	Dan Marriott (R)	194,885	67.0
	Arthur L. Monson (D)	87,967	30.3

VERMONT

#	Candidates	Votes	%
AL	James M. Jeffords (R)	154,274	79.2
	Robin Lloyd (CIT)	24,758	12.7
	Peter Diamondstone (LU)	15,218	7.8

VIRGINIA

	Candidates	Votes	%
1	Paul S. Trible Jr. (R)	130,130	90.5
	Sharon D. Grant (I)	13,688	9.5
2	G. William Whitehurst (R)	97,319	89.8
	Kenneth Morrison (LIBERT)	11,003	10.2
3	Thomas J. Bliley Jr. (R)	96,524	51.6
	John A. Mapp (D)	60,962	32.6
	Howard H. Carwile (I)	19,549	10.5
	James B. Turney (LIBERT)	9,852	5.3
4	Robert W. Daniel Jr. (R)	92,557	60.7
	Cecil Y. Jenkins (D)	59,930	39.3
5	Dan Daniel (D)	112,143	99.9
6	M. Caldwell Butler (R)	123,125	99.2
7	J. Kenneth Robinson (R)	139,957	99.7
8	Stanford E. Parris (R)	95,624	48.8
	Herbert E. Harris II (D)	94,530	48.3
9	William C. Wampler (R)	119,196	69.4
	Roosevelt Ferguson (D)	52,636	30.6
10	Frank R. Wolf (R)	110,840	51.1
	Joseph L. Fisher (D)	105,883	48.9

WASHINGTON

	Candidates	Votes	%
1	Joel Pritchard (R)	180,475	78.3
	Robin Drake (D)	41,830	18.1
2	Al Swift (D)	162,002	63.9

	Candidates	Votes	%
	Neal Snider (R)	82,639	32.6
3	Don Bonker (D)	155,906	62.7
	Rod Culp (R)	92,872	37.3
4	Sid Morrison (R)	134,691	57.4
	Mike McCormack (D)	100,114	42.6
5	Thomas S. Foley (D)	120,530	51.9
	John Sonneland (R)	111,705	48.1
6	Norman D. Dicks (D)	122,903	53.6
	Jim Beaver (R)	106,236	46.4
7	Mike Lowry (D)	112,848	57.3
	Ron Dunlap (R)	84,218	42.7

WEST VIRGINIA

	Candidates	Votes	%
1	Robert H. Mollohan (D)	107,471	63.6
	Joe Bartlett (R)	61,438	36.4
2	Cleve Benedict (R)	102,805	55.9
	Pat R. Hamilton (D)	80,940	44.1
3	Mick Staton (R)	94,583	52.7
	John G. Hutchinson (D)	84,980	47.3
4	Nick J. Rahall (D)	117,595	76.6
	Winton G. Covey Jr. (R)	36,020	23.4

Special Election

	Candidates	Votes	%
3	John G. Hutchinson (D)	51,169	53.8
	David Staton (R)	43,950	46.2

WISCONSIN

	Candidates	Votes	%
1	Les Aspin (D)	126,222	56.2
	Kathryn H. Canary (R)	96,047	42.8
2	Robert W. Kastenmeier (D)	142,037	54.0
	James A. Wright (R)	119,514	45.4
3	Steven Gunderson (R)	132,001	51.0
	Alvin Baldus (D)	126,859	49.0
4	Clement J. Zablocki (D)	146,437	70.0
	Elroy C. Honadel (R)	61,027	29.2
5	Henry S. Reuss (D)	129,574	77.0
	David Bathke (R)	37,267	22.2
6	Thomas E. Petri (R)	148,980	59.3
	Gary R. Goyke (D)	98,628	40.7
7	David R. Obey (D)	164,340	64.7
	Vinton A. Vesta (R)	89,745	35.3
8	Toby Roth (R)	169,664	67.7
	Michael R. Monfils (D)	81,043	32.3
9	F. James Sensenbrenner (R)	206,227	78.4
	Gary C. Benedict (D)	56,838	21.6

WYOMING

	Candidates	Votes	%
AL	Richard B. Cheney (R)	116,361	68.6
	Jim Rogers (D)	53,338	31.4
	David G. Glancy (D)	24,390	42.8

1. For the 1980 House elections in Louisiana, an open primary election was held with candidates from all parties running on the same ballot. Any candidate who received a majority was elected unopposed, with no further appearance on the general election ballot. If no candidate received 50 percent, a runoff was held between the two top finishers.

2. In Minnesota the Democratic Party is known as the Democratic-Farmer-Labor Party and the Republican Party as the Independent-Republican Party; candidates appear on the ballot with these designations.

1981 House Elections

MARYLAND

Special Election

	Candidates	Votes	%
5	Steny H. Hoyer (D)	42,573	55.2
	Audrey Scott (R)	33,708	43.5

MICHIGAN

Special Election

	Candidates	Votes	%
4	Mark Siljander (R)	36,046	72.6
	Johnie Rodebush (D)	12,461	25.1

MISSISSIPPI

Special Election

	Candidates	Votes	%
4	Wayne Dowdy (D)	55,656	50.4
	Liles Williams (R)	54,744	49.6

OHIO

Special Election

	Candidates	Votes	%
4	Michael Oxley (R)	41,987	50.2
	Dale Locker (D)	41,646	49.8

PENNSYLVANIA

Special Election

	Candidates	Votes	%
3	Joseph F. Smith (R, I)	29,907	52.5
	David G. Glancy (D)	24,390	42.8

1982 House Elections

ALABAMA

	Candidates	Votes	%
1	Jack Edwards (R)	87,901	61.0
	Steve Gudac (D)	54,315	37.7
2	William L. Dickinson (R)	83,290	50.4
	Billy Joe Camp (D)	81,904	49.6
3	Bill Nichols (D)	100,864	96.3
4	Tom Bevill (D)	118,595	100.0
5	Ronnie G. Flippo (D)	108,807	80.7
	Leopold Yambrek (R)	24,593	18.2
6	Ben Erdreich (D)	88,029	53.2
	Albert Lee Smith Jr. (R)	76,726	46.4
7	Richard C. Shelby (D)	124,070	96.8

ALASKA

	Candidates	Votes	%
AL	Don Young (R)	128,274	70.8
	Dave Carlson (D)	52,001	28.7

ARIZONA

	Candidates	Votes	%
1	John McCain (R)	89,116	65.9
	William E. Hegarty (D)	41,261	30.5
2	Morris K. Udall (D)	73,468	70.9
	Roy B. Laos (R)	28,407	27.4
3	Bob Stump (R)	101,198	63.3
	Pat Bosch (D)	58,644	36.7
4	Eldon Rudd (R)	95,620	65.7
	Wayne O. Earley (D)	44,182	30.4
5	Jim McNulty (D)	82,938	49.7
	Jim Kolbe (R)	80,531	48.3

ARKANSAS

	Candidates	Votes	%
1	Bill Alexander (D)	124,208	64.8
	Chuck Banks (R)	67,427	35.2
2	Ed Bethune (R)	96,775	53.9
	Charles L. George (D)	82,913	46.1
3	John Paul Hammerschmidt (R)	133,909	66.0
	Jim McDougal (D)	69,089	34.0
4	Beryl Anthony Jr. (D)	121,256	65.6
	Bob Leslie (R)	63,661	34.4

CALIFORNIA

	Candidates	Votes	%
1	Douglas H. Bosco (D)	107,749	49.8
	Don H. Clausen (R)	102,043	47.2
2	Gene Chappie (R)	116,172	57.9
	John A. Newmeyer (D)	81,314	40.5
3	Robert T. Matsui (D)	194,680	89.6
	Bruce A. Daniel (LIBERT)	16,222	7.5
4	Vic Fazio (D)	118,476	63.9
	Roger B. Canfield (R)	67,047	36.1
5	Phillip Burton (D)	103,268	57.9
	Milton Marks (R)	72,139	40.5
6	Barbara Boxer (D)	96,379	52.4
	Dennis McQuaid (R)	82,128	44.6
7	George Miller (D)	126,952	67.2
	Paul E. Vallely (R)	56,960	30.2
8	Ronald V. Dellums (D)	121,537	55.9
	Claude B. Hutchison Jr. (R)	95,694	44.0
9	Fortney H. (Pete) Stark (D)	104,393	60.7
	Bill J. Kennedy (R)	67,702	39.3
10	Don Edwards (D)	77,263	62.7
	Bob Herriott (R)	41,506	33.7
11	Tom Lantos (D)	109,812	57.1
	Bill Royer (R)	76,462	39.7
12	Ed Zschau (R)	115,365	62.9
	Emmett Lynch (D)	61,372	33.5
13	Norman Y. Mineta (D)	110,805	65.9
	Tom Kelly (R)	52,806	31.4
14	Norman D. Shumway (R)	134,225	63.4
	Baron Reed (D)	77,400	36.6
15	Tony Coelho (D)	86,022	63.7
	Ed Bates (R)	45,948	34.0

	Candidates	Votes	%
16	Leon E. Panetta (D)	142,630	83.5
	G. Richard Arnold (R)	24,448	14.3
17	Charles Pashayan Jr. (R)	80,271	54.0
	Gene Tackett (D)	68,364	46.0
18	Richard Lehman (D)	92,762	59.5
	Adrian C. Fondse (R)	59,664	38.3
19	Robert J. Lagomarsino (R)	112,486	61.1
	Frank Frost (D)	66,042	35.8
20	William M. Thomas (R)	123,312	68.1
	Robert J. Bethea (D)	57,769	31.9
21	Bobbi Fiedler (R)	138,474	71.8
	George Henry Margolis (D)	46,412	24.1
22	Carlos J. Moorhead (R)	145,831	73.6
	Harvey L. Goldhammer (D)	46,521	23.5
23	Anthony C. Beilenson (D)	120,788	59.6
	David Armor (R)	82,031	40.4
24	Henry A. Waxman (D)	88,516	65.1
	Jerry Zerg (R)	42,133	31.0
25	Edward R. Roybal (D)	71,106	85.5
	Daniel John Gorham (LIBERT)	12,060	14.5
26	Howard L. Berman (D)	97,383	59.6
	Hal Phillips (R)	66,072	40.4
27	Mel Levine (D)	108,347	59.5
	Bart W. Christensen (R)	67,479	37.0
28	Julian C. Dixon (D)	103,469	78.9
	David Goerz (R)	24,473	18.7
29	Augustus F. Hawkins (D)	97,028	79.8
	Milton R. MacKaig (R)	24,568	20.2
30	Matthew G. (Marty) Martinez (D)	60,905	53.9
	John H. Rousselot (R)	52,177	46.1
31	Mervyn M. Dymally (D)	86,718	72.4
	Henry C. Minturn (R)	33,043	27.6
32	Glenn M. Anderson (D)	84,663	58.0
	Brian Lungren (R)	57,863	39.6
33	David Dreier (R)	112,362	65.2
	Paul Servelle (D)	55,514	32.2
34	Esteban Torres (D)	68,316	57.2
	Paul R. Jackson (R)	51,026	42.8
35	Jerry Lewis (R)	112,786	68.3
	Robert E. Erwin (D)	52,349	31.7
36	George E. Brown Jr. (D)	76,546	54.3
	John Paul Stark (R)	64,361	45.7
37	Al McCandless (R)	105,065	59.1
	Curtis P. (Sam) Cross (D)	68,510	38.5
38	Jerry M. Patterson (D)	73,914	52.4
	William F. Dohr (R)	61,279	43.4
39	William E. Dannemeyer (R)	129,539	72.2
	Frank G. Verges (D)	46,681	26.0
40	Robert E. Badham (R)	144,228	71.5
	Paul Haseman (D)	52,546	26.1
41	Bill Lowery (R)	140,130	68.9
	Tony Brandenburg (D)	58,677	28.8
42	Dan Lungren (R)	142,845	69.0
	James P. Spellman (D)	58,690	28.3
43	Ron Packard (R WRITE-IN)	66,444	36.8
	Roy (Pat) Archer (D)	57,995	32.1
	Johnnie R. Crean (R)	56,297	31.1
44	Jim Bates (D)	78,474	64.9
	Shirley M. Gissendanner (R)	38,447	31.8
45	Duncan L. Hunter (R)	117,771	68.6
	Richard Hill (D)	50,148	29.2

Special Election

		Votes	%
30	Matthew G. (Marty) Martinez (D)	22,572	32.0
	Dennis S. Kazarian (D)	20,313	29.0
	Ralph Ramirez (R)	11,033	16.0

Special Runoff Election

		Votes	%
30	Matthew G. (Marty) Martinez (D)	14,593	51.0
	Ralph Ramirez (R)	14,043	49.0

COLORADO

	Candidates	Votes	%
1	Patricia Schroeder (D)	94,969	60.3
	Arch Decker (R)	59,009	37.4
2	Timothy E. Wirth (D)	101,202	61.8
	John C. Buechner (R)	59,590	36.4
3	Ray Kogovsek (D)	92,384	53.4
	Tom Wiens (R)	77,410	44.8
4	Hank Brown (R)	105,550	69.8
	Charles L. (Bud) Bishopp (D)	45,750	30.2
5	Ken Kramer (R)	84,479	59.5
	Tom Cronin (D)	57,392	40.5
6	Jack Swigert (R)	98,909	62.2
	Steve Hogan (D)	56,598	35.6

CONNECTICUT

	Candidates	Votes	%
1	Barbara B. Kennelly (D)	126,798	68.1
	Herschel A. Klein (R)	58,075	31.2
2	Sam Gejdenson (D)	95,254	55.8
	Tony Guglielmo (R)	74,294	43.5
3	Bruce A. Morrison (D)	90,638	49.9
	Lawrence J. DeNardis (R)	88,951	49.0
4	Stewart B. McKinney (R)	93,660	56.5
	John A. Phillips (D)	71,110	42.9
5	William R. Ratchford (D)	101,362	58.5
	Neal B. Hanlon (R)	70,808	40.8
6	Nancy L. Johnson (R)	99,703	51.7
	William E. Curry Jr. (D)	92,178	47.8

Special Election

		Votes	%
1	Barbara B. Kennelly (D)	51,431	58.8
	Ann P. Uccello (R)	36,085	41.2

DELAWARE

	Candidates	Votes	%
AL	Thomas R. Carper (D)	98,533	52.4
	Thomas B. Evans Jr. (R)	87,153	46.3

FLORIDA

	Candidates	Votes	%
1	Earl Hutto (D)	82,569	74.4
	J. Terry Bechtol (R)	28,373	25.6
2	Don Fuqua (D)	79,143	61.7
	Ron McNeil (R)	49,101	38.3
3	Charles E. Bennett (D)	73,802	84.1
	George Grimsley (R)	13,972	15.9
4	Bill Chappell Jr. (D)	83,895	66.9
	Larry Gaudet (R)	41,457	33.1
5	Bill McCollum (R)	69,993	58.8
	Dick Batchelor (D)	49,070	41.2
6	Kenneth H. (Buddy) MacKay (D)	85,825	61.3
	Ed Havill (R)	54,059	38.6
7	Sam Gibbons (D)	85,331	74.2
	Ken Ayers (R)	29,632	25.8
8	C. W. Bill Young (R)		100.0
9	Michael Bilirakis (R)	95,009	51.2
	George H. Sheldon (D)	90,697	48.8
10	Andy Ireland (D)		100.0
11	Bill Nelson (D)	101,746	70.6
	Joel Robinson (R)	42,422	29.4
12	Tom Lewis (R)	81,893	52.6
	Brad Culverhouse (D)	73,913	47.4
13	Connie Mack III (R)	132,951	65.1
	Dana N. Stevens (D)	71,239	34.9
14	Daniel A. Mica (D)	128,646	73.0
	Steve Mitchell (R)	47,560	27.0
15	E. Clay Shaw Jr. (R)	89,158	57.1
	Edward J. Stack (D)	67,083	42.9
16	Larry Smith (D)	91,888	67.9
	Maurice Berkowitz (R)	43,458	32.1
17	William Lehman (D)		100.0
18	Claude Pepper (D)	72,183	71.2
	Ricardo Nunez (R)	29,196	28.8

Candidates	Votes	%
19 Dante B. Fascell (D)	74,312	58.8
Glenn Rinker (R)	51,969	41.2

GEORGIA

Candidates	Votes	%
1 Lindsay Thomas (D)	65,625	64.1
Herb Jones (R)	36,799	35.9
2 Charles Hatcher (D)	73,897	100.0
3 Richard Ray (D)	74,626	71.0
Tyron Elliott (R)	30,537	29.0
4 Elliott H. Levitas (D)	38,758	65.5
Dick Winder (R)	20,418	34.5
5 Wyche Fowler Jr. (D)	53,264	80.8
J. E. (Billy) McKinney (I)	9,049	13.7
Paul Jones (R)	3,633	5.5
6 Newt Gingrich (R)	62,352	55.3
Jim wood (D)	50,459	44.7
7 Larry P. McDonald (D)	71,647	61.1
Dave Sellers (R)	45,569	38.9
8 J. Roy Rowland (D)	75,009	100.0
9 Ed Jenkins (D)	86,514	77.0
Charles Sherwood (R)	25,907	23.0
10 Doug Barnard Jr. (D)	80,311	100.0

HAWAII

Candidates	Votes	%
1 Cecil Heftel (D)	134,779	89.9
Rockne H. Johnson (LIBERT)	15,128	10.1
2 Daniel K. Akaka (D)	132,072	89.2
Gregory B. Mills (NP)	9,080	6.2

IDAHO

Candidates	Votes	%
1 Larry E. Craig (R)	86,277	53.7
Larry LaRocco (D)	74,388	46.3
2 George Hansen (R)	83,873	52.3
Richard Stallings (D)	76,608	47.7

ILLINOIS

Candidates	Votes	%
1 Harold Washington (D)	172,641	97.3
2 Gus Savage (D)	140,827	87.0
Kevin Walker Sparks (R)	20,670	12.8
3 Marty Russo (D)	137,391	74.0
Richard D. Murphy (R)	48,268	26.0
4 George M. O'Brien (R)	79,842	54.6
Michael A. Murer (D)	66,323	45.4
5 William O. Lipinski (D)	110,351	75.4
Daniel J. Partyka (R)	35,970	24.6
6 Henry J. Hyde (R)	97,918	68.4
Leroy E. Kennel (D)	45,237	31.6
7 Cardiss Collins (D)	133,978	86.5
Dansby Cheeks (R)	20,994	13.5
8 Dan Rostenkowski (D)	124,318	83.4
Bonnie Hickey (R)	24,666	16.6
9 Sidney R. Yates (D)	114,083	66.5
Catherine Bertini (R)	54,851	32.0
10 John Edward Porter (R)	90,750	59.0
Eugenia S. Chapman (D)	63,115	41.0
11 Frank Annunzio (D)	134,755	72.6
James F. Moynihan (R)	50,967	27.4
12 Philip M. Crane (R)	86,487	66.2
Daniel G. DeFosse (R)	40,108	30.7
13 John N. Erlenborn (R)	113,423	69.8
Robert Bily (D)	49,105	30.2
14 Tom Corcoran (R)	98,262	64.6
Dan McGrath (D)	53,914	35.4
15 Edward R. Madigan (R)	105,038	66.3
Tim L. Hall (D)	53,303	33.7
16 Lynn Martin (R)	89,405	57.2
Carl R. Schwerdtfeger (D)	66,877	42.8
17 Lane Evans (D)	94,483	52.8
Kenneth G. McMillan (R)	84,347	47.2
18 Robert H. Michel (R)	97,406	51.6
G. Douglas Stephens (D)	91,281	48.4
19 Daniel B. Crane (R)	94,833	52.1
John Gwinn (D)	87,231	47.9
20 Richard J. Durbin (D)	100,758	50.4
Paul Findley (R)	99,348	49.6
21 Melvin Price (D)	89,500	63.7
Robert H. Gaffner (R)	46,764	33.3
22 Paul Simon (D)	123,693	66.2
Peter G. Prineas (R)	63,279	33.8

INDIANA

Candidates	Votes	%
1 Katie Hall (D)	87,369	56.3
Thomas H. Krieger (R)	66,921	43.1
2 Philip R. Sharp (D)	107,298	56.2
Ralph W. Van Natta (R)	83,593	43.8
3 John Hiler (R)	86,958	51.2
Richard C. Bodine (D)	83,046	48.8
4 Dan Coats (R)	110,155	64.3
Roger M. Miller (D)	60,054	35.1
5 Elwood Hillis (R)	105,469	61.1
Allen B. Maxwell (D)	67,238	38.9
6 Dan Burton (R)	131,100	64.9
George E. Grabianowski (D)	70,764	35.1
7 John T. Myers (R)	115,884	62.3
Stephen S. Bonney (D)	70,249	37.7
8 Francis X. McCloskey (D)	100,592	51.4
Joel Deckard (R)	94,127	48.1
9 Lee H. Hamilton (D)	121,094	67.1
Floyd E. Coates (R)	58,532	32.4
10 Andrew Jacobs Jr. (D)	114,674	66.7
Michael A. Carroll (R)	56,992	33.2

IOWA

Candidates	Votes	%
1 Jim Leach (R)	89,585	59.2
William E. Gluba (D)	61,734	40.8
2 Tom Tauke (R)	99,478	58.8
Brent Appel (D)	69,539	41.1
3 Cooper Evans (R)	104,072	55.5
Lynn G. Cutler (D)	83,581	44.5
4 Neal Smith (D)	118,849	66.0
Dave Readinger (R)	60,534	33.6
5 Tom Harkin (D)	93,333	58.9
Arlyn E. Danker (R)	65,200	41.1
6 Berkley Bedell (D)	101,690	64.3
Al Bremer (R)	56,487	35.7

KANSAS

Candidates	Votes	%
1 Pat Roberts (R)	115,749	68.4
Kent Roth (D)	51,079	30.2
2 Jim Slattery (D)	86,286	57.4
Morris Kay (R)	63,942	42.6
3 Larry Winn Jr. (R)	82,117	59.2
William L. Kostar (D)	53,140	38.3
4 Dan Glickman (D)	107,326	73.9
Gerald Caywood (R)	35,478	24.4
5 Bob Whittaker (R)	103,551	67.6
Lee Rowe (D)	47,676	31.1

KENTUCKY

Candidates	Votes	%
1 Carroll Hubbard Jr. (D)	48,342	100.0
2 William H. Natcher (D)	49,571	73.8
Mark T. Watson (R)	17,561	26.2
3 Romano L. Mazzoli (D)	92,849	65.1
Carl Brown (R)	45,900	32.2
4 Gene Snyder (R)	74,109	54.2
Terry L. Mann (D)	61,937	45.3
5 Harold Rogers (R)	52,928	65.2
Doye Davenport (D)	28,285	34.8
6 Larry J. Hopkins (R)	68,418	56.8
Don Mills (D)	49,839	41.4
7 Carl D. Perkins (D)	82,463	79.4
Tom Hamby (R)	21,436	20.6

LOUISIANA[1]

Candidates	Votes	%
1 Bob Livingston (R)		100.0
2 Lindy (Mrs. Hale) Boggs (D)		100.0
3 W. J. (Billy) Tauzin (D)		100.0
4 Buddy Roemer (D)		100.0
5 Jerry Huckaby (D)		100.0
6 Henson Moore (R)		100.0
7 John B. Breaux (D)		100.0
8 Gillis W. Long (D)		100.0

MAINE

Candidates	Votes	%
1 John R. McKernan Jr. (R)	124,850	50.3
John M. Kerry (D)	118,884	47.9
2 Olympia J. Snowe (R)	136,075	66.6
James Patrick Dunleavy (D)	68,086	33.3

MARYLAND

Candidates	Votes	%
1 Roy Dyson (D)	89,503	69.3
C.A. Porter Hopkins (R)	39,656	30.7
2 Clarence D. Long (D)	83,318	52.6
Helen Delich Bentley (R)	75,062	47.4
3 Barbara A. Mikulski (D)	110,042	74.2
H. Robert Scherr (R)	38,259	25.8
4 Marjorie S. Holt (R)	75,617	61.2
Patricia O'Brien Aiken (D)	47,947	38.8
5 Steny H. Hoyer (D)	83,937	79.6
William P. Guthrie (R)	21,533	20.4
6 Beverly B. Byron (D)	102,596	74.4
Roscoe Bartlett (R)	35,321	25.6
7 Parren J. Mitchell (D)	103,496	87.9
M. Leonora Jones (R)	14,203	12.1
8 Michael D. Barnes (D)	121,761	71.3
Elizabeth W. Spencer (R)	48,910	28.7

MASSACHUSETTS

Candidates	Votes	%
1 Silvio O. Conte (R, D)	145,417	100.0
2 Edward P. Boland (D)	118,215	72.6
Thomas P. Swank (R)	44,544	27.4
3 Joseph D. Early (D)	142,611	100.0
4 Barney Frank (D)	121,802	59.5
Margaret M. Heckler (R)	82,804	40.5
5 James M. Shannon (D)	140,177	84.6
Angelo Laudani (LIBERT)	25,224	15.2
6 Nicholas Mavroules (D)	117,723	57.8
Thomas H. Trimarco (R)	85,849	42.2
7 Edward J. Markey (D)	151,305	77.8
David Basile (R)	43,063	22.2
8 Thomas P. O'Neill Jr. (D)	123,296	74.9
Frank Luke McNamara Jr. (R)	41,370	25.1
9 Joe Moakley (D)	102,665	64.1
Deborah R. Cochran (R)	55,030	34.3
10 Gerry E. Studds (D)	138,418	68.7
John E. Conway (R)	63,014	31.3
11 Brian J. Donnelly (D)	144,132	100.0

MICHIGAN

Candidates	Votes	%
1 John Conyers Jr. (D)	125,517	96.7
2 Carl D. Pursell (R)	106,960	65.5
George Wahr Sallade (D)	53,040	32.5
3 Howard Wolpe (D)	96,842	56.3
Richard L. Milliman (R)	73,315	42.6
4 Mark Siljander (R)	87,489	59.7
David A. Masiokas (D)	56,877	38.8
5 Harold S. Sawyer (R)	98,650	53.1
Stephen V. Monsma (D)	87,229	46.9
6 Bob Carr (D)	84,778	51.4
Jim Dunn (R)	78,388	47.5
7 Dale E. Kildee (D)	118,538	75.4
George R. Darrah (R)	36,303	23.1
8 Bob Traxler (D)	113,515	91.0
Sheila M. Hart (LIBERT)	11,219	9.0
9 Guy Vander Jagt (R)	112,504	64.9
Gerald D. Warner (D)	60,932	35.1
10 Don Albosta (D)	102,048	60.1
Lawrence W. Reed (R)	66,080	38.9
11 Robert W. Davis (R)	106,039	60.5
Kent Bourland (D)	69,181	39.5
12 David E. Bonior (D)	103,851	65.9
Ray Contesti (R)	52,312	33.2
13 George W. Crockett Jr. (D)	108,351	88.0
Letty Gupta (R)	13,732	11.1
14 Dennis M. Hertel (D)	116,421	94.9
Harold H. Dunn (LIBERT)	6,175	5.0

	Candidates	Votes	%
15	William D. Ford (D)	94,950	72.8
	Mitchell Moran (R)	33,904	26.0
16	John D. Dingell (D)	114,006	73.7
	David K. Haskins (R)	39,227	25.3
17	Sander Levin (D)	116,901	66.6
	Gerald E. Rosen (R)	55,620	31.7
18	Allen J. Sipher (D)	46,545	25.7
	William S. Broomfield (R)	132,902	73.3

MINNESOTA

	Candidates	Votes	%
1	Timothy J. Penny (DFL)	109,257	51.2
	Tom Hagedorn (I-R)	102,298	47.9
2	Vin Weber (I-R)	123,508	54.5
	James W. Nichols (DFL)	103,243	45.5
3	Bill Frenzel (I-R)	166,891	72.2
	Joel Sailterman (DFL)	60,993	26.4
4	Bruce F. Vento (DFL)	153,494	73.2
	Bill James (I-R)	56,248	26.8
5	Martin Olav Sabo (DFL)	136,634	65.5
	Keith W. Johnson (I-R)	61,184	29.4
6	Gerry Sikorski (DFL)	109,246	50.8
	Arlen Erdahl (I-R)	105,734	49.2
7	Arlan Stangeland (I-R)	108,254	50.3
	Gene Wenstrom (DFL)	107,062	49.7
8	James L. Oberstar (DFL)	176,392	76.7
	Marjory L. Luce (I-R)	53,467	23.3

MISSISSIPPI

	Candidates	Votes	%
1	Jamie L. Whitten (D)	79,726	70.9
	Fran Fawcett (R)	32,750	29.1
2	Webb Franklin (R)	74,450	50.3
	Robert G. Clark (D)	71,536	48.4
3	G. V. (Sonny) Montgomery (D)	114,530	93.1
	James Bradshaw (I)	8,519	6.9
4	Wayne Dowdy (D)	79,977	52.5
	Liles Williams (R)	69,469	45.6
5	Trent Lott (R)	82,884	78.5
	Arlon (Blackie) Coate (D)	22,634	21.5

MISSOURI

	Candidates	Votes	%
1	William Clay (D)	102,656	66.1
	William E. White (R)	52,599	33.9
2	Robert A. Young (D)	100,770	56.5
	Harold L. Dielmann (R)	77,433	43.5
3	Richard A. Gephardt (D)	131,566	77.9
	Richard Foristel (R)	37,388	22.1
4	Ike Skelton (D)	96,388	54.8
	Wendell Bailey (R)	79,565	45.2
5	Alan Wheat (D)	96,059	57.9
	John A. Sharp (R)	66,664	40.2
6	E. Thomas Coleman (R)	97,993	55.3
	Jim Russell (D)	79,053	44.7
7	Gene Taylor (R)	91,391	50.5
	David A. Geisler (D)	89,549	49.5
8	Bill Emerson (R)	86,493	53.1
	Jerry Ford (D)	76,413	46.9
9	Harold L. Volkmer (D)	99,228	60.8
	Larry E. Mead (R)	63,942	39.2

MONTANA

	Candidates	Votes	%
1	Pat Williams (D)	100,087	59.7
	Bob Davies (R)	62,402	37.2
2	Howard Lyman (D)	65,815	44.2
	Ron Marlenee (R)	79,968	53.7

NEBRASKA

	Candidates	Votes	%
1	Douglas K. Bereuter (R)	137,675	75.1
	Curt Donaldson (D)	45,676	24.9
2	Hal Daub (R)	92,639	56.7
	Richard M. Fellman (D)	70,431	43.1
3	Virginia Smith (R)	171,853	100.0

NEVADA

	Candidates	Votes	%
1	Harry Reid (D)	61,901	57.5
	Peggy Cavnar (R)	45,675	42.5
2	Barbara Vucanovich (R)	70,188	55.5
	Mary Gojack (D)	52,265	41.3

NEW HAMPSHIRE

	Candidates	Votes	%
1	Norman E. D'Amours (D)	76,281	54.9
	Robert C. Smith (R)	61,876	44.5
2	Judd Gregg (R)	92,098	70.8
	Robert L. Dupay (D)	37,906	29.2

NEW JERSEY

	Candidates	Votes	%
1	James J. Florio (D)	110,570	73.3
	John A. Dramesi (R)	39,501	26.2
2	William J. Hughes (D)	102,826	68.0
	John J. Mahoney (R)	47,069	31.1
3	James J. Howard (D)	104,055	62.3
	Marie Sheehan Muhler (R)	60,515	36.2
4	Christopher H. Smith (R)	85,660	52.7
	Joseph P. Merlino (D)	75,658	46.5
5	Marge Roukema (R)	104,695	65.3
	Fritz Cammerzell (D)	53,659	33.5
6	Bernard J. Dwyer (D)	100,419	68.1
	Bertram L. Buckler (R)	46,095	31.3
7	Matthew J. Rinaldo (R)	91,837	56.0
	Adam K. Levin (D)	70,978	43.3
8	Robert A. Roe (D)	89,980	70.7
	Norm Robertson (R)	36,317	28.5
9	Robert G. Torricelli (D)	99,090	53.0
	Harold C. Hollenbeck (R)	86,022	46.0
10	Peter W. Rodino Jr. (D)	76,684	82.6
	Timothy Lee Jr. (R)	14,551	15.7
11	Joseph G. Minish (D)	105,607	64.3
	Rey Redington (R)	57,099	34.8
12	Jim Courter (R)	117,793	66.8
	Jeff Connor (D)	57,049	32.3
13	Edwin B. Forsythe (R)	100,061	59.5
	George Callas (D)	65,820	39.1
14	Frank J. Guarini (D)	94,021	74.3
	Charles J. Catrillo (R)	28,257	22.3

NEW MEXICO

	Candidates	Votes	%
1	Manuel Lujan Jr. (R)	74,459	52.4
	Jan Alan Hartke (D)	67,534	47.6
2	Joe Skeen (R)	71,021	58.4
	Caleb Chandler (D)	50,599	41.6
3	Bill Richardson (D)	84,669	64.5
	Marjorie Bell Chambers (R)	46,466	35.4

NEW YORK

	Candidates	Votes	%
1	William Carney (R, C, RTL)	88,234	63.9
	Ethan C. Eldon (D)	49,787	36.1
2	Thomas J. Downey (D)	80,951	63.9
	Paul G. Costello (R, C)	42,790	33.8
3	Robert J. Mrazek (D)	93,846	51.8
	John LeBoutillier (R, C)	83,238	46.0
4	Norman F. Lent (R, C)	105,241	60.4
	Robert P. Zimmerman (D, L)	63,390	36.4
5	Raymond J. McGrath (R, C)	100,485	58.1
	Arnold J. Miller (D, L)	67,002	38.8
6	Joseph P. Addabbo (D, R, L)	95,483	95.9
7	Benjamin S. Rosenthal (D, L)	84,013	77.2
	Albert Lemishow (R, C, RTL)	24,832	22.8
8	James H. Scheuer (D, L)	91,830	89.5
	John T. Blume (C)	10,741	10.5
9	Geraldine A. Ferraro (D)	75,286	73.2
	John J. Weigandt (R)	20,352	19.8
	Ralph G. Groves (C, RTL)	6,011	5.9
10	Charles E. Schumer (D, L)	89,852	79.2
	Stephen Marks (R, C)	21,726	19.2
11	Edolphus Towns (D)	39,357	83.7
	James W. Smith (R)	4,449	9.5
12	Major R. Owens (D, L)	44,586	90.5
	David Katan Sr. (R)	3,215	6.5

	Candidates	Votes	%
13	Stephen J. Solarz (D, L)	68,549	80.5
	Leon F. Nadrowski (R, RTL)	14,257	16.7
14	Guy V. Molinari (R, C, RTL)	67,626	56.1
	Leo C. Zeferetti (D)	51,728	42.9
15	Bill Green (R)	66,262	53.6
	Betty G. Lall (D, L)	55,483	44.9
16	Charles B. Rangel (D, R, L)	76,626	97.5
17	Ted Weiss (D, L)	113,172	85.0
	Louis S. Antonelli (R, C, RTL)	19,928	15.0
18	Robert Garcia (D, R, L)	57,009	98.9
19	Mario Biaggi (D, R, L, RTL)	118,803	93.7
	Michael J. McSherry (C)	7,438	5.9
20	Richard L. Ottinger (D)	98,425	56.5
	Jon S. Fossel (R, C)	72,005	41.3
21	Hamilton Fish Jr. (R, C)	117,460	75.2
	J. Morgan Strong (D)	38,664	24.8
22	Benjamin A. Gilman (R)	92,266	52.9
	Peter A. Peyser (D)	73,124	42.0
23	Samuel S. Stratton (D)	164,427	76.1
	Frank Wicks (R, NF)	41,386	19.2
24	Gerald B. H. Solomon (R, C, RTL)	140,296	73.9
	Roy Esiason (D)	49,441	26.1
25	Sherwood L. Boehlert (R)	93,071	55.8
	Anita Maxwell (D)	70,793	42.4
26	David O'B. Martin (R, C)	108,962	71.6
	David P. Landy (D)	43,208	28.4
27	George C. Wortley (R)	95,290	53.2
	Elaine Lytel (D, L)	79,209	44.2
28	Matthew F. McHugh (D, L)	100,665	56.3
	David F. Crowley (R, C)	75,991	42.5
29	Frank Horton (R)	104,412	66.4
	William C. Larsen (D)	47,463	30.2
30	Barber B. Conable Jr. (R)	119,105	68.2
	Bill Benet (D)	48,764	27.9
31	Jack F. Kemp (R, C)	133,462	75.3
	James A. Martin (D, L)	43,843	24.7
32	John J. LaFalce (D, L)	116,386	91.4
	Raymond R. Walker (R, C)	8,638	6.8
33	Henry J. Nowak (D, L)	126,091	84.1
	Walter J. Pillich (R, C)	19,791	13.2
34	Stanley N. Lundine (D)	99,502	60.2
	James J. Snyder (R, C)	63,972	38.7

NORTH CAROLINA

	Candidates	Votes	%
1	Walter B. Jones (D)	79,954	81.3
	James F. McIntyre III (R)	17,478	17.8
2	I. T. (Tim) Valentine Jr. (D)	59,617	53.6
	John W. Marin (R)	34,293	30.8
	H. M. Michaux Jr. (WRITE IN)	15,990	14.4
3	Charles Whitley (D)	68,936	63.6
	Eugene (Red) McDaniel (R)	39,046	36.0
4	Ike Andrews (D)	70,369	51.3
	William Cobey Jr. (R)	64,955	47.4
5	Stephen L. Neal (D)	87,819	60.3
	Anne Bagnal (R)	57,083	39.2
6	Charles Robin Britt (D)	68,696	53.8
	Eugene Johnston (R)	58,244	45.6
7	Charlie Rose (D)	68,529	71.0
	Edward Johnson (R)	27,015	28.0
8	W. G. (Bill) Hefner (D)	71,691	57.4
	Harris D. Blake (R)	52,417	42.0
9	James G. Martin (R)	64,297	57.0
	Preston Cornelius (D)	47,258	41.9
10	James T. Broyhill (R)	80,904	92.7
	Jhon Rankin (LIBERT)	6,360	7.3
11	James McClure Clarke (D)	85,410	49.9
	Bill Hendon (R)	84,085	49.2

NORTH DAKOTA

	Candidates	Votes	%
AL	Byron L. Dorgan (D)	186,534	71.6
	Kent H. Jones (R)	72,241	27.7

OHIO

	Candidates	Votes	%
1	Thomas A. Luken (D)	99,143	63.5
	John (Jake) Held (R)	52,658	33.7
2	Bill Gradison (R)	97,434	62.7

Candidates	Votes	%
William J. Luttmer (D)	53,169	34.2
3 Tony P. Hall (D)	119,926	87.7
Kathryn E. Brown (LIBERT)	16,828	12.3
4 Michael G. Oxley (R)	105,087	64.6
Robert W. Moon (D)	57,564	35.4
5 Delbert L. Latta (R)	86,450	55.2
James R. Sherck (D)	70,120	44.8
6 Bob McEwen (R)	92,135	59.2
Lynn Alan Grimshaw (D)	63,435	40.8
7 Michael Dewine (R)	87,842	56.3
Roger D. Tackett (D)	65,543	42.0
8 Thomas N. Kindness (R)	98,527	66.4
John W. Griffin (D)	49,877	33.6
9 Marcy Kaptur (D)	95,162	57.9
Ed Weber (R)	64,459	39.3
10 Clarence E. Miller (R)	100,044	63.3
John M. Buchanan (D)	57,983	36.7
11 Dennis E. Eckart (D)	93,302	60.9
Glen W. Warner (R)	56,616	36.9
12 John R. Kasich (R)	88,335	50.5
Bob Shamansky (D)	82,753	47.3
13 Don J. Pease (D)	92,296	61.2
Timothy Paul Martin (R)	53,376	35.4
14 John F. Seiberling (D)	115,629	70.5
Louis A. Mangels (R)	48,421	29.5
15 Chalmers P. Wylie (R)	104,678	66.3
Greg Kostelac (D)	47,070	29.8
16 Ralph Regula (R)	110,485	65.8
Jeffrey R. Orenstein (D)	57,386	34.2
17 Lyle Williams (R)	98,476	55.1
George D. Tablack (D)	80,375	44.9
18 Douglas Applegate (D)	128,665	100.0
19 Edward F. Feighan (D)	111,760	58.8
Richard G. Anter II (R)	72,682	38.3
20 Mary Rose Oakar (D)	133,603	85.6
Paris T. LeJeune (R)	17,675	11.3
21 Louis Stokes (D)	132,544	86.1
Alan G. Shatteen (R)	21,332	13.9

Special Election

	Votes	%
17 Jean Ashbrook (R)	18,106	73.4
Jack Koelbe (D)	6,385	25.9

OKLAHOMA

Candidates	Votes	%
1 James R. Jones (D)	76,379	54.1
Richard C. Freeman (R)	64,704	45.9
2 Mike Synar (D)	111,895	72.6
Lou Striegel (R)	42,298	27.4
3 Wes Watkins (D)	121,670	82.2
Patrick K. Miller (R)	26,335	17.8
4 Dave McCurdy (D)	84,205	65.0
Howard Rutledge (R)	44,351	34.2
5 Mickey Edwards (R)	98,979	67.2
Dan Lane (D)	42,453	28.8
6 Glenn English (D)	102,811	75.4
Ed Moore (R)	33,519	24.6

OREGON

Candidates	Votes	%
1 Les AuCoin (D)	118,638	53.8
Bill Moshofsky (R)	101,720	46.2
2 Bob Smith (R)	106,912	55.6
Larryann Willis (D)	85,495	44.4
3 Ron Wyden (D)	159,416	78.3
Thomas H. Phelan (R)	44,162	21.7
4 James Weaver (D)	115,448	59.0
Ross Anthony (R)	80,054	40.9
5 Denny Smith (R)	103,906	51.2
J. Ruth McFarland (D)	98,952	48.8

PENNSYLVANIA

Candidates	Votes	%
1 Thomas M. Foglietta (D)	103,626	72.3
Michael Marino (R)	38,155	26.6
2 William H. Gray III (D)	120,744	76.1
Milton Street (I)	35,205	22.2
3 Robert A. Borski (D)	97,161	50.1
Charles F. Dougherty (R)	94,497	48.7
4 Joseph P. Kolter (D)	100,481	60.1
Eugene V. Atkinson (R)	64,539	38.6
5 Richard T. Schulze (R)	90,648	67.2
Bob Burger (D)	44,170	32.8
6 Gus Yatron (D)	108,230	72.0
Harry B. Martin (R)	42,155	28.0
7 Robert W. Edgar (D)	105,775	55.4
Steve Joachim (R)	85,023	44.6
8 Peter H. Kostmayer (D)	83,242	50.3
Jim Coyne (R)	80,928	48.9
9 Bud Shuster (R)	92,322	65.1
Eugene J. Duncan (D)	49,583	34.9
10 Joseph M. McDade (R)	103,617	67.5
Robert J. Rafalko (D)	49,868	32.5
11 Frank Harrison (D)	90,371	53.5
James L. Nelligan (R)	78,485	46.5
12 John P. Murtha (D)	96,369	61.1
William N. Tuscano (R)	54,212	34.4
13 Lawrence Coughlin (R)	109,198	64.3
Martin J. Cunningham Jr. (D)	59,709	35.2
14 William J. Coyne (D)	120,980	74.9
John R. Clark (R)	32,780	20.3
15 Don Ritter (R)	79,455	57.8
Richard J. Orloski (D)	58,002	42.2
16 Robert S. Walker (R)	93,034	71.3
Jean D. Mowery (D)	37,364	28.7
17 George W. Gekas (R)	84,291	57.6
Larry J. Hochendoner (D)	61,974	42.4
18 Doug Walgren (D)	101,807	54.2
Ted Jacob (R)	84,428	45.0
19 Bill Goodling (R)	101,163	70.8
Larry Becker (D)	41,787	29.2
20 Joseph M. Gaydos (D)	127,281	76.0
Terry T. Ray (R)	38,212	22.8
21 Thomas J. Ridge (R)	80,180	50.2
Anthony (Buzz) Andrezeski (D)	79,451	49.8
22 Austin J. Murphy (D)	123,716	78.7
Frank J. Paterra (R)	32,176	20.5
23 William F. Clinger Jr. (R)	92,424	65.2
Joseph J. Calla Jr. (D)	49,297	34.8

RHODE ISLAND

Candidates	Votes	%
1 Fernand J. St Germain (D)	97,254	60.7
Burton Stallwood (R)	61,253	38.3
2 Claudine Schneider (R)	96,282	55.6
James V. Aukerman (D)	76,769	44.4

SOUTH CAROLINA

Candidates	Votes	%
1 Thomas F. Hartnett (R)	63,945	54.3
W. Mullins McLeod (D)	52,916	44.9
2 Floyd Spence (R)	71,569	58.5
Ken Mosely (D)	50,749	41.5
3 Butler Derrick (D)	77,125	90.4
Gordon T. Davis (LIBERT)	8,214	9.6
4 Carroll A. Campbell Jr. (R)	69,802	63.3
Marion E. Tyus (D)	40,394	36.7
5 John Spratt (D)	69,345	67.6
John S. Wilkerson (R)	33,191	32.4
6 Robert M. Tallon Jr. (D)	62,582	52.5
John L. Napier (R)	56,653	47.5

SOUTH DAKOTA

Candidates	Votes	%
AL Thomas A. Daschle (D)	142,122	51.6
Clint Roberts (R)	133,530	48.4

TENNESSEE

Candidates	Votes	%
1 James H. Quillen (R)	89,497	74.1
Jessie J. Cable (D)	27,580	22.8
2 John J. Duncan (R)	109,045	100.0
3 Marilyn Lloyd Bouquard (D)	84,967	61.8
Glen Byers (R)	49,885	36.3
4 Jim Cooper (D)	93,453	66.1
Cissy Baker (R)	47,865	33.9
5 Bill Boner (D)	109,282	80.1
Laural Steinhice (R)	27,061	19.8
6 Albert Gore Jr. (D)	104,094	100.0
7 Don Sundquist (R)	73,835	50.5
Bob Clement (D)	72,359	49.5
8 Ed Jones (D)	93,945	74.9
Bruce Benson (R)	31,527	25.1
9 Harold E. Ford (D)	112,143	72.4
Joe Crawford (R)	40,812	26.4

TEXAS

Candidates	Votes	%
1 Sam B. Hall Jr. (D)	100,685	97.5
2 Charles Wilson (D)	91,762	94.3
Ed Richbourg (LIBERT)	5,584	5.7
3 Steve Bartlett (R)	99,852	77.1
James L. McNees Jr. (D)	28,223	21.8
4 Ralph M. Hall (D)	94,134	73.8
Peter J. Collumb (R)	32,221	25.3
5 John Bryant (D)	52,214	64.8
Joe Devaney (R)	27,121	33.7
6 Phil Gramm (D)	91,546	94.5
Ron Hard (LIBERT)	5,288	5.5
7 Bill Archer (R)	108,718	85.0
Dennis Scoggins (D)	17,866	14.0
8 Jack Fields (R)	50,630	56.7
Henry E. Allee (D)	38,041	42.6
9 Jack Brooks (D)	78,965	67.6
John W. Lewis (R)	35,422	30.3
10 J. J. Pickle (D)	121,030	90.1
William G. Kelsey (LIBERT)	8,735	6.5
11 Marvin Leath (D)	83,236	96.3
12 Jim Wright (D)	78,913	68.9
Jim Ryan (R)	34,879	30.5
13 Jack Hightower (D)	86,376	63.6
Ron Slover (R)	47,877	35.3
14 Bill Patman (D)	76,851	60.7
Joe Wyatt Jr. (R)	48,942	38.6
15 E. (Kika) de la Garza (D)	76,544	95.7
16 Ronald Coleman (D)	44,024	53.9
Pat B. Haggerty (R)	36,064	44.2
17 Charles W. Stenholm (D)	109,359	97.1
18 Mickey Leland (D)	68,014	82.6
C. Leon Pickett (R)	12,104	14.7
19 Kent Hance (D)	89,702	81.6
E. L. Hicks (R)	19,062	17.3
20 Henry B. Gonzalez (D)	68,544	91.5
Roger V. Gary (LIBERT)	4,163	5.6
21 Tom Loeffler (R)	106,515	74.6
Charles S. Stough (D)	35,112	24.6
22 Ron Paul (R)	66,536	100.0
23 Abraham Kazen Jr. (D)	51,690	55.3
Jeff Wentworth (R)	41,363	44.2
24 Martin Frost (D)	63,857	72.9
Lucy P. Patterson (R)	22,798	26.0
25 Mike Andrews (D)	63,974	60.4
Mike Faubion (R)	40,112	37.9
26 Tom Vandergriff (D)	69,782	50.1
Jim Bradshaw (R)	69,438	49.9
27 Solomon P. Ortiz (D)	66,604	64.0
Jason Luby (R)	35,209	33.8

UTAH

Candidates	Votes	%
1 James V. Hansen (R)	111,416	62.8
A. Stephen Dirks (D)	66,006	37.2
2 Dan Marriott (R)	92,109	53.8
Frances Farley (D)	78,981	46.2
3 Howard C. Nielson (R)	108,478	76.9
Henry A. Huish (I)	32,661	23.1

VERMONT

Candidates	Votes	%
AL James M. Jeffords (R)	114,191	69.2
Mark A. Kaplan (D)	38,296	23.2

VIRGINIA

Candidates	Votes	%
1 Herbert H. Bateman (R)	76,926	53.9
John J. McGlennon (D)	62,379	43.7
2 G. William Whitehurst (R)	78,108	99.9
3 Thomas J. Bliley Jr. (R)	92,928	59.2
John A. Waldrop Jr. (D)	63,946	40.8

	Candidates	Votes	%
4	Norman Sisisky (D)	80,695	54.4
	Robert W. Daniel Jr. (R)	67,708	45.6
5	Dan Daniel (D)	88,293	100.0
6	James R. Olin (D)	68,192	49.7
	Kevin G. Miller (R)	66,537	48.5
7	J. Kenneth Robinson (R)	76,752	59.9
	Lindsay G. Dorrier Jr. (D)	46,514	36.3
8	Stan Parris (R)	69,620	49.7
	Herbert E. Harris II (D)	68,071	48.6
9	Frederick C. Boucher (D)	76,205	50.4
	William C. Wampler (R)	75,082	49.6
10	Frank R. Wolf (R)	86,506	52.7
	Ira M. Lechner (D)	75,361	45.9

WASHINGTON

	Candidates	Votes	%
1	Joel Pritchard (R)	123,956	67.6
	Brian Long (D)	59,444	32.4
2	Al Swift (D)	101,383	59.6
	Joan Houchen (R)	68,622	40.4
3	Don Bonker (D)	97,323	60.1
	J.T. Quigg (R)	59,686	36.8

	Candidates	Votes	%
4	Sid Morrison (R)	112,148	69.8
	Charles D. Kilbury (D)	45,990	28.6
5	Thomas S. Foley (D)	109,549	64.3
	John Sonneland (R)	60,816	35.7
6	Norman D. Dicks (D)	89,985	62.5
	Ted Haley (R)	47,720	33.2
7	Mike Lowry (D)	126,313	70.9
	Bob Dorse (R)	51,759	29.1
8	Rodney Chandler (R)	79,209	57.0
	Beth Bland (D)	59,824	43.0

WEST VIRGINIA

	Candidates	Votes	%
1	Alan B. Mollohan (D)	79,529	53.2
	John F. McCuskey (R)	70,069	46.8
2	Harley O. Staggers Jr. (D)	87,904	64.0
	J. D. Hinkle Jr. (R)	49,413	36.0
3	Bob Wise (D)	84,619	57.9
	David Michael Staton (R)	60,844	41.6
4	Nick J. Rahall II (D)	91,184	80.5
	Homer L. Harris (R)	22,054	19.5

	Candidates	Votes	%
	WISCONSIN		
1	Les Aspin (D)	95,055	61.0
	Peter N. Jannson (R)	59,309	38.1
2	Robert W. Kastenmeier (D)	112,677	60.6
	Jim Johnson (R)	71,989	38.7
3	Steve Gunderson (R)	99,304	56.6
	Paul Offner (D)	75,132	42.8
4	Clement J. Zablocki (D)	129,557	94.6
5	Jim Moody (D)	99,713	63.5
	Rod K. Johnston (R)	54,826	34.9
6	Thomas E. Petri (R)	111,348	65.0
	Gordon E. Loehr (D)	59,922	35.0
7	David R. Obey (D)	122,124	68.0
	Bernard A. Zimmerman (R)	57,535	32.0
8	Toby Roth (R)	101,379	57.2
	Ruth C. Clusen (D)	74,436	42.0
9	F. James Sensenbrenner Jr. (R)	111,503	100.0

WYOMING

	Candidates	Votes	%
AL	Dick Cheney (R)	113,236	71.1
	Ted Hommel (D)	46,041	28.9

1. For the 1982 House elections in Louisiana, an open primary election was held with candidates from all parties running on the same ballot. Any candidate who received a majority was elected unopposed, with no further appearance on the general election ballot. If no candidate received 50 percent, a runoff was held between the two top finishers.

1983 House Elections

CALIFORNIA

Special Election

	Candidates	Votes	%
5	Sala Burton (D)	44,790	56.9
	Dunan Howard (R)	18,305	23.3
	Richard Doyle (D)	6,582	8.4

COLORADO

Special Election

	Candidates	Votes	%
6	Daniel S. Schaefer (R)	49,816	63.3
	Steve Hogan (D)	27,779	35.3

GEORGIA

Special Election (Nonpartisan)

	Candidates	Votes	%
7	Kathryn McDonald	25,468	30.6
	George W. (Buddy) Darden	22,894	27.6
	George A. Sellers	20,970	25.2
	George Pullen	4,578	5.5
	Dan H. Fincher	4,278	5.1

Special Runoff Election (Nonpartisan)

	Candidates	Votes	%
7	George W. (Buddy) Darden	56,267	59.1
	Kathryn McDonald	38,949	40.9

ILLINOIS

Special Election

	Candidates	Votes	%
1	Charles A. Hayes (D)	39,623	93.7
	Diane Preacely (R)	2,272	5.4

NEW YORK

Special Election

	Candidates	Votes	%
7	Gary L. Ackerman (D, L)	18,388	48.7
	Albert Lemishow (R, C)	8,331	22.1
	Douglas F. Schoen (NEIGH)	5,997	15.9
	Sheldon Loeffler (I)	4,318	11.4

TEXAS

Special Election

	Candidates	Votes	%
6	Phil Gramm (R)	46,371	55.3
	Den Kubiak (D)	33,201	39.6

1984 House Elections

ALABAMA

	Candidates	Votes	%
1	Sonny Callahan (R)	102,479	51.0
	Frank McRight (D)	98,455	49.0
2	William L. Dickinson (R)	118,153	60.3
	Larry Lee (D)	75,506	38.6
3	Bill Nichols (D)	120,357	96.2
4	Tom Bevill (D)	120,106	100.0
5	Ronnie G. Flippo (D)	140,542	95.9
6	Ben Erdreich (D)	130,973	59.6
	J. T. (Jabo) Waggoner (R)	87,550	39.8
7	Richard C. Shelby (D)	135,834	96.8

ALASKA

		Votes	%
AL	Don Young (R)	113,582	55.0
	Pegge Begich (D)	86,052	41.7

ARIZONA

		Votes	%
1	John McCain (R)	162,418	78.1
	Harry W. Braun III (D)	45,609	21.9
2	Morris K. Udall (D)	106,332	87.7
	Lorenzo Torrez (I)	14,869	12.3
3	Bob Stump (R)	156,686	71.8
	Bob Schuster (D)	57,748	26.4
4	Eldon Rudd (R)	167,558	100.0
5	Jim Kolbe (R)	116,075	50.9
	James F. McNulty Jr. (D)	109,871	48.2

ARKANSAS

		Votes	%
1	Bill Alexander (D)	121,047	97.2
2	Tommy F. Robinson (D)	103,165	47.1
	Judy Petty (R)	90,841	41.5
	Jim Taylor (I)	25,073	11.4
3	John Paul Hammerschmidt (R)		100.0
4	Beryl Anthony Jr. (D)	117,123	97.9

CALIFORNIA

		Votes	%
1	Douglas H. Bosco (D)	157,037	62.3
	David Redick (R)	95,186	37.7
2	Gene Chappie (R)	158,679	69.5
	Harry Cozad (D)	69,793	30.5
3	Robert T. Matsui (D)	131,369	100.0
4	Vic Fazio (D)	130,109	61.4
	Roger Canfield (R)	77,773	36.7
5	Sala Burton (D)	139,692	72.3
	Tom Spinosa (R)	45,930	23.8
6	Barbara Boxer (D)	162,511	68.0
	Douglas Binderup (R)	71,011	29.7
7	George Miller (D)	158,306	66.7
	Rosemary Thakar (R)	78,985	33.3
8	Ronald V. Dellums (D)	144,316	60.3
	Charles Connor (R)	94,907	39.7
9	Fortney H. (Pete) Stark (D)	136,511	69.9
	J. T. Eager Beaver (R)	51,399	26.3
10	Don Edwards (D)	102,469	62.4
	Robert P. Herriott (R)	56,256	34.3
11	Tom Lantos (D)	147,607	69.9
	John J. Hickey (R)	59,625	28.3
12	Ed Zschau (R)	155,795	61.7
	Martin Carnoy (D)	91,026	36.0
13	Norman Y. Mineta (D)	139,851	65.2
	John D. Williams (R)	70,666	33.0
14	Norman D. Shumway (R)	179,238	73.3
	Ruth (Paula) Carlson (D)	58,384	23.9
15	Tony Coelho (D)	109,590	65.5
	Carol Harner (R)	54,730	32.7
16	Leon E. Panetta (D)	153,377	70.8
	Patricia Smith Ramsey (R)	60,065	27.7
17	Charles Pashayan Jr. (R)	128,802	72.5
	Simon Lakritz (D)	48,888	27.5
18	Richard H. Lehman (D)	128,186	67.3

	Candidates	Votes	%
	Dale L. Ewen (R)	62,339	32.7
19	Robert J. Lagomarsino (R)	153,187	67.3
	James C. Carey Jr. (D)	70,278	30.9
20	William M. Thomas (R)	151,732	70.9
	Mike LeSage (D)	62,307	29.1
21	Bobbi Fiedler (R)	173,504	72.3
	Charles Davis (D)	62,085	25.9
22	Carlos J. Moorhead (R)	184,981	85.2
	Michael B. Yauch (LIBERT)	32,036	14.8
23	Anthony C. Beilenson (D)	140,461	61.6
	Claude Parrish (R)	84,093	36.9
24	Henry A. Waxman (D)	97,340	63.4
	Jerry Zerg (R)	51,010	33.2
25	Edward R. Roybal (D)	74,261	71.7
	Roy D. (Bill) Bloxom (R)	24,968	24.1
26	Howard L. Berman (D)	117,080	62.8
	Miriam Ojeda (R)	69,372	37.2
27	Mel Levine (D)	116,933	54.9
	Robert B. Scribner (R)	88,896	41.8
28	Julian C. Dixon (D)	113,076	75.6
	Beatrice M. Jett (R)	33,511	22.4
29	Augustus F. Hawkins (D)	108,777	86.6
	Echo Y. Goto (R)	16,781	13.4
30	Matthew G. Martinez (D)	64,378	51.8
	Richard Gomez (R)	53,900	43.3
31	Mervyn M. Dymally (D)	100,658	70.7
	Henry C. Minturn (R)	41,691	29.3
32	Glenn M. Anderson (D)	102,961	60.7
	Roger E. Fiola (R)	62,176	36.6
33	David Dreier (R)	147,363	70.6
	Claire K. McDonald (D)	54,147	26.0
34	Esteban Edward Torres (D)	87,060	59.8
	Paul R. Jackson (R)	58,467	40.2
35	Jerry Lewis (R)	176,477	85.5
	Kevin Akin (PFP)	29,990	14.5
36	George E. Brown Jr. (D)	104,438	56.6
	John Paul Stark (R)	80,212	43.4
37	Al McCandless (R)	149,951	63.6
	David E. Skinner (D)	85,908	36.4
38	Bob Dornan (R)	86,545	53.2
	Jerry M. Patterson (D)	73,231	45.0
39	William E. Dannemeyer (R)	175,788	76.2
	Robert E. Ward (D)	54,889	23.8
40	Robert E. Badham (R)	164,257	64.4
	Carol Ann Bradford (D)	86,748	34.0
41	Bill Lowery (R)	161,068	63.4
	Robert L. Simmons (D)	85,475	33.7
42	Dan Lungren (R)	177,783	73.0
	Mary Lou Brophy (D)	60,025	24.6
43	Ron Packard (R)	165,643	74.1
	Lois E. Humphreys (D)	50,996	22.8
44	Jim Bates (D)	99,378	69.7
	Neill Campbell (R)	39,977	28.0
45	Duncan L. Hunter (R)	149,011	75.1
	David W. Guthrie (D)	45,325	22.9

COLORADO

		Votes	%
1	Patricia Schroeder (D)	126,348	62.0
	Mary Downs (R)	73,993	36.3
2	Timothy E. Wirth (D)	118,580	53.2
	Michael J. Norton (R)	101,488	45.5
3	Mike Strang (R)	122,669	57.1
	W. Mitchell (D)	90,063	41.9
4	Hank Brown (R)	146,469	71.1
	Mary Fagan Bates (D)	56,462	27.4
5	Ken Kramer (R)	163,654	78.6
	William Geffen (D)	44,588	21.4
6	Dan L. Schaefer (R)	171,427	89.4
	John Heckman (I)	20,333	10.6

CONNECTICUT

		Votes	%
1	Barbara B. Kennelly (D)	147,748	61.7
	Herschel A. Klein (R)	90,823	37.9
2	Sam Gejdenson (D)	124,110	54.4

	Candidates	Votes	%
	Roberta F. Koontz (R)	103,119	45.2
3	Bruce A. Morrison (D)	129,230	52.6
	Lawrence J. DeNardis (R)	115,939	47.2
4	Stewart B. McKinney (R)	165,644	70.4
	John M. Ormon (D)	69,666	29.6
5	John G. Rowland (R)	130,700	54.3
	William R. Ratchford (D)	109,425	45.5
6	Nancy L. Johnson (R)	155,422	64.0
	Arthur H. House (D)	87,489	36.0

DELAWARE

		Votes	%
AL	Thomas R. Carper (D)	142,070	58.5
	Elise R. W. du Pont (R)	100,650	41.4

FLORIDA

		Votes	%
1	Earl Hutto (D)		100.0
2	Don Fuqua (D)		100.0
3	Charles E. Bennett (D)		100.0
4	Bill Chappell Jr. (D)	134,694	64.8
	Alton H. (Bill) Starling (R)	73,218	35.2
5	Bill McCollum (R)		100.0
6	Buddy MacKay (D)	167,409	99.3
7	Sam Gibbons (D)	100,430	58.8
	Michael N. Kavouklis (R)	70,280	41.2
8	C. W. Bill Young (R)	184,553	80.3
	Robert Kent (D)	45,393	19.7
9	Michael Bilirakis (R)	191,343	78.6
	Jack Wilson (D)	52,150	21.4
10	Andy Ireland (R)	126,206	61.9
	Patricia M. Glass (D)	77,635	38.1
11	Bill Nelson (D)	145,764	60.5
	Rob Quartel (R)	95,115	39.5
12	Tom Lewis (R)		100.0
13	Connie Mack (R)		100.0
14	Daniel A. Mica (D)	153,935	55.4
	Don Ross (R)	123,926	44.6
15	E. Clay Shaw Jr. (R)	128,097	65.7
	Bill Humphrey (D)	65,833	34.3
16	Larry Smith (D)	108,410	56.4
	Tom Bush (R)	83,903	43.6
17	William Lehman (D)		100.0
18	Claude Pepper (D)	76,404	60.5
	Ricardo Nunez (R)	49,818	39.5
19	Dante B. Fascell (D)	115,631	64.3
	Bill Flanagan (R)	64,317	35.7

GEORGIA

		Votes	%
1	Robert Lindsay Thomas (D)	126,082	81.6
	Erie Lee Downing (R)	28,460	18.4
2	Charles Hatcher (D)	110,561	100.0
3	Richard Ray (D)	111,061	81.4
	Mitchell Cantu (R)	25,410	18.6
4	Pat Swindall (R)	120,456	53.1
	Elliott H. Levitas (D)	106,376	46.9
5	Wyche Fowler Jr. (D)	151,233	100.0
6	Newt Gingrich (R)	116,655	69.1
	Gerald Johnson (D)	52,061	30.9
7	George (Buddy) Darden (D)	106,586	55.2
	William E. Bronson (R)	86,431	44.8
8	J. Roy Rowland (D)	100,936	100.0
9	Ed Jenkins (D)	109,422	67.5
	Frank H. Cofer Jr. (R)	52,731	32.5
10	Doug Barnard Jr. (D)	116,364	100.0

HAWAII

		Votes	%
1	Cecil Heftel (D)	114,844	82.7
	William F. Beard (R)	20,608	14.8
2	Daniel K. Akaka (D)	112,377	82.2
	A. D. Shipley (R)	20,000	14.6

IDAHO

	Candidates	Votes	%
1	Larry E. Craig (R)	139,085	68.6
	Bill Hellar (D)	63,591	31.4
2	Richard H. Stallings (D)	101,287	50.0
	George Hansen (R)	101,117	50.0

ILLINOIS

	Candidates	Votes	%
1	Charles A. Hayes (D)	177,438	95.6
2	Gus Savage (D)	155,349	83.0
	Dale F. Harman (R)	31,865	17.0
3	Marty Russo (D)	143,363	64.4
	Richard D. Murphy (R)	79,218	35.6
4	George M. O'Brien (R)	121,744	64.0
	Dennis E. Marlow (D)	68,547	36.0
5	William O. Lipinski (D)	106,597	63.6
	John M. Paczkowski (R)	61,109	36.4
6	Henry J. Hyde (R)	157,370	75.1
	Robert H. Renshaw (D)	52,189	24.9
7	Cardiss Collins (D)	135,493	78.4
	James L. Bevel (R)	37,411	21.6
8	Dan Rostenkowski (D)	114,385	71.3
	Spiro F. Georgeson (R)	46,030	28.7
9	Sidney R. Yates (D)	144,879	67.5
	Herbert Sohn (R)	69,613	32.5
10	John Edward Porter (R)	153,330	72.6
	Ruth C. Braver (D)	57,809	27.4
11	Frank Annunzio (D)	138,171	62.6
	Charles J. Theusch (R)	82,518	37.4
12	Philip M. Crane (R)	159,582	77.8
	Edward J. LaFlamme (D)	45,537	22.2
13	Harris W. Fawell (R)	157,603	67.0
	Michael J. Donohue (D)	77,623	33.0
14	John E. Grotberg (R)	135,967	62.2
	Dan McGrath (D)	82,756	37.8
15	Edward R. Madigan (R)	149,096	73.2
	John M. Hoffman (D)	54,516	26.8
16	Lynn Martin (R)	127,684	58.4
	Carl R. Schwerdfieger (D)	90,850	41.6
17	Lane Evans (D)	128,273	56.7
	Kenneth G. McMillan (R)	98,069	43.3
18	Robert H. Michel (R)	136,183	61.0
	Gerald A. Bradley (D)	86,884	38.9
19	Terry L. Bruce (D)	117,634	52.3
	Daniel B. Crane (R)	107,463	47.7
20	Richard J. Durbin (D)	145,092	61.3
	Richard G. Austin (R)	91,728	38.7
21	Melvin Price (D)	127,046	60.2
	Robert H. Gaffner (R)	84,148	39.8
22	Kenneth J. Gray (D)	116,952	50.3
	Randy Patchett (R)	115,775	49.7

INDIANA

	Candidates	Votes	%
1	Peter J. Visclosky (D)	147,035	70.7
	Joseph B. Grenchik (R)	59,986	28.8
2	Philip R. Sharp (D)	118,965	53.4
	Ken MacKenzie (R)	103,061	46.3
3	John Hiler (R)	115,139	52.4
	Michael P. Barnes (D)	103,961	47.3
4	Dan Coats (R)	129,674	60.8
	Michael H. Barnard (D)	82,053	38.5
5	Elwood Hillis (R)	143,560	67.9
	Allen B. Maxwell (D)	66,631	31.5
6	Dan Burton (R)	178,814	72.7
	Howard O. Campbell (D)	65,772	26.8
7	John T. Myers (R)	147,787	67.3
	Arthur E. Smith (D)	69,097	31.5
8	Richard D. McIntyre (R)[1]	114,278	49.9
	Frank McCloskey (D)	113,860	49.8
9	Lee H. Hamilton (D)	137,018	65.1
	Floyd E. Coates (R)	72,652	34.5
10	Andrew Jacobs Jr. (D)	115,274	59.0
	Joseph P. Watkins (R)	79,342	40.6

IOWA

	Candidates	Votes	%
1	Jim Leach (R)	131,182	66.8
	Kevin Ready (D)	65,293	33.2
2	Tom Tauke (R)	136,893	63.9
	Joe Welsh (D)	77,335	36.1
3	Cooper Evans (R)	133,737	60.7
	Joe Johnston (D)	86,574	39.3
4	Neal Smith (D)	136,922	60.7
	Robert R. Lockard (R)	88,717	39.3
5	Jim Lightfoot (R)	104,632	50.8
	Jerome D. Fitzgerald (D)	101,435	49.2
6	Berkley Bedell (D)	127,706	62.0
	Darrel Rensink (R)	78,182	38.0

KANSAS

	Candidates	Votes	%
1	Pat Roberts (R)	159,931	76.0
	Darrell Ringer (D)	49,015	23.3
2	Jim Slattery (D)	112,263	60.0
	Jim Van Slyke (R)	73,045	39.1
3	Jan Meyers (R)	117,159	54.8
	John E. Reardon (D)	85,441	39.9
	John S. Ralph Jr. (I)	11,302	5.3
4	Dan Glickman (D)	138,917	74.4
	William V. Krause (R)	47,776	25.6
5	Bob Whittaker (R)	144,075	73.5
	John A. Barnes (D)	49,435	25.2

KENTUCKY

	Candidates	Votes	%
1	Carroll Hubbard Jr. (D)	112,180	100.0
2	William H. Natcher (D)	93,042	62.1
	Timothy A. Morrison (R)	56,700	37.9
3	Romano L. Mazzoli (D)	145,680	67.7
	Suzanne M. Warner (R)	68,185	31.7
4	Gene Snyder (R)	108,398	53.7
	William P. Mulloy II (D)	93,640	46.3
5	Harold Rogers (R)	125,164	75.9
	Sherman W. McIntosh (D)	39,783	24.1
6	Larry J. Hopkins (R)	126,525	71.4
	Jerry Hammond (D)	49,657	28.0
7	Carl C. (Chris) Perkins (D)[2]	122,679	73.7
	Aubrey Russell (R)	43,890	26.3

LOUISIANA[3]

		Votes	%
1	Bob Livingston (R)		100.0
2	Lindy (Mrs. Hale) Boggs (D)		100.0
3	W. J. (Billy) Tauzin (D)		100.0
4	Buddy Roemer (D)		100.0
5	Jerry Huckaby (D)		100.0
6	W. Henson Moore (R)		100.0
7	John B. Breaux (D)		100.0
8	Gillis W. Long (D)		100.0

MAINE

		Votes	%
1	John R. McKernan Jr. (R)	182,785	63.5
	Barry J. Hobbins (D)	104,972	36.5
2	Olympia J. Snowe (R)	192,166	75.7
	Chipman C. Bull (D)	57,347	22.6

MARYLAND

		Votes	%
1	Roy Dyson (D)	96,673	58.4
	Harlan C. Williams (R)	68,865	41.6
2	Helen Delich Bentley (R)	111,517	51.4
	Clarence D. Long (D)	105,571	48.6
3	Barbara A. Mikulski (D)	133,189	68.2
	Ross Z. Pierpont (R)	59,493	30.5
4	Marjorie S. Holt (R)	114,430	66.2
	Howard M. Greenebaum (D)	58,312	33.8
5	Steny H. Hoyer (D)	116,310	72.2
	John E. Ritchie (R)	44,839	27.8
6	Beverly B. Byron (D)	123,383	65.1
	Robin Ficker (R)	66,056	34.9
7	Parren J. Mitchell (D)	139,488	100.0
8	Michael D. Barnes (D)	181,947	71.5
	Albert Ceccone (R)	70,715	27.8

MASSACHUSETTS

	Candidates	Votes	%
1	Silvio O. Conte (R)	162,646	72.9
	Mary L. Wentworth (D)	60,372	27.1
2	Edward P. Boland (D)	132,693	68.7
	Thomas P. Swank (R)	60,463	31.3
3	Joseph D. Early (O)	148,461	67.4
	Kenneth R. Redding (R)	71,765	32.6
4	Barney Frank (D)	172,903	74.2
	Jim Forte (R)	60,121	25.8
5	Chester G. Atkins (D)	120,008	53.4
	Gregory S. Hyatt (R)	104,912	46.6
6	Nicholas Mavroules (D)	168,662	70.4
	Frederick S. Leber (R)	63,363	26.4
7	Edward J. Markey (D)	167,211	71.4
	S. Lester Ralph (R)	66,930	28.6
8	Thomas P. O'Neill Jr. (D)	179,617	91.8
	Laura Ross (COM)	15,810	8.1
9	Joe Moakley (D)	153,132	99.9
10	Gerry E. Studds (D)	143,062	55.7
	Lewis Crampton (R)	113,745	44.3
11	Brian J. Donnelly (D)	172,010	100.0

MICHIGAN

	Candidates	Votes	%
1	John Conyers Jr. (D)	152,432	89.4
	Edward J. Mack (R)	17,393	10.2
2	Carl D. Pursell (R)	140,688	68.6
	Mike McCauley (D)	62,374	30.4
3	Howard Wolpe (D)	106,505	52.9
	Jackie McGregor (R)	94,714	47.1
4	Mark D. Siljander (R)	127,907	66.9
	Charles S. Rodebaugh (D)	63,159	33.1
5	Paul B. Henry (R)	140,131	61.8
	Gary J. McInerney (D)	85,232	37.6
6	Bob Carr (D)	106,705	52.4
	Tom Ritter (R)	95,113	46.7
7	Dale E. Kildee (D)	145,070	93.1
	Samuel Johnston (I)	10,663	6.8
8	Bob Traxler (D)	126,161	64.4
	John Heussner (R)	69,683	35.6
9	Guy Vander Jagt (R)	150,885	70.9
	John M. Senger (D)	61,233	28.8
10	Bill Schuette (R)	104,950	50.1
	Donald J. Albosta (D)	103,636	49.4
11	Robert W. Davis (R)	126,992	58.6
	Tom Stewart (D)	89,640	41.4
12	David E. Bonior (D)	113,772	58.3
	Eugene J. Tyza (R)	79,824	40.9
13	George W. Crockett Jr. (D)	132,222	86.6
	Robert Murphy (R)	20,416	13.4
14	Dennis M. Hertel (D)	113,610	59.1
	John Lauve (D)	77,427	40.3
15	William D. Ford (D)	98,973	59.9
	Gerald R. Carlson (R)	66,172	40.1
16	John D. Dingell (D)	121,463	63.7
	Frank Grzywacki (R)	68,116	35.7
17	Sander M. Levin (D)	133,064	100.0
18	William S. Broomfield (R)	186,505	79.4
	Vivian H. Smargon (D)	46,191	19.7

MINNESOTA[4]

	Candidates	Votes	%
1	Timothy J. Penny (DFL)	140,095	57.0
	Keith Spicer (I-R)	105,723	43.0
2	Vin Weber (I-R)	153,308	63.1
	Todd Lundquist (DFL)	89,770	36.9
3	Bill Frenzel (I-R)	207,819	73.2
	Dave Peterson (DFL)	76,132	26.8
4	Bruce F. Vento (DFL)	167,678	73.5
	Mary Jane Rachner (I-R)	57,450	25.2
5	Martin Olav Sabo (DFL)	165,075	70.1
	Richard D. Wieblen (I-R)	62,642	26.6
6	Gerry Sikorski (DFL)	154,603	60.5
	Patrick Trueman (I-R)	101,058	39.5
7	Arlan Stangeland (I-R)	135,087	57.0
	Collin C. Peterson (DFL)	101,720	42.9
8	James L. Oberstar (DFL)	165,727	67.2
	Dave Rued (I-R)	79,181	32.1

MISSISSIPPI

#	Candidates	Votes	%
1	Jamie L. Whitten (D)	136,530	88.4
	John Hargett (I)	17,991	11.6
2	Webb Franklin (R)	92,392	50.6
	Robert G. Clark (D)	89,154	48.9
3	G. V. (Sonny) Montgomery (D)	158,002	100.0
4	Wayne Dowdy (D)	113,635	55.3
	David Armstrong (R)	91,797	45.6
5	Trent Lott (R)	142,637	84.7
	Arlon (Blackie) Coate (D)	25,840	15.3

MISSOURI

#	Candidates	Votes	%
1	William L. Clay (D)	147,436	68.3
	Eric Rathbone (R)	68,538	31.7
2	Robert A. Young (D)	139,123	51.8
	John Buechner (R)	127,710	47.5
3	Richard A. Gephardt (D)	193,537	100.0
4	Ike Skelton (D)	150,624	66.9
	Carl D. Russell (R)	74,434	33.1
5	Alan Wheat (D)	150,675	66.0
	Jim Kenworthy (R)	72,477	31.8
6	E. Thomas Coleman (R)	150,996	64.8
	Kenneth C. Hensley (D)	81,917	35.2
7	Gene Taylor (R)	164,586	69.6
	Ken Young (D)	71,867	30.4
8	Bill Emerson (R)	134,186	65.4
	Bill Blue (D)	70,922	34.6
9	Harold L. Volkmer (D)	123,588	52.9
	Carrie Francke (R)	110,100	47.1

MONTANA

#	Candidates	Votes	%
1	Pat Williams (D)	126,998	65.6
	Gary K. Carlson (R)	61,794	31.9
2	Ron Marlenee (R)	116,932	65.9
	Chet Blaylock (D)	60,445	34.1

NEBRASKA

#	Candidates	Votes	%
1	Doug Bereuter (R)	158,836	74.1
	Monica Bauer (D)	55,508	25.9
2	Hal Daub (R)	139,384	64.9
	Thomas F. Cavanaugh (D)	75,210	35.0
3	Virginia Smith (R)	183,901	83.3
	Tom Vickers (D)	36,899	16.7

NEVADA

#	Candidates	Votes	%
1	Harry Reid (D)	73,242	56.1
	Peggy Cavnar (R)	55,391	42.4
2	Barbara F. Vucanovich (R)	99,775	71.2
	Andrew Barbano (D)	36,130	25.8

NEW HAMPSHIRE

#	Candidates	Votes	%
1	Robert C. Smith (R)	111,627	58.6
	Dudley Dudley (D)	76,854	40.3
2	Judd Gregg (R)	138,975	76.2
	Larry Converse (D)	42,257	23.2

NEW JERSEY

#	Candidates	Votes	%
1	James J. Florio (D)	152,125	71.9
	Frederick A. Busch Jr. (R)	58,800	27.8
2	William J. Hughes (D)	132,841	63.2
	Raymond G. Massie (R)	77,231	36.7
3	James J. Howard (D)	122,291	53.3
	Brian T. Kennedy (R)	105,028	45.8
4	Christopher H. Smith (R)	139,295	61.3
	James C. Hedden (D)	87,908	38.7
5	Marge Roukema (R)	171,979	71.2
	Rose Brunetto (D)	69,666	28.8
6	Bernard J. Dwyer (D)	118,532	55.9
	Dennis Adams (R)	90,862	42.8
7	Matthew J. Rinaldo (R)	165,685	74.2
	John F. Feeley (D)	56,798	25.4
8	Robert A. Roe (D)	118,793	62.7
	Marguerite A. Page (R)	69,973	36.9
9	Robert G. Torricelli (D)	149,493	62.6
	Neil Romano (R)	89,166	37.4
10	Peter W. Rodino Jr. (D)	111,244	83.7
	Howard E. Berkeley (R)	21,712	16.3
11	Dean A. Gallo (R)	133,662	55.8
	Joseph G. Minish (D)	106,038	44.2
12	Jim Courter (R)	148,042	65.0
	Peter Bearse (D)	78,167	34.3
13	H. James Saxton (R)[5]	141,136	60.7
	James B. Smith (D)	89,307	38.4
14	Frank J. Guarini (D)	115,117	65.7
	Edward T. Magee (R)	58,265	33.3

NEW MEXICO

#	Candidates	Votes	%
1	Manuel Lujan Jr. (R)	115,808	64.9
	Charles Ted Asbury (D)	60,598	34.0
2	Joe Skeen (R)	116,006	74.3
	Peter R. York (D)	40,063	25.7
3	Bill Richardson (D)	100,470	60.8
	Louis H. Gallegos (R)	62,351	37.7

NEW YORK

#	Candidates	Votes	%
1	William Carney (R, C, RTL)	107,029	53.1
	George J. Hochbrueckner (D, RP)	94,551	46.9
2	Thomas J. Downey (D, IP)	97,648	54.7
	Paul Aniboli (R, C, RTL)	80,855	45.3
3	Robert J. Mrazek (D)	120,191	51.0
	Robert P. Quinn (R, C)	112,909	47.9
4	Norman F. Lent (R, C)	154,875	68.9
	Sheldon Engelhard (D, L)	65,678	29.2
5	Raymond J. McGrath (R, C)	138,560	62.4
	Michael d'Innocenzo (D, IV)	78,429	35.3
6	Joseph P. Addabbo (D, L)	120,098	82.7
	Philip J. Veltre (R, C, RTL)	25,040	17.3
7	Gary L. Ackerman (D, L)	97,674	69.3
	Gustave A. Reifenkugel (R, C)	43,370	30.7
8	James H. Scheuer (D, L)	104,558	62.8
	Robert L. Brandofino (R, C)	62,015	37.2
9	Thomas J. Manton (D)	71,420	52.8
	Serphin R. Maltese (R, C, RTL)	63,910	47.2
10	Charles E. Schumer (D, L)	115,867	72.4
	John H. Fox (R, C)	42,000	26.3
11	Edolphus Towns (D, L)	81,002	85.2
	Nathaniel Hendricks (R)	12,494	13.1
12	Major R. Owens (D, L)	82,047	90.5
	Joseph N. O. Caesar (R, C, RTL)	8,609	9.5
13	Stephen J. Solarz (D, L)	82,610	65.9
	Lew Y. Levin (R, C, RTL)	42,737	34.1
14	Guy V. Molinari (R, C, RTL)	117,041	70.2
	Kevin L. Sheehy (D)	49,776	29.8
15	Bill Green (R, I)	107,644	56.1
	Andrew J. Stein (D, L)	84,404	43.9
16	Charles B. Rangel (D, R)	117,759	97.0
17	Ted Weiss (D, L)	162,489	81.5
	Kenneth Katzman (R)	33,316	16.7
18	Robert Garcia (D, L)	85,960	89.2
	Curtis Johnson (R)	8,970	9.3
19	Mario Biaggi (D, R, L, RTL)	155,067	94.8
	Alice Farrell (C)	8,472	5.2
20	Joseph J. DioGuardi (R, C)	106,958	50.1
	Oren J. Teicher (D)	102,842	48.2
21	Hamilton Fish Jr. (R, C, RTL)	160,053	78.3
	Lawrence W. Grunberger (D)	44,274	21.7
22	Benjamin A. Gilman (R)	144,278	68.5
	Bruce M. Levine (D, L)	57,934	27.5
23	Samuel S. Stratton (D)	188,144	77.8
	Frank Wicks (R, NF)	53,060	21.9
24	Gerald B. H. Solomon (R, C, RTL)	164,019	73.2
	Edward J. Bloch (D)	60,188	26.8
25	Sherwood Boehlert (R)	140,256	72.8
	James J. Ball (D)	52,434	27.2
26	David O'B. Martin (R, C)	131,257	70.6
	Bernard J. Lammers (D)	54,663	29.4
27	George C. Wortley (R, C)	122,215	56.6
	Thomas C. Buckel Jr. (D, L)	93,601	43.4
28	Matthew F. McHugh (D)	123,334	56.6
	Constance E. Cook (R)	90,324	41.4
29	Frank Horton (R)	138,362	69.6
	James R. Toole (D)	48,301	24.3
30	Fred J. Eckert (R, C, RTL)	119,844	54.4
	W. Douglas Call (D)	100,066	45.4
31	Jack F. Kemp (R, C, RTL)	168,332	75.0
	Peter J. Martinelli (D, L)	56,156	25.0
32	John J. LaFalce (D, L)	139,979	69.4
	Anthony J. Murty (R, C, RTL)	61,797	30.6
33	Henry J. Nowak (D, L)	155,198	77.6
	David S. Lewandowski (R, C, RTL)	44,880	22.4
34	Stan Lundine (D)	110,902	54.2
	Jill Houghton Emery (R, C)	91,016	44.5

NORTH CAROLINA

#	Candidates	Votes	%
1	Walter B. Jones (D)	122,815	67.1
	Herbert W. Lee (R)	60,153	32.9
2	Tim Valentine (D)	122,292	67.7
	Frank H. Hill (R)	58,312	32.3
3	Charles Whitley (D)	100,185	64.1
	Danny G. Moody (R)	56,096	35.9
4	Bill Cobey (R)	117,436	50.6
	Ike Andrews (D)	114,462	49.4
5	Stephen L. Neal (D)	109,831	50.7
	Stuart Epperson (R)	106,599	49.3
6	Howard Coble (R)	102,925	50.6
	Robin Britt (D)	100,263	49.3
7	Charlie Rose (D)	92,157	59.2
	S. Thomas Rhodes (R)	63,625	40.8
8	W. G. (Bill) Hefner (D)	99,731	50.9
	Harris D. Blake (R)	96,354	49.1
9	J. Alex McMillan (R)	109,420	50.1
	D. G. Martin (D)	109,099	49.9
10	James T. Broyhill (R)	142,873	73.4
	Ted A. Poovey (D)	51,860	26.6
11	Bill Hendon (R)	112,598	51.0
	James McClure Clarke (D)	108,284	49.0

NORTH DAKOTA

#	Candidates	Votes	%
AL	Byron L. Dorgan (D)	242,968	78.7
	Lois Ivers Altenburg (R)	65,761	21.3

OHIO

#	Candidates	Votes	%
1	Thomas A. Luken (D)	121,577	55.1
	Norman A. Murdock (R)	88,859	40.3
2	Bill Gradison (R)	149,856	68.6
	Thomas D. Porter (D)	68,597	31.4
3	Tony P. Hall (D)	151,398	100.0
4	Michael G. Oxley (R)	162,199	77.5
	William O. Sutton (D)	47,018	22.5
5	Delbert L. Latta (R)	132,582	62.7
	James R. Sherck (D)	78,809	37.3
6	Bob McEwen (R)	150,101	74.0
	Bob Smith (D)	52,727	26.0
7	Michael DeWine (R)	147,885	76.7
	Donald E. Scott (D)	40,621	21.1
8	Thomas N. Kindness (R)	155,200	76.9
	John T. Francis (D)	46,673	23.1
9	Marcy Kaptur (D)	117,985	54.9
	Frank Venner (R)	93,210	43.4
10	Clarence E. Miller (R)	149,337	73.0
	John M. Buchanan (D)	55,172	27.0
11	Dennis E. Eckart (D)	133,096	66.8
	Dean Beagle (R)	66,278	33.2
12	John R. Kasich (R)	148,899	69.5
	Richard Sloan (D)	65,215	30.5
13	Don J. Pease (D)	131,923	66.4
	William G. Schaffner (R)	59,610	30.0
14	John F. Seiberling (D)	155,729	71.4
	Jean E. Bender (R)	62,366	28.6
15	Chalmers P. Wylie (R)	148,311	71.6
	Duane Jager (D)	58,870	28.4
16	Ralph Regula (R)	152,399	72.4

Candidates	Votes	%
James Gwin (D)	58,048	27.6
17 James A. Traficant Jr. (D)	123,014	53.3
Lyle Williams (R)	105,449	45.7
18 Douglas Applegate (D)	155,759	75.9
Kenneth P. Burt Jr. (R)	49,356	24.1
19 Edward F. Feighan (D)	139,605	55.2
Matthew J. Hatchadorian (R)	107,957	42.7
20 Mary Rose Oakar (D)	167,115	100.0
21 Louis Stokes (D)	165,247	82.4
Robert L. Woodall (R)	29,500	14.7

OKLAHOMA

Candidates	Votes	%
1 James R. Jones (D)	113,919	52.2
Frank Keating (R)	103,098	47.3
2 Mike Synar (D)	148,124	74.1
Gary K. Rice (R)	51,889	25.9
3 Wes Watkins (D)	137,964	77.8
Patrick K. Miller (R)	39,454	22.2
4 Dave McCurdy (D)	109,447	63.6
Jerry Smith (R)	60,844	35.4
5 Mickey Edwards (R)	135,167	75.6
Allen Greeson (D)	39,089	21.9
6 Glenn English (D)	96,994	58.9
Craig Dodd (R)	67,601	41.1

OREGON

Candidates	Votes	%
1 Les AuCoin (D)	138,393	53.1
Bill Moshofsky (R)	122,247	46.9
2 Robert F. Smith (R)	132,649	57.0
Larryann C. Willis (D)	100,152	43.0
3 Ron Wyden (D)	173,438	72.3
Drew Davis (R)	66,394	27.7
4 James Weaver (D)	134,190	58.2
Bruce Long (R)	96,487	41.8
5 Denny Smith (R)	130,424	54.5
Ruth McFarland (D)	108,919	45.5

PENNSYLVANIA

Candidates	Votes	%
1 Thomas M. Foglietta (D)	148,123	74.9
Carmine DiBiase (R)	49,559	25.1
2 William H. Gray III (D)	200,484	91.0
Ronald J. Sharper (R)	18,224	8.3
3 Robert A. Borski (D)	152,598	63.9
Flora L. Becker (R)	85,358	35.7
4 Joe Kolter (D)	114,040	56.8
James Kunder (R)	86,769	43.2
5 Richard T. Schulze (R)	141,965	72.6
Louis J. Fanti (D)	53,586	27.4
6 Gus Yatron (D)	181,165	100.0
7 Bob Edgar (D)	124,458	50.1
Curt Weldon (R)	124,046	49.9
8 Peter H. Kostmayer (D)	112,648	50.9
David A. Christian (R)	108,696	49.1
9 Bud Shuster (R)	118,437	66.5
Nancy Kulp (D)	59,549	33.5
10 Joseph M. McDade (R)	150,166	77.1
Gene Basalyga (D)	44,571	22.9
11 Paul E. Kanjorski (D)	108,430	58.6
Robert P. Hudock (R)	76,692	41.4
12 John P. Murtha (D)	134,384	69.1
Thomas J. Fullard III (R)	57,466	29.5
13 Lawrence Coughlin (R)	133,948	56.1
Joseph M. Hoeffel (D)	104,756	43.9
14 William J. Coyne (D)	163,818	76.6
John Robert Clark (R)	42,616	19.9
15 Don Ritter (R)	110,338	58.1
Jane Wells-Schooley (D)	79,490	41.9
16 Robert S. Walker (R)	138,477	77.8
Martin L. Bard (D)	39,515	22.2
17 George W. Gekas (R)	129,716	80.3
Stephen A. Anderson (D)	31,770	19.7
18 Doug Walgren (D)	149,628	62.7
John G. Maxwell (R)	87,521	36.7
19 Bill Goodling (R)	141,196	75.6
F. John Rarig (D)	44,117	23.6

Candidates	Votes	%
20 Joseph M. Gaydos (D)	158,751	76.0
Daniel Lloyd (R)	50,247	24.0
21 Tom Ridge (R)	125,730	65.4
James A. Young (D)	65,594	34.1
22 Austin J. Murphy (D)	153,514	79.0
Nancy S. Pryor (R)	39,752	20.0
23 William F. Clinger Jr. (R)	94,952	51.6
Bill Wachob (D)	88,957	48.4

RHODE ISLAND

Candidates	Votes	%
1 Fernand J. St Germain (D)	130,584	68.5
Alfred Rego Jr. (R)	60,026	31.5
2 Claudine Schneider (R)	135,161	67.7
Richard Sinapi (D)	64,341	32.3

SOUTH CAROLINA

Candidates	Votes	%
1 Thomas F. Hartnett (R)	103,288	61.7
Ed Pendarvis (D)	64,022	38.3
2 Floyd Spence (R)	108,085	62.1
Ken Mosely (D)	63,932	36.7
3 Butler Derrick (D)	88,917	58.4
Clarence E. Taylor (R)	61,739	40.6
4 Carroll A. Campbell Jr. (R)	105,139	63.9
Jeff Smith (D)	57,854	35.2
5 John M. Spratt Jr. (D)	98,513	96.3
6 Robin Tallon (D)	97,329	59.9
Lois Eargle (R)	63,005	38.8

SOUTH DAKOTA

Candidates	Votes	%
AL Thomas A. Daschle (D)	181,401	57.4
Dale Bell (R)	134,821	42.6

TENNESSEE

Candidates	Votes	%
1 James H. Quillen (R)	113,407	100.0
2 John J. Duncan (R)	132,604	77.3
John F. Bowen (D)	38,846	22.7
3 Marilyn Lloyd (D)	99,465	52.4
John Davis (R)	90,216	47.6
4 Jim Cooper (D)	93,848	75.2
James Beau Seigneur (R)	31,011	24.8
5 Bill Boner (D)	138,233	100.0
6 Bart Gordon (D)	103,989	62.8
Joe Simpkins (R)	61,559	37.2
7 Don Sundquist (R)	107,257	100.0
8 Ed Jones (D)	118,653	100.0
9 Harold E. Ford (D)	133,428	71.5
William B. Thompson Jr. (R)	53,064	28.5

TEXAS

Candidates	Votes	%
1 Sam B. Hall Jr. (D)	139,829	100.0
2 Charles Wilson (D)	113,225	59.3
Louis Dugas Jr. (R)	77,842	40.7
3 Steve Bartlett (R)	228,819	83.0
Jim Westbrook (D)	46,890	17.0
4 Ralph M. Hall (D)	120,749	58.0
Thomas Blow (R)	87,553	42.0
5 John Bryant (D)	94,391	100.0
6 Joe L. Barton (R)	131,482	56.6
Dan Kubiak (D)	100,799	43.4
7 Bill Archer (R)	213,480	86.7
Billy Willibey (D)	32,835	13.3
8 Jack Fields (R)	113,031	64.6
Don Buford (D)	62,072	35.4
9 Jack Brooks (D)	120,559	58.9
Jim Mahan (R)	84,306	41.2
10 J. J. Pickle (D)	186,447	99.8
11 Marvin Leath (D)	112,940	100.0
12 Jim Wright (D)	106,299	100.0
13 Beau Boulter (R)	107,600	53.0
Jack Hightower (D)	95,367	47.0
14 Mac Sweeney (R)	104,181	51.3
Bill Patman (D)	98,885	48.7
15 E. (Kika) de la Garza (D)	104,863	100.0
16 Ronald D. Coleman (D)	76,375	57.4
Jack Hammond (R)	56,589	42.6

Candidates	Votes	%
17 Charles W. Stenholm (D)	143,012	100.0
18 Mickey Leland (D)	109,626	78.8
Glen E. Beaman (R)	26,400	19.0
19 Larry Combest (R)	102,805	58.1
Don R. Richards (D)	74,044	41.9
20 Henry B. Gonzalez (D)	100,443	100.0
21 Tom Loeffler (R)	199,909	80.6
Joe Sullivan (D)	48,039	19.4
22 Thomas D. DeLay (R)	125,225	65.3
Doug Williams (D)	66,495	34.7
23 Albert G. Bustamante (D)	95,721	100.0
24 Martin Frost (D)	105,210	59.5
Bob Burk (R)	71,703	40.5
25 Michael A. Andrews (D)	113,946	64.0
Jerry Patterson (R)	63,974	36.0
26 Dick Armey (R)	126,641	51.3
Tom Vandergriff (D)	120,451	48.7
27 Solomon P. Ortiz (D)	105,516	63.6
Richard Moore (R)	60,283	36.4

UTAH

Candidates	Votes	%
1 James V. Hansen (R)	142,952	71.2
Milton C. Abrams (D)	56,619	28.2
2 David S. Monson (R)	105,540	49.4
Frances Farley (D)	105,044	49.1
3 Howard C. Nielson (R)	138,918	74.5
Bruce R. Baird (D)	46,560	25.0

VERMONT

Candidates	Votes	%
AL James M. Jeffords (R)	148,025	65.4
Anthony Pollina (D)	60,360	26.7

VIRGINIA

Candidates	Votes	%
1 Herbert H. Bateman (R)	118,085	59.1
John McGlennon (D)	79,577	39.8
2 G. William Whitehurst (R)	136,632	99.8
3 Thomas J. Bliley Jr. (R)	169,987	85.6
Roger L. Coffey (I)	28,556	14.4
4 Norman Sisisky (D)	120,093	99.9
5 Dan Daniel (D)	117,738	100.0
6 James R. Olin (D)	105,207	53.5
Ray Garland (R)	91,344	46.5
7 D. French Slaughter Jr. (R)	109,110	56.5
Lewis M. Costello (D)	77,624	40.2
8 Stan Parris (R)	125,015	55.8
Richard L. Saslaw (D)	97,250	43.4
9 Frederick C. Boucher (D)	102,446	52.0
Jefferson Stafford (R)	94,510	48.0
10 Frank R. Wolf (R)	158,528	62.5
John P. Flannery II (D)	95,074	37.5

WASHINGTON

Candidates	Votes	%
1 John R. Miller (R)	147,926	56.3
Brock Evans (D)	115,001	43.7
2 Al Swift (D)	142,065	58.6
Jim Klauder (R)	93,472	38.6
3 Don Bonker (D)	150,432	71.1
Herb Elder (R)	61,219	28.9
4 Sid Morrison (R)	150,322	76.1
Mark Epperson (D)	47,158	23.9
5 Thomas S. Foley (D)	154,988	69.7
Jack Hebner (R)	67,438	30.3
6 Norman D. Dicks (D)	124,367	66.1
Mike Lonergan (R)	60,721	32.3
7 Mike Lowry (D)	174,560	70.4
Robert O. Dorse (R)	71,576	28.9
8 Rod Chandler (R)	146,891	62.4
Bob Lamson (D)	88,379	37.6

WEST VIRGINIA

Candidates	Votes	%
1 Alan B. Mollohan (D)	104,639	54.4
James Altmeyer (R)	87,622	45.6
2 Harley O. Staggers Jr. (D)	100,345	56.0
Cleve Benedict (R)	78,936	44.0
3 Bob Wise (D)	125,306	67.9

Candidates	Votes	%
Margaret Miller (R)	59,128	32.1
4 Nick J. Rahall II (D)	98,919	66.7
Jess T. Shumate (R)	49,474	33.3

WISCONSIN

Candidates	Votes	%
1 Les Aspin (D)	127,184	56.2
Pete Jansson (R)	99,080	43.8
2 Robert W. Kastenmeier (D)	159,987	63.6
Albert E. Wiley Jr. (R)	91,345	36.3
3 Steve Gunderson (R)	160,437	68.4
Charles F. Dahl (D)	74,253	31.6

Candidates	Votes	%
4 Gerald D. Kleczka (D)	158,722	66.6
Robert V. Nolan (R)	78,056	32.8
5 Jim Moody (D)	175,243	98.0
6 Thomas E. Petri (R)	170,271	75.8
David L. Iaquinta (D)	54,266	24.2
7 David R. Obey (D)	146,131	61.2
Mark G. Michaelsen (R)	92,507	38.8
8 Toby Roth (R)	161,005	67.9
Paul Willems (D)	73,090	30.8
9 F. James Sensenbrenner Jr. (R)	180,247	73.4
John Krause (D)	64,157	26.1

Special Election

Candidates	Votes	%
4 Gerald D. Kleczka (D)	76,384	65.0
Robert V. Nolan (R)	41,007	34.9

WYOMING

	Candidates	Votes	%
AL	Dick Cheney (R)	138,234	73.6
	Hugh B. McFadden Jr. (D)	45,857	24.4

1. Contested election. A recount by a House Administration Committee task force determined that McCloskey defeated McIntyre by a four-vote margin, 116,645 (50.00085 percent) to 116, 841 (49.99914 percent). On May 1, 1985, the House voted 236-190 to seat McCloskey.

2. A special election was held in conjunction with the November election. Perkins was elected to fill both the unexpired term of his father, Rep. Carl D. Perkins, D, who died Aug. 3, 1984, and the two-year term beginning Jan. 3, 1985.

3. For the 1984 House elections in Louisiana, an open primary election was held with candidates from all parties running on the same ballot. Any candidate who received a majority was elected unopposed, with no further appearance on the general election ballot. If no candidate received 50 percent, a runoff was held between the two top finishers.

4. In Minnesota the Democratic Party is known as the Democratic-Farmer-Labor Party and the Republican Party as the Independent-Republican Party; candidates appear on the ballot with these designations.

5. A special election was held in conjunction with the November election. Saxton was elected to serve both the unexpired term of Rep. Edwin B. Forsythe, R, who died March 29, 1984, and the two-year term beginning Jan. 3. 1985.

1985 House Elections

LOUISIANA

Special Election[1]

Candidates	Votes	%
8 Cathy (Mrs. Gillis) Long (D)	61,791	55.7
John E. (Jock) Scott (D)	27,138	24.5
Clyde C. Holloway (R)	18,013	16.3

TEXAS

Special Election[2]

Candidates	Votes	%
1 Edd Hargett (R)	29,720	42.0
Jim Chapman (D)	21,382	30.2
Sam Russell (D)	13,090	18.5

Special Runoff Election

Candidates	Votes	%
1 Jim Chapman (D)	52,665	50.9
Edd Hargett (R)	50,741	50.9

1. Long was elected to serve the unexpired term of her husband, Rep. Gillis W. Long, D, who died Jan. 20, 1985.

2. A special election was held to fill the unexpired term of Rep. Sam B. Hall Jr., D, who resigned May 27, 1985, to accept a federal judgeship.

1986 House Elections

ALABAMA

	Candidates	Votes	%
1	Sonny Callahan (R)	96,469	100.0
2	William L. Dickinson (R)	115,302	66.7
	Mercer Stone (D)	57,568	33.3
3	Bill Nichols (D)	115,127	80.6
	Whit Guerin (R)	27,769	19.4
4	Tom Bevill (D)	132,881	77.5
	Al DeShazo (R)	38,588	22.5
5	Ronnie G. Flippo (D)	125,406	78.9
	Herb McCarley (R)	33,528	21.1
6	Ben Erdreich (D)	139,608	72.7
	L. Morgan Williams (R)	51,924	27.1
7	Claude Harris (D)	108,126	59.8
	Bill McFarland (R)	72,777	40.2

ALASKA

	Candidates	Votes	%
AL	Don Young (R)	101,799	56.5
	Pegge Begich (D)	74,053	41.1

ARIZONA

	Candidates	Votes	%
1	John J. Rhodes III (R)	127,370	71.3
	Harry Braun III (D)	51,163	28.7
2	Morris K. Udall (D)	77,239	73.3
	Sheldon Clark (R)	24,522	23.3
3	Bob Stump (R)	146,462	100.0
4	Jon Kyl (R)	121,939	43.6
	Philip R. Davis (D)	66,894	35.4
5	Jim Kolbe (R)	119,647	64.9
	Joel Ireland (D)	64,848	35.1

ARKANSAS

	Candidates	Votes	%
1	Bill Alexander (D)	105,773	64.2
	Rick H. Albin (R)	58,937	35.8
2	Tommy F. Robinson (D)	128,814	75.7
	Keith Hamaker (R)	41,244	24.2
3	John Hammerschmidt (R)	145,113	79.8
	Su Sargent (D)	36,726	20.2
4	Beryl Anthony Jr. (D)	115,335	77.5
	Lamar Keels (R)	22,980	15.4
	Stephen A. Bltely (I)	10,604	7.1

CALIFORNIA

	Candidates	Votes	%
1	Douglas H. Bosco (D)	138,174	67.5
	Floyd G. Sampson (R)	54,436	26.6
	Elden McFarland (PFP)	12,149	5.9
2	Wally Herger (R)	109,758	58.3
	Stephen C. Swendiman (D)	74,602	39.6
3	Robert T. Matsui (D)	158,709	75.9
	Lowell P. Landowski (R)	50,265	24.1
4	Vic Fazio (D)	128,364	70.2
	Jack D. Hite (R)	54,596	29.8
5	Sala Burton (D)	122,688	75.1
	Mike Garza (R)	36,039	22.1
6	Barbara Boxer (D)	142,946	73.9
	Franklin H. Ernst III (R)	50,606	26.1
7	George Miller (D)	124,174	66.6
	Rosemary Thakar (R)	62,379	33.4
8	Ronald V. Dellums (D)	121,790	60.0
	Steven Eigenberg (R)	76,850	37.9
9	Fortney H. Stark (D)	113,490	69.7
	David M. Williams (R)	49,300	30.3
10	Don Edwards (D)	84,240	70.5
	Michael R. La Crone (R)	31,826	26.6
11	Tom Lantos (D)	112,380	74.1
	G. M. "Bill" Quraishi (R)	39,315	25.9
12	Ernest L. Konnyu (R)	111,252	59.5
	Lance T. Weil (D)	69,564	37.2
13	Norman Y. Mineta (D)	107,696	69.7
	Bob Nash (R)	46,754	30.3
14	Norman D. Shumway (R)	146,906	71.6
	Bill Steele (D)	53,597	26.1

	Candidates	Votes	%
15	Tony Coelho (D)	93,600	71.0
	Carol Harner (R)	35,793	27.2
16	Leon E. Panetta (D)	128,151	78.4
	Louis Darrigo (R)	31,386	19.2
17	Charles Pashayan Jr. (R)	88,787	60.2
	John Hartnett (D)	58,682	39.8
18	Richard H. Lehman (D)	101,480	71.3
	David C. Crevelt (R)	40,907	28.7
19	Robert J. Lagomarsino (R)	122,578	71.9
	Wayne B. Norris (D)	45,619	26.7
20	William M. Thomas (R)	129,989	72.6
	Jules H. Moquin (D)	49,027	27.4
21	Elton Gallegly (R)	132,090	68.4
	Gilbert R. Saldana (D)	54,497	28.2
22	Carlos J. Moorheed (R)	141,096	73.8
	John G. Simmons (D)	44,036	23.1
23	Anthony C. Beilenson (D)	121,468	65.7
	George Woolverton (R)	58,746	31.8
24	Henry A. Waxman (D)	103,914	87.9
	George Abrahams (LIBERT)	8,871	7.5
25	Edward R. Roybal (D)	62,692	76.1
	Gregory L. Hardy (R)	17,558	21.3
26	Howard L. Berman (D)	98,091	65.1
	Robert M. Kerns (R)	52,662	34.9
27	Mel Levine (D)	110,403	63.7
	Robert B. Scribner (R)	59,410	34.3
28	Julian C. Dixon (D)	92,635	76.4
	George Z. Adams (R)	25,858	21.3
29	Augustus F. Hawkins (D)	78,132	84.6
	John Van de Brooke (R)	13,432	14.5
30	Matthew G. Martinez (D)	59,369	62.5
	John W. Almquist (R)	33,705	35.5
31	Mervyn M. Dymally (D)	77,126	70.3
	Jack McMurray (R)	30,322	27.6
32	Glenn M. Anderson (D)	90,739	68.5
	Joyce M. Robertson (R)	39,003	29.4
33	David Dreier (R)	118,541	71.7
	Monty Hempel (D)	44,312	26.8
34	Esteban E. Torres (D)	66,404	60.3
	Charles M. House (R)	43,659	39.7
35	Jerry Lewis (R)	127,235	76.9
	R. "Sarge" Hall (D)	38,322	23.1
36	George E. Brown Jr. (D)	78,118	57.1
	Bob Henley (R)	58,660	42.9
37	Al McCandless (R)	122,416	63.7
	David E. Skinner (D)	69,808	36.3
38	Bob Dornan (R)	66,032	55.3
	Richard Robinson (D)	50,625	42.4
39	William E. Dannemeyer (R)	137,603	74.5
	David D. Vest (D)	42,377	24.0
40	Robert E. Badham (R)	119,829	59.8
	Bruce W. Sumner (D)	75,664	37.7
41	Bill Lowery (R)	133,566	67.8
	Dan Kripke (D)	59,816	30.4
42	Dan Lungren (R)	140,364	72.8
	Michael P. Blackburn (D)	47,586	24.7
43	Ron Packard (R)	137,341	73.1
	Joseph Chirra (D)	45,078	24.0
44	Jim Bates (D)	70,557	64.3
	Bill Mitchell (R)	36,359	33.1
45	Duncan Hunter (R)	118,900	76.9
	Hewitt Fitts Ryan (D)	32,800	21.2

COLORADO

	Candidates	Votes	%
1	Patricia Schroeder (D)	106,113	68.4
	Joy Wood (R)	49,095	31.6
2	David E. Skaggs (D)	91,223	51.5
	Michael J. Norton (R)	86,032	48.5
3	Ben Nighthorse Campbell (D)	95,353	51.9
	Mike Strang (R)	88,508	48.1
4	Hank Brown (R)	117,089	69.8
	David Sprague (D)	50,672	30.2
5	Joel Hefley (R)	121,153	69.8
	Bill Story (D)	52,488	30.2
6	Dan Schaefer (R)	104,359	65.0

	Candidates	Votes	%
	Chuck Norris (D)	53,834	33.5

CONNECTICUT

	Candidates	Votes	%
1	Barbara B. Kennelly (D)	128,930	74.2
	Herschel A. Klein (R)	44,122	25.4
2	Sam Gejdenson (D)	109,229	67.4
	Francis M. "Bud" Mullen (R)	52,889	32.6
3	Bruce A. Morrison (D)	114,276	69.6
	Ernest J. Diette Jr. (R)	49,806	30.4
4	Stewart B. McKinney (R)	77,212	53.5
	Christine M. Niedermeier (D)	66,999	46.5
5	John G. Rowland (R)	98,664	60.9
	Jim Cohen (D)	63,371	39.1
6	Nancy L. Johnson (R)	111,304	64.2
	Paul S. Amenta (D)	63,133	35.8

DELAWARE

	Candidates	Votes	%
AL	Thomas R. Carper (D)	106,351	66.2
	Thomas Stephen Neuberger (R)	53,767	33.4

FLORIDA

	Candidates	Votes	%
1	Earl Hutto (D)	97,465	63.8
	Greg Neubeck (R)	55,415	36.2
2	Bill Grant (D)	110,120	99.4
3	Charles E. Bennett (D)		100.0
4	Bill Chappell Jr. (D)		100.0
5	Bill McCollum (R)		100.0
6	Buddy MacKay (D)	143,583	70.2
	Larry Gallagher (R)	61,053	29.8
7	Sam Gibbons (D)		100.0
8	C. W. Bill Young (R)		100.0
9	Michael Bilirakis (R)	166,504	70.8
	Gabe Cazares (D)	68,574	29.2
10	Andy Ireland (R)	122,368	71.2
	David B. Higginbottom (D)	49,559	28.8
11	Bill Nelson (D)	149,036	72.7
	Scott Ellis (R)	55,904	27.3
12	Tom Lewis (R)	150,222	99.4
13	Connie Mack (R)	187,794	75.0
	Addison S. Gilbert III (D)	62,694	25.0
14	Daniel A. Mica (D)	171,961	73.8
	Rick Martin (R)	61,185	26.2
15	E. Clay Shaw Jr. (R)		100.0
16	Lawrence J. Smith (D)	121,213	69.7
	Mary Collins (R)	52,807	30.3
17	William Lehman (D)		100.0
18	Claude Pepper (D)	80,047	73.5
	Tom Brodie (R)	28,803	26.5
19	Dante B. Fascell (D)	99,203	69.1
	Bill Flanagan (R)	44,455	30.9

GEORGIA

	Candidates	Votes	%
1	Lindsay Thomas (D)	69,440	100.0
2	Charles Hatcher (D)	72,482	100.0
3	Richard Ray (D)	75,850	99.7
4	Pat Swindall (R)	86,366	53.2
	Ben Jones (D)	75,892	46.8
5	John Lewis (D)	93,229	75.3
	Portia A. Scott (R)	30,562	24.7
6	Newt Gingrich (R)	75,583	59.5
	Crandle Bray (D)	51,352	40.5
7	George "Buddy" Darden (D)	88,636	66.4
	Joe Morecraft (R)	44,891	33.6
8	J. Roy Rowland (D)	82,254	86.4
	Eddie McDowell (R)	12,952	13.6
9	Ed Jenkins (D)	84,303	100.0
10	Doug Barnard Jr. (D)	79,548	67.3
	Jim Hill (R)	38,714	32.7

HAWAII

	Candidates	Votes	%
1	Patricia Saiki (R)	99,683	59.2
	Mufi Hannemann (D)	63,061	37.5
2	Daniel K. Akaka (D)	123,830	76.1
	Maria M. Hustace (R)	35,371	21.7

Special Election[1]

1	Neil Abercrombie (D)	42,031	29.9
	Patricia Saiki (R)	41,067	29.2
	Mufi Hannemann (D)	39,800	28.3
	Steve Cobb (D)	16,721	11.9

IDAHO

1	Larry E. Craig (R)	120,553	65.1
	Bill Currie (D)	59,723	32.3
2	Richard H. Stallings (D)	103,035	54.4
	Mel Richardson (R)	86,528	45.6

ILLINOIS

1	Charles A. Hayes (D)	122,376	96.4
2	Gus Savage (D)	99,268	83.8
	Ron Taylor (R)	19,149	16.2
3	Marty Russo (D)	102,949	66.2
	James J. Tierney (R)	52,618	33.8
4	Jack Davis (R)	61,633	51.6
	Shawn Collins (D)	57,925	48.4
5	William O. Lipinski (D)	82,466	70.4
	Daniel John Sobieski (R)	34,738	29.6
6	Henry J. Hyde (R)	98,196	75.4
	Robert H. Renshaw (D)	32,064	24.6
7	Cardiss Collins (D)	90,761	80.2
	Caroline K. Kallas (R)	21,055	18.6
8	Dan Rostenkowski (D)	82,873	78.7
	Thomas J. DeFazio (R)	22,383	21.3
9	Sidney R. Yates (D)	92,738	71.6
	Herbert Sohn (R)	36,715	28.4
10	John Edward Porter (R)	87,530	75.1
	Robert A. Cleland (D)	28,990	24.9
11	Frank Annunzio (D)	106,970	70.7
	George S. Gottlieb (R)	44,341	29.3
12	Philip M. Crane (R)	89,044	77.7
	John A. Leonardi (D)	25,536	22.3
13	Harris W. Fawell (R)	107,227	73.4
	Dominick J. Jeffrey (D)	38,874	26.6
14	Dennis Hastert (R)	77,288	52.4
	Mary Lou Kearns (D)	70,293	47.6
15	Edward R. Madigan (R)	115,284	100.0
16	Lynn Martin (R)	92,982	66.9
	Kenneth F. Bohnsack (D)	46,087	33.1
17	Lane Evans (D)	85,442	55.6
	Sam McHard (R)	68,101	44.4
18	Robert H. Michel (R)	94,308	62.6
	Jim Dawson (D)	56,331	37.4
19	Terry L. Bruce (D)	111,105	66.4
	Al Salvi (R)	56,186	33.6
20	Richard J. Durbin (D)	126,556	68.1
	Kevin B. McCarthy (R)	59,291	31.9
21	Melvin Price (D)	65,722	50.4
	Robert H. Gaffner (R)	64,779	49.6
22	Kenneth J. Gray (D)	97,585	53.2
	Randy Patchett (R)	85,733	46.8

INDIANA

1	Peter J. Visclosky (D)	86,983	73.4
	William Costas (R)	30,395	25.7
2	Philip R. Sharp (D)	102,456	61.9
	Donald J. Lynch (R)	62,013	37.4
3	John Hiler (R)	75,979	49.8
	Thomas W. Ward (D)	75,932	49.8
4	Daniel R. Coats (R)	99,865	69.6
	Gregory Alan Scher (D)	43,105	30.0
5	Jim Jontz (D)	80,772	51.4
	James R. Butcher (R)	75,507	48.1
6	Dan Burton (R)	118,363	68.3
	Thomas F. McKenna (D)	53,431	30.9
7	John T. Myers (R)	104,965	66.8

Candidates	Votes	%
L. Eugene Smith (D)	49,675	31.6

8	Frank McCloskey (D)	106,662	53.0
	Richard D. McIntyre (R)	93,586	46.5
9	Lee H. Hamilton (D)	120,586	71.9
	Robert Walter Kilroy (R)	46,398	27.7
10	Andrew Jacobs Jr. (D)	68,817	57.7
	Jim Eynon (R)	49,064	41.2

IOWA

1	Jim Leach (R)	86,834	66.4
	John R. Whitaker (D)	43,985	33.6
2	Tom Tauke (R)	88,708	61.3
	Eric Tabor (D)	55,903	38.7
3	David R. Nagle (D)	83,504	54.6
	John McIntee (R)	69,386	45.4
4	Neal Smith (D)	107,271	68.4
	Bob Lockard (R)	49,641	31.6
5	Jim Ross Lightfoot (R)	85,025	59.2
	Scott Hughes (D)	58,552	40.8
6	Fred Grandy (R)	81,861	50.9
	Clayton Hodgson (D)	78,807	49.0

KANSAS

1	Pat Roberts (R)	141,297	76.5
	Dale Lyon (D)	43,359	23.5
2	Jim Slattery (D)	110,737	70.6
	Phill Kline (R)	46,029	29.4
3	Jan Meyers (R)	109,266	100.0
4	Dan Glickman (D)	111,164	64.5
	Bob Knight (R)	61,178	35.5
5	Bob Whittaker (R)	116,800	71.1
	Kym E. Myers (D)	47,540	28.9

KENTUCKY

1	Carroll Hubbard Jr. (D)	64,315	100.0
2	William H. Natcher (D)	57,644	100.0
3	Romano L. Mazzoli (D)	81,943	73.0
	Lee Holmes (R)	29,348	26.2
4	Jim Bunning (R)	67,626	55.1
	Terry L. Mann (D)	53,906	43.9
5	Harold Rogers (R)	56,760	100.0
6	Larry J. Hopkins (R)	75,906	74.3
	Jerry W. Hammond (D)	26,315	25.7
7	Carl C. Perkins (D)	90,619	79.6
	James T. Polley (R)	23,209	20.4

LOUISIANA[2]

1	Robert L. Livingston (R)		100.0
2	Lindy (Mrs. Hale) Boggs (D)		100.0
3	W. J. "Billy" Tauzin (D)		100.0
4	Buddy Roemer (D)		100.0
5	Jerry Huckaby (D)		100.0
6	Richard H. Baker (R)		100.0
7	Jimmy Hayes (D)	109,205	57.0
	Margaret Lowenthal (D)	82,293	43.0
8	Clyde C. Holloway (R)	102,276	51.4
	Faye Williams (D)	96,864	48.6

MAINE

1	Joseph E. Brennan (D)	121,848	53.2
	H. Rollin Ives (R)	100,260	43.7
2	Olympia J. Snowe (R)	148,770	77.3
	Richard R. Charette (D)	43,614	22.7

MARYLAND

1	Roy Dyson (D)	88,113	66.8
	Harlan C. Williams (R)	43,764	33.2
2	Helen Delich Bentley (R)	96,745	58.7
	Kathleen Kennedy Townsend (D)	68,200	41.3
3	Benjamin L. Cardin (D)	100,161	79.1
	Ross Z. Pierpont (R)	26,452	20.9
4	Tom McMillen (D)	65,075	50.2
	Robert R. Neall (R)	64,651	49.8

5	Steny H. Hoyer (D)	82,098	81.9
	John Eugene Sellner (R)	18,102	18.1
6	Beverly B. Byron (D)	102,975	72.2
	John Vandenberge (R)	39,600	27.8
7	Kweisi Mfume (D)	79,226	86.7
	Saint George I. B. Crosse III (R)	12,170	13.3
8	Constance A. Morella (R)	92,917	52.9
	Stewart Bainum Jr. (D)	82,825	47.1

MASSACHUSETTS

1	Silvio O. Conte (R)	113,653	77.8
	Robert S. Weiner (D)	32,396	22.2
2	Edward P. Boland (D)	91,033	65.9
	Brian P. Lees (R)	47,022	34.1
3	Joseph D. Early (D)	120,222	100.0
4	Barney Frank (D)	134,387	88.8
	Thomas D. DeVisscher (AM)	16,857	11.2
5	Chester G. Atkins (D)	113,690	99.9
6	Nicholas Mavroules (D)	131,051	99.9
7	Edward J. Markey (D)	124,183	100.0
8	Joseph P. Kennedy II (D)	104,651	72.0
	Clark C. Abt (R)	40,259	27.7
9	Joe Moakley (D)	110,026	83.8
	Robert W. Horan (I)	21,292	16.2
10	Gerry E. Studds (D)	121,578	65.1
	Ricardo M. Barros (R)	49,451	26.5
	Alexander Byron (I)	15,687	8.4
11	Brian J. Donnelly (D)	114,926	100.0

MICHIGAN

1	John Conyers Jr. (D)	94,307	89.2
	Bill Ashe (R)	10,407	9.8
2	Carl D. Pursell (R)	79,567	59.0
	Dean Baker (D)	55,204	41.0
3	Howard Wolpe (D)	78,720	60.4
	Jackie McGregor (R)	51,678	39.6
4	Fred Upton (R)	70,331	61.9
	Dan Roche (D)	41,624	36.6
5	Paul B. Henry (R)	100,577	71.2
	Teresa S. Decker (D)	40,608	28.8
6	Bob Carr (D)	74,927	56.7
	Jim Dunn (R)	57,283	43.3
7	Dale E. Kildee (D)	101,225	79.6
	Trudie Callihan (R)	24,848	19.5
8	Bob Traxler (D)	97,406	72.6
	John A. Levi (R)	36,695	27.4
9	Guy Vander Jagt (R)	89,991	64.4
	Richard J. Anderson (D)	49,702	35.6
10	Bill Schuette (R)	78,475	51.2
	Donald J. Albosta (D)	74,941	48.8
11	Robert W. Davis (R)	91,575	63.0
	Robert C. Anderson (D)	53,180	36.6
12	David E. Bonior (D)	87,643	66.4
	Candice S. Miller (R)	44,442	33.6
13	George W. Crockett Jr. (D)	76,435	85.2
	Mary Griffin (R)	12,395	13.8
14	Dennis M. Hertel (D)	92,328	72.9
	Stanley T. Grot (R)	33,831	26.7
15	William D. Ford (D)	77,950	75.2
	Glen Kassel (R)	25,078	24.2
16	John D. Dingell (D)	101,659	77.8
	Frank W. Grzywacki (R)	28,971	22.2
17	Sander M. Levin (D)	105,031	76.4
	Calvin Williams (R)	30,879	22.5
18	William S. Broomfield (R)	110,099	73.8
	Gary L. Kohut (D)	39,144	26.2

MINNESOTA[3]

1	Timothy J. Penny (DFL)	125,115	72.4
	Paul H. Grawe (I-R)	47,750	27.6
2	Vin Weber (I-R)	100,249	51.6
	Dave Johnson (DFL)	94,048	48.4
3	Bill Frenzel (I-R)	127,434	70.1
	Ray Stock (DFL)	54,261	29.9
4	Bruce F. Vento (DFL)	112,662	72.9
	Harold Stassen (I-R)	41,926	27.1
5	Martin Olav Sabo (DFL)	105,410	72.7

Candidates	Votes	%
Rick Serra (I-R)	37,583	25.9
6 Gerry Sikorski (DFL)	110,598	65.8
Barbara Zwach Sykora (I-R)	57,460	34.2
7 Arlan Stangeland (I-R)	94,024	49.7
Collin C. Peterson (DFL)	93,903	49.6
8 James L. Oberstar (DFL)	135,718	72.6
Dave Rued (I-R)	51,315	27.4

MISSISSIPPI

1 Jamie L. Whitten (D)	59,870	66.4
Larry Cobb (R)	30,267	33.6
2 Mike Espy (D)	73,119	51.7
Webb Franklin (R)	68,292	48.3
3 G. V. "Sonny" Montgomery (D)	80,575	100.0
4 Wayne Dowdy (D)	85,819	71.5
Gail Healy (R)	34,190	28.5
5 Trent Lott (R)	75,288	82.3
Larry L. Albritton (D)	16,143	17.7

MISSOURI

1 William L. Clay (D)	91,044	66.1
Robert J. Wittmann (R)	46,599	33.9
2 Jack Buechner (R)	101,010	51.9
Robert A. Young (D)	93,538	48.1
3 Richard A. Gephardt (D)	116,403	69.0
4 Ike Skelton (D)	129,471	100.0
5 Alan Wheat (D)	101,030	70.9
Greg Fisher (R)	39,340	27.6
6 E. Thomas Coleman (R)	95,865	56.7
Doug R. Hughes (D)	73,155	43.3
7 Gene Taylor (R)	114,210	67.0
Ken Young (D)	56,291	33.0
8 Bill Emerson (R)	79,142	52.5
Wayne Cryts (D)	71,532	47.5
9 Harold L. Volkmer (D)	95,939	57.5
Ralph Uthlaut Jr. (R)	70,972	42.5

MONTANA

1 Pat Williams (D)	98,501	61.7
Don Allen (R)	61,230	38.3
2 Ron Marlenee (R)	84,548	53.5
Richard "Buck" O'Brien (D)	73,583	46.5

NEBRASKA

1 Doug Bereuter (R)	121,772	64.4
Steve Burns (D)	67,137	35.5
2 Hal Daub (R)	99,569	58.5
Walter M. Calinger (D)	70,372	41.3
3 Virginia Smith (R)	136,985	69.8
Scott E. Sidwell (D)	59,182	30.2

NEVADA

1 James H. Bilbray (D)	61,830	54.1
Bob Ryan (R)	50,342	44.0
2 Barbara F. Vucanovich (R)	83,479	58.4
Pete Sferrazza (D)	59,433	41.6

NEW HAMPSHIRE

1 Robert C. Smith (R)	70,739	56.4
James M. Demers (D)	54,787	43.6
2 Judd Gregg (R)	85,479	74.2
Laurence Craig-Green (D)	29,688	25.8

NEW JERSEY

1 James J. Florio (D)	93,497	75.6
Fred A. Busch (R)	29,175	23.6
2 William J. Hughes (D)	83,821	68.3
Alfred J. Bennington Jr. (R)	35,167	28.6
3 James J. Howard (D)	73,743	58.7
Brian T. Kennedy (R)	51,882	41.3
4 Christopher H. Smith (R)	78,699	61.1
Jeffrey Laurenti (D)	49,290	38.3
5 Marge Roukema (R)	94,253	74.6
H. Vernon Jolley (D)	32,145	25.4
6 Bernard J. Dwyer (D)	67,460	69.0

Candidates	Votes	%
John D. Scalamonti (R)	28,286	28.9
7 Matthew J. Rinaldo (R)	92,254	79.0
June S. Fischer (D)	24,462	21.0
8 Robert A. Roe (D)	57,820	62.8
Thomas P. Zampino (R)	34,268	37.2
9 Robert G. Torricelli (D)	89,634	69.0
Arthur F. Jones (R)	40,226	31.0
10 Peter W. Rodino Jr. (D)	46,666	95.9
11 Dean A. Gallo (R)	75,037	68.0
Frank Askin (D)	35,280	32.0
12 Jim Courter (R)	72,966	63.5
David B. Crabiel (D)	41,967	36.5
13 H. James Saxton (R)	82,866	65.4
John Wydra (D)	43,920	34.6
14 Frank J. Guarini (D)	63,057	70.7
Albio Sires (R)	23,822	26.7

NEW MEXICO

1 Manuel Lujan Jr. (R)	90,476	70.9
Manny Garcia (D)	37,138	29.1
2 Joe Skeen (R)	77,787	62.9
Mike Runnels (D)	45,924	37.1
3 Bill Richardson (D)	95,760	71.3
David F. Cargo (R)	38,552	28.7

NEW YORK

1 George J. Hochbrueckner (D)	67,139	51.2
Gregory J. Blass (R)	55,413	42.3
2 Thomas J. Downey (D)	69,771	64.3
Jeffrey A. Butzke (R, C)	35,132	32.4
3 Robert J. Mrazek (D)	83,985	56.4
Joseph A. Guarino (R, C)	60,367	40.6
4 Norman F. Lent (R, C)	92,214	64.8
Patricia Sullivan (D, L)	43,581	30.6
5 Raymond J. McGrath (R, C)	93,473	65.3
Michael T. Sullivan (D, L, RTL)	49,728	34.7
6 Floyd H. Flake (D)	58,317	67.7
Richard Dietl (R, C)	27,773	32.3
7 Gary L. Ackerman (D)	62,836	77.4
Edward Nelson Rodriguez (R, C)	18,384	22.6
8 James H. Scheuer (D, L)	70,605	90.2
Gustave Reifenkugel (C)	7,679	9.8
9 Thomas J. Manton (D)	50,738	69.4
Salvatore J. Calise (R)	18,040	24.7
Thomas V. Ognibene (C)	4,348	5.9
10 Charles E. Schumer (D, L)	76,318	93.3
Alice E. Gaffney (C)	5,472	6.7
11 Edolphus Towns (D, L)	41,689	89.4
Nathaniel Hendricks (R)	4,053	8.7
12 Major R. Owens (D, L)	42,138	91.5
Owen Augustin (R)	2,752	6.0
13 Stephen J. Solarz (D, L)	61,089	82.4
Leon Nadrowski (R)	10,941	14.8
14 Guy V. Mollnari (R, C)	64,647	68.8
Barbara Walla (D)	27,950	29.7
15 Bill Green (R)	58,214	58.0
George A. Hirsch (D, L)	42,147	42.0
16 Charles B. Rangel (D, R, L)	61,262	96.4
17 Ted Weiss (D, L)	95,094	85.5
Thomas A. Chorba (R, C)	15,587	14.0
18 Robert Garcia (D, L)	43,343	93.5
Melanie Chase (R)	2,479	5.4
19 Mario Biaggi (D, R, L)	87,774	90.2
Alice Farrell (C)	6,906	7.1
20 Joseph J. DioGuardi (R, C)	80,220	53.9
Bella S. Abzug (D)	66,359	44.5
21 Hamilton Fish Jr. (R, C)	102,070	76.5
Lawrence W. Grunberger (D)	28,339	21.3
22 Benjamin A. Gilman (R)	94,244	69.5
Eleanor F. Burlingham (D)	36,852	27.2
23 Samuel S. Stratton (D)	140,759	96.4
24 Gerald B. H. Solomon (R, C, RTL)	117,285	70.4
Ed Bloch (D)	49,225	29.6
25 Sherwood Boehlert (R)	104,216	69.0
Kevin J. Conway (D)	33,864	22.4
Robert S. Barstow (C, RTL)	12,999	8.6

Candidates	Votes	%
26 David O'B. Martin (R, C)	94,840	100.0
27 George C. Wortley (R, C)	83,430	49.7
Rosemary S. Pooler (D)	82,491	49.1
28 Matthew F. McHugh (D)	103,908	68.3
Mark R. Masterson (R, C, RTL)	48,213	31.7
29 Frank Horton (R)	99,704	70.7
James R. Vogel (D)	34,194	24.2
30 Louise M. Slaughter (D)	86,777	51.0
Fred J. Eckert (R, C)	83,402	49.0
31 Jack F. Kemp (R, C, RTL)	92,508	57.4
James P. Keane (D)	67,574	42.0
32 John J. LaFalce (D, L)	99,745	91.0
Dean L. Walker (C)	6,234	5.7
33 Henry J. Nowak (D, L)	109,256	85.1
Charles A. Walker (R, C)	19,147	14.9
34 Amo Houghton (R, C)	85,856	60.1
Larry M. Himelein (D)	56,898	39.9

Special Election[4]

6 Alton R. Waldon Jr. (D)	12,654	31.0
Floyd H. Flake (UT)	12,376	30.3
Richard Dietl (R, C)	8,700	21.3
Kevin McCabe (GOOD GOV)	3,738	9.2
Andrew Jenkins (L)	3,323	8.1

NORTH CAROLINA

1 Walter B. Jones (D)	91,122	69.5
Howard Moye (R)	39,912	30.5
2 Tim Valentine (D)	95,320	74.6
Bud McElhaney (R)	32,515	25.4
3 H. Martin Lancaster (D)	71,460	64.5
Gerald B. Hurst (R)	39,408	35.5
4 David E. Price (D)	92,216	55.7
William Cobey Jr. (R)	73,469	44.3
5 Stephen L. Neal (D)	86,410	54.1
Stuart Epperson (R)	73,261	45.9
6 Howard Coble (R)	72,329	50.0
Robin Britt (D)	72,250	50.0
7 Charlie Rose (D)	70,471	64.2
Thomas J. Harrelson (R)	39,289	35.8
8 W. G. "Bill" Hefner (D)	80,959	57.9
William G. Hamby Jr. (R)	58,941	42.1
9 Alex McMillan (R)	80,352	51.3
D. G. Martin (D)	76,240	48.7
10 Cass Ballenger (R)	83,902	57.5
Lester D. Roark (D)	62,035	42.5
11 James McClure Clarke (D)	91,575	50.7
Bill Hendon (R)	89,069	49.3

Special Election[5]

10 Cass Ballenger (R)	82,973	57.5
Lester D. Roark (D)	61,205	42.5

NORTH DAKOTA

AL Byron L. Dorgan (D)	216,258	75.5
Syver Vinje (R)	66,989	23.4

OHIO

1 Thomas A. Luken (D)	90,477	61.7
Fred E. Morr (R)	56,100	38.3
2 Bill Gradison (R)	105,061	70.7
William F. Stineman (D)	43,448	29.3
3 Tony P. Hall (D)	98,311	73.7
Ron Crutcher (R)	35,167	26.3
4 Michael G. Oxley (R)	115,751	75.1
Clem T. Cratty (D)	26,320	17.1
Raven L. Workman (I)	11,997	7.8
5 Delbert L. Latta (R)	102,016	65.0
Tom Murray (D)	54,864	35.0
6 Bob McEwen (R)	106,354	70.3
Gordon Roberts (D)	42,155	27.8
7 Michael DeWine (R)	119,238	100.0
8 Donald E. Lukens (R)	98,475	68.1
John W. Griffin (D)	46,195	31.9
9 Marcy Kaptur (D)	105,646	77.5
Mike Shufeldt (R)	30,643	22.5

Candidates	Votes	%
10 Clarence E. Miller (R)	106,870	70.4
John M. Buchanan (D)	44,847	29.6
11 Dennis E. Eckart (D)	104,740	72.4
Margaret Mueller (R)	35,944	24.9
12 John R. Kasich (R)	117,905	73.4
Timothy C. Jochim (D)	42,727	26.6
13 Don J. Pease (D)	88,612	62.8
William D. Nielsen (R)	52,452	37.2
14 Thomas C. Sawyer (D)	83,257	53.7
Lynn Slaby (R)	71,713	46.3
15 Chalmers P. Wylie (R)	97,745	63.7
David L. Jackson (D)	55,750	36.3
16 Ralph Regula (R)	118,206	76.3
William J. Kennick (D)	36,639	23.7
17 James A. Traficant Jr. (D)	112,855	72.3
James H. Fulks (R)	43,334	27.7
18 Douglas Applegate (D)	126,526	100.0
19 Edward F. Feighan (D)	97,814	54.8
Gary C. Suhadolnik (R)	80,743	45.2
20 Mary Rose Oakar (D)	110,976	84.9
Bill Smith (R)	19,794	15.1
21 Louis Stokes (D)	99,878	81.6
Franklin H. Roski (R)	22,594	18.4

OKLAHOMA

Candidates	Votes	%
1 James M. Inhofe (R)	78,919	54.8
Gary D. Allison (D)	61,663	42.8
2 Mike Synar (D)	114,543	73.3
Gary K. Rice (R)	41,795	26.7
3 Wes Watkins (D)	114,008	78.1
Patrick K. Miller (R)	31,913	21.9
4 Dave McCurdy (D)	94,984	76.2
Larry Humphreys (R)	29,697	23.8
5 Mickey Edwards (R)	108,774	70.6
Donna Compton (D)	45,256	29.4
6 Glenn English (D)		100.0

OREGON

Candidates	Votes	%
1 Les AuCoin (D)	141,585	61.7
Tony Meeker (R)	87,874	38.3
2 Robert F. Smith (R)	113,566	60.2
Larry Tuttle (D)	75,124	39.8
3 Ron Wyden (D)	180,067	85.9
Thomas H. Phelan (R)	29,321	14.0
4 Peter A. DeFazio (D)	105,697	54.1
Bruce Long (R)	89,795	45.9
5 Denny Smith (R)	125,906	60.5
Barbara Ross (D)	82,290	39.5

PENNSYLVANIA

Candidates	Votes	%
1 Thomas M. Foglietta (D)	88,224	74.7
Anthony J. Mucciolo (R)	29,811	25.3
2 William H. Gray III (D)	128,399	98.4
3 Robert A. Borski (D)	107,804	61.8
Robert A. Rovner (R)	66,693	38.2
4 Joe Kolter (D)	86,133	60.4
Al Lindsay (R)	55,165	38.7
5 Richard T. Schulze (R)	87,593	65.7
Tim Ringgold (D)	45,648	34.3
6 Gus Yatron (D)	98,142	69.1
Norm Bertasavage (R)	43,858	30.9
7 Curt Weldon (R)	110,118	61.3
Bill Spingler (D)	69,557	38.7
8 Peter H. Kostmayer (D)	85,731	55.0
David A. Christian (R)	70,047	45.0
9 Bud Shuster (R)	120,890	100.0
10 Joseph M. McDade (R)	118,603	74.7
Robert C. Bolus (D)	40,248	25.3
11 Paul E. Kanjorski (D)	112,405	70.6
Marc Holtzman (R)	46,785	29.4
12 John P. Murtha (D)	97,135	67.4
Kathy Holtzman (R)	46,937	32.6
13 Lawrence Coughlin (R)	100,701	58.5
Joseph M. Hoeffel (D)	71,381	41.5
14 William J. Coyne (D)	104,726	89.6
Richard Edward Caligiuri (LIBERT)	6,058	5.2

Candidates	Votes	%
15 Don Ritter (R)	74,829	56.8
Joe Simonetta (D)	56,972	43.2
16 Robert S. Walker (R)	100,784	74.6
James D. Hagelgans (D)	34,399	25.4
17 George W. Gekas (R)	101,027	73.6
Michael S. Ogden (D)	36,157	26.4
18 Doug Walgren (D)	104,164	63.0
Ernie Buckman (R)	61,164	37.0
19 Bill Goodling (R)	100,055	72.9
Richard F. Thornton (D)	37,223	27.1
20 Joseph M. Gaydos (D)	136,638	98.5
21 Tom Ridge (R)	111,148	80.9
Joylyn Blackwell (D)	26,324	19.1
22 Austin J. Murphy (D)	131,650	100.0
23 William F. Clinger Jr. (R)	79,595	55.5
Bill Wachob (D)	63,875	44.5

RHODE ISLAND

Candidates	Votes	%
1 Fernand J. St Germain (D)	85,077	57.7
John A. Holmes Jr. (R)	62,397	42.3
2 Claudine Schneider (R)	113,603	71.8
Donald J. Ferry (D)	44,586	28.2

SOUTH CAROLINA

Candidates	Votes	%
1 Arthur Ravenel Jr. (R)	59,969	52.0
Jimmy Stuckey (D)	55,262	48.0
2 Floyd D. Spence (R)	73,455	53.6
Fred Zeigler (D)	63,592	46.4
3 Butler Derrick (D)	79,109	68.4
Richard Dickison (R)	36,495	31.5
4 Liz J. Patterson (D)	67,012	51.4
Bill Workman (R)	61,648	47.3
5 John M. Spratt Jr. (D)	95,859	99.7
6 Robin Tallon (D)	92,398	75.5
Robbie Cunningham (R)	29,922	24.5

SOUTH DAKOTA

Candidates	Votes	%
AL Tim Johnson (D)	171,462	59.2
Dale Bell (R)	118,261	40.8

TENNESSEE

Candidates	Votes	%
1 James H. Quillen (R)	80,289	68.9
John B. Russell (D)	36,278	31.1
2 John J. Duncan (R)	96,396	76.2
John F. Bowen (D)	30,088	23.8
3 Marilyn Lloyd (D)	75,034	53.9
Jim Golden (R)	64,084	46.1
4 Jim Cooper (D)	86,997	100.0
5 Bill Boner (D)	85,126	57.9
Terry Holcomb (R)	58,701	39.9
6 Bart Gordon (D)	102,180	76.8
Fred Vail (R)	30,823	23.2
7 Don Sundquist (R)	93,902	72.3
M. Lloyd Hiler (D)	35,966	27.7
8 Ed Jones (D)	101,699	80.4
Dan H. Campbell (R)	24,792	19.6
9 Harold E. Ford (D)	83,006	83.4
Isaac Richmond (I)	16,221	16.3

TEXAS

Candidates	Votes	%
1 Jim Chapman (D)	84,445	100.0
2 Charles Wilson (D)	78,529	56.7
Julian Gordon (R)	55,986	40.5
3 Steve Bartlett (R)	143,381	94.1
4 Ralph M. Hall (D)	97,540	71.7
Thomas Blow (R)	38,578	28.3
5 John Bryant (D)	57,410	58.5
Tom Carter (R)	39,945	40.7
6 Joe L. Barton (R)	86,190	55.8
Pete Geren (D)	68,270	44.2
7 Bill Archer (R)	129,673	87.4
Harry Kniffen (D)	17,635	11.9
8 Jack Fields (R)	66,280	68.4
Blaine Mann (D)	30,617	31.6
9 Jack Brooks (D)	73,285	61.5

Candidates	Votes	%
Lisa D. Duperier (R)	45,834	38.5
10 J. J. "Jake" Pickle (D)	135,863	72.3
Carole Keeton Rylandar (R)	52,000	27.7
11 Marvin Leath (D)	84,201	100.0
12 Jim Wright (D)	84,831	68.7
Don McNeil (R)	38,620	31.3
13 Beau Boulter (R)	84,980	64.9
Doug Seal (D)	45,907	35.1
14 Mac Sweeney (R)	74,471	52.3
Greg H. Laughlin (D)	67,852	47.7
15 E. "Kika" de la Garza (D)	70,777	100.0
16 Ronald D. Coleman (D)	50,590	65.7
Roy Gillia (R)	26,421	34.3
17 Charles W. Stenholm (D)	97,791	100.0
18 Mickey Leland (D)	63,335	90.2
Joanne Kuniansky (I)	6,884	9.8
19 Larry Combest (R)	68,695	62.0
Gerald McCathern (D)	42,129	38.0
20 Henry B. Gonzalez (D)	55,363	100.0
21 Lamar Smith (R)	100,346	60.6
Pete Snelson (D)	63,779	38.5
22 Thomas D. DeLay (R)	76,459	71.8
Susan Director (D)	30,079	28.2
23 Albert G. Bustamante (D)	68,131	90.7
Ken Hendrix (LIBERT)	7,001	9.3
24 Martin Frost (D)	69,368	67.2
Bob Burk (R)	33,819	32.8
25 Michael A. Andrews (D)	67,435	100.0
26 Dick Armey (R)	101,735	68.1
George Richardson (D)	47,651	31.9
27 Solomon P. Ortiz (D)	64,165	100.0

UTAH

Candidates	Votes	%
1 James V. Hansen (R)	82,151	51.6
Gunn McKay (D)	77,180	48.4
2 Wayne Owens (D)	76,921	55.2
Tom Shimizu (R)	60,967	43.7
3 Howard C. Nielson (R)	86,599	66.6
Dale F. Gardiner (D)	42,582	32.7

VERMONT

Candidates	Votes	%
AL James M. Jeffords (R)	168,403	89.1

VIRGINIA

Candidates	Votes	%
1 Herbert H. Bateman (R)	80,713	56.0
Robert C. Scott (D)	63,364	44.0
2 Owen B. Pickett (D)	54,491	49.5
A. J. "Joe" Canada Jr. (R)	46,137	41.9
Stephen P. Shao (I)	9,492	8.6
3 Thomas J. Bliley Jr. (R)	74,525	67.0
Kenneth E. Powell (D)	32,961	29.7
4 Norman Sisisky (D)	64,699	99.8
5 Dan Daniel (D)	73,085	81.5
J. F. "Frank" Cole (I)	16,551	18.5
6 Jim Olin (D)	88,230	69.9
Flo Neher Traywick (R)	38,051	30.1
7 D. French Slaughter Jr. (R)	58,927	98.3
8 Stan Parris (R)	72,670	61.8
James H. Boren (D)	44,965	38.2
9 Rick Boucher (D)	59,864	99.0
10 Frank R. Wolf (R)	95,724	60.2
John G. Milliken (D)	63,292	39.8

WASHINGTON

Candidates	Votes	%
1 John R. Miller (R)	97,969	51.4
Reese Lindquist (D)	92,697	48.6
2 Al Swift (D)	124,840	72.2
Thomas S. Talman (R)	48,077	27.8
3 Don Bonker (D)	114,775	73.6
Joe Illing (R)	41,275	26.4
4 Sid Morrison (R)	107,593	72.1
Robert Goedecke (D)	41,709	27.9
5 Thomas S. Foley (D)	121,732	74.7
Floyd L. Wakefield (R)	41,179	25.3
6 Norm Dicks (D)	90,063	71.2
Kenneth W. Branten (R)	36,410	28.8

	Candidates	Votes	%
7	Mike Lowry (D)	124,317	72.6
	Don McDonald (R)	46,831	27.4
8	Rod Chandler (R)	107,824	65.2
	David E. Giles (D)	57,545	34.8

WEST VIRGINIA

		Votes	%
1	Alan B. Mollohan (D)	90,715	100.0
2	Harley O. Staggers Jr. (D)	76,355	69.5
	Michele Golden (R)	33,554	30.5
3	Bob Wise (D)	73,669	64.9
	Tim Sharp (R)	39,820	35.1
4	Nick J. Rahall II (D)	58,217	71.3

	Candidates	Votes	%
	Martin Miller (R)	23,490	28.7

WISCONSIN

		Votes	%
1	Les Aspin (D)	106,288	74.3
	Iris Peterson (R)	34,495	24.1
2	Robert W. Kastenmeier (D)	106,919	55.6
	Ann J. Haney (R)	85,156	44.2
3	Steve Gunderson (R)	104,393	64.1
	Leland E. Mulder (D)	58,445	35.9
4	Gerald D. Kleczka (D)	120,354	99.6
5	Jim Moody (D)	109,506	99.0
6	Thomas E. Petri (R)	124,328	96.7

	Candidates	Votes	%
7	David R. Obey (D)	106,700	62.2
	Kevin J. Hermening (R)	63,408	36.9
8	Toby Roth (R)	118,162	67.4
	Paul F. Willems (D)	57,265	32.6
9	F. James Sensenbrenner Jr. (R)	138,766	78.2
	Thomas G. Popp (D)	38,636	21.8

WYOMING

		Votes	%
AL	Dick Cheney (R)	111,007	69.5
	Rick Gilmore (D)	48,780	30.5

1. A special election was held to fill the unexpired term of Rep. Cecil Heftel (D), who resigned July 11, 1986.

2. For the 1986 House elections in Louisiana, an open primary election was held with candidates from all parties running on the same ballot. Any candidate who received a majority was elected unopposed, with no further appearance on the general election ballot. If no candidate received 50 percent, a runoff was held between the two top finishers.

3. In Minnesota the Democratic Party is known as the Democratic-Farmer-Labor Party and the Republican Party as the Independent-Republican Party; candidates appear on the ballot with these designations.

4. A special election was held to fill the unexpired term of Rep. Joseph P. Addabbo (D), who died April 10, 1986.

5. A special election was held to fill the unexpired term of Rep. James T. Broyhill (R), who resigned in July 1986, having been appointed to the Senate.

1987 House Elections

CALIFORNIA

Special Election[1]

	Candidates	Votes	%
5	Nancy Pelosi (D)	46,428	63.3
	Harriet Ross (R)	22,478	30.7

CONNECTICUT

Special Election[2]

		Votes	%
4	Christopher Shays (R)	50,518	57.2
	Christine M. Niedermeier (D)	37,293	42.2

1. A special election was held to fill the unexpired term of Rep. Sala Burton (D), who died Feb.1, 1987.

2. A special election was held to fill the unexpired term of Rep. Stewart B. Mckinney (R), who died May 7, 1987.

1988 House Elections

ALABAMA

	Candidates	Votes	%
1	Sonny Callahan (R)	115,173	59.2
	John M. Tyson Jr. (D)	77,670	40.0
2	Bill Dickinson (R)	120,408	94.2
	Brooke King (LIBERT)	7,352	5.8
3	Bill Nichols (D)	117,514	96.1
	Shockley (LIBERT)	4,793	3.9
4	Tom Bevill (D)	131,880	96.2
	John Sebastian (LIBERT)	5,264	3.8
5	Ronnie G. Flippo (D)	120,142	64.4
	Stan McDonald (R)	64,491	34.5
6	Ben Erdreich (D)	138,920	66.5
	Charles Caddis (R)	68,788	32.9
7	Claude Harris (D)	136,074	67.7
	James E. "Jim" Bacon (R)	63,372	31.5

ALASKA

	Candidates	Votes	%
AL	Don Young (R)	120,595	62.5
	Peter Gruenstein (D)	71,881	37.3

ARIZONA

	Candidates	Votes	%
1	John J. Rhodes III (R)	184,639	72.1
	John M. Fillmore (D)	71,388	27.9
2	Morris K. Udall (D)	99,895	73.3
	Joseph D. Sweeney (R)	36,309	26.7
3	Bob Stump (R)	174,453	68.9
	Dave Moss (D)	72,417	28.6
4	Jon Kyl (R)	206,248	87.1
	Gary Sprunk (LIBERT)	30,430	12.9
5	Jim Kolbe (R)	164,462	67.8
	Judith E. Belcher (D)	78,115	32.2

ARKANSAS

	Candidates	Votes	%
1	Bill Alexander (D)		100.0
2	Tommy F. Robinson (D)	168,889	83.5
	Warren D. Carpenter (R)	33,475	16.5
3	John Paul Hammerschmidt (R)	161,623	74.7
	David Stewart (D)	54,767	25.3
4	Beryl Anthony Jr. (D)	129,508	69.2
	Roger N. Bell (R)	57,658	30.8

CALIFORNIA

	Candidates	Votes	%
1	Douglas H. Bosco (D)	159,815	62.9
	Samuel "Mark" Vanderbilt (R)	72,189	28.4
	Eric Fried (PFP)	22,150	8.7
2	Wally Herger (R)	139,010	58.8
	Wayne Meyer (D)	91,088	38.5
3	Robert T. Matsui (D)	183,470	71.2
	Lowell P. Landowski (R)	74,296	28.8
4	Vic Fazio (D)	181,184	99.3
5	Nancy Pelosi (D)	133,530	76.4
	Bruce Michael O'Neill (R)	33,692	19.3
6	Barbara Boxer (D)	176,645	73.4
	William Steinmetz (R)	64,174	26.6
7	George Miller (D)	170,006	68.4
	Jean Last (R)	78,478	31.6
8	Ronald V. Dellums (D)	163,221	66.6
	John J. Cuddihy Jr. (R)	76,531	31.2
9	Pete Stark (D)	152,866	73.0
	Howard Hertz (R)	56,656	27.0
10	Don Edwards (D)	142,500	86.2
	Kennita Watson (LIBERT)	22,801	13.8
11	Tom Lantos (D)	145,484	71.0
	G.M. "Bill" Quraishi (R)	50,050	24.4
12	Tom Campbell (R)	136,384	51.7
	Anna G. Eshoo (D)	121,523	46.0
13	Norman Y. Mineta (D)	143,980	67.1
	Luke Sommer (R)	63,959	29.8
14	Norman D. Shumway (R)	173,876	62.6
	Patricia Malberg (D)	103,899	37.4
15	Tony Coelho (D)	118,710	69.7

	Candidates	Votes	%
	Carol Harner (R)	47,957	28.2
16	Leon E. Panetta (D)	177,452	78.6
	Stanley Monteith (R)	48,375	21.4
17	Charles Pashayan Jr. (R)	129,568	71.5
	Vincent Lavery (D)	51,730	28.5
18	Richard H. Lehman (D)	125,715	69.9
	David A. Linn (R)	54,034	30.1
19	Robert J. Lagomarsino (R)	116,026	50.2
	Gary K. Hart (D)	112,033	48.5
20	William M. Thomas (R)	162,779	71.1
	Lita Reid (D)	62,037	27.1
21	Elton Gallegly (R)	181,413	69.1
	Donald E. Stevens (D)	75,739	28.8
22	Carlos J. Moorhead (R)	164,699	69.5
	John G. Simmons (D)	61,555	26.0
23	Anthony C. Beilenson (D)	147,858	63.5
	Jim Salomon (R)	77,184	33.1
24	Henry A. Waxman (D)	112,038	72.3
	John N. Cowles (R)	36,835	23.7
25	Edward R. Roybal (D)	85,378	85.5
	Raul Reyes (PFP)	8,746	8.8
	John C. Thie (LIBERT)	5,752	5.8
26	Howard L. Berman (D)	126,930	70.3
	G. C. "Brodie" Broderson (R)	53,518	29.7
27	Mel Levine (D)	148,814	67.5
	Dennis Galbraith (R)	65,307	29.6
28	Julian C. Dixon (D)	109,801	76.1
	George Z. Adams (R)	28,645	19.8
29	Augustus F. Hawkins (D)	88,169	82.8
	Reuben D. Franco (R)	14,543	13.7
30	Matthew G. Martinez (D)	72,253	59.9
	Ralph R. Ramirez (R)	43,833	36.3
31	Mervyn M. Dymally (D)	100,919	71.6
	Arnold C. May (R)	36,017	25.5
32	Glenn M. Anderson (D)	114,666	66.9
	Sanford W. Kahn (R)	50,710	29.6
33	David Dreier (R)	151,704	69.2
	Nelson Gentry (D)	57,586	26.2
34	Esteban E. Torres (D)	92,087	63.2
	Charles M. House (R)	50,954	35.0
35	Jerry Lewis (R)	181,203	70.4
	Paul Sweeney (D)	71,186	27.7
36	George E. Brown Jr. (D)	103,493	54.0
	John Paul Stark (R)	81,413	42.5
37	Al McCandless (R)	174,284	64.3
	Johnny Pearson (D)	89,666	33.1
38	Robert K. Dornan (R)	87,690	59.5
	Jerry Yudelson (D)	52,399	35.6
39	William E. Dannemeyer (R)	169,360	73.8
	Don E. Marquis (D)	52,162	22.7
40	C. Christopher Cox (R)	181,269	67.0
	Lida Lenney (D)	80,782	29.9
41	Bill Lowery (R)	187,380	65.6
	Dan Kripke (D)	88,192	30.8
42	Dana Rohrabacher (R)	153,280	64.2
	Guy K. Kimbrough (D)	78,778	33.0
43	Ron Packard (R)	202,478	71.7
	Howard Greenebaum (D)	72,499	25.6
44	Jim Bates (D)	90,796	59.7
	Rob Butterfield (R)	55,511	36.5
45	Duncan Hunter (R)	166,451	74.0
	Pete Lepiscopo (D)	54,012	24.0

COLORADO

	Candidates	Votes	%
1	Patricia Schroeder (D)	133,922	69.9
	Joy Wood (R)	57,587	30.1
2	David E. Skaggs (D)	147,437	62.7
	David Bath (R)	87,578	37.3
3	Ben Nighthorse Campbell (D)	169,284	78.0
	Jim Zartman (R)	47,625	22.0
4	Hank Brown (R)	156,202	73.1
	Charles S. Vigil (D)	57,552	26.9
5	Joel Hefley (R)	181,612	75.1
	John J. Mitchell (D)	60,116	24.9

	Candidates	Votes	%
6	Dan Schaefer (R)	136,487	63.0
	Martha M. Ezzard (D)	77,158	35.6

CONNECTICUT

	Candidates	Votes	%
1	Barbara B. Kennelly (D)	176,463	77.2
	Mario Robles Jr. (R)	51,985	22.8
2	Sam Gejdenson (D)	143,326	63.6
	Glenn Carberry (R)	81,965	36.4
3	Bruce A. Morrison (D)	147,394	66.5
	Gerard B. Patton (R)	74,275	33.5
4	Christopher Shays (R)	147,843	71.8
	Roger Pearson (D)	55,751	27.1
5	John G. Rowland (R)	163,729	73.6
	Joseph Marinan Jr. (D)	58,612	26.4
6	Nancy L. Johnson (R)	157,020	66.3
	James L. Griffin (D)	78,814	33.3

DELAWARE

	Candidates	Votes	%
AL	Thomas R. Carper (D)	158,338	67.5
	James P. Krapf Sr. (R)	76,179	32.5

FLORIDA

	Candidates	Votes	%
1	Earl Hutto (D)	142,449	66.9
	E. D. Armbruster (R)	70,534	33.1
2	Bill Grant (D)	134,269	99.7
3	Charles E. Bennett (D)		100.0
4	Craig T. James (R)	125,608	50.2
	Bill Chappell Jr. (D)	124,817	49.8
5	Bill McCollum (R)		100.0
6	Cliff Stearns (R)	136,415	53.5
	Jon Mills (D)	118,756	46.5
7	Sam Gibbons (D)		100.0
8	C. W. Bill Young (R)	169,165	73.0
	C. Bette Wimbish (D)	62,539	27.0
9	Michael Bilirakis (R)	223,925	99.9
10	Andy Ireland (R)	156,563	73.5
	David B. Higginbottom (D)	56,536	26.5
11	Bill Nelson (D)	168,390	60.8
	Bill Tolley (R)	108,373	39.2
12	Tom Lewis (R)		100.0
13	Porter J. Goss (R)	231,170	71.2
	Jack Conway (D)	93,700	28.8
14	Harry A. Johnston (D)	173,292	54.9
	Ken Adams (R)	142,635	45.1
15	E. Clay Shaw Jr. (R)	132,090	66.1
	Michael A. "Mike" Kuhle (D)	67,746	33.9
16	Lawrence J. Smith (D)	153,032	69.4
	Joseph Smith (R)	67,461	30.6
17	William Lehman (D)		100.0
18	Claude Pepper (D)		100.0
19	Dante B. Fascell (D)	135,355	72.4
	Ralph Carlos Rocheteau (R)	51,628	27.6

GEORGIA

	Candidates	Votes	%
1	Lindsay Thomas (D)	94,531	67.0
	Chris Meredith (R)	46,552	33.0
2	Charles Hatcher (D)	85,029	61.7
	Ralph T. Hudgens (R)	52,807	38.3
3	Richard Ray (D)	97,663	100.0
4	Ben Jones (D)	148,394	60.3
	Pat Swindall (R)	97,745	39.7
5	John Lewis (D)	135,194	78.2
	J. W. Tibbs Jr. (R)	37,693	21.8
6	Newt Gingrich (R)	110,169	58.9
	David Worley (D)	76,824	41.1
7	George "Buddy" Darden (D)	135,056	64.8
	Robert Lamutt (R)	73,425	35.2
8	J. Roy Rowland (D)	102,696	100.0
9	Ed Jenkins (D)	121,800	62.9
	Joe Hoffman (R)	71,905	37.1
10	Doug Barnard Jr. (D)	118,156	64.0
	Mark Myers (R)	66,521	36.0

HAWAII

Candidates	Votes	%
1 Patricia Saiki (R)	96,848	54.7
Mary Bitterman (D)	76,394	43.2
2 Daniel K. Akaka (D)	144,802	88.9
Lloyd "Jeff" Mallan (LIBERT)	18,006	11.1

IDAHO

	Votes	%
1 Larry E. Craig (R)	135,221	65.8
Jeanne Givens (D)	70,328	34.2
2 Richard H. Stallings (D)	127,956	63.4
Dane Watkins (R)	68,226	33.8

ILLINOIS

	Votes	%
1 Charles A. Hayes (D)	164,125	96.0
2 Gus Savage (D)	138,256	82.7
William T. Hespel (R)	28,831	17.3
3 Marty Russo (D)	132,111	62.2
Joseph J. McCarthy (R)	80,181	37.8
4 George E. Sangmeister (D)	91,282	50.3
Jack Davis (R)	90,243	49.7
5 William O. Lipinski (D)	93,567	61.3
John J. Holowinski (R)	59,128	38.7
6 Henry J. Hyde (R)	153,425	73.7
William J. Andrie (D)	54,804	26.3
7 Cardiss Collins (D)	135,331	100.0
8 Dan Rostenkowski (D)	107,728	74.6
V. Stephen Vetter (R)	34,659	24.0
9 Sidney R. Yates (D)	135,583	66.1
Herbert Sohn (R)	67,604	32.9
10 John Edward Porter (R)	158,519	72.5
Eugene F. Friedman (D)	60,187	27.5
11 Frank Annunzio (D)	131,753	64.5
George S. Gottlieb (R)	72,489	35.5
12 Philip M. Crane (R)	165,913	75.2
John A. Leonardi (D)	54,769	24.8
13 Harris W. Fawell (R)	174,992	70.2
Evelyn E. Craig (D)	74,424	29.8
14 Dennis Hastert (R)	161,146	73.7
Stephen Youhanaie (D)	57,482	26.3
15 Edward R. Madigan (R)	140,171	71.7
Thomas J. "Tom" Curl (D)	55,260	28.3
16 Lynn Martin (R)	128,365	63.9
Steven E. Mahan (D)	72,431	36.1
17 Lane Evans (D)	132,130	64.9
William E. Stewart (R)	71,560	35.1
18 Robert H. Michel (R)	114,458	54.7
G. Douglas Stephens (D)	94,763	45.3
19 Terry L. Bruce (D)	132,889	64.2
Robert F. Kerans (R)	73,981	35.8
20 Richard J. Durbin (D)	153,341	68.9
Paul E. Jurgens (R)	69,303	31.1
21 Jerry F. Costello (D)	105,836	52.6
Robert H. Gaffner (R)	95,385	47.4
22 Glenn Poshard (D)	139,392	64.9
Patrick J. Kelley (R)	75,462	35.1

Special Election[1]

	Votes	%
21 Jerry F. Costello (D)	33,144	51.5
Robert H. Gaffner (R)	31,257	48.5

INDIANA

	Votes	%
1 Peter J. Visclosky (D)	138,251	77.1
Owen W. Crumpacker (R)	41,076	22.9
2 Philip R. Sharp (D)	116,915	53.2
Mike Pence (R)	102,846	46.8
3 John Hiler (R)	116,309	54.3
Thomas W. Ward (D)	97,934	45.7
4 Daniel R. Coats (R)	132,843	62.1
Jill Long (D)	80,915	37.9
5 Jim Jontz (D)	116,240	56.3
Patricia L. Williams (R)	90,163	43.7
6 Dan Burton (R)	192,064	72.9
George Thomas Holland (D)	71,447	27.1
7 John T. Myers (R)	130,578	61.8

Candidates	Votes	%
Mark Richard Waterfill (D)	80,738	38.2
8 Frank McCloskey (D)	141,355	61.8
John L. Myers (R)	87,321	38.2
9 Lee H. Hamilton (D)	147,193	70.7
Floyd Eugene Coates (R)	60,946	29.3
10 Andrew Jacobs Jr. (D)	105,846	60.5
James C. Cummings (R)	68,978	39.5

IOWA

	Votes	%
1 Jim Leach (R)	112,746	60.7
Bill Gluba (D)	71,280	38.4
2 Tom Tauke (R)	113,543	56.8
Eric Tabor (D)	86,438	43.2
3 Dave Nagle (D)	129,204	63.4
Donald B. Redfern (R)	74,682	36.6
4 Neal Smith (D)	157,065	71.6
Paul Lunde (R)	62,056	28.3
5 Jim Ross Lightfoot (R)	117,761	63.9
Gene Freund (D)	66,599	36.1
6 Fred Grandy (R)	125,859	64.4
Dave O'Brien (D)	69,614	35.6

KANSAS

	Votes	%
1 Pat Roberts (R)	168,700	100.0
2 Jim Slattery (D)	135,694	73.3
Phil Meinhardt (R)	49,498	26.7
3 Jan Meyers (R)	150,223	73.6
Lionel Kunst (D)	53,959	26.4
4 Dan Glickman (D)	122,777	64.0
Lee Thompson (R)	69,165	36.0
5 Bob Whittaker (R)	127,722	70.2
John A. Barnes (D)	54,327	29.8

KENTUCKY

	Votes	%
1 Carroll Hubbard Jr. (D)	117,288	95.0
2 William H. Natcher (D)	92,184	60.6
Martin A. Tori (R)	59,907	39.4
3 Romano L. Mazzoli (D)	131,981	69.7
Philip Dunnagan (R)	57,387	30.3
4 Jim Bunning (R)	145,609	74.2
Richard V. Beliles (D)	50,575	25.8
5 Harold Rogers (R)	104,467	100.0
6 Larry J. Hopkins (R)	128,898	74.0
Milton Patton (D)	45,339	26.0
7 Carl C. Perkins (D)	96,946	58.7
Will T. Scott (R)	68,165	41.3

LOUISIANA[2]

	Votes	%
1 Robert L. Livingston (R)		100.0
2 Lindy (Mrs. Hale) Boggs (D)		100.0
3 W. J. "Billy" Tauzin (D)		100.0
4 Jim McCrery (R)		100.0
5 Jerry Huckaby (D)		100.0
6 Richard H. Baker (R)		100.0
7 Jimmy Hayes (D)		100.0
8 Clyde C. Holloway (R)	116,241	56.8
Faye Williams (D)	88,564	43.2

Special Election[3]

	Votes	%
4 Jim McCrery (R)	63,590	50.5
Foster Campbell (D)	62,214	49.5

MAINE

	Votes	%
1 Joseph E. Brennan (D)	190,989	63.2
Edward S. O'Meara Jr. (R)	111,125	36.8
2 Olympia J. Snowe (R)	167,229	66.2
Kenneth P. Hayes (D)	85,346	33.8

MARYLAND

	Votes	%
1 Roy Dyson (D)	96,128	50.4
Wayne T. Gilchrest (R)	94,588	49.6
2 Helen Delich Bentley (R)	157,956	71.5
Joseph Bartenfelder (D)	63,114	28.5

Candidates	Votes	%
3 Benjamin L. Cardin (D)	133,779	72.9
Ross Z. Pierpont (R)	49,733	27.1
4 Tom McMillen (D)	128,624	68.3
Bradlyn McClanahan (R)	59,688	31.7
5 Steny H. Hoyer (D)	128,437	78.6
John Eugene Sellner (R)	34,909	21.4
6 Beverly B. Byron (D)	166,753	75.4
Kenneth W. Halsey (R)	54,528	24.6
7 Kweisi Mfume (D)	117,650	100.0
8 Constance A. Morella (R)	172,619	62.7
Peter Franchot (D)	102,478	37.3

MASSACHUSETTS

	Votes	%
1 Silvio O. Conte (R)	186,356	82.7
John R. Arden (D)	38,907	17.3
2 Richard E. Neal (D)	156,262	80.2
Louis R. Godena (I)	38,446	19.7
3 Joseph D. Early (D)	191,005	99.8
4 Barney Frank (D)	169,729	70.3
Debra R. Tucker (R)	71,661	29.7
5 Chester G. Atkins (D)	181,860	84.1
T. David Hudson (LIBERT)	34,339	15.9
6 Nicholas Mavroules (D)	177,643	69.6
Paul McCarthy (R)	77,186	30.3
7 Edward J. Markey (D)	188,647	100.0
8 Joseph P. Kennedy II (D)	165,745	80.4
Glenn W. Fiscus (R)	40,316	19.6
9 Joe Moakley (D)	160,799	99.8
10 Gerry E. Studds (D)	187,178	66.7
Jon L. Bryan (D)	93,564	33.3
11 Brian J. Donnelly (D)	169,692	80.8
Michael C. Gilleran (R)	40,277	19.2

MICHIGAN

	Votes	%
1 John Conyers Jr. (D)	127,800	91.2
Bill Ashe (R)	10,979	7.8
2 Carl D. Pursell (R)	120,070	54.7
Lana Pollack (D)	98,290	44.7
3 Howard Wolpe (D)	112,605	57.3
Cal Allgaier (R)	83,769	42.7
4 Fred Upton (R)	132,270	70.8
Norman J. Rivers (D)	54,428	29.2
5 Paul B. Henry (R)	166,569	72.6
James M. Catchick (D)	62,868	27.4
6 Bob Carr (D)	120,581	58.9
Scott Schultz (R)	81,079	39.6
7 Dale E. Kildee (D)	150,832	75.8
Jeff Coad (R)	47,071	23.6
8 Bob Traxler (D)	139,904	72.1
Lloyd F. Buhl (R)	54,195	27.9
9 Guy Vander Jagt (R)	149,748	69.8
David John Gawron (D)	64,843	30.2
10 Bill Schuette (R)	152,646	72.7
Mathias G. Forbes (D)	55,398	26.4
11 Robert W. Davis (R)	129,085	59.6
Mitch Irwin (D)	86,526	40.0
12 David E. Bonior (D)	108,158	53.6
Douglas Carl (R)	91,780	45.5
13 George W. Crockett Jr. (D)	99,751	87.0
John Wright Savage II (R)	13,196	11.5
14 Dennis M. Hertel (D)	111,612	62.6
Kenneth C. McNealy (R)	64,750	36.3
15 William D. Ford (D)	104,596	63.8
Burl A. Adkins (R)	56,963	34.8
16 John D. Dingell (D)	132,775	97.4
17 Sander M. Levin (D)	135,493	70.2
Dennis M. Flessland (R)	55,197	28.6
18 William S. Broomfield (R)	195,579	76.0
Gary L. Kohut (D)	57,643	22.4

MINNESOTA[4]

	Votes	%
1 Timothy J. Penny (DFL)	161,118	70.1
Curt Schrimpf (I-R)	67,709	29.5
2 Vin Weber (I-R)	131,639	57.8
Doug Peterson (DFL)	96,016	42.2
3 Bill Frenzel (I-R)	215,322	68.2
Dave Carlson (DFL)	99,770	31.6

Candidates	Votes	%
4 Bruce F. Vento (DFL)	181,227	72.4
Ian Maitland (I-R)	67,073	26.8
5 Martin Olav Sabo (DFL)	174,416	72.1
Raymond C. Gilbertson (I-R)	60,646	25.1
6 Gerry Sikorski (DFL)	169,486	65.4
Ray Ploetz (I-R)	89,209	34.4
7 Arlan Stangeland (I-R)	121,396	54.6
Marv Hanson (DFL)	101,011	45.4
8 James L. Oberstar (DFL)	165,656	74.5
Jerry Shuster (I-R)	56,630	25.5

MISSISSIPPI

Candidates	Votes	%
1 Jamie L. Whitten (D)	137,445	78.2
Jim Bush (R)	38,381	21.8
2 Mike Espy (D)	112,401	64.7
Jack Coleman (R)	59,827	34.5
3 G.V. "Sonny" Montgomery (D)	164,651	88.8
Jimmie Ray Bourland (R)	20,729	11.2
4 Mike Parker (D)	110,184	54.8
Thomas Collins (R)	88,433	44.0
5 Larkin Smith (R)	100,185	55.0
Gene Taylor (D)	82,034	45.0

MISSOURI

Candidates	Votes	%
1 William L. Clay (D)	140,751	71.6
Joseph A. Schwan (R)	53,109	27.0
2 Jack Buechner (R)	186,450	66.3
Bob Feigenbaum (D)	91,645	32.6
3 Richard A. Gephardt (D)	150,205	62.8
Mark F. "Thor" Hearne (R)	86,763	36.3
4 Ike Skelton (D)	166,480	71.8
David Eyerly (R)	65,393	28.2
5 Alan Wheat (D)	149,166	70.3
Mary Ellen Lobb (R)	60,453	28.5
6 E. Thomas Coleman (R)	135,883	59.3
Doug R. Hughes (D)	93,128	40.7
7 Mel Hancock (R)	127,939	53.1
Max E. Bacon (D)	111,244	46.2
8 Bill Emerson (R)	117,601	58.1
Wayne Cryts (D)	84,801	41.9
9 Harold L. Volkmer (D)	160,872	67.9
Ken Dudley (R)	76,008	32.1

MONTANA

Candidates	Votes	%
1 Pat Williams (D)	115,278	60.8
Jim Fenlason (R)	74,405	39.2
2 Ron Marlenee (R)	97,465	55.5
Richard "Buck" O'Brien (D)	78,069	44.5

NEBRASKA

Candidates	Votes	%
1 Doug Bereuter (R)	146,231	66.9
Corky Jones (D)	72,167	33.0
2 Peter Hoagland (D)	112,174	50.5
Jerry Schenken (R)	109,193	49.1
3 Virginia Smith (R)	170,302	79.0
John D. Racek (D)	45,183	21.0

NEVADA

Candidates	Votes	%
1 James H. Bilbray (D)	101,764	64.0
Lucille Lusk (R)	53,588	33.7
2 Barbara F. Vucanovich (R)	105,981	57.3
James Spoo (D)	75,163	40.6

NEW HAMPSHIRE

Candidates	Votes	%
1 Robert C. Smith (R)	131,824	60.3
Joseph F. Keefe (D)	86,623	39.6
2 Chuck Douglas (R)	119,742	56.8
James W. Donchess (D)	89,677	42.5

NEW JERSEY

Candidates	Votes	%
1 James J. Florio (D)	141,988	69.9
Frank A. Cristaudo (R)	60,037	29.5

Candidates	Votes	%
2 William J. Hughes (D)	134,505	65.7
Kirk W. Conover (R)	67,759	33.1
3 Frank Pallone Jr. (D)	117,024	51.6
Joseph Azzolina (R)	107,479	47.4
4 Christopher H. Smith (R)	155,283	65.7
Betty Holland (D)	79,006	33.4
5 Marge Roukema (R)	175,562	75.7
Lee Monaco (D)	54,828	23.6
6 Bernard J. Dwyer (D)	120,125	61.1
Peter J. Sica (R)	74,824	38.1
7 Matthew J. Rinaldo (R)	153,350	74.6
James Hely (D)	52,189	25.4
8 Robert A. Roe (D)	96,036	100.0
9 Robert G. Torricelli (D)	142,012	67.1
Roger J. Lane (R)	68,363	32.3
10 Donald M. Payne (D)	84,681	77.4
Michael Webb (R)	13,848	12.6
Anthony Imperiale (I)	5,422	5.0
11 Dean A. Gallo (R)	154,654	70.5
John C. Shaw (D)	64,773	29.5
12 Jim Courter (R)	165,918	69.3
Norman J. Weinstein (D)	71,596	29.9
13 H. James Saxton (R)	167,470	69.5
James B. Smith (D)	73,561	30.5
14 Frank J. Guarini (D)	104,001	67.3
Fred J. Theemling Jr. (R)	47,293	30.6

Special Election[5]

Candidates	Votes	%
3 Frank Pallone Jr. (D)	116,988	52.0
Joseph Azzolina (R)	106,489	47.3

NEW MEXICO

Candidates	Votes	%
1 Steven H. Schiff (R)	89,985	50.6
Tom Udall (D)	84,138	47.3
2 Joe Skeen (R)	100,324	100.0
3 Bill Richardson (D)	124,938	73.1
Cecilia M. Salazar (R)	45,954	26.9

NEW YORK

Candidates	Votes	%
1 George J. Hochbrueckner (D)	105,624	50.8
Edward P. Romaine (R, C, RTL)	102,327	49.2
2 Thomas J. Downey (D)	107,646	61.6
Joseph Cardino Jr. (R, C, RTL)	66,972	38.4
3 Robert J. Mrazek (D)	128,336	57.2
Robert Previdi (R, C)	91,122	40.6
4 Norman F. Lent (R, C)	151,038	70.1
Francis T. Goban (D, L)	59,479	27.6
5 Raymond J. McGrath (R, C)	134,881	65.1
William G. Kelly (D)	68,930	33.2
6 Floyd H. Flake (D, L)	94,506	85.9
Robert L. Brandofino (C)	15,547	14.1
7 Gary L. Ackerman (D, L)	93,120	100.0
8 James H. Scheuer (D, L)	100,240	100.0
9 Thomas J. Manton (D)	72,851	100.0
10 Charles E. Schumer (D, L)	107,056	78.4
George S. Popielarski (R)	24,313	17.8
11 Edolphus Towns (D, L)	73,755	88.7
Riaz B. Hussain (R)	7,418	8.9
12 Major R. Owens (D, L)	74,304	93.0
Owen Augustin (R, C)	5,582	7.0
13 Stephen J. Solarz (D, L)	81,305	74.7
Anthony M. Curci (R, C)	27,536	25.3
14 Guy V. Molinari (R, C, RTL)	99,179	63.3
Jerome X. O'Donovan (D)	57,503	36.7
15 Bill Green (R)	107,599	61.3
Peter G. Doukas (D)	64,425	36.7
16 Charles B. Rangel (D, R, L)	107,620	97.1
17 Ted Weiss (D, L)	157,339	84.4
Myrna C. Albert (R, C)	29,156	15.6
18 Robert Garcia (D, L)	75,459	91.1
Fred Brown (R)	5,764	6.9
19 Eliot L. Engel (D, L)	77,158	56.0
Mario Biaggi (R)	37,454	27.2
Martin J. O'Grady (RTL)	11,271	8.2
Robert Blumetti (C)	11,182	8.1
20 Nita M. Lowey (D)	102,235	50.3
Joseph J. DioGuardi (R, C)	96,465	47.5

Candidates	Votes	%
21 Hamilton Fish Jr. (R, C)	150,443	74.6
Lawrence W. Grunberger (D)	47,294	23.5
22 Benjamin A. Gilman (R)	144,227	70.8
Eleanor F. Burlingham (D)	54,312	26.7
23 Michael R. McNulty (D)	145,040	61.7
Peter M. Bakal (R, C)	89,858	38.3
24 Gerald B. H. Solomon (R, C, RTL)	162,962	72.4
Fred Baye (D)	62,177	27.6
25 Sherwood Boehlert (R)	130,122	100.0
26 David O'B. Martin (R, C)	131,043	75.0
Donald R. Ravenscroft (D)	43,585	25.0
27 James T. Walsh (R)	124,928	57.5
Rosemary S. Pooler (D)	90,854	41.8
28 Matthew F. McHugh (D)	141,976	93.2
Mary C. Dixon (RTL)	10,395	6.8
29 Frank Horton (R)	132,608	68.8
James R. Vogel (D)	51,243	26.6
30 Louise M. Slaughter (D)	128,364	56.9
John D. Bouchard (R)	89,126	39.5
31 Bill Paxon (R, C, RTL)	117,710	53.4
David J. Swarts (D, L)	102,777	46.6
32 John J. LaFalce (D, L)	133,917	72.7
Emil K. Everett (R, C, RTL)	50,229	27.3
33 Henry J. Nowak (D, L)	139,604	100.0
34 Amo Houghton (R, C)	131,078	96.5

NORTH CAROLINA

Candidates	Votes	%
1 Walter B. Jones (D)	118,027	65.2
Howard Moye (R)	63,013	34.8
2 Tim Valentine (D)	128,832	100.0
3 H. Martin Lancaster (D)	95,323	100.0
4 David E. Price (D)	131,896	58.0
Tom Fetzer (R)	95,482	42.0
5 Stephen L. Neal (D)	110,516	52.6
Lyons Gray (R)	99,540	47.4
6 Howard Coble (R)	116,534	62.5
Tom Gilmore (R)	70,008	37.5
7 Charlie Rose (D)	102,392	67.3
George "Jerry" Thompson (R)	49,855	32.7
8 W. G. "Bill" Hefner (D)	99,214	51.5
Ted Blanton (R)	93,463	48.5
9 Alex McMillan (R)	139,014	65.9
Mark Sholander (D)	71,802	34.1
10 Cass Ballenger (R)	112,554	61.0
Jack L. Rhyne (D)	71,865	39.0
11 James McClure Clarke (D)	108,436	50.4
Charles H. Taylor (R)	106,907	49.6

NORTH DAKOTA

Candidates	Votes	%
AL Byron L. Dorgan (D)	212,583	70.9
Steve Sydness (R)	84,475	28.1

OHIO

Candidates	Votes	%
1 Thomas A. Luken (D)	117,682	56.5
Steve Chabot (R)	90,738	43.5
2 Bill Gradison (R)	153,162	72.3
Chuck R. Stidham (D)	58,637	27.7
3 Tony P. Hall (D)	141,953	76.9
Ron Crutcher (R)	42,664	23.1
4 Michael G. Oxley (R)	160,099	99.7
5 Paul E. Gillmor (R)	123,838	60.7
Tom Murray (D)	80,292	39.3
6 Bob McEwen (R)	152,235	74.3
Gordon Roberts (D)	52,635	25.7
7 Michael DeWine (R)	142,597	73.9
Jack Schira (D)	50,423	26.1
8 Donald E. Lukens (R)	154,164	75.9
John W. Griffin (D)	49,084	24.1
9 Marcy Kaptur (D)	157,557	81.3
Al Hawkins (R)	36,183	18.7
10 Clarence E. Miller (R)	143,673	71.6
John M. Buchanan (D)	56,894	28.4
11 Dennis E. Eckart (D)	124,600	61.5
Margaret Mueller (R)	78,028	38.5
12 John R. Kasich (R)	154,727	79.0
Mark P. Brown (D)	41,178	21.0

Candidates	Votes	%
13 Don J. Pease (D)	137,074	69.8
Dwight Brown (R)	59,287	30.2
14 Thomas C. Sawyer (D)	148,951	74.7
Loretta A. Lang (R)	50,356	25.3
15 Chalmers P. Wylie (R)	146,854	74.8
Mark S. Froehlich (D)	49,441	25.2
16 Ralph Regula (R)	158,824	78.6
Melvin J. Gravely (D)	43,356	21.4
17 James A. Traficant Jr. (D)	162,526	77.2
Frederick W. Lenz (R)	47,929	22.8
18 Douglas Applegate (D)	151,306	76.6
William C. Abraham (R)	46,130	23.4
19 Edward F. Feighan (D)	168,065	70.5
Noel F. Roberts (R)	70,359	29.5
20 Mary Rose Oakar (D)	146,715	82.6
Michael Sajna (R)	30,944	17.4
21 Louis Stokes (D)	148,388	85.7
Franklin H. Roski (R)	24,804	14.3

OKLAHOMA

Candidates	Votes	%
1 James M. Inhofe (R)	103,458	52.6
Kurt Glassco (D)	93,101	47.4
2 Mike Synar (D)	136,009	64.9
Ira Phillips (R)	73,659	35.1
3 Wes Watkins (D)		100.0
4 Dave McCurdy (D)		100.0
5 Mickey Edwards (R)	139,182	72.2
Terry J. Montgomery (D)	53,668	27.8
6 Glenn English (D)	122,887	73.1
Mike Brown (R)	45,239	26.9

OREGON

Candidates	Votes	%
1 Les AuCoin (D)	179,915	69.6
Earl Molander (R)	78,626	30.4
2 Robert F. Smith (R)	125,366	62.7
Larry Tuttle (D)	74,700	37.3
3 Ron Wyden (D)	190,684	99.4
4 Peter A. DeFazio (D)	108,483	72.0
Jim Howard (R)	42,220	28.0
5 Denny Smith (R)	111,489	50.2
Mike Kopetski (D)	110,782	49.8

PENNSYLVANIA

Candidates	Votes	%
1 Thomas M. Foglietta (D)	128,076	76.3
William J. O'Brien (R)	39,749	23.7
2 William H. Gray III (D)	184,322	93.7
Richard L. Harsch (R)	12,365	6.3
3 Robert A. Borski (D)	135,590	63.2
Mark Matthews (R)	78,909	36.8
4 Joe Kolter (D)	124,041	69.8
Gordon R. Johnston (R)	52,402	29.5
5 Richard T. Schulze (R)	153,453	78.2
Donald A. Hadley (D)	42,758	21.8
6 Gus Yatron (D)	114,119	63.1
James R. Erwin (R)	65,278	36.1
7 Curt Weldon (R)	155,387	67.8
David Landau (D)	73,745	32.2
8 Peter H. Kostmayer (D)	128,153	56.8
Ed Howard (R)	93,648	41.5
9 Bud Shuster (R, D)	158,702	100.0
10 Joseph M. McDade (R)	140,096	73.2
Robert C. Cordaro (D)	51,179	26.8
11 Paul E. Kanjorski (D)	120,706	100.0
12 John P. Murtha (D)	133,081	100.0
13 Lawrence Coughlin (R)	152,191	66.6
Bernard Tomkin (D)	76,424	33.4
14 William J. Coyne (D)	135,181	78.6
Richard Edward Caligiuri (R)	36,719	21.4
15 Don Ritter (R)	106,951	57.5
Ed Reibman (D)	79,127	42.5
16 Robert S. Walker (R)	136,944	74.0
Ernest Eric Guyll (D)	48,169	26.0
17 George W. Gekas (R, D)	166,289	100.0
18 Doug Walgren (D)	136,924	62.7
John A. Newman (R)	80,975	37.0
19 Bill Goodling (R)	145,381	77.2
Paul E. Ritchey (D)	42,819	22.8

Candidates	Votes	%
20 Joseph M. Gaydos (D)	137,472	98.5
21 Tom Ridge (R)	141,832	78.7
George R. H. Elder (D)	38,288	21.3
22 Austin J. Murphy (D)	123,428	72.4
William Hodgkiss (R)	47,039	27.6
23 William F. Clinger Jr. (R)	105,575	62.0
Howard Shakespeare (D)	63,476	37.3

RHODE ISLAND

Candidates	Votes	%
1 Ronald K. Machtley (R)	105,506	55.6
Fernand J. St Germain (D)	84,141	44.4
2 Claudine Schneider (R)	145,218	72.1
Ruth S. Morgenthau (D)	56,129	27.9

SOUTH CAROLINA

Candidates	Votes	%
1 Arthur Ravenel Jr. (R)	101,572	63.8
Wheeler Tillman (D)	57,691	36.2
2 Floyd D. Spence (R)	94,960	52.8
Jim Leventis (D)	83,978	46.6
3 Butler Derrick (D)	89,071	53.7
Henry S. Jordan (R)	75,571	45.6
4 Liz J. Patterson (D)	90,234	52.2
Knox White (R)	82,793	47.8
5 John M. Spratt Jr. (D)	107,959	69.8
Robert K. "Bob" Carley (R)	46,622	30.2
6 Robin Tallon (D)	120,719	76.1
Robert Cunningham Sr. (R)	37,958	23.9

SOUTH DAKOTA

Candidates	Votes	%
AL Tim Johnson (D)	223,759	71.7
David Volk (R)	88,157	28.3

TENNESSEE

Candidates	Votes	%
1 James H. Quillen (R)	119,526	80.2
Sidney S. Smith (D)	29,469	19.8
2 John J. Duncan (R)	99,631	56.2
Dudley W. Taylor (R)	77,540	43.8
3 Marilyn Lloyd (D)	108,264	57.4
Harold L. Coker (R)	80,372	42.6
4 Jim Cooper (D)	94,129	100.0
5 Bob Clement (D)	155,068	100.0
6 Bart Gordon (D)	123,652	76.5
Wallace Embry (R)	38,033	23.5
7 Don Sundquist (R)	142,025	80.1
Ken Bloodworth (D)	35,237	19.9
8 John Tanner (D)	94,571	62.4
Ed Bryant (R)	56,893	37.6
9 Harold E. Ford (D)	126,280	81.6
Isaac Richmond (I)	28,522	18.4

Special Elections

Candidates	Votes	%
2 John J. "Jimmy" Duncan Jr.[6]		
(R)	92,929	56.1
Dudley W. Taylor (D)	70,576	42.6
5 Bob Clement (D)[7]	56,323	62.2
Terry Holcomb (R)	32,847	36.3

TEXAS

Candidates	Votes	%
1 Jim Chapman (D)	122,566	62.2
Horace McQueen (R)	74,357	37.8
2 Charles Wilson (D)	145,614	87.7
Gary W. Nelson (LIBERT)	20,475	12.3
3 Steve Bartlett (R)	227,882	81.8
Blake Cowden (D)	50,627	18.2
4 Ralph M. Hall (D)	139,379	66.4
Randy Sutton (R)	67,337	32.1
5 John Bryant (D)	95,376	60.7
Lon Williams (R)	59,877	38.1
6 Joe L. Barton (R)	164,692	67.6
N. P. "Pat" Kendrick (D)	78,786	32.4
7 Bill Archer (R)	185,203	79.1
Diane Richards (D)	48,824	20.9
8 Jack Fields (R)	90,503	100.0
9 Jack Brooks (D)	137,270	100.0

Candidates	Votes	%
10 J. J. "Jake" Pickle (D)	232,213	93.4
Vincent J. May (LIBERT)	16,281	6.6
11 Marvin Leath (D)	134,207	95.4
12 Jim Wright (D)	135,459	99.3
13 Bill Sarpalius (D)	98,345	52.5
Larry S. Milner (R)	89,105	47.5
14 Greg H. Laughlin (D)	111,395	53.2
Mac Sweeney (R)	96,042	45.9
15 E. "Kika" de la Garza (D)	93,672	93.9
Gloria Joyce Hendrix (LIBERT)	6,133	6.1
16 Ronald D. Coleman (D)	104,514	100.0
17 Charles W. Stenholm (D)	149,064	100.0
18 Mickey Leland (D)	94,408	92.9
J. Alejandro Snead (LIBERT)	7,235	7.1
19 Larry Combest (R)	113,068	67.7
Gerald McCathern (D)	53,932	32.3
20 Henry B. Gonzalez (D)	94,527	70.7
Lee Trevino (R)	36,801	27.5
21 Lamar Smith (R)	203,989	93.2
James A. Robinson (LIBERT)	14,801	6.8
22 Thomas D. DeLay (R)	125,733	67.4
Wayne Walker (D)	58,471	31.4
23 Albert G. Bustamante (D)	116,423	64.5
Jerome L. Gonzales (R)	60,559	33.6
24 Martin Frost (D)	135,794	92.6
Leo Sadovy (LIBERT)	10,841	7.4
25 Michael A. Andrews (D)	113,499	71.4
George H. Loefflor Jr. (R)	44,043	27.7
26 Dick Armey (R)	194,944	69.3
Jo Ann Reyes (D)	86,490	30.7
27 Solomon P. Ortiz (D)	105,085	100.0

UTAH

Candidates	Votes	%
1 James V. Hansen (R)	130,893	59.8
Gunn McKay (D)	87,976	40.2
2 Wayne Owens (D)	112,129	57.4
Richard Snelgrove (R)	80,212	41.1
3 Howard C. Nielson (R)	129,951	66.8
Robert W. Stringham (D)	60,018	30.9

VERMONT

Candidates	Votes	%
AL Peter Smith (R)	98,937	41.2
Bernard Sanders (I)	90,026	37.5
Paul N. Poirier (D)	45,330	18.9

VIRGINIA

Candidates	Votes	%
1 Herbert H. Bateman (R)	135,937	73.3
James S. Ellenson (D)	49,614	26.7
2 Owen B. Pickett (D)	106,666	60.5
Jerry R. Curry (R)	62,564	35.5
Stephen P. Shao (I)	4,255	2.4
Robert A. Smith (I)	2,691	1.5
3 Thomas J. Bliley Jr. (R)	187,354	99.7
4 Norman Sisisky (D)	134,786	99.9
5 Lewis F. Payne Jr. (D)	97,242	54.2
Charles Hawkins (R)	78,396	43.7
6 Jim Olin (D)	118,369	63.9
Charles E. Judd (R)	66,935	36.1
7 D. French Slaughter Jr. (R)	136,988	99.6
8 Stan Parris (R)	154,761	62.3
David G. Brickley (D)	93,561	37.7
9 Rick Boucher (D)	113,309	63.4
John C. Brown (R)	65,410	36.6
10 Frank R. Wolf (R)	188,550	68.1
Robert L. Weinberg (D)	88,284	31.9

Special Election[8]

Candidates	Votes	%
5 Lewis F. Payne Jr. (D)	55,469	59.3
Linda Arey (R)	38,063	40.7

WASHINGTON

Candidates	Votes	%
1 John R. Miller (R)	152,265	55.4
Reese Lindquist (D)	122,646	44.6
2 Al Swift (D)	175,191	100.0
3 Jolene Unsoeld (D)	109,412	50.1

	Candidates	Votes	%
	Bill Wight (R)	108,794	49.9
4	Sid Morrison (R)	142,938	74.5
	J. Richard Golob (D)	48,850	25.5
5	Thomas S. Foley (D)	160,654	76.4
	Marlyn A. Derby (R)	49,657	23.6
6	Norm Dicks (D)	125,904	67.6
	Kevin P. Cook (R)	60,346	32.4
7	Jim McDermott (D)	173,809	76.3
	Robert Edwards (R)	53,902	23.7
8	Rod Chandler (R)	174,942	70.9
	Jim Kean (D)	71,920	29.1

WEST VIRGINIA

	Candidates	Votes	%
1	Alan B. Mollohan (D)	119,256	74.5
	Howard K. Tuck (R)	40,732	25.5

	Candidates	Votes	%
2	Harley O. Staggers Jr. (D)	118,356	100.0
3	Bob Wise (D)	120,192	74.3
	Paul W. Hart (R)	41,478	25.7
4	Nick J. Rahall II (D)	78,812	61.3
	Marianne R. Brewster (R)	49,753	38.7

WISCONSIN

	Candidates	Votes	%
1	Les Aspin (D)	158,552	76.2
	Bernie Weaver (R)	49,620	23.8
2	Robert W. Kastenmeier (D)	151,501	58.5
	Ann J. Haney (R)	107,457	41.5
3	Steve Gunderson (R)	157,513	68.3
	Karl E. Krueger (D)	72,935	31.6
4	Gerald D. Kleczka (D)	177,283	99.7
5	Jim Moody (D)	140,518	64.1

	Candidates	Votes	%
	Helen Barnhill (R)	78,307	35.7
6	Thomas E. Petri (R)	165,923	74.2
	Joe Garrett (D)	57,552	25.8
7	David R. Obey (D)	142,197	61.8
	Kevin J. Hermening (R)	86,077	37.4
8	Toby Roth (R)	167,275	69.7
	Robert Baron (D)	72,708	30.3
9	F. James Sensenbrenner Jr. (R)	185,093	74.9
	Tom Hickey (D)	62,003	25.1

WYOMING

	Candidates	Votes	%
AL	Dick Cheney (R)	118,350	66.6
	Bryan Sharratt (D)	56,527	31.8

1. A special election was held to fill the unexpired term of Rep. Melvin Price (D), who died April 22, 1988.

2. For the 1988 House elections in Louisiana, an open primary election was held with candidates from all parties running on the same ballot. Any candidate who received a majority was elected unopposed, with no further appearance on the general election ballot. If no candidate received 50 percent, a runoff was held betweeen the two top finishers.

3. A special election was held to fill the unexpired term of Rep. Buddy Roemer (D), who resigned March 14, 1988, having been elected governor.

4. In Minnesota the Democratic Party is known as the Democratic-Farmer-Labor Party and the Republican Party as the Independent-Republican Party; candidates appear on the ballot with these designations.

5. A special election was held to fill the unexpired term of Rep. James J. Howard (D), who died March 25, 1988.

6. A special election was held to fill the unexpired term of Rep. John J. Duncan (R), who died June 21, 1988.

7. A special election was held to fill the unexpired term of Rep. Bill Bonor (D), who resigned Oct. 5, 1987, having been elected mayor of Nashville.

8. A special election was held to fill the unexpired term of Rep. W. C. Daniel (D), who died Jan. 23, 1988.

1989 House Elections

ALABAMA

Special Election[1]

	Candidates	Votes	%
3	Glen Browder (D)	47,294	65.3
	John Rice (R)	25,142	34.7

CALIFORNIA

Special Election[2]

	Candidates	Votes	%
15	Gary Condit (D)	51,543	57.1
	Clare Berryhill (R)	1,592	35.0

FLORIDA

Special Election[3]

	Candidates	Votes	%
18	Ileana Ros-Lehtinen (R)	49,298	53.3
	Gerald Richman (D)	43,274	46.7

INDIANA

Special Election[4]

	Candidates	Votes	%
4	Jill L. Long (D)	65,272	50.7
	Dan Heath (R)	63,494	49.3

MISSISSIPPI

Special Election[5]

	Candidates	Votes	%
5	Gene Taylor (D)	51,561	42.0
	Tom Anderson Jr. (R)	45,727	37.2
	Mike Moore (D)	25,579	20.8

Special Runoff Election

	Candidates	Votes	%
5	Gene Taylor (D)	83,296	65.2
	Tom Anderson Jr. (R)	44,494	34.8

TEXAS[6]

Special Election[7]

	Candidates	Votes	%
12	Bob Lanier (R)	21,978	39.4
	Pete Geren (D)	17,751	31.8
	Jim Lane (D)	12,308	22.1

Special Runoff Election

	Candidates	Votes	%
12	Pete Geren (D)	40,210	51.0
	Bob Lanier (R)	38,590	49.0

Special Election[8]

	Candidates	Votes	%
18	Craig Washington (D)	27,367	41.3
	Anthony Hall (D)	22,797	34.4
	Ron Wilson (D)	4,948	7.5

Special Runoff Election

	Candidates	Votes	%
18	Craig Washington (D)	24,140	56.6
	Anthony Hall (D)	18,484	43.4

WYOMING

Special Election[9]

	Candidates	Votes	%
AL	Craig Thomas (R)	74,384	52.5
	John P. Vinich (D)	60,845	43.0

1. A special election was held to fill the unexpired term of Rep. Bill Nichols (D), who died Dec. 13, 1988.

2. A special election was held to fill the unexpired term of Rep. Tony Coelho (D), who resigned June 15, 1989.

3. A special election was held to fill the unexpired term of Rep. Claude Pepper (D), who died May 30, 1989.

4. A special election was held to fill the unexpired term of Rep. Daniel R. Coats (R), who resigned in January 1989, having been appointed to the U.S. Senate.

5. A special election was held to fill the unexpired term of Rep. Larkin Smith (R), who died Aug. 15, 1989.

6. Texas election law requires all candidates in special elections to run against each other, regardless of party. If no candidate received a majority, a special runoff election was held between the two candidates receiving the most votes in the special election.

7. A special election was held to fill the unexpired term of Rep. Jim Wright (D), who resigned June 30, 1989.

8. A special election was held to fill the unexpired term of Rep. Mickey Leland (D), who died Aug. 7, 1989.

9. A special election was held to fill the unexpired term of Rep. Dick Cheney (R), who resigned March 17, 1989, having been appointed defense secretary.

1990 House Elections

ALABAMA

	Candidates	Votes	%
1	Sonny Callahan (R)	82,185	99.6
2	Bill Dickinson (R)	87,649	51.3
	Faye Baggiano (D)	83,243	48.7
3	Glen Browder (D)	101,923	73.7
	Don Sledge (R)	36,317	26.3
4	Tom Bevill (D)	129,872	99.7
5	Robert E. "Bud" Cramer (D)	113,047	67.1
	Albert McDonald (R)	55,326	32.9
6	Ben Erdreich (D)	134,412	92.8
	David A. Alvarez (I)	8,640	6.0
7	Claude Harris (D)	127,490	70.5
	Michael D. Barker (R)	53,258	29.5

ALASKA

	Candidates	Votes	%
AL	Don Young (R)	99,003	51.7
	John E. Devens (D)	91,677	47.8

ARIZONA

	Candidates	Votes	%
1	John J. Rhodes III (R)	166,223	99.5
2	Morris K. Udall (D)	76,549	65.9
	Joseph D. Sweeney (R)	39,586	34.1
3	Bob Stump (R)	134,279	56.6
	Roger Hartstone (D)	103,018	43.4
4	Jon Kyl (R)	141,843	61.3
	Mark Ivey Jr. (D)	89,395	38.7
5	Jim Kolbe (R)	138,975	64.8
	Chuck Phillips (D)	75,642	35.2

ARKANSAS

	Candidates	Votes	%
1	Bill Alexander (D)	101,026	64.3
	Terry Hayes (R)	56,071	35.7
2	Ray Thornton (D)	103,471	60.4
	Jim Keet (R)	67,800	39.6
3	John Paul Hammerschmidt (R)	129,876	70.5
	Dan Ivy (D)	54,332	29.5
4	Beryl Anthony Jr. (D)	110,365	72.4
	Roy Rood (R)	42,130	27.6

CALIFORNIA

	Candidates	Votes	%
1	Frank Riggs (R)	99,782	43.3
	Douglas H. Bosco (D)	96,468	41.9
	Darlene G. Comingore (PF)	34,011	14.8
2	Wally Herger (R)	133,315	63.7
	Erwin E. "Bill" Rush (D)	65,333	31.2
	Ross Crain (LIBERT)	10,753	5.1
3	Robert T. Matsui (D)	132,143	60.3
	Lowell P. Landowski (R)	76,148	34.8
4	Vic Fazio (D)	115,090	54.7
	Mark Baughman (R)	82,738	39.3
	Bryce Bigwood (LIBERT)	12,626	6.0
5	Nancy Pelosi (D)	120,633	77.2
	Alan Nichols (R)	35,671	22.8
6	Barbara Boxer (D)	137,306	68.1
	Bill Boerum (R)	64,402	31.9
7	George Miller (D)	121,080	60.5
	Roger A. Payton (R)	79,031	39.5
8	Ronald V. Dellums (D)	119,645	61.3
	Barbara Galewski (R)	75,544	38.7
9	Pete Stark (D)	94,739	58.4
	Victor Romero (R)	67,412	41.6
10	Don Edwards (D)	81,875	62.7
	Mark Patrosso (R)	48,747	37.3
11	Tom Lantos (D)	105,029	65.9
	G. M. "Bill" Quraishi (R)	45,818	28.8
	June R. Genis (LIBERT)	8,518	5.3
12	Tom Campbell (R)	125,157	60.8
	Robert Palmer (D)	69,270	33.7
	Chuck Olson (LIBERT)	11,271	5.5
13	Norman Y. Mineta (D)	97,286	58.0

	Candidates	Votes	%
	David E. Smith (R)	59,773	35.7
	John H. Webster (LIBERT)	10,587	6.3
14	John T. Doolittle (R)	128,309	51.5
	Patricia Malberg (D)	120,742	48.5
15	Gary Condit (D)	97,147	66.2
	Cliff Burris (R)	49,634	33.8
16	Leon E. Panetta (D)	134,236	74.2
	Jerry M. Reiss (R)	39,885	22.0
17	Calvin Dooley (D)	82,611	54.5
	Charles Pashayan Jr. (R)	68,848	45.5
18	Richard H. Lehman (D)	98,804	100.0
19	Robert J. Lagomarsino (R)	94,599	54.6
	Anita Perez Ferguson (D)	76,991	44.4
20	William M. Thomas (R)	112,962	59.8
	Michael A. Thomas (D)	65,101	34.4
	William H. Dilbeck (LIBERT)	10,555	5.6
21	Elton Gallegly (R)	118,326	58.4
	Richard D. Freiman (D)	68,921	34.0
	Peggy Christensen (LIBERT)	15,364	7.6
22	Carlos J. Moorhead (R)	108,634	60.0
	David Bayer (D)	61,630	34.1
23	Anthony C. Beilenson (D)	103,141	61.7
	Jim Salomon (R)	57,118	34.2
24	Henry A. Waxman (D)	71,562	68.9
	John N. Cowles (R)	26,607	25.6
	Maggie Phair (PF)	5,706	5.5
25	Edward R. Roybal (D)	48,120	70.0
	Steven J. Renshaw (R)	17,021	24.8
	Robert H. Scott (LIBERT)	3,576	5.2
26	Howard L. Berman (D)	78,031	61.1
	Roy Dahlson (R)	44,492	34.8
27	Mel Levine (D)	90,857	58.2
	David Barrett Cohen (R)	58,140	37.2
28	Julian C. Dixon (D)	69,482	72.7
	George Z. Adams (R)	21,245	22.2
29	Maxine Waters (D)	51,350	79.4
	Bill DeWitt (R)	12,054	18.6
30	Matthew G. Martinez (D)	45,456	58.2
	Reuben D. Franco (R)	28,914	37.0
31	Mervyn M. Dymally (D)	56,394	67.1
	Eunice A. Sato (R)	27,593	32.9
32	Glenn M. Anderson (D)	68,268	61.5
	Sanford W. Kahn (R)	42,692	38.5
33	David Dreier (R)	101,336	63.7
	Georgia Houston Webb (D)	49,981	31.4
34	Esteban E. Torres (D)	55,646	60.7
	John Eastman (R)	36,024	39.3
35	Jerry Lewis (R)	121,602	60.6
	Barry Norton (D)	66,100	32.9
	Jerry Johnson (LIBERT)	13,020	6.5
36	George E. Brown Jr. (D)	72,409	52.7
	Robert Hammock (R)	64,961	47.3
37	Al McCandless (R)	115,469	49.7
	Ralph Waite (D)	103,961	44.8
38	Robert K. Dornan (R)	60,561	58.1
	Barbara Jackson (D)	43,693	41.9
39	William E. Dannemeyer (R)	113,849	65.3
	Francis X. Hoffman (D)	53,670	30.8
40	C. Christopher Cox (R)	142,299	67.6
	Eugene C. Gratz (D)	68,087	32.4
41	Bill Lowery (R)	105,723	49.2
	Dan Kripke (D)	93,586	43.6
	Karen S. R. Works (PF)	15,428	7.2
42	Dana Rohrabacher (R)	109,353	59.3
	Guy C. Kimbrough (D)	67,189	36.5
43	Ron Packard (R)	151,206	68.1
	Doug Hansen (PF)	40,212	18.1
	Richard L. Arnold (LIBERT)	30,720	13.8
44	Randy "Duke" Cunningham (R)	50,377	46.3
	Jim Bates (D)	48,712	44.8
45	Duncan Hunter (R)	123,591	72.8
	Joe Shea (LIBERT)	46,068	27.2

COLORADO

	Candidates	Votes	%
1	Patricia Schroeder (D)	82,176	63.7
	Gloria Gonzales Roemer (R)	46,802	36.3
2	David E. Skaggs (D)	105,248	60.7
	Jason Lewis (R)	68,226	39.3
3	Ben Nighthorse Campbell (D)	124,487	70.2
	Bob Ellis (R)	49,961	28.2
4	Wayne Allard (R)	89,285	54.1
	Dick Bond (D)	75,901	45.9
5	Joel Hefley (R)	127,740	66.4
	Cal Johnston (D)	57,776	30.0
6	Dan Schaefer (R)	105,312	64.5
	Don Jarrett (D)	57,961	35.5

CONNECTICUT

	Candidates	Votes	%
1	Barbara B. Kennelly (D)	126,566	71.4
	James M. Garvey (R)	50,690	28.6
2	Sam Gejdenson (D)	105,085	59.7
	John M. Ragsdale (R)	70,922	40.3
3	Rosa DeLauro (D)	90,772	52.1
	Thomas Scott (R)	83,440	47.9
4	Christopher Shays (R)	105,682	76.5
	Al Smith (D)	32,352	23.4
5	Gary Franks (R)	93,912	51.7
	Toby Moffett (D)	85,803	47.2
6	Nancy L. Johnson (R)	141,105	74.4
	Paul Kulas (D)	48,628	25.6

DELAWARE

	Candidates	Votes	%
AL	Thomas R. Carper (D)	116,274	65.5
	Ralph O. Williams (R)	58,037	32.7

FLORIDA

	Candidates	Votes	%
1	Earl Hutto (D)	88,416	52.2
	Terry Ketchel (R)	80,851	47.8
2	Pete Peterson (D)	103,032	56.9
	Bill Grant (R)	77,939	43.1
3	Charles E. Bennett (D)	84,280	72.7
	Rod Sullivan (R)	31,727	27.3
4	Craig T. James (R)	120,895	55.9
	Reid Hughes (D)	95,320	44.1
5	Bill McCollum (R)	94,453	59.9
	Bob Fletcher (D)	63,253	40.1
6	Cliff Stearns (R)	138,588	59.2
	Art Johnson (D)	95,421	40.8
7	Sam Gibbons (D)	99,464	67.6
	Charles D. Prout (R)	47,765	32.4
8	C. W. Bill Young (R)		100.0
9	Michael Bilirakis (R)	142,163	58.1
	Cheryl Davis Knapp (D)	102,503	41.9
10	Andy Ireland (R)		100.0
11	Jim Bacchus (D)	120,991	51.9
	Bill Tolley (R)	111,970	48.1
12	Tom Lewis (R)		100.0
13	Porter J. Goss (R)		100.0
14	Harry A. Johnston (D)	156,055	66.0
	Scott Shore (R)	80,249	34.0
15	E. Clay Shaw Jr. (R)	104,295	97.8
16	Lawrence J. Smith (D)		100.0
17	William Lehman (D)	79,569	78.3
	Earl Rodney (R)	22,029	21.7
18	Ileana Ros-Lehtinen (R)	56,364	60.4
	Bernard Anscher (D)	36,978	39.6
19	Dante B. Fascell (D)	87,696	62.0
	Bob Allen (R)	53,796	38.0

GEORGIA

	Candidates	Votes	%
1	Lindsay Thomas (D)	80,515	71.2
	Chris Meredith (R)	32,532	28.8
2	Charles Hatcher (D)	77,910	73.0
	Jonathan Perry Waters (R)	28,781	27.0

Candidates	Votes	%
3 Richard Ray (D)	72,961	63.2
Paul Broun (R)	42,561	36.8
4 Ben Jones (D)	96,526	52.4
John Linder (R)	87,569	47.6
5 John Lewis (D)	86,037	75.6
J. W. Tibbs Jr. (R)	27,781	24.4
6 Newt Gingrich (R)	78,768	50.3
David Worley (D)	77,794	49.7
7 George "Buddy" Darden (D)	95,817	60.1
Al Beverly (R)	63,588	39.9
8 J. Roy Rowland (D)	81,344	68.7
Bob Cunningham (R)	36,980	31.3
9 Ed Jenkins (D)	96,197	55.8
Joe Hoffman (R)	76,121	44.2
10 Doug Barnard Jr. (D)	89,683	58.3
Sam Jones (R)	64,184	41.7

HAWAII

Candidates	Votes	%
1 Neil Abercrombie (D)	97,622	60.0
Mike Liu (R)	62,982	38.7
2 Patsy T. Mink (D)	118,155	66.3
Andy Poepoe (R)	54,625	30.6

Special Election[1]

2 Patsy T. Mink (D)	51,841	37.4
Mufi Hannemann (D)	50,164	36.1
Ron Menor (D)	23,629	17.0
Andy Poepoe (R)	8,872	6.4

IDAHO

1 Larry LaRocco (D)	85,054	53.0
C. A. "Skip" Smyser (R)	75,406	47.0
2 Richard H. Stallings (D)	98,008	63.6
Sean McDevitt (R)	56,044	36.4

ILLINOIS

1 Charles A. Hayes (D)	100,890	93.8
Babette Peyton (R)	6,708	6.2
2 Gus Savage (D)	80,245	78.2
William T. Hespel (R)	22,350	21.8
3 Marty Russo (D)	110,512	70.9
Carl L. Klein (R)	45,299	29.1
4 George E. Sangmeister (D)	77,290	59.2
Manny Hoffman (R)	53,258	40.8
5 William O. Lipinski (D)	73,805	66.3
David J. Shestokas (R)	34,440	31.0
6 Henry J. Hyde (R)	96,410	66.7
Robert J. Cassidy (D)	48,155	33.3
7 Cardiss Collins (D)	80,021	79.9
Michael Dooley (R)	20,099	20.1
8 Dan Rostenkowski (D)	70,151	79.1
Robert Marshall (LIBERT)	18,529	20.9
9 Sidney R. Yates (D)	96,557	71.2
Herbert Sohn (R)	39,031	28.8
10 John Edward Porter (R)	104,070	67.7
Peg McNamara (D)	47,286	30.8
11 Frank Annunzio (D)	82,703	53.6
Walter W. Dudycz (R)	68,850	44.6
Larry Saska (IS)	2,692	1.7
12 Philip M. Crane (R)	113,081	82.2
Steve Pedersen (IS)	24,450	17.8
13 Harris W. Fawell (R)	116,048	65.8
Steven Thomas (D)	60,305	34.2
14 Dennis Hastert (R)	112,383	66.9
Donald J. Westphal (D)	55,592	33.1
15 Edward R. Madigan (R)	119,812	100.0
16 John W. Cox Jr. (D)	83,061	54.6
John W. Hallock Jr. (R)	69,105	45.4
17 Lane Evans (D)	102,062	66.5
Dan Lee (R)	51,380	33.5
18 Robert H. Michel (R)	105,693	98.4
19 Terry L. Bruce (D)	113,958	66.3
Robert F. Kerans (R)	55,680	32.4
20 Richard J. Durbin (D)	130,114	66.2
Paul E. Jurgens (R)	66,433	33.8
21 Jerry F. Costello (D)	95,208	66.0

Candidates	Votes	%
Robert H. Gaffner (R)	48,949	34.0
22 Glenn Poshard (D)	138,425	83.7
Jim Wham (I)	26,896	16.3

INDIANA

1 Peter J. Visclosky (D)	68,920	66.0
William Costas (R)	35,450	34.0
2 Philip R. Sharp (D)	93,495	59.4
Mike Pence (R)	63,980	40.6
3 Tim Roemer (D)	80,740	50.9
John Hiler (R)	77,911	49.1
4 Jill Long (D)	99,347	60.7
Rick Hawks (R)	64,415	39.3
5 Jim Jontz (D)	81,373	53.1
John A. Johnson (R)	71,750	46.9
6 Dan Burton (R)	116,470	63.5
James P. Fadely (D)	67,024	36.5
7 John T. Myers (R)	88,598	57.6
John W. Riley Sr. (D)	65,248	42.4
8 Frank McCloskey (D)	97,465	54.7
Richard E. Mourdock (R)	80,645	45.3
9 Lee H. Hamilton (D)	107,526	69.0
Floyd Eugene Coates (R)	48,325	31.0
10 Andrew Jacobs Jr. (D)	69,362	66.4
Janos Horvath (R)	35,049	33.6

IOWA

1 Jim Leach (R)	90,042	99.8
2 Jim Nussle (R)	82,650	49.8
Eric Tabor (D)	81,008	48.8
3 David R. Nagle (D)	100,947	99.2
4 Neal Smith (D)	127,812	97.9
5 Jim Ross Lightfoot (R)	99,978	68.0
Rod Powell (D)	47,022	32.0
6 Fred Grandy (R)	112,333	71.8
Mike O. Earll (D)	44,063	28.2

KANSAS

1 Pat Roberts (R)	102,974	62.6
Duane West (D)	61,396	37.4
2 Jim Slattery (D)	99,093	62.8
Scott Morgan (R)	58,643	37.2
3 Jan Meyers (R)	88,725	60.1
Leroy Jones (D)	58,923	39.9
4 Dan Glickman (D)	112,015	70.8
Roger M. Grund (R)	46,283	29.2
5 Dick Nichols (R)	90,555	59.3
George Wingert (D)	62,244	40.7

KENTUCKY

1 Carroll Hubbard Jr. (D)	85,323	86.9
Marvin H. Seat (POP)	12,879	13.1
2 William H. Natcher (D)	77,057	66.0
Martin A. Tori (R)	39,624	34.0
3 Romano L. Mazzoli (D)	84,750	60.6
Al Brown (R)	55,188	39.4
4 Jim Bunning (R)	101,680	69.3
Galen Martin (D)	44,979	30.7
5 Harold Rogers (R)	64,660	100.0
6 Larry J. Hopkins (R)	76,859	100.0
7 Carl C. Perkins (D)	61,330	50.8
Will T. Scott (R)	59,377	49.2

LOUISIANA[2]

1 Bob Livingston (R)		100.0
2 William J. Jefferson (D)	55,621	52.5
Marc H. Morial (D)	50,232	47.5
3 W. J. "Billy" Tauzin (D)		100.0
4 Jim McCrery (R)		100.0
5 Jerry Huckaby (D)		100.0
6 Richard H. Baker (R)		100.0
7 Jimmy Hayes (D)		100.0
8 Clyde C. Holloway (R)		100.0

MAINE

Candidates	Votes	%
1 Thomas H. Andrews (D)	167,623	60.1
David F. Emery (R)	110,836	39.7
2 Olympia J. Snowe (R)	121,704	51.0
Patrick K. McGowan (D)	116,798	49.0

MARYLAND

1 Wayne T. Gilchrest (R)	88,920	56.8
Roy Dyson (D)	67,518	43.2
2 Helen Delich Bentley (R)	115,398	74.4
Ronald P. Bowers (D)	39,785	25.6
3 Benjamin L. Cardin (D)	82,545	69.7
Harwood Nichols (R)	35,841	30.3
4 Tom McMillen (D)	85,601	58.9
Robert P. Duckworth (R)	59,846	41.1
5 Steny H. Hoyer (D)	84,747	80.7
Lee F. Breuer (R)	20,314	19.3
6 Beverly B. Byron (D)	106,502	65.3
Christopher P. Flotes Jr. (R)	56,479	34.7
7 Kweisi Mfume (D)	59,628	85.0
Kenneth Kondner (R)	10,529	15.0
8 Constance A. Morella (R)	130,059	73.5
James Walker Jr. (D)	39,343	22.2

MASSACHUSETTS

1 Silvio O. Conte (R)	150,748	77.5
John R. Arden (D)	43,611	22.4
2 Richard E. Neal (D)	134,152	99.8
3 Joseph D. Early (D)	150,992	99.4
4 Barney Frank (D)	143,473	65.5
John R. Soto (R)	75,454	34.5
5 Chester G. Atkins (D)	110,232	52.2
John F. MacGovern (R)	101,017	47.8
6 Nicholas Mavroules (D)	149,284	65.0
Edgar L. Kelley (R)	80,177	34.9
7 Edward J. Markey (D)	155,380	99.9
8 Joseph P. Kennedy II (D)	125,479	72.2
Glenn W. Fiscus (R)	39,310	22.6
Susan C. Davies (NA)	8,806	5.1
9 Joe Moakley (D)	124,534	70.3
Robert W. Horan (I)	52,660	29.7
10 Larry E. Studds (D)	137,805	53.4
Jon L. Bryan (R)	120,217	46.6
11 Brian J. Donnelly (D)	145,480	99.7

MICHIGAN

1 John Conyers Jr. (D)	76,556	89.3
Ray Shoulders (R)	7,298	8.5
2 Carl D. Pursell (R)	95,962	64.1
Elmer White (D)	49,678	33.2
3 Howard Wolpe (D)	82,376	57.9
Brad Haskins (R)	60,007	42.1
4 Fred Upton (R)	75,850	57.8
JoAnne McFarland (D)	55,449	42.2
5 Paul B. Henry (R)	126,308	75.4
Thomas Trzybinskl (D)	41,170	24.6
6 Bob Carr (D)	97,547	99.8
7 Dale E. Kildee (D)	90,307	68.4
David J. Morrill (R)	41,759	31.6
8 Bob Traxler (D)	98,903	68.6
James White (R)	45,259	31.4
9 Guy Vander Jagt (R)	89,078	54.8
Geraldine Greene (D)	73,604	45.2
10 Dave Camp (R)	99,952	65.0
Joan Louise Dennison (D)	50,923	33.1
11 Robert W. Davis (R)	94,555	61.3
Marcia Gould (D)	59,759	38.7
12 David E. Bonior (D)	98,232	64.7
Jim Dingeman (R)	51,119	33.7
13 Barbara-Rose Collins (D)	54,345	80.1
Carl R. Edwards Sr. (R)	11,203	16.5
14 Dennis M. Hertel (D)	78,506	63.6
Kenneth C. McNealy (R)	40,499	32.8
15 William D. Ford (D)	68,742	61.2
Burl C. Adkins (R)	41,092	36.6

	Candidates	Votes	%
16	John D. Dingell (D)	88,962	66.6
	Frank Beaumont (R)	42,629	31.9
17	Sander M. Levin (D)	92,205	69.7
	Blaine L. Lankford (R)	40,100	30.3
18	William S. Broomfield (R)	126,629	66.4
	Walter Briggs (D)	64,185	33.6

MINNESOTA[3]

	Candidates	Votes	%
1	Timothy J. Penny (DFL)	156,749	78.1
	Doug Andersen (I-R)	43,856	21.9
2	Vin Weber (I-R)	126,367	61.8
	Jim Stone (DFL)	77,935	38.1
3	Jim Ramstad (I-R)	195,833	66.9
	Lewis DeMars (DFL)	96,395	32.9
4	Bruce F. Vento (DFL)	143,353	64.7
	Ian Maitland (I-R)	77,639	35.1
5	Martin Olav Sabo (DFL)	144,682	72.9
	Raymond C. Gilbertson (I-R)	53,720	27.1
6	Gerry Sikorski (DFL)	164,816	64.6
	Bruce D. Anderson (I-R)	90,138	35.3
7	Collin C. Peterson (DFL)	107,126	53.5
	Arlan Stangeland (I-R)	92,876	46.4
8	James L. Oberstar (DFL)	151,145	72.9
	Jerry Shuster (I-R)	56,068	27.0

MISSISSIPPI

	Candidates	Votes	%
1	Jamie L. Whitten (D)	43,668	64.9
	Bill Bowlin (R)	23,650	35.1
2	Mike Espy (D)	59,393	84.1
	Dorothy Benford (R)	11,224	15.9
3	G.V. "Sonny" Montgomery (D)	49,162	100.0
4	Mike Parker (D)	57,137	80.6
	Jerry "Rev" Parks (R)	13,754	19.4
5	Gene Taylor (D)	89,926	81.4
	Sheila Smith (R)	20,588	18.6

MISSOURI

	Candidates	Votes	%
1	William L. Clay (D)	62,550	60.9
	Wayne G. Piotrowski (R)	40,160	39.1
2	Joan Kelly Horn (D)	94,378	50.0
	Jack Buechner (R)	94,324	50.0
3	Richard A. Gephardt (D)	88,950	56.8
	Malcolm L. Holekamp (R)	67,659	43.2
4	Ike Skelton (D)	105,527	61.8
	David Eyerly (R)	65,095	38.2
5	Alan Wheat (D)	71,890	62.1
	Robert H. Gardner (R)	43,897	37.9
6	E. Thomas Coleman (R)	78,956	51.9
	Bob McClure (D)	73,093	48.1
7	Mel Hancock (R)	83,609	52.1
	Thomas Patrick Deaton (D)	76,725	47.9
8	Bill Emerson (R)	81,452	57.3
	Russ Carnahan (D)	60,751	42.7
9	Harold L. Volkmer (D)	94,156	57.5
	Don Curtis (R)	69,514	42.5

MONTANA

	Candidates	Votes	%
1	Pat Williams (D)	100,409	61.1
	Brad Johnson (R)	63,837	38.9
2	Ron Marlenee (R)	96,449	63.0
	Don Burris (D)	56,739	37.0

NEBRASKA

	Candidates	Votes	%
1	Doug Bereuter (R)	129,654	64.7
	Larry Hall (D)	70,587	35.2
2	Peter Hoagland (D)	111,903	57.9
	Ally Milder (R)	80,845	41.8
3	Bill Barrett (R)	98,607	51.1
	Sandra K. Scofield (D)	94,234	48.8

NEVADA

	Candidates	Votes	%
1	James H. Bilbray (D)	84,650	61.4
	Bob Dickinson (R)	47,377	34.4

	Candidates	Votes	%
2	Barbara F. Vucanovich (R)	103,508	59.1
	Jane Wisdom (D)	59,581	34.0
	Dan Becan (LIBERT)	12,120	6.9

NEW HAMPSHIRE

	Candidates	Votes	%
1	Bill Zeliff (R)	81,684	55.1
	Joseph F. Keefe (D)	66,176	44.6
2	Dick Swett (D)	74,829	52.7
	Chuck Douglas (R)	67,063	47.2

NEW JERSEY

	Candidates	Votes	%
1	Robert E. Andrews (D)	73,522	54.3
	Daniel J. Mangini (R)	57,801	42.7
2	William J. Hughes (D)	98,734	88.2
	William A. Kanengiser (POP)	13,246	11.8
3	Frank Pallone Jr. (D)	77,709	49.1
	Paul A. Kapalko (R)	73,451	46.4
4	Christopher H. Smith (R)	101,508	62.9
	Mark Setaro (D)	55,454	34.4
5	Marge Roukema (R)	118,101	75.7
	Lawrence Wayne Olsen (D)	35,010	22.4
6	Bernard J. Dwyer (D)	63,696	50.5
	Paul Danielczyk (R)	58,209	46.2
7	Matthew J. Rinaldo (R)	100,274	74.6
	Bruce H. Bergen (D)	31,114	23.2
8	Robert A. Roe (D)	55,212	76.9
	Stephen Sibilia (IC)	13,239	18.4
9	Robert G. Torricelli (D)	82,736	57.0
	Peter J. Russo (R)	59,759	41.2
10	Donald M. Payne (D)	42,616	81.5
	Howard E. Berkeley (R)	9,072	17.3
11	Dean A. Gallo (R)	95,198	64.9
	Michael Gordon (D)	47,782	32.6
12	Dick Zimmer (R)	108,173	64.0
	Marguerite Chandler (D)	52,498	31.1
13	H. James Saxton (R)	100,537	58.1
	John H. Adler (D)	68,286	39.5
14	Frank J. Guarini (D)	57,581	66.1
	Fred J. Theemling Jr. (R)	25,473	29.2

Special Election[4]

	Candidates	Votes	%
1	Robert E. Andrews (D)	72,324	55.3
	Daniel J. Mangini (R)	58,671	44.7

NEW MEXICO

	Candidates	Votes	%
1	Steven H. Schiff (R)	97,375	70.2
	Rebecca Vigil-Giron (D)	41,306	29.8
2	Joe Skeen (R)	80,677	100.0
3	Bill Richardson (D)	104,225	74.5
	Phil T. Archuletta (R)	35,751	25.5

NEW YORK

	Candidates	Votes	%
1	George J. Hochbrueckner (D, Tax Break)	75,211	56.3
	Francis W. Creighton (R)	46,380	34.7
	Clayton Baldwin Jr. (C)	6,883	5.2
2	Thomas J. Downey (D)	56,722	55.8
	John W. Bugler (R, RTL, Tax Cut)	36,859	36.2
	Dominic A. Curcio (C)	8,150	8.0
3	Robert J. Mrazek (D, L)	73,029	53.3
	Robert Previdi (R, C)	59,089	43.1
4	Norman F. Lent (R, C)	79,304	61.2
	Francis T. Goban (D)	41,308	31.8
	John J. Dunkle (RTL)	6,706	5.2
5	Raymond J. McGrath (R, C)	71,948	54.6
	Mark S. Epstein (D, L)	53,920	40.9
6	Floyd H. Flake (D, L)	44,306	73.1
	William Sampol (R)	13,224	21.8
	John Cronin (RTL)	3,111	5.1
7	Gary L. Ackerman (D, L)	51,091	100.0
8	James H. Scheuer (D, L)	56,396	72.3
	Gustave Reifenkugel (R)	21,646	27.7
9	Thomas J. Manton (D)	35,177	64.4
	Ann Pfoser Darby (R, AC)	13,330	24.4

	Candidates	Votes	%
	Thomas V. Ognibene (C)	6,137	11.2
10	Charles E. Schumer (D, L)	61,468	80.4
	Patrick J. Kinsella (R, C)	14,963	19.6
11	Edolphus Towns (D, L)	36,286	92.9
12	Major R. Owens (D, L)	40,570	94.9
13	Stephen J. Solarz (D, L)	47,446	80.4
	Edwin Ramos (R, C)	11,557	19.6
14	Susan Molinari (R, C)	58,616	60.0
	Anthony J. Pocchia (D, L, SIS)	34,625	35.5
15	Bill Green (R)	52,919	58.8
	Frances L. Reiter (D)	33,464	37.2
16	Charles B. Rangel (D, R, L)	55,882	97.2
	Alvaader Frazier (NA)	1,592	2.8
17	Ted Weiss (D, L)	79,161	80.4
	William W. Koeppel (R)	15,219	15.5
18	Jose E. Serrano (D, L)	38,024	93.2
19	Eliot L. Engel (D, L)	45,758	61.2
	William J. Gouldman (R)	17,135	22.9
	Kevin Brawley (C, RTL)	11,868	15.9
20	Nita M. Lowey (D)	82,203	62.8
	Glenn D. Belitto (R)	35,575	27.2
	John M. Schafer (C, RTL)	13,030	10.0
21	Hamilton Fish Jr. (R, C)	99,866	71.4
	Richard L. Barbuto (D)	34,128	24.4
22	Benjamin A. Gilman (R)	95,495	68.6
	John G. Dow (D)	37,034	26.6
23	Michael R. McNulty (D, C)	117,239	64.1
	Margaret B. Buhrmaster (R)	65,760	35.9
24	Gerald B. H. Solomon (R, C, RTL)	121,206	68.1
	Bob Lawrence (D)	56,671	31.9
25	Sherwood Boehlert (R)	91,348	83.9
	William L. Griffen (L)	17,481	16.1
26	David O'B. Martin (R, C)	97,340	100.0
27	James T. Walsh (R, C)	95,220	63.2
	Peggy L. Murray (D, L)	52,438	34.8
28	Matthew F. McHugh (D)	97,815	64.8
	Seymour Krieger (R)	53,077	35.2
29	Frank Horton (R)	89,105	63.0
	Alton F. Eber (D)	34,835	24.6
	Peter DeMauro (C)	12,599	8.9
30	Louise M. Slaughter (D)	97,280	59.0
	John M. Regan Jr. (R, C, RTL)	67,534	41.0
31	Bill Paxon (R, C, RTL)	90,237	56.6
	Kevin P. Gaughan (D, L)	69,328	43.4
32	John J. LaFalce (D, L)	68,367	55.0
	Michael T. Waring (R)	39,053	31.4
	Kenneth J. Kowalski (C, RTL)	16,853	13.6
33	Henry J. Nowak (D, L)	84,905	77.5
	Thomas K. Kepfer (R)	18,181	16.6
	Louis P. Corrigan Jr. (C)	6,460	5.9
34	Amo Houghton (R, C)	89,831	69.6
	Joseph P. Leahey (D)	37,421	29.0

Special Elections

	Candidates	Votes	%
14	Susan Molinari (R)[5]	29,336	59.0
	Robert Gigante (D)	17,302	34.8
	Barbara Bollaert (RTL)	2,649	5.3
18	Jose E. Serrano (D, L)[6]	26,928	92.4
	Simeon Golar (R)	2,079	7.1

NORTH CAROLINA

	Candidates	Votes	%
1	Walter B. Jones (D)	105,832	64.8
	Howard Moye (R)	57,526	35.2
2	Tim Valentine (D)	130,979	74.7
	Hal C. Sharpe (R)	44,263	25.3
3	H. Martin Lancaster (D)	83,930	59.3
	Don Davis (R)	57,605	40.7
4	David E. Price (D)	139,396	58.1
	John Carrington (R)	100,661	41.9
5	Stephen L. Neal (D)	113,814	59.1
	Ken Bell (R)	78,747	40.9
6	Howard Coble (R)	125,392	66.6
	Helen R. Allegrone (D)	62,913	33.4
7	Charlie Rose (D)	94,946	65.6
	Robert C. Anderson (R)	49,681	34.4
8	W. G. "Bill" Hefner (D)	98,700	55.0
	Ted Blanton (R)	80,852	45.0

Candidates	Votes	%
9 Alex McMillan (R)	131,936	62.0
David P. McKnight (D)	80,802	38.0
10 Cass Ballenger (R)	106,400	61.8
Daniel R. Green Jr. (D)	65,710	38.2
11 Charles H. Taylor (R)	101,991	50.7
James McClure Clarke (D)	99,318	49.3

NORTH DAKOTA

Candidates	Votes	%
AL Byron L. Dorgan (D)	152,530	65.2
Edward T. Schafer (R)	81,443	34.8

OHIO

Candidates	Votes	%
1 Charles Luken (D)	83,932	51.1
J. Kenneth Blackwell (R)	80,362	48.9
2 Bill Gradison (R)	103,817	64.4
Tyrone K. Yates (D)	57,345	35.6
3 Tony P. Hall (D)	116,797	100.0
4 Michael G. Oxley (R)	103,897	61.7
Thomas E. Burkhart (D)	64,467	38.3
5 Paul E. Gillmor (R)	113,615	68.5
P. Scott Mange (D)	41,693	25.1
John E. Jackson (I)	10,612	6.4
6 Bob McEwen (R)	117,220	71.2
Ray Mitchell (D)	47,415	28.8
7 David L. Hobson (R)	97,123	62.1
Jack Schira (D)	59,349	37.9
8 John A. Boehner (R)	99,955	61.1
Gregory V. Jolivette (D)	63,584	38.9
9 Marcy Kaptur (D)	117,681	77.7
Jerry D. Lammers (R)	33,791	22.3
10 Clarence E. Miller (R)	106,009	63.2
John M. Buchanan (D)	61,656	36.8
11 Dennis E. Eckart (D)	111,923	65.7
Margaret Mueller (R)	58,372	34.3
12 John R. Kasich (R)	130,495	72.0
Mike Gelpi (D)	50,784	28.0
13 Don J. Pease (D)	93,431	56.7
William D. Nielsen (R)	60,925	36.9
John Michael Ryan (I)	10,506	6.4
14 Thomas C. Sawyer (D)	97,875	59.6
Jean E. Bender (R)	66,460	40.4
15 Chalmers P. Wylie (R)	99,251	59.1
Thomas V. Erney (D)	68,510	40.8
16 Ralph Regula (R)	101,097	58.9
Warner D. Mendenhall (D)	70,516	41.1
17 James A. Traficant Jr. (D)	133,207	77.7
Robert R. DeJulio Jr. (R)	38,199	22.3
18 Douglas Applegate (D)	120,782	74.3
John A. Hales (R)	41,823	25.7
19 Edward F. Feighan (D)	132,951	64.8
Susan M. Lawko (R)	72,315	35.2
20 Mary Rose Oakar (D)	109,390	73.3
Bill Smith (R)	39,749	26.7
21 Louis Stokes (D)	103,338	80.0
Franklin H. Roski (R)	25,906	20.0

OKLAHOMA

Candidates	Votes	%
1 James M. Inhofe (R)	75,618	56.0
Kurt Glassco (D)	59,521	44.0
2 Mike Synar (D)	90,820	61.3
Terry M. Gorham (R)	57,331	38.7
3 Bill Brewster (D)	107,641	80.4
Patrick K. Miller (R)	26,261	19.6
4 Dave McCurdy (D)	100,879	73.6
Howard Bell (R)	36,232	26.4
5 Mickey Edwards (R)	114,608	69.6
Bryce Baggett (D)	50,086	30.4
6 Glenn English (D)	110,100	80.0
Robert Burns (R)	27,540	20.0

OREGON

Candidates	Votes	%
1 Les AuCoin (D)	150,292	63.1
Earl Molander (R)	72,382	30.4
Rick Livingston (I)	15,585	6.5
2 Robert F. Smith (R)	127,998	68.0
Jim Smiley (D)	60,131	32.0
3 Ron Wyden (D)	169,731	80.8
Philip E. Mooney (R)	40,216	19.1
4 Peter A. DeFazio (D)	162,494	85.8
Tonie Nathan (LIBERT)	26,432	14.0
5 Mike Kopetski (D)	124,610	55.0
Denny Smith (R)	101,650	44.9

PENNSYLVANIA

Candidates	Votes	%
1 Thomas M. Foglietta (D)	73,423	79.4
James Love Jackson (R)	19,018	20.6
2 William H. Gray III (D)	94,584	92.1
Donald Bakove (R)	8,118	7.9
3 Robert A. Borski (D)	89,908	60.0
Joseph Marc McColgan (R)	59,901	40.0
4 Joe Kolter (D)	74,114	55.9
Gordon R. Johnston (R)	58,469	44.1
5 Richard T. Schulze (R)	75,097	57.1
Samuel C. Stretton (D)	50,597	38.5
6 Gus Yatron (D)	74,394	57.0
John F. Hicks (R)	56,093	43.0
7 Curt Weldon (R)	105,868	65.3
John Innelli (D)	56,292	34.7
8 Peter H. Kostmayer (D)	85,015	56.6
Audrie Zettick Schaller (R)	65,100	43.4
9 Bud Shuster (R, D)	106,632	100.0
10 Joseph M. McDade (R, D)	113,490	100.0
11 Paul E. Kanjorski (D)	88,219	100.0
12 John P. Murtha (D)	80,686	61.7
William Choby (R)	50,007	38.3
13 Lawrence Coughlin (R)	89,577	60.3
Bernard Tomkin (D)	58,967	39.7
14 William J. Coyne (D)	77,636	71.8
Richard Edward Caligiuri (R)	30,497	28.2
15 Don Ritter (R)	77,178	60.6
Richard J. Orloski (D)	50,233	39.4
16 Robert S. Walker (R)	85,596	66.1
Ernest Eric Guyll (D)	43,849	33.9
17 George W. Gekas (R, D)	110,317	100.0
18 Rick Santorum (R)	85,697	51.4
Doug Walgren (D)	80,880	48.6
19 Bill Goodling (R)	96,336	100.0
20 Joseph M. Gaydos (D)	82,080	65.6
Robert C. Lee (R)	43,054	34.4
21 Tom Ridge (R)	92,732	100.0
22 Austin J. Murphy (D)	78,375	63.3
Suzanne Hayden (R)	45,509	36.7
23 William F. Clinger Jr. (R)	78,189	59.4
Daniel J. Shannon (D)	53,465	40.6

RHODE ISLAND

Candidates	Votes	%
1 Ronald K. Machtley (R)	89,963	55.2
Scott Wolf (D)	73,131	44.8
2 Jack Reed (D)	108,818	59.2
Gertrude M. "Trudy" Coxe (R)	74,953	40.8

SOUTH CAROLINA

Candidates	Votes	%
1 Arthur Ravenel Jr. (R)	80,839	65.5
Eugene Platt (D)	42,555	34.5
2 Floyd D. Spence (R)	90,054	88.7
Geb Sommer (LIBERT)	11,101	10.9
3 Butler Derrick (D)	72,561	58.0
Ray Haskett (R)	52,419	41.9
4 Liz J. Patterson (D)	81,927	61.4
Terry E. Haskins (R)	51,338	38.4
5 John M. Spratt Jr. (D)	91,775	99.9
6 Robin Tallon (D)	94,121	99.6

SOUTH DAKOTA

Candidates	Votes	%
AL Tim Johnson (D)	173,814	67.6
Don Frankenfeld (R)	83,484	32.4

TENNESSEE

Candidates	Votes	%
1 James H. Quillen (R)	47,796	99.9
2 John J. Duncan (R)	62,797	80.6
Peter Hebert (I)	15,127	19.4
3 Marilyn Lloyd (D)	49,662	53.0
Grady L. Rhoden (R)	36,855	39.3
Peter T. Melcher (I)	5,598	6.0
4 Jim Cooper (D)	52,101	67.4
Claiborne "Clay" Sanders (R)	22,890	29.6
5 Bob Clement (D)	55,607	72.4
Tom Stone (I)	13,577	17.7
Al Borgman (I)	5,383	7.0
6 Bart Gordon (D)	60,538	66.7
Gregory Cochran (R)	26,424	29.1
7 Don Sundquist (R)	66,141	62.0
Ken Bloodworth (D)	40,516	38.0
8 John Tanner (D)	62,241	100.0
9 Harold E. Ford (D)	48,629	58.1
Aaron C. Davis (R)	25,730	30.8
Thomas M. Davidson (I)	7,249	8.7

TEXAS

Candidates	Votes	%
1 Jim Chapman (D)	89,241	61.0
Hamp Hodges (R)	56,954	39.0
2 Charles Wilson (D)	76,974	55.6
Donna Peterson (R)	61,555	44.4
3 Steve Bartlett (R)	153,857	99.6
4 Ralph M. Hall (D)	108,300	99.6
5 John Bryant (D)	65,228	59.6
Jerry Rucker (R)	41,307	37.7
6 Joe L. Barton (R)	125,049	66.5
John E. Welch (D)	62,344	33.1
7 Bill Archer (R)	114,254	100.0
8 Jack Fields (R)	60,603	100.0
9 Jack Brooks (D)	79,786	57.7
Maury Meyers (R)	58,399	42.3
10 J. J. "Jake" Pickle (D)	152,784	64.9
David Beilharz (R)	73,766	31.3
11 Chet Edwards (D)	73,810	53.5
Hugh D. Shine (R)	64,269	46.5
12 Pete Geren (D)	98,026	71.3
Mike McGinn (R)	39,438	28.7
13 Bill Sarpalius (D)	81,815	56.5
Dick Waterfield (R)	63,045	43.5
14 Greg H. Laughlin (D)	89,251	54.3
Joe Dial (R)	75,098	45.7
15 E. "Kika" de la Garza (D)	72,461	100.0
16 Ronald D. Coleman (D)	62,455	95.6
17 Charles W. Stenholm (D)	104,100	100.0
18 Craig Washington (D)	54,477	99.6
19 Larry Combest (D)	83,795	100.0
20 Henry B. Gonzalez (D)	56,318	100.0
21 Lamar Smith (R)	144,570	74.8
Kirby J. Roberts (D)	48,585	25.2
22 Thomas D. DeLay (R)	93,425	71.2
Bruce Director (D)	37,721	28.8
23 Albert G. Bustamante (D)	71,052	63.5
Jerome L. Gonzales (R)	40,856	36.5
24 Martin Frost (D)	86,297	100.0
25 Michael A. Andrews (D)	67,427	100.0
26 Dick Armey (R)	147,856	70.4
John Wayne Caton (D)	62,158	29.6
27 Solomon P. Ortiz (D)	62,822	100.0

UTAH

Candidates	Votes	%
1 James V. Hansen (R)	82,746	52.1
Kenley Brunsdale (D)	69,491	43.8
2 Wayne Owens (D)	85,167	57.6
Genevieve Atwood (R)	58,869	39.8
3 Bill Orton (D)	79,163	58.3
Karl Snow (R)	49,452	36.4

VERMONT

Candidates	Votes	%
AL Bernard Sanders (I)	117,522	56.0
Peter Smith (R)	82,938	39.5

VIRGINIA

Candidates	Votes	%
1 Herbert H. Bateman (R)	72,000	51.0
Andrew H. Fox (D)	69,194	49.0

	Candidates	Votes	%
2	Owen B. Pickett (D)	55,179	75.0
	Harry G. Broskie (I)	15,915	21.6
3	Thomas J. Bliley Jr. (R)	77,125	65.3
	Jay Starke (D)	36,253	30.7
4	Norman Sisisky (D)	71,051	78.3
	Don L. Reynolds (I)	12,295	13.6
	Loretta F. Chandler (I)	7,102	7.8
5	Lewis F. Payne Jr. (D)	66,532	99.4
6	Jim Olin (D)	92,968	82.7
	Gerald E. Berg (I)	18,148	16.1
7	D. French Slaughter Jr. (R)	81,688	58.1
	David M. Smith (D)	58,684	41.7
8	James P. Moran Jr. (D)	88,475	51.7
	Stan Parris (R)	76,367	44.6
9	Rick Boucher (D)	67,215	97.1
10	Frank R. Wolf (R)	103,761	61.5
	N. MacKenzie Canter III (D)	57,249	33.9

WASHINGTON

	Candidates	Votes	%
1	John R. Miller (R)	100,339	52.0
	Cynthia Sullivan (D)	92,447	48.0
2	Al Swift (D)	92,837	50.5
	Doug Smith (R)	75,669	41.2

	Candidates	Votes	%
	William L. McCord (LIBERT)	15,165	8.3
3	Jolene Unsoeld (D)	95,645	53.8
	Bob Williams (R)	82,269	46.2
4	Sid Morrison (R)	106,545	70.7
	Ole Hougen (D)	44,241	29.3
5	Thomas S. Foley (D)	110,234	68.8
	Marlyn A. Derby (R)	49,965	31.2
6	Norm Dicks (D)	79,079	61.4
	Norbert Mueller (R)	49,786	38.6
7	Jim McDermott (D)	106,761	72.3
	Larry Penberthy (R)	35,511	24.1
8	Rod Chandler (R)	96,323	56.2
	David E. Giles (D)	75,031	43,8

WEST VIRGINIA

		Votes	%
1	Alan B. Mollohan (D)	72,849	67.1
	Howard K. Tuck (R)	35,657	32.9
2	Harley O. Staggers Jr. (D)	63,174	55.5
	Oliver Luck (R)	50,708	44.5
3	Bob Wise (D)	75,327	100.0
4	Nick J. Rahall II (D)	39,948	52.0
	Marianne R. Brewster (R)	36,946	48.0

WISCONSIN

	Candidates	Votes	%
1	Les Aspin (D)	93,961	99.4
2	Scott L. Klug (R)	96,938	53.2
	Robert W. Kastenmeier (D)	85,156	46.8
3	Steve Gunderson (R)	94,509	61.0
	James L. Ziegeweid (D)	60,409	39.0
4	Gerald D. Kleczka (D)	96,981	69.2
	Joseph L. Cook (R)	43,001	30.7
5	Jim Moody (D)	77,557	68.0
	Donalda Hammersmith (R)	31,255	27.4
6	Thomas E. Petri (R)	111,036	99.5
7	David R. Obey (D)	100,069	62.1
	John L. McEwen (R)	60,961	37.9
8	Toby Roth (R)	95,902	53.5
	Jerome Van Sistine (D)	83,199	46.4
9	F. James Sensenbrenner Jr. (R)	117,967	99.7

WYOMING

		Votes	%
AL	Craig Thomas (R)	87,078	55.1
	Pete Maxfield (D)	70,977	44.9

1. A special election was held to fill the unexpired term of Rep. Daniel K. Akaka (D), who resigned May 16, 1990, having been appointed to the U.S. Senate.

2. For the 1990 House elections in Louisiana, an open primary election was held with candidates from all parties running on the same ballot. Any candidate who received a majority was elected unopposed, with no further appearance on the general election ballot. If no candidate received 50 percent, a runoff was held between the two top finishers.

3. In Minnesota the Democratic Party is known as the Democratic-Farmer-Labor Party and the Republican Party as the Independent-Republican Party; candidates appear on the ballot with these designations.

4. A special election was held to fill the unexpired term of Rep. James J. Florio (D), who resigned Jan. 16, 1990, having been elected governor.

5. A special election was held to fill the unexpired term of Rep. Guy V. Molinari (R), who resigned Jan. 1, 1990.

6. A special election was held to fill the unexpired term of Rep. Robert Garcia (D), who resigned Jan. 7, 1990.

1991 House Elections

ARIZONA

Special Election[1]

	Candidates	Votes	%
2	Ed Pastor (D)	32,289	55.5
	Pat Conner (R)	25,814	44.4

ILLINOIS

Special Election[2]

		Votes	%
15	Thomas W. Ewing (R)	25,675	66.4
	Gerald Bradley (D)	13,011	33.6

MASSACHUSETTS

Special Election[3]

	Candidates	Votes	%
1	John Olver (D)	70,022	49.6
	Steven D. Pierce (R)	68,052	48.2

PENNSYLVANIA

Special Election[4]

		Votes	%
2	Lucien E. Blackwell (D)	51,820	39.2
	Chaka Fattah (D)	37,068	28.0
	John F. White Jr. (D)	36,469	27.6
	Nadine G. Smith-Bulford (R)	6,928	5.2

TEXAS

Special Election[5]

	Candidates	Votes	%
3	Sam Johnson (R)	24,004	52.6
	Tom Pauken (R)	21,647	47.4

VIRGINIA

Special Election[6]

		Votes	%
7	George F. Allen (R)	106,745	62.0
	Kay Slaughter (D)	59,655	34.7

1. A special election was held to fill the unexpired term of Rep. Morris K. Udall (D), who resigned May 4, 1991.

2. A special election was held to fill the unexpired term of Rep. Edward R. Madigan (R), who resigned March 8, 1991, having been appointed agriculture secretary.

3. A special election was held to fill the unexpired term of Rep. Silvio O. Conte (R), who died Feb. 8, 1991.

4. A special election was held to fill the unexpired term of Rep. William H. Gray III (D), who resigned Sept. 11, 1991.

5. A special election was held to fill the unexpired term of Rep. Steve Bartlett (R), who resigned March 11, 1991.

6. A special election was held to fill the unexpired term of Rep. D. French Slaughter Jr. (R), who resigned Nov. 5, 1991.

1992 House Elections

ALABAMA

	Candidates	Votes	%
1	Sonny Callahan (R)	128,874	60.2
	William A. Brewer (D)	78,742	36.8
2	Terry Everett (R)	112,906	49.5
	George C. Wallace Jr. (D)	109,335	47.9
3	Glen Browder (D)	119,175	60.3
	Don Sledge (R)	73,800	37.4
4	Tom Bevill (D)	157,907	68.5
	Mickey Strickland (R)	66,934	29.0
5	Robert E. "Bud" Cramer (D)	160,060	65.6
	Terry Smith (R)	77,951	31.9
6	Spencer Bachus (R)	146,599	52.4
	Ben Erdreich (D)	126,062	45.0
7	Earl F. Hilliard (D)	144,320	69.5
	Kervin Jones (R)	36,086	17.4
	James M. Lewis (I)	12,461	6.0
	James Chambliss (I)	11,466	5.5

ALASKA

	Candidates	Votes	%
AL	Don Young (R)	111,849	46.8
	John E. Devens (D)	102,378	42.8
	Michael A. States (ALI)	15,049	6.3

ARIZONA

	Candidates	Votes	%
1	Sam Coppersmith (D)	130,715	51.3
	John J. Rhodes III (R)	113,613	44.6
2	Ed Pastor (D)	90,693	66.0
	Don Shooter (R)	41,257	30.0
3	Bob Stump (R)	158,906	61.5
	Roger Hartstone (D)	88,830	34.4
4	Jon Kyl (R)	156,330	59.2
	Walter R. Mybeck II (D)	70,572	26.7
	Debbie Collings (I)	25,553	9.7
5	Jim Kolbe (R)	172,867	66.5
	Jim Toevs (D)	77,256	29.7
6	Karan English (D)	124,251	53.0
	Doug Wead (R)	97,074	41.4
	Sarah Stannard (I)	13,047	5.6

ARKANSAS

	Candidates	Votes	%
1	Blanche Lambert (D)	149,558	69.8
	Terry Hayes (R)	64,618	30.2
2	Ray Thornton (D)	154,946	74.2
	Dennis Scott (R)	53,978	25.8
3	Tim Hutchinson (R)	125,295	50.2
	John VanWinkle (D)	117,775	47.2
4	Jay Dickey (R)	113,009	52.3
	W. J. "Bill" McCuen (D)	102,918	47.7

CALIFORNIA

	Candidates	Votes	%
1	Dan Hamburg (D)	119,676	47.6
	Frank Riggs (R)	113,266	45.1
2	Wally Herger (R)	167,247	65.2
	Elliot Roy Freedman (D)	71,780	28.0
	Harry H. Pendery (LIBERT)	17,529	6.8
3	Vic Fazio (D)	122,149	51.2
	H. L. "Bill" Richardson (R)	96,092	40.3
	Ross Crain (LIBERT)	20,444	8.6
4	John T. Doolittle (R)	141,155	49.8
	Patricia Malberg (D)	129,489	45.7
5	Robert T. Matsui (D)	158,250	68.6
	Robert S. Dinsmore (R)	58,698	25.5
6	Lynn Woolsey (D)	190,322	65.2
	Bill Filante (R)	98,171	33.6
7	George Miller (D)	153,320	70.3
	Dave Scholl (R)	54,822	25.1
8	Nancy Pelosi (D)	191,906	82.5
	Marc Wolin (R)	25,693	11.0
9	Ronald V. Dellums (D)	164,265	71.9
	G. William Hunter (R)	53,707	23.5

	Candidates	Votes	%
10	Bill Baker (R)	145,702	52.0
	Wendell H. Williams (D)	134,635	48.0
11	Richard W. Pombo (R)	94,453	47.6
	Patricia Garamendi (D)	90,539	45.6
	Christine Roberts (LIBERT)	13,498	6.8
12	Tom Lantos (D)	157,205	68.8
	Jim Tomlin (R)	53,278	23.3
13	Pete Stark (D)	123,795	60.2
	Verne Teyler (R)	64,953	31.6
	Roslyn A. Allen (PFP)	16,768	8.2
14	Anna G. Eshoo (D)	146,873	56.7
	Tom Huening (R)	101,202	39.0
15	Norman Y. Mineta (D)	168,617	63.5
	Robert Wick (R)	82,875	31.2
	Duggan Dieterly (LIBERT)	13,293	5.0
16	Don Edwards (D)	96,661	62.0
	Ted Bundesen (R)	49,843	32.0
	Amani S. Kuumba (PFP)	9,370	6.0
17	Leon E. Panetta (D)	151,565	72.0
	Bill McCampbell (R)	49,947	23.7
18	Gary Condit (D)	139,704	84.7
	Kim R. Almstrom (LIBERT)	25,307	15.3
19	Richard H. Lehman (D)	101,619	46.9
	Tal L. Cloud (R)	100,590	46.4
	Dorothy L. Wells (PFP)	13,334	6.2
20	Calvin Dooley (D)	72,679	64.9
	Ed Hunt (R)	39,388	35.1
21	William M. Thomas (R)	127,758	65.2
	Deborah A. Vollmer (D)	68,058	34.7
22	Michael Huffington (R)	131,242	52.5
	Gloria Ochoa (D)	87,328	34.9
	Mindy Lorenz (GREEN)	23,699	9.5
23	Elton Gallegly (R)	115,504	54.3
	Anita Perez Ferguson (D)	88,225	41.4
24	Anthony C. Beilenson (D)	141,742	55.5
	Tom McClintock (R)	99,835	39.1
	John Paul Lindblad (PFP)	13,690	5.4
25	Howard P. "Buck" McKeon (R)	113,611	51.9
	James H. "Gil" Gilmartin (D)	72,233	33.0
	Rick Pamplin (I)	13,930	6.4
26	Howard L. Berman (D)	73,807	61.0
	Gary Forsch (R)	36,453	30.1
	Margery Hinds (PFP)	7,180	5.9
27	Carlos J. Moorhead (R)	105,521	49.7
	Doug Kahn (D)	83,805	39.4
	Jesse A. Moorman (GREEN)	11,003	5.2
28	David Dreier (R)	122,353	58.4
	Al Wachtel (D)	76,525	36.5
29	Henry A. Waxman (D)	160,312	61.3
	Mark A. Robbins (R)	67,141	25.7
	David Davis (I)	15,445	5.9
	Susan C. Davies (PFP)	13,888	5.3
30	Xavier Becerra (D)	48,800	58.4
	Morry Waksberg (R)	20,034	24.0
	Blase Bonpane (GREEN)	6,315	7.6
	Elizabeth A. Nakano (PFP)	6,173	7.4
31	Matthew G. Martinez (D)	68,324	62.6
	Reuben D. Franco (R)	40,873	37.4
32	Julian C. Dixon (D)	150,644	87.2
	Bob Weber (LIBERT)	12,384	7.2
	William R. Williams (PFP)	9,782	5.7
33	Lucille Roybal-Allard (D)	32,010	63.0
	Robert Guzman (R)	15,428	30.4
34	Esteban E. Torres (D)	91,738	61.3
	J. "Jay" Hernandez (R)	50,907	34.0
35	Maxine Waters (D)	102,941	82.5
	Nate Truman (R)	17,417	14.0
36	Jane Harman (D)	125,751	48.4
	Joan Milke Flores (R)	109,684	42.2
	Richard H. Greene (GREEN)	13,297	5.1
37	Walter R. Tucker (D)	97,159	85.7
	B. Kwaku Duren (PFP)	16,178	14.3
38	Steve Horn (R)	92,038	48.6
	Evan Anderson Braude (D)	82,108	43.4
39	Ed Royce (R)	122,472	57.3

	Candidates	Votes	%
	Molly McClanahan (D)	81,728	38.2
40	Jerry Lewis (R)	129,563	63.1
	Donald M. Rusk (D)	63,881	31.1
	Margie Akin (PFP)	11,839	5.8
41	Jay C. Kim (R)	101,753	59.6
	Bob Baker (D)	58,777	34.4
	Mike Noonan (PFP)	10,136	5.9
42	George E. Brown Jr. (D)	79,780	50.7
	Dick Rutan (R)	69,251	44.0
	Fritz R. Ward (LIBERT)	8,424	5.4
43	Ken Calvert (R)	88,987	46.7
	Mark A. Takano (D)	88,468	46.4
44	Al McCandless (R)	110,333	54.2
	Georgia Smith (D)	81,693	40.1
	Phil Turner (LIBERT)	11,515	5.7
45	Dana Rohrabacher (R)	123,731	54.5
	Patricia McCabe (D)	88,508	39.0
	Gary D. Copeland (LIBERT)	14,777	6.5
46	Robert K. Dornan (R)	55,659	50.2
	Robert John Banuelos (D)	45,435	41.0
	Richard G. Newhouse (LIBERT)	9,712	8.8
47	C. Christopher Cox (R)	165,004	64.9
	John F. Anwiler (D)	76,924	30.3
48	Ron Packard (R)	140,935	61.1
	Michael Farber (D)	67,415	29.2
	Donna White (PFP)	13,396	5.8
49	Lynn Schenk (D)	127,280	51.1
	Judy Jarvis (R)	106,170	42.7
50	Bob Filner (D)	77,293	56.6
	Tony Valencia (R)	39,531	28.9
	Barbara Hutchinson (LIBERT)	15,489	11.3
51	Randy "Duke" Cunningham (R)	141,890	56.1
	Bea Herbert (D)	85,148	33.7
52	Duncan Hunter (R)	112,995	52.9
	Janet M. Gastil (D)	88,076	41.2

COLORADO

	Candidates	Votes	%
1	Patricia Schroeder (D)	156,629	68.8
	Raymond Diaz Aragon (R)	70,902	31.2
2	David E. Skaggs (D)	164,790	60.7
	Bryan Day (R)	88,470	32.6
	Vern Tharp (AGA)	18,101	6.7
3	Scott McInnis (R)	143,293	54.7
	Mike Callihan (D)	114,480	43.7
4	Wayne Allard (R)	139,884	57.8
	Tom Redder (D)	101,957	42.2
5	Joel Hefley (R)	173,096	71.1
	Charles A. Oriez (D)	62,550	25.7
6	Dan Schaefer (R)	142,021	60.9
	Tom Kolbe (D)	91,073	39.1

CONNECTICUT

	Candidates	Votes	%
1	Barbara B. Kennelly (D, ACP)	164,735	67.1
	Philip L. Steele (R)	75,113	30.6
2	Sam Gejdenson (D, ACP)	123,291	50.8
	Edward W. Munster (R)	119,416	49.2
3	Rosa DeLauro (D, ACP)	162,568	65.7
	Thomas Scott (R)	84,952	34.3
4	Christopher Shays (R)	147,816	67.3
	Dave Schropfer (D)	58,666	26.7
	Al Smith (ACP)	11,679	5.3
5	Gary Franks (R)	104,891	43.7
	James J. Lawlor (D)	74,791	31.1
	Lynn H. Taborsak (ACP)	54,022	22.5
6	Nancy L. Johnson (R)	166,967	69.7
	Eugene F. Slason (D)	60,373	25.2

DELAWARE

	Candidates	Votes	%
AL	Michael N. Castle (R)	153,037	55.4
	S. B. Woo (D)	117,426	42.5

FLORIDA

	Candidates	Votes	%
1	Earl Hutto (D)	118,941	52.0
	Terry Ketchel (R)	100,349	43.9
2	Pete Peterson (D)	167,215	73.4
	Ray Wagner (R)	60,425	26.5
3	Corrine Brown (D)	91,915	59.3
	Don Weidner (R)	63,115	40.7
4	Tillie Fowler (R)	135,883	56.7
	Mattox Hair (D)	103,531	43.2
5	Karen L. Thurman (D)	129,698	49.2
	Tom Hogan (R)	114,356	43.4
	Cindy Munkittrick (I)	19,462	7.4
6	Cliff Stearns (R)	144,195	65.4
	Phil Denton (D)	76,419	34.6
7	John L. Mica (R)	125,823	56.4
	Dan Webster (D)	96,945	43.5
8	Bill McCollum (R)	141,977	68.5
	Chuck Kovaleski (D)	65,145	31.5
9	Michael Bilirakis (R)	158,028	58.9
	Cheryl Davis Knapp (D)	110,135	41.1
10	C. W. Bill Young (R)	149,606	56.6
	Karen Moffitt (D)	114,809	43.4
11	Sam Gibbons (D)	100,984	52.8
	Mark Sharpe (R)	77,640	40.6
	Joe De Minico (I)	12,730	6.7
12	Charles T. Canady (R)	100,484	52.1
	Tom Mims (D)	92,346	47.9
13	Dan Miller (R)	158,881	57.8
	Rand Snell (D)	115,767	42.2
14	Porter J. Goss (R)	220,351	82.1
	James H. King (I)	48,160	17.9
15	Jim Bacchus (D)	132,412	50.7
	Bill Tolley (R)	128,873	49.3
16	Tom Lewis (R)	157,322	60.8
	John P. Comerford (D)	101,237	39.2
17	Carrie Meek (D)	102,784	100.0
18	Ileana Ros-Lehtinen (R)	104,755	66.8
	Magda Montiel Davis (D)	52,142	33.2
19	Harry A. Johnston (D)	177,423	63.1
	Larry Metz (R)	103,867	36.9
20	Peter Deutsch (D)	130,959	55.1
	Beverly Kennedy (R)	91,589	38.5
	James M. Blackburn (I)	15,341	6.4
21	Lincoln Diaz-Balart (R)		100.0
22	E. Clay Shaw Jr. (R)	128,400	52.0
	Gwen Margolis (D)	91,625	37.1
	Richard "Even" Stephens (I)	15,469	6.3
23	Alcee L. Hastings (D)	84,249	58.5
	Ed Fielding (R)	44,807	31.1
	Al Woods (I)	14,879	10.3

GEORGIA

	Candidates	Votes	%
1	Jack Kingston (R)	103,932	57.8
	Barbara Christmas (D)	75,808	42.2
2	Sanford Bishop (D)	95,789	63.7
	Jim Dudley (R)	54,593	36.3
3	Mac Collins (R)	114,107	54.8
	Richard Ray (D)	94,271	45.2
4	John Linder (R)	126,495	50.5
	Cathey Steinberg (D)	123,819	49.5
5	John Lewis (D)	147,445	72.1
	Paul R. Stabler (R)	56,960	27.9
6	Newt Gingrich (R)	158,761	57.7
	Tony Center (D)	116,196	42.3
7	George "Buddy" Darden (D)	111,374	57.3
	Al Beverly (R)	82,915	42.7
8	J. Roy Rowland (D)	108,472	55.7
	Bob Cunningham (R)	86,220	44.3
9	Nathan Deal (D)	113,024	59.2
	Daniel Becker (R)	77,919	40.8
10	Don Johnson (D)	108,426	53.8
	Ralph T. Hudgens (R)	93,059	46.2
11	Cynthia McKinney (D)	120,168	73.1
	Woodrow Lovett (R)	44,221	26.9

HAWAII

	Candidates	Votes	%
1	Neil Abercrombie (D)	129,332	72.9
	Warner C. Kimo Sutton (R)	41,575	23.4
2	Patsy T. Mink (D)	131,454	72.6
	Kamuela Price (R)	40,070	22.1
	Lloyd "Jeff" Mallan (LIBERT)	9,431	5.2

IDAHO

	Candidates	Votes	%
1	Larry LaRocco (D)	140,985	58.1
	Rachel S. Gilbert (R)	90,983	37.5
2	Michael D. Crapo (R)	139,783	60.8
	J. D. Williams (D)	81,450	35.4

ILLINOIS

	Candidates	Votes	%
1	Bobby L. Rush (D)	209,258	82.8
	Jay Walker (R)	43,453	17.2
2	Mel Reynolds (D)	182,614	78.1
	Ron Blackstone (R)	31,957	13.7
	Louanner Peters (I)	19,293	8.2
3	William O. Lipinski (D)	162,165	63.5
	Harry C. Lepinske (R)	93,128	36.5
4	Luis V. Gutierrez (D)	90,452	77.6
	Hildegarde Rodriguez-Schieman (R)	26,154	22.4
5	Dan Rostenkowski (D)	132,889	57.3
	Elias R. Zenkich (R)	90,738	39.1
6	Henry J. Hyde (R)	165,009	65.5
	Barry W. Watkins (D)	86,891	34.5
7	Cardiss Collins (D)	182,811	81.1
	Norman G. Boccio (R)	35,346	15.7
8	Philip M. Crane (R)	132,887	55.7
	Sheila A. Smith (D)	96,419	40.4
9	Sidney R. Yates (D)	162,942	68.0
	Herbert Sohn (R)	64,760	27.0
	Sheila A. Jones (ECR)	12,001	5.0
10	John Edward Porter (R)	155,230	64.5
	Michael J. Kennedy (D)	85,400	35.5
11	George E. Sangmeister (D)	135,387	55.7
	Robert T. Herbolsheimer (R)	107,860	44.3
12	Jerry F. Costello (D)	168,762	71.2
	Mike Starr (R)	68,115	28.8
13	Harris W. Fawell (R)	179,257	68.4
	Dennis Michael Temple (D)	82,985	31.6
14	Dennis Hastert (R)	155,271	67.3
	Jonathan Abram Reich (D)	75,294	32.6
15	Thomas W. Ewing (R)	142,167	59.3
	Charles D. Mattis (D)	97,190	40.6
16	Donald Manzullo (R)	142,388	55.6
	John W. Cox Jr. (D)	113,555	44.4
17	Lane Evans (D)	156,233	60.1
	Ken Schloemer (R)	103,719	39.9
18	Robert H. Michel (R)	156,533	57.8
	Ronald C. Hawkins (D)	114,413	42.2
19	Glenn Poshard (D)	187,156	69.1
	Douglas E. Lee (R)	83,526	30.9
20	Richard J. Durbin (D)	154,869	56.5
	John M. Shimkus (R)	119,219	43.5

INDIANA

	Candidates	Votes	%
1	Peter J. Visclosky (D)	147,054	69.4
	David J. Vucich (R)	64,770	30.6
2	Philip R. Sharp (D)	130,881	57.1
	William G. Frazier (R)	90,593	39.5
3	Tim Roemer (D)	121,269	57.4
	Carl H. Baxmeyer (R)	89,834	42.6
4	Jill Long (D)	134,907	62.1
	Charles W. Pierson (R)	82,468	37.9
5	Steve Buyer (R)	112,492	51.0
	Jim Jontz (D)	107,973	49.0
6	Dan Burton (R)	186,499	72.2
	Natalie M. Bruner (D)	71,952	27.8
7	John T. Myers (R)	129,189	59.5
	Ellen E. Wedum (D)	88,005	40.5
8	Frank McCloskey (D)	125,244	52.5
	Richard E. Mourdock (R)	108,054	45.3

	Candidates	Votes	%
9	Lee H. Hamilton (D)	160,980	69.7
	Michael E. Bailey (R)	70,057	30.3
10	Andrew Jacobs Jr. (D)	117,604	64.0
	Janos Horvath (R)	64,378	35.0

IOWA

	Candidates	Votes	%
1	Jim Leach (R)	178,042	68.1
	Jan J. Zonneveld (D)	81,600	31.2
2	Jim Nussle (R)	134,536	50.2
	David R. Nagle (D)	131,570	49.1
3	Jim Ross Lightfoot (R)	125,931	48.9
	Elaine Baxter (D)	121,063	47.1
4	Neal Smith (D)	158,610	61.6
	Paul Lunde (R)	94,045	36.5
5	Fred Grandy (R)	196,942	99.3

KANSAS

	Candidates	Votes	%
1	Pat Roberts (R)	194,912	68.3
	Duane West (D)	83,620	29.3
2	Jim Slattery (D)	151,019	56.2
	Jim Van Slyke (R)	109,801	40.8
3	Jan Meyers (R)	169,929	58.0
	Tom Love (D)	110,076	37.6
4	Dan Glickman (D)	143,671	51.7
	Eric R. Yost (R)	117,070	42.1
	Seth L. Warren (LIBERT)	17,275	6.2

KENTUCKY

	Candidates	Votes	%
1	Tom Barlow (D)	128,524	60.5
	Steve Hamrick (R)	83,088	39.1
2	William H. Natcher (D)	126,894	61.4
	Bruce R. Bartley (R)	79,684	38.6
3	Romano L. Mazzoli (D)	148,066	52.7
	Susan B. Stokes (R)	132,689	47.3
4	Jim Bunning (R)	139,634	61.6
	Dr. Floyd G. Poore (D)	86,890	38.4
5	Harold Rogers (R)	115,255	54.6
	John Doug Hays (D)	95,760	45.4
6	Scotty Baesler (D)	135,613	60.7
	Charles W. Ellinger (R)	87,816	39.3

LOUISIANA[1]

	Candidates	Votes	%
1	Robert L. Livingston (R)		100.0
2	William J. Jefferson (D)		100.0
3	W. J. "Billy" Tauzin (D)		100.0
4	Cleo Fields (D)	143,980	73.9
	Charles Jones (D)	50,851	26.1
5	Jim McCrery (R)	153,501	63.0
	Jerry Huckaby (D)	90,079	37.0
6	Richard H. Baker (R)	123,953	50.6
	Clyde C. Holloway (R)	121,225	49.4
7	Jimmy Hayes (D)		100.0

MAINE

	Candidates	Votes	%
1	Thomas H. Andrews (D)	232,696	65.0
	Linda Bean (R)	125,236	35.0
2	Olympia J. Snowe (R)	153,022	49.1
	Patrick K. McGowan (D)	130,824	42.0
	Jonathan K. Carter (GREEN)	27,526	8.8

MARYLAND

	Candidates	Votes	%
1	Wayne T. Gilchrest (R)	120,084	51.6
	Tom McMillen (D)	112,771	48.4
2	Helen Delich Bentley (R)	165,443	65.1
	Michael C. Hickey Jr. (D)	88,658	34.9
3	Benjamin L. Cardin (D)	163,354	73.5
	William T. S. Bricker (R)	58,869	26.5
4	Albert R. Wynn (D)	136,902	75.2
	Michele Dyson (R)	45,166	24.8
5	Steny H. Hoyer (D)	118,312	53.0
	Lawrence J. Hogan Jr. (R)	97,982	43.9
6	Roscoe G. Bartlett (R)	125,564	54.2
	Thomas H. Hattery (D)	106,224	45.8

Candidates	Votes	%
7 Kweisi Mfume (D)	152,689	85.3
Kenneth Kondner (R)	26,304	14.7
8 Constance A. Morella (R)	203,377	72.5
Edward J. Heffernan (D)	77,042	27.5

MASSACHUSETTS

Candidates	Votes	%
1 John W. Olver (D)	135,049	51.5
Patrick Larkin (R)	113,828	43.4
2 Richard E. Neal (D)	131,215	53.1
Anthony W. Ravosa Jr. (R)	76,795	31.1
Thomas R. Sheehan (FTP)	38,963	15.8
3 Peter I. Blute (R)	131,473	50.4
Joseph D. Early (D)	115,587	44.3
4 Barney Frank (D)	182,633	67.7
Edward J. McCormick III (R)	70,665	26.2
Luke Lumina (IV)	13,670	5.1
5 Martin T. Meehan (D)	133,844	52.2
Paul W. Cronin (R)	96,206	37.5
Mary J. Farinelli (I)	19,077	7.4
6 Peter G. Torkildsen (R)	159,165	54.8
Nicholas Mavroules (D)	130,248	44.9
7 Edward J. Markey (D)	174,837	62.1
Stephen A. Sohn (R)	78,262	27.8
Robert B. Antonelli (I)	28,421	10.1
8 Joseph P. Kennedy II (D)	149,903	83.1
Alice Harriett Nakash (I)	30,402	16.8
9 Joe Moakley (D)	175,550	69.2
Martin D. Conboy (R)	54,291	21.4
Lawrence C. Mackin (I)	15,637	6.2
10 Gerry E. Studds (D)	189,342	60.8
Daniel W. Daly (R)	75,887	24.4
Jon L. Bryan (I)	39,265	12.6

MICHIGAN

Candidates	Votes	%
1 Bart Stupak (D)	144,857	53.9
Philip E. Ruppe (R)	117,056	43.6
2 Peter Hoekstra (R)	155,577	63.0
John H. Miltner (D)	86,265	35.0
3 Paul B. Henry (R)	162,451	61.3
Carol S. Kooistra (D)	95,927	36.2
4 Dave Camp (R)	157,337	62.5
Lisa A. Donaldson (D)	87,573	34.8
5 James A. Barcia (D)	147,618	60.3
Keith Muxlow (R)	93,098	38.0
6 Fred Upton (R)	144,083	61.8
Andy Davis (D)	89,020	38.2
7 Nick Smith (R)	133,992	87.6
Kenneth Proctor (LIBERT)	18,751	12.3
8 Bob Carr (D)	135,517	47.6
Dick Chrysler (R)	131,906	46.3
9 Dale E. Kildee (D)	133,956	53.7
Megan O'Neill (R)	111,798	44.8
10 David E. Bonior (D)	138,193	53.1
Douglas Carl (R)	114,918	44.2
11 Joe Knollenberg (R)	168,940	57.6
Walter Briggs (D)	117,725	40.2
12 Sander M. Levin (D)	137,514	52.6
John Pappageorge (R)	119,357	45.7
13 William D. Ford (D)	127,642	51.9
R. Robert Geake (R)	105,169	42.8
14 John Conyers Jr. (D)	165,496	82.4
John W. Gordon (R)	32,036	15.9
15 Barbara-Rose Collins (D)	148,908	80.5
Charles C. Vincent (R)	31,849	17.2
16 John D. Dingell (D)	156,964	65.1
Frank Beaumont (R)	75,694	31.4

MINNESOTA[2]

Candidates	Votes	%
1 Timothy J. Penny (DFL)	206,369	73.9
Timothy R. Droogsma (I-R)	72,367	25.9
2 David Minge (DFL)	132,156	47.8
Cal R. Ludeman (I-R)	131,587	47.6
3 Jim Ramstad (I-R)	200,240	63.6
Paul Mandell (DFL)	104,606	33.2
4 Bruce F. Vento (DFL)	159,796	57.5
Ian Maitland (I-R)	101,744	36.6
5 Martin Olav Sabo (DFL)	174,139	62.8

Candidates	Votes	%
Stephen A. Moriarty (I-R)	77,093	27.8
6 Rod Grams (I-R)	133,564	44.4
Gerry Sikorski (DFL)	100,016	33.2
Dean Barkley (I)	48,329	16.1
James H. Peterson (IFP)	16,411	5.5
7 Collin C. Peterson (DFL)	133,886	50.4
Bernie Omann (I-R)	130,396	49.1
8 James L. Oberstar (DFL)	167,104	59.0
Phil Herwig (I-R)	83,823	29.6
Harry Robb Welty (Perot Choice)	22,619	8.0

MISSISSIPPI

Candidates	Votes	%
1 Jamie L. Whitten (D)	121,664	59.5
Clyde E. Whitaker (R)	82,952	40.5
2 Mike Espy (D)	133,361	76.4
Dorothy Benford (R)	41,248	23.6
3 G. V. "Sonny" Montgomery (D)	162,864	81.2
Michael E. Williams (R)	37,710	18.8
4 Mike Parker (D)	130,927	67.3
Jack L. McMillan (R)	43,705	22.5
Liz Gilchrist (I)	10,523	5.4
5 Gene Taylor (D)	120,766	63.2
Paul Harvey (R)	67,619	35.4

MISSOURI

Candidates	Votes	%
1 William L. Clay (D)	158,693	68.1
Arthur S. Montgomery (R)	74,482	31.9
2 James M. Talent (R)	157,594	50.4
Joan Kelly Horn (D)	148,729	47.6
3 Richard A. Gephardt (D)	174,000	64.0
Malcolm L. Holekamp (R)	90,006	33.1
4 Ike Skelton (D)	176,977	70.4
John Carley (R)	74,475	29.6
5 Alan Wheat (D)	151,014	59.1
Edward "Gomer" Moody (R)	93,562	36.6
6 Pat Danner (D)	148,887	55.4
E. Thomas Coleman (R)	119,637	44.6
7 Mel Hancock (R)	160,303	61.6
Thomas Patrick Deaton (D)	99,762	38.4
8 Bill Emerson (R)	147,398	62.9
Thad Bullock (D)	86,730	37.0
9 Harold L. Volkmer (D)	124,694	47.7
Rick Hardy (R)	118,811	45.5

MONTANA

Candidates	Votes	%
AL Pat Williams (D)	203,711	50.5
Ron Marlenee (R)	189,570	47.0

NEBRASKA

Candidates	Votes	%
1 Doug Bereuter (R)	142,713	59.7
Gerry Finnegan (D)	96,309	40.3
2 Peter Hoagland (D)	119,512	51.2
Ronald L. Staskiewicz (R)	113,828	48.8
3 Bill Barrett (R)	170,857	71.7
Lowell Fisher (D)	67,457	28.3

NEVADA

Candidates	Votes	%
1 James H. Bilbray (D)	128,278	57.9
J. Coy Pettyjohn (R)	84,217	38.0
2 Barbara F. Vucanovich (R)	129,575	47.9
Pete Sferrazza (D)	117,199	43.3

NEW HAMPSHIRE

Candidates	Votes	%
1 Bill Zeliff (R)	135,936	53.1
Bob Preston (D)	108,578	42.4
2 Dick Swett (D)	157,328	61.7
Bill Hatch (R)	91,126	35.7

NEW JERSEY

Candidates	Votes	%
1 Robert E. Andrews (D)	153,525	67.3
Lee A. Solomon (R)	65,123	28.6
2 William J. Hughes (D)	132,465	55.9
Frank A. LoBiondo (R)	98,315	41.5

Candidates	Votes	%
3 H. James Saxton (R)	151,368	59.2
Timothy E. Ryan (D)	94,012	36.8
4 Christopher H. Smith (R)	149,095	61.8
Brian M. Hughes (D)	84,514	35.0
5 Marge Roukema (R)	196,198	71.5
Frank R. Lucas (D)	67,579	24.6
6 Frank Pallone Jr. (D)	118,266	52.3
Joseph M. Kyrillos (R)	100,949	44.6
7 Bob Franks (R)	132,174	53.3
Leonard R. Sendelsky (D)	105,761	42.6
8 Herbert C. Klein (D)	96,742	47.0
Joseph L. Bubba (R)	84,674	41.1
Gloria J. Kolodziej (IFC)	16,170	7.9
9 Robert G. Torricelli (D)	139,188	58.3
Patrick J. Roma (R)	88,179	36.9
10 Donald M. Payne (D)	117,287	78.4
Alfred D. Palermo (R)	30,160	20.2
11 Dean A. Gallo (R)	188,165	70.1
Ona Spiridellis (D)	68,871	25.7
12 Dick Zimmer (R)	174,216	63.9
Frank Abate (D)	83,035	30.4
13 Robert Menendez (D)	93,670	64.3
Fred J. Theemling Jr. (R)	44,529	30.6

NEW MEXICO

Candidates	Votes	%
1 Steven H. Schiff (R)	128,426	62.6
Robert J. Aragon (D)	76,600	37.3
2 Joe Skeen (R)	94,838	56.4
Dan Sosa Jr. (D)	73,157	43.5
3 Bill Richardson (D)	122,850	67.4
F. Gregg Bemis Jr. (R)	54,569	29.9

NEW YORK

Candidates	Votes	%
1 George J. Hochbrueckner (D, LIF)	117,940	51.7
Edward P. Romaine (R, C, RTL, TCP-LI)	110,043	48.3
2 Rick A. Lazio (R, C, TCP-LI)	109,386	53.2
Thomas J. Downey (D, LIF)	96,328	46.8
3 Peter T. King (R, C)	124,727	49.6
Steve A. Orlins (D)	116,915	46.5
4 David A. Levy (R, C)	110,710	50.2
Philip Schiliro (D, L)	100,386	45.5
5 Gary L. Ackerman (D, L)	110,476	52.4
Allan E. Binder (R, C)	94,907	45.0
6 Floyd H. Flake (D)	96,972	81.0
Dianand D. Bhagwandin (R, C)	22,687	19.0
7 Thomas J. Manton (D)	72,280	56.9
Dennis C. Shea (R, C)	54,639	43.1
8 Jerrold Nadler (D, L)	138,296	81.2
David L. Askren (R)	25,548	15.0
9 Charles E. Schumer (D, L)	116,545	88.6
Alice E. Gaffney (C)	14,985	11.4
10 Edolphus Towns (D, L)	97,509	95.8
11 Major R. Owens (D, L)	80,028	93.6
Michael Gaffney (C)	4,287	5.0
12 Nydia M. Velázquez (D)	55,926	76.5
Angel Diaz (R, C, RTL)	14,976	20.5
13 Susan Molinari (R, C)	107,903	56.1
Sal F. Albanese (D, L)	73,520	38.2
Kathleen M. Murphy (RTL)	10,825	5.6
14 Carolyn B. Maloney (D, L)	101,662	50.4
Bill Green (R, INS)	97,215	48.2
15 Charles B. Rangel (D)	105,011	94.9
16 Jose E. Serrano (D, L)	85,222	91.4
Michael Walters (R, C)	7,975	8.6
17 Eliot L. Engel (D, L)	98,068	80.1
Martin Richman (R)	16,511	13.5
18 Nita M. Lowey (D)	115,841	55.6
Joseph J. DioGuardi (R, C, RTL)	92,687	44.4
19 Hamilton Fish Jr. (R, C)	139,610	60.1
Neil McCarthy (D)	92,854	39.9
20 Benjamin A. Gilman (R)	150,301	66.1
Jonathan L. Levine (D)	66,826	29.4
21 Michael R. McNulty (D, C)	166,371	62.7
Nancy Norman (R, L)	91,184	34.4

Candidates	Votes	%
22 Gerald B. H. Solomon (R, C, RTL)	164,436	65.4
David Roberts (D)	86,896	34.6
23 Sherwood Boehlert (R)	139,774	63.6
Paula DiPerna (D)	61,835	28.2
24 John M. McHugh (R, VR)	122,257	60.8
Margaret M. Ravenscroft (D)	47,675	23.7
Morrison J. Hosley Jr. (C, RTL)	26,763	13.3
25 James T. Walsh (R, C)	135,076	55.7
Rhea Jezer (D, CS)	107,310	44.3
26 Maurice D. Hinchey (D, L)	119,557	50.4
Bob Moppert (R, C)	110,738	46.7
27 Bill Paxon (R, C, RTL)	156,596	63.5
W. Douglas Call (D)	89,906	36.5
28 Louise M. Slaughter (D)	140,908	55.2
William P. Polito (R, C)	112,273	44.0
29 John J. LaFalce (D, L)	128,230	54.5
William E. Miller Jr. (R, C)	98,031	41.6
30 Jack Quinn (R, CC)	125,734	51.7
Dennis Gorski (D, C)	111,445	45.8
31 Amo Houghton (R, C)	150,696	70.6
Joseph P. Leahey (D)	52,010	24.4
Gretchen S. McManus (RTL)	10,848	5.1

Special Election[3]

17 Jerrold Nadler (D, L)	151,122	100.0

NORTH CAROLINA

1 Eva Clayton (D)	116,078	67.0
Ted Tyler (R)	54,457	31.4
2 Tim Valentine (D)	113,693	53.7
Don Davis (R)	93,893	44.4
3 H. Martin Lancaster (D)	101,739	54.4
Tommy Pollard (R)	80,759	43.2
4 David E. Price (D)	171,299	64.6
LaVinia "Vicky" Rothrock Goudie (R)	89,345	33.7
5 Stephen L. Neal (D)	117,835	52.7
Richard M. Burr (R)	102,086	45.6
6 Howard Coble (R)	162,822	70.8
Robin Hood (D)	67,200	29.2
7 Charlie Rose (D)	92,414	56.7
Robert C. Anderson (R)	66,536	40.8
8 W. G. "Bill" Hefner (D)	113,162	59.3
Coy C. Privette (R)	71,842	37.6
9 Alex McMillan (R)	153,650	67.3
Rory Blake (D)	74,583	32.7
10 Cass Ballenger (R)	149,033	63.4
Ben Neill (D)	79,206	33.7
11 Charles H. Taylor (R)	130,158	54.7
John S. Stevens (D)	108,003	45.3
12 Melvin Watt (D)	127,262	70.4
Barbara Gore Washington (R)	49,402	27.3

Special Election[4]

1 Eva Clayton (D)	118,324	56.7
Ted Tyler (R)	86,273	41.3

NORTH DAKOTA

AL Earl Pomeroy (D)	169,273	56.8
John T. Korsmo (R)	117,442	39.4

OHIO

1 David Mann (D)	120,190	51.3
Steve Grote (I)	101,498	43.3
James A. Berns (I)	12,734	5.4
2 Bill Gradison (R)	177,720	70.1
Thomas R. Chandler (D)	75,924	29.9
3 Tony P. Hall (D)	146,072	59.7
Peter W. Davis (R)	98,733	40.3
4 Michael G. Oxley (R)	147,346	61.3
Raymond M. Ball (D)	92,608	38.5
5 Paul E. Gillmor (R)	187,860	100.0
6 Ted Strickland (D)	122,720	50.7
Bob McEwen (R)	119,252	49.3

Candidates	Votes	%
7 David L. Hobson (R)	164,195	71.3
Clifford S. Heskett (D)	66,237	28.7
8 John A. Boehner (R)	176,362	74.0
Fred Sennet (D)	62,033	26.0
9 Marcy Kaptur (D)	178,879	73.6
Ken D. Brown (R)	53,011	21.8
10 Martin R. Hoke (R)	136,433	56.8
Mary Rose Oakar (D)	103,788	43.2
11 Louis Stokes (D)	154,718	69.2
Beryl E. Rothschild (R)	43,866	19.6
Edmund Gudenas (I)	19,773	8.8
12 John R. Kasich (R)	170,297	71.2
Bob Fitrakis (D)	68,761	28.8
13 Sherrod Brown (D)	134,486	53.3
Margaret Mueller (R)	88,889	35.2
Mark Miller (I)	20,320	8.1
14 Thomas C. Sawyer (D)	165,335	67.8
Robert Morgan (R)	78,659	32.2
15 Deborah Pryce (R)	110,390	44.1
Richard Cordray (D)	94,907	37.9
Linda S. Reidelbach (I)	44,906	17.9
16 Ralph Regula (R)	158,489	63.7
Warner D. Mendenhall (D)	90,224	36.3
17 James A. Traficant Jr. (D)	216,503	84.2
Salvatore Pansino (R)	40,743	15.8
18 Douglas Applegate (D)	166,189	68.3
Bill Ress (R)	77,229	31.7
19 Eric D. Fingerhut (D)	138,465	52.6
Robert A. Gardner (R)	124,606	47.4

OKLAHOMA

1 James M. Inhofe (R)	119,211	52.8
John Selph (D)	106,619	47.2
2 Mike Synar (D)	118,542	55.5
Jerry Hill (R)	87,657	41.1
3 Bill Brewster (D)	155,934	75.1
Robert W. Stokes (R)	51,725	24.9
4 Dave McCurdy (D)	140,841	70.7
Howard Bell (R)	58,235	29.3
5 Ernest Jim Istook (R)	123,237	53.4
Laurie Williams (D)	107,579	46.6
6 Glenn English (D)	134,734	67.8
Bob Anthony (R)	64,068	32.2

OREGON

1 Elizabeth Furse (D)	152,917	52.0
Tony Meeker (R)	140,986	47.9
2 Robert F. Smith (R)	184,163	67.1
Denzel Ferguson (D)	90,036	32.8
3 Ron Wyden (D)	208,028	77.1
Al Ritter (R)	50,235	18.6
4 Peter A. DeFazio (D)	199,372	71.4
Richard L. Schulz (R)	79,733	28.5
5 Mike Kopetski (D)	174,443	63.9
Jim Seagraves (R)	97,984	35.9

PENNSYLVANIA

1 Thomas M. Foglietta (D)	150,172	80.9
Craig Snyder (R)	35,419	19.1
2 Lucien E. Blackwell (D)	164,355	76.8
Larry Hollin (R)	47,906	22.4
3 Robert A. Borski (D)	130,828	58.9
Charles F. Dougherty (R)	86,787	39.1
4 Ron Klink (D)	186,684	78.5
Gordon R. Johnston (R)	48,484	20.4
5 William F. Clinger Jr. (R, D)	188,911	100.0
6 Tim Holden (D)	108,312	52.1
John E. Jones (R)	99,694	47.9
7 Curt Weldon (R)	180,648	66.0
Frank Daly (D)	91,623	33.5
8 Jim Greenwood (R)	129,593	51.9
Peter H. Kostmayer (D)	114,095	45.7
9 Bud Shuster (R, D)	182,406	100.0
10 Joseph M. McDade (R, D)	189,414	90.4
Albert A. Smith (LIBERT)	20,134	9.6
11 Paul E. Kanjorski (D)	138,875	67.1
Michael A. Fescina (R)	68,112	32.9

Candidates	Votes	%
12 John P. Murtha (D)	166,916	100.0
13 Marjorie Margolies-Mezvinsky (D)	127,685	50.3
Jon D. Fox (R)	126,312	49.7
14 William J. Coyne (D)	165,633	72.3
Byron W. King (R)	61,311	26.8
15 Paul McHale (D)	111,419	52.2
Don Ritter (R)	99,520	46.7
16 Robert S. Walker (R)	137,823	64.8
Robert Peters (D)	74,741	35.2
17 George W. Gekas (R)	150,158	69.5
Bill Sturges (D)	65,881	30.5
18 Rick Santorum (R)	154,024	60.6
Frank A. Pecora (D)	96,655	38.0
19 Bill Goodling (R)	98,599	45.3
Paul V. Kilker (D)	74,798	34.4
Thomas M. Humbert (I)	44,190	20.3
20 Austin J. Murphy (D)	114,898	50.7
Bill Townsend (R)	111,591	49.3
21 Tom Ridge (R)	150,729	68.0
John C. Harkins (D)	70,802	32.0

RHODE ISLAND

1 Ronald K. Machtley (R)	135,982	70.1
David R. Carlin Jr. (D)	48,092	24.8
Frederick E. Dick (RPI)	6,012	3.1
Norman J. Jacques (I)	4,003	2.1
2 Jack Reed (D)	144,450	70.7
James W. Bell (R)	49,998	24.5

SOUTH CAROLINA

1 Arthur Ravenel Jr. (R)	121,938	66.1
Bill Oberst Jr. (D)	59,908	32.5
2 Floyd D. Spence (R)	148,667	87.6
Geb Sommer (LIBERT)	20,816	12.3
3 Butler Derrick (D)	119,119	61.1
Jim Bland (R)	75,660	38.8
4 Bob Inglis (R)	99,879	50.3
Liz J. Patterson (D)	94,182	47.5
5 John M. Spratt Jr. (D)	112,031	61.2
Bill Horne (R)	70,866	38.7
6 James E. Clyburn (D)	120,647	65.3
John Chase (R)	64,149	34.7

SOUTH DAKOTA

AL Tim Johnson (D)	230,070	69.1
John Timmer (R)	89,375	26.8

TENNESSEE

1 James H. Quillen (R)	114,797	67.5
J. Carr "Jack" Christian (D)	47,809	28.1
2 John J. Duncan (R)	148,377	72.2
Troy Goodale (R)	52,887	25.7
3 Marilyn Lloyd (D)	105,693	48.8
Zach Wamp (R)	102,763	47.5
4 Jim Cooper (D)	98,984	64.1
Dale Johnson (R)	50,340	32.6
5 Bob Clement (D)	125,233	66.8
Tom Stone (R)	49,417	26.3
6 Bart Gordon (D)	120,177	56.6
Marsha Blackburn (R)	86,289	40.6
7 Don Sundquist (R)	125,101	61.7
David R. Davis (D)	72,062	35.5
8 John Tanner (D)	136,852	83.7
Lawrence J. Barnes (I)	9,605	5.9
9 Harold E. Ford (D)	123,276	57.9
Charles L. Black (R)	60,606	28.5
Richard Liptock (I)	14,075	6.6
James Vandergriff (I)	12,265	5.8

TEXAS

1 Jim Chapman (D)	152,209	100.0
2 Charles Wilson (D)	118,625	56.1
Donna Peterson (R)	92,176	43.6
3 Sam Johnson (R)	201,569	86.1
Noel Kopala (LIBERT)	32,570	13.9

	Candidates	Votes	%
4	Ralph M. Hall (D)	128,008	58.1
	David L. Bridges (R)	83,875	38.1
5	John Bryant (D)	98,567	58.9
	Richard Stokley (R)	62,419	37.3
6	Joe L. Barton (R)	189,140	71.9
	John Dietrich (D)	73,933	28.1
7	Bill Archer (R)	169,407	100.0
8	Jack Fields (R)	179,349	77.0
	Chas. Robinson (D)	53,473	23.0
9	Jack Brooks (D)	118,690	53.6
	Steve Stockman (R)	96,270	43.5
10	J. J. "Jake" Pickle (D)	177,233	67.7
	Herbert Spiro (R)	68,646	26.2
11	Chet Edwards (D)	119,999	67.4
	James W. Broyles (R)	58,033	32.6
12	Pete Geren (D)	125,492	62.8
	David Hobbs (R)	74,432	37.2
13	Bill Sarpalius (D)	117,892	60.3
	Beau Boulter (R)	77,514	39.7
14	Greg H. Laughlin (D)	135,930	68.1
	Humberto J. Garza (R)	54,412	27.3
15	E. "Kika" de la Garza (D)	86,351	60.4
	Tom Haughey (R)	56,549	39.6
16	Ronald D. Coleman (D)	66,731	51.9
	Chip Taberski (R)	61,870	48.1
17	Charles W. Stenholm (D)	136,213	66.1
	Jeannie Sadowski (R)	69,958	33.9
18	Craig Washington (D)	111,422	64.7
	Edward Blum (R)	56,080	32.6
19	Larry Combest (R)	162,057	77.4
	Terry Lee Moser (D)	47,325	22.6
20	Henry B. Gonzalez (D)	103,755	100.0
21	Lamar Smith (R)	190,979	72.2
	James M. Gaddy (D)	62,827	23.7
22	Thomas D. DeLay (R)	150,221	68.9
	Richard Konrad (D)	67,812	31.1
23	Henry Bonilla (R)	98,259	59.1
	Albert G. Bustamante (D)	63,797	38.4
24	Martin Frost (D)	104,174	59.8
	Steve Masterson (R)	70,042	40.2
25	Michael A. Andrews (D)	98,975	56.0
	Dolly Madison McKenna (R)	73,192	41.4
26	Dick Armey (R)	150,209	73.1
	John Wayne Caton (D)	55,237	26.9
27	Solomon P. Ortiz (D)	87,022	55.5
	Jay Kimbrough (R)	66,853	42.6
28	Frank Tejeda (D)	122,457	87.1
	David C. Slatter (LIBERT)	18,128	12.9
29	Gene Green (D)	64,064	64.9

	Candidates	Votes	%
	Clark Kent Ervin (R)	34,609	35.1
30	Eddie Bernice Johnson (D)	107,831	71.5
	Lucy Cain (R)	37,853	25.1

UTAH

	Candidates	Votes	%
1	James V. Hansen (R)	160,037	65.3
	Ron Holt (D)	68,712	28.0
	William J. Lawrence (IP)	16,505	6.7
2	Karen Shepherd (D)	127,738	50.5
	Enid Greene (R)	118,307	46.8
3	Bill Orton (D)	135,029	58.9
	Richard R. Harrington (R)	84,019	36.7

VERMONT

	Candidates	Votes	%
AL	Bernard Sanders (I)	162,724	57.8
	Tim Philbin (R)	86,901	30.9
	Lewis E. Young (D)	22,279	7.9

VIRGINIA

	Candidates	Votes	%
1	Herbert H. Bateman (R)	133,537	57.5
	Andrew H. Fox (D)	89,814	38.7
2	Owen B. Pickett (D)	99,253	56.0
	J. L. "Jim" Chapman IV (R)	77,797	43.9
3	Robert C. Scott (D)	132,432	78.6
	Daniel Jenkins (R)	35,780	21.2
4	Norman Sisisky (D)	147,649	68.4
	A. J. "Tony" Zevgolis (R)	68,286	31.6
5	Lewis F. Payne Jr. (D)	133,031	68.9
	W. A. "Bill" Hurlburt (R)	60,030	31.1
6	Robert W. Goodlatte (R)	127,309	60.0
	Stephen Alan Musselwhite (D)	84,618	39.9
7	Thomas J. Bliley Jr. (R)	211,618	82.9
	Gerald E. Berg (I)	43,267	16.9
8	James P. Moran Jr. (D)	138,542	56.1
	Kyle E. McSlarrow (R)	102,717	41.6
9	Rick Boucher (D)	133,284	63.1
	L. Garrett Weddle (R)	77,985	36.9
10	Frank R. Wolf (R)	144,471	63.6
	Raymond E. Vickery (D)	75,775	33.4
11	Leslie L. Byrne (D)	114,172	50.0
	Henry N. Butler (R)	103,119	45.2

WASHINGTON

	Candidates	Votes	%
1	Maria Cantwell (D)	148,844	54.9
	Gary Nelson (R)	113,897	42.0

	Candidates	Votes	%
2	Al Swift (D)	133,207	52.1
	Jack Metcalf (R)	107,365	42.0
3	Jolene Unsoeld (D)	138,043	56.0
	Pat Fiske (R)	108,583	44.0
4	Jay Inslee (D)	106,556	50.8
	Richard "Doc" Hastings (R)	103,028	49.2
5	Thomas S. Foley (D)	135,965	55.2
	John Sonneland (R)	110,443	44.8
6	Norm Dicks (D)	152,933	64.2
	Lauri J. Phillips (R)	66,664	28.0
	Tom Donnelly (I)	14,490	6.1
7	Jim McDermott (D)	222,604	78.4
	Glenn C. Hampson (R)	54,149	19.1
8	Jennifer Dunn (R)	155,874	60.4
	George O. Tamblyn (D)	87,611	33.9
	Bob Adams (I)	14,686	5.7
9	Mike Kreidler (D)	110,902	52.1
	Pete von Reichbauer (R)	91,910	43.2

WEST VIRGINIA

	Candidates	Votes	%
1	Alan B. Mollohan (D)	172,924	100.0
2	Bob Wise (D)	143,988	70.9
	Samuel A. Cravotta (R)	59,102	29.1
3	Nick J. Rahall II (D)	122,279	65.6
	Ben Waldman (R)	64,012	34.4

WISCONSIN

	Candidates	Votes	%
1	Les Aspin (D)	147,495	57.6
	Mark Neumann (R)	104,352	40.7
2	Scott L. Klug (R)	183,366	62.6
	Ada E. Deer (D)	108,291	37.0
3	Steve Gunderson (R)	146,903	56.4
	Paul Sacia (D)	108,664	41.7
4	Gerald D. Kleczka (D)	173,482	65.8
	Joseph L. Cook (R)	84,872	32.2
5	Thomas M. Barrett (D)	162,344	69.3
	Donalda Hammersmith (R)	71,085	30.4
6	Thomas E. Petri (R)	143,875	52.9
	Peggy A. Lautenschlager (D)	128,232	47.1
7	David R. Obey (D)	166,200	64.4
	Dale R. Vannes (R)	91,772	35.6
8	Toby Roth (R)	191,704	70.1
	Catherine L. Helms (D)	81,792	29.9
9	F. James Sensenbrenner Jr. (R)	192,898	69.7
	Ingrid K. Buxton (D)	77,362	28.0

WYOMING

1994 House Elections

ALABAMA

	Candidates	Votes	%
1	Sonny Callahan (R)	103,431	67.3
	Don Womack (D)	50,227	32.7
2	Terry Everett (R)	124,465	73.6
	Brian Dowling (D)	44,694	26.4
3	Glen Browder (D)	93,924	63.6
	Ben Hand (R)	53,757	36.4
4	Tom Bevill (D)	119,436	98.5
5	Robert E. "Bud Cramer (D)	88,693	50.5
	Wayne Parker (R)	86,923	49.5
6	Spencer Bachus (R)	155,047	79.0
	Larry Fortenberry (D)	41,030	20.9
7	Earl F. Hilliard (D)	116,150	76.9
	Alfred J. MiddletonSr. (R)	34,814	23.0

ALASKA

	Candidates	Votes	%
AL	Don Young (R)	118,537	56.9
	Tony Smith (D)	68,172	32.7
	Jonni Whitmore (GREEN)	21,277	10.2

ARIZONA

	Candidates	Votes	%
1	Matt Salmon (R)	101,350	56.0
	Chuck Blanchard (D)	70,627	39.0
2	Ed Pastor (D)	62,589	62.3
	Robert MacDonald (R)	32,797	32.7
	James Bertrand (LIBERT)	5,060	5.0
3	Bob Stump (R)	145,396	70.1
	Howard Lee Sprague (D)	61,939	29.9
4	John Shadegg (R)	116,714	60.2
	Carol Cure (D)	69,760	36.0
5	Jim Kolbe (R)	149,514	67.7
	Gary Auerbach (D)	63,436	28.7
6	J.D. Hayworth (R)	107,060	54.6
	Karan English (D)	81,321	41.5

ARKANSAS

	Candidates	Votes	%
1	Blanche Lambert (D)	95,290	53.4
	Warren Dupwe (R)	83,147	46.6
2	Ray Thornton (D)	97,580	57.4
	Bill Powell (R)	72,473	42.6
3	Tim Hutchinson (R)	129,800	67.7
	Berta L. Seitz (D)	61,883	32.3
4	Jay Dickey (R)	87,469	51.8
	Jay Bradford (D)	81,370	48.2

CALIFORNIA

	Candidates	Votes	%
1	Frank Riggs (R)	106,870	53.3
	Dan Hamburg (D)	93,717	46.7
2	Wally Herger (R)	137,863	64.2
	Mary Jacobs (D)	55,958	26.1
	Devvy Kidd (AMI)	15,569	7.2
3	Vic Fazio (D)	97,093	49.8
	Tim Lefever (R)	89,964	46.1
4	John T. Doolittle (R)	144,936	61.3
	Katie Hirning (D)	82,505	34.9
5	Robert T. Matsui (D)	125,042	68.5
	Robert S. Dinsmore (R)	52,905	29.0
6	Lynn Woolsey (D)	137,642	58.1
	Michael J. Nugent (R)	88,940	37.6
7	George Miller (D)	116,105	69.7
	Charles V. Hughes (R)	45,698	27.4
8	Nancy Pelosi (D)	137,642	81.8
	Elsa C. Cheung (R)	30,528	18.2
9	Ronald V. Dellums (D)	129,233	72.2
	Deborah Wright (R)	40,448	22.6
	Emma Wong Mar (PFP)	9,194	5.1
10	Bill Baker (R)	138,916	59.3
	Ellen Schwartz (D)	90,523	38.6
11	Richard W. Pombo (R)	99,302	62.1
	Randy A. Perry (D)	55,794	34.9
12	Tom Lantos (D)	118,408	67.4

	Candidates	Votes	%
	Deborah Wilder (R)	57,228	32.6
13	Pete Stark (D)	97,344	64.6
	Larry Molton (R)	45,555	30.2
	Robert "Bob" Gough (LIBERT)	7,743	5.1
14	Anna G. Eshoo (D)	120,713	60.6
	Ben Brink (R)	78,475	39.4
15	Norman Y. Mineta (D)	119,921	59.9
	Robert Wick (R)	80,266	40.1
16	Zoe Lofgren (D)	74,935	65.0
	Lyle J. Smith (R)	40,409	35.0
17	Sam Farr (D)	87,222	52.2
	Bill McCampbell (R)	74,380	44.5
18	Gary A. Condit (D)	91,105	65.5
	Tom Carter (R)	44,046	31.7
19	George P. Radanovich (R)	104,435	56.8
	Richard H. Lehman (D)	72,912	39.6
20	Cal Dooley (D)	57,394	56.7
	Paul Young (R)	43,836	43.3
21	Bill Thomas (R)	116,874	68.1
	John L. Evans (D)	47,517	27.7
22	Andrea Seastrand (R)	102,987	49.3
	Walter Holden Capps (D)	101,424	48.5
23	Elton Gallegly (R)	114,043	66.2
	Kevin Ready (D)	47,345	27.5
24	Anthony C. Beilenson (D)	95,342	49.4
	Rich Sybert (R)	91,806	47.5
25	Howard P. "Buck" McKeon (R)	110,301	64.9
	James H. Gilmartin (D)	53,445	31.4
26	Howard L. Berman (D)	55,145	62.6
	Gary E. Forsch (R)	28,423	32.2
	Erich D. Miller (LIBERT)	4,570	5.2
27	Carlos J. Moorhead (R)	88,341	53.0
	Doug Kahn (D)	70,267	42.1
28	David Dreier (R)	110,179	67.1
	Tommy Randle (D)	50,022	30.4
29	Henry A. Waxman (D)	129,413	68.0
	Paul Stepanek (R)	53,801	28.3
30	Xavier Becerra (D)	43,943	66.2
	David A. Ramirez (R)	18,741	28.2
	R. William Weilburg (LIBERT)	3,741	5.6
31	Matthew G. Martinez (D)	50,541	59.1
	John V. Flores (R)	34,926	40.9
32	Julian C. Dixon (D)	98,017	77.6
	Ernie A. Farhat (R)	22,190	17.6
33	Lucille Roybal-Allard (D)	33,814	81.5
	Kermit Booker (PFP)	7,694	18.5
34	Esteban E. Torres (D)	72,439	61.7
	Albert J. Nunez (R)	40,068	34.1
35	Maxine Waters (D)	65,688	78.1
	Nate Truman (R)	18,390	21.9
36	Jane Harman (D)	93,939	48.0
	Susan M. Brooks (R)	93,127	47.6
37	Walter R. Tucker III (D)	64,166	77.4
	Guy Wilson (LIBERT)	18,502	22.3
38	Steve Horn (R)	85,225	58.5
	Peter Mathews (D)	53,681	36.8
39	Ed Royce (R)	113,037	66.4
	R.O. "Bob" Davis (D)	49,459	29.0
40	Jerry Lewis (R)	115,728	70.7
	Donald M. "Don" Rusk (D)	48,003	29.3
41	Jay C. Kim (R)	81,854	62.1
	Ed Tessier (D)	49,924	37.9
42	George E. Brown Jr. (D)	58,888	51.1
	Rob Guzman (R)	56,259	48.8
43	Ken Calvert (R)	84,500	54.7
	Mark A. Takano (D)	59,342	38.4
	Gene L. Berkman (LIBERT)	9,636	6.2
44	Sonny Bono (R)	95,521	55.6
	Steve Clute (D)	65,370	38.1
	Donald Cochran (AMI)	10,885	6.3
45	Dana Rohrabacher (R)	124,006	69.1
	Brett Williamson (D)	55,489	30.9
46	Robert K. Dornan (R)	50,126	57.1
	Michael Farber (D)	32,577	37.1

	Candidates	Votes	%
	Richard G. Newhouse (LIBERT)	5,018	5.7
47	Christopher Cox (R)	152,413	71.7
	Gary Kingsbury (D)	53,035	24.9
48	Ron Packard (R)	143,275	73.4
	Andrei Leschick (D)	43,446	22.3
49	Brian P. Bilbray (R)	90,283	48.5
	Lynn Schenk (D)	85,597	46.0
50	Bob Filner (D)	59,214	56.7
	Mary Alice Acevedo (R)	36,955	35.4
51	Randy "Duke" Cunningham (R)	138,547	66.9
	Rita K. Tamerius (D)	57,374	27.7
52	Duncan Hunter (R)	109,201	64.0
	Janet M. Gastil (D)	53,024	31.1

COLORADO

	Candidates	Votes	%
1	Patricia Schroeder (D)	93,123	60.0
	William Eggert (R)	61,978	39.9
2	David E. Skaggs (D)	105,938	56.8
	Patricia "Pat" Miller (R)	80,723	43.2
3	Scott McInnis (R)	145,365	69.6
	Linda Powers (D)	63,427	30.4
4	Wayne Allard (R)	136,251	72.3
	Cathy Kipp (D)	52,202	27.7
5	Joel Hefley (R)		100.0
6	Dan Schaefer (R)	124,079	69.8
	John Hallen (D)	49,701	28.0

CONNECTICUT

	Candidates	Votes	%
1	Barbara B. Kennelly (D,ACP)	138,637	73.4
	Douglas T. Putnam (R)	46,865	24.8
2	Sam Gejdenson (D)	79,188	42.6
	Edward W. Munster (R)	79,167	42.5
	David Bingham (ACP)	27,716	14.9
3	Rosa L. DeLauro (D)	111,261	63.4
	Susan E. Johnson (R,ACP)	64,094	36.6
4	Christopher Shays (R)	109,436	74.4
	Jonathan D. Kantrowitz (D)	34,962	23.8
5	Gary A. Franks (R)	93,471	52.2
	James H. Maloney (D,ACP)	81,523	45.5
6	Nancy L. Johnson (R)	123,101	63.9
	Charlotte Koskoff (D,ACP)	60,701	31.5

DELAWARE

	Candidates	Votes	%
AL	Michael N. Castle (R)	137,960	70.7
	Carol Ann DeSantis (D)	51,803	26.6

FLORIDA

	Candidates	Votes	%
1	Joe Scarborough (R)	112,901	61.6
	Vince Whibbs Jr. (D)	70,389	38.4
2	Pete Peterson (D)	117,404	61.3
	Carole Griffin (R)	74,011	38.7
3	Corrine Brown (D)	63,845	57.7
	Marc Little (R)	46,895	42.3
4	Tillie Fowler (R)		100.0
5	Karen L. Thurman (D)	125,780	57.2
	"Big Daddy" Don Garlits (R)	94,093	42.8
6	Cliff Stearns (R)	148,698	99.1
7	John L. Mica (R)	131,711	73.4
	Edward D. Goddard (D)	47,747	26.6
8	Bill McCollum (R)	131,376	99.7
9	Michael Bilirakis (R)	177,253	99.9
10	C.W. Bill Young (R)		100.0
11	Sam M. Gibbons (D)	76,814	51.6
	Mark Sharpe (R)	72,119	48.4
12	Charles T. Canady (R)	106,123	65.0
	Robert Connors (D)	57,203	35.0
13	Dan Miller (R)		100.0
14	Porter J. Goss (R)		100.0
15	Dave Weldon (R)	117,027	53.7
	Sue Munsey (D)	100,513	46.1

Candidates	Votes	%
16 Mark Foley (R)	122,734	58.1
John Comerford (D)	88,646	41.9
17 Carrie P. Meek (D)		100.0
18 Ileana Ros-Lehtinen (R)		100.0
19 Harry A. Johnston (D)	147,591	66.1
Peter J. Tsakanikas (R)	75,779	33.9
20 Peter Deutsch (D)	114,615	61.2
Beverly "Bev" Kennedy (R)	72,516	38.8
21 Lincoln Diaz-Balart (R)		100.0
22 E. Clay Shaw Jr. (R)	119,690	63.4
Hermine L. Wiener (D)	69,215	36.6
23 Alcee L. Hastings (D)		100.0

GEORGIA

Candidates	Votes	%
1 Jack Kingston (R)	88,788	76.6
Raymond Beckworth (D)	27,197	23.4
2 Sanford D. Bishop Jr. (D)	65,383	66.2
John Clayton (R)	33,429	33.8
3 Mac Collins (R)	94,717	65.5
Fred Overby (D)	49,828	34.5
4 John Linder (R)	90,063	57.9
Comer Yates (D)	65,566	42.1
5 John Lewis (D)	85,094	69.1
Dale Dixon (R)	37,999	30.9
6 Newt Gingrich (R)	119,432	64.2
Ben Jones (D)	66,700	35.8
7 Bob Barr (R)	71,265	51.9
George "Buddy" Darden (D)	65,978	48.1
8 Saxby Chambliss (R)	89,591	62.7
Craig Mathis (D)	53,408	37.3
9 Nathan Deal (D)	79,145	57.9
Robert L. Castello (R)	57,568	42.1
10 Charlie Norwood (R)	96,099	65.2
Don Johnson (D)	51,192	34.8
11 Cynthia A. McKinney (D)	71,560	65.6
Woodrow Lovett (R)	37,533	34.4

HAWAII

Candidates	Votes	%
1 Neil Abercrombie (D)	94,754	53.6
Orson Swindle (R)	76,623	43.4
2 Patsy T. Mink (D)	124,431	70.1
Robert H. Garner (R)	42,891	24.2
Lawrence R. Bartley (LIBERT)	10,074	5.7

IDAHO

Candidates	Votes	%
1 Helen Chenoweth (R)	111,728	55.4
Larry LaRocco (D)	89,826	44.6
2 Michael D. Crapo (R)	143,593	75.0
Penny Fletcher (D)	47,936	25.0

ILLINOIS

Candidates	Votes	%
1 Bobby L. Rush (D)	112,474	75.7
William J. Kelly (R)	36,038	24.3
2 Mel Reynolds (D)	93,998	98.1
3 William O. Lipinski (D)	92,353	54.2
Jim Nalepa (R)	78,163	45.8
4 Luis V. Gutierrez (D)	46,695	75.2
Steven Valtierra (R)	15,384	24.8
5 Michael Patrick Flanagan (R)	75,328	54.4
Dan Rostenkowski (D)	63,065	45.6
6 Henry J. Hyde (R)	115,664	73.5
Tom Berry (D)	37,163	23.6
7 Cardiss Collins (D)	93,457	79.6
Charles "Chuck" Mobley (R)	24,011	20.4
8 Philip M. Crane (R)	88,225	64.9
Robert C. Walberg (D)	47,654	35.1
9 Sidney R. Yates (D)	94,404	66.1
George Edward Larney (R)	48,419	33.9
10 John Edward Porter (R)	114,884	75.1
Andrew M. Krupp (D)	38,191	24.9
11 Gerald C. "Jerry" Weller (R)	97,241	60.6
Frank Giglio (D)	63,150	39.4
12 Jerry F. Costello (D)	101,391	65.9
Jan Morris (R)	52,419	34.1
13 Harris W. Fawell (R)	124,312	73.1

Candidates	Votes	%
William A. Riley (D)	45,709	26.9
14 Dennis Hastert (R)	110,204	76.5
Steve Denari (D)	33,891	23.5
15 Thomas W. Ewing (R)	108,857	68.2
Paul Alexander (D)	50,874	31.8
16 Donald Manzullo (R)	117,238	70.6
Pete Sullivan (D)	48,736	29.4
17 Lane Evans (D)	95,312	54.5
Jim Anderson (R)	79,471	45.5
18 Ray LaHood (R)	119,838	60.2
G. Douglas Stephens (D)	78,332	39.3
19 Glenn Poshard (D)	115,045	58.4
Brent Winters (R)	81,995	41.6
20 Richard J. Durbin (D)	108,034	54.8
Bill Owens (R)	88,964	45.2

INDIANA

Candidates	Votes	%
1 Peter J. Visclosky (D)	68,612	56.5
John Larson (R)	52,920	43.5
2 David M. McIntosh (R)	93,592	54.5
Joseph H. Hogsett (D)	78,241	45.5
3 Tim Roemer (D)	72,497	55.2
Richard Burkett (R)	58,878	44.8
4 Mark Edward Souder (R)	88,584	55.4
Jill L. Long (D)	71,235	44.6
5 Steve Buyer (R)	111,031	69.5
J.D. Beatty (D)	45,224	28.3
6 Dan Burton (R)	136,876	77.0
Natalie M. Bruner (D)	40,815	23.0
7 John T. Myers (R)	104,359	65.1
Michael M. Harmless (D)	55,941	34.9
8 John Hostettler (R)	93,529	52.4
Frank McCloskey (D)	84,857	47.6
9 Lee H. Hamilton (D)	91,459	52.0
Jean Leising (R)	84,315	48.0
10 Andrew Jacobs Jr. (D)	58,573	53.5
Marvin Bailey Scott (R)	50,998	46.5

IOWA

Candidates	Votes	%
1 Jim Leach (R)	110,448	60.2
Glen Winekauf (D)	69,461	37.9
2 Jim Nussle (R)	111,076	56.0
Dave Nagle (D)	86,087	43.4
3 Jim Ross Lightfoot (R)	111,862	57.8
Elaine Baxter (D)	79,310	41.0
4 Greg Ganske (R)	111,935	52.5
Neal Smith (D)	98,824	46.4
5 Tom Latham (R)	114,796	60.8
Sheila McGuire (D)	73,627	39.0

KANSAS

Candidates	Votes	%
1 Pat Roberts (R)	169,531	77.4
Terry L. Nichols (D)	49,477	22.6
2 Sam Brownback (R)	135,725	65.6
John Carlin (D)	71,025	34.4
3 Jan Meyers (R)	102,218	56.6
Judy Hancock (D)	78,401	43.4
4 Todd Tiahrt (R)	111,653	52.9
Dan Glickman (D)	99,366	47.1

KENTUCKY

Candidates	Votes	%
1 Edward Whitfield (R)	64,849	51.0
Tom Barlow (D)	62,387	49.0
2 Ron Lewis (R)	90,535	59.8
David Adkisson (D)	60,867	40.2
3 Mike Ward (D)	67,663	44.4
Susan B. Stokes (R)	67,238	44.1
Richard Lewis (KTAX)	17,591	11.5
4 Jim Bunning (R)	96,695	74.1
Sally Harris Skaggs (D)	33,717	25.9
5 Harold Rogers (R)	82,291	79.4
Walter "Doc" Blevins (D)	21,318	20.6
6 Scotty Baesler (D)	70,085	58.8
Matthew Eric Wills (R)	49,032	41.2

Candidates	Votes	%
2 Ron Lewis (R)	40,126	55.2
Joseph E. Prather (D)	32,625	44.8

LOUISIANA[2]

Candidates	Votes	%
1 Robert L. Livingston (R)		100.0
2 William J. Jefferson (D)		100.0
3 W.J. "Billy" Tauzin (D)		100.0
4 Cleo Fields (D)		100.0
5 Jim McCrery (R)		100.0
6 Richard H. Baker (R)		100.0
7 Jimmy Hayes (D)		100.0

MAINE

Candidates	Votes	%
1 James B. Longley Jr. (R)	136,316	51.9
Dennis L. Dutremble (D)	126,373	48.1
2 John Baldacci (D)	109,615	45.7
Richard A. Bennett (R)	97,754	40.7
John M. Michael (I)	21,117	8.8

MARYLAND

Candidates	Votes	%
1 Wayne T. Gilchrest (R)	120,975	67.7
Ralph T. Gies (D)	57,712	32.3
2 Robert L. Ehrlich Jr. (R)	125,162	62.7
Gerry L. Brewster (D)	74,275	37.2
3 Benjamin L. Cardin (D)	117,269	71.0
Robert Ryan Tousey (R)	47,966	29.0
4 Albert R. Wynn (D)	93,148	75.0
Michele Dyson (R)	30,999	25.0
5 Steny H. Hoyer (D)	98,821	58.8
Donald Devine (R)	69,211	41.2
6 Roscoe G. Bartlett (R)	122,809	65.9
Paul Muldowney (D)	63,411	34.1
7 Kwesi Mfume (D)	97,016	81.5
Kenneth Kondner (R)	22,007	18.5
8 Constance A. Morella (R)	143,449	70.3
Steven Van Grack (D)	60,660	29.7

MASSACHUSETTS

Candidates	Votes	%
1 John W. Olver (D)	150,047	99.4
2 Richard E. Neal (D)	117,178	58.6
John M. Briare (R)	72,732	36.3
Kate Ross (NL)	10,167	5.1
3 Peter I. Blute (R)	115,810	54.6
Kevin O'Sullivan (D)	93,689	44.2
4 Barney Frank (D)	168,942	99.5
5 Martin T. Meehan (D)	140,725	69.8
David E. Coleman (R)	60,734	30.1
6 Peter G. Torkildsen (R)	120,952	50.5
John F. Tierney (D)	113,481	47.4
7 Edward J. Markey (D)	146,246	64.4
Brad Bailey (R)	80,674	35.5
8 Joseph P. Kennedy II (D)	113,224	99.0
9 Joe Moakley (D)	146,287	69.8
Michael M. Murphy (R)	63,369	30.2
10 Gerry E. Studds (D)	172,753	68.7
Keith Jason Hemeon (R)	78,487	31.2

MICHIGAN

Candidates	Votes	%
1 Bart Stupak (D)	121,433	56.9
Gil Ziegler (R)	89,660	42.0
2 Peter Hoekstra (R)	146,164	75.3
Marcus Pete Hoover (D)	46,097	23.7
3 Vernon J. Ehlers (R)	136,711	73.9
Betsy J. Flory (D)	43,580	23.5
4 Dave Camp (R)	145,176	73.1
Damion Frasier (D)	50,544	25.5
5 James A. Barcia (D)	126,456	65.5
William T. Anderson (R)	61,342	31.8
6 Fred Upton (R)	121,923	73.5
David Taylor (D)	42,348	25.5
7 Nick Smith (R)	115,621	65.1
Kim McCaughtry (D)	57,326	32.3
8 Dick Chrysler (R)	109,663	51.6

Candidates	Votes	%
Bob Mitchell (D)	95,383	44.9
9 Dale E. Kildee (D)	97,096	51.2
Megan O'Neill (R)	89,148	47.0
10 David E. Bonior (D)	121,876	62.2
Donald J. Lobsinger (R)	73,862	37.7
11 Joe Knollenberg (R)	154,696	68.2
Mike Breshgold (D)	69,168	30.5
12 Sander M. Levin (D)	103,508	52.0
John Pappageorge (R)	92,762	46.6
13 Lynn Nancy Rivers (D)	89,573	51.9
John A. Schall (R)	77,908	45.1
14 John Conyers Jr. (D)	128,463	81.5
Richard Charles Fornier (R)	26,215	16.6
15 Barbara-Rose Collins (D)	119,442	84.1
John W. Savage II (R)	20,074	14.1
16 John D. Dingell (D)	105,849	59.1
Ken Larkin (R)	71,159	39.8

MINNESOTA

Candidates	Votes	%
1 Gil Gutknecht (R)	117,613	55.2
John C. Hottinger (D)	95,328	44.7
2 David Minge (D)	114,289	52.0
Gary B. Revier (R)	98,881	45.0
3 Jim Ramstad (R)	173,223	73.2
Bob Olson (D)	62,211	26.3
4 Bruce F. Vento (D)	115,638	54.9
Dennis Newinski (R)	88,344	41.9
5 Martin Olav Sabo (D)	121,515	61.9
Dorothy LeGrand (R)	73,258	37.3
6 William P. "Bill" Luther (D)	113,740	49.9
Tad Jude (R)	113,190	49.7
7 Collin C. Peterson (D)	108,023	51.2
Bernie Omann (R)	102,623	48.6
8 James L. Oberstar (D)	153,161	65.7
Phil Herwig (R)	79,818	34.2

MISSISSIPPI

Candidates	Votes	%
1 Roger Wicker (R)	80,553	63.1
Bill Wheeler (D)	47,192	36.9
2 Bennie Thompson (D)	68,014	53.7
Bill Jordan (R)	49,270	38.9
Vince Thornton (MSTAX)	9,408	7.4
3 G.V. "Sonny" Montgomery (D)	83,163	67.6
Dutch Dabbs (R)	39,826	32.4
4 Mike Parker (D)	82,939	68.5
Mike Wood (R)	38,200	31.5
5 Gene Taylor (D)	73,179	60.1
George Barlos (R)	48,575	39.9

MISSOURI

Candidates	Votes	%
1 William L. Clay (D)	97,061	63.4
Donald R. Counts (R)	50,303	32.9
2 James M. Talent (R)	154,882	67.3
Pat Kelly (D)	70,480	30.6
3 Richard A. Gephardt (D)	117,601	57.7
Gary Gill (R)	80,977	39.7
4 Ike Skelton (D)	137,876	67.8
James A. Noland Jr. (R)	65,616	32.2
5 Karen McCarthy (D)	100,391	56.6
Ron Freeman (R)	77,120	43.4
6 Pat Danner (D)	140,108	66.1
Tina Tucker (R)	71,709	33.9
7 Mel Hancock (R)	112,228	57.3
James R. Fossard (D)	77,836	39.7
8 Bill Emerson (R)	129,320	70.1
James L. "Jay" Thompson (D)	48,987	26.5
9 Harold L. Volkmer (D)	103,443	50.5
Kenny Hulshof (R)	92,301	45.0

MONTANA

Candidates	Votes	%
AL Pat Williams (D)	171,372	48.7
Cy Jamison (R)	148,715	42.2
Steve Kelly (I)	32,046	9.1

NEBRASKA

Candidates	Votes	%
1 Doug Bereuter (R)	117,967	62.6
Patrick Combs (D)	70,369	37.3
2 Jon Christensen (R)	92,516	49.9
Peter Hoagland (D)	90,750	49.0
3 Bill Barrett (R)	154,919	78.7
Gil Chapin (D)	41,943	21.3

NEVADA

Candidates	Votes	%
1 John Ensign (R)	73,769	48.5
James Bilbray (D)	72,333	47.5
2 Barbara F. Vucanovich (R)	142,202	63.5
Janet Greeson (D)	65,390	29.2

NEW HAMPSHIRE

Candidates	Votes	%
1 Bill Zeliff (R)	97,017	65.6
Bill Verge (D)	42,481	28.7
2 Charles Bass (R)	83,121	51.4
Dick Swett (D)	74,243	46.0

NEW JERSEY

Candidates	Votes	%
1 Robert E. Andrews (D)	108,155	72.3
James N. Hogan (R)	41,505	27.7
2 Frank A. LoBiondo (R)	102,566	64.6
Louis N. Magazzu (D)	56,151	35.4
3 H. James Saxton (R)	115,750	66.4
James Smith (D)	54,441	31.2
4 Christopher H. Smith (R)	109,818	67.9
Ralph Walsh (D)	49,537	30.6
5 Marge Roukema (R)	139,964	74.2
Bill Auer (D)	41,275	21.9
6 Frank Pallone Jr. (D)	88,922	60.4
Mike Herson (D)	55,287	37.5
7 Bob Franks (R)	98,814	59.6
Karen Carroll (D)	64,231	38.7
8 Bill Martini (R)	70,494	49.9
Herb Klein (D)	68,661	48.6
9 Robert G. Torricelli (D)	99,984	62.5
Peter J. Russo (R)	57,651	36.1
10 Donald M. Payne (D)	74,622	75.9
Jim Ford (R)	21,524	21.9
11 Rodney Frelinghuysen (R)	127,868	71.2
Frank Herbert (D)	50,211	28.0
12 Dick Zimmer (R)	125,939	68.3
Joseph D. Youssouf (D)	55,977	30.4
13 Robert Menendez (D)	67,688	70.9
Fernando A. Alonso (R)	24,071	25.2

NEW MEXICO

Candidates	Votes	%
1 Steven H. Schiff (R)	119,996	73.9
Peter L. Zollinger (D)	42,316	26.1
2 Joe Skeen (R)	89,966	63.3
Benjamin Anthony Chavez (R)	45,316	31.9
3 Bill Richardson (D)	99,900	63.6
F. Gregg Bemis Jr. (R)	53,515	34.1

NEW YORK

Candidates	Votes	%
1 Michael P. Forbes (R,C,RTL, WTP)	90,491	52.5
George J. Hochbrueckner (D,LIF)	80,146	46.5
2 Rick A. Lazio (R,C,WTP)	100,107	68.2
James Manfre (D,LIF)	41,102	28.0
3 Peter T. King (R,C)	115,236	59.2
Norma Grill (D)	77,774	40.0
4 Daniel Frisa (R)	87,815	50.2
Philip M. Schiliro (D)	65,286	37.3
David A. Levy (C)	15,173	8.7
5 Gary Ackerman (D,L)	93,896	55.0
Grant M. Lally (R,C)	73,884	43.3
6 Floyd H. Flake (D)	68,596	80.4
Denny D. Bhagwandin (R,C)	16,675	19.6
7 Thomas J. Manton (D)	58,935	87.1
Robert E. Hurley (C)	8,698	12.9

Candidates	Votes	%
8 Jerrold Nadler (D,L)	109,946	82.0
David L. Askren (R)	21,132	15.8
9 Charles E. Schumer (D,L)	95,139	72.6
James McCall (R,C)	35,880	27.4
10 Edolphus Towns (D,L)	77,026	89.0
Amelia Smith Parker (R)	7,995	9.2
11 Major R. Owens (D,L)	61,945	88.9
Gary S. Popkin (R,LIBERT)	6,605	9.5
12 Nydia M. Velazquez (D,L)	39,929	92.3
Genevieve R. Brennan (C)	2,747	6.3
13 Susan Molinari (R,C)	96,491	71.4
Tyrone G. Butler (D)	33,937	25.1
14 Carolyn B. Maloney (D,IN)	98,479	64.2
Charles Millard (R,L)	54,277	35.4
15 Charles B. Rangel (D,L)	77,830	96.5
16 Jose E. Serrano (D,L)	58,572	96.3
17 Eliot L. Engel (D,L)	73,321	77.6
Edward T. Marshall (R)	16,896	17.9
18 Nita M. Lowey (D)	91,663	57.3
Andrew C. Hartzell Jr. (R,C)	65,517	40.9
19 Sue W. Kelly (R)	100,173	52.1
Hamilton Fish Jr. (D)	70,696	36.8
Joseph J. DioGuardi (C,RTL)	19,761	10.3
20 Benjamin A. Gilman (R)	120,334	67.5
Gregory B. Julian (D)	52,345	29.4
21 Michael R. McNulty (D,C)	147,804	67.0
Joseph A. Gomez (R)	68,745	31.2
22 Gerald B.H. Solomo (R,C,RTL)	157,717	73.4
L. Robert Lawrence (D)	57,064	26.6
23 Sherwood Boehlert (R)	124,486	70.5
Charles W. Skeele Jr. (D)	40,786	23.1
Donald J. Thomas (RTL)	11,216	6.4
24 John M. McHugh (R,C)	124,645	78.6
Danny M. Francis (D)	34,032	21.4
25 James T. Walsh (R,C)	113,949	57.6
Rhea Jezer (D,CHGC)	83,853	42.4
26 Maurice D. Hinchey (D,L)	95,492	49.1
Bob Moppert (R,C)	94,244	48.5
27 Bill Paxon (R,C,RTL)	152,610	74.5
William A. Long Jr. (D)	52,160	25.5
28 Louise M. Slaughter (D)	110,987	56.6
Renee Forgensi Davison (R,C)	78,516	40.1
29 John J. LaFalce (D,L)	103,053	55.2
William E. Miller (R,C)	80,355	43.0
30 Jack Quinn (R,C)	124,738	67.0
David A. Franczyk (D,L)	61,392	33.0
31 Amo Houghton (R,C)	121,178	84.8
Gretchen S. McManus (RTL)	21,747	15.2

NORTH CAROLINA

Candidates	Votes	%
1 Eva Clayton (D)	66,827	61.1
Ted Tyler (R)	42,602	38.9
2 David Funderburk (R)	79,207	56.0
Richard Moore (D)	62,122	44.0
3 Walter B. Jones Jr. (R)	72,464	52.7
H. Martin Lancaster (D)	65,013	47.3
4 Frederick Kenneth Heineman (R)	77,773	50.4
David Price (D)	76,558	49.6
5 Richard Burr (R)	84,741	57.3
A.P. "Sandy" Sands (D)	63,194	42.7
6 Howard Coble (R)		100.0
7 Charlie Rose (D)	62,670	51.6
Robert C. Anderson (R)	58,849	48.4
8 W.G. "Bill" Hefner (D)	62,845	52.4
Sherrill Morgan (R)	57,140	47.6
9 Sue Myrick (R)	82,374	65.0
Rory Blake (D)	44,379	35.0
10 Cass Ballenger (R)	107,829	71.5
Robert Wayne Avery (D)	42,939	28.5
11 Charles H. Taylor (R)	115,826	60.1
Maggie Palmer Lauterer (D)	76,862	39.9
12 Melvin Watt (D)	57,655	65.8
Joseph A. "Joe" Martino (R)	29,933	34.2

NORTH DAKOTA

	Candidates	Votes	%
AL	Earl Pomeroy (D)	123,134	52.3
	Gary Porter (R)	105,988	45.0

OHIO

	Candidates	Votes	%
1	Steve Chabot (R)	92,997	56.1
	David Mann (D)	72,822	43.9
2	Rob Portman (R)	150,128	77.4
	Les Mann (D)	43,730	22.6
3	Tony P. Hall (D)	105,342	59.3
	David A. Westbrock (R)	72,314	40.7
4	Michael G. Oxley (R)		100.0
5	Paul E. Gillmor (R)	135,879	73.4
	Jarrod Tudor (D)	49,335	26.6
6	Frank A. Cremeans (R)	91,263	50.9
	Ted Strickland (D)	87,861	49.1
7	David L. Hobson (R)		100.0
8	John A. Boehner (R)	148,338	99.9
9	Marcy Kaptur (D)	118,120	75.3
	R. Randy Whitman (R)	38,665	24.7
10	Martin R. Hoke (R)	95,226	51.9
	Francis E. Gaul (D)	70,918	38.6
	Joseph J. Jacobs Jr. (I)	17,495	9.5
11	Louis Stokes (D)	114,220	77.2
	James J. Sykora (R)	33,705	22.8
12	John R. Kasich (R)	114,608	66.5
	Cynthia L. Ruccia (D)	57,294	33.2
13	Sherrod Brown (D)	93,147	49.1
	Gregory A. White (R)	86,422	45.5
14	Tom Sawyer (D)	96,274	51.9
	Lynn Slaby (R)	89,106	48.1
15	Deborah Pryce (R)	112,912	70.7
	Bill Buckel (D)	46,480	29.1
16	Ralph Regula (R)	137,322	75.0
	J. Michael Finn (D)	45,781	25.0
17	James A. Traficant Jr. (D)	149,004	77.4
	Mike G. Meister (R)	43,490	22.6
18	Bob Ney (R)	103,115	54.0
	Greg L. DiDonato (D)	87,926	46.0
19	Steven C. LaTourette (R)	99,997	48.5
	Eric D. Fingerhut (D)	89,701	43.5
	Ronald E. Young (I)	11,364	5.5

OKLAHOMA

	Candidates	Votes	%
1	Steve Largent (R)	107,085	62.7
	Stuart Price (D)	63,753	37.3
2	Tom Coburn (R)	82,479	52.1
	Virgil R. Cooper (D)	75,943	47.9
3	Bill Brewster (D)	115,731	73.8
	Darrel Dewayne Tallant (R)	41,147	26.2
4	J.C. Watts (R)	80,251	51.6
	David Perryman (D)	67,237	43.3
	Bill Tiffee (I)	7,913	5.1
5	Ernest Jim Istook (R)	136,877	78.1
	Tom Keith (I)	38,270	21.9
6	Frank D. Lucas (R)	106,961	70.2
	Jeffrey S. Tollett (D)	45,399	29.8

Special Election[3]

	Candidates	Votes	%
6	Frank D. Lucas (R)	71,354	54.2
	Dan Webber Jr. (D)	60,411	45.8

OREGON

	Candidates	Votes	%
1	Elizabeth Furse (D)	121,147	47.7
	Bill Witt (R)	120,846	47.6
2	Wes Cooley (R)	134,255	57.3
	Sue C. Kupillas (D)	90,822	38.7
3	Ron Wyden (D)	161,624	72.5
	Everett Hall (R)	43,211	19.4
	Mark Brunelle (I)	13,550	6.1
4	Peter A. DeFazio (D)	158,981	66.8
	John D. Newkirk (R)	78,947	33.2
5	Jim Bunn (R)	121,369	49.8
	Catherine Webber (D)	114,015	46.8

PENNSYLVANIA

	Candidates	Votes	%
1	Thomas M. Foglietta (D)	99,669	81.5
	Roger F. Gordon (R)	22,595	18.5
2	Chaka Fattah (D)	120,553	85.9
	Lawrence R. Watson (R)	19,824	14.1
3	Robert A. Borski (D)	92,702	62.7
	James C. Hasher (R)	55,209	37.3
4	Ron Klink (D)	119,115	64.2
	Ed Peglow (R)	66,509	35.8
5	William F. Clinger (R)	145,335	99.9
6	Tim Holden (D)	90,023	56.7
	Fred Levering (R)	68,610	43.3
7	Curt Weldon (R)	137,480	69.7
	Sara Nichols (D)	59,845	30.3
8	James C. Greenwood (R)	110,499	66.1
	John P. Murray (D)	44,559	26.7
9	Bud Shuster (R)	146,688	99.7
10	Joseph M. McDade (R)	106,992	65.7
	Daniel J. Schreffler (D)	50,635	31.1
11	Paul E. Kanjorski (D)	101,966	66.5
	J. Andrew Podolak (R)	51,295	33.5
12	John P. Murtha (D)	117,825	68.9
	Bill Choby (R)	53,147	31.1
13	Jon D. Fox (R)	96,254	49.4
	Marjorie Margolies-Mezvinsky (D)	88,073	45.2
14	William J. Coyne (D)	105,310	64.1
	John Robert Clark (R)	53,221	32.4
15	Paul McHale (D)	72,073	47.8
	Jim Yeager (R)	71,602	47.4
16	Robert S. Walker (R)	109,759	69.7
	Bill Chertok (D)	47,680	30.3
17	George W. Gekas (R)	133,788	99.9
18	Mike Doyle (D)	101,784	54.8
	John McCarty (R)	83,881	45.2
19	Bill Goodling (R)	124,496	99.5
20	Frank R. Mascara (D)	95,251	53.1
	Mike McCormick (R)	84,156	46.9
21	Phil English (R)	89,439	49.5
	Bill Leavens (D)	84,796	46.9

RHODE ISLAND

	Candidates	Votes	%
1	Patrick J. Kennedy (D)	89,832	54.1
	Kevin Vigilante (R)	76,069	45.9
2	Jack Reed (D)	119,659	68.0
	A. John Elliot (R)	56,348	32.0

SOUTH CAROLINA

	Candidates	Votes	%
1	Marshall "Mark" Sanford (R)	973,03	66.3
	Robert Barber (D)	47,769	32.4
2	Floyd D. Spence (R)	133,307	99.8
3	Lindsey Graham (R)	90,123	60.1
	James Bryan (D)	59,932	39.9
4	Bob Inglis (R)	109,626	73.5
	Jerry Fowler (D)	39,396	26.4
5	John M. Spratt Jr. (D)	77,311	52.1
	Larry Bigham (R)	70,967	47.8
6	James E. Clyburn (D)	88,635	63.8
	Gary McLeod (R)	50,259	36.2

SOUTH DAKOTA

	Candidates	Votes	%
AL	Tim Johnson (D)	183,036	59.8
	Jan Berkhout (R)	112,054	36.6

TENNESSEE

	Candidates	Votes	%
1	James H. Quillen (R)	102,947	72.9
	J. Carr "Jack" Christian (D)	34,691	24.6
2	John J. "Jimmy" Duncan Jr. (R)	128,937	90.5
3	Zach Wamp (R)	84,583	52.3
	Randy Button (D)	73,839	45.6
4	Van Hilleary (R)	81,539	56.6
	Jeff Whorley (D)	60,489	42.0
5	Bob Clement (D)	95,953	60.2
	John Osborne (R)	61,692	38.7
6	Bart Gordon (D)	90,933	50.6

	Candidates	Votes	%
	Steve Gill (R)	88,759	49.4
7	Ed Bryant (R)	102,587	60.2
	Harold Byrd (D)	65,851	38.6
8	John Tanner (D)	97,951	63.8
	Neal R. Morris (R)	55,573	36.2
9	Harold E. Ford (D)	94,805	57.8
	Rod DeBerry (R)	69,226	42.2

TEXAS

	Candidates	Votes	%
1	Jim Chapman (D)	86,480	55.3
	Mike Blankenship (R)	63,911	40.9
2	Charles Wilson (D)	87,709	57.0
	Donna Peterson (R)	66,071	43.0
3	Sam Johnson (R)	157,011	91.0
	Tom Donahue (LIBERT)	15,611	9.0
4	Ralph M. Hall (D)	99,303	58.8
	David L. Bridges (R)	67,267	39.8
5	John Bryant (D)	61,877	50.1
	Pete Sessions (R)	58,521	47.3
6	Joe L. Barton (R)	152,038	75.6
	Terry Jesmore (D)	44,286	22.0
7	Bill Archer (R)		100.0
8	Jack Fields (R)	148,473	92.0
	Russ Klecka (I)	12,831	8.0
9	Steve Stockman (R)	81,353	51.9
	Jack Brooks (D)	71,643	45.7
10	Lloyd Doggett (D)	113,738	56.3
	A. Jo Baylor (R)	80,382	39.8
11	Chet Edwards (D)	76,667	59.2
	Jim Broyles (R)	52,876	40.8
12	Pete Geren (D)	96,372	68.7
	Ernest J. Anderson Jr. (R)	43,959	31.3
13	William M. "Mac" Thornberry (R)	79,466	55.4
	Bill Sarpalius (D)	63,923	44.6
14	Greg Laughlin (D)	86,175	55.6
	Jim Deats (R)	68,793	44.4
15	E. "Kika" de la Garza (D)	61,527	59.0
	Tom Haughey (R)	41,119	39.4
16	Ronald D. Coleman (D)	49,815	57.1
	Bobby Ortiz (R)	37,409	42.9
17	Charles W. Stenholm (D)	83,497	53.7
	Phil Boone (R)	72,108	46.3
18	Sheila Jackson Lee (D)	84,790	73.5
	Jerry Burley (R)	28,153	24.4
19	Larry Combest (R)		100.0
20	Henry B. Gonzalez (D)	60,114	62.5
	Carl Bill Colyer (R)	36,035	37.5
21	Lamar Smith (R)	165,595	90.0
	Kerry Lowry (I)	18,480	10.0
22	Tom DeLay (R)	120,302	73.7
	Scott Douglas Cunningham (D)	38,826	23.8
23	Henry Bonilla (R)	73,815	62.6
	Rolando L. Rios (D)	44,101	37.4
24	Martin Frost (D)	65,019	52.8
	Ed Harrison (R)	58,062	47.2
25	Ken Bentsen (D)	61,959	52.3
	Gene Fontenot (R)	53,321	45.0
26	Dick Armey (R)	135,398	76.4
	LeEarl Ann Bryant (D)	39,763	22.4
27	Solomon P. Ortiz (D)	65,325	59.4
	Erol A. Stone (R)	44,693	40.6
28	Frank Tejeda (D)	73,986	70.9
	David C. Slatter (R)	28,777	27.6
29	Gene Green (D)	44,102	73.4
	Harold "Oilman" Eide (R)	15,952	26.6
30	Eddie Bernice Johnson (D)	73,166	72.6
	Lucy Cain (R)	25,848	25.7

UTAH

	Candidates	Votes	%
1	James V. Hansen (R)	104,954	64.5
	Bobbie Coray (D)	57,644	35.5
2	Enid Greene Waldholtz (R)	85,507	45.8
	Karen Shepherd (D)	66,911	35.9
	Merrill Cook (I)	34,167	18.3
3	Bill Orton (D)	91,505	59.0

Candidates	Votes	%
Dixie Thompson (R)	61,839	39.9

VERMONT

	Candidates	Votes	%
AL	Bernard Sanders (I)	105,502	49.9
	John Carroll (R)	98,523	46.6

VIRGINIA

	Candidates	Votes	%
1	Herbert H. Bateman (R)	142,930	74.3
	Mary Sinclair (D)	45,173	23.5
2	Owen Pickett (D)	81,372	59.0
	Jim Chapman (R)	56,375	40.9
3	Robert C. Scott (D)	108,532	79.4
	Tom Ward (R)	28,080	20.6
4	Norman Sisisky (D)	115,055	61.6
	George Sweet (R)	71,678	38.4
5	Lewis F. Payne Jr. (D)	95,308	53.3
	George C. Landrith III (R)	83,555	46.7
6	Robert W. Goodlatte (R)	126,455	99.9
7	Thomas J. Bliley Jr. (R)	176,941	84.0
	Gerald E. "Jerry" Berg (I)	33,220	15.8
8	James P. Moran (D)	120,281	59.3
	Kyle E. McSlarrow (R)	79,568	39.3
9	Rick Boucher (D)	102,876	58.8
	Steve Fast (R)	72,133	41.2
10	Frank R. Wolf (R)	153,311	87.3
	Alan R. Ogden (I)	13,687	7.8
11	Thomas M. Davis III (R)	98,216	52.9
	Leslie L. Byrne (D)	84,104	45.3

WASHINGTON

	Candidates	Votes	%
1	Rick White (R)	100,554	51.7
	Maria Cantwell (D)	94,110	48.3
2	Jack Metcalf (R)	107,430	54.7
	Harriet A. Spanel (D)	89,096	45.3
3	Linda Smith (R)	100,188	52.0
	Jolene Unsoeld (D)	85,826	44.6
4	Doc Hastings (R)	92,828	53.3
	Jay Inslee (D)	81,198	46.7
5	George Nethercutt (R)	110,057	50.9
	Thomas S. Foley (D)	106,074	49.1
6	Norm Dicks (D)	105,480	58.3
	Benjamin Gregg (R)	75,322	41.7
7	Jim McDermott (D)	148,353	75.1
	Keith Harris (R)	49,091	24.9
8	Jennifer Dunn (R)	140,409	76.1
	Jim Wyrick (D)	44,165	23.9
9	Randy Tate (R)	77,833	51.8
	Mike Kreidler (D)	72,451	48.2

WEST VIRGINIA

	Candidates	Votes	%
1	Alan B. Mollohan (D)	103,177	70.3
	Sally Rossy Riley (R)	43,590	29.7
2	Bob Wise (D)	90,757	63.7
	Sam Cravotta (R)	51,691	36.3
3	Nick J. Rahall II (D)	74,967	63.9
	Ben Waldman (R)	42,382	36.1

WISCONSIN

	Candidates	Votes	%
1	Mark W. Neumann (R)	83,937	49.4
	Peter W. Barca (D)	82,817	48.8
2	Scott L. Klug (R)	133,734	69.2
	Thomas C. Hecht (D)	55,406	28.7
3	Steve Gunderson (R)	89,338	55.7
	Harvey Stower (D)	65,758	41.0
4	Gerald D. Kleczka (D)	93,789	53.7
	Tom Reynolds (R)	78,225	44.8
5	Thomas M. Barrett (D)	87,806	62.4
	Stephen B. Hollingshead (R)	51,145	36.4
6	Tom Petri (R)	119,384	99.5
7	David R. Obey (D)	97,184	54.3
	Scott West (R)	81,706	45.7
8	Toby Roth (R)	114,319	63.7
	Stan Gruszynski (D)	65,065	36.3
9	F. James Sensenbrenner (R)	141,617	99.8

WYOMING

	Candidates	Votes	%
AL	Barbara Cubin (R)	104,426	53.2
	Bob Schuster (D)	81,022	41.3
	Dave Dawson (LIBERT)	10,749	5.5

1. A special election was held to fill the unexpired term of Rep. William H. Natcher (D), who died March 29, 1994.

2. For the 1994 House elections in Louisiana, an open primary election was held with candidates from all parties running on the same ballot. Any candidate who received a majority was elected unopposed, with no further appearance on the general election ballot. If no candidate received 50 percent, a runoff was held between the two top finishers.

3. A special election was held to fill the unexpired term of Rep. Glen English (D), who resigned Jan. 7, 1994.

1995 House Elections

CALIFORNIA

Special Election[1]

	Candidates	Votes	%
15	Tom Campbell (R)	54,372	58.9
	Jerry Estruth (D)	33,051	35.8
	Linh Kieu Dao (I)	4,922	5.3

ILLINOIS

Special Election[2]

	Candidates	Votes	%
2	Jesse Jackson Jr. (D)	48,145	76.0
	Thomas "T. J." Somer (R)	15,171	24.0

1. A special election was held to fill the unexpired term of Rep. Norman Y. Mineta (D), who resigned Oct. 10, 1995.

2. A special election was held to fill the unexpired term of Rep. Mel Reynolds (D), who resigned Oct. 1, 1995.

1996 House Elections

ALABAMA

	Candidates	Votes	%
1	Sonny Callahan (R)	132,206	64.4
	Don Womack (D)	69,470	33.8
2	Terry Everett (R)	132,563	63.2
	Bob E. Gaines (D)	74,317	35.4
3	Bob Riley (R)	98,353	50.4
	T.D "Ted" Little (D)	92,325	47.3
4	Robert B. Aderholt (R)	102,741	49.9
	Robert T. "Bob" Wilson (D)	99,250	48.2
5	Robert E. "Bud" Cramer (D)	114,442	55.7
	Wayne Parker (R)	86,727	42.2
6	Spencer Bachus (R)	180,781	70.9
	Mary Lynn Bates (D)	69,592	27.3
7	Earl F. Hilliard (D)	136,651	71.1
	Joe Powell (R)	52,142	27.1

ALASKA

	Candidates	Votes	%
AL	Don Young (R)	138,834	59.4
	Georgianna Lincoln (D)	85,114	36.4

ARIZONA

	Candidates	Votes	%
1	Matt Salmon (R)	135,634	60.2
	John Cox (D)	89,738	39.8
2	Ed Pastor (D)	81,982	65.0
	Jim Buster (R)	38,786	30.8
3	Bob Stump (R)	175,231	66.5
	Alexander "Big Al" Schneider (D)	88,214	33.5
4	John Shadegg (R)	150,486	66.8
	Maria Elena Milton (D)	74,857	33.2
5	Jim Kolbe (R)	179,349	68.7
	Mort Nelson (D)	67,597	25.9
6	J.D Hayworth (R)	121,431	47.6
	Steve Owens (D)	118,957	46.6
	Robert Anderson (LIBERT)	14,899	5.8

ARKANSAS

	Candidates	Votes	%
1	Marion Berry (D)	105,280	52.8
	Warren Dupwe (R)	88,436	44.3
2	Vic Snyder (D)	114,841	52.3
	Bud Cummins (R)	104,548	47.7
3	Asa Hutchinson (R)	137,093	55.7
	Ann Henry (D)	102,994	41.8
4	Jay Dickey (R)	125,956	63.5
	Vincent Tolliver (D)	72,391	36.5

CALIFORNIA

	Candidates	Votes	%
1	Frank Riggs (R)	110,242	49.6
	Michela Alioto (D)	96,522	43.5
	Emil Rossi (LIBERT)	15,354	6.9
2	Wally Herger (R)	144,913	60.8
	Roberts A. Braden (D)	80,401	33.7
3	Vic Fazio (D)	118,663	53.5
	Tim LeFever (R)	91,134	41.1
4	John T. Doolittle (R)	164,048	60.5
	Katie Hirning (D)	97,948	36.1
5	Robert T. Matsui (D)	142,618	70.4
	Robert S. Dinsmore (R)	52,940	26.1
6	Lynn Woolsey (D)	156,958	61.8
	Duane C. Hughes (R)	86,278	34.0
7	George Miller (D)	137,089	71.8
	Norman H. Reece (R)	42,542	22.3
8	Nancy Pelosi (D)	175,216	84.3
	Justin Raimondo (R)	25,739	12.4
9	Ronald V. Dellums (D)	154,806	77.0
	Deborah Wright (R)	37,126	18.5
10	Ellen O. Tauscher (D)	137,726	48.6
	Bill Baker (R)	133,633	47.2
11	Richard W. Pombo (R)	107,477	59.3
	Jason Silva (D)	65,536	36.2
12	Tom Lantos (D)	149,052	71.7

	Candidates	Votes	%
	Storm Jenkins (R)	49,278	23.7
13	Pete Stark (D)	114,408	65.2
	James S. Fay (R)	53,385	30.4
14	Anna G. Eshoo (D)	149,313	64.9
	Ben Brink (R)	71,573	31.1
15	Tom Campbell (R)	132,737	58.5
	Dick Lane (D)	79,048	34.8
16	Zoe Lofgren (D)	94,020	65.7
	Chuck Wojslaw (R)	43,191	30.2
17	Sam Farr (D)	115,116	58.9
	Jess Brown (R)	73,856	37.8
18	Gary A. Condit (D)	108,827	65.7
	Bill Conrad (R)	52,695	31.8
19	George P. Radanovich (R)	137,402	66.6
	Paul Barile (D)	58,452	28.3
20	Cal Dooley (D)	65,381	56.5
	Trice Harvey (R)	45,276	39.1
21	Bill Thomas (R)	125,916	65.8
	Deborah A. Vollmer (D)	50,694	26.5
22	Walter Holden Capps (D)	118,299	48.4
	Andrea Seastrand (R)	107,987	44.2
23	Elton Gallegly (R)	118,880	59.6
	Robert R. Unruhe (D)	70,035	35.1
24	Brad Sherman (D)	106,193	49.4
	Rich Sybert (R)	93,629	43.6
25	Howard P. "Buck" McKeon (R)	122,428	62.4
	Diane Trautman (D)	65,089	33.2
26	Howard L. Berman (D)	67,525	65.9
	Bill Glass (R)	29,332	28.6
27	James E. Rogan (R)	95,310	50.2
	Doug Kahn (D)	82,014	43.2
28	David Dreier (R)	113,389	60.7
	David Levering (D)	69,037	36.9
29	Henry A. Waxman (D)	145,278	67.6
	Paul Stepanek (R)	52,857	24.6
30	Xavier Becerra (D)	58,283	72.3
	Patricia Jean Parker (R)	15,078	18.7
31	Matthew G. Martinez (D)	69,285	67.5
	John V. Flores (R)	28,705	28.0
32	Julian C. Dixon (D)	124,712	82.4
	Larry Ardito (R)	18,768	12.4
33	Lucille Roybal-Allard (D)	47,478	82.1
	John P. Leonard (R)	8,147	14.1
34	Esteban E. Torres (D)	94,730	68.4
	David G. Nunez (R)	36,852	26.6
35	Maxine Waters (D)	92,762	85.5
	Eric Carlson (R)	13,116	12.1
36	Jane Harman (D)	117,752	52.5
	Susan Brooks (R)	98,538	43.9
37	Juanita Millender McDonald (D)	87,247	85.0
	Michael E. Voetee (R)	15,399	15.0
38	Steve Horn (R)	88,136	52.6
	Rick Zbur (D)	71,627	42.7
39	Ed Royce (R)	120,761	62.8
	R.O "Bob" Davis (D)	61,392	31.9
	Jack Dean (LIBERT)	10,137	5.3
40	Jerry Lewis (R)	98,821	64.9
	Robert "Bob" Conaway (D)	44,102	29.0
41	Jay C. Kim (R)	83,934	58.5
	Richard L. Waldron (D)	47,346	33.0
42	George E. Brown Jr. (D)	52,166	50.5
	Linda M. Wilde (R)	51,170	49.5
43	Ken Calvert (R)	97,247	54.7
	Guy C. Kimbrough (D)	67,422	37.9
44	Sonny Bono (R)	110,643	57.7
	Anita Rufus (D)	73,844	38.5
45	Dana Rohrabacher (R)	125,326	61.0
	Sally J. Alexander (D)	68,312	33.2
46	Loretta Sanchez (D)	47,964	46.8
	Robert K. Dornan (R)	46,980	45.8
47	Christopher Cox (R)	160,078	65.7
	Tina Louise Laine (D)	70,362	28.9
48	Ron Packard (R)	145,814	65.9
	Dan Farrell (D)	59,558	26.9

	Candidates	Votes	%
49	Brian P. Bilbray (R)	108,806	52.6
	Peter Navarro (D)	86,657	41.9
50	Bob Filner (D)	73,200	61.9
	Jim Baize (R)	38,351	32.4
51	Randy "Duke" Cunningham (R)	149,032	65.1
	Rita Tamerius (D)	66,250	28.9
52	Duncan Hunter (R)	116,746	65.5
	Darity Wesley (D)	53,104	29.8

Special Election[1]

		Votes	%
37	Juanita Millender-McDonald (D)	13,868	27.3
	Willard H. Murray Jr. (D)	10,396	20.4
	Omar Bradley (D)	6,975	13.7
	Paul H. Richards (D)	6,035	11.9
	Robert M. Sausedo (D)	4,495	8.8
	Robin Tucker (D)	3,661	7.2
	Charles Davis (D)	2,555	5.0

COLORADO

	Candidates	Votes	%
1	Diana DeGette (D)	112,631	56.9
	Joe Rogers (R)	79,540	40.2
2	David E. Skaggs (D)	145,894	57.0
	Pat Miller (R)	97,865	38.3
3	Scott McInnis (R)	183,523	68.9
	Al Gurule (D)	82,953	31.1
4	Bob Schaffer (R)	137,012	56.1
	Guy Kelley (D)	92,837	38.1
5	Joel Hefley (R)	188,805	71.9
	Mike Robinson (D)	73,660	28.1
6	Dan Schaefer (R)	146,018	62.2
	Joan Fitz-Gerald (D)	88,600	37.8

CONNECTICUT

	Candidates	Votes	%
1	Barbara B. Kennelly (D,ACP)	158,222	73.5
	Kent Sleath (R)	53,666	24.9
2	Sam Gejdenson (D,ACP)	115,175	51.6
	Edward W. Munster (R)	100,332	44.9
3	Rosa DeLauro (D,ACP)	150,798	71.3
	John Coppola (R)	59,335	28.1
4	Christopher Shays (R)	121,949	60.5
	Bill Finch (D)	75,902	37.6
5	Jim Maloney (D,ACP)	111,974	52.0
	Gary A. Franks (R)	98,782	45.9
6	Nancy L. Johnson (R)	113,020	49.6
	Charlotte Koskoff (D,ACP)	111,433	48.9

DELAWARE

	Candidates	Votes	%
AL	Michael N. Castle (R)	185,576	69.5
	Dennis E. Williams (D)	73,253	27.5

FLORIDA

	Candidates	Votes	%
1	Joe Scarborough (R)	175,946	72.5
	Kevin Beck (D)	66,495	27.4
2	Allen Boyd (D)	138,151	59.4
	Bill Sutton (R)	94,122	40.5
3	Corrine Brown (D)	98,085	61.2
	Preston James Fields (R)	62,196	38.8
4	Tillie Fowler (R)		100.0
5	Karen L. Thurman (D)	161,050	61.7
	Dave Gentry (R)	100,051	38.3
6	Cliff Stearns (R)	161,527	67.2
	Newell O'Brien (D)	78,908	32.8
7	John L. Mica (R)	143,667	62.0
	George Stuart Jr. (D)	87,832	37.9
8	Bill McCollum (R)	136,515	67.5
	Al Krulick (D)	65,794	32.5
9	Michael Bilirakis (R)	161,708	68.7
	Jerry Provenzano (D)	73,809	31.3

	Candidates	Votes	%
10	C.W Bill Young (R)	114,443	66.6
	Henry Green (D)	57,375	33.4
11	Jim Davis (D)	108,522	57.9
	Mark Sharpe (R)	78,881	42.0
12	Charles T. Canady (R)	122,584	61.6
	Mike Canady (D)	76,513	38.4
13	Dan Miller (R)	173,671	64.3
	Sanford Gordon (D)	96,098	35.6
14	Porter J. Goss (R)	176,992	73.5
	Jim Nolan (D)	63,842	26.5
15	Dave Weldon (R)	139,014	51.4
	John L. Byron (D)	115,981	42.9
	David Golding (I)	15,349	5.7
16	Mark Foley (R)	175,714	64.0
	Jim Stuber (D)	98,827	36.0
17	Carrie P. Meek (D)	114,638	88.8
	Wellington Rolle (R)	14,525	11.2
18	Ileana Ros-Lehtinen (R)	123,659	100.0
19	Robert Wexler (D)	188,766	65.6
	Beverly "Bev" Kennedy (R)	99,101	34.4
20	Peter Deutsch (D)	159,256	65.0
	Jim Jacobs (R)	85,777	35.0
21	Lincoln Diaz-Balart (R)	125,469	100.0
22	E. Clay Shaw Jr. (R)	137,098	61.9
	Kenneth D. Cooper (D)	84,517	38.1
23	Alcee L. Hastings (D)	102,161	73.5
	Robert Paul Brown (R)	36,907	26.5

GEORGIA

	Candidates	Votes	%
1	Jack Kingston (R)	108,616	68.2
	Rosemary Kaszans (D)	50,622	31.8
2	Sanford D. Bishop Jr. (D)	88,256	54.0
	Darrel Ealum (R)	75,282	46.0
3	Mac Collins (R)	120,251	61.1
	Jim Chafin (D)	76,538	38.9
4	Cynthia A. McKinney (D)	127,157	57.8
	John Mitnick (R)	92,985	42.2
5	John Lewis (D)	136,555	100.0
6	Newt Gingrich (R)	174,155	57.8
	Michael Coles (D)	127,135	42.2
7	Bob Barr (R)	112,009	57.8
	Charlie Watts (D)	81,765	42.2
8	Saxby Chambliss (R)	93,619	52.6
	Jim Wiggins (D)	84,506	47.4
9	Nathan Deal (R)	132,532	65.5
	McCracken "Ken" Poston (D)	69,662	34.5
10	Charlie Norwood (R)	96,723	52.3
	David Bell (D)	88,054	47.7
11	John Linder (R)	145,821	64.3
	Tommy Stephenson (D)	80,940	35.7

HAWAII

	Candidates	Votes	%
1	Neil Abercrombie (D)	86,732	50.4
	Orson Swindle (R)	80,053	46.5
2	Patsy T. Mink (D)	109,178	60.3
	Tom Pico Jr. (R)	55,729	30.8

IDAHO

	Candidates	Votes	%
1	Helen Chenoweth (R)	132,344	50.0
	Dan Williams (D)	125,899	47.5
2	Michael D. Crapo (R)	157,646	68.8
	John D. Seidl (D)	67,625	29.5

ILLINOIS

	Candidates	Votes	%
1	Bobby L. Rush (D)	174,005	85.7
	Noel Naughton (R)	25,659	12.6
2	Jesse L. Jackson Jr. (D)	172,648	94.1
	Frank H. Stratman (LIBERT)	10,880	5.9
3	William O. Lipinski (D)	137,153	65.3
	Jim Nalepa (R)	67,214	32.0
4	Luis V. Gutierrez (D)	85,278	93.6
	William Passmore (LIBERT)	5,857	6.4
5	Rod R. Blagojevich (D)	117,544	64.1
	Michael Patrick Flanagan (R)	65,768	35.9
6	Henry J. Hyde (R)	132,401	64.3

	Candidates	Votes	%
	Stephen de la Rosa (D)	68,807	33.4
7	Danny K. Davis (D)	149,568	82.6
	Randy Borow (R)	27,241	15.0
8	Philip M. Crane (R)	127,763	62.2
	Elizabeth Ann "Betty" Hull (D)	74,068	36.1
9	Sidney R. Yates (D)	124,319	63.4
	Joseph Walsh (R)	71,763	36.6
10	John Edward Porter (R)	145,626	69.1
	Philip R. Torf (D)	65,144	30.9
11	Gerald C. "Jerry" Weller (R)	109,896	51.8
	Clem Balanoff (D)	102,388	48.2
12	Jerry F. Costello (D)	150,005	71.6
	Shapley R. Hunter (R)	55,690	26.6
13	Harris W. Fawell (R)	141,651	59.9
	Susan W. Hynes (D)	94,693	40.1
14	Dennis Hastert (R)	134,432	64.4
	Doug Mains (D)	74,332	35.6
15	Thomas W. Ewing (R)	121,019	57.3
	Laurel Lunt Prussing (D)	90,065	42.7
16	Donald Manzullo (R)	137,523	60.3
	Catherine M. Lee (D)	90,575	39.7
17	Lane Evans (D)	120,008	51.9
	Mark Baker (R)	109,240	47.3
18	Ray LaHood (R)	143,110	59.3
	Mike Curran (D)	98,413	40.7
19	Glenn Poshard (D)	158,668	66.7
	Brent Winters (R)	75,751	31.8
20	John M. Shimkus (R)	120,926	50.3
	Jay C. Hoffman (D)	119,688	49.7

INDIANA

	Candidates	Votes	%
1	Peter J. Visclosky (D)	133,553	69.2
	Michael Edward Petyo (R)	56,418	29.2
2	David M. McIntosh (R)	123,113	57.8
	R. Marc "Marc" Carmichael (D)	85,105	40.0
3	Tim Roemer (D)	114,288	57.9
	Joe Zakas (R)	80,699	40.9
4	Mark E. Souder (R)	121,344	58.4
	Gerald L. Houseman (D)	81,740	39.3
5	Steve Buyer (R)	125,191	59.3
	Douglas L. Clark (D)	63,578	30.1
6	Dan Burton (R)	193,193	74.9
	Carrie J. Dillard Trammell (D)	59,661	23.1
7	Ed Pease (R)	130,010	62.0
	Robert F. Hellmann (D)	72,705	34.6
8	John Hostettler (R)	109,860	50.0
	Jonathan Weinzapfel (D)	106,201	48.3
9	Lee H. Hamilton (D)	128,123	56.5
	Jean Leising (R)	96,442	42.5
10	Julia Carson (D)	85,965	52.9
	Virginia Blankenbaker (R)	72,796	44.8

IOWA

	Candidates	Votes	%
1	Jim Leach (R)	129,242	52.8
	Bob Rush (D)	111,595	45.6
2	Jim Nussle (R)	127,827	53.4
	Donna L. Smith (D)	109,731	45.9
3	Leonard L. Boswell (D)	115,914	49.4
	Mike Mahaffey (R)	111,895	47.6
4	Greg Ganske (R)	133,419	52.0
	Connie McBurney (D)	119,790	46.7
5	Tom Latham (R)	147,576	65.5
	MacDonald Smith (D)	75,785	33.6

KANSAS

	Candidates	Votes	%
1	Jerry Moran (R)	191,899	73.5
	John Divine (D)	63,948	24.5
2	Jim Ryun (R)	131,592	52.2
	John Frieden (D)	114,644	45.5
3	Vince Snowbarger (R)	139,169	49.8
	Judy Hancock (D)	126,848	45.4
4	Todd Tiahrt (R)	128,486	50.1
	Randy Rathbun (D)	119,544	46.6

KENTUCKY

	Candidates	Votes	%
1	Edward Whitfield (R)	111,473	53.6
	Dennis L. Null (D)	96,684	46.4
2	Ron Lewis (R)	125,433	58.1
	Joe Wright (D)	90,483	41.9
3	Anne M. Northup (R)	126,625	50.3
	Mike Ward (D)	125,326	49.7
4	Jim Bunning (R)	149,135	68.4
	Denny Bowman (D)	68,939	31.6
5	Harold Rogers (R)	117,842	100.0
6	Scotty Baesler (D)	125,999	55.7
	Ernest Fletcher (R)	100,231	44.3

LOUISIANA[2]

	Candidates	Votes	%
1	Robert L. Livingston (R)		100.0
2	William J. Jefferson (D)		100.0
3	W.J "Billy" Tauzin (R)		100.0
4	Jim McCrery (R)		100.0
5	John Cooksey (R)	135,990	58.3
	Francis Thompson (D)	97,363	41.7
6	Richard H. Baker (R)		100.0
7	Chris John (D)	128,449	53.1
	Hunter Lundy (D)	113,351	46.9

MAINE

	Candidates	Votes	%
1	Tom Allen (D)	173,745	55.3
	James B. Longley Jr. (R)	140,354	44.7
2	John Baldacci (D)	205,439	71.9
	Paul R. Young (R)	70,856	24.8

MARYLAND

	Candidates	Votes	%
1	Wayne T. Gilchrest (R)	131,033	61.6
	Steven R. Eastaugh (D)	81,825	38.4
2	Robert L. Ehrlich Jr. (R)	143,075	61.8
	Connie Galiazzo DeJuliis (D)	88,344	38.2
3	Benjamin L. Cardin (D)	130,204	67.3
	Patrick L. McDonough (R)	63,229	32.7
4	Albert R. Wynn (D)	142,094	85.2
	John B. Kimble (R)	24,700	14.8
5	Steny H. Hoyer (D)	121,288	56.9
	John S. Morgan (R)	91,806	43.1
6	Roscoe G. Bartlett (R)	132,853	56.8
	Stephen Crawford (D)	100,910	43.2
7	Elijah E. Cummings (D)	115,764	83.5
	Kenneth Kondner (R)	22,929	16.5
8	Constance A. Morella (R)	152,538	61.2
	Don Mooers (D)	96,229	38.6

Special Election[3]

	Candidates	Votes	%
7	Elijah E. Cummings (D)	18,870	80.9
	Kenneth Konder (R)	4,449	19.1

MASSACHUSETTS

	Candidates	Votes	%
1	John W. Olver (D)	129,232	52.7
	Jane Swift (R)	115,801	47.2
2	Richard E. Neal (D)	162,995	71.7
	Mark Steele (R)	49,885	21.9
3	Jim McGovern (D)	135,047	52.9
	Peter I. Blute (R)	115,695	45.4
4	Barney Frank (D)	183,854	71.6
	Jonathan Raymond (R)	72,707	28.3
5	Martin T. Meehan (D)	183,457	99.1
6	John F. Tierney (D)	133,684	48.2
	Peter G. Torkildsen (R)	132,318	48.1
7	Edward J. Markey (D)	177,053	69.8
	Patricia Long (R)	76,407	30.1
8	Joseph P. Kennedy II (D)	147,246	84.3
	R. Philip Hyde (R)	27,315	15.6
9	Joe Moakley (D)	172,012	72.2
	Paul Gryska (R)	66,080	27.7
10	Bill Delahunt (D)	160,747	54.3
	Edward Teague (R)	123,523	41.7

MICHIGAN

	Candidates	Votes	%
1	Bart Stupak (D)	181,486	70.7
	Bob Carr (R)	69,957	27.2
2	Peter Hoekstra (R)	165,608	65.3
	Dan Kruszynski (D)	83,603	33.0
3	Vernon J. Ehlers (R)	169,466	68.6
	Betsy J. Flory (D)	72,791	29.5
4	Dave Camp (R)	159,561	65.5
	Lisa A. Donaldson (D)	79,691	32.7
5	James A. Barcia (D)	162,675	70.0
	Lawrence Sims	65,542	28.2
6	Fred Upton (R)	146,170	67.7
	Clarence J. Annen (D)	66,243	30.7
7	Nick Smith (R)	120,227	55.0
	Kim H. Tunnicliff (D)	93,725	42.9
8	Debbie Stabenow (D)	141,086	53.8
	Dick Chrysler (R)	115,836	44.1
9	Dale E. Kildee (D)	136,856	59.2
	Patrick M. Nowak (R)	89,733	38.8
10	David E. Bonior (D)	132,829	54.4
	Susy Heintz (R)	106,444	43.6
11	Joe Knollenberg (R)	169,165	61.2
	Morris Frumin (D)	99,303	35.9
12	Sander M. Levin (D)	133,436	57.4
	John Pappageorge (R)	94,235	40.5
13	Lynn Rivers (D)	123,133	56.6
	Joe Fitzsimmons (R)	89,907	41.3
14	John Conyers Jr. (D)	157,722	85.9
	William A. Ashe (R)	22,152	12.1
15	Carolyn Cheeks Kilpatrick (D)	143,683	88.4
	Stephen Hume (R)	16,009	9.8
16	John D. Dingell (D)	136,854	62.0
	James R. DeSana (R)	78,723	35.7

MINNESOTA

		Votes	%
1	Gil Gutknecht (R)	137,545	52.7
	Mary Rieder (D)	123,188	47.2
2	David Minge (D)	144,083	54.9
	Gary B. Revier (R)	107,807	41.1
3	Jim Ramstad (R)	205,845	70.1
	Stanley J. Leino (D)	87,359	29.8
4	Bruce F. Vento (D)	145,831	57.0
	Dennis Newinski (R)	94,110	36.8
5	Martin Olav Sabo (D)	158,275	64.3
	Jack Uldrich (R)	70,115	28.5
	Erika Anderson (GR)	13,102	5.3
6	William P. "Bill" Luther (D)	164,921	55.8
	Tad Jude (R)	129,989	44.0
7	Collin C. Peterson (D)	170,936	67.9
	Darrell McKigney (R)	80,132	31.8
8	James L. Oberstar (D)	185,333	67.3
	Andy Larson (R)	69,460	25.2
	Stan Estes (REF)	16,639	6.0

MISSISSIPPI

		Votes	%
1	Roger Wicker (R)	123,724	67.6
	Henry Boyd Jr. (D)	55,998	30.6
2	Bennie Thompson (D)	102,503	59.6
	Danny Covington (R)	65,263	38.0
3	Charles W. "Chip" Pickering Jr. (R)	115,443	61.4
	John Arthur Eaves Jr. (D)	68,658	36.5
4	Mike Parker (R)	112,444	61.2
	Kevin Antoine (D)	66,836	36.4
5	Gene Taylor (D)	103,415	58.3
	Dennis Dollar (R)	71,114	40.1

MISSOURI

		Votes	%
1	William L. Clay (D)	131,659	70.2
	Daniel F. O'Sullivan Jr. (R)	51,857	27.6
2	James M. Talent (R)	165,999	61.3
	Joan Kelly Horn (D)	100,372	37.1
3	Richard A. Gephardt (D)	137,300	59.0
	Deborah Lynn Wheelehan (R)	90,202	38.8
4	Ike Skelton (D)	153,566	63.8

Candidates	Votes	%
Bill Phelps (R)	81,650	33.9
5 Karen McCarthy (D)	144,223	67.4
Penny Bennett (R)	61,803	28.9
6 Pat Danner (D)	169,006	68.6
Jeff Bailey (R)	72,064	29.3
7 Roy Blunt (R)	162,558	64.9
Ruth Bamberger (D)	79,306	31.6
8 Jo Ann Emerson (I)	112,472	50.5
Emily Firebaugh (R)	83,084	37.3
Richard A. Kline (D)	23,477	10.5
9 Kenny Hulshof (R)	123,580	49.4
Harold L. Volkmer (D)	117,685	47.0

Special Election[4]

	Votes	%
8 Jo Ann Emerson (R)	132,804	63.3
Emily Firebaugh (D)	71,625	34.1

MONTANA

		Votes	%
AL	Rick Hill (R)	211,975	52.4
	Bill Yellowtail (D)	174,516	43.2

NEBRASKA

		Votes	%
1	Doug Bereuter (R)	157,108	70.0
	Patrick J. Combs (D)	67,152	29.9
2	Jon Christensen (R)	125,201	56.8
	James Martin Davis (D)	88,447	40.1
3	Bill Barrett (R)	167,758	77.4
	John Webster (D)	48,833	22.5

NEVADA

		Votes	%
1	John Ensign (R)	86,472	50.1
	Bob Coffin (D)	75,081	43.5
2	Jim Gibbons (R)	162,310	58.6
	Thomas Wilson (D)	97,742	35.3

NEW HAMPSHIRE

		Votes	%
1	John E. Sununu (R)	123,939	50.0
	Joseph F. Keefe (D)	115,462	46.6
2	Charles Bass (R)	123,001	50.5
	Deborah "Arnie" Arnesen (D)	105,867	43.5

NEW JERSEY

		Votes	%
1	Robert E. Andrews (D)	160,415	76.1
	Mel Suplee (R)	44,286	21.0
2	Frank A. LoBiondo (R)	133,130	60.3
	Ruth Katz (D)	83,912	38.0
3	H. James Saxton (R)	157,503	64.2
	John Leonardi (D)	81,590	33.3
4	Christopher H. Smith (R)	146,440	63.6
	Kevin John Meara (D)	77,565	33.7
5	Marge Roukema (R)	181,323	71.3
	Bill Auer (D)	62,956	24.8
6	Frank Pallone Jr. (D)	124,635	61.3
	Steven J. Corodemus (R)	73,402	36.1
7	Bob Franks (R)	128,817	55.4
	Larry Lerner (D)	97,283	41.8
8	Bill J. Pascrell Jr. (D)	98,853	51.2
	Bill Martini (R)	92,604	47.7
9	Steve R. Rothman (D)	117,646	55.8
	Kathleen A. Donovan (R)	89,005	42.2
10	Donald M. Payne (D)	127,126	84.2
	Vanessa Williams (R)	22,086	14.6
11	Rodney Frelinghuysen (R)	169,091	66.3
	Chris Evangel (D)	78,742	30.9
12	Michael Pappas (R)	135,811	50.4
	David N. Del Vecchio (D)	125,594	46.7
13	Robert Menendez (D)	115,457	78.8
	Carlos E. Munoz (R)	25,426	17.4

NEW MEXICO

	Candidates	Votes	%
1	Steven H. Schiff (R)	109,290	56.6
	John Wertheim (D)	71,635	37.1
2	Joe Skeen (R)	95,091	55.9
	E. Shirley Baca (D)	74,915	44.1
3	Bill Richardson (D)	124,594	67.2
	Bill Redmond (R)	56,580	30.5

NEW YORK

		Votes	%
1	Michael P. Forbes (R,C,INDC,RTL)	116,620	54.7
	Nora Bredes (D,SM)	96,496	45.3
2	Rick A. Lazio (R,C)	112,135	64.2
	Kenneth J. Herman (D,INDC)	57,953	33.2
3	Peter T. King (R,C,FDM)	127,972	55.3
	Dal LaMagna (D,INDC)	97,518	42.1
4	Carolyn McCarthy (D,INDC)	127,060	57.5
	Daniel Frisa (R,C,FDM)	89,542	40.5
5	Gary L. Ackerman (D,L,INDC)	125,918	63.7
	Grant M. Lally (R,C,FDM)	69,244	35.0
6	Floyd H. Flake (D)	102,799	84.9
	Jorawar Misir R,C,INDC,FDM	18,348	15.1
7	Thomas J. Manton (D)	78,848	71.1
	Rose Birtley (R,C,INDC)	32,092	28.9
8	Jerrold Nadler (D,L)	131,943	82.3
	Michael Benjamin (R,FDM)	26,028	16.2
9	Charles E. Schumer (D,L)	107,107	74.8
	Robert J. Verga (R,INDC,FDM)	30,488	21.3
10	Edolphus Towns (D,L)	99,889	91.3
	Amelia Smith Parker (R,C,FDM)	8,660	7.9
11	Major R. Owens (D,L)	89,905	92.0
	Claudette Hayle (R,C,INDC,FDM)	7,866	8.0
12	Nydia M. Velazquez (D,L)	61,913	84.6
	Miguel I. Prado (R,C,FDM)	9,978	13.6
13	Susan Molinari (R,C,FDM)	94,660	61.6
	Tyrone G. Butler (D,L)	53,376	34.7
14	Carolyn B. Maloney (D,L)	130,175	72.4
	Jeffrey E. Livingston (R)	42,641	23.7
15	Charles B. Rangel (D,L)	113,898	91.3
16	Jose E. Serrano (D,L)	95,568	96.3
17	Eliot L. Engel (D,L)	101,287	85.0
	Denis McCarthy (R,C,RTL)	15,892	13.3
18	Nita M. Lowey (D)	118,194	63.6
	Kerry J. Katsorhis (R,C)	59,487	32.0
19	Sue W. Kelly (R,FDM)	102,142	46.3
	Richard S. Klein (D,L)	86,926	39.4
	Joseph J. DioGuardi (C,RTL)	27,424	12.4
20	Benjamin A. Gilman (R)	122,479	57.1
	Yash P. Aggarwal (D,L)	80,761	37.6
21	Michael R. McNulty (D,C,INDC)	158,491	66.1
	Nancy Norman (R,FDM)	64,471	26.9
	Lee H. Wasserman (L)	16,794	7.0
22	Gerald B.H Solomon (R,C,RTL,FDM)	144,125	60.5
	Steve James (D)	94,192	39.5
23	Sherwood Boehlert (R,FDM)	124,626	64.3
	Bruce W. Hapanowicz (D)	50,436	26.0
	Thomas E. Loughlin Jr. (INDC)	10,835	5.6
24	John M. McHugh (R,C)	124,240	71.1
	Donald Ravenscroft (D)	43,692	25.0
25	James T. Walsh (R,C,INDC,FDM)	126,691	55.1
	Marty Mack (D)	103,199	44.9
26	Maurice D. Hinchey (D,L)	122,850	55.2
	Sue Wittig (R,C,RTL,FDM)	94,125	42.3
27	Bill Paxon (R,C,RTL,FDM)	142,568	59.9
	Thomas M. Fricano (D,SM)	95,503	40.1
28	Louise M. Slaughter (D)	133,084	57.3
	Geoffrey Rosenberger (R,C,FDM)	99,366	42.7
29	John J. LaFalce (D,L)	132,317	62.0

	Candidates	Votes	%
	David B. Callard (R,C,RTL,FDM)	81,135	38.0
30	Jack Quinn (R,C,INDC,FDM)	121,369	54.8
	Francis Pordum (D,PS)	100,040	45.2
31	Amo Houghton (R,C,FDM)	139,734	71.6
	Bruce D. MacBain (D)	49,502	25.4

NORTH CAROLINA

	Candidates	Votes	%
1	Eva Clayton (D)	108,759	65.9
	Ted Tyler (R)	54,666	33.1
2	Bob Etheridge (D)	113,820	52.5
	David Funderburk (R)	98,951	45.7
3	Walter B. Jones Jr. (R)	118,159	62.7
	George Parrott (D)	68,887	36.5
4	David E. Price (D)	157,194	54.4
	Fred Heineman (R)	126,466	43.8
5	Richard M. Burr (R)	130,177	62.1
	Neil Grist Cashion Jr. (D)	74,320	35.4
6	Howard Coble (R)	167,828	73.4
	Mark Costley (D)	58,022	25.4
7	Mike McIntyre (D)	87,487	52.9
	Bill Caster (R)	75,811	45.8
8	W.G "Bill" Hefner (D)	103,129	55.2
	Curtis Blackwood (R)	81,676	43.7
9	Sue Myrick (R)	147,755	63.0
	Michel C. "Mike" Daisley (D)	83,078	35.4
10	Cass Ballenger (R)	158,585	70.0
	Ben Neill (D)	65,103	28.7
11	Charles H. Taylor (R)	132,860	58.3
	James Mark Ferguson (D)	91,257	40.0
12	Melvin Watt (D)	124,675	71.5
	Joseph A. "Joe" Martino Jr. (R)	46,581	26.7

NORTH DAKOTA

	Candidates	Votes	%
AL	Earl Pomeroy (D)	144,833	55.1
	Kevin Cramer (R)	113,684	43.2

OHIO

	Candidates	Votes	%
1	Steve Chabot (R)	118,324	54.2
	Mark P. Longabaugh (D)	94,719	43.4
2	Rob Portman (R)	186,853	72.0
	Thomas R. Chandler (D)	58,715	22.6
	Kathleen M. McKnight (NL)	13,905	5.4
3	Tony P. Hall (D)	144,583	63.6
	David A. Westbrock (R)	75,732	33.3
4	Michael G. Oxley (R)	147,608	64.8
	Paul McClain (D)	69,096	30.3
5	Paul E. Gillmor (R)	145,692	61.1
	Annie Saunders (D)	81,170	34.1
6	Ted Strickland (D)	118,003	51.3
	Frank A. Cremeans (R)	111,907	48.7
7	David L. Hobson (R)	158,087	67.8
	Richard K. Blain (D)	61,419	26.4
	Dawn Marie Johnson (NL)	13,478	5.8
8	John A. Boehner (R)	165,815	70.3
	Jeffrey D. Kitchen (D)	61,515	26.1
9	Marcy Kaptur (D)	170,617	77.1
	Randy Whitman (R)	46,040	20.8
10	Dennis J. Kucinich (D)	110,723	49.1
	Martin R. Hoke (R)	104,546	46.3
11	Louis Stokes (D)	153,546	81.2
	James J. Sykora (R)	28,821	15.2
12	John R. Kasich (R)	151,667	63.9
	Cynthia L. Ruccia (D)	78,762	33.2
13	Sherrod Brown (D)	146,690	60.5
	Kenneth C. Blair Jr. (R)	87,108	35.9
14	Tom Sawyer (D)	124,136	54.3
	Joyce George (R)	95,307	41.7
15	Deborah Pryce (R)	156,776	70.8
	Cliff Arnebeck (D)	64,665	29.2
16	Ralph Regula (R)	159,314	68.7
	Thomas E. Burkhart (D)	64,902	28.0
17	James A. Traficant Jr. (D)	218,283	91.0
	James M. Cahaney (NL)	21,685	9.0
18	Bob Ney (R)	117,365	50.2

	Candidates	Votes	%
	Robert L. Burch (D)	108,332	46.3
19	Steven C. LaTourette (R)	135,012	54.7
	Tom Coyne Jr. (D)	101,152	41.0

OKLAHOMA

	Candidates	Votes	%
1	Steve Largent (R)	143,415	68.2
	Randolph John Amen (D)	57,996	27.6
2	Tom Coburn (R)	112,273	55.5
	Glen D. Johnson (D)	90,120	44.5
3	Wes Watkins (R)	98,526	51.4
	Darryl Roberts (D)	86,647	45.2
4	J.C Watts (R)	106,923	57.7
	Ed Crocker (D)	73,950	39.9
5	Ernest Jim Istook Jr. (R)	148,362	69.7
	James L. Forsythe (D)	57,594	27.1
6	Frank D. Lucas (R)	113,499	63.9
	Paul M. Barby (D)	64,173	36.1

OREGON

	Candidates	Votes	%
1	Elizabeth Furse (D)	144,588	51.9
	Bill Witt (R)	126,146	45.3
2	Bob Smith (R)	164,062	61.7
	Mike Dugan (D)	97,195	36.5
3	Earl Blumenauer (D)	165,922	66.9
	Scott Bruun (R)	65,259	26.3
4	Peter A. DeFazio (D)	177,270	65.7
	John D. Newkirk (R)	76,649	28.4
5	Darlene Hooley (D)	139,521	51.2
	Jim Bunn (R)	125,409	46.0

Special Election[5]

	Candidates	Votes	%
3	Earl Blumenauer (D)	50,125	69.9
	Mark Brunelle (R)	17,085	23.8

PENNSYLVANIA

	Candidates	Votes	%
1	Thomas M. Foglietta (D)	145,210	87.5
	James D. Cella (R)	20,734	12.5
2	Chaka Fattah (D)	168,887	88.0
	Larry G. Murphy (R)	23,047	12.0
3	Robert A. Borski (D)	121,120	68.9
	Joseph M. McColgan (R)	54,681	31.1
4	Ron Klink (D)	142,621	64.2
	Paul T. Adametz (R)	79,448	35.8
5	John E. Peterson (R)	116,303	60.2
	Ruth C. Rudy (D)	76,627	39.7
6	Tim Holden (D)	115,193	58.6
	Christian Y. Leinbach (R)	80,061	40.7
7	Curt Weldon (R)	165,087	66.9
	John Innelli (D)	79,875	32.4
8	James C. Greenwood (R)	133,749	59.1
	John P. Murray (D)	79,856	35.3
9	Bud Shuster (R)	142,105	73.7
	Monte Kemmler (D)	50,650	26.3
10	Joseph M. McDade (R)	124,670	59.8
	Joe Cullen (D)	75,536	36.2
11	Paul E. Kanjorski (D)	128,258	68.0
	Stephen A. Urban (R)	60,339	32.0
12	John P. Murtha (D)	136,815	70.0
	Bill Choby (R)	58,643	30.0
13	Jon D. Fox (R)	120,304	48.9
	Joseph M. Hoeffel (D)	120,220	48.9
14	William J. Coyne (D)	122,922	60.7
	Bill Ravotti (R)	78,921	39.0
15	Paul McHale (D)	109,812	54.8
	Bob Kilbanks (R)	82,803	41.3
16	Joseph R. Pitts (R)	124,511	59.4
	James G. Blaine (D)	78,598	37.5
17	George W. Gekas (R)	150,678	72.2
	Paul Kettl (D)	57,911	27.8
18	Mike Doyle (D)	120,410	56.0
	David B. Fawcett (R)	86,829	40.4
19	Bill Goodling (R)	130,716	62.6
	Scott L. Chronister (D)	74,944	35.9
20	Frank R. Mascara (D)	113,394	53.9
	Mike McCormick (R)	97,004	46.1
21	Phil English (R)	106,875	50.7

	Candidates	Votes	%
	Ronald A. DiNicola (D)	104,004	49.3

RHODE ISLAND

	Candidates	Votes	%
1	Patrick J. Kennedy (D)	121,781	69.4
	Giovanni D. Cicione (R)	49,199	28.0
2	Bob Weygand (D)	118,827	64.5
	Rick Wild (R)	58,458	31.7

SOUTH CAROLINA

	Candidates	Votes	%
1	Mark Sanford (R)	138,467	96.4
2	Floyd D. Spence (R)	158,229	89.8
	Maurice T. Raiford (NL)	17,713	10.0
3	Lindsey Graham (R)	114,273	60.3
	Debbie Dorn (D)	73,417	38.7
4	Bob Inglis (R)	138,165	70.9
	Darrell E. Curry (D)	54,126	27.8
5	John M. Spratt Jr. (D)	97,335	54.1
	Larry L. Bigham (R)	81,455	45.3
6	James E. Clyburn (D)	120,132	69.4
	Gary McLeod (R)	51,974	30.0

SOUTH DAKOTA

	Candidates	Votes	%
AL	John Thune (R)	186,393	57.7
	Rick Weiland (D)	119,547	37.0

TENNESSEE

	Candidates	Votes	%
1	Bill Jenkins (R)	117,676	64.8
	Kay C. Smith (D)	58,657	33.3
2	John J. "Jimmy" Duncan Jr. (R)	150,953	70.7
	Stephen Smith (D)	61,020	28.6
3	Zach Wamp (R)	113,408	56.3
	Charles "Chuck" Jolly (D)	85,714	42.6
4	Van Hilleary (R)	103,091	57.9
	Mark Stewart (D)	73,331	41.2
5	Bob Clement (D)	140,264	72.4
	Steven L. Edmondson (R)	46,201	23.8
6	Bart Gordon (D)	123,846	54.4
	Steve Gill (R)	94,599	41.6
7	Ed Bryant (R)	136,643	64.1
	Don Trotter (D)	73,629	34.6
8	John Tanner (D)	123,681	67.3
	Tom Watson (R)	55,024	29.9
9	Harold E. Ford Jr. (D)	116,345	61.1
	Rod DeBerry (R)	70,951	37.3

TEXAS[6]

	Candidates	Votes	%
1	Max Sandlin (D)	102,697	51.6
	Ed Merritt (R)	93,105	46.7
2	Jim Turner (D)	102,908	52.2
	Brian Babin (R)	89,838	45.6
3	Sam Johnson (R)	142,325	73.0
	Lee Cole (D)	47,654	24.4
4	Ralph M. Hall (D)	132,126	63.8
	Jerry Ray Hall (R)	71,065	34.3
5	Pete Sessions (R)	80,196	53.1
	John Pouland (D)	70,922	47.0
6	Joe L. Barton (R)	160,800	77.1
	Janet Carroll "Skeet" Richardson (I)	26,713	12.8
	Catherine A. Anderson (L)	14,456	6.9
7	Bill Archer (R)	152,024	81.4
	Al J.K Siegmund (D)	28,187	15.1
86	Kevin Brady (R)	80,325	41.5
	Gene Fontenot (R)	75,399	38.9
	Cynthia "C.J" Newman (D)	26,246	13.6
	Robert Musemeche (D)	11,689	6.0
96	Steve Stockman (R)	88,171	46.4
	Nick Lampson (D)	83,782	44.1
	Geraldine Sam (D)	17,887	9.4
10	Lloyd Doggett (D)	132,066	56.2
	Teresa Doggett (R)	97,204	41.4
11	Chet Edwards (D)	99,990	56.8
	Jay Mathis (R)	74,549	42.4
12	Kay Granger (R)	98,349	57.8
	Hugh Parmer (D)	69,859	41.0

Candidates	Votes	%
13 William M. "Mac"		
Thornberry (R)	116,098	66.9
Samuel Brown		
Silverman (D)	56,066	32.3
14 Ron Paul (R)	99,961	51.1
Charles "Lefty" Morris (D)	93,200	47.6
15 Ruben Hinojosa (D)	86,347	62.3
Tom Haughey (R)	50,914	36.7
16 Silvestre Reyes (D)	90,260	70.6
Rick Ledesma (R)	35,271	27.6
17 Charles W. Stenholm (D)	99,678	51.6
Rudy Izzard (R)	91,429	47.4
18 Sheila Jackson-Lee (D)	106,111	77.1
Larry White (R)	13,956	10.1
Jerry Burley (R)	7,877	5.7
19 Larry Combest (R)	156,910	80.4
John W. Sawyer (D)	38,316	19.6
20 Henry B. Gonzalez (D)	88,190	63.7
James D. Walker (R)	47,616	34.4
21 Lamar Smith (R)	205,830	76.4
Gordon H. Wharton (D)	60,338	22.4
22 Tom DeLay (R)	126,056	68.1
Scott Douglas		
Cunningham (D)	59,030	31.9
23 Henry Bonilla (R)	101,332	61.8
Charles P. Jones (D)	59,596	36.4
24 Martin Frost (D)	77,847	55.7
Ed Harrison (R)	54,551	39.1
25 Ken Bentsen (D)	43,701	34.0
Dolly Madison McKenna (R)	21,898	17.1
Beverley Clark (D)	21,699	16.9
Brent Perry (R)	16,737	13.0
John Devine (R)	9,070	7.1
John M. Sanchez (R)	8,984	7.0
26 Dick Armey (R)	163,708	73.6
Jerry Frankel (D)	58,623	26.4
27 Solomon P. Ortiz (D)	97,350	64.6
Joe Gardner (R)	50,964	33.8
28 Frank Tejeda (D)	110,148	75.4
Mark Lynn Cude (R)	34,191	23.4
29 Gene Green (D)	61,751	67.5
Jack Rodriguez (R)	28,381	31.0
30 Eddie Bernice Johnson (D)	61,723	54.6
John Hendry (R)	20,664	18.3
James L. Sweatt (D)	9,909	8.8
Marvin E. Crenshaw (D)	7,765	6.9
Lisa Anne Kitterman (R)	7,761	6.9

Special Runoff Elections[6]

Candidates	Votes	%
8 Kevin Brady (R)	30,366	59.1
Gene Fontenot (R)	21,004	40.9
9 Nick Lampson (D)	59,225	52.8

Candidates	Votes	%
Steve Stockman (R)	52,870	47.2
25 Ken Bentsen (D)	29,396	57.3
Dolly Madison McKenna (R)	21,892	42.7

UTAH

Candidates	Votes	%
1 James V. Hansen (R)	150,126	68.3
Gregory J. Sanders (D)	65,866	30.0
2 Merrill Cook (R)	129,963	55.0
Ross Anderson (D)	100,283	42.4
3 Christopher B. Cannon (R)	106,220	51.1
Bill Orton (D)	98,178	47.3

VERMONT

Candidates	Votes	%
AL Bernard Sanders (I)	140,678	55.2
Susan Sweetser (R)	83,021	32.6
Jack Long (D)	23,830	9.4

VIRGINIA

Candidates	Votes	%
1 Herbert H. Bateman (R)	165,574	99.0
2 Owen B. Pickett (D)	106,215	64.8
John Tate (R)	57,586	35.1
3 Robert C. Scott (D)	118,603	82.1
Elsie Holland (R)	25,781	17.9
4 Norman Sisisky (D)	160,100	78.6
A.J "Tony" Zevgolis (R)	43,516	21.4
5 Virgil H. Goode Jr. (D)	120,323	60.8
George C. Landrith III (R)	70,869	35.8
6 Robert W. Goodlatte (R)	133,576	67.0
Jeffrey Grey (D)	61,485	30.8
7 Thomas J. Bliley Jr. (R)	189,644	75.1
Roderic H. Slayton (D)	51,206	20.3
8 James P. Moran (D)	152,334	66.4
John Otey (R)	64,562	28.1
9 Rick Boucher (D)	122,908	65.0
Patrick Muldoon (R)	58,055	30.7
10 Frank R. Wolf (R)	169,266	72.0
Robert L. Weinberg (D)	59,145	25.2
11 Thomas M. Davis III (R)	138,758	64.1
Tom Horton (D)	74,701	34.5

WASHINGTON

Candidates	Votes	%
1 Rick White (R)	141,948	53.7
Jeffrey Coopersmith (D)	122,187	46.3
2 Jack Metcalf (R)	124,655	48.5
Kevin Quigley (D)	122,728	47.8
3 Linda Smith (R)	123,117	50.2
Brian Baird (D)	122,230	49.8
4 Richard "Doc"		
Hastings (R)	108,647	53.0

Candidates	Votes	%
Rick Locke (D)	96,502	47.0
5 George Nethercutt (R)	131,618	55.6
Judy Olson (D)	105,166	44.4
6 Norm Dicks (D)	155,467	65.9
Bill Tinsley (R)	71,337	30.2
7 Jim McDermott (D)	209,753	81.0
Frank Kleschen (R)	49,341	19.0
8 Jennifer Dunn (R)	170,691	65.4
Dave Little (D)	90,340	34.6
9 Adam Smith (D)	105,236	50.1
Randy Tate (R)	99,199	47.3

WEST VIRGINIA

Candidates	Votes	%
1 Alan B. Mollohan (D)	171,334	100.0
2 Bob Wise (D)	141,551	68.9
Greg Morris (R)	63,933	31.1
3 Nick J. Rahall II (D)	145,550	100.0

WISCONSIN

Candidates	Votes	%
1 Mark W. Neumann (R)	118,408	50.9
Lydia C. Spottswood (D)	114,148	49.0
2 Scott L. Klug (R)	154,557	57.4
Paul R. Soglin (D)	110,467	41.0
3 Ron Kind (D)	121,967	52.0
Jim Harsdorf (R)	112,146	47.8
4 Gerald D. Kleczka (D)	134,470	57.6
Tom Reynolds (R)	98,438	42.2
5 Thomas M. Barrett (D)	141,179	73.3
Paul D. Melotik (R)	47,384	24.6
6 Tom Petri (R)	169,213	73.0
Alver Lindskoog (D)	55,377	23.9
7 David R. Obey (D)	137,428	57.0
Scott West (R)	103,365	42.9
8 Jay W. Johnson (D)	129,551	52.0
David T. Prosser Jr. (R)	119,398	48.0
9 F. James Sensenbrenner		
Jr. (R)	197,910	74.4
Floyd Brenholt (D)	67,740	25.5

WYOMING

Candidates	Votes	%
AL Barbara Cubin (R)	116,004	55.2
Pete Maxfield (D)	85,724	40.8

1. A special election was held to fill the unexpired term of Rep. Walter R. Tucker III (D), who resigned Dec. 15, 1995. No runoff was required because only Democrats filed for the primary.

2. For the 1996 House elections in Louisiana, an open primary election was held with candidates from all parties running on the same ballot. Any candidate who received a majority was elected unopposed, with no further appearance on the general election ballot. If no candidate received 50 percent, a runoff was held between the two top finishers.

3. A special election was held to fill the unexpired term of Rep. Kweisi Mfume (D), who resigned Feb. 15, 1996.

4. A special election was held in conjunction with the November election. Emerson was elected to serve both the unexpired term of Bill Emerson (R), who died June 22, 1996, and the two-year term beginning Jan. 7, 1997.

5. A special election was held to fill the unexpired term of Ron Wyden (D), who resigned Feb. 5, 1996, having been elected to the U.S. Senate.

6. In July 1996 a panel of federal judges declared that three Texas districts were unconstitutionally drawn. The three districts and an additional ten surrounding ones were redrawn, invalidating the March 1996 primary results for the districts. In November, candidates in the thirteen districts ran in open primaries, with only those capturing a majority of the vote winning outright. Special runoff elections were held in December for the top two finishers in the districts where no candidate received a majority of the votes cast.

1997 House Elections

	NEW MEXICO		
	Special Election[1]		
	Candidates	**Votes**	**%**
3	Bill Redmond (R)	43,559	*42.7*
	Eric P. Serna (D)	40,542	*39.8*
	Carol A. Miller (GREEN)	17,101	*16.8*

	NEW YORK		
	Special Election[2]		
	Candidates	**Votes**	**%**
13	Vito J. Fossella (R, RTL, C)	79,838	*61.3*
	Eric N. Vitaliano (D)	50,373	*38.7*

	TEXAS		
	Special Runoff Election[3]		
	Candidates	**Votes**	**%**
28	Ciro D. Rodriguez (D)	19,992	*66.7*
	Juan F. Solis III (D)	9,990	*33.3*

1. A special election was held to fill the unexpired term of Rep. Bill Richardson (D), who resigned Feb. 13, 1997, to become U.S. representative to the United Nations.

2. A special election was held to fill the unexpired term of Rep. Susan Molinari (R), who resigned Aug. 1, 1997.

3. A special all-party primary was held to fill the unexpired term of Rep. Fred Tejeda (D), who died Jan. 30, 1997. With no candidate receiving the majority vote, a special runoff election of the top two finishers was held.

1998 House Elections

ALABAMA

	Candidates	Votes	%
1	Sonny Callahan (R)	112,872	100.0
2	Terry Everett (R)	131,428	69.3
	Joe Fondren (D)	58,136	30.7
3	Bob Riley (R)	101,731	58.1
	Joe Turnham (D)	73,357	41.9
4	Robert B. Aderholt (R)	106,297	56.4
	Donald Bevill (D)	82,065	43.5
5	Robert E. "Bud" Cramer (D)	134,819	69.7
	Gil Aust (R)	58,536	30.3
6	Spencer Bachus (R)	154,761	71.8
	Donna Wesson Smalley (D)	60,657	28.1
7	Earl F. Hilliard (D)	136,431	100.0

ALASKA

	Candidates	Votes	%
AL	Don Young (R)	139,676	62.6
	James W. "Jim" Duncan (D)	77,232	34.6

ARIZONA

	Candidates	Votes	%
1	Matt Salmon (R)	98,840	64.6
	David Mendoza (D)	51,108	35.4
2	Ed Pastor (D)	57,178	67.6
	Edward Clyde "Ed" Barron (R)	23,628	28.0
3	Bob Stump (R)	137,618	67.3
	Stuart Marc Starky (D)	66,979	32.7
4	John Shadegg (R)	102,722	64.7
	Eric Ehst (D)	49,538	31.2
5	Jim Kolbe (R)	103,952	51.6
	Thomas John Volgy (D)	91,030	45.2
6	J. D. Hayworth (R)	106,891	53.0
	Steve Owens (D)	88,001	43.7

ARKANSAS

	Candidates	Votes	%
1	Marion Berry (D)		100.0
2	Vic Snyder (D)	100,334	58.0
	Phil Wyrick (R)	72,737	42.0
3	Asa Hutchinson (R)	154,780	80.8
	Ralph Forbes (REF)	36,917	19.3
4	Jay Dickey (R)	92,346	57.5
	Judy Smith (D)	68,194	42.5

CALIFORNIA

	Candidates	Votes	%
1	Mike Thompson (D)	121,713	61.9
	Mark Luce (R)	64,622	32.8
2	Wally Herger (R)	128,372	62.5
	Roberts "Rob" Braden (D)	70,837	34.5
3	Doug Ose (R)	100,621	52.4
	Sandie Dunn (D)	86,471	45.0
4	John T. Doolittle (R)	155,306	62.6
	David Shapiro (D)	85,394	34.4
5	Robert T. Matsui (D)	130,715	71.9
	Robert S. Dinsmore (R)	47,307	26.0
6	Lynn Woolsey (D)	158,446	68.0
	Ken McAuliffe (R)	69,295	29.7
7	George Miller (D)	125,842	76.7
	Norman H. Reece (R)	38,290	23.3
8	Nancy Pelosi (D)	148,027	85.8
	David J. Martz (R)	20,781	12.0
9	Barbara Lee (D)	140,722	82.8
	Claiborne "Clay" Sanders (R)	22,431	13.2
10	Ellen O. Tauscher (D)	127,134	53.5
	Charles Ball (R)	103,299	43.4
11	Richard W. Pombo (R)	95,496	61.4
	Robert L. Figueroa (D)	56,345	36.2
12	Tom Lantos (D)	128,135	74.0
	Robert H. Evans Jr. (R)	36,562	21.1
13	Pete Stark (D)	101,671	71.2
	James R. Goetz (R)	38,050	26.6
14	Anna G. Eshoo (D)	129,663	68.6
	John C. "Chris" Haugen (R)	53,719	28.4
15	Tom Campbell (R)	111,876	60.5

	Candidates	Votes	%
	Dick Lane (D)	70,059	37.9
16	Zoe Lofgren (D)	85,503	72.8
	Horace Eugene Thayn (R)	27,494	23.4
17	Sam Farr (D)	103,719	64.5
	Bill McCampbell (R)	52,470	32.7
18	Gary A. Condit (D)	118,842	86.8
	Linda M. DeGroat (LIBERT)	18,089	13.2
19	George P. Radanovich (R)	131,105	79.4
	Jonathan Richter (LIBERT)	34,044	20.6
20	Cal Dooley (D)	60,599	60.7
	Cliff Unruh (R)	39,183	39.3
21	William Thomas (R)	115,989	78.9
	John Evans (REF)	30,994	21.1
22	Lois Capps (D)	111,388	55.1
	Tom Bordonaro (R)	86,921	43.0
23	Elton W. Gallegly (R)	96,362	60.1
	Daniel Gonzalez (D)	64,068	39.9
24	Brad Sherman (D)	103,491	57.3
	Randy Hoffman (R)	69,501	38.5
25	Howard P. "Buck" McKeon (R)	114,013	74.7
	Bruce Acker (LIBERT)	38,669	25.3
26	Howard L. Berman (D)	69,000	82.5
	Juan Carlos Ros (LIBERT)	6,556	7.8
	Maria Armoudian (GREEN)	4,858	5.8
27	James E. Rogan (R)	80,702	50.7
	Barry Gordon (D)	73,875	46.4
28	David Dreier (R)	90,607	57.6
	Janice Nelson (D)	61,721	39.3
29	Henry A. Waxman (D)	131,561	73.9
	Mike Gottlieb (R)	40,282	22.6
30	Xavier Becerra (D)	58,230	81.2
	Patricia Jean Parker (R)	13,441	18.8
31	Matthew G. Martinez (D)	61,173	70.0
	Frank Moreno (R)	19,786	22.6
	Krista Lieberg-Wong (GREEN)	4,377	5.0
32	Julian C. Dixon (D)	112,253	86.7
	Laurence Ardito (R)	14,622	11.3
33	Lucille Roybal-Allard (D)	43,310	87.2
	Wayne Miller (R)	6,364	12.8
34	Grace Napolitano (D)	76,471	67.6
	Ed Perez (R)	32,321	28.6
35	Maxine Waters (D)	78,732	89.3
	Gordon Michael Mego (AM I)	9,413	10.7
36	Steve Kuykendall (R)	88,843	48.9
	Janice Hahn (D)	84,624	46.6
37	Juanita Millender-McDonald (D)	70,026	85.1
	Saul E. Lankster (R)	12,301	14.9
38	Steve Horn (R)	71,386	52.9
	Peter Mathews (D)	59,767	44.3
39	Ed Royce (R)	97,366	62.6
	A. R. Groom (D)	52,815	34.0
40	Jerry Lewis (R)	97,406	64.9
	Robert Conaway (D)	47,897	31.9
41	Gary Miller (R)	68,310	53.2
	Eileen Ansari (D)	52,264	40.7
42	George E. Brown Jr. (D)	62,207	55.3
	Elia Pirozzi (R)	45,328	40.3
43	Ken Calvert (R)	83,012	55.7
	Mike Rayburn (D)	56,373	37.8
44	Mary Bono (R)	97,013	60.1
	Ralph Waite (D)	57,697	35.7
45	Dana Rohrabacher (R)	94,296	58.7
	Patricia Neal (D)	60,022	37.3
46	Loretta Sanchez (D)	47,964	56.4
	Robert Dornan (R)	33,388	39.3
47	Christopher Cox (R)	132,711	67.6
	Christina Avalos (D)	57,938	29.5
48	Ron Packard (R)	138,948	76.9
	Sharon Miles (NL)	23,262	12.9
	Daniel Muhe (LIBERT)	18,509	10.2
49	Brian P. Bilbray (R)	90,516	48.8
	Christine Kehoe (D)	86,400	46.6
50	Bob Filner (D)	77,354	99.2
51	Randy "Duke" Cunningham (R)	126,229	61.0
	Dan Kripke (D)	71,706	34.7

	Candidates	Votes	%
52	Duncan Hunter (R)	116,251	75.7
	Lynn Badler (LIBERT)	21,933	14.3
	Adrienne Pelton (NL)	15,380	10.0

COLORADO

	Candidates	Votes	%
1	Diana DeGette (D)	116,628	66.9
	Nancy McClanahan (R)	52,452	30.1
2	Mark Udall (D)	113,946	49.9
	Bob Greenlee (R)	108,385	47.4
3	Scott McInnis (R)	156,501	66.1
	Robert Reed Kelley (D)	74,479	31.5
4	Bob Schaffer (R)	131,318	59.3
	Susan Kirkpatrick (D)	89,973	40.7
5	Joel Hefley (R)	155,790	72.7
	Ken Alford (D)	55,609	26.0
6	Tom Tancredo (R)	111,374	55.9
	Henry L. Strauss (D)	82,662	41.5

Special Primary[1]

		Votes	%
9	Barbara Lee (D)	33,497	66.8
	Greg Harper (D)	8,048	16.1
	Claiborne "Clay" Sanders (R)	6,114	12.2

Special Election[2]

		Votes	%
22	Lois Capps (D)	93,392	53.5
	Tom J. Bordonaro (R)	78,224	44.8

Special Primary[3]

		Votes	%
44	Mary Bono (R)	53,755	64.0
	Ralph Waite (D)	24,228	28.8

CONNECTICUT

	Candidates	Votes	%
1	John B. Larson (D)	97,681	58.1
	Kevin O'Connor (R)	69,668	41.4
2	Sam Gejdenson (D)	99,567	61.0
	Gary M. Koval (R)	57,860	35.5
3	Rosa DeLauro (D)	109,726	71.3
	Martin Reust (R)	42,090	27.4
4	Christopher Shays (R)	94,767	69.1
	Jonathan Kantrowitz (D)	40,988	29.9
5	Jim Maloney (D)	78,394	49.9
	Mark Nielsen (R)	76,051	48.4
6	Nancy L. Johnson (R)	101,630	58.1
	Charlotte Koskoff (D)	69,201	39.6

DELAWARE

	Candidates	Votes	%
AL	Michael N. Castle (R)	119,811	66.4
	Dennis E. Williams (D)	57,446	31.8

FLORIDA

	Candidates	Votes	%
1	Joe Scarborough (R)	140,525	99.5
2	Allen Boyd (D)	138,440	95.2
3	Corrine Brown (D)	66,621	55.4
	Bill Randall (R)	53,530	44.6
4	Tillie Fowler (R)		100.0
5	Karen L. Thurman (D)	132,005	66.3
	Jack "THRO" Gargan (REF)	67,147	33.7
6	Cliff Stearns (R)		100.0
7	John L. Mica (R)		100.0
8	Bill McCollum (R)	104,298	65.8
	Al Krulick (D)	54,245	34.2
9	Michael Bilirakis (R)		100.0
10	C. W. Bill Young (R)		100.0
11	Jim Davis (D)	85,262	64.9
	Joe Chillura (R)	46,176	35.1
12	Charles T. Canady (R)		100.0
13	Dan Miller (R)		100.0
14	Porter J. Goss (R)		100.0

	Candidates	Votes	%
15	Dave Weldon (R)	129,278	63.1
	David R. Golding (D)	75,654	36.9
16	Mark Foley (R)		100.0
17	Carrie P. Meek (D)		100.0
18	Ileana Ros-Lehtinen (R)		100.0
19	Robert Wexler (D)		100.0
20	Peter Deutsch (D)		100.0
21	Lincoln Diaz-Balart (R)	84,018	74.8
	Patrick Cusack (D)	28,378	25.2
22	E. Clay Shaw Jr. (R)		100.0
23	Alcee L. Hastings (D)		100.0

GEORGIA

	Candidates	Votes	%
1	Jack Kingston (R)	92,229	100.0
2	Sanford D. Bishop (D)	77,953	56.8
	Joe McCormick (R)	59,305	43.2
3	Mac Collins (R)	123,064	100.0
4	Cynthia A. McKinney (D)	100,622	61.1
	Sunny Warren (R)	64,146	38.9
5	John Lewis (D)	109,177	78.5
	John H. Lewis Sr. (R)	29,877	21.5
6	Newt Gingrich (R)	164,996	70.7
	Gary "Bats" Pelphrey (D)	68,366	29.3
7	Bob Barr (R)	85,982	55.4
	James F. Williams (D)	69,293	44.6
8	Saxby Chambliss (R)	87,993	62.4
	Ronald L. Cain (D)	53,079	37.6
9	Nathan Deal (R)	122,713	100.0
10	Charlie Norwood (R)	88,527	59.6
	Marion Spencer "Denise" Freeman (D)	60,004	40.4
11	John Linder (R)	120,909	69.3
	Vincent Littman (D)	53,510	30.7

HAWAII

	Candidates	Votes	%
1	Neil Abercrombie (D)	116,693	61.6
	Gene Ward (R)	68,905	36.3
2	Patsy T. Mink (D)	144,254	69.4
	Carol J. Douglass (R)	50,423	24.3

IDAHO

	Candidates	Votes	%
1	Helen Chenoweth (R)	113,231	55.3
	Dan Williams (D)	91,653	44.7
2	Mike Simpson (R)	91,337	52.5
	Richard H. Stallings (D)	77,736	44.7

ILLINOIS

	Candidates	Votes	%
1	Bobby L. Rush (D)	151,890	87.1
	Marlene White Ahimaz (R)	18,429	10.6
2	Jesse L. Jackson Jr. (D)	148,985	89.4
	Robert Gordon III (R)	16,075	9.6
3	William O. Lipinski (D)	115,887	72.5
	Robert Marshall (R)	44,012	27.5
4	Luis V. Gutierrez (D)	54,244	81.7
	John Birch (R)	10,529	15.9
5	Rod R. Blagojevich (D)	95,738	74.0
	Alan Spitz (R)	33,687	26.0
6	Henry J. Hyde (R)	111,603	67.3
	Thomas A. Cramer (D)	49,906	30.1
7	Danny K. Davis (D)	130,984	92.9
	Dorn E. Van Cleave III (LIBERT)	9,984	7.1
8	Philip M. Crane (R)	104,242	68.6
	Mike Rothman (D)	47,614	31.4
9	Janice D. "Jan" Schakowsky (D)	107,878	74.6
	Herbert Sohn (R)	33,448	23.1
10	John E. Porter (R)	138,429	100.0
11	Gerald C. "Jerry" Weller (R)	100,597	58.8
	Gary S. Mueller (D)	70,458	41.2
12	Jerry F. Costello (D)	99,665	60.4
	Bill Price (R)	65,409	39.6
13	Judy Biggert (R)	121,889	61.0
	Susan W. Hynes (D)	77,878	39.0
14	J. Dennis Hastert (R)	117,304	69.8
	Robert A. Cozzi Jr. (D)	50,844	30.2
15	Thomas W. Ewing (R)	104,255	61.6
	Laurel Lunt Prussing (D)	65,054	38.4
16	Donald Manzullo (R)	143,868	100.0
17	Lane Evans (D)	100,128	51.6
	Mark Baker (R)	94,072	48.4
18	Ray LaHood (R)	158,175	100.0
19	David Phelps (D)	122,430	58.3
	Brent Winters (R)	87,614	41.7
20	John M. Shimkus (R)	121,103	61.3
	Rick Verticchio (D)	76,475	38.7

INDIANA

	Candidates	Votes	%
1	Peter J. Visclosky (D)	92,634	72.5
	Michael Petyo (R)	33,503	26.2
2	David M. McIntosh (R)	99,608	60.6
	Sherman A. Boles (D)	62,452	38.0
3	Tim Roemer (D)	84,625	58.1
	Daniel A. Holtz (R)	61,041	41.9
4	Mark E. Souder (R)	93,671	63.3
	Mark J. Wehrle (D)	54,286	36.7
5	Steve Buyer (R)	101,567	62.5
	David F. Steele III (D)	58,504	36.0
6	Dan Burton (R)	135,240	72.0
	Bob Kern (D)	31,472	16.8
	Joe Hauptmann (LIBERT)	21,015	11.2
7	Edward A. Pease (R)	109,712	68.9
	Samuel "Dutch" Hillenberg (D)	44,823	28.1
8	John N. Hostettler (R)	92,785	52.1
	Gail Riecken (D)	81,871	46.0
9	Baron Hill (D)	92,973	50.8
	Jean Leising (R)	87,797	47.9
10	Julia M. Carson (D)	69,682	58.3
	Gary A. Hofmeister (R)	47,017	39.4

IOWA

	Candidates	Votes	%
1	Jim Leach (R)	106,419	56.5
	Bob Rush (D)	79,529	42.3
2	Jim Nussle (R)	104,613	55.2
	Rob Tully (D)	83,405	44.0
3	Leonard L. Boswell (D)	107,947	56.9
	Larry McKibben (R)	78,063	41.1
4	Greg Ganske (R)	129,942	65.2
	Jon Dvorak (D)	67,550	33.9
5	Tom Latham (R)	132,730	99.2

KANSAS

	Candidates	Votes	%
1	Jerry Moran (R)	152,775	80.7
	Jim Phillips (D)	36,618	19.3
2	Jim Ryun (R)	108,527	61.0
	Jim Clark (D)	69,521	39.0
3	Dennis Moore (D)	103,376	52.4
	Vince Snowbarger (R)	93,938	47.6
4	Todd Tiahrt (R)	94,785	58.3
	Jim Lawing (D)	62,737	38.6

KENTUCKY

	Candidates	Votes	%
1	Edward Whitfield (R)	95,308	55.2
	Tom Barlow (D)	77,402	44.8
2	Ron Lewis (R)	113,285	63.7
	Bob Evans (D)	62,848	35.3
3	Anne Meagher Northup (R)	100,690	51.5
	Chris Gorman (D)	92,865	47.5
4	Ken Lucas (D)	93,485	53.4
	Gex Williams (R)	81,547	46.6
5	Harold Rogers (R)	142,215	78.2
	Sidney Bailey-Bamer (D)	39,585	21.8
6	Ernie Fletcher (R)	104,046	53.1
	Ernesto Scorsone (D)	90,033	46.0

LOUISIANA

	Candidates	Votes	%
1	Robert L. Livingston (R)		100.0
2	William J. Jefferson (D)	102,247	86.0
	David Reed (D)	10,803	9.1
	Don-Terry Veal (D)	5,899	5.0
3	W. J. "Billy" Tauzin (R)		100.0
4	Jim McCrery (R)		100.0
5	John C. Cooksey (R)		100.0
6	Richard H. Baker (R)	97,044	50.7
	Marjorie McKeithen (D)	94,201	49.3
7	Chris John (D)		100.0

MAINE

	Candidates	Votes	%
1	Tom Allen (D)	134,335	60.3
	Ross J. Connelly (R)	79,160	35.5
2	John Baldacci (D)	146,202	76.2
	Jonathan Reisman (R)	45,674	23.8

MARYLAND

	Candidates	Votes	%
1	Wayne T. Gilchrest (R)	135,771	69.2
	Irving Pinder (D)	60,450	30.8
2	Robert L. Ehrlich Jr. (R)	145,711	69.3
	Kenneth T. Bosley (D)	64,474	30.7
3	Benjamin L. Cardin (D)	137,501	77.6
	Colin Felix Harby (R)	39,667	22.4
4	Albert R. Wynn (D)	129,139	85.7
	John B. Kimble (R)	21,518	14.3
5	Steny H. Hoyer (D)	126,792	65.4
	Robert B. Ostrom (R)	67,176	34.6
6	Roscoe G. Bartlett (R)	127,802	63.4
	Timothy D. McCown (D)	73,728	36.6
7	Elijah E. Cummings (D)	112,699	85.7
	Kenneth Kondner (R)	18,742	14.3
8	Constance A. Morella (R)	133,145	60.3
	Ralph G. Neas (D)	87,497	39.6

MASSACHUSETTS

	Candidates	Votes	%
1	John W. Olver (D)	121,863	71.7
	Gregory L. Morgan (R)	48,055	28.3
2	Richard E. Neal (D)	130,550	99.0
3	James McGovern (D)	108,613	56.9
	Matthew J. Amorello (R)	79,174	41.5
4	Barney Frank (D)	148,340	98.4
5	Martin T. Meehan (D)	127,418	70.7
	David E. Coleman (R)	52,725	29.3
6	John F. Tierney (D)	117,132	54.6
	Peter G. Torkildsen (R)	90,986	42.4
7	Edward J. Markey (D)	137,178	70.6
	Patricia H. Long (R)	56,977	29.3
8	Michael E. Capuano (D)	99,603	81.7
	Philip Hyde III (R)	14,125	11.6
9	Joe Moakley (D)	150,667	99.4
10	Bill Delahunt (D)	164,917	70.0
	Eric V. Bleicken (R)	70,466	29.9

MICHIGAN

	Candidates	Votes	%
1	Bart Stupak (D)	130,129	58.7
	Michelle A. McManus (R)	87,630	39.5
2	Peter Hoekstra (R)	146,854	68.7
	Bob Shrauger (D)	63,573	29.8
3	Vernon Ehlers (R)	146,364	73.1
	John Ferguson Jr. (D)	49,489	24.7
4	Dave Camp (R)	155,343	91.3
	Dan Marsh (LIBERT)	10,404	6.1
5	James A. Barcia (D)	135,254	71.2
	Donald W. Brewster (R)	51,442	27.1
6	Fred Upton (R)	113,292	70.1
	Clarence J. Annen (D)	45,358	28.1
7	Nick Smith (R)	104,656	57.7
	Jim Berryman (D)	72,998	40.1
8	Debbie Stabenow (D)	125,169	57.4
	Susan Grimes Munsell (R)	84,254	38.6
9	Dale E. Kildee (D)	105,457	55.9
	Tom McMillin (R)	79,062	41.9
10	David E. Bonior (D)	108,770	52.4
	Brian Palmer (R)	94,027	45.3
11	Joe Knollenberg (R)	144,264	63.9
	Travis M. Reeds (D)	76,107	33.7
12	Sander Levin (D)	105,824	55.9
	Leslie A. Touma (R)	79,619	42.0
13	Lynn Nancy Rivers (D)	99,935	58.1

	Candidates	Votes	%
	Tom Hickey (R)	68,328	39.8
14	John Conyers Jr. (D)	126,321	86.9
	Vendella M. Collins (R)	16,140	11.1
15	Carolyn Cheeks Kilpatrick (D)	108,582	87.0
	Chrysanthea D. Boyd-Fields (R)	12,887	10.3
16	John D. Dingell (D)	116,145	66.6
	William Morse (R)	54,121	31.0

MINNESOTA

1	Gil Gutknecht (R)	131,233	54.7
	Tracy L. Beckman (D)	108,420	45.2
2	David Minge (D)	148,933	57.0
	Craig Duehring (R)	99,490	38.1
3	Jim Ramstad (R)	203,731	71.9
	Stanley J. Leino (D)	66,505	23.5
4	Bruce Vento (D)	128,726	53.7
	Dennis R. Newinski (R)	95,388	39.8
5	Martin Olav Sabo (D)	145,535	66.9
	Frank Taylor (R)	60,035	27.6
6	William P. "Bill" Luther (D)	148,728	50.0
	John Kline (R)	136,866	46.0
7	Collin C. Peterson (D)	169,907	71.7
	Aleta Edin (R)	66,562	28.1
8	James L. Oberstar (D)	173,734	66.0
	Jerry Shuster (R)	69,667	26.5
	Stan "The Man" Estes (REF)	15,137	6.4

MISSISSIPPI

1	Roger Wicker (R)	66,738	67.2
	Rex Weathers (D)	30,438	30.6
2	Bennie Thompson (D)	80,507	71.2
	Will Chipman (LIBERT)	32,533	28.8
3	Charles W. "Chip" Pickering Jr. (R)	84,785	84.6
	C. T. Scarborough (LIBERT)	15,465	15.4
4	Ronnie Shows (D)	73,252	53.4
	Delbert Hosemann (R)	61,551	44.9
5	Gene Taylor (D)	78,661	77.8
	Randy McDonnell (R)	19,341	19.1

MISSOURI

1	William L. Clay (D)	90,840	72.6
	Richmond A. Soulade Sr. (R)	30,635	24.5
2	James M. Talent (R)	142,313	70.0
	John Ross (D)	57,565	28.3
3	Richard A. Gephardt (D)	98,287	55.8
	William J. Federer (R)	74,005	42.0
4	Ike Skelton (D)	133,173	71.0
	Cecilia D. Noland (R)	51,005	27.2
5	Karen McCarthy (D)	101,313	65.9
	Penny Bennett (R)	47,582	31.0
6	Pat Danner (D)	136,774	70.9
	Jeff Bailey (R)	51,679	26.8
7	Roy Blunt (R)	129,746	72.6
	Marc Perkel (D)	43,416	24.3
8	Jo Ann Emerson (R)	104,271	62.6
	Anthony J. "Tony" Heckemeyer (D)	59,426	35.7
9	Kenny Hulshof (R)	117,196	62.2
	Linda Vogt (D)	66,861	35.5

MONTANA

AL	Rick Hill (R)	175,748	53.0
	Robert "Dusty" Deschamps (D)	147,073	44.4

NEBRASKA

1	Doug Bereuter (R)	136,058	73.5
	Don Eret (D)	48,826	26.4
2	Lee Terry (R)	106,782	65.5
	Michael Scott (D)	55,722	34.2
3	Bill Barrett (R)	149,896	84.3
	Jerry Hickman (LIBERT)	27,278	15.3

NEVADA

	Candidates	Votes	%
1	Shelley Berkley (D)	79,315	49.2
	Don Chairez (R)	73,540	45.7
2	Jim Gibbons (R)	201,623	81.1
	Christopher Horne (IA)	20,738	8.3
	Louis R. Tomburello (LIBERT)	18,561	7.5

NEW HAMPSHIRE

1	John E. Sununu (R)	104,430	66.8
	Peter Flood (D)	51,783	33.1
2	Charles Bass (R)	85,740	53.1
	Mary Rauh (D)	72,217	44.8

NEW JERSEY

1	Robert E. Andrews (D)	90,279	73.2
	Ronald L. Richards (R)	27,855	22.6
2	Frank A. LoBiondo (R)	93,248	65.9
	Derek Hunsberger (D)	43,563	30.8
3	H. James Saxton (R)	97,508	62.0
	Steven J. Polansky (D)	55,248	35.1
4	Christopher H. Smith (R)	92,991	62.0
	Larry Schneider (D)	52,281	35.0
5	Marge Roukema (R)	106,304	63.7
	Mike Schneider (D)	55,487	33.3
6	Frank Pallone Jr. (D)	78,102	57.0
	Michael Ferguson (R)	55,180	40.3
7	Bob Franks (R)	77,751	52.5
	Maryanne S. Connelly (D)	65,776	44.4
8	Bill Pascrell Jr. (D)	81,068	62.1
	Matthew J. Kirnan (R)	46,289	35.4
9	Steven R. Rothman (D)	91,330	64.6
	Steve Lonegan (R)	47,817	33.8
10	Donald M. Payne (D)	82,244	83.5
	William Stanley Wnuck (R)	10,678	10.8
11	Rodney Frelinghuysen (R)	100,910	67.7
	John P. Scollo (D)	44,160	29.6
12	Rush Holt (D)	92,528	50.1
	Michael Pappas (R)	87,221	47.2
13	Robert Menendez (D)	70,308	80.1
	Theresa de Leon (R)	14,615	16.6

NEW MEXICO

1	Heather A. Wilson (R)	86,784	48.3
	Phillip J. Maloof (D)	75,040	41.9
	Robert L. Anderson (GREEN)	17,266	9.6
2	Joe Skeen (R)	85,077	57.9
	E. Shirley Baca (D)	61,796	42.1
3	Tom Udall (D)	91,248	53.2
	Bill Redmond (R)	74,266	43.3

Special Election[4]

1	Heather A. Wilson (R)	54,853	44.5
	Phillip J. Maloof (D)	48,747	39.6
	Robert L. Anderson (GREEN)	18,108	14.7

NEW YORK

1	Michael P. Forbes (R, RTL, C)	99,460	64.1
	William G. Holst (D)	55,630	35.9
2	Rick A. Lazio (R, C)	85,089	66.2
	John C. Bace (D)	37,949	29.5
3	Peter T. King (R, RTL)	117,258	64.3
	Kevin N. Langberg (D)	63,628	34.9
4	Carolyn McCarthy (D)	90,256	52.6
	Gregory R. Becker (R)	79,984	46.6
5	Gary L. Ackerman (D, INDEP, L)	97,404	65.0
	David C. Pinzon (R, C)	49,586	33.1
6	Gregory W. Meeks (D)	76,122	100.0
7	Joseph Crowley (D)	50,924	69.0
	James J. Dillon (R)	18,896	25.6
	Richard Retcho (C)	3,960	5.4
8	Jerrold Nadler (D, L)	112,948	86.0
	Ted Howard (R)	18,383	14.0
9	Anthony Weiner (D, INDEP)	69,439	66.4

	Candidates	Votes	%
	Louis Telano (R)	24,486	23.4
	Melinda Katz (L)	5,698	5.5
10	Edolphus Towns (D, L)	83,528	92.3
	Ernestine M. Brown (R)	5,577	6.2
11	Major R. Owens (D, L)	75,773	90.0
	David Greene (R, C)	7,284	8.7
12	Nydia M. Velázquez (D)	53,269	83.6
	Rosemarie Markgraf (R)	7,405	11.6
13	Vito J. Fossella (R, C, RTL)	76,138	64.8
	Eugene V. "Gene" Prisco (D, L)	40,167	34.2
14	Carolyn B. Maloney (D, L, INDEP)	111,072	77.4
	Stephanie Kupferman (R)	32,458	22.6
15	Charles B. Rangel (D, L)	90,424	93.1
	David E. Cunningham (R)	5,633	5.8
16	Jose E. Serrano (D, L)	67,367	95.4
17	Eliot L. Engel (D, L)	80,947	88.0
	Peter Fiumefreddo (R, C, INDEP)	11,037	12.0
18	Nita M. Lowey (D)	91,623	82.8
	Daniel McMahon (C)	12,594	11.4
19	Sue W. Kelly (R, C)	98,512	62.5
	Dick Collins (D)	52,503	33.3
20	Benjamin A. Gilman (R)	98,546	58.3
	Paul J. Feiner (D, INDEP, L)	65,589	38.8
21	Michael R. McNulty (D, C, INDEP)	146,639	74.2
	Lauren Ayers (R)	50,931	25.8
22	John E. Sweeney (R, C, INDEP)	106,919	55.3
	Jean Parvin Bordewich (D)	81,296	42.1
23	Sherwood L. Boehlert (R)	111,242	80.8
	David Vickers (C, INDEP)	26,493	19.2
24	John M. McHugh (R, C)	116,682	79.0
	Neil P. Tallon (D)	31,011	21.0
25	James T. Walsh (R, C)	121,204	69.4
	Yvonne Rothenberg (D, L, GREEN)	53,461	30.6
26	Maurice D. Hinchey (D, INDEP, L)	108,204	61.8
	William H. "Bud" Walker (R, C)	54,776	31.2
	Randall Terry (RTL)	12,160	6.9
27	Thomas M. Reynolds (R, C)	102,042	57.3
	Bill Cook (D, INDEP, RTL)	75,978	42.7
28	Louise Slaughter (D)	118,856	64.8
	Richard A. "Dick" Kaplan (R, INDEP)	56,443	30.8
29	John J. LaFalce (D, INDEP, L)	97,235	57.0
	Chris Collins (R, C)	69,481	40.7
30	Jack Quinn (R, C, INDEP)	116,093	67.8
	Crystal D. Peoples (D)	55,199	32.2
31	Amo Houghton (R, C)	107,615	68.1
	Caleb Rossiter (D)	40,091	25.3
	James R. Pierce Sr. (RTL)	10,546	6.7

Special Election[5]

6	Gregory W. Meeks (D, L)	14,224	56.5
	Alton R. Waldon Jr. (C, I)	5,229	20.8
	Barbara M. Clark (TFC)	3,305	13.1
	Celestine V. Miller (R)	2,209	8.8

NORTH CAROLINA

1	Eva Clayton (D)	85,125	62.2
	Ted Tyler (R)	50,578	37.0
2	Bob Etheridge (D)	100,550	57.4
	Dan Page (R)	72,997	41.7
3	Walter B. Jones (R)	83,529	61.9
	Jon Williams (D)	50,041	37.1
4	David E. Price (D)	129,157	57.4
	Tom Roberg (R)	93,469	41.6
5	Richard M. Burr (R)	119,103	67.6
	Mike Robinson (D)	55,806	31.7
6	Howard Coble (R)	112,740	88.6
	Jeffrey D. Bentley (LIBERT)	14,454	11.4
7	Mike McIntyre (D)	124,366	91.3
	Paul Meadows (LIBERT)	11,924	8.7

Candidates	Votes	%
8 Robin Hayes (R)	67,505	50.7
Mike Taylor (D)	64,127	48.2
9 Sue Myrick (R)	120,570	69.3
Rory Blake (D)	51,345	29.5
10 Cass Ballenger (R)	118,541	85.6
Deborah Garrett Eddins (LIBERT)	19,970	14.4
11 Charles H. Taylor (R)	112,908	56.6
David Young (D)	84,256	42.2
12 Melvin Watt (D)	82,305	56.0
Scott Keadle (R)	62,070	42.2

NORTH DAKOTA

	Candidates	Votes	%
AL	Earl Pomeroy (D)	119,668	56.2
	Kevin Cramer (R)	87,511	41.1

OHIO

Candidates	Votes	%
1 Steve Chabot (R)	92,421	53.0
Roxanne Qualls (D)	82,003	47.0
2 Rob Portman (R)	154,344	75.8
Charles W. Sanders (D)	49,293	24.2
3 Tony P. Hall (D)	114,198	69.3
John Shondel (R)	50,544	30.7
4 Michael G. Oxley (R)	112,011	63.8
Paul A. McClain (D)	63,529	36.2
5 Paul E. Gillmor (R)	123,979	66.7
Susan Davenport Darrow (D)	61,926	33.3
6 Ted Strickland (D)	102,852	57.0
Nancy P. Hollister (R)	77,711	43.0
7 David L. Hobson (R)	120,765	67.2
Donald E. Minor Jr. (D)	49,780	27.7
James Schrader (LIBERT)	9,146	5.1
8 John A. Boehner (R)	127,979	70.7
John W. Griffin (D)	52,912	29.3
9 Marcy Kaptur (D)	130,793	81.1
Edward Emery (R)	30,312	18.8
10 Dennis Kucinich (D)	110,552	66.8
Joe Slovenic (R)	55,537	33.2
11 Stephanie Tubbs Jones (D)	115,226	80.4
James D. Hereford (R)	18,592	13.0
Jean Murrell Capers (I)	9,477	6.6
12 John R. Kasich (R)	124,197	67.2
Edward S. Brown (D)	60,694	32.8
13 Sherrod Brown (D)	116,309	61.5
Grace L. Drake (R)	72,666	38.5
14 Thomas C. Sawyer (D)	106,046	62.7
Tom Watkins (R)	63,027	37.3
15 Deborah Pryce (R)	113,846	65.7
Adam Clay Miller (D)	49,334	28.5
Kevin Nestor (I)	9,996	5.7
16 Ralph Regula (R)	117,426	64.0
Peter D. Ferguson (D)	66,047	36.0
17 James A. Traficant Jr. (D)	123,718	68.2
Paul H. Alberty (R)	57,703	31.8
18 Bob Ney (R)	113,119	60.3
Robert Burch (D)	74,571	39.7
19 Steven C. LaTourette (R)	126,786	66.4
Elizabeth Kelley (D)	64,090	33.6

OKLAHOMA

Candidates	Votes	%
1 Steve Largent (R)	91,031	61.8
Howard Plowman (D)	56,309	38.2
2 Tom Coburn (R)	85,581	57.7
Kent Pharaoh (D)	59,042	39.8
3 Wes Watkins (R)	89,832	62.0
Walt Roberts (D)	55,163	38.0
4 J. C. Watts Jr. (R)	83,272	61.5
Ben Odom (D)	52,107	38.5
5 Ernest Istook (R)	103,217	68.2
Mary Catherine "M. C." Smothermon (D)	48,182	31.8
6 Frank D. Lucas (R)	85,261	65.0
Paul M. Barby (D)	43,555	33.2

OREGON

Candidates	Votes	%
1 David Wu (D)	119,993	50.1
Molly Bordonaro (R)	112,827	47.1
2 Greg Walden (R)	132,316	61.5
Kevin M. Campbell (D)	74,924	34.8
3 Earl Blumenauer (D)	153,889	83.9
Bruce Alexander Knight (LIBERT)	16,930	9.2
Walter F. "Walt" Brown (S)	10,199	5.6
4 Peter A. DeFazio (D)	157,524	70.1
Steve J. Webb (R)	64,143	28.6
5 Darlene Hooley (D)	124,916	54.9
Marylin Shannon (R)	92,215	40.5

PENNSYLVANIA

Candidates	Votes	%
1 Robert A. Brady (D)	77,788	81.2
William M. Harrison (R)	15,898	16.6
2 Chaka Fattah (D)	102,763	86.5
Anne Marie Mulligan (R)	16,001	13.5
3 Robert A. Borski (D)	66,270	59.3
Charles F. Dougherty (R)	45,390	40.7
4 Ron Klink (D)	103,183	63.8
Mike Turzai (R)	58,485	36.2
5 John E. Peterson (R)	99,502	84.8
William M. Belitskus (GREEN)	17,734	15.1
6 Tim Holden (D)	83,374	61.0
John Meckley (R)	54,579	39.0
7 Curt Weldon (R)	119,491	71.8
Martin J. D'Urso (D)	46,920	28.2
8 Jim Greenwood (R)	93,697	63.3
Bill Tuthill (D)	48,320	32.6
9 Bud Shuster (R)	125,409	99.5
10 Donald L. Sherwood (R)	84,275	48.7
Patrick Casey (D)	83,760	48.4
11 Paul E. Kanjorski (D)	88,933	66.8
Stephen A. Urban (R)	44,123	33.2
12 John P. Murtha (D)	100,528	68.5
Timothy E. Holloway (R)	46,239	31.5
13 Joseph M. Hoeffel III (D)	95,105	51.6
Jon D. Fox (R)	85,915	46.6
14 William J. Coyne (D)	83,355	60.5
Bill Ravotti (R)	52,745	38.3
15 Pat Toomey (R)	81,755	55.0
Roy C. Afflerbach (D)	66,930	45.0
16 Joseph E. Pitts (R)	95,979	70.5
Robert S. Yorczyk (D)	40,092	29.5
17 George W. Gekas (R)	114,931	99.8
18 Mike Doyle (D)	98,363	67.7
Dick Walker (R)	46,945	32.3
19 Bill Goodling (R)	96,284	67.6
Linda G. Ropp (D)	40,674	28.5
20 Frank Mascara (D)	97,885	99.8
21 Phil English (R)	94,518	63.4
Larry Klemens (D)	54,591	36.6

Special Election[6]

Candidates	Votes	%
1 Robert A. Brady (D)	13,923	73.6
William M. Harrison (R)	2,436	12.9
Juanita Norwood (REF)	1,993	10.5

RHODE ISLAND

Candidates	Votes	%
1 Patrick J. Kennedy (D)	92,788	66.8
Ronald G. Santa (R)	38,460	27.7
2 Bob Weygand (D)	110,917	72.0
John O. Matson (R)	38,170	24.8

SOUTH CAROLINA

Candidates	Votes	%
1 Mark Sanford (R)	118,414	91.0
Joseph F. Innella (NL)	11,586	8.9
2 Floyd D. Spence (R)	119,583	57.8
Jane Frederick (D)	84,864	41.0
3 Lindsey Graham (R)	129,047	99.7
4 Jim DeMint (R)	105,264	57.7
Glenn Gilbert Reese (D)	73,314	40.2
5 John M. Spratt (D)	95,105	57.9
Mike Burkhold (R)	66,299	40.4
6 James "Jim" Clyburn (D)	116,507	72.6
Gary McLeod (R)	41,421	25.8

SOUTH DAKOTA

	Candidates	Votes	%
AL	John Thune (R)	194,157	75.1
	Jeff Moser (D)	64,433	24.9

TENNESSEE

Candidates	Votes	%
1 Bill Jenkins (R)	68,904	69.1
Kay C. White (D)	30,710	30.8
2 John J. "Jimmy" Duncan Jr. (R)	90,860	88.6
3 Zach Wamp (R)	75,100	66.0
James D. "Jim" Lewis Jr. (D)	37,144	32.6
4 Van Hilleary (R)	62,829	59.6
Jerry W. Cooper (D)	42,627	40.4
5 Bob Clement (D)	74,611	82.8
William M. Lancaster (I)	6,162	6.8
Al Borgman (I)	4,983	5.5
6 Bart Gordon (D)	75,055	54.6
Walt R. Massey Jr. (R)	62,277	45.3
7 Ed Bryant (R)	91,980	99.5
8 John Tanner (D)	76,803	100.0
9 Harold E. Ford Jr. (D)	75,428	78.7
Claude Burdikoff (R)	18,078	18.9

TEXAS

Candidates	Votes	%
1 Max Sandlin (D)	80,788	59.4
Dennis Boerner (R)	55,191	40.6
2 Jim Turner (D)	81,556	58.4
Brian Babin (R)	56,891	40.8
3 Sam Johnson (R)	106,690	91.2
Ken Ashby (LIBERT)	10,288	8.8
4 Ralph M. Hall (D)	82,989	57.6
Jim Lohmeyer (R)	58,954	40.9
5 Pete Sessions (R)	61,714	55.8
Victor M. Morales (D)	48,073	43.4
6 Joe Barton (R)	112,957	72.9
Ben B. Boothe (D)	40,112	25.9
7 Bill Archer (R)	111,010	93.3
Drew Parks (LIBERT)	7,889	6.6
8 Kevin Brady (R)	123,372	92.8
Don L. Richards (LIBERT)	9,576	7.2
9 Nick Lampson (D)	86,055	63.7
Tom Cottar (R)	49,107	36.3
10 Lloyd Doggett (D)	116,127	85.2
Vincent J. May (LIBERT)	20,155	14.8
11 Chet Edwards (D)	71,142	82.4
Vince Hanke (LIBERT)	15,161	17.6
12 Kay Granger (R)	66,740	61.9
Tom Hall (D)	39,084	36.3
13 William M. "Mac" Thornberry (R)	81,141	67.9
Mark Harmon (D)	37,027	31.0
14 Ron Paul (R)	84,459	55.3
Loy Sneary (D)	68,014	44.5
15 Rubén Hinojosa (D)	47,957	59.4
Tom Haughey (R)	34,221	41.6
16 Silvestre Reyes (D)	67,486	87.9
Stu Nance (LIBERT)	5,329	6.9
Lorenzo Morales (I)	3,952	5.1
17 Charles W. Stenholm (D)	75,367	53.6
Rudy Izzard (R)	63,700	45.3
18 Sheila Jackson-Lee (D)	82,091	89.9
James Galvan (LIBERT)	9,176	10.1
19 Larry Combest (R)	108,266	83.6
Sidney Blankenship (D)	21,162	16.4
20 Charlie Gonzalez (D)	50,356	63.2
James Walker (R)	28,347	35.6
21 Lamar Smith (R)	165,047	91.4
Jeffrey C. Blunt (LIBERT)	15,561	8.6
22 Tom DeLay (R)	87,840	65.2
Hill Kemp (D)	45,386	33.7
23 Henry Bonilla (R)	73,177	63.8
Charlie Urbina Jones (D)	40,281	35.1
24 Martin Frost (D)	56,321	57.5
Shawn Terry (R)	40,105	40.9
25 Ken Bentsen (D)	58,591	57.9
John Sanchez (R)	41,848	41.3
26 Dick Armey (R)	120,332	88.1
Joe Turner (LIBERT)	16,182	11.9

	Candidates	Votes	%
27	Solomon P. Ortiz (D)	61,638	63.3
	Erol A. Stone (R)	34,284	35.2
28	Ciro D. Rodriguez (D)	71,849	90.5
	Edward Elmer (LIBERT)	7,504	9.5
29	Gene Green (D)	44,179	92.8
30	Eddie Bernice Johnson (D)	57,603	72.2
	Carrie Kelleher (R)	21,338	27.0

UTAH

	Candidates	Votes	%
1	James V. Hansen (R)	109,708	67.7
	Steve Beierlein (D)	49,307	30.4
2	Merrill Cook (R)	93,718	52.8
	Lily Eskelsen (D)	77,198	43.5
3	Christopher B. Cannon (R)	100,830	76.9
	Will Christensen (IA)	20,720	15.8
	Kitty K. Burton (LIBERT)	9,553	7.3

VERMONT

	Candidates	Votes	%
AL	Bernard Sanders (I)	136,403	63.4
	Mark Candon (R)	70,740	32.9

VIRGINIA

	Candidates	Votes	%
1	Herbert H. Bateman (R)	76,474	77.1
	Bradford L. Phillips (I)	13,235	13.2
	Josh Billings (I)	9,492	9.5
2	Owen B. Pickett (D)	67,975	94.3
3	Robert C. Scott (D)	48,129	76.0
	Robert S. "Bob" Barnett (I)	14,453	22.8
4	Norman Sisisky (D)	64,563	97.0
5	Virgil H. Goode Jr. (D)	73,097	98.9
6	Robert W. Goodlatte (R)	89,177	69.3
	David Bowers (D)	39,487	30.7

	Candidates	Votes	%
7	Thomas J. Bliley Jr. (R)	77,044	78.7
	Bradley E. Evans (I)	20,293	20.7
8	James P. Moran (D)	97,545	66.7
	Demaris Miller (R)	48,352	33.1
9	Rick Boucher (D)	87,163	60.9
	Joe Barta (R)	55,918	39.1
10	Frank R. Wolf (R)	103,648	71.6
	Cornell W. Brooks (D)	36,476	25.2
11	Thomas M. Davis III (R)	91,603	81.7
	C. W. Levi Levy (I)	18,807	16.8

WASHINGTON

	Candidates	Votes	%
1	Jay Inslee (D)	112,726	49.8
	Rick White (R)	99,919	44.1
	Bruce Craswell (AMH)	13,837	6.1
2	Jack Metcalf (R)	124,125	55.2
	Grethe Cammermeyer (D)	100,776	44.8
3	Brian Baird (D)	120,364	54.7
	Don Benton (R)	99,855	45.3
4	Richard "Doc" Hastings (R)	121,684	69.1
	Gordon Allen Pross (D)	43,043	24.4
	Peggy McKerlie (REF)	11,363	6.5
5	George Nethercutt (R)	110,040	56.9
	Brad Lyons (D)	73,545	38.1
	John Beal (AMH)	9,673	5.0
6	Norm Dicks (D)	143,308	68.4
	Bob Lawrence (R)	66,291	31.6
7	Jim McDermott (D)	183,076	88.2
	Stan Lippmann (REF)	19,545	9.4
8	Jennifer Dunn (R)	135,539	59.7
	Heidi Behrens-Benedict (D)	91,371	40.3
9	Adam Smith (D)	111,948	64.7
	Ron Taber (R)	61,108	35.3

WEST VIRGINIA

	Candidates	Votes	%
1	Alan B. Mollohan (D)	105,101	84.7
	Richard Kerr (LIBERT)	19,013	15.3
2	Bob Wise (D)	99,357	73.0
	Sally Anne Kay (R)	29,136	21.4
	John Brown (LIBERT)	7,660	5.6
3	Nick J. Rahall II (D)	78,814	86.6
	Joe Whelan (LIBERT)	12,196	13.4

WISCONSIN

	Candidates	Votes	%
1	Paul Ryan (R)	108,475	57.1
	Lydia Spottswood (D)	81,164	42.7
2	Tammy Baldwin (D)	116,377	52.5
	Josephine Musser (R)	103,528	46.7
3	Ron Kind (D)	128,256	71.5
	Troy A. Brechler (R)	51,001	28.4
4	Gerald D. Kleczka (D)	105,841	57.9
	Tom Reynolds (R)	76,666	42.0
5	Thomas M. Barrett (D)	121,129	78.2
	Jack Melvin (R)	33,506	21.6
6	Tom Petri (R)	144,144	92.6
	Timothy Farness (TAX)	11,267	7.2
7	David R. Obey (D)	115,613	60.6
	Scott West (R)	75,049	39.3
8	Mark Green (R)	112,418	54.6
	Jay Johnson (D)	93,441	45.4
9	F. James Sensenbrenner Jr. (R)	175,533	91.3
	Jeffrey M. Gonyo (INDEP)	16,419	8.5

WYOMING

	Candidates	Votes	%
AL	Barbara Cubin (R)	100,687	57.8
	Scott Farris (D)	67,399	38.7

1. A special all-party primary was held to fill the unexpired term of Rep. Ronald V. Dellums (D), who resigned Feb. 6, 1998. Because Lee won a majority of the vote in the first-round balloting, no runoff election was held.

2. A special election was held to fill the unexpired term of Rep. Walter Capps (D), who died Oct. 28, 1997.

3. A special all-party primary was held to fill the unexpired term of Sony Bono (R), who died Jan. 5, 1998. Because Bono won a majority of the vote in the first-round balloting, no runoff election was held.

4. A special election was held to fill the unexpired term of Rep. Steven H. Schiff (R), who died March 25, 1998.

5. A special election was held to fill the unexpired term of Rep. Floyd H. Flake (D), who resigned Nov. 15, 1997.

6. A special election was held to fill the unexpired term of Rep. Thomas M. Foglietta (D), who resigned Nov. 12, 1997.

1999 House Elections

CALIFORNIA

Special Election[1]

	Candidates	Votes	%
42	Joe Baca (D)	23,690	50.5
	Elia Pirozzi (R)	21,018	44.9

GEORGIA

Special Primary[2]

	Candidates	Votes	%
6	Johnny Jackson (R)	51,548	66.3
	Christina Jefferey (R)	20,155	38.7
	Gary Pelphrey (D)	4,014	5.1

LOUISIANA

Special Runoff Election[3]

	Candidates	Votes	%
1	David Vitter (R)	61,661	50.7
	David Conner Treen (D)	59,849	49.3

1. A special election was held to fill the unexpired term of Rep. George E. Brown Jr. (D), who died July 15, 1999.

2. A special all-party primary was held to fill the unexpired term of Speaker Newt Gingrich (R), who resigned Jan. 3, 1999. Because Jackson won a majority of the vote in the first-round balloting, no runoff election was held.

3. A special all-party primary was held to fill the unexpired term of Rep. Bob Livingston (D), who resigned Feb. 8, 1999. With no candidate receiving the majority vote, a special runoff election of the top two finishers was held.

2000 House Elections

ALABAMA

	Candidates	Votes	%
1	Sonny Callahan (R)	151,188	91.3
	Richard M. "Dick" Coffee (LIBERT)	14,031	8.5
2	Terry Everett (R)	151,830	68.2
	Charles Woods (D)	64,958	29.2
3	Bob Riley (R)	147,317	86.9
	John P. Sophocleus (LIBERT)	21,119	12.4
4	Robert B. Aderholt (R)	140,009	60.6
	Marsha Folsom (D)	86,400	37.4
5	Robert E. "Bud" Cramer (D)	186,059	88.8
	Alan Fulton Barksdale (LIBERT)	22,110	10.6
6	Spencer Bachus (R)	212,751	87.9
	Terry Reagin Sr. (LIBERT)	28,189	11.7
7	Earl F. Hilliard (D)	148,243	74.6
	Ed Martin (R)	46,134	23.2

ALASKA

	Candidates	Votes	%
AL	Don Young (R)	190,862	69.6
	Clifford Mark Greene (D)	45,372	16.5
	Anna C. Young (GREEN)	22,440	8.2

ARIZONA

	Candidates	Votes	%
1	Jeff Flake (R)	123,289	53.6
	David Mendoza (D)	97,455	42.4
2	Ed Pastor (D)	84,034	68.5
	Bill Barenholtz (R)	32,990	26.9
3	Bob Stump (R)	198,367	65.7
	Gene Scharer (D)	94,676	31.4
4	John Shadegg (R)	140,396	64.0
	Ben Jankowski (D)	71,803	32.7
5	Jim Kolbe (R)	172,986	60.1
	George Cunningham (D)	101,564	35.3
6	J. D. Hayworth (R)	186,687	61.4
	Larry Nelson (D)	108,317	35.6

ARKANSAS

	Candidates	Votes	%
1	Marion Berry (D)	120,266	60.1
	Susan Myshka (R)	79,437	39.7
2	Vic Snyder (D)	126,957	57.5
	Bob Thomas (R)	93,692	42.5
3	Asa Hutchinson (R)		100.0
4	Mike Ross (D)	108,143	51.0
	Jay Dickey (R)	104,017	49.0

CALIFORNIA

	Candidates	Votes	%
1	Mike Thompson (D)	155,638	65.0
	Russell J. "Jim" Chase (R)	66,987	28.0
2	Wally Herger (R)	168,172	65.7
	Stan Morgan (D)	72,075	28.2
3	Doug Ose (R)	129,254	56.2
	Bob Kent (D)	93,067	40.4
4	John T. Doolittle (R)	197,503	63.4
	Mark Norberg (D)	97,974	31.5
5	Robert T. Matsui (D)	147,025	68.9
	Ken Payne (R)	55,945	26.1
6	Lynn Woolsey (D)	182,116	64.3
	Ken McAuliffe (R)	80,169	28.3
7	George Miller (D)	159,692	76.5
	Christopher Hoffman (R)	44,154	21.1
8	Nancy Pelosi (D)	181,847	84.4
	Adam Sparks (R)	25,298	11.7
9	Barbara Lee (D)	182,352	85.0
	Arneze Washington (R)	21,033	9.8
10	Ellen O. Tauscher (D)	160,429	52.6
	Claude B. Hutchison Jr. (R)	134,863	44.2
11	Richard W. Pombo (R)	120,635	57.8
	Tom Santos (D)	79,539	38.1
12	Tom Lantos (D)	158,404	74.5
	Mike Garza (R)	44,162	20.8

	Candidates	Votes	%
13	Pete Stark (D)	129,012	70.4
	James Goetz (R)	44,499	24.3
14	Anna G. Eshoo (D)	161,720	70.2
	Bill Quraishi (R)	59,338	25.8
15	Mike Honda (D)	128,545	54.3
	Jim Cunneen (R)	99,866	42.2
16	Zoe Lofgren (D)	115,118	72.1
	Horace Thayn (R)	37,213	23.3
17	Sam Farr (D)	143,219	68.6
	Clint Engler (R)	51,557	24.7
18	Gary A. Condit (D)	121,003	67.1
	Steve Wilson (R)	56,465	31.3
19	George P. Radanovich (R)	144,517	64.9
	Daniel Rosenberg (D)	70,578	31.7
20	Cal Dooley (D)	66,235	52.3
	Rich Rodriguez (R)	57,563	45.5
21	Bill Thomas (R)	142,539	71.6
	Pedro Martinez (D)	49,318	24.8
22	Lois Capps (D)	135,538	53.1
	Mike Stoker (R)	113,094	44.3
23	Elton Gallegly (R)	119,479	54.1
	Michael Case (D)	89,918	40.7
24	Brad Sherman (D)	155,398	66.0
	Jerry Doyle (R)	70,169	29.8
25	Howard P. "Buck" McKeon (R)	138,628	62.2
	Sid Gold (D)	73,921	33.2
26	Howard L. Berman (D)	96,500	84.1
	Bill Farley (LIBERT)	13,052	11.4
27	Adam Schiff (D)	113,708	52.7
	James E. Rogan (R)	94,518	43.8
28	David Dreier (R)	116,557	56.8
	Janice M. Nelson (D)	81,804	39.9
29	Henry A. Waxman (D)	180,295	75.7
	Jim Scileppi (R)	45,784	19.2
30	Xavier Becerra (D)	83,223	83.3
	Tony Goss (R)	11,788	11.8
31	Hilda Solis (D)	89,600	79.4
	Krista Lieberg-Wong (GREEN)	10,294	9.1
	Michael McGuire (LIBERT)	7,138	6.3
	Richard Griffin (NL)	5,882	5.2
32	Julian C. Dixon (D)	137,447	83.5
	Kathy Williamson (R)	19,924	12.1
33	Lucille Roybal-Allard (D)	60,510	84.5
	Wayne Miller (R)	8,260	11.5
34	Grace F. Napolitano (D)	105,980	71.3
	Robert Arthur Canales (R)	33,445	22.5
	Julia F. Simon (NL)	9,262	6.2
35	Maxine Waters (D)	100,569	86.5
	Carl McGill (R)	12,582	10.8
36	Jane Harman (D)	115,651	48.4
	Steven T. Kuykendall (R)	111,199	46.5
37	Juanita Millender-McDonald (D)	93,269	82.3
	Vernon Van (R)	12,762	11.3
38	Steve Horn (R)	87,266	48.4
	Gerrie Schipske (D)	85,498	47.5
39	Ed Royce (R)	129,294	62.7
	Gill G. Kanel (D)	64,938	31.5
40	Jerry Lewis (R)	151,069	79.9
	Frank Schmit (NL)	19,029	10.1
	Jay Lindberg (LIBERT)	18,924	10.0
41	Gary G. Miller (R)	104,695	58.9
	Rodolfo "Rudy" Favila (D)	66,361	37.4
42	Joe Baca (D)	90,585	59.8
	Elia Pirozzi (R)	53,239	35.1
43	Ken Calvert (R)	140,201	73.7
	Bill Reed (LIBERT)	29,755	15.6
	Nathaniel Adam (NL)	20,376	10.7
44	Mary Bono (R)	123,738	59.2
	Ron Oden (D)	79,302	37.9
45	Dana Rohrabacher (R)	136,275	62.1
	Ted Crisell (D)	71,066	32.4
46	Loretta Sanchez (D)	70,381	60.2
	Gloria Matta Tuchman (R)	40,928	35.0

	Candidates	Votes	%
47	Christopher Cox (R)	181,365	65.6
	John L. Graham (D)	83,186	30.1
48	Darrell Issa (R)	160,627	61.4
	Peter Kouvelis (D)	74,073	28.3
49	Susan A. Davis (D)	113,400	49.6
	Brian P. Bilbray (R)	105,515	46.2
50	Bob Filner (D)	95,191	68.3
	Bob Divine (R)	38,526	27.6
51	Randy "Duke" Cunningham (R)	172,291	64.3
	George "Jorge" Barraza (D)	81,408	30.4
52	Duncan Hunter (R)	131,345	64.7
	Craig B. Barkacs (D)	63,537	31.3

COLORADO

	Candidates	Votes	%
1	Diana DeGette (D)	141,831	68.7
	Jesse L. Thomas (R)	56,291	27.3
2	Mark Udall (D)	155,725	55.0
	Carolyn Cox (R)	109,338	38.6
3	Scott McInnis (R)	199,204	65.8
	Curtis Imrie (D)	87,921	29.1
4	Bob Schaffer (R)	209,078	79.5
	Dan Sewell Ward (NL)	19,721	7.5
	Kordon Baker (LIBERT)	19,713	7.5
5	Joel Hefley (R)	253,330	82.7
	Kerry Kantor (LIBERT)	37,719	12.3
	Randy MacKenzie (NL)	15,260	5.0
6	Tom Tancredo (R)	141,410	53.9
	Ken Toltz (D)	110,568	42.1

CONNECTICUT

	Candidates	Votes	%
1	John B. Larson (D)	151,932	71.9
	Bob Backlund (R)	59,331	28.1
2	Rob Simmons (R)	114,380	50.6
	Sam Gejdenson (D)	111,520	49.4
3	Rosa DeLauro (D)	156,910	71.9
	June Gold (R)	60,037	27.5
4	Christopher Shays (R)	119,155	57.6
	Stephanie Sanchez (D)	84,472	40.9
5	Jim Maloney (D)	118,932	53.6
	Mark D. Nielsen (R)	98,229	44.3
6	Nancy L. Johnson (R)	143,698	62.6
	Paul Vincent Valenti (D)	75,471	32.9

DELAWARE

	Candidates	Votes	%
AL	Michael N. Castle (R)	211,797	67.6
	Mike Miller (D)	96,488	30.8

FLORIDA

	Candidates	Votes	%
1	Joe Scarborough (R)	226,473	99.5
2	Allen Boyd (D)	185,579	72.1
	Doug Dodd (R)	71,754	27.9
3	Corrine Brown (D)	102,143	57.6
	Jennifer Carroll (R)	75,228	42.4
4	Ander Crenshaw (R)	203,090	67.0
	Tom Sullivan (D)	94,587	31.2
5	Karen L. Thurman (D)	180,338	64.3
	Peter C. K. "Pete" Enwall (R)	100,244	35.7
6	Cliff Stearns (R)	178,789	99.9
7	John L. Mica (R)	171,018	63.2
	Daniel Vaughen (D)	99,531	36.8
8	Richard "Ric" Keller (R)	125,253	50.8
	Linda Chapin (D)	121,295	49.2
9	Michael Bilirakis (R)	210,318	81.9
	Jon Scott Duffey (REF)	46,474	18.1
10	C. W. Bill Young (R)	146,799	75.7
	Josette Green (NL)	26,908	13.9
	Randy Heine (NP)	20,296	10.5
11	Jim Davis (D)	149,465	84.6
	Charlie Westlake (LIBERT)	27,197	15.4
12	Adam Putnam (R)	125,224	57.0
	Michael Stedem (D)	94,395	43.0

Candidates	Votes	%
13 Dan Miller (R)	175,918	63.8
Daniel E. Dunn (D)	99,568	36.1
14 Porter J. Goss (R)	242,614	85.2
Sam Farling (NL)	41,988	14.8
15 Dave Weldon (R)	176,189	58.8
Patsy Ann Kurth (D)	117,511	39.2
16 Mark Foley (R)	176,153	60.2
Jean Elliott Brown (D)	108,782	37.2
17 Carrie P. Meek (D)	100,715	100.0
18 Ileana Ros-Lehtinen (R)	112,968	100.0
19 Robert Wexler (D)	171,080	71.6
Morris Kent Thompson (R)	67,789	28.4
20 Peter Deutsch (D)	156,765	99.9
21 Lincoln Diaz-Balart (R)	132,317	100.0
22 E. Clay Shaw Jr. (R)	105,855	50.1
Elaine Bloom (D)	105,256	49.9
23 Alcee L. Hastings (D)	89,179	76.3
Bill Lambert (R)	27,630	23.7

GEORGIA

Candidates	Votes	%
1 Jack Kingston (R)	131,684	69.1
Joyce Marie Griggs (D)	58,776	30.9
2 Sanford D. Bishop Jr. (D)	96,430	53.5
Dylan Glenn (R)	83,870	46.5
3 Mac Collins (R)	150,200	63.5
Gail Notti (D)	86,309	36.5
4 Cynthia A. McKinney (D)	139,579	60.7
Sunny Warren (R)	90,277	39.3
5 John Lewis (D)	137,333	77.2
Hank Schwab (R)	40,606	22.8
6 Johnny Isakson (R)	256,595	74.8
Brett DeHart (D)	86,666	25.2
7 Bob Barr (R)	126,312	55.3
Roger Kahn (D)	102,272	44.7
8 Saxby Chambliss (R)	113,380	58.9
Jim Marshall (D)	79,051	41.1
9 Nathan Deal (R)	183,171	75.2
James Harrington (D)	60,360	24.8
10 Charlie Norwood (R)	122,590	63.2
Marion Spencer "Denise" Freeman (D)	71,309	36.8
11 John Linder (R)	199,652	100.0

HAWAII

Candidates	Votes	%
1 Neil Abercrombie (D)	108,517	69.0
Philip L. Meyers (R)	44,989	28.6
2 Patsy T. Mink (D)	112,856	61.6
Russell R. Francis (R)	65,906	36.0

IDAHO

Candidates	Votes	%
1 C. L. "Butch" Otter (R)	173,743	64.8
Linda Pall (D)	84,080	31.4
2 Mike Simpson (R)	158,912	70.7
Craig Williams (D)	58,265	25.9

ILLINOIS

Candidates	Votes	%
1 Bobby L. Rush (D)	172,271	87.8
Raymond G. Wardingley (R)	23,915	12.2
2 Jesse L. Jackson Jr. (D)	175,995	89.8
Robert Gordon III (R)	19,906	10.2
3 William O. Lipinski (D)	145,498	75.6
Karl Groth (R)	47,005	24.4
4 Luis V. Gutierrez (D)	89,487	88.6
Stephanie Sailor (LIBERT)	11,476	11.4
5 Rod R. Blagojevich (D)	142,161	87.3
Matthew Joseph Beauchamp (LIBERT)	20,728	12.7
6 Henry J. Hyde (R)	133,327	58.9
Brent Christensen (D)	92,880	41.1
7 Danny K. Davis (D)	164,155	85.9
Robert Dallas (R)	26,872	14.1
8 Philip M. Crane (R)	141,918	61.0
Lance Pressl (D)	90,777	39.0
9 Jan Schakowsky (D)	147,002	76.4
Dennis J. Driscoll (R)	45,344	23.6

Candidates	Votes	%
10 Mark Steven Kirk (R)	121,582	51.2
Lauren Beth Gash (D)	115,924	48.8
11 Jerry Weller (R)	132,384	56.4
James P. Stevenson (D)	102,485	43.6
12 Jerry F. Costello (D)	183,208	100.0
13 Judy Biggert (R)	193,250	66.2
Thomas Mason (D)	98,768	33.8
14 J. Dennis Hastert (R)	188,597	74.0
Vern Deljonson (D)	66,309	26.0
15 Timothy V. Johnson (R)	125,943	53.2
Mike Kelleher (D)	110,679	46.8
16 Donald Manzullo (R)	178,174	66.7
Charles W. Hendrickson (D)	88,781	33.2
17 Lane Evans (D)	132,494	54.9
Mark Baker (R)	108,853	45.1
18 Ray LaHood (R)	173,706	67.1
Joyce Harant (D)	85,317	32.9
19 David D. Phelps (D)	155,101	64.6
James E. "Jim" Eatherly (R)	85,137	35.4
20 John Shimkus (R)	161,393	63.1
Jeffrey Cooper (D)	94,382	36.9

INDIANA

Candidates	Votes	%
1 Peter J. Visclosky (D)	148,683	71.6
Jack Reynolds (R)	56,200	27.0
2 Mike Pence (R)	106,023	50.9
Bob Rock (D)	80,885	38.8
William G. Frazier (I)	19,077	9.2
3 Tim Roemer (D)	107,438	51.6
Chris Chocola (R)	98,822	47.4
4 Mark Souder (R)	131,051	62.3
Mike Foster (D)	74,492	35.4
5 Steve Buyer (R)	132,051	60.9
Greg Goodnight (D)	81,427	37.5
6 Dan Burton (R)	199,207	70.3
Darin Patrick Griesey (D)	74,881	26.4
7 Brian D. Kerns (R)	135,869	64.8
Michael Graf (D)	66,764	31.8
8 John Hostettler (R)	116,879	52.7
Paul Perry (D)	100,488	45.3
9 Baron P. Hill (D)	126,420	54.2
Michael Everett Bailey (R)	102,219	43.8
10 Julia Carson (D)	91,689	58.5
Marvin B. Scott (R)	62,233	39.7

IOWA

Candidates	Votes	%
1 Jim Leach (R)	164,972	61.8
Bob Simpson (D)	96,283	36.1
2 Jim Nussle (R)	139,906	55.4
Donna L. Smith (D)	110,327	43.7
3 Leonard L. Boswell (D)	156,327	62.8
Jay B. Marcus (R)	83,810	33.7
4 Greg Ganske (R)	169,267	61.4
Michael L. Huston (D)	101,112	36.7
5 Tom Latham (R)	159,367	68.8
Mike Palecek (D)	67,593	29.2

KANSAS

Candidates	Votes	%
1 Jerry Moran (R)	216,484	89.3
Jack W. Warner (LIBERT)	25,843	10.7
2 Jim Ryun (R)	164,951	67.4
Stanley Wiles (D)	71,709	29.3
3 Dennis Moore (D)	154,505	50.0
Phill Kline (R)	144,672	46.9
4 Todd Tiahrt (R)	131,871	54.4
Carlos Nolla (D)	101,980	42.0

KENTUCKY

Candidates	Votes	%
1 Edward Whitfield (R)	132,115	58.0
Brian Roy (D)	95,806	42.0
2 Ron Lewis (R)	160,800	67.7
Brian Pedigo (D)	74,537	31.4
3 Anne M. Northup (R)	142,106	52.9
Eleanor Jordan (D)	118,875	44.2
4 Ken Lucas (D)	125,872	54.3
Don Bell (R)	100,943	43.5

Candidates	Votes	%
5 Harold Rogers (R)	145,980	73.6
Sidney "Jane" Bailey-Bamer (D)	52,495	26.4
6 Ernie Fletcher (R)	142,971	52.8
Scotty Baesler (D)	94,167	34.8
Gatewood Galbraith (I)	32,436	12.0

LOUISIANA

Candidates	Votes	%
1 David Vitter (R)	191,379	80.5
Michael A. Armato (D)	40,917	17.2
2 William J. Jefferson (D)		100.0
3 W. J. "Billy" Tauzin (R)	143,446	78.0
Edwin J. "Eddie" Albares (I)	16,908	9.2
Anita Rosenthal (NL)	13,488	7.3
Dion Bourque (LIBERT)	10,118	5.5
4 Jim McCrery (R)	122,678	70.5
Phillip R. Green (D)	43,600	25.1
5 John Cooksey (R)	123,975	69.1
Roger Beall (D)	50,163	28.0
6 Richard H. Baker (R)	165,637	68.0
Kathy J. Rogillio (D)	72,192	29.7
7 Chris John (D)	152,796	83.3
Michael P. Harris (LIBERT)	30,687	16.7

MAINE

Candidates	Votes	%
1 Tom Allen (D)	202,823	59.8
Jane Amero (R)	123,915	36.5
2 John Baldacci (D)	219,783	73.4
Richard Campbell (R)	79,522	26.6

MARYLAND

Candidates	Votes	%
1 Wayne T. Gilchrest (R)	165,293	64.4
Bennett Bozman (D)	91,022	35.5
2 Robert L. Ehrlich Jr. (R)	178,556	68.6
Kenneth T. Bosley (D)	81,591	31.3
3 Benjamin L. Cardin (D)	169,347	75.7
Colin Harby (R)	53,827	24.0
4 Albert R. Wynn (D)	172,624	87.2
John B. Kimble (R)	24,973	12.6
5 Steny H. Hoyer (D)	166,231	65.1
Thomas E. "Tim" Hutchins (R)	89,019	34.9
6 Roscoe G. Bartlett (R)	168,624	60.6
Donald DeArmon (D)	109,136	39.3
7 Elijah E. Cummings (D)	134,066	87.1
Kenneth Kondner (R)	19,773	12.8
8 Constance A. Morella (R)	156,241	52.0
Terry Lierman (D)	136,840	45.5

MASSACHUSETTS

Candidates	Votes	%
1 John W. Olver (D)	169,375	68.2
Pete Abair (R)	73,580	29.6
2 Richard E. Neal (D)	196,670	98.9
3 Jim McGovern (D)	213,065	98.8
4 Barney Frank (D)	200,638	74.9
Martin D. Travis (R)	56,553	21.1
5 Martin T. Meehan (D)	199,601	98.0
6 John F. Tierney (D)	205,324	71.0
Paul McCarthy (R)	83,501	28.9
7 Edward J. Markey (D)	211,543	98.9
8 Michael E. Capuano (D)	144,031	99.3
9 Joe Moakley (D)	193,020	77.6
Janet E. Jeghelian (R)	48,672	19.6
10 Bill Delahunt (D)	234,675	74.1
Eric V. Bleichen (R)	81,192	25.6

MICHIGAN

Candidates	Votes	%
1 Bart Stupak (D)	169,649	58.4
Chuck Yob (R)	117,300	40.4
2 Peter Hoekstra (R)	186,762	64.4
Bob Shrauger (D)	96,370	33.2
3 Vernon J. Ehlers (R)	179,539	65.0
Tim Steele (D)	91,309	33.1
4 Dave Camp (R)	182,128	68.0
Lawrence D. Hollenbeck (D)	78,019	29.1

Candidates	Votes	%
5 James A. Barcia (D)	184,048	74.3
Ronald G. Actis (R)	59,274	23.9
6 Fred Upton (R)	159,373	67.9
James Bupp (D)	68,532	29.2
7 Nick Smith (R)	147,369	61.1
Jennie Crittendon (D)	86,080	35.7
8 Mike Rogers (R)	145,190	48.8
Dianne Byrum (D)	145,079	48.7
9 Dale E. Kildee (D)	158,184	61.1
Grant Garrett (R)	92,926	35.9
10 David E. Bonior (D)	181,818	64.4
Thomas Turner (R)	93,713	33.2
11 Joe Knollenberg (R)	170,790	55.8
Matthew Frumin (D)	124,053	40.5
12 Sander M. Levin (D)	157,720	64.3
Bart Baron (R)	78,795	32.1
13 Lynn Rivers (D)	160,084	64.7
Carl F. Barry (R)	79,445	32.1
14 John Conyers Jr. (D)	168,982	89.1
William A. Ashe (R)	17,582	9.3
15 Carolyn Cheeks Kilpatrick (D)	140,609	88.6
Chrysanthea D. Boyd-Fields (R)	14,336	9.0
16 John D. Dingell (D)	167,142	71.0
William Morse (R)	62,469	26.5

MINNESOTA

1 Gil Gutknecht (R)	159,835	56.4
Mary Rieder (D)	117,946	41.6
2 Mark Kennedy (R)	138,957	48.1
David Minge (D)	138,802	48.0
3 Jim Ramstad (R)	222,571	67.6
Sue Shuff (D)	98,219	29.8
4 Betty McCollum (D)	130,403	48.0
Linda Runbeck (R)	83,852	30.9
Tom Foley (INDEP)	55,899	20.6
5 Martin Olav Sabo (D)	176,629	69.2
Frank Taylor (R)	58,191	22.8
6 Bill Luther (D)	176,340	49.6
John Kline (R)	170,900	48.0
7 Collin C. Peterson (D)	185,771	68.7
Glen Menze (R)	79,175	29.3
8 James L. Oberstar (D)	210,094	67.8
Robert Lemen (R)	79,890	25.8

MISSISSIPPI

1 Roger Wicker (R)	145,967	69.8
Joey Grist (D)	59,763	28.6
2 Bennie Thompson (D)	112,777	65.1
Hardy Caraway (R)	54,090	31.2
3 Charles W. "Chip" Pickering Jr. (R)	153,899	73.2
William Clay Thrash (D)	54,151	25.7
4 Ronnie Shows (D)	115,732	58.1
Dunn Lampton (R)	79,218	39.8
5 Gene Taylor (D)	153,264	78.8
Randy McDonnell (R)	35,309	18.2

MISSOURI

1 William Lacy Clay Jr. (D)	149,173	75.2
Zellner Dwight Billingsly (R)	42,730	21.5
2 Todd Akin (R)	164,926	55.3
Ted House (D)	126,441	42.4
3 Richard A. Gephardt (D)	147,222	57.8
William J. Federer (R)	100,967	39.7
4 Ike Skelton (D)	180,634	66.9
James A. Noland Jr. (R)	84,406	31.3
5 Karen McCarthy (D)	159,826	68.8
Steve Gordon (R)	66,439	28.6
6 Sam Graves (R)	138,925	50.9
Steve Danner (D)	127,792	46.8
7 Roy Blunt (R)	202,305	73.9
Charles Christrup (D)	65,510	23.9
8 Jo Ann Emerson (R)	162,239	69.3
Bob Camp (D)	67,760	28.9
9 Kenny Hulshof (R)	172,787	59.3
Steven R. Carroll (D)	111,662	38.3

MONTANA

Candidates	Votes	%
AL Denny Rehberg (R)	211,418	51.5
Nancy Keenan (D)	189,971	46.3

NEBRASKA

1 Doug Bereuter (R)	155,485	66.2
Alan Jacobsen (D)	72,859	31.0
2 Lee Terry (R)	148,911	65.8
Shelley Kiel (D)	70,268	31.1
3 Tom Osborne (R)	182,117	82.0
Rollie Reynolds (D)	34,944	15.7

NEVADA

1 Shelley Berkley (D)	118,469	51.7
Jon Porter (R)	101,276	44.2
2 Jim Gibbons (R)	229,608	64.5
Tierney Cahill (D)	106,379	29.9

NEW HAMPSHIRE

1 John E. Sununu (R)	150,609	52.9
Martha Fuller Clark (D)	128,387	45.1
2 Charles Bass (R)	152,581	56.2
Barney Brannen (D)	110,367	40.6

NEW JERSEY

1 Robert E. Andrews (D)	167,327	76.2
Charlene Cathcart (R)	46,455	21.2
2 Frank A. LoBiondo (R)	155,187	66.4
Edward G. Janosik (D)	74,632	31.9
3 H. James Saxton (R)	157,053	57.3
Susan Bass Levin (D)	112,848	41.2
4 Christopher H. Smith (R)	158,515	63.2
Reed Gusciora (D)	87,956	35.1
5 Marge Roukema (R)	175,546	65.4
Linda Mercurio (D)	81,715	30.4
6 Frank Pallone Jr. (D)	141,698	67.5
Brian T. Kennedy (R)	62,454	29.8
7 Mike Ferguson (R)	128,434	51.6
Maryanne S. Connelly (D)	113,479	45.6
8 Bill Pascrell Jr. (D)	134,074	67.0
Anthony Fusco Jr. (R)	60,606	30.3
9 Steven R. Rothman (D)	140,462	67.9
Joseph Tedeschi (R)	61,984	30.0
10 Donald M. Payne (D)	133,073	87.5
Dirk B. Weber (R)	18,436	12.1
11 Rodney Frelinghuysen (R)	186,140	68.0
John P. Scollo (D)	80,958	29.6
12 Rush D. Holt (D)	146,162	48.7
Dick Zimmer (R)	145,511	48.5
13 Robert Menendez (D)	117,856	78.7
Theresa de Leon (R)	27,849	18.6

NEW MEXICO

1 Heather A. Wilson (R)	107,296	50.3
John Kelly (D)	92,187	43.3
Daniel Kerlinsky (GREEN)	13,656	6.4
2 Joe Skeen (R)	100,742	58.1
Michael A. Montoya (D)	72,614	41.9
3 Tom Udall (D)	135,040	67.2
Lisa L. Lutz (R)	65,979	32.8

NEW YORK

1 Felix J. Grucci Jr. (R, INDEP, C, RTL)	133,020	55.5
Regina Seltzer (D)	97,299	40.6
2 Steven Israel (D)	90,438	47.9
Joan B. Johnson (R)	65,880	34.9
Robert T. Walsh Sr. (RTL)	11,224	6.0
Richard Thompson (C)	10,824	5.7
David Bishop (INDEP, GREEN, WF)	10,266	5.4
3 Peter T. King (R, INDEP, C, RTL)	143,126	59.5

Candidates	Votes	%
Dal LaMagna (D, GREEN, WF)	95,787	39.8
4 Carolyn McCarthy (D, INDEP, WF)	136,703	60.6
Greg R. Becker (R, C, RTL)	87,830	38.9
5 Gary L. Ackerman (D, INDEP, L, WF)	137,684	68.0
Edward Elkowitz (R, C)	61,084	30.1
6 Gregory W. Meeks (D, WF)	120,818	100.0
7 Joseph Crowley (D)	78,207	71.7
Rose Robles Birtley (R)	24,592	22.5
8 Jerrold Nadler (D, L, WF)	150,273	81.2
Marian S. Henry (R)	27,057	14.6
9 Anthony Weiner (D, L)	98,983	68.4
Noach Dear (R, C)	45,649	31.6
10 Edolphus Towns (D, L)	120,700	90.2
Ernestine M. Brown (R)	6,852	5.1
11 Major R. Owens (D, WF)	112,050	87.0
Susan Cleary (R)	8,406	6.5
Una Clarke (D, L)	7,366	5.7
12 Nydia M. Velazquez (D, WF)	86,288	87.1
Rosemary Markgraf (R)	10,052	10.1
13 Vito J. Fossella (R, C, RTL)	109,806	64.6
Katina M. Johnstone (D, WF)	57,603	33.9
14 Carolyn B. Maloney (D, L)	148,080	73.9
Carla Rhodes (R)	45,453	22.7
15 Charles B. Rangel (D, L, WF)	130,161	91.9
Jose A. Suero (R)	7,346	5.2
16 Jose E. Serrano (D, L)	103,041	95.8
17 Eliot L. Engel (D, L)	115,093	89.7
Patrick McManus (C, R)	13,201	10.3
18 Nita M. Lowey (D)	126,878	67.3
John G. Vonglis (R, C)	58,022	30.8
19 Sue W. Kelly (R, C)	145,532	60.9
Larry Otis Graham (D, L, WF)	85,871	35.9
20 Benjamin A. Gilman (R)	136,016	57.6
Paul J. Feiner (D, L, GREEN, WF)	94,646	40.1
21 Michael R. McNulty (D, INDEP, C)	175,339	74.4
Thomas G. Pillsworth (R)	60,333	25.6
22 John E. Sweeney (R, C)	167,368	67.9
Kenneth F. McCallion (D, GREEN, WF)	79,111	32.1
23 Sherwood Boehlert (R, INDEP)	124,132	60.5
David Vickers (C, RTL)	42,854	20.9
Richard W. Englebrecht (D)	38,049	18.6
24 John M. McHugh (R, C)	138,322	74.3
Neil P. Tallon (D)	42,698	22.9
25 James T. Walsh (R, INDEP, C)	151,880	69.0
Francis J. Gavin (D)	64,533	29.3
26 Maurice D. Hinchey (D, INDEP, WF, L)	140,395	62.0
Bob Moppert (R, C)	83,856	37.0
27 Thomas M. Reynolds (R, C)	157,694	69.3
Thomas W. Pecoraro (D)	69,870	30.7
28 Louise M. Slaughter (D)	151,688	65.7
Mark C. Johns (R, C)	75,348	32.6
29 John J. LaFalce (D, INDEP, L)	128,328	61.3
Brett M. Sommer (R, C, RTL)	81,159	38.7
30 Jack Quinn (R, C, INDEP)	138,452	67.1
John Fee (D, L, WF)	67,819	32.9
31 Amory Houghton (R, C)	154,238	77.3
Kisun J. Peters (D)	45,193	22.7

NORTH CAROLINA

1 Eva Clayton (D)	124,171	65.6
Duane E. Kratzer Jr. (R)	62,198	32.9
2 Bob Etheridge (D)	146,733	58.3
Doug Haynes (R)	103,011	40.9
3 Walter B. Jones Jr. (R)	121,940	61.4
Leigh Harvey McNairy (D)	74,058	37.3
4 David E. Price (D)	200,885	61.6
Jess Ward (R)	119,412	36.6
5 Richard M. Burr (R)	172,489	92.8
Steven Francis LeBoeuf (LIBERT)	13,366	7.2
6 Howard Coble (R)	195,727	91.0
Jeffrey D. Bentley (LIBERT)	18,726	8.7

	Candidates	Votes	%
7	Mike McIntyre (D)	160,185	69.7
	James Adams (R)	66,463	28.9
8	Robin Hayes (R)	111,950	55.0
	Mike Taylor (D)	89,505	44.0
9	Sue Myrick (R)	264,220	68.6
	Ed McGuire (D)	79,382	30.0
10	Cass Ballenger (R)	164,182	68.2
	Delmas Parker (D)	70,877	29.5
11	Charles H. Taylor (R)	146,677	55.1
	Sam Neill (D)	112,234	42.1
12	Melvin Watt (D)	135,570	64.8
	Joshua "Chad" Mitchell (R)	69,596	33.3

NORTH DAKOTA

		Votes	%
AL	Earl Pomeroy (D)	151,173	52.9
	John Dorso (R)	127,251	44.5

OHIO

		Votes	%
1	Steve Chabot (R)	116,768	53.0
	John Cranley (D)	98,328	44.6
2	Rob Portman (R)	204,184	73.6
	Charles W. Sanders (D)	64,091	23.1
3	Tony P. Hall (D)	177,731	83.0
	Regina Burch (NL)	36,516	17.0
4	Michael G. Oxley (R)	156,510	67.4
	Daniel J. Dickman (D)	67,330	29.0
5	Paul E. Gillmor (R)	169,857	69.8
	Dannie Edmon (D)	62,138	25.5
6	Ted Strickland (D)	138,849	57.7
	Michael Azinger (R)	96,966	40.3
7	David L. Hobson (R)	163,646	67.6
	Donald E. Minor Jr. (D)	60,755	25.1
	John R. Mitchel (I)	13,983	5.8
8	John A. Boehner (R)	179,756	71.0
	John G. Parks (D)	66,293	26.2
9	Marcy Kaptur (D)	168,547	74.8
	Dwight E. Bryan (R)	49,446	21.9
10	Dennis J. Kucinich (D)	167,063	75.0
	Bill Smith (R)	48,930	22.0
11	Stephanie Tubbs Jones (D)	164,134	84.8
	James Sykora (R)	21,630	11.2
12	Pat Tiberi (R)	139,242	52.9
	Maryellen O'Shaughnessy (D)	115,432	43.8
13	Sherrod Brown (D)	170,058	64.6
	Rick H. Jeric (R)	84,295	32.0
14	Tom Sawyer (D)	149,184	64.8
	Rick Wood (R)	71,432	31.0
15	Deborah Pryce (R)	156,792	67.5
	Bill Buckel (D)	64,805	27.9
16	Ralph Regula (R)	162,294	69.2
	William Smith (D)	62,709	26.8
17	James A. Traficant Jr. (D)	120,333	50.0
	Paul Alberty (R)	54,751	22.7
	Randy D. Walter (I)	51,793	21.5
18	Bob Ney (R)	152,325	64.4
	Marc D. Guthrie (D)	79,232	33.5
19	Steven C. LaTourette (R)	174,262	69.2
	Dale Virgil Blanchard (D)	70,429	28.0

OKLAHOMA

1	Steve Largent (R)	138,528	69.3
	Dan Lowe (D)	58,493	29.2
2	Brad Carson (D)	107,273	54.9
	Andy Ewing (R)	81,672	41.8
3	Wes Watkins (R)	137,826	86.6
	Argus W. Yandell Jr. (I)	14,660	9.2
4	J. C. Watts Jr. (R)	114,000	64.9
	Larry Weatherford (D)	54,808	31.2
5	Ernest Istook (R)	134,159	68.4
	Garland McWatters (D)	53,275	27.2
6	Frank D. Lucas (R)	95,635	59.3
	Randy Beutler (D)	63,106	39.2

OREGON

1	David Wu (D)	176,902	58.3
	Charles Starr (R)	115,303	38.0

	Candidates	Votes	%
2	Greg Walden (R)	220,086	73.6
	Walter A. Ponsford (D)	78,101	26.1
3	Earl Blumenauer (D)	181,049	66.8
	Jeffrey L. Pollock (R)	64,128	23.6
4	Peter A. DeFazio (D)	197,998	68.0
	John Lindsey (R)	88,950	30.6
5	Darlene Hooley (D)	156,315	56.8
	Brian Boquist (R)	118,631	43.1

PENNSYLVANIA

1	Robert A. Brady (D)	149,621	88.3
	Steven N. Kush (R)	19,920	11.7
2	Chaka Fattah (D)	180,021	98.0
3	Robert A. Borski (D)	130,528	68.7
	Charles F. Dougherty (R)	59,343	31.3
4	Melissa Hart (R)	145,390	59.0
	Terry Van Horne (D)	100,995	41.0
5	John E. Peterson (R)	147,570	85.5
	William M. Belitskus (GREEN)	13,857	8.0
	Thomas A. Martin (LIBERT)	11,020	6.4
6	Tim Holden (D)	140,084	66.3
	Thomas G. Kopel (R)	71,227	33.7
7	Curt Weldon (R)	172,569	64.8
	Peter A. Lennon (D)	93,687	35.2
8	James C. Greenwood (R)	154,090	59.1
	Ron Strouse (D)	100,617	38.6
9	Bud Shuster (R)	184,401	99.4
10	Donald L. Sherwood (R)	124,830	52.6
	Patrick Casey (D)	112,580	47.4
11	Paul E. Kanjorski (D)	131,948	66.4
	Stephen A. Urban (R)	66,699	33.6
12	John P. Murtha (D)	145,538	70.8
	Bill Choby (R)	56,575	27.5
13	Joseph M. Hoeffel (D)	146,026	52.8
	Stewart Greenleaf (R)	126,501	45.7
14	William J. Coyne (D)	147,533	99.9
15	Patrick J. Toomey (R)	118,307	53.2
	Ed O'Brien (D)	103,864	46.7
16	Joseph R. Pitts (R)	162,403	66.9
	Robert S. Yorczyk (D)	80,177	33.1
17	George W. Gekas (R)	166,236	71.5
	Leslye Hess Herrmann (D)	66,190	28.5
18	Mike Doyle (D)	156,131	69.4
	Craig C. Stephens (R)	68,798	30.6
19	Todd Platts (R)	168,722	72.5
	Jeff Sanders (D)	61,538	26.5
20	Frank R. Mascara (D)	145,131	64.4
	Ronald J. Davis (R)	80,312	35.6
21	Phil English (R)	135,164	60.8
	Mark Flitter (D)	87,018	39.2

RHODE ISLAND

1	Patrick J. Kennedy (D)	123,442	66.7
	Steve Cabral (R)	61,522	33.2
2	Jim Langevin (D)	123,805	62.2
	Rodney D. Driver (I)	42,625	21.4
	Robert G. "Bob" Tingle (R)	27,932	14.0

SOUTH CAROLINA

1	Henry Brown (R)	139,597	60.3
	Andy Brack (D)	82,622	35.7
2	Floyd D. Spence (R)	154,338	57.0
	Jane Frederick (D)	110,672	40.8
3	Lindsey Graham (R)	150,176	67.8
	George Brightharp (D, UC)	67,174	30.3
4	Jim DeMint (R)	150,436	79.6
	Ted Adams (CONST)	16,532	8.7
	April Bishop (LIBERT)	12,757	6.7
5	John M. Spratt Jr. (D)	126,877	58.8
	Carl Gullick (R)	85,247	39.5
6	James E. Clyburn (D)	138,053	71.8
	Vince Ellison (R)	50,005	26.0

SOUTH DAKOTA

AL	John Thune (R)	231,083	73.4
	Curt M. Hohn (D)	78,321	24.9

TENNESSEE

	Candidates	Votes	%
1	Bill Jenkins (R)	157,828	100.0
2	John J. "Jimmy" Duncan Jr. (R)	187,154	89.3
	Kevin J. Rowland (LIBERT)	22,304	10.6
3	Zach Wamp (R)	139,840	63.9
	Will Callaway (D)	75,785	34.6
4	Van Hilleary (R)	133,622	65.8
	David H. Dunaway (D)	67,165	33.1
5	Bob Clement (D)	149,277	72.5
	Stan Scott (R)	50,386	24.5
6	Bart Gordon (D)	168,861	62.1
	David Charles (R)	97,169	35.7
7	Ed Bryant (R)	171,056	69.6
	Richard P. Sims (D)	71,587	29.1
8	John Tanner (D)	143,127	72.3
	Billy Yancy (R)	54,929	27.7
9	Harold E. Ford Jr. (D)	143,298	100.0

TEXAS

1	Max Sandlin (D)	118,157	55.8
	Noble Willingham (R)	91,912	43.4
2	Jim Turner (D)	162,891	91.1
	Gary Lyndon Dye (LIBERT)	15,939	8.9
3	Sam Johnson (R)	187,486	71.6
	Billy Wayne Zachary (D)	67,233	25.7
4	Ralph M. Hall (D)	145,887	60.3
	Jon Newton (R)	91,574	37.9
5	Pete Sessions (R)	100,487	54.0
	Regina Montoya Coggins (D)	82,629	44.4
6	Joe L. Barton (R)	222,685	88.1
	Frank Brady (LIBERT)	30,056	11.9
7	John Culberson (R)	183,712	73.9
	Jeff Sell (D)	60,694	24.4
8	Kevin Brady (R)	233,848	91.6
	Gil Guillory (LIBERT)	21,368	8.4
9	Nick Lampson (D)	130,143	59.2
	Paul Williams (R)	87,165	39.7
10	Lloyd Doggett (D)	203,628	84.6
	Michael Davis (LIBERT)	37,203	15.4
11	Chet Edwards (D)	105,782	54.8
	Ramsey W. Farley (R)	85,546	44.3
12	Kay Granger (R)	117,739	62.7
	Mark Greene (D)	67,612	36.0
13	William M. "Mac" Thornberry (R)	117,995	67.6
	Curtis Clinesmith (D)	54,343	31.1
14	Ron Paul (R)	137,370	59.7
	Loy Sneary (D)	92,689	40.3
15	Ruben Hinojosa (D)	106,570	88.5
	Frank L. Jones (LIBERT)	13,167	10.9
16	Silvestre Reyes (D)	92,669	68.3
	Daniel Power (R)	40,921	30.2
17	Charles W. Stenholm (D)	120,670	59.0
	Darrell Clements (R)	72,535	35.5
	Debra Monde (LIBERT)	11,180	5.5
18	Sheila Jackson-Lee (D)	131,857	76.5
	Bob Levy (R)	38,191	22.2
19	Larry Combest (R)	170,319	91.6
	John M. Turnbow (LIBERT)	15,579	8.4
20	Charlie Gonzalez (D)	107,487	87.7
	Alejandro "Alex" DePena (LIBERT)	15,087	12.3
21	Lamar Smith (R)	251,049	75.9
	Jim Green (D)	73,326	22.2
22	Tom DeLay (R)	154,662	60.4
	Jo Ann Matranga (D)	92,645	36.2
23	Henry Bonilla (R)	119,769	59.3
	Isidro Garza Jr. (D)	78,274	38.8
24	Martin Frost (D)	103,152	61.8
	Bryndan Wright (R)	61,235	36.7
25	Ken Bentsen (D)	106,112	60.1
	Phil Sudan (R)	68,010	38.5
26	Dick Armey (R)	214,025	72.5
	Steve Love (D)	75,601	25.6
27	Solomon P. Ortiz (D)	102,088	63.4
	Pat Ahumada (R)	54,660	33.9

	Candidates	Votes	%
28	Ciro D. Rodriguez (D)	123,104	89.0
	William A. "Bill" Stallknecht (LIBERT)	15,156	11.0
29	Gene Green (D)	84,665	73.3
	Joe Vu (R)	29,606	25.6
30	Eddie Bernice Johnson (D)	109,163	91.8
	Kelly Rush (LIBERT)	9,798	8.2

UTAH

	Candidates	Votes	%
1	James V. Hansen (R)	180,591	69.0
	Kathleen Collinwood (D)	71,229	27.2
2	Jim Matheson (D)	145,021	55.9
	Derek W. Smith (R)	107,114	41.3
3	Christopher B. Cannon (R)	138,943	58.5
	Donald Dunn (D)	88,547	37.3

VERMONT

	Candidates	Votes	%
AL	Bernard Sanders (I)	196,118	69.2
	Karen Kerin (R)	51,977	18.3
	Peter Diamondstone (D)	14,918	5.3

VIRGINIA

	Candidates	Votes	%
1	Jo Ann Davis (R)	151,344	57.5
	Lawrence Davies (D)	97,399	37.0
2	Edward L. Schrock (R)	97,856	52.0
	Jody Wagner (D)	90,328	48.0
3	Robert C. Scott (D)	137,527	97.7
4	Norman Sisisky (D)	189,787	98.9
5	Virgil H. Goode Jr. (I)	143,312	67.3
	John Boyd (D)	65,387	30.7
6	Robert W. Goodlatte (R)	153,338	99.3
7	Eric I. Cantor (R)	192,652	66.9
	Warren A. Stewart (D)	94,935	33.0

	Candidates	Votes	%
8	James P. Moran (D)	164,178	63.3
	Demaris Miller (R)	88,262	34.1
9	Rick Boucher (D)	137,488	69.8
	Michael D. "Oz" Osborne (R)	59,335	30.1
10	Frank R. Wolf (R)	238,817	84.2
	Brian M. Brown (LIBERT)	28,107	9.9
	Marc A. Rossi (I)	16,031	5.7
11	Thomas M. Davis III (R)	150,395	61.9
	Mike Corrigan (D)	83,455	34.3

WASHINGTON

	Candidates	Votes	%
1	Jay Inslee (D)	155,820	54.6
	Dan McDonald (R)	121,823	42.6
2	Rick Larsen (D)	146,617	50.0
	John Koster (R)	134,660	45.9
3	Brian Baird (D)	159,428	56.4
	Trent Matson (R)	114,861	40.6
4	Richard "Doc" Hastings (R)	143,259	60.9
	Jim Davis (D)	87,585	37.3
5	George Nethercutt (R)	144,038	57.3
	Tom Keefe (D)	97,703	38.9
6	Norm Dicks (D)	164,853	64.7
	Bob Lawrence (R)	79,215	31.1
7	Jim McDermott (D)	193,470	72.8
	Joe Szwaja (GREEN)	52,142	19.6
	Joel Grus (LIBERT)	20,197	7.6
8	Jennifer Dunn (R)	183,255	62.2
	Heidi Behrens-Benedict (D)	104,944	35.6
9	Adam Smith (D)	135,452	61.7
	Chris Vance (R)	76,766	35.0

WEST VIRGINIA

	Candidates	Votes	%
1	Alan B. Mollohan (D)	170,974	87.8
	Richard Kerr (LIBERT)	23,797	12.2

	Candidates	Votes	%
2	Shelley Moore Capito (R)	108,769	48.5
	Jim Humphreys (D)	103,003	45.9
	John Brown (LIBERT)	12,543	5.6
3	Nick J. Rahall II (D)	146,807	91.3
	Jeff Robinson (LIBERT)	13,979	8.7

WISCONSIN

	Candidates	Votes	%
1	Paul D. Ryan (R)	177,612	66.6
	Jeffrey C. Thomas (D)	88,885	33.3
2	Tammy Baldwin (D)	163,534	51.4
	John Sharpless (R)	154,632	48.6
3	Ron Kind (D)	173,505	63.7
	Susan Tully (R)	97,741	35.9
4	Gerald D. Kleczka (D)	163,622	60.8
	Tim Riener (R)	101,811	37.8
5	Thomas M. Barrett (D)	173,893	77.7
	Jonathan Smith (R)	49,296	22.0
6	Tom Petri (R)	179,205	65.0
	Daniel Flaherty (D)	96,125	34.9
7	David R. Obey (D)	173,007	63.3
	Sean Cronin (R)	100,264	36.7
8	Mark Green (R)	211,388	74.6
	Dean Reich (D)	71,575	25.3
9	F. James Sensenbrenner Jr. (R)	239,498	74.0
	Mike Clawson (D)	83,720	25.9

WYOMING

	Candidates	Votes	%
AL	Barbara Cubin (R)	141,848	66.8
	Michael Allen Green (D)	60,638	28.6

House Returns: Other Sources

In the preceding pages of House popular election returns (829–1226) the symbol # is used to denote returns for the years 1824–1973 that were taken from a source other than the Inter-University Consortium for Political and Social Research (ICPSR). This page lists the source for each of those returns. *(See box, ICPSR Historical Election Returns File, p. xvi in Vol. I.)*

The two most frequently used alternative sources were *Statistics of the Congressional Elections of* _____, published by the Clerk of the House of Representatives for every general election year since 1920, and the Elections Research Center, which compiled for Congressional Quarterly the biennial *America Votes* series under the direction of Richard M. Scammon and Alice V. McGillivray beginning in 1956.

1840—Georgia (at-large special):
Georgia Secretary of State.

1844—Ohio (10th District special):
Ohio Historical Society Archives.

1845—Tennessee (8th District):
Tennessee Secretary of State.

1872—Georgia (4th District special):
Georgia Secretary of State.

1872—Pennsylvania (13th District special):
Pennsylvania Secretary of State.

1873—Louisiana (4th District special):
Louisiana State University Library.

1874—Tennessee (4th District special):
Tennessee Secretary of State.

1884—Pennsylvania (19th District special):
Pennsylvania Secretary of State.

1884—South Carolina (4th District special):
South Carolina Secretary of State.

1886—Louisiana (2nd District special):
Biographical Directory of the American Congress, 1774–1996 (Washington, D.C.: CQ Staff Directories, 1997).

1892—Texas (9th District special):
Official Texas Election Register.

1908—Nebraska (5th District):
1910 World Almanac, published by *The New York World* newspaper.

1922—New Jersey (8th District):
Statistics of the Congressional Election of Nov. 7, 1922.

1924—Georgia (9th District) **Ohio** (22nd District):
Statistics of the Congressional and Presidential Election of Nov. 4, 1924.

1926—Massachusetts (8th District special); **Minnesota** (4th District):
Statistics of the Congressional Election of Nov. 2, 1926.

1928—New Jersey (8th District); **Oregon** (3rd District); **Tennessee** (5th District):
Statistics of the Congressional and Presidential Election of Nov. 6, 1928.

1930—California (3rd District); **Georgia** (8th and 11th Districts); **Kentucky** (2nd District special); **Wisconsin** (5th District):
Statistics of the Congressional Election of Nov. 4, 1930.

1937—New York (17th District special):
New York Secretary of State.

1944—Wisconsin (8th District):
Statistics of the Presidential and Congressional Election of Nov. 7, 1944.

1946—Georgia (5th District); **Nebraska** (3rd District):
Statistics of the Congressional Election of Nov. 5, 1946.

1950—Tennessee (5th District):
Statistics of the Congressional Election of Nov. 4, 1958.

1950—Texas (18th District special):
Texas Secretary of State.

1951—Missouri (11th District special):
Missouri Secretary of State.

1959—Iowa (4th District special):
Iowa Secretary of State.

1960—Indiana (5th District):
Richard M. Scammon (ed.), *America Votes 4* (Pittsburgh: University of Pittsburgh Press, 1962), p. 123.

1961—Arizona, Arkansas, Michigan, Tennessee (special elections):
Elections Research Center.

1962—Michigan (14th District special); **New York** (6th District special); **South Carolina** (2nd District special):
Elections Research Center.

1963—North Dakota, Pennsylvania, Texas (special elections):
Elections Research Center.

1964—Pennsylvania (5th District special); **Tennessee** (2nd District special):
Elections Research Center.

1964—Pennsylvania (6th District):
Pennsylvania Secretary of State.

1965—South Carolina (special):
Elections Research Center.

1966—California (4th District special); **Texas** (8th District special):
Elections Research Center.

1967—California (11th District special primary):
California Secretary of State.

1967—California (11th District special):
Elections Research Center.

1967—New York; Rhode Island (special elections):
Elections Research Center.

1968—New York (7th District):
Richard M. Scammon (ed.), *America Votes 8* (Washington, D.C.: Congressional Quarterly, 1970), p. 274.

1968—New York (13th District special): **Texas** (3rd District special):
Elections Research Center.

1968—Mississippi (3rd District special):
Mississippi Secretary of State.

1969—California (27th District special primary):
California Secretary of State.

1969—Massachusetts; Montana; Tennessee (special elections):
Elections Research Center.

1970—Texas (2nd District):
Texas Secretary of State.

1971—Kentucky (special):
Kentucky Secretary of State.

1972—Pennsylvania (27th District special):
Pennsylvania Secretary of State.

1972—Vermont (special):
Elections Research Center.

1973—Illinois (special):
Illinois Secretary of State.

CHAPTER 24

Senate Elections

THE CREATION OF THE UNITED STATES SENATE was a result of the so-called "great compromise" at the Constitutional Convention in 1787. The small states wanted equal representation in Congress, fearing domination by the larger states under a population formula. The larger states, however, naturally wished for a legislature based on population, where their strength would prevail.

In compromising this dispute, delegates simply split the basis for representation between the two houses—population for the House of Representatives, equal representation by state for the Senate. By the terms of the compromise, each state was entitled to two senators. In a sense, they were conceived to be ambassadors from the states, representing the sovereign interests of the states to the federal government.

Election by State Legislatures

To elect these "ambassadors," the Founders chose the state legislatures instead of the people themselves. The argument was that legislatures would be able to give more sober and reflective thought than the people at large to the kind of persons needed to represent the states' interests to the federal government. The delegates also thought the state legislatures and thus the states would take a greater interest in the fledgling national government if they were involved in its operations this way. Furthermore, the state legislatures had chosen the members of the Continental Congress (the Congress under the Articles of Confederation), as well as the members of the Constitutional Convention itself, so the procedure was familiar to the delegates.

In choosing the state legislatures as the instruments of election for senators, the Constitutional Convention considered and abandoned several alternatives. Some delegates had suggested that the senators be elected by the House or appointed by the president from a list of nominees selected by the state legislatures. These ideas were discarded as making the Senate too dependent on another part of the federal government. Also turned down was a scheme for a system of electors, similar to presidential electors, to choose the senators in each state. And popular election was rejected as being too radical and inconvenient.

So deeply entrenched was the ambassadorial aspect of a senator's duty that state legislatures sometimes took it upon themselves to instruct senators on how to vote. This occasionally raised severe problems of conscience among senators and resulted in several resignations.

For example, in 1836 future president John Tyler was serving as a U.S. senator from Virginia. That year the Virginia legislature instructed him to vote for a resolution to expunge the Senate censure of President Andrew Jackson for his removal of the federal deposits from the Bank of the United States. Tyler, who had voted for the censure resolution, resigned from the Senate rather than comply.

In another instance, Sen. Hugh L. White of Tennessee, a Whig, resigned from the Senate in 1840 after being instructed by his state legislature to vote for the subtreasury bill, an economic measure supported by the Democratic Van Buren administration.

Another problem for the Founders was the length of the senatorial term. The framers of the Constitution tried to balance two principles: the belief that relatively frequent elections were necessary to promote good behavior and the need for steadiness and continuity in government.

Delegates proposed terms of three, four, five, six, seven, and nine years. They finally settled on six-year staggered terms, with one-third of the members coming up for election every two years. (See "Sessions and Terms," p. 1231.)

Changing Election Procedures

At first each state made its own arrangements for its state legislature to elect the senators. Many states required an election by the two chambers of the legislature sitting separately. That is, each chamber had to vote for the same candidate for him to be elected. Other states, however, provided for election by a joint ballot of the two chambers sitting together.

However, the Constitution specifically authorized Congress to regulate senatorial elections if it so chose. Article I, Section 4, Paragraph 1 states, "The times, places and manner of holding elections for Senators and Representatives shall be prescribed in each state by the legislature thereof; but the Congress may at any time by law make or alter such regulations, except as to the place of chusing Senators."

1866 ACT OF CONGRESS

In 1866 Congress decided to exercise its authority. Procedures in some states, particularly those requiring concurrent majorities in both houses of the state legislature for election to the Senate, had resulted in numerous delays and vacancies.

The new federal law set up the following procedure: the first ballot for senator was to be taken by the two chambers of each state legislature voting separately. If no candidate received a majority of the vote in both houses, then the two chambers were to meet and ballot jointly until a majority choice emerged.

Also included in the 1866 law were provisions for roll-call votes in the state legislatures (secret ballots had been taken in

several states) and for a definite timetable. The law directed that the first vote take place on the second Tuesday after the meeting and organization of the legislature, followed by a minimum of a single ballot on every legislative day thereafter until election of a senator resulted.

But the new uniform system did not have the desired effect. The requirement for a majority vote continued the frequency of deadlock. In fact one of the worst deadlocks in senatorial election history happened under the 1866 federal law.

The case occurred in Delaware at the end of the nineteenth century. In 1899, with the legislature divided between two factions of the Republican Party and the Democrats in the minority, no majority selection could be made for the senatorial term beginning March 4, 1899. So bitter was the Republican factional dispute that neither side would support a candidate acceptable to the other; nor would the Democrats play kingmaker by siding with one or the other Republican group. The dispute continued throughout the life of the Fifty-sixth Congress (1899–1901), leaving a seat unfilled.

Furthermore, the term of Delaware's other Senate seat ended in 1901, necessitating another election. The same pattern continued, with the legislature unable to fill either seat, leaving Delaware totally unrepresented in the Senate from March 4, 1901, until March 1, 1903, when two senators were finally elected in the closing days of the Fifty-seventh Congress (1901–1903). The deadlock was broken when the two Republican factions split the state's two seats between them.

ABUSES OF ELECTION BY LEGISLATURES

Besides the frequent deadlocks, critics pointed to what they saw as other faults in the system. They charged that the party caucuses in the state legislatures, as well as individual members, were subject to intense and unethical lobbying practices by supporters of various senatorial candidates. The relatively small size of the electing body and the high stakes involved—a seat in the Senate—often tempted the use of questionable methods in conducting the elections.

Allegations that such methods were used involved the Senate itself in election disputes. The Constitution makes Congress the judge of its own members. Article I, Section 5, Paragraph 1 states, "Each House shall be the judge of the elections, returns and qualifications of its own members. . . ."

One of the most sensational cases concerned the election of William Lorimer, R-Ill. Lorimer won on the ninety-ninth ballot taken by the Illinois legislature in 1909. A year after he had taken his seat, the Senate cleared Lorimer of charges that he had won election by bribery. But the revelation of new evidence prompted another investigation, and in 1912 the Senate voted that Lorimer's election was invalid and that he was not entitled to his seat.

Critics had still another grievance against the legislative method of choosing senators. They contended that elections to the state legislatures were often overshadowed by senatorial contests. Thus when voters went to the polls to choose their state legislators, they sometimes would be urged to disregard state and local issues and vote for a legislator who promised to

Before 1913 senators were selected by the legislatures of each state. Public disapproval of the role of party bosses and vested interests in this selection process ultimately led to the passage of the Seventeenth Amendment, which mandated direct election of senators.

support a certain candidate for the U.S. Senate. This, the critics said, led to neglect of state government and issues. Moreover, drawn-out Senate contests tended to hold up the consideration of state business.

Demands for Popular Elections

But the main criticism of legislative elections was that they distorted or even blocked the will of the people. Throughout the nineteenth century, the movement toward popular election had taken away from the legislatures the right to elect presidential electors in states that had such provisions. Now attention focused on the Senate.

Five times around the turn of the century the House passed constitutional amendments to provide for Senate elections by popular vote—in the Fifty-second Congress on Jan. 16, 1893; in the Fifty-third Congress on July 21, 1894; in the Fifty-fifth Congress on May 11, 1898; in the Fifty-sixth Congress on April 13, 1900, and in the Fifty-seventh Congress on Feb. 13, 1902. But each time the Senate refused to act.

Frustrated in their desire for direct popular elections, reformers began implementing various formulas for preselecting Senate candidates, attempting to reduce the legislative balloting to something approaching a mere formality. In some cases party conventions endorsed nominees for the Senate, allowing the voters at least to know who the members of the legislature were likely to support. Southern states early in the century adopted the party primary to choose Senate nominees. However, legislators never could be legally bound to support anyone because the Constitution gave them the unfettered power of electing to the Senate whomever they chose.

Oregon took the lead in instituting nonbinding popular elections. Under a 1901 law, voters expressed their choice for senator in popular ballots. While the election results had no legal force, the law required that the popular returns be formally announced to the state legislature before it elected a senator.

At first the law did not work—the winner of the informal popular vote in 1902 was not chosen senator by the legislature. But the reformers increased their pressure, demanding that candidates for the legislature sign a pledge to vote for the winner of the popular vote. By 1908 the plan was successful. The Republican legislature elected to the Senate Democrat George Chamberlain, the winner of the popular contest. Several other states—including Colorado, Kansas, Minnesota, Montana, Nevada and Oklahoma—adopted the Oregon method.

THE SEVENTEENTH AMENDMENT

Despite these palliatives, pressures continued to mount for a switch to straight popular elections. Frustrated at the failure of the Senate to act, proponents of change began pushing for a convention to propose this and perhaps other amendments to the Constitution. (Article V of the Constitution provides two methods of proposing amendments—either passage by two-thirds of both houses of Congress or through the calling of a special convention if requested by the legislatures of two-thirds of the states. In either case any amendment proposed by Congress or by a special convention must be ratified by three-fourths of the states.)

Conservatives began to fear a convention more than they did popular election of senators. There was no precedent for an amending convention and conservatives worried that it might be dominated by liberals and progressives who would propose numerous amendments and change the very nature of the government. Consequently, their opposition to popular election of senators diminished.

At the same time progressives of both parties made strong gains in the midterm elections of 1910. Some successful Senate candidates had made pledges to work for adoption of a constitutional amendment providing for popular election. In this atmosphere the Senate debated and finally passed the amendment on June 12, 1911, by a vote of 64–24. The House concurred in the Senate version on May 13, 1912, by a vote of 238–39. Ratification of the Seventeenth Amendment was completed by the requisite number of states on April 8, 1913, and was proclaimed a part of the Constitution by Secretary of State William Jennings Bryan on May 31, 1913.

The first popularly elected senator was chosen in a special election in November 1913. He was Sen. Blair Lee, D-Md. (1914–1917), elected for the remaining three years of the unexpired term of Democratic Sen. Isidor Rayner (1905–1912), who had died in office.

There was no wholesale changeover in membership when the Seventeenth Amendment became effective. In fact every one of the twenty-three senators elected by state legislatures for their previous terms, and running for reelection to full terms in November 1914, was successful. Seven had retired or died, and two had been defeated for renomination.

The changeover in method of electing senators ended the frequent legislative stalemates in choosing members of the Senate. Otherwise many things remained the same. There were still election disputes, including charges of corruption, as well as miscounting of votes.

ELECTION DISPUTES

Election disputes continued to occupy the Senate. A bitter contest for a New Hampshire Senate seat in 1974 between Republican representative Louis C. Wyman and Democrat John A. Durkin wound up in the Senate after a seesaw battle between New Hampshire authorities over who had won. The state Ballot Law Commission had finally awarded the victory to Wyman by two votes, but Durkin took his case to the Senate. After wrestling with the problem for seven months, the Senate gave up and declared the seat vacant. A new election was held Sept. 16, 1975, which Durkin won decisively.

Senate's Three Classes

The Senate is divided into three classes or groups of members. A member's class depends on the year in which he or she is elected. Article I, Section 3, Paragraph 2 of the Constitution, relating to the classification of senators in the first and succeeding Congresses, provides that "Immediately after they shall be assembled in consequence of the first election, they shall be divided as equally as may be into three classes. The seats of the Senators of the first class shall be vacated at the expiration of the second year, of the second class at the expiration of the fourth year and of the third class at the expiration of the sixth year, so that one-third may be chosen every second year. . . ."

Thus senators belonging to class one began their regular terms in the years 1789, 1791, 1797, 1803, etc., continuing through the present day to 1989, 1995, 2001 and were to be up for reelection in 2006. Senators belonging to class two began their regular terms in 1789, 1793, 1799, 1805, etc., continuing through to the present day in 1985, 1991, 1997 and were to be up for reelection in 2002. And senators belonging to class three began their regular terms in 1789, 1795, 1801, 1807, etc., continuing through the present day to 1987, 1993, 1999 and coming up for reelection in 2004.

Sessions and Terms

In the fall of 1788, the expiring Continental Congress established a schedule for the incoming government under the new

Senate Appointments and Special Elections

Governors were given specific authority in the Constitution to make temporary appointments to the Senate. Article I, Section 3, Paragraph 2 states: "If vacancies happen by resignation, or otherwise, during the recess of the legislature of any state, the executive thereof may make temporary appointments until the next meeting of the legislature, which shall then fill such vacancies."

The principle was established as early as 1794 that a vacancy created solely because a state legislature had failed to elect a new senator could not be filled by appointment, because the vacancy had not occurred "during the recess of the legislature."

For example, the term of Sen. Matthew Quay, R-Pa. (1887–1899, 1901–1904) expired March 3, 1899. The legislature was in session but had not reelected him. Nor did it elect anyone before adjourning that April 20. Thereupon, the governor appointed Quay to the vacancy; but the Senate did not allow Quay to take the seat, because the vacancy had occurred during the meeting of the legislature. In 1901 the legislature elected Quay for the remainder of the term.

On the other hand, if a senator's term expired and the legislature was *not* in session, a governor was able to make an appointment—but only until the legislature either elected a successor or adjourned without electing one. For example, on March 3, 1809, the term of Sen. Samuel Smith, D-R-Md. (1803–1815, 1822–1833) expired. The legislature was not then in session and had not elected a successor. Therefore, the governor appointed Smith to fill the vacancy until the next meeting of the legislature, which was scheduled for June 5, 1809. The Senate ruled that he was entitled to the seat. During the subsequent meeting of the state legislature that year, Smith was elected to a full term.

Whatever the condition under which an appointment had been made, it was to last only through the next state legislative session. Even if a legislature failed to elect a new senator, the appointed senator's service was to expire with the adjournment of the state legislature.

This principle was confirmed in the case of Sen. Samuel Phelps, Whig-Vt. (1839–1851, 1853–1854). Phelps was appointed in January 1853 to a vacancy caused by the death of Sen. William Upham, Whig-Vt. (1843–1853), whose term was to run through March 3, 1855. As the legislature was in recess, Phelps continued to serve until the expiration of the Thirty-Second Congress on March 3, 1853, and also during a special session of the Thirty-Third Congress in March and April 1853. The Vermont legislature met during October and December without electing a senator to fill the unexpired term. Phelps then showed up for the regular session of the Thirty-Third Congress in December, but the Senate in March 1854 decided he was not entitled to retain his seat, because the legislature had met and adjourned without electing a new senator.

17th Amendment and Special Elections

The adoption of the Seventeenth Amendment in 1913, providing for popular election of senators, altered the provision for gubernatorial appointment of senators to fill vacancies. The amendment provided that, in case of a vacancy, "the executive authority of such state shall issue writs of election to fill such vacancies: *Provided*, that the legislature of any state may empower the executive thereof to make temporary appointments until the people fill the vacancies by election as the legislature may direct." Under this provision, state legislatures allowed governors to make temporary appointments until the vacancy could be filled by a special election. Special elections—elections held to fill unexpired terms—were usually held in November of an even-numbered year. Some states, however, provided for special elections to be held within just a few months after the vacancy occurred.

Before ratification of the Seventeenth Amendment the term of an appointee generally ended when a successor was elected to fill the unexpired term or at the end of the six-year term, whichever occurred first. After the ratification of the Seventeenth Amendment but before ratification of the Twentieth Amendment in 1933, senators who were elected to fill lengthy unexpired terms usually could take office immediately, displacing an appointee. If an appointee was serving near the close of a six-year term, most states would hold simultaneous elections to fill both the six-year term and the four-month "lame-duck" term. Sometimes different persons would be elected to each term.

To eliminate the lame-duck sessions that ran from December of an even-numbered year through March 3 of the next year, the Twentieth Amendment changed the March 3 beginning date of the terms for Congress to Jan. 3. After the so-called lame-duck amendment took effect, senators elected to fill vacancies in terms that had several years to run would take office immediately, as before, but, if a vacancy occurred near the end of a six-year term, an appointee would often serve until the Jan. 3 expiration date, eliminating the necessity for a special election.

Some states, however, have held elections in November for the remaining two months of a term. Georgia voters in 1972, for example, found on the ballot two Senate elections, one for a six-year term and one for a two-month term to fill the unexpired term of Democratic Sen. Richard B. Russell (1933–1971), who died in office.

Dates of Service

Title II, Section 36 of the U.S. Code sets the dates on which senators appointed or elected to fill unexpired terms formally begin service and go on the payroll. The service of an appointee commences the day of appointment and continues until a successor is elected and qualified. If the Senate is in sine die adjournment when a new senator is elected to succeed an appointee, he will take office and begin receiving his salary on the day after the election.

If the Senate is in session when a new senator is elected to succeed an appointee, the new senator may take office when he or she presents him or herself before the Senate to take the oath; the appointee may continue in office until this occurs or the Senate adjourns sine die, whichever happens first. The term of the newly elected senator would then begin at sine die adjournment.

Constitution. The Congress decided that the new government was to commence on the first Wednesday in March 1789—March 4. Even though the House did not achieve a quorum until April 1 and the Senate April 6, and President George Washington was not inaugurated until April 30, Senate, House and presidential terms were still considered to have begun March 4. The term of the first Congress continued through March 3, 1791. Because congressional and presidential terms were fixed at exactly two, four, and six years, March 4 became the official date of transition from one administration to another every four years and from one Congress to another every two years.

'LONG' AND 'SHORT' SESSIONS

The Constitution did not mandate a regular congressional session to begin March 4. Instead, Article I, Section 4, Paragraph 2 called for at least one congressional session every year, to convene on the first Monday in December unless Congress by law set a different day. Consequently, except when called by the president for special sessions, or when Congress itself set a different day, Congress convened in regular session each December, until the passage of the Twentieth Amendment in 1933.

The December date resulted in a long and short session. The first (long) session would meet in December of an odd-numbered year and continue into the next year, usually adjourning some time the next summer. The second (short) session began in December of an even-numbered year and continued through March 3 of the next year, when its term ran out. It also became customary for the Senate to meet in brief special session on March 4 or March 5, especially in years when a new president was inaugurated, to act on presidential nominations.

To illustrate with an example of a typical Congress, the Twenty-ninth (1845–1847): President James K. Polk, a Democrat, was inaugurated on March 4, 1845. The Senate met in special session from March 4 to March 20 to confirm Polk's cabinet and other appointments. Then the first regular session convened Dec. 1, 1845, working until Aug. 10, 1846, when it adjourned. The second, a short session, lasted from Dec. 7, 1846, through March 3, 1847.

Since it was not clear whether terms of members of Congress ended at midnight March 3 or noon March 4, the custom evolved of extending the legislative day of March 3, in odd-numbered years, to noon March 4.

THE TWENTIETH AMENDMENT

The political consequence of the short session was to encourage filibusters and other delaying tactics by members determined to block legislation that would die upon the automatic adjournment of Congress on March 3. Moreover, the Congresses that met in short session always included a substantial number of "lame-duck" members who had been defeated at the polls, yet were able quite often to determine the legislative outcome of the session.

Dissatisfaction with the short session began to mount after 1900. During the Wilson administration (1913–1921), each of four such sessions ended with a Senate filibuster and the loss of important bills including several funding bills. Sen. George W. Norris, R-Neb. (1913–1943), became the leading advocate of a constitutional amendment to abolish the short session by starting the terms of Congress and the president in January instead of March. The Senate approved the Norris amendment five times during the 1920s, only to see it blocked in the House each time. It was finally approved by both chambers in 1932 and became the Twentieth Amendment upon ratification by the thirty-sixth state in 1933.

The amendment provided that the terms of senators and representatives would begin and end at noon on the third day of January of the year following the election. However, according to the Senate Manual (2000 edition, p. 997), "In view of the impracticality of dealing with split days, . . . it has been the long established practice for payment of salaries, computation of allowances and recording of service to credit a Member for the full day of the third of January he takes office and consider his term as ended at the close of business on the second of January six years later." Congressional Quarterly has retained this convention in the list of senators in this volume, with dates of service shown as beginning on Jan. 3 and ending on Jan. 2.

The Twentieth Amendment also established noon Jan. 20 as the day on which the president and vice president take office. It provided also that Congress should meet annually on Jan. 3 "unless they shall by law appoint a different day." The second session of the Seventy-third Congress was the first to convene on the new date, Jan. 3, 1934. Franklin D. Roosevelt was the first president and John N. Garner the first vice president to be inaugurated on Jan. 20, at the start of their second terms in 1937.

The amendment was intended to permit Congress to extend its first session for as long as necessary and to complete the work of its second session before the next election, thereby obviating legislation by a lame-duck body.

The Modern Senate

The Senate is often called the nation's most exclusive club, even though the House of Representatives has equal power. One reason for the Senate's greater prestige is its smaller size. Out of a nation of more than 280 million (as of the 2000 census), only 100 men and women can be senators, compared with 435 representatives. And a state's two senators each represent the entire state, while all but the least populated states are carved into multiple House districts.

As a result of the Senate's compact size and an individual's greater opportunity to affect legislation, there is often intense competition and hefty expenditures to capture a seat.

In the election of 2000, former Wall Street financier Jon Corzine set a record for a Senate race by spending more than $60 million to win his contest in New Jersey. Nearly all of the money came out of Corzine's pocket. In neighboring New York, First Lady Hillary Rodham Clinton, a Democrat, and Republican Rep. Rick A. Lazio combined to spend roughly $70 million in a race that Clinton ultimately won. Altogether, according to totals tabulated by the Federal Election Commission shortly after the 2000 election, a total of nineteen Senate candidates spent more than $5 million on their campaigns. Eleven of these candidates won, eight lost.

Shortly after the 1996 congressional elections, newly elected senators Robert Torricelli, D-N.J., and Susan Collins, R-Maine, shake hands as Senate Majority Leader Trent Lott, R-Miss (center), and Minority Leader Tom Daschle, D-S.D. (right), look on.

Those numbers underscore the fact that senators tend to be much more vulnerable at the ballot box than House members. In the general election of 2000, six incumbents lost their reelection bids in each chamber. But 400 House incumbents were on the November ballot compared to just twenty-nine Senate incumbents.

That disparity between the reelection rates in each chamber is not unusual. In nearly half of the elections from 1968 through 2000, at least 95 percent of all House incumbents seeking reelection were victorious. But in that same time period, the Senate reelection rate topped 95 percent in just one election (1990) and often fell below 75 percent.

From 1980 into June 2001, partisan control of the Senate changed four times. In 1980 the strong showing of Republican presidential candidate Ronald Reagan helped the GOP pick up a net of twelve Senate seats and wrest control of the upper chamber from the Democrats for the first time in twenty-six years. But in the midterm election of 1986, without Reagan on the ballot, Democrats regained control, picking up a net of eight seats and ousting many of the Senate freshmen who had been elected with Reagan's help six years earlier.

In 1994, though, the tide turned again in favor of the Republicans, as they picked up a net of seven seats. Unlike the GOP's

success in 1980, though, which was basically nationwide, the party's Senate gains in the 1990s were largely concentrated in the South. By the beginning of the twenty-first century, Republicans in both the Senate and the House held a larger proportion of seats in the once solidly Democratic South than in any other region.

Republicans were able to maintain a clear-cut majority in the Senate from 1994 until the end of the century. But in the election of 2000, Democrats gained a net of four seats to produce a 50–50 tie. It was the first partisan deadlock in the Senate since the election of 1880—but it lasted only six months until a Republican moderate, Sen. James Jeffords of Vermont, decided to leave the Republican Party and become an Independent, and to caucus with the Democrats. Jeffords said he was no longer comfortable with the GOP's increasingly conservative stand on many issues. His decision gave the Democrats a 50–49 margin and allowed them to organize the chamber, including taking over the chairs of committees and setting the legislative agenda.

The 2000 election also created several other unusual situations. Since the 107th Congress convened on Jan. 3, 2001, when there was still a Democratic vice president (Al Gore) to cast the tie-breaking vote, Democrats were in nominal control of the Senate for the first seventeen days. When the new GOP administration was sworn in Jan. 20, and Republican Vice President Dick Cheney took his seat as the presiding officer who could cast a tie-breaking vote if necessary, Senate Republicans regained the upper hand. They remained in command until June 5, when Jeffords became an Independent. But during this six months with a tenuous advantage, they entered into a unique power-sharing arrangement with the Democrats, which resulted in the two parties evenly dividing membership on committees as well as agreeing to committee staffs and budgets of equal size. Republicans, though, chaired the committees.

Throughout its history, the Senate has been an almost exclusive preserve of white males. Only four blacks have served in the Senate since ratification of the Fifteenth Amendment in 1870 gave former slaves the right to vote. And the Senate never had more than two female members at the same time until 1993. The number of women senators, though, has grown steadily since then, reaching a total of thirteen as a result of the election of 2000.

## CHAPTER 25

U.S. Senators, 1789–2001

THIS CHAPTER (pages 1236–1266) contains a listing of United States senators who served from March 4, 1789, through July 2001—from the First Congress to the first session of the 107th Congress. Arranged alphabetically by state, the lists provide the name, political affiliation, and dates of service of each senator in chronological order within each class. *(See "Senate's Three Classes," p. 1231.)*

The primary source for the names, classes, and dates of service of senators is the *Senate Manual* (Washington, D.C.: Government Printing Office, 2000). Congressional Quarterly obtained additional information in certain cases from the *Biographical Directory of the American Congress, 1774–1996* (Washington, D.C.: CQ Staff Directories, 1997). Congressional Quarterly editors updated the list from state secretaries of state through the 2000 elections. Footnotes were derived from all sources.

PARTY AFFILIATION

Determinations of senators' party affiliations were based on three sources. From 1913, when the Seventeenth Amendment established popular election of senators, to 1972 party designations were taken from the Inter-University Consortium for Political and Social Research (ICPSR) popular vote returns (pages 1268–1303). However, if a senator was elected in any one election with the support of more than one political party, only the major party is indicated in the listing. For example, Sen. Robert F. Kennedy of New York, who in 1964 was the nominee of both the Democratic and Liberal parties, appears as a Democrat (D).

Also from 1913 on, whenever senators switched parties during their period of service, each party is listed even if the senator was not formally elected as a nominee of the new party. For example, Sen. Wayne Morse of Oregon (1945–1969) is listed as a Republican, Independent, and Democrat (R, I, D). He was elected twice as a Republican in 1944 and 1950, left that party in 1952 and called himself an Independent until 1955, and then became a Democrat. He was reelected as a Democrat in 1956 and 1962. *(See "Political Party Abbreviations," p. 1596, in Reference Materials.)*

For the period before popular election of senators (1789–1913), party affiliations were taken from the *Biographical Directory of the American Congress, 1774–1996* and the *Dictionary of American Biography*, 20 volumes (New York: Scribner's, 1928–1958). Because political parties did not formally exist in the early years of the Republic, classification of senators by party during this period can be difficult or misleading. In cases where party affiliation was not appropriate or could not be determined, no party designation appears.

Except where otherwise noted, senators were elected to office by state legislatures or, after ratification of the Seventeenth Amendment in 1913, by popular vote.

Footnotes have been used to indicate the following circumstances:

• The appointment of a senator by the governor of his state to fill an unexpired term. In such cases the service of an appointee ended at the expiration of the six-year term, or when a new senator was elected, or after the recess of the state legislature. *(See box, Senate Appointments and Special Elections, p. 1232.)* In many cases, the appointee was elected to the Senate while serving there by appointment. In these cases, the footnote states that the senator was appointed and "subsequently elected."

• The death or resignation of a senator before the expiration of the term for which he was elected or appointed. In a number of instances, retiring or defeated senators resigned shortly before the start of a new congressional session. This enabled the succeeding senator to take office early by appointment, thereby giving him seniority over other newly elected senators. The practice has become less common in the modern era due to changes in seniority rules. Resignations are footnoted but subsequent appointments are not. However, the dates of service shown in the main listing account for the complete period served.

• The expulsion of a senator by the Senate, and certain cases of disputed elections. Information on these was obtained from *Senate Election, Expulsion and Censure Cases* (S Doc 92-7), a publication prepared in 1972 by the Senate Rules and Administration Committee.

• A change in political party affiliation by a senator, if it could be determined that the senator was elected or appointed as a member of one political party but was subsequently reelected as a nominee of a different party.

United States Senators, 1789–2001

ALABAMA

(Became a state Dec. 14, 1819)

Class 2

Senators	Dates of Service	
William R. King (D-R, D)[1]	Dec. 14, 1819	April 15, 1844
Dixon H. Lewis (D)[2]	April 22, 1844	Oct. 25, 1848
Benjamin Fitzpatrick (D)[3]	Nov. 25, 1848	Nov. 30, 1849
Jeremiah Clemens (D)	Nov. 30, 1849	March 3, 1853
Clement Claiborne Clay Jr. (D)[4]	March 4, 1853	March 14, 1861
Willard Warner (R)	July 25, 1868	March 3, 1871
George Goldthwaite (D)[5]	March 4, 1871	March 3, 1877
John T. Morgan (D)[6]	March 4, 1877	June 11, 1907
John H. Bankhead (D)[7]	June 18, 1907	March 1, 1920
Braxton B. Comer (D)[8]	March 5, 1920	Nov. 2, 1920
J. Thomas Heflin (D)	Nov. 2, 1920	March 3, 1931
John H. Bankhead II (D)[9]	March 4, 1931	June 12, 1946
George R. Swift (D)[10]	June 15, 1946	Nov. 5, 1946
John Sparkman (D)	Nov. 6, 1946	Jan. 2, 1979
Howell Heflin (D)	Jan. 3, 1979	Jan. 2, 1997
Jeff Sessions (R)	Jan. 3, 1997	

Class 3

Senators	Dates of Service	
John W. Walker (D-R)[11]	Dec. 14, 1819	Dec. 12, 1822
William Kelly (D-R)	Dec. 12, 1822	March 3, 1825
Henry H. Chambers (D-R)[12]	March 4, 1825	Jan. 25, 1826
Israel Pickens (D-R)[13]	Feb. 17, 1826	Nov. 27, 1826
John McKinley (D-R, D)	Nov. 27, 1826	March 3, 1831
Gabriel Moore (D)	March 4, 1831	March 3, 1837
John McKinley (D)[14]	March 4, 1837	April 22, 1837
Clement Comer Clay (D)[15]	June 19, 1837	Nov. 15, 1841
Arthur P. Bagby (D)[16]	Nov. 24, 1841	June 16, 1848
William R. King (D)[17]	July 1, 1848	Dec. 20, 1852
Benjamin Fitzpatrick (D)[18]	Jan. 14, 1853	Jan. 21, 1861
George E. Spencer (R)	July 25, 1868	March 3, 1879
George S. Houston (D)[19]	March 4, 1879	Dec. 31, 1879
Luke Pryor (D)[20]	Jan. 7, 1880	Nov. 23, 1880
James L. Pugh (D)	Nov. 24, 1880	March 3, 1897
Edmund W. Pettus (D)[21]	March 4, 1897	July 27, 1907
Joseph F. Johnston (D)[22]	Aug. 6, 1907	Aug. 8, 1913
Francis S. White (D)	May 11, 1914	March 3, 1915
Oscar W. Underwood (D)	March 4, 1915	March 3, 1927
Hugo Black (D)[23]	March 4, 1927	Aug. 19, 1937
Dixie Bibb Graves (D)[24]	Aug. 20, 1937	Jan. 10, 1938
Lister Hill (D)[25]	Jan. 11, 1938	Jan. 2, 1969
James B. Allen (D)[26]	Jan. 3, 1969	June 1, 1978
Maryon Pittman Allen (D)[27]	June 8, 1978	Nov. 7, 1978
Donald W. Stewart (D)[28]	Nov. 8, 1978	Jan. 1, 1981
Jeremiah Denton (R)	Jan. 2, 1981	Jan. 2, 1987
Richard C. Shelby (D, R)[29]	Jan. 3, 1987	

Alabama
1. Resigned April 15, 1844.
2. Appointed by governor to fill vacancy. Subsequently elected. Died Oct. 25, 1848.
3. Appointed by governor to fill vacancy.
4. Seat declared vacant March 14, 1861. Vacancy lasted until July 25, 1868, because of Civil War.
5. Not sworn in until Jan. 15, 1872, because of protest.
6. Died June 11, 1907.
7. Appointed by governor to fill vacancy. Subsequently elected. Died March 1, 1920.
8. Appointed by governor to fill vacancy.
9. Died June 12, 1946.
10. Appointed by governor to fill vacancy. Resigned Nov. 5, 1946.
11. Resigned Dec. 12, 1822.
12. Died Jan. 25, 1826.
13. Appointed by governor to fill vacancy.
14. Resigned April 22, 1837.
15. Resigned Nov. 15, 1841.
16. Resigned June 16, 1848.
17. Appointed by governor to fill vacancy. Subsequently elected. Resigned Dec. 20, 1852, having been elected vice president of the United States.
18. Appointed by governor to fill vacancy. Subsequently elected. Withdrew from Senate Jan. 21, 1861, because of Civil War. Seat remained vacant until July 25, 1868.
19. Died Dec. 31, 1879.
20. Appointed by governor to fill vacancy.
21. Died July 27, 1907.
22. Died Aug. 8, 1913.
23. Resigned Aug. 19, 1937.
24. Appointed by governor to fill vacancy. Resigned Jan. 10, 1938.
25. Appointed by governor to fill vacancy. Subsequently elected.
26. Died June 1, 1978.
27. Appointed by governor to fill vacancy.
28. Resigned Jan. 1, 1981.
29. Elected as a Democrat in 1986 and 1992. Shelby became a Republican on Nov. 9, 1994.

ALASKA

(Became a state Jan. 3, 1959)

Class 2

Senators	Dates of Service	
E. L. Bartlett (D)[1]	Jan. 3, 1959	Dec. 11, 1968
Ted Stevens (R)[2]	Dec. 24, 1968	

Class 3

Ernest Gruening (D)	Jan. 3, 1959	Jan. 2, 1969
Mike Gravel (D)	Jan. 3, 1969	Jan. 2, 1981
Frank H. Murkowski (R)	Jan. 3, 1981	

Alaska
1. Died Dec. 11, 1968.
2. Appointed by governor to fill vacancy. Subsequently elected

ARIZONA

(Became a state Feb. 14, 1912)

Class 1

Senators	Dates of Service	
Henry Fountain Ashurst (D)	March 27, 1912	Jan. 2, 1941
Ernest W. McFarland (D)	Jan. 3, 1941	Jan. 2, 1953
Barry Goldwater (R)	Jan. 3, 1953	Jan. 2, 1965
Paul J. Fannin (R)	Jan. 3, 1965	Jan. 2, 1977
Dennis DeConcini (D)	Jan. 3, 1977	Jan. 2, 1995
Jon Kyl (R)	Jan. 3, 1995	

Class 3

Marcus A. Smith (D)	March 27, 1912	March 3, 1921
Ralph H. Cameron (R)	March 4, 1921	March 3, 1927
Carl Hayden (D)	March 4, 1927	Jan. 2, 1969
Barry Goldwater (R)	Jan. 3, 1969	Jan. 2, 1987
John McCain (R)	Jan. 3, 1987	

ARKANSAS

(Became a state June 15, 1836)

Class 2

Senators	Dates of Service	
William S. Fulton (D)[1]	Sept. 18, 1836	Aug. 15, 1844
Chester Ashley (D)[2]	Nov. 8, 1844	April 29, 1848
William K. Sebastian (D)[3]	May 12, 1848	July 11, 1861
Alexander McDonald (R)	June 23, 1868	March 3, 1871
Powell Clayton (R)	March 14, 1871	March 3, 1877
Augustus H. Garland (D)[4]	March 4, 1877	March 6, 1885
James H. Berry (D)	March 20, 1885	March 3, 1907
Jeff Davis (D)[5]	March 4, 1907	Jan. 3, 1913
John N. Heiskell (D)[6]	Jan. 6, 1913	Jan. 29, 1913
William M. Kavanaugh (D)	Jan. 29, 1913	March 3, 1913
Joseph T. Robinson (D)[7]	March 10, 1913	July 14, 1937
John E. Miller (D)[8]	Nov. 15, 1937	March 31, 1941
Lloyd Spencer (D)[9]	April 1, 1941	Jan. 2, 1943
John L. McClellan (D)[10]	Jan. 3, 1943	Nov. 28, 1977
Kaneaster Hodges Jr. (D)[11]	Dec. 10, 1977	Jan. 2, 1979
David Pryor (D)	Jan. 3, 1979	Jan. 2, 1997
Tim Hutchinson (R)	Jan. 3, 1997	

Class 3

Ambrose H. Sevier (D)[12]	Sept. 18, 1836	March 15, 1848
Solon Borland (D)[13]	March 30, 1848	April 3, 1853
Robert W. Johnson (D)[14]	July 6, 1853	March 3, 1861
Charles B. Mitchel (D)[15]	March 4, 1861	July 11, 1861
Benjamin F. Rice (R)	June 23, 1868	March 3, 1873
Stephen W. Dorsey (R)	March 4, 1873	March 3, 1879
James D. Walker (D)	March 4, 1879	March 3, 1885
James K. Jones (D)	March 4, 1885	March 3, 1903
James P. Clarke (D)[16]	March 4, 1903	Oct. 1, 1916
William F. Kirby (D)	Nov. 8, 1916	March 2, 1921
Thaddeus H. Caraway (D)[17]	March 4, 1921	Nov. 6, 1931
Hattie W. Caraway (D)[18]	Nov. 13, 1931	Jan. 2, 1945

J. William Fulbright (D)[19]	Jan. 3, 1945	Dec. 31, 1974
Dale Bumpers (D)	Jan. 3, 1975	Jan. 3, 1999
Blanche Lincoln (D)	Jan. 3, 1999	

Arkansas
1. Died Aug. 15, 1844.
2. Died April 29, 1848.
3. Appointed by governor to fill vacancy. Subsequently elected. Expelled July 11, 1861. Seat remained vacant until June 23, 1868, because of Civil War.
4. Resigned March 6, 1885.
5. Died Jan. 3, 1913.
6. Appointed by governor to fill vacancy.
7. Died July 14, 1937.
8. Resigned March 31, 1941.
9. Appointed by governor to fill vacancy.
10. Died Nov. 28, 1977.
11. Appointed by governor to fill vacancy.
12. Resigned March 15, 1848.
13. Appointed by governor to fill vacancy. Subsequently elected. Resigned April 3, 1853.
14. Appointed by governor to fill vacancy. Subsequently elected.
15. Expelled July 11, 1861. Vacancy until June 23, 1868, because of Civil War.
16. Died Oct. 1, 1916.
17. Died Nov. 6, 1931.
18. Appointed by governor to fill vacancy. Subsequently elected.
19. Resigned Dec. 31, 1974.

CALIFORNIA

(Became a state Sept. 9, 1850)

Class 1

Senators	Dates of Service	
John C. Frémont (D)	Sept. 9, 1850	March 3, 1851
John B. Weller (D)	Jan. 30, 1852	March 3, 1857
David C. Broderick (D)[1]	March 4, 1857	Sept. 16, 1859
Henry P. Haun (D)[2]	Nov. 3, 1859	March 4, 1860
Milton S. Latham (D)	March 5, 1860	March 3, 1863
John Conness (UN R)	March 4, 1863	March 3, 1869
Eugene Casserly (D)[3]	March 4, 1869	Nov. 29, 1873
John S. Hager (A-MON D)	Dec. 23, 1873	March 3, 1875
Newton Booth (A-MONOPT)	March 4, 1875	March 3, 1881
John F. Miller (R)[4]	March 4, 1881	March 8, 1886
George Hearst (D)[5]	March 23, 1886	Aug. 4, 1886
Abram P. Williams (R)	Aug. 4, 1886	March 3, 1887
George Hearst (D)[6]	March 4, 1887	Feb. 28, 1891
Charles N. Felton (R)	March 19, 1891	March 3, 1893
Stephen M. White (D)	March 4, 1893	March 3, 1899
Thomas R. Bard (R)	Feb. 7, 1900	March 3, 1905
Frank P. Flint (R)	March 4, 1905	March 3, 1911
John D. Works (R)	March 4, 1911	March 3, 1917
Hiram W. Johnson (R)[7]	April 2, 1917	Aug. 6, 1945
William F. Knowland (R)[8]	Aug. 26, 1945	Jan. 2, 1959
Clair Engle (D)[9]	Jan. 3, 1959	July 30, 1964
Pierre Salinger (D)[10]	Aug. 4, 1964	Dec. 31, 1964
George Murphy (R)[11]	Jan. 1, 1965	Jan. 2, 1971
John V. Tunney (D)[12]	Jan. 2, 1971	Jan. 1, 1977
S. I. Hayakawa (R)	Jan. 2, 1977	Jan. 2, 1983
Pete Wilson (R)[13]	Jan. 3, 1983	Jan. 7, 1991
John Seymour (R)[14]	Jan. 10, 1991	Nov. 3, 1992
Dianne Feinstein (D)	Nov. 10, 1992	

Class 3

William M. Gwin (D)	Sept. 9, 1850	March 3, 1855
William M. Gwin (D)[15]	Jan. 13, 1857	March 3, 1861
James A. McDougall (D)	March 4, 1861	March 3, 1867
Cornelius Cole (R)	March 4, 1867	March 3, 1873
Aaron A. Sargent (R)	March 4, 1873	March 3, 1879
James T. Farley (D)	March 4, 1879	March 3, 1885
Leland Stanford (R)[16]	March 4, 1885	June 21, 1893
George C. Perkins (R)[17]	July 26, 1893	March 3, 1915
James D. Phelan (D)	March 4, 1915	March 3, 1921
Samuel M. Shortridge (R)	March 4, 1921	March 3, 1933
William Gibbs McAdoo (D)[18]	March 4, 1933	Nov. 8, 1938
Thomas M. Storke (D)[19]	Nov. 9, 1938	Jan. 2, 1939
Sheridan Downey (D)[20]	Jan. 3, 1939	Nov. 30, 1950
Richard M. Nixon (R)[21]	Dec. 4, 1950	Jan. 1, 1953
Thomas H. Kuchel (R)[22]	Jan. 2, 1953	Jan. 2, 1969
Alan Cranston (D)	Jan. 3, 1969	Jan. 2, 1993
Barbara Boxer (D)	Jan. 3, 1993	

California
1. Died Sept. 16, 1859.
2. Appointed by governor to fill vacancy.
3. Resigned Nov. 29, 1873.
4. Died March 8, 1886.
5. Appointed by governor to fill vacancy.
6. Died Feb. 28, 1891.
7. Died Aug. 6, 1945.
8. Appointed by governor to fill vacancy. Subsequently elected.
9. Died July 30, 1964.
10. Appointed by governor to fill vacancy. Resigned Dec. 31, 1964.
11. Resigned Jan. 2, 1971.
12. Resigned Jan. 1, 1977.
13. Resigned Jan. 7, 1991, having been elected governor.
14. Appointed by governor to fill vacancy. Resigned Nov. 3, 1992.
15. Vacancy from March 4, 1855, to Jan. 12, 1857, because of failure of legislature to elect.
16. Died June 21, 1893.
17. Appointed by governor to fill vacancy. Subsequently elected.
18. Resigned Nov. 8, 1938.
19. Appointed by governor to fill vacancy.
20. Resigned Nov. 30, 1950.
21. Resigned Jan. 1, 1953, having been elected U.S. vice president.
22. Appointed by governor to fill vacancy. Subsequently elected.

COLORADO

(Became a state Aug. 1, 1876)

Class 2

Senators	Dates of Service	
Henry M. Teller (R)[1]	Nov. 15, 1876	April 17, 1882
George M. Chilcott (R)[2]	April 17, 1882	Jan. 27, 1883
Horace A. W. Tabor (R)	Jan. 27, 1883	March 3, 1883
Thomas M. Bowen (R)	March 4, 1883	March 3, 1889
Edward O. Wolcott (R)	March 4, 1889	March 3, 1901
Thomas M. Patterson (D)	March 4, 1901	March 3, 1907
Simon Guggenheim (R)	March 4, 1907	March 3, 1913
John F. Shafroth (D)	March 4, 1913	March 3, 1919
Lawrence C. Phipps (R)	March 4, 1919	March 3, 1931
Edward P. Costigan (D)	March 4, 1931	Jan. 2, 1937
Edwin C. Johnson (D)	Jan. 3, 1937	Jan. 2, 1955
Gordon Allott (R)	Jan. 3, 1955	Jan. 2, 1973
Floyd K. Haskell (D)	Jan. 3, 1973	Jan. 2, 1979
William L. Armstrong (R)	Jan. 3, 1979	Jan. 2, 1991

Hank Brown (R)	Jan. 3, 1991	Jan. 2, 1997
Wayne Allard (R)	Jan. 3, 1997	

Class 3

Jerome B. Chaffee (R)	Nov. 15, 1876	March 3, 1879
Nathaniel P. Hill (R)	March 4, 1879	March 3, 1885
Henry M. Teller (R, I SIL R, D)[3]	March 4, 1885	March 3, 1909
Charles J. Hughes Jr. (D)[4]	March 4, 1909	Jan. 11, 1911
Charles S. Thomas (D)	Jan. 15, 1913	March 3, 1921
Samuel D. Nicholson (R)[5]	March 4, 1921	March 24, 1923
Alva B. Adams (D)[6]	May 17, 1923	Nov. 30, 1924
Rice W. Means (R)	Dec. 1, 1924	March 3, 1927
Charles W. Waterman (R)[7]	March 4, 1927	Aug. 27, 1932
Walter Walker (D)[8]	Sept. 26, 1932	Dec. 6, 1932
Karl C. Schuyler (R)	Dec. 7, 1932	March 3, 1933
Alva B. Adams (D)[9]	March 4, 1933	Dec. 1, 1941
Eugene D. Millikin (R)[10]	Dec. 20, 1941	Jan. 2, 1957
John A. Carroll (D)	Jan. 3, 1957	Jan. 2, 1963
Peter H. Dominick (R)	Jan. 3, 1963	Jan. 2, 1975
Gary Hart (D)	Jan. 3, 1975	Jan. 2, 1987
Timothy E. Wirth (D)	Jan. 3, 1987	Jan. 2, 1993
Ben Nighthorse Campbell (D, R)[11]	Jan. 3, 1993	

Colorado
1. Resigned April 17, 1882.
2. Appointed by governor to fill vacancy.
3. Elected as a Republican in 1885 and 1891, an Independent Silver Republican in 1897 and a Democrat in 1903.
4. Died Jan. 11, 1911. Vacancy until Jan. 15, 1913, because of failure of legislature to elect.
5. Died March 24, 1923.
6. Appointed by governor to fill vacancy.
7. Died Aug. 27, 1932.
8. Appointed by governor to fill vacancy.
9. Died Dec. 1, 1941.
10. Appointed by governor to fill vacancy. Subsequently elected.
11. Elected as a Democrat in 1992. Campbell became a Republican on March 3, 1995.

CONNECTICUT

(Ratified the Constitution Jan. 9, 1788)

Class 1

Senators	Dates of Service	
Oliver Ellsworth (FED)[1]	March 4, 1789	March 8, 1796
James Hillhouse (FED)[2]	May 12, 1796	May 10, 1810
Samuel W. Dana (FED)	May 10, 1810	March 3, 1821
Elijah Boardman (D-R)[3]	March 4, 1821	Aug. 18, 1823
Henry W. Edwards (D-R)[4]	Oct. 8, 1823	March 3, 1827
Samuel A. Foote (D-R)	March 4, 1827	March 3, 1833
Nathan Smith (W)[5]	March 4, 1833	Dec. 6, 1835
John M. Niles (D)[6]	Dec. 14, 1835	March 3, 1839
Thaddeus Betts (W)[7]	March 4, 1839	April 7, 1840
Jabez W. Huntington (W)[8]	May 4, 1840	Nov. 2, 1847
Roger S. Baldwin (W)[9]	Nov. 11, 1847	March 3, 1851
Isaac Toucey (D)[10]	May 12, 1852	March 3, 1857
James Dixon (R)	March 4, 1857	March 3, 1869
William A. Buckingham (R)[11]	March 4, 1869	Feb. 5, 1875

William W. Eaton (D)[12]	Feb. 5, 1875	March 3, 1881
Joseph R. Hawley (R)	March 4, 1881	March 3, 1905
Morgan G. Bulkeley (R)	March 4, 1905	March 3, 1911
George P. McLean (R)	March 4, 1911	March 3, 1929
Frederic C. Walcott (R)	March 4, 1929	Jan. 2, 1935
Francis Maloney (D)[13]	Jan. 3, 1935	Jan. 16, 1945
Thomas C. Hart (R)[14]	Feb. 15, 1945	Nov. 5, 1946
Raymond E. Baldwin (R)[15]	Dec. 27, 1946	Dec. 17, 1949
William Benton (D)[16]	Dec. 17, 1949	Jan. 2, 1953
William A. Purtell (R)	Jan. 3, 1953	Jan. 2, 1959
Thomas J. Dodd (D)	Jan. 3, 1959	Jan. 2, 1971
Lowell P. Weicker Jr. (R)	Jan. 3, 1971	Jan. 2, 1989
Joseph I. Lieberman (D)	Jan. 3, 1989	

Class 3

William S. Johnson[17]	March 4, 1789	March 4, 1791
Roger Sherman[18]	June 13, 1791	July 23, 1793
Stephen M. Mitchell	Dec. 2, 1793	March 3, 1795
Jonathan Trumbull[19]	March 4, 1795	June 10, 1796
Uriah Tracy (FED)[20]	Oct. 13, 1796	July 19, 1807
Chauncey Goodrich (FED)[21]	Oct. 25, 1807	May 1813
David Daggett (FED)	May 13, 1813	March 3, 1819
James Lanman (D-R)	March 4, 1819	March 3, 1825
Calvin Willey (D-R)	May 4, 1825	March 3, 1831
Gideon Tomlinson (D)	March 4, 1831	March 3, 1837
Perry Smith (D)	March 4, 1837	March 3, 1843
John M. Niles (D)	March 4, 1843	March 3, 1849
Truman Smith (W)[22]	March 4, 1849	May 24, 1854
Francis Gillette (F SOIL W)	May 25, 1854	March 3, 1855
Lafayette S. Foster (R)	March 4, 1855	March 3, 1867
Orris S. Ferry (R)[23]	March 4, 1867	Nov. 21, 1875
James E. English (D)[24]	Nov. 27, 1875	May 17, 1876
William H. Barnum (D)	May 17, 1876	March 3, 1879
Orville H. Platt (R)[25]	March 4, 1879	April 21, 1905
Frank B. Brandegee (R)[26]	May 10, 1905	Oct. 14, 1924
Hiram Bingham (R)	Dec. 17, 1924	March 3, 1933
Augustine Lonergan (D)	March 4, 1933	Jan. 2, 1939
John A. Danaher (R)	Jan. 3, 1939	Jan. 2, 1945
Brien McMahon (D)[27]	Jan. 3, 1945	July 28, 1952
William A. Purtell (R)[28]	Aug. 29, 1952	Nov. 4, 1952
Prescott Bush (R)	Nov. 5, 1952	Jan. 2, 1963
Abraham Ribicoff (D)	Jan. 3, 1963	Jan. 2, 1981
Christopher J. Dodd (D)	Jan. 3, 1981	

Connecticut
1. Resigned March 8, 1796.
2. Resigned June 10, 1810.
3. Died Aug. 18, 1823.
4. Appointed by governor to fill vacancy. Subsequently elected.
5. Died Dec. 6, 1835.
6. Appointed by governor to fill vacancy. Subsequently elected.
7. Died April 7, 1840.
8. Died Nov. 2, 1847.
9. Appointed by governor to fill vacancy. Subsequently elected.
10. Vacant from March 4, 1851, to May 11, 1852, because of failure of governor to appoint.
11. Died Feb. 5, 1875.
12. Appointed by governor to fill vacancy. Subsequently elected.
13. Died Jan. 16, 1945.
14. Appointed by governor to fill vacancy.
15. Resigned Dec. 17, 1949.
16. Appointed by governor to fill vacancy. Subsequently elected.
17. Resigned March 4, 1791.

18. Died July 23, 1793.
19. Resigned June 10, 1796.
20. Died July 19, 1807.
21. Resigned May 1813.
22. Resigned May 24, 1854.
23. Died Nov. 21, 1875.
24. Appointed by governor to fill vacancy.
25. Died April 21, 1905.
26. Died Oct. 14, 1924.
27. Died July 28, 1952.
28. Appointed by governor to fill vacancy.

DELAWARE

(Ratified the Constitution Dec. 7, 1787)

Class 1

Senators	Dates of Service	
George Read (FED)[1]	March 4, 1789	Sept. 18, 1793
Henry Latimer (FED)[2]	Feb. 7, 1795	Feb. 28, 1801
Samuel White (FED)[3]	Feb. 28, 1801	Nov. 4, 1809
Outerbridge Horsey (FED)	Jan. 12, 1810	March 3, 1821
Caesar A. Rodney (D-R)[4]	Jan. 10, 1822	Jan. 29, 1823
Thomas Clayton (FED)	Jan. 8, 1824	March 3, 1827
Louis McLane (D-R)[5]	March 4, 1827	April 16, 1829
Arnold Naudain (NR)[6]	Jan. 7, 1830	June 16, 1836
Richard H. Bayard (W)[7]	June 17, 1836	Sept. 19, 1839
Richard H. Bayard (W)	Jan. 12, 1841	March 3, 1845
John M. Clayton (W)[8]	March 4, 1845	Feb. 23, 1849
John Wales (W)	Feb. 23, 1849	March 3, 1851
James A. Bayard Jr. (W, D)[9]	March 4, 1851	Jan. 29, 1864
George Read Riddle (D)[10]	Jan. 29, 1864	March 29, 1867
James A. Bayard Jr. (D)[11]	April 5, 1867	March 3, 1869
Thomas F. Bayard Sr. (D)[12]	March 4, 1869	March 6, 1885
George Gray (D)	March 18, 1885	March 3, 1899
L. Heisler Ball (R)[13]	March 2, 1903	March 3, 1905
Henry A. du Pont (R)[14]	June 13, 1906	March 3, 1917
Josiah O. Wolcott (D)[15]	March 4, 1917	July 2, 1921
T. Coleman du Pont (R)[16]	July 7, 1921	Nov. 6, 1922
Thomas F. Bayard Jr. (D)	Nov. 7, 1922	March 3, 1929
John G. Townsend Jr. (R)	March 4, 1929	Jan. 2, 1941
James M. Tunnell (D)	Jan. 3, 1941	Jan. 2, 1947
John J. Williams (R)[17]	Jan. 3, 1947	Dec. 31, 1970
William V. Roth Jr. (R)	Jan. 1, 1971	Jan. 3, 2001
Thomas R. Carper (D)	Jan. 3, 2001	

Class 2

Richard Bassett (FED)	March 4, 1789	March 3, 1793
John Vining (FED)[18]	March 4, 1793	Jan. 19, 1798
Joshua Clayton (FED)[19]	Jan. 19, 1798	Aug. 11, 1798
William Hill Wells (FED)[20]	Jan. 17, 1799	Nov. 6, 1804
James A. Bayard Sr. (FED)[21]	Nov. 13, 1804	March 3, 1813
William Hill Wells (FED)	May 28, 1813	March 3, 1817
Nicholas Van Dyke (FED)[22]	March 4, 1817	May 21, 1826
Daniel Rodney (FED)[23]	Nov. 8, 1826	Jan. 12, 1827
Henry M. Ridgeley	Jan. 12, 1827	March 3, 1829
John M. Clayton (NR, W)[24]	March 4, 1829	Dec. 29, 1836
Thomas Clayton (W)	Jan. 9, 1837	March 3, 1847
Presley Spruance (W)	March 4, 1847	March 3, 1853
John M. Clayton (W)[25]	March 4, 1853	Nov. 9, 1856

Joseph P. Comegys (W)[26]	Nov. 19, 1856	Jan. 14, 1857
Martin W. Bates (D)	Jan. 14, 1857	March 3, 1859
Willard Saulsbury Sr. (D)	March 4, 1859	March 3, 1871
Eli Saulsbury (D)	March 4, 1871	March 3, 1889
Anthony Higgins (R)	March 4, 1889	March 3, 1895
Richard R. Kenney (D)[27]	Jan. 19, 1897	March 3, 1901
James F. Allee (R)[28]	March 2, 1903	March 3, 1907
Harry A. Richardson (R)	March 4, 1907	March 3, 1913
Willard Saulsbury Jr. (D)	March 4, 1913	March 3, 1919
L. Heisler Ball (R)	March 4, 1919	March 3, 1925
T. Coleman du Pont (R)[29]	March 4, 1925	Dec. 9, 1928
Daniel O. Hastings (R)[30]	Dec. 10, 1928	Jan. 2, 1937
James H. Hughes (D)	Jan. 3, 1937	Jan. 2, 1943
C. Douglass Buck (R)	Jan. 3, 1943	Jan. 2, 1949
J. Allen Frear Jr. (D)	Jan. 3, 1949	Jan. 2, 1961
J. Caleb Boggs (R)	Jan. 3, 1961	Jan. 2, 1973
Joseph R. Biden Jr. (D)	Jan. 3, 1973	

Delaware

1. Resigned Sept. 18, 1793.
2. Resigned Feb. 28, 1801.
3. Appointed by governor to fill vacancy. Subsequently elected. Died Nov. 4, 1809.
4. Resigned Jan. 29, 1823.
5. Resigned April 16, 1829.
6. Resigned June 16, 1836.
7. Resigned Sept. 19, 1839. Vacant until Jan. 12, 1841.
8. Resigned Feb. 23, 1849.
9. Resigned Jan. 29, 1864.
10. Died March 29, 1867.
11. Appointed by governor to fill vacancy. Subsequently elected.
12. Resigned March 6, 1885.
13. Vacant until March 2, 1903, because of failure of legislature to elect.
14. Vacant until June 13, 1906, because of failure of legislature to elect.
15. Resigned July 2, 1921.
16. Appointed by governor to fill vacancy.
17. Resigned Dec. 31, 1970.
18. Resigned Jan. 19, 1798.
19. Died Aug. 11, 1798.
20. Resigned Nov. 6, 1804.
21. Resigned March 3, 1813.
22. Died May 21, 1826.
23. Appointed by governor to fill vacancy.
24. Resigned Dec. 29, 1836.
25. Died Nov. 9, 1856.
26. Appointed by governor to fill vacancy.
27. Vacancy until Jan. 19, 1897, because of failure of legislature to elect.
28. Vacancy until March 2, 1903, because of failure of legislature to elect.
29. Resigned Dec. 9, 1928.
30. Appointed by governor to fill vacancy. Subsequently elected.

FLORIDA

(Became a state March 3, 1845)

Class 1

Senators	Dates of Service	
David Levy Yulee (D)	July 1, 1845	March 3, 1851
Stephen R. Mallory (D)[1]	March 4, 1851	March 14, 1861
Adonijah S. Welch (R)	July 2, 1868	March 3, 1869
Abijah Gilbert (R)	March 4, 1869	March 3, 1875
Charles W. Jones (D)	March 4, 1875	March 3, 1887
Samuel Pasco (D)[2]	May 19, 1887	April 18, 1899
James P. Taliaferro (D)[3]	April 19, 1899	March 3, 1911
Nathan P. Bryan (D)[4]	March 4, 1911	March 3, 1917
Park Trammell (D)[5]	March 4, 1917	May 8, 1936

Scott M. Loftin (D)[6]	May 26, 1936	Nov. 3, 1936
Charles O. Andrews (D)[7]	Nov. 4, 1936	Sept. 18, 1946
Spessard L. Holland (D)[8]	Sept. 25, 1946	Jan. 2, 1971
Lawton Chiles (D)	Jan. 3, 1971	Jan. 2, 1989
Connie Mack (R)	Jan. 3, 1989	Jan. 3, 2001
Bill Nelson (D)	Jan. 3, 2001	

Class 3

James D. Westcott Jr. (D)	July 1, 1845	March 3, 1849
Jackson Morton (W)	March 4, 1849	March 3, 1855
David Levy Yulee (D)[9]	March 4, 1855	Jan. 21, 1861
Thomas W. Osborn (R)	June 30, 1868	March 3, 1873
Simon B. Conover (R)	March 4, 1873	March 3, 1879
Wilkinson Call (D)	March 4, 1879	March 3, 1897
Stephen R. Mallory (D)[10]	May 24, 1897	Dec. 23, 1907
William J. Bryan (D)[11]	Dec. 26, 1907	March 22, 1908
William H. Milton (D)[12]	March 27, 1908	March 3, 1909
Duncan U. Fletcher (D)[13]	March 4, 1909	June 17, 1936
William L. Hill (D)[14]	July 1, 1936	Nov. 3, 1936
Claude Pepper (D)	Nov. 4, 1936	Jan. 2, 1951
George A. Smathers (D)	Jan. 3, 1951	Jan. 2, 1969
Edward J. Gurney (R)[15]	Jan. 3, 1969	Dec. 31, 1974
Richard Stone (D)[16]	Jan. 2, 1975	Dec. 31, 1980
Paula Hawkins (R)	Jan. 1, 1981	Jan. 2, 1987
Bob Graham (D)	Jan. 3, 1987	

Florida

1. Seat declared vacant March 14, 1861. Vacancy lasted until July 2, 1868, because of Civil War.
2. Pasco served continuously through this period, twice by appointment of the governor and twice by election.
3. Taliaferro served twice by election and once by appointment during his term of office.
4. Appointed by governor to fill vacancy. Subsequently elected.
5. Died May 8, 1936.
6. Appointed by governor to fill vacancy.
7. Died Sept. 18, 1946.
8. Appointed by governor to fill vacancy. Subsequently elected.
9. Retired from the Senate Jan. 21, 1861, because of Civil War. Seat remained vacant until June 30, 1868.
10. Mallory served twice by election and once by appointment during his term of office. Died Dec. 23, 1907.
11. Appointed by governor to fill vacancy. Died March 22, 1908.
12. Appointed by governor to fill vacancy.
13. Appointed by governor to fill vacancy. Subsequently elected. Died June 17, 1936.
14. Appointed by governor to fill vacancy.
15. Resigned Dec. 31, 1974.
16. Resigned Dec. 31, 1980.

GEORGIA

(Ratified the Constitution Jan. 2, 1788)

Class 2

Senators	Dates of Service	
William Few (D-R)	March 4, 1789	March 3, 1793
James Jackson (D-R)[1]	March 4, 1793	1795
George Walton[2]	Nov. 16, 1795	Feb. 20, 1796
Josiah Tattnall	Feb. 20, 1796	March 3, 1799
Abraham Baldwin (D-R)[3]	March 4, 1799	March 4, 1807
George Jones[4]	Aug. 27, 1807	Nov. 7, 1807
William H. Crawford (D-R)[5]	Nov. 7, 1807	March 23, 1813

William B. Bulloch (D-R)[6]	April 8, 1813	Nov. 6, 1813
William Wyatt Bibb (D-R)[7]	Nov. 6, 1813	Nov. 9, 1816
George M. Troup (D-R)[8]	Nov. 13, 1816	Sept. 23, 1818
John Forsyth (D-R)[9]	Nov. 23, 1818	Feb. 17, 1819
Freeman Walker (D-R)[10]	Nov. 6, 1819	Aug. 8, 1821
Nicholas Ware (D-R)[11]	Nov. 10, 1821	Sept. 7, 1824
Thomas W. Cobb (D-R)[12]	Nov. 4, 1824	1828
Oliver H. Prince (D-R)	Nov. 7, 1828	March 3, 1829
George M. Troup (D)[13]	March 4, 1829	March 2, 1833
John Pendleton King (D)[14]	Nov. 21, 1833	Nov. 1, 1837
Wilson Lumpkin (D)	Nov. 22, 1837	March 3, 1841
John M. Berrien (W)[15]	March 4, 1841	May 1845
John M. Berrien (W)	Nov. 14, 1845	March 3, 1847
John M. Berrien (W)[16]	Nov. 13, 1847	May 28, 1852
Robert M. Charlton[17]	May 31, 1852	March 3, 1853
Robert Toombs (D)[18]	March 4, 1853	March 14, 1861
Homer V. M. Miller (D)	Feb. 24, 1871	March 3, 1871
Thomas M. Norwood (D)	Nov. 14, 1871	March 3, 1877
Benjamin H. Hill (D)[19]	March 4, 1877	Aug. 16, 1882
Pope Barrow (D)	Nov. 15, 1882	March 3, 1883
Alfred H. Colquitt (D)[20]	March 4, 1883	March 26, 1894
Patrick Walsh (D)[21]	April 2, 1894	March 3, 1895
Augustus O. Bacon (D)[22]	March 4, 1895	Feb. 14, 1914
William S. West (D)[23]	March 2, 1914	Nov. 3, 1914
Thomas W. Hardwick (D)	Nov. 4, 1914	March 3, 1919
William J. Harris (D)[24]	March 4, 1919	April 18, 1932
John S. Cohen (D)[25]	April 25, 1932	Jan. 11, 1933
Richard B. Russell (D)[26]	Jan. 12, 1933	Jan. 21, 1971
David H. Gambrell (D)[27]	Feb. 1, 1971	Nov. 7, 1972
Sam Nunn (D)	Nov. 8, 1972	Jan. 2, 1997
Max Cleland (D)	Jan. 3, 1997	

Class 3

James Gunn	March 4, 1789	March 3, 1801
James Jackson (D-R)[28]	March 4, 1801	March 19, 1806
John Milledge (D-R)[29]	June 19, 1806	Nov. 14, 1809
Charles Tait (D-R)	Nov. 27, 1809	March 3, 1819
John Elliott (D-R)	March 4, 1819	March 3, 1825
John M. Berrien (D-R)[30]	March 4, 1825	March 9, 1829
John Forsyth (D)[31]	Nov. 9, 1829	June 27, 1834
Alfred Cuthbert (D)	Jan. 12, 1835	March 3, 1843
Walter T. Colquitt (D)[32]	March 4, 1843	February 1848
Herschel V. Johnson (D)[33]	Feb. 4, 1848	March 3, 1849
William C. Dawson (W)	March 4, 1849	March 3, 1855
Alfred Iverson (D)[34]	March 4, 1855	Jan. 28, 1861
Joshua Hill (UN R)	Feb. 1, 1871	March 3, 1873
John B. Gordon (D)[35]	March 4, 1873	May 26, 1880
Joseph E. Brown (D)[36]	May 26, 1880	March 3, 1891
John B. Gordon (D)	March 4, 1891	March 3, 1897
Alexander S. Clay (D)[37]	March 4, 1897	Nov. 13, 1910
Joseph M. Terrell (D)[38]	Nov. 17, 1910	July 14, 1911
Hoke Smith (D)	Dec. 4, 1911	March 3, 1921
Thomas E. Watson (D)[39]	March 4, 1921	Sept. 26, 1922
Rebecca L. Felton (D)[40]	Oct. 3, 1922	Nov. 21, 1922
Walter F. George (D)	Nov. 22, 1922	Jan. 2, 1957
Herman E. Talmadge (D)	Jan. 3, 1957	Jan. 2, 1981
Mack Mattingly (R)	Jan. 3, 1981	Jan. 2, 1987
Wyche Fowler (D)	Jan. 3, 1987	Jan. 2, 1993

Paul Coverdell (R)[41]	Jan. 3, 1993	July 18, 2000
Zell Miller (D)[42]	July 27, 2000	

Georgia
1. Resigned.
2. Appointed by governor to fill vacancy.
3. Died March 4, 1807.
4. Appointed by governor to fill vacancy.
5. Resigned March 23, 1813.
6. Appointed by governor to fill vacancy.
7. Resigned Nov. 9, 1816.
8. Resigned declared Sept. 23, 1818.
9. Resigned Feb. 17, 1819.
10. Resigned Aug. 8, 1821.
11. Died Sept. 7, 1824.
12. Resigned.
13. Resigned March 2, 1833.
14. Resigned Nov. 1, 1837.
15. Resigned in May 1845. Seat vacant until Nov. 14, 1845, because of failure of legislature to elect.
16. Vacant from March 4, 1847, to Nov. 13, 1847, because of failure of legislature to elect. Resigned May 28, 1952.
17. Appointed by governor to fill vacancy.
18. Seat declared vacant March 14, 1861. Remained vacant until Feb. 24, 1871, because of Civil War.
19. Died Aug. 16, 1882.
20. Died March 26, 1894.
21. Appointed by governor to fill vacancy. Subsequently elected.
22. Bacon was elected three times and appointed twice during his term of service. Died Feb. 14, 1914.
23. Appointed by governor to fill vacancy.
24. Died April 18, 1932.
25. Appointed by governor to fill vacancy.
26. Died Jan. 21, 1971.
27. Appointed by governor to fill vacancy.
28. Died March 19, 1806.
29. Resigned Nov. 14, 1809.
30. Resigned March 9, 1829.
31. Resigned June 27, 1834.
32. Resigned in February 1848.
33. Appointed by governor to fill vacancy.
34. Retired from Senate Jan. 28, 1861. Vacancy until Feb. 1, 1871, because of Civil War.
35. Resigned May 26, 1880.
36. Appointed by governor to fill vacancy. Subsequently elected.
37. Died Nov. 13, 1910.
38. Appointed by governor to fill vacancy. Resigned July 14, 1911.
39. Died Sept. 26, 1922.
40. Appointed by governor to fill vacancy.
41. Died July 18, 2000.
42. Appointed by governor to fill vacancy. Subsequently elected.

HAWAII

(Became a state Aug. 21, 1959)

Class 1

Senators	Dates of Service	
Hiram L. Fong (R)	Aug. 21, 1959	Jan. 2, 1977
Spark M. Matsunaga (D)[1]	Jan. 3, 1977	April 15, 1990
Daniel K. Akaka (D)[2]	May 16, 1990	

Class 3

Oren E. Long (D)	Aug. 21, 1959	Jan. 2, 1963
Daniel K. Inouye (D)	Jan. 3, 1963	

Hawaii
1. Died April 15, 1990.
2. Appointed by governor to fill vacancy. Subsequently elected.

IDAHO

(Became a state July 3, 1890)

Class 2

Senators	Dates of Service	
George L. Shoup (R)	Dec. 18, 1890	March 3, 1901
Fred T. Dubois (D)	March 4, 1901	March 3, 1907
William E. Borah (R)[1]	March 4, 1907	Jan. 19, 1940
John Thomas (R)[2]	Jan. 27, 1940	Nov. 10, 1945
Charles C. Gossett (D)[3]	Nov. 17, 1945	Nov. 5, 1946
Henry C. Dworshak (R)	Nov. 6, 1946	Jan. 2, 1949
Bert H. Miller (D)[4]	Jan. 3, 1949	Oct. 8, 1949
Henry C. Dworshak (R)[5]	Oct. 14, 1949	July 23, 1962
Len B. Jordan (R)[6]	Aug. 6, 1962	Jan. 2, 1973
James A. McClure (R)	Jan. 3, 1973	Jan. 2, 1991
Larry E. Craig (R)	Jan. 3, 1991	

Class 3

William J. McConnell (R)	Dec. 18, 1890	March 3, 1891
Fred T. Dubois (R)	March 4, 1891	March 3, 1897
Henry Heitfeld (POP)	March 4, 1897	March 3, 1903
Weldon B. Heyburn (R)[7]	March 4, 1903	Oct. 17, 1912
Kirtland I. Perky (D)[8]	Nov. 18, 1912	Feb. 5, 1913
James H. Brady (R)[9]	Feb. 6, 1913	Jan. 13, 1918
John F. Nugent (D)[10]	Jan. 22, 1918	Jan. 14, 1921
Frank R. Gooding (R)[11]	Jan. 15, 1921	June 24, 1928
John Thomas (R)[12]	June 30, 1928	March 3, 1933
James P. Pope (D)	March 4, 1933	Jan. 2, 1939
D. Worth Clark (D)	Jan. 3, 1939	Jan. 2, 1945
Glen H. Taylor (D)	Jan. 3, 1945	Jan. 2, 1951
Herman Welker (R)	Jan. 3, 1951	Jan. 2, 1957
Frank Church (D)	Jan. 3, 1957	Jan. 2, 1981
Steven D. Symms (R)	Jan. 3, 1981	Jan. 2, 1993
Dirk Kempthorne (R)	Jan. 3, 1993	Jan. 3, 1999
Michael D. Crapo (R)	Jan. 3, 1999	

Idaho
1. Died Jan. 19, 1940.
2. Appointed by governor to fill vacancy. Subsequently elected. Died Nov. 10, 1945.
3. Appointed by governor to fill vacancy.
4. Died Oct. 8, 1949.
5. Appointed by governor to fill vacancy. Subsequently elected. Died July 23, 1962.
6. Appointed by governor to fill vacancy. Subsequently elected.
7. Died Oct. 17, 1912.
8. Appointed by governor to fill vacancy.
9. Died Jan. 13, 1918.
10. Appointed by governor to fill vacancy. Subsequently elected. Resigned Jan. 14, 1921.
11. Appointed by governor to fill vacancy. Subsequently elected. Died June 24, 1928.
12. Appointed by governor to fill vacancy. Subsequently elected.

ILLINOIS

(Became a state Dec. 3, 1818)

Class 2

Senators	Dates of Service	
Jesse B. Thomas (D-R)	Dec. 3, 1818	March 3, 1829
John McLean (D)[1]	March 4, 1829	Oct. 14, 1830
David J. Baker (D)[2]	Nov. 12, 1830	Dec. 11, 1830
John M. Robinson (D)	Dec. 11, 1830	March 3, 1841
Samuel McRoberts (D)[3]	March 4, 1841	March 27, 1843
James Semple (D)[4]	Aug. 16, 1843	March 3, 1847
Stephen A. Douglas (D)[5]	March 4, 1847	June 3, 1861
Orville H. Browning (R)[6]	June 26, 1861	Jan. 12, 1863
William A. Richardson (D)	Jan. 12, 1863	March 3, 1865
Richard Yates (R)	March 4, 1865	March 3, 1871
John A. Logan (R)	March 4, 1871	March 3, 1877
David Davis (I)	March 4, 1877	March 3, 1883
Shelby M. Cullom (R)	March 4, 1883	March 3, 1913
James Hamilton Lewis (D)	March 26, 1913	March 3, 1919
Medill McCormick (R)[7]	March 4, 1919	Feb. 25, 1925
Charles S. Deneen (R)[8]	Feb. 26, 1925	March 3, 1931
James Hamilton Lewis (D)[9]	March 4, 1931	April 9, 1939
James M. Slattery (D)[10]	April 14, 1939	Nov. 21, 1940
C. Wayland Brooks (R)	Nov. 22, 1940	Jan. 2, 1949
Paul H. Douglas (D)	Jan. 3, 1949	Jan. 2, 1967
Charles H. Percy (R)	Jan. 3, 1967	Jan. 2, 1985
Paul Simon (D)	Jan. 3, 1985	Jan. 2, 1997
Richard J. Durbin (D)	Jan. 3, 1997	

Class 3

Ninian Edwards (D-R)[11]	Dec. 3, 1818	March 4, 1824
John McLean (D-R)	Nov. 23, 1824	March 3, 1825
Elias K. Kane (D)[12]	March 4, 1825	Dec. 11, 1835
William Lee D. Ewing (D)	Dec. 30, 1835	March 3, 1837
Richard M. Young (D)	March 4, 1837	March 3, 1843
Sidney Breese (D)	March 4, 1843	March 3, 1849
James Shields (D)	March 4, 1849	March 15, 1849
James Shields (D)[13]	Dec. 3, 1849	March 3, 1855
Lyman Trumbull (R)	March 4, 1855	March 3, 1873
Richard J. Oglesby (R)	March 4, 1873	March 3, 1879
John A. Logan (R)[14]	March 4, 1879	Dec. 26, 1886
Charles B. Farwell (R)	Jan. 19, 1887	March 3, 1891
John McAuley Palmer (D)	March 4, 1891	March 3, 1897
William E. Mason (R)	March 4, 1897	March 3, 1903
Albert J. Hopkins (R)	March 4, 1903	March 3, 1909
William Lorimer (R)[15]	June 18, 1909	July 13, 1912
Lawrence Y. Sherman (R)	March 26, 1913	March 3, 1921
William B. McKinley (R)[16]	March 4, 1921	Dec. 7, 1926
Frank L. Smith (R)[17]		
Otis F. Glenn (R)	Dec. 3, 1928	March 3, 1933
William H. Dietrich (D)	March 4, 1933	Jan. 2, 1939
Scott W. Lucas (D)	Jan. 3, 1939	Jan. 2, 1951
Everett McKinley Dirksen (R)[18]	Jan. 3, 1951	Sept. 7, 1969
Ralph Tyler Smith (R)[19]	Sept. 17, 1969	Nov. 16, 1970
Adlai E. Stevenson III (D)	Nov. 17, 1970	Jan. 2, 1981
Alan J. Dixon (D)	Jan. 3, 1981	Jan. 2, 1993
Carol Moseley Braun (D)	Jan. 3, 1993	Jan. 3, 1999
Peter G. Fitzgerald (R)	Jan. 3, 1999	

Illinois
1. Died Oct. 14, 1830.
2. Appointed by governor to fill vacancy.
3. Died March 27, 1843.
4. Appointed by governor to fill vacancy. Subsequently elected.
5. Died June 3, 1861.
6. Appointed by governor to fill vacancy.
7. Died Feb. 25, 1925.

Illinois (continued)

8. Appointed by governor to fill vacancy. Subsequently elected.

9. Died April 9, 1939.

10. Appointed by governor to fill vacancy.

11. Resigned March 4, 1824.

12. Died Dec. 11, 1835.

13. Shields was seated but his election was declared void by the Senate March 15, 1849, because he had not been a citizen of the United States for the requisite number of years prior to his election. Subsequently elected to fill the vacancy and, having in the interim met the constitutional requirement, took his seat Dec. 3, 1849.

14. Died Dec. 26, 1886.

15. Lorimer was accused of bribery and other corrupt practices in securing his election to the Senate. After lengthy investigation, the Senate voted on July 13, 1912, to declare his election invalid.

16. Died Dec. 7, 1926.

17. Smith was appointed by the governor Dec. 6, 1926, to fill the remaining three months of McKinley's term. He had previously been elected for a full six-year term. He was not permitted to take the oath for either term. The Committee on Privileges and Elections recommended on Jan. 17, 1928, that Smith not be allowed to take his seat because of fraud and corruption during the campaign. The Senate adopted this resolution Jan. 19, 1928, and the seat was declared vacant. According to the Biographical Directory, Smith "resigned Feb. 9, 1928," but since the seat was already vacant, this action was apparently meaningless.

18. Died Sept. 7, 1969.

19. Appointed by governor to fill vacancy.

INDIANA

(Became a state Dec. 11, 1816)

Class 1

Senators	Dates of Service	
James Noble (D-R)[1]	Dec. 11, 1816	Feb. 26, 1831
Robert Hanna (W)[2]	Aug. 19, 1831	Jan. 3, 1832
John Tipton (D)	Jan. 4, 1832	March 3, 1839
Albert S. White (W)	March 4, 1839	March 3, 1845
Jesse D. Bright (D)[3]	March 4, 1845	Feb. 5, 1862
Joseph A. Wright (D)[4]	Feb. 24, 1862	Jan. 14, 1863
David Turpie (D)	Jan. 14, 1863	March 3, 1863
Thomas A. Hendricks (D)	March 4, 1863	March 3, 1869
Daniel D. Pratt (R)	March 4, 1869	March 3, 1875
Joseph E. McDonald (D)	March 4, 1875	March 3, 1881
Benjamin Harrison (R)	March 4, 1881	March 3, 1887
David Turpie (D)	March 4, 1887	March 3, 1899
Albert J. Beveridge (R)	March 4, 1899	March 3, 1911
John W. Kern (D)	March 4, 1911	March 3, 1917
Harry S. New (R)	March 4, 1917	March 3, 1923
Samuel M. Ralston (D)[5]	March 4, 1923	Oct. 14, 1925
Arthur R. Robinson (R)[6]	Oct. 20, 1925	Jan. 2, 1935
Sherman Minton (D)	Jan. 3, 1935	Jan. 2, 1941
Raymond E. Willis (R)	Jan. 3, 1941	Jan. 2, 1947
William E. Jenner (R)	Jan. 3, 1947	Jan. 2, 1959
Vance Hartke (D)	Jan. 3, 1959	Jan. 2, 1977
Richard G. Lugar (R)	Jan. 3, 1977	

Class 3

Waller Taylor (R)	Dec. 16, 1816	March 4, 1825
William Hendricks (D)	March 4, 1825	March 3, 1837
Oliver H. Smith (W)	March 4, 1837	March 3, 1843
Edward A. Hannegan (D)	March 4, 1843	March 3, 1849
James Whitcomb (D)[7]	March 4, 1849	Oct. 4, 1852
Charles W. Cathcart (D)[8]	Nov. 23, 1852	Jan. 11, 1853
John Petit (D)	Jan. 11, 1853	March 3, 1855

Graham N. Fitch (D)[9]	Feb. 4, 1857	March 3, 1861
Henry S. Lane (R)	March 4, 1861	March 3, 1867
Oliver H. P. T. Morton (R)[10]	March 4, 1867	Nov. 1, 1877
Daniel W. Voorhees (D)[11]	Nov. 6, 1877	March 3, 1897
Charles W. Fairbanks (R)[12]	March 4, 1897	March 3, 1905
James A. Hemenway (R)	March 4, 1905	March 3, 1909
Benjamin F. Shively (D)[13]	March 4, 1909	March 14, 1916
Thomas Taggart (D)[14]	March 20, 1916	Nov. 7, 1916
James E. Watson (R)	Nov. 8, 1916	March 3, 1933
Frederick Van Nuys (D)[15]	March 4, 1933	Jan. 25, 1944
Samuel D. Jackson (D)[16]	Jan. 28, 1944	Nov. 13, 1944
William E. Jenner (R)	Nov. 14, 1944	Jan. 2, 1945
Homer E. Capehart (R)	Jan. 3, 1945	Jan. 2, 1963
Birch Bayh (D)	Jan. 3, 1963	Jan. 2, 1981
Dan Quayle (R)[17]	Jan. 3, 1981	Jan. 3, 1989
Daniel R. Coats (R)[18]	Jan. 3, 1989	Jan. 3, 1999
Evan Bayh (D)	Jan. 3, 1999	

Indiana

1. Died Feb. 26, 1831.

2. Appointed by governor to fill vacancy.

3. Expelled Feb. 5, 1862, for writing a letter to Jefferson Davis addressing him as "President of the Confederate States." (Biographical Directory, p. 637).

4. Appointed by governor to fill vacancy.

5. Died Oct. 14, 1925.

6. Appointed by governor to fill vacancy. Subsequently elected.

7. Died Oct. 4, 1852.

8. Appointed by governor to fill vacancy.

9. Vacancy from March 4, 1855, to Feb. 4, 1857.

10. Died Nov. 1, 1877.

11. Appointed by governor to fill vacancy. Subsequently elected.

12. Resigned March 3, 1905, having been electeed vice president of the United States.

13. Died March 14, 1916.

14. Appointed by governor to fill vacancy.

15. Died Jan. 25, 1944.

16. Appointed by governor to fill vacancy.

17. Resigned Jan. 3, 1989, having been elected vice president of the United States.

18. Appointed by governor to fill vacancy. Subsequently elected.

IOWA

(Became a state Dec. 28, 1846)

Class 2

Senators	Dates of Service	
George W. Jones (D)	Dec. 7, 1848	March 3, 1859
James W. Grimes (R)[1]	March 4, 1859	Dec. 6, 1869
James B. Howell (R)	Jan. 18, 1870	March 3, 1871
George G. Wright (R)	March 4, 1871	March 3, 1877
Samuel J. Kirkwood (R)[2]	March 4, 1877	March 7, 1881
James W. McDill (R)[3]	March 8, 1881	March 3, 1883
James F. Wilson (R)	March 4, 1883	March 3, 1895
John H. Gear (R)[4]	March 4, 1895	July 14, 1900
Jonathan P. Dolliver (R)[5]	Aug. 22, 1900	Oct. 15, 1910
Lafayette Young (R)[6]	Nov. 12, 1910	April 11, 1911
William S. Kenyon (R)[7]	April 12, 1911	Feb. 24, 1922
Charles A. Rawson (R)[8]	Feb. 24, 1922	Dec. 1, 1922
Smith W. Brookhart (R)[9]	Dec. 2, 1922	April 12, 1926
Daniel F. Steck (D)[10]	April 12, 1926	March 3, 1931
L. J. Dickinson (R)	March 4, 1931	Jan. 2, 1937
Clyde L. Herring (D)	Jan. 19, 1937	Jan. 2, 1943

George A. Wilson (R)	Jan. 14, 1943	Jan. 2, 1949
Guy M. Gillette (D)	Jan. 3, 1949	Jan. 2, 1955
Thomas E. Martin (R)	Jan. 3, 1955	Jan. 2, 1961
Jack Miller (R)	Jan. 3, 1961	Jan. 2, 1973
Dick Clark (D)	Jan. 3, 1973	Jan. 2, 1979
Roger W. Jepsen (R)	Jan. 3, 1979	Jan. 2, 1985
Tom Harkin (D)	Jan. 3, 1985	

Class 3

Augustus C. Dodge (D)[11]	Dec. 7, 1848	Feb. 22, 1855
James Harlan (R)[12]	March 4, 1855	Jan. 12, 1857
James Harlan (R)[13]	Jan. 29, 1857	May 15, 1865
Samuel J. Kirkwood (R)	Jan. 13, 1866	March 3, 1867
James Harlan (R)	March 4, 1867	March 3, 1873
William B. Allison (R)[14]	March 4, 1873	Aug. 4, 1908
Albert B. Cummins (R)[15]	Nov. 24, 1908	July 30, 1926
David W. Stewart (R)[16]	Aug. 7, 1926	March 3, 1927
Smith W. Brookhart (R)	March 4, 1927	March 3, 1933
Richard Louis Murphy (D)[17]	March 4, 1933	July 16, 1936
Guy M. Gillette (D)	Nov. 4, 1936	Jan. 2, 1945
Bourke B. Hickenlooper (R)	Jan. 3, 1945	Jan. 2, 1969
Harold E. Hughes (D)	Jan. 3, 1969	Jan. 2, 1975
John C. Culver (D)	Jan. 3, 1975	Jan. 2, 1981
Charles E. Grassley (R)	Jan. 3, 1981	

Iowa
1. Resigned Dec. 6, 1869.
2. Resigned March 7, 1881.
3. Appointed by governor to fill vacancy. Subsequently elected.
4. Died July 14, 1900.
5. Appointed by governor to fill vacancy. Subsequently elected. Died Oct. 15, 1910.
6. Appointed by governor to fill vacancy.
7. Resigned Feb. 24, 1922.
8. Appointed by governor to fill vacancy.
9. Elected to fill vacancy in term expiring March 3, 1925. Presented credentials for term expiring March 3, 1931, and was seated. Steck challenged Brookhart's right to the seat, alleging that ballots cast for Steck had either been rejected or counted for Brookhart, and that illegal votes had been cast for Brookhart. The Senate voted to unseat Brookhart and award the seat to Steck, who took the oath April 12, 1926, and served for the remainder of the term.
10. Successfully contested the election of Smith W. Brookhart.
11. Resigned Feb. 22, 1855.
12. Harlan was elected by the legislature for the term beginning March 4, 1855, and took his seat. The Senate voted Jan. 12, 1857, to deny him a seat, following protests that the legislature that elected him had not been properly constituted.
13. Elected to fill the vacancy caused by the Senate's having declared the seat vacant, and took his seat Jan. 29, 1857. Resigned May 15, 1865.
14. Died Aug. 4, 1908.
15. Died July 30, 1926.
16. Appointed by governor to fill vacancy. Subsequently elected.
17. Died July 16, 1936.

KANSAS

(Became a state Jan. 29, 1861)

Class 2

Senators	Dates of Service	
James H. Lane (R)[1]	April 4, 1861	July 11, 1866
Edmund G. Ross (R)[2]	July 19, 1866	March 3, 1871
Alexander Caldwell (R)[3]	March 4, 1871	March 24, 1873
Robert Crozier (R)[4]	Nov. 24, 1873	Feb. 2, 1874
James M. Harvey (R)	Feb. 2, 1874	March 3, 1877

Preston B. Plumb (R)[5]	March 4, 1877	Dec. 20, 1891
Bishop W. Perkins (R)[6]	Jan. 1, 1892	March 3, 1893
John Martin (D)	March 4, 1893	March 3, 1895
Lucien Baker (R)	March 4, 1895	March 3, 1901
Joseph R. Burton (R)[7]	March 4, 1901	June 4, 1906
Alfred W. Benson (R)[8]	June 11, 1906	Jan. 23, 1907
Charles Curtis (R)	Jan. 23, 1907	March 3, 1913
William H. Thompson (D)	March 4, 1913	March 3, 1919
Arthur Capper (R)	March 4, 1919	Jan. 2, 1949
Andrew F. Schoeppel (R)[9]	Jan. 3, 1949	Jan. 21, 1962
James B. Pearson (R)[10]	Jan. 31, 1962	Dec. 23, 1978
Nancy Landon Kassebaum (R)	Dec. 23, 1978	Jan. 2, 1997
Pat Roberts (R)	Jan. 3, 1997	

Class 3

Samuel C. Pomeroy (R)	April 4, 1861	March 3, 1873
John J. Ingalls (R)	March 4, 1873	March 3, 1891
William A. Peffer (POP)	March 4, 1891	March 3, 1897
William A. Harris (D)	March 4, 1897	March 3, 1903
Chester I. Long (R)	March 4, 1903	March 3, 1909
Joseph L. Bristow (R)	March 4, 1909	March 3, 1915
Charles Curtis (R)[11]	March 4, 1915	March 3, 1929
Henry J. Allen (R)[12]	April 1, 1929	Nov. 30, 1930
George McGill (D)	Dec. 1, 1930	Jan. 2, 1939
Clyde M. Reed (R)[13]	Jan. 3, 1939	Nov. 8, 1949
Harry Darby (R)[14]	Dec. 2, 1949	Nov. 28, 1950
Frank Carlson (R)	Nov. 29, 1950	Jan. 2, 1969
Robert Dole (R)[15]	Jan. 3, 1969	June 11, 1996
Sheila Frahm (R)[16]	June 11, 1996	Nov. 27, 1996
Sam Brownback (R)	Nov. 27, 1996	

Kansas
1. Died July 11, 1866.
2. Appointed by governor to fill vacancy. Subsequently elected.
3. Resigned March 24, 1873.
4. Appointed by governor to fill vacancy.
5. Died Dec. 20, 1891.
6. Appointed by governor to fill vacancy.
7. Resigned June 4, 1906.
8. Appointed by governor to fill vacancy.
9. Died Jan. 21, 1962.
10. Appointed by governor to fill vacancy. Subsequently elected. Resigned Dec. 23, 1978.
11. Resigned March 3, 1929.
12. Appointed by governor to fill vacancy.
13. Died Nov. 8, 1949.
14. Appointed by governor to fill vacancy.
15. Resigned June 11, 1996.
16. Appointed by governor to fill vacancy. Resigned Nov. 27, 1996.

KENTUCKY

(Became a state June 1, 1792)

Class 2

Senators	Dates of Service	
John Brown (D-R)	June 18, 1792	March 3, 1805
Buckner Thruston (D-R)[1]	March 4, 1805	Dec. 18, 1809
Henry Clay (D-R)	Jan. 4, 1810	March 3, 1811
George M. Bibb (D-R)[2]	March 4, 1811	Aug. 23, 1814
George Walker (D-R)[3]	Aug. 30, 1814	Dec. 16, 1814

William T. Barry (D-R)[4]	Dec. 16, 1814	May 1, 1816
Martin D. Hardin (D-R)[5]	Nov. 13, 1816	March 3, 1817
John J. Crittenden (D-R)[6]	March 4, 1817	March 3, 1819
Richard M. Johnson (D-R)	Dec. 10, 1819	March 3, 1829
George M. Bibb (D-R)	March 4, 1829	March 3, 1835
John J. Crittenden (W)	March 4, 1835	March 3, 1841
James T. Morehead (W)	March 4, 1841	March 3, 1847
Joseph R. Underwood (W)	March 4, 1847	March 3, 1853
John B. Thompson (W)	March 4, 1853	March 3, 1859
Lazarus W. Powell (D)	March 4, 1859	March 3, 1865
James Guthrie (D)[7]	March 4, 1865	Feb. 7, 1868
Thomas C. McCreery (D)	Feb. 19, 1868	March 3, 1871
John W. Stevenson (D)	March 4, 1871	March 3, 1877
James B. Beck (D)[8]	March 4, 1877	May 3, 1890
John G. Carlisle (D)[9]	May 17, 1890	Feb. 4, 1893
William Lindsay (D)	Feb. 15, 1893	March 3, 1901
Joseph C. S. Blackburn (D)	March 4, 1901	March 3, 1907
Thomas H. Paynter (D)	March 4, 1907	March 3, 1913
Ollie M. James (D)[10]	March 4, 1913	Aug. 28, 1918
George B. Martin (D)[11]	Sept. 7, 1918	March 3, 1919
A. Owsley Stanley (D)	March 4, 1919	March 3, 1925
Fred M. Sackett (R)[12]	March 4, 1925	Jan. 9, 1930
John M. Robsion (R)[13]	Jan. 9, 1930	Nov. 30, 1930
Ben M. Williamson (D)	Dec. 1, 1930	March 3, 1931
Marvel M. Logan (D)[14]	March 4, 1931	Oct. 3, 1939
Albert B. Chandler (D)[15]	Oct. 10, 1939	Nov. 1, 1945
William A. Stanfill (R)[16]	Nov. 19, 1945	Nov. 5, 1946
John Sherman Cooper (R)	Nov. 6, 1946	Jan. 2, 1949
Virgil Chapman (D)[17]	Jan. 3, 1949	March 8, 1951
Thomas R. Underwood (D)[18]	March 19, 1951	Nov. 4, 1952
John Sherman Cooper (R)	Nov. 5, 1952	Jan. 2, 1955
Alben W. Barkley (D)[19]	Jan. 3, 1955	April 30, 1956
Robert Humphreys (D)[20]	June 21, 1956	Nov. 6, 1956
John Sherman Cooper (R)	Nov. 7, 1956	Jan. 2, 1973
Walter D. Huddleston (D)	Jan. 3, 1973	Jan. 2, 1985
Mitch McConnell (R)	Jan. 3, 1985	

Class 3

John Edwards (D-R)	June 18, 1792	March 3, 1795
Humphrey Marshall (FED)	March 4, 1795	March 3, 1801
John Breckinridge (D-R)[21]	March 4, 1801	Aug. 7, 1805
John Adair (D-R)[22]	Nov. 8, 1805	Nov. 18, 1806
Henry Clay (D-R)	Dec. 29, 1806	March 3, 1807
John Pope (D-R)	March 4, 1807	March 3, 1813
Jesse Bledsoe (D-R)[23]	March 4, 1813	Dec. 24, 1814
Isham Talbot (D-R)	Jan. 5, 1815	March 3, 1819
William Logan (D-R)[24]	March 4, 1819	May 28, 1820
Isham Talbot (D-R)	Oct. 19, 1820	March 3, 1825
John Rowan (D-R)	March 4, 1825	March 3, 1831
Henry Clay (NR, W)[25]	Nov. 10, 1831	March 31, 1842
John J. Crittenden (W)[26]	March 31, 1842	June 12, 1848
Thomas Metcalfe[27]	June 23, 1848	March 3, 1849
Henry Clay (W)[28]	March 4, 1849	June 29, 1852
David Meriwether (D)[29]	July 6, 1852	Sept. 1, 1852
Archibald Dixon (W)	Sept. 1, 1852	March 3, 1855
John J. Crittenden (W)	March 4, 1855	March 3, 1861

John C. Breckinridge (D)[30]	March 4, 1861	Dec. 4, 1861
Garrett Davis (D)[31]	Dec. 10, 1861	Sept. 22, 1872
Willis B. Machen (D)[32]	Sept. 27, 1872	March 3, 1873
Thomas C. McCreery (D)	March 4, 1873	March 3, 1879
John Stuart Williams (D)	March 4, 1879	March 3, 1885
Joseph C. S. Blackburn (D)	March 4, 1885	March 3, 1897
William J. Deboe (R)	March 4, 1897	March 3, 1903
James B. McCreary (D)	March 4, 1903	March 3, 1909
William O. Bradley (R)[33]	March 4, 1909	May 23, 1914
Johnson N. Camden Jr. (D)[34]	June 16, 1914	March 3, 1915
John C. W. Beckham (D)	March 4, 1915	March 3, 1921
Richard P. Ernst (R)	March 4, 1921	March 3, 1927
Alben W. Barkley (D)[35]	March 4, 1927	Jan. 19, 1949
Garrett L. Withers (D)[36]	Jan. 20, 1949	Nov. 26, 1950
Earle C. Clements (D)	Nov. 27, 1950	Jan. 2, 1957
Thruston B. Morton (R)[37]	Jan. 3, 1957	Dec. 16, 1968
Marlow W. Cook (R)[38]	Dec. 17, 1968	Dec. 27, 1974
Wendell H. Ford (D)	Dec. 28, 1974	Jan. 3, 1999
Jim Bunning (R)	Jan. 3, 1999	

Kentucky

1. Resigned Dec. 18, 1809.
2. Resigned Aug. 23, 1814.
3. Appointed by governor to fill vacancy.
4. Resigned May 1, 1816.
5. Appointed by governor to fill vacancy. Subsequently elected.
6. Resigned March 3, 1819.
7. Resigned Feb. 7, 1868.
8. Died May 3, 1890.
9. Resigned Feb. 4, 1893.
10. Died Aug. 28, 1918.
11. Appointed by governor to fill vacancy.
12. Resigned Jan. 9, 1930.
13. Appointed by governor to fill vacancy.
14. Died Oct. 3, 1939.
15. Appointed by governor to fill vacancy. Subsequently elected. Resigned Nov. 1, 1945.
16. Appointed by governor to fill vacancy.
17. Died March 8, 1951.
18. Appointed by governor to fill vacancy.
19. Died April 30, 1956.
20. Appointed by governor to fill vacancy.
21. Resigned Aug. 7, 1805.
22. Resigned Nov. 18, 1806.
23. Resigned Dec. 24, 1814.
24. Resigned May 28, 1820.
25. Resigned March 31, 1842.
26. Resigned June 12, 1848.
27. Appointed by governor to fill vacancy. Subsequently elected.
28. Died June 29, 1852.
29. Appointed by governor to fill vacancy.
30. Expelled Dec. 4, 1861.
31. Died Sept. 22, 1872.
32. Appointed by governor to fill vacancy. Subsequently elected.
33. Died May 23, 1914.
34. Appointed by governor to fill vacancy. Subsequently elected.
35. Resigned Jan. 19, 1949, to become vice president of the United States.
36. Appointed by governor to fill vacancy.
37. Resigned Dec. 16, 1968.
38. Resigned Dec. 27, 1974.

LOUISIANA

(Became a state April 30, 1812)

Class 2

Senators	Dates of Service	
John N. Destrehan (D-R)[1]		
Thomas Posey (D-R)[2]	Oct. 8, 1812	Feb. 4, 1813
James Brown (D-R)	Feb. 5, 1813	March 3, 1817
William C. C. Claiborne (D-R)[3]	March 4, 1817	Nov. 23, 1817
Henry Johnson (D-R)[4]	Jan. 12, 1818	May 27, 1824
Dominique Bouligny (D-R)	Nov. 19, 1824	March 3, 1829
Edward Livingston (D)[5]	March 4, 1829	May 24, 1831
George A. Waggaman (NR)	Nov. 15, 1831	March 3, 1835
Robert C. Nicholas (D)	Jan. 13, 1836	March 3, 1841
Alexander Barrow (W)[6]	March 4, 1841	Dec. 29, 1846
Pierre Soulé (D)	Jan. 21, 1847	March 3, 1847
Solomon W. Downs (D)	March 4, 1847	March 3, 1853
Judah P. Benjamin (W, D)[7]	March 4, 1853	March 14, 1861
John S. Harris (R)	July 17, 1868	March 3, 1871
J. Rodman West (R)	March 4, 1871	March 3, 1877
William P. Kellogg (R)	March 4, 1877	March 3, 1883
Randall L. Gibson (D)[8]	March 4, 1883	Dec. 15, 1892
Donelson Caffery (D)[9]	Dec. 31, 1892	March 3, 1901
Murphy J. Foster (D)	March 4, 1901	March 3, 1913
Joseph E. Ransdell (D)	March 4, 1913	March 3, 1931
Huey P. Long (D)[10]	Jan. 25, 1932	Sept. 10, 1935
Rose McConnell Long (D)[11]	Jan. 31, 1936	Jan. 2, 1937
Allen J. Ellender (D)[12]	Jan. 3, 1937	July 27, 1972
Elaine S. Edwards (D)[13]	Aug. 1, 1972	Nov. 13, 1972
J. Bennett Johnston (D)	Nov. 14, 1972	Jan. 2, 1997
Mary L. Landrieu (D)	Jan. 3, 1997	

Class 3

Allan B. Magruder (D-R)	Sept. 3, 1812	March 3, 1813
Eligius Fromentin (D-R)	March 4, 1813	March 3, 1819
James Brown (D-R)[14]	March 4, 1819	Dec. 10, 1823
Josiah S. Johnston (D-R)[15]	Jan. 15, 1824	May 19, 1833
Alexander Porter (W)[16]	Dec. 19, 1833	Jan. 5, 1837
Alexander Mouton (D)[17]	Jan. 12, 1837	March 1, 1842
Charles M. Conrad (W)	April 14, 1842	March 3, 1843
Henry Johnson (W)[18]	Feb. 12, 1844	March 3, 1849
Pierre Soulé (D)[19]	March 4, 1849	April 11, 1853
John Slidell (D)[20]	April 28, 1853	Feb. 4, 1861
William P. Kellogg (R)[21]	July 17, 1868	Nov. 1, 1872
James B. Eustis (D)	Jan. 12, 1876	March 3, 1879
Benjamin F. Jonas (D)	March 4, 1879	March 3, 1885
James B. Eustis (D)	March 4, 1885	March 3, 1891
Edward D. White (D)[22]	March 4, 1891	March 12, 1894
Newton C. Blanchard (D)[23]	March 12, 1894	March 3, 1897
Samuel D. McEnery (D)[24]	March 4, 1897	June 28, 1910
John R. Thornton (D)	Dec. 7, 1910	March 3, 1915
Robert F. Broussard (D)[25]	March 4, 1915	April 12, 1918
Walter Guion (D)[26]	April 22, 1918	Nov. 5, 1918
Edward J. Gay (D)	Nov. 6, 1918	March 3, 1921
Edwin S. Broussard (D)	March 4, 1921	March 3, 1933
John H. Overton (D)[27]	March 4, 1933	May 14, 1948

William C. Feazel (D)[28]	May 18, 1948	Dec. 30, 1948
Russell B. Long (D)	Dec. 31, 1948	Jan. 2, 1987
John B. Breaux (D)	Jan. 3, 1987	

Louisiana
1. Elected Sept. 3, 1812, but did not take oath. Resigned Oct. 1, 1812.
2. Appointed by governor to fill vacancy.
3. Died Nov. 23, 1817.
4. Resigned May 27, 1824.
5. Resigned May 24, 1831.
6. Died Dec. 29, 1846.
7. Seat declared vacant March 14, 1861. Vacancy until July 17, 1868, because of Civil War.
8. Died Dec. 15, 1892.
9. Appointed by governor to fill vacancy. Subsequently elected.
10. Elected Nov. 4, 1930, but did not take oath until Jan. 25, 1932. Governor during interim. Died Sept. 10, 1935.
11. Appointed by governor to fill vacancy. Subsequently elected.
12. Died July 27, 1972.
13. Appointed by governor to fill vacancy. Resigned Nov. 13, 1972.
14. Resigned Dec. 10, 1823.
15. Died May 19, 1833.
16. Resigned Jan. 5, 1837.
17. Resigned March 1, 1842.
18. Vacancy from March 4, 1843, to Feb. 12, 1844.
19. Resigned April 11, 1853.
20. Retired Feb. 4, 1861. Vacancy until July 17, 1868, because of Civil War.
21. Resigned Nov. 1, 1872. Vacancy from Nov. 1, 1872, until Jan. 12, 1876.
22. Resigned March 12, 1894.
23. Appointed by governor to fill vacancy. Subsequently elected.
24. Died June 28, 1910.
25. Died April 12, 1918.
26. Appointed by governor to fill vacancy.
27. Died May 14, 1948.
28. Appointed by governor to fill vacancy.

MAINE

(Became a state March 15, 1820)

Class 1

Senators	Dates of Service	
John Holmes (D-R)	June 13, 1820	March 3, 1827
Albion K. Parris (D-R)[1]	March 4, 1827	Aug. 26, 1828
John Holmes (NR)	Jan. 15, 1829	March 3, 1833
Ether Shepley (D)[2]	March 4, 1833	March 3, 1836
Judah Dana (D)[3]	Dec. 7, 1836	Feb. 22, 1837
Reuel Williams (D)[4]	Feb. 22, 1837	Feb. 15, 1843
John Fairfield (D)[5]	March 3, 1843	Dec. 24, 1847
Wyman B. S. Moor (D)[6]	Jan. 5, 1848	May 26, 1848
Hannibal Hamlin (D)[7]	June 8, 1848	Jan. 7, 1857
Amos Nourse	Jan. 16, 1857	March 3, 1857
Hannibal Hamlin (R)[8]	March 4, 1857	Jan. 17, 1861
Lot Myrick Morrill (R)	Jan. 17, 1861	March 3, 1869
Hannibal Hamlin (R)	March 4, 1869	March 3, 1881
Eugene Hale (R)	March 4, 1881	March 3, 1911
Charles F. Johnson (D)	March 4, 1911	March 3, 1917
Frederick Hale (R)	March 4, 1917	Jan. 2, 1941
Ralph O. Brewster (R)	Jan. 3, 1941	Jan. 2, 1953
Frederick G. Payne (R)	Jan. 3, 1953	Jan. 2, 1959
Edmund S. Muskie (D)[9]	Jan. 3, 1959	May 7, 1980
George J. Mitchell (D)[10]	May 17, 1980	Jan. 2, 1995
Olympia J. Snowe (R)	Jan. 3, 1995	

Class 2

John Chandler (D-R)	June 14, 1820	March 3, 1829
Peleg Sprague (NR)[11]	March 4, 1829	Jan. 1, 1835
John Ruggles (D)	Jan. 20, 1835	March 3, 1841
George Evans (W)	March 4, 1841	March 3, 1847
James W. Bradbury (D)	March 4, 1847	March 3, 1853
William P. Fessenden (R)[12]	Feb. 10, 1854	July 1, 1864
Nathan A. Farwell (R)[13]	Oct. 27, 1864	March 3, 1865
William P. Fessenden (R)[14]	March 4, 1865	Sept. 9, 1869
Lot Myrick Morrill (R)[15]	Oct. 30, 1869	July 7, 1876
James G. Blaine (R)[16]	July 10, 1876	March 5, 1881
William P. Frye (R)[17]	March 18, 1881	Aug. 8, 1911
Obadiah Gardner (D)[18]	Sept. 23, 1911	March 3, 1913
Edwin C. Burleigh (R)[19]	March 4, 1913	June 16, 1916
Bert M. Fernald (R)[20]	Sept. 12, 1916	Aug. 23, 1926
Arthur R. Gould (R)	Nov. 30, 1926	March 3, 1931
Wallace H. White Jr. (R)	March 4, 1931	Jan. 2, 1949
Margaret Chase Smith (R)	Jan. 3, 1949	Jan. 2, 1973
William D. Hathaway (D)	Jan. 3, 1973	Jan. 2, 1979
William S. Cohen (R)	Jan. 3, 1979	Jan. 2, 1997
Susan Collins (R)	Jan. 3, 1997	

Maine
 1. Resigned Aug. 26, 1828.
 2. Resigned March 3, 1836.
 3. Appointed by governor to fill vacancy.
 4. Resigned Feb. 15, 1843.
 5. Died Dec. 24, 1847.
 6. Appointed by governor to fill vacancy.
 7. Resigned Jan. 7, 1857.
 8. Resigned Jan. 17, 1861, to become vice president of the United States.
 9. Resigned May 7, 1980.
 10. Appointed by governor to fill vacancy. Subsequently elected.
 11. Resigned Jan. 1, 1835.
 12. Resigned July 1, 1864.
 13. Appointed by governor to fill vacancy. Subsequently elected.
 14. Died Sept. 9, 1869.
 15. Appointed by governor to fill vacancy. Subsequently elected. Resigned July 7, 1876.
 16. Appointed by governor to fill vacancy. Subsequently elected. Resigned March 5, 1881.
 17. Died Aug. 8, 1911.
 18. Appointed by governor to fill vacancy. Subsequently elected.
 19. Died June 16, 1916.
 20. Died Aug. 23, 1926.

MARYLAND

(Ratified the Constitution April 28, 1788)

Class 1

Senators	Dates of Service	
Charles Carroll (FED)[1]	March 4, 1789	Nov. 30, 1792
Richard Potts (FED)[2]	Jan. 10, 1793	Oct. 24, 1796
John E. Howard (FED)	Nov. 30, 1796	March 3, 1803
Samuel Smith (D-R)[3]	March 4, 1803	March 3, 1815
Robert G. Harper[4]	Jan. 29, 1816	Dec. 6, 1816
Alexander C. Hanson (FED)[5]	Dec. 20, 1816	April 23, 1819
William Pinkney (D-R)[6]	Dec. 21, 1819	Feb. 25, 1822
Samuel Smith (D-R)	Dec. 17, 1822	March 3, 1833
Joseph Kent (NR)[7]	March 4, 1833	Nov. 24, 1837

William D. Merrick (W)	Jan. 4, 1838	March 3, 1845
Reverdy Johnson (W)[8]	March 4, 1845	March 7, 1849
David Stewart (W)[9]	Dec. 6, 1849	Jan. 12, 1850
Thomas G. Pratt (W)	Jan. 12, 1850	March 3, 1857
Anthony Kennedy (UN)	March 4, 1857	March 3, 1863
Reverdy Johnson (D)[10]	March 4, 1863	July 10, 1868
William Pinkney Whyte (D)[11]	July 13, 1868	March 3, 1869
William T. Hamilton (D)	March 4, 1869	March 3, 1875
William Pinkney Whyte (D)	March 4, 1875	March 3, 1881
Arthur P. Gorman (D)	March 4, 1881	March 3, 1899
Louis E. McComas (R)	March 4, 1899	March 3, 1905
Isidor Rayner (D)[12]	March 4, 1905	Nov. 25, 1912
William P. Jackson (R)[13]	Nov. 29, 1912	Jan. 28, 1914
Blair Lee (D)	Jan. 29, 1914	March 3, 1917
Joseph I. France (R)	March 4, 1917	March 3, 1923
William Cabell Bruce (D)	March 4, 1923	March 3, 1929
Phillips Lee Goldsborough (R)	March 4, 1929	Jan. 2, 1935
George W. Radcliffe (D)	Jan. 3, 1935	Jan. 2, 1947
Herbert R. O'Conor (D)	Jan. 3, 1947	Jan. 2, 1953
J. Glenn Beall (R)	Jan. 3, 1953	Jan. 2, 1965
Joseph D. Tydings (D)	Jan. 3, 1965	Jan. 2, 1971
J. Glenn Beall Jr. (R)	Jan. 3, 1971	Jan. 2, 1977
Paul S. Sarbanes (D)	Jan. 3, 1977	

Class 3

John Henry (D-R)[14]	March 4, 1789	Dec. 10, 1797
James Lloyd (D-R)[15]	Dec. 11, 1797	Dec. 1, 1800
William Hindman (FED)[16]	Dec. 12, 1800	Nov. 19, 1801
Robert Wright (D-R)[17]	Nov. 19, 1801	Nov. 12, 1806
Philip Reed (D-R)	Nov. 25, 1806	March 3, 1813
Robert H. Goldsborough (FED)	May 21, 1813	March 3, 1819
Edward Lloyd (D-R)[18]	Dec. 21, 1819	Jan. 14, 1826
Ezekiel F. Chambers (W)[19]	Jan. 24, 1826	Dec. 20, 1834
Robert H. Goldsborough (W)[20]	Jan. 13, 1835	Oct. 5, 1836
John S. Spence (W)[21]	Dec. 31, 1836	Oct. 24, 1840
John Leeds Kerr (W)	Jan. 5, 1841	March 3, 1843
James A. Pearce (W, D)[22]	March 4, 1843	Dec. 20, 1862
Thomas H. Hicks (R)[23]	Dec. 29, 1862	Feb. 14, 1865
John A. J. Creswell (R)	March 9, 1865	March 3, 1867
George Vickers (D)[24]	March 7, 1868	March 3, 1873
George R. Dennis (D)	March 4, 1873	March 3, 1879
James B. Groome (D)	March 4, 1879	March 3, 1885
Ephraim King Wilson (D)[25]	March 4, 1885	Feb. 24, 1891
Charles H. Gibson (D)[26]	Nov. 19, 1891	March 3, 1897
George L. Wellington (R)	March 4, 1897	March 3, 1903
Arthur P. Gorman (D)[27]	March 4, 1903	June 4, 1906
William Pinkney Whyte (D)[28]	June 8, 1906	March 17, 1908
John Walter Smith (D)	March 25, 1908	March 3, 1921
Ovington E. Weller (R)	March 4, 1921	March 3, 1927
Millard E. Tydings (D)	March 4, 1927	Jan. 2, 1951
John Marshall Butler (R)	Jan. 3, 1951	Jan. 2, 1963
Daniel B. Brewster (D)	Jan. 3, 1963	Jan. 2, 1969
Charles Mathias Jr. (R)	Jan. 3, 1969	Jan. 2, 1987
Barbara A. Mikulski (D)	Jan. 3, 1987	

Maryland
1. Resigned Nov. 30, 1792.
2. Resigned Oct. 24, 1796.
3. Served continuously during this period, twice by election, once by appointment of the governor.
4. Resigned Dec. 6, 1816.
5. Died April 23, 1819.
6. Died Feb. 25, 1822.
7. Died Nov. 24, 1837.
8. Resigned March 7, 1849.
9. Appointed by governor to fill vacancy.
10. Resigned July 10, 1868.
11. Appointed by governor to fill vacancy.
12. Died Nov. 25, 1912.
13. Appointed by governor to fill vacancy.
14. Resigned Dec. 10, 1797.
15. Resigned Dec. 1, 1800.
16. Served first by election and subsequently by appointment of the governor during this period.
17. Resigned Nov. 12, 1806.
18. Resigned Jan. 14, 1826.
19. Resigned Dec. 20, 1834.
20. Died Oct. 5, 1836.
21. Died Oct. 24, 1840.
22. Died Dec. 20, 1862.
23. Appointed by governor to fill vacancy. Subsequently elected. Died Feb. 14, 1865.
24. Vacancy from March 4, 1867, to March 7, 1868.
25. Died Feb. 24, 1891.
26. Appointed by governor to fill vacancy. Subsequently elected.
27. Died June 4, 1906.
28. Appointed by governor to fill vacancy. Subsequently elected. Died March 17, 1908.

MASSACHUSETTS

(Ratified the Constitution Feb. 6, 1788)

Class 1

Senators	Dates of Service	
Tristram Dalton (FED)	March 4, 1789	March 3, 1791
George Cabot (FED)[1]	March 4, 1791	June 9, 1796
Benjamin Goodhue (FED)[2]	June 11, 1796	Nov. 8, 1800
Jonathan Mason (FED)	Nov. 14, 1800	March 3, 1803
John Quincy Adams (FED, D-R)[3]	March 4, 1803	June 8, 1808
James Lloyd (FED)[4]	June 9, 1808	May 1, 1813
Christopher Gore (FED)[5]	May 5, 1813	May 30, 1816
Eli P. Ashmun (FED)[6]	June 12, 1816	May 10, 1818
Prentiss Mellen (FED)[7]	June 5, 1818	May 15, 1820
Elijah H. Mills (FED)	June 12, 1820	March 3, 1827
Daniel Webster (D-R, NR, W)[8]	May 30, 1827	Feb. 22, 1841
Rufus Choate (W)	Feb. 23, 1841	March 3, 1845
Daniel Webster (W)[9]	March 4, 1845	July 22, 1850
Robert C. Winthrop (W)[10]	July 30, 1850	Feb. 1, 1851
Robert Rantoul (D)	Feb. 1, 1851	March 3, 1851
Charles Sumner (F SOIL, R)[11]	March 4, 1851	March 11, 1874
William B. Washburn (R)	April 17, 1874	March 3, 1875
Henry L. Dawes (R)	March 4, 1875	March 3, 1893
Henry Cabot Lodge (R)[12]	March 4, 1893	Nov. 9, 1924
William M. Butler (R)[13]	Nov. 13, 1924	Dec. 5, 1926
David I. Walsh (D)	Dec. 6, 1926	Jan. 2, 1947
Henry Cabot Lodge Jr. (R)	Jan. 3, 1947	Jan. 2, 1953
John F. Kennedy (D)[14]	Jan. 3, 1953	Dec. 22, 1960
Benjamin A. Smith II (D)[15]	Dec. 27, 1960	Nov. 6, 1962
Edward M. Kennedy (D)	Nov. 7, 1962	

Class 2

Caleb Strong (FED)[16]	March 4, 1789	June 1, 1796
Theodore Sedgwick (FED)	June 11, 1796	March 3, 1799
Samuel Dexter (FED)[17]	March 4, 1799	May 30, 1800
Dwight Foster (FED)[18]	June 6, 1800	March 3, 1803
Timothy Pickering (FED)	March 4, 1803	March 3, 1811
Joseph B. Varnum (D-R)	June 8, 1811	March 3, 1817
Harrison Gray Otis (FED)[19]	March 4, 1817	May 30, 1822
James Lloyd (FED)[20]	June 5, 1822	May 23, 1826
Nathaniel Silsbee (D-R, NR)	May 31, 1826	March 3, 1835
John Davis (W)[21]	March 4, 1835	Jan. 5, 1841
Isaac C. Bates (W)[22]	Jan. 13, 1841	March 16, 1845
John Davis (W)	March 24, 1845	March 3, 1853
Edward Everett (W)[23]	March 4, 1853	June 1, 1854
Julius Rockwell[24]	June 3, 1854	Jan. 31, 1855
Henry Wilson (R)[25]	Jan. 31, 1855	March 3, 1873
George S. Boutwell (R)	March 12, 1873	March 3, 1877
George F. Hoar (R)[26]	March 4, 1877	Sept. 30, 1904
Winthrop Murray Crane (R)[27]	Oct. 12, 1904	March 3, 1913
John W. Weeks (R)	March 4, 1913	March 3, 1919
David I. Walsh (D)	March 4, 1919	March 3, 1925
Frederick H. Gillett (R)	March 4, 1925	March 3, 1931
Marcus A. Coolidge (D)	March 4, 1931	March 3, 1937
Henry Cabot Lodge Jr. (R)[28]	Jan. 3, 1937	Feb. 3, 1944
Sinclair Weeks (R)[29]	Feb. 8, 1944	Dec. 19, 1944
Leverett Saltonstall (R)	Jan. 10, 1945	Jan. 2, 1967
Edward W. Brooke (R)	Jan. 3, 1967	Jan. 2, 1979
Paul E. Tsongas (D)[30]	Jan. 3, 1979	Jan. 2, 1985
John F. Kerry (D)	Jan. 2, 1985	

Massachusetts
1. Resigned June 9, 1796.
2. Resigned Nov. 8, 1800.
3. Resigned June 8, 1808.
4. Resigned May 1, 1813.
5. Appointed by governor to fill vacancy. Subsequently elected. Resigned May 30, 1816.
6. Resigned May 10, 1818.
7. Resigned May 15, 1820.
8. Resigned Feb. 22, 1841.
9. Resigned July 22, 1850.
10. Appointed by governor to fill vacancy.
11. Died March 11, 1874.
12. Died Nov. 9, 1924.
13. Appointed by governor to fill vacancy.
14. Resigned Dec. 22, 1960, having been elected president of the United States.
15. Appointed by governor to fill vacancy.
16. Resigned June 1, 1796.
17. Resigned May 30, 1800.
18. Resigned March 3, 1803.
19. Resigned May 30, 1822.
20. Resigned May 23, 1826.
21. Resigned Jan. 5, 1841.
22. Died March 16, 1845.
23. Resigned June 1, 1854.
24. Appointed by governor to fill vacancy.
25. Resigned March 3, 1873.
26. Died Sept. 30, 1904.
27. Appointed by governor to fill vacancy. Subsequently elected.
28. Resigned Feb. 3, 1944.
29. Appointed by governor to fill vacancy.
30. Resigned Jan. 2, 1985.

MICHIGAN

(Became a state Jan. 26, 1837)

Class 1

Senators	Dates of Service	
Lucius Lyon (D)	Jan. 26, 1837	March 3, 1839
Augustus S. Porter (W)	Jan. 20, 1840	March 3, 1845
Lewis Cass (D)[1]	March 4, 1845	May 29, 1848
Thomas Fitzgerald (D)[2]	June 8, 1848	March 3, 1849
Lewis Cass (D)	March 4, 1849	March 3, 1857
Zachariah Chandler (R)	March 4, 1857	March 3, 1875
Isaac P. Christiancy (R)[3]	March 4, 1875	Feb. 10, 1879
Zachariah Chandler (R)[4]	Feb. 19, 1879	Nov. 1, 1879
Henry P. Baldwin (R)[5]	Nov. 17, 1879	March 3, 1881
Omar D. Conger (R)	March 4, 1881	March 3, 1887
Francis B. Stockbridge (R)[6]	March 4, 1887	April 30, 1894
John Patton Jr. (R)[7]	May 5, 1894	Jan. 14, 1895
Julius C. Burrows (R)	Jan. 23, 1895	March 3, 1911
Charles E. Townsend (R)	March 4, 1911	March 3, 1923
Woodbridge N. Ferris (D)[8]	March 4, 1923	March 23, 1928
Arthur H. Vandenberg (R)[9]	March 31, 1928	April 18, 1951
Blair Moody (D)[10]	April 22, 1951	Nov. 4, 1952
Charles E. Potter (R)	Nov. 5, 1952	Jan. 2, 1959
Philip A. Hart (D)[11]	Jan. 3, 1959	Dec. 26, 1976
Donald W. Riegle Jr. (D)	Dec. 30, 1976	Jan. 2, 1995
Spencer Abraham (R)	Jan. 3, 1995	Jan. 3, 2001
Debbie Stabenow (D)	Jan. 3, 2001	

Class 2

John Norvell (D)	Jan. 26, 1837	March 3, 1841
William Woodbridge (W)	March 4, 1841	March 3, 1847
Alpheus Felch (D)	March 4, 1847	March 3, 1853
Charles E. Stuart (D)	March 4, 1853	March 3, 1859
Kinsley S. Bingham (R)[12]	March 4, 1859	Oct. 5, 1861
Jacob M. Howard (R)	Jan. 4, 1862	March 3, 1871
Thomas W. Ferry (R)	March 4, 1871	March 3, 1883
Thomas W. Palmer (R)	March 4, 1883	March 3, 1889
James McMillan (R)[13]	March 4, 1889	Aug. 10, 1902
Russell A. Alger (R)[14]	Sept. 27, 1902	Jan. 24, 1907
William Alden Smith (R)	Feb. 6, 1907	March 3, 1919
Truman H. Newberry (R)[15]	March 4, 1919	Nov. 18, 1922
James Couzens (R)[16]	Nov. 29, 1922	Oct. 22, 1936
Prentiss M. Brown (D)	Nov. 19, 1936	Jan. 2, 1943
Homer Ferguson (R)	Jan. 3, 1943	Jan. 2, 1955
Patrick V. McNamara (D)[17]	Jan. 3, 1955	April 30, 1966
Robert P. Griffin (R)[18]	May 11, 1966	Jan. 2, 1979
Carl Levin (D)	Jan. 3, 1979	

Michigan
1. Resigned May 29, 1848.
2. Appointed by governor to fill vacancy.
3. Resigned Feb. 10, 1879.
4. Died Nov. 1, 1879.
5. Appointed by governor to fill vacancy. Subsequently elected.
6. Died April 30, 1894.
7. Appointed by governor to fill vacancy.
8. Died March 23, 1928.
9. Appointed by governor to fill vacancy. Subsequently elected. Died April 18, 1951.
10. Appointed by governor to fill vacancy.
11. Died Dec. 26, 1976.

12. Died Oct. 5, 1861.
13. Died Aug. 10, 1902.
14. Appointed by governor to fill vacancy. Subsequently elected. Died Jan. 24, 1907.
15. Resigned Nov. 18, 1922.
16. Appointed by governor to fill vacancy. Subsequently elected. Died Oct. 22, 1936.
17. Died April 30, 1966.
18. Appointed by governor to fill vacancy. Subsequently elected.

MINNESOTA

(Became a state May 11, 1858)

Class 1

Senators	Dates of Service	
Henry M. Rice (D)	May 11, 1858	March 3, 1863
Alexander Ramsey (R)	March 4, 1863	March 3, 1875
Samuel J. R. McMillan (R)	March 4, 1875	March 3, 1887
Cushman K. Davis (R)[1]	March 4, 1887	Nov. 27, 1900
Charles A. Towne (D)[2]	Dec. 5, 1900	Jan. 23, 1901
Moses E. Clapp (R)	Jan. 23, 1901	March 3, 1917
Frank B. Kellogg (R)	March 4, 1917	March 3, 1923
Henrik Shipstead (F-LAB, R)[3]	March 4, 1923	Jan. 2, 1947
Edward J. Thye (R)	Jan. 3, 1947	Jan. 2, 1959
Eugene J. McCarthy (DFL)	Jan. 3, 1959	Jan. 2, 1971
Hubert H. Humphrey (DFL)[4]	Jan. 3, 1971	Jan. 13, 1978
Muriel Humphrey (DFL)[5]	Jan. 25, 1978	Nov. 7, 1978
Dave Durenberger (I-R)	Nov. 8, 1978	Jan. 2, 1995
Rod Grams (R)	Jan. 3, 1995	Jan. 3, 2001
Mark Dayton (D)	Jan. 3, 2001	

Class 2

James Shields (D)	May 11, 1858	March 3, 1859
Morton S. Wilkinson (R)	March 4, 1859	March 3, 1865
Daniel S. Norton (R)[6]	March 4, 1865	July 13, 1870
William Windom (R)[7]	July 15, 1870	Jan. 22, 1871
Ozora P. Stearns (R)	Jan. 23, 1871	March 3, 1871
William Windom (R)[8]	March 4, 1871	March 4, 1881
A. J. Edgerton (R)[9]	March 12, 1881	Oct. 26, 1881
William Windom (R)	Oct. 27, 1881	March 3, 1883
Dwight M. Sabin (R)	March 4, 1883	March 3, 1889
William D. Washburn (R)	March 4, 1889	March 3, 1895
Knute Nelson (R)[10]	March 4, 1895	April 28, 1923
Magnus Johnson (F-LAB)	July 16, 1923	March 3, 1925
Thomas D. Schall (R)[11]	March 4, 1925	Dec. 22, 1935
Elmer A. Benson (F-LAB)[12]	Dec. 27, 1935	Nov. 3, 1936
Guy V. Howard (R)	Nov. 4, 1936	Jan. 2, 1937
Ernest Lundeen (F-LAB)[13]	Jan. 3, 1937	Aug. 31, 1940
Joseph H. Ball (R)[14]	Oct. 14, 1940	Nov. 17, 1942
Arthur E. Nelson (R)	Nov. 18, 1942	Jan. 2, 1943
Joseph H. Ball (R)	Jan. 3, 1943	Jan. 2, 1949
Hubert H. Humphrey (DFL)[15]	Jan. 3, 1949	Dec. 29, 1964
Walter F. Mondale (DFL)[16]	Dec. 30, 1964	Dec. 30, 1976
Wendell R. Anderson (DFL)[17]	Dec. 30, 1976	Dec. 29, 1978

Rudy Boschwitz (I-R)	Dec. 30, 1978	Jan. 2, 1991
Paul Wellstone (DFL)	Jan. 3, 1991	

Minnesota
  1. Died Nov. 27, 1900.
  2. Appointed by governor to fill vacancy.
  3. Elected as a Farmer-Laborite in 1922, 1928, and 1934, as a Republican in 1940.
  4. Died Jan. 13, 1978.
  5. Appointed by governor to fill vacancy.
  6. Died July 13, 1870.
  7. Appointed by governor to fill vacancy.
  8. Resigned March 4, 1881.
  9. Appointed by governor to fill vacancy.
  10. Died April 28, 1923.
  11. Died Dec. 22, 1935.
  12. Appointed by governor to fill vacancy.
  13. Died Aug. 31, 1940.
  14. Appointed by governor to fill vacancy.
  15. Resigned Dec. 29, 1964, having been elected vice president of the United States.
  16. Appointed by governor to fill vacancy. Subsequently elected. Resigned Dec. 30, 1976, having been elected vice president of the United States.
  17. Appointed by governor to fill vacancy. Resigned Dec. 29, 1978.

MISSISSIPPI

(Became a state Dec. 10, 1817)

Class 1

Senators	Dates of Service	
Walter Leake (D-R)[1]	Dec. 10, 1817	May 15, 1820
David Holmes (D-R)[2]	Aug. 30, 1820	Sept. 25, 1825
Powhatan Ellis (D-R)[3]	Sept. 28, 1825	Jan. 28, 1826
Thomas B. Reed (D-R)	Jan. 28, 1826	March 3, 1827
Powhatan Ellis (D-R)[4]	March 4, 1827	July 10, 1832
John Black (D, W)[5]	Nov. 12, 1832	Jan. 22, 1838
James F. Trotter (D)[6]	Jan. 22, 1838	July 10, 1838
Thomas Hickman Williams (D)[7]	Nov. 12, 1838	March 3, 1839
John Henderson (W)	March 4, 1839	March 3, 1845
Jesse Speight (D)[8]	March 4, 1845	May 1, 1847
Jefferson Davis (D)[9]	Aug. 10, 1847	Sept. 23, 1851
John J. McRae (D)[10]	Dec. 1, 1851	March 17, 1852
Stephen Adams (D)	March 17, 1852	March 3, 1857
Jefferson Davis (D)[11]	March 4, 1857	March 14, 1861
Adelbert Ames (R)[12]	April 1, 1870	Jan. 10, 1874
Henry R. Pease (R)	Feb. 3, 1874	March 3, 1875
Blanche K. Bruce (R)	March 4, 1875	March 3, 1881
James Z. George (D)[13]	March 4, 1881	Aug. 14, 1897
Hernando D. Money (D)[14]	Oct. 8, 1897	March 3, 1911
John Sharp Williams (D)	March 4, 1911	March 3, 1923
Hubert D. Stephens (D)	March 4, 1923	Jan. 2, 1935
Theodore G. Bilbo (D)[15]	Jan. 3, 1935	Jan. 2, 1947
John C. Stennis (D)	Nov. 5, 1947	Jan. 2, 1989
Trent Lott (R)	Jan. 3, 1989	

Class 2

Thomas Hill Williams (D-R)	Dec. 10, 1817	March 3, 1829
Thomas B. Reed (D)[16]	March 4, 1829	Nov. 26, 1829
Robert H. Adams (D)[17]	Jan. 6, 1830	July 2, 1830
George Poindexter (D)[18]	Oct. 15, 1830	March 3, 1835
Robert J. Walker (D)[19]	March 4, 1835	March 5, 1845
Joseph W. Chalmers (D)[20]	Nov. 3, 1845	March 3, 1847
Henry Stuart Foote (W)[21]	March 4, 1847	Jan. 8, 1852
Walker Brooke (W)	Feb. 18, 1852	March 3, 1853
Albert G. Brown (D)[22]	March 4, 1853	March 14, 1861
Hiram R. Revels (R)	Feb. 25, 1870	March 3, 1871
James L. Alcorn (R)[23]	Dec. 4, 1871	March 3, 1877
Lucius Q. C. Lamar (D)[24]	March 4, 1877	March 6, 1885
Edward C. Walthall (D)[25]	March 9, 1885	Jan. 24, 1894
Anselm J. McLaurin (D)	Feb. 7, 1894	March 3, 1895
Edward C. Walthall (D)[26]	March 4, 1895	April 21, 1898
William V. Sullivan (D)[27]	May 31, 1898	March 3, 1901
Anselm J. McLaurin (D)[28]	March 4, 1901	Dec. 22, 1909
James Gordon (D)[29]	Dec. 27, 1909	Feb. 22, 1910
Le Roy Percy (D)	Feb. 23, 1910	March 3, 1913
James K. Vardaman (D)	March 4, 1913	March 3, 1919
Pat Harrison (D)[30]	March 4, 1919	June 22, 1941
James O. Eastland (D)[31]	June 30, 1941	Sept. 28, 1941
Wall Doxey (D)	Sept. 29, 1941	Jan. 2, 1943
James O. Eastland (D)[32]	Jan. 3, 1943	Dec. 27, 1978
Thad Cochran (R)	Dec. 27, 1978	

Mississippi
  1. Resigned May 15, 1820.
  2. Appointed by governor to fill vacancy. Subsequently elected. Resigned Sept. 25, 1825.
  3. Appointed by governor to fill vacancy.
  4. Resigned July 10, 1832.
  5. Appointed by governor to fill vacancy. Subsequently elected. Resigned Jan. 22, 1838.
  6. Resigned July 10, 1838.
  7. Appointed by governor to fill vacancy. Subsequently elected.
  8. Died May 1, 1847.
  9. Appointed by governor to fill vacancy. Subsequently elected. Resigned Sept. 23, 1851.
  10. Appointed by governor to fill vacancy.
  11. Seat declared vacant March 14, 1861. Vacancy until April 1, 1870, because of Civil War.
  12. Resigned Jan. 10, 1874.
  13. Died Aug. 14, 1897.
  14. Appointed by governor to fill vacancy. Subsequently elected.
  15. Elected for term beginning Jan. 3, 1947, but was never sworn in. Died Aug. 21, 1947.
  16. Died Nov. 26, 1829.
  17. Died July 2, 1830.
  18. Appointed by governor to fill vacancy. Subsequently elected.
  19. Resigned March 5, 1845.
  20. Appointed by governor to fill vacancy. Subsequently elected.
  21. Resigned Jan. 8, 1852.
  22. Seat declared vacant March 14, 1861. Vacancy until Feb. 25, 1870, because of Civil War.
  23. Elected Jan. 18, 1870. Took oath Dec. 4, 1871. Governor during interim.
  24. Resigned March 6, 1885.
  25. Appointed by governor to fill vacancy. Subsequently elected. Resigned Jan. 24, 1894.
  26. Died April 21, 1898.
  27. Appointed by governor to fill vacancy. Subsequently elected.
  28. Died Dec. 22, 1909.
  29. Appointed by governor to fill vacancy.
  30. Died June 22, 1941.
  31. Appointed by governor to fill vacancy.
  32. Resigned Dec. 27, 1978.

MISSOURI

(Became a state Aug. 10, 1821)

Class 1

Senators	Dates of Service	
Thomas H.		
Benton (D-R, D)	Aug. 10, 1821	March 3, 1851
Henry S. Geyer (D)	March 4, 1851	March 3, 1857
Trusten Polk (D)[1]	March 4, 1857	Jan. 10, 1862
John B. Henderson (D)[2]	Jan. 17, 1862	March 3, 1869
Carl Schurz (R)	March 4, 1869	March 3, 1875
Francis M. Cockrell (D)	March 4, 1875	March 3, 1905
William Warner (R)	March 18, 1905	March 3, 1911
James A. Reed (D)	March 4, 1911	March 3, 1929
Roscoe C. Patterson (R)	March 4, 1929	Jan. 2, 1935
Harry S Truman (D)[3]	Jan. 3, 1935	Jan. 18, 1945
Frank P. Briggs (D)[4]	Jan. 18, 1945	Jan. 2, 1947
James P. Kem (R)	Jan. 3, 1947	Jan. 2, 1953
Stuart Symington (D)[5]	Jan. 3, 1953	Dec. 27, 1976
John C. Danforth (R)	Dec. 27, 1976	Jan. 2, 1995
John Ashcroft (R)	Jan. 3, 1995	Jan. 3, 2001
Jean Carnahan (D)[6]	Jan. 3, 2001	

Class 3

David Barton (D-R)	Aug. 10, 1821	March 3, 1831
Alexander Buckner (D)[7]	March 4, 1831	June 6, 1833
Lewis F. Linn (D)[8]	Oct. 25, 1833	Oct. 3, 1843
David R. Atchison (D)[9]	Oct. 14, 1843	March 3, 1855
James S. Green (D)	Jan. 12, 1857	March 3, 1861
Waldo P. Johnson (D)[10]	March 17, 1861	Jan. 10, 1862
Robert Wilson (UN)[11]	Jan. 17, 1862	Nov. 13, 1863
B. Gratz Brown (D)	Nov. 13, 1863	March 3, 1867
Charles D. Drake (R)[12]	March 4, 1867	Dec. 19, 1870
Daniel T. Jewett (R)[13]	Dec. 19, 1870	Jan. 20, 1871
Francis P. Blair (D)	Jan. 20, 1871	March 3, 1873
Lewis V. Bogy (D)[14]	March 4, 1873	Sept. 20, 1877
David H. Armstrong (D)[15]	Sept. 29, 1877	Jan. 26, 1879
James Shields (D)	Jan. 27, 1879	March 3, 1879
George G. Vest (D)	March 4, 1879	March 3, 1903
William J. Stone (D)[16]	March 4, 1903	April 14, 1918
Xenophon P. Wilfley (D)[17]	April 30, 1918	Nov. 5, 1918
Selden P. Spencer (R)[18]	Nov. 6, 1918	May 16, 1925
George H. Williams (R)[19]	May 25, 1925	Dec. 5, 1926
Harry B. Hawes (D)[20]	Dec. 6, 1926	Feb. 3,1933
J. Bennett Champ Clark (D)	Feb. 3, 1933	Jan. 2, 1945
Forrest C. Donnell (R)	Jan. 3, 1945	Jan. 2, 1951
Thomas C.		
Hennings Jr. (D)[21]	Jan. 3, 1951	Sept. 13, 1960
Edward V. Long (D)[22]	Sept. 23, 1960	Dec. 27, 1968
Thomas F. Eagleton (D)	Dec. 28, 1968	Jan. 2, 1987
Christopher S. Bond (R)	Jan. 3, 1987	

Missouri
1. Expelled Jan. 10, 1862.
2. Appointed by governor to fill vacancy. Subsequently elected.
3. Resigned Jan. 18, 1945, having been elected vice president of the United States.
4. Appointed by governor to fill vacancy.
5. Resigned Dec. 27, 1976.

6. Appointed by governor to fill vacancy created when her husband Mel Carnahan died before winning election to the office.
7. Died June 6, 1833.
8. Appointed by governor to fill vacancy. Subsequently elected. Died Oct. 3, 1843.
9. Appointed by governor to fill vacancy. Subsequently elected.
10. Expelled Jan. 10, 1862.
11. Appointed by governor to fill vacancy.
12. Resigned Dec. 19, 1870.
13. Appointed by governor to fill vacancy.
14. Died Sept. 20, 1877.
15. Appointed by governor to fill vacancy.
16. Died April 14, 1918.
17. Appointed by governor to fill vacancy.
18. Died May 16, 1925.
19. Appointed by governor to fill vacancy.
20. Resigned Feb. 3, 1933.
21. Died Sept. 13, 1960.
22. Appointed by governor to fill vacancy. Subsequently elected. Resigned Dec. 27, 1968.

MONTANA

(Became a state Nov. 8, 1889)

Class 1

Senators	Dates of Service	
Wilbur F. Sanders (R)	Jan. 1, 1890	March 3, 1893
Lee Mantle (R)[1]	Jan. 16, 1895	March 3, 1899
William A. Clark (D)[2]	March 4, 1899	May 15, 1900
Paris Gibson (D)	March 7, 1901	March 3, 1905
Thomas H. Carter (R)	March 4, 1905	March 3, 1911
Henry L. Myers (D)	March 4, 1911	March 3, 1923
Burton K. Wheeler (D)	March 4, 1923	Jan. 2, 1947
Zales N. Ecton (R)	Jan. 3, 1947	Jan. 2, 1953
Mike Mansfield (D)	Jan. 3, 1953	Jan. 2, 1977
John Melcher (D)	Jan. 3, 1977	Jan. 2, 1989
Conrad Burns (R)	Jan. 3, 1989	

Class 2

Thomas C. Power (R)	Jan. 2, 1890	March 3, 1895
Thomas H. Carter (R)	March 4, 1895	March 3, 1901
William A. Clark (D)	March 4, 1901	March 3, 1907
Joseph M. Dixon (R)	March 4, 1907	March 3, 1913
Thomas J. Walsh (D)[3]	March 4, 1913	March 2, 1933
John E. Erickson (D)[4]	March 13, 1933	Nov. 6, 1934
James E. Murray (D)	Nov. 7, 1934	Jan. 2, 1961
Lee Metcalf (D)[5]	Jan. 3, 1961	Jan. 12, 1978
Paul G. Hatfield (D)[6]	Jan. 22, 1978	Dec. 14, 1978
Max Baucus (D)	Dec. 15, 1978	

Montana
1. Vacancy from March 4, 1893, to Jan. 16, 1895, because of failure of legislature to elect.
2. Resigned May 15, 1900.
3. Died March 2, 1933.
4. Appointed by governor to fill vacancy.
5. Died Jan. 12, 1978.
6. Appointed by governor to fill vacancy. Resigned Dec. 14, 1978.

NEBRASKA

(Became a state March 1, 1867)

Class 1

Senators	Dates of Service	
Thomas W. Tipton (R)	March 1, 1867	March 3, 1875
Algernon S. Paddock (R)	March 4, 1875	March 3, 1881
Charles H. Van Wyck (R)	March 4, 1881	March 3, 1887
Algernon S. Paddock (R)	March 4, 1887	March 3, 1893
William V. Allen (POP)	March 4, 1893	March 3, 1899
Monroe L. Hayward (R)[1]	March 8, 1899	Dec. 5, 1899
William V. Allen (POP)[2]	Dec. 13, 1899	March 28, 1901
Charles H. Dietrich (R)	March 28, 1901	March 3, 1905
Elmer J. Burkett (R)	March 4, 1905	March 3, 1911
Gilbert M. Hitchcock (D)	March 4, 1911	March 3, 1923
Robert B. Howell (R)[3]	March 4, 1923	March 11, 1933
William H. Thompson (D)[4]	May 24, 1933	Nov. 6, 1934
Richard C. Hunter (D)	Nov. 7, 1934	Jan. 2, 1935
Edward R. Burke (D)	Jan. 3, 1935	Jan. 2, 1941
Hugh Butler (R)[5]	Jan. 3, 1941	July 1, 1954
Sam W. Reynolds (R)[6]	July 3, 1954	Nov. 7, 1954
Roman L. Hruska (R)[7]	Nov. 8, 1954	Dec. 27, 1976
Edward Zorinsky (D)[8]	Dec. 28, 1976	March 6, 1987
David Karnes (R)[9]	March 13, 1987	Jan. 2, 1989
Bob Kerrey (D)	Jan. 3, 1989	Jan. 3, 2001
Ben Nelson (D)	Jan. 3, 2001	

Class 2

Senators	Dates of Service	
John M. Thayer (R)	March 1, 1867	March 3, 1871
Phineas W. Hitchcock (R)	March 4, 1871	March 3, 1877
Alvin Saunders (R)	March 4, 1877	March 3, 1883
Charles F. Manderson (R)	March 4, 1883	March 3, 1895
John M. Thurston (R)	March 4, 1895	March 3, 1901
Joseph H. Millard (R)	March 28, 1901	March 3, 1907
Norris Brown (R)	March 4, 1907	March 3, 1913
George W. Norris (R, I)[10]	March 4, 1913	Jan. 2, 1943
Kenneth S. Wherry (R)[11]	Jan. 3, 1943	Nov. 29, 1951
Fred A. Seaton (R)[12]	Dec. 10, 1951	Nov. 4, 1952
Dwight Griswold (R)[13]	Nov. 5, 1952	Apr. 12, 1954
Eva Bowring (R)[14]	April 16, 1954	Nov. 7, 1954
Hazel H. Abel (R)[15]	Nov. 8, 1954	Dec. 31, 1954
Carl T. Curtis (R)	Jan. 1, 1955	Jan. 2, 1979
J. James Exon (D)	Jan. 3, 1979	Jan. 2, 1997
Chuck Hagel (R)	Jan. 3, 1997	

Nebraska
1. Died Dec. 5, 1899.
2. Appointed by governor to fill vacancy.
3. Died March 11, 1933.
4. Appointed by governor to fill vacancy.
5. Died July 1, 1954.
6. Appointed by governor to fill vacancy.
7. Resigned Dec. 27, 1976.
8. Died March 6, 1987
9. Appointed by governor to fill vacancy.
10. Norris elected as Republican in 1912, 1918, 1924 and 1930. Elected as Independent in 1936.
11. Died Nov. 29, 1951.
12. Appointed by governor to fill vacancy.
13. Died April 12, 1954.
14. Appointed by governor to fill vacancy.
15. Resigned Dec. 31, 1954.

NEVADA

(Became a state Oct. 31, 1864)

Class 1

Senators	Dates of Service	
William M. Stewart (R)	Dec. 15, 1864	March 3, 1875
William Sharon (R)	March 4, 1875	March 3, 1881
James G. Fair (D)	March 4, 1881	March 3, 1887
William M. Stewart (R)	March 4, 1887	March 3, 1905
George S. Nixon (R)[1]	March 4, 1905	June 5, 1912
William A. Massey (R)[2]	July 1, 1912	Jan. 29, 1913
Key Pittman (D)[3]	Jan. 29, 1913	Nov. 10, 1940
Berkeley L. Bunker (D)[4]	Nov. 27, 1940	Dec. 6, 1942
James G. Scrugham (D)[5]	Dec. 7, 1942	June 23, 1945
E. P. Carville (D)[6]	July 25, 1945	Jan. 2, 1947
George W. Malone (R)	Jan. 3, 1947	Jan. 2, 1959
Howard W. Cannon (D)	Jan. 3, 1959	Jan. 2, 1983
Chic Hecht (R)	Jan. 3, 1983	Jan. 2, 1989
Richard H. Bryan (D)	Jan. 3, 1989	Jan. 3, 2001
John Ensign (R)	Jan. 3, 2001	

Class 3

Senators	Dates of Service	
James W. Nye (R)	Dec. 16, 1864	March 3, 1873
John P. Jones (R)	March 4, 1873	March 3, 1903
Francis G. Newlands (D)[7]	March 4, 1903	Dec. 24, 1917
Charles B. Henderson (D)[8]	Jan. 12, 1918	March 3, 1921
Tasker L. Oddie (R)	March 4, 1921	March 3, 1933
Patrick A. McCarran (D)[9]	March 4, 1933	Sept. 28, 1954
Ernest S. Brown (R)[10]	Oct. 1, 1954	Dec. 1, 1954
Alan Bible (D)[11]	Dec. 2, 1954	Dec. 17, 1974
Paul Laxalt (R)	Dec. 18, 1974	Jan. 2, 1987
Harry Reid (D)	Jan. 3, 1987	

Nevada
1. Died June 5, 1912.
2. Appointed by governor to fill vacancy.
3. Died Nov. 10, 1940.
4. Appointed by governor to fill vacancy.
5. Died June 23, 1945.
6. Appointed by governor to fill vacancy.
7. Died Dec. 24, 1917.
8. Appointed by governor to fill vacancy. Subsequently elected.
9. Died Sept. 28, 1954.
10. Appointed by governor to fill vacancy.
11. Resigned Dec. 17, 1974.

NEW HAMPSHIRE

(Ratified the Constitution June 21, 1788)

Class 2

Senators	Dates of Service	
Paine Wingate (FED)	March 4, 1789	March 3, 1793
Samuel Livermore[1]	March 4, 1793	June 12, 1801
Simeon Olcott (FED)	June 17, 1801	March 3, 1805
Nicholas Gilman (D-R)[2]	March 4, 1805	May 2, 1814
Thomas W. Thompson	June 24, 1814	March 3, 1817
David L. Morrill (D-R)	March 4, 1817	March 3, 1823
Samuel Bell (D-R, NR, W)	March 4, 1823	March 3, 1835

Henry Hubbard (D)	March 4, 1835	March 3, 1841
Levi Woodbury (D)[3]	March 4, 1841	Nov. 20, 1845
Benning W. Jenness (D)[4]	Dec. 1, 1845	June 13, 1846
Joseph Cilley (D)	June 13, 1846	March 3, 1847
John P. Hale (D)	March 4, 1847	March 3, 1853
Charles G. Atherton (D)[5]	March 4, 1853	Nov. 15, 1853
Jared W. Williams[6]	Nov. 29, 1853	Aug. 3, 1854
John P. Hale (R)	July 30, 1855	March 3, 1865
Aaron H. Cragin (R)	March 4, 1865	March 3, 1877
Edward H. Rollins (R)	March 4, 1877	March 3, 1883
Austin F. Pike (R)[7]	March 4, 1883	Oct. 8, 1886
Person C. Cheney (R)[8]	Nov. 24, 1886	June 14, 1887
William E. Chandler (R)	June 14, 1887	March 3, 1889
Gilman Marston (R)[9]	March 4, 1889	June 18, 1889
William E. Chandler (R)	June 19, 1889	March 3, 1901
Henry E. Burnham (R)	March 4, 1901	March 3, 1913
Henry F. Hollis (D)	March 13, 1913	March 3, 1919
Henry W. Keyes (R)	March 4, 1919	Jan. 2, 1937
Styles Bridges (R)[10]	Jan. 3, 1937	Nov. 26, 1961
Maurice J. Murphy Jr. (R)[11]	Dec. 7, 1961	Nov. 6, 1962
Thomas J. McIntyre (D)	Nov. 7, 1962	Jan. 2, 1979
Gordon J. Humphrey (R)[12]	Jan. 3, 1979	Dec. 4, 1990
Robert C. Smith (R, I, R)	Dec. 7, 1990	

Class 3

John Langdon (D-R)	March 4, 1789	March 3, 1801
James Sheafe (FED)[13]	March 4, 1801	June 14, 1802
William Plumer (FED)	June 17, 1802	March 3, 1807
Nahum Parker[14]	March 4, 1807	June 1, 1810
Charles Cutts (FED)[15]	June 21, 1810	June 10, 1813
Jeremiah Mason (FED)[16]	June 10, 1813	June 16, 1817
Clement Storer	June 27, 1817	March 3, 1819
John F. Parrott (D-R)	March 4, 1819	March 3, 1825
Levi Woodbury (D-R)	June 16, 1825	March 3, 1831
Isaac Hill (D)[17]	March 4, 1831	May 30, 1836
John Page (D)	June 8, 1836	March 3, 1837
Franklin Pierce (D)[18]	March 4, 1837	Feb. 28, 1842
Leonard Wilcox (D)[19]	March 1, 1842	March 3, 1843
Charles G. Atherton (D)	March 4, 1843	March 3, 1849
Moses Norris Jr. (D)[20]	March 4, 1849	Jan. 11, 1855
John S. Wells[21]	Jan. 16, 1855	March 3, 1855
James Bell (R)[22]	July 30, 1855	May 26, 1857
Daniel Clark (R)[23]	June 27, 1857	July 27, 1866
George G. Fogg (R)[24]	Aug. 31, 1866	March 3, 1867
James E. Patterson (R)	March 4, 1867	March 3, 1873
Bainbridge Wadleigh (R)	March 4, 1873	March 3, 1879
Charles H. Bell (R)[25]	March 13, 1879	June 16, 1879
Henry W. Blair (R)[26]	June 17, 1879	March 3, 1891
Jacob H. Gallinger (R)[27]	March 4, 1891	Aug. 17, 1918
Irving W. Drew (R)[28]	Sept. 2, 1918	Nov. 5, 1918
George H. Moses (R)	Nov. 6, 1918	March 3, 1933
Fred H. Brown (D)	March 4, 1933	Jan. 2, 1939
Charles W. Tobey (R)[29]	Jan. 3, 1939	July 24, 1953
Robert W. Upton (R)[30]	Aug. 14, 1953	Nov. 7, 1954
Norris Cotton (R)[31]	Nov. 8, 1954	Dec. 31, 1974
Louis C. Wyman (R)[32]	Jan. 1, 1975	Jan. 2, 1975
Norris Cotton (R)[33]	Aug. 8, 1975	Sept. 18, 1975
John A. Durkin (D)[34]	Sept. 18, 1975	Dec. 29, 1980
Warren B. Rudman (R)	Dec. 29, 1980	Jan. 2, 1993
Judd Gregg (R)	Jan. 3, 1993	

New Hampshire
1. Resigned June 12, 1801.
2. Died May 2, 1814.
3. Resigned Nov. 20, 1845.
4. Appointed by governor to fill vacancy.
5. Died Nov. 15, 1853.
6. Appointed by governor to fill vacancy. Senate resolution of Aug. 3, 1854, declared that representation under the appointment had expired. Vacancy from Aug. 4, 1854, to July 29, 1855.
7. Died Oct. 8, 1886.
8. Appointed by governor to fill vacancy.
9. Appointed by governor to fill vacancy.
10. Died Nov. 26, 1961.
11. Appointed by governor to fill vacancy.
12. Resigned Dec. 4, 1990.
13. Resigned June 14, 1802.
14. Resigned June 1, 1810.
15. Elected, subsequently appointed by governor to fill vacancy.
16. Resigned June 16, 1817.
17. Resigned May 30, 1836.
18. Resigned Feb. 28, 1842.
19. Appointed by governor to fill vacancy. Subsequently elected.
20. Died Jan. 11, 1855.
21. Appointed by governor to fill vacancy.
22. Died May 26, 1857.
23. Resigned July 27, 1866.
24. Appointed by governor to fill vacancy.
25. Appointed by governor to fill vacancy.
26. Served continuously during this period; twice by election, once by appointment of the governor.
27. Died Aug. 17, 1918.
28. Appointed by governor to fill vacancy.
29. Died July 24, 1953.
30. Appointed by governor to fill vacancy.
31. Resigned Dec. 31, 1974.
32. Appointed by governor to fill vacancy. Wyman and John A. Durkin (D) both claimed to have been elected to the seat for a six-year term beginning Jan. 3, 1975. Neither was seated. After unsuccessfully attempting for seven months to determine the winner, the Senate July 30, 1975, voted to declare the seat vacant effective Aug. 8, 1975.
33. Appointed by governor to fill vacancy.
34. Resigned Dec. 29, 1980.

NEW JERSEY

(Ratified the Constitution Dec. 18, 1787)

Class 1

Senators	Dates of Service	
Jonathan Elmer (FED)	March 4, 1789	March 3, 1791
John Rutherfurd (FED)[1]	March 4, 1791	Nov. 26, 1798
Franklin Davenport[2]	Dec. 5, 1798	March 3, 1799
James Schureman[3]	March 4, 1799	Feb. 16, 1801
Aaron Ogden (FED)	Feb. 28, 1801	March 3, 1803
John Condit (D-R)[4]	Sept. 1, 1803	March 3, 1809
John Lambert	March 4, 1809	March 3, 1815
James J. Wilson (D-R)[5]	March 4, 1815	Jan. 8, 1821
Samuel L. Southard (D-R)[6]	Jan. 26, 1821	March 3, 1823
Joseph McIlvaine (D-R)[7]	Nov. 12, 1823	Aug. 19, 1826
Ephraim Bateman (D-R)[8]	Nov. 10, 1826	Jan. 12, 1829
Mahlon Dickerson (D)	Jan. 30, 1829	March 3, 1833
Samuel L. Southard (NR, W)[9]	March 4, 1833	June 26, 1842
William L. Dayton (W)[10]	July 2, 1842	March 3, 1851
Robert F. Stockton (D)[11]	March 4, 1851	Jan. 10, 1853

John R. Thomson (D)[12]	March 4, 1853	Sept. 12, 1862
Richard S. Field (R)[13]	Nov. 21, 1862	Jan. 14, 1863
James W. Wall (D)	Jan. 14, 1863	March 3, 1863
William Wright (D)[14]	March 4, 1863	Nov. 1, 1866
Frederick T. Frelinghuysen (R)[15]	Nov. 12, 1866	March 3, 1869
John P. Stockton (D)	March 4, 1869	March 3, 1875
Theodore F. Randolph (D)	March 4, 1875	March 3, 1881
William J. Sewell (R)	March 4, 1881	March 3, 1887
Rufus Blodgett (D)	March 4, 1887	March 3, 1893
James Smith Jr. (D)	March 4, 1893	March 3, 1899
John Kean (R)	March 4, 1899	March 3, 1911
James E. Martine (D)	March 4, 1911	March 3, 1917
Joseph S. Frelinghuysen (R)	March 4, 1917	March 3, 1923
Edward I. Edwards (D)	March 4, 1923	March 3, 1929
Hamilton F. Kean (R)	March 4, 1929	Jan. 2, 1935
A. Harry Moore (D)[16]	Jan. 3, 1935	Jan. 18, 1938
John Milton (D)[17]	Jan. 18, 1938	Nov. 8, 1938
W. Warren Barbour (R)[18]	Nov. 9, 1938	Nov. 22, 1943
Arthur Walsh (D)[19]	Nov. 26, 1943	Dec. 6, 1944
H. Alexander Smith (R)	Dec. 7, 1944	Jan. 2, 1959
Harrison A. Williams Jr. (D)[20]	Jan. 3, 1959	March 11, 1982
Nicholas F. Brady (R)[21]	April 12, 1982	Dec. 26, 1982
Frank R. Lautenberg (D)	Dec. 27, 1982	Jan. 3, 2001
Jon Corzine (D)	Jan. 3, 2001	

Class 2

William Paterson (FED)[22]	March 4, 1789	Nov. 13, 1790
Philemon Dickinson	Nov. 23, 1790	March 3, 1793
Frederick Frelinghuysen (FED)[23]	March 4, 1793	Nov. 12, 1796
Richard Stockton (FED)	Nov. 12, 1796	March 3, 1799
Jonathan Dayton	March 4, 1799	March 3, 1805
Aaron Kitchell[24]	March 4, 1805	March 12, 1809
John Condit (D-R)[25]	March 21, 1809	March 3, 1817
Mahlon Dickerson (D-R)[26]	March 4, 1817	Jan. 30, 1829
Theodore Frelinghuysen (NR)	March 4, 1829	March 3, 1835
Garret D. Wall (D)	March 4, 1835	March 3, 1841
Jacob W. Miller (W)	March 4, 1841	March 3, 1853
William Wright (D)	March 4, 1853	March 3, 1859
John C. Ten Eyck (R)	March 4, 1859	March 3, 1865
John P. Stockton (D)[27]	March 4, 1865	March 27, 1866
Alexander G. Cattell (R)	Sept. 19, 1866	March 3, 1871
Frederick T. Frelinghuysen (R)	March 4, 1871	March 3, 1877
John R. McPherson (D)	March 4, 1877	March 3, 1895
William J. Sewell (R)[28]	March 4, 1895	Dec. 27, 1901
John F. Dryden (R)	Jan. 29, 1902	March 3, 1907
Frank O. Briggs (R)	March 4, 1907	March 3, 1913
Wililam Hughes (D)[29]	March 4, 1913	Jan. 30, 1918
David Baird (R)[30]	Feb. 23, 1918	March 3, 1919
Walter E. Edge (R)[31]	March 4, 1919	Nov. 21, 1929
David Baird Jr. (R)[32]	Nov. 30, 1929	Dec. 2, 1930
Dwight W. Morrow (R)[33]	Dec. 3, 1930	Oct. 5, 1931
W. Warren Barbour (R)[34]	Dec. 1, 1931	Jan. 2, 1937

William H. Smathers (D)	April 15, 1937	Jan. 2, 1943
Albert W. Hawkes (R)	Jan. 3, 1943	Jan. 2, 1949
Robert C. Hendrickson (R)	Jan. 3, 1949	Jan. 2, 1955
Clifford P. Case (R)	Jan. 3, 1955	Jan. 2, 1979
Bill Bradley (D)	Jan. 3, 1979	Jan. 2, 1997
Robert G. Torricelli (D)	Jan. 3, 1997	

New Jersey
1. Resigned Nov. 26, 1798.
2. Appointed by governor to fill vacancy.
3. Resigned Feb. 16, 1801.
4. Appointed by governor to fill vacancy. Subsequently elected.
5. Resigned Jan. 8, 1821.
6. Appointed by governor to fill vacancy. Subsequently elected. Resigned March 3, 1823.
7. Died Aug. 19, 1826.
8. Resigned Jan. 12, 1829.
9. Died June 26, 1842.
10. Appointed by governor to fill vacancy. Subsequently elected.
11. Resigned Jan. 10, 1853.
12. Died Sept. 12, 1862.
13. Appointed by governor to fill vacancy.
14. Died Nov. 1, 1866.
15. Appointed by governor to fill vacancy. Subsequently elected.
16. Resigned Jan. 18, 1938.
17. Appointed by governor to fill vacancy.
18. Died Nov. 22, 1943.
19. Appointed by governor to fill vacancy.
20. Resigned March 11, 1982.
21. Appointed by governor to fill vacancy. Resigned Dec. 26, 1982.
22. Resigned Nov. 13, 1790.
23. Resigned Nov. 12, 1796.
24. Resigned March 12, 1809.
25. Appointed by governor to fill vacancy. Subsequently elected.
26. Resigned Jan. 30, 1829.
27. Seat declared vacant March 27, 1866.
28. Died Dec. 27, 1901.
29. Died Jan. 30, 1918.
30. Appointed by governor to fill vacancy. Subsequently elected.
31. Resigned Nov. 21, 1929.
32. Appointed by governor to fill vacancy.
33. Died Oct. 5, 1931.
34. Appointed by governor to fill vacancy. Subsequently elected.

NEW MEXICO

(Became a state Jan. 6, 1912)

Class 1

Senators	Dates of Service	
Thomas B. Catron (R)	March 27, 1912	March 3, 1917
Andrieus A. Jones (D)[1]	March 4, 1917	Dec. 20, 1927
Bronson Cutting (R)[2]	Dec. 29, 1927	Dec. 6, 1928
Octaviano A. Larrazolo (R)	Dec. 7, 1928	March 3, 1929
Bronson Cutting (R)[3]	March 4, 1929	May 6, 1935
Dennis Chavez (D)[4]	May 11, 1935	Nov. 18, 1962
Edwin L. Mechem (R)[5]	Nov. 30, 1962	Nov. 3, 1964
Joseph M. Montoya (D)	Nov. 4, 1964	Jan. 2, 1977
Harrison (Jack) Schmitt (R)	Jan. 3, 1977	Jan. 2, 1983
Jeff Bingaman (D)	Jan. 3, 1983	

Class 2

Albert B. Fall (R)[6]	March 27, 1912	March 4, 1921
Holm O. Bursum (R)[7]	March 11, 1921	March 3, 1925
Sam G. Bratton (D)[8]	March 4, 1925	June 24, 1933
Carl A. Hatch (D)[9]	Oct. 10, 1933	Jan. 2, 1949

Clinton P. Anderson (D)	Jan. 3, 1949	Jan. 2, 1973
Pete V. Domenici (R)	Jan. 3, 1973	

New Mexico
1. Died Dec. 20, 1927.
2. Appointed by governor to fill vacancy.
3. Died May 6, 1935.
4. Appointed by governor to fill vacancy. Subsequently elected. Died Nov. 18, 1962.
5. Appointed by governor to fill vacancy.
6. Resigned March 4, 1921.
7. Appointed by governor to fill vacancy. Subsequently elected.
8. Resigned June 24, 1933.
9. Appointed by governor to fill vacancy. Subsequently elected.

NEW YORK

(Ratified the Constitution July 26, 1788)

Class 1

Senators	Dates of Service	
Philip Schuyler (FED)	July 15, 1789	March 3, 1791
Aaron Burr (D-R)	March 4, 1791	March 3, 1797
Philip Schuyler (FED)[1]	March 4, 1797	Jan. 3, 1798
John S. Hobart (FED)[2]	Jan. 11, 1798	April 16, 1798
William North (FED)[3]	May 5, 1798	Aug. 17, 1798
James Watson (FED)[4]	Aug. 17, 1798	March 19, 1800
Gouverneur Morris (FED)	April 3, 1800	March 3, 1803
Theodorus Bailey (D-R)[5]	March 4, 1803	Jan. 16, 1804
John Armstrong (D-R)[6]	Feb. 4, 1804	June 30, 1804
Samuel L. Mitchill (D-R)	Nov. 9, 1804	March 3, 1809
Obadiah German (D-R)	March 4, 1809	March 3, 1815
Nathan Sanford (D-R)	March 4, 1815	March 3, 1821
Martin Van Buren (D-R)[7]	March 4, 1821	Dec. 20, 1828
Charles E. Dudley (D)	Jan. 15, 1829	March 3, 1833
Nathaniel P. Tallmadge (D)[8]	March 4, 1833	June 17, 1844
Daniel S. Dickinson (D)[9]	Nov. 30, 1844	March 3, 1851
Hamilton Fish (W)	March 4, 1851	March 3, 1857
Preston King (R)	March 4, 1857	March 3, 1863
Edwin D. Morgan (R)	March 4, 1863	March 3, 1869
Reuben E. Fenton (R)	March 4, 1869	March 3, 1875
Francis Kernan (D)	March 4, 1875	March 3, 1881
Thomas C. Platt (R)[10]	March 4, 1881	May 16, 1881
Warner Miller (R)	July 16, 1881	March 3, 1887
Frank Hiscock (R)	March 4, 1887	March 3, 1893
Edward Murphy Jr. (D)	March 4, 1893	March 3, 1899
Chauncey M. Depew (R)	March 4, 1899	March 3, 1911
James A. O'Gorman (D)	March 31, 1911	March 3, 1917
William M. Calder (R)	March 4, 1917	March 3, 1923
Royal S. Copeland (D)[11]	March 4, 1923	June 17, 1938
James M. Mead (D)	Dec. 3, 1938	Jan. 2, 1947
Irving M. Ives (R)	Jan. 3, 1947	Jan. 2, 1959
Kenneth B. Keating (R)	Jan. 3, 1959	Jan. 2, 1965
Robert F. Kennedy (D)[12]	Jan. 3, 1965	June 6, 1968
Charles E. Goodell (R)[13]	Sept. 10, 1968	Jan. 2, 1971
James L. Buckley (C-R)	Jan. 3, 1971	Jan. 2, 1977
Daniel Patrick Moynihan (D)	Jan. 3, 1977	Jan. 3, 2001
Hillary Rodham Clinton (D)	Jan. 3, 2001	

Class 3

Rufus King (FED)[14]	July 16, 1789	May 23, 1796
John Laurance (FED)[15]	Nov. 9, 1796	Aug. 1800

John Armstrong (D-R)[16]	Nov. 6, 1800	Feb. 5, 1802
De Witt Clinton (D-R)[17]	Feb. 9, 1802	Nov. 4, 1803
John Armstrong (D-R)[18]	Nov. 10, 1803	Feb. 4, 1804
John Smith (D-R)	Feb. 4, 1804	March 3, 1813
Rufus King (FED)	March 4, 1813	March 3, 1825
Nathan Sanford (D-R)	Jan. 14, 1826	March 3, 1831
William L. Marcy (D)[19]	March 4, 1831	Jan. 1, 1833
Silas Wright Jr. (D)[20]	Jan. 4, 1833	Nov. 26, 1844
Henry A. Foster (D)[21]	Nov. 30, 1844	Jan. 18, 1845
John A. Dix (D)	Jan. 18, 1845	March 3, 1849
William H. Seward (W)	March 4, 1849	March 3, 1861
Ira Harris (R)	March 4, 1861	March 3, 1867
Roscoe Conkling (R)[22]	March 4, 1867	May 16, 1881
Elbridge G. Lapham (R)	July 22, 1881	March 3, 1885
William M. Evarts (R)	March 4, 1885	March 3, 1891
David B. Hill (D)	Jan. 7, 1892	March 3, 1897
Thomas C. Platt (R)	March 4, 1897	March 3, 1909
Elihu Root (R)	March 4, 1909	March 3, 1915
James W. Wadsworth Jr. (R)	March 4, 1915	March 3, 1927
Robert F. Wagner (D)[23]	March 4, 1927	June 28, 1949
John Foster Dulles (R)[24]	July 7, 1949	Nov. 8, 1949
Herbert H. Lehman (D)	Nov. 9, 1949	Jan. 2, 1957
Jacob K. Javits (R)	Jan. 9, 1957	Jan. 2, 1981
Alfonse M. D'Amato (R)	Jan. 3, 1981	Jan. 3, 1999
Charles E. Schumer (D)	Jan. 3, 1999	

New York
1. Resigned Jan. 3, 1798.
2. Resigned April 16, 1798.
3. Appointed by governor to fill vacancy.
4. Resigned March 19, 1800.
5. Resigned Jan. 16, 1804.
6. Resigned June 30, 1804.
7. Resigned Dec. 20, 1828.
8. Resigned June 17, 1844.
9. Appointed by governor to fill vacancy. Subsequently elected.
10. Resigned May 16, 1881.
11. Died June 17, 1938.
12. Died June 6, 1968.
13. Appointed by governor to fill vacancy.
14. Resigned May 23, 1796.
15. Resigned in August 1800.
16. Resigned Feb. 5, 1802.
17. Resigned Nov. 4, 1803.
18. Appointed by governor to fill vacancy.
19. Resigned Jan. 1, 1833.
20. Resigned Nov. 26, 1844.
21. Appointed by governor to fill vacancy.
22. Resigned May 16, 1881.
23. Resigned June 28, 1949.
24. Appointed by governor to fill vacancy.

NORTH CAROLINA

(Ratified the Constitution Nov. 21, 1789)

Class 2

Senators	Dates of Service	
Samuel Johnston (FED)	Nov. 27, 1789	March 3, 1793
Alexander Martin (D-R)	March 4, 1793	March 3, 1799
Jesse Franklin (D-R)	March 4, 1799	March 3, 1805
James Turner (D-R)[1]	March 4, 1805	Nov. 21, 1816
Montfort Stokes (D-R)	Dec. 4, 1816	March 3, 1823
John Branch (D-R)[2]	March 4, 1823	March 9, 1829
Bedford Brown (D)[3]	Dec. 9, 1829	Nov. 11, 1840

Willie P. Mangum (W)	Nov. 25, 1840	March 3, 1853
David S. Reid (D)[4]	Dec. 6, 1854	March 3, 1859
Thomas Bragg (D)[5]	March 4, 1859	July 11, 1861
Joseph C. Abbott (R)	July 17, 1868	March 3, 1871
Matt W. Ransom (D)	Jan. 30, 1872	March 3, 1895
Marion Butler (POP)	March 4, 1895	March 3, 1901
Furnifold M. Simmons (D)	March 4, 1901	March 3, 1931
Josiah W. Bailey (D)[6]	March 4, 1931	Dec. 15, 1946
William B. Umstead (D)[7]	Dec. 18, 1946	Dec. 30, 1948
J. Melville Broughton (D)[8]	Dec. 31, 1948	March 6, 1949
Frank P. Graham (D)[9]	March 29, 1949	Nov. 26, 1950
Willis Smith (D)[10]	Nov. 27, 1950	June 23, 1953
Alton A. Lennon (D)[11]	July 10, 1953	Nov. 28, 1954
W. Kerr Scott (D)[12]	Nov. 29, 1954	April 16, 1958
B. Everett Jordan (D)[13]	April 19, 1958	Jan. 2, 1973
Jesse Helms (R)	Jan. 3, 1973	

Class 3

Benjamin Hawkins (FED)	Nov. 27, 1789	March 3, 1795
Timothy Bloodworth (D-R)	March 4, 1795	March 3, 1801
David Stone (D-R)[14]	March 4, 1801	Feb. 17, 1807
Jesse Franklin (D-R)	March 4, 1807	March 3, 1813
David Stone (D-R)[15]	March 4, 1813	Dec. 24, 1814
Francis Locke (D-R)[16]		
Nathaniel Macon (D-R)[17]	Dec. 5, 1815	Nov. 14, 1828
James Iredell (D-R)	Dec. 15, 1828	March 3, 1831
Willie P. Mangum (D)[18]	March 4, 1831	Nov. 26, 1836
Robert Strange (D)[19]	Dec. 5, 1836	Nov. 16, 1840
William A. Graham (W)	Nov. 25, 1840	March 3, 1843
William H. Haywood Jr. (D)[20]	March 4, 1843	July 25, 1846
George E. Badger (W)	Nov. 25, 1846	March 3, 1855
Asa Biggs (D)[21]	March 4, 1855	May 5, 1858
Thomas L. Clingman (D)[22]	May 6, 1858	July 11, 1861
John Pool (R)	July 17, 1868	March 3, 1873
Augustus S. Merrimon (D)	March 4, 1873	March 3, 1879
Zebulon B. Vance (D)[23]	March 4, 1879	April 14, 1894
Thomas J. Jarvis (D)[24]	April 19, 1894	Jan. 23, 1895
Jeter C. Pritchard (R)	Jan. 23, 1895	March 3, 1903
Lee S. Overman (D)[25]	March 4, 1903	Dec. 12, 1930
Cameron Morrison (D)[26]	Dec. 13, 1930	Dec. 4, 1932
Robert R. Reynolds (D)	Dec. 5, 1932	Jan. 2, 1945
Clyde R. Hoey (D)[27]	Jan. 3, 1945	May 12, 1954
Sam J. Ervin Jr. (D)[28]	June 5, 1954	Dec. 31, 1974
Robert Morgan (D)	Jan. 3, 1975	Jan. 2, 1981
John P. East (R)[29]	Jan. 3, 1981	June 29, 1986
James T. Broyhill (R)[30]	July 14, 1986	Nov. 4, 1986
Terry Sanford (D)[31]	Nov. 5, 1986	Jan. 2, 1993
Lauch Faircloth (R)	Jan. 3, 1993	Jan. 3, 1999
John Edwards (D)	Jan. 3, 1999	

North Carolina
1. Resigned Nov. 21, 1816.
2. Resigned March 9, 1829.
3. Resigned Nov. 11, 1840.
4. Vacancy from March 4, 1853, to Dec. 6, 1854.
5. Expelled July 11, 1861. Vacancy until July 17, 1868, because of Civil War.
6. Died Dec. 15, 1946.
7. Appointed by governor to fill vacancy.
8. Died March 6, 1949.

9. Appointed by governor to fill vacancy.
10. Died June 23, 1953.
11. Appointed by governor to fill vacancy.
12. Died April 16, 1958.
13. Appointed by governor to fill vacancy. Subsequently elected.
14. Approximate date of resignation, Feb. 17, 1807.
15. Resigned Dec. 24, 1814.
16. Elected in 1814 but never seated. Did not qualify. Resigned Dec. 5, 1815.
17. Resigned Nov. 14, 1828.
18. Resigned Nov. 26, 1836.
19. Resigned Nov. 16, 1840.
20. Resigned July 25, 1846.
21. Resigned May 5, 1858.
22. Appointed by governor to fill vacancy. Subsequently elected. Expelled July 11, 1861. Vacancy until July 17, 1868, because of Civil War.
23. Died April 14, 1894.
24. Appointed by governor to fill vacancy.
25. Died Dec. 12, 1930.
26. Appointed by governor to fill vacancy.
27. Died May 12, 1954.
28. Appointed by governor to fill vacancy. Subsequently elected. Resigned Dec. 31, 1974.
29. Died June 29, 1986.
30. Appointed by governor to fill vacancy.
31. Officially sworn in on Dec. 10, 1986.

NORTH DAKOTA

(Became a state Nov. 2, 1889)

Class 1

Senators	Dates of Service	
Lyman R. Casey (R)	Nov. 25, 1889	March 3, 1893
William N. Roach (D)	March 4, 1893	March 3, 1899
Porter J. McCumber (R)	March 4, 1899	March 3, 1923
Lynn J. Frazier (R)	March 4, 1923	Jan. 2, 1941
William Langer (R)[1]	Jan. 3, 1941	Nov. 8, 1959
C. Norman Brunsdale (R)[2]	Nov. 19, 1959	Aug. 7, 1960
Quentin N. Burdick (D)[3]	Aug. 8, 1960	Sept. 8, 1992
Jocelyn B. Burdick (D)[4]	Sept. 12, 1992	Dec. 4, 1992
Kent Conrad (D)	Dec. 5, 1992	

Class 3

Gilbert A. Pierce (R)	Nov. 21, 1889	March 3, 1891
Henry C. Hansbrough (R)	March 4, 1891	March 3, 1909
Martin N. Johnson (R)[5]	March 4, 1909	Oct. 21, 1909
Fountain L. Thompson (D)[6]	Nov. 10, 1909	Jan. 31, 1910
William E. Purcell (D)[7]	Feb. 1, 1910	Feb. 1, 1911
Asle J. Gronna (R)	Feb. 2, 1911	March 3, 1921
Edwin F. Ladd (R)[8]	March 4, 1921	June 22, 1925
Gerald P. Nye (R)[9]	Nov. 14, 1925	Jan. 2, 1945
John Moses (D)[10]	Jan. 3, 1945	March 3, 1945
Milton R. Young (R)[11]	March 12, 1945	Jan. 2, 1981
Mark Andrews (R)	Jan. 3, 1981	Jan. 2, 1987
Kent Conrad (D)[12]	Jan. 3, 1987	Dec. 4, 1992
Byron L. Dorgan (D)	Dec. 15, 1992	

North Dakota
1. Died Nov. 8, 1959.
2. Appointed by governor to fill vacancy.
3. Died Sept. 8, 1992.
4. Appointed by governor to fill vacancy.
5. Died Oct. 21, 1909.
6. Appointed by governor to fill vacancy. Resigned Jan. 31, 1910.
7. Appointed by governor to fill vacancy.
8. Died June 22, 1925.

North Dakota (continued)
9. Appointed by governor to fill vacancy. Subsequently elected.
10. Died March 3, 1945.
11. Appointed by governor to fill vacancy. Subsequently elected.
12. Resigned Dec. 4, 1992.

OHIO

(Became a state March 1, 1803)

Class 1

Senators	Dates of Service	
John Smith (D-R)[1]	April 1, 1803	April 25, 1808
Return J. Meigs Jr. (D-R)[2]	Dec. 12, 1808	May 10, 1810
Thomas Worthington (D-R)[3]	Dec. 15, 1810	Dec. 1, 1814
Joseph Kerr (D-R)	Dec. 10, 1814	March 3, 1815
Benjamin Ruggles (D-R)	March 4, 1815	March 3, 1833
Thomas Morris (D)	March 4, 1833	March 3, 1839
Benjamin Tappan (D)	March 4, 1839	March 3, 1845
Thomas Corwin (W)[4]	March 4, 1845	July 20, 1850
Thomas Ewing (W)[5]	July 20, 1850	March 3, 1851
Benjamin F. Wade (W, R)	March 15, 1851	March 3, 1869
Allen G. Thurman (D)	March 4, 1869	March 3, 1881
John Sherman (R)[6]	March 4, 1881	March 5, 1897
Marcus A. Hanna (R)[7]	March 5, 1897	Feb. 15, 1904
Charles W. F. Dick (R)	March 2, 1904	March 3, 1911
Atlee Pomerene (D)	March 4, 1911	March 3, 1923
Simeon D. Fess (R)	March 4, 1923	Jan. 2, 1935
Vic Donahey (D)	Jan. 3, 1935	Jan. 2, 1941
Harold H. Burton (R)[8]	Jan. 3, 1941	Sept. 30, 1945
James W. Huffman (D)[9]	Oct. 8, 1945	Nov. 5, 1946
Kingsley A. Taft (R)	Nov. 6, 1946	Jan. 2, 1947
John W. Bricker (R)	Jan. 3, 1947	Jan. 2, 1959
Stephen M. Young (D)	Jan. 3, 1959	Jan. 2, 1971
Robert Taft Jr. (R)[10]	Jan. 3, 1971	Dec. 28, 1976
Howard M. Metzenbaum (D)	Dec. 29, 1976	Jan. 2, 1995
Mike DeWine (R)	Jan. 3, 1995	

Class 3

Senators	Dates of Service	
Thomas Worthington (D-R)	April 1, 1803	March 3, 1807
Edward Tiffin (D-R)[11]	March 4, 1807	March 3, 1809
Stanley Griswold (D-R)[12]	May 18, 1809	Dec. 11, 1809
Alexander Campbell (D-R)	Dec. 11, 1809	March 3, 1813
Jeremiah Morrow (D-R)	March 4, 1813	March 3, 1819
William A. Trimble (D-R)[13]	March 4, 1819	Dec. 13, 1821
Ethan Allen Brown (D-R)	Jan. 3, 1822	March 3, 1825
William H. Harrison (D-R)[14]	March 4, 1825	May 20, 1828
Jacob Burnet	Dec. 10, 1828	March 3, 1831
Thomas Ewing (NR, W)	March 4, 1831	March 3, 1837
William Allen (D)	March 4, 1837	March 3, 1849
Salmon P. Chase (F SOIL D)	March 4, 1849	March 3, 1855
George E. Pugh (D)	March 4, 1855	March 3, 1861
Salmon P. Chase (R)[15]	March 4, 1861	March 6, 1861
John Sherman (R)[16]	March 21, 1861	March 8, 1877
Stanley Matthews (R)	March 21, 1877	March 3, 1879
George H. Pendleton (D)	March 4, 1879	March 3, 1885

Henry B. Payne (D)	March 4, 1885	March 3, 1891
Calvin S. Brice (D)	March 4, 1891	March 3, 1897
Joseph B. Foraker (R)	March 4, 1897	March 3, 1909
Theodore E. Burton (R)	March 4, 1909	March 3, 1915
Warren G. Harding (R)[17]	March 4, 1915	Jan. 13, 1921
Frank B. Willis (R)[18]	Jan. 14, 1921	March 30, 1928
Cyrus Locher (D)[19]	April 4, 1928	Dec. 14, 1928
Theodore E. Burton (R)[20]	Dec. 15, 1928	Oct. 28, 1929
Roscoe C. McCulloch (R)[21]	Nov. 5, 1929	Nov. 30, 1930
Robert J. Bulkley (D)	Dec. 1, 1930	Jan. 2, 1939
Robert A. Taft (R)[22]	Jan. 3, 1939	July 31, 1953
Thomas A. Burke (D)[23]	Nov. 10, 1953	Dec. 2, 1954
George H. Bender (R)	Dec. 16, 1954	Jan. 2, 1957
Frank J. Lausche (D)	Jan. 3, 1957	Jan. 2, 1969
William B. Saxbe (R)[24]	Jan. 3, 1969	Jan. 4, 1974
Howard M. Metzenbaum (D)[25]	Jan. 4, 1974	Dec. 23, 1974
John Glenn (D)	Dec. 24, 1974	Jan. 3, 1999
George V. Voinovich (R)	Jan. 3, 1999	

Ohio
1. Resigned April 25, 1808.
2. Resigned May 10, 1810.
3. Resigned Dec. 1, 1814.
4. Resigned July 20, 1850.
5. Appointed by governor to fill vacancy.
6. Resigned March 5, 1897.
7. Appointed by governor to fill vacancy. Subsequently elected. Died Feb. 15, 1904.
8. Resigned Sept. 30, 1945.
9. Appointed by governor to fill vacancy.
10. Resigned Dec. 28, 1976.
11. Resigned March 3, 1809.
12. Appointed by governor to fill vacancy.
13. Died Dec. 13, 1821.
14. Resigned May 20, 1828.
15. Resigned March 6, 1861.
16. Resigned March 8, 1877.
17. Resigned Jan. 13, 1921, to become president of the United States.
18. Died March 30, 1928.
19. Appointed by governor to fill vacancy.
20. Died Oct. 28, 1929.
21. Appointed by governor to fill vacancy.
22. Died July 31, 1953.
23. Appointed by governor to fill vacancy.
24. Resigned Jan. 4, 1974.
25. Appointed by governor to fill vacancy. Resigned Dec. 23, 1974.

OKLAHOMA

(Became a state Nov. 16, 1907)

Class 2

Senators	Dates of Service	
Robert L. Owen (D)	Dec. 11, 1907	March 3, 1925
William B. Pine (R)	March 4, 1925	March 3, 1931
Thomas P. Gore (D)	March 4, 1931	Jan. 2, 1937
Josh Lee (D)	Jan. 3, 1937	Jan. 2, 1943
Edward H. Moore (R)	Jan. 3, 1943	Jan. 2, 1949
Robert S. Kerr (D)[1]	Jan. 3, 1949	Jan. 1, 1963
J. Howard Edmondson (D)[2]	Jan. 7, 1963	Nov. 3, 1964
Fred R. Harris (D)	Nov. 4, 1964	Jan. 2, 1973
Dewey F. Bartlett (R)	Jan. 3, 1973	Jan. 2, 1979
David L. Boren (D)[3]	Jan. 3, 1979	Nov. 15, 1994
James M. Inhofe (R)	Nov. 17, 1994	

Class 3

Thomas P. Gore (D)	Dec. 11, 1907	March 3, 1921
John W. Harreld (R)	March 4, 1921	March 3, 1927
Elmer Thomas (D)	March 4, 1927	Jan. 2, 1951
A. S. Mike Monroney (D)	Jan. 3, 1951	Jan. 2, 1969
Henry Bellmon (R)	Jan. 3, 1969	Jan. 2, 1981
Don Nickles (R)	Jan. 3, 1981	

Oklahoma
1. Died Jan. 1, 1963.
2. Appointed by governor to fill vacancy.
3. Resigned Nov. 15, 1994.

OREGON

(Became a state Feb. 14, 1859)

Class 2

Senators	Dates of Service	
Delazon Smith (D)	Feb. 14, 1859	March 3, 1859
Edward D. Baker (R)[1]	Oct. 2, 1860	Oct. 21, 1861
Benjamin Stark (D)[2]	Oct. 29, 1861	Sept. 12, 1862
Benjamin F. Harding (R)	Sept. 12, 1862	March 3, 1865
George H. Williams (R)	March 4, 1865	March 3, 1871
James K. Kelly (D)	March 4, 1871	March 3, 1877
La Fayette Grover (D)	March 4, 1877	March 3, 1883
Joseph N. Dolph (R)	March 4, 1883	March 3, 1895
George W. McBride (R)	March 4, 1895	March 3, 1901
John H. Mitchell (R)[3]	March 4, 1901	Dec. 8, 1905
John M. Gearin (D)[4]	Dec. 13, 1905	Jan. 23, 1907
Frederick W. Mulkey (R)	Jan. 23, 1907	March 3, 1907
Jonathan Bourne Jr. (R)	March 4, 1907	March 3, 1913
Harry Lane (D)[5]	March 4, 1913	May 23, 1917
Charles L. McNary (R)[6]	May 29, 1917	Nov. 5, 1918
Frederick W. Mulkey (R)[7]	Nov. 6, 1918	Dec. 17, 1918
Charles L. McNary (R)[8]	Dec. 18, 1918	Feb. 25, 1944
Guy Cordon (R)[9]	March 4, 1944	Jan. 2, 1955
Richard L. Neuberger (D)[10]	Jan. 3, 1955	March 9, 1960
Hall S. Lusk (D)[11]	March 16, 1960	Nov. 8, 1960
Maurine B. Neuberger (D)	Nov. 9, 1960	Jan. 2, 1967
Mark O. Hatfield (R)	Jan. 10, 1967	Jan. 2, 1997
Gordon H. Smith (R)	Jan. 3, 1997	

Class 3

Joseph Lane (D)	Feb. 14, 1859	March 3, 1861
James W. Nesmith (D)	March 4, 1861	March 3, 1867
Henry W. Corbett (R)	March 4, 1867	March 3, 1873
John H. Mitchell (R)	March 4, 1873	March 3, 1879
James H. Slater (D)	March 4, 1879	March 3, 1885
John H. Mitchell (R)	Nov. 18, 1885	March 3, 1897
Joseph Simon (R)[12]	Oct. 8, 1898	March 3, 1903
Charles W. Fulton (R)	March 4, 1903	March 3, 1909
George E. Chamberlain (D)	March 4, 1909	March 3, 1921
Robert N. Stanfield (R)	March 4, 1921	March 3, 1927
Frederick Steiwer (R)[13]	March 4, 1927	Jan. 31, 1938
Alfred Evan Reames (D)[14]	Feb. 1, 1938	Nov. 8, 1938
Alexander G. Barry (R)	Nov. 9, 1938	Jan. 2, 1939
Rufus C. Holman (R)	Jan. 3, 1939	Jan. 2, 1945
Wayne L. Morse (R, I, D)[15]	Jan. 3, 1945	Jan. 2, 1969
Bob Packwood (R)[16]	Jan. 3, 1969	Oct. 1, 1995
Ron Wyden (D)	Feb. 6, 1996	

Oregon
1. Vacancy from March 4, 1859, to Oct. 2, 1860. Died Oct. 21, 1861.
2. Appointed by governor to fill vacancy.
3. Died Dec. 8, 1905.
4. Appointed by governor to fill vacancy.
5. Died May 23, 1917.
6. Appointed by governor to fill vacancy.
7. Resigned Dec. 17, 1918.
8. Appointed by governor to fill vacancy. Subsequently elected. Died Feb. 25, 1944.
9. Appointed by governor to fill vacancy. Subsequently elected.
10. Died March 9, 1960.
11. Appointed by governor to fill vacancy.
12. Vacancy from March 4, 1897, to Oct. 7, 1898, because of failure of legislature to elect.
13. Resigned Jan. 31, 1938.
14. Appointed by governor to fill vacancy.
15. Elected as a Republican in 1944 and 1950, as a Democrat in 1956 and 1962. Morse was also an Independent from Oct. 24, 1952, to Feb. 17, 1955.
16. Resigned Oct. 1, 1995.

PENNSYLVANIA

(Ratified the Constitution Dec. 12, 1787)

Class 1

Senators	Dates of Service	
William Maclay (D-R)[1]	March 4, 1789	March 3, 1791
Albert Gallatin (D-R)[2]	Feb. 28, 1793	Feb. 28, 1794
James Ross (FED)	April 1, 1794	March 3, 1803
Samuel Maclay (D-R)[3]	March 4, 1803	Jan. 4, 1809
Michael Leib (D-R)[4]	Jan. 9, 1809	Feb. 14, 1814
Jonathan Roberts (D-R)	Feb. 24, 1814	March 3, 1821
William Findlay (D-R)	Dec. 10, 1821	March 3, 1827
Isaac D. Barnard[5]	March 4, 1827	Dec. 6, 1831
George M. Dallas (D)	Dec. 13, 1831	March 3, 1833
Samuel McKean (D)	Dec. 7, 1833	March 3, 1839
Daniel Sturgeon (D)	Jan. 14, 1840	March 3, 1851
Richard Brodhead (D)	March 4, 1851	March 3, 1857
Simon Cameron (R)[6]	March 4, 1857	March 4, 1861
David Wilmot (R)	March 14, 1861	March 3, 1863
Charles R. Buckalew (D)	March 4, 1863	March 3, 1869
John Scott (R)	March 4, 1869	March 3, 1875
William A. Wallace (D)	March 4, 1875	March 3, 1881
John I. Mitchell (R)	March 4, 1881	March 3, 1887
Matthew S. Quay (R)[7]	March 4, 1887	March 3, 1899
Matthew S. Quay (R)[8]	Jan. 17, 1901	May 28, 1904
Philander C. Knox (R)[9]	June 10, 1904	March 4, 1909
George T. Oliver (R)	March 17, 1909	March 3, 1917
Philander C. Knox (R)[10]	March 4, 1917	Oct. 12, 1921
William E. Crow (R)[11]	Oct. 24, 1921	Aug. 2, 1922
David A. Reed (R)[12]	Aug. 8, 1922	Jan. 2, 1935
Joseph F. Guffey (D)	Jan. 3, 1935	Jan. 2, 1947
Edward Martin (R)	Jan. 3, 1947	Jan. 2, 1959
Hugh Scott (R)	Jan. 3, 1959	Jan. 2, 1977
John Heinz (R)[13]	Jan. 3, 1977	April 4, 1991
Harris Wofford (D)[14]	May 9, 1991	Jan. 2, 1995
Rick Santorum (R)	Jan. 3, 1995	

Class 3

Robert Morris (FED)	March 4, 1789	March 3, 1795
William Bingham (FED)	March 4, 1795	March 3, 1801
John P. G. Muhlenberg (D-R)[15]	March 4, 1801	June 30, 1801
George Logan (D-R)[16]	July 13, 1801	March 3, 1807
Andrew Gregg (D-R)	March 4, 1807	March 3, 1813
Abner Lacock (D-R)	March 4, 1813	March 3, 1819
Walter Lowrie (D-R)	March 4, 1819	March 3, 1825
William Marks (D-R)	March 4, 1825	March 3, 1831
William Wilkins (D & A-MAS)[17]	March 4, 1831	June 30, 1834
James Buchanan (D)[18]	Dec. 6, 1834	March 5, 1845
Simon Cameron (D)	March 13, 1845	March 3, 1849
James Cooper (W)	March 4, 1849	March 3, 1855
William Bigler (D)	Jan. 14, 1856	March 3, 1861
Edgar Cowan (R)	March 4, 1861	March 3, 1867
Simon Cameron (R)[19]	March 4, 1867	March 3, 1877
J. Donald Cameron (R)	March 20, 1877	March 3, 1897
Boies Penrose (R)[20]	March 4, 1897	Dec. 31, 1921
George Wharton Pepper (R)[21]	Jan. 9, 1922	March 3, 1927
William S. Vare (R)[22]		
Joseph R. Grundy (R)[23]	Dec. 11, 1929	Dec. 1, 1930
James J. Davis (R)	Dec. 2, 1930	Jan. 2, 1945
Francis J. Myers (D)	Jan. 3, 1945	Jan. 2, 1951
James H. Duff (R)	Jan. 16, 1951	Jan. 2, 1957
Joseph S. Clark (D)	Jan. 3, 1957	Jan. 2, 1969
Richard S. Schweiker (R)	Jan. 3, 1969	Jan. 2, 1981
Arlen Specter (R)	Jan. 3, 1981	

Pennsylvania

1. Vacancy from March 4, 1791, to Feb. 28, 1793, because of failure of legislature to elect.

2. Senate resolution of Feb. 28, 1794, declared that Gallatin had not been a citizen for the nine years required by the Constitution for Senate membership.

3. Resigned Jan. 4, 1809.

4. Resigned Feb. 14, 1814.

5. Resigned Dec. 6, 1831.

6. Resigned March 4, 1861.

7. Quay was elected for two six-year terms, his second term expiring March 3, 1899. The legislature adjourned without electing a senator for the new term beginning March 4, 1899. Quay was appointed by the governor to fill the vacancy on April 21, 1899. When the Senate convened, he presented his credentials Dec. 25, 1899, but was not permitted to take his seat. On April 24, 1900, the seat was declared vacant. Quay was elected to fill the vacancy and took his seat Jan. 17, 1901.

8. Died May 28, 1904.

9. Appointed by governor to fill vacancy. Subsequently elected. Resigned March 4, 1909.

10. Died Oct. 12, 1921.

11. Appointed by governor to fill vacancy. Died Aug. 2, 1922.

12. Appointed by governor to fill vacancy. Subsequently elected.

13. Died April 4, 1991.

14. Appointed by governor to fill vacancy. Subsequently elected.

15. Resigned June 30, 1801.

16. Appointed by governor to fill vacancy. Subsequently elected.

17. Resigned June 30, 1834.

18. Resigned March 5, 1845.

19. Resigned March 3, 1877.

20. Died Dec. 31, 1921.

21. Appointed by governor to fill vacancy. Subsequently elected.

22. Credentials as senator-elect were presented and referred to the Committee on Privileges and Elections. Meanwhile Vare was not permitted to take his seat and on Dec. 6, 1929, was declared not entitled to a seat.

23. Appointed by governor to fill vacancy.

RHODE ISLAND

(Ratified the Constitution May 29, 1790)

Class 1

Senators	Dates of Service	
Theodore Foster (LAW ORD)	June 7, 1790	March 3, 1803
Samuel J. Potter[1]	March 4, 1803	Oct. 14, 1804
Benjamin Howland (D-R)	Oct. 29, 1804	March 3, 1809
Francis Malbone[2]	March 4, 1809	June 4, 1809
Christopher G. Champlin[3]	June 26, 1809	Oct. 2, 1811
William Hunter (FED)	Oct. 28, 1811	March 3, 1821
James De Wolf (D-R)[4]	March 4, 1821	Oct. 31, 1825
Asher Robbins (D-R, NR, W)	Oct. 31, 1825	March 3, 1839
Nathan F. Dixon (W)[5]	March 4, 1839	Jan. 29, 1842
William Sprague (W)[6]	Feb. 5, 1842	Jan. 17, 1844
John B. Francis (LAW ORD)	Jan. 25, 1844	March 3, 1845
Albert C. Greene (W)	March 4, 1845	March 3, 1851
Charles T. James (D)	March 4, 1851	March 3, 1857
James F. Simmons (R)[7]	March 4, 1857	Aug. 15, 1862
Samuel G. Arnold (R)	Sept. 5, 1862	March 3, 1863
William Sprague (R)[8]	March 4, 1863	March 3, 1875
Ambrose E. Burnside (R)[9]	March 4, 1875	Sept. 13, 1881
Nelson W. Aldrich (R)	Oct. 5, 1881	March 3, 1911
Henry F. Lippitt (R)	March 4, 1911	March 3, 1917
Peter G. Gerry (D)	March 4, 1917	March 3, 1929
Felix Hebert (R)	March 4, 1929	Jan. 2, 1935
Peter G. Gerry (D)	Jan. 3, 1935	Jan. 2, 1947
J. Howard McGrath (D)[10]	Jan. 3, 1947	Aug. 23, 1949
Edward L. Leahy (D)[11]	Aug. 24, 1949	Dec. 18, 1950
John O. Pastore (D)[12]	Dec. 19, 1950	Dec. 28, 1976
John H. Chafee (R)[13]	Dec. 29, 1976	Oct. 24, 1999
Lincoln D. Chafee (R)[14]	Nov. 4, 1999	

Class 2

Joseph Stanton Jr. (D-R)	June 7, 1790	March 3, 1793
William Bradford[15]	March 4, 1793	October 1797
Ray Greene (FED)[16]	Nov. 13, 1797	March 5, 1801
Christopher Ellery (D-R)	May 6, 1801	March 3, 1805
James Fenner (D-R)[17]	March 4, 1805	Sept. 1807
Elisha Mathewson (D-R)	Oct. 26, 1807	March 3, 1811
Jeremiah B. Howell (FED)	March 4, 1811	March 3, 1817
James Burrill Jr. (D-R)[18]	March 4, 1817	Dec. 25, 1820
Nehemiah R. Knight (D-R, D)	Jan. 9, 1821	March 3, 1841
James F. Simmons (W)	March 4, 1841	March 3, 1847
John H. Clarke (W)	March 4, 1847	March 3, 1853
Philip Allen (D)	July 20, 1853	March 3, 1859
Henry B. Anthony (R)[19]	March 4, 1859	Sept. 2, 1884
William P. Sheffield (R)[20]	Nov. 19, 1884	Jan. 20, 1885
Jonathan Chace (R)[21]	Jan. 20, 1885	April 9, 1889
Nathan F. Dixon III (R)	April 10, 1889	March 3, 1895
George Peabody Wetmore (R)	March 4, 1895	March 3, 1907
George Peabody Wetmore (R)[22]	Jan. 22, 1908	March 3, 1913

LeBaron B. Colt (R)[23]	March 4, 1913	Aug. 18, 1924
Jesse H. Metcalf (R)	Nov. 5, 1924	Jan. 2, 1937
Theodore F. Green (D)	Jan. 3, 1937	Jan. 2, 1961
Claiborne Pell (D)	Jan. 3, 1961	Jan. 2, 1997
Jack Reed (D)	Jan. 3, 1997	

Rhode Island
1. Died Oct. 14, 1804.
2. Died June 4, 1809.
3. Resigned Oct. 2, 1811.
4. Resigned Oct. 31, 1825.
5. Died Jan. 29, 1842.
6. Resigned Jan. 17, 1844.
7. Resigned Aug. 15, 1862.
8. Nephew of William Sprague, listed above with footnote 6.
9. Died Sept. 13, 1881.
10. Resigned Aug. 23, 1949.
11. Appointed by governor to fill vacancy.
12. Resigned Dec. 28, 1976.
13. Died Oct. 24, 1999.
14. Appointed by governor to fill vacancy. Subsequently elected.
15. Resigned in October 1797.
16. Resigned March 5, 1801.
17. Resigned in September 1807.
18. Died Dec. 25, 1820.
19. Died Sept. 2, 1884.
20. Appointed by governor to fill vacancy.
21. Resigned April 9, 1889.
22. Vacant March 4, 1907 to Jan. 22, 1908, because of failure of legislature to elect.
23. Died Aug. 18, 1924.

SOUTH CAROLINA

(Ratified the Constitution May 23, 1788)

Class 2

Senators	Dates of Service	
Pierce Butler (D-R)[1]	March 4, 1789	Oct. 25, 1796
John Hunter (FED)[2]	Dec. 8, 1796	Nov. 26, 1798
Charles Pinckney (D-R)[3]	Dec. 6, 1798	1801
Thomas Sumter (D-R)[4]	Dec. 15, 1801	Dec. 16, 1810
John Taylor (D-R)[5]	Dec. 31, 1810	Nov. 1816
William Smith (D-R)	Dec. 4, 1816	March 3, 1823
Robert Y. Hayne (D-R)[6]	March 4, 1823	Dec. 13, 1832
John C. Calhoun (D)[7]	Dec. 29, 1832	March 3, 1843
Daniel Elliott Huger (D)[8]	March 4, 1843	March 3, 1845
John C. Calhoun (D)[9]	Nov. 26, 1845	March 31, 1850
Franklin H. Elmore (D)[10]	April 11, 1850	May 29, 1850
Robert W. Barnwell (D)[11]	June 4, 1850	Dec. 18, 1850
R. Barnwell Rhett (D)[12]	Dec. 18, 1850	May 7, 1852
William F. DeSaussure (D)[13]	May 10, 1852	March 3, 1853
Josiah J. Evans (D)[14]	March 4, 1853	May 6, 1858
Arthur P. Hayne (D)[15]	May 11, 1858	Dec. 2, 1858
James Chestnut Jr. (D)[16]	Dec. 3, 1858	July 11, 1861
Thomas J. Robertson (R)	July 15, 1868	March 3, 1877
Matthew C. Butler (D)	March 4, 1877	March 3, 1895
Benjamin R. Tillman (D)[17]	March 4, 1895	July 3, 1918
Christie Bénet (D)[18]	July 6, 1918	Nov. 5, 1918
William P. Pollock (D)	Nov. 6, 1918	March 3, 1919
Nathaniel B. Dial (D)	March 4, 1919	March 3, 1925
Coleman L. Blease (D)	March 4, 1925	March 3, 1931
James F. Byrnes (D)[19]	March 4, 1931	July 8, 1941
Alva M. Lumpkin (D)[20]	July 17, 1941	Aug. 1, 1941

Roger C. Peace (D)[21]	Aug. 5, 1941	Nov. 4, 1941
Burnet R. Maybank (D)[22]	Nov. 5, 1941	Sept. 1, 1954
Charles E. Daniel (D)[23]	Sept. 6, 1954	Dec. 23, 1954
Strom Thurmond (D)[24]	Dec. 24, 1954	April 4, 1956
Thomas A. Wofford (D)[25]	April 5, 1956	Nov. 6, 1956
Strom Thurmond (D, R)[26]	Nov. 7, 1956	

Class 3

Ralph Izard (FED)	March 4, 1789	March 3, 1795
Jacob Read (FED)	March 4, 1795	March 3, 1801
John E. Colhoun (D-R)[27]	March 4, 1801	Oct. 26, 1802
Pierce Butler (D-R)[28]	Nov. 4, 1802	Nov. 21, 1804
John Gaillard (D-R)[29]	Dec. 6, 1804	Feb. 26, 1826
William Harper (D-R)[30]	March 8, 1826	Nov. 29, 1826
William Smith (D-R)	Nov. 29, 1826	March 3, 1831
Stephen D. Miller D)[31]	March 4, 1831	March 2, 1833
William C. Preston (D)[32]	Nov. 26, 1833	Nov. 29, 1842
George McDuffie (D)[33]	Dec. 2, 1842	Aug. 17, 1846
Andrew P. Butler (D)[34]	Dec. 4, 1846	May 25, 1857
James H. Hammond (D)[35]	Dec. 7, 1857	Nov. 11, 1860
Frederick A. Sawyer (R)	July 16, 1868	March 3, 1873
John J. Patterson (R)	March 4, 1873	March 3, 1879
Wade Hampton (D)	March 4, 1879	March 3, 1891
John L. M. Irby (D)	March 4, 1891	March 3, 1897
Joseph H. Earle (D)[36]	March 4, 1897	May 20, 1897
John L. McLaurin (D)[37]	May 27, 1897	March 3, 1903
Asbury C. Latimer (D)[38]	March 4, 1903	Feb. 20, 1908
Frank B. Gary (D)	March 6, 1908	March 3, 1909
Ellison D. Smith (D)[39]	March 4, 1909	Nov. 17, 1944
Wilton E. Hall (D)[40]	Nov. 20, 1944	Jan. 2, 1945
Olin D. Johnston (D)[41]	Jan. 3, 1945	April 18, 1965
Donald Russell (D)[42]	April 22, 1965	Nov. 8, 1966
Ernest F. Hollings (D)	Nov. 9, 1966	

South Carolina
1. Resigned Oct. 25, 1796.
2. Resigned Nov. 26, 1798.
3. Resigned in 1801.
4. Resigned Dec. 16, 1810.
5. Resigned in November 1816.
6. Resigned Dec. 13, 1832.
7. Resigned March 3, 1843.
8. Resigned March 3, 1845. Seat vacant until Nov. 26, 1845.
9. Died March 31, 1850.
10. Appointed by governor to fill vacancy. Died May 29, 1850.
11. Appointed by governor to fill vacancy.
12. Resigned May 7, 1852.
13. Appointed by governor to fill vacancy. Subsequently elected.
14. Died May 6, 1858.
15. Appointed by governor to fill vacancy.
16. Expelled July 11, 1861. Vacancy until July 15, 1868, because of Civil War.
17. Died July 3, 1918.
18. Appointed by governor to fill vacancy.
19. Resigned July 8, 1941.
20. Appointed by governor to fill vacancy. Died Aug. 1, 1941.
21. Appointed by governor to fill vacancy.
22. Died Sept. 1, 1954.
23. Appointed by governor to fill vacancy. Resigned Dec. 23, 1954.
24. Resigned April 4, 1956.
25. Appointed by governor to fill vacancy.
26. Became a Republican on Sept. 16, 1964.
27. Died Oct. 26, 1802.
28. Resigned Nov. 21, 1804.
29. Died Feb. 26, 1826.
30. Appointed by governor to fill vacancy.
31. Resigned March 2, 1833.

South Carolina (continued)
32. Resigned Nov. 29, 1842.
33. Resigned Aug. 17, 1846.
34. Died May 25, 1857.
35. Did not attend sessions of the Senate after Nov. 11, 1860. Vacancy until July 16, 1868, because of Civil War.
36. Died May 20, 1897.
37. Appointed by governor to fill vacancy. Subsequently elected.
38. Died Feb. 20, 1908.
39. Died Nov. 17, 1944.
40. Appointed by governor to fill vacancy.
41. Died April 18, 1965.
42. Appointed by governor to fill vacancy.

SOUTH DAKOTA

(Became a state Nov. 2, 1889)

Class 2

Senators	Dates of Service	
Richard F. Pettigrew (R)	Nov. 2, 1889	March 3, 1901
Robert J. Gamble (R)	March 4, 1901	March 3, 1913
Thomas Sterling (R)	March 4, 1913	March 3, 1925
William H. McMaster (R)	March 4, 1925	March 3, 1931
William J. Bulow (D)	March 4, 1931	Jan. 2, 1943
Harlan J. Bushfield (R)[1]	Jan. 3, 1943	Sept. 27, 1948
Vera C. Bushfield (R)[2]	Oct. 6, 1948	Dec. 26, 1948
Karl E. Mundt (R)	Dec. 31, 1948	Jan. 2, 1973
James Abourezk (D)	Jan. 3, 1973	Jan. 2, 1979
Larry Pressler (R)	Jan. 3, 1979	Jan. 2, 1997
Tim Johnson (D)	Jan. 3, 1997	

Class 3

Gideon C. Moody (R)	Nov. 2, 1889	March 3, 1891
James H. Kyle (I)[3]	March 4, 1891	July 1, 1901
Alfred B. Kittredge (R)[4]	July 11, 1901	March 3, 1909
Coe I. Crawford (R)	March 4, 1909	March 3, 1915
Edwin S. Johnson (D)	March 4, 1915	March 3, 1921
Peter Norbeck (R)[5]	March 4, 1921	Dec. 20, 1936
Herbert E. Hitchcock (D)[6]	Dec. 29, 1936	Nov. 8, 1938
Gladys Pyle (R)	Nov. 9, 1938	Jan. 2, 1939
J. Chandler Gurney (R)	Jan. 3, 1939	Jan. 2, 1951
Francis Case (R)[7]	Jan. 3, 1951	June 22, 1962
Joe H. Bottum (R)[8]	July 9, 1962	Jan. 2, 1963
George McGovern (D)	Jan. 3, 1963	Jan. 2, 1981
James Abdnor (R)	Jan. 3, 1981	Jan. 2, 1987
Thomas A. Daschle (D)	Jan. 3, 1987	

South Dakota
1. Died Sept. 27, 1948.
2. Appointed by governor to fill vacancy. Resigned Dec. 26, 1948.
3. Died July 1, 1901.
4. Appointed by governor to fill vacancy. Subsequently elected.
5. Died Dec. 20, 1936.

6. Appointed by governor to fill vacancy.
7. Died June 22, 1962.
8. Appointed by governor to fill vacancy.

TENNESSEE

(Became a state June 1, 1796)

Class 1

Senators	Dates of Service	
William Cocke (D-R)	Aug. 2, 1796	March 3, 1797
William Cocke (D-R)[1]	April 22, 1797	Sept. 26, 1797
Andrew Jackson (D-R)[2]	Sept. 26, 1797	April 1798
Daniel Smith (D-R)[3]	Oct. 6, 1798	Dec. 12, 1798
Joseph Anderson (D-R)[4]	March 4, 1799	March 3, 1815
George W. Campbell (D-R)[5]	Oct. 10, 1815	April 20, 1818
John H. Eaton (D-R)[6]	Sept. 5, 1818	March 9, 1829
Felix Grundy (D)[7]	Oct. 19, 1829	July 4, 1838
Ephraim H. Foster (W)[8]	Sept. 17, 1838	March 3, 1839
Felix Grundy (D)[9]	Dec. 14, 1839	Dec. 19, 1840
Alfred O. P. Nicholson (D)[10]	Dec. 25, 1840	Feb. 7, 1942
Ephraim H. Foster (W)	Oct. 17, 1843	March 3, 1845
Hopkins L. Turney (W)	March 4, 1845	March 3, 1851
James C. Jones (W)	March 4, 1851	March 3, 1857
Andrew Johnson (D)[11]	Oct. 8, 1857	March 4, 1862
David T. Patterson (D)	July 28, 1866	March 3, 1869
William G. Brownlow (R)	March 4,1869	March 3, 1875
Andrew Johnson (D)[12]	March 4, 1875	July 31, 1875
David M. Key (D)[13]	Aug. 18, 1875	Jan. 19, 1877
James E. Bailey (D)	Jan. 19, 1877	March 3, 1881
Howell E. Jackson (D)[14]	March 4, 1881	April 14, 1886
W. C. Whitthorne (D)[15]	April 16, 1886	March 3, 1887
William B. Bate (D)[16]	March 4, 1887	March 9, 1905
James B. Frazier (D)	March 21, 1905	March 3, 1911
Luke Lea (D)	March 4, 1911	March 3, 1917
Kenneth D. McKellar (D)	March 4, 1917	Jan. 2, 1953
Albert Gore (D)	Jan. 3, 1953	Jan. 2, 1971
Bill Brock (R)	Jan. 3, 1971	Jan. 2, 1977
Jim Sasser (D)	Jan. 3, 1977	Jan. 2, 1995
Bill Frist (R)	Jan. 3, 1995	

Class 2

William Blount (D-R)[17]	Aug. 2, 1796	July 8, 1797
Joseph Anderson (D-R)	Sept. 26, 1797	March 3, 1799
William Cocke (D-R)	March 4, 1799	March 3, 1805
Daniel Smith (D-R)[18]	March 4, 1805	March 31, 1809
Jenkin Whiteside (D-R)[19]	April 11, 1809	Oct. 8, 1811
George W. Campbell (D-R)[20]	Oct. 8, 1811	Feb. 11, 1814
Jesse Wharton (D-R)[21]	March 17, 1814	Oct. 10, 1815
John Williams (D-R)[22]	Oct. 10, 1815	March 3, 1823
Andrew Jackson (D-R)[23]	March 4, 1823	Oct. 14, 1825
Hugh Lawson White (D-R, D)	Oct. 28, 1825	March 3, 1835
Hugh Lawson White (D)[24]	Oct. 6, 1835	Jan. 13, 1840
Alexander Anderson (D)	Jan. 27, 1840	March 4, 1841
Spencer Jarnagin (W)[25]	Oct. 17, 1843	March 3, 1847
John Bell (W)	Nov. 22, 1847	March 3, 1853

John Bell (W)	Oct. 29, 1853	March 3, 1859
Alfred O. P. Nicholson (D)[26]	March 4, 1859	July 11, 1861
Joseph S. Fowler (UN R)	July 25, 1866	March 3, 1871
Henry Cooper (D)	March 4, 1871	March 3, 1877
Isham G. Harris (D)[27]	March 4, 1877	July 8, 1897
Thomas B. Turley (D)[28]	July 20, 1897	March 3, 1901
Edward W. Carmack (D)	March 4, 1901	March 3, 1907
Robert L. Taylor (D)[29]	March 4, 1907	March 31, 1912
Newell Sanders (R)[30]	April 8, 1912	Jan. 24, 1913
William R. Webb (D)	Jan. 24, 1913	March 3, 1913
John K. Shields (D)	March 4, 1913	March 3, 1925
Lawrence D. Tyson (D)[31]	March 4, 1925	Aug. 24, 1929
William E. Brock (D)[32]	Sept. 2, 1929	March 3, 1931
Cordell Hull (D)[33]	March 4, 1931	March 3, 1933
Nathan L. Bachman (D)[34]	March 4, 1933	April 23, 1937
George L. Berry (D)[35]	May 6, 1937	Nov. 8, 1938
Tom Stewart (D)	Jan. 16, 1939	Jan. 2, 1949
Estes Kefauver (D)[36]	Jan. 3, 1949	Aug. 10, 1963
Herbert S. Walters (D)[37]	Aug. 20, 1963	Nov. 3, 1964
Ross Bass (D)	Nov. 4, 1964	Jan. 2, 1967
Howard H. Baker Jr. (R)	Jan. 3, 1967	Jan. 2, 1985
Albert Gore Jr. (D)[38]	Jan. 3, 1985	Jan. 1, 1993
Harlan Mathews (D)[39]	Jan. 2, 1993	Dec. 2, 1994
Fred Thompson (R)	Dec. 9, 1994	

Tennessee

1. Appointed by governor to fill vacancy.
2. Resigned in April 1798.
3. Appointed by governor to fill vacancy.
4. Served twice through election and once by appointment of the governor during this period.
5. Resigned April 20, 1818.
6. Appointed by governor to fill vacancy. Subsequently elected. Resigned March 9, 1829.
7. Resigned July 4, 1838.
8. Appointed by governor to fill vacancy. Subsequently elected for term beginning March 4, 1839, but resigned March 3, 1839. Vacancy until Dec. 14, 1839.
9. Died Dec. 19, 1840.
10. Appointed by governor to fill vacancy.
11. Resigned March 4, 1862. Vacancy until July 28, 1866, because of Civil War.
12. Died July 31, 1875.
13. Appointed by governor to fill vacancy.
14. Resigned April 14, 1886.
15. Appointed by governor to fill vacancy.
16. Died March 9, 1905.
17. Expelled July 8, 1797.
18. Resigned March 31, 1809.
19. Resigned Oct. 8, 1811.
20. Resigned Feb. 11, 1814.
21. Appointed by governor to fill vacancy.
22. Williams served twice by election and once by appointment of the governor during this period.
23. Resigned Oct. 14, 1825.
24. White's seat was vacant between March 4, 1835, and Oct. 5, 1835. Resigned Jan. 13, 1840.
25. Vacancy from March 4, 1841, to Oct. 17, 1843.
26. Expelled July 11, 1861. Vacant until July 25, 1866, because of Civil War.
27. Died July 8, 1897.
28. Appointed by governor to fill vacancy. Subsequently elected.
29. Died March 31, 1912.
30. Appointed by governor to fill vacancy.
31. Died Aug. 24, 1929.
32. Appointed by governor to fill vacancy. Subsequently elected.
33. Resigned March 3, 1933.
34. Appointed by governor to fill vacancy. Subsequently elected. Died April 23, 1937.
35. Appointed by governor to fill vacancy.

36. Died Aug. 10, 1963.
37. Appointed by governor to fill vacancy.
38. Resigned Jan. 1, 1993, having been elected vice president of the United States.
39. Appointed by governor to fill vacancy.

TEXAS

(Became a state Dec. 29, 1845)

Class 1

Senators	Dates of Service	
Thomas J. Rusk (D)[1]	Feb. 21, 1846	July 29, 1857
J. P. Henderson (D)[2]	Nov. 9, 1857	June 4, 1858
Matthias Ward (D)[3]	Sept. 27, 1858	Dec. 5, 1859
Louis T. Wigfall (D)[4]	Dec. 5, 1859	July 11, 1861
J. W. Flanagan (R)	March 31, 1870	March 3, 1875
Samuel B. Maxey (D)	March 4, 1875	March 3, 1887
John H. Reagan (D)[5]	March 4, 1887	June 10, 1891
Horace Chilton (D)[6]	June 10, 1891	March 22, 1892
Roger Q. Mills (D)	March 23, 1892	March 3, 1899
Charles A. Culberson (D)	March 4, 1899	March 3, 1923
Earle B. Mayfield (D)	March 4, 1923	March 3, 1929
Tom Connally (D)	March 4, 1929	Jan. 2, 1953
Price Daniel (D)[7]	Jan. 3, 1953	Jan. 14, 1957
William A. Blakley (D)[8]	Jan. 15, 1957	April 28, 1957
Ralph Yarborough (D)	April 29, 1957	Jan. 2, 1971
Lloyd Bentsen (D)[9]	Jan. 3, 1971	Jan. 20, 1993
Bob Krueger (D)[10]	Jan. 21, 1993	June 14, 1993
Kay Bailey Hutchison (R)	June 14, 1993	

Class 2

Sam Houston (D)	Feb. 21, 1846	March 3, 1859
John Hemphill (D)[11]	March 4, 1859	July 11, 1861
Morgan C. Hamilton (R)	March 31, 1870	March 3, 1877
Richard Coke (D)	March 4, 1877	March 3, 1895
Horace Chilton (D)	March 4, 1895	March 3, 1901
Joseph W. Bailey (D)[12]	March 4, 1901	Jan. 3, 1913
Rienzi M. Johnston (D)[13]	Jan. 4, 1913	Jan. 29, 1913
Morris Sheppard (D)[14]	Jan. 29, 1913	April 9, 1941
Andrew Jackson Houston (D)[15]	April 21, 1941	June 26, 1941
W. Lee O'Daniel (D)	Aug. 4, 1941	Jan. 2, 1949
Lyndon B. Johnson (D)[16]	Jan. 3, 1949	Jan. 3, 1961
William A. Blakley (D)[17]	Jan. 3, 1961	June 14, 1961
John Tower (R)	June 15, 1961	Jan. 2, 1985
Phil Gramm (R)	Jan. 3, 1985	

Texas

1. Died July 29, 1857.
2. Died June 4, 1858.
3. Appointed by governor to fill vacancy.
4. Expelled July 11, 1861. Vacant until March 31, 1870, because of Civil War.
5. Resigned June 10, 1891.
6. Appointed by governor to fill vacancy.
7. Resigned Jan. 14, 1957.
8. Appointed by governor to fill vacancy.
9. Resigned Jan. 20, 1993.
10. Appointed by governor to fill vacancy.
11. Expelled July 11, 1861. Vacant until March 31, 1870, because of Civil War.

Texas (continued)
12. Resigned Jan. 3, 1913.
13. Appointed by governor to fill vacancy.
14. Died April 9, 1941.
15. Appointed by governor to fill vacancy. Died June 26, 1941.
16. Resigned Jan. 3, 1961, immediately after taking oath of office, having been elected vice president of the United States.
17. Appointed by governor to fill vacancy.

UTAH

(Became a state Jan. 4, 1896)

Class 1

Senators	Dates of Service	
Frank J. Cannon (R)	Jan. 22, 1896	March 3, 1899
Thomas Kearns (R)[1]	Jan. 23, 1901	March 3, 1905
George Sutherland (R)	March 4, 1905	March 3, 1917
William H. King (D)	March 4, 1917	Jan. 2, 1941
Abe Murdock (D)	Jan. 3, 1941	Jan. 2, 1947
Arthur V. Watkins (R)	Jan. 3, 1947	Jan. 2, 1959
Frank E. Moss (D)	Jan. 3, 1959	Jan. 2, 1977
Orrin G. Hatch (R)	Jan. 3, 1977	

Class 3

Arthur Brown (R)	Jan. 22, 1896	March 3, 1897
Joseph L. Rawlins (D)	March 4, 1897	March 3, 1903
Reed Smoot (R)	March 4, 1903	March 3, 1933
Elbert D. Thomas (D)	March 4, 1933	Jan. 2, 1951
Wallace F. Bennett (R)[2]	Jan. 3, 1951	Dec. 20, 1974
Jake Garn (R)	Dec. 21, 1974	Jan. 2, 1993
Robert F. Bennett (R)	Jan. 3, 1993	

Utah
1. Vacancy from March 4, 1899, to Jan. 22, 1901, because of failure of Legislature to elect.
2. Resigned Dec. 20, 1974.

VERMONT

(Became a state March 4, 1791)

Class 1

Senators	Dates of Service	
Moses Robinson (D-R)[1]	Oct. 17, 1791	Oct. 15, 1796
Isaac Tichenor (FED)[2]	Oct. 18, 1796	Oct. 17, 1797
Nathaniel Chipman (FED)	Oct. 17, 1797	March 3, 1803
Israel Smith (D-R)[3]	March 4, 1803	Oct. 1, 1807
Jonathan Robinson	Oct. 10, 1807	March 3, 1815
Isaac Tichenor (FED)	March 4, 1815	March 3, 1821
Horatio Seymour (D-R)	March 4, 1821	March 3, 1833
Benjamin Swift (W)	March 4, 1833	March 3, 1839
Samuel S. Phelps (W)	March 4, 1839	March 3, 1851
Solomon Foot (W, R)[4]	March 4, 1851	March 28, 1866
George F. Edmunds (R)[5]	April 3, 1866	Nov. 1, 1891
Redfield Proctor (R)[6]	Nov. 2, 1891	March 4, 1908
John W. Stewart (R)[7]	March 24, 1908	Oct. 20, 1908
Carroll S. Page (R)	Oct. 21, 1908	March 3, 1923
Frank L. Greene (R)[8]	March 4, 1923	Dec. 17, 1930

Frank C. Partridge (R)[9]	Dec. 23, 1930	March 31, 1931
Warren R. Austin (R)[10]	April 1, 1931	Aug. 2, 1946
Ralph E. Flanders (R)[11]	Nov. 1, 1946	Jan. 2, 1959
Winston L. Prouty (R)[12]	Jan. 3, 1959	Sept. 10, 1971
Robert T. Stafford (R)[13]	Sept. 16, 1971	Jan. 2, 1989
James M. Jeffords (R, I)[14]	Jan. 3, 1989	

Class 3

Stephen R. Bradley (D-R)	Oct. 17, 1791	March 3, 1795
Elijah Paine (FED)[15]	March 4, 1795	Sept. 1, 1801
Stephen R. Bradley (D-R)	Oct. 15, 1801	March 3, 1813
Dudley Chase (D-R)[16]	March 4, 1813	Nov. 3, 1817
James Fisk (D-R)[17]	Nov. 4, 1817	Jan. 8, 1818
William A. Palmer (D-R)	Oct. 20, 1818	March 3, 1825
Dudley Chase (D-R)	March 4, 1825	March 3, 1831
Samuel Prentiss (W)[18]	March 4, 1831	April 11, 1842
Samuel C. Crafts (W)[19]	Apr. 23, 1842	March 3, 1843
William Upham (W)[20]	March 4, 1843	Jan. 14, 1853
Samuel S. Phelps (W)[21]	Jan. 17, 1853	March 16, 1854
Lawrence Brainerd	Oct. 14, 1854	March 3, 1855
Jacob Collamer (R)[22]	March 4, 1855	Nov. 9, 1865
Luke P. Poland (R)[23]	Nov. 21, 1865	March 3, 1867
Justin S. Morrill (R)[24]	March 4, 1867	Dec. 28, 1898
Jonathan Ross (R)[25]	Jan. 11, 1899	Oct. 17, 1900
William P. Dillingham (R)[26]	Oct. 18, 1900	July 12, 1923
Porter H. Dale (R)[27]	Nov. 6, 1923	Oct. 6, 1933
Ernest W. Gibson (R)[28]	Nov. 21, 1933	June 20, 1940
Ernest W. Gibson Jr. (R)[29]	June 24, 1940	Jan. 2, 1941
George D. Aiken (R)	Jan. 10, 1941	Jan. 2, 1975
Patrick J. Leahy (D)	Jan. 3, 1975	

Vermont
1. Resigned Oct. 15, 1796.
2. Resigned Oct. 17, 1797.
3. Resigned Oct. 1, 1807.
4. Died March 28, 1866.
5. Appointed by governor to fill vacancy. Subsequently elected. Resigned Nov. 1, 1891.
6. Appointed by governor to fill vacancy. Subsequently elected. Died March 4, 1908.
7. Appointed by governor to fill vacancy.
8. Died Dec. 17, 1930.
9. Appointed by governor to fill vacancy.
10. Resigned Aug. 2, 1946.
11. Appointed by governor to fill vacancy. Subsequently elected.
12. Died Sept. 10, 1971.
13. Appointed by governor to fill vacancy. Subsequently elected.
14. Elected as a Republican in 1988, 1994, and 2000. Jeffords became an Independent on June 5, 2001.
15. Resigned Sept. 1, 1801.
16. Resigned Nov. 3, 1817.
17. Resigned Jan. 8, 1818.
18. Resigned April 11, 1842.
19. Appointed by governor to fill vacancy. Subsequently elected.
20. Died Jan. 14, 1853.
21. Appointed by governor to fill vacancy. By resolution of March 16, 1854, the Senate declared that he was not entitled to retain his seat. Seat remained vacant until Oct. 14, 1854.
22. Died Nov. 9, 1865.
23. Appointed by governor to fill vacancy. Subsequently elected.
24. Died Dec. 28, 1898.
25. Appointed by governor to fill vacancy.
26. Died July 12, 1923.
27. Died Oct. 6, 1933.
28. Appointed by governor to fill vacancy. Subsequently elected. Died June 20, 1940.
29. Appointed by governor to fill vacancy.

VIRGINIA

(Ratified the Constitution June 25, 1788)

Class 1

Senators	Dates of Service	
William Grayson (A-FED)[1]	March 4, 1789	March 12, 1790
John Walker[2]	March 31, 1790	Nov. 9, 1790
James Monroe (D-R)[3]	Nov. 9, 1790	Nov. 18, 1794
Stevens T. Mason (D-R)[4]	Nov. 18, 1794	May 10, 1803
John Taylor (D-R)[5]	June 4, 1803	Dec. 7, 1803
Abraham B. Venable (D-R)[6]	Dec. 7, 1803	June 7, 1804
William B. Giles (D-R)[7]	Aug. 11, 1804	Dec. 4, 1804
Andrew Moore (D-R)	Dec. 4, 1804	March 3, 1809
Richard Brent (D-R)[8]	March 4, 1809	Dec. 30, 1814
James C. Barbour (D-R)[9]	Jan. 2, 1815	March 27, 1825
John Randolph (D-R)	Dec. 9, 1825	March 3, 1827
John Tyler (D-R, D)[10]	March 4, 1827	Feb. 29, 1836
William C. Rives (D)[11]	March 4, 1836	March 3, 1839
William C. Rives (W)	Jan. 18, 1841	March 3, 1845
Isaac S. Pennybacker (D)[12]	Dec. 3, 1845	Jan. 12, 1847
James M. Mason (D)[13]	Jan. 21, 1847	July 11, 1861
Waitman T. Willey (R)[14]	July 13, 1861	March 3, 1863
Lemuel J. Bowden (R)[15]	March 4, 1863	Jan. 2, 1864
John F. Lewis (R)	Jan. 27, 1870	March 3, 1875
Robert W. Withers (C)	March 4, 1875	March 3, 1881
William Mahone (R)	March 4, 1881	March 3, 1887
John W. Daniel (D)[16]	March 4, 1887	June 29, 1910
Claude A. Swanson (D)[17]	Aug. 1, 1910	March 3, 1933
Harry F. Byrd (D)[18]	March 4, 1933	Nov. 10, 1965
Harry F. Byrd Jr. (D, I)[19]	Nov. 12, 1965	Jan. 2, 1983
Paul S. Trible Jr. (R)	Jan. 3, 1983	Jan. 2, 1989
Charles S. Robb (D)	Jan. 3, 1989	Jan. 3, 2001
George F. Allen (R)	Jan. 3, 2001	

Class 2

Richard Henry Lee (A-FED)[20]	March 4, 1789	Oct. 8, 1792
John Taylor (D-R)[21]	Oct. 18, 1792	May 11, 1794
Henry Tazewell (D-R)[22]	Nov. 18, 1794	Jan. 24, 1799
Wilson C. Nicholas (D-R)[23]	Dec. 5, 1799	May 22, 1804
Andrew Moore (D-R)[24]	Aug. 11, 1804	Dec. 4, 1804
William B. Giles (D-R)[25]	Dec. 4, 1804	March 3, 1815
Armistead T. Mason (D-R)	Jan. 3, 1816	March 3, 1817
John W. Eppes (D-R)[26]	March 4, 1817	Dec. 4, 1819
James Pleasants (D-R)[27]	Dec. 10, 1819	Dec. 15, 1822
John Taylor (D-R)[28]	Dec. 18, 1822	Aug. 20, 1824
Littleton W. Tazewell (D-R, D)[29]	Dec. 7, 1824	July 16, 1832
William C. Rives (D)[30]	Dec. 10, 1832	Feb. 22, 1834
Benjamin W. Leigh (D)[31]	Feb. 26, 1834	July 4, 1836
Richard E. Parker (D)[32]	Dec. 12, 1836	March 13, 1837
William H. Roane (D)	March 14, 1837	March 3, 1841
William S. Archer (W)	March 4, 1841	March 3, 1847
Robert M. T. Hunter (D)[33]	March 4, 1847	July 11, 1861
John S. Carlile (UN)[34]	July 13, 1861	March 3, 1865
John W. Johnston (C)[35]	Jan. 28, 1870	March 3, 1883
H. H. Riddleberger (R)	March 4, 1883	March 3, 1889
John S. Barbour Jr. (D)[36]	March 4, 1889	May 14, 1892
Eppa Hunton (D)[37]	May 28, 1892	March 3, 1895
Thomas S. Martin (D)[38]	March 4, 1895	Nov. 12, 1919
Carter Glass (D)[39]	Feb. 2, 1920	May 28, 1946
Thomas G. Burch (D)[40]	May 31, 1946	Nov. 5, 1946
A. Willis Robertson (D)[41]	Nov. 6, 1946	Dec. 30, 1966
William B. Spong Jr. (D)	Dec. 31, 1966	Jan. 2, 1973
William Lloyd Scott (R)[42]	Jan. 3, 1973	Jan. 1, 1979
John W. Warner (R)	Jan. 2, 1979	

Virginia

1. Died March 12, 1790.
2. Appointed by governor to fill vacancy.
3. Resigned Nov. 18, 1794.
4. Died May 10, 1803.
5. Appointed by governor to fill vacancy.
6. Resigned June 7, 1804.
7. Appointed by governor to fill vacancy.
8. Died Dec. 30, 1814.
9. Resigned March 27, 1825.
10. Resigned Feb. 29, 1836.
11. The seat was vacant between the expiration of Rives' first term March 3, 1839, and his re-election and subsequent service beginning Jan. 18, 1841.
12. Died Jan. 12, 1847.
13. Expelled July 11, 1861. Vacant until July 13, 1861.
14. Willey was elected by a "rump" state legislature which supported the Union and represented territory which was later to become West Virginia.
15. Died Jan. 2, 1864. Bowden, like Willey, his predecessor, was elected to represent Virginia by a "rump" state legislature which supported the Union. After his death, the seat remained vacant until Jan. 27, 1870, because of the Civil War.
16. Died June 29, 1910.
17. Appointed by governor to fill vacancy. Subsequently elected. Resigned March 3, 1933.
18. Appointed by governor to fill vacancy. Subsequently elected. Resigned Nov. 10, 1965.
19. Appointed by governor to fill vacancy. Subsequently elected as a Democrat in 1966, as an Independent in 1970.
20. Resigned Oct. 8, 1792.
21. Resigned May 11, 1794.
22. Died Jan. 24, 1799.
23. Resigned May 22, 1804.
24. Appointed by governor to fill vacancy.
25. Resigned March 3, 1815.
26. Resigned Dec. 4, 1819.
27. Resigned Dec. 15, 1822.
28. Died Aug. 20, 1824.
29. Resigned July 16, 1832.
30. Resigned Feb. 22, 1834.
31. Resigned July 4, 1836.
32. Resigned March 13, 1837.
33. Expelled July 11, 1861. Vacant until July 13, 1861.
34. Carlile was elected by a "rump" state legislature which supported the Union and represented territory which was later to become West Virginia. After the expiration of his term, the seat remained vacant until Jan. 28, 1870, because of Civil War.
35. The seat was vacant between the expiration of Johnston's first term March 3, 1871, and his re-election and subsequent seating March 15, 1871.
36. Died May 14, 1892.
37. Appointed by governor to fill vacancy. Subsequently elected.
38. Died Nov. 12, 1919.
39. Appointed by governor to fill vacancy. Subsequently elected. Died May 28, 1946.
40. Appointed by governor to fill vacancy.
41. Resigned Dec. 30, 1966.
42. Resigned Jan. 1, 1979.

WASHINGTON

(Became a state Nov. 11, 1889)

Class 1

Senators	Dates of Service	
John B. Allen (R)	Nov. 20, 1889	March 3, 1893
John L. Wilson (R)[1]	Feb. 1, 1895	March 3, 1899
Addison G. Foster (R)	March 4, 1899	March 3, 1905
Samuel H. Piles (R)	March 4, 1905	March 3, 1911
Miles Poindexter (R)	March 4, 1911	March 3, 1923
Clarence C. Dill (D)	March 4, 1923	Jan. 2, 1935
L. B. Schwellenbach (D)[2]	Jan. 3, 1935	Dec. 16, 1940
Mon C. Wallgren (D)[3]	Dec. 19, 1940	Jan. 10, 1945
Hugh B. Mitchell (D)[4]	Jan. 10, 1945	Dec. 25, 1946
Harry P. Cain (R)	Dec. 26, 1946	Jan. 2, 1953
Henry M. Jackson (D)[5]	Jan. 3, 1953	Sept. 1, 1983
Daniel J. Evans (R)[6]	Sept. 12, 1983	Jan. 2, 1989
Slade Gorton (R)	Jan. 3, 1989	Jan. 3, 2001
Maria Cantwell (D)	Jan. 3, 2001	

Class 3

Watson C. Squire (R)	Nov. 20, 1889	March 3, 1897
George Turner (D)	March 4, 1897	March 3, 1903
Levi Ankeny (R)	March 4, 1903	March 3, 1909
Wesley L. Jones (R)[7]	March 4, 1909	Nov. 19, 1932
Elijah S. Grammer (R)[8]	Nov. 22, 1932	March 3, 1933
Homer T. Bone (D)[9]	March 4, 1933	Nov. 13, 1944
Warren G. Magnuson (D)	Dec. 14, 1944	Jan. 2, 1981
Slade Gorton (R)	Jan. 3, 1981	Jan. 2, 1987
Brock Adams (D)	Jan. 3, 1987	Jan. 2, 1993
Patty Murray (D)	Jan. 3, 1993	

Washington
1. Vacancy from March 4, 1893, to Feb. 1, 1895, because of failure of legislature to elect. John B. Allen was appointed by governor March 10, 1893, to fill vacancy, but by Senate resolution of Aug. 28, 1893, was declared not entitled to a seat.
2. Resigned Dec. 16, 1940.
3. Resigned Jan. 10, 1945.
4. Appointed by governor to fill vacancy. Resigned Dec. 25, 1946.
5. Died Sept. 1, 1983.
6. Appointed by governor to fill vacancy. Subsequently elected.
7. Died Nov. 19, 1932.
8. Appointed by governor to fill vacancy.
9. Resigned Nov. 13, 1944.

WEST VIRGINIA

(Became a state June 19, 1863)

Class 1

Senators	Dates of Service	
Peter G. Van Winkle (R)	Aug. 4, 1863	March 3, 1869
Arthur I. Boreman (R)	March 4, 1869	March 3, 1875
Allen T. Caperton (D)[1]	March 4, 1875	July 26, 1876
Samuel Price[2]	Aug. 26, 1876	Jan. 26, 1877
Frank Hereford (D)	Jan. 26, 1877	March 3, 1881
Johnson N. Camden (D)	March 4, 1881	March 3, 1887
Charles J. Faulkner (D)	March 4, 1887	March 3, 1899
Nathan B. Scott (R)	March 4, 1899	March 3, 1911
William E. Chilton (D)	March 4, 1911	March 3, 1917
Howard Sutherland (R)	March 4, 1917	March 3, 1923
Matthew M. Neely (D)	March 4, 1923	March 3, 1929
Henry D. Hatfield (R)	March 4, 1929	Jan. 2, 1935
Rush D. Holt (D)[3]	June 21, 1935	Jan. 2, 1941
Harley M. Kilgore (D)[4]	Jan. 3, 1941	Feb. 28, 1956
William R. Laird III (D)[5]	March 13, 1956	Nov. 6, 1956
Chapman Revercomb (R)	Nov. 7, 1956	Jan. 2, 1959
Robert C. Byrd (D)	Jan. 3, 1959	

Class 2

Waitman T. Willey (R)	Aug. 4, 1863	March 3, 1871
Henry G. Davis (D)	March 4, 1871	March 3, 1883
John E. Kenna (D)[6]	March 4, 1883	Jan. 11, 1893
Johnson N. Camden (D)	Jan. 25, 1893	March 3, 1895
Stephen B. Elkins (R)[7]	March 4, 1895	Jan. 4, 1911
Davis Elkins (R)[8]	Jan. 9, 1911	Jan. 31, 1911
Clarence W. Watson (D)	Feb. 1, 1911	March 3, 1913
Nathan Goff (R)	March 4, 1913	March 3, 1919
Davis Elkins (R)	March 4, 1919	March 3, 1925
Guy D. Goff (R)	March 4, 1925	March 3, 1931
Matthew M. Neely (D)[9]	March 4, 1931	Jan. 12, 1941
Joseph Rosier (D)[10]	Jan. 13, 1941	Nov. 17, 1942
Hugh Ike Shott (R)	Nov. 18, 1942	Jan. 2, 1943
Chapman Revercomb (R)	Jan. 3, 1943	Jan. 2, 1949
Matthew M. Neely (D)[11]	Jan. 3, 1949	Jan. 18, 1958
John D. Hoblitzell Jr. (R)[12]	Jan. 25, 1958	Nov. 4, 1958
Jennings Randolph (D)	Nov. 5, 1958	Jan. 2, 1985
John D. Rockefeller IV (D)	Jan. 15, 1985	

West Virginia
1. Died July 26, 1876.
2. Appointed by governor to fill vacancy.
3. Elected Nov. 6, 1934, to a six-year term, but did not reach the age of 30—required by the Constitution for service in the Senate—until June 19, 1935. Took his seat June 21, 1935.
4. Died Feb. 28, 1956.
5. Appointed by governor to fill vacancy.
6. Died Jan. 11, 1893.
7. Died Jan. 4, 1911.
8. Appointed by governor to fill vacancy.
9. Resigned Jan. 12, 1941.
10. Appointed by governor to fill vacancy.
11. Died Jan. 18, 1958.
12. Appointed by governor to fill vacancy.

WISCONSIN

(Became a state May 29, 1848)

Class 1

Senators	Dates of Service	
Henry Dodge (D)	June 8, 1848	March 3, 1857
James R. Doolittle (R)	March 4, 1857	March 3, 1869
Matthew H. Carpenter (R)	March 4, 1869	March 3, 1875
Angus Cameron (R)	March 4, 1875	March 3, 1881
Philetus Sawyer (R)	March 4, 1881	March 3, 1893
John L. Mitchell (D)	March 4, 1893	March 3, 1899
Joseph V. Quarles (R)	March 4, 1899	March 3, 1905
Robert M. La Follette (R)[1]	Jan. 4, 1906	June 18, 1925
R. M. La Follette Jr. (R, PROG)[2]	Sept. 30, 1925	Jan. 2, 1947

Joseph R. McCarthy (R)[3]	Jan. 3, 1947	May 2, 1957
William Proxmire (D)	Aug. 28, 1957	Jan. 2, 1989
Herbert H. Kohl (D)	Jan. 3, 1989	

Class 3

Senators	Dates of Service	
Isaac P. Walker (D)	June 8, 1848	March 3, 1855
Charles Durkee (R)	March 4, 1855	March 3, 1861
Timothy O. Howe (R)	March 4, 1861	March 3, 1879
Matthew H. Carpenter (R)[4]	March 4, 1879	Feb. 24, 1881
Angus Cameron (R)	March 10, 1881	March 3, 1885
John Coit Spooner (R)	March 4, 1885	March 3, 1891
William F. Vilas (D)	March 4, 1891	March 3, 1897
John Coit Spooner (R)[5]	March 4, 1897	May 1, 1907
Isaac Stephenson (R)	May 17, 1907	March 3, 1915
Paul O. Husting (D)[6]	March 4, 1915	Oct. 21, 1917
Irvine L. Lenroot (R)	April 18, 1918	March 3, 1927
John J. Blaine (R)	March 4, 1927	March 3, 1933
F. Ryan Duffy (D)	March 4, 1933	Jan. 2, 1939
Alexander Wiley (R)	Jan. 3, 1939	Jan. 2, 1963
Gaylord Nelson (D)	Jan. 3, 1963	Jan. 2, 1981
Bob Kasten (R)	Jan. 3, 1981	Jan. 2, 1993
Russell D. Feingold (D)	Jan. 3, 1993	

Wisconsin

1. Elected Jan. 25, 1905. Took oath Jan. 4, 1906. Governor during interim. Died June 18, 1925. Vacancy from June 19 to Sept. 29, 1925.

2. Elected as a Republican in 1925 and 1928, as a Progressive in 1934 and 1940.

3. Died May 2, 1957.

4. Died Feb. 24, 1881.

5. Resigned effective May 1, 1907.

6. Died Oct. 21, 1917. Seat vacant until April 18, 1918.

WYOMING

(Became a state July 10, 1890)

Class 1

Senators	Dates of Service	
Francis E. Warren (R)	Nov. 18, 1890	March 3, 1893
Clarence D. Clark (R)[1]	Jan. 23, 1895	March 3, 1917

John B. Kendrick (D)[2]	March 4, 1917	Nov. 3, 1933
Joseph C. O'Mahoney (D)[3]	Jan. 1, 1934	Jan. 2, 1953
Frank A. Barrett (R)	Jan. 3, 1953	Jan. 2, 1959
Gale W. McGee (D)	Jan. 3, 1959	Jan. 2, 1977
Malcolm Wallop (R)	Jan. 3, 1977	Jan. 2, 1995
Craig Thomas (R)	Jan. 3, 1995	

Class 2

Joseph M. Carey (R)	Nov. 15, 1890	March 3, 1895
Francis E. Warren (R)[4]	March 4, 1895	Nov. 24, 1929
Patrick J. Sullivan (R)[5]	Dec. 5, 1929	Nov. 30, 1930
Robert D. Carey (R)	Dec. 1, 1930	Jan. 2, 1937
Harry H. Schwartz (D)	Jan. 3, 1937	Jan. 2, 1943
E. V. Robertson (R)	Jan. 3, 1943	Jan. 2, 1949
Lester C. Hunt (D)[6]	Jan. 3, 1949	June 19, 1954
Edward D. Crippa (R)[7]	June 24, 1954	Nov. 28, 1954
Joseph C. O'Mahoney (D)	Nov. 29, 1954	Jan. 2, 1961
John Joseph Hickey (D)[8]	Jan. 3, 1961	Nov. 6, 1962
Milward L. Simpson (R)	Nov. 7, 1962	Jan. 2, 1967
Clifford P. Hansen (R)[9]	Jan. 3, 1967	Dec. 31, 1978
Alan K. Simpson (R)	Jan. 1, 1979	Jan. 2, 1997
Michael B. Enzi (R)	Jan. 3, 1997	

Wyoming

1. Vacancy from March 4, 1893, to Jan. 23, 1895, because of failure of legislature to elect.

2. Died Nov. 3, 1933. Vacancy from Nov. 4, 1933, to Jan. 1, 1934.

3. Appointed by governor to fill vacancy. Subsequently elected.

4. Died Nov. 24, 1929.

5. Appointed by governor to fill vacancy.

6. Died June 19, 1954.

7. Appointed by governor to fill vacancy.

8. Keith Thomson (R), who had been elected Nov. 8, 1960, to a full six-year term beginning Jan. 3, 1961, died Dec. 9, 1960. Hickey, the incumbent governor, resigned and was appointed by his successor to fill the vacancy.

9. Resigned Dec. 31, 1978.

Senate General Election Returns, 1913–2000

SENATORIAL GENERAL ELECTION RETURNS for all fifty states are presented in this chapter (pages 1268–1303). The major source for returns for the years 1913 through 1973 was the Inter-University Consortium for Political and Social Research (ICPSR) at the University of Michigan. The symbol # next to returns before 1974 indicates that Congressional Quarterly obtained the returns from a source other than the ICPSR. A complete set of other sources used appears on page 1304.

Prior to ratification of the Seventeenth Amendment, April 8, 1913, a number of states conducted nonbinding popular polls for Senate candidates, designed to guide the state legislatures in choosing between candidates. The ICPSR obtained some of the returns for these polls, and they are published within this chapter. *(See "Demands for Popular Elections," p. 1230.)* While the complete source annotations for the ICPSR collection are too extensive to publish here, information on the sources for specific election returns can be obtained through the ICPSR. *(See box, ICPSR Historical Election Returns File, p. xvi, Vol. I.)*

For Senate elections from 1974 to 2000, the source was the *America Votes* series, compiled biennially by Congressional Quarterly in Washington, D.C. Richard M. Scammon and Alice V. McGillivray of the Elections Research Center, Washington, D.C., created the series first published in 1956. Since 1996 the series has been compiled by Rhodes Cook. Returns for the 1975 special election in New Hampshire were obtained form the New Hampshire secretary of state. A Senate Candidates Index is located on pages I-113 TO I-119.

PRESENTATION OF RETURNS

The senate returns are arranged alphabetically by state and in chronological order by class of senator within each state listing. *(see "Senate's Three Classes," p. 1231.)* the candidates receiving the greatest number of popular votes is listed first with his or her vote total and percentage of the total vote cast, followed in descending order of votes received by all other candidates who received *at least 5 percent* of the total vote cast.

Special elections to fill vacancies are designated in the returns. *(See box, Senate Appointments and Special Elections, p. 1232.)*

When a state *simultaneously* held a special election to fill the remaining few months of an unexpired term and a general election for the next full six-year term, the special election is listed *after* the general election. For example, see page 1271 where the 1946 California general and special election returns appear.

Where a state had a special election and a general election for the same class in the same year, but not simultaneously, the elections appear in the order they occurred. For example, see page 1280 where the 1936 Louisiana special election, held in April, precedes the general election, held in November.

VOTE TOTALS AND PERCENTAGES

The ICPSR collection includes all candidates receiving popular votes. In the *Guide to U.S. Elections,* fourth edition, only Senate candidates receiving *at least 5 percent of the total vote* for that election are included. For example, the ICPSR data collection for the 1944 New York senatorial election, 6,209,317 votes were cast, with Robert F. Wagner receiving 3,294,576 votes (53.05 percent), Thomas J. Curran receiving 2,899,497 votes (46.69 percent) and a third candidate, Eric Haas, receiving the remaining 15,244 votes (0.25 percent). The returns for the 1944 New York Senate election appear on page 1290. Returns for Haas are not listed because he received less than 5 percent of the total vote. The percentage listed for Wagner is 53.1 and for Curran is 46.7.

The procedure used throughout this section was to calculate percentages to two decimal places on the basis of the total number of votes cast in the election and round each percentage to one decimal place. Due to rounding and scattered votes for other candidates, percentages do not add to 100 percent.

PARTY DESIGNATIONS

In the ICPSR returns, the distinct—and in many cases, *multiple*—party designations appearing in the original sources are preserved. In many cases party labels represent combinations of multiparty support received by individual candidates. If, for example, on the ballot and official returns more than one party name was listed next to a candidate's name, then the party designation appearing in the election returns for that candidate will be a unique abbreviation for that combination of parties. *(See "Political Party Abbreviations," p. 1596, in Reference Materials.)*

In the special case of a candidate's name listed separately on the original ballot under more than one party—where returns were reported *separately* for each party—Congressional Quarterly has summed the votes recorded under the several parties and that figure appears as the candidate's total vote. Whenever separate party totals have been summed, a *comma* separates the abbreviations of the parties contributing the largest and second largest share of the total vote.

Most cases of this special situation occurred in New York and Pennsylvania during this century. For example, in the 1944 New York election cited above, Wagner's total vote of 3,294,576 was comprised of 2,485,735 as the Democratic Party nominee, 483,785 votes as American Labor Party candidate and 325,056 votes as Liberal Party nominee. On page 1290, only Wagner's to-

tal vote of 3,294,576 appears. Congressional Quarterly has also included party abbreviations for the two parties that contributed the most votes to Wagner's total—separated by a comma. Thus, immediately following his name appear the abbreviations—

D, AM LAB—indicating that Wagner was a candidate of at least two parties and that the greatest number of votes he received was as a Democrat.

Senate General Election Returns, 1913–2000

ALABAMA

Candidates	Votes	%
Class 2		
1918 John H. Bankhead (D)	54,880	100.0
Special Election		
1920 J. Thomas Heflin (D)	161,531	71.4
C. P Lunsford (R)	62,020	27.4
1924 J. Thomas Heflin (D)	120,017	75.2
F. H Lathrop (R)	39,623	24.8
1930 John H. Bankhead II (D)	150,985	59.7
J. Thomas Heflin (I)	101,862	40.3
1936 John H. Bankhead II (D)	239,632	87.0
H. E Berkstresser (R)	33,698	12.2
1942 John H. Bankhead II (D)	69,212	100.0
Special Election		
1946 John Sparkman (D)	163,217	100.0
1948 John Sparkman (D)	185,534	84.0
Paul G. Parsons (R)	35,341	16.0
1954 John Sparkman (D)	259,348	82.5
J. Foy Guin Jr. (R)	55,110	17.5
1960 John Sparkman (D)	389,196	70.2
Julian Elgin (R)	164,868	29.8
1966 John Sparkman (D)	482,138	60.1
John Grenier (R)	313,018	39.0
1972 John Sparkman (D)	654,491	62.3
Winton M. Blount (R)	347,523	33.1
1978 Howell Heflin (D)	547,054	94.0
Jerome B. Couch (P)	34,951	6.0
1984 Howell Heflin (D)	860,535	62.8
Albert Lee Smith Jr. (R)	498,508	36.3
1990 Howell Heflin (D)	717,814	60.6
Bill Cabaniss (R)	467,190	39.4
1996 Jeff Sessions (R)	786,436	52.5
Roger Bedford (D)	681,651	45.6
Class 3		
1914 Oscar W. Underwood (D)	63,338	78.1
Alex C. Birch (R)	12,320	15.2
A. P Longshore (PROG)	4,263	5.3

	Candidates	Votes	%
Special Election			
1914	Frank S. White (D)	102,326	99.9
1920	Oscar W. Underwood (D)	155,664	68.0
	L. H Reynolds (R)	71,334	31.2
1926	Hugo L. Black (D)	91,843	80.9
	E. H Dryer (R)	21,722	19.1
1932	Hugo L. Black (D)	209,614	86.3
	J. Theodore Johnson (R)	33,425	13.8
Special Election			
1938	Lister Hill (D)	113,413#	86.4
	J. M Pennington (R)	17,885#	13.6
1944	Lister Hill (D)	202,604	81.8
	John A. Posey (R)	41,983	17.0
1950	Lister Hill (D)	125,534	76.5
	John G. Crommelin Jr. (I)	38,477	23.5
1956	Lister Hill (D)	330,182	100.0
1962	Lister Hill (D)	201,937	50.9
	James D. Martin (R)	195,134	49.1
1968	Jim Allen (D)	638,774	70.0
	Perry Hooper (R)	201,227	22.1
	Robert Schwenn (NDPA)	72,699	8.0
1974	Jim Allen (D)	501,541	95.8
Special Election			
1978	Donald W. Stewart (D)	401,852	54.9
	James D. Martin (R)	316,170	43.2
1980	Jeremiah Denton (R)	650,362	50.2
	James E. Folsom Jr. (D)	610,175	47.1
1986	Richard C. Shelby (D)	609,360	50.3
	Jeremiah Denton (R)	602,537	49.7
1992	Richard C. Shelby (D)	1,022,698	64.9
	Richard Sellers (R)	522,015	33.1
1998	Richard C. Shelby (R)	817,973	63.2
	Clayton Suddith (D)	474,568	36.7

ALASKA

	Candidates	Votes	%
Class 2			
1958	E. L Bartlett (D)	40,939	83.8
	R. E Robertson (R)	7,299	15.0

1960	E. L Bartlett (D)	38,041	63.4
	Lee L. McKinley (R)	21,937	36.6
1966	E. L Bartlett (D)	49,289	75.5
	Lee L. McKinley (R)	15,961	24.5

Special Election

1970	Ted Stevens (R)	47,908	59.6
	Wendell P. Kay (D)	32,456	40.4
1972	Ted Stevens (R)	74,216	77.3
	Gene Guess (D)	21,791	22.7
1978	Ted Stevens (R)	92,783	75.6
	Donald W. Hobbs (D)	29,574	24.1
1984	Ted Stevens (R)	146,919	71.2
	John E. Havelock (D)	58,804	28.5
1990	Ted Stevens (R)	125,806	66.2
	Michael Beasley (D)	61,152	32.2
1996	Ted Stevens (R)	177,893	76.7
	Jed Whittaker (GREEN)	29,037	12.5
	Theresa Nangle Obermeyer (D)	23,977	10.3

Class 3

1958	Ernest Gruening (D)	26,063	52.6
	Mike Stepovich (R)	23,462	47.4
1962	Ernest Gruening (D)	33,827	58.1
	Ted Stevens (R)	24,354	41.9
1968	Mike Gravel (D)	36,527	45.1
	Elmer Rasmuson (R)	30,286	37.4
	Ernest Gruening (I)	14,118	17.4
1974	Mike Gravel (D)	54,361	58.3
	C. R Lewis (R)	38,914	41.7
1980	Frank H. Murkowski (R)	84,159	53.7
	Clark S. Gruening (D)	72,007	45.9
1986	Frank H. Murkowski (R)	97,674	54.0
	Glenn Olds (D)	79,727	44.1
1992	Frank H. Murkowski (R)	127,163	53.0
	Tony Smith (D)	92,065	38.4
	Mary E. Jordan (GREEN)	20,019	8.4
1998	Frank H. Murkowski (R)	165,227	74.5
	Joseph Sonneman (D)	43,743	19.7

ARIZONA

Candidates	Votes	%

Class 1

1916	Henry F. Ashurst (D)	29,882	55.4
	Joseph H. Kibbey (R)	21,261	39.4
	W. S Bradford (SOC)	2,827	5.2
1922	Henry F. Ashurst (D)	39,722	65.0
	James H. McClintock (R)	21,358	35.0
1928	Henry F. Ashurst (D)	47,013	54.3
	Ralph H. Cameron (R)	39,651	45.8
1934	Henry F. Ashurst (D)	67,648	72.0
	J. E Thompson (R)	24,075	25.6
1940	Ernest W. McFarland (D)	101,495	71.6
	I. A Jennings (R)	39,657	28.0
1946	Ernest W. McFarland (D)	80,415	69.2

	Ward S. Powers (R)	35,022	30.1
1952	Barry Goldwater (R)	132,063	51.3
	Ernest W. McFarland (D)	125,338	48.7
1958	Barry Goldwater (R)	164,593	56.1
	Ernest W. McFarland (D)	129,030	43.9
1964	Paul Fannin (R)	241,084	51.4
	Roy Elson (D)	227,704	48.6
1970	Paul Fannin (R)	228,284	56.0
	Sam Grossman (D)	179,512	44.0
1976	Dennis DeConcini (D)	400,334	54.0
	Sam Steiger (R)	321,236	43.3
1982	Dennis DeConcini (D)	411,970	56.9
	Pete Dunn (R)	291,749	40.3
1988	Dennis DeConcini (D)	660,403	56.7
	Keith DeGreen (R)	478,060	41.1
1994	Jon Kyl (R)	600,999	53.7
	Sam Coppersmith (D)	442,510	39.5
	Scott Grainger (LIBERT)	75,493	6.7
2000	Jon Kyl (R)	1,108,196	79.3
	William Toel (I)	109,230	7.8
	Vance Hansen (GREEN)	108,926	7.8
	Barry J. Hess II (LIBERT)	70,724	5.1

Class 3

1914	Marcus A. Smith (D)	25,800	53.2
	J. L Hubbell (R)	9,182	19.0
	Eugene W. Chafin (IP)	7,293	15.1
	Bert Davis (SOC)	3,582	7.4
	J. Bernard Nelson (PROG)	2,606	5.4
1920	Ralph H. Cameron (R)	35,893	55.2
	Marcus A. Smith (D)	29,169	44.8
1926	Carl Hayden (D)	44,591	58.3
	Ralph H. Cameron (R)	31,845	41.7
1932	Carl Hayden (D)	74,310	66.7
	Ralph H. Cameron (R)	35,737	32.1

Explanation of Symbols

In the returns for Senate elections *symbols* are used to denote special circumstances. In cases where no symbol is used, the candidate who received the most votes won the election to the Senate. The following is a key to the symbols used:

✔ Elected to the Senate, but the number of votes and the percentage of the total vote received by the winner are not available.

* The symbol is used in two kinds of situations: (1) When the winner of the election died before the term of office was to begin; (2) When the apparent winner was not permitted to take office. *(For an explanation of specific cases, consult the appropriate state in the list of senators, pp. 1236–1266.)*

Information was obtained from a source other than the Inter-University Consortium for Political and Social Research (ICPSR). *(See "Senate Returns: Other Sources," p. 1304.)*

1938	Carl Hayden (D)	82,714	76.5
	B. H Clingan (R)	25,378	23.5
1944	Carl Hayden (D)	90,335	69.4
	Fred W. Fickett (R)	39,891	30.6
1950	Carl Hayden (D)	116,246	62.8
	Bruce Brockett (R)	68,846	37.2
1956	Carl Hayden (D)	170,816	61.4
	Ross F. Jones (R)	107,447	38.6
1962	Carl Hayden (D)	199,217	54.9
	Evan Mecham (R)	163,388	45.1
1968	Barry M. Goldwater (R)	274,607	57.2
	Roy Elson (D)	205,338	42.8
1974	Barry M. Goldwater (R)	320,396	58.3
	Jonathan Marshall (D)	229,523	41.7
1980	Barry M. Goldwater (R)	432,371	49.5
	Bill Schulz (D)	422,972	48.4
1986	John McCain (R)	521,850	60.5
	Richard Kimball (D)	340,965	39.5
1992	John McCain (R)	771,395	55.8
	Claire Sargent (D)	436,321	31.6
	Evan Mecham (I)	145,361	10.5
1998	John McCain (R)	696,577	68.7
	Ed Ranger (D)	275,224	27.2

ARKANSAS

Candidates	Votes	%
Class 2		

1918	Joseph T. Robinson (D)	78,386	100.0
1924	Joseph T. Robinson (D)	100,408#	73.5
	Charles F. Cole (R)	36,163#	26.5
1930	Joseph T. Robinson (D)	141,806	100.0
1936	Joseph T. Robinson (D)	155,075	81.8
	G. C Ledbetter (R)	30,997	16.4

Special Election

| 1937 | John E. Miller (I) | 66,990 | 60.7 |
| | Carl E. Bailey (D) | 43,406 | 39.3 |

1942	John L. McClellan (D)	99,126	100.0
1948	John L. McClellan (D)	216,401	93.3
	R. Walter Tucker (I)	15,521	6.7
1954	John L. McClellan (D)	291,058	100.0
1960	John L. McClellan (D)	✔	
1966	John L. McClellan (D)	✔	
1972	John L. McClellan (D)	386,398	60.8
	Wayne H. Babbitt (R)	248,238	39.1
1978	David H. Pryor (D)	399,916	76.6
	Tom Kelly (R)	84,722	16.2
	John G. Black (I)	37,488	7.2
1984	David Pryor (D)	502,341	57.3
	Ed Bethune (R)	373,615	42.7
1990	David Pryor (D)	493,910	99.8
1996	Tim Hutchinson (R)	445,942	52.7
	Winston Bryant (D)	400,241	47.3

| **Class 3** | | | |

| 1914 | James P. Clarke (D) | 33,449# | 74.9 |
| | Meyers (R) | 11,222# | 25.1 |

Special Election

| 1916 | William F. Kirby (D) | 110,293 | 69.3 |
| | H. L Remmel (R) | 48,922 | 30.7 |

1920	Thaddeus H. Caraway (D)	126,577	65.9
	Charles F. Cole (R)	65,381	34.1
1926	Thaddeus H. Caraway (D)	28,064	82.8
	R. A Jones (R)	5,848	17.2

Special Election

| 1932 | Hattie W. Caraway (D) | 31,133# | 91.6 |
| | Rex Floyd (I) | 1,752# | 5.2 |

1932	Hattie W. Caraway (D)	183,795	89.5
	John W. White (R)	21,597	10.5
1938	Hattie W. Caraway (D)	122,871	89.6
	C. D Atkinson (R)	14,240	10.4
1944	J. William Fulbright (D)	182,529	85.1
	Victor M. Wade (R)	31,942	14.9
1950	J. William Fulbright (D)	302,582	100.0
1956	J. William Fulbright (D)	331,679	83.0
	Ben C. Henley (R)	68,016	17.0
1962	J. William Fulbright (D)	214,867	68.7
	Kenneth Jones (R)	98,013	31.3
1968	J. William Fulbright (D)	349,965	59.2
	Charles Bernard (R)	241,739	40.9
1974	Dale Bumpers (D)	461,056	84.9
	John Harris Jones (R)	82,026	15.1
1980	Dale Bumpers (D)	477,905	59.1
	Bill Clark (R)	330,576	40.9
1986	Dale Bumpers (D)	433,092	62.3
	Asa Hutchinson (R)	262,300	37.7
1992	Dale Bumpers (D)	553,635	60.2
	Mike Huckabee (R)	366,373	39.8
1998	Blanche Lincoln (D)	385,878	55.1
	Fay Boozman (R)	295,870	42.2

CALIFORNIA

Candidates	Votes	%
Class 1		

1916	Hiram W. Johnson (R & PROG)	574,667	61.1
	George S. Patton (D)	277,852	29.5
	Walter Thomas Mills (SOC)	49,341	5.2
1922	Hiram W. Johnson (R)	564,422	62.2
	William J. Pearson (D)	215,748	23.8
	H. Clay Needham (P)	70,748	7.8
	Upton Sinclair (SOC)	56,982	6.3
1928	Hiram W. Johnson (R)	1,148,397	74.1
	Minor Moore (D)	282,411	18.2
	Charles H. Randall (P)	92,106	5.9
1934	Hiram W. Johnson (R-D-PR-C)	1,946,572	94.5
	George R. Kirkpatrick (SOC)	108,748	5.3
1940	Hiram W. Johnson (R-D-PROG)	2,238,899	82.5
	Fred Dyster (P)	366,044	13.5

1946	William F. Knowland (R)	1,428,067	54.1
	Will Rogers Jr. (D)	1,167,161	44.2

Special Election

1946	William F. Knowland (R)	425,273	74.3
	Will Rogers Jr. (D)	90,723	15.9
1952	William F. Knowland (R-D)	3,982,448	87.7
	Reuben W. Borough (I PROG)	542,270	11.9
1958	Clair Engle (D)	2,927,693	57.0
	Goodwin J. Knight (R)	2,204,337	42.9
1964	George Murphy (R)	3,628,555	51.5
	Pierre Salinger (D)	3,411,912	48.5
1970	John V. Tunney (D)	3,496,558	53.9
	George Murphy (R)	2,877,617	44.3
1976	S. I Hayakawa (R)	3,748,973	50.2
	John V. Tunney (D)	3,502,862	46.9
1982	Pete Wilson (R)	4,022,565	51.5
	Edmund G. Brown Jr. (D)	3,494,968	44.8
1988	Pete Wilson (R)	5,143,409	52.8
	Leo T. McCarthy (D)	4,287,253	44.0

Special Election

1992	Dianne Feinstein (D)	5,853,651	54.3
	John Seymour (R)	4,093,501	38.0
1994	Dianne Feinstein (D)	3,977,063	46.8
	Michael Huffington (R)	3,811,501	44.8
2000	Dianne Feinstein (D)	5,932,522	55.8
	Tom Campbell (R)	3,886,853	36.6

Class 3

1914	James D. Phelan (D)	279,896	31.6
	Francis J. Heney (PROG)	255,232	28.8
	Joseph R. Knowland (R)	254,159	28.7
	Ernest Untermann (SOC)	56,805	6.4
1920	Samuel M. Shortridge (R)	447,835	49.0
	James D. Phelan (D)	371,580	40.7
	James S. Edwards (P)	57,768	6.3
1926	Samuel M. Shortridge (R)	670,128	63.1
	John B. Elliott (D)	391,599	36.9
1932	William Gibbs McAdoo (D)	943,164	43.4
	Tallant Tubbs (R)	669,676	30.8
	Robert P. Shuler (P)	560,088	25.8
1938	Sheridan Downey (D-PRO-TN)	1,372,314	54.4
	Philip Bancroft (R)	1,126,240	44.7
1944	Sheridan Downey (D)	1,728,155	52.3
	Frederick F. Houser (R)	1,576,553	47.7
1950	Richard M. Nixon (R)	2,183,454	59.2
	Helen Gahagan Douglas (D)	1,502,507	40.8

Special Election

1954	Thomas H. Kuchel (R)	2,090,836	53.2
	Samuel William Yorty (D)	1,788,071	45.5
1956	Thomas H. Kuchel (R)	2,892,918	54.0
	Richard Richards (D)	2,445,816	45.6
1962	Thomas H. Kuchel (R)	3,180,483	56.3
	Richard Richards (D)	2,452,839	43.4
1968	Alan Cranston (D)	3,680,352	51.8

	Max Rafferty (R)	3,329,148	46.9
1974	Alan Cranston (D)	3,693,160	60.5
	H. L "Bill" Richardson (R)	2,210,267	36.2
1980	Alan Cranston (D)	4,705,399	56.5
	Paul Gann (R)	3,093,426	37.1
1986	Alan Cranston (D)	3,646,672	49.3
	Ed Zschau (R)	3,541,804	47.9
1992	Barbara Boxer (D)	5,173,467	47.9
	Bruce Herschensohn (R)	4,644,182	43.0
1998	Barbara Boxer (D)	4,411,705	53.1
	Matt Fong (R)	3,576,351	43.0

COLORADO

Candidates	Votes	%

Class 2

1912	John F. Shafroth (D)	118,260	47.3
	Clyde C. Dawson (R)	66,949	26.8
	Frank D. Catlin (PROG-BMR)	58,649	23.5
1918	Lawrence C. Phipps (R)	107,726	49.5
	John F. Shafroth (D)	104,347	47.9
1924	Lawrence C. Phipps (R)	159,698	50.2
	Alva B. Adams (D)	139,660	43.9
	Morton Alexander (F-LAB)	16,039	5.0
1930	Edward P. Costigan (D)	180,028	55.9
	George H. Shaw (R)	137,487	42.7
1936	Edwin C. Johnson (D)	299,376	63.5
	Raymond L. Sauter (R)	166,308	35.3
1942	Edwin C. Johnson (D)	174,612	50.2
	Ralph L. Carr (R)	170,970	49.2
1948	Edwin C. Johnson (D)	340,719	66.8
	Will F. Nicholson (R)	165,069	32.4
1954	Gordon Allott (R)	248,502	51.3
	John A. Carroll (D)	235,686	48.7
1960	Gordon Allott (R)	389,428	53.5
	Robert L. Knous (D)	334,854	46.0
1966	Gordon Allott (R)	368,307	58.0
	Roy Romer (D)	266,198	41.9
1972	Floyd K. Haskell (D)	457,545	49.4
	Gordon Allott (R)	447,957	48.4
1978	William L. Armstrong (R)	480,596	58.7
	Floyd K. Haskell (D)	330,247	40.3
1984	William L. Armstrong (R)	833,821	64.2
	Nancy Dick (D)	449,327	34.6
1990	Hank Brown (R)	569,048	55.7
	Josie Heath (D)	425,746	41.7
1996	Wayne Allard (R)	750,325	51.1
	Tom Strickland (D)	677,600	46.1

Class 3

Special Election

1912	Charles S. Thomas (D)	111,633	44.9
	Charles W. Waterman (R)	66,627	26.8
	I. N Stevens (PROG-BMR)	64,405	25.9
1914	Charles S. Thomas (D)	102,037	40.3
	Hubert Work (R)	98,728	39.0

	Benjamin Griffith (PROG)	27,072	10.7
	J. C Griffiths (SOC)	13,943	5.5
1920	Samuel D. Nicholson (R)	156,577	54.5
	Tully Scot (D)	112,890	39.3

Special Election

| 1924 | Rice W. Means (R) | 159,353 | 50.2 |
| | Morrison Shafroth (D) | 138,714 | 43.7 |

	Charles T. Philp (F-LAB)	17,542	5.5
1926	Charles W. Waterman (R)	149,585	50.3
	William E. Sweet (D)	138,113	46.4
1932	Alva B. Adams (D)	226,516	51.9
	Karl C. Schuyler (R)	198,519	45.5

Special Election

| 1932 | Karl C. Schuyler (R) | 207,540 | 48.8 |
| | Walter Walker (D) | 206,475 | 48.5 |

| 1938 | Alva B. Adams (D) | 262,806 | 58.2 |
| | Archibald A. Lee (R) | 181,297 | 40.2 |

Special Election

| 1942 | Eugene D. Millikin (R) | 191,517 | 56.1 |
| | James A. Marsh (D) | 143,817 | 42.1 |

1944	Eugene D. Millikin (R)	277,410#	56.1
	Barney L. Whatley (D)	214,335#	43.0
1950	Eugene D. Millikin (R)	239,734	53.3
	John A. Carroll (D)	210,442	46.8
1956	John A. Carroll (D)	319,872	50.2
	Dan Thornton (R)	317,102	49.8
1962	Peter H. Dominick (R)	328,655	53.6
	John A. Carroll (D)	279,586	45.6
1968	Peter H. Dominick (R)	459,952	58.6
	Stephen L. R McNichols (D)	325,584	41.5
1974	Gary Hart (D)	471,691	57.2
	Peter H. Dominick (R)	325,508	39.5
1980	Gary Hart (D)	590,501	50.3
	Mary E. Buchanan (R)	571,295	48.7
1986	Timothy E. Wirth (D)	529,449	49.9
	Ken Kramer (R)	512,994	48.4
1992	Ben Nighthorse Campbell (D)	803,725	51.8
	Terry Considine (R)	662,893	42.7
1998	Ben Nighthorse Campbell (R)	829,370	62.5
	Dottie Lamm (D)	464,754	35.0

CONNECTICUT

Candidates	Votes	%

Class 1

1916	George P. McLean (R)	107,020	50.2
	Homer Cummings (D)	98,649	46.2
1922	George P. McLean (R)	169,524	52.3
	Thomas J. Spellacy (D)	147,276	45.5
1928	Frederic C. Walcott (R)	296,958	53.9
	Augustine Lonergan (D)	251,429	45.6

1934	Francis T. Maloney (D)	265,552	51.8
	Frederic C. Walcott (R)	247,623	48.3
1940	Francis T. Maloney (D)	416,740	53.2
	Paul L. Cornell (R, UN)	358,313	45.7
1946	Raymond E. Baldwin (R)	381,328	56.1
	Joseph M. Tone (D)	276,424	40.7

Special Election

| 1946 | Raymond E. Baldwin (R) | 378,707 | 55.8 |
| | Wilbur L. Cross (D) | 278,188 | 41.0 |

Special Election

| 1950 | William Benton (D) | 431,413 | 49.2 |
| | Prescott S. Bush (R) | 430,311 | 49.1 |

1952	William A. Purtell (R)	573,854	52.5
	William Benton (D)	485,066	44.4
1958	Thomas J. Dodd (D)	554,841	57.5
	William A. Purtell (R)	410,622	42.5
1964	Thomas J. Dodd (D)	781,008	64.6
	John Lodge (R)	426,939	35.3
1970	Lowell P. Weicker Jr. (R)	454,721	41.7
	Joseph D. Duffey (D)	368,111	33.8
	Thomas J. Dodd (DODD I)	266,497	24.5
1976	Lowell P. Weicker Jr. (R)	785,683	57.7
	Gloria Schaffer (D)	561,018	41.2
1982	Lowell P. Weicker Jr. (R)	545,987	50.4
	Anthony T. Moffett (D)	499,146	46.1
1988	Joseph I. Lieberman (D)	688,499	49.8
	Lowell P. Weicker Jr. (R)	678,454	49.0
1994	Joseph I. Lieberman (D,ACP)	723,842	67.0
	Jerry Labriola (R)	334,833	31.0
2000	Joseph I. Lieberman (D)	828,902	63.2
	Philip A. Giordano (R)	448,077	34.2

Class 3

1914	Frank B. Brandegee (R)	89,983	49.8
	Simeon Baldwin (D)	76,081	42.1
1920	Frank B. Brandegee (R)	216,792	59.4
	Augustine Lonergan (D)	131,824	36.1

Special Election

| 1924 | Hiram Bingham (R) | 112,400# | 60.4 |
| | Hamilton Holt (D) | 71,871# | 38.6 |

1926	Hiram Bingham (R)	191,401	63.3
	Rollin U. Tyler (D)	107,753	35.6
1932	Augustine Lonergan (D)	282,327	48.5
	Hiram Bingham (R)	278,061	47.7
1938	John A. Danaher (R)	270,413	42.9
	Augustine Lonergan (D, UN)	252,426	40.0
	Bellani Trombley (SOC)	99,282	15.8
1944	Brien McMahon (D)	430,716	52.0
	John A. Danaher (R)	391,748	47.3
1950	Brien McMahon (D)	453,646	51.7
	Joseph E. Talbot (R)	409,053	46.6

Special Election

| 1952 | Prescott S. Bush (R) | 559,465 | 51.2 |
| | Abraham A. Ribicoff (D) | 530,505 | 48.5 |

1956	Prescott S. Bush (R)	610,829	54.8
	Thomas J. Dodd (D)	479,460	43.1
1962	Abraham A. Ribicoff (D)	527,522	51.3
	Horace Seely-Brown (R)	501,694	48.8
1968	Abraham A. Ribicoff (D)	655,043	54.3
	Edwin H. May (R)	551,455	45.7
1974	Abraham A. Ribicoff (D)	690,820	63.7
	James H. Brannen III (R)	372,055	34.3
1980	Christopher J. Dodd (D)	763,969	56.3
	James L. Buckley (R)	581,884	42.9
1986	Christopher J. Dodd (D)	632,695	64.8
	Roger W. Eddy (R)	340,438	34.8
1992	Christopher J. Dodd (D, ACP)	882,569	58.8
	Brook Johnson (R)	572,036	38.1
1998	Christopher J. Dodd (D)	628,306	65.1
	Gary A. Franks (R)	312,177	32.4

DELAWARE

Candidates	Votes	%
Class 1		

1916	Josiah O. Wolcott (D)	25,434	49.7
	Henry A. du Pont (R)	22,925	44.8
1922	Thomas F. Bayard (D)	37,304	49.8
	T. Coleman du Pont (R)	36,979	49.4

Special Election

| 1922 | Thomas F. Bayard (D) | 36,954 | 49.7 |
| | T. Coleman du Pont (R) | 36,894 | 49.6 |

1928	John G. Townsend Jr. (R)	63,725	61.0
	Thomas F. Bayard (D)	40,828	39.1
1934	John G. Townsend Jr. (R)	52,829	53.3
	Wilbur L. Adams (D)	45,771	46.2
1940	James M. Tunnell (D)	68,294	50.6
	John G. Townsend Jr. (R)	63,799	47.3
1946	John J. Williams (R)	62,603	55.2
	James M. Tunnell (D)	50,910	44.9
1952	John J. Williams (R)	93,020	54.5
	A. I du Pont Bayard (D)	77,685	45.5
1958	John J. Williams (R)	82,280	53.3
	Elbert N. Carvel (D)	72,152	46.7
1964	John J. Williams (R)	103,782	51.7
	Elbert N. Carvel (D)	96,850	48.3
1970	William V. Roth Jr. (R)	94,979	58.8
	Jacob Zimmerman (D)	64,740	40.1
1976	William V. Roth Jr. (R)	125,502	55.8
	Thomas C. Maloney (D)	98,055	43.6
1982	William V. Roth Jr. (R)	105,357	55.2
	David N. Levinson (D)	84,413	44.2
1988	William V. Roth Jr. (R)	151,115	62.1
	S. B Woo (D)	92,378	37.9
1994	William V. Roth Jr. (R)	111,088	55.8
	Charles M. Oberly (D)	84,554	42.5
2000	Thomas R. Carper (D)	181,566	55.5
	William V. Roth Jr. (R)	142,891	43.7

	Class 2		
1918	Lewis Heisler Ball (R)	21,519	51.2
	Willard Saulsbury (D)	20,113	47.8
1924	T. Coleman du Pont (R)	52,731	59.4
	James M. Tunnell (D & PROG)	36,085	40.6
1930	Daniel O. Hastings (R)	47,909	54.5
	Thomas F. Bayard (D)	39,881	45.4

Special Election

| 1930 | Daniel O. Hastings (R) | 47,665 | 54.8 |
| | Thomas F. Bayard (D) | 39,279 | 45.1 |

1936	James H. Hughes (D)	67,136	53.0
	Daniel O. Hastings (R)	52,460	41.4
	Robert G. Houston (IR)	6,897	5.4
1942	Clayton Douglass Buck (R)	46,210	54.2
	E. Ennals Berl (D)	38,322	44.9
1948	J. Allen Frear Jr. (D)	71,888	50.9
	Clayton Douglass Buck (R)	68,246	48.3
1954	J. Allen Frear Jr. (D)	82,511	56.9
	Herbert B. Warburton (R)	62,389	43.1
1960	J. Caleb Boggs (R)	98,874	50.7
	J. Allen Frear Jr. (D)	96,090	49.3
1966	J. Caleb Boggs (R)	97,268	59.1
	James M. Tunnell Jr. (D)	67,263	40.9
1972	Joseph R. Biden Jr. (D)	116,006	50.5
	J. Caleb Boggs (R)	112,844	49.1
1978	Joseph R. Biden Jr. (D)	93,930	58.0
	James H. Baxter (R)	66,479	41.0
1984	Joseph R. Biden Jr. (D)	147,831	60.1
	John M. Burris (R)	98,101	39.1
1990	Joseph R. Biden Jr. (D)	112,918	62.7
	M. Jane Brady (R)	64,554	35.8
1996	Joseph R. Biden Jr. (D)	165,465	60.0
	Raymond J. Clatworthy (R)	105,088	38.1

FLORIDA

Candidates	Votes	%
Class 1		

1916	Park Trammell (D)	58,391	82.9
	W. R O'Neal (R)	8,774	12.5
1922	Park Trammell (D)	45,707	88.0
	W. C Lawson (IR)	6,074	11.7
1928	Park Trammell (D)	153,816	68.5
	Barclay H. Warburton (R)	70,633	31.5
1934	Park Trammell (D)	131,780	100.0

Special Election

| 1936 | Charles O. Andrews (D) | 241,528 | 80.9 |
| | Howard C. Babcock (R) | 57,016 | 19.1 |

1940	Charles O. Andrews (D)	323,216	100.0
1946	Spessard L. Holland (D)	156,232	78.7
	J. Harry Schad (R)	42,413	21.4
1952	Spessard L. Holland (D)	616,665	99.8
1958	Spessard L. Holland (D)	386,113	71.2
	Leland Hyzer (R)	155,956	28.8

1964	Spessard L. Holland (D)	997,585	63.9
	Claude R. Kirk Jr. (R)	562,212	36.0
1970	Lawton Chiles (D)	902,438	53.9
	William C. Cramer (R)	772,817	46.1
1976	Lawton Chiles (D)	1,799,518	63.0
	John Grady (R)	1,057,886	37.0
1982	Lawton Chiles (D)	1,637,667	61.7
	Van B. Poole (R)	1,015,330	38.3
1988	Connie Mack (R)	2,051,071	50.4
	Buddy MacKay (D)	2,016,553	49.6
1994	Connie Mack (R)	2,894,726	70.5
	Hugh E. Rodham (D)	1,210,412	29.5
2000	Bill Nelson (D)	2,989,487	51.0
	Bill McCollum (R)	2,705,348	46.2

Class 3

1914	Duncan U. Fletcher (D)	22,761	99.5
1920	Duncan U. Fletcher (D)	98,966	74.3
	John M. Cheney (R)	27,914	21.0
1926	Duncan U. Fletcher (D)	51,054	77.9
	John M. Lindsay (RDC)	8,381	12.8
	W. R O'Neal (R)	6,133	9.4
1932	Duncan U. Fletcher (D)	204,651	99.8

Special Election

| 1936 | Claude Pepper (D) | 246,050 | 100.0 |

1938	Claude Pepper (D)	145,757	82.5
	Thomas E. Swanson (R)	31,035	17.6
1944	Claude Pepper (D)	335,685	71.3
	Miles H. Draper (R)	135,258	28.7
1950	George A. Smathers (D)	238,987	76.2
	John P. Booth (R)	74,228	23.7
1956	George A. Smathers (D)	655,418	100.0
1962	George A. Smathers (D)	657,633	70.0
	Emerson Rupert (R)	281,381	30.0
1968	Edward J. Gurney (R)	1,131,499	55.9
	Leroy Collins (D)	892,637	44.1
1974	Richard Stone (D)	781,031	43.4
	Jack Eckerd (R)	736,674	40.9
	John Grady (AM)	282,659	15.7
1980	Paula Hawkins (R)	1,822,460	51.7
	Bill Gunter (D)	1,705,409	48.3
1986	Bob Graham (D)	1,877,231	54.7
	Paula Hawkins (R)	1,551,888	45.3
1992	Bob Graham (D)	3,244,299	65.4
	Bill Grant (R)	1,715,156	34.6
1998	Bob Graham (D)	2,436,407	62.5
	Charlie Crist (R)	1,463,755	37.5

GEORGIA

Candidates	Votes	%

Class 2

Special Election

| 1914 | Thomas W. Hardwick (D) | 62,239 | 68.9 |
| | Hutch (PROG) | 28,163 | 31.2 |

1918	William J. Harris (D)	53,731	88.4
	Williams (R)	7,078	11.6
1924	William J. Harris (D)	155,497#	100.0
1930	William J. Harris (D)	55,606	100.0

Special Election

| 1932 | Richard B. Russell (D) | 238,931 | 100.0 |

1936	Richard B. Russell (D)	263,468	100.0
1942	Richard B. Russell (D)	59,870	96.9
1948	Richard B. Russell (D)	362,104	99.9
1954	Richard B. Russell (D)	333,917	100.0
1960	Richard B. Russell (D)	576,140	99.9
1966	Richard B. Russell (D)	631,002	100.0
1972	Sam Nunn (D)	635,970	54.0
	Fletcher Thompson (R)	542,331	46.0

Special Election

| 1972 | Sam Nunn (D) | 404,890 | 52.0 |
| | Fletcher Thompson (R) | 362,501 | 46.5 |

1978	Sam Nunn (D)	536,320	83.1
	John W. Stokes (R)	108,808	16.9
1984	Sam Nunn (D)	1,344,104	79.9
	Jon Michael Hicks (R)	337,196	20.1
1990	Sam Nunn (D)	1,033,439	100.0
1996	Max Cleland (D)	1,103,993	48.9
	Guy Millner (R)	1,073,969	47.5

Class 3

1914	Hoke Smith (D)	61,489	68.4
	McClure (PROG)	28,435	31.6
1920	Thomas Watson (D)	124,630	94.9
	Harvey S. Edwards (I)	6,700	5.1

Special Election

| 1922 | Walter F. George (D) | 75,860 | 100.0 |

1926	Walter F. George (D)	47,446	100.0
1932	Walter F. George (D)	234,590	92.8
	James W. Arnold (R)	18,151	7.2
1938	Walter F. George (D)	66,897	95.1
1944	Walter F. George (D)	272,541	100.0
1950	Walter F. George (D)	261,290	100.0
1956	Herman E. Talmadge (D)	541,094	100.0
1962	Herman E. Talmadge (D)	306,250	100.0
1968	Herman E. Talmadge (D)	885,103	77.5
	E. Earl Patton (R)	256,796	22.5
1974	Herman E. Talmadge (D)	627,376	71.7
	Jerry Johnson (R)	246,866	28.2
1980	Mack Mattingly (R)	803,686	50.9
	Herman E. Talmadge (D)	776,143	49.1
1986	Wyche Fowler Jr. (D)	623,707	50.9
	Mack Mattingly (R)	601,241	49.1
1992[1]	Wyche Fowler Jr. (D)	1,108,416	49.2
	Paul Coverdell (R)	1,073,282	47.7

Runoff Election[1]

| 1992 | Paul Coverdell (R) | 635,114 | 50.6 |
| | Wyche Fowler Jr. (D) | 618,877 | 49.4 |

		Votes	%
1998	Paul Coverdell (R)	918,540	52.4
	Michael Coles (D)	791,904	45.2

Special Election

		Votes	%
2000	Zell Miller (D)	1,413,224	58.2
	Matt Mattingly (R)	920,478	37.9

Georgia

1. Georgia law in 1992 required election by a majority of the popular vote and provided for a runoff between the two top finishers when neither gained a majority in the regular election. The majority-vote provision was later repealed.

HAWAII

Candidates	Votes	%

Class 1

1959	Hiram L. Fong (R)	87,161	52.9
	Frank F. Fasi (D)	77,647	47.1
1964	Hiram L. Fong (R)	110,747	53.0
	Thomas P. Gill (D)	96,789	46.4
1970	Hiram L. Fong (R)	124,163	51.6
	Cecil Heftel (D)	116,597	48.4
1976	Spark M. Matsunaga (D)	162,305	53.7
	William F. Quinn (R)	122,724	40.6
1982	Spark M. Matsunaga (D)	245,386	80.1
	Clarence J. Brown (R)	52,071	17.0
1988	Spark M. Matsunaga (D)	247,941	76.5
	Maria M. Hustace (R)	66,987	20.7

Special Election

1990	Daniel K. Akaka (D)	188,901	54.0
	Patricia Saiki (R)	155,978	44.6
1994	Daniel K. Akaka (D)	256,189	71.8
	Maria M. Hustace (R)	86,320	24.2
2000	Daniel K. Akaka (D)	251,215	72.7
	John S. Carroll (R)	84,701	24.5

Class 3

1959	Oren E. Long (D)	83,700	51.1
	Wilfred C. Tsukiyama (R)	79,123	48.3
1962	Daniel K. Inouye (D)	136,294	69.4
	Ben Dillingham (R)	60,067	30.6
1968	Daniel K. Inouye (D)	189,248	83.4
	Wayne C. Thiessen (R)	34,008	15.0
1974	Daniel K. Inouye (D)	207,454	82.9
	James D. Kimmel (PP)	42,767	17.1
1980	Daniel K. Inouye (D)	224,485	77.9
	Cooper Brown (R)	53,068	18.4
1986	Daniel K. Inouye (D)	241,887	73.6
	Frank Hutchinson (R)	86,910	26.4
1992	Daniel K. Inouye (D)	208,266	57.3
	Rick Reed (R)	97,928	26.9
	Linda B. Martin (GREEN)	49,921	13.7
1998	Daniel K. Inouye (D)	315,252	79.2
	Crystal Young (R)	70,964	17.8

IDAHO

Candidates	Votes	%

Class 2

1918	William E. Borah (R)	63,587	67.2
	Frank L. Moore (D)	31,018	32.8
1924	William E. Borah (R)	99,846	79.5
	Frank Martin (D)	25,199	20.1
1930	William E. Borah (R)	94,938	72.4
	Joseph M. Tyler (D)	36,162	27.6
1936	William E. Borah (R)	128,723	63.4
	C. Ben Ross (D)	74,444	36.6

Special Election

1940	John Thomas (R)	124,535	53.0
	Glen H. Taylor (D)	110,664	47.1
1942	John Thomas (R)	73,353	51.5
	Glen H. Taylor (D)	68,989	48.5

Special Election

1946	Henry C. Dworshak (R)	105,523	58.6
	George E. Donart (D)	74,629	41.4
1948	Bert C. Miller (D)	107,000	50.0
	Henry C. Dworshak (R)	103,868	48.5

Special Election

1950	Henry C. Dworshak (R)	104,608	51.9
	Claude J. Burtenshaw (D)	97,092	48.1
1954	Henry C. Dworshak (R)	142,269	62.8
	Glen H. Taylor (D)	84,139	37.2
1960	Henry C. Dworshak (R)	152,648	52.3
	R. F "Bob" McLaughlin (D)	139,448	47.7

Special Election

1962	Len B. Jordan (R)	131,279	51.0
	Gracie Pfost (D)	126,398	49.1
1966	Len B. Jordan (R)	139,819	55.4
	Ralph R. Harding (D)	112,637	44.6
1972	James A. McClure (R)	161,804	52.3
	William E. "Bud" Davis (D)	140,913	45.5
1978	James A. McClure (R)	194,412	68.4
	Dwight Jensen (D)	89,635	31.6
1984	James A. McClure (R)	293,193	72.2
	Peter M. Busch (D)	105,591	26.0
1990	Larry E. Craig (R)	193,641	61.3
	Ron J. Twilegar (D)	122,295	38.7
1996	Larry E. Craig (R)	283,532	57.0
	Walt Minnick (D)	198,422	39.9

Class 3

1914	James H. Brady (R)	47,486	43.9
	James H. Hawley (D)	41,266	38.1
	Paul Clagstone (EP)	10,321	9.5
	C. W Cooper (SOC)	7,888	7.3

Special Election

1918	John F. Nugent (D)	48,467	50.5
	Frank R. Gooding (R)	47,497	49.5
1920	Frank R. Gooding (R)	75,985	54.1
	John F. Nugent (D)	64,513	45.9
1926	Frank R. Gooding (R)	56,847	45.4
	H. F Samuels (PROG)	37,047	29.6
	John F. Nugent (D)	31,285	25.0

Special Election

1928	John Thomas (R)	90,922	62.6
	Chase Clark (D)	53,399	36.7

1932	James Pope (D)	103,020	55.7
	John Thomas (R)	78,225	42.3
1938	D. Worth Clark (D)	99,801	54.7
	Donald A. Callahan (R)	81,939	44.9
1944	Glen H. Taylor (D)	107,096	51.1
	C. A Bottolfsen (R)	102,373	48.9
1950	Herman Welker (R)	124,237	61.7
	D. Worth Clark (D)	77,180	38.3
1956	Frank Church (D)	149,096	56.2
	Herman Welker (R)	102,781	38.7
	Glen H. Taylor (WRITE IN)	13,415	5.1
1962	Frank Church (D)	141,657	54.7
	Jack Hawley (R)	117,129	45.3
1968	Frank Church (D)	173,482	60.3
	George V. Hansen (R)	114,394	39.7
1974	Frank Church (D)	145,140	56.1
	Robert L. Smith (R)	109,072	42.1
1980	Steven D. Symms (R)	218,701	49.7
	Frank Church (D)	214,439	48.8
1986	Steven D. Symms (R)	196,958	51.6
	John V. Evans (D)	185,066	48.4
1992	Dirk Kempthorne (R)	270,468	56.5
	Richard Stallings (D)	208,036	43.5
1998	Michael D. Crapo (R)	262,966	69.5
	Bill Mauk (D)	107,375	28.4

ILLINOIS

Candidates	Votes	%

Class 2

1918	Medill McCormick (R)	479,957	50.5
	James Hamilton Lewis (D)	426,943	44.9
1924	Charles S. Deneen (R)	1,449,180	63.5
	Albert A. Sprague (D)	806,702	35.4
1930	James Hamilton Lewis (D)	1,432,216	64.0
	Ruth Hanna McCormick (R)	687,469	30.7
1936	James Hamilton Lewis (D)	2,142,887	56.5
	Otis F. Glenn (R)	1,545,160	40.7

Special Election

1940	C. Wayland Brooks (R)	2,045,924	50.1
	James M. Slattery (D)	2,025,097	49.6

1942	C. Wayland Brooks (R)	1,582,887	53.2
	Raymond S. McKeough (D)	1,380,011	46.4

1948	Paul H. Douglas (D)	2,147,754	55.1
	C. Wayland Brooks (R)	1,740,026	44.6
1954	Paul H. Douglas (D)	1,804,338	53.6
	Joseph T. Meek (R)	1,563,683	46.4
1960	Paul H. Douglas (D)	2,530,943	54.6
	Samuel W. Witwer (R)	2,093,846	45.2
1966	Charles H. Percy (R)	2,100,449	55.0
	Paul H. Douglas (D)	1,678,147	43.9
1972	Charles H. Percy (R)	2,867,078	62.2
	Roman Pucinski (D)	1,721,031	37.4
1978	Charles H. Percy (R)	1,698,711	53.3
	Alex Seith (D)	1,448,187	45.5
1984	Paul Simon (D)	2,397,303	50.1
	Charles H. Percy (R)	2,308,039	48.2
1990	Paul Simon (D)	2,115,377	65.1
	Lynn Martin (R)	1,135,628	34.9
1996	Richard J. Durbin (D)	2,384,028	56.1
	Al Salvi (R)	1,728,824	40.7

Class 3

1914	Lawrence Y. Sherman (R)	390,661	38.5
	Roger C. Sullivan (D)	373,403	36.8
	Raymond Robins (PROG)	203,027	20.0
1920	William B. McKinley (R)	1,381,384	66.8
	Peter A. Waller (D)	554,372	26.8
1926	Frank L. Smith (R)	842,273*	46.9
	George E. Brennan (D)	774,943	43.1
	Hugh S. Magill (IR)	156,245	8.7

Special Election

1928	Otis F. Glenn (R)	1,594,031	54.5
	Anton J. Cermak (D)	1,315,338	44.9

1932	William H. Dieterich (D)	1,670,466	52.2
	Otis F. Glenn (R)	1,471,841	46.0
1938	Scott W. Lucas (D)	1,638,162	51.3
	Richard J. Lyons (R)	1,542,574	48.3
1944	Scott W. Lucas (D)	2,059,023	52.6
	Richard J. Lyons (R)	1,841,793	47.1
1950	Everett McKinley Dirksen (R)	1,951,984	53.9
	Scott W. Lucas (D)	1,657,630	45.8
1956	Everett McKinley Dirksen (R)	2,307,352	54.1
	Richard Stengel (D)	1,949,883	45.7
1962	Everett McKinley Dirksen (R)	1,961,202	52.9
	Sidney R. Yates (D)	1,748,007	47.1
1968	Everett McKinley Dirksen (R)	2,358,947	53.0
	William G. Clark (D)	2,073,242	46.6

Special Election

1970	Adlai E. Stevenson III (D)	2,065,054	57.4
	Ralph Tyler Smith (R)	1,519,718	42.2

1974	Adlai E. Stevenson III (D)	1,811,496	62.2
	George M. Burditt (R)	1,084,884	37.2
1980	Alan J. Dixon (D)	2,565,302	56.0
	David C. O'Neal (R)	1,946,296	42.5
1986	Alan J. Dixon (D)	2,033,926	65.1
	Judy Koehler (R)	1,053,793	33.7
1992	Carol Moseley-Braun (D)	2,631,229	53.3
	Richard S. Williamson (R)	2,126,833	43.1

| 1998 | Peter G. Fitzgerald (R) | 1,709,041 | 47.4 |
| | Carol Moseley-Braun (D) | 1,610,496 | 50.3 |

INDIANA

	Candidates	Votes	%
	Class 1		
1916	Harry S. New (R)	337,089	47.8
	John W. Kern (D)	325,588	46.1
1922	Samuel M. Ralston (D)	558,169	50.9
	Albert J. Beveridge (R)	524,558	47.8

Special Election

| 1926 | Arthur R. Robinson (R) | 519,401 | 50.6 |
| | Evans Woollen (D) | 496,540 | 48.4 |

1928	Arthur R. Robinson (R)	782,144	55.3
	Albert Stump (D)	623,996	44.1
1934	Sherman Minton (D)	758,801	51.5
	Arthur R. Robinson (R)	700,103	47.5
1940	Raymond E. Willis (R)	888,070	50.5
	Sherman Minton (D)	864,803	49.1
1946	William E. Jenner (R)	739,809	54.9
	M. Clifford Townsend (D)	584,288	43.4
1952	William E. Jenner (R)	1,020,605	52.4
	Henry F. Schricker (D)	911,169	46.8
1958	R. Vance Hartke (D)	973,636	56.5
	Harold W. Handley (R)	731,635	42.4
1964	R. Vance Hartke (D)	1,128,505	54.3
	D. Russell Bontrager (R)	941,519	45.3
1970	R. Vance Hartke (D)	870,990	50.1
	Richard L. Roudebush (R)	866,707	49.9
1976	Richard G. Lugar (R)	1,275,833	58.8
	R. Vance Hartke (D)	878,522	40.5
1982	Richard G. Lugar (R)	978,301	53.8
	Floyd Fithian (D)	828,400	45.6
1988	Richard G. Lugar (R)	1,430,525	68.1
	Jack Wickes (D)	668,778	31.9
1994	Richard G. Lugar (R)	1,039,625	67.4
	Jim Jontz (D)	470,799	30.5
2000	Richard G. Lugar (R)	1,427,944	66.6
	David L. Johnson (D)	683,273	31.9
	Class 3		
1914	Benjamin F. Shively (D)	272,249	42.1
	Hugh Miller (R)	226,766	35.1
	Albert J. Beveridge (PROG)	108,581	16.8

Special Election

| 1916 | James E. Watson (R) | 335,193 | 47.7 |
| | Thomas Taggart (D) | 325,607 | 46.3 |

1920	James E. Watson (R)	681,854	54.6
	Thomas Taggart (D)	514,191	41.2
1926	James E. Watson (R)	522,737	50.0
	Albert Stump (D)	511,454	49.0
1932	Frederick Van Nuys (D)	870,053	55.6
	James E. Watson (R)	661,750	42.3

| 1938 | Frederick Van Nuys (D) | 788,386 | 49.8 |
| | Raymond E. Willis (R) | 783,189 | 49.5 |

Special Election

| 1944 | William E. Jenner (R) | 857,250 | 52.1 |
| | Cornelius O'Brien (D) | 775,417 | 47.1 |

1944	Homer E. Capehart (R)	829,489	50.2
	Henry F. Schricker (D)	807,766	48.9
1950	Homer E. Capehart (R)	844,303	52.8
	Alex M. Campbell (D)	741,025	46.4
1956	Homer E. Capehart (R)	1,084,262	55.2
	Claude R. Wickard (D)	871,781	44.4
1962	Birch Bayh (D)	905,491	50.3
	Homer E. Capehart (R)	894,547	49.7
1968	Birch Bayh (D)	1,060,456	51.7
	William D. Ruckelshaus (R)	988,571	48.2
1974	Birch Bayh (D)	889,269	50.7
	Richard G. Lugar (R)	814,117	46.4
1980	Dan Quayle (R)	1,182,414	53.8
	Birch Bayh (D)	1,015,962	46.2
1986	Dan Quayle (R)	936,143	60.6
	Jill Long (D)	595,192	38.5

Special Election

| 1990 | Daniel R. Coats (R) | 806,048 | 53.6 |
| | Baron P. Hill (D) | 696,639 | 46.4 |

1992	Daniel R. Coats (R)	1,267,972	57.3
	Joseph H. Hogsett (D)	900,148	40.7
1998	Evan Bayh (D)	1,012,244	63.7
	Paul Helmke (R)	552,732	34.8

IOWA

	Candidates	Votes	%
	Class 2		
1918	William S. Kenyon (R)	230,264	65.4
	Charles R. Keyes (D)	121,830	34.6

Special Election

| 1922 | Smith W. Brookhart (R) | 389,751 | 63.1 |
| | Clyde L. Herring (D) | 227,833 | 36.9 |

1924[1]	Smith W. Brookhart (R)	447,594	50.0
	Daniel F. Steck (D)	446,840	50.0
1930	Lester J. Dickinson (R)	307,613	56.3
	Daniel F. Steck (D)	235,186	43.0
1936	Clyde L. Herring (D)	539,555	50.5
	Lester J. Dickinson (R)	503,635	47.1
1942	George A. Wilson (R)	410,333	58.0
	Clyde L. Herring (D)	295,194	41.7
1948	Guy M. Gillette (D)	578,226	57.8
	George A. Wilson (R)	415,778	41.6
1954	Thomas E. Martin (R)	442,409	52.2
	Guy M. Gillette (D)	402,712	47.5
1960	Jack Miller (R)	642,463	51.9
	Herschel C. Loveless (D)	595,119	48.1

1966	Jack Miller (R)	522,339	60.9
	E. B Smith (D)	324,114	37.8
1972	Dick Clark (D)	662,637	55.1
	Jack Miller (R)	530,525	44.1
1978	Roger W. Jepsen (R)	421,598	51.1
	Dick Clark (D)	395,066	47.9
1984	Tom Harkin (D)	716,883	55.5
	Roger W. Jepsen (R)	564,381	43.7
1990	Tom Harkin (D)	535,975	54.5
	Tom Tauke (R)	446,869	45.4
1996	Tom Harkin (D)	634,166	51.8
	Jim Ross Lightfoot (R)	571,807	46.7

Class 3

1914	Albert B. Cummins (R)	205,832	48.2
	Connolly (D)	167,251	39.2
	Spurgeon (I)	24,490	5.7
1920	Albert B. Cummins (R)	528,499	61.4
	Claude R. Porter (D)	322,015	37.4
1926	Smith W. Brookhart (R)	323,409	56.5
	Claude R. Porter (D)	247,869	43.3

Special Election

1926	David W. Stewart (R)	336,410	100.0
1932	Richard Louis Murphy (D)	538,422	54.9
	Henry Field (R)	399,929	40.8

Special Election

1936	Guy M. Gillette (D)	536,075	51.9
	Berry F. Halden (R)	481,521	46.6
1938	Guy M. Gillette (D)	413,788	49.7
	Lester J. Dickinson (R)	410,983	49.4
1944	Bourke B. Hickenlooper (R)	523,963	51.3
	Guy M. Gillette (D)	494,229	48.4
1950	Bourke B. Hickenlooper (R)	470,613	54.8
	Albert J. Loveland (D)	383,766	44.7
1956	Bourke B. Hickenlooper (R)	635,499	53.9
	R. M Evans (D)	543,156	46.1
1962	Bourke B. Hickenlooper (R)	431,364	53.4
	E. B Smith (D)	376,602	46.6
1968	Harold E. Hughes (D)	574,884	50.3
	David M. Stanley (R)	568,469	49.7
1974	John C. Culver (D)	462,947	52.0
	David M. Stanley (R)	420,546	47.3
1980	Charles E. Grassley (R)	683,014	53.5
	John C. Culver (D)	581,545	45.5
1986	Charles E. Grassley (R)	588,880	66.0
	John P. Roehrick (D)	299,406	33.6
1992	Charles E. Grassley (R)	899,761	69.6
	Jean Lloyd-Jones (D)	351,561	27.2
1998	Charles E. Grassley (R)	648,480	68.4
	David Osterberg (D)	289,049	30.5

Iowa
1. Disputed election. See list of senators, Iowa, p. 1243.

KANSAS

	Candidates	Votes	%
	Class 2		
1912	William H. Thompson (D)	172,601	49.3
	W. R Stubbs (R)	151,647	43.3
	Allan W. Ricker (SOC)	25,610	7.3
1918	Arthur Capper (R)	281,931	63.7
	William H. Thompson (D)	149,300	33.7
1924	Arthur Capper (R)	428,494	70.1
	James Malone (D)	154,189	25.2
1930	Arthur Capper (R)	364,548	61.1
	Jonathan M. Davis (D)	232,161	38.9
1936	Arthur Capper (R)	417,873	51.0
	Omar B. Ketchum (D)	396,685	48.4
1942	Arthur Capper (R)	284,059	57.1
	George McGill (D)	200,437	40.3
1948	Andrew F. Schoeppel (R)	393,412	54.9
	George McGill (D)	305,987	42.7
1954	Andrew F. Schoeppel (R)	348,144	56.3
	George McGill (D)	258,575	41.8
1960	Andrew F. Schoeppel (R)	485,499	54.6
	Frank Theis (D)	388,895	43.8

Special Election

1962	James B. Pearson (R)	344,689	56.2
	Paul L. Aylward (D)	260,756	42.5
1966	James B. Pearson (R)	350,077	52.2
	J. Floyd Breeding (D)	303,223	45.2
1972	James B. Pearson (R)	622,591	71.4
	Arch Tetzlaff (D)	200,764	23.0
1978	Nancy Landon Kassebaum (R)	403,354	53.9
	William R. Roy (D)	317,602	42.4
1984	Nancy Landon Kassebaum (R)	757,402	76.0
	James R. Maher (D)	211,664	21.2
1990	Nancy Landon Kassebaum (R)	578,605	73.6
	Dick Williams (D)	207,491	26.4
1996	Pat Roberts (R)	652,677	62.0
	Sally Thompson (D)	362,380	34.4

Class 3

1914	Charles Curtis (R)	180,823	35.5
	George A. Neeley (D)	176,929	34.8
	Victor Murdock (PROG)	116,755	22.9
1920	Charles Curtis (R)	327,072	64.0
	George H. Hodges (D)	170,443	33.4
1926	Charles Curtis (R)	308,222	63.6
	Charles Stephens (D)	168,446	34.7

Special Election

1930	George McGill (D)	288,889	50.0
	Henry J. Allen (R)	276,833	48.0
1932	George McGill (D)	328,992	45.7
	Ben S. Paulen (R)	302,809	42.0
	George Alfred Brown (I)	65,583	9.1
1938	Clyde M. Reed (R)	419,532	56.2
	George McGill (D)	326,774	43.8

1944	Clyde M. Reed (R)	387,090	*57.8*
	Thurman Hill (D)	272,053	*40.7*
1950	Frank Carlson (R)	335,880	*54.3*
	Paul Aiken (D)	271,365	*43.8*

Special Election

1950	Frank Carlson (R)	321,718	*55.2*
	Paul Aiken (D)	261,405	*44.8*

1956	Frank Carlson (R)	477,822	*57.9*
	George Hart (D)	333,939	*40.5*
1962	Frank Carlson (R)	388,500	*62.4*
	K. L Smith (D)	223,630	*35.9*
1968	Robert Dole (R)	490,911	*60.1*
	William I. Robinson (D)	315,911	*38.7*
1974	Robert Dole (R)	403,983	*50.9*
	William R. Roy (D)	390,451	*49.1*
1980	Robert Dole (R)	598,686	*63.8*
	John Simpson (D)	340,271	*36.2*
1986	Robert Dole (R)	576,902	*70.0*
	Guy MacDonald (D)	246,664	*30.0*
1992	Robert Dole (R)	706,246	*62.7*
	Gloria O'Dell (D)	349,525	*31.0*

Special Election

1996	Sam Brownback (R)	574,021	*53.9*
	Jill Docking (D)	461,344	*43.3*

1998	Sam Brownback (R)	474,639	*65.3*
	Paul Feleciano Jr. (D)	229,718	*31.6*

KENTUCKY

Candidates	Votes	%

Class 2

1918	Augustus Owsley Stanley (D)	184,385	*50.8*
	Ben L. Bruner (R)	178,797	*49.2*
1924	Frederic M. Sackett (R)	406,123	*51.6*
	Augustus Owsley Stanley (D)	381,605	*48.4*
1930	Marvel M. Logan (D)	336,748	*52.1*
	John M. Robsion (R)	309,180	*47.9*
1936	Marvel M. Logan (D)	539,968	*58.8*
	Robert M. Lucas (R)	365,850	*39.8*

Special Election

1940	Albert B. "Happy" Chandler (D)	561,151	*58.3*
	Walter B. Smith (R)	401,812	*41.7*

1942	Albert B. "Happy" Chandler (D)	216,958	*55.3*
	Richard J. Colbert (R)	175,081	*44.7*

Special Election

1946	John Sherman Cooper (R)	327,652	*53.3*
	John Young Brown (D)	285,829	*46.5*

1948	Virgil Chapman (D)	408,256	*51.4*
	John Sherman Cooper (R)	383,776	*48.3*

Special Election

1952	John Sherman Cooper (R)	494,576	*51.5*
	Thomas R. Underwood (D)	465,652	*48.5*

1954	Alben W. Barkley (D)	434,109	*54.5*
	John Sherman Cooper (R)	362,948	*45.5*

Special Election

1956	John Sherman Cooper (R)	538,505	*53.2*
	Lawrence W. Wetherby (D)	473,140	*46.8*

1960	John Sherman Cooper (R)	644,087	*59.2*
	Keen Johnson (D)	444,290	*40.8*
1966	John Sherman Cooper (R)	483,805	*64.5*
	John Young Brown (D)	266,079	*35.5*
1972	Walter D. Huddleston (D)	528,550	*50.9*
	Louie B. Nunn (R)	494,337	*47.6*
1978	Walter D. Huddleston (D)	290,730	*61.0*
	Louie Guenthner (R)	175,766	*36.9*
1984	Mitch McConnell (R)	644,990	*49.9*
	Walter D. Huddleston (D)	639,721	*49.5*
1990	Mitch McConnell (R)	478,034	*52.2*
	Harvey Sloane (D)	437,976	*47.8*
1996	Mitch McConnell (R)	724,794	*55.5*
	Steven L. Beshear (D)	560,012	*42.8*

Class 3

1914	John C. W Beckham (D)	175,999	*51.8*
	Willson (R)	144,758	*42.6*

Special Election

1914	Johnson N. Camden Jr. (D)	177,797	*54.0*
	Bullitt (R)	133,139	*40.4*

1920	Richard P. Ernst (R)	454,226	*50.3*
	John C. W Beckham (D)	449,244	*49.7*
1926	Alben W. Barkley (D)	286,997	*51.8*
	Richard P. Ernst (R)	266,657	*48.2*
1932	Alben W. Barkley (D)	574,977	*59.2*
	M. H Thatcher (R)	393,865	*40.5*
1938	Alben W. Barkley (D)	346,735	*62.0*
	John P. Haswell (R)	212,266	*38.0*
1944	Alben W. Barkley (D)	464,053	*54.8*
	James Park (R)	380,425	*44.9*
1950	Earle C. Clements (D)	334,249	*54.2*
	Charles I. Dawson (R)	278,368	*45.1*

Special Election

1950	Earle C. Clements (D)	317,320#	*54.4*
	Charles I. Dawson (R)	265,994#	*45.6*

1956	Thruston B. Morton (R)	506,903	*50.4*
	Earle C. Clements (D)	499,922	*49.7*
1962	Thruston B. Morton (R)	432,648	*52.8*
	Wilson W. Wyatt (D)	387,440	*47.2*
1968	Marlow W. Cook (R)	484,260	*51.4*
	Katherine Peden (D)	448,960	*47.6*
1974	Wendell H. Ford (D)	399,406	*53.5*
	Marlow W. Cook (R)	328,982	*44.1*

1980	Wendell H. Ford (D)	720,861	65.1
	Mary Louise Foust (R)	386,029	34.9
1986	Wendell H. Ford (D)	503,775	74.4
	Jackson M. Andrews (R)	173,330	25.6
1992	Wendell H. Ford (D)	836,888	62.9
	David L. Williams (R)	476,604	35.8
1998	Jim Bunning (R)	569,817	49.7
	Scotty Baesler (D)	563,051	49.2

LOUISIANA

	Candidates	Votes	%
	Class 2		
1918	Joseph E. Ransdell (D)	44,224	100.0
1924	Joseph E. Ransdell (D)	94,939	100.0
1930	Huey P. Long (D)	130,536	100.0

Special Election

1936	Rose McConnell Long (D)	131,930#	100.0

1936	Allen J. Ellender (D)	293,256	100.0
1942	Allen J. Ellender (D)	85,488	100.0
1948	Allen J. Ellender (D)	330,315	100.0
1954	Allen J. Ellender (D)	207,115	100.0
1960	Allen J. Ellender (D)	432,228	79.8
	George W. Reese Jr. (R)	109,698	20.2
1966	Allen J. Ellender (D)	437,695	100.0
1972	J. Bennett Johnston (D)	598,987	55.2
	John J. McKeithen (I)	250,161	23.1
	Ben C. Toledano (R)	206,846	19.1
1978[1]	J. Bennett Johnston (D)	—	—
1984[1]	J. Bennett Johnston (D)	—	—
1990[1]	J. Bennett Johnston (D)	—	—
1996	Mary L. Landrieu (D)	852,945	50.2
	Louis "Woody" Jenkins (R)	847,157	49.8
	Class 3		
1914	Robert F. Broussard (D)	✔	

Special Election

1918	Edward J. Gay (D)	44,345	100.0

1920	Edwin S. Broussard (D)	94,944#	100.0
1926	Edwin S. Broussard (D)	54,180	100.0
1932	John H. Overton (D)	249,189	100.0
1938	John H. Overton (D)	151,585	99.8
1944	John H. Overton (D)	286,365	100.0

Special Election

1948	Russell B. Long (D)	305,346	74.9
	Clem S. Clarke (R)	102,339	25.1

1950	Russell B. Long (D)	220,907	87.7
	Charles S. Gerth (R)	30,931	12.3
1956	Russell B. Long (D)	335,564	100.0
1962	Russell B. Long (D)	318,838	75.6
	Taylor Walters O'Hearn (R)	103,066	24.4
1968	Russell B. Long (D)	518,586	100.0
1974	Russell B. Long (D)	434,643	100.0

1980[1]	Russell B. Long (D)	—	—
1986	John B. Breaux (D)	723,586	52.8
	W. Henson Moore (R)	646,311	47.2
1992[1]	John B. Breaux (D)	—	—
1998	John B. Breaux (D)	620,502	64.0
	Jim Donelon (R)	306,616	31.6

Louisiana

1. Dash (—) indicates candidate elected in primary. Since 1978, Louisiana has held an open-primary election with candidates from all parties running on the same ballot. Any candidate who receives a majority is elected; if no candidate receives 50 percent, there is a runoff election in November between the two top finishers.

MAINE

	Candidates	Votes	%
	Class 1		
1916	Frederick Hale (R)	79,841	52.8
	Charles Johnson (D)	69,486	46.0
1922	Frederick Hale (R)	101,026	57.5
	Oakley C. Curtis (D)	74,659	42.5
1928	Frederick Hale (R)	145,501	69.6
	Herbert E. Holmes (D)	63,429	30.4
1934	Frederick Hale (R)	139,773	50.1
	F. Harold Dubord (D)	138,573	49.7
1940	Ralph O. Brewster (R)	150,149	58.6
	Louis J. Brann (D)	105,740	41.3
1946	Ralph O. Brewster (R)	111,215	63.6
	Peter M. MacDonald (D)	63,799	36.5
1952	Frederick G. Payne (R)	139,205	58.7
	Roger P. Dube (D)	82,665	34.9
	Earl S. Grant (I)	15,294#	6.4
1958	Edmund S. Muskie (D)	172,842	60.8
	Frederick G. Payne (R)	111,522	39.2
1964	Edmund S. Muskie (D)	253,511	66.6
	Clifford G. McIntire (R)	127,040	33.4
1970	Edmund S. Muskie (D)	199,954	61.9
	Neil S. Bishop (R)	123,906	38.3
1976	Edmund S. Muskie (D)	292,704	60.2
	Robert A. G Monks (R)	193,489	39.8
1982	George J. Mitchell (D)	279,819	60.9
	David F. Emery (R)	179,882	39.1
1988	George J. Mitchell (D)	452,590	81.2
	Jasper S. Wyman (R)	104,758	18.8
1994	Olympia J. Snowe (R)	308,244	60.3
	Thomas H. Andrews (D)	186,042	36.4
2000	Olympia J. Snowe (R)	437,689	68.9
	Mark Lawrence (D)	197,183	31.1
	Class 2		

Special Election

1916	Bert M. Fernald (R)	81,369	54.3
	Kenneth Sills (D)	68,201	45.5

1918	Bert M. Fernald (R)	66,858	55.6
	Earl Newbert (D)	53,460	44.4
1924	Bert M. Fernald (R)	148,783	60.4
	Fulton J. Redman (D)	97,428	39.6

Special Election

1926	Arthur R. Gould (R)	79,498	71.8
	Fulton J. Redman (D)	31,225	28.2
1930	Wallace H. White Jr. (R)	88,262	60.9
	Frank H. Haskell (D)	56,561	39.1
1936	Wallace H. White Jr. (R)	158,068	50.8
	Louis J. Brann (D)	153,420	49.3
1942	Wallace H. White Jr. (R)	111,520	66.7
	Fulton J. Redman (D)	55,754	33.3
1948	Margaret Chase Smith (R)	159,182	71.3
	Adrian H. Scolten (D)	64,074	28.7
1954	Margaret Chase Smith (R)	144,530	58.6
	Paul A. Fullam (D)	102,075	41.4
1960	Margaret Chase Smith (R)	256,890	61.7
	Lucia M. Cormier (D)	159,809	38.4
1966	Margaret Chase Smith (R)	188,291	59.0
	Elmer H. Violette (D)	131,136	41.1
1972	William D. Hathaway (D)	224,270	53.2
	Margaret Chase Smith (R)	197,040	46.8
1978	William S. Cohen (R)	212,294	56.6
	William D. Hathaway (D)	127,327	33.9
	Hayes E. Gahagan (I)	27,824	7.4
1984	William S. Cohen (R)	404,414	73.3
	Elizabeth H. Mitchell (D)	142,626	25.9
1990	William S. Cohen (R)	319,167	61.3
	Neil Rolde (D)	201,053	38.6
1996	Susan Collins (R)	298,422	49.2
	Joseph E. Brennan (D)	266,226	43.9

MARYLAND

Candidates	Votes	%
Class 1		

Special Election

1913	Blair Lee (D)	112,485#	56.8
	Thomas Parran (R)	73,300#	37.0
1916	Joseph Irwin France (R)	113,662	49.3
	David J. Lewis (D)	109,740	47.6
1922	William Cabell Bruce (D)	160,947	52.6
	Joseph Irwin France (R)	139,581	45.6
1928	Phillips Lee Goldsborough (R)	256,224	54.1
	William Cabell Bruce (D)	214,447	45.2
1934	George L. Radcliffe (D)	264,279	56.1
	Joseph Irwin France (R)	197,643	42.0
1940	George L. Radcliffe (D)	394,239#	64.7
	Harry W. Nice (R)	203,912#	33.5
1946	Herbert R. O'Conor (D)	237,232#	50.2
	David John Markey (R)	235,000#	49.8
1952	J. Glenn Beall (R)	449,823	52.5
	George P. Mahoney (D)	406,370	47.5
1958	J. Glenn Beall (R)	382,021	51.0
	Thomas D'Alesandro Jr. (D)	367,270	49.0
1964	Joseph D. Tydings (D)	678,649	62.8
	J. Glenn Beall (R)	402,393	37.2
1970	J. Glenn Beall Jr. (R)	484,960	50.7
	Joseph D. Tydings (D)	460,442	48.1

1976	Paul S. Sarbanes (D)	772,101	56.5
	J. Glenn Beall Jr. (R)	530,439	38.8
1982	Paul S. Sarbanes (D)	707,356	63.5
	Lawrence J. Hogan (R)	407,334	36.5
1988	Paul S. Sarbanes (D)	999,166	61.8
	Alan L. Keyes (R)	617,537	38.2
1994	Paul S. Sarbanes (D)	809,125	59.1
	William Brock (R)	559,908	40.9
2000	Paul S. Sarbanes (D)	1,230,013	63.2
	Paul Rappaport (R)	715,178	36.7

Class 3

1914	John Walter Smith (D)	110,204	51.0
	Edward C. Carrington Jr. (R)	94,864	43.9
1920	Ovington E. Weller (R)	184,999	47.3
	John Walter Smith (D)	169,200	43.3
	George D. Iverson Jr. (I)	21,345	5.5
1926	Millard E. Tydings (D)	195,410	57.6
	Ovington E. Weller (R)	139,995	41.3
1932	Millard E. Tydings (D)	293,389	66.2
	Wallace Williams (R)	138,266	31.2
1938	Millard E. Tydings (D)	357,245	68.3
	Oscar Leser (R)	153,253	29.3
1944	Millard E. Tydings (D)	344,725	61.7
	Blanchard Randall Jr. (R)	213,705	38.3
1950	John Marshall Butler (R)	326,291	53.0
	Millard E. Tydings (D)	283,180	46.0
1956	John Marshall Butler (R)	473,059	53.0
	George P. Mahoney (D)	419,108	47.0
1962	Daniel B. Brewster (D)	439,723	62.0
	Edward T. Miller (R)	269,131	38.0
1968	Charles McC. Mathias Jr. (R)	541,893	47.8
	Daniel B. Brewster (D)	443,367	39.1
	George P. Mahoney (I)	148,467	13.1
1974	Charles McC. Mathias Jr. (R)	503,223	57.3
	Barbara A. Mikulski (D)	374,563	42.7
1980	Charles McC. Mathias Jr. (R)	850,970	66.2
	Edward T. Conroy (D)	435,118	33.8
1986	Barbara A. Mikulski (D)	675,229	60.7
	Linda Chavez (R)	437,419	39.3
1992	Barbara A. Mikulski (D)	1,307,610	71.0
	Alan L. Keyes (R)	533,688	29.0
1998	Barbara A. Mikulski (D)	1,062,810	70.5
	Ross Z. Pierpont (R)	444,637	29.5

MASSACHUSETTS

Candidates	Votes	%
Class 1		

1916	Henry Cabot Lodge (R)	267,177	51.7
	John F. Fitzgerald (D)	234,238	45.3
1922	Henry Cabot Lodge (R)	414,130	47.6
	William A. Gaston (D)	406,776	46.8

Special Election

1926	David I. Walsh (D)	525,303	52.0
	William M. Butler (R)	469,989	46.5

1928	David I. Walsh (D)	818,055	53.6
	Benjamin Loring Young (R)	693,563	45.5
1934	David I. Walsh (D)	852,776	59.4
	Robert M. Washburn (R)	536,692	37.4
1940	David I. Walsh (D)	1,088,838	55.6
	Henry Parkman Jr. (R)	838,122	42.8
1946	Henry Cabot Lodge Jr. (R)	989,736	59.6
	David I. Walsh (D)	660,200	39.7
1952	John F. Kennedy (D)	1,211,984	51.4
	Henry Cabot Lodge Jr. (R)	1,141,247	48.4
1958	John F. Kennedy (D)	1,362,926	73.2
	Vincent J. Celeste (R)	488,318	26.2

Special Election

1962	Edward M. Kennedy (D)	1,162,611	55.4
	George C. Lodge (R)	877,669	41.9

1964	Edward M. Kennedy (D)	1,716,907	74.3
	Howard Whitmore Jr. (R)	587,663	25.4
1970	Edward M. Kennedy (D)	1,202,856	62.1
	Josiah A. Spaulding (R)	715,978	37.0
1976	Edward M. Kennedy (D)	1,726,657	69.3
	Michael Robertson (R)	722,641	29.0
1982	Edward M. Kennedy (D)	1,247,084	60.8
	Raymond Shamie (R)	784,602	38.3
1988	Edward M. Kennedy (D)	1,693,344	65.0
	Joseph D. Malone (R)	884,267	33.9
1994	Edward M. Kennedy (D)	1,265,997	58.1
	W. Mitt Romney (R)	894,000	41.0
2000	Edward M. Kennedy (D)	1,889,494	72.7
	Jack E. Robinson (R)	334,341	12.9
	Carla Howell (LIBERT)	308,748	11.8

Class 2

1918	David I. Walsh (D)	207,478	49.7
	John W. Weeks (R)	188,287	45.1
	Thomas W. Lawson (I)	21,985	5.3
1924	Frederick H. Gillett (R)	566,188	50.3
	David I. Walsh (D)	547,600	48.6
1930	Marcus A. Coolidge (D)	651,939	54.0
	William M. Butler (R)	539,226	44.7
1936	Henry Cabot Lodge Jr. (R)	875,160	48.5
	James M. Curley (D)	739,751	41.0
	Thomas C. O'Brien (UN)	134,245	7.4
1942	Henry Cabot Lodge Jr. (R)	721,239	52.4
	Joseph E. Casey (D)	641,042	46.6

Special Election

1944	Leverett Saltonstall (R)	1,228,754	64.3
	John H. Corcoran (D)	667,086	34.9

1948	Leverett Saltonstall (R)	1,088,475	53.0
	John I. Fitzgerald (D)	954,398	46.4
1954	Leverett Saltonstall (R)	956,605	50.5
	Foster Furcolo (D)	927,899	49.0
1960	Leverett Saltonstall (R)	1,358,556	56.2
	Thomas J. O'Connor Jr. (D)	1,050,725	43.5
1966	Edward W. Brooke (R)	1,213,473	60.7
	Endicott Peabody (D)	774,761	38.7
1972	Edward W. Brooke (R)	1,505,932	63.5
	John J. Droney (D)	823,278	34.7

1978	Paul E. Tsongas (D)	1,093,283	55.1
	Edward W. Brooke (R)	890,584	44.8
1984	John F. Kerry (D)	1,393,150	55.1
	Raymond Shamie (R)	1,136,913	44.9
1990	John F. Kerry (D)	1,321,712	57.1
	Jim Rappaport (R)	992,917	42.9
1996	John F. Kerry (D)	1,334,345	52.2
	William F. Weld (R)	1,142,837	44.7

MICHIGAN

Candidates	Votes	%

Class 1

1916	Charles E. Townsend (R)	364,657	56.3
	Lawrence Price (D)	257,954	39.9
1922	Woodbridge N. Ferris (D)	294,932	50.6
	Charles E. Townsend (R)	281,843	48.4
1928	Arthur H. Vandenberg (R)	977,893	71.8
	John W. Bailey (D)	376,592	27.7

Special Election

1928	Arthur H. Vandenberg (R)	974,203	72.0
	John W. Bailey (D)	375,673	27.8

1934	Arthur H. Vandenberg (R)	626,017	51.3
	Frank A. Picard (D)	573,574	47.0
1940	Arthur H. Vandenberg (R)	1,053,104	52.7
	Frank Fitzgerald (D)	939,740	47.0
1946	Arthur H. Vandenberg (R)	1,085,570	67.1
	James H. Lee (D)	517,923	32.0
1952	Charles E. Potter (R)	1,428,352	50.6
	Blair Moody (D)	1,383,416	49.0

Special Election

1952	Charles E. Potter (R)	1,417,032	51.2
	Blair Moody (D)	1,347,705	48.7

1958	Philip A. Hart (D)	1,216,966	53.6
	Charles E. Potter (R)	1,046,963	46.1
1964	Philip A. Hart (D)	1,996,912	64.4
	Elly M. Peterson (R)	1,096,272	35.3
1970	Philip A. Hart (D)	1,744,672	66.8
	Lenore Romney (R)	858,438	32.9
1976	Donald W. Riegle Jr. (D)	1,831,031	52.5
	Marvin L. Esch (R)	1,635,087	46.8
1982	Donald W. Riegle Jr. (D)	1,728,793	57.7
	Philip E. Ruppe (R)	1,223,288	40.9
1988	Donald W. Riegle Jr. (D)	2,116,865	60.4
	Jim Dunn (R)	1,348,219	38.5
1994	Spencer Abraham (R)	1,578,770	51.9
	Bob Carr (D)	1,300,960	42.7
2000	Debbie Stabenow (D)	2,061,952	49.5
	Spencer Abraham (R)	1,994,693	47.9

Class 2

1918	Truman H. Newberry (R)	220,054	50.2
	Henry Ford (D)	212,487	48.5
1924	James Couzens (R)	858,934	74.3
	Mortimer E. Cooley (D)	284,609	24.6

Special Election

1924	James Couzens (R)	839,569	75.0
	Mortimer E. Cooley (D)	266,851	23.9
1930	James Couzens (R)	634,577	78.2
	Thomas A. E Weadock (D)	169,757	20.9
1936	Prentiss M. Brown (D)	910,937	53.3
	Wilber M. Brucker (R)	714,602	41.8
1942	Homer Ferguson (R)	589,652	49.6
	Prentiss M. Brown (D)	561,595	47.2
1948	Homer Ferguson (R)	1,045,156	50.7
	Frank E. Hook (D)	1,000,329	48.5
1954	Patrick V. McNamara (D)	1,088,550	50.8
	Homer Ferguson (R)	1,049,420	48.9
1960	Patrick V. McNamara (D)	1,669,179	51.7
	Alvin M. Bentley (R)	1,548,873	48.0
1966	Robert P. Griffin (R)	1,363,530	55.9
	G. Mennen Williams (D)	1,069,484	43.8

Special Election

1966	Robert P. Griffin (R)	1,321,222	56.0
	G. Mennen Williams (D)	1,031,138	43.7
1972	Robert P. Griffin (R)	1,781,065	52.3
	Frank J. Kelley (D)	1,577,178	46.3
1978	Carl Levin (D)	1,484,193	52.1
	Robert P. Griffin (R)	1,362,165	47.9
1984	Carl Levin (D)	1,915,831	51.8
	Jack Lousma (R)	1,745,302	47.2
1990	Carl Levin (D)	1,471,753	57.5
	Bill Schuette (R)	1,055,695	41.2
1996	Carl Levin (D)	2,195,738	58.4
	Ronna Romney (R)	1,500,106	39.9

MINNESOTA

Candidates	Votes	%

Class 1

1916	Frank B. Kellogg (R)	185,159	48.6
	Daniel W. Lawler (D)	117,541	30.8
	W. G Calderwood (P)	78,425	20.6
1922	Henrik Shipstead (F-LAB)	325,372	47.1
	Frank B. Kellogg (R)	241,833	35.0
	Anna D. Olesen (D)	123,624	17.9
1928	Henrik Shipstead (F-LAB)	665,169	65.4
	Arthur E. Nelson (R)	342,992	33.7
1934	Henrik Shipstead (F-LAB)	503,379	49.9
	Einar Hoidale (D)	294,757	29.2
	N. J Holmberg (R)	200,083	19.8
1940	Henrik Shipstead (R)	641,049	53.0
	Elmer A. Benson (F-LAB)	310,875	25.7
	John E. Regan (D)	248,658	20.6
1946	Edward J. Thye (R)	517,775	58.9
	Theodore Jorgenson (DFL)	349,520	39.8
1952	Edward J. Thye (R)	785,649	56.6
	William E. Carlson (DFL)	590,011	42.5
1958	Eugene J. McCarthy (DFL)	608,847	52.9
	Edward J. Thye (R)	536,629	46.6

1964	Eugene J. McCarthy (DFL)	931,363	60.3
	Wheelock Whitney (R)	605,933	39.3
1970	Hubert H. Humphrey (DFL)	788,256	57.8
	Clark MacGregor (R)	568,025	41.6
1976	Hubert H. Humphrey (DFL)	1,290,736	67.5
	Gerald W. Brekke (R)	478,611	25.0
	Paul Helm (AM)	125,612	6.6

Special Election

1978	Dave Durenberger (I-R)	957,908	61.4
	Robert E. Short (DFL)	538,675	34.5
1982	Dave Durenberger (I-R)	949,207	52.6
	Mark Dayton (DFL)	840,401	46.6
1988	Dave Durenberger (I-R)	1,176,210	56.2
	Hubert H. Humphrey III (DFL)	1,856,694	40.9
1994	Rod Grams (R)	869,653	49.1
	Ann Wynia (D)	781,860	44.1
	Dean M. Barkley (I)	95,400	5.4
2000	Mark Dayton (D)	1,181,553	48.8
	Rod Grams (R)	1,047,474	43.3
	James Gibson (INDEP)	140,583	5.8

Class 2

1912	Knute Nelson (R)	173,074	62.8
	Daniel W. Lawler (D)	102,691	37.2
1918	Knute Nelson (R)	206,687	60.1
	W. G Calderwood (N)	137,294	39.9

Special Election

1923	Magnus Johnson (F-LAB)	290,165#	57.5
	J. A O. Preus (R)	195,319#	38.7
1924	Thomas D. Schall (R)	388,594	46.5
	Magnus Johnson (F-LAB)	380,646	45.5
	John J. Farrell (D)	53,709	6.4
1930	Thomas D. Schall (R)	293,626	37.6
	Einar Hoidale (D)	282,018	36.1
	Ernest Lundeen (F-LAB)	178,671	22.9
1936	Ernest Lundeen (F-LAB)	663,363	62.2
	Theodore Christianson (R)	402,404	37.8

Special Election

1936	Guy V. Howard (R)	317,457	42.9
	N. J Holmberg (I)	210,364	28.4
	Andrew Olaf Devolt (I PROG)	147,858	20.0
	John G. Alexander (I)	64,493	8.7
1942	Joseph H. Ball (R)	356,297	47.0
	Elmer A. Benson (F-LAB)	213,965	28.2
	Martin A. Nelson (I PROG)	109,231	14.4
	Ed Murphy (D)	78,959	10.4

Special Election

1942	Arthur E. Nelson (R)	372,240	56.1
	Al Hansen (F-LAB)	177,008	26.7
	John E. O'Rourke (D)	114,086	17.2
1948	Hubert H. Humphrey (DFL)	729,494	59.9
	Joseph H. Ball (R)	482,801	39.7

1954	Hubert H. Humphrey (DFL)	642,193	56.4
	Val Bjornson (R)	479,619	42.1
1960	Hubert H. Humphrey (DFL)	884,168	57.5
	P. Kenneth Peterson (R)	648,586	42.2
1966	Walter F. Mondale (DFL)	685,840	53.9
	Robert A. Forsythe (R)	574,868	45.2
1972	Walter F. Mondale (DFL)	981,320	56.7
	Phil Hansen (R)	742,121	42.9
1978	Rudy Boschwitz (I-R)	894,092	56.6
	Wendell R. Anderson (DFL)	638,375	40.4
1984	Rudy Boschwitz (I-R)	1,199,926	58.1
	Joan Anderson Growe (DFL)	852,844	41.3
1990	Paul Wellstone (DFL)	911,999	50.4
	Rudy Boschwitz (I-R)	864,375	47.8
1996	Paul Wellstone (DFL)	1,098,493	50.3
	Rudy Boschwitz (R)	901,282	41.3
	Dean Barkley (REF)	152,333	7.0

MISSISSIPPI

	Candidates	Votes	%
	Class 1		
1916	John Sharp Williams (D)	74,290	100.0
1922	Hubert D. Stephens (D)	63,636	93.2
1928	Hubert D. Stephens (D)	111,210	100.0
1934	Theodore G. Bilbo (D)	51,709	100.0
1940	Theodore G. Bilbo (D)	143,333	100.0
1946	Theodore G. Bilbo (D)	46,747*	100.0

Special Election

1947	John C. Stennis (D)	52,068	26.9
	William M. Colmer (D)	45,725	23.6
	Forrest B. Jackson (D)	43,642	22.5
	Paul B. Johnson Jr. (D)	27,159	14.0
	John E. Rankin (D)	24,492	12.6
1952	John C. Stennis (D)	233,919	100.0
1958	John C. Stennis (D)	61,039	100.0
1964	John C. Stennis (D)	343,364	100.0
1970	John C. Stennis (D)	286,622	88.4
	William R. Thompson (I)	37,593	11.6
1976	John C. Stennis (D)	554,433	100.0
1982	John C. Stennis (D)	414,099	64.2
	Haley Barbour (R)	230,927	35.8
1988	Trent Lott (R)	510,380	53.9
	Wayne Dowdy (D)	436,339	46.1
1994	Trent Lott (R)	418,333	68.8
	Ken Harper (D)	189,752	31.2
2000	Trent Lott (R)	654,941	65.9
	Troy Brown (D)	314,090	31.6

	Class 2		
1918	Pat Harrison (D)	30,055	95.0
	Sumner W. Rose (S)	1,569	5.0
1924	Pat Harrison (D)	97,257	100.0
1930	Pat Harrison (D)	33,953	100.0
1936	Pat Harrison (D)	140,570	100.0

Special Election

1941	Wall Doxey (D)	59,485	50.3
	Ross Collins (D)	58,809	49.7
1942	James O. Eastland (D)	51,355	100.0
1948	James O. Eastland (D)	151,478	100.0
1954	James O. Eastland (D)	100,848	95.6
1960	James O. Eastland (D)	244,341	91.8
	Joe A. Moore (R)	21,807	8.2
1966	James O. Eastland (D)	258,248	65.5
	Prentiss Walker (R)	105,652	26.8
	Clifton R. Whitley (I)	30,641	7.8
1972	James O. Eastland (D)	375,102	58.1
	Gil Carmichael (R)	249,779	38.7
1978	Thad Cochran (R)	263,089	45.1
	Maurice Dantin (D)	185,454	31.8
	Charles Evers (I)	133,646	22.9
1984	Thad Cochran (R)	580,314	60.9
	William D. Winter (D)	371,926	39.1
1990	Thad Cochran (R)	274,244	100.0
1996	Thad Cochran (R)	624,154	71.0
	James W. Hunt (D)	240,647	27.4

MISSOURI

	Candidates	Votes	%
	Class 1		
1916	James A. Reed (D)	396,166	50.6
	Dickey (R)	371,710	47.4
1922	James A. Reed (D)	506,267	51.9
	R. R Brewster (R)	462,009	47.3
1928	Roscoe C. Patterson (R)	787,499	51.9
	Charles M. Hay (D)	726,322	47.9
1934	Harry S Truman (D)	787,110	59.5
	Roscoe C. Patterson (R)	524,954	39.7
1940	Harry S Truman (D)	930,775	51.2
	Manvel H. Davis (R)	886,376	48.7
1946	James P. Kem (R)	572,556	52.7
	Frank Briggs (D)	511,544	47.1
1952	Stuart Symington (D)	1,008,523	54.0
	James P. Kem (R)	858,170	45.9
1958	Stuart Symington (D)	780,083	66.5
	Hazel Palmer (R)	393,847	33.6
1964	Stuart Symington (D)	1,186,666	66.6
	Jean Paul Bradshaw (R)	596,377	33.5
1970	Stuart Symington (D)	655,431	51.1
	John C. Danforth (R)	617,903	48.2
1976	John C. Danforth (R)	1,090,067	56.9
	Warren E. Hearnes (D)	813,571	42.5
1982	John C. Danforth (R)	784,876	50.8
	Harriett Woods (D)	758,629	49.1
1988	John C. Danforth (R)	1,407,416	67.7
	Jay Nixon (D)	660,045	31.8
1994	John Ashcroft (R)	1,060,149	59.7
	Alan Wheat (D)	633,697	35.7
2000	Mel Carnahan (D) [1]	1,191,812	50.5
	John Ashcroft (R)	1,142,852	48.4

Class 3

1914	William J. Stone (D)	311,616	50.4
	Thomas J. Akins (R)	257,054	41.6

Special Election

1918	Selden P. Spencer (R)	302,680	52.4
	Joseph Folk (D)	267,397	46.3
1920	Selden P. Spencer (R)	711,161	53.7
	Breckinridge Long (D)	589,498	44.5
1926	Harry B. Hawes (D)	506,015	51.3
	George H. Williams (R)	470,654	47.7

Special Election

1926	Harry B. Hawes (D)	509,439	51.9
	George H. Williams (R)	473,128	48.2
1932	J. Bennett "Champ" Clark (D)	1,017,046	63.2
	Henry W. Kiel (R)	577,184	35.9
1938	J. Bennett "Champ" Clark (D)	757,587	60.7
	Henry S. Caulfield (R)	488,687	39.2
1944	Forrest C. Donnell (R)	779,029	50.0
	Roy McKittrick (D)	777,229	49.9
1950	Thomas C. Hennings Jr. (D)	685,732	53.6
	Forrest C. Donnell (R)	593,139	46.4
1956	Thomas C. Hennings Jr. (D)	1,015,936	56.4
	Herbert Douglas (R)	785,048	43.6

Special Election

1960	Edward V. Long (D)	999,656	53.2
	Lon Hocker (R)	880,576	46.8
1962	Edward V. Long (D)	666,929	54.6
	Crosby Kemper (R)	555,330	45.4
1968	Thomas F. Eagleton (D)	887,414	51.1
	Thomas B. Curtis (R)	850,544	48.9
1974	Thomas F. Eagleton (D)	735,433	60.1
	Thomas B. Curtis (R)	480,900	39.3
1980	Thomas F. Eagleton (D)	1,074,859	52.0
	Gene McNary (R)	985,399	47.7
1986	Christopher S. Bond (R)	777,612	52.6
	Harriett Woods (D)	699,624	47.4
1992	Christopher S. Bond (R)	1,221,901	51.9
	Geri Rothman-Serot (D)	1,057,967	44.9
1998	Christopher S. Bond (R)	830,625	52.7
	Jeremiah W. Nixon (D)	690,208	43.8

Missouri
1. Carnahan died three weeks before the election, but his name remained on the ballot. His widow, Jean Carnahan, was appointed to the seat by the governor.

MONTANA

Candidates	Votes	%

Class 1

1916	Henry L. Myers (D)	85,585	51.1
	Charles N. Pray (R)	72,753	43.4
	Henry Labeau (SOC)	9,292	5.5
1922	Burton K. Wheeler (D)	88,205	55.4
	Carl W. Riddick (R)	69,464	43.6
1928	Burton K. Wheeler (D)	103,655	53.2
	Joseph M. Dixon (R)	91,185	46.8
1934	Burton K. Wheeler (D)	142,823	70.1
	George M. Bourquin (R)	58,519	28.7
1940	Burton K. Wheeler (D)	176,753	73.4
	E. K. Cheadle (R)	63,941	26.6
1946	Zales N. Ecton (R)	101,901	53.5
	Leif Erickson (D)	86,476	45.4
1952	Mike Mansfield (D)	133,109	50.8
	Zales N. Ecton (R)	127,360	48.6
1958	Mike Mansfield (D)	174,910	76.2
	Lou W. Welch (R)	54,573	23.8
1964	Mike Mansfield (D)	180,643	64.5
	Alex Blewett (R)	99,367	35.5
1970	Mike Mansfield (D)	150,060	60.5
	Harold E. Wallace (R)	97,809	39.5
1976	John Melcher (D)	206,232	64.2
	Stanley C. Burger (R)	115,213	35.8
1982	John Melcher (D)	174,861	54.5
	Larry Williams (R)	133,789	41.7
1988	Conrad Burns (R)	189,445	51.9
	John Melcher (D)	175,809	48.1
1994	Conrad Burns (R)	218,542	62.4
	Jack Mudd (D)	131,845	37.6
2000	Conrad Burns (R)	208,082	50.6
	Brian Schweitzer (D)	194,430	47.2

Class 2

1912	Thomas J. Walsh (D)	28,421	41.2
	Joseph M. Dixon (PROG)	22,161	32.1
	Henry C. Smith (R)	18,450	26.7
1918	Thomas J. Walsh (D)	46,160	41.1
	Oscar M. Lanstrum (R)	40,229	35.8
	Jeanette Rankin (N)	26,013	23.1
1924	Thomas J. Walsh (D)	89,681	52.8
	Frank B. Linderman (R)	72,005	42.4
1930	Thomas J. Walsh (D)	106,274	60.3
	Albert J. Galen (R)	66,724	37.9

Special Election

1934	James E. Murray (D)	116,965	59.6
	Scott Leavitt (R)	77,370	39.5
1936	James E. Murray (D)	121,769	55.0
	T. O. Larson (R)	60,038	27.1
	Joseph P. Monaghan (I)	39,655	17.9
1942	James E. Murray (D)	83,673	49.1
	Wellington D. Rankin (R)	82,461	48.4
1948	James E. Murray (D)	125,193	56.7
	Tom J. Davis (R)	94,458	42.7
1954	James E. Murray (D)	114,591	50.4
	Wesley A. D'Ewart (R)	112,863	49.6
1960	Lee Metcalf (D)	140,331	50.7
	Orvin B. Fjare (R)	136,281	49.3
1966	Lee Metcalf (D)	138,166	53.2
	Tim Babcock (R)	121,697	46.8
1972	Lee Metcalf (D)	163,609	52.0
	Henry S. Hibbard (R)	151,316	48.1

1978	Max Baucus (D)	160,353	55.7
	Larry Williams (R)	127,589	44.3
1984	Max Baucus (D)	215,704	56.9
	Chuck Cozzens (R)	154,308	40.7
1990	Max Baucus (D)	217,563	68.1
	Allen C. Kolstad (R)	93,836	29.4
1996	Max Baucus (D)	201,935	49.6
	Dennis Rehberg (R)	182,111	44.7

NEBRASKA

	Candidates	Votes	%
	Class 1		
1916	Gilbert M. Hitchcock (D & PRI)	143,082	50.0
	John L. Kennedy (R & PROG)	131,359	45.9
1922	Robert Beecher Howell (R)	220,350	56.8
	Gilbert M. Hitchcock (D)	148,265	38.2
1928	Robert Beecher Howell (R)	324,014	61.3
	Richard L. Metcalfe (D)	204,737	38.7
1934	Edward R. Burke (D)	305,858	55.3
	Robert G. Simmons (R)	237,126	42.9

Special Election

1934	Richard C. Hunter (D)	281,421	56.5
	J. H Kemp (R)	216,846	43.5

1940	Hugh Butler (R)	340,250	57.0
	R. L Cochran (D)	247,659	41.5
1946	Hugh Butler (R)	271,208	70.8
	John E. Mekota (D)	111,751	29.2
1952	Hugh Butler (R)	408,971	69.1
	Stanley D. Long (D)	164,660	27.8

Special Election

1954	Roman L. Hruska (R)	250,341	60.9
	James F. Green (D)	160,881	39.1

1958	Roman L. Hruska (R)	232,227	55.6
	Frank B. Morrison (D)	185,152	44.4
1964	Roman L. Hruska (R)	345,772	61.4
	Raymond W. Arndt (D)	217,605	38.6
1970	Roman L. Hruska (R)	240,894	52.5
	Frank B. Morrison (D)	217,681	47.4
1976	Edward Zorinsky (D)	313,809	52.4
	John Y. McCollister (R)	284,284	47.5
1982	Edward Zorinsky (D)	363,350	66.6
	Jim Keck (R)	155,760	28.5
1988	Bob Kerrey (D)	378,717	56.7
	David Karnes (R)	278,250	41.7
1994	Bob Kerrey (D)	317,297	54.8
	Jan Stoney (R)	260,668	45.0
2000	Ben Nelson (D)	353,097	51.0
	Don Stenberg (R)	337,967	48.8

	Class 2		
1918	George W. Norris (R)	119,486	54.5
	John H. Morehead (D)	99,696	45.5
1924	George W. Norris (R)	274,640	62.4
	J. J. Thomas (D & PROG)	165,370	37.6
1930	George W. Norris (R)	247,118	56.8
	Gilbert M. Hitchcock (D)	172,795	39.7
1936	George W. Norris (I)	258,700	43.8
	Robert G. Simmons (R)	223,276	37.8
	Terry Carpenter (D)	108,391	18.4
1942	Kenneth S. Wherry (R)	186,207	49.0
	George W. Norris (I)	108,851	28.6
	Foster May (D)	83,763	22.0
1948	Kenneth S. Wherry (R)	267,575	56.7
	Terry Carpenter (D)	204,320	43.3

Special Election

1952	Dwight Griswold (R)	369,841	63.6
	William Ritchie (D)	211,898	36.4
1954	Carl T. Curtis (R)	255,695	61.1
	Keith Neville (D)	162,990	38.9

Special Election

1954	Hazel H. Abel (R)	233,589	57.8
	William H. Meier (D)	170,828	42.2

1960	Carl T. Curtis (R)	352,748	58.9
	Robert B. Conrad (D)	245,837	41.1
1966	Carl T. Curtis (R)	296,116	61.2
	Frank B. Morrison (D)	187,950	38.8
1972	Carl T. Curtis (R)	301,841	53.1
	Terry Carpenter (D)	265,922	46.8
1978	J. James Exon (D)	334,276	67.6
	Donald Shasteen (R)	159,806	32.3
1984	J. James Exon (D)	332,217	51.9
	Nancy Hoch (R)	307,147	48.0
1990	J. James Exon (D)	349,779	58.9
	Hal Daub (R)	243,013	40.9
1996	Chuck Hagel (R)	379,933	56.1
	Ben Nelson (D)	281,904	41.7

NEVADA

	Candidates	Votes	%
	Class 1		
1910	George S. Nixon (R)	9,779	48.0
	Key Pittman (D)	8,624	42.4
	Jud Harris (SOC)	1,959	9.6

Special Election

1912	Key Pittman (D)	7,942	39.8
	W. A. Massey (R)	7,853	39.3
	G. A. Steele (SOC)	2,740	13.7
	S. Summerfield (PROG)	1,428	7.2

1916	Key Pittman (D)	12,765	38.8
	Samuel Platt (R)	10,618	32.3
	A. Grant Miller (SOC)	9,507	28.9
1922	Key Pittman (D)	18,201	62.8
	Charles S. Chandler (R)	10,770	37.2

1928	Key Pittman (D)	19,515	59.3
	Samuel Platt (R)	13,414	40.7
1934	Key Pittman (D)	27,581	64.5
	George W. Malone (R)	14,273	33.4
1940	Key Pittman (D)	31,351	60.5
	Samuel Platt (R)	20,488	39.5

Special Election

1942	J. G. Scrugham (D)	23,805	58.7
	Cecil W. Creel (R)	16,735	41.3
1946	George W. Malone (R)	27,801	55.2
	Berkeley L. Bunker (D)	22,553	44.8
1952	George W. Malone (R)	41,906	51.7
	Thomas B. Mechling (D)	39,184	48.3
1958	Howard W. Cannon (D)	48,732	57.7
	George W. Malone (R)	35,760	42.3
1964	Howard W. Cannon (D)	67,336	50.0
	Paul Laxalt (R)	67,288	50.0
1970	Howard W. Cannon (D)	85,187	57.7
	William J. Raggio (R)	60,838	41.2
1976	Howard W. Cannon (D)	127,295	63.0
	David Towell (R)	63,471	31.4
1982	Chic Hecht (R)	120,377	50.1
	Howard W. Cannon (D)	114,720	47.7
1988	Richard H. Bryan (D)	175,548	50.2
	Chic Hecht (R)	161,336	46.1
1994	Richard H. Bryan (D)	193,804	52.7
	Hal Furman (R)	156,020	42.4
2000	John Ensign (R)	330,687	55.1
	Ed Bernstein (D)	238,260	39.7

Class 3

1908	Francis G. Newlands (D)	12,473	53.4
	P. L. Flanigan (R)	8,972	38.4
	T. C. Lutz (SOC)	1,929	8.3
1914	Francis G. Newlands (D)	8,078	37.5
	Samuel Platt (R)	8,038	37.3
	A. Grant Miller (SOC)	5,451	25.3

Special Election

1918	Charles B. Henderson (D)	12,197	47.7
	E. E. Roberts (R)	8,053	31.5
	Anne Martin (I)	4,603	18.0
1920	Tasker L. Oddie (R)	11,550	42.1
	Charles B. Henderson (D)	10,402	37.9
	Anne Martin (I)	4,981	18.2
1926	Tasker L. Oddie (R)	17,430	55.8
	Ray T. Baker (D)	13,273	42.5
1932	Patrick A. McCarran (D)	21,398	52.1
	Tasker L. Oddie (R)	19,706	47.9
1938	Patrick A. McCarran (D)	27,406	59.0
	Tasker L. Oddie (R)	19,078	41.0
1944	Patrick A. McCarran (D)	30,595	58.4
	George W. Malone (R)	21,816	41.6
1950	Patrick A. McCarran (D)	35,829	58.0
	George E. Marshall (R)	25,933	42.0

Special Election

1954	Alan Bible (D)	45,043	58.1
	Ernest S. Brown (R)	32,470	41.9
1956	Alan Bible (D)	50,677	52.6
	Cliff Young (R)	45,712	47.4
1962	Alan Bible (D)	63,443	65.3
	William B. Wright (R)	33,749	34.7
1968	Alan Bible (D)	83,622	54.8
	Ed Fike (R)	69,068	45.2
1974	Paul Laxalt (R)	79,605	47.0
	Harry Reid (D)	78,981	46.6
1980	Paul Laxalt (R)	144,224	58.5
	Mary Gojack (D)	92,129	37.4
1986	Harry Reid (D)	130,955	50.0
	Jim Santini (R)	116,606	44.5
1992	Harry Reid (D)	253,150	51.0
	Demar Dahl (R)	199,413	40.2
1998	Harry Reid (D)	208,650	47.9
	John Ensign (R)	208,222	47.8

NEW HAMPSHIRE

	Candidates	Votes	%
	Class 2		
1918	Henry W. Keyes (R)	37,787	53.6
	Eugene E. Reed (D)	32,763	46.4
1924	Henry W. Keyes (R)	94,432	59.8
	George E. Farrand (D)	63,596	40.2
1930	Henry W. Keyes (R)	72,225	57.9
	Albert W. Noone (D)	52,284	41.9
1936	Styles Bridges (R)	107,923	51.9
	William N. Rogers (D)	99,195	47.7
1942	Styles Bridges (R)	88,601	54.6
	Francis P. Murphy (D)	73,656	45.4
1948	Styles Bridges (R)	129,600	58.1
	Alfred E. Fortin (D)	91,760	41.2
1954	Styles Bridges (R)	117,150	60.2
	Gerard L. Morin (D)	77,386	39.8
1960	Styles Bridges (R)	173,521	60.4
	Herbert W. Hill (D)	114,024	39.7

Special Election

1962	Thomas J. McIntyre (D)	117,612	52.3
	Perkins Bass (R)	107,199	47.7
1966	Thomas J. McIntyre (D)	123,888	54.0
	Harrison R. Thyng (R)	105,241	45.9
1972	Thomas J. McIntyre (D)	184,495	56.9
	Wesley Powell (R)	139,852	43.1
1978	Gordon J. Humphrey (R)	133,745	50.7
	Thomas J. McIntyre (D)	127,945	48.5
1984	Gordon J. Humphrey (R)	225,828	58.7
	Norman E. D'Amours (D)	157,447	41.0
1990	Robert C. Smith (R)	189,792	65.1
	John A. Durkin (D)	91,299	31.3
1996	Robert C. Smith (R)	242,304	49.2
	Dick Swett (D)	227,397	46.2

Class 3

1914	Jacob H. Gallinger (R)	42,113	51.7
	Raymond B. Stevens (D)	36,382	44.6

Special Election

1918	George H. Moses (R)	35,528	50.8
	John B. Jameson (D)	34,459	49.2

1920	George H. Moses (R)	90,173	57.7
	Raymond B. Stevens (D)	65,035	41.6
1926	George H. Moses (R)	79,279	62.3
	Robert C. Murchie (D)	47,935	37.7
1932	Fred H. Brown (D)	98,766	50.4
	George H. Moses (R)	96,649	49.3
1938	Charles W. Tobey (R)	100,633	54.2
	Fred H. Brown (D)	84,920	45.8
1944	Charles W. Tobey (R)	110,549	50.9
	Joseph J. Betley (D)	106,508	49.1
1950	Charles W. Tobey (R)	106,142	55.7
	Emmet J. Kelley (D)	72,473	38.0
	Wesley Powell (I)	11,958	6.3

Special Election

1954	Norris Cotton (R)	114,068	60.2
	Stanley J. Betley (D)	75,490	39.8

1956	Norris Cotton (R)	161,424	64.1
	Laurence M. Pickett (D)	90,519	35.9
1962	Norris Cotton (R)	134,035	59.7
	Alfred Catalfo Jr. (D)	90,444	40.3
1968	Norris Cotton (R)	170,163	59.3
	John W. King (D)	116,816	40.7
1974[1]	Louis C. Wyman (R)	110,926*	49.7
	John A. Durkin (D)	110,924	49.7

Special Election[1]

1975	John A. Durkin (D)	140,778	53.6
	Louis C. Wyman (R)	113,007	43.1
	Carmen C. Chimento (AM)	8,787	3.3

1980	Warren B. Rudman (R)	195,563	52.1
	John A. Durkin (D)	179,455	47.8
1986	Warren B. Rudman (R)	154,090	62.9
	Endicott Peabody (D)	79,222	32.4
1992	Judd Gregg (R)	249,591	48.1
	John Rauh (D)	234,982	45.3
1998	Judd Gregg (R)	213,477	67.8
	George Condodemetraky (D)	88,883	28.2

New Hampshire

1. Wyman's two-vote margin was challenged by Durkin. The Senate refused to seat either candidate. After seven months of fruitless efforts to decide a winner, the Senate voted July 30, 1975, to declare the seat vacant effective Aug. 8, 1975. In a special election Sept. 16, 1975, Durkin defeated Wyman.

NEW JERSEY

	Candidates	Votes	%

Class 1

1916	Joseph S. Frelinghuysen (R)	244,715	56.0
	James Martine (D)	170,019	38.9

1922	Edward I. Edwards (D)	451,832	54.9
	Joseph S. Frelinghuysen (R)	362,699	44.1
1928	Hamilton F. Kean (R)	841,752	57.9
	Edward I. Edwards (D)	608,623	41.8
1934	A. Harry Moore (D)	785,971	57.9
	Hamilton F. Kean (R)	554,483	40.9

Special Election

1938	W. Warren Barbour (R)	816,667	53.0
	William H. J Ely (D)	704,159	45.7

1940	W. Warren Barbour (R)	1,029,331	55.1
	James H. R Cromwell (D)	823,893	44.1

Special Election

1944	H. Alexander Smith (R)	939,987	50.4
	Elmer H. Wene (D)	910,096	48.8

1946	H. Alexander Smith (R)	799,808	58.5
	George E. Brunner (D)	548,458	40.1
1952	H. Alexander Smith (R)	1,286,782	55.5
	Archibald S. Alexander (D)	1,011,187	43.6
1958	Harrison A. Williams Jr. (D)	966,832	51.4
	Robert Winthrop Kean (R)	882,287	46.9
1964	Harrison A. Williams Jr. (D)	1,677,515	61.9
	Bernard M. Shanley (R)	1,011,280	37.3
1970	Harrison A. Williams Jr. (D)	1,157,074	54.0
	Nelson G. Gross (R)	903,026	42.2
1976	Harrison A. Williams Jr. (D)	1,681,140	60.7
	David F. Norcross (R)	1,054,508	38.0
1982	Frank R. Lautenberg (D)	1,117,549	50.9
	Millicent Fenwick (R)	1,047,626	47.8
1988	Frank R. Lautenberg (D)	1,599,905	53.5
	Pete Dawkins (R)	1,349,937	45.2
1994	Frank R. Lautenberg (D)	1,033,487	50.3
	Garabed "Chuck" Haytaian (R)	966,244	47.0
2000	Jon Corzine (D)	1,511,237	50.1
	Bob Franks (R)	1,420,267	47.1

Class 2

1918	Walter E. Edge (R)	179,022	50.3
	George M. Lamonte (D)	153,743	43.2

Special Election

1918	David Baird (R)	170,414	49.2
	Charles O'Connor Hennessy (D)	154,734	44.6

1924	Walter E. Edge (R)	608,020	61.8
	Frederick W. Donnelly (D)	331,034	33.7
1930	Dwight W. Morrow (R)	601,497	58.5
	Alexander Simpson (D)	401,007	39.0

Special Elections

1930	Dwight W. Morrow (R)	571,006	59.1
	Thelma Parkinson (D)	372,739	38.6

1932	W. Warren Barbour (R)	741,734	49.6
	Percy H. Stewart (D)	725,511	48.5
1936	William H. Smathers (D)	916,414	54.9
	W. Warren Barbour (R)	740,088	44.3

1942	Albert W. Hawkes (R)	648,855	53.1
	William H. Smathers (D)	559,851	45.8
1948	Robert C. Hendrickson (R)	934,720	50.0
	Archibald S. Alexander (D)	884,414	47.3
1954	Clifford P. Case (R)	861,528	48.7
	Charles R. Howell (D)	858,158	48.5
1960	Clifford P. Case (R)	1,483,832	55.7
	Thorn Lord (D)	1,151,385	43.2
1966	Clifford P. Case (R)	1,278,843	60.0
	Warren W. Wilentz (D)	788,021	37.0
1972	Clifford P. Case (R)	1,743,854	62.5
	Paul J. Krebs (D)	963,573	34.5
1978	Bill Bradley (D)	1,082,960	55.3
	Jeffrey Bell (R)	844,200	43.1
1984	Bill Bradley (D)	1,986,644	64.2
	Mary V. Mochary (R)	1,080,100	35.2
1990	Bill Bradley (D)	977,810	50.4
	Christine Todd Whitman (R)	918,874	47.4
1996	Robert G. Torricelli (D)	1,519,328	52.7
	Dick Zimmer (R)	1,227,817	42.6

NEW MEXICO

Candidates	Votes	%
Class 1		

1916	Andrieus A. Jones (D)	34,142	51.1
	Frank A. Hubbell (R)	30,622	45.8
1922	Andrieus A. Jones (D)	60,969	55.2
	S. B Davis Jr. (R)	48,721	44.1
1928	Bronson M. Cutting (R)	68,070	57.7
	Jethro S. Vaught (D)	49,913	42.3

Special Election

| 1928 | Octaviano A. Larrazolo (R) | 64,623 | 55.7 |
| | Juan N. Vigil (D) | 51,495 | 44.4 |

| 1934 | Bronson M. Cutting (R) | 76,228 | 50.2 |
| | Dennis Chavez (D) | 74,944 | 49.4 |

Special Election

| 1936 | Dennis Chavez (D) | 94,585 | 55.7 |
| | M. A Otero Jr. (R) | 75,030 | 44.2 |

1940	Dennis Chavez (D)	103,194	56.0
	Albert K. Mitchell (R)	81,257	44.1
1946	Dennis Chavez (D)	68,650	51.5
	Patrick J. Hurley (R)	64,632	48.5
1952	Dennis Chavez (D)	122,543	51.1
	Patrick J. Hurley (R)	117,168	48.9
1958	Dennis Chavez (D)	127,496	62.7
	Forrest S. Atchley (R)	75,827	37.3
1964	Joseph M. Montoya (D)	178,209	54.7
	Edwin L. Mechem (R)	147,562	45.3
1970	Joseph M. Montoya (D)	151,486	52.3
	Anderson Carter (R)	135,004	46.6
1976	Harrison "Jack" Schmitt (R)	234,681	56.8
	Joseph M. Montoya (D)	176,382	42.7
1982	Jeff Bingaman (D)	217,682	53.8
	Harrison "Jack" Schmitt (R)	187,128	46.2

1988	Jeff Bingaman (D)	321,983	63.3
	Bill Valentine (R)	186,579	36.7
1994	Jeff Bingaman (D)	249,989	54.0
	Colin R. McMillan (R)	213,025	46.0
2000	Jeff Bingaman (D)	363,744	61.7
	Bill Redmond (R)	225,517	38.3

Class 2

| 1918 | Albert B. Fall (R) | 24,322 | 51.4 |
| | W. B Walton (D) | 22,470 | 47.5 |

Special Election

| 1921 | Holm O. Bursum (R) | 36,868 | 51.4 |
| | R. H Hanna (D) | 31,353 | 43.7 |

1924	Sam G. Bratton (D)	57,355	49.9
	Holm O. Bursum (R)	54,558	47.4
1930	Sam G. Bratton (D)	69,356	58.6
	Herbert B. Holt (R)	48,699	41.2

Special Election

| 1934 | Carl A. Hatch (D) | 81,934 | 54.5 |
| | Richard C. Dillon (R) | 67,577 | 45.0 |

1936	Carl A. Hatch (D)	104,550	61.7
	Ernest W. Everly (R)	64,817	38.3
1942	Carl A. Hatch (D)	63,301	59.2
	J. Benson Newell (R)	43,704	40.8
1948	Clinton P. Anderson (D)	108,269	57.2
	Patrick J. Hurley (R)	80,226	42.4
1954	Clinton P. Anderson (D)	111,351	57.3
	Edwin L. Mechem (R)	83,071	42.7
1960	Clinton P. Anderson (D)	190,654	63.4
	William Colwes (R)	109,897	36.6
1966	Clinton P. Anderson (D)	137,205	53.1
	Anderson Carter (R)	120,988	46.9
1972	Pete V. Domenici (R)	204,253	54.0
	Jack Daniels (D)	173,815	46.0
1978	Pete V. Domenici (R)	183,442	53.4
	Toney Anaya (D)	160,045	46.6
1984	Pete V. Domenici (R)	361,371	71.9
	Judith A. Pratt (D)	141,253	28.1
1990	Pete V. Domenici (R)	296,712	72.9
	Tom R. Benavides (D)	110,033	27.1
1996	Pete V. Domenici (R)	357,171	64.7
	Art Trujillo (D)	164,356	29.8

NEW YORK

Candidates	Votes	%
Class 1		

1916	William M. Calder (R)	839,314	54.3
	William F. McCombs (D & AM)	605,933	39.2
1922	Royal S. Copeland (D)	1,276,667	52.6
	William M. Calder (R)	995,421	41.0
1928	Royal S. Copeland (D)	2,084,273	49.1
	Alanson B. Houghton (R)	2,034,014	47.9
1934	Royal S. Copeland (D)	2,046,377	55.3
	E. Harold Cluett (R)	1,363,440	36.9
	Norman Thomas (SOC)	194,952	5.3

Special Election

1938	James M. Mead (D, AM LAB)	2,438,904	53.6
	Edward F. Corsi (R, I PROG)	2,083,666	45.8
1940	James M. Mead (D, AM LAB)	3,274,766	53.3
	Bruce Barton (R)	2,868,852	46.7
1946	Irving M. Ives (R)	2,559,365	52.6
	Herbert H. Lehman (D, AM LAB)	2,308,112	47.4
1952	Irving M. Ives (R)	3,853,934	55.2
	John Cashmore (D)	2,521,736	36.1
	George S. Counts (L)	489,775	7.0
1958	Kenneth B. Keating (R)	2,842,942	50.8
	Frank S. Hogan (D, L)	2,709,950	48.4
1964	Robert F. Kennedy (D, L)	3,823,749	53.5
	Kenneth B. Keating (R)	3,104,056	43.4
1970	James L. Buckley (C, I ALNC)	2,288,190	38.8
	Richard L. Ottinger (D)	2,171,232	36.8
	Charles E. Goodell (R, L)	1,434,472	24.3
1976	Daniel Patrick Moynihan (D, L)	3,422,594	54.2
	James L. Buckley (R, C)	2,836,633	44.9
1982	Daniel Patrick Moynihan (D, L)	3,232,146	65.1
	Florence M. Sullivan (R, C)	1,696,766	34.2
1988	Daniel Patrick Moynihan (D, L)	4,048,649	67.0
	Robert R. McMillan (R, C)	1,875,784	31.1
1994	Daniel Patrick Moynihan (D,L)	2,646,541	55.2
	Bernadette Castro (R,C,TCN)	1,988,308	41.5
2000	Hillary Rodham Clinton (D,L)	3,747,310	55.3
	Rick A. Lazio (R,C,TCN)	2,915,730	43.0

Class 3

1914	James W. Wadsworth Jr. (R)	639,112	47.0
	James W. Gerard (D, I LEAGUE)	571,419	42.1
1920	James W. Wadsworth Jr. (R)	1,434,393	52.4
	Harry C. Walker (D)	901,310	32.9
	Jacob Panken (SOC)	208,155	7.6
	Ella A. Boole (P)	159,623	5.8
1926	Robert F. Wagner (D)	1,321,463	46.5
	James W. Wadsworth Jr. (R)	1,205,246	42.4
	F. W Cristman (IR)	231,906	8.2
1932	Robert F. Wagner (D)	2,532,905	55.8
	George Z. Medalie (R)	1,751,186	38.6
1938	Robert F. Wagner (D, AM LAB)	2,497,029	54.5
	John Lord O'Brian (R, I PROG)	2,058,615	45.0
1944	Robert F. Wagner (D, AM LAB)	3,294,576	53.1
	Thomas J. Curran (R)	2,899,497	46.7

Special Election

1949	Herbert H. Lehman (D, L)	2,582,438	52.0
	John Foster Dulles (R)	2,384,381	48.0

1950	Herbert H. Lehman (D, L)	2,632,313	50.3
	Joe R. Hanley (R)	2,367,353	45.3
1956	Jacob K. Javits (R)	3,723,933	53.3
	Robert F. Wagner Jr. (D, L)	3,265,159	46.7
1962	Jacob K. Javits (R)	3,272,417	57.4
	James B. Donovan (D, L)	2,289,323	40.1
1968	Jacob K. Javits (R, L)	3,269,772	49.7
	Paul O'Dwyer (D)	2,150,695	32.7
	James L. Buckley (C)	1,139,402	17.3
1974	Jacob K. Javits (R, L)	2,340,188	45.3
	Ramsey Clark (D)	1,973,781	38.2
	Barbara A. Keating (C)	822,584	15.9
1980	Alfonse M. D'Amato (R, C)	2,699,652	44.9
	Elizabeth Holtzman (D)	2,618,661	43.5
	Jacob K. Javits (L)	664,544	11.0
1986	Alfonse M. D'Amato (R, C)	2,378,197	56.9
	Mark Green (D)	1,723,216	41.2
1992	Alfonse M. D'Amato (R, C)	3,166,994	49.0
	Robert Abrams (D, L)	3,086,200	47.8
1998	Charles E. Schumer (D)	2,551,065	54.6
	Alfonse M. D'Amato (R)	2,058,988	44.1

NORTH CAROLINA

Candidates	Votes	%

Class 2

1918	Furnifold M. Simmons (D)	143,519	60.5
	John M. Morehead (R)	93,707	39.5
1924	Furnifold M. Simmons (D)	295,344	61.6
	A. A Whitener (R)	184,493	38.5
1930	Josiah W. Bailey (D)	324,293	60.6
	George M. Pritchard (R)	210,761	39.4
1936	Josiah W. Bailey (D)	564,088	70.8
	Frank R. Patton (R)	233,000	29.2
1942	Josiah W. Bailey (D)	230,427	65.9
	Sam J. Morris (R)	119,165	34.1
1948	J. Melville Broughton (D)	540,762	70.7
	John A. Wilkinson (R)	220,307	28.8

Special Election

1948	J. Melville Broughton (D)	534,917#	100.0

Special Election

1950	Willis Smith (D)	364,912	67.0
	E. L Gavin (R)	177,753	32.6

Special Election

1954	W. Kerr Scott (D)	408,312	65.9
	Paul C. West (R)	211,322	34.1

Special Election

1954	W. Kerr Scott (D)	402,268	100.0

Special Election

1958	B. Everett Jordan (D)	431,492	70.0
	Richard C. Clarke Jr. (R)	184,977	30.0
1960	B. Everett Jordan (D)	793,521	61.4
	Kyle Hayes (R)	497,964	38.6

1966	B. Everett Jordan (D)	501,440	55.6
	John S. Shallcross (R)	400,502	44.4
1972	Jesse Helms (R)	795,248	54.0
	Nick Galifianakis (D)	677,293	46.0
1978	Jesse Helms (R)	619,151	54.5
	John Ingram (D)	516,663	45.5
1984	Jesse Helms (R)	1,156,768	51.7
	James B. Hunt, Jr. (D)	1,070,488	47.8
1990	Jesse Helms (R)	1,087,331	52.5
	Harvey B. Gantt (D)	981,573	47.4
1996	Jesse Helms (R)	1,345,833	52.6
	Harvey B. Gantt (D)	1,173,875	45.9

Class 3

1914	Lee S. Overman (D)	121,342	58.1
	A. A Whitener (R)	87,101	41.7
1920	Lee S. Overman (D)	310,504	57.5
	A. E Holton (R)	229,343	42.5
1926	Lee S. Overman (D)	218,934	60.5
	Johnson J. Hayes (R)	142,891	39.5
1932	Robert R. Reynolds (D)	476,048	68.3
	Jake F. Newell (R)	221,392	31.7
1938	Robert R. Reynolds (D)	316,685	63.8
	Charles A. Jonas (R)	179,461	36.2
1944	Clyde R. Hoey (D)	533,813	70.3
	A. I Ferree (R)	226,037	29.8
1950	Clyde R. Hoey (D)	376,473	68.7
	Halsey B. Leavitt (R)	171,804	31.3

Special Election

1954	Sam J. Ervin Jr. (D)	410,574	100.0
1956	Sam J. Ervin Jr. (D)	731,353	66.6
	Joel A. Johnson (R)	367,475	33.4
1962	Sam J. Ervin Jr. (D)	491,520	60.5
	Claude L. Greene Jr. (R)	321,635	39.6
1968	Sam J. Ervin Jr. (D)	870,406	60.6
	Robert Vance Somers (R)	566,934	39.4
1974	Robert B. Morgan (D)	633,775	62.1
	William E. Stevens (R)	377,618	37.0
1980	John P. East (R)	898,064	50.0
	Robert Morgan (D)	887,653	49.4
1986	Terry Sanford (D)	823,662	51.8
	James T. Broyhill (R)	767,668	48.2
1992	Lauch Faircloth (R)	1,297,892	50.3
	Terry Sanford (D)	1,194,015	46.3
1998	John Edwards (D)	1,029,237	51.2
	Lauch Faircloth (R)	945,943	47.0

NORTH DAKOTA

	Candidates	Votes	%
	Class 1		
1916	Porter J. McCumber (R)	57,714	53.9
	John Burke (D)	40,988	38.2
	E. R Fry (SOC)	8,472	7.9
1922	Lynn J. Frazier (R & NP)	101,312	52.3
	J. F T. O'Connor (D & I)	92,464	47.7

1928	Lynn J. Frazier (R)	159,940	79.6
	F. F Burchard (D)	38,856	19.4
1934	Lynn J. Frazier (R)	151,205	58.2
	Henry Holt (D)	104,477	40.2
1940	William Langer (R)	100,647	38.1
	William Lemke (I)	92,593	35.1
	Charles V. Vogel (D)	69,847	26.5
1946	William Langer (R)	88,210	53.3
	Arthur E. Thompson (I)	38,804	23.5
	Abner B. Larson (D)	38,368	23.2
1952	William Langer (R)	157,907	66.4
	Harold A. Morrison (D)	55,347	23.3
	Fred G. Aandahl (I)	24,741	10.4
1958	William Langer (R)	117,070	57.2
	Raymond Vendsel (D)	84,892	41.5

Special Election

1960	Quentin N. Burdick (D)	104,593	49.7
	John E. Davis (R)	103,475	49.2
1964	Quentin N. Burdick (D)	149,264	57.6
	Thomas S. Kleppe (R)	109,681	42.4
1970	Quentin N. Burdick (D)	134,519	61.3
	Thomas S. Kleppe (R)	82,996	37.8
1976	Quentin N. Burdick (D)	175,772	62.1
	Richard Stroup (R)	103,466	36.6
1982	Quentin N. Burdick (D)	164,873	62.8
	Gene Knorr (R)	89,304	34.0
1988	Quentin N. Burdick (D)	171,899	59.4
	Earl Strinden (R)	112,937	39.1

Special Election

1992	Kent Conrad (D)	102,887	63.3
	Jack Dalrymple (R)	54,726	33.7
1994	Kent Conrad (D)	137,157	58.0
	Ben Clayburgh (R)	99,390	42.0
2000	Kent Conrad (D)	176,470	61.4
	Duane Sand (R)	111,069	38.6

Class 3

1914	Asle J. Gronna (R)	48,732	55.8
	W. E Purcell (D)	29,640	34.0
	W. H Brown (SOC)	6,231	7.1
1920	Edwin F. Ladd (R & NP)	130,614	59.8
	H. H Perry (D & I)	87,765	40.2
1926	Gerald P. Nye (R)	107,921	69.6
	Norris H. Nelson (I)	18,951	12.2
	F. F Burchard (D)	13,519	8.7
	C. P Stone (R)	9,738	6.3

Special Election

1926	Gerald P. Nye (R)	79,709	50.2
	L. B Hanna	59,499	37.5
	C. P Stone	19,586	12.3
1932	Gerald P. Nye (R)	172,796	72.3
	P. W Lanier (D)	65,575	27.5
1938	Gerald P. Nye (R)	131,907	50.1
	William Langer (I)	112,007	42.6
	J. J Nygaard (D)	19,244	7.3

1944	John Moses (D)	95,102	45.2
	Gerald P. Nye (R)	69,530	33.0
	Lynn U. Stambaugh (IR)	44,596	21.2

Special Election

1946	Milton R. Young (R)	75,998	55.5
	William Lanier (D)	37,507	27.4
	Gerald P. Nye (I)	20,848	15.2

1950	Milton R. Young (R)	126,209	67.6
	Harry O'Brien (D)	60,507	32.4
1956	Milton R. Young (R)	155,305	63.6
	Quentin N. Burdick (D)	87,919	36.0
1962	Milton R. Young (R)	135,705	60.7
	William Lanier (D)	88,032	39.4
1968	Milton R. Young (R)	154,968	64.6
	Herschel Lashkowitz (D)	80,815	33.7
1974	Milton R. Young (R)	114,117	48.4
	William L. Guy (D)	113,931	48.3
1980	Mark Andrews (R)	210,347	70.3
	Kent Johanneson (D)	86,658	29.0
1986	Kent Conrad (D)	143,932	49.8
	Mark Andrews (R)	141,797	49.1
1992	Byron L. Dorgan (D)	179,347	59.0
	Steve Sydness (R)	118,162	38.9
1998	Byron L. Dorgan (D)	134,747	63.2
	Donna Nalewaja (R)	75,013	35.2

OHIO

Candidates	Votes	%
Class 1		

1916	Atlee Pomerene (D)	571,488	49.3
	Myron T. Herrick (R)	535,391	46.2
1922	Simeon D. Fess (R)	794,149	50.9
	Atlee Pomerene (D)	744,558	47.7
1928	Simeon D. Fess (R)	1,412,805	60.7
	Charles V. Truax (D)	908,952	39.1
1934	Vic Donahey (D)	1,276,206	60.0
	Simeon D. Fess (R)	839,068	39.4
1940	Harold H. Burton (R)	1,602,567	52.4
	John McSweeney (D)	1,457,359	47.6
1946	John W. Bricker (R)	1,275,774	57.0
	James W. Huffman (D)	947,610	42.4

Special Election

1946	Kingsley A. Taft (R)	1,193,942	56.2
	Henry P. Webber (D)	929,584	43.8

1952	John W. Bricker (R)	1,878,961	54.6
	Michael V. DiSalle (D)	1,563,330	45.4
1958	Stephen M. Young (D)	1,652,211	52.5
	John W. Bricker (R)	1,497,199	47.5
1964	Stephen M. Young (D)	1,923,608	50.2
	Robert Taft Jr. (R)	1,906,781	49.8
1970	Robert Taft Jr. (R)	1,565,682	49.7
	Howard M. Metzenbaum (D)	1,495,262	47.5

1976	Howard M. Metzenbaum (D)	1,941,113	49.5
	Robert A. Taft Jr. (R)	1,823,774	46.5
1982	Howard M. Metzenbaum (D)	1,923,767	56.7
	Paul E. Pfeifer (R)	1,396,790	41.1
1988	Howard M. Metzenbaum (D)	2,480,038	57.0
	George V. Voinovich (R)	1,872,716	43.0
1994	Mike DeWine (R)	1,836,556	53.4
	Joel Hyatt (D)	1,348,213	39.2
	Joseph J. Slovenec (I)	252,031	7.3
2000	Mike DeWine (R)	2,665,512	59.9
	Ted Celeste (D)	1,595,066	35.9

Class 3

1914	Warren G. Harding (R)	526,115	49.2
	Timothy S. Hogan (D)	423,742	39.6
	Arthur L. Garford (PROG)	67,509	6.3
1920	Frank B. Willis (R)	1,134,953	59.1
	W. A Julian (D)	782,650	40.8
1926	Frank B. Willis (R)	711,359	53.2
	Atlee Pomerene (D)	623,221	46.6

Special Election

1928	Theodore E. Burton (R)	1,429,534	62.4
	Graham P. Hunt (D)	856,807	37.4

Special Election

1930	Robert J. Bulkley (D)	1,046,561#	54.8
	Roscoe C. McCulloch (R)	863,944#	45.2
1932	Robert J. Bulkley (D)	1,290,175	52.5
	Gilbert Bettman (R)	1,126,830	45.8
1938	Robert A. Taft (R)	1,257,412	53.6
	Robert J. Bulkley (D)	1,086,815	46.4
1944	Robert A. Taft (R)	1,500,809	50.3
	William G. Pickrel (D)	1,483,069	49.7
1950	Robert A. Taft (R)	1,645,643	57.5
	Joseph T. Ferguson (D)	1,214,459	42.5

Special Election

1954	George H. Bender (R)	1,257,874	50.1
	Thomas A. Burke (D)	1,254,899	49.9
1956	Frank J. Lausche (D)	1,864,589	52.9
	George H. Bender (R)	1,660,910	47.1
1962	Frank J. Lausche (D)	1,843,813	61.6
	John Marshall Briley (R)	1,151,292	38.4
1968	William B. Saxbe (R)	1,928,964	51.5
	John J. Gilligan (D)	1,814,152	48.5
1974	John Glenn (D)	1,930,670	64.6
	Ralph J. Perk (R)	918,133	30.7
1980	John Glenn (D)	2,770,786	68.8
	James E. Betts (R)	1,137,695	28.2
1986	John Glenn (D)	1,949,208	62.5
	Thomas N. Kindness (R)	1,171,893	37.5
1992	John Glenn (D)	2,444,419	51.0
	Mike DeWine (R)	2,028,300	42.3
	Martha K. Grevatt (I)	321,234	6.7

| 1998 | George V. Voinovich (R) | 1,922,087 | 56.5 |
| | Mary O. Boyle (D) | 1,482,054 | 43.5 |

OKLAHOMA

	Candidates	Votes	%
	Class 2		
1912	Robert L. Owen (D)	126,407	50.4
	Dickerson (R)	83,448	33.3
1918	Robert L. Owen (D)	105,050	55.4
	Johnson (R)	77,188	40.7
1924	William B. Pine (R)	341,720	61.6
	John Calloway Walton (D)	196,527	35.4
1930	Thomas P. Gore (D)	255,838	52.3
	William B. Pine (R)	232,589	47.5
1936	Josh Lee (D)	493,407	68.0
	Herbert K. Hyde (R)	229,004	31.6
1942	Edward H. Moore (R)	204,163	54.8
	Josh Lee (D)	166,653	44.8
1948	Robert S. Kerr (D)	441,654	62.3
	Ross Rizley (R)	265,169	37.4
1954	Robert S. Kerr (D)	335,127	55.8
	Fred M. Mock (R)	262,013	43.7
1960	Robert S. Kerr (D)	474,116	54.8
	B. Hayden Crawford (R)	385,646	44.6

Special Election

| 1964 | Fred R. Harris (D) | 466,782 | 51.2 |
| | Bud Wilkinson (R) | 445,392 | 48.8 |

1966	Fred R. Harris (D)	343,157	53.7
	Pat J. Patterson (R)	295,585	46.3
1972	Dewey F. Bartlett (R)	516,934	51.4
	Ed Edmondson (D)	478,212	47.6
1978	David L. Boren (D)	493,953	65.5
	Robert B. Kamm (R)	247,857	32.9
1984	David L. Boren (D)	906,131	75.6
	Will E. Crozier (R)	280,638	23.4
1990	David L. Boren (D)	735,684	83.2
	Stephen Jones (R)	148,814	16.8

Special Election

| 1994 | James M. Inhofe (R) | 542,390 | 55.2 |
| | Dave McCurdy (D) | 392,488 | 40.0 |

1996	James M. Inhofe (R)	670,610	56.7
	Jim Boren (D)	474,162	40.1
	Class 3		
1914	Thomas P. Gore (D)	119,443	48.0
	Burford (R)	73,292	29.4
	P. S Nagle (SOC)	52,259	21.0
1920	John W. Harreld (R)	247,721	50.6
	Scott Ferris (D)	218,371	44.6
1926	Elmer Thomas (D)	195,307	54.8
	John W. Harreld (R)	159,287	44.7
1932	Elmer Thomas (D)	426,130	65.6
	Wirt Franklin (R)	218,854	33.7
1938	Elmer Thomas (D)	307,936	65.4
	Harry G. Glasser (R)	159,734	33.9

1944	Elmer Thomas (D)	390,851	55.7
	William J. Otjen (R)	309,222	44.0
1950	A. S Mike Monroney (D)	345,953	54.8
	W. H "Bill" Alexander (R)	285,224	45.2
1956	A. S Mike Monroney (D)	459,996	55.4
	Douglas McKeever (R)	371,146	44.7
1962	A. S Mike Monroney (D)	353,890	53.2
	B. Hayden Crawford (R)	307,966	46.3
1968	Henry Bellmon (R)	470,120	51.7
	A. S Mike Monroney (D)	419,658	46.2
1974	Henry Bellmon (R)	390,997	49.4
	Ed Edmondson (D)	387,162	48.9
1980	Don Nickles (R)	587,252	53.5
	Andrew Coats (D)	478,283	43.5
1986	Don Nickles (R)	493,436	55.2
	James R. Jones (D)	400,230	44.8
1992	Don Nickles (R)	757,876	58.5
	Steve Lewis (D)	494,350	38.2
1998	Don Nickles (R)	570,682	66.4
	Don E. Carroll (D)	268,898	31.3

OREGON

	Candidates	Votes	%
	Class 2		
1912	Harry Lane (D)	40,172	30.1
	Ben Selling (R)	38,453	28.8
	Jonathan Bourne Jr. (POPU GOV)	25,929	19.4
	B. F Ramp (SOC)	11,093	8.3
	A. E Clark (PROG)	11,083	8.3
	B. Lee Paget (P)	6,848	5.1
1918	Charles L. McNary (R)	82,360	54.2
	Oswald West (D)	64,303	42.3

Special Election

| 1918 | Fred W. Mulkey (R) | 103,913 | 84.5 |
| | Martha E. Bean (SOC) | 19,014 | 15.5 |

1924	Charles L. McNary (R)	174,672	66.0
	Milton A. Miller (D)	65,340	24.7
	F. E Coulter (PROG)	20,379	7.7
1930	Charles L. McNary (R)	137,231	58.1
	Elton Watkins (D)	66,028	27.9
	L. A Banks (I)	17,488	7.4
1936	Charles L. McNary (R)	199,332	49.7
	Willis Mahoney (D)	193,822	48.3
1942	Charles L. McNary (R)	214,755	77.1
	Walter W. Whitbeck (D)	63,946	22.9

Special Election

| 1944 | Guy Cordon (R) | 260,631 | 57.5 |
| | Willis Mahoney (D) | 192,305 | 42.5 |

1948	Guy Cordon (R)	299,295	60.0
	Manley J. Wilson (D)	199,275	40.0
1954	Richard L. Neuberger (D)	285,775	50.2
	Guy Cordon (R)	283,313	49.8

1960	Maurine B. Neuberger (D)	412,757	54.6
	Elmo Smith (R)	343,009	45.4

Special Election

1960	Maurine B. Neuberger (D)	422,024	55.0
	Elmo Smith (R)	345,464	45.0

1966	Mark O. Hatfield (R)	354,391	51.7
	Robert B. Duncan (D)	330,374	48.2
1972	Mark O. Hatfield (R)	494,671	53.7
	Wayne Morse (D)	425,036	46.2
1978	Mark O. Hatfield (R)	550,165	61.6
	Vernon Cook (D)	341,616	38.3
1984	Mark O. Hatfield (R)	808,152	66.5
	Margie Hendricksen (D)	406,122	33.4
1990	Mark O. Hatfield (R)	590,095	53.7
	Harry Lonsdale (D)	507,743	46.2
1996	Gordon H. Smith (R)	677,336	49.8
	Tom Bruggere (D)	624,370	45.9

Class 3

1908	George E. Chamberlain (D)	52,421	46.7
	H. M Cake (R)	50,899	45.3
1914	George E. Chamberlain (D)	111,748	45.5
	R. A Booth (R)	88,297	36.0
	William Hanley (PROG)	26,220	10.7
1920	Robert N. Stanfield (R)	116,696	50.7
	George E. Chamberlain (D)	100,124	43.5
1926	Frederick Steiwer (R)	89,007	39.8
	Bert E. Haney (D)	81,301	36.3
	Robert N. Stanfield (I)	50,246	22.5
1932	Frederick Steiwer (R)	186,210	52.7
	Walter B. Gleason (D)	137,237	38.9
1938	Rufus C. Holman (R)	203,120	54.9
	Willis Mahoney (D)	167,135	45.1

Special Election

1938	Alexander G. Barry (R)	180,815	54.2
	Robert A. Miller (D)	152,773	45.8

1944	Wayne Morse (R)	269,095	60.7
	Edgar W. Smith (D)	174,140	39.3
1950	Wayne Morse (R)	376,510	74.8
	Howard Latourette (D)	116,780	23.2
1956	Wayne Morse (D)	396,849	54.2
	Douglas McKay (R)	335,405	45.8
1962	Wayne Morse (D)	344,716	54.2
	Sig Unander (R)	291,587	45.8
1968	Bob Packwood (R)	408,825	50.2
	Wayne Morse (D)	405,380	49.8
1974	Bob Packwood (R)	420,984	54.9
	Betty Roberts (D)	338,591	44.2
1980	Bob Packwood (R)	594,290	52.1
	Ted Kulongoski (D)	501,963	44.0
1986	Bob Packwood (R)	656,317	63.0
	Rick Bauman (D)	375,735	36.0
1992	Bob Packwood (R)	717,455	52.1
	Les AuCoin (D)	639,851	46.5

Special Election

1996	Ron Wyden (D)	571,739	48.4
	Gordon H. Smith (R)	553,519	46.8

1998	Ron Wyden (D)	682,425	61.1
	John Lim (D)	377,739	33.8

PENNSYLVANIA

Candidates	Votes	%

Class 1

1916	Philander C. Knox (R, RO PROG)	680,447	56.3
	Ellis L. Orvis (D)	450,112	37.3
1922	David A. Reed (R)	802,146	56.0
	Samuel E. Shull (D)	423,583	29.6
	William J. Burke (PROG)	127,180	8.9

Special Election

1922	David A. Reed (R)	860,483#	86.1
	Rachel C. Robinson (P)	60,390#	6.0
	William J. VanEssen (SOC)	55,703#	5.6

1928	David A. Reed (R)	1,948,646	64.4
	William N. McNair (D)	1,029,055	34.0
1934	Joseph F. Guffey (D)	1,494,001	50.8
	David A. Reed (R)	1,366,877	46.5
1940	Joseph F. Guffey (D)	2,069,980	51.8
	Jay Cooke (R)	1,893,104	47.4
1946	Edward Martin (R)	1,853,458	59.3
	Joseph F. Guffey (D)	1,245,338	39.8
1952	Edward Martin (R)	2,331,034	51.6
	Guy Kurtz Bard (D)	2,168,546	48.0
1958	Hugh Scott (R)	2,042,586	51.2
	George M. Leader (D)	1,929,821	48.4
1964	Hugh Scott (R)	2,429,858	50.6
	Genevieve Blatt (D)	2,359,223	49.1
1970	Hugh Scott (R)	1,874,106	51.4
	William G. Sesler (D)	1,653,774	45.4
1976	John Heinz (R)	2,381,891	52.4
	William J. Green III (R)	2,126,977	46.8
1982	John Heinz (R)	2,136,418	59.3
	Cyril H. Wecht (D)	1,412,965	39.2
1988	John Heinz (R)	2,901,715	66.5
	Joseph C. Vignola (D)	1,416,764	32.4

Special Election

1991	Harris Wofford (D)	1,860,760	55.0
	Dick Thornburgh (R)	1,521,986	45.0

1994	Rick Santorum (R)	1,735,691	49.4
	Harris Wofford (D)	1,648,481	46.9
2000	Rick Santorum (R)	2,481,962	52.4
	Ron Klink (D)	2,154,908	45.5

Class 3

1914	Boies Penrose (R, PERS LIB)	519,801	46.8
	Gifford Pinchot		
	(WASH,B MOOSE)	269,175	24.2
	A. Mitchell Palmer (D)	266,415	24.0
1920	Boies Penrose (R)	1,068,985	59.9
	John A. Farrell (D)	484,862	27.2
	Leah Cobb Marion (P)	132,610	7.4

Special Election

1922	George Wharton Pepper (R)	819,507	57.6
	Fred B. Kerr (D)	468,330	32.9
1926	William S. Vare (R)	822,187*	54.6
	William B. Wilson (D, LAB)	648,680	43.1

Special Election

1930	James J. Davis (R)	1,462,186	71.5
	Sedgwick Kistler (D)	523,338	25.6
1932	James J. Davis (R)	1,371,844	49.3
	Lawrence H. Rupp (D)	1,200,767	43.2
1938	James J. Davis (R)	2,086,932	54.7
	George H. Earle		
	(D, ROYAL OAK)	1,694,464	44.4
1944	Francis J. Myers (D)	1,864,735	50.0
	James J. Davis (R)	1,840,943	49.4
1950	James H. Duff (R)	1,820,400	51.3
	Francis J. Myers (D)	1,694,076	47.7
1956	Joseph S. Clark (D)	2,268,641	50.1
	James H. Duff (R)	2,250,671	49.7
1962	Joseph S. Clark (D)	2,238,383	51.1
	James E. Van Zandt (R)	2,134,649	48.7
1968	Richard S. Schweiker (R)	2,399,762	51.9
	Joseph S. Clark (D)	2,117,662	45.8
1974	Richard S. Schweiker (R)	1,843,317	53.0
	Peter Flaherty (D)	1,596,121	45.9
1980	Arlen Specter (R)	2,230,404	50.5
	Peter Flaherty (D)	2,122,391	48.0
1986	Arlen Specter (R)	1,906,537	56.4
	Bob Edgar (D)	1,448,219	42.9
1992	Arlen Specter (R)	2,358,125	49.1
	Lynn Yeakel (D)	2,224,966	46.3
1998	Arlen Specter (R)	1,814,180	61.3
	Bill Lloyd (D)	1,028,839	34.8

RHODE ISLAND

Candidates	Votes	%

Class 1

1916	Peter G. Gerry (D)	47,048	52.9
	Henry Lippitt (R)	39,211	44.1
1922	Peter G. Gerry (D)	82,889	52.2
	R. Livingston Beeckman (R)	68,930	43.4
1928	Felix Hebert (R)	119,228	50.6
	Peter G. Gerry (D)	116,234	49.3
1934	Peter G. Gerry (D)	140,700	57.1
	Felix Hebert (R)	105,545	42.9

1940	Peter G. Gerry (D)	173,847	55.2
	James O. McManus (R)	141,312	44.8
1946	J. Howard McGrath (D)	150,748	55.1
	W. Gurnee Dyer (R)	122,780	44.9

Special Election

1950	John O. Pastore (D)	184,520	61.6
	Austin T. Levy (R)	114,890	38.4
1952	John O. Pastore (D)	225,128	54.8
	Bayard Ewing (R, CLEAN GV)	185,850	45.2
1958	John O. Pastore (D)	222,166	64.5
	Bayard Ewing (R)	122,353	35.5
1964	John O. Pastore (D)	319,607	82.7
	Ronald R. Lagueux (R)	66,715	17.3
1970	John O. Pastore (D)	230,469	67.5
	John McLaughlin (R)	107,351	31.5
1976	John H. Chafee (R)	230,329	57.7
	Richard P. Lorber (D)	167,665	42.0
1982	John H. Chafee (R)	175,495	51.2
	Julius C. Michaelson (D)	167,283	48.8
1988	John H. Chafee (R)	217,273	54.6
	Richard A. Licht (D)	180,717	45.4
1994	John H. Chafee (R)	222,856	64.5
	Linda J. Kushner (D)	122,532	35.5
2000	Lincoln Chafee (R)	222,588	56.8
	Bob Weygand (D)	161,023	41.1

Class 2

1918	LeBaron B. Colt (R)	42,055	51.8
	George O'Shaunessy (D)	37,573	46.2
1924	Jesse H. Metcalf (R)	120,815	57.6
	William S. Flynn (D)	87,620	41.8

Special Election

1924	Jesse H. Metcalf (R)	116,572	56.4
	William S. Flynn (D)	88,138	42.6
1930	Jesse H. Metcalf (R)	112,202	50.3
	Peter G. Gerry (D)	109,687	49.2
1936	Theodore F. Green (D)	149,157	48.6
	Jesse H. Metcalf (R)	136,174	44.4
	Lapointe (UN)	21,501	7.0
1942	Theodore F. Green (D)	138,239	58.0
	Ira Lloyd Letts (R)	100,236	42.0
1948	Theodore F. Green (D)	190,284	59.3
	Thomas P. Hazard (R)	130,668	40.7
1954	Theodore F. Green (D)	193,654	59.3
	Walter I. Sundlun (R)	132,970	40.7
1960	Claiborne Pell (D)	275,575	68.9
	Raoul Archambault (R)	124,408	31.1
1966	Claiborne Pell (D)	219,331	67.7
	Ruth M. Briggs (R)	104,838	32.3
1972	Claiborne Pell (D)	221,942	53.7
	John H. Chafee (R)	188,990	45.7
1978	Claiborne Pell (D)	229,557	75.1
	James G. Reynolds (R)	76,061	24.9
1984	Claiborne Pell (D)	286,780	72.6
	Barbara Leonard (R)	108,492	27.4

1990	Claiborne Pell (D)	225,105	61.8
	Claudine Schneider (R)	138,947	38.2
1996	Jack Reed (D)	230,676	63.5
	Nancy J. Mayer (R)	127,368	35.1

SOUTH CAROLINA

	Candidates	Votes	%
	Class 2		
1918	Nathaniel B. Dial (D)	25,792	100.0

Special Election

1918	William P. Pollock (D)	✔	
1924	Coleman L. Blease (D)	49,060	100.0
1930	James F. Byrnes (D)	16,213	100.0
1936	James F. Byrnes (D)	113,696	98.6

Special Election

1941	Burnet R. Maybank (D)	✔	
1942	Burnet R. Maybank (D)	23,356	100.0
1948	Burnet R. Maybank (D)	135,998	96.5
1954	Strom Thurmond (WRITE IN)	143,442	63.1
	Edgar A. Brown (D)	83,525	36.8

Special Election

1956	Strom Thurmond (D)	245,371	100.0
1960	Strom Thurmond (D)	330,164	100.0
1966	Strom Thurmond (R)	271,297	62.2
	Bradley Morrah (D)	164,955	37.8
1972	Strom Thurmond (R)	415,806	63.3
	Eugene N. Zeigler (D)	241,056	36.7
1978	Strom Thurmond (R)	351,733	55.6
	Charles D. Ravenel (D)	281,119	44.4
1984	Strom Thurmond (R)	644,815	66.8
	Melvin Purvis Jr. (R)	306,982	31.8
1990	Strom Thurmond (R)	482,032	64.2
	Bob Cunningham (D)	244,112	32.5
1996	Strom Thurmond (R)	619,859	53.4
	Elliott Close (D)	510,951	44.0
	Class 3		
1914	Ellison D. Smith (D)	32,950	99.8
1920	Ellison D. Smith (D)	64,388	100.0
1926	Ellison D. Smith (D)	14,560	100.0
1932	Ellison D. Smith (D)	104,472	98.1
1938	Ellison D. Smith (D)	45,751	98.9
1944	Olin D. Johnston (D)	94,556	92.9
1950	Olin D. Johnston (D)	50,240	99.9
1956	Olin D. Johnston (D)	230,150	82.2
	L. P Crawford (R)	49,695	17.8
1962	Olin D. Johnston (D)	178,712	57.2
	W. D Workman Jr. (R)	133,930	42.8

Special Election

1966	Ernest F. Hollings (D)	223,790	51.4
	Marshall Parker (R)	212,032	48.7
1968	Ernest F. Hollings (D)	404,060	61.9

	Marshall Parker (R)	248,780	38.1
1974	Ernest F. Hollings (D)	356,126	69.5
	Gwenyfred Bush (R)	146,645	28.6
1980	Ernest F. Hollings (D)	612,554	70.4
	Marshall T. Mays (R)	257,946	29.6
1986	Ernest F. Hollings (D)	465,500	63.1
	Henry D. McMaster (R)	262,886	35.6
1992	Ernest F. Hollings (D)	591,030	50.1
	Thomas F. Hartnett (R)	554,175	46.9
1998	Ernest F. Hollings (D)	562,791	52.7
	Robert D. Inglis (R)	488,132	45.7

SOUTH DAKOTA

	Candidates	Votes	%
	Class 2		
1918	Thomas Sterling (R)	51,198	55.1
	Rinehart (D)	36,210	39.0
	Rafferty (I)	5,560	6.0
1924	William H. McMaster (R)	90,006	44.1
	U. S G. Cherry (D)	63,548	31.2
	Tom Ayres (F-LAB)	21,136	10.4
	George W. Egan (I)	14,484	7.1
1930	William J. Bulow (D)	106,317	51.6
	William H. McMaster (R)	99,595	48.4
1936	William J. Bulow (D)	141,509	48.8
	Chandler Gurney (R)	135,461	46.8
1942	Harlan J. Bushfield (R)	106,704	58.7
	Tom Berry (D)	74,945	41.3
1948	Karl E. Mundt (R)	144,084	59.3
	John A. Engel (D)	98,749	40.7
1954	Karl E. Mundt (R)	135,071	57.3
	Kenneth Holum (D)	100,674	42.7
1960	Karl E. Mundt (R)	160,181	52.4
	George McGovern (D)	145,261	47.6
1966	Karl E. Mundt (R)	150,517	66.3
	Donn H. Wright (D)	76,563	33.7
1972	James Abourezk (D)	174,773	57.0
	Robert W. Hirsch (R)	131,613	42.9
1978	Larry Pressler (R)	170,832	66.8
	Don Barnett (D)	84,767	33.2
1984	Larry Pressler (R)	235,176	74.5
	George V. Cunningham (D)	80,537	25.5
1990	Larry Pressler (R)	135,682	52.4
	Ted Muenster (D)	116,727	45.1
1996	Tim Johnson (D)	166,533	51.3
	Larry Pressler (R)	157,954	48.7
	Class 3		
1914	Edwin S. Johnson (D)	47,668	48.1
	Charles H. Burke (R)	44,244	44.7
1920	Peter Norbeck (R)	92,267	50.1
	Tom Ayres (NON PART)	44,309	24.1
	U. S G. Cherry (D)	36,833	20.0
	R. O Richards (I)	10,032	5.5
1926	Peter Norbeck (R)	105,756	59.5
	C. J Gunderson (D)	59,128	33.3
	Howard Platt (F-LAB)	12,797	7.2

1932	Peter Norbeck (R)	151,845	53.8
	U. S G. Cherry (D)	125,731	44.6
1938	Chandler Gurney (R)	146,813	52.5
	Tom Berry (D)	133,064	47.5

Special Election

| 1938 | Gladys Pyle (R) | 155,292 | 58.1 |
| | John T. McCullen Sr. (D) | 112,177 | 41.9 |

1944	Chandler Gurney (R)	145,248	63.9
	George M. Bradshaw (D)	82,199	36.1
1950	Francis Case (R)	160,670	63.9
	John A. Engel (D)	90,692	36.1
1956	Francis Case (R)	147,621	50.8
	Kenneth Holum (D)	143,001	49.2
1962	George McGovern (D)	127,458	50.1
	Joe Bottum (R)	126,861	49.9
1968	George McGovern (D)	158,961	56.8
	Archie Gubbrud (R)	120,951	43.2
1974	George McGovern (D)	147,929	53.0
	Leo K. Thorsness (R)	130,955	47.0
1980	James Abdnor (R)	190,594	58.2
	George McGovern (D)	129,018	39.4
1986	Thomas Daschle (D)	152,657	51.6
	James Abdnor (R)	143,173	48.4
1992	Thomas Daschle (D)	217,095	64.9
	Charlene Haar (R)	108,733	32.5
1998	Thomas Daschle (D)	162,884	62.1
	Ron Schmidt (R)	95,431	36.4

TENNESSEE

Candidates	Votes	%

Class 1

1916	Kenneth D. McKellar (D)	143,718	54.4
	Ben W. Hooper (R)	118,174	44.8
1922	Kenneth D. McKellar (D)	151,523	68.0
	Newell Sanders (R)	71,199	32.0
1928	Kenneth D. McKellar (D)	175,431	59.3
	J. A Fowler (R)	120,289	40.7
1934	Kenneth D. McKellar (D)	195,430	63.4
	Ben W. Hooper (R)	110,401	35.8
1940	Kenneth D. McKellar (D)	295,440	70.8
	Howard Baker (R)	121,790	29.2
1946	Kenneth D. McKellar (D)	145,654	66.6
	W. B Ladd (R)	57,237	26.2
	John R. Neal (I)	11,516	5.3
1952	Albert Gore (D)	545,432	74.2
	Hobart F. Atkins (R)	153,479	20.9
1958	Albert Gore (D)	317,324	79.0
	Hobart F. Atkins (R)	76,371	19.0
1964	Albert Gore (D)	570,542	53.6
	Dan H. Kuykendall (R)	493,475	46.4
1970	Bill Brock (R)	562,645	51.3
	Albert Gore (D)	519,858	47.4
1976	Jim Sasser (D)	751,180	52.5
	Bill Brock (R)	673,231	47.0

1982	Jim Sasser (D)	780,113	61.9
	Robin L. Beard (D)	479,642	38.1
1988	Jim Sasser (D)	1,020,061	65.1
	Bill Andersen (R)	541,033	34.5
1994	Bill Frist (R)	834,226	56.4
	Jim Sasser (D)	623,164	42.1
2000	Bill Frist (R)	1,255,444	65.1
	Jeff Clark (D)	621,152	32.2

Class 2

1918	John K. Shields (D)	98,605	62.2
	H. Clay Evans (R)	59,989	37.8
1924	Lawrence D. Tyson (D)	147,821	57.3
	H. B Lindsay (R)	109,863	42.6
1930	Cordell Hull (D)	154,071	71.3
	Paul E. Divine (R)	58,550	27.1

Special Election

| 1930 | William E. Brock (D) | 144,021 | 74.4 |
| | F. Todd Meacham (R) | 49,634 | 25.6 |

Special Election

| 1934 | Nathan L. Bachman (D) | 200,249 | 80.1 |
| | John R. Neal (I) | 49,773 | 19.9 |

| 1936 | Nathan L. Bachman (D) | 273,298 | 76.4 |
| | Dwayne D. Maddox (R) | 67,238 | 18.8 |

Special Election

| 1938 | A. Tom Stewart (D) | 194,026 | 70.5 |
| | Harley G. Fowler (R) | 72,098 | 26.2 |

1942	A. Tom Stewart (D)	109,881	68.9
	F. Todd Meacham (R)	34,324	21.5
	John R. Neal (I)	15,317	9.6
1948	Estes Kefauver (D)	326,062	65.3
	B. Carroll Reece (R)	166,947	33.5
1954	Estes Kefauver (D)	249,121	70.0
	Tom Wall (R)	106,971	30.0
1960	Estes Kefauver (D)	594,460	71.8
	A. Bradley Frazier (R)	234,053	28.3

Special Election

| 1964 | Ross Bass (D) | 568,905 | 52.1 |
| | Howard H. Baker Jr. (R) | 517,330 | 47.4 |

1966	Howard H. Baker Jr. (R)	483,063	55.7
	Frank G. Clement (D)	383,843	44.3
1972	Howard H. Baker Jr. (R)	716,539	61.6
	Ray Blanton (D)	440,599	37.9
1978	Howard H. Baker Jr. (R)	642,644	55.5
	Jane Eskind (D)	466,228	40.3
1984	Albert Gore Jr. (D)	1,000,607	60.7
	Victor Ashe (R)	557,016	33.8
	Ed McAteer (I)	87,234	5.3
1990	Albert Gore Jr. (D)	530,898	67.7
	William R. Hawkins (R)	233,703	29.8

Special Election

| 1994 | Fred Thompson (R) | 885,998 | 60.4 |
| | Jim Cooper (D) | 565,930 | 38.6 |

1996	Fred Thompson (R)	1,091,554	61.4
	Houston Gordon (D)	654,937	36.8

TEXAS

	Candidates	Votes	%
	Class 1		
1916	Charles A. Culberson (D)	303,035	81.3
	Alex W. Atcheson (R)	48,788	13.1
1922	Earle B. Mayfield (D)	261,063	66.6
	George E. B Peddy (R)	130,731	33.4
1928	Tom Connally (D)	566,139	81.2
	T. M Kennerly (R)	130,172	18.7
1934	Tom Connally (D)	437,254	96.7
1940	Tom Connally (D)	993,974	94.3
	George I. Shannon (R)	60,051	5.7
1946	Tom Connally (D)	336,931	88.5
	Murray C. Sells (R)	43,619	11.5
1952	Price Daniel (D, R)	1,894,671	100.0

Special Election

1957	Ralph Yarborough (D)	364,878	38.1
	Martin Dies (D)	290,869	30.4
	Thad Hutcheson (R)	219,591	22.9
1958	Ralph Yarborough (D)	587,030	74.6
	Roy Whittenburg (R)	185,926	23.6
1964	Ralph Yarborough (D)	1,463,958	56.2
	George Bush (R)	1,134,337	43.6
1970	Lloyd Bentsen (D)	1,193,814	53.5
	George Bush (R)	1,036,045	46.4
1976	Lloyd Bentsen (D)	2,199,956	56.8
	Alan Steelman (R)	1,636,370	42.2
1982	Lloyd Bentsen (D)	1,818,223	58.6
	James M. Collins (R)	1,256,759	40.5
1988	Lloyd Bentsen (D)	3,149,806	59.2
	Beau Boulter (R)	2,129,228	40.0

Special Primary[1]

1993	Kay Bailey Hutchison (R)	593,338	29.0
	Bob Krueger (D)	593,239	29.0
	Joe L. Barton (R)	284,135	13.9
	Jack Fields (R)	277,560	13.6
	Richard Fisher (D)	165,564	8.1

Special Runoff Election[1]

1993	Kay Bailey Hutchison (R)	1,188,716	67.3
	Bob Krueger (D)	576,538	32.7
1994	Kay Bailey Hutchison (R)	2,604,218	60.8
	Richard Fisher (D)	1,639,615	38.3
2000	Kay Bailey Hutchison (R)	4,082,091	65.0
	Gene Kelly (D)	2,030,315	32.2

	Class 2		
1918	Morris Sheppard (D)	155,178	86.7
	J. Webs Flanagan (R)	22,214	12.4
1924	Morris Sheppard (D)	592,057	85.4
	T. M Kennerly (R)	101,252	14.6

1930	Morris Sheppard (D)	266,562	86.9
	D. J Haesly (R)	39,053	12.7
1936	Morris Sheppard (D)	773,574	92.6
	Carlos G. Watson (R)	59,491	7.1

Special Election

1941	W. Lee O'Daniel (D)	175,590	30.5
	Lyndon B. Johnson (D)	174,284	30.3
	Gerald C. Mann (D)	140,807	24.5
	Martin Dies (D)	80,551	14.0
1942	W. Lee O'Daniel (D)	260,629	94.9
1948	Lyndon B. Johnson (D)	702,785	66.2
	Jack Porter (R)	349,665	32.9
1954	Lyndon B. Johnson (D)	539,319	84.7
	Carlos G. Watson (R)	94,131	14.8
1960	Lyndon B. Johnson (D)	1,306,605	58.0
	John G. Tower (R)	926,653	41.1

Special Primary[1]

1961	John G. Tower (R)	327,308#	30.9
	William A. Blakley (D)	190,818#	18.1
	Jim Wright (D)	171,328#	16.2
	Will Wilson (D)	121,961#	11.5
	Maury Maverick Jr. (D)	104,992#	9.9
	Henry B. Gonzalez (D)	97,659#	9.2

Special Runoff Election[1]

1961	John G. Tower (R)	448,217	50.6
	William A. Blakley (D)	437,874	49.4
1966	John G. Tower (R)	842,501	56.4
	Waggoner Carr (D)	643,855	43.1
1972	John G. Tower (R)	1,822,877	53.4
	Barefoot Sanders (D)	1,511,985	44.3
1978	John G. Tower (R)	1,151,376	49.8
	Bob Krueger (D)	1,139,149	49.3
1984	Phil Gramm (R)	3,111,348	58.5
	Lloyd Doggett (D)	2,202,557	41.4
1990	Phil Gramm (R)	2,302,357	60.2
	Hugh Parmer (D)	1,429,986	37.4
1996	Phil Gramm (R)	3,027,680	54.8
	Victor M. Morales (D)	2,428,776	43.9

Texas

1. Under Texas law passed after the 1957 special election, candidates in special elections for the Senate would all run together in a primary with party affiliation. If none received a majority of the vote in the first primary, a runoff would be held between the top two contenders.

UTAH

Candidates	Votes	%
Class 1		

1916	William H. King (D)	81,057	56.9
	George Sutherland (R)	56,862	39.9
1922	William H. King (D)	58,749	48.6
	Ernest Bamberger (R)	58,188	48.2
1928	William H. King (D)	97,436	55.5
	Ernest Bamberger (R)	77,073	43.9

Year	Candidate	Votes	%
1934	William H. King (D)	95,931	53.1
	Don B. Colton (R)	82,154	45.4
1940	Abe Murdock (D)	155,499	62.9
	Philo T. Farnsworth Jr. (R)	91,931	37.2
1946	Arthur V. Watkins (R)	101,142	51.2
	Abe Murdock (D)	96,257	48.8
1952	Arthur V. Watkins (R)	177,435	54.3
	Walter K. Granger (D)	149,598	45.7
1958	Frank E. Moss (D)	112,827	38.7
	Arthur V. Watkins (R)	101,471	34.8
	J. Bracken Lee (I)	77,013	26.4
1964	Frank E. Moss (D)	227,822	57.3
	Ernest L. Wilkinson (R)	169,562	42.7
1970	Frank E. Moss (D)	210,207	56.2
	Laurence J. Burton (R)	159,004	42.5
1976	Orrin G. Hatch (R)	290,221	53.7
	Moss E. Frank (D)	241,948	44.8
1982	Orrin G. Hatch (R)	309,332	58.3
	Ted Wilson (D)	219,482	41.3
1988	Orrin G. Hatch (R)	430,089	67.1
	Brian H. Moss (D)	203,364	31.7
1994	Orrin G. Hatch (R)	357,297	68.8
	Patrick A. Shea (D)	146,938	28.3
2000	Orrin G. Hatch (R)	504,803	65.6
	Scott N. Howell (D)	242,569	31.5

Class 3

Year	Candidate	Votes	%
1914	Reed Smoot (R)	56,282	49.1
	James H. Moyle (D & PROG)	53,127	46.3
1920	Reed Smoot (R)	82,566	56.6
	Milton H. Welling (D)	56,280	38.6
1926	Reed Smoot (R)	88,101	61.5
	Ashby Snow (D)	53,809	37.6
1932	Elbert D. Thomas (D)	116,909	56.7
	Reed Smoot (R)	86,066	41.7
1938	Elbert D. Thomas (D)	102,353	55.8
	Franklin S. Harris (R)	81,071	44.2
1944	Elbert D. Thomas (D)	148,748	59.9
	Adam S. Bennion (R)	99,532	40.1
1950	Wallace F. Bennett (R)	142,427	53.9
	Elbert D. Thomas (D)	121,198	45.8
1956	Wallace F. Bennett (R)	178,261	54.0
	Alonzo F. Hopkin (D)	152,120	46.0
1962	Wallace F. Bennett (R)	166,755	52.4
	David S. King (D)	151,656	47.6
1968	Wallace F. Bennett (R)	225,075	53.7
	Milton L. Weilenmann (D)	192,168	45.8
1974	Jake Garn (R)	210,299	50.0
	Wayne Owens (D)	185,377	44.1
1980	Jake Garn (R)	437,675	73.6
	Dan Berman (D)	151,454	25.5
1986	Jake Garn (R)	314,608	72.3
	Craig Oliver (D)	115,523	26.6
1992	Robert F. Bennett (R)	420,069	55.4
	Wayne Owens (D)	301,228	39.7
1998	Robert F. Bennett (R)	316,652	64.0
	Scott Leckman (D)	163,172	33.0

VERMONT

	Candidates	Votes	%

Class 1

Year	Candidate	Votes	%
1916	Carroll S. Page (R)	47,362	74.2
	Oscar C. Miller (D)	14,956	23.4
1922	Frank L. Greene (R)	45,284	67.9
	William B. Mayo (D)	21,375	32.1
1928	Frank L. Greene (R)	93,136	71.6
	Fred C. Martin (D)	37,030	28.5

Special Election

Year	Candidate	Votes	%
1931	Warren R. Austin (R)	27,661#	64.3
	Stephen M. Driscoll (D)	15,360#	35.7
1934	Warren R. Austin (R)	67,146	51.0
	Fred C. Martin (D)	63,632	48.4
1940	Warren R. Austin (R)	93,283	66.5
	Ona S. Searles (D)	47,101	33.6
1946	Ralph E. Flanders (R)	54,729	74.6
	Charles P. McDevitt (D)	18,594	25.4
1952	Ralph E. Flanders (R)	111,406	72.3
	Allan R. Johnston (D)	42,630	27.7
1958	Winston L. Prouty (R)	64,900	52.2
	Frederick J. Fayette (D)	59,536	47.8
1964	Winston L. Prouty (R, I)	87,879	53.5
	Frederick J. Fayette (D)	76,457	46.5
1970	Winston L. Prouty (R)	91,198	58.9
	Philip H. Hoff (D)	62,271	40.2

Special Election

Year	Candidate	Votes	%
1972	Robert T. Stafford (R)	45,888#	64.3
	Randolph T. Major (D)	23,842#	33.4
1976	Robert T. Stafford (R)	94,481	50.0
	Thomas P. Salmon (D)	85,682	45.3
1982	Robert T. Stafford (R)	84,450	50.3
	James A. Guest (D)	79,340	47.2
1988	James M. Jeffords (R)	163,183	67.9
	William Gray (D)	71,460	29.8
1994	James M. Jeffords (R)	106,505	50.3
	Jan Backus (D)	85,868	40.6
	Gavin T. Mills (I)	12,465	5.9
2000	James M. Jeffords (R)	189,133	65.6
	Ed Flanagan (D)	73,352	25.4

Class 3

Year	Candidate	Votes	%
1914	William P. Dillingham (R)	35,137	56.0
	Charles A. Prouty (PROG D & P)	26,776	42.7
1920	William P. Dillingham (R)	69,650	78.0
	Howard E. Shaw (D)	19,580	21.9

Special Election

1923	Porter H. Dale (R)	30,582	66.2
	Park H. Pollard (D)	15,621	33.8
1926	Porter H. Dale (R, P)	52,286	73.4
	James E. Kennedy (D)	18,878	26.5
1932	Porter H. Dale (R)	74,319	55.1
	Fred C. Martin (D)	60,453	44.9

Special Election

1934	Ernest W. Gibson (R)	28,436#	58.2
	Harry W. Witters (D)	20,382#	41.8
1938	Ernest W. Gibson (R)	73,990	65.7
	John McGrath (D)	38,673	34.3

Special Election

1940	George D. Aiken (R)	87,150	61.6
	Herbert B. Comings (D)	54,263	38.4
1944	George D. Aiken (R)	81,094	65.8
	Harry W. Witters (D)	42,136	34.2
1950	George D. Aiken (R)	69,543	78.0
	James E. Bigelow (D)	19,608	22.0
1956	George D. Aiken (R)	103,101	66.4
	Bernard G. O'Shea (D)	52,184	33.6
1962	George D. Aiken (R)	81,241	66.9
	W. Robert Johnson (D)	40,134	33.1
1968	George D. Aiken (R, D)	157,154	99.9
1974	Patrick J. Leahy (D, I VT)	70,629	49.5
	Richard W. Mallary (R)	66,223	46.4
1980	Patrick J. Leahy (D)	104,176	49.8
	Stewart M. Ledbetter (R)	101,421	48.5
1986	Patrick J. Leahy (D)	124,123	63.2
	Richard A. Snelling (R)	67,798	34.5
1992	Patrick J. Leahy (D)	154,762	54.2
	James H. Douglas (R)	123,854	43.3
1998	Patrick J. Leahy (D)	154,567	72.2
	Fred H. Tuttle (R)	48,051	22.4

VIRGINIA

Candidates	Votes	%

Class 1

1916	Claude A. Swanson (D)	133,091	99.9
1922	Claude A. Swanson (D)	116,393	71.9
	J. W McGavock (R)	42,903	26.5
1928	Claude A. Swanson (D)	275,425	99.8

Special Election

1933	Harry F. Byrd (D)	119,377	71.3
	Henry A. Wise (R)	44,648	26.7
1934	Harry F. Byrd (D)	109,963	76.0
	Lawrence C. Page (R)	30,289	20.9
1940	Harry F. Byrd (D)	274,260	93.3
1946	Harry F. Byrd (D)	163,960	64.9
	Lester S. Parsons (R)	77,005	30.5

1952	Harry F. Byrd (D)	398,677	73.4
	H. M Vise Sr. (ID)	69,133	12.7
	Clarke T. Robb (SOCIAL D)	67,281	12.4
1958	Harry F. Byrd (D)	317,221	69.3
	Louise Wensel (I)	120,224	26.3
1964	Harry F. Byrd (D)	592,260	63.8
	Richard A. May (R)	176,624	19.0
	James W. Respess (I)	95,526	10.3

Special Election

1966	Harry F. Byrd Jr. (D)	389,028	53.3
	Lawrence M. Traylor (R)	272,804	37.4
	John W. Carter (C)	57,692	7.9
1970	Harry F. Byrd Jr. (I)	506,623	53.5
	George C. Rawlings Jr. (D)	295,057	31.2
	Ray Garland (R)	145,031	15.3
1976	Harry F. Byrd Jr. (I)	890,778	57.2
	Elmo R. Zumwalt (D)	596,009	38.3
1982	Paul S. Trible Jr. (R)	724,571	51.2
	Richard Davis (D)	690,839	48.8
1988	Charles S. Robb (D)	1,474,086	71.2
	Maurice A. Dawkins (R)	593,652	28.7
1994	Charles S. Robb (D)	938,376	45.6
	Oliver L. North (R)	882,213	42.9
	J. Marshall Coleman (I)	235,324	11.4
2000	George F. Allen (R)	1,420,460	52.3
	Charles S. Robb (D)	1,296,093	47.7

Class 2

1918	Thomas S. Martin (D)	40,403	99.7

Special Election

1920	Carter Glass (D)	184,646#	91.3
	J. R Pollard (R)	17,576#	8.7
1924	Carter Glass (D)	151,498	73.1
	Carroll Livingston Ricker (SOC)	50,092	24.2
1930	Carter Glass (D)	112,002	76.7
	J. Cloyd Byars (I)	26,091	17.9
	Joe C. Morgan (SOC)	7,954	5.4
1936	Carter Glass (D)	244,518	91.7
1942	Carter Glass (D)	79,421	91.1
	Lawrence S. Wilkes (SOC)	5,690	6.5

Special Election

1946	A. Willis Robertson (D)	169,680	68.2
	Robert H. Woods (R)	72,253	29.0
1948	A. Willis Robertson (D)	253,865	65.6
	Robert H. Woods (R)	119,366	30.8
1954	A. Willis Robertson (D)	244,844	79.9
	Charles William Lewis Jr. (ID)	32,681	10.7
	Clarke T. Robb (SOCIAL D)	28,922	9.4
1960	A. Willis Robertson (D)	506,169	81.3
	Stuart D. Baker (ID)	88,718	14.2
1966	William B. Spong Jr. (D)	429,855	58.6
	James P. Ould Jr. (R)	245,681	33.5
	F. Lee Hawthorne (C)	58,251	7.9

1972	William Lloyd Scott (R)	718,337	51.5
	William B. Spong Jr. (D)	643,963	46.1
1978	John W. Warner (R)	613,232	50.2
	Andrew P. Miller (D)	608,511	49.8
1984	John W. Warner (R)	1,406,194	70.0
	Edythe C. Harrison (D)	601,142	29.9
1990	John W. Warner (R)	876,782	80.9
	Nancy B. Spannaus (I)	196,755	18.2
1996	John W. Warner (R)	1,235,744	52.5
	Mark Warner (D)	1,115,982	47.4

WASHINGTON

Candidates		Votes	%
Class 1			
1916	Miles Poindexter (R)	202,287	55.4
	George Turner (D)	135,339	37.1
	Bruce Rogers (SOC)	21,709	5.9
1922	Clarence C. Dill (D)	130,375	44.2
	Miles Poindexter (R)	126,556	43.0
	James A. Duncan (F-LAB)	35,352	12.0
1928	Clarence C. Dill (D)	261,524	53.4
	Kenneth Mackintosh (R)	227,415	46.5
1934	Lewis B. Schwellenbach (D)	302,606	60.9
	Reno Odlin (R)	168,994	34.0
1940	Mon C. Wallgren (D)	404,718	54.2
	Stephen F. Chadwick (R)	342,589	45.8
1946	Harry P. Cain (R)	358,847	54.3
	Hugh B. Mitchell (D)	298,683	45.2
1952	Henry M. Jackson (D)	595,288	56.2
	Harry P. Cain (R)	460,884	43.5
1958	Henry M. Jackson (D)	597,040	67.3
	William B. Bantz (R)	278,271	31.4
1964	Henry M. Jackson (D)	875,950	72.2
	Lloyd J. Andrews (R)	337,138	27.8
1970	Henry M. Jackson (D)	879,385	82.4
	Charles W. Elicker (R)	170,790	16.0
1976	Henry M. Jackson (D)	1,071,219	71.8
	George M. Brown (R)	361,546	24.2
1982	Henry M. Jackson (D)	943,655	69.0
	Doug Jewett (R)	332,273	24.3
	King Lysen (I)	72,297	5.3

Special Election

1983	Daniel J. Evans (R)	617,699	55.4
	Mike Lowry (D)	496,393	44.6
1988	Slade Gorton (R)	944,359	51.1
	Mike Lowry (D)	904,183	48.9
1994	Slade Gorton (R)	947,821	55.7
	Ron Sims (D)	752,352	44.3
2000	Maria Cantwell (D)	1,199,437	48.7
	Slade Gorton (R)	1,197,208	48.6

Class 3

1914	Wesley L. Jones (R)	130,479	37.8
	W. W Black (D)	91,733	26.6
	Ole Hanson (PROG)	83,282	24.1
	Adam H. Barth (SOC)	30,234	8.8

1920	Wesley L. Jones (R)	217,069	56.4
	C. L France (F-LAB)	99,309	25.8
	George F. Cotterill (D)	68,488	17.8
1926	Wesley L. Jones (R)	164,130	51.3
	A. Scott Bullitt (D)	148,792	46.5
1932	Homer T. Bone (D)	365,949	60.6
	Wesley L. Jones (R)	197,450	32.7
1938	Homer T. Bone (D)	371,535	62.6
	Ewing D. Colvin (R)	220,204	37.1
1944	Warren G. Magnuson (D)	452,013	55.1
	Harry P. Cain (R)	364,356	44.4
1950	Warren G. Magnuson (D)	397,719	53.4
	Walter Williams (R)	342,464	46.0
1956	Warren G. Magnuson (D)	685,565	61.1
	Arthur B. Langlie (R)	436,652	38.9
1962	Warren G. Magnuson (D)	491,365	52.1
	Richard G. Christensen (R)	446,204	47.3
1968	Warren G. Magnuson (D)	796,183	64.4
	Jack Metcalf (R)	435,894	35.3
1974	Warren G. Magnuson (D)	611,811	60.7
	Jack Metcalf (R)	363,626	36.1
1980	Slade Gorton (R)	936,317	54.2
	Warren G. Magnuson (D)	792,052	45.8
1986	Brock Adams (D)	677,471	50.6
	Slade Gorton (R)	650,931	48.7
1992	Patty Murray (D)	1,197,973	54.0
	Rod Chandler (R)	1,020,829	46.0
1998	Patty Murray (D)	1,103,184	58.6
	Linda Smith (R)	785,377	41.6

WEST VIRGINIA

Candidates		Votes	%
Class 1			
1916	Howard Sutherland (R)	144,243	50.1
	William E. Chilton (D)	138,585	48.2
1922	Matthew M. Neely (D)	198,853	51.2
	Howard Sutherland (R)	185,046	47.6
1928	Henry D. Hatfield (R)	327,266	50.7
	Matthew M. Neely (D)	317,620	49.2
1934	Rush D. Holt (D)	349,882	55.1
	Henry D. Hatfield (R)	281,756	44.4
1940	Harley M. Kilgore (D)	492,413	56.3
	Thomas Sweeney (R)	381,806	43.7
1946	Harley M. Kilgore (D)	273,151	50.3
	Thomas Sweeney (R)	269,617	49.7
1952	Harley M. Kilgore (D)	470,019	53.6
	Chapman Revercomb (R)	406,554	46.4

Special Election

1956	Chapman Revercomb (R)	432,123	53.7
	William C. Marland (D)	373,051	46.3
1958	Robert C. Byrd (D)	381,745	59.2
	Chapman Revercomb (R)	263,172	40.8
1964	Robert C. Byrd (D)	515,015	67.7
	Cooper P. Benedict (R)	246,072	32.3
1970	Robert C. Byrd (D)	345,965	77.6
	Elmer H. Dodson (R)	99,658	22.4

1976	Robert C. Byrd (D)	566,423	99.9
1982	Robert C. Byrd (D)	387,170	68.5
	Cleve K. Benedict (R)	173,910	30.8
1988	Robert C. Byrd (D)	410,983	64.8
	M. Jay Wolfe (R)	223,564	35.2
1994	Robert C. Byrd (D)	290,495	69.0
	Stan Klos (R)	130,441	31.0
2000	Robert C. Byrd (D)	469,215	77.8
	David T. Gallaher (R)	121,635	20.2

Class 2

1918	David Elkins (R)	115,216	53.5
	Clarence W. Watson (D)	97,715	45.4
1924	Guy D. Goff (R)	290,004	50.9
	William E. Chilton (D)	271,809	47.7
1930	Matthew M. Neely (D)	342,467	61.9
	James Ellwood Jones (R)	209,427	37.9
1936	Matthew M. Neely (D)	488,620	59.1
	Hugh Ike Shott (R)	338,363	40.9
1942	Chapman Revercomb (R)	256,816	55.4
	Matthew M. Neely (D)	207,045	44.6

Special Election

| 1942 | Hugh Ike Shott (R) | 227,469 | 52.3 |
| | Joseph Rosier (D) | 207,678 | 47.7 |

1948	Matthew M. Neely (D)	435,354	57.0
	Chapman Revercomb (R)	328,534	43.0
1954	Matthew M. Neely (D)	325,263	54.8
	Thomas Sweeney (R)	268,066	45.2

Special Election

| 1958 | Jennings Randolph (D) | 374,167 | 59.3 |
| | John D. Hoblitzell Jr. (R) | 256,510 | 40.7 |

1960	Jennings Randolph (D)	458,355	55.3
	Cecil H. Underwood (R)	369,935	44.7
1966	Jennings Randolph (D)	292,325	59.5
	Francis J. Love (R)	198,891	40.5
1972	Jennings Randolph (D)	486,310	66.5
	Louise Leonard (R)	245,531	33.6
1978	Jennings Randolph (D)	249,034	50.5
	Arch A. Moore Jr. (R)	244,317	49.5
1984	John D. "Jay" Rockefeller IV (D)	374,233	51.8
	John R. Raese (R)	344,680	47.7
1990	John D. "Jay" Rockefeller IV (D)	276,234	68.3
	John Yoder (R)	128,071	31.7
1996	John D. "Jay" Rockefeller IV (D)	456,526	76.6
	Betty A. Burks (R)	139,088	23.4

WISCONSIN

Candidates	Votes	%

Class 1

1916	Robert M. La Follette (R)	251,303	60.5
	William F. Wolfe (D)	135,144	32.5
	Richard Elsner (SOCIAL D)	28,908	7.0

| 1922 | Robert M. La Follette (R) | 379,494 | 80.6 |
| | Jessie Jack Hooper (ID) | 78,029 | 16.6 |

Special Election

1925	Robert M. La Follette Jr. (R)	237,719	67.5
	Edward F. Dithmar (IR)	91,318	25.9
1928	Robert M. La Follette Jr. (R)	635,376	85.6
	William H. Markham (IR)	81,302	11.0
1934	Robert M. La Follette Jr. (PROG)	440,513	47.8
	John M. Callahan (D)	223,438	24.2
	John B. Chapple (R)	210,569	22.8
1940	Robert M. La Follette Jr. (PROG)	605,609	45.3
	Fred H. Clausen (R)	553,692	41.4
	James E. Finnegan (D)	176,688	13.2
1946	Joseph R. McCarthy (R)	620,430	61.3
	Howard J. McMurray (D)	378,772	37.4
1952	Joseph R. McCarthy (R)	870,444	54.2
	Thomas E. Fairchild (D)	731,402	45.6

Special Election

| 1957 | William Proxmire (D) | 435,985 | 56.4 |
| | Walter J. Kohler Jr. (R) | 312,931 | 40.5 |

1958	William Proxmire (D)	682,440	57.1
	Roland J. Steinle (R)	510,398	42.7
1964	William Proxmire (D)	892,013	53.3
	Wilbur N. Renk (R)	780,116	46.6
1970	William Proxmire (D)	948,445	70.8
	John E. Erickson (R)	381,297	28.5
1976	William Proxmire (D)	1,396,970	72.2
	Stanley York (R)	521,902	27.0
1982	William Proxmire (D)	983,311	63.6
	Scott McCallum (R)	527,355	34.1
1988	Herb Kohl (D)	1,128,625	52.1
	Susan Engeleiter (R)	1,030,440	47.5
1994	Herb Kohl (D)	912,662	58.3
	Robert T. Welch (R)	636,989	40.7
2000	Herb Kohl (D)	1,563,238	61.5
	John Gillespie (R)	940,744	37.0

Class 3

1914	Paul O. Husting (D)	134,925	43.8
	Francis E. McGovern (R)	133,969	43.5
	Emil Seidel (SOCIAL D)	29,774	9.7

Special Election

1918	Irvine L. Lenroot (R)	163,980#	38.7
	John Davies (D)	148,714#	35.1
	Victor L. Berger (SOC)	110,487#	26.1

1920	Irvine L. Lenroot (R)	281,576	41.6
	James Thompson (I)	235,029	34.7
	Paul S. Reinsch (D)	89,265	13.2
	Frank J. Weber (SOC)	66,172	9.8
1926	John J. Blaine (R)	300,759	55.0
	Charles D. Rosa (I-PROG-R)	111,122	20.3
	Thomas M. Kearney (D)	66,672	12.2
	Leo Krzycki (SOC)	31,317	5.7
1932	F. Ryan Duffy (D)	610,236	57.0
	John B. Chapple (R)	387,668	36.2
	Emil Seidel (SOC)	65,807	6.1

1938	Alexander Wiley (R)	446,770	47.7
	Herman L. Ekern (PROG)	249,209	26.6
	F. Ryan Duffy (D)	231,976	24.7
1944	Alexander Wiley (R)	634,513	50.5
	Howard J. McMurray (D)	537,144	42.8
	Harry Sauthoff (PROG)	73,089	5.8
1950	Alexander Wiley (R)	595,283	53.3
	Thomas E. Fairchild (D)	515,539	46.2
1956	Alexander Wiley (R)	892,473	58.6
	Henry W. Maier (D)	627,903	41.2
1962	Gaylord Nelson (D)	662,342	52.6
	Alexander Wiley (R)	594,846	47.2
1968	Gaylord Nelson (D)	1,020,931	61.7
	Jerris Leonard (R)	633,910	38.3
1974	Gaylord Nelson (D)	740,700	61.8
	Thomas E. Petri (R)	429,327	35.8
1980	Bob Kasten (R)	1,106,311	50.2
	Gaylord Nelson (D)	1,065,487	48.3
1986	Bob Kasten (R)	754,573	50.9
	Ed Garvey (D)	702,963	47.4
1992	Russell D. Feingold (D)	1,290,662	52.6
	Bob Kasten (R)	1,129,599	46.0
1998	Russell D. Feingold (D)	890,059	50.5
	Mark W. Neumann (R)	852,272	48.4

WYOMING

	Candidates	Votes	%
	Class 1		
1916	John B. Kendrick (D)	26,324	51.5
	Clarence D. Clark (R)	23,258	45.5
1922	John B. Kendrick (D)	35,734	57.3
	F. W Mondell (R)	26,627	42.7
1928	John B. Kendrick (D)	43,032	53.5
	Charles E. Winter (R)	37,076	46.1
1934	Joseph C. O'Mahoney (D)	53,806	56.6
	Vincent Carter (R)	40,819	43.0
Special Election			
1934	Joseph C. O'Mahoney (D)	53,859	56.9
	Vincent Carter (R)	40,825	43.1
1940	Joseph C. O'Mahoney (D)	65,022	58.7
	Milward L. Simpson (R)	45,682	41.3
1946	Joseph C. O'Mahoney (D)	45,843	56.2
	Harry B. Henderson (R)	35,714	43.8
1952	Frank A. Barrett (R)	67,176	51.6
	Joseph C. O'Mahoney (D)	62,921	48.4
1958	Gale McGee (D)	58,035	50.8
	Frank A. Barrett (R)	56,122	49.2
1964	Gale McGee (D)	76,485	54.0
	John S. Wold (R)	65,185	46.0
1970	Gale McGee (D)	67,207	55.8
	John S. Wold (R)	53,279	44.2

1976	Malcolm Wallop (R)	84,810	54.6
	Gale McGee (D)	70,558	45.4
1982	Malcolm Wallop (R)	94,725	56.7
	Rodger McDaniel (D)	72,466	43.3
1988	Malcolm Wallop (R)	91,143	50.4
	John Vinich (D)	89,821	49.6
1994	Craig Thomas (R)	118,754	58.9
	Mike Sullivan (D)	79,287	39.3
2000	Craig Thomas (R)	157,622	73.8
	Mel Logan (D)	47,087	22.0
	Class 2		
1918	Francis E. Warren (R)	23,975	57.8
	John E. Osborne (D)	17,528	42.2
1924	Francis E. Warren (R)	41,293	55.2
	Robert R. Rose (D)	33,536	44.8
1930	Robert D. Carey (R)	43,626	59.1
	Harry H. Schwartz (D)	30,259	41.0
Special Election			
1930	Robert D. Carey (R)	42,726#	58.8
	Harry H. Schwartz (D)	29,904#	41.2
1936	Harry H. Schwartz (D)	53,919	53.8
	Robert D. Carey (R)	45,483	45.4
1942	Edward V. Robertson (R)	41,486	54.6
	Harry H. Schwartz (D)	34,503	45.4
1948	Lester C. Hunt (D)	57,953	57.1
	Edward V. Robertson (R)	43,527	42.9
1954	Joseph C. O'Mahoney (D)	57,845	51.5
	William Henry Harrison (R)	54,407	48.5
Special Election			
1954	Joseph C. O'Mahoney (D)	57,163	51.6
	William Henry Harrison (R)	53,705	48.4
1960	Keith Thomson (R)	78,103*	56.4
	Raymond B. Whitaker (D)	60,447	43.6
Special Election			
1962	Milward L. Simpson (R)	69,043	57.8
	J. J Hickey (D)	50,329	42.2
1966	Clifford P. Hansen (R)	63,548	51.8
	Teno Roncalio (D)	59,141	48.2
1972	Clifford P. Hansen (R)	101,314	71.3
	Mike Vinich (D)	40,753	28.7
1978	Alan K. Simpson (R)	82,908	62.2
	Raymond B. Whitaker (D)	50,456	37.8
1984	Alan K. Simpson (R)	146,373	78.3
	Victor A. Ryan (D)	40,525	21.7
1990	Alan K. Simpson (R)	100,784	63.9
	Kathy Helling (D)	56,848	36.1
1996	Michael B. Enzi (R)	114,116	54.1
	Kathy Karpan (D)	89,103	42.2

Senate Returns: Other Sources

In the preceding pages of Senate popular election returns (1268–1303) the symbol # is used to denote 1913–1975 returns taken from a source other than the election data provided by the Inter-University Consortium for Political and Social Research (ICPSR). This page lists the source for each of those returns.

Alabama

1938: *Statistics of the Congressional Election of Nov. 8. 1938.*

Arkansas

1924: *Statistics of the Congressional and Presidential Election of Nov. 4, 1924.*

1914/1916 *World Almanac,* published by the *New York World* newspaper.

1932 special election: Alexander Heard and Donald S. Strong, *Southern Primaries and Elections, 1920–1949,* p. 31.

Colorado

1944: *Statistics of the Congressional and Presidential Election of Nov. 7, 1944.*

Connecticut

1924 special election: *Statistics of the Congressional Election of Nov. 4, 1924.*

Georgia

1924: *Statistics of the Congressional and Presidential Election of Nov. 4, 1924.*

Kentucky

1950 special election: *Statistics of the Congressional Election of Nov. 7, 1950.*

Louisiana

1936 special election: Louisiana secretary of state.

1920: *Statistics of the Congressional and Presidential Election of Nov. 2, 1920.*

Maine

1952: *Statistics of the Congressional and Presidential Election of Nov. 4, 1952.*

Maryland

1913 special election: Maryland secretary of state.

1940: *Statistics of the Congressional and Presidential Election of Nov. 5, 1940.*

1946: *Statistics of the Congressional Election of Nov. 5, 1946.*

Minnesota

1923 special election: 1924 *World Almanac,* published by the *New York World* newspaper.

North Carolina

1948 special election: *Statistics of the Congressional and Presidential Election of Nov. 2, 1948.*

Ohio

1930 special election: *Statistics of the Congressional Election of Nov. 4, 1930.*

Pennsylvania

1922 special election: *Statistics of the Congressional Election of Nov. 7, 1922.*

Texas

1961 special primary: Richard M. Scammon, ed., *America Votes 5* (Pittsburgh, 1964), p. 401.

Vermont

1931 special election: Vermont secretary of state.

1972 special election: Richard M. Scammon, ed., *America Votes 10* (Washington, D.C.: Congressional Quarterly, 1973), p. 372.

1934 special election: Vermont secretary of state.

Virginia

1920 special election: *Statistics of the Congressional and Presidential Election of Nov. 2, 1920.*

Wisconsin

1918 special election: Seward W. Livermore, *Politics Is Adjourned: Woodrow Wilson and the War Congress* (Middletown, Conn.: Wesleyan University Press, 1966), p. 271.

Wyoming

1930 special election: *Statistics of the Congressional Election of Nov. 4, 1930.*

The most frequently used alternative source was *Statistics of the Congressional Elections of _____ ,* published by the Clerk of the House of Representatives for every general election year since 1920.

## CHAPTER 27

Senate Primary Election Returns, 1920–2000

Senatorial primary returns for all fifty states are presented in this chapter (pages 1306–1374). For all nonsouthern states, primary returns go back to 1956; for eleven southern states (Alabama, Arkansas, Florida, Georgia, Louisiana, Mississippi, North Carolina, South Carolina, Tennessee, Texas, and Virginia), primary returns go back to 1920 where available. The vast majority of southern primaries during the period of 1920 to 1973 were held to nominate candidates of the dominant Democratic Party. In most cases, the winner of the Democratic primary went into the general election facing no Republican opponent and almost certain of victory.

The major source for primary election returns for all nonsouthern states from 1956 to 2000 was the *America Votes* series, compiled biennially by Congressional Quarterly in Washington, D.C. Richard M. Scammon and Alice V. McGillivray of the Elections Research Center, Washington, D.C., created the series first published in 1956. Since 1996 the series has been compiled under the direction of Rhodes Cook. Other sources were the returns obtained by Congressional Quarterly after each federal election from the state secretaries of state. In cases of discrepancies, Congressional Quarterly accepted the *America Votes* figure. The first year for which *America Votes* reported primary returns, 1956, was chosen as the starting point for most states because senatorial primary votes for earlier years are not readily available.

For the eleven southern states the primary election returns presented for the years 1920 through 1973 were obtained, except where indicted by a footnote, from the Inter-University Consortium for Political and Social Research (ICPSR) at the University of Michigan. Major sources for returns since 1973 were the *America Votes* series and state secretaries of state.

COMPILATION OF ICPSR DATA FILE

Statewide candidate totals for southern primary elections for senator were prepared by the ICPSR staff from several sources. Election returns for the years prior to 1949 were obtained from *Southern Primaries and Elections* (University: University of Alabama Press, 1950), edited by Alexander Heard and Donald S. Strong. It should be noted that, although they transcribed their data from official returns, professors Heard and Strong found that many of the returns contained errors and discrepancies between the sum of county totals and the state total, or returns published as final in newspapers and secretary of state reports. No attempt was made by Heard and Strong to correct these discrepancies because the source of the error could not be determined.

For the period from 1949 to 1972, candidate totals were acquired from two sources. The first was a collection of southern primary electoral statistics prepared from official returns by Hugh Davis Graham, chairman, division of social sciences, University of Maryland (Baltimore County), and Numan V. Bartley, department of history, University of Georgia (Athens). In addition, reference was made to official returns supplied to ICPSR by the various secretaries of state in conjunction with the ICPSR effort to maintain its continuing collection of election materials. The returns obtained from Bartley and Graham, and the secretary of state offices, were compared with published reports of the election outcomes (notably state manuals and the *America Votes* series) to verify the completeness and accuracy of the returns.

PRESENTATION OF RETURNS

The returns for Senate primaries are arranged alphabetically by state and in chronological order by class of senator within each state listing. *(See "Senate's Three Classes," p. 1231.)* Candidates are listed in descending order, with the candidate receiving the greatest number of popular votes listed first. Percentage of the total vote is listed for each candidate who received *at least 5 percent* of the total vote cast.

Primaries for special elections to fill vacancies and runoff primaries are designated in the returns. For southern states prior to 1974, Republican primary results have been included, whenever available.

NAMES, VOTE TOTALS, AND PERCENTAGES

The names of senatorial primary candidates are listed as they appeared in the source materials. In a few cases, first names are not known. In some cases the full names of candidates (instead of shortened forms) have been used for consistency across elections.

For pre-1976 primary elections included in this section, the ICPSR computed statewide vote totals for each candidate. *(See box, ICPSR Historical Election Returns File, p. xvi.)* Percentages of the total vote were calculated on the basis of each candidate's proportion of the *total number of votes cast* for all candidates. Percentages have been calculated to two decimal places and rounded to one place. Due to rounding and the scattered votes of minor candidates, percentages in individual primary races may not add up to 100.

If no vote is shown for a candidate but the percentage of total vote is listed as 100 percent, in most cases the candidates in question ran unopposed and state election officials either did not bother to put the candidate's name on the ballot or simply did not make an effort to record the total number of votes.

When Senate primary elections were held under a preferential voting system and the use of second choice votes was required to determine a winner, the symbol ✔ appears next to the winner's name. *(See "Preferential Primaries, p. 130, Vol. I.)*

There were a number of unusual cases in the history of southern Senate primaries in which the nominee of one or both major parties was chosen by a party committee rather than in a primary. In these cases, the names of the nominees will appear in the primary returns along with a footnote indicating the particular circumstances. Where no primary is indicated for a year in which a state elected a senator, it generally means that party conventions chose the nominees. Notes at the end of a state's listing explain other unusual circumstances.

A Senate Primary Candidates Index is located on pages I-120 to I-128.

Senate Primary Election Returns, 1920–2000

ALABAMA

Candidates	Votes	%
Class 2		

1920   Democratic Special Primary

J. Thomas Heflin (D)	49,554✔	37.9
White (D)	34,854	26.6
O'Neal (D)	33,174	25.4
Rushton (D)	13,232	10.1

Democratic Second Choice

White (D)	12,699	36.5
J. Thomas Heflin (D)	11,062	31.8
Rushton (D)	7,316	21.0
O'Neal (D)	3,691	10.6

1924   Democratic Primary

J. Thomas Heflin (D)		100.0

1930   Democratic Primary

John H. Bankhead II (D)	102,462	63.9
Fred I. Thompson (D)	57,809	36.1

1936   Democratic Primary

John H. Bankhead II (D)	178,500	81.1
H. L. Anderson (D)	41,673	18.9

1942   Democratic Primary

John H. Bankhead II (D)		100.0

1946   Democratic Special Primary

John Sparkman (D)	85,049	50.1
James A. Simpson (D)	46,762	27.6
Frank W. Boykin (D)	35,982	21.2

1948   Democratic Primary

John Sparkman (D)	235,464	75.7
Philip J. Hamm (D)	61,308	19.7

1954   Democratic Primary

John Sparkman (D)	323,877	58.3
Laurie C. Battle (D)	208,166	37.4

1960   Democratic Primary

John Sparkman (D)	335,722	83.1
John G. Crommelin Jr. (D)	51,571	12.8

1966   Democratic Primary

John Sparkman (D)	378,295	57.0
Frank E. Dixon (D)	133,139	20.1
John G. Crommelin Jr. (D)	114,622	17.3
Mrs. Frank R. Stewart (D)	37,889	5.7

1972   Republican Primary

Winton M. "Red" Blount (R)	27,736	54.2
James D. Martin (R)	16,800	32.8
Bert Nettles (R)	5,765	11.3

Democratic Primary

John Sparkman (D)	331,818	50.3
Melba T. Allen (D)	194,690	29.5
Lambert C. Mims (D)	87,461	13.3

1978   Republican Primary

James D. Martin (R)[1]		100.0

Democratic Primary

Howell Heflin (D)	369,270	43.3
Walter Flowers (D)	236,894	27.8
John Baker (D)	191,110	22.4

Democratic Runoff

Howell Heflin (D)	556,685	64.9
Walter Flowers (D)	300,654	35.1

1984   Republican Primary

Albert Lee Smith Jr. (R)	27,304	61.8
Doug Carter (R)	8,067	18.3
Joseph Keith (R)	5,171	11.7
Clint Wilkes (R)	3,644	8.2

Democratic Primary

Howell Heflin (D)	399,817	83.2
Charles Wayne Borden (D)	47,462	9.9
Mrs. Frank Ross Stewart (D)	33,114	6.9

1990	**Republican Primary**		
	Bill Cabaniss (R)		*100.0*
	Democratic Primary		
	Howell Heflin (D)	540,876	*81.4*
	Mrs. Frank Ross Stewart (D)	123,508	*18.6*
1996	**Republican Primary**		
	Jeff Sessions (R)	82,373	*37.8*
	Sid McDonald (R)	47,320	*21.7*
	Charles Woods (R)	24,409	*11.2*
	Frank McRight (R)	21,964	*10.1*
	Walter D. Clark (R)	18,745	*8.6*
	Jimmy Blake (R)	15,385	*7.1*
	Republican Runoff		
	Jeff Sessions (R)	81,622	*59.3*
	Sid McDonald (R)	56,131	*40.7*
	Democratic Primary		
	Roger Bedford (D)	141,360	*44.8*
	Glen Browder (D)	91,203	*28.9*
	Natalie Davis (D)	71,588	*22.7*
	Democratic Runoff		
	Roger Bedford (D)	141,747	*61.6*
	Glen Browder (D)	88,415	*38.4*

Class 3

1920	**Democratic Primary**		
	Oscar W. Underwood (D)	66,916	*50.3*
	Musgrove (D)	56,257	*42.3*
	Weakley (D)	9,766	*7.4*
	Democratic Second Choice		
	Weakley (D)	21,199	*74.4*
	Musgrove (D)	5,172	*18.2*
	Oscar W. Underwood (D)	2,129	*7.5*
1926	**Democratic Primary**		
	Hugo L. Black (D)	71,916✔	*33.4*
	John H. Bankhead II (D)	49,841	*23.1*
	Mayfield (D)	34,326	*15.9*
	Musgrove (D)	30,454	*14.1*
	Thomas E. Kilby (D)	29,123	*13.5*
	Democratic Second Choice		
	Mayfield (D)	16,668	*24.9*
	John H. Bankhead II (D)	14,024	*21.0*
	Hugo L. Black (D)	12,961	*19.4*
	Musgrove (D)	12,598	*18.9*
	Thomas E. Kilby (D)	10,587	*15.8*
1932	**Democratic Primary**		
	Hugo L. Black (D)	92,930	*49.7*
	Thomas E. Kilby (D)	57,875	*30.9*
	John Morgan Burns (D)	15,528	*8.3*

	Charles C. McCall (D)	11,376	*6.1*
	Henry L. Anderson (D)	9,467	*5.1*
	Democratic Runoff		
	Hugo L. Black (D)	103,453	*58.3*
	Thomas E. Kilby (D)	74,039	*41.7*
1938	**Democratic Special Primary**		
	Lister Hill (D)	90,601	*61.8*
	J. Thomas Heflin (D)	50,189	*34.3*
1938	**Democratic Primary**		
	Lister Hill (D)		*100.0*
1944	**Democratic Primary**		
	Lister Hill (D)	126,372	*55.5*
	James A. Simpson (D)	101,176	*44.5*
1950	**Democratic Primary**		
	Lister Hill (D)	✔	
1956	**Democratic Primary**		
	Lister Hill (D)	247,519	*68.2*
	John G. Crommelin Jr. (D)	115,440	*31.8*
1962	**Democratic Primary**		
	Lister Hill (D)	363,613	*73.7*
	Donald G. Hallmark (D)	72,855	*14.8*
	John G. Crommelin Jr. (D)	56,822	*11.5*
1968	**Democratic Primary**		
	James B. Allen (D)	224,483	*41.9*
	Armistead I. Selden (D)	190,283	*35.5*
	Bob Smith (D)	72,928	*13.6*
	James E. Folsom (D)	32,004	*6.0*
	Democratic Runoff		
	James B. Allen (D)	196,511	*50.5*
	Armistead I. Selden (D)	192,448	*49.5*
1974	**Democratic Primary**		
	James B. Allen (D)	572,584	*82.8*
	John Taylor (D)	118,848	*17.2*
1978[2]	**Republican Special Primary**		
	George Nichols (R)[3]	15,637	*72.5*
	Elvin McCary (R)	5,941	*27.5*
	Democratic Special Primary		
	Maryon Pittman Allen (D)	334,758	*44.6*
	Donald W. Stewart (D)	259,795	*34.6*
	Ted Taylor (D)	70,894	*9.4*
	Dan Wiley (D)	66,689	*8.9*
	Democratic Special Runoff		
	Donald W. Stewart (D)	502,346	*57.2*
	Maryon Pittman Allen (D)	375,894	*42.8*

1980	Republican Primary		
	Jeremiah Denton (R)	73,708	63.8
	Armistead Selden (R)	41,825	36.2
	Democratic Primary		
	Donald W. Stewart (D)	222,540	48.6
	Jim Folsom Jr. (D)	163,196	35.7
	Finis St. John (D)	51,260	11.2
	Democratic Runoff		
	Jim Folsom Jr. (D)	204,486	50.6
	Donald W. Stewart (D)	199,428	49.4
1986	**Republican Primary**		
	Jeremiah Denton (R)	29,805	88.5
	Richard W. Vickers (R)	3,854	11.5
	Democratic Primary		
	Richard C. Shelby (D)	420,155	51.3
	James B. Allen Jr. (D)	284,206	34.7
	Ted McLaughlin (D)	70,784	8.6
1992	**Republican Primary**		
	Richard Sellers (R)		100.0
	Democratic Primary		
	Richard C. Shelby (D)	304,957	61.5
	Chris McNair (D)	136,836	27.6
	Bob Miller (D)	28,432	5.7
	Mrs. Frank Ross Stewart (D)	25,956	5.2
1998	**Republican Primary**		
	Richard C. Shelby (R)		100.0
	Democratic Primary		
	Clayton Suddith (D)		100.0

Alabama

1. Martin withdrew after the primary to run for the short-term Senate seat. He was not replaced.

2. A special election was held in 1978 to fill the remaining two years of the term of Sen. James B. Allen (D), who died June 1, 1978.

3. Nichols withdrew after the primary and James D. Martin was substituted by the state committee.

ALASKA[1]

	Candidates	Votes	%
	Class 2		
1958[2]	**Republican Primary**		
	R. E. Robertson (R)		100.0
	Democratic Primary		
	E. L. Bartlett (D)		100.0
1960	**Republican Primary**		
	Lee L. McKinley (R)	8,867	68.2
	Lawrence M. Brayton (R)	4,131	31.8

	Democratic Primary		
	E. L. Bartlett (D)		100.0
1966	**Republican Primary**		
	Lee L. McKinley (R)	9,310	55.8
	Lawrence M. Brayton (R)	5,492	32.9
	Maxine B. Whaley (R)	1,866	11.2
	Democratic Primary		
	E. L. Bartlett (D)	27,994	87.2
	T. J. Bichsel (D)	1,864	5.8
1970[3]	**Republican Special Primary**		
	Ted Stevens (R)	39,062	96.7
	Democratic Special Primary		
	Wendell P. Kay (R)	16,729	56.8
	Joe Josephson (R)	12,730	43.2
1972	**Republican Primary**		
	Ted Stevens (R)		100.0
	Democratic Primary		
	Gene Guess (D)		100.0
1978	**Republican Primary**		
	Ted Stevens (R)		100.0
	Democratic Primary		
	Donald W. Hobbs (D)	10,589	55.0
	Joseph A. Sonneman (D)	8,662	45.0
1984	**Republican Primary**		
	Ted Stevens (R)	65,552	100.0
	Democratic Primary		
	John E. Havelock (D)	19,074	65.5
	Dave Carlson (D)	4,620	15.9
	Michael Beasley (D)	2,443	8.4
	Joe Tracanna (D)	1,661	5.7
1990	**Republican Primary**		
	Ted Stevens (R)	81,968	70.2
	Robert M. Bird (R)	34,824	29.8
	Democratic Primary		
	Michael Beasley (D)	12,371	57.0
	Tom Taggart (D)	9,329	43.0
1996	**Republican Primary**		
	Ted Stevens (R)	71,043	67.7
	Dave W. Cuddy (R)	32,994	31.5
	Democratic Primary		
	Theresa Obermeyer (D)	4,072	33.8
	Joseph A. Sonneman (D)	2,643	21.9
	Michael Beasley (D)	1,968	16.3
	Henry J. Blake Jr. (D)	1,157	9.6

Lawrence Freiberger (D)	921	*7.6*
Frank Vondersaar (D)	655	*5.4*
Robert Alan Gigler (D)	631	*5.2*

Green Primary

Jed Whittaker (GREEN)	3,751	*100.0*

Class 3

1958[2]   **Republican Primary**

Mike Stepovich (R)		100.0

Democratic Primary

Ernest Gruening (D)		*100.0*

1962   **Republican Primary**

Ted Stevens (R)	11,000	*72.5*
Frank Cook (R)	4,175	*27.5*

Democratic Primary

Ernest Gruening (D)	18,525	*86.3*
R. L. Veach (D)	2,946	*13.7*

1968   **Republican Primary**

Elmer Rasmuson (R)	10,320	*53.1*
Ted Stevens (R)	9,111	*46.9*

Democratic Primary

Mike Gravel (D)	17,971	*52.9*
Ernest Gruening (D)	16,015	*47.1*

1974   **Republican Primary**

C. R. Lewis (R)	21,065	*52.7*
Terry Miller (R)	16,336	*40.8*
Red Stevens (R)	2,207	*5.5*

Democratic Primary

Mike Gravel (D)	22,834	*54.3*
Gene Guess (D)	15,090	*35.9*
Richard J. Greuel (D)	3,367	*8.0*

1980   **Republican Primary**

Frank H. Murkowski (R)	16,292	*59.0*
Arthur R. Kennedy (R)	5,527	*20.0*
Morris Thompson (R)	3,635	*13.2*

Democratic Primary

Clark S. Gruening (D)	39,719	*54.9*
Mike Gravel (D)	31,504	*43.5*

1986   **Republican Primary**

Frank H. Murkowski (R)		*100.0*

Democratic Primary

Glenn Olds (D)	36,995	*75.0*
Bill Barnes (D)	4,871	*9.9*
Dave Carlson (D)	4,211	*8.5*

Libertarian Primary

Chuck House (LIBERT)		*100.0*

1992[4]   **Republican Primary**

Frank H. Murkowski (R)	37,486	*80.5*
Jed Whittaker (R)	9,065	*19.5*

Democratic Primary

Tony Smith (D)	33,162	*48.8*
William L. Hensley (D)	29,586	*43.5*

Green Primary

Mary E. Jodan (GREEN)	5,989	*100.0*

1998   **Republican Primary**

Frank H. Murkowski (R)	76,649	*71.8*
William L. Hale (R)	6,313	*5.9*

Democratic Primary

Joseph A. Sonneman (D)	10,721	*10.0*
Frank Vondersaar (D)	6,342	*5.9*

Green Primary

Jefferey Gottlieb (GREEN)	5,989	*100.0*

Alaska

1. In Alaska's so-called "jungle" primaries, all candidates for an office appeared together on the same ballot with their parties designated. Nominations went to the Republican and Democrat receiving the most votes for the office. Percentages were calculated here as if candidates had run in separate party primaries.

2. Alaska became a state Jan. 3, 1959. The first Senate elections for that state were for unspecified terms. The Senate later determined that Sen. Bartlett would serve two years (Class 2) and Sen. Gruening, four (Class 3).

3. A special election was held in 1970 to fill the remaining two years of the term of Sen. E. L. Bartlett (D), who died Dec. 11, 1968. The first two years of the vacancy were filled by appointee Ted Stevens (R).

4. In 1992 the Republican primary was a closed primary with only candidates from that party on the ballot. All other parties ran on a multiparty ballot with nominations going to the candidate with the highest vote in each party.

ARIZONA

Candidates	Votes	%

Class 1

1958   **Republican Primary**

Barry Goldwater (R)		*100.0*

Democratic Primary

Ernest W. McFarland (D)	111,429	*72.5*
Stephen W. Langmade (D)	42,199	*27.5*

1964   **Republican Primary**

Paul Fannin (R)		*100.0*

Democratic Primary

Roy L. Elson (D)	76,697	*41.4*
Renz L. Jennings (D)	64,331	*34.7*
Howard V. Peterson (D)	22,424	*12.1*
George Gavin (D)	10,291	*5.6*

1970	**Republican Primary**		
	Paul Fannin (R)		100.0
	Democratic Primary		
	Sam Grossman (D)	78,006	65.2
	John Kruglick (D)	27,324	22.8
	H. L. Kelly (D)	14,238	11.9
1976	**Republican Primary**		
	Sam Steiger (R)	102,843	52.5
	John B. Conlan (R)	93,033	47.5
	Democratic Primary		
	Dennis DeConcini (D)	121,423	53.4
	Carolyn Warner (D)	71,612	31.5
	Wade Church (D)	34,266	15.1
	Libertarian Primary		
	Allan Norwitz (LIBERT)		100.0
1982	**Republican Primary**		
	Pete Dunn (R)	97,391	55.1
	Dean Sellers (R)	79,375	44.9
	Democratic Primary		
	Dennis DeConcini (D)	140,328	84.4
	Caroline P. Killeen (D)	25,909	15.6
	Libertarian Primary		
	Randall Clamons (LIBERT)		100.0
1988	**Republican Primary**		
	Keith DeGreen (R)		100.0
	Democratic Primary		
	Dennis DeConcini (D)		100.0
1994	**Republican Primary**		
	Jon Kyl (R)	231,275	99.0
	Democratic Primary		
	Sam Coopersmith (D)	82,057	32.2
	Richard Mahoney (D)	81,998	32.1
	Cindy Resnick (D)	75,563	29.6
	Dave Moss (D)	15,612	6.1
	Libertarian Primary		
	Scott Grainger (LIBERT)	5,424	100.0
2000	**Republican Primary**		
	Jon Kyl (R)	255,659	100.0
	Democratic Primary[1]		
	Stuart Starky	3,245	67.7
	Ronald E. Maynard	1,545	32.3

Class 3

1956	**Republican Primary**		
	Ross F. Jones (R)	31,246	79.3
	Albert H. Mackenzie (R)	8,147	20.7
	Democratic Primary		
	Carl Hayden (D)	99,859	82.4
	Robert E. Miller (D)	21,370	17.6
1962	**Republican Primary**		
	Evan Mecham (R)	40,300	59.0
	Stephen Shadegg (R)	27,965	41.0
	Democratic Primary		
	Carl Hayden (D)	117,688	76.5
	W. Lee McLane (D)	36,158	23.5
1968	**Republican Primary**		
	Barry Goldwater (R)		100.0
	Democratic Primary		
	Roy L. Elson (D)	95,231	62.8
	Bob Kennedy (D)	41,397	27.3
	Dick Herbert (D)	15,061	9.9
1974	**Republican Primary**		
	Barry Goldwater (R)		100.0
	Democratic Primary		
	Jonathan Marshall (D)	79,225	53.6
	George Oglesby (D)	36,262	24.5
	William M. Feighan (D)	32,449	21.9
1980	**Republican Primary**		
	Barry Goldwater (R)		100.0
	Democratic Primary		
	Bill Schulz (D)	97,520	55.4
	James F. McNulty Jr. (D)	58,894	33.4
	Frank DePaoli (D)	19,259	10.9
	Libertarian Primary		
	Fred Esser (LIBERT)		100.0
1986	**Republican Primary**		
	John McCain (R)		100.0
	Democratic Primary		
	Richard Kimball (D)		100.0
1992	**Republican Primary**		
	John McCain (R)		100.0
	Democratic Primary		
	Claire Sargent (D)	124,174	56.8
	Truman Spangrud (D)	94,326	43.2

		Votes	%

1998   **Republican Primary**

John McCain (R) — 206,490 — 99.7

Democratic Primary

Ed Ranger (D) — 100,822 — 100.0

Arizona
1. Democrats only had write-in candidates in 2000.

ARKANSAS

Candidates	Votes	%

Class 2

1924   **Democratic Primary**

Joseph T. Robinson (D) — — 100.0

1930   **Democratic Primary**

Joseph T. Robinson (D) — 167,167 — 76.6
Tom W. Campbell (D) — 51,085 — 23.4

1936   **Democratic Primary**

Joseph T. Robinson (D) — 170,356 — 72.7
Cleveland Holland (D) — 42,541 — 18.2
J. Rosser Venable (D) — 21,352 — 9.1

1937   **Democratic Primary**

Carl E. Bailey (D)[1]

1942   **Democratic Primary**

Jack Holt (D) — 54,185 — 32.1
John L. McClellan (D) — 53,729 — 31.8
Clyde Ellis (D) — 34,264 — 20.3
David D. Terry (D) — 26,911 — 15.9

Democratic Runoff

John L. McClellan (D) — 134,277 — 61.7
Jack Holt (D) — 83,516 — 38.4

1948   **Democratic Primary**

John L. McClellan (D) — — 100.0

1954   **Democratic Primary**

John L. McClellan (D) — — 100.0

1960   **Democratic Primary**

John L. McClellan (D) — — 100.0

1966   **Democratic Primary**

John L. McClellan (D) — 310,526 — 77.2
Foster Johnson (D) — 91,746 — 22.8

1972   **Republican Primary**

Wayne H. Babbitt (R) — — 100.0

Democratic Primary

John L. McClellan (D) — 220,588 — 44.7
David Pryor (D) — 204,058 — 41.4
Ted Boswell (D) — 62,496 — 12.7

Democratic Runoff

John L. McClellan (D) — 242,983 — 52.0
David Pryor (D) — 224,262 — 48.0

1978   **Republican Primary**

Tom Kelly (R) — — 100.0

Democratic Primary

David Pryor (D) — 198,039 — 34.3
Jim Guy Tucker (D) — 187,568 — 32.5
Ray Thornton (D) — 184,095 — 31.9

Democratic Runoff

David Pryor (D) — 265,525 — 54.9
Jim Guy Tucker (D) — 218,026 — 45.1

1984   **Republican Primary**

Ed Bethune (R) — — 100.0

Democratic Primary

David Pryor (D) — — 100.0

1990   **Democratic Primary**

David Pryor (D) — — 100.0

1996   **Republican Primary**

Mike Huckabee (R)[2] — — 100.0

Democratic Primary

Winston Bryant (D) — 129,328 — 39.3
Lu Hardin (D) — 71,889 — 21.9
Bill Bristow (D) — 58,093 — 17.7
Sandy McMath (D) — 42,303 — 12.9
Kevin Smith (D) — 21,774 — 6.6

Democratic Runoff

Winston Bryant (D) — 123,273 — 54.7
Lu Hardin (D) — 101,901 — 45.3

Class 3

1920   **Democratic Primary**

Thaddeus H. Caraway (D) — 92,411 — 62.9
Charles F. Kirby (D) — 54,527 — 37.1

1926   **Democratic Primary**

Thaddeus H. Caraway (D) — — 100.0

1932   **Democratic Primary**

Hattie W. Caraway (D) — 127,702 — 44.7
O. L. Bodenhamer (D) — 63,858 — 22.4
Vincent M. Miles (D) — 30,423 — 10.7
Charles H. Brough (D) — 26,207 — 9.2
William F. Kirby (D) — 21,448 — 7.5

1938   **Democratic Primary**

Hattie W. Caraway (D) — 145,472 — 51.0
John L. McClellan (D) — 134,708 — 47.3

1944   **Democratic Primary**

J. William Fulbright (D)	67,228	36.2
Homer M. Adkins (D)	49,795	26.8
T. H. Barton (D)	43,053	23.2
Hattie W. Caraway (D)	24,881	13.4

Democratic Runoff

J. William Fulbright (D)	117,121	57.9
Homer M. Adkins (D)	85,163	42.1

1950   **Democratic Primary**

J. William Fulbright (D)	189,200	100.0

1956   **Republican Primary**

Kenneth G. Jones (R)		100.0

Democratic Primary

J. William Fulbright (D)		100.0

1962   **Democratic Primary**

J. William Fulbright (D)	253,751	66.1
Winston G. Chandler (D)	129,987	33.9

1968   **Republican Primary**

Charles T. Bernard (R)		100.0

Democratic Primary

J. William Fulbright (D)	220,684	52.9
James Johnson (D)	132,038	31.7
Bobby K. Hayes (D)	52,906	12.7

1974   **Republican Primary**

John H. Jones (R)		100.0

Democratic Primary

Dale Bumpers (D)	380,748	65.0
J. William Fulbright (D)	204,630	35.0

1980   **Republican Primary**

Bill Clark (R)		100.0

Democratic Primary

Dale Bumpers (D)		100.0

1986   **Republican Primary**

Asa Hutchinson (R)		100.0

Democratic Primary

Dale Bumpers (D)		100.0

1992   **Republican Primary**

Mike Huckabee (R)	41,346	79.1
David Busby (R)	10,892	20.9

Democratic Primary

Dale Bumpers (D)	322,458	64.5
Julia H. Jones (D)	177,273	35.5

1998   **Republican Primary**

Fay Boozman (R)	42,621	77.8
Tom Prince (R)	12,156	22.2

Democratic Primary

Blanche Lambert Lincoln (D)	145,009	45.5
Winston Bryant (D)	87,183	27.3
Scott Ferguson (D)	44,761	14.0
Nate Coulter (D)	41,848	13.1

Arkansas

1. Robinson died July 14, 1937, a few months into his new six-year term. The state committee of the Democratic Party in Arkansas selected Gov. Carl E. Bailey as the Democratic nominee to run in an Oct. 19 special election; no Democratic primary was held. Bailey lost the special election to Rep. John E. Miller, a Democrat running as an Independent. (See p. 1270.)

2. Huckabee withdrew from the Senate race May 30 to become governor. The state Republican Party selected Rep. Tim Hutchinson as the Republican nominee to run in the general election.

CALIFORNIA

Candidates	Votes	%
Class 1		

1958[1]   **Republican Primary**

Goodwin J. Knight (R)	790,939	49.1
George Christopher (R)	558,245	34.7
Clair Engle (D)	173,845	10.8

Democratic Primary

Clair Engle (D)	1,558,622	70.8
Goodwin J. Knight (R)	385,170	17.5
George Christopher (R)	221,783	10.1

1964   **Republican Primary**

George Murphy (R)	1,121,591	54.1
Leland M. Kaiser (R)	689,323	33.3
Fred Hall (R)	261,036	12.6

Democratic Primary

Pierre Salinger (D)	1,177,517	44.3
Alan Cranston (D)	1,037,748	39.0
George McLain (D)	180,405	6.8

1970   **Republican Primary**

George Murphy (R)	1,325,271	64.3
Norton Simon (R)	670,702	32.5

Democratic Primary

John V. Tunney (D)	1,010,812	41.6
George E. Brown (D)	812,463	33.4
Kenneth Hahn (D)	417,970	17.2

American Independent Primary

Charles C. Ripley (AM I)	14,115	65.0
John Ortman (AM I)	7,600	34.9

Peace and Freedom Primary

Robert Scheer (PFP)		100.0

1976 Republican Primary

S. I. Hayakawa (R)	886,743	38.2
Robert H. Finch (R)	614,240	26.5
Alphonzo E. Bell (R)	532,969	23.0
John L. Harmer (R)	197,252	8.5

Democratic Primary

John V. Tunney (D)	1,774,879	53.8
Tom Hayden (D)	1,210,637	36.7

American Independent Primary

Jack McCoy (AM I)		100.0

Peace and Freedom Primary

David Wald (PFP)		100.0

1982 Republican Primary

Pete Wilson (R)	851,292	37.5
Paul N. McCloskey (R)	577,267	25.5
Barry M. Goldwater Jr. (R)	408,308	18.0
Robert K. Dornan (R)	181,970	8.0

Democratic Primary

Edmund G. Brown Jr. (D)	1,392,660	50.7
Gore Vidal (D)	415,366	15.1
Paul B. Carpenter (D)	415,198	15.1
Daniel K. Whitehurst (D)	167,574	6.1

American Independent Primary

Theresa Dietrich (AM I)		100.0

Peace and Freedom Primary

David Wald (PFP)		100.0

Libertarian Primary

Joseph Fuhrig (LIBERT)		100.0

1988 Republican Primary

Pete Wilson (R)		100.0

Democratic Primary

Leo T. McCarthy (D)	2,367,067	81.7
John H. Abbott (D)	220,331	7.6
Robert J. Banuelos (D)	163,882	5.7
Charles Greene (D)	146,307	5.0

American Independent Primary

Merton D. Short (AM I)		100.0

Libertarian Primary

Jack Dean (LIBERT)		100.0

Peace and Freedom Primary

M. Elizabeth Munoz (PFP)	3,701	58.5
Gloria Garcia (PFP)	2,623	41.5

1992[2] Republican Special Primary

John Seymour (R)	1,216,096	51.2
William E. Dannemeyer (R)	638,279	26.9
Jim Trinity (R)	306,182	12.9
William B. Allen (R)	216,177	9.1

Democratic Special Primary

Dianne Feinstein (D)	1,775,730	57.8
Gray Davis (D)	1,009,761	32.8

American Independent Special Primary

Paul Meeuwenberg (AM I)		100.0

Libertarian Special Primary

Richard B. Boddie (LIBERT)		100.0

Peace and Freedom Special Primary

Gerald Horne (PFP)	5,681	64.0
Jamie Mangia (PFP)	3,195	36.0

1994 Republican Primary

Michael Huffington (R)	1,072,558	55.4
William E. Dannemeyer (R)	565,864	29.3
Kate Squires (R)	202,387	10.5

Democratic Primary

Dianne Feinstein (D)	1,635,837	74.2
Ted J. Andromidas (D)	297,128	13.5
Daniel D. O'Dowd (D)	271,615	12.3

American Independent Primary

Paul Meeuwenberg (AM I)	17,747	100.0

Libertarian Primary

Richard B. Boddie (LIBERT)	13,596	100.0

Green Primary

Barbara Blong (GREEN)	9,006	52.8
Kent W. Smith (GREEN)	3,846	22.6
"None of the above"	4,203	24.6

Peace and Freedom Primary

Elizabeth Cervantes Barron (PFP)	3,487	70.7
Larry D. Hampshire (PFP)	1,445	29.3

2000[3] Republican Primary

Tom Campbell (R)	1,697,208	56.2
Ron Haynes (R)	679,034	22.5
Bill Horn (R)	453,630	15.0

Democratic Primary

Dianne Feinstein (D)	3,759,560	95.4
Michael Schmier (D)	181,104	4.6

Libertarian Primary

Gail Katherine Lightfoot (LIBERT)	120,622	100.0

Green Primary

Medea Susan Benjamin (GREEN)	99,716	74.0
Jan B. Tucker (GREEN)	35,124	26.0

Reform Primary

Jose Luis "Joe" Camahort (REF)	46,278	70.3
Valli Sharpe-Geisier (REF)	19,516	29.7

American Independent Primary

Diane Beall Templin (AM I)	38,836	100.0

Natural Law

Brian M. Rees (NL)	26,382	100.0

Class 3

1956[1] **Republican Primary**

Thomas H. Kuchel (R)	1,332,074	90.4

Democratic Primary

Richard Richards (D)	1,004,336	53.4
Thomas H. Kuchel (R)	494,066	26.2
Samuel W. Yorty (D)	383,813	20.4

Prohibition Party Primary

Ray Gourley (P)		100.0

1962 **Republican Primary**

Thomas H. Kuchel (R)	1,357,975	75.0
Lloyd Wright (R)	247,300	13.7
Howard Jarvis (R)	180,768	10.0

Democratic Primary

Richard Richards (D)	1,674,563	82.6
Gabriel Green (D)	171,379	8.5
J. F. Coleman (D)	170,296	8.4

1968 **Republican Primary**

Max Rafferty (R)	1,112,947	50.1
Thomas H. Kuchel (R)	1,043,315	46.9

Democratic Primary

Alan Cranston (D)	1,681,825	59.0
Anthony C. Beilenson (D)	644,844	22.6
Walter R. Buchanan (D)	227,798	8.0
William M. Bennett (D)	207,720	7.3

Peace and Freedom Primary

Paul Jacobs (PFP)		100.0

1974 **Republican Primary**

H. L. "Bill" Richardson (R)	1,061,986	64.6
Earl W. Brian (R)	273,636	16.7
James E. Johnson (R)	118,715	7.2
William H. Reinholz (R)	107,217	6.5

Democratic Primary

Alan Cranston (D)	2,262,574	83.5
Howard L. Gifford (D)	318,080	11.7

American Independent Primary

Jack McCoy (AM I)		100.0

Peace and Freedom Primary

Gayle M. Justice (PFP)		100.0

1980 **Republican Primary**

Paul Gann (R)	934,433	40.0
Samuel W. Yorty (R)	668,583	28.6
John G. Schmitz (R)	442,839	19.0

Democratic Primary

Alan Cranston (D)	2,608,746	79.9
Richard Morgan (D)	350,394	10.7

American Independent Primary

James C. Griffin (AM I)		100.0

Peace and Freedom Primary

David Wald (PFP)		100.0

Libertarian Primary

David Bergland (LIBERT)		100.0

1986 **Republican Primary**

Ed Zschau (R)	737,384	37.1
Bruce Herschensohn (R)	587,852	29.6
Michael D. Antonovich (R)	180,010	9.1
Bobbi Fiedler (R)	143,032	7.2
Ed Davis (R)	130,309	6.6

Democratic Primary

Alan Cranston (D)	1,807,242	80.7
Charles Greene (D)	165,594	7.4
John H. Abbott (D)	124,218	5.5

American Independent Primary

Edward B. Vallen (AM I)		100.0

Libertarian Primary

Breck McKinley (LIBERT)		100.0

Peace and Freedom Primary

Paul Kangas (PFP)	2,495	51.6
Lenni Brenner (PFP)	2,344	48.4

1992 **Republican Primary**

Bruce Herschensohn (R)	956,146	38.2
Tom Campbell (R)	895,970	35.8
Sonny Bono (R)	417,848	16.7

Democratic Primary

Barbara Boxer (D)	1,339,126	43.7
Leo T. McCarthy (D)	935,209	30.5
Mel Levine (D)	667,359	21.8

American Independent Primary

Jerome McCready (AM I)		100.0

	Candidates	Votes	%
	Libertarian Primary		
	June R. Genis (LIBERT)		*100.0*
	Peace and Freedom Primary		
	Genevieve Torres (PFP)	5,492	*60.3*
	Shirley Lee (PFP)	3,610	*39.7*
1998[3]	**Republican Primary**		
	Matt Fong (R)	1,292,662	*45.3*
	Darrell Issa (R)	1,143,107	*40.0*
	Frank Riggs (R)	295,886	*10.4*
	Democratic Primary		
	Barbara Boxer (D)	2,574,284	*92.2*
	John Pinkerton (D)	219,250	*7.8*
	Libertarian Primary		
	Ted Brown (LIBERT)	67,408	*100.0*
	Peace and Freedom Primary		
	Ophie C. Beltran (PFP)	52,306	*100.0*
	Reform		
	Timothy R. Erich (REF)	45,601	*100.0*
	American Independent Primary		
	H. Joseph Perrin Sr. (AM I)	24,026	*100.0*
	Natural Law		
	Brian M. Rees (NL)	23,943	*100.0*

California

1. California's cross-filing law permitted a candidate to enter both the Democratic and Republican primaries. The law was repealed after 1958.

2. A special election was held in 1992 to fill the remaining two years of the term of Sen. Pete Wilson (R), who resigned Jan. 7, 1991, after he was elected governor. The first two years of the vacancy were filled by appointee John Seymour (R).

3. In 1998 California instituted an open primary with all candidates running on a single, multiparty ballot with their parties designated. Nominations went to the candidate with the highest vote in each party. Percentages were calculated here as if candidates had run in separate party primaries.

COLORADO

	Candidates	Votes	%
	Class 2		
1960	**Republican Primary**		
	Gordon Allott (R)		*100.0*
	Democratic Primary		
	Robert L. Knous (D)		*100.0*
1966	**Republican Primary**		
	Gordon Allott (R)		*100.0*
	Democratic Primary		
	Roy Romer (D)		*100.0*

	Candidates	Votes	%
1972	**Republican Primary**		
	Gordon Allott (R)		*100.0*
	Democratic Primary		
	Floyd K. Haskell (D)	77,574	*58.8*
	Anthony F. Vollack (D)	54,298	*41.2*
1978	**Republican Primary**		
	William L. Armstrong (R)	108,573	*73.4*
	Jack Swigert (R)	39,247	*26.6*
	Democratic Primary		
	Floyd K. Haskell (D)		*100.0*
1984	**Republican Primary**		
	William L. Armstrong (R)	105,870	*100.0*
	Democratic Primary		
	Nancy Dick (D)	78,248	*51.0*
	Carlos F. Lucero (D)	75,277	*49.0*
1990	**Republican Primary**		
	Hank Brown (R)		*100.0*
	Democratic Primary		
	Josie Heath (D)	116,099	*58.6*
	Carlos F. Lucero (D)	82,173	*41.4*
1996	**Republican Primary**		
	Wayne Allard (R)	115,064	*56.8*
	Gale Norton (R)	87,394	*43.2*
	Democratic Primary		
	Tom Strickland (D)	87,294	*66.1*
	Gene Nichol (D)	44,709	*33.9*
	Class 3		
1956	**Republican Primary**		
	Dan Thornton (R)		*100.0*
	Democratic Primary		
	John A. Carroll (D)	62,688	*50.8*
	Charles Brannan (D)	60,701	*49.2*
1962	**Republican Primary**		
	Peter H. Dominick (R)		*100.0*
	Democratic Primary		
	John A. Carroll (D)		*100.0*
1968	**Republican Primary**		
	Peter H. Dominick (R)		*100.0*
	Democratic Primary		
	Stephen McNichols (D)	92,250	*58.5*
	Kenneth Montfort (D)	65,347	*41.5*

1974   **Republican Primary**

Peter H. Dominick (R)   *100.0*

Democratic Primary

Gary Hart (D)	81,161	*39.9*
Herrick S. Roth (D)	66,819	*32.9*
Martin P. Miller (D)	55,339	*27.2*

1980   **Republican Primary**

Mary E. Buchanan (R)	65,803	*30.8*
Howard W. Callaway (R)	64,256	*30.1*
Sam Zakhem (R)	42,629	*20.0*
John M. Cogswell (R)	40,651	*19.0*

Democratic Primary

Gary Hart (D)   *100.0*

1986   **Republican Primary**

Ken Kramer (R)   *100.0*

Democratic Primary

Timothy E. Wirth (D)   *100.0*

1992   **Republican Primary**

Terry Considine (R)   122,427   *100.0*

Democratic Primary

Ben Nighthorse Campbell (D)	117,634	*45.5*
Richard D. Lamm (D)	93,599	*36.2*
Josie Heath (D)	47,418	*18.3*

1998   **Republican Primary**

Ben Nighthorse Campbell (R)	154,702	*70.6*
Bill Eggert (R)	64,347	*29.4*

Democratic Primary

Dottie Lamm (D)	84,929	*58.0*
Gil Romero (D)	61,548	*42.0*

CONNECTICUT[1]

Candidates	Votes	%
Class 1		

1970   **Republican Primary**

Lowell P. Weicker Jr. (R)	77,057	*60.3*
John M. Lupton (R)	50,657	*39.7*

Democratic Primary

Joseph D. Duffey (D)	79,166	*43.7*
Alphonsus J. Donahue (D)	66,916	*36.8*
Edward L. Marcus (D)	35,715	*19.7*

1994   **Republican Primary**

Jerry Labriola (R)	69,972	*66.8*
Joe Bentivegna (R)	34,733	*33.2*

Class 3

1980   **Republican Primary**

James L. Buckley (R)	64,962	*56.5*
Richard C. Buzzuto (R)	50,096	*43.5*

1992   **Republican Primary**

Brook Johnson (R)	50,305	*59.4*
Christopher Burnham (R)	40,542	*40.6*

Connecticut
1. In Connecticut, party conventions nominated candidates subject to a system of "challenge" primaries that allowed defeated candidates to petition for a popular vote if they received at least 20 percent of the convention vote.

DELAWARE

Candidates	Votes	%
Class 1		

1982   **Republican Primary**

William V. Roth Jr. (R)   *100.0*

Democratic Primary

David N. Levinson (D)   *100.0*

1988   **Republican Primary**

William V. Roth Jr. (R)   *100.0*

Democratic Primary[1]

S. B. Woo (D)	20,225	*50.0*
Samuel S. Beard (D)	20,154	*50.0*

1994   **Republican Primary**

William V. Roth Jr. (R)   *100.0*

Democratic Primary

2000   **Republican Primary**

William V. Roth Jr.   *100.0*

Democratic Primary

Thomas R. Carper (D)   *100.0*

Class 2

1978[2]   **Republican Primary**

James H. Baxter (R)	12,107	*53.7*
James E. Venema (R)	10,422	*46.3*

1984   **Republican Primary**

John M. Burris (R)   *100.0*

Democratic Primary

Joseph R. Biden (D)   *100.0*

1990   **Republican Primary**

M. Jane Brady (R)   *100.0*

Democratic Primary		
Joseph R. Biden (D)		100.0

1996   Republican Primary

| Raymond J. Clatworthy (R) | 18,638 | 82.2 |
| Vance Phillips (R) | 3,307 | 14.6 |

Democratic Primary		
Joseph R. Biden (D)		100.0

Delaware
1. Data are given for the recount vote.
2. From 1972 through 1978 Delaware used a system of "challenge" primaries, in which a candidate for statewide office who received at least 35 percent of the convention vote could challenge the endorsed candidate in a primary. There was no Senate election in Delaware in 1980, the first year that the state used the direct primary system.

FLORIDA

Candidates	Votes	%
Class 1		

1922   Democratic Primary

| Park Trammell (D) | 59,232 | 66.7 |
| Albert W. Gilchrist (D) | 29,527 | 33.3 |

1928   Democratic Primary

| Park Trammell (D) | 138,534 | 58.0 |
| John W. Martin (D) | 100,454 | 42.0 |

1934   Democratic Primary

Park Trammell (D)	81,321	38.0
Claude Pepper (D)	79,396	37.1
Charles A. Mitchell (D)	30,455	14.2
James F. Sikes (D)	14,558	6.8

Democratic Runoff

| Park Trammell (D) | 103,028 | 51.0 |
| Claude Pepper (D) | 98,978 | 49.0 |

1936   Democratic Special Primary

| Charles O. Andrews (D) | 67,387 | 51.9 |
| Doyle E. Carlton (D) | 62,530 | 48.1 |

1940   Democratic Primary

Charles O. Andrews (D)	179,195	40.9
Jerry W. Carter (D)	80,869	18.5
B. MacFadden (D)	71,487	16.3
Fred P. Cone (D)	68,584	15.7
Charles F. Coe (D)	33,463	7.6

Democratic Runoff

| Charles O. Andrews (D) | 312,293 | 69.4 |
| Jerry W. Carter (D) | 137,641 | 30.6 |

1946   Democratic Primary

| Spessard L. Holland (D) | 204,352 | 60.7 |
| Robert A. "Lex" Green (D) | 109,040 | 32.4 |

1952   Democratic Primary

| Spessard L. Holland (D) | 485,515 | 84.2 |
| William A. Gaston (D) | 91,011 | 15.8 |

1958   Republican Primary

| Leland Hyzer (R) | | 100.0 |

Democratic Primary

| Spessard L. Holland (D) | 408,084 | 55.9 |
| Claude Pepper (D) | 321,377 | 44.1 |

1964   Republican Primary

| Claude R. Kirk Jr. (R) | | 100.0 |

Democratic Primary

| Spessard L. Holland (D) | 676,014 | 70.0 |
| Brailey Odham (D) | 289,454 | 30.0 |

1970   Republican Primary

| William C. Cramer (R) | 220,553 | 62.5 |
| G. Harrold Carswell (R) | 121,281 | 34.4 |

Democratic Primary

Farris Bryant (D)	240,222	32.9
Lawton Chiles (D)	188,300	25.8
Fred Schultz (D)	175,745	24.1
Al Hastings (D)	91,948	12.6

Democratic Runoff

| Lawton Chiles (D) | 474,420 | 65.7 |
| Farris Bryant (D) | 247,211 | 34.3 |

1976   Republican Primary

John Grady (R)	164,644	54.5
Walter Sims (R)	74,684	24.7
Helen S. Hansel (R)	62,718	20.8

Democratic Primary

| Lawton Chiles (D) | | 100.0 |

1982   Republican Primary

Van B. Poole	154,158	41.6
David H. Bludworth	116,030	31.3
George Snyder	100,607	27.1

Republican Runoff

| Van B. Poole | 131,638 | 58.1 |
| David H. Bludworth | 95,024 | 41.9 |

Democratic Primary

| Lawton Chiles (D) | | 100.0 |

1988   Republican Primary

| Connie Mack (R) | 405,296 | 61.8 |
| Robert W. Merkle (R) | 250,730 | 38.2 |

Democratic Primary

| Bill Gunter (D) | 383,721 | 38.0 |
| Buddy McKay (D) | 263,946 | 26.1 |

Dan Mica (D)	179,524	17.8
Patricia Prank (D)	119,277	11.8
Claude R. Kirk Jr. (D)	51,387	5.0

Democratic Runoff

Buddy McKay (D)	369,266	52.0
Bill Gunter (D)	340,918	48.0

1994 **Republican Primary**

Connie Mack (R)		100.0

Democratic Primary

Hugh E. Rodham (D)	255,605	33.8
Mike Wiley (D)	188,551	24.9
Ellis Rubin (D)	161,386	21.3
Arturo Perez (D)	151,121	20.0

2000 **Republican Primary**

Bill McCollum (R)	660,592	81.1
Hamilton A. S. Bartlett (R)	153,613	18.9

Democratic Primary

Bill Nelson (D)	692,147	77.5
Newall Jerome Daughtrey (D)	105,650	11.8
David B. Higginbottom (D)	95,492	10.7

Class 3

1920 **Democratic Primary**

Duncan U. Fletcher (D)	62,304	71.4
Sidney J. Catts (D)	25,007	28.6

1926 **Democratic Primary**

Duncan U. Fletcher (D)	63,760	59.5
Jerry W. Carter (D)	39,143	36.5

Democratic Second Choice

Jerry W. Carter (D)	932	53.4
Duncan U. Fletcher (D)	812	46.6

1932 **Democratic Primary**

Duncan U. Fletcher (D)		100.0

1936 **Democratic Special Primary**

Claude Pepper (D)		100.0

1938 **Democratic Primary**

Claude Pepper (D)	242,350	58.4
J. Mark Wilcox (D)	110,675	26.7
David Sholtz (D)	52,785	12.7

1944 **Republican Primary**

Miles H. Draper (R)	5,289	53.3
H. K. Gibson (R)	4,628	46.7

Democratic Primary

Claude Pepper (D)	194,445	51.3
J. Ollie Edmunds (D)	127,158	33.5
Millard B. Conklin (D)	33,317	8.8

1950 **Democratic Primary**

George A. Smathers (D)	387,215	54.8
Claude Pepper (D)	319,754	45.2

1956 **Democratic Primary**

George A. Smathers (D)	614,663	87.5
Erle Griffis (D)	87,525	12.5

1962 **Republican Primary**

Emerson H. Rupert (R)		100.0

Democratic Primary

George A. Smathers (D)	587,562	84.2
Roger L. Davis (D)	74,565	10.7
Douglas Randolph Voorhees (D)	35,832	5.1

1968 **Republican Primary**

Edward J. Gurney (R)	169,805	80.0
Herman W. Goldner (R)	42,347	20.0

Democratic Primary

Leroy Collins (D)	426,096	49.5
Earl Faircloth (D)	397,642	46.2

Democratic Runoff

Leroy Collins (D)	410,689	50.2
Earl Faircloth (D)	407,696	49.8

1974 **Republican Primary**

Jack M. Eckerd (R)	186,897	67.5
Paula Hawkins (R)	90,049	32.5

Democratic Primary

Bill Gunter (D)	236,185	29.8
Richard Stone (D)	157,301	19.8
Richard A. Pettigrew (D)	146,728	18.5
Mallory E. Horne (D)	90,684	11.4
Glenn W. Turner (D)	51,326	6.5

Democratic Runoff

Richard Stone (D)	321,683	50.8
Bill Gunter (D)	311,044	49.2

1980 **Republican Primary**

Paula Hawkins (R)	209,856	48.1
Louis Frey (R)	119,834	27.5
Ander Crenshaw (R)	54,767	12.6

Republican Runoff

Paula Hawkins (R)	293,600	61.6
Louis Frey (R)	182,911	38.4

Democratic Primary

Richard Stone (D)	355,287	32.1
Bill Gunter (D)	335,859	30.3
Buddy MacKay (D)	272,538	24.6
Richard A. Pettigrew (D)	108,154	9.8

	Democratic Runoff		
	Bill Gunter (D)	594,676	51.8
	Richard Stone (D)	554,268	48.2
1986	**Republican Primary**		
	Paula Hawkins (R)	491,953	88.7
	Jon L. Shudlick (R)	62,474	11.3
	Democratic Primary		
	Bob Graham (D)	851,586	85.0
	Robert P. Kunst (D)	149,797	15.0
1992	**Republican Primary**		
	Bill Grant (R)	413,457	56.1
	Rob Quartel (R)	196,524	26.7
	Hugh Brotherton (R)	126,878	17.2
	Democratic Primary		
	Bob Graham (D)	968,618	84.3
	Jim Mahorner (D)	180,405	15.7
1998	**Republican Primary**		
	Charlie Crist (R)	365,894	66.4
	Andy Martin (R)	184,739	33.6
	Democratic Primary		
	Bob Graham (D)		100.0

GEORGIA

	Candidates	Votes	%
	Class 2		
1924	**Democratic Primary**		
	William J. Harris (D)	144,740	65.7
	Thomas W. Hardwick (D)	75,713	34.3
1930	**Democratic Primary**		
	William J. Harris (D)	162,169	77.9
	John M. Slaton (D)	46,095	22.1
1932	**Democratic Special Primary**		
	Richard B. Russell (D)	162,745	57.7
	Charles R. Crisp (D)	119,193	42.3
1936	**Democratic Primary**		
	Richard B. Russell (D)	256,154	65.5
	Eugene Talmadge (D)	134,695	34.5
1942	**Democratic Primary**		
	Richard B. Russell (D)	232,084	80.6
	Will D. Upshaw (D)	55,845	19.4
1948	**Democratic Primary**		
	Richard B. Russell (D)	703,048	100.0
1954	**Democratic Primary**		
	Richard B. Russell (D)	619,129	100.0

1960	**Democratic Primary**		
	Richard B. Russell (D)	560,256	100.0
1966	**Democratic Primary**		
	Richard B. Russell (D)	596,209	90.6
	Harry L. Hyde (D)	61,922	9.4
1972[1]	**Republican Special Primary**		
	Fletcher Thompson (R)	70,859	100.0
	Republican Primary		
	Fletcher Thompson (R)	71,464	91.1
	Democratic Special Primary		
	David H. Gambrell (D)	258,216	34.3
	Sam Nunn (D)	170,689	22.7
	S. Ernest Vandiver (D)	151,908	20.2
	Hosea Williams (D)	45,613	6.1
	J. B. Stoner (D)	38,261	5.1
	Democratic Special Runoff		
	Sam Nunn (D)	326,186	52.1
	David H. Gambrell (D)	299,919	47.9
	Democratic Primary		
	David H. Gambrell (D)	225,470	31.5
	Sam Nunn (D)	166,035	23.2
	S. Ernest Vandiver (D)	147,135	20.5
	Hosea Williams (D)	46,153	6.4
	J. B. Stoner (D)	40,675	5.7
	Democratic Runoff		
	Sam Nunn (D)	334,670	54.2
	David H. Gambrell (D)	283,414	45.9
1978	**Republican Primary**		
	John W. Stokes (R)	14,443	58.5
	Dean Parkison (R)	10,250	41.5
	Democratic Primary		
	Sam Nunn (D)	525,703	80.0
	Jack Dorsey (D)	71,223	10.8
1984	**Republican Primary**		
	Mike Hicks (R)	27,547	41.1
	Kelly Stratton Brown (R)	26,657	39.7
	J. W. Tibbs Jr. (R)	12,849	19.2
	Republican Runoff		
	Mike Hicks (R)	16,987	67.1
	J. W. Tibbs Jr. (R)	8,336	32.9
	Democratic Primary		
	Sam Nunn (D)	801,412	90.2
	Jim Boyd (D)	86,973	9.8
1990	**Democratic Primary**		
	Sam Nunn (D)		100.0

1996   **Republican Primary**

Guy Millner (R)	187,177	41.9
Johnny Isakson (R)	155,141	34.7
Clint Day (R)	83,610	18.7

Republican Runoff

Guy Millner (R)	169,240	52.8
Johnny Isakson (R)	151,560	47.2

Democratic Primary

Max Cleland (D)	517,697	100.0

Class 3

1920   **Democratic Primary**

Thomas Watson (D)	102,647	45.0
Dorsey (D)	68,220	29.9
Smith (D)	56,357	24.7

1922   **Democratic Special Primary**

Walter F. George (D)	60,436	54.6
Thomas W. Hardwick (D)	36,328	32.9
Wright (D)	12,820	11.6

1926   **Democratic Primary**

Walter F. George (D)	128,179	67.4
Richard B. Russell (D)	61,911	32.6

1932   **Democratic Primary**

Walter F. George (D)		100.0

1938   **Democratic Primary**

Walter F. George (D)	141,235	44.0
Eugene Talmadge (D)	103,075	32.1
L. S. Camp (D)	76,778	23.9

1944   **Democratic Primary**

Walter F. George (D)	211,081	86.0
John W. Goolsby (D)	34,465	14.0

1950   **Democratic Primary**

Walter F. George (D)	470,156	82.5
Alex McLennan (D)	79,886	14.0

1956   **Democratic Primary**

Herman E. Talmadge (D)	498,327	80.3
M. E. Thompson (D)	122,152	19.7

1962   **Democratic Primary**

Herman E. Talmadge (D)	673,782	88.0
Henry M. Henderson (D)	91,664	12.0

1968   **Republican Primary**

E. Earl Patton (R)	20,316	59.5
Jack Sells (R)	13,805	40.5

Democratic Primary

Herman E. Talmadge (D)	697,915	77.1
Maynard H. Jackson Jr. (D)	207,171	22.9

1974   **Republican Primary**

Jerry R. Johnson (R)		100.0

Democratic Primary

Herman E. Talmadge (D)	523,133	81.5
Carlton Myers (D)	119,011	18.5

1980   **Republican Primary**

Mack Mattingly (R)	28,191	59.8
E. J. Bagley (R)	6,082	12.9
Hulon M. Madeley (R)	3,999	8.5
Dean Parkison (R)	3,219	6.8
Nick M. Belluso (R)	2,947	6.3
J. W. Tibbs Jr. (R)	2,700	5.7

Democratic Primary

Herman E. Talmadge (D)	432,215	42.0
Zell Miller (D)	247,766	24.1
Norman Underwood (D)	183,683	17.8
Dawson Mathis (D)	133,729	13.0

Democratic Runoff

Herman E. Talmadge (D)	559,615	58.6
Zell Miller (D)	395,773	41.4

1986   **Republican Primary**

Mack Mattingly (R)	74,743	95.0

Democratic Primary

Wyche Fowler (D)	314,787	50.2
Hamilton Jordan (D)	196,307	31.3
John D. Russell (D)	100,881	16.1

1992   **Republican Primary**

Paul Coverdell (R)	100,016	37.1
Bob Barr (R)	65,471	24.3
John Knox (R)	64,514	23.9
Charles Tanksley (R)	32,590	12.1

Republican Runoff

Paul Coverdell (R)	80,435	50.5
Bob Barr (R)	78,887	49.5

Democratic Primary

Wyche Fowler (D)	683,274	100.0

1998   **Republican Primary**

Paul Coverdell (R)	323,350	100.0

Democratic Primary

Michael Coles (D)	312,765	76.1
Jim Boyd (D)	98,020	23.9

Georgia

1. Two Senate primaries were held simultaneously in 1972: a special primary for the remainder of the term of Richard B. Russell (D), who died Jan. 21, 1971, and a regular primary for the full term beginning in January 1973. Gambrell, who was appointed to the Senate seat in 1971, led candidates in both parties, but lost both primary runoffs to Nunn. Returns for the special primary from the Elections Research Center, Washington, D.C.

HAWAII

Candidates	Votes	%
Class 1		

1959[1] **Republican Primary**

Hiram L. Fong (R)		100.0

Democratic Primary

Frank F. Fasi (D)	46,868	59.9
William H. Heen (D)	31,317	40.0

1964 **Republican Primary**

Hiram L. Fong (R)	31,770	95.2

Democratic Primary

Thomas P. Gill (D)	71,298	64.0
Nadao Yoshinaga (D)	37,253	33.4

1970 **Republican Primary**

Hiram L. Fong (R)		100.0

Democratic Primary

Cecil Heftel (D)	78,934	62.4
Tony N. Hodges (D)	30,430	24.1
Neil Abercrombie (D)	17,058	13.5

1976 **Republican Primary**

William F. Quinn (R)	32,058	93.7
Spencer J. Cabral (R)	2,170	6.3

Democratic Primary

Spark M. Matsunaga (D)	105,731	51.0
Patsy Mink (D)	84,732	40.9

Libertarian Primary

Rockne Johnson (LIBERT)		100.0

Non-Partisan Primary

James D. Kimmel (NON PART)		100.0

People's Primary

Anthony N. Hodges (PP)		100.0

1982 **Republican Primary**

Clarence J. Brown (R)	6,142	65.2
Arbis D. Shipley (R)	3,279	34.8

Democratic Primary

Spark M. Matsunaga (D)		100.0

Independent Democratic Primary

E. F. Bernier-Nachtwey (ID)		100.0

1988 **Republican Primary**

Maria M. Hustace (R)	18,124	48.7
Leonard Mednick (R)	13,590	36.4
Susanne Sydney (R)	5,526	14.8

Democratic Primary

Spark M. Matsunaga (D)	180,853	86.9
Robert Zimmerman (D)	27,360	13.1

Libertarian Primary

Ken Schoolland (LIBERT)		100.0

1990[2] **Republican Special Primary**

Patricia Saiki (R)	39,847	85.8
Richard I. C. Sutton (R)	2,443	5.3

Democratic Special Primary

Daniel K. Akaka (D)	180,235	90.7
Paul Snider (D)	18,427	9.3

Libertarian Special Primary

Ken Schoolland (LIBERT)		100.0

1994 **Republican Primary**

Maria M. Hustace (R)	16,647	40.9
Richard C. S. Ho (R)	9,069	22.3
Frances D. Bollinger (R)	7,869	19.3
Paul A. Manner (R)	2,640	6.5
Robert H. Harker (R)	2,454	6.0
James DeLuze (R)	2,046	5.0

Democratic Primary

Daniel K. Akata (D)	168,877	100.0

Libertarian Primary

Richard Rowland (LIBERT)	351	100.0

2000 **Republican Primary**

John Carroll (R)	33,349	71.5
Eugene F. Douglass (R)	6,117	13.1
James R. DeLuze (R)	3,910	8.4
Harry J. Friel (R)	3,277	7.0

Democratic Primary

Daniel K. Akaka (D)	150,507	90.2
Art P. Reyes (D)	16,312	9.8

Libertarian Primary

Lloyd Mallan (LIBERT)	664	84.7

Natural Law Primary

Lauri A. Clegg (NL)	469	98.3

Constitution Primary

David Porter (CONST)	122	61.3
Paul Manner (CONST)	76	38.2

Class 3		

1959[1] **Republican Primary**

Wilfred C. Tsukiyama (R)		100.0

Democratic Primary

Oren E. Long (D)	61,345	83.9
Kenneth E. Young (D)	9,036	12.3

Commonwealth Primary

Eugene Ressencourt (CP)		100.0

1962   **Republican Primary**

Ben F. Dillingham (R)		100.0

Democratic Primary

Daniel K. Inouye (D)	80,707	93.6
Frank Troy (D)	5,476	6.3

1968   **Republican Primary**

Wayne C. Thiessen (R)		100.0

Democratic Primary

Daniel K. Inouye (D)	111,135	87.5
William Lampard (D)	14,357	11.3

Peace and Freedom Primary

Oliver Lee (PFP)		100.0

1974   **Democratic Primary**

Daniel K. Inouye (D)		100.0

Peoples Primary

James D. Kimmel (PP)	61	64.9
Floyd Nachtwey (PP)	33	35.1

1980   **Republican Primary**

Cooper Brown (R)	3,219	39.0
Lawrence I. Weisman (R)	2,586	31.4
Dan Dew (R)	1,854	22.5
E. F. Bernier-Nachtwey (R)	584	7.1

Democratic Primary

Daniel K. Inouye (D)	198,468	87.5
Kamuela Price (D)	15,361	6.8
John P. Fritz (D)	12,929	5.7

Libertarian Primary

H. E. Shasteen (LIBERT)		100.0

1986   **Republican Primary**

Frank Hutchinson (R)	20,375	67.7
Marvin Franklin (R)	9,714	32.3

Democratic Primary

Daniel K. Inouye (D)		100.0

1992   **Republican Primary**

Rick Reed (R)	33,250	74.1
Maria M. Hustace (R)	9,348	20.8
John James (R)	2,250	5.0

Democratic Primary

Daniel K. Inouye (D)	141,273	76.1
Wayne K. Nishiki (D)	44,505	24.0

Green Primary

Linda B. Martin (GREEN)		100.0

Libertarian Primary

Richard O. Rowland (LIBERT)		100.0

1998   **Republican Primary**

Crystal Young (R)	26,920	28.1
Jay Lawrence Friedheim (R)	18,969	19.8
Eugene F. Douglass (R)	10,417	10.9
James R. DeLuze (R)	8,995	9.4
William Fenton Sink (R)	7,519	7.9
Randolph John Amen (R)	7,476	7.8
Stuart Gregory (R)	6,368	6.7
Harry J. Friel (R)	5,358	5.6

Democratic Primary

Daniel K. Inouye (D)	108,891	92.8
Richard Thompson (D)	8,468	7.2

Libertarian Primary

Lloyd Mallan (LIBERT)	300	88.5

Hawaii

1. Hawaii became a state Aug. 21, 1959. The first Senate elections for that state were for unspecified terms. The Senate later determined that Sen. Fong would serve the long term (Class 1) and Sen. Long, the short term (Class 3).

2. A special election was held in 1990 to fill the remaining four years of the term of Sen. Spark Matsunaga (D), who died April 15, 1990.

IDAHO

Candidates	Votes	%
Class 2		

1960   **Republican Primary**

Henry C. Dworshak (R)		100.0

Democratic Primary

Gregg Potvin (D)	16,524	23.7
Bob McLaughlin (D)	14,694	21.1
Compton White (D)	14,515	20.8
A. W. Brunt (D)	13,015	18.7
Joseph R. Garry (D)	10,899	15.6

Democratic Runoff

R. F. "Bob" McLaughlin	13,117	51.9
Gregg Potvin	12,174	48.1

1966   **Republican Primary**

Len B. Jordan (R)		100.0

Democratic Primary

Ralph R. Harding (D)		100.0

1972	**Republican Primary**		
	James A. McClure (R)	46,522	36.1
	George Hansen (R)	35,412	27.4
	Glen Wegner (R)	24,582	19.1
	Robert E. Smylie (R)	22,497	17.4
	Democratic Primary		
	William E. "Bud" Davis (D)	23,953	36.1
	W. Anthony Park (D)	17,636	26.5
	Byron Johnson (D)	15,526	23.4
	Rose Bowman (D)	9,327	14.0
1978	**Republican Primary**		
	James A. McClure (R)		100.0
	Democratic Primary		
	Dwight Jensen (D)		100.0
1984	**Republican Primary**		
	James A. McClure (R)	102,125	100.0
	Democratic Primary		
	Peter M. Busch (D)	27,871	62.0
	Louis A. Hatheway (D)	17,065	38.0
1990	**Republican Primary**		
	Larry E. Craig (R)	65,830	59.0
	Jim Jones (R)	45,733	41.0
	Democratic Primary		
	Ron J. Twilegar (D)	30,154	64.5
	David C. Steed (D)	16,587	35.5
1996	**Republican Primary**		
	Larry E. Craig (R)	106,817	100.0
	Democratic Primary		
	Walt Minnick (D)	34,551	100.0

Class 3

1956	**Republican Primary**		
	Herman Welker (R)	31,399	42.5
	William S. Holden (R)	21,081	28.5
	Ray J. Davis (R)	12,349	16.7
	John C. Sanborn (R)	8,261	11.2
	Democratic Primary		
	Frank Church (D)	27,942	37.7
	Glen H. Taylor (D)	27,742	37.5
	Claude Burtenshaw (D)	11,738	15.9
	Alvin McCormack (D)	6,596	8.9
1962	**Republican Primary**		
	Jack Hawley (R)	38,210	60.2
	George Hansen (R)	25,223	39.8
	Democratic Primary		
	Frank Church (D)		100.0

1968	**Republican Primary**		
	George Hansen (R)		100.0
	Democratic Primary		
	Frank Church (D)		100.0
1974	**Republican Primary**		
	Robert L. Smith (R)	45,553	72.0
	Donald L. Winder (R)	13,406	21.2
	Charles Bolstridge (R)	4,331	6.8
	Democratic Primary		
	Frank Church (D)	53,659	85.8
	Leon R. Olson (D)	8,904	14.2
	American Primary		
	Jean L. Stoddard (AM)		100.0
1980	**Republican Primary**		
	Steven D. Symms (R)		100.0
	Democratic Primary		
	Frank Church (D)		100.0
	Libertarian Primary		
	Larry Fullmer (LIBERT)		100.0
1986	**Republican Primary**		
	Steven D. Symms (R)		100.0
	Democratic Primary		
	John V. Evans (D)		100.0
1992	**Republican Primary**		
	Dirk Kempthorne (R)	67,001	57.4
	Rodney W. Beck (R)	26,977	23.1
	Milton E. Erhart (R)	22,682	19.4
	Democratic Primary		
	Richard Stallings (D)	40,102	71.7
	Matt Schaffer (D)	8,976	16.0
	David W. Shepherd (D)	6,882	12.3
1998	**Republican Primary**		
	Michael Crapo (R)	110,205	87.3
	Matt Lambert (R)	16,075	12.7
	Democratic Primary		
	Bill Mauk (D)	22,503	100.0

ILLINOIS

Candidates	Votes	%
Class 2		

1960	**Republican Primary**		
	Samuel W. Witwer (R)	249,849	31.5
	Warren E. Wright (R)	226,449	28.6

William H. Rentschler (R)	202,600	25.6
John W. Lewis (R)	48,989	6.2

Democratic Primary

Paul H. Douglas (D)		100.0

1966   Republican Primary

Charles H. Percy (R)	605,815	90.6
Howard J. Doyle (R)	38,636	5.8

Democratic Primary

Paul H. Douglas (D)		100.0

1972   Republican Primary

Charles H. Percy (R)		100.0

Democratic Primary

Roman C. Pucinski (D)	859,890	70.6
W. Dakin Williams (D)	357,744	29.4

1978   Republican Primary

Charles H. Percy (R)	401,409	84.2
Lar Daly (R)	74,739	15.7

Democratic Primary

Alex Seith (D)	483,196	69.5
Anthony R. Martin-Trigona (D)	212,105	30.5

1984   Republican Primary

Charles H. Percy (R)	387,865	59.3
Tom Corcoran (R)	239,847	36.7

Democratic Primary

Paul Simon (D)	556,757	35.6
Roland W. Burris (D)	360,182	23.0
Alex Seith (D)	327,125	20.9
Philip J. Rock (D)	303,397	19.4

1990   Republican Primary

Lynn Martin (R)		100.0

Democratic Primary

Paul Simon (D)		100.0

1996   Republican Primary

Al Salvi (R)	377,141	47.6
Bob Kustra (R)	342,935	43.3
Robert Marshall (R)	43,937	5.6

Democratic Primary

Richard J. Durbin (D)	512,520	64.9
Pat Quinn (D)	233,138	29.5

Libertarian Primary

Robin J. Miller (LIBERT)	1,258	73.7
David F. Hoscheidt (LIBERT)	448	26.3

Class 3

1956   Republican Primary

Everett McKinley Dirksen (R)		100.0

Democratic Primary

Richard Stengel (D)		100.0

1962   Republican Primary

Everett McKinley Dirksen (R)	742,973	87.1
Harley D. Jones (R)	109,574	12.8

Democratic Primary

Sidney R. Yates (D)	744,128	77.2
Lar Daly (D)	219,169	22.7

1968   Republican Primary

Everett McKinley Dirksen (R)	622,710	92.1
Roy C. Johnson (R)	53,069	7.8

Democratic Primary

William G. Clark (D)		100.0

1970   Republican Special Primary

Ralph Tyler Smith (R)	414,489	58.9
William H. Rentschler (R)	271,648	38.6

Democratic Special Primary

Adlai E. Stevenson III (D)		100.0

1974   Republican Primary

George M. Burditt (R)	432,796	84.7
Lar Daly (R)	78,146	15.3

Democratic Primary

Adlai E. Stevenson III (D)	822,248	82.9
W. Dakin Williams (D)	169,662	17.1

1980   Republican Primary

David C. O'Neal (R)	424,634	41.5
William J. Scott (R)	352,138	34.4
Richard E. Carver (R)	245,668	24.1

Democratic Primary

Alan J. Dixon (D)	671,746	66.9
Alex Seith (D)	190,339	18.9
Robert A. Wallace (D)	64,037	6.4

1986   Republican Primary

Judy Koehler (R)	266,214	55.0
George A. Ranney (R)	217,720	45.0

Democratic Primary

Alan J. Dixon (D)	720,571	84.8
Sheila Jones (D)	129,474	15.2

1992   Republican Primary

Richard S. Williamson (R)	608,079	100.0

Democratic Primary		
Carol Moseley-Braun (D)	557,694	38.3
Alan J. Dixon (D)	504,077	34.6
Albert F. Hofeld (D)	394,497	27.1

1998

Republican Primary		
Peter G. Fitzgerald (R)	372,916	51.8
Loleta Didrickson (R)	346,606	48.2

Democratic Primary		
Carol Moseley-Braun (D)	666,419	100.0

INDIANA

Candidates	Votes	%
Class 1		

1976[1]

Republican Primary		
Richard G. Lugar (R)	393,064	65.5
Edgar D. Whitcomb (R)	179,203	29.8

Democratic Primary		
R. Vance Hartke (D)	304,076	53.1
Philip H. Hayes (D)	268,790	46.9

1982

Republican Primary		
Richard G. Lugar (R)		100.0

Democratic Primary		
Floyd Fithian (D)	262,644	59.5
Michael Kendall (D)	178,702	40.5

1988

Republican Primary		
Richard G. Lugar (R)		100.0

Democratic Primary		
Jack Wickes (D)		100.0

1994

Republican Primary		
Richard G. Lugar (R)	398,111	100.0

Democratic Primary		
Jim Jontz (D)	191,619	54.8
John W. Taylor (D)	158,159	45.2

2000

Republican Primary		
Richard G. Lugar (R)	356,888	100.0

Democratic Primary		
David L. Johnson (D)	192,531	100.0

Class 3		

1980

Republican Primary		
Dan Quayle (R)	397,273	77.1
Roger F. Marsh (R)	118,273	22.9

Democratic Primary		
Birch Bayh (D)		100.0

1986

Republican Primary		
Dan Quayle (R)		100.0

Democratic Primary		
Jill Long (D)	258,085	73.5
Georgia D. Irey (D)	93,079	26.5

1990[2]

Republican Special Primary		
Daniel R. Coats (R)		100.0

Democratic Special Primary		
Baron P. Hill (D)		100.0

1992

Republican Primary		
Daniel R. Coats (R)	389,119	100.0

Democratic Primary		
Joseph H. Hogsett (D)	320,732	100.0

1998

Republican Primary		
Paul Helmke (R)	138,960	35.2
John Price (R)	131,327	33.2
Peter Rusthoven (R)	124,711	31.6

Democratic Primary		
Evan Bayh (D)	324,923	100.0

Indiana

1. Before 1976, when Indiana adopted a primary system, party conventions nominated candidates for statewide office.

2. A special election was held in 1990 to fill the remaining two years of the term of Sen. Dan Quayle (R), who resigned Jan. 3, 1989, after he was elected vice president. The first two years of the vacancy were filled by appointee Daniel R. Coats (R).

IOWA

Candidates	Votes	%
Class 2		

1960[1]

Republican Primary		
Jack Miller (R)	66,455	30.8
Dayton Countryman (R)	62,500	29.0
Rollo Bergeson (R)	31,559	14.6
Ken Stringer (R)	29,927	13.9
Oliver J. Reeve (R)	14,414	6.7
Ernest J. Seemann (R)	10,931	5.1

Democratic Primary		
Herschel C. Loveless (D)		100.0

1966

Republican Primary		
Jack Miller (R)	141,141	83.9
Herbert H. Hoover (R)	27,007	16.1

Democratic Primary		
E. B. Smith (D)	39,870	50.1
Gary L. Cameron (D)	22,650	28.5
Ernest J. Seeman (D)	8,646	10.9
Robert L. Nereim (D)	8,343	10.5

1972   Republican Primary

Jack Miller (R)	170,590	*84.4*
Ralph Scott (R)	31,607	*15.6*

Democratic Primary

Dick Clark (D)		*100.0*

American Independent Primary

William A. Rocap (AMI)		*100.0*

1978   Republican Primary

Roger W. Jepsen (R)	87,397	*57.3*
Maurie Van Nostrand (R)	54,189	*35.5*
Joe Bertroche (R)	10,860	*7.1*

Democratic Primary

Dick Clark (D)	87,880	*80.5*
Gerald Baker (D)	13,132	*12.0*
Robert L. Nereim (D)	8,176	*7.5*

1984   Republican Primary

Roger W. Jepsen (R)	113,996	*100.0*

Democratic Primary

Tom Harkin (D)	106,005	*100.0*

1990   Republican Primary

Tom Tauke (R)		*100.0*

Democratic Primary

Tom Harkin (D)		*100.0*

1996   Republican Primary

Jim Ross Lightfoot (R)	101,608	*61.5*
Maggie Tinsman (R)	40,955	*24.8*
Steve Grubbs (R)	22,554	*13.6*

Democratic Primary

Tom Harkin (D)	98,737	*99.2*

Class 3

1956   Republican Primary

Bourke B. Hickenlooper (R)	157,652	*67.7*
Dayton Countryman (R)	75,264	*32.3*

Democratic Primary

R. M. Evans (D)	64,195	*63.1*
Lumund Wilcox (D)	37,590	*36.9*

1962   Republican Primary

Bourke B. Hickenlooper (R)	164,535	*85.4*
Herbert H. Hoover (R)	28,095	*14.6*

Democratic Primary

E. B. Smith (D)		*100.0*

1968   Republican Primary

David M. Stanley (R)	143,854	*58.7*
James E. Bromwell (R)	65,509	*26.7*

Dayton Countryman (R)	22,049	*9.0*
William N. Plymat (R)	13,485	*5.5*

Democratic Primary

Harold E. Hughes (D)	103,936	*86.8*
Robert L. Nereim (D)	15,772	*13.2*

1974   Republican Primary

David M. Stanley (R)	87,464	*66.9*
George F. Milligan (R)	43,206	*33.1*

Democratic Primary

John C. Culver (D)		*100.0*

1980   Republican Primary

Charles E. Grassley (R)	170,120	*66.7*
Tom Stoner (R)	89,409	*33.3*

Democratic Primary

John C. Culver (D)		*100.0*

1986   Republican Primary

Charles E. Grassley (R)		*100.0*

Democratic Primary

John P. Roehrick (D)	88,347	*83.8*
Juan Cortez (D)	16,987	*16.1*

1992   Republican Primary

Charles E. Grassley (R)	109,273	*99.7*

Democratic Primary

Jean Lloyd-Jones (D)	60,615	*60.8*
Rosanne Freeburg (D)	38,774	*38.9*

1998   Republican Primary

Charles E. Grassley (R)	149,943	*99.7*

Democratic Primary

David Osterberg (D)	86,064	*99.4*

Iowa

1. Because no candidate in Iowa's 1960 Republican primary received the minimum percentage required for Senate nomination, a state convention was held, resulting in the nomination of Miller.

KANSAS

Candidates	Votes	%

Class 2

1960   Republican Primary

Andrew F. Schoeppel (R)	201,753	*80.0*
Henry P. Cleaver (R)	50,507	*20.0*

Democratic Primary

Frank Theis (D)	88,194	*59.1*
Joseph W. Henkle (D)	60,942	*40.9*

1962[1]   **Republican Special Primary**

James B. Pearson (R)	124,854	62.3
Edward F. Arn (R)	75,524	37.7

Democratic Special Primary

Paul L. Aylward (D)		100.0

1966   **Republican Primary**

James B. Pearson (R)	101,523	50.3
R. F. Ellsworth (R)	83,083	41.1
Ava A. Anderson (R)	10,095	5.0

Democratic Primary

J. Floyd Breeding (D)	51,860	49.9
K. L. Smith (D)	19,433	18.7
Harold S. Herd (D)	16,963	16.3
Leigh Warner (D)	15,625	15.0

1972   **Republican Primary**

James B. Pearson (R)	229,908	82.2
Harlan D. House (R)	49,825	17.8

Democratic Primary

Arch O. Tezlaff (D)		100.0

1978   **Republican Primary**

Nancy Landon Kassebaum (R)	67,324	30.6
Wayne Angell (R)	54,161	24.6
Sam Hardage (R)	30,248	13.7
Jan Meyers (R)	20,933	9.5
Deryl K. Schuster (R)	18,568	8.5
Norman E. Gaar (R)	14,502	6.6

Democratic Primary

William R. Roy (D)	100,508	76.7
Dorothy K. White (D)	13,865	10.6
James R. Maher (D)	11,556	8.8

1984   **Republican Primary**

Nancy Landon Kassebaum (R)	214,429	100.0

Democratic Primary

James R. Maher (D)	97,843	100.0

1990   **Republican Primary**

Nancy Landon Kassebaum (R)	267,946	87.2
R. Gregory Walstrom (R)	39,379	12.8

Democratic Primary

William R. Roy (D)[2]	86,174	56.9
Dick Williams (D)	65,395	43.1

1996   **Republican Primary**

Pat Roberts (R)	245,411	78.2
Tom Little (R)	25,052	8.0
Thomas L. Oyler (R)	23,266	7.4
Richard L. Cooley (R)	20,060	6.4

Democratic Primary

Sally Thompson (D)	121,476	100.0

Class 3

1956   **Republican Primary**

Frank Carlson (R)	215,364	77.9
Walter I. Biddle (R)	61,053	22.1

Democratic Primary

George Hart (D)	54,553	40.4
Paul L. Aylward (D)	54,085	40.0
Fred Kilian (D)	16,384	12.1
Marlyn Korf (D)	10,176	7.5

1962   **Republican Primary**

Frank Carlson (R)	167,498	86.9
Joe Corpstein (R)	25,168	13.1

Democratic Primary

K. L. Smith (D)	65,876	62.5
Joseph J. Poizner (D)	39,458	37.5

1968   **Republican Primary**

Robert Dole (R)	190,782	68.5
William H. Avery (R)	87,801	31.5

Democratic Primary

William I. Robinson (D)	56,242	40.9
James K. Logan (D)	50,709	36.9
K. L. Smith (D)	13,698	10.0

1974   **Republican Primary**

Robert Dole (R)		100.0

Democratic Primary

William R. Roy (D)	125,634	85.0
George Hart (D)	22,109	15.0

1980   **Republican Primary**

Robert Dole (R)	201,484	81.9
Jim H. Grainge (R)	44,674	18.1

Democratic Primary

John Simpson (D)	52,004	35.8
James R. Maher (D)	46,322	31.9
John A. Barnes (D)	16,466	11.3
Ken North (D)	14,218	9.8
Ed Phillips (D)	8,838	6.1
Howard C. Lee (D)	7,461	5.1

1986   **Republican Primary**

Robert Dole (R)	228,301	84.4
Shirley J. A. Landis (R)	42,237	15.6

Democratic Primary

Guy MacDonald (D)	31,942	27.7
Darrell T. Ringer (D)	30,483	26.4

	W. H. Addington (D)	21,082	18.3
	Lionel Kunst (D)	18,795	16.3
	Jim Oyler (D)	13,201	11.4
1992	**Republican Primary**		
	Robert Dole (R)	244,480	80.4
	Richard W. Rodewald (R)	59,589	19.6
	Democratic Primary		
	Gloria O'Dell (D)	111,015	69.2
	Fred Phelps (D)	49,416	30.8
1996[3]	**Republican Special Primary**		
	Sam Brownback (R)	187,914	54.8
	Sheila Frahm (R)	142,487	41.6
	Democratic Special Primary		
	Jill Docking (D)	127,012	74.4
	Joan Finney (D)	43,726	25.6
1998	**Republican Primary**		
	Sam Brownback (R)	255,747	100.0
	Democratic Primary		
	Paul Feleciano Jr. (D)	58,097	58.7
	Todd Covault (D)	40,825	41.3

Kansas

1. A special election was held in 1962 to fill the remaining four years of the term of Sen. Andrew Schoeppel (R), who died Jan. 21, 1962.

2. Roy withdrew after the primary and Williams was substituted by the state party committee.

3. A special election was held to fill the remaining two years of the term of Sen. Robert Dole (R), who resigned June 11, 1996, to run for president. Sheila Frahm was appointed by the governor to fill vacancy until the election; she resigned Nov. 27, 1996.

KENTUCKY

	Candidates	Votes	%
	Class 2		
1960	**Republican Primary**		
	John Sherman Cooper (R)	50,896	96.3
	Democratic Primary		
	Keen Johnson (D)	112,797	58.0
	John Young Brown (D)	75,897	39.0
1966	**Republican Primary**		
	John Sherman Cooper (R)	65,023	92.8
	Democratic Primary		
	John Young Brown (D)	71,759	75.6
	Gaines P. Wilson (D)	12,921	13.6
	James Ward Lentz (D)	5,399	5.7
	J. N. R. Cecil (D)	4,861	5.1

1972	**Republican Primary**		
	Louie B. Nunn (R)	57,348	69.7
	Robert E. Gable (R)	18,107	22.0
	Democratic Primary		
	Walter D. Huddleston (D)	106,144	71.6
	Sandy Hockensmith (D)	14,786	10.0
	James E. Wallace (D)	11,290	7.6
	Willis V. Johnson (D)	8,727	5.9
1978	**Republican Primary**		
	Louie Guenthner (R)	14,218	47.2
	Oline Carmical (R)	9,346	31.0
	Thurman J. Hamlin (R)	6,550	21.8
	Democratic Primary		
	Walter D. Huddleston (D)	89,333	75.6
	Jack A. Watson (D)	13,177	11.1
	William J. Taylor (D)	8,710	7.4
	George W. Tolhurst (D)	6,921	5.9
1984	**Republican Primary**		
	Mitch McConnell (R)	39,465	79.2
	C. Roger Harker (R)	3,798	7.6
	T. William "Tommy" Klein (R)	3,352	6.7
	Thurman Hamlin (R)	3,202	6.4
	Democratic Primary		
	Walter D. Huddleston (D)		100.0
1990	**Republican Primary**		
	Mitch McConnell (R)	64,063	88.5
	T. William "Tommy" Klein (R)	8,310	11.5
	Democratic Primary		
	Harvey Sloane (D)	183,789	59.3
	John Brock (D)	126,318	40.7
1996	**Republican Primary**		
	Mitch McConnell (R)	88,620	88.6
	Democratic Primary		
	Steven L. Beshear (D)	177,859	66.4
	Tom Barlow (D)	64,235	24.0
	Shelby Lanier Jr. (D)	25,856	9.6
	Class 3		
1956[1]	**Republican Primary**		
	Thruston B. Morton (R)	42,038	70.6
	Julian H. Golden (R)	12,976	21.8
	Granville Thomas (R)	4,495	7.6
	Democratic Primary		
	Earle C. Clements (D)	218,353	60.8
	Joe B. Bates (D)	136,533	38.0

1962	Republican Primary		
	Thruston B. Morton (R)	41,892	91.2
	Thurman J. Hamlin (R)	4,048	8.8
	Democratic Primary		
	Wilson W. Wyatt (D)	127,403	77.0
	Marion Vance (D)	28,513	17.2
	James L. Delk (D)	9,483	5.7
1968	Republican Primary		
	Marlow W. Cook (R)	73,171	62.0
	Eugene Siler (R)	39,743	33.7
	Democratic Primary		
	Katherine Peden (D)	86,317	43.8
	John Young Brown (D)	51,509	26.2
	Foster Ockerman (D)	25,602	13.0
	Ted Osborn (D)	20,049	10.2
1974	Republican Primary		
	Marlow W. Cook (R)	35,904	87.6
	Thurman J. Hamlin (R)	2,826	6.9
	T. William "Tommy" Klein (R)	2,256	5.5
	Democratic Primary		
	Wendell H. Ford (D)	136,458	84.8
	Harvey E. Brazin (D)	24,436	15.2
	American Primary		
	William E. Parker (AM)		100.0
1980	Republican Primary		
	Mary Louise Foust (R)	25,717	42.0
	Granville Thomas (R)	10,246	16.7
	Jackson M. Andrews (R)	8,382	13.7
	T. William "Tommy" Klein (R)	6,418	10.5
	Yale J. Lubkin (R)	5,669	9.2
	DeSota Vaught (R)	4,848	7.9
	Democratic Primary		
	Wendell H. Ford (D)	188,047	87.0
	Flora T. Stuart (D)	28,202	13.0
1986	Republican Primary		
	Jackson M. Andrews (R)	16,211	39.0
	Carl W. Brown (R)	9,724	23.3
	T. William "Tommy" Klein (R)	8,595	20.6
	Thurman J. Hamlin (R)	7,062	17.0
	Democratic Primary		
	Wendell H. Ford (D)		100.0
1992	Republican Primary		
	David L. Williams (R)	49,880	60.9
	Philip Thompson (R)	25,026	30.5
	Denny Ormerod (R)	7,066	8.6

	Democratic Primary		
	Wendell H. Ford (D)		100.0
1998	Republican Primary		
	Jim Bunning (R)	152,493	74.3
	Barry Metcalf (R)	52,798	25.7
	Democratic Primary		
	Scotty Baesler (D)	194,125	34.2
	Charlie Owen (D)	166,472	29.2
	Steve L. Henry (D)	156,576	27.6

Kentucky

1. Candidates for the special election to fill the unexpired term of Sen. Alben W. Barkley (D), who died April 30, 1956, were nominated by the Democratic and Republican state committees, not by primaries. The 1956 Senate primary in Kentucky was for the Class 3 seat that was slated to be filled that year.

LOUISIANA[1]

Candidates	Votes	%
Class 2		

1924	Democratic Primary		
	Joseph E. Ransdell (D)	104,312	54.9
	Lee E. Thomas (D)	85,547	45.1
1930	Democratic Primary		
	Huey P. Long (D)	149,640	57.3
	Joseph E. Ransdell (D)	111,451	42.7
1936	Democratic Special Primary		
	Oscar K. Allen (D)[2]	368,115	68.7
	Frank J. Looney (D)	160,566	30.0
1936	Democratic Primary		
	Allen J. Ellender (D)	364,931	68.0
	John N. Sandlin (D)	167,471	31.2
1942	Democratic Primary		
	Allen J. Ellender (D)	218,141	68.0
	E. A. Stephens (D)	102,900	32.1
1948	Democratic Primary		
	Allen J. Ellender (D)	284,293	61.7
	James Domengeaux (D)	119,459	25.9
	Charles S. Gerth (D)	57,047	12.4
1954	Democratic Primary		
	Allen J. Ellender (D)	268,064	59.2
	Frank B. Ellis (D)	162,775	35.9
1960	Republican Primary		
	George W. Reese Jr. (R)	726	72.3
	William Dane (R)	278	27.7
	Democratic Primary		
	Allen J. Ellender (D)		100.0

1966	Democratic Primary		
	Allen J. Ellender (D)	494,519	74.2
	J. D. Deblieux (D)	94,154	14.1
	Troyce E. Guice (D)	78,137	11.7
1972	Republican Primary		
	C. M. McLean (R)[3]		100.0
	Democratic Primary		
	J. Bennett Johnston (D)	623,078	79.4
	Frank Tunney Allen (D)	88,198	11.2
	Allen J. Ellender (D)[4]	73,088	9.3
1978	Open Primary		
	J. Bennett Johnston (D)	498,773	59.4
	Louis "Woody" Jenkins (D)	340,896	40.6
1984	Open Primary		
	J. Bennett Johnston (D)	838,181	85.7
	Robert M. Ross (R)	86,546	8.9
	Larry N. "Boo-ga-loo" Cooper (R)	52,746	5.4
1990	Open Primary		
	J. Bennett Johnston (D)	752,902	53.9
	David E. Duke (R)	607,391	43.5
1996	Open Primary		
	Louis "Woody" Jenkins (R)	322,244	26.2
	Mary L. Landrieu (D)	264,268	21.5
	Richard P. Ieyoub (D)	250,682	20.4
	David E. Duke (R)	141,489	11.5
	Jimmy Hayes (R)	71,699	5.8

Class 3

1920	Democratic Primary		
	Edwin S. Broussard (D)	49,718✔	45.7
	Jared Y. Sanders (D)	43,425	40.0
	D. Caffery (D)	15,563	14.3
	Democratic Second Choice		
	D. Caffery (D)	3,328	38.6
	Edwin S. Broussard (D)	2,931	34.0
	Jared Y. Sanders (D)	2,374	27.5
1926	Democratic Primary		
	Edwin S. Broussard (D)	84,041	51.1
	Jared Y. Sanders (D)	80,562	48.9
1932	Democratic Primary		
	John H. Overton (D)	181,464	59.2
	Edwin S. Broussard (D)	124,935	40.8
1938	Democratic Primary		
	John H. Overton (D)		100.0
1944	Democratic Primary		
	John H. Overton (D)	151,886	61.6
	E. A. Stephens (D)	68,408	27.8
	Griffin T. Hawkins (D)	19,087	7.7

1948	Democratic Special Primary		
	Russell B. Long (D)	264,143	51.0
	Robert F. Kennon (D)	253,668	49.0
1950	Democratic Primary		
	Russell B. Long (D)	359,330	68.5
	Malcolm E. LaFargue (D)	156,918	29.9
1956	Democratic Primary		
	Russell B. Long (D)		100.0
1962	Republican Primary		
	Taylor W. O'Hearn (R)		100.0
	Democratic Primary		
	Russell B. Long (D)	407,162	80.2
	Philemon A. Stamant (D)	100,843	19.9
1968	Republican Primary		
	Richard H. Kilbourne (R)[5]		100.0
	Democratic Primary		
	Russell B. Long (D)	494,467	87.0
	Maurice P. Blanche (D)	73,791	13.0
1974	Democratic Primary		
	Russell B. Long (D)	520,606	74.7
	Sherman A. Bernard (D)	131,540	18.9
	Annie Smart (D)	44,341	6.4
1980	Open Primary		
	Russell B. Long (D)	484,770	57.6
	Louis "Woody" Jenkins (D)	325,922	38.8
1986	Open Primary		
	W. Henson Moore (R)	529,433	44.2
	John B. Breaux (D)	447,328	37.3
	Samuel B. Nunez (D)	73,505	6.1
1992	Open Primary		
	John B. Breaux (D)	616,021	73.1
	John Khachturian (I)	74,785	8.9
	Lyle Stockstill (R)	69,986	8.3
	Nick J. Accardo (D)	45,839	5.4
1998	Open Primary		
	John B. Breaux (D)	620,502	64.0
	Jim Donelon (R)	306,616	31.6

Louisiana

1. In 1978 Louisiana eliminated the partisan primary for U.S. senator and instituted an open primary with candidates from all parties on the same ballot. Any candidate who receives a majority appears in the general election unopposed. If no candidate receives 50 percent of the vote, there is a runoff election, without regard to party affiliation, between the top two finishers.

2. Allen, the incumbent governor of Louisiana, died Jan. 28, 1936, just one week after winning the Democratic nomination for the Senate for the term ending Jan. 3, 1937. The Senate seat had been vacant since the assassination Sept. 10, 1935, of Sen. Huey P. Long, D (1932–1935). The new governor appointed Long's widow, Rose McConnell Long, to the Senate seat and she took office Jan. 31, 1936. She was also designated the Democratic nominee to replace Allen in the April 20 special election, which she won without opposition.

Louisiana (continued)

3. McLean withdrew from the race after the primary. The Republican state central committee substituted Ben C. Toledano as the candidate for the general election.

4. Ellender died July 27, 1972, before the Aug. 19 primary in which he was a candidate for renomination to a seventh term. But Ellender's name remained on the ballot for the primary, which Johnston won without a runoff.

5. Kilbourne withdrew from the race after the primary. The Republicans did not choose any substitute candidate, thus allowing Long to run unopposed in the November election.

MAINE

Candidates	Votes	%

Class 1

1958   Republican Primary

Frederick G. Payne (R)	82,448	83.6
Herman D. Sahagian (R)	16,133	16.4

Democratic Primary

Edmund S. Muskie (D)		100.0

1964   Republican Primary

Clifford McIntire (R)		100.0

Democratic Primary

Edmund S. Muskie (D)		100.0

1970   Republican Primary

Neil S. Bishop (R)	45,216	59.8
Abbott O. Greene (R)	30,201	40.0

Democratic Primary

Edmund S. Muskie (D)		100.0

1976   Republican Primary

Robert A. G. Monks (R)	65,224	83.9
Plato Truman (R)	12,552	16.1

Democratic Primary

Edmund S. Muskie (D)		100.0

1982   Republican Primary

David F. Emery (R)		100.0

Democratic Primary

George J. Mitchell (D)		100.0

1988   Republican Primary

Jaspar S. Wyman (R)		100.0

Democratic Primary

George J. Mitchell (D)		100.0

1994   Republican Primary

Olympia J. Snowe (R)	80,686	99.9

Democratic Primary

Thomas H. Andrews (D)	83,108	99.8

2000   Republican Primary

Olympia J. Snowe (R)	34,757	100.0

Democratic Primary

Mark W. Lawrence (D)	26,543	100.0

Class 2

1960   Republican Primary

Margaret Chase Smith (R)		100.0

Democratic Primary

Lucia M. Cormier (D)		100.0

1966   Republican Primary

Margaret Chase Smith (R)		100.0

Democratic Primary

Elmer H. Violette (D)	23,259	45.2
Plato Truman (D)	19,844	38.5
Jack L. Smith (D)	8,386	16.3

1972   Republican Primary

Margaret Chase Smith (R)	76,964	66.7
Robert A. G. Monks (R)	38,345	33.3

Democratic Primary

William D. Hathaway (D)	61,921	90.8
Jack L. Smith (D)	6,263	9.2

1978   Republican Primary

William S. Cohen (R)		100.0

Democratic Primary

William D. Hathaway (D)		100.0

1984   Republican Primary

William S. Cohen (R)		100.0

Democratic Primary

Elizabeth H. Mitchell (D)		100.0

1990   Republican Primary

William S. Cohen (R)		100.0

Democratic Primary

Neil Rolde (D)		100.0

1996   Republican Primary

Susan M. Collins (R)	53,339	55.5
W. John Hathaway (R)	29,792	31.0
Robert A. G. Monks (R)	12,943	13.5

Democratic Primary

Joseph E. Brennan (D)	48,335	56.7
Sean F. Faircloth (D)	21,204	24.9
Richard A. Spencer (D)	10,236	12.0
Jean Hay (D)	4,524	5.3

MARYLAND[1]

Candidates	Votes	%

Class 1

1958 Republican Primary

J. Glenn Beall (R)	67,580	89.6
Henry J. Laque (R)	7,826	10.4

Democratic Primary

Thomas D'Alesandro Jr. (D)	125,408	34.7
George P. Mahoney (D)	119,796	33.2
James Bruce (D)	53,365	14.8
Clarence D. Long (D)	47,290	13.1

1964 Republican Primary

J. Glenn Beall (R)	68,930	59.8
James P. Gleason (R)	35,645	30.9
William A. Albaugh (R)	8,352	7.2

Democratic Primary

Joseph D. Tydings (D)	279,564	64.5
Louis L. Goldstein (D)	155,086	26.6
John J. Harbaugh (D)	22,665	5.2

1970 Republican Primary

J. Glenn Beall Jr. (R)	99,687	83.5
Harry L. Simms (R)	9,927	8.3
Wainwright Dawson (R)	9,786	8.2

Democratic Primary

Joseph D. Tydings (D)	242,874	52.7
George P. Mahoney (D)	173,157	37.6
Walter G. Finch (D)	33,361	7.2

1976 Republican Primary

J. Glenn Beall Jr. (R)		100.0

Democratic Primary

Paul S. Sarbanes (D)	302,983	56.5
Joseph D. Tydings (D)	191,875	35.8

1982 Republican Primary

Lawrence J. Hogan (R)	79,375	65.5
Donovan B. Finch (R)	25,290	20.8
William A. Albaugh (R)	16,599	13.7

Democratic Primary

Paul S. Sarbanes (D)	432,931	81.1

1988 Republican Primary

Thomas L. Blair (R)[2]	68,268	45.6
James G. Bennett (R)	19,720	13.2
Patrick L. McDonough (R)	16,305	10.9
E. Robert Zarwell (R)	10,725	7.2
Albert Ceccone (R)	9,601	6.4
John C. Webb (R)	8,405	5.6
Horace S. Rich (R)	8,031	5.4

Democratic Primary

Paul S. Sarbanes (D)	309,919	85.8
B. Emerson Sweatt (D)	25,932	7.2
A. Robert Kaufman (D)	25,450	7.0

1994 Republican Primary

William E. Brock (R)	82,223	37.8
Ruthann Aron (R)	56,369	25.9
Ronald Franks (R)	38,213	17.6
Ross Z. Pierpont (R)	17,306	8.0
John C. Webb (R)	12,179	5.6

Democratic Primary

Paul S. Sarbanes (D)	382,115	78.9
John B. Liston (D)	52,031	10.7
Dennard A. Gayle (D)	30,665	6.3

2000 Republican Primary

Paul H. Rappaport (R)	70,231	22.7
Ron Sobhani (R)	53,084	17.1
Ross Z. Pierpont (R)	52,052	16.8
Robin Ficker (R)	46,995	15.2
Kenneth R. Timmerman (R)	30,146	9.7
Ken Wayman (R)	28,461	9.2
John Stafford (R)	18,656	6.0

Democratic Primary

Paul S. Sarbanes (D)	384,748	83.2
George English (D)	45,984	9.9
Sidney Altman (D)	31,502	6.8

Class 3

1956 Republican Primary

John Marshall Butler (R)	58,642	86.6
Earl E. Knepper (R)	5,376	7.9
Henry J. Laque (R)	3,696	5.5

Democratic Primary

Millard E. Tydings (D)[3]	142,238	47.5
George P. Mahoney (D)	134,246	44.8

1962 Republican Primary

Edward T. Miller (R)	43,437	48.1
James P. Gleason (R)	34,523	38.3
Harry L. Simms (R)	7,689	8.5
Henry J. Laque (R)	4,565	5.1

Democratic Primary

Daniel B. Brewster (D)	182,272	52.2
Blair Lee (D)	100,915	28.9
Elbert M. Byrd (D)	32,147	9.2
Herbert J. Hoover (D)	19,719	5.6

1968 Republican Primary

Charles McC. Mathias Jr. (R)	66,777	80.0
Harry L. Simms (R)	11,927	14.3
Paul F. Wattay (R)	4,790	5.7

Democratic Primary

Daniel B. Brewster (D)	150,481	*67.4*
Ross Z. Pierpont (D)	38,555	*17.3*
Walter G. Finch (D)	19,829	*8.9*
Richard R. Howes (D)	14,224	*6.4*

1974   Republican Primary

Charles McC. Mathias Jr. (R)	79,823	*75.8*
Ross Z. Pierpont (R)	25,512	*24.2*

Democratic Primary

Barbara A. Mikulski (D)	132,658	*40.9*
Bernard L. Talley (D)	79,080	*24.4*
Walter G. Finch (D)	32,068	*9.9*
Xavier A. Aragona (D)	17,668	*5.4*

1980   Republican Primary

Charles McC. Mathias Jr. (R)	82,430	*55.0*
John M. Brennan (R)	24,848	*16.6*
V. Dallas Merrell (R)	23,073	*15.4*
Roscoe G. Bartlett (R)	10,970	*7.3*

Democratic Primary

Edward T. Conroy (D)	79,033	*22.4*
Victor L. Crawford (D)	52,803	*15.0*
Robert L. Douglass (D)	43,035	*12.2*
Dennis C. McCoy (D)	40,510	*11.5*
R. Spencer Oliver (D)	35,407	*10.4*
John A. Kennedy (D)	20,255	*5.7*
Frank J. Broschart (D)	19,455	*5.5*

1986   Republican Primary

Linda Chavez (R)	100,888	*73.1*
Michael Schaefer (R)	16,902	*12.2*

Democratic Primary

Barbara A. Mikulski (D)	307,876	*49.5*
Michael D. Barnes (D)	195,086	*31.4*
Harry Hughes (D)	88,908	*14.3*

1992   Republican Primary

Alan L. Keyes (R)	95,831	*45.9*
Martha S. Klima (R)	20,758	*10.0*
Joseph I. Cassilly (R)	16,091	*7.7*
Ross Z. Pierpont (R)	12,658	*6.1*
S. Rob Sobhani (R)	12,423	*6.0*

Democratic Primary

Barbara A. Mikulski (D)	376,444	*76.8*
Thomas M. Wheatley (D)	31,214	*6.4*
Walter Boyd (D)	26,467	*5.4*

1998   Republican Primary

Ross Z. Pierpont (R)	32,691	*18.4*
John Taylor (R)	22,855	*12.9*
Michael Gloth (R)	19,926	*11.2*
Kenneth Wayman (R)	16,505	*9.3*

Bradlyn McClanahan (R)	16,439	*9.3*
Howard David Greyber (R)	16,177	*9.1*
John Stafford (R)	15,031	*8.5*
George Liebmann (R)	14,440	*8.1*
Barry Steve Asbury (R)	11,881	*6.7*
Thomas Scott (R)	11,707	*6.6*

Democratic Primary

Barbara A. Mikulski (D)	349,382	*84.4*
Ann L. Mallory (D)	43,120	*10.4*
Kauko H. Kokkonen (D)	21,658	*5.2*

Maryland

1. Until 1962 Maryland used a system of convention unit votes, with each county (and each of the six legislative districts into which Baltimore city was divided) being allocated as many unit votes as it had members of the state legislature, ranging from three to seven. These unit votes were automatically credited to the candidate carrying the county or legislative district.

2. Blair withdrew after the Republican primary. Alan L. Keyes was substituted by the party state central committee.

3. In 1956, because Tydings and Mahoney tied in unit votes at 76 each, Tydings won the nomination with the higher popular vote. But illness forced him to retire from the campaign and Mahoney was substituted by the party state committee.

MASSACHUSETTS

Candidates	Votes	%
Class 1		

1958   Republican Primary

Vincent J. Celeste (R)		*100.0*

Democratic Primary

John F. Kennedy (D)		*100.0*

1962[1]   Republican Special Primary

George C. Lodge (R)	244,921	*55.5*
Laurence Curtis (R)	196,444	*44.5*

Democratic Special Primary

Edward M. Kennedy (D)	559,303	*72.9*
Edward J. McCormack (D)	247,403	*27.1*

1964   Republican Primary

Howard Whitmore (R)		*100.0*

Democratic Primary

Edward M. Kennedy (D)		*100.0*

1970   Republican Primary

Josiah A. Spaulding (R)	109,306	*57.3*
John J. McCarthy (R)	81,356	*42.7*

Democratic Primary

Edward M. Kennedy (D)		*100.0*

1976   Republican Primary

Michael Robertson (R)		*100.0*

Democratic Primary

Edward M. Kennedy (D)	534,725	73.9
Robert E. Dinsmore (D)	117,496	16.2
Frederick C. Langone (D)	59,315	8.2

1982   Republican Primary

Raymond Shamie (R)		100.0

Democratic Primary

Edward M. Kennedy (D)		100.0

1988   Republican Primary

Joseph Malone (R)		100.0

Democratic Primary

Edward M. Kennedy (D)		100.0

1994   Republican Primary

W. Mitt Romney (R)	188,280	82.0
John R. Lakian (R)	40,898	17.8

Democratic Primary

Edward M. Kennedy (D)	391,637	98.9

2000   Republican Primary

Jack E. Robinson III (R)	42,263	96.6

Democratic Primary

Edward M. Kennedy (D)	236,883	99.0

Class 2

1960   Republican Primary

Leverett Saltonstall (R)		100.0

Democratic Primary

Thomas J. O'Connor (D)	270,081	48.3
Foster Furcolo (D)	217,939	39.0
Edmund C. Buckley (D)	70,744	12.7

1966   Republican Primary

Edward W. Brooke (R)		100.0

Democratic Primary

Endicott Peabody (D)	320,967	50.3
John F. Collins (D)	265,016	41.6
Thomas B. Adams (D)	51,435	8.1

1972   Republican Primary

Edward W. Brooke (R)		100.0

Democratic Primary

John J. Droney (D)	215,523	45.1
Gerald O'Leary (D)	169,876	35.5
John P. Lynch (D)	92,979	19.4

1978   Republican Primary

Edward W. Brooke (R)	146,351	53.3
Avi Nelson (R)	128,388	46.7

Democratic Primary

Paul E. Tsongas (D)	296,915	35.6
Paul Guzzi (D)	258,960	31.0
Kathleen Sullivan Alioto (D)	161,036	19.3
Howard Phillips (D)	65,397	7.8
Elaine Noble (D)	52,464	6.3

1984   Republican Primary

Raymond Shamie (R)	173,851	62.4
Elliot L. Richardson (R)	104,761	37.6

Democratic Primary

John F. Kerry (D)	322,470	40.8
James M. Shannon (D)	297,941	37.7
David M. Bartley (D)	85,910	10.9
Michael Joseph Connolly (D)	82,999	10.5

1990   Republican Primary

Jim Rappaport (R)	265,093	66.2
Daniel W. Daly (R)	135,647	33.8

Democratic Primary

John F. Kerry (D)		100.0

1996   Republican Primary

William F. Weld (R)	72,600	98.6

Democratic Primary

John Kerry (D)	221,213	98.6

Massachusetts

1. A special election was held in 1962 to fill the remaining two years of the term of Sen. John F. Kennedy (D), who resigned Dec. 22, 1960, after he was elected president. The first two years of the vacancy were filled by appointee Benjamin A. Smith.

MICHIGAN

Candidates	Votes	%

Class 1

1958   Republican Primary

Charles E. Potter (R)		100.0

Democratic Primary

Philip A. Hart (D)	297,767	80.2
Homer Martin (D)	73,334	19.8

1964   Republican Primary

Elly M. Peterson (R)	219,883	39.0
James F. O'Neil (R)	192,825	34.2
Edward A. Meany (R)	151,498	26.8

Democratic Primary

Philip A. Hart (D)		100.0

1970   Republican Primary

Lenore Romney (R)	277,086	51.3
Robert J. Huber (R)	262,938	48.7

Democratic Primary

Philip A. Hart (D)		100.0

1976 **Republican Primary**

Marvin L. Esch (R)	209,250	44.2
Thomas E. Brennan (R)	129,917	27.5
Robert J. Huber (R)	82,092	17.3
Deane Baker (R)	51,852	11.0

Democratic Primary

Donald W. Riegle Jr. (D)	325,705	44.3
Richard H. Austin (D)	208,310	28.3
James G. O'Hara (D)	170,473	23.2

1982 **Republican Primary**

Philip E. Ruppe (R)	253,082	46.0
William S. Ballenger (R)	122,523	22.3
Robert J. Huber (R)	102,693	18.7
Deane Baker (R)	71,902	13.0

Democratic Primary

Donald W. Riegle Jr. (D)		100.0

1988 **Republican Primary**

Jim Dunn (R)	245,275	61.1
Robert J. Huber (R)	155,984	38.9

Democratic Primary

Donald W. Riegle (D)		100.0

1994 **Republican Primary**

Spencer Abraham (R)	292,399	51.9
Ronna E. Romney (R)	270,304	48.0

Democratic Primary

M. Robert Carr (D)	157,585	24.0
Lana Pollack (D)	151,323	23.1
Joel Ferguson (D)	130,125	19.8
William M. Brodhead (D)	94,601	14.4
John F. Kelley (D)	71,964	11.0
Carl J. Marlinga (D)	50,329	7.7

2000 **Republican Primary**

Spencer Abraham (R)	527,278	100.0

Democratic Primary

Debbie Stabenow (D)	417,503	100.0

Class 2

1960 **Republican Primary**

Alvin M. Bentley (R)	344,043	72.0
Donald S. Leonard (R)	133,562	28.0

Democratic Primary

Patrick V. McNamara (D)		100.0

1966[1] **Republican Special Primary**

Robert P. Griffin (R)	356,700	100.0

Democratic Special Primary

G. Mennen Williams (D)	381,496	59.6
Jerome P. Cavanagh (D)	258,822	40.4

1966 **Republican Primary**

Robert P. Griffin (R)	387,892	100.0

Democratic Primary

G. Mennen Williams (D)	437,438	60.1
Jerome P. Cavanagh (D)	290,465	39.9

1972 **Republican Primary**

Robert P. Griffin (R)		100.0

Democratic Primary

Frank J. Kelley (D)		100.0

1978 **Republican Primary**

Robert P. Griffin (R)	322,530	78.3
L. Brooks Patterson (R)	89,383	21.7

Democratic Primary

Carl Levin (D)	226,584	38.9
Phil Power (D)	115,117	19.8
Richard F. Vander Veen (D)	89,257	15.3
Anthony Derezinski (D)	53,696	9.2
John Otterbacher (D)	50,860	8.7
Paul Rosenbaum (D)	46,892	8.1

1984 **Republican Primary**

Jack Lousma (R)	328,002	62.7
Jim Dunn (R)	194,657	37.2

Democratic Primary

Carl Levin (D)	376,873	100.0

1990 **Republican Primary**

Bill Schuette (R)	270,434	59.7
Clark Durant (R)	182,592	40.3

Democratic Primary

Carl Levin (D)		100.0

1996 **Republican Primary**

Ronna E. Romney (R)	355,583	52.1
Jim Nicholson (R)	326,835	47.9

Democratic Primary

Carl Levin (D)	405,580	99.9

Michigan

1. Robert P. Griffin (R) was appointed in May 1966 to fill the vacancy caused by the death of Sen. Patrick V. McNamara (D) on April 30. On Aug. 2 two Senate primaries were held simultaneously, a special primary for the remainder of McNamara's term and a regular primary for the full term beginning in January 1967. Griffin, who was unopposed for the Republican nomination, and G. Mennen Williams (D) won both primaries. In the November general election Griffin defeated Williams for both the short and the full terms. Returns for the special primary from the Elections Research Center, Washington, D.C.

MINNESOTA[1]

Candidates	Votes	%

Class 1

1958   Republican Primary

| Edward J. Thye (R) | 202,241 | 91.0 |
| E. C. Slettedahl (R) | 13,734 | 6.2 |

Democratic Primary

| Eugene J. McCarthy (DFL) | 279,796 | 75.7 |
| Hjalmar Petersen (DFL) | 76,340 | 20.6 |

1964   Republican Primary

| Wheelock Whitney (R) | | 100.0 |

Democratic Primary

| Eugene J. McCarthy (DFL) | 245,068 | 90.5 |
| R. H. Underdahl (DFL) | 14,562 | 5.4 |

1970   Republican Primary

| Clark MacGregor (R) | 220,353 | 93.3 |
| John D. Baucom (R) | 15,797 | 6.7 |

Democratic Primary

| Hubert H. Humphrey (DFL) | 338,705 | 79.2 |
| Earl D. Craig (DFL) | 88,709 | 20.8 |

1976   Republican Primary

Gerald W. Brekke (I-R)	76,183	54.5
Richard Franson (I-R)	32,115	23.0
John H. Glover (I-R)	13,014	9.3
Roland Riemers (I-R)	9,307	6.7
Bea Mooney (I-R)	9,150	6.5

Democratic Primary

| Hubert H. Humphrey (DFL) | 317,632 | 91.3 |
| Dick Bullock (DFL) | 30,262 | 8.7 |

1978[2]   Republican Special Primary

Dave Durenberger (I-R)	139,187	67.3
Malcolm Moos (I-R)	32,314	15.6
Ken Nordstrom (I-R)	14,635	7.1
Will Lundquist (I-R)	12,261	5.9

Democratic Special Primary

| Robert E. Short (DFL) | 257,269 | 48.0 |
| Donald M. Fraser (DFL) | 253,818 | 47.4 |

American Special Primary

| Paul Helm (AM) | | 100.0 |

1982   Republican Primary

| Dave Durenberger (I-R) | 287,651 | 93.4 |
| Mary Jane Rachner (I-R) | 20,401 | 6.6 |

Democratic Primary

| Mark Dayton (DFL) | 359,014 | 69.1 |
| Eugene J. McCarthy (DFL) | 125,229 | 24.1 |

1988   Republican Primary

| Dave Durenberger (I-R) | 112,413 | 93.5 |

Democratic Primary

| Hubert H. Humphrey III (DFL) | 153,808 | 90.6 |
| Kent S. Herschbach (DFL) | 15,994 | 9.4 |

1994   Republican Primary

| Rod Grams (I-R) | 269,931 | 58.2 |
| Joanell M. Dyrstad (I-R) | 163,205 | 35.2 |

Democratic Primary

| Ann Wynia (D) | 236,476 | 61.6 |
| Tom Foley (D) | 126,756 | 33.0 |

2000   Republican Primary

| Rod Grams (R) | 112,335 | 89.1 |
| Bill Dahn (R) | 13,728 | 10.9 |

Democratic Primary

Mark Dayton (D)	178,972	41.3
Mike Ciresi (D)	96,874	22.4
Jerry R. Janezich (D)	90,074	20.8
Rebecca Yanisch (D)	63,289	14.6

Class 2

1960   Republican Primary

| P. K. Peterson (R) | 256,641 | 89.5 |
| James Malcolm Williams (R) | 30,242 | 10.5 |

Democratic Primary

| Hubert H. Humphrey (D) | | 100.0 |

1966   Republican Primary

| Robert A. Forsythe (R) | 211,282 | 81.2 |
| Henry A. Johnsen (R) | 48,941 | 18.8 |

Democratic Primary

| Walter F. Mondale (DFL) | 410,841 | 91.0 |
| Ralph E. Franklin (DFL) | 40,785 | 9.0 |

1972   Republican Primary

| Philip Hansen (R) | | 100.0 |

Democratic Primary

| Walter F. Mondale (DFL) | 230,679 | 89.9 |

1978   Republican Primary

| Rudy Boschwitz (I-R) | 185,393 | 86.8 |
| Harold E. Stassen (I-R) | 28,170 | 13.2 |

Democratic Primary

| Wendell R. Anderson (DFL) | 286,209 | 56.9 |
| John S. Connolly (DFL) | 159,974 | 31.8 |

American Primary

| Sal Carlone (AM) | | 100.0 |

1984

Republican Primary

Rudy Boschwitz (I-R)	162,555	96.6

Democratic Primary

Joan Anderson Growe (DFL)	238,190	75.9
Robert W. "Bob" Mattson (DFL)	61,489	19.6

1990

Republican Primary

Rudy Boschwitz (I-R)	293,619	86.9
John J. Zeleniak (I-R)	44,202	13.1

Democratic Primary

Paul D. Wellstone (DFL)	226,306	60.4
James W. Nichols (DFL)	129,302	34.5
Gene Schenk (DFL)	19,379	5.2

1996

Republican Primary

Rudy Boschwitz (R)	158,678	80.6
Stephen Young (R)	16,324	8.3
Bert McKasy (R)	12,711	6.5

Democratic Primary

Paul Wellstone (DFL)	194,699	86.4
Dick Franson (DFL)	16,465	7.3

Reform Primary

Dean Barkley (REF)	3,553	100.0

Minnesota

1. In Minnesota, the Democratic Party is known as the Democratic-Farmer-Labor Party (DFL). From 1976 to 1994, Republican Party was known as the Independent Republican Party (I-R).

2. A special election was held to fill the unexpired term of Sen. Hubert H. Humphrey (DFL), who died Jan. 13, 1978.

MISSISSIPPI

Candidates	Votes	%
Class 1		

1922

Democratic Primary

James K. Vardaman (D)	74,597	47.0
Hubert D. Stephens (D)	65,980	41.5
Bell Kearney (D)	18,303	11.5

Democratic Runoff

Hubert D. Stephens (D)	95,351	52.3
James K. Vardaman (D)	86,853	47.7

1928

Democratic Primary

Hubert D. Stephens (D)	62,850	52.6
T. Webber Wilson (D)	56,641	47.4

1934

Democratic Primary

Hubert D. Stephens (D)	64,035	37.3
Theodore G. Bilbo (D)	63,752	37.2
Ross A. Collins (D)	42,209	24.6

Democratic Runoff

Theodore G. Bilbo (D)	101,702	51.8
Hubert D. Stephens (D)	94,587	48.2

1940

Democratic Primary

Theodore G. Bilbo (D)	91,334	59.3
Hugh L. White (D)	62,641	40.7

1946

Democratic Primary

Theodore G. Bilbo (D)	97,820	51.0
Ellis (D)	58,005	30.2
Ross A. Collins (D)	18,875	9.8
Levings (D)	15,720	8.2

1952

Democratic Primary

John C. Stennis (D)	191,380	89.4
William P. Davis (D)	22,802	10.7

1958

Democratic Primary

John C. Stennis (D)		100.0

1964

Democratic Primary

John C. Stennis (D)	173,764	97.4

1970

Democratic Primary

John C. Stennis (D)		100.0

1976

Democratic Primary

John C. Stennis (D)	157,943	85.4
E. Michael Marks (D)	27,016	14.6

1982

Republican Primary

Haley Barbour (R)	30,636	74.2
Bobby Richard (R)	10,651	25.8

Democratic Primary

John C. Stennis (D)	145,817	75.1
Charles Pittman (D)	33,651	17.3
Colon Johnston (D)	14,696	7.6

1988

Republican Primary

Trent Lott (R)		100.0

Democratic Primary

Wayne Dowdy (D)	189,954	53.4
Dick Molpus (D)	152,126	42.8

1994

Republican Primary

Trett Lott (R)	72,543	95.4

Democratic Primary

Ken Harper (D)	62,963	46.7
Hiram Eastland (D)	38,976	28.9
Jorja P. Turnipseed (D)	17,873	13.3
James W. Hunt (D)	7,843	5.8
Shawn O'Hara (D)	7,189	5.3

		Votes	%
2000	**Republican Primary**		
	Trent Lott (R)	107,127	*100.0*
	Democratic Primary		
	Troy Brown (D)	27,457	*36.6*
	Rickey L. Cole (D)	15,449	*20.6*
	Clinton Allison (D)	14,671	*19.6*
	Robert R. Richmond Jr. (D)	8,809	*11.7*
	James "Bootie" Hunt (D)	8,616	*11.5*
	Democratic Runoff		
	Troy Brown (D)	20,358	*66.9*
	Rickey L. Cole (D)	10,080	*33.1*

Class 2

		Votes	%
1924	**Democratic Primary**		
	Pat Harrison (D)	80,371	*82.1*
	Earl Brewer (D)	17,496	*17.9*
1930	**Democratic Primary**		
	Pat Harrison (D)		*100.0*
1936	**Democratic Primary**		
	Pat Harrison (D)	128,729	*65.5*
	M. S. Conner (D)	65,296	*33.2*
1942	**Democratic Primary**		
	James O. Eastland (D)	50,112	*37.6*
	Wall Doxey (D)	37,756	*28.3*
	Ross A. Collins (D)	36,511	*27.4*
	Wall (D)	8,077	*6.1*
	Democratic Runoff		
	James O. Eastland (D)	74,747	*56.8*
	Wall Doxey (D)	56,748	*43.2*
1948	**Democratic Primary**		
	James O. Eastland (D)		*100.0*
1954	**Democratic Primary**		
	James O. Eastland (D)	136,836	*62.0*
	Carroll Gartin (D)	83,761	*38.0*
1960	**Democratic Primary**		
	James O. Eastland (D)	136,735	*94.2*
	Ance Blakeney (D)	8,397	*5.8*
1966	**Republican Primary**		
	Prentiss Walker (R)		*100.0*
	Democratic Primary		
	James O. Eastland (D)	240,171	*83.1*
	Clifton Whitley (D)	34,323	*11.9*
	Charles P. Mosby (D)	14,591	*5.1*
1972	**Republican Primary**		
	Gil Carmichael (R)	18,369	*79.1*
	James H. Meredith (R)	4,859	*20.9*

		Votes	%
	Democratic Primary		
	James O. Eastland (D)	203,847	*70.2*
	Taylor Webb (D)	67,656	*23.3*
	Louis Fondren (D)	18,753	*6.5*
1978	**Republican Primary**		
	Thad Cochran (R)	51,212	*69.1*
	Charles W. Pickering (R)	22,949	*30.9*
	Democratic Primary		
	Maurice Dantin (D)	102,968	*27.2*
	Cliff Finch (D)	98,751	*26.1*
	Charles Sullivan (D)	78,702	*20.8*
	William L. Waller (D)	74,465	*19.7*
	Democratic Runoff		
	Maurice Dantin (D)	235,904	*65.3*
	Cliff Finch (D)	125,109	*34.7*
1984	**Republican Primary**		
	Thad Cochran (R)		*100.0*
	Democratic Primary		
	William Winter (D)	88,883	*69.5*
	W. W. Easley III (D)	15,363	*12.0*
	William L. Gilbert (D)	13,843	*10.8*
	Billy Taylor (D)	9,786	*7.6*
1990	**Republican Primary**		
	Thad Cochran (R)		*100.0*
1996	**Republican Primary**		
	Thad Cochran (R)	138,813	*95.4*
	Democratic Primary		
	James W. Hunt (D)	47,483	*58.8*
	Shawn O'Hara (D)	33,336	*41.2*

MISSOURI

Candidates	Votes	%

Class 1

		Votes	%
1958	**Republican Primary**		
	Hazel Palmer (R)	61,481	*44.6*
	William M. Thomas (R)	36,438	*26.5*
	Homer S. Cotton (R)	27,023	*19.6*
	Hiram Grosby (R)	12,818	*9.3*
	Democratic Primary		
	Stuart Symington (D)	365,470	*92.2*
	Lawrence L. Hastings (D)	19,954	*5.0*
1964	**Republican Primary**		
	Jean P. Bradshaw (R)	165,048	*78.2*
	Morris D. Duncan (R)	46,030	*21.8*

Democratic Primary		
Stuart Symington (D)	563,313	92.0
William M. Thomas (D)	35,509	5.8

1970   **Republican Primary**

John C. Danforth (R)	165,728	72.6
Doris M. Bass (R)	45,049	19.7
Morris D. Duncan (R)	17,670	7.7

Democratic Primary

Stuart Symington (D)	392,670	89.3

American Primary

Gene Chapman (AM)	684	47.1
Lawrence Petty (AM)	400	27.5
Ralph A. DePugh (AM)	368	25.4

1976   **Republican Primary**

John C. Danforth (R)	284,025	93.5
Gregory Hansman (R)	19,796	6.5

Democratic Primary

Jerry Litton (D)[1]	401,822	45.4
Warren E. Hearnes (D)	233,544	26.4
James W. Symington (D)	222,681	25.2

1982   **Republican Primary**

John C. Danforth (R)	217,162	73.9
Mel Hancock (R)	61,378	20.9

Democratic Primary

Harriett Woods (D)	263,259	44.8
Burleigh Arnold (D)	140,446	23.9
Tom Ryan (D)	75,599	12.9
Thomas E. Zych (D)	35,876	6.1

1988   **Republican Primary**

John C. Danforth (R)		100.0

Democratic Primary

Jeremiah W. Nixon (D)		100.0

1994   **Republican Primary**

John Ashcroft (R)	260,065	83.2

Democratic Primary

Alan Wheat (D)	215,171	41.0
Marsha Murphy (D)	200,937	38.3
Jim Thomas (D)	60,204	11.5

Libertarian Primary

Bill Johnson (LIBERT)	1,604	69.7
Rickey Jamerson (LIBERT)	698	30.4

2000   **Republican Primary**

John Ashcroft (R)	327,442	89.6
Marc Perkel (R)	38,103	10.4

Democratic Primary		
Mel Carnahan (D)	323,841	78.2
Ronald William Wagganer (D)	90,251	21.8

Class 3

1956   **Republican Primary**

Herbert Douglas (R)	83,458	40.8
Albert E. Schoenbeck (R)	78,747	38.5
William M. Thomas (R)	28,924	14.1
William E. Van Taay (R)	13,556	6.6

Democratic Primary

Thomas C. Hennings Jr. (D)[2]	389,986	95.9

1962   **Republican Primary**

Crosby Kemper (R)	119,136	66.6
Duane Cox (R)	23,606	13.2
Morris D. Duncan (R)	15,109	8.5
William M. Thomas (R)	14,131	7.9

Democratic Primary

Edward V. Long (D)	370,826	86.5
Lewis E. Morris (D)	37,507	8.8

1968   **Republican Primary**

Thomas B. Curtis (R)	192,028	84.5
Morris D. Duncan (R)	24,418	10.8

Democratic Primary

Thomas F. Eagleton (D)	224,017	36.6
Edward V. Long (D)	198,901	32.5
True Davis (D)	178,961	29.3

1974   **Republican Primary**

Thomas B. Curtis (R)	136,447	81.9
Paul M. Robinett (R)	16,882	10.1
Gregory Hansman (R)	13,285	8.0

Democratic Primary

Thomas F. Eagleton (D)	420,681	87.5
Pat O'Brien (D)	30,389	6.3
Lee C. Sutton (D)	29,835	6.2

1980   **Republican Primary**

Gene McNary (R)	197,060	61.5
David Doctorian (R)	82,332	25.7
Morris D. Duncan (R)	21,959	6.9
Gregory Hansman (R)	18,893	5.9

Democratic Primary

Thomas F. Eagleton (D)	553,392	82.8
Lee C. Sutton (D)	53,280	8.2
Herb Fillmore (D)	38,677	6.0

1986   **Republican Primary**

Christopher Bond (R)	239,961	88.9

Democratic Primary

Harriett Woods (D)	362,287	75.6
James J. Askew (D)	44,292	9.2
Oren L. Staley (D)	34,009	7.1

1992   Republican Primary

Christopher Bond (R)	337,795	82.7
Wes Hummel (R)	70,626	17.3

Democratic Primary

Geri Rothman-Serot (D)	224,984	35.6
Bill Peacock (D)	67,723	10.7
Mert Bernstein (D)	59,290	9.4
George D. Weber (D)	57,254	9.1
Barbara M. Manson (D)	50,091	7.9
Carol A. Coe (D)	48,634	7.7
David Westfall (D)	38,509	6.1

1998   Republican Primary

Christopher Bond (R)	213,569	86.9

Democratic Primary

Jeremiah W. "Jay" Nixon (D)	200,339	66.5
James J. Askew (D)	57,364	19.1
Daniel Dodson (D)	19,257	6.4

Missouri

1. Litton, the winner of the Democratic Senate primary on Aug. 3, 1976, died the same day and the Missouri Democratic central committee substituted Hearnes, the second-place finisher, as the party's nominee.

2. Candidates for the short-term Senate seat vacated by the death of Sen. Thomas C. Hennings Jr. (D) in September 1960 were nominated by the Democratic and Republican state committees of Missouri.

MONTANA

Candidates	Votes	%
Class 1		

1958   Republican Primary

Lou W. Welch (R)	19,860	50.8
Blanche Anderson (R)	19,264	49.2

Democratic Primary

Mike Mansfield (D)	97,207	91.7

1964   Republican Primary

Alex Blewett (R)	31,934	59.4
Lyman Brewster (R)	12,375	23.0
Antoinette Rosell (R)	9,480	17.6

Democratic Primary

Mike Mansfield (D)	109,904	85.5
Joseph P. Monaghan (D)	18,630	14.5

1970   Republican Primary

Harold E. Wallace (R)		100.0

Democratic Primary

Mike Mansfield (D)	68,146	77.2
Tom McDonald (D)	10,733	12.2
John W. Lawlor (D)	9,384	10.6

1976   Republican Primary

Stanley C. Burger (R)	32,313	40.4
Dave Drum (R)	27,257	34.1
John F. Tierney (R)	15,129	18.9
Larry L. Gilbert (R)	5,258	6.6

Democratic Primary

John Melcher (D)	84,413	87.9
Ray E. Gulick (D)	11,593	12.1

1982   Republican Primary

Larry Williams (R)	49,615	88.1
Willie D. Morris (R)	6,696	11.9

Democratic Primary

John Melcher (D)	83,539	68.3
Michael A. Bond (D)	33,565	27.4

1988   Republican Primary

Conrad Burns (R)	63,330	84.7
Tom Faranda (R)	11,427	15.3

Democratic Primary

John Melcher (D)	88,457	74.5
Robert C. Kelleher (D)	30,212	25.5

1994   Republican Primary

Conrad Burns (R)	82,827	100.0

Democratic Primary

Jack Mudd (D)	58,371	47.2
John Melcher (D)	39,607	32.0
Becky Shaw (D)	25,688	20.8

2000   Republican Primary

Conrad Burns (R)	102,125	100.0

Democratic Primary

Brian Schweitzer (D)	59,189	66.2
John Driscoll (D)	30,242	33.8

Class 2

1960   Republican Primary

Orvin B. Fjare (R)	25,899	38.5
Sumner Gerard (R)	17,932	26.6
Wayne Montgomery (R)	13,527	20.1
James H. Morrow (R)	5,261	7.8

Democratic Primary

Lee Metcalf (D)	45,339	35.1
John W. Bonner (D)	33,246	25.8

		Votes	%
	Le Roy Anderson (D)	26,152	20.3
	John W. Mahan (D)	24,208	18.8
1966	**Republican Primary**		
	Tim M. Babcock (R)		100.0
	Democratic Primary		
	Lee Metcalf (D)		100.0
1972	**Republican Primary**		
	Henry S. Hibbard (R)	43,028	49.7
	Harold E. Wallace (R)	26,463	30.6
	Norman C. Wheeler (R)	13,826	16.0
	Democratic Primary		
	Lee Metcalf (D)	106,491	86.4
	Jerome Peters (D)	16,729	13.6
1978	**Republican Primary**		
	Larry Williams (R)	35,479	61.6
	Bill Osborne (R)	16,436	28.6
	Clancy Rich (R)	5,622	9.8
	Democratic Primary		
	Max S. Baucus (D)	87,085	65.3
	Paul Hatfield (D)	25,789	19.3
	John Driscoll (D)	18,184	13.6
1984	**Republican Primary**		
	Chuck Cozzens (R)	33,661	50.7
	Ralph Bouma (R)	17,900	27.0
	Aubyn Curtiss (R)	14,729	22.2
	Democratic Primary		
	Max S. Baucus (D)	80,726	79.4
	Bob Ripley (D)	20,979	20.6
1990	**Republican Primary**		
	Allen C. Kolstad (R)	38,097	43.6
	Bruce Vorhauer (R)	30,837	35.3
	Bill Farrell (R)	11,833	13.5
	John Domenech (R)	6,654	7.6
	Democratic Primary		
	Max S. Baucus (D)	81,687	82.8
	John Driscoll (D)	12,622	12.8
1996	**Republican Primary**		
	Dennis Rehberg (R)	82,158	73.8
	Ed Borcherdt (R)	14,670	13.2
	John K. McDonald (R)	14,485	13.0
	Democratic Primary		
	Max S. Baucus (D)	85,976	100.0
	Reform Primary		
	Becky Shaw (REF)	930	68.0
	Webb Sullivan (REF)	437	32.0

NEBRASKA

	Candidates	Votes	%
	Class 1		
1958	**Republican Primary**		
	Roman L. Hruska (R)		100.0
	Democratic Primary		
	Frank B. Morrison (D)	35,482	51.9
	Eugene O'Sullivan (D)	26,436	38.6
	Mike F. Kracher (D)	6,500	9.5
1964	**Republican Primary**		
	Roman L. Hruska (R)		100.0
	Democratic Primary		
	Raymond W. Arndt (D)		100.0
1970	**Republican Primary**		
	Roman L. Hruska (R)	159,057	85.6
	Otis Glebe (R)	26,627	14.3
	Democratic Primary		
	Frank B. Morrison (D)	85,293	67.2
	Wallace C. Peterson (D)	34,856	27.5
	David J. Thomas (D)	6,610	5.2
1976	**Republican Primary**		
	John Y. McCollister (R)	150,732	78.3
	Richard F. Proud (R)	41,519	21.6
	Democratic Primary		
	Edward Zorinsky (D)	79,988	48.6
	Hess Dyas (D)	77,384	47.0
1982	**Republican Primary**		
	Jim Keck (R)	104,550	66.0
	Ken Cameron (R)	53,453	33.8
	Democratic Primary		
	Edward Zorinsky (D)		100.0
1988	**Republican Primary**		
	David Karnes (R)	117,439	54.8
	Harold J. Daub (R)	96,436	45.0
	Democratic Primary		
	Bob Kerrey (D)	156,498	91.4
	Ken L. Michaelis (D)	14,248	8.3
	New Alliance Primary		
	Ernest Chambers (NA)		100.0
1994	**Republican Primary**		
	Gene Spence (R)	69,529	38.1
	Ralph Knobel (R)	57,719	31.6

Alan Jacobsen (R)	27,374	15.0
John DeCamp (R)	24,414	13.4

Democratic Primary

Bob Kerry (D)	107,137	99.3

2000 **Republican Primary**

Don Stenberg (R)	94,394	50.0
Scott Moore (R)	41,120	21.8
David Hergert (R)	32,228	17.1

Democratic Primary

Ben Nelson (D)	105,661	92.1
Al Hamburg (D)	8,482	7.4

Class 2

1960 **Republican Primary**

Carl T. Curtis (R)		100.0

Democratic Primary

Ralph G. Brooks (D)[1]	41,777	42.4
Clair A. Callan (D)	34,052	34.5
Albert J. Baker (D)	14,355	14.6
Mike F. Kracher (D)	8,424	8.5

1966 **Republican Primary**

Carl T. Curtis (R)		100.0

Democratic Primary

Frank B. Morrison (D)	91,178	78.0
Raymond W. Arndt (D)	25,657	21.9

1972 **Republican Primary**

Carl T. Curtis (R)	141,213	74.0
Ronald L. Blauvelt (R)	30,138	15.8
Christine M. Kneifl (R)	10,941	5.7

Democratic Primary

Terry Carpenter (D)	52,779	29.0
Wallace C. Peterson (D)	49,569	27.2
Wayne W. Ziebarth (D)	42,181	23.1
Donald Searcy (D)	25,854	14.2

1978 **Republican Primary**

Donald Shasteen (R)	127,525	78.4
Lenore R. Etchison (R)	34,916	21.5

Democratic Primary

J. James Exon (D)		100.0

1984 **Republican Primary**

Nancy Hoch (R)	61,009	40.5
John W. DeCamp (R)	24,730	16.4
Richard N. Thompson (R)	23,720	15.7
Fred A. Lockwood (R)	21,115	14.0
Ken Cameron (R)	16,123	10.7

Democratic Primary

J. James Exon (D)	135,242	100.0

1990 **Republican Primary**

Harold J. Daub (R)	178,232	91.3
Otis Glebe (R)	16,367	8.4

Democratic Primary

J. James Exon (D)		100.0

1996 **Republican Primary**

Chuck Hagel (R)	112,953	62.2
Don Stenberg (R)	67,974	37.5

Democratic Primary

Ben Nelson (D)	93,140	97.0

Nebraska

1. Brooks, winner of the Senate primary, died in September 1960 and the Nebraska Democratic state committee substituted Robert Conrad as the party's nominee. Conrad had been a candidate for the Democratic gubernatorial nomination.

NEVADA[1]

Candidates	Votes	%

Class 1

1958 **Republican Primary**

George W. Malone (R)		100.0

Democratic Primary

Howard W. Cannon (D)	22,787	51.7
Fred Anderson (D)	21,319	48.3

1964 **Republican Primary**

Paul Laxalt (R)	25,220	90.3
Wilford Owen Woodruff (R)	1,433	5.1

Democratic Primary

Howard W. Cannon (D)	36,320	59.6
William A. Galt (D)	12,054	19.8
Harry Claiborne (D)	10,807	17.7

1970 **Republican Primary**

William J. Raggio (R)	32,816	90.5
Wilford O. Woodruff (R)	3,456	9.5

Democratic Primary

Howard W. Cannon (D)	54,320	89.3
Walter D. Duesenberg (D)	4,350	7.1

1976 **Republican Primary**

David Towell (R)	25,960	67.4
S. M. Cavnar (R)	5,964	15.5
"None of these candidates"	5,164	13.4

Democratic Primary

Howard W. Cannon (D)	61,407	*85.8*
"None of these candidates"	4,817	*6.7*

1982   Republican Primary

Chic Hecht (R)	26,940	*39.1*
Rick Fore (R)	17,065	*24.8*
Jack Kenney (R)	12,191	*17.7*
S. M. Cavnar (R)	6,327	*9.2*
"None of these candidates"	5,411	*7.8*

Democratic Primary

Howard W. Cannon (D)	54,288	*49.7*
James Santini (D)	49,735	*45.5*

1988   Republican Primary

Chic Hecht (R)	55,473	*82.1*
Larry Scheffler (R)	5,618	*8.3*
"None of these candidates"	6,460	*9.6*

Democratic Primary

Richard H. Bryan (D)	62,278	*79.5*
Patrick M. Fitzpatrick (D)	4,721	*6.0*
"None of these candidates"	7,035	*9.0*

1994   Republican Primary

Hal Furman (R)	58,521	*50.5*
Charles Woods (R)	29,601	*25.5*

Democratic Primary

Richard H. Bryan (D)		*100.0*

2000   Republican Primary

John Ensign (R)	95,904	*88.0*
Richard Hamzik (R)	6,202	*5.7*

Democratic Primary

Ed Bernstein (D)		*100.0*

Class 3

1956   Republican Primary

Clifton Young (R)		*100.0*

Democratic Primary

Alan Bible (D)	26,784	*68.2*
Mahlon Brown (D)	8,043	*20.5*
Harvey Dickerson (D)	2,436	*6.2*
Jay Sourwine (D)	2,020	*5.1*

1962   Republican Primary

William B. Wright (R)	17,478	*69.7*
Charles B. Grant (R)	6,811	*27.1*

Democratic Primary

Alan Bible (D)	38,556	*76.2*
Jack Streeter (D)	10,703	*21.1*

1968   Republican Primary

Ed Fike (R)	20,585	*53.0*
William J. Raggio (R)	17,634	*45.4*

Democratic Primary

Alan Bible (D)		*100.0*

1974   Republican Primary

Paul Laxalt (R)	33,660	*81.3*
Jim Talbert (R)	3,984	*9.6*
S. M. Cavnar (R)	3,752	*9.1*

Democratic Primary

Harry Reid (D)	44,768	*58.6*
Maya Miller (D)	25,738	*33.7*
Dan Miller (D)	5,869	*7.7*

1980   Republican Primary

Paul Laxalt (R)	45,857	*90.3*
Richard A. Glister (R)	2,509	*5.0*

Democratic Primary

Mary Gojack (D)		*100.0*

1986   Republican Primary

James Santini (R)	55,947	*80.3*
Richard Gilster (R)	3,544	*5.1*
"None of these candidates"	8,214	*11.8*

Democratic Primary

Harry Reid (D)	74,275	*82.7*
Manny Beals (D)	7,039	*7.8*
"None of these candidates"	8,486	*9.4*

1992   Republican Primary

Demar Dahl (R)	37,667	*36.9*
Bob Gore (R)	31,963	*31.3*
"None of these candidates"	13,523	*13.2*
Andy Anderson (R)	8,351	*8.2*

Democratic Primary

Harry Reid (D)	64,828	*52.8*
Charles Wood (D)	48,364	*39.4*

1998   Republican Primary

John Ensign (R)	105,263	*80.6*
Ralph W. Stephens (R)	13,679	*10.5*
"None of these candidates"	13,523	*9.0*

Democratic Primary

Harry Reid (D)		*100.0*

Nevada

1. In Nevada, primary voters may vote for "None of these candidates." The "None of these candidates" vote is given here only where it amounted to 5 percent or more of the total.

NEW HAMPSHIRE

Candidates	Votes	%

Class 2

1960 **Republican Primary**

| Styles Bridges (R) | 87,629 | 92.9 |
| Albert Levitt (R) | 6,681 | 7.1 |

Democratic Primary

Herbert W. Hill (D)	16,198	40.2
Alphonse Roy (D)	13,782	34.3
Frank L. Sullivan (D)	10,266	25.5

1962[1] **Republican Special Primary**

Perkins Bass (R)	31,037	31.3
Doloris Bridges (R)	29,345	29.6
Maurice J. Murphy (R)	24,204	24.4
Chester E. Merrow (R)	14,417	14.6

Democratic Special Primary

| Thomas J. McIntyre (D) | | 100.0 |

1966 **Republican Primary**

Harrison R. Thyng (R)	22,741	29.5
Wesley Powell (R)	18,145	23.5
William R. Johnson (R)	17,410	22.6
Lane Dwinell (R)	10,781	14.0
Doloris Bridges (R)	7,613	9.9

Democratic Primary

| Thomas J. McIntyre (D) | | 100.0 |

1972 **Republican Primary**

Wesley Powell (R)	42,837	48.0
Peter J. Booras (R)	19,714	22.1
David A. Brock (R)	16,326	18.3
Marshall W. Cobleigh (R)	10,106	11.3

Democratic Primary

| Thomas J. McIntyre (D) | | 100.0 |

1978 **Republican Primary**

Gordon J. Humphrey (R)	35,503	50.4
James A. Masiello (R)	18,371	26.1
Alf E. Jacobson (R)	13,619	19.4

Democratic Primary

| Thomas J. McIntyre (D) | 31,796 | 80.7 |
| Raymond J. Coughlan (D) | 7,605 | 19.3 |

1984 **Republican Primary**

| Gordon J. Humphrey (R) | 57,763 | 99.1 |

Democratic Primary

| Norman E. D'Amours (D) | 42,371 | 99.3 |

1990 **Republican Primary**

| Robert C. Smith (R) | 56,215 | 65.0 |
| Tom Christo (R) | 25,286 | 29.2 |

Democratic Primary

John A. Durkin (D)	20,222	41.4
James W. Donchess (D)	15,205	31.1
John Rauh (D)	12,935	26.5

1996 **Republican Primary**

| Robert C. Smith (R) | 85,223 | 97.3 |

Democratic Primary

| Dick Swett (D) | 32,461 | 52.0 |
| John Rauh (D) | 29,395 | 47.1 |

Libertarian Primary

| Ken Blevens (LIBERT) | 663 | 86.0 |

Class 3

1956 **Republican Primary**

| Norris Cotton (R) | 61,673 | 89.5 |
| Joseph Moore (R) | 7,264 | 10.5 |

Democratic Primary

| Laurence M. Pickett (D) | | 100.0 |

1962 **Republican Primary**

| Norris Cotton (R) | 87,445 | 94.4 |
| Norman LePage (R) | 5,167 | 5.6 |

Democratic Primary

| Alfred Catalfo (D) | | 100.0 |

1968 **Republican Primary**

| Norris Cotton (R) | 78,058 | 92.4 |
| John C. Mongan (R) | 6,279 | 7.4 |

Democratic Primary

| John W. King (D) | | 100.0 |

1974 **Republican Primary**

| Louis C. Wyman (R) | 66,749 | 83.0 |
| Leslie R. Babb (R) | 13,670 | 17.0 |

Democratic Primary

John A. Durkin (D)	22,258	50.0
Laurence I. Radway (D)	14,646	32.9
Dennis J. Sullivan (D)	6,330	14.2

1980 **Republican Primary**

Warren B. Rudman (R)	20,206	20.3
John H. Sununu (R)	16,885	16.9
Wesley Powell (R)	14,861	14.9
Edward B. Hager (R)	9,821	9.9
Lawrence J. Brady (R)	9,426	9.5
David H. Bradley (R)	9,361	9.4

Anthony Campaigne (R)	8,495	8.6
George B. Roberts (R)	7,397	7.4

Democratic Primary

John A. Durkin (D)	36,933	79.6
William F. Sullivan (D)	9,486	20.4

1986 Republican Primary

Warren B. Rudman (R)		100.0

Democratic Primary

Endicott Peabody (D)	20,568	61.2
Robert L. Dupay (D)	6,108	18.2
Robert A. Patton (D)	3,721	11.1
Andrew D. Tempelman (D)	2,601	7.8

1992 Republican Primary

Judd Gregg (R)	57,141	49.8
Harold Eckman (R)	43,264	37.7
Jean T. White (R)	10,642	9.3

Democratic Primary

John Rauh (D)	41,923	50.5
Brenda J. Elias (D)	15,943	19.2
Terry Bennett (D)	11,699	14.1
Jeanne Stapleton (D)	7,804	9.4

1998 Republican Primary

Judd Gregg (R)	63,729	85.2
Phil Weber (R)	10,784	14.4

Democratic Primary

George Condodemetraky (D)	22,988	96.7

New Hampshire

1. A special election was held to fill the unexpired term of Sen. Styles Bridges (R), who died Nov. 26, 1961.

NEW JERSEY

Candidates	Votes	%

Class 1

1958 Republican Primary

Robert W. Kean (R)	152,884	43.0
Bernard M. Shanley (R)	128,990	36.3
Robert Morris (R)	73,658	20.7

Democratic Primary

Harrison A. Williams Jr. (D)	152,413	43.1
John J. Grogan (D)	139,605	39.5
Joseph E. McLean (D)	61,478	17.4

1964 Republican Primary

Bernard M. Shanley (R)		100.0

Democratic Primary

Harrison A. Williams Jr. (D)		100.0

1970 Republican Primary

Nelson G. Gross (R)	150,662	65.4
James A. Quaremba (R)	43,547	18.9
Joseph T. Gavin (R)	36,208	15.7

Democratic Primary

Harrison A. Williams Jr. (D)	190,692	65.6
Frank J. Guarini (D)	100,045	34.4

1976 Republican Primary

David F. Norcross (R)	196,457	68.3
Martin E. Wendelken (R)	45,472	15.8
James E. Parker (R)	27,672	9.6
N. Leonard Smith (R)	17,892	6.2

Democratic Primary

Harrison A. Williams Jr. (D)	378,553	85.1
Stephen J. Foley (D)	66,178	14.9

1982 Republican Primary

Millicent Fenwick (R)	193,683	54.3
Jeffrey Bell (R)	163,145	45.7

Democratic Primary

Frank R. Lautenberg (D)	104,666	26.0
Andrew Maguire (D)	92,878	23.0
Joseph A. LeFante (D)	81,440	20.2
Barbara B. Sigmund (D)	45,708	11.3
Howard Rosen (D)	28,427	7.0

1988 Republican Primary

Peter M. Dawkins (R)		100.0

Democratic Primary

Frank R. Lautenberg (D)	362,072	79.5
Elnardo J. Webster (D)	51,938	11.4
Harold J. Young (D)	41,303	9.1

1994 Republican Primary

Garabed Haytaian (R)	126,768	67.3
Brian T. Kennedy (R)	61,532	32.7

Democratic Primary

Frank R. Lautenberg (D)	151,416	81.0
Bill Campbell (D)	26,066	13.9
Lynne A. Speed (D)	9,563	5.1

2000 Republican Primary

Bob Franks (R)	98,370	35.7
William L. Gormley (R)	94,010	34.1
James W. Treffinger (R)	48,674	17.7
Murray Sabrin (R)	34,629	12.6

Democratic Primary

Jon S. Corzine (D)	251,216	58.0
Jim Florio (D)	182,212	42.0

Class 2

1960   **Republican Primary**

Clifford P. Case (R)	230,802	63.7
Robert Morris (R)	120,729	33.3

Democratic Primary

Thorn Lord (D)	177,429	81.6
Richard M. Glassner (D)	40,134	18.4

1966   **Republican Primary**

Clifford P. Case (R)		100.0

Democratic Primary

Warren W. Wilentz (D)	197,428	72.7
David Frost (D)	31,289	11.5
John J. Winberry (D)	19,745	7.3
Clarence Coggins (D)	16,775	6.2

1972   **Republican Primary**

Clifford P. Case (R)	187,268	70.1
James W. Ralph (R)	79,776	29.9

Democratic Primary

Paul J. Krebs (D)	135,000	43.2
Daniel M. Gaby (D)	86,213	27.6
Joseph T. Karcher (D)	51,321	16.4
Henry Kielbasa (D)	40,235	12.9

1978   **Republican Primary**

Jeffrey Bell (R)	118,555	50.7
Clifford P. Case (R)	115,082	49.3

Democratic Primary

Bill Bradley (D)	217,502	58.9
Richard C. Leone (D)	97,667	26.4
Alexander J. Menza (D)	32,386	8.8

1984   **Republican Primary**

Mary V. Mochary (R)	111,851	61.4
Robert Morris (R)	70,418	38.6

Democratic Primary

Bill Bradley (D)	404,301	92.9
Elliot Greenspan (D)	30,680	7.0

1990   **Republican Primary**

Christine Todd Whitman (R)		100.0

Democratic Primary

Bill Bradley (D)	197,454	92.4
Daniel Z. Seyler (D)	16,287	7.6

1996   **Republican Primary**

Dick Zimmer (R)	144,121	68.0
Richard A. Du Haime (R)	42,155	19.9
Dick La Rossa (R)	25,608	12.1

Democratic Primary

Robert G. Torricelli (D)	223,444	100.0

NEW MEXICO

Candidates	Votes	%

Class 1

1958   **Republican Primary**

Forrest S. Atchley (R)	10,384	51.3
Reginaldo Espinoza (R)	9,861	48.7

Democratic Primary

Dennis Chavez (D)	68,689	65.7
E. S. Walker (D)	35,927	34.3

1964   **Republican Primary**

Edwin L. Mechem (R)		100.0

Democratic Primary

Joseph M. Montoya (D)		100.0

1970   **Republican Primary**

Anderson Carter (R)	32,122	57.8
David F. Cargo (R)	17,951	32.3
Harold G. Thompson (R)	5,544	10.0

Democratic Primary

Joseph M. Montoya (D)	85,285	73.1
Richard B. Edwards (D)	31,381	26.9

1976   **Republican Primary**

Harrison "Jack" Schmitt (R)	34,074	71.7
Eugene W. Pierce (R)	10,965	23.1
Arthur A. Lavine (R)	2,481	5.2

Democratic Primary

Joseph M. Montoya (D)	96,063	66.3
Robert R. Sims (D)	48,824	33.7

1982   **Republican Primary**

Harrison "Jack" Schmitt (R)		100.0

Democratic Primary

Jeff Bingaman (D)	91,780	54.4
Jerry Apodaca (D)	66,598	39.4
Virginia R. Keehan (D)	10,466	6.2

1988   **Republican Primary**

William Valentine (R)	35,809	43.4
Rick Montoya (R)	23,162	28.1
Corky Morris (R)	16,539	20.1
Joseph J. Carraro (R)	6,928	8.4

Democratic Primary

Jeff Bingaman (D)		100.0

1994	Republican Primary		
	Colin R. McMillan (R)	65,119	*72.6*
	Bill Turner (R)	13,178	*14.7*
	Robin D. Otten (R)	11,439	*12.7*
	Democratic Primary		
	Jeff Bingaman (D)	165,148	*100.0*
2000	**Republican Primary**		
	Bill Redmond (R)	43,780	*60.4*
	Steve Pearce (R)	15,628	*21.6*
	William F. Davis (R)	13,083	*18.0*
	Democratic Primary		
	Jeff Bingaman (D)	124,887	*100.0*

Class 2

1960	Republican Primary		
	William F. Colwes (R)	18,884	*53.0*
	Joseph Rendon (R)	11,866	*33.3*
	Frederic W. Airy (R)	4,859	*13.6*
	Democratic Primary		
	Clinton P. Anderson (D)	98,037	*81.3*
	James P. Speer (D)	9,360	*7.8*
	N. Tito Quintana (D)	8,981	*7.4*
1966	**Republican Primary**		
	Anderson Carter (R)		*100.0*
	Democratic Primary		
	Clinton P. Anderson (D)		*100.0*
1972	**Republican Primary**		
	Pete V. Domenici (R)	37,337	*63.2*
	David F. Cargo (R)	12,522	*21.2*
	E. Lee Francis (R)	4,583	*7.8*
	Democratic Primary		
	Jack Daniels (D)	45,648	*29.7*
	Robert A. Mondragon (D)	29,603	*19.3*
	David L. Norvell (D)	24,917	*16.2*
	Thomas G. Morris (D)	22,849	*14.9*
1978	**Republican Primary**		
	Pete V. Domenici (R)		*100.0*
	Democratic Primary		
	Toney Anaya (D)		*100.0*
1984	**Republican Primary**		
	Pete V. Domenici (R)	42,760	*100.0*
	Democratic Primary		
	Judith A. Pratt (D)	67,722	*45.5*
	Nick Franklin (D)	56,434	*37.9*
	Anselmo A. Chavez (D)	24,694	*16.6*

1990	Republican Primary		
	Pete V. Domenici (R)		*100.0*
	Democratic Primary		
	Tom R. Benavides (D)		*100.0*
1996	**Republican Primary**		
	Pete V. Domenici (R)	69,394	*100.0*
	Democratic Primary		
	Art Trujillo (D)	84,721	*70.6*
	Eric Treisman (D)	35,363	*29.4*
	Green Primary		
	Abraham J. Gutmann (GREEN)	952	*61.5*
	Sam Hitt (GREEN)	597	*38.6*

NEW YORK[1]

	Candidates	Votes	%

Class 1

1970	Republican Primary		
	Charles E. Goodell (R)		*100.0*
	Democratic Primary		
	Richard L. Ottinger (D)	366,789	*39.6*
	Paul O'Dwyer (D)	302,438	*32.7*
	Theodore C. Sorensen (D)	154,434	*16.7*
	Richard D. McCarthy (D)	102,224	*11.0*
	Conservative Primary		
	James L. Buckley (C)		*100.0*
	Liberal Primary		
	Charles E. Goodell (L)		*100.0*
1976	**Republican Primary**		
	James L. Buckley (R)	242,527	*70.5*
	Peter A. Peyser (R)	101,629	*29.5*
	Democratic Primary		
	Daniel Patrick Moynihan (D)	333,697	*36.4*
	Bella S. Abzug (D)	323,705	*35.3*
	Ramsey Clark (D)	94,191	*10.3*
	Paul O'Dwyer (D)	82,689	*9.0*
	Abraham J. Hirschfeld (D)	82,331	*9.0*
	Conservative Primary		
	James L. Buckley (C)		*100.0*
	Liberal Primary		
	Henry S. Stern (L)[2]		*100.0*
1982	**Republican Primary**		
	Florence M. Sullivan (R)	216,486	*42.4*
	Muriel Siebert (R)	157,446	*30.8*
	Whitney N. Seymour (R)	136,974	*26.8*

Democratic Primary

Daniel Patrick Moynihan (D)	922,059	85.1
Melvin Klenetsky (D)	161,012	14.9

Conservative Primary

Florence M. Sullivan (C)		100.0

Liberal Primary

Daniel Patrick Moynihan (L)		100.0

Right to Life Primary

Florence M. Sullivan (RTL)		100.0

1988   Republican Primary

Robert McMillan (R)		100.0

Democratic Primary

Daniel Patrick Moynihan (D)		100.0

Conservative Primary

Robert McMillan (R)		100.0

Liberal Primary

Daniel Patrick Moynihan (L)		100.0

Right to Life Primary

Adelle R. Nathanson (RTL)		100.0

1994   Republican Primary

Bernadette Castro (R)		100.0

Democratic Primary

Daniel Patrick Moynihan (D)	526,766	74.7
Al Sharpton (D)	178,231	25.3

Conservative Primary

Bernadette Castro (R)	12,300	62.9
Henry F. Lewes (R)	7,251	37.1

Liberal Primary

Daniel Patrick Moynihan (L)		100.0

Right to Life Primary

Henry F. Lewes (RTL)		100.0

2000   Republican Primary

Rick A. Lazio (R)		100.0

Democratic Primary

Hillary Rodham Clinton (D)	565,353	82.0
Mark S. McMahon (D)	124,315	18.0

Conservative Primary

Rick A. Lazio (R)		100.0

Liberal Primary

Hillary Rodham Clinton (D)		100.0

Right to Life Primary

John O. Adefope (RTL)		100.0

Class 3

1968   Republican Primary

Jacob K. Javits (R)		100.0

Democratic Primary

Paul O'Dwyer (D)	275,877	36.1
Eugene H. Nickerson (D)	257,639	33.7
Joseph Y. Resnick (D)	229,893	30.1

Conservative Primary

James L. Buckley (C)		100.0

Liberal Primary

Jacob K. Javits (L)	10,277	72.1
Murray Baron (L)	3,969	27.8

1974   Republican Primary

Jacob K. Javits (R)		100.0

Democratic Primary

Ramsey Clark (D)	414,327	48.0
Lee Alexander (D)	255,250	29.6
Abraham J. Hirschfeld (D)	194,076	22.5

Conservative Primary

Barbara A. Keating (C)		100.0

Liberal Primary

Jacob K. Javits (L)		100.0

1980   Republican Primary

Alfonse M. D'Amato (R)	323,468	55.7
Jacob K. Javits (R)	257,433	44.3

Democratic Primary

Elizabeth Holtzman (D)	378,567	40.7
Bess Myerson (D)	292,767	31.5
John V. Lindsay (D)	146,815	15.8
John Santucci (D)	111,129	12.0

Conservative Primary

Alfonse M. D'Amato (C)		100.0

Liberal Primary

Jacob K. Javits (R)		100.0

Right to Life Primary

Alfonse M. D'Amato (RTL)		100.0

1986   Republican Primary

Alfonse M. D'Amato (R)		100.0

Democratic Primary

John S. Dyson (D)		100.0

	Right to Life Primary		
	Alfonse M. D'Amato (RTL)		100.0
1992	**Republican Primary**		
	Alfonse M. D'Amato (R)		100.0
	Democratic Primary		
	Robert Abrams (D)	426,904	37.0
	Geraldine A. Ferraro (D)	415,650	36.0
	Al Sharpton (D)	166,665	14.5
	Elizabeth Holtzman (D)	144,026	12.5
	Conservative Primary		
	Alfonse M. D'Amato (C)		100.0
	Liberal Primary		
	Robert Abrams (L)		100.0
	Right to Life Primary		
	Alfonse M. D'Amato (RTL)		100.0
1998	**Republican Primary**		
	Alfonse M. D'Amato (R)		100.0
	Democratic Primary		
	Charles E. Schumer (D)	388,701	50.8
	Geraldine A. Ferraro (D)	201,625	26.4
	Mark Green (D)	145,819	19.1
	Conservative Primary		
	Alfonse M. D'Amato (C)		100.0
	Liberal Primary		
	Charles E. Schumer (L)		100.0
	Right to Life Primary		
	Alfonse M. D'Amato (RTL)		100.0

New York

1. Until 1968, when New York adopted a primary system, party conventions or state central committees nominated candidates for statewide office.

2. Stern withdrew after the primary and the Liberal Party's state committee substituted Daniel Patrick Moynihan (D) as the Liberal nominee.

NORTH CAROLINA

Candidates	Votes	%

Class 2

1924	**Democratic Primary**		
	Furnifold M. Simmons (D)		100.0
1930	**Republican Primary**		
	George M. Pritchard (R)	22,287	56.9
	G. E. Butler (R)	9,098	23.2
	I. B. Tucker (R)	6,277	16.0

	Democratic Primary		
	Josiah W. Bailey (D)	200,242	60.2
	Furnifold M. Simmons (D)	129,875	39.0
1936	**Democratic Primary**		
	Josiah W. Bailey (D)	247,365	52.5
	Richard T. Fountain (D)	184,197	39.1
	W. H. Griffin (D)	26,171	5.6
1942	**Democratic Primary**		
	Josiah W. Bailey (D)	211,038	65.8
	Richard T. Fountain (D)	94,581	29.5
1948	**Democratic Primary**		
	J. Melville Broughton (D)	207,981	53.1
	William B. Umstead (D)	183,865	46.9
	Democratic Special Primary		
	J. Melville Broughton (D)	206,605	52.3
	William B. Umstead (D)	188,420	47.7
1950	**Democratic Special Primary**		
	Frank P. Graham (D)	303,605	49.1
	Willis Smith (D)	250,222	40.5
	Robert R. Reynolds (D)	58,752	9.5
	Democratic Special Runoff		
	Willis Smith (D)	281,114	51.8
	Frank P. Graham (D)	261,789	48.2
1954	**Democratic Primary**		
	W. Kerr Scott (D)	312,053	50.8
	Alton Lennon (D)	286,730	46.7
	Democratic Special Primary		
	W. Kerr Scott (D)	274,674	49.4
	Alton Lennon (D)	264,265	47.5
1958	B. Everett Jordan (D)[1]		
	Richard C. Clarke Jr. (R)		
1960	**Republican Primary**		
	Kyle Hayes (R)		100.0
	Democratic Primary		
	B. Everett Jordan (D)	324,188	54.3
	Addison Hewlett (D)	217,899	36.5
	Robert W. Gregory (D)	31,463	5.3
1966	**Republican Primary**		
	John S. Shallcross (R)		100.0
	Democratic Primary		
	B. Everett Jordan (D)	445,454	79.3
	Hubert E. Seymour (D)	116,548	20.7
1972	**Republican Primary**		
	Jesse Helms (R)	92,496	60.1
	James C. Johnson (R)	45,303	29.5
	William H. Booe (R)	16,032	10.4

Democratic Primary

Nick Galifianakis (D)	377,993	*49.3*
B. Everett Jordan (D)	340,391	*44.4*

Democratic Runoff

Nick Galifianakis (D)	333,558	*55.5*
B. Everett Jordan (D)	267,997	*44.6*

1978 Republican Primary

Jesse Helms (R)		*100.0*

Democratic Primary

Luther H. Hodges Jr. (D)	260,868	*40.1*
John Ingram (D)	170,715	*26.2*
Lawrence Davis (D)	105,381	*16.2*
McNeill Smith (D)	82,703	*12.7*

Democratic Runoff

John Ingram (D)	244,469	*54.2*
Luther H. Hodges Jr. (D)	206,223	*45.8*

1984 Republican Primary

Jesse Helms (R)	134,675	*90.6*
George Wimbish (R)	13,899	*9.4*

Democratic Primary

James B. Hunt Jr. (D)	655,429	*77.5*
Thomas L. Allred (D)	126,841	*15.0*
Harrill Jones (D)	63,676	*7.5*

1990 Republican Primary

Jesse Helms (R)	157,345	*84.3*
L. C. Nixon (R)	15,355	*8.2*
George Wimbish (R)	13,895	*7.4*

Democratic Primary

Harvey B. Gantt (D)	260,179	*37.5*
Mike Easley (D)	209,934	*30.3*
John Ingram (D)	120,990	*17.4*
R. P. Thomas (D)	82,883	*12.0*

Democratic Runoff

Harvey B. Gantt (D)	273,567	*56.9*
Mike Easley (D)	207,283	*43.1*

1996 Republican Primary

Jesse Helms (R)		*100.0*

Democratic Primary

Harvey B. Gantt (D)	308,837	*52.4*
Charlie Sanders (D)	245,297	*41.6*
Ralph M. McKinney Jr. (D)	34,829	*5.9*

Class 3

1920 Democratic Primary

Lee S. Overman (D)	94,806	*79.9*
A. L. Brooks (D)	23,869	*20.1*

1926 Democratic Primary

Lee S. Overman (D)	140,260	*60.4*
Robert R. Reynolds (D)	91,914	*39.6*

1932 Republican Primary

Jake F. Newell (R)	29,906	*86.5*
G. W. DePriest (R)	4,668	*13.5*

Democratic Primary

Robert R. Reynolds (D)	156,548	*42.5*
Cameron Morrison (D)	143,179	*38.9*
Bowie (D)	37,748	*10.2*
Grist (D)	31,010	*8.4*

Democratic Runoff

Robert R. Reynolds (D)	227,864	*65.4*
Cameron Morrison (D)	120,428	*34.6*

1938 Democratic Primary

Robert R. Reynolds (D)	315,316	*61.5*
Frank Hancock (D)	197,154	*38.5*

1944 Democratic Primary

Clyde R. Hoey (D)	211,049	*68.9*
Cameron Morrison (D)	80,154	*26.2*

1950 Democratic Primary

Clyde R. Hoey (D)		*100.0*
Sam J. Ervin Jr. (D)[2]		

1956 Republican Primary

Joel A. Johnson (R)		*100.0*

Democratic Primary

Sam J. Ervin Jr. (D)	360,967	*84.6*
Marshall C. Kurfees (D)	65,512	*15.4*

1962 Republican Primary

Claude L. Greene Jr. (R)	31,756	*61.1*
C. H. Babcock (R)	20,246	*38.9*

Democratic Primary

Sam J. Ervin Jr. (D)		*100.0*

1968 Republican Primary

Robert V. Somers (R)	48,351	*36.6*
J. L. Zimmerman (R)	43,644	*33.1*
Edwin W. Tenney (R)	40,023	*30.3*

Republican Runoff

Robert V. Somers (R)	8,816	*60.0*
J. L. Zimmerman (R)	5,734	*39.4*

Democratic Primary

Sam J. Ervin Jr. (D)	499,392	*78.3*
Charles A. Pratt (D)	60,362	*9.5*
John T. Gathings (D)	48,357	*7.6*

1974	Republican Primary		
	William E. Stevens (R)	62,419	65.1
	Wood Hall Young (R)	26,918	28.1
	B. E. "Bee" Sweatt (R)	6,520	6.8
	Democratic Primary		
	Robert Morgan (D)	294,986	50.4
	Nick Galifianakis (D)	189,815	32.4
	Henry Hall Wilson (D)	67,247	11.5
1980	**Republican Primary**		
	John P. East (R)		100.0
	Democratic Primary		
	Robert Morgan (D)		100.0
1986	**Republican Primary**		
	James T. Broyhill (R)	139,570	66.5
	David B. Funderburk (R)	63,593	30.3
	Democratic Primary		
	Terry Sanford (D)	409,394	60.2
	John Ingram (D)	111,557	16.4
	Fountain Odom (D)	49,689	7.3
	William I. Belk (D)	33,821	5.0
1992	**Republican Primary**		
	Lauch Faircloth (R)	129,159	47.7
	Sue Myrick (R)	81,801	30.2
	Eugene Johnston (R)	46,112	17.0
	Larry E. Harrington (R)	13,496	5.0
	Democratic Primary		
	Terry Sanford (D)		100.0
1998	**Republican Primary**		
	Lauch Faircloth (R)	217,035	81.8
	Steve Franks (R)	34,459	13.0
	Leonard D. Plyler (R)	13.794	5.2
	Democratic Primary		
	John Edwards (D)	277,468	51.4
	D. G. Martin (D)	149,049	27.6
	Ella Scarborough (D)	55,486	10.3

North Carolina

1. Sen. W. Kerr Scott (D 1954–1958) died April 16, 1958. Jordan was appointed to succeed him. Jordan and Clarke were designated by the state committee of their respective parties to run in the Nov. 4 special election for the remaining two years of Scott's term. Jordan won.

2. Sen. Clyde R. Hoey (D 1945–1954) died May 12, 1954. Ervin was appointed to replace him and was also named by the Democratic state executive committee to run in a Nov. 2 special election for the remaining two years of the term.

NORTH DAKOTA

	Candidates	Votes	%
	Class 1		
1958	**Republican Primary**		
	William Langer (R)[1]	68,541	65.5
	Clyde Duffy (R)	34,152	32.6
	Democratic Primary		
	Raymond Vendsel (D)	30,775	65.8
	Anson Anderson (D)	15,999	34.2
1964	**Republican Primary**		
	Tom Kleppe (R)		100.0
	Democratic Primary		
	Quentin N. Burdick (D)		100.0
1970	**Republican Primary**		
	Tom Kleppe (R)		100.0
	Democratic Primary		
	Quentin N. Burdick (D)		100.0
1976	**Republican Primary**		
	Richard Stroup (R)		100.0
	Democratic Primary		
	Quentin N. Burdick (D)		100.0
	American Primary		
	Clarence Haggard (AM)		100.0
1982	**Republican Primary**		
	Gene Knorr (R)		100.0
	Democratic Primary		
	Quentin N. Burdick (D)		100.0
1988	**Republican Primary**		
	Earl Strinden (R)		100.0
	Democratic Primary		
	Quentin N. Burdick (D)[2]		100.0
	Libertarian Primary		
	Kenneth C. Gardner (LIBERT)		100.0
1994	**Republican Primary**		
	Ben Clayburgh (R)	49,493	100.0
	Democratic Primary		
	Kent Conrad (D)	66,265	100.0
2000	**Republican Primary**		
	Duane Sand (R)	37,878	100.0

Democratic Primary

Kent Conrad (D)	36,585	*100.0*

Class 3

1956   **Republican Primary**

Milton R. Young (R)	88,738	*88.6*
Ray R. Lake (R)	11,398	*11.4*

Democratic Primary

Quentin N. Burdick (D)		*100.0*

1962   **Republican Primary**

Milton R. Young (R)	67,938	*92.2*
Roger Vorachek (R)	5,729	*7.8*

Democratic Primary

William Lanier (D)		*100.0*

1968   **Republican Primary**

Milton R. Young (R)		*100.0*

Democratic Primary

Herschel Lashkowitz (D)		*100.0*

1974   **Republican Primary**

Milton R. Young (R)		*100.0*

Democratic Primary

William L. Guy (D)	55,269	*83.0*
Robert P. McCarney (D)	11,286	*17.0*

1980   **Republican Primary**

Mark Andrews (R)		*100.0*

Democratic Primary

Kent Johanneson (D)	30,789	*77.4*
Michael P. Saba (D)	9,013	*22.6*

1986   **Republican Primary**

Mark Andrews (R)		*100.0*

Democratic Primary

Kent Conrad (R)		*100.0*

1992[2]   **Republican Primary**

Steve Sydness (R)	45,611	*100.0*

Democratic Primary

Byron L. Dorgan (D)	68,113	*100.0*

1998   **Republican Primary**

Donna Nalewaja (R)	24,666	*67.1*
Larry D. Solar (R)	12,104	*32.9*

Democratic Primary

Byron L. Dorgan (D)	43,494	*100.0*

North Dakota

1. No primaries were held for the June 1960 special election in North Dakota to fill the vacancy caused by Langer's death. Nominees were selected by state conventions.

2. A special election was also held in 1992 to fill the remaining two years of the term of Sen. Quentin N. Burdick (D), who died Sept. 8, 1992. Both major-party candidates were nominated by the state party committees and no primaries were held.

OHIO

Candidates	Votes	%
Class 1		

1958   **Republican Primary**

John W. Bricker (R)		*100.0*

Democratic Primary

Stephen M. Young (D)		*100.0*

1964   **Republican Primary**

Robert A. Taft Jr. (R)	606,944	*79.1*
Ted W. Brown (R)	160,263	*20.9*

Democratic Primary

Stephen M. Young (D)	520,641	*66.5*
John Glenn (D)	206,956	*26.4*

1970   **Republican Primary**

Robert A. Taft Jr. (R)	472,202	*50.3*
James A. Rhodes (R)	466,932	*49.7*

Democratic Primary

Howard M. Metzenbaum (D)	430,469	*46.3*
John Glenn (D)	417,027	*44.9*
Kenneth W. Clement (D)	50,375	*5.4*

American Independent Primary

Richard B. Kay (AMI)		*100.0*

1976   **Republican Primary**

Robert A. Taft Jr. (R)		*100.0*

Democratic Primary

Howard M. Metzenbaum (D)	576,124	*53.6*
James V. Stanton (D)	400,552	*37.3*
James D. Nolan (D)	62,979	*5.8*

1982   **Republican Primary**

Paul E. Pfeifer (R)	364,579	*60.0*
Walter E. Beckjord (R)	180,198	*29.7*
Bill Ress (WRITE IN)	62,446	*10.3*

Democratic Primary

Howard M. Metzenbaum (D)	810,785	*82.9*
Norbert G. Dennerll (D)	167,778	*17.1*

Libertarian Primary

Philip Herzing (LIBERT)		*100.0*

1988	Republican Primary		
	George Voinovich (R)		100.0
	Democratic Primary		
	Howard Metzenbaum (D)	1,070,934	83.6
	Ralph A. Applegate (D)	210,508	16.4
1994	**Republican Primary**		
	Mike DeWine (R)	422,366	52.0
	Bernadine Healy (R)	263,559	32.5
	Gene Watts (R)	83,103	10.2
	George H. Rhodes (R)	42,633	5.3
	Democratic Primary		
	Joel Hyatt (D)	432,360	46.2
	Mary O. Boyle (D)	415,851	44.5
	Ralph A. Applegate (D)	86,677	9.3
2000	**Republican Primary**		
	Mike DeWine (R)	1,029,860	79.5
	Ronald Richard Dickson (R)	161,185	12.4
	Frank A. Cremeans (R)	104,219	8.0
	Democratic Primary		
	Theodore S. Celeste (D)	375,205	43.9
	Marvin A. McMickle (D)	208,291	24.3
	Richard Cordray (D)	202,345	23.7
	Daniel I. Radakovich (D)	69,620	8.1

Class 3

1956	Republican Primary		
	George H. Bender (R)		100.0
	Democratic Primary		
	Frank J. Lausche (D)		100.0
1962	**Republican Primary**		
	John M. Briley (R)	177,987	35.3
	Charles E. Fry (R)	143,320	28.4
	John S. Ballard (R)	132,924	26.3
	Ross Pepple (R)	50,221	10.0
	Democratic Primary		
	Frank J. Lausche (D)	437,902	74.0
	Albert T. Ball (D)	90,609	15.3
	Raymond Warren Beringer (D)	63,543	10.7
1968	**Republican Primary**		
	William B. Saxbe (R)	575,178	82.3
	William L. White (R)	71,191	10.2
	Albert E. Payne (R)	52,393	7.5
	Democratic Primary		
	John J. Gilligan (D)	544,814	55.4
	Frank J. Lausche (D)	438,588	44.6

1974	Republican Primary		
	Ralph J. Perk (R)	341,078	64.8
	Peter E. Voss (R)	185,342	35.2
	Democratic Primary		
	John Glenn (D)	571,871	54.4
	Howard M. Metzenbaum (D)	480,123	45.6
1980	**Republican Primary**		
	James E. Betts (R)		100.0
	Democratic Primary		
	John Glenn (D)	934,230	85.9
	Frances A. Waterman (D)	88,506	8.1
	Francis Hunstiger (D)	64,270	5.9
1986	**Republican Primary**		
	Thomas N. Kindness (R)		100.0
	Democratic Primary		
	John H. Glenn (D)	678,171	87.6
	Don Scott (D)	96,309	12.4
1992	**Republican Primary**		
	Mike DeWine (R)	583,805	70.3
	George H. Rhodes (R)	246,625	29.7
	Democratic Primary		
	John H. Glenn (D)	859,622	100.0
1998	**Republican Primary**		
	George V. Voinovich (R)	543,833	72.3
	David McCollough (R)	208,011	27.7
	Democratic Primary		
	Mary O. Boyle (D)	680,626	100.0

OKLAHOMA

Candidates	Votes	%

Class 2

1960	Republican Primary		
	B. Hayden Crawford (R)	37,508	70.4
	Herbert K. Hyde (R)	15,743	29.6
	Democratic Primary		
	Robert S. Kerr (D)	300,061	77.6
	Thomas C. Dunn (D)	65,139	16.8
	D. R. Condo (D)	21,420	5.5
1964[1]	**Republican Special Primary**		
	Bud Wilkinson (R)	100,544	79.2
	Thomas J. Harris (R)	19,170	15.1
	Forest W. Beall (R)	7,211	5.7

Democratic Special Primary

J. Howard Edmondson (D)	215,455	36.4
Fred R. Harris (D)	190,868	32.3
Raymond Gary (D)	170,869	28.9

Democratic Special Runoff

Fred R. Harris (D)	277,362	60.9
J. Howard Edmondson (D)	178,051	39.1

1966   Republican Primary

Pat J. Patterson (R)	36,036	42.5
Don Kinkaid (R)	32,137	37.9
Gustav K. Brandborg (R)	16,617	19.6

Republican Runoff

Pat J. Patterson (R)	42,550	58.3
Don Kinkaid (R)	30,452	41.7

Democratic Primary

Fred R. Harris (D)	359,747	83.6
W. R. Owens (D)	41,580	9.7
Billy E. Brown (D)	29,184	6.8

1972   Republican Primary

Dewey F. Bartlett (R)	94,935	93.1
C. W. Wood (R)	7,029	6.9

Democratic Primary

Ed Edmondson (D)	249,729	56.3
Charles Nesbitt (D)	92,101	20.8
Al Terrill (D)	33,520	7.6
Jed Johnson (D)	28,795	6.5

1978   Republican Primary

Robert B. Kamm (R)		100.0

Democratic Primary

David L. Boren (D)	252,560	45.8
Ed Edmondson (D)	155,626	28.2
Gene Stipe (D)	114,423	20.8

Democratic Runoff

David L. Boren (D)	281,587	60.5
Ed Edmondson (D)	184,175	39.5

1984   Republican Primary

George L. Mothershed (R)	46,933	39.3
Will E. "Bill" Crozier (R)	39,581	33.1
Gar Graham (R)	32,901	27.6

Democratic Primary

David L. Boren (D)	432,534	89.9
Marshall Luse (D)	48,761	10.1

1990   Republican Primary

Stephen Jones (R)		100.0

Democratic Primary

David L. Boren (D)	445,969	84.3
Virginia Jenner (D)	57,909	10.9

1994[2]   Republican Special Primary

James M. Inhofe (R)	159,001	77.8
Tony Caldwell (R)	45,359	22.2

Democratic Special Primary

Dave McCurdy (D)	283,095	64.9
Cody L. Graves (D)	153,367	35.1

1996   Republican Primary

James M. Inhofe (R)	116,241	75.3
Dan Lowe (R)	38,044	24.7

Democratic Primary

Jim Boren (D)	186,611	55.5
Don McCorkell (D)	122,635	36.5
David Louis Annanders (D)	26,794	8.0

Libertarian Primary

Agnes Marie Regier (LIBERT)	1,511	51.4
Michael A. Clem (LIBERT)	1,429	48.6

Class 3

1956   Republican Primary

Douglas McKeever (R)	24,447	55.5
Paul V. Beck (R)	7,666	17.4
Ernest G. Albright (R)	6,539	14.8
Dan M. Madrano (R)	5,379	12.2

Democratic Primary

A. S. Mike Monroney (D)	245,572	71.1
H. O. Doenges (D)	54,546	15.8
Ora J. Fox (D)	29,825	8.6

1962   Republican Primary

B. Hayden Crawford (R)		100.0

Democratic Primary

A. S. Mike Monroney (D)	335,922	74.3
Wilson Wallace (D)	64,996	14.4
Billy E. Brown (D)	26,440	5.8
Woodrow W. Bussey (D)	24,725	5.5

1968   Republican Primary

Henry Bellmon (R)		100.0

Democratic Primary

A. S. Mike Monroney (D)	281,697	76.3
W. R. Owens (D)	32,823	8.9
Jesse L. Leeds (D)	22,843	6.2
Billy E. Brown (D)	20,681	5.6

American Primary

George Washington (AM)	414	57.6
Landis B. Hiniker (AM)	305	42.4

1974	**Republican Primary**		
	Henry Bellmon (R)	132,888	*87.1*
	Warner M. Hornbeck (R)	19,733	*12.9*
	Democratic Primary		
	Ed Edmondson (D)	288,665	*48.7*
	Charles Nesbitt (D)	222,727	*37.5*
	Wilburn Cartwright (D)	35,107	*5.9*
	Democratic Runoff		
	Ed Edmondson (D)	306,178	*58.7*
	Charles Nesbitt (D)	215,685	*41.3*
1980	**Republican Primary**		
	Don Nickles (R)	47,879	*34.7*
	John Zink (R)	45,914	*33.3*
	Ed Noble (R)	39,839	*28.9*
	Republican Runoff		
	Don Nickles (R)	81,697	*65.6*
	John Zink (R)	42,818	*34.4*
	Democratic Primary		
	Robert S. Kerr Jr. (D)	156,666	*34.0*
	Andrew Coats (D)	154,762	*33.6*
	Gene Howard (D)	55,503	*12.1*
	James E. Hamilton (D)	49,369	*10.7*
	Democratic Runoff		
	Andrew Coats (D)	209,952	*53.0*
	Robert S. Kerr Jr. (D)	185,814	*46.9*
	Libertarian Primary		
	Robert Murphy (LIBERT)		*100.0*
1986	**Republican Primary**		
	Don Nickles (R)		*100.0*
	Democratic Primary		
	James R. Jones (R)	324,907	*67.4*
	George Gentry (R)	157,141	*32.6*
1992	**Republican Primary**		
	Don Nickles (R)		*100.0*
	Democratic Primary		
	Steve Lewis (D)		*100.0*
1998	**Republican Primary**		
	Don Nickles (R)		*100.0*
	Democratic Primary		
	Don E. Carroll (D)	120,759	*45.9*
	Jacquelyn Morrow Lewis Ledgerwood (D)	56,393	*21.4*
	Jerry Kobyluk (D)	54,196	*20.6*
	Arlie Nixon (D)	31,860	*12.1*

	Democratic Special Runoff		
	Don E. Carroll (D)	117,442	*75.2*
	Jacquelyn Morrow Lewis Ledgerwood (D)	38,817	*24.8*

Oklahoma
1. A special election was held to fill the unexpired term of Sen. Robert S. Kerr (D), who died Jan. 1, 1963.
2. A special election was held to fill the unexpired term of Sen. David L. Boren (D), who resigned Nov. 15, 1994.

OREGON

	Candidates	Votes	%
	Class 2		
1960[1]	**Republican Special Primary**		
	Elmo E. Smith (R)	201,024	*85.5*
	George Altvater (R)	33,022	*14.0*
	Democratic Special Primary		
	Maurine B. Neuberger (D)	244,865	*99.5*
1960	**Republican Primary**		
	Elmo E. Smith (R)	179,575	*76.5*
	George Altvater (R)	20,438	*8.7*
	R. F. Cook (R)	19,443	*8.3*
	Thomas Killam (R)	14,490	*6.2*
	Democratic Primary		
	Maurine B. Neuberger (D)	211,961	*77.9*
	Harry C. Fowler (D)	28,032	*10.3*
	William B. Murphy (D)	16,245	*6.0*
1966	**Republican Primary**		
	Mark O. Hatfield (R)	178,782	*75.9*
	Walter Huss (R)	30,906	*13.1*
	James Bacaloff (R)	19,699	*8.4*
	Democratic Primary		
	Robert B. Duncan (D)	161,189	*62.2*
	Howard Morgan (D)	89,174	*34.4*
1972	**Republican Primary**		
	Mark O. Hatfield (R)	171,594	*61.1*
	Lynn Engdahl (R)	63,859	*22.8*
	Kenneth A. Brown (R)	30,826	*11.0*
	Democratic Primary		
	Wayne L. Morse (D)	173,147	*43.7*
	Robert B. Duncan (D)	130,845	*33.0*
	Don Willner (D)	74,060	*18.7*
1978	**Republican Primary**		
	Mark O. Hatfield (R)	159,617	*65.7*
	Bert W. Hawkins (R)	43,350	*17.8*
	Robert D. Maxwell (R)	24,294	*10.0*
	Richard L. Schnepel (R)	15,628	*6.4*

Democratic Primary

Vernon Cook (D)	151,754	58.3
John Sweeney (D)	41,599	16.0
Jack A. Brown (D)	35,211	13.5
Steve Anderson (D)	30,066	11.6

1984   Republican Primary

Mark O. Hatfield (R)	214,114	78.6
John T. Schiess (R)	26,848	9.9
Sherry Reynolds (R)	18,590	6.8

Democratic Primary

Margie Hendriksen (D)	249,142	75.8
Sam Kahl (D)	79,317	24.1

1990   Republican Primary

Mark Hatfield (R)	220,449	78.3
Randy Prince (R)	59,970	21.3

Democratic Primary

Harry Lonsdale (D)	162,529	64.1
Steve Anderson (D)	34,305	13.5
Neale S. Hyatt (D)	20,684	8.2
Brooks Washburne (D)	13,766	5.4

1996   Republican Primary

Gordon Smith (R)	224,428	78.1
Lon Mabon (R)	23,479	8.2
Kirby Brumfield (R)	15,744	5.5

Democratic Primary

Tom Bruggere (D)	151,288	49.6
Harry Lonsdale (D)	76,059	24.9
Bill Dwyer (D)	30,871	10.1
Jerry Rust (D)	27,773	9.1
Anna Nevenich (D)	16,827	5.5

Class 3

1956   Republican Primary

Douglas McKay (R)	123,281	49.5
Phil Hitchcock (R)	99,296	39.8
Elmer Deetz (R)	23,170	9.3

Democratic Primary

Wayne L. Morse (D)	195,784	83.4
Woody Smith (D)	38,959	16.6

1962   Republican Primary

Sig Ulander (R)	106,821	50.1
Edwin R. Durno (R)	72,955	34.2
Harold M. Livingston (R)	16,880	7.9

Democratic Primary

Wayne L. Morse (D)	183,385	79.8
Charles E. Gilbert (D)	46,171	20.1

1968   Republican Primary

Bob Packwood (R)	241,464	88.0
John S. Boyd (R)	32,807	12.0

Democratic Primary

Wayne L. Morse (D)	185,091	49.0
Robert B. Duncan (D)	174,795	46.3

1974   Republican Primary

Bob Packwood (R)		100.0

Democratic Primary

Wayne L. Morse (D)[2]	155,729	49.0
Jason Boe (D)	125,055	39.3
Robert T. Daly (D)	21,881	6.9

1980   Republican Primary

Bob Packwood (R)	191,127	62.4
Brenda Jose (R)	45,973	15.0
Kenneth A. Brown (R)	23,599	7.7
Rosalie Huss (R)	22,929	7.5
Willard D. Severn (R)	22,281	7.3

Democratic Primary

Ted Kulongoski (D)	161,153	47.7
Charles O. Porter (D)	69,649	20.6
Jack Sumner (D)	46,107	13.6
John Sweeney (D)	39,691	11.7
Gene Arvidson (D)	20,548	6.1

1986   Republican Primary

Bob Packwood (R)	171,985	57.6
Joe P. Lutz (R)	126,315	42.3

Democratic Primary

James Weaver (D)[3]	183,334	61.6
Rod Monroe (D)	44,553	15.0
Rick Bauman (D)	41,939	14.1
Steve Anderson (D)	26,130	8.8

1992   Republican Primary

Bob Packwood (R)	176,939	59.1
John DeZell (R)	61,128	20.4
Stephanie J. Salvey (R)	27,088	9.0
Randy Prince (R)	20,358	6.8

Democratic Primary

Les AuCoin (D)	153,029	42.2
Harry Lonsdale (D)	152,699	42.1
Joseph Wetzel (D)	32,183	8.9
Bob Bell (D)	23,700	6.5

1995[4]   Republican Special Primary

Gordon Smith (R)	246,060	63.0
Norma Paulus (R)	98,158	25.1
Jack Roberts (R)	29,687	7.6

Democratic Special Primary

Ron Wyden (D)	212,532	49.7
Peter A. DeFazio (D)	187,411	43.8

1998	Republican Primary		
	John Lim (R)	135,048	*62.4*
	John Michael Fitzpatrick (R)	58,139	*26.9*
	Valentine Christian (R)	20,569	*9.5*
	Democratic Primary		
	Ron Wyden (D)	283,654	*91.5*
	John Sweeney (D)	25,456	*8.2*

Oregon

1. A special election to fill the unexpired term of Sen. Richard L. Neuberger (D), who died March 9, 1960, was held in conjunction with the election for the full term, beginning Jan. 3, 1961. His widow, Maurine B. Neuberger (D), and Elmo Smith (R), won both primaries and Maurine Neuberger went on to defeat Smith in the November general election for both the short and full terms. The short term had been filled until the election by Hall Lusk. Returns for the special primary from the Elections Research Center, Washington, D.C.

2. Sen. Morse died after winning the primary and the Democratic state central committee substituted Betty Roberts as the party's nominee.

3. Weaver withdrew after the Democratic primary. Bauman was substituted by the party state central committee.

4. A special election was held to fill the unexpired term of Sen. Bob Packwood (R), who resigned Oct. 1, 1995.

PENNSYLVANIA

	Candidates	Votes	%
	Class 1		
1958	**Republican Primary**		
	Hugh Scott (R)	766,102	*74.0*
	Weldon B. Heyburn (R)	160,857	*15.5*
	Harrison A. Moyer (R)	108,179	*10.4*
	Democratic Primary		
	George M. Leader (D)	724,645	*74.2*
	Clarence P. Bowers (D)	252,468	*25.8*
1964	**Republican Primary**		
	Hugh Scott (R)	869,774	*88.9*
	W. Henry McFarland (R)	106,376	*10.9*
	Democratic Primary		
	Genevieve Blatt (D)	461,111	*45.4*
	Michael A. Musmanno (D)	460,620	*45.4*
	David B. Roberts (D)	93,311	*9.2*
1970	**Republican Primary**		
	Hugh Scott (R)		*100.0*
	Democratic Primary		
	William G. Sesler (D)	477,680	*53.8*
	Norval D. Reece (D)	241,731	*27.3*
	Frank Mesaros (D)	167,779	*18.9*
	American Independent Primary		
	W. Henry McFarland (AMI)		*100.0*
	Constitution Primary		
	Frank W. Gaydosh (CONST)		*100.0*

1976	Republican Primary		
	John Heinz (R)	358,715	*37.7*
	Arlen Specter (R)	332,513	*35.0*
	George R. Packard (R)	160,379	*16.9*
	Democratic Primary		
	William J. Green III (D)	762,733	*68.8*
	Jeanette Reibman (D)	345,264	*31.1*
	Constitution Primary		
	Andrew J. Watson (CONST)		*100.0*
1982	**Republican Primary**		
	John Heinz (R)		*100.0*
	Democratic Primary		
	Cyril H. Wecht (D)	426,625	*57.2*
	John J. Logue (D)	166,078	*22.3*
	Cyril E. Sagan (D)	152,631	*20.5*
1988	**Republican Primary**		
	H. John Heinz (R)[1]		*100.0*
	Democratic Primary		
	Joseph C. Vignola (D)	492,153	*45.4*
	Susan S. Kefover (D)	371,443	*34.2*
	Steve Douglas (D)	145,614	*13.4*
	John J. Logue (D)	76,020	*7.0*
1994	**Republican Primary**		
	Rick Santorum (R)	667,115	*81.5*
	Joe Watkins (R)	150,969	*18.5*
	Democratic Primary		
	Harris Wofford (D)	714,930	*100.0*
2000	**Republican Primary**		
	Rick Santorum (R)	545,687	*100.0*
	Democratic Primary		
	Ron Klink (D)	299,219	*40.7*
	Allyson Y. Schwartz (D)	194,783	*26.5*
	Tom Foley (D)	184,003	*25.0*
	Class 3		
1956	**Republican Primary**		
	James H. Duff (R)	803,971	*85.0*
	Paul E. Sanger (R)	141,820	*15.0*
	Democratic Primary		
	Joseph S. Clark (D)		*100.0*
1962	**Republican Primary**		
	James E. Van Zandt (R)		*100.0*
	Democratic Primary		
	Joseph S. Clark (D)		*100.0*

1968	Republican Primary		
	Richard S. Schweiker (R)		100.0
	Democratic Primary		
	Joseph S. Clark (D)	460,380	53.3
	John H. Dent (D)	402,799	46.7
1974	Republican Primary		
	Richard S. Schweiker (R)		100.0
	Democratic Primary		
	Peter Flaherty (D)	485,361	47.1
	Herbert S. Denenberg (D)	447,081	43.3
	Frank Mesaros (D)	64,070	6.2
	Constitution Primary		
	George W. Shankey (CONST)		100.0
1980	Republican Primary		
	Arlen Specter (R)	419,372	36.4
	Bud Haabestad (R)	382,281	33.2
	Edward L. Howard (R)	148,200	12.9
	Democratic Primary		
	Peter Flaherty (D)	771,119	53.2
	Joseph Rhodes (D)	179,107	12.4
	Peter Liacouras (D)	116,975	8.1
	C. Delores Tucker (D)	107,483	7.4
	Ed Mezvinsky (D)	100,841	7.0
	Tom Anderson (D)	89,656	6.2
1986	Republican Primary		
	Arlen Specter (R)	434,623	76.2
	Richard A. Stokes (R)	135,673	23.8
	Democratic Primary		
	Robert W. Edgar (D)	432,940	47.3
	Don Bailey (D)	408,460	44.7
	George R. H. Elder (D)	46,663	5.1
1992	Republican Primary		
	Arlen Specter (R)	683,118	65.1
	Stephen F. Freind (R)	366,608	34.9
	Democratic Primary		
	Lynn Yeakel (D)	556,372	44.8
	Mark S. Singel (D)	403,656	32.5
	Bob Colville (D)	172,845	13.9
1998	Republican Primary		
	Arlen Specter (R)	376,322	67.2
	Larry Murphy (R)	101,120	18.1
	Tom Lingenfelter (R)	82,168	14.7
	Democratic Primary		
	Bill Lloyd (D)	236,435	49.5
	Richard J. Orloski (D)	121,669	25.5
	Richard J. Cusick (D)	118,684	24.9

Pennsylvania

1. Heinz died April 4, 1991. A special election was held in 1991 to fill the vacancy. Candidates were nominated by state party committees, therefore no primaries were held.

RHODE ISLAND

	Candidates	Votes	%
	Class 1		
1958	Republican Primary		
	Bayard Ewing (R)		100.0
	Democratic Primary		
	John O. Pastore (D)		100.0
1964	Republican Primary		
	Ronald R. Lagueux (R)		100.0
	Democratic Primary		
	John O. Pastore (D)		100.0
1970	Republican Primary		
	John McLaughlin (R)		100.0
	Democratic Primary		
	John O. Pastore (D)	54,090	88.1
	John Quattrocchi (D)	7,332	11.9
1976	Republican Primary		
	John H. Chafee (R)		100.0
	Democratic Primary		
	Richard P. Lorber (D)	60,118	37.8
	Philip W. Noel (D)	60,018	37.7
	John P. Hawkins (D)	25,456	16.0
1982	Republican Primary		
	John H. Chafee (R)		100.0
	Democratic Primary		
	Julius C. Michaelson (D)	56,800	82.4
	Helen E. Flynn (D)	12,159	17.6
1988	Republican Primary		
	John H. Chafee (R)		100.0
	Democratic Primary		
	Richard A. Licht (D)		100.0
1994	Republican Primary		
	John H. Chafee (R)	27,906	69.0
	Thomas R. Post Jr. (R)	12,517	31.0
	Democratic Primary		
	Linda J. Kushner (D)	45,718	100.0
2000	Republican Primary		
	Lincoln D. Chafee (R)	2,221	100.0

Democratic Primary		
Robert A. Weygand (D)	51,769	57.5
Richard A. Licht (D)	38,281	42.5

Class 2

1960   Republican Primary

Raoul Archambault (R)		100.0

Democratic Primary

Claiborne Pell (D)	83,184	61.3
Dennis J. Roberts (D)	44,924	33.1
Howard McGrath (D)	7,535	5.6

1966   Republican Primary

Ruth M. Briggs (R)	15,451	82.1
Charles H. Eden (R)	3,363	17.9

Democratic Primary

Claiborne Pell (D)		100.0

1972   Republican Primary

John H. Chafee (R)		100.0

Democratic Primary

Claiborne Pell (D)		100.0

1978   Republican Primary

James G. Reynolds (R)		100.0

Democratic Primary

Claiborne Pell (D)	69,729	87.0
Raymond J. Greiner (D)	6,076	7.6
Francis P. Kelley (D)	4,330	5.4

1984   Republican Primary

Barbara Leonard (R)	108,492	100.0

Democratic Primary

Claiborne Pell (D)	82,394	100.0

1990   Republican Primary

Claudine Schneider (R)		100.0

Democratic Primary

Claiborne Pell (D)		100.0

1996   Republican Primary

Nancy J. Mayer (R)	11,600	77.5
Thomas R. Post Jr. (R)	2,302	15.4
Theodore Leonard (R)	1,072	7.2

Democratic Primary

Jack Reed (D)	59,336	86.1
Don Gil (D)	9,554	13.9

SOUTH CAROLINA

Candidates	Votes	%

Class 2

1924   Democratic Primary

Coleman L. Blease (D)	83,738	41.8
James F. Byrnes (D)	67,727	33.8
Nathan B. Dial (D)	44,425	22.2

Democratic Runoff

Coleman L. Blease (D)	100,686	50.6
James F. Byrnes (D)	98,465	49.4

1930   Democratic Primary

Coleman L. Blease (D)	111,989	45.6
James F. Byrnes (D)	94,242	38.4
Harris (D)	39,512	16.1

Democratic Runoff

James F. Byrnes (D)	120,755	51.0
Coleman L. Blease (D)	116,264	49.1

1936   Democratic Primary

James F. Byrnes (D)	257,247	87.1
Stoney (D)	25,672	8.7

1941   Democratic Special Primary

Burnet R. Maybank (D)	59,017	47.4
Olin D. Johnston (D)	40,296	32.4
Bryson (D)	25,257	20.3

Democratic Special Runoff

Burnet R. Maybank (D)	92,100	56.6
Olin D. Johnston (D)	70,687	43.4

1942   Democratic Primary

Burnet R. Maybank (D)	120,731	51.4
Eugene Blease (D)	114,241	48.6

1948   Democratic Primary

Burnet R. Maybank (D)	172,611	51.6
William Jennings Bryan Dorn (D)	83,068	24.9
Bennett (D)	45,068	13.5
Johnstone (D)	18,184	5.4

1954   Democratic Primary

Burnet R. Maybank (D)[1]		100.0

1956   Democratic Special Primary

Strom Thurmond (D)		100.0

1960   Democratic Primary

Strom Thurmond (D)	273,795	89.5
R. B. Herbert (D)	32,136	10.5

1966   **Democratic Primary**

| Bradley Morrah (D) | 167,401 | 55.9 |
| John B. Culbertson (D) | 131,870 | 44.1 |

1972   **Democratic Primary**

| Eugene N. Ziegler (D) | 201,170 | 58.7 |
| John B. Culbertson (D) | 141,757 | 41.3 |

1978   **Republican Primary**

| Strom Thurmond (R) | | 100.0 |

Democratic Primary

Charles D. Ravenel (D)	205,348	55.9
John B. Culbertson (D)	69,184	18.8
James T. Triplett (D)	50,951	13.9
William T. McElveen (D)	41,550	11.3

1984   **Republican Primary**

| Strom Thurmond (R) | 44,662 | 94.3 |
| R. H. Cunningham (R) | 2,693 | 5.7 |

Democratic Primary

| Melvin Pervis Jr. (D) | 149,730 | 50.2 |
| Cecil J. Williams (D) | 148,586 | 49.8 |

1990   **Republican Primary**

| Strom Thurmond (R) | | 100.0 |

Democratic Primary

| Bob Cunningham (D) | | 100.0 |

1996   **Republican Primary**

Strom Thurmond (R)	132,157	60.6
Harold Worley (R)	65,670	30.1
Charlie Thompson (R)	20,188	9.3

Democratic Primary

| Elliott Springs Close (D) | 102,988 | 62.1 |
| Cecil J. Williams (D) | 62,794 | 37.9 |

Class 3

1920   **Democratic Primary**

Ellison D. Smith (D)	57,423	48.7
George Warren (D)	36,272	30.8
W. P. Pollock (D)	15,678	13.3
W. C. Irby (D)	8,454	7.2

Democratic Runoff

| Ellison D. Smith (D) | 65,880 | 60.7 |
| George Warren (D) | 42,735 | 39.3 |

1926   **Democratic Primary**

Ellison D. Smith (D)	72,015	42.0
Edgar Brown (D)	65,331	38.1
Nathan B. Dial (D)	34,114	19.9

Democratic Runoff

| Ellison D. Smith (D) | 82,783 | 51.6 |
| Edgar Brown (D) | 77,559 | 48.4 |

1932   **Democratic Primary**

Ellison D. Smith (D)	100,270	37.0
Coleman L. Blease (D)	81,297	30.0
Williams (D)	48,084	17.7
Harris (D)	41,748	15.4

Democratic Runoff

| Ellison D. Smith (D) | 150,468 | 56.7 |
| Coleman L. Blease (D) | 114,840 | 43.3 |

1938   **Democratic Primary**

| Ellison D. Smith (D) | 186,519 | 55.4 |
| Olin D. Johnston (D) | 150,437 | 44.7 |

1944   **Democratic Primary**

Olin D. Johnston (D)	138,440	55.2
Ellison D. Smith (D)	88,045	35.1
Daniel (D)	14,572	5.8

1950   **Democratic Primary**

| Olin D. Johnston (D) | 186,180 | 54.0 |
| Strom Thurmond (D) | 158,904 | 46.1 |

1956   **Democratic Primary**

| Olin D. Johnston (D) | | 100.0 |

1962   **Democratic Primary**

| Olin D. Johnston (D) | 210,918 | 65.7 |
| Ernest F. Hollings (D) | 110,023 | 34.3 |

1966   **Democratic Special Primary**

| Ernest F. Hollings (D) | 196,405 | 60.8 |
| Donald S. Russell (D) | 126,595 | 39.2 |

1968   **Democratic Primary**

| Ernest F. Hollings (D) | 307,561 | 78.3 |
| John B. Culbertson (D) | 85,219 | 21.7 |

1974   **Republican Primary**

| Gwenyfred Bush (R) | | 100.0 |

Democratic Primary

| Ernest F. Hollings (D) | | 100.0 |

1980   **Republican Primary**

Marshall T. Mays (R)	14,075	42.6
Charles F. Rhodes (R)	11,395	34.5
Robert K. Carley (R)	7,575	22.9

Republican Runoff

| Marshall T. Mays (R) | 6,853 | 64.8 |
| Charles F. Rhodes (R) | 3,717 | 35.2 |

Democratic Primary

Ernest F. Hollings (D)	266,796	81.2
Nettie D. Dickerson (D)	34,720	10.6
William P. Kreml (D)	27,049	8.2

1986	**Republican Primary**		
	Henry D. McMaster (R)	27,695	*53.4*
	Henry S. Jordan (R)	24,164	*46.6*
	Democratic Primary		
	Ernest F. Hollings (D)		*100.0*
1992	**Republican Primary**		
	Thomas F. Hartnett (R)	123,572	*76.8*
	Charlie E. Thompson (R)	37,352	*23.2*
	Democratic Primary		
	Ernest F. Hollings (D)		*100.0*
1998	**Republican Primary**		
	Bob Inglis (R)	115,029	*74.6*
	Stephen Brown (R)	33,530	*21.7*
	Democratic Primary		
	Ernest F. Hollings (D)		*100.0*

South Carolina

1. Maybank had been renominated July 13, 1954, but died Sept. 1. Officials of the South Carolina Democratic Party, charged with replacing him on the ballot for the November general election, declined to order a new primary and selected state Sen. Edgar A. Brown as their candidate. He was defeated in the election by former governor Strom Thurmond (D 1947–1951), who waged a successful write-in campaign.

SOUTH DAKOTA

	Candidates	Votes	%
	Class 2		
1960	**Republican Primary**		
	Karl E. Mundt (R)		*100.0*
	Democratic Primary		
	George McGovern (D)		*100.0*
1966	**Republican Primary**		
	Karl E. Mundt (R)	66,758	*82.1*
	Richard R. Murphy (R)	14,593	*17.9*
	Democratic Primary		
	Donn H. Wright (D)		*100.0*
1972	**Republican Primary**[1]		
	Robert W. Hirsch (R)	27,322	*27.4*
	Gordon Mydland (R)	22,297	*22.3*
	Chuck Lien (R)	21,995	*22.0*
	Kenneth D. Stofferahn (R)	16,615	*16.6*
	Tom Reardon (R)	11,592	*11.6*
	Democratic Primary		
	James Abourezk (D)	46,931	*79.4*
	George Blue (D)	12,163	*20.6*

1978	**Republican Primary**		
	Larry Pressler (R)	66,893	*73.9*
	Ronald F. Williamson (R)	23,646	*26.1*
	Democratic Primary		
	Don Barnett (D)	37,319	*55.1*
	Kenneth D. Stofferahn (D)	30,384	*44.9*
1984	**Republican Primary**		
	Larry Pressler (R)		*100.0*
	Democratic Primary		
	George V. Cunningham (D)	31,376	*68.1*
	Dean L. Sinclair (D)	14,672	*31.8*
1990	**Republican Primary**		
	Larry Pressler (R)		*100.0*
	Democratic Primary		
	Ted Muenster (D)		*100.0*
1996	**Republican Primary**		
	Larry Pressler (R)		*100.0*
	Democratic Primary		
	Tim Johnson (D)		*100.0*
	Class 3		
1956	**Republican Primary**		
	Francis Case (R)		*100.0*
	Democratic Primary		
	Kenneth Holum (D)	23,464	*60.8*
	Merton B. Tice (D)	15,099	*39.1*
1962	**Republican Primary**		
	Francis Case (R)[2]	57,583	*83.5*
	A. C. Miller (R)	11,414	*16.5*
	Democratic Primary		
	George McGovern (D)		*100.0*
1968	**Republican Primary**		
	Archie M. Gubbrud (R)		*100.0*
	Democratic Primary		
	George McGovern (D)		*100.0*
1974	**Republican Primary**		
	Leo K. Thorsness (R)	49,716	*52.3*
	Al Schock (R)	35,406	*37.3*
	Barbara B. Gunderson (R)	9,852	*10.4*
	Democratic Primary		
	George McGovern (D)		*100.0*
1980	**Republican Primary**		
	James Abdnor (R)	68,196	*72.9*
	Dale Bell (R)	25,314	*27.1*

Democratic Primary		
George McGovern (D)	44,822	62.4
Larry Schumaker (D)	26,958	37.6

1986   Republican Primary

James Abdnor (R)	63,414	54.5
William J. Janklow (R)	52,924	45.5

Democratic Primary		
Thomas A. Daschle (D)		100.0

1992   Republican Primary

Charlene Haar (R)		100.0

Democratic Primary		
Thomas A. Daschle (D)		100.0

1998   Republican Primary

Ron Schmidt (R)	26,540	52.0
Alan Aker (R)	19,200	37.6
John M. Sanders (R)	5,292	10.4

Democratic Primary		
Thomas A. Daschle (D)		100.0

South Dakota

1. A state Republican convention was held June 26 because no one received the 35 percent required for nomination under the South Dakota primary law. Hirsch was nominated at this convention.

2. Case died shortly after winning the primary and the Republican state committee substituted Joe H. Bottum as the party's nominee.

TENNESSEE

Candidates	Votes	%

Class 1

1922   Democratic Primary

Kenneth D. McKellar (D)	102,692	64.0
Fitzhugh (D)	47,627	29.7
Cooper (D)	9,480	5.9

1928   Democratic Primary

Kenneth D. McKellar (D)	120,298	63.3
Finis Garrett (D)	64,470	33.9

1934   Democratic Primary

Kenneth D. McKellar (D)	212,226	84.0
John R. Neal (D)	40,463	16.0

1940   Democratic Primary

Kenneth D. McKellar (D)	230,033	91.5
John R. Neal (D)	14,583	5.8

1946   Republican Primary

William B. Ladd (R)	30,954	100.0

Democratic Primary		
Kenneth D. McKellar (D)	188,805	62.0
Edward W. Carmack (D)	107,363	35.2

1952   Democratic Primary

Albert Gore (D)	334,957	56.5
Kenneth D. McKellar (D)	245,054	41.4

1958   Republican Primary

Hobart F. Atkins (R)		100.0

Democratic Primary		
Albert Gore (D)	375,439	59.0
Prentice Cooper (D)	253,191	39.8

1964   Republican Primary

Dan H. Kuykendall (R)		100.0

Democratic Primary		
Albert Gore (D)	401,163	84.7
Sam J. Galloway (D)	37,974	8.0

1970   Republican Primary

Bill Brock (R)	176,703	74.9
Tex Ritter (R)	54,401	23.0

Democratic Primary		
Albert Gore (D)	269,770	51.0
Hudley Crockett (D)	238,767	45.2

1976   Republican Primary

Bill Brock (R)		100.0

Democratic Primary		
James R. Sasser (D)	244,930	44.2
John J. Hooker (D)	171,716	31.0
Harry Sadler (D)	54,125	9.8
David Bolin (D)	44,056	8.0
Lester Kefauver (D)	29,864	5.4

1982   Republican Primary

Robin L. Beard (R)	205,271	91.4
William B. Thompson (R)	19,277	8.6

Democratic Primary		
James R. Sasser (D)	511,059	88.9
Charles G. Vick (D)	13,488	11.1

1988   Republican Primary

Bill Anderson (R)	115,341	72.9
Alice W. Algood (R)	34,413	21.8
Hubert D. Patty (R)	8,358	5.3

Democratic Primary		
James R. Sasser (D)		100.0

1994   Republican Primary

Bill Frist (R)	197,734	44.4
Bob Corker (R)	143,808	32.3
Steve Wilson (R)	50,274	11.3
Harold Sterling (R)	28,425	6.4

Democratic Primary

James R. Sasser (D)	402,610	100.0

2000   **Republican Primary**

Bill Frist (R)	186,882	99.8

Democratic Primary

Jeff Clark (D)	64,851	34.2
John Jay Hooker (D)	64,041	33.8
Mary Taylor-Shelby (D)	28,604	15.1
Shannon Wood (D)	25,372	13.4

Class 2

1924   **Democratic Primary**

Lawrence D. Tyson (D)	72,496	41.9
John K. Shields (D)	54,990	31.8
Nathan L. Bachman (D)	44,946	26.0

1930   **Democratic Primary**

Cordell Hull (D)	140,802	62.9
A. L. Todd (D)	79,649	35.6

Democratic Special Primary

William E. Brock (D)	113,492	70.7
John R. Neal (D)	47,110	29.3

1934   **Democratic Special Primary**

Nathan L. Bachman (D)	166,293	57.9
Gordon Browning (D)	121,169	42.2

1936   **Democratic Primary**

Nathan L. Bachman (D)	217,531	82.9
John R. Neal (D)	44,830	17.1

1938   **Democratic Special Primary**

A. Tom Stewart (D)	174,940	49.3
George Berry (D)	101,966	28.7
J. Ridley Mitchell (D)	70,393	19.8

1942   **Democratic Primary**

A. Tom Stewart (D)	136,415	51.9
Edward W. Carmack (D)	116,841	44.4

1948   **Republican Primary**

B. Carroll Reece (R)	82,522	81.7
Allen J. Strawbridge (R)	18,526	18.3

Democratic Primary

Estes Kefauver (D)	171,791	42.4
A. Tom Stewart (D)	129,873	32.1
John A. Mitchell (D)	96,192	23.7

1954   **Democratic Primary**

Estes Kefauver (D)	440,497	68.2
Pat Sutton (D)	186,363	28.9

1960   **Republican Primary**

A. Bradley Frazier (R)	16,633	58.8
Hansel Proffitt (R)	11,667	41.2

Democratic Primary

Estes Kefauver (D)	463,848	64.6
Andrew T. Taylor (D)	249,336	34.7

1964[1]   **Republican Special Primary**

Howard H. Baker Jr. (R)	93,301	85.0
Charles Moffett (R)	10,596	9.6
Hubert D. Patty (R)	5,947	5.4

Democratic Special Primary

Ross Bass (D)	330,213	50.8
Frank G. Clement (D)	233,245	35.9
M. M. Bullard (D)	86,718	13.3

1966   **Republican Primary**

Howard H. Baker Jr. (R)	112,617	75.7
Kenneth Roberts (R)	36,043	24.2

Democratic Primary

Frank G. Clement (D)	384,322	51.2
Ross Bass (D)	366,079	48.8

1972   **Republican Primary**

Howard H. Baker Jr. (R)	242,373	97.0

Democratic Primary

Ray Blanton (D)	292,249	76.4
Don Palmer (D)	40,700	10.6

1978   **Republican Primary**

Howard H. Baker Jr. (R)	205,680	83.4
Harvey D. Howard (R)	21,154	8.6

Democratic Primary

Jane Eskind (D)	196,156	34.5
Bill Bruce (D)	170,795	30.1
J. D. Lee (D)	89,939	15.8
James Boyd (D)	48,458	8.5

1984   **Republican Primary**

Victor Ashe (R)	145,774	86.5
Jack McNeil (R)	17,970	10.7

Democratic Primary

Albert Gore Jr. (D)	345,527	100.0

1990   **Republican Primary**

William R. Hawkins (R)	54,317	38.9
Ralph Brown (R)	53,873	38.5
Patrick K. Hales (R)	31,515	22.5

Democratic Primary

Albert Gore Jr. (D)		100.0

1994[2]	Republican Special Primary		
	Fred Thompson (R)	235,386	64.2
	John Baker (R)	131,431	35.8
	Democratic Special Primary		
	Jim Cooper (D)	375,615	100.0
1996	Republican Primary		
	Fred Thompson (R)	266,549	94.1
	Jim F. Counts (R)	16,715	5.9
	Democratic Primary		
	Houston Gordon (D)	156,704	63.5
	Ashley M. King (D)	89,887	36.4

Tennessee

1. A special election was held to fill the remaining two years of the term of Sen. Estes Kefauver (D), who died Aug. 10, 1963. The first year of the vacancy was filled by appointee Herbert S. Walker (D).

2. A special election was held to fill the remaining two years of the term of Sen. Albert Gore Jr. (D), who resigned Jan 1, 1993, having been elected vice president. The governor appointed Harlan Mathews (D) senator for the two years prior to the election.

TEXAS

Candidates	Votes	%
Class 1		

1922	Democratic Primary		
	Earle B. Mayfield (D)	153,538	26.8
	James E. Ferguson (D)	127,071	22.2
	Charles A. Culberson (D)	99,635	17.4
	Cullen F. Thomas (D)	88,026	15.4
	Clarence Ousley (D)	62,451	10.9
	Robert L. Henry (D)	41,567	7.3
	Democratic Runoff		
	Earle B. Mayfield (D)	273,308	54.4
	James E. Ferguson (D)	228,701	45.6
1928	Democratic Primary		
	Earle B. Mayfield (D)	200,246	29.7
	Tom Connally (D)	178,091	26.4
	Alvin Owsley (D)	131,755	19.5
	Thomas L. Blanton (D)	126,758	18.8
	Democratic Runoff		
	Tom Connally (D)	320,071	55.4
	Earle B. Mayfield (D)	257,747	44.6
1934	Republican Primary		
	U. S. Goen (R)	1,148	100.0
	Democratic Primary		
	Tom Connally (D)	567,139	58.8
	J. W. Bailey (D)	355,963	36.9

1940	Democratic Primary		
	Tom Connally (D)	923,219	84.8
	Guy B. Fisher (D)	98,125	9.0
	A. P. Belcher (D)	66,962	6.2
1946	Democratic Primary		
	Tom Connally (D)	823,818	75.4
	Floyd E. Ryan (D)	85,292	7.8
	Cyclone Davis (D)	74,252	6.8
	Terrell Sledge (D)	66,947	6.1
1952	Democratic Primary		
	Price Daniel (D)	940,770	72.6
	Lindley Beckworth (D)	285,842	22.0
	E. W. Napier (D)	70,132	5.4
1958	Republican Primary		
	Roy Whittenburg (R)		100.0
	Democratic Primary		
	Ralph Yarborough (D)	761,511	58.7
	William A. Blakley (D)	535,418	41.3
1964	Republican Primary		
	George Bush (R)	62,985	44.1
	Jack Cox (R)	45,561	31.9
	Robert Morris (R)	28,279	19.8
	Republican Runoff		
	George Bush (R)	49,751	62.1
	Jack Cox (R)	30,333	37.9
	Democratic Primary		
	Ralph Yarborough (D)	904,811	57.4
	Gordon McLendon (D)	672,573	42.6
1970	Republican Primary		
	George Bush (R)	96,806	87.6
	Robert Morris (R)	13,654	12.4
	Democratic Primary		
	Lloyd Bentsen (D)	816,641	53.0
	Ralph Yarborough (D)	724,122	47.0
1976	Republican Primary		
	Alan Steelman (R)	251,252	70.5
	Hugh Sweeney (R)	64,404	18.1
	Louis Leman (R)	40,651	11.4
	Democratic Primary		
	Lloyd Bentsen (D)	970,983	63.5
	Phil Gramm (D)	427,597	28.0
	Hugh Wilson (D)	10,715	7.2
1982	Republican Primary		
	James M. Collins (R)	152,469	58.0
	Walter H. Mengden (R)	91,780	34.9
	Don L. Richardson (R)	18,616	7.1

Democratic Primary

Lloyd Bentsen (D)	987,153	*78.1*
Joe Sullivan (D)	276,314	*21.9*

1988   Republican Primary

Wes Gilbreath (R)	275,080	*36.7*
Beau Boulter (R)	228,676	*30.5*
Milton E. Fox (R)	138,031	*18.4*
Ned Snead (R)	107,560	*14.4*

Republican Runoff

Beau Boulter (R)	111,134	*60.2*
Wes Gilbreath (R)	73,573	*40.0*

Democratic Primary

Lloyd Bentsen (D)	1,365,736	*84.8*
Joe Sullivan (D)	244,805	*15.2*

1994   Republican Primary

Kay Bailey Hutchison (R)	467,975	*84.3*
Stephen Hopkins (R)	34,703	*6.2*

Democratic Primary

Jim Mattox (D)	416,503	*40.5*
Richard Fisher (D)	388,090	*37.8*
Michael A. Andrews (D)	159,793	*15.5*
Evelyn K. Lantz (D)	63,523	*6.2*

2000   Republican Primary

Kay Bailey Hutchison (R)	955,033	*100.0*

Democratic Primary

Gene Kelly (D)	220,531	*35.7*
Charles Gandy (D)	140,636	*22.8*
Don Clark (D)	139,243	*22.5*
Bobby Wightman (D)	83,643	*13.5*

Democratic Runoff

Gene Kelly (D)	143,366	*58.4*
Charles Gandy (D)	101,983	*41.6*

Class 2

1924   Democratic Primary

Morris Sheppard (D)	440,511	*64.8*
Fred W. Davis (D)	159,663	*23.5*
John F. Maddox (D)	80,070	*11.8*

1930   Republican Primary

Doran John Haesly (R)	3,645	*40.5*
C. O. Harris (R)	2,784	*31.0*
Harve H. Haines (R)	2,568	*28.5*

Democratic Primary

Morris Sheppard (D)	526,293	*71.1*
Robert L. Henry (D)	174,260	*23.5*
C. A. Mitchner (D)	40,130	*5.4*

1936   Democratic Primary

Morris Sheppard (D)	616,293	*64.6*
Joe H. Eagle (D)	136,718	*14.3*
Guy B. Fisher (D)	89,215	*9.4*

1942   Democratic Primary

W. Lee O'Daniel (D)	475,541	*48.3*
James Allred (D)	317,501	*32.3*
Moody (D)	178,471	*18.1*

Democratic Runoff

W. Lee O'Daniel (D)	451,359	*51.0*
James Allred (D)	433,203	*49.0*

1948   Democratic Primary

Coke R. Stevenson (D)	477,077	*39.7*
Lyndon B. Johnson (D)	405,617	*33.7*
George Peddy (D)	237,195	*19.7*

Democratic Runoff

Lyndon B. Johnson (D)	494,191	*50.0*
Coke R. Stevenson (D)	494,104	*50.0*

1954   Democratic Primary

Lyndon B. Johnson (D)	883,264	*71.4*
Dudley T. Dougherty (D)	354,188	*28.6*

1960   Democratic Primary

Lyndon B. Johnson (D)		*100.0*

1966   Republican Primary

John Tower (R)		*100.0*

Democratic Primary

Waggoner Carr (D)	899,523	*79.9*
John R. Willoughby (D)	226,598	*20.1*

1972   Republican Primary

John Tower (R)		*100.0*

Democratic Primary

Ralph Yarborough (D)	1,032,606	*50.0*
Barefoot Sanders (D)	787,504	*38.1*
Hugh Wilson (D)	125,460	*6.1*

Democratic Runoff

Barefoot Sanders (D)	1,008,499	*52.1*
Ralph Yarborough (D)	928,132	*47.9*

1978   Republican Primary

John Tower (R)		*100.0*

Democratic Primary

Robert Krueger (D)	853,460	*54.7*
Joe Christie (D)	707,738	*45.3*

1984	**Republican Primary**		
	Phil Gramm (R)	246,716	73.2
	Ron Paul (R)	55,431	16.4
	Rob Mosbacher (R)	26,279	7.8

	Democratic Primary		
	Kent Hance (D)	456,446	31.2
	Lloyd Doggett (D)	456,173	31.2
	Robert Krueger (D)	454,886	31.1

	Democratic Runoff		
	Lloyd Doggett (D)	489,932	50.0
	Kent Hance (D)	489,834	50.0

	Democratic Runoff Recount		
	Lloyd Doggett (D)	491,251	50.1
	Kent Hance (D)	489,906	50.0

1990	**Republican Primary**		
	Phil Gramm (R)		100.0

	Democratic Primary		
	Hugh Parmer (D)	766,284	75.4
	Harley Schlanger (D)	249,445	24.6

1996	**Republican Primary**		
	Phil Gramm (R)	838,339	85.0
	David Young (R)	75,463	7.7
	Henry C. "Hank" Grover (R)	72,400	7.3

	Democratic Primary		
	Victor M. Morales (D)	322,218	36.2
	John Bryant (D)	267,545	30.0
	Jim Chapman (D)	239,427	26.9
	John Will Odam (D)	61,433	6.9

	Democratic Runoff		
	Victor M. Morales (D)	246,614	51.2
	John Bryant (D)	235,281	48.8

UTAH[1]

	Candidates	Votes	%
	Class 1		

1958	**Republican Primary**		
	Arthur V. Watkins (R)	39,593	68.1
	Carvel Mattsson (R)	18,563	31.9

	Democratic Primary		
	Frank E. Moss (D)	35,862	59.2
	Brigham E. Roberts (D)	24,736	40.8

1964	**Republican Primary**		
	Ernest L. Wilkinson (R)	61,167	50.7
	Sherman P. Lloyd (R)	59,398	49.3

	Democratic Primary		
	Frank E. Moss (D)		100.0

1970	**Republican Primary**		
	Laurence J. Burton (R)		100.0

	Democratic Primary		
	Frank E. Moss (D)		100.0

1976	**Republican Primary**		
	Orrin G. Hatch (R)	104,490	64.6
	Jack Carlson (R)	57,249	35.4

	Democratic Primary		
	Frank E. Moss (D)		100.0

1994	**Independent Primary**		
	Craig Oliver (I)	818	56.9
	Bill Rigley (I)	620	43.1

	Class 3		

1956	**Republican Primary**		
	Wallace F. Bennett (R)		100.0

	Democratic Primary		
	Alonzo F. Hopkin (D)	44,980	56.8
	Herbert B. Maw (D)	34,246	43.2

1962	**Republican Primary**		
	Wallace F. Bennett (R)	70,519	59.2
	J. Bracken Lee (R)	48,606	40.8

	Democratic Primary		
	David S. King (D)	55,965	77.4
	Calvin L. Rampton (D)	16,327	22.6

1968	**Republican Primary**		
	Wallace F. Bennett (R)	81,945	60.9
	Mark E. Anderson (R)	52,689	39.1

	Democratic Primary		
	Milton Weilenmann (D)	47,908	50.7
	Phil L. Hansen (D)	46,579	49.3

1974	**Republican Primary**		
	Jake Garn (R)		100.0

	Democratic Primary		
	Wayne Owens (D)		100.0

	American Primary		
	Bruce Bangerter (AM)	2,254	50.9
	Kenneth R. Larsen (AM)	2,173	49.1

1980	**Democratic Primary**		
	Dan Berman (D)	28,930	50.2
	A. Stephen Dirks (D)	28,643	49.7

American Primary		
George M. Batchelor (AM)	675	54.5
Larry Topham (AM)	563	45.5

1986   **Democratic Primary**

Craig Oliver (D)	14,654	50.5
Terry Williams (D)	14,379	49.5

1992   **Republican Primary**

Robert F. Bennett (R)	135,514	51.4
Joe Cannon (R)	128,125	48.6

Democratic Primary

Wayne Owens (D)	74,124	61.4
Doug Anderson (D)	46,622	38.6

Utah

1. From 1980 to 1998, some Democratic and Republican candidates were nominated by convention.

VERMONT

Candidates	Votes	%
Class 1		

1958   **Republican Primary**

Winston L. Prouty (R)	31,866	64.6
Lee E. Emerson (R)	17,468	35.4

Democratic Primary

Frederick J. Fayette (D)		100.0

1964   **Republican Primary**

Winston L. Prouty (R)		100.0

Democratic Primary

Frederick J. Fayette (D)	12,388	71.0
William H. Meyer (D)	4,913	28.2

1970   **Republican Primary**

Winston L. Prouty (R)		100.0

Democratic Primary

Philip H. Hoff (D)	23,082	69.7
Fiore L. Bove (D)	7,941	24.0
William H. Meyer (D)	2,024	6.1

1972[1]   **Republican Special Primary**

Robert T. Stafford (R)		100.0

Democratic Special Primary

Randolph T. Major (D)		100.0

1976   **Republican Primary**

Robert T. Stafford (R)	24,338	68.7
John J. Welch (R)	10,911	30.8

Democratic Primary

Thomas P. Salmon (D)	21,674	52.7
Scott Skinner (D)	19,238	46.8

Liberty Union Primary

Nancy Kaufman (LU)	362	69.6
John Medeiros (LU)	146	28.1

1982   **Republican Primary**

Robert T. Stafford (R)	26,323	46.2
Stewart M. Ledbetter (R)	19,743	34.7
John M. McClaughry (R)	10,692	18.8

Democratic Primary

James A. Guest (D)	11,352	67.1
Thomas E. McGregor (D)	3,749	22.1
Earl S. Gardner (D)	1,281	7.6

Citizens Primary

Ion Laskaris (CIT)		100.0

Liberty Union Primary

Jerry Levy (LU)		100.0

1988   **Republican Primary**

James M. Jeffords (R)	30,555	60.8
Mike Griffes (R)	19,593	39.0

Democratic Primary

William Gray (D)		100.0

Liberty Union Primary

Jerry Levy (LU)		100.0

1994   **Republican Primary**

James M. Jeffords (R)	24,766	91.6

Democratic Primary

Jan Backus (D)	16,217	53.6
Doug Costle (D)	13,139	43.5

Liberty Union Primary

Jerry Levy (LU)	289	90.0

2000   **Republican Primary**

James M. Jeffords (R)	60,234	77.8
Rick Hubbard (R)	15,991	20.7

Democratic Primary

Ed Flanagan (D)	17,440	49.2
Jan Backus (D)	16,444	46.4

Class 3

1956   **Republican Primary**

George D. Aiken (R)		100.0

	Democratic Primary		
	Bernard G. O'Shea (D)		100.0
1962	**Republican Primary**		
	George D. Aiken (R)		100.0
	Democratic Primary		
	W. Robert Johnson (D)	5,718	54.7
	William H. Meyer (D)	4,741	45.3
1968	**Republican Primary**		
	George D. Aiken (R)	42,248	72.8
	William K. Tufts (R)	15,786	27.2
	Democratic Primary		
	George D. Aiken (WRITE IN)	1,354	61.8
	Others (WRITE IN)	438	20.0
	Philip H. Hoff (WRITE IN)	400	18.2
1974	**Republican Primary**		
	Richard W. Mallary (R)	27,221	59.1
	Charles R. Ross (R)	16,479	35.8
	Democratic Primary		
	Patrick J. Leahy (D)	19,801	83.9
	Nathaniel Frothingham (D)	3,703	15.7
1980	**Republican Primary**		
	Stewart M. Ledbetter (R)	16,518	35.3
	James E. Mullin (R)	12,256	26.2
	Tom Evslin (R)	8,575	18.3
	T. Garry Buckley (R)	5,209	11.1
	Robert Schuettinger (R)	3,450	7.4
	Democratic Primary		
	Patrick J. Leahy (D)		100.0
	Liberty Union Primary		
	Earl S. Gardner (LU)		100.0
1986	**Republican Primary**		
	Richard A. Snelling (R)	21,477	75.1
	Anthony N. Doria (R)	6,493	22.7
	Democratic Primary		
	Patrick J. Leahy (D)		100.0
	Liberty Union Primary		
	Jerry Levy (LU)		100.0
1992	**Republican Primary**		
	James H. Douglas (R)	28,693	78.2
	John L. Gropper (R)	7,395	20.2
	Democratic Primary		
	Patrick J. Leahy (D)	24,721	97.6
	Liberty Union Primary		
	Jerry Levy (LU)		100.0

1998	**Republican Primary**		
	Fred Tuttle (R)	28,355	53.7
	Jack McMullen (R)	23,321	44.2
	Democratic Primary		
	Patrick J. Leahy (D)	18,643	96.6
	Vermont Grassroots Primary		
	Bob Melamede (VG)	137	59.5

Vermont
1. A special election was held in 1972 to fill the unexpired term of Sen. Winston L. Prouty (R), who died Sept. 10, 1971. Robert T. Stafford had been appointed to fill the vacancy on an interim basis.

VIRGINIA[1]

	Candidates	Votes	%
	Class 1		
1922	**Democratic Primary**		
	Claude A. Swanson (D)	102,045	73.0
	Davis (D)	37,671	27.0
1928	**Democratic Primary**		
	Claude A. Swanson (D)	✔	
1933	**Democratic Special Primary**		
	Harry F. Byrd (D)		100.0
1934	**Democratic Primary**		
	Harry F. Byrd (D)		100.0
1940	**Democratic Primary**		
	Harry F. Byrd (D)		100.0
1946	**Democratic Primary**		
	Harry F. Byrd (D)	141,923	63.5
	Martin A. Hutchinson (D)	81,605	36.5
1952	**Democratic Primary**		
	Harry F. Byrd (D)	216,438	62.7
	Francis Pickens Miller (D)	128,869	37.3
1958	**Democratic Primary**		
	Harry F. Byrd (D)		100.0
1964	**Democratic Primary**		
	Harry F. Byrd (D)		100.0
1966[2]	**Democratic Special Primary**		
	Harry F. Byrd Jr. (D)	221,221	51.0
	Armistead L. Boothe (D)	212,996	49.1
1970	**Democratic Primary[3]**		
	George C. Rawlings (D)	58,874	45.7
	Clive L. DuVal (D)	58,174	45.1
	Milton Colvin (D)	11,911	9.2

1976	Democratic Primary		
	Elmo R. Zumwalt (D)		100.0
1994	Republican Primary		
	Oliver L. North (R)		100.0
	Democratic Primary		
	Charles S. Robb (D)	154,561	57.9
	Virgil H. Goode (D)	90,547	33.9
	Sylvia L. Clute (D)	17,329	6.5

Class 2

1920	Democratic Special Primary		
	Carter Glass (D)		100.0
1924	Democratic Primary		
	Carter Glass (D)		100.0
1930	Democratic Primary		
	Carter Glass (D)		100.0
1936	Democratic Primary		
	Carter Glass (D)		100.0
1942	Democratic Primary		
	Carter Glass (D)		100.0
1946	Democratic Special Primary		
	A. Willis Robertson (D)	✔	
1948	Democratic Primary		
	A. Willis Robertson (D)	80,340	70.3
	James P. Hart Jr. (D)	33,928	29.7
1954	Democratic Primary		
	A. Willis Robertson (D)		100.0
1960	Democratic Primary		
	A. Willis Robertson (D)		100.0
1966	Democratic Primary		
	William B. Spong Jr. (D)	216,885	50.1
	A. Willis Robertson (D)	216,274	49.9
1972	Democratic Primary		
	William B. Spong Jr. (D)		100.0
1996	Republican Primary		
	John W. Warner (R)	323,520	65.6
	James C. "Jim" Miller (R)	170,015	34.4

Virginia
1. Following 1976, candidates were nominated by state party convention.
2. A special election was held in 1966 to fill the remaining four years of the term of Sen. Harry F. Byrd (D), who resigned Nov. 10, 1965. The first year of the vacancy was filled by Byrd's son, Harry F. Byrd Jr. (D), who went on to win the primary and election.
3. Rawlings became the Democratic nominee when DuVal did not request a runoff.

WASHINGTON

	Candidates	Votes	%

Class 1

1958	Republican Primary		
	William B. Bantz (R)		100.0
	Democratic Primary		
	Henry M. Jackson (D)	334,862	85.8
	Alice F. Bryant (D)	55,200	14.1
1964	Republican Primary		
	Lloyd J. Andrews (R)	216,616	81.2
	David J. Williams (R)	37,450	14.0
	Democratic Primary		
	Henry M. Jackson (D)	478,892	90.6
	Alice F. Bryant (D)	29,052	5.5
1970	Republican Primary		
	Charles W. Elicker (R)	33,262	37.1
	Howard S. Reed (R)	22,293	24.9
	R. J. Odman (R)	14,856	16.6
	William H. Davis (R)	11,207	12.5
	Bill Patrick (R)	7,976	8.9
	Democratic Primary		
	Henry M. Jackson (D)	497,309	84.3
	Carl Maxey (D)	79,201	13.4
1976	Republican Primary		
	George M. Brown (R)	51,885	29.5
	Warren Hanson (R)	43,905	25.0
	Harry C. Nielsen (R)	28,030	15.9
	Wilbur R. Parkin (R)	21,639	12.3
	William H. Davis (R)	16,881	9.6
	Clarice L. R. Privette (R)	13,526	7.7
	Democratic Primary		
	Henry M. Jackson (D)	549,974	87.4
	Dennis Kelley (D)	54,470	8.7
1982	Republican Primary		
	Doug Jewett (R)	73,616	46.3
	Larry Penberthy (R)	46,037	28.9
	Ken Talbott (R)	15,581	9.8
	Patrick S. McGowan (R)	13,054	8.2
	Democratic Primary		
	Henry M. Jackson (D)	450,580	94.9
1983[1]	Republican Special Primary		
	Dan Evans (R)	250,046	64.3
	Lloyd E. Cooney (R)	133,799	34.4

Democratic Special Primary

Mike Lowry (D)	179,509	*61.5*
Charles Royer (D)	103,304	*35.4*

1988   Republican Primary

Slade Gorton (R)	335,846	*85.3*
Doug Smith (R)	31,512	*8.0*
William C. Goodloe (R)	26,224	*6.7*

Democratic Primary

Mike Lowry (D)	297,399	*55.2*
Don Bonker (D)	241,170	*44.8*

1994   Republican Primary

Slade Gorton (R)	492,251	*92.8*
Warren E. Hanson (R)	26,628	*5.0*

Democratic Primary

Ron Sims (D)	162,382	*42.0*
Mike James (D)	138,005	*35.7*
Scott Hardman (D)	29,973	*7.7*
Jesse Wineberry (D)	24,698	*6.4*

2000   Republican Primary

Slade Gorton (R)	560,787	*93.3*

Democratic Primary

Maria Cantwell (D)	472,609	*70.6*
Deborah Senn (D)	168,110	*25.1*

Class 3

1956   Republican Primary

Arthur B. Langlie (R)		*100.0*

Democratic Primary

Warren G. Magnuson (D)		*100.0*

1962   Republican Primary

Richard G. Christensen (R)	178,616	*82.1*
Ben Larson (R)	38,759	*17.8*

Democratic Primary

Warren G. Magnuson (D)	280,981	*93.7*
John Patric (D)	18,849	*6.3*

1968   Republican Primary

Jack Metcalf (R)	210,981	*73.6*
Harvey L. Cole (R)	40,844	*14.2*
Ralph O. Westlake (R)	25,756	*9.0*

Democratic Primary

Warren G. Magnuson (D)	373,303	*92.9*
Arthur DeWitt (D)	28,683	*7.1*

1974   Republican Primary

Jack Metcalf (R)	103,616	*61.0*
Jesse Chiang (R)	31,193	*18.4*

Donald C. Knutson (R)	13,738	*8.1*
June Riggs (R)	8,491	*5.0*

Democratic Primary

Warren G. Magnuson (D)	288,038	*92.5*
John Patric (D)	23,438	*7.5*

1980   Republican Primary

Slade Gorton (R)	313,560	*55.6*
Lloyd E. Cooney (R)	229,178	*40.7*

Democratic Primary

Warren G. Magnuson (D)	348,471	*92.4*

1986   Republican Primary

Slade Gorton (R)	291,735	*93.0*

Democratic Primary

Brock Adams (D)	287,258	*91.7*

Socialist Workers Primary

Jill Fein (SOC WORK)		*100.0*

1992   Republican Primary

Rod Chandler (R)	228,083	*42.1*
Leo K. Thorsness (R)	185,498	*34.2*
Tim Hill (R)	128,232	*23.7*

Democratic Primary

Patty Murray (D)	318,455	*56.7*
Don Bonker (D)	208,321	*37.1*

1998[2]   Republican Primary

Linda Smith (R)	337,407	*64.2*
Chris Bayley (R)	155,864	*29.7*

Democratic Primary

Patty Murray (D)	479,009	*95.2*

Socialist Workers Primary

Nan Bailey (SOC WORK)	3,709	*100.0*

Reform Primary

Mike The Mover (REF)	6,596	*54.1*
Steve Thompson (REF)	3,371	*27.6*
Charlie R. Jackson (REF)	2,234	*18.3*

Washington

1. A special election was held to fill the five-year unexpired term of Sen. Henry M. Jackson (D), who died Sept. 1, 1983. Under Washington's so-called "jungle" primary, all 33 candidates appeared on the same Oct. 11 ballot with their party designations. The two highest vote getters, Dan Evans (R) and Mike Lowry (D), won ballot positions for the special election. Percentages are calculated here as if candidates had run in separate party primaries.

2. In 1998 Washington instituted an open primary with all candidates running on a single, multiparty ballot with their parties designated. Nominations went to the candidate with the highest vote in each party. Percentages were calculated here as if candidates had run in separate party primaries.

WEST VIRGINIA

Candidates	Votes	%
Class 1		

1956[1]   **Republican Special Primary**

Chapman Revercomb (R)	79,106	41.5
Tom Sweeney (R)	57,556	30.2
Philip H. Hill (R)	37,574	19.7
A. J. Carey (R)	11,268	5.9

Democratic Special Primary

William C. Marland (D)	118,159	37.2
John G. Fox (D)	104,869	33.1
Byron B. Randolph (D)	56,945	17.9
Walter G. Crichton (D)	26,972	8.5

1958   **Republican Primary**

Chapman Revercomb (R)		100.0

Democratic Primary

Robert C. Byrd (D)	170,686	80.2
Fleming N. Alderson (D)	23,915	11.2
Jack R. Delligatti (D)	18,235	8.6

1964   **Republican Primary**

Cooper P. Benedict (R)		100.0

Democratic Primary

Robert C. Byrd (D)	268,368	85.4
William F. Champe (D)	45,738	14.6

1970[2]   **Democratic Primary**

Robert C. Byrd (D)	195,725	89.0
John J. McOwen (D)	24,286	11.0

1976[2]   **Democratic Primary**

Robert C. Byrd (D)		100.0

1982   **Republican Primary**

Cleveland K. Benedict (R)	73,638	80.9
James A. Washburn (R)	9,877	10.8
Frederick A. Weiland (R)	7,531	8.3

Democratic Primary

Robert C. Byrd (D)		100.0

1988   **Republican Primary**

M. Jay Wolfe (R)	81,286	70.3
Bernie Lumbert (R)	34,273	29.7

Democratic Primary

Robert C. Byrd (D)	252,767	80.8
Bobbie E. Myers (D)	60,186	19.2

1994   **Republican Primary**

Stan Klos (R)	46,709	60.2
Arthur Gindin (R)	30,824	39.8

Democratic Primary

Robert C. Byrd (D)	190,061	85.4
James M. Fuller (D)	20,057	9.0
Paul Nuchims (D)	12,381	5.6

2000   **Republican Primary**

David T. Gallaher (R)	42,446	52.0
Garry P. Adkins (R)	39,254	48.0

Democratic Primary

Robert C. Byrd (D)	251,438	100.0

Class 2		

1958[3]   **Republican Special Primary**

John D. Hoblitzell (R)		100.0

Democratic Special Primary

Jennings Randolph (D)	102,547	47.2
William C. Marland (D)	77,901	35.8
Arnold M. Vickers (D)	25,439	11.7
W. R. Wilson (D)	11,540	5.3

1960   **Republican Primary**

Cecil H. Underwood (R)		100.0

Democratic Primary

Jennings Randolph (R)		100.0

1966   **Republican Primary**

Francis J. Love (R)	61,479	63.4
Harold G. Cutright (R)	35,530	36.6

Democratic Primary

Jennings Randolph (D)		100.0

1972   **Republican Primary**

Louise Leonard (R)		100.0

Democratic Primary

Jennings Randolph (D)		100.0

1978   **Republican Primary**

Arch A. Moore Jr. (R)	90,406	90.6
Donald G. Michels (R)	9,414	9.4

Democratic Primary

Jennings Randolph (D)	181,480	80.5
Sharon Rogers (D)	43,991	19.5

1984   **Republican Primary**

John R. Raese (R)	61,389	47.8
Samuel N. Kusic (R)	44,820	34.9
J. Frank Deem (R)	13,707	10.7

Democratic Primary

John D. "Jay" Rockefeller IV (D)	240,559	66.3
Lacy Wright (D)	51,591	14.2

Ken Auvil (D)	41,408	*11.4*
Homer L. Harris (D)	29,138	*8.0*

1990   **Republican Primary**

John Yoder (R)		*100.0*

Democratic Primary

John D. "Jay" Rockefeller IV (D)	200,161	*84.7*
Ken B. Thompson (D)	21,669	*9.2*

1996   **Republican Primary**

Betty A. Burks (R)	90,446	*100.0*

Democratic Primary

John D. "Jay" Rockefeller IV (D)	280,303	*88.4*
Bruce Barilla (D)	36,637	*11.6*

West Virginia

1. A special election was held to fill the seat vacated by the death of Sen. Harley M. Kilgore (D) on Feb. 28, 1956.

2. No Republican candidates entered the 1970 and 1976 Senate primaries. After the primary date in 1970, the party designated Elmer H. Dodson as the Republican candidate. No Republican candidate was designated in 1976.

3. A special election was held to fill the seat of Sen. Matthew M. Neely (D), who died Jan. 18, 1958.

WISCONSIN

Candidates	Votes	%

Class 1

1957[1]   **Republican Special Primary**

Walter J. Kohler (R)	109,256	*34.4*
Glenn R. Davis (R)	100,532	*31.7*
Alvin E. O'Konski (R)	66,784	*21.0*
Warren P. Knowles (R)	23,996	*7.6*

Democratic Special Primary

William Proxmire (D)	86,341	*60.3*
Clement J. Zablocki (D)	56,817	*39.7*

1958   **Republican Primary**

Roland J. Steinle (R)		*100.0*

Democratic Primary

William Proxmire (D)	220,146	*85.6*
Harry Halloway (D)	20,880	*8.1*
Arthur J. McGurn (D)	16,014	*6.2*

1964   **Republican Primary**

Wilbur N. Renk (R)		*100.0*

Democratic Primary

William Proxmire (D)	295,676	*88.8*
Kenneth F. Klinkert (D)	20,022	*6.0*
Arlyn F. Wollenburg (D)	17,333	*5.2*

1970   **Republican Primary**

John E. Erickson (R)		*100.0*

Democratic Primary

William Proxmire (D)		*100.0*

American Primary

Edmond E. Hou-Seye (AM)		*100.0*

1976   **Republican Primary**

Stanley York (R)		*100.0*

Democratic Primary

William Proxmire (D)		*100.0*

1982   **Republican Primary**

Scott McCallum (R)	182,043	*67.7*
Paul T. Brewer (R)	86,728	*32.3*

Democratic Primary

William Proxmire (D)	467,214	*86.1*
Marcel Dandeneau (D)	75,258	*13.9*

Libertarian Primary

George Liljenfeldt (LIBERT)		*100.0*

Constitution Primary

Sanford G. Knapp (CONST)		*100.0*

1988   **Republican Primary**

Susan Engeleiter (R)	209,025	*57.0*
Stephen B. King (R)	148,601	*40.5*

Democratic Primary

Herbert H. Kohl (D)	249,226	*46.8*
Anthony S. Earl (D)	203,479	*38.2*
Edward R. Garvey (D)	55,225	*10.4*

1994   **Republican Primary**

Robert T. Welch (R)	157,109	*47.4*
Matthew Gunderson (R)	74,460	*22.4*
Cate Zeuske (R)	56,248	*17.0*
Thomas M. Fitzpatrick (R)	43,695	*13.2*

Democratic Primary

Herbert H. Kohl (D)	135,982	*89.6*
Edmond Hou-Seye (D)	15,579	*10.3*

Libertarian Primary

James Dean (LIBERT)	1,030	*100.0*

2000   **Republican Primary**

John Gillespie (R)	135,364	*68.0*
Bill Lorge (R)	41,026	*20.6*
Marc Gumz (R)	21,698	*10.9*

Democratic Primary

Herbert H. Kohl (D)	184,920	*89.8*
Jim Sigl (D)	20,858	*10.1*

Class 3

1956   **Republican Primary**

Alexander Wiley (R)	221,042	48.9
Glenn R. Davis (R)	211,016	46.7

Democratic Primary

Henry W. Maier (D)	169,999	66.9
Elliot N. Walstead (D)	83,801	33.0

1962   **Republican Primary**

Alexander Wiley (R)	347,155	80.3
Arlyn F. Wollenburg (R)	85,044	19.7

Democratic Primary

Gaylord Nelson (D)		100.0

1968   **Republican Primary**

Jerris Leonard (R)	133,060	50.7
Robert I. Johnson (R)	73,344	28.0
James J. Donohue (R)	45,523	17.4

Democratic Primary

Gaylord Nelson (D)		100.0

1974   **Republican Primary**

Thomas E. Petri (R)	130,523	85.2
James A. Sigl (R)	22,714	14.8

Democratic Primary

Gaylord Nelson (D)		100.0

American Primary

Gerald L. McFarren (AM)		100.0

1980   **Republican Primary**

Robert W. Kasten (R)	134,586	36.8
Terry J. Kohler (R)	106,270	29.0
Douglass Cofrin (R)	84,355	23.0
Russell A. Olson (R)	40,823	11.1

Democratic Primary

Gaylord Nelson (D)		100.0

Constitution Primary

James P. Wickstrom (CONST)		100.0

Libertarian Primary

Bervin J. Larson (LIBERT)		100.0

1986   **Republican Primary**

Robert W. Kasten (R)		100.0

Democratic Primary

Edward R. Garvey (D)	126,408	47.6
Matthew J. Flynn (D)	101,777	38.3
Gary R. George (D)	29,485	11.1

1992   **Republican Primary**

Robert W. Kasten (R)	197,488	80.5
Roger W. Faulkner (R)	47,804	19.5

Democratic Primary

Russell D. Feingold (D)	367,746	69.7
Jim Moody (D)	74,472	14.1
Joseph W. Checota (D)	71,570	13.6

1998   **Republican Primary**

Mark W. Neumann (R)	217,527	99.7

Democratic Primary

Russell D. Feingold (D)	193,505	99.7

Wisconsin

1. A special election was held to fill the unexpired term of Sen. Joseph R. McCarthy (R), who died May 2, 1957.

WYOMING

Candidates	Votes	%

Class 1

1958   **Republican Primary**

Frank A. Barrett (R)		100.0

Democratic Primary

Gale McGee (D)	22,098	59.5
Hepburn T. Armstrong (D)	15,024	40.5

1964   **Republican Primary**

John S. Wold (R)	23,278	52.0
K. L. Sailors (R)	21,522	48.0

Democratic Primary

Gale McGee (D)	39,140	89.6
I. Wayne Kinney (D)	4,535	10.4

1970   **Republican Primary**

John S. Wold (R)	40,276	88.0
Arthur E. Linde (R)	5,479	12.0

Democratic Primary

Gale McGee (D)	32,956	79.6
D. P. Svilar (D)	8,448	20.4

1976   **Republican Primary**

Malcolm Wallop (R)	41,445	76.6
Nels T. Larson (R)	6,965	12.9
Doyle W. Henry (R)	5,727	10.6

Democratic Primary

Gale McGee (D)		100.0

1982   **Republican Primary**

Malcolm Wallop (R)	61,650	80.9
Richard Redland (R)	14,543	19.1

Democratic Primary		
Rodger McDaniel (D)		100.0

1988   Republican Primary

Malcolm Wallop (R)	55,752	83.2
Nora M. Lewis (R)	3,933	5.9
I. W. Kinney (R)	3,716	5.5

Democratic Primary		
John P. Vinich (D)	23,214	47.2
Pete Maxfield (D)	14,613	29.7
Lynn Simons (D)	11,350	23.1

1994   Republican Primary

Craig Thomas (R)	81,381	100.0

Democratic Primary		
Mike Sullivan (D)	39,563	100.0

2000   Republican Primary

Craig Thomas (R)	68,132	100.0

Democratic Primary		
Mel Logan (D)	16,530	64.6
Sheldon Sumey (D)	9,062	35.4

Class 2

1960   Republican Primary

E. Keith Thomson (R)	31,596	69.1
Frank A. Barrett (R)	13,380	29.2

Democratic Primary		
Raymond B. Whitaker (D)	18,031	44.1
Velma Linford (D)	13,792	33.8
Carl A. Johnson (D)	5,370	13.1
Charles B. Chittim (D)	3,653	8.9

1962[1]   Republican Special Primary

Milward L. Simpson (R)	30,124	59.6
K. L. Sailors (R)	20,383	40.4

Democratic Special Primary		
J. J. Hickey (D)		100.0

1966   Republican Primary

Clifford P. Hansen (R)	40,102	86.1
I. Wayne Kinney (R)	6,468	13.9

Democratic Primary		
Teno Roncalio (D)		100.0

1972   Republican Primary

Clifford P. Hansen (R)		100.0

Democratic Primary		
Mike Vinich (D)	16,148	52.5
Doyle W. Henry (D)	5,642	18.4
Patrick E. Shanklin (D)	4,665	15.2
William E. Fritchell (D)	4,281	13.9

1978   Republican Primary

Alan K. Simpson (R)	37,332	54.7
Hugh Binford (R)	20,768	30.4
Gordon H. Barrows (R)	8,494	12.4

Democratic Primary		
Raymond B. Whitaker (D)	19,854	47.6
Dean M. Larson (D)	11,039	26.5
Charles Carroll (D)	10,797	25.9

1984   Republican Primary

Alan K. Simpson (R)	66,178	87.9
Stephen Tarver (R)	9,137	12.1

Democratic Primary		
Victor A. Ryan (D)	17,608	45.3
Al Hamburg (D)	12,088	31.1
Michael J. Dee (D)	9,187	23.6

1990   Republican Primary

Alan K. Simpson (R)	69,142	84.4
Nora M. Lewis (R)	6,577	8.0
Douglas W. Crook (R)	6,201	7.6

Democratic Primary		
Kathy Helling (D)	12,103	35.1
Howard O'Connor (D)	7,196	20.9
Al Hamburg (D)	6,483	18.8
Emmett Jones (D)	4,455	12.9
Dale Bulman (D)	2,291	6.6
Don C. Jolliffe (D)	1,983	5.7

1996   Republican Primary

Michael B. Enzi (R)	27,056	32.5
John Barrasso (R)	24,918	29.9
Curt Meier (R)	14,739	17.7
Nimi McConigley (R)	6,005	7.2
Kevin P. Meenan (R)	6,000	7.2

Democratic Primary		
Kathy Karpan (D)	32,419	86.1
Mickey Kalinay (D)	5,245	13.9

Wyoming

1. A special election was held to fill the unexpired term of E. Keith Thomson (R), who died after winning the Senate seat in 1960. J. J. Hickey (D), the incumbent governor, resigned in January 1961 and his successor appointed him to the seat, where he served until after the special election was held, in November 1962.

Gubernatorial Elections

## CHAPTER 28

Introduction

NEXT TO THE PRESIDENT, governors are the most powerful elected officials in the United States. Some preside over states that are larger than many foreign countries. Every governor but Nebraska's must deal with a legislature that is partisan and bicameral in nature, just like the U.S. Congress.

Over the years, many voters have regarded executive experience as a governor more akin to that of the president than service as a legislator, military commander, or business leader, which helps to explain why four of the five presidents since 1977 have been governors or former governors. (The exception was George Bush, and his son was governor of Texas when he won the presidency in 2000.)

In all, seventeen of the nation's forty-three presidents (or 40 percent) have first been governors—including Ronald Reagan of California; Calvin Coolidge of Massachusetts; Woodrow Wilson of New Jersey; Grover Cleveland, Theodore Roosevelt, and Franklin D. Roosevelt of New York; and George W. Bush of Texas. More recently, though, it is not only big-state governors who have made the leap to the White House, but executives from smaller states as well, including Jimmy Carter of Georgia and Bill Clinton of Arkansas.

But in recent years, many politicians wanting an active role in fashioning policy have found their state capital and not Washington, D.C., to be the place to be. The downsizing of the federal government in the late twentieth century shifted power to the states, as they became laboratories of government experimentation on issues from education to welfare reform.

As a consequence, there have been a noticeable number of politicians in recent years who have aborted promising careers on Capitol Hill to return to state government. In 1998 Republican senator Dirk Kempthorne exchanged his U.S. Senate seat for the governorship of his home state of Idaho. In 2000 three members of the U.S. House ran for governor in their home states, although only one—Democrat Bob Wise of West Virginia—was successful.

For all their power today, though, governors still are on a tighter leash than most other officials elected under our federal system of government. Presidents have been limited to two terms since 1951 by constitutional amendment, but the Supreme Court has nullified state efforts to impose term limits on their members of Congress. By contrast, roughly three-fourths of the states limit their governors to a single term or two consecutive terms, although in many states governors may serve again after a one-term hiatus.

The election of governors by popular vote goes back to the early years of the Republic in the late eighteenth century. But the first female governors were not elected until 1924, four years af-

ter the Nineteenth Amendment granted women's suffrage in every state. Elected that year to succeed their husbands were Nellie Tayloe Ross of Wyoming and Miriam "Ma" Ferguson of Texas, both Democrats.

The first two Hispanic governors were elected in 1974, Democrats Jerry Apodaca in New Mexico and Raul Castro in neighboring Arizona. The first popularly elected African American governor was Democrat L. Douglas Wilder of Virginia, who was narrowly elected in 1989. Gary Locke, a Democrat of Chinese descent, became the first Asian American governor with his election in Washington in 1996.

Throughout most of the period since the end of World War II, Democrats have held a majority of the nation's governorships, cresting at thirty-seven after the Watergate crisis in the mid-1970s. But Republicans have held the upper hand since the election of 1994. After the 2000 election, twenty-nine governors were Republicans, nineteen were Democrats, and two (in Maine and Minnesota) were independents. One of the independent governors, former professional wrestler Jesse Ventura, won the governorship of Minnesota in 1998 on the Reform Party line, but bolted the party in early 2000.

Gubernatorial duties vary in detail from state to state, but basically they are the same. Most state constitutions today have the "strong governor, weak legislature" system, which is the reverse of the situation that prevailed at the dawn of the American Republic.

The newly freed states looked with suspicion on the office of governor. In the colonial era, the British-appointed governors were the symbols of the mother country's control and, the revolutionaries argued, of tyranny. Colonial assemblies, however, were able to gain control over appropriations and thus became the champions of colonial rights against the governors. After the Revolutionary War, when drawing up their constitutions, states gave most of the power to the legislative bodies and imposed restrictions on governors, including the length of the term of office and the method of election.

Length of Terms

As of 1789 the four New England states—Connecticut, Massachusetts, New Hampshire, and Rhode Island—held gubernatorial elections every year. Some of the Middle Atlantic states favored somewhat longer terms; New York and Pennsylvania had three-year terms for their governors, although New Jersey instituted a one-year term. The border and southern states had a mix: Maryland and North Carolina governors served a one-year term; South Carolina had a two-year term; and Delaware,

Table 28-1			
Party Lineup of Governors			
Year	Democrat	Republican	Other
1950	23	25	0
1952	18	30	0
1954	27	21	0
1956	29	19	0
1958	35	14	0
1960	34	16	0
1962	34	16	0
1964	33	17	0
1966	25	25	0
1968	19	31	0
1970	29	21	0
1972	31	19	0
1974	36	13	1
1976	37	12	1
1978	32	18	0
1980	26	24	0
1982	34	16	0
1964	34	16	0
1986	26	24	0
1988	28	22	0
1990	27	21	2
1992	30	18	2
1994	19	30	1
1996	17	32	1
1998	17	31	2
2000	19	29	2

Note: The figures above show the number of governorships held by the two parties after each even-numbered election since 1950. They do not reflect midterm changes or the results of elections in odd-numbered years.

Virginia, and Georgia had three-year terms. No state had a four-year term.

Over the years states have changed the length of gubernatorial terms. With some occasional back and forth movement, the general trend has been toward lengthening terms. New York, for example, has changed the term of office of its governor four times. Beginning in 1777 with a three-year term, the state switched to a two-year term in 1820, back to a three-year term in 1876, back to a two-year term in 1894, and to a four-year term beginning in 1938.

Maryland provides another example of a state that has changed its gubernatorial term several times. Beginning with one year in 1776, the state extended the term to three years in 1838, then to four years in 1851. Regular gubernatorial elections were held every second odd year from then through 1923, when the state had one three-year term so that future elections would be held in even-numbered years, beginning in 1926. Thus, the state held gubernatorial elections in 1919, 1923, and 1926 and then every four years after that.

The trend toward longer gubernatorial terms shows up clearly by comparing the length of terms in 1900 and 2000. Of the forty-five states in the Union in 1900, twenty-two, almost half, had two-year terms. One (New Jersey) had a three-year term, while Rhode Island and Massachusetts were the only states left with one-year terms. The remaining twenty states had four-year gubernatorial terms. (*See Table 28-2, p. 1379.*)

As of January 2001, forty-three of those same states had four-year terms, and the five states admitted to the Union after 1900—Oklahoma (1907), Arizona and New Mexico (1912), Alaska and Hawaii (1959)—had four-year gubernatorial terms. This left only two states with two-year terms: New Hampshire and Vermont.

Arkansas, one of the last holdouts, voted in 1984 to switch to a four-year term, effective in 1986. Rhode Island voters in 1992 approved a constitutional change to a four-year term beginning with the 1994 election. New Hampshire voters, on the other hand, in 1984 rejected a proposal for a four-year gubernatorial term.

Elections in Nonpresidential Years

Along with the change to longer terms for governors came another trend—away from holding gubernatorial elections in presidential election years. Except for North Dakota, every state that switched in the twentieth century to four-year gubernatorial terms scheduled its elections in nonpresidential years. Moreover, Florida, which held its quadrennial gubernatorial elections in presidential years, changed to nonpresidential years in 1966. To make the switch, the state shortened to two years the term of the governor elected in 1964, then resumed the four-year term in 1966. Louisiana switched its gubernatorial election to nonpresidential years in 1975. Illinois made a similar switch in 1976. All of these states held one election on a shorter than regular cycle and then resumed their regular four-year rotation. Arkansas switched from a two-year to a four-year term in 1984 and chose to select its governors in nonpresidential election years beginning in 1986.

These changes left only nine states—Delaware, Indiana, Missouri, Montana, North Carolina, North Dakota, Utah, Washington, and West Virginia—holding quadrennial gubernatorial elections at the same time as the presidential election. New Hampshire and Vermont still had two-year terms, so every other gubernatorial election in these two states occurred in a presidential year. Five states—Kentucky, Louisiana, Mississippi, New Jersey, and Virginia—elect governors in odd-numbered years.

Methods of Election

Yet another way in which Americans of the early federal period restricted their governors was by the method of election. In 1789 only in New York and the four New England states did the people directly choose their governors by popular vote. In the remaining eight states, governors were chosen by the state legislatures, thus enhancing the power of the legislatures in their dealings with the governors. But several factors—including the democratic trend to elect public officials directly, the increasing trust in the office of governor, and the need for a stronger and more independent chief executive—led to the gradual introduction of popular votes in all the states.

By the 1860s the remaining eight original states had switched to popular ballots. Pennsylvania was first, in 1790, and was followed by Delaware in 1792, Georgia in 1825, North Carolina in

Table 28-2
Length of Governor Terms (in years)

State	1900	2000	Year of change	State	1900	2000	Year of change
Alabama	2	4	1901	Montana	4	4	—
Alaska[1]	—	4	—	Nebraska	2	4	1966
Arizona[1]	—	4	1970	Nevada	4	4	—
Arkansas	2	4	1986	New Hampshire	2	2	—
California	4	4	—	New Jersey	3	4	1949
Colorado	2	4	1958	New Mexico[1]	—	4	1970
Connecticut	2	4	1950	New York	2	4	1938
Delaware	4	4	—	North Carolina	4	4	—
Florida	4	4	—	North Dakota	2	4	1964
Georgia	2	4	1942	Ohio	2	4	1958
Hawaii[1]	—	4	—	Oklahoma[1]	—	4	—
Idaho	2	4	1946	Oregon	4	4	—
Illinois	4	4	—	Pennsylvania	4	4	—
Indiana	4	4	—	Rhode Island[3]	1	4	1912, 1994
Iowa	2	4	1974	South Carolina	2	4	1926
Kansas	2	4	1974	South Dakota	2	4	1974
Kentucky	4	4	—	Tennessee	2	4	1954
Louisiana	4	4	—	Texas	2	4	1974
Maine	2	4	1958	Utah	4	4	—
Maryland	4	4	—	Vermont	2	2	—
Massachusetts[2]	1	4	1920, 1966	Virginia	4	4	—
Michigan	2	4	1966	Washington	4	4	—
Minnesota	2	4	1962	West Virginia	4	4	—
Mississippi	4	4	—	Wisconsin	2	4	1970
Missouri	4	4	—	Wyoming	4	4	—

1. Oklahoma was admitted to the Union in 1907, Arizona and New Mexico in 1912, and Alaska and Hawaii in 1959. Oklahoma, Alaska, and Hawaii always have had four-year gubernatorial terms; Arizona began with a two-year term and switched to four years in 1970. New Mexico (1912) began with a four-year term, changed to two years in 1916, and went back to four years in 1970.
2. Massachusetts switched from a one- to a two-year term in 1920 and to a four-year term in 1966.
3. Rhode Island switched from a one- to a two-year term in 1912 and to a four-year term in 1994.

Source: Book of the States, 2000–01, vol. 33 (Lexington, Ky.: Council of State Governments, 2000); Philip D. Duncan and Brian Nutting, eds. *Politics in America 2002: The 107th Congress* (Washington, D.C.: Congressional Quarterly, 2001); state secretaries of state.

1835, Maryland in 1838, New Jersey in 1844, Virginia in 1851, and South Carolina in 1865, after the Civil War.

All the states admitted to the Union after the original thirteen, with one exception, made provision from the very beginning for popular election of their governors. The exception was Louisiana, which from its admission in 1812 until a change in the state constitution in 1845 had a unique system of gubernatorial elections. The people participated by voting in a first-step popular election. In a second step, the legislature was to select the governor from the two candidates receiving the highest popular vote.

Number of Terms

Another limitation placed on governors is a restriction on the number of terms they are allowed to serve. In the early years at least three states had such limitations: governors of Maryland were eligible to serve three consecutive one-year terms and then were required to retire for at least one year; Pennsylvania allowed its governors three consecutive three-year terms and then forced retirement for at least one term; and in New Jersey, according to the constitution of 1844, a governor could serve only one three-year term before retiring for at least one term.

In the last decades of the twentieth century, increasing voter discontent with government performance and with politicians stoked a movement to limit the number of years a person could serve in public office. The movement was especially pronounced at the gubernatorial level. By the beginning of the twenty-first century, only eleven states did not impose some term limits on their governors: Connecticut, Illinois, Iowa, Massachusetts, Minnesota, New Hampshire, New York, North Dakota, Texas, Vermont, and Wisconsin.

The lack of a term limit has resulted in some long gubernatorial tenures in some of these states. New York's Mario M. Cuomo, a Democrat, was beaten trying for a fourth term as governor in 1994. Wisconsin's Tommy G. Thompson, a Republican, was in the middle of his fourth term when he was tapped to be the secretary of health and human services after the 2000 election. And Vermont's Howard B. Dean, a Democrat, was elected to a fifth two-year term in 2000. Most of the other states have placed a limit of two consecutive terms on their governor, which has meant eight years continuously in office. A few states had variations on this theme. *(See Table 28-3, p. 1380.)*

Table 28-3
Limitations on Governor Terms

State	Term limit	State	Term limit
Alabama	2	Montana[4]	2
Alaska[1]	2	Nebraska[1]	2
Arizona[1]	2	Nevada	2
Arkansas	2	New Hampshire	None
California	2	New Jersey[1]	2
Colorado	2	New Mexico[1]	2
Connecticut	None	New York	None
Delaware[2]	2	North Carolina[1]	2
Florida[3]	2	North Dakota	None
Georgia[1]	2	Ohio[1]	2
Hawaii	2	Oklahoma[1]	2
Idaho[1]	2	Oregon[5]	2
Illinois	None	Pennsylvania	2
Indiana[1]	2	Rhode Island	2
Iowa	None	South Carolina[1]	2
Kansas	2	South Dakota[1]	2
Kentucky	2	Tennessee[1]	2
Louisiana[1]	2	Texas	None
Maine[1]	2	Utah	3
Maryland[1]	2	Vermont	None
Massachusetts	None	Virginia[6]	1
Michigan	2	Washington	2
Minnesota	None	West Virginia	2
Mississippi[2]	2	Wisconsin	None
Missouri[2]	2	Wyoming[5]	2

Notes: Gubernatorial term limits as of 2000.

1. After two consecutive terms, must wait four years and/or one full term before being eligible again.
2. Absolute two-term limitation, but not necessarily consecutive.
3. Eligible for eight consecutive years.
4. Eligible for eight out of 16 years.
5. Eligible for eight out of any period of twelve years.
6. Cannot serve consecutive terms, but after a four-year respite can seek reelection.

Source: Book of the States, 2000–01, vol. 33 (Lexington, Ky.: Council of State Governments, 2000), Table 2.9.

Majority Vote Requirement

A peculiarity of gubernatorial voting that has almost disappeared from the American political scene is the requirement that the winning gubernatorial candidate receive a majority of the popular vote. Otherwise, the choice devolves upon the state legislature or, in some cases, a runoff between the two leading candidates is required. Centered in New England, this practice was used mainly in the nineteenth century. All six present-day New England states as well as Arizona, Georgia, and Mississippi had such a provision governing their gubernatorial election at one time or another. New Hampshire, Vermont, Massachusetts, and Connecticut already had the provision when they entered the Union between 1789 and 1791.

Rhode Island required a majority election but did not adopt a provision for legislative election until 1842; Maine adopted a majority provision when it split off from Massachusetts to form a separate state in 1820. Georgia put the majority provision in its constitution when it switched from legislative to popular election of governors in 1825 but, instead of legislative elections, provides for a runoff between the top two contenders three weeks after the general election. Mississippi wrote the majority

provision into its constitution in 1890. Arizona adopted a runoff in 1990.

The purpose of the majority provision appears to have been to safeguard against a candidate's winning with a small fraction of the popular vote in a multiple field. In most of New England, the provision was part of the early state constitutions, formed largely in the 1780s, before the development of the two-party system.

The prospect of multiple-candidate fields diminished with the coming of the two-party system. Nevertheless, each of these states had occasion to use the provision at least once. Sometimes, in an extremely close election, minor-party candidates received enough of a vote to keep the winner from getting a majority of the total vote. And at other times strong third-party movements or disintegration of the old party structure resulted in the election's being thrown into the state legislature.

Vermont retains the majority vote provision, and its legislature chose the governor in January 1987, the first time it had done so since 1912. Georgia maintains the requirement for a majority vote for governor but, instead of legislative election, provides for a runoff between the top two contenders three weeks after the general election. Mississippi has a majority vote provision that was not used until 1999, when neither major party candidate received a majority of the vote, throwing the election into the Democratically controlled House of the legislature. On Jan. 4, 2000, as expected, the House elected the Democratic candidate, Lt. Gov. Ronnie Musgrove, who had edged Republican Mike Parker in the popular vote, 49.6 percent to 48.5 percent.

Following are the states that had the majority vote provision for governor, the years in which the choice devolved on the legislature because of it, and the year, if any, in which the requirement was repealed or changed:

• Arizona. Arizona adopted and used a runoff provision in 1990 following impeachment of a governor elected with less than a majority.

• Connecticut. No gubernatorial candidate received a majority of the popular vote, thus throwing the election into the legislature, in the following years subsequent to 1824: 1833, 1834, 1842, 1844, 1846, 1849, 1850, 1851, 1854, 1855, 1856, 1878, 1884, 1886, 1888, and 1890. Following the election of 1890, the legislature was unable to choose a new governor, so the outgoing governor, Morgan G. Bulkeley, R, continued to serve through the entire new term (1891–1893). The provision was repealed in 1901. The years prior to 1824 in which the provision was used, if any, were unavailable from the Connecticut secretary of state's office.

• Georgia. Although the majority vote requirement was contained in the constitution as early as 1825, it was not used until the twentieth century. In 1966, with an emerging Republican Party, a controversial Democratic nominee, and an Independent Democrat all affecting the gubernatorial race, no candidate received a majority. The legislature chose Democrat Lester Maddox, who trailed Republican Howard H. Callaway by 3,039 votes in the election tally. Controversy surrounding this experience led to the change from legislative choice to a runoff between the top two contenders. Earlier, in 1946, the Georgia legislature also

Removal of a Governor from Office

Term limits ensure a steady turnover of governors in most states. Elections every four years also enable the voters to replace an unpopular governor. In addition, governors guilty of unethical conduct or crimes and misdemeanors may be removed from office in the midst of their term through impeachment or recall.

The recall of a governor, which requires the holding of a special election if enough voters petition for removal, is an option in roughly one-third of the states. But it has been used only once against a governor. In 1921 North Dakota voters ousted Lynn J. Frazier of the Republican and National Prohibition Party, who had been forced into a special election with Ragnvald A. Nestos, an Independent Republican, which Neston won. Frazier was in his third two-year term when he was removed, along with two cabinet members. The following year Frazier was elected to the U.S. Senate, where he served until 1941.

Impeachment by the state legislature, similar to the federal system in which the House impeaches (charges) and the Senate acquits or convicts, was used five times in the twentieth century to remove governors. The most recent case was that of Arizona governor Evan Mecham, a Republican, who was impeached and convicted in January 1988. He was found guilty of obstructing an investigation and improperly using official funds. Mecham's removal through impeachment ended a recall movement against him.

Other governors have resigned after being convicted in the judicial system. Among such cases is that of Maryland governor Marvin Mandel, a Democrat, who served time in prison while suspended from office after his 1977 conviction on federal mail fraud charges. After his conviction was reversed, Mandel served the remaining few hours of his term.

Alabama governor Guy Hunt, a Republican, was removed from office in 1993 after he was convicted of diverting inaugural funds to personal use. Jim Guy Tucker, who as governor of Arkansas, resigned in 1996 after being convicted of bank fraud conspiracy in connection with the Whitewater real estate scandal. In September 1997 Arizona governor Fife Symington, a Republican, resigned after being convicted of making false statements to obtain loans for his real estate business.

attempted to choose the governor, under unusual circumstances not covered by the majority vote requirement. The governor-elect, Eugene Talmadge, D, died before taking office. When it met, the legislature chose Talmadge's son, Herman E. Talmadge, as the new governor. Herman Talmadge was eligible for consideration on the basis that he received enough write-in votes in the general election to make him the second-place candidate. But the state supreme court voided the legislature's choice and declared that the lieutenant governor–elect, Melvin E. Thompson, D, should be governor.

• Maine. Maine entered statehood in 1820 with a majority vote provision for governor but repealed it in 1880. During this sixty-year span, the Legislature was called on to choose the governor nine times, in 1840, 1846, 1848, 1852, 1853, 1854, 1855, 1878, and 1879.

• Massachusetts. Like the other New England states, Massachusetts originally had a requirement for majority voting in gubernatorial elections. However, after the legislature was forced to choose the governor for six straight elections from 1848 to 1853, Massachusetts repealed the provision in 1855. The years in which it was used were 1785, 1833, 1842, 1843, 1845, 1848, 1849, 1850, 1851, 1852, and 1853.

• Mississippi. This state had a majority voting requirement since its 1890 constitution but the provision was never needed for more than a century. In 1999, for the first time, no candidate received a majority, throwing the election into the Mississippi House, which chose a Democrat.

• New Hampshire. New Hampshire's mandated majority vote for governor was in force from 1784 through 1912, when it was repealed. The outcome of the following gubernatorial elections was determined by the Legislature: 1785, 1787, 1789, 1790, 1812, 1824, 1846, 1851, 1856, 1863, 1871, 1874, 1875, 1886, 1888, 1890, 1906, and 1912.

• Rhode Island. Under the constitution of 1842, Rhode Island required a majority to win the gubernatorial election. Under this mandate, the legislature chose the governor in the years 1846, 1875, 1876, 1880, 1889, 1890, and 1891. Because of a disagreement between the two houses of the state legislature, the ballots for governor were not counted in 1893, and Gov. D. Russell Brown, R, continued in office for another term of one year. The provision for majority voting then was repealed.

Before 1842 there also was a requirement for a popular majority, but the legislature was not allowed to choose a new governor if no candidate achieved a majority. Three times—in 1806, 1832, and 1839—there was a lack of a majority in a gubernatorial election, with a different outcome each time. In 1806 the lieutenant governor–elect served as acting governor for the term. In 1832 the legislature mandated a new election, but still no majority choice was reached; three more elections were held, all without a majority being achieved, so the same state officers were continued until the next regular election. And in 1839, when neither the gubernatorial nor lieutenant governor's race yielded a winner by majority, the senior state senator acted as governor for the term.

• Vermont. Vermont's provision for majority gubernatorial election resulted in the legislature's picking the governor twenty times: 1789, 1797, 1813, 1814, 1830, 1831, 1832, 1834, 1841, 1843, 1845, 1846, 1847, 1848, 1849, 1852, 1853, 1902, 1912, and 1987 (when the legislature elected Democrat Madeleine M. Kunin, who had won the popular vote the previous November with 47.0 percent of the vote). On a twenty-first occasion, 1835, the legislature failed to choose a new governor because of a deadlock and the lieutenant governor–elect served as governor for the term. The Vermont provision remains in force.

## CHAPTER 29

Governors of the States, 1776–2001

THIS CHAPTER (pages 1384–1414) contains a listing of state governors from the 1776 to 2001. Arranged alphabetically by state, the lists provide the name, political affiliation, and dates of service of each state's governors in chronological order. New to this edition is the addition of revolutionary governors during the period beginning with the Declaration of Independence in 1776 to the original thirteen states' ratification of the Constitution. The date when a state ratified the Constitution or entered the union is listed below the state's name.

The primary sources used for the names, party affiliations, and dates of service for governors were Joseph E. Kallenbach and Jessamine S. Kallenbach, *American State Governors, 1776–1976*, 3 vols. (Dobbs Ferry, N.Y.: Oceana Publishing, 1977); William W. Hunt, *The Book of Governors* (Los Angeles: Washington Typographers, 1935); Samuel R. Solomon, *Governors of the States 1900–1974* (Lexington, Ky.: Council of State Governments, 1974); gubernatorial election returns provided by the Inter-University Consortium for Political and Social Research (ICPSR), appearing on pages 1415–1477; *The Encyclopedia Americana*, 30 vols. (Danbury, Conn.: Grolier Education, 1982); issues of *CQ Weekly*; state manuals published by the state governments; and state governors' offices and Internet sites.

NAMES, PARTY AFFILIATION, AND DATES OF SERVICE

For the revolutionary period from 1776 to 1787, the Kallenbachs' *American State Governors, 1776–1976* was used for names of state governors and dates of service. In some cases the Kallenbachs provide complete dates (month, day, and year), in other cases only month and year. A few states during this period called their early chief executives "presidents." These chief executives are included in the list and footnoted.

Because political parties did not exist formally in the early years of the Republic, classification of governors by party during this period can be difficult or misleading. In cases where party affiliation was not appropriate or could not be determined, no party designation appears. After 1824, the starting date for the ICPSR gubernatorial election returns, the ICPSR data were used where they provided information on party affiliation. While the complete source annotations for the ICPSR collection are too extensive to publish here, information on the sources for specific election returns can be obtained through the ICPSR. *(See box, ICPSR Historical Election Returns File, p. xvi, Vol. I.)* State manuals and *The Encyclopedia Americana*, which gives governors' party affiliation for some states, were also consulted.

For the eighteenth and nineteenth centuries, Hunt's *The Book of Governors* and state manuals were used for names and dates of service. Hunt provides the names of state governors and dates of service—in some cases complete dates (month, day, and year), in other cases only month and year and in still other cases only the dates of gubernatorial elections. Congressional Quarterly has used the most precise dates available from Hunt and state manuals.

For the twentieth century, *The Governors of the States 1900–1974* was the primary source for the names of governors and dates of service. The party designations appearing in the ICPSR election returns were used to assign party affiliation. Where the ICPSR returns indicated two or more party designations, only the major party is listed. *(See "Political Party Abbreviations," p. 1596.)*

FOOTNOTES

Footnotes, based on information from the above sources, have been used to indicate the following circumstances:

• Deaths, resignations, or removals from office and succession of lieutenant governors or other officials to governorships.

• Circumstances surrounding disputed elections.

In the twentieth century the trend was toward longer gubernatorial terms and limitations on the number of consecutive terms, as well as unusual gubernatorial election procedures in some states. *(See Chapter 28, Introduction.)*

Governors of the States, 1776–2001

ALABAMA

(Became a state Dec. 14, 1819)

Governors	Dates of Service	
William W. Bibb (D-R)	Nov. 9, 1819	July 15, 1820
Thomas Bibb (D-R)	July 15, 1820	Nov. 9, 1821
Israel Pickens (D-R)	Nov. 9, 1821	Nov. 25, 1825
John Murphy (JAC D)	Nov. 25, 1825	Nov. 25, 1829
Gabriel Moore (JAC D)	Nov. 25, 1829	March 3, 1831
Samuel B. Moore (D)	March 3, 1832	Nov. 26, 1831
John Gayle (D)	Nov. 26, 1831	Nov. 21, 1835
Clement C. Clay (D)	Nov. 21, 1835	July 17, 1837
Hugh McVay (D)	July 17, 1837	Nov. 21, 1837
Arthur P. Bagby (D)	Nov. 21, 1837	Nov. 22, 1841
Benjamin Fitzpatrick (D)	Nov. 22, 1841	Dec. 10, 1845
Joshua L. Martin (I)	Dec. 10, 1845	Dec. 16, 1847
Reuben Chapman (D)	Dec. 16, 1847	Dec. 17, 1849
Henry W. Collier (D)	Dec. 17, 1849	Dec. 20, 1853
John A. Winston (D)	Dec. 20, 1853	Dec. 1, 1857
Andrew B. Moore (D)	Dec. 1, 1857	Dec. 2, 1861
John Gill Shorter (D)	Dec. 2, 1861	Dec. 1, 1863
Thomas H. Watts (W)	Dec. 1, 1863	May 1865
Lewis E. Parsons[1]	June 21, 1865	Dec. 20, 1865
Robert M. Patton (W)	Dec. 20, 1865	July 14, 1868
William Hugh Smith (R)	July 14, 1868	Nov. 26, 1870
Robert B. Lindsay (D)	Nov. 26, 1870	Nov. 17, 1872
David P. Lewis (R)	Nov. 17, 1872	Nov. 24, 1874
George S. Houston (D)	Nov. 24, 1874	Nov. 28, 1878
Rufus W. Cobb (D)	Nov. 28, 1878	Dec. 1, 1882
Edward A. O'Neal (D)	Dec. 1, 1882	Dec. 1, 1886
Thomas Seay (D)	Dec. 1, 1886	Dec. 1, 1890
Thomas G. Jones (D)	Dec. 1, 1890	Dec. 1, 1894
William C. Oates (D)	Dec. 1, 1894	Dec. 1, 1896
Joseph F. Johnston (D)	Dec. 1, 1896	Dec. 1, 1900
William D. Jelks (D)[2]	Dec. 1, 1900	Dec. 26, 1900
William J. Samford (D)[3]	Dec. 26, 1900	June 11, 1901
William D. Jelks (D)[4]	June 11, 1901	April 25, 1904
Russell M. Cunningham (D)[5]	April 25, 1904	March 5, 1905
William D. Jelks (D)	March 5, 1905	Jan. 14, 1907
Braxton B. Comer (D)	Jan. 14, 1907	Jan. 17, 1911
Emmet O'Neal (D)	Jan. 17, 1911	Jan. 18, 1915
Charles Henderson (D)	Jan. 18, 1915	Jan. 20, 1919
Thomas E. Kilby (D)	Jan. 20, 1919	Jan. 15, 1923
William W. Brandon (D)	Jan. 15, 1923	Jan. 17, 1927
Bibb Graves (D)	Jan. 17, 1927	Jan. 19, 1931
Benjamin M. Miller (D)	Jan. 19, 1931	Jan. 14, 1935
Bibb Graves (D)	Jan. 14, 1935	Jan. 17, 1939
Frank M. Dixon (D)	Jan. 17, 1939	Jan. 19, 1943
Chauncey M. Sparks (D)	Jan. 19, 1943	Jan. 20, 1947
James E. Folsom (D)	Jan. 20, 1947	Jan. 15, 1951
Gordon Persons (D)	Jan. 15, 1951	Jan. 17, 1955
James E. Folsom (D)	Jan. 17, 1955	Jan. 19, 1959
John M. Patterson (D)	Jan. 19, 1959	Jan. 14, 1963
George C. Wallace (D)	Jan. 14, 1963	Jan. 16, 1967
Lurleen B. Wallace (D)[6]	Jan. 16, 1967	May 7, 1968
Albert P. Brewer (D)[7]	May 7, 1968	Jan. 18, 1971
George C. Wallace (D)	Jan. 18, 1971	Jan. 15, 1979
Forrest H. "Fob" James Jr. (D)	Jan. 15, 1979	Jan. 17, 1983
George C. Wallace (D)	Jan. 17, 1983	Jan. 19, 1987
Guy Hunt (R)[8]	Jan. 19, 1987	April 22, 1993
James E. Folsom Jr. (D)[9]	April 22, 1993	Jan. 16, 1995
Forrest H. "Fob" James Jr. (R)[10]	Jan. 16, 1995	Jan. 18, 1999
Don Siegelman (D)	Jan. 18, 1999	

Alabama
1. Provisional governor, appointed by president.
2. Jelks, as president of the state Senate, took office as acting governor due to the illness of governor-elect Samford.
3. Died June 11, 1901.
4. As president of the state Senate, Jelks became governor on Samford's death. Subsequently reelected in 1902.
5. As lieutenant governor, he became acting governor due to the illness of Jelks.
6. Died May 7, 1968.
7. As lieutenant governor, he succeeded to office.
8. Removed from office upon conviction of misusing campaign funds.
9. As lieutenant governor, he succeeded to office.
10. Switched to Republican Party in 1994.

ALASKA

(Became a state Jan. 3, 1959)

Governors	Dates of Service	
William A. Egan (D)	Jan. 3, 1959	Dec. 5, 1966
Walter J. Hickel (R)[1]	Dec. 5, 1966	Jan. 29, 1969
Keith H. Miller (R)[2]	Jan. 29, 1969	Dec. 5, 1970
William A. Egan (D)	Dec. 5, 1970	Dec. 2, 1974
Jay S. Hammond (R)	Dec. 2, 1974	Dec. 6, 1982
Bill Sheffield (D)	Dec. 6, 1982	Dec. 1, 1986
Steve C. Cowper (D)	Dec. 1, 1986	Dec. 3, 1990
Walter J. Hickel (ALI)	Dec. 3, 1990	Dec. 5, 1994
Tony Knowles (D)	Dec. 5, 1994	

Alaska
1. Resigned Jan. 29, 1969.
2. As secretary of state, he succeeded to office.

ARIZONA

(Became a state Feb. 14, 1912)

Governors	Dates of Service	
George W. P. Hunt (D)	Feb. 14, 1912	Jan. 1, 1917
Thomas E. Campbell (R)[1]	Jan. 1, 1917	Dec. 25, 1917

George W. P. Hunt (D)[2]	Dec. 25, 1917	Jan. 6, 1919
Thomas E. Campbell (R)	Jan. 6, 1919	Jan. 1, 1923
George W. P. Hunt (D)	Jan. 1, 1923	Jan. 7, 1929
John C. Phillips (R)	Jan. 7, 1929	Jan. 5, 1931
George W. P. Hunt (D)	Jan. 5, 1931	Jan. 2, 1933
Benjamin B. Moeur (D)	Jan. 2, 1933	Jan. 4, 1937
Rawghile C. Stanford (D)	Jan. 4, 1937	Jan. 2, 1939
Robert T. Jones (D)	Jan. 2, 1939	Jan. 6, 1941
Sidney P. Osborn (D)[3]	Jan. 6, 1941	May 25, 1948
Dan E. Garvey (D)[4]	May 25, 1948	Jan. 1, 1951
J. Howard Pyle (R)	Jan. 1, 1951	Jan. 3, 1955
Ernest W. McFarland (D)	Jan. 3, 1955	Jan. 5, 1959
Paul J. Fannin (R)	Jan. 5, 1959	Jan. 4, 1965
Sam Goddard (D)	Jan. 4, 1965	Jan. 2, 1967
Jack Williams (R)	Jan. 2, 1967	Jan. 6, 1975
Raul Castro (D)[5]	Jan. 6, 1975	Oct. 20, 1977
Wesley Bolin (D)[6]	Oct. 20, 1977	March 4, 1978
Bruce Babbitt (D)[7]	March 4, 1978	Jan. 5, 1987
Evan Mecham (R)[8]	Jan. 5, 1987	April 4, 1988
Rose Mofford (D)[9]	April 5, 1988	March 6, 1991
Fife Symington (R)[10]	March 6, 1991	Sept. 5, 1997
Jane D. Hull (R)[11]	Sept. 5, 1997	

Arizona
1. Campbell was initially declared the winner, but the election was contested. After an extended recount, Hunt was declared the winner by 43 votes.
2. Hunt served out the remainder of the term following his successful challenge to Campbell's election.
3. Died May 25, 1948.
4. As secretary of state, he succeeded to office. Subsequently elected.
5. Resigned Oct. 20, 1977, to become ambassador to Argentina.
6. As secretary of state, he succeeded to office. Died March 4, 1978.
7. As attorney general, he succeeded to office. Subsequently elected.
8. Impeached; removed from office April 4, 1988.
9. As secretary of state, she succeeded to office.
10. Resigned Sept. 5, 1997.
11. As secretary of state, she succeeded to office.

ARKANSAS

(Became a state June 15, 1836)

Governors	Dates of Service	
James S. Conway (D)	Sept. 13, 1836	Nov. 4, 1840
Archibald Yell (D)[1]	Nov. 4, 1840	April 29, 1844
Samuel Adams (D)[2]	April 24, 1844	Nov. 5, 1844
Thomas S. Drew (D)[3]	Nov. 5, 1844	Jan. 10, 1849
Richard C. Byrd (D)[4]	Jan. 11, 1849	April 19, 1849
John S. Roane (D)	April 19, 1849	Nov. 15, 1852
Elias N. Conway (D)	Nov. 15, 1852	Nov. 16, 1860
Henry M. Rector (ID)	Nov. 16, 1860	Nov. 4, 1862
Thomas Fletcher[5]	Nov. 4, 1862	Nov. 15, 1862
Harris Flannigan (D)	Nov. 15, 1862	April 18, 1864
Isaac Murphy (UN)	April 18, 1864	July 2, 1868
Powell Clayton (R)[6]	July 2, 1868	March 17, 1871
Ozra A. Hadley (R)[7]	March 17, 1871	Jan. 6, 1873
Elisha Baxter (R)	Jan. 6, 1873	Nov. 12, 1874
Augustus H. Garland (D)	Nov. 12, 1874	Jan. 11, 1877
William R. Miller (D)	Jan. 11, 1877	Jan. 13, 1881
Thomas J. Churchill (D)	Jan. 13, 1881	Jan. 13, 1883
James H. Berry (D)	Jan. 13, 1883	Jan. 17, 1885

Simon P. Hughes (D)	Jan. 17, 1885	Jan. 17, 1889
James P. Eagle (D)	Jan. 17, 1889	Jan. 10, 1893
William M. Fishback (D)	Jan. 10, 1893	Jan. 18, 1895
James P. Clarke (D)	Jan. 18, 1895	Jan. 12, 1897
Daniel Webster Jones (D)	Jan. 12, 1897	Jan. 8, 1901
Jeff Davis (D)	Jan. 8, 1901	Jan. 8, 1907
John S. Little (D)[8]	Jan. 8, 1907	Feb. 11, 1907
John I. Moore (D)[9]	Feb. 11, 1907	May 11, 1907
Xenophon O. Pindall (D)[10]	May 14, 1907	Jan. 11, 1909
George W. Donaghey (D)	Jan. 11, 1909	Jan. 15, 1913
Joseph T. Robinson (D)[11]	Jan. 15, 1913	March 10, 1913
William K. Oldham (D)[12]	March 10, 1913	March 13, 1913
Junius M. Futrell (D)[13]	March 13, 1913	July 23, 1913
George W. Hays (D)	July 23, 1913	Jan. 9, 1917
Charles H. Brough (D)	Jan. 9, 1917	Jan. 11, 1921
Thomas C. McRae (D)	Jan. 11, 1921	Jan. 13, 1925
Thomas J. Terrall (D)	Jan. 13, 1925	Jan. 11, 1927
John E. Martineau (D)[14]	Jan. 11, 1927	March 4, 1928
Harvey Parnell (D)[15]	March 4, 1928	Jan. 10, 1933
Junius M. Futrell (D)	Jan. 10, 1933	Jan. 12, 1937
Carl E. Bailey (D)	Jan. 12, 1937	Jan. 14, 1941
Homer M. Adkins (D)	Jan. 14, 1941	Jan. 9, 1945
Benjamin T. Laney (D)	Jan. 9, 1945	Jan. 11, 1949
Sidney S. McMath (D)	Jan. 11, 1949	Jan. 13, 1953
Frances A. Cherry (D)	Jan. 13, 1953	Jan. 11, 1955
Orval E. Faubus (D)	Jan. 11, 1955	Jan. 10, 1967
Winthrop Rockefeller (R)	Jan. 10, 1967	Jan. 12, 1971
Dale Bumpers (D)[16]	Jan. 12, 1971	Jan. 3, 1975
Bob Riley (D)[17]	Jan. 3, 1975	Jan. 14, 1975
David Pryor (D)[18]	Jan. 14, 1975	Jan. 3, 1979
Joe Purcell (D)[19]	Jan. 3, 1979	Jan. 9, 1979
Bill Clinton (D)	Jan. 9, 1979	Jan. 19, 1981
Frank D. White (R)	Jan. 19, 1981	Jan. 11, 1983
Bill Clinton (D)[20]	Jan. 11, 1983	Dec. 12, 1992
Jim Guy Tucker Jr. (D)[21]	Dec. 12, 1992	July 15, 1996
Mike Huckabee (R)[22]	July 15, 1996	

Arkansas
1. Resigned April 29, 1844.
2. As president of the state Senate, he succeeded to office.
3. Resigned Jan. 10, 1849.
4. As president of the state Senate, he succeeded to office.
5. Acting governor.
6. Resigned March 17, 1871.
7. Succeeded to office.
8. Resigned Feb. 11, 1907.
9. Acting governor.
10. Elected president of the state Senate, he then succeeded to office as governor.
11. Resigned March 10, 1913.
12. As president of the state Senate, he succeeded to office.
13. As president of the state Senate, he succeeded to office.
14. Resigned March 4, 1928.
15. As lieutenant governor, he succeeded to office. Subsequently elected.
16. Resigned Jan. 3, 1975.
17. As lieutenant governor, he succeeded to office.
18. Resigned Jan. 3, 1979.
19. As lieutenant governor, he succeeded to office.
20. Resigned Dec. 12, 1992, having been elected president of the United States.
21. As lieutenant governor, he succeeded to office. Resigned July 15, 1996
22. As lieutenant governor, he succeeded to office.

CALIFORNIA

(Became a state Sept. 9, 1850)

Governors	Dates of Service	
Peter H. Burnett (ID)[1]	Dec. 20, 1849	Jan. 9, 1851
John McDougal (ID)[2]	Jan. 9, 1851	Jan. 8, 1852
John Bigler (D)	Jan. 8, 1852	Jan. 9, 1856
J. Neely Johnson (AM)	Jan. 9, 1856	Jan. 8, 1858
John B. Weller (D)	Jan. 8, 1858	Jan. 9, 1860
Milton S. Latham (D)[3]	Jan. 9, 1860	Jan. 14, 1860
John G. Downey (D)[4]	Jan. 14, 1860	Jan. 10, 1862
Leland Stanford (R)	Jan. 10, 1862	Dec. 10, 1863
Frederick F. Low (UN R)	Dec. 10, 1863	Dec. 5, 1867
Henry H. Haight (D)	Dec. 5, 1867	Dec. 8, 1871
Newton Booth (R)[5]	Dec. 8, 1871	Feb. 27, 1875
Romualdo Pacheco (R)[6]	Feb. 27, 1875	Dec. 9, 1875
William Irwin (D)	Dec. 9, 1875	Jan. 8, 1880
George C. Perkins (R)	Jan. 8, 1880	Jan. 10, 1883
George Stoneman (D)	Jan. 10, 1883	Jan. 8, 1887
Washington Bartlett (D)[7]	Jan. 8, 1887	Sept. 13, 1887
Robert W. Waterman (R)[8]	Sept. 13, 1887	Jan. 8, 1891
Henry H. Markham (R)	Jan. 8, 1891	Jan. 11, 1895
James H. Budd (D)	Jan. 11, 1895	Jan. 3, 1899
Henry T. Gage (R & UL)	Jan. 3, 1899	Jan. 6, 1903
George C. Pardee (R)	Jan. 6, 1903	Jan. 8, 1907
James N. Gillett (R)	Jan. 8, 1907	Jan. 3, 1911
Hiram W. Johnson (R, PROG)[9]	Jan. 3, 1911	March 15, 1917
William D. Stephens (RP & PROG)[10]	March 15, 1917	Jan. 9, 1923
Friend William Richardson (R)	Jan. 9, 1923	Jan. 4, 1927
Clement C. Young (R)	Jan. 4, 1927	Jan. 6, 1931
James Rolph Jr. (R)[11]	Jan. 6, 1931	June 2, 1934
Frank F. Merriam (R)[12]	June 2, 1934	Jan. 2, 1939
Culbert L. Olson (D)	Jan. 2, 1939	Jan. 4, 1943
Earl Warren (R)[13]	Jan. 4, 1943	Oct. 5, 1953
Goodwin J. Knight (R)[14]	Oct. 5, 1953	Jan. 5, 1959
Edmund G. Brown (D)	Jan. 5, 1959	Jan. 2, 1967
Ronald Reagan (R)	Jan. 1, 1967	Jan. 6, 1975
Edmund G. Brown Jr. (D)	Jan. 6, 1975	Jan. 3, 1983
George Deukmejian (R)	Jan. 3, 1983	Jan. 7, 1991
Peter B. "Pete" Wilson (R)	Jan. 7, 1991	Jan. 4, 1999
Gray Davis (D)	Jan. 4, 1999	

California
1. Resigned Jan. 9, 1851.
2. As lieutenant governor, he succeeded to office.
3. Resigned Jan. 14, 1860.
4. As lieutenant governor, he succeeded to office.
5. Resigned Feb. 27, 1875.
6. As lieutenant governor, he succeeded to office.
7. Died Sept. 13, 1887.
8. As lieutenant governor, he succeeded to office.
9. Elected as Republican in 1910. Elected as Progressive in 1914. Resigned March 15, 1917.
10. As lieutenant governor, he succeeded to office. Subsequently elected.
11. Died June 2, 1934.
12. As lieutenant governor, he succeeded to office. Subsequently elected.
13. Resigned Oct. 5, 1953.
14. As lieutenant governor, he succeeded to office. Subsequently elected.

COLORADO

(Became a state Aug. 1, 1876)

Governors	Dates of Service	
John L. Routt (R)	Nov. 3, 1876	Jan. 14, 1879
Frederick W. Pitkin (R)	Jan. 14, 1879	Jan. 9, 1883
James B. Grant (D)	Jan. 9, 1883	Jan. 13, 1885
Benjamin H. Eaton (R)	Jan. 13, 1885	Jan. 11, 1887
Alva Adams (D)	Jan. 11, 1887	Jan. 10, 1889
Job A. Cooper (R)	Jan. 10, 1889	Jan. 13, 1891
John L. Routt (R)	Jan. 13, 1891	Jan. 10, 1893
Davis H. Waite (POP & SL D)	Jan. 10, 1893	Jan. 8, 1895
Albert W. McIntire (R)	Jan. 8, 1895	Jan. 12, 1897
Alva Adams (D)	Jan. 12, 1897	Jan. 10, 1899
Charles S. Thomas (FUS)	Jan. 10, 1899	Jan. 8, 1901
James B. Orman (FUS)	Jan. 8, 1901	Jan. 13, 1903
James H. Peabody (R)	Jan. 13, 1903	Jan. 10, 1905
Alva Adams (D)[1]	Jan. 10, 1905	March 16, 1905
James H. Peabody (R)	March 16, 1905	March 17, 1905
Jesse F. McDonald (R)[2]	March 17, 1905	Jan. 8, 1907
Henry A. Buchtel (R)	Jan. 8, 1907	Jan. 12, 1909
John F. Shafroth (D)	Jan. 12, 1909	Jan. 14, 1913
Elias M. Ammons (D)	Jan. 14, 1913	Jan. 12, 1915
George A. Carlson (R)	Jan. 12, 1915	Jan. 9, 1917
Julius C. Gunter (D)	Jan. 9, 1917	Jan. 14, 1919
Oliver H. Shoup (R)	Jan. 14, 1919	Jan. 9, 1923
William E. Sweet (D)	Jan. 9, 1923	Jan. 13, 1925
Clarence J. Morley (R)	Jan. 13, 1925	Jan. 11, 1927
William H. Adams (D)	Jan. 11, 1927	Jan. 10, 1933
Edwin C. Johnson (D)[3]	Jan. 10, 1933	Jan. 3, 1937
Ray H. Talbot (D)[4]	Jan. 3, 1937	Jan. 12, 1937
Teller Ammons (D)	Jan. 12, 1937	Jan. 10, 1939
Ralph L. Carr (R)	Jan. 10, 1939	Jan. 12, 1943
John C. Vivian (R)	Jan. 12, 1943	Jan. 14, 1947
William L. Knous (D)[5]	Jan. 14, 1947	April 15, 1950
Walter W. Johnson (D)[6]	April 15, 1950	Jan. 9, 1951
Dan Thornton (R)	Jan. 9, 1951	Jan. 11, 1955
Edwin C. Johnson (D)	Jan. 11, 1955	Jan. 8, 1957
Stephen L. R. McNichols (D)	Jan. 8, 1957	Jan. 8, 1963
John A. Love (R)[7]	Jan. 8, 1963	July 16, 1973
John D. Vanderhoof (R)[8]	July 16, 1973	Jan. 14, 1975
Richard D. Lamm (D)	Jan. 14, 1975	Jan. 13, 1987
Roy Romer (D)	Jan. 13, 1987	Jan. 12, 1999
Bill Owens (R)	Jan. 12, 1999	

Colorado
1. The 1904 election between Alva Adams (D) and James H. Peabody (R) caused a dispute surrounding charges of fraud that had to be settled by the legislature. Both contenders were asked to withdraw. Adams served as governor for sixty-six days and Peabody for one day.
2. As lieutenant governor, he succeeded to office.
3. Resigned Jan. 3, 1937.
4. As lieutenant governor, he succeeded to office.
5. Resigned April 15, 1950.
6. As lieutenant governor, he succeeded to office.
7. Resigned July 16, 1973.
8. As lieutenant governor, he succeeded to office.

CONNECTICUT

(Ratified the Constitution Jan. 9, 1788)

Governors	Dates of Service	
Jonathan Trumbull	October 2, 1769	May 13, 1784
Matthew Griswold	May 13, 1784	May 11, 1786
Samuel Huntington[1]	May 11, 1786	Jan. 5, 1796
Oliver Wolcott (FED)[2]	Jan. 5, 1796	Dec. 1, 1797
Jonathan Trumbull II (FED)[3]	Dec. 1, 1797	Aug. 7, 1809
John Treadwell (FED)	Aug. 7, 1809	May 9, 1811
Roger Griswold (FED)[4]	May 9, 1811	Oct. 25, 1812
John Cotton Smith (FED)	Oct. 25, 1812	May 8, 1817
Oliver Wolcott Jr. (D-R)	May 8, 1817	May 2, 1827
Gideon Tomlinson (D-R, NR)[5]	May 2, 1827	March 1831
John S. Peters (NR)	March 1831	May 4, 1833
Henry W. Edwards (D)	May 4, 1833	May 7, 1834
Samuel A. Foote (NR)	May 7, 1834	May 6, 1835
Henry W. Edwards (D)	May 6, 1835	May 2, 1838
William W. Ellsworth (W)	May 2, 1838	May 4, 1842
Chauncey F. Cleveland (D)	May 4, 1842	May 1844
Roger S. Baldwin (W)	May 1844	May 6, 1846
Isaac Toucey (D)	May 6, 1846	May 5, 1847
Clark Bissell (W)	May 5, 1847	May 2, 1849
Joseph Trumbull (W)	May 2, 1849	May 4, 1850
Thomas H. Seymour (D)[6]	May 4, 1850	Oct. 13, 1853
Charles H. Pond (D)[7]	Oct. 13, 1853	May 1854
Henry Dutton (W)	May 3, 1854	May 1855
William T. Minor (AM)	May 3, 1855	May 6, 1857
Alexander H. Holley (R)	May 6, 1857	May 5, 1858
William A. Buckingham (R)	May 5, 1858	May 2, 1866
Joseph R. Hawley (R)	May 2, 1866	May 1, 1867
James E. English (D)	May 1, 1867	May 5, 1869
Marshall Jewell (R)	May 5, 1869	May 4, 1870
James E. English (D)	May 4, 1870	May 1871
Marshall Jewell (R)	May 16, 1871	May 7, 1873
Charles R. Ingersoll (D)	May 7, 1873	Jan. 3, 1877
Richard D. Hubbard (D)	Jan. 3, 1877	Jan. 9, 1879
Charles B. Andrews (R)	Jan. 9, 1879	Jan. 5, 1881
Hobart B. Bigelow (R)	Jan. 5, 1881	Jan. 3, 1883
Thomas M. Waller (D)	Jan. 3, 1883	Jan. 8, 1885
Henry B. Harrison (R)	Jan. 8, 1885	Jan. 7, 1887
Phineas C. Lounsbury (R)	Jan. 7, 1887	Jan. 10, 1889
Morgan G. Bulkeley (R)[8]	Jan. 10, 1889	Jan. 4, 1893
Luzon B. Morris (D)	Jan. 4, 1893	Jan. 9, 1895
O. Vincent Coffin (R)	Jan. 9, 1895	Jan. 6, 1897
Lorrin A. Cooke (R)	Jan. 6, 1897	Jan. 4, 1899
George E. Lounsbury (R)	Jan. 4, 1899	Jan. 9, 1901
George P. McLean (R)	Jan. 9, 1901	Jan. 7, 1903
Abiram Chamberlain (R)	Jan. 7, 1903	Jan. 4, 1905
Henry Roberts (R)	Jan. 4, 1905	Jan. 9, 1907
Rollin S. Woodruff (R)	Jan. 9, 1907	Jan. 6, 1909
George L. Lilley (R)[9]	Jan. 6, 1909	April 21, 1909
Frank B. Weeks (R)[10]	April 21, 1909	Jan. 4, 1911
Simeon E. Baldwin (D)	Jan. 4, 1911	Jan. 6, 1915
Marcus H. Holcomb (R)	Jan. 6, 1915	Jan. 5, 1921
Everett J. Lake (R)	Jan. 5, 1921	Jan. 3, 1923
Charles A. Templeton (R)	Jan. 3, 1923	Jan. 7, 1925
Hiram Bingham (R)[11]	Jan. 7, 1925	Jan. 8, 1925
John H. Trumbull (R)[12]	Jan. 8, 1925	Jan. 7, 1931
Wilbur L. Cross (D)	Jan. 7, 1931	Jan. 4, 1939
Raymond E. Baldwin (R)	Jan. 4, 1939	Jan. 8, 1941
Robert A. Hurley (D)	Jan. 8, 1941	Jan. 6, 1943
Raymond E. Baldwin (R)[13]	Jan. 6, 1943	Dec. 27, 1946
Wilbert Snow (D)[14]	Dec. 27, 1946	Jan. 8, 1947
James L. McConaughy (R)[15]	Jan. 8, 1947	March 7, 1948
James C. Shannon (R)[16]	March 7, 1948	Jan. 5, 1949
Chester Bowles (D)	Jan. 5, 1949	Jan. 3, 1951
John D. Lodge (R)	Jan. 3, 1951	Jan. 5, 1955
Abraham Ribicoff (D)[17]	Jan. 5, 1955	Jan. 21, 1961
John Dempsey (D)[18]	Jan. 21, 1961	Jan. 6, 1971
Thomas J. Meskill (R)	Jan. 6, 1971	Jan. 8, 1975
Ella T. Grasso (D)[19]	Jan. 8, 1975	Dec. 31, 1980
William A. O'Neill (D)[20]	Dec. 31, 1980	Jan. 9, 1991
Lowell P. Weicker Jr. (I)	Jan. 9, 1991	Jan. 4, 1995
John G. Rowland (R)	Jan. 4, 1995	

Connecticut
1. Died Jan. 5, 1796.
2. Died Dec. 1, 1797.
3. Died Aug. 7, 1809.
4. Died Oct. 25, 1812.
5. Resigned in 1831 to become U.S. senator.
6. Resigned Oct. 13, 1853.
7. As lieutenant governor, he succeeded to office.
8. The 1890 election was disputed, with Democrats claiming that Luzon Morris had won a majority of the popular vote and been elected governor, and Republicans claiming that he had not and demanding an election by the legislature. Since control of the legislature was divided, the two houses could not agree on what to do, so Bulkeley remained in office for the term.
9. Died April 21, 1909.
10. As lieutenant governor, he succeeded to office.
11. Resigned Jan. 8, 1925.
12. As lieutenant governor, he succeeded to office. Subsequently elected.
13. Resigned Dec. 27, 1946.
14. As lieutenant governor, he succeeded to office.
15. Died March 7, 1948.
16. As lieutenant governor, he succeeded to office.
17. Resigned Jan. 21, 1961.
18. As lieutenant governor, he succeeded to office. Subsequently elected.
19. Resigned Dec. 31, 1980.
20. As lieutenant governor, he succeeded to office. Subsequently elected.

DELAWARE

(Ratified the Constitution Dec. 7, 1787)

Governors	Dates of Service	
John McKinley[1]	Feb. 21, 1777	Sept. 12, 1777
Thomas McKean	Sept. 12, 1777	Oct. 20, 1777
George Read	Oct. 20, 1777	March 30, 1778
Caesar Rodney	March 31, 1778	Nov. 6, 1781
John Dickinson[2]	Nov. 13, 1781	Nov. 4, 1782
John Cook[3]	Nov. 4, 1782	Feb. 8, 1783
Nicholas Van Dyke	Feb. 8, 1783	Oct. 27, 1786
Thomas Collins[4]	Oct. 27, 1786	March 29, 1789
Jehu Davis[5]	March 29, 1789	June 2, 1789
Joshua Clayton (FED)[6]	June 2, 1789	Jan. 13, 1796
Gunning Bedford Sr. (FED)[7]	Jan. 13, 1796	Sept. 28, 1797
Daniel Rogers (FED)[8]	Sept. 28, 1797	Jan. 9, 1799
Richard Bassett (FED)[9]	Jan. 1799	March 1801

James Sykes (FED)[10]	March 1801	Jan. 1802
David Hall (D-R)	Jan. 1802	Jan. 1805
Nathaniel Mitchell (FED)	Jan. 1805	Jan. 1808
George Truitt (FED)	Jan. 1808	Jan. 1811
Joseph Haslet (D-R)	Jan. 1811	Jan. 1814
Daniel Rodney (FED)	Jan. 1814	Jan. 1817
John Clark (FED)	Jan. 1817	Jan. 1820
Henry Molleston[11]		
Jacob Stout (FED)[12]	Jan. 1820	Jan. 1821
John Collins (D-R)[13]	Jan. 1821	April 1822
Caleb Rodney (D-R)[14]	April 1822	Jan. 1823
Joseph Haslet (D-R)[15]	Jan. 1823	June 20, 1823
Charles Thomas (D-R)[16]	June 20, 1823	Jan. 1824
Samuel Paynter (FED)	Jan. 1824	Jan. 1827
Charles Polk (FED)	Jan. 1827	Jan. 1830
David Hazzard (D)	Jan. 1830	Jan. 1833
Caleb P. Bennett (D)[17]	Jan. 1833	April 9, 1836
Charles Polk[18]	April 9, 1836	Jan. 1837
Cornelius P. Comegys (W)	Jan. 1837	Jan. 1841
William B. Cooper (W)	Jan. 1841	Jan. 1845
Thomas Stockton (W)[19]	Jan. 1845	March 2, 1846
Joseph Maull (W)[20]	March 2, 1846	May 1, 1846
William Temple (W)[21]	May 1, 1846	Jan. 1847
William Tharp (D)	Jan. 1847	Jan. 1851
William H. Ross (D)	Jan. 1851	Jan. 1855
Peter F. Causey (AM)	Jan. 1855	Jan. 1859
William Burton (D)	Jan. 1859	Jan. 1863
William Cannon (UN)[22]	Jan. 1863	March 1, 1865
Gove Saulsbury (D)[23]	March 1, 1865	Jan. 1871
James Ponder (D)	Jan. 1871	Jan. 1875
John P. Cochran (D)	Jan. 1875	Jan. 1879
John W. Hall (D)	Jan. 1879	Jan. 1883
Charles C. Stockley (D)	Jan. 1883	Jan. 1887
Benjamin T. Biggs (D)	Jan. 1887	Jan. 1891
Robert J. Reynolds (D)	Jan. 1891	Jan. 1895
Joshua H. Marvel (R)[24]	Jan. 1895	April 8, 1895
William T. Watson (D)[25]	April 8, 1895	Jan. 19, 1897
Ebe W. Tunnell (D)	Jan. 19, 1897	Jan. 15, 1901
John Hunn (R)	Jan. 15, 1901	Jan. 17, 1905
Preston Lea (R)	Jan. 17, 1905	Jan. 19, 1909
Simeon S. Pennewill (R)	Jan. 19, 1909	Jan. 21, 1913
Charles R. Miller (R)	Jan. 21, 1913	Jan. 17, 1917
John G. Townsend Jr. (R)	Jan. 17, 1917	Jan. 18, 1921
William D. Denney (R)	Jan. 18, 1921	Jan. 20, 1925
Robert P. Robinson (R)	Jan. 20, 1925	Jan. 15, 1929
C. Douglass Buck (R)	Jan. 15, 1929	Jan. 19, 1937
Richard C. McMullen (D)	Jan. 19, 1937	Jan. 21, 1941
Walter W. Bacon (R)	Jan. 21, 1941	Jan. 18, 1949
Elbert N. Carvel (D)	Jan. 18, 1949	Jan. 20, 1953
J. Caleb Boggs (R)[26]	Jan. 20, 1953	Dec. 30, 1960
David P. Buckson (R)[27]	Dec. 30, 1960	Jan. 17, 1961
Elbert N. Carvel (D)	Jan. 17, 1961	Jan. 19, 1965
Charles L. Terry Jr. (D)	Jan. 19, 1965	Jan. 21, 1969
Russell W. Peterson (R)	Jan. 21, 1969	Jan. 16, 1973
Sherman W. Tribbitt (D)	Jan. 16, 1973	Jan. 18, 1977
Pierre duPont (R)	Jan. 18, 1977	Jan. 15, 1985
Michael N. Castle (R)[28]	Jan. 15, 1985	Dec. 31, 1992
Dale E. Wolf (R)[29]	Jan. 1, 1993	Jan. 19, 1993
Thomas R. Carper (D)	Jan. 19, 1993	Jan. 3, 2001
Ruth Ann Miner (D)	Jan. 3, 2001	

Delaware
1. Delaware's first ten chief executives were called presidents.
2. Resigned Nov. 4, 1782.
3. As speaker of the Council, he succeeded to office.
4. Died March 29, 1789.
5. As speaker of the Assembly, he succeeded to office.
6. Joshua Clayton was president of Delaware from 1789 to 1793 and governor from 1793 to 1796.
7. Died Sept. 28, 1797.
8. Acting governor.
9. Resigned in March 1801.
10. Acting governor.
11. Died before taking office.
12. Acting governor.
13. Died in April 1822.
14. Acting governor.
15. Died June 20, 1823.
16. Acting governor.
17. Died April 9, 1836.
18. Acting governor.
19. Died March 2, 1846.
20. Acting governor. Died May 1, 1846.
21. Acting governor.
22. Died March 1, 1865.
23. Acting governor. Subsequently elected.
24. Died April 8, 1895.
25. Acting governor.
26. Resigned Dec. 30, 1960.
27. As lieutenant governor, he succeeded to office.
28. Resigned Dec. 31, 1992, having been elected to the U.S. House.
29. As lieutenant governor, he succeeded to office.

FLORIDA

(Became a state March 3, 1845)

Governors	Dates of Service	
William D. Moseley (D)	June 25, 1845	Oct. 1, 1849
Thomas Brown (W)	Oct. 1, 1849	Oct. 3, 1853
James E. Broome (D)	Oct. 3, 1853	Oct. 5, 1857
Madison S. Perry (D)	Oct. 5, 1857	Oct. 7, 1861
John Milton (D)[1]	Oct. 7, 1861	April 1, 1865
William Marvin[2]	July 13, 1865	Dec. 20, 1865
David S. Walker (C)	Dec. 20, 1865	July 9, 1868
Harrison Reed (R)	July 9, 1868	Jan. 7, 1873
Ossian B. Hart (R)[3]	Jan. 7, 1873	March 18, 1874
Marcellus L. Stearns (R)[4]	March 18, 1874	Jan. 2, 1877
George F. Drew (D)	Jan. 2, 1877	Jan. 4, 1881
William D. Bloxham (D)	Jan. 4, 1881	Jan. 6, 1885
Edward A. Perry (D)	Jan. 6, 1885	Jan. 8, 1889
Francis P. Fleming (D)	Jan. 8, 1889	Jan. 3, 1893
Henry L. Mitchell (D)	Jan. 3, 1893	Jan. 5, 1897
William D. Bloxham (D)	Jan. 5, 1897	Jan. 8, 1901
William S. Jennings (D)	Jan. 8, 1901	Jan. 3, 1905
Napoleon B. Broward (D)	Jan. 3, 1905	Jan. 5, 1909
Albert W. Gilchrist (D)	Jan. 5, 1909	Jan. 7, 1913
Park Trammell (D)	Jan. 7, 1913	Jan. 2, 1917
Sidney J. Catts (IP)	Jan. 2, 1917	Jan. 4, 1921
Cary A. Hardee (D)	Jan. 4, 1921	Jan. 6, 1925
John W. Martin (D)	Jan. 6, 1925	Jan. 8, 1929
Doyle E. Carlton (D)	Jan. 8, 1929	Jan. 3, 1933
David Sholtz (D)	Jan. 3, 1933	Jan. 5, 1937
Frederick P. Cone (D)	Jan. 5, 1937	Jan. 7, 1941

Spessard L. Holland (D)	Jan. 7, 1941	Jan. 2, 1945
Millard F. Caldwell (D)	Jan. 2, 1945	Jan. 4, 1949
Fuller Warren (D)	Jan. 4, 1949	Jan. 6, 1953
Daniel T. McCarty (D)[5]	Jan. 6, 1953	Sept. 28, 1953
Charley E. Johns (D)[6]	Sept. 18, 1953	Jan. 4, 1955
LeRoy Collins (D)[7]	Jan. 4, 1955	Jan. 3, 1961
Farris Bryant (D)	Jan. 3, 1961	Jan. 5, 1965
Haydon Burns (D)	Jan. 5, 1965	Jan. 3, 1967
Claude R. Kirk Jr. (R)	Jan. 3, 1967	Jan. 5, 1971
Reubin Askew (D)	Jan. 5, 1971	Jan. 2, 1979
Robert Graham (D)[8]	Jan. 2, 1979	Jan. 3, 1987
John W. Mixon (D)[9]	Jan. 3, 1987	Jan. 6, 1987
Bob Martinez (R)	Jan. 6, 1987	Jan. 8, 1991
Lawton M. Chiles Jr. (D)[10]	Jan. 8, 1991	Dec. 12, 1998
Buddy MacKay (D)[11]	Dec. 13, 1998	Jan. 5, 1999
Jeb Bush (R)	Jan. 5, 1999	

Florida
1. Died April 1, 1865.
2. Acting governor, appointed by president.
3. Died March 18, 1874.
4. As lieutenant governor, he succeeded to office.
5. Died Sept. 28, 1953.
6. As president of the state Senate, he succeeded to office for the remainder of the first half of McCarty's term.
7. Elected in a special election to serve the last two years of McCarty's term. Subsequently reelected.
8. Resigned Jan. 3, 1987, having been elected to the U.S. Senate.
9. As lieutenant governor, he succeeded to office.
10. Died Dec. 12, 1998.
11. As lieutenant governor, he succeeded to office.

GEORGIA

(Ratified the Constitution Jan. 2, 1788)

Governors	Dates of Service	
Archibald Bulloch[1]	Jan. 22, 1776	Feb. 22, 1777
Button Gwinnett[2]	March 4, 1777	May 8, 1777
John Adam Treutlen	May 8, 1777	Jan. 10, 1778
John Houstoun	Jan. 10, 1778	Jan. 1779
John Wereat[3]	Aug. 6, 1779	Jan. 4, 1780
George Walton	Nov. 4, 1779	Jan. 4, 1780
Richard Howley[4]	Jan. 4, 1780	Feb. 18, 1780
Stephen Heard[5]	May 24, 1780	Aug. 16, 1781
Nathan Brownson[6]	Aug. 18, 1781	Jan. 3, 1782
John Martin	Jan. 3, 1782	Jan. 8, 1783
Lyman Hall	Jan. 8, 1783	Jan. 8, 1784
John Houstoun	Jan. 9, 1784	Jan. 6, 1785
Samuel Elbert	Jan. 6, 1785	Jan. 9, 1786
Edward Telfair	Jan. 9, 1786	Jan. 9, 1787
George Mathews	Jan. 9, 1787	Jan. 9, 1788
George Handley	Jan. 26, 1788	Jan. 7, 1789
George Walton (D-R)	Jan. 7, 1789	Nov. 9, 1789
Edward Telfair (D-R)	Nov. 9, 1789	Nov. 7, 1793
George Mathews (D-R)	Nov. 7, 1793	Jan. 15, 1796
Jared Irwin (D-R)	Jan. 15, 1796	Jan. 12, 1798
James Jackson (D-R)	Jan. 12, 1798	March 3, 1801
David Emanuel (D-R)	March 3, 1801	Nov. 7, 1801
Josiah Tattnall Jr. (D-R)	Nov. 7, 1801	Nov. 4, 1802
John Milledge (D-R)	Nov. 4, 1802	Sept. 23, 1806

Jared Irwin (D-R)	Sept. 23, 1806	Nov. 10, 1809
David B. Mitchell (D-R)	Nov. 10, 1809	Nov. 5, 1813
Peter Early (D-R)	Nov. 5, 1813	Nov. 10, 1815
David B. Mitchell (D-R)	Nov. 10, 1815	March 4, 1817
William Rabun (D-R)	March 4, 1817	Oct. 24, 1819
Matthew Talbot (D-R)	Oct. 24, 1819	Nov. 5, 1819
John Clark (D-R)	Nov. 5, 1819	Nov. 7, 1823
George M. Troup (D-R)	Nov. 7, 1823	Nov. 7, 1827
John Forsyth (D-R)	Nov. 7, 1827	Nov. 4, 1829
George R. Gilmer (D)	Nov. 4, 1829	Nov. 9, 1831
Wilson Lumpkin (UN D)	Nov. 9, 1831	Nov. 4, 1835
William Schley (D)	Nov. 4, 1835	Nov. 8, 1837
George R. Gilmer (W)	Nov. 8, 1837	Nov. 6, 1839
Charles J. McDonald (D)	Nov. 6, 1839	Nov. 8, 1843
George W. Crawford (W)	Nov. 8, 1843	Nov. 3, 1847
George W. Towns (D)	Nov. 3, 1847	Nov. 5, 1851
Howell Cobb (UN D)	Nov. 5, 1851	Nov. 9, 1853
Herschel V. Johnson (D)	Nov. 9, 1853	Nov. 6, 1857
Joseph E. Brown (D)	Nov. 6, 1857	June 17, 1865
James Johnson (D)	June 17, 1865	Dec. 14, 1865
Charles J. Jenkins (D)	Dec. 14, 1865	Jan. 13, 1868
Gen. Thomas H. Ruger[7]	Jan. 13, 1868	July 4, 1868
Rufus Brown Bullock (R)[8]	July 4, 1868	Oct. 23, 1871
Benjamin Conley (R)[9]	Oct. 30, 1871	Jan. 12, 1872
James M. Smith (LR)	Jan. 12, 1872	Jan. 12, 1877
Alfred Holt Colquitt (D)	Jan. 12, 1877	Nov. 4, 1882
Alexander H. Stephens (D)[10]	Nov. 4, 1882	March 4, 1883
James H. Boynton (D)[11]	March 5, 1883	May 10, 1883
Henry D. McDaniel (D)	May 10, 1883	Nov. 9, 1886
John B. Gordon (D)	Nov. 9, 1886	Nov. 8, 1890
William J. Northen (D)	Nov. 8, 1890	Oct. 27, 1894
William Y. Atkinson (D)	Oct. 27, 1894	Oct. 29, 1898
Allen D. Candler (D)	Oct. 29, 1898	Oct. 25, 1902
Joseph M. Terrell (D)	Oct. 25, 1902	June 29, 1907
Hoke Smith (D)	June 29, 1907	June 26, 1909
Joseph M. Brown (D)	June 26, 1909	July 1, 1911
Hoke Smith (D)[12]	July 1, 1911	Nov. 16, 1911
John M. Slaton (D)[13]	Nov. 16, 1911	Jan. 25, 1912
Joseph M. Brown (D)	Jan. 25, 1912	June 28, 1913
John M. Slaton (D)	June 28, 1913	June 26, 1915
Nathaniel E. Harris (D)	June 26, 1915	June 30, 1917
Hugh M. Dorsey (D)	June 30, 1917	June 25, 1921
Thomas W. Hardwick (D)	June 25, 1921	June 30, 1923
Clifford M. Walker (D)	June 30, 1923	June 25, 1927
Lamartine G. Hardman (D)	June 25, 1927	June 27, 1931
Richard B. Russell (D)[14]	June 27, 1931	Jan. 10, 1933
Eugene Talmadge (D)	Jan. 10, 1933	Jan. 12, 1937
Eurith D. Rivers (D)	Jan. 12, 1937	Jan. 14, 1941
Eugene Talmadge (D)	Jan. 14, 1941	Jan. 12, 1943
Ellis G. Arnall (D)	Jan. 12, 1943	Jan. 14, 1947
Eugene Talmadge (D)[15]		
Herman E. Talmadge (D)[16]	Jan. 14, 1947	March 18, 1947
Melvin E. Thompson (D)	March 18, 1947	Nov. 17, 1948
Herman E. Talmadge (D)	Nov. 17, 1948	Jan. 11, 1955
S. Marvin Griffin (D)	Jan. 11, 1955	Jan. 13, 1959
S. Ernest Vandiver Jr. (D)	Jan. 13, 1959	Jan. 15, 1963
Carl Edward Sanders (D)	Jan. 15, 1963	Jan. 10, 1967

Lester G. Maddox (D)[17]	Jan. 10, 1967	Jan. 12, 1971
Jimmy Carter (D)	Jan. 12, 1971	Jan. 14, 1975
George Busbee (D)	Jan. 14, 1975	Jan. 11, 1983
Joe Frank Harris (D)	Jan. 11, 1983	Jan. 14, 1991
Zell Miller (D)	Jan. 14, 1991	Jan. 11, 1999
Roy Barnes (D)	Jan. 11, 1999	

Georgia

1. Georgia's first two chief executives were called "president and commander in chief." Bulloch died Feb. 22, 1777.

2. Succeeded to office.

3. The revolutionaries were briefly split into two factions, one electing Wereat and the other Walton. The two factions came together in 1780 and elected Howley.

4. Howley was elected both governor and representative to the Continental Congress. He chose to go to Congress in February.

5. Succeeded to office. Resigned Aug. 16, 1781.

6. Succeeded to office.

7. Military governor.

8. Resigned Oct. 23, 1871.

9. As president of the state Senate, he succeeded to office.

10. Died March 4, 1883.

11. As president of the state Senate, he succeeded to office.

12. Resigned Nov. 16, 1911.

13. As president of the state Senate, he succeeded to office.

14. Resigned Jan. 10, 1933.

15. Died Dec. 21, 1946, before his inauguration.

16. Eugene Talmadge's death led to a famous controversy that lasted several months, during which three different men claimed office as governor. The Talmadge-dominated legislature elected Herman Talmadge, Eugene's son, to serve out his term, but this action was disputed by outgoing governor Ellis Arnall and Lieutenant Governor-elect Melvin E. Thompson. Herman Talmadge seized the governor's mansion by force, but was thrown out after sixty-seven days in office by the Georgia Supreme Court, which ruled his election by the legislature unconstitutional. Thompson then assumed office as governor until 1948, when a special election was held. He lost the Democratic Georgia nomination to Talmadge, who then won the special election for the remaining two years of the term. Talmadge was reelected in 1950.

17. Republican candidate Howard Callaway led in the popular vote, but failed to win a majority because of write-in votes cast for former governor Ellis Arnall, who had lost the Democratic primary to Lester Maddox. The legislature elected Maddox as governor.

HAWAII

(Became a state Aug. 21, 1959)

Governors	Dates of Service	
William F. Quinn (R)	Aug. 21, 1959	Dec. 3, 1962
John A. Burns (D)	Dec. 3, 1962	Dec. 2, 1974
George R. Ariyoshi (D)	Dec. 2, 1974	Dec. 1, 1986
John Waihee (D)	Dec. 1, 1986	Dec. 5, 1994
Benjamin J. Cayetano (D)	Dec. 5, 1994	

IDAHO

(Became a state July 3, 1890)

Governors	Dates of Service	
George L. Shoup (R)[1]	Oct. 1, 1890	Dec. 1890
N. B. Willey (R)[2]	Dec. 19, 1890	Jan. 1, 1893
William J. McConnell (R)	Jan. 1893	Jan. 4, 1897
Frank Steunenberg (D)	Jan. 4, 1897	Jan. 7, 1901
Frank W. Hunt (D-FUS)	Jan. 7, 1901	Jan. 5, 1903
John T. Morrison (R)	Jan. 5, 1903	Jan. 2, 1905
Frank R. Gooding (R)	Jan. 2, 1905	Jan. 4, 1909

James H. Brady (R)	Jan. 4, 1909	Jan. 2, 1911
James H. Hawley (D)	Jan. 2, 1911	Jan. 6, 1913
John M. Haines (R)	Jan. 6, 1913	Jan. 4, 1915
Moses Alexander (D)	Jan. 4, 1915	Jan. 6, 1919
David W. Davis (R)	Jan. 6, 1919	Jan. 1, 1923
Charles C. Moore (R)	Jan. 1, 1923	Jan. 3, 1927
H. Clarence Baldridge (R)	Jan. 3, 1927	Jan. 5, 1931
C. Ben Ross (D)	Jan. 5, 1931	Jan. 4, 1937
Barzilla W. Clark (D)	Jan. 4, 1937	Jan. 2, 1939
Clarence A. Bottolfsen (R)	Jan. 2, 1939	Jan. 6, 1941
Chase A. Clark (D)	Jan. 6, 1941	Jan. 4, 1943
Clarence A. Bottolfsen (R)	Jan. 4, 1943	Jan. 1, 1945
Charles C. Gossett (D)[3]	Jan. 1, 1945	Nov. 17, 1945
Arnold Williams (D)[4]	Nov. 17, 1945	Jan. 6, 1947
Charles A. Robins (R)	Jan. 6, 1947	Jan. 1, 1951
Len B. Jordan (R)	Jan. 1, 1951	Jan. 3, 1955
Robert E. Smylie (R)	Jan. 3, 1955	Jan. 2, 1967
Don Samuelson (R)	Jan. 2, 1967	Jan. 4, 1971
Cecil D. Andrus (D)[5]	Jan. 4, 1971	Jan. 24, 1977
John V. Evans (D)[6]	Jan. 24, 1977	Jan. 5, 1987
Cecil D. Andrus (D)	Jan. 5, 1987	Jan. 2, 1995
Philip E. Batt (R)	Jan. 2, 1995	Jan. 8, 1999
Dirk Kempthorne (R)	Jan. 8, 1999	

Idaho

1. Resigned in December 1890.

2. As lieutenant governor, he succeeded to office.

3. Resigned Nov. 17, 1945.

4. As lieutenant governor, he succeeded to office.

5. Resigned Jan. 24, 1977.

6. As lieutenant governor, he succeeded to office. Subsequently elected.

ILLINOIS

(Became a state Dec. 3, 1818)

Governors	Dates of Service	
Shadrach Bond (D-R)	Oct. 6, 1818	Dec. 5, 1822
Edward Coles (D-R)	Dec. 5, 1822	Dec. 6, 1826
Ninian Edwards (NR)	Dec. 6, 1826	Dec. 6, 1830
John Reynolds (NR)[1]	Dec. 6, 1830	Nov. 17, 1834
William L. D. Ewing[2]	Nov. 17, 1834	Dec. 3, 1834
Joseph Duncan (W)	Dec. 3, 1834	Dec. 7, 1838
Thomas Carlin (D)	Dec. 7, 1838	Dec. 8, 1842
Thomas Ford (D)	Dec. 8, 1842	Dec. 9, 1846
Augustus C. French (D)	Dec. 9, 1846	Jan. 10, 1853
Joel A. Matteson (D)	Jan. 10, 1853	Jan. 12, 1857
William H. Bissell (R)[3]	Jan. 12, 1857	March 18, 1860
John Wood (R)[4]	March 21, 1860	Jan. 14, 1861
Richard Yates (R)	Jan. 14, 1861	Jan. 16, 1865
Richard J. Oglesby (R)	Jan. 16, 1865	Jan. 11, 1869
John M. Palmer (R)	Jan. 11, 1869	Jan. 13, 1873
Richard J. Oglesby (R)[5]	Jan. 13, 1873	Jan. 23, 1873
John L. Beveridge (R)[6]	Jan. 23, 1873	Jan. 8, 1877
Shelby M. Cullom (R)[7]	Jan. 8, 1877	Feb. 8, 1883
John M. Hamilton (R)[8]	Feb. 16, 1883	Jan. 30, 1885
Richard J. Oglesby (R)	Jan. 30, 1885	Jan. 14, 1889
Joseph W. Fifer (R)	Jan. 14, 1889	Jan. 10, 1893
John P. Altgeld (D)	Jan. 10, 1893	Jan. 11, 1897
John R. Tanner (R)	Jan. 11, 1897	Jan. 14, 1901

Richard Yates (R)	Jan. 14, 1901	Jan. 9, 1905
Charles S. Deneen (R)	Jan. 9, 1905	Feb. 3, 1913
Edward F. Dunne (D)	Feb. 3, 1913	Jan. 8, 1917
Frank O. Lowden (R)	Jan. 8, 1917	Jan. 10, 1921
Len Small (R)	Jan. 10, 1921	Jan. 14, 1929
Louis L. Emmerson (R)	Jan. 14, 1929	Jan. 9, 1933
Henry Horner (D)[9]	Jan. 9, 1933	Oct. 6, 1940
John H. Stelle (D)[10]	Oct. 6, 1940	Jan. 13, 1941
Dwight H. Green (R)	Jan. 13, 1941	Jan. 10, 1949
Adlai E. Stevenson (D)	Jan. 10, 1949	Jan. 12, 1953
William G. Stratton (R)	Jan. 12, 1953	Jan. 9, 1961
Otto Kerner (D)[11]	Jan. 9, 1961	May 22, 1968
Samuel H. Shapiro (D)[12]	May 22, 1968	Jan. 13, 1969
Richard B. Ogilvie (R)	Jan. 13, 1969	Jan. 8, 1973
Daniel Walker (D)	Jan. 8, 1973	Jan. 10, 1977
James R. Thompson (R)	Jan. 10, 1977	Jan. 14, 1991
Jim Edgar (R)	Jan. 14, 1991	Jan. 11, 1999
George Ryan (R)	Jan. 11, 1999	

Illinois
1. Resigned Nov. 17, 1834.
2. Ewing was acting lieutenant governor and succeeded to office as governor following Reynolds' resignation.
3. Died March 18, 1860.
4. As lieutenant governor, he succeeded to office.
5. Resigned Jan. 23, 1873.
6. As lieutenant governor, he succeeded to office.
7. Resigned Feb. 8, 1883.
8. As lieutenant governor, he succeeded to office.
9. Died Oct. 6, 1940.
10. As lieutenant governor, he succeeded to office.
11. Resigned May 22, 1968.
12. As lieutenant governor, he succeeded to office.

INDIANA

(Became a state Dec. 11, 1816)

Governors	Dates of Service	
Jonathan Jennings (D-R)[1]	Nov. 7, 1816	Sept. 12, 1822
Ratliff Boon (D-R)[2]	Sept. 12, 1822	Dec. 4, 1822
William Hendricks (D-R)[3]	Dec. 5, 1822	Feb. 12, 1825
James B. Ray (CLAY R)[4]	Feb. 12, 1825	Dec. 7, 1831
Noah Noble (NR, W)	Dec. 7, 1831	Dec. 6, 1837
David Wallace (W)	Dec. 6, 1837	Dec. 9, 1840
Samuel Bigger (W)	Dec. 9, 1840	Dec. 6, 1843
James Whitcomb (D)[5]	Dec. 6, 1843	Dec. 27, 1848
Paris C. Dunning (D)[6]	Dec. 27, 1848	Dec. 5, 1849
Joseph A. Wright (D)	Dec. 5, 1849	Jan. 12, 1857
Ashbel P. Willard (D)[7]	Jan. 12, 1857	Oct. 4, 1860
Abraham A. Hammond (D)[8]	Oct. 4, 1860	Jan. 14, 1861
Henry S. Lane (R)[9]	Jan. 14, 1861	Jan. 16, 1861
Oliver P. Morton (R)[10]	Jan. 16, 1861	Jan. 23, 1867
Conrad Baker (R)[11]	Jan. 24, 1867	Jan. 13, 1873
Thomas A. Hendricks (D)	Jan. 13, 1873	Jan. 8, 1877
James D. Williams (D)[12]	Jan. 8, 1877	Nov. 20, 1880
Isaac P. Gray (D)[13]	Nov. 20, 1880	Jan. 10, 1881
Albert G. Porter (R)	Jan. 10, 1881	Jan. 12, 1885
Isaac P. Gray (D)	Jan. 12, 1885	Jan. 14, 1889
Alvin P. Hovey (R)[14]	Jan. 14, 1889	Nov. 21, 1891
Ira Joy Chase (R)[15]	Nov. 21, 1891	Jan. 9, 1893
Claude Matthews (D)	Jan. 1893	Jan. 11, 1897
James A. Mount (R)	Jan. 11, 1897	Jan. 14, 1901
Winfield T. Durbin (R)	Jan. 14, 1901	Jan. 9, 1905
J. Frank Hanly (R)	Jan. 9, 1905	Jan. 11, 1909
Thomas R. Marshall (D)	Jan. 11, 1909	Jan. 13, 1913
Samuel M. Ralston (D)	Jan. 13, 1913	Jan. 8, 1917
James Putnam Goodrich (R)	Jan. 8, 1917	Jan. 10, 1921
Warren T. McCray (R)[16]	Jan. 10, 1921	April 30, 1924
Emmett F. Branch (R)[17]	April 30, 1924	Jan. 12, 1925
Edward Jackson (R)	Jan. 12, 1925	Jan. 14, 1929
Harry G. Leslie (R)	Jan. 14, 1929	Jan. 9, 1933
Paul V. McNutt (D)	Jan. 9, 1933	Jan. 11, 1937
M. Clifford Townsend (D)	Jan. 11, 1937	Jan. 13, 1941
Henry F. Schricker (D)	Jan. 13, 1941	Jan. 8, 1945
Ralph F. Gates (R)	Jan. 8, 1945	Jan. 10, 1949
Henry F. Schricker (D)	Jan. 10, 1949	Jan. 12, 1953
George N. Craig (R)	Jan. 12, 1953	Jan. 14, 1957
Harold W. Handley (R)	Jan. 14, 1957	Jan. 9, 1961
Matthew E. Welsh (D)	Jan. 9, 1961	Jan. 11, 1965
Roger D. Branigin (D)	Jan. 11, 1965	Jan. 13, 1969
Edgar D. Whitcomb (R)	Jan. 13, 1969	Jan. 8, 1973
Otis R. Bowen (R)	Jan. 8, 1973	Jan. 12, 1981
Robert D. Orr (R)	Jan. 12, 1981	Jan. 9, 1989
Evan Bayh (D)	Jan. 9, 1989	Jan. 13, 1997
Frank L. O'Bannon (D)	Jan. 13, 1997	

Indiana
1. Resigned Sept. 12, 1822.
2. Acting governor.
3. Resigned Feb. 12, 1825.
4. Acting governor. Subsequently elected.
5. Resigned Dec. 27, 1848.
6. Acting governor.
7. Died Oct. 4, 1860.
8. Acting governor.
9. Resigned Jan. 16, 1861.
10. Acting governor. Subsequently elected. Resigned in 1867.
11. Acting governor. Subsequently elected.
12. Died Nov. 20, 1880.
13. Acting governor.
14. Died Nov. 21, 1891.
15. Acting governor.
16. Resigned April 30, 1924.
17. As lieutenant governor, he succeeded to office.

IOWA

(Became a state Dec. 28, 1846)

Governors	Dates of Service	
Ansel Briggs (D)	Dec. 3, 1846	Dec. 4, 1850
Stephen P. Hempstead (D)	Dec. 4, 1850	Dec. 9, 1854
James W. Grimes (R)	Dec. 9, 1854	Jan. 13, 1858
Ralph P. Lowe (R)	Jan. 13, 1858	Jan. 11, 1860
Samuel J. Kirkwood (R)	Jan. 11, 1860	Jan. 14, 1864
William M. Stone (UN R)	Jan. 14, 1864	Jan. 16, 1868
Samuel Merrill (R)	Jan. 16, 1868	Jan. 11, 1872
Cyrus C. Carpenter (R)	Jan. 11, 1872	Jan. 13, 1876
Samuel J. Kirkwood (R)[1]	Jan. 13, 1876	Feb. 1, 1877
Joshua G. Newbold (R)[2]	Feb. 1, 1877	Jan. 17, 1878
John H. Gear (R)	Jan. 17, 1878	Jan. 12, 1882
Buren R. Sherman (R)	Jan. 12, 1882	Jan. 14, 1886
William Larrabee (R)	Jan. 14, 1886	Feb. 26, 1890

Horace Boies (D)	Feb. 27, 1890	Jan. 11, 1894
Frank D. Jackson (R)	Jan. 11, 1894	Jan. 16, 1896
Francis M. Drake (R)	Jan. 16, 1896	Jan. 13, 1898
Leslie M. Shaw (R)	Jan. 13, 1898	Jan. 16, 1902
Albert B. Cummins (R)[3]	Jan. 16, 1902	Nov. 24, 1908
Warren Garst (R)[4]	Nov. 24, 1908	Jan. 14, 1909
Beryl F. Carroll (R)	Jan. 14, 1909	Jan. 16, 1913
George W. Clarke (R)	Jan. 16, 1913	Jan. 11, 1917
William L. Harding (R)	Jan. 11, 1917	Jan. 13, 1921
Nathan E. Kendall (R)	Jan. 13, 1921	Jan. 15, 1925
John Hammill (R)	Jan. 15, 1925	Jan. 15, 1931
Daniel W. Turner (R)	Jan. 15, 1931	Jan. 12, 1933
Clyde L. Herring (D)	Jan. 12, 1933	Jan. 14, 1937
Nelson G. Kraschel (D)	Jan. 14, 1937	Jan. 12, 1939
George A. Wilson (R)	Jan. 12, 1939	Jan. 14, 1943
Bourke B. Hickenlooper (R)	Jan. 14, 1943	Jan. 11, 1945
Robert D. Blue (R)	Jan. 11, 1945	Jan. 13, 1949
William S. Beardsley (R)[5]	Jan. 13, 1949	Nov. 21, 1954
Leo Elthon (R)[6]	Nov. 22, 1954	Jan. 13, 1955
Leo Arthur Hoegh (R)	Jan. 13, 1955	Jan. 17, 1957
Herschel C. Loveless (D)	Jan. 17, 1957	Jan. 12, 1961
Norman A. Erbe (R)	Jan. 12, 1961	Jan. 17, 1963
Harold E. Hughes (D)[7]	Jan. 17, 1963	Jan. 1, 1969
Robert D. Fulton (D)[8]	Jan. 1, 1969	Jan. 16, 1969
Robert D. Ray (R)	Jan. 16, 1969	Jan. 14, 1983
Terry E. Branstad (R)	Jan. 14, 1983	Jan. 15, 1999
Tom Vilsack (D)	Jan. 15, 1999	

Iowa
1. Resigned Feb. 1, 1877.
2. As lieutenant governor, he succeeded to office.
3. Resigned Nov. 24, 1908.
4. As lieutenant governor, he succeeded to office.
5. Died Nov. 21, 1954.
6. As lieutenant governor, he succeeded to office.
7. Resigned Jan. 1, 1969
8. As lieutenant governor, he succeeded to office.

KANSAS

(Became a state Jan. 29, 1861)

Governors	Dates of Service	
Charles Robinson (R)	Feb. 9, 1861	Jan. 12, 1863
Thomas Carney (R)	Jan. 12, 1863	Jan. 9, 1865
Samuel J. Crawford (R)[1]	Jan. 9, 1865	Nov. 4, 1868
Nehemiah Green (R)[2]	Nov. 4, 1868	Jan. 11, 1869
James Madison Harvey (R)	Jan. 11, 1869	Jan. 13, 1873
Thomas A. Osborn (R)	Jan. 13, 1873	Jan. 18, 1877
George T. Anthony (R)	Jan. 18, 1877	Jan. 13, 1879
John P. St. John (R)	Jan. 13, 1879	Jan. 8, 1883
George Washington Glick (D)	Jan. 8, 1883	Jan. 13, 1885
John A. Martin (R)	Jan. 13, 1885	Jan. 14, 1889
Lyman U. Humphrey (R)	Jan. 14, 1889	Jan. 9, 1893
Lorenzo D. Lewelling (POP)	Jan. 9, 1893	Jan. 14, 1895
Edmund N. Morrill (R)	Jan. 14, 1895	Jan. 11, 1897
John W. Leedy (D-PP)	Jan. 11, 1897	Jan. 9, 1899
William E. Stanley (R)	Jan. 9, 1899	Jan. 12, 1903
Willis J. Bailey (R)	Jan. 12, 1903	Jan. 9, 1905

Edward W. Hoch (R)	Jan. 9, 1905	Jan. 11, 1909
Walter R. Stubbs (R)	Jan. 11, 1909	Jan. 13, 1913
George H. Hodges (D)	Jan. 13, 1913	Jan. 11, 1915
Arthur Capper (R)	Jan. 11, 1915	Jan. 13, 1919
Henry J. Allen (R)	Jan. 13, 1919	Jan. 8, 1923
Jonathan McM. Davis (D)	Jan. 8, 1923	Jan. 12, 1925
Ben S. Paulen (R)	Jan. 12, 1925	Jan. 14, 1929
Clyde M. Reed (R)	Jan. 14, 1929	Jan. 12, 1931
Harry W. Woodring (D)	Jan. 12, 1931	Jan. 9, 1933
Alfred M. Landon (R)	Jan. 9, 1933	Jan. 11, 1937
Walter A. Huxman (D)	Jan. 11, 1937	Jan. 9, 1939
Payne H. Ratner (R)	Jan. 9, 1939	Jan. 11, 1943
Andrew F. Schoeppel (R)	Jan. 11, 1943	Jan. 13, 1947
Frank Carlson (R)[3]	Jan. 13, 1947	Nov. 28, 1950
Frank L. Hagaman (R)[4]	Nov. 28, 1950	Jan. 8, 1951
Edward F. Arn (R)	Jan. 8, 1951	Jan. 10, 1955
Frederick L. Hall (R)[5]	Jan. 10, 1955	Jan. 3, 1957
John McCuish (R)[6]	Jan. 3, 1957	Jan. 14, 1957
George Docking (D)	Jan. 14, 1957	Jan. 9, 1961
John Anderson Jr. (R)	Jan. 9, 1961	Jan. 11, 1965
William H. Avery (R)	Jan. 11, 1965	Jan. 9, 1967
Robert B. Docking (D)	Jan. 9, 1967	Jan. 13, 1975
Robert F. Bennett (R)	Jan. 13, 1975	Jan. 8, 1979
John Carlin (D)	Jan. 8, 1979	Jan. 12, 1987
Mike Hayden (R)	Jan. 12, 1987	Jan. 14, 1991
Joan Finney (D)	Jan. 14, 1991	Jan. 9, 1995
Bill Graves (R)	Jan. 9, 1995	

Kansas
1. Resigned Nov. 4, 1868.
2. Succeeded to office.
3. Resigned Nov. 28, 1950.
4. As lieutenant governor, he succeeded to office.
5. Resigned Jan. 3, 1957.
6. As lieutenant governor, he succeeded to office.

KENTUCKY

(Became a state June 1, 1792)

Governors	Dates of Service	
Isaac Shelby (D-R)	June 4, 1792	June 7, 1796
James Garrard (D-R)	June 7, 1796	June 1, 1804
Christopher Greenup (D-R)	June 1, 1804	June 1, 1808
Charles Scott (D-R)	June 1, 1808	June 1, 1812
Isaac Shelby (D-R)	June 1, 1812	June 1, 1816
George Madison (D-R)[1]	June 1, 1816	Oct. 21, 1816
Gabriel Slaughter (D-R)[2]	Oct. 21, 1816	June 1, 1820
John Adair (D-R)	June 1, 1820	June 1, 1824
Joseph Desha (D-R)	June 1, 1824	June 1, 1828
Thomas Metcalfe (NR)	June 1, 1828	June 1, 1832
John Breathitt (D)[3]	June 1, 1832	Feb. 22, 1834
James Morehead (NR)[4]	Feb. 22, 1834	June 1, 1836
James Clark (W)[5]	June 1, 1836	Oct. 5, 1839
Charles A. Wickliffe (W)[6]	Oct. 5, 1839	June 1, 1840
Robert P. Letcher (W)	June 1, 1840	June 1, 1844
William Owsley (W)	June 1, 1844	June 1, 1848
John J. Crittenden (W)[7]	June 1, 1848	July 31, 1850
John L. Helm (W)[8]	July 31, 1850	Sept. 2, 1851
Lazarus W. Powell (D)	Sept. 1851	Sept. 2, 1855

Charles S. Morehead (AM)	Sept. 1855	Sept. 1859
Beriah Magoffin (D)[9]	Sept. 1859	Aug. 18, 1862
James F. Robinson (UN)[10]	Aug. 18, 1862	Sept. 1863
Thomas E. Bramlette (UN)	Sept. 1863	Sept. 1867
John L. Helm (D)[11]	Sept. 3, 1867	Sept. 13, 1867
John W. Stevenson (D)[12]	Sept. 13, 1867	March 4, 1871
Preston H. Leslie (D)[13]	March 4, 1871	Sept. 1875
James B. McCreary (D)	Sept. 1875	Sept. 1879
Luke P. Blackburn (D)	Sept. 1879	Sept. 1883
J. Procter Knott (D)	Sept. 1883	Sept. 1887
Simon B. Buckner (D)	Sept. 1887	Sept. 1891
John Y. Brown (D)	Sept. 1891	Dec. 1895
William O. Bradley (R)	Dec. 1895	Dec. 12, 1899
William S. Taylor (R)[14]	Dec. 12, 1899	Jan. 31, 1900
William Goebel (D)[15]	Jan. 31, 1900	Feb. 3, 1900
John C. W. Beckham (D)[16]	Feb. 3, 1900	Dec. 10, 1907
August E. Willson (R)	Dec. 10, 1907	Dec. 12, 1911
James B. McCreary (D)	Dec. 12, 1911	Dec. 7, 1915
Augustus O. Stanley (D)[17]	Dec. 7, 1915	May 19, 1919
James D. Black (D)[18]	May 19, 1919	Dec. 9, 1919
Edwin P. Morrow (R)	Dec. 9, 1919	Dec. 11, 1923
William J. Fields (D)	Dec. 11, 1923	Dec. 13, 1927
Flem D. Sampson (R)	Dec. 13, 1927	Dec. 8, 1931
Ruby Lafoon (D)	Dec. 8, 1931	Dec. 10, 1935
Albert B. (Happy) Chandler (D)[19]	Dec. 10, 1935	Oct. 9, 1939
Keen Johnson (D)[20]	Oct. 9, 1939	Dec. 7, 1943
Simeon S. Willis (R)	Dec. 7, 1943	Dec. 9, 1947
Earle C. Clements (D)[21]	Dec. 9, 1947	Nov. 27, 1950
Lawrence W. Wetherby (D)[22]	Nov. 27, 1950	Dec. 13, 1955
Albert B. (Happy) Chandler (D)	Dec. 13, 1955	Dec. 9, 1959
Bert T. Combs (D)	Dec. 9, 1959	Dec. 10, 1963
Edward T. Breathitt (D)	Dec. 10, 1963	Dec. 12, 1967
Louie B. Nunn (R)	Dec. 12, 1967	Dec. 7, 1971
Wendell H. Ford (D)[23]	Dec. 7, 1971	Dec. 28, 1974
Julian Carroll (D)[24]	Dec. 28, 1974	Dec. 11, 1979
John Y. Brown Jr. (D)	Dec. 11, 1979	Dec. 13, 1983
Martha Layne Collins (D)	Dec. 13, 1983	Dec. 8, 1987
Wallace G. Wilkinson (D)	Dec. 8, 1987	Dec. 10, 1991
Brereton C. Jones (D)	Dec. 10, 1991	Dec. 12, 1995
Paul E. Patton (D)	Dec. 12, 1995	

Kentucky
1. Died Oct. 21, 1816.
2. As lieutenant governor, he succeeded to office.
3. Died Feb. 22, 1834.
4. As lieutenant governor, he succeeded to office.
5. Died Oct. 5, 1839.
6. As lieutenant governor, he succeeded to office.
7. Resigned July 31, 1850.
8. As lieutenant governor, he succeeded to office.
9. Resigned Aug. 18, 1862.
10. As president of the state Senate, he succeeded to office.
11. Died Sept. 13, 1867.
12. As lieutenant governor, he succeeded to office. Subsequently elected. Resigned March 4, 1871.
13. As president of the state Senate, he succeeded to office. Subsequently elected.
14. Taylor was removed by the legislature following an election challenge by his Democratic opponent, William Goebel.
15. Successfully challenged the election of William S. Taylor. Died Feb. 3, 1900.

16. As lieutenant governor, he succeeded to office. Subsequently elected.
17. Resigned May 19, 1919.
18. As lieutenant governor, he succeeded to office.
19. Resigned Oct. 9, 1939.
20. As lieutenant governor, he succeeded to office. Subsequently elected.
21. Resigned Nov. 27, 1950.
22. As lieutenant governor, he succeeded to office. Subsequently elected.
23. Resigned Dec. 28, 1974.
24. As lieutenant governor, he succeeded to office. Subsequently elected.

LOUISIANA

(Became a state April 30, 1812)

Governors	Dates of Service	
William C. C. Claiborne	July 30, 1812	Dec. 16, 1816
Jacques Philippe Villere	Dec. 17, 1816	Dec. 17, 1820
Thomas B. Robertson[1]	Dec. 18, 1820	Nov. 15, 1824
Henry S. Thibodeaux[2]	Nov. 15, 1824	Dec. 13, 1824
Henry S. Johnson (AM FAC)	Dec. 13, 1824	Dec. 15, 1828
Pierre Derbigny (NR)[3]	Dec. 15, 1828	Oct. 6, 1829
Armand Beauvais[4]	Oct. 6, 1829	Jan. 14, 1830
Jacques Dupre	Jan. 14, 1830	Jan. 31, 1831
Andre B. Roman (NR)	Jan. 31, 1831	Feb. 4, 1835
Edward E. White (W)	Feb. 4, 1835	Feb. 4, 1839
Andre B. Roman (W)	Feb. 4, 1839	Jan. 30, 1843
Alexander Mouton (D)	Jan. 30, 1843	Feb. 11, 1846
Isaac Johnson (D)	Feb. 12, 1846	Jan. 27, 1850
Joseph M. Walker (D)	Jan. 28, 1850	Jan. 17, 1853
Paul O. Hebert (D)	Jan. 18, 1853	Jan. 21, 1856
Robert C. Wickliffe (D)	Jan. 22, 1856	Jan. 22, 1860
Thomas O. Moore (D)	Jan. 23, 1860	Jan. 25, 1864
George F. Shepley[5]	July 2, 1862	March 4, 1864
Henry W. Allen[6]	Jan. 25, 1864	June 2, 1865
Michael Hahn[7]	March 4, 1864	March 4, 1865
James M. Wells (D)[8]	March 4, 1865	June 3, 1867
Benjamin F. Flanders[9]	June 3, 1867	Jan. 8, 1868
Joshua Baker[10]	Jan. 8, 1868	June 27, 1868
Henry C. Warmoth (R)	June 27, 1868	Dec. 9, 1872
Pinckney B. S. Pinchback[11]	Dec. 9, 1872	Jan. 13, 1873
William P. Kellogg (R)[12]	Jan. 13, 1873	Jan. 5, 1877
Francis T. Nicholls (D)[13]	Jan. 8, 1877	Jan. 13, 1880
Louis A. Wiltz (D)[14]	Jan. 14, 1880	Oct. 16, 1881
Samuel D. McEnery (D)[15]	Oct. 16, 1881	May 20, 1888
Francis T. Nicholls (D)	May 21, 1888	May 10, 1892
Murphy J. Foster (A-LOT D, D)	May 10, 1892	May 8, 1900
William W. Heard (D)	May 8, 1900	May 10, 1904
Newton C. Blanchard (D)	May 10, 1904	May 12, 1908
Jared Y. Sanders (D)	May 12, 1908	May 14, 1912
Luther E. Hall (D)	May 14, 1912	May 9, 1916
Ruffin G. Pleasant (D)	May 9, 1916	May 11, 1920
John M Parker (D)	May 11, 1920	May 13, 1924
Henry L. Fuqua (D)[16]	May 13, 1924	Oct. 11, 1926
Oramel H. Simpson (D)[17]	Oct. 11, 1926	May 21, 1928
Huey P. Long Jr. (D)[18]	May 21, 1928	Jan. 25, 1932
Alvin O. King (D)[19]	Jan. 25, 1932	May 10, 1932
Oscar K. Allen (D)[20]	May 10, 1932	Jan. 28, 1936
James A. Noe (D)[21]	Jan. 28, 1936	May 12, 1936
Richard W. Leche (D)[22]	May 12, 1936	June 26, 1939

Earl K. Long (D)[23]	June 26, 1939	May 14, 1940
Sam H. Jones (D)	May 14, 1940	May 9, 1944
James H. Davis (D)	May 9, 1944	May 11, 1948
Earl K. Long (D)	May 11, 1948	May 13, 1952
Robert F. Kennon (D)	May 13, 1952	May 8, 1956
Earl K. Long (D)	May 8, 1956	May 10, 1960
James H. Davis (D)	May 10, 1960	May 12, 1964
John J. McKeithen (D)	May 12, 1964	May 9, 1972
Edwin W. Edwards (D)	May 9, 1972	March 10, 1980
David C. Treen (R)	March 10, 1980	March 12, 1984
Edwin W. Edwards (D)	March 12, 1984	March 14, 1988
Charles Roemer (D, R)[24]	March 14, 1988	Jan. 8, 1992
Edwin W. Edwards (D)	Jan. 8, 1992	Jan. 8, 1996
Mike Foster (R)	Jan. 8, 1996	

Louisiana

1. Resigned Nov. 15, 1824.
2. As president of the state Senate, he succeeded to office.
3. Died Oct. 1, 1829.
4. As president of the state Senate, he succeeded to office.
5. Military governor within Union lines.
6. Last elected Confederate governor.
7. Elected within Union lines. Resigned March 4, 1865.
8. As lieutenant governor, he succeeded to office. Subsequently elected. Removed June 3, 1867.
9. Under military authority.
10. Under military authority.
11. Acting governor.
12. The 1872 gubernatorial election in Louisiana set off a bitter dispute between Republicans backing Kellogg and Democrats supporting his opponent, John McEnery. Each side organized its own boards to canvass the vote, resulting in two separate sets of election returns, one showing Kellogg the winner, the other McEnery. To add to the confusion, two rival legislatures assumed office, each claiming legitimacy, and Kellogg and McEnery were both inaugurated as governor by their respective factions. President Ulysses S. Grant (R) finally stepped in and recognized Kellogg as the legitimate governor on May 22, 1873.
13. The 1876 election set off a dispute similar to that of 1872. Nicholls, the Democrat, and Packard, the Republican, each had election returns showing him the winner. There were also two legislatures, each controlled by a different party. Nicholls set up a de facto state government and was recognized by federal authorities.
14. Died in October 1881.
15. As lieutenant governor, he succeeded to office. Subsequently elected.
16. Died Oct. 11, 1926.
17. As lieutenant governor, he succeeded to office.
18. Resigned Jan. 25, 1932.
19. As lieutenant governor, he succeeded to office.
20. Died Jan. 28, 1936.
21. As lieutenant governor, he succeeded to office.
22. Resigned June 26, 1939.
23. As lieutenant governor, he succeeded to office.
24. Elected in 1987 as a Democrat. Became a Republican in March 1991.

MAINE

(Became a state March 15, 1820)

Governors	Dates of Service	
William King (D-R)[1]	May 31, 1820	May 28, 1821
William D. Williamson (D-R)[2]	May 29, 1821	Dec. 25, 1821
Benjamin Ames (D-R)[3]	Dec. 25, 1821	Jan. 2, 1821
Daniel Rose (D-R)[4]	Jan. 2, 1822	Jan. 4, 1822
Albion K. Parris (D-R)	Jan. 5, 1822	Jan. 3, 1827
Enoch Lincoln (D-R)[5]	Jan. 3, 1827	Oct. 8, 1829
Nathan Cutler (D)[6]	Oct. 12, 1829	Feb. 5, 1830

Joshua Hall (D)[7]	Feb. 5, 1830	Feb. 10, 1830
Jonathan G. Hunton (NR)	Feb. 10, 1830	Jan. 5, 1831
Samuel E. Smith (JAC D)	Jan. 5, 1831	Jan. 1, 1834
Robert P. Dunlap (D)	Jan. 1, 1834	Jan. 3, 1838
Edward Kent (W)	Jan. 3, 1838	Jan. 2, 1839
John Fairfield (D)	Jan. 2, 1839	Jan. 6, 1841
Richard H. Vose[8]	Jan. 12, 1841	Jan. 13, 1841
Edward Kent (W)	Jan. 13, 1841	Jan. 5, 1842
John Fairfield (D)[9]	Jan. 5, 1842	March 7, 1843
Edward Kavanagh (D)[10]	March 7, 1843	Jan. 1, 1844
David Dunn (D)	Jan. 2, 1844	Jan. 3, 1844
John W. Dana (D)	Jan. 3, 1844	Jan. 5, 1844
Hugh J. Anderson (D)	Jan. 5, 1844	May 12, 1847
John W. Dana (D)	May 13, 1847	May 8, 1850
John Hubbard (D)	May 9, 1850	Jan. 5, 1853
William G. Crosby (W)	Jan. 5, 1853	Jan. 3, 1855
Anson P. Morrill (R)	Jan. 3, 1855	Jan. 2, 1856
Samuel Wells (D)	Jan. 2, 1856	Jan. 8, 1857
Hannibal Hamlin (R)[11]	Jan. 8, 1857	Feb. 25, 1857
Joseph H. Williams (R)[12]	Feb. 26, 1857	Jan. 8, 1858
Lot M. Morrill (R)	Jan. 8, 1858	Jan. 2, 1861
Israel Washburn Jr. (R)	Jan. 2, 1861	Jan. 7, 1863
Abner Coburn (R)	Jan. 7, 1863	Jan. 6, 1864
Samuel Cony (UN R)	Jan. 6, 1864	Jan. 2, 1867
Joshua L. Chamberlain (R)	Jan. 2, 1867	Jan. 4, 1871
Sidney Perham (R)	Jan. 4, 1871	Jan. 7, 1874
Nelson Dingley Jr. (R)	Jan. 7, 1874	Jan. 5, 1876
Selden Connor (R)	Jan. 5, 1876	Jan. 8, 1879
Alonzo Garcelon (D)	Jan. 8, 1879	Jan. 1880
Daniel F. Davis (R)	Jan. 17, 1880	Jan. 1881
Harris M. Plaisted (D)	Jan. 13, 1881	Jan. 3, 1883
Frederick Robie (R)	Jan. 3, 1883	Jan. 5, 1887
Joseph R. Bodwell (R)[13]	Jan. 5, 1887	Dec. 15, 1887
Sebastian S. Marble (R)[14]	Dec. 16, 1887	Jan. 2, 1889
Edwin C. Burleigh (R)	Jan. 2, 1889	Jan. 4, 1893
Henry B. Cleaves (R)	Jan. 4, 1893	Jan. 6, 1897
Llewellyn Powers (R)	Jan. 6, 1897	Jan. 2, 1901
John F. Hill (R)	Jan. 2, 1901	Jan. 4, 1905
William T. Cobb (R)	Jan. 4, 1905	Jan. 6, 1909
Bert M. Fernald (R)	Jan. 6, 1909	Jan. 4, 1911
Frederick W. Plaisted (D)	Jan. 4, 1911	Jan. 1, 1913
William T. Haines (R)	Jan. 1, 1913	Jan. 6, 1915
Oakley C. Curtis (D)	Jan. 6, 1915	Jan. 3, 1917
Carl E. Milliken (R)	Jan. 3, 1917	Jan. 5, 1921
Frederic H. Parkhurst (R)[15]	Jan. 5, 1921	Jan. 31, 1921
Percival P. Baxter (R)[16]	Jan. 31, 1921	Jan. 8, 1925
Ralph O. Brewster (R)	Jan. 8, 1925	Jan. 2, 1929
William T. Gardiner (R)	Jan. 2, 1929	Jan. 4, 1933
Louis J. Brann (D)	Jan. 4, 1933	Jan. 6, 1937
Lewis O. Barrows (R)	Jan. 6, 1937	Jan. 1, 1941
Sumner Sewall (R)	Jan. 1, 1941	Jan. 3, 1945
Horace A. Hildreth (R)	Jan. 3, 1945	Jan. 5, 1949
Frederick G. Payne (R)[17]	Jan. 5, 1949	Dec. 25, 1952
Burton M. Cross (R)[18]	Dec. 26, 1952	Jan. 5, 1955
Edmund S. Muskie (D)[19]	Jan. 5, 1955	Jan. 3, 1959
Robert N. Haskell (R)[20]	Jan. 3, 1959	Jan. 8, 1959
Clinton A. Clauson (D)[21]	Jan. 8, 1959	Dec. 30, 1959
John H. Reed (R)[22]	Dec. 30, 1959	Jan. 5, 1967

Kenneth M. Curtis (D)	Jan. 5, 1967	Jan. 1, 1975
James B. Longley (I)	Jan. 2, 1975	Jan. 3, 1979
Joseph E. Brennan (D)	Jan. 3, 1979	Jan. 7, 1987
John R. McKernan Jr. (R)	Jan. 7, 1987	Jan. 5, 1995
Angus King Jr. (I)	Jan. 5, 1995	

Maine

1. Resigned May 28, 1821.
2. Acting governor. Resigned Dec. 25, 1821.
3. Acting governor.
4. Acting governor.
5. Died Oct. 8, 1829.
6. Acting governor.
7. Acting governor.
8. As president of the state Senate, acted as governor while an inconclusive popular election result was being resolved in the legislature.
9. Resigned March 7, 1843.
10. Acting governor.
11. Resigned Feb. 25, 1857.
12. Acting governor.
13. Died Dec. 15, 1887.
14. Acting governor.
15. Died Jan. 31, 1921.
16. As president of the state Senate, he succeeded to office. Subsequently elected.
17. Resigned Dec. 25, 1952.
18. As president of the state Senate, he succeeded to office. He had previously been elected for a two-year term beginning Jan. 1953.
19. Resigned Jan. 3, 1959.
20. As president of the state Senate, he succeeded to office.
21. Died Dec. 30, 1959.
22. As president of the state Senate, he succeeded to office. Subsequently elected in a special election for the remainder of Clauson's term. Reelected in 1962.

MARYLAND

(Ratified the Constitution April 28, 1788)

Governors	Dates of Service	
Thomas Johnson	March 21, 1777	Nov. 12, 1779
Thomas S. Lee	Nov. 12, 1779	Nov. 22, 1782
William Paca	Nov. 22, 1782	Nov. 26, 1785
William Smallwood	Nov. 26, 1785	Nov. 24, 1788
John Eager Howard (FED)	Nov. 24, 1788	Nov. 14, 1791
George Plater (FED)[1]	Nov. 14, 1791	Feb. 10, 1792
James Brice (FED)[2]	Feb. 13, 1792	April 5, 1792
Thomas Sim Lee (FED)	April 5, 1792	Nov. 14, 1794
John H. Stone (FED)	Nov. 14, 1794	Nov. 17, 1797
John Henry (FED)	Nov. 17, 1797	Nov. 14, 1798
Benjamin Ogle (FED)	Nov. 14, 1798	Nov. 10, 1801
John Francis Mercer (D-R)	Nov. 10, 1801	Nov. 15, 1803
Robert Bowie (D-R)	Nov. 15, 1803	Nov. 10, 1806
Robert Wright (D-R)[3]	Nov. 12, 1806	May 6, 1809
James Butcher (D-R)[4]	May 6, 1809	June 9, 1809
Edward Lloyd (D-R)	June 9, 1809	Nov. 16, 1811
Robert Bowie (D-R)	Nov. 16, 1811	Nov. 25, 1812
Levin Winder (FED)	Nov. 25, 1812	Jan. 2, 1816
Charles Ridgely (FED)	Jan. 2, 1816	Jan. 8, 1819
Charles Goldsborough (FED)	Jan. 8, 1819	Dec. 20, 1819
Samuel Sprigg (D-R)	Dec. 20, 1819	Dec. 16, 1822
Samuel Stevens Jr. (D-R)	Dec. 16, 1822	Jan. 9, 1826
Joseph Kent (D-R)	Jan. 9, 1826	Jan. 15, 1829
Daniel Martin (A-JAC D)	Jan. 15, 1829	Jan. 15, 1830
Thomas King Carroll (D)	Jan. 15, 1830	Jan. 13, 1831
Daniel Martin (A-JAC D)[5]	Jan. 13, 1831	July 11, 1831
George Howard (A-JAC D)[6]	July 11, 1831	Jan. 17, 1833
James Thomas (A-JAC D)	Jan. 17, 1833	Jan. 14, 1836
Thomas W. Veazey (W)	Jan. 14, 1836	Jan. 7, 1839
William Grason (D)	Jan. 7, 1839	Jan. 3, 1842
Francis Thomas (D)	Jan. 3, 1842	Jan. 6, 1845
Thomas G. Pratt (W)	Jan. 6, 1845	Jan. 3, 1848
Philip Francis Thomas (D)	Jan. 3, 1848	Jan. 6, 1851
Enoch L. Lowe (D)	Jan. 6, 1851	Jan. 11, 1854
Thomas W. Ligon (D)	Jan. 11, 1854	Jan. 13, 1858
Thomas H. Hicks (AM)	Jan. 13, 1858	Jan. 8, 1862
Augustus W. Bradford (UN R)	Jan. 8, 1862	Jan. 10, 1866
Thomas Swann (UN R)	Jan. 10, 1866	Jan. 13, 1869
Oden Bowie (D)	Jan. 13, 1869	Jan. 10, 1872
William P. Whyte (D)[7]	Jan. 10, 1872	March 4, 1874
James B. Groome (D)[8]	March 4, 1874	Jan. 12, 1876
John Lee Carroll (D)	Jan. 12, 1876	Jan. 14, 1880
William T. Hamilton (D)	Jan. 14, 1880	Jan. 9, 1884
Robert M. McLane (D)[9]	Jan. 9, 1884	March 27, 1885
Henry Lloyd (D)[10]	March 27, 1885	Jan. 11, 1888
Elihu E. Jackson (D)	Jan. 11, 1888	Jan. 13, 1892
Frank Brown (D)	Jan. 13, 1892	Jan. 8, 1896
Lloyd Lowndes (R)	Jan. 8, 1896	Jan. 10, 1900
John W. Smith (D)	Jan. 10, 1900	Jan. 13, 1904
Edwin Warfield (D)	Jan. 1, 1904	Jan. 8, 1908
Austin L. Crothers (D)	Jan. 8, 1908	Jan. 10, 1912
Phillips L. Goldsborough (R)	Jan. 10, 1912	Jan. 12, 1916
Emerson C. Harrington (D)	Jan. 12, 1916	Jan. 14, 1920
Albert C. Ritchie (D)	Jan. 14, 1920	Jan. 9, 1935
Harry W. Nice (R)	Jan. 9, 1935	Jan. 11, 1939
Herbert R. O'Conor (D)[11]	Jan. 11, 1939	Jan. 3, 1947
William P. Lane Jr. (D)[12]	Jan. 3, 1947	Jan. 10, 1951
Theodore R. McKeldin (R)	Jan. 10, 1951	Jan. 14, 1959
J. Millard Tawes (D)	Jan. 14, 1959	Jan. 25, 1967
Spiro T. Agnew (R)[13]	Jan. 25, 1967	Jan. 7, 1969
Marvin Mandel (D)[14]	Jan. 7, 1969	Jan. 15, 1979
Blair Lee (D)[15]	Oct. 7, 1977	Jan. 15, 1979
Harry Hughes (D)	Jan. 17, 1979	Jan. 20, 1987
William D. Schaefer (D)	Jan. 21, 1987	Jan. 18, 1995
Parris N. Glendening (D)	Jan. 18, 1995	

Maryland

1. Died Feb. 10, 1792.
2. Acting governor.
3. Resigned May 6, 1809.
4. Acting governor.
5. Died July 11, 1831.
6. Acting governor. Subsequently elected by the legislature.
7. Resigned March 4, 1874.
8. Acting governor. Subsequently elected by the legislature.
9. Resigned March 27, 1885.
10. Acting governor. Subsequently elected by the legislature.
11. Resigned Jan. 3, 1947.
12. Elected by the legislature to complete the remaining five days of O'Conor's term. Had previously been elected for a four-year term beginning Jan. 8, 1947.
13. Resigned Jan. 7, 1969.
14. Elected by the legislature to complete Agnew's term. Subsequently reelected in 1970 and 1974. Suspended from office Oct. 7, 1977 to Jan. 15, 1979.
15. As lieutenant governor, served as acting governor.

MASSACHUSETTS

(Ratified the Constitution Feb. 6, 1788)

Governors	Dates of Service	
John Hancock[1]	Oct. 25, 1780	March 1785
Thomas Cushing[2]	March 1785	May 26, 1785
James Bowdoin	May 26, 1785	May 30, 1787
John Hancock	May 30, 1787	Oct. 8, 1793
Samuel Adams	Oct. 8, 1793	June 2, 1797
Increase Sumner (FED)	June 2, 1797	June 7, 1799
Moses Gill (FED)[3]	June 7, 1799	May 20, 1800
Caleb Strong (FED)	May 30, 1800	May 29, 1807
James Sullivan (D-R)	May 29, 1807	Dec. 10, 1808
Levi Lincoln (D-R)[4]	Dec. 10, 1808	May 1, 1809
Christopher Gore (FED)	May 1809	June 1810
Elbridge Gerry (D-R)	June 1810	June 1812
Caleb Strong (FED)	June 1812	May 30, 1816
John Brooks (FED)	May 30, 1816	May 31, 1823
William Eustis (D-R)	May 31, 1823	Feb. 6, 1825
Marcus Morton (D-R)[5]	Feb. 6, 1825	May 26, 1825
Levi Lincoln (AR, NR)[6]	May 26, 1825	Jan. 9, 1834
John Davis (NR, W)	Jan. 9, 1834	March 1, 1835
Samuel T. Armstrong (W)[7]	March 1, 1835	Jan. 13, 1836
Edward Everett (W)	Jan. 13, 1836	Jan. 18, 1840
Marcus Morton (D)	Jan. 18, 1840	Jan. 7, 1841
John Davis (W)	Jan. 7, 1841	Jan. 17, 1843
Marcus Morton (D)	Jan. 17, 1843	Jan. 1844
George N. Briggs (W)	Jan. 1844	Jan. 11, 1851
George S. Boutwell (D)	Jan. 11, 1851	Jan. 14, 1853
John H. Clifford (W)	Jan. 14, 1853	Jan. 12, 1854
Emory Washburn (W)	Jan. 12, 1854	Jan. 4, 1855
Henry J. Gardner (AM)	Jan. 4, 1855	Jan. 7, 1858
Nathaniel P. Banks (R)	Jan. 7, 1858	Jan. 3, 1861
John A. Andrew (R)	Jan. 3, 1861	Jan. 4, 1866
Alexander H. Bullock (UN)	Jan. 4, 1866	Jan. 7, 1869
William Claflin (R)	Jan. 7, 1869	Jan. 4, 1872
William B. Washburn (R)[8]	Jan. 4, 1872	April 29, 1874
Thomas Talbot (R)[9]	April 29, 1874	Jan. 7, 1875
William Gaston (D)	Jan. 7, 1875	Jan. 6, 1876
Alexander H. Rice (R)	Jan. 6, 1876	Jan. 2, 1879
Thomas Talbot (R)	Jan. 2, 1879	Jan. 8, 1880
John Davis Long (R)	Jan. 8, 1880	Jan. 4, 1883
Benjamin F. Butler (D)	Jan. 4, 1883	Jan. 3, 1884
George D. Robinson (R)	Jan. 3, 1884	Jan. 6, 1887
Oliver Ames (R)	Jan. 6, 1887	Jan. 7, 1890
John Q. A. Brackett (R)	Jan. 7, 1890	Jan. 8, 1891
William E. Russell (D)	Jan. 8, 1891	Jan. 4, 1894
Frederic T. Greenhalge (R)[10]	Jan. 4, 1894	March 5, 1896
Roger Wolcott (R)[11]	March 5, 1896	Jan. 4, 1900
Winthrop M. Crane (R)	Jan. 4, 1900	Jan. 8, 1903
John L. Bates (R)	Jan. 8, 1903	Jan. 5, 1905
William L. Douglas (D)	Jan. 5, 1905	Jan. 4, 1906
Curtis Guild Jr. (R)	Jan. 4, 1906	Jan. 7, 1909
Eban Sumner Draper (R)	Jan. 7, 1909	Jan. 5, 1911
Eugene N. Foss (D)	Jan. 5, 1911	Jan. 8, 1914
David I. Walsh (D)	Jan. 8, 1914	Jan. 6, 1916
Samuel W. McCall (R)	Jan. 6, 1916	Jan. 2, 1919
Calvin Coolidge (R)	Jan. 2, 1919	Jan. 6, 1921
Channing H. Cox (R)	Jan. 6, 1921	Jan. 8, 1925
Alvan T. Fuller (R)	Jan. 8, 1925	Jan. 3, 1929
Frank G. Allen (R)	Jan. 3, 1929	Jan. 8, 1931
Joseph B. Ely (D)	Jan. 8, 1931	Jan. 3, 1935
James M. Curley (D)	Jan. 3, 1935	Jan. 7, 1937
Charles F. Hurley (D)	Jan. 7, 1937	Jan. 5, 1939
Leverett Saltonstall (R)	Jan. 5, 1939	Jan. 3, 1945
Maurice J. Tobin (D)	Jan. 3, 1945	Jan. 2, 1947
Robert F. Bradford (R)	Jan. 2, 1947	Jan. 6, 1949
Paul A. Dever (D)	Jan. 6, 1949	Jan. 8, 1953
Christian A. Herter (R)	Jan. 8, 1953	Jan. 3, 1957
Foster J. Furcolo (D)	Jan. 3, 1957	Jan. 5, 1961
John A. Volpe (R)	Jan. 5, 1961	Jan. 3, 1963
Endicott Peabody (D)	Jan. 3, 1963	Jan. 7, 1965
John A. Volpe (R)[12]	Jan. 7, 1965	Jan. 22, 1969
Francis W. Sargent (R)[13]	Jan. 22, 1969	Jan. 2, 1975
Michael S. Dukakis (D)	Jan. 2, 1975	Jan. 4, 1979
Edward J. King (D)	Jan. 4, 1979	Jan. 6, 1983
Michael S. Dukakis (D)	Jan. 6, 1983	Jan. 3, 1991
William F. Weld (R)[14]	Jan. 3, 1991	July, 29, 1997
Argeo "Paul" Cellucci (R)[15]	July 29, 1997	April 11, 2001
Jane Swift (R)[16]	April 11, 2001	

Massachusetts
1. Resigned in March 1785.
2. As lieutenant governor, he succeeded to office.
3. Acting governor.
4. Acting governor.
5. Acting governor.
6. ICPSR data shows that there were two elections for governor in Massachusetts in 1831, and returns for both have been provided. The winner both times was incumbent Levi Lincoln. An explanation was obtained from Albert Bushnell Hart's *Commonwealth of Massachusetts*, vol. 4 (New York: States History Company, 1930), 82. Massachusetts had a one-year term for its governors during this period. Apparently the state decided in 1831 to move its gubernatorial election from April to November to coincide with presidential elections in 1832 and succeeding years. As a consequence, Lincoln was required to run twice within the same year to make the adjustment.
7. Acting governor.
8. Resigned May 1, 1874.
9. Acting governor.
10. Died March 5, 1896.
11. As lieutenant governor, he succeeded to office. Subsequently elected.
12. Resigned Jan. 22, 1969.
13. As lieutenant governor, he succeeded to office. Subsequently elected.
14. Resigned July 29, 1997.
15. As lieutenant governor, he succeeded to office. Subsequently elected. Resigned April 11, 2001.
16. As lieutenant governor, she succeeded to office.

MICHIGAN

(Became a state Jan. 26, 1837)

Governors	Dates of Service	
Stevens T. Mason (D)	Nov. 3, 1835	Jan. 7, 1840
Edward Mundy (D)[1]	April 3, 1838	June 12, 1838
William Woodbridge (W)[2]	Jan. 7, 1840	Feb. 23, 1841
James W. Gordon (W)[3]	Feb. 23, 1841	Jan. 3, 1842
John S. Barry (D)	Jan. 3, 1842	Jan. 5, 1846
Alpheus Felch (D)[4]	Jan. 5, 1846	March 3, 1847
William L. Greenly (D)[5]	March 3, 1847	Jan. 3, 1848
Epaphroditus Ransom (D)	Jan. 3, 1848	Jan. 7, 1850

John S. Barry (D)	Jan. 7, 1850	Jan. 1, 1851
Robert McClelland (D)[6]	Jan. 1, 1851	March 7, 1853
Andrew Parsons (D)[7]	March 7, 1853	Jan. 3, 1855
Kinsley S. Bingham (R)	Jan. 3, 1855	Jan. 5, 1859
Moses Wisner (R)	Jan. 5, 1859	Jan. 2, 1861
Austin Blair (R)	Jan. 2, 1861	Jan. 4, 1865
Henry H. Crapo (UN R)	Jan. 4, 1865	Jan. 6, 1869
Henry P. Baldwin (R)	Jan. 6, 1869	Jan. 1, 1873
John J. Bagley (R)	Jan. 1, 1873	Jan. 3, 1877
Charles M. Croswell (R)	Jan. 3, 1877	Jan. 1, 1881
David H. Jerome (R)	Jan. 1, 1881	Jan. 1, 1883
Josiah W. Begole (D)	Jan. 1, 1883	Jan. 1, 1885
Russell A. Alger (R)	Jan. 1, 1885	Jan. 1, 1887
Cyrus G. Luce (R)	Jan. 1, 1887	Jan. 1, 1891
Edward B. Winans (D)	Jan. 1, 1891	Jan. 1, 1893
John T. Rich (R)	Jan. 1, 1893	Jan. 1, 1897
Hazen S. Pingree (R)	Jan. 1, 1897	Jan. 1, 1901
Aaron T. Bliss (R)	Jan. 1, 1901	Jan. 1, 1905
Fred M. Warner (R)	Jan. 1, 1905	Jan. 1, 1911
Chase S. Osborn (R)	Jan. 1, 1911	Jan. 1, 1913
Woodbridge N. Ferris (D)	Jan. 1, 1913	Jan. 1, 1917
Albert E. Sleeper (R)	Jan. 1, 1917	Jan. 1, 1921
Alexander J. Groesbeck (R)	Jan. 1, 1921	Jan. 1, 1927
Fred W. Green (R)	Jan. 1, 1927	Jan. 1, 1931
Wilber M. Brucker (R)	Jan. 1, 1931	Jan. 1, 1933
William A. Comstock (D)	Jan. 1, 1933	Jan. 1, 1935
Frank D. Fitzgerald (R)	Jan. 1, 1935	Jan. 1, 1937
Frank Murphy (D)	Jan. 1, 1937	Jan. 1, 1939
Frank D. Fitzgerald (R)[8]	Jan. 1, 1939	March 16, 1939
Luren D. Dickinson (R)[9]	March 16, 1939	Jan. 1, 1941
Murray D. Van Wagoner (D)	Jan. 1, 1941	Jan. 1, 1943
Harry F. Kelly (R)	Jan. 1, 1943	Jan. 1, 1947
Kim Sigler (R)	Jan. 1, 1947	Jan. 1, 1949
G. Mennen Williams (D)	Jan. 1, 1949	Jan. 1, 1961
John B. Swainson (D)	Jan. 1, 1961	Jan. 1, 1963
George W. Romney (R)[10]	Jan. 1, 1963	Jan. 22, 1969
William G. Milliken (R)[11]	Jan. 22, 1969	Jan. 1, 1983
James J. Blanchard (D)	Jan. 1, 1983	Jan. 1, 1991
John Engler (R)	Jan. 1, 1991	

Michigan

1. Lieutenant governor, serving as acting governor for several months in 1838.
2. Resigned Feb. 23, 1841.
3. As lieutenant governor, he succeeded to office.
4. Resigned March 3, 1847.
5. As lieutenant governor, he succeeded to office.
6. Resigned March 7, 1853.
7. As lieutenant governor, he succeeded to office.
8. Died March 16, 1939.
9. As lieutenant governor, he succeeded to office.
10. Resigned Jan. 22, 1969.
11. As lieutenant governor, he succeeded to office. Subsequently elected.

MINNESOTA

(Became a state May 11, 1858)

Governors	Dates of Service	
Henry H. Sibley (D)	May 24, 1858	Jan. 2, 1860
Alexander Ramsey (R)[1]	Jan. 2, 1860	July 10, 1863

Henry A. Swift (R)[2]	July 10, 1863	Jan. 11, 1864
Stephen Miller (UN)	Jan. 11, 1864	Jan. 8, 1866
William R. Marshall (R)	Jan. 8, 1866	Jan. 9, 1870
Horace Austin (R)	Jan. 9, 1870	Jan. 7, 1874
Cushman K. Davis (R)	Jan. 7, 1874	Jan. 7, 1876
John S. Pillsbury (R)	Jan. 7, 1876	Jan. 10, 1882
Lucius F. Hubbard (R)	Jan. 10, 1882	Jan. 5, 1887
Andrew R. McGill (R)	Jan. 5, 1887	Jan. 9, 1889
William R. Merriam (R)	Jan. 9, 1889	Jan. 4, 1893
Knute Nelson (R)	Jan. 4, 1893	Jan. 31, 1895
David M. Clough (R)	Jan. 31, 1895	Jan. 2, 1899
John Lind (D & POP)	Jan. 2, 1899	Jan. 7, 1901
Samuel R. Van Sant (R)	Jan. 7, 1901	Jan. 4, 1905
John A. Johnson (D)[3]	Jan. 4, 1905	Sept. 21, 1909
Adolph O. Eberhart (R)[4]	Sept. 21, 1909	Jan. 5, 1915
Winfield S. Hammond (D)[5]	Jan. 5, 1915	Dec. 30, 1915
Joseph A. A. Burnquist (R)[6]	Dec. 30, 1915	Jan. 5, 1921
Jacob A. O. Preus (R)	Jan. 5, 1921	Jan. 6, 1925
Theodore Christianson (R)	Jan. 6, 1925	Jan. 6, 1931
Floyd B. Olson (F-LAB)[7]	Jan. 6, 1931	Aug. 22, 1936
Hjalmar Petersen (F-LAB)[8]	Aug. 22, 1936	Jan. 4, 1937
Elmer A. Benson (F-LAB)	Jan. 4, 1937	Jan. 2, 1939
Harold E. Stassen (R)[9]	Jan. 2, 1939	April 27, 1943
Edward J. Thye (R)[10]	April 27, 1943	Jan. 8, 1947
Luther W. Youngdahl (R)[11]	Jan. 8, 1947	Sept. 27, 1951
C. Elmer Anderson (R)[12]	Sept. 27, 1951	Jan. 5, 1955
Orville L. Freeman (DFL)	Jan. 5, 1955	Jan. 2, 1961
Elmer L. Andersen (R)[13]	Jan. 2, 1961	March 25, 1963
Karl F. Rolvaag (DFL)[14]	March 25, 1963	Jan. 2, 1967
Harold LeVander (R)	Jan. 2, 1967	Jan. 4, 1971
Wendell R. Anderson (DFL)[15]	Jan. 4, 1971	Dec. 29, 1976
Rudy Perpich (DFL)[16]	Dec. 29, 1976	Jan. 1, 1979
Albert H. Quie (I-R)	Jan. 1, 1979	Jan. 3, 1983
Rudy Perpich (DFL)	Jan. 3, 1983	Jan. 7, 1991
Arne H. Carlson (I-R)	Jan. 7, 1991	Jan. 5, 1999
Jesse Ventura (REF)	Jan. 4, 1999	

Minnesota

1. Resigned July 10, 1863.
2. As lieutenant governor, he succeeded to office.
3. Died Sept. 21, 1909.
4. As lieutenant governor, he succeeded to office. Subsequently elected.
5. Died Dec. 30, 1915.
6. As lieutenant governor, he succeeded to office. Subsequently elected.
7. Died Aug. 22, 1936.
8. As lieutenant governor, he succeeded to office.
9. Resigned April 27, 1943.
10. As lieutenant governor, he succeeded to office. Subsequently elected.
11. Resigned Sept. 27, 1951.
12. As lieutenant governor, he succeeded to office. Subsequently elected.
13. The 1962 election between incumbent Governor Andersen (R) and Lieutenant Governor Karl Rolvaag (DFL) was disputed. Andersen served for almost three months of the term before the Minnesota Supreme Court ruled that Rolvaag had won by 91 votes.
14. Served the remainder of the four-year term after the removal of Governor Andersen.
15. Resigned Dec. 29, 1976, having been appointed to the U.S. Senate.
16. As lieutenant governor, he succeeded to office.

MISSISSIPPI

(Became a state Dec. 10, 1817)

Governors	Dates of Service	
David Holmes (D-R)	Dec. 10, 1817	Jan. 5, 1820
George Poindexter (D-R)	Jan. 5, 1820	Jan. 7, 1822
Walter Leake (D-R)[1]	Jan. 7, 1822	Nov. 17, 1825
Gerard C. Brandon (D-R)[2]	Nov. 17, 1825	Jan. 7, 1826
David Holmes (D-R)[3]	Jan. 7, 1826	July 25, 1826
Gerard C. Brandon (D)[4]	July 25, 1826	Jan. 9, 1832
Abram M. Scott (NR)[5]	Jan. 9, 1832	June 12, 1833
Charles Lynch (NR)[6]	June 12, 1833	Nov. 20, 1833
Hiram G. Runnels (D)[7]	Nov. 20, 1833	Nov. 20, 1835
John A. Quitman (W)[8]	Dec. 3, 1835	Jan. 7, 1836
Charles Lynch (W)	Jan. 7, 1836	Jan. 8, 1838
Alexander G. McNutt (D)	Jan. 8, 1838	Jan. 10, 1842
Tilgham M. Tucker (D)	Jan. 10, 1842	Jan. 10, 1844
Albert G. Brown (D)	Jan. 10, 1844	Jan. 10, 1848
Joseph M. Matthews (D)	Jan. 10, 1848	Jan. 10, 1850
John A. Quitman (D)[9]	Jan. 10, 1850	Feb. 3, 1851
John I. Guion (D)[10]	Feb. 3, 1851	Nov. 4, 1851
James Whitfield (D)[11]	Nov. 24, 1851	Jan. 10, 1852
Henry S. Foote (UN)[12]	Jan. 10, 1852	Jan. 5, 1854
John J. Pettus (D)[13]	Jan. 5, 1854	Jan. 10, 1854
John J. McRae (D)	Jan. 10, 1854	Nov. 16, 1857
William McWillie (D)	Nov. 16, 1857	Nov. 21, 1859
John J. Pettus (D)	Nov. 21, 1859	Nov. 16, 1863
Charles Clark (D)[14]	Nov. 16, 1863	May 22, 1865
William L. Sharkey	June 13, 1865	Oct. 16, 1865
Benjamin G. Humphreys[15]	Oct. 16, 1865	June 15, 1868
Adelbert Ames	June 15, 1868	March 10, 1870
James L. Alcorn (R)[16]	March 10, 1870	Nov. 30, 1871
Ridgley C. Powers (R)[17]	Nov. 30, 1871	Jan. 4, 1874
Adelbert Ames (R)[18]	Jan. 4, 1874	March 29, 1876
John M. Stone (D)[19]	March 29, 1876	Jan. 29, 1882
Robert Lowry (D)	Jan. 29, 1882	Jan. 13, 1890
John M. Stone (D)	Jan. 13, 1890	Jan. 20, 1896
Anselm J. McLaurin (D)	Jan. 20, 1896	Jan. 16, 1900
Andrew H. Longino (D)	Jan. 16, 1900	Jan. 19, 1904
James Kimble Vardaman (D)	Jan. 19, 1904	Jan. 21, 1908
Edmond Favor Noel (D)	Jan. 21, 1908	Jan. 16, 1912
Earl LeRoy Brewer (D)	Jan. 16, 1912	Jan. 18, 1916
Theodore Gilmore Bilbo (D)	Jan. 18, 1916	Jan. 20, 1920
Lee Maurice Russell (D)	Jan. 20, 1920	Jan. 22, 1924
Henry Lewis Whitfield (D)[20]	Jan. 22, 1924	March 18, 1927
Dennis Murphree (D)[21]	March 18, 1927	Jan. 17, 1928
Theodore Gilmore Bilbo (D)	Jan. 17, 1928	Jan. 19, 1932
Martin Sennett Conner (D)	Jan. 19, 1932	Jan. 21, 1936
Hugh L. White (D)	Jan. 21, 1936	Jan. 16, 1940
Paul B. Johnson (D)[22]	Jan. 16, 1940	Dec. 26, 1943
Dennis Murphree (D)[23]	Dec. 26, 1943	Jan. 18, 1944
Thomas L. Bailey (D)[24]	Jan. 18, 1944	Nov. 2, 1946
Fielding L. Wright (D)[25]	Nov. 2, 1946	Jan. 22, 1952
Hugh L. White (D)	Jan. 22, 1952	Jan. 17, 1956
J. P. Coleman (D)	Jan. 17, 1956	Jan. 19, 1960
Ross R. Barnett (D)	Jan. 19, 1960	Jan. 21, 1964
Paul B. Johnson Jr. (D)	Jan. 21, 1964	Jan. 16, 1968
John Bell Williams (D)	Jan. 16, 1968	Jan. 18, 1972
William Lowe Waller (D)	Jan. 18, 1972	Jan. 20, 1976
Cliff Finch (D)	Jan. 20, 1976	Jan. 22, 1980
William Winter (D)	Jan. 22, 1980	Jan. 10, 1984
Bill Allain (D)	Jan. 10, 1984	Jan. 12, 1988
Ray Mabus (D)	Jan. 12, 1988	Jan. 14, 1992
Kirk Fordice (R)	Jan. 14, 1992	Jan. 11, 2000
Ronnie Musgrove (D)	Jan. 11, 2000	

Mississippi
1. Died Nov. 17, 1825.
2. As lieutenant governor, he succeeded to office.
3. Resigned July 25, 1826.
4. As lieutenant governor, he succeeded to office. Subsequently elected.
5. Died June 12, 1833.
6. As president of the state Senate, he succeeded to office.
7. Resigned Nov. 20, 1835.
8. As president of the state Senate, he succeeded to office.
9. Resigned Feb. 3, 1851.
10. As president of the state Senate, he succeeded to office.
11. As president of the state Senate, he succeeded to office.
12. Resigned Jan. 5, 1854.
13. As president of the state Senate, he succeeded to office.
14. Removed from office May 22, 1865.
15. Removed from office June 15, 1868.
16. Resigned Nov. 30, 1871.
17. As lieutenant governor, he succeeded to office.
18. Resigned March 29, 1876.
19. As president of the state Senate, he succeeded to office. Subsequently elected.
20. Died March 18, 1927.
21. As lieutenant governor, he succeeded to office.
22. Died Dec. 26, 1943.
23. As lieutenant governor, he succeeded to office.
24. Died Nov. 2, 1946.
25. As lieutenant governor, he succeeded to office. Subsequently elected.

MISSOURI

(Became a state Aug. 10, 1821)

Governors	Dates of Service	
Alexander McNair (D-R)	Aug. 10, 1821	Nov. 15, 1824
Frederick Bates (AR)[1]	Nov. 15, 1824	Aug. 4, 1825
Abraham J. Williams (D-R)[2]	Aug. 4, 1825	Jan. 20, 1826
John Miller (JAC D)	Jan. 20, 1826	Nov. 14, 1832
Daniel Dunklin (D)	Nov. 14, 1832	Sept. 13, 1836
Lilburn W. Boggs (D)	Sept. 13, 1836	Nov. 16, 1840
Thomas Reynolds (D)[3]	Nov. 16, 1840	Feb. 9, 1844
Meredith M. Marmaduke (D)[4]	Feb. 9, 1844	Nov. 20, 1844
John C. Edwards (D)	Nov. 20, 1844	Dec. 27, 1848
Austin A. King (D)	Dec. 27, 1848	Jan. 3, 1853
Sterling Price (D)	Jan. 3, 1853	Jan. 5, 1857
Trusten Polk (D)[5]	Jan. 5, 1857	Feb. 27, 1857
Hancock Lee Jackson (D)[6]	Feb. 27, 1857	Oct. 22, 1857
Robert Marcellus Stewart (D)	Oct. 22, 1857	Jan. 3, 1861
Claiborne Fox Jackson (D)[7]	Jan. 31, 1861	July 30, 1861
Hamilton R. Gamble (UN)[8]	July 31, 1861	Jan. 31, 1864
Willard Preble Hall (UN)[9]	Jan. 31, 1864	Jan. 2, 1865
Thomas C. Fletcher (UN R)	Jan. 2, 1865	Jan. 12, 1869
Joseph W. McClurg (R)	Jan. 12, 1869	Jan. 9, 1871
Benjamin G. Brown (R)	Jan. 9, 1871	Jan. 8, 1873
Silas Woodson (D)	Jan. 8, 1873	Jan. 12, 1875

Charles Henry Hardin (D)	Jan. 12, 1875	Jan. 8, 1877
John S. Phelps (D)	Jan. 8, 1877	Jan. 10, 1881
Thomas T. Crittenden (D)	Jan. 10, 1881	Jan. 12, 1885
John S. Marmaduke (D)[10]	Jan. 12, 1885	Dec. 28, 1887
Albert P. Morehouse (D)[11]	Dec. 28, 1887	Jan. 14, 1889
David R. Francis (D)	Jan. 14, 1889	Jan. 9, 1893
William J. Stone (D)	Jan. 9, 1893	Jan. 11, 1897
Lawrence Vest Stephens (D)	Jan. 11, 1897	Jan. 14, 1901
Alexander M. Dockery (D)	Jan. 14, 1901	Jan. 9, 1905
Joseph W. Folk (D)	Jan. 9, 1905	Jan. 11, 1909
Herbert S. Hadley (R)	Jan. 11, 1909	Jan. 13, 1913
Elliot W. Major (D)	Jan. 13, 1913	Jan. 8, 1917
Frederick D. Gardner (D)	Jan. 8, 1917	Jan. 10, 1921
Arthur M. Hyde (R)	Jan. 10, 1921	Jan. 12, 1925
Samuel A. Baker (R)	Jan. 12, 1925	Jan. 14, 1929
Henry S. Caulfield (R)	Jan. 14, 1929	Jan. 9, 1933
Guy B. Park (D)	Jan. 9, 1933	Jan. 11, 1937
Lloyd C. Stark (D)	Jan. 11, 1937	Jan. 13, 1941
Forrest C. Donnell (R)	Jan. 13, 1941	Jan. 8, 1945
Phil M. Donnelly (D)	Jan. 8, 1945	Jan. 10, 1949
Forrest Smith (D)	Jan. 10, 1949	Jan. 12, 1953
Phil M. Donnelly (D)	Jan. 12, 1953	Jan. 14, 1957
James T. Blair Jr. (D)	Jan. 14, 1957	Jan. 9, 1961
John M. Dalton (D)	Jan. 9, 1961	Jan. 11, 1965
Warren E. Hearnes (D)	Jan. 11, 1965	Jan. 8, 1973
Christopher S. Bond (R)	Jan. 8, 1973	Jan. 10, 1977
Joseph P. Teasdale (D)	Jan. 10, 1977	Jan. 12, 1981
Christopher S. Bond (R)	Jan. 12, 1981	Jan. 14, 1985
John Ashcroft (R)	Jan. 14, 1985	Jan. 11, 1993
Mel E. Carnahan (D)[12]	Jan. 11, 1993	Oct. 15, 2000
Roger B. Wilson (D)[13]	Oct. 16, 2000	Jan. 8, 2001
Bob Holden (D)	Jan. 8, 2001	

Missouri
1. Died Aug. 4, 1825.
2. Acting governor.
3. Died in 1844.
4. Acting governor.
5. Resigned Feb. 27, 1857.
6. Acting governor.
7. Removed from office in 1861 by convention.
8. Appointed governor by convention. Died Jan. 31, 1864.
9. Acting governor.
10. Died Dec. 28, 1887.
11. Acting governor.
12. Died Oct. 15, 2000.
13. As lieutenant governor, he succeeded to office.

MONTANA

(Became a state Nov. 8, 1889)

Governors	Dates of Service	
Joseph K. Toole (D)	Nov. 8, 1889	Jan. 1, 1893
John E. Rickards (R)	Jan. 2, 1893	Jan. 3, 1897
Robert B. Smith (PP & D)	Jan. 4, 1897	Jan. 7, 1901
Joseph K. Toole (D)[1]	Jan. 7, 1901	April 1, 1908
Edwin L. Norris (D)[2]	April 1, 1908	Jan. 5, 1913
Samuel V. Stewart (D)	Jan. 6, 1913	Jan. 2, 1921
Joseph M. Dixon (R)	Jan. 3, 1921	Jan. 4, 1925
John E. Erickson (D)[3]	Jan. 4, 1925	March 13, 1933

Frank H. Cooney (D)[4]	March 13, 1933	Dec. 15, 1935
William E. Holt (D)[5]	Dec. 16, 1935	Jan. 4, 1937
Roy E. Ayers (D)	Jan. 4, 1937	Jan. 6, 1942
Samuel C. Ford (R)	Jan. 6, 1941	Jan. 3, 1949
John W. Bonner (D)	Jan. 3, 1949	Jan. 4, 1953
J. Hugo Aronson (R)	Jan. 4, 1953	Jan. 4, 1961
Donald G. Nutter (R)[6]	Jan. 4, 1961	Jan. 25, 1962
Tim M. Babcock (R)[7]	Jan. 26, 1962	Jan. 6, 1969
Forrest H. Anderson (D)	Jan. 6, 1969	Jan. 1, 1973
Thomas L. Judge (D)	Jan. 1, 1973	Jan. 5, 1981
Ted Schwinden (D)	Jan. 5, 1981	Jan. 2, 1989
Stan Stephens (R)	Jan. 2, 1989	Jan. 4, 1993
Marc F. Racicot (R)	Jan. 4, 1993	Jan. 2, 2001
Judy Martz (R)	Jan. 2, 2001	

Montana
1. Resigned April 1, 1908.
2. As lieutenant governor, he succeeded to office. Subsequently elected.
3. Resigned March 13, 1933.
4. As lieutenant governor, he succeeded to office. Died Dec. 15, 1935.
5. As president of the state Senate, he succeeded to office.
6. Died Jan. 25, 1962.
7. As lieutenant governor, he succeeded to office. Subsequently elected.

NEBRASKA

(Became a state March 1, 1867)

Governors	Dates of Service	
David Butler (R)[1]	March 27, 1867	June 2, 1871
William H. James (R)[2]	June 2, 1871	Jan. 13, 1873
Robert W. Furnas (R)	Jan. 13, 1873	Jan. 1875
Silas Garber (R)	Jan. 1875	Jan. 1879
Albinus Nance (R)	Jan. 1879	Jan. 1883
James W. Dawes (R)	Jan. 1883	Jan. 15, 1887
John M. Thayer (R)	Jan. 15, 1887	Jan. 15, 1891
James E. Boyd (D)[3]	Jan. 15, 1891	May 5, 1891
John M. Thayer (R)[4]	May 5, 1891	Feb. 8, 1892
James E. Boyd (D)[5]	Feb. 8, 1892	Jan. 1893
Lorenzo Crounse (R)	Jan. 1893	Jan. 1895
Silas A. Holcomb (D & PPI)	Jan. 1895	Jan. 5, 1899
William A. Poynter (FUS)[6]	Jan. 5, 1899	Jan. 3, 1901
Charles H. Dietrich (R)[7]	Jan. 3, 1901	May 1, 1901
Ezra P. Savage (R)[8]	May 1, 1901	Jan. 8, 1903
John H. Mickey (R)	Jan. 8, 1903	Jan. 3, 1907
George L. Sheldon (R)	Jan. 3, 1907	Jan. 7, 1909
Ashton C. Shallenberger (D)	Jan. 7, 1909	Jan. 5, 1911
Chester H. Aldrich (R)	Jan. 5, 1911	Jan. 9, 1913
John H. Morehead (D)	Jan. 9, 1913	Jan. 4, 1917
Keith Neville (D)	Jan. 4, 1917	Jan. 9, 1919
Samuel R. McKelvie (R)	Jan. 9, 1919	Jan. 3, 1923
Charles W. Bryan (D)	Jan. 4, 1923	Jan. 8, 1925
Adam McMullen (R)	Jan. 8, 1925	Jan. 3, 1929
Arthur J. Weaver (R)	Jan. 3, 1929	Jan. 8, 1931
Charles W. Bryan (D)	Jan. 8, 1931	Jan. 3, 1935
Robert L. Cochran (D)	Jan. 3, 1935	Jan. 9, 1941
Dwight P. Griswold (R)	Jan. 9, 1941	Jan. 9, 1947
Val Peterson (R)	Jan. 9, 1947	Jan. 8, 1953
Robert Berkey Crosby (R)	Jan. 8, 1953	Jan. 6, 1955
Victor E. Anderson (R)	Jan. 6, 1955	Jan. 8, 1959

Ralph G. Brooks (D)[9]	Jan. 8, 1959	Sept. 9, 1960
Dwight W. Burney (R)[10]	Sept. 9, 1960	Jan. 5, 1961
Frank B. Morrison (D)	Jan. 5, 1961	Jan. 5, 1967
Norbert T. Tiemann (R)	Jan. 5, 1967	Jan. 7, 1971
J. James Exon (D)	Jan. 7, 1971	Jan. 3, 1979
Charles Thone (R)	Jan. 4, 1979	Jan. 6, 1983
Bob Kerrey (D)	Jan. 6, 1983	Jan. 9, 1987
Kay A. Orr (R)	Jan. 9, 1987	Jan. 9, 1991
Earl "Ben" Nelson (D)	Jan. 9, 1991	Jan. 7, 1999
Mike Johanns (R)	Jan. 7, 1999	

Nebraska

1. Impeached. Removed from office June 2, 1871.
2. As lieutenant governor, he succeeded to office.
3. The election of Boyd was challenged by Governor Thayer on the grounds that Boyd had been born in Ireland and was not an American citizen and was thus ineligible to be governor. Boyd was removed by the Nebraska Supreme Court May 5, 1891.
4. Following the removal of Boyd, Thayer returned to office.
5. U.S. Supreme Court declared that Boyd was a citizen, and he returned to office Feb. 18, 1892, and served out the remainder of his term.
6. Fusion composed of Democrats and Populists.
7. Resigned May 1, 1901.
8. As lieutenant governor, he succeeded to office.
9. Died Sept. 9, 1960.
10. As lieutenant governor, he succeeded to office.

NEVADA

(Became a state Oct. 31, 1864)

Governors	Dates of Service	
H. G. Blasdel (UN R)	Dec. 5, 1864	Jan. 2, 1871
Lewis R. Bradley (D)	Jan. 3, 1871	Jan. 6, 1879
John H. Kinkead (R)	Jan. 7, 1879	Jan. 1, 1883
Jewett W. Adams (D)	Jan. 2, 1883	Jan. 3, 1887
Charles C. Stevenson (R)[1]	Jan. 4, 1887	Sept. 2, 1890
Frank Bell (R)[2]	Sept. 21, 1890	Jan. 5, 1891
Roswell K. Colcord (R)	Jan. 6, 1891	Jan. 7, 1895
John S. Jones (D SIL)[3]	Jan. 8, 1895	April 10, 1896
Reinhold Sadler (SIL R)[4]	April 10, 1896	Jan. 1, 1903
John Sparks (D & SILVER)[5]	Jan. 1, 1903	May 22, 1908
Denver S. Dickerson (D)[6]	May 22, 1908	Jan. 2, 1911
Tasker L. Oddie (R)	Jan. 2, 1911	Jan. 4, 1915
Emmet D. Boyle (D)	Jan. 4, 1915	Jan. 1, 1923
James G. Scrugham (D)	Jan. 1, 1923	Jan. 3, 1927
Frederick B. Balzar (R)[7]	Jan. 3, 1927	March 21, 1934
Morley I. Griswold (R)[8]	March 21, 1934	Jan. 7, 1935
Richard Kirman Sr. (D)	Jan. 7, 1935	Jan. 2, 1939
Edward P. Carville (D)[9]	Jan. 2, 1939	July 24, 1945
Vail M. Pittman (D)[10]	July 24, 1945	Jan. 1, 1951
Charles H. Russell (R)	Jan. 1, 1951	Jan. 5, 1959
Grant Sawyer (D)	Jan. 5, 1959	Jan. 2, 1967
Paul D. Laxalt (R)	Jan. 2, 1967	Jan. 4, 1971
Mike O'Callaghan (D)	Jan. 4, 1971	Jan. 1, 1979
Robert F. List (R)	Jan. 1, 1979	Jan. 3, 1983
Richard H. Bryan (D)[11]	Jan. 3, 1983	Jan. 3, 1989
Bob J. Miller (D)[12]	Jan. 3, 1989	Jan. 4, 1999
Kenny Guinn (R)	Jan. 4, 1999	

Nevada

1. Left office due to disability, Sept. 1, 1890. Died Sept. 21, 1890.
2. As lieutenant governor, he succeeded to office.

3. Died April 10, 1896.
4. As lieutenant governor, he succeeded to office. Subsequently elected.
5. Died May 22, 1908.
6. As lieutenant governor, he succeeded to office.
7. Died March 21, 1934.
8. As lieutenant governor, he succeeded to office.
9. Resigned July 24, 1945.
10. As lieutenant governor, he succeeded to office. Subsequently elected.
11. Resigned Jan. 3, 1989, having been elected to the U.S. Senate.
12. As lieutenant governor, he succeeded to office. Subsequently elected.

NEW HAMPSHIRE

(Ratified the Constitution June 21, 1788)

Governors	Dates of Service	
Meshesh Weare[1]	June 2, 1784	June 8, 1785
John Langdon	June 8, 1785	June 9, 1786
John Sullivan	June 9, 1786	June 5, 1788
John Langdon[2]	June 6, 1788	Jan. 22, 1789
John Pickering[3]	Jan. 22, 1789	June 6, 1789
John Sullivan (FED)	June 6, 1789	June 5, 1790
Josiah Bartlett (D-R)[4]	June 5, 1790	June 5, 1794
Joseph T. Gilman (FED)	June 5, 1794	June 6, 1805
John Langdon (D-R)	June 6, 1805	June 8, 1809
Jeremiah Smith (FED)	June 8, 1809	June 7, 1810
John Langdon (D-R)	June 7, 1810	June 5, 1812
William Plumer (D-R)	June 5, 1812	June 3, 1813
John T. Gilman (FED)	June 13, 1813	June 6, 1816
William Plumer (D-R)	June 6, 1816	June 3, 1819
Samuel Bell (D-R)	June 3, 1819	June 5, 1823
Levi Woodbury (D-R)	June 5, 1823	June 2, 1824
David L. Morrill (D-R)	June 3, 1824	June 7, 1827
Benjamin Pierce (D-R)	June 7, 1827	June 5, 1828
John Bell (NR)	June 5, 1828	June 4, 1829
Benjamin Pierce (JAC D)	June 4, 1829	June 3, 1830
Matthew Harvey (JAC D)[5]	June 3, 1830	Feb. 28, 1831
Joseph M. Harper (D)[6]	Feb. 28, 1831	June 2, 1831
Samuel Dinsmoor (JAC D)	June 2, 1831	June 5, 1834
William Badger (D)	June 5, 1834	June 2, 1836
Isaac Hill (D)	June 2, 1836	June 5, 1839
John Page (D)	June 5, 1839	June 2, 1842
Henry Hubbard (D)	June 2, 1842	June 6, 1844
John H. Steele (D)	June 6, 1844	June 4, 1846
Anthony Colby (W)	June 4, 1846	June 3, 1847
Jared W. Williams (D)	June 3, 1847	June 7, 1849
Samuel Dinsmoor Jr. (D)	June 7, 1849	June 3, 1852
Noah Martin (D)	June 3, 1852	June 8, 1854
Nathaniel B. Baker (D)	June 8, 1854	June 7, 1855
Ralph Metcalf (AM)	June 7, 1855	June 4, 1857
William Haile (R)	June 4, 1857	June 2, 1859
Ichabod Goodwin (R)	June 2, 1859	June 6, 1861
Nathaniel S. Berry (R)	June 6, 1861	June 3, 1863
Joseph A. Gilmore (R)	June 3, 1863	June 8, 1865
Frederick Smyth (UN)	June 8, 1865	June 6, 1867
Walter Harriman (R)	June 6, 1867	June 2, 1869
Onslow Stearns (R)	June 3, 1869	June 8, 1871
James A. Weston (D)	June 14, 1871	June 6, 1872
Ezekiel A. Straw (R)	June 6, 1872	June 3, 1874
James A. Weston (D)	June 3, 1874	June 10, 1875

Person C. Cheney (R)	June 10, 1875	June 6, 1877
Benjamin F. Prescott (R)	June 7, 1877	June 5, 1879
Natt Head (R)	June 5, 1879	June 2, 1881
Charles H. Bell (R)	June 2, 1881	June 7, 1883
Samuel W. Hale (R)	June 7, 1883	June 4, 1885
Moody Currier (R)	June 4, 1885	June 2, 1887
Charles H. Sawyer (R)	June 2, 1887	June 6, 1889
David H. Goodell (R)	June 6, 1889	Jan. 8, 1891
Hiram A. Tuttle (R)	Jan. 8, 1891	Jan. 5, 1893
John B. Smith (R)	Jan. 5, 1893	Jan. 3, 1895
Charles A. Busiel (R)	Jan. 3, 1895	Jan. 7, 1897
George A. Ramsdell (R)	Jan. 7, 1897	Jan. 5, 1899
Frank W. Rollins (R)	Jan. 5, 1899	Jan. 3, 1901
Chester B. Jordan (R)	Jan. 3, 1901	Jan. 1, 1903
Nahum J. Batchelder (R)	Jan. 1, 1903	Jan. 5, 1905
John McLane (R)	Jan. 5, 1905	Jan. 3, 1907
Charles M. Floyd (R)	Jan. 3, 1907	Jan. 7, 1909
Henry B. Quinby (R)	Jan. 7, 1909	Jan. 5, 1911
Robert P. Bass (R)	Jan. 5, 1911	Jan. 2, 1913
Samuel D. Felker (D)	Jan. 2, 1913	Jan. 7, 1915
Rolland H. Spaulding (R)	Jan. 7, 1915	Jan. 3, 1917
Henry Wilder Keyes (R)[7]	Jan. 3, 1917	Jan. 2, 1919
John H. Bartlett (R)	Jan. 2, 1919	Jan. 6, 1921
Albert O. Brown (R)	Jan. 6, 1921	Jan. 4, 1923
Fred H. Brown (D)	Jan. 4, 1923	Jan. 1, 1925
John G. Winant (R)	Jan. 1, 1925	Jan. 6, 1927
Huntley N. Spaulding (R)	Jan. 6, 1927	Jan. 3, 1929
Charles W. Tobey (R)	Jan. 3, 1929	Jan. 1, 1931
John G. Winant (R)	Jan. 1, 1931	Jan. 3, 1935
H. Styles Bridges (R)	Jan. 3, 1935	Jan. 7, 1937
Francis P. Murphy (R)	Jan. 7, 1937	Jan. 2, 1941
Robert O. Blood (R)	Jan. 2, 1941	Jan. 4, 1945
Charles M. Dale (R)	Jan. 4, 1945	Jan. 6, 1949
Sherman Adams (R)	Jan. 6, 1949	Jan. 1, 1953
Hugh Gregg (R)	Jan. 1, 1953	Jan. 6, 1955
Lane Dwinell (R)	Jan. 6, 1955	Jan. 1, 1959
Wesley Powell (R)	Jan. 1, 1959	Jan. 3, 1963
John W. King (D)	Jan. 3, 1963	Jan. 2, 1969
Walter Peterson (R)	Jan. 2, 1969	Jan. 4, 1973
Meldrim Thomson Jr. (R)	Jan. 4, 1973	Jan. 4, 1979
Hugh J. Gallen (D)[8]	Jan. 4, 1979	Nov. 11, 1982
Robert B. Monier (D)[9]	Nov. 11, 1982	Nov. 30, 1982
William M. Gardner (D)[10]	Nov. 30, 1982	Dec. 1, 1982
Vesta M. Roy (D)[11]	Dec. 1, 1982	Jan. 6, 1983
John H. Sununu (R)	Jan. 6, 1983	Jan. 4, 1989
Judd Gregg (R)	Jan. 4, 1989	Jan. 7, 1993
Steve Merrill (R)	Jan. 7, 1993	Jan. 9, 1997
Jeanne Shaheen (D)	Jan. 9, 1997	

New Hampshire
1. New Hampshire's first seven chief executives were called presidents.
2. Resigned Jan. 22, 1789.
3. Acting president of New Hampshire.
4. Josiah Bartlett was president of New Hampshire from 1790 to 1792 and governor from 1792 to 1794.
5. Resigned Feb. 28, 1831.
6. Acting governor in 1831.
7. Keyes was disqualified at the end of his term by illness, and Jesse M. Barton, president of the state Senate, became acting governor.
8. Hospitalized Nov. 20, 1982. Died Dec. 29, 1982.
9. As president of the state Senate, served as acting governor until the legislature dissolved on Nov. 30, 1982.
10. As secretary of state, served as acting governor until new members of the legislature were sworn in.
11. As new president of the state Senate, served as acting governor.

NEW JERSEY

(Ratified the Constitution Dec. 18, 1787)

Governors	Dates of Service	
William Livingston (FED)[1]	Aug. 27, 1776	July 25, 1790
Elisha Lawrence (FED)[2]	July 25, 1790	Oct. 30, 1790
William Paterson (FED)[3]	Oct. 30, 1790	March 4, 1793
Thomas Henderson (FED)	March 30, 1793	June 3, 1793
Richard Howell (FED)	June 3, 1793	Oct. 31, 1801
Joseph Bloomfield (D-R)	Oct. 31, 1801	Oct. 28, 1802
John Lambert (D-R)[4]	Nov. 15, 1802	Oct. 29, 1803
Joseph Bloomfield (D-R)	Oct. 29, 1803	Oct. 29, 1812
Aaron Ogden (FED)	Oct. 29, 1812	Oct. 29, 1813
William S. Pennington (D-R)[5]	Oct. 29, 1813	June 19, 1815
William Kennedy (D-R)[6]	June 19, 1815	Oct. 25, 1815
Mahlon Dickerson (D-R)[7]	Oct. 26, 1815	Feb. 1, 1817
Isaac H. Williamson (FED)	Feb. 6, 1817	Oct. 30, 1829
Peter D. Vroom (D)	Nov. 6, 1829	Oct. 26, 1832
Samuel L. Southard (W)	Oct. 26, 1832	Feb. 1833
Elias P. Seeley (W)	Feb. 27, 1833	Oct. 23, 1833
Peter D. Vroom (D)	Oct. 25, 1833	Oct. 28, 1836
Philemon Dickerson (D)	Nov. 3, 1836	Oct. 27, 1837
William Pennington (W)	Oct. 27, 1837	Oct. 27, 1843
Daniel Haines (D)	Oct. 27, 1843	Jan. 21, 1845
Charles C. Stratton (W)	Jan. 21, 1845	Jan. 18, 1848
Daniel Haines (D)	Jan. 18, 1848	Jan. 20, 1851
George F. Fort (D)	Jan. 21, 1851	Jan. 17, 1854
Rodman M. Price (D)	Jan. 17, 1854	Jan. 20, 1857
William A. Newell (FUS)	Jan. 20, 1857	Jan. 17, 1860
Charles S. Olden (R)	Jan. 17, 1860	Jan. 20, 1863
Joel Parker (D)	Jan. 20, 1863	Jan. 16, 1866
Marcus L. Ward (UN)	Jan. 16, 1866	Jan. 19, 1869
Theodore F. Randolph (D)	Jan. 19, 1869	Jan. 16, 1872
Joel Parker (D)	Jan. 16, 1872	Jan. 19, 1875
Joseph D. Bedle (D)	Jan. 19, 1875	Jan. 15, 1878
George B. McClellan (D)	Jan. 15, 1878	Jan. 18, 1881
George C. Ludlow (D)	Jan. 18, 1881	Jan. 15, 1884
Leon Abbett (D)	Jan. 15, 1884	Jan. 18, 1887
Robert S. Green (D)	Jan. 18, 1887	Jan. 21, 1890
Leon Abbett (D)	Jan. 21, 1890	Jan. 17, 1893
George T. Werts (D)	Jan. 17, 1893	Jan. 21, 1896
John W. Griggs (R)[8]	Jan. 21, 1896	Jan. 31, 1898
Foster M. Voorhees (R)[9]	Feb. 1, 1898	Oct. 18, 1898
David O. Watkins (R)[10]	Oct. 18, 1898	Jan. 17, 1899
Foster M. Voorhees (R)	Jan. 17, 1899	Jan. 21, 1902
Franklin Murphy (R)	Jan. 21, 1902	Jan. 17, 1905
Edward C. Stokes (R)	Jan. 17, 1905	Jan. 21, 1908
John F. Fort (R)	Jan. 21, 1908	Jan. 17, 1911
Woodrow Wilson (D)[11]	Jan. 17, 1911	March 1, 1913
James F. Fielder (D)[12]	March 1, 1913	Oct. 28, 1913
Leon R. Taylor (D)[13]	Oct. 28, 1913	Jan. 20, 1914
James F. Fielder (D)	Jan. 20, 1914	Jan. 15, 1917
Walter E. Edge (R)[14]	Jan. 15, 1917	May 16, 1919

William N. Runyon (R)[15]	May 16, 1919	Jan. 13, 1920
Clarence E. Case (R)[16]	Jan. 13, 1920	Jan. 20, 1920
Edward I. Edwards (D)	Jan. 20, 1920	Jan. 15, 1923
George S. Silzer (D)	Jan. 15, 1923	Jan. 19, 1926
Arthur Harry Moore (D)	Jan. 19, 1926	Jan. 15, 1929
Morgan F. Larson (R)	Jan. 15, 1929	Jan. 19, 1932
Arthur Harry Moore (D)[17]	Jan. 19, 1932	Jan. 3, 1935
Clifford R. Powell (R)[18]	Jan. 3, 1935	Jan. 8, 1935
Horace G. Prall (R)[19]	Jan. 8, 1935	Jan. 15, 1935
Harold G. Hoffman (R)	Jan. 15, 1935	Jan. 18, 1938
Arthur Harry Moore (D)	Jan. 18, 1938	Jan. 21, 1941
Charles Edison (D)	Jan. 21, 1941	Jan. 18, 1944
Walter E. Edge (R)	Jan. 18, 1944	Jan. 21, 1947
Alfred E. Driscoll (R)	Jan. 21, 1947	Jan. 19, 1954
Robert B. Meyner (D)	Jan. 19, 1954	Jan. 16, 1962
Richard J. Hughes (D)	Jan. 16, 1962	Jan. 20, 1970
William T. Cahill (R)	Jan. 20, 1970	Jan. 15, 1974
Brendan T. Byrne (D)	Jan. 15, 1974	Jan. 19, 1982
Thomas H. Kean (R)	Jan. 19, 1982	Jan. 16, 1990
James J. Florio (D)	Jan. 16, 1990	Jan. 18, 1994
Christine Todd Whitman (R)[20]	Jan. 18, 1994	Jan. 31, 2001
Donald T. DiFrancesco (R)[21]	Jan. 31, 2001	

New Jersey
1. Died in office.
2. As vice president of the Legislative Council, he succeeded to office.
3. Resigned March 4, 1793.
4. Acting governor.
5. Resigned June 19, 1815.
6. As vice president of the Legislative Council, he succeeded to office.
7. Resigned Feb. 1, 1817.
8. Resigned Jan. 31, 1898.
9. Acting governor.
10. Acting governor.
11. Resigned March 1, 1913, having been elected president of the United States.
12. As president of the state Senate, he succeeded to office. Resigned Oct. 28, 1913.
13. Acting governor.
14. Resigned May 16, 1919.
15. As president of the state Senate, he succeeded to office. Service ended Jan. 13, 1920.
16. Acting governor.
17. Resigned Jan. 3, 1935.
18. As president of the state Senate, he succeeded to office. Service ended Jan. 8, 1935.
19. Acting governor.
20. Resigned Jan. 31, 2001.
21. As president of the state Senate, he succeeded to office.

NEW MEXICO

(Became a state Jan. 6, 1912)

Governors	Dates of Service	
William C. McDonald (D)	Jan. 6, 1912	Jan. 1, 1917
Ezequiel C. de Baca (D)[1]	Jan. 1, 1917	Feb. 18, 1917
Washington E. Lindsey (R)[2]	Feb. 19, 1917	Jan. 1, 1919
Octaviano A. Larrazolo (R)	Jan. 1, 1919	Jan. 1, 1921
Merritt C. Mechem (R)	Jan. 1, 1921	Jan. 1, 1923
James F. Hinkle (D)	Jan. 1, 1923	Jan. 1, 1925
Arthur T. Hannett (D)	Jan. 1, 1925	Jan. 1, 1927
Richard C. Dillon (R)	Jan. 1, 1927	Jan. 1, 1931

Arthur Seligman (D)[3]	Jan. 1, 1931	Sept. 25, 1933
Andrew W. Hockenhull (D)[4]	Sept. 25, 1933	Jan. 1, 1935
Clyde Tingley (D)	Jan. 1, 1935	Jan. 1, 1939
John E. Miles (D)	Jan. 1, 1939	Jan. 1, 1943
John J. Dempsey (D)	Jan. 1, 1943	Jan. 1, 1947
Thomas J. Mabry (D)	Jan. 1, 1947	Jan. 1, 1951
Edwin L. Mechem (R)	Jan. 1, 1951	Jan. 1, 1955
John F. Simms (D)	Jan. 1, 1955	Jan. 1, 1957
Edwin L. Mechem (R)	Jan. 1, 1957	Jan. 1, 1959
John Burroughs (D)	Jan. 1, 1959	Jan. 1, 1961
Edwin L. Mechem (R)[5]	Jan. 1, 1961	Nov. 30, 1962
Tom Bolack (R)[6]	Nov. 30, 1962	Jan. 1, 1963
Jack M. Campbell (D)	Jan. 1, 1963	Jan. 1, 1967
David F. Cargo (R)	Jan. 1, 1967	Jan. 1, 1971
Bruce King (D)	Jan. 1, 1971	Jan. 1, 1975
Jerry Apodaca (D)	Jan. 1, 1975	Jan. 1, 1979
Bruce King (D)	Jan. 1, 1979	Jan. 1, 1983
Toney Anaya (D)	Jan. 1, 1983	Jan. 1, 1987
Garrey E. Carruthers (R)	Jan. 1, 1987	Jan. 1, 1991
Bruce King (D)	Jan. 1, 1991	Jan. 1, 1995
Gary E. Johnson (R)	Jan. 1, 1995	

New Mexico
1. Died Feb. 18, 1917.
2. As lieutenant governor, he succeeded to office.
3. Died Sept. 25, 1933.
4. As lieutenant governor, he succeeded to office.
5. Resigned Nov. 30, 1962.
6. As lieutenant governor, he succeeded to office.

NEW YORK

(Ratified the Constitution July 26, 1788)

Governors	Dates of Service	
George Clinton (D-R)	July 30, 1777	June 30, 1795
John Jay (FED)	July 1, 1795	July 1, 1801
George Clinton (D-R)	July 1, 1801	July 1, 1804
Morgan Lewis (D-R)	July 1, 1804	July 1, 1807
Daniel D. Tompkins (D-R)[1]	July 1, 1807	Feb. 24, 1817
John Tayler (D-R)[2]	Feb. 24, 1817	July 1, 1817
De Witt Clinton (D-R)	July 1, 1817	Jan. 1, 1823
Joseph C. Yates (D-R)	Jan. 1, 1823	Jan. 1, 1825
De Witt Clinton (CLINT R)[3]	Jan. 1, 1825	Feb. 11, 1828
Nathaniel Pitcher (D-R)[4]	Feb. 11, 1828	Jan. 1, 1829
Martin Van Buren (JAC D)[5]	Jan. 1, 1829	March 12, 1829
Enos T. Throop (JAC D)[6]	March 12, 1829	Jan. 1, 1833
William L. Marcy (D)	Jan. 1, 1833	Jan. 1, 1839
William H. Seward (W)	Jan. 1, 1839	Jan. 1, 1843
William C. Bouck (D)	Jan. 1, 1843	Jan. 1, 1845
Silas Wright (D)	Jan. 1, 1845	Jan. 1, 1847
John Young (W)	Jan. 1, 1847	Jan. 1, 1849
Hamilton Fish (W)	Jan. 1, 1849	Jan. 1, 1851
Washington Hunt (W-A-RENT)	Jan. 1, 1851	Jan. 1, 1853
Horatio Seymour (D)	Jan. 1, 1853	Jan. 1, 1855
Myron H. Clark (FUS R)	Jan. 1, 1855	Jan. 1, 1857
John A. King (R)	Jan. 1, 1857	Jan. 1, 1859
Edwin D. Morgan (R)	Jan. 1, 1859	Jan. 1, 1863

CH. 29 GOVERNORS OF THE STATES 1403

Horatio Seymour (D)	Jan. 1, 1863	Jan. 1, 1865	Thomas Burke	June 26, 1781	April 26, 1782
Reuben E. Fenton (UN)	Jan. 1, 1865	Jan. 1, 1869	Alexander Martin	April 26, 1782	April 1, 1785
John T. Hoffman (D)	Jan. 1, 1869	Jan. 1, 1873	Richard Caswell	April 1, 1785	Dec. 20, 1787
John A. Dix (R)	Jan. 1, 1873	Jan. 1, 1875	Samuel Johnston (FED)	Dec. 20, 1787	Dec. 17, 1789
Samuel J. Tilden (D)	Jan. 1, 1875	Jan. 1, 1877	Alexander Martin (FED)	Dec. 17, 1789	Dec. 14, 1792
Lucius Robinson (D)[7]	Jan. 1, 1877	Jan. 1, 1880	Richard D. Spaight (D-R)	Dec. 14, 1792	Nov. 19, 1795
Alonzo B. Cornell (R)	Jan. 1, 1880	Jan. 1, 1883	Samuel Ashe (D-R)	Nov. 19, 1795	Dec. 7, 1798
Grover Cleveland (D)[8]	Jan. 1, 1883	Jan. 6, 1885	William R. Davie (FED)	Dec. 7, 1798	Nov. 23, 1799
David B. Hill (D)[9]	Jan. 6, 1885	Jan. 1, 1892	Benjamin Williams (D-R)	Nov. 23, 1799	Dec. 6, 1802
Roswell P. Flower (D)	Jan. 1, 1892	Jan. 1, 1895	James Turner (D-R)	Dec. 6, 1802	Dec. 10, 1805
Levi P. Morton (R)[10]	Jan. 1, 1895	Jan. 1, 1897	Nathaniel Alexander (D-R)	Dec. 10, 1805	Dec. 1, 1807
Frank S. Black (R)	Jan. 1, 1897	Jan. 1, 1899	Benjamin Wiliams (D-R)	Dec. 1, 1807	Dec. 12, 1808
Theodore Roosevelt (R)	Jan. 1, 1899	Jan. 1, 1901	David Stone (D-R)	Dec. 12, 1808	Dec. 5, 1810
Benjamin B. Odell Jr. (R)	Jan. 1, 1901	Jan. 1, 1905	Benjamin Smith (D-R)	Dec. 5, 1810	Dec. 9, 1811
Frank W. Higgins (R)	Jan. 1, 1905	Jan. 1, 1907	William Hawkins (D-R)	Dec. 9, 1811	Nov. 29, 1814
Charles Evans Hughes (R)[11]	Jan. 1, 1907	Oct. 6, 1910	William Miller (D-R)	Dec. 7, 1814	Dec. 3, 1817
Horace White (R)[12]	Oct. 6, 1910	Jan. 1, 1911	John Branch (D-R)	Dec. 6, 1817	Dec. 7, 1820
John A. Dix (D)	Jan. 1, 1911	Jan. 1, 1913	Jesse Franklin (D-R)	Dec. 7, 1820	Dec. 7, 1821
William Sulzer (D)[13]	Jan. 1, 1913	Oct. 17, 1913	Gabriel Holmes (D-R)	Dec. 7, 1821	Dec. 7, 1824
Martin H. Glynn (D)[14]	Oct. 17, 1913	Jan. 1, 1915	Hutchins G. Burton (D-R)	Dec. 7, 1824	Dec. 8, 1827
Charles S. Whitman (R)	Jan. 1, 1915	Jan. 1, 1919	James Iredell (D-R)	Dec. 8, 1827	Dec. 12, 1828
Alfred E. Smith (D)	Jan. 1, 1919	Jan. 1, 1921	John Owen (D)	Dec. 12, 1828	Dec. 18, 1830
Nathan L. Miller (R)	Jan. 1, 1921	Jan. 1, 1923	Montfort Stokes (D)	Dec. 18, 1830	Dec. 6, 1832
Alfred E. Smith (D)	Jan. 1, 1923	Jan. 1, 1929	David L. Swain (D)	Dec. 6, 1832	Dec. 10, 1835
Franklin D. Roosevelt (D)	Jan. 1, 1929	Jan. 1, 1933	Richard D. Spaight Jr. (D)	Dec. 10, 1835	Dec. 31, 1836
Herbert H. Lehman (D)[15]	Jan. 1, 1933	Dec. 3, 1942	Edward B. Dudley (W)	Dec. 31, 1836	Jan. 1, 1841
Charles Poletti (D)[16]	Dec. 3, 1942	Jan. 1, 1943	John M. Morehead (W)	Jan. 1, 1841	Jan. 1, 1845
Thomas E. Dewey (R)	Jan. 1, 1943	Jan. 1, 1955	William A. Graham (W)	Jan. 1, 1845	Jan. 1, 1849
W. Averell Harriman (D)	Jan. 1, 1955	Jan. 1, 1959	Charles Manly (W)	Jan. 1, 1849	Jan. 1, 1851
Nelson A. Rockefeller (R)[17]	Jan. 1, 1959	Dec. 18, 1973	David S. Reid (D)[1]	Jan. 1, 1851	Dec. 6, 1854
Malcolm Wilson (R)[18]	Dec. 18, 1973	Jan. 1, 1975	Warren Winslow (D)[2]	Dec. 6, 1854	Jan. 1, 1855
Hugh Carey (D)	Jan. 1, 1975	Jan. 1, 1983	Thomas Bragg (D)	Jan. 1, 1855	Jan. 1, 1859
Mario M. Cuomo (D)	Jan. 1, 1983	Jan. 1, 1995	John W. Ellis (D)[3]	Jan. 1, 1859	July 7, 1861
George E. Pataki (R)	Jan. 1, 1995		Henry T. Clark (D)[4]	July 7, 1861	Sept. 8, 1862
			Zebulon B. Vance (C)[5]	Sept. 8, 1862	May 29, 1865

New York

1. Resigned Feb. 24, 1817, having been elected vice president of the United States.
2. As lieutenant governor, he succeeded to office.
3. Died Feb. 11, 1828.
4. As lieutenant governor, he succeeded to office.
5. Resigned March 12, 1829.
6. As lieutenant governor, he succeeded to office. Subsequently elected.
7. Term of office changed from two years to three years.
8. Resigned Jan. 6, 1885, having been elected president of the United States.
9. As lieutenant governor, he succeeded to office. Subsequently elected.
10. Term of office changed from three years to two years.
11. Resigned Oct. 6, 1910.
12. As lieutenant governor, he succeeded to office.
13. Impeached; removed from office Oct. 17, 1913.
14. As lieutenant governor, he succeeded to office.
15. First governor elected to a four-year term (in 1938). Resigned Dec. 3, 1942.
16. As lieutenant governor, he succeeded to office.
17. Resigned Dec. 18, 1973.
18. As lieutenant governor, he succeeded to office.

NORTH CAROLINA

(Ratified the Constitution Nov. 21, 1789)

Governors	Dates of Service	
Richard Caswell	Dec. 19, 1776	April 1780
Abner Nash	April 1780	June 26, 1781

William W. Holden[6]	May 29, 1865	Dec. 15, 1865
Jonathan Worth (C)[7]	Dec. 15, 1865	July 1, 1868
William W. Holden (R)[8]	July 1, 1868	Dec. 15, 1870
Tod R. Caldwell (R)[9]	Dec. 15, 1870	July 11, 1874
Curtis H. Brogden (R)[10]	July 11, 1874	Jan. 1, 1877
Zebulon B. Vance (D)[11]	Jan. 1, 1877	Feb. 5, 1879
Thomas J. Jarvis (D)[12]	Feb. 5, 1879	Jan. 21, 1885
Alfred M. Scales (D)	Jan. 21, 1885	Jan. 17, 1889
Daniel G. Fowle (D)[13]	Jan. 17, 1889	April 8, 1891
Thomas M. Holt (D)[14]	April 8, 1891	Jan. 18, 1893
Elias Carr (D)	Jan. 18, 1893	Jan. 12, 1897
Daniel L. Russell (D)	Jan. 12, 1897	Jan. 15, 1901
Charles B. Aycock (D)	Jan. 15, 1901	Jan. 11, 1905
Robert B. Glenn (D)	Jan. 11, 1905	Jan. 12, 1909
William W. Kitchin (D)	Jan. 12, 1909	Jan. 15, 1913
Locke Craig (D)	Jan. 15, 1913	Jan. 11, 1917
Thomas W. Bickett (D)	Jan. 11, 1917	Jan. 12, 1921
Carmeron Morrison (D)	Jan. 12, 1921	Jan. 14, 1925
Angus Wilton McLean (D)	Jan. 14, 1925	Jan. 11, 1929
O. Max Gardner (D)	Jan. 11, 1929	Jan. 5, 1933
John C. B. Ehringhaus (D)	Jan. 5, 1933	Jan. 7, 1937
Clyde R. Hoey (D)	Jan. 7, 1937	Jan. 9, 1941
J. Melville Broughton (D)	Jan. 9, 1941	Jan. 4, 1945
R. Gregg Cherry (D)	Jan. 4, 1945	Jan. 6, 1949
W. Kerr Scott (D)	Jan. 6, 1949	Jan. 8, 1953

William B. Umstead (D)[15]	Jan. 8, 1953	Nov. 7, 1954
Luther H. Hodges (D)[16]	Nov. 7, 1954	Jan. 5, 1961
Terry Sanford (D)	Jan. 5, 1961	Jan. 8, 1965
Dan K. Moore (D)	Jan. 8, 1965	Jan. 3, 1969
Robert W. Scott (D)	Jan. 3, 1969	Jan. 5, 1973
James E. Holshouser Jr. (R)	Jan. 5, 1973	Jan. 8, 1977
James B. Hunt Jr. (D)	Jan. 8, 1977	Jan. 5, 1985
James G. Martin (R)	Jan. 5, 1985	Jan. 9, 1993
James B. Hunt Jr. (D)	Jan. 9, 1993	Jan. 6, 2001
Michael F. Easley (D)	Jan. 6, 2001	

North Carolina
1. Resigned Dec. 6, 1854.
2. Acting governor.
3. Died July 7, 1861.
4. Acting governor.
5. Removed from office. Last Confederate governor.
6. Provisional governor appointed by President Johnson.
7. Removed July 1, 1868.
8. Impeached. Removed from office Dec. 15, 1870.
9. As lieutenant governor, he succeeded to office. Subsequently elected. Died July 11, 1874.
10. As lieutenant governor, he succeeded to office.
11. Resigned Feb. 5, 1879.
12. As lieutenant governor, he succeeded to office. Subsequently elected.
13. Died April 8, 1891.
14. As lieutenant governor, he succeeded to office.
15. Died Nov. 7, 1954.
16. As lieutenant governor, he succeeded to office. Subsequently elected.

NORTH DAKOTA

(Became a state Nov. 2, 1889)

Governors	Dates of Service	
John Miller (R)	Nov. 4, 1889	Jan. 6, 1891
Andrew H. Burke (R)	Jan. 7, 1891	Jan. 4, 1893
Eli C. D. Shortridge (FUS)	Jan. 4, 1893	Jan. 7, 1895
Roger Allin (R)	Jan. 7, 1895	Jan. 5, 1897
Frank A. Briggs (R)[1]	Jan. 5, 1897	Aug. 9, 1898
Joseph M. Devine (R)[2]	Aug. 9, 1898	Jan. 3, 1899
Frederick B. Fancher (R)	Jan. 3, 1899	Jan. 10, 1901
Frank White (R)	Jan. 10, 1901	Jan. 4, 1905
Elmore Y. Sarles (R)	Jan. 5, 1905	Jan. 9, 1907
John Burke (D)	Jan. 9, 1907	Jan. 8, 1913
Louis B. Hanna (R)	Jan. 8, 1913	Jan. 3, 1917
Lynn J. Frazier (R)[3]	Jan. 3, 1917	Nov. 23, 1921
Ragnvald A. Nestos (R)[4]	Nov. 23, 1921	Jan. 5, 1925
Arthur G. Sorlie (R)[5]	Jan. 7, 1925	Aug. 28, 1928
Walter J. Maddock (R)[6]	Aug. 28, 1928	Jan. 9, 1929
George F. Shafer (R)	Jan. 9, 1929	Dec. 31, 1932
William Langer (R)[7]	Dec. 31, 1932	July 17, 1934
Ole H. Olson (R)[8]	July 17, 1934	Jan. 7, 1935
Thomas H. Moodie (D)[9]	Jan. 7, 1935	Feb. 2, 1935
Walter Welford (R)[10]	Feb. 2, 1935	Jan. 6, 1937
William Langer (I)	Jan. 6, 1937	Jan. 5, 1939
John Moses (D)	Jan. 5, 1939	Jan. 4, 1945
Fred G. Aandahl (R)	Jan. 4, 1945	Jan. 3, 1951
C. Norman Brunsdale (R)	Jan. 3, 1951	Jan. 9, 1957
John E. Davis (R)	Jan. 9, 1957	Jan. 4, 1961
William L. Guy (D)	Jan. 4, 1961	Jan. 2, 1973
Arthur A. Link (D)	Jan. 2, 1973	Jan. 7, 1981
Allen I. Olson (R)[11]	Jan. 7, 1981	Jan. 8, 1985
George Sinner (D)[11]	Jan. 8, 1985	Jan. 5, 1993
Edward T. Schafer (R)	Jan. 5, 1993	Dec. 15, 2000
John Hoeven (R)	Dec. 15, 2000	

North Dakota
1. Died in 1898.
2. As lieutenant governor, he succeeded to office.
3. Recalled in election of Oct. 28, 1921; removed Nov. 23, 1921.
4. Elected in recall election of 1921, which removed Governor Frazier. Subsequently elected for a full two-year term.
5. Died Aug. 28, 1928.
6. As lieutenant governor, he succeeded to office.
7. Removed by North Dakota Supreme Court July 17, 1934.
8. As lieutenant governor, he succeeded to office.
9. Disqualified by North Dakota Supreme Court Feb. 2, 1935.
10. As lieutenant governor, he succeeded to office.
11. Although Olson relinquished his office on Jan. 5 and Sinner assumed it Jan. 8, the North Dakota Supreme Court held that Sinner's term began Jan. 1.

OHIO

(Became a state March 1, 1803)

Governors	Dates of Service	
Edward Tiffin (D-R)[1]	March 3, 1803	March 4, 1807
Thomas Kirker (D-R)[2]	March 4, 1807	Dec. 12, 1808
Samuel Huntington (D-R)	Dec. 12, 1808	Dec. 8, 1810
Return Jonathan Meigs (D-R)[3]	Dec. 8, 1810	March 24, 1814
Othneil Looker (D-R)[4]	March 24, 1814	Dec. 8, 1814
Thomas Worthington (D-R)	Dec. 8, 1814	Dec. 14, 1818
Ethan Allen Brown (D-R)[5]	Dec. 14, 1818	Jan. 4, 1822
Allen Trimble (D-R)[6]	Jan. 4, 1822	Dec. 28, 1822
Jeremiah Morrow (JAC D)	Dec. 28, 1822	Dec. 19, 1826
Allen Trimble (NR)	Dec. 19, 1826	Dec. 18, 1830
Duncan McArthur (NR)	Dec. 18, 1830	Dec. 7, 1832
Robert Lucas (D)	Dec. 7, 1832	Dec. 12, 1836
Joseph Vance (W)	Dec. 12, 1836	Dec. 13, 1838
Wilson Shannon (D)	Dec. 13, 1838	Dec. 16, 1840
Thomas Corwin (W)	Dec. 16, 1840	Dec. 14, 1842
Wilson Shannon (D)[7]	Dec. 14, 1842	April 15, 1844
Thomas W. Bartley (D)[8]	April 15, 1844	Dec. 3, 1844
Mordecai Bartley (W)	Dec. 3, 1844	Dec. 12, 1846
William Bebb (W)	Dec. 12, 1846	Jan. 22, 1849
Seabury Ford (W)[9]	Jan. 22, 1849	Dec. 12, 1850
Reuben Wood (D)[10]	Dec. 12, 1850	July 13, 1853
William Medill (D)[11]	July 13, 1853	Jan. 14, 1856
Salmon P. Chase (R)	Jan. 14, 1856	Jan. 9, 1860
William Dennison Jr. (R)	Jan. 9, 1860	Jan. 13, 1862
David Tod (UN)	Jan. 13, 1862	Jan. 11, 1864
John Brough (UN)[12]	Jan. 11, 1864	Aug. 29, 1865
Charles Anderson (UN)[13]	Aug. 29, 1865	Jan. 8, 1866
Jacob D. Cox (UN)	Jan. 8, 1866	Jan. 13, 1868
Rutherford B. Hayes (R)	Jan. 13, 1868	Jan. 8, 1872
Edward F. Noyes (R)	Jan. 8, 1872	Jan. 12, 1874
William Allen (D)	Jan. 12, 1874	Jan. 10, 1876
Rutherford B. Hayes (R)[14]	Jan. 10, 1876	March 2, 1877
Thomas L. Young (R)[15]	March 2, 1877	Jan. 14, 1878
Richard M. Bishop (D)	Jan. 14, 1878	Jan. 12, 1880
Charles Foster (R)	Jan. 12, 1880	Jan. 14, 1884

George Hoadly (D)	Jan. 14, 1884	Jan. 11, 1886		Robert L. Williams (D)	Jan. 11, 1915	Jan. 13, 1919
Joseph B. Foraker (R)	Jan. 11, 1886	Jan. 13, 1890		James B. A. Robertson (D)	Jan. 13, 1919	Jan. 8, 1923
James E. Campbell (D)	Jan. 13, 1890	Jan. 11, 1892		John C. Walton (D)[1]	Jan. 8, 1923	Nov. 19, 1923
William McKinley Jr. (R)	Jan. 11, 1892	Jan. 13, 1896		Martin E. Trapp (D)[2]	Nov. 19, 1923	Jan. 10, 1927
Asa S. Bushnell (R)	Jan. 13, 1896	Jan. 8, 1900		Henry S. Johnston (D)[3]	Jan. 10, 1927	March 20, 1929
George K. Nash (R)	Jan. 8, 1900	Jan. 11, 1904		William J. Holloway (D)[4]	March 20, 1929	Jan. 12, 1931
Myron T. Herrick (R)	Jan. 11, 1904	Jan. 8, 1906		William H. Murray (D)	Jan. 12, 1931	Jan. 14, 1935
John M. Pattison (D)[16]	Jan. 8, 1906	June 18, 1906		Ernest W. Marland (D)	Jan. 14, 1935	Jan. 9, 1939
Andrew L. Harris (R)[17]	June 18, 1906	Jan. 11, 1909		Leon C. Phillips (D)	Jan. 9, 1939	Jan. 11, 1943
Judson Harmon (D)	Jan. 11, 1909	Jan. 13, 1913		Robert S. Kerr (D)	Jan. 11, 1943	Jan. 13, 1947
James M. Cox (D)	Jan. 13, 1913	Jan. 11, 1915		Roy J. Turner (D)	Jan. 13, 1947	Jan. 8, 1951
Frank B. Willis (R)	Jan. 11, 1915	Jan. 8, 1917		Johnston Murray (D)	Jan. 8, 1951	Jan. 10, 1955
James M. Cox (D)	Jan. 8, 1917	Jan. 10, 1921		Raymond D. Gary (D)	Jan. 10, 1955	Jan. 12, 1959
Harry L. Davis (R)	Jan. 10, 1921	Jan. 8, 1923		J. Howard Edmondson (D)[5]	Jan. 12, 1959	Jan. 6, 1963
Alvin Victor Donahey (D)	Jan. 8, 1923	Jan. 14, 1929		George P. Nigh (D)[6]	Jan. 6, 1963	Jan. 14, 1963
Myers Y. Cooper (R)	Jan. 14, 1929	Jan. 12, 1931		Henry L. Bellmon (R)	Jan. 14, 1963	Jan. 9, 1967
George White (D)	Jan. 12, 1931	Jan. 14, 1935		Dewey F. Bartlett (R)	Jan. 9, 1967	Jan. 11, 1971
Martin L. Davey (D)	Jan. 14, 1935	Jan. 9, 1939		David Hall (D)	Jan. 11, 1971	Jan. 13, 1975
John W. Bricker (R)	Jan. 9, 1939	Jan. 8, 1945		David L. Boren (D)	Jan. 13, 1975	Jan. 3, 1979
Frank J. Lausche (D)	Jan. 8, 1945	Jan. 13, 1947		George Nigh (D)	Jan. 3, 1979	Jan. 12, 1987
Thomas J. Herbert (R)	Jan. 13, 1947	Jan. 10, 1949		Henry L. Bellmon (R)	Jan. 12, 1987	Jan. 14, 1991
Frank J. Lausche (D)[18]	Jan. 10, 1949	Jan. 3, 1957		David Walters (D)	Jan. 14, 1991	Jan. 9, 1995
John W. Brown (R)[19]	Jan. 3, 1957	Jan. 14, 1957		Frank Keating (R)	Jan. 9, 1995	
C. William O'Neill (R)	Jan. 14, 1957	Jan. 12, 1959				
Michael V. DiSalle (D)	Jan. 12, 1959	Jan. 14, 1963				
James A. Rhodes (R)	Jan. 14, 1963	Jan. 11, 1971				
John J. Gilligan (D)	Jan. 11, 1971	Jan. 13, 1975				
James A. Rhodes (R)	Jan. 13, 1975	Jan. 10, 1983				
Richard F. Celeste (D)	Jan. 10, 1983	Jan. 14, 1991				
George V. Voinovich (R)[20]	Jan. 14, 1991	Dec. 31, 1998				
Nancy Hollister (R)[21]	Dec. 31, 1998	Jan. 11, 1999				
Robert A. Taft II (R)	Jan. 11, 1999					

Oklahoma

1. Impeached; removed from office, Nov. 19, 1923.
2. As lieutenant governor, he succeeded to office.
3. Impeached; removed from office, March 20, 1929.
4. As lieutenant governor, he succeeded to office.
5. Resigned Jan. 6, 1963.
6. As lieutenant governor, he succeeded to office.

Ohio

1. Resigned March 4, 1807.
2. As Speaker of the state Senate, he succeeded to office.
3. Resigned March 24, 1814.
4. As Speaker of the state Senate, he succeeded to office.
5. Resigned Jan. 4, 1822.
6. As Speaker of the state Senate, he succeeded to office.
7. Resigned April 15, 1844.
8. As Speaker of the state Senate, he succeeded to office.
9. The election of 1848 was disputed, and Ford's election was delayed until Jan. 22, 1849.
10. Resigned July 13, 1853.
11. As lieutenant governor, he succeeded to office. Subsequently elected.
12. Died Aug. 29, 1865.
13. As lieutenant governor, he succeeded to office.
14. Resigned March 2, 1877, having been elected president of the United States.
15. As lieutenant governor, he succeeded to office.
16. Died June 18, 1906.
17. As lieutenant governor, he succeeded to office.
18. Resigned Jan. 3, 1957.
19. As lieutenant governor, he succeeded to office.
20. Resigned Dec. 31, 1998, having been elected to the U.S. Senate.
21. As lieutenant governor, she succeeded to office.

OKLAHOMA

(Became a state Nov. 16, 1907)

Governors	Dates of Service	
Charles N. Haskell (D)	Nov. 16, 1907	Jan. 9, 1911
Lee Cruce (D)	Jan. 9, 1911	Jan. 11, 1915

OREGON

(Became a state Feb. 14, 1859)

Governors	Dates of Service	
John Whiteaker (D)	March 3, 1859	Sept. 10, 1862
Addison C. Gibbs (UN R)	Sept. 10, 1862	Sept. 12, 1866
George L. Woods (R)	Sept. 12, 1866	Sept. 14, 1870
La Fayette Grover (D)[1]	Sept. 14, 1870	Feb. 1, 1877
Stephen F. Chadwick (D)[2]	Feb. 1, 1877	Sept. 11, 1878
William Wallace Thayer (D)	Sept. 11, 1878	Sept. 13, 1882
Zenas F. Moody (R)	Sept. 13, 1882	Jan. 12, 1887
Sylvester Pennoyer (D)	Jan. 12, 1887	Jan. 14, 1895
William P. Lord (R)	Jan. 14, 1895	Jan. 9, 1899
Theodore T. Geer (R)	Jan. 9, 1899	Jan. 14, 1903
George E. Chamberlain (D)[3]	Jan. 15, 1903	March 1, 1909
Frank W. Benson (R)[4]	March 1, 1909	June 16, 1910
Jay Bowerman (R)[5]	June 16, 1910	Jan. 8, 1911
Oswald West (D)	Jan. 11, 1911	Jan. 12, 1915
James Withycombe (R)[6]	Jan. 12, 1915	March 3, 1919
Ben W. Olcott (R)[7]	March 3, 1919	Jan. 8, 1923
Walter M. Pierce (D)	Jan. 8, 1923	Jan. 10, 1927
Isaac L. Patterson (R)[8]	Jan. 10, 1927	Dec. 21, 1929
A. W. Norblad (R)[9]	Dec. 22, 1929	Jan. 12, 1931
Julius L. Meier (I)	Jan. 12, 1931	Jan. 14, 1935
Charles H. Martin (D)	Jan. 14, 1935	Jan. 9, 1939
Charles A. Sprague (R)	Jan. 9, 1939	Jan. 11, 1943
Earl Snell (R)[10]	Jan. 11, 1943	Oct. 28, 1947
John H. Hall (R)[11]	Oct. 30, 1947	Jan. 10, 1949

Douglas McKay (R)[12]	Jan. 10, 1949	Dec. 27, 1952
Paul L. Patterson (R)[13]	Dec. 27, 1952	Jan. 31, 1956
Elmo Smith (R)[14]	Feb. 1, 1956	Jan. 14, 1957
Robert D. Holmes (D)[15]	Jan. 14, 1957	Jan. 12, 1959
Mark O. Hatfield (R)	Jan. 12, 1959	Jan. 9, 1967
Tom McCall (R)	Jan. 9, 1967	Jan. 13, 1975
Robert W. Straub (D)	Jan. 13, 1975	Jan. 8, 1979
Victor Atiyeh (R)	Jan. 8, 1979	Jan. 12, 1987
Neil Goldschmidt (D)	Jan. 12, 1987	Jan. 14, 1991
Barbara Roberts (D)	Jan. 14, 1991	Jan. 9, 1995
John Kitzhaber (D)	Jan. 9, 1995	

Oregon
1. Resigned Feb. 1, 1877.
2. As secretary of state, he succeeded to office.
3. Resigned March 1, 1909.
4. As secretary of state, he succeeded to office. Resigned June 17, 1910.
5. As president of the state Senate, he succeeded to office.
6. Died March 3, 1919.
7. As secretary of state, he succeeded to office.
8. Died Dec. 21, 1929.
9. As president of the state Senate, he succeeded to office.
10. Died Oct. 28, 1947.
11. As speaker of the House, he succeeded to office for the remainder of the first two years of Snell's term.
12. Elected for the last two years of Snell's term in a special election. Subsequently reelected. Resigned Dec. 27, 1952.
13. As president of the state senate, he succeeded to office. Subsequently elected. Died Jan. 31, 1956.
14. As president of the state Senate, he succeeded to office for the remainder of the first two years of Patterson's term.
15. Elected in a special election for the last two years of Patterson's term.

PENNSYLVANIA

(Ratified the Constitution Dec. 12, 1787)

Governors	Dates of Service	
Thomas Wharton Jr.[1]	March 5, 1777	May 23, 1778
George Bryan	May 23, 1778	Dec. 22, 1778
Joseph Reed	Dec. 22, 1778	Nov. 15, 1781
William Moore	Nov. 15, 1781	Nov. 7, 1782
John Dickinson	Nov. 7, 1782	Oct. 18, 1785
Benjamin Franklin	Oct. 18, 1785	Nov. 5, 1788
Thomas Mifflin[2]	Nov. 5, 1788	Dec. 17, 1799
Thomas McKean (D-R)	Dec. 17, 1799	Dec. 20, 1808
Simon Snyder (D-R)	Dec. 20, 1808	Dec. 16, 1817
William Findlay (D-R)	Dec. 16, 1817	Dec. 19, 1820
Joseph Hiester (D-R)	Dec. 19, 1820	Dec. 16, 1823
John A. Shulze (JAC D)	Dec. 16, 1823	Dec. 15, 1829
George Wolfe (JAC D)	Dec. 15, 1829	Dec. 15, 1835
Joseph Ritner (D)	Dec. 15, 1835	Jan. 15, 1839
David R. Porter (D)	Jan. 15, 1839	Jan. 21, 1845
Francis R. Shunk (D)[3]	Jan. 21, 1845	July 9, 1848
William F. Johnston (W)[4]	July 26, 1848	Jan. 20, 1852
William Bigler (D)	Jan. 20, 1852	Jan. 16, 1855
James Pollock (W)	Jan. 16, 1855	Jan. 19, 1858
William F. Packer (D)	Jan. 19, 1858	Jan. 15, 1861
Andrew G. Curtin (R)	Jan. 15, 1861	Jan. 15, 1867
John W. Geary (R)	Jan. 15, 1867	Jan. 21, 1873
John F. Hartranft (R)	Jan. 21, 1873	Jan. 18, 1879
Henry M. Hoyt (R)	Jan. 21, 1879	Jan. 16, 1883
Robert E. Pattison (D)	Jan. 16, 1883	Jan. 18, 1887

James A. Beaver (R)	Jan. 18, 1887	Jan. 20, 1891
Robert E. Pattison (D)	Jan. 20, 1891	Jan. 15, 1895
Daniel H. Hastings (R)	Jan. 15, 1895	Jan. 17, 1899
William A. Stone (R)	Jan. 17, 1899	Jan. 20, 1903
Samuel W. Pennypacker (R)	Jan. 20, 1903	Jan. 15, 1907
Edwin S. Stuart (R)	Jan. 15, 1907	Jan. 17, 1911
John K. Tener (R)	Jan. 17, 1911	Jan. 19, 1915
Martin G. Brumbaugh (R)	Jan. 19, 1915	Jan. 21, 1919
William C. Sproul (R)	Jan. 21, 1919	Jan. 16, 1923
Gifford Pinchot (R)	Jan. 16, 1923	Jan. 18, 1927
John S. Fisher (R)	Jan. 18, 1927	Jan. 20, 1931
Gifford Pinchot (R, PROG)	Jan. 20, 1931	Jan. 15, 1935
George H. Earle (D)	Jan. 15, 1935	Jan. 17, 1939
Arthur H. James (R)	Jan. 17, 1939	Jan. 19, 1943
Edward Martin (R)[5]	Jan. 19, 1943	Jan. 2, 1947
John C. Bell Jr. (R)[6]	Jan. 2, 1947	Jan. 21, 1947
James H. Duff (R)	Jan. 21, 1947	Jan. 16, 1951
John S. Fine (R)	Jan. 16, 1951	Jan. 18, 1955
George M. Leader (D)	Jan. 18, 1955	Jan. 20, 1959
David L. Lawrence (D)	Jan. 20, 1959	Jan. 15, 1963
William W. Scranton (R)	Jan. 15, 1963	Jan. 17, 1967
Raymond P. Shafer (R)	Jan. 17, 1967	Jan. 19, 1971
Milton J. Shapp (D)	Jan. 19, 1971	Jan. 16, 1979
Richard L. Thornburgh (R)	Jan. 16, 1979	Jan. 20, 1987
Robert P. Casey (D)	Jan. 20, 1987	Jan. 17, 1995
Tom Ridge (R)	Jan. 17, 1995	

Pennsylvania
1. Pennsylvania's first seven chief executives were called presidents.
2. Thomas Mifflin was president of Pennsylvania from 1788 to 1790 and governor from 1790 to 1799.
3. Resigned July 9, 1848.
4. Interregnum from July 9 to July 26, 1848. Johnston became acting governor. Subsequently elected.
5. Resigned Jan. 2, 1947.
6. As lieutenant governor, he succeeded to office.

RHODE ISLAND

(Ratified the Constitution May 29, 1790)

Governors	Dates of Service	
Nicholas Cooke	May 4, 1776	May 6, 1778
William Greene	May 6, 1778	May 3, 1786
John Collins (FED)	May 3, 1786	May 5, 1790
Arthur Fenner (D-R)[1]	May 5, 1790	Oct. 15, 1805
Henry Smith (D-R)[2]	Oct. 15, 1805	May 7, 1806
Isaac Wilbur (D-R)[3]	May 7, 1806	May 6, 1807
James Fenner	May 6, 1807	May 1, 1811
William Jones (FED)	May 1, 1811	May 7, 1817
Nehemiah R. Knight (D-R)[4]	May 7, 1817	Jan. 9, 1821
Edward Wilcox (D-R)[5]	Jan. 9, 1821	May 2, 1821
William C. Gibbs (D-R)	May 2, 1821	May 5, 1824
James Fenner (D-R)	May 5, 1824	May 4, 1831
Lemuel H. Arnold (D)[6]	May 4, 1831	May 1, 1833
John Brown Francis (D)	May 1, 1833	May 2, 1838
William Sprague (W)	May 2, 1838	May 1, 1839
Samuel Ward King (W)[7]	May 2, 1839	May 2, 1843
James Fenner (L & O W)	May 2, 1843	May 6, 1845
Charles Jackson (LIBER W)	May 6, 1845	May 6, 1846
Byron Diman (L & O W)	May 6, 1846	May 4, 1847

Elisha Harris (W)	May 4, 1847	May 1, 1849
Henry B. Anthony (W)	May 1, 1849	May 6, 1851
Philip Allen (D)[8]	May 6, 1851	July 20, 1853
Francis M. Dimond (D)[9]	July 20, 1853	May 2, 1854
William W. Hoppin (W, R)	May 2, 1854	May 26, 1857
Elisha Dyer (R)	May 26, 1857	May 31, 1859
Thomas G. Turner	May 31, 1859	May 29, 1860
William Sprague (FUS, UN)[10]	May 29, 1860	March 3, 1863
William C. Cozzens[11]	March 3, 1863	May 26, 1863
James Y. Smith (UN R)	May 26, 1863	May 29, 1866
Ambrose E. Burnside (R)	May 29, 1866	May 25, 1869
Seth Padelford (R)	May 25, 1869	May 27, 1873
Henry Howard (R)	May 27, 1873	May 25, 1875
Henry Lippitt (R)	May 25, 1875	May 29, 1877
Charles Van Zandt (R & TEMP)	May 29, 1877	May 25, 1880
Alfred H. Littlefield (R)	May 25, 1880	May 29, 1883
Augustus O. Bourn (R)	May 29, 1883	May 26, 1885
George P. Wetmore (R)	May 26, 1885	May 31, 1887
John W. Davis (D)	May 31, 1887	May 29, 1888
Royal C. Taft (R)	May 29, 1888	May 28, 1889
Herbert W. Ladd (R)	May 28, 1889	May 27, 1890
John W. Davis (D)	May 27, 1890	May 26, 1891
Herbert W. Ladd (R)	May 26, 1891	May 31, 1892
D. Russell Brown (R)[12]	May 31, 1892	May 29, 1895
Charles W. Lippitt (R)	May 29, 1895	May 25, 1897
Elisha Dyer (R)	May 25, 1897	May 29, 1900
William Gregory (R)[13]	May 29, 1900	Dec. 16, 1901
Charles D. Kimball (R)[14]	Dec. 16, 1901	Jan. 6, 1903
Lucius F. C. Garvin (D)	Jan. 6, 1903	Jan. 3, 1905
George H. Utter (R)	Jan. 3, 1905	Jan. 1, 1907
James H. Higgins (D)	Jan. 1, 1907	Jan. 5, 1909
Aram J. Pothier (R)	Jan. 5, 1909	Jan. 5, 1915
R. Livingston Beeckman (R)	Jan. 5, 1915	Jan. 4, 1921
Emery J. San Souci (R)	Jan. 4, 1921	Jan. 2, 1923
William S. Flynn (D)	Jan. 2, 1923	Jan. 6, 1925
Aram J. Pothier (R)[15]	Jan. 6, 1925	Feb. 4, 1928
Norman S. Case (R)[16]	Feb. 4, 1928	Jan. 3, 1933
Theodore F. Green (D)	Jan. 3, 1933	Jan. 5, 1937
Robert E. Quinn (D)	Jan. 5, 1937	Jan. 3, 1939
William H. Vanderbilt (R)	Jan. 3, 1939	Jan. 7, 1941
J. Howard McGrath (D)[17]	Jan. 7, 1941	Oct. 6, 1945
John O. Pastore (D)[18]	Oct. 6, 1945	Dec. 19, 1950
John S. McKiernan (D)[19]	Dec. 19, 1950	Jan. 2, 1951
Dennis J. Roberts (D)	Jan. 2, 1951	Jan. 6, 1959
Christopher Del Sesto (R)	Jan. 6, 1959	Jan. 3, 1961
John A. Notte Jr. (D)	Jan. 3, 1961	Jan. 1, 1963
John H. Chafee (R)	Jan. 1, 1963	Jan. 7, 1969
Frank Licht (D)	Jan. 7, 1969	Jan. 2, 1973
Philip W. Noel (D)	Jan. 2, 1973	Jan. 4, 1977
Joseph J. Garrahy (D)	Jan. 4, 1977	Jan. 1, 1985
Edward D. DiPrete (R)	Jan. 1, 1985	Jan. 1, 1991
Bruce Sundlun (D)	Jan. 1, 1991	Jan. 3, 1995
Lincoln C. Almond (R)	Jan. 3, 1995	

Rhode Island

1. Died Oct. 15, 1805.
2. Smith, as first senator, served as governor.
3. No governor was elected in 1806. Wilbur, the lieutenant governor, served as acting governor.

4. Resigned Jan. 9, 1821.
5. As lieutenant governor, he succeeded to office.
6. In the 1832 election no candidate for governor received the majority of the total vote cast that was required for election. Elections were held four more times—on May 16, July 18, Aug. 28, and Nov. 21—each one resulting without choice. Arnold was continued in office until 1833. (The returns for this election, p. 000, show only the first election.)
7. No governor was elected in 1839, no candidate having received a majority of the vote. In addition, no lieutenant governor was elected. King, as first senator, became acting governor for the term. Subsequently reelected three times.
8. Resigned July 20, 1853.
9. As lieutenant governor, he succeeded to office.
10. Resigned March 3, 1863.
11. As president of the state Senate, he succeeded to office.
12. No candidate received a majority of the vote in the election of 1893, and under the law the legislature was required to elect the governor. However, because of a dispute between the two houses no choice was made. Governor Brown continued in office for the term. He was reelected in 1894. The controversy over the election resulted in repeal of the majority-vote requirement in 1893.
13. Died Dec. 16, 1901.
14. As lieutenant governor, he succeeded to office.
15. Died Feb. 4, 1928.
16. As lieutenant governor, he succeeded to office. Subsequently elected.
17. Resigned Oct. 6, 1945.
18. As lieutenant governor, he succeeded to office. Subsequently elected. Resigned Dec. 19, 1950.
19. As lieutenant governor, he succeeded to office.

SOUTH CAROLINA

(Ratified the Constitution May 23, 1788)

Governors	Dates of Service	
John Rutledge[1]	March 26, 1776	March 5, 1778
Rawlins Lowndes[2]	March 7, 1778	Jan. 9, 1779
John Rutledge	Jan. 9, 1779	Jan. 31, 1782
John Mathews	Jan. 31, 1782	Feb. 1783
Benjamin Guerard	Feb. 4, 1783	Feb. 10, 1785
William Moultrie	Feb. 10, 1785	Feb. 20, 1787
Thomas Pinckney (FED)	Feb. 20, 1787	Jan. 26, 1789
Charles Pinckney (FED)	Jan. 26, 1789	Dec. 5, 1792
William Moultrie (FED)	Dec. 5, 1792	Dec. 1794
Arnoldus Vander Horst (FED)	Dec. 1794	Dec. 1796
Charles Pinckney (D-R)	Dec. 1796	Dec. 6, 1798
Edward Rutledge (FED)[3]	Dec. 18, 1798	Jan. 23, 1800
John Drayton (D-R)[4]	Jan. 23, 1800	Dec. 1802
James B. Richardson (D-R)	Dec. 1802	Dec. 1804
Paul Hamilton (D-R)	Dec. 1804	Dec. 1806
Charles Pinckney (D-R)	Dec. 1806	Dec. 10, 1808
John Drayton (D-R)	Dec. 10, 1808	Dec. 1810
Henry Middleton (D-R)	Dec. 10, 1810	Dec. 1812
Joseph Alston (D-R)	Dec. 1812	Dec. 1814
David R. Williams (D-R)	Dec. 1814	Dec. 1816
Andrew Pickens (D-R)	Dec. 1816	Dec. 1818
John Geddes (D-R)	Dec. 1818	Dec. 1820
Thomas Bennett (D-R)	Dec. 1820	Dec. 1822
John Lyde Wilson (D-R)	Dec. 1822	Dec. 1824
Richard I. Manning (D-R)	Dec. 1824	Dec. 1826
John Taylor (D-R)	Dec. 1826	Dec. 1828
Stephen D. Miller (D)	Dec. 1828	Dec. 1830
James Hamilton Jr. (D)	Dec. 1830	Dec. 13, 1832
Robert Y. Hayne (D)	Dec. 13, 1832	Dec. 11, 1834
George McDuffie (D)	Dec. 11, 1834	Dec. 1836

Pierce M. Butler (D)	Dec. 1836	Dec. 10, 1838
Patrick Noble (D)[5]	Dec. 10, 1838	April 7, 1840
B. K. Henagan (D)[6]	April 7, 1840	Dec. 10, 1840
John P. Richardson (D)	Dec. 10, 1840	Dec. 1842
James H. Hammond (D)	Dec. 1842	Dec. 1844
William Aiken (D)	Dec. 1844	Dec. 1846
David Johnson (D)	Dec. 1846	Dec. 1848
Whitmarsh B. Seabrook (D)	Dec. 1848	Dec. 1850
John Hugh Means (D)	Dec. 16, 1850	Dec. 1852
John Laurence Manning (D)	Dec. 1852	Dec. 1854
James H. Adams (D)	Dec. 1854	Dec. 1856
Robert F. W. Alston (D)	Dec. 1856	Dec. 1858
William H. Gist (D)	Dec. 1858	Dec. 1860
Francis W. Pickens (D)	Dec. 1860	Dec. 1862
Milledge L. Bonham (D)	Dec. 1862	Dec. 1864
Andrew G. Magrath (D)[7]	Dec. 20, 1864	May 25, 1865
Benjamin F. Perry[8]	June 30, 1865	Nov. 29, 1865
James L. Orr (C)[9]	Nov. 29, 1865	July 6, 1868
Robert K. Scott (R)	July 9, 1868	Dec. 7, 1872
Franklin J. Moses Jr. (R)	Dec. 7, 1872	Dec. 1, 1874
Daniel H. Chamberlain (R)[10]	Dec. 1, 1874	April 10, 1877
Wade Hampton (D)[11]	Dec. 14, 1876	Feb. 26, 1879
William D. Simpson (D)[12]	Feb. 26, 1879	Sept. 1, 1880
Thomas B. Jeter (D)[13]	Sept. 1, 1880	Nov. 30, 1880
Johnson Hagood (D)	Nov. 30, 1880	Dec. 1882
Hugh Smith Thompson (D)[14]	Dec. 1882	July 10, 1886
John C. Sheppard (D)[15]	July 10, 1886	Nov. 30, 1886
John P. Richardson (D)	Nov. 30, 1886	Dec. 4, 1890
Benjamin Ryan Tillman (D)	Dec. 4, 1890	Dec. 1894
John Gary Evans (D)	Dec. 4, 1894	Jan. 18, 1897
William H. Ellerbe (D)[16]	Jan. 18, 1897	June 2, 1899
Miles B. McSweeney (D)[17]	June 2, 1899	Jan. 20, 1903
Duncan C. Heyward (D)	Jan. 20, 1903	Jan. 15, 1907
Martin F. Ansel (D)	Jan. 15, 1907	Jan. 17, 1911
Coleman L. Blease (D)[18]	Jan. 17, 1911	Jan. 14, 1915
Charles A. Smith (D)[19]	Jan. 14, 1915	Jan. 19, 1915
Richard I. Manning (D)	Jan. 19, 1915	Jan. 21, 1919
Robert A. Cooper (D)[20]	Jan. 21, 1919	May 20, 1922
Wilson G. Harvey (D)[21]	May 20, 1922	Jan. 16, 1923
Thomas G. McLeod (D)	Jan. 16, 1923	Jan. 18, 1927
John G. Richards (D)	Jan. 18, 1927	Jan. 20, 1931
Ibra C. Blackwood (D)	Jan. 20, 1931	Jan. 15, 1935
Olin D. Johnston (D)	Jan. 15, 1935	Jan. 17, 1939
Burnet R. Maybank (D)[22]	Jan. 17, 1939	Nov. 4, 1941
Joseph E. Harley (D)[23]	Nov. 4, 1941	Feb. 27, 1942
Richard M. Jeffries (D)[24]	March 2, 1942	Jan. 19, 1943
Olin D. Johnston (D)[25]	Jan. 19, 1943	Jan. 2, 1945
Ransome J. Williams (D)[26]	Jan. 2, 1945	Jan. 21, 1947
J. Strom Thurmond (D)	Jan. 21, 1947	Jan. 16, 1951
James F. Byrnes (D)	Jan. 16, 1951	Jan. 18, 1955
George Bell Timmerman Jr. (D)	Jan. 18, 1955	Jan. 20, 1959
Ernest F. Hollings (D)	Jan. 20, 1959	Jan. 15, 1963
Donald S. Russell (D)[27]	Jan. 15, 1963	April 22, 1965
Robert E. McNair (D)[28]	April 22, 1965	Jan. 19, 1971
John C. West (D)	Jan. 19, 1971	Jan. 21, 1975
James Edwards (R)	Jan. 21, 1975	Jan. 10, 1979
Richard Riley (D)	Jan. 10, 1979	Jan. 14, 1987
Carroll Campbell (R)	Jan. 14, 1987	Jan. 11, 1995
David Beasley (R)	Jan. 11, 1995	Jan. 13, 1999
Jim Hodges (D)	Jan. 13, 1999	

South Carolina

1. South Carolina's first two chief executives were called presidents. Rutledge resigned March 5, 1778.

2. Chosen by the legislature, he succeeded to office.

3. Died Jan. 23, 1800.

4. As lieutenant governor, he succeeded to office. Subsequently elected.

5. Died April 7, 1840.

6. As lieutenant governor, he succeeded to office.

7. Last Confederate governor. Removed by federal authorities.

8. Provisional governor appointed by President Johnson.

9. Deposed by act of Congress.

10. There was a dispute between two factions in the state house over the elections and seating of eight of its members following the 1876 election. The pro-Chamberlain (R) faction declared Chamberlain to have been re-elected and he was reinaugurated on Dec. 7. The pro-Hampton (D) faction also organized as the state house of representatives and on Dec. 14 declared Hampton to have been elected. He was inaugurated on the same day. For a time there were two rival state governments. In several cases arising later, raising the question of Hampton's authority to act as governor, the supreme court of the state declared him to be the lawfully elected chief executive of the state. Chamberlain dropped his claim to the office on April 10, 1877, following the withdrawal of federal troops from the state in March 1877 by President Hayes.

11. Resigned Feb. 26, 1879.

12. As lieutenant governor, he succeeded to office. Resigned in September 1880.

13. As president of the state Senate, he succeeded to office.

14. Resigned July 10, 1886.

15. As lieutenant governor, he succeeded to office.

16. Died June 2, 1899.

17. As lieutenant governor, he succeeded to office. Subsequently elected.

18. Resigned Jan. 14, 1915.

19. As lieutenant governor, he succeeded to office.

20. Resigned May 20, 1922.

21. As lieutenant governor, he succeeded to office.

22. Resigned Nov. 4, 1941.

23. As lieutenant governor, he succeeded to office. Died Feb. 27, 1942.

24. As president of the state Senate, he succeeded to office.

25. Resigned Jan. 2, 1945.

26. As lieutenant governor, he succeeded to office.

27. Resigned April 22, 1965.

28. As lieutenant governor, he succeeded to office. Subsequently elected.

SOUTH DAKOTA

(Became a state Nov. 2, 1889)

Governors	Dates of Service	
Arthur C. Mellette (R)	Nov. 2, 1889	Jan. 1893
Charles H. Sheldon (R)	Jan. 1893	Jan. 1, 1897
Andrew E. Lee (PP, FUS)	Jan. 1, 1897	Jan. 8, 1901
Charles N. Herreid (R)	Jan. 8, 1901	Jan. 3, 1905
Samuel H. Elrod (R)	Jan. 3, 1905	Jan. 8, 1907
Coe I. Crawford (R)	Jan. 8, 1907	Jan. 5, 1909
Robert S. Vessey (R)	Jan. 5, 1909	Jan. 7, 1913
Frank M. Byrne (R)	Jan. 7, 1913	Jan. 2, 1917
Peter Norbeck (R)	Jan. 2, 1917	Jan. 4, 1921
William H. McMaster (R)	Jan. 4, 1921	Jan. 6, 1925
Carl Gunderson (R)	Jan. 6, 1925	Jan. 4, 1927
William J. Bulow (D)	Jan. 4, 1927	Jan. 6, 1931
Warren E. Green (R)	Jan. 6, 1931	Jan. 3, 1933
Tom Berry (D)	Jan. 3, 1933	Jan. 5, 1937
Leslie Jensen (R)	Jan. 5, 1937	Jan. 3, 1939
Harlan J. Bushfield (R)	Jan. 3, 1939	Jan. 5, 1943

Merrell Q. Sharpe (R)	Jan. 5, 1943	Jan. 7, 1947
George T. Mickelson (R)	Jan. 7, 1947	Jan. 2, 1951
Sigurd Anderson (R)	Jan. 2, 1951	Jan. 4, 1955
Joe Foss (R)	Jan. 4, 1955	Jan. 6, 1959
Ralph E. Herseth (D)	Jan. 6, 1959	Jan. 3, 1961
Archie M. Gubbrud (R)	Jan. 3, 1961	Jan. 5, 1965
Nils A. Boe (R)	Jan. 5, 1965	Jan. 7, 1969
Frank L. Farrar (R)	Jan. 7, 1969	Jan. 5, 1971
Richard F. Kneip (D)[1]	Jan. 5, 1971	July 24, 1978
Harvey L. Wollman (D)[2]	July 24, 1978	Jan. 1, 1979
William J. Janklow (R)	Jan. 1, 1979	Jan. 6, 1987
George S. Mickelson (R)[3]	Jan. 6, 1987	April 19, 1993
Walter D. Miller (R)[4]	April 20, 1993	Jan. 7, 1995
William J. Janklow (R)	Jan. 7, 1995	

South Dakota
1. Resigned July 24, 1978.
2. As lieutenant governor, he succeeded to office.
3. Died April 19, 1993.
4. As lieutenant governor, he succeeded to office.

TENNESSEE

(Became a state June 1, 1796)

Governors	Dates of Service	
John Sevier (D-R)	March 30, 1796	Sept. 23, 1801
Archibald Roane (D-R)	Sept. 23, 1801	Sept. 23, 1803
John Sevier (D-R)	Sept. 23, 1803	Sept. 20, 1809
William Blount (D-R)	Sept. 20, 1809	Sept. 27, 1815
Joseph McMinn (D-R)	Sept. 27, 1815	Oct. 1, 1821
William Carroll (D-R)	Oct. 1, 1821	Oct. 1, 1827
Sam Houston (D-R)[1]	Oct. 1, 1827	April 16, 1829
William Hall (D-R)[2]	April 16, 1829	Oct. 1, 1829
William Carroll (D)	Oct. 1, 1829	Oct. 12, 1835
Newton Cannon (W)	Oct. 12, 1835	Oct. 14, 1839
James K. Polk (D)	Oct. 14, 1839	Oct. 15, 1841
James C. Jones (W)	Oct. 15, 1841	Oct. 14, 1845
Aaron V. Brown (D)	Oct. 14, 1845	Oct. 17, 1847
Neill S. Brown (W)	Oct. 17, 1847	Oct. 16, 1849
William Trousdale (D)	Oct. 16, 1849	Oct. 16, 1851
William B. Campbell	Oct. 16, 1851	Oct. 17, 1853
Andrew Johnson (D)	Oct. 17, 1853	Nov. 3, 1857
Isham G. Harris (D)	Nov. 3, 1857	March 12, 1862
Andrew Johnson[3]	March 12, 1862	March 4, 1865
William G. Brownlow (W, R)[4]	April 5, 1865	Oct. 1867
DeWitt Clinton Senter (CR)[5]	Oct. 11, 1867	Oct. 10, 1871
John C. Brown (D, LR)	Oct. 10, 1871	Jan. 18, 1875
James D. Porter Jr. (D)	Jan. 18, 1875	Feb. 16, 1879
Albert S. Marks (D)	Feb. 16, 1879	Jan. 17, 1881
Alvin Hawkins (R)	Jan. 17, 1881	Jan. 15, 1883
William B. Bate (LOWTAX D, D)	Jan. 15, 1883	Jan. 17, 1887
Robert L. Taylor (D)	Jan. 17, 1887	Jan. 19, 1891
John P. Buchanan (D)	Jan. 19, 1891	Jan. 16, 1893
Peter Turney (D)[6]	Jan. 16, 1893	Jan. 21, 1897
Robert L. Taylor (D)	Jan. 21, 1897	Jan. 16, 1899
Benton McMillin (D)	Jan. 16, 1899	Jan. 19, 1903

James B. Frazier (D)[7]	Jan. 19, 1903	March 21, 1905
John I. Cox (D)[8]	March 21, 1905	Jan. 17, 1907
Malcolm R. Patterson (D)	Jan. 17, 1907	Jan. 26, 1911
Ben W. Hooper (R)	Jan. 26, 1911	Jan. 17, 1915
Thomas C. Rye (D)	Jan. 17, 1915	Jan. 15, 1919
Albert H. Roberts (D)	Jan. 15, 1919	Jan. 15, 1921
Alfred A. Taylor (R)	Jan. 15, 1921	Jan. 16, 1923
Austin Peay (D)[9]	Jan. 16, 1923	Oct. 2, 1927
Henry H. Horton (D)[10]	Oct. 3, 1927	Jan. 17, 1933
Hill McAlister (D)	Jan. 17, 1933	Jan. 15, 1937
Gordon Browning (D)	Jan. 15, 1937	Jan. 16, 1939
Prentice Cooper (D)	Jan. 16, 1939	Jan. 16, 1945
James N. McCord (D)	Jan. 16, 1945	Jan. 17, 1949
Gordon Browning (D)	Jan. 17, 1949	Jan. 15, 1953
Frank G. Clement (D)	Jan. 15, 1953	Jan. 19, 1959
Buford Ellington (D)	Jan. 19, 1959	Jan. 15, 1963
Frank G. Clement (D)	Jan. 15, 1963	Jan. 16, 1967
Buford Ellington (D)	Jan. 16, 1967	Jan. 16, 1971
Winfield Dunn (R)	Jan. 16, 1971	Jan. 18, 1975
Ray Blanton (D)	Jan. 18, 1975	Jan. 17, 1979
Lamar Alexander (R)	Jan. 17, 1979	Jan. 17, 1987
Ned R. McWherter (D)	Jan. 17, 1987	Jan. 21, 1995
Don Sundquist (R)	Jan. 21, 1995	

Tennessee
1. Resigned April 16, 1829.
2. As Speaker of the state Senate, he succeeded to office.
3. Appointed military governor by President Lincoln.
4. Resigned in October 1867.
5. As Speaker of the state Senate, he succeeded to office. Subsequently elected.
6. Governor Turney ran for reelection in 1894, but his Republican opponent, H. Clay Evans, appeared to have won a narrow victory. There were allegations of fraud, however, resulting in a recount of the votes by the legislature. The legislature's count made Turney the winner, and he took office for a second term.
7. Resigned March 21, 1905.
8. As Speaker of the state Senate, he succeeded to office.
9. Died Oct. 2, 1927.
10. As Speaker of the state Senate, he succeeded to office. Subsequently elected.

TEXAS

(Became a state Dec. 29, 1845)

Governors	Dates of Service	
Anson Jones (D)	Dec. 9, 1844	Feb. 19, 1846
J. Pinckney Henderson (D)	Feb. 19, 1846	Dec. 21, 1847
George T. Wood (D)	Dec. 21, 1847	Dec. 21, 1849
P. Hansbrough Bell (D)[1]	Dec. 21, 1849	Nov. 23, 1853
J. W. Henderson (D)[2]	Nov. 23, 1853	Dec. 21, 1853
Elisha M. Pease (D)	Dec. 21, 1853	Dec. 21, 1857
Hardin R. Runnels (D)	Dec. 21, 1857	Dec. 21, 1859
Sam Houston (ID)[3]	Dec. 21, 1859	March 16, 1861
Edward Clark (D)[4]	March 16, 1861	Nov. 7, 1861
Francis R. Lubbock[5]	Nov. 7, 1861	Nov. 5, 1863
Pendleton Murrah[6]	Nov. 5, 1863	June 17, 1865
Andrew J. Hamilton[7]	June 17, 1865	Aug. 9, 1866
James W. Throckmorton (C)	Aug. 9, 1866	Aug. 8, 1867
Elisha M. Pease[8]	Aug. 8, 1867	Sept. 30, 1869
Edmund J. Davis (R)	Jan. 8, 1870	Jan. 15, 1874

Richard Coke (D)[9]	Jan. 15, 1874	Dec. 1, 1876
Richard B. Hubbard (D)[10]	Dec. 1, 1876	Jan. 21, 1879
Oran M. Roberts (D)	Jan. 21, 1879	Jan. 16, 1883
John Ireland (D)	Jan. 16, 1883	Jan. 18, 1887
Lawrence S. Ross (D)	Jan. 18, 1887	Jan. 20, 1891
James S. Hogg (D)	Jan. 20, 1891	Jan. 15, 1895
Charles A. Culberson (D)	Jan. 15, 1895	Jan. 17, 1899
Joseph D. Sayers (D)	Jan. 17, 1899	Jan. 20, 1903
Samuel W. T. Lanham (D)	Jan. 20, 1903	Jan. 15, 1907
Thomas M. Campbell (D)	Jan. 15, 1907	Jan. 17, 1911
Oscar B. Colquitt (D)	Jan. 17, 1911	Jan. 19, 1915
James E. Ferguson (D)[11]	Jan. 19, 1915	Aug. 25, 1917
William P. Hobby (D)[12]	Aug. 25, 1917	Jan. 18, 1921
Pat M. Neff (D)	Jan. 18, 1921	Jan. 20, 1925
Miriam A. Ferguson (D)	Jan. 20, 1925	Jan. 18, 1927
Dan Moody (D)	Jan. 18, 1927	Jan. 20, 1931
Ross M. Sterling (D)	Jan. 20, 1931	Jan. 17, 1933
Miriam A. Ferguson (D)	Jan. 17, 1933	Jan. 15, 1935
James V. Allred (D)	Jan. 15, 1935	Jan. 17, 1939
W. Lee O'Daniel (D)[13]	Jan. 17, 1939	Aug. 4, 1941
Coke R. Stevenson (D)[14]	Aug. 4, 1941	Jan. 21, 1947
Beauford H. Jester (D)[15]	Jan. 21, 1947	July 11, 1949
Allan Shivers (D)[16]	July 11, 1949	Jan. 15, 1957
Price Daniel (D)	Jan. 15, 1957	Jan. 15, 1963
John B. Connally (D)	Jan. 15, 1963	Jan. 21, 1969
Preston Smith (D)	Jan. 21, 1969	Jan. 16, 1973
Dolph Briscoe (D)	Jan. 16, 1973	Jan. 16, 1979
William P. Clements (R)	Jan. 16, 1979	Jan. 18, 1983
Mark White (D)	Jan. 18, 1983	Jan. 20, 1987
William P. Clements (R)	Jan. 20, 1987	Jan. 15, 1991
Ann W. Richards (D)	Jan. 15, 1991	Jan. 17, 1995
George W. Bush (R)[17]	Jan. 17, 1995	Dec. 21, 2000
Rick Perry (R)[18]	Dec. 21, 2000	

Texas
1. Resigned Nov. 23, 1853.
2. As lieutenant governor, he succeeded to office.
3. Resigned March 16, 1861.
4. As lieutenant governor, he succeeded to office.
5. Resigned Nov. 5, 1863.
6. Administration terminated June 17, 1865, due to fall of the Confederacy.
7. Provisional governor appointed by the president.
8. Appointed under martial law. Vacated office Sept. 30, 1869. Governorship is considered to have remained vacant until inauguration of Edmund J. Davis.
9. Resigned Dec. 1, 1876.
10. As lieutenant governor, he succeeded to office.
11. Impeached. Removed from office Aug. 25, 1917.
12. As lieutenant governor, he succeeded to office. Subsequently elected.
13. Resigned Aug. 4, 1941.
14. As lieutenant governor, he succeeded to office. Subsequently elected.
15. Died July 11, 1949.
16. As lieutenant governor, he succeeded to office. Subsequently elected.
17. Resigned Dec. 21, 2000.
18. As lieutenant governor, he succeeded to office.

UTAH

(Became a state Jan. 4, 1896)

Governors	Dates of Service	
Heber Manning Wells (R)	Jan. 6, 1896	Jan. 2, 1905
John C. Cutler (R)	Jan. 2, 1905	Jan. 4, 1909

William Spry (R)	Jan. 4, 1909	Jan. 1, 1917
Simon Bamberger (D)	Jan. 1, 1917	Jan. 3, 1921
Charles R. Mabey (R)	Jan. 3, 1921	Jan. 5, 1925
George H. Dern (D)	Jan. 5, 1925	Jan. 2, 1933
Henry H. Blood (D)	Jan. 2, 1933	Jan. 6, 1941
Herbert B. Maw (D)	Jan. 6, 1941	Jan. 3, 1949
J. Bracken Lee (R)	Jan. 3, 1949	Jan. 7, 1957
George Dewey Clyde (R)	Jan. 7, 1957	Jan. 4, 1965
Calvin L. Rampton (D)	Jan. 4, 1965	Jan. 3, 1977
Scott M. Matheson (D)	Jan. 3, 1977	Jan. 7, 1985
Norman H. Bangerter (R)	Jan. 7, 1985	Jan. 3, 1993
Mike O. Leavitt (R)	Jan. 3, 1993	

VERMONT

(Became a state March 4, 1791)

Governors	Dates of Service	
Thomas Chittenden[1]	March 4, 1791	Aug. 25, 1797
Paul Brigham[2]	Aug. 25, 1797	Oct. 16, 1797
Isaac Tichenor (FED)	Oct. 16, 1797	Oct. 9, 1807
Israel Smith (D-R)	Oct. 9, 1807	Oct. 14, 1808
Isaac Tichenor (FED)	Oct. 14, 1808	Oct. 14, 1809
Jonas Galusha (D-R)	Oct. 14, 1809	Oct. 23, 1813
Martin Chittenden (FED)	Oct. 23, 1813	Oct. 14, 1815
Jonas Galusha (D-R)	Oct. 14, 1815	Oct. 13, 1820
Richard Skinner (D-R)	Oct. 13, 1820	Oct. 10, 1823
Cornelius P. Van Ness (D-R)	Oct. 10, 1823	Oct. 13, 1826
Ezra Butler (D-R)	Oct. 13, 1826	Oct. 10, 1828
Samuel C. Crafts (NR)	Oct. 10, 1828	Oct. 18, 1831
William A. Palmer (A-MAS)	Oct. 18, 1831	Nov. 2, 1835
Silas H. Jennison (W)[3]	Nov. 2, 1835	Oct. 15, 1841
Charles Paine (W)	Oct. 15, 1841	Oct. 13, 1843
John Mattocks (W)	Oct. 13, 1843	Oct. 11, 1844
William Slade (W)	Oct. 11, 1844	Oct. 9, 1846
Horace Eaton (W)	Oct. 9, 1846	Oct. 1848
Carlos Coolidge (W)	Oct. 1848	Oct. 11, 1850
Charles K. Williams (W)	Oct. 11, 1850	Oct. 1852
Erastus Fairbanks (W)	Oct. 1852	Oct. 1853
John S. Robinson (D)	Oct. 1853	Oct. 13, 1854
Stephen Royce (W, R)	Oct. 13, 1854	Oct. 10, 1856
Ryland Fletcher (R)	Oct. 10, 1856	Oct. 10, 1858
Hiland Hall (R)	Oct. 10, 1858	Oct. 12, 1860
Erastus Fairbanks (R)	Oct. 12, 1860	Oct. 11, 1861
Frederick Holbrook (R)	Oct. 11, 1861	Oct. 9, 1863
John Gregory Smith (R)	Oct. 9, 1863	Oct. 13, 1865
Paul Dillingham (R)	Oct. 13, 1865	Oct. 13, 1867
John B. Page (R)	Oct. 13, 1867	Oct. 15, 1869
Peter T. Washburn (R)[4]	Oct. 15, 1869	Feb. 7, 1870
George W. Hendee (R)[5]	Feb. 7, 1870	Oct. 6, 1870
John W. Stewart (R)	Oct. 6, 1870	Oct. 3, 1872
Julius Converse (R)	Oct. 3, 1872	Oct. 8, 1874
Asahel Peck (R)	Oct. 8, 1874	Oct. 5, 1876
Horace Fairbanks (R)	Oct. 5, 1876	Oct. 3, 1878
Redfield Proctor (R)	Oct. 3, 1878	Oct. 7, 1880
Roswell Farnham (R)	Oct. 7, 1880	Oct. 5, 1882
John L. Barstow (R)	Oct. 5, 1882	Oct. 2, 1884
Samuel E. Pingree (R)	Oct. 2, 1884	Oct. 7, 1886

Ebenezer J. Ormsbee (R)	Oct. 7, 1886	Oct. 4, 1888
William P. Dillingham (R)	Oct. 4, 1888	Oct. 2, 1890
Carroll S. Page (R)	Oct. 2, 1890	Oct. 6, 1892
Levi K. Fuller (R)	Oct. 6, 1892	Oct. 4, 1894
Urban A. Woodbury (R)	Oct. 4, 1894	Oct. 8, 1896
Josiah Grout (R)	Oct. 8, 1896	Oct. 6, 1898
Edward C. Smith (R)	Oct. 6, 1898	Oct. 4, 1900
William W. Stickney (R)	Oct. 4, 1900	Oct. 3, 1902
John G. McCullough (R)	Oct. 3, 1902	Oct. 6, 1904
Charles J. Bell (R)	Oct. 6, 1904	Oct. 4, 1906
Fletcher D. Proctor (R)	Oct. 4, 1906	Oct. 8, 1908
George H. Prouty (R)	Oct. 8, 1908	Oct. 5, 1910
John A. Mead (R)	Oct. 5, 1910	Oct. 3, 1912
Allen M. Fletcher (R)	Oct. 3, 1912	Jan. 7, 1915
Charles W. Gates (R)	Jan. 7, 1915	Jan. 4, 1917
Horace F. Graham (R)	Jan. 4, 1917	Jan. 9, 1919
Percival W. Clement (R)	Jan. 9, 1919	Jan. 6, 1921
James Hartness (R)	Jan. 6, 1921	Jan. 4, 1923
Redfield Proctor (R)	Jan. 4, 1923	Jan. 8, 1925
Franklin S. Billings (R)	Jan. 8, 1925	Jan. 6, 1927
John E. Weeks (R)	Jan. 6, 1927	Jan. 8, 1931
Stanley C. Wilson (R)	Jan. 8, 1931	Jan. 10, 1935
Charles M. Smith (R)	Jan. 10, 1935	Jan. 7, 1937
George D. Aiken (R)	Jan. 7, 1937	Jan. 9, 1941
William H. Wills (R)	Jan. 9, 1941	Jan. 4, 1945
Mortimer R. Proctor (R)	Jan. 4, 1945	Jan. 9, 1947
Ernest W. Gibson (R)[6]	Jan. 9, 1947	Jan. 16, 1950
Harold J. Arthur (R)[7]	Jan. 16, 1950	Jan. 4, 1951
Lee E. Emerson (R)	Jan. 4, 1951	Jan. 6, 1955
Joseph B. Johnson (R)	Jan. 6, 1955	Jan. 8, 1959
Robert T. Stafford (R)	Jan. 8, 1959	Jan. 5, 1961
Frank Ray Keyser Jr. (R)	Jan. 5, 1961	Jan. 10, 1963
Philip H. Hoff (D)	Jan. 10, 1963	Jan. 9, 1969
Deane C. Davis (R)	Jan. 9, 1969	Jan. 4, 1973
Thomas P. Salmon (D)	Jan. 4, 1973	Jan. 6, 1977
Richard A. Snelling (R)	Jan. 6, 1977	Jan. 10, 1985
Madeleine M. Kunin (D)	Jan. 10, 1985	Jan. 10, 1991
Richard A. Snelling (R)[8]	Jan. 10, 1991	Aug. 14, 1991
Howard Dean (D)[9]	Aug. 14, 1991	

Vermont
1. Died Aug. 25, 1797.
2. As lieutenant governor, he succeeded to office.
3. No candidate received a majority of the vote and the legislature failed to elect a governor in 1835. Silas H. Jennison, the lieutenant governor, served as governor for the term and was subsequently elected.
4. Died Feb. 7, 1870.
5. As lieutenant governor, he succeeded to office.
6. Resigned Jan. 16, 1950.
7. As lieutenant governor, he succeeded to office.
8. Died Aug. 14, 1991.
9. As lieutenant governor, he succeeded to office. Subsequently elected.

VIRGINIA

(Ratified the Constitution June 25, 1788)

Governors	Dates of Service	
Patrick Henry	June 29, 1776	June 1, 1779
Thomas Jefferson[1]	June 1, 1779	June 1, 1781
William Fleming[2]	June 2, 1781	June 12, 1781

Thomas Nelson Jr.[3]	June 12, 1781	Nov. 30, 1781
Benjamin Harrison[4]	Nov. 30, 1781	Nov. 29, 1784
Patrick Henry	Nov. 30, 1784	Nov. 29, 1786
Edmund Randolph	Dec. 1, 1786	Dec. 1, 1788
Beverley Randolph	Dec. 3, 1788	Dec. 1, 1791
Henry Lee (FED)	Dec. 1, 1791	Dec. 1, 1794
Robert Brooke	Dec. 1, 1794	Dec. 1, 1796
James Wood (D-R)	Dec. 1, 1796	Dec. 1, 1799
James Monroe (D-R)	Dec. 1, 1799	Dec. 1, 1802
John Page (D-R)	Dec. 1, 1802	Dec. 1, 1805
William H. Cabell (D-R)	Dec. 7, 1805	Dec. 1, 1808
John Tyler Sr. (D-R)	Dec. 1, 1808	Jan. 1811
James Monroe (D-R)[5]	Jan. 16, 1811	April 5, 1811
George William Smith (D-R)[6]	April 6, 1811	Dec. 26, 1811
Peyton Randolph (D-R)[7]	Dec. 27, 1811	Jan. 3, 1812
James Barbour (D-R)	Jan. 3, 1812	Dec. 1, 1814
Wilson Carey Nicholas (D-R)	Dec. 1, 1814	Dec. 1, 1816
James P. Preston (D-R)	Dec. 1, 1816	Dec. 1, 1819
Thomas M. Randolph (D-R)	Dec. 1, 1819	Dec. 1, 1822
James Pleasants (D-R)	Dec. 1, 1822	Dec. 1825
John Tyler Jr. (D-R)	Dec. 10, 1825	March 4, 1827
William B. Giles (D)	March 4, 1827	March 4, 1830
John Floyd (D)	March 4, 1830	March 31, 1834
Littleton W. Tazewell (D)[8]	March 31, 1834	April 30, 1836
Wyndham Robertson (D)[9]	April 30, 1836	March 31, 1837
David Campbell (D)	March 31, 1837	March 31, 1840
Thomas W. Gilmer (W)[10]	March 31, 1840	March 1841
John Mercer Patton (W)[11]	March 18, 1841	March 31, 1841
John Rutherford (W)[12]	March 31, 1841	March 31, 1842
John M. Gregory (W)[13]	March 31, 1842	Jan. 1, 1843
James McDowell (W)	Jan. 1, 1843	Jan. 1, 1846
William Smith (D)	Jan. 1, 1846	Jan. 1, 1849
John B. Floyd (D)	Jan. 1, 1849	Jan. 16, 1852
Joseph Johnson (D)	Jan. 16, 1852	Dec. 31, 1855
Henry A. Wise (D)	Jan. 1, 1856	Dec. 31, 1859
John Letcher (D)	Jan. 1, 1860	Dec. 31, 1863
William Smith (D)[14]	Jan. 1, 1864	April 1865
Francis H. Peirpoint[15]	June 20, 1861	April 4, 1868
Henry H. Wells[16]	April 4, 1868	Sept. 21, 1869
Gilbert C. Walker (C)[17]	Sept. 21, 1869	Jan. 1, 1874
James Lawson Kemper (D)	Jan. 1, 1874	Jan. 1, 1878
Frederick W. M. Holliday (D)	Jan. 1, 1878	Jan. 1, 1882
William E. Cameron (READJ)	Jan. 1, 1882	Jan. 1, 1886
Fitzhugh Lee (D)	Jan. 1, 1886	Jan. 1, 1890
Philip W. McKinney (D)	Jan. 1, 1890	Jan. 1, 1894
Charles T. O'Ferrall (D)	Jan. 1, 1894	Jan. 1, 1898
James Hoge Tyler (D)	Jan. 1, 1898	Jan. 1, 1902
Andrew J. Montague (D)	Jan. 1, 1902	Feb. 1, 1906
Claude A. Swanson (D)	Feb. 1, 1906	Feb. 1, 1910
William H. Mann (D)	Feb. 1, 1910	Feb. 1, 1914
Henry C. Stuart (D)	Feb. 1, 1914	Feb. 1, 1918
Westmoreland Davis (D)	Feb. 1, 1918	Feb. 1, 1922
E. Lee Trinkle (D)	Feb. 1, 1922	Feb. 1, 1926
Harry F. Byrd (D)	Feb. 1, 1926	Jan. 15, 1930
John G. Pollard (D)	Jan. 15, 1930	Jan. 17, 1934

George C. Peery (D)	Jan. 17, 1934	Jan. 19, 1938
James H. Price (D)	Jan. 19, 1938	Jan. 21, 1942
Colgate W. Darden Jr. (D)	Jan. 21, 1942	Jan. 16, 1946
William M. Tuck (D)	Jan. 16, 1946	Jan. 18, 1950
John S. Battle (D)	Jan. 18, 1950	Jan. 20, 1954
Thomas B. Stanley (D)	Jan. 20, 1954	Jan. 11, 1958
James Lindsay Almond Jr. (D)	Jan. 11, 1958	Jan. 13, 1962
Albertis S. Harrison Jr. (D)	Jan. 13, 1962	Jan. 15, 1966
Mills E. Godwin Jr. (D)	Jan. 16, 1966	Jan. 17, 1970
Linwood Holton (R)	Jan. 17, 1970	Jan. 12, 1974
Mills E. Godwin Jr. (R)	Jan. 12, 1974	Jan. 14, 1978
John Dalton (R)	Jan. 14, 1978	Jan. 16, 1982
Charles S. Robb (D)	Jan. 16, 1982	Jan. 18, 1986
Gerald L. Baliles (D)	Jan. 18, 1986	Jan. 14, 1990
L. Douglas Wilder (D)	Jan. 14, 1990	Jan. 15, 1994
George F. Allen (R)	Jan. 15, 1994	Jan. 17, 1998
James S. Gilmore III (R)	Jan. 17, 1998	

Virginia
1. Refused reelection and vacated office before end of term.
2. As member of the Privy Council, he succeeded to office.
3. Resigned Nov. 30, 1781.
4. Succeeded to office.
5. Resigned April 5, 1811.
6. As senior member of the Council of State, became acting governor. Died Dec. 1811.
7. As senior member of the Council of State, became acting governor.
8. Resigned April 30, 1836.
9. As senior member of the Council of State, became acting governor.
10. Resigned in March 1841.
11. As senior member of the Council of State, became acting governor. Following Gilmer's resignation, the legislature did not elect a new governor for twenty-one months. Patton, Rutherford, and Gregory took turns as acting governor.
12. As senior member of the Council of State, became acting governor.
13. As senior member of the Council of State, became acting governor.
14. Last Confederate governor.
15. Became Union governor June 20, 1861. Appointed provisional governor May 9, 1865.
16. Provisional governor.
17. Provisional governor from September 1869 to Jan. 1, 1870. Elected to four-year term beginning Jan. 1, 1870.

WASHINGTON

(Became a state Nov. 11, 1889)

Governors	Dates of Service	
Elisha P. Ferry (R)	Nov. 11, 1889	Jan. 9, 1893
John H. McGraw (R)	Jan. 9, 1893	Jan. 11, 1897
John R. Rogers (PP, D)[1]	Jan. 11, 1897	Dec. 26, 1901
Henry McBride (R)[2]	Dec. 26, 1901	Jan. 9, 1905
Albert E. Mead (R)	Jan. 9, 1905	Jan. 27, 1909
Samuel G. Cosgrove (R)[3]	Jan. 27, 1909	March 28, 1909
Marion E. Hay (R)[4]	March 29, 1909	Jan. 11, 1913
Ernest Lister (D)[5]	Jan. 11, 1913	June 14, 1919
Louis F. Hart (R)[6]	June 14, 1919	Jan. 12, 1925
Roland H. Hartley (R)	Jan. 12, 1925	Jan. 9, 1933
Clarence D. Martin (D)	Jan. 9, 1933	Jan. 13, 1941
Arthur B. Langlie (R)	Jan. 13, 1941	Jan. 8, 1945
Monrad C. Wallgren (D)	Jan. 8, 1945	Jan. 10, 1949
Arthur B. Langlie (R)	Jan. 10, 1949	Jan. 14, 1957
Albert D. Rosellini (D)	Jan. 14, 1957	Jan. 11, 1965

Daniel J. Evans (R)	Jan. 11, 1965	Jan. 12, 1977
Dixy Lee Ray (D)	Jan. 12, 1977	Jan. 14, 1981
John D. Spellman (R)	Jan. 14, 1981	Jan. 16, 1985
Booth Gardner (D)	Jan. 16, 1985	Jan. 13, 1993
Mike Lowry (D)	Jan. 13, 1993	Jan. 15, 1997
Gary Locke (D)	Jan. 15, 1997	

Washington
1. Elected as a Populist in 1896. Elected as a Democrat in 1900. Died Dec. 26, 1901.
2. As lieutenant governor, he succeeded to office.
3. Died March 28, 1909.
4. As lieutenant governor, he succeeded to office.
5. Died June 14, 1919.
6. As lieutenant governor, he succeeded to office. Subsequently elected.

WEST VIRGINIA

(Became a state June 19, 1863)

Governors	Dates of Service	
Arthur I. Boreman (UN R, R)[1]	June 20, 1863	Feb. 26, 1869
Daniel D. T. Farnsworth (R)[2]	Feb. 27, 1869	March 3, 1869
William E. Stevenson (R)	March 4, 1869	March 3, 1871
John Jeremiah Jacob (D, I)	March 4, 1871	March 3, 1877
Henry Mason Mathews (D)	March 4, 1877	March 3, 1881
Jacob B. Jackson (D)	March 4, 1881	March 3, 1885
Emanuel Willis Wilson (D)[3]	March 4, 1885	Feb. 5, 1890
Aretas Brooks Fleming (D)[4]	Feb. 6, 1890	March 3, 1893
William A. MacCorkle (D)	March 4, 1893	March 3, 1897
George W. Atkinson (R)	March 4, 1897	March 4, 1901
Albert B. White (R)	March 4, 1901	March 4, 1905
William M. O. Dawson (R)	March 4, 1905	March 4, 1909
William E. Glasscock (R)	March 4, 1909	March 4, 1913
Harry D. Hatfield (R)	March 4, 1913	March 4, 1917
John J. Cornwell (D)	March 4, 1917	March 4, 1921
Ephraim F. Morgan (R)	March 4, 1921	March 4, 1925
Howard M. Gore (R)	March 4, 1925	March 4, 1929
William G. Conley (R)	March 4, 1929	March 4, 1933
Herman G. Kump (D)	March 4, 1933	Jan. 18, 1937
Homer A. Holt (D)	Jan. 18, 1937	Jan. 13, 1941
Matthew M. Neely (D)	Jan. 13, 1941	Jan. 15, 1945
Clarence W. Meadows (D)	Jan. 15, 1945	Jan. 17, 1949
Okey L. Patteson (D)	Jan. 17, 1949	Jan. 19, 1953
William C. Marland (D)	Jan. 19, 1953	Jan. 14, 1957
Cecil H. Underwood (R)	Jan. 14, 1957	Jan. 16, 1961
William W. Barron (D)	Jan. 16, 1961	Jan. 18, 1965
Hulett C. Smith (D)	Jan. 18, 1965	Jan. 13, 1969
Arch A. Moore Jr. (R)	Jan. 13, 1969	Jan. 17, 1977
John D. Rockefeller (D)	Jan. 17, 1977	Jan. 14, 1985
Arch A. Moore Jr. (R)	Jan. 14, 1985	Jan. 16, 1989
Gaston Caperton (D)	Jan. 16, 1989	Jan. 13, 1997
Cecil H. Underwood (R)	Jan. 13, 1997	Jan. 15, 2001
Bob Wise (D)	Jan. 15, 2001	

West Virginia
1. Resigned Feb. 26, 1869.
2. As president of the state Senate, he succeeded to office.
3. Wilson continued in office for almost one year beyond the expiration of his term pending a settlement of the disputed election of 1888.
4. The 1888 election between Democrat Aretas Brooks Fleming and ReW

West Virginia (continued)
publican Nathan Goff was very close, and the final outcome was in dispute. After almost one year of investigation, the West Virginia legislature declared Fleming the winner, and he took office Feb. 6, 1890.

WISCONSIN

(Became a state May 29, 1848)

Governors	Dates of Service	
Nelson Dewey (D)	June 7, 1848	Jan. 5, 1852
Leonard J. Farwell (W)	Jan. 5, 1852	Jan. 2, 1854
William A. Barstow (D)[1]	Jan. 2, 1854	March 21, 1856
Arthur MacArthur (D)[2]	March 21, 1856	March 25, 1856
Coles Bashford (R)[3]	March 25, 1856	
Alexander W. Randall (R)	Jan. 4, 1858	Jan. 6, 1862
Louis P. Harvey (R)[4]	Jan. 6, 1862	April 19, 1862
Edward Salomon (R)[5]	April 19, 1862	Jan. 4, 1864
James T. Lewis (R)	Jan. 4, 1864	Jan. 1, 1866
Lucius Fairchild (R)	Jan. 1, 1866	Jan. 1, 1872
Cadwallader C. Washburn (R)	Jan. 1, 1872	Jan. 5, 1874
William R. Taylor (D)	Jan. 5, 1874	Jan. 3, 1876
Harrison Ludington (R)	Jan. 3, 1876	Jan. 7, 1878
William E. Smith (R)	Jan. 7, 1878	Jan. 2, 1882
Jeremiah M. Rusk (R)	Jan. 2, 1882	Jan. 7, 1889
William D. Hoard (R)	Jan. 7, 1889	Jan. 5, 1891
George W. Peck (D)	Jan. 5, 1891	Jan. 7, 1895
William H. Upham (R)	Jan. 7, 1895	Jan. 4, 1897
Edward Scofield (R)	Jan. 4, 1897	Jan. 7, 1901
Robert M. La Follette (R)[6]	Jan. 7, 1901	Jan. 1, 1906
James O. Davidson (R)[7]	Jan. 1, 1906	Jan. 2, 1911
Francis E. McGovern (R)	Jan. 2, 1911	Jan. 4, 1915
Emanuel L. Philipp (R)	Jan. 4, 1915	Jan. 3, 1921
John J. Blaine (R)	Jan. 3, 1921	Jan. 3, 1927
Fred R. Zimmerman (R)	Jan. 3, 1927	Jan. 7, 1929
Walter J. Kohler Sr. (R)	Jan. 7, 1929	Jan. 5, 1931
Philip F. La Follette (R)	Jan. 5, 1931	Jan. 2, 1933
Albert G. Schmedeman (D)	Jan. 2, 1933	Jan. 7, 1935
Philip F. La Follette (PROG)	Jan. 7, 1935	Jan. 2, 1939
Julius P. Heil (R)	Jan. 2, 1939	Jan. 4, 1943
Orland S. Loomis (PROG)[8]		
Walter S. Goodland (R)[9]	Jan. 4, 1943	March 12, 1947
Oscar Rennebohm (R)[10]	March 12, 1947	Jan. 1, 1951
Walter J. Kohler Jr. (R)	Jan. 1, 1951	Jan. 7, 1957
Vernon W. Thomson (R)	Jan. 7, 1957	Jan. 5, 1959
Gaylord A. Nelson (D)	Jan. 5, 1959	Jan. 7, 1963
John W. Reynolds (D)	Jan. 7, 1963	Jan. 4, 1965
Warren P. Knowles (R)	Jan. 4, 1965	Jan. 4, 1971
Patrick J. Lucey (D)[11]	Jan. 4, 1971	July 7, 1977
M. J. Schreiber (D)[12]	July 7, 1977	Jan. 1, 1979
Lee S. Dreyfus (R)	Jan. 1, 1979	Jan. 3, 1983
Anthony S. Earl (D)	Jan. 3, 1983	Jan. 5, 1987
Tommy G. Thompson (R)[13]	Jan. 5, 1987	Feb. 1, 2001
Scott McCallum (R)[14]	Feb. 1, 2001	

Wisconsin
1. Barstow's election to a second term in 1855 was disputed by his opponent, Coles Bashford, who charged fraud. Barstow took office, but resigned while the case was pending in court. The office was awarded to Bashford several days later.

2. Acting governor.
3. Successfully contested the election of William Augustus Barstow and served out the remainder of the term.
4. Died April 19, 1862.
5. Acting governor.
6. Resigned Jan. 1, 1906.
7. As lieutenant governor, he succeeded to office. Subsequently elected.
8. Elected in 1942 for a two-year term, but died Dec. 7, 1942, before inauguration.
9. As lieutenant governor, he succeeded to office. Subsequently elected. Died March 12, 1947.
10. As lieutenant governor, he succeeded to office. Subsequently elected.
11. Resigned July 7, 1977.
12. As lieutenant governor, he succeeded to office.
13. Resigned Feb. 1, 2001.
14. As lieutenant governor, he succeeded to office.

WYOMING

(Became a state July 10, 1890)

Governors	Dates of Service	
Francis E. Warren (R)[1]	Oct. 11, 1890	Nov. 24, 1890
Amos W. Barber (R)[2]	Nov. 24, 1890	Jan. 2, 1893
John E. Osborne (D)[3]	Jan. 2, 1893	Jan. 7, 1895
William A. Richards (R)	Jan. 7, 1895	Jan. 2, 1899
DeForest Richards (R)[4]	Jan. 2, 1899	April 28, 1903
Fenimore C. Chatterton (R)[5]	April 28, 1903	Jan. 2, 1905
Bryant B. Brooks (R)[6]	Jan. 2, 1905	Jan. 2, 1911
Joseph M. Carey (D)	Jan. 2, 1911	Jan. 4, 1915
John B. Kendrick (D)[7]	Jan. 4, 1915	Feb. 26, 1917
Frank L. Houx (D)[8]	Feb. 26, 1917	Jan. 6, 1919
Robert D. Carey (R)	Jan. 6, 1919	Jan. 1, 1923
William B. Ross (D)[9]	Jan. 1, 1923	Oct. 2, 1924
Frank E. Lucas (R)[10]	Oct. 2, 1924	Jan. 5, 1925
Nellie T. Ross (D)[11]	Jan. 5, 1925	Jan. 3, 1927
Frank C. Emerson (R)[12]	Jan. 3, 1927	Feb. 18, 1931
Alonzo M. Clark (R)[13]	Feb. 18, 1931	Jan. 2, 1933
Leslie A. Miller (D)[14]	Jan. 2, 1933	Jan. 2, 1939
Nels H. Smith (R)	Jan. 2, 1939	Jan. 4, 1943
Lester C. Hunt (D)[15]	Jan. 4, 1943	Jan. 3, 1949
Arthur G. Crane (R)[16]	Jan. 3, 1949	Jan. 1, 1951
Frank A. Barrett (R)[17]	Jan. 1, 1951	Jan. 3, 1953
Clifford Joy Rogers (R)[18]	Jan. 3, 1953	Jan. 3, 1955
Milward L. Simpson (R)	Jan. 3, 1955	Jan. 5, 1959
John J. Hickey (D)[19]	Jan. 5, 1959	Jan. 2, 1961
Jack R. Gage (D)[20]	Jan. 2, 1961	Jan. 6, 1963
Clifford P. Hansen (R)	Jan. 7, 1963	Jan. 2, 1967
Stanley K. Hathaway (R)	Jan. 2, 1967	Jan. 6, 1975
Ed Herschler (D)	Jan. 6, 1975	Jan. 5, 1987
Michael J. Sullivan (D)	Jan. 5, 1987	Jan. 2, 1995
Jim Geringer (R)	Jan. 2, 1995	

Wyoming
1. Resigned Nov. 24, 1890.
2. As secretary of state, he succeeded to office for the remainder of the first half of Gov. Warren's term.
3. Elected in a special election for the second half of Warren's term.
4. Died April 28, 1903.
5. As secretary of state, he succeeded to office for the remainder of the first half of Richards' term.
6. Elected in a special election for second half of Richards' term. Subsequently reelected.
7. Resigned Feb. 26, 1917.
8. As secretary of state, he succeeded to office.
9. Died Oct. 2, 1924.

Wyoming (continued)

10. As secretary of state, he succeeded to office for the remainder of the first half of Ross's term.

11. Elected in a special election for the second half of Ross' (her husband's) term.

12. Died Feb. 18, 1931.

13. As secretary of state, he succeeded to office for the remainder of the first half of Gov. Emerson's term.

14. Elected in a special election for the second half of Emerson's term. Subsequently reelected.

15. Resigned Jan. 3, 1949.

16. As secretary of state, he succeeded to office.

17. Resigned Jan. 3, 1953.

18. As secretary of state, he succeeded to office.

19. Resigned Jan. 2, 1961.

20. As secretary of state, he succeeded to office.

## CHAPTER 30

Gubernatorial General Election Returns, 1776–2000

GUBERNATORIAL GENERAL ELECTION RETURNS for all fifty states are presented in this section (pages 1416–1477). In previous editions of *Guide to U.S. Elections*, gubernatorial returns were only provided back to 1787, when the original thirteen states began ratifying the Constitution. For this edition, returns for the thirteen original states during the revolutionary period (1776–1787) have been provided where possible. In a few states during this time governors were appointed rather than elected. In states where elections were held, returns were not always available. The returns added to this edition were provided by elections historian Michael J. Dubin, who conducted original research, including examining newspaper reports, manuscript election returns, and other firsthand sources provided by the states' secretaries of state and historical offices.

Returns for the years 1787 through 1823 were obtained from *American State Governors, 1776–1976*, by Joseph E. Kallenbach and Jessamine S. Kallenbach (Dobbs Ferry, N.Y.: Oceana Publishing, 1977). Those for 1824 through 1973 were obtained from the Inter-University Consortium for Political and Social Research (ICPSR) at the University of Michigan. *(See box, ICPSR Historical Returns File, p. xvi, Vol. I.)* Major sources for returns from 1974 to 1997 were Congressional Quarterly, which obtained them from the state secretaries of state, and the biennial *America Votes* series, compiled biennially by Congressional Quarterly in Washington, D.C. Richard M. Scammon and Alice V. McGillivray of the Elections Research Center, Washington, D.C., created the series first published in 1956. Since 1996 the series has been compiled under the direction of Rhodes Cook.

The symbol # next to returns before 1974 indicates that Congressional Quarterly obtained the returns from a source other than Kallenbach or the ICPSR. A complete list of other sources used appears on page 1477. A "Gubernatorial Candidates Index" is located on pages I-129 to I-142.

In addition to these sources, new elections data research uncovered by Dubin supplements the original material in this edition. CQ editors felt the new data was of scholarly merit and worthy of inclusion—much of it filling the gaps of missing names or returns in previous editions of *Guide to U.S. Elections*.

PRESENTATION OF RETURNS

The gubernatorial returns are arranged alphabetically by state and in chronological order of election within each state listing. The candidate receiving the greatest number of popular votes is listed first with his or her vote total and percentage of the total vote cast, followed in descending order of votes received by all other candidates receiving *at least 5 percent* of the total vote cast.

Special elections to fill vacancies are designated in the returns.

VOTE TOTALS AND PERCENTAGES

The ICPSR collection includes all candidates receiving popular votes, only gubernatorial candidates receiving *at least 5 percent of the total popular vote* for that election are included. For example, the ICPSR data collection for the 1908 Illinois gubernatorial election shows that 1,154,612 votes were cast, with Republican Charles S. Deneen receiving 550,076 votes (47.64 percent), Democrat Adlai E. Stevenson receiving 526,912 votes (45.64 percent), and four other candidates receiving the remaining 77,624 votes (6.72 percent). These four candidates do not appear on page 1429 of this book because none of them received 5 percent or more of the vote.

The percentages used in this section were calculated to two decimal places on the basis of the total number of votes cast in the election and rounded to one place. Thus, on page 1429, for the 1908 Illinois election, Deneen's percentage of the total vote is listed as 47.6 percent and Stevenson's as 45.6 percent. The percentages are rounded to one decimal place and do not add to 100 percent because of the scattered votes for the other four candidates.

NAMES AND PARTY DESIGNATIONS

Names are listed as they were recorded in the official returns or other source documentation. In some instances, particularly in the nineteenth century, candidate names in the ICPSR file are incomplete. First names were the most commonly missing elements in the original sources consulted by the scholars and archivists who gathered the ICPSR returns. Congressional Quarterly has added full names when they could be determined and has corrected obvious misspellings. For this edition, elections scholar Michael J. Dubin assisted in finding missing names and correcting the misspellings of previous editions.

In the ICPSR returns, the distinct—and in many cases, *multiple*—party designations appearing in the original sources are preserved. In many cases party labels represent combinations of multiparty support received by individual candidates. If, for example, on the ballot and official returns more than one party name was listed next to a candidate's name, then the party designation appearing in the election returns for that candidate will be a unique abbreviation for that combination of parties. *(See "Political Party Abbreviations," p. 1596.)*

In the special case of a candidate's name listed separately on the original ballot under more than one party—where returns were reported *separately* for each party—Congressional Quar-

terly has summed the votes recorded under the several parties and that figure appears as the candidate's total vote. Whenever separate party totals have been summed, a *comma* separates the abbreviations of the parties contributing the largest and second largest share of the total vote.

Most cases of this special situation occurred in New York and Pennsylvania during this century. For example, in the original ICPSR returns for New York's 1946 gubernatorial election, James M. Mead received 1,532,161 votes as Democratic Party candidate, 428,903 votes as American Labor Party candidate, and 177,418 votes as Liberal Party candidate for a total of 2,138,482 votes.

In organizing the ICPSR data for publication, Congressional Quarterly has summed all votes Mead received from these three parties. Thus, on page 1454 only Mead's total vote of 2,138,482 appears.

Congressional Quarterly has also included party abbreviations for the two parties that contributed the most votes to Mead's total—separated by a comma. Thus, immediately following his name appear the abbreviations—D, AM LAB—indicating that Mead was a candidate of at least two parties and that the greatest number of votes he received was as a Democrat.

Gubernatorial General Election Returns, 1776–2000

ALABAMA

(Became a state Dec. 14, 1819)

	Candidates	Votes	%
1819	William Wyatt Bibb (D-R)	8,321	53.9
	W. D. Williams	7,140	46.1
1821	Israel Pickens (D-R)	9,616	57.4
	Henry Chambers	7,129	42.6
1823	Israel Pickens (D-R)	13,580	57.5
	Henry Chambers	10,033	42.5
1825	John Murphy (JAC D)	12,184	100.0
1827	John Murphy (JAC D)	8,334	99.2
1829	Gabriel Moore (JAC D)	10,956	100.0
1831	John Gayle (D)	14,403	55.0
	Nicholas Davis (NR)	8,137	31.1
	Samuel B. Moore	3,643	13.9
1833	John Gayle (D)	9,750	100.0
1835	Clement Comer Clay (D)	23,279	65.6
	Enoch Parsons (SR W)	12,209	34.4
1837	Arthur P. Bagby (D)	24,419	54.8
	Samuel W. Oliver (A-VB D)	20,152	45.2
1839	Arthur P. Bagby (D)	20,451	92.3
	Arthur F. Hopkins (W)	1,708	7.7
1841	Benjamin Fitzpatrick (D)	27,974	56.9
	James W. McClung (IW)	21,219	43.1
1843	Benjamin Fitzpatrick (D)	✔	
1845	Joshua L. Martin (I)	30,261	53.6
	Nathaniel Terry (D)	25,587	45.3
1847	Reuben Chapman (D)	30,622	56.8
	Nicholas Davis (W)	23,247	43.2
1849	Henry Watkins Collier (D)	36,350	98.1
1851	Henry Watkins Collier (D)	37,480	85.7
	James Shields (W)	5,749	13.2
1853	John A. Winston (D)	29,476	62.3
	William S. Earnest (W)	10,871	23.0
	Alvis Q. Nicks (UN D)	5,128	10.8

1855	John A. Winston (D)	43,930	57.8
	George D. Shortridge (AM)	32,086	42.2
1857	Andrew B. Moore (D)	41,871	94.5
1859	Andrew B. Moore (D)	52,786	72.8
	William F. Samford (SO RTS D)	19,745	27.2
1861	John Gill Shorter (D)	38,221	57.5
	Thomas Hill Watts (W)	28,117	42.3
1863	Thomas Hill Watts (W)	28,201	71.7
	John Gill Shorter (D)	9,664	24.6
1865	Robert Miller Patton (W)	20,611	45.2
	Michael J. Bulger (D)	16,380	35.9
	William R. Smith (UN)	8,557	18.8
1868	William Hugh Smith (R)	62,067	100.0
1870	Robert B. Lindsay (D)	77,723	50.5
	William Hugh Smith (R)	76,282	49.5
1872	David P. Lewis (R)	89,868	52.5
	Thomas H. Herndon (LR)	81,371	47.5
1874	George S. Houston (D)	107,118	53.3
	David P. Lewis (R)	93,928	46.7
1876	George S. Houston (D)	96,401	63.4
	Noadiah Woodruff (R)	55,682	36.6
1878	Rufus W. Cobb (D)	88,255	100.0
1880	Rufus W. Cobb (D)	134,905	76.1
	J. M. Pickens (G)	42,363	23.9
1882	Edward A. O'Neal (D)	102,617	68.7
	James L. Sheffield (R)	46,742	31.3
1884	Edward A. O'Neal (D)	143,229	99.7
1886	Thomas Seay (D)	145,095	79.4
	Arthur Bingham (R)	36,793	20.1
1888	Thomas Seay (D)	155,973	77.6
	W. T. Ewing (R)	44,707	22.2
1890	Thomas G. Jones (D)	139,912	76.1
	Benjamin M. Long (R)	42,391	23.1
1892	Thomas G. Jones (D)	126,955	52.2
	Reuben F. Kolb (ID)	115,732	47.5

1894	W. C. Oates (D)	110,875	57.1
	Reuben F. Kolb (POP)	83,292	42.9
1896	Joseph F. Johnston (D)	128,549	59.0
	Albert T. Goodwyn (POP)	89,290	41.0
1898	Joseph F. Johnston (D)	110,551	67.0
	Gilbert B. Dean (POP)	50,052	30.3
1900	William J. Samford (D)	115,167	71.0
	John A. Steele (R)	28,305	17.5
	G. B. Crowe (POP)	17,444	10.8
1902	William D. Jelks (D)	67,748	73.7
	John A. W. Smith (R)	24,150	26.3
1906	Braxton B. Comer (D)	61,223	85.5
	Asa E. Stratton (R)	9,981	13.9
1910	Emmet O'Neal (D)	77,694	78.7
	Joseph O. Thompson (R)	19,210	19.5
1914	Charles Henderson (D)	61,307	78.7
	John B. Shields (R)	11,773	15.1
1918	Thomas E. Kilby (D)	54,746	80.2
	Dallas B. Smith	13,497	19.8
1922	William W. Brandon (D)	113,605	77.6
	O. D. Street (R)	31,175	21.3
1926	Bibb Graves (D)	93,432	81.2
	J. A. Bingham (R)	21,605	18.8
1930	B. M. Miller (D)	155,034	61.8
	Hugh A. Locke (I)	95,745	38.2
1934	Bibb Graves (D)	155,197	86.9
	Edmund H. Dryer (R)	22,621	12.7
1938	Frank Dixon (D)	115,761	87.4
	W. A. Clardy (R)	16,513	12.5
1942	Chauncey Sparks (D)	69,048	89.0
	Hugh McEniry (R)	8,167	10.5
1946	James E. Folsom (D)	174,959	88.7
	Lyman Ward (R)	22,362	11.3
1950	Gordon Persons (D)	155,414	91.1
	John S. Crowder (R)	15,177	8.9
1954	James E. Folsom (D)	244,401	73.4
	Tom Abernethy (R)	88,688	26.6
1958	John Patterson (D)	239,633	88.4
	William L. Longshore Jr. (R)	30,415	11.2
1962	George C. Wallace (D)	303,987	96.3
1966	Lurleen B. Wallace (D)	537,505	63.4
	James Martin (R)	262,943	31.0
	Carl R. Robinson (I)	47,653	5.6
1970	George C. Wallace (D)	637,046	74.5
	John Logan Cashin (NDPA)	125,491	14.7
	A. C. Shelton (I)	75,679	8.9
1974	George C. Wallace (D)	497,574	83.2
	Elvin McCary (R)	88,381	14.8
1978	Forrest H. "Fob" James Jr. (D)	551,886	72.6
	Guy Hunt (R)	196,963	25.9
1982	George C. Wallace (D)	650,538	57.6
	Emory Folmar (R)	440,815	39.1
1986	Guy Hunt (R)	696,203	56.4
	Bill Baxley (D)	537,163	43.5
1990	Guy Hunt (R)	633,520	52.1
	Paul Hubbert (D)	582,106	47.9
1994	Forrest H. "Fob" James Jr. (R)	604,926	50.3
	James E. Folsom Jr. (D)	594,169	49.4
1998	Don Siegelman (D)	760,155	57.7
	Forrest H. "Fob" James Jr. (R)	554,746	42.1

ALASKA

(Became a state Jan. 3, 1959)

1958	William A. Egan (D)	29,189	59.6
	John Butrovich Jr. (R)	19,299	39.4
1962	William A. Egan (D)	29,627	52.3
	Mike Stepovich (R)	27,054	47.7
1966	Walter J. Hickel (R)	33,145	50.0
	William A. Egan (D)	32,065	48.4
1970	William A. Egan (D)	42,309	52.4
	Keith H. Miller (R)	37,264	46.1
1974	Jay S. Hammond (R)	45,840	47.7
	William A. Egan (D)	45,553	47.4
	Joseph E. Vogler (ALI)	4,770	5.0
1978	Jay S. Hammond (R)	49,580	39.1
	Walter J. Hickel (WRITE IN)	33,555	26.4
	Chancy Croft (D)	25,656	20.2
	Tom Kelly (I)	15,656	12.3

Explanation of Symbols

In the returns for gubernatorial elections, *symbols* are used to denote special circumstances. Where no symbol is used, the candidate who received the most votes won the election on the basis of the popular vote and served as governor. The following is a key to the symbols used:

✔ Elected and served as governor, but the number of votes and the percentage of the total received were not available.

† Elected governor by the state legislature because no candidate received a majority of the popular vote as required by state law at the time of the election. *(See p. 1380 for an explanation of the election of governors by state legislatures.)*

* Symbol used for two types of situations: (1) the candidate who won the election did not serve as governor because he died before assuming office; (2) none of the candidates running qualified to become governor on the basis of the election returns or action by the state legislature. *(For an explanation of a specific case, consult the appropriate state listed in Chapter 29, "Governors of the States, 1776–2001," pp. 1383–1414.)*

‡ Disputed election. The symbol is used in a variety of circumstances such as an election dispute resulting in the unseating of a governor after he assumed office or resulting in rival governors each claiming to have been legitimately elected. *(For an explanation of a specific case, consult the appropriate state listed in the selection, "Governors of the States, 1776–2001," pp. 1383–1414.)*

Information was obtained from a source other than Congressional Quarterly's basic sources for this volume. *(For a list of the other sources used, see p. 1477.)*

1982	Bill Sheffield (D)	89,918	46.1
	Tom Fink (R)	72,291	37.1
	Richard L. Randolph (LIBERT)	29,067	14.9
1986	Steve C. Cowper (D)	84,943	47.3
	Arliss Sturgulewski (R)	76,515	42.6
	Joe Vogler (ALI)	10,013	5.6
1990	Walter J. Hickel (ALI)	75,721	38.9
	Tony Knowles (D)	60,201	30.9
	Arliss Sturgulewski (R)	50,991	26.2
1994	Tony Knowles (D)	87,693	41.1
	James O. "Jim" Campbell (R)	87,157	40.8
	John B. "Jack" Coghill (ALI)	27,838	13.0
1998	Tony Knowles (D)	112,879	51.3
	Robin Taylor (WRITE IN)	40,209	18.3
	John Lindauer (R)	39,331	17.9
	Ray Metcalfe (MOD R)	13,540	6.2

ARIZONA

(Became a state Feb. 14, 1912)

1911	George W. P. Hunt (D)	11,123	51.5
	Edward W. Wells (R)	9,166	42.4
	P. W. Gallentine (SOC)	1,247	5.8
1914	George W. P. Hunt (D)	25,226	49.5
	Ralph H. Cameron (R)	17,602	34.5
	George U. Young (PROG)	5,206	10.2
	J. R. Barnette (SOC)	2,973	5.8
1916	Thomas E. Campbell (R)	27,976‡	48.0
	George W. P. Hunt (D)	27,946	47.9
1918	Thomas E. Campbell (R)	25,927	49.9
	Fred T. Colter (D)	25,588	49.3
1920	Thomas E. Campbell (R)	37,060	54.2
	Mit Simms (D)	31,385	45.9
1922	George W. P. Hunt (D)	37,310	54.9
	Thomas E. Campbell (R)	30,599	45.1
1924	George W. P. Hunt (D)	38,372	50.5
	Dwight B. Heard (R)	37,571	49.5
1926	George W. P. Hunt (D)	39,979	50.3
	E. S. Clark (R)	39,580	49.8
1928	John C. Phillips (R)	47,829	51.7
	George W. P. Hunt (D)	44,553	48.2
1930	George W. P. Hunt (D)	48,875	51.4
	John C. Phillips (R)	46,231	48.6
1932	Benjamin B. Moeur (D)	75,314	63.2
	J. C. Kinney (R)	42,202	35.4
1934	Benjamin B. Moeur (D)	61,355	59.7
	Thomas Maddock (R)	39,242	38.2
1936	Rawghile C. Stanford (D)	87,678	70.7
	Thomas E. Campbell (R)	36,114	29.1
1938	Robert T. Jones (D)	80,350	68.6
	Jerrie W. Lee (R)	32,022	27.3
1940	Sidney P. Osborn (D)	97,606	65.5
	Jerrie W. Lee (R)	50,358	33.8
1942	Sidney P. Osborn (D)	63,484	72.5
	Jerrie W. Lee (R)	23,562	26.9
1944	Sidney P. Osborn (D)	100,220	77.9
	Jerrie W. Lee (R)	27,261	21.2
1946	Sidney P. Osborn (D)	73,595	60.1
	Bruce D. Brockett (R)	48,867	39.9

1948	Dan E. Garvey (D)	104,008	59.2
	Bruce D. Brockett (R)	70,419	40.1
1950	Howard Pyle (R)	99,109	50.8
	Ana Frohmiller (D)	96,118	49.2
1952	Howard Pyle (R)	156,592	60.2
	Joe C. Haldiman (D)	103,693	39.8
1954	Ernest W. McFarland (D)	128,104	52.5
	Howard Pyle (R)	115,866	47.5
1956	Ernest W. McFarland (D)	171,848	59.6
	Horace B. Griffen (R)	116,744	40.5
1958	Paul Fannin (R)	160,136	55.1
	Robert Morrison (D)	130,329	44.9
1960	Paul Fannin (R)	235,502	59.3
	Lee Ackerman (D)	161,605	40.7
1962	Paul Fannin (R)	200,578	54.8
	Sam Goddard (D)	165,263	45.2
1964	Sam Goddard (D)	252,098	53.2
	Richard Kleindienst (R)	221,404	46.8
1966	Jack Williams (R)	203,438	53.8
	Sam Goddard (D)	174,904	46.2
1968	Jack Williams (R)	279,923	57.8
	Sam Goddard (D)	204,075	42.2
1970	Jack Williams (R)	209,356	50.9
	Raul H. Castro (D)	202,053	49.1
1974	Raul H. Castro (D)	278,375	50.4
	Russell Williams (R)	273,674	49.6
1978	Bruce Babbitt (D)	282,605	52.5
	Evan Mecham (R)	241,093	44.8
1982	Bruce Babbitt (D)	453,795	62.5
	Leo Corbet (R)	235,877	32.5
	Sam Steiger (LIBERT)	36,649	5.0
1986	Evan Mecham (R)	343,913	39.7
	Carolyn Warner (D)	298,986	34.5
	Bill Schulz (I)	224,085	25.8
1990	Fife Symington (R)	523,984	49.6
	Terry Goddard (D)	519,691	49.2

Runoff Election

| 1991 | Fife Symington (R) | 492,569 | 52.4 |
| | Terry Goddard (D) | 448,168 | 47.6 |

1994	Fife Symington (R)	593,492	52.5
	Eddie Basha (D)	500,702	44.3
1998	Jane Dee Hull (R)	620,188	60.9
	Paul Johnson (D)	361,552	35.5

ARKANSAS

(Became a state June 15, 1836)

1836	James S. Conway (D)	4,855	61.6
	Absalom Fowler (W)	3,024	38.4
1840	Archibald Yell (D)	10,554	96.4
1844	Thomas S. Drew (D)	8,859	47.6
	Lorenzo Gibson (W)	7,244	38.9
	Richard Byrd (I)	2,507	13.5
1848	Thomas S. Drew (D)	15,962	96.6
1849	John S. Roane (D)	3,290	50.5
	C. Wilson (W)	3,228	49.5

1852	Elias N. Conway (D)	15,442	55.4
	B. H. Smithson (W)	12,414	44.6
1856	Elias N. Conway (D)	27,612	64.4
	James Yell (AM)	15,249	35.6
1860	Henry M. Rector (ID)	32,048	52.5
	Richard H. Johnson (D)	28,969	47.5
1872	Elisha Baxter (R)	41,808	51.8
	Joseph Brooks (D)	38,909	48.2
1874	Augustus H. Garland (D)	76,552	100.0
1876	William R. Miller (D)	69,775	65.6
	A. Bishop (R)	36,272	34.1
1878	William R. Miller (D)	88,726	100.0
1880	Thomas J. Churchill (D)	84,185	72.8
	W. P. Parks (G)	31,424	27.2
1882	James H. Berry (D)	87,669	59.6
	W. D. Slack (R)	49,372	33.5
	R. K. Garland (G)	10,142	6.9
1884	Simon P. Hughes (D)	100,875	64.6
	Thomas Boles (R)	55,388	35.5
1886	Simon P. Hughes (D)	90,650	55.3
	S. Gregg (R)	54,063	33.0
	C. E. Cunningham (AG WHEEL)	19,169	11.7
1888	James P. Eagle (D)	99,229	54.1
	C. M. Norwood (LAB)	84,273	45.9
1890	James P. Eagle (D)	106,267	55.5
	N. B. Fizer (R)	85,181	44.5
1892	William M. Fishback (D)	90,115	57.7
	William G. Whipple (R)	33,634	21.5
	J. P. Carnahan (POP)	31,116	19.9
1894	James P. Clarke (D)	74,809	59.1
	H. L. Remmel (R)	26,085	20.6
	D. E. Barker (POP)	24,181	19.1
1896	Daniel Webster Jones (D)	91,114	64.3
	H. L. Remmel (R)	35,837	25.3
	A. W. Files (POP)	13,980	9.9
1898	Daniel Webster Jones (D)	75,354	67.4
	H. F. Auten (R)	27,524	24.6
	W. S. Morgan (POP)	8,332	7.5
1900	Jefferson Davis (D)	88,636	66.7
	H. L. Remmel (R)	40,701	30.6
1902	Jefferson Davis (D)	77,354	64.6
	Harry H. Meyers (R)	29,251	24.4
	Charles D. Greaves (POP)	8,345	7.0
1904	Jefferson Davis (D)	90,263	61.0
	Harry H. Myers (R)	53,898	36.4
1906	John S. Little (D)	105,586	69.1
	John I. Worthington (R)	41,689	27.3
1908	George W. Donaghey (D)	110,418	68.1
	John I. Worthington (R)	44,863	27.7
1910	George W. Donaghey (D)	101,612	67.4
	Andrew I. Roland (R)	39,870	26.5
	Dan Hogan (SOC)	9,196	6.1
1912	Joseph T. Robinson (D)	109,825	64.7
	Andrew I. Roland (R)	46,440	27.4
	G. E. Mikel (SOC)	13,384	7.9

Special Election

1913	George W. Hays (D)	53,655	64.3
	Harry H. Meyers (R)	17,040	20.4

	George W. Murphy (PROG)	8,431	10.1
	J. Emil Webber (SOC)	4,378	5.2
1914	George W. Hays (D)	94,143	69.5
	Audrey L. Kinney (R)	30,947	22.8
	Dan Hogan (SOC)	10,434	7.7
1916	Charles H. Brough (D)	122,041	69.5
	Wallace Townsend (R)	43,963	25.0
	William Davis (SOC)	9,730	5.5
1918	Charles H. Brough (D)	68,192	93.4
	Clay Fulks (SOC)	4,792	6.6
1920	Thomas C. McRae (D)	123,637	65.0
	Wallace Townsend (R)	46,350	24.4
	J. H. Blount (NEG I)	15,627	8.2
1922	Thomas C. McRae (D)	99,987	78.1
	John W. Grabiel (R)	28,055	21.9
1924	Thomas J. Terral (D)	99,598	79.8
	John W. Grabiel (R)	25,152	20.2
1926	John E. Martineau (D)	116,735	76.5
	M. D. Bowers (R)	35,969	23.6
1928	Harvey J. Parnell (D)	151,743	77.3
	M. D. Bowers (R)	44,545	22.7
1930	Harvey J. Parnell (D)	112,847	81.2
	J. O. Livesay (R)	26,162	18.8
1932	Julius M. Futrell (D)	200,096	90.4
	J. O. Livesay (R)	19,717	8.9
1934	Julius M. Futrell (D)	123,918	89.2
	C. C. Ledbetter (R)	13,083	9.4
1936	Carl E. Bailey (D)	155,152	84.9
	Osro Cobb (R)	26,875	14.7
1938	Carl E. Bailey (D)	118,696	86.3
	Charles S. Cole (I)	12,077	8.8
1940	Homer M. Adkins (D)	184,578	91.4
	H. C. Stump (R)	16,600	8.2
1942	Homer M. Adkins (D)	98,871	100.0
1944	Ben Laney (D)	186,401	86.0
	H. C. Stump (R)	30,442	14.0
1946	Ben Laney (D)	128,029	84.1
	W. T. Mills (R)	24,133	15.9
1948	Sidney S. McMath (D)	217,771	89.2
	Charles R. Black (R)	26,500	10.9
1950	Sidney S. McMath (D)	266,778	84.1
	Jefferson W. Speck (R)	50,303	15.9
1952	Francis Cherry (D)	342,292	87.4
	Jefferson W. Speck (R)	49,292	12.6
1954	Orval E. Faubus (D)	208,121	62.1
	Pratt C. Remmel (R)	127,004	37.9
1956	Orval E. Faubus (D)	321,797	80.7
	Roy Mitchell (R)	77,215	19.4
1958	Orval E. Faubus (D)	236,598	82.5
	George W. Johnson (R)	50,288	17.5
1960	Orval E. Faubus (D)	292,064	69.2
	Henry M. Britt (R)	129,921	30.8
1962	Orval E. Faubus (D)	225,743	73.3
	Willis Ricketts (R)	82,349	26.7
1964	Orval E. Faubus (D)	337,489	57.0
	Winthrop Rockefeller (R)	254,561	43.0
1966	Winthrop Rockefeller (R)	306,324	54.4
	James Johnson (D)	257,203	45.6

1968	Winthrop Rockefeller (R)	322,782	52.4
	Marion Crank (D)	292,813	47.6
1970	Dale Bumpers (D)	375,648	61.7
	Winthrop Rockefeller (R)	197,418	32.4
	Walter L. Carruth (AM)	36,132	5.9
1972	Dale Bumpers (D)	488,892	75.4
	Len E. Blaylock (R)	159,177	24.6
1974	David H. Pryor (D)	358,018	65.6
	Ken Coon (R)	187,872	34.4
1976	David H. Pryor (D)	605,083	83.2
	Leon Griffith (R)	121,716	16.7
1978	Bill Clinton (D)	335,101	63.4
	A. Lynn Lowe (R)	193,746	36.6
1980	Frank D. White (R)	435,684	51.9
	Bill Clinton (D)	403,241	48.1
1982	Bill Clinton (D)	431,855	54.7
	Frank D. White (R)	357,496	45.3
1984	Bill Clinton (D)	554,561	62.6
	Woody Freeman (R)	331,987	37.4
1986	Bill Clinton (D)	439,851	63.9
	Frank White (R)	248,415	36.1
1990	Bill Clinton (D)	400,386	57.5
	Sheffield Nelson (R)	295,925	42.5
1994	Jim Guy Tucker (D)	428,936	59.8
	Sheffield Nelson (R)	287,904	40.2
1998	Mike Huckabee (R)	421,989	59.8
	Bill Bristow (D)	272,923	38.7

CALIFORNIA

(Became a state Sept. 9, 1850)

1849	Peter H. Burnett (ID)	6,716	47.3
	Winfield S. Sherwood	3,188	22.5
	John A. Sutter	2,201	15.5
	John W. Geary	1,475	10.4
1851	John Bigler (D)	23,175	50.5
	Pierson B. Reading (W)	22,732	49.5
1853	John Bigler (D)	38,940	51.0
	William Waldo (W)	37,464	49.0
1855	J. Neeley Johnson (AM)	51,976	52.5
	John Bigler (D)	46,935	47.5
1857	John B. Weller (D)	49,096	56.8
	Edward Stanly (R)	17,723	20.5
	George W. Bowie (AM)	19,481	20.8
1859	Milton S. Latham (D)	44,023	57.4
	John Currey (A-LEC D)	24,180	31.5
	Leland Stanford (R)	8,466	11.0
1861	Leland Stanford (R)	56,036	46.8
	John R. McConnell (SEC D)	32,751	27.4
	John Conness (UN D)	30,944	25.8
1863	Frederick F. Low (UN R)	64,283	59.0
	John G. Downey (D)	44,622	41.0
1867	Henry H. Haight (D)	49,905	54.0
	George C. Gurham (R)	40,359	43.7
1871	Newton Booth (R)	62,581	52.1
	Henry H. Haight (D)	57,520	47.9

1875	William Irwin (D)	61,509	50.0
	Timothy G. Phelps (R)	31,322	25.5
	John Bidwell (I)	29,752	24.2
1879	George C. Perkins (R)	67,965	42.4
	Hugh J. Glenn (D)	47,647	29.8
	William F. White (WMP/L)	44,482	27.8
1882	George Stoneman (D)	90,694	55.1
	Morris M. Estee (R)	67,175	40.8
1886	Washington Bartlett (D)	84,970	43.4
	John F. Swift (R)	84,316	43.1
	C. C. O'Donnell (I)	12,227	6.3
1890	Henry H. Markham (R)	125,129	49.6
	E. B. Pond (D)	117,184	46.4
1894	James H. Budd (D)	111,944	39.3
	Morris M. Estee (R)	110,738	38.9
	J. V. Webster (PP)	51,304	18.0
1898	Henry T. Gage (R & UL)	148,354	51.7
	James G. Maguire (D & POP)	129,261	45.0
1902	George C. Pardee (R)	146,332	48.1
	Franklin K. Lane (D)	143,783	47.2
1906	James N. Gillett (R)	125,887	40.4
	Theodore A. Bell (D)	117,645	37.7
	William H. Langdon (I LEAGUE)	45,008	14.4
	Austin Lewis (SOC)	16,036	5.1
1910	Hiram W. Johnson (R)	177,191	45.9
	Theodore A. Bell (D)	154,835	40.1
	J. Stitt Wilson (SOC)	47,819	12.4
1914	Hiram W. Johnson (PROG)	460,495	49.7
	John D. Fredericks (R)	271,990	29.4
	J. B. Curtin (D)	116,121	12.5
	Noble A. Richardson (SOC)	50,716	5.5
1918	William D. Stephens (RP&PROG)	387,547	56.3
	Theodore A. Bell (I)	251,189	36.5
1922	Friend William Richardson (R)	576,445	59.7
	Thomas Lee Woolwine (D)	347,530	36.0
1926	Clement C. Young (R)	814,815	71.2
	Justus S. Wardell (D)	282,451	24.7
1930	James Rolph Jr. (R)	999,393	72.2
	Milton K. Young (D)	333,973	24.1
1934	Frank F. Merriam (R)	1,138,620	48.9
	Upton Sinclair (D)	879,537	37.8
	Raymond L. Haight (C PROG)	302,519	13.0
1938	Culbert L. Olson (D)	1,391,734	52.5
	Frank F. Merriam (R)	1,171,019	44.2
1942	Earl Warren (R)	1,275,237	57.1
	Culbert L. Olson (D)	932,995	41.8
1946	Earl Warren (R-D)	2,344,542	91.6
	Henry R. Schmidt (P)	180,579	7.1
1950	Earl Warren (R)	2,461,754	64.9
	James Roosevelt (D)	1,333,856	35.1
1954	Goodwin J. Knight (R)	2,290,519	56.8
	Richard Perrin Graves (D)	1,739,368	43.2
1958	Edmund G. Brown (D)	3,140,076	59.8
	William F. Knowland (R)	2,110,911	40.2
1962	Edmund G. Brown (D)	3,037,109	51.9
	Richard M. Nixon (R)	2,740,351	46.8
1966	Ronald Reagan (R)	3,742,913	57.6
	Edmund G. Brown (D)	2,749,174	42.3

1970	Ronald Reagan (R)	3,439,664	*52.8*
	Jess Unruh (D)	2,938,607	*45.1*
1974	Edmund G. "Jerry" Brown Jr. (D)	3,131,648	*50.1*
	Houston I. Flournoy (R)	2,952,954	*47.3*
1978	Edmund G. "Jerry" Brown Jr. (D)	3,878,812	*56.0*
	Evelle J. Younger (R)	2,526,534	*36.5*
	Ed Clark (I)	377,960	*5.5*
1982	George Deukmejian (R)	3,881,014	*49.3*
	Tom Bradley (D)	3,787,669	*48.1*
1986	George Deukmejian (R)	4,506,601	*60.5*
	Tom Bradley (D)	2,781,714	*37.4*
1990	Pete Wilson (R)	3,791,904	*49.2*
	Dianne Feinstein (D)	3,525,197	*45.8*
1994	Pete Wilson (R)	4,781,766	*55.2*
	Kathleen Brown (D)	3,519,799	*40.6*
1998	Gray Davis (D)	4,860,702	*58.0*
	Dan Lungren (R)	3,218,030	*38.4*

COLORADO

(Became a state Aug. 1, 1876)

1876	John L. Routt (R)	14,154	*51.5*
	Bela M. Hughes (D)	13,316	*48.5*
1878	Frederick W. Pitkin (R)	14,308	*50.0*
	W. A. H. Loveland (D)	11,535	*40.3*
	R. G. Buckingham (G)	2,783	*9.7*
1880	Frederick W. Pitkin (R)	28,465	*53.3*
	John S. Hough (D)	23,547	*44.1*
1882	James B. Grant (D)	31,375	*51.1*
	E. L. Campbell (R)	28,820	*46.9*
1884	Benjamin H. Eaton (R)	33,845	*50.7*
	Alva Adams (D)	30,743	*46.1*
1886	Alva Adams (D)	29,234	*49.7*
	William H. Meyer (R)	26,816	*45.6*
1888	Job A. Cooper (R)	49,490	*53.8*
	Thomas M. Patterson (D)	39,197	*42.6*
1890	John L. Routt (R)	41,827	*50.1*
	Caldwell Yeaman (D)	35,359	*42.4*
	John G. Coy (F ALNC)	5,199	*6.2*
1892	Davis H. Waite (POP & SL D)	43,342	*46.7*
	Joseph C. Helm (R)	38,806	*41.8*
	Joseph H. Maupin (D)	8,944	*9.6*
1894	Albert W. McIntire (R)	93,502	*52.0*
	Davis H. Waite (POP)	73,894	*41.1*
1896	Alva Adams (D)	87,387	*46.2*
	M. S. Bailey (N SILVER)	71,808	*38.0*
	George H. Allen (R)	23,945	*12.7*
1898	Charles S. Thomas (FUS)	93,966	*62.8*
	Henry R. Wolcott (R)	51,051	*34.1*
1900	James B. Orman (FUS)	118,647	*53.8*
	Frank C. Goudy (R)	96,027	*43.5*
1902	James H. Peabody (R)	87,684	*46.9*
	E. C. Stimson (D)	80,727	*43.2*
1904	Alva Adams (D)	123,092‡	*50.6*
	James H. Peabody (R)	113,754	*46.8*
1906	Henry A. Buchtel (R)	92,602	*45.6*
	Alva Adams (D)	74,416	*36.6*

	Ben B. Lindsey (I)	18,014	*8.9*
	William D. Haywood (SOC)	16,015	*7.9*
1908	John F. Shafroth (D)	130,141	*49.4*
	Jesse F. McDonald (R)	118,953	*45.2*
1910	John F. Shafroth (D)	114,676	*54.0*
	John B. Stephen (R)	97,691	*46.0*
1912	Elias M. Ammons (D)	114,044	*42.9*
	Edward P. Costigan (PROG-BMR)	66,132	*24.9*
	C. C. Parks (R)	63,061	*23.7*
	Charles A. Ashelstrom (SOC)	16,189	*6.1*
1914	George A. Carlson (R)	129,096	*48.7*
	Thomas M. Patterson (D)	90,640	*34.2*
	Edward P. Costigan (PROG)	32,920	*12.4*
1916	Julius C. Gunter (D)	151,912	*53.3*
	George A. Carlson (R)	117,723	*41.3*
1918	Oliver H. Shoup (R)	112,693	*51.1*
	Thomas J. Tynan (D)	102,397	*46.5*
1920	Oliver H. Shoup (R)	174,488	*59.6*
	James M. Collins (D)	108,738	*37.1*
1922	William E. Sweet (D)	138,098	*49.6*
	Benjamin Griffith (R)	134,353	*48.3*
1924	Clarence J. Morley (R)	178,078	*51.9*
	William E. Sweet (D)	151,041	*44.0*
1926	William H. Adams (D)	183,342	*59.8*
	Oliver H. Shoup (R)	116,756	*38.1*
1928	William H. Adams (D)	240,160	*61.9*
	William L. Boatright (R)	144,067	*37.1*
1930	William H. Adams (D)	197,067	*60.4*
	Robert F. Rockwell (R)	124,164	*38.1*
1932	Edwin C. Johnson (D)	257,188	*57.2*
	James D. Parriott (R)	183,258	*40.8*
1934	Edwin C. Johnson (D)	237,026	*58.1*
	Nate C. Warren (R)	162,791	*39.9*
1936	Teller Ammons (D)	263,311	*54.6*
	Charles M. Armstrong (R)	210,614	*43.7*
1938	Ralph L. Carr (R)	255,159	*55.8*
	Teller Ammons (D)	199,562	*43.7*
1940	Ralph L. Carr (R)	296,671	*54.4*
	George E. Saunders (D)	245,292	*45.0*
1942	John C. Vivian (R)	193,501	*56.2*
	Homer F. Bedford (D)	149,402	*43.4*
1944	John C. Vivian (R)	259,862	*52.4*
	Roy Best (D)	236,086	*47.6*
1946	William Lee Knous (D)	174,604	*52.1*
	Leon E. Lavington (R)	160,483	*47.9*
1948	William Lee Knous (D)	332,752	*66.3*
	David A. Hamil (R)	168,928	*33.7*
1950	Dan Thornton (R)	236,472	*52.4*
	Walter W. Johnson (D)	212,976	*47.2*
1952	Dan Thornton (R)	349,924	*57.1*
	John W. Metzger (D)	260,044	*42.4*
1954	Edwin C. Johnson (D)	262,205	*53.6*
	Donald G. Brotzman (R)	227,335	*46.4*
1956	Stephen L. R. McNichols (D)	331,283	*51.3*
	Donald G. Brotzman (R)	313,950	*48.7*
1958	Stephen L. R. McNichols (D)	321,165	*58.4*
	Palmer L. Burch (R)	228,643	*41.6*

1962	John A. Love (R)	349,342	56.7
	Stephen L. R. McNichols (D)	262,890	42.6
1966	John A. Love (R)	356,730	54.0
	Robert L. Knous (D)	287,132	43.5
1970	John A. Love (R)	350,690	52.5
	Mark Hogan (D)	302,432	45.2
1974	Richard D. Lamm (D)	441,408	53.2
	John D. Vanderhoof (R)	378,698	45.7
1978	Richard D. Lamm (D)	483,985	58.7
	Ted Strickland (R)	317,292	38.5
1982	Richard D. Lamm (D)	627,960	65.7
	John D. Fuhr (R)	302,740	31.7
1986	Roy Romer (D)	616,325	58.2
	Ted Strickland (R)	434,420	41.0
1990	Roy Romer (D)	626,032	61.9
	John Andrews (R)	358,403	35.4
1994	Roy Romer (D)	619,205	55.5
	Bruce Benson (R)	432,042	38.7
1998	Bill Owens (R)	648,202	49.1
	Gail Schoettler (D)	639,905	48.4

CONNECTICUT

(Ratified the Constitution Jan. 9, 1788)

1776	Jonathan Trumbull	✔	
1777	Jonathan Trumbull	✔	
1778	Jonathan Trumbull	2,306	100.0
1779	Jonathan Trumbull	2,108	100.0
1780	Jonathan Trumbull	3,598†	49.3
1781	Jonathan Trumbull	2,636†	38.8
	William Pitkin	1,225	18.0
	Richard Law	810	11.9
	Matthew Griswold	651	9.6
	Samuel Huntington	649	9.5
	Oliver Wolcott	384	5.6
1782	Jonathan Trumbull	3,025	50.2
1783	Jonathan Trumbull	2,209†	31.3
	William Pitkin	2,080	29.5
	Oliver Wolcott	918	13.0
	Samuel Huntington	896	12.7
1784	Matthew Griswold	2,192†	32.0
	William Pitkin	1,689	24.6
	Samuel Huntington	1,177	17.2
	Oliver Wolcott	1,053	15.4
1785	Matthew Griswold	✔	
1786	Samuel Huntington	✔	
1787–1795	Samuel Huntington	✔	
1796	Oliver Wolcott Sr.	3,805†	48.8
	Jonathan Trumbull II	1,187	15.2
	Jonathan Ingersoll	937	12.0
	Oliver Ellsworth	629	8.1
	Richard Law	485	6.2
1797	Oliver Wolcott Sr.	✔	
1798–1800	Jonathan Trumbull II	✔	
1801	Jonathan Trumbull II	11,156	83.8
	Richard Law	1,056	7.9

1802	Jonathan Trumbull II (FED)	11,398	69.9
	Ephraim Kirby (D-R)	4,523	27.7
1803	Jonathan Trumbull II (FED)	14,375	64.0
	Ephraim Kirby (D-R)	7,848	35.0
1804	Jonathan Trumbull II (FED)	11,936	61.8
	William Hart (D-R)	7,376	38.2
1805	Jonathan Trumbull II (FED)	13,689	62.5
	William Hart (D-R)	8,223	37.5
1806	Jonathan Trumbull II (FED)	13,413	58.6
	William Hart (D-R)	9,460	41.4
1807	Jonathan Trumbull II (FED)	11,959	60.0
	William Hart (D-R)	7,971	40.0
1808	Jonathan Trumbull II (FED)	12,146	61.6
	William Hart (D-R)	7,566	38.4
1809	Jonathan Trumbull II (FED)	14,650	64.2
	Asa Spalding (D-R)	8,159	35.8
1810	John Treadwell (FED)	10,265†	49.5
	Asa Spalding (D-R)	7,185	34.6
	Roger Griswold (FED)	3,110	15.0
1811	Roger Griswold (FED)	10,148	53.8
	John Treadwell (FED)	8,727	46.2
1812	Roger Griswold (FED)	11,721	86.1
	Elijah Boardman (D-R)	1,487	10.9
1813	John C. Smith (FED)	11,893	59.1
	Elijah Boardman (D-R)	7,201	35.8
1814	John C. Smith (FED)	9,415	72.9
	Elijah Boardman (D-R)	2,619	20.3
1815	John C. Smith (FED)	8,176	59.3
	Elijah Boardman (D-R)	4,876	35.3
1816	John C. Smith (FED)	11,575	52.7
	Oliver Wolcott Jr. (D-R, AM, TOL[1])	10,184	46.4
1817	Oliver Wolcott Jr. (TOL[1], REF)	13,655	50.2
	John C. Smith (FED)	13,321	49.0
1818	Oliver Wolcott Jr. (CONST, REF)	16,432	87.0
1819	Oliver Wolcott Jr. (TOL[1], REF)	22,539	86.8
1820	Oliver Wolcott Jr. (D-R)	15,738	78.4
1821	Oliver Wolcott Jr. (D-R)	10,064	86.6
1822	Oliver Wolcott Jr. (D-R)	8,568	85.5
	Zephaniah Swift (FED)	570	5.8
1823	Oliver Wolcott Jr. (D-R)	9,090	88.9
1824	Oliver Wolcott Jr. (D-R)	6,637	92.1
	Timothy Pitkin (OPP R)	466	6.5
1825	Oliver Wolcott Jr. (D-R)	7,147	68.8
	David Daggett (FED)	1,342	12.9
	Nathan Smith (OPP R)	863	8.3
	Timothy Pitkin (OPP R)	525	5.1
1826	Oliver Wolcott Jr. (D-R)	6,780	57.8
	David Daggett (FED)	4,340	37.0
1827	Gideon Tomlinson (OLD R)	7,681	56.7
	Oliver Wolcott (OPP R)	5,295	39.1
1828	Gideon Tomlinson (NR)	9,297	97.3
1829	Gideon Tomlinson (NR)	9,612	95.8
1830	Gideon Tomlinson (NR)	12,988	95.6
1831	John S. Peters (NR)	12,819	65.4
	Zalmon Storrs (A-MASC)	4,778	24.4
1832	John S. Peters (NR)	11,971	70.3
	Calvin Willey (D)	4,463	26.2

Year	Candidate	Votes	%
1833	John S. Peters (NR)	9,212	42.3
	Henry W. Edwards (D)	9,030†	41.5
	Zalmon Storrs (A-MASC)	3,250	14.9
1834	Samuel A. Foot (NR)	18,411†	49.8
	Henry W. Edwards (D)	15,834	42.9
	Zalmon Storrs (A-MASC)	2,398	6.5
1835	Henry W. Edwards (D)	22,129	52.1
	Samuel A. Foot (W)	19,835	46.7
1836	Henry W. Edwards (D)	20,360	53.6
	Gideon Tomlinson (W)	17,393	45.8
1837	Henry W. Edwards (D)	23,805	52.5
	William W. Ellsworth (W)	21,508	47.5
1838	William W. Ellsworth (W)	27,115	54.1
	Seth P. Beers (D)	21,489	42.9
1839	William W. Ellsworth (W)	26,358	51.5
	John M. Niles (D)	23,728	46.4
1840	William W. Ellsworth (W)	29,870	54.2
	John M. Niles (D)	25,270	45.8
1841	William W. Ellsworth (W)	26,986	55.8
	Francis H. Nicoll (D)	21,388	44.2
1842	Chauncey F. Cleveland (D)	25,564†	49.9
	William W. Ellsworth (W)	23,700	46.2
1843	Chauncey F. Cleveland (D)	27,416	50.1
	Roger S. Baldwin (W)	25,401	46.4
1844	Roger S. Baldwin (W)	30,093†	49.4
	Chauncey F. Cleveland (D)	28,846	47.3
1845	Roger S. Baldwin (W)	29,508	51.0
	Isaac Toucey (D)	26,258	45.3
1846	Clark Bissell (W)	27,822	48.6
	Isaac Toucey (D)	27,203†	47.5
1847	Clark Bissell (W)	30,137	50.5
	Whittlesey (D)	27,402	45.9
1848	Clark Bissell (W)	30,717	50.4
	George S. Catlin (D)	28,525	46.8
1849	Joseph Trumbull (W)	27,800†	49.4
	Thomas H. Seymour (D)	25,018	44.4
	John M. Niles (F SOIL)	3,520	6.3
1850	Thomas H. Seymour (D)	28,428†	48.1
	Lafayette S. Foster (W)	27,780	47.0
1851	Thomas H. Seymour (D)	30,077†	49.0
	Lafayette S. Foster (W)	28,756	46.9
1852	Thomas H. Seymour (D)	31,624	50.4
	Green Kendrick (W)	28,241	45.0
1853	Thomas H. Seymour (D)	30,814	51.0
	Henry Dutton (W)	20,671	34.2
	Francis Gillette (F SOIL)	8,926	14.8
1854	Samuel Ingham (D)	28,338	46.4
	Henry Dutton (W)	19,465†	31.9
	Charles Chapman (TEMP)	10,672	17.5
1855	William T. Minor (AM)	28,080†	43.5
	Samuel Ingham (D)	27,291	42.3
	Henry Dutton (W)	9,162	14.2
1856	Samuel Ingham (D)	32,704	49.0
	William T. Minor (AM)	26,008†	39.0
	Gideon Wells (R)	6,740	10.1
1857	Alexander H. Holley (R)	31,709	50.4
	Samuel Ingham (D)	31,156	49.5
1858	William A. Buckingham (R)	36,298	51.8
	James T. Pratt (D)	33,544	47.8
1859	William A. Buckingham (R)	40,247	51.1
	James T. Pratt (D)	38,369	48.7
1860	William A. Buckingham (R)	44,458	50.3
	Thomas H. Seymour (D)	43,920	49.7
1861	William A. Buckingham (R)	43,013	51.2
	James C. Loomis (D)	40,986	48.8
1862	William A. Buckingham (R)	39,782	56.5
	James C. Loomis (D)	30,634	43.5
1863	William A. Buckingham (R)	41,033	51.6
	Thomas H. Seymour (D)	38,397	48.3
1864	William A. Buckingham (UN R)	39,820	53.8
	Origen S. Seymour (D)	34,162	46.2
1865	William A. Buckingham (UN R)	42,374	57.5
	Origen S. Seymour (D)	31,339	42.5
1866	Joseph R. Hawley (R)	43,888	50.3
	James E. English (D)	43,433	49.7
1867	James E. English (D)	47,565	50.5
	Joseph R. Hawley (R)	46,578	49.5
1868	James E. English (D)	50,541	50.9
	Marshall Jewell (R)	48,777	49.1
1869	Marshall Jewell (R)	45,493	50.2
	James E. English (D)	45,082	49.8
1870	James E. English (D)	44,128	50.5
	Marshall Jewell (R)	43,285	49.5
1871	Marshall Jewell (R)	47,473	50.1
	James E. English (D)	47,370	49.9
1872	Marshall Jewell (R)	46,563	50.0
	Richard D. Hubbard (D)	44,562	47.9
1873	Charles R. Ingersoll (D)	45,059	51.9
	Henry P. aven (R)	39,245	45.2
1874	Charles R. Ingersoll (D)	46,755	51.1
	Henry B. Harrison (R)	39,973	43.5
	Henry D. Smith (TEMP)	4,960	5.4
1875	Charles R. Ingersoll (D)	53,752	53.2
	James L. Greene (R)	44,272	43.9
1876	Charles R. Ingersoll (D)	51,138	51.9
	Henry C. Robinson (R)	43,510	44.1
1876	Richard D. Hubbard (D)	61,934	50.8
	Henry C. Robinson (R)	58,514	48.0
1878	Charles B. Andrews (R)	48,867†	46.7
	Richard D. Hubbard (D)	46,385	44.3
	Charles Atwater (N)	8,314	7.9
1880	Hobart B. Bigelow (R)	67,070	50.5
	James E. English (D)	64,293	48.4
1882	Thomas M. Waller (D)	59,014	51.0
	Morgan G. Bulkeley (R)	54,853	47.4
1884	Thomas M. Waller (D)	67,910	49.3
	Henry B. Harrison (R)	66,274†	48.1
1886	Edward C. Cleveland (D)	58,818	47.7
	Phineas C. Lounsbury (R)	56,920†	46.2
1888	Luzon B. Morris (D)	75,074	48.9
	Morgan G. Bulkeley (R)	73,659†	47.9
1890	Luzon B. Morris (D)	67,658*	50.0
	Samuel E. Merwin (R)	63,975	47.3
1892	Luzon B. Morris (D)	82,787	50.3
	Samuel E. Merwin (R)	76,745	46.6
1894	O. Vincent Coffin (R)	83,975	54.2
	Ernest Cady (D)	66,287	42.8

1896	Lorrin A. Cooke (R)	108,807	62.5		1948	Chester Bowles (D)	431,746	49.3
	Joseph B. Sargent (D)	56,524	32.5			James C. Shannon (R)	429,071	49.0
1898	George E. Lounsbury (R)	81,015	54.2		1950	John D. Lodge (R)	436,418	49.7
	Daniel A. Morgan (D)	64,227	42.9			Chester Bowles (D)	419,404	47.7
1900	George P. McLean (R)	95,822	53.0		1954	Abraham A. Ribicoff (D)	463,643	49.5
	Samuel L. Bronson (D)	81,421	45.1			John D. Lodge (R)	460,528	49.2
1902	Abiram Chamberlain (R)	85,338	53.4		1958	Abraham A. Ribicoff (D)	607,012	62.3
	Melbert B. Cary (D)	69,330	43.4			Fred R. Zeller (R)	360,644	37.0
1904	Henry Roberts (R)	104,736	54.9		1962	John N. Dempsey (D)	549,027	53.2
	A. Heaton Robertson (D)	79,164	41.5			John Alsop (R)	482,852	46.8
1906	Rollin S. Woodruff (R)	88,384	54.8		1966	John N. Dempsey (D)	561,599	55.7
	Charles Thayer (D)	67,776	42.1			E. Clayton Gengras (R)	446,536	44.3
1908	George L. Lilley (R)	98,179	51.9		1970	Thomas J. Meskill (R)	582,160	53.8
	A. Heaton Robertson (D)	82,260	43.5			Emilio Q. Daddario (D)	500,561	46.2
1910	Simeon E. Baldwin (D)	77,243	46.5		1974	Ella T. Grasso (D)	643,490	58.4
	Charles A. Goodwin (R)	73,528	44.3			Robert H. Steele (R)	440,169	39.9
	Robert Hunter (SOC)	12,179	7.3		1978	Ella T. Grasso (D)	613,109	59.1
1912	Simeon E. Baldwin (D)	78,264	41.1			Ronald A. Sarasin (R)	422,316	40.7
	John P. Studley (R)	67,531	35.5		1982	William A. O'Neill (D)	578,264	53.3
	Herbert K. Smith (PROG)	31,020	16.3			Lewis B. Rome (R)	497,773	45.9
	Samuel E. Beardsley (SOC)	10,236	5.4		1986	William A. O'Neill (D)	575,638	57.9
1914	Marcus H. Holcomb (R)	91,262	50.4			Julie D. Belaga (R)	408,489	41.1
	Lyman Tingier (D)	73,888	40.8		1990	Lowell P. Weicker Jr. (ACP)	460,576	40.4
1916	Marcus H. Holcomb (R)	109,293	51.1			John G. Rowland (R)	427,840	37.5
	Morris Beardsley (D)	96,787	45.3			Bruce A. Morrison (D)	236,641	20.7
1918	Marcus H. Holcomb (R)	84,891	50.7		1994	John G. Rowland (R)	415,201	36.2
	Thomas Spellacy (D)	76,773	45.9			Bill Curry (D)	375,133	32.7
1920	Everett J. Lake (R)	230,792	63.0			Eunice Strong Groark (ACP)	216,585	18.9
	Rollin U. Tyler (D)	119,912	32.8			Tom Scott (I)	130,128	11.3
1922	Charles A. Templeton (R)	170,231	52.4		1998	John G. Rowland (R)	628,707	62.9
	David Fitzgerald (D)	148,641	45.7			Barbara B. Kennelly (D)	354,187	35.4
1924	Hiram Bingham (R)	246,336	66.2					
	Charles Morris (D)	118,676	31.9					

Connecticut
1. Toleration Party.

1926	John H. Trumbull (R)	192,425	63.6
	Charles Morris (D)	107,045	35.4

DELAWARE

(Ratified the Constitution Dec. 7, 1787)

1928	John H. Trumbull (R)	296,216	53.6		1792[1]	Joshua Clayton	2,209	48.3
	Charles Morris (D)	252,209	45.6			Thomas Montgomery	1,902	41.6
1930	Wilbur L. Cross (D)	215,072	49.9			George Mitchell	458	10.0
	Ernest E. Rogers (R)	209,607	48.6		1795	Gunning Bedford Jr.	2,352	52.3
1932	Wilbur L. Cross (D)	288,347	49.0			Archibald Alexander	2,142	47.7
	John H. Trumbull (R)	277,503	47.1		1798	Richard Bassett (FED)	2,490	52.5
1934	Wilbur L. Cross (D)	257,996	46.7			David Hall (D-R)	2,068	43.6
	Hugh Meade Alcorn (R)	249,397	45.2		1801	David Hall (D-R)	3,475	50.1
	Jasper McLevy (SOC)	38,438	7.0			Nathanael Mitchell (FED)	3,457	49.9
1936	Wilbur L. Cross (D)	372,953#	55.3		1804	Nathanael Mitchell (FED)	4,391	52.0
	Arthur M. Brown (R)	277,190#	41.1			Joseph Hazlett (D-R)	4,050	48.0
1938	Raymond E. Baldwin (R, UN)	230,237	36.4		1807	George Truitt (FED)	3,309	51.9
	Wilbur L. Cross (D)	227,549	36.0			Joseph Hazlett (D-R)	3,062	48.1
	Jasper McLevy (SOC)	166,253	26.3		1810	Joseph Hazlett (D-R)	3,664	50.5
1940	Robert A. Hurley (D)	388,361	49.5			Daniel Rodney (FED)	3,593	49.5
	Raymond E. Baldwin (R, UN)	374,581	47.8		1813	Daniel Rodney (FED)	4,643	55.2
1942	Raymond E. Baldwin (R)	281,362	48.9			James Riddle (D-R)	3,768	44.8
	Robert A. Hurley (D)	255,166	44.4		1816	John Clarke (FED)	4,008	53.3
	Jasper McLevy (SOC)	34,537	6.0			Mansen Bull (D-R)	3,517	46.7
1944	Raymond E. Baldwin (R)	418,289	50.5					
	Robert A. Hurley (D)	392,417	47.4					
1946	James L. McConaughy (R)	371,852	54.4					
	Wilbert Snow (D)	276,335	40.4					

1819	Henry Molleston (FED)	3,823*	54.6
	Mansen Bull (D-R)	3,185	45.4
1820	John Collins (D-R)	3,970	53.1
	Jesse Green (FED)	3,520	47.0
1822	Joseph Hazlett (D-R)	3,784	50.1
	James Booth (FED)	3,762	49.9
1823	Samuel Paynter (FED)	4,348	51.8
	Daniel Hazzard (D-R)	4,051	48.2
1826	Charles Polk (FED)	4,344#	50.6
	David Hazzard (D-R)	4,238#	49.4
1829	David Hazzard (AM D-R)	4,215#	51.0
	Alan Thompson (JAC D)	4,046#	49.0
1832	Caleb P. Bennett (D)	4,220	50.3
	Arnold Naudain (NR)	4,166	49.7
1836	Cornelius P. Comegys (W)	4,693	52.3
	Nehemiah Clark (D)	4,276	47.7
1840	William B. Cooper (W)	5,855	53.8
	Warren Jefferson (D)	5,024	46.2
1844	Thomas Stockton (W)	6,140	50.2
	William Tharp (D)	6,095	49.8
1846	William Tharp (D)	6,148	50.6
	Peter F. Causey (W)	6,012	49.4
1850	William H. Ross (D)	6,001	48.3
	Peter F. Causey (W)	5,978	48.1
1854	Peter F. Causey (AM)	6,941	52.6
	William Burton (D)	6,244	47.4
1858	William Burton (D)	7,758	50.7
	James Buckmaster	7,554	49.3
1862	William Cannon (UN)	8,155	50.3
	Samuel L. Jefferson (D)	8,044	49.7
1866	Gove Saulsbury (D)	9,810	53.3
	James Riddle (R)	8,598	46.7
1870	James Ponder (D)	12,459	55.6
	Thomas B. Coursey (R)	9,942	44.4
1874	John P. Cochran (D)	12,488	52.6
	Isaac Jump (R)	11,259	47.4
1878	John W. Hall (D)	10,730	79.1
	Kensey J. Stewart (NG)	2,835	20.9
1882	Charles C. Stockley (D)	16,558	53.1
	Albert Curry (R)	14,620	46.9
1886	Benjamin T. Biggs (D)	13,942	63.6
	James R. Hoffecker (TEMP REF)	7,835	35.8
1890	Robert J. Reynolds (D)	17,801	50.4
	Harry A. Richardson (R)	17,258	48.9
1894	Joshua H. Marvel (R)	19,880	50.8
	Ebe W. Tunnell (D)	18,659	47.7
1896	Ebe W. Tunnell (D)	15,507	44.2
	John H. Hoffecker (R)	11,014	31.4
	John C. Higgins (A-AK R)	7,154	20.4
1900	John Hunn (R)	22,421	53.6
	Peter J. Ford (D)	18,808	44.9
1904	Preston Lea (R)	22,532	51.4
	Caleb S. Pennewill (D)	19,780	45.1
1908	Simeon S. Pennewill (R)	24,905	52.0
	Rowland G. Paynter (D)	22,794	47.6
1912	Charles R. Miller (R & PROG)	22,745	47.0
	Thomas M. Monaghan (D)	21,460	44.3
	George B. Hynson (PROG)	3,019	6.2

1916	John G. Townsend Jr. (R)	26,648	52.1
	James H. Hughes (D)	24,053	47.0
1920	William E. Denney (R)	51,895	55.2
	Andrew J. Lynch (D)	41,038	43.7
1924	Robert P. Robinson (R)	53,046	59.6
	Joseph Bancroft (D)	34,830	39.2
1928	C. Douglass Buck (R)	63,683	60.9
	Charles M. Wharton (D)	40,824	39.1
1932	Clayton Douglass Buck (R)	60,903	54.2
	Landreth L. Layton (D)	50,401	44.9
1936	Richard C. McMullen (D)	65,509	51.6
	Harry L. Cannon (R)	52,879	41.7
	Isaac Dolphus Short (IR)	8,282	6.5
1940	Walter W. Bacon (R)	70,629	52.4
	Josiah Marvel Jr. (D)	61,237	45.4
1944	Walter W. Bacon (R)	63,829	50.5
	Isaac J. MacCollum (D)	62,156	49.2
1948	Elbert N. Carvel (D)	75,339	53.7
	Hyland P. George (R)	64,996	46.3
1952	J. Caleb Boggs (R)	88,977	52.1
	Elbert N. Carvel (D)	81,772	47.9
1956	J. Caleb Boggs (R)	91,965	52.0
	J. H. Tyler McConnell (D)	85,047	48.1
1960	Elbert N. Carvel (D)	100,792	51.7
	John W. Rollins (R)	94,043	48.3
1964	Charles L. Terry Jr. (D)	102,797	51.4
	David P. Buckson (R)	97,374	48.7
1968	Russell W. Peterson (R)	104,474	50.5
	Charles L. Terry Jr. (D)	102,360	49.5
1972	Sherman W. Tribbitt (D)	117,274	51.3
	Russell W. Peterson (R)	109,583	47.9
1976	Pierre S. "Pete" du Pont IV (R)	130,531	56.9
	Sherman W. Tribbitt (D)	97,480	42.5
1980	Pierre S. "Pete" du Pont IV (R)	159,004	70.6
	William J. Gordy (D)	64,217	28.5
1984	Michael N. Castle (R)	132,250	55.5
	William T. Quillen (D)	108,315	44.5
1988	Michael N. Castle (R)	169,733	70.7
	Jacob Kreshtool (D)	70,236	29.3
1992	Thomas R. Carper (D)	179,365	64.7
	B. Gary Scott (R)	90,725	32.7
1996	Thomas R. Carper (D)	188,300	69.5
	Janet C. Rzewnicki (R)	82,654	30.5
2000	Ruth Ann Minner (D)	191,695	59.2
	John M. Burris (R)	128,603	39.7

Delaware
1. Before 1792 governor chosen by legislature.

FLORIDA

(Became a state March 3, 1845)

1845	William D. Moseley (D)	3,292	55.1
	Richard K. McCall (W)	2,679	44.9
1848	Thomas S. Brown (W)	4,145	52.5
	William Bailey (D)	3,746	47.5
1852	James E. Broome (D)	4,457	51.2
	George T. Ward (W)	4,246	48.8

1856	Madison S. Perry (D)	6,208	51.3
	David S. Walker (AM)	5,894	48.7
1860	John Milton (D)	7,302	55.4
	Edward Hopkins (CST U)	5,882	44.6
1865	David S. Walker (D)	5,873#	100.0
1868	Harrison Reed (R)	14,421#	59.1
	George W. Scott (D)	7,731#	31.7
	Samuel Walker (RAD R)	2,251#	9.2
1872	Ossian B. Hart (R)	17,603	52.4
	William D. Bloxham (LR)	16,004	47.6
1876	George F. Drew (D)	24,613	50.5
	Marcellus L. Stearns (R)	24,116	49.5
1880	William D. Bloxham (D)	28,372	54.9
	Simon B. Conover (R)	23,307	45.1
1884	Edward A. Perry (D)	32,096	53.5
	Frank Pope (R)	27,865	46.5
1888	Francis P. Fleming (D)	40,195	60.4
	V. J. Shipman (R)	26,385	39.6
1892	Henry L. Mitchell (D)	32,064	78.7
	Alonzo P. Baskin (FLA PP)	8,379	20.6
1896	William D. Bloxham (D)	27,171	66.6
	Edward R. Gunby (R)	8,290	20.3
	William A. Wicks (POP)	5,370	13.2
1900	William S. Jennings (D)	29,251	82.0
	M. B. MacFarlane (R)	6,438	18.0
1904	Napoleon B. Broward (D)	28,971	79.2
	M. B. MacFarlane (R)	6,357	17.4
1908	Albert W. Gilchrist (D)	33,036	78.8
	John M. Cheney (R)	6,453	15.4
	A. J. Pettigrew (SOC)	2,427	5.8
1912	Park Trammell (D)	38,377	80.2
	Thomas W. Cox (SOC)	3,467	7.2
	William R. O'Neal (R)	2,646	5.5
1916	Sidney J. Catts (IP)	39,546#	47.7
	William V. Knott (D)	30,343	36.6
	George W. Allen (R)	10,333	12.5
1920	Cary A. Hardee (D)	103,407	77.9
	George E. Gay (R)	23,788	17.9
1924	John W. Martin (D)	84,181	82.8
	W. O'Neal	17,499	17.2
1928	Doyle E. Carlton (D)	148,455	61.0
	W. J. Howey (R)	95,018	39.0
1932	David Sholtz (D)	186,270	66.6
	W. J. Howey (R)	93,323	33.4
1936	Fred P. Cone (D)	253,638	80.9
	E. E. Callaway (R)	59,832	19.1
1940	Spessard L. Holland (D)	334,152	100.0
1944	Millard F. Caldwell (D)	361,077	78.9
	Bert Lee Acker (R)	96,321	21.1
1948	Fuller Warren (D)	381,459	83.4
	Bert Lee Acker (R)	76,153	16.6
1952	Daniel T. McCarty (D)	624,463	74.8
	Harry S. Swan (R)	210,009	25.2

Special Election

| 1954 | Leroy Collins (D) | 287,769 | 80.5 |
| | J. Tom Watson (R) | 69,852 | 19.5 |

1956	Leroy Collins (D)	747,753	73.7
	William A. Washburn Jr. (R)	266,980	26.3
1960	Farris Bryant (D)	849,407	59.9
	George C. Petersen (R)	569,936	40.2
1964	Haydon Burns (D)	933,554	56.1
	Charles R. Holley (R)	686,297	41.3
1966	Claude R. Kirk Jr. (R)	821,190	55.1
	Robert King High (D)	668,233	44.9
1970	Reubin Askew (D)	984,305	56.8
	Claude R. Kirk Jr. (R)	746,243	43.0
1974	Reubin Askew (D)	1,118,954	61.2
	Jerry Thomas (R)	709,438	38.8
1978	Robert Graham (D)	1,406,580	55.6
	Jack M. Eckerd (R)	1,123,888	44.4
1982	Robert Graham (D)	1,739,553	64.7
	L. A. "Skip" Bafalis (R)	949,013	35.3
1986	Bob Martinez (R)	1,847,525	54.6
	Steve Pajcic (D)	1,538,620	45.4
1990	Lawton Chiles (D)	1,995,206	56.5
	Bob Martinez (R)	1,535,068	43.5
1994	Lawton Chiles (D)	2,135,008	50.8
	Jeb Bush (R)	2,071,068	49.2
1998	Jeb Bush (R)	2,191,105	55.3
	Buddy MacKay (D)	1,773,054	44.7

GEORGIA

(Ratified the Constitution Jan. 2, 1788)

1825[1]	George M. Troup	20,550	50.9
	John Clark	18,862	49.2
1827	John Forsyth	22,774	70.1
1829	George R. Gilmer	24,204	69.3
	Joel Crawford	10,718	30.7
1831	Wilson Lumpkin	27,305	51.4
	George R. Gilmer	25,863	48.6
1833	Wilson Lumpkin	30,861	51.9
	Joel Crawford	28,565	48.1
1835	William Schley (D)	31,177	52.1
	Charles Dougherty (W)	28,606	47.9
1837	George R. Gilmer (W)	34,179	50.5
	William Schley (D)	33,417	49.5
1839	Charles James McDonald (D)	34,634	51.4
	Charles Dougherty (W)	32,807	48.6
1841	Charles James McDonald (D)	37,847	52.9
	William C. Dawson (W)	33,703	47.1
1843	George Walker Crawford (W)	38,713	52.3
	Mark A. Cooper (D)	35,325	47.7
1845	George Walker Crawford (W)	41,514	51.1
	Matthew McAllister (D)	39,763	48.9
1847	George Washington Towns (D)	43,220	50.8
	Duncan L. Clinch (W)	41,931	49.3
1849	George Washington Towns (D)	46,514	51.8
	Edward Y. Hill (W)	43,222	48.2
1851	Howell Cobb (UN)	57,397	59.7
	Charles J. McDonald (SOR W)	38,824	40.3
1853	Hershel Vespasian Johnson (D)	47,638	50.3
	Charles J. Jenkins (W)	47,128	49.7

1855	Hershel Vespasian Johnson (D)	53,478	51.9
	Garnett Andrews (AM)	43,228	42.0
	B. H. Overby (TEMP)	6,284	6.1
1857	Joseph Emerson Brown (D)	57,067	55.2
	Benjamin H. Hill (AM)	46,295	44.8
1859	Joseph Emerson Brown (D)	63,784	60.4
	Warren Akin (OPP)	41,830	39.6
1865	Charles J. Jenkins (D)	✔	
1868	Rufus B. Bullock (R)	83,107	52.1
	John B. Gordon (D)	76,539	47.9
1872	James Milton Smith (LR)	104,539	69.2
	Dawson A. Walker (R)	46,475	30.8
1876	Alfred Holt Colquitt (D)	110,624	76.2
	Jonathan Norcross (R)	34,492	23.8
1880	Alfred Holt Colquitt (D)	117,803	64.9
	Thomas M. Norwood (ID)	63,631	35.1
1882	Alexander H. Stephens (D)	107,649	70.6
	Lucius J. Gartrell (ID)	44,893	29.4

Special Election

1883	Henry D. McDaniel (D)	✔	

1884	Henry D. McDaniel (D)	119,880	100.0
1886	John B. Gordon (D)	101,159	99.2
1888	John B. Gordon (D)	121,999	100.0
1890	William J. Northen (D)	105,365	100.0
1892	William J. Northen (D)	136,543	66.7
	William L. Peck (PP)	68,093	33.3
1894	William Y. Atkinson (D)	121,249	55.6
	James K. Hines (POP)	96,990	44.4
1896	William Y. Atkinson (D)	123,206	58.9
	Seaborn Wright (POP)	85,981	41.1
1898	Allen D. Candler (D)	118,028	69.8
	J. R. Hogan (POP)	51,191	30.3
1900	Allen D. Candler (D)	92,729	78.6
	George W. Trayler (POP)	25,285	21.4
1902	Joseph M. Terrell (D)	81,548	93.6
	James K. Hines (POP)	5,566	6.4
1904	Joseph M. Terrell (D)	67,523	100.0
1906	Hoke Smith (D)	94,223	99.9
1908	Joseph M. Brown (D)	112,292	90.5
	Yancy Carter (I)	11,746	9.5
1910	Hoke Smith (D)	✔	
	Joseph M. Brown (D)		

Special Election

1912	Joseph M. Brown (D)	✔	
	Pope Brown		
	Richard Russell Sr. (D)		

1912	John M. Slaton (D)	✔	
1914	Nathaniel E. Harris (D)	✔	
1916	Hugh M. Dorsey (D)	59,526	100.0
1918	Hugh M. Dorsey (D)	70,621	100.0
1920	Thomas W. Hardwick (D)	✔	
1922	Clifford M. Walker (D)	75,000	100.0
1924	Clifford M. Walker (D)	152,367	100.0
1926	Lamartine G. Hardman (D)	47,300	100.0
1928	Lamartine G. Hardman (D)	✔	

1930	Richard B. Russell (D)	✔	
1932	Eugene Talmadge (D)	240,242	100.0
1934	Eugene Talmadge (D)	53,101	100.0
1936	Eurith D. Rivers (D)	263,140	99.7
1938	Eurith D. Rivers (D)	66,863	94.3
1940	Eugene Talmadge (D, ID)	286,277	99.6
1942	Ellis Arnall (D)	62,220	96.3
1946	Eugene Talmadge (D)	144,067*	99.1

Special Election

1948	Herman E. Talmadge (D)	354,712	97.5
1950	Herman E. Talmadge (D)	230,771	98.4
1954	S. Marvin Griffin (D)	331,899	100.0
1958	S. Ernest Vandiver (D)	168,414	100.0
1962	Carl E. Sanders (D)	311,524	100.0
1966	Howard H. Callaway (R)	453,665	47.8
	Lester Maddox (D)	450,626†	47.4
1970	Jimmy Carter (D)	620,419	59.3
	Hal Suit (R)	424,983	40.6
1974	George Busbee (D)	646,777	69.1
	Ronnie Thompson (R)	289,113	30.9
1978	George Busbee (D)	534,572	80.6
	Rodney M. Cook (R)	128,139	19.3
1982	Joe Frank Harris (D)	734,090	62.8
	Robert H. Bell (R)	434,496	37.2
1986	Joe Frank Harris (D)	828,465	70.5
	Guy Davis (R)	346,512	29.5
1990	Zell Miller (D)	766,662	52.9
	Johnny Isakson (R)	645,625	44.5
1994	Zell Miller (D)	788,926	51.1
	Guy Millner (R)	756,371	48.9
1998	Roy E. Barnes (D)	941,076	52.5
	Guy Millner (R)	790,201	44.1

Georgia
1. Before 1825 governor chosen by legislature.

HAWAII

(Became a state Aug. 21, 1959)

1959	William F. Quinn (R)	86,213	51.1
	John A. Burns (D)	82,074	48.7
1962	John A. Burns (D)	114,308	58.3
	William F. Quinn (R)	81,707	41.7
1966	John A. Burns (D)	108,840	51.1
	Randolph Crossley (R)	104,324	48.9
1970	John A. Burns (D)	137,812	57.7
	Sam King (R)	101,249	42.4
1974	George R. Ariyoshi (D)	136,262	54.6
	Randolph Crossley (R)	113,388	45.4
1978	George R. Ariyoshi (D)	153,394	54.5
	John Leopold (R)	124,610	44.3
1982	George R. Ariyoshi (D)	141,043	45.2
	Frank F. Fasi (ID)	89,303	28.6
	D. G. "Andy" Anderson (R)	81,507	26.1
1986	John Waihee (D)	173,655	52.0
	D. G. "Andy" Anderson (R)	160,460	48.0

1990	John Waihee (D)	203,491	59.8
	Fred Hemmings (R)	131,310	38.6
1994	Benjamin J. Cayetano (D)	134,978	36.6
	Frank F. Fasi (BP)	113,158	30.7
	Patricia F. Saiki (R)	107,908	29.2
1998	Benjamin J. Cayetano (D)	204,206	50.1
	Linda Lingle (R)	198,952	48.8

IDAHO

(Became a state July 3, 1890)

1890	George L. Shoup (R)	10,262	56.4
	Wilson (D)	7,948	43.7
1892	William J. McConnell (R)	8,178	40.7
	John M. Burke (D)	6,769	33.7
	Abraham J. Crook (PP)	4,865	24.2
1894	William J. McConnell (R)	10,208	41.5
	James W. Ballantine (PP)	7,121	29.0
	Edward A. Stevenson (D)	7,057	28.7
1896	Frank Steunenberg (PP-D-S-R)	22,096	76.8
	David H. Budlong (R)	6,441	22.4
1898	Frank Steunenberg (FUS)	19,407	48.8
	A. B. Moss (R)	13,794	34.7
	J. H. Anderson (PP)	5,371	13.5
1900	Frank W. Hunt (D-FUS)	28,628	52.0
	D. W. Standrod (R)	26,468	48.0
1902	John T. Morrison (R)	31,874	52.9
	Frank W. Hunt (D)	26,021	43.2
1904	Frank R. Gooding (R)	41,877	58.7
	Henry Heitfeld (D)	24,252	34.0
	Theodore B. Shaw (SOC)	4,000	5.6
1906	Frank R. Gooding (R)	38,386	52.2
	Charles O. Stockslager (D)	29,496	40.1
	Thomas F. Kelley (SOC)	4,650	6.3
1908	James H. Brady (R)	47,864	49.6
	Moses Alexander (D)	40,145	41.6
	Ernest Untermann (SOC)	6,155	6.4
1910	James H. Hawley (D)	40,856	47.4
	James H. Brady (R)	39,961	46.4
	S. W. Motley (SOC)	5,342	6.2
1912	John M. Haines (R)	35,074	33.2
	James H. Hawley (D)	33,992	32.2
	G. H. Martin (PROG)	24,325	23.1
	L. A. Coblentz (SOC)	11,094	10.5
1914	Moses Alexander (D)	47,618	44.1
	John M. Haines (R)	40,349	37.4
	Hugh E. McElroy (EP)	10,583	9.8
	L. A. Coblentz (SOC)	7,967	7.4
1916	Moses Alexander (D)	63,877	47.5
	David W. Davis (R)	63,305	47.1
	Annie E. Triplow (SOC)	7,321	5.4
1918	David W. Davis (R)	57,626	60.0
	H. F. Samuels (D)	38,499	40.1
1920	David W. Davis (R)	75,748	53.0
	Ted A. Walters (D)	38,509	26.9
	Sherman D. Fairchild (I)	28,752	20.1

1922	Charles C. Moore (R)	50,538	39.5
	H. F. Samuels (PROG)	40,516	31.7
	M. Alexander (D)	36,810	28.8
1924	Charles C. Moore (R)	65,408	43.9
	H. F. Samuels (PROG)	58,163	39.0
	A. L. Freehafer (D)	25,081	16.8
1926	H. C. Baldridge (R)	61,575	51.1
	W. Scott Hall (PROG)	34,208	28.4
	Asher B. Wilson (D)	24,837	20.6
1928	H. C. Baldridge (R)	87,681	57.8
	C. Ben Ross (D)	63,046	41.6
1930	C. Ben Ross (D)	73,896	56.0
	John McMurray (R)	58,002	44.0
1932	C. Ben Ross (D)	116,663	61.7
	Defenbach (R)	68,863	36.4
1934	C. Ben Ross (D)	93,313	54.6
	Frank L. Stephan (R)	75,659	44.3
1936	Barzilla W. Clark (D)	115,098	57.2
	Frank L. Stephan (R)	83,430	41.5
1938	C. A. Bottolfsen (R)	106,268	57.3
	C. Ben Ross (D)	77,697	41.9
1940	Chase A. Clark (D)	120,420	50.5
	C. A. Bottolfsen (R)	118,117	49.5
1942	C. A. Bottolfsen (R)	72,260	50.2
	Chase A. Clark (D)	71,826	49.9
1944	Charles C. Gossett (D)	109,527	52.6
	W. H. Detweiler (R)	98,532	47.4
1946	Charles A. Robins (R)	102,233	56.4
	Arnold Williams (D)	79,131	43.6
1950	Len B. Jordan (R)	107,642	52.6
	Calvin E. Wright (D)	97,150	47.4
1954	Robert E. Smylie (R)	124,038	54.2
	Clark Hamilton (D)	104,647	45.8
1958	Robert E. Smylie (R)	121,810	51.0
	A. M. Derr (D)	117,236	49.0
1962	Robert E. Smylie (R)	139,578	54.6
	Vernon K. Smith (D)	115,876	45.4
1966	Don Samuelson (R)	104,586	41.4
	Cecil D. Andrus (D)	93,744	37.1
	Perry Swisher (I)	30,913	12.2
	Philip W. Jungert (I)	23,139	9.2
1970	Cecil D. Andrus (D)	128,004	52.2
	Don Samuelson (R)	117,108	47.8
1974	Cecil D. Andrus (D)	184,142	70.9
	Jack M. Murphy (R)	68,731	26.5
1978	John V. Evans (D)	169,540	58.8
	Allan Larsen (R)	114,149	39.6
1982	John V. Evans (D)	165,365	50.6
	Philip Batt (R)	161,157	49.4
1986	Cecil D. Andrus (D)	193,429	49.9
	David H. Leroy (R)	189,794	49.0
1990	Cecil D. Andrus (D)	218,673	68.2
	Roger Fairchild (R)	101,937	31.8
1994	Phil Batt (R)	216,123	52.3
	Larry EchoHawk (D)	181,363	43.9
1998	Dirk Kempthorne (R)	258,095	67.7
	Robert C. Huntley (D)	110,815	29.1

ILLINOIS

(Became a state Dec. 3, 1818)

1818	Shadrach Bond	3,427	
1822	Edward Coles	2,854	33.2
	Joseph B. Phillips	2,687	31.2
	Thomas C. Browne	2,443	28.4
	James B. Moore	622	7.2
1826	Ninian Edwards (NR)	6,280	49.4
	Thomas Sloo Jr. (JAC D)	5,833	45.9
1830	John Reynolds (NR)	12,837	59.0
	William Kinney (JAC D)	8,938	41.1
1834	Joseph Duncan (W)	17,340	52.9
	William Kinney (D)	10,224	31.2
	Robert H. McLaughlin	4,315	13.2
1838	Thomas Carlin (D)	30,668	50.8
	Cyrus Edwards (W)	29,722	49.2
1842	Thomas Ford (D)	46,507	53.8
	Joseph Duncan (W)	39,030	45.1
1846	Augustus C. French (D)	58,656	58.2
	Thomas M. Kilpatrick (W)	37,033	36.7
	Richard Eels (LIB)	5,157	5.1
1848	Augustus C. French (D)	67,828	86.8
	W. S. D. Morison	5,659	7.2
	Charles V. Dyer	4,692	6.0
1852	Joel A. Matteson (D)	80,709	52.4
	Edwin B. Webb (W)	64,408	41.8
	D. A. Knowlton (F SOIL)	9,024	5.9
1856	William H. Bissell (R)	111,466	47.0
	William A. Richardson (D)	106,769	45.0
	Buckner S. Morris (AM)	19,078	8.0
1860	Richard Yates (R)	172,218	51.2
	James C. Allen (D)	159,293	47.3
1864	Richard J. Oglesby (UN R)	190,376	54.5
	James C. Robinson (D)	158,711	45.5
1868	John M. Palmer (R)	250,467	55.5
	John R. Eden (D)	200,813	44.5
1872	Richard J. Oglesby (R)	237,777	54.4
	Gust Koener (LR)	197,083	45.1
1876	Shelby M. Cullom (R)	279,263	50.6
	Lewis Steward (D & G)	272,495	49.4
1880	Shelby M. Cullom (R)	314,565	50.4
	Lyman Trumbull (D)	277,562	44.5
1884	Richard J. Oglesby (R)	334,234	49.6
	Carter H. Harrison (D)	319,645	47.5
1888	Joseph W. Fifer (R)	367,856	49.2
	John M. Palmer (D)	355,313	47.5
1892	John P. Altgeld (D)	425,498	48.7
	Joseph W. Fifer (R)	402,666	46.1
1896	John R. Tanner (R)	587,637	54.1
	John P. Altgeld (R)	474,256	43.7
1900	Richard Yates (R)	580,200	51.5
	Samuel Alschuler (D)	518,966	46.1
1904	Charles S. Deneen (R)	634,029	59.1
	Lawrence B. Stringer (D)	334,880	31.2
	John Collins (SOC)	59,062	5.5
1908	Charles S. Deneen (R)	550,076	47.6
	Adlai E. Stevenson (D)	526,912	45.6

1912	Edward F. Dunne (D)	443,120	38.1
	Charles S. Deneen (R)	318,469	27.4
	Frank H. Funk (PROG)	303,401	26.1
	John C. Kennedy (SOC)	78,679	6.8
1916	Frank O. Lowden (R)	696,535	52.7
	Edward F. Dunne (D)	556,654	42.1
1920	Len Small (R)	1,243,148	58.9
	James Hamilton Lewis (D)	731,541	34.6
1924	Len Small (R)	1,366,436	56.7
	Norman L. Jones (D)	1,021,408	42.4
1928	Louis L. Emmerson (R)	1,709,818	56.8
	Floyd E. Thompson (D)	1,284,897	42.7
1932	Henry Horner (D)	1,930,330	57.6
	Len Small (R)	1,364,043	40.7
1936	Henry Horner (D)	2,067,861	53.1
	C. Wayland Brooks (R)	1,682,674	43.2
1940	Dwight H. Green (R)	2,197,778	52.9
	Harry B. Hershey (D)	1,940,833	46.7
1944	Dwight H. Green (R)	2,013,270	50.8
	Thomas J. Courtney (D)	1,940,999	48.9
1948	Adlai E. Stevenson (D)	2,250,074	57.1
	Dwight H. Green (R)	1,678,007	42.6
1952	William G. Stratton (R)	2,317,363	52.5
	Sherwood Dixon (D)	2,089,721	47.3
1956	William G. Stratton (R)	2,171,786	50.3
	Richard B. Austin (D)	2,134,909	49.5
1960	Otto Kerner (D)	2,594,731	55.5
	William G. Stratton (R)	2,070,479	44.3
1964	Otto Kerner (D)	2,418,394	51.9
	Charles H. Percy (R)	2,239,095	48.1
1968	Richard B. Ogilvie (R)	2,307,295	51.2
	Samuel H. Shapiro (D)	2,179,501	48.4
1972	Daniel Walker (D)	2,371,303	50.7
	Richard B. Ogilvie (R)	2,293,809	49.0
1976	James R. Thompson (R)	3,000,395	64.7
	Michael J. Howlett (D)	1,610,258	34.7
1978	James R. Thompson (R)	1,859,684	59.0
	Michael Bakalis (D)	1,263,134	40.1
1982	James R. Thompson (R)	1,816,101	49.4
	Adlai E. Stevenson III (D)	1,811,027	49.3
1986	James R. Thompson (R)	1,655,945	52.7
	Adlai E. Stevenson III (IS)	1,256,725	40.0
	"Democrat" (no candidate)	208,841	6.6
1990	Jim Edgar (R)	1,653,126	50.7
	Neil F. Hartigan (D)	1,569,217	48.2
1994	Jim Edgar (R)	1,984,318	63.9
	Dawn Clark Netsch (D)	1,069,850	34.4
1998	George H. Ryan (R)	1,714,094	51.0
	Glenn Poshard (D)	1,594,191	47.5

INDIANA

(Became a state Dec. 11, 1816)

1816	Jonathan Jennings	5,211	57.0
	Thomas Posey	3,934	43.0
1819	Jonathan Jennings	9,168	81.4
	Christopher Harrison	2,007	17.8

Year	Candidate	Votes	%
1822	William Hendricks	18,340	100.0
1825	James Brown Ray (CLAY R)	13,040	56.1
	Isaac Blackford (NR)	10,218	43.9
1828	James Brown Ray (CLAY R)	15,131	39.5
	Israel T. Canby (JAC D)	12,251	32.0
	Harbin H. Moore (NR)	10,898	28.5
1831	Noah Noble (NR)	23,518	45.6
	James G. Read (JAC D)	21,002	40.7
	Milton Stapp (I)	6,984	13.5
1834	Noah Noble (W)	36,773	57.4
	James G. Read (D)	27,257	42.6
1837	David Wallace (W)	46,067	55.5
	John Dumont (W)	36,915	44.5
1840	Samuel Bigger (W)	62,932	53.7
	Tilghman A. Howard (D)	54,274	46.3
1843	James Whitcomb (D)	60,784	50.2
	Samuel Bigger (W)	58,721	48.5
1846	James Whitcomb (D)	64,104	50.7
	Joseph G. Marshall (W)	60,138	47.5
1849	Joseph A. Wright (D)	76,996	52.3
	John A. Matson (W)	67,218	45.6
1852	Joseph A. Wright (D)	92,576	54.7
	Nicholas McCarty (W)	73,641	43.3
1856	Ashbel P. Willard (D)	117,971	51.3
	Oliver P. Morton (R)	112,039	48.7
1860	Henry S. Lane (R)	136,736	51.9
	Thomas Andrews Hendricks (D)	126,767	48.2
1864	Oliver P. Morton (R)	152,275	53.7
	Joseph E. McDonald (D)	131,200	46.3
1868	Conrad Baker (R)	171,523	50.1
	Thomas Andrews Hendricks (D)	170,602	49.9
1872	Thomas Andrews Hendricks (D)	189,424	50.1
	Thomas McClelland Browne (R)	188,276	49.8
1876	James Douglas Williams (D)	213,164	49.1
	Benjamin Harrison (R)	208,080	47.9
1880	Albert Gallatin Porter (R)	231,405	49.2
	Franklin Landers (D)	224,452	47.7
1884	Isaac P. Gray (D)	245,130	49.5
	William H. Calkins (R)	237,748	48.0
1888	Alvin P. Hovey (R)	263,194	49.0
	Courtland C. Matson (D)	260,994	48.6
1892	Claude Matthews (D)	260,601	47.5
	Ira J. Chase (R)	253,625	46.2
1896	James A. Mount (R)	320,936	50.9
	Benjamin F. Shively (D)	294,855	46.8
1900	Winfield T. Durbin (R)	331,531	50.5
	John W. Kern (D)	306,368	46.7
1904	J. Frank Hanly (R)	359,362	53.5
	John W. Kern (D)	274,998	41.0
1908	Thomas R. Marshall (D)	348,843	49.0
	James E. Watson (R)	334,040	46.9
1912	Samuel M. Ralston (D)	275,357	42.9
	Albert J. Beveridge (PROG)	166,124	25.9
	Winfield T. Durbin (R)	142,850	22.3
	Stephen N. Reynolds (SOC)	35,464	5.5
1916	James P. Goodrich (R)	337,831	47.8
	John A. M. Adair (D)	325,060	46.0
1920	Warren T. McCray (R)	683,253	54.6
	Carleton B. McCulloch (D)	515,253	41.2
1924	Ed Jackson (R)	654,784	52.9
	Carleton B. McCulloch (D)	572,303	46.3
1928	Harry G. Leslie (R)	728,203	51.3
	Frank C. Dailey (D)	683,545	48.1
1932	Paul V. McNutt (D)	862,127	55.0
	Raymond S. Springer (R)	669,797	42.8
1936	Maurice Clifford Townsend (D)	908,494	55.4
	Raymond S. Springer (R)	727,526	44.3
1940	Henry F. Schricker (D)	889,620	49.9
	Glenn R. Hillis (R)	885,657	49.7
1944	Ralph F. Gates (R)	849,346	51.0
	Samuel D. Jackson (D)	802,765	48.2
1948	Henry F. Schricker (D)	884,995	53.6
	Hobart Creighton (R)	745,892	45.1
1952	George N. Craig (R)	1,075,685	55.7
	John A. Watkins (D)	841,984	43.6
1956	Harold W. Handley (R)	1,086,868	55.6
	Ralph Tucker (D)	859,393	44.0
1960	Matthew E. Welsh (D)	1,072,717	50.4
	Crawford F. Parker (R)	1,049,540	49.3
1964	Roger D. Branigin (D)	1,164,763	56.2
	Richard O. Ristine (R)	901,342	43.5
1968	Edgar D. Whitcomb (R)	1,080,271	52.7
	Robert L. Rock (D)	965,816	47.1
1972	Otis R. Bowen (R)	1,203,903	56.8
	Matthew E. Welsh (D)	900,489	42.5
1976	Otis R. Bowen (R)	1,236,555	56.8
	Larry A. Conrad (D)	927,243	42.6
1980	Robert D. Orr (R)	1,257,383	57.7
	John A. Hillenbrand (D)	913,116	41.9
1984	Robert D. Orr (R)	1,146,497	52.2
	W. Wayne Townsend (D)	1,036,832	47.2
1988	Evan Bayh (D)	1,138,574	53.2
	John M. Mutz (R)	1,002,207	46.8
1992	Evan Bayh (D)	1,382,151	62.0
	Linley E. Pearson (R)	822,533	36.9
1996	Frank L. O'Bannon (D)	1,087,128	51.5
	Stephen Goldsmith (R)	986,982	46.8
2000	Frank L. O'Bannon (D)	1,232,525	56.6
	David M. McIntosh (R)	908,285	41.7

IOWA

(Became a state Dec. 28, 1846)

Year	Candidate	Votes	%
1846	Ansel Briggs (ER)	7,626	50.8
	Thomas McKnight (W)	7,379	49.2
1850	Stephen Hempstead (D)	13,486	52.9
	James L. Thompson (W)	11,403	44.8
1854	James W. Grimes (R)	23,312	52.4
	Curtis Bates (NEB)	21,192	47.6
1857	Ralph P. Lowe (R)	38,498	50.9
	Ben M. Samuels (D)	36,088	47.7
1859	Samuel J. Kirkwood (R)	56,502	51.4
	Augustus C. Dodge (D)	53,332	48.6
1861	Samuel J. Kirkwood (R)	60,303	55.5
	William H. Merritt (D)	43,245	39.8
1863	William M. Stone (UN)	86,107	60.5
	James M. Tuttle (D)	56,132	39.5

Year	Candidate	Votes	%	Year	Candidate	Votes	%
1865	William M. Stone (UN R)	70,461	56.4	1918	William L. Harding (R)	192,662	50.6
	Thomas H. Benton (D)	54,090	43.3		Claude R. Porter (D)	178,815	46.9
1867	Samuel Merrill (R)	90,204	58.9	1920	Nathan E. Kendall (R)	513,118	58.7
	Charles Mason (D)	62,966	41.1		Clyde L. Herring (D)	338,108	38.7
1869	Samuel Merrill (R)	97,243	62.9	1922	Nathan E. Kendall (R)	419,648	70.5
	George Gillaspie (D)	57,287	37.1		J. R. Files (D)	175,252	29.5
1871	Cyrus Clay Carpenter (R)	109,328	61.6	1924	John Hammill (R)	604,624	72.7
	Joseph C. Knapp (D)	68,199	38.4		J. C. Murtagh (D)	226,850	27.3
1873	Cyrus Clay Carpenter (R)	105,132	56.5	1926	John Hammill (R)	377,330	71.3
	J. G. Vale (A-MONOP)	81,020	43.5		Alex R. Miller (D)	150,374	28.4
1875	Samuel Jordan Kirkwood (R)	124,855	57.0	1928	John Hammill (R)	591,720	62.8
	Shepherd Leffler (D)	93,270	42.6		L. W. Housel (D)	350,722	37.2
1877	John Henry Gear (R)	121,316	49.4	1930	Dan W. Turner (R)	364,036	65.7
	John P. Irish (D)	79,304	32.3		Fred P. Hageman (D)	186,039	33.6
	Daniel P. Stubbs (G)	34,316	14.0	1932	Clyde L. Herring (D)	508,573	52.8
1879	John Henry Gear (R)	157,408	53.9		Dan W. Turner (R)	455,145	47.2
	Henry H. Trimble (D)	85,364	29.3	1934	Clyde L. Herring (D)	468,921	54.3
	Daniel Campbell (G)	45,674	15.7		Dan W. Turner (R)	394,634	45.7
1881	Buren R. Sherman (R)	133,328	56.7	1936	Nelson G. Kraschel (D)	524,178	48.7
	L. G. Kinne (D)	73,344	31.2		George Wilson (R)	521,747	48.4
	D. M. Clark (G)	28,112	12.0	1938	George Wilson (R)	447,061	52.7
1883	Buren R. Sherman (R)	164,095	50.1		Nelson G. Kraschel (D)	387,779	45.7
	L. G. Kinne (D)	140,012	42.8	1940	George Wilson (R)	620,480	52.7
	James B. Weaver (G)	23,089	7.1		John Valentine (D)	553,941	47.1
1885	William Larrabee (R)	175,605	50.8	1942	Bourke B. Hickenlooper (R)	438,547	62.8
	Charles Whiting (D)	168,619	48.7		Nelson G. Kraschel (D)	258,310	37.0
1887	William Larrabee (R)	169,596	50.1	1944	Robert D. Blue (R)	561,827	56.0
	T. J. Anderson (D)	153,706	45.4		R. F. Mitchell (D)	437,684	43.6
1889	Horace Boies (D)	180,106	49.9	1946	Robert D. Blue (R)	362,592	57.4
	Joseph Hutchinson (R)	173,450	48.1		Frank Miles (D)	266,190	42.1
1891	Horace Boies (D)	207,594	49.4	1948	William Beardsley (R)	553,900	55.7
	Herman C. Wheeler (R)	199,381	47.5		Carroll O. Switzer (D)	434,432	43.7
1893	Frank D. Jackson (R)	206,821	49.7	1950	William Beardsley (R)	506,642	59.1
	Horace Boies (D)	174,656	42.0		Lester S. Gillette (D)	347,176	40.5
	J. M. Joseph (PP)	23,980	5.8	1952	William Beardsley (R)	638,388	51.9
1895	Francis M. Drake (R)	208,708	52.0		Herschel C. Loveless (D)	587,671	47.8
	W. I. Babb (D)	149,428	37.2	1954	Leo A. Hoegh (R)	435,944	51.4
	Sylvanus B. Crane (PP)	32,189	8.0		Clyde E. Herring (D)	410,255	48.4
1897	Leslie M. Shaw (R)	224,729	51.3	1956	Herschel C. Loveless (D)	616,852	51.2
	Fred E. White (D)	194,853	44.5		Leo A. Hoegh (R)	587,383	48.8
1899	Leslie M. Shaw (R)	239,464	55.3	1958	Herschel C. Loveless (D)	465,024	54.1
	Fred E. White (D)	183,301	42.3		William G. Murray (R)	394,071	45.9
1901	Albert B. Cummins (R)	226,902	58.1	1960	Norman A. Erbe (R)	645,026	52.1
	T. J. Phillips (D)	143,783	36.8		E. J. McManus (D)	592,063	47.9
1903	Albert B. Cummins (R)	238,804	57.1	1962	Harold E. Hughes (D)	430,899	52.6
	J. B. Sullivan (D)	159,725	38.2		Norman A. Erbe (R)	388,955	47.4
1906	Albert B. Cummins (R)	216,995	50.2	1964	Harold E. Hughes (D)	794,610	68.1
	Claude R. Porter (D)	196,123	45.4		Evan Hultman (R)	365,131	31.3
1908	Beryl F. Carroll (R)	256,980	54.6	1966	Harold E. Hughes (D)	494,259	55.3
	Fred E. White (D)	196,929	41.8		William G. Murray (R)	394,518	44.2
1910	Beryl F. Carroll (R)	205,678	49.8	1968	Robert D. Ray (R)	614,328	54.1
	Claude R. Porter (D)	187,353	45.4		Paul Franzenburg (D)	521,216	45.9
1912	George W. Clarke (R)	184,150	39.9	1970	Robert D. Ray (R)	403,394	51.0
	Edward G. Dunn (D)	182,449	39.6		Robert D. Fulton (D)	368,911	46.6
	John L. Stevens (PROG)	71,879	15.6	1972	Robert D. Ray (R)	707,177	58.4
1914	George W. Clarke (R)	207,881	49.3		Paul Franzenburg (D)	487,282	40.3
	John T. Hamilton (D)	181,036	42.9	1974	Robert D. Ray (R)	534,518	58.1
1916	William L. Harding (R)	313,586	61.0		James F. Schaben (D)	377,553	41.0
	E. T. Meredith (D)	186,832	36.4				

1978	Robert D. Ray (R)	491,713	58.3
	Jerome D. Fitzgerald (D)	345,519	41.0
1982	Terry E. Branstad (R)	548,313	52.8
	Roxanne Conlin (D)	483,291	46.5
1986	Terry E. Branstad (R)	472,712	51.9
	Lowell L. Junkins (D)	436,987	48.0
1990	Terry E. Branstad (R)	591,852	60.6
	Donald D. Avenson (D)	379,372	38.9
1994	Terry E. Branstad (R)	566,395	56.8
	Bonnie J. Campbell (D)	414,453	41.6
1998	Tom Vilsack (D)	500,231	52.3
	Jim Ross Lightfoot (R)	444,787	46.5

KANSAS

(Became a state Jan. 29, 1861)

1859[1]	Charles Robinson (R)	7,848	59.2
	Samuel Medary (D)	5,401	40.8
1862	Thomas Carney (R)	9,990	64.7
	W. R. Wagstaff (UN R)	5,456	35.3
1864	Samuel J. Crawford (R)	12,711	60.7
	Solon O. Thacher (R-UNION)	8,244	39.3
1866	Samuel J. Crawford (R)	19,370	70.4
	J. L. McDowell (N UNION)	8,151	29.6
1868	James M. Harvey (R)	29,795	68.2
	George W. Glick (D)	13,881	31.8
1870	James M. Harvey (R)	40,667	66.4
	Isaac Sharp (D)	20,496	33.5
1872	Thomas A. Osborn (R)	66,715	65.8
	Thaddeus H. Walker (LR)	34,698	34.2
1874	Thomas A. Osborn (R)	48,794	56.4
	James C. Cusey (D)	35,301	40.8
1876	George T. Anthony (R)	69,176	56.8
	John Martin (D)	46,201	37.9
1878	John P. St. John (R)	74,020	53.5
	John R. Goodin (D)	37,208	26.9
	D. P. Mitchell (G)	27,057	19.6
1880	John P. St. John (R)	115,144	57.9
	Edmund G. Ross (D)	63,557	32.0
	H. P. Vrooman (G LAB)	19,481	9.8
1882	George W. Glick (D)	83,232	46.4
	John P. St. John (R)	75,158	41.9
	Charles Robinson (G LAB)	20,933	11.7
1884	John A. Martin (R)	146,777	55.3
	George W. Glick (D)	108,284	40.8
1886	John A. Martin (R)	149,715	54.7
	Thomas Moonlight (D)	115,667	42.3
1888	Lyman U. Humphrey (R)	180,841	54.7
	John Martin (D)	107,582	32.5
	Peter P. Elder (UN LAB)	35,847	10.8
1890	Lyman U. Humphrey (R)	115,024	39.1
	J. F. Willits (ALNC D)	106,945	36.3
	Charles Robinson (D & RESUB)	71,357	24.2
1892	Lorenzo D. Lewelling (POP)	162,507	50.0
	Abram W. Smith (R)	158,075	48.7
1894	Edmund N. Morrill (R)	148,700	49.5
	Lorenzo D. Lewelling (D-PP)	118,329	39.4
	David Overmyer (STAL D)	27,709	9.2

1896	John W. Leedy (D-PP)	167,941	50.5
	Edmund N. Morrill (R)	160,507	48.3
1898	William E. Stanley (R)	149,312	51.8
	John W. Leedy (D-PP)	134,158	46.6
1900	William E. Stanley (R)	181,897	51.9
	John W. Breidenthal (D-PP)	164,793	47.0
1902	Willis J. Bailey (R)	159,242	55.5
	W. H. Craddock (D)	117,148	40.8
1904	Edward W. Hoch (R)	186,731	57.9
	David M. Dale (D)	116,991	36.3
1906	Edward W. Hoch (R)	152,147	48.2
	William A. Harris (D)	150,024	47.6
1908	Walter R. Stubbs (R)	196,692	52.5
	Jeremiah D. Botkin (D)	162,385	43.3
1910	Walter R. Stubbs (R)	162,181	49.8
	George H. Hodges (D)	146,014	44.8
1912	George H. Hodges (D)	167,437	46.6
	Arthur Capper (R)	167,408	46.5
	George W. Kleihege (SOC)	24,767	6.9
1914	Arthur Capper (R)	209,543	39.7
	George H. Hodges (D)	161,696	30.6
	Henry J. Allen (PROG)	84,060	15.9
	J. B. Billard (I)	47,201	8.9
1916	Arthur Capper (R)	353,169	60.8
	W. C. Lansdon (D)	192,037	33.1
1918	Henry J. Allen (R)	287,957	66.4
	W. C. Lansdon (D)	133,054	30.7
1920	Henry J. Allen (R)	319,914	58.4
	Jonathan M. Davis (D)	214,940	39.3
1922	Jonathan M. Davis (D)	271,058	50.9
	W. Y. Morgan (R)	252,602	47.4
1924	Ben S. Paulen (R)	323,402	49.0
	Jonathan M. Davis (D)	182,861	27.7
	William Allen White (I)	149,811	22.7
1926	Ben S. Paulen (R)	321,540	63.3
	Jonathan M. Davis (D)	179,308	35.3
1928	Clyde M. Reed (R)	433,395	65.6
	Chauncey B. Little (D)	219,327	33.2
1930	Harry H. Woodring (D)	217,171	35.0
	Frank Haucke (R)	216,920	34.9
	John R. Brinkley (I)	183,278	29.5
1932	Alfred M. Landon (R)	278,581	34.8
	Harry H. Woodring (D)	272,944	34.1
	John R. Brinkley (I)	244,607	30.6
1934	Alfred M. Landon (R)	422,030	53.5
	Omar B. Ketchum (D)	359,877	45.6
1936	Walter A. Huxman (D)	433,319	51.1
	Will G. West (R)	411,446	48.5
1938	Payne Ratner (R)	393,989	52.1
	Walter A. Huxman (D)	341,271	45.1
1940	Payne Ratner (R)	425,928	49.6
	William H. Burke (D)	425,498	49.6
1942	Andrew F. Schoeppel (R)	287,895	56.7
	William H. Burke (D)	212,071	41.8
1944	Andrew F. Schoeppel (R)	463,110	65.7
	Robert S. Lemon (D)	231,410	32.8
1946	Frank Carlson (R)	309,064	53.5
	Harry H. Woodring (D)	254,283	44.0

1948	Frank Carlson (R)	433,396	*57.0*
	Randolph Carpenter (D)	307,485	*40.4*
1950	Edward F. Arn (R)	333,001	*53.8*
	Kenneth T. Anderson (D)	275,494	*44.5*
1952	Edward F. Arn (R)	491,338	*56.3*
	Charles Rooney (D)	363,482	*41.7*
1954	Fred Hall (R)	329,868	*53.0*
	George Docking (D)	286,218	*46.0*
1956	George Docking (D)	479,701	*55.5*
	Warren W. Shaw (R)	364,340	*42.1*
1958	George Docking (D)	415,506	*56.5*
	Clyde M. Reed (R)	313,036	*42.5*
1960	John Anderson Jr. (R)	511,534	*55.5*
	George Docking (D)	402,261	*43.6*
1962	John Anderson Jr. (R)	341,257	*53.4*
	Dale E. Saffels (D)	291,285	*45.6*
1964	William H. Avery (R)	432,667	*50.9*
	Harry G. Wiles (D)	400,264	*47.1*
1966	Robert Docking (D)	380,030	*54.8*
	William H. Avery (R)	304,325	*43.9*
1968	Robert Docking (D)	447,269	*51.9*
	Rick Harman (R)	410,673	*47.6*
1970	Robert Docking (D)	404,611	*54.3*
	Kent Frizzell (R)	333,227	*44.7*
1972	Robert Docking (D)	571,256	*62.0*
	Morris Kay (R)	341,440	*37.1*
1974	Robert F. Bennett (R)	387,792	*49.5*
	Vern Miller (D)	384,115	*49.0*
1978	John Carlin (D)	363,835	*49.4*
	Robert F. Bennett (R)	348,015	*47.3*
1982	John Carlin (D)	405,772	*53.2*
	Sam Hardage (R)	339,356	*44.5*
1986	Mike Hayden (R)	436,267	*51.9*
	Tom Docking (D)	404,338	*48.1*
1990	Joan Finney (D)	380,609	*48.6*
	Mike Hayden (R)	333,589	*42.6*
	Christina Campbell-Cline (I)	69,127	*8.8*
1994	Bill Graves (R)	526,113	*64.1*
	Jim Slattery (D)	294,733	*35.9*
1998	Bill Graves (R)	544,882	*73.4*
	Tom Sawyer (D)	168,243	*22.7*

Kansas

1. Election was held on December 6, 1859, in anticipation of statehood, which was not granted until 1861. Robinson was sworn in as the state's first governor based on this election.

KENTUCKY

(Became a state June 1, 1792)

1800[1]	James Garrard	8,390	*39.4*
	Christopher Greenup	6,745	*31.7*
	Benjamin Logan	3,995	*18.8*
	Thomas Todd	2,166	*10.2*
1804	Christopher Greenup	25,917	*100.0*
1808	Charles Scott	22,050	*61.3*
	John Allen	8,430	*23.4*
	Green Clay	5,516	*15.3*

1812	Isaac Shelby	30,362	*70.9*
	Gabriel Slaughter	12,464	*29.1*
1816	George Madison	47,442	*100.0*
1820	John Adair	20,493	*32.8*
	William Logan	19,947	*31.9*
	Joseph Desha	12,518	*20.0*
	Anthony Butler	9,585	*15.3*
1824	Joseph Desha	38,463	*59.5*
	Christopher Tompkins	22,300	*34.5*
	William Russell	3,899	*6.0*
1828	Thomas Metcalfe (NR)	38,940	*50.5*
	William T. Barry (D)	38,231	*49.5*
1832	John Breathitt (D)	40,715	*50.8*
	Richard A. Buckner (NR)	39,473	*49.2*
1836	James Clark (W)	38,587	*55.8*
	Martin Flournoy (D)	30,491	*44.2*
1840	Robert P. Letcher (W)	55,370	*58.3*
	Richard French (D)	39,659	*41.7*
1844	William Owsley (W)	59,680	*52.0*
	William O. Butler (D)	55,506	*48.0*
1848	John J. Crittenden (W)	66,466	*53.4*
	Lazarus W. Powell (D)	58,045	*46.6*
1851	Lazarus W. Powell (D)	54,821	*48.8*
	Archibald Dixon (W)	54,023	*48.1*
1855	Charles S. Morehead (AM)	69,816	*51.6*
	Beverly L. Clark (D)	65,413	*48.4*
1859	Beriah Magoffin (D)	76,187	*53.1*
	Joshua F. Bell (OPP)	67,283	*46.9*
1863	Thomas E. Branlette (UN)	67,586	*79.6*
	Charles A. Wickliffe (D)	17,344	*20.4*
1867	John Larue Helm (D)	90,216	*65.7*
	Sidney M. Barnes (R)	33,939	*24.7*
	William B. Kinkead (C)	13,167	*9.6*

Special Election

1868	John W. Stevenson (D)	114,412	*81.6*
	R. Tarvin Baker (R)	26,610	*18.7*

1871	Preston H. Leslie (D)	126,445	*58.6*
	George M. Thomas (R)	89,298	*41.4*
1875	James B. McCreary (D)	126,976	*58.3*
	John M. Harlan (R)	90,795	*41.7*
1879	Luke P. Blackburn (D)	125,399	*55.4*
	Walter Evans (R)	81,881	*36.2*
	C. W. Cook (G)	18,954	*8.4*
1883	J. Procter Knott (D)	133,615	*60.0*
	Thomas Z. Morrow (R)	89,181	*40.0*
1887	Simon B. Buckner (D)	143,466	*50.7*
	William O. Bradley (R)	126,754	*44.8*
1891	John Young Brown (D)	144,168	*49.9*
	Andrew T. Wood (R)	116,087	*40.1*
	S. B. Erwin (POP)	25,631	*8.9*
1895	William O. Bradley (R)	172,436	*48.3*
	P. Watt Hardin (D)	163,524	*45.8*
1899	William S. Taylor (R)	193,727‡	*48.1*
	William Goebel (D)	191,331	*47.5*

Special Election

1900	John C. W. Beckham (D)	233,197	49.9
	John W. Yerkes (R)	229,468	49.1
1903	John C. W. Beckham (D)	229,014	52.1
	Morris B. Belknap (R)	202,862	46.2
1907	August E. Willson (R)	214,478	51.2
	Samuel W. Hager (D)	196,428	46.9
1911	James B. McCreary (D)	226,549	53.7
	Edward C. O'Rear (R)	195,672	46.3
1915	Augustus Owsley Stanley (D)	219,991	49.1
	Edwin P. Morrow (R)	219,520	49.0
1919	Edwin P. Morrow (R)	254,472	53.8
	James D. Black (D)	214,134	45.3
1923	William J. Fields (D)	356,045	53.3
	Charles I. Dawson (R)	306,277	45.8
1927	Flem D. Sampson (R)	399,698	52.1
	John C. W. Beckham (D)	367,576	47.9
1931	Ruby Lafoon (D)	438,513	54.3
	William B. Harrison (R)	366,982	45.4
1935	Albert B. "Happy" Chandler (D)	556,262	54.5
	King Swope (R)	461,104	45.1
1939	Keen Johnson (D)	460,834	56.5
	King Swope (R)	354,704	43.5
1943	Simeon S. Willis (R)	279,144	50.5
	J. Lyter Donaldson (D)	270,525	48.9
1947	Earle C. Clements (D)	387,795	57.2
	Eldon S. Dummit (R)	287,756	42.5
1951	Lawrence W. Wetherby (D)	346,345	54.6
	Eugene Siler (R)	288,014	45.4
1955	Albert B. "Happy" Chandler (D)	451,647	58.0
	Edwin R. Denney (R)	322,671	41.5
1959	Bert T. Combs (D)	516,549	60.6
	John M. Robsion (R)	336,456	39.4
1963	Edward T. Breathitt (D)	449,551	50.7
	Louie B. Nunn (R)	436,496	49.3
1967	Louie B. Nunn (R)	454,123	51.2
	Henry Ward (D)	425,674	48.0
1971	Wendell H. Ford (D)	470,720	50.6
	Tom Emberton (R)	412,653	44.3
1975	Julian Carroll (D)	470,159	62.8
	Robert E. Gable (R)	277,998	37.2
1979	John Y. Brown Jr. (D)	558,088	59.4
	Louie B. Nunn (R)	381,278	40.6
1983	Martha Layne Collins (D)	561,674	54.6
	Jim Bunning (R)	454,650	44.2
1987	Wallace G. Wilkinson (D)	504,674	64.5
	John Harper (R)	273,141	34.9
1991	Brereton Jones (D)	540,468	64.7
	Larry J. Hopkins (R)	294,452	35.3
1995	Paul E. Patton (D)	500,787	50.9
	Larry E. Forgy (R)	479,227	48.7
1999	Paul E. Patton (D)	352,099	60.7
	Peppy Martin (R)	128,788	22.2
	Gatewood Galbraith (REF)	88,930	15.3

Kentucky

1. Governors were chosen by a specially elected body of electors in 1792 and 1796.

LOUISIANA

(Became a state April 30, 1812)

1812[1]	William C. C. Claiborne (AM FAC)[2]	2,757	71.2
	Jacques Villeré (CREOLE)	946	24.4
1816[1]	Jacques Villeré (CREOLE)	2,314	51.9
	Joshua Lewis (AM FAC)[2]	2,145	48.1
1820[1]	Thomas B. Robertson (AM FAC)[2]	1,903	40.1
	Pierre Derbigny (CREOLE)	1,187	25.0
	Abner L. Duncan (AM FAC)[2]	1,031	21.7
	Jean Noel Destrehan (CREOLE)	627	13.2
1824[1]	Henry Johnson (AM FAC)[2]	2,847	43.6
	Jacques Villeré (CREOLE)	1,831	28.1
	Bernard Marigny (CREOLE)	1,427	21.9
1828[1]	Pierre Derbigny (NR)	3,041	42.8
	Thomas Butler (JAC D)	1,639	23.1
	Bernard Marigny (JAC D)	1,247	17.6
	Philemon Thomas (NR)	1,172	16.5
1831[1]	Andre B. Roman (NR)	3,733	44.3
	William S. Hamilton (JAC D)	2,730	32.4
	Arnaud Beauvais (NR)	1,475	17.5
	David Randall (JAC D)	455	5.4
1834[1]	Edward D. White (W)	6,973	62.7
	John B. Dawson (D)	4,149	37.3
1838[1]	Andre B. Roman (W)	7,588	52.8
	Denis Prieur (D)	6,776	47.2
1842[1]	Alexander Mouton (D)	9,666	54.0
	Henry Johnson (W)	8,204	46.0
1846	Isaac Johnson (D)	12,629	54.1
	De Buys (W)	10,138	43.4
1849	Joseph Walker (D)	18,566	51.4
	Alexander Declouet (W)	17,553	48.6
1852	Paul O. Hebert (D)	17,813	53.0
	Louis Bordelon (W)	15,781	47.0
1855	Robert C. Wickliffe (D)	22,952	53.7
	Charles De7rbigny (AM)	19,755	46.3
1859	Thomas O. Moore (D)	25,454	62.0
	Thomas J. Wells (OPP)	15,587	38.0
1863	Henry W. Allen	7,497	87.5
	Leroy Stafford	807	9.4
1864	Michael Hahn	6,171	54.3
	J. Q. Fellows	2,959	26.1
	Benjamin Flanders	2,225	19.6
1865	James Madison Wells (D)	22,532	78.2
	Henry W. Allen	6,297	21.8
1868	Henry C. Warmoth (R)	64,271	62.8
	James G. Taliaferro (D)	38,118	37.2
1872	William Pitt Kellogg (R)	72,890‡	57.4
	John McEnery (D)	54,079	42.6
1876	Francis T. Nicholls (D)	84,487‡	52.5
	Stephen B. Packard (R)	76,476	47.5
1879	Louis A. Wiltz (D)	73,623	64.6
	Taylor Beattie (R)	40,415	35.4

1884	Samuel D. McEnery (D)	88,780	67.1
	John A. Stevenson (R)	43,502	32.9
1888	Francis T. Nicholls (D)	136,747	72.5
	Henry C. Warmoth (R)	51,993	27.6
1892	Murphy J. Foster (A-LOT D)	79,407	44.5
	Samuel D. McEnery (D)	47,046	26.4
	A. H. Leonard (R)	29,648	16.6
	John E. Breaux (IR)	12,409	7.0
	R. H. Tannehill (POP)	9,792	5.5
1896	Murphy J. Foster (D)	116,116	56.9
	John N. Pharr (R POP FU)	87,698	43.0
1900	William Wright Heard (D)	60,206	78.3
	Don Caffery Jr. (R FUS, PP)	14,215	18.5
1904	Newton C. Blanchard (D)	47,745	89.0
	W. J. Behan (R)	5,877	11.0
1908	Jared Y. Sanders (D)	60,066	87.1
	Henry N. Pharr (R)	7,617	11.1
1912	Luther E. Hall (D)	50,581	89.5
	H. S. Suthon (R)	4,961	8.8
1916	Ruffin G. Pleasant (D)	80,807	62.5
	John M. Parker (PROG)	48,085	37.2
1920	John M. Parker (D)	53,792#	97.6
1924	Henry L. Fuqua (D)	66,203	97.9
1928	Huey P. Long (D)	92,941	96.1
1932	Oscar K. Allen (D)	110,193	100.0
1936	Richard W. Leche (D)	131,999	100.0
1940	Sam H. Jones (D)	225,841	99.4
1944	Jimmie H. Davis (D)	51,604	100.0
1948	Earl K. Long (D)	76,566	100.0
1952	Robert F. Kennon (D)	118,723	96.0
1956	Earl K. Long (D)	172,291	100.0
1960	Jimmie H. Davis (D)	407,907	80.5
	F. C. Grevemberg (R)	86,135	17.0
1964	John J. McKeithen (D)	469,589	60.7
	Charlton H. Lyons Sr. (R)	297,753	38.5
1968	John J. McKeithen (D)	372,762	100.0
1972	Edwin W. Edwards (D)	641,146	57.2
	David C. Treen (R)	480,424	42.8
1975	Edwin W. Edwards (D)	430,095	100.0
1979	David C. Treen (R)	690,691	50.3
	Louis Lambert (D)	681,134	49.7
1983	Edwin W. Edwards (D)	1,008,282	62.4
	David C. Treen (R)	586,643	36.3
1991[3]	Edwin W. Edwards (D)	1,057,031	61.2
	David Duke (R)	671,009	38.8
1995	M. J. "Mike" Foster (R)	984,499	63.5
	Cleo Fields (D)	565,861	36.5
1999	M. J. "Mike" Foster (R)	805,203	62.2
	William J. Jefferson (D)	382,445	29.5

Louisiana

1. Until 1845 the governor was elected by joint vote of the two houses of the legislature, which could choose one of the two who received the most popular votes. In all nine elections under this system the candidate receiving a popular plurality was subsequently chosen by the legislature. Thereafter elections were determined by a plurality of the popular vote.

2. Until 1828, contests were essentially between candidates supported by the "American" and "Creole" factions of the Jeffersonian Republican party.

3. The 1987 election was decided in the all-party primary unique to Louisiana. The candidate who finished second withdrew.

MAINE

(Became a state March 15, 1820)

1820	William King (D-R)	21,083	95.3
1821	Albion K. Parris (D-R)	12,887	52.8
	Ezekiel Whitman (FED)	6,811	27.9
	Joshua Wingate Jr. (D-R)	3,879	15.9
1822	Albion K. Parris (D-R)	15,476	69.8
	Ezekiel Whitman (FED)	5,795	26.1
1823	Albion K. Parris (D-R)	18,550	95.6
1824	Albion K. Parris (D-R)	19,759	96.8
1825	Albion K. Parris (D-R)	14,206	93.1
1826	Enoch Lincoln (D-R)	20,689	98.2
1827	Enoch Lincoln (D-R)	19,969	97.6
1828	Enoch Lincoln (D-R)	25,745	91.6
1829	Jonathan G. Hunton (NR)	23,315	50.1
	Samuel E. Smith (JAC D)	22,991	49.4
1830	Samuel E. Smith (JAC D)	30,215	51.1
	Jonathan G. Hunton (NR)	28,639	48.5
1831	Samuel E. Smith (D)	28,292	56.3
	Daniel Goodenow (NR)	21,821	43.5
1832	Samuel E. Smith (D)	31,987	52.8
	Daniel Goodenow (NR)	27,651	45.6
1833	Robert P. Dunlap (D)	25,731	52.1
	Daniel Goodenow (W)	18,112	36.7
	Samuel E. Smith (DISS D)	3,024	6.1
1834	Robert P. Dunlap (D)	38,133	52.1
	Peleg Sprague (W)	33,912	46.3
1835	Robert P. Dunlap (D)	27,733	61.4
	William King (W)	16,860	37.3
1836	Robert P. Dunlap (D)	31,837	58.2
	Edward Kent (W)	22,703	41.5
1837	Edward Kent (W)	34,358	50.1
	Gorham Parks (D)	33,879	49.4
1838	John Fairfield (D)	46,216	51.6
	Edward Kent (W)	42,897	47.9
1839	John Fairfield (D)	39,221	54.1
	Edward Kent (W)	33,339	45.9
1840	Edward Kent (W)	45,574†	50.0
	John Fairfield (D)	45,507	49.9
1841	John Fairfield (D)	47,354	55.0
	Edward Kent (W)	36,780	42.7
1842	John Fairfield (D)	40,855	56.9
	Edward Robinson (W)	26,745	37.3
	James Appleton (LIB)	4,080	5.7
1843	Hugh J. Anderson (D)	32,034	50.9
	Edward Robinson (W)	20,975	33.3
	James Appleton (LIB & SC)	6,746	10.7
	Edward Kavanaugh (CALH D)	3,221	5.1
1844	Hugh J. Anderson (D)	48,942	51.8
	Edward Robinson (W)	38,501	41.1
	James Appleton (LIB & SC)	6,245	6.7
1845	Hugh J. Anderson (D)	34,711	51.9
	Freeman H. Morse (W)	26,341	39.4
	Samuel Fessenden (LIB)	5,867	8.8
1846	John W. Dana (D)	34,715†	47.3
	David Bronson (W)	29,100	39.7
	Samuel Fessenden (LIB & SC)	9,550	13.0

1847	John W. Dana (D)	33,429	51.4
	David Bronson (W)	24,246	37.3
	Samuel Fessenden (LIB & SC)	7,352	11.3
1848	John W. Dana (D)	38,720†	48.4
	Elijah L. Hamlin (W)	29,738	37.2
	Samuel Fessenden (F SOIL)	11,484	14.4
1849	John Hubbard (D)	37,534	50.9
	Elijah L. Hamlin (W)	28,260	38.3
	George F. Talbot (FS & SC)	8,025	10.9
1850	John Hubbard (D)	41,220	51.0
	William G. Crosby (W)	32,308	40.0
	George F. Talbot (F SOIL)	7,271	9.0
1852	John Hubbard (D)	41,999†	44.4
	William G. Crosby (W)	29,127	30.8
	Anson G. Chandler (A-MAINE)	21,774	23.0
1853	Albert Pillsbury (D)	36,127	43.3
	William G. Crosby (W)	27,259†	32.7
	Anson P. Morrill (WILDCAT)	11,012	13.2
	Ezekiel Holmes (FS & SC)	9,039	10.8
1854	Anson P. Morrill (R)	44,565†	49.2
	Albion K. Parris (D)	28,462	31.5
	Isaac Reed (W)	14,001	15.5
1855	Anson P. Morrill (R)	51,441	46.6
	Samuel Wells (D)	48,341†	43.8
	Isaac Reed (W)	10,610	9.6
1856	Hannibal Hamlin (R)	69,574	58.1
	Samuel Wells (D)	43,628	36.4
	George F. Patten (W)	6,554	5.5
1857	Lot M. Morrill (R)	54,655	56.0
	Manassah H. Smith (D)	42,968	44.0
1858	Lot M. Morrill (R)	60,360	53.5
	Manassah H. Smith (D)	52,440	46.5
1859	Lot M. Morrill (R)	57,230	55.8
	Manassah H. Smith (D)	45,387	44.3
1860	Israel Washburn Jr. (R)	70,030	56.4
	Ephraim Smart (D)	52,350	42.2
1861	Israel Washburn Jr. (R)	57,475	58.7
	Charles D. Jameson (D)	21,119	21.6
	John W. Dana (OPP D)	19,363	19.8
1862	Abner Coburn (R)	46,689	53.3
	Bion Bradbury (D)	33,645	38.4
	Charles D. Jameson (D)	7,302	8.3
1863	Samuel Cony (UN R)	68,339	57.4
	Bion Bradbury (D)	50,676	42.6
1864	Samuel Cony (UN R)	65,583	58.6
	Joseph Howard (D)	46,403	41.4
1865	Samuel Cony (UN R)	54,430	63.3
	Joseph Howard (D)	31,609	36.7
1866	Joshua L. Chamberlain (R)	69,636	62.4
	Eben F. Pillsbury (D)	41,947	37.6
1867	Joshua L. Chamberlain (R)	57,713	55.6
	Eben F. Pillsbury (D)	45,990	44.3
1868	Joshua L. Chamberlain (R)	75,523	57.3
	Eben F. Pillsbury (D)	56,207	42.7
1869	Joshua L. Chamberlain (R)	51,314	54.0
	Franklin Smith (D)	39,033	41.1
	N. G. Hichborn (TEMP)	4,735	5.0
1870	Sidney Perham (R)	54,019	54.1
	Charles W. Roberts (D)	45,732	45.8

1871	Sidney Perham (R)	58,285	55.1
	Charles P. Kimball (D)	47,578	44.9
1872	Sidney Perham (R)	71,883	56.5
	Charles P. Kimball (D)	55,343	43.5
1873	Nelson Dingley Jr. (R)	45,239	55.9
	Joseph Titcomb (D)	32,924	40.7
1874	Nelson Dingley Jr. (R)	50,865	53.4
	Joseph Titcomb (D)	41,898	44.0
1875	Selden Connor (R)	57,812	51.8
	Charles W. Roberts (D)	53,807	48.2
1876	Selden Connor (R)	75,867	55.5
	John C. Talbot (D)	60,423	44.2
1877	Selden Connor (R)	53,584	52.5
	Joseph H. Williams (D)	42,311	41.5
	Henry C. Munson (G)	5,291	5.2
1878	Selden Connor (R)	56,559	44.8
	Joseph L. Smith (G)	41,371	32.8
	Alonzo Garcelon (D)	28,218†	22.4
1879	Daniel F. Davis (R)	68,967†	49.7
	Joseph L. Smith (NG)	47,643	34.3
	Alonzo Garcelon (D)	21,851	15.8
1880	Harris M. Plaisted (D & G)	73,713	49.9
	Daniel F. Davis (R)	73,544	49.8
1882	Frederick Robie (R)	72,481	52.4
	Harris M. Plaisted (FUS)	63,921	46.2
1884	Frederick Robie (R)	78,318	55.5
	John B. Redman (D)	58,503	41.5
1886	Joseph R. Bodwell (R)	68,850	53.7
	Clark S. Edwards (D)	55,289	43.1
1888	Edwin C. Burleigh (R)	79,401	54.6
	William L. Putnam (D)	61,348	42.2
1890	Edwin C. Burleigh (R)	64,264	56.4
	William P. Thompson (D)	45,370	39.8
1892	Henry B. Cleaves (R)	67,900	52.1
	Charles F. Johnson (D)	55,392	42.5
1894	Henry B. Cleaves (R)	69,322	64.3
	Charles F. Johnson (D)	30,405	28.2
1896	Llewellyn Powers (R)	82,596	66.9
	Melvin P. Frank (D)	34,350	27.8
1898	Llewellyn Powers (R)	53,900	62.2
	Samuel L. Lord (D)	29,485	34.0
1900	John F. Hill (R)	73,470	62.3
	Samuel L. Lord (D)	40,086	34.0
1902	John F. Hill (R)	65,354	59.5
	Samuel W. Gould (D)	38,107	34.7
1904	William T. Cobb (R)	76,962	58.5
	Cyrus W. Davis (D)	50,146	38.1
1906	William T. Cobb (R)	69,427	52.0
	Cyrus W. Davis (D)	61,363	46.0
1908	Bert M. Fernald (R)	73,551	51.6
	Obadiah Gardner (D)	66,278	46.5
1910	Frederick W. Plaisted (D)	73,304	52.0
	Bert M. Fernald (R)	64,644	45.9
1912	William T. Haines (R)	70,931	50.0
	Frederick W. Plaisted (D)	67,702	47.7
1914	Oakley C. Curtis (D)	62,076	43.8
	William T. Haines (R)	58,887	41.6
	Halbert P. Gardner (PROG)	18,226	12.9

Candidate	Votes	%
enry J. Gardner (AM)	51,497	37.7
lius Rockwell (R)	36,715	26.9
asmus D. Beach (D)	34,728	25.5
amuel H. Walley (W)	13,296	9.7
enry J. Gardner (FREM AM)	92,467	58.9
asmus D. Beach (D)	40,082	25.5
eorge W. Gordon (FILL AM)	10,385	6.6
athaniel P. Banks (R)	60,797	46.6
enry J. Gardner (AM)	37,596	28.8
rasmus D. Beach (D)	31,760	24.3
athaniel P. Banks (R)	68,700	57.6
Erasmus D. Beach (D)	38,298	32.1
Amos A. Lawrence (AM)	12,084	10.1
Nathaniel P. Banks (R)	58,780	54.0
Benjamin F. Butler (D)	35,334	32.5
George N. Briggs (AM)	14,365	13.2
John A. Andrew (R)	104,527	61.6
Erasmus D. Beach (D)	35,191	20.8
Amos A. Lawrence (CST U)	23,816	14.0
John A. Andrew (R)	65,261	67.1
Isaac Davis (D)	31,266	32.1
John A. Andrew (R)	79,835	59.5
Charles Devens Jr. (PP)	54,167	40.4
John A. Andrew (UN R)	70,483	70.7
Henry W. Paine (D)	29,207	29.3
John A. Andrew (UN)	125,281	71.8
Henry W. Paine (D)	49,190	28.2
Alexander H. Bullock (UN)	69,912	76.6
Darius N. Couch (D)	21,245	23.3
Alexander H. Bullock (R)	91,980	77.5
Theodore H. Sweetser (D)	26,671	22.5
Alexander H. Bullock (R)	98,306	58.3
John Quincy Adams (D)	70,360	41.7
William Claflin (R)	132,121	67.6
John Quincy Adams (D)	63,266	32.4
William Claflin (R)	74,106	53.5
John Quincy Adams (D)	50,735	36.6
Edwin M. Chamberlain (LAB REF)	13,567	9.8
William Claflin (R)	79,549	53.0
John Quincy Adams (D)	48,680	32.3
Wendell Phillips (LAB REF & P)	21,946	14.6
William B. Washburn (R)	75,129	54.9
John Quincy Adams (D)	47,725	34.9
Edwin M. Chamberlain (LAB REF)	6,848	5.0
William B. Washburn (R)	133,900	69.1
Francis W. Bird (LR)	59,626	30.8
William B. Washburn (R)	72,183	54.6
William Gaston (D)	59,360	44.9
William Gaston (D)	96,376	51.8
Thomas Talbot (R)	89,344	48.0
Alexander H. Rice (R)	83,639	48.3
William Gaston (D)	78,333	45.2
John I. Baker (TEMP)	9,124	5.3
Alexander H. Rice (R)	137,665	53.6
Charles Francis Adams (D)	106,850	41.6
Alexander H. Rice (R)	91,255	49.5
William Gaston (D)	73,185	39.7
Robert C. Pitman (P)	16,354	8.9

Year	Candidate	Votes	%
1878	Thomas Talbot (R)	134,725	52.6
	Benjamin F. Butler (BUT D & R)	109,435	42.7
1879	John D. Long (R)	122,751	50.4
	Benjamin F. Butler (BUT D & R)	109,149	44.8
1880	John D. Long (R)	164,926	58.4
	Charles P. Thompson (D)	111,410	39.5
1881	John D. Long (R)	96,609	61.2
	Charles P. Thompson (D)	54,586	34.6
1882	Benjamin F. Butler (D-NG LAB)	133,946	52.3
	Robert R. Bishop (R)	119,997	46.8
1883	George D. Robinson (R)	160,092	51.3
	Benjamin F. Butler (D & G)	150,228	48.1
1884	George D. Robinson (R)	159,345	52.4
	William C. Endicott (D)	111,829	36.8
	Matthew J. McCafferty (G)	24,363	8.0
1885	George D. Robinson (R)	112,243	53.5
	Frederick O. Prince (D)	90,346	43.1
1886	Oliver Ames (R)	122,346	50.2
	John F. Andrew (D)	112,883	46.3
1887	Oliver Ames (R)	136,000	51.1
	Henry B. Lovering (D)	118,394	44.5
1888	Oliver Ames (R)	180,849	52.7
	William E. Russell (D)	152,780	44.5
1889	John Q. A. Brackett (R)	127,357	48.4
	William E. Russell (D)	120,582	45.8
	John Blackmer (P)	15,108	5.7
1890	William E. Russell (D)	140,507	49.2
	John Q. A. Brackett (R)	131,454	46.0
1891	William E. Russell (D)	157,982	49.1
	Charles H. Allen (R)	151,515	47.1
1892	William E. Russell (D)	186,377	49.0
	William H. Haile (R)	183,843	48.4
1893	Frederic T. Greenhalge (R)	192,613	52.8
	John E. Russell (D)	156,916	43.0
1894	Frederic T. Greenhalge (R)	189,307	56.5
	John E. Russell (D)	123,930	37.0
1895	Frederic T. Greenhalge (R)	186,280	56.8
	George Fred Williams (D)	121,599	37.1
1896	Roger Wolcott (R)	258,204	67.1
	George Fred Williams (D, BRYAN D)	103,662	27.0
1897	Roger Wolcott (R)	165,095	61.2
	George Fred Williams (D)	79,552	29.5
	William Everett (DN)	13,879	5.1
1898	Roger Wolcott (R)	191,146	60.2
	Alexander B. Bruce (D)	107,960	34.0
1899	Winthrop Murray Crane (R)	168,902	56.5
	Robert Treat Paine (D)	103,802	34.7
1900	Winthrop Murray Crane (R)	228,054	59.1
	Robert Treat Paine (D)	130,078	33.7
1901	Winthrop Murray Crane (R)	185,809	57.3
	Josiah Quincy (D)	114,362	35.2
1902	John L. Bates (R)	196,276	49.2
	William A. Gaston (D)	159,156	39.9
	John C. Chase (SOC)	33,629	8.4
1903	John L. Bates (R)	199,684	50.4
	William A. Gaston (D)	163,700	41.3
	John C. Chase (SOC)	25,251	6.4

Year	Candidate	Votes	%
1916	Carl E. Milliken (R)	81,760	54.0
	Oakley C. Curtis (D)	67,930	44.9
1918	Carl E. Milliken (R)	64,069	52.0
	Bertrand G. McIntire (D)	59,050	48.0
1920	Frederick H. Parkhurst (R)	135,393	65.9
	Bertrand G. McIntire (D)	70,047	34.1
1922	Percival P. Baxter (R)	103,713	58.0
	William R. Pattangall (D)	75,226	42.0
1924	Ralph O. Brewster (R)	145,281	57.2
	William R. Pattangall (D)	108,626	42.8
1926	Ralph O. Brewster (R)	100,776	55.5
	Ernest L. McLean (D)	80,748	44.5
1928	William Tudor Gardiner (R)	148,053	69.3
	Edward C. Moran Jr. (D)	65,572	30.7
1930	William Tudor Gardiner (R)	82,310	55.1
	Edward C. Moran Jr. (D)	67,172	44.9
1932	Louis J. Brann (D)	121,158	50.3
	Burleigh Martin (R)	118,800	49.3
1934	Louis J. Brann (D)	156,917	54.0
	Alfred K. Ames (R)	133,414	45.9
1936	Lewis O. Barrows (R)	173,716	56.0
	F. Harold Dubord (D)	130,466	42.1
1938	Lewis O. Barrows (R)	157,206	52.9
	Louis J. Brann (D)	139,745	47.0
1940	Sumner Sewall (R)	162,719	63.8
	Fulton J. Redman (D)	92,053	36.1
1942	Sumner Sewall (R)	118,047	66.8
	George W. Lane Jr. (D)	58,558	33.2
1944	Horace A. Hildreth (R)	131,849	70.3
	Paul J. Jullien (D)	55,781	29.7
1946	Horace A. Hildreth (R)	110,327	61.3
	F. Davis Clark (D)	69,624	38.7
1948	Frederick G. Payne (R)	145,956	65.6
	Louis B. Lausier (D)	76,544	34.4
1950	Frederick G. Payne (R)	145,823	60.5
	Earle S. Grant (D)	94,304	39.1
1952	Burton M. Cross (R)	128,532	52.1
	James C. Oliver (D)	82,538	33.4
	Neil Bishop (IR)	35,732	14.5
1954	Edmund S. Muskie (D)	135,673	54.5
	Burton M. Cross (R)	113,298	45.5
1956	Edmund S. Muskie (D)	180,254	59.2
	Willis A. Trafton Jr. (R)	124,395	40.8
1958	Clinton A. Clauson (D)	145,673	52.0
	Horace A. Hildreth (R)	134,572	48.0

Special Election

Year	Candidate	Votes	%
1960	John H. Reed (R)	219,768	52.7
	Frank M. Coffin (D)	197,447	47.3
1962	John H. Reed (R)	146,604	50.1
	Maynard C. Dolloff (D)	146,121	49.9
1966	Kenneth M. Curtis (D)	172,036	53.1
	John H. Reed (R)	151,802	46.9
1970	Kenneth M. Curtis (D)	163,138	50.1
	James S. Erwin (R)	162,248	49.9
1974	James B. Longley (I)	142,464	39.1
	George J. Mitchell (D)	132,219	36.3
	James S. Erwin (R)	84,176	23.1

Year	Candidate	Votes	%
1978	Joseph E. Brennan (D)	176,493	47.7
	Linwood E. Palmer (R)	126,862	34.3
	Herman C. Frankland (I)	65,889	17.8
1982	Joseph E. Brennan (D)	281,066	61.1
	Charles R. Cragin (R)	172,949	37.6
1986	John R. McKernan Jr. (R)	170,312	39.9
	James Tierney (D)	128,744	30.1
	Sherry E. Huber (I)	64,317	15.1
	John E. Menario (I)	63,474	14.9
1990	John R. McKernan Jr. (R)	243,766	46.7
	Joseph E. Brennan (D)	230,038	44.0
	Andrew Adam (Unenrolled)	48,377	9.3
1994	Angus King (I)	180,829	35.4
	Joseph E. Brennan (D)	172,951	33.8
	Susan M. Collins (R)	117,990	23.1
	Jonathan K. Carter (I)	32,695	6.4
1998	Angus King (I)	246,772	58.6
	James B. Longley Jr. (R)	79,716	18.9
	Thomas J. Connolly (D)	50,506	12.0
	Patricia H. LaMarche (GREEN)	28,722	6.8

MARYLAND

(Ratified the Constitution April 28, 1788)

Year	Candidate	Votes	%
1838[1]	William Grayson (D)	27,722	50.3
	John L. Steele (W)	27,409	49.7
1841	Francis Thomas (D)	28,959	50.6
	William C. Johnson (W)	28,320	49.4
1844	Thomas G. Pratt (W)	35,040	50.4
	James Carroll (D)	34,495	49.6
1847	Philip Francis Thomas (D)	34,388	50.5
	William T. Goldsborough (W)	33,676	49.5
1850	Enoch L. Lowe (D)	36,340	51.0
	William B. Clarke (W)	34,858	49.0
1853	Thomas Watkins Ligon (D)	39,087	52.8
	Richard J. Bowie (W)	34,939	47.2
1857	Thomas Holliday Hicks (AM)	47,141	54.9
	John C. Groome (D)	38,681	45.1
1861	Augustus W. Bradford (UN R)	57,472	68.8
	Benjamin C. Howard (PEACE D)	26,045	31.2
1864	Thomas Swann (UN R)	40,579	55.9
	Ezekiel F. Chambers (D)	32,068	44.1
1867	Oden Bowie (D)	63,694	74.3
	Hugh L. Bond (R)	22,050	25.7
1871	William P. Whyte (D)	73,959	55.7
	Jacob Tome (R)	58,824	44.3
1875	John Lee Carroll (D)	85,454	54.1
	J. Morrison Harris (R)	72,530	45.9
1879	William T. Hamilton (D)	90,771	56.9
	James A. Carey (R)	68,609	43.1
1883	Robert M. McLane (D)	92,694	53.5
	Hart B. Holton (R)	80,707	46.6
1887	Elihu E. Jackson (D)	99,038	52.1
	Walter B. Brooks (R)	86,622	45.6
1891	Frank Brown (D)	108,539	56.5
	William J. Vannort (R)	78,388	40.8

1895	Lloyd Lowndes (R)	124,936	52.0
	John E. Hurst (D)	106,169	44.2
1899	John Walter Smith (D)	128,409	51.1
	Lloyd Lowndes (R)	116,286	46.3
1903	Edwin Warfield (D)	108,548	52.0
	Stephenson A. Williams (R)	95,923	46.0
1907	Austin L. Crothers (D)	102,051	50.7
	George A. Gaither (R)	94,300	46.8
1911	Phillips Lee Goldsborough (R)	106,392	49.3
	Arthur Pue Gorman (D)	103,395	47.9
1915	Emerson C. Harrington (D)	119,317	49.6
	Ovington E. Weller (R)	116,136	48.2
1919	Albert C. Ritchie (D)	112,240	49.1
	Harry W. Nice (R)	112,075	49.0
1923	Albert C. Ritchie (D)	177,871	56.0
	Alexander Armstrong (R)	137,471	43.3
1926	Albert C. Ritchie (D)	207,435	57.9
	Addison E. Mullikin (R)	148,145	41.4
1930	Albert C. Ritchie (D)	283,639	56.0
	William F. Broening (R)	216,864	42.8
1934	Harry W. Nice (R)	253,813	49.5
	Albert C. Ritchie (D)	247,664	48.3
1938	Herbert R. O'Conor (D)	308,372	54.6
	Harry W. Nice (R)	242,095	42.9
1942	Herbert R. O'Conor (D)	198,486	52.6
	Theodore R. McKeldin (R)	179,206	47.5
1946	William Preston Lane Jr. (D)	268,084	54.7
	Theodore R. McKeldin (R)	221,752	45.3
1950	Theodore R. McKeldin (R)	369,807	57.3
	William Preston Lane Jr. (D)	275,824	42.7
1954	Theodore R. McKeldin (R)	381,451	54.5
	Harry Clifton Byrd (D)	319,033	45.5
1958	J. Millard Tawes (D)	485,061	63.6
	James Patrick Devereux (R)	278,173	36.5
1962	J. Millard Tawes (D)	428,071	55.6
	Frank Small Jr. (R)	341,271	44.4
1966	Spiro T. Agnew (R)	455,318	49.5
	George P. Mahoney (D)	373,543	40.6
	Hyman A. Pressman (I)	90,899	9.9
1970	Marvin Mandel (D)	639,579	65.7
	C. Stanley Blair (R)	314,336	32.3
1974	Marvin Mandel (D)	602,648	63.5
	Louise Gore (R)	346,449	36.5
1978	Harry Hughes (D)	718,328	71.0
	J. Glenn Beall Jr. (R)	293,635	29.0
1982	Harry Hughes (D)	705,910	62.0
	Robert A. Pascal (R)	432,826	38.0
1986	William D. Schaefer (D)	907,291	82.4
	Thomas J. Mooney (R)	194,185	17.6
1990	William D. Schaefer (D)	664,015	59.8
	William S. Shepard (R)	446,980	40.2
1994	Parris N. Glendening (D)	708,094	50.2
	Ellen R. Sauerbrey (R)	702,101	49.8
1998	Parris N. Glendening (D)	846,972	55.1
	Ellen R. Sauerbrey (R)	688,357	44.8

Maryland
1. Before 1838 governor chosen by General Assembly.

MASSACHUSETTS

(Ratified the Constitution Feb. 6, 1788)

1780	John Hancock	11,207	91.6
	James Bowdoin	1,033	8.4
1781	John Hancock	7,996	93.1
1782	John Hancock	5,855	83.8
	Thomas Cushing	1,129	16.2
1783	John Hancock	6,693	73.5
1784	John Hancock	5,160	67.6
1785	James Bowdoin	3,510	44.1
	Thomas Cushing	3,005	37.7
	Benjamin Lincoln	1,152	14.5
1786	James Bowdoin	6,001	82.5
	John Hancock	1,272	17.5
1787	John Hancock	18,459	77.4
	James Bowdoin	5,395	22.6
1788	John Hancock	17,841	80.5
	Elbridge Gerry	4,145	18.9
1789	John Hancock	17,264	80.7
	James Bowdoin	3,457	16.7
1790	John Hancock	14,283	86.5
	James Bowdoin	1,880	11.6
1791	John Hancock	15,996	93.9
1792	John Hancock	14,628	86.6
	Francis Dana	825	5.1
1793	John Hancock	16,428	89.9
1794	Samuel Adams	14,425	61.5
	William Cusing	7,199	33.7
1795	Samuel Adams	15,976	90.2
1796[1]	Samuel Adams	15,195	57.4
	Increase Sumner (FED)	10,204	38.5
1797[1]	Increase Sumner (FED)	14,540	56.7
	James Sullivan (D-R)	7,125	27.8
	Moses Gill (FED)	3,553	13.8
1798[1]	Increase Sumner (FED)	18,245	85.8
	James Sullivan (D-R)	1,933	9.1
1799	Increase Sumner (FED)	24,069	72.9
	William Heath (D-R)	8,694	26.3
1800	Caleb Strong (FED)	19,630	50.3
	Elbridge Gerry (D-R)	17,019	43.6
	Moses Gill (FED)	2,019	5.2
1801	Caleb Strong (FED)	25,452	55.3
	Elbridge Gerry (D-R)	20,184	43.9
1802	Caleb Strong (FED)	29,983	60.5
	Elbridge Gerry (D-R)	19,443	43.9
1803	Caleb Strong (FED)	29,199	67.3
	Elbridge Gerry (D-R)	13,910	32.3
1804	Caleb Strong (FED)	30,011	55.1
	James Sullivan (D-R)	23,996	44.0
1805	Caleb Strong (FED)	35,204	51.0
	James Sullivan (D-R)	33,518	48.6
1806	Caleb Strong (FED)	37,740	50.2
	James Sullivan (D-R)	37,109	49.4
1807	James Sullivan (D-R)	41,954	51.5
	Caleb Strong (FED)	39,224	48.1
1808	James Sullivan (D-R)	41,193	50.8
	Christopher Gore (FED)	39,643	48.9

1809	Christopher Gore (FED)	47,916	51.3	1834	John Davis (W)
	Levi Lincoln I (D-R)	45,118	48.3		Marcus Morton (D
1810	Elbridge Gerry (D-R)	46,541	51.2		John Bailey (A-MA!
	Christopher Gore (FED)	44,079	48.5	1835	Edward Everett (W]
1811	Elbridge Gerry (D-R)	43,328	51.6		Marcus Morton (D)
	Christopher Gore (FED)	40,142	47.8	1836	Edward Everett (W)
1812	Caleb Strong (FED)	52,696	50.6		Marcus Morton (D)
	Elbridge Gerry (D-R)	51,326	49.3	1837	Edward Everett (W)
1813	Caleb Strong (FED)	56,754	56.6		Marcus Morton (D)
	Joseph B. Varnum (D-R)	42,789	42.7	1838	Edward Everett (W)
1814	Caleb Strong (FED)	56,374	55.0		Marcus Morton (D)
	Lemuel Dexter (D-R)	45,953	44.8	1839	Marcus Morton (D)
1815	Caleb Strong (FED)	50,921	53.6		Edward Everett (W)
	Lemuel Dexter (D-R)	43,938	46.2	1840	John Davis (W)
1816	John Brooks (FED)	49,527	51.1		Marcus Morton (D)
	Lemuel Dexter (D-R)	47,321	48.8	1841	John Davis (W)
1817	John Brooks (FED)	46,160	54.6		Marcus Morton (D)
	Henry Dearborn (D-R)	38,129	45.1	1842	Marcus Morton (D)
1818	John Brooks (FED)	39,538	55.7		John Davis (W)
	Benjamin W. Crowninshield (D-R)	30,041	42.4		Samuel E. Sewall (LIB)
1819	John Brooks (FED)	42,875	53.7	1843	George N. Briggs (W)
					Marcus Morton (D)
	Benjamin W. Crowninshield (D-R)	35,277	44.2	1844	Samuel E. Sewall (LIB)
1820	John Brooks (FED)	31,072	58.3		George N. Briggs (W)
	William Eustis (D-R)	21,927	41.1		George Bancroft (D)
1821	John Brooks (FED)	28,608	58.3	1845	Samuel E. Sewall (LIB)
	William Eustis (D-R)	20,268	41.3		George N. Briggs (W)
1822	John Brooks (FED)	28,487	57.1		Isaac Davis (D)
	William Eustis (D-R)	21,177	42.5	1846	Samuel E. Sewall (LIB)
1823	William Eustis (D-R)	34,402	52.7		George N. Briggs (W)
	Harrison G. Otis (FED)	30,171	46.2		Henry Shaw (AM R)
1824	William Eustis (D-R)	38,650	52.9		Isaac Davis (D)
	Samuel Lathrop (FED)	34,210	46.8	1847	Samuel E. Sewall (LIB)
1825	Levi Lincoln (R-FF)	35,221	94.1		George N. Briggs (W)
1826	Levi Lincoln (AR)	27,884	68.0		Caleb Cushing (D)
	Samuel Hubbard (FED)	9,044	22.1	1848	Samuel E. Sewall (LIB)
	James Lloyd (FED)	2,212	5.4		George N. Briggs (W)
1827	Levi Lincoln (AR)	29,029	74.2		Stephen C. Phillips (F SOIL)
	William C. Jarvis (FB R)	7,130	18.2	1849	Caleb Cushing (D)
1828	Levi Lincoln (AR)	27,981	81.5		George N. Briggs (W)
	Marcus Morton (JAC R)	4,423	12.9		George S. Boutwell (D)
1829	Levi Lincoln (NR)	25,217	71.6	1850	Stephen C. Phillips (F SOIL)
	Marcus Morton (JAC R)	6,864	19.5		George N. Briggs (W)
1830	Levi Lincoln (NR)	30,908	65.5		George S. Boutwell (D)
	Marcus Morton (JAC R)	14,440	30.6	1851	Stephen C. Phillips (F SOIL)
1831	Levi Lincoln (NR)	31,875	65.2		Robert C. Winthrop (W)
	Marcus Morton (JAC R)	12,694	26.0		George S. Boutwell (D)
1831	Levi Lincoln (NR)	28,804	53.9		John G. Palfrey (F SOIL)
	Samuel Lathrop (A-MAS)	13,357	25.0	1852	John H. Clifford (W)
	Marcus Morton (D)	10,975	20.6		Henry W. Bishop (D)
1832	Levi Lincoln (NR)	33,946	52.9		Horace Mann (F SOIL)
	Marcus Morton (D)	15,197	23.7	1853	Emory Washburn (W)
	Samuel Lathrop (A-MAS)	14,755	23.0		Henry W. Bishop (D)
1833	John Davis (NR)	25,149†	40.3		Henry Wilson (F SOIL)
	John Quincy Adams (A-MAS)	18,274	29.3	1854	Henry J. Gardner (AM)
	Marcus Morton (D)	15,493	24.8		Emory Washburn (W)
	Samuel L. Allen (WM)	3,459	5.5		Henry W. Bishop (D)
					Henry Wilson (F SOIL)

(Right-edge partial column, years: 1855, 1856, 1857, 1858, 1859, 1860, 1861, 1862, 1863, 1864, 1865, 1866, 1867, 1868, 1869, 1870, 1871, 1872, 1873, 1874, 1875, 1876, 1876, 187)

1904	William L. Douglas (D)	234,670	52.1		1940	Leverett Saltonstall (R)	999,223	49.7
	John L. Bates (R)	198,681	44.1			Paul A. Dever (D)	993,635	49.5
1905	Curtis Guild Jr. (R)	197,469	50.5		1942	Leverett Saltonstall (R)	758,402	54.1
	Charles W. Bartlett (D)	174,911	44.7			Roger L. Putnam (D)	630,265	45.0
1906	Curtis Guild Jr. (R)	222,528	52.0		1944	Maurice J. Tobin (D)	1,048,284	53.6
	John B. Moran (D, I LEAGUE)	192,295	44.9			Horace T. Cahill (R)	897,708	45.9
1907	Curtis Guild Jr. (R)	188,068	50.3		1946	Robert F. Bradford (R)	911,152	54.1
	Henry M. Whitney (D, D CIT)	84,379	22.6			Maurice J. Tobin (D)	762,743	45.3
	Thomas L. Hisgen (I LEAGUE)	75,499	20.2		1948	Paul A. Dever (D)	1,239,247	59.0
1908	Eben S. Draper (R)	228,318	51.6			Robert F. Bradford (R)	849,895	40.5
	James H. Vahey (D)	168,162	38.0		1950	Paul A. Dever (D)	1,074,570	56.3
	William N. Osgood (I LEAGUE)	23,101	5.2			Arthur W. Coolidge (R)	824,069	43.1
1909	Eben S. Draper (R)	190,186	48.6		1952	Christian A. Herter (R)	1,175,955	49.9
	James H. Vahey (D)	182,252	46.6			Paul A. Dever (D)	1,161,499	49.3
1910	Eugene N. Foss (D, D & PROG)	229,352	52.0		1954	Christian A. Herter (R)	985,339	51.8
	Eben S. Draper (R)	194,173	44.1			Robert F. Murphy (D)	910,087	47.8
1911	Eugene N. Foss (D, D & PROG)	214,897	48.8		1956	Foster Furcolo (D)	1,234,618	52.8
	Louis A. Frothingham (R)	206,795	47.0			Sumner G. Whittier (R)	1,096,759	46.9
1912	Eugene N. Foss (D)	193,184	40.6		1958	Foster Furcolo (D)	1,067,020	56.2
	Joseph Walker (R)	143,597	30.2			Charles Gibbons (R)	818,463	43.1
	Charles S. Bird (PROG)	122,602	25.8		1960	John A. Volpe (R)	1,269,295	52.5
1913	David I. Walsh (D)	183,267	39.8			Joseph D. Ward (D)	1,130,810	46.8
	Charles S. Bird (PROG)	127,755	27.7		1962	Endicott Peabody (D)	1,053,322	49.9
	Augustus P. Gardner (R)	116,705	25.3			John A. Volpe (R)	1,047,891	49.7
1914	David I. Walsh (D)	210,442	45.9		1964	John A. Volpe (R)	1,176,462	50.3
	Samuel W. McCall (R)	198,627	43.4			Francis X. Bellotti (D)	1,153,416	49.3
	Joseph Walker (PROG)	32,145	7.0		1966	John A. Volpe (R)	1,277,358	62.6
1915	Samuel W. McCall (R)	235,863	47.0			Edward J. McCormack (D)	752,720	36.9
	David I. Walsh (D)	229,550	45.7		1970	Francis W. Sargent (R)	1,058,623	56.7
1916	Samuel W. McCall (R)	276,123	52.5			Kevin H. White (D)	799,269	42.8
	Frederick W. Mansfield (D)	229,883	43.7		1974	Michael S. Dukakis (D)	992,284	53.5
1917	Samuel W. McCall (R)	226,145	58.3			Francis W. Sargent (R)	784,353	42.3
	Frederick W. Mansfield (D)	135,676	35.0		1978	Edward J. King (D)	1,030,294	52.5
1918	Calvin Coolidge (R)	214,863	50.9			Francis W. Hatch (R)	926,072	47.2
	Richard H. Long (D)	197,828	46.8		1982	Michael S. Dukakis (D)	1,219,109	59.5
1919	Calvin Coolidge (R)	317,774	60.9			John W. Sears (R)	749,679	36.6
	Richard H. Long (D)	192,673	37.0		1986	Michael S. Dukakis (D)	1,157,786	68.7
1920	Channing H. Cox (R)	643,869	67.0			George Kariotis (R)	525,364	31.2
	John J. Walsh (D)	290,350	30.2		1990	William F. Weld (R)	1,175,817	50.2
1922	Channing H. Cox (R)	464,873	52.2			John Silber (D)	1,099,878	46.9
	John F. Fitzgerald (D)	404,192	45.4		1994	William F. Weld (R)	1,533,430	70.9
1924	Alvan T. Fuller (R)	650,817	56.0			Mark Roosevelt (D)	611,650	28.3
	James M. Curley (D)	490,010	42.2		1998	Paul Cellucci (R)	967,160	50.8
1926	Alvan T. Fuller (R)	595,006	58.8			Scott Harshbarger (D)	901,843	47.4
	William A. Gaston (D)	407,389	40.3					
1928	Frank G. Allen (R)	769,372	50.1					
	Charles H. Cole (D)	750,137	48.8					
1930	Joseph B. Ely (D)	606,902	49.5					
	Frank G. Allen (R)	590,238	48.2					
1932	Joseph B. Ely (D)	825,479	52.8					
	William Sterling Youngman (R)	704,576	45.0					
1934	James M. Curley (D)	736,463	49.7					
	Gaspar G. Bacon (R)	627,413	42.3					
	Frank A. Goodwin (E TAX)	94,141	6.4					
1936	Charles F. Hurley (D)	867,743	47.6					
	John W. Haigis (R)	839,740	46.1					
1938	Leverett Saltonstall (R)	941,465	53.3					
	James M. Curley (D)	793,884	45.0					

Massachusetts

1. Totals for losing candidates in these elections include some votes for other candidates.

MICHIGAN

(Became a state Jan. 26, 1837)

1835	Stevens T. Mason (D)	8,461	91.2
	John Biddle (W)	814	8.8
1837	Stevens T. Mason (D)	15,314	50.9
	Charles C. Trowbridge (W)	14,780	49.1
1839	William Woodbridge (W)	18,195	51.6
	Elon Farnsworth (D)	17,037	48.4

1841	John S. Barry (D)	21,001	55.8	1890	Edward B. Winans (D)	183,725	46.2
	Philo C. Fuller (W)	15,449	41.1		James M. Turner (R)	172,205	43.3
1843	John S. Barry (D)	21,392	54.8		Azariah S. Partridge (P)	28,681	7.2
	Zind Pilcher (W)	14,899	38.1	1892	John T. Rich (R)	221,228	47.2
	James G. Birney (LIB)	2,776	7.1		Allen B. Morse (D)	205,138	43.8
1845	Alpheus Felch (D)	20,123	51.0	1894	John T. Rich (R)	237,215	56.9
	Stephen Vickery (W)	16,316	41.4		Spencer O. Fisher (D)	130,823	31.4
	James G. Birney (LIB)	3,023	7.7		Alva W. Nichols (PP)	30,008	7.2
1847	Epaphroditus Ransom (D)	24,639	53.2	1896	Hazen S. Pingree (R)	304,431	56.1
	James M. Edmunds (W)	18,990	41.0		Charles R. Sligh (D & POP)	221,022	40.7
	Chester Gurney (LIB)	2,585	5.6	1898	Hazen S. Pingree (R)	243,239	57.8
1849	John S. Barry (D)	27,619	54.2		Justin R. Whiting (DPUS)	168,142	39.9
	Flavius Littlejohn (W FS)	23,320	45.8	1900	Aaron T. Bliss (R)	305,612	55.8
1851	Robert McClelland (D)	23,827	58.3		William C. Maybury (D)	226,208	41.3
	Townsend E. Gidley (W FS)	16,901	41.3	1902	Aaron T. Bliss (R)	211,261	52.5
1852	Robert McClelland (D)	42,798	51.1		Lorenzo T. Durand (D)	174,077	43.3
	Zacharaiah Chandler (W)	34,660	41.4	1904	Fred M. Warner (R)	283,799	54.1
	Isaac P. Christiancy (F SOIL)	6,350	7.6		Woodbridge N. Ferris (D)	223,571	42.6
1854	Kinsley S. Bingham (R)	43,652	53.0	1906	Fred M. Warner (R)	227,567	60.9
	John S. Barry (NEB D)	38,676	47.0		Charles H. Kimmerle (D)	130,018	34.8
1856	Kinsley S. Bingham (R)	71,402	56.9	1908	Fred M. Warner (R)	262,141	48.4
	Alpheus Felch (D)	54,085	43.1		Lawton T. Hemans (D)	252,611	46.6
1858	Moses Wisner (R)	65,201	53.8	1910	Chase S. Osborn (R)	202,803	52.9
	Charles E. Stuart (D)	56,067	46.2		Lawton T. Hemans (D)	159,770	41.6
1860	Austin Blair (R)	87,780	56.7	1912	Woodbridge N. Ferris (D)	194,017	35.4
	John S. Barry (D)	67,053	43.3		Amos S. Musselman (R)	169,963	31.0
1862	Austin Blair (R)	68,716	52.5		Lucius W. Watkins (N PROG)	152,909	27.9
	Byron G. Stout (D)	62,102	47.5	1914	Woodbridge N. Ferris (D)	212,063	48.2
1864	Henry H. Crapo (UN R)	91,353	55.2		Chase S. Osborn (R)	176,254	40.0
	William H. Fenton (D)	74,293	44.9		Henry R. Pattengill (N PROG)	36,747	8.3
1866	Henry H. Crapo (R)	97,112	58.6	1916	Albert E. Sleeper (R)	363,724	55.8
	Alpheus S. Williams (D)	68,650	41.4		Edwin F. Sweet (D)	264,440	40.6
1868	Henry P. Baldwin (R)	128,042	56.8	1918	Albert E. Sleeper (R)	266,738	61.4
	John Moore (D)	97,290	43.2		John W. Bailey (D)	158,142	36.4
1870	Henry P. Baldwin (R)	100,176	53.8	1920	Alexander J. Groesbeck (R)	703,180	66.4
	Charles C. Comstock (D)	83,391	44.8		Woodbridge N. Ferris (D)	310,566	29.3
1872	John J. Bagley (R)	137,602	63.0	1922	Alexander J. Groesbeck (R)	356,933	61.2
	Austin L. Blair (L)	80,958	37.0		Alva M. Cummins (D)	218,252	37.4
1874	John J. Bagley (R)	111,519	50.5	1924	Alexander J. Groesbeck (R)	799,225	68.8
	Henry Chamberlain (D)	105,550	47.8		Edward Frensdorf (D)	343,577	29.6
1876	Charles M. Croswell (R)	165,926	52.3	1926	Fred W. Green (R)	399,564	63.4
	William L. Webber (D)	142,493	44.9		William A. Comstock (D)	227,155	36.0
1878	Charles M. Croswell (R)	126,280	45.4	1928	Fred W. Green (R)	961,179	69.9
	Orlando M. Barnes (D)	78,503	28.2		William A. Comstock (D)	404,546	29.4
	Henry S. Smith (NG)	73,313	26.4	1930	Wilber M. Brucker (R)	483,990	56.9
1880	David H. Jerome (R)	178,944	51.3		William A. Comstock (D)	357,664	42.0
	Frederick M. Holloway (D)	137,671	39.4	1932	William A. Comstock (D)	887,672	54.9
	David Woodman (G)	31,085	8.9		Wilber M. Brucker (R)	696,935	43.1
1882	Josiah W. Begole (D & G)	154,269	49.5	1934	Frank D. Fitzgerald (R)	659,743	52.4
	David H. Jerome (R)	149,697	48.0		Arthur J. Lacy (D)	577,044	45.8
1884	Russell A. Alger (R)	190,840	47.7	1936	Frank Murphy (D)	892,774	51.0
	Josiah W. Begole (D & G)	186,887	46.7		Frank D. Fitzgerald (R)	843,855	48.2
	David Preston (P)	22,207	5.5	1938	Frank D. Fitzgerald (R)	847,245	52.8
1886	Cyrus G. Luce (R)	181,474	47.7		Frank Murphy (D)	753,752	47.0
	George L. Yaple (D)	174,042	45.7	1940	Murray D. Van Wagoner (D)	1,077,065	53.1
	Samuel Dickie (P)	25,179	6.6		Luren D. Dickinson (R)	945,784	46.6
1888	Cyrus G. Luce (R)	233,580	49.2	1942	Harry F. Kelly (R)	645,335	52.6
	Wellington R. Burt (D)	216,450	45.6		Murray D. Van Wagoner (D)	573,314	46.7

1944	Harry F. Kelly (R)	1,208,859	54.7
	Edward J. Fry (D)	989,307	44.8
1946	Kim Sigler (R)	1,003,878	60.3
	Murray D. Van Wagoner (D)	644,540	38.7
1948	G. Mennen Williams (D)	1,128,664	53.4
	Kim Sigler (R)	964,810	45.7
1950	G. Mennen Williams (D)	935,152	49.8
	Harry F. Kelly (R)	933,998	49.7
1952	G. Mennen Williams (D)	1,431,893	50.0
	Fred M. Alger Jr. (R)	1,423,275	49.7
1954	G. Mennen Williams (D)	1,216,308	55.6
	Donald S. Leonard (R)	963,300	44.1
1956	G. Mennen Williams (D)	1,666,689	54.7
	Albert E. Cobo (R)	1,376,376	45.1
1958	G. Mennen Williams (D)	1,225,533	53.0
	Paul D. Bagwell (R)	1,078,089	46.6
1960	John B. Swainson (D)	1,643,634	50.5
	Paul D. Bagwell (R)	1,602,022	49.2
1962	George Romney (R)	1,420,086	51.4
	John B. Swainson (D)	1,339,513	48.5
1964	George Romney (R)	1,764,355	55.9
	Neil Staebler (D)	1,381,442	43.7
1966	George Romney (R)	1,490,430	60.5
	Zolton A. Ferency (D)	963,383	39.1
1970	William G. Milliken (R)	1,338,711	50.4
	Sander Levin (D)	1,294,600	48.7
1974	William G. Milliken (R)	1,356,865	51.1
	Sander Levin (D)	1,242,247	46.8
1978	William G. Milliken (R)	1,628,485	56.8
	William Fitzgerald (D)	1,237,256	43.2
1982	James J. Blanchard (D)	1,561,291	51.4
	Richard H. Headlee (R)	1,369,582	45.1
1986	James J. Blanchard (D)	1,632,138	68.1
	William Lucas (R)	753,647	31.4
1990	John Engler (R)	1,276,134	49.8
	James J. Blanchard (D)	1,258,539	49.1
1994	John Engler (R)	1,899,101	61.5
	Howard Wolpe (D)	1,188,438	38.5
1998	John Engler (R)	1,883,005	62.2
	Geoffrey Fieger (D)	1,143,574	37.8

MINNESOTA

(Became a state May 11, 1858)

1857	Henry H. Sibley (D)	17,790	50.3
	Alexander Ramsey (R)	17,550	49.7
1859	Alexander Ramsey (R)	21,335	54.8
	George L. Becker (D)	17,583	45.2
1861	Alexander Ramsey (R)	16,274#	60.9
	Edward O. Hamlin (D)	10,448#	39.1
1863	Stephen Miller (UN)	19,628	60.6
	Henry T. Wells (D)	12,739	39.4
1865	William R. Marshall (R)	17,318	55.6
	Henry M. Rice (D)	13,842	44.5
1867	William R. Marshall (R)	34,874	54.2
	Charles E. Flandrau (D)	29,511	45.8
1869	Horace Austin (R)	27,348	50.2
	George L. Otis (D)	25,401	46.6

1871	Horace Austin (R)	46,669	59.9
	Winthrop Young (D)	31,212	40.1
1873	Cushman K. Davis (R)	40,741#	52.9
	Ara Barton (IR & D)	35,245#	45.8
1875	John S. Pillsbury (R)	45,073#	53.6
	David L. Buell (D)	35,275#	41.9
1877	John S. Pillsbury (R)	57,071#	57.9
	William L. Banning (D)	39,147#	39.7
1879	John S. Pillsbury (R)	57,522	54.0
	Edmund Rice (D)	41,844	39.3
1881	Lucius F. Hubbard (R)	65,025	63.6
	Richard W. Johnson (D)	37,168	36.4
1883	Lucius F. Hubbard (R)	72,462	53.4
	Adolph Bierman (D)	58,251	42.9
1886	Andrew R. McGill (R)	106,966	48.5
	Albert A. Ames (D)	104,483	47.4
1888	William R. Merriam (R)	134,355	51.3
	Eugene M. Wilson (D)	110,251	42.1
	Hugh Harrison (P)	17,150	6.6
1890	William R. Merriam (R)	88,111	36.6
	Thomas Wilson (D)	85,844	35.6
	Sidney M. Owen (ALNC)	58,513	24.3
1892	Knute Nelson (R)	109,220	42.7
	Daniel W. Lawler (D)	94,600	37.0
	Ignatius Donnelly (PP)	39,860	15.6
1894	Knute Nelson (R)	147,943	49.9
	Sidney M. Owen (PP)	87,898	29.7
	George L. Becker (D)	53,583	18.1
1896	David M. Clough (R)	165,906	49.2
	John Lind (PP & D)	162,254	48.1
1898	John Lind (D & POP)	131,980	52.3
	William H. Eustis (R)	111,796	44.3
1900	Samuel R. Van Sant (R)	152,905	48.7
	John Lind (PP & D)	150,651	48.0
1902	Samuel R. Van Sant (R)	155,849	57.5
	Leonard A. Rosing (D)	99,362	36.7
1904	John A. Johnson (D)	147,992	48.7
	Robert C. Dunn (R)	140,130	46.1
1906	John A. Johnson (D)	168,480	60.9
	A. L. Cole (R)	96,162	34.8
1908	John A. Johnson (D)	175,136	52.0
	Jacob F. Jacobson (R)	147,357	43.7
1910	Adolph O. Eberhart (R)	164,185	55.7
	James Gray (D)	103,779	35.2
1912	Adolph O. Eberhart (R)	129,688	40.7
	Peter M. Ringdal (D)	99,659	31.3
	Paul L. Collins (PROG)	33,455	10.5
	Engebret E. Lobeck (P)	29,876	9.4
	David Morgan (PUB OWN)	25,769	8.1
1914	Winfield S. Hammond (D)	156,304	45.5
	William E. Lee (R)	143,730	41.9
	Willis G. Calderwood (P)	18,582	5.4
	Tom J. Lewis (SOC)	17,325	5.1
1916	Joseph A. A. Burnquist (R)	245,841	62.9
	Thomas P. Dwyer (D)	93,112	23.8
	J. O. Bentall (SOC)	26,306	6.7
	Thomas J. Anderson (P)	19,884	5.1

1918	Joseph A. A. Burnquist (R)	166,615	45.1
	David H. Evans (F-LAB)	111,966	30.3
	Fred E. Wheaton (D)	76,838	20.8
1920	Jacob A. O. Preus (R)	415,805	53.1
	Henrik Shipstead (I)	281,406	35.9
	L. C. Hodgson (D)	81,291	10.4
1922	Jacob A. O. Preus (R)	309,756	45.2
	Magnus Johnson (F-LAB)	295,479	43.1
	Edward Indrehus (D)	79,903	11.7
1924	Theodore Christianson (R)	406,692	48.7
	Floyd B. Olson (F-LAB)	366,029	43.8
	Carlos Avery (D)	49,353	5.9
1926	Theodore Christianson (R)	395,779	56.5
	Magnus Johnson (F-LAB)	266,845	38.1
	Alfred Jaques (D)	38,008	5.4
1928	Theodore Christianson (R)	549,857	55.0
	Ernest Lundeen (F-LAB)	227,193	22.7
	Andrew Nelson (D)	213,734	21.4
1930	Floyd B. Olson (F-LAB)	473,154	59.3
	Ray P. Chase (R)	289,528	36.4
1932	Floyd B. Olson (F-LAB)	522,438	50.6
	Earle Brown (R)	334,081	32.3
	John E. Regan (D)	169,859	16.4
1934	Floyd B. Olson (F-LAB)	468,812	44.6
	Martin A. Nelson (R)	396,359	37.7
	John E. Regan (D)	176,928	16.8
1936	Elmer A. Benson (F-LAB)	680,342	60.7
	Martin A. Nelson (R)	431,841	38.6
1938	Harold E. Stassen (R)	678,839	59.9
	Elmer A. Benson (F-LAB)	387,263	34.2
	Thomas Gallagher (D)	65,875	5.8
1940	Harold E. Stassen (R)	654,686	52.1
	Hjalmar Petersen (F-LAB)	459,609	36.5
	Ed Murphy (D)	140,021	11.1
1942	Harold E. Stassen (R)	409,800	51.6
	Hjalmar Petersen (F-LAB)	299,917	37.8
	John D. Sullivan (D)	75,151	9.5
1944	Edward J. Thye (R)	701,185	61.1
	Byron G. Allen (DFL)	440,132	38.3
1946	Luther W. Youngdahl (R)	519,067	59.0
	Harold H. Barker (DFL)	349,565	39.7
1948	Luther W. Youngdahl (R)	643,572	53.2
	Charles L. Halsted (DFL)	545,746	45.1
1950	Luther W. Youngdahl (R)	635,800	60.8
	Harry H. Peterson (DFL)	400,637	38.3
1952	C. Elmer Anderson (R)	785,125	55.3
	Orville L. Freeman (DFL)	624,480	44.0
1954	Orville L. Freeman (DFL)	607,099	52.7
	C. Elmer Anderson (R)	538,865	46.8
1956	Orville L. Freeman (DFL)	731,180	51.4
	Ancher Nelsen (R)	685,196	48.2
1958	Orville L. Freeman (DFL)	658,326	56.8
	George Mackinnon (R)	490,731	42.3
1960	Elmer L. Andersen (R)	783,813	50.6
	Orville L. Freeman (DFL)	760,934	49.1
1962	Karl F. Rolvaag (DFL)	619,842‡	49.7
	Elmer L. Andersen (R)	619,751	49.7
1966	Harold Levander (R)	680,593	52.6
	Karl F. Rolvaag (DFL)	607,943	46.9

1970	Wendell R. Anderson (DFL)	737,921	54.3
	Douglas M. Head (R)	621,780	45.7
1974	Wendell R. Anderson (DFL)	786,787	62.8
	John W. Johnson (R)	367,722	29.3
1978	Albert H. Quie (I-R)	830,019	52.3
	Rudy Perpich (DFL)	718,244	45.3
1982	Rudy Perpich (DFL)	1,049,104	58.6
	Wheelock Whitney (I-R)	715,796	40.0
1986	Rudy Perpich (DFL)	790,138	55.8
	Cal R. Ludeman (I-R)	606,755	42.9
1990	Arne Carlson (I-R)	895,988	49.6
	Rudy Perpich (DFL)	836,218	46.3
1994	Arne H. Carlson (I-R)	1,094,165	62.0
	John Marty (DFL)	589,344	33.4
1998	Jesse Ventura (REF)	773,403	37.0
	Norm Coleman (R)	716,880	34.3
	Hubert H. Humphrey III (DFL)	587,060	28.1

MISSISSIPPI

(Became a state Dec. 10, 1817)

1817	David Holmes	4,108	100.0
1819	George Poindexter	2,721	61.5
	Thomas Hinds	1,702	38.5
1821	Walter Leake	4,789	77.1
	Charles B. Green	1,269	20.4
1823	Walter Leake	3,996	47.1
	David Dickson	2,511	29.6
	William Lattimore	1,986	23.4
1825	David Holmes (OLD R)	7,850	84.0
	Cowles Mead (OLD R)	1,499	16.0
1827	Gerard C. Brandon	5,482	51.0
	Daniel Williams	3,392	31.6
	Beverly R. Grayson	1,866	17.4
1829	Gerard C. Brandon (JAC D)	7,344	64.8
	George W. Winchester (NR)	3,991	35.2
1831	Abram M. Scott (NR)	3,953	31.6
	Hiram G. Runnels (JAC D)	3,711	29.7
	Charles Lynch (JAC D)	2,902	23.2
	Wiley Harris (JAC D)	1,449	11.6
1833	Hiram G. Runnels (D)	6,705	52.3
	Abram M. Scott (W)	6,117	47.7
1835	Charles Lynch (W)	9,877	51.1
	Hiram G. Runnels (D)	9,451	48.9
1837	Alexander G. McNutt (D)	12,936	46.5
	J. B. Morgan (SR W)	9,896	35.6
	John A. Grimball (SR W)	4,974	17.9
1839	Alexander G. McNutt (D)	18,880	54.3
	Edward Turner (W)	15,886	45.7
1841	Tilgham M. Tucker (D)	19,059	53.2
	D. O. Shattuck (W)	16,783	46.8
1843	Albert G. Brown (A-RPT D)	21,035	53.0
	G. R. Clayton (W)	17,322	43.6
1845	Albert G. Brown (D)	28,310	66.2
	Thomas Coopwood (W)	12,852	30.0
1847	Joseph W. Matthews (D)	26,995	64.8
	Alexander B. Bradford (W)	13,997	33.6

1849	John A. Quitman (D)	33,117	*59.0*
	Luke Lea (W)	22,996	*40.9*
1851	Henry S. Foote (UN)	29,358	*50.9*
	Jefferson Davis (SO RTS)	28,359	*49.1*
1853	John J. McCrae (D)	32,116	*54.0*
	Franics M. Rogers (W)	27,279	*46.0*
1855	John J. McCrae (D)	32,669	*54.2*
	Charles D. Fontaine (AM)	27,578	*45.8*
1857	William McWillie (D)	27,376	*66.0*
	William Yerger (AM)	14,085	*34.0*
1859	John J. Pettus (D)	34,559	*77.0*
	Harvey W. Walter (OPP)	10,308	*23.0*
1861	John J. Pettus	29,959	*86.9*
	Jacob Thompson	3,556	*10.3*
1863	Charles Clark	16,050	*69.8*
	A. M. West	4,914	*21.4*
	Reuben Davis	2,021	*8.8*
1865	Benjamin G. Humphreys (SEC W)	19,037	*42.2*
	E. S. Fisher (UN)	15,557	*34.5*
	William S. Patton	10,519	*23.3*
1868	Benjamin G. Humphreys (D)	62,321	*52.6*
	Beriah B. Eggleston (R)	56,072	*47.4*
1869	James L. Alcorn (R)	76,186	*66.7*
	Louis Dent (C)	38,097	*33.3*
1873	Adelbert Ames (R)	73,324	*58.1*
	James L. Alcorn (I)	52,857	*41.9*
1877	John M. Stone (D)	96,376	*98.8*
1881	Robert Lowry (D)	76,805	*59.6*
	Benjamin King (G & R)	51,994	*40.4*
1885	Robert Lowry (D)	88,783	*100.0*
1889	John M. Stone (D)	84,929	*100.0*
1895	Anselm J. McLaurin (D)	46,870	*72.1*
	Frank Burkitt (PP)	18,167	*27.9*
1899	Andrew H. Longino (D)	42,273	*87.6*
	R. K. Prewitt (POP)	6,007	*12.4*
1903	James K. Vardaman (D)	32,191	*100.0*
1907	Edmund F. Noel (D)	29,528	*100.0*
1911	Earl Brewer (D)	40,471	*95.2*
1915	Theodore G. Bilbo (D)	50,541	*92.6*
	J. T. Lester (SOC)	4,046	*7.4*
1919	Lee M. Russell (D)	39,239	*96.9*
1923	Henry L. Whitfield (D)	29,138	*100.0*
1927	Theodore G. Bilbo (D)	31,717	*100.0*
1931	Martin S. Conner (D)	44,931	*100.0*
1935	Hugh L. White (D)	45,881	*100.0*
1939	Paul B. Johnson (D)	61,614	*100.0*
1943	Thomas L. Bailey (D)	50,488	*100.0*
1947	Fielding L. Wright (D)	161,993	*97.5*
1951	Hugh L. White (D)	43,422	*100.0*
1955	James P. Coleman (D)	40,707	*100.0*
1959	Ross R. Barnett (D)	57,671	*100.0*
1963	Paul B. Johnson Jr. (D)	225,456	*61.9*
	Rubel L. Phillips (R)	138,515	*38.1*
1967	John Bell Williams (D)	315,318	*70.3*
	Rubel L. Phillips (R)	133,379	*29.7*
1971	William L. Waller (D)	601,222	*77.0*
	James Charles Evers (I)	172,762	*22.1*

1975	Cliff Finch (D)	369,568	*52.2*
	Gil Carmichael (R)	319,632	*45.1*
1979	William F. Winter (D)	413,620	*61.1*
	Gil Carmichael (R)	263,702	*38.9*
1983	Bill Allain (D)	409,209#	*55.1*
	Leon Bramlett (R)	288,764#	*38.9*
1987	Ray Mabus (D)	387,346	*53.8*
	Jack Reed (R)	332,985	*46.3*
1991	Kirk Fordice (R)	361,500	*50.8*
	Ray Mabus (D)	338,435	*47.6*
1995	Kirk Fordice (R)	455,261	*55.6*
	Dick Molpus (D)	364,210	*44.4*
1999	Ronnie Musgrove (D)	379,034	*49.6*
	Mike Parker (R)	370,691	*48.5*

MISSOURI

(Became a state Aug. 10, 1821)

1820	Alexander McNair (D-R)	6,576	*72.0*
	William Clark (D-R)	2,556	*28.0*
1824	Frederick Bates (AR)	6,165	*57.1*
	William H. Ashley (CLAY R)	4,636	*42.9*
1825	John Miller (JAC D)	2,793	*48.4*
	William Carr (JAC D)	1,610	*27.9*
	David Todd (NR)	1,291	*22.4*
1828	John Miller	11,958	*100.0*
1832	Daniel Dunklin (D)	9,141	*50.9*
	John Bull (A-JAC)	8,132	*45.2*
1836	Lilburn W. Boggs (D)	14,315	*52.3*
	William H. Ashley (I)	13,055	*47.7*
1840	Thomas Reynolds (D)	29,656	*57.2*
	John B. Clark (W)	22,205	*42.8*
1844	John Cummins Edwards (D)	36,978	*54.1*
	Charles H. Allen (W)	31,357	*45.9*
1848	Austin A. King (D)	48,921	*59.0*
	James S. Rollins (W)	33,942	*41.0*
1852	Sterling Price (D)	46,494	*58.7*
	James Winston (W)	32,706	*41.3*
1856	Trusten Polk (D)	47,066	*40.8*
	Robert C. Ewing (AM)	40,620	*35.2*
	Thomas Hart Benton (BENTON D)	27,615	*24.0*

Special Election

1857	Robert M. Stewart (D)	47,975	*50.2*
	James S. Rollins (AM)	47,619	*49.8*

1860	Claiborne Fox Jackson (D)	74,446	*47.0*
	Sample Orr (CST U)	66,583	*42.0*
	Hancock Jackson (BRECK D)	11,415	*7.2*
1864	Thomas C. Fletcher (UN R)	73,600	*70.3*
	Thomas L. Price (D)	31,064	*29.7*
1868	Joseph W. McClurg (R)	82,090	*56.7*
	John S. Phelps (D)	62,778	*43.3*
1870	Benjamin Gratz Brown (D)	104,374	*62.3*
	Joseph W. McClurg (R)	63,235	*37.7*
1872	Silas Woodson (D & L)	156,767	*56.3*
	John B. Henderson (R)	121,889	*43.7*

1874	Charles H. Hardin (D)	149,566	57.2
	William Gentry (R)	112,104	42.8
1876	John S. Phelps (D)	199,583	57.0
	Gustavus A. Finkelnburg (R)	147,684	42.2
1880	Thomas T. Crittenden (D)	207,670	52.2
	D. P. Dyer (R)	153,636	38.6
	L. A. Brown (G)	36,340	9.1
1884	John Sappington Marmaduke (D)	218,885	50.1
	Nicholas Ford (G & R)	207,939	47.5
1888	David Rowland Francis (D)	255,764	49.4
	E. E. Kimball (R)	242,531	46.8
1892	William Joel Stone (D)	265,044	49.0
	William Warner (R)	235,383	43.5
	Leverett Leonard (PP)	37,262	6.9
1896	Lawrence Vest Stephens (D)	351,062	52.9
	Robert E. Lewis (R)	307,729	46.4
1900	Alexander Monroe Dockery (D)	350,045	51.2
	Joseph Flory (R)	317,905	46.5
1904	Joseph Wingate Folk (D)	326,652	50.7
	Cyrus P. Walbridge (R)	296,552	46.1
1908	Herbert Spencer Hadley (R)	355,932	49.7
	William Cowherd (D)	340,053	47.5
1912	Elliott Woolfolk Major (D)	337,019	48.2
	John C. McKinley (R)	217,819	31.2
	Albert D. Nortoni (PROG)	109,146	15.6
1916	Frederick Dozier Gardner (D)	382,355	48.7
	Henry Lamm (R)	380,092	48.4
1920	Arthur Mastick Hyde (R)	722,020	54.3
	John M. Atkinson (D)	580,726	43.6
1924	Samuel Aaron Baker (R)	640,135	49.4
	Arthur W. Nelson (D)	634,263	48.9
1928	Henry Stewart Caulfield (R)	784,311	51.6
	Francis M. Wilson (D)	731,783	48.2
1932	Guy Brasfield Park (D)	968,551	60.2
	Edward H. Winter (R)	629,428	39.1
1936	Lloyd Crow Stark (D)	1,037,133	57.1
	Jesse W. Barrett (R)	772,934	42.5
1940	Forrest C. Donnell (R)	911,530	50.1
	Larry McDaniel (D)	907,917	49.9
1944	Phil M. Donnelly (D)	793,490	50.9
	Jean Paul Bradshaw (R)	762,908	49.0
1948	Forrest Smith (D)	893,092	57.0
	Murray E. Thompson (R)	670,064	42.8
1952	Phil M. Donnelly (D)	983,169	52.6
	Howard Elliott (R)	886,270	47.4
1956	James T. Blair Jr. (D)	941,528	52.1
	Lon Hocker (R)	866,810	47.9
1960	John M. Dalton (D)	1,095,195	58.0
	Edward G. Farmer (R)	792,131	42.0
1964	Warren E. Hearnes (D)	1,110,651	62.1
	Ethan A. H. Shepley (R)	678,949	37.9
1968	Warren E. Hearnes (D)	1,072,805	60.8
	Lawrence K. Roos (R)	691,797	39.2
1972	Christopher S. Bond (R)	1,029,451	55.2
	Edward L. Dowd (D)	832,751	44.6
1976	Joseph P. Teasdale (D)	971,184	50.2
	Christopher S. Bond (R)	958,110	49.6
1980	Christopher S. Bond (R)	1,098,950	52.6
	Joseph P. Teasdale (D)	981,884	47.0
1984	John Ashcroft (R)	1,194,506	56.7
	Kenneth J. Rothman (D)	913,700	43.3
1988	John Ashcroft (R)	1,339,531	64.2
	Betty Hearnes (D)	724,919	34.8
1992	Mel Carnahan (D)	1,375,425	58.7
	William L. Webster (R)	968,574	41.3
1996	Mel Carnahan (D)	1,224,801	57.2
	Margaret Kelly (R)	866,268	40.4
2000	Bob Holden (D)	1,152,752	49.1
	James M. Talent (R)	1,131,307	48.2

MONTANA

(Became a state Nov. 8, 1889)

1889	Joseph K. Toole (D)	19,735	51.0
	Thomas C. Power (R)	18,991	49.0
1892	John E. Rickards (R)	18,187	41.2
	Timothy E. Collins (D)	17,650	40.0
	William Kennedy (PP)	7,794	17.6
1896	Robert B. Smith (PP & D)	36,688	71.0
	Alexander C. Botkin (R-SIL R)	14,993	29.0
1900	Joseph K. Toole (D)	31,419	49.3
	David S. Folsom (R)	22,691	35.6
	Thomas S. Hogan (ID)	9,188	14.4
1904	Joseph K. Toole (D-LAB-PP)	35,377	53.8
	William Lindsay (R)	26,957	41.0
	Malcolm A. O'Malley (SOC)	3,431	5.2
1908	Edwin L. Norris (D)	32,282	47.3
	Edward Donlan (R)	30,792	45.2
	Harry Hazelton (SOC)	5,112	7.5
1912	Samuel V. Stewart (D)	25,371	31.7
	Harry L. Wilson (R)	22,950	28.7
	Frank J. Edwards (PROG)	18,881	23.6
	Lewis J. Duncan (SOC)	12,766	16.0
1916	Samuel V. Stewart (D)	85,683	49.4
	Frank J. Edwards (R)	76,556	44.1
	Lewis J. Duncan (SOC)	11,342	6.5
1920	Joseph M. Dixon (R)	111,113	59.7
	Burton K. Wheeler (D)	74,875	40.3
1924	John E. Erickson (D)	88,801	51.0
	Joseph M. Dixon (R)	74,126	42.6
	Frank J. Edwards (F-LAB)	10,576	6.1
1928	John E. Erickson (D)	114,256	58.7
	Wellington D. Rankin (R)	79,777	41.0
1932	John E. Erickson (D)	104,949	48.5
	Frank A. Hazelbaker (R)	101,105	46.7
1936	Roy E. Ayers (D)	115,310	51.0
	Frank A. Hazelbaker (R)	108,854	48.1
1940	Samuel C. Ford (R)	124,435	50.7
	Roy E. Ayers (D)	119,453	48.6
1944	Samuel C. Ford (R)	116,461	56.4
	Leif Erickson (D)	89,224	43.2
1948	John W. Bonner (D)	124,267	55.7
	Samuel C. Ford (R)	97,792	43.9
1952	John Hugo Aronson (R)	134,423	51.0
	John W. Bonner (D)	129,369	49.0

1956	John Hugo Aronson (R)	138,878	51.4
	Arnold H. Olsen (D)	131,488	48.6
1960	Donald G. Nutter (R)	154,230	55.1
	Paul Cannon (D)	125,651	44.9
1964	Tim Babcock (R)	144,113	51.3
	Roland Renne (D)	136,862	48.7
1968	Forrest H. Anderson (D)	150,481	54.1
	Tim Babcock (R)	116,432	41.9
1972	Thomas L. Judge (D)	172,523	54.1
	Ed Smith (R)	146,231	45.9
1976	Thomas L. Judge (D)	195,420	61.7
	Robert Woodahl (R)	115,848	36.6
1980	Ted Schwinden (D)	199,574	55.4
	Jack Ramirez (R)	160,892	44.6
1984	Ted Schwinden (D)	266,578	70.3
	Pat M. Goodover (R)	100,070	26.4
1988	Stan Stephens (R)	190,604	51.9
	Thomas L. Judge (D)	169,313	46.1
1992	Marc Racicot (R)	209,401	51.3
	Dorothy Bradley (D)	198,421	48.7
1996	Marc Racicot (R)	320,768	79.6
	Judy Jacobson (D)	84,407	20.4
2000	Judy Martz (R)	209,135	51.0
	Mark O'Keefe (D)	193,131	47.1

NEBRASKA

(Became a state March 1, 1867)

1866	David Butler (R)	4,083	50.4
	J. S. Morton (D)	4,001	49.4
1868	David Butler (R)	8,576	57.5
	T. R. Porter (D)	6,349	42.5
1870	David Butler (R)	11,126	56.3
	J. H. Croxton (D)	8,648	43.7
1872	Robert W. Furnas (R)	16,543	59.6
	H. C. Lett (D)	11,227	40.4
1874	Silas Garber (R)	21,548	59.9
	Albert Tuxbury (D)	8,946	24.9
	J. F. Gardner (PP I)	4,159	11.6
1876	Silas Garber (R)	31,947	61.2
	Paren England (D)	17,219	33.0
	J. F. Gardner (G)	3,022	5.8
1878	Albinus Nance (R)	29,269	56.1
	W. H. Webster (D)	13,471	25.8
	Levi G. Todd (G)	9,484	18.2
1880	Albinus Nance (R)	55,237	63.2
	T. W. Tipton (D)	28,167	32.3
1882	James W. Dawes (R)	43,495	48.8
	J. S. Morton (D)	28,562	32.1
	E. P. Ingersoll (G)	16,991	19.1
1884	James W. Dawes (R)	72,835	54.5
	J. S. Morton (D)	57,634	43.2
1886	John M. Thayer (R)	76,456	55.2
	J. E. North (D)	52,456	37.9
	H. W. Hardy (P)	8,198	5.9
1888	John M. Thayer (R)	103,982	51.3
	J. A. McShane (D)	85,420	42.1

1890	James E. Boyd (D)	71,331‡	33.3
	J. H. Powers (PP I)	70,187	32.8
	L. D. Richards (R)	68,878	32.2
1892	Lorenzo Crounse (R)	78,426	39.7
	Charles Henry Van Wyck (PP I)	68,617	34.8
	J. S. Morton (D)	44,195	22.4
1894	Silas A. Holcomb (D & PPI)	97,825	48.0
	T. J. Majors (R)	94,613	46.4
1896	Silas A. Holcomb (D & PPI)	116,415	53.5
	J. H. McColl (R)	94,724	43.5
1898	William A. Poynter (FUS)	95,703	50.2
	M. L. Hayward (R)	92,982	48.8
1900	Charles H. Dietrich (R)	113,879	48.9
	William A. Poynter (FUS)	113,018	48.5
1902	John H. Mickey (R)	96,471	49.7
	William H. Thompson (FUS)	91,116	46.9
1904	John H. Mickey (R)	111,711	49.7
	George W. Berge (FUS)	102,568	45.6
1906	George L. Sheldon (R)	97,858	51.3
	Ashton Shallenberger (D & PPI)	84,885	44.5
1908	Ashton Shallenberger (D & PPI)	132,960	49.9
	George L. Sheldon (R)	125,967	47.3
1910	Chester H. Aldrich (R)	123,070	51.9
	James C. Dahlman (D)	107,760	45.5
1912	John H. Morehead (D & PPI)	123,997	49.3
	Chester H. Aldrich (R & PROG)	114,075	45.3
1914	John H. Morehead (D & PPI)	120,201	50.4
	R. B. Howell (R)	101,229	42.4
1916	Keith Neville (D & PPI)	143,564	49.3
	Abraham L. Sutton (R & PROG)	136,811	47.0
1918	Samuel R. McKelvie (R)	121,188	54.5
	Keith Neville (D)	97,886	44.0
1920	Samuel R. McKelvie (R)	152,863	40.4
	John H. Morehead (D)	130,433	34.5
	Arthur G. Wray (NON PL)	88,905	23.5
1922	Charles W. Bryan (D)	214,070	54.6
	Charles H. Randall (R)	164,435	42.0
1924	Adam McMullen (R)	229,067	51.1
	J. N. Norton (D)	183,709	41.0
	Dan Butler (PROG)	35,594	7.9
1926	Adam McMullen (R)	206,120	49.8
	Charles W. Bryan (D)	202,688	49.0
1928	Arthur J. Weaver (R)	308,262	57.0
	Charles W. Bryan (D)	230,640	42.6
1930	Charles W. Bryan (D)	222,161	50.8
	Arthur J. Weaver (R)	215,615	49.3
1932	Charles W. Bryan (D)	296,117	52.5
	Dwight Griswold (R)	260,888	46.3
1934	Robert L. Cochran (D)	284,095	50.8
	Dwight Griswold (R)	266,707	47.7
1936	Robert L. Cochran (D)	333,412	55.9
	Dwight Griswold (R)	257,279	43.1
1938	Robert L. Cochran (D)	218,787	44.0
	Charles J. Warner (R)	201,898	40.6
	Charles W. Bryan	76,258	15.4
1940	Dwight Griswold (R)	365,638	60.9
	Terry Carpenter (D)	235,167	39.1
1942	Dwight Griswold (R)	283,271	74.8
	Charles W. Bryan (D)	95,231	25.2

1944	Dwight Griswold (R)	410,136	76.1
	George W. Olsen (D)	128,760	23.9
1946	Val Peterson (R)	249,468	65.5
	Frank Sorrell (D)	131,367	34.5
1948	Val Peterson (R)	286,119	60.1
	Frank Sorrell (D)	190,214	39.9
1950	Val Peterson (R)	247,089	54.9
	Walter R. Raecke (D)	202,638	45.1
1952	Robert B. Crosby (R)	365,409	61.4
	Walter R. Raecke (D)	229,400	38.6
1954	Victor E. Anderson (R)	250,080	60.3
	William Ritchie (D)	164,753	39.7
1956	Victor E. Anderson (R)	308,285	54.3
	Frank Sorrell (D)	228,048	40.2
	George L. Morris	31,583	5.6
1958	Ralph G. Brooks (D)	211,345	50.2
	Victor E. Anderson (R)	209,705	49.8
1960	Frank B. Morrison (D)	311,344	52.0
	John R. Cooper (R)	287,302	48.0
1962	Frank B. Morrison (D)	242,669	52.2
	Fred A. Seaton (R)	221,885	47.8
1964	Frank B. Morrison (D)	347,026	60.0
	Dwight W. Burney (R)	231,029	40.0
1966	Norbert T. Tiemann (R)	299,245	61.5
	Philip C. Sorensen (D)	186,985	38.5
1970	J. James Exon (D)	248,552	53.8
	Norbert T. Tiemann (R)	201,994	43.8
1974	J. James Exon (D)	267,012	59.2
	Richard D. Marvel (R)	159,780	35.4
	Ernest W. Chambers (I)	24,320	5.4
1978	Charles Thone (R)	275,473	55.9
	Gerald T. Whelan (D)	216,754	44.0
1982	Robert Kerrey (D)	277,436	50.6
	Charles Thone (R)	270,203	49.3
1986	Kay A. Orr (R)	298,325	52.9
	Helen Boosalis (D)	265,156	47.0
1990	Ben Nelson (D)	292,771	49.9
	Kay A. Orr (R)	288,741	49.2
1994	Ben Nelson (D)	423,270	73.0
	Gene Spence (R)	148,230	25.6
1998	Mike Johanns (R)	293,910	53.9
	Bill Hoppner (D)	250,678	46.0

NEVADA

(Became a state Oct. 31, 1864)

1864	Henry G. Blasdel (UN R)	9,834	60.0
	David E. Buell (D)	6,555	40.0
1866	Henry G. Blasdel (R)	5,125	55.5
	John D. Winters (D)	4,105	44.5
1870	Lewis R. Bradley (D)	7,200	53.9
	F. A. Tritte (R)	6,147	46.1
1874	Lewis R. Bradley (D)	10,310	56.7
	J. C. Hazlett (R)	7,785	43.3
1878	John H. Kinkead (R)	9,747	51.3
	Lewis R. Bradley (D)	9,252	48.7
1882	Jewett W. Adams (D)	7,770	54.3
	Enoch Strother (R)	6,535	45.7

1886	Charles C. Stevenson (R)	6,463	52.4
	Jewett W. Adams (D)	5,869	47.6
1890	Roswell K. Colcord (R)	6,601	53.3
	Thomas Winters (D)	5,791	46.7
1894	John E. Jones (D SIL)	5,223	49.9
	A. C. Cleveland (R)	3,861	36.9
	George E. Peckham (POP)	711	6.8
	Theodore Winters (D)	678	6.5
1898	Reinhold Sadler (SIL R)	3,570	35.7
	William McMillan (R)	3,548	35.5
	George Russell (D)	2,057	20.6
	J. B. McCullough (PP)	833	8.3
1902	John Sparks (D & SILVER)	6,540	57.8
	A. C. Cleveland (R)	4,778	42.2
1906	John Sparks (D & SILVER)	8,686	58.5
	James F. Mitchell (R)	5,336	36.0
	Thomas B. Casey (SOC)	815	5.5
1910	Tasker L. Oddie (R)	10,435	50.6
	D. S. Dickerson (D)	8,798	42.7
	Henry F. Gegax (SOC)	1,393	6.8
1914	Emmet D. Boyle (D)	9,623	44.7
	Tasker L. Oddie (R)	8,537	39.6
	W. A. Morgan (SOC)	3,391	15.7
1918	Emmet D. Boyle (D)	12,875	52.1
	Tasker L. Oddie (R)	11,845	47.9
1922	James G. Scrugham (D)	15,437	53.9
	John H. Miller (R)	13,215	46.1
1926	Fred B. Balzar (R)	16,374	53.0
	James G. Scrugham (D)	14,521	47.0
1930	Fred B. Balzar (R)	18,442	53.3
	C. L. Richards (D)	16,192	46.8
1934	Richard Kirman Sr. (D)	23,088	53.9
	Morley Griswold (R)	14,778	34.5
	L. C. Branson (I)	4,940	11.5
1938	Edward P. Carville (D)	28,528	61.9
	John A. Fulton (R)	17,586	38.1
1942	Edward P. Carville (D)	24,505	60.3
	A. V. Tallman (R)	16,164	39.8
1946	Vail Pittman (D)	28,655	57.4
	Melvin E. Jepson (R)	21,247	42.6
1950	Charles H. Russell (R)	35,609	57.6
	Vail Pittman (D)	26,164	42.4
1954	Charles H. Russell (R)	41,665	53.1
	Vail Pittman (D)	36,797	46.9
1958	Grant Sawyer (D)	50,864	59.9
	Charles H. Russell (R)	34,025	40.1
1962	Grant Sawyer (D)	64,784	66.8
	Oran K. Gragson (R)	32,145	33.2
1966	Paul Laxalt (R)	71,807	52.2
	Grant Sawyer (D)	65,870	47.8
1970	Mike O'Callaghan (D)	70,697	48.1
	Ed Fike (R)	64,400	43.8
1974	Mike O'Callaghan (D)	114,114	67.4
	Shirley Crumpler (R)	28,959	17.1
	James Ray Houston (IA)	26,285	15.5
1978	Robert F. List (R)	108,097	56.2
	Robert E. Rose (D)	76,361	39.7
1982	Richard H. Bryan (D)	128,132	53.4
	Robert F. List (R)	100,104	41.8

1986	Richard H. Bryan (D)	187,268	71.9
	Patty Cafferata (R)	65,081	25.0
1990	Bob J. Miller (D)	207,878	64.8
	Jim Gallaway (R)	95,789	29.9
1994	Bob J. Miller (D)	200,026	53.9
	Jim Gibbons (R)	156,875	42.3
1998	Kenny Guinn (R)	223,892	51.6
	Jan Laverty Jones (D)	182,281	42.0

NEW HAMPSHIRE

(Ratified the Constitution June 21, 1788)

1784	Meshech Ware	✔	
1785	George Atkinson	2,755	40.8
	John Langdon	2,497†	30.0
	John Sullivan	777	11.5
	Josiah Barlett	720	10.7
1786	John Sullivan	4,309	50.2
	John Langdon	3,600	42.0
1787	John Langdon	4,034	45.3
	John Sullivan	3,642†	40.9
	Josiah Barlett	628	7.1
	Samuel Livermore	603	6.8
1788	John Langdon	4,421	50.0
	John Sullivan	3,664	41.5
1789	John Sullivan	3,657†	42.9
	John Pickering	3,488	40.9
	Josiah Bartlett	968	11.3
1790	John Pickering	3,189	41.0
	Joshua Wentworth	2,369	30.4
	Josiah Bartlett	1,676†	21.5
1791	Josiah Bartlett	8,679	96.8
1792	Josiah Bartlett	8,092	96.5
1793	Josiah Bartlett	7,388	75.0
	John Langdon	1,306	13.3
	John T. Gilman	708	7.2
1794	John T. Gilman	7,629	72.9
1795	John T. Gilman	9,340	98.9
1796	John T. Gilman (FED)	7,809	72.5
1797	John T. Gilman (FED)	9,625	88.9
1798	John T. Gilman (FED)	9,397	77.3
	Oliver Peabody (D-R)	1,189	9.8
	Timothy Walker	734	6.0
1799	John T. Gilman (FED)	10,138	86.4
1800	John T. Gilman (FED)	10,362	61.8
	Timothy Walker (D-R)	6,039	36.0
1801	John T. Gilman (FED)	10,898	65.5
	Timothy Walker (D-R)	5,249	31.5
1802	John T. Gilman (FED)	10,377	54.1
	John Langdon (D-R)	8,753	45.7
1803	John T. Gilman (FED)	12,263	57.5
	John Langdon (D-R)	9,011	42.3
1804	John T. Gilman (FED)	12,246	50.4
	John Langdon (D-R)	12,009	49.5
1805	John Langdon (D-R)	16,097	56.6
	John T. Gilman (FED)	12,287	43.2

1806	John Langdon (D-R)	15,277	74.3
	Timothy Farrar (FED)	1,720	8.4
	John T. Gilman (FED)	1,553	7.5
1807	John Langdon (D-R)	13,912	82.5
1808	John Langdon (D-R)	12,641	79.5
	John T. Gilman (FED)	1,261	7.9
1809	Jeremiah Smith (FED)	15,610	50.4
	John Langdon (D-R)	15,241	49.2
1810	John Langdon (D-R)	16,482	52.1
	Jeremiah Smith (FED)	15,166	47.9
1811	John Langdon (D-R)	17,554	54.7
	Jeremiah Smith (FED)	14,477	45.1
1812	John T. Gilman (FED)	15,613	48.8
	William Plumer (D-R)	15,492†	48.4
1813	John T. Gilman (FED)	18,107	50.7
	William Plumer (D-R)	17,410	48.7
1814	John T. Gilman (FED)	19,695	51.1
	William Plumer (D-R)	18,794	48.7
1815	John T. Gilman (FED)	18,357	50.7
	William Plumer (D-R)	17,799	49.2
1816	William Plumer (D-R)	20,338	53.0
	James Sheafe (FED)	17,994	46.9
1817	William Plumer (D-R)	19,088	54.0
	James Sheafe (FED)	12,029	34.0
	Jeremiah Mason (FED)	3,607	10.2
1818	William Plumer (D-R)	18,674	59.3
	Jeremiah Mason (FED)	6,850	21.8
	William Hale (FED)	5,019	16.0
1819	Samuel Bell (D-R)	13,761	56.7
	William Hale (FED)	8,660	35.7
1820	Samuel Bell (D-R)	22,212	89.7
1821	Samuel Bell (D-R)	22,582	92.4
1822	Samuel Bell (D-R)	22,934	95.6
1823	Levi Woodbury (D-R)	16,985	56.7
	Samuel Dinsmoor Sr. (D-R)	12,718	42.5
1824	David L. Morrill	14,899†	49.7
	Levi Woodbury	11,741	39.1
	Jeremiah Smith	3,360	11.2
1825	David L. Morrill (NR)	29,770	97.6
1826	David L. Morrill	17,528	58.8
	Benjamin Pierce	12,287	41.2
1827	Benjamin Pierce (JAC D)	23,695	86.1
	David L. Morrill (NR)	2,541	9.2
1828	John Bell (NR)	21,149	53.1
	Benjamin Pierce (JAC D)	18,672	46.9
1829	Benjamin Pierce (JAC D)	22,615	54.0
	John Bell (NR)	19,583	46.0
1830	Matthew Harvey (JAC D)	23,214	54.9
	Timothy Upham (NR)	19,040	45.1
1831	Samuel Dinsmoor (JAC D)	23,503	55.6
	Ichabod Bartlett (NR)	18,681	44.2
1832	Samuel Dinsmoor (D)	24,167	61.8
	Ichabod Bartlett	14,920	38.2
1833	Samuel Dinsmoor (D)	28,270	84.5
	Arthur Livermore (NR)	3,959	11.9
1834	William Badger (D)	28,542	95.1
1835	William Badger (D)	25,767	63.4
	Joseph Healy (W)	14,825	36.6

Year	Candidate	Votes	%	Year	Candidate	Votes	%
1836	Isaac Hill (D)	24,904	81.2	1858	William Haile (R)	36,215	53.3
	Joseph Healy (W)	2,566	8.4		Asa P. Cate (D)	31,677	46.7
	George Sullivan	2,230	7.3	1859	Ichabod Goodwin (R)	36,326	52.6
1837	Isaac Hill (D)	22,361	91.2		Asa P. Cate (D)	32,802	47.4
1838	Isaac Hill (D)	28,687	53.2	1860	Ichabod Goodwin (R)	38,031	53.1
	James Wilson Jr. (W)	25,244	46.8		Asa P. Cate (D)	33,543	46.9
1839	John Page (D)	30,518	55.9	1861	Nathaniel S. Berry (R)	35,467	52.9
	James Wilson Jr. (W)	23,928	43.8		George Stark (D)	31,452	46.9
1840	John Page (D)	29,521	58.1	1862	Nathaniel S. Berry (R)	32,150	51.5
	Enos Stevens (W)	20,716	40.8		George Stark (D)	28,566	45.8
1841	John Page (D)	29,116	56.4	1863	Ira A. Eastman (D)	32,833	49.6
	Enos Stevens (W)	21,230	41.1		Joseph A. Gilmore (R)	29,035†	43.8
1842	Henry Hubbard (D)	26,831	56.2		Walter Harriman (UN)	4,372	6.6
	Enos Stevens (W)	12,234	25.6	1864	Joseph A. Gilmore (UN)	37,006	54.2
	John H. White (ID)	5,869	12.3		Edward W. Harrington (D)	31,340	45.9
	Daniel Hoit (LIB)	2,812	5.9	1865	Frederick Smyth (UN)	33,167	54.5
1843	Henry Hubbard (D)	23,050	51.7		Edward W. Harrington (D)	27,735	45.5
	Anthony Colby (W)	12,551	28.0	1866	Frederick Smyth (R)	35,137	53.5
	John H. White (C)	5,767	12.9		John G. Sinclair (D)	30,481	46.4
	Daniel Hoit (LIB)	3,402	7.6	1867	Walter Harriman (R)	35,809	52.2
1844	John H. Steele (D)	25,986	53.6		John G. Sinclair (D)	32,663	47.6
	Anthony Colby (W)	14,750	30.3	1868	Walter Harriman (R)	39,724	51.7
	Daniel Hoit (LIB)	5,767	11.8		John G. Sinclair (D)	37,098	48.3
1845	John H. Steele (D)	23,406	51.1	1869	Onslow Stearns (R)	35,777	52.8
	Anthony Colby (W)	15,585	34.1		John Bedell (D)	32,004	47.2
	Daniel Hoit (LIB)	5,786	12.6	1870	Onslow Stearns (R)	34,847	51.1
1846	Jared W. Williams (D)	26,740	48.7		John Bedell (D)	25,058	36.7
	Anthony Colby (W)	17,787†	32.0		Samuel Flint (LAB REF)	7,363	10.8
	Nathaniel S. Berry (LIB)	10,379	18.7	1871	James A. Weston (D)	34,799†	49.9
1847	Jared W. Williams (D)	30,806	50.9		James Pike (R)	33,892	48.6
	Anthony Colby (W)	21,109	34.9	1872	Ezekiel A. Straw (R)	38,751	50.8
	Nathaniel S. Berry (AB)	8,531	14.1		James A. Weston (D)	36,584	47.9
1848	Jared W. Williams (D)	32,245	52.8	1873	Ezekiel A. Straw (R)	34,023	50.2
	Nathaniel S. Berry (W FS)	28,829	47.2		James A. Weston (D)	32,016	47.2
1849	Samuel Dinsmoor Jr. (D)	30,107	53.8	1874	James A. Weston (D)	35,608†	49.6
	Levi Chamberlain (W)	18,764	33.6		Luther McCutchins (R)	34,143	47.5
	Nathaniel S. Berry (FS & SC)	7,045	12.6	1875	Person C. Cheney (R)	39,293†	49.6
1850	Samuel Dinsmoor Jr. (D)	30,751	55.2		Hiram R. Roberts (D)	39,121	49.4
	Levi Chamberlain (W)	18,512	33.2	1876	Person C. Cheney (R)	41,761	52.0
	Nathaniel S. Berry (F SOIL)	6,472	11.6		Marcy (D)	38,133	47.5
1851	Samuel Dinsmoor Jr. (D)	27,425†	47.3	1877	Benjamin F. Prescott (R)	40,757	52.3
	Thomas E. Sawyer (W)	18,458	31.8		Marcy (D)	36,726	47.2
	John Atwood (F SOIL)	12,049	20.9	1878	Benjamin F. Prescott (R)	39,372	50.6
1852	Noah Martin (D)	30,807	51.2		McKean (D)	37,860	48.7
	Thomas E. Sawyer (W)	19,850	33.0	1878	Natt Head (R)	38,075	50.4
	John Atwood (F SOIL)	9,479	15.8		Frank A. McKean (D)	31,138	41.2
1853	Noah Martin (D)	30,924	54.7		Warren G. Brown (G)	6,407	8.5
	James Bell (W)	17,580	31.1	1880	Charles H. Bell (R)	44,434	51.6
	John H. White (F SOIL)	7,997	14.1		Frank Jones (D)	40,815	47.4
1854	Nathaniel B. Baker (D)	29,788	51.3	1882	Samuel W. Hale (R)	38,402	50.4
	James Bell (W)	16,941	29.3		Martin V. B. Edgerly (D)	36,916	48.5
	Jared Perkins (F SOIL)	11,080	19.2	1884	Moody Currier (R)	42,514	50.3
1855	Ralph Metcalf (AM)	32,783	50.7		George Hill (D)	39,637	46.9
	Nathaniel B. Baker (D)	27,055	41.8	1886	Charles H. Sawyer (R)	37,796†	48.8
	James Bell (W)	3,436	5.3		Thomas Cogswell (D)	37,338	48.3
1856	Ralph Metcalf (AM)	32,119†	48.2	1888	David H. Goodell (R)	44,809†	49.5
	John S. Wells (D)	32,031	48.0		Charles H. Amsden (D)	44,217	48.8
1857	William Haile (R)	34,214	51.9	1890	Hiram A. Tuttle (R)	42,479†	49.3
	John S. Wells (D)	31,209	47.4		Charles H. Amsden (D)	42,386	49.2

Year	Candidate	Votes	%
1892	John B. Smith (R)	43,676	50.2
	Luther F. McKinney (D)	41,501	47.7
1894	Charles A. Busiel (R)	46,491	56.0
	Henry O. Kent (D)	33,959	40.9
1896	George A. Ramsdell (R)	48,387	61.4
	Henry O. Kent (D)	28,333	36.0
1898	Frank W. Rollins (R)	44,730	54.2
	Charles F. Stone (D)	35,653	43.2
1900	Chester B. Jordan (R)	53,891	59.4
	Frederick E. Potter (D)	34,956	38.5
1902	Nahum J. Bachelder (R)	42,115	53.2
	Henry F. Hollis (D)	33,844	42.8
1904	John McLane (R)	51,171	57.8
	Henry F. Hollis (D)	35,437	40.1
1906	Charles M. Floyd (R)	40,581†	49.8
	Nathan C. Jameson (D)	37,672	46.2
1908	Henry B. Quinby (R)	44,630	50.4
	Clarence E. Carr (D)	41,386	46.7
1910	Robert P. Bass (R)	44,908	53.4
	Clarence E. Carr (D)	37,737	44.8
1912	Samuel D. Felker (D)	34,203†	41.1
	Franklin Worcester (R)	32,504	39.0
	Winston Churchill (PROG)	14,401	17.3
1914	Rolland H. Spaulding (R)	46,413	55.2
	Albert W. Noone (D)	33,674	40.0
1916	Henry W. Keyes (R)	45,899	53.2
	John C. Hutchins (D)	38,853	45.1
1918	John H. Bartlett (R)	38,465	54.1
	Nathaniel E. Martin (D)	32,605	45.9
1920	Albert O. Brown (R)	93,273	59.6
	Charles E. Tilton (D)	62,174	39.7
1922	Fred H. Brown (D)	70,160	53.3
	Windsor H. Goodnow (R)	61,526	46.7
1924	John G. Winant (R)	88,650	53.9
	Fred H. Brown (D)	75,691	46.1
1926	Huntley N. Spaulding (R)	77,394	59.7
	Eaton D. Sargent (D)	52,236	40.3
1928	Charles W. Tobey (R)	108,431	57.5
	Eaton D. Sargent (D)	79,798	42.3
1930	John G. Winant (R)	75,518	58.0
	Albert W. Noone (D)	54,441	41.8
1932	John G. Winant (R)	106,777	54.2
	Henri Ledoux (D)	89,487	45.4
1934	H. Styles Bridges (R)	89,481	50.6
	John L. Sullivan (D)	87,019	49.2
1936	Francis P. Murphy (R)	118,178	56.6
	Amos Blandin (D)	89,011	42.6
1938	Francis P. Murphy (R)	107,841	57.1
	John L. Sullivan (D)	80,847	42.8
1940	Robert O. Blood (R)	112,386	50.7
	F. Clyde Keefe (D)	109,093	49.3
1942	Robert O. Blood (R)	83,766	52.2
	William J. Neal (D)	76,782	47.8
1944	Charles M. Dale (R)	115,799	53.1
	James J. Powers (D)	102,232	46.9
1946	Charles M. Dale (R)	103,204	63.1
	F. Clyde Keefe (D)	60,247	36.9
1948	Sherman Adams (R)	116,212	52.2
	Herbert W. Hill (D)	105,207	47.3
1950	Sherman Adams (R)	108,907	57.0
	Robert P. Bingham (D)	82,258	43.0
1952	Hugh Gregg (R)	167,791	63.2
	William H. Craig (D)	97,924	36.9
1954	Lane Dwinell (R)	107,287	55.1
	John Shaw (D)	87,344	44.9
1956	Lane Dwinell (R)	141,578	54.7
	John Shaw (D)	117,117	45.3
1958	Wesley Powell (R)	106,790	51.7
	Bernard L. Boutin (D)	99,955	48.4
1960	Wesley Powell (R)	161,123	55.5
	Bernard L. Boutin (D)	129,404	44.5
1962	John W. King (D)	135,481	58.9
	John Pillsbury (R)	94,567	41.1
1964	John W. King (D)	190,863	66.8
	John Pillsbury (R)	94,824	33.2
1966	John W. King (D)	125,882	53.9
	Hugh Gregg (R)	107,259	45.9
1968	Walter Peterson (R)	149,902	52.5
	Emile R. Bussiere (D)	135,378	47.4
1970	Walter Peterson (R)	102,298	46.0
	Roger J. Crowley Jr. (D)	98,098	44.1
	Meldrim Thomson Jr. (AM)	22,033	9.9
1972	Meldrim Thomson Jr. (R)	133,702	41.4
	Roger J. Crowley Jr. (D)	126,107	39.0
	Malcolm McLane (I)	63,199	19.6
1974	Meldrim Thomson Jr. (R)	115,933	51.1
	Richard W. Leonard (D)	110,591	48.8
1976	Meldrim Thomson Jr. (R)	197,589	57.7
	Harry V. Spanos (D)	144,655	42.3
1978	Hugh J. Gallen (D)	133,133	49.4
	Meldrim Thomson Jr. (R)	122,464	45.4
1980	Hugh J. Gallen (D)	226,436	59.0
	Meldrim Thomson Jr. (R)	156,178	40.7
1982	John H. Sununu (R)	145,389	51.4
	Hugh J. Gallen (D)	132,317	46.8
1984	John H. Sununu (R)	256,571	66.8
	Chris Spirou (D)	127,156	33.1
1986	John H. Sununu (R)	134,824	53.7
	Paul McEachern (D)	116,142	46.3
1988	Judd Gregg (R)	267,064	60.4
	Paul McEachern (D)	172,543	39.1
1990	Judd Gregg (R)	177,611	60.2
	J. Joseph Grandmaison (D)	101,886	34.6
1992	Steve Merrill (R)	289,170	56.0
	Deborah "Arnie" Arnesen (D)	206,232	40.0
1994	Steven Merrill (R)	218,134	69.9
	Wayne D. King (D)	79,686	25.6
1996	Jeanne Shaheen (D)	284,175	57.2
	Ovide M. Lamontagne (R)	196,321	39.5
1998	Jeanne Shaheen (D)	210,769	66.1
	Jay Lucas (R)	98,473	30.9
2000	Jeanne Shaheen (D)	275,038	48.7
	Gordon Humphrey (R)	246,952	43.7
	Mary Brown (I)	35,904	6.4

NEW JERSEY

(Ratified the Constitution Dec. 18, 1787)

1844[1]	Charles C. Stratton (W)	37,985	50.9
	John R. Thompson (D)	36,581	49.1
1847	Daniel Haines (D)	34,765	51.9
	William Wright (W)	32,251	48.1
1849	George F. Fort (D)	39,723	53.8
	John Runk (W)	34,054	46.2
1853	Rodman M. Price (D)	38,312	52.6
	Joel Haywood (W)	34,530	47.4
1856	William A. Newell (FUS)	50,803	51.3
	William C. Alexander (D)	48,246	48.7
1859	Charles S. Olden (R)	53,315	50.8
	Edwin V. Wright (D)	51,714	49.2
1862	Joel Parker (D)	61,307	56.8
	Marcus L. Ward (UN)	46,710	43.2
1865	Marcus L. Ward (UN)	67,525	51.1
	Theodore Runyon (D)	64,706	48.9
1868	Theodore F. Randolph (D)	83,619	51.4
	John I. Blair (R)	79,072	48.6
1871	Joel Parker (D)	82,362	51.9
	Cornelius Walsh (R)	76,383	48.1
1874	Joseph D. Bedle (D)	97,283	53.7
	George A. Halsey (R)	84,050	46.4
1878	George B. McClellan (D)	97,837	51.7
	William A. Newell (R)	85,094	44.9
1880	George C. Ludlow (D)	121,666	49.5
	Frederick A. Potts (R)	121,015	49.3
1883	Leon Abbett (D)	103,856	49.9
	Jonathan Dixon (R)	97,047	46.7
1886	Robert S. Green (D)	109,939	47.4
	Benjamin F. Howey (R)	101,919	44.0
	Clinton B. Fisk (P)	19,808	8.6
1889	Leon Abbett (D)	138,245	51.4
	Edward B. Grubb (R)	123,992	46.1
1892	George T. Werts (D)	167,257	49.7
	John Kean Jr. (R)	159,632	47.4
1895	John W. Griggs (R)	162,900	52.3
	Alexander T. McGill (D)	136,000	43.6
1898	Foster M. Voorhees (R)	164,051	48.9
	Elvin W. Crane (D & CD)	158,552	47.3
1901	Franklin Murphy (R)	183,814	50.9
	James M. Seymour (D)	166,681	46.1
1904	Edward C. Stokes (R)	231,363	53.5
	Charles C. Black (D)	179,719	41.6
1907	John Franklin Fort (R)	194,313	49.3
	Frank Katzenbach (D)	186,300	47.3
1910	Woodrow Wilson (D)	233,682	53.9
	Vivian M. Lewis (R)	184,626	42.6
1913	James F. Fielder (D)	173,148	46.1
	Edward C. Stokes (R)	140,298	37.4
	Everett Colby (PROG)	41,132	11.0
1916	Walter E. Edge (R)	247,343	55.4
	H. Otto Wittpenn (D)	177,696	39.8
1919	Edward I. Edwards (D)	217,486	49.2
	Newton A. K. Bugbee (R)	202,976	45.9
1922	George S. Silzer (D)	427,206	52.2
1925	William N. Runyon (R)	383,312	46.8
	Arthur Harry Moore (D)	471,549	51.9
	Arthur Whitney (R)	433,121	47.6
1928	Morgan F. Larson (R)	824,005	54.9
	William L. Dill (D)	671,728	44.7
1931	Arthur Harry Moore (D)	735,504	57.8
	David Baird Jr. (R)	505,451	39.7
1934	Harold G. Hoffman (R)	686,530	49.9
	William L. Dill (D)	674,096	49.0
1937	Arthur Harry Moore (D)	746,033	50.8
	Lester H. Clee (R)	700,767	47.8
1940	Charles Edison (D)	984,407	51.4
	Robert C. Hendrickson (R)	920,512	48.0
1943	Walter E. Edge (R)	634,364	55.2
	Vincent J. Murphy (D)	506,604	44.1
1946	Alfred E. Driscoll (R)	807,378	57.1
	Lewis G. Hansen (D)	585,960	41.4
1949	Alfred E. Driscoll (R)	885,882	51.5
	Elmer H. Wene (D)	810,022	47.1
1953	Robert B. Meyner (D)	962,710	53.2
	Paul L. Troast (R)	809,068	44.7
1957	Robert B. Meyner (D)	1,101,130	54.6
	Malcolm S. Forbes (R)	897,321	44.5
1961	Richard J. Hughes (D)	1,084,194	50.4
	James P. Mitchell (R)	1,049,274	48.7
1965	Richard J. Hughes (D)	1,279,568	57.4
	Wayne Dumont Jr. (R)	915,996	41.1
1969	William T. Cahill (R)	1,411,905	59.7
	Robert B. Meyner (D)	911,003	38.5
1973	Brendan T. Byrne (D)	1,397,613	66.4
	Charles W. Sandman Jr. (R)	676,235	32.1
1977	Brendan T. Byrne (D)	1,184,564	55.7
	Raymond H. Bateman (R)	888,880	41.8
1981	Thomas H. Kean (R)	1,145,999	49.5
	James J. Florio (D)	1,144,202	49.4
1985	Thomas H. Kean (R)	1,372,631	70.3
	Peter Shapiro (D)	578,402	29.7
1989	James J. Florio (D)	1,379,937	61.2
	Jim Courter (R)	838,553	37.2
1993	Christine Todd Whitman (R)	1,236,124	49.3
	James J. Florio (D)	1,210,031	48.3
1997	Christine Todd Whitman (R)	1,126,927	46.9
	James McGreevey (D)	1,100,239	45.8

New Jersey
1. Before 1844 governor chosen by legislature.

NEW MEXICO

(Became a state Jan. 6, 1912)

1911	William C. McDonald (D)	31,036	51.0
	Holm O. Bursum (R)	28,019	46.1
1916	Ezequiel C. deBaca (D)	32,875	49.4
	Holm O. Bursum (R)	31,552	47.4
1918	Octaviano A. Larrazolo (R)	23,752	50.5
	Felix Garcia (D)	22,433	47.7
1920	Merritt C. Mechem (R)	54,426	51.3
	Richard H. Hanna (D)	50,755	47.8

1922	James F. Hinkle (D)	60,317	54.6
	Charles I. Hill (R)	49,363	44.7
1924	Arthur T. Hannett (D)	56,183	48.8
	Manuel B. Otero (R)	55,984	48.6
1926	Richard C. Dillon (R)	56,294	51.6
	Arthur T. Hannett (D)	52,523	48.2
1928	Richard C. Dillon (R)	65,967	55.6
	Robert C. Dow (D)	52,550	44.3
1930	Arthur Seligman (D)	62,789	53.2
	Clarence M. Botts (R)	55,026	46.6
1932	Arthur Seligman (D)	83,612	54.8
	Richard C. Dillon (R)	67,406	44.2
1934	Clyde Tingley (D)	78,390	51.9
	Jaffa Miller (R)	71,899	47.6
1936	Clyde Tingley (D)	97,090	57.2
	Jaffa Miller (R)	72,539	42.8
1938	John E. Miles (D)	82,344	52.2
	Albert K. Mitchell (R)	75,017	47.6
1940	John E. Miles (D)	103,035	55.6
	Maurice Miera (R)	82,306	44.4
1942	John J. Dempsey (D)	59,258	54.6
	Joseph F. Tondre (R)	49,380	45.5
1944	John J. Dempsey (D)	76,443	51.8
	Carroll G. Gunderson (R)	71,113	48.2
1946	Thomas J. Mabry (D)	70,055	52.8
	Edward L. Safford (R)	62,575	47.2
1948	Thomas J. Mabry (D)	103,969	54.7
	Manuel Lujan (R)	86,023	45.3
1950	Edwin L. Mechem (R)	96,846	53.7
	John E. Miles (D)	83,359	46.3
1952	Edwin L. Mechem (R)	129,116	53.8
	Everett Grantham (D)	111,034	46.2
1954	John F. Simms Jr. (D)	110,583	57.0
	Alvin Stockton (R)	83,373	43.0
1956	Edwin L. Mechem (R)	131,488	52.2
	John F. Simms Jr. (D)	120,263	47.8
1958	John Burroughs (D)	103,481	50.5
	Edwin L. Mechem (R)	101,567	49.5
1960	Edwin L. Mechem (R)	153,765	50.3
	John Burroughs (D)	151,777	49.7
1962	Jack M. Campbell (D)	130,933	53.0
	Edwin L. Mechem (R)	116,184	47.0
1964	Jack M. Campbell (D)	191,497	60.2
	Merle H. Tucker (R)	126,540	39.8
1966	David F. Cargo (R)	134,625	51.7
	T. E. Lusk (D)	125,587	48.3
1968	David F. Cargo (R)	160,140	50.5
	Fabian Chavez Jr. (D)	157,230	49.5
1970	Bruce King (D)	148,835	51.3
	Pete V. Domenici (R)	134,640	46.4
1974	Jerry Apodaca (D)	164,172	49.9
	Joseph R. Skeen (R)	160,430	48.8
1978	Bruce King (D)	174,631	50.5
	Joseph R. Skeen (R)	170,848	49.4
1982	Toney Anaya (D)	215,840	53.0
	John B. Irick (R)	191,626	47.0
1986	Garrey E. Carruthers (R)	209,455	53.0
	Ray B. Powell (D)	185,378	47.0

1990	Bruce King (D)	224,564	54.6
	Frank M. Bond (R)	185,692	45.2
1994	Gary E. Johnson (R)	232,945	49.8
	Bruce King (D)	186,686	39.9
	Roberto Mondragon (GREEN)	47,990	10.3
1998	Gary E. Johnson (R)	271,948	54.5
	Martin J. Chavez (D)	226,755	45.5

NEW YORK

(Ratified the Constitution July 26, 1788)

1777	George Clinton	1,828	48.6
	Philip Schuyer	1,199	31.9
	John M. Scott	368	9.8
	John Jay	367	9.8
1780	George Clinton	3,264✔	
1783	George Clinton	3,584	75.5
	Philip Schuyer	643	13.6
	Ephraim Paine	520	11.0
1786	George Clinton	✔	
1789	George Clinton	6,391	51.7
	Robert Yates	5,962	48.3
1792	George Clinton (ANTI-FED)[1]	8,440	50.3
	John Jay (FED)	8,332	49.7
1795	John Jay (FED)	13,481	53.1
	Robert Yates (ANTI-FED)[1]	11,892	46.9
1798	John Jay (FED)	16,012	54.0
	Robert R. Livingston (ANTI-FED)[1]	13,632	46.0
1801	George Clinton (D-R)	24,808	54.3
	Stephen Van Rensselaer (FED)	20,843	45.7
1804	Morgan Lewis (FED)	30,829	58.2
	Aaron Burr (D-R)	22,139	41.8
1807	Daniel Tompkins (D-R)	35,074	53.1
	Morgan Lewis (ANTI-CLINT)[2]	30,989	46.9
1810	Daniel Tompkins (D-R)	43,094	54.2
	Jonas Platt (ANTI-CLINT)[2]	36,484	45.8
1813	Daniel Tompkins (D-R)	43,324	52.2
	Stephen Van Rensselaer (FED)	39,718	47.8
1816	Daniel Tompkins (D-R)	45,412	54.0
	Rufus King (FED)	38,647	46.0

Special Election

1817	De Witt Clinton (D-R)	43,310	96.7
1820	De Witt Clinton (CLINT R)	47,447	50.8
	Daniel Tompkins (BUCK R)	45,990	49.2
1822	Joseph C. Yates (BUCK R)	128,493	97.8
1824	De Witt Clinton (CLINT R)	103,684	54.1
	Samuel Young (VB R)	88,037	45.9
1826	De Witt Clinton (CLINT R)	99,808	51.0
	William B. Rochester (BUCK R)	96,080	49.1
1828	Martin Van Buren (JAC D)	136,795	49.5
	Smith Thompson (NR)	106,415	38.5
	Solomon Southwick (A-MAS)	33,335	12.1
1830	Enos T. Throop (JAC D)	128,947	51.7
	Francis Granger (NR)	120,667	48.3
1832	William L. Marcy (JAC D)	166,410	51.5
	Francis Granger (NR)	156,672	48.5

1834	William L. Marcy (D)	181,900	51.8	1891	Roswell P. Flower (D)	582,893	50.1
	William H. Seward (W)	169,008	48.2		Jacob Sloat Fassett (R)	534,956	46.0
1836	William L. Marcy (D)	166,218	54.9	1894	Levi P. Morton (R)	673,818	53.1
	Jesse Buel (W)	136,653	45.1		David B. Hill (D)	517,710	40.8
1838	William H. Seward (W)	192,882	51.4	1896	Frank S. Black (R)	787,516	55.3
	William L. Marcy (D)	182,461	48.6		Wilbur E. Porter (D)	574,524	40.3
1840	Wiliam H. Seward (W)	222,011	50.3	1898	Theodore Roosevelt (R)	661,707	49.0
	William C. Bouck (D)	216,726	49.1		Augustus Van Wyck (D)	643,921	47.7
1842	William C. Bouck (D)	208,062	51.8	1900	Benjamin B. Odell Jr. (R)	804,859	52.0
	Luther Bradish (W)	186,089	46.4		John B. Stanchfield (D)	693,733	44.8
1844	Silas Wright (D)	241,087	49.5	1902	Benjamin B. Odell Jr. (R)	665,150	48.1
	Millard Fillmore (W)	231,060	47.4		Bird S. Coler (D)	655,398	47.4
1846	John Young (W)	198,878	48.9	1904	Frank W. Higgins (R)	813,264	50.3
	Silas Wright (D)	187,306	46.1		D. Cady Herrick (D)	732,704	45.3
1848	Hamilton Fish (W)	218,776	47.6	1906	Charles Evans Hughes (R)	749,002	50.5
	John Dix (F SOIL)	122,811	26.7		William R. Hearst (D, I LEAGUE)	691,105	46.6
	Reuben Walworth (D)	116,811	25.4	1908	Charles Evans Hughes (R)	804,651	49.1
1850	Washington Hunt (W-A-RENT)	214,614	49.6		Lewis Stuyvesant Chanler (D)	735,189	44.8
	Horatio Seymour (D)	214,352	49.6	1910	John A. Dix (D)	689,700	48.0
1852	Horatio Seymour (D)	264,121	50.3		Henry L. Stimson (R)	622,299	43.3
	Washington Hunt (W)	241,525	46.0	1912	William Sulzer (D)	649,559	41.5
1854	Myron H. Clark (FUS R)	156,804	33.4		Job E. Hedges (R)	444,105	28.3
	Horatio Seymour (SOFT D)	156,495	33.3		Oscar S. Straus (IL & NPR)	393,183	25.1
	Daniel Ullman (AM)	122,282	26.1	1914	Charles S. Whitman (R)	686,701	47.7
	Greene C. Bronson (HARD D)	33,850	7.2		Martin H. Glynn (D, I LEAGUE)	541,269	37.5
1856	John A. King (R)	264,400	44.5		William Sulzer (AM, P)	126,270	8.8
	Amasa J. Parker (D)	198,616	33.4	1916	Charles S. Whitman (R, N PROG)	850,020	52.6
	Erastus Brooks (AM)	130,870	22.0		Samuel Seabury (D)	686,862	42.5
1858	Edwin D. Morgan (R)	247,953	45.5	1918	Alfred E. Smith (D)	1,009,936	47.4
	Amasa J. Parker (D)	230,513	42.3		Charles S. Whitman (R, P)	995,094	46.6
	Lorenzo Burrows (AM)	60,880	11.2		Charles W. Ervin (SOC)	121,705	5.7
1860	Edwin D. Morgan (R)	358,002	53.2	1920	Nathan L. Miller (R)	1,335,878	46.6
	William Kelly (DOUG D)	294,803	43.8		Alfred E. Smith (D)	1,261,812	44.0
1862	Horatio Seymour (D)	306,649	50.9		Joseph D. Cannon (SOC)	159,804	5.6
	James S. Wadsworth (UN)	295,897	49.1	1922	Alfred E. Smith (D)	1,397,657	55.2
1864	Reuben E. Fenton (UN)	369,557	50.6		Nathan L. Miller (R)	1,011,725	40.0
	Horatio Seymour (D)	361,264	49.4	1924	Alfred E. Smith (D)	1,627,111	50.0
1866	Reuben E. Fenton (UN)	366,315	50.9		Theodore Roosevelt Jr. (R)	1,518,552	46.6
	John T. Hoffman (D)	352,526	49.0	1926	Alfred E. Smith (D)	1,523,813	52.3
1868	John T. Hoffman (D)	439,301	51.6		Ogden L. Mills (R)	1,276,137	43.8
	John A. Griswold (R)	411,355	48.4	1928	Franklin D. Roosevelt (D)	2,130,238	49.0
1870	John T. Hoffman (D)	399,552	51.9		Albert Ottinger (R)	2,104,630	48.4
	Stewart L. Woodford (R)	366,436	47.6	1930	Franklin D. Roosevelt (D)	1,770,342	56.1
1872	John A. Dix (R)	447,806	53.3		Charles H. Tuttle (R)	1,045,231	33.1
	Francis Kernan (LR)	392,350	46.8		Robert P. Carroll (LAW PRES)	190,666	6.1
1874	Samuel J. Tilden (D)	416,391	52.4	1932	Herbert H. Lehman (D)	2,659,597	56.7
	John A. Dix (R)	366,074	46.1		William J. Donovan (R)	1,812,002	38.6
1876	Lucius Robinson (D)	519,832	51.3	1934	Herbert H. Lehman (D)	2,201,727	57.8
	Edwin D. Morgan (R)	489,371	48.3		Robert Moses (R)	1,393,744	36.6
1879	Alonzo B. Cornell (R)	418,567	46.7	1936	Herbert H. Lehman (D, AM LAB)	2,970,595	53.5
	Lucius Robinson (D)	375,790	41.9		William F. Bleakley (R)	2,450,105	44.1
	John Kelly (TAM D)	77,566	8.7	1938	Herbert H. Lehman (D, AM LAB)	2,391,331	50.4
1882	Grover Cleveland (D)	535,318	58.5		Thomas E. Dewey (R, I PROG)	2,326,892	49.0
	Charles J. Folger (R)	342,464	37.4	1942	Thomas E. Dewey (R)	2,148,546	52.1
1885	David B. Hill (D)	501,456	48.9		John J. Bennett Jr. (D)	1,501,039	36.4
	Ira Davenport (R)	490,331	47.9		Dean Alfange (AM LAB)	403,626	9.8
1888	David B. Hill (D)	650,464	49.4	1946	Thomas E. Dewey (R)	2,825,633	56.9
	Warner Miller (R)	631,303	48.0		James M. Mead (D, AM LAB)	2,138,482	43.1

1950	Thomas E. Dewey (R)	2,819,523	*53.1*
	Walter A. Lynch (D, L)	2,246,855	*42.3*
1954	Averell Harriman (D, L)	2,560,738	*49.6*
	Irving M. Ives (R)	2,549,613	*49.4*
1958	Nelson A. Rockefeller (R)	3,126,929	*54.7*
	Averell Harriman (D, L)	2,553,895#	*44.7*
1962	Nelson A. Rockefeller (R)	3,081,587	*53.1*
	Robert M. Morgenthau (D, L)	2,552,418	*44.0*
1966	Nelson A. Rockefeller (R)	2,690,626	*44.6*
	Frank O'Connor (D)	2,298,363	*38.1*
	Paul L. Adams (C)	510,023	*8.5*
	Franklin Roosevelt Jr. (L)	507,234	*8.4*
1970	Nelson A. Rockefeller (R, CSI)	3,151,432	*52.4*
	Arthur J. Goldberg (D, L)	2,421,426	*40.3*
	Paul L. Adams (C)	422,514	*7.0*
1974	Hugh L. Carey (D, L)	3,028,503	*57.2*
	Malcolm Wilson (R, C)	2,219,667	*41.9*
1978	Hugh L. Carey (D, L)	2,429,272	*50.9*
	Perry B. Duryea (R, C)	2,156,404	*45.2*
1982	Mario M. Cuomo (D, L)	2,675,213	*50.9*
	Lew Lehrman (R, C)	2,494,827	*47.5*
1986	Mario M. Cuomo (D, L)	2,775,229	*64.6*
	Andrew P. O'Rourke (R, C)	1,363,810	*31.8*
1990	Mario M. Cuomo (D, L)	2,157,087	*53.2*
	Pierre A. Rinfret (R)	865,948	*21.3*
	Herbert I. London (C)	827,614	*20.4*
1994	George E. Pataki (R, C, TCN)	2,538,702	*48.8*
	Mario M. Cuomo (D, L)	2,364,904	*45.4*
1998	George E. Pataki (R, C)	2,571,991	*54.3*
	Peter F. Vallone (D, WF)	1,570,317	*33.2*
	Tom Golisano (IND)	364,056	*7.7*

New York
1. Anti-Federalist Party
2. Anti-Clinton Party

NORTH CAROLINA

(Ratified the Constitution Nov. 21, 1789)

1836[1]	Edward B. Dudley (W)	33,993	*53.2*
	Richard D. Spaight (D)	29,950	*46.8*
1838	Edward B. Dudley (W)	34,329	*63.0*
	John Branch (D)	20,153	*37.0*
1840	John M. Morehead (W)	45,581	*56.8*
	Romulus M. Saunders (D)	34,716	*43.2*
1842	John M. Morehead (W)	37,943	*52.4*
	Louis D. Henry (D)	34,411	*47.6*
1844	William A. Graham (W)	42,586	*51.9*
	Michael Hoke (D)	39,433	*48.1*
1846	William A. Graham (W)	43,486	*55.0*
	James B. Shepard (D)	35,627	*45.0*
1848	Charles Manly (W)	42,536	*50.5*
	David S. Reid (D)	41,682	*49.5*
1850	David S. Reid (D)	45,058	*51.6*
	Charles Manly (W)	42,341	*48.5*
1852	David S. Reid (D)	48,484	*53.0*
	John Kerr (W)	42,993	*47.0*
1854	Thomas Bragg (D)	48,705	*51.1*
	Alfred Dockery (W)	46,644	*48.9*

1856	Thomas Bragg (D)	57,698	*56.2*
	John A. Gilmer (AM)	44,970	*43.8*
1858	John W. Ellis (D)	56,429	*58.5*
	Duncan K. McCrae (DISTRIB)	40,036	*41.5*
1860	John W. Ellis (D)	59,463	*52.8*
	John Pool (W)	53,123	*47.2*
1862	Zebulon B. Vance	55,282	*72.7*
	William J. Johnston	20,813	*27.4*
1864	Zebulon B. Vance	58,070	*80.0*
	William W. Holden	14,491	*20.0*
1865	Jonathan Worth	32,539	*55.7*
	William W. Holden	25,809	*44.2*
1866	Jonathan Worth (C)	34,250	*75.9*
	Alfred Dockery (NC R)	10,759	*23.8*
1868	William W. Holden (R)	92,235	*55.5*
	Thomas S. Ashe (C)	73,600	*44.3*
1872	Tod R. Caldwell (R)	98,630	*50.5*
	Augustus S. Merrimon (D)	96,731	*49.5*
1876	Zebulon B. Vance (D)	123,265	*52.8*
	Thomas Settle (R)	110,061	*47.2*
1880	Thomas J. Jarvis (D)	121,837	*51.3*
	Ralph P. Buxton (R)	115,559	*48.7*
1884	Alfred M. Scales (D)	143,249	*53.8*
	Tyre York (R)	122,795	*46.1*
1888	Daniel G. Fowle (D)	148,405	*52.0*
	Oliver H. Dockery (R)	134,035	*46.9*
1892	Elias Carr (D)	135,327	*48.3*
	David M. Furches (R)	94,681	*33.8*
	Wyatt P. Exum (PP)	47,747	*17.0*
1896	Daniel L. Russell (R)	154,025	*46.5*
	Cyrus B. Watson (D)	145,286	*43.9*
	William A. Guthrie (PP)	30,943	*9.4*
1900	Charles B. Aycock (D)	186,650	*59.6*
	Spencer B. Adams (R)	126,296	*40.3*
1904	Robert B. Glenn (D)	128,761	*61.7*
	C. J. Harris (R)	79,505	*38.1*
1908	William W. Kitchin (D)	145,102	*57.3*
	J. Elwood Cox (R)	107,760	*42.6*
1912	Locke Craig (D)	149,972	*61.4*
	Iredell Meares (PROG)	49,925	*20.4*
	Thomas Settle (R)	43,627	*17.9*
1916	Thomas W. Bickett (D)	167,664	*58.1*
	Frank A. Linney (R)	120,157	*41.7*
1920	Cameron Morrison (D)	308,151	*57.2*
	John J. Parker (R)	230,193	*42.8*
1924	Angus Wilton McLean (D)	294,441	*61.3*
	I. M. Meekins (R)	185,578	*38.7*
1928	O. Max Gardner (D)	362,009	*55.6*
	Herbert F. Seawell (R)	289,415	*44.4*
1932	J. C. B. Ehringhaus (D)	497,708	*70.1*
	Clifford Frazier (R)	212,561	*29.9*
1936	Clyde R. Hoey (D)	542,139	*66.7*
	Gilliam Grissom (R)	270,943	*33.3*
1940	J. Melville Broughton (D)	608,744	*75.7*
	Robert H. McNeill (R)	195,402	*24.3*
1944	R. Gregg Cherry (D)	528,995	*69.6*
	Frank C. Patton (R)	230,968	*30.4*
1948	W. Kerr Scott (D)	570,995	*73.2*
	George M. Pritchard (R)	206,166	*26.4*

1952	William B. Umstead (D)	796,306	67.5
	Herbert F. Seawell Jr. (R)	383,329	32.5
1956	Luther H. Hodges (D)	760,480	67.0
	Kyle Hayes (R)	375,379	33.1
1960	Terry Sanford (D)	735,248	54.5
	Robert L. Gavin (R)	613,975	45.5
1964	Dan K. Moore (D)	790,343	56.6
	Robert L. Gavin (R)	606,165	43.4
1968	Robert W. Scott (D)	821,232	52.7
	James C. Gardner (R)	737,075	47.3
1972	James C. Holshouser Jr. (R)	767,470	51.0
	Hargrove Bowles Jr. (D)	729,104	48.5
1976	James B. Hunt Jr. (D)	1,081,293	65.0
	David T. Flaherty (R)	564,102	33.9
1980	James B. Hunt Jr. (D)	1,143,145	61.9
	Beverly Lake (R)	691,449	37.4
1984	James G. Martin (R)	1,208,167	54.3
	Rufus Edmisten (D)	1,011,209	45.4
1988	James G. Martin (R)	1,222,338	56.1
	Robert B. Jordan III (D)	957,687	43.9
1992	James B. Hunt Jr. (D)	1,368,246	52.7
	Jim Gardner (R)	1,121,955	43.2
1996	James B. Hunt Jr. (D)	1,436,638	56.0
	Robin Hayes (R)	1,097,053	42.8
2000	Mike Easley (D)	1,530,324	52.0
	Richard Vinroot (R)	1,360,960	46.3

North Carolina
1. Before 1836 governor chosen by General Assembly.

NORTH DAKOTA

(Became a state Nov. 2, 1889)

1889	John Miller (R)	25,365	66.6
	William Roach (D)	12,733	33.4
1890	Andrew H. Burke (R)	19,053	52.2
	William Roach (D)	12,604	34.6
	Muir (I)	4,821	13.2
1892	Eli C. D. Shortridge (FUS)	18,943	52.4
	Andrew H. Burke (R)	17,203	47.6
1894	Roger Allin (R)	23,723	55.8
	Wallace (POP)	9,354	22.0
	Kinter (D)	8,188	19.2
1896	Frank A. Briggs (R)	25,918	55.6
	R. B. Richardson (FUS)	20,690	44.4
1898	Frederick B. Fancher (R)	27,308	58.4
	Holmes (FUS)	19,496	41.7
1900	Frank White (R)	34,052	59.2
	M. A. Wipperman (D & I)	22,275	38.7
1902	Frank White (R)	31,613	62.7
	Cronan (D)	17,576	34.9
1904	Elmore Y. Sarles (R)	48,026	70.7
	M. F. Hegge (D)	16,744	24.7
1906	John Burke (D)	34,424	53.2
	Elmore Y. Sarles (R)	29,309	45.3
1908	John Burke (D)	49,398	51.1
	C. A. Johnson (R)	46,849	48.4

1910	John Burke (D)	47,005	50.0
	C. A. Johnson (R)	44,555	47.4
1912	Louis B. Hanna (R)	39,811	45.5
	F. O. Hellstrom (D)	31,544	36.0
	W. D. Sweet (PROG)	9,406	10.7
	A. E. Bowen Jr. (SOC)	6,835	7.8
1914	Louis B. Hanna (R)	44,279	49.6
	F. O. Hellstrom (D)	34,746	38.9
	J. A. Williams (SOC)	6,019	6.7
1916	Lynn J. Frazier (R)	87,665	79.2
	D. H. McArthur (D)	20,351	18.4
1918	Lynn J. Frazier (R & NP)	54,517	59.7
	S. J. Doyle (D & I)	36,733	40.3
1920	Lynn J. Frazier (R & NP)	117,018	51.0
	J. F. T. O'Connor (D & I)	112,488	49.0

Special Election

1921	Ragnvald A. Nestos (IR)	111,434	50.9
	Lynn J. Frazier (R & NP)	107,332	49.1
1922	Ragnvald A. Nestos (R)	110,321	57.7
	William Lemke (NON PART)	81,048	42.4
1924	Arthur G. Sorlie (R)	101,170	53.9
	Halvor L. Halvorson (D)	86,414	46.1
1926	Arthur G. Sorlie (R)	131,003	81.7
	D. M. Holmes (D)	24,287	15.2
1928	George F. Shafer (R)	131,193	56.5
	Walter Maddock (D)	100,205	43.2
1930	George F. Shafer (R)	133,264	73.6
	Pierce Blewett (D)	41,988	23.2
1932	William Langer (R)	134,231	54.8
	Herbert C. Depuy (D)	110,263	45.0
1934	Thomas H. Moodie (D)	145,433	53.0
	Lydia Langer (R)	127,954	46.6
1936	William Langer (I)	98,750	35.8
	Walter Welford (R)	95,697	34.7
	John Moses (D)	80,726	29.3
1938	John Moses (D)	138,270	52.5
	John N. Hagan (R)	125,246	47.5
1940	John Moses (D)	173,278	63.1
	Jack A. Patterson (R)	101,287	36.9
1942	John Moses (D)	101,390	57.6
	Oscar W. Hagen (R)	74,577	42.4
1944	Fred G. Aandahl (R)	107,863	52.0
	William T. Depuy (D)	59,961	28.9
	Alvin C. Strutz (IR)	38,997	18.8
1946	Fred G. Aandahl (R)	116,672	68.9
	Quentin Burdick (D)	52,719	31.1
1948	Fred G. Aandahl (R)	131,764	61.3
	Howard Henry (D)	80,655	37.5
1950	Norman Brunsdale (R)	121,822	66.3
	Clyde G. Byerly (D)	61,950	33.7
1952	Norman Brunsdale (R)	199,944	78.7
	Ole S. Johnson (D)	53,990	21.3
1954	Norman Brunsdale (R)	124,253	64.2
	Cornelius Bymers (D)	69,248	35.8
1956	John E. Davis (R)	147,566	58.5
	Wallace E. Warner (D)	104,869	41.5

1958	John E. Davis (R)	111,836	*53.1*
	John F. Lord (D)	98,763	*46.9*
1960	William L. Guy (D)	136,148	*49.4*
	C. P. Dahl (R)	122,486	*44.5*
	Herschel Lashkowitz (I)	16,741	*6.1*
1962	William L. Guy (D)	115,258	*50.4*
	Mark Andrews (R)	113,251	*49.6*
1964	William L. Guy (D)	146,414	*55.7*
	Don Halcrow (R)	116,247	*44.3*
1968	William L. Guy (D)	135,955	*54.8*
	Robert P. McCarney (R)	108,382	*43.7*
1972	Arthur A. Link (D)	143,899	*51.0*
	Richard Larsen (R)	138,032	*49.0*
1976	Arthur A. Link (D)	153,309	*51.6*
	Richard Elkin (R)	138,321	*46.5*
1980	Allen I. Olson (R)	162,230	*53.6*
	Arthur A. Link (D)	140,391	*46.4*
1984	George Sinner (D)	173,922	*55.3*
	Allen I. Olson (R)	140,460	*44.7*
1988	George Sinner (D)	179,094	*59.9*
	Leon Mallberg (R)	119,986	*40.1*
1992	Edward T. Schafer (R)	176,398	*57.9*
	Nicholas Spaeth (D)	123,845	*40.6*
1996	Edward T. Schafer (R)	174,937	*66.2*
	Lee Kaldor (D)	89,349	*33.8*
2000	John Hoeven (R)	159,255	*55.0*
	Heidi Heitkamp (D)	130,144	*45.0*

OHIO

(Became a state March 1, 1803)

1803	Edward Tiffin (D-R)	4,614	*94.2*
	Benjamin Gilman (D-R)	246	*5.0*
1805	Edward Tiffin (D-R)	4,783	
1807[1]	Return J. Meigs Jr. (D-R)	3,299	*58.7*
	Nathanael Massie (D-R)	2,317	*41.3*
1808	Samuel Huntington (D-R)	7,293	*44.8*
	Thomas Worthington (D-R)	5,601	*34.4*
	Thomas Kirker (D-R)	3,397	*20.9*
1810	Return J. Meigs Jr. (D-R)	9,924	*56.2*
	Thomas Worthington (D-R)	7,731	*43.8*
1812	Return J. Meigs Jr. (FED)	11,859	*60.0*
	Thomas Scott (D-R)	7,903	*40.0*
1814	Thomas Worthington (D-R)	15,879	*72.0*
	Othniel Looker (FED)	6,171	*28.0*
1816	Thomas Worthington (D-R)	22,931	*74.4*
	James Dunlap (D-R)	6,295	*20.4*
	Ethan A. Brown (FED)	1,607	*5.2*
1818	Ethan A. Brown (D-R)	30,194	*78.9*
	James Dunlap (D-R)	8,075	*21.1*
1820	Ethan A. Brown (D-R)	34,836	*71.3*
	Jeremiah Morrow (D-R)	9,426	*19.3*
	William H. Harrison (D-R)	4,348	*8.9*
1822	Jeremiah Morrow (D-R)	26,059	*43.4*
	Allen Trimble (FED)	22,889	*38.1*
	William W. Irwin (D-R)	11,060	*18.4*

1824	Jeremiah Morrow (JAC D)	38,328	*51.0*
	Allen Trimble (NR)	36,869	*49.0*
1826	Allen Trimble (NR)	70,475	*84.2*
	Alex Campbell	4,765	*5.7*
	Benjamin Tappan	4,209	*5.0*
1828	Allen Trimble (NR)	53,971	*51.9*
	John W. Campbell (JAC D)	51,951	*48.1*
1830	Duncan McArthur (NR)	49,677	*50.1*
	Robert Lucas (JAC D)	49,186	*49.6*
1832	Robert Lucas (D)	71,038	*52.9*
	Darius Lyman (NR)	63,213	*47.1*
1834	Robert Lucas (D)	70,738	*51.2*
	James Findlay (W)	67,414	*48.8*
1836	Joseph Vance (W)	91,742	*51.7*
	Eli Baldwin (D)	85,851	*48.3*
1838	Wilson Shannon (D)	107,884	*51.4*
	Joseph Vance (W)	102,146	*48.6*
1840	Thomas Corwin (W)	145,643	*53.0*
	Wilson Shannon (D)	129,054	*47.0*
1842	Wilson Shannon (D)	119,774	*49.3*
	Thomas Corwin (W)	117,902	*48.6*
1844	Mordecai Bartley (W)	146,333	*48.7*
	David Tod (D)	145,062	*48.3*
1846	William Bebb (W)	118,857	*48.3*
	David Tod (D)	116,554	*47.3*
1848	Seabury Ford (W)	148,766‡	*49.9*
	John B. Weller (D)	148,452	*49.8*
1850	Reuben Wood (D)	133,093	*49.7*
	William Johnston (W)	121,105	*45.2*
	Edward Smith (F SOIL)	13,747	*5.1*
1851	Reuben Wood (D)	145,656	*51.6*
	Samuel F. Vinton (W)	119,550	*42.4*
	Samuel Lewis (F SOIL)	16,910	*6.0*
1853	William Medill (D)	147,663	*52.0*
	Nelson Barrere (W)	85,843	*30.2*
	Samuel Lewis (F SOIL)	50,346	*17.7*
1855	Salmon P. Chase (R)	146,720	*48.6*
	William Medill (D)	131,019	*43.4*
	Allen Trimble (W)	24,276	*8.0*
1857	Salmon P. Chase (R)	160,685	*48.6*
	Henry B. Payne (D)	159,294	*48.2*
1859	William Dennison Jr. (R)	184,502	*51.9*
	Rufus P. Ranney (D)	171,266	*48.1*
1861	David Tod (UN)	206,997	*57.7*
	Hugh J. Jewett (D)	151,774	*42.3*
1863	John Brough (UN)	288,856	*60.6*
	Clement L. Vallandigham (D)	187,728	*39.4*
1865	Jacob D. Cox (UN)	223,642	*53.5*
	George W. Morgan (D)	193,791	*46.4*
1867	Rutherford B. Hayes (R)	243,811	*50.3*
	Allen G. Thurman (D)	240,622	*49.7*
1869	Rutherford B. Hayes (R)	236,092	*50.7*
	George H. Pendleton (D)	228,703	*49.1*
1871	Edward F. Noyes (R)	238,273	*51.8*
	George W. McCook (D)	218,105	*47.4*
1873	William Allen (D)	214,654	*47.8*
	Edward F. Noyes (R)	213,837	*47.6*
1875	Rutherford B. Hayes (R)	297,817	*50.3*
	William Allen (D)	292,279	*49.3*

1877	Richard M. Bishop (D)	271,642	48.9
	William H. West (R)	249,105	44.9
1879	Charles Foster (R)	336,321	50.3
	Thomas Ewing (D)	319,132	47.7
1881	Charles Foster (R)	312,785	50.1
	John W. Bookwalter (D)	288,426	46.2
1883	George Hoadly (D)	359,693	50.1
	Joseph B. Foraker (R)	347,164	48.3
1885	Joseph B. Foraker (R)	359,281	49.1
	George Hoadly (D)	341,830	46.8
1887	Joseph B. Foraker (R)	356,534	47.9
	Thomas E. Powell (D)	333,205	44.8
1889	James E. Campbell (D)	379,423	48.9
	Joseph B. Foraker (R)	368,551	47.5
1891	William McKinley Jr. (R)	386,739	48.6
	James E. Campbell (D)	365,228	45.9
1893	William McKinley Jr. (R)	433,342	52.6
	Lawrence T. Neal (D)	352,347	42.8
1895	Asa S. Bushnell (R)	427,141	51.0
	James E. Campbell (D)	334,519	40.0
	Jacob S. Coxey (PP)	52,625	6.3
1897	Asa S. Bushnell (R)	429,915	50.3
	Horace L. Chapman (D)	401,750	47.0
1899	George K. Nash (R)	417,199	45.9
	John R. McLean (D)	368,176	40.5
	Samuel M. Jones (NON PART)	106,721	11.8
1901	George K. Nash (R)	436,092	52.7
	James Kilbourne (D)	368,525	44.5
1903	Myron T. Herrick (R)	475,560	54.9
	Tom L. Johnson (D)	361,748	41.8
1905	John M. Pattison (D)	473,264	50.5
	Myron T. Herrick (R)	430,617	46.0
1908	Judson Harmon (D)	552,569	49.2
	Andrew L. Harris (R)	533,197	47.5
1910	Judson Harmon (D)	477,077	51.6
	Warren G. Harding (R)	376,700	40.8
	Tom Clifford (SOC)	60,637	6.6
1912	James M. Cox (D)	439,023	42.4
	Robert B. Brown (R)	272,500	26.3
	Arthur L. Garford (PROG)	217,903	21.0
	C. E. Ruthenberg (SOC)	87,709	8.5
1914	Frank B. Willis (R)	523,074	46.3
	James M. Cox (D)	493,804	43.7
	James R. Garfield (PROG)	60,904	5.4
1916	James M. Cox (D)	568,218	48.4
	Frank B. Willis (R)	561,602	47.8
1918	James M. Cox (D)	486,403	50.6
	Frank B. Willis (R)	474,559	49.4
1920	Harry L. Davis (R)	1,039,835	51.9
	Vic Donahey (D)	918,962	45.9
1922	Vic Donahey (D)	821,948	50.6
	Carmi A. Thompson (R)	803,300	49.4
1924	Vic Donahey (D)	1,064,981	54.0
	Harry L. Davis (R)	888,139	45.0
1926	Vic Donahey (D)	707,733	50.5
	Myers Y. Cooper (R)	685,897	49.0
1928	Myers Y. Cooper (R)	1,355,517	54.8
	Martin L. Davey (D)	1,106,739	44.7

1930	George White (D)	1,033,168	52.8
	Myers Y. Cooper (R)	923,538	47.2
1932	George White (D)	1,356,518	52.8
	David S. Ingalls (R)	1,151,933	44.9
1934	Martin L. Davey (D)	1,118,257	51.1
	Clarence J. Brown (R)	1,052,851	48.1
1936	Martin L. Davey (D)	1,539,461	52.0
	John W. Bricker (R)	1,412,773	47.7
1938	John W. Bricker (R)	1,265,548	52.5
	Charles Sawyer (D)	1,147,323	47.6
1940	John W. Bricker (R)	1,824,863	55.6
	Martin L. Davey (D)	1,460,396	44.5
1942	John W. Bricker (R)	1,086,937	60.5
	John McSweeney (D)	709,599	39.5
1944	Frank J. Lausche (D)	1,603,809	51.8
	James Garfield Stewart (R)	1,491,450	48.2
1946	Thomas J. Herbert (R)	1,166,550	50.6
	Frank J. Lausche (D)	1,125,997	48.9
1948	Frank J. Lausche (D)	1,619,775	53.7
	Thomas J. Herbert (R)	1,398,514	46.3
1950	Frank J. Lausche (D)	1,522,249	52.6
	Don H. Ebright (R)	1,370,570	47.4
1952	Frank J. Lausche (D)	2,015,110	55.9
	Charles P. Taft (R)	1,590,058	44.1
1954	Frank J. Lausche (D)	1,405,262	54.1
	James A. Rhodes (R)	1,192,528	45.9
1956	C. William O'Neill (R)	1,984,988	56.0
	Michael V. DiSalle (D)	1,557,103	44.0
1958	Michael V. DiSalle (D)	1,869,260	56.9
	C. William O'Neill (R)	1,414,874	43.1
1962	James A. Rhodes (R)	1,836,432	58.9
	Michael V. DiSalle (D)	1,280,521	41.1
1966	James A. Rhodes (R)	1,795,277	62.2
	Frazier Reams Jr. (D)	1,092,054	37.8
1970	John J. Gilligan (D)	1,725,560	54.2
	Roger Cloud (R)	1,382,659	43.4
1974	James A. Rhodes (R)	1,493,679	48.6
	John J. Gilligan (D)	1,482,191	48.2
1978	James A. Rhodes (R)	1,402,167	49.3
	Richard F. Celeste (D)	1,354,631	47.6
1982	Richard F. Celeste (D)	1,981,882	59.0
	Clarence Brown Jr. (R)	1,303,962	38.8
1986	Richard F. Celeste (D)	1,858,372	60.6
	James A. Rhodes (R)	1,207,264	39.4
1990	George V. Voinovich (R)	1,928,103	55.7
	Anthony J. Celebrezze Jr. (D)	1,539,416	44.3
1994	George V. Voinovich (R)	2,401,572	71.8
	Robert L. Burch Jr. (D)	835,849	25.0
1998	Robert A. Taft II (R)	1,678,721	50.0
	Lee Fisher (D)	1,498,956	44.7

Ohio

1. The election was challenged by Massie. The legislature eventually declared Meigs ineligible and arranged for a new election in 1808. Pending the outcome of that election, Speaker of the Senate Thomas Kirker was acting governor.

OKLAHOMA

(Became a state Nov. 16, 1907)

Year	Candidate	Votes	%
1907	Charles N. Haskell (D)	137,633	53.4
	Frank Frantz (R)	110,296	42.8
1910	Lee Cruce (D)	119,873	48.6
	J. W. McNeal (R)	99,319	40.2
	J. T. Crumbie (SOC)	24,457	9.9
1914	Robert L. Williams (D)	100,596	39.7
	John Fields (R)	95,909	37.8
	Fred W. Holt (SOC)	52,704	20.8
1918	James B. A. Robertson (D)	104,132	53.5
	Horace G. McKeever (R)	82,905	42.6
1922	John C. Walton (D)	280,207	54.5
	John Fields (R)	230,469	44.8
1926	Henry S. Johnston (D)	213,162	54.9
	Omer K. Benedict (R)	171,710	44.2
1930	William H. Murray (D)	301,921	59.1
	Ira A. Hill (R)	208,575	40.8
1934	Ernest W. Marland (D)	365,992	58.2
	William B. Pine (R)	243,936	38.8
1938	Leon C. Phillips (D)	355,740	70.0
	Ross Rizley (R)	148,861	29.3
1942	Robert S. Kerr (D)	196,565	51.9
	William J. Otjen (R)	180,454	47.6
1946	Roy J. Turner (D)	259,491	52.5
	Olney F. Flynn (R)	227,426	46.0
1950	Johnston Murray (D)	329,308	51.1
	Jo O. Ferguson (R)	313,205	48.6
1954	Raymond Gary (D)	357,386	58.7
	Reuben K. Sparks (R)	251,808	41.3
1958	J. Howard Edmondson (D)	399,504	74.1
	Phil Ferguson (R)	107,495	20.0
	D. A. Jelly Boyce (I)	31,840	5.9
1962	Henry L. Bellmon (R)	392,316	55.3
	W. P. Atkinson (D)	315,357	44.4
1966	Dewey F. Bartlett (R)	377,078	55.7
	Preston J. Moore (D)	296,328	43.8
1970	David Hall (D)	338,338	48.4
	Dewey F. Bartlett (R)	336,157	48.1
1974	David L. Boren (D)	514,389	63.9
	James M. Inhofe (R)	290,459	36.1
1978	George Nigh (D)	402,240	51.7
	Ron Shotts (R)	367,055	47.2
1982	George Nigh (D)	548,159	62.1
	Tom Daxon (R)	332,207	37.6
1986	Henry L. Bellmon (R)	431,762	47.5
	David Walters (D)	405,295	44.5
	Jerry Brown (I)	60,115	6.6
1990	David Walters (D)	523,196	57.4
	Bill Price (R)	297,584	32.7
	Thomas D. Ledgerwood II (I)	90,534	9.9
1994	Frank Keating (R)	466,740	46.9
	Jack Mildren (D)	294,936	29.6
	Wes Watkins (I)	233,336	23.5
1998	Frank Keating (R)	505,498	57.9
	Laura Boyd (D)	357,552	40.9

OREGON

(Became a state Feb. 14, 1859)

Year	Candidate	Votes	%
1858	John Whiteaker (D)	5,134	54.7
	E. M. Barnum (OPP)	4,213	44.9
1862	Addison C. Gibbs (UN R)	7,039	67.1
	John F. Miller (D)	3,450	32.9
1866	George L. Woods (R)	10,316	50.7
	James K. Kelly (D)	10,039	49.3
1870	La Fayette Grover (D)	11,726	51.4
	Joel Palmer (R)	11,095	48.6
1874	La Fayette Grover (D)	9,713	38.2
	J. C. Tolman (R)	9,163	36.1
	Thomas F. Campbell (I)	6,532	25.7
1878	William Wallace Thayer (D)	16,213	48.0
	C. C. Beekman (R)	16,152	47.8
1882	Zenas F. Moody (R)	21,481	51.8
	Joseph S. Smith (D)	20,029	48.3
1886	Sylvester Pennoyer (D)	27,901	50.9
	T. R. Cornelius (R)	24,199	44.1
1890	Sylvester Pennoyer (D)	38,920	53.6
	David P. Thompson (R)	33,765	46.5
1894	William P. Lord (R)	40,403	46.7
	Nathan Pierce (PP)	26,255	30.4
	William Galloway (D)	17,865	20.5
1898	Theodore Thurston Geer (R)	45,094	53.2
	William R. King (D-PP)	34,542	40.8
1902	George E. Chamberlain (D)	41,857	46.2
	W. J. Furnish (R)	41,611	45.9
1906	George E. Chamberlain (D)	46,002	47.6
	James Withycombe (R)	43,508	45.0
	C. W. Barzee (SOC)	4,468	5.0
1910	Oswald West (D)	54,853	46.6
	Jay Bowerman (R)	48,751	41.4
	W. S. Richards (SOC)	8,040	6.8
	A. E. Eaton (P)	6,046	5.1
1914	James Withycombe (R)	121,037	48.8
	C. J. Smith (D)	94,594	38.1
	W. J. Smith (SOC)	14,284	5.8
1918	James Withycombe (R)	81,067	53.0
	Walter M. Pierce (D)	65,440	42.8
1922	Walter M. Pierce (D)	133,969	57.4
	Ben W. Olcott (R)	99,164	42.6
1926	I. L. Patterson (R)	120,073	53.1
	Walter M. Pierce (D)	93,470	41.4
	H. H. Stallard (I)	12,402	5.5
1930	Julius L. Meier (I)	135,608	54.5
	Ed F. Bailey (D)	62,434	25.1
	Phil Metschan (R)	46,840	18.8
1934	Charles H. Martin (D)	116,677	38.6
	Peter Zimmerman (I)	95,519	31.6
	Joe E. Dunne (R)	86,923	28.7
1938	Charles A. Sprague (R)	214,062	57.4
	Henry L. Hess (D)	158,744	42.6
1942	Earl Snell (R)	220,188	77.9
	Lew Wallace (D)	62,561	22.1
1946	Earl Snell (R)	237,681	69.1
	Carl C. Donaugh (D)	106,474	30.9

Special Election

1948	Douglas McKay (R)	271,295	53.2
	Lew Wallace (D)	226,949	44.5
1950	Douglas McKay (R)	334,160	66.1
	Austin F. Flegal (D)	171,750	34.0
1954	Paul Patterson (R)	322,522	56.9
	Joseph K. Carson Jr. (D)	244,179	43.1

Special Election

1956	Robert D. Holmes (D)	369,439	50.5
	Elmo Smith (R)	361,840	49.5
1958	Mark O. Hatfield (R)	331,900	55.3
	Robert D. Holmes (D)	267,934	44.7
1962	Mark O. Hatfield (R)	345,497	54.2
	Robert Y. Thornton (D)	265,359	41.6
1966	Tom McCall (R)	377,346	55.3
	Robert W. Straub (D)	305,008	44.7
1970	Tom McCall (R)	369,964	55.6
	Robert W. Straub (D)	293,892	44.2
1974	Robert W. Straub (D)	444,812	57.7
	Victor Atiyeh (R)	324,751	42.1
1978	Victor Atiyeh (R)	498,452	54.9
	Robert W. Straub (D)	409,411	44.9
1982	Victor Atiyeh (R)	639,841	61.4
	Ted Kulongoski (D)	374,316	35.9
1986	Neil Goldschmidt (D)	549,456	51.9
	Norma Paulus (R)	506,986	47.8
1990	Barbara Roberts (D)	508,749	45.7
	Dave Frohnmayer (R)	444,646	40.0
	Al Mobley (I)	144,062	12.9
1994	John Kitzhaber (D)	622,083	50.9
	Denny Smith (R)	517,874	42.4
1998	John Kitzhaber (D)	717,061	64.4
	Bill Sizemore (R)	334,001	30.0

PENNSYLVANIA

(Ratified the Constitution Dec. 12, 1787)

1790	Thomas Mifflin	27,725	90.8
	Arthur St. Clair (FED)	2,802	9.2
1793	Thomas Mifflin (D-R)	18,590	63.5
	Frederick A. Muhlenberg (FED)	10,706	36.5
1796	Thomas Mifflin (D-R)	30,020	96.7
1799	Thomas McKean (D-R)	37,244	53.3
	James Ross (FED)	32,643	46.7
1802	Thomas McKean (D-R)	47,849	73.6
	James Ross (FED)	17,037	26.2
1805	Thomas McKean (I D-R)[1]	43,644	52.9
	Simon Snyder (D-R)	38,833	47.1
1808	Simon Snyder (D-R)	67,975	60.9
	James Ross (FED)	39,575	35.5
1811	Simon Snyder (D-R)	52,319	90.8
	William Tilghman (FED)	3,609	6.3
1814	Simon Snyder (D-R)	51,009	62.6
	Isaac Wayne (FED)	29,566	36.3

1817	William Findlay (D-R)	66,331	52.8
	Joseph Hiester (D-R/FED)	59,272	47.2
1820	Joseph Hiester (D-R)	67,905	50.6
	William Findlay (D-R)	66,300	49.4
1823	John Andrew Schulze (D-R)	89,928	58.3
	Andrew Gregg (FED)	64,211	41.7
1826	John Andrew Schulze (JAC D)	72,710	96.9
1829	George Wolf (JAC D)	78,138	60.1
	Joseph Ritner (A-MAS)	51,776	39.9
1832	George Wolf (D)	91,385	50.9
	Joseph Ritner (A-MAS)	88,115	49.1
1835	Joseph Ritner (D)	94,023	46.9
	George Wolf (W)	65,804	32.8
	Henry Muhlenburgh	40,586	20.3
1838	David R. Porter (D)	127,821	51.1
	Joseph Ritner (A-MASC)	122,325	48.9
1841	David R. Porter (D)	136,504	54.4
	John Banks (W)	113,453	45.3
1844	Francis R. Shunk (D)	160,322	50.3
	Joseph Markle (W)	156,041	48.9
1847	Francis R. Shunk (D)	146,081	50.8
	James Irwin (W)	128,148	44.6
1848	William F. Johnston (W)	168,522	50.0
	Morris Longstreth (D)	168,225	50.0
1851	William Bigler (D)	186,499	50.9
	William F. Johnston (W)	178,034	48.6
1854	James Pollock (W)	203,822	54.6
	William Bigler (D)	166,991	44.8
1857	William F. Packer (D)	188,836	52.0
	David Wilmot (R)	146,139	40.2
	Isaac Hazlehurst (AM)	28,168	7.8
1860	Andrew G. Curtin (R)	262,403	53.3
	Henry D. Foster (D)	230,269	46.7
1863	Andrew G. Curtin (R)	269,496	51.5
	George W. Woodward (D)	254,171	48.5
1866	John White Geary (R)	307,274	51.4
	Hiester Clymer (D)	290,096	48.6
1869	John White Geary (R)	290,552	50.4
	Asa Packer (D)	285,956	49.6
1872	John Frederick Hartranft (R)	353,387	52.6
	Charles B. Buckalew (D)	317,823	47.3
1875	John Frederick Hartranft (R)	304,175	49.9
	Cyrus L. Pershing (D)	292,136	47.9
1878	Henry Martyn Hoyt (R)	319,567	45.5
	Andrew H. Dill (D)	297,060	42.3
	Samuel R. Mason (G)	81,758	11.6
1882	Robert E. Pattison (D)	355,791	47.8
	James A. Beaver (R)	315,589	42.4
	John Stewart (IR)	43,743	5.9
1886	James A. Beaver (R)	412,285	50.3
	Chauncey F. Black (D)	369,634	45.1
1890	Robert E. Pattison (D)	464,209	50.0
	George W. Delamater (R)	447,655	48.2
1894	Daniel H. Hastings (R)	574,801	60.3
	William M. Singerly (D)	333,404	35.0
1898	William A. Stone (R)	476,206	49.0
	George A. Jenks (D)	358,300	36.9
	Silas C. Swallow (P, HG)	132,931	13.7

1902	Samuel W. Pennypacker (R, CIT)	593,828	54.2
	Robert E. Pattison		
	(D, A-MACH, BALLOT)	450,978	41.2
1906	Edwin S. Stuart (R, CIT)	506,418	50.3
	Lewis Emery Jr.		
	(D, LINCOLN, CP, UN LAB)	458,064	45.5
1910	John K. Tener (R, WML)	415,614	41.6
	William H. Berry (KEY)	382,127	38.3
	Webster Grim (D)	129,395	13.0
	John W. Slayton (SOC)	53,055	5.3
1914	Martin G. Brumbaugh (		
	R, KEY, PERS LIB)	588,705	53.0
	Vance C. McCormick		
	(D, WASH)	453,880	40.8
1918	William Sproul (R, WASH)	552,537	61.1
	Eugene C. Bonniwell		
	(D, F PLAY)	305,315	33.7
1922	Gifford Pinchot (R)	831,696	56.8
	John A. McSparran (D)	581,625	39.7
1926	John S. Fisher (R)	1,102,823	73.3
	Eugene C. Bonniwell		
	(D, LAB)	365,280	24.3
1930	Gifford Pinchot (R, P, I)	1,068,874	50.8
	John M. Hemphill (D, L, I)	1,010,204	47.7
1934	George H. Earle (D)	1,476,377	50.0
	William A. Schnader (R)	1,410,138	47.8
1938	Arthur H. James (R)	2,036,345	53.4
	Charles Jones		
	(D, ROYAL OAK)	1,756,280	46.1
1942	Edward Martin (R)	1,367,531	53.7
	F. Clair Ross (D)	1,149,897	45.1
1946	James H. Duff (R)	1,828,462	58.5
	John S. Rice (D)	1,270,947	40.7
1950	John S. Fine (R)	1,796,119	50.7
	Richardson Dilworth (D)	1,710,355	48.3
1954	George M. Leader (D)	1,996,266	53.7
	Lloyd H. Wood (R)	1,717,070	46.2
1958	David L. Lawrence (D)	2,024,852	50.8
	Arthur T. McGonigle (R)	1,948,769	48.9
1962	William W. Scranton (R)	2,424,918	55.4
	Richardson Dilworth (D)	1,938,627	44.3
1966	Raymond P. Shafer (R)	2,110,349	52.1
	Milton Shapp (D)	1,868,719	46.1
1970	Milton Shapp (D)	2,043,029	55.2
	Raymond J. Broderick (R)	1,542,854	41.7
1974	Milton Shapp (D)	1,878,252	53.8
	Andrew "Drew" L.		
	Lewis Jr. (R)	1,578,917	45.2
1978	Richard L. Thornburgh (R)	1,966,042	52.5
	Peter Flaherty (D)	1,737,888	46.4
1982	Richard L. Thornburgh (R)	1,872,784	50.8
	Allen E. Ertel (D)	1,772,353	48.1
1986	Robert P. Casey (D)	1,717,484	50.7
	William W. Scranton (R)	1,638,268	48.3
1990	Robert P. Casey (D)	2,065,244	67.7
	Barbara Hafer (R)	987,516	32.3
1994	Tom J. Ridge (R)	1,627,976	45.4
	Mark S. Singel (D)	1,430,099	39.9
	Peg Luksik (CST)	460,269	12.8

1998	Tom J. Ridge (R)	1,736,844	57.4
	Ivan Itkin (D)	938,745	31.0
	Peg Luksik (CST)	315,761	10.4

Pennsylvania
1. Independent Democratic-Republican.

RHODE ISLAND

(Ratified the Constitution May 29, 1790)

1776–1777	Nicholas Cooke	✔	
1778–1785	William Greene	✔	
1786–1789	John Collins	✔	
1790–1796	Arthur Fenner	✔	
1797–1798	Arthur Fenner	1,204	100.0
1800	Arthur Fenner	✔	
1801	Arthur Fenner	3,760	100.0
1802	Arthur Fenner	3,802	66.3
	William Greene	1,934	33.7
1803–1805	Arthur Fenner	✔	
1806	Richard Jackson Jr. (FED)	1,662*	43.1
	Henry Smith (D-R)	1,097	28.4
	Peleg Arnold (D-R)	1,094	28.3
1807	James Fenner (D-R)	2,564	65.9
	Seth Wheaton (FED)	1,268	32.6
1808–1810	James Fenner (D-R)	✔	
1811	William Jones (FED)	3,885	51.1
	James Fenner (D-R)	3,651	48.1
1812	William Jones (FED)	4,122	51.5
	James Fenner (D-R)	3,874	48.4
1813	William Jones (FED)	3,350	
1814	William Jones (FED)	2,710	76.6
1815	William Jones (FED)	3,372	56.6
	Peleg Arnold (D-R)	2,588	43.4
1816	William Jones (FED)	3,591	52.4
	Nehemiah R. Knight (D-R)	3,259	47.6
1817	Nehemiah R. Knight (D-R)	3,949	50.4
	William Jones (FED)	3,878	49.5
1818	Nehemiah R. Knight (D-R)	4,509	53.7
	Elisha R. Potter (FED)	3,893	46.3
1819	Nehemiah R. Knight (D-R)	2,664	100.0
1820	Nehemiah R. Knight (D-R)	1,981	100.0
1821	William C. Gibbs (D-R)	3,801	57.6
	Samuel W. Bridgham (F)	2,801[1]	
1822	William C. Gibbs	2,092	100.0
1823	William C. Gibbs	1,647	100.0
1824	James Fenner (D-R)	2,146	78.3
	Wheeler Martin (D-R)	594	21.7
1825	James Fenner	1,731	100.0
1826	James Fenner	1,731	100.0
1827	James Fenner	2,421	100.0
1828	James Fenner	4,233	100.0

Year	Candidate	Votes	%
1829	James Fenner (JAC)	3,584	100.0
1830	James Fenner (JAC)	2,793	63.1
	Asa Messer	1,455	32.9
1831	Lemuel H. Arnold (NR)	3,780	56.8
	James Fenner (JAC)	2,877	43.2
1832[2]	Lemuel H. Arnold (NR)	2,730*	48.5
	James Fenner (D)	2,290	40.7
	William Sprague (A-MAS)	610	10.8
1833	John Brown Francis (D)	4,025	55.0
	Lemuel H. Arnold (NR)	3,292	45.0
1834	John Brown Francis (D)	3,676	51.0
	Nehemiah R. Knight (W)	3,520	48.9
1835	John Brown Francis (D)	3,880	50.7
	Nehemiah R. Knight (W)	3,774	49.3
1836	John Brown Francis (D)	4,020	56.2
	Tristam Burges (W)	2,984	41.7
1837	John Brown Francis (D)	2,716	73.1
	William Peckham (CONST)	946	25.5
1838	William Sprague (W)	3,984	52.5
	John Brown Francis (D)	3,504	46.2
1839	William Sprague (W)	2,908*	47.4
	Nathaniel Bullock (D)	2,771	45.2
	Tristam Burges (AB)	457	7.4
1840	Samuel Ward King (W)	4,797	58.4
	Thomas F. Carpenter (D)	3,418	41.6
1841	Samuel Ward King (W)	2,648	97.7
1842	Samuel Ward King (W)	4,864	67.9
	Thomas F. Carpenter (W)	2,281	32.1
1843	James Fenner (L & O W)	9,107	55.2
	Thomas F. Carpenter (D)	7,392	44.8
1844	James Fenner (LAW ORD)	5,560	96.4
1845	Charles Jackson (LIBER W)	8,010	50.6
	James Fenner (L & O W)	7,800	49.4
1846	Byron Diman (L & O W)	7,477†	49.8
	Charles Jackson (D & LIBN)	7,391	49.2
1847	Elisha Harris (W)	6,300	55.3
	Olney Ballou (D)	4,350	38.2
1848	Elisha Harris (W)	5,695	58.0
	Adnah Sackett (D)	3,683	37.5
1849	Henry B. Anthony (W)	5,081	59.0
	Adnah Sackett (D)	2,964	34.4
	Edward Harris (F SOIL)	458	5.3
1850	Henry B. Anthony (W)	3,629	80.2
	Edward Harris (F SOIL)	761	16.8
1851	Philip Allen (D)	6,935	52.4
	Josiah Chapin (W)	6,106	46.2
1852	Philip Allen (D)	9,151	51.1
	Elisha Harris (W)	8,749	48.9
1853	Philip Allen (D)	10,361	54.2
	William W. Hoppin (W)	8,228	43.0
1854	William W. Hoppin (W)	9,216	58.6
	Francis M. Dimond (D)	6,523	41.4
1855	William W. Hoppin (W & AM)	11,130	80.0
	Americus V. Potter (D)	2,729	19.6
1856	William W. Hoppin (AM & R)	9,865	58.0
	Americus V. Potter (D)	7,131	41.9
1857	Elisha Dyer (R)	9,591	64.3
	Americus V. Potter (D)	5,323	35.7
1858	Elisha Dyer (R)	7,934	69.0
	Elisha R. Potter (D)	3,572	31.0
1859	Thomas G. Turner (R)	8,938	71.5
	Elisha R. Potter (D)	3,536	28.3
1860	William Sprague (FUS)	12,278	53.0
	Seth Padelford (R)	10,740	46.7
1861	William Sprague (UN)	12,005	53.7
	James Y. Smith (R)	10,326	46.3
1862	William Sprague (UN)	11,199	99.4
1863	James Y. Smith (R)	10,749	57.4
	William C. Cozzens (D & CST)	7,672	41.0
1864	James Y. Smith (UN R)	8,836	50.4
	George H. Browne (D)	7,312	41.7
	Amos C. Barstow (CONST)	1,348	7.7
1865	James Y. Smith (UN R)	10,153	92.4
1866	Ambrose E. Burnside (R)	7,724	72.3
	Lymon Pierce (D)	2,796	26.2
1867	Ambrose E. Burnside (R)	7,569	69.4
	Lymon Pierce (D)	3,339	30.6
1868	Ambrose E. Burnside (R)	10,054	63.8
	Lymon Pierce (D)	5,709	36.2
1869	Seth Padelford (R)	7,359	68.4
	Lymon Pierce (D)	3,390	31.5
1870	Seth Padelford (R)	10,337	61.2
	Lymon Pierce (D)	6,295	37.3
1871	Seth Padelford (R)	8,721	61.4
	Thomas Steere (D)	5,367	37.7
1872	Seth Padelford (R)	9,463	53.0
	Olney Arnold (D)	8,308	46.5
1873	Henry Howard (R)	9,656	71.8
	Benjamin G. Chace (D)	3,786	28.2
1874	Henry Howard (R)	12,335	87.5
	Lymon Pierce (D)	1,589	11.3
1875	Rowland Hazard (I)	8,724	39.2
	Henry Lippitt (R)	8,368†	37.6
	Charles R. Cutler (D)	5,166	23.2
1876	Henry Lippitt (R)	8,689†	45.6
	Albert C. Howard (P)	6,733	35.4
	William B. Beach (D)	3,599	18.9
1877	Charles C. Van Zandt (R & TEMP)	12,455	50.9
	Jerothmul B. Barnaby (D)	11,783	48.2
1878	Charles C. Van Zandt (R & TEMP)	11,454	58.1
	Isaac Lawrence (D)	7,639	38.8
1879	Charles C. Van Zandt (R & TEMP)	9,717	62.1
	Thomas W. Segar (D)	5,506	35.2
1880	Alfred H. Littlefield (R)	10,224†	44.8
	Horace A. Kimball (D)	7,440	32.6
	Albert C. Howard (IR & P)	5,047	22.1
1881	Alfred H. Littlefield (R)	10,849	67.0
	Horace A. Kimball (D)	4,756	29.4
1882	Alfred H. Littlefield (R)	10,056	64.8
	Horace A. Kimball (D)	5,311	34.2
1883	Augustus O. Bourn (R)	13,078	54.5
	William Sprague (D)	10,201	42.5
1884	Augustus O. Bourn (R)	15,936	62.4
	Thomas W. Segar (D)	9,592	37.6

1885	George Peabody Wetmore (R)	12,563	56.0	1909	Aram J. Pothier (R)	37,107	57.0
	Ziba O. Slocum (D)	8,674	38.6		Olney Arnold (D)	25,338	38.9
	George H. Slade (P)	1,206	5.4	1910	Aram J. Pothier (R)	33,540	49.6
1886	George Peabody Wetmore (R)	14,340	53.4		Lewis A. Waterman (D)	32,400	47.9
	Amasa Sprague (D)	9,944	37.0	1911	Aram J. Pothier (R)	37,969	53.4
	George H. Slade (P)	2,585	9.6		Lewis A. Waterman (D)	30,575	43.0
1887	John W. Davis (D)	18,095	51.5	1912	Aram J. Pothier (R)	34,133	43.7
	George Peabody Wetmore (R)	15,111	43.0		Theodore Francis Green (D)	32,725	41.9
	Thomas H. Peabody (P)	1,895	5.4		Albert H. Humes (PROG)	8,457	10.8
1888	Royal C. Taft (R)	20,744	52.3	1914	R. Livingston Beeckman (R)	41,996	53.8
	John W. Davis (D)	17,556	44.3		Patrick H. Quinn (D)	32,182	41.3
1889	John W. Davis (D)	21,289	49.4	1916	R. Livingston Beeckman (R)	49,524	55.9
	Herbert W. Ladd (R)	16,870†	39.1		Addison P. Munroe (D)	36,158	40.8
	James H. Chace (LAW ENF)	3,596	8.3	1918	R. Livingston Beeckman (R)	42,682	53.1
1890	John W. Davis (D)	20,548†	48.8		Alberic A. Archambault (D)	36,031	44.8
	Herbert W. Ladd (R)	18,988	45.1	1920	Emery J. San Souci (R)	109,138	64.6
1891	John W. Davis (D)	22,249	49.0		Edward M. Sullivan (D)	55,963	33.2
	Herbert W. Ladd (R)	20,995†	46.2	1922	William S. Flynn (D)	81,935	51.7
1892	D. Russell Brown (R)	27,461	50.2		Harold J. Gross (R)	74,724	47.2
	William T. C. Wardwell (D)	25,433	46.5	1924	Aram J. Pothier (R)	122,749	58.6
1893	David S. Baker (D)	22,015*	46.7		Felix A. Toupin (D)	85,942	41.0
	D. Russell Brown (R)	21,830	46.3	1926	Aram J. Pothier (R)	89,574	53.9
	Metcalf (P)	3,265	6.9		Joseph H. Gainer (D)	75,882	45.7
1894	D. Russell Brown (R)	29,157	53.2	1928	Norman S. Case (R)	121,748	51.6
	David S. Baker Jr. (D)	22,650	41.3		Alberic A. Archambault (D)	113,594	48.1
1895	Charles Warren Lippitt (R)	25,098	56.9	1930	Norman S. Case (R)	112,070	50.5
	George L. Littlefield (D)	14,289	32.4		Theodore Francis Green (D)	108,558	48.9
	Smith Quimby (P)	2,624	6.0	1932	Theodore Francis Green (D)	146,474	55.2
1896	Charles Warren Lippitt (R)	28,472	56.4		Norman S. Case (R)	115,438	43.5
	George L. Littlefield (D)	17,061	33.8	1934	Theodore Francis Green (D)	140,258	56.6
	Thomas H. Peabody (P)	2,950	5.8		Luke H. Callan (R)	105,139	42.4
1897	Elisha Dyer (R)	24,309	58.1	1936	Robert E. Quinn (D)	160,776	53.7
	Daniel T. Church (D)	13,675	32.7		Charles P. Sisson (R)	137,369	45.9
	Thomas H. Peabody (P)	2,096	5.0	1938	William H. Vanderbilt (R)	167,003	53.7
1898	Elisha Dyer (R)	24,743	57.7		Robert E. Quinn (D)	129,603	41.6
	Daniel T. Church (D)	13,224	30.9	1940	J. Howard McGrath (D)	177,937	55.8
	James P. Reid (SOC LAB)	2,877	6.7		William H. Vanderbilt (R)	140,474	44.1
1899	Elisha Dyer (R)	24,308	56.4	1942	J. Howard McGrath (D)	139,407	58.5
	George W. Greene (D)	14,602	33.9		James O. McManus (R)	98,741	41.5
	Thomas F. Herrick (SOC LAB)	2,941	6.8	1944	J. Howard McGrath (D)	179,010	60.7
1900	William Gregory (R)	26,043	54.3		Norman D. Macleod (R)	116,158	39.4
	Nathan W. Littlefield (D)	17,184	35.9	1946	John O. Pastore (D)	148,885	54.1
	James P. Reid (SOC LAB)	2,858	6.0		John G. Murphy (R)	126,456	45.9
1901	William Gregory (R)	25,575	53.6	1948	John O. Pastore (D)	198,056	61.2
	Lucius F. C. Garvin (D)	19,038	39.9		Albert P. Ruerat (R)	124,441	38.4
1902	Lucius F. C. Garvin (D)	32,279	54.0	1950	Dennis J. Roberts (D)	176,125	59.3
	Charles Dean Kimball (R)	24,541	41.0		Eugene J. Lachapelle (R)	120,683	40.7
1903	Lucius F. C. Garvin (D)	30,578	49.3	1952	Dennis J. Roberts (D)	215,587	52.6
	Samuel Pomeroy Colt (R)	29,275	47.2		Raoul Archambault Jr. (R)	194,102	47.4
1904	George H. Utter (R)	33,821	48.9	1954	Dennis J. Roberts (D)	189,595	57.7
	Lucius F. C. Garvin (D)	32,965	47.7		Dean J. Lewis (R)	137,131	41.7
1905	George H. Utter (R)	31,311	53.3	1956	Dennis J. Roberts (D)	192,315	50.1
	Lucius F. C. Garvin (D)	25,816	44.0		Christopher Del Sesto (R)	191,604	49.9
1906	James H. Higgins (D)	33,195	49.9	1958	Christopher Del Sesto (R)	176,505	50.9
	George H. Utter (R)	31,877	47.9		Dennis J. Roberts (D)	170,275	49.1
1907	James H. Higgins (D)	33,300	50.4	1960	John A. Notte Jr. (D)	227,318	56.6
	Frederick H. Jackson (R)	31,005	46.9		Christopher Del Sesto (R)	174,044	43.4
1908	Aram J. Pothier (R)	38,676	52.6	1962	John H. Chafee (R)	163,952	50.1
	Olney Arnold (D)	31,406	42.7		John A. Notte Jr. (D)	163,554	49.9

1964	John H. Chafee (R)	239,501	61.2
	Edward P. Gallogly (D)	152,165	38.9
1966	John H. Chafee (R)	210,202	63.3
	Horace E. Hobbs (D)	121,862	36.7
1968	Frank Licht (D)	195,766	51.0
	John H. Chafee (R)	187,958	49.0
1970	Frank Licht (D)	173,420	50.1
	Herbert F. DeSimone (R)	171,549	49.5
1972	Philip W. Noel (D)	216,953	52.6
	Herbert F. DeSimone (R)	194,315	47.1
1974	Philip W. Noel (D)	252,436	78.5
	James W. Nugent (R)	69,224	21.5
1976	J. Joseph Garrahy (D)	218,561	54.8
	James L. Taft (R)	178,254	44.7
1978	J. Joseph Garrahy (D)	197,386	62.8
	Lincoln Almond (R)	96,596	30.7
	Joseph A. Doorley Jr. (I)	20,381	6.5
1980	J. Joseph Garrahy (D)	299,174	73.7
	Vincent A. Cianci (R)	106,729	26.3
1982	J. Joseph Garrahy (D)	247,208	73.3
	Vincent Mazullo (R)	79,602	23.6
1984	Edward D. DiPrete (R)	245,059	60.0
	Anthony J. Solomon (D)	163,311	40.0
1986	Edward D. DiPrete (R)	208,822	64.7
	Bruce Sundlun (D)	104,508	32.4
1988	Edward D. DiPrete (R)	203,550	50.8
	Bruce Sundlun (D)	196,936	49.2
1990	Bruce Sundlun (D)	264,411	74.2
	Edward D. DiPrete (R)	92,177	25.8
1992	Bruce Sundlun (D)	261,484	61.6
	Elizabeth Ann Leonard (R)	145,590	34.3
1994	Lincoln C. Almond (R)	171,194	47.4
	Myrth York (D)	157,361	43.5
	Robert J. Healey Jr. (I)	32,822	9.1
1998	Lincoln C. Almond (R)	156,180	51.0
	Myrth York (D)	129,105	42.1
	Robert J. Healey Jr. (I)	19,250	6.3

Rhode Island
1. Includes votes for other candidates.
2. The General Assembly ordered additional elections because no candidate had achieved a majority of the vote. Second election: Arnold, 3,909; Fenner, 2,940; Sprague, 698. Third election: Arnold, 2,729; Fenner, 2,341; Sprague, 792. Fourth election: Arnold, 3,062; Fenner, 2,715; Sprague, 967. Fifth election: Arnold, 2,880; Fenner, 2,306; Sprague, 832. With no candidate achieving a majority, Arnold, the incumbent, served the full term.

SOUTH CAROLINA

(Ratified the Constitution May 23, 1788)

1865[1]	James L. Orr	9,771	51.8
	Wade Hampton	9,109	48.3
1868	Robert K. Scott (R)	69,693	75.0
	W. D. Porter	23,087	24.8
1870	Robert K. Scott (R)	85,071	62.3
	R. B. Carpenter (D)	51,537	37.7
1872	Franklin J. Moses Jr. (R)	69,838	65.4
	Reuben Tomlinson (ID)	36,553	34.2

1874	Daniel H. Chamberlain (R)	80,403	53.9
	John T. Green (I REF D)	68,818	46.1
1876	Wade Hampton (D)	92,261	50.3
	Daniel H. Chamberlain (R)	91,127	49.7
1878	Wade Hampton (D)	119,550	99.8
1880	Johnson Hagood (D)	117,432	96.4
1882	Hugh S. Thompson (D)	67,158	79.5
	J. McLane (G)	17,319	20.5
1884	Hugh S. Thompson (D)	67,895	100.0
1886	John P. Richardson (D)	33,114	100.0
1888	John P. Richardson (D)	58,730	100.0
1890	Benjamin Ryan Tillman (D)	59,159	79.8
	A. C. Haskell (ID)	14,828	20.0
1892	Benjamin Ryan Tillman (D)	56,673	99.9
1894	John Gary Evans (D)	39,507	69.6
	Sampson Pope (POP)	17,278	30.4
1896	William H. Ellerbe (D)	59,424	89.1
	Sampson Pope (LW R)	4,432	6.7
1898	William H. Ellerbe (D)	28,225	100.0
1900	Miles B. McSweeney (D)	46,457	100.0
1902	Duncan C. Heyward (D)	31,817	100.0
1904	Duncan C. Heyward (D)	51,917	100.0
1906	Martin F. Ansel (D)	30,251	99.9
1908	Martin F. Ansel (D)	61,060	100.0
1910	Coleman L. Blease (D)	30,739	99.8
1912	Coleman L. Blease (D)	44,122	99.5
1914	Richard I. Manning (D)	34,600	99.8
1916	Richard I. Manning (D)	60,396	97.9
1918	Robert A. Cooper (D)	25,267	100.0
1920	Robert A. Cooper (D)	58,050	100.0
1922	Thomas G. McLeod (D)	34,065	100.0
1924	Thomas G. McLeod (D)	53,545	100.0
1926	John G. Richards (D)	16,589	100.0
1930	Ibra C. Blackwood (D)	17,790	100.0
1934	Olin D. Johnston (D)	23,177	100.0
1938	Burnet R. Maybank (D)	49,009	99.4
1942	Olin D. Johnston (D)	23,859	100.0
1946	J. Strom Thurmond (D)	26,520	100.0
1950	James F. Byrnes (D)	50,633	100.0
1954	George Bell Timmerman Jr. (D)	214,204	100.0
1958	Ernest F. Hollings (D)	77,714	100.0
1962	Donald Russell (D)	253,704	100.0
1966	Robert E. McNair (D)	255,854	58.2
	Joseph O. Rogers Jr. (R)	184,088	41.8
1970	John C. West (D)	250,551	51.7
	Albert Watson (R)	221,233	45.6
1974	James B. Edwards (R)	266,109	50.9
	W. J. Bryan Dorn (D)	248,938	47.6
1978	Richard W. Riley (D)	384,898	61.4
	Edward L. Young (R)	236,946	37.8
1982	Richard W. Riley (D)	468,819	69.8
	W. D. Workman (R)	202,806	30.2
1986	Carroll Campbell (R)	384,565	51.0
	Mike Daniel (D)	361,325	47.9
1990	Carroll Campbell (R)	528,831	69.5
	Theo Mitchell (D)	212,034	27.9
1994	David Beasley (R)	470,756	50.4
	Nick A. Theodore (D)	447,002	47.9

1998	James H. Hodges (D)	570,070	53.2
	David Beasley (R)	484,088	45.2

South Carolina
1. Before 1865 governor chosen by legislature.

SOUTH DAKOTA

(Became a state Nov. 2, 1889)

1889	Arthur C. Mellette (R)	53,964	69.3
	P. F. McClure (D)	23,840	30.6
1890	Arthur C. Mellette (R)	34,487	44.5
	H. L. Loucks (I)	24,591	31.7
	Maris Taylor (D)	18,484	23.8
1892	Charles H. Sheldon (R)	33,214	47.2
	A. L. Vanosdel (I)	22,323	31.7
	Peter Couchman (D)	14,872	21.1
1894	Charles H. Sheldon (R)	40,402	52.0
	Isaac Howe (I)	27,568	35.5
	James A. Ward (D)	8,756	11.3
1896	Andrew E. Lee (PP)	41,177	49.8
	A. O. Ringsrud (R)	40,869	49.4
1898	Andrew E. Lee (FUS)	37,319	49.6
	Kirk G. Phillips (R)	36,980	49.2
1900	Charles N. Herreid (R)	53,788	56.3
	Burre H. Lien (FUS)	40,091	42.0
1902	Charles N. Herreid (R)	48,195	64.7
	John W. Martin (D)	21,396	28.7
1904	Samuel H. Elrod (R)	68,561	68.3
	Louis N. Crill (D)	24,772	24.7
1906	Coe I. Crawford (R)	48,709	65.3
	John A. Stransky (D)	19,923	26.7
1908	Robert S. Vessey (R)	62,989	55.3
	Andrew E. Lee (D)	44,876	39.4
1910	Robert S. Vessey (R)	61,744	58.4
	Chauncey L. Wood (D)	37,983	35.9
1912	Frank M. Byrne (R)	57,161	48.5
	Edwin S. Johnson (D)	53,850	45.7
1914	Frank M. Byrne (R)	49,138	50.1
	J. W. McCarter (D)	34,542	35.2
	R. O. Richards (I)	9,725	9.9
1916	Peter Norbeck (R)	72,789	56.6
	Orville Rinehart (D)	50,545	39.3
1918	Peter Norbeck (R)	51,175	53.2
	Mark P. Bates (NON PART)	25,118	26.1
	James B. Bird (D)	17,858	18.6
1920	William H. McMaster (R)	103,592	56.3
	Mark P. Bates (NON PART)	48,426	26.3
	W. W. Howes (D)	31,870	17.3
1922	William H. McMaster (R)	78,984	45.0
	Louis N. Crill (D)	50,409	28.7
	Lorraine Daly (NON PART)	46,033	26.2
1924	Carl Gunderson (R)	109,914	53.9
	William J. Bulow (D)	46,613	22.9
	A. L. Putnam (F-LAB)	27,027	13.3
	R. O. Richards (I)	20,359	10.0
1926	William J. Bulow (D)	87,076	47.4
	Carl Gunderson (R)	74,101	40.3

	Tom Ayres (F-LAB)	11,958	6.5
	John E. Hipple (I)	10,637	5.8
1928	William J. Bulow (D)	136,016	52.5
	Buell F. Jones (R)	121,643	46.9
1930	Warren E. Green (R)	107,643	53.0
	D. A. McCullough (D)	93,954	46.2
1932	Tom Berry (D)	158,058	55.6
	Warren E. Green (R)	120,473	42.4
1934	Tom Berry (D)	172,228	58.6
	William C. Allen (R)	119,477	40.7
1936	Leslie Jensen (R)	151,659	51.6
	Tom Berry (D)	142,255	48.4
1938	Harlan J. Bushfield (R)	149,362	54.0
	Oscar Fosheim (D)	127,485	46.1
1940	Harlan J. Bushfield (R)	167,686	55.1
	Lewis W. Bicknell (D)	136,428	44.9
1942	Merrell Q. Sharpe (R)	109,786	61.5
	Lewis B. Bicknell (D)	68,706	38.5
1944	Merrell Q. Sharpe (R)	148,646	65.5
	Lynn Fellows (D)	78,276	34.5
1946	George T. Mickelson (R)	108,998	67.2
	Richard Haeder (D)	53,294	32.8
1948	George T. Mickelson (R)	149,883	61.1
	Harold J. Volz (D)	95,489	38.9
1950	Sigurd Anderson (R)	154,254	60.9
	Joe Robbie (D)	99,062	39.1
1952	Sigurd Anderson (R)	203,102	70.2
	Sherman A. Iverson (D)	86,412	29.9
1954	Joe Foss (R)	133,878	56.7
	Ed C. Martin (D)	102,377	43.3
1956	Joe Foss (R)	158,819	54.4
	Ralph Herseth (D)	133,198	45.6
1958	Ralph Herseth (D)	132,761	51.4
	Phil Saunders (R)	125,520	48.6
1960	Archie M. Gubbrud (R)	154,530	50.7
	Ralph Herseth (D)	150,095	49.3
1962	Archie M. Gubbrud (R)	143,682	56.1
	Ralph Herseth (D)	112,438	43.9
1964	Nils A. Boe (R)	150,151	51.7
	John F. Lindley (D)	140,419	48.3
1966	Nils A. Boe (R)	131,710	57.7
	Robert Chamberlin (D)	96,504	42.3
1968	Frank L. Farrar (R)	159,646	57.7
	Robert Chamberlin (D)	117,260	42.4
1970	Richard F. Kneip (D)	131,616	54.9
	Frank L. Farrar (R)	108,347	45.2
1972	Richard F. Kneip (D)	185,012	60.0
	Carveth Thompson (R)	123,165	40.0
1974	Richard F. Kneip (D)	149,151	53.6
	John E. Olson (R)	129,077	46.4
1978	William J. Janklow (R)	147,116	56.6
	Roger McKellips (D)	112,679	43.4
1982	William J. Janklow (R)	197,426	70.9
	Michael J. O'Connor (D)	81,136	29.1
1986	George S. Mickelson (R)	152,543	51.8
	R. Lars Herseth (D)	141,898	48.2
1990	George S. Mickelson (R)	151,198	58.9
	Bob L. Samuelson (D)	105,525	41.1

1994	William J. Janklow (R)	172,515	55.4		1851	William B. Campbell (W)	63,333	50.7
	Jim Beddow (D)	126,273	40.5			William Trousdale (D)	61,673	49.3
1998	William J. Janklow (R)	166,621	64.0		1853	Andrew Johnson (D)	63,413	50.9
	Bernie Hunhoff (D)	85,473	32.9			Gustavus H. Henry (W)	61,163	49.1

TENNESSEE

(Became a state June 1, 1796)

1796[1]	John Sevier	✔			1855	Andrew Johnson (D)	67,499	50.8
1797	John Sevier	✔				Meredith P. Gentry (AM)	65,332	49.2
1799[2]	John Sevier	5,295	99.7		1857	Isham G. Harris (D)	71,178	54.3
1801	Archibald Roane	8,438	99.9			Robert Hatton (AM)	59,807	45.7
1803	John Sevier	6,786	58.0		1859	Isham G. Harris (D)	76,073	52.8
	Archibald Roane	4,923	42.0			John H. Netherland (OPP)	68,042	47.2
1805	John Sevier	10,293	63.7		1861	Isham G. Harris (D)	74,973	63.4
	Archibald Roane	5,855	36.3			William H. Polk	43,342	36.6
1807	John Sevier	✔			1863	Robert L. Caruthers	7,050	98.4
	William Cocke				1865	William G. Brownlow (W, R)	22,814	99.9
1809	Willie Blount	13,686	61.9		1867	William G. Brownlow (R)	74,484	76.9
	William Cocke	8,435	38.1			Emerson Etheridge (C)	22,440	23.2
1811	Willie Blount	19,980	100.0		1869	De Witt Clinton Senter (CR)	120,333	68.6
1813[3]	Willie Blount	21,510				William B. Stokes (RAD R)	55,036	31.4
1815	Joseph McMinn	16,354	42.7		1870	John C. Brown (D)	76,666	65.0
	Robert Weakley	7,642	19.9			William H. Wisener (R)	41,278	35.0
	Jesse Wharton	7,060	18.4		1872	John C. Brown (LR)	97,689	53.7
	Robert C. Foster	4,225	11.0			A. A. Freeman (R)	84,100	46.3
	Thomas Johnson	3,106	8.1		1874	James D. Porter Jr. (D)	103,061	64.9
1817	Joseph McMinn	27,882	64.3			Horace Maynard (R)	55,836	35.1
	Robert C. Foster	15,480	35.7		1876	James D. Porter Jr. (D)	123,740	58.8
1819	Joseph McMinn	36,470	79.2			Dorsey B. Thomas (I)	73,695	35.0
	Enoch Parsons	9,148	20.8		1878	Albert S. Marks (D)	89,097	60.3
1821	William Carroll	43,310	79.6			E. M. Wight (R)	43,175	29.2
	Edward Ward	11,130	20.4			R. M. Edwards (G)	15,470	10.5
1823	William Carroll	32,597			1880	Alvin Hawkins (R)	103,966	42.6
1825[4]	William Carroll	34,284	100.0			Wright (STC D)	79,081	32.4
1827	Samuel Houston	44,243	56.0			Wilson (LOWTAX D)	57,568	23.6
	Newton Cannon	32,929	41.7		1882	William B. Bate (LOWTAX D)	120,091	52.9
1829[5]	William Carroll	58,917	99.8			Alvin Hawkins (R)	93,182	41.0
1831[6]	William Carroll (D)	63,894	97.3		1884	William B. Bate (D)	132,201	51.3
1833[7]	William Carroll (D)	52,335	97.8			Frank T. Reid (R)	125,276	48.7
1835	Newton Cannon (W)	41,862	50.4		1886	Robert L. Taylor (D)	126,491	53.5
	William Carroll	33,180	40.0			Alfred A. Taylor (R)	109,842	46.5
	West H. Humphries	7,999	9.6		1888	Robert L. Taylor (D)	156,799	51.8
1837	Newton Cannon (W)	51,341	60.2			Samuel W. Hawkins (R)	139,014	45.9
	Robert Armstrong (D)	33,954	39.8		1890	John P. Buchanan (D)	113,536	56.6
1839	James K. Polk (D)	54,012	51.2			Lewis T. Baxter (R)	76,071	37.9
	Newton Cannon (W)	51446	48.8			David C. Kelly (P)	11,011	5.5
1841	James C. Jones (W)	53,586	51.6		1892	Peter Turney (D)	126,248	47.9
	James K. Polk (D)	50,343	48.4			George W. Winsted (R)	100,599	38.1
1843	James C. Jones (W)	57,008	52.4			John P. Buchanan (PP)	31,515	12.0
	James K. Polk (D)	51,819	47.6		1894	H. Clay Evans (R)	105,164‡	45.2
1845	Aaron V. Brown (D)	58,269	50.7			Peter Turney (D)	104,350	44.9
	Ephraim H. Foster (W)	56,646	49.3			A. L. Mills (POP)	23,129	9.9
1847	Neill S. Brown (W)	61,372	50.6		1896	Robert L. Taylor (D)	156,227	48.8
	Aaron V. Brown (D)	60,004	49.4			George N. Tillman (R)	149,374	46.6
1849	William Trousdale (D)	61,740	50.6		1898	Benton McMillin (D)	105,640	57.9
	Neill S. Brown (W)	60,340	49.4			James A. Fowler (R)	72,611	39.8
					1900	Benton McMillin (D)	145,708	53.9
						John E. McCall (R)	119,831	44.3
					1902	James B. Frazier (D)	98,951	61.8
						Henry T. Campbell (R)	59,002	36.8
					1904	James B. Frazier (D)	131,503	55.7
						Jesse H. Littleton (R)	103,409	43.8

Year	Candidate	Votes	%
1906	Malcolm R. Patterson (D)	111,876	54.4
	H. Clay Evans (R)	92,804	45.2
1908	Malcolm R. Patterson (D)	133,176	53.7
	George N. Tillman (R)	113,269	45.7
1910	Ben W. Hooper (R)	133,076	51.9
	Robert L. Taylor (D)	121,694	47.5
1912	Ben W. Hooper (R)	124,641	50.2
	Benton McMillin (D)	116,610	46.9
1914	Tom C. Rye (D)	137,636	53.6
	Ben W. Hooper (R)	117,717	45.8
1916	Tom C. Rye (D)	146,759	55.0
	John W. Overall (R)	117,819	44.2
1918	Albert H. Roberts (D)	98,628	62.4
	H. B. Lindsay (R)	59,518	37.6
1920	Alfred A. Taylor (R)	229,133	54.9
	Albert H. Roberts (D)	185,890	44.6
1922	Austin Peay (D)	141,012	57.9
	Alfred A. Taylor (R)	102,586	42.1
1924	Austin Peay (D)	162,002	57.2
	T. F. Peck (R)	121,228	42.8
1926	Austin Peay (D)	84,979	64.7
	Walter White (R)	46,238	35.2
1928	Henry H. Horton (D)	195,546	61.1
	Raleigh Hopkins (R)	124,733	39.0
1930	Henry H. Horton (D)	153,341	63.8
	C. Arthur Bruce (R)	85,558	35.6
1932	Hill McAlister (D)	169,075	42.8
	John E. McCall (R)	117,797	29.8
	Lewis S. Pope (I)	106,990	27.1
1934	Hill McAlister (D)	198,743	61.8
	Lewis S. Pope (FUS)	122,965	38.2
1936	Gordon Browning (D)	332,523	80.4
	P. H. Thach (R)	77,392	18.7
1938	Prentice Cooper (D)	210,567	71.7
	Howard H. Baker (R)	83,031	28.3
1940	Prentice Cooper (D)	323,466	72.1
	C. Arthur Bruce (R)	125,245	27.9
1942	Prentice Cooper (D)	120,148	70.2
	C. N. Frazier (R)	51,120	29.9
1944	James N. McCord (D)	275,746	62.5
	J. W. Kilgo (R)	158,742	36.0
1946	James N. McCord (D)	149,937	65.3
	W. O. Lowe (R)	73,222	31.9
1948	Gordon Browning (D)	363,903	66.9
	Roy Acuff (R)	179,957	33.1
1950	Gordon Browning (D)	184,437	78.1
	John R. Neal (R)	51,757	21.9
1952	Frank G. Clement (D)	640,290	79.4
	R. Beecher Witt (R)	166,377	20.6
1954	Frank G. Clement (D)	281,291	87.2
	John R. Neal (I)	39,574	12.3
1958	Buford Ellington (D)	248,874	57.5
	James N. McCord (I)	136,406	31.5
	Thomas P. Wall (R)	35,938	8.3
1962	Frank G. Clement (D)	315,648	50.9
	William R. Anderson (I)	203,765	32.8
	Hubert D. Patty (R)	99,884	16.1
1966	Buford Ellington (D)	532,998	81.2
	H. L. Crowder (I)	64,602	9.8
	Charles Moffett (I)	50,221	7.7
1970	Winfield Dunn (R)	575,777	52.0
	John J. Hooker Jr. (D)	509,521	46.0
1974	Ray Blanton (D)	576,833	55.4
	Lamar Alexander (R)	455,467	43.8
1978	Lamar Alexander (R)	661,959	55.6
	Jake Butcher (D)	523,495	44.0
1982	Lamar Alexander (R)	737,963	59.6
	Randy Tyree (D)	500,937	40.4
1986	Ned R. McWherter (D)	656,602	54.3
	Winfield Dunn (R)	553,449	45.7
1990	Ned R. McWherter (D)	480,885	60.8
	Dwight Henry (R)	289,348	36.6
1994	Don Sundquist (R)	807,104	54.3
	Phil Bredesen (D)	664,252	44.7
1998	Don Sundquist (R)	669,973	68.6
	John J. Hooker (D)	287,750	29.5

Tennessee

1. Until the 1830s contests were essentially on a personal popularity basis among members of the Democratic-Republican Party.
2. Returns are incomplete; five counties are missing.
3. Returns are incomplete; ten counties are missing.
4. Returns are incomplete; twenty-three counties are missing.
5. Returns are incomplete; six counties are missing.
6. Returns are incomplete; two counties are missing.
7. Returns are incomplete; five counties are missing.

TEXAS

(Became a state Dec. 29, 1845)

Year	Candidate	Votes	%
1845	J. Pinckney Henderson	8,190#	83.1
	James B. Miller	1,672#	16.9
1847	George T. Wood (D)	7,088	50.3
	James B. Miller (D)	5,105	36.2
	Nicholas H. Darnell	1,437	10.2
1849	P. Hansbrough Bell (D)	10,319	47.5
	George T. Wood	8,764	40.4
	John T. Mills	2,632	12.1
1851	P. Hansbrough Bell	13,595	48.2
	Middletown T. Johnson	5,262	18.7
	John A. Greer	4,061	14.4
	Benjamin H. Epperson	2,971	10.5
	Thomas J. Chambers	2,320	8.2
1853	Elisha M. Pease (D)	13,099	36.2
	William B. Ochiltree (W)	9,180	25.4
	George T. Wood (D)	5,983	16.5
	L. D. Evans (D)	4,679	12.9
	Thomas J. Chambers (D)	2,449	6.8
1855	Elisha M. Pease (D)	26,336	56.8
	D. C. Dickson (KN)	18,968	40.9
1857	Hardin R. Runnels (D)	32,552	57.9
	Sam Houston (AM)	23,628	42.1
1859	Sam Houston (ID)	36,227	56.8
	Hardin R. Runnels (D)	27,500	43.2
1861	Francis R. Lubbock	21,860	38.1
	Edward Clark	21,675	37.8
	Thomas J. Chambers	13,759	24.0

Year	Candidate	Votes	%
1863	Pendleton Murrah	17,486	56.6
	Thomas J. Chambers	12,254	39.7
1865	James W. Throckmorton (C)	49,277	80.3
	Elisha M. Pease (R)	12,068	19.7
1866	James W. Throckmorton	48,631	80.1
	Elisha M. Pease (R)	12,051	19.9
1869	Edmund J. Davis (R)	39,838	50.2
	Andrew J. Hamilton (D)	39,046	49.2
1873	Richard Coke (D)	98,906	66.0
	Edmund J. Davis (R)	51,049	34.0
1875	Richard Coke (D)	149,974	75.0
	William Chambers (R)	49,994	25.0
1878	Oran M. Roberts (D)	158,960	67.1
	William H. Hamman (NG)	55,004	23.2
	Anthony B. Norton (R)	22,941	9.7
1880	Oran M. Roberts (D)	165,949	62.9
	E. J. Davis (R)	64,372	24.4
	William H. Hamman (G)	33,699	12.8
1882	John Ireland (D)	150,811	58.0
	George W. Jones (R-G-FUS)	108,988	41.9
1884	John Ireland (D)	210,691	63.2
	George W. Jones (R)	98,031	29.4
	Anthony B. Norton (G)	23,464	7.0
1886	Lawrence S. Ross (D)	229,806	73.0
	A. M. Cochran (R)	66,456	21.1
	E. L. Dahoney (P)	18,556	5.9
1888	Lawrence S. Ross (D)	249,361	70.8
	Marion Martin (P & F ALNC)	102,807	29.2
1890	James S. Hogg (D)	261,998	76.7
	Webster Flanagan (R)	76,932	22.5
1892	James S. Hogg (D)	190,386	43.7
	George Clark (R)	133,434	30.7
	Thomas L. Nugent (POP)	108,483	24.9
1894	Charles A. Culberson (D)	207,171	48.9
	Thomas L. Nugent (POP)	151,595	35.8
	W. K. Makemson (R)	54,525	12.9
1896	Charles A. Culberson (D)	298,568	55.3
	Jerome C. Kearby (POP)	238,688	44.2
1898	Joseph D. Sayers (D)	291,548	71.2
	Barnett Gibbs (POP)	114,865	28.1
1900	Joseph D. Sayers (D)	303,548	67.6
	R. E. Hannay (R)	112,864	25.1
	T. J. McMinn (POP)	26,579	5.9
1902	Samuel W. T. Lanham (D)	269,076	74.9
	George W. Burkett (R)	65,706	18.3
1904	Samuel W. T. Lanham (D)	204,961	73.6
	J. G. Lowden (R)	56,499	20.3
1906	Thomas M. Campbell (D)	149,263	81.2
	C. A. Gray (R)	23,779	12.9
1908	Thomas M. Campbell (D)	220,996	72.9
	John N. Simpson (R)	73,309	24.2
1910	Oscar B. Colquitt (D)	174,578	79.8
	J. O. Terrell (R)	26,176	12.0
	Reddin Andrews (SOC)	11,536	5.3
1912	Oscar B. Colquitt (D)	233,073	77.8
	Reddin Andrews (SOC)	25,238	8.4
	C. W. Johnson (R)	22,914	7.6
	Ed C. Lasater (PROG)	15,754	5.3
1914	James E. Ferguson (D)	176,601	82.0
	E. R. Meitzen (SOC)	24,977	11.6
	John W. Philip (R)	11,405	5.3
1916	James E. Ferguson (D)	297,177	80.5
	R. B. Creager (R)	49,117	13.3
	E. R. Meitzen (SOC)	19,278	5.2
1918	William P. Hobby (D)	148,982	84.0
	Charles A. Boynton (R)	26,713	15.1
1920	Pat M. Neff (D)	290,672	60.2
	John G. Culbertson (R)	90,102	18.7
	T. H. McGregor (AM)	69,380	14.4
	H. Capers (B & T R)	26,128	5.4
1922	Pat M. Neff (D)	332,676	81.9
	W. H. Atwell (R)	73,569	18.1
1924	Miriam A. Ferguson (D)	422,563	58.9
	George C. Butte (R)	294,920	41.1
1926	Dan Moody (D)	233,002	87.5
	H. H. Haines (R)	32,434	12.2
1928	Dan Moody (D)	582,897	82.4
	W. H. Holmes (R)	123,337	17.4
1930	Ross Sterling (D)	253,732	80.0
	W. E. Talbot (R)	62,334	19.7
1932	Miriam A. Ferguson (D)	521,395	61.6
	Orville Bullington (R)	322,589	38.1
1934	James V. Allred (D)	428,755	96.4
1936	James V. Allred (D)	780,442	92.9
	C. O. Harris (R)	58,744	7.0
1938	W. Lee O'Daniel (D)	358,943	96.8
1940	W. Lee O'Daniel (D)	1,040,358	94.7
	G. C. Hopkins (R)	57,971	5.3
1942	Coke R. Stevenson (D)	280,735	96.8
1944	Coke R. Stevenson (D)	1,006,778	90.9
	B. J. Peasley (R)	101,110	9.1
1946	Beauford H. Jester (D)	345,507	91.2
	Eugene Nolte Jr. (R)	33,277	8.8
1948	Beauford H. Jester (D)	1,024,160	84.7
	Alvin H. Lane (R)	177,399	14.7
1950	Allan Shivers (D)	367,345	90.2
	Ralph W. Currie (R)	39,793	9.8
1952	Allan Shivers (D, R)	1,853,863	99.9
1954	Allan Shivers (D)	569,533	89.4
	Tod R. Adams (R)	66,154	10.4
1956	Price Daniel (D)	1,433,051	78.4
	William R. Bryant (R)	271,088	14.8
	W. Lee O'Daniel (WRITE IN)	122,103	6.7
1958	Price Daniel (D)	695,035	88.1
	Edwin S. Mayer (R)	94,098	11.9
1960	Price Daniel (D)	1,637,755	72.8
	William M. Steger (R)	612,963	27.2
1962	John B. Connally (D)	847,036	54.0
	Jack Cox (R)	715,025	45.6
1964	John B. Connally (D)	1,877,793	73.8
	Jack Crichton (R)	661,675	26.0
1966	John B. Connally (D)	1,037,517	72.8
	T. E. Kennerly (R)	368,025	25.8
1968	Preston Smith (D)	1,662,019	57.0
	Paul Eggers (R)	1,254,333	43.0
1970	Preston Smith (D)	1,197,726	53.6
	Paul Eggers (R)	1,037,723	46.4

Year	Candidate	Votes	%
1950	Lee E. Emerson (R)	64,915	74.5
	J. Edward Moran (D)	22,227	25.5
1952	Lee E. Emerson (R)	78,338	51.9
	Robert W. Larrow (D)	60,051	39.8
	Henry W. Vail (IR)	12,447	8.3
1954	Joseph B. Johnson (R)	59,778	52.3
	E. Frank Branon (D)	54,554	47.7
1956	Joseph B. Johnson (R)	88,379	57.5
	E. Frank Branon (D)	65,420	42.5
1958	Robert T. Stafford (R)	62,222	50.3
	Bernard J. Leddy (D)	61,503	49.7
1960	F. Ray Keyser Jr. (R)	92,861	56.4
	Russell F. Niquette (D)	71,755	43.6
1962	Philip H. Hoff (D, I)	61,383	50.6
	F. Ray Keyser Jr. (R)	60,035	49.4
1964	Philip H. Hoff (D)	106,611	64.9
	Ralph A. Foote (R, I)	57,576	35.1
1966	Philip H. Hoff (D)	78,669	57.7
	Richard A. Snelling (R)	57,577	42.3
1968	Deane C. Davis (R)	89,387	55.5
	John J. Daley (D)	71,656	44.5
1970	Deane C. Davis (R)	87,458	57.0
	Leo O'Brien Jr. (D)	66,028	43.0
1972	Thomas P. Salmon (D, I VT)	104,533	55.2
	Luther F. Hackett (R)	82,491	43.6
1974	Thomas P. Salmon (D, I VT)	79,842	56.6
	Walter L. Kennedy (R)	53,672	38.0
	Martha Abbott (LU)	7,629	5.4
1976	Richard A. Snelling (R)	99,268	53.4
	Stella B. Hackel (D)	75,262	40.5
	Bernard J. Sanders (LU)	11,317	6.1
1978	Richard A. Snelling (R)	78,181	62.8
	Edwin C. Granai (D)	42,482	34.1
1980	Richard A. Snelling (R)	123,229	58.7
	J. Jerome Diamond (D)	76,826	36.6
1982	Richard A. Snelling (R)	93,111	55.0
	Madeleine M. Kunin (D)	74,394	44.0
1984	Madeleine M. Kunin (D)	116,938	50.0
	John J. Easton (R)	113,264	48.5
1986	Madeleine M. Kunin[1] (D)	92,379	47.0
	Peter Smith (R)	75,162	38.2
	Bernard Sanders (I)	28,430	14.5
1988	Madeleine M. Kunin (D)	134,438	55.4
	Michael Bernhardt (R)	105,191	43.3
1990	Richard A. Snelling (R)	109,540	51.8
	Peter Welch (D)	97,321	46.0
1992	Howard Dean (D)	213,523	74.7
	John McClaughry (R)	65,837	23.0
1994	Howard Dean (D)	145,661	68.7
	David Kelley (R)	40,292	19.0
	Thomas J. Morse (I)	15,000	7.1
1996	Howard Dean (D)	179,544	70.5
	John L. Gropper (R)	57,161	22.4
1998	Howard Dean (D)	121,425	55.7
	Ruth Dwyer (R)	89,726	41.1
2000	Howard Dean (D)	148,059	50.5
	Ruth Dwyer (R)	111,359	37.9
	Anthony Pollina (PROG)	28,116	9.6

Vermont

1. Since no candidate won a clear majority of the total vote cast for governor, the election passed to the state legislature. Sitting in joint assembly in January 1987, the legislature elected Kunin with 139 votes to 39 for Smith and 1 for Sanders.

VIRGINIA

(Ratified the Constitution June 25, 1788)

Year	Candidate	Votes	%
1851[1]	Joseph Johnson (D)	65,527	53.5
	George W. Summers (W)	57,040	46.5
1855	Henry A. Wise (D)	83,275	53.2
	Thomas S. Flournoy (AM)	73,354	46.8
1859	John Letcher (D)	77,229	52.0
	William L. Goggin (OPP)	71,427	48.0
1861	John Letcher	✔	
1862	Francis H. Pierpont (UN)	14,824	99.2
1863	William Smith	28,613	48.1
	Thomas S. Flournoy	23,453	39.4
	George W. Munford	7,478	12.6
1869	Gilbert C. Walker (C)	119,535	54.2
	H. H. Wells (RAD)	101,204	45.9
1873	James L. Kemper (D)	119,672	56.2
	Robert W. Hughes (R)	93,413	43.8
1877	Frederick W. M. Holliday (D)	101,873	95.9
1881	William E. Cameron (READJ)	113,464	53.0
	John W. Daniel (D)	100,757	47.0
1885	Fitzhugh Lee (D)	152,547	52.8
	John S. Wise (R)	136,508	47.2
1889	Philip W. McKinney (D)	163,180	57.2
	William Mahone (R)	121,240	42.5
1893	Charles T. O'Ferrall (D)	128,144	59.7
	Edmund R. Cocke (POP)	79,653	37.1
1897	James Hoge Tyler (D)	110,253	64.6
	Patrick H. McCaull (R)	56,739	33.2
1901	Andrew J. Montague (D)	116,691	58.2
	J. Hampton Hoge (R)	81,366	40.6
1905	Claude A. Swanson (D)	84,235	64.5
	Lunsford L. Lewis (R)	45,815	35.1
1909	William Hodges Mann (D)	70,759	63.4
	William P. Kent (R)	40,357	36.1
1913	Henry C. Stuart (D)	66,518	91.9
	C. Campbell (SOC)	3,789	5.2
1917	Westmoreland Davis (D)	64,226	71.5
	T. J. Muncy (R)	24,957	27.8
1921	Elbert Lee Trinkle (D)	139,416	66.2
	Henry W. Anderson (R)	65,833	31.2
1925	Harry F. Byrd (D)	107,378	74.1
	S. Harris Hoge (R)	37,592	25.9
1929	John Garland Pollard (D)	169,329	62.8
	William Moseley Brown (R)	99,650	36.9
1933	George C. Peery (D)	122,820	73.7
	Fred W. McWane (R)	40,377	24.2
1937	James H. Price (D)	124,145	82.8
	J. Powell Royall	23,670	15.8
1941	Colgate W. Darden Jr. (D)	98,680	80.6
	B. Muse (R)	21,896	17.9
1945	William M. Tuck (D)	112,355	66.6
	S. Lloyd Landreth (R)	52,386	31.0

Year	Candidate	Votes	%
1972	Dolph Briscoe (D)	1,633,493	47.9
	Hank C. Grover (R)	1,533,986	45.0
	Ramsey Muniz (LRU)	214,118	6.3
1974	Dolph Briscoe (D)	1,016,334	61.4
	Jim Granberry (R)	514,725	31.1
	Ramsey Muniz (LRU)	93,295	5.6
1978	William P. Clements (R)	1,183,839	50.0
	John Hill (D)	1,166,979	49.2
1982	Mark White (D)	1,697,870	53.2
	William P. Clements (R)	1,465,937	45.9
1986	William P. Clements (R)	1,813,779	52.7
	Mark White (D)	1,584,515	46.1
1990	Ann W. Richards (D)	1,925,670	49.5
	Clayton Williams (R)	1,826,431	46.9
1994	George W. Bush (R)	2,350,994	53.5
	Ann Richards (D)	2,016,928	45.9
1998	George W. Bush (R)	2,551,454	68.2
	Gary Mauro (D)	1,165,444	31.2

UTAH

(Became a state Jan. 4, 1896)

Year	Candidate	Votes	%
1896	Heber M. Wells (R)	20,833	50.3
	J. T. Caine (D)	18,519	44.7
1900	Heber M. Wells (R)	47,600	51.7
	James H. Moyle (D)	44,447	48.3
1904	John C. Cutler (R)	50,837	50.0
	James H. Moyle (D)	38,047	37.4
	William M. Ferry (AM)	7,959	7.8
1908	William Spry (R)	52,913	47.5
	Jesse William Knight (D)	43,266	38.8
	James A. Street (AM)	11,404	10.2
1912	William Spry (R)	42,552	38.2
	John F. Tolton (D)	36,076	32.4
	Nephi L. Morris (PROG)	23,590	21.2
	Homer P. Burt (SOC)	8,797	7.9
1916	Simon Bamberger (D)	78,298	55.0
	Nephi L. Morris (R)	59,522	41.8
1920	Charles R. Mabey (R)	83,518	58.2
	T. N. Taylor (D)	54,913	38.3
1924	George H. Dern (D)	81,308	53.0
	Charles R. Mabey (R)	72,127	47.0
1928	George H. Dern (D)	102,953	58.5
	William H. Wattis (R)	72,306	41.1
1932	Henry H. Blood (D)	116,031	56.4
	William W. Seegmiller (R)	85,913	41.8
1936	Henry H. Blood (D)	109,656	51.0
	Ray E. Dillman (R)	80,118	37.2
	Harman W. Peery	24,754	11.5
1940	Herbert B. Maw (D)	128,519	52.1
	Don B. Colton (R)	117,713	47.7
1944	Herbert B. Maw (D)	123,907	50.2
	J. Bracken Lee (R)	122,851	49.8
1948	J. Bracken Lee (R)	151,253	55.0
	Herbert B. Maw (D)	123,814	45.0
1952	J. Bracken Lee (R)	180,516	55.1
	Earl J. Glade (D)	147,188	44.9

Year	Candidate	Votes	%
1956	George Dewey Clyde (R)	127,164	38.2
	L. C. Romney (D)	111,297	33.4
	J. Bracken Lee (I)	94,428	28.4
1960	George Dewey Clyde (R)	195,634	52.7
	William A. Barlocker (D)	175,855	47.3
1964	Calvin L. Rampton (D)	226,956	57.0
	Mitchell Melich (R)	171,300	43.0
1968	Calvin L. Rampton (D)	289,283	68.7
	Carl W. Buehner (R)	131,729	31.3
1972	Calvin L. Rampton (D)	331,998	69.7
	Nicholas L. Strike (R)	144,449	30.3
1976	Scott M. Matheson (D)	280,706	52.0
	Vernon B. Romney (R)	248,027	46.0
1980	Scott M. Matheson (D)	330,974	55.2
	Bob Wright (R)	266,578	44.4
1984	Norman H. Bangerter (R)	351,792	55.9
	Wayne Owens (D)	275,669	43.8
1988	Norman H. Bangerter (R)	260,462	40.1
	Ted Wilson (D)	249,321	38.4
	Merrill Cook (I)	136,651	21.0
1992	Michael O. Leavitt (R)	321,713	42.2
	Merrill Cook (IP)	255,753	33.3
	Stewart Hanson (D)	177,181	23.2
1996	Michael O. Leavitt (R)	503,693	75.0
	Jim Bradley (D)	156,616	23.3
2000	Michael O. Leavitt (R)	424,837	55.8
	Bill Orton (D)	321,979	42.3

VERMONT

(Became a state March 4, 1791)

Year	Candidate	Votes	%
1778–			
1788	Thomas Chittenden	✔	
1789	Thomas Chittenden	1,263†	43.3
	Moses Robinson	746	25.6
	Samuel Safford	478	16.4
1790	Thomas Chittenden	✔	
1791	Thomas Chittenden	✔	
1792	Thomas Chittenden	✔	
1793	Thomas Chittenden	3,184	51.7
	Isaac Tichenor	2,712	44.1
1794	Thomas Chittenden	2,643	52.1
	Isaac Tichenor	2,000	39.4
1795	Thomas Chittenden	4,260	60.7
	Isaac Tichenor	2,038	29.1
1796	Thomas Chittenden	✔	
1797	Isaac Tichenor (FED)	†	
	Moses Robinson (D-R)		
	Gideon Olin		
1798	Isaac Tichenor (FED)	6,211	66.4
	Moses Robinson (D-R)	2,805	30.0
1799	Isaac Tichenor (FED)	7,454	65.6
	Israel Smith (D-R)	3,915	34.4
1800	Isaac Tichenor (FED)	6,444	65.9
	Israel Smith (D-R)	3,339	34.1
1801	Isaac Tichenor (FED)	✔	
	Israel Smith (D-R)		

Year	Candidate	Votes	%
1802	Isaac Tichenor (FED)	7,823	60.5
	Israel Smith (D-R)	5,085	39.3
1803	Isaac Tichenor (FED)	7,940	59.5
	Jonathan Robinson (D-R)	5,408	40.5
1804	Isaac Tichenor (FED)	8,075	56.6
	Jonathan Robinson (D-R)	6,184	43.4
1805	Isaac Tichenor (FED)	8,682	60.9
	Jonathan Robinson (D-R)	5,056	35.5
1806	Isaac Tichenor (FED)	9,435	56.6
	Israel Smith (D-R)	7,241	43.9
1807	Israel Smith (D-R)	9,903	53.0
	Isaac Tichenor (FED)	8,571	45.9
1808	Isaac Tichenor (FED)	13,634	50.8
	Israel Smith (D-R)	12,775	47.6
1809	Jonas Galusha (D-R)	14,583	51.1
	Isaac Tichenor (FED)	13,467	47.2
1810	Jonas Galusha (D-R)	13,810	57.3
	Isaac Tichenor (FED)	9,912	41.2
1811	Jonas Galusha (D-R)	13,828	54.0
	Martin Chittenden (FED)	11,214	43.8
1812	Jonas Galusha (D-R)	19,158	53.6
	Martin Chittenden (FED)	15,950	44.6
1813	Jonas Galusha (D-R)	16,828	49.5
	Martin Chittenden (FED)	16,532†	48.7
1814	Martin Chittenden (FED)	17,466†	49.4
	Jonas Galusha (D-R)	17,411	49.3
1815	Jonas Galusha (D-R)	18,055	51.3
	Martin Chittenden (FED)	16,698	47.3
1816	Jonas Galusha (D-R)	17,262	55.2
	Samuel Strong (FED)	13,888	44.4
1817	Jonas Galusha (D-R)	13,756	64.3
	Isaac Tichenor (FED)	7,430	34.7
1818	Jonas Galusha (D-R)	15,243	95.3
1819	Jonas Galusha (D-R)	12,628	81.2
	William C. Bradley (D-R)	1,053	6.8
1820	Richard Skinner (D-R)	13,152	93.4
1821	Richard Skinner (D-R)	12,434	98.7
1822	Richard Skinner (D-R)	11,520	100.0
1823	Cornelius P. Van Ness (D-R)	11,479	85.6
	Dudley Chase	1,088	8.1
1824	Cornelius P. Van Ness (D-R)	13,485	85.4
	Joel Doolittle	1,962	12.4
1825	Cornelius P. Van Ness (D-R)	12,229	98.4
1826	Ezra Butler (D-R)	8,966	63.3
	Joel Doolittle	3,157	22.3
1827	Ezra Butler (D-R)	13,699	85.2
	Joel Doolittle	1,951	12.1
1828	Samuel C. Crafts (NR)	16,285	91.8
	Joel Doolittle	933	5.3
1829	Samuel C. Crafts (NR)	14,325#	55.7
	Heman Allen (A-MASC)	7,376#	28.7
	Joel Doolittle (JAC)	3,973#	15.4
1830	Samuel C. Crafts (OPP)-	13,476#	43.9
	William A. Palmer (A-MAS)	10,923#	35.6
	Ezra Meech (JAC)	6,285#	20.5
1831	William A. Palmer (A-MAS)-	15,258#	44.0
	Heman Allen (NR)	12,990#	37.5
	Ezra Meech (JAC)	6,158#	17.8

Year	Candidate	Votes	%
1832	William A. Palmer (A-MAS)	17,318†	42.2
	Samuel C. Crafts (NR)	15,499	37.7
	Ezra Meech (D)	8,210	20.0
1833	William A. Palmer (A-MAS)	20,565	52.9
	Ezra Meech (FUS)	15,683	40.3
1834	William A. Palmer (A-MAS)	17,131†	45.4
	William C. Bradley (D)	10,385	27.5
	Horatio Seymour (W)	10,159	26.9
1835	William A. Palmer (A-MAS)	16,210*	46.4
	William C. Bradley (D)	13,254	37.9
	Charles Paine (W)	5,435	15.6
1836	Silas H. Jennison (W & A-MASC)	20,371	55.8
	William C. Bradley (D)	16,134	44.2
1837	Silas H. Jennison (W)	22,257	55.7
	William C. Bradley (D)	17,722	44.3
1838	Silas H. Jennison (W)	22,169	56.0
	William C. Bradley (D)	17,416	44.0
1839	Silas H. Jennison (W)	24,611	52.5
	Nathan Smilie (D)	22,251	47.5
1840	Silas H. Jennison (W)	33,435	59.6
	Paul Dillingham Jr. (D)	22,637	40.4
1841	Charles Paine (W)	23,353†	48.7
	Nathan Smilie (D)	21,302	44.4
	Titus Hutchinson (LIB)	3,039	6.3
1842	Charles Paine (W)	27,167	50.9
	Nathan Smilie (D)	24,130	45.2
1843	John Mattocks (W)	24,465†	48.7
	Daniel Kellogg (D)	21,982	43.8
	Charles K. Williams (LIB)	3,766	7.5
1844	William Slade (W)	28,265	51.5
	Daniel Kellogg (D)	20,930	38.2
	William R. Shafter (LIB)	5,618	10.2
1845	William Slade (W)	22,770†	47.2
	Daniel Kellogg (D)	18,591	38.5
	William R. Shafter (LIB)	6,534	13.5
1846	Horace Eaton (W)	23,638†	48.5
	John Smith (D)	17,877	36.7
	Lawrence Brainerd (F SOIL)	7,118	14.6
1847	Horace Eaton (W)	22,455†	46.7
	Paul Dillingham Jr. (D)	18,601	38.7
	Lawrence Brainerd (F SOIL)	6,926	14.4
1848	Carlos Coolidge (W)	22,014†	43.7
	Oscar L. Shafter (F SOIL D)	14,934	29.6
	Paul Dillingham (CASS D)	13,420	26.6
1849	Carlos Coolidge (W)	26,238†	49.6
	Horatio Needham (F SOIL D)	23,250	44.0
	Jonas Clark (D)	4,142	8.7
1850	Charles K. Williams (W)	24,483	51.5
	Lucius B. Peck (F SOIL D)	18,856	39.7
	John Roberts (HUNKER D)	4,379	9.1
1851	Charles K. Williams (W)	22,676	51.1
	Timothy B. Redfield (F SOIL)	14,950	33.7
	John S. Robinson (HUNKER D)	6,686	15.1
1852	Erastus Fairbanks (W)	23,795†	49.4
	John S. Robinson (D)	14,938	31.0
	Lawrence Brainerd (F SOIL)	9,445	19.6
1853	Erastus Fairbanks (W)	21,118	44.1
	John S. Robinson (D)	18,287†	38.2
	Lawrence Brainerd (F SOIL)	8,370	17.5

Year	Candidate	Votes	%
1854	Stephen Royce (W)	27,926	62.6
	Merritt Clark (D)	15,084	33.8
1855	Stephen Royce (R)	25,699#	59.0
	Merritt Clark (D)	12,800#	29.4
	James M. Slade (AM)	3,631#	8.3
1856	Ryland Fletcher (R)	34,052	74.1
	Henry Keyes (D)	11,661	25.4
1857	Ryland Fletcher (R)	26,719	67.0
	Henry Keyes (D)	12,869	32.3
1858	Hiland Hall (R)	29,660	68.7
	Henry Keyes (D)	13,338	30.9
1859	Hiland Hall (R)	31,045	68.4
	John G. Saxe (D)	14,328	31.6
1860	Erastus Fairbanks (R)	34,188	71.0
	John G. Saxe (DOUG D)	11,796	24.6
1861	Frederick Holbrook (UN R)	33,155	78.8
	Andrew Tracy (UN D)	5,722	13.6
	B. H. Smalley (BRECK D)	3,190	7.6
1862	Frederick Holbrook (R)	30,032	88.5
	B. H. Smalley (D)	3,843	11.3
1863	John Gregory Smith (R)	29,228	71.0
	Timothy P. Redfield (D)	11,917	29.0
1864	John Gregory Smith (UN)	32,052	71.5
	Timothy P. Redfield (D)	12,637	28.2
1865	Paul Dillingham (R)	27,586	75.7
	Charles N. Davenport (D)	8,857	24.3
1866	Paul Dillingham (R)	34,117	75.1
	Charles N. Davenport (D)	11,292	24.9
1867	John B. Page (R)	31,694	73.3
	John L. Edwards (D)	11,510	26.6
1868	John B. Page (R)	42,615	73.6
	John L. Edwards (D)	15,289	26.4
1869	Peter T. Washburn (R)	31,834	73.5
	Homer W. Heaton (D)	11,455	26.5
1870	John W. Stewart (R)	33,367	73.5
	Homer W. Heaton (D)	12,058	26.5
1872	Julius Converse (R)	41,946	71.6
	A. B. Gardner (LR)	16,613	28.4
1874	Asahel Peck (R)	33,582	71.7
	W. H. H. Bingham (D)	13,257	28.3
1876	Horace Fairbanks (R)	44,723	68.0
	W. H. H. Bingham (D)	20,988	31.9
1878	Redfield Proctor (R)	37,312	64.3
	W. H. H. Bingham (D)	17,274	29.8
1880	Roswell Farnham (R)	47,848	67.7
	Edward J. Phelps (D)	21,245	30.1
1882	John L. Barstow (R)	35,839	69.1
	George E. Eaton (D)	14,466	27.9
1884	Samuel E. Pingree (R)	42,524	67.3
	Lyman W. Redington (D)	19,820	31.4
1886	Ebenezer J. Ormsbee (R)	37,709	66.0
	Stephen C. Shurtleff (D)	17,187	30.1
1888	William P. Dillingham (R)	48,522	69.9
	Stephen C. Shurtleff (D)	19,527	28.1
1890	Carroll S. Page (R)	33,462	62.1
	Herbert F. Brigham (D)	19,299	35.8
1892	Levi K. Fuller (R)	38,918	65.2
	B. B. Smalley (D)	19,216	32.2

Year	Candidate	Votes	%
1894	Urban A. Woodbury (R)	42,663	73
	George W. Smith (D)	14,142	24
1896	Josiah Grout (R)	53,426	76
	J. Henry Jackson (D)	14,855	21
1898	Edward C. Smith (R)	38,555	71
	Thomas W. Moloney (D)	14,686	2
1900	William W. Stickney (R)	48,441	7
	John H. Center (D)	17,129	2.
1902	John G. McCullough (R)	31,864†	4.
	Percival W. Clement (H LIC)	28,201	4
	Felix W. McGettrick (D)	7,364	1
1904	Charles J. Bell (R)	48,115	7
	Eli H. Porter (D)	16,556	2
1906	Fletcher D. Proctor (R)	42,332	6
	Percival W. Clement (ID)	26,912	3
1908	George H. Prouty (R)	45,598	
	James E. Burke (D)	15,953	2
1910	John A. Mead (R)	35,263	
	Charles D. Watson (D)	17,425	
1912	Allen M. Fletcher (R)	26,237†	
	Harland B. Howe (D)	20,001	
	Frazer Metzger (PROG)	15,629	
1914	Charles W. Gates (R)	36,972	
	Harland B. Howe (D)	16,191	
	Walter J. Aldrich (PROG)	6,929	
1916	Horace F. Graham (R)	43,265	
	William B. Mayo (D)	15,789	
1918	Percival W. Clement (R)	28,358	
	William B. Mayo (D, P)	13,859	
1920	James Hartness (R, P)	67,674	
	Fred C. Martin (D)	18,917	
1922	Redfield Proctor (R, P)	51,104	
	J. Holmes Jackson (D)	17,059	
1924	Franklin S. Billings (R)	75,510	
	Fred C. Martin (D)	18,263	
1926	John E. Weeks (R)	44,564	
	Herbert C. Comings (D, P)	28,651	
1928	John E. Weeks (R)	94,974	
	Harry C. Shurtleff (D)	33,563	
1930	Stanley C. Wilson (R)	52,836	
	Park H. Pollard (D)	21,540	
1932	Stanley C. Wilson (R)	81,656	
	James P. Leamy (D)	49,247	
1934	Charles M. Smith (R)	73,620	
	James P. Leamy (D)	54,159	
1936	George D. Aiken (R)	83,602	
	Alfred H. Heininger (D)	53,218	
1938	George D. Aiken (R)	75,098	
	Fred C. Martin (D)	37,404	
1940	William H. Wills (R)	87,346	
	John McGrath (D)	49,068	
1942	William H. Wills (R)	44,804	
	Park H. Pollard (D)	12,708	
1944	Mortimer R. Proctor (R)	78,907	
	Ernest H. Bailey (D)	40,835	
1946	Ernest W. Gibson (R)	57,849	
	Berthold C. Coburn (D)	14,096	
1948	Ernest W. Gibson (R)	86,394	
	Charles F. Ryan (D)	33,588	

1949	John S. Battle (D)	184,772	70.4
	Walter Johnson (R)	71,991	27.4
1953	Thomas B. Stanley (D)	226,998	54.8
	Ted Dalton (R)	183,328	44.3
1957	J. Lindsay Almond Jr. (D)	326,921	63.2
	Ted Dalton (R)	188,628	36.4
1961	Albertis S. Harrison Jr. (D)	251,861	63.8
	H. Clyde Pearson (R)	142,567	36.1
1965	Mills E. Godwin Jr. (D)	269,526	47.9
	Linwood Holton (R)	212,207	37.7
	William J. Story Jr. (C)	75,307	13.4
1969	Linwood Holton (R)	480,869	52.5
	William C. Battle (D)	415,695	45.4
1973	Mills E. Godwin Jr. (R)	525,075	50.7
	Henry Howell (I)	510,103	49.3
1977	John Dalton (R)	699,302	55.9
	Henry Howell (D)	541,319	43.3
1981	Charles S. Robb (D)	760,357	53.5
	J. Marshall Coleman (R)	659,398	46.4
1985	Gerald L. Baliles (D)	741,438	55.2
	Wyatt B. Durrette (R)	601,652	44.8
1989	L. Douglas Wilder (D)	896,936	50.1
	J. Marshall Coleman (R)	890,195	49.8
1993	George F. Allen (R)	1,045,319	58.3
	Mary Sue Terry (D)	733,527	40.9
1997	James S. Gilmore (R)	969,062	55.8
	Donald. S. Breyer (D)	738,971	42.6

Virginia
1. Before 1851 governor was elected by General Assembly.

WASHINGTON

(Became a state Nov. 11, 1889)

1889	Elisha P. Ferry (R)	33,711	57.7
	Eugene Scruple (D)	24,732	42.3
1892	John H. McGraw (R)	33,281	37.0
	Henry J. Snively (D)	28,959	32.2
	C. W. Young (PP)	23,750	26.4
1896	John R. Rogers (PP)	50,849	55.6
	P. C. Sullivan (R)	38,154	41.7
1900	John R. Rogers (D)	52,048	48.9
	J. M. Frink (R)	49,860	46.8
1904	Albert E. Mead (R)	74,278	51.3
	George Turner (D)	59,119	40.9
	D. Burgess (SOC)	7,421	5.1
1908	Samuel G. Cosgrove (R)	110,190	62.6
	John Pattison (D)	58,126	33.0
1912	Ernest Lister (D)	97,251	30.6
	M. E. Hay (R)	96,629	30.4
	Robert T. Hodge (PROG)	77,731	24.4
	Anna A. Maley (SOC)	37,155	11.7
1916	Ernest Lister (D)	181,745	48.1
	Henry McBride (R)	167,809	44.4
	L. E. Katterfeld (SOC)	21,117	5.6
1920	Louis F. Hart (R)	210,662	52.7
	Robert Bridges (F-LAB)	121,371	30.4
	W. W. Black (D)	66,079	16.5

1924	Roland H. Hartley (R)	220,162	56.4
	Ben F. Hill (D)	126,447	32.4
	J. R. Oman (F-LAB)	40,073	10.3
1928	Roland H. Hartley (R)	281,991	56.2
	Scott Bullitt (D)	214,334	42.7
1932	Clarence D. Martin (D)	352,215	57.3
	John A. Gellatly (R)	207,497	33.8
	L. C. Hicks (LIB)	41,710	6.8
1936	Clarence D. Martin (D)	466,550	69.4
	Roland H. Hartley (R)	189,141	28.1
1940	Arthur B. Langlie (R)	392,522	50.2
	Clarence C. Dill (D)	386,706	49.5
1944	Monrad C. Wallgren (D)	428,834	51.5
	Arthur B. Langlie (R)	400,604	48.1
1948	Arthur B. Langlie (R)	445,958	50.5
	Monrad C. Wallgren (D)	417,035	47.2
1952	Arthur B. Langlie (R)	567,822	52.7
	Hugh B. Mitchell (D)	510,675	47.4
1956	Albert D. Rosellini (D)	616,773	54.6
	Emmett T. Anderson (R)	508,041	45.0
1960	Albert D. Rosellini (D)	611,987	50.3
	Lloyd Andrews (R)	594,122	48.9
1964	Daniel J. Evans (R)	697,256	55.8
	Albert D. Rosellini (D)	548,692	43.9
1968	Daniel J. Evans (R)	692,378	54.7
	John J. O'Connell (D)	560,262	44.3
1972	Daniel J. Evans (R)	747,825	50.8
	Albert D. Rosellini (D)	630,613	42.8
	Vick Gould (TPCT)	86,843	5.9
1976	Dixy Lee Ray (D)	821,797	53.1
	John D. Spellman (R)	687,039	44.4
1980	John D. Spellman (R)	981,083	56.7
	James A. McDermott (D)	749,813	43.3
1984	Booth Gardner (D)	1,006,993	53.3
	John D. Spellman (R)	881,994	46.7
1988	Booth Gardner (D)	1,166,448	62.2
	Bob Williams (R)	708,481	37.8
1992	Mike Lowry (D)	1,184,315	52.2
	Ken Eikenberry (R)	1,086,216	47.8
1996	Gary Locke (D)	1,296,492	58.0
	Ellen Craswell (R)	940,538	42.0
2000	Gary Locke (D)	1,441,973	58.4
	John Carlson (R)	980,060	39.7

WEST VIRGINIA

(Became a state June 19, 1863)

1863	Arthur I. Boreman (UN R)	25,797	100.0
1864	Arthur I. Boreman (UN R)	19,353	100.0
1866	Arthur I. Boreman (R)	23,802	58.1
	Benjamin H. Smith (D)	17,158	41.9
1868	William E. Stevenson (R)	26,935	54.6
	James M. Camden (D)	22,358	45.4
1870	John J. Jacob (D)	29,097	51.9
	William E. Stevenson (R)	26,924	48.1
1872	John J. Jacob (I)	42,888	51.6
	Johnson N. Camden (D)	40,305	48.5

1876	Henry M. Mathews (D)	56,206	56.2
	Nathan Goff (R)	43,477	43.5
1880	Jacob B. Jackson (D)	60,991	51.3
	George C. Sturgiss (R)	44,855	37.7
	N. B. French (G)	13,027	11.0
1884	E. Willis Wilson (D)	71,408	52.0
	Edwin Maxwell (R)	66,059	48.1
1888	Nathan Goff (R)	78,904‡	50.0
	A. Brooks Fleming (D)	78,798	50.0
1892	William A. MacCorkle (D)	84,585	49.4
	Thomas E. Davis (R)	80,658	47.1
1896	George W. Atkinson (R)	105,588	52.4
	Cornelius C. Watts (D)	93,558	46.4
1900	Albert B. White (R)	118,798	53.8
	John H. Holt (D)	100,233	45.4
1904	William M. O. Dawson (R)	121,540	50.8
	John J. Cornwell (D)	112,538	47.0
1908	William E. Glasscock (R)	130,807	50.7
	Louis Bennett (D)	118,909	46.1
1912	Harry D. Hatfield (R)	128,062	47.7
	William R. Thompson (D)	119,292	44.5
	Walter B. Hilton (SOC)	15,048	5.6
1916	John J. Cornwell (D)	143,324	49.5
	Ira E. Robinson (R)	140,558	48.6
1920	Ephraim F. Morgan (R)	242,237	47.3
	Arthur B. Koontz (D)	185,662	36.3
	S. B. Montgomery (NON PART)	81,330	15.9
1924	Howard M. Gore (R)	302,987	53.0
	Jake Fisher (D)	261,846	45.8
1928	William G. Conley (R)	345,729	53.7
	J. Alfred Taylor (D)	296,637	46.1
1932	Herman G. Kump (D)	402,316	53.8
	T. C. Townsend (R)	342,660	45.8
1936	Homer A. Holt (D)	492,333	59.2
	Summers H. Sharp (R)	339,890	40.8
1940	Matthew M. Neely (D)	496,028	56.4
	Daniel Boone Dawson (R)	383,698	43.6
1944	Clarence W. Meadows (D)	395,122	54.4
	Daniel Boone Dawson (R)	330,649	45.6
1948	Okey L. Patteson (D)	438,752	57.1
	Herbert S. Boreman (R)	329,309	42.9
1952	William C. Marland (D)	454,898	51.5
	Rush D. Holt (R)	427,629	48.5
1956	Cecil H. Underwood (R)	440,502	53.9
	Robert H. Mollohan (D)	377,121	46.1
1960	William W. Barron (D)	446,755	54.0
	Harold E. Neely (R)	380,665	46.0
1964	Hulett Smith (D)	433,023	54.9
	Cecil H. Underwood (R)	355,559	45.1
1968	Arch A. Moore Jr. (R)	378,315	50.9
	James M. Sprouse (D)	365,530	49.1
1972	Arch A. Moore Jr. (R)	423,817	54.7
	John D. Rockefeller IV (D)	350,462	45.3
1976	John D. Rockefeller IV (D)	495,661	66.2
	Cecil H. Underwood (R)	253,420	33.8
1980	John D. Rockefeller IV (D)	401,863	54.1
	Arch A. Moore Jr. (R)	337,240	45.4
1984	Arch A. Moore Jr. (R)	394,937	53.3
	Clyde M. See Jr. (D)	346,565	46.7

1988	Gaston Caperton (D)	382,421	58.9
	Arch A. Moore Jr. (R)	267,172	41.1
1992	Gaston Caperton (D)	368,302	56.0
	Cleve Benedict (R)	240,390	36.6
	Charlotte Jean Pritt (WRITE IN)	48,501	7.4
1996	Cecil H. Underwood (R)	324,518	51.6
	Charlotte Jean Pritt (D)	287,870	45.8
2000	Bob Wise (D)	324,822	50.1
	Cecil H. Underwood (R)	305,926	47.2

WISCONSIN

(Became a state May 29, 1848)

1848	Nelson Dewey (D)	19,538	55.6
	Tweedy (W)	14,449	41.1
1849	Nelson Dewey (D)	16,649	52.5
	Alexander L. Collins (W)	11,317	35.7
	Warren Chase (F SOIL)	3,761	11.9
1851	Leonard J. Farwell (W)	22,319	50.6
	Don Alonzo J. Upham (D)	21,812	49.4
1853	William Augustus Barstow (D)	30,405	54.7
	Edward D. Holton (W)	21,886	39.4
	Henry S. Baird (W)	3,304	6.0
1855	William Augustus Barstow (D)	36,355‡	50.1
	Coles Bashford (R)	36,198	49.9
1857	Alexander W. Randall (R)	44,693	50.3
	James B. Cross (D)	44,239	49.7
1859	Alexander W. Randall (R)	59,999	53.3
	Harrison C. Hobart (D)	52,539	46.7
1861	Louis P. Harvey (R)	53,777	54.2
	Benjamin Ferguson (D)	45,456	45.8
1863	James T. Lewis (R)	78,470	58.8
	Henry L. Palmer (D)	55,049	41.2
1865	Lucius Fairchild (R)	58,332	54.7
	Harrison C. Hobart (D)	48,330	45.3
1867	Lucius Fairchild (R)	73,637	51.7
	John J. Tallmadge (D)	68,873	48.3
1869	Lucius Fairchild (R)	69,502	53.2
	Charles D. Robinson (D)	61,239	46.8
1871	Cadwallader C. Washburn (R)	78,301	53.2
	James R. Doolittle (D)	68,920	46.8
1873	William R. Taylor (D)	81,599	55.2
	Cadwallader C. Washburn (R)	66,224	44.8
1875	Harrison Ludington (R)	85,155	50.2
	William R. Taylor (D)	84,314	49.8
1877	William E. Smith (R)	78,759	44.9
	James Mallory (D)	70,486	40.2
	Edward P. Allis (G)	26,216	14.9
1879	William E. Smith (R)	100,535	53.2
	James G. Jenkins (D)	75,030	39.7
	Reuben May (G)	12,996	6.9
1881	Jeremiah M. Rusk (R)	81,754	47.6
	Nicholas D. Fratt (D)	69,797	40.6
	Theodore D. Kanouse (P)	13,225	7.7
1884	Jeremiah M. Rusk (R)	163,210	51.0
	Nicholas D. Fratt (D)	143,943	45.0
1886	Jeremiah M. Rusk (R)	133,247	46.5
	Gilbert M. Woodward (D)	114,525	40.0

	John Cochrane (LAB)	21,467	7.5	1930	Philip F. La Follette (R)	392,958	64.8
	John M. Olin (P)	17,089	6.0		Charles E. Hammersley (D)	170,020	28.0
1888	William D. Hoard (R)	175,696	49.5	1932	Albert G. Schmedeman (D)	590,114	52.5
	James Morgan (D)	155,423	43.8		Walter J. Kohler Sr. (R)	470,805	41.9
1890	George W. Peck (D)	160,388	51.9		Frank B. Metcalfe (SOC)	56,965	5.1
	William D. Hoard (R)	132,074	42.7	1934	Philip F. La Follette (PROG)	373,083	39.1
1892	George W. Peck (D)	178,095	47.9		Albert G. Schmedeman (D)	359,467	37.7
	John C. Spooner (R)	170,497	45.9		Howard T. Greene (R)	172,980	18.1
1894	William H. Upham (R)	196,151	52.3	1936	Philip F. La Follette (PROG)	573,724	46.4
	George W. Peck (D)	142,250	37.9		Alexander Wiley (R)	363,973	29.4
	D. Frank Powell (PP)	25,604	6.8		William L. Lueck (D)	268,530	21.7
1896	Edward Scofield (R)	264,981	59.7	1938	Julius P. Heil (R)	543,675	55.4
	Willis C. Silverthorn (D)	169,257	38.1		Philip F. La Follette (PROG)	353,381	36.0
1898	Edward Scofield (R)	173,137	52.6		Harry W. Bolens (D)	78,446	8.0
	Hiram Wilson Sawyer (D)	135,353	41.1	1940	Julius P. Heil (R)	558,678	40.7
1900	Robert M. La Follette (R)	264,419	59.8		Orland S. Loomis (PROG)	546,436	39.8
	Louis G. Bomrich (D)	160,674	36.4		McGovern (D)	264,985	19.3
1902	Robert M. La Follette (R)	193,407	52.9	1942	Orland S. Loomis (PROG)	397,664*	49.7
	David S. Rose (D)	145,820	39.9		Julius P. Heil (R)	291,945	36.5
1904	Robert M. La Follette (R)	227,253	50.6		William C. Sullivan (D)	98,153	12.3
	George W. Peck (D)	176,301	39.2	1944	Walter S. Goodland (R)	697,740	52.8
	William A. Arnold (SOCIAL D)	24,857	5.5		Daniel W. Hoan (D)	536,357	40.6
1906	James O. Davidson (R)	183,558	57.4		Alexander O. Benz (PROG)	76,028	5.8
	John A. Aylward (D)	103,311	32.3	1946	Walter S. Goodland (R)	621,970	59.8
	Winfield R. Gaylord (SOCIAL D)	24,435	7.6		Daniel W. Hoan (D)	406,499	39.1
1908	James O. Davidson (R)	242,963	54.0	1948	Oscar Rennebohm (R)	684,839	54.1
	John A. Aylward (D)	165,977	36.9		Carl W. Thompson (D)	558,497	44.1
	Harvey D. Brown (SOCIAL D)	28,583	6.4	1950	Walter J. Kohler Jr. (R)	605,649	53.2
1910	Francis E. McGovern (R)	161,619	50.6		Carl W. Thompson (D)	525,319	46.2
	Adolph H. Schmitz (D)	110,446	34.6	1952	Walter J. Kohler Jr. (R)	1,009,171	62.5
	William A. Jacobs (SOCIAL D)	39,547	12.4		William Proxmire (D)	601,844	37.3
1912	Francis E. McGovern (R)	179,360	45.5	1954	Walter J. Kohler Jr. (R)	596,158	51.5
	John C. Karel (D)	167,316	42.5		William Proxmire (D)	560,747	48.4
	Carl D. Thompson (SOCIAL D)	34,468	8.8	1956	Vernon W. Thomson (R)	808,273	51.9
1914	Emanuel L. Philipp (R)	140,787	43.3		William Proxmire (D)	749,421	48.1
	John C. Karel (D)	119,509	36.7	1958	Gaylord A. Nelson (D)	644,296	53.6
	John J. Blaine (I)	32,560	10.0		Vernon W. Thomson (R)	556,391	46.3
	Oscar Ameringer (SOCIAL D)	25,917	8.0	1960	Gaylord A. Nelson (D)	890,868	51.6
1916	Emanuel L. Philipp (R)	229,889	52.9		Philip G. Kuehn (R)	837,123	48.4
	Burt Williams (D)	164,555	37.9	1962	John W. Reynolds (D)	637,491	50.4
	Rae Weaver (SOC)	30,649	7.1		Philip G. Kuehn (R)	625,536	49.4
1918	Emanuel L. Philipp (R)	155,799	47.0	1964	Warren P. Knowles (R)	856,779	50.6
	Harry A. Moehlenpah (D)	112,576	34.0		John W. Reynolds (D)	837,901	49.4
	Emil Seidel (SOC)	57,532	17.4	1966	Warren P. Knowles (R)	626,041	53.5
1920	John J. Blaine (R)	366,247	53.0		Patrick J. Lucey (D)	539,258	46.1
	McCoy (D)	247,746	35.8	1968	Warren P. Knowles (R)	893,463	52.9
	Coleman (SOC)	71,103	10.3		Bronson C. La Follette (D)	791,100	46.8
1922	John J. Blaine (R)	367,929	76.4	1970	Patrick J. Lucey (D)	728,403	54.2
	Arthur A. Bentley (ID)	51,061	10.6		Jack B. Olson (R)	602,617	44.9
	Louis A. Arnold (SOC)	39,570	8.2	1974	Patrick J. Lucey (D)	628,639	53.2
1924	John J. Blaine (R)	412,255	51.8		William D. Dyke (R)	497,189	42.1
	Martin L. Lueck (D)	317,550	39.9	1978	Lee S. Dreyfus (R)	816,056	54.4
	William F. Quick (SOC)	45,268	5.7		Martin J. Schreiber (D)	673,813	44.9
1926	Fred R. Zimmerman (R)	350,927	63.5	1982	Anthony S. Earl (D)	896,872	56.7
	Charles B. Perry (I)	76,507	13.8		Terry J. Kohler (R)	662,738	41.9
	Virgil H. Cady (D)	72,627	13.1	1986	Tommy G. Thompson (R)	805,090	52.7
	Herman O. Kent (SOC)	40,293	7.3		Anthony S. Earl (D)	705,578	46.2
1928	Walter J. Kohler Sr. (R)	547,738	55.4	1990	Tommy G. Thompson (R)	802,321	58.2
	Albert G. Schmedeman (D)	394,368	39.9		Thomas Loftus (D)	576,280	41.8

1994	Tommy G. Thompson (R)	1,051,326	67.2
	Chuck Chvala (D)	482,850	30.9
1998	Tommy G. Thompson (R)	1,047,716	59.7
	Edward R. Garvey (D)	679,553	38.7

WYOMING

(Became a state July 10, 1890)

1890	Francis E. Warren (R)	8,879	55.4
	George W. Baxter (D)	7,153	44.6

Special Election

1892	John E. Osborne (D)	9,290	53.8
	Edward Ivinson (R)	7,509	43.5

1894	William A. Richards (R)	10,149	52.6
	William H. Holliday (D)	6,965	36.1
	Lewis C. Tidball (POP)	2,176	11.3
1898	DeForest Richards (R)	10,383	52.4
	Horace C. Alger (D)	8,989	45.4
1902	DeForest Richards (R)	14,483	57.8
	George T. Beck (D)	10,017	40.0

Special Election

1904	Bryant B. Brooks (R)	17,765	57.5
	John E. Osborne (D)	12,137	39.3

1906	Bryant B. Brooks (R)	16,317	60.2
	Stephen A. D. Keister (D)	9,444	34.8
1910	Joseph M. Carey (D)	21,086	55.6
	W. E. Mullen (R)	15,235	40.2
1914	John B. Kendrick (D)	22,387	51.6
	Hilliard S. Ridgely (R)	19,174	44.2
1918	Robert D. Carey (R)	23,825	56.1
	Frank L. Houx (D)	18,640	43.9
1922	William B. Ross (D)	31,110	50.6
	John W. Hay (R)	30,387	49.4

Special Election

1924	Nellie T. Ross (D)	43,323	55.1
	E. J. Sullivan (R)	35,275	44.9

1926	Frank C. Emerson (R)	35,651	50.9
	Nellie T. Ross (D)	34,286	49.0
1930	Frank C. Emerson (R)	38,058	50.6
	Leslie A. Miller (D)	37,188	49.4

Special Election

1932	Leslie A. Miller (D)	48,130	50.9
	Harry R. Weston (R)	44,692	47.2

1934	Leslie A. Miller (D)	54,305	57.9
	A. M. Clark (R)	38,792	41.4
1938	Nels H. Smith (R)	57,288	59.8
	Leslie A. Miller (D)	38,501	40.2
1942	Lester C. Hunt (D)	39,599	51.3
	Nels H. Smith (R)	37,568	48.7
1946	Lester C. Hunt (D)	43,020	52.9
	Earl Wright (R)	38,333	47.1
1950	Frank A. Barrett (R)	54,441	56.2
	John J. McIntyre (D)	42,518	43.9
1954	Milward L. Simpson (R)	56,275	50.5
	William Jack (D)	55,163	49.5
1958	John J. Hickey (D)	55,070	48.9
	Milward L. Simpson (R)	52,488	46.6
1962	Clifford P. Hansen (R)	64,970	54.5
	Jack R. Gage (D)	54,298	45.5
1966	Stanley K. Hathaway (R)	65,624	54.3
	Ernest Wilkerson (D)	55,249	45.7
1970	Stanley K. Hathaway (R)	74,249	62.8
	John J. Rooney (D)	44,008	37.2
1974	Ed Herschler (D)	71,741	55.9
	Dick Jones (R)	56,645	44.1
1978	Ed Herschler (D)	69,972	50.9
	John C. Ostlund (R)	67,595	49.1
1982	Ed Herschler (D)	106,427	63.1
	Warren A. Morton (R)	62,128	36.9
1986	Michael J. Sullivan (D)	88,879	54.0
	Pete Simpson (R)	75,841	46.0
1990	Michael J. Sullivan (D)	104,638	65.4
	Mary Mead (R)	55,471	34.6
1994	Jim Geringer (R)	118,016	58.7
	Kathy Karpan (D)	80,747	40.2
1998	Jim Geringer (R)	97,235	55.6
	John P. Vinich (D)	70,754	40.5

Governor Returns: Other Sources

In the preceding pages (ooo-ooo), the symbol # is used to denote returns taken from a source other than Congressional Quarterly's principal sources of historical gubernatorial popular election returns: the Inter-University Consortium for Political and Social Research (ICPSR) for 1824–1974 returns; Joseph E. Kallenbach and Jessamine S. Kallenbach, *American State Governors, 1776–1976*, vol. 1 (Dobbs Ferry, N.Y.: Oceana Publications, 1977) for pre-1824 returns; and Congressional Quarterly's biennial series *America Votes* (Washington, D.C.: Congressional Quarterly) for elections since 1975. This page lists the source for elections where the symbol # appears. *(For a description of the ICPSR collection, see p. 000.)*

Delaware

1928: Secretary of State of Delaware.

Florida

1868: Morris, Allen, *The Florida Handbook 1975–1976* (Tallahassee, Fla.: Peninsular Publishing, 1975), p. 532.

1916: *Governors of the States 1900–1974* (Lexington, Ky.: Council of State Governments), p. 16.

Louisiana

1920: Secretary of State of Louisiana.

Minnesota

1861, 1873, 1875, 1877: *The Minnesota Legislative Manual 1973–1974* (St. Paul, Minn.: State of Minnesota), pp. 507–508.

Mississippi

1983: Secretary of State of Mississippi.

New York

1958: Scammon, Richard M., *America Votes 3* (Pittsburgh: University of Pittsburgh, 1959), p. 272.

Texas

1845: Kallenbach, Joseph E., and Jessamine S. Kallenbach, *American State Governors, 1776–1976*, vol. 1 (Dobbs Ferry, N.Y.: Oceana Publications, 1977), p. 572.

Vermont

1829, 1830, 1831, 1855: *Vermont State Manual and Legislative Directory*, pp. 314–315.

## CHAPTER 31

Gubernatorial Primary Election Returns

GUBERNATORIAL PRIMARY ELECTION RETURNS for all fifty states are presented in this section (pp. 1480-1542). Returns for most states go back to 1956. Primary returns for eleven southern states (Alabama, Arkansas, Florida, Georgia, Louisiana, Mississippi, North Carolina, South Carolina, Tennessee, Texas, and Virginia) go back to 1919 where available. The vast majority of southern primaries during the period of 1919 to 1973 were held to nominate candidates of the dominant Democratic Party. In many cases, the winner of the Democratic primary went into the general election facing no Republican opponent. *(See Chapter 6, The Historical Significance of Southern Primaries, Vol. I.)*

The major source for primary election returns for all non-southern states was the *America Votes* series, compiled biennially by Congressional Quarterly in Washington, D.C. Richard M. Scammon and Alice V. McGillivray of the Elections Research Center, Washington, D.C., created the series first published in 1956. Since 1996 the series has been compiled under the direction of Rhodes Cook. Other sources were the returns obtained by Congressional Quarterly after each federal and gubernatorial election from the state secretaries of state. In cases of discrepancies, Congressional Quarterly accepted the *America Votes* figure. The first year for which *America Votes* reported primary returns, 1956, was chosen as the starting point because gubernatorial primary votes for earlier years are not readily available.

For the eleven southern states that were members of the Civil War Confederacy, the primary election returns presented for the years 1919 through 1973 were obtained, except where indicted by a footnote, from the Inter-University Consortium for Political and Social Research (ICPSR) at the University of Michigan. Major sources for returns since 1973 were Congressional Quarterly, which obtained them from the state secretaries of state and the *America Votes* series.

COMPILATION OF ICPSR DATA FILE

Statewide candidate totals for southern primary elections for governor were prepared by the ICPSR staff from several sources. Election returns for the years prior to 1949 were obtained from *Southern Primaries and Elections* (University: University of Alabama Press, 1950), edited by Alexander Heard and Donald S. Strong. It should be noted that, although they transcribed their data from official returns, Professors Heard and Strong found that many of the returns contained errors and discrepancies between the sum of county totals and the state total, or returns published as final in newspapers and secretary of state reports. No attempt was made by Heard and Strong to correct these discrepancies because the source of the error could not be determined.

For the period from 1949 to 1973, candidate totals were acquired from two sources. The first was a collection of southern primary electoral statistics prepared from official returns by Hugh Davis Graham, chair, division of social sciences, University of Maryland (Baltimore County), and Numan V. Bartley, department of history, University of Georgia (Athens). In addition, reference was made to official returns supplied to ICPSR by the various secretaries of state in conjunction with the ICPSR effort to maintain its continuing collection of election materials. The returns obtained from Bartley and Graham, and the secretary of state offices, were compared with published reports of the election outcomes (notably state manuals and the *America Votes* series) to verify the completeness and accuracy of the returns.

PRESENTATION OF RETURNS

The gubernatorial primary returns are arranged alphabetically by state and in chronological order of election within each state listing.

Candidates are listed in descending order, with the candidate receiving the greatest number of popular votes listed first. Percentage of the total vote is listed for each candidate who received *at least 5 percent* of the total vote cast.

Primaries for special elections to fill vacancies and runoff primaries are designated in the returns. For southern states prior to 1974, Republican primary results have been included, whenever available.

NAMES, VOTE TOTALS, AND PERCENTAGES

The names of gubernatorial primary candidates are listed as they appeared in the source materials. In a few cases, first names are not known.

For pre-1976 southern primary elections included in this section, the ICPSR computed statewide vote totals for each candidate. *(See box, ICPSR Historical Election Returns File, p. xvi, Vol. I.)*

Percentages of the total vote were calculated on the basis of each candidate's proportion of the *total number of votes cast* for all candidates. Percentages have been calculated to two decimal places and rounded to one place. Due to rounding and the scattered votes of minor candidates, percentages in individual primary races may not add up to 100.

If no vote is shown for a candidate but the percentage of total vote is listed as 100 percent, in most cases the candidates in

question ran unopposed and state election officials either did not bother to put the candidate's name on the ballot or simply did not make an effort to record the total number of votes.

When gubernatorial primary elections were held under a preferential voting system and the use of second choice votes was required to determine a winner, the symbol ✔ appears next to the winner's name. *(See "Preferential Primaries," p. 130, Vol. I.)*

Where no primary is indicated for a year in which a state elected a governor, it generally means that party conventions chose the nominees. Notes at the end of a state's listing explain other unusual circumstances.

A Gubernatorial Primary Candidates Index is located on pages I-143 to I-150.

Gubernatorial Primary Election Returns, 1919–2000

ALABAMA

	Candidates	Votes	%
1922	**Democratic Primary**		
	William W. Brandon (D)	163,217	78.7
	Bibb Graves (D)	44,151	21.3
1926	**Democratic Primary**		
	Bibb Graves (D)	61,493✔	27.6
	McDowell (D)	59,699	26.8
	Carmichael (D)	54,072	24.3
	Patterson (D)	47,411	21.3
	Democratic Second Choice		
	Bibb Graves (D)	21,978	31.0
	Patterson (D)	20,893	29.5
	Carmichael (D)	20,061	28.3
	McDowell (D)	7,943	11.2
1930	**Democratic Primary**		
	B. M. Miller (D)	77,066✔	39.2
	W. C. Davis (D)	70,966	36.1
	W. Finnell (D)	19,320	9.8
	Charles C. McCall (D)	19,004	9.7
	Democratic Second Choice		
	W. C. Davis (D)	10,673	25.8
	B. M. Miller (D)	9,994	24.2
	W. Finnell (D)	9,867	23.9
	Charles C. McCall (D)	6,467	15.7
	J. A. Carnley (D)	2,819	6.8
1934	**Democratic Primary**		
	Bibb Graves (D)	132,462	43.4
	Frank M. Dixon (D)	97,508	32.0
	Leon McCord (D)	75,208	24.6
	Democratic Runoff		
	Bibb Graves (D)	157,140	53.7
	Frank M. Dixon (D)	135,309	46.3

		Votes	%
1938	**Democratic Primary**		
	Frank M. Dixon (D)	152,860	48.6
	Chauncey Sparks (D)[1]	74,554	23.7
	R. J. Goode (D)	70,287	22.4
1942	**Democratic Primary**		
	Chauncey Sparks (D)	145,798	52.2
	James E. Folsom (D)	73,306	26.2
	Chris J. Sherlock (D)	53,448	19.1
1946	**Democratic Primary**		
	James E. Folsom (D)	104,152	28.5
	Handy Ellis (D)	88,459	24.2
	Joe N. Poole (D)	70,925	19.4
	Elbert Boozer (D)	58,134	15.9
	Gordon Persons (D)	43,843	12.0
	Democratic Runoff		
	James E. Folsom (D)	205,168	58.7
	Handy Ellis (D)	144,126	41.3
1950	**Democratic Primary**		
	Gordon Persons (D)	137,055	34.1
	Philip J. Hamm (D)[2]	56,395	14.0
	Elbert Boozer (D)	48,021	11.9
	J. Bruce Henderson (D)	38,867	9.7
	Chauncey Sparks (D)	27,404	6.8
	Eugene "Bull" Connor (D)	20,629	5.1
	Robert K. "Buster" Bell (D)	20,171	5.0
1954	**Democratic Primary**		
	James E. Folsom (D)	305,384	51.4
	Jimmy Faulkner (D)	151,925	25.6
	Jim Allen (D)	61,530	10.4
	J. Bruce Henderson (D)	47,969	8.1
1958	**Democratic Primary**		
	John Patterson (D)	196,859	31.8
	George C. Wallace (D)	162,435	26.3
	Jimmy Faulkner (D)	91,512	14.8

	A. W. Todd (D)	59,240	9.6
	Laurie C. Battle (D)	38,955	6.3

Democratic Runoff

	John Patterson (D)	315,353	55.7
	George C. Wallace (D)	250,451	44.3

1962   Democratic Primary

	George C. Wallace (D)	207,062	32.5
	Ryan deGraffenried (D)	160,704	25.2
	James E. Folsom (D)	159,640	25.1
	Macdonald Gallion (D)	80,374	12.6

Democratic Runoff

	George C. Wallace (D)	340,730	55.9
	Ryan deGraffenried (D)	269,122	44.1

1966   Democratic Primary

	Lurleen B. Wallace (D)	480,841	54.1
	Richmond M. Flowers (D)	172,386	19.4
	Carl Elliott (D)	71,972	8.1
	Bob Gilchrist (D)	49,502	5.6

1970   Democratic Primary

	Albert Brewer (D)	428,146	42.0
	George C. Wallace (D)	416,443	40.8
	Charles Woods (D)	149,887	14.7

Democratic Runoff

	George C. Wallace (D)	559,832	51.6
	Albert Brewer (D)	525,951	48.4

1974   Republican Primary

	Elvin McCary (R)		100.0

Democratic Primary

	George C. Wallace (D)	536,235	64.7
	Gene McLain (D)	249,695	30.1

1978   Republican Primary

	Guy Hunt (R)	21,499	83.2
	Bert Hayes (R)	2,817	10.9
	Julian Elgin (R)	1,534	5.9

Democratic Primary

	Forrest H. "Fob" James Jr. (D)	256,196	28.5
	Bill Baxley (D)	210,089	23.3
	Albert Brewer (D)	193,479	21.5
	Sid McDonald (D)	143,930	16.0
	Jere Beasley (D)	77,202	8.6

Democratic Runoff

	Forrest H. "Fob" James Jr. (D)	515,520	55.2
	Bill Baxley (D)	418,932	44.8

1982   Republican Primary

	Emory Folmar (R)		100.0

Democratic Primary

	George C. Wallace (D)	425,469	42.5
	George McMillan (D)	296,262	29.6
	Joe C. McCorquodale (D)	250,614	25.1

Democratic Runoff

	George C. Wallace (D)	512,203	51.2
	George McMillan (D)	488,444	48.8

1986   Republican Primary

	Guy Hunt (R)	20,823	71.3
	Doug Carter (R)	8,371	28.7

Democratic Primary

	Bill Baxley (D)	345,985	36.8
	Charles Graddick (D)	275,714	29.3
	Forrest H. James (D)	195,844	20.8
	George McMillan (D)	117,258	12.5

Democratic Runoff[3]

	Charles Graddick (D)	470,051	50.5
	Bill Baxley (D)	461,295	49.5

1990   Republican Primary

	Guy Hunt (R)	119,877	95.8

Democratic Primary

	Paul R. Hubbert (D)	233,808	31.5
	Don Siegelman (D)	184,635	24.9
	Forrest H. "Fob" James Jr. (D)	160,121	21.6
	Ronnie G. Flippo (D)	128,105	17.3

Democratic Runoff

	Paul R. Hubbert (D)	309,609	53.6
	Don Siegelman (D)	267,588	46.4

1994   Republican Primary

	Forrest H. "Fob" James Jr. (R)	84,019	39.5
	Ann Bedsole (R)	54,449	25.6
	Winton Blount (R)	51,785	24.4
	Mickey Kirkland (R)	18,538	8.7

Democratic Primary

	James E. Folsom Jr. (D)	380,227	54.0
	Paul R. Hubbert (D)	285,554	40.6

Republican Runoff

	Forrest H. "Fob" James Jr. (R)	130,233	62.4
	Ann Bedsole (R)	78,338	37.6

1998   Republican Primary

	Forrest H. "Fob" James Jr. (R)	172,145	47.9
	Winton Blount (R)	147,958	41.2
	Guy Hunt (R)	28,652	8.0

Democratic Primary

	Don Siegelman (D)	280,181	78.2
	Lenora Pate (D)	59,300	16.6

Republican Runoff		
Forrest H. "Fob" James Jr. (R)	256,702	55.8
Winton Blount (R)	203,658	44.2

Alabama

1. Sparks withdrew from the race May 11, 1938, declining a runoff with Dixon, who became the Democratic nominee.

2. Hamm withdrew May 12, 1950, declining a runoff with Persons, who became the Democratic nominee.

3. After the Democratic runoff primary a subcommittee of Alabama's Democratic party declared Baxley the nominee, deciding that voters who voted in the Republican primary had crossed over and voted in the Democratic runoff primary for Graddick, against party rules. This decision was contested through the courts, but the Democratic Party decision was upheld.

ALASKA[1]

	Candidates	Votes	%
1958	**Republican Primary**		
	John Butrovich (R)		100.0
	Democratic Primary		
	William A. Egan (D)	22,735	61.1
	Victor Rivers (D)	8,845	23.7
	J. G. Williams (D)	5,656	15.2
1962	**Republican Primary**		
	Mike Stepovich (R)	6,415	38.1
	Howard W. Pollock (R)	5,247	31.2
	John B. Coghill (R)	2,295	13.6
	Verne O. Martin (R)	1,504	8.9
	Milo H. Fritz (R)	1,371	8.1
	Democratic Primary		
	William A. Egan (D)	13,698	62.3
	George H. Byer (D)	5,275	24.0
	Warren A. Taylor (D)	2,386	10.8
1966	**Republican Primary**		
	Walter J. Hickel (R)	10,580	55.3
	Bruce Kendall (R)	4,511	23.6
	Mike Stepovich (R)	4,039	21.1
	Democratic Primary		
	William A. Egan (D)	19,801	61.0
	Wendell P. Kay (D)	12,660	39.0
1970	**Republican Primary**		
	Keith Miller (R)	19,153	53.4
	Howard W. Pollock (R)	16,691	46.5
	Democratic Primary		
	William A. Egan (D)	23,973	67.5
	Larry Carr (D)	11,350	31.9
1974	**Republican Primary**		
	Jay S. Hammond (R)	28,602	47.2
	Walter J. Hickel (R)	20,728	34.2
	Keith Miller (R)	10,864	17.9

	Candidates	Votes	%
	Democratic Primary		
	William A. Egan (D)	20,356	91.0
1978[2]	**Republican Primary**		
	Jay S. Hammond (R)	31,896	39.1
	Walter J. Hickel (R)	31,798	38.9
	Tom Fink (R)	17,487	21.4
	Democratic Primary		
	Chancy Croft (D)	8,911	36.1
	Edward A. Merdes (D)	8,639	35.0
	Jalmar M. Kerttula (D)	7,125	28.9
1982	**Republican Primary**		
	Tom Fink (R)	41,911	51.3
	Terry Miller (R)	36,594	44.8
	Democratic Primary		
	Bill Sheffield (D)	21,940	39.7
	Steve Cowper (D)	21,680	39.2
	H. A. Boucher (D)	8,584	15.5
1986	**Republican Primary**		
	Arliss Sturgulewski (R)	25,740	30.6
	Walter J. Hickel (R)	23,733	28.3
	Richard Randolph (R)	18,164	21.6
	Joe L. Hayes (R)	7,989	9.5
	Bob Richards (R)	4,973	5.9
	Democratic Primary		
	Steve Cowper (D)	36,233	54.5
	Bill Sheffield (D)	29,935	45.0
	Alaskan Independent Primary		
	Joe Vogler (ALI)		100.0
	Libertarian Primary		
	Mary O'Brannon (LIBERT)	205	53.5
	Ed Hoch (LIBERT)	178	46.5
1990	**Republican Primary[3]**		
	Arliss Sturgulewski (R)	26,906	36.4
	James O. Campbell (R)	23,442	31.7
	Rick Halford (R)	22,466	30.4
	Democratic Primary		
	Tony Knowles (D)	36,019	56.1
	Stephen McAlpine (D)	27,656	43.0
	Alaskan Independence Primary		
	John Lindauer (ALI)[4]	3,505	87.7
	William DeRushe (ALI)	492	12.3
1994	**Republican Primary**		
	James O. "Jim" Campbell (R)	24,854	49.8
	Tom Fink (R)	23,586	47.2

Democratic Primary

Tony Knowles (D)	24,727	*43.6*
Stephen McAlpine (D)	17,482	*30.9*
Sam Cotten (D)	13,899	*24.5*

Alaskan Independence Primary

John B. "Jack" Coghill (ALI)	4,213	*80.1*
Jude Henzler (ALI)	465	*8.8*
Al Rowe (ALI)	348	*6.6*

Green Primary

Jim Sykes (GREEN)	2,505	*100.0*

1998   ### Republican Primary

John Lindauer (R)	25,070	*41.6*
Robin Taylor (R)	17,679	*29.4*
Wayne Ross (R)	17,445	*29.0*

Democratic Primary

Tony Knowles (D)	38,788	*88.8*
Nels Anderson Jr. (D)	3,387	*7.8*

Alaskan Independence Primary

Sylvia Sullivan (ALI)	981	*54.9*
Harold Haldane (ALI)	466	*26.1*
Roger Gigler (ALI)	339	*19.0*

Republican Moderate Primary

Ray Metcalfe (R)	1,157	*100.0*

Green Primary

Jim Sykes (GREEN)	2,251	*100.0*

Alaska

1. In Alaska's so-called "jungle" primaries, all candidates for an office appeared together on the same ballot with their parties designated. Nominations went to the Republican and Democrat receiving the most votes for the office. Percentages were calculated here as if candidates had run in separate party primaries.

2. There were recounts of the votes received by the two top finishers in both primaries. In the Republican recount, Hammond's vote was 31,921 (50.0 percent) and Hickel's was 31,823 (49.9 percent). In the Democratic recount, Croft's vote was 8,910 (50.7 percent) and Merdes's was 8,655 (49.3 percent).

3. The Republican primary ballot was a single-ballot and only registered Republican, Non Partisan, and Undeclared voters could participate in the primary. All other parties ran on a multiparty ballot and the primary was open to all registered voters except Republicans.

4. Lindauer withdrew after the primary and Walter J. Hickel was substituted by the party committee.

ARIZONA

	Candidates	Votes	%
1956	**Republican Primary**		
	Horace B. Griffen (R)	20,471	*46.0*
	O. D. Miller (R)	17,858	*40.1*
	Fred Trump (R)	6,199	*13.9*

	Democratic Primary		
	Ernest W. McFarland (D)		*100.0*
1958	**Republican Primary**		
	Paul Fannin (R)		*100.0*
	Democratic Primary		
	Robert Morrison (D)	77,931	*50.4*
	Dick Searles (D)	58,699	*37.9*
	Marvin L. Burton (D)	18,122	*11.7*
1960	**Republican Primary**		
	Paul Fannin (R)		*100.0*
	Democratic Primary		
	Lee Ackerman (D)		*100.0*
1962	**Republican Primary**		
	Paul Fannin (R)		*100.0*
	Democratic Primary		
	Sam Goddard (D)	91,661	*59.8*
	Joe Haldiman (D)	41,645	*27.2*
	J. M. Morris (D)	19,850	*13.0*
1964	**Republican Primary**		
	Richard Kleindienst (R)	64,310	*62.8*
	Evan Mecham (R)	38,131	*37.2*
	Democratic Primary		
	Sam Goddard (D)	114,377	*60.0*
	Art Brock (D)	57,067	*30.0*
	J. M. Morris (D)	11,303	*5.9*
1966	**Republican Primary**		
	John R. Williams (R)	37,409	*44.3*
	John Haugh (R)	25,905	*30.6*
	Robert W. Pickrell (R)	21,192	*25.1*
	Democratic Primary		
	Sam Goddard (D)	63,180	*45.5*
	Norman Green (D)	53,921	*38.9*
	Andrew J. Gilbert (D)	23,637	*17.0*
1968	**Republican Primary**		
	John R. Williams (R)		*100.0*
	Democratic Primary		
	Sam Goddard (D)	112,948	*73.4*
	Currin V. Shields (D)	30,337	*19.7*
	Jack DeVault (D)	10,613	*6.9*
1970	**Republican Primary**		
	John R. Williams (R)		*100.0*
	Democratic Primary		
	Raul H. Castro (D)	63,294	*52.0*
	Jack Ross (D)	30,921	*25.4*
	George Nader (D)	27,534	*22.6*

1974   **Republican Primary**

Russell Williams (R)	53,132	35.6
Evan Mecham (R)	30,266	20.3
William C. Jacquin (R)	27,138	18.2
John R. Driggs (R)	23,519	15.7
Milton H. Graham (R)	15,315	10.2

Democratic Primary

Raul H. Castro (D)	115,268	67.2
Jack Ross (D)	31,250	18.2
David R. Moss (D)	19,143	11.2

1978   **Republican Primary**

Evan Mecham (R)	50,713	44.1
Jack Londen (R)	40,116	34.9

Democratic Primary

Bruce Babbitt (D)	108,548	76.8
David R. Moss (D)	32,785	23.2

Libertarian Primary

V. Gene Lewter (LIBERT)		100.0

Socialist Worker Primary

Jessica Sampson (SOC WORK)		100.0

1982   **Republican Primary**

Leo Corbet (R)	108,766	61.7
Evan Mecham (R)	67,456	38.3

Democratic Primary

Bruce Babbitt (D)	142,559	85.8
Steve Jancek (D)[1]	23,492	14.1

Libertarian Primary

Sam Stelger (LIBERT)		100.0

1986   **Republican Primary**

Evan Mecham (R)	121,614	53.7
Burton S. Barr (R)	104,682	46.3

Democratic Primary

Carolyn Warner (D)	106,687	50.6
Tony Mason (D)	92,413	43.9
Dave Moss (D)	11,588	5.5

1990   **Republican Primary**

Fife Symington (R)	163,010	43.8
Evan Mecham (R)	91,136	24.5
Fred Koory (R)	61,487	16.5
Sam Steiger (R)	49,019	13.2

Democratic Primary

Terry Goddard (D)	212,579	84.0
Dave Moss (D)	40,478	16.0

1994   **Republican Primary**

Fife Symington (R)	202,588	68.1
Barbara Barrett (R)	94,740	31.9

Democratic Primary

Eddie Basha (D)	96,613	36.8
Terry Goddard (D)	92,239	35.2
Paul Johnson (D)	73,512	16.0

Libertarian Primary

John Buttrick (LIBERT)	5,052	100.0

1998   **Republican Primary**

Jane Dee Hull (R)	177,324	76.5
Jim Howl (R)	30,699	13.2
Charles Brown (R)	23,710	10.2

Democratic Primary

Paul Johnson (D)	109,044	100.0

Arizona
1. Jancek died before the primary, but his name remained on the ballot.

ARKANSAS

Candidates	Votes	%

1920   **Democratic Primary**

Thomas C. McRae (D)	41,907	26.9
Smead Powell (D)	32,263	20.7
Thomas J. Terral (D)	29,303	18.8
J. C. Floyd (D)	21,596	13.9
G. R. Haynie (D)	16,747	10.8

1922   **Democratic Primary**

Thomas C. McRae (D)	127,728	70.5
E. P. Toney (D)	53,572	29.6

1924   **Democratic Primary**

Thomas J. Terral (D)	54,533	26.3
Lee Cazort (D)	43,466	21.0
John E. Martineau (D)	35,438	17.1
Jim G. Ferguson (D)	27,155	13.1
Hamp Williams (D)	23,785	11.5
Jacob R. Willson (D)	22,626	10.9

1926   **Democratic Primary**

John E. Martineau (D)	117,232	53.5
Thomas J. Terral (D)	101,981	46.5

1928   **Democratic Primary**

Harvey J. Parnell (D)	94,207	41.7
Brooks Hays (D)	57,497	25.4
Thomas J. Terral (D)	34,476	15.2
J. Carrol Cone (D)	31,786	14.1

1930   **Democratic Primary**

Harvey J. Parnell (D)	133,870	54.2
Brooks Hays (D)	88,541	35.8
J. C. Sheffield (D)	20,133	8.2

Democratic Primary

Candidate	Votes	%
Tom Bradley (D)	1,726,985	61.1
John Garamendi (D)	712,161	25.2

American Independent Primary

Candidate	Votes	%
James C. Griffin (AMI)		100.0

Peace and Freedom Primary

Candidate	Votes	%
Elizabeth Martinez (PFP)	4,353	55.1
Jan B. Tucker (PFP)	3,552	44.9

Libertarian Primary

Candidate	Votes	%
Dan P. Dougherty (LIBERT)		100.0

1986

Republican Primary

Candidate	Votes	%
George Deukmejian (R)	1,927,288	93.6
William H. R. Clark (R)	132,125	6.4

Democratic Primary

Candidate	Votes	%
Tom Bradley (D)	1,768,042	81.5
Hugh G. Bagley (D)	141,217	6.5
Charles Pineda (D)	109,001	5.0

American Independent Primary

Candidate	Votes	%
Gary V. Miller (AMI)		100.0

Peace and Freedom Primary

Candidate	Votes	%
Maria E. Munoz (PFP)	3,508	69.8
Cheryl Zuur (PFP)	1,519	30.2

Libertarian Primary

Candidate	Votes	%
Joseph Fuhrig (LIBERT)		100.0

1990

Republican Primary

Candidate	Votes	%
Pete Wilson (R)	1,856,613	87.5
David M. Williams (R)	107,397	5.1

Democratic Primary

Candidate	Votes	%
Dianne Feinstein (D)	1,361,361	52.3
John Van de Kamp (D)	1,067,899	41.0

American Independent Primary

Candidate	Votes	%
Jerome McCready (AMI)	8,921	54.1
Chuck Morsa (AMI)	7,563	45.9

Libertarian Primary

Candidate	Votes	%
Dennis Thompson (LIBERT)		100.0

Peace and Freedom Primary

Candidate	Votes	%
Maria E. Munoz (PFP)	3,461	56.7
Merle Woo (PFP)	2,647	43.3

1994

Republican Primary

Candidate	Votes	%
Pete Wilson (R)	1,266,832	61.4
Ron K. Unz (R)	707,431	34.3

Democratic Primary

Candidate	Votes	%
Kathleen Brown (D)	1,110,372	48.4
John Garamendi (D)	755,876	32.9
Tom Hayden (D)	318,777	13.9

American Independent Primary

Candidate	Votes	%
Jerome McCready (AMI)	18,984	100.0

Libertarian Primary

Candidate	Votes	%
Richard Rider (LIBERT)	13,757	81.1

Peace and Freedom Primary

Candidate	Votes	%
Gloria Estela La Riva (PFP)	4,633	62.3

Green Primary

Candidate	Votes	%
John T. Selawsky (GREEN)	3,688	16.6
James Ogle (GREEN)	2,930	13.2
John Lewallen (GREEN)	2,923	13.1

1998

Republican Primary

Candidate	Votes	%
Dan Lungren (R)	2,023,618	93.4

Democratic Primary

Candidate	Votes	%
Gray Davis (D)	2,083,396	57.5
Al Checchi (D)	748,828	20.7
Jane Harman (D)	741,251	20.5

Green Primary

Candidate	Votes	%
Dan Hamburg (GREEN)	92,118	100.0

Libertarian Primary

Candidate	Votes	%
Steve W. Kubby (LIBERT)	47,025	100.0

Peace and Freedom Primary

Candidate	Votes	%
Gloria Estela La Riva (PFP)	21,505	58.0
Marsha Feinland (PFP)	15,572	42.0

American Independent Primary

Candidate	Votes	%
Nathan E. Johnson (AMI)	19,540	100.0

Natural Law Primary

Candidate	Votes	%
Harold H. Bloomfield (NL)	12,422	100.0

COLORADO

Candidates	Votes	%

1956

Republican Primary

Candidate	Votes	%
Donald G. Brotzman (R)		100.0

1932

Democratic Primary

Candidate	Votes	%
J. Marion Futrell (D)	124,239	44.0
Thomas J. Terral (D)	59,066	21.0
A. B. Priddy (D)	37,134	13.2
D. H. Blackwood (D)	33,147	11.8

1934

Democratic Primary

Candidate	Votes	%
J. Marion Futrell (D)	167,917	65.9
Howard Reed (D)	86,894	34.1

1936

Democratic Primary

Candidate	Votes	%
Carl E. Bailey (D)	76,014	32.0
Ed F. McDonald (D)	72,075	30.3
R. A. Cook (D)	60,768	25.6
Thomas J. Terral (D)	23,663	10.0

1938

Democratic Primary

Candidate	Votes	%
Carl E. Bailey (D)	146,472	51.5
R. A. Cook (D)	131,791	46.3

1940

Democratic Primary

Candidate	Votes	%
Homer M. Adkins (D)	142,247	56.2
Carl E. Bailey (D)	110,613	43.7

1942

Democratic Primary

Candidate	Votes	%
Homer M. Adkins (D)	120,811	71.8
Fred Keller (D)	44,304	26.3

1944

Democratic Primary

Candidate	Votes	%
Ben Laney (D)	70,965	38.6
J. Bryan Sims (D)[1]	63,454	34.5
David L. Terry (D)	49,685	27.0

1946

Democratic Primary

Candidate	Votes	%
Ben Laney (D)	125,444	64.6
J. M. Malone (D)	63,601	32.8

1948

Democratic Primary

Candidate	Votes	%
Sidney S. McMath (D)	87,829	34.1
Jack Holt (D)	60,313	23.4
James McKrell (D)	57,030	22.1
Horace Thompson (D)	48,674	18.9

Democratic Runoff

Candidate	Votes	%
Sidney S. McMath (D)	157,137	51.7
Jack Holt (D)	146,880	48.3

1950

Democratic Primary

Candidate	Votes	%
Sidney S. McMath (D)	209,559	64.0
Ben T. Laney (D)	112,651	34.4

1952

Democratic Primary

Candidate	Votes	%
Sidney S. McMath (D)	100,858	30.7
Francis Cherry (D)	91,195	27.7
Tackett (D)	63,827	19.4
Jack Holt (D)	45,233	13.8
Murry (D)	27,937	8.5

Democratic Runoff

Candidate	Votes	%
Francis Cherry (D)	237,448	63.1
Sidney S. McMath (D)	139,052	36.9

1954

Democratic Primary

Candidate	Votes	%
Francis Cherry (D)	154,879	47.7
Orval E. Faubus (D)	109,614	33.8
Guy Jones (D)	41,249	12.7
McMillan (D)	18,857	5.8

Democratic Runoff

Candidate	Votes	%
Orval E. Faubus (D)	191,328	50.9
Francis Cherry (D)	184,509	49.1

1956

Democratic Primary

Candidate	Votes	%
Orval E. Faubus (D)	180,760	58.1
James Johnson (D)	83,856	26.9
Jim Snoddy (D)	43,630	14.0

1958

Republican Primary

Candidate	Votes	%
George W. Johnson (R)	3,147	72.7
Donald D. Layne (R)	1,273	28.8

Democratic Primary

Candidate	Votes	%
Orval E. Faubus (D)	264,346	68.9
Chris Finkbeiner (D)	60,173	15.7
Lee Ward (D)	59,385	15.5

1960

Republican Primary

Candidate	Votes	%
Henry M. Britt (R)		100.0

Democratic Primary

Candidate	Votes	%
Orval E. Faubus (D)	238,997	58.8
Joe C. Hardin (D)	66,499	16.4
Bruce Bennett (D)	58,400	14.4
H. E. Williams (D)	33,374	8.2

1962

Republican Primary

Candidate	Votes	%
Willis Ricketts (R)		100.0

Democratic Primary

Candidate	Votes	%
Orval E. Faubus (D)	208,996	51.6
Sidney S. McMath (D)	83,473	20.6
Dale Alford (D)	82,815	20.4
Vernon H. Whitten (D)	22,377	5.5

1964

Republican Primary

Candidate	Votes	%
Winthrop Rockefeller (R)		100.0

Democratic Primary

Candidate	Votes	%
Orval E. Faubus (D)	239,890	65.7
Ervin Odell Dorsey (D)	69,638	19.1
Joe Hubbard (D)	39,199	10.7

1966

Republican Primary

Candidate	Votes	%
Winthrop Rockefeller (R)	19,646	98.5

Democratic Primary

James Johnson (D)	105,607	25.1
Frank Holt (D)	92,711	22.1
Brooks Hays (D)	64,814	15.4
Dale Alford (D)	53,531	12.7
Sam Boyce (D)	49,744	11.8
Raymond Rebsamen (D)	35,607	8.5

Democratic Runoff

James Johnson (D)	210,543	51.9
Frank Holt (D)	195,442	48.1

1968 ## Republican Primary

Winthrop Rockefeller (R)	27,913	95.5

Democratic Primary

Marion Crank (D)	106,092	25.6
Virginia Johnson (D)	86,038	20.7
Ted Boswell (D)	85,629	20.6
Bruce Bennett (D)	65,095	15.7
Frank Whitbeck (D)	61,758	14.9

Democratic Runoff

Marion Crank (D)	215,087	63.3
Virginia Johnson (D)	124,880	36.7

1970 ## Republican Primary

Winthrop Rockefeller (R)	58,197	96.8

Democratic Primary

Orval E. Faubus (D)	156,578	36.4
Dale Bumpers (D)	86,156	20.0
Joe Purcell (D)	81,566	18.9
Hayes C. McClerkin (D)	45,011	10.5
Bill Wells (D)	32,543	7.6

Democratic Runoff

Dale Bumpers (D)	259,780	58.7
Orval E. Faubus (D)	182,732	41.3

1972 ## Republican Primary

Len E. Blaylock (R)		100.0

Democratic Primary

Dale Bumpers (D)	330,088	66.7
Q. Byrum Hurst (D)	81,239	16.4
Mack Harbour (D)	55,172	11.2

1974 ## Republican Primary

Ken Coon (R)	3,698	81.9
Joseph Weston (R)	815	18.1

Democratic Primary

David Pryor (D)	297,673	51.0
Orval E. Faubus (D)	193,105	33.1
Bob Riley (D)	92,612	15.9

1976 ## Republican Primary

Leon Griffith (R)	13,044	57.2
Joseph Weston (R)	9,753	42.8

Democratic Primary

David Pryor (D)	312,865	59.5
Jim Lindsey (D)	171,031	32.5
Frank Lady (D)	36,832	7.0

1978 ## Republican Primary

A. Lynn Lowe (R)		100.0

Democratic Primary

Bill Clinton (D)	341,118	59.7
Joe D. Woodward (D)	123,674	21.6
Frank Lady (D)	76,026	13.1

1980 ## Republican Primary

Frank D. White (R)	5,867	71.8
Marshall Chrisman (R)	2,310	28.2

Democratic Primary

Bill Clinton (D)	306,735	68.9
Monroe A. Schwarzlose (D)	138,660	31.1

1982 ## Republican Primary

Frank D. White (R)	11,111	83.2
Marshall Chrisman (R)	1,410	10.6
Connie Voll (R)	826	6.2

Democratic Primary

Bill Clinton (D)	236,961	41.8
Joe Purcell (D)	166,066	29.3
Jim Guy Tucker (D)	129,362	22.8

Democratic Runoff

Bill Clinton (D)	239,209	53.7
Joe Purcell (D)	206,358	46.3

1984 ## Republican Primary

Woody Freeman (R)	13,030	68.4
Erwin Davis (R)	6,010	31.2

Democratic Primary

Bill Clinton (D)	317,577	64.4
Lonnie Turner (D)	119,266	24.2
Kermit Moss (D)	31,727	6.4

1986 ## Republican Primary

Frank D. White (R)	13,831	61.9
Wayne Lanier (R)	4,576	20.5
Maurice Britt (R)	3,116	13.9

Democratic Primary

Bill Clinton (D)	315,397	60.6
Orval E. Faubus (D)	174,402	33.5
Dean Goldsby (D)	30,829	5.9

1990 ## Republican Primary

Sheffield Nelson (R)	47,246	54.3
Tommy F. Robinson (R)	39,731	45.7

Democratic Primary

Bill Clinton (D)	269,329	54.8
Tom McRae (D)	190,887	38.9

1994 ## Republican Primary

Sheffield Nelson (R)	24,054	50.8
Steve Luelf (R)	20,953	44.2
William L. Jones (R)	2,346	5.0

1998 ## Republican Primary

Mike Huckabee (R)	51,627	90.2
Gene McVay (R)	5,581	9.8

Democratic Primary

Bill Bristow (D)		100.0

Arkansas
1. Sims withdrew from a runoff, and Laney became the Democratic nominee.

CALIFORNIA

Candidates	Votes	%

1958 ## Republican Primary

William F. Knowland (R)	1,290,106	77.5
Edmund G. Brown (D)	374,879	22.5

Democratic Primary

Edmund G. Brown (D)	1,890,622	82.6
William F. Knowland (R)	313,385	13.7

1962 ## Republican Primary

Richard M. Nixon (R)	1,285,151	65.4
Joseph C. Shell (R)	656,542	33.4

Democratic Primary

Edmund G. Brown (D)	1,739,792	81.4

Prohibition Primary

Robert L. Wyckoff		100.0

1966 ## Republican Primary

Ronald Reagan (R)	1,417,623	64.7
George Christopher (R)	675,683	30.8

Democratic Primary

Edmund G. Brown (D)	1,355,262	51.9
Samuel W. Yorty (D)	981,088	37.6

1970 ## Republican Primary

Ronald Reagan (R)		100.0

Democratic Primary

Jess Unruh (D)	1,602,690	64.0
Samuel W. Yorty (D)	659,494	26.3

American Independent Primary

William K. Shearer (AMI)	14,069	61.4
Keith H. Greene (AMI)	8,827	38.5

Peace and Freedom Primary

Ricardo Romo (PFP)	6,214	63.5
Warren A. Nielsen (PFP)	3,569	36.5

1974 ## Republican Primary

Houston I. Flournoy (R)	1,164,015	63.0
Ed Reinecke (R)	556,259	30.1

Democratic Primary

Edmund G. Brown Jr. (D)	1,085,752	37.7
Joseph L. Alioto (D)	544,007	18.9
Robert Moretti (D)	478,469	16.6
William M. Roth (D)	293,686	10.2
Jerome R. Waldie (D)	227,489	7.9

American Independent Primary

Edmon V. Kaiser (AMI)		100.0

Peace and Freedom Primary

Elizabeth Keathley (PFP)	2,111	28.1
Lester H. Higby (PFP)	1,855	24.7
C. T. Weber (PFP)	1,822	24.2
Trudy Saposhnek (PFP)	1,417	18.8

1978 ## Republican Primary

Evelle J. Younger (R)	1,008,087	40.0
Ed Davis (R)	738,741	29.3
Ken Maddy (R)	484,583	19.2
Pete Wilson (R)	230,146	9.1

Democratic Primary

Edmund G. Brown Jr. (D)	2,567,067	77.5

American Independent Primary

Theresa F. Dietrich (AMI)	12,278	57.4
Laszlo Kecskemethy (AMI)	9,112	42.6

Peace and Freedom Primary

Marilyn Seals (PFP)		100.0

1982 ## Republican Primary

George Deukmejian (R)	1,165,266	51.
Mike Curb (R)	1,020,935	44.

Democratic Primary

Stephen McNichols (D)		100.0

1958   **Republican Primary**

Palmer L. Burch (R)		100.0

Democratic Primary

Stephen McNichols (D)		100.0

1962   **Republican Primary**

John A. Love (R)	66,027	59.6
David A. Hamil (R)	44,693	40.4

Democratic Primary

Stephen McNichols (D)		100.0

1966   **Republican Primary**

John A. Love (R)		100.0

Democratic Primary

Robert L. Knous (D)		100.0

1970   **Republican Primary**

John A. Love (R)		100.0

Democratic Primary

Mark Hogan (D)		100.0

1974   **Republican Primary**

John D. Vanderhoof (R)	94,334	60.5
Robert W. Daniels (R)	61,691	39.5

Democratic Primary

Richard D. Lamm (D)	120,452	58.7
Thomas Farley (D)	84,796	41.3

1978   **Republican Primary**

Ted Strickland (R)	87,248	59.0
Richard Plock (R)	60,597	41.0

Democratic Primary

Richard D. Lamm (D)		100.0

1982   **Republican Primary**

John D. Fuhr (R)		100.0

Democratic Primary

Richard D. Lamm (D)		100.0

1986   **Republican Primary**

Ted Strickland (R)	66,796	35.6
Steve Schuck (R)	64,245	34.2
Bob Kirscht (R)	56,779	30.2

Democratic Primary

Roy Romer (D)		100.0

1990   **Republican Primary**

John Andrews (R)		100.0

Democratic Primary

Roy Romer (D)		100.0

1994   **Republican Primary**

Bruce Benson (R)	109,462	61.2
Michael C. Bird (R)	38,571	21.6
Dick Sargent (R)	30,326	17.0

Democratic Primary

Roy Romer (D)	61,686	100.0

1998   **Republican Primary**

Bill Owens (R)	126,613	59.2
Tom Norton (R)	87,269	40.8

Democratic Primary

Gail Schoettler (D)	79,607	55.3
Mike Feeley (D)	64,466	44.7

CONNECTICUT[1]

Candidates	Votes	%
1970 **Republican Primary**		
Thomas J. Meskill (R)	93,419	71.4
Wallace Barnes (R)	37,383	28.6
1978 **Democratic Primary**		
Ella T. Grasso (D)	137,904	67.3
Robert K. Killian (D)	66,924	32.7
1986 **Republican Primary**		
Julie D. Belaga (R)	39,074	41.3
Richard C. Bozzuto (R)	33,852	35.8
Gerald Labriola (R)	21,610	22.9
1990 **Democratic Primary**		
Bruce A. Morrison (D)	84,771	64.7
William J. Cibes (D)	46,294	35.3
1994 **Republican Primary**		
John G. Rowland (R)	78,051	67.8
Pauline R. Kezer (R)	37,010	32.2
Democratic Primary		
Bill Curry (D)	93,241	54.7
John B. Larson (D)	77,165	45.3

Connecticut

1. In Connecticut, party conventions nominated candidates subject to a system of "challenge" primaries that allowed defeated candidates to petition for a popular vote if they received at least 20 percent of the convention vote. Returns are given here for challenge primaries held for the governorship nomination between 1956 and 1990.

DELAWARE[1]

	Candidates	Votes	%
1972	**Republican Primary**		
	Russell W. Peterson (R)	23,929	54.3
	David P. Buckson (R)	20,138	45.7
1980	**Republican Primary**		
	Pierre S. "Pete" du Pont IV (R)		100.0
	Democratic Primary		
	William J. Gordy (D)		100.0
1984	**Republican Primary**		
	Michael N. Castle (R)		100.0
	Democratic Primary		
	William T. Quillen (D)	20,473	59.1
	Sherman W. Tribbitt (D)	14,185	40.9
1988	**Republican Primary**		
	Michael N. Castle (R)		100.0
	Democratic Primary		
	Jacob Kreshtool (D)		100.0
1992	**Republican Primary**		
	B. Gary Scott (R)	23,994	81.8
	Wilfred Plomis (R)	5,346	18.2
	Democratic Primary		
	Thomas R. Carper (D)	36,600	89.2
	Daniel D. Rappa (D)	4,434	10.8
1996	**Republican Primary**		
	Janet C. Rzewnicki (R)		100.0
	Democratic Primary		
	Thomas R. Carper (D)		100.0
2000	**Republican Primary**		
	John M. Burris (R)	13,893	50.1
	William Swain Lee (R)	13,847	49.9
	Democratic Primary		
	Ruth Ann Minner (D)		100.0

Delaware

1. From 1972 through 1992 Delaware used a system of "challenge" primaries, in which a candidate for statewide office who received at least 35 percent of the convention vote could challenge the endorsed candidate in a primary.

FLORIDA

	Candidates	Votes	%
1920	**Democratic Primary**		
	Cary E. Hardee (D)	52,591	59.5
	V. C. Swearingen (D)	30,240	34.2
	Lincoln Hulley (D)	5,591	6.3
	Democratic Second Choice		
	Cary A. Hardee (D)	1,559	51.7
	V. C. Swearingen (D)	1,459	48.3
1924	**Democratic Primary**		
	John W. Martin (D)	55,715 ✔	38.0
	Sidney J. Catts (D)	43,230	29.5
	Frank E. Jennings (D)	37,962	25.9
	Worth W. Trammell (D)	8,381	5.7
	Democratic Second Choice		
	John W. Martin (D)	17,339	74.1
	Sidney J. Catts (D)	6,067	25.9
1928	**Democratic Primary**		
	Doyle E. Carlton (D)	77,569 ✔	30.4
	Sidney J. Catts (D)	68,984	27.1
	Fons A. Hathaway (D)	67,849	26.6
	John S. Taylor (D)	37,304	14.6
	Democratic Second Choice		
	Doyle E. Carlton (D)	28,471	75.9
	Sidney J. Catts (D)	9,066	24.2
1932	**Democratic Primary**		
	John W. Martin (D)	66,940	24.2
	David Sholtz (D)	55,406	20.0
	Cary A. Hardee (D)	50,427	18.2
	Stafford Caldwell (D)	44,938	16.2
	Charles M. Durrance (D)	36,291	13.1
	Democratic Runoff		
	David Sholtz (D)	173,540	62.8
	John W. Martin (D)	102,805	37.2
1936	**Democratic Primary**		
	Raleigh Pettaway (D)	51,705	15.7
	Fred P. Cone (D)	46,842	14.3
	William C. Hodges (D)	46,471	14.1
	Jerry W. Carter (D)	35,578	10.8
	B. F. Paty (D)	34,153	10.4
	Dan Chappell (D)	29,494	9.0
	Grady Burton (D)	24,985	7.6
	Peter Thomasello Jr. (D)	22,355	6.8
	Stafford Caldwell (D)	19,789	6.0
	Democratic Runoff		
	Fred P. Cone (D)	184,540	58.8
	Raleigh Pettaway (D)	129,150	41.2
1940	**Democratic Primary**		
	Spessard L. Holland (D)	118,962	24.7
	Francis P. Whitehair (D)	95,431	19.8

	Fuller Warren (D)	83,316	*17.3*
	B. F. Paty (D)	75,608	*15.7*
	W. B. Fraser (D)	36,855	*7.7*
	James Barbee (D)	33,699	*7.0*

Democratic Runoff

Spessard L. Holland (D)	272,718	*57.0*
Francis P. Whitehair (D)	206,158	*43.1*

1944   Republican Primary

Bert L. Acker (R)	5,954	*61.3*
Edward T. Keenan (R)	3,766	*38.7*

Democratic Primary

Millard F. Caldwell (D)	116,111	*28.6*
Robert A. "Lex" Green (D)	113,300	*27.9*
E. R. Graham (D)	91,174	*22.5*
F. D. Upchurch (D)	30,524	*7.5*
Raymond Sheldon (D)	27,940	*6.9*
J. Edwin Baker (D)	27,028	*6.6*

Democratic Runoff

Millard F. Caldwell (D)	215,485	*55.3*
Robert A. "Lex" Green (D)	174,100	*44.7*

1948   Republican Primary

Bert L. Acker (R)	10,807	*64.0*
John L. Cogdill (R)	6,079	*36.0*

Democratic Primary

Fuller Warren (D)	183,326	*32.7*
Daniel T. McCarty (D)	161,788	*28.9*
Colin English (D)	85,158	*15.2*
W. A. Shands (D)	62,358	*11.1*
J. Tom Watson (D)	51,505	*9.2*

Democratic Runoff

Fuller Warren (D)	299,641	*52.0*
Daniel T. McCarty (D)	276,425	*48.0*

1952   Republican Primary[1]

Harry S. Swan (R)	11,148	*43.0*
Bert L. Acker (R)	9,728	*37.5*
Elmore F. Kitzmiller (R)	5,050	*19.5*

Republican Runoff

Harry S. Swan (R)	10,217	*63.0*
Bert L. Acker (R)	5,995	*37.0*

Democratic Primary

Daniel T. McCarty (D)	316,427	*48.9*
Brailey Odham (D)	232,565	*31.5*
Alto Adams (D)	126,426	*17.1*

Democratic Runoff

Daniel T. McCarty (D)	384,200	*53.3*
Brailey Odham (D)	336,716	*46.7*

1954[1]   Republican Special Primary

J. Tom Watson (R)	24,429	*68.0*
Charles E. Compton (R)	11,552	*32.0*

Democratic Special Primary

Charley E. Johns (D)	255,787	*38.4*
Leroy Collins (D)	222,791	*33.4*
Brailey Odham (D)	187,782	*28.2*

Democratic Special Runoff

Leroy Collins (D)	380,323	*54.8*
Charley E. Johns (D)	314,198	*45.2*

1956   Republican Primary

W. A. Washburn Jr. (R)		*100.0*

Democratic Primary

Leroy Collins (D)	434,274	*51.7*
Sumter L. Lowery (D)	179,019	*21.3*
Farris Bryant (D)	110,469	*13.2*
Fuller Warren (D)	107,990	*12.9*

1960   Republican Primary

George C. Peterson (R)	65,202	*72.7*
Emerson H. Rupert (R)	24,484	*27.3*

Democratic Primary

Farris Bryant (D)	193,507	*20.7*
Doyle E. Carlton Jr. (D)	186,228	*19.9*
Haydon Burns (D)	166,352	*17.8*
John M. McCarty (D)	144,750	*15.5*
Fred Dickinson (D)	115,520	*12.3*
Thomas E. David (D)	80,057	*8.5*

Democratic Runoff

Farris Bryant (D)	512,757	*55.2*
Doyle E. Carlton Jr. (D)	416,052	*44.8*

1964   Republican Primary

Charles R. Holley (R)	70,573	*53.9*
H. B. Foster (R)	33,563	*25.6*
Ken Folks (R)	26,815	*20.5*

Democratic Primary

Haydon Burns (D)	312,453	*27.5*
Robert King High (D)	207,280	*18.3*
Scott Kelly (D)	205,078	*18.1*
Fred Dickinson (D)	184,865	*16.3*
John E. Mathews (D)	140,210	*12.3*
Frederick B. Karl (D)	85,953	*7.6*

Democratic Runoff

Haydon Burns (D)	648,093	*58.2*
Robert King High (D)	465,547	*41.8*

1966   **Republican Primary**

Claude R. Kirk Jr. (R)	100,838	*80.8*
Richard B. Muldrew (R)	23,953	*19.2*

Democratic Primary

Haydon Burns (D)	372,451	*35.4*
Robert King High (D)	338,281	*32.1*
Scott Kelly (D)	331,580	*31.5*

Democratic Runoff

Robert King High (D)	596,471	*53.9*
Haydon Burns (D)	509,271	*46.1*

1970   **Republican Primary**

Claude R. Kirk Jr. (R)	172,888	*48.1*
Jack M. Eckerd (R)	137,731	*38.4*
L. A. "Skip" Bafalis (R)	48,378	*13.5*

Republican Runoff

Claude R. Kirk Jr. (R)	199,943	*56.8*
Jack M. Eckerd (R)	152,327	*43.2*

Democratic Primary

Earl Faircloth (D)	227,413	*30.0*
Reubin Askew (D)	206,333	*27.2*
John E. Matthews (D)	186,053	*24.5*
Chuck Hall (D)	139,384	*18.4*

Democratic Runoff

Reubin Askew (D)	447,025	*57.7*
Earl Faircloth (D)	328,038	*42.3*

1974   **Republican Primary**

Jerry Thomas (R)		*100.0*

Democratic Primary

Reubin Askew (D)	597,137	*68.8*
Ben Hill Griffin (D)	137,008	*16.3*
Tom Adams (D)	85,557	*10.2*

1978   **Republican Primary**

Jack M. Eckerd (R)	244,394	*63.8*
Louis Frey (R)	138,437	*36.2*

Democratic Primary

Robert L. Shevin (D)	364,732	*35.2*
Bob Graham (D)	261,972	*25.2*
Hans G. Tanzler (D)	124,706	*12.0*
Jim Williams (D)	124,427	*12.0*
Bruce A. Smathers (D)	85,298	*8.2*
Claude R. Kirk Jr. (D)	62,534	*6.0*

Democratic Runoff

Bob Graham (D)	482,535	*53.5*
Robert L. Shevin (D)	418,636	*46.5*

1982   **Republican Primary**

L. A. "Skip" Bafalis (R)	325,108	*86.4*
Vernon Davids (R)	51,340	*13.6*

Democratic Primary

Bob Graham (D)	839,320	*84.5*
Fred Kuhn (D)	93,078	*9.4*
Robert P. Kunst (D)	61,136	*6.2*

1986   **Republican Primary**

Bob Martinez (R)	244,499	*44.1*
Louis Frey (R)	138,017	*24.9*
Tom Gallagher (R)	127,709	*23.0*
Chester Clem (R)	44,438	*8.0*

Republican Runoff

Bob Martinez (R)	259,333	*66.3*
Louis Frey (R)	131,652	*33.7*

Democratic Primary

Steve Pajcic (D)	361,359	*35.9*
Jim Smith (D)	310,479	*30.8*
Harry Johnston (D)	258,038	*25.6*
Mark K. Goldstein (D)	54,077	*5.4*

Democratic Runoff

Steve Pajcic (D)	429,427	*50.6*
Jim Smith (D)	418,614	*49.4*

1990   **Republican Primary**

Bob Martinez (R)	460,718	*69.0*
Marlene Howard (R)	132,565	*19.8*
John Davis (R)	34,720	*5.2*

Democratic Primary

Lawton Chiles (D)	746,325	*69.5*
Bill Nelson (D)	327,731	*30.5*

1994   **Republican Primary**

John Ellis "Jeb" Bush (R)	411,680	*45.7*
Jim Smith (R)	165,869	*18.4*
Tom Gallagher (R)	117,067	*13.0*
Ander Crenshaw (R)	109,148	*12.1*
Kenneth L. Connor (R)	83,945	*9.3*

Democratic Primary

Lawton Chiles (D)	603,657	*72.2*
Jack Gargan (D)	232,757	*27.8*

1998   **Republican Primary**

John Ellis "Jeb" Bush (R)		*100.0*

Democratic Primary

Kenneth H. "Buddy" MacKay (D)		*100.0*

Florida

1. Returns from *Florida Handbook, 1975–76*, p. 534.

HAWAII

Candidates	Votes	%
1959 Republican Primary		
William F. Quinn (R)		100.0
Democratic Primary		
John A. Burns (D)	69,152	89.8
E. D. Hitchcock (D)	7,828	10.2
Commonwealth Primary		
David Kihei (CP)	65	64.4
Epifanio Taok (CP)	36	35.6
1962 Republican Primary		
William F. Quinn (R)	44,205	57.1
James K. Kealoha (R)	33,272	49.9
Democratic Primary		
John A. Burns (D)	71,540	90.2
Hyman Greenstein (D)	7,781	9.8
1966 Republican Primary		
Randolph Crossley (R)	35,311	98.1
Democratic Primary		
John A. Burns (D)	86,825	79.5
G. J. Fontes (D)	22,401	20.5
1970 Republican Primary		
Samuel P. King (R)	20,605	49.3
Hebden Porteus (R)	17,880	42.8
David Watumull (R)	3,318	7.9
Democratic Primary		
John A. Burns (D)	82,441	53.2
Thomas P. Gill (D)	69,209	44.7
1974 Republican Primary		
Randolph Crossley (R)	25,425	82.5
Joseph K. Hao (R)	5,405	17.5
Democratic Primary		
George R. Ariyoshi (D)	71,319	36.2
Frank F. Fasi (D)	62,023	31.5
Thomas P. Gill (D)	59,280	30.1
1978 Republican Primary		
John Leopold (R)	20,524	91.6
Democratic Primary		
George R. Ariyoshi (D)	130,527	50.3
Frank F. Fasi (D)	126,903	48.9
Aloha Democrat Primary		
John Moore (A-D)		100.0

Candidates	Votes	%
Libertarian Primary		
Gregory Reeser (LIBERT)		100.0
Non Partisan Primary		
Alema Leota (NON PART)	236	58.9
Frank Pore (NON PART)	165	41.1
1982 Republican Primary		
D. G. Anderson (R)	11,997	96.8
Democratic Primary		
George R. Ariyoshi (D)	128,993	53.9
Jean King (D)	106,935	44.7
Independent Democratic Primary		
Frank F. Fasi (ID)		100.0
Non Partisan Primary		
BraDa Ji Price (NON PART)[1]		100.0
1986 Republican Primary		
D. G. Anderson (R)	38,790	94.6
Democratic Primary		
John Waihee (D)	105,579	45.6
Cecil Heftel (D)	83,939	36.2
Patsy T. Mink (D)	37,998	16.4
1990 Republican Primary		
Fred Hemmings (R)	38,827	90.1
Democratic Primary		
John Waihee (D)	179,383	88.5
Libertarian Primary		
Triaka-Don Smith (LIBERT)		100.0
1994 Republican Primary		
Patricia F. Saiki (R)	49,953	85.7
Democratic Primary		
Benjamin J. Cayetano (D)	110,782	52.2
John Lewin (D)	76,666	36.1
Libertarian Primary		
George Peabody (LIBERT)	312	63.2
Green Primary		
Michael Kioni Dudley (GREEN)	753	30.5
Edwina A. Wong (GREEN)	637	25.8
Gregory Goodwin (GREEN)	391	15.9
Best Primary		
Frank F. Fasi (BP)	30,879	95.3

1998 **Republican Primary**

Linda Lingle (R)	109,061	*69.2*
Frank F. Fasi (R)	48,488	*30.8*

Democratic Primary

Benjamin J. Cayetano (D)	95,797	*86.4*
Jim Brewer (D)	6,169	*5.6*

Libertarian Primary

George Peabody (LIBERT)	300	*88.5*

Hawaii
1. Price withdrew and no substitution was made.

IDAHO

Candidates	Votes	%

1958 **Republican Primary**

Robert E. Smylie (R)		*100.0*

Democratic Primary

A. M. Derr (D)	25,599	*34.5*
H. Max Hanson (D)	25,477	*34.3*
John Glasby (D)	21,207	*28.6*

1962 **Republican Primary**

Robert E. Smylie (R)	37,761	*57.2*
Elvin A. Lindquist (R)	16,565	*25.1*
George L. Crookham (R)	11,669	*17.7*

Democratic Primary

Vernon K. Smith (D)	35,574	*43.1*
Charles Herndon (D)	18,072	*21.9*
John G. Walters (D)	13,186	*16.0*
Howard D. Hechtner (D)	7,952	*9.6*
Conley Ward (D)	5,427	*6.6*

1966 **Republican Primary**

Don Samuelson (R)	52,891	*61.0*
Robert E. Smylie (R)	33,753	*39.0*

Democratic Primary

Charles Herndon (D)[1]	28,926	*40.7*
Cecil D. Andrus (D)	27,649	*39.0*
William J. Dee (D)	14,409	*20.3*

1970 **Republican Primary**

Don Samuelson (R)	46,719	*58.4*
Dick Smith (R)	33,339	*41.6*

Democratic Primary

Cecil D. Andrus (D)	29,036	*46.0*
Vernon Ravenscroft (D)	23,369	*37.1*
Lloyd Walker (D)	10,664	*16.9*

1974 **Republican Primary**

Jack M. Murphy (R)		*100.0*

Democratic Primary

Cecil D. Andrus (D)		*100.0*

1978 **Republican Primary**

Allan Larsen (R)	33,778	*28.7*
Vernon Ravenscroft (D)	32,455	*27.6*
C. L. Otter (R)	30,523	*26.0*
Larry Jackson (R)	13,510	*11.5*

Democratic Primary

John V. Evans (D)		*100.0*

American Primary

Wayne L. Loveless (AM)		*100.0*

1982 **Republican Primary**

Phillip Batt (R)	63,622	*63.9*
Ralph Olmstead (R)	35,932	*36.1*

Democratic Primary

John V. Evans (D)		*100.0*

1986 **Republican Primary**

David H. Leroy (R)		*100.0*

Democratic Primary

Cecil D. Andrus (D)		*100.0*

1990 **Republican Primary**

Roger Fairchild (R)	37,728	*37.1*
Rachel S. Gilbert (R)	33,483	*32.9*
Milton E. Erhart (R)	30,514	*30.0*

Democratic Primary

Cecil D. Andrus (D)		*100.0*

1994 **Republican Primary**

Phil Batt (R)	57,066	*48.0*
Larry Eastland (R)	38,664	*32.5*
Charles L. Winder (R)	16,063	*13.5*
Doug Dorn (R)	7,098	*6.0*

Democratic Primary

Larry EchoHawk (D)	42,661	*73.8*
Ron Beitelspacher (D)	12,377	*21.4*

1998 **Republican Primary**

Dirk Kempthorne (R)	111,658	*87.2*
David Shepherd (R)	16,332	*12.8*

Democratic Primary

Robert C. Huntley (D)	14,638	*54.3*
William G. Tamasky (D)	4,769	*17.7*
Jack Wayne Chappell (D)	4,666	*17.3*
Donald McMurrian (D)	2,900	*10.8*

Idaho
1. Herndon died after the primary and the Democratic state central committee substituted Andrus as the nominee.

ILLINOIS

Candidates	Votes	%
1956 **Republican Primary**		
William G. Stratton (R)	556,909	69.8
Warren E. Wright (R)	187,645	23.5
Democratic Primary		
Herbert C. Paschen (D)[1]	475,813	57.8
Morris B. Sachs (D)	347,458	42.2
1960 **Republican Primary**		
William G. Stratton (R)	499,365	59.1
Hayes Robertson (R)	345,340	40.9
Democratic Primary		
Otto Kerner (D)	649,253	60.9
Joseph D. Lohman (D)	232,345	21.8
Stephen A. Mitchell (D)	184,651	17.3
1964 **Republican Primary**		
Charles H. Percy (R)	626,111	60.3
William J. Scott (R)	388,903	37.4
Democratic Primary		
Otto Kerner (D)		100.0
1968 **Republican Primary**		
Richard B. Ogilvie (R)	335,727	47.5
John H. Altofer (R)	288,904	40.9
William G. Stratton (R)	50,041	7.1
Democratic Primary		
Samuel H. Shapiro (D)		100.0
1972 **Republican Primary**		
Richard B. Ogilvie (R)	442,323	75.5
John Mathis (D)	143,053	24.4
Democratic Primary		
Daniel Walker (D)	735,193	51.4
Paul Simon (D)	694,900	48.6
1976 **Republican Primary**		
James R. Thompson (R)	625,457	86.4
Richard H. Cooper (R)	97,937	13.5
Democratic Primary		
Michael J. Howlett (D)	811,721	53.8
Daniel Walker (D)	696,380	46.2
1978 **Republican Primary**		
James R. Thompson (R)		100.0
Democratic Primary		
Michael Bakalis (D)	601,045	82.8
W. Dakin Williams (D)	124,406	17.2

Candidates	Votes	%
1982 **Republican Primary**		
James R. Thompson (R)	507,893	83.7
John E. Roche (R)	54,858	9.0
V. A. Kelley (R)	43,627	7.2
Democratic Primary		
Adlai E. Stevenson III (D)		100.0
1986 **Republican Primary**		
James R. Thompson (R)	452,685	90.9
Peter Bowen (R)	45,236	9.1
Democratic Primary		
Adlai E. Stevenson III (D)[2]	735,249	92.9
Larry Burgess (D)	55,930	7.1
1990 **Republican Primary**		
Jim Edgar (R)	482,441	62.8
Steven Baer (R)	256,889	33.5
Democratic Primary		
Neil F. Hartigan (D)		100.0
1994 **Republican Primary**		
Jim Edgar (R)	521,590	75.0
Jack Roeser (R)	173,742	25.0
Democratic Primary		
Dawn C. Netsch (D)	487,364	44.3
Roland W. Burris (D)	401,142	36.5
Richard Phelan (D)	160,576	14.6
1998 **Republican Primary**		
George H. Ryan (R)	608,940	86.1
Chad Koppie (R)	98,466	13.9
Democratic Primary		
Glenn W. Poshard (D)	357,342	37.6
Roland W. Burris (D)	290,393	30.6
John R. Schmidt (D)	236,309	24.9
Jim Burns (D)	55,233	5.8

Illinois

1. Paschen withdrew after the primary and the Democratic state committee substituted Richard B. Austin as the party's nominee.

2. Stevenson withdrew after the primary on the ground that the nominated candidate for lieutenant governor was a known supporter of Lyndon LaRouche, whose views were so different from Stevenson's as to make a joint candidacy impossible. No replacement candidate was named by the Democratic party. A new party, Illinois Solidarity, was formed with Stevenson as its gubernatorial candidate.

INDIANA

Candidates	Votes	%
1976[1] **Republican Primary**		
Otis R. Bowen (R)		100.0

Democratic Primary

Larry A. Conrad (D)	358,421	64.5
Jack L. New (D)	105,965	19.1
Robert J. Fair (D)	91,606	16.5

1980   Republican Primary

Robert D. Orr (R)		100.0

Democratic Primary

John A. Hillenbrand (D)	284,182	52.4
W. Wayne Townsend (D)	257,779	47.6

1984   Republican Primary

Robert D. Orr (R)	319,889	71.6
John Snyder (R)	126,778	28.4

Democratic Primary

W. Wayne Townsend (D)	347,948	56.9
Virginia Dill McCarty (D)	219,806	35.9
Donald W. Mantooth (D)	43,507	7.1

1988   Republican Primary

John M. Mutz (R)		100.0

Democratic Primary

Evan Bayh (D)	493,198	83.1
Stephen J. Daily (D)	66,242	11.2
Frank L. O'Bannon (D)	34,360	5.8

1992   Republican Primary

Linley E. Pearson (R)	223,373	48.9
H. Dean Evans (R)	153,089	33.5
John A. Johnson (R)	80,784	17.7

Democratic Primary

Evan Bayh (D)	390,938	100.0

1996   Republican Primary

Stephen Goldsmith (R)	298,532	54.1
Rex Early (R)	204,301	37.0
George Witwer (R)	48,749	8.8

Democratic Primary

Frank O'Bannon (D)	305,589	100.0

2000   Republican Primary

David McIntosh (R)	279,920	71.0
John Price (R)	114,580	29.0

Democratic Primary

Frank O'Bannon (D)	272,213	100.0

Indiana

1. Until 1976 all nominations for statewide office in Indiana were made by state party conventions.

IOWA

Candidates	Votes	%
1956 Republican Primary		
Leo A. Hoegh (R)		100.0
Democratic Primary		
Herschel C. Loveless (D)	77,206	70.0
Lawrence E. Plummer (D)	33,103	30.0
1958 Republican Primary		
William G. Murray (R)	112,496	56.6
W. H. Nicholas (R)	86,154	43.4
Democratic Primary		
Herschel C. Loveless (D)		100.0
1960 Republican Primary		
Norman A. Erbe (R)	81,869	36.3
Jack Schroeder (R)	75,599	33.5
W. H. Nicholas (R)	68,037	30.2
Democratic Primary		
E. J. McManus (D)	74,990	61.7
Harold E. Hughes (D)	46,542	38.3
1962 Republican Primary		
Norman A. Erbe (R)	134,010	67.7
W. H. Nicholas (R)	63,966	32.3
Democratic Primary		
Harold E. Hughes (D)	66,624	78.9
Lewis E. Lint (D)	17,770	21.1
1964 Republican Primary		
Evan Hultman (R)		100.0
Democratic Primary		
Harold E. Hughes (D)		100.0
1966 Republican Primary		
William G. Murray (R)	87,371	50.5
Robert K. Beck (R)	85,733	49.5
Democratic Primary		
Harold E. Hughes (D)		100.0
1968 Republican Primary		
Robert Ray (R)	108,744	43.2
Donald E. Johnson (R)	77,715	30.8
Robert K. Beck (R)	65,439	26.0
Democratic Primary		
Paul Franzenburg		100.0
1970 Republican Primary		
Robert Ray (R)		100.0

Democratic Primary

Robert Fulton (D)	48,459	46.7
William Gannon (D)	46,524	44.8
Robert L. Nereim (D)	8,796	8.5

1972   Republican Primary

Robert Ray (R)		100.0

Democratic Primary

Paul Franzenburg (D)	85,807	57.5
John Tapscott (D)	63,284	42.4

American Independent Primary

Robert D. Dilley (AMI)		100.0

1974   Republican Primary

Robert Ray (R)		100.0

Democratic Primary

James F. Schaben (D)	59,840	44.8
William Gannon (D)	52,420	39.3
Clark Rasmussen (D)	21,240	15.9

1978   Republican Primary

Robert Ray (R)	136,517	87.5
Donovan D. Nelson (R)	19,486	12.5

Democratic Primary

Jerome D. Fitzgerald (D)	58,039	55.5
Tom Whitney (D)	37,132	35.5
Warren D. Strait (D)	9,443	9.0

1982   Republican Primary

Terry Branstad (R)		100.0

Democratic Primary

Roxanne Conlin (D)	94,481	48.2
Jerome D. Fitzgerald (D)	61,340	31.3
Edward L. Campbell (D)	40,233	20.5

1986   Republican Primary

Terry E. Branstad (R)		100.0

Democratic Primary

Lowell L. Junkins (D)	70,605	52.6
Bob Anderson (D)	44,550	33.2
George R. Kinley (D)	15,473	11.5

1990   Republican Primary

Terry E. Branstad (R)		100.0

Democratic Primary

Donald D. Avenson (D)	79,022	39.5
Tom Miller (D)	63,364	31.6
John Chrystal (D)	52,170	26.0

1994   Republican Primary

Terry E. Branstad (R)	161,228	51.8
Fred Grandy (R)	149,809	48.1

Democratic Primary

Bonnie J. Campbell (D)	99,718	77.7
William J. Reichardt (D)	24,630	19.2

1998   Republican Primary

Jim Ross Lightfoot (R)	113,499	69.9
David A. Oman (R)	35,402	21.8
Paul D. Pate (R)	13,299	8.2

Democratic Primary

Tom Vilsack (D)	59,130	51.2
Mark McCormick (D)	55,950	48.4

KANSAS

Candidates	Votes	%

1956   Republican Primary

Warren W. Shaw (R)	156,476	52.7
Fred Hall (R)	123,398	41.5

Democratic Primary

George Docking (D)	76,544	50.3
Harry H. Woodring (D)	75,548	49.7

1958   Republican Primary

Clyde M. Reed (R)	142,247	72.6
Fred Hall (R)	35,632	18.2

Democratic Primary

George Docking (D)		100.0

1960   Republican Primary

John Anderson (R)	128,081	48.7
McDill Boyd (R)	116,725	44.4
William H. Addington (R)	18,169	6.9

Democratic Primary

George Docking (D)		100.0

1962   Republican Primary

John Anderson (R)	164,888	84.1
Harvey F. Crouch (R)	31,221	15.9

Democratic Primary

Dale E. Saffels (D)	69,728	59.7
George Hart (D)	47,055	40.3

1964   Republican Primary

William H. Avery (R)	85,746	30.4
McDill Boyd (R)	75,451	26.7
Paul R. Wunsch (R)	71,601	25.4
William M. Ferguson (R)	36,622	13.0

Democratic Primary

Harry G. Wiles (D)	50,590	32.4
Jules V. Doty (D)	37,305	23.9
George Hart (D)	30,973	19.8
Joseph W. Henkle (D)	21,304	13.6
J. Donald Coffin (D)	9,140	5.9

1966   Republican Primary

William H. Avery (R)	144,842	75.1
Dell Crozier (R)	48,051	24.9

Democratic Primary

Robert Docking (D)	96,414	85.5
George Hart (D)	16,385	14.5

1968   Republican Primary

Rick Harman (R)	133,454	48.9
John Crutcher (R)	128,635	47.1

Democratic Primary

Robert Docking (D)		100.0

1970   Republican Primary

Kent Frizzell (R)	141,298	60.5
Rick Harman (R)	78,086	33.4

Democratic Primary

Robert Docking (D)		100.0

1972   Republican Primary

Morris Kay (R)	138,815	46.6
John Anderson (R)	88,088	29.6
Ray E. Frisbie (R)	46,125	15.5
Reynolds Shultz (R)	24,911	8.4

Democratic Primary

Robert Docking (D)		100.0

1974   Republican Primary

Robert F. Bennett (R)	67,347	32.4
Donald O. Concannon (R)	66,817	32.1
Forrest J. Robinson (R)	56,440	27.2
Robert W. Clack (R)	17,333	8.3

Democratic Primary

Vern Miller (D)		100.0

1978   Republican Primary

Robert F. Bennett (R)	142,239	69.2
Robert R. Sanders (R)	40,542	19.7
Harold Knight (R)	22,671	11.1

Democratic Primary

John Carlin (D)	71,366	55.2
Bert Chaney (D)	34,132	26.4
Harry G. Wiles (D)	23,762	18.4

1982   Republican Primary

Sam Hardage (R)	86,692	36.8
Dave Owen (R)	79,770	33.8
Wendell Lady (R)	61,419	26.0

Democratic Primary

John Carlin (D)	103,780	78.9
Jimmy D. Montgomery (D)	27,785	21.1

1986   Republican Primary

Mike Hayden (R)	99,669	36.1
Larry Jones (R)	85,989	31.1
Jack H. Brier (R)	37,410	13.6
Gene Bicknell (R)	25,733	9.3
Richard J. Peckham (R)	18,876	6.8

Democratic Primary

Thomas R. Docking (D)		100.0

1990   Republican Primary

Mike Hayden (R)	138,467	44.7
Nestor Weigand (R)	130,816	42.3
Richard Peckham (R)	29,033	9.4

Democratic Primary

Joan Finney (D)	81,250	47.2
John Carlin (D)	79,406	46.1
Fred Phelps (D)	11,572	6.7

1994   Republican Primary

Bill Graves (R)	115,608	40.9
Gene Bicknell (R)	79,816	28.2
Fred Kerr (R)	63,495	22.5

Democratic Primary

Jim Slattery (D)	84,389	53.0
Joan Wagnon (D)	42,115	26.5
James L. Francisco (D)	16,048	10.1
Leslie Kitchenmaster (D)	11,253	7.1

1998   Republican Primary

Bill Graves (R)	225,782	72.8
David Miller (R)	84,368	27.2

Democratic Primary

Tom Sawyer (D)	88,248	85.3
Fred Phelps (D)	15,233	14.7

KENTUCKY

Candidates	Votes	%
1959 Republican Primary		
John M. Robsion (R)	63,130	86.3
Thurman J. Hamlin (R)	6,019	8.2
Granville Thomas (R)	3,991	5.5

Democratic Primary

Bert T. Combs (D)	292,462	53.0
Harry Lee Waterfield (D)	259,461	45.6

1963   Republican Primary

Louie B. Nunn (R)	77,455	88.5
J. N. R. Cecil (R)	10,039	11.5

Democratic Primary

Edward T. Breathitt (D)	318,858	53.8
Albert B. Chandler (D)	256,451	43.2

1967   Republican Primary

Louie B. Nunn (R)	90,216	50.4
Marlow W. Cook (R)	86,397	48.3

Democratic Primary

Henry Ward (D)	207,797	52.4
Albert B. Chandler (D)	111,782	28.2
Harry Lee Waterfield (D)	42,583	10.7

1971   Republican Primary

Thomas Emberton (R)	84,863	84.1
Ried Martin (R)	6,379	6.3
Thurman J. Hamlin (R)	5,469	5.4

Democratic Primary

Wendell H. Ford (D)	237,815	53.0
Bert T. Combs (D)	195,678	43.6

1975   Republican Primary

Robert E. Gable (R)	38,113	51.3
Elmer Begley (R)	16,885	22.7
T. William Klein (R)	10,844	14.6
Granville Thomas (R)	8,426	11.3

Democratic Primary

Julian Carroll (D)	263,965	66.3
Todd Hollenbach (D)	113,285	28.5

1979   Republican Primary

Louie B. Nunn (R)	106,006	79.6
Ray B. White (R)	18,514	13.9

Democratic Primary

John Y. Brown Jr. (D)	165,158	29.1
Harvey Sloane (D)	139,713	24.6
Terry McBrayer (D)	131,530	23.2
Carroll Hubbard (D)	68,577	12.1
Thelma L. Stovall (D)	47,633	8.4

1983   Republican Primary

Jim Bunning (R)	72,808	74.4
Lester Burns (R)	7,340	7.5
Donald Wiggins (R)	5,464	5.6
Elizabeth Wickham (R)	5,174	5.3

Democratic Primary

Martha Layne Collins (D)	223,692	34.0
Harvey Sloane (D)	219,160	33.3
Grady Strumbo (D)	199,795	30.3

1987   Republican Primary

John Harper (R)	37,432	41.4
Joseph E. Johnson (R)	22,396	24.8
Leonard W. Beasley (R)	21,067	23.3
Thurman J. Hamlin (R)	9,475	10.5

Democratic Primary

Wallace G. Wilkinson (D)	221,138	34.9
John Y. Brown, Jr. (D)	163,204	25.8
Steven L. Beshear (D)	114,439	18.1
Grady Stumbo (D)	84,613	13.4
Julian Carroll (D)	42,137	6.6

1991   Republican Primary

Larry J. Hopkins (R)	81,526	50.6
Larry E. Forgy (R)	79,581	49.4

Democratic Primary

Brereton C. Jones (D)	184,703	37.5
Scott Baesler (D)	149,352	30.4
Floyd G. Poore (D)	132,060	26.8
Gatewood Galbraith (D)	25,834	5.3

1995   Republican Primary

Larry E. Forgy (R)	97,099	82.4
Robert E. Gable (R)	17,054	14.5

Democratic Primary

Paul E. Patton (D)	152,203	44.9
Bob Babbage (D)	81,352	24.0
John "Eck" Rose (D)	71,740	21.2
Gatewood Galbraith (D)	29,039	8.6

1999   Republican Primary

Peppy Martin (R)	19,248	51.3
David L. Williams (R)	18,295	48.7

Democratic Primary

Paul Patton (D)		100.0

LOUISIANA

Candidates	Votes	%

1920   Democratic Primary

John M. Parker (D)	77,868	54.2
Frank P. Stubbs (D)	65,685	45.8

1924   Democratic Primary

Hewitt Bouanchaud (D)	84,162	35.1
Henry L. Fuqua (D)	81,382	34.0
Huey P. Long (D)	73,985	30.9

	Democratic Runoff		
	Henry L. Fuqua (D)	125,880	*57.8*
	Hewitt Bouanchaud (D)	92,006	*42.2*
1928	**Democratic Primary**		
	Huey P. Long (D)	126,842	*43.9*
	Riley J. Wilson (D)[1]	81,747	*28.3*
	O. H. Simpson (D)	80,326	*27.8*
1932	**Democratic Primary**		
	Oscar K. Allen (D)	214,699	*56.5*
	Dudley J. LeBlanc (D)	110,048	*29.0*
	George Seth Guion (D)	53,756	*14.2*
1936	**Democratic Primary**		
	Richard W. Leche (D)	362,502	*67.1*
	Cleveland Dear (D)	176,150	*32.6*
1940	**Democratic Primary**		
	Earl K. Long (D)	226,385	*40.9*
	Sam H. Jones (D)	154,936	*28.0*
	J. A. Noe (D)	116,564	*21.1*
	James H. Morrison (D)	48,243	*8.7*
	Democratic Runoff		
	Sam H. Jones (D)	284,437	*51.7*
	Earl K. Long (D)	265,403	*48.3*
1944	**Democratic Primary**		
	Jimmie H. Davis (D)	167,434	*34.9*
	Lewis L. Morgan (D)	131,682	*27.5*
	James H. Morrison (D)	76,081	*15.9*
	Dudley J. LeBlanc (D)	40,392	*8.4*
	Sam S. Caldwell (D)	34,335	*7.2*
	Democratic Runoff		
	Jimmie H. Davis (D)	251,228	*53.6*
	Lewis L. Morgan (D)	217,915	*46.5*
1948	**Democratic Primary**		
	Earl K. Long (D)	267,253	*41.5*
	Sam H. Jones (D)	147,329	*22.9*
	Robert F. Kennon (D)	127,569	*19.8*
	James H. Morrison (D)	101,754	*15.8*
	Democratic Runoff		
	Earl K. Long (D)	432,528	*65.9*
	Sam H. Jones (D)	223,971	*34.1*
1952	**Democratic Primary**		
	Carlos G. Spaht (D)	173,987	*22.8*
	Robert F. Kennon (D)	163,434	*21.5*
	Hale Boggs (D)	142,542	*18.7*
	James M. McLemore (D)	116,405	*15.3*
	William J. Dodd (D)	90,925	*11.9*
	Dudley J. LeBlanc (D)	62,906	*8.3*

	Democratic Runoff		
	Robert F. Kennon (D)	482,302	*61.4*
	Carlos G. Spaht (D)	302,743	*38.6*
1956	**Democratic Primary**		
	Earl K. Long (D)	421,681	*51.4*
	deLesseps S. Morrison (D)	191,576	*23.4*
	Frederick T. Preaus (D)	95,955	*11.7*
	Francis C. Grevemberg (D)	62,309	*7.6*
	James M. McLemore (D)	48,188	*5.9*
1959[2]	**Republican Primary**		
	F. C. Grevemberg (R)		*100.0*
	Democratic Primary		
	deLesseps S. Morrison (D)	278,956	*33.1*
	Jimmie H. Davis (D)	213,551	*25.3*
	William M. Rainach (D)	143,095	*17.0*
	James A. Noe (D)	97,654	*11.6*
	William J. Dodd (D)	85,436	*10.1*
	Democratic Runoff		
	Jimmie H. Davis (R)	487,681	*54.1*
	deLesseps S. Morrison (D)	414,110	*45.9*
1963[3]	**Republican Primary**		
	Charlton H. Lyons Sr. (R)		*100.0*
	Democratic Primary		
	deLesseps S. Morrison (D)	299,702	*33.1*
	John J. McKeithen (D)	157,304	*17.4*
	Gillis W. Long (D)	137,778	*15.2*
	Robert F. Kennon (D)	127,870	*14.1*
	Shelby M. Jackson (D)	103,949	*11.5*
	Democratic Runoff		
	John J. McKeithen (D)	492,905	*52.2*
	deLesseps S. Morrison (D)	451,161	*47.8*
1967	**Democratic Primary**		
	John J. McKeithen (D)	836,304	*80.6*
	John R. Rarick (D)	179,846	*17.3*
1971	**Republican Primary**		
	David C. Treen (R)	9,732	*92.1*
	Robert Ross (R)	839	*7.9*
	Democratic Primary		
	Edwin W. Edwards (D)	276,397	*23.5*
	J. Bennett Johnston (D)	208,830	*17.8*
	Gillis W. Long (D)	164,276	*14.0*
	Jimmie H. Davis (D)	138,756	*11.8*
	John G. Schwegmann (D)	92,072	*7.8*
	A. A. Aycock (D)	88,465	*7.5*
	Samuel Bell (D)	72,486	*6.2*
	Speedy O. Long (D)	61,359	*5.2*

Democratic Runoff

Edwin W. Edwards (D)	584,262	*50.2*
J. Bennett Johnston (D)	579,774	*49.8*

1975[4] Open Primary

Edwin W. Edwards (D)	750,107	*62.3*
Robert C. Jones (D)	292,220	*24.3*
Wade O. Martin (D)	146,368	*12.2*

1979[5] Open Primary

David C. Treen (R)	297,674	*21.8*
Louis Lambert (D)	283,266	*20.7*
James E. Fitzmorris (D)	280,760	*20.6*
Paul Hardy (D)	227,026	*16.6*
E. L. Henry (D)	135,769	*9.9*
Edgar G. Mouton (D)	124,333	*9.1*

1987 Open Primary

Charles "Buddy" Roemer (D)	516,078	*33.1*
Edwin W. Edwards (D)[6]	437,801	*28.0*
Bob Livingston (R)	287,780	*18.5*
W. J. Tauzin (D)	154,079	*9.9*
James H. Brown (D)	138,223	*8.8*

1991 Open Primary

Edwin W. Edwards (D)	523,195	*33.8*
David E. Duke (R)	491,342	*31.7*
Charles "Buddy" Roemer (R)	410,690	*26.5*
Clyde C. Holloway (R)	82,683	*5.3*

1995 Open Primary

M. J. "Mike" Foster (R)	385,267	*26.1*
Cleo Fields (D)	280,921	*19.0*
Mary L. Landrieu (D)	271,938	*18.4*
Charles "Buddy" Roemer (R)	263,330	*17.8*
Phil Preis (D)	133,271	*9.0*

1999 Open Primary

M. J. "Mike" Foster (R)		*100.0*

Louisiana

1. Wilson declined a runoff with Long, who became the Democratic nominee.

2. The Democratic and Republican primaries were held Dec. 5, 1959; the Democratic runoff was held Jan. 9, 1960.

3. The Democratic and Republican primaries were held Dec. 7, 1963; the Democratic runoff was held Jan. 11, 1964.

4. In 1975 Louisiana eliminated the partisan primary for governor and instituted an open primary with candidates from all parties running on the same ballot. Any candidate who received a majority appeared in the general election unopposed. If no candidate received 50 percent, a runoff was held between the two top finishers.

5. In 1979 there was a court-ordered recount of the votes for the top three candidates. Results were as follows: Treen: 297,469 votes, 34.6 percent; Lambert: 282,708, 32.8 percent; and Fitzmorris: 280,412, 32.6 percent.

6. Edwards withdrew and no runoff election was held in November.

MAINE

Candidates	Votes	%

1956 Republican Primary

Willis A Trafton (R)	42,901	*51.0*
Philip F. Chapman (R)	24,787	*29.4*
Alexander A. LaFleur (R)	16,479	*19.6*

Democratic Primary

Edmund S. Muskie (D)		*100.0*

1958 Republican Primary

Horace A. Hildreth (R)	63,424	*62.0*
Philip F. Chapman (R)	38,865	*38.0*

Democratic Primary

Clinton A. Clauson (D)	20,736	*51.8*
Maynard C. Dolloff (D)	19,301	*48.2*

1960 Republican Primary

John H. Reed (R)		*100.0*

Democratic Primary

Frank M. Coffin (D)		*100.0*

1962 Republican Primary

John H. Reed (R)		*100.0*

Democratic Primary

Maynard C. Dolloff (D)	18,234	*50.3*
Richard J. Dubord (D)	18,007	*49.7*

1966 Republican Primary

John H. Reed (R)	55,924	*59.7*
James S. Erwin (R)	37,765	*40.3*

Democratic Primary

Kenneth M. Curtis (D)	30,879	*55.6*
Carlton D. Reed (D)	13,839	*24.9*
Dana W. Childs (D)	10,793	*19.4*

1970 Republican Primary

James S. Erwin (R)	72,760	*89.1*
Calvin F. Grass (R)	8,898	*10.9*

Democratic Primary

Kenneth M. Curtis (D)	33,052	*63.2*
Plato Truman (D)	19,266	*36.8*

1974 Republican Primary

James S. Erwin (R)	38,044	*39.3*
Harrison L. Richardson (R)	36,693	*37.9*
Wakine G. Tanous (R)	18,786	*19.4*

Democratic Primary

George J. Mitchell (D)	33,312	*37.5*
Joseph E. Brennan (D)	23,443	*26.4*

Peter S. Kelley (D)	21,358	*24.1*
Lloyd P. LaFountain (D)	7,954	*9.0*

1978   Republican Primary

Linwood E. Palmer (R)	35,976	*48.7*
Charles L. Cragin (R)	28,244	*38.3*
Jerrold B. Speers (R)	9,603	*13.0*

Democratic Primary

Joseph E. Brennan (D)	38,361	*52.0*
Philip L. Merrill (D)	26,803	*36.3*
Richard J. Carey (D)	8,588	*11.6*

1982   Republican Primary

Charles L. Cragin (R)	32,235	*38.0*
Sherry F. Huber (R)	27,739	*32.7*
Richard H. Pierce (R)	24,820	*29.3*

Democratic Primary

Joseph E. Brennan (D)	56,990	*76.8*
Georgette B. Berube (D)	17,219	*23.2*

1986   Republican Primary

John R. McKernan (R)	79,393	*68.4*
Porter D. Leighton (R)	36,705	*31.6*

Democratic Primary

James Tierney (D)	44,087	*37.2*
Severin M. Beliveau (D)	27,991	*23.6*
G. William Diamond (D)	24,693	*20.8*
David E. Redmond (D)	17,598	*14.9*

1990   Republican Primary

John R. McKernan (R)		*100.0*

Democratic Primary

Joseph E. Brennan (D)		*100.0*

1994   Republican Primary

Susan M. Collins (R)	19,477	*21.5*
Sumner H. Lipman (R)	15,282	*16.9*
Jasper S. Wyman (R)	14,418	*15.9*
Judith C. Foss (R)	11,780	*13.0*
Paul R. Young (R)	10,119	*11.2*
Mary Adams (R)	7,854	*8.7*
Charles M. Webster (R)	6,239	*6.9*
Pamela A. Cahill (R)	5,218	*5.8*

Democratic Primary

Joseph E. Brennan (D)	56,932	*56.3*
Thomas H. Allen (D)	24,095	*23.8*
Richard E. Barringer (D)	9,191	*9.1*
Robert L. Woodbury (D)	8,243	*8.1*

1998   Republican Primary

James B. Longley Jr. (R)	38,192	*66.0*
Henry L. Joy (R)	11,411	*19.7*
Leo G. Martin (R)	8,229	*14.2*

Democratic Primary

Thomas J. Connolly (D)	36,954	*81.7*
Joseph J. Ricci (D)	8,264	*18.3*

MARYLAND

Candidates	Votes	%

1958   Republican Primary

James Devereux (R)		*100.0*

Democratic Primary

J. Millard Tawes (D)	261,594	*82.0*
Bruce S. Campbell (D)	24,953	*7.8*
Morgan L. Amaimo (D)	16,459	*5.2*
Joseph A. Phillips (D)	15,836	*5.0*

1962   Republican Primary

Frank Small (R)	71,791	*77.8*
Karla Balentine (R)	11,504	*12.5*
Joseph L. Pavlock (R)	8,972	*9.7*

Democratic Primary

J. Millard Tawes (D)	178,792	*40.4*
George P. Mahoney (D)	125,966	*28.5*
David Hume (D)	118,295	*26.7*

1966   Republican Primary

Spiro T. Agnew (R)	98,531	*83.2*
Andrew J. Groszer (R)	9,987	*8.4*

Democratic Primary

George P. Mahoney (D)	148,446	*30.2*
Carlton R. Sickles (D)	146,507	*29.8*
Thomas B. Finan (D)	134,216	*27.3*
Clarence W. Miles (D)	42,304	*8.6*

1970   Republican Primary

C. Stanley Blair (R)	101,541	*81.5*
Peter James (R)	15,790	*12.8*
John C. Webb (R)	7,194	*5.7*

Democratic Primary

Marvin Mandel (D)	414,160	*89.1*

1974   Republican Primary

Louise Gore (R)	57,626	*53.6*
Lawrence J. Hogan (R)	49,887	*46.4*

Democratic Primary

Marvin Mandel (D)	254,509	*65.7*
Wilson K. Barnes (D)	96,902	*25.0*

1978   Republican Primary

J. Glenn Beall Jr. (R)	76,011	*57.7*
Carlton Beall (R)	30,119	*22.8*
Louise Gore (R)	20,690	*15.7*

Democratic Primary

Harry R. Hughes (D)	213,457	37.2
Blair Lee (D)	194,236	33.9
Theodore G. Venetoulis (D)	140,486	24.5

1982 Republican Primary

Robert A. Pascal (R)	113,425	84.3
Ross Z. Pierpont (R)	21,165	15.7

Democratic Primary

Harry R. Hughes (D)	393,244	59.8
Harry J. McGuirk (D)	129,049	26.3
Harry W. Kelley (D)	61,271	12.5

1986 Republican Primary

Thomas J. Mooney (R)		100.0

Democratic Primary

William D. Schaefer (D)	395,170	61.7
Stephen H. Sachs (D)	224,755	35.1

1990 Republican Primary

William S. Shepard (R)	66,966	52.7
Ross Z. Pierpont (R)	60,065	47.3

Democratic Primary

William D. Schaefer (D)	358,534	78.1
Frederick M. Griisser (D)	100,816	21.9

1994 Republican Primary

Ellen R. Sauerbrey (R)	123,676	52.2
Helen D. Bentley (R)	89,821	37.9
William S. Shepard (R)	23,505	9.9

Democratic Primary

Parris N. Glendening (D)	293,314	53.6
American Joe Miedusiewski (D)	100,326	18.3
Melvin A. Steinberg (D)	82,308	15.0
Don Allensworth (D)	46,888	8.6

1998 Republican Primary

Ellen R. Sauerbrey (R)	175,633	81.0
Charles I. Ecker (R)	41,126	19.0

Democratic Primary

Parris N. Glendening (D)	296,863	70.1
Eileen M. Rehrmann (D)	56,806	13.4
Terence McGuire (D)	46,124	10.9
Lawrence K. Freeman (D)	23,752	5.6

MASSACHUSETTS

Candidates	Votes	%

1956 Republican Primary

Sumner G. Whittier (R)		100.0

Democratic Primary

Foster Furcolo (D)	358,051	73.1
Thomas H. Buckley (D)	131,496	26.9

1958[1] Republican Primary

Charles Gibbons (R)	158,944	84.3
George Fingold (R)	23,031	12.2

Democratic Primary

Foster Furcolo (D)		100.0

1960 Republican Primary

John A. Volpe (R)		100.0

Democratic Primary

Joseph D. Ward (D)	180,848	30.2
Endicott Peabody (D)	152,762	25.5
Francis E. Kelly (D)	98,107	16.4
Robert F. Murphy (D)	76,577	12.8
John F. Kennedy (D)[2]	52,972	8.8

1962 Republican Primary

John A. Volpe (R)		100.0

Democratic Primary

Endicott Peabody (D)	596,553	80.0
Clement A. Riley (D)	149,499	20.0

1964 Republican Primary

John A. Volpe (R)		100.0

Democratic Primary

Francis X. Bellotti (D)	363,675	49.6
Endicott Peabody (D)	336,780	45.9

1966 Republican Primary

John A. Volpe (R)		100.0

Democratic Primary

Edward J. McCormack (D)	343,381	55.1
Kenneth P. O'Donnell (D)	279,541	44.9

1970 Republican Primary

Francis W. Sargent (R)		100.0

Democratic Primary

Kevin H. White (D)	231,605	34.3
Maurice A. Donahue (D)	218,665	32.4
Francis X. Bellotti (D)	164,313	24.4
Kenneth P. O'Donnell (D)	59,970	8.9

1974 Republican Primary

Francis W. Sargent (R)	124,250	63.3
Carroll P. Sheehan (R)	71,936	36.7

Democratic Primary

Michael S. Dukakis (D)	444,590	57.7
Robert H. Quinn (D)	326,385	42.3

MICHIGAN

1978	Republican Primary		
	Francis W. Hatch (R)	141,070	*56.0*
	Edward F. King (R)	110,932	*44.0*
	Democratic Primary		
	Edward J. King (D)	442,174	*51.1*
	Michael S. Dukakis (D)	365,417	*42.2*
	Barbara Ackermann (D)	58,220	*6.7*
1982	Republican Primary		
	John W. Sears (R)	90,617	*50.7*
	John R. Lakian (R)	46,675	*26.1*
	Andrew H. Card (R)	40,899	*22.9*
	Democratic Primary		
	Michael S. Dukakis (D)	631,911	*53.5*
	Edward J. King (D)	549,335	*46.5*
1986	Republican Primary		
	Gregory S. Hyatt (R)[3]	31,021	*48.2*
	Royall H. Switzler (R)	20,802	*32.3*
	George Kariotis (R)	11,787	*18.3*
	Democratic Primary		
	Michael S. Dukakis (D)		*100.0*
1990	Republican Primary		
	William F. Weld (R)	270,455	*60.5*
	Steven D. Pierce (R)	176,184	*39.4*
	Democratic Primary		
	John Silber (D)	562,222	*53.4*
	Francis X. Bellotti (D)	459,128	*43.6*
1994	Republican Primary		
	William F. Weld (R)	211,325	*99.7*
	Democratic Primary		
	Mark Roosevelt (D)	215,061	*47.9*
	George A. Bachrach (D)	120,567	*26.9*
	Michael J. Barrett (D)	111,199	*24.8*
1998	Republican Primary		
	Argeo Paul Cellucci (R)	136,258	*58.6*
	Joseph D. Malone (R)	95,963	*41.2*
	Democratic Primary		
	Scott Harshberger (D)	306,883	*51.1*
	Patricia McGovern (D)	189,686	*31.6*
	Brian J. Donnelly (D)	101,984	*17.0*

Massachusetts

1. Fingold died a few days before the primary. Charles Gibbons, supported by the Republican state committee, polled 158,944 sticker and write-in votes, followed by 23,031 for Fingold, whose name remained on the ballot, and 6,535 other write-ins.

2. John F. Kennedy of Canton, Mass.; not to be confused with Sen. John F. Kennedy, D-Mass., then a candidate for president.

3. Hyatt withdrew after the primary, and Kariotis was substituted by the Republican state central committee.

	Candidates	Votes	%
1956	**Republican Primary**		
	Albert E. Cobo (R)	348,652	*69.0*
	Donald S. Leonard (R)	156,822	*31.0*
	Democratic Primary		
	G. Mennen Williams (D)		*100.0*
1958	**Republican Primary**		
	Paul D. Bagwell (R)		*100.0*
	Democratic Primary		
	G. Mennen Williams (D)	385,864	*85.5*
	W. L. Johnson (D)	65,614	*14.5*
1960	**Republican Primary**		
	Paul D. Bagwell (R)		*100.0*
	Democratic Primary		
	John B. Swainson (D)	274,743	*50.8*
	James M. Hare (D)	205,086	*37.9*
	Edward Connor (D)	60,895	*11.3*
1962	**Republican Primary**		
	George W. Romney (R)		*100.0*
	Democratic Primary		
	John B. Swainson (D)		*100.0*
1964	**Republican Primary**		
	George W. Romney (R)	583,356	*87.9*
	George N. Higgins (R)	80,608	*12.1*
	Democratic Primary		
	Neil Staebler (D)		*100.0*
1966	**Republican Primary**		
	George W. Romney (R)		*100.0*
	Democratic Primary		
	Zoltan A. Ferency (D)		*100.0*
1970	**Republican Primary**		
	William G. Milliken (R)	416,491	*77.8*
	James C. Turner (R)	119,140	*22.2*
	Democratic Primary		
	Sander Levin (D)	304,343	*54.1*
	Zolton A. Ferency (D)	167,442	*29.8*
	George N. Parris (D)	49,559	*8.8*
	George F. Montgomery (D)	41,218	*7.3*

American Independent Primary

James L. McCormick (WRITE IN)

1974   **Republican Primary**

William G. Milliken (R)   100.0

Democratic Primary

Sander M. Levin (D)	445,273	61.3
Jerome P. Cavanagh (D)	199,361	27.4
James E. Wells (D)	81,844	11.3

1978   **Republican Primary**

William G. Milliken (R)   100.0

Democratic Primary

William Fitzgerald (D)	240,641	39.8
Zolton A. Ferency (D)	151,062	25.0
Patrick McCullough (D)	108,742	18.0
William Ralls (D)	104,364	17.2

1982   **Republican Primary**

Richard H. Headlee (R)	220,378	34.4
James H. Brickley (R)	194,429	30.3
L. Brooks Patterson (R)	180,065	28.1
Jack Welborn (R)	46,505	7.2

Democratic Primary

James J. Blanchard (D)	406,941	50.2
William Fitzgerald (D)	138,453	17.1
David A. Plawecki (D)	95,805	11.8
Zolton A. Ferency (D)	85,088	10.5
Edward C. Pierce (D)	44,894	5.5

1986   **Republican Primary**

William Lucas (R)	259,153	44.5
Dick Chrysler (R)	198,174	34.0
Colleen Engler (R)	63,927	11.0
Dan Murphy (R)	61,073	10.5

Democratic Primary

James J. Blanchard (D)	428,125	93.7
Henry Wilson (D)	28,940	6.3

1990   **Republican Primary**

John Engler (R)	409,747	86.6
John Lauve (R)	63,457	13.4

Democratic Primary

James J. Blanchard (D)   100.0

1994   **Republican Primary**

John Engler (R)	549,565	99.8

Democratic Primary

Howard Wolpe (D)	242,847	35.2
Debbie Stabenow (D)	209,641	30.4
Larry Owen (D)	176,675	25.6
Lynn Jondahl (D)	59,127	8.6

1998   **Republican Primary**

John Engler (R)	477,628	89.6
Gary Artinian (R)	55,453	10.4

Democratic Primary

Geoffrey Fieger (D)	300,458	41.2
Larry Owen (D)	272,360	37.3
Doug Ross (D)	156,847	21.5

MINNESOTA[1]

Candidates	Votes	%

1956   **Republican Primary**

Ancher Nelsen (R)	283,844	94.4

Democratic Primary

Orville L. Freeman (DFL)	269,740	89.5

1958   **Republican Primary**

George MacKinnon (R)	202,833	85.3
Glenn B. Brown (R)	34,878	14.7

Democratic Primary

Orville L. Freeman (DFL)	331,822	87.6
Harold Strom (DFL)	47,041	12.4

1960   **Republican Primary**

Elmer L. Andersen (R)		100.0

Democratic Primary

Orville L. Freeman (DFL)	264,571	88.8
Belmont Tudisco (DFL)	33,452	11.2

1962   **Republican Primary**

Elmer L. Andersen (R)		100.0

Democratic Primary

Karl F. Rolvaag (DFL)	271,818	92.5
Belmont Tudisco (DFL)	22,042	7.5

1966   **Republican Primary**

Harold LeVander (R)	276,403	97.9

Democratic Primary

Karl F. Rolvaag (DFL)	336,656	66.3
A. M. Keith (DFL)	157,661	31.0

1970   **Republican Primary**

Douglas M. Head (R)	210,621	87.5
John C. Peterson (R)	19,737	8.2

Democratic Primary

Wendell R. Anderson (DFL)		100.0

1974   **Republican Primary**

John W. Johnson (R)		100.0

Democratic Primary

Wendell R. Anderson (DFL)	254,671	78.2
Thomas E. McDonald (DFL)	70,871	21.8

1978

Republican Primary

Albert H. Quie (I-R)	174,799	83.6
Robert W. Johnson (I-R)	34,406	16.4

Democratic Primary

Rudy Perpich (DFL)	390,069	80.0
Alice Tripp (DFL)	97,247	20.0

American Primary

Richard Pedersen (AM)		100.0

1982

Republican Primary

Wheelock Whitney (I-R)	185,801	60.1
Lou Wangberg (I-R)	105,696	34.2
Harold E. Stassen (I-R)	17,795	5.7

Democratic Primary

Rudy Perpich (DFL)	275,920	51.2
Warren Spannaus (DFL)	248,218	46.1

1986

Republican Primary

Cal R. Ludeman (I-R)	147,674	76.9
James H. Lindau (I-R)	30,768	16.0

Democratic Primary

Rudy Perpich (DFL)	293,426	57.5
George Latimer (DFL)	207,198	40.6

1990

Republican Primary

Jon Grunseth (I-R)[2]	169,451	49.4
Arne Carlson (I-R)	108,446	31.6
Doug Kelley (I-R)	57,872	16.9

Democratic Primary

Rudy Perpich (DFL)	218,410	55.5
Mike Hatch (DFL)	166,183	42.2

1994

Republican Primary

Arne Carlson (I-R)	321,084	66.5
Allen Quist (I-R)	161,670	33.5

Democratic Primary

John Marty (DFL)	144,462	37.8
Mike Hatch (DFL)	139,109	36.4
Tony Bouza (DFL)	93,841	24.6

1998

Republican Primary

Norm Coleman (R)	127,957	91.3
Bill Dahn (R)	12,167	8.7

Democratic Primary

Hubert H. "Skip" Humphrey III (DFL)	182,562	37.0
Mike Freeman (DFL)	93,714	19.0
Doug Johnson (DFL)	91,888	18.6
Mark Dayton (DFL)	88,070	17.8
Ted Mondale (DFL)	36,237	7.3

Minnesota

1. In Minnesota, the Democratic Party is known as the Democratic-Farmer-Labor Party (DFL). From 1976 to 1994, Republican Party was known as the Independent Republican Party (I-R).

2. Grunseth withdrew after the primary and Carlson was substituted by the state party committee.

MISSISSIPPI

Candidates	Votes	%

1919

Democratic Primary

Lee M. Russell (D)	48,348	32.6
Oscar Johnston (D)	39,206	26.4
A. H. Longino (D)	30,831	20.8
Ross A. Collins (D)	30,026	20.2

Democratic Runoff

Lee M. Russell (D)	77,427	52.7
Oscar Johnston (D)	69,565	47.3

1923

Democratic Primary

Henry L. Whitfield (D)	85,328	33.6
Theodore G. Bilbo (D)	65,105	25.6
Martin S. Conner (D)	48,739	19.2
L. C. Franklin (D)	37,245	14.7
Percey Bell (D)	17,724	7.0

Democratic Runoff

Henry L. Whitfield (D)	134,715	53.3
Theodore G. Bilbo (D)	118,143	46.7

1927

Democratic Primary

Theodore G. Bilbo (D)	135,065	46.9
Dennis Murphree (D)	71,836	25.0
Martin S. Conner (D)	57,402	19.9
A. C. Anderson (D)	23,528	8.2

Democratic Runoff

Theodore G. Bilbo (D)	153,669	52.8
Dennis Murphree (D)	137,130	47.2

1931

Democratic Primary

Hugh L. White (D)	108,022	34.5
Martin S. Conner (D)	92,089	29.4
Paul B. Johnson (D)	58,668	18.7
Mitchell (D)	54,202	17.3

Democratic Runoff

Martin S. Conner (D)	170,690	54.1
Hugh L. White (D)	144,918	45.9

1935

Democratic Primary

Paul B. Johnson (D)	111,523	31.5
Hugh L. White (D)	110,825	31.3
Dennis Murphree (D)	92,997	26.2
Franklin (D)	34,700	9.8

Democratic Runoff

Hugh L. White (D)	182,771	51.7
Paul B. Johnson (D)	170,705	48.3

1939   **Democratic Primary**

Paul B. Johnson (D)	103,099	33.5
Martin S. Conner (D)	79,305	25.8
Thomas L. Bailey (D)	58,987	19.2
Franklin (D)	31,845	10.4
Snider (D)	24,244	7.9

Democratic Runoff

Paul B. Johnson (D)	163,620	54.7
Martin S. Conner (D)	135,724	45.3

1943   **Democratic Primary**

Martin S. Conner (D)	110,917	38.8
Thomas L. Bailey (D)	68,963	24.1
Dennis Murphree (D)	68,510	24.0
Franklin (D)	37,240	13.0

Democratic Runoff

Thomas L. Bailey (D)	143,153	53.2
Martin S. Conner (D)	125,882	46.8

1947   **Democratic Primary**

Fielding L. Wright (D)	202,014	55.3
Paul B. Johnson Jr. (D)	112,123	30.7
Jesse M. Byrd (D)	37,997	10.4

1951   **Democratic Primary**

Hugh L. White (D)	94,820	23.3
Paul B. Johnson Jr. (D)	86,150	21.1
Sam Lumpkin (D)	84,451	20.7
Ross R. Barnett (D)	81,674	20.0
Mary D. Cain (D)	24,756	6.1
Jesse M. Byrd (D)	22,783	5.6

Democratic Runoff

Hugh L. White (D)	201,222	51.2
Paul B. Johnson Jr. (D)	191,966	48.8

1955   **Democratic Primary**

Paul B. Johnson Jr. (D)	122,423	28.1
James P. Coleman (D)	104,140	23.9
Fielding L. Wright (D)	94,410	21.6
Ross R. Barnett (D)	92,785	21.3
Mary D. Cain (D)	22,469	5.2

Democratic Runoff

James P. Coleman (D)	233,237	55.6
Paul B. Johnson Jr. (D)	185,924	44.4

1959   **Democratic Primary**

Ross R. Barnett (D)	155,508	35.3
Carroll Gartin (D)	151,043	34.3
Charles L. Sullivan (D)	131,792	29.9

Democratic Runoff

Ross R. Barnett (D)	230,557	54.3
Carroll Gartin (D)	193,706	45.7

1963   **Republican Primary**

Rubel L. Phillips (R)		100.0

Democratic Primary

Paul B. Johnson Jr. (D)	182,540	38.5
James P. Coleman (D)	156,296	33.0
Charles L. Sullivan (D)	132,321	27.9

Democratic Runoff

Paul B. Johnson Jr. (D)	261,493	57.3
James P. Coleman (D)	194,958	42.7

1967   **Republican Primary**

Rubel L. Phillips (R)		100.0

Democratic Primary

William Winter (D)	222,001	32.5
John Bell Williams (D)	197,778	28.9
James E. "Jimmy" Swan (D)	124,361	18.2
Ross R. Barnett (D)	76,053	11.1
William L. Waller (D)	60,090	8.8

Democratic Runoff

John Bell Williams (D)	371,815	54.5
William Winter (D)	310,527	45.5

1971   **Democratic Primary**

Charles L. Sullivan (D)	288,219	37.8
William L. Waller (D)	227,424	29.8
James E. "Jimmy" Swan (D)	128,946	16.9
Roy C. Adams (D)	45,445	6.0
Ed Pittman (D)	38,170	5.0

Democratic Runoff

William L. Waller (D)	389,952	54.2
Charles L. Sullivan (D)	329,236	45.8

1975   **Democratic Primary**

William Winter (D)	286,652	36.3
Cliff Finch (D)	253,829	32.1
Maurice Dantin (D)	179,472	22.7
John Arthur Eaves (D)	50,606	6.4

Democratic Runoff

Cliff Finch (D)	442,865	57.7
William Winter (D)	324,749	42.3

1979   **Republican Primary**

Gil Carmichael (R)	17,216	53.1
Leon Bramlett (R)	15,236	46.9

Democratic Primary

Evelyn Gandy (D)	224,746	30.5
William Winter (D)	183,944	25.0
John A. Eaves (D)	143,411	19.5
Jim Herring (D)	135,812	18.4

Democratic Runoff

William Winter (D)	386,174	56.6
Evelyn Gandy (D)	295,835	43.4

1983 ### Republican Primary

Leon Bramlett (R)		100.0

Democratic Primary

Evelyn Gandy (D)	316,304	38.2
William A. Allain (D)	293,348	35.4
Mike P. Sturdivant (D)	172,526	21.0

Democratic Runoff

William A. Allain (D)	405,348	52.4
Evelyn Gandy (D)	367,953	47.5

1987 ### Republican Primary

Jack Reed (R)	14,798	78.5
Doug Lemon (R)	4,057	21.5

Democratic Primary

Ray Mabus (D)	304,559	35.7
Mike P. Sturdivant (D)	131,180	16.2
William L. Waller (D)	105,056	13.0
John A. Eaves (D)	98,517	12.2
Maurice Dantin (D)	83,603	10.3
Ed Pittman (D)	73,667	9.1

Democratic Runoff

Ray Mabus (D)	428,883	64.3
Mike P. Sturdivant (D)	238,039	35.7

1991 ### Republican Primary

Kirk Fordice (R)	28,411	44.7
Pete Johnson (R)	27,561	43.4
Bobby Clanton (R)	7,589	11.9

Republican Runoff

Kirk Fordice (R)	31,753	60.6
Pete Johnson (R)	20,622	39.4

Democratic Primary

Ray Mabus (D)	368,679	50.7
Wayne Dowdy (D)	299,172	41.2
George Blair (D)	58,614	8.1

1995 ### Republican Primary

Kirk Fordice (R)	117,907	93.7

Democratic Primary

Dick Molpus (D)	396,816	77.1
Shawn O'Hara (D)	117,833	22.9

1999 ### Republican Primary

Mike Parker (R)	77,674	50.7
Eddie Briggs (R)	42,763	27.9
Charlie Williams (R)	17,176	11.2
Dan M. Gibson (R)	11,348	7.4

Democratic Primary

Ronnie Musgrove (D)	309,519	56.7
James "Jimmy" Roberts Jr. (D)	142,617	26.1
Richard Barrett (D)	32,383	5.9

MISSOURI

Candidates	Votes	%
1956 **Republican Primary**		
Lon Hocker (R)	136,388	66.9
Joseph M. Whealen (R)	53,811	26.4
Winford Sidebotham (R)	13,710	6.7
Democratic Primary		
James T. Blair (D)	387,330	88.1
Charles A. Lee (D)	34,107	7.7
1960 **Republican Primary**		
Edward G. Farmer (R)	107,637	54.1
William B. Ewald (R)	57,953	29.1
Harry C. Timmerman (R)	33,388	16.8
Democratic Primary		
John M. Dalton (D)	466,984	86.4
1964 **Republican Primary**		
Ethan Shepley (R)	161,327	75.7
Harry C. Timmerman (R)	17,510	8.2
William B. Ewald (R)	17,170	8.1
Joseph M. Badgett (R)	17,156	8.0
Democratic Primary		
Warren E. Hearnes (D)	334,708	51.9
Hilary A. Bush (D)	283,640	44.0
1968 **Republican Primary**		
Lawrence K. Roos (R)	170,428	76.4
Harry C. Timmerman (R)	41,549	18.6
Harvey F. Euge (R)	10,994	5.0
Democratic Primary		
Warren E. Hearnes (D)	497,056	85.5
Robert B. Curtis (D)	42,971	7.4
Milton Morris (D)	41,506	7.1
1972 **Republican Primary**		
Christopher S. "Kit" Bond (R)	265,467	75.1
Gene McNary (R)	56,652	16.0
R. J. King (R)	21,422	6.1
Democratic Primary		
Edward L. Dowd (D)	265,011	40.8
William S. Morris (D)	152,055	23.4
Joseph P. Teasdale (D)	135,965	20.9
Earl R. Blackwell (D)	72,212	11.1

	Non Partisan Primary		
	Paul J. Leonard (NON PART)	606	55.4
	Charles S. Miller (NON PART)	487	44.6
1976	**Republican Primary**		
	Christopher S. "Kit" Bond (R)	286,377	92.0
	Harvey F. Euge (R)	24,975	8.0
	Democratic Primary		
	Joseph P. Teasdale (D)	419,656	48.6
	William Cason (D)	340,208	39.4
1980	**Republican Primary**		
	Christopher S. "Kit" Bond (R)	223,678	63.5
	William Phelps (R)	122,867	34.9
	Democratic Primary		
	Joseph P. Teasdale (D)	359,263	54.0
	James I. Spainhower (D)	294,917	44.3
1984	**Republican Primary**		
	John Ashcroft (R)	245,308	67.4
	Gene McNary (R)	115,516	31.8
	Democratic Primary		
	Kenneth J. Rothman (D)	288,543	56.0
	Mel Carnahan (D)	104,368	20.3
	Norman L. Merrell (D)	97,973	19.0
1988	**Republican Primary**		
	John Ashcroft (R)		100.0
	Democratic Primary		
	Betty C. Hearnes (D)	375,564	81.5
	Lavoy Reed (D)	85,409	18.5
1992	**Republican Primary**		
	William L. Webster (R)	183,968	43.8
	Roy D. Blunt (R)	163,719	39.0
	Wendell Bailey (R)	63,481	15.1
	Democratic Primary		
	Mel Carnahan (D)	388,098	55.4
	Vince Schoemehl (D)	235,652	33.6
	Sharon Rogers (D)	35,104	5.0
1996	**Republican Primary**		
	Margaret Kelly (R)	219,435	77.7
	John M. Swenson (R)	29,675	10.5
	David Andrew Brown (R)	18,755	6.6
	Lester W. "Les" Duggan Jr. (R)	14,448	5.1
	Democratic Primary		
	Mel Carnahan (D)	347,488	81.6
	Ruth Redel (D)	33,452	7.9
	Edwin W. Howald (D)	29,890	7.0

	Libertarian Primary		
	J Mark Ogelsby (LIBERT)	1,627	63.7
	Martin Lindstedt (LIBERT)	926	36.3
2000	**Republican Primary**		
	Jim Talent (R)	296,159	84.5
	Jennie Lee Sievers (R)	33,674	9.6
	Elgar Macy (R)	20,681	5.9
	Democratic Primary		
	Bob Holden (D)	362,457	100.0

MONTANA

	Candidates	Votes	%
1956	**Republican Primary**		
	J. Hugo Aronson (R)		100.0
	Democratic Primary		
	Arnold H. Olsen (D)	55,269	44.9
	John W. Bonner (D)	51,306	41.7
	Danny O'Neill (D)	14,777	12.0
1960	**Republican Primary**		
	Donald G. Nutter (R)	33,099	50.4
	Wesley A. D'Ewart (R)	32,538	49.6
	Democratic Primary		
	Paul Cannon (D)	44,690	34.9
	Jack Toole (D)	40,537	31.6
	Mike Kuchera (D)	33,216	25.9
	Willard E. Fraser (D)	6,505	5.1
1964	**Republican Primary**		
	Tim M. Babcock (R)		100.0
	Democratic Primary		
	Roland Renne (D)	71,967	55.9
	Mike Kuchera (D)	56,710	44.1
1968	**Republican Primary**		
	Tim M. Babcock (R)	50,369	55.1
	Ted James (R)	36,664	40.1
	Democratic Primary		
	Forrest H. Anderson (D)	39,057	38.3
	Eugene H. Mahoney (D)	35,562	34.9
	LeRoy Anderson (D)	16,476	16.2
	Willard E. Fraser (D)	8,525	8.3
1972	**Republican Primary**		
	Ed Smith (R)	39,552	40.6
	Frank Dunkle (R)	37,375	38.4
	Tom A. Selstad (R)	18,046	18.5

Democratic Primary

Thomas L. Judge (D)	75,917	59.9
Dick Dzivi (D)	38,639	30.5

1976   Republican Primary

Robert Woodahl (R)	47,629	56.7
John K. McDonald (R)	36,420	43.3

Democratic Primary

Thomas L. Judge (D)		100.0

1980   Republican Primary

Jack Ramirez (R)	48,926	68.4
Al Bishop (R)	14,522	20.3
Florence Haegen (R)	8,118	11.3

Democratic Primary

Ted Schwinden (D)	69,051	50.6
Thomas L. Judge (D)	57,946	42.5

1984   Republican Primary

Pat M. Goodover (R)	56,199	100.0

Democratic Primary

Ted Schwinden (D)	80,633	81.4
Robert Carlson Kelleher (D)	18,423	18.6

1988   Republican Primary

Stan Stephens (R)	44,022	50.1
Cal Winslow (R)	37,875	43.1
Jim Waltermire (R)[1]	6,024	6.9

Democratic Primary

Thomas L. Judge (D)	46,412	39.3
Frank Morrison (D)	32,124	27.2
Mike Greely (D)	26,827	22.7
Ted Neuman (D)	7,297	6.2

1992   Republican Primary

Marc Racicot (R)	68,013	68.7
Andrea Bennett (R)	31,038	31.3

Democratic Primary

Dorothy Bradley (D)	54,453	41.2
Mike McGrath (D)	44,323	33.5
Frank Morrison (D)	23,883	18.1

1996   Republican Primary

Marc Racicot (R)	92,644	76.4
Rob Natelson (R)	28,672	23.6

Democratic Primary

Chet Blaylock (D)[2]	55,120	74.6
Bob Kelleher (D)	18,761	25.4

2000   Republican Primary

Judy Martz (R)	64,278	56.9
Rob Natelson (R)	48,738	43.1

Democratic Primary

Mark O'Keefe (D)	46,294	48.0
Joseph Mazurek (D)	34,385	35.7
Mike Cooney (D)	15,677	16.3

Montana
1. Waltermire died two months before the primary.
2. Blaylock died Oct. 23 and was succeeded as the party's gubernatorial candidate by Judy Jacobson.

NEBRASKA

Candidates	Votes	%

1956   Republican Primary

Victor E. Anderson (R)	86,168	82.6
Edwin L. Hart (R)	18,202	17.4

Democratic Primary

Frank Sorrell (D)	43,301	69.9
Ted Baum (D)	18,667	30.1

1958   Republican Primary

Victor E. Anderson (R)	90,150	76.4
Louis H. Hector (R)	27,768	23.5

Democratic Primary

Ralph G. Brooks (D)	37,816	54.8
Edward A. Dosek (D)	31,221	45.2

1960   Republican Primary

John R. Cooper (R)	61,286	37.7
Hazel Abel (R)	39,109	24.1
Terry Carpenter (R)	25,659	15.8
Dwain Williams (R)	23,545	14.5
Del Lienemann (R)	9,390	5.8

Democratic Primary

Frank B. Morrison (D)	51,335	48.0
Robert Conrad (D)	44,486	41.6
Charles A. Bates (D)	5,477	5.1

1962   Republican Primary

Fred A. Seaton (R)	130,816	85.3
George A. Clarke (R)	17,368	11.3

Democratic Primary

Frank B. Morrison (D)	78,817	76.6
Mrs. Ralph G. Brooks (D)	15,565	15.1
Tony Mangiamelli (D)	8,464	8.3

1964   Republican Primary

Dwight W. Burney (R)	82,256	58.8
Jack Romans (R)	44,102	31.5

Democratic Primary

Frank B. Morrison (D)	83,362	88.8
Charles A. Bates (D)	6,543	7.0

1966 **Republican Primary**

Norbert T. Tiemann (R)	78,338	*44.0*
Val Peterson (R)	63,589	*35.7*
Bruce Hagemeister (R)	22,574	*12.7*
Henry E. Kuhlmann (R)	12,052	*6.8*

Democratic Primary

Philip C. Sorensen (D)	65,051	*56.8*
J. W. Burbach (D)	35,439	*30.9*
Henry E. Ley (D)	13,819	*12.1*

1970 **Republican Primary**

Norbert T. Tiemann (R)	97,616	*50.5*
Clifton B. Batchelder (R)	89,355	*46.2*

Democratic Primary

J. James Exon (D)	54,783	*44.6*
J. W. Burbach (D)	51,760	*42.2*
Richard R. Larsen (D)	15,602	*12.7*

1974 **Republican Primary**

Richard D. Marvel (R)		*100.0*

Democratic Primary

J. James Exon (D)	125,690	*87.4*
Richard D. Schmitz (D)	17,889	*12.4*

1978 **Republican Primary**

Charles Thone (R)	89,378	*45.3*
Robert A. Phares (R)	48,402	*24.5*
Stanley R. Juelfs (R)	43,828	*22.2*
Vance D. Rogers (R)	14,076	*7.1*

Democratic Primary

Gerald T. Whelan (D)	104,178	*79.4*
Robert V. Hansen (D)	26,509	*20.2*

1982 **Republican Primary**

Charles Thone (R)	115,750	*62.5*
Stan DeBoer (R)	55,983	*30.2*
Barton E. Chandler (R)	13,086	*7.1*

Democratic Primary

Bob Kerrey (D)	87,913	*71.0*
George Burrows (D)	35,426	*28.6*

1986 **Republican Primary**

Kay Orr (R)	75,914	*39.4*
Kermit Brashear (R)	60,308	*31.3*
Nancy Hoch (R)	42,649	*22.1*

Democratic Primary

Helen Boosalis (D)	63,833	*44.0*
David A. Domina (D)	37,975	*26.2*
Chris Beutler (D)	31,605	*21.8*

1990 **Republican Primary**

Kay Orr (R)	130,045	*68.1*
Mort Sullivan (R)	59,048	*30.9*

Democratic Primary[1]

Ben Nelson (D)	44,721	*26.8*
Bill Hoppner (D)	44,679	*26.7*
Mike Boyle (D)	41,227	*24.7*
Bill Harris (D)	31,527	*18.9*

1994 **Republican Primary**

Gene Spence (R)	69,529	*38.1*
Ralph Knobel (R)	57,719	*31.6*
Alan Jacobsen (R)	27,374	*15.0*
John DeCamp (R)	24,414	*13.4*

Democratic Primary

Ben Nelson (D)	101,422	*88.1*
Robert F. Winingar (D)	6,993	*6.1*
Robb Nimic (D)	6,373	*5.5*

1998 **Republican Primary**

Mike Johanns (R)	88,173	*40.0*
John Breslow (R)	65,806	*29.9*
Jon Christensen (R)	62,107	*28.2*

Democratic Primary

Bill Hoppner (D)	72,887	*65.4*
James D. McFarland (D)	33,890	*30.4*

Nebraska
1. The figures for Nelson and Hoppner are for the recount.

NEVADA

Candidates	Votes	%

1958 **Republican Primary**

Charles H. Russell (R)		*100.0*

Democratic Primary

Grant Sawyer (D)	20,711	*46.3*
Harvey Dickerson (D)	13,372	*29.9*
George E. Franklin (D)	10,175	*22.7*

1962 **Republican Primary**

Oran K. Gragson (R)	16,538	*64.3*
H. M. Greenspun (R)	9,176	*35.7*

Democratic Primary

Grant Sawyer (D)	40,168	*81.4*
Gene Austin (D)	5,017	*10.2*

1966 **Republican Primary**

Paul Laxalt (R)	32,768	*94.7*
John P. Screen (R)	1,834	*5.3*

Democratic Primary

Grant Sawyer (D)	40,982	*58.6*
Edward G. Marshall (D)	13,858	*19.8*
Charles E. Springer (D)	13,270	*19.0*

1970   **Republican Primary**

Ed Fike (R)	31,931	88.2
Margie Dyer (R)	4,281	11.8

Democratic Primary

Mike O'Callaghan (D)	41,185	68.8
Hank Thornley (D)	16,107	26.9

1974   **Republican Primary**

Shirley Crumpler (R)	17,076	49.4
William Bickerstaff (R)	13,632	39.5
Gilbert D. Buck (R)	2,405	7.0

Democratic Primary

Mike O'Callaghan (D)	69,089	90.8

1978   **Republican Primary**

Robert F. List (R)	39,997	82.4
William C. Allen (R)	3,038	6.3
"None of these candidates"[1]	3,570	7.3

Democratic Primary

Robert E. Rose (D)	41,672	48.1
John Foley (D)	20,186	23.3
Jack Schofield (D)	18,414	21.3

1982   **Republican Primary**

Robert F. List (R)	39,319	57.0
Mike Moody (R)	13,849	20.1
"None of these candidates"[1]	13,252	19.2

Democratic Primary

Richard H. Bryan (D)	55,261	51.1
Myron E. Leavitt (D)	34,783	32.1
Stan Colton (D)	10,830	10.0

1986   **Republican Primary**

Patty Cafferata (R)	31,430	46.1
Jim Stone (R)	12,296	18.0
Marcia J. Wines (R)	5,599	8.2
"None of these candidates"[1]	15,116	22.2

Democratic Primary

Richard H. Bryan (D)	71,920	79.9
Herb Tobman (D)	13,776	15.3

1990   **Republican Primary**

Jim Gallaway (R)	37,467	49.3
"None of these candidates"[1]	16,565	21.8
Charlie Brown (R)	16,067	21.1

Democratic Primary

Robert J. Miller (D)	71,537	81.0
"None of these candidates"[1]	7,394	8.4

1994   **Republican Primary**

Jim Gibbons (R)	59,705	51.2
Cheryl A. Lau (R)	37,749	32.3
"None of these candidates"[1]	10,391	8.9

Democratic Primary

Robert J. Miller (D)	75,311	62.7
Jan L. Jones (D)	33,566	27.9
"None of these candidates"[1]	6,917	5.8

1998   **Republican Primary**

Kenny Guinn (R)	76,953	58.1
Aaron Russo (R)	34,251	25.9
Lonnie Hammargren (R)	13,410	10.1

Democratic Primary

Jan Laverty Jones (D)	62,495	59.6
Joe Neal (D)	16,646	15.9
"None of these candidates"[1]	12,857	12.3

Nevada
1. Nevada provided space on the ballot for a vote against the candidates listed.

NEW HAMPSHIRE

Candidates	Votes	%

1956   **Republican Primary**

Lane Dwinell (R)	38,734	53.1
Wesley Powell (R)	33,408	45.8

Democratic Primary

John Shaw (D)		100.0

1958   **Republican Primary**

Wesley Powell (R)	39,761	47.5
Hugh Gregg (R)	39,365	47.1

Democratic Primary

Bernard L. Boutin (D)	16,646	47.0
John Shaw (D)	12,783	36.1
Alfred J. Champagne (D)	4,586	13.0

1960   **Republican Primary**

Wesley Powell (R)	49,119	49.9
Hugh Gregg (R)	48,108	48.8

Democratic Primary

Bernard L. Boutin (D)	31,650	77.6
John Shaw (D)	7,151	17.5

1962   **Republican Primary**

John Pillsbury (R)	55,784	56.4
Wesley Powell (R)	42,005	42.4

Democratic Primary

John W. King (D)	27,933	93.2
Elmer E. Bussey (D)	2,039	6.8

1964   **Republican Primary**

John Pillsbury (R)	32,200	51.4
Wesley Powell (R)	21,764	34.7
John W. King (WRITE IN)	3,608	5.8
John C. Mongan (R)	3,532	5.6

Democratic Primary

John W. King (D)		*100.0*

1966   Republican Primary

Hugh Gregg (R)	33,946	*44.9*
James J. Barry (R)	20,791	*27.5*
Alexander M. Taft (R)	14,845	*19.6*

Democratic Primary

John W. King (D)		*100.0*

1968   Republican Primary

Walter R. Peterson (R)	29,262	*34.1*
Wesley Powell (R)	26,498	*30.9*
Meldrim Thomson (R)	25,275	*29.5*

Democratic Primary

Emile R. Bussiere (D)	12,021	*32.7*
Henry P. Sullivan (D)	10,895	*29.6*
Vincent P. Dunn (D)	10,412	*28.3*

1970   Republican Primary

Walter R. Peterson (R)	43,667	*50.9*
Meldrim Thomson Jr. (R)	41,392	*48.2*

Democratic Primary

Roger J. Crowley (D)	17,089	*47.5*
Charles F. Whittemore (D)	13,354	*37.1*
Dennis J. Sullivan (D)	4,747	*13.2*

1972   Republican Primary

Meldrim Thomson Jr. (R)	43,611	*47.9*
Walter R. Peterson (R)	41,252	*45.3*

Democratic Primary

Roger J. Crowley (D)	29,326	*61.4*
Robert E. Raiche (D)	16,216	*33.9*

1974   Republican Primary

Meldrim Thomson Jr. (R)	47,244	*54.9*
David L. Nixon (R)	37,286	*43.3*

Democratic Primary

Richard W. Leonard (D)	16,503	*37.8*
Harry V. Spanos (D)	14,149	*32.4*
Hugh Gallen (D)	13,030	*29.8*

1976   Republican Primary

Meldrim Thomson Jr. (R)	52,968	*64.6*
Gerald J. Zeiller (R)	26,728	*32.6*

Democratic Primary

Harry V. Spanos (D)	21,589	*41.3*
James A. Connor (D)	15,758	*30.2*
Hugh Gallen (D)	13,629	*26.1*

1978   Republican Primary

Meldrim Thomson Jr. (R)	45,069	*59.7*
Wesley Powell (R)	28,286	*37.4*

Democratic Primary

Hugh Gallen (D)	26,217	*73.0*
Delbert F. Downing (D)	9,688	*27.0*

1980   Republican Primary

Meldrim Thomson Jr. (R)	55,554	*56.4*
Louis C. D'Allesandro (R)	40,060	*40.7*

Democratic Primary

Hugh Gallen (D)	37,786	*81.3*
Thomas B. Wingate (D)	8,689	*18.7*

1982   Republican Primary

John H. Sununu (R)	26,617	*31.9*
Robert B. Monier (R)	24,823	*29.7*
Louis C. D'Allesandro (R)	24,163	*29.0*

Democratic Primary

Hugh Gallen (D)		*100.0*

1984   Republican Primary

John H. Sununu (R)	52,737	*84.1*
James F. Fallon (R)	8,994	*14.3*

Democratic Primary

Chris Spirou (D)	22,835	*49.5*
Paul McEachern (D)	18,460	*40.0*
Robert L. Dupay (D)	4,060	*8.8*

1986   Republican Primary

John H. Sununu (R)	44,906	*77.3*
Roger L. Easton (R)	12,702	*21.9*

Democratic Primary

Paul McEachern (D)	19,731	*54.6*
Paul M. Gagnon (D)	9,790	*27.1*
Bruce Anderson (D)	5,816	*16.1*

1988   Republican Primary

Judd Gregg (R)	65,777	*79.0*
Robert F. Shaw (R)	15,133	*18.2*

Democratic Primary

Paul McEachern (D)		*100.0*

1990   Republican Primary

Judd Gregg (R)	67,934	*80.8*
Robert A. Bonser (R)	15,207	*18.1*

Democratic Primary

J. Joseph Grandmaison (D)	22,246	*45.7*
Robert F. Preston (D)	21,653	*44.5*
Paul Blacketor (D)	3,923	*8.1*

1992   Republican Primary

Steve Merrill (R)	60,809	*52.7*
Edward C. du Pont (R)	25,530	*22.1*
Elizabeth Hager (R)	24,433	*21.2*

Democratic Primary		
Deborah A. Arnesen (D)	41,770	47.7
Norman E. D'Amours (D)	23,919	27.3
Ned Helms (D)	19,792	22.6

1994 **Republican Primary**

Steve Merrill (R)	68,340	87.9
Fred Bramante (R)	6,623	8.5

Democratic Primary

Wayne D. King (D)	24,867	89.5

Libertarian Primary

Steve Winter (LIBERT)	773	76.7
Calvin Warburton (LIBERT)	235	23.3

1996 **Republican Primary**

Ovide M. Lamontagne (R)	47,628	46.7
Bill Zeliff (R)	43,407	42.5
Al Rubega (R)	6,062	5.9

Democratic Primary

Jeanne Shaheen (D)	52,293	85.7
Sid Lovett (D)	4,289	7.0

Libertarian Primary

Robert Kingsbury (LIBERT)	325	46.0
Clarence G. Blevens (LIBERT)	222	31.4
Finlay Rotthaus (LIBERT)	159	22.5

1998 **Republican Primary**

Jay Lucas (R)	24,796	33.9
Jim Rubens (R)	22,444	30.7
Fred Bramante (R)	14,367	19.7
Emile D. Beaulieu (R)	8,521	11.7

Democratic Primary

Jeanne Shaheen (D)	28,628	93.8

2000 **Republican Primary**

Gordon Humphrey (R)	54,134	51.9
James Squires (R)	23,582	22.6
Jeffrey Howard (R)	21,734	20.8

Democratic Primary

Jeanne Shaheen (D)	45,249	60.4
Mark D. Fernald (D)	28,488	38.0

NEW JERSEY

Candidates	Votes	%

1957 **Republican Primary**

Malcolm S. Forbes (R)	216,677	63.7
Wayne Dumont (R)	123,350	36.3

Democratic Primary

Robert B. Meyner (D)		100.0

1961 **Republican Primary**

James P. Mitchell (R)	202,188	43.7
Walter H. Jones (R)	160,553	34.7
Wayne Dumont (R)	95,761	20.7

Democratic Primary

Richard J. Hughes (D)	222,789	84.2
Weldon R. Sheets (D)	21,285	8.0
Eugene E. Demarest (D)	20,487	7.7

1965 **Republican Primary**

Wayne Dumont (R)	167,402	50.3
Charles W. Sandman (R)	154,491	46.5

Democratic Primary

Richard J. Hughes (D)	236,518	90.9
William J. Clark (D)	23,722	9.1

1969 **Republican Primary**

William T. Cahill (R)	158,980	39.3
Charles W. Sandman (R)	144,877	35.8
Harry L. Sears (R)	46,778	11.6
Francis X. McDermott (R)	35,503	8.8

Democratic Primary

Robert B. Meyner (D)	173,801	44.8
William F. Kelly (D)	87,888	22.6
Henry Hellstoski (D)	60,483	15.6
D. Louis Tonti (D)	34,810	9.0
Ned J. Parsekian (D)	24,908	6.4

1973 **Republican Primary**

Charles W. Sandman (R)	209,657	57.5
William T. Cahill (R)	148,034	40.6

Democratic Primary

Brendan T. Byrne (D)	193,120	45.3
Ann Klein (D)	116,705	27.4
Ralph C. DeRose (D)	95,085	22.3

1977 **Republican Primary**

Raymond H. Bateman (R)	196,592	54.7
Thomas H. Kean (R)	129,982	36.2
C. Robert Sarcone (R)	20,861	5.8

Democratic Primary

Brendan T. Byrne (D)	175,448	30.3
Robert A. Roe (D)	134,116	23.2
Ralph C. DeRose (D)	99,948	17.3
James J. Florio (D)	87,743	15.1
Joseph A. Hoffman (D)	58,835	10.2

1981 **Republican Primary**

Thomas H. Kean (R)	122,512	30.7
Lawrence F. Kramer (R)	83,565	21.0
Joseph Sullivan (R)	67,651	17.0
Jim Wallwork (R)	61,816	15.5
Barry T. Parker (R)	26,040	6.5

Democratic Primary		
James J. Florio (D)	164,179	25.9
Robert A. Roe (D)	98,660	15.6
Kenneth A. Gibson (D)	95,212	15.0
Joseph P. Merlino (D)	70,910	11.2
John J. Degnan (D)	65,844	10.4
Thomas F. X. Smith (D)	57,479	9.1

1985 Republican Primary

Thomas H. Kean (R)		100.0

Democratic Primary		
Peter Shapiro (D)	101,243	31.0
John F. Russo (D)	86,827	26.6
Kenneth A. Gibson (D)	85,293	26.1
Stephen B. Wiley (D)	27,914	8.6
Robert J. Del Tufo (D)	19,742	6.0

1989 Republican Primary

James A. Courter (R)	112,326	29.0
Cary Edwards (R)	85,313	22.0
Chuck Hardwick (R)	82,392	21.3
Bill Gormley (R)	66,430	17.2
Gerald Cardinale (R)	32,250	8.3

Democratic Primary		
James J. Florio (D)	251,979	68.2
Barbara Boggs Sigmund (D)	61,033	16.5
Alan J. Karcher (D)	56,311	15.2

1993 Republican Primary

Christine Todd Whitman (R)	159,765	40.0
Cary Edwards (R)	131,578	32.9
Bill Wallwork (R)	96,034	24.0

Democratic Primary		
James J. Florio (D)		100.0

1997 Republican Primary

Christine Todd Whitman (R)	147,731	100.0

Democratic Primary		
James McGreevey (D)	148,153	39.9
Robert E. Andrews (D)	138,160	37.2
Michael Murphy (D)	79,172	21.3

NEW MEXICO

Candidates	Votes	%

1956 Republican Primary

Edwin L. Mechem (R)		100.0

Democratic Primary		
John F. Simms (D)	46,722	48.3
Ingram B. Pickett (D)	43,937	45.4
Robert F. Stephens (D)	6,067	6.3

1958 Republican Primary

Edwin L. Mechem (R)		100.0

Democratic Primary		
John Burroughs (D)	46,344	43.8
Joseph A. Bursey (D)	33,623	31.7
Ingram B. Pickett (D)	18,150	17.1
Robert C. Dow (D)	5,569	5.2

1960 Republican Primary

Edwin L. Mechem (R)	29,486	76.0
Paul W. Robinson (R)	9,331	24.0

Democratic Primary		
John Burroughs (D)	66,541	53.7
Joseph A. Bursey (D)	48,841	39.4
Thomas E. Holland (D)	8,413	6.8

1962 Republican Primary

Edwin L. Mechem (R)		100.0

Democratic Primary		
Jack M. Campbell (D)	47,873	38.7
Ed V. Mead (D)	44,385	35.9
Leo T. Murphy (D)	28,755	23.3

1964 Republican Primary

Merle H. Tucker (R)		100.0

Democratic Primary		
Jack M. Campbell (D)		100.0

1966 Republican Primary

David F. Cargo (R)	17,836	51.8
Clifford J. Hawley (R)	16,588	48.2

Democratic Primary		
Thomas E. Lusk (D)	85,211	59.9
John Burroughs (D)	57,143	40.1

1968 Republican Primary

David F. Cargo (R)	28,014	54.9
Clifford J. Hawley (R)	23,052	45.1

Democratic Primary		
Fabian Chavez (D)	41,348	30.9
Bruce King (D)	24,658	18.4
Calvin Horn (D)	24,376	18.2
Mack Easley (D)	21,436	16.0
Bobby M. Mayfield (D)	19,528	14.6

1970 Republican Primary

Pete V. Domenici (R)	25,881	46.0
Stephen C. Helbing (R)	13,265	23.6
Edward M. Hartman (R)	5,309	9.4
Tom Clear (R)	5,262	9.3
Junio Lopez (R)	4,272	7.6

Democratic Primary

Bruce King (D)	62,718	48.9
Jack Daniels (D)	47,523	37.1
Alexander F. Sceresse (D)	17,918	14.0

1974   Republican Primary

Joe Skeen (R)	28,227	55.4
John P. Eastham (R)	15,003	29.5
James L. Hughes (R)	4,758	9.3
Walter E. Bruce (R)	2,913	5.7

Democratic Primary

Jerry Apodaca (D)	45,447	30.6
Tibo J. Chavez (D)	35,090	23.6
Odis Echols (D)	25,760	17.3
Bobby M. Mayfield (D)	22,806	15.3
Drew Cloud (D)	12,707	8.6

1978   Republican Primary

Joe Skeen (R)	38,638	81.2
Philip R. Grant (R)	8,966	18.8

Democratic Primary

Bruce King (D)	92,432	61.3
Robert E. Ferguson (D)	58,334	38.7

1982   Republican Primary

John B. Irick (R)	35,789	54.5
William A. Sego (R)	27,220	41.5

Democratic Primary

Toney Anaya (D)	101,077	56.9
Aubrey L. Dunn (D)	60,866	34.3
Fabian Chavez (D)	11,874	6.7

1986   Republican Primary

Garrey E. Carruthers (R)	27,671	31.1
Joseph H. Mercer (R)	23,560	26.4
Colin R. McMillan (R)	19,807	22.2
Frank M. Bond (R)	10,619	11.9
Paul F. Becht (R)	6,566	7.4

Democratic Primary

Ray B. Pohwell (D)		100.0

1990   Republican Primary

Frank M. Bond (R)	44,928	55.5
Les Houston (R)	27,073	33.4
James A. Caudell (R)	4,681	5.8
Harry F. Kinney (R)	4,289	5.3

Democratic Primary

Bruce King (D)	95,884	52.9
Paul Bardacke (D)	70,169	38.7

1994   Republican Primary

Gary E. Johnson (R)	32,091	34.5
Dick Cheney (R)	30,811	33.1

John Dendahl (R)	18,007	19.3
David F. Cargo (R)	12,105	13.0

Democratic Primary

Bruce King (D)	76,039	38.8
Casey E. Luna (D)	71,364	36.4
Jim Baca (D)	48,401	24.7

1998   Republican Primary

Gary E. Johnson (R)	64,669	100.0

Democratic Primary

Martin J. Chavez (D)	82,147	48.1
Gary K. King (D)	51,847	30.4
Jerry Apodaca (D)	16,303	9.5
Robert E. Vigil (D)	10,483	6.1

NEW YORK

Candidates	Votes	%

1970[1]   Republican Primary

Nelson A. Rockefeller (R)		100.0

Democratic Primary

Arthur J. Goldberg (D)	493,295	52.2
Howard J. Samuels (D)	451,703	47.8

Conservative Primary

Paul L. Adams (C)		100.0

Liberal Primary

Arthur J. Goldberg (L)		100.0

1974   Republican Primary

Malcolm Wilson (R)		100.0

Democratic Primary

Hugh L. Carey (D)	600,283	60.8
Howard J. Samuels (D)	387,369	39.2

Conservative Primary

Malcolm Wilson (C)		100.0

Liberal Primary

Edward Morrison (L)[2]		100.0

1978   Republican Primary

Perry B. Duryea (R)		100.0

Democratic Primary

Hugh L. Carey (D)	376,457	52.0
Mary Anne Krupsak (D)	244,252	33.7
Jeremiah B. Bloom (D)	103,479	14.3

Conservative Primary

Perry B. Duryea (C)		100.0

Liberal Primary

Hugh L. Carey (L)		100.0

1982 **Republican Primary**

Lew Lehrman (R)	464,231	80.6
Paul J. Curran (R)	111,814	19.4

Democratic Primary

Mario M. Cuomo (D)	678,900	52.3
Edward I. Koch (D)	618,356	47.7

Conservative Primary

Lew Lehrman (R)		100.0

Liberal Primary

Mario M. Cuomo (L)		100.0

Right to Life Primary

Robert J. Bohner (RTL)		100.0

1986 **Republican Primary**

Andrew P. O'Rouke (R)		100.0

Democratic Primary

Mario M. Cuomo (D)		100.0

Conservative Primary

Andrew P. O'Rouke (C)		100.0

Liberal Primary

Mario M. Cuomo (L)		100.0

Right to Life Primary

Denis E. Dillon (RTL)		100.0

1990 **Republican Primary**

Pierre A. Rinfret (R)		100.0

Democratic Primary

Mario M. Cuomo (D)		100.0

Conservative Primary

Herbert I. London (C)		100.0

Liberal Primary

Mario M. Cuomo (L)		100.0

Right to Life Primary

Louis P. Wein (RTL)		100.0

1994 **Republican Primary**

George E. Pataki (R)	273,620	75.6
Richard M. Rosenbaum (R)	88,302	24.4

Democratic Primary

Mario M. Cuomo (D)	548,762	79.5
Lenora B. Fulani (D)	141,918	20.5

Conservative Primary

George E. Pataki (C)	17,649	78.4
Robert G. Relph (C)	4,862	21.6

1998 **Republican Primary**

George E. Pataki (R)		100.0

Democratic Primary

Peter F. Vallone (D)	416,147	56.4
Beth McCaughey Ross (D)	156,592	21.2
Charles J. Hynes (D)	109,333	14.8
James L. Larocca (D)	56,011	7.6

New York
1. Until 1970, candidates for state office in New York were nominated by state party conventions or central committees.
2. Morrison withdrew after the primary and the Liberal state committee substituted Hugh L. Carey as the party's nominee.

NORTH CAROLINA

	Candidates	Votes	%
1920	**Democratic Primary**		
	Cameron Morrison (D)	49,070	38.3
	O. Max Gardner (D)	48,983	38.2
	R. N. Page (D)	30,180	23.5
	Democratic Runoff		
	Cameron Morrison (D)	70,332	53.5
	O. Max Gardner (D)	61,073	46.5
1924	**Democratic Primary**		
	Angus Wilton McLean (D)	151,197	64.4
	Josiah W. Bailey (D)	83,573	35.6
1928	**Democratic Primary**		
	O. Max Gardner (D)		100.0
1932	**Democratic Primary**		
	J. C. B. Ehringhaus (D)	162,498	42.8
	R. T. Fountain (D)	115,127	30.3
	Allen J. Maxwell (D)	102,032	26.9
	Democratic Runoff		
	J. C. B. Ehringhaus (D)	182,005	51.9
	R. T. Fountain (D)	168,971	48.1
1936	**Democratic Primary**		
	Clyde R. Hoey (D)	193,972	37.5
	Ralph McDonald (D)	189,504	36.7
	A. H. Graham (D)	126,782	24.5
	Democratic Runoff		
	Clyde R. Hoey (D)	266,354	55.4
	Ralph McDonald (D)	214,414	44.6

1940   **Republican Primary**

Robert H. McNeill (R)	13,190	47.3
Pritchard (R)	11,847	42.7
Hoffman (R)	2,773	10.0

Democratic Primary

J. Melville Broughton (D)	147,386	31.4
W. P. Horton (D)[1]	105,916	22.6
A. J. Maxwell (D)	102,095	21.8
Lee Gravely (D)	63,030	13.4
Thomas E. Cooper (D)	33,176	7.1

1944   **Democratic Primary**

R. Gregg Cherry (D)	185,027	57.5
Ralph McDonald (D)	134,661	41.9

1948   **Democratic Primary**

Charles M. Johnson (D)	170,141	40.2
W. Kerr Scott (D)	161,293	38.1
R. Mayne Albright (D)	76,281	18.0

Democratic Runoff

W. Kerr Scott (D)	217,620	54.4
Charles M. Johnson (D)	182,684	45.6

1952   **Democratic Primary**

William B. Ulmstead (D)	294,170	52.1
Hubert E. Olive (D)	265,675	47.1

1956   **Republican Primary**

Kyle Hayes (R)		100.0

Democratic Primary

Luther H. Hodges (D)	401,082	86.0
Tom Sawyer (D)	29,248	6.3
Harry P. Stokely (D)	24,416	5.2

1960   **Republican Primary**

Robert L. Gavin (R)		100.0

Democratic Primary

Terry Sanford (D)	269,463	41.3
I. Beverly Lake (D)	181,692	27.8
Malcolm B. Seawell (D)	101,148	15.5
John D. Larkins (D)	100,757	15.4

Democratic Runoff

Terry Sanford (D)	352,133	56.1
I. Beverly Lake (D)	275,905	43.9

1964   **Republican Primary**

Robert L. Gavin (R)	53,145	83.3
Charles W. Strong (R)	8,652	13.6

Democratic Primary

Richardson Preyer (D)	281,430	36.6
Dan K. Moore (D)	257,872	33.5
I. Beverly Lake (D)	217,172	28.2

Democratic Runoff

Dan K. Moore (D)	480,431	62.1
Richardson Preyer (D)	293,863	38.0

1968   **Republican Primary**

James C. Gardner (R)	113,584	72.7
John L. Stikley (R)	42,483	27.3

Democratic Primary

Robert W. Scott (D)	337,368	48.1
J. Melville Broughton Jr. (D)[2]	233,924	33.4
Reginald A. Hawkins (D)	129,808	18.5

1972   **Republican Primary**

James C. Gardner (R)	84,906	49.8
James E. Holshouser Jr. (R)	83,637	49.0

Republican Runoff

James E. Holshouser Jr. (R)	69,916	50.6
James C. Gardner (R)	68,134	49.4

Democratic Primary

Hargrove "Skipper" Bowles Jr. (D)	367,433	45.5
H. P. "Pat" Taylor (D)	304,910	37.7
Reginald A. Hawkins (D)	65,950	8.2
Wilbur Hobby (D)	58,990	7.3

Democratic Runoff

Hargrove "Skipper" Bowles Jr. (D)	336,034	54.3
H. P. "Pat" Taylor (D)	282,345	45.7

1976   **Republican Primary**

David T. Flaherty (R)	57,663	49.8
Coy C. Privette (R)	37,573	32.4
J. F. Alexander (R)	16,149	13.9

Republican Runoff

David T. Flaherty (R)	45,661	60.5
Coy C. Privette (R)	29,810	39.5

Democratic Primary

James B. "Jim" Hunt Jr. (D)	362,102	53.4
Edward M. O'Herron (D)	157,815	23.2
George Wood (D)	121,673	17.9

1980   **Republican Primary**

I. Beverly Lake Jr. (R)	119,255	80.8
C. J. Carstens (R)	28,354	19.2

Democratic Primary

James B. "Jim" Hunt Jr. (D)	524,844	69.6
Robert W. Scott (D)	217,289	28.8

1984   **Republican Primary**

James G. Martin (R)	128,714	91.7
Ruby T. Hooper (R)	11,640	8.3

Democratic Primary

Rufus Edmisten (D)	295,051	30.9
H. Edward Knox (D)	249,286	26.1
D. M. Faircloth (D)	153,210	16.0
Thomas O. Gilmore (D)	82,299	8.6
James C. Green (D)	80,775	8.4
John Ingram (D)	75,248	7.9

Democratic Runoff

Rufus Edmisten (D)	352,351	51.9
H. Edward Knox (D)	326,278	48.1

1988 Republican Primary

James G. Martin (R)		100.0

Democratic Primary

Robert B. Jordan (D)	403,145	79.7
Billy Martin (D)	60,770	12.0

1992 Republican Primary

James C. Gardner (R)	215,528	82.0
Ruby T. Hooper (R)	26,179	10.0
Gary M. Dunn (R)	21,256	8.1

Democratic Primary

James B. "Jim" Hunt Jr. (D)	459,300	65.5
Lacy H. Thornburg (D)	188,806	26.9

1996 Republican Primary

Robin Hayes (R)	140,351	50.2
Richard Vinroot (R)	127,916	45.7

Democratic Primary

James B. "Jim" Hunt Jr. (D)		100.0

2000 Republican Primary

Richard Vinroot (R)	142,820	45.5
Leo Daughtry (R)	116,115	37.0
Charles B. Neely (R)	48,101	15.3

Democratic Primary

Mike Easley (D)	330,764	58.9
Dennis A. Wicker (D)	203,723	36.3

North Carolina
1. Horton declined a runoff with Broughton, who became the Democratic nominee.
2. J. Melville Broughton Jr. declined a runoff with Scott, who became the Democratic nominee.

NORTH DAKOTA

	Candidates	Votes	%

1956 Republican Primary

John E. Davis (R)	55,149	53.3
Ray Schnell (R)	48,296	46.7

Democratic Primary

Wallace E. Warner (D)		100.0

1958 Republican Primary

John E. Davis (R)		100.0

Democratic Primary

John F. Lord (D)	26,447	55.4
Art Ford (D)	21,271	44.6

1960 Republican Primary

C. P. Dahl (R)	86,900	77.6
Orris G. Nordhougen (R)	25,132	22.4

Democratic Primary

William L. Guy (D)		100.0

1962 Republican Primary

Mark Andrews (R)		100.0

Democratic Primary

William L. Guy (D)		100.0

1964 Republican Primary

Donald M. Halcrow (R)	43,089	55.0
Robert P. McCarney (R)	35,269	45.0

Democratic Primary

William L. Guy (D)		100.0

1968 Republican Primary

Robert P. McCarney (R)	47,324	52.5
Edward W. Doherty (R)	42,845	47.5

Democratic Primary

William L. Guy (D)		100.0

1972 Republican Primary

Richard Larsen (R)	66,045	67.8
Robert P. McCarney (R)	31,377	32.2

Democratic Primary

Arthur A. Link (D)	29,979	93.1
Edward P. Burns (D)	2,231	6.9

1976 Republican Primary

Richard Elkin (R)	54,427	81.9
Herb Geving (R)	12,013	18.1

Democratic Primary

Arthur A. Link (D)		100.0

American Primary

Martin Vaaler (AM)		100.0

1980 Republican Primary

Allen I. Olson (R)	60,016	75.7
Orville W. Hagen (R)	19,306	24.3

Democratic Primary

Arthur A. Link (D)		100.0

1984 Republican Primary

Allen I. Olson (R)	41,191	100.0

Democratic Primary

George A. Sinner (D)	36,461	87.6
Anna Belle Bourgois (D)	5,180	12.4

1988 Republican Primary

Leon L. Mallberg (R)		100.0

Democratic Primary

George A. Sinner (D)		100.0

1992 Republican Primary

Edward T. Schafer (R)	47,300	100.0

Democratic Primary

Nicholas Spaeth (D)	50,607	65.1
Bill Heigaard (D)	27,161	34.9

1996 Republican Primary

Edward T. Schafer (R)	48,412	100.0

Democratic Primary

Lee Kaldor (D)	46,049	100.0

2000 Republican Primary

John Hoeven (R)	40,308	100.0

Democratic Primary

Heidi Heitkamp (D)	34,851	100.0

OHIO

Candidates	Votes	%

1956 Republican Primary

C. William O'Neill (R)	425,947	72.5
John W. Brown (R)	161,826	27.5

Democratic Primary

Michael V. DiSalle (D)	279,831	57.4
John E. Sweeney (D)	106,071	21.8
Robert W. Reider (D)	41,224	8.5
Frank X. Kryzan (D)	37,290	7.6

1958 Republican Primary

C. William O'Neill (R)	346,660	63.6
Charles P. Taft (R)	198,173	36.4

Democratic Primary

Michael V. DiSalle (D)	242,830	37.7
Anthony J. Celebrezze (D)	140,453	21.8
Albert S. Porter (D)	108,498	16.8

Robert N. Gorman (D)	57,694	9.0
M. E. Sensenbrenner (D)	52,350	8.1
Clingan Jackson (D)	35,175	5.5

1962 Republican Primary

James A. Rhodes (R)	520,868	89.6
William L. White (R)	59,916	10.3

Democratic Primary

Michael V. DiSalle (D)	331,463	50.3
Mark McElroy (D)	299,207	45.4

1966 Republican Primary

James A. Rhodes (R)	577,827	88.7
William L. White (R)	73,428	11.3

Democratic Primary

Frazier Reams Jr. (D)	326,419	58.5
Harry H. McIlwain (D)	231,406	41.5

1970 Republican Primary

Roger Cloud (R)	468,369	50.5
Donald E. Lukens (R)	283,257	30.5
Paul W. Brown (R)	164,672	17.7

Democratic Primary

John J. Gilligan (D)	547,675	59.7
Robert E. Sweeney (D)	216,195	23.6
Mark McElroy (D)	153,702	16.7

American Independent Primary

Edwin G. Lawton (AMI)	3,463	64.9
Robert W. Annable (AMI)	1,870	35.1

1974 Republican Primary

James A. Rhodes (R)	385,669	62.8
Charles E. Fry (R)	183,899	29.9
Bert Dawson (R)	44,938	7.3

Democratic Primary

John J. Gilligan (D)	713,488	70.6
James D. Nolan (D)	297,244	29.4

1978 Republican Primary

James A. Rhodes (R)	393,632	67.7
Charles F. Kurfess (R)	187,544	32.3

Democratic Primary

Richard F. Celeste (D)	491,524	84.6
Dale Reusch (D)	88,314	15.2

1982 Republican Primary

Clarence Brown Jr. (R)	347,176	51.5
Seth Taft (R)	153,806	22.8
Thomas A. Van Meter (R)	136,761	20.3
Robert W. Teater (R)	35,821	5.3

Democratic Primary		
Richard F. Celeste (D)	436,887	42.4
William J. Brown (D)	383,007	37.2
Jerry Springer (D)	210,524	20.4

Libertarian Primary		
Phyllis Goetz (LIBERT)		100.0

1986 Republican Primary

James A. Rhodes (R)	352,261	48.2
Paul E. Gillmor (R)	281,737	38.5
Paul E. Pfeifer (R)	96,948	13.3

Democratic Primary		
Richard F. Celeste (D)		100.0

1990 Republican Primary

George Voinovich (R)		100.0

Democratic Primary		
Anthony J. Celebrezze (D)	683,932	83.9
Michael H. Lord (D)	131,564	16.1

1994 Republican Primary

George Voinovich (R)	750,779	100.0

Democratic Primary		
Robert L. Burch (D)	408,159	58.8
Peter M. Schuller (D)	286,275	41.2

1998 Republican Primary

Robert A. Taft II (R)	691,946	100.0

Democratic Primary		
Lee Fisher (D)	663,832	100.0

OKLAHOMA

Candidates	Votes	%

1958 Republican Primary

Phil Ferguson (R)	31,602	51.4
Clarence E. Barnes (R)	21,075	34.3
Carmon C. Harris (R)	5,941	9.7

Democratic Primary		
J. Howard Edmondson (D)	108,358	21.1
W. P. Atkinson (D)	107,616	20.9
George Miskovsky (D)	87,766	17.1
William O. Coe (D)	72,763	14.2
Bill Doenges (D)	57,990	11.3
Jim A. Rinehart (D)	39,279	7.6

Democratic Runoff		
J. Howard Edmondson (D)	363,742	69.6
W. P. Atkinson (D)	158,780	30.4

1962 Republican Primary

Henry L. Bellmon (R)	56,560	91.4
Leslie C. Skoien (R)	5,313	8.6

Democratic Primary		
Raymond Gary (D)	176,525	33.0
W. P. Atkinson (D)	91,182	17.1
Preston J. Moore (D)	85,248	16.0
George Nigh (D)	84,404	15.8
Fred R. Harris (D)	78,476	14.7

Democratic Runoff		
W. P. Atkinson (D)	231,994	50.0
Raymond Gary (D)	231,545	49.9

1966 Republican Primary

Dewey F. Bartlett (R)	46,053	49.0
John N. H. Camp (R)	45,185	48.1

Democratic Primary		
Raymond Gary (D)	160,825	31.6
Preston J. Moore (D)	104,081	20.4
David Hall (D)	94,309	18.5
Cleeta J. Rogers (D)	71,248	14.0
Charles Nesbitt (D)	26,546	5.2

Republican Runoff		
Dewey F. Bartlett (R)	46,916	55.2
John N. H. Camp (R)	38,043	44.8

Democratic Runoff		
Preston J. Moore (D)	228,625	53.7
Raymond Gary (D)	196,835	46.3

1970 Republican Primary

Dewey F. Bartlett (R)		100.0

Democratic Primary		
David Hall (D)	198,976	49.5
Bryce Baggett (D)	96,069	23.9
Joe Cannon (D)	56,842	14.1
Wilburn Cartwright (D)	50,396	12.5

Democratic Runoff		
David Hall (D)	179,902	57.5
Bryce Baggett (D)	132,952	42.5

1974 Republican Primary

James M. Inhofe (R)	88,594	58.8
Denzil D. Garrison (R)	62,188	41.2

Democratic Primary		
Clem R. McSpadden (D)	238,534	37.7
David L. Boren (D)	225,321	35.6
David Hall (D)	169,290	26.7

Democratic Runoff

David L. Boren (D)	286,171	53.5
Clem R. McSpadden (D)	248,623	46.5

1978 Republican Primary

Ron Shotts (R)	82,895	76.8
Jerry L. Mash (R)	13,145	12.2
Jim Head (R)	11,826	11.0

Democratic Primary

George Nigh (D)	276,910	49.9
Larry Derryberry (D)	208,055	37.5
Bob Funston (D)	69,475	12.5

Democratic Runoff

George Nigh (D)	269,681	57.7
Larry Derryberry (D)	197,457	42.3

1982 Republican Primary

Tom Daxon (R)	73,677	64.7
Neal A. McCaleb (R)	35,379	31.1

Democratic Primary

George Nigh (D)	379,301	82.6
Howard L. Bell (D)	79,735	17.4

1986 Republican Primary

Henry L. Bellmon (R)	111,665	70.3
Mike Fair (R)	33,266	20.9

Democratic Primary

David Walters (D)	238,165	46.0
Mike Turpen (D)	207,357	40.0
Leslie Fisher (D)	33,639	6.5

Democratic Runoff

David Walters (D)	235,373	50.4
Mike Turpen (D)	231,390	49.6

1990 Republican Primary

Vince Orza (R)	75,992	40.1
Bill Price (R)	51,355	27.1
Burns Hargis (R)	33,641	17.8
Jerry Brown (R)	25,670	13.5

Republican Runoff

Bill Price (R)	94,682	50.8
Vince Orza (R)	91,599	49.2

Democratic Primary

Wes Watkins (D)	175,568	32.3
David Walters (D)	171,730	31.6
Steve Lewis (D)	160,455	29.5

Democratic Runoff

David Walters (D)	243,252	50.7
Wes Watkins (D)	236,597	49.3

1994 Republican Primary

Frank Keating (R)	117,265	56.9
Jerry Pierce (R)	60,280	29.3
Virginia Hale (R)	15,229	7.4

Democratic Primary

Jack Mildren (D)	214,765	48.6
Bernice Shedrick (D)	165,066	37.3
Danny Williams (D)	46,571	10.5

1998 Republican Primary

Frank Keating (R)		100.0

Democratic Primary

Laura Boyd (D)	171,121	60.2
James Hager (D)	112,941	39.8

OREGON

Candidates	Votes	%
1956 Republican Primary		
Elmo E. Smith (R)	225,748	91.0
Earl L. Dickson (R)	22,306	9.0
Democratic Primary		
Robert D. Holmes (D)	112,307	50.8
Lew Wallace (D)	108,822	49.2
1958 Republican Primary		
Mark O. Hatfield (R)	106,687	47.9
Sig Unander (R)	65,180	29.2
Warren Gill (R)	40,489	18.2
Democratic Primary		
Robert D. Holmes (D)	129,491	62.0
Lew Wallace (D)	59,992	28.7
Wiley W. Smith (D)	18,484	8.8
1962 Republican Primary		
Mark O. Hatfield (R)	174,811	82.2
George Altvater (R)	37,306	17.5
Democratic Primary		
Robert Y. Thornton (D)	149,000	66.2
Walter J. Pearson (D)	62,331	27.7
1966 Republican Primary		
Tom McCall (R)	215,959	91.4
John L. Reynolds (R)	20,286	8.6
Democratic Primary		
Robert W. Straub (D)	182,697	72.5
Ben Musa (D)	41,610	16.5
Emmet T. Rogers (D)	17,618	7.0

1970	**Republican Primary**		
	Tom McCall (R)	183,298	74.4
	Robert H. Wampler (R)	38,322	15.6
	Andrew R. Gigler (R)	24,797	10.1
	Democratic Primary		
	Robert W. Straub (D)	182,683	65.9
	Art Pearl (D)	33,716	12.2
	Gracie Hansen (D)	20,329	7.3
	Al Holdiman (D)	18,180	6.6
1974	**Republican Primary**		
	Victor G. Atiyeh (R)	144,454	60.7
	Clay Myers (R)	79,003	33.2
	Democratic Primary		
	Robert W. Straub (D)	107,205	33.6
	Betty Roberts (D)	98,654	30.9
	Jim Redden (D)	88,795	27.8
1978	**Republican Primary**		
	Victor G. Atiyeh (R)	115,593	46.4
	Tom McCall (R)	83,568	33.5
	Roger Martin (R)	42,644	17.1
	Democratic Primary		
	Robert W. Straub (D)	144,761	51.0
	Marvin J. Hollingsworth (D)	52,901	18.7
	Emily Ashworth (D)	49,201	17.3
1982	**Republican Primary**		
	Victor G. Atiyeh (R)	208,333	82.4
	Clif Everett (R)	17,741	7.0
	Walter Huss (R)	16,892	6.7
	Democratic Primary		
	Ted Kulongoski (D)	186,580	59.5
	Don Clark (D)	60,850	19.4
	Jerry Rust (D)	22,962	7.3
1986	**Republican Primary**		
	Norma Paulus (R)	219,505	77.0
	Betty Freauf (R)	36,384	12.8
	Democratic Primary		
	Neil Goldschmidt (D)	214,148	67.4
	Edward N. Fadeley (D)	81,300	25.6
1990	**Republican Primary**		
	Dave Frohnmayer (R)	227,867	79.1
	John K. Lim (R)	32,397	11.2
	Democratic Primary		
	Barbara Roberts (D)		100.0
1994	**Republican Primary**		
	Denny Smith (R)	135,330	49.5
	Craig Berkman (R)	110,821	40.5
	Jack Feder (R)	15,055	5.5

	Democratic Primary		
	John Kitzhaber (D)	250,514	88.5
	Paul D. Wells (D)	30,052	10.6
1998	**Republican Primary**		
	Bill Sizemore (R)	108,036	50.4
	Walter Huss (R)	39,186	18.3
	Jeffrey Brady (R)	34,460	16.1
	Bill Spidal (R)	25,373	11.8
	Democratic Primary		
	John Kitzhaber (D)	271,781	87.7
	Dave Foley (D)	23,870	7.7

PENNSYLVANIA

	Candidates	**Votes**	**%**
1958	**Republican Primary**		
	A. T. McGonigle (R)	578,286	53.3
	Harold E. Stassen (R)	344,043	31.7
	William S. Livengood (R)	138,284	12.7
	Democratic Primary		
	David Lawrence (D)	730,229	74.4
	Roy E. Furman (D)	194,464	19.8
	Edward P. Lavelle (D)	56,188	5.7
1962	**Republican Primary**		
	William W. Scranton (R)	743,785	78.0
	J. Collins McSparran (R)	209,041	21.9
	Democratic Primary		
	Richardson Dilworth (D)	651,096	72.9
	Harvey F. Johnston (D)	143,243	16.0
	Charles J. Schmitt (D)	96,899	10.9
1966	**Republican Primary**		
	Raymond P. Shafer (R)	835,768	78.0
	Harold E. Stassen (R)	172,150	16.1
	George J. Brett (R)	63,366	5.9
	Democratic Primary		
	Milton Shapp (D)	543,057	48.6
	Robert P. Casey (D)	493,886	44.2
	Erwin L. Murray (D)	80,803	7.2
1970	**Republican Primary**		
	Raymond Broderick (R)		100.0
	Democratic Primary		
	Milton Shapp (D)	519,161	49.1
	Robert P. Casey (D)	480,944	45.5
	American Independent Primary		
	Francis T. McGeever (AMI)		100.0

Constitutional Primary

Andrew J. Watson (CST)		100.0

1974   Republican Primary

Andrew L. Lewis (R)	534,637	76.9
Alvin J. Jacobson (R)	97,072	14.0
Leonard M. Strunk (R)	63,868	9.2

Democratic Primary

Milton Shapp (D)	729,201	70.4
Martin P. Mullen (D)	199,613	19.3
Harvey F. Johnston (D)	106,474	10.3

Constitutional Primary

Stephen Depue (CST)	1,006	52.8
Norah M. Cope (CST)	898	47.2

1978   Republican Primary

Richard L. Thornburgh (R)	325,376	32.6
Arlen Specter (R)	206,802	20.7
Bob Butera (R)	190,653	19.1
David W. Marston (R)	161,813	16.2
Henry Hager (R)	57,119	5.7

Democratic Primary

Peter Flaherty (D)	574,889	44.9
Robert P. Casey (D)	445,146	34.7
Ernest P. Kline (D)	223,811	17.5

1982   Republican Primary

Richard L. Thornburgh (R)		100.0

Democratic Primary

Allen E. Ertel (D)	436,251	57.6
Steve Douglas (D)	143,762	19.0
Earl S. McDowell (D)	116,880	15.4
Eugene Knox (D)	59,925	7.9

1986   Republican Primary

William W. Scranton (R)		100.0

Democratic Primary

Robert Casey (D)	549,376	56.4
Edward G. Rendell (D)	385,539	39.6

1990   Republican Primary

Barbara Hafer (R)	321,026	54.4
Marguerite A. Luksik (R)	268,773	45.6

Democratic Primary

Robert Casey (D)	636,594	77.5
Philip J. Berg (D)	184,365	22.5

1994   Republican Primary

Tom J. Ridge (R)	344,708	34.6
Ernie Preate (R)	287,400	28.8
Sam Katz (R)	156,895	15.7

Mike Fisher (R)	139,712	14.0
John F. Perry (R)	68,069	6.8

Democratic Primary

Mark S. Singel (D)	346,334	31.2
Dwight Evans (D)	234,285	21.1
Catherine B. Knoll (D)	217,267	19.6
Lynn Yeakel (D)	153,966	13.9
Charles Vope (D)	122,627	11.0

1998   Republican Primary

Tom J. Ridge (R)	501,532	99.2

Democratic Primary

Ivan Itkin (D)	255,555	49.1
Don Bailey (D)	200,451	38.5
William Keisling (D)	63,696	12.2

RHODE ISLAND

Candidates	Votes	%
1956 Republican Primary		
Christopher Del Sesto (R)		100.0
Democratic Primary		
Dennis J. Roberts (D)		100.0
1958 Republican Primary		
Christopher Del Sesto (R)		100.0
Democratic Primary		
Dennis J. Roberts (D)	53,121	56.1
Armand H. Coté (D)	41,536	43.9
1960 Republican Primary		
Christopher Del Sesto (R)		100.0
Democratic Primary		
John A. Notte (D)	73,607	56.3
Armand H. Coté (D)	57,200	43.7
1962 Republican Primary		
John H. Chafee (R)	17,756	62.5
Louis Jackvony (R)	10,459	36.8
Democratic Primary		
John A. Notte (D)	49,204	53.1
Kevin Coleman (D)	41,658	45.0
1964 Republican Primary		
John H. Chafee (R)		100.0
Democratic Primary		
Edward P. Gallogly (D)	55,282	56.7
Alexander R. Walsh (D)	25,457	26.1
John L. Rego (D)	16,715	17.2

1966	**Republican Primary**		
	John H. Chafee (R)		100.0
	Democratic Primary		
	Horace E. Hobbs (D)		100.0
1968	**Republican Primary**		
	John H. Chafee (R)		100.0
	Democratic Primary		
	Frank Licht (D)		100.0
1970	**Republican Primary**		
	Herbert F. DeSimone (R)	11,826	96.0
	Democratic Primary		
	Frank Licht (D)		100.0
1972	**Republican Primary**		
	Herbert F. DeSimone (R)		100.0
	Democratic Primary		
	Philip W. Noel (D)		100.0
1974	**Republican Primary**		
	James W. Nugent (R)		100.0
	Democratic Primary		
	Philip W. Noel (D)		100.0
1976	**Republican Primary**		
	James L. Taft (R)		100.0
	Democratic Primary		
	J. Joseph Garrahy (D)	113,625	82.4
	Giovani Folcarelli (D)	24,314	17.6
1978	**Republican Primary**		
	Lincoln Almond (R)		100.0
	Democratic Primary		
	J. Joseph Garrahy (D)		100.0
1982	**Republican Primary**		
	Vincent Marzullo (R)		100.0
	Democratic Primary		
	J. Joseph Garrahy (D)		100.0
1984	**Republican Primary**		
	Edward D. DiPrete (R)	245,059	100.0
	Democratic Primary		
	Anthony J. Solomon (D)	73,090	57.9
	Joseph W. Walsh (D)	53,041	42.0
1986	**Republican Primary**		
	Edward D. DiPrete (R)		100.0

	Democratic Primary		
	Bruce G. Sundlun (D)	43,120	75.3
	Steve White (D)	14,124	24.7
1988	**Republican Primary**		
	Edward D. DiPrete (R)		100.0
	Democratic Primary		
	Bruce G. Sundlun (D)	68,065	90.3
	Peter Van Daam (D)	7,328	9.7
1990	**Republican Primary**		
	Edward D. DiPrete (R)	7,644	70.8
	Steve White (R)	3,157	29.2
	Democratic Primary		
	Bruce G. Sundlun (D)	68,021	40.5
	Francis X. Flaherty (D)	53,821	32.1
	Joseph R. Paolino (D)	46,074	27.4
1992	**Republican Primary**		
	Elizabeth Ann Leonard (R)	7,534	52.1
	J. Michael Levesque (R)	6,926	47.9
	Democratic Primary		
	Bruce G. Sundlun (D)	78,735	52.2
	Francis X. Flaherty (D)	72,011	47.8
1994	**Republican Primary**		
	Lincoln C. Almond (R)	24,873	57.8
	Ronald K. Machtley (R)	18,150	42.2
	Democratic Primary		
	Myrth York (D)	56,719	57.2
	Bruce G. Sundlun (D)	27,432	27.7
	Louise Durfee (D)	11,914	12.0
1998	**Republican Primary**		
	Lincoln C. Almond (R)	5,510	100.0
	Democratic Primary		
	Myrth York (D)	53,561	82.9
	Jack Dennison Potter (D)	11,055	17.1

SOUTH CAROLINA

	Candidates	Votes	%
1920	**Democratic Primary**		
	Robert A. Cooper (D)		100.0
1922	**Democratic Primary**		
	Coleman L. Blease (D)	77,798	44.8
	Thomas G. McLeod (D)	65,768	37.9
	George K. Laney (D)	23,164	13.4
	Democratic Runoff		
	Thomas G. McLeod (D)	100,114	53.8
	Coleman L. Blease (D)	85,834	46.2

1924[1]   **Democratic Primary**

Thomas G. McLeod (D)	107,356	61.2
J. T. Duncan (D)	68,155	38.8

1926   **Democratic Primary**

John G. Richards (D)	44,806	25.8
Ibra C. Blackwood (D)	34,870	20.1
Edmund B. Jackson (D)	33,804	19.5
Carroll D. Nance (D)	16,970	9.8
George K. Laney (D)	13,386	7.7
Thomas H. Peeples (D)	10,636	6.1
D. A. G. Ouzts (D)	10,570	6.1

Democratic Runoff

John G. Richards (D)	95,007	58.2
Ibra C. Blackwood (D)	68,224	41.8

1930   **Democratic Primary**

Olin D. Johnston (D)	58,653	24.9
Ibra C. Blackwood (D)	43,859	18.6
Lever (D)	39,477	16.8
Williams (D)	36,488	15.5
Keith (D)	28,780	12.2
Herbert (D)	17,102	7.3

Democratic Runoff

Ibra C. Blackwood (D)	118,721	50.2
Olin D. Johnston (D)	117,752	49.8

1934   **Democratic Primary**

Olin D. Johnston (D)	104,799	35.2
Coleman L. Blease (D)	85,795	28.9
Wyndham Manning (D)	55,767	18.8
Pearce (D)	36,328	12.2

Democratic Runoff

Olin D. Johnston (D)	157,673	56.2
Coleman L. Blease (D)	122,876	43.8

1938   **Democratic Primary**

Burnet R. Maybank (D)	177,900	44.9
Wyndham Manning (D)	74,356	18.8
Coleman L. Blease (D)	60,823	15.4
Bennett (D)	47,882	12.1
Adams (D)	26,376	6.7

Democratic Runoff

Burnet R. Maybank (D)	163,947	52.3
Wyndham Manning (D)	149,368	47.7

1942   **Democratic Primary**

Olin D. Johnston (D)	121,465	51.8
Wyndham Manning (D)	113,014	48.2

1946   **Democratic Primary**

Strom Thurmond (D)	96,691	33.4
James C. McLeod (D)	83,464	28.9
Williams (D)	35,813	12.4

Taylor (D)	22,447	7.8
O'Neal (D)	16,574	5.7
Long (D)	16,503	5.7

Democratic Runoff

Strom Thurmond (D)	144,420	57.0
James C. McLeod (D)	109,169	43.1

1950   **Democratic Primary**

James F. Byrnes (D)	248,069	71.6
Bates (D)	63,143	18.2
Pope (D)	29,622	8.6

1954   **Democratic Primary**

George Bell Timmerman Jr. (D)	185,541	61.3
Bates (D)	116,942	38.7

1958   **Democratic Primary**

Ernest F. Hollings (D)	158,159	41.9
Donald S. Russell (D)	132,099	35.0
William C. Johnston (D)	86,981	23.1

Democratic Runoff

Ernest F. Hollings (D)	190,691	56.8
Donald S. Russell (D)	145,162	43.2

1962   **Democratic Primary**

Donald S. Russell (D)	199,619	60.8
Burnet R. Maybank (D)	103,015	31.4
A. W. Bethea (D)	17,251	5.3

1966   **Democratic Primary**

Robert E. McNair (D)		100.0

1970   **Democratic Primary**

John C. West (D)		100.0

1974   **Republican Primary**

James B. Edwards (R)	20,177	57.7
William C. Westmoreland (R)	14,777	42.3

Democratic Primary

Charles D. Ravenel (D)	107,345	33.6
William Jennings Bryan Dorn (D)	105,734	33.1
Earle E. Morris Jr. (D)	80,292	25.2

Democratic Runoff

Charles D. Ravenel (D)[2]	186,985	54.8
William Jennings Bryan Dorn (D)	154,187	45.2

1978   **Republican Primary**

Edward L. Young (R)	12,172	51.4
Raymond Finch (R)	11,499	48.6

Democratic Primary

W. Brantley Harvey (D)	142,785	37.5
Richard Riley (D)	125,185	32.9
William Jennings Bryan Dorn (D)	112,793	29.6

Democratic Runoff		
Richard Riley (D)	180,882	53.3
W. Brantley Harvey (D)	158,665	46.7

1982 Republican Primary

W. D. Workman (R)	17,128	81.8
Roddy T. Martin (R)	3,816	18.2

Democratic Primary

Richard Riley (D)		100.0

1986 Republican Primary

Carroll Campbell (R)		100.0

Democratic Primary[3]

Mike Daniel (D)	156,077	47.4
Phil Lader (D)	86,136	26.1
Frank Eppes (D)	59,125	17.9
Hugh Leatherman (D)	28,158	8.5

1990 Republican Primary

Carroll Campbell (R)		100.0

Democratic Primary

Theo Mitchell (D)	116,471	60.1
Ernie Passailaigue (D)	77,429	39.9

1994 Republican Primary

David Beasley (R)	119,724	47.2
Arthur Ravenel (R)	81,129	32.0
Thomas F. Hartnett (R)	52,866	20.8

Democratic Primary

Nick A. Theodore (D)	129,572	49.6
Joe Riley (D)	99,967	38.2
T. Travis Medlock (D)	22,468	8.6

Republican Runoff

David Beasley (R)	134,297	57.6
Arthur Ravenel (R)	98,915	42.4

Democratic Runoff

Nick A. Theodore (D)	113,127	50.4
Joe Riley (D)	111,517	49.6

1998 Republican Primary

David Beasley (R)	114,082	72.2
William "Bill" Able (R)	43,967	27.8

Democratic Primary

James H. Hodges (D)		100.0

South Carolina

1. The *New York Times* of Aug. 28, 1924, provided the returns given for McLeod and Duncan. Gov. McLeod was renominated and subsequently re-elected to a second term.

2. Charles D. Ravenel was ruled ineligible by the state Supreme Court because he did not meet the state's residency requirement for gubernatorial candidates. At a special state party convention, Dorn was designated to replace Ravenel as the Democratic candidate.

3. Neither Lader nor the other two candidates requested a runoff primary, and Daniel was declared the nominee.

SOUTH DAKOTA

Candidates	Votes	%

1956 Republican Primary

Joe J. Foss (R)		100.0

Democratic Primary

Ralph Herseth (D)		100.0

1958 Republican Primary

Phil Saunders (R)	49,746	61.6
L. R. Houck (R)	21,621	26.8
Charles Lacey (R)	9,384	11.6

Democratic Primary

Ralph Herseth (D)		100.0

1960 Republican Primary

Archie M. Gubbrud (R)		100.0

Democratic Primary

Ralph Herseth (D)		100.0

1962 Republican Primary

Archie M. Gubbrud (R)		100.0

Democratic Primary

Ralph Herseth (D)		100.0

1964 Republican Primary

Nils A. Boe (R)	50,335	53.5
Sigurd Anderson (R)	43,809	46.5

Democratic Primary

John F. Lindley (D)	27,071	65.8
Merton B. Tice (D)	14,051	34.2

1966 Republican Primary

Nils A. Boe (R)		100.0

Democratic Primary

Robert Chamberlin (D)		100.0

1968 Republican Primary

Frank Farrar (R)		100.0

Democratic Primary

Robert Chamberlin (D)		100.0

1970 Republican Primary

Frank Farrar (R)	48,520	58.2
Frank E. Henderson (R)	34,893	41.8

Democratic Primary

Richard F. Kneip (D)		100.0

1972 Republican Primary

Carveth Thompson (R)	65,538	72.4
Simon W. Chance (R)	24,975	27.6

Democratic Primary

Richard K. Kneip (D)		100.0

1974 **Republican Primary**

John E. Olson (R)	49,973	55.6
Ronald F. Williamson (R)	25,509	28.4
Oscar W. Hagen (R)	14,444	16.1

Democratic Primary

Richard F. Kneip (D)	45,932	66.2
Bill Dougherty (D)	23,467	33.8

1978 **Republican Primary**

William J. Janklow (R)	46,423	50.9
LeRoy G. Hoffman (R)	30,026	32.9
Clint Roberts (R)	14,774	16.2

Democratic Primary

Roger McKellips (D)	34,160	49.1
Harvey Wollman (D)	32,690	47.0

1982 **Republican Primary**

William J. Janklow (R)		100.0

Democratic Primary

Michael J. O'Connor (D)	24,101	58.8
Elvern R. Varilek (D)	16,916	41.2

1986 **Republican Primary**

George S. Mickelson (R)	40,979	35.3
Clint Roberts (R)	37,250	32.1
Lowell Hansen (R)	21,884	18.8
Alice Kundert (R)	15,985	13.8

Democratic Primary

R. Lars Herseth (D)	30,801	42.8
Richard F. Kneip (D)	27,811	38.7
Kenneth D. Stofferahn (D)	13,332	18.5

1990 **Republican Primary**

George S. Mickelson (R)		100.0

Democratic Primary

Bob L. Samuelson (D)		100.0

1994 **Republican Primary**

William J. Janklow (R)	57,221	54.0
Walter D. Miller (R)	48,754	46.0

Democratic Primary

Jim Beddow (D)	29,082	55.5
Carrol V. "Red" Allen (D)	12,184	23.2
Jim Burg (D)	11,181	21.3

1998 **Republican Primary**

William J. Janklow (R)		100.0

Democratic Primary

Bernie Hunhoff (D)		100.0

TENNESSEE

Candidates	Votes	%

1920 **Democratic Primary**

Albert H. Roberts (D)	67,886	59.6
W. R. Crabtree (D)	44,853	39.4

1922 **Democratic Primary**

Austin Peay (D)	63,940	39.2
Benton McMillin (D)	59,922	36.8
Harvey Hannah (D)	24,062	14.8
L. E. Gwinn (D)	15,137	9.3

1924 **Democratic Primary**

Austin Peay (D)	125,031	79.0
John R. Neal (D)	33,199	21.0

1926 **Democratic Primary**

Austin Peay (D)	96,545	51.6
Hill McAlister (D)	88,488	47.3

1928 **Democratic Primary**

Henry H. Horton (D)	97,333	44.7
Hill McAlister (D)	92,017	42.3
Lewis S. Pope (D)	27,779	12.8

1930 **Democratic Primary**

Henry H. Horton (D)	144,990	58.9
L. E. Gwinn (D)	101,285	41.1

1932 **Democratic Primary**

Hill McAlister (D)	116,020	40.9
Lewis S. Pope (D)	106,450	37.5
M. R. Patterson (D)	58,915	20.8

1934 **Democratic Primary**

Hill McAlister (D)	191,460	58.3
Lewis S. Pope (D)	137,253	41.8

1936 **Democratic Primary**

Gordon Browning (D)	243,463	68.0
Burgin E. Dossett (D)	109,170	30.5

1938 **Democratic Primary**

Prentice Cooper (D)	237,853	59.5
Gordon Browning (D)	158,854	39.7

1940 **Democratic Primary**

Prentice Cooper (D)	240,427	83.6
Dempster (D)	44,122	15.3

1942 **Democratic Primary**

Prentice Cooper (D)	171,259	57.6
J. Ridley Mitchell (D)	124,037	41.7

1944 **Republican Primary**

John W. Kilgo (R)	33,979	63.9
W. O. Lowe (R)	13,425	25.2
H. C. Lowery (R)	3,681	6.9

Democratic Primary

James N. McCord (D)	132,466	87.4
John R. Neal (D)	11,659	7.7

1946 **Republican Primary**

W. O. Lowe (R)	33,269	100.0

Democratic Primary

James N. McCord (D)	187,119	59.8
Gordon Browning (D)	120,535	38.5

1948 **Republican Primary**

Roy Acuff (R)	90,140	80.6
Robert M. McMurry (R)	21,765	19.5

Democratic Primary

Gordon Browning (D)	240,676	55.8
James N. McCord (D)	183,948	42.6

1950 **Democratic Primary**

Gordon Browning (D)	267,855	55.7
Clifford R. Allen (D)	208,634	43.4

1952 **Democratic Primary**

Frank G. Clement (D)	302,491	46.7
Gordon Browning (D)	245,166	37.9
Clifford R. Allen (D)	75,269	11.6

1954 **Democratic Primary**

Frank G. Clement (D)	481,808	68.2
Gordon Browning (D)	195,156	27.6

1958 **Republican Primary**

Robert L. Peters (R)	18,323	59.3
Hansell Proffitt (R)	12,565	40.7

Democratic Primary

Buford Ellington (D)	213,415	31.1
Andrew T. Taylor (D)	204,629	29.9
Edmund Orgill (D)	204,382	29.8
Clifford R. Allen (D)	56,854	8.3

1962 **Republican Primary**

Hubert D. Patty		100.0

Democratic Primary

Frank G. Clement (D)	309,333	42.5
P. R. Olgiati (D)	211,812	29.1
William W. Farris (D)	202,813	27.9

1966 **Democratic Primary**

Buford Ellington (D)	413,950	53.5
John J. Hooker (D)	360,105	46.5

1970 **Republican Primary**

Winfield Dunn (R)	81,475	33.2
Maxey Jarman (R)	70,420	28.7
William Jenkins (R)	50,910	20.8
Claude Robertson (R)	40,547	16.5

Democratic Primary

John J. Hooker (D)	261,580	44.3
Stanley Snodgrass (D)	193,199	32.7
Robert L. Taylor (D)	90,009	15.3

1974 **Republican Primary**

Lamar Alexander (R)	120,773	48.5
Nat Winston (R)	90,980	36.5
Dortch Oldham (R)	35,683	14.3

Democratic Primary

Ray Blanton (D)	148,062	22.7
Jake Butcher (D)	131,412	20.2
Tom Wiseman (D)	89,061	13.7
Hudley Crockett (D)	86,852	13.2
Franklin Haney (D)	84,155	12.9
Stanley Snodgrass (D)	40,211	6.2

1978 **Republican Primary**

Lamar Alexander (R)	230,922	86.0
Harold Sterling (R)	34,037	12.7

Democratic Primary

Jake Butcher (D)	320,329	40.9
Bob Clement (D)	288,577	36.9
Richard Fulton (D)	122,101	15.6
Roger Murray (D)	40,871	5.2

1982 **Republican Primary**

Lamar Alexander (R)		100.0

Democratic Primary

Randy Tyree (D)	318,205	50.0
Anna Belle Clement O'Brien (D)	254,500	40.0

1986 **Republican Primary**

Winfield Dunn (R)	222,458	94.2

Democratic Primary

Ned McWherter (D)	314,449	42.5
Jane Eskind (D)	225,551	30.5
Richard Fulton (D)	190,016	25.7

1990 **Republican Primary**

Dwight Henry (R)	92,100	53.5
Charles R. Moffett (R)	26,363	15.3
Terry A. Williams (R)	18,153	10.6
Carroll Turner (R)	16,293	9.5
Hubert D. Patty (R)	10,097	5.9
Robert O. Watson (R)	8,893	5.2

Democratic Primary

Ned McWherter (D)		100.0

1994 **Republican Primary**

Don Sunquist (R)	386,696	83.3
David Y. Copeland (R)	69,773	15.0

Democratic Primary

Phil Bredesen (D)	284,803	*53.0*
Bill Morris (D)	103,869	*19.3*
Steve Hewlett (D)	43,478	*8.1*
Frank Cochran (D)	41,097	*7.7*

1998   Republican Primary

Don Sunquist (R)	358,786	*92.5*
Shirley Beck-Vosse (R)	28,951	*7.5*

Democratic Primary

John J. Hooker (D)	123,384	*41.3*
Mike Whitaker (D)	83,542	*28.0*
Sherry Whittenberg (D)	28,822	*9.7*
Luther Best (D)	25,565	*8.6*
Donald Jackson (D)	18,458	*6.2*

TEXAS

Candidates	Votes	%

1920   Democratic Primary

Joseph W. Bailey (D)	152,340	*33.9*
Pat M. Neff (D)	149,818	*33.3*
Robert E. Thomason (D)	99,002	*22.0*
Ben F. Looney (D)	48,640	*10.8*

Democratic Runoff

Pat M. Neff (D)	264,075	*58.8*
Joseph W. Bailey (D)	184,702	*41.2*

1922   Democratic Primary

Pat M. Neff (D)	318,000	*53.9*
Fred S. Rogers (D)	195,941	*33.2*
Harry T. Warner (D)	57,617	*9.8*

1924   Democratic Primary

F. D. Robertson (D)	193,508	*27.5*
Miriam A. Ferguson (D)	146,424	*20.8*
Lynch Davidson (D)	141,208	*20.1*
T. W. Davidson (D)	125,011	*17.8*

Democratic Runoff

Miriam A. Ferguson (D)	413,751	*56.7*
F. D. Robertson (D)	316,019	*43.3*

1926   Republican Primary

H. H. Haines (R)	11,215	*73.4*
E. P. Scott (R)	4,074	*26.7*

Democratic Primary

Dan Moody (D)	409,732	*49.9*
Miriam A. Ferguson (D)	283,482	*34.5*
Lynch Davidson (D)	122,449	*14.9*

Democratic Runoff

Dan Moody (D)	495,723	*64.7*
Miriam A. Ferguson (D)	270,595	*35.3*

1928   Democratic Primary

Dan Moody (D)	442,080	*59.9*
Louis J. Wardlaw (D)	245,508	*33.3*

1930   Republican Primary

George C. Butte (R)	5,001	*51.2*
H. E. Exum (R)	2,773	*28.4*
John F. Grant (R)	1,800	*18.4*

Democratic Primary

Miriam A. Ferguson (D)	242,959	*29.2*
Ross S. Sterling (D)	170,754	*20.5*
Clint C. Small (D)	138,934	*16.7*
T. B. Love (D)	87,068	*10.5*
James Young (D)	73,385	*8.8*
Barry Miller (D)	54,652	*6.6*
E. B. Mayfield (D)	54,459	*6.5*

Democratic Runoff

Ross S. Sterling (D)	473,371	*55.2*
Miriam A. Ferguson (D)	384,402	*44.8*

1932   Democratic Primary

Miriam A. Ferguson (D)	402,238	*41.8*
Ross S. Sterling (D)	296,383	*30.8*
Tom F. Hunter (D)	220,391	*22.9*

Democratic Runoff

Miriam A. Ferguson (D)	477,644	*50.2*
Ross S. Sterling (D)	473,846	*49.8*

1934   Republican Primary

D. E. Waggoner (R)	13,043	*100.0*

Democratic Primary

James V. Allred (D)	298,903	*29.9*
Tom F. Hunter (D)	243,254	*24.3*
C. C. McDonald (D)	207,200	*20.7*
Clint C. Small (D)	125,324	*12.5*
Edgar E. Witt (D)	62,476	*6.2*
Maury Hughes (D)	58,815	*5.9*

Democratic Runoff

James V. Allred (D)	499,343	*52.1*
Tom F. Hunter (D)	459,106	*47.9*

1936   Democratic Primary

James V. Allred (D)	553,219	*52.5*
Tom F. Hunter (D)	239,460	*22.7*
F. W. Fischer (D)	145,877	*13.9*
Roy Sanderford (D)	81,170	*7.7*

Democratic Primary		
W. A. Barlocker (D)	74,424	70.6
Ira A. Huggins (D)	31,045	29.4

1964   Republican Primary

Mitchell Melich (R)	63,108	53.0
D. James Cannon (R)	55,938	47.0

Democratic Primary		
Calvin L. Rampton (D)	57,848	62.7
Ernest Howard Dean (D)	34,470	37.3

1968   Republican Primary

Carl W. Buehner (R)	93,635	70.1
Lamar A. Rawlings (R)	39,907	29.9

Democratic Primary		
Calvin L. Rampton (D)		100.0

1972   Republican Primary

Nicholas L. Strike (R)		100.0

Democratic Primary		
Calvin L. Rampton (D)		100.0

1976   Republican Primary

Vernon B. Romney (R)	87,251	53.4
Dixie L. Leavitt (R)	76,139	46.6

Democratic Primary		
Scott M. Matheson (D)	50,505	59.0
John P. Creer (D)	35,154	41.0

1984   Republican Primary

Norman H. Bangerter (R)	94,347	56.4
Dan Marriott (R)	72,940	43.6

Democratic Primary		
Wayne Owens (D)	51,302	62.0
Kem C. Gardner (D)	31,421	38.0

1992   Republican Primary

Michael O. Leavitt (R)	143,514	56.0
Richard M. Eyre (R)	112,881	44.0

Democratic Primary		
Stewart Hanson (D)	64,084	56.8
Patrick Shea (D)	48,758	43.2

2000   Republican Primary

Michael O. Leavitt (R)	122,289	61.8
Glen P. Davis (R)	75,719	38.2

VERMONT

Candidates	Votes	%

1956   Republican Primary

Joseph B. Johnson (R)		100.0

Democratic Primary		
E. Frank Branon (D)		100.0

1958   Republican Primary

Robert T. Stafford (R)		100.0

Democratic Primary		
Bernard J. Leddy (D)		100.0

1960   Republican Primary

F. Ray Keyser (R)	17,491	29.6
Robert S. Babcock (R)	16,762	28.4
A. Luke Crispe (R)	14,874	25.2
W. A. Simpson (R)	9,916	16.8

Democratic Primary		
Russell F. Niquette (D)		100.0

1962   Republican Primary

F. Ray Keyser (R)		100.0

Democratic Primary		
Philip H. Hoff (D)		100.0

1964   Republican Primary

Ralph A. Foote (R)	19,121	42.8
Robert S. Babcock (R)	16,225	36.3
Roger MacBride (R)	9,265	20.7

Democratic Primary		
Philip H. Hoff (D)		100.0

1966   Republican Primary

Richard A. Snelling (R)	22,069	59.0
Thomas L. Hayes (R)	15,286	40.9

Democratic Primary		
Philip H. Hoff (D)		100.0

1968   Republican Primary

Deane C. Davis (R)	36,719	62.7
James L. Oakes (R)	21,791	37.2

Democratic Primary		
John J. Daley (D)		100.0

1970   Republican Primary

Deane C. Davis (R)	31,549	79.3
Thomas L. Hayes (R)	8,048	20.2

Democratic Primary

Leo O'Brien (D)	18,058	*54.7*
John J. Daley (D)	14,795	*44.8*

1972   Republican Primary

Luther F. Hackett (R)	33,323	*54.4*
James M. Jeffords (R)	27,902	*45.5*

Democratic Primary

Thomas P. Salmon (D)		*100.0*

1974   Republican Primary

Walter L. Kennedy (R)	23,738	*55.5*
Harry R. Montague (R)	13,901	*32.5*
T. James Lannon (R)	4,667	*10.9*

Democratic Primary

Thomas P. Salmon (D)	18,498	*83.6*
John F. Reilly (D)	3,537	*16.0*

1976   Republican Primary

Richard Snelling (R)	24,279	*70.8*
William G. Craig (R)	9,429	*27.5*

Democratic Primary

Stella B. Hackel (D)	18,522	*44.0*
Brian D. Burns (D)	14,725	*34.9*
Robert O'Brien (D)	8,809	*20.9*

Liberty Union Primary

Bernard Sanders (LU)		*100.0*

1978   Republican Primary

Richard A. Snelling (R)		*100.0*

Democratic Primary

Edwin C. Granai (D)	8,572	*64.6*
Bernard G. O'Shea (D)	4,570	*34.4*

Liberty Union Primary

Earl S. Gardner (LU)		*100.0*

1980   Republican Primary

Richard A. Snelling (R)	38,228	*85.0*
Clifford Thompson (R)	3,432	*7.6*
Kirk E. Faryniasz (R)	2,273	*5.0*

Democratic Primary

M. Jerome Diamond (D)	15,738	*50.3*
Timothy J. O'Connor (D)	14,857	*47.5*

1982   Republican Primary

Richard A. Snelling (R)		*100.0*

Democratic Primary

Madeleine M. Kunin (D)	16,002	*90.7*
Clifford Thompson (D)	1,433	*8.1*

Liberty Union Primary

Richard F. Gottlieb (LU)		*100.0*

1984   Republican Primary

John J. Easton (R)	30,436	*61.3*
Hilton Wick (R)	19,170	*38.2*

Democratic Primary

Madeleine M. Kunin (D)	17,138	*100.0*

Liberty Union Primary

Richard F. Gottlieb (LU)		*100.0*

1986   Republican Primary

Peter Smith (R)		*100.0*

Democratic Primary

Madeleine M. Kunin (D)		*100.0*

Liberty Union Primary

Richard F. Gottlieb (LU)		*100.0*

1988   Republican Primary

Michael Bernhardt (R)		*100.0*

Democratic Primary

Madeleine M. Kunin (D)		*100.0*

Liberty Union Primary

Richard F. Gottlieb (LU)		*100.0*

1990   Republican Primary

Richard A. Snelling (R)	38,881	*86.7*
Richard F. Gottlieb (R)	5,503	*12.3*

Democratic Primary

Peter Welch (D)	14,656	*86.6*
William Gwin (D)	1,719	*10.2*

Libertarian Primary

David Atkinson (LIBERT)		*100.0*

1992   Republican Primary

John McClaughry (R)	28,026	*92.5*

Democratic Primary

Howard B. Dean (D)	25,504	*98.5*

Liberty Union Primary

Richard F. Gottlieb (LU)		*100.0*

1994   Republican Primary

David F. Kelley (R)	9,864	*33.5*
Thomas J. Morse (R)	8,508	*28.9*
John L. Gropper (R)	7,675	*26.1*
August Jaccaci (R)	1,626	*5.5*

Democratic Primary

Howard B. Dean (D)	25,544	95.6

Liberty Union Primary

Richard F. Gottlieb (LU)	278	91.0

1996   **Republican Primary**

John L. Gropper (R)	12,626	62.2
Thomas J. Morse (LIBERT)	6,710	33.1

Democratic Primary

Howard B. Dean (D)	18,112	97.8

Liberty Union Primary

Mary Alice Herbert (LU)	237	92.2

1998   **Republican Primary**

Ruth Dwyer (R)	30,224	57.5
Bernie Rome (R)	21,196	40.3

Democratic Primary

Howard B. Dean (D)	16,798	93.6

Vermont Grassroots Primary

Joel W. Williams (LU)	3,305	100.0

Libertarian Primary

Amy Berkey (LIBERT)	2,141	100.0

Liberty Union Primary

Richard Gottlieb (LU)	1,177	100.0

2000   **Republican Primary**

Ruth Dwyer (R)	46,611	57.9
William Meub (R)	33,105	41.1

Democratic Primary

Howard B. Dean (D)	31,366	84.4
Brian Pearl (D)	4,357	11.7

VIRGINIA[1]

Candidates	Votes	%

1921   **Democratic Primary**

Elbert Lee Trinkle (D)	86,812	57.5
Henry St. George Tucker (D)	64,286	42.6

1925   **Democratic Primary**

Harry F. Byrd (D)	107,317	61.4
G. Walter Mapp (D)	67,579	38.6

1929   **Democratic Primary**

John Garland Pollard (D)	104,310	75.5
G. Walter Mapp (D)	29,386	21.3

1933   **Democratic Primary**

George C. Peery (D)	116,837	61.6
J. T. Deal (D)	40,268	21.2
W. Worth Smith (D)	32,518	17.2

1937   **Democratic Primary**

James H. Price (D)	166,319	86.1
Vivian L. Page (D)	26,955	14.0

1941   **Democratic Primary**

Colgate W. Darden Jr. (D)	105,655	76.6
Vivian L. Page (D)	19,526	14.2
Hudson Cary (D)	12,793	9.3

1945   **Democratic Primary**

William M. Tuck (D)	97,304	70.1
Moss A. Plunkett (D)	41,484	29.9

1949   **Democratic Primary**

John S. Battle (D)	135,426	42.8
Francis P. Miller (D)	111,697	35.3
Horace H. Edwards (D)	47,435	15.0
Remmie L. Arnold (D)	22,054	7.0

1953   **Democratic Primary**

Thomas B. Stanley (D)	150,499	65.9
Charles R. Fenwick (D)	77,715	34.1

1957   **Democratic Primary**

J. Lindsay Almond Jr. (D)	119,307	79.5
Howard H. Carwile (D)	30,794	20.5

1961   **Democratic Primary**

Albertis S. Harrison Jr. (D)	199,519	56.7
A. E. S. Stephens (D)	152,639	43.3

1965   **Democratic Primary**

Mills E. Godwin Jr. (D)		100.0

1969   **Democratic Primary**

William C. Battle (D)	158,956	38.9
Henry Howell (D)	154,617	37.8
Fred G. Pollard (D)	95,057	23.3

Democratic Runoff

William C. Battle (D)	226,108	52.5
Henry Howell (D)	207,505	47.9

1977   **Democratic Primary**

Henry Howell (D)	253,373	51.4
Andrew P. Miller (D)	239,735	48.6

1989   **Republican Primary**

J. Marshall Coleman (R)	147,941	36.8
Paul S. Trible (R)	141,120	35.1
Stanford E. Parris (R)	112,826	28.1

Virginia

1. After 1977, candidates were chosen by convention rather than through primaries, except for the Republican nomination in 1989.

WASHINGTON[1]

	Candidates	Votes	%
1956	**Republican Primary**		
	Emmett T. Anderson (R)	192,500	59.6
	Don Eastvold (R)	99,020	30.7
	Democratic Primary		
	Albert D. Rosellini (D)	236,291	55.7
	Earl S. Coe (D)	140,882	33.2
	Roderick Lindsay (D)	39,072	9.2
1960	**Republican Primary**		
	Lloyd J. Andrews (R)	263,897	64.6
	Newman Clark (R)	144,440	35.4
	Democratic Primary		
	Albert D. Rosellini (D)	244,579	82.2
	John Patric (D)	28,970	9.7
	Bruce M. Sigman (D)	24,031	8.1
1964	**Republican Primary**		
	Daniel J. Evans (R)	323,152	59.9
	Richard G. Christensen (R)	213,217	39.5
	Democratic Primary		
	Albert D. Rosellini (D)	243,220	84.9
	Jessop McDonnell (D)	17,262	6.0
1968	**Republican Primary**		
	Daniel J. Evans (R)	305,897	89.4
	Democratic Primary		
	John J. O'Connell (D)	182,969	50.5
	Martin J. Durkan (D)	162,382	44.8
1972	**Republican Primary**		
	Daniel J. Evans (R)	224,953	67.9
	Perry B. Woodall (R)	100,372	30.3
	Democratic Primary		
	Albert D. Rosellini (D)	276,121	47.5
	Martin J. Durkan (D)	195,931	33.7
	James A. McDermott (D)	99,155	17.1
1976	**Republican Primary**		
	John Spellman (R)	185,439	60.5
	Harley Hoppe (R)	111,957	36.5
	Democratic Primary		
	Dixy Lee Ray (D)	205,232	37.6
	Wes Uhlman (D)	198,336	36.4
	Marvin Durning (D)	136,290	25.0

	Candidates	Votes	%
1980	**Republican Primary**		
	John Spellman (R)	162,426	40.6
	Duane Berentson (R)	154,724	38.7
	Bruce Chapman (R)	70,875	17.7
	Democratic Primary		
	James A. McDermott (D)	321,256	56.4
	Dixy Lee Ray (D)	234,252	41.1
1984	**Republican Primary**		
	John Spellman (R)	239,463	95.5
	Democratic Primary		
	Booth Gardner (D)	421,087	64.4
	Jim McDermott (D)	209,435	32.0
1988	**Republican Primary**		
	Bob Williams (R)	187,797	56.4
	Norm Maleng (R)	139,274	41.4
	Democratic Primary		
	Booth Gardner (D)	539,243	90.6
	Jeanne Dixon (D)	31,917	5.4
1992	**Republican Primary**		
	Ken Eikenberry (R)	258,553	39.1
	Sid Morrison (R)	250,418	37.9
	Dan McDonald (R)	144,050	21.8
	Democratic Primary		
	Mike Lowry (D)	337,783	70.1
	Joe King (D)	96,480	20.0
	Sally McQuown (D)	31,175	6.5
1996	**Republican Primary**		
	Ellen Craswell (R)	185,680	31.9
	Dale Foreman (R)	162,615	28.0
	Norm Maleng (R)	109,088	18.8
	Jim Waldo (R)	63,854	11.0
	Pam Roach (R)	29,533	5.1
	Democratic Primary		
	Gary Locke (D)	287,762	45.6
	Norman Rice (D)	212,888	33.7
	Jay Inslee (D)	118,571	18.8
2000	**Republican Primary**		
	John Carlson (R)	446,142	82.7
	Harold Hochstatter (R)	93,467	17.3
	Democratic Primary		
	Gary Locke (D)	701,929	96.1

Washington

1. In Washington's so-called "jungle" primaries, all candidates for an office appeared together on the same ballot with their parties designated. Nominations went to the Republican and Democrat receiving the most votes for the office. Independents and minor party candidates gained a place on the general election ballot by obtaining at least 1 percent of the total vote cast in the primary. Percentages were calculated here as if candidates had run in separate party primaries.

WEST VIRGINIA

Candidates	Votes	%

1956 **Republican Primary**

| Cecil H. Underwood (R) | 98,344 | 50.5 |
| John T. Copenhaver (R) | 91,088 | 46.8 |

Democratic Primary

Robert H. Mollohan (D)	148,557	42.6
Milton J. Ferguson (D)	95,869	27.5
J. Howard Myers (D)	75,606	21.7
Joe F. Burdett (D)	24,913	7.1

1960 **Republican Primary**

| Harold E. Neely (R) | 102,618 | 55.3 |
| Chapman Revercomb (R) | 83,028 | 44.7 |

Democratic Primary

W. W. Barron (D)	187,501	51.0
Hulett C. Smith (D)	140,079	38.1
Orel J. Skeen (D)	39,907	10.9

1964 **Republican Primary**

| Cecil H. Underwood (R) | 152,573 | 89.7 |
| Harry H. Cupp (R) | 11,325 | 6.7 |

Democratic Primary

Hulett C. Smith (D)	186,273	53.3
Bonn Brown (D)	85,527	24.4
Julius W. Singleton (D)	47,845	13.7
Harold G. Cutright (D)	30,119	8.6

1968 **Republican Primary**

| Arch A. Moore Jr. (R) | 106,299 | 57.0 |
| Cecil H. Underwood (R) | 76,659 | 41.1 |

Democratic Primary

James M. Sprouse (D)	123,181	37.6
C. Donald Robertson (D)	118,637	36.2
Paul J. Kaufman (D)	72,917	22.3

1972 **Republican Primary**

| Arch A. Moore Jr. (R) | | 100.0 |

Democratic Primary

John D. "Jay" Rockefeller IV (D)	262,613	72.2
Lee M. Kenna (D)	63,514	17.5
Robert Myers (D)	37,616	10.3

1976 **Republican Primary**

| Cecil H. Underwood (R) | 97,671 | 64.4 |
| Ralph D. Albertazzie (R) | 44,393 | 29.3 |

Democratic Primary

| John D. "Jay" Rockefeller IV (D) | 206,732 | 49.7 |
| James M. Sprouse (D) | 118,707 | 28.5 |

| Ken Hechler (D) | 52,791 | 12.7 |
| John G. Hutchinson (D) | 26,222 | 6.3 |

1980 **Republican Primary**

| Arch A. Moore Jr. (R) | | 100.0 |

Democratic Primary

| John D. "Jay" Rockefeller IV (D) | 250,550 | 78.0 |
| H. John Rogers (D) | 70,452 | 21.9 |

1984 **Republican Primary**

| Arch A. Moore Jr. (R) | 135,887 | 100.0 |

Democratic Primary

Clyde M. See (D)	148,049	39.8
Warren R. McGraw (D)	104,138	28.0
Chauncey H. Browning (D)	101,712	27.4

1988 **Republican Primary**

| Arch A. Moore Jr. (R) | 78,495 | 53.2 |
| John R. Raese (R) | 68,973 | 46.8 |

Democratic Primary

Gaston Caperton (D)	132,435	38.0
Clyde M. See (D)	94,364	27.0
Mario J. Palumbo (D)	51,722	14.8
Gus R. Douglass (D)	48,748	14.0

1992 **Republican Primary**

| Cleveland K. Benedict (R) | 104,169 | 86.4 |
| Vernon Criss (R) | 16,350 | 13.6 |

Democratic Primary

Gaston Caperton (D)	142,261	42.7
Charlotte Pritt (D)	115,498	34.7
Mario J. Palumbo (D)	66,984	20.1

1996 **Republican Primary**

Cecil H. Underwood (R)	54,628	40.8
Jon McBride (R)	44,255	33.0
David McKinley (R)	35,089	26.2

Democratic Primary

Charlotte Pritt (D)	130,107	39.5
Joe Manchin III (D)	107,124	32.6
Jim Lees (D)	64,100	19.5

2000 **Republican Primary**

Cecil H. Underwood (R)	87,910	81.0
Joseph Oliverio (R)	11,590	10.7
Donna H. McCase (R)	5,902	5.4

Democratic Primary

| Bob Wise (D) | 174,202 | 63.1 |
| Jim Lees (D) | 101,774 | 36.9 |

WISCONSIN

Candidates	Votes	%
1956 Republican Primary		
Vernon W. Thomson (R)		100.0
Democratic Primary		
William Proxmire (D)		100.0
1958 Republican Primary		
Vernon W. Thomson (R)		100.0
Democratic Primary		
Gaylord Nelson (D)		100.0
1960 Republican Primary		
Philip G. Kuehn (R)		100.0
Democratic Primary		
Gaylord Nelson (D)		100.0
1962 Republican Primary		
Philip G. Kuehn (R)	250,539	53.8
Wilbur N. Renk (R)	199,616	42.9
Democratic Primary		
John W. Reynolds (D)		100.0
1964 Republican Primary		
Warren P. Knowles (R)	246,760	71.9
Milo G. Knutson (R)	96,421	28.1
Democratic Primary		
John W. Reynolds (D)	241,170	70.3
Dominic H. Frinzi (D)	102,066	29.7
1966 Republican Primary		
Warren P. Knowles (R)		100.0
Democratic Primary		
Patrick J. Lucey (D)	128,359	45.2
David Carley (D)	95,803	33.7
Dominic H. Frinzi (D)	44,344	15.6
Abe L. Swed (D)	15,362	5.4
1968 Republican Primary		
Warren P. Knowles (R)		100.0
Democratic Primary		
Bronson C. LaFollette (D)	173,458	84.4
Floyd L. Wille (D)	31,778	15.5
1970 Republican Primary		
Jack B. Olson (R)	203,434	91.4
Roman R. Blenski (R)	19,061	8.6

Candidates	Votes	%
Democratic Primary		
Patrick J. Lucey (D)	177,584	60.6
Donald O. Peterson (D)	105,849	36.1
American Primary		
Leo J. McDonald (AM)		100.0
1974 Republican Primary		
William D. Dyke (R)		100.0
Democratic Primary		
Patrick J. Lucey (D)	259,001	78.2
Edmond E. Hou-Seye (D)	72,113	21.8
American Primary		
William H. Upham (AM)		100.0
1978 Republican Primary		
Lee Sherman Dreyfus (R)	197,279	57.9
Bob Kasten (R)	143,361	42.1
Democratic Primary		
Martin J. Schreiber (D)	217,572	60.4
David Carley (D)	132,901	36.9
Conservative Primary		
Eugene R. Zimmerman (C)		100.0
1982 Republican Primary		
Terry J. Kohler (R)	227,844	68.2
Lowell B. Jackson (R)	106,413	31.8
Democratic Primary		
Anthony S. Earl (D)	268,857	45.9
Martin J. Schreiber (D)	245,952	42.0
James B. Wood (D)	71,282	12.2
Libertarian Primary		
Larry Smiley (LIBERT)		100.0
Constitution Primary		
James P. Wickstrom (CONST)		100.0
Socialist Workers Primary		
Peter Seidman (SOC WORK)		100.0
1986 Republican Primary		
Tommy G. Thompson (R)	156,875	52.1
Jonathan B. Barry (R)	67,114	22.3
George Watts (R)	58,424	19.4
Albert L. Wiley (R)	15,233	5.1
Democratic Primary		
Anthony S. Earl (D)	215,183	80.2
Edmond Hou-Seye (D)	52,784	19.7
Labor-Farm Primary		
Kathryn A. Christensen (LAB F)		100.0

1990	**Republican Primary**		
	Tommy G. Thompson (R)	201,467	92.5
	Bennett A. Masel (R)	11,230	5.2
	Democratic Primary		
	Thomas Loftus (D)		100.0
1994	**Republican Primary**		
	Tommy G. Thompson (R)	321,487	99.8
	Democratic Primary		
	Chuck Chvala (D)	121,916	99.8
	Libertarian Primary		
	David S. Harmon (LIBERT)	1,109	99.6
	U.S. Taxpayers Primary		
	Edward J. Frami (USTAX)	856	99.3
	Independent Primary		
	Michael J. Mangan (I)	554	100.0
1998	**Republican Primary**		
	Tommy G. Thompson (R)	229,916	83.4
	Jeffrey A. Hyslop (R)	45,252	16.4
	Democratic Primary		
	Ed Garvey (D)	175,082	79.8
	Gary R. George (D)	43,830	20.0

WYOMING

	Candidates	Votes	%
1958	**Republican Primary**		
	Milward L. Simpson (R)	28,749	77.6
	Stanley Edwards (R)	8,294	22.4
	Democratic Primary		
	J. J. Hickey (D)		100.0
1962	**Republican Primary**		
	Clifford P. Hansen (R)	28,494	57.0
	Charles M. Crowell (R)	16,906	33.8
	R. E. Cheever (R)	4,575	9.1
	Democratic Primary		
	Jack R. Gage (D)	21,051	55.5
	William Jack (D)	16,875	44.5
1966	**Republican Primary**		
	Stan Hathaway (R)	26,110	55.2
	Joe Burke (R)	19,815	41.9
	Democratic Primary		
	Ernest Wilkerson (D)	13,145	31.1
	Bill Nation (D)	9,834	23.2

	Jack R. Gage (D)	8,661	20.5
	Raymond B. Whitaker (D)	6,238	14.7
	Howard L. Burke (D)	4,426	10.5
1970	**Republican Primary**		
	Stan Hathaway (R)		100.0
	Democratic Primary		
	John J. Rooney (D)		100.0
1974	**Republican Primary**		
	Dick Jones (R)	15,502	26.5
	Malcolm Wallop (R)	14,688	25.1
	Roy Peck (R)	14,217	24.3
	Clarence Brimmer (R)	14,014	24.0
	Democratic Primary		
	Ed Herschler (D)	19,997	46.6
	Harry E. Leimback (D)	15,255	35.5
	John J. Rooney (D)	7,674	17.9
1978	**Republican Primary**		
	John C. Ostlund (R)	40,251	58.9
	Gus Fleischli (R)	24,824	36.4
	Democratic Primary		
	Ed Herschler (D)	28,406	65.3
	Margaret McKinstry (D)	15,111	34.7
1982	**Republican Primary**		
	Warren A. Morton (R)	52,536	74.3
	Rex G. Welty (R)	9,106	12.9
	Carl A. Johnson (R)	9,025	12.8
	Democratic Primary		
	Ed Herschler (D)	44,396	85.2
	Pat McGuire (D)	7,720	14.8
1986	**Republican Primary**		
	Peter Simpson (R)	25,948	27.6
	Bill Budd (R)	25,495	27.1
	Fred Schroeder (R)	15,013	16.0
	Russ Donley (R)	12,979	13.8
	David R. Nicholas (R)	11,092	11.8
	Democratic Primary		
	Mike Sullivan (D)	29,266	70.9
	Pat McGuire (D)	5,406	13.1
	Keith B. Goodenough (D)	4,039	9.8
	Al Hamburg (D)	2,554	6.2
1990	**Republican Primary**		
	Mary Mead (R)	51,160	67.3
	Nyla Murphy (R)	24,916	32.7
	Democratic Primary		
	Mike Sullivan (D)	38,447	88.4
	Ron Clingman (D)	5,026	11.6

1994

Republican Primary

Jim Geringer (R)	37,847	42.7
John Perry (R)	28,019	31.6
Charles K. Scott (R)	19,305	21.8

Democratic Primary

Kathy Karpan (D)	39,824	100.0

1998

Republican Primary

Jim Geringer (R)	56,015	66.5
Bill Taliaferro (R)	28,164	33.5

Democratic Primary

John P. Vinich (D)	18,054	53.9
Keith Goodenough (D)	9,033	27.0
Phil Roberts (D)	6,415	19.1

Reference Materials

Constitutional Provisions and Amendments on Elections

ARTICLE I

Section 2: The House of Representatives shall be composed of Members chosen every second Year by the People of the several States, and the Electors in each State shall have the Qualifications requisite for Electors of the most numerous Branch of the State Legislature.

No Person shall be a Representative who shall not have attained to the age of twenty five Years, and been seven Years a Citizen of the United States, and who shall not, when elected, be an Inhabitant of that State in which he shall be chosen.

Representatives and direct Taxes shall be apportioned among the several States which may be included within this Union, according to their respective Numbers, which shall be determined by adding to the whole Number of free Persons, including those bound to Service for a Term of Years, and excluding Indians not taxed, three fifths of all other Persons. The actual Enumeration shall be made within three Years after the first Meeting of the Congress of the United States, and within every subsequent Term of ten Years, in such Manner as they shall by Law direct. The Number of Representatives shall not exceed one for every thirty thousand, but each State shall have at least one Representative. . . .

When vacancies happen in the Representation from any State, the Executive Authority thereof shall issue Writs of Election to fill such Vacancies.

Section 3: The Senate of the United States shall be composed of two Senators from each State, chosen by the Legislature thereof, for six Years, and each Senator shall have one Vote.

Immediately after they shall be assembled in Consequence of the first Election, they shall be divided as equally as may be into three Classes. The Seats of the Senators of the first Class shall be vacated at the Expiration of the second Year, of the second Class at the Expiration of the fourth Year, and of the third Class at the Expiration of the sixth Year, so that one third may be chosen every second Year; and if Vacancies happen by Resignation, or otherwise, during the Recess of the Legislature of any State, the Executive thereof may make temporary Appointments until the next Meeting of the Legislature, which shall then fill such Vacancies.

No Person shall be a Senator who shall not have attained to the Age of thirty Years, and been nine Years a Citizen of the United States, and who shall not, when elected, be an Inhabitant of that State for which he shall be chosen. . . .

Section 4: The Times, Places and Manner of holding Elections for Senators and Representatives, shall be prescribed in each State by the Legislature thereof; but the Congress may at any time by Law make or alter such Regulations, except as to the Place of Chusing Senators.

The Congress shall assemble at least once in every Year, and such Meeting shall be on the first Monday in December, unless they shall by Law appoint a different Day.

Section 5: Each House shall be the Judge of the Elections, Returns and Qualifications of its own Members, and a Majority of each shall constitute a Quorum to do Business. . . .

ARTICLE II

Section 1: The executive Power shall be vested in a President of the United States of America. He shall hold his Office during the Term of four Years, and, together with the Vice President, chosen for the same term, be elected, as follows.

Each State shall appoint, in such Manner as the Legislature thereof may direct, a Number of Electors, equal to the whole Number of Senators and Representatives to which the State may be entitled in the Congress: but no Senator or Representative, or Person holding an Office of Trust or Profit under the United States, shall be appointed an Elector.

[The Electors shall meet in their respective States, and vote by Ballot for two Persons, of whom one at least shall not be an Inhabitant of the same State with themselves. And they shall make a List of all the Persons voted for, and of the Number of Votes for each; which List they shall sign and certify, and transmit sealed to the Seat of the Government of the United States, directed to the President of the Senate. The President of the Senate shall, in the Presence of the Senate and House of Representatives, open all the Certificates, and the Votes shall then be counted. The Person having the greatest Number of Votes shall be the President, if such Number be a Majority of the whole Number of Electors appointed; and if there be more than one who have such Majority, and have an equal Number of Votes, then the House of Representatives shall immediately chuse by Ballot one of them for President; and if no Person have a Majority, then from the five highest on the List the said House shall in like Manner chuse the President. But in chusing the President, the Votes shall be taken by States, the Representation from each State having one Vote; a quorum for this Purpose shall consist of a Member or Members from two thirds of the States, and a Majority of all the States shall be necessary to a Choice. In every Case, after the Choice of the President, the Person having the greatest Number of Votes of the Electors shall be the Vice President. But if there should remain two or more who have equal Votes, the Senate shall chuse from them by Ballot the Vice-President.][1]

The Congress may determine the Time of chusing the Electors, and the Day on which they shall give their Votes; which

Day shall be the same throughout the United States.

No person except a natural born Citizen, or a Citizen of the United States, at the time of the Adoption of this Constitution, shall be eligible to the Office of President; neither shall any Person be eligible to that Office who shall not have attained to the Age of thirty five Years, and been fourteen Years a Resident within the United States.

AMENDMENT XII
(Ratified July 27, 1804)

The Electors shall meet in their respective states and vote by ballot for President and Vice-President, one of whom, at least, shall not be an inhabitant of the same state with themselves; they shall name in their ballots the person voted for as President, and in distinct ballots the person voted for as Vice-President, and they shall make distinct lists of all persons voted for as President, and of all persons voted for as Vice-President, and of the number of votes for each, which lists they shall sign and certify, and transmit sealed to the seat of the government of the United States, directed to the President of the Senate; . . . The person having the greatest number of votes for President, shall be the President, if such number be a majority of the whole number of Electors appointed; and if no person have such majority, then from the persons having the highest numbers not exceeding three on the list of those voted for as President, the House of Representatives shall choose immediately, by ballot, the President. But in choosing the President, the votes shall be taken by states, the representation from each state having one vote; a quorum for this purpose shall consist of a member or members from two-thirds of the states, and a majority of all the states shall be necessary to a choice. [And if the House of Representatives shall not choose a President whenever the right of choice shall devolve upon them, before the fourth day of March next following, then the Vice-President shall act as President, as in the case of the death or other constitutional disability of the President.—][2] The person having the greatest number of votes as Vice-President, shall be the Vice-President, if such number be a majority of the whole number of Electors appointed, and if no person have a majority, then from the two highest numbers on the list, the Senate shall choose the Vice President; a quorum for the purpose shall consist of two-thirds of the whole number of Senators, and a majority of the whole number shall be necessary to a choice. But no person constitutionally ineligible to the office of President shall be eligible to that of Vice-President of the United States.

AMENDMENT XIV
(Ratified July 9, 1868)

Section 2: Representatives shall be apportioned among the several States according to their respective numbers, counting the whole number of persons in each State, excluding Indians not taxed. But when the right to vote at any election for the choice of electors for President and Vice President of the United States, Representatives in Congress, the Executive and Judicial officers of a State, or the members of the Legislature thereof, is denied to any of the male inhabitants of such State, being twenty-one years of age,[3] and citizens of the United States, or in any

way abridged, except for participation in rebellion, or other crime, the basis of representation therein shall be reduced in the proportion which the number of such male citizens shall bear to the whole number of male citizens twenty-one years of age in such State.

Section 3: No person shall be a Senator or Representative in Congress, or elector of President and Vice President, or hold any office, civil or military, under the United States, or under any State, who, having previously taken an oath, as a member of Congress, or as an officer of the United States, or as a member of any State legislature, or as an executive or judicial officer of any State, to support the Constitution of the United States, shall have engaged in insurrection or rebellion against the same, or given aid or comfort to the enemies thereof. But Congress may by a vote of two-thirds of each House, remove such disability.

AMENDMENT XV
(Ratified February 3, 1870)

The right of citizens of the United States to vote shall not be denied or abridged by the United States or by any State on account of race, color, or previous condition of servitude.

AMENDMENT XVII
(Ratified April 8, 1913)

The Senate of the United States shall be composed of two Senators from each State, elected by the people thereof, for six years; and each Senator shall have one vote. The electors in each State shall have the qualification requisite for electors of the most numerous branch of the State legislatures.

When vacancies happen in the representation of any State in the Senate, the executive authority of such State shall issue writs of election to fill such vacancies: *Provided,* That the legislature of any State may empower the executive thereof to make temporary appointments until the people fill the vacancies by election as the legislature may direct.

This amendment shall not be so construed as to affect the election or term of any Senator chosen before it becomes valid as part of the Constitution.

AMENDMENT XIX
(Ratified August 18, 1920)

The right of citizens of the United States to vote shall not be denied or abridged by the United States or by any State on account of sex.

AMENDMENT XX
(Ratified January 23, 1933)

Section 1: The terms of the President and Vice President shall end at noon on the 20th day of January, and the terms of the Senators and Representatives at noon on the 3d day of January, of the years in which such terms would have ended if this article had not been ratified; and the terms of their successors shall then begin.

Section 2: The Congress shall assemble at least once in every year, and such meeting shall begin at noon on the 3d day of January, unless they by law appoint a different day.

Section 3: If, at the time fixed for the beginning of the term of the President, the President elect shall have died, the Vice President elect shall become President. If a President shall not have been chosen before the time fixed for the beginning of his term, or if the President elect shall have failed to qualify, then the Vice President elect shall act as President until a President shall have qualified; and the Congress may by law provide for the case wherein neither a President elect nor a Vice President elect shall have qualified, declaring who shall then act as President, or the manner in which one who is to act shall be selected, and such person shall act accordingly until a President or Vice President shall have qualified.

Section 4: The Congress may by law provide for the case of the death of any of the persons from whom the House of Representatives may choose a President whenever the right of choice shall have devolved upon them, and for the case of the death of any of the persons from whom the Senate may choose a Vice President whenever the right of choice shall have devolved upon them. . . .

AMENDMENT XXII
(Ratified February 27, 1951)

No person shall be elected to the office of the President more than twice, and no person who has held the office of President, or acted as President, for more than two years of a term to which some other person was elected President shall be elected to the office of the President more than once. But this Article shall not apply to any person holding the office of President, when this Article was proposed by the Congress, and shall not prevent any person who may be holding the office of President, or acting as President, during the term within which this Article becomes operative form holding the office of President or acting as President during the remainder of such term.

AMENDMENT XXIV
(Ratified January 23, 1964)

The right of citizens of the United States to vote in any primary or other election for President or Vice President, for electors for President or Vice President, or for Senator or Representative in Congress, shall not be denied or abridged by the United States or by any State on by reason of failure to pay any poll tax or other tax.

AMENDMENT XXV
(Ratified Feb. 10, 1967)

Section 1: In case of the removal of the President from office or of his death or resignation, the Vice President shall become President.

Section 2: Whenever there is a vacancy in the office of the Vice President, the President shall nominate a Vice President who shall take office upon confirmation by a majority vote of both Houses of Congress.

Section 3: Whenever the President transmits to the President pro tempore of the Senate and the Speaker of the House of Representatives his written declaration that he is unable to discharge the powers and duties of his office, and until he transmits to them a written declaration to the contrary, such powers and duties shall be discharged by the Vice President as Acting President.

Section 4: Whenever the Vice President and a majority of either the principal officers of the executive departments or of such other body as Congress may by law provide, transmit to the President pro tempore of the Senate and the Speaker of the House of Representatives their written declaration that the President is unable to discharge the powers and duties of his office, the Vice President shall immediately assume the powers and duties of the office as Acting President.

Thereafter, when the President transmits to the President pro tempore of the Senate and the Speaker of the House of Representatives his written declaration that no inability exists, he shall resume the powers and duties of his office unless the Vice President and a majority of either the principal officers of the executive departments or of such other body as Congress may by law provide, transmit within four days to the President pro tempore of the Senate and the Speaker of the House of Representatives their written declaration that the President is unable to discharge the powers and duties of his office. Thereupon Congress shall decide the issue, assembling within forty-eight hours for that purpose if not in session. If the Congress, within twenty-one days after receipt of the latter written declaration, or, if Congress is not in session, within twenty-one days after Congress is required to assemble, determines by two-thirds vote of both houses that the President is unable to discharge the powers and duties of his office, the Vice President shall continue to discharge the same as Acting President; otherwise, the President shall resume the powers and duties of his office.

AMENDMENT XXVI
(Ratified July 1, 1971)

Section 1: The right of citizens of the United States, who are eighteen years of age or older, to vote shall not be denied or abridged by the United States or by any State on account of age.

Notes

1. Superseded by the Twelve Amendment.
2. Changed to January 20 by the Twentieth Amendment.
3. Superseded by the Nineteenth and Twenty-Sixth Amendments.

Population of the United States and Puerto Rico: 1790 to 2000

	1790	1800	1810	1820	1830	1840	1850	1860	1870	1880	1890
Alabama		1,250 [1]	9,046 [1]	127,901	309,527	590,756	771,623	964,201	996,992	1,262,505	1,513,401
Alaska										33,426	32,052
Arizona									9,658	40,440	88,243
Arkansas			1,062	14,273	30,388	97,574	209,897	435,450	484,471	802,525	1,128,211
California							92,597	379,994	560,247	864,694	1,213,398
Colorado								34,277	39,864	194,327	413,249
Connecticut	237,946	251,002	261,942	275,248	297,675	309,978	370,792	460,147	537,454	622,700	746,258
Delaware	59,096	64,273	72,674	72,749	76,748	78,085	91,532	112,216	125,015	146,608	168,493
District of Columbia		8,144	15,471	23,336	30,261	33,745	51,687	75,080	131,700	177,624	230,392
Florida					34,730	54,477	87,445	140,424	187,748	269,493	391,422
Georgia	82,548	162,686	252,433	340,989	516,823	691,392	906,185	1,057,286	1,184,109	1,542,180	1,837,353
Hawaii											
Idaho									14,999	32,610	88,548
Illinois			12,282 [3]	55,211	157,445	476,183	851,470	1,711,951	2,539,891	3,077,871	3,826,352
Indiana		5,641 [4]	24,520 [4]	147,178	343,031	685,866	988,416	1,350,428	1,680,637	1,978,301	2,192,404
Iowa						43,112 [5]	192,214	674,913	1,194,020	1,624,615	1,912,297
Kansas								107,206	364,399	996,096	1,428,108
Kentucky	73,677	220,955	406,511	564,317	687,917	779,828	982,405	1,155,684	1,321,011	1,648,690	1,858,635
Louisiana			76,556	153,407	215,739	352,411	517,762	708,002	726,915	939,946	1,118,588
Maine	96,540	151,719	228,705	298,335	399,455	501,793	583,169	628,279	626,915	648,936	661,086
Maryland	319,728	341,548	380,546	407,350	447,040	470,019	583,034	687,049	780,894	934,943	1,042,390
Massachusetts	378,787	422,845	472,040	523,287	610,408	737,699	994,514	1,231,066	1,457,351	1,783,085	2,238,947
Michigan			4,762 [6]	8,896 [6]	31,639 [6]	212,267	397,654	749,113	1,184,059	1,636,937	2,093,890
Minnesota							6,077	172,023	439,706	780,773	1,310,283
Mississippi		7,600 [7]	31,306 [7]	75,448	136,621	375,651	606,526	791,305	827,922	1,131,597	1,289,600
Missouri			19,783	66,586	140,455	383,702	682,044	1,182,012	1,721,295	2,168,380	2,679,185
Montana									20,595	39,159	142,924
Nebraska								28,841	122,993	452,402	1,062,656
Nevada								6,857 [8]	42,491	62,266	47,355
New Hampshire	141,885	183,858	214,460	244,161	269,328	284,574	317,976	326,073	318,300	346,991	376,530
New Jersey	184,139	211,149	245,562	277,575	320,823	373,306	489,555	672,035	906,096	1,131,116	1,444,933
New Mexico							61,547 [9]	93,516 [9]	91,874	119,565	160,282
New York	340,120	589,051	959,049	1,372,812	1,918,608	2,428,921	3,097,394	3,880,735	4,382,759	5,082,871	6,003,174
North Carolina	393,751	478,103	555,500	638,829	737,987	753,419	869,039	992,622	1,071,361	1,399,750	1,617,949
North Dakota								4,837 [10]	2,405	36,909	190,983
Ohio		45,365 [11]	230,760	581,434	937,903	1,519,467	1,980,329	2,339,511	2,665,260	3,198,062	3,672,329
Oklahoma											258,657
Oregon							12,093	52,465	90,923	174,768	317,704
Pennsylvania	434,373	602,365	810,091	1,049,458	1,348,233	1,724,033	2,311,786	2,906,215	3,521,951	4,282,891	5,258,113
Puerto Rico											
Rhode Island	68,825	69,122	76,931	83,059	97,199	108,830	147,545	174,620	217,353	276,531	345,506
South Carolina	249,073	345,591	415,115	502,741	581,185	594,398	688,507	703,708	705,606	995,577	1,151,149
South Dakota								4,837 [10]	11,776	98,268	348,600
Tennessee	35,691	105,602	261,727	422,823	681,904	829,210	1,002,717	1,109,801	1,258,520	1,542,359	1,767,518
Texas							212,592	604,215	818,579	1,591,749	2,235,527
Utah							11,380	40,273 [13]	86,786	143,963	210,779
Vermont	85,425	154,465	217,895	235,981	280,652	291,948	314,120	315,098	330,551	332,286	332,422
Virginia	691,737	807,557	877,683	938,261	1,044,054	1,025,227	1,119,348	1,219,630	1,225,163	1,512,565	1,655,980
Washington							1,201	11,594 [14]	23,955	75,116	357,232
West Virginia	55,873	78,592	105,469	136,808	176,924	224,537	302,313	376,688	442,014	618,457	762,794
Wisconsin						30,945 [15]	305,391	775,881	1,054,670	1,315,497	1,693,330
Wyoming									9,118	20,789	62,555
Total	3,929,214	5,308,483	7,239,881	9,638,453	12,866,020 [16]	17,069,453 [16]	23,191,876	31,443,321	38,558,371 [17]	50,189,209	62,979,766 [17]

1. Alabama. Population of those parts of Mississippi Territory now in Alabama.
2. Alaska. 1940 Census taken as of Oct. 1, 1939; 1930 Census, as of Oct. 1, 1929.
3. Illinois. Population of Illinois Territory, which comprised area constituting State of Illinois, almost all of Wisconsin, the western part of the upper peninsula of Michigan and the northeastern part of Minnesota.
4. Indiana. 1810 figure includes population of area separated in 1816; 1800 figure includes population (3,124) of those portions of Indiana Territory which were taken to form Michigan and Illinois Territories in 1805 and 1809, respectively, and that portion which was separated in 1816.

5. Iowa. Includes population of area constituting that part of Minnesota lying west of the Mississippi River and a line drawn from it source northwards to the Canadian boundary.
6. Michigan. Population of Michigan Territory as then constituted; boundaries changed in 1816, 1818, 1834 and 1836.
7. Mississippi. Population of those parts of present state included in Mississippi Territory as then constituted.
8. Nevada. Population of Nevada Territory as organized in 1861.
9. New Mexico. 1860 figure includes population of area taken to form part of Arizona Territory in 1863. 1850 figure is for Territory of New Mexico which included greater

1900	1910	1920	1930	1940	1950	1960	1970	1980	1990	2000
1,828,697	2,138,093	2,348,174	1,646,248	2,832,961	3,061,743	3,266,740	3,444,354	3,893,888	4,040,587	4,447,100
63,592	64,356	55,036	59,278 [2]	72,524 [2]	128,643	226,167	302,583	401,851	550,043	626,932
122,931	204,354	334,162	435,573	499,261	749,587	1,302,161	1,775,399	2,718,215	3,665,228	5,130,632
1,311,564	1,574,449	1,752,204	1,854,482	1,949,387	1,909,511	1,786,272	1,923,322	2,286,435	2,350,725	2,673,400
1,485,053	2,377,549	3,426,861	5,677,251	6,907,387	10,586,223	15,717,204	19,971,069	23,667,902	29,760,021	33,871,648
539,700	799,024	939,629	1,035,791	1,123,296	1,325,089	1,753,947	2,209,596	2,889,964	3,294,394	4,301,261
908,420	1,114,756	1,380,631	1,606,903	1,709,242	2,007,280	2,535,234	3,032,217	3,107,576	3,287,116	3,405,565
184,735	202,322	223,003	238,380	266,505	318,085	446,292	548,104	594,338	666,168	783,600
278,718	331,069	437,571	486,869	663,091	802,178	763,956	756,668	638,333	606,900	572,059
528,542	752,619	968,470	1,468,211	1,897,414	2,771,305	4,951,560	6,791,418	9,746,324	12,937,926	15,982,378
2,216,331	2,609,121	2,895,832	2,908,506	3,123,723	3,444,578	3,943,116	4,587,930	5,463,105	6,478,216	8,186,453
154,001	191,874	255,881	368,300	422,770	499,794	632,772	769,913	964,691	1,108,229	1,211,537
161,772	325,594	431,866	445,032	524,873	588,637	667,191	713,015	943,935	1,006,749	1,293,953
4,821,550	5,638,591	6,485,280	7,630,654	7,897,241	8,712,176	10,081,158	11,110,285	11,426,518	11,430,602	12,419,293
2,516,462	2,700,876	2,930,390	3,238,503	3,427,796	3,934,224	4,662,498	5,195,392	5,490,224	5,544,159	6,080,485
2,231,853	2,224,771	2,404,021	2,470,939	2,538,268	2,621,073	2,757,537	2,825,368	2,913,808	2,776,755	2,926,324
1,470,495	1,690,949	1,769,257	1,880,999	1,801,028	1,905,299	2,178,611	2,249,071	2,363,679	2,477,574	2,688,418
2,147,174	2,289,905	2,416,630	2,614,589	2,845,627	2,944,806	3,038,156	3,220,711	3,660,777	3,685,296	4,041,769
1,381,625	1,656,388	1,798,509	2,101,593	2,363,880	2,683,516	3,257,022	3,644,637	4,205,900	4,219,973	4,468,976
694,466	742,371	768,014	797,423	847,226	913,774	969,265	993,722	1,124,660	1,227,928	1,274,923
1,188,044	1,295,346	1,449,661	1,631,526	1,821,244	2,343,001	3,100,689	3,923,897	4,216,975	4,781,468	5,296,486
2,805,346	3,366,416	3,852,356	4,249,614	4,316,721	4,690,514	5,148,578	5,689,170	5,737,037	6,016,425	6,349,097
2,420,982	2,810,173	3,668,412	4,842,325	5,256,106	6,371,766	7,823,194	8,881,826	9,262,078	9,295,297	9,938,444
1,751,394	2,075,708	2,387,125	2,563,953	2,792,300	2,982,483	3,413,864	3,806,103	4,075,970	4,375,099	4,919,479
1,551,270	1,797,114	1,790,618	2,009,821	2,183,796	2,178,914	2,178,141	2,216,994	2,520,638	2,573,216	2,844,658
3,106,665	3,293,335	3,404,055	3,629,367	3,784,664	3,954,653	4,319,813	4,677,623	4,916,686	5,117,073	5,595,211
243,329	376,053	548,889	537,606	559,456	591,024	674,767	694,409	786,690	799,065	902,195
1,066,300	1,192,214	1,296,372	1,377,963	1,315,834	1,325,510	1,411,330	1,485,333	1,569,825	1,578,385	1,711,263
42,335	81,875	77,407	91,058	110,247	160,083	285,278	488,738	800,493	1,201,833	1,998,257
411,588	430,572	443,083	465,293	491,524	533,242	606,921	737,681	920,610	1,109,252	1,235,786
1,883,669	2,537,167	3,155,900	4,041,334	4,160,165	4,835,329	6,066,782	7,171,112	7,364,823	7,730,188	8,414,350
195,310	327,301	360,350	423,317	531,818	681,187	951,023	1,017,055	1,302,894	1,515,069	1,819,046
7,268,894	9,113,614	10,385,227	12,588,066	13,479,142	14,830,192	16,782,304	18,241,391	17,558,072	17,990,455	18,976,457
1,893,810	2,206,287	2,559,123	3,170,276	3,571,623	4,061,929	4,556,155	5,084,411	5,881,766	6,628,637	8,049,313
319,146	577,056	646,872	680,845	641,935	619,636	632,446	617,792	652,717	638,800	642,200
4,157,545	4,767,121	5,759,394	6,646,697	6,907,612	7,946,627	9,706,397	10,657,423	10,797,630	10,847,115	11,353,140
790,391	1,657,155	2,028,283	2,396,040	2,336,434	2,233,351	2,328,284	2,559,463	3,025,290	3,145,585	3,450,654
413,536	672,765	783,389	953,786	1,089,684	1,521,341	1,768,687	2,091,533	2,633,105	2,842,321	3,421,399
6,302,115	7,665,111	8,720,017	9,631,350	9,900,180	10,498,012	11,319,366	11,800,766	11,863,895	11,881,632	12,281,054
953,243 [12]	1,118,012	1,299,809	1,543,913	1,869,255	2,210,703	2,349,544	2,712,033	3,196,520	3,522,037	3,808,610
428,556	542,610	604,397	687,497	713,346	791,896	859,488	949,723	947,154	1,003,464	1,048,319
1,340,316	1,515,400	1,683,724	1,738,765	1,899,804	2,117,027	2,382,594	2,590,713	3,121,820	3,486,703	4,012,012
401,570	583,888	636,547	692,849	642,961	652,740	680,514	666,257	690,768	696,004	754,844
2,020,616	2,184,789	2,337,885	2,616,556	2,915,841	3,291,718	3,567,089	3,926,018	4,591,120	4,877,185	5,689,283
3,048,710	3,896,542	4,663,228	5,824,715	6,414,824	7,711,194	9,579,677	11,198,655	14,229,191	16,986,510	20,851,820
276,749	373,351	449,396	507,847	550,310	688,862	890,627	1,059,273	1,461,037	1,722,850	2,233,169
343,641	355,956	352,428	359,611	359,231	377,747	389,881	444,732	511,456	562,758	608,827
1,854,184	2,061,612	2,309,187	2,421,851	2,677,773	3,318,680	3,966,949	4,651,448	5,346,818	6,187,358	7,078,515
518,103	1,141,990	1,356,621	1,563,396	1,736,191	2,378,963	2,853,214	3,413,244	4,132,156	4,866,692	5,894,121
958,800	1,221,119	1,463,701	1,729,205	1,901,974	2,005,552	1,860,421	1,744,237	1,949,644	1,793,477	1,808,344
2,069,042	2,333,860	2,632,067	2,939,006	3,137,587	3,434,575	3,951,777	4,417,821	4,705,767	4,891,769	5,363,675
92,531	145,965	194,402	225,565	250,742	290,529	330,066	332,416	469,557	453,588	493,782
76,212,168	92,228,496	106,021,537	123,202,624	132,164,569	151,325,79	179,323,175	203,302,031	226,545,805	252,231,910	285,230,516

parts of present states of Arizona and New Mexico and smaller parts of Colorado and Nevada.

10. Dakotas. Population of Dakota Territory.

11. Ohio. Population of Territory northwest of the River Ohio.

12. Puerto Rico. Census taken as of Nov. 10, 1899 by War Department.

13. Utah. Population of Utah Territory exclusive of that part of present state of Colorado taken to form Colorado Territory in 1861.

14. Washington. 1860 figure includes population of Idaho and parts of Montana and Wyoming. 1850 figure of population of those parts of Oregon Territory taken to form part of Washington Territory in 1853 and 1859.

15. Wisconsin. Includes population of that part of Minnesota northeast of the Mississippi River.

16. Includes persons (6,100 in 1840 and 5,318 in 1830) on public ships in the service of the United States, not credited to any region, division, or state.

17. Includes population (325,464) of Indian Territory and Indian reservations specially enumerated in 1890 but not included in general report on population for 1890.

Source: Bureau of the Census.

Changing Methods of Electing Presidential Electors: 1788–1836

This chart shows the changing methods used by the states to elect presidential electors from 1788 to 1836. (See "Methods of Choosing Electors," p. 703, Vol. I.)

State	1788–1789	1792	1796	1800	1804	1808
Alabama	—	—	—	—	—	—
Arkansas	—	—	—	—	—	—
Connecticut	L	L	L	L	L	L
Delaware	D(3)[1]	L	L	L	L	L
Georgia	L	L	GT	L	L	L
Illinois	—	—	—	—	—	—
Indiana	—	—	—	—	—	—
Kentucky	—	D(4)	D(4)	D(4)	D(2)[2]	D(2)[2]
Louisiana	—	—	—	—	—	—
Maine	—	—	—	—	—	—
Maryland	GT	GT	D(10)	D(10)	D(9)[4]	D(9)[4]
Massachusetts	D(8) & L[6]	D(4) & L[7]	D(14) & L[8]	L	D(17) & A(2)	L
Michigan	—	—	—	—	—	—
Mississippi	—	—	—	—	—	—
Missouri	—	—	—	—	—	—
New Hampshire	GT & L[10]	GT[11]	GT & L[10]	L	GT	GT
New Jersey	L	L	L	L	GT	GT
New York	—	L	L	L	L	L
North Carolina	—	L[13]	D(12)	D(12)	D(14)	D(14)
Ohio	—	—	—	—	GT	GT
Pennsylvania	GT	GT	GT	L	GT	GT
Rhode Island	—	L	L	GT	GT	GT
South Carolina	L	L	L	L	L	L
Tennessee	—	—	E[14]	E[14]	D(5)	D(5)
Vermont	—	L	L	L	L	L
Virginia	D(12)	D(21)	D(21)	GT	GT	GT

Explanation of symbols: L—by Legislature; GT—by people, on general ticket; D—by people in districts; A—by people, in the state at large; E—by electors. The number in parentheses following the symbol "D" is the number of districts into which the state was divided. As a rule, each district elected 1 elector. The number in parentheses following the symbol "A" is the number of electors elected at large.

1. Each qualified voter voted for 1 elector. The 3 electors who received most votes in the state were elected.
2. Each district elected 4 electors.
3. Two districts chose 5 electors each, and one chose 4 electors.
4. During the years 1804–1828, Maryland chose 11 electors in nine districts, two of the districts elected two members each.
5. One district chose 4 electors; one district, 2 electors; and one district, 1 elector.
6. Each of the eight districts chose 2 electors, from which the General Court (the legislature) selected 1. It also elected 2 electors at large.
7. Two of the districts voted for five members each, and two for three members each. A majority of votes was necessary for a choice. In case of failure to elect by popular vote the General Court supplied the deficiency. In the election of 1972, the people chose 5 electors and the General Court chose 11.

	1812	1816	1820	1824	1828	1832	1836
Alabama	—	—	L	GT	GT	GT	GT
Arkansas	—	—	—	—	—	—	GT
Connecticut	L	L	GT	GT	GT	GT	GT
Delaware	L	L	L	L	L	GT	GT
Georgia	L	L	L	L	GT	GT	GT
Illinois	—	—	D(3)	D(3)	GT	GT	GT
Indiana	—	L	L	GT	GT	GT	GT
Kentucky	D(3)[2]	D(3)[2]	D(3)[3]	GT	GT	GT	GT
Louisiana	L	L	L	L	GT	GT	GT
Maine	—	—	D(7) & A(2)	D(7) & A(2)	D(7) &A(2)	GT	GT
Maryland	D(9)[4]	D(9)[4]	D(9)[4]	D(9)[4]	D(9)[4]	D(4)[5]	GT
Massachusetts	D(6)[9]	L	D(13) & A(2)	GT	GT	GT	GT
Michigan	—	—	—	—	—	—	GT
Mississippi	—	—	GT	GT	GT	GT	GT
Missouri	—	—	L	D(3)	GT	GT	GT
New Hampshire	GT	GT	GT	GT	GT	GT	GT
New Jersey	L	GT	GT	GT	GT	GT	GT
New York	L	L	L	L	D(30) & E[12]	GT	GT
North Carolina	L	GT	GT	GT	GT	GT	GT
Ohio	GT	GT	GT	GT	GT	GT	GT
Pennsylvania	GT	GT	GT	GT	GT	GT	GT
Rhode Island	GT	GT	GT	GT	GT	GT	GT
South Carolina	L	L	L	L	L	L	L
Tennessee	D(8)	D(8)	D(8)	D(11)	D(11)	GT	GT
Vermont	L	L	L	L	GT	GT	GT
Virginia	GT	GT	GT	GT	GT	GT	GT

8. A majority of votes was necessary for a popular choice. Deficiencies were filled by the General Court, as in 1792. It also chose 2 electors at large. In 1796 it chose 9 electors, and the people, 7 electors.

9. One district chose 6 electors; one district, 5 electors; one district, 4 electors each; two districts, 3 electors each; and one district, 1 elector.

10. A majority of the popular vote was necessary for a choice. In case of a failure to elect, the legislature supplied the deficiency.

11. A majority of votes was necessary for a choice. In case of a failure to elect 1 or more electors a second election was held by the people, at which choice was made from the first election who had the most votes. The number of candidates in the second election was limited to twice the number of electors wanted.

12. One district elected 3 electors; two districts, 2 electors each; and twenty-seven districts, 1 elector each. The 34 electors thus elected chose 2 presidential electors.

13. The state was divided into four districts, and the members of the legislature residing in each district chose 3 electors.

14. In 1796 and 1800, Tennessee choose 3 presidential electors—1 each for the districts of Washington, Hamilton, and Metro; 3 "electors" for each county in the state were appointed by the legislature; and the "electors" residing in each of the three districts chose 1 of the 3 presidential electors.

Source: Bureau of the Census, *Historical Statistics of the United States; Colonial Times to 1970* (Washington, D.C.: Government Printing Office, 1975).

Presidential Nominating
Campaign Lengths, 1968–2000

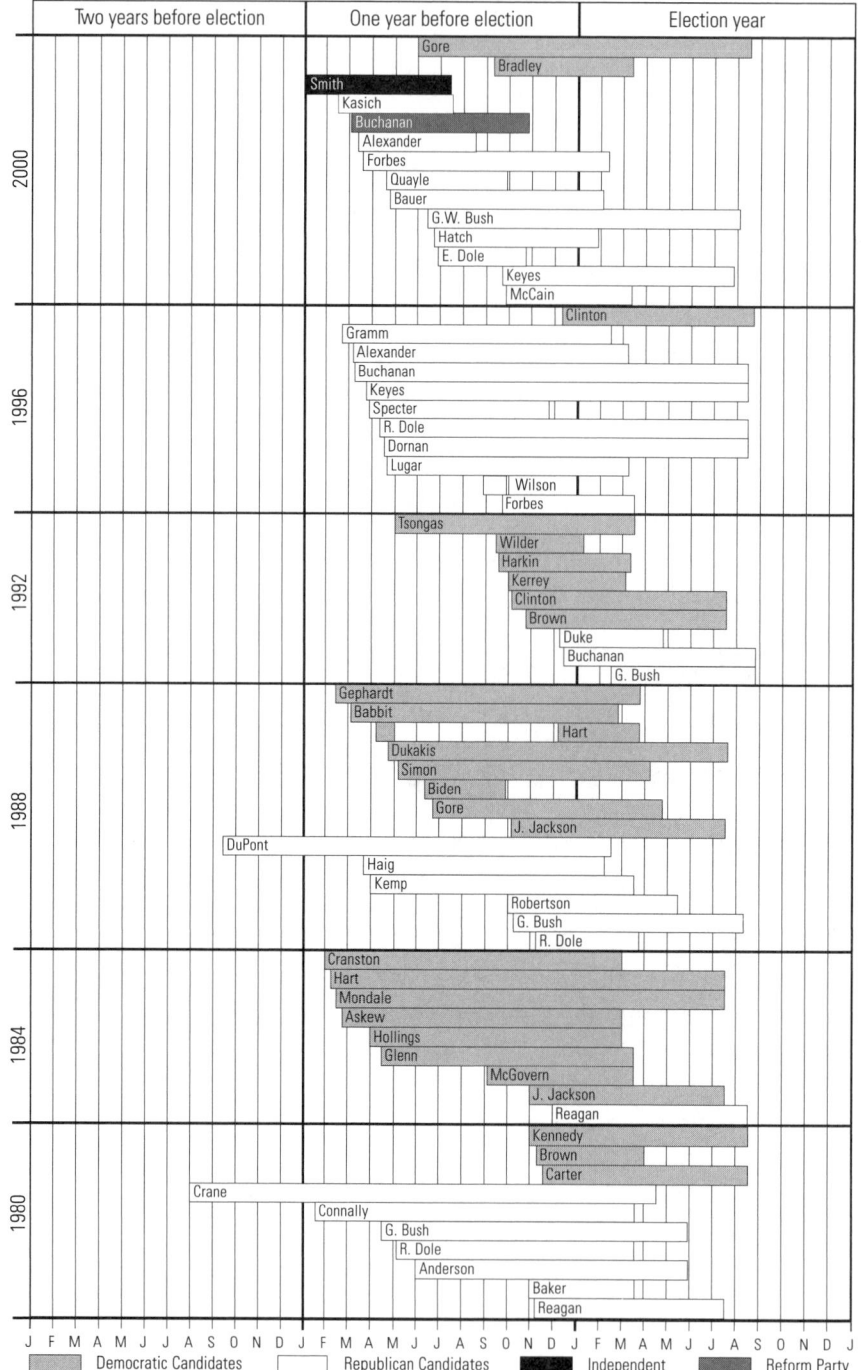

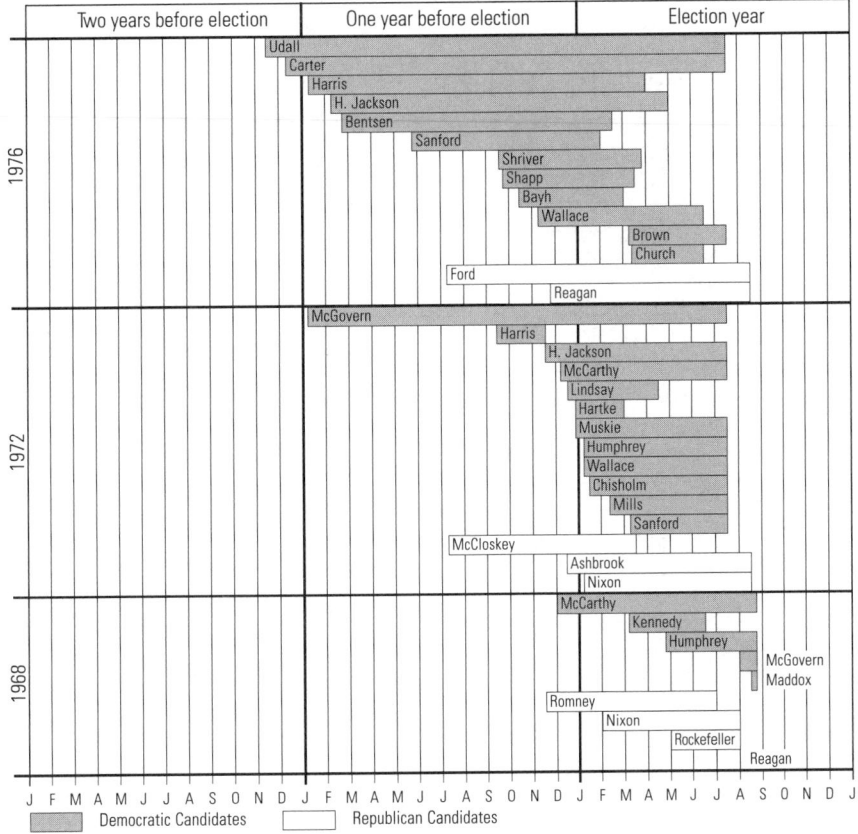

Note: Beginning of campaigns is determined by date of the formal announcement.

Sources: 1968–1984: Congressional Quarterly, *Elections '80* (Washington, D.C.: Congressional Quarterly, 1980), and Congressional Quarterly, *Congressional Quarterly's Guide to U.S. Elections,* 2d ed. (Washington, D.C.: Congressional Quarterly, 1985), 387; 1988–1996: *Congressional Quarterly Weekly Report* (1987), 2732; (1988), 1894, 1896, 1899; (1991), 3735; (1992), 66, 361, 556, 633, 1086; (1995), 2, 13, 15, 3025, 3606; (1996), 641, 716; 2000: compiled by the editors from news reports, various sources.

Victorious Party in Presidential Races, 1860–2000

State	1860	1864	1868	1872	1876	1880	1884	1888	1892	1896	1900	1904	1908	1912	1916	1920	1924	1928
Alabama	SD	[2]	R	R	D	D	D	D	D	D	D	D	D	D	D	D	D	D
Alaska																		
Arizona														D	D	R	R	R
Arkansas	SD	[2]	R	[4]	D	D	D	D	D	D	D	D	D	D	D	D	D	D
California	R	R	R	R	R	D[6]	R	R	D[7]	R[12]	R	R	R	PR	D	R	R	R
Colorado					R	R	R	R	PP	D	D	R	D	D	D	R	R	R
Connecticut	R	R	R	R	D	R	D	D	D	R	R	R	R	D	R	R	R	R
Delaware	SD	D	D	R	D	D	D	D	D	R	R	R	R	D	R	R	R	R
Dist. of Columbia																		
Florida	SD	[2]	R	R	D	D	D	D	D	D	D	D	D	D	D	D	D	R
Georgia	SD	[2]	D	D[5]	D	D	D	D	D	D	D	D	D	D	D	D	D	D
Hawaii																		
Idaho									PP	D	D	R	R	D	D	R	R	R
Illinois	R	R	R	R	R	R	R	R	D	R	R	R	R	D	R	R	R	R
Indiana	R	R	R	R	D	R	D	R	D	R	R	R	R	D	R	R	R	R
Iowa	R	R	R	R	R	R	R	R	R	R	R	R	R	D	R	R	R	R
Kansas		R	R	R	R	R	R	R	PP	D	R	R	R	D	D	R	R	R
Kentucky	CU	D	D	D	D	D	D	D	D	R[13]	D	D	D	D	D	D	R	R
Louisiana	SD	[2]	D	[4]	R	D	D	D	D	D	D	D	D	D	D	D	D	D
Maine	R	R	R	R	R	R	R	R	R	R	R	R	R	D	R	R	R	R
Maryland	SD	R	D	D	D	D	D	D	D	R	R	D[14]	D[15]	D	D	R	R	R
Massachusetts	R	R	R	R	R	R	R	R	R	R	R	R	R	D	R	R	R	D
Michigan	R	R	R	R	R	R	R	R	R[8]	R	R	R	R	PR	R	R	R	R
Minnesota	R	R	R	R	R	R	R	R	R	R	R	R	R	PR	R	R	R	R
Mississippi	SD	[2]	[3]	R	D	D	D	D	D	D	D	D	D	D	D	D	D	D
Missouri	D	R	R	D	D	D	D	D	D	D	D	R	R	D	D	R	R	R
Montana									R	D	D	R	R	D	D	R	R	R
Nebraska			R	R	R	R	R	R	R	D	R	R	D	D	D	R	R	R
Nevada		R	R	R	R	R	R	R	PP	D	D	R	D	D	D	R	R	R
New Hampshire	R	R	R	R	R	R	R	R	R	R	R	R	R	D	D	R	R	R
New Jersey	R[1]	D	D	R	D	D	D	D	D	R	R	R	R	D	R	R	R	R
New Mexico														D	D	R	R	R
New York	R	R	D	R	D	R	D	R	D	R	R	R	R	D	R	R	R	R
North Carolina	SD	[2]	R	R	D	D	D	D	D	D	D	D	D	D	D	D	D	R
North Dakota									[9]	R	R	R	R	D	D	R	R	R
Ohio	R	R	R	R	R	R	R	R	R[10]	R	R	R	R	D	D	R	R	R
Oklahoma													D	D	D	R	D	R
Oregon	R	R	D	R	R	R	R	R	R[11]	R	R	R	R	D	R	R	R	R
Pennsylvania	R	R	R	R	R	R	R	R	R	R	R	R	R	PR	R	R	R	R
Rhode Island	R	R	R	R	R	R	R	R	R	R	R	R	R	D	R	R	R	D
South Carolina	SD	[2]	R	R	D	D	D	D	D	D	D	D	D	D	D	D	D	D
South Dakota									R	D	R	R	R	PR	R	R	R	R
Tennessee	CU	[2]	R	D	D	D	D	D	D	D	D	D	D	D	D	R	D	R
Texas	SD	[2]	[3]	D	D	D	D	D	D	D	D	D	D	D	D	D	D	R
Utah										D	R	R	R	R	D	R	R	R
Vermont	R	R	R	R	R	R	R	R	R	R	R	R	R	R	R	R	R	R
Virginia	CU	[2]	[3]	R	D	D	D	D	D	D	D	D	D	D	D	D	D	R
Washington									R	D	R	R	R	PR	D	R	R	R
West Virginia		R	R	R	D	D	D	D	D	R	R	R	R	D	R[16]	R	R	R
Wisconsin	R	R	R	R	R	R	R	R	D	R	R	R	R	D	R	R	PR	R
Wyoming									R	D	R	R	R	D	D	R	R	R
Winning Party	R	R	R	R	R	R	D	R	D	R	R	R	R	D	D	R	R	R

Note: With the exception of the District of Columbia, blanks indicate states not yet admitted to the Union. The District of Columbia received the presidential vote in 1961.

Key: AI-American Independent Party; CU-Constitutional Union Party; D-Democratic Party; PP-People's Party; PR-Progressive (Bull Moose) Party; R-Republican Party; SD-Southern Democratic Party; SR-States' Rights Democratic Party.

1. Four electors voted Republican; three, Democratic.
2. Confederate states did not vote in 1864.
3. Did not vote in 1868.
4. Votes were not counted.
5. Three votes for Greeley not counted.
6. Five electors voted Democratic; one, Republican.
7. Eight electors voted Democratic; one, Republican.
8. Nine electors voted Republican; five, Democratic.
9. One vote each for Democratic, Republican and People's parties.
10. Twenty-two electors voted Republican; one, Democratic.

1932	1936	1940	1944	1948	1952	1956	1960	1964	1968	1972	1976	1980	1984	1988	1992	1996	2000	Dems.	Reps.	Other
D	D	D	D	SR	D	D[18]	D[19]	R	AI	R	D	R	R	R	R	R	R	22	10	3
							R	D	R	R	R	R	R	R	R	R	R	1	10	0
D	D	D	D	D	R	R	R	R	R	R	R	R	R	R	R	D	R	8	15	0
D	D	D	D	D	D	D	D	D	AI	R	R	R	R	R	D	D	R	26	6	2
D	D	D	D	D	D	R	R	D	R	R	R	R	R	D	D	D	D	12	23	1
D	D	D	D	D	R	R	R	D	R	R	R	R	R	D	R	R	R	10	21	1
R	D	D	D	R	R	R	D	D	D	R	R	R	R	R	D	D	D	14	22	0
R	D	D	D	R	R	R	D	D	R	R	D	R	R	R	D	D	D	17	18	1
								D	D	D	D	D	D	D	D	D	D[26]	10	0	0
D	D	D	D	D	R	R	R	D	R	D	R	R	R	R	D	R	D	20	14	1
D	D	D	D	D	D	D	D	R	AI	R	D	D	R	R	D	R	R	27	6	2
							D	D	R	D	D	R	D	D	D	D	D	9	2	0
D	D	D	D	D	R	R	R	D	R	R	R	R	R	R	R	R	R	10	17	1
D	D	D	D	D	R	R	D	D	R	R	R	R	R	R	D	D	D	12	24	0
D	D	R	R	R	R	R	R	D	R	R	R	R	R	R	R	R	R	7	29	0
D	D	R	D	D	R	R	R	D	R	R	D	R	R	R	D	D	D	9	27	0
R	R	R	R	R	R	R	R	D	R	R	R	R	R	R	R	R	R	6	28	1
D	D	D	D	D	D	D	R	D	R	R	D	R	R	D	D	D	R	24	11	1
D	D	D	D	SR	D	R	D	R	AI	R	D	R	R	R	D	D	R	23	8	3
R	R	R	R	R	R	R	R	D	D	R	R	R	R	R	D	D	D	6	30	0
D	D	D	D	D	R	R	D	D	D	R	D	D	R	D	D	D	D	23	12	1
D	D	D	D	D	R	R	D	D	D	D	D	R	R	D	D	D	D	16	20	0
D	D	D	D	D	R	R	D	D	D	R	R	R	R	R	D	D	D	9	26	1
D	D	D	D	D	R	R	D	D	D	R	D	D	D	D	D	D	D	15	20	1
D	D	D	D	SR	D	D	[20]	R	AI	R	D	R	R	R	R	R	R	21	9	4
D	D	D	D	D	R	D	D	D	R	D	R	R	R	D	D	R	R	22	14	0
D	D	D	D	D	R	R	R	D	R	R	R	R	R	R	D	R	R	11	17	0
D	D	D	D	R	R	R	D	R	R	R	R	R	R	R	R	R	R	7	27	0
D	D	R	R	D	R	R	D	D	R	R	R	R	R	R	D	D	R	15	19	1
R	D	D	D	D	R	R	R	D	R	R	R	R	R	R	D	D	R	8	28	0
D	D	D	D	R	R	R	D	D	R	R	R	R	R	D	D	D	D	17	19	0
D	D	D	D	D	R	R	D	D	R	R	R	R	R	D	D	D	D	12	11	0
D	D	D	D	R	R	R	D	D	D	R	D	R	R	D	D	D	D	17	19	0
D	D	D	D	D	D	D	D	D	R[22]	R	D	R	R	R	R	R	R	23	11	1
D	D	R	R	R	R	R	R	D	R	R	R	R	R	R	R	R	R	5	22	1
D	D	D	R	R	R	R	R	D	R	R	D	R	R	R	D	D	R	10	26	0
D	D	D	D	D	R	R	R[21]	D	R	R	R	R	R	R	R	R	R	10	14	0
D	D	D	D	R	R	R	R	D	R	R	R	R	R	D	D	D	D	11	25	0
R	D	D	D	R	R	R	D	D	D	R	D	R	R	D	D	D	D	10	25	1
D	D	D	D	D	R	R	D	D	D	R	D	D	R	D	D	D	D	16	20	0
D	D	D	D	SR	D	D	D	R	R	R	D	R	R	R	R	R	R	21	12	2
D	D	R	R	R	R	R	R	D	R	R	R	R	R	R	R	R	R	4	23	1
D	D	D	D	D[17]	R	R	D	D	R	R	D	R	R	R	D	D	R	22	12	1
D	D	D	D	D	R	R	D	D	D	R	D	R	R	R	R	R	R	23	10	1
D	D	D	D	D	R	R	R	D	R	R	R	R	R	R	R	R	R	8	19	0
R	R	R	R	R	R	R	R	D	R	R	R	R	R	D	D	D	D	4	32	0
D	D	D	D	D	R	D	D	D	D	R[23]	R	R	R	R	R	R	R	19	14	1
D	D	D	D	D	R	R	D	D	R	R[24]	R	R	D	D	D	D	D	13	14	1
D	D	D	D	D	D	R	D	D	D	R	D	D	R	D[25]	D	D	R	20	15	0
D	D	R	D	D	R	R	D	D	R	R	D	R	R	D	D	D	D	12	23	1
D	D	D	D	R	R	R	R	D	R	R	R	R	R	R	R	R	R	8	20	0
D	D	D	D	D	R	R	D	D	R	D	R	R	R	R	R	R	R	14	22	0

11. Three electors voted Republican; one, People's Party.
12. Eight electors voted Republican; one, Democratic.
13. Twelve electors voted Republican; one, Democratic.
14. Seven electors voted Democratic; one, Republican.
15. Six electors voted Democratic; two, Republican.
16. Seven electors voted Republican; one, Democratic.
17. Eleven electors voted Democratic; one, States' Rights.
18. One elector voted for Walter B. Jones.
19. Six of eleven electors voted for Harry F. Byrd.
20. Eight independent electors voted for Byrd.
21. One vote cast for Byrd.
22. Twelve electors voted Republican; one, American Independent.
23. One elector voted Libertarian.
24. One elector voted for Ronald Reagan.
25. One elector voted for Lloyd Bentsen.
26. One elector did not vote.

Distribution of House Seats and Electoral Votes, 1952–2000

State	U.S. House Seats									Electoral Votes					
	1963–1973	1970 Census Changes	1973–1983	1980 Census Changes	1983–1993	1990 Census Changes	1993–2003	2000 Census Changes	2003–2013	1952, 1956, 1960	1964, 1968	1972, 1976, 1980	1984, 1988	1992, 1996, 2000	2004, 2008
Alabama	8	−1	7	—	7	—	7	—	7	11	10	9	9	9	9
Alaska	1	—	1	—	1	—	1	—	1	3	3	3	3	3	3
Arizona	3	+1	4	+1	5	+1	6	+2	8	4	5	6	7	8	10
Arkansas	4	—	4	—	4	—	4	—	4	8	6	6	6	6	6
California	38	+5	43	+2	45	+7	52	+1	53	32	40	45	47	54	55
Colorado	4	+1	5	+1	6	—	6	+1	7	6	6	7	8	8	9
Connecticut	6	—	6	—	6	—	6	−1	5	8	8	8	8	8	7
Delaware	1	—	1	—	1	—	1	—	1	3	3	3	3	3	3
Dist. of Col.	—	—	—	—	—	—	—	—	—	—	3	3	3	3	3
Florida	12	+3	15	+4	19	+4	23	+2	25	10	14	17	21	25	27
Georgia	10	—	10	—	10	+1	11	+2	13	12	12	12	12	13	15
Hawaii	2	—	2	—	2	—	2	—	2	3	4	4	4	4	4
Idaho	2	—	2	—	2	—	2	—	2	4	4	4	4	4	4
Illinois	24	—	24	−2	22	−2	20	−1	19	27	26	26	24	22	21
Indiana	11	—	11	−1	10	—	10	−1	9	13	13	13	12	12	11
Iowa	7	−1	6	—	6	−1	5	—	5	10	9	8	8	7	7
Kansas	5	—	5	—	5	−1	4	—	4	8	7	7	7	6	6
Kentucky	7	—	7	—	7	−1	6	—	6	10	9	9	9	8	8
Louisiana	8	—	8	—	8	−1	7	—	7	10	10	10	10	9	9
Maine	2	—	2	—	2	—	2	—	2	5	4	4	4	4	4
Maryland	8	—	8	—	8	—	8	—	8	9	10	10	10	10	10
Massachusetts	12	—	12	−1	11	−1	10	—	10	16	14	14	13	12	12
Michigan	19	—	19	−1	18	−2	16	−1	15	20	21	21	20	18	17
Minnesota	8	—	8	—	8	—	8	—	8	11	10	10	10	10	10
Mississippi	5	—	5	—	5	—	5	−1	4	8	7	7	7	7	6
Missouri	10	—	10	−1	9	—	9	—	9	13	12	12	11	11	11
Montana	2	—	2	—	2	−1	1	—	1	4	4	4	4	3	3
Nebraska	3	—	3	—	3	—	3	—	3	6	5	5	5	5	5
Nevada	1	—	1	+1	2	—	2	+1	3	3	3	3	4	4	5
New Hampshire	2	—	2	—	2	—	2	—	2	4	4	4	4	4	4
New Jersey	15	—	15	−1	14	−1	13	—	13	16	17	17	16	15	15
New Mexico	2	—	2	+1	3	—	3	—	3	4	4	4	5	5	5
New York	41	−2	39	−5	34	−3	31	−2	29	45	43	41	36	33	31
North Carolina	11	—	11	—	11	+1	12	+1	13	14	13	13	13	14	15
North Dakota	2	−1	1	—	1	—	1	—	1	4	4	3	3	3	3
Ohio	24	−1	23	−2	21	−2	19	−1	18	25	26	25	23	21	20
Oklahoma	6	—	6	—	6	—	6	−1	5	8	8	8	8	8	7
Oregon	4	—	4	+1	5	—	5	—	5	6	6	6	7	7	7
Pennsylvania	27	−2	25	−2	23	−2	21	−2	19	32	29	27	25	23	21
Rhode Island	2	—	2	—	2	—	2	—	2	4	4	4	4	4	4
South Carolina	6	—	6	—	6	—	6	—	6	8	8	8	8	8	8
South Dakota	2	—	2	−1	1	—	1	—	1	4	4	4	3	3	3
Tennessee	9	−1	8	+1	9	—	9	—	9	11	11	10	11	11	11
Texas	23	+1	24	+3	27	+3	30	+2	32	24	25	26	29	32	34
Utah	2	—	2	+1	3	—	3	—	3	4	4	4	5	5	5
Vermont	1	—	1	—	1	—	1	—	1	3	3	3	3	3	3
Virginia	10	—	10	—	10	+1	11	—	11	12	12	12	12	13	13
Washington	7	—	7	+1	8	+1	9	—	9	9	9	9	10	11	11
West Virginia	5	−1	4	—	4	−1	3	—	3	8	7	6	6	5	5
Wisconsin	10	−1	9	—	9	—	9	−1	8	12	12	11	11	11	10
Wyoming	1	—	1	—	1	—	1	—	1	3	3	3	3	3	3

Note: Table is based on the censuses of 1950, 1960, 1970, 1980, 1990, and 2000.

Bush v. Gore: Excerpts from the 2000 Supreme Court Decision on the Florida Recount

B Y A 5–4 VOTE divided along conservative-liberal lines, the Supreme Court on December 12, 2000, put an end to the five-week dispute over the presidential election results in Florida and effectively elected Republican George W. Bush as the nation's forty-third president. The decision stopped the manual count of several thousand contested ballots that had been ordered by the Florida Supreme Court, leaving Bush the certified winner by 537 votes of the state's twenty-five electoral votes, enough to give him the presidency. Although the U.S. Supreme Court sent the case back to the Florida court for further consideration, the decision left Vice President Al Gore's attorneys little maneuvering room to pursue his challenge, and the Democratic nominee conceded the election to Bush on December 13. It was a painful decision for Gore, who had won the nationwide popular vote by approximately 577,000 votes.

The Court's decision capped the most extraordinary period in U.S. presidential politics in more than a century. The November 7 election left Gore with 267 electoral votes—just 3 short of the 270 needed under the Constitution for election as president. Bush had 246 electoral votes coming out of the election. In doubt were Florida's 25 electoral votes, which would provide the margin of victory. There Bush had a slim advantage, and for five weeks lawyers and partisans for the two sides clashed in the courts, at local elections headquarters, and even in the streets. Bush sought to preserve his slim lead by erecting legal roadblocks to the recounting of thousands of ballots that were in dispute. Needing every vote he could get, Gore demanded that all disputed votes be counted.

Throughout the ordeal, the nation and the world watched as election workers peered at ballots looking for signs of voter intent, and as judges struggled with Florida's sometimes conflicting laws to determine the state legislature's intent. It was the closest the United States had come to a constitutional crisis over a presidential election since 1876, when an election dispute dragged on for months and was finally resolved by a contentious vote in the House of Representatives.

In the end Bush won because he had two important allies working in tandem: the calendar and the Supreme Court. Under a federal law enacted in 1887, a state's electors had to be selected by December 12 if they were to be free from challenge in the U.S. Congress. Although nothing in the law prevented electors from being selected after December 12—in 1960 Hawaii did not select its electors until January 4—the Bush team argued that the Florida legislature had intended December 12 to be the deadline for selecting electors. Bush's attorneys then used every legal maneuver they could muster to prevent or delay voter recounts until this deadline had passed and it was too late to overturn the Bush lead. As the December 12 date approached, the final arbiter of whether additional votes would be counted was the Supreme Court, which for the first time in U.S. history found itself in the position of being able to determine who would become president. On the key decision in the case of *Bush v. Gore*, the Court's five most conservative justices sided with Bush, the conservative candidate, and the four most liberal justices sided with Gore, the liberal candidate.

The coincidence of this split did not go unnoticed. Editorial writers and legal experts said that the Court should have refused to review the dispute and left it for Congress to resolve. By injecting the Supreme Court into a political issue, the Court had weakened its own legitimacy as well as Bush's claim to the White House, those critics said. John Paul Stevens, one of the dissenting justices, said the Court's ruling "can only lend credence to the most cynical appraisal of the work of judges throughout the land." Another dissenter, Justice Stephen G. Breyer, referred to the Court action as "this self-inflicted wound." Nor did it escape public notice that the Republican nominee who had campaigned on states' rights had turned to the federal judiciary to overrule the Florida state courts or that his promises of inclusion did not extend to disputed ballots cast primarily by blacks, the urban poor, and the elderly.

Although most Americans accepted the Court's decision and Gore's concession calmly, it remained to be seen to what extent the controversy had damaged the public's trust in its governing institutions and in the electoral process. Some observers predicted that the incident would discourage voter turnout in the future, especially among African Americans and other minorities who were already skeptical about the voting process. Several news organizations immediately announced plans to perform their own recounts of the Florida ballots, while politicians and election officials across the country promised to review election laws and procedures to prevent similar situations in the future.

On December 14 Florida governor Jeb Bush announced that he was creating a special task force to investigate the integrity of Florida's election process. He also said he would welcome an investigation by the U.S. Commission on Civil Rights into allegations into voting irregularities, including incidents of intimidation directed at black voters. Bush, the younger brother of the president-elect, and Florida secretary of state Katherine Harris, an acknowledged Bush supporter, had been accused by Gore partisans of using their offices to help thwart the recount.

THE FIRST PHASE: PROTESTING THE COUNT

Pollsters and political pundits had predicted that the presidential race would be close, but no one could have predicted the precise, sometimes bizarre, twists and turns that would occur

before the outcome of the 2000 election was determined. The dispute over Florida's ballots began early on election evening, November 7, when television networks first projected that Gore would win Florida and then put the state back into the undecided column. Early in the morning of November 8, both Bush and Gore were projected to be within reach of an electoral college majority—with Florida's twenty-five electoral votes enough to clinch the victory for either candidate. After several news organizations declared Bush the winner in Florida, Gore called him to concede. A half hour later, the Gore campaign determined Florida was too close to call, and Gore called Bush to retract his concession.

After the first statewide count, which did not include thousands of absentee ballots, Bush was ahead by 1,784 votes out of more than 6 million cast statewide. A mandatory machine recount of the close vote whittled Bush's lead down to 327 votes. By this time Democratic voters in several counties were complaining about broken voting machines and confusing ballots that may have caused them to vote for a candidate other than Gore. Many voters said there was so much confusion and such long lines at some precincts that they left without voting. Some black voters said that police roadblocks prevented then from even getting to the polls. On November 10, three days after the balloting was completed and with the presidential election outcome still uncertain, the Gore campaign formally asked for a manual recount of the ballots in the four Florida counties where most of the complaints originated. The following day, the Bush campaign filed suit in federal district court to stop the recounts.

For the next ten days the dispute centered on the secretary of state's certification of the vote, with the Bush forces pushing election officials to hold to certification deadlines established in state law and the Gore forces trying to extend those deadlines so that the manual recounts could be completed. The recount process was slow, as vote counters wrangled over whether to count the "hanging chads" and "dimples" left in ballots that were not cleanly punched through by the voting machines. Election officials in Miami-Dade County eventually abandoned their recount because they did not think they could meet a court-imposed deadline. Vote counters in Palm Beach and Broward counties continued, despite uncertainties about whether their efforts would ever be counted in the state's final tally. In at least one case, vote counters were threatened by Republican partisans monitoring the count.

On November 18 absentee ballots were counted, raising Bush's official lead to 930 votes. But the Florida Supreme Court had barred the secretary of state from certifying the election until it could hear arguments on whether the ballots counted by hand should be included in the final tally. On November 21 the seven-member court unanimously ruled that the hand counts had to be included and extended the deadline for certification of the vote from November 14 to November 26. Bush immediately appealed the decision to the U.S. Supreme Court, arguing that the Florida Supreme Court had violated federal election law by rewriting the state election law after the election had taken place. In the first of several controversial decisions involving the

recount, the U.S. Supreme Court agreed on November 24 to review the case.

THE SECOND PHASE:
CONTESTING THE CERTIFICATION

The second, or contest, phase of the dispute began November 26, when Harris certified Bush the winner with 537 votes. The following day Gore filed suit in state court, contesting the results of the certification on the grounds that there were still enough uncounted votes to change the outcome of the election. Throughout this phase the Gore attorneys argued that the will of the people could not be fully known until all the ballots were counted; while the Bush attorneys argued that recounts using different standards were unfair and a violation of the Constitution's equal protection clause.

On December 1 the U.S. Supreme Court heard arguments in the suit brought by Bush challenging the extended certification deadline. Three days later, on December 4, the Court issued an unsigned opinion setting aside the Florida Supreme Court's decision extending the deadline for manual recounts and asked the Florida court to clarify two issues regarding its original decision. On the same day, Florida judge N. Sanders Sauls rejected Gore's suit contesting the election results.

Gore appealed Sauls's ruling to the state supreme court. By a 4–3 decision on December 8 the state supreme court ordered an immediate manual recount of all the "undervotes"—some 45,000 ballots that had not been counted because machines had not detected a vote for president. The ruling revived Gore's flagging hopes for the White House and sent Bush's lawyers back to the U.S. Supreme Court, where they sought a stay of the recount while they appealed the state supreme court ruling. On December 9 the Court granted the stay and agreed to hear the appeal. On December 11 the Court heard oral argument, and on December 12, at about 10:00 p.m., it handed down its historic ruling.

THE DECISION: EQUAL PROTECTION
UNDER A DEADLINE

The majority opinion was unsigned, but it was obvious from the four dissents that the main opinion had been supported by the five conservative justices—Chief Justice William H. Rehnquist, and Justices Sandra Day O'Connor, Anthony M. Kennedy, Antonin Scalia, and Clarence Thomas. Rehnquist wrote a concurring opinion that was joined by Scalia and Thomas. Justices Stevens, Breyer, David H. Souter, and Ruth Bader Ginsburg each wrote dissents that were joined in part by the other dissenters. Court reporters said the unsigned or "per curiam" Court opinion appeared to be largely the work of O'Connor and Kennedy, neither of whose name appeared on any of the signed opinions. O'Connor and Kennedy were the most moderate justices on the Court and often were the decisive votes in close cases. The majority opinion itself appeared to be a failed effort at finding a compromise that would draw the support of both liberal and conservative justices. In its main finding, the majority ruled that the state supreme court's failure to establish uniform standards for manually counting the undervotes denied Florida voters

their constitutionally guaranteed right to equal protection of the laws.

Breyer and Souter indicated in their dissents that they, too, were troubled by the equal protection problems associated with standards that varied from county to county and even among teams of counters. Whereas Breyer and Souter would have sent the case back to the state supreme court with instructions to establish uniform standards and proceed with the recount, the majority said there was no time for that to happen before December 12, the deadline for the state to obtain the so-called safe harbor for its electors protecting them from challenge in Congress. Because the Florida Supreme Court held that the state legislature had intended to obtain that safe harbor, the majority said, the remedy proposed by the dissenters to extend the count beyond that deadline "contemplates action in violation of the Florida election code" and was therefore inappropriate.

In their separate opinions, the four dissenters argued that the federal questions involved were insubstantial and the Court should never have agreed to review the case in the first place. "Of course, the selection of the President is of fundamental national importance," Breyer wrote. "But that importance is political, not legal. And this Court should resist the temptation unnecessarily to resolve tangential legal disputes, where doing so threatens to determine the outcome of the election." Stevens was blunter in his criticism: "What must underlie petitioners' entire federal assault on the Florida election procedures is an unstated lack of confidence in the impartiality and capacity of the state judges who would make the critical decision if the vote count were to proceed. Otherwise their position is without merit," Stevens wrote.

In their concurring opinion, Rehnquist, Scalia, and Thomas acknowledged that "in most cases, comity and respect for federalism compel us to defer" to state courts on interpretations of state law. But the three justices said there were a "few exceptional cases in which the Constitution imposes a duty or confers a power on a particular branch of a state's government" and thus presented a "federal question" that was appropriate for the Supreme Court to address. *Bush v. Gore* was one of those exceptional cases, Rehnquist wrote, because it involved a presidential election, and because the Constitution specifically delegated authority to oversee presidential elections to state legislatures. Having justified their intervention in the case, the three then found the state supreme court's interpretation of the Florida election law to be "absurd."

Both Stevens and Ginsburg rejected the equal protection argument advanced by the majority. "We live in an imperfect world, one in which thousands of votes have not been counted," Ginsburg said. "I cannot agree that the recount adopted by the Florida court, awed as it may be, would yield a result any less fair or precise than the certification that preceded that recount." All four dissenters lambasted the majority for hinging the outcome of the case on the December 12 safe-harbor deadline. No state was required to meet that deadline, Souter said. The only penalty for failing to meet it was loss of the safe harbor and "even that determination is to be made, if made anywhere, in the Congress."

Although the impact of the Supreme Court's controversial ruling on the courts and on the legitimacy of Bush's presidency could not be assessed for years to come, legal experts warned that the majority's application of equal protection notions to the voting booth may have opened a big can of worms. Even though the majority explicitly stated that its ruling was limited to the case before it, said Kathleen Sullivan, dean of Stanford University Law School, "theoretically any voter in America going to court tomorrow" could challenge differences in the voting procedures in the same state or county under the equal protection clause. Someone, for example, could protest the use of punch-card machines in one precinct and optical scanners in another, she said. A. E. Dick Howard, a professor at the University of Virginia Law School, agreed that the "spirit and philosophy of the equal protection discussion [in the *Bush v. Gore* ruling] would be one that could invite other attacks in other contexts. Once an idea is unleashed, it's not easily contained. . . . I'm not prepared to say the court can keep that particular genie in the bottle."

Following are excerpts from the unsigned majority opinion, a concurring opinion, and four dissenting opinions, in the case of *Bush v. Gore*, in which the Supreme Court by a vote of 5–4 ruled on December 12, 2000, that the Florida Supreme Court had failed to guarantee equal protection of the laws when it ordered a manual count of several thousand disputed votes cast in the presidential election and ruled further that the error could not be remedied in time to meet a December 12 deadline for selecting electors. The decision had the effect of naming Republican George W. Bush, governor of Texas, the president-elect of the United States. The document was obtained from the Internet at http://frwebgate.access.gpo.gov/supremecourt/00-949_dec12.fdf.

Bush v. Gore

CHIEF JUSTICE REHNQUIST'S OPINION OF THE COURT

On December 8, 2000, the Supreme Court of Florida ordered that the Circuit Court of Leon County tabulate by hand 9,000 ballots in Miami-Dade County. It also ordered the inclusion in the certified vote totals of 215 votes identified in Palm Beach County and 168 votes identified in Miami-Dade County for Vice President Albert Gore, Jr., and Senator Joseph Lieberman, Democratic Candidates for President and Vice President. The Supreme Court noted that petitioner, Governor George W. Bush asserted that the net gain for Vice President Gore in Palm Beach County was 176 votes, and directed the Circuit Court to resolve that dispute on remand. The court further held that relief would require manual recounts in all Florida counties where so-called "undervotes" had not been subject to manual tabulation. The court ordered all manual recounts to begin at once. Governor Bush and Richard Cheney, Republican Candidates for the Presidency and Vice Presidency, filed an emergency application for a stay of this mandate. On December 9, we granted the application, treated the application as a petition for a writ of certiorari, and granted certiorari.

REFERENCE MATERIALS

.... On November 8, 2000, the day following the Presidential election, the Florida Division of Elections reported that petitioner, Governor Bush, had received 2,909,135 votes, and respondent, Vice President Gore, had received 2,907,351 votes, a margin of 1,784 for Governor Bush. Because Governor Bush's margin of victory was less than "one-half of a percent. . . of the votes cast," an automatic machine recount was conducted under. . . the Florida Election Code, the results of which showed Governor Bush still winning the race but by a diminished margin. Vice President Gore then sought manual recounts in Volusia, Palm Beach, Broward, and Miami-Dade Counties, pursuant to Florida's election protest provisions. A dispute arose concerning the deadline for local county canvassing boards to submit their returns to the Secretary of State (Secretary). The Secretary declined to waive the November 14 deadline imposed by statute. The Florida Supreme Court, however, set the deadline at November 26. We granted certiorari and vacated the Florida Supreme Court's decision, finding considerable uncertainty as to the grounds on which it was based. On December 11, the Florida Supreme Court issued a decision on remand reinstating that date. On November 26, the Florida Elections Canvassing Commission certified the results of the election and declared Governor Bush the winner of Florida's 25 electoral votes. On November 27, Vice President Gore, pursuant to Florida's contest provisions, filed a complaint in Leon County Circuit Court contesting the certification. He sought relief pursuant to Section 102.168 (3) (c), which provides that "[r]eceipt of a number of illegal votes or rejection of a number of legal votes sufficient to change or place in doubt the result of the election" shall be grounds for a contest. The Circuit Court denied relief, stating that Vice President Gore failed to meet his burden of proof. He appealed to the First District Court of Appeal, which certified the matter to the Florida Supreme Court.

Accepting jurisdiction, the Florida Supreme Court affirmed in part and reversed in part. The court held that the Circuit Court had been correct to reject Vice President Gore's challenge to the results certified in Nassau County and his challenge to the Palm Beach County Canvassing Board's determination that 3,300 ballots cast in that county were not, in the statutory phrase, "legal votes." The Supreme Court held that Vice President Gore had satisfied his burden of proof. . . with respect to his challenge to Miami-Dade County's failure to tabulate, by manual count, 9,000 ballots on which the machines had failed to detect a vote for President ("undervotes"). Noting the closeness of the election, the Court explained that "[o]n this record, there can be no question that there are legal votes within the 9,000 uncounted votes sufficient to place the results of this election in doubt." A "legal vote," as determined by the Supreme Court, is "one in which there is a 'clear indication of the intent of the voter.'" The court therefore ordered a hand recount of the 9,000 ballots in Miami-Dade County. Observing that the contest provisions vest broad discretion in the circuit judge to "provide any relief appropriate under such circumstances," the Supreme Court further held that the Circuit Court could order "the Supervisor of Elections and the Canvassing Boards, as well as the necessary public officials, in all counties

that have not conducted a manual recount or tabulation of the undervotes. . . to do so forthwith, said tabulation to take place in the individual counties where the ballots are located." The Supreme Court also determined that Palm Beach County and Miami-Dade County, in their earlier manual recounts, had identified a net gain of 215 and 168 legal votes, respectively, for Vice President Gore. Rejecting the Circuit Court's conclusion that Palm Beach County lacked the authority to include the 215 net votes submitted past the November 26 deadline, the Supreme Court explained that the deadline was not intended to exclude votes identified after that date through ongoing manual recounts. As to Miami-Dade County, the Court concluded that although the 168 votes identified were the result of a partial recount, they were "legal votes [that] could change the outcome of the election." The Supreme Court therefore directed the Circuit Court to include those totals in the certified results, subject to resolution of the actual vote total from the Miami-Dade partial recount.

The petition presents the following questions: whether the Florida Supreme Court established new standards for resolving Presidential election contests, thereby violating Art. II, Section 1, cl. 2, of the United States Constitution and failing to comply with 3 U.S.C. Section 5, and whether the use of standardless manual recounts violates the Equal Protection and Due Process Clauses. With respect to the equal protection question, we find a violation of the Equal Protection Clause.

. . . . The individual citizen has no federal constitutional right to vote for electors for the President of the United States unless and until the state legislature chooses a statewide election as the means to implement its power to appoint members of the Electoral College. This is the source for the statement in *McPherson v. Blacker* (1892) that the State legislature's power to select the manner for appointing electors is plenary; it may, if it so chooses, select the electors itself, which indeed was the manner used by State legislatures in several States for many years after the Framing of our Constitution. History has now favored the voter, and in each of the several States the citizens themselves vote for Presidential electors. When the state legislature vests the right to vote for President in its people, the right to vote as the legislature has prescribed is fundamental; and one source of its fundamental nature lies in the equal weight accorded to each vote and the equal dignity owed to each voter. The State, of course, after granting the franchise in the special context of Article II, can take back the power to appoint electors. . . .

The right to vote is protected in more than the initial allocation of the franchise. Equal protection applies as well to the manner of its exercise. Having once granted the right to vote on equal terms, the State may not, by later arbitrary and disparate treatment, value one person's vote over that of another. . . .

There is no difference between the two sides of the present controversy on these basic propositions. Respondents say that the very purpose of vindicating the right to vote justifies the recount procedures now at issue. The question before us, however, is whether the recount procedures the Florida Supreme Court has adopted are consistent with its obligation to avoid arbitrary and disparate treatment of the members of its electorate.

Much of the controversy seems to revolve around ballot cards designed to be perforated by a stylus but which, either through error or deliberate omission, have not been perforated with sufficient precision for a machine to count them. In some cases a piece of the card—a chad—is hanging, say by two corners. In other cases there is no separation at all, just an indentation. The Florida Supreme Court has ordered that the intent of the voter be discerned from such ballots. For purposes of resolving the equal protection challenge, it is not necessary to decide whether the Florida Supreme Court had the authority under the legislative scheme for resolving election disputes to define what a legal vote is and to mandate a manual recount implementing that definition. The recount mechanisms implemented in response to the decisions of the Florida Supreme Court do not satisfy the minimum requirement for nonarbitrary treatment of voters necessary to secure the fundamental right. Florida's basic command for the count of legally cast votes is to consider the "intent of the voter." This is unobjectionable as an abstract proposition and a starting principle. The problem inheres in the absence of specific standards to ensure its equal application. The formulation of uniform rules to determine intent based on these recurring circumstances is practicable and, we conclude, necessary.

. . . . The want of those rules here has led to unequal evaluation of ballots in various respects. As seems to have been acknowledged at oral argument, the standards for accepting or rejecting contested ballots might vary not only from county to county but indeed within a single county from one recount team to another. . . .

The State Supreme Court ratified this uneven treatment. It mandated that the recount totals from two counties, Miami-Dade and Palm Beach, be included in the certified total. The court also appeared to hold *sub silentio* that the recount totals from Broward County, which were not completed until after the original November 14 certification by the Secretary of State, were to be considered part of the new certified vote totals even though the county certification was not contested by Vice President Gore. Yet each of the counties used varying standards to determine what was a legal vote. Broward County used a more forgiving standard than Palm Beach County, and uncovered almost three times as many new votes, a result markedly disproportionate to the difference in population between the counties. In addition, the recounts in these three counties were not limited to so-called undervotes but extended to all of the ballots. The distinction has real consequences. A manual recount of all ballots identifies not only those ballots which show no vote but also those which contain more than one, the so-called overvotes. Neither category will be counted by the machine. This is not a trivial concern.

At oral argument, respondents estimated there are as many as 110,000 overvotes statewide. As a result, the citizen whose ballot was not read by a machine because he failed to vote for a candidate in a way readable by a machine may still have his vote counted in a manual recount; on the other hand, the citizen who marks two candidates in a way discernable by the machine will not have the same opportunity to have his vote count, even if a manual examination of the ballot would reveal the requisite indicia of intent. Furthermore, the citizen who marks two candidates, only one of which is discernable by the machine, will have his vote counted even though it should have been read as an invalid ballot. The State Supreme Court's inclusion of vote counts based on these variant standards exemplifies concerns with the remedial processes that were under way.

That brings the analysis to yet a further equal protection problem. The votes certified by the court included a partial total from one county, Miami-Dade. The Florida Supreme Court's decision thus gives no assurance that the recounts included in a final certification must be complete. Indeed, it is respondent's submission that it would be consistent with the rules of the recount procedures to include whatever partial counts are done by the time of final certification, and we interpret the Florida Supreme Court's decision to permit this. . . . The press of time does not diminish the constitutional concern. A desire for speed is not a general excuse for ignoring equal protection guarantees.

In addition to these difficulties the actual process by which the votes were to be counted under the Florida Supreme Court's decision raises further concerns. That order did not specify who would recount the ballots. The county canvassing boards were forced to pull together ad hoc teams comprised of judges from various Circuits who had no previous training in handling and interpreting ballots. Furthermore, while others were permitted to observe, they were prohibited from objecting during the recount.

The recount process, in its features here described, is inconsistent with the minimum procedures necessary to protect the fundamental right of each voter in the special instance of a statewide recount under the authority of a single state judicial officer. Our consideration is limited to the present circumstances, for the problem of equal protection in election processes generally presents many complexities.

The question before the Court is not whether local entities, in the exercise of their expertise, may develop different systems for implementing elections. Instead, we are presented with a situation where a state court with the power to assure uniformity has ordered a statewide recount with minimal procedural safeguards. When a court orders a statewide remedy, there must be at least some assurance that the rudimentary requirements of equal treatment and fundamental fairness are satisfied. Given the Court's assessment that the recount process underway was probably being conducted in an unconstitutional manner, the Court stayed the order directing the recount so it could hear this case and render an expedited decision. The contest provision, as it was mandated by the State Supreme Court, is not well calculated to sustain the confidence that all citizens must have in the outcome of elections. The State has not shown that its procedures include the necessary safeguards. . . .

Upon due consideration of the difficulties identified to this point, it is obvious that the recount cannot be conducted in compliance with the requirements of equal protection and due process without substantial additional work. It would require not only the adoption (after opportunity for argument) of adequate statewide standards for determining what is a legal vote,

and practicable procedures to implement them, but also orderly judicial review of any disputed matters that might arise. . . .

The Supreme Court of Florida has said that the legislature intended the State's electors to "participat[e] fully in the federal electoral process," as provided in 3 U.S.C. Section 5.

That statute, in turn, requires that any controversy or contest that is designed to lead to a conclusive selection of electors be completed by December 12. That date is upon us, and there is no recount procedure in place under the State Supreme Court's order that comports with minimal constitutional standards. Because it is evident that any recount seeking to meet the December 12 date will be unconstitutional for the reasons we have discussed, we reverse the judgment of the Supreme Court of Florida ordering a recount to proceed. Seven Justices of the Court agree that there are constitutional problems with the recount ordered by the Florida Supreme Court that demand a remedy. The only disagreement is as to the remedy.

Because the Florida Supreme Court has said that the Florida Legislature intended to obtain the safe-harbor benefits of 3 U.S.C. Section 5, Justice Breyer's proposed remedy—remanding to the Florida Supreme Court for its ordering of a constitutionally proper contest until December 18—contemplates action in violation of the Florida election code, and hence could not be part of an "appropriate" order authorized by Fla. Stat. Section 102.168 (8) (2000) . . . .

None are more conscious of the vital limits on judicial authority than are the members of this Court, and none stand more in admiration of the Constitution's design to leave the selection of the President to the people, through their legislatures, and to the political sphere. When contending parties invoke the process of the courts, however, it becomes our unsought responsibility to resolve the federal and constitutional issues the judicial system has been forced to confront. The judgment of the Supreme Court of Florida is reversed, and the case is remanded for further proceedings not inconsistent with this opinion.

Pursuant to this Court's Rule 45.2, the Clerk is directed to issue the mandate in this case forthwith.

It is so ordered.

JUSTICES SCALIA'S AND THOMAS'S ADDITIONAL GROUNDS

We deal here not with an ordinary election, but with an election for the President of the United States. . . .

In most cases, comity and respect for federalism compel us to defer to the decisions of state courts on issues of state law. That practice reflects our understanding that the decisions of state courts are definitive pronouncements of the will of the States as sovereigns. Of course, in ordinary cases, the distribution of powers among the branches of a State's government raises no questions of federal constitutional law, subject to the requirement that the government be republican in character. . . . But there are a few exceptional cases in which the Constitution imposes a duty or confers a power on a particular branch of a State's government. This is one of them.

Article II, Section 1, cl. 2, provides that "[e]ach State shall appoint, in such Manner as the Legislature thereof may direct," electors for President and Vice President. Thus, the text of the election law itself, and not just its interpretation by the courts of the States, takes on independent significance. . . . A significant departure from the legislative scheme for appointing Presidential electors presents a federal constitutional question.

3 U.S.C. Section 5 informs our application of Art. II, Section 1, cl. 2, to the Florida statutory scheme, which, as the Florida Supreme Court acknowledged, took that statute into account. Section 5 provides that the State's selection of electors "shall be conclusive, and shall govern in the counting of the electoral votes" if the electors are chosen under laws enacted prior to election day, and if the selection process is completed six days prior to the meeting of the electoral college. . . .

If we are to respect the legislature's Article II powers, therefore, we must ensure that postelection state-court actions do not frustrate the legislative desire to attain the "safe harbor" provided by Section 5.

In Florida, the legislature has chosen to hold statewide elections to appoint the State's 25 electors. Importantly, the legislature has delegated the authority to run the elections and to oversee election disputes to the Secretary of State (Secretary), and to state circuit courts. Isolated sections of the code may well admit of more than one interpretation, but the general coherence of the legislative scheme may not be altered by judicial interpretation so as to wholly change the statutorily provided apportionment of responsibility among these various bodies. In any election but a Presidential election, the Florida Supreme Court can give as little or as much deference to Florida's executives as it chooses, so far as Article II is concerned, and this Court will have no cause to question the court's actions. But, with respect to a Presidential election, the court must be both mindful of the legislature's role under Article II in choosing the manner of appointing electors and deferential to those bodies expressly empowered by the legislature to carry out its constitutional mandate.

In order to determine whether a state court has infringed upon the legislature's authority, we necessarily must examine the law of the State as it existed prior to the action of the court. Though we generally defer to state courts on the interpretation of state law. . . there are of course areas in which the Constitution requires this Court to undertake an independent, if still deferential, analysis of state law. . . .

This inquiry does not imply a disrespect for state courts but rather a respect for the constitutionally prescribed role of state legislatures. To attach definitive weight to the pronouncement of a state court, when the very question at issue is whether the court has actually departed from the statutory meaning, would be to abdicate our responsibility to enforce the explicit requirements of Article II.

. . . . Acting pursuant to its constitutional grant of authority, the Florida Legislature has created a detailed, if not perfectly crafted, statutory scheme that provides for appointment of Presidential electors by direct election. Under the statute, "[v]otes cast for the actual candidates for President and Vice President shall be counted as votes cast for the presidential electors supporting such candidates." The legislature has designated

the Secretary of State as the "chief election officer," with the responsibility to "[o]btain and maintain uniformity in the application, operation, and interpretation of the election laws."

The state legislature has delegated to county canvassing boards the duties of administering elections. Those boards are responsible for providing results to the state Elections Canvassing Commission, comprising the Governor, the Secretary of State, and the Director of the Division of Elections. . . .

After the election has taken place, the canvassing boards receive returns from precincts, count the votes, and in the event that a candidate was defeated by .5% or less, conduct a mandatory recount. The county canvassing boards must file certified election returns with the Department of State by 5 p.m. on the seventh day following the election. The Elections Canvassing Commission must then certify the results of the election. The state legislature has also provided mechanisms both for protesting election returns and for contesting certified election results. . . . Any protest must be filed prior to the certification of election results by the county canvassing board. Once a protest has been filed, "the county canvassing board may authorize a manual recount." If a sample recount . . . "indicates an error in the vote tabulation which could affect the outcome of the election," the county canvassing board is instructed to: "(a) Correct the error and recount the remaining precincts with the vote tabulation system; (b) Request the Department of State to verify the tabulation software; or (c) Manually recount all ballots." In the event a canvassing board chooses to conduct a manual recount of all ballots, [state law] prescribes procedures for such a recount.

. . . . The grounds for contesting an election include "[r]eceipt of a number of illegal votes or rejection of a number of legal votes sufficient to change or place in doubt the result of the election." Any contest must be filed in the appropriate Florida circuit court, and the canvassing board or election board is the proper party defendant. [Florida law] provides that "[t]he circuit judge to whom the contest is presented may fashion such orders as he or she deems necessary to ensure that each allegation in the complaint is investigated, examined, or checked, to prevent or correct any alleged wrong, and to provide any relief appropriate under such circumstances." In Presidential elections, the contest period necessarily terminates on the date set by 3 U.S.C. Section 5 for concluding the State's "final determination" of election controversies.

In its first decision. . . the Florida Supreme Court extended the 7-day statutory certification deadline established by the legislature. This modification of the code, by lengthening the protest period, necessarily shortened the contest period for Presidential elections. Underlying the extension of the certification deadline and the shortchanging of the contest period was, presumably, the clear implication that certification was a matter of significance: The certified winner would enjoy presumptive validity, making a contest proceeding by the losing candidate an uphill battle. In its latest opinion, however, the court empties certification of virtually all legal consequence during the contest, and in doing so departs from the provisions enacted by the Florida Legislature. The court determined that canvassing

boards' decisions regarding whether to recount ballots past the certification deadline (even the certification deadline established by Harris I) are to be reviewed de novo, although the election code clearly vests discretion whether to recount in the boards, and sets strict deadlines subject to the Secretary's rejection of late tallies and monetary fines for tardiness. . . . Moreover, the Florida court held that all late vote tallies arriving during the contest period should be automatically included in the certification regardless of the certification deadline (even the certification deadline established by Harris I), thus virtually eliminating both the deadline and the Secretary's discretion to disregard recounts that violate it.

Moreover, the court's interpretation of "legal vote," and hence its decision to order a contest-period recount, plainly departed from the legislative scheme. Florida statutory law cannot reasonably be thought to require the counting of improperly marked ballots. Each Florida precinct before election day provides instructions on how properly to cast a vote, Section 101.46; each polling place on election day contains a working model of the voting machine it uses, Section 101.5611; and each voting booth contains a sample ballot, Section 101.46. In precincts using punch-card ballots, voters are instructed to punch out the ballot cleanly. . . .

No reasonable person would call it "an error in the vote tabulation," or a "rejection of legal votes," when electronic or electromechanical equipment performs precisely in the manner designed, and fails to count those ballots that are not marked in the manner that these voting instructions explicitly and prominently specify. The scheme that the Florida Supreme Court's opinion attributes to the legislature is one in which machines are required to be "capable of correctly counting votes," but which nonetheless regularly produces elections in which legal votes are predictably not tabulated, so that in close elections manual recounts are regularly required. This is of course absurd. The Secretary of State, who is authorized by law to issue binding interpretations of the election code, rejected this peculiar reading of the statutes. . . . The Florida Supreme Court, although it must defer to the Secretary's interpretations, . . . rejected her reasonable interpretation and embraced the peculiar one.

But as we indicated in our remand of the earlier case, in a Presidential election the clearly expressed intent of the legislature must prevail. And there is no basis for reading the Florida statutes as requiring the counting of improperly marked ballots, as an examination of the Florida Supreme Court's textual analysis shows. . . . The State's Attorney General (who was supporting the Gore challenge) confirmed in oral argument here that never before the present election had a manual recount been conducted on the basis of the contention that "undervotes" should have been examined to determine voter intent. For the court to step away from this established practice, prescribed by the Secretary of State, the state official charged by the legislature with "responsibility to. . . .[o]btain and maintain uniformity in the application, operation, and interpretation of the election laws," Section 97.012 (1), was to depart from the legislative scheme.

. . . . The scope and nature of the remedy ordered by the Florida Supreme Court jeopardizes the "legislative wish" to take advantage of the safe harbor provided by 3 U.S.C. Section 5. December 12, 2000, is the last date for a final determination of the Florida electors that will satisfy Section 5. Yet in the late afternoon of December 8th—four days before this deadline—the Supreme Court of Florida ordered recounts of tens of thousands of so-called "undervotes" spread through 64 of the State's 67 counties. This was done in a search for elusive—perhaps delusive—certainty as to the exact count of 6 million votes. But no one claims that these ballots have not previously been tabulated; they were initially read by voting machines at the time of the election, and thereafter reread by virtue of Florida's automatic recount provision. No one claims there was any fraud in the election. The Supreme Court of Florida ordered this additional recount under the provision of the election code giving the circuit judge the authority to provide relief that is "appropriate under such circumstances."

Surely when the Florida Legislature empowered the courts of the State to grant "appropriate" relief, it must have meant relief that would have become final by the cut-off date of 3 U.S.C. Section 5. In light of the inevitable legal challenges and ensuing appeals to the Supreme Court of Florida and petitions for certiorari to this Court, the entire recounting process could not possibly be completed by that date. . . .

As the dissent noted: "In [the four days remaining], all questionable ballots must be reviewed by the judicial officer appointed to discern the intent of the voter in a process open to the public. Fairness dictates that a provision be made for either party to object to how a particular ballot is counted. Additionally, this short time period must allow for judicial review. I respectfully submit this cannot be completed without taking Florida's presidential electors outside the safe harbor provision, creating the very real possibility of disenfranchising those nearly 6 million voters who are able to correctly cast their ballots on election day." . . . Given all these factors, and in light of the legislative intent identified by the Florida Supreme Court to bring Florida within the "safe harbor" provision of 3 U.S.C. Section 5, the remedy prescribed by the Supreme Court of Florida cannot be deemed an "appropriate" one as of December 8.

It significantly departed from the statutory framework in place on November 7, and authorized open-ended further proceedings which could not be completed by December 12, thereby preventing a final determination by that date.n to those given in the per curiam, we would reverse.

JUSTICE STEVENS'S DISSENT

The Constitution assigns to the States the primary responsibility for determining the manner of selecting the Presidential electors. . . . When questions arise about the meaning of state laws, including election laws, it is our settled practice to accept the opinions of the highest courts of the States as providing the final answers. On rare occasions, however, either federal statutes or the Federal Constitution may require federal judicial intervention in state elections. This is not such an occasion.

The federal questions that ultimately emerged in this case are

not substantial. Article II provides that "[e]ach State shall appoint, in such Manner as the Legislature thereof may direct, a Number of Electors." It does not create state legislatures out of whole cloth, but rather takes them as they come—as creatures born of, and constrained by, their state constitutions. Lest there be any doubt, we stated over 100 years ago in *McPherson v. Blacker* (1892), that "[w]hat is forbidden or required to be done by a State" in the Article II context "is forbidden or required of the legislative power under state constitutions as they exist." In the same vein, we also observed that "[t]he [State's] legislative power is the supreme authority except as limited by the constitution of the State." The legislative power in Florida is subject to judicial review pursuant to Article V of the Florida Constitution, and nothing in Article II of the Federal Constitution frees the state legislature from the constraints in the state constitution that created it. Moreover, the Florida Legislature's own decision to employ a unitary code for all elections indicates that it intended the Florida Supreme Court to play the same role in Presidential elections that it has historically played in resolving electoral disputes. The Florida Supreme Court's exercise of appellate jurisdiction therefore was wholly consistent with, and indeed contemplated by, the grant of authority in Article II.

It hardly needs stating that Congress, pursuant to 3 U.S.C. Section 5, did not impose any affirmative duties upon the States that their governmental branches could "violate." Rather, Section 5 provides a safe harbor for States to select electors in contested elections "by judicial or other methods" established by laws prior to the election day. Section 5, like Article II, assumes the involvement of the state judiciary in interpreting state election laws and resolving election disputes under those laws. Neither Section 5 nor Article II grants federal judges any special authority to substitute their views for those of the state judiciary on matters of state law.

Nor are petitioners correct in asserting that the failure of the Florida Supreme Court to specify in detail the precise manner in which the "intent of the voter," is to be determined rises to the level of a constitutional violation. We found such a violation when individual votes within the same State were weighted unequally. . . but we have never before called into question the substantive standard by which a State determines that a vote has been legally cast. And there is no reason to think that the guidance provided to the fact-finders, specifically the various canvassing boards, by the "intent of the voter" standard is any less sufficient—or will lead to results any less uniform—than, for example, the "beyond a reasonable doubt" standard employed everyday by ordinary citizens in courtrooms across this country.

Admittedly, the use of differing substandards for determining voter intent in different counties employing similar voting systems may raise serious concerns. Those concerns are alleviated—if not eliminated—by the fact that a single impartial magistrate will ultimately adjudicate all objections arising from the recount process. Of course, as a general matter, "[t]he interpretation of constitutional principles must not be too literal. We must remember that the machinery of government would not work if it were not allowed a little play in its joints." *Bain Peanut Co. of Tex. v. Pinson* (1931) (Holmes, J.). If it were other-

wise, Florida's decision to leave to each county the determination of what balloting system to employ—despite enormous differences in accuracy—might run afoul of equal protection. So, too, might the similar decisions of the vast majority of state legislatures to delegate to local authorities certain decisions with respect to voting systems and ballot design. Even assuming that aspects of the remedial scheme might ultimately be found to violate the Equal Protection Clause, I could not subscribe to the majority's disposition of the case. As the majority explicitly holds, once a state legislature determines to select electors through a popular vote, the right to have one's vote counted is of constitutional stature. As the majority further acknowledges, Florida law holds that all ballots that reveal the intent of the voter constitute valid votes. Recognizing these principles, the majority nonetheless orders the termination of the contest proceeding before all such votes have been tabulated. Under their own reasoning, the appropriate course of action would be to remand to allow more specific procedures for implementing the legislature's uniform general standard to be established.

In the interest of finality, however, the majority effectively orders the disenfranchisement of an unknown number of voters whose ballots reveal their intent—and are therefore legal votes under state law—but were for some reason rejected by ballot-counting machines. It does so on the basis of the deadlines set forth in Title 3 of the United States Code. But, as I have already noted, those provisions merely provide rules of decision for Congress to follow when selecting among conflicting slates of electors. They do not prohibit a State from counting what the majority concedes to be legal votes until a bona fide winner is determined. Indeed, in 1960, Hawaii appointed two slates of electors and Congress chose to count the one appointed on January 4, 1961, well after the Title 3 deadlines. . . . Thus, nothing prevents the majority, even if it properly found an equal protection violation, from ordering relief appropriate to remedy that violation without depriving Florida voters of their right to have their votes counted. As the majority notes, "[a] desire for speed is not a general excuse for ignoring equal protection guarantees." Finally, neither in this case, nor in its earlier opinion in *Palm Beach County Canvassing Bd. v. Harris,* did the Florida Supreme Court make any substantive change in Florida electoral law. Its decisions were rooted in long-established precedent and were consistent with the relevant statutory provisions, taken as a whole. It did what courts do—it decided the case before it in light of the legislature's intent to leave no legally cast vote uncounted. In so doing, it relied on the sufficiency of the general "intent of the voter" standard articulated by the state legislature, coupled with a procedure for ultimate review by an impartial judge, to resolve the concern about disparate evaluations of contested ballots. If we assume—as I do—that the members of that court and the judges who would have carried out its mandate are impartial, its decision does not even raise a colorable federal question.

What must underlie petitioners' entire federal assault on the Florida election procedures is an unstated lack of confidence in the impartiality and capacity of the state judges who would make the critical decisions if the vote count were to proceed. Otherwise, their position is wholly without merit. The endorsement of that position by the majority of this Court can only lend credence to the most cynical appraisal of the work of judges throughout the land. It is confidence in the men and women who administer the judicial system that is the true backbone of the rule of law. Time will one day heal the wound to that confidence that will be inflicted by today's decision. One thing, however, is certain. Although we may never know with complete certainty the identity of the winner of this year's Presidential election, the identity of the loser is perfectly clear. It is the Nation's confidence in the judge as an impartial guardian of the rule of law. I respectfully dissent.

JUSTICE SOUTER CONCURS EXCEPTING ONE PART

The Court should not have reviewed either *Bush v. Palm Beach County Canvassing Bd.* or this case, and should not have stopped Florida's attempt to recount all undervote ballots by issuing a stay of the Florida Supreme Court's orders during the period of this review. If this Court had allowed the State to follow the course indicated by the opinions of its own Supreme Court, it is entirely possible that there would ultimately have been no issue requiring our review, and political tension could have worked itself out in the Congress following the procedure provided in 3 U.S.C. Section 15. The case being before us, however, its resolution by the majority is another erroneous decision.

As will be clear, I am in substantial agreement with the dissenting opinions of Justice Stevens, Justice Ginsburg and Justice Breyer. I write separately only to say how straightforward the issues before us really are.

There are three issues: whether the State Supreme Court's interpretation of the statute providing for a contest of the state election results somehow violates 3 U.S.C. Section 5; whether that court's construction of the state statutory provisions governing contests impermissibly changes a state law from what the State's legislature has provided, in violation of Article II, Section 1, cl. 2, of the national Constitution; and whether the manner of interpreting markings on disputed ballots failing to cause machines to register votes for President (the undervote ballots) violates the equal protection or due process guaranteed by the Fourteenth Amendment. None of these issues is difficult to describe or to resolve.

. . . . The 3 U.S.C. Section 5 issue is not serious. That provision sets certain conditions for treating a State's certification of Presidential electors as conclusive in the event that a dispute over recognizing those electors must be resolved in the Congress under 3 U.S.C. Section 15. Conclusiveness requires selection under a legal scheme in place before the election, with results determined at least six days before the date set for casting electoral votes. But no State is required to conform to Section 5 if it cannot do that (for whatever reason); the sanction for failing to satisfy the conditions of Section 5 is simply loss of what has been called its "safe harbor." And even that determination is to be made, if made anywhere, in the Congress.

.... The second matter here goes to the State Supreme Court's interpretation of certain terms in the state statute governing election "contests." The issue is whether the judgment of the state supreme court has displaced the state legislature's provisions for election contests: is the law as declared by the court different from the provisions made by the legislature, to which the national Constitution commits responsibility for determining how each State's Presidential electors are chosen? ...

Bush does not, of course, claim that any judicial act interpreting a statute of uncertain meaning is enough to displace the legislative provision and violate Article II; statutes require interpretation, which does not without more affect the legislative character of a statute within the meaning of the Constitution. What Bush does argue, as I understand the contention, is that the interpretation of Section 102.168 was so unreasonable as to transcend the accepted bounds of statutory interpretation, to the point of being a nonjudicial act and producing new law untethered to the legislative act in question.

The starting point for evaluating the claim that the Florida Supreme Court's interpretation effectively rewrote Section 102.168 must be the language of the provision on which Gore relies to show his right to raise this contest: that the previously certified result in Bush's favor was produced by "rejection of a number of legal votes sufficient to change or place in doubt the result of the election."

None of the state court's interpretations is unreasonable to the point of displacing the legislative enactment quoted. As I will note below, other interpretations were of course possible, and some might have been better than those adopted by the Florida court's majority; the two dissents from the majority opinion of that court and various briefs submitted to us set out alternatives. But the majority view is in each instance within the bounds of reasonable interpretation, and the law as declared is consistent with Article II.

. . . . The statute does not define a "legal vote," the rejection of which may affect the election. The State Supreme Court was therefore required to define it, and in doing that the court looked to another election statute, dealing with damaged or defective ballots, which contains a provision that no vote shall be disregarded "if there is a clear indication of the intent of the voter as determined by a canvassing board." The court read that objective of looking to the voter's intent as indicating that the legislature probably meant "legal vote" to mean a vote recorded on a ballot indicating what the voter intended.

It is perfectly true that the majority might have chosen a different reading... But even so, there is no constitutional violation in following the majority view; Article II is unconcerned with mere disagreements about interpretive merits.

The Florida court next interpreted "rejection" to determine what act in the counting process may be attacked in a contest. Again, the statute does not define the term. The court majority read the word to mean simply a failure to count. That reading is certainly within the bounds of common sense, given the objective to give effect to a voter's intent if that can be determined. . . .

The same is true about the court majority's understanding of the phrase "votes sufficient to change or place in doubt" the re-

sult of the election in Florida. The court held that if the uncounted ballots were so numerous that it was reasonably possible that they contained enough "legal" votes to swing the election, this contest would be authorized by the statute. While the majority might have thought (as the trial judge did) that a probability, not a possibility, should be necessary to justify a contest, that reading is not required by the statute's text, which says nothing about probability. Whatever people of good will and good sense may argue about the merits of the Florida court's reading, there is no warrant for saying that it transcends the limits of reasonable statutory interpretation to the point of supplanting the statute enacted by the "legislature" within the meaning of Article II. . . .

It is only on the third issue before us that there is a meritorious argument for relief, as this Court's Per Curiam opinion recognizes. It is an issue that might well have been dealt with adequately by the Florida courts if the state proceedings had not been interrupted, and if not disposed of at the state level it could have been considered by the Congress in any electoral vote dispute. But because the course of state proceedings has been interrupted, time is short, and the issue is before us, I think it sensible for the Court to address it.

Petitioners have raised an equal protection claim (or, alternatively, a due process claim. . . in the charge that unjustifiably disparate standards are applied in different electoral jurisdictions to otherwise identical facts. It is true that the Equal Protection Clause does not forbid the use of a variety of voting mechanisms within a jurisdiction, even though different mechanisms will have different levels of effectiveness in recording voters' intentions; local variety can be justified by concerns about cost, the potential value of innovation, and so on. But evidence in the record here suggests that a different order of disparity obtains under rules for determining a voter's intent that have been applied (and could continue to be applied) to identical types of ballots used in identical brands of machines and exhibiting identical physical characteristics (such as "hanging" or "dimpled" chads).

I can conceive of no legitimate state interest served by these differing treatments of the expressions of voters' fundamental rights. The differences appear wholly arbitrary. In deciding what to do about this, we should take account of the fact that electoral votes are due to be cast in six days. I would therefore remand the case to the courts of Florida with instructions to establish uniform standards for evaluating the several types of ballots that have prompted differing treatments, to be applied within and among counties when passing on such identical ballots in any further recounting (or successive recounting) that the courts might order.

Unlike the majority, I see no warrant for this Court to assume that Florida could not possibly comply with this requirement before the date set for the meeting of electors, December 18.

. . . . To recount these [ballots] manually would be a tall order, but before this Court stayed the effort to do that the courts of Florida were ready to do their best to get that job done. There is no justification for denying the State the opportunity to try to count all disputed ballots now. I respectfully dissent.

JUSTICE GINSBURG'S DISSENT

The Chief Justice acknowledges that provisions of Florida's Election Code "may well admit of more than one interpretation." But instead of respecting the state high court's province to say what the State's Election Code means, the chief justice maintains that Florida's Supreme Court has veered so far from the ordinary practice of judicial review that what it did cannot properly be called judging. . . . I might join the chief justice were it my commission to interpret Florida law. But disagreement with the Florida court's interpretation of its own State's law does not warrant the conclusion that the justices of that court have legislated. There is no cause here to believe that the members of Florida's high court have done less than "their mortal best to discharge their oath of office," and no cause to upset their reasoned interpretation of Florida law. . . .

The extraordinary setting of this case has obscured the ordinary principle that dictates its proper resolution: Federal courts defer to state high courts' interpretations of their State's own law. This principle reflects the core of federalism, on which all agree. . . .

The Chief Justice's solicitude for the Florida Legislature comes at the expense of the more fundamental solicitude we owe to the legislature's sovereign.

Were the other members of this Court as mindful as they generally are of our system of dual sovereignty, they would affirm the judgment of the Florida Supreme Court.

. . . . I agree with Justice Stevens that petitioners have not presented a substantial equal protection claim. Ideally, perfection would be the appropriate standard for judging the recount. But we live in an imperfect world, one in which thousands of votes have not been counted. I cannot agree that the recount adopted by the Florida court, awed as it may be, would yield a result any less fair or precise than the certification that preceded that recount. . . .

Even if there were an equal protection violation, I would agree with Justice Stevens, Justice Souter, and Justice Breyer that the Court's concern about the December 12 date is misplaced. Time is short in part because of the Court's entry of a stay on December 9, several hours after an able circuit judge in Leon County had begun to superintend the recount process. More fundamentally, the Court's reluctance to let the recount go forward. . . . ultimately turns on its own judgment about the practical realities of implementing a recount, not the judgment of those much closer to the process.

. . . . In sum, the Court's conclusion that a constitutionally adequate recount is impractical is a prophecy the Court's own judgment will not allow to be tested. Such an untested prophecy should not decide the Presidency of the United States.

I dissent.

JUSTICE BREYER'S DISSENT

The Court was wrong to take this case. It was wrong to grant a stay. It should now vacate that stay and permit the Florida Supreme Court to decide whether the recount should resume.

The political implications of this case for the country are momentous. But the federal legal questions presented, with one exception, are insubstantial.

The majority raises three Equal Protection problems with the Florida Supreme Court's recount order: first, the failure to include overvotes in the manual recount; second, the fact that all ballots, rather than simply the undervotes, were recounted in some, but not all, counties; and third, the absence of a uniform, specific standard to guide the recounts. As far as the first issue is concerned, petitioners presented no evidence, to this Court or to any Florida court, that a manual recount of overvotes would identify additional legal votes. The same is true of the second, and, in addition, the majority's reasoning would seem to invalidate any state provision for a manual recount of individual counties in a statewide election.

The majority's third concern does implicate principles of fundamental fairness. The majority concludes that the Equal Protection Clause requires that a manual recount be governed not only by the uniform general standard of the "clear intent of the voter," but also by uniform subsidiary standards. . . . I agree that, in these very special circumstances, basic principles of fairness should have counseled the adoption of a uniform standard to address the problem. In light of the majority's disposition, I need not decide whether, or the extent to which, as a remedial matter, the Constitution would place limits upon the content of the uniform standard.

Nonetheless, there is no justification for the majority's remedy, which is simply to reverse the lower court and halt the recount entirely. An appropriate remedy would be, instead, to remand this case with instructions that, even at this late date, would permit the Florida Supreme Court to require recounting all undercounted votes in Florida, including those from Broward, Volusia, Palm Beach, and Miami-Dade Counties, whether or not previously recounted prior to the end of the protest period, and to do so in accordance with a single-uniform substandard.

The majority justifies stopping the recount entirely on the ground that there is no more time. In particular, the majority relies on the lack of time for the Secretary to review and approve equipment needed to separate undervotes. But the majority reaches this conclusion in the absence of any record evidence that the recount could not have been completed in the time allowed by the Florida Supreme Court. The majority finds facts outside of the record on matters that state courts are in a far better position to address. Of course, it is too late for any such recount to take place by December 12, the date by which election disputes must be decided if a State is to take advantage of the safe harbor provisions of 3 U.S.C. Section 5.

Whether there is time to conduct a recount prior to December 18, when the electors are scheduled to meet, is a matter for the state courts to determine. And whether, under Florida law, Florida could or could not take further action is obviously a matter for Florida courts, not this Court, to decide. . . .

By halting the manual recount, and thus ensuring that the uncounted legal votes will not be counted under any standard, this Court crafts a remedy out of proportion to the asserted

harm. And that remedy harms the very fairness interests the Court is attempting to protect. The manual recount would itself redress a problem of unequal treatment of ballots. As Justice Stevens points out, the ballots of voters in counties that use punch-card systems are more likely to be disqualified than those in counties using optical-scanning systems. According to recent news reports, variations in the undervote rate are even more pronounced. . . . Thus, in a system that allows counties to use different types of voting systems, voters already arrive at the polls with an unequal chance that their votes will be counted. I do not see how the fact that this results from counties' selection of different voting machines rather than a court order makes the outcome any more fair. Nor do I understand why the Florida Supreme Court's recount order, which helps to redress this inequity, must be entirely prohibited based on a deficiency that could easily be remedied.

The remainder of petitioners' claims, which are the focus of the Chief Justice's concurrence, raise no significant federal questions. I cannot agree that the Chief Justice's unusual review of state law in this case is justified by reference either to Art. II, Section 1, or to 3 U.S.C. Section 5.

Moreover, even were such review proper, the conclusion that the Florida Supreme Court's decision contravenes federal law is untenable. . . .

Despite the reminder that this case involves "an election for the President of the United States," no preeminent legal concern, or practical concern related to legal questions, required this Court to hear this case, let alone to issue a stay that stopped Florida's recount process in its tracks. With one exception, petitioners' claims do not ask us to vindicate a constitutional provision designed to protect a basic human right. Petitioners invoke fundamental fairness, namely, the need for procedural fairness, including finality. But with the one "equal protection" exception, they rely upon law that focuses, not upon that basic need, but upon the constitutional allocation of power. Respondents invoke a competing fundamental consideration—the need to determine the voter's true intent. But they look to state law, not to federal constitutional law, to protect that interest.

Neither side claims electoral fraud, dishonesty, or the like. And the more fundamental equal protection claim might have been left to the state court to resolve if and when it was discovered to have mattered. It could still be resolved through a remand conditioned upon issuance of a uniform standard; it does not require reversing the Florida Supreme Court. Of course, the selection of the President is of fundamental national importance. But that importance is political, not legal. And this Court should resist the temptation unnecessarily to resolve tangential legal disputes, where doing so threatens to determine the outcome of the election.

The Constitution and federal statutes themselves make clear that restraint is appropriate. They set forth a road map of how to resolve disputes about electors, even after an election as close as this one. That road map foresees resolution of electoral disputes by state courts. . . . But it nowhere provides for involvement by the United States Supreme Court. To the contrary, the Twelfth Amendment commits to Congress the authority and re-

sponsibility to count electoral votes. A federal statute, the Electoral Count Act, enacted after the close 1876 Hayes-Tilden Presidential election, specifies that, after States have tried to resolve disputes (through "judicial" or other means), Congress is the body primarily authorized to resolve remaining disputes. . . .

Given this detailed, comprehensive scheme for counting electoral votes, there is no reason to believe that federal law either foresees or requires resolution of such a political issue by this Court. Nor, for that matter, is there any reason to. . . .think [that] the Constitution's Framers would have reached a different conclusion. Madison, at least, believed that allowing the judiciary to choose the presidential electors "was out of the question." The decision by both the Constitution's Framers and the 1886 Congress to minimize this Court's role in resolving close federal presidential elections is as wise as it is clear.

However awkward or difficult it may be for Congress to resolve difficult electoral disputes, Congress, being a political body, expresses the people's will far more accurately than does an unelected Court. And the people's will is what elections are about.

. . . . I think it not only legally wrong, but also most unfortunate, for the Court simply to have terminated the Florida recount. Those who caution judicial restraint in resolving political disputes have described the quintessential case for that restraint as a case marked, among other things, by the "strangeness of the issue," its "intractability to principled resolution," its "sheer momentousness. . . which tends to unbalance judicial judgment," and "the inner vulnerability, the self-doubt of an institution which is electorally irresponsible and has no earth to draw strength from." Those characteristics mark this case.

At the same time, as I have said, the Court is not acting to vindicate a fundamental constitutional principle, such as the need to protect a basic human liberty. No other strong reason to act is present. Congressional statutes tend to obviate the need. And, above all, in this highly politicized matter, the appearance of a split decision runs the risk of undermining the public's confidence in the Court itself. That confidence is a public treasure. It has been built slowly over many years, some of which were marked by a Civil War and the tragedy of segregation. It is a vitally necessary ingredient of any successful effort to protect basic liberty and, indeed, the rule of law itself. We run no risk of returning to the days when a President (responding to this Court's efforts to protect the Cherokee Indians) might have said, "John Marshall has made his decision; now let him enforce it!" But we do risk a self-inflicted wound—a wound that may harm not just the Court, but the Nation.

I fear that in order to bring this agonizingly long election process to a definitive conclusion, we have not adequately attended to that necessary "check upon our own exercise of power," "our own sense of self-restraint." *United States v. Butler* (1936) (Stone, J., dissenting). Justice Brandeis once said of the Court, "The most important thing we do is not doing." What it does today, the Court should have left undone. I would repair the damage as best we now can, by permitting the Florida recount to continue under uniform standards. I respectfully dissent.

Election Results, Congress and Presidency, 1860–2000

Election year	Congress	House Members elected Dem.	House Members elected Rep.	House Members elected Misc.	House Gains/losses Dem.	House Gains/losses Rep.	Senate Members elected Dem.	Senate Members elected Rep.	Senate Members elected Misc.	Senate Gains/losses Dem.	Senate Gains/losses Rep.	Presidency Popular vote Elected	Presidency Popular vote Plurality
1860	37th	42	106	28	−59	−7	11	31	7	−27	+5	Lincoln (R)	485,706
1862	38th	80	103		+38	−3	12	39		+1	+8		
1864	39th	46	145		−34	+42	10	42		−2	+3	Lincoln (R)	405,581
1866	40th	49	143		+3	−2	11	42		+1	0	Johnson (R)	
1868	41st	73	170		+24	+27	11	61		0	+19	Grant (R)	304,906
1870	42nd	104	139		+31	−31	17	57		+6	−4		
1872	43rd	88	203		−16	+64	19	54		+2	−3	Grant (R)	763,474
1874	44th	181	107	3	+93	−96	29	46		+10	−8		
1876	45th	156	137		−25	+30	36	39	1	+7	−7	Hayes (R)	−254,235
1878	46th	150	128	14	−6	−9	43	33		+7	−6		
1880	47th	130	152	11	−20	+24	37	37	2	−6	+4	Garfield (R)	1,898
1882	48th	200	119	6	+70	−33	36	40		−1	+3	Arthur (R)	
1884	49th	182	140	2	−18	+21	34	41		−2	+2	Cleveland (D)	25,685
1886	50th	170	151	4	−12	+11	37	39		+3	−2		
1888	51st	156	173	1	−14	+22	37	47		0	+8	Harrison (R)	−90,596
1890	52nd	231	88	14	+75	−85	39	47	2	+2	0		
1892	53rd	220	126	8	−11	+38	44	38	3	+5	−9	Cleveland (D)	372,639
1894	54th	104	246	7	−116	+120	30	44	5	−5	+6		
1896	55th	134	206	16	+30	−40	34	46	10	−5	+2	McKinley (R)	596,985
1898	56th	163	185	9	+29	−21	26	53	11	−8	+7		
1900	57th	153	198	5	−10	+13	29	56	3	+3	+3	McKinley (R)	859,694
1902	58th	178	207		+25	+9	32	58		+3	+2	Roosevelt (R)	
1904	59th	136	250		−42	+43	32	58		0	0	Roosevelt (R)	2,543,695
1906	60th	164	222		+28	−28	29	61		−3	−3		
1908	61st	172	219		+8	−3	32	59		+3	−2	Taft (R)	1,269,457
1910	62nd	228	162	1	+56	−57	42	49		+10	−10		
1912	63rd	290	127	18	+62	−35	51	44	1	+9	−5	Wilson (D)	2,173,945
1914	64th	231	193	8	−59	+66	56	39	1	+5	−5		
1916	65th	210	216	9	−21	+23	53	42	1	−3	+3	Wilson (D)	579,511
1918	66th	191	237	7	−19	+21	47	48	1	−6	+6		
1920	67th	132	300	1	−59	+63	37	59		−10	+11	Harding (R)	7,020,023
1922	68th	207	225	3	+75	−75	43	51	2	+6	−8	Coolidge (R)	
1924	69th	183	247	5	−24	+22	40	54	1	−3	+3	Coolidge (R)	7,333,217

Election Year	Congress	House — Members elected			House — Gains/losses		Senate — Members elected			Senate — Gains/losses		Presidency — Popular vote	
		Dem.	Rep.	Misc.	Dem.	Rep.	Dem.	Rep.	Misc.	Dem.	Rep.	Elected	Plurality
1926	70th	195	237	3	+12	−10	47	48	1	+7	−6		
1928	71st	167	267	1	−28	+30	39	56	1	−8	+8	Hoover (R)	6,429,579
1930	72nd	220	214	1	+53	−53	47	48	1	+8	−8		
1932	73rd	313	117	5	+97	−101	59	36	1	+12	−12	Roosevelt (D)	7,068,817
1934	74th	322	103	10	+9	−14	69	25	2	+10	−11		
1936	75th	333	89	13	+11	−14	75	17	4	+6	−8	Roosevelt (D)	11,073,102
1938	76th	262	169	4	−71	+80	69	23	4	−6	+6		
1940	77th	267	162	6	+5	−7	66	28	2	−3	+5	Roosevelt (D)	4,964,561
1942	78th	222	209	4	−45	+47	57	38	1	−9	+10		
1944	79th	243	190	2	+21	−19	57	38	1	0	0	Roosevelt (D)	3,594,993
1946	80th	188	246	1	−55	+56	45	51		−12	+13	Truman (D)	
1948	81st	263	171	1	+75	−75	54	42		+9	−9	Truman (D)	2,188,054
1950	82nd	234	199	2	−29	+28	48	47	1	−6	+5		
1952	83rd	213	221	1	−21	+22	47	48	1	−1	+1	Eisenhower (R)	6,621,242
1954	84th	232	203		+19	−18	48	47	1	+1	−1		
1956	85th	234	201		+2	−2	49	47		+1	0	Eisenhower (R)	9,567,720
1958	86th	283	154		+49	−47	64	34		+17	−13		
1960	87th	263	174		−20	+20	64	36		−2	+2	Kennedy (D)	118,574[1]
1962	88th	258	176	1[2]	−4	+2	67	33		+4	−4		
1964	89th	295	140		+38	−38	68	32		+2	−2	Johnson (D)	15,951,378
1966	90th	248	187		−47	+47	64	36		−3	+3		
1968	91st	243	192		−4	+4	58	42		−5	+5	Nixon (R)	510,314
1970	92nd	255	180		+12	−12	55	45		−4	+2		
1972	93rd	243	192		−12	+12	57	43		+2	−2	Nixon (R)	17,999,528
1974	94th	291	144		+43	−43	61	38		+3	−3		
1976	95th	292	143		+1	−1	62	38		0	0	Carter (D)	1,682,970
1978	96th	277	158		−11	+11	59	41		−3	+3		
1980	97th	243	192		−33	+33	47	53		−12	+12	Reagan (R)	8,420,270
1982	98th	269	166		+26	−26	46	54		0	0		
1984	99th	253	182		−14	+14	47	53		+2	−2	Reagan (R)	16,877,890
1986	100th	258	177		+5	−5	55	45		+8	−8		
1988	101st	259	174		+2	−2	55	45		+1	−1	Bush (R)	7,077,023
1990	102nd	267	167	1	+9	−8	56	44		+1	−1		
1992	103rd	258	176	1	−9	+9	57	43		+1	−1	Clinton (D)	5,805,444
1994	104th	204	230	1	−52	+52	47	53		−8	+8[3]		
1996	105th	207	227	1	+3	−3	45	55		−2	+2	Clinton (D)	8,203,602
1998	106th	211	223	1	+5	−5	45	55		0	0		
2000	107th	212	221	2	+1	−2	50	50		+4	−4	G. W. Bush (R)	−539,898

Notes: The seats totals reflect the makeup of the House and Senate at the start of each Congress. Special elections that shifted party ratios inbetween elections are not noted.

    1 Includes divided Alabama elector slate votes.

    2. Vacancy—Rep. Clem Miller, D–Calif. (1959–62) died Oct. 6, 1962, but his name remained on the ballot and he received a plurality.

    3. Sen. Richard Shelby (Ala.) switched from the Democratic to the Republican Party the day after the election, bringing the total Republican gain to nine.

The Partisan Landscape, 2000:
Presidential Voting by Congressional District

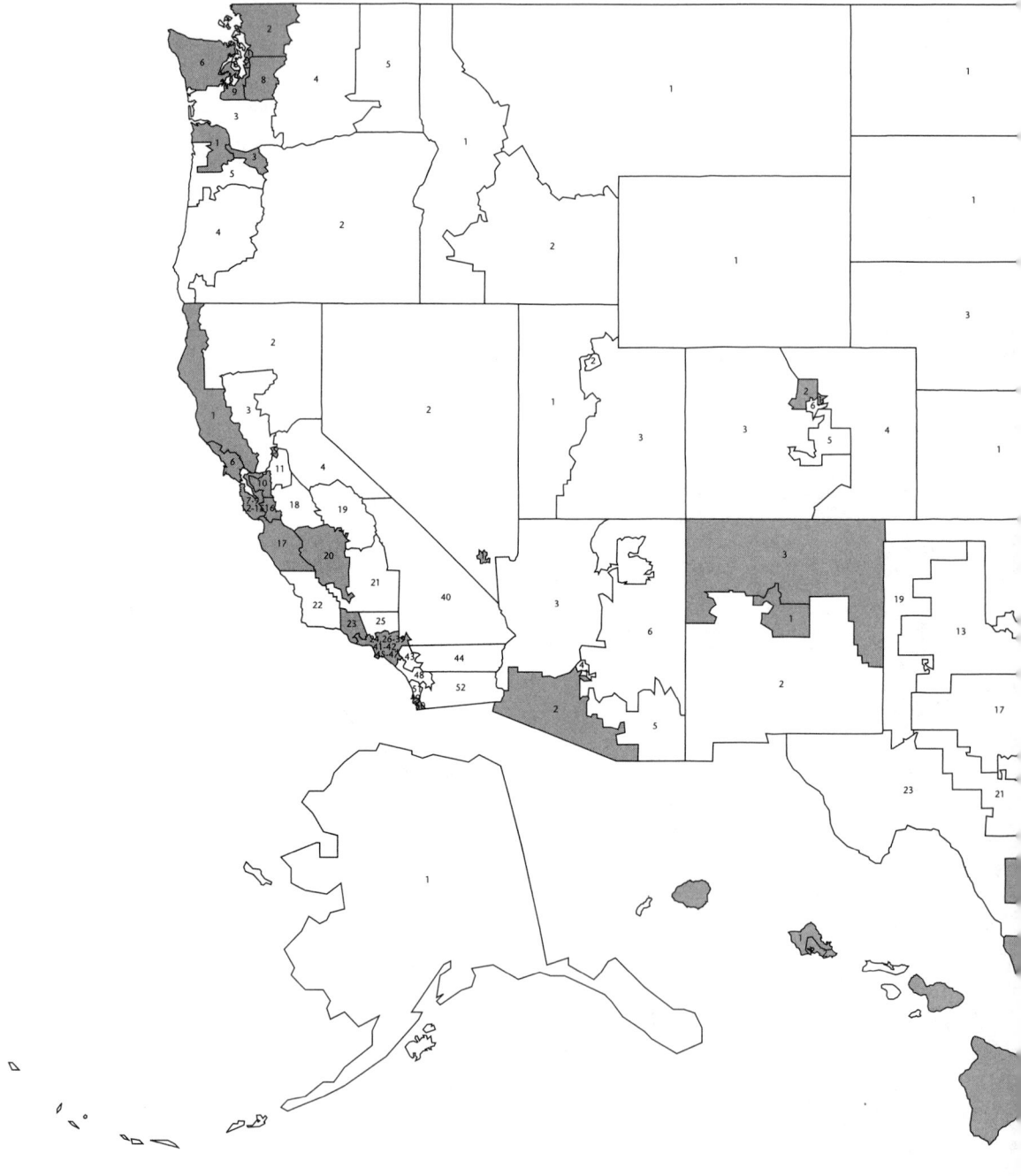

Sources: Map provided by Marilyn Gates-Davis and Christopher M. Karlsten, Congressional Quarterly; election results supplied by Greg Giroux, Congressional Quarterly.

Notes: Map shows which presidential candidate won a plurality in each of the 435 congressional districts. George W. Bush carried 228 districts; Al Gore, 207. Following are election results by congressional district for populous areas: *California:* Bay area: Congressional districts numbered 8-9 (Gore), 12-14 (Gore); Los Angeles and Orange County: 24 (Gore), 26-38 (Gore), 39 (Bush), 41 (Bush), 45 (Bush), 46 (Gore), 47-48 (Bush); *Florida:* Miami area: 17 (Gore), 18 (Bush), 19 (Gore), 21 (Bush), 22 (Gore); Tampa–St. Petersburg area: 10-11 (Gore); *Illinois:* Chicago area: 1-5

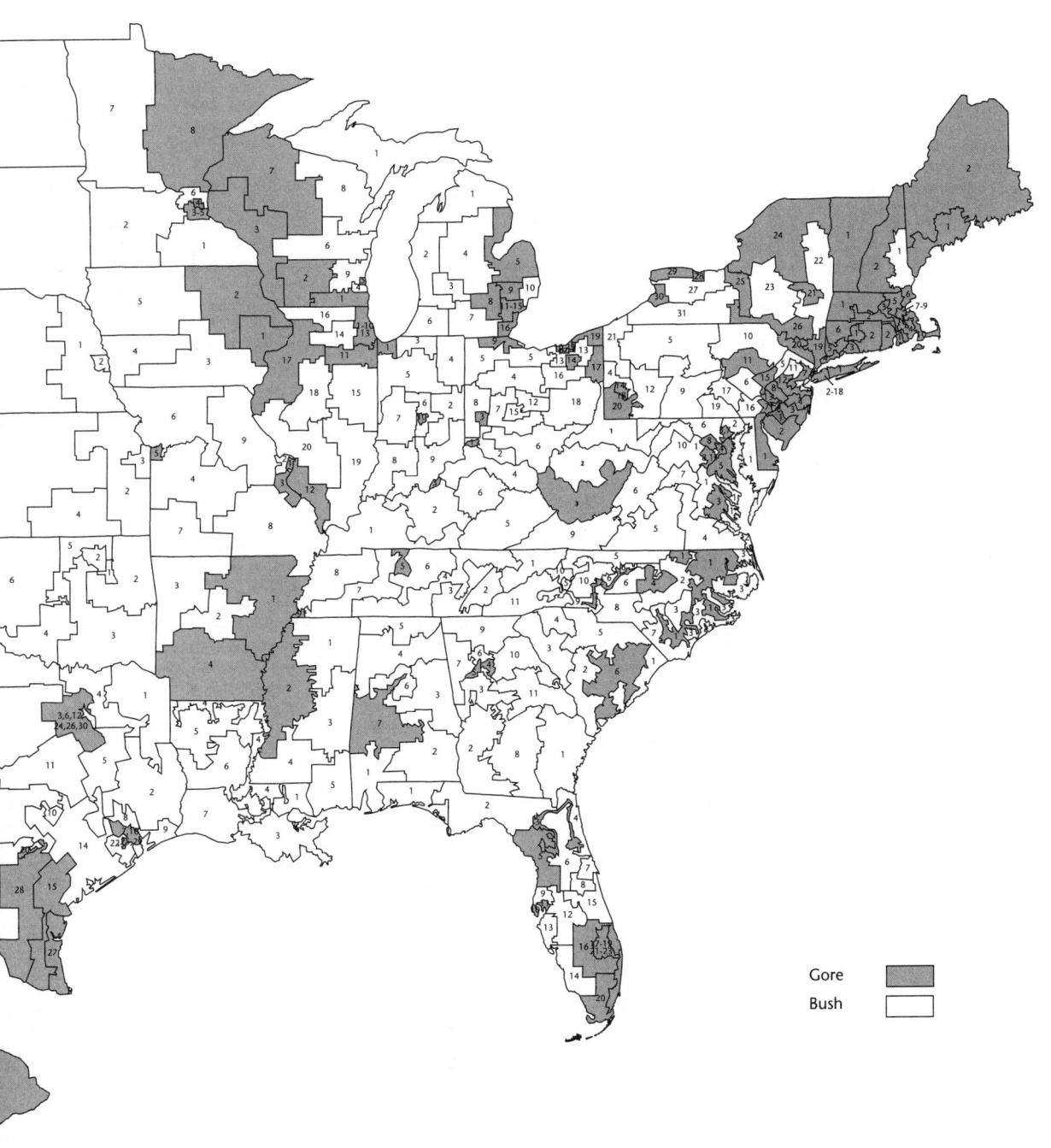

(Gore), 6 (Bush), 7 (Gore), 8 (Bush), 9-10 (Gore); *Maryland:* Baltimore area: 3 (Gore), 7 (Gore); *Massachusetts:* Boston and coastal areas: 4 (Gore), 6-10 (Gore); *Michigan:* Detroit area: 12 (Gore), 14-15 (Gore); *Minnesota:* Minneapolis–St. Paul area: 4-5 (Gore); *Missouri:* St. Louis area: 1 (Gore), 2 (Bush), 3 (Gore); *New Jersey:* Northern New Jersey area: 7-10 (Gore); *New York:* New York City area: 2-18 (Gore); *Ohio:* Cincinnati area: 1 (Gore), 2 (Bush); Cleveland area: 10-11 (Gore); *Pennsylvania:* Philadelphia area: 1-3 (Gore); Pittsburgh area: 14 (Gore), 18 (Gore); *Texas:* Dallas area: 3-4 (Bush), 6 (Bush), 24 (Gore), 26 (Bush), 30 (Gore); Fort Worth area: 6 (Bush), 12 (Bush), 24 (Gore), 26 (Bush); Houston area: 7-9 (Bush), 18 (Gore), 22 (Bush), 25 (Gore), 29 (Gore); San Antonio area: 20 (Gore), 21 (Bush), 23 (Bush), 28 (Gore); *Virginia:* Northern Virginia area: 8 (Gore), 11 (Gore); *Wisconsin:* Milwaukee area: 4 (Bush), 5 (Gore).

Results of House Elections, 1928–2000

	1928	1930	1932	1934	1936	1938	1940	1942	1944	1946	1948	1950	1952	1954	1956	1958	1960	1962	1964
Totals																			
Democrats	165	217	313	322	334	262	268	222	242	188	263	235	213	232	234	283	263	259	295
Republicans	269	217	117	103	88	169	162	209	191	246	171	199	221	203	201	153	174	176	140
Alabama																			
Democrats	10	10	9¹	9	9	9	9	9	9	9	9	9	9	9	9	9	9	8¹	3
Republicans	0	0	0	0	0	0	0	0	0	0	0	0	0	0	0	0	0	0	5
Alaska																			
Democrats	—	—	—	—	—	—	—	—	—	—	—	—	—	—	—	1	1	1	1
Republicans	—	—	—	—	—	—	—	—	—	—	—	—	—	—	—	0	0	0	0
Arizona																			
Democrats	1	1	1	1	1	1	1	2²	2	2	2	2	1	1	1	1	1	2²	2
Republicans	0	0	0	0	0	0	0	0	0	0	0	0	1	1	1	1	1	1	1
Arkansas																			
Democrats	7	7	7	7	7	7	7	7	7	7	7	7	6¹	6	6	6	6	4¹	4
Republicans	0	0	0	0	0	0	0	0	0	0	0	0	0	0	0	0	0	0	0
California																			
Democrats	1	1	11²	13	15	12	11	12²	16	9	10	10	11²	11	13	16	16	25^{2,3}	23
Republicans	10	10	9	7	4	8	9	11	7	14	13	13	19	19	17	14	14	13	15
Colorado																			
Democrats	1	1	4	4	4	4	2	1	0	1	3	2	2	2	2	3	2	2	4
Republicans	3	3	0	0	0	0	2	3	4	3	1	2	2	2	2	1	2	2	0
Connecticut																			
Democrats	0	2	2²	4	6	2	6	0	4	0	3	2	1	1	0	6	4	5	6
Republicans	5	3	4	2	0	4	0	6	2	6	3	4	5	5	6	0	2	1	0
Delaware																			
Democrats	0	0	1	0	1	0	1	0	1	0	0	0	0	1	0	1	1	1	1
Republicans	1	1	0	1	0	1	0	1	0	1	1	0	1	0	0	0	0	0	0
Florida																			
Democrats	4	4	5²	5	5	5	5	6²	6	6	6	6	8²	7	7	7	7	10²	10
Republicans	0	0	0	0	0	0	0	0	0	0	0	0	0	1	1	1	1	2	2
Georgia																			
Democrats	12	12	10¹	10	10	10	10	10	10	10	10	10	10	10	10	10	10	10	9
Republicans	0	0	0	0	0	0	0	0	0	0	0	0	0	0	0	0	0	0	1
Hawaii																			
Democrats	—	—	—	—	—	—	—	—	—	—	—	—	—	—	—	—	1	2²	2
Republicans	—	—	—	—	—	—	—	—	—	—	—	—	—	—	—	—	0	0	0
Idaho																			
Democrats	0	0	2	2	2	1	1	1	1	0	1	0	1	1	1	1	2	2	1
Republicans	2	2	0	0	0	1	1	1	1	2	1	2	1	1	1	1	0	0	1
Illinois																			
Democrats	6	13⁴	19	21	21	17	11	7¹	11	6	12	8	9¹	12	11	14	14	12¹	13
Republicans	21	14	8	6	6	10	16	19	15	20	14	18	16	13	14	11	11	12	11
Indiana																			
Democrats	3	9	12¹	11	11	5	4	2¹	2	2	7	2	1	2	2	8	4⁴	4	6
Republicans	10	4	0	1	1	7	8	9	9	9	4	9	10	9	9	3	7	7	5
Iowa																			
Democrats	0	1	6¹	6	5	2	2	0¹	0	0	0	0	0	0	1	4	2	1¹	6
Republicans	11	10	3	3	4	7	7	8	8	8	8	8	8	8	7	4	6	6	1
Kansas																			
Democrats	1	1	3¹	3	2	1	1	0¹	0	0	0	0	1	0	1	3	1	0¹	0
Republicans	7	7	4	4	5	6	6	6	6	6	6	6	5	6	5	3	5	5	5
Kentucky																			
Democrats	2	9	9¹	8	8	8	8	8	8	6	7	7	6¹	6	6	7	7	5¹	6
Republicans	9	2	0	1	1	1	1	1	1	3	2	2	2	2	2	1	1	2	1
Louisiana																			
Democrats	8	8	8	8	8	8	8	8	8	8	8	8	8	8	8	8	8	8	8
Republicans	0	0	0	0	0	0	0	0	0	0	0	0	0	0	0	0	0	0	0
Maine																			
Democrats	0	0	2¹	2	0	0	0	0	0	0	0	0	0	0	1	2	0	0¹	1
Republicans	4	4	1	1	3	3	3	3	3	3	3	3	3	3	2	1	3	2	1
Maryland																			
Democrats	4	6	6	6	6	6	6	4	5	4	4	3	3²	4	4	7	6	6²	6
Republicans	2	0	0	0	0	0	0	2	1	2	2	3	4	3	3	0	1	2	2
Massachusetts																			
Democrats	3	4	5¹	7	5	5	6	4¹	4	5	4	6	6	7	7	8	8	7¹	7
Republicans	13	12	10	8	10	10	9	10	10	9	8	8	8	7	7	6	6	5	5
Michigan																			
Democrats	0	0	10²	6	8	5	6	5	6	3	5	5	5²	7	6	7	7	8²	12
Republicans	13	13	7	11	9	12	11	12	11	14	12	12	13	11	12	11	11	11	7
Minnesota																			
Democrats	0	0	1¹	1	1	1	0	0	2	1	4	4	4	5	5	4	3	4¹	4
Republicans	9	9	3	5	3	7	8	8	7	8	5	5	5	4	4	5	6	4	4
Mississippi																			
Democrats	8	8	7¹	7	7	7	7	7	7	7	7	7	6¹	6	6	6	6	5¹	4
Republicans	0	0	0	0	0	0	0	0	0	0	0	0	0	0	0	0	0	0	1
Missouri																			
Democrats	6	12	13¹	12	12	12	10	5	7	4	12	10	7	9	10	10	9	8¹	8
Republicans	10	4	0	1	1	1	3	8	6	9	1	3	4	2	1	1	2	2	2

1. State lost seats due to reapportionment.

2. State gained seats due to reapportionment.

3. Alaska 1972, California 1962, and Louisiana 1972: national and state totals reflect the reelection of a Democrat who died before the election but whose name remained on the ballot.

4. Illinois 1930, Indiana 1960 and 1984, and New Hampshire 1936: national and state totals reflect the final outcome of a contested election in which a Republican was first certified the winner, but the House decided to seat the Democrat.

	1966	1968	1970	1972	1974	1976	1978	1980	1982	1984	1986	1988	1990	1992	1994	1996	1998	2000
Totals																		
Democrats	248	243	255	243	291	292	277	243	269	253	258	260	267	258	204	207	211	212
Republicans	187	192	180	192	144	143	158	192	166	182	177	175	167	176	230	227	223	221
Alabama																		
Democrats	5	5	5	4¹	4	4	4	4	5	5	5	5	5	4	4	2	2	2
Republicans	3	3	3	3	3	3	3	3	2	2	2	2	2	3	3	5	5	5
Alaska																		
Democrats	0	0	1	1³	0	0	0	0	0	0	0	0	0	0	0	0	0	0
Republicans	1	1	0	0	1	1	1	1	1	1	1	1	1	1	1	1	1	1
Arizona																		
Democrats	1	1	1	1²	1	2	2	2	2²	1	1	1	1	3²	1	1	1	1
Republicans	2	2	2	3	3	2	2	2	3	4	4	4	4	3	5	5	5	5
Arkansas																		
Democrats	3	3	3	3	3	3	2	2	2	3	3	3	3	2	2	2	2	3
Republicans	1	1	1	1	1	1	2	2	2	1	1	1	1	2	2	2	2	1
California																		
Democrats	21	21	20	23²	28	29	26	22	28²	27	27	27	26	30²	27	29	28	32
Republicans	17	17	18	20	15	14	17	21	17	18	18	18	19	22	25	23	24	20
Colorado																		
Democrats	3	3	2	2²	3	3	3	3	3²	2	3	3	3	2	2	2	2	2
Republicans	1	1	2	3	2	2	2	2	3	4	3	3	3	4	4	4	4	4
Connecticut																		
Democrats	5	4	3	3	4	4	5	4	4	3	3	3	3	3	3	4	4	3
Republicans	1	2	2	3	2	2	1	2	2	3	3	3	3	3	3	2	2	3
Delaware																		
Democrats	0	0	0	0	0	0	0	0	1	1	1	1	1	0	0	0	0	0
Republicans	1	1	1	1	1	1	1	1	0	0	0	0	0	1	1	1	1	1
Florida																		
Democrats	9	9	9	11²	10	10	12	11	13²	12	12	10	9	10²	8	8	8	8
Republicans	3	3	3	4	5	5	3	4	6	7	7	9	10	13	15	15	15	15
Georgia																		
Democrats	8	8	8	9	10	10	9	9	9	8	8	9	9	7²	4	3	3	3
Republicans	2	2	2	1	0	0	1	1	1	2	2	1	1	4	7	8	8	8
Hawaii																		
Democrats	2	2	2	2	2	2	2	2	2	2	1	1	2	2	2	2	2	2
Republicans	0	0	0	0	0	0	0	0	0	0	1	1	0	0	0	0	0	0
Idaho																		
Democrats	0	0	0	0	0	0	0	0	0	1	1	1	2	1	0	0	0	0
Republicans	2	2	2	2	2	2	2	2	2	1	1	1	0	1	2	2	2	2
Illinois																		
Democrats	12	12	12	10	13	12	11	10	12¹	13	13	14	15	12¹	10	10	10	10
Republicans	12	12	12	14	11	12	13	14	10	9	9	8	7	8	10	10	10	10
Indiana																		
Democrats	5	4	5	4	9	8	7	6	5¹	5⁴	6	6	8	7	4	4	4	4
Republicans	6	7	6	7	2	3	4	5	5	5	4	4	2	3	6	6	6	6
Iowa																		
Democrats	2	2	2	3¹	5	4	3	3	3	2	2	2	2	1¹	0	1	1	1
Republicans	5	5	5	3	1	2	3	3	3	4	4	4	4	4	5	4	4	4
Kansas																		
Democrats	0	0	1	1	1	2	1	1	2	2	2	2	2	2¹	0	0	1	1
Republicans	5	5	4	4	4	3	4	4	3	3	3	3	3	2	4	4	3	3
Kentucky																		
Democrats	4	4	5	5	5	5	4	4	4	4	4	4	4	4¹	2	1	1	1
Republicans	3	3	2	2	2	2	3	3	3	3	3	3	3	2	4	5	5	5
Louisiana																		
Democrats	8	8	8	7³	6⁵	6	5	6	6	6	5	4	4	4¹	4	2	2	2
Republicans	0	0	0	1	2	2	3	2	2	2	3	4	4	3	3	5	5	5
Maine																		
Democrats	2	2	2	1	0	0	0	0	0	0	1	1	1	1	1	2	2	2
Republicans	0	0	0	1	2	2	2	2	2	2	1	1	1	1	1	0	0	0
Maryland																		
Democrats	5	4	5	4	5	5	6	7	7	6	6	6	5	4	4	4	4	4
Republicans	3	4	3	4	3	3	2	1	1	2	2	2	3	4	4	4	4	4
Massachusetts																		
Democrats	7	7	8	9⁶	10	10	10	10	10¹	10	10	10	10	8¹	8	10	10	10
Republicans	5	5	4	3	2	2	2	2	1	1	1	1	1	2	2	0	0	0
Michigan																		
Democrats	7	7	7	7	12	11	13	12	12¹	11	11	11	11	10¹	9	10	10	9
Republicans	12	12	12	12	7	8	6	7	6	7	7	7	7	6	7	6	6	7
Minnesota																		
Democrats	3	3	4	4	5	5	4	3	5	5	5	5	6	6	6	6	6	5
Republicans	5	5	4	4	3	3	4	5	3	3	3	3	2	2	2	2	2	3
Mississippi																		
Democrats	5	5	5	3	3	3	3	3	3	3	4	4	5	5	4	2	3	3
Republicans	0	0	0	2	2	2	2	2	2	2	1	1	0	0	1	3	2	2
Missouri																		
Democrats	8	9	9	9	9	8	8	6	6¹	6	5	5	6	6	6	5	5	4
Republicans	2	1	1	1	1	2	2	4	3	3	4	4	3	3	3	4	4	5

5. Louisiana 1974: national and state totals reflect the final outcome of a contested election in which no winner was declared, followed by a special election won by the Republican.

6. Massachusetts 1972 and Pennsylvania 1980: national and state Democratic totals reflect the election of an Independent candidate who previously announced he would serve as a Democrats.

Results of House Elections, 1928–2000 (continued)

	1928	1930	1932	1934	1936	1938	1940	1942	1944	1946	1948	1950	1952	1954	1956	1958	1960	1962	1964
Montana																			
Democrats	1	1	2	2	2	1	1	2	1	1	1	1	1	1	2	2	1	1	1
Republicans	1	1	0	0	0	1	1	0	1	1	1	1	1	1	0	0	1	1	1
Nebraska																			
Democrats	2	4	5¹	4	4	2	2	0¹	0	0	1	0	0	0	0	2	0	0¹	1
Republicans	4	2	0	1	1	3	3	4	4	4	3	4	4	4	4	2	4	3	2
Nevada																			
Democrats	0	0	1	1	1	1	1	1	1	0	1	1	0	0	1	1	1	1	1
Republicans	1	1	0	0	0	0	0	0	0	1	0	0	1	1	0	0	0	0	0
New Hampshire																			
Democrats	0	0	1	1	1⁴	0	0	0	0	0	0	0	0	0	0	0	0	0	1
Republicans	2	2	1	1	1	2	2	2	2	2	2	2	2	2	2	2	2	2	1
New Jersey																			
Democrats	2	3	4²	4	7	3	4	3	2	2	5	5	5	6	4	5	6	7²	11
Republicans	10	9	10	10	7	11	10	11	12	12	9	9	9	8	10	9	8	8	4
New Mexico																			
Democrats	0	1	1	1	1	1	1	2²	2	2	2	2	2	2	2	2	2	2	2
Republicans	1	0	0	0	0	0	0	0	0	0	0	0	0	0	0	0	0	0	0
New York																			
Democrats	23	23	29²	29	29	25	25	23	22	16	24	23	16¹	17	17	19	22	20¹	27
Republicans	20	20	16	16	16	19	19	21	22	28	20	22	27	26	26	24	21	21	14
North Carolina																			
Democrats	8	10	11²	11	11	11	11	12²	12	12	12	12	11	11	11	11	11	9¹	9
Republicans	2	0	0	0	0	0	0	0	0	0	0	0	1	1	1	1	1	2	2
North Dakota																			
Democrats	0	0	0¹	0	0	0	0	0	0	0	0	0	0	0	0	1	0	0	1
Republicans	3	3	2	2	2	2	2	2	2	2	2	2	2	2	2	1	2	2	1
Ohio																			
Democrats	3	9	18²	18	22	9	12	3¹	6	4	12	7	6	6	6	9	7	6²	10
Republicans	19	13	6	6	2	15	12	20	17	19	11	15	16	17	17	14	16	18	14
Oklahoma																			
Democrats	5	7	9²	9	9	9	8	7¹	6	6	8	6	5¹	5	5	5	5	5	5
Republicans	3	1	0	0	0	0	1	1	2	2	0	2	1	1	1	1	1	1	1
Oregon																			
Democrats	0	1	2	1	2	1	1	0²	0	0	0	0	0	1	3	3	2	3	3
Republicans	3	2	1	2	1	2	2	4	4	4	4	4	4	3	1	1	2	1	1
Pennsylvania																			
Democrats	1	3	11¹	23	27	15	19	14¹	15	5	16	13	11¹	14	13	16	14	13¹	15
Republicans	35	33	23	11	7	9	15	19	18	28	19	20	19	16	17	14	16	14	12
Rhode Island																			
Democrats	1	1	2¹	2	2	0	2	2	2	2	2	2	2	2	2	2	2	2	2
Republicans	2	2	0	0	0	2	0	0	0	0	0	0	0	0	0	0	0	0	0
South Carolina																			
Democrats	7	7	6¹	6	6	6	6	6	6	6	6	6	6	6	6	6	6	6	6
Republicans	0	0	0	0	0	0	0	0	0	0	0	0	0	0	0	0	0	0	0
South Dakota																			
Democrats	0	0	2¹	2	1	0	0	0	0	0	0	0	0	0	1	1	0	0	0
Republicans	3	3	0	0	1	2	2	2	2	2	2	2	2	2	1	1	2	2	2
Tennessee																			
Democrats	8	8	7¹	7	7	7	7	8²	8	8	8	8	7¹	7	7	7	7	6	6
Republicans	2	2	2	2	2	2	2	2	2	2	2	2	2	2	2	2	2	3	3
Texas																			
Democrats	17	17	21²	21	21	21	21	21	21	21	21	21	22²	21	21	21	21	21²	23
Republicans	1⁷	1	0	0	0	0	0	0	0	0	0	0	0	1	1	1	1	2	0
Utah																			
Democrats	0	0	2	2	2	2	2	2	2	1	2	2	0	0	0	1	2	0	1
Republicans	2	2	0	0	0	0	0	0	0	1	0	0	2	2	2	1	0	2	1
Vermont																			
Democrats	0	0	0¹	0	0	0	0	0	0	0	0	0	0	0	0	1	0	0	0
Republicans	2	2	1	1	1	1	1	1	1	1	1	1	1	1	1	0	1	1	1
Virginia																			
Democrats	8	9	9¹	9	9	9	9	9	9	9	9	9	7²	8	8	8	8	8	8
Republicans	2	1	0	0	0	0	0	0	0	0	0	0	3	2	2	2	2	2	2
Washington																			
Democrats	1	1	6²	6	6	6	6	3	4	1	2	2	1²	1	1	1	2	1	5
Republicans	4	4	0	0	0	0	0	3	2	5	4	4	6	6	6	6	5	6	2
West Virginia																			
Democrats	1	2	6	6	6	5	6	3	5	2	6	6	5	6	4	5	5	4¹	4
Republicans	5	4	0	0	0	1	0	3	1	4	0	0	1	0	2	1	1	1	1
Wisconsin																			
Democrats	0	1	5¹	3	3	0	1	3	2	0	2	1	1	3	3	5	4	4	5
Republicans	11	10	5	0	0	8	6	5	7	10	8	9	9	7	7	5	6	6	5
Wyoming																			
Democrats	0	0	0	1	1	0	1	0	0	0	0	0	0	0	0	0	0	1	0
Republicans	1	1	1	0	0	1	0	1	1	1	1	1	1	1	1	1	1	0	1

Notes: State totals reflect the number of Democrats and Republicans in each House delegation at the start of each Congress. The above totals do not include "other" representatives elected as independent or third-party candidates. Those numbers are California: Progressive 1936 (1). (No formal party. The representative became a Democrat in 1938.) Minnesota: Farmer-Labor 1928– 1930 (1), 1932 (5), 1934 (3), 1936 (5), 1938–1942 (1). (Merged with D in 1944.) New York: American Labor 1938–1948 (1). (Party disbanded after 1954.) Ohio: Independent 1950–1952 (1). (Defeated by Democrat in 1954.) Wisconsin: Progressive 1934 (7), 1936–1938 (2), 1940 (3), 1942 (2) and 1944 (1). (Disbanded after 1944. The last Progressive became a Republican in 1946.) Vermont: Independent 1990–2000 (1). Virginia: Independent 2000 (1). National totals: 1928–1930 (1), 1932 (5), 1934 (10), 1936 (13), 1938 (4), 1940 (5), 1942 (4), 1944 (2), 1946–1952 (1), 1990–1998 (1), and 2000 (2).

	1966	1968	1970	1972	1974	1976	1978	1980	1982	1984	1986	1988	1990	1992	1994	1996	1998	2000
Montana																		
Democrats	1	1	1	1	2	1	1	1	1	1	1	1	1	1[1]	1	1	0	0
Republicans	1	1	1	1	0	1	1	1	1	1	1	1	1	0	0	0	1	1
Nebraska																		
Democrats	0	0	0	0	0	1	1	0	0	0	0	1	1	1	0	0	0	0
Republicans	3	3	3	3	3	2	2	3	3	3	3	2	2	2	3	3	3	3
Nevada																		
Democrats	1	1	1	0	1	1	1	1	1[2]	1	1	1	1	1	0	0	1	1
Republicans	0	0	0	1	0	0	0	0	1	1	1	1	1	1	2	2	1	1
New Hampshire																		
Democrats	0	0	0	0	1	1	1	1	1	0	0	0	1	1	0	0	0	0
Republicans	2	2	2	2	1	1	1	1	1	2	2	2	1	1	2	2	2	2
New Jersey																		
Democrats	9	9	9	8	12	11	10	8	9[1]	8	8	8	8	7[1]	5	6	7	7
Republicans	6	6	6	7	3	4	5	7	5	6	6	6	6	6	8	7	6	6
New Mexico																		
Democrats	2	0	1	1	1	1	1	0	1[2]	1	1	1	1	1	1	1	1	1
Republicans	0	2	1	1	1	1	1	2	2	2	2	2	2	2	2	2	2	2
New York																		
Democrats	26	26	24	22[1]	27	28	26	22	20[1]	19	20	21	21	18[1]	17	18	18	19
Republicans	15	15	17	17	12	11	13	17	14	15	14	13	13	13	14	13	13	12
North Carolina																		
Democrats	8	7	7	7	9	9	9	7	9	6	8	8	7	8[2]	4	6	5	5
Republicans	3	4	4	4	2	2	2	4	2	5	3	3	4	4	8	6	7	7
North Dakota																		
Democrats	0	0	1	0[1]	0	0	0	1	1	1	1	1	1	1	1	1	1	1
Republicans	2	2	1	1	1	1	1	0	0	0	0	0	0	0	0	0	0	0
Ohio																		
Democrats	5	6	7	7[1]	8	10	10	11	10[1]	11	11	11	11	10[1]	6	8	8	8
Republicans	19	18	17	16	15	13	13	12	11	10	10	10	10	9	13	11	11	11
Oklahoma																		
Democrats	4	4	4	5	6	5	5	5	5	5	4	4	4	4	1	0	0	1
Republicans	2	2	2	1	0	1	1	1	1	1	2	2	2	2	5	6	6	5
Oregon																		
Democrats	2	2	2	2	4	4	4	3	3[2]	3	3	3	4	4	3	4	4	4
Republicans	2	2	2	2	0	0	0	1	2	2	2	2	1	1	2	1	1	1
Pennsylvania																		
Democrats	14	14	14	13[1]	14	17	15	13[6]	13[1]	13	12	12	11	11[1]	11	11	11	10
Republicans	13	13	13	12	11	8	10	12	10	10	11	11	12	10	10	10	10	11
Rhode Island																		
Democrats	2	2	2	2	2	2	2	1	1	1	1	0	1	1	2	2	2	2
Republicans	0	0	0	0	0	0	0	1	1	1	1	2	1	1	0	0	0	0
South Carolina																		
Democrats	5	5	5	4	5	5	4	2	3	3	4	4	4	3	2	2	2	2
Republicans	1	1	1	2	1	1	2	4	3	3	2	2	2	3	4	4	4	4
South Dakota																		
Democrats	0	0	2	1	0	0	1	1	1[1]	1	1	1	1	1	1	0	0	0
Republicans	2	2	0	1	2	2	1	1	0	0	0	0	0	0	0	1	1	1
Tennessee																		
Democrats	5	5	5	3[1]	5	5	5	5	6[2]	6	6	6	6	6	4	4	4	4
Republicans	4	4	4	5	3	3	3	3	3	3	3	3	3	3	5	5	5	5
Texas																		
Democrats	21	20	20	20[2]	21	22	20	19	22[2]	17	17	19	19	21[2]	19	17	17	17
Republicans	2	3	3	4	3	2	4	5	5	10	10	8	8	9	11	13	13	13
Utah																		
Democrats	0	0	1	2	2	1	1	0	0[2]	0	1	1	2	2	1	0	0	1
Republicans	2	2	1	0	0	1	1	2	3	3	2	2	1	1	2	3	3	2
Vermont																		
Democrats	0	0	0	0	0	0	0	0	0	0	0	0	0	0	0	0	0	0
Republicans	1	1	1	1	1	1	1	1	1	1	1	1	0	0	0	0	0	0
Virginia																		
Democrats	6	5	4	3	5	4	4	1	4	4	5	5	6	7[2]	6	6	6	4
Republicans	4	5	6	7	5	6	6	9	6	6	5	5	4	4	5	5	5	6
Washington																		
Democrats	5	5	6	6	6	6	6	5	5[2]	5	5	5	5	8[2]	2	3	5	6
Republicans	2	2	1	1	1	1	1	2	3	3	3	3	3	1	7	6	4	3
West Virginia																		
Democrats	4	5	5	4[1]	4	4	4	2	4	4	4	4	4	3[1]	3	3	3	2
Republicans	1	0	0	0	0	0	0	2	0	0	0	0	0	0	0	0	0	1
Wisconsin																		
Democrats	3	3	5	5[1]	7	7	6	5	5	5	5	5	4	4	3	5	4	5
Republicans	7	7	5	4	2	2	3	4	4	4	4	4	5	5	6	4	5	4
Wyoming																		
Democrats	0	1	1	1	1	0	0	0	0	0	0	0	0	0	0	0	0	0
Republicans	1	1	0	0	0	0	1	1	1	1	1	1	1	1	1	1	1	1

7. Texas 1928: national and state totals reflect the final outcome of a contested election in which a Democrats was at first certified the winner, but the House decided to seat the Republican.

Sessions of the U.S. Congress, 1789–2000

Congress	Session	Date of beginning[1]	Date of adjournment[2]	Length in days	President pro tempore of the Senate[3]	Speaker of the House of Representatives
1st	1	Mar. 4, 1789	Sept. 29, 1789	210	John Langdon of New Hampshire	Frederick A. C. Muhlenberg of Pennsylvania
	2	Jan. 4, 1790	Aug. 12, 1790	221		
	3	Dec. 6, 1790	Mar. 3, 1791	88		
2nd	1	Oct. 24, 1791	May 8, 1792	197	Richard Henry Lee of Virginia	Jonathan Trumbull of Connecticut
	2	Nov. 5, 1792	Mar. 2, 1793	119	John Langdon of New Hampshire	
3rd	1	Dec. 2, 1793	June 9, 1794	190	Langdon Ralph Izard of South Carolina	Frederick A. C. Muhlenberg of Pennsylvania
	2	Nov. 3, 1794	Mar. 3, 1795	121	Henry Tazewell of Virginia	
4th	1	Dec. 7, 1795	June 1, 1796	177	Tazewell Samuel Livermore of New Hampshire	Jonathan Dayton of New Jersey
	2	Dec. 5, 1796	Mar. 3, 1797	89	William Bingham of Pennsylvania	
5th	1	May 15, 1797	July 10, 1797	57	William Bradford of Rhode Island	Dayton
	2	Nov. 13, 1797	July 16, 1798	246	Jacob Read of South Carolina Theodore Sedgwick of Massachusetts	George Dent of Maryland[5]
	3	Dec. 3, 1798	Mar. 3, 1799	91	John Laurence of New York James Ross of Pennsylvania	
6th	1	Dec. 2, 1799	May 14, 1800	164	Samuel Livermore of New Hampshire Uriah Tracy of Connecticut	Theodore Sedgwick of Massachusetts
	2	Nov. 17, 1800	Mar. 3, 1801	107	John E. Howard of Maryland James Hillhouse of Connecticut	
7th	1	Dec. 7, 1801	May 3, 1802	148	Abraham Baldwin of Georgia	Nathaniel Macon of North Carolina
	2	Dec. 6, 1802	Mar. 3, 1803	88	Stephen R. Bradley of Vermont	
8th	1	Oct. 17, 1803	Mar. 27, 1804	163	John Brown of Kentucky Jesse Franklin of North Carolina	Macon
	2	Nov. 5, 1804	Mar. 3, 1805	119	Joseph Anderson of Tennessee	
9th	1	Dec. 2, 1805	Apr. 21, 1806	141	Samuel Smith of Maryland	Macon
	2	Dec. 1, 1806	Mar. 3, 1807	93	Smith	
10th	1	Oct. 26, 1807	Apr. 25, 1808	182	Smith	Joseph B. Varnum of Massachusetts
	2	Nov. 7, 1808	Mar. 3, 1809	117	Stephen R. Bradley of Vermont John Milledge of Georgia	

(Continued)

Congress	Session	Date of beginning[1]	Date of adjournment[2]	Length in days	President pro tempore of the Senate[3]	Speaker of the House of Representatives
11th	1	May 22, 1809	June 28, 1809	38	Andrew Gregg of Pennsylvania	Varnum
	2	Nov. 27, 1809	May 1, 1810	156	John Gaillard of South Carolina	
	3	Dec. 3, 1810	Mar. 3, 1811	91	John Pope of Kentucky	
12th	1	Nov. 4, 1811	July 6, 1812	245	William H. Crawford of Georgia	Henry Clay of Kentucky
	2	Nov. 2, 1812	Mar. 3, 1813	122	Crawford	
13th	1	May 24, 1813	Aug. 2, 1813	71	Crawford	Clay
	2	Dec. 6, 1813	Apr. 18, 1814	134	Joseph B. Varnum of Massachusetts	
	3	Sept. 19, 1814	Mar. 3, 1815	166	John Gaillard of South Carolina	Langdon Cheves of South Carolina [6]
14th	1	Dec. 4, 1815	Apr. 30, 1816	148	Gaillard	Henry Clay of Kentucky
	2	Dec. 2, 1816	Mar. 3, 1817	92	Gaillard	
15th	1	Dec. 1, 1817	Apr. 20, 1818	141	Gaillard	Clay
	2	Nov. 16, 1818	Mar. 3, 1819	108	James Barbour of Virginia	
16th	1	Dec. 6, 1819	May 15, 1820	162	John Gaillard of South Carolina	Clay
	2	Nov. 13, 1820	Mar. 3, 1821	111	Gaillard	John W. Taylor of New York [7]
17th	1	Dec. 3, 1821	May 8, 1822	157	Gaillard	Philip P. Barbour of Virginia
	2	Dec. 2, 1822	Mar. 3, 1823	92	Gaillard	
18th	1	Dec. 1, 1823	May 27, 1824	178	Gaillard	Henry Clay of Kentucky
	2	Dec. 6, 1824	Mar. 3, 1825	88	Gaillard	
19th	1	Dec. 5, 1825	May 22, 1826	169	Nathaniel Macon of North Carolina	John W. Taylor of New York
	2	Dec. 4, 1826	Mar. 3, 1827	90	Macon	
20th	1	Dec. 3, 1827	May 26, 1828	175	Samuel Smith of Maryland	Andrew Stevenson of Virginia
	2	Dec. 1, 1828	Mar. 3, 1829	93	Smith	
21st	1	Dec. 7, 1829	May 31, 1830	176	Smith	Stevenson
	2	Dec. 6, 1830	Mar. 3, 1831	88	Littleton Waller Tazewell of Virginia	
22nd	1	Dec. 5, 1831	July 16, 1832	225	Tazewell	Stevenson
	2	Dec. 3, 1832	Mar. 2, 1833	91	Hugh Lawson White of Tennessee	
23rd	1	Dec. 2, 1833	June 30, 1834	211	George Poindexter of Mississippi	Stevenson
	2	Dec. 1, 1834	Mar. 3, 1835	93	John Tyler of Virginia	John Bell of Tennessee [8]
24th	1	Dec. 7, 1835	July 4, 1836	211	William R. King of Alabama	James K. Polk of Tennessee
	2	Dec. 5, 1836	Mar. 3, 1837	89	King	
25th	1	Sept. 4, 1837	Oct. 16, 1837	43	King	Polk
	2	Dec. 4, 1837	July 9, 1838	218	King	
	3	Dec. 3, 1838	Mar. 3, 1839	91	King	
26th	1	Dec. 2, 1839	July 21, 1840	233	King	Robert M. T. Hunter of Virginia
	2	Dec. 7, 1840	Mar. 3, 1841	87	King	
27th	1	May 31, 1841	Sept. 13, 1841	106	Samuel L. Southard of New Jersey	John White of Kentucky
	2	Dec. 6, 1841	Aug. 31, 1842	269	Willie P. Mangum of North Carolina	
	3	Dec. 5, 1842	Mar. 3, 1843	89	Mangum	

(Continued)

Congress	Session	Date of beginning[1]	Date of adjournment[2]	Length in days	President pro tempore of the Senate[3]	Speaker of the House of Representatives
28th	1	Dec. 4, 1843	June 17, 1844	196	Mangum	John W. Jones of Virginia
	2	Dec. 2, 1844	Mar. 3, 1845	92	Mangum	
29th	1	Dec. 1, 1845	Aug. 10, 1846	253	David R. Atchison of Missouri	John W. Davis of Indiana
	2	Dec. 7, 1846	Mar. 3, 1847	87	Atchison	
30th	1	Dec. 6, 1847	Aug. 14, 1848	254	Atchison	Robert C. Winthrop of Massachusetts
	2	Dec. 4, 1848	Mar. 3, 1849	90	Atchison	
31st	1	Dec. 3, 1849	Sept. 30, 1850	302	William R. King of Alabama	Howell Cobb of Georgia
	2	Dec. 2, 1850	Mar. 3, 1851	92	King	
32nd	1	Dec. 1, 1851	Aug. 31, 1852	275	King	Linn Boyd of Kentucky
	2	Dec. 6, 1852	Mar. 3, 1853	88	David R. Atchison of Missouri	
33rd	1	Dec. 5, 1853	Aug. 7, 1854	246	Atchison	Boyd
	2	Dec. 4, 1854	Mar. 3, 1855	90	Jesse D. Bright of Indiana Lewis Cass of Michigan	
34th	1	Dec. 3, 1855	Aug. 18, 1856	260	Jesse D. Bright of Indiana	Nathaniel P. Banks of Massachusetts
	2	Aug. 21, 1856	Aug. 30, 1856	10	Bright	
	3	Dec. 1, 1856	Mar. 3, 1857	93	James M. Mason of Virginia Thomas J. Rusk of Texas	
35th	1	Dec. 7, 1857	June 14, 1858	189	Benjamin Fitzpatrick of Alabama	James L. Orr of South Carolina
	2	Dec. 6, 1858	Mar. 3, 1859	88	Fitzpatrick	
36th	1	Dec. 5, 1859	June 25, 1860	202	Fitzpatrick Jesse D. Bright of Indiana	William Pennington of New Jersey
	2	Dec. 3, 1860	Mar. 3, 1861	93	Solomon Foot of Vermont	
37th	1	July 4, 1861	Aug. 6, 1861	34	Foot	Galusha A. Grow of Pennsylvania
	2	Dec. 2, 1861	July 17, 1862	228	Foot	
	3	Dec. 1, 1862	Mar. 3, 1863	93	Foot	
38th	1	Dec. 7, 1863	July 4, 1864	209	Foot Daniel Clark of New Hampshire	Schuyler Colfax of Indiana
	2	Dec. 5, 1864	Mar. 3, 1865	89	Clark	
39th	1	Dec. 4, 1865	July 28, 1866	237	Lafayette S. Foster of Connecticut	Colfax
	2	Dec. 3, 1866	Mar. 3, 1867	91	Benjamin F. Wade of Ohio	
40th	1	Mar. 4, 1867[9]	Dec. 2, 1867	274	Wade	Colfax
	2	Dec. 2, 1867[10]	Nov. 10, 1868	345	Wade	
	3	Dec. 7, 1868	Mar. 3, 1869	87	Wade	Theodore M. Pomeroy of New York [11]
41st	1	Mar. 4, 1869	Apr. 10, 1869	38	Henry B. Anthony of Rhode Island	James G. Blaine of Maine
	2	Dec. 6, 1869	July 15, 1870	222	Anthony	
	3	Dec. 5, 1870	Mar. 3, 1871	89	Anthony	
42nd	1	Mar. 4, 1871	Apr. 20, 1871	48	Anthony	Blaine
	2	Dec. 4, 1871	June 10, 1872	190	Anthony	
	3	Dec. 2, 1872	Mar. 3, 1873	92	Anthony	
43rd	1	Dec. 1, 1873	June 23, 1874	204	Matthew H. Carpenter of Wisconsin	Blaine
	2	Dec. 7, 1874	Mar. 3, 1875	87	Carpenter Henry B. Anthony of Rhode Island	

(Continued)

Congress	Session	Date of beginning[1]	Date of adjournment[2]	Length in days	President pro tempore of the Senate[3]	Speaker of the House of Representatives
44th	1	Dec. 6, 1875	Aug. 15, 1876	254	Thomas W. Ferry of Michigan	Michael C. Kerr of Indiana[12]
						Samuel S. Cox of New York, pro tempore[13]
						Milton Sayler of Ohio, pro tempore[14]
	2	Dec. 4, 1876	Mar. 3, 1877	90	Ferry	Samuel J. Randall of Pennsylvania
45th	1	Oct. 15, 1877	Dec. 3, 1877	50	Ferry	Randall
	2	Dec. 3, 1877	June 20, 1878	200	Ferry	
	3	Dec. 2, 1878	Mar. 3, 1879	92	Ferry	
46th	1	Mar. 18, 1879	July 1, 1879	106	Allen G. Thurman of Ohio	Randall
	2	Dec. 1, 1879	June 16, 1880	199	Thurman	
	3	Dec. 6, 1880	Mar. 3, 1881	88	Thurman	
47th	1	Dec. 5, 1881	Aug. 8, 1882	247	Thomas F. Bayard of Delaware	J. Warren Keifer of Ohio
					David Davis of Illinois	
	2	Dec. 4, 1882	Mar. 3, 1883	90	George F. Edmunds of Vermont	
48th	1	Dec. 3, 1883	July 7, 1884	218	Edmunds	John G. Carlisle of Kentucky
	2	Dec. 1, 1884	Mar. 3, 1885	93	Edmunds	
49th	1	Dec. 7, 1885	Aug. 5, 1886	242	John Sherman of Ohio	Carlisle
	2	Dec. 6, 1886	Mar. 3, 1887	88	John J. Ingalls of Kansas	
50th	1	Dec. 5, 1887	Oct. 20, 1888	321	Ingalls	Carlisle
	2	Dec. 3, 1888	Mar. 3, 1889	91	Ingalls	
51st	1	Dec. 2, 1889	Oct. 1, 1890	304	Ingalls	Thomas B. Reed of Maine
	2	Dec. 1, 1890	Mar. 3, 1891	93	Charles F. Manderson of Nebraska	
52nd	1	Dec. 7, 1891	Aug. 5, 1892	251	Manderson	Charles F. Crisp of Georgia
	2	Dec. 5, 1892	Mar. 3, 1893	89	Isham G. Harris of Tennessee	
53rd	1	Aug. 7, 1893	Nov. 3, 1893	89	Harris	Crisp
	2	Dec. 4, 1893	Aug. 28, 1894	268	Harris	
	3	Dec. 3, 1894	Mar. 3, 1895	97	Matt W. Ransom of North Carolina	
					Isham G. Harris of Tennessee	
54th	1	Dec. 2, 1895	June 11, 1896	193	William P. Frye of Maine	Thomas B. Reed of Maine
	2	Dec. 7, 1896	Mar. 3, 1897	87	Frye	
55th	1	Mar. 15, 1897	July 24, 1897	131	Frye	Reed
	2	Dec. 6, 1897	July 8, 1898	215	Frye	
	3	Dec. 5, 1898	Mar. 3, 1899	89	Frye	
56th	1	Dec. 4, 1899	June 7, 1900	186	Frye	David B. Henderson of Iowa
	2	Dec. 3, 1900	Mar. 3, 1901	91	Frye	
57th	1	Dec. 2, 1901	July 1, 1902	212	Frye	Henderson
	2	Dec. 1, 1902	Mar. 3, 1903	93	Frye	
58th	1	Nov. 9, 1903	Dec. 7, 1903	29	Frye	Joseph G. Cannon of Illinois
	2	Dec. 7, 1903	Apr. 28, 1904	144	Frye	
	3	Dec. 5, 1904	Mar. 3, 1905	89	Frye	
59th	1	Dec. 4, 1905	June 30, 1906	209	Frye	Cannon
	2	Dec. 3, 1906	Mar. 3, 1907	91	Frye	
60th	1	Dec. 2, 1907	May 30, 1908	181	Frye	Cannon
	2	Dec. 7, 1908	Mar. 3, 1909	87	Frye	

(Continued)

Congress	Session	Date of beginning[1]	Date of adjournment[2]	Length in days	President pro tempore of the Senate[3]	Speaker of the House of Representatives
61st	1	Mar. 15, 1909	Aug. 5, 1909	144	Frye	Cannon
	2	Dec. 6, 1909	June 25, 1910	202	Frye	
	3	Dec. 5, 1910	Mar. 3, 1911	89	Frye	
62nd	1	Apr. 4, 1911	Aug. 22, 1911	141	Frye[15]	Champ Clark of Missouri
	2	Dec. 4, 1911	Aug. 26, 1912	267	Augustus O. Bacon of Georgia[16]	
					Frank B. Brandegee of Connecticut[17]	
					Charles Curtis of Kansas[18]	
					Jacob H. Gallinger of New Hampshire[19]	
					Henry Cabot Lodge of Massachusetts[20]	
	3	Dec. 2, 1912	Mar. 3, 1913	92	Bacon;[21] Gallinger[22]	
63rd	1	Apr. 7, 1913	Dec. 1, 1913	239	James P. Clarke of Arkansas	Clark
	2	Dec. 1, 1913	Oct. 24, 1914	328	Clarke	
	3	Dec. 7, 1914	Mar. 3, 1915	87	Clarke	
64th	1	Dec. 6, 1915	Sept. 8, 1916	278	Clarke[23]	Clark
	2	Dec. 4, 1916	Mar. 3, 1917	90	Willard Saulsbury of Delaware	
65th	1	Apr. 2, 1917	Oct. 6, 1917	188	Saulsbury	Clark
	2	Dec. 3, 1917	Nov. 21, 1918	354	Saulsbury	
	3	Dec. 2, 1918	Mar. 3, 1919	92	Saulsbury	
66th	1	May 19, 1919	Nov. 19, 1919	185	Albert B. Cummins of Iowa	Frederick H. Gillett of Massachusetts
	2	Dec. 1, 1919	June 5, 1920	188	Cummins	
	3	Dec. 6, 1920	Mar. 3, 1921	88	Cummins	
67th	1	Apr. 11, 1921	Nov. 23, 1921	227	Cummins	Gillett
	2	Dec. 5, 1921	Sept. 22, 1922	292	Cummins	
	3	Nov. 20, 1922	Dec. 4, 1922	15	Cummins	
	4	Dec. 4, 1922	Mar. 3, 1923	90	Cummins	
68th	1	Dec. 3, 1923	June 7, 1924	188	Cummins	Gillett
	2	Dec. 1, 1924	Mar. 3, 1925	93	Cummins	
69th	1	Dec. 7, 1925	July 3, 1926	209	George H. Moses of New Hampshire	Nicholas Longworth of Ohio
	2	Dec. 6, 1926	Mar. 3, 1927	88	Moses	
70th	1	Dec. 5, 1927	May 29, 1928	177	Moses	Longworth
	2	Dec. 3, 1928	Mar. 3, 1929	91	Moses	
71st	1	Apr. 15, 1929	Nov. 22, 1929	222	Moses	Longworth
	2	Dec. 2, 1929	July 3, 1930	214	Moses	
	3	Dec. 1, 1930	Mar. 3, 1931	93	Moses	
72nd	1	Dec. 7, 1931	July 16, 1932	223	Moses	John N. Garner of Texas
	2	Dec. 5, 1932	Mar. 3, 1933	89	Moses	
73rd	1	Mar. 9, 1933	June 15, 1933	99	Key Pittman of Nevada	Henry T. Rainey of Illinois[24]
	2	Jan. 3, 1934	June 18, 1934	167	Pittman	
74th	1	Jan. 3, 1935	Aug. 26, 1935	236	Pittman	Joseph W. Byrns of Tennessee[25]
	2	Jan. 3, 1936	June 20, 1936	170	Pittman	William B. Bankhead of Alabama[26]
75th	1	Jan. 5, 1937	Aug. 21, 1937	229	Pittman	Bankhead
	2	Nov. 15, 1937	Dec. 21, 1937	37	Pittman	
	3	Jan. 3, 1938	June 16, 1938	165	Pittman	

(Continued)

Congress	Session	Date of beginning[1]	Date of adjournment[2]	Length in days	President pro tempore of the Senate[3]	Speaker of the House of Representatives
76th	1	Jan. 3, 1939	Aug. 5, 1939	215	Pittman	Bankhead [27]
	2	Sept. 21, 1939	Nov. 3, 1939	44	Pittman	
	3	Jan. 3, 1940	Jan. 3, 1941	367	Pittman [28]	Sam Rayburn of Texas [29]
					William H. King of Utah [30]	
77th	1	Jan. 3, 1941	Jan. 2, 1942	365	Pat Harrison of Mississippi[31]	Rayburn
					Carter Glass of Virginia [32]	
	2	Jan. 5, 1942	Dec. 16, 1942	346		
78th	1	Jan. 6, 1943 [33]	Dec. 21, 1943	350	Glass	Rayburn
	2	Jan. 10, 1944 [34]	Dec. 19, 1944	345	Glass	
79th	1	Jan. 3, 1945 [35]	Dec. 21, 1945	353	Kenneth McKellar of Tennessee	Rayburn
	2	Jan. 14, 1946 [36]	Aug. 2, 1946	201	McKellar	
80th	1	Jan. 3, 1947 [37]	Dec. 19, 1947	351	Arthur H. Vandenberg of Michigan	Joseph W. Martin Jr. of Massachusetts
	2	Jan. 6, 1948 [38]	Dec. 31, 1948	361	Vandenberg	
81st	1	Jan. 3, 1949	Oct. 19, 1949	290	Kenneth McKellar of Tennessee	Sam Rayburn of Texas
	2	Jan. 3, 1950 [39]	Jan. 2, 1951	365	McKellar	
82nd	1	Jan. 3, 1951 [40]	Oct. 20, 1951	291	McKellar	Rayburn
	2	Jan. 8, 1952 [41]	July 7, 1952	182	McKellar	
83rd	1	Jan. 3, 1953 [42]	Aug. 3, 1953	213	Styles Bridges of New Hampshire	Joseph W. Martin Jr. of Massachusetts
	2	Jan. 6, 1954 [43]	Dec. 2, 1954	331	Bridges	
84th	1	Jan. 5, 1955 [44]	Aug. 2, 1955	210	Walter F. George of Georgia	Sam Rayburn of Texas
	2	Jan. 3, 1956 [45]	July 27, 1956	207	George	
85th	1	Jan. 3, 1957 [46]	Aug. 30, 1957	239	Carl Hayden of Arizona	Rayburn
	2	Jan. 7, 1958 [47]	Aug. 24, 1958	230	Hayden	
86th	1	Jan. 7, 1959 [48]	Sept. 15, 1959	252	Hayden	Rayburn
	2	Jan. 6, 1960 [49]	Sept. 1, 1960	240	Hayden	
87th	1	Jan. 3, 1961 [50]	Sept. 27, 1961	268	Hayden	Rayburn [51]
	2	Jan. 10, 1962 [52]	Oct. 13, 1962	277	Hayden	John W. McCormack of Massachusetts [53]
88th	1	Jan. 9, 1963 [54]	Dec. 30, 1963	356	Hayden	McCormack
	2	Jan. 7, 1964 [55]	Oct. 3, 1964	270	Hayden	
89th	1	Jan. 4, 1965	Oct. 23, 1965	293	Hayden	McCormack
	2	Jan. 10, 1966 [56]	Oct. 22, 1966	286	Hayden	
90th	1	Jan. 10, 1967 [57]	Dec. 15, 1967	340	Hayden	McCormack
	2	Jan. 15, 1968 [58]	Oct. 14, 1968	274	Hayden	
91st	1	Jan. 3, 1969 [59]	Dec. 23, 1969	355	Richard B. Russell of Georgia	McCormack
	2	Jan. 19, 1970 [60]	Jan. 2, 1971	349	Russell	
92nd	1	Jan. 21, 1971 [61]	Dec. 17, 1971	331	Russell[62]	Carl Albert of Oklahoma
					Allen J. Ellender of Louisiana[63]	
	2	Jan. 18, 1972 [64]	Oct. 18, 1972	275	Ellender [65]	
					James O. Eastland of Mississippi [66]	
93rd	1	Jan. 3, 1973 [67]	Dec. 22, 1973	354	Eastland	Albert
	2	Jan. 21, 1974 [68]	Dec. 20, 1974	334	Eastland	
94th	1	Jan. 14, 1975 [69]	Dec. 19, 1975	340	Eastland	Albert
	2	Jan. 19, 1976 [70]	Oct. 1, 1976	257	Eastland	

(Continued)

Congress	Session	Date of beginning[1]	Date of adjournment[2]	Length in days	President pro tempore of the Senate[3]	Speaker of the House of Representatives
95th	1	Jan. 4, 1977 [71]	Dec. 15, 1977	346	Eastland	Thomas P. O'Neill Jr. of Massachusetts
	2	Jan. 19, 1978 [72]	Oct. 15, 1978	270	Eastland	
96th	1	Jan. 15, 1979 [73]	Jan. 3, 1980	354	Warren G. Magnuson of Washington	O'Neill
	2	Jan. 3, 1980 [74]	Dec. 16, 1980	349	Magnuson	
97th	1	Jan. 5, 1981 [75]	Dec. 16, 1981	347	Strom Thurmond of South Carolina	O'Neill
	2	Jan. 25, 1982 [76]	Dec. 23, 1982	333	Thurmond	
98th	1	Jan. 3, 1983 [77]	Nov. 18, 1983	320	Thurmond	O'Neill
	2	Jan. 23, 1984 [78]	Oct. 12, 1984	264	Thurmond	
99th	1	Jan. 3, 1985 [79]	Dec. 20, 1985	352	Thurmond	O'Neill
	2	Jan. 21, 1986 [80]	Oct. 18, 1986	278	Thurmond	
100th	1	Jan. 6, 1987 [81]	Dec. 22, 1987	351	John C. Stennis of Mississippi	Jim Wright of Texas
	2	Jan. 25, 1988 [82]	Oct. 22, 1988	272	Stennis	
101st	1	Jan. 3, 1989 [83]	Nov. 22, 1989	324	Robert C. Byrd of West Virginia	Wright; Thomas S. Foley of Washington [84]
	2	Jan. 23, 1990 [85]	Oct. 28, 1990	260	Byrd	Foley
102nd	1	Jan. 3, 1991 [86]	Jan. 3, 1992	366	Byrd	Foley
	2	Jan. 3, 1992 [87]	Oct. 9, 1992	281	Byrd	
103rd	1	Jan. 5, 1993[88]	Nov. 26, 1993	326	Byrd	Foley
	2	Jan. 25, 1994[89]	Dec. 1, 1994	311	Byrd	
104th	1	Jan. 4, 1995[90]	Jan. 3, 1996	365	Strom Thurmond of South Carolina	Newt Gingrich of Georgia
	2	Jan. 3, 1996[91]	Oct. 4, 1996	276	Thurmond	
105th	1	Jan. 7, 1997[92]	Nov. 13, 1997	311	Thurmond	Gingrich
	2	Jan. 27, 1998[93]	Dec. 19, 1998	327	Thurmond	
106th	1	Jan. 6, 1999[94]	Nov. 22, 1999	313	Thurmond	J. Dennis Hastert
	2	Jan. 24, 2000[95]	Dec. 15, 2000	339	Thurmond	of Illinois

Notes:

1. The Constitution (art. I, sec. 4) provided that "The Congress shall assemble at least once in every year . . . on the first Monday in December, unless they shall by law appoint a different day." Pursuant to a resolution of the Continental Congress, the first session of the First Congress convened March 4, 1789. Up to and including May 20, 1820, 18 acts were passed providing for the meeting of Congress on other days in the year. After 1820 Congress met regularly on the first Monday in December until 1934, when the Twentieth Amendment to the Constitution became effective changing the meeting date to Jan. 3. (Until then, brief special sessions of the Senate only were held at the beginning of each presidential term to confirm Cabinet and other nominations—and occasionally at other times for other purposes. The Senate last met in special session from March 4 to March 6, 1933.) The first and second sessions of the First Congress were held in New York City. Subsequently, including the first session of the Sixth Congress, Philadelphia was the meeting place; since then, Congress has convened in Washington.

2. Until adoption of the Twentieth Amendment, the deadline for adjournment of Congress in odd-numbered years was March 3. However, the expiring Congress often extended the "legislative day" of March 3 up to noon of March 4, when the new Congress came officially into being. After ratification of the Twentieth Amendment, the deadline for adjournment of Congress in odd-numbered years was noon on Jan. 3.

3. At one time, the appointment or election of a president pro tempore was considered by the Senate to be for the occasion only, so that more than one appear in several sessions, and in others none was chosen. Since March 12, 1890, they have served until "the Senate otherwise ordered."

4. Elected to count the vote for president and vice president, which was done April 6, 1789, because there was a quorum of the Senate for the first time. John Adams, vice president, appeared April 21, 1789, and took his seat as president of the Senate.

5. Elected Speaker pro tempore for April 20, 1798, and again for May 28, 1798.

6. Elected Speaker Jan. 19, 1814, to succeed Henry Clay, who resigned Jan. 19, 1814.

7. Elected Speaker Nov. 15, 1820, to succeed Henry Clay, who resigned Oct. 28, 1820.

8. Elected Speaker June 2, 1834, to succeed Andrew Stevenson of Virginia, who resigned.

9. There were recesses in this session from Saturday, Mar. 30, to Wednesday, July 1, and from Saturday, July 20, to Thursday, Nov. 21.

10. There were recesses in this session from Monday, July 27, to Monday, Sept. 21, to Friday, Oct. 16, and to Tuesday, Nov. 10. No business was transacted subsequent to July 27.

11. Elected Speaker Mar. 3, 1869, and served one day.

12. Died Aug. 19, 1876.

13. Appointed Speaker pro tempore Feb. 17, May 12, June 19.

14. Appointed Speaker pro tempore June 4.

15. Resigned as president pro tempore Apr. 27, 1911.

16. Elected to serve Jan. 11–17, Mar. 11–12, Apr. 8, May 10, May 30 to June 1 and 3, June 13 to July 5, Aug. 1–10, and Aug. 27 to Dec. 15, 1912.

17. Elected to serve May 25, 1912.

18. Elected to serve Dec. 4–12, 1911.

19. Elected to serve Feb. 12–14, Apr. 26–27, May 7, July 6–31, Aug. 12–26, 1912.

20. Elected to serve Mar. 25–26, 1912.

21. Elected to serve Aug. 27 to Dec. 15, 1912, Jan. 5–18, and Feb. 2–15, 1913.

22. Elected to serve Dec. 16, 1912, to Jan. 4, 1913, Jan. 19 to Feb. 1, and Feb. 16 to Mar. 3, 1913.

23. Died Oct. 1, 1916.

24. Died Aug. 19, 1934.

25. Died June 4, 1936.

26. Elected June 4, 1936.

27. Died Sept. 15, 1940.

28. Died Nov. 10, 1940.

29. Elected Sept. 16, 1940.

30. Elected Nov. 19, 1940.

31. Elected Jan. 6, 1941; died June 22, 1941.

32. Elected July 10, 1941.

33. There was a recess in this session from Thursday, July 8, to Tuesday, Sept. 14.

34. There were recesses in this session from Saturday, Apr. 1, to Wednesday, Apr. 12; from Friday, June 23, to Tuesday, Aug. 1; and from Thursday, Sept. 21, to Tuesday, Nov. 14.

35. The House was in recess in this session from Saturday, July 21, 1945, to Wednesday, Sept. 5, 1945, and the Senate from Wednesday, Aug. 1, 1945, to Wednesday, Sept. 5, 1945.

36. The House was in recess in this session from Thursday, Apr. 18, 1946, to Tuesday, Apr. 30, 1946.

37. There was a recess in this session from Sunday, July 27, 1947, to Monday, Nov. 17, 1947.

38. There were recesses in this session from Sunday, June 20, 1948, to Monday, July 26, 1948, and from Saturday, Aug. 7, 1948, to Friday, Dec. 31, 1948.

39. The House was in recess in this session from Thursday, Apr. 6, 1950, to Tuesday, Apr. 18, 1950, and both the Senate and the House were in recess from Saturday, Sept. 23, 1950, to Monday, Nov. 27, 1950.

40. The House was in recess in this session from Thursday, Mar. 22, 1951, to Monday, Apr. 2, 1951, and from Thursday, Aug. 23, 1951, to Wednesday, Sept. 12, 1951.

41. The House was in recess in this session from Thursday, Apr. 10, 1952, to Tuesday, Apr. 22, 1952.

42. The House was in recess in this session from Thursday, Apr. 2, 1953, to Monday, Apr. 13, 1953.

43. The House was in recess in this session from Thursday, Apr. 15, 1954, to Monday, Apr. 26, 1954, and adjourned sine die Aug. 20, 1954. The Senate was in recess in this session from Friday, Aug. 20, 1954, to Monday, Nov. 8, 1954; from Thursday, Nov. 18, 1954, to Monday, Nov. 29, 1954, and adjourned sine die Dec. 2, 1954.

44. There was a recess in this session from Monday, Apr. 4, 1955, to Wednesday, Apr. 13, 1955.

45. There was a recess in this session from Thursday, Mar. 29, 1956, to Monday, Apr. 9, 1956.

46. There was a recess in this session from Thursday, Apr. 18, 1957, to Monday, Apr. 29, 1957.

47. There was a recess in this session from Thursday, Apr. 3, 1958, to Monday, Apr. 14, 1958.

48. There was a recess in this session from Thursday, Mar. 26, 1959, to Tuesday, Apr. 7, 1959.

49. The Senate was in recess in this session from Thursday, Apr. 14, 1960, to Monday, Apr. 18, 1960; from Friday, May 27, 1960, to Tuesday, May 31, 1960, and from Sunday, July 3, 1960, to Monday, Aug. 8, 1960. The House was in recess in this session from Thursday, Apr. 14, 1960, to Monday, Apr. 18, 1960; from Friday, May 27, 1960, to Tuesday, May 31, 1960, and from Sunday, July 3, 1960, to Monday, Aug. 15, 1960.

50. The House was in recess in this session from Thursday, Mar. 30, 1961, to Monday, Apr. 10, 1961.

51. Died Nov. 16, 1961.

52. The House was in recess in this session from Thursday, Apr. 19, 1962, to Monday, Apr. 30, 1962.

53. Elected Jan. 10, 1962.

54. The House was in recess in this session from Thursday, Apr. 11, 1963, to Monday, Apr. 22, 1963.

55. The House was in recess in this session from Thursday, Mar. 26, 1964, to Monday, Apr. 6, 1964; from Thursday, July 2, 1964, to Monday, July 20, 1964; from Friday, Aug. 21, 1964, to Monday, Aug. 31, 1964. The Senate was in recess in this session from Friday, July 10, 1964, to Monday, July 20, 1964; from Friday, Aug. 21, 1964, to Monday, Aug. 31, 1964.

56. The House was in recess in this session from Thursday, Apr. 7, 1966, to Monday, Apr. 18, 1966; from Thursday, June 30, 1966, to Monday, July 11, 1966. The Senate was in recess in this session from Thursday, Apr. 7, 1966, to Wednesday, Apr. 13, 1966; from Thursday, June 30, 1966, to Monday, July 11, 1966.

57. There was a recess in this session from Thursday, Mar. 23, 1967, to Monday, Apr. 3, 1967; from Thursday, June 29, 1967, to Monday, July 10, 1967; from Thursday, Aug. 31, 1967, to Monday, Sept. 11, 1967; and from Wednesday, Nov. 22, 1967, to Monday, Nov. 27, 1967.

58. The House was in recess this session from Thursday, Apr. 11, 1968, to Monday, Apr. 22, 1968; from Wednesday, May 29, 1968, to Monday, June 3, 1968; from Wednesday, July 3, 1968, to Monday, July 8, 1968; from Friday, Aug. 2, 1968, to Wednesday, Sept. 4, 1968. The Senate was in recess this session from Thursday, Apr. 11, 1968, to Wednesday, Apr. 17, 1968; from Wednesday, May 29, 1968, to Monday, June 3, 1968; from Wednesday, July 3, 1968, to Monday, July 8, 1968; from Friday, Aug. 2, 1968, to Wednesday, Sept. 4, 1968.

59. The House was in recess this session from Friday, Feb. 7, 1969, to Monday, Feb. 17, 1969; from Thursday, Apr. 3, 1969, to Monday, Apr. 14, 1969; from Wednesday, May 28, 1969, to Monday, June 2, 1969; from Wednesday, July 2, 1969, to Monday, July 7, 1969; from Wednesday, Aug. 13, 1969, to Wednesday, Sept. 3, 1969; from Thursday, Nov. 6, 1969, to Wednesday, Nov. 12, 1969; from Wednesday, Nov. 26, 1969, to Monday, Dec. 1, 1969. The Senate was in recess this session from Friday, Feb. 7, 1969, to Monday, Feb. 17, 1969; from Thursday, Apr. 3, 1969, to Monday, Apr. 14, 1969; from Wednesday, July 2, 1969, to Monday, July 7, 1969; from Wednesday, Aug. 13, 1969, to Wednesday, Sept. 3, 1969; from Wednesday, Nov. 26, 1969, to Monday, Dec. 1, 1969.

60. The House was in recess this session from Tuesday, Feb. 10, 1970, to Monday, Feb. 16, 1970; from Thursday, Mar. 26, 1970, to Tuesday, Mar. 31, 1970; from Wednesday, May 27, 1970, to Monday, June 1, 1970; from Wednesday, July 1, 1970, to Monday, July 6, 1970; from Friday, Aug. 14, 1970, to Wednesday, Sept. 9, 1970; from Wednesday, Oct. 14, 1970, to Monday, Nov. 16, 1970; from Wednesday, Nov. 25, 1970, to Monday, Nov. 30, 1970; from Tuesday, Dec. 22, 1970, to Tuesday, Dec. 29, 1970. The Senate was in recess this session from Tuesday, Feb. 10, 1970, to Monday, Feb. 16, 1970; from Thursday, Mar. 26, 1970, to Tuesday, Mar. 31, 1970; from Wednesday, Sept. 2, 1970, to Tuesday, Sept. 8, 1970; from Wednesday, Oct. 14, 1970, to Monday, Nov. 16, 1970; from Wednesday, Nov. 25, 1970, to Monday, Nov. 30, 1970; from Tuesday, Dec. 22, 1970, to Monday, Dec. 28, 1970.

61. The House was in recess this session from Wednesday, Feb. 10, 1971, to Wednesday, Feb. 17, 1971; from Wednesday, Apr. 7, 1971, to Monday, Apr. 19, 1971; from Thursday, May 27, 1971, to Tuesday, June 1, 1971; from Thursday, July 1, 1971, to Tuesday, July 6, 1971; from Friday, Aug. 6, 1971, to Wednesday, Sept. 8, 1971; from Thursday, Oct. 7, 1971, to Tuesday, Oct. 12, 1971; from Thursday, Oct. 21, 1971, to Tuesday, Oct. 26, 1971; from Friday, Nov. 19, 1971, to Monday, Nov. 29, 1971. The Senate was in recess this session from Thursday, Feb. 11, 1971, to Wednesday, Feb. 17, 1971; from Wednesday, Apr. 7, 1971, to Wednesday, Apr. 14, 1971; from Wednesday, May 26, 1971, to Tuesday, June 1, 1971; from Wednesday, June 30, 1971, to Tuesday, July 6, 1971; from Friday, Aug. 6, 1971, to Wednesday, Sept. 8, 1971; from Thursday, Oct. 21, 1971, to Tuesday, Oct. 26, 1971; from Wednesday, Nov. 24, 1971, to Monday, Nov. 29, 1971.

62. Died Jan. 21, 1971.

63. Elected Jan. 22, 1971.

64. The House was in recess this session from Wednesday, Feb. 9, 1972, to Wednesday, Feb. 16, 1972; from Wednesday, Mar. 29, 1972, to Monday, Apr. 10, 1972; from Wednesday, May 24, 1972, to Tuesday, May 30, 1972; from Friday, June 30, 1972, to Monday, July 17, 1972; from Friday, Aug. 18, 1972, to Tuesday, Sept. 5, 1972. The Senate was in recess this session from Wednesday, Feb. 9, 1972, to Monday, Feb. 14, 1972; from Thursday, Mar. 30, 1972, to Tuesday, Apr. 4, 1972; from Thursday, May 25, 1972, to Tuesday, May 30, 1972; from Friday, June 30, 1972, to Monday, July 17, 1972; from Friday, Aug. 18, 1972, to Tuesday, Sept. 5, 1972.

65. Died July 27, 1972.

66. Elected July 28, 1972.

67. The House was in recess this session from Thursday, Feb. 8, 1973, to Monday, Feb. 19, 1973; from Thursday, Apr. 19, 1973, to Monday, Apr. 30, 1973; from Thursday, May 24, 1973, to Tuesday, May 29, 1973; from Saturday, June 30, 1973, to Tuesday, July 10, 1973; from Friday, Aug. 3, 1973, to Wednesday, Sept. 5, 1973; from Thursday, Oct. 4, 1973, to Tuesday, Oct. 9, 1973; from Thursday, Oct. 18, 1973, to Tuesday, Oct. 23, 1973; from Thursday, Nov. 15, 1973 to Monday, Nov. 26, 1973. The Senate was in recess this session from Thursday, Feb. 8, 1973, to Thursday, Feb. 15, 1973; from Wednesday, Apr. 18, 1973, to Monday, Apr. 30, 1973; from Wednesday, May 23, 1973, to Tuesday, May 29, 1973; from Saturday, June 30, 1973, to Monday, July 9, 1973; from Friday, Aug. 3, 1973, to Wednesday, Sept. 5, 1973; from Thursday, Oct. 18, 1973, to Tuesday, Oct. 23, 1973; from Wednesday, Nov. 21, 1973, to Monday, Nov. 26, 1973.

68. The House was in recess this session from Thursday, Feb. 7, 1974, to Wednesday, Feb. 13, 1974; from Thursday, Apr. 11, 1974, to Monday, Apr. 22, 1974; from Thursday, May 23, 1974, to Tuesday, May 28, 1974; from Thursday, Aug. 22, 1974, to Wednesday, Sept. 11, 1974; from Thursday, Oct. 17, 1974, to Monday, Nov. 18, 1974; from Tuesday, Nov. 26, 1974, to Tuesday, Dec. 3, 1974. The Senate was in recess this session from Friday, Feb. 8, 1974, to Monday, Feb. 18, 1974; from Wednesday, Mar. 13, 1974, to Tuesday, Mar. 19, 1974; from Thursday, Apr. 11, 1974, to Monday, Apr. 22, 1974; from Wednesday, May 23, 1974, to Tuesday, May 28, 1974; from Thursday, Aug. 22, 1974, to Wednesday, Sept. 4, 1974; from Thursday, Oct. 17, 1974, to Monday, Nov. 18, 1974; from Tuesday, Nov. 26, 1974, to Monday, Dec. 2, 1974.

69. The House was in recess this session from Wednesday, Mar. 26, 1975, to Monday, Apr. 7, 1975; from Thursday, May 22, 1975, to Monday, June 2, 1975; from Thursday, June 26, 1975, to Tuesday, July 8, 1975; from Friday, Aug. 1, 1975, to Wednesday, Sept. 3, 1975; from Thursday, Oct. 9, 1975, to Monday, Oct. 20, 1975; from Thursday, Oct. 23, 1975, to Tuesday, Oct. 28, 1975; from Thursday, Nov. 20, 1975, to Monday, Dec. 1, 1975. The Senate was in recess this session from Wednesday, Mar. 26, 1975, to Monday, Apr. 7, 1975; from Thursday, May 22, 1975, to Monday, June 2, 1975; from Friday, June 27, 1975, to Monday, July 7, 1975; from Friday, Aug. 1, 1975, to Wednesday, Sept. 3, 1975; from Thursday, Oct. 9, 1975, to Monday, Oct. 20,

1975; from Thursday, Oct. 23, 1975, to Tuesday, Oct. 28, 1975; from Thursday, Nov. 20, 1975, to Monday, Dec. 1, 1975.

70. The House was in recess this session from Wednesday, Feb. 11, 1976, to Monday, Feb. 16, 1976; from Wednesday, Apr. 14, 1976, to Monday, Apr. 26, 1976; from Thursday, May 27, 1976, to Tuesday, June 1, 1976; from Friday, July 2, 1976, to Monday, July 19, 1976; from Tuesday, Aug. 10, 1976, to Monday, Aug. 23, 1976; from Thursday, Sept. 2, 1976, to Wednesday, Sept. 8, 1976. The Senate was in recess this session from Friday, Feb. 6, 1976, to Monday, Feb. 16, 1976; from Wednesday, Apr. 14, 1976, to Monday, Apr. 26, 1976; from Friday, May 28, 1976, to Wednesday, June 2, 1976; from Friday, July 2, 1976, to Monday, July 19, 1976; from Tuesday, Aug. 10, 1976, to Monday, Aug. 23, 1976; from Wednesday, Sept. 1, 1976, to Tuesday, Sept. 7, 1976.

71. The House was in recess this session from Wednesday, Feb. 9, 1977, to Wednesday, Feb. 16, 1977; from Wednesday, Apr. 6, 1977, to Monday, Apr. 18, 1977; from Thursday, May 26, 1977, to Wednesday, June 1, 1977; from Thursday, June 30, 1977, to Monday, July 11, 1977; from Friday, Aug. 5, 1977, to Wednesday, Sept. 7, 1977; from Thursday, Oct. 6, 1977, to Tuesday, Oct. 11, 1977. The Senate was in recess this session from Friday, Feb. 11, 1977, to Monday, Feb. 21, 1977; from Thursday, Apr. 7, 1977, to Monday, Apr. 18, 1977; from Friday, May 27, 1977, to Monday, June 6, 1977; from Friday, July 1, 1977, to Monday, July 11, 1977; from Saturday, Aug. 6, 1977, to Wednesday, Sept. 7, 1977.

72. The House was in recess this session from Thursday, Feb. 9, 1978, to Tuesday, Feb. 14, 1978; from Wednesday, Mar. 22, 1978, to Monday, Apr. 3, 1978; from Thursday, May 25, 1978, to Wednesday, May 31, 1978; from Thursday, June 29, 1978, to Monday, July 10, 1978; from Thursday, Aug. 17, 1978, to Wednesday, Sept. 6, 1978. The Senate was in recess this session from Friday, Feb. 10, 1978, to Monday, Feb. 20, 1978; from Thursday, Mar. 23, 1978, to Monday, Apr. 3, 1978; from Friday, May 26, 1978, to Monday, June 5, 1978; from Thursday, June 29, 1978, to Monday, July 10, 1978; from Friday, Aug. 25, 1978, to Wednesday, Sept. 6, 1978.

73. The House was in recess this session from Thursday, Feb. 8, 1979, to Tuesday, Feb. 13, 1979; from Tuesday, Apr. 10, 1979, to Monday, Apr. 23, 1979; from Thursday, May 24, 1979, to Wednesday, May 30, 1979; from Friday, June 29, 1979, to Monday, July 9, 1979; from Thursday, Aug. 2, 1979, to Wednesday, Sept. 5, 1979; from Tuesday, Nov. 20, 1979, to Monday, Nov. 26, 1979. The Senate was in recess this session from Friday, Feb. 9, 1979, to Monday, Feb. 19, 1979; from Tuesday, Apr. 10, 1979, to Monday, Apr. 23, 1979; from Friday, May 25, 1979, to Monday, June 4, 1979; from Friday, Aug. 3, 1979, to Wednesday, Sept. 5, 1979; from Tuesday, Nov. 20, 1979, to Monday, Nov. 26, 1979.

74. The House was in recess this session from Wednesday, Feb. 13, 1980, to Tuesday, Feb. 19, 1980; from Wednesday, Apr. 2, 1980, to Tuesday, Apr. 15, 1980; from Thursday, May 22, 1980, to Wednesday, May 28, 1980; from Wednesday, July 2, 1980, to Monday, July 21, 1980; from Friday, Aug. 1, 1980, to Monday, Aug. 18, 1980; from Thursday, Aug. 28, 1980, to Wednesday, Sept. 13, 1980. The Senate was in recess this session from Monday, Feb. 11, 1980, to Thursday, Feb. 14, 1980; from Thursday, Apr. 3, 1980, to Tuesday, Apr. 15, 1980; from Thursday, May 22, 1980, to Wednesday, May 28, 1980; from Wednesday, July 2, 1980, to Monday, July 21, 1980; from Wednesday, Aug. 6, 1980, to Monday, Aug. 18, 1980; from Wednesday, Aug. 27, 1980, to Wednesday, Sept. 3, 1980; from Wednesday, Oct. 1, 1980, to Wednesday, Nov. 12, 1980; from Monday, Nov. 24, 1980, to Monday, Dec. 1, 1980.

75. The House was in recess this session from Friday, Feb. 6, 1981, to Tuesday, Feb. 17, 1981; from Friday, Apr. 10, 1981, to Monday, Apr. 27, 1981; from Friday, June 26, 1981, to Wednesday, July 8, 1981; from Tuesday, Aug. 4, 1981, to Wednesday, Sept. 9, 1981; from Wednesday, Oct. 7, 1981, to Tuesday, Oct. 13, 1981; from Monday, Nov. 23, 1981, to Monday, Nov. 30, 1981. The Senate was in recess this session from Friday, Feb. 6, 1981, to Monday, Feb. 16, 1981; from Friday, Apr. 10, 1981, to Monday, Apr. 27, 1981; from Thursday, June 25, 1981, to Wednesday, July 8, 1981; from Monday, Aug. 3, 1981, to Wednesday, Sept. 9, 1981; from Wednesday, Oct. 7, 1981, to Wednesday, Oct. 14, 1981; from Tuesday, Nov. 24, 1981, to Monday, Nov. 30, 1981.

76. The House was in recess this session from Wednesday, Feb. 10, 1982, to Monday, Feb. 22, 1982; from Tuesday, Apr. 6, 1982, to Tuesday, Apr. 20, 1982; from Thursday, May 27, 1982, to Wednesday, June 2, 1982; from Thursday, July 1, 1982, to Monday, July 12, 1982; from Friday, Aug. 20, 1982, to Wednesday, Sept. 8, 1982; from Friday, Oct. 1, 1982, to Monday, Nov. 29, 1982. The Senate was in recess this session from Thursday, Feb. 11, 1982, to Monday, Feb. 22, 1982; from Thursday, Apr. 1, 1982, to Tuesday, Apr. 13, 1982; from Thursday, May 27, 1982, to Tuesday, June 8, 1982; from Thursday, July 1, 1982, to Monday, July 12, 1982; from Friday, Aug. 20, 1982, to Wednesday, Sept. 8, 1982; from Friday, Oct. 1, 1982, to Monday, Nov. 29, 1982.

77. The House adjourned for recess this session Friday, Jan. 7, 1983, to Tuesday, Jan. 25, 1983; Thursday, Feb. 17, 1983, to Tuesday, Feb. 22, 1983; Thursday, March 24, 1983, to Tuesday, Apr. 5, 1983; Thursday, May 26, 1983, to Wednesday, June 1, 1983; Thursday, June 30, 1983, to Monday, July 11, 1983; Friday, Aug. 5, 1983, to Monday, Sept. 12, 1983; Friday, Oct. 7, 1983, to Monday, Oct. 17, 1983. The Senate adjourned for recess this session Monday, Jan. 3, 1983, to Tuesday, Jan. 25, 1983; Friday, Feb. 4, 1983, to Monday, Feb. 14, 1983; Friday, March 25, 1983, to Tuesday, Apr. 5, 1983; Friday, May 27, 1983, to Monday, June 6, 1983; Friday, July 1, 1983, to Monday, July 11, 1983; Friday, Aug. 5, 1983, to Monday, Sept. 12, 1983; Monday Oct. 10, 1983, to Monday, Oct. 17, 1983.

78. The House adjourned for recess this session Thursday, Feb. 9, 1984, to Tuesday, Feb. 21, 1984; Friday, Apr. 13, 1984, to Tuesday, Apr. 24, 1984; Friday, May 25, 1984, to Wednesday, May 30, 1984; Friday, June 29, 1984, to Monday, July 23, 1984; Friday, Aug. 10, 1984, to Wednesday, Sept. 5, 1984. The Senate adjourned for recess this session Friday, Feb. 10, 1984, to Monday, Feb. 20, 1984; Friday, Apr. 13, 1984, to Tuesday, Apr. 24, 1984; from Friday, May 25, 1984, to Thursday, May 31, 1984; from Friday, June 29, 1984, to Monday, July 23, 1984; Friday, Aug. 10, 1984, to Wednesday, Sept. 5, 1984.

79. The House adjourned for recess this session Monday, Jan. 7, 1985, to Monday, Jan. 21, 1985; Thursday, Feb. 7, 1985, to Tuesday, Feb. 19, 1985; Thursday, March 7, 1985, to Tuesday, March 19, 1985; Thursday, Apr. 4, 1985, to Monday, Apr. 15, 1985; Thursday, May 23, 1985, to Monday, June 3, 1985; Thursday, June 27, 1985, to Monday, July 8, 1985; Thursday, Aug. 1, 1985, to Wednesday, Sept. 4, 1985; Thursday, Nov. 21, 1985, to Monday, Dec. 2, 1985. The Senate adjourned for recess this session Monday, Jan. 7, 1985, to Monday, Jan. 21, 1985; Thursday, Feb. 7, 1985, to Monday, Feb. 18, 1985; Tuesday, March 12, 1985, to Thursday, March 14, 1985; Thursday, Apr. 4, 1985, to Monday, Apr. 15, 1985; Friday, May 24, 1985, to Monday, June 3, 1985; Thursday, June 27, 1985, to Monday, July 8, 1985; Thursday, Aug. 1, 1985, to Monday, Sept. 9, 1985; Saturday, Nov. 23, 1985, to Monday, Dec. 2, 1985.

80. The House adjourned for recess this session Tuesday, Jan. 7, 1986, to Tuesday, Jan. 21, 1986; Friday, Feb. 7, 1986, to Tuesday, Feb. 18, 1986; Tuesday, March 25, 1986, to Tuesday, Apr. 8, 1986; Thursday, May 22, 1986, to Tuesday, June 3, 1986; Thursday, June 26, 1986, to Monday, July 14, 1986; Friday, Aug. 15, 1986, to Monday, Sept. 8, 1986. The Senate adjourned for recess this session Tuesday, Jan. 7, 1986, to Tuesday, Jan. 21, 1986; Friday, Feb. 7, 1986, to Monday, Feb. 17, 1986; Thursday, March 27, 1986, to Tuesday, Apr. 8, 1986; Wednesday, May 21, 1986, to Monday, June 2, 1986; Thursday, June 26, 1986, to Monday, July 14, 1986; Friday, Aug. 15, 1986, to Monday, Sept. 8, 1986.

81. The House adjourned for recess this session Thursday, Jan. 8, 1987, to Tuesday, Jan. 20, 1987; Wednesday, Feb. 11, 1987, to Wednesday, Feb. 18, 1987; Thursday, Apr. 9, 1987, to Tuesday, Apr. 21, 1987; Thursday, May 21, 1987, to Wednesday, May 27, 1987; Wednesday, July 1, 1987, to Tuesday, July 7, 1987; Wednesday, July 15, 1987, to Monday, July 20, 1987; Friday, Aug. 7, 1987, to Wednesday, Sept. 9, 1987; Tuesday, Nov. 10, 1987, to Monday, Nov. 16, 1987; Friday, Nov. 20, 1987, to Monday, Nov. 30, 1987. The Senate adjourned for recess this session Tuesday, Jan. 6, 1987, to Monday, Jan. 12, 1987; Thursday, Feb. 5, 1987, to Monday, Feb. 16, 1987; Friday, Apr. 10, 1987, to Tuesday, Apr. 21, 1987; Thursday, May 21, 1987, to Wednesday, May 27, 1987; Wednesday, July 1, 1987, to Tuesday, July 7, 1987; Friday, Aug. 7, 1987, to Wednesday, Sept. 9, 1987; Friday, Nov. 20, 1987, to Monday, Nov. 30, 1987.

82. The House adjourned for recess this session Tuesday, Feb. 9, 1988, to Tuesday, Feb. 16, 1988; Thursday, March 31, 1988, to Monday, Apr. 11, 1988; Thursday, May 26, 1988, to Wednesday, June 1, 1988; Thursday, June 30, 1988, to Thursday, July 7, 1988; Thursday, July 14, 1988, to Tuesday, July 26, 1988; Thursday, Aug. 11, 1988, to Wednesday, Sept. 7, 1988. The Senate adjourned for recess this session Thursday, Feb. 4, 1988, to Monday, Feb. 15, 1988; Friday, March 4, 1988, to Monday, March 14, 1988; Thursday, March 31, 1988, to Monday, Apr. 11, 1988; Friday, Apr. 29, 1988, to Monday, May 9, 1988; Friday, May 27, 1988, to Monday, June 6, 1988; Wednesday, June 29, 1988, to Wednesday, July 6, 1988; Thursday, July 14, 1988, to Monday, July 25, 1988, Thursday, Aug. 11, 1988, to Wednesday, Sept. 7, 1988.

83. The House adjourned for recess this session Wednesday, Jan. 4, 1989, to Thursday, Jan. 19, 1989; Thursday, Feb. 9, 1989, to Tuesday, Feb. 21, 1989; Thursday, March 23, 1989, to Monday, Apr. 3, 1989; Tuesday, Apr. 18, 1989, to Tuesday, Apr. 25, 1989; Thursday, May 25, 1989, to Wednesday, May 31, 1989; Thursday, June 29, 1989, to Monday, July 10, 1989; Saturday, Aug. 5, 1989, to Wednesday, Sept. 6, 1989. The Senate adjourned for recess this session Wednesday, Jan. 4, 1989, to Friday, Jan. 20, 1989; Friday, Jan. 20, 1989, to Wednesday, Jan. 25, 1989; Thursday, Feb. 9, 1989, to Tuesday, Feb. 21, 1989; Friday, March 17, 1989, to Tuesday, Apr. 4, 1989; Wednesday, Apr. 19, 1989, to Monday, May 1, 1989; Thursday, May 18, 1989, to Wednesday, May 31, 1989; Friday, June 23, 1989, to Tuesday, July 11, 1989; Friday, Aug. 4, 1989, to Wednesday, Sept. 6, 1989.

84. Elected Speaker June 6, 1989, to succeed Jim Wright, who resigned the Speakership that day.

85. The House adjourned for recess this session Wednesday, Feb. 7, 1990, to Tuesday, Feb. 20, 1990; Wednesday, Apr. 4, 1990, to Wednesday, Apr. 18, 1990; Friday, May 25, 1990, to Tuesday, June 5, 1990; Thursday, June 28, 1990, to Tuesday, July 10, 1990; Saturday, Aug. 4, 1990, to Wednesday, Sept. 5, 1990. The Senate adjourned for recess this session Thursday, Feb. 8, 1990, to Tuesday, Feb. 20, 1990; Friday, March 9, 1990, to Tuesday, March 20, 1990; Thursday, Apr. 5, 1990, to Wednesday, Apr. 18, 1990; Thursday, May 24, 1990, to Tuesday, June 5, 1990; Thursday, June 28, 1990, to Tuesday, July 10, 1990; Saturday, Aug. 4, 1990, to Monday, Sept. 10, 1990.

86. The House adjourned for recess this session Wednesday, Feb. 6, 1991, to Tuesday, Feb. 19, 1991; Friday, March 22, 1991, to Tuesday, Apr. 9, 1991; Thursday, June 27, 1991, to Tuesday, July 9, 1991; Friday, Aug. 2, 1991, to Wednesday, Sept. 11, 1991. The Senate adjourned for recess this session Wednesday, Feb. 6, 1991, to Tuesday, Feb. 19, 1991; Friday, March 22, 1991, to Tuesday, Apr. 9, 1991; Thursday, Apr. 25, 1991, to Monday, May 6, 1991; Friday, May 24, 1991, to Monday, June 3, 1991; Friday, June 28, 1991, to Monday, July 8, 1991; Friday, Aug. 2, 1991, to Tuesday, Sept. 10, 1991.

87. The House adjourned for recess this session Friday, Jan. 3, 1992, to Wednesday, Jan. 22, 1992; Friday, Apr. 10, 1992, to Tuesday, April 28, 1992; Thursday, July 2, 1992, to Tuesday, July 7, 1992; Friday, July 9, 1992, to Tuesday, July 21, 1992; Wednesday, Aug. 12, 1992, to Wednesday, Sept. 9, 1992. The Senate adjourned for recess this session Monday, Jan. 6, 1992, to Monday, Jan. 20, 1992; Monday, Feb. 10, 1992, to Monday, Feb. 17, 1992; Monday, Apr. 13, 1992, to Friday, Apr. 24, 1992; Monday, May 25, 1992, to Friday, May 29, 1992; Monday, July 6, 1992, to Friday, July 17, 1992; Thursday, Aug. 13, 1992, to Monday, Sept. 7, 1992.

88. The House adjourned for recess this session Thursday, Jan. 7, 1993, to Tuesday, Jan. 19, 1993; Friday, Feb. 5, 1993, to Monday, Feb. 15, 1993; Thursday, Apr. 8, 1993, to Sunday, Apr. 18, 1993; Friday, May 28, 1993, to Monday, June 7, 1993; Friday, July 2, 1993, to Monday, July 12, 1993; Saturday, Aug. 7, 1993, to Tuesday, Sept. 7, 1993. The Senate adjourned for recess this session Friday, Jan. 8, 1993, to Tuesday, Jan. 19, 1993; Friday, Feb. 5, 1993, to Monday, Feb. 15, 1993; Monday, Apr. 5, 1993, to Friday, Apr. 16, 1993; Monday, May 31, 1993, to Friday, June 4, 1993; Friday, July 2, 1993, to Friday, July 9, 1993; Monday, Aug. 9, 1993, to Monday, Sept. 6, 1993; Friday, Oct. 8, 1993, to Tuesday, Oct. 12, 1993; Friday, Nov. 12, 1993, to Monday Nov. 15, 1993.

89. The House adjourned for recess this session Thursday, Jan. 27, 1994, to Monday, Jan. 31, 1994; Saturday, Feb. 12, 1994, to Monday, Feb. 21, 1994; Friday, March 25, 1994, to Monday, Apr. 11, 1994; Friday, May 27, 1994, to Tuesday, June 7, 1994; Friday, July 1, 1994, to Monday, July 11, 1994; Saturday, Aug. 27, 1994, to Sunday, Sept. 11, 1994. The Senate adjourned for recess this session Monday, Feb. 14, 1994, to Monday, Feb. 21, 1994; Monday, March 28, 1994, to Friday, Apr. 8, 1994; Monday, May 30, 1994, to Monday, June 6, 1994; Monday, July 4, 1994, to Friday, July 8, 1994; Friday, Aug. 26, 1994, to Friday, Sept. 9, 1994.

90. The House adjourned for recess this session Saturday, Apr. 8, 1995, to Sunday, Apr. 30, 1995; Friday, May 26, 1995, to Monday, June 5, 1995; Saturday, July 1, 1995, to Sunday, July 9, 1995; Saturday, Aug. 5, 1995, to Tuesday, Sept. 5, 1995; Saturday, Sept. 30, 1995, to Thursday, Oct. 5, 1995. The Senate adjourned for recess this session Friday, Feb. 17, 1995, to Tuesday, Feb. 21,

1995; Saturday, Apr. 8, 1995, to Sunday, Apr. 23, 1995; Saturday, May 27, 1995, to Sunday, June 4, 1995; Saturday, July 1, 1995, to Sunday, July 9, 1995; Saturday, Aug. 12, 1995, to Monday, Sept. 4, 1995; Sunday, Oct. 1, 1995, to Monday, Oct. 9, 1995; Saturday, Nov. 21, 1995, to Sunday, Nov. 26, 1995.

91. The House adjourned for recess this session Wednesday, Jan. 10, 1996, to Sunday, Jan. 21, 1996; Saturday, March 30, 1996, to Sunday, Apr. 14, 1996; Saturday, June 29, 1996, to Sunday, July 7, 1996; Saturday, Aug. 3, 1996, to Tuesday, Sept. 3, 1996. The Senate adjourned for recess this session Thursday, Jan. 11, 1996, to Sunday, Jan. 21, 1996; Saturday, March 30, 1996, to Saturday, Apr. 14, 1996; Saturday, May 25, 1996, to Sunday, June 2, 1996; Saturday, June 29, 1996, to Sunday, July 7, 1996; Saturday, Aug. 3, 1996, to Monday, Sept. 2, 1996.

92. The House adjourned for recess this session Friday, Jan. 10, 1997, to Sunday, Jan. 19, 1997; Wednesday, Jan. 22, 1997, to Monday, Feb. 3, 1997; Friday, Feb. 14, 1997, to Monday, Feb. 24, 1997; Saturday, March 22, 1997, to Monday, Apr. 7, 1997; Friday, June 27, 1997, to Monday, July 7, 1997; Saturday, Aug. 2, 1997, to Tuesday, Sept. 2, 1997; Friday, Oct. 10, 1997, to Monday, Oct. 20, 1997. The Senate adjourned for recess this session Friday, Jan. 10, 1997, to Monday, Jan. 20, 1997; Friday, Feb. 14, 1997, to Sunday, Feb. 23, 1997; Saturday, March 22, 1997, to Sunday, Apr. 6, 1997; Saturday, May 24, 1997, to Sunday, June 1, 1997; Saturday, June 28, 1997, to Sunday, July 6, 1997; Saturday, Aug. 2, 1997, to Monday, Sept. 1, 1997; Friday, Oct. 10, 1997, to Sunday, Oct. 19, 1997.

93. The House adjourned for recess this session Friday, Feb. 13, 1998, to Monday, Feb. 23, 1998; Thursday, Apr. 2, 1998, to Monday, Apr. 20, 1998; Saturday, May 23, 1998, to Tuesday, June 2, 1998; Friday, June 26, 1998, to Monday, July 13, 1998; Saturday, Aug. 8, 1998, to Tuesday, Sept. 8, 1998. The House adjourned Oct. 21, 1998, and was called back by the Speaker for a resumption of the second session Thursday, Dec. 17, 1998, to Saturday, Dec. 19, 1998. The Senate adjourned for recess this session Thursday, Jan. 1, 1998, to Monday, Jan. 26, 1998; Saturday, Feb. 14, 1998, to Sunday, Feb. 22, 1998; Saturday, Apr. 4, 1998, to Sunday, Apr. 19, 1998; Saturday, May 23, 1998, to Sunday, May 31, 1998; Saturday, June 27, 1998, to Sunday, July 5, 1998; Saturday, Aug. 1, 1998, to Sunday, Aug. 30, 1998; Saturday, Sept. 5, 1998, to Monday, Sept. 7, 1998.

94. The House adjourned for recess this session Wednesday, Jan. 6, 1999, to Tuesday, Jan. 19, 1999; Tuesday, Jan. 19, 1999, to Tuesday, Feb. 2, 1999; Friday, Feb. 12, 1999, to Tuesday, Feb. 23, 1999; Thursday, March 25, 1999, to Monday, April 12, 1999; Thursday, May 27, 1999, to Monday, June 7, 1999; Saturday, July 3, 1999, to Sunday, July 11, 1999; Saturday, Aug. 7, 1999, to Tuesday, Sept. 7, 1999. The Senate adjourned for recess this session Friday, Feb. 12, 1999, to Monday, Feb. 22, 1999; Thursday, March 25, 1999, to Monday, Apr. 12, 1999; Thursday, May 27, 1999, to Monday, June 7, 1999; Saturday, July 3, 1999, to Sunday, July 11, 1999; Saturday, Aug. 7, 1999, to Tuesday, Sept. 7, 1999; Saturday, Oct. 9, 1999, to Monday, Oct. 11, 1999.

95. The House adjourned for recess this session Saturday, Feb. 19, 2000, to Sunday, Feb. 27, 2000; Saturday, April 15, 2000, to Sunday, April 30, 2000; Saturday, May 27, 2000, to Sunday, June 4, 2000; Saturday, July 1, 2000, to Sunday, July 9, 2000; Monday July 31, 2000, to Tuesday, Sept. 5, 2000. The Senate adjourned for recess this session Saturday, Feb. 12, 2000, to Monday, Feb. 21, 2000; Saturday, March 11, 2000, to Sunday, March 19, 2000; Saturday, April 15, 2000, to Sunday, April 24, 2000; Saturday, May 27, 2000, to Sunday, June 4, 2000; Saturday, July 1, 2000, to Sunday, July 9, 2000; Saturday, July 29, 2000, to Monday, Sept. 4, 2000; Friday, Sept. 29, 2000, to Sunday, Oct. 1, 2000.

Sources: For 1789–1990: *Official Congressional Directory.* For 1991–2000: Calendars of the U.S. House of Representatives and the U.S. Senate.

Speakers of the House of Representatives, 1789–2001

Congress		Speaker	Congress		Speaker
1st	(1789–1791)	Frederick A. C. Muhlenberg, Pa.	50th	(1887–1889)	Carlisle
2nd	(1791–1793)	Jonathan Trumbull, F-Conn.	51st	(1889–1891)	Thomas Brackett Reed, R-Maine
3rd	(1793–1795)	Muhlenberg	52nd	(1891–1893)	Charles F. Crisp, D-Ga.
4th	(1795–1797)	Jonathan Dayton, F-N.J.	53rd	(1893–1895)	Crisp
5th	(1797–1799)	Dayton	54th	(1895–1897)	Reed
6th	(1799–1801)	Theodore Sedgwick, F-Mass.	55th	(1897–1899)	Reed
7th	(1801–1803)	Nathaniel Macon, D-N.C.	56th	(1899–1901)	David B. Henderson, R-Iowa
8th	(1803–1805)	Macon	57th	(1901–1903)	Henderson
9th	(1805–1807)	Macon	58th	(1903–1905)	Joseph G. Cannon, R-Ill.
10th	(1807–1809)	Joseph B. Varnum, Mass.	59th	(1905–1907)	Cannon
11th	(1809–1811)	Varnum	60th	(1907–1909)	Cannon
12th	(1811–1813)	Henry Clay, R-Ky.	61st	(1909–1911)	Cannon
13th	(1813–1814)	Clay	62nd	(1911–1913)	James B. "Champ" Clark, D-Mo.
	(1814–1815)	Langdon Cheves, D-S.C.	63rd	(1913–1915)	Clark
14th	(1815–1817)	Clay	64th	(1915–1917)	Clark
15th	(1817–1819)	Clay	65th	(1917–1919)	Clark
16th	(1819–1820)	Clay	66th	(1919–1921)	Frederick H. Gillett, R-Mass.
	(1820–1821)	John W. Taylor, D-N.Y.	67th	(1921–1923)	Gillett
17th	(1821–1823)	Philip P. Barbour, D-Va.	68th	(1923–1925)	Gillett
18th	(1823–1825)	Clay	69th	(1925–1927)	Nicholas Longworth, R-Ohio
19th	(1825–1827)	Taylor	70th	(1927–1929)	Longworth
20th	(1827–1829)	Andrew Stevenson, D-Va.	71st	(1929–1931)	Longworth
21st	(1829–1831)	Stevenson	72nd	(1931–1933)	John Nance Garner, D-Texas
22nd	(1831–1833)	Stevenson	73rd	(1933–1934)	Henry T. Rainey, D-Ill.[1]
23rd	(1833–1834)	Stevenson	74th	(1935–1936)	Joseph W. Byrns, D-Tenn.
	(1834–1835)	John Bell, W-Tenn.		(1936–1937)	William B. Bankhead, D-Ala.
24th	(1835–1837)	James K. Polk, D-Tenn.	75th	(1937–1939)	Bankhead
25th	(1837–1839)	Polk	76th	(1939–1940)	Bankhead
26th	(1839–1841)	Robert M. T. Hunter, D-Va.		(1940–1941)	Sam Rayburn, D-Texas
27th	(1841–1843)	John White, W-Ky.	77th	(1941–1943)	Rayburn
28th	(1843–1845)	John W. Jones, D-Va.	78th	(1943–1945)	Rayburn
29th	(1845–1847)	John W. Davis, D-Ind.	79th	(1945–1947)	Rayburn
30th	(1847–1849)	Robert C. Winthrop, W-Mass.	80th	(1947–1949)	Joseph W. Martin Jr., R-Mass.
31st	(1849–1851)	Howell Cobb, D-Ga.	81st	(1949–1951)	Rayburn
32nd	(1851–1853)	Linn Boyd, D-Ky.	82nd	(1951–1953)	Rayburn
33rd	(1853–1855)	Boyd	83rd	(1953–1955)	Martin
34th	(1855–1857)	Nathaniel P. Banks, R-Mass.	84th	(1955–1957)	Rayburn
35th	(1857–1859)	James L. Orr, D-S.C.	85th	(1957–1959)	Rayburn
36th	(1859–1861)	William Pennington, R-N.J.	86th	(1959–1961)	Rayburn
37th	(1861–1863)	Galusha A. Grow, R-Pa.	87th	(1961)	Rayburn
38th	(1863–1865)	Schuyler Colfax, R-Ind.		(1962–1963)	John W. McCormack, D-Mass.
39th	(1865–1867)	Colfax	88th	(1963–1965)	McCormack
40th	(1867–1869)	Colfax	89th	(1965–1967)	McCormack
	(1869)	Theodore M. Pomeroy, R-N.Y.	90th	(1967–1969)	McCormack
41st	(1869–1871)	James G. Blaine, R-Maine	91st	(1969–1971)	McCormack
42nd	(1871–1873)	Blaine	92nd	(1971–1973)	Carl Albert, D-Okla.
43rd	(1873–1875)	Blaine	93rd	(1973–1975)	Albert
44th	(1875–1876)	Michael C. Kerr, D-Ind.	94th	(1975–1977)	Albert
	(1876–1877)	Samuel J. Randall, D-Pa.	95th	(1977–1979)	Thomas P. O'Neill Jr., D-Mass.
45th	(1877–1879)	Randall	96th	(1979–1981)	O'Neill
46th	(1879–1881)	Randall	97th	(1981–1983)	O'Neill
47th	(1881–1883)	Joseph Warren Keifer, R-Ohio	98th	(1983–1985)	O'Neill
48th	(1883–1885)	John G. Carlisle, D-Ky.			
49th	(1885–1887)	Carlisle			

Congress		Speaker	Congress		Speaker
99th	(1985–1987)	O'Neill	103rd	(1993–1995)	Foley
100th	(1987–1989)	Jim Wright, D-Texas	104th	(1995–1997)	Newt Gingrich, R-Ga.
101st	(1989)	Wright[2]	105th	(1997–1999)	Gingrich
	(1989–1991)	Thomas S. Foley, D-Wash.	106th	(1999– 2001)	J. Dennis Hastert, R-Ill.
102nd	(1991–1993)	Foley	107th	(2001–)	Hastert

Notes: Key to abbreviations: D—Democrat; F—Federalist; R— Republican; W—Whig.

1. Rainey died in 1934, but was not replaced until the next Congress.

2. Wright resigned and was succeeded by Foley on June 6, 1989.

Sources: 1999–2000 Congressional Directory, 106th Congress (Washington, D.C.: Government Printing OYce, 1999); *CQ Weekly,* selected issues.

House Floor Leaders, 1899–2001

Congress		Majority	Minority
6th	(1899–1901)	Sereno E. Payne, R-N.Y.	James D. Richardson, D-Tenn.
57th	(1901–1903)	Payne	Richardson
58th	(1903–1905)	Payne	John Sharp Williams, D-Miss.
59th	(1905–1907)	Payne	Williams
60th	(1907–1909)	Payne	Williams/Champ Clark, D-Mo.[1]
61st	(1909–1911)	Payne	Clark
62nd	(1911–1913)	Oscar W. Underwood, D-Ala.	James R. Mann, R-Ill.
63rd	(1913–1915)	Underwood	Mann
64th	(1915–1917)	Claude Kitchin, D-N.C.	Mann
65th	(1917–1919)	Kitchin	Mann
66th	(1919–1921)	Franklin W. Mondell, R-Wyo.	Clark
67th	(1921–1923)	Mondell	Claude Kitchin, D-N.C.
68th	(1923–1925)	Nicholas Longworth, R-Ohio	Finis J. Garrett, D-Tenn.
69th	(1925–1927)	John Q. Tilson, R-Conn.	Garrett
70th	(1927–1929)	Tilson	Garrett
71st	(1929–1931)	Tilson	John N. Garner, D-Texas
72nd	(1931–1933)	Henry T. Rainey, D-Ill.	Bertrand H. Snell, R-N.Y.
73rd	(1933–1935)	Joseph W. Byrns, D-Tenn.	Snell
74th	(1935–1937)	William B. Bankhead, D-Ala.[2]	Snell
75th	(1937–1939)	Sam Rayburn, D-Texas	Snell
76th	(1939–1941)	Rayburn/John W. McCormack, D-Mass.[3]	Joseph W. Martin Jr., R-Mass.
77th	(1941–1943)	McCormack	Martin
78th	(1943–1945)	McCormack	Martin
79th	(1945–1947)	McCormack	Martin
80th	(1947–1949)	Charles A. Halleck, R-Ind.	Sam Rayburn, D-Texas
81st	(1949–1951)	McCormack	Martin
82nd	(1951–1953)	McCormack	Martin
83rd	(1953–1955)	Halleck	Rayburn
84th	(1955–1957)	McCormack	Martin
85th	(1957–1959)	McCormack	Martin
86th	(1959–1961)	McCormack	Charles A. Halleck, R-Ind.
87th	(1961–1963)	McCormack/Carl Albert, D-Okla.[4]	Halleck
88th	(1963–1965)	Albert	Halleck
89th	(1965–1967)	Albert	Gerald R. Ford, R-Mich.
90th	(1967–1969)	Albert	Ford
91st	(1969–1971)	Albert	Ford
92nd	(1971–1973)	Hale Boggs, D-La.	Ford
93rd	(1973–1975)	Thomas P. O'Neill Jr., D-Mass.	Ford/John J. Rhodes, R-Ariz.[5]
94th	(1975–1977)	O'Neill	Rhodes
95th	(1977–1979)	Jim Wright, D-Texas	Rhodes
96th	(1979–1981)	Wright	Rhodes
97th	(1981–1983)	Wright	Robert H. Michel, R Ill.
98th	(1983–1985)	Wright	Michel
99th	(1985–1987)	Wright	Michel
100th	(1987–1989)	Thomas S. Foley, D-Wash.	Michel

Congress		Majority	Minority
101st	(1989–1991)	Foley/Richard A. Gephardt, D-Mo.[6]	Michel
102nd	(1991–1993)	Gephardt	Michel
103rd	(1993–1995)	Gephardt	Michel
104th	(1995–1997)	Dick Armey, R-Texas	Richard A. Gephardt, D-Mo.
105th	(1997–1999)	Armey	Gephardt
106th	(1999–2001)	Armey	Gephardt
107th	(2001–)	Armey	Gephardt

1. Clark became minority leader in 1908.

2. Bankhead became Speaker of the House on June 4, 1936. The post of majority leader remained vacant until the next Congress.

3. McCormack became majority leader on Sept. 26, 1940, filling the vacancy caused by the elevation of Rayburn to the post of Speaker of the House on Sept. 16, 1940.

4. Albert became majority leader on Jan. 10, 1962, filling the vacancy caused by the elevation of McCormack to the post of Speaker of the House on Jan. 10, 1962.

5. Rhodes became minority leader on Dec. 7, 1973, filling the vacancy caused by the resignation of Ford on Dec. 6, 1973, to become vice president.

6. Gephardt became majority leader on June 14, 1989, filling the vacancy created when Foley succeeded Wright as Speaker of the House on June 6, 1989.

Sources: Randall B. Ripley, *Party Leaders in the House of Representatives* (Washington, D.C.: Brookings Institution, 1967); *Biographical Directory of the American Congress, 1774–1996* (Alexandria, Va.: CQ StaV Directories, 1997); *CQ Weekly*, selected issues.

Senate Floor Leaders, 1911–2001

Congress		Majority	Minority
62nd	(1911–1913)	Shelby M. Cullom, R-Ill.	Thomas S. Martin, D-Va.
63rd	(1913–1915)	John W. Kern, D-Ind.	Jacob H. Gallinger, R-N.H.
64th	(1915–1917)	Kern	Gallinger
65th	(1917–1919)	Thomas S. Martin, D-Va.	Gallinger/Henry Cabot Lodge, R-Mass.[1]
66th	(1919–1921)	Henry Cabot Lodge, R-Mass.	Martin/Oscar W. Underwood, D-Ala.[2]
67th	(1921–1923)	Lodge	Underwood
68th	(1923–1925)	Lodge/Charles Curtis, R-Kan.[3]	Joseph T. Robinson, D-Ark.
69th	(1925–1927)	Curtis	Robinson
70th	(1927–1929)	Curtis	Robinson
71st	(1929–1931)	James E. Watson, R-Ind.	Robinson
72nd	(1931–1933)	Watson	Robinson
73rd	(1933–1935)	Joseph T. Robinson, D-Ark.	Charles L. McNary, R-Ore.
74th	(1935–1937)	Robinson	McNary
75th	(1937–1939)	Robinson/Alben W. Barkley, D-Ky.[4]	McNary
76th	(1939–1941)	Barkley	McNary
77th	(1941–1943)	Barkley	McNary
78th	(1943–1945)	Barkley	McNary
79th	(1945–1947)	Barkley	Wallace H. White Jr., R-Maine
80th	(1947–1949)	Wallace H. White Jr., R-Maine	Alben W. Barkley, D-Ky.
81st	(1949–1951)	Scott W. Lucas, D-Ill.	Kenneth S. Wherry, R-Neb.
82nd	(1951–1953)	Ernest W. McFarland, D-Ariz.	Wherry/Styles Bridges, R-N.H.[5]
83rd	(1953–1955)	Robert A. Taft, R-Ohio/ William F. Knowland, R-Calif.[6]	Lyndon B. Johnson, D-Texas
84th	(1955–1957)	Lyndon B. Johnson, D-Texas	William F. Knowland, R-Calif.
85th	(1957–1959)	Johnson	Knowland
86th	(1959–1961)	Johnson	Everett McKinley Dirksen, R-Ill.
87th	(1961–1963)	Mike Mansfield, D-Mont.	Dirksen
88th	(1963–1965)	Mansfield	Dirksen
89th	(1965–1967)	Mansfield	Dirksen
90th	(1967–1969)	Mansfield	Dirksen
91st	(1969–1971)	Mansfield	Dirksen/Hugh Scott, R-Pa.[7]
92nd	(1971–1973)	Mansfield	Scott
93rd	(1973–1975)	Mansfield	Scott
94th	(1975–1977)	Mansfield	Scott
95th	(1977–1979)	Robert C. Byrd, D-W.Va.	Howard H. Baker Jr., R-Tenn.
96th	(1979–1981)	Byrd	Baker
97th	(1981–1983)	Howard H. Baker Jr., R-Tenn.	Robert C. Byrd, D-W.Va.
98th	(1983–1985)	Baker	Byrd
99th	(1985–1987)	Bob Dole, R-Kan.	Byrd
100th	(1987–1989)	Byrd	Bob Dole, R-Kan.
101st	(1989–1991)	George J. Mitchell, D-Maine	Dole
102nd	(1991–1993)	Mitchell	Dole
103rd	(1993–1995)	Mitchell	Dole
104th	(1995–1997)	Bob Dole, R-Kan./Trent Lott, R-Miss.[8]	Tom Daschle, D-S.D.
105th	(1997–1999)	Lott	Daschle

106th	(1999–2001)	Lott	Daschle
107th	(2001–)	Lott/Tom Daschle, D-SD[9]	Daschle/Trent Lott, R-Miss.[9]

1. Lodge became minority leader on Aug. 24, 1918, filling the vacancy caused by the death of Gallinger on Aug. 17, 1918.

2. Underwood became minority leader on April 27, 1920, filling the vacancy caused by the death of Martin on Nov. 12, 1919. Gilbert M. Hitchcock, D-Neb., served as acting minority leader in the interim.

3. Curtis became majority leader on Nov. 28, 1924, filling the vacancy caused by the death of Lodge on Nov. 9, 1924.

4. Barkley became majority leader on July 22, 1937, filling the vacancy caused by the death of Robinson on July 14, 1937.

5. Bridges became minority leader on Jan. 8, 1952, filling the vacancy caused by the death of Wherry on Nov. 29, 1951.

6. Knowland became majority leader on Aug. 4, 1953, filling the vacancy caused by the death of Taft on July 31, 1953. Taft's vacant seat was filled by Democrat Thomas Burke on Nov. 10, 1953. The division of the Senate changed to 48 Democrats, 47 Republicans, and 1 Independent, thus giving control of the Senate to the Democrats. However, Knowland remained as majority leader until the end of the 83rd Congress.

7. Scott became minority leader on Sept. 24, 1969, filling the vacancy caused by the death of Dirksen on Sept. 7, 1969.

8. Lott became majority leader on June 12, 1996, following the resignation of Dole on June 11.

9. Daschle became majority leader on June 5, 2001, when Republican Jim Jeffords became an Independent. Lott became minority leader.

Sources: Biographical Directory of the American Congress, 1774–1996 (Alexandria, Va.: CQ Staff Directories, 1997); Majority and Minority Leaders of the Senate, comp. Floyd M. Riddick, 94th Cong., 1st sess., 1975, S Doc 66; *CQ Weekly,* selected issues.

Election-Related Web Sites

THOUSANDS OF Internet sites provide information about elections and politics. These Web sites are operated by candidates, political parties, interest groups, think tanks, trade associations, labor unions, businesses, government agencies, news organizations, polling firms, universities, and individuals.

Election-oriented sites can have very short lives. Many spring up just before a particular election and then go dark once the ballots are counted. The sites listed below, however, have proven themselves to be stable sources of ongoing election information—at least as of July 2001.

BALLOT ACCESS NEWS

http://www.ballot-access.org

The full text of the newsletter *Ballot Access News* from early 1994 to the present is available at this site. The newsletter publishes news about efforts around the country to overturn laws that restrict ballot access by candidates.

BALLOT WATCH

http://www.ballotwatch.org

A database at Ballot Watch has details about initiatives and referendums that are moving toward qualification on state ballots or that have already qualified in states around the country. You can search the database by subject, status, state, and type of measure.

THE BROOKINGS INSTITUTION: CAMPAIGN FINANCE REFORM

http://www.brook.edu/GS/CF/CF_HP.HTM

This page at the Brookings Institution's Web site has updates about campaign finance reform legislation in Congress, analyses of recent court decisions in campaign finance cases, links to related sites, and background information about topics such as campaign finance laws, First Amendment issues, soft money, and issue advocacy.

CENSUS: VOTING AND REGISTRATION DATA

http://www.census.gov/population/www/socdemo/voting.html

The U.S. Census Bureau operates this site, which has data about registration and voting by various demographic and socioeconomic groups. Data are available from 1964 to the present.

ELECNET

http://www.debexar.com/elecnet/index.cfm

ELECnet provides more than 400 links to Web sites operated by state, county, and city elections offices around the country.

The links are arranged by state. It also has links to federal agencies that provide election information and national organizations that host election-oriented Web sites.

ELECTION NOTES

http://www.klipsan.com/elecnews.htm

This site's highlight is its links to current election news stories from around the world. It also has the full text of a book titled *Atlas of United States Presidential Elections,* links to worldwide election calendars, links to election results, and much more. It's operated by Klipsan Press.

ELECTORAL COLLEGE HOME PAGE

http://www.nara.gov/fedreg/elctcoll/index.html

Background information about how the electoral college operates is available at this site. It also has results for popular votes and electoral college votes in presidential elections from 1789 to the present, and provisions of the U.S. Constitution and federal law pertaining to presidential elections.

FEDERAL ELECTION COMMISSION

http://www.fec.gov

This site's main feature is a database of campaign finance reports filed from May 1996 to the present by House and presidential candidates, political action committees, and political party committees. Senate reports are not included because they're filed with the Secretary of the Senate. Another valuable resource is the *Combined Federal/State Disclosure and Election Directory,* which provides detailed information about every federal and state office that collects campaign finance data or regulates election spending. For each office, the publication lists the types of data that are available and complete contact information, including a link to the office's Web site.

INTERNATIONAL FOUNDATION FOR ELECTION SYSTEMS

http://www.ifes.org/index.htm

One of this site's highlights is its collection of links to Web sites operated by election commissions and other election-related organizations in countries around the world. It also provides a worldwide election calendar, links to news about current elections, and a newsletter titled *Elections Today.*

THE NEW YORK TIMES: POLITICS

http://www.nytimes.com/pages/politics/index.html

Political stories from the current day's issue of the *New York Times* are available through this site. It also offers breaking Washington news stories from the Associated Press, archived

Times stories about specific political topics, results from political polls, and political cartoons by a variety of artists.

OPENSECRETS.ORG

http://www.opensecrets.org

Both raw data about money in politics and reports that analyze all the numbers are available at this site. It's operated by the Center for Responsive Politics, a nonprofit research group. Numerous databases provide detailed campaign finance data for federal candidates and information about contributions by political action committees. The site also has lists of the top federal contributors by industry, profiles of every political action committee registered with the Federal Election Commission, data about soft money contributions, links to sources of state campaign finance data, reports with titles such as *Influence Inc.: The Bottom Line on Washington Lobbyists* and *The Politics of Sugar*, and much more.

THE PEW RESEARCH CENTER FOR THE PEOPLE & THE PRESS

http://www.people-press.org

The Pew site presents the results of polls regarding the press, politics, and public policy issues conducted from 1995 to the present. The polls measure public attitudes about topics such as China policy, Congress, the economy, elections, and the Internet's impact in elections.

POLITICAL MONEY LINE

http://www.tray.com/fecinfo

Political Money Line, which is operated by a private company, offers an extraordinary collection of federal campaign finance data. The site has lists of the top contributors from each state, lists of the leading political action committees in various categories, data on soft money contributions, numerous databases that provide itemized information about receipts and expenditures by federal candidates and political action committees, and much more. Most of the information is free, although some sections of the site are limited to subscribers.

POLITICAL RESOURCES ON THE NET

http://www.politicalresources.net

Links to more than 24,000 election and politics-related sites Web sites around the world are presented at this site. The links lead to sites operated by political parties, organizations, governments, media outlets, and others. You can browse the links by region or country, and you also can search the whole site.

POLITICAL SCIENCE RESOURCES: UNITED STATES POLITICS

http://www.lib.umich.edu/libhome/Documents.center/psusp.html

This site from the University of Michigan Documents Center offers links to hundreds of Web sites about politics and elections. The listings are divided into more than two dozen categories, including campaign finances, cybercitizenry, elections, foreign policy, lobby groups, news sources, political parties, primaries, public opinion, public policy issues, statistics, and think tanks, among others.

POLITICS1

http://www.politics1.com

Politics1 provides a huge set of annotated links to Web sites operated by candidates, political parties, election offices, and election news sources in states around the country. It also has links to sites for presidential candidates, the two major parties, third parties, and political news sources.

POLITICSONLINE

http://www.politicsonline.com

This site's highlight is its large collection of links to news stories about how the Internet is being used in elections and politics around the world.

PROJECT VOTE SMART

http://www.vote-smart.org

The Project Vote Smart site provides biographies of thousands of candidates and elected officials in offices ranging from state legislator to president, voting records for members of Congress, detailed campaign finance data for members of Congress, the texts of ballot initiatives from states around the country, links to thousands of other political Web sites, and lots more.

WASHINGTONPOST.COM: ON POLITICS

http://www.washingtonpost.com/wp-dyn/politics

The latest political news from the *Washington Post* and the Associated Press highlights this page. It also has archived stories about dozens of political issues such as gun control and health care, election coverage, and more.

YAHOO! NEWS: ELECTORAL REFORM AND REDISTRICTING

http://fullcoverage.yahoo.com/fc/US/US_Elections

Hundreds of news stories about elections, election reform, and redistricting are available through this Yahoo! page. Sources include the *New York Times, Chicago Tribune, Washington Post, Boston Globe, Denver Post, Dallas Morning News, Los Angeles Times, Christian Science Monitor, Philadelphia Inquirer, Roll Call,* CNN, and the BBC, among others.

Political Party Abbreviations

THE FOLLOWING LIST provides a key to the political party abbreviations used in *Guide to U.S. Elections*, Fourth Edition. This list was developed by Congressional Quarterly from two sources for party designations: the Inter-University Consortium for Political and Social Research (ICPSR), for most election returns up to 1973; and the *America Votes* series (compiled biennially by Congressional Quarterly in Washington, D.C.) for most election returns after 1974. In cases of discrepancy, the ICPSR party designation was used.

The election data obtained from the ICPSR contain nearly 1,500 different party labels. In many cases the party labels represent combinations of multiparty support received by individual candidates. However, in preparing the returns for publication, approximately 1,000 of the party labels were eliminated because the candidate(s) did not receive at least 5 percent of the votes cast. The names of the parties appear below in the form they were obtained from ICPSR and *America Votes*.

A-A	Anti-Adams	A-LOT D	Anti-Lottery Democrat	A VB D	Anti-Van Buren Democrat
A-AK R	Anti-Addicks Republican	AM	American		
AB	Abolition	A-MACH	Anti-Machine	A-WOLF D	Anti-Wolf Democrat
A-BANK	Anti-Bank	A-MAINE	Anti-Maine Law	BALLOT	Ballot Reform
AB-D	Abolition-Democrat	A-MAS	Anti-Mason	BARN D	Barnburner Democrat
A-BEN D	Anti-Benton Democrat	A-MASC	Anti-Masonic	BC	Butter Congressional
A-BOSS	Anti-Boss	A-MASDNR	Anti-Mason-Democrat-	BENTON D	Benton Democrat
A-BROD D	Anti-Broderick Democrat		National Republican	B MOOSE	Bull Moose
AC	Anti-corruption	AM & EMANC	American and	BOLT D	Bolting Democrat
A-CB	Anti Carpet-Baggers		Emancipationist	BRECK D	Breckinridge Democrat
ACP	A Connecticut Party	AMH	American Heritage	BROD D	Broderick Democrat
AD	Adams Democrat	AM I	American Independent	BRYAN	Bryan Party
A-D-FUS	Anti-Democrat-Fusion	AM LAB	American Labor	BRYAN D	Bryan Democrat
AGA	American Grassroots	AM MO	American Party of	B-T R	Brindle-Tail Republican
	Alternative		Missouri	B & T R	Black and Tan Republican
AG WHEEL	Agricultural Wheeler	AM NAT	American National	BUCK R	Bucktail Republican
A JAC	Andrew Jackson	A-MON D	Anti-Monopoly	BUSINESS	Business Med
A-JAC	Anti-Jackson		Democrat	BUT D & N	Butler Democrat and
A-JAC D	Anti-Jackson Democrat	A-MONOP	Anti-Monopoly		National
A-KN D	Anti-Know Nothing	AM R	American Republican	BUT D & R	Butler Democrat and
	Democrat	AM&R	American and Republican		Greenback
A-KN I	Anti-Know Nothing	A-NEB	Anti-Nebraska	BUT R	But. Republican
	Independent	A-NEB D	Anti-Nebraska Democrat	C	Conservative
A-KN I D	Anti-Know Nothing	ANTI-CLINT	Anti-Clinton	CALH D	Calhoun Democrat
	Independent Democrat	ANTI-CL R	Anti-Clinton Republican	CASS D	Cass Democrat
AK R	Addicks Republican	ANTI-FED	Anti-Federalist	CC	Change Congress
A-LD D	Anti-Land Distribution	AP	Action Party	CD	Conservative Democrat
	Democrat	APOLLO	Apollo Hall	CI/IC	Citizen Independent or
A-LEC D	Anti-Lecompton	AR	Adams Republican		Independent Citizen
	Democrat	A-RENT	Anti-Rent	CIT	Citizens
A-LEC DR	Anti-Lecompton	A-RPT D	Anti-Redemption	CIT & CO D	Citizen and County
	Democrat and		Democrat		Democrat
	Republican	A-TAM	Anti-Tammany	CITY	City Party
ALI	Alaskan Independent	A-TARIFF	Anti-Tariff	CITY FUS	City Fusion
ALL PP	All Peoples	A-TAX	Anti-Tax	CIV A	'Civ. A'
ALNC	Alliance	A-TRUST	Anti-Trust (A.T.)	CLAY D	Clay Democrat

1596

NEW DEAL	New Deal	PPL DR S	People's Party Labor, Democratic Republican, Silver	R-D-PROG	Republican-Democratic-Progressive
NEW I	New Independent			R D P T	Republican, Democrat, Progressive, Townsend
NEW LEAD	New Leadership	PP & R	Peoples and Republican		
NF	Nuclear Freeze	PRC TOWN	PRC, Townsend	R D T	Republican, Democrat, Townsend
NG	National Greenback	PRG SOC	Progressive Social		
NL	Natural Law	PRI R	Primary Republican	READJ	Readjuster
NON PART	Non Partisan	PRO-BANK	Pro-Bank	REDEM D	Redemption Democrat
NON PL	Nonpartisan League	PROG	Progressive	REF	Reform
NP	National Prohibition	PROG-BMR	Progressive-Bull Moose-Roosevelt	REF D	Reform Democrat
N PROG	National Progressive			REG	Regular
NR	National Republican	PROG & BUS	Progressive and Businessmen's	REG D	Regular Democrat
NR-A-MAS	National Republican-Anti-Mason			REPEAL	Repeal
		PROG D	Progressive Democrat	REPEAL L	Repeal League
N SILVER	National Silver	PROG D & P	Progressive-Democrat and Prohibition	R & F ALNC	Republican and Farmer's Alliance
N SR	National States Rights				
NULL	Nullifier	PROG & IL	Progressive and Independence League	R-FF	Republican-Federalist Fusion
NULL D	Nullifier Democrat				
NULL NR	Nullification-National Republican	PROG-P	Progressive-Prohibition	R-F-LAB	Republican-Farmer Labor
		PROG R	Progressive Republican	R F-L-P	Republican, Farmer-Labor-Prohibition
N UNION	National Union	PT	Protectionist		
OB	Open Book	PUB OWN	Public Ownership	RG	Republican Greenback
OLD AGE	Old Age Pension	PURE POL	Pure Politics	R-G-FUS	Republican-Greenback-Fusion
OLD R	Old Republican	R	Republican		
OP	Occion Popular	RAD	Radical	R-GOLD D	Republican-Gold Democrat
OPP	Opposition	RAD R	Radical Republican		
OPP D	Opposition Democrat	R AM	Republican American	R & ID	Republican and Independent Democrat
OPP R	Opposition Republican	R & A-MONO	Republican and Anti-Monopoly		
OPP & SC	Opposition and Scattering			R & IL	Republican and Independence League
		R AM & PR	Republican, American and Progressive	RIL A NP	Republican Ind League, Amer. Nat'l Progressive
P	Prohibition				
P & D	Prohibition and Democrat	R & A-TAM	Republican and Anti-Tammany	RIL & NPR	Republican, Independent League and National Progressive
P D-R & PR	Prohibition, Democrat-Republican and Progressive	R & A-TR	Republican and Anti-Trust Republican		
		R & BM	Republican and Bull Moose	RIL P NP	Republican, Independent League, Prohibition, Nat'l Progressive
P D SOC	Prohibition, Democrat, Socialist	RBM & PR	Republican, Bull Moose and Progressive		
PEACE D	Peace Democrat			R IL PR	Republican, Independence League and Progressive
PERS LIB	Personal Liberty	R & CF	Republican and City Fusion		
P & F ALNC	Prohibition and Farmer's Alliance	RCF & LP	Republican City Fusion and Law Preservation		
				R & IV	Republican and Independent Voters
PFP	Peace and Freedom	R CF & REC	Republican, City Fusion, and Recovery		
P-LAB	Population-Labor			R K & WASH	Republican, Keystone, and Washington
POP	Populist	RCI	Rich County Independent		
POP & D	Populist and Democrat	R CIT	Republican Citizens	RKW & ROPR	Republican, Keystone, Washington and Roosevelt Progressive
POP I	Populist Independent	R CST & CF	Republican, Constitutional, and City Fusion		
POP & R	Populist and Republican				
POP SIL	Populist Silver			R & LAB	Republican and Labor
POP & SL D	Populist and Silver Democrat	R-D¹	Republican-Democrat	R & LP	Republican and Law Preservation
		RDC	Republican Delegate Convention		
POPU GOV	Popular Government			R MCK CIT	Republican, McKinley Citizen
PP	People's	R-D-P	Republican-Democrat-Prohibition		
PP CAND	People's Candidate, The			R & ND	Republican and National Democrat
PP & D	People's and Democrat	R-D-PR-C	Republican-Democrat-Progressive-Commonwealth		
PP-D-S-R	Peoples-Democrat-Silver-Republican			R & NG	Republican and National Greenback
PP I	People's Independent				

R & NP	Republican and Nonpartisan	SIL-R-D	Silver-Republican-Democrat	TOWN-SJD	Townsend-Social Justice, Democratic
R NPR	Republican, Nat'l Progressive	SINGLE T	Single Tax	TCPT	Taxpayers Party to Cut Taxes
R NPR AM	Republican, Nat'l Progressive, American	SIS	Staten Island Secession	U	United
		SM D	Sound Money Democrat	U CIT	United Citizen
RO	Roosevelt	SOC	Socialist	U LAB	United Labor
ROBINSON	Robinson Citizens Party	SOC & F-L	Socialist and Farmer-Labor	ULTRA AB	Ultra Abolitionist
ROB R	Rob. Republican			UN	Union
R-OP	Republican-Other Parties	SOCIAL D	Social Democrat	UN D	Union Democrat
RO PROG	Roosevelt Progressive	SOC LAB	Socialist Labor	UN LAB	Union Labor
RO SOC D	Roosevelt Social Democrat	SOC & LP	Socialist and Law Preservation	UN LAB & D	Union Labor and Democrat
ROYAL OAK	Royal Oak	SOC & PROG	Socialist and Progressive	UNP R	Unpledged Republican
RP	Rate Payers Against LILCO	SOC WORK	Socialist Workers	UN PROG	Union Progressive
		SO D	Southern Democrat	UN R	Union Republican
R & P	Republican and Prohibition	SOFT D	Soft Democrat	UN & SQD	Union and Square Deal
		SOFT D & AM	Soft Democrat and American	UNT	Unionist
RP & DC	Republican Party and Delegate Convention	SOJ	Scales of Justice	UN W	Union Whig
RPI	Ross Perot Independent	SO RTS	Southern Rights	USLP	U.S. Labor Party
R P NPR	Republican, Prohibition, Nat'l Progressive	SO RTS D	Southern Rights Democrat	UT	Unity
				U TAX	United Taxpayers
R POP FU	Republican Populist Fusion	SOR W	Southern Rights Whig	UVD	Ultra-Veto Democrat
		SPP	Straight People Party	VB D	Van Buren Democrat
RP & PROG	Republican, Prohibition, and Progressive	SR	State Rights	VB R	Van Buren Republican
		SR D	State Rights Democrat	VETS F	Veterans Farmer
R PR IL	Republican, Progressive, Independence League	SR FT	State Rights Free Trader	VETS V	Veterans Victory
		SR W	State Rights Whig	VG	Vermont Grassroots
R & PROG	Republican and Progressive	SSR D	State's Rights Democrat	VI	Voice of Independence
		SSR NULL	State's Rights Nullifier	VL	Voters League
R-SIL R	Republican-Silver Republican	STAL D	Stalwart Democrat	VR	Voter Rights
		STAL SIL	Stalwart Silver	W	Whig
R & SOC	Republican and Socialist	STATE D	State Democrat	W & AM	Whig and American
R SOC & LP	Republican, Socialist, and Law Preservation	STC D	State Credit Democrat	W & A-MASC	Whig and Anti-Masonic
		STICKER	Sticker	W-A-RENT	Whig Anti-Rent
R & SQDEAL	Republican and Square Deal	TAFT	'Taft for President'	WASH	Washington
		TAM	Tammany	WCP AM	Workers (Communist) Party of America
RT	Republican, Townsend	TAM D	Tammany Democrat		
R & TEMP	Republican and Temperance	TAM D & UL	Tammany Democrat and Union Labor	WELFARE	Welfare
				WF	Working Families
RTL	Right to Life	TAM & NY D	Tammany and New York Democracy	W FS	Whig Free Soil
R & UL	Republican and Union Labor			WILDCAT	Wildcat
		TAX	U.S. Taxpayers	WILSON I	Wilson Independent
R-UNION	Republican-Union	TAYLOR W	Taylor Whig	WL	Workers League
R & VIC	Republican and 'Vic'	TCP-LI	Tax Cut Party-Long Island	WM	Workingmen
R VIC & CF	Republican, 'Vic,' and City Fusion			WM PENN	William Penn
		TEMP	Temperance	WMP/L	Workingman's Party or League
R & WASH	Republican and Washington	TEMP REF	Temperance Reform		
		TFC	Twenty-First Century	WOLF-D	Wolf Democrat
R & YD	Republican and Young Democracy	THIRD	The Third Party	WP AM	Workers Party of America
		TOL	Toleration		
SEC	Secessionist	TOWN	Townsend	WRITE IN	Write In
SEC D	Secession Democrat	TOWN-C-L	Townsend-Coughlin-Labor	YD	Young Democracy
SEC W	Secessionist Whig			YD & R	Young Democrat and Republican
SILENT	Silent Majority	TOWN OAP	Townsend Old Age Pension		
SIL-R	Silver Republican	TOWN SJ	Townsend Social Justice	YOUNGMAN	Youngman

Selected Bibliography

Part I Elections in America

Abramson, Paul R., John H. Aldrich, and David W. Rohde. *Change and Continuity in the 1996 and 1998 Elections.* Washington, D.C.: CQ Press, 1999.

Alvarez, R. Michael. *Information and Elections.* Ann Arbor: University of Michigan Press, 1997.

Avey, Michael J. *The Demobilization of American Voters: A Comprehensive Theory of Voter Turnout.* Westport, Conn.: Greenwood, 1989.

Berelson, Bernard, Paul F. Lazerfeld, and William A. McPhee. *Voting: A Study of Opinion Formation in a Presidential Campaign.* Chicago: University of Chicago Press, 1954.

Black, Earl, and Merle Black. *The Vital South: How Presidents Are Elected.* Cambridge: Harvard University Press, 1992.

Buchanan, Bruce. *Renewing Presidential Politics: Campaigns, Media, and the Public Interest.* Lanham, Md.: Rowman and Littlefield, 1996.

Campbell, Angus, Gerald Gurin, and Warren E. Miller. *The Voter Decides.* Evanston, Ill.: Row, Peterson, 1954.

Campbell, Angus, Philip E. Converse, Warren E. Miller, and Donald E. Stokes. *The American Voter.* New York: Wiley, 1960.

Campbell, Angus, et al. *Elections and the Political Order.* New York: Wiley, 1966.

Campbell, James E. *The Presidential Pulse of Congressional Elections.* 2nd ed. Lexington: University of Kentucky Press, 1997.

Campbell, James E., and James C. Garand. *Before the Vote: Forecasting American National Elections.* Thousand Oaks, Calif.: Sage Publications, 2000.

Carmines, Edward G., and James A. Stimson. *Issue Evolution: Race and the Transformation of American Politics.* Princeton, N.J.: Princeton University Press, 1989.

Chen, Kevin. *Political Alienation and Voting Turnout in the United States, 1960–1988.* San Francisco: Mellon Research University Press, 1992.

Claude, Richard. *The Supreme Court and the Electoral Process.* Baltimore: Johns Hopkins University Press, 1970.

Conway, M. Margaret. *Political Participation in the United States.* 3rd ed. Washington, D.C.: CQ Press, 2000.

Cummings, Milton C. *Congressmen and the Electorate: Elections for the U.S. House and the President, 1920–1964.* New York: Free Press, 1966.

Davies, Philip J. *U.S. Elections Today.* 2nd ed. New York: Manchester University Press, 1999.

DiClerico, Robert E. *Political Parties, Campaigns and Elections.* Upper Saddle River, N.J.: Prentice Hall, 2000.

Dinkin, Robert J. *Voting in Revolutionary America: A Study of Elections in the Original Thirteen States, 1776–1789.* Westport, Conn.: Greenwood Press, 1982.

Doppelt, Jack C., and Ellen Shearer. *Nonvoters: America's No-Shows.* Thousand Oaks, Calif.: Sage Publications, 1999.

Downs, Anthony. *An Economic Theory of Democracy.* New York: Harper, 1957.

Dunham, Pat. *Electoral Behavior in the United States.* Englewood Cliffs, N.J.: Prentice-Hall, 1991.

Edsall, Thomas B., and Mary D. Edsall. *Chain Reaction: The Impact of Race, Rights, and Taxes on American Politics.* New York: Norton, 1991.

Enelow, James M., and Melvin J. Hinich. *The Spatial Theory of Voting: An Introduction.* New York: Cambridge University Press, 1984.

Farrand, Max, ed. *The Records of the Federal Convention of 1787.* 4 vols. New Haven, Conn.: Yale University Press, 1966.

Fiorina, Morris P. *Retrospective Voting in American National Elections.* New Haven, Conn.: Yale University Press, 1981.

Flanigan, William H., and Nancy H. Zingale. *Political Behavior of the American Electorate.* 9th ed. Washington, D.C.: CQ Press, 1998.

Garrow, David J. *Protest at Selma: Martin Luther King, Jr., and the Voting Rights Act of 1965.* New Haven, Conn.: Yale University Press, 1978.

Ginsberg, Benjamin, and Martin Shefter. *Politics by Other Means: The Declining Importance of Elections in America.* New York: Basic Books, 1990.

Goehlert, Robert U., and Fenton S. Martin. *CQ's Guide to Modern Elections: An Annotated Bibliography, 1960–1996.* Washington, D.C.: CQ Press, 1999.

Graham, Gene. *One Man, One Vote: Baker vs. Carr and the American Levelers.* Boston: Little, Brown, 1972.

Grofman, Bernard, and Chandler Davidson, eds. *Controversies in Minority Voting: The Voting Rights Act in Perspective.* Washington, D.C.: Brookings Institution Press, 1992.

Grofman, Bernard, Lisa Handley, and Richard G. Niemi. *Minority Representation and the Quest for Voting Equality.* New York: Cambridge University Press, 1992.

Hamilton, Alexander, James Madison, and John Jay. *The Federalist Papers.* New York: New American Library, 1961.

Haynes, George H. *The Election of Senators.* New York: Henry Holt, 1906.

Heard, Alexander, and Donald S. Strong. *Southern Primaries and Elections, 1920–1949.* University: University of Alabama Press, 1950.

Herrnson, Paul S. *Congressional Elections: Campaigning at Home and in Washington.* 3rd ed. Washington, D.C.: CQ Press, 2000.

Holbrook, Thomas M. *Do Campaigns Matter?* Thousand Oaks, Calif.: Sage Publications, 1996.

Huckfeldt, Robert, and Carol W. Kohfeld. *Race and the Decline of Class in American Politics.* Urbana: University of Illinois Press, 1989.

Hutson, James H. *Supplement to Max Farrand's the Records of the Federal Convention of 1787.* New Haven, Conn.: Yale University Press, 1987.

Jacobson, Gary C. *The Politics of Congressional Elections.* 5th ed. New York: Longman, 2001.

Key, V. O., Jr., and Milton C. Cummings Jr. *The Responsible Electorate: Rationality in Presidential Voting, 1936–1960.* Cambridge: Harvard University Press, 1966.

Kleppner, Paul. *Who Voted? The Dynamics of Electoral Turnout, 1870–1980.* New York: Praeger, 1982.

Kornbluh, Mark L. *Why America Stopped Voting: The Decline of Participatory Democracy and the Emergence of Modern American Politics.* New York: New York University Press, 2000

Lawson, Steven F. *In Pursuit of Power: Southern Blacks and Electoral Politics, 1965–1982.* New York: Columbia University Press, 1985.

Lewinson, Paul. *Race, Class and Party: A History of Negro Suffrage and White Politics in the South.* New York: Oxford University Press, 1932.

Mann, Thomas E. *Unsafe at Any Margin: Interpreting Congressional Elections.* Washington, D.C.: American Enterprise Institute, 1978.

Mayhew, David R. *Congress: The Electoral Connection.* New Haven, Conn.: Yale University Press, 1974.

McGovney, Dudley O. *The American Suffrage Medley.* Chicago: University of Chicago Press, 1949.

Miller, Warren E., and J. Merrill Shanks. *The New American Voter.* Cambridge: Harvard University Press, 1996.

Moreland, Laurence W., Robert P. Steed, and Tod A. Baker, eds. *Blacks in Southern Politics.* New York: Praeger, 1987.

Myrdal, Gunnar. *An American Dilemma: The Negro Problem and Modern Democracy.* New York: Harper & Row, 1944.

Nie, Norman H., Sidney Verba, and John R. Petrocik. *The Changing American Voter.* Cambridge: Harvard University Press, 1976.

Niemi, Richard G., and Herbert F. Weisberg, eds. *Classics in Voting Behavior.* Washington, D.C.: CQ Press, 1993.

___. *Controversies in Voting Behavior.* 3rd ed. Washington, D.C.: CQ Press, 1993.

Ogden, Frederic D. *The Poll Tax in the South.* University: University of Alabama Press, 1958.

Piven, Frances F., and Richard A. Cloward. *Why Americans Don't Vote.* New York: Pantheon Books, 1989.

Pomper, Gerald M. *Voter's Choice: Varieties of American Electoral Behavior.* New York: Dodd, Mead, 1975.

Pomper, Gerald M., et al. *The Election of 1996: Reports and Interpretations.* Chatham, N.J.: Chatham House, 1997.

Popkin, Samuel L. *The Reasoning Voter: Communication and Persuasion in Presidential Campaigns.* 2nd ed. Chicago: University of Chicago Press, 1994.

Prendergast, William B. *The Catholic Voter in American Politics: The Passing of the Democratic Monolith.* Washington, D.C.: Georgetown University Press, 1999.

Rosenstone, Steven J., and John Mark Hansen. *Mobilization, Participation, and Democracy in America.* New York: Macmillan, 1993.

Rozell, Mark J., and Clyde Wilcox, eds. *God at the Grass Roots 1996: The Christian Right in the American Elections.* Lanham, Md.: Rowman and Littlefield, 1997.

Smith, Eric R. A. N. *The Unchanging American Voter.* Berkeley: University of California Press, 1989.

Stanley, Harold W. *Voter Mobilization and the Politics of Race: The South and Universal Suffrage, 1952–1984.* New York: Praeger, 1987.

Swain, Carol M. *Black Faces, Black Interests: The Representation of African Americans in Congress.* Cambridge: Harvard University Press, 1993.

Tate, Katherine. *From Protest to Politics: The New Black Voters in American Elections.* Cambridge: Harvard University Press, 1993.

Teixeira, Ruy A. *The Disappearing American Voter.* Washington, D.C.: Brookings Institution, 1992.

Teixeira, Ruy A., and Joel Rogers. *America's Forgotten Majority: Why the White Working Class Still Matters.* New York: Basic Books, 2000.

Thernstrom, Abigail M. *Whose Votes Count? Affirmative Action and Minority Voting Rights.* Cambridge: Harvard University Press, 1987.

Verba, Sidney, and Norman H. Nie. *Participation in America: Political Democracy and Social Equality.* New York: Harper and Row, 1972.

Weisberg, Herbert F., ed. *Democracy's Feast: Elections in America.* Chatham, N.J.: Chatham House, 1995.

Wilcox, Clyde. *The Latest American Revolution? The 1994 Elections and Their Implications for Governance.* New York: St. Martin's, 1994.

Wolfinger, Raymond E., and Steven J. Rosenstone. *Who Votes?* New Haven, Conn.: Yale University Press, 1980.

Part II Political Parties

Alexander, Herbert E. *Financing Politics: Money, Elections, and Political Reform.* 4th ed. Washington, D.C.: CQ Press, 1992.

Arnett, A. M. *The Populist Movement in Georgia.* New York: Columbia University Press, 1922.

Bass, Harold F. *Historical Dictionary of United States Political Parties.* Lanham, Md.: Scarecrow Press, 2000.

Beck, Paul A., and Marjorie R. Hershey. *Party Politics in America.* 9th ed. New York: Longman, 2001.

Bibby, John F. *Politics, Parties, and Elections in America.* 4th ed. Chicago: Nelson-Hall, 1999.

Bibby, John F., and L. Sandy Maisel. *Two Parties—Or More? The American Party System.* Boulder, Colo.: Westview, 1998.

Biersack, Robert, Paul S. Herrnson, and Clyde Wilcox. *After the Revolution: PACs, Lobbies, and the Republican Congress.* Boston: Allyn and Bacon, 1999.

Biersack, Robert, Paul S. Herrnson, and Clyde Wilcox, eds. *Risky Business: PAC Decisionmaking in Congressional Elections.* Armonk, N.Y.: Sharpe, 1994.

Binning, William C., Larry E. Esterly, and Paul A. Sracic. *Encyclopedia of American Parties, Campaigns, and Elections.* Westport, Conn.: Greenwood Press, 1999.

Birnbaum, Jeffrey H. *The Money Men: The Real Story of Fund-Raising's Influence on Political Power in America.* New York: Crown, 2000.

Blue, Frederick J. *The Free Soilers: Third Party Politics, 1848–1854.* Urbana: University of Illinois Press, 1973.

Borden, Morton. *Parties and Politics in the Early Republic, 1789–1815.* Arlington Heights, Ill.: Davidson, Harlan, 1967.

Brennan, Mary C. *Turning Right in the Sixties: The Conservative Capture of the GOP.* Chapel Hill: University of North Carolina Press, 1995.

Brenner, Lenni. *The Lesser Evil.* Secaucus, N.J.: Lyle Stuart, 1988.

Brock, William. *Parties and Political Conscience: American Dilemmas, 1840–1850.* Millwood, N.Y.: Kraus International Publications, 1979.

Brown, Clifford W., Jr., Lynda W. Powell, and Clyde Wilcox. *Serious Money: Fundraising and Contributing in Presidential Nomination Campaigns.* New York: Cambridge University Press, 1995.

Brown, Stuart G. *First Republicans: Political Philosophy and Public Policy in the Party of Jefferson and Madison.* Syracuse, N.Y.: Syracuse University Press, 1954.

Burner, David. *The Politics of Provincialism: The Democratic Party in Transition, 1918–1932.* Cambridge, Mass.: Harvard University Press, 1986.

Campaign Finance Institute. "Issue Ad Disclosure: Recommendations for a New Approach." Washington, D.C.: Campaign Finance Institute, Task Force on Disclosure, February 2001.

Campbell, Colton C., and Nicol C. Rae, eds. *The Contentious Senate: Partisanship, Ideology, and the Myth of Cool Judgment.* Lanham, Md.: Rowman & Littlefield, 2001.

Campbell, James E. *Cheap Seats: The Democratic Party's Advantage in U.S. House Elections.* Columbus: Ohio State University Press, 1996.

Cantor, Joseph E. "Campaign Finance in the 2000 Federal Elections: Overview and Estimates of the Flow of Money." Report. No. RL30884. Library of Congress, Congressional Research Service, March 16, 2001.

Carmines, Edward G., and James A. Stimson. *Issue Evolution: Race and the Transformation of American Politics.* Princeton, N.J.: Princeton University Press, 1989.

Chambers, William N., and Walter D. Burnham, eds. *The American Party System: Stages of Political Development.* 2nd ed. New York: Oxford University Press, 1975.

Cigler, Allan J., and Burdett A. Loomis, eds. *Interest Group Politics.* 5th ed. Washington, D.C.: CQ Press, 1998.

Clawson, Dan, Alan Neustadtl, and Denise Scott. *Money Talks: Corporate PACs and Political Influence.* New York: Basic Books, 1992.

Clawson, Dan, Alan Neustadtl, and Mark Weller. *Dollars and Votes: How Business Campaign Contributions Subvert Democracy.* Philadelphia: Temple University Press, 1998.

Congressional Quarterly. *Political Parties in America.* Washington, D.C.: CQ Press, 2001.

Converse, Philip E. *The Dynamics of Party Support: Cohort-Analyzing Party Identification.* Beverly Hills, Calif.: Sage Publications, 1976.

Corrado, Anthony. *Campaign Finance Reform: Beyond the Basics.* New York: Century Foundation Press, 2000.

Cummings, Milton C., Jr. *Congressmen and the Electorate: Elections for the U.S. House and President, 1920–1964.* New York: Free Press, 1966.

Cunningham, Noble E. *Jeffersonian Republicans: The Formation of Party Organization, 1789–1801.* Chapel Hill: University of North Carolina Press, 1967.

David, Paul T. *Party Strength in the United States, 1872–1970.* Charlottesville: University Press of Virginia, 1972.

Haskell, John. *Fundamentally Flawed: Understanding and Reforming Presidential Primaries.* Lanham, Md.: Rowman and Littlefield, 1996.

Havel, James T. *U.S. Presidential Candidates and the Elections: A Biographical and Historical Guide.* New York: Macmillan Library Reference, 1996.

Haworth, Paul L. *The Hayes-Tilden Disputed Presidential Election of 1876.* 1906. Reprint, New York: AMS Press, 1979.

Heale, M. J. *The Presidential Quest: Candidates and Images in American Political Culture, 1787–1852.* New York: Longman, 1982.

Herzke, Allen D. *Echoes of Discontent: Jesse Jackson, Pat Robertson, and the Resurgence of Populism.* Washington, D.C.: CQ Press, 1993.

Huckfeldt, Robert, and John Sprague. *Citizens, Politics, and Social Communication: Information and Influence in an Election Campaign.* New York: Cambridge University Press, 1995.

Jackson, John S., and William Crotty. *The Politics of Presidential Selection.* New York: HarperCollins, 1996.

Jamieson, Kathleen Hall. *Packaging the Presidency: A History and Criticism of Presidential Campaign Advertising.* 3rd ed. New York: Oxford University Press, 1996.

Jensen, Merrill, ed. *The Documentary History of the First Federal Elections, 1788–1790.* Madison, Wis.: Madison House, 1991.

Johnson, Donald B. *National Party Platforms.* Rev. ed. Urbana: University of Illinois Press, 1978.

Just, Marion R., et al. *Crosstalk: Citizens, Candidates, and the Media in a Presidential Campaign.* Chicago: University of Chicago Press, 1996.

Keech, William R., and Donald R. Matthews. *The Party's Choice.* Washington, D.C.: Brookings Institution Press, 1976.

Kessel, John H. *Presidential Campaign Politics.* 4th ed. Pacific Grove, Calif.: Brooks-Cole, 1992.

Key, V. O., Jr. *The Responsible Electorate: Rationality in Presidential Voting, 1936–1960.* Cambridge, Mass.: Harvard University Press, 1966.

Kleppner, Paul. *Who Voted? The Dynamics of Electoral Turnout, 1870–1980.* New York: Praeger, 1982.

Kleppner, Paul, and Walter D. Burnham. *The Evolution of American Electoral Systems.* Westport, Conn.: Greenwood Press, 1982.

Kraus, Sidney. *Televised Presidential Debates and Public Policy.* 2nd ed. Mahwah, N.J.: Lawrence Erlbaum Associates, 2000.

League of Women Voters of the United States. *Choosing the President: A Citizen's Guide to the 2000 Election.* Washington, D.C.: Lyons Press, 1999.

Longley, Lawrence D. *The Politics of Electoral College Reform.* New Haven, Conn.: Yale University Press, 1972.

Longley, Lawrence D., and Neal R. Peirce. *The Electoral Primer.* New Haven, Conn.: Yale University Press, 1996.

Maisel, L. Sandy. *Parties and Elections in America: The Electoral Process.* 3rd ed. Lanham, Md.: Rowman and Littlefield, 1999.

Mayer, William G., ed. *In Pursuit of the White House 2000: How We Choose Our Presidential Nominees.* Chatham, N.J.: Chatham House, 1999.

Mayhew, David R. *Divided We Govern: Party Control, Lawmaking & Investigations.* New Haven, Conn.: Yale University Press, 1991.

McCubbins, Matthew D., ed. *Under the Watchful Eye: Managing Presidential Campaigns in the Television Era.* Washington, D.C.: CQ Press, 1992.

McGillivray, Alice V. *Presidential Primaries and Caucuses: 1992, A Handbook of Election Statistics.* Washington, D.C.: Congressional Quarterly, 1992.

McKee, Thomas H. *The National Conventions and Platforms of All Political Parties, 1789–1905: Convention, Popular and Electoral Vote.* New York: AMS Press, 1971.

Menefee-Libey, David. *The Triumph of Campaign-Centered Politics.* New York: Chatham House, 2000.

Miller, Arthur H., and Bruce E. Gronbeck, eds. *Presidential Campaigns and American Self Images.* Boulder, Colo.: Westview, 1994.

Miller, Warren E., and Teresa E. Levitin. *Leadership and Change: Presidential Elections from 1952 to 1976.* Cambridge, Mass.: Winthrop, 1976.

Moore, John L. *Elections A to Z.* Washington, D.C.: CQ Press, 1999.

Nelson, Michael, ed. *Historical Documents on Presidential Elections, 1787–1988.* Washington, D.C.: Congressional Quarterly, 1991.

———. *The Presidency and the Political System.* 6th ed. Washington, D.C.: CQ Press, 2000.

———, ed. *The Elections of 2000.* Washington, D.C.: CQ Press, 2001.

Newman, Bruce I. *The Marketing of the President: Political Marketing as a Campaign Strategy.* Thousand Oaks, Calif.: Sage, 1994.

Nimmo, Dan. *The Political Persuaders: The Technique of Modern Election Campaigns.* Englewood Cliffs, N.J.: Transaction Publishers, 1999.

Norrander, Barbara. *Super Tuesday: Regional Politics and Presidential Primaries.* Lexington: University Press of Kentucky, 1992.

Peirce, Neal, and Lawrence D. Longley. *The People's President: The Electoral College and the Emerging Consensus for a Direct Vote Alternative.* Rev. ed. New Haven, Conn.: Yale University Press, 1981.

Pika, Joseph H., and Richard Watson. *The Presidential Contest.* 5th ed. Washington, D.C.: CQ Press, 1995.

Polsby, Nelson W., and Aaron Wildavsky. *Presidential Elections: Strategies and Structures of American Politics.* 10th ed. New York: Chatham House, 2000.

Pomper, Gerald M., et al. *The Election of 1996: Reports and Interpretations.* Chatham, N.J.: Chatham House, 1997.

Robinson, Edgar E. *The Presidential Vote, 1896–1932.* Stanford, Calif.: Stanford University Press, 1947.

———. *They Voted for Roosevelt: The Presidential Vote, 1932–1944.* Stanford, Calif.: Stanford University Press, 1947.

Roseboom, Eugene H. *A History of Presidential Elections: From George Washington to Jimmy Carter.* 4th ed. New York: Macmillan, 1979.

Rosenstone, Steven J., Roy L. Behr, and Edward Lazarus. *Third Parties in America: Citizen Response to Major Party Failure.* Princeton, N.J.: Princeton University Press, 1984.

Runyon, John H. *Source Book of American Presidential Campaign and Election Statistics, 1948–1968.* New York: Ungar, 1971.

Scammon, Richard M. *America Votes: A Handbook of Contemporary Election Statistics.* Vols. 1–2. New York: Macmillan, 1956–58. *America Votes.* Vols. 3–5. Pittsburgh: University of Pittsburgh, 1959–64. *America Votes.* Vols. 6–11. Washington, D.C.: Congressional Quarterly, 1966–1975.

Scammon, Richard M., and Alice V. McGillivray. *America Votes.* Vols. 12–21. Washington, D.C.: Congressional Quarterly, 1977–1995.

Scammon, Richard M., Alice V. McGillivray, and Rhodes Cook. *America Votes.* Vols. 22–24. Washington, D.C.: CQ Press, 1997–2001.

Schantz, Harvey L., ed. *American Presidential Elections: Process, Policy, and Political Change.* Albany: State University of New York Press, 1996.

Scher, Richard K. *The Modern Political Campaign: Mudslinging, Bombast, and the Vitality of American Politics.* Armonk, N.Y.: Sharpe, 1997.

Schlesinger, Arthur M., Jr., *The Coming to Power: Critical Presidential Elections in American History.* New York: Chelsea House, 1981.

———, ed. *History of American Presidential Elections.* 4 vols. New York: McGraw Hill, 1971.

———, ed. *Running for President: The Candidates and Their Images.* New York: Simon and Schuster, 1994.

Shafer, Byron. *Bifurcated Politics: Evolution and Reform in the National Party Convention.* Cambridge, Mass.: Harvard University Press, 1988.

Shields-West, Eileen. *World Almanac of Presidential Campaigns.* New York: World Almanac, 1992.

Singer, Aaron, ed. *Campaign Speeches of American Presidential Candidates, 1928–1972.* New York: Ungar, 1976.

———. *Campaign Speeches of American Presidential Candidates, 1948–1984.* New York: Ungar, 1985.

Squire, Peverill, ed. *The Iowa Caucuses and the Presidential Nominating Process.* Boulder, Colo.: Westview, 1989.

Stephenson, D. Grier, Jr. *Campaigns and the Court: The U.S. Supreme Court in Presidential Elections.* New York: Columbia University Press, 1999.

Sullivan, Denis G., Jeffrey L. Pressman, and F. Christopher Arterton. *Explorations in Convention Decision-Making: The Democratic Party in the 1970s.* San Francisco: Freeman, 1974.

Tenpas, Kathryn D. *Presidents as Candidates: Inside the White House for the Presidential Campaign.* New York: Garland, 1997.

Thurber, James A., and Candice J. Nelson, eds. *Campaigns and Elections American Style.* Boulder, Colo.: Westview, 1995.

Troy, Gil. *See How They Ran: The Changing Role of the Presidential Candidate.* Rev. ed. Cambridge, Mass.: Harvard University Press, 1996.

Tugwell, Rexford G. *How They Became President: Thirty-Five Ways to the White House.* New York: Simon and Schuster, 1965.

Wattenberg, Martin P. *The Rise of Candidate-Centered Politics: Presidential Elections of the 1980s.* Cambridge, Mass.: Harvard University Press, 1991.

Wayne, Stephen J. *The Road to the White House 2000: The Politics of Presidential Elections.* New York: St. Martin's, 1999.

West, Darrell M. *Air Wars: Television Advertising in Election Campaigns, 1952–1996.* 2nd ed. Washington, D.C.: CQ Press, 1997.

White, Theodore H. *America in Search of Itself: The Making of the President, 1956–1980.* New York: Harper and Row, 1982.

Witcover, Jules. *No Way to Pick a President.* New York: Farrar, Straus, and Giroux, 1999.

Part IV Congressional Elections

Abramowitz, Alan I., and Jeffrey A. Segal. *Senate Elections.* Ann Arbor: University of Michigan Press, 1992.

The Almanac of American Politics. Washington, D.C.: National Journal, 1972– .

America Votes: A Handbook of Contemporary American Election Statistics. Washington, D.C.: CQ Press, 1956–.

Ansolabehere, Stephen, and Shanto Iyengar. *Going Negative: How Political Ads Shrink and Polarize the Electorate.* New York: Free Press, 1995.

Baker, Gordon E. *The Reapportionment Revolution: Representation, Political Power, and the Supreme Court.* New York: Random House, 1966.

Bartels, Larry M., and Lynn Vavreck, eds. *Campaign Reform: Insights and Evidence.* Ann Arbor: University of Michigan Press, 2000.

Bass, Jack, and Walter DeVries. *Transformation of Southern Politics: Social Change and Political Consequence since 1945.* Athens: University of Georgia Press, 1995.

Benjamin, Gerald, and Michael J. Malbin, eds. *Limiting Legislative Terms.* Washington, D.C.: CQ Press, 1992.

Brady, David W. *Critical Elections and Congressional Policy Making.* Stanford: Stanford University Press, 1988.

Brady, David W., John F. Cogan, and Morris B. Fiorina, eds. *Continuity and Change in House Elections.* Stanford: Hoover Institution Press, 2000.

Burrell, Barbara C. *A Woman's Place Is in the House: Campaigning for Congress in the Feminist Era.* Ann Arbor: University of Michigan Press, 1994.

Butler, David, and Bruce E. Cain. *Congressional Redistricting: Comparative and Theoretical Perspectives.* New York: Macmillan, 1992.

Campbell, James E. *The Presidential Pulse of Congressional Elections.* 2nd ed. Lexington: University Press of Kentucky, 1997.

Carroll, Susan J. *Women as Candidates in American Politics.* 2nd ed. Bloomington: Indiana University Press, 1994.

Congressional Quarterly. *Congressional Districts in the 1990s.* Washington, D.C.: Congressional Quarterly, 1993.

Congressional Quarterly. *Congressional Elections: 1946–1996.* Washington, D.C.: Congressional Quarterly, 1997.

Congressional Quarterly. *Guide to Congress.* 5th ed. Washington, D.C.: CQ Press, 2000.

Congressional Quarterly. *Politics in America.* Washington, D.C.: Congressional Quarterly Press, 1965–1987.

Congressional Quarterly's Politics in America. Washington, D.C.: CQ Press, 1989– .

Cook, Rhodes. *How Congress Gets Elected.* Washington, D.C.: CQ Press, 2000.

Cook, Rhodes, and Alice V. McGillivray, comps. *U.S. Primary Elections: 1997–1998: Congress and Governors: A Handbook of Election Statistics.* Washington, D.C.: Congressional Quarterly, 1999.

Cortner, Richard C. *The Apportionment Cases.* Knoxville: University of Tennessee Press, 1970.

Davidson, Roger H., and Walter J. Oleszek. *Congress and Its Members.* 7th ed. Washington, D.C.: CQ Press, 2000.

Dixon, Robert G., Jr. *Democratic Representation: Reapportionment in Law and Politics.* New York: Oxford University Press, 1968.

Dodd, Lawrence D., and Bruce I. Oppenheimer, eds. *Congress Reconsidered.* 6th ed. Washington, D.C.: CQ Press, 1997.

Doron, Gideon, and Michael Harris. *Term Limits.* Lanham, Md.: Lexington Books, 2000.

Dubin, Michael J. *United States Congressional Elections, 1788–1997: The Official Results of the Elections of the 1st through 105th Congresses.* Jefferson, N.C.: McFarland, 1998.

Election Data Book: A Statistical Portrait of Voting in America. Lanham, Md.: Bernan Press, 1993.

Fenno, Richard F., Jr. *Home Style: House Members in Their Districts.* Boston: Little, Brown, 1978.

___. *The Making of a Senator: Dan Quayle.* Washington, D.C.: CQ Press, 1989.

___. *Senators on the Campaign Trail: The Politics of Representation.* Norman: University of Oklahoma Press, 1996.

Fiorina, Morris P. *Congress: Keystone of the Washington Establishment.* 2nd ed. New Haven, Conn.: Yale University Press, 1989.

Fowler, Linda L. *Candidates, Congress, and the American Democracy.* Ann Arbor: University of Michigan Press, 1993.

Fox, Richard L. *Gender Dynamics in Congressional Elections.* Thousand Oaks, Calif.: Sage Publications, 1997.

Galderisi, Peter F., Marni Ezra, and Michael Lyons, eds. *Congressional Primaries and the Politics of Representation.* Lanham, Md.: Rowman & Littlefield, 2001.

Galloway, George B. *History of the House of Representatives.* 2nd ed. New York: Crowell, 1976.

Ginsberg, Benjamin, and Alan Stone, eds. *Do Elections Matter?* 3rd ed. Armonk, N.Y.: M.E. Sharpe, 1996.

Grofman, Bernard, ed. *Race and Redistricting in the 1990s.* New York: Agathon Press, 1998.

Herrnson, Paul S. *Congressional Elections: Campaigning at Home and in Washington.* 3rd ed. Washington, D.C.: CQ Press, 2000.

___. *Playing Hardball: Campaigning for the U.S. Congress.* Upper Saddle River, N.J.: Prentice Hall, 2001.

Jacobson, Gary C. *The Electoral Origins of Divided Government: Competition in U.S. House Elections, 1946–1988.* Boulder, Colo.: Westview Press, 1990.

___. *The Politics of Congressional Elections.* 5th ed. New York: Longman, 2001.

Kahn, Kim F., and Patrick J. Kenney. *The Spectacle of U.S. Senate Campaigns.* Princeton: Princeton University Press, 1999.

Krousser, J. Morgan. *Colorblind Justice: Minority Voting Rights and the Undoing of the Second Reconstruction.* Chapel Hill: University of North Carolina Press, 1999.

Lublin, David. *The Paradox of Representation: Racial Gerrymandering and Minority Interests in Congress.* Princeton: Princeton University Press, 1997.

Luce, Robert. *Legislative Principles: The Historic Theory of Lawmaking by Representative Government.* New York: Houghton Mifflin, 1930.

Magleby, David B., ed. *Outside Money: Soft Money and Issue Advocacy in the 1998 Congressional Elections.* Lanham, Md.: Rowman & Littlefield, 2000.

Makinson, Larry, and Joshua F. Goldstein. *Open Secrets: The Encyclopedia of Congressional Money and Politics.* 4th ed. Washington, D.C.: Congressional Quarterly, 1996.

Mann, Thomas E., and Norman J. Ornstein. *Renewing Congress.* Washington, D.C.: Brookings Institution, 1993.

Martin, Fenton S., and Robert U. Goehlert. *How to Research Congress.* Washington, D.C.: Congressional Quarterly, 1996.

Martis, Kenneth C. *The Historical Atlas of United States Congressional Districts 1789–1983.* New York: Free Press, 1982.

Matteson, David M. *The Organization of the Government under the Constitution.* New York: Da Capo Press, 1970.

Matthews, Donald R. *U.S. Senators and Their World.* New York: Norton, 1973.

Mayhew, David R. *Congress: The Electoral Connection.* New Haven, Conn.: Yale University Press, 1974.

McGillivray, Alice V. *Congressional and Gubernatorial Primaries: 1991–1992: A Handbook of Election Statistics.* Washington, D.C.: Congressional Quarterly, 1993.

___. *Congressional and Gubernatorial Primaries: 1993–1994: A Handbook of Election Statistics.* Washington, D.C.: Congressional Quarterly, 1995.

Merriner, James L., and Thomas P. Senter. *Against Long Odds: Citizens Who Challenge Congressional Incumbents.* Westport, Conn.: Praeger, 1999.

Miller, Warren, Arthur Miller, and Edward Schneider. *American National Data Sourcebook, 1952–1986.* Cambridge: Harvard University Press, 1989.

Monmonier, Mark. *Bushmanders and Bullwinkles: How Politicians Manipulate Electronic Maps and Census Data to Win Elections.* Chicago: University of Chicago Press, 2001.

O'Rourke, Timothy. *The Impact of Reapportionment.* New Brunswick, N.J.: Transaction Books, 1980.

Rohde, David W. *Parties and Leaders in the Postreform House.* Chicago: University of Chicago Press, 1991.

Rush, Mark E. *Does Redistricting Make a Difference? Partisan Representation and Electoral Behavior.* Baltimore: Johns Hopkins University Press, 1993.

Scher, Richard K., Jon L. Mills, and John J. Hotaling. *Voting Rights and Democracy: The Law and Politics of Districting.* Chicago: Nelson-Hall, 1997.

Schwab, Larry M. *The Impact of Congressional Reapportionment and Redistricting.* Lanham, Md.: University Press of America, 1988.

Silbey, Joel H., ed. *The United States Congress: The Electoral Connection, 1789–1989.* Brooklyn, N.Y.: Carlson Publishing, 1991.

Thernstrom, Abigail M. *Whose Votes Count? Affirmative Action and Minority Voting Rights.* Cambridge: Harvard University Press, 1987.

Thomas, Sue, and Clyde Wilcox, eds. *Women and Elective Office: Past, Present, and Future.* New York: Oxford University Press, 1998.

Vital Statistics on Congress. Washington, D.C.: Congressional Quarterly, 1980– .

Westlye, Mark C. *Senate Elections and Campaign Intensity.* Baltimore: Johns Hopkins University Press, 1991.

Part V Gubernatorial Elections

America Votes: A Handbook of Contemporary Election Statistics. Washington, D.C.: Congressional Quarterly, 1956– .

Bartley, Numan V. *From Thurmond to Wallace: Political Tendencies in Georgia, 1948–1968.* Baltimore: Johns Hopkins University Press, 1970.

Bartley, Numan V., and Hugh D. Graham. *Southern Elections: County and Precinct Data, 1950–1972.* Baton Rouge: Louisiana State University Press, 1977.

Bass, Jack, and Walter DeVries. *Transformation of Southern Politics: Social Change and Political Consequence Since 1945.* New York: New American Library, 1977.

Book of the States. Lexington, Ky.: Council of State Governments, 1935– .

Bryce, James. *The American Commonwealth.* 1922. Reprint. New York: AMS Press, 1973.

Carsey, Thomas M. *Campaign Dynamics: The Race for Governor.* Ann Arbor: University of Michigan Press, 2000.

Ceaser, James, and Andrew Busch. *Upside Down and Inside Out: The 1992 Elections and American Politics.* Lanham, Md.: Rowman and Littlefield, 1993.

Congressional Quarterly. *The People Speak: American Elections in Focus.* Washington, D.C.: Congressional Quarterly, 1990.

Congressional Quarterly. *American Political Leaders 1789–2000.* Washington, D.C.: Congressional Quarterly, 2000.

Cook, Rhodes, and Alice V. McGillivray, eds. *U.S. Primary Elections, 1995–1996: President, Congress, Governors: A Handbook of Election Statistics.* Washington, D.C.: Congressional Quarterly, 1997.

___, eds. *U.S. Primary Elections, 1997–1998: President, Congress, Governors: A Handbook of Election Statistics.* Washington, D.C.: Congressional Quarterly, 1999.

Cosman, Bernard. *Five States for Goldwater: Continuity and Change in Southern Voting Patterns 1920–1964.* University: University of Alabama Press, 1965.

Council of State Governments. *State Elective Officials and the Legislatures.* Lexington, Ky.: Council of State Governments, 1977– .

Election Data Book: A Statistical Portrait of Voting in America. Lanham, Md.: Bernan Press, 1993.

Engel, Michael. *State and Local Government: Fundamentals and Perspectives.* New York: P. Lang, 1999.

Ewing, Cortez A. *Primary Elections in the South: Study in Uniparty Politics.* 1953. Reprint. Westport, Conn.: Greenwood Press, 1980.

Germond, Jack W., and Jules Witcover. *Mad as Hell: Revolt at the Ballot Box, 1992.* New York: Warner Books, 1993.

Grantham, Dewey W. *Democratic South.* Athens: University of Georgia Press, 1963.

Gray, Virginia, Russell L. Hanson, and Herbert Jacob, eds. *Politics in the American States.* 7th ed. Washington, D.C.: CQ Press, 1999.

Heard, Alexander, and Donald S. Strong. *Southern Primaries and Elections 1920–1949.* University: University of Alabama Press, 1950.

Hollingsworth, Harold M., ed. *Essays on Recent Southern Politics.* Austin: University of Texas Press, 1970.

Jacobstein, Helen L. *The Segregation Factor in the Florida Democratic Gubernatorial Primary Election of 1956.* Gainesville: University of Florida Press, 1972.

Jewell, Malcolm E. *Parties and Primaries: Nominating State Governors.* New York: Praeger, 1984.

Kallenbach, Joseph E., and Jessamine S. Kallenbach. *American State Governors, 1776–1976.* 3 vols. Dobbs Ferry, N.Y.: Oceana, 1977.

Key, V. O., Jr. *Southern Politics in State and Nation.* New York: Knopf, 1949.

Kousser, J. Morgan. *The Shaping of Southern Politics: Suffrage Restrictions and the Establishment of the One Party South, 1880–1910.* New Haven, Conn.: Yale University Press, 1974.

Kurland, Gerald. *George Wallace: Southern Governor and Presidential Candidate.* Charlotteville, N.Y.: Sam Har Press, 1972.

Lamis, Alexander P. *The Two-Party South.* 2nd ed. New York: Oxford University Press, 1990.

McGillivray, Alice V. *Congressional and Gubernatorial Primaries: 1991–1992: A Handbook of Election Statistics.* Washington, D.C.: Congressional Quarterly, 1993.

___. *Congressional and Gubernatorial Primaries: 1993–1994: A Handbook of Election Statistics.* Washington, D.C.: Congressional Quarterly, 1995.

Moreland, Laurence W., et al. *Contemporary Southern Political Attitudes and Behavior: Studies and Essays.* New York: Praeger, 1982.

Mullaney, Marie M. *Biographical Directory of the Governors of the United States 1983–1988.* Westport, Conn.: Meckler, 1989.

___. *Biographical Directory of the Governors of the United States 1988–1994.* Westport, Conn.: Greenwood Press, 1994.

Raimo, John, ed. *Biographical Directory of the Governors of the United States, 1978–1982.* Westport, Conn.: Meckler, 1983.

Ransone, Coleman B., Jr. *The American Governorship.* Westport, Conn.: Greenwood Press, 1982.

___. *The Office of the Governor in the United States.* 1956. Reprint. Salem, N.C.: Ayer.

Rusk, Jerrold G. *A Statistical History of the American Electorate.* Washington, D.C.: CQ Press, 2001.

Sabato, Larry. *Goodbye to Good-time Charlie: The American Governorship Transformed.* 2nd ed. Washington, D.C.: CQ Press, 1983.

Sale, Kirkpatrick. *Power Shift: The Rise of the Southern Rim and Its Challenge to the Eastern Establishment.* New York: Random House, 1975.

Sindler, Allan P. *Huey Long's Louisiana: State Politics 1920–1952.* Baltimore: Johns Hopkins University Press, 1956.

Sindler, Allan P., ed. *Change in the Contemporary South.* Durham, N.C.: Duke University Press, 1963.

Sobel, Robert, and John Raimo, eds. *Biographical Directory of the Governors of the United States, 1789–1978.* 4 vols. Westport, Conn.: Meckler, 1978.

Spence, James R. *The Making of a Governor: The Moore-Preyer-Lake Primaries of 1964.* Winston-Salem, N.C.: John H. Blair, 1968.

State and Local Government. Washington, D.C.: Congressional Quarterly, 1999- .

Steed, Robert P., and Laurence W. Moreland, eds. *Party Politics in the South.* New York: Praeger, 1980.

Tindale, George B. *The Disruption of the Solid South.* New York: Norton, 1972.

Woodward, C. Vann. *Origins of the New South, 1877–1913.* Baton Rouge: Louisiana State University Press, 1951.

___. *Reunion and Reaction: The Compromise of 1877 and the End to Reconstruction.* 1985. Reprint. New York: Oxford University Press, 1991.

Illustration Credits and Acknowledgments

VOLUME I

1. The Evolution of American Elections
1 Courtesy of the League of Women Voters   6 Library of Congress
7 (left) The Bettmann Archive, (right) Franklin D. Roosevelt Library
9 National Archives   11 Herblock, *Washington Post*   14 Library of Congress   16 AP/Wide World Photos   19 Patt Chishom, Congressional Quarterly

2. Elections: An Expanding Franchise
24 Library of Congress   27 National Archives   32 Library of Congress
34 AARP News Bulletin   38 Win McNamee, Reuters

3. Political Party Development
41 Fred Sons, Congressional Quarterly 44 Library of Congress
45 Library of Congress   46 no credit   49 Library of Congress

4. Historical Profiles of American Political Parties
53 Library of Congress   56 Library of Congress   58 Library of Congress
60 Congressional Quarterly   62 Library of Congress   64 Library of Congress   67 Library of Congress   70 Library of Congress   72 Library of Congress   74 Library of Congress   75 Library of Congress   78 National Republican Congressional Committee   81 Library of Congress

5. Campaign Finance
88 Scott J. Ferrell, Congressional Quarterly   93 Douglas Graham, Congressional Quarterly   102 Herblock, *Washington Post*   109 Library of Congress   115 no credit   116 Gerald R. Ford Library   117 no credit
123 R. Michael Jenkins, Congressional Quarterly

7. Politics and Issues, 1945–2000
135 Senate Historical Office   139 National Archives   146 U.S. Information Agency   150 Dwight D. Eisenhower Library   156 John F. Kennedy Library   159 National Park Service   165 AP/Wide World Photos   174 Senate Historical Office   180 White House   185 no credit   192 Congressional Quarterly   201 Rick Wilking, Reuters   206 AP/Wide World Photos

8. Introduction to Presidential Elections
207 no credit   210 AFP Photos   213 UPI Bettmann Newsphotos
221 Library of Congress

9. Chronology of Presidential Elections
226 John Frost, *History of the United States, 1836;* The New York Public Library   227 Library of Congress   229 Courtesy of the New-York Historical Society, New York City   233 Library of Congress   242 The Bettmann Archive   243 Library of Congress   244 Library of Congress   245 Library of Congress   249 Library of Congress   251 Library of Congress   252 Library of Congress   255 (left) Library of Congress, Theodore Roosevelt Collection, (right) Harvard College Library   257 Library of Congress   259 Franklin D. Roosevelt Library   260 Smithsonian Institute   262 The Bettmann Archive   263 Franklin D. Roosevelt Library   266 (left) Library of Congress, (center) Library of Congress, (right) courtesy of the New-York Historical Society, New York City   270 From the collection of the St. Louis Mercantile Library Association   274 Charleston Gazette   277 Library of Congress   279 AP/Wide World Photos   282 Sygma   285 UPI/Bettmann Newsphotos

287 David Valdez, White House   291 Reuters/Bettmann   293 MTV
295 Reuters   297 Reuters   300 AP/Wide World Photos

10 Presidential Primaries
No credit

12 Nominating Conventions
427 R. Michael Jenkins, Congressional Quarterly

14 Convention Chronology
442 Library of Congress   443 Library of Congress   444 Library of Congress   446 Library of Congress   448 Library of Congress   450 Library of Congress   453 Library of Congress   456 Library of Congress
459 Library of Congress   461 Library of Congress   463 Library of Congress   465 Library of Congress   467 Library of Congress   470 Library of Congress   472 Library of Congress   474 Library of Congress
477 (left) Library of Congress, (right) National Portrait Gallery, Smithsonian Institution, Washington, D.C.   479 (left) Library of Congress, (right) National Portrait Gallery, Smithsonian Institution, Washington, D.C.   481 Library of Congress   483 (left, center) Library of Congress, (right) National Portrait Gallery, Smithsonian Institution, Washington, D.C.   485 Library of Congress   490 Library of Congress   492 Library of Congress   495 Library of Congress   498 Library of Congress
501 Library of Congress   504 Library of Congress   506 Library of Congress   508 (left) New York State Historical Society, (right) Library of Congress   511 (left) New York State Historical Society, (left center) Harry S. Truman Library, (right center, right) Library of Congress
515 Library of Congress   518 Library of Congress   521 Library of Congress   525 Library of Congress   529 Library of Congress   533 (left) Library of Congress, (right) White House   537 White House   542 (left, center) White House, (right) no credit   548 White House   552 (left) no credit, (right) White House   556 (left, center) White House, (right) no credit   561 (left) White House, (center, right) no credit   566 (right) no credit, (center) Billy Suratt, UPI, (left), no credit.

17 The Electoral College
715 AP/Wide World Photos

VOLUME II

20 Introduction to Congressional Elections
789 James Watts, Congressional Quarterly   792 Scott J. Ferrell, Congressional Quarterly

21 House Elections
801 Library of Congress   804 Douglas Graham, Congressional Quarterly

23. Reapportionment and Redistricting
811 National Portrait Gallery   817 Library of Congress   822 R. Michael Jenkins, Congressional Quarterly

24 Senate Elections
1230 Library of Congress   1234 Scott J. Ferrell, Congressional Quarterly

28 Introduction to Gubernatorial Elections
1375 AP/World Wide Photos

House Candidates Index

The House Candidates Index includes all candidates appearing in House General Election Returns, 1824–2000 (pp. 829–1227). The index includes candidates' names followed by state abbreviations and the years of candidacy. To locate a candidate's re-turns, turn to pages 830 to 1226 where the returns are arranged chronologically by year and alphabetically by state for each year. State abbreviations appear below.

A

Aaker (MN) - 1900
Aandahl, Fred G. (ND) - 1950
Aaron, Samuel (NJ) - 1840
Aaron, Ward (NY) - 1824
Aarons, Morris (NY) - 1960
Abair, Pete (MA) - 2000
Abate, Frank (NJ) - 1992
Abbett, Edwin L. (NY) - 1890
Abbey, Frank E. (IL) - 1914
Abbey, George W. (MI) - 1886
Abbey, James B. (CA) - 1942, 1944
Abbitt, Watkins M. (VA) - 1948, 1950, 1952, 1954, 1956, 1958, 1960, 1962, 1964, 1966, 1968, 1970
Abbot, William S. (MA) - 1968
Abbott (WI) - 1852
Abbott, Amos (MA) - 1842, 1844, 1846
Abbott, Burnett J. (MI) - 1928
Abbott, Israel B. (NC) - 1886
Abbott, Jo (TX) - 1886, 1888, 1890, 1892, 1894
Abbott, Josiah G. (MA) - 1862, 1864, 1874
Abbott, Nehemiah (ME) - 1856
Abdella, James (NY) - 1980
Abdnor, James (SD) - 1972, 1974, 1976, 1978
Abele, Homer E. (OH) - 1958, 1962, 1964
Abercrombie, C. H. (OR) - 1912
Abercrombie, James (AL) - 1851, 1853
Abercrombie, James F. (AL) - 1914
Abercrombie, John W. (AL) - 1912, 1914
Abercrombie, Neil (HI) - 1986, 1990, 1992, 1994, 1996, 1998, 2000
Abernethy, Charles L. (NC) - 1922, 1924, 1926, 1928, 1930, 1932
Abernethy, Thomas G. (MS) - 1942, 1944, 1946, 1948, 1950, 1952, 1954, 1956, 1958, 1960, 1962, 1964, 1966, 1968, 1970
Abernethy, Tom (AL) - 1962
Abourezk, James (SD) - 1970
Abraham, William C. (OH) - 1988
Abrahams, George (CA) - 1986
Abrams, Milton C. (UT) - 1984
Abrams, Samuel (MA) - 1930

Abramson, Irving (NJ) - 1942
Abramson, R. S. (LA) - 1972
Abt, Clark C. (MA) - 1986
Abzug, Bella S. (NY) - 1970, 1972, 1974, 1978, 1986
Acee (MS) - 1837
Acer, Christopher T. (NY) - 1970, 1974
Acers, N. F. (KS) - 1882
Acevedo, Mary Alice (CA) - 1994
Acheson, A. W. (TX) - 1898, 1920
Acheson, Ernest F. (PA) - 1892, 1894, 1896, 1898, 1900, 1902, 1904, 1906
Achison, A. W. (TX) - 1890
Acker, Bert L. (FL) - 1940, 1942
Acker, Bruce (CA) - 1998
Acker, Ephraim L. (PA) - 1870, 1874
Ackerman, Edwin D. (NY) - 1908
Ackerman, Ernest R. (NJ) - 1918, 1920, 1922, 1924, 1926, 1928, 1930
Ackerman, Gary L. (NY) - 1983, 1984, 1986, 1988, 1990, 1992, 1994, 1996, 1998, 2000
Ackerman, J. Waldo Jr. (IL) - 1960
Ackerman, Johann S. (IL) - 1956
Ackerman, Luther H. (PA) - 1958
Ackerson, Nels J. (IN) - 1980
Ackerty, Merrick W. (IN) - 1892
Acklen, Joseph H. (LA) - 1876, 1878, 1882
Acklen, William (AL) - 1847
Ackley, Charles W. (NJ) - 1934
Acklin, George W. (PA) - 1998
Acklin, J. A. (LA) - 1884
Actis, Ronald G. (MI) - 2000
Acuff, Judd (TN) - 1938
Adair, Charles R. (MI) - 1922, 1940
Adair, Clark W. (NE) - 1904
Adair, E. Ross (IN) - 1950, 1952, 1954, 1956, 1958, 1960, 1962, 1964, 1966, 1968, 1970
Adair, J. Carlton (NV) - 1962
Adair, J. Leroy (IL) - 1932, 1934
Adair, John (KY) - 1831
Adair, John A. M. (IN) - 1906, 1908, 1910, 1912, 1914, 1924
Adair, Verdell (MD) - 1972
Adam, Nathaniel (CA) - 2000

Adametz, Paul T. (PA) - 1996
Adamowski, Benjamin S. (IL) - 1942
Adams (GA) - 1916
Adams (MO) - 1858
Adams (NJ) - 1912
Adams (NY) - 1842, 1872
Adams (PA) - 1848, 1850
Adams (VT) - 1872
Adams, Alfred (TN) - 1972
Adams, Allen C. (OK) - 1916
Adams, Allison L. (NY) - 1918
Adams, Alva (CO) - 1902
Adams, Alva B. (CO) - 1954, 1956
Adams, Augustus (IL) - 1878
Adams, Billy (GA) - 1976
Adams, Bob (WA) - 1992
Adams, Brock (WA) - 1964, 1966, 1968, 1970, 1972, 1974, 1976
Adams, C. E. (NE) - 1898
Adams, C. P. (MN) - 1882
Adams, Charles D. (OH) - 1880
Adams, Charles F. (MA) - 1852, 1858, 1860
Adams, Charles H. (NY) - 1874
Adams, Clifford R. (MN) - 1970
Adams, Clyde (FL) - 1976
Adams, David (TN) - 1835
Adams, Dennis (NJ) - 1984
Adams, Dennis Sr. (NJ) - 1976
Adams, Edson (CA) - 1974
Adams, Edward R. (NY) - 1996
Adams, Francis A. (NY) - 1908
Adams, G. (KY) - 1845
Adams, George (OH) - 1892, 1900
Adams, George E. (IL) - 1882, 1884, 1886, 1888, 1890
Adams, George M. (KY) - 1867, 1868, 1870, 1872, 1882
Adams, George Z. (CA) - 1986, 1988, 1990
Adams, Green (KY) - 1847, 1859
Adams, Henry C. (WI) - 1902, 1904
Adams, J. A. (WA) - 1900
Adams, J. M. (AL) - 1855
Adams, James (NC) - 2000
Adams, James A. (WI) - 1972

Adams, James F. (MO) - 1926
Adams, John (NH) - 1976
Adams, John (NY) - 1832
Adams, John J. (NY) - 1882, 1884
Adams, John Q. (NY) - 1896
Adams, John Quincy (MA) - 1830, 1833, 1834, 1836, 1838, 1840, 1842, 1844, 1846
Adams, Joseph S. (NC) - 1896
Adams, Ken (FL) - 1988
Adams, L. S. (AZ) - 1954
Adams, Mike (TN) - 1980
Adams, Monroe (NC) - 1938, 1940
Adams, Norman W. (OH) - 1946
Adams, Parmenio (NY) - 1824
Adams, Paul L. (MI) - 1942
Adams, Percy D. (NY) - 1890
Adams, Robert Jr. (PA) - 1893, 1894, 1896, 1898, 1900, 1902, 1904
Adams, S. C. (VA) - 1890
Adams, Samuel (PA) - 1878
Adams, Seth (MA) - 1870
Adams, Sherman (NH) - 1944
Adams, Silas R. (KY) - 1892, 1894
Adams, Spencer B. (NC) - 1898
Adams, Stanley G. (VA) - 1948
Adams, Stephen (MS) - 1845
Adams, Ted (SC) - 2000
Adams, Thomas J. (NY) - 1968
Adams, W. P. C. (WA) - 1894
Adams, Wayne N. (WA) - 1968
Adams, Wilbur (DE) - 1932
Adams, William (PA) - 1908, 1916, 1922
Adamson, William C. (GA) - 1896, 1898, 1900, 1902, 1904, 1906, 1908, 1910, 1912, 1914, 1916
Adanti, Michael J. (CT) - 1976
Addabbo, Joseph P. (NY) - 1960, 1962, 1964, 1966, 1968, 1970, 1972, 1974, 1976, 1978, 1980, 1982, 1984
Addams, William (PA) - 1824, 1826, 1828
Addonizio, G. George (NJ) - 1956, 1958
Addonizio, Hugh J. (NJ) - 1948, 1950, 1952, 1954, 1956, 1958, 1960
Ade, William H. (IN) - 1914

State Abbreviations

Alabama	AL	Indiana	IN	Nebraska	NE	South Carolina	SC
Alaska	AK	Iowa	IA	Nevada	NV	South Dakota	SD
Arizona	AZ	Kansas	KS	New Hampshire	NH	Tennessee	TN
Arkansas	AR	Kentucky	KY	New Jersey	NJ	Texas	TX
California	CA	Louisiana	LA	New Mexico	NM	Utah	UT
Colorado	CO	Maine	ME	New York	NY	Vermont	VT
Connecticut	CT	Maryland	MD	North Carolina	NC	Virginia	VA
Delaware	DE	Massachusetts	MA	North Dakota	ND	Washington	WA
Florida	FL	Michigan	MI	Ohio	OH	West Virginia	WV
Georgia	GA	Minnesota	MN	Oklahoma	OK	Wisconsin	WI
Hawaii	HI	Mississippi	MS	Oregon	OR	Wyoming	WY
Idaho	ID	Missouri	MO	Pennsylvania	PA		
Illinois	IL	Montana	MT	Rhode Island	RI		

Bowdon, Franklin W. (AL) - 1846, 1847, 1849
Bowe, John (MN) - 1932
Bowen (NY) - 1850, 1852
Bowen (PA) - 1856
Bowen, A. H. (SC) - 1882
Bowen, A. M. (ID) - 1910
Bowen, C. D. (FL) - 1920
Bowen, Christopher (SC) - 1868, 1870
Bowen, David R. (MS) - 1972, 1974, 1976, 1978, 1980
Bowen, Edna (WI) - 1952
Bowen, Elizabeth Ann (WV) - 1966
Bowen, Ephriam F. (IN) - 1932
Bowen, Henry (VA) - 1882, 1886, 1888
Bowen, James (ME) - 1843
Bowen, John F. (FL) - 1972
Bowen, John F. (TN) - 1984, 1986
Bowen, Lester W. (MA) - 1944, 1946
Bowen, M. A. (NY) - 1914
Bowen, Rees T. (VA) - 1872
Bowen, Sam (PA) - 1896
Bowen, T. M. (CO) - 1894
Bowen, William F. (OH) - 1978
Bower (PA) - 1866, 1888
Bower, Andrew P. (PA) - 1930
Bower, Charles C. (IN) - 1900
Bower, Gustavus M. (MO) - 1842
Bower, H. O. (LA) - 1916
Bower, William H. (NC) - 1892, 1894
Bowers, Claude G. (IN) - 1904, 1906
Bowers, David (VA) - 1998
Bowers, Eaton J. (MS) - 1902, 1904, 1906, 1908
Bowers, G. Roger (PA) - 1978
Bowers, George H. (IN) - 1958, 1960
Bowers, George M. (WV) - 1914, 1916, 1918, 1920, 1922
Bowers, John O. (IN) - 1912
Bowers, M. D. (AR) - 1924
Bowers, O. C. (PA) - 1904
Bowers, Quinton (AL) - 1968
Bowers, Ronald P. (MD) - 1990
Bowers, Varnum J. (MI) - 1916, 1924, 1928
Bowers, William W. (CA) - 1890, 1892, 1894, 1896
Bowersock, Justin D. (KS) - 1898, 1900, 1902, 1904
Bowes, Henry W. (NY) - l896
Bowie (MD) - 1843
Bowie, G. W. (CA) - 1854
Bowie, Richard J. (MD) - 1849, 1851
Bowie, Stuart S. (PA) - 1972
Bowie, Sydney J. (AL) - 1900, 1902, 1904
Bowie, Thomas F. (MD) - 1851, 1855, 1857
Bowler (MN) - 1916
Bowler, J. M. (MN) - 1894
Bowler, James B. (IL) - 1953, 1954, 1956
Bowler, Robert B. (OH) - 1892
Bowles, C. J. (IN) - 1874
Bowles, Charles (MI) - 1932, 1934
Bowles, Chester (CT) - 1958
Bowles, Elihu (WA) - 1922
Bowles, Henry L. (MA) - 1926
Bowles, Thomas P. Jr. (CA) - 1978
Bowlin, Bill (MS) - 1990
Bowlin, James B. (MO) - 1842, 1844, 1846, 1848, 1850
Bowling, William B. (AL) - 1920, 1922, 1924, 1926
Bowman (MO) - 1850
Bowman, C. A. (KS) - 1920
Bowman, Charles C. (PA) - 1910, 1912
Bowman, Charles M. (PA) - 1920
Bowman, Denny (KY) - 1996
Bowman, Frank (NY) - 1928
Bowman, Frank L. (WV) - 1924, 1926, 1928, 1930, 1932
Bowman, Ivan L. (MI) - 1942
Bowman, J. G. (SC) - 1836
Bowman, John (IA) - 1874
Bowman, Kenneth (IN) - 1966
Bowman, Leroy (NY) - 1958
Bowman, Noah (KS) - 1902
Bowman, Ralph Waldo (NY) - 1916, 1918
Bowman, Selwyn Z. (MA) - 1878, 1880, 1882
Bowman, Stuart H. (WV) - 1918
Bowman, Thomas (IA) - 1938

Bowman, W. C. (CA) - 1894
Bowne, Obadiah (NY) - 1850
Bowne, Samuel (NY) - 1840
Box, John C. (TX) - 1918, 1920, 1922, 1924, 1926, 1928
Boxer, Barbara (CA) - 1982, 1984, 1986, 1988, 1990
Boyarsky, Harry (NY) - 1942
Boyce, James A. (IN) - 1894
Boyce, William H. (DE) - 1922, 1924
Boyce, William W. (SC) - 1853, 1854, 1856, 1858, 1860
Boyd (KY) - 1849
Boyd (TN) - 1865
Boyd, Allen (FL) - 1996, 1998, 2000
Boyd, F. W. (KS) - 1922
Boyd, George D. (NC) - 1853
Boyd, Harrison N. (PA) - 1922, 1924
Boyd, Henry Jr. (MS) - 1996
Boyd, Hugh J. (SC) - 1968
Boyd, J. F. (NE) - 1908, 1910
Boyd, James (MO) - 1878
Boyd, James E. (NC) - 1876
Boyd, James E. (NE) - 1894
Boyd, Jim (TN) - 1966
Boyd, John (VA) - 2000
Boyd, John F. (NE) - 1906
Boyd, John H. (NY) - 1846, 1850
Boyd, Joseph H. (NY) - 1972
Boyd, Linn (KY) - 1833, 1835, 1837, 1839, 1841, 1843, 1845, 1847, 1851, 1853
Boyd, Robert (KY) - 1876
Boyd, Sempronius H. (MO) - 1862, 1864, 1868
Boyd, Thomas A. (IL) - 1876, 1878
Boyd, W. R. (OK) - 1940, 1942
Boyd, Weir (GA) - 1870
Boyd, William M. (OH) - 1946
Boyd-Fields, Chrysanthea D. (MI) - 1998, 2000
Boyden, Jesse S. (MI) - 1886
Boyden, Nathaniel (NC) - 1847, 1868
Boyden, Willard E. (MA) - 1928
Boye (NJ) - 1852
Boyer, Arthur O. (NY) - 1960
Boyer, Benjamin M. (PA) - 1864, 1866
Boyer, Daniel B. Jr. (PA) - 1966
Boyer, James S. (NY) - 1900
Boyer, Lewis L. (IL) - 1936, 1938
Boyer, Selwyn L. (IL) - 1966
Boyett, T. R. (CA) - 1958
Boyhan (NY) - 1888
Boykin, Frank W. (AL) - 1936, 1938, 1940, 1942, 1944, 1946, 1948, 1950, 1952, 1954, 1956, 1958, 1960
Boylan, John J. (NY) - 1922, 1924, 1926, 1928, 1930, 1932, 1934, 1936
Boylan, John J. Jr. (VT) - 1954
Boylan, John P. (PA) - 1930
Boyle, Charles A. (IL) - 1954, 1956, 1958
Boyle, Charles E. (PA) - 1882, 1884
Boyle, Eugene Jr. (NJ) - 1969
Boyle, J. T. (KY) - 1863
Boyle, James P. (NY) - 1924
Boyle, John F. (MI) - 1968
Boyle, John J. (WI) - 1932
Boyle, Lawrence P. (IL) - 1912
Boyle, Patrick J. (RI) - 1920
Boyle, St. John (KY) - 1890
Boyle, Walter Durley (IL) - 1950
Boyles, Aubrey (AL) - 1926
Boyles, Henry (OH) - 1874
Boynton (MA) - 1880
Boynton (ME) - 1862, 1874
Boynton, Charles C. (CA) - 1906
Boynton, E. Moody (MA) - 1878, 1882, 1896, 1898
Boynton, G. W. (TX) - 1908
Bozeman, C. Howard (TN) - 1954
Bozman, Bennett (MD) - 2000
Bozzone, Richard T. (NJ) - 1972
Bozzuffi, William J. (NJ) - 1952
Braaten (MN) - 1908
Braaten, Kenneth W. (WA) - 1986
Brabson, Reese B. (TN) - 1859
Brace, T. K. (CT) - 1843
Bracewell, H. B. (IA) - 1916
Brack, Andy (SC) - 2000

Bracken, John P. (PA) - 1920, 1921
Brackenridge, Henry M. (PA) - 1840
Bracklin, James (WI) - 1886
Bradbury (ME) - 1858, 1860, 1874
Bradbury, E. L. (TN) - 1928, 1930, 1936
Braddock, John S. (OH) - 1888
Brademas, John (IN) - 1954, 1956, 1958, 1960, 1962, 1964, 1966, 1968, 1970, 1972, 1974, 1976, 1978, 1980
Braden (IN) - 1880
Braden, Roberts A. "Rob (CA) - 1996, 1998
Braden, W. Wallace (CA) - 1948
Bradfield, George H. (CO) - 1932, 1934, 1936
Bradford (AL) - 1849
Bradford (MA) - 1878
Bradford (MO) - 1912
Bradford (MS) - 1849, 1853
Bradford (RI) - 1865
Bradford, A. C. (NV) - 1864
Bradford, Carol Ann (CA) - 1984
Bradford, J. M. (LA) - 1834
Bradford, Jay (AR) - 1994
Bradford, Naomi (CO) - 1980
Bradford, Robert E. (OR) - 1930
Bradford, T. F. (TN) - 1833
Bradford, Taul (AL) - 1847
Bradford, William J. A. (MA) - 1834
Bradhst (NY) - 1848
Bradish, Luther (NY) - 1830, 1832
Bradley (AR) - 1878
Bradley (IN) - 1852
Bradley (NJ) - 1862
Bradley (NY) - 1844, 1858
Bradley (RI) - 1863
Bradley (VT) - 1846
Bradley, A. A. (GA) - 1870
Bradley, C. D. (KY) - 1865
Bradley, Charles S. (RI) - 1886, 1887
Bradley, Daniel (NY) - 1894
Bradley, David O. (NY) - 1868
Bradley, Edward (MI) - 1846
Bradley, Fred (MI) - 1938, 1940, 1942, 1944, 1946
Bradley, George (MI) - 1852
Bradley, Gerald A. (IL) - 1984, 1991
Bradley, J. M. (AR) - 1872
Bradley, James O. (OH) - 1958
Bradley, John F. (PA) - 1976
Bradley, Michael J. (PA) - 1934, 1936, 1938, 1940, 1942, 1944
Bradley, Nathan B. (MI) - 1872, 1874
Bradley, Omar (CA) - 1996
Bradley, Paul (CO) - 1968
Bradley, Richard (NH) - 1837
Bradley, Thomas J. (NY) - 1896, 1898
Bradley, Thomas W. (NY) - 1902, 1904, 1906, 1908, 1910
Bradley, Vernon E. (MA) - 1954
Bradley, W. O. (KY) - 1872, 1876
Bradley, W. S. (IA) - 1926
Bradley, William C. (VT) - 1824
Bradley, Willis W. (CA) - 1946, 1948
Bradshaw, Charles (SC) - 1968
Bradshaw, James (MS) - 1982
Bradshaw, Jim (TX) - 1980, 1982
Bradshaw, Samuel C. (PA) - 1854, 1856
Bradstreet (CT) - 1912
Bradt, Mary A. (NY) - 1976
Brady, Chuck (CO) - 1972
Brady, David (CT) - 1954
Brady, Francis M. (KS) - 1904, 1906, 1912
Brady, Frank (TX) - 2000
Brady, Fred D. (SD) - 1970
Brady, Hugh E. (OR) - 1932
Brady, J. L. (KS) - 1912, 1914
Brady, J. T. (TX) - 1880
Brady, James D. (VA) - 1884
Brady, Jasper E. (PA) - 1846, 1848
Brady, Jim (TX) - 1972, 1974
Brady, John E. (NY) - 1912
Brady, Kevin (TX) - 1996, 1998, 2000
Brady, Philip E. (MA) - 1898
Brady, Robert A. (PA) - 1998, 2000
Brady, S. (MD) - 1843
Brady, Thomas J. (MN) - 1920
Brady, William (TN) - 1833

Bragg (WI) - 1862
Bragg, Edward S. (WI) - 1876, 1878, 1880, 1884
Bragg, John (AL) - 1851
Bragg, Merl J. (OH) - 1946
Brainard, F. W. (CO) - 1912
Brainard, Robert L. (ID) - 1944
Brainerd, Clarence J. (MI) - 1936
Braman, Isaac G. (NY) - 1932
Bramback (OH) - 1856
Bramble, A. F. (KS) - 1968
Bramblett, Ernest K. (CA) - 1946, 1948, 1950, 1952
Bramhall, Ronald O. (IA) - 1956
Bramlage, Ervin L. (KY) - 1936
Bramlett, Lunsford M. (TN) - 1825, 1827
Bramlette, Thomas E. (KY) - 1853
Bramwell, Arthur (NY) - 1978
Branagan, W. J. (IA) - 1904
Branagan, William T. (IA) - 1932
Branch (MO) - 1862
Branch, H. B. (MO) - 1864
Branch, John (NC) - 1831
Branch, Lawrence Ob (NC) - 1855, 1857, 1859
Branch, William A. B. (NC) - 1890, 1892, 1884
Branch, William McKinley (AL) - 1968
Branch, Wilson (CA) - 1980
Brand, Charles (OH) - 1922, 1924, 1926, 1928, 1930
Brand, Charles H. (GA) - 1916, 1918, 1920, 1922, 1924, 1926, 1928, 1930, 1932
Brandau, John P. (MD) - 1928
Brandegee, Augustus (CT) - 1863, 1865
Brandegee, Frank B. (CT) - 1902, 1904
Brandenburg, C. W. (KS) - 1894
Brandenburg, Tony (CA) - 1982
Brandofino, Robert L. (NY) - 1984, 1988
Brandon, Doug (AR) - 1978
Brandon, Martin O. (MN) - 1934, 1936, 1938
Brandon, Rodney H. (IL) - 1926
Brandreth (NY) - 1876
Brandreth, George A. (NY) - 1892
Brandt (MO) - 1914
Brandt, Charles F. (NY) - 1896
Brandt, J. Seldon (PA) - 1926
Branham (GA) - 1832
Branine, Ezra (KS) - 1914
Brann, Louis J. (ME) - 1942
Brannan, Charles I. (GA) - 1900
Brannan, W. F. (IA) - 1878
Brannen, Barney (NH) - 2000
Brannon, John (WV) - 1884
Branscum, Truman T. (OK) - 1966
Bransford (TN) - 1843
Branson, David (PA) - 1874
Bransrator, Charles W. (IN) - 1922, 1924
Branth (NY) - 1854
Brantley, Hobart (NC) - 1926, 1934
Brantley, William G. (GA) - 1896, 1898, 1900, 1902, 1904, 1906, 1908
Branyan, James C. (IN) - 1886
Brasco, Frank J. (NY) - 1966, 1968, 1970, 1972
Brasnears, J. (PA) - 1838
Brass, E. E. (IL) - 1912
Bratcher, Rhodes (KY) - 1964
Brathwaite, Peter L. W. (FL) - 1978
Bratten, Robert F. (MD) - 1892
Brattland, M. A. (MN) - 1912, 1914
Bratton, John (SC) - 1884
Bratton, U. S. (AR) - 1900
Braude, Evan Anderson (CA) - 1992
Braun, Ernst A. (WI) - 1924
Braun, Harry W. III (AZ) - 1984, 1986
Brauner, William I. (ID) - 1970
Braunstein, Alexander (NY) - 1916, 1923
Braver, Ruth C. (IL) - 1984
Brawley, Kevin (NY) - 1990
Brawley, William H. (SC) - 1890, 1892
Braxton (VA) - 1829, 1831, 1841
Braxton, Elliott M. (VA) - 1870, 1872
Braxton, Thomas N. (IN) - 1888
Bray (NY) - 1882
Bray, Crandle (GA) - 1986
Bray, Everett L. (MI) - 1900
Bray, W. S. (SD) - 1908

Houk, David A. (OH) - 1864
Houk, George W. (OH) - 1888, 1890, 1892
Houk, John (PA) - 1910, 1912
Houk, John C. (TN) - 1891, 1892
Houk, Leonidas C. (TN) - 1878, 1880, 1882, 1884, 1886, 1888, 1890
Houk, William G. (NY) - 1946
Houlihan (CT) - 1896
Houlihan, John J. (IL) - 1972, 1974
Hourian, George (WV) - 1890
Hourihan, James L. (MA) - 1916
Hourwich, Isaac A. (NY) - 1912
House (NY) - 1884
House (OH) - 1832
House, Arthur H. (CT) - 1984
House, Charles M. (CA) - 1986, 1988
House, Earl E. (CO) - 1928
House, George (OH) - 1840
House, J. E. (SD) - 1926
House, John F. (TN) - 1874, 1876, 1878, 1880
House, Ted (MO) - 2000
Houseman, Gerald L. (IN) - 1996
Houseman, Julius (MI) - 1882
Houser, Frederick F. (CA) - 1932, 1934, 1936
Houser, William W. (IL) - 1904
Housholder, E. D. (FL) - 1926
Houst (PA) - 1872
Housten, L. E. (MS) - 1855
Houston (DE) - 1880
Houston (KY) - 1849
Houston (MO) - 1916
Houston, A. J. (TX) - 1898, 1904
Houston, A. W. (TX) - 1894
Houston, D. F. (PA) - 1874
Houston, E. C. (NE) - 1924
Houston, George S. (AL) - 1841, 1843, 1845, 1847, 1851, 1853, 1855, 1857, 1859
Houston, H. H. (KY) - 1872, 1876, 1882, 1884
Houston, Henry A. (DE) - 1902
Houston, James E. (OH) - 1976
Houston, Jefferson Earle (IL) - 1920
Houston, John M. (KS) - 1934, 1936, 1938, 1940, 1942
Houston, John W. (DE) - 1844, 1846, 1848, 1852
Houston, Robert G. (DE) - 1896, 1924, 1926, 1928, 1930
Houston, Samuel (PA) - 1824
Houston, Samuel (TN) - 1825
Houston, Sid (TN) - 1916
Houston, Syd (TN) - 1896
Houston, W. T. (LA) - 1884
Houston, William (IN) - 1912
Houston, William C. (TN) - 1904, 1906, 1908, 1910, 1912, 1914, 1916
Hout, J. N. (AR) - 1922
Hout, J. N. Jr. (AR) - 1936
Houton, Daniel J. (MA) - 1970
Hove, John (ND) - 1963
Hovey (CT) - 1857
Hovey (IN) - 1858
Hovey, Alvin P. (IN) - 1886
How (NY) - 1852
Howard (MD) - 1833
Howard (MS) - 1843
Howard (OH) - 1858, 1870
Howard (RI) - 1837, 1886
Howard, Arthur (MA) - 1916
Howard, B. F. (WV) - 1942
Howard, Benjamin C. (MD) - 1829, 1831, 1835, 1837
Howard, Bert (NE) - 1940
Howard, Charles F. (IN) - 1918
Howard, Duncan (CA) - 1983
Howard, E. E. (MN) - 1926
Howard, E. J. (KY) - 1890
Howard, Ed (PA) - 1988
Howard, Edgar (NE) - 1900, 1922, 1924, 1926, 1928, 1930, 1932, 1934, 1938
Howard, Edward (MA) - 1892
Howard, Edward J. (PA) - 1944
Howard, Ernest Linoln (VA) - 1904
Howard, Everette B. (OK) - 1918, 1920, 1922, 1926, 1928
Howard, Francis (MO) - 1958

Howard, Francis E. (MO) - 1952
Howard, Frank E. (IA) - 1926
Howard, Frederick A. (PA) - 1912
Howard, Harry C. (MA) - 1914
Howard, Jacob M. (MI) - 1840, 1843
Howard, James J. (NJ) - 1964, 1966, 1968, 1970, 1972, 1974, 1976, 1978, 1980, 1982, 1984, 1986
Howard, Jim (OR) - 1976, 1988
Howard, John (OH) - 1876
Howard, John A. (CA) - 1966
Howard, John A. (WV) - 1894
Howard, John C. (NY) - 1894
Howard, Jonas G. (IN) - 1884, 1886
Howard, Laurence E. (MI) - 1968
Howard, M. R. (KS) - 1932
Howard, M. W. (AL) - 1910
Howard, Mary Giles (TN) - 1924
Howard, Milford W. (AL) - 1894, 1896
Howard, R. A. (OK) - 1932
Howard, Robert (MA) - 1894
Howard, Ted (NY) - 1998
Howard, Theodore R. M. (IL) - 1958
Howard, Tilghman A. (IN) - 1839
Howard, Timothy J. (NH) - 1900
Howard, Volney E. (TX) - 1849, 1851
Howard, W. G. (KY) - 1918
Howard, William (GA) - 1910
Howard, William (OH) - 1866
Howard, William A. (MI) - 1852, 1854, 1856, 1858
Howard, William M. (GA) - 1896, 1898, 1900, 1902, 1904, 1906, 1908
Howard, William S. (GA) - 1910, 1912, 1914, 1916
Howe (NY) - 1878, 1888
Howe (WI) - 1848
Howe, Albert R. (MS) - 1872, 1875
Howe, Allan T. (UT) - 1974, 1976
Howe, Appleton (MA) - 1844, 1846, 1848
Howe, Ben (NY) - 1922
Howe, Church (NE) - 1886
Howe, Harland B. (VT) - 1904
Howe, James R. (NY) - 1894, 1896, 1902
Howe, John W. (PA) - 1848, 1850
Howe, Samuel G. (MA) - 1846
Howe, Thomas M. (PA) - 1850, 1852
Howe, Thomas Y. Jr. (NY) - 1850
Howe, William S. (MA) - 1934, 1936
Howell (NY) - 1854
Howell (PA) - 1872
Howell, Benjamin F. (NJ) - 1894, 1896, 1898, 1900, 1902, 1904, 1906, 1908, 1910
Howell, Charles R. (NJ) - 1946, 1948, 1950, 1952
Howell, Edward (NY) - 1832
Howell, Elias (OH) - 1834
Howell, Evan (IL) - 1940, 1942, 1944, 1946
Howell, George (PA) - 1902, 1904
Howell, Herbert H. (NC) - 1968, 1970
Howell, Hynek M. (IL) - 1924
Howell, James A. (IL) - 1932, 1934
Howell, John H. (IA) - 1898
Howell, John W. (FL) - 1912
Howell, Joseph (UT) - 1902, 1904, 1906, 1908, 1910, 1912, 1914
Howell, Melvin C. (PA) - 1964
Howell, William E. (LA) - 1902
Hower, Robert E. (NY) - 1936
Hower, Robert J. (NY) - 1968
Howes, Frederick (MA) - 1824
Howey (NJ) - 1892
Howey, Benjamin F. (NJ) - 1882, 1884
Howie (NY) - 1886
Howland, Abraham H. (MA) - 1848, 1852, 1854
Howland, L. (WI) - 1882
Howland, Paul (OH) - 1906, 1908, 1910, 1912
Howland, Weston (MA) - 1884
Howley, Joseph (PA) - 1912
Howth (TX) - 1857
Hoxie (NY) - 1852
Hoxie, John R. (IL) - 1876
Hoxworth, Stephen A. (IL) - 1912
Hoy, James P. (MI) - 1972

Hoyer, Steny H. (MD) - 1981, 1982, 1984, 1986, 1988, 1990, 1992, 1994, 1996, 1998, 2000
Hoyle, George V. (NY) - 1866
Hoynes, William (IN) - 1888
Hoyt (MI) - 1878
Hoyt (NY) - 1888
Hoyt (WI) - 1854
Hoyt, Elihu (MA) - 1828
Hoyt, Eugene (TX) - 1970
Hoyt, Ferdinand A. (NY) - 1942
Hoyt, John C. (OH) - 1978
Hoyt, Jonathan (NY) - 1832
Hoyt, Thaddeus E. (OH) - 1886, 1890, 1906
Hoyt, Timothy C. (UT) - 1916
Hoyt, William T. (CT) - 1924
Hruby, Otto Joseph Jr. (IL) - 1944
Hruska, Roman L. (NE) - 1952
Hubard, Edmund W. (VA) - 1841, 1843, 1845
Hubard, Robert T. (VA) - 1884, 1898, 1900
Hubbard (CT) - 1857, 1875, 1890
Hubbard (OH) - 1858
Hubbard, Asahel W. (IA) - 1862, 1864, 1866
Hubbard, Carroll Jr. (KY) - 1974, 1976, 1978, 1980, 1982, 1984, 1986, 1988, 1990
Hubbard, Chester D. (WV) - 1864, 1866
Hubbard, David (AL) - 1839, 1847, 1849, 1851, 1857
Hubbard, Demas Jr. (NY) - 1864
Hubbard, E. B. (AL) - 1902
Hubbard, Elbert H. (IA) - 1904, 1906, 1908, 1910
Hubbard, Frank C. (OK) - 1907
Hubbard, Frederick W. (NY) - 1864
Hubbard, Garland R. (KY) - 1944
Hubbard, George Denys (MD) - 1956
Hubbard, H. Warren (NY) - 1926
Hubbard, Henry (NH) - 1829, 1831, 1833
Hubbard, J. R. (WV) - 1878
Hubbard, Joel D. (MO) - 1894, 1896
Hubbard, John (ME) - 1838, 1840
Hubbard, John C. (OH) - 1878
Hubbard, John H. (CT) - 1863, 1865
Hubbard, Kyle (KY) - 1974
Hubbard, R. B. (MA) - 1846
Hubbard, R. T. (VA) - 1898
Hubbard, Richard (CT) - 1833, 1834, 1835
Hubbard, Richard D. (CT) - 1867
Hubbard, Robert (CT) - 1876
Hubbard, Rudolphius B. (MA) - 1844
Hubbard, Samuel D. (CT) - 1843, 1845, 1847
Hubbard, William P. (WV) - 1890, 1906, 1908
Hubbell, Edwin N. (NY) - 1864
Hubbell, Homer E. (VT) - 1846
Hubbell, J. Felipe (NM) - 1924
Hubbell, James R. (OH) - 1864, 1870
Hubbell, Jay A. (MI) - 1872, 1874, 1876, 1878, 1880
Hubbell, Walter (OK) - 1940
Hubbell, William S. (NY) - 1842
Hubble, M. J. (MO) - 1864
Hubbs, Orlando (NC) - 1880
Hubbs, Stanley (IL) - 1952, 1956
Huber, Harry I. (PA) - 1902
Huber, J. David (IN) - 1970
Huber, Robert J. (MI) - 1972, 1974
Huber, S. C. (IA) - 1910, 1912
Huber, Walter B. (OH) - 1944, 1946, 1948, 1950, 1952
Hubert, John (IL) - 1920
Hubler, Eugene W. (PA) - 1972
Hubley, Edward B. (PA) - 1834, 1836
Hubschmitt, Frank (NJ) - 1920
Huck, Winnifred Mason (IL) - 1922
Huckaba, G. M. (AL) - 1924
Huckaby, Jerry (LA) - 1976, 1978, 1980, 1982, 1984, 1986, 1988, 1990, 1992
Huckell, Benjamin (PA) - 1870
Huckenstine, John (PA) - 1900
Huckleberry (AR) - 1876
Huckleberry, Roy (IN) - 1942
Hudd, Thomas R. (WI) - 1886
Huddleson (PA) - 1843
Huddleston, George (AL) - 1914, 1916, 1918, 1920, 1922, 1924, 1926, 1928, 1930, 1932, 1934

Huddleston, George Jr. (AL) - 1954, 1956, 1958, 1960, 1962, 1964
Hudec, James S. (OH) - 1946
Hudgens, Ralph T. (GA) - 1988, 1992
Hudnut, William H. III (IN) - 1972, 1974
Hudock, Robert P. (PA) - 1978, 1984
Hudson (MO) - 1904
Hudson, Charles (MA) - 1841, 1842, 1844, 1846, 1848
Hudson, Edward (NY) - 1944
Hudson, Fred (TX) - 1978
Hudson, Grant M. (MI) - 1922, 1924, 1926, 1928, 1932
Hudson, Hiram B. (MI) - 1888, 1894
Hudson, J. K. (KS) - 1874
Hudson, John (MT) - 1906
Hudson, John H. (OH) - 1876
Hudson, Leslie H. (MI) - 1958
Hudson, Richard R. (OH) - 1872
Hudson, Roy (NY) - 1936
Hudson, Samuel E. (PA) - 1896
Hudson, T. David (MI) - 1988
Hudson, T. J. (KS) - 1908
Hudson, Thomas B. (MO) - 1844
Hudson, Thomas J. (KS) - 1892
Hudspeth, Claude B. (TX) - 1918, 1920, 1922, 1924, 1926, 1928
Hudspeth, Emmett L. (TX) - 1978
Huening, Tom (CA) - 1992
Huff, Charles F. (LA) - 1976
Huff, George F. (PA) - 1890, 1894, 1902, 1904, 1906, 1908
Huff, George W. (PA) - 1896
Huff, Richard H. (AZ) - 1980
Huffington, Michael (CA) - 1992
Huffman, Marion (OH) - 1900, 1922
Hufford, Tom (VA) - 1968
Huger, Alfred (SC) - 1834
Huggins, Edward N. (OH) - 1892, 1898
Huggins, Walter F. (IL) - 1906, 1912, 1916
Hughes (MN) - 1904
Hughes (MO) - 1920
Hughes (NH) - 1853
Hughes (NY) - 1854, 1874
Hughes (OK) - 1914
Hughes (PA) - 1860
Hughes (TN) - 1878, 1880, 1904
Hughes (VA) - 1906
Hughes, A. M. (TN) - 1837
Hughes, A. M. Jr. (TN) - 1890, 1896, 1920
Hughes, Bernard J. (IL) - 1964, 1966
Hughes, Brian M. (NJ) - 1992
Hughes, C. M. (TX) - 1916
Hughes, Charles (CA) - 1978
Hughes, Charles (NY) - 1852
Hughes, Charles B. (CO) - 1924
Hughes, Charles V. (CA) - 1980, 1994
Hughes, D. D. (MI) - 1870
Hughes, Daniel M. (NH) - 1978
Hughes, David A. (WA) - 1970
Hughes, Doug R. (MO) - 1986, 1988
Hughes, Duane C. (CA) - 1996
Hughes, Dudley M. (GA) - 1908, 1910, 1912, 1914
Hughes, E. J. (ND) - 1922
Hughes, Edward (VA) - 1898
Hughes, George A. (TX) - 1972
Hughes, George R. Jr. (PA) - 1970
Hughes, George W. (MD) - 1859
Hughes, Gordon F. (MA) - 1958, 1962, 1964, 1966, 1970
Hughes, Harry R. (MD) - 1964
Hughes, James (IN) - 1856, 1858
Hughes, James (PA) - 1902
Hughes, James (WI) - 1932
Hughes, James A. (WV) - 1902, 1904, 1906, 1908, 1910, 1912, 1926, 1928
Hughes, James E. (WI) - 1940
Hughes, James H. (WV) - 1900
Hughes, James M. (MO) - 1842
Hughes, Miller (KY) - 1920, 1928
Hughes, Nicholas (NJ) - 1920
Hughes, Norman R. (MI) - 1978, 1980
Hughes, Peter J. (PA) - 1900
Hughes, Reid (FL) - 1990
Hughes, Richard J. (NJ) - 1938

Hughes, Robert H. (TX) - 1968
Hughes, Robert M. (VA) - 1902, 1904
Hughes, Robert W. (VA) - 1870, 1872
Hughes, S. (MD) - 1826
Hughes, Scott (IA) - 1986
Hughes, Thomas H. (NJ) - 1828, 1830
Hughes, W. G. (KY) - 1855
Hughes, William (NJ) - 1902, 1904, 1906,
  1908, 1910
Hughes, William J. (NJ) - 1970, 1974, 1976,
  1978, 1980, 1982, 1984, 1986, 1988, 1990,
  1992
Hughey, R. M. (OH) - 1912
Hughey, William (OH) - 1932
Hughson, Jonas A. (NY) - 1854
Hugunin, Daniel Jr. (NY) - 1824
Huhn, Kenneth (NY) - 1978
Huiet, Ben T. (GA) - 1946
Huish, Henry A. (UT) - 1982
Hukriede, Theodore W. (MO) - 1920, 1922
Hulbert, Murray (NY) - 1914, 1916
Hulburd, Calvin T. (NY) - 1862, 1864, 1866
Hulette, Frank P. (NY) - 1896
Hulick, George W. (OH) - 1892, 1894
Hulin, H. Frank (NC) - 1946
Huling, Cyrus (OH) - 1902
Huling, James H. (WV) - 1894
Hulings, Willis J. (PA) - 1912, 1914, 1917, 1918,
  1920
Hull (CT) - 1912
Hull, Charles J. (MD) - 1918
Hull, Cordell (TN) - 1906, 1908, 1910, 1912,
  1914, 1916, 1918, 1920, 1922, 1924, 1926,
  1928
Hull, Elizabeth Ann "Betty" (IL) - 1996
Hull, Harry E. (IA) - 1914, 1916, 1918, 1920,
  1922
Hull, John A. T. (IA) - 1890, 1892, 1894, 1896,
  1898, 1900, 1902, 1904, 1906, 1908
Hull, John W. (MN) - 1978
Hull, Lewis W. (OH) - 1892
Hull, Matthew R. (IN) - 1845
Hull, Merlin (WI) - 1928, 1930, 1934, 1936,
  1938, 1940, 1942, 1944, 1946, 1948, 1950,
  1952
Hull, Morton D. (IL) - 1923, 1924, 1926, 1928,
  1930
Hull, Moses (WI) - 1906
Hull, Noble A. (FL) - 1878
Hull, Perry M. (WI) - 1960
Hull, W. R. Jr. (MO) - 1954, 1956, 1958, 1960,
  1962, 1964, 1966, 1968, 1970
Hull, William E. (IL) - 1922, 1924, 1926, 1928,
  1930
Hulle, Charles F. (WI) - 1906
Hulme, John (PA) - 1866
Hulshart, George (PA) - 1980
Hulshof, Kenny (MO) - 1994, 1996, 1998,
  2000
Hultman, Cal (IA) - 1980
Human, I. J. (TN) - 1912
Humbert, Thomas M. (PA) - 1992
Hume, Frank (VA) - 1890
Hume, Stephen (MI) - 1996
Humes, John N. (VA) - 1837
Humes, Ted (PA) - 1976
Hummel, Valentine (PA) - 1828, 1830
Hummer, George P. (MI) - 1896, 1907
Humphrey (OH) - 1832
Humphrey, Alex P. (KY) - 1950
Humphrey, Bill (FL) - 1984
Humphrey, Calvin P. (OH) - 1888
Humphrey, Charles (NY) - 1824, 1826, 1830
Humphrey, D. C. (TX) - 1936
Humphrey, Edward (IL) - 1834
Humphrey, Frank L. (OH) - 1928
Humphrey, Herman L. (WI) - 1876, 1878,
  1880
Humphrey, James M. (NY) - 1858, 1860, 1862,
  1864, 1866
Humphrey, L. U. (KS) - 1892
Humphrey, Lott W. (NC) - 1870
Humphrey, Watts S. (MI) - 1890
Humphrey, William E. (WA) - 1902, 1904,
  1906, 1908, 1910, 1912, 1914
Humphreys, Andrew (IN) - 1876

Humphreys, Benjamin G. (MS) - 1902, 1904,
  1906, 1908, 1910, 1912, 1914, 1916, 1918,
  1920, 1922
Humphreys, George (NY) - 1866
Humphreys, Harry D. (WV) - 1966
Humphreys, Jim (WV) - 2000
Humphreys, Larry (OK) - 1986
Humphreys, Lois E. (CA) - 1984
Humphreys, Raymond V. (WV) - 1936, 1938
Humphreys, Richard C. (MA) - 1892
Humphries, Elijah (MA) - 1902
Humphries, Gene (OK) - 1970
Humphries, R. M. (TX) - 1888
Hundley, Oscar R. (AL) - 1896
Hungate, J. H. (IL) - 1876
Hungate, William L. (MO) - 1964, 1966, 1968,
  1970, 1972, 1974
Hungerford, John N. (NY) - 1876
Hungerford, Orville (NY) - 1842, 1844, 1846
Hungness, Marshall (IL) - 1974
Hunnicut, J. W. (VA) - 1869
Hunsberger, Derek (NJ) - 1998
Hunsicker, Thomas C. (OH) - 1924
Hunston, Walter J. (OH) - 1954, 1960
Hunt (LA) - 1855
Hunt (MO) - 1896
Hunt (NY) - 1842, 1856, 1862
Hunt (OH) - 1843
Hunt, Alvah (NY) - 1834
Hunt, C. Everett (CA) - 1964
Hunt, Caleb S. (LA) - 1868
Hunt, Carleton (LA) - 1882, 1884
Hunt, D. G. (TX) - 1902
Hunt, Douglas P. (MN) - 1954
Hunt, Ed (CA) - 1992
Hunt, Francis M. (OH) - 1896
Hunt, George (IL) - 1872
Hunt, Herschel (OH) - 1944
Hunt, Hiram P. (NY) - 1834, 1836, 1838, 1840
Hunt, J. L. N. (NY) - 1880
Hunt, James B. (MI) - 1843, 1844
Hunt, John E. (NJ) - 1966, 1968, 1970, 1972,
  1974
Hunt, John H. (MA) - 1916
Hunt, John J. (NC) - 1976
Hunt, John T. (MO) - 1902, 1904
Hunt, Jonathan (VT) - 1826, 1828, 1830
Hunt, Nat B. (TX) - 1914
Hunt, Samuel F. (OH) - 1880
Hunt, T. (NC) - 1825
Hunt, T. J. (AR) - 1894
Hunt, Theodore G. (LA) - 1853
Hunt, Washington (NY) - 1836, 1842, 1844,
  1846
Hunt, William R. (PA) - 1972
Hunt, William T. (OH) - 1962
Hunter (CT) - 1908, 1912
Hunter (NY) - 1842
Hunter (OH) - 1828
Hunter, A. Oakley (CA) - 1950, 1952, 1954
Hunter, Andrew J. (IL) - 1870, 1882, 1892,
  1896
Hunter, Clay (KS) - 1980
Hunter, Duncan L. (CA) - 1980, 1982, 1984,
  1986, 1988, 1990, 1992, 1994, 1996, 1998,
  2000
Hunter, E. T. (IL) - 1928
Hunter, Edward C. (IL) - 1938
Hunter, G. William (CA) - 1992
Hunter, Harold (OK) - 1978
Hunter, Jack C. (OH) - 1976
Hunter, James T. (NY) - 1902
Hunter, James W. (IL) - 1892
Hunter, Joe W. (KS) - 1960
Hunter, John (AL) - 1849
Hunter, John (NY) - 1824, 1830
Hunter, John F. (OH) - 1936, 1938, 1940, 1942,
  1944
Hunter, John W. (NY) - 1866
Hunter, Morton C. (IN) - 1866, 1872, 1874,
  1876, 1878
Hunter, Nicholas (PA) - 1870
Hunter, Robert M. T. (VA) - 1837, 1839, 1841,
  1843, 1845, 1847
Hunter, Robert O. (CA) - 1968
Hunter, Shapley R. (IL) - 1996

Hunter, W. Godfrey (KY) - 1878, 1882, 1886,
  1888, 1892, 1894, 1896
Hunter, William (RI) - 1825
Hunter, William F. (OH) - 1848, 1850
Hunter, Wm. H. (OH) - 1836
Huntingdon, Abel (NY) - 1834
Huntington (NY) - 1854, 1884, 1886
Huntington, Abel (NY) - 1832
Huntington, Hugh (OH) - 1916
Huntington, Jabez (CT) - 1829, 1831, 1833
Huntington, Roger (CT) - 1829
Huntington, Roger W. (NY) - 1920
Huntley (NY) - 1878
Hunton (VA) - 1827
Hunton, Eppa (VA) - 1872, 1874, 1876, 1878
Hunton, William E. Jr. (VA) - 1876
Huntsman, Adam (TN) - 1835
Huntsman, Bishop S. (KY) - 1918
Huot, J. Oliva (NH) - 1962, 1964, 1966
Huppuch, Milton K. (NY) - 1912
Huppuch, Winfield A. (NY) - 1908
Hurd, Frank H. (OH) - 1872, 1874, 1876, 1878,
  1880, 1882, 1884, 1886
Hurd, M. Michael (MI) - 1980
Hurlburt, R. H. (OH) - 1874
Hurlburt, W. A. "Bill" (VA) - 1992
Hurlbut, Elisha P. (NY) - 1834
Hurlbut, Stephen A. (IL) - 1872, 1874, 1876
Hurley (TN) - 1851
Hurley, David (PA) - 1838
Hurley, Denis M. (NY) - 1894, 1896, 1898
Hurley, Francis X. (MA) - 1950
Hurley, Frank (MA) - 1942
Hurley, George A. (OH) - 1956
Hurley, J. A. (TX) - 1892
Hurley, James M. (MA) - 1926
Hurley, James R. (NJ) - 1976
Hurley, John (TX) - 1902
Hurley, Robert E. (NY) - 1994
Hurley, Rodger L. (NY) - 1980
Hurley, S. R. (VA) - 1926
Hurst, Alfred (IA) - 1896
Hurst, Gerald B. (NC) - 1986
Hurst, J. E. (OH) - 1904
Hurst, Julius (TN) - 1964, 1966
Hurst, William L. (KY) - 1886
Hurt, J. Smith (KY) - 1865
Hurt, Leslie Raymond (IL) - 1932
Hurt, Z. Smith (KY) - 1882
Hurteau, Oscar J. V. (RI) - 1948
Husband, W. C. (MT) - 1938
Husch, George S. (NY) - 1910
Hussain, Riaz B. (NY) - 1988
Husselman, Calvin (IN) - 1892
Hussey, Erastus (MI) - 1846
Hustace, Maria M. (HI) - 1986
Husted, Earl W. (WA) - 1914
Husted, James W. (NY) - 1912, 1914, 1916,
  1918, 1920
Husting (WI) - 1918
Huston, Alfred D. (IL) - 1940, 1942
Huston, Michael L. (IA) - 2000
Huston, Paul (OK) - 1932, 1934
Hutchens, W. R. (AL) - 1916
Hutcheson, Gene (CO) - 1978
Hutcheson, Joseph C. (TX) - 1892, 1894
Hutchings, C. F. (KS) - 1904
Hutchings, Robert L. (TX) - 1978, 1980
Hutchins (MI) - 1866
Hutchins (OH) - 1858
Hutchins, E. S. (KY) - 1912
Hutchins, Edward (MI) - 1891
Hutchins, John (OH) - 1846, 1860
Hutchins, John C. (OH) - 1880
Hutchins, Thomas E. "Tim" (MD) - 2000
Hutchins, Waldo (NY) - 1879, 1880, 1882
Hutchins, Wells A. (OH) - 1862
Hutchins, William A. (OH) - 1864, 1880
Hutchinson (OH) - 1860
Hutchinson, Asa (AR) - 1996, 1998, 2000
Hutchinson, Barbara (CA) - 1992
Hutchinson, Edward (MI) - 1962, 1964, 1966,
  1968, 1970, 1972, 1974
Hutchinson, Elijah C. (NJ) - 1914, 1916, 1918,
  1920, 1922
Hutchinson, John G. (WV) - 1980

Hutchinson, John H. (WV) - 1880, 1886
Hutchinson, Joseph Henry (ID) - 1902
Hutchinson, Tim (AR) - 1992, 1994
Hutchinson, Titus (VT) - 1843, 1844, 1846
Hutchinson, W. O. (TX) - 1872, 1886
Hutchison, A. P. (PA) - 1914
Hutchison, Claude B. Jr. (CA) - 1982, 2000
Hutchison, R. H. Jr. (KY) - 1952
Hutchison, Ralph (MO) - 1938, 1944
Hutchison, W. O. (TX) - 1894
Huth, Clarence F. (PA) - 1900
Huth, Lloyd N. (PA) - 1946
Hutner, Joseph L. (NY) - 1966
Hutt, James B. Jr. (VA) - 1976
Hutto, Earl D. (FL) - 1978, 1980, 1982, 1984,
  1986, 1988, 1990, 1992
Hutton, Harry W. (CA) - 1928
Hutton, John E. (MO) - 1884, 1886
Huyler, John (NJ) - 1856, 1858
Huza, Stephen H. (WA) - 1964
Hyatt, Gregory S. (MA) - 1984
Hyatt, William S. (KS) - 1916
Hyde (CT) - 1861, 1863, 1886, 1896
Hyde (NY) - 1848, 1856
Hyde, Alvan P. (CT) - 1859
Hyde, C. H. (OK) - 1918, 1926
Hyde, DeWitt S. (MD) - 1952, 1954, 1956,
  1958
Hyde, Henry J. (IL) - 1962, 1974, 1976, 1978,
  1980, 1982, 1984, 1986, 1988, 1990, 1992,
  1994, 1996, 1998, 2000
Hyde, Ira B. (MO) - 1872, 1874
Hyde, Philip III (MA) - 1998
Hyde, R. Philip (MA) - 1996
Hyde, Samuel C. (WA) - 1894, 1896
Hyde, William P. (CA) - 1964
Hyder, Elton M. (TX) - 1946, 1948
Hyer, Fred C. (NJ) - 1932
Hyman, John A. (NC) - 1874
Hyman, Samuel M. (NY) - 1912
Hymes, Alex (LA) - 1908
Hynes, Susan W. (IL) - 1996, 1998
Hynes, William J. (AR) - 1872, 1874
Hyzer, Leland (FL) - 1956

I

Iams, Franklin P. (PA) - 1898
Iandiorio, Antonio (NY) - 1950
Iannelli, Gerard (PA) - 1958
Iannitti, Thomas V. (RI) - 1976
Iannucci, James (PA) - 1952
Iaquinta, David L. (WI) - 1984
Icenhour, James O. (NC) - 1980
Ichord, Richard (MO) - 1960, 1962, 1964,
  1966, 1968, 1970, 1972, 1974, 1976, 1978
Ide, M. (MA) - 1852
Ide, O. Z. (MI) - 1938
Igoe, James T. (IL) - 1926, 1928, 1930
Igoe, Kevin R. (MD) - 1980
Igoe, Michael L. (IL) - 1934
Igoe, William L. (MO) - 1912, 1914, 1916,
  1918
Ihnen, Edward H. (NJ) - 1964
Ihrie, Peter Jr. (PA) - 1830
Ikard, Frank (TX) - 1951, 1952, 1954, 1956,
  1958, 1960
Ikeler, Fred (PA) - 1918
Ikirt, George P. (OH) - 1888, 1892
Ikola, Roger A. (CA) - 1974
Illing, Joe (WA) - 1986
Imhoff, Lawrence E. (OH) - 1932, 1934, 1936,
  1938, 1940, 1942
Imle, Albert R. (IL) - 1954, 1956
Imperiale, Anthony (NJ) - 1988
Imrie, Curtis (CO) - 2000
Indyke, Joseph S. (NJ) - 1976
Ingalls (ME) - 1856
Ingalls, J. S. (MN) - 1912
Ingalls, Sheffield (KS) - 1914
Ingalls, William (MA) - 1828
Inge, Samuel W. (AL) - 1847, 1849
Inge, William M. (TN) - 1833
Ingersoll (CT) - 1910
Ingersoll (PA) - 1837, 1860
Ingersoll, Charles (CT) - 1841
Ingersoll, Charles E. (PA) - 1902

Kenefick, Thomas W. (MA) - 1900
Kenkle (IN) - 1860
Kenly, John R. (MD) - 1849
Kenna, John E. (WV) - 1876, 1878, 1880, 1882
Kennamer, Charles B. (AL) - 1906, 1920
Kennedy (CT) - 1904, 1914, 1916
Kennedy (MD) - 1837, 1839, 1845, 1847
Kennedy (NJ) - 1840
Kennedy (NY) - 1854
Kennedy (PA) - 1884
Kennedy (VA) - 1847
Kennedy, Alfred J. (NY) - 1920
Kennedy, Ambrose (RI) - 1912, 1914, 1916, 1918, 1920
Kennedy, Ambrose J. (MD) - 1932, 1934, 1936, 1938
Kennedy, Andrew (IN) - 1841, 1843, 1845
Kennedy, B. F. (OH) - 1926
Kennedy, Basil G. (WI) - 1954, 1958
Kennedy, Beverly "Bev" (FL) - 1992, 1994, 1996
Kennedy, Bill J. (CA) - 1982
Kennedy, Brian T. (NJ) - 1984, 1986, 2000
Kennedy, C. L. (TX) - 1980
Kennedy, Charles A. (IA) - 1906, 1908, 1910, 1912, 1914, 1916, 1918
Kennedy, E. C. (WI) - 1894
Kennedy, Ed. N. (OH) - 1924
Kennedy, Edward H. (IN) - 1904
Kennedy, Francis M. (MA) - 1904, 1906
Kennedy, Frank P. (WI) - 1928
Kennedy, Hugh T. (MN) - 1932
Kennedy, J. R. (ND) - 1944
Kennedy, James (OH) - 1902, 1904, 1906, 1908, 1910, 1920, 1926
Kennedy, James A. (PA) - 1948
Kennedy, James E. (VT) - 1922
Kennedy, James T. (NC) - 1912
Kennedy, John (MD) - 1826
Kennedy, John A. (IL) - 1962
Kennedy, John A. (WI) - 1942
Kennedy, John F. (MA) - 1946, 1948, 1950
Kennedy, John F. (NY) - 1912
Kennedy, John L. (NE) - 1904, 1906
Kennedy, John P. (MD) - 1838, 1841, 1843
Kennedy, Joseph P. II (MA) - 1986, 1988, 1990, 1992, 1994, 1996
Kennedy, Mark (MN) - 2000
Kennedy, Martin J. (NY) - 1930, 1932, 1934, 1936, 1938, 1940, 1942
Kennedy, Mary (MA) - 1960
Kennedy, Michael J. (IL) - 1992
Kennedy, Michael J. (NY) - 1938, 1940
Kennedy, Michael T. (IA) - 1912
Kennedy, O. W. (CA) - 1916
Kennedy, Orram W. (PA) - 1902
Kennedy, P. (LA) - 1868
Kennedy, Patrick J. (RI) - 1994, 1996, 1998, 2000
Kennedy, R. E. (TX) - 1948, 1850, 1956
Kennedy, Richard D. (OH) - 1962
Kennedy, Robert P. (OH) - 1886, 1888
Kennedy, Roger G. (MN) - 1952
Kennedy, T. (MD) - 1826
Kennedy, Thomas F. (PA) - 1908, 1912
Kennedy, Thomas P. (PA) - 1958
Kennedy, Walter P. (NJ) - 1960
Kennedy, William (CT) - 1912
Kennedy, William (NJ) - 1826
Kennedy, William J. (CA) - 1980
Kennedy, William J. (MI) - 1966
Kennel, Leroy E. (IL) - 1980, 1982
Kennelly, Barbara B. (CT) - 1982, 1984, 1986, 1988, 1990, 1992, 1994, 1996
Kennelly, John W. (NY) - 1940
Kennelly, William (NY) - 1920
Kennerly, T. Everton (TX) - 1958
Kennerly, T. M. (TX) - 1908
Kennett, Luther M. (MO) - 1854, 1856
Kenneweg, C. F. (MD) - 1902
Kenney, Edward A. (NJ) - 1932, 1934, 1936
Kenney, John N. (PA) - 1976
Kenney, Melvin R. (MD) - 1960
Kenney, Thomas S. (FL) - 1964
Kennick, Joseph M. (CA) - 1952, 1954
Kennick, William J. (OH) - 1986

Kennish (MO) - 1900
Kennon, David C. (OH) - 1886
Kennon, William Jr. (OH) - 1846, 1848
Kennon, William Sr. (OH) - 1828, 1830, 1834, 1836
Kenny, Eugene P. (NJ) - 1962
Kenny, Raymond (WV) - 1922
Kent (NH) - 1875, 1877, 1878
Kent, Bob (CA) - 2000
Kent, Edward (ME) - 1834
Kent, Everett (PA) - 1922, 1924, 1926, 1928, 1930
Kent, Henry S. (PA) - 1896
Kent, Herman O. (WI) - 1932
Kent, Joseph (MD) - 1824
Kent, K. Wayne (IN) - 1968
Kent, Robert (FL) - 1984
Kent, Roger (CA) - 1950
Kent, W. E. (MT) - 1914
Kent, William (CA) - 1910, 1912, 1914
Kenworthy, Jim (MO) - 1984
Kenyon, William S. (NY) - 1858
Keogh, Eugene J. (NY) - 1936, 1938, 1940, 1942, 1944, 1946, 1948, 1950, 1952, 1954, 1956, 1958, 1960, 1962, 1964
Keogh, Thomas B. (NC) - 1880
Kepfer, Thomas K. (NY) - 1990
Kepple, George E. (TX) - 1928
Kepple, Minerva D. (MA) - 1926
Ker, A. J. (LA) - 1880
Kerans, Robert F. (IL) - 1988, 1990
Kercheval (VA) - 1825, 1829
Kercheval, Samuel (VA) - 1827
Kerigan, Joseph E. (MA) - 1922, 1924
Kerin, Karen (VT) - 2000
Kerlinsky, Daniel (NM) - 2000
Kern (MO) - 1896, 1898
Kern, Bob (IN) - 1998
Kern, Frederick J. (IL) - 1898, 1900, 1902
Kernan, Francis (NY) - 1862, 1864
Kernochan, H. P. (LA) - 1894
Kerns, Brian D. (IN) - 2000
Kerns, Robert M. (CA) - 1986
Kerr (NJ) - 1886
Kerr (PA) - 1852, 1860
Kerr, Charles (IL) - 1888
Kerr, Daniel (IA) - 1886, 1888, 1900
Kerr, Dempsey A. (OH) - 1970
Kerr, E. C. (MO) - 1876
Kerr, Frederick B. (PA) - 1932
Kerr, Gordon E. (IL) - 1960
Kerr, J. (VA) - 1837
Kerr, James (PA) - 1888
Kerr, John (IL) - 1846
Kerr, John (NC) - 1847, 1853, 1855
Kerr, John Bozman (MD) - 1849
Kerr, John H. (NC) - 1924, 1926, 1928, 1930, 1932, 1934, 1936, 1938, 1940, 1942, 1944, 1946, 1948, 1950
Kerr, John Leeds (MD) - 1824, 1826, 1829, 1831
Kerr, Josiah L. (MD) - 1900
Kerr, Marion J. (ID) - 1916
Kerr, Michael C. (IN) - 1864, 1866, 1868, 1870, 1872, 1874
Kerr, Richard (WV) - 1998, 2000
Kerr, Robert M. (AL) - 1968, 1972
Kerr, W. S. (OH) - 1912
Kerr, William W. (PA) - 1892
Kerr, Winfield S. (OH) - 1894, 1896, 1898
Kerraghan, Henry (MS) - 1888
Kerrigan (NY) - 1876
Kerrigan, James E. (NY) - 1860
Kerry, John F. (MA) - 1972
Kerry, John M. (ME) - 1982
Kerschner, William H. (PA) - 1926
Kershaw, J. B. (SC) - 1874
Kershaw, William J. (WI) - 1908, 1910, 1926, 1928, 1930
Kershner, Howard E. (KS) - 1916
Kershner, William (OH) - 1846
Kershot (NJ) - 1916
Kersteen, Herman C. (PA) - 1958
Kersten, Charles J. (WI) - 1946, 1948, 1950, 1952, 1954
Kerwick, William (NY) - 1954, 1958

Kerwin, John M. Jr. (IL) - 1950, 1954
Kesel, John J. (NY) - 1924
Kespohl, Julius (IL) - 1914
Kesselring, Leo J. (NY) - 1968, 1978
Kessinger, Albert R. (NY) - 1924
Ketcham, Henry B. (NY) - 1900
Ketcham, John C. (MI) - 1920, 1922, 1924, 1926, 1928, 1930, 1932
Ketcham, John H. (NY) - 1864, 1866, 1868, 1870, 1876, 1878, 1880, 1882, 1884, 1886, 1888, 1890, 1896, 1898, 1900, 1902, 1904
Ketcham, William M. (NY) - 1894
Ketcham, Winthrop W. (PA) - 1864, 1874
Ketchel, Terry (FL) - 1990, 1992
Ketchim (NY) - 1872
Ketchum, William M. (CA) - 1972, 1974, 1976
Ketola, Jerry H. (MN) - 1960, 1962
Ketter, Henry (OH) - 1900
Kettl, Paul (PA) - 1996
Kettner, William (CA) - 1912, 1914, 1916, 1918
Keuffner, W. C. (IL) - 1882
Keusterman, G. (WI) - 1886
Kewen, E. J. C. (CA) - 1849, 1851, 1872
Key (MD) - 1839, 1845
Key (TN) - 1872
Key, B. C. (KY) - 1892
Key, John A. (OH) - 1912, 1914, 1916, 1918
Keyes, E. W. (WI) - 1882
Keyes, Perley (NY) - 1828
Keys (KY) - 1900
Keys, B. F. (KY) - 1896
Keys, Ben C. (KY) - 1894
Keys, J. Grant (OH) - 1962
Keys, Martha E. (KS) - 1974, 1976, 1978
Keys, Sam (KS) - 1980
Kibbe, Frederick A. (FL) - 1962
Kidd, Bill (WY) - 1972
Kidd, Devvy (CA) - 1994
Kidd, Joe P. (TN) - 1906
Kidd, Meredith H. (IN) - 1884
Kidd, Robert F. (WV) - 1920
Kidd, Robert H. (WV) - 1924
Kidd, William M. (WV) - 1966
Kidder, David (ME) - 1824
Kidder, Jefferson P. (VT) - 1850
Kidwell, Zedekiah (VA) - 1853, 1855
Kiefer, Andrew R. (MN) - 1892
Kiefer, W. Jonathon (PA) - 1910
Kiefner, Charles E. (MO) - 1924, 1926, 1928, 1930
Kiel, Shelley (NE) - 2000
Kiernan, John F. (NY) - 1938
Kiernan, Luke A. Jr. (NJ) - 1944
Kiernan, Vincent P. (CT) - 1948
Kiernan, William C. (WI) - 1928
Kiess, Edgar R. (PA) - 1912, 1914, 1916, 1918, 1920, 1922, 1924, 1926, 1928
Kiest, Charles F. (IL) - 1904
Kiggin, James (MA) - 1974
Kij, Daniel J. (NY) - 1962
Kilbanks, Bob (NY) - 1996
Kilbourne, Richard C. (CT) - 1970
Kilbride, L. J. (MN) - 1944, 1946
Kilburn, Clarence E. (NY) - 1940, 1942, 1944, 1946, 1948, 1950, 1952, 1954, 1956, 1958, 1960, 1962
Kilbury, Charles D. (WA) - 1982
Kilday, Paul J. (TX) - 1938, 1940, 1942, 1944, 1946, 1948, 1950, 1952, 1954, 1956, 1958, 1960
Kildee, Dale E. (MI) - 1976, 1978, 1980, 1982, 1984, 1986, 1988, 1990, 1992, 1994, 1996, 1998, 2000
Kilgore, Constantine B. (TX) - 1886, 1888, 1890, 1892
Kilgore, Daniel (OH) - 1834, 1836
Kilgore, David (IN) - 1849, 1856, 1858
Kilgore, James (KY) - 1878
Kilgore, Joe M. (TX) - 1954, 1956, 1958, 1960, 1962
Kilker, Paul V. (PA) - 1992
Kille, Joseph (NJ) - 1838, 1840
Killeen, George (MI) - 1900
Killen, Marcella F. (MN) - 1948, 1950
Killgrew, John F. (NY) - 1946

Killinger, John W. (PA) - 1858, 1860, 1870, 1872, 1876, 1878
Kilpatrick (NJ) - 1880
Kilpatrick, Carolyn Cheeks (MI) - 1996, 1998, 2000
Kilpatrick, Robert J. (OH) - 1952
Kilpatrick, W. B. (OH) - 1922, 1930
Kilroy, Robert Walter (IN) - 1986
Kilso, M. A. (IA) - 1888
Kiltz, Walter K. (IL) - 1966
Kim, Jay C. (CA) - 1992, 1994, 1996
Kimball (ME) - 1852
Kimball (MO) - 1886
Kimball, Alanson M. (WI) - 1874, 1876
Kimball, George E. (MO) - 1938
Kimball, Henry M. (MI) - 1934
Kimball, J. Chillis (MA) - 1870
Kimball, John Clark (IL) - 1962, 1964
Kimball, W. S. (WY) - 1928
Kimball, William (ME) - 1854
Kimball, William P. (KY) - 1906
Kimberly, Dennis (CT) - 1825
Kimberly, Lewis R. (KY) - 1942
Kimble, John B. (MD) - 1996, 1998, 2000
Kimble, William E. (AZ) - 1964
Kimbly, J. T. (KY) - 1892
Kimbrell (MO) - 1912, 1916
Kimbrough, Calvin (NY) - 1976
Kimbrough, Guy C. (CA) - 1988, 1990, 1996
Kimbrough, Jay (TX) - 1992
Kimmel (MD) - 1865, 1882
Kimmel, N. (Toni) (CA) - 1970
Kimmel, William (MD) - 1878
Kimmell (MD) - 1837, 1841
Kimmell, Fran M. (PA) - 1868, 1882
Kimmell, William (MD) - 1864, 1876
Kimmerle, Charles H. (MI) - 1908
Kincaid, D. H. (KY) - 1922
Kincaid, Randall R. (NC) - 1980
Kincaid, William M. (MO) - 1846
Kincaid, William W. (PA) - 1916
Kincaide, Henry L. (MA) - 1912, 1914, 1916
Kincannon, A. A. (TN) - 1835, 1837
Kincheloe, Charles F. (IL) - 1912
Kincheloe, David H. (KY) - 1914, 1916, 1918, 1920, 1922, 1924, 1926, 1928
Kind, Ron (WI) - 1996, 1998, 2000
Kindel, George J. (CO) - 1910, 1912, 1916
Kindleberger, E. Crosby (NY) - 1912
Kindness, Thomas N. (OH) - 1974, 1976, 1978, 1980, 1982, 1984
Kindred, C. F. (MN) - 1882
Kindred, James M. (TX) - 1904
Kindred, John J. (NY) - 1910, 1920, 1922, 1924, 1926
Kindrick, William D. (TN) - 1845
Kindschi, Ivan H. (WI) - 1962
Kinett, James P. (TN) - 1938
King (CT) - 1912
King (GA) - 1826
King (MO) - 1852
King (ND) - 1902
King (NY) - 1826, 1842, 1852, 1876
King (PA) - 1860, 1872
King (RI) - 1837
King (TN) - 1884
King (WI) - 1878
King, Adam (PA) - 1826, 1828, 1830
King, Adam E. (MD) - 1868
King, Andrew (MO) - 1870
King, Arthur F. (CT) - 1938
King, Austin A. (MO) - 1862, 1864
King, Byron W. (PA) - 1992
King, Carleton J. (NY) - 1960, 1962, 1964, 1966, 1968, 1970, 1972, 1974
King, Cecil R. (CA) - 1942, 1944, 1946, 1948, 1950, 1952, 1954, 1956, 1958, 1960, 1962, 1964, 1966
King, Charles A. (OH) - 1882
King, Charles F. (MA) - 1900
King, Daniel P. (MA) - 1842, 1844, 1846, 1848
King, David (NM) - 1980
King, David S. (UT) - 1958, 1960, 1964, 1966
King, Edward A. (OH) - 1844
King, Edward J. (IL) - 1914, 1916, 1918, 1920, 1922, 1924, 1926, 1928

Lucas, Wingate H. (TX) - 1946, 1948, 1950, 1952
Lucca, Mariano A. (NY) - 1954, 1958, 1960
Luce, Charles T. (MA) - 1898, 1900, 1902
Luce, Clare Boothe (CT) - 1942, 1944
Luce, J. G. (VA) - 1908
Luce, John C. (OR) - 1892
Luce, Marjory L. (MN) - 1982
Luce, Mark (CA) - 1998
Luce, Robert (MA) - 1918, 1920, 1922, 1924, 1926, 1928, 1930, 1932, 1934, 1936, 1938, 1940
Lucero, Antonio (NM) - 1920
Lucey, Dennis B. (NY) - 1912
Lucey, Patrick J. (WI) - 1950
Lucier, Alvin A. (NH) - 1938
Luck, Charles W. (ID) - 1914
Luck, Oliver (WV) - 1990
Luckey, Henry C. (NE) - 1934, 1936, 1938, 1940
Luckey, Hugh M. (IL) - 1936
Luckey, James B. (OH) - 1878
Lucking, Alfred (MI) - 1902, 1904
Luckow, Edward L. (WI) - 1900
Lucy, Dennis B. (NY) - 1898
Ludeman, Cal R. (MN) - 1992
Ludington (WI) - 1874
Ludling, J. T. (LA) - 1878
Ludlow, C. O. (IL) - 1912
Ludlow, Louis (IN) - 1928, 1930, 1932, 1934, 1936, 1938, 1940, 1942, 1944, 1946
Ludlow, Willis H. (ID) - 1972
Ludwig, Carl J. (WI) - 1934
Ludwig, Earl (OH) - 1944, 1948
Ludwig, William H. (WI) - 1944
Luecke, John (MI) - 1936, 1938
Lufkin, Willfred W. (MA) - 1918, 1920
Luhring, Oscar R. (IN) - 1918, 1920, 1922
Lujan, Manuel (NM) - 1944
Lujan, Manuel Jr. (NM) - 1968, 1970, 1972, 1974, 1976, 1978, 1980, 1982, 1984, 1986
Luke, George W. (NJ) - 1968
Luken, Charles (OH) - 1990
Luken, Thomas A. (OH) - 1974, 1976, 1978, 1980, 1982, 1984, 1986, 1988
Lukens, Donald E. (OH) - 1966, 1968, 1986, 1988
Lukson, Lee (WA) - 1968
Luling, Charles (WI) - 1884, 1886
Luman (OH) - 1843
Lumina, Luke (MA) - 1992
Lumpkin, John H. (GA) - 1840, 1842, 1844, 1846, 1855
Lumpkin, S. H. (TX) - 1900, 1902
Lumpkin, Wilson (GA) - 1826, 1828, 1830
Lund, Arnold L. (FL) - 1956
Lund, Arnold L. (IL) - 1934
Lund, Frank J. (IA) - 1940
Lund, Wendell L. (MI) - 1940
Lundblad, Henry R. (IL) - 1930
Lunde, Paul (IA) - 1988, 1992
Lundeen, B. A. (MN) - 1970
Lundeen, Ernest (MN) - 1916, 1920, 1926, 1932, 1934
Lundin, Frederick (IL) - 1908, 1910
Lundine, Stanley N. (NY) - 1976, 1978, 1980, 1982, 1984
Lundquist, Carl Hjalmar (IL) - 1916
Lundquist, Todd (MN) - 1984
Lundstrom, Milton A. (IL) - 1958
Lundy (PA) - 1850
Lundy, Daniel F. (NJ) - 1970
Lundy, Hunter (LA) - 1996
Lundy, Rayfield (CA) - 1964, 1968, 1972
Lungren, Brian (CA) - 1982
Lungren, Dan (CA) - 1980, 1984, 1986
Lungren, Daniel E. (CA) - 1976, 1978
Lunn, George R. (NY) - 1912, 1916, 1918
Lunsford, Charles P. (AL) - 1912
Lunsford, Charles P. G. (AL) - 1930
Lupton, John M. (CT) - 1962
Lupton, S. (VA) - 1910
Lupton, William R. (NY) - 1946
Lurry (OK) - 1914
Lusch, A. T. (IA) - 1872
Lusk, Georgia L. (NM) - 1946

Lusk, John W. (IL) - 1902
Lusk, Lucille (NV) - 1988
Lustig, Wayne (VA) - 1964
Luther, Ernest M. (NE) - 1954
Luther, William P. "Bill" (MN) - 1994, 1996, 1998, 2000
Luthringer (NJ) - 1912
Luttmer, William J. (OH) - 1982
Lutton, John M. (CA) - 1980
Luttrell, Hiram A. (CA) - 1912
Luttrell, John K. (CA) - 1872, 1875, 1876
Lutz, Earle (VA) - 1946
Lutz, Lisa L. (NM) - 2000
Lutz, Ralph C. (OH) - 1940
Luxford, Richard (CO) - 1950
Lybarger, Edwin L. (OH) - 1888
Lybrand, Archibald (OH) - 1896, 1898
Lybrand, Samuel (OH) - 1872
Lyerle, William D. (IL) - 1910
Lyford, Joseph P. (CT) - 1952, 1954
Lyle (TN) - 1882, 1902
Lyle, Cy H. (TN) - 1910, 1914
Lyle, John E. Jr. (TX) - 1944, 1946, 1948, 1950, 1952
Lyle, R. J. (MS) - 1894
Lyman (CT) - 1898, 1900
Lyman (GA) - 1824
Lyman (OH) - 1852
Lyman, A. P. (VT) - 1850
Lyman, Arthur (MA) - 1902
Lyman, Asael (ID) - 1948
Lyman, Howard (MT) - 1982
Lyman, Joseph (IA) - 1884, 1886
Lyman, Theodore (MA) - 1833, 1882, 1884
Lynch (KY) - 1900
Lynch (MD) - 1841, 1851
Lynch (MS) - 1882, 1884, 1886
Lynch, Charles W. (OH) - 1942
Lynch, Daniel C. (NB) - 1974
Lynch, David J. (MI) - 1920
Lynch, Donald J. (IN) - 1986
Lynch, Emmett (CA) - 1982
Lynch, Eugene A. (MA) - 1926
Lynch, J. Gregory (CT) - 1950
Lynch, James (NY) - 1824
Lynch, Joe D. (CA) - 1886
Lynch, John (ME) - 1864, 1866, 1868, 1870
Lynch, John (PA) - 1886, 1888
Lynch, John D. (MA) - 1902
Lynch, John F. (CT) - 1936
Lynch, John F. (ME) - 1884, 1886
Lynch, John J. (ME) - 1900
Lynch, John R. (MS) - 1872, 1875, 1876, 1880
Lynch, P. J. (IN) - 1914
Lynch, Patrick H. (PA) - 1914, 1916
Lynch, Ralph N. (IA) - 1944
Lynch, T. Joseph (NY) - 1956, 1958, 1960, 1962
Lynch, Thomas (WI) - 1890, 1892, 1894
Lynch, W. A. (SD) - 1904
Lynch, W. D. (ND) - 1932
Lynch, Walter A. (NY) - 1940, 1942, 1944, 1946, 1948
Lynch, Walter A. Jr. (NY) - 1958
Lynch, William A. (SD) - 1894
Lynch, William D. (ND) - 1934
Lynde, John (NY) - 1824
Lynde, Tilly (NY) - 1828, 1832
Lynde, William P. (WI) - 1848, 1874, 1876
Lynn, James F. (MN) - 1922, 1928
Lynn, John D. (NY) - 1894
Lynn, William H. (NY) - 1908
Lyon (AL) - 1839
Lyon (MS) - 1882
Lyon (NY) - 1858, 1878
Lyon (TN) - 1849
Lyon (WI) - 1870
Lyon, Caleb (NY) - 1852
Lyon, Chittenden (KY) - 1826, 1827, 1829, 1831, 1833
Lyon, Dale (KS) - 1986
Lyon, David Greenhill (AL) - 1837
Lyon, Frances (AL) - 1835, 1837
Lyon, Frank (VA) - 1932
Lyon, Homer L. (NC) - 1920, 1922, 1924, 1926
Lyon, J. L. (CA) - 1892

Lyon, Judson W. (GA) - 1888
Lyon, Lucius (MI) - 1843
Lyon, T. J. (MS) - 1920
Lyons, Brad (WA) - 1998
Lyons, Charlton H. (LA) - 1961
Lyons, Hall M. (LA) - 1966
Lyons, J. A. (IA) - 1898
Lyons, J. Walter (VT) - 1902
Lyons, James (VA) - 1902
Lytel, Elaine (NY) - 1982
Lytle (GA) - 1859
Lytle, Reynold K. (OH) - 1874
Lytle, Robert T. (OH) - 1832, 1834

M

Maas, Melvin J. (MN) - 1926, 1928, 1930, 1932, 1934, 1936, 1938, 1940, 1942, 1944
Mabee, Wallace F. (ME) - 1936
Mabey, Charles R. (UT) - 1916
Mabie, J. Frank (MT) - 1910, 1912
Mabry (TN) - 1874
Mabson (AL) - 1884
Mabson, A. A. (AL) - 1880
Macaluso, Michael (NY) - 1976
MacArthur, Walter (CA) - 1910
MacBain, Bruce D. (NY) - 1996
Macchio, Nicholas R. (NY) - 1972
MacCracken, Henry F. (OH) - 1904
MacCrate, John (NY) - 1918
MacDevitt, James C. (NY) - 1930
MacDonald, Marie (NY) - 1912, 1920
MacDonald, Moses (ME) - 1850
MacDonald, Robert (AZ) - 1994
MacDonald, Torbert H. (MA) - 1954, 1956, 1958, 1960, 1962, 1964, 1966, 1968, 1970, 1972, 1974
MacDonald, William J. (MI) - 1914, 1916
MacDougall, Clinton D. (NY) - 1872, 1874
MacDougall, Curtis D. (IL) - 1944
Mace, Daniel (IN) - 1851, 1852, 1854
Mace, Lawson (IN) - 1914
Macey, C. C. (SC) - 1884
MacFarland, Grenville S. (MA) - 1902
MacFarlane, William (NY) - 1928
MacGovern, John F. (MA) - 1990
MacGregor, Clarence (NY) - 1918, 1920, 1922, 1924, 1926
MacGregor, Clark (MN) - 1960, 1962, 1964, 1966, 1968
Machen, Hervey G. (MD) - 1964, 1966, 1968
Machrowicz, Thaddeus M. (MI) - 1950, 1952, 1954, 1956, 1958, 1960
Machtley, Ronald K. (RI) - 1988, 1990, 1992
Maciejewski, A. F. (IL) - 1938, 1940
MacIntyre, N. J. (PA) - 1908
Maciora, Lucien J. (CT) - 1940, 1942
Mack, Bill (NY) - 1970, 1974, 1978
Mack, Charles C. (KS) - 1918
Mack, Connie (FL) - 1982, 1984, 1986
Mack, Edward J. (MI) - 1984
Mack, H. C. (TX) - 1886
Mack, Joseph S. (MI) - 1956, 1958
Mack, Mansfield E. (WA) - 1934
Mack, Marty (NY) - 1996
Mack, Peter F. Jr. (IL) - 1948, 1950, 1952, 1954, 1956, 1958, 1960, 1962, 1974, 1976
Mack, Russell V. (WA) - 1934, 1940, 1948, 1950, 1952, 1954, 1956, 1958
MacKaig, Milton R. (CA) - 1982
MacKay, Buddy (FL) - 1986
MacKay, J. Alan (MA) - 1974
MacKay, James A. (GA) - 1964, 1966, 1968
MacKay, Kenneth H. (Buddy) (FL) - 1982, 1984
Macken, Terry R. (CA) - 1966
MacKenzie, A. E. (NV) - 1950
MacKenzie, Charles S. (NJ) - 1934, 1936
MacKenzie, Ken (IN) - 1984
MacKenzie, Randy (CO) - 2000
Mackey (NY) - 1888
Mackey (PA) - 1884, 1886
Mackey, Cyms H. (IA) - 1866, 1882
Mackey, Edmund W. M. (SC) - 1874, 1878, 1880, 1882
Mackey, Harry A. (PA) - 1912
Mackey, Levi A. (PA) - 1868, 1874, 1876

Mackie, John C. (MI) - 1964, 1966
Mackie, John G. (CO) - 1958
Mackin, Lawrence C. (MA) - 1992
MacKinnon Daniel F. (CT) - 1978
MacKinnon, George (MN) - 1946, 1948
MacKintosh (MN) - 1914
MacKintosh, George L. (IN) - 1928
Macklin, Joseph (NC) - 1837
MacLafferty, James H. (CA) - 1922
MacLaren, Joseph R. (NY) - 1954
Maclay, William B. (NY) - 1842, 1844, 1846, 1848, 1856, 1858, 1864
MacLean, Andrew A. (NY) - 1930
MacLean, John P. (OH) - 1896
MacLeod, Charles Kevin (MA) - 1978
Macleod, Kenneth P. (ME) - 1964
Maclin, Earl (TN) - 1964
Macmillan, J. H. (NV) - 1886
Macmillan, Thomas C. (IL) - 1892
MacMullen, Arthur H. J. (NY) - 1938
MacMullen, Leon C. (PA) - 1950
MacNeil, L. W. (IL) - 1906
Macomber (NY) - 1854
Macon, Robert B. (AR) - 1902, 1904, 1906, 1908, 1910
Macon, Thomas (CO) - 1888
MacRae, Colin D. (NY) - 1936
MacVicar, James A. (ME) - 1948
Macy, John B. (WI) - 1852, 1854
Macy, W. Kingsland (NY) - 1946, 1948, 1950
Madden, Charles F. Jr. (OH) - 1966
Madden, John (KS) - 1896
Madden, Martin B. (IL) - 1902, 1904, 1906, 1908, 1910, 1912, 1914, 1916, 1918, 1920, 1922, 1924, 1926
Madden, Ray J. (IN) - 1942, 1944, 1946, 1948, 1950, 1952, 1954, 1956, 1958, 1960, 1962, 1964, 1966, 1968, 1970, 1972, 1974
Madden, Thomas M. (NJ) - 1938
Madden, William C. (MA) - 1960
Madden, William E. Jr. (PA) - 1928
Madden, William F. (MA) - 1936
Maddock, Thomas (AZ) - 1918
Maddox, Fletcher (MT) - 1914
Maddox, Henry J. (MS) - 1952
Maddox, John W. (GA) - 1892, 1894, 1896, 1898, 1900, 1902
Maddox, P. W. (TN) - 1942
Maddox, Samuel T. (NY) - 1864
Madigan (ME) - 1864
Madigan, Edward R. (IL) - 1972, 1974, 1976, 1978, 1980, 1982, 1984, 1986, 1988, 1990
Madison, Edmond H. (KS) - 1906, 1908, 1910
Madoo, William (NY) - 1908
Madrid, Jim (CA) - 1976
Maffett, James T. (PA) - 1886
Magazzu, Louis N. (NJ) - 1994
Magee, Clare (MO) - 1948, 1950
Magee, David F. (PA) - 1890, 1920
Magee, Edward T. (NJ) - 1984
Magee, Hugh (NY) - 1846
Magee, James M. (PA) - 1922, 1924, 1926
Magee, John (NY) - 1826, 1828, 1830, 1864
Magee, John A. (PA) - 1872
Magee, Walter W. (NY) - 1914, 1916, 1918, 1920, 1922, 1924, 1926
Magill, Frank S. (PA) - 1936
Maginness, Edmund A. (IN) - 1902
Maginnis, John J. (MA) - 1948
Maginnis, Martin (MT) - 1889
Magisen, Robert C. (IL) - 1910
Magli, Vito (NY) - 1952
Magner, Thomas F. (NY) - 1888, 1890, 1892
Magnuson, Don (WA) - 1952, 1954, 1956, 1958, 1960, 1962
Magnuson, Warren G. (WA) - 1936, 1938, 1940, 1942
Magoon, Henry S. (WI) - 1874
Magove (NY) - 1876
Magrady, Frederick W. (PA) - 1924, 1926, 1928, 1930
Magrann, Thomas J. (PA) - 1980
Magraw, S. M. (MD) - 1849
Magruder, Bernard F. (WI) - 1942
Maguire, Andrew (NJ) - 1974, 1976, 1978, 1980

Metcalf, Randall (OH) - 1964
Metcalf, Victor H. (CA) - 1898, 1900, 1902
Metcalfe, Henry B. (NY) - 1874
Metcalfe, Lyne S. (MO) - 1876
Metcalfe, Ralph H. (IL) - 1970, 1972, 1974, 1976
Metcalfe, Theodore W. (NE) - 1940
Metcalfe, Thomas (KY) - 1824, 1827
Metton, L. D. (SC) - 1894
Metz, Herman A. (NY) - 1912, 1922
Metz, Larry (FL) - 1992
Metzenbaum, James (OH) - 1942
Metzerott, Oliver (MD) - 1928
Metzger, Bruce A. (PA) - 1928
Metzger, Charles J. (IL) - 1924
Metzger, Donald L. (IL) - 1974
Metzger, Fraser (VT) - 1914
Metzger, Tom (CA) - 1980
Metzler, Gottfried (PA) - 1894
Mewboorne, James M. (NC) - 1890
Meyer, Adolph (LA) - 1890, 1892, 1894, 1896, 1898, 1900, 1902, 1904, 1906
Meyer, Alvin P. (IA) - 1952
Meyer, Ben F. (NM) - 1944, 1948
Meyer, Conrad J. (NY) - 1914
Meyer, Donald D. (MO) - 1978
Meyer, Ed J. (OH) - 1914
Meyer, F. B. (MO) - 1938, 1940
Meyer, Fred W. (NY) - 1926
Meyer, G. A. (IA) - 1912, 1914
Meyer, G. E. H. (TX) - 1920
Meyer, Henry (PA) - 1894
Meyer, Herbert A. (KS) - 1946, 1948
Meyer, Howard M. (IN) - 1942
Meyer, J. Edward (NY) - 1976
Meyer, John A. (MD) - 1940
Meyer, John H. (OH) - 1906
Meyer, Kathleen M. (PA) - 1978, 1980
Meyer, Lee S. (MD) - 1902, 1904
Meyer, Wayne (CA) - 1988
Meyer, William H. (VT) - 1958, 1960, 1972
Meyer, William X. (IL) - 1926
Meyerhoeffer (VA) - 1833
Meyers, Benjamin F. (PA) - 1870, 1872
Meyers, George Jr. (IN) - 1980
Meyers, Jan (KS) - 1984, 1986, 1988, 1990, 1992, 1994
Meyers, Jerome M. (PA) - 1960
Meyers, Joseph J. (IA) - 1934
Meyers, Leonard (PA) - 1872
Meyers, Mahlon (PA) - 1900
Meyers, Maury (TX) - 1990
Meyers, Meredith (PA) - 1924, 1932
Meyers, O. P. (IA) - 1920
Meyers, Philip L. (HI) - 2000
Meyers, Robert M. (PA) - 1954, 1960
Meyers, Victor A. (WA) - 1958
Meyner, Helen S. (NJ) - 1972, 1974, 1976, 1978
Meyner, Robert B. (NJ) - 1946
Mezger, Irving H. (MD) - 1938
Mezvinsky, Edward (IA) - 1970, 1972, 1974, 1976
Mfume, Kweisi (MD) - 1986, 1988, 1990, 1992, 1994
Mgrath (NY) - 1850
Mica, Daniel A. (FL) - 1978, 1980, 1982, 1984, 1986
Mica, John L. (FL) - 1992, 1994, 1996, 1998, 2000
Michael, George W. (IN) - 1898
Michael, John M. (ME) - 1994
Michael, Lawrence (VA) - 1944, 1946
Michael, W. E. (TN) - 1948
Michaels, Ernest E. (IL) - 1962
Michaels, Mortimer H. (NY) - 1936
Michaelson, M. Alfred (IL) - 1920, 1922, 1924, 1926, 1928, 1932
Michaelson, Mark G. (WI) - 1984
Michal, Charles J. (IL) - 1950
Michalek, Anthony (IL) - 1904, 1906, 1908
Michales, William H. (NY) - 1918
Michalowski, Edward S. (PA) - 1928, 1930
Michaux, H. M. Jr. (NC) - 1982
Michel, Robert H. (IL) - 1956, 1958, 1960, 1962, 1964, 1966, 1968, 1970, 1972, 1974,

1976, 1978, 1980, 1982, 1984, 1986, 1988, 1990, 1992
Michelson, Adolph (ND) - 1940
Michener, Earl C. (MI) - 1918, 1920, 1922, 1924, 1926, 1928, 1930, 1932, 1934, 1936, 1938, 1940, 1942, 1944, 1946, 1948
Michener, James A. (PA) - 1962
Michener, Ross (OH) - 1944
Michler, P. S. (PA) - 1838
Micich, Michael (IA) - 1956, 1958
Mickelson, Grace (SD) - 1976
Mickey, J. Ross (IL) - 1900
Mickle (NJ) - 1830
Middlesworth, Ner (PA) - 1852
Middleton, Alfred J. Sr. (AL) - 1994
Middleton, Clyde (KY) - 1962, 1964
Middleton, George (NJ) - 1862, 1864
Middleton, J. O. (AL) - 1924
Middleton, J. Osmond (AL) - 1908
Middleton, Larry (MI) - 1956
Midton (NY) - 1854
Miel, Lucas S. (MI) - 1958
Miele, Alphonse A. (NJ) - 1960
Miera, M. F. (NM) - 1934
Miers, Robert W. (IN) - 1896, 1898, 1902, 1904
Miglionico, Nina (AL) - 1974
Mihaly, John H. (OH) - 1960
Mihelich, John L. (OH) - 1936
Mihlbaugh, Robert H. (OH) - 1964, 1966
Mikan, George (MN) - 1956
Mikels, LeRoy (PA) - 1954
Mikulski, Barbara A. (MD) - 1976, 1978, 1980, 1982, 1984
Mikuria, Tom (CA) - 1980
Mikva, Abner J. (IL) - 1968, 1970, 1972, 1974, 1976, 1978
Milano, Salvatore J. (NY) - 1954
Milbourn, James G. (PA) - 1918
Milburn, William (MO) - 1846
Milby, Robert L. (KY) - 1954
Milder, Ally (NE) - 1990
Miles (CT) - 1886, 1890
Miles, Arthur A. (IL) - 1932
Miles, B. P. (MD) - 1894
Miles, Clarence G. (NE) - 1950
Miles, D. (MD) - 1892
Miles, Frederick (CT) - 1878, 1880, 1888, 1892
Miles, J. B. (AR) - 1882
Miles, John (MD) - 1896
Miles, John E. (NM) - 1948
Miles, John F. (WI) - 1894
Miles, Joshua W. (MD) - 1894
Miles, N. D. (KY) - 1904
Miles, Rowland (NY) - 1900
Miles, Sharon (CA) - 1998
Miles, W. Porcher (SC) - 1856, 1858, 1860
Miley (MO) - 1898
Milford, Dale (TX) - 1972, 1974, 1976
Milias, George W. (CA) - 1974
Milio, Louis R. (MD) - 1950
Milius, William B. (MO) - 1966
Millard, Charles (NY) - 1994
Millard, Charles D. (NY) - 1930, 1932, 1934, 1936
Millard, Stephen C. (NY) - 1882, 1884
Millen (AL) - 1882
Millen, John (GA) - 1842
Millender-McDonald, Juanita (CA) - 1996, 1998, 2000
Miller (GA) - 1844, 1857
Miller (IN) - 1880
Miller (NY) - 1852
Miller (PA) - 1843, 1888
Miller (VA) - 1829, 1831, 1865
Miller, A. B. (PA) - 1898
Miller, A. Grant (NV) - 1922
Miller, A. M. (NC) - 1956
Miller, Adam Clay (OH) - 1998
Miller, Albert (MI) - 1910
Miller, Allen (OH) - 1884
Miller, Arnold J. (NY) - 1982
Miller, Arthur L. (NE) - 1942, 1944, 1946, 1948, 1950, 1952, 1954, 1956, 1958
Miller, Ashley Grant (NV) - 1910
Miller, Bert H. (ID) - 1914, 1938

Miller, C. W. (SC) - 1860
Miller, Candice S. (MI) - 1986
Miller, Carol A. (NM) - 1997
Miller, Celestine V. (NY) - 1998
Miller, Charles (OR) - 1894
Miller, Charles A. (OH) - 1904
Miller, Charles E. (NY) - 1934
Miller, Charles E. (OH) - 1934
Miller, Charles H. (OH) - 1908
Miller, Charles H. (WA) - 1908
Miller, Charles W. (IN) - 1908
Miller, Clarence A. (TX) - 1924
Miller, Clarence B. (MN) - 1908, 1910, 1912, 1914, 1916, 1918
Miller, Clarence C. (OH) - 1940, 1942
Miller, Clarence E. (OH) - 1966, 1968, 1970, 1972, 1974, 1976, 1978, 1980, 1982, 1984, 1986, 1988, 1990
Miller, Clement (CA) - 1960, 1962
Miller, Clement W. (CA) - 1956, 1958
Miller, Clifford L. (NY) - 1932
Miller, Clyde W. (KS) - 1916
Miller, Dan (FL) - 1992, 1994, 1996, 1998, 2000
Miller, Daniel F. (IA) - 1848, 1850
Miller, Daniel H. (PA) - 1824, 1826, 1828, 1830
Miller, David (NY) - 1832
Miller, David J. (CO) - 1944
Miller, David L. (KS) - 1980
Miller, Dee D. (TX) - 1966
Miller, Demaris (VA) - 1998, 2000
Miller, E. B. (TX) - 1914
Miller, E. Spencer (PA) - 1906
Miller, Edward E. (IL) - 1922
Miller, Edward T. (MD) - 1946, 1948, 1950, 1952, 1954, 1956, 1958, 1960
Miller, Elijah (NY) - 1826
Miller, Elizabeth T. (NY) - 1974, 1976
Miller, Erich D. (CA) - 1994
Miller, Ernest M. (IA) - 1940
Miller, Eugene A. (MO) - 1952
Miller, Frank (WA) - 1938, 1940
Miller, Franklin (NY) - 1968
Miller, Fred (WA) - 1920
Miller, Frieda S. (PA) - 1920
Miller, G. M. (OR) - 1886
Miller, Gary G. (CA) - 1998, 2000
Miller, George (CA) - 1974, 1976, 1978, 1980, 1982, 1984, 1986, 1988, 1990, 1992, 1994, 1996, 1998, 2000
Miller, George A. (NJ) - 1902
Miller, George C. (NJ) - 1948
Miller, George F. (PA) - 1864, 1866
Miller, George Fraser (NY) - 1918
Miller, George G. (NY) - 1896
Miller, George H. (GA) - 1896
Miller, George H. (MO) - 1956
Miller, George P. (CA) - 1944, 1946, 1948, 1950, 1952, 1954, 1956, 1958, 1960, 1962, 1964, 1966, 1968, 1970
Miller, George T. (PA) - 1880
Miller, George W. (PA) - 1874
Miller, Guy E. (CO) - 1906
Miller, Harold O. (VA) - 1970, 1972
Miller, Harris (VT) - 1902
Miller, Henry W. (NC) - 1843, 1851
Miller, Herman (NY) - 1896
Miller, Howard A. (MA) - 1966
Miller, Howard A. Jr. (MA) - 1968, 1970
Miller, Howard M. (MA) - 1972
Miller, Howard S. (KS) - 1936, 1952, 1954, 1956
Miller, Hugh (KY) - 1910
Miller, Izetta Jewel (NY) - 1930
Miller, J. (MO) - 1850
Miller, J. Clyde (AL) - 1902
Miller, J. E. (PA) - 1924
Miller, J. R. (TN) - 1865
Miller, Jack L. (WV) - 1964
Miller, Jacob F. (WI) - 1920
Miller, James (NH) - 1824
Miller, James F. (TX) - 1882, 1884
Miller, James H. (WV) - 1902
Miller, James Monroe (KS) - 1898, 1900, 1902, 1904, 1906, 1908
Miller, James W. (MD) - 1948, 1950

Miller, Jedediah (NY) - 1832, 1840
Miller, Jeff N. (TX) - 1912
Miller, Jesse (PA) - 1832, 1834
Miller, Jesse M. (MI) - 1882
Miller, John (MO) - 1836, 1838, 1840
Miller, John (NY) - 1824, 1826, 1838
Miller, John A. (NJ) - 1960
Miller, John E. (AR) - 1930, 1932, 1934, 1936
Miller, John F. (PA) - 1896, 1900
Miller, John F. (WA) - 1916, 1918, 1920, 1922, 1924, 1926, 1928, 1932
Miller, John G. (MO) - 1846, 1850, 1852, 1854
Miller, John J. (NY) - 1948
Miller, John K. (OH) - 1846, 1848
Miller, John R. (WA) - 1984, 1986, 1988, 1990
Miller, Joseph (OH) - 1856, 1858
Miller, Joseph (OH) - 1956
Miller, Joseph S. (WV) - 1906
Miller, Kenneth C. (NJ) - 1972
Miller, Kevin G. (VA) - 1982
Miller, Killian (NY) - 1834, 1854
Miller, Les (AZ) - 1980
Miller, Lewis (OH) - 1878
Miller, Lloyd D. (OH) - 1968
Miller, Locke (PA) - 1928, 1934
Miller, Louis E. (MO) - 1932, 1942, 1944
Miller, Lucas M. (WI) - 1890
Miller, Margaret (WV) - 1984
Miller, Mark (OH) - 1992
Miller, Martin (WV) - 1986
Miller, Matt (CA) - 1980
Miller, Mayne W. (TN) - 1958
Miller, Mike (DE) - 2000
Miller, Milton S. (CA) - 1970
Miller, Nathaniel (NY) - 1838
Miller, Orrin L. (KS) - 1894
Miller, P. H. (ND) - 1936
Miller, Pat (CO) - 1994, 1996
Miller, Patrick K. (OK) - 1982, 1984, 1986, 1990
Miller, Paul G. (OH) - 1910
Miller, Peter H. (FL) - 1916
Miller, Richard T. (NJ) - 1902
Miller, Riley V. (NY) - 1892
Miller, Robert A. (OR) - 1890
Miller, Robert C. (IL) - 1970
Miller, Robert E. (AZ) - 1968
Miller, Robert H. (PA) - 1976, 1978
Miller, Robert Lowell (IN) - 1964
Miller, Roger M. (IN) - 1982
Miller, Roy O. (MO) - 1940
Miller, Russell R. (CA) - 1970
Miller, S. (CA) - 1910
Miller, S. E. (PA) - 1920
Miller, Sam James (CA) - 1948
Miller, Samuel A. (OH) - 1886
Miller, Samuel F. (NY) - 1862, 1874
Miller, Samuel H. (NY) - 1940
Miller, Samuel H. (PA) - 1880, 1882, 1914
Miller, Samuel H. Jr. (NY) - 1944
Miller, Seth (NY) - 1838
Miller, Silas F. (KY) - 1882
Miller, Smith (IN) - 1852, 1854
Miller, T. C. (NC) - 1837
Miller, Thomas (OH) - 1866
Miller, Thomas Byron (PA) - 1942, 1944
Miller, Thomas E. (SC) - 1888, 1890
Miller, Thomas W. (DE) - 1914, 1916
Miller, W. D. (MS) - 1896
Miller, W. H. (PA) - 1864
Miller, Ward M. (OH) - 1960
Miller, Warner (NY) - 1878, 1880
Miller, Warren (WV) - 1894, 1896
Miller, Wayne (CA) - 1998, 2000
Miller, Wayne (MI) - 1968
Miller, William (OH) - 1912
Miller, William E. (NY) - 1950, 1952, 1954, 1956, 1958, 1960, 1962
Miller, William E. Jr. (NY) - 1992, 1994
Miller, William H. (PA) - 1862
Miller, William J. (CT) - 1938, 1940, 1942, 1944, 1946, 1948
Miller, William S. (NY) - 1844
Millett, James M. (MN) - 1920
Millett, Jeremy J. (LA) - 1974
Millhol (PA) - 1872

Milligan (MD) - 1878
Milligan, Jacob L. (MO) - 1920, 1922, 1924, 1926, 1928, 1930, 1932
Milligan, John E. (HI) - 1964
Milligan, John J. (DE) - 1830, 1832, 1834, 1836, 1838
Milligan, Vanche F. (NY) - 1942
Milliken (PA) - 1834
Milliken, Benjamin (GA) - 1896
Milliken, Charles W. (KY) - 1872
Milliken, J. A. (ME) - 1854
Milliken, John G. (VA) - 1986
Milliken, Seth L. (ME) - 1880, 1882, 1884, 1886, 1888, 1890, 1892, 1894, 1896
Milliken, William H. Jr. (PA) - 1958, 1960, 1962
Millikin (MD) - 1882
Millikin, Charles W. (KY) - 1874
Milliman, Nathaniel B. (NY) - 1866
Milliman, Richard L. (MI) - 1982
Millington, Charles S. (NY) - 1908, 1910
Mills (GA) - 1874
Mills (NJ) - 1876
Mills (OK) - 1914
Mills, Annie D. (NY) - 1934
Mills, Benjamin (IL) - 1834
Mills, Charles S. (VA) - 1876
Mills, Daniel W. (IL) - 1896, 1898, 1900
Mills, Don (KY) - 1982
Mills, Francis Jones (KY) - 1964
Mills, George T. (VA) - 1890
Mills, Gregory B. (HI) - 1982
Mills, Isaac R. (IL) - 1898
Mills, James K. (CA) - 1976
Mills, John (MA) - 1828, 1830
Mills, Jon (FL) - 1988
Mills, Louis V. (NY) - 1966
Mills, Merrill I. (MI) - 1868
Mills, Newton V. (LA) - 1936, 1938, 1940
Mills, Ogden L. (NY) - 1912, 1920, 1922, 1924
Mills, Roger Q. (TX) - 1872, 1874, 1876, 1878, 1880, 1882, 1884, 1886, 1888, 1890
Mills, W. T. (AR) - 1908
Mills, Walter S. (OK) - 1924, 1926, 1928
Mills, Wilbur D. (AR) - 1938, 1940, 1942, 1944, 1946, 1948, 1950, 1952, 1954, 1956, 1958, 1960, 1962, 1964, 1966, 1968, 1970, 1972, 1974
Mills, William (IA) - 1868
Mills, William O. (MD) - 1972
Mills, William Wirt (NY) - 1912
Millson, John S. (VA) - 1849, 1851, 1853, 1855, 1857, 1589, 1865
Millspaugh, Frank C. (MO) - 1918, 1920, 1922, 1924
Millward, William (PA) - 1854, 1856, 1858
Milner (GA) - 1884
Milner, Albert R. (OH) - 1912
Milner, Larry S. (TX) - 1988
Milnes, Alfred (MI) - 1895, 1896
Milnes, William Jr. (VA) - 1869
Milstead, Andrew J. (AL) - 1900
Miltner, John H. (MI) - 1992
Milton (GA) - 1832
Milton, Maria Elena (AZ) - 1996
Mims, Tom (FL) - 1992
Minahan, Daniel F. (NJ) - 1918, 1920, 1922, 1924, 1930
Mincker, Jeremiah F. (OH) - 1916
Minckler, J. A. (ND) - 1912
Mindnich, Martin S. (NY) - 1900
Minehart, T. Z. (PA) - 1930
Minehart, Thomas Z. (PA) - 1942
Miner (CT) - 1873
Miner (NY) - 1854
Miner, A. L. (VT) - 1850
Miner, Charles (PA) - 1824, 1826
Miner, George F. (NY) - 1910
Miner, Henry C. (NY) - 1894
Miner, Phineas (CT) - 1834, 1837
Miner, Simeon (CT) - 1831
Mineta, Norman Y. (CA) - 1974, 1976, 1978, 1980, 1982, 1984, 1986, 1988, 1990, 1992, 1994
Minge, David (MN) - 1992, 1994, 1996, 1998, 2000

Minger, Irwin W. (CA) - 1940
Minick, William H. (PA) - 1894
Minico, Joe De (FL) - 1992
Minier, Philip N. (IL) - 1882
Minish, Joseph G. (NJ) - 1962, 1964, 1966, 1968, 1970, 1972, 1974, 1976, 1978, 1980, 1982, 1984
Miniter, Patrick J. (IL) - 1894
Mink, Patsy T. (HI) - 1964, 1966, 1968, 1970, 1972, 1974, 1990, 1992, 1994, 1996
Mink, Patsy T. (HI) - 1998, 2000
Minney, Michael J. (PA) - 1974, 1976
Minor, Charles E. (IA) - 1976, 1978
Minor, Donald E. Jr. (OH) - 1998, 2000
Minor, Edward S. (WI) - 1894, 1896, 1898, 1900, 1902, 1904
Minor, F. W. (TX) - 1872
Minor, George W. K. (PA) - 1880
Minor, Robert (IL) - 1924
Minshall, William E. Jr. (OH) - 1954, 1956, 1958, 1960, 1962, 1964, 1966, 1968, 1970, 1972
Minturn, Henry C. (CA) - 1982, 1984
Mirza, G. S. (IL) - 1964
Mish, Frank W. (MD) - 1920, 1922, 1926
Misir, Jorawar (NY) - 1996
Miska, Walter J. (RI) - 1970
Misner, E. H. (CA) - 1908
Missemer (MO) - 1894
Mister, Matthew K. (MS) - 1888
Mitchel, John R. (OH) - 2000
Mitchel, Peter (NY) - 1846
Mitchell (AR) - 1860, 1884
Mitchell (CT) - 1865
Mitchell (MI) - 1878
Mitchell (MO) - 1860
Mitchell (NY) - 1878
Mitchell (PA) - 1860, 1872
Mitchell (WI) - 1868
Mitchell, Alexander (WI) - 1870, 1872
Mitchell, Alexander C. (KS) - 1910
Mitchell, Anderson (NC) - 1843
Mitchell, Andrew D. (AL) - 1910
Mitchell, Arthur W. (IL) - 1934, 1936, 1938, 1940
Mitchell, Bill (CA) - 1986
Mitchell, Bob (MI) - 1994
Mitchell, Charles (NY) - 1836, 1838
Mitchell, Charles L. (CT) - 1882, 1884
Mitchell, D. P. (KS) - 1880
Mitchell, Donald J. (NY) - 1972, 1974, 1976, 1978, 1980
Mitchell, Donnell (OR) - 1954
Mitchell, Edward (PA) - 1976
Mitchell, Edward A. (IN) - 1946, 1948
Mitchell, Ernest S. (CA) - 1938
Mitchell, George E. (MD) - 1824, 1829, 1831
Mitchell, H. K. (NV) - 1865, 1866
Mitchell, Harlan Erwin (GA) - 1958
Mitchell, Harry (MI) - 1932
Mitchell, Harry B. (MT) - 1916, 1918, 1926
Mitchell, Harry B. (PA) - 1928
Mitchell, Harry W. (OH) - 1948
Mitchell, Henry (NY) - 1832
Mitchell, Hugh B. (WA) - 1948, 1950, 1954, 1958
Mitchell, Ira C. (IA) - 1864
Mitchell, J. Ridley (TN) - 1934, 1936
Mitchell, James C. (MN) - 1920
Mitchell, James C. (TN) - 1825, 1827
Mitchell, James S. (PA) - 1824
Mitchell, John (PA) - 1824, 1826
Mitchell, John C. Jr. (CO) - 1970
Mitchell, John E. (IN) - 1962
Mitchell, John F. (NC) - 1912
Mitchell, John I. (PA) - 1876, 1878
Mitchell, John J. (CO) - 1988
Mitchell, John J. (MA) - 1908, 1910, 1912, 1914
Mitchell, John L. (WI) - 1890, 1892
Mitchell, John Murray (NY) - 1894, 1896, 1898
Mitchell, John R. (TN) - 1930, 1932
Mitchell, John W. (MO) - 1940, 1942, 1944
Mitchell, Joseph J. (MN) - 1960
Mitchell, Joshua "Chad" (NC) - 2000
Mitchell, Leland D. (MI) - 1962

Mitchell, Lewis Z. (PA) - 1868
Mitchell, Lex N. (PA) - 1914
Mitchell, Parren J. (MD) - 1970, 1972, 1974, 1976, 1978, 1980, 1982, 1984
Mitchell, Perry (ID) - 1924
Mitchell, Perry W. (ID) - 1912
Mitchell, Poppy X. (IL) - 1964
Mitchell, R. B. (KS) - 1872
Mitchell, R. F. (IA) - 1924
Mitchell, Ray (OH) - 1990
Mitchell, Robbins (TX) - 1974
Mitchell, Robert (OH) - 1832, 1834
Mitchell, Robert W. (PA) - 1966
Mitchell, Steve (FL) - 1982
Mitchell, Ted (PA) - 1980
Mitchell, Thomas R. (SC) - 1824, 1826, 1828, 1830, 1833
Mitchell, W. (CO) - 1984
Mitchell, Wendell (AL) - 1978
Mitchell, William (IN) - 1860, 1862
Mitchell, William (NY) - 1836, 1838
Mitchell, William C. (PA) - 1910
Mitchner, C. H. (OH) - 1866
Mitnick, John (GA) - 1996
Mix (NY) - 1860
Mix, C. E. (WA) - 1896
Mixon, Billy (GA) - 1966
Mize, Chester L. (KS) - 1964, 1966, 1968, 1970
Mizell, Wilmer D. (NC) - 1968, 1970, 1972, 1974, 1976
Mizer, George Alfred Jr. (OK) - 1974
Mkee (WI) - 1852
Mlain, Thomas J. (OH) - 1840
Moakley, Joe (MA) - 1972, 1974, 1976, 1978, 1980, 1982, 1984, 1986, 1988, 1990, 1992, 1994, 1996, 1998, 2000
Moats, W. O. (KY) - 1922
Moberly, William E. (IL) - 1878
Mobley, Charles "Chuck" (IL) - 1994
Mobley, Russell G. (KY) - 1968
Mock, Ira J. (AR) - 1932
Modica, Louis J. (NY) - 1980
Moe, I, J. (ND) - 1936
Moe, Joseph P. (FL) - 1946
Moehlenpah, H. A. (WI) - 1908
Moeller, Walter H. (OH) - 1958, 1960, 1962, 1964, 1966
Moen (MN) - 1902
Moffatt, Seth C. (MI) - 1884, 1886
Moffet, David (PA) - 1894, 1904
Moffet, John (PA) - 1868, 1870
Moffett, George Lee (IN) - 1922
Moffett, T. K. (MS) - 1978, 1980
Moffett, Toby (CT) - 1974, 1976, 1978, 1980, 1990
Moffitt, John H. (NY) - 1886, 1888
Moffitt, Karen (FL) - 1992
Mohan, Richard A. (IL) - 1954
Mohney, Foster M. (PA) - 1912
Moise, E. M. (SC) - 1892
Molander, Earl (OR) - 1988, 1990
Molesworth, Jack E. (MA) - 1964
Molinari, Guy V. (NY) - 1980, 1982, 1984, 1986, 1988
Molinari, Susan (NY) - 1990, 1992, 1994, 1996
Molineaux, R. O. (PA) - 1900
Mollette, John B. (KY) - 1936
Mollohan, Alan B. (WV) - 1982, 1984, 1986, 1988, 1990, 1992, 1994, 1996, 1998, 2000
Mollohan, Robert H. (WV) - 1952, 1954, 1958, 1968, 1970, 1972, 1974, 1976, 1978, 1980
Molly, Edwin H. (PA) - 1900
Molone, John L. (WI) - 1914
Moloney, Maurice T. (IL) - 1898
Moloney, Thomas W. (VT) - 1890
Molony, Richard S. (IL) - 1850
Molton, Larry (CA) - 1994
Monaco, Lee (NJ) - 1988
Monagan, John S. (CT) - 1958, 1960, 1962, 1964, 1966, 1968, 1970, 1972
Monaghan, Joseph P. (MT) - 1932, 1934
Monaghan, R. J. (PA) - 1880
Monaghan, Robert C. (PA) - 1868
Monahan, James G. (WI) - 1918
Monahan, Thomas G. (MT) - 1978
Monahan, Tom (MT) - 1980

Monast, Louis (RI) - 1924, 1926, 1928
Monde, Debra (TX) - 2000
Mondell, Frank W. (WY) - 1894, 1896, 1898, 1900, 1902, 1904, 1906, 1908, 1910, 1912, 1914, 1916, 1918, 1920
Mondragon, Robert A. (NM) - 1974
Monell, John (NY) - 1846
Monell, Robert (NY) - 1826, 1828
Money (OH) - 1858
Money, Hernando D. (MS) - 1875, 1876, 1878, 1880, 1882, 1892, 1894
Monfils, Michael R. (WI) - 1980
Monfils, Owen F. (WI) - 1962
Monkiewicz, Boleslaus J. (CT) - 1938, 1940, 1942, 1944
Monnett, Frank S. (OH) - 1910
Monohan, Barry F. (MA) - 1974
Monro, Donald L. (PA) - 1900
Monroe (KY) - 1837
Monroe, A. T. (TX) - 1884
Monroe, H. H. (ME) - 1900
Monroe, H. Lee (TX) - 1928
Monroe, James (NY) - 1836, 1838, 1840, 1846
Monroe, James (OH) - 1870, 1872, 1874, 1876, 1878
Monroe, James M. (OH) - 1886
Monroe, James O. (IL) - 1902, 1904
Monroe, Robert G. (NY) - 1894
Monroney, A. S. Mike (OK) - 1938, 1940, 1942, 1944, 1946, 1948
Monrose, Herbert M. (FL) - 1974
Monsma, Stephen V. (MI) - 1982
Monson, Arthur L. (UT) - 1980
Monson, David S. (UT) - 1984
Montague, Andrew J. (VA) - 1914, 1920, 1928, 1932
Montague, Andrew Jackson (VA) - 1912, 1916, 1918, 1922, 1924, 1926, 1930, 1934, 1936
Montanus, P. E. (OH) - 1904
Montegut (LA) - 1847
Monteith, Stanley (CA) - 1988
Montelli, Anthony L. (NJ) - 1934
Montet, Numa F. (LA) - 1929, 1930, 1932, 1934
Montgomery (PA) - 1854
Montgomery, Alexander B. (KY) - 1886, 1888, 1890, 1892, 1894
Montgomery, Arthur S. (MO) - 1992
Montgomery, B. F. (IA) - 1870
Montgomery, D. (OK) - 1920
Montgomery, G. V. (Sonny) (MS) - 1966, 1968, 1970, 1972, 1974, 1976, 1978, 1980, 1982, 1984, 1986, 1988, 1990, 1992, 1994
Montgomery, George F. (MI) - 1972, 1974
Montgomery, Harry C. (IL) - 1936
Montgomery, J. R. (PA) - 1948, 1950
Montgomery, James R. (PA) - 1972, 1974
Montgomery, John (KS) - 1964
Montgomery, John D. (KS) - 1956
Montgomery, John G. (PA) - 1856
Montgomery, M. A. (MS) - 1896
Montgomery, Place (OK) - 1940
Montgomery, Rex (KS) - 1926
Montgomery, Samuel (KY) - 1851
Montgomery, Samuel J. (OK) - 1924, 1926
Montgomery, Seaborn S. (GA) - 1896
Montgomery, Terry (MN) - 1970
Montgomery, Terry J. (OK) - 1988
Montgomery, W. (PA) - 1866
Montgomery, Wayne (MT) - 1962, 1964
Montgomery, William (NC) - 1835, 1837, 1839
Montgomery, William (PA) - 1856, 1858
Montgomery, William P. (RI) - 1980
Montieth, Hugh (NC) - 1952
Montoya, Anthony J. (NY) - 1968
Montoya, Joseph M. (NM) - 1958, 1960, 1962
Montoya, Michael A. (NM) - 2000
Montoya, Nestor (NM) - 1920
Monuh, Thomas (MS) - 1894
Monyek, Rose Zeidwerg (NJ) - 1980
Monypeny, William W. (KS) - 1954
Moody, C. H. (KS) - 1886
Moody, Charles H. (KS) - 1882
Moody, Danny G. (NC) - 1984
Moody, Edward "Gomer" (MO) - 1992
Moody, Harold (IN) - 1962

Morrison, J. T. (ID) - 1900
Morrison, James H. (LA) - 1942, 1944, 1946, 1948, 1950, 1952, 1954, 1956, 1958, 1960, 1962, 1964
Morrison, John A. (PA) - 1850
Morrison, John D. (OK) - 1934, 1936
Morrison, John E. (MI) - 1942
Morrison, John H. (ID) - 1904
Morrison, John H. (NY) - 1902
Morrison, John T. (ID) - 1896
Morrison, Kenneth (VA) - 1980
Morrison, Martin A. (IN) - 1908, 1910, 1912, 1914
Morrison, Mrs. Frank B. (NE) - 1968
Morrison, Robert S. (CO) - 1880
Morrison, Royd E. (PA) - 1916
Morrison, Sid (WA) - 1980, 1982, 1984, 1986, 1988, 1990
Morrison, Timothy A. (KY) - 1984
Morrison, William R. (IL) - 1862, 1864, 1866, 1872, 1874, 1876, 1878, 1880, 1882, 1884, 1886
Morrissey, John (NY) - 1866, 1868
Morrissey, John P. (NY) - 1948
Morrissey, Joseph F. (CT) - 1934
Morrissey, Patrick H. (IL) - 1924
Morrissey, Richard J. (MA) - 1912
Morrow (NJ) - 1886
Morrow, Jeremiah (OH) - 1840
Morrow, John (NM) - 1922, 1924, 1926, 1928
Morrow, Robert D. (MD) - 1972
Morrow, Thomas H. (OH) - 1920
Morrow, William (KY) - 1859
Morrow, William E. (NC) - 1958
Morrow, William W. (CA) - 1882, 1884, 1886, 1888
Morroway (MO) - 1912, 1914
Morse (CT) - 1902, 1904
Morse (MA) - 1886
Morse (MO) - 1884
Morse, Bushrod (MA) - 1890
Morse, Charles A. (NH) - 1906
Morse, D. A. (CA) - 1849
Morse, Elijah A. (MA) - 1888, 1890, 1892, 1894
Morse, Elmer A. (WI) - 1906, 1908, 1910, 1912
Morse, F. Bradford (MA) - 1960, 1962, 1964, 1966, 1968, 1970
Morse, Freeman H. (ME) - 1843, 1844, 1847, 1856, 1858
Morse, I. Porter (MA) - 1896, 1898
Morse, Isaac E. (LA) - 1847, 1849
Morse, Issac E. (LA) - 1844, 1847, 1849, 1851
Morse, Jenner E. (MI) - 1908
Morse, Leopold (MA) - 1870, 1872, 1876, 1878, 1880, 1882, 1886
Morse, Oliver A. (NY) - 1856
Morse, Roy L. (WI) - 1904
Morse, William (MI) - 1998, 2000
Morsey (MO) - 1892
Morss, Joseph B. (MA) - 1864
Morten, Stanley W. (IL) - 1952
Morton, Eskridge H. (WV) - 1922
Morton, Frank L. (PA) - 1916
Morton, Howard A. (MA) - 1924
Morton, Isaac (OH) - 1878
Morton, J. Sterling (NE) - 1888
Morton, Jeremiah (VA) - 1849
Morton, Levi P. (NY) - 1876, 1878, 1880
Morton, Minor G. (OH) - 1922
Morton, Nathaniel (MA) - 1848
Morton, Richard (NY) - 1906
Morton, Rogers C. B. (MD) - 1962, 1964, 1966, 1968, 1970
Morton, Thomas B. (AL) - 1900
Morton, Thruston B. (KY) - 1946, 1948, 1950
Morton, W. O. (CA) - 1904
Mosby (VA) - 1865
Moseley (VA) - 1853
Moseley, Edna D. (NY) - 1948
Moseley, James Brady (MA) - 1972
Moseley, Nicholas (CT) - 1928
Moseley, Ralph S. (NE) - 1930
Moseley, William A. (NY) - 1842, 1844
Moseley, William D. (NC) - 1837
Mosely, J. H. (WI) - 1888

Mosely, Ken (SC) - 1982, 1984
Moser, Guy L. (PA) - 1936, 1938, 1940
Moser, Jeff (SD) - 1998
Moser, Terry Lee (TX) - 1992
Moses (SC) - 1853
Moses, Charles L. (GA) - 1890, 1892, 1894
Moses, David (NY) - 1938, 1940
Moses, Halsey H. (OH) - 1864
Moses, Joel (NY) - 1922
Mosgrove, James (PA) - 1878, 1880
Mosher, Charles (MI) - 1884
Mosher, Charles A. (OH) - 1960, 1962, 1964, 1966, 1968, 1970, 1972, 1974
Mosher, H. S. (IA) - 1914
Mosher, Orris (IA) - 1912
Mosher, Richard T. (NY) - 1948
Moshofsky, Bill (OR) - 1982, 1984
Mosier, Harold G. (OH) - 1936
Moskowitz, Henry (NY) - 1912
Mosley (GA) - 1846
Moss (MO) - 1856
Moss, C. V. (NC) - 1944
Moss, D. S. (NC) - 1896
Moss, Dave (AZ) - 1988
Moss, David (IN) - 1878
Moss, Edward F. (NY) - 1940
Moss, Hunter H. Jr. (WV) - 1912, 1914
Moss, J. McKenzie (KY) - 1900, 1902
Moss, John E. (CA) - 1952, 1954, 1956, 1958, 1960, 1962, 1964, 1966, 1968, 1970, 1972, 1974, 1976
Moss, M. J. Jr. (FL) - 1946, 1948
Moss, Mrs. St. Clair (MO) - 1922
Moss, Norman H. (IL) - 1892
Moss, Preston B. (MT) - 1922
Moss, Ralph W. (IN) - 1908, 1910, 1912, 1914, 1916, 1918
Moss, William R. (OH) - 1976
Mosser, Charles M. (PA) - 1944
Mossholder, Max (TX) - 1960
Most, Amicus (NY) - 1942
Mostyn, William H. (NY) - 1956
Motley, Joseph (TN) - 1868
Motlow, George (TN) - 1930
Motsinger, Newel H. (IN) - 1896
Mott, Frank H. (NY) - 1918
Mott, George (NY) - 1870
Mott, James W. (OR) - 1932, 1934, 1936, 1938, 1940, 1942, 1944
Mott, Luther W. (NY) - 1910, 1912, 1914, 1916, 1918, 1920, 1922
Mott, Richard (OH) - 1854, 1856
Mottashed, J. Charles (MI) - 1946
Mottl, Ronald M. (OH) - 1970, 1974, 1976, 1978, 1980
Mottley, E. L. (KY) - 1876
Mottola, Rudolph E. (MA) - 1956
Mottola, Vincent (MA) - 1942
Moulder, Garret (PA) - 1898
Moulder, Morgan M. (MO) - 1948, 1950, 1952, 1954, 1956, 1958, 1960
Mouln (NY) - 1852
Moulton (MO) - 1916
Moulton (NH) - 1847
Moulton (NY) - 1882
Moulton, Arthur L. (OR) - 1914
Moulton, Mace (NH) - 1845
Moulton, Samuel W. (IL) - 1862, 1864, 1880, 1882
Mount, James A. (IN) - 1890
Mourdock, Richard E. (IN) - 1990, 1992
Mouser, Grant E. (OH) - 1904, 1906, 1908
Mouser, Grant E. Jr. (OH) - 1928, 1930, 1932, 1936
Mouton, Robert L. (LA) - 1936, 1938
Mowery, Jean D. (PA) - 1982
Mowery, Wes (TX) - 1976
Mowery, Wesley H. (TX) - 1978
Mowry (RI) - 1916
Mowry, Sumner (RI) - 1928
Moxley, William J. (IL) - 1909, 1910
Moye, Charles A. Jr. (GA) - 1954
Moye, Howard (NC) - 1986, 1988, 1990
Moye, James M. (MS) - 1966
Moyer, Charles W. (PA) - 1942
Moyer, William B. (PA) - 1974

Moynihan, James F. (IL) - 1982
Moynihan, Joseph A. Jr. (MI) - 1954
Moynihan, P. H. (IL) - 1932, 1934, 1936, 1940
Mozley (MO) - 1900
Mozley, Norman A. (MO) - 1894
Mrazek, Robert J. (NY) - 1982, 1984, 1986, 1988, 1990
Mrozinski, Phillip D. (WI) - 1970, 1972
Mruk, Joseph (NY) - 1942
Mton (VA) - 1851
Mucci, Henry A. (CT) - 1946
Mucciolo, Anthony J. (PA) - 1986
Mudd, John E. (MD) - 1968
Mudd, Sydney E. (MD) - 1888, 1890, 1896, 1898, 1900, 1902, 1904, 1906, 1908, 1914, 1916, 1918, 1920, 1922
Mudd, Thomas Brackett Reed (MD) - 1924, 1926
Mudd, W. S. (AL) - 1851
Mudge (NY) - 1878
Mudge, D. H. (IL) - 1916
Mudge, Ezra (MA) - 1828
Mueller, Alfred C. (IA) - 1938
Mueller, Gary S. (IL) - 1998
Mueller, Margaret (OH) - 1986, 1988, 1990, 1992
Mueller, Norbert (WA) - 1990
Mufsey, Benjamin B. (MA) - 1850
Mugford, James E. (PA) - 1976
Muhe, Daniel (CA) - 1998
Muhlenberg, Francis S. (OH) - 1828
Muhlenberg, Frederick A. (PA) - 1946, 1948
Muhlenberg, H. A. (PA) - 1892
Muhlenberg, Henry A. (PA) - 1852
Muhlenburg, Henry A. P. (PA) - 1828, 1830, 1832, 1834, 1836
Muhler, Marie Sheehan (NJ) - 1980, 1982
Muir (ND) - 1894
Muir, Robert (NY) - 1836
Mulder, Leland E. (WI) - 1986
Muldoon, Hugh (IL) - 1972
Muldoon, Patrick (VA) - 1996
Muldowney, Michael J. (PA) - 1932, 1934
Muldowney, Paul (MD) - 1994
Muldrow, Henry L. (MS) - 1876, 1878, 1880, 1882
Mulford (NJ) - 1854
Mulhern, Joseph J. (MA) - 1960
Mulholland, Frank L. (OH) - 1916, 1934
Mulkey, William O. (AL) - 1900, 1914
Mullaney, T. W. (IA) - 1948, 1952
Mullen, C. N. (ME) - 1912
Mullen, C. W. (ME) - 1914
Mullen, Francis M. "Bud" (CT) - 1986
Mullen, John (NY) - 1910
Mullen, John F. (MA) - 1902
Muller, Gustav A. (PA) - 1894
Muller, Nicholas (NY) - 1876, 1878, 1880, 1882, 1884, 1898, 1900
Muller, Paul Jr. (NY) - 1910
Mullholland (NY) - 1884
Mulligan, Anne Marie (PA) - 1998
Mulligan, Thomas J. (OH) - 1908
Mullikin, Addison E. (MD) - 1910
Mullin, Joseph (NY) - 1846
Mullins, Fenton P. F. (PA) - 1896
Mullins, James (TN) - 1867, 1870
Mulloy, William P. (KY) - 1984
Muloaney, William (IA) - 1900
Mulrenan, John P. (PA) - 1930
Multer, Abraham J. (NY) - 1947, 1948, 1950, 1952, 1954, 1956, 1958, 1960, 1962, 1964, 1966
Mulvaney, John T. (IA) - 1904, 1914
Mulvaney, M. F. (NE) - 1938
Mulvany (PA) - 1856
Mumma, Walter M. (PA) - 1950, 1952, 1954, 1956, 1958, 1960
Muncaster, Robert (CA) - 1964
Munday, James A. (WA) - 1892, 1913
Mundt, Karl E. (SD) - 1936, 1938, 1940, 1942, 1944, 1946
Mundy (NY) - 1852
Mundy, Roy (WA) - 1960
Mungen (OH) - 1858
Mungen, William (OH) - 1866, 1868

Munger, Frank Sr. (MN) - 1930
Munger, W. H. (NE) - 1882
Munkittrick, Cindy (FL) - 1992
Munly, M. G. (OR) - 1912
Munn, Charles (MN) - 1942
Munn, Daniel W. (IL) - 1870
Munn, James (WA) - 1966
Munoz, Carlos E. (NJ) - 1996
Munro, Donald L. (PA) - 1898
Munro, William (WI) - 1894
Munroe, John H. (IA) - 1894
Munsell, Susan Grimes (MI) - 1998
Munsey, Sue (FL) - 1994
Munster, Edward W. (CT) - 1992, 1994, 1996
Muntzing, Melvin C. (WV) - 1944
Munyon, LeRoy (IA) - 1924
Mur (PA) - 1852
Murback, Jacob F. (MD) - 1912
Murch, Thompson H. (ME) - 1878, 1880, 1882
Murchison, Carmack (TN) - 1928
Murchison, Roderick (NC) - 1839, 1841
Murdock (WI) - 1892
Murdock, Abe (UT) - 1932, 1934, 1936, 1938
Murdock, Allen C. (WV) - 1904
Murdock, John R. (AZ) - 1936, 1938, 1940, 1942, 1944, 1946, 1948, 1950, 1952
Murdock, Norman A. (OH) - 1984
Murdock, Victor (KS) - 1904, 1906, 1908, 1910, 1912
Murer, Michael A. (IL) - 1980, 1982
Murkowski, Frank H. (AK) - 1970
Murphey (AL) - 1839
Murphey, Archibald D. (NC) - 1827
Murphey, Charles (GA) - 1851
Murphey, Walter W. (MS) - 1974
Murphy (AR) - 1880
Murphy (MO) - 1892, 1906 ,1910
Murphy (NY) - 1844, 1852, 1854, 1862, 1881
Murphy (OH) - 1860
Murphy, A. A. (GA) - 1896
Murphy, Arthur P. (MO) - 1904, 1908
Murphy, Austin J. (PA) - 1976, 1978, 1980, 1982, 1984, 1986, 1988, 1990, 1992
Murphy, B. Frank (OH) - 1918, 1920, 1922, 1924, 1926, 1928, 1930, 1932, 1934
Murphy, Bartholomew F. (NY) - 1938
Murphy, Charles J. (IN) - 1930
Murphy, D. W. B. (PA) - 1912
Murphy, Daniel D. (IA) - 1910
Murphy, Edward M. (PA) - 1924
Murphy, Eva Morley (KS) - 1914
Murphy, Everett J. (IL) - 1894, 1896
Murphy, Francis (NY) - 1894
Murphy, Francis L. (MN) - 1940
Murphy, Francis T. (WI) - 1940
Murphy, Frank (MI) - 1920
Murphy, George B. (NY) - 1962
Murphy, Henry (NY) - 1846
Murphy, Henry C. (NY) - 1842
Murphy, J. Palmer (NJ) - 1964
Murphy, J. W. (WI) - 1908
Murphy, James J. (MA) - 1974, 1978
Murphy, James J. (NY) - 1948, 1950, 1952
Murphy, James W. (WI) - 1906, 1920
Murphy, Jeremiah (AL) - 1908
Murphy, Jeremiah Henry (IA) - 1876, 1882, 1884
Murphy, John (AL) - 1831, 1833
Murphy, John (NY) - 1894
Murphy, John (PA) - 1908, 1924, 1926, 1930
Murphy, John F. (MI) - 1914
Murphy, John M. (NY) - 1960, 1962, 1964, 1966, 1968, 1970, 1972, 1974, 1976, 1978, 1980
Murphy, John V. (NY) - 1938
Murphy, John W. (PA) - 1942, 1944
Murphy, Joseph (CA) - 1980
Murphy, Joseph (PA) - 1972
Murphy, Joseph J. (OH) - 1960
Murphy, Kathleen M. (NY) - 1992
Murphy, Larry G. (PA) - 1996
Murphy, Lewis J. (IN) - 1954
Murphy, Michael M. (MA) - 1994
Murphy, Morgan F. (IL) - 1970, 1972, 1974, 1976, 1978
Murphy, Pat W. (AR) - 1934

Murphy, Patrick J. (NY) - 1918, 1920, 1926
Murphy, R. B. (ND) - 1932
Murphy, Richard D. (IL) - 1982, 1984
Murphy, Robert (AL) - 1851
Murphy, Robert (MI) - 1984
Murphy, W. M. (AL) - 1847
Murphy, Wilbur J. (NY) - 1920, 1932
Murphy, William (IL) - 1920, 1922
Murphy, William E. (KS) - 1942
Murphy, William H. (MA) - 1916
Murphy, William J. (MA) - 1930
Murphy, William K. (IL) - 1882
Murphy, William M. (NY) - 1948
Murphy, William T. (IL) - 1958, 1960, 1962, 1964, 1966, 1968
Murray (MD) - 1841
Murray (NY) - 1870, 1872
Murray (TN) - 1872
Murray, Ambrose S. (NY) - 1854, 1856, 1864
Murray, David W. (MA) - 1906, 1922, 1924
Murray, Dennis (CA) - 1972
Murray, Donald W. (IA) - 1962
Murray, Elizabeth Chilton (VA) - 1944
Murray, Esther (CA) - 1950
Murray, Frank X. (PA) - 1946
Murray, George W. (SC) - 1892, 1894, 1896, 1898
Murray, James C. (IL) - 1954, 1956
Murray, John H. (PA) - 1924
Murray, John J. (IN) - 1962
Murray, John J. (PA) - 1928
Murray, John L. (KY) - 1837
Murray, John P. (PA) - 1994, 1996
Murray, Joseph (CO) - 1886
Murray, Mervin (NJ) - 1968
Murray, Peggy L. (NY) - 1990
Murray, Ray (IA) - 1936
Murray, Reid F. (WI) - 1938, 1940, 1942, 1944, 1946, 1948, 1950
Murray, Richard D. (WI) - 1968
Murray, Robert F. (IN) - 1934
Murray, Robert J. (OH) - 1910
Murray, Robert M. (OH) - 1882, 1886
Murray, Robert N. (IL) - 1860
Murray, Samuel G. (MT) - 1900
Murray, Samuel P. (WI) - 1960
Murray, Thomas A. (NH) - 1942
Murray, Thomas H. (PA) - 1880
Murray, Thomas R. (CT) - 1920
Murray, Tom (OH) - 1986, 1988
Murray, Tom (TN) - 1942, 1944, 1946, 1948, 1950, 1952, 1954, 1956, 1958, 1960, 1962, 1964
Murray, Troy T. (MA) - 1952
Murray, Willard H. Jr. (CA) - 1996
Murray, William (NY) - 1850, 1852
Murray, William F. (MA) - 1910, 1912
Murray, William H. (OK) - 1912, 1914
Murrey, S. E. (TN) - 1910
Murtagh, James C. (IA) - 1906, 1914, 1916
Murtha, James A. Jr. (NY) - 1894
Murtha, John P. (PA) - 1968, 1974, 1976, 1978, 1980, 1982, 1984, 1986, 1988, 1990, 1992, 1994, 1996, 1998, 2000
Murty, Anthony J. (NY) - 1984
Muse (TN) - 1874
Musemeche, Robert (TX) - 1996
Mushat, John (NC) - 1827
Musick (MO) - 1888
Musselwhite, Harry W. (MI) - 1932, 1934
Musselwhite, Stephen Alan (VA) - 1992
Musser, C. S. (WV) - 1936
Musser, E. S. (PA) - 1912
Musser, Frank C. (PA) - 1922, 1924
Musser, J. Edward (FL) - 1960
Musser, Josephine (WI) - 1998
Musser, Virgil L. (OH) - 1968, 1970, 1972
Musson, J. J. (OH) - 1872
Musto, Frank A. (NJ) - 1958, 1960
Musto, Raphael (PA) - 1980
Mutaker, Edgar K. (MA) - 1848
Mutari, George J. (NY) - 1940
Mutchler, Howard (PA) - 1893, 1900
Mutchler, William (PA) - 1874, 1880, 1882, 1888, 1890, 1892
Muxlow, Keith (MI) - 1992

Muzyka, Richard A. (PA) - 1974
Muzzicato, Charles (NY) - 1942
Muzzicato, Charles (NY) - 1960
Mybeck, Walter R. II (AZ) - 1992
Myer, Gilbert F. (PA) - 1924
Myer, Philip (NY) - 1954, 1956
Myer, Rolla (ID) - 1910
Myers (NJ) - 1916
Myers (PA) - 1854, 1856
Myers, Amos (PA) - 1862
Myers, Carlton H. Dr. (IL) - 1958
Myers, Dick (IA) - 1978
Myers, F. W. (IA) - 1892
Myers, Francis J. (PA) - 1938, 1940, 1942
Myers, Fred (NC) - 1956
Myers, Gary A. (PA) - 1972, 1974, 1976
Myers, H. H. (AR) - 1894, 1908
Myers, Harvey (KY) - 1872
Myers, Henry F. (PA) - 1916
Myers, Herbert E. (KY) - 1970
Myers, Isaac (SC) - 1904
Myers, Jacob F. (OH) - 1954
Myers, Jefferson (OR) - 1896
Myers, John (OR) - 1884
Myers, John H. (PA) - 1928
Myers, John L. (IN) - 1988
Myers, John T. (IN) - 1966, 1968, 1970, 1972, 1974, 1976, 1978, 1980, 1982, 1984, 1986, 1988, 1990, 1992, 1994
Myers, Kym E. (KS) - 1986
Myers, Leonard (PA) - 1862, 1864, 1866, 1868, 1870, 1874
Myers, Mark (GA) - 1988
Myers, Michael J. (Ozzie) (PA) - 1976, 1978, 1980
Myers, Robert L. (PA) - 1968
Myers, W. W. (OR) - 1906
Myers, Wade A. (KS) - 1962
Myers, William H. (IN) - 1926
Myers, William R. (NC) - 1880
Myers, William Ralph (IN) - 1878, 1880
Myerson, Joseph G. (NY) - 1930
Myhra, Norman L. (WI) - 1966
Myre, R. L. (KY) - 1924
Myrick, John E. (GA) - 1898
Myrick, Sue (NC) - 1994, 1996, 1998, 2000
Myrland, Richard G. (IL) - 1946
Myrowitz, Paul (NY) - 1970
Myshka, Susan (AR) - 2000

N

Nabers, Benjamin D. (MS) - 1851, 1853
Nabers, Zoe S. Mrs. (IA) - 1940
Nadell, Mel (CA) - 1974
Nadler, Jerrold (NY) - 1992, 1994, 1996, 1998, 2000
Nadrowski, Leon F. (NY) - 1958, 1960, 1962, 1966, 1982, 1986
Nagel, Charles W. (KY) - 1910
Nagel, Fredric H. Jr. (CA) - 1960, 1962
Nager, Charles J. (NY) - 1948
Nagle, David R. (IA) - 1986, 1988, 1990, 1992, 1994
Nagler, Isidore (NY) - 1938
Nahra, Joseph J. (OH) - 1980
Nail, Vern W. (IA) - 1942
Nair, C. P. (VA) - 1916
Nair, Lois V. (MI) - 1958, 1960, 1962
Nakano, Elizabeth A. (CA) - 1992
Nakash, Alice Harriett (MA) - 1992
Nakasian, Samuel (NY) - 1968
Nalepa, Jim (IL) - 1994, 1996
Nalle, William M. (MO) - 1870
Nalley, George M. (WA) - 1974
Nally, James T. (IL) - 1960
Nance, A. H. (Bob) (UT) - 1970
Nance, E. L. (KY) - 1932
Nance, Stu (TX) - 1998
Nanney, C. Y. Jr. (NC) - 1946
Napear, Matthew (NY) - 1940
Naphen, Henry F. (MA) - 1898, 1900
Napier (TN) - 1898
Napier, John L. (SC) - 1980, 1982
Napieralski, E. F. (IL) - 1914
Napolitano, Grace F. (CA) - 1998, 2000
Narick, Steven D. (WV) - 1960

Nash (NY) - 1888
Nash, Bob (CA) - 1986
Nash, Charles E. (LA) - 1874, 1876
Nash, Charles E. (ME) - 1882
Nash, Francis D. (IL) - 1962
Nash, George K. (OH) - 1876
Nash, Henry K. (NC) - 1843, 1849
Nash, John B. (NH) - 1894, 1896
Nash, John F. (NY) - 1920
Nash, John W. (WI) - 1944
Nash, L. B. (AR) - 1868
Nash, Lyman J. (WI) - 1908
Nash, Merle W. (TX) - 1980
Nash, Samuel A. (OH) - 1872
Nash, Willis G. (NY) - 1934
Nason, Arthur L. (MA) - 1912
Nast, Charles Coudert (NY) - 1932
Natcher, William H. (KY) - 1954, 1956, 1958, 1960, 1962, 1964, 1966, 1968, 1970, 1972, 1974, 1976, 1978, 1980, 1982, 1984, 1986, 1988, 1990, 1992
Nathan, Theodora (OR) - 1976
Nathan, Tonie (OR) - 1990
Nations, Henry T. (AL) - 1908
Naudain, Arnold (DE) - 1824, 1826
Naughton, Noel (IL) - 1996
Nauman, George (PA) - 1876
Nauman, Ralph A. (SD) - 1962
Navarro, Peter (CA) - 1996
Nave, Forest Jr. (MO) - 1966
Naylor (VA) - 1833
Naylor, Charles (PA) - 1837, 1838
Neaf, Martin L. (MO) - 1942
Neal (PA) - 1843
Neal, Everett E. (IN) - 1910
Neal, Fred W. (CA) - 1968
Neal, George B. (OH) - 1902
Neal, George I. (WV) - 1898
Neal, George S. (WV) - 1914
Neal, Henry S. (OH) - 1876, 1878, 1880
Neal, Joe (WV) - 1972
Neal, John R. (TN) - 1884, 1886
Neal, Jurius E. (IA) - 1861
Neal, Lawrence T. (OH) - 1872, 1874, 1882, 1888
Neal, Patricia (CA) - 1998
Neal, Richard E. (MA) - 1988, 1990, 1992, 1994, 1996, 1998, 2000
Neal, Stephen L. (NC) - 1974, 1976, 1978, 1980, 1982, 1984, 1986, 1988, 1990, 1992
Neal, T. V. (TN) - 1892
Neal, W. H. (AR) - 1896
Neal, Will E. (WV) - 1952, 1954, 1956, 1958
Neale, Raphael (MD) - 1824
Neall, Robert R. (MD) - 1986
Nearing, Scott (NY) - 1918
Neas, Ralph G. (MD) - 1998
Neat (KY) - 1916
Nebg (PA) - 1858
Neddy, Tom (CA) - 1974
Nedzi, Lucien N. (MI) - 1961, 1962, 1964, 1966, 1968, 1970, 1972, 1974, 1976, 1978
Neece, William H. (IL) - 1872, 1882, 1884, 1886, 1896
Needham (MO) - 1888
Needham, Daniel (MA) - 1854
Needham, Henry Clay (CA) - 1898, 1900, 1902, 1904, 1906, 1908, 1910, 1912, 1914
Needham, Thomas H. (RI) - 1956
Needhm (VT) - 1856
Needles, Thomas B. (IL) - 1884
Neeley, George A. (KS) - 1910, 1912
Neely, H. G. (TX) - 1950
Neely, Matthew M. (WV) - 1914, 1916, 1918, 1920, 1944, 1946
Neese, John A. (GA) - 1898
Neff (MO) - 1896
Neff, Harold H. (WV) - 1946
Neff, John E. (IN) - 1872
Neff, Samuel G. (PA) - 1944, 1946
Neff, Samuel Gunnett (PA) - 1950
Negley, James S. (PA) - 1868, 1870, 1872, 1874, 1884
Neighbors, B. G. (TX) - 1920
Neihart, C. T. (KS) - 1928
Neil, Helen Nolan (NY) - 1952

Neil, Henry (IL) - 1920
Neil, John B. (OH) - 1888
Neil, John F. (IN) - 1912
Neil, Robert (AR) - 1892, 1894
Neill, Ben (NC) - 1992, 1996
Neill, Sam (NC) - 2000
Neilly, J. W. (PA) - 1914
Nellermoe, Arthur F. (MN) - 1944
Nelligan, James L. (PA) - 1980, 1982
Nellis (NY) - 1848
Nelsen, Ancher (MN) - 1958, 1960, 1962, 1964, 1966, 1968, 1970, 1972
Nelson (GA) - 1838
Nelson (IN) - 1860
Nelson (MD) - 1884
Nelson (MN) - 1904, 1914
Nelson (MO) - 1894
Nelson (NY) - 1860
Nelson (TN) - 1874
Nelson, Adolphus P. (WI) - 1918, 1920
Nelson, Bill (FL) - 1978, 1980, 1982, 1984, 1986, 1988
Nelson, Charles L. (TN) - 1845
Nelson, Charles P. (ME) - 1948, 1950, 1952, 1954
Nelson, Ed (AL) - 1972
Nelson, Edwin M. (IL) - 1960
Nelson, Frank J. (NY) - 1900
Nelson, Fred N. (WA) - 1922
Nelson, G. M. (FL) - 1956
Nelson, Gary (WA) - 1992
Nelson, Gary W. (TX) - 1988
Nelson, Gaylord A. (WI) - 1954
Nelson, H. J. (PA) - 1920
Nelson, Homer A. (NY) - 1862, 1864
Nelson, Janice A. (CA) - 1998, 2000
Nelson, Jeremiah (MA) - 1830
Nelson, John C. (IN) - 1902
Nelson, John E. (ME) - 1922, 1924, 1926, 1928, 1930, 1932
Nelson, John M. (WI) - 1906, 1908, 1910, 1912, 1914, 1916, 1920, 1922, 1924, 1930
Nelson, John Mandt (WI) - 1926, 1928
Nelson, Knute (MN) - 1882, 1884, 1886
Nelson, Larry (AZ) - 2000
Nelson, Mort (AZ) - 1996
Nelson, Norris J. (CA) - 1940
Nelson, O. M. (WA) - 1924, 1928
Nelson, Oscar F. (IL) - 1914
Nelson, Patrick L. (OH) - 1974
Nelson, Philip E. (WI) - 1936
Nelson, Robert L. (NY) - 1964
Nelson, Thomas A. R. (TN) - 1859
Nelson, Thomas F. (WI) - 1962
Nelson, Thomas T. (PA) - 1912
Nelson, V. C. (TX) - 1928
Nelson, Verner (MN) - 1946
Nelson, Will L. Jr. (MO) - 1946
Nelson, William (IL) - 1872
Nelson, William (NY) - 1846, 1848
Nelson, William L. (MO) - 1918, 1920, 1924, 1926, 1928, 1930, 1934, 1936, 1938, 1940, 1942
Nelson, William O. (IN) - 1938
Nemanich, Anton Jr. (IL) - 1920
Nero, Frank R. (NJ) - 1976
Nes, Henry (PA) - 1843, 1846, 1848
Nesbit (GA) - 1836
Nesbit, Fred (PA) - 1902
Nesbit, John F. (NE) - 1926
Nesbit, Walter (IL) - 1930, 1932, 1934
Nesemeier, Edward (ND) - 1952
Nesmith (NH) - 1845
Nesmith, James W. (OR) - 1873
Nesmith, Robert (TX) - 1958, 1960
Nestor, Kevin (OH) - 1998
Nethercutt, George (WA) - 1994, 1996, 1998, 2000
Neubauer, Bruce J. (GA) - 1980
Neubeck, Greg (FL) - 1986
Neuberger, Thomas Stephen (DE) - 1986
Neuman, Mortimer (NJ) - 1932
Neumann, Mark W. (WI) - 1992, 1993, 1994, 1996
Neumann, Paul (CA) - 1882
Neumann, William (IL) - 1920

Olson, Robert C. (MN) - 1954
Olson, Robert C. Jr. (MN) - 1976
Olson, Virgil L. (KS) - 1976
Olver, John W. (MA) - 1991, 1992, 1994, 1996, 1998, 2000
O'Malley (MO) - 1900
O'Malley, Matthew V. (NY) - 1931
O'Malley, Patrick J. (MA) - 1948
O'Malley, Thomas (WI) - 1928, 1930, 1932, 1934, 1936, 1938
Omann, Bernie (MN) - 1992, 1994
O'Mara, Bill (NV) - 1978
O'Mara, Eugene J. (NJ) - 1928
O'Mauleby, William (MD) - 1866
Omdahl, John (ND) - 1940
Omdahl, Lloyd (ND) - 1976
O'Meara, Edward S. Jr. (ME) - 1988
O'Meara, John R. (MI) - 1958
O'Meara, Thomas J. (IA) - 1841
O'Merberg, Maynard J. (CA) - 1948
O'Neal (AL) - 1849
O'Neal (GA) - 1874
O'Neal, Emmet (KY) - 1934, 1936, 1938, 1940, 1942, 1944, 1946
O'Neal, H. F. (TX) - 1880
O'Neal, I. C. (VA) - 1876
O'Neal, James (NY) - 1918, 1920
O'Neal, John H. (IN) - 1886
O'Neal, Maston (GA) - 1964, 1966, 1968
O'Neal, Weden (KY) - 1890, 1892
O'Neal, William R. (FL) - 1908
O'Neall, John H. (IN) - 1888
O'Neil (CT) - 1902
O'Neil, A. F. (OH) - 1928
O'Neil, Frank M. (PA) - 1962
O'Neil, James F. (MI) - 1962
O'Neil, Joseph B. (CA) - 1942
O'Neil, Joseph H. (MA) - 1884, 1888, 1890, 1892
O'Neil, Patrick M. (NY) - 1972
O'Neil, Thomas J. (KS) - 1894
O'Neill (TX) - 1878
O'Neill, Bruce Michael (CA) - 1988
O'Neill, Charles (PA) - 1862, 1864, 1866, 1868, 1870, 1872, 1874, 1876, 1878, 1880, 1882, 1884, 1886, 1888, 1890, 1892
O'Neill, Edward L. (NJ) - 1934, 1936, 1938
O'Neill, Eugene T. (NY) - 1946
O'Neill, Francis A. (NY) - 1912
O'Neill, Francis G. (MA) - 1940
O'Neill, Francis P. (MA) - 1942
O'Neill, Harry P. (PA) - 1948, 1950, 1952
O'Neill, James F. (MA) - 1952, 1954
O'Neill, John (OH) - 1862
O'Neill, John J. (MO) - 1882, 1884, 1886, 1888, 1890, 1892
O'Neill, Megan (MI) - 1992, 1994
O'Neill, Paul J. (FL) - 1964
O'Neill, Thomas P. Jr. (MA) - 1952, 1954, 1956, 1958, 1960, 1962, 1964, 1966, 1968, 1972, 1974, 1976, 1978, 1980, 1982, 1984
O'Neill, Vincent E. (MI) - 1952
O'Neill, William E. (IL) - 1900
Oppenheim, J. Philip (IN) - 1978
Orchard, Ernest R. (MN) - 1952
Orchard, Ernie (MN) - 1954
Ordway, Albert (VA) - 1870
O'Reilly, Daniel (NY) - 1878, 1880
O'Reilly, Gerald (NY) - 1946
O'Reilly, Kathleen F. (MI) - 1980
O'Reilly, Maurice (IA) - 1950
O'Reilly, T. Bronson (NY) - 1956
O'Reilly, Timothy I. (CA) - 1954
Orenstein, Jeffrey R. (OH) - 1982
Organ, Rollin B. (IL) - 1898
Oriez, Charles A. (CO) - 1992
Orlikoski, Walter J. (IL) - 1940
Orlins, Steve A. (NY) - 1992
Orloski, Richard J. (PA) - 1982, 1990
Ormon, John M. (CT) - 1984
Ormsby, Caleb N. (MI) - 1848
Ormsby, Walter M. (NY) - 1962
Ornstein, Franklin (NY) - 1974
O'Rourke, Hugh (MA) - 1914
O'Rourke, James S. (IL) - 1926, 1928
O'Rourke, Jerome F. (MI) - 1960

O'Rourke, Peter (MI) - 1968
O'Rourke, Philip A. (CA) - 1954
O'Rourke, Vernon A. (PA) - 1942, 1944, 1946
O'Rourke, William J. (PA) - 1932
Orozco, Bill (CA) - 1966, 1968
Orr (MO) - 1914
Orr, Emmett (KY) - 1914
Orr, George (NY) - 1920
Orr, Jackson (IA) - 1870, 1872
Orr, James A. (CO) - 1910
Orr, James L. (SC) - 1848, 1850, 1853, 1854, 1856
Orr, James W. (TX) - 1964
Orr, Robert Jr. (PA) - 1826
Orr, Sample (MO) - 1864
Orr, Samuel (NY) - 1926, 1930, 1932, 1934
Orr, William (IL) - 1834
Orr, William P. (OH) - 1890
Orrick (MD) - 1841
Orth, Godlove S. (IN) - 1862, 1864, 1866, 1868, 1872, 1878, 1880, 1882
Ortiz, Bobby (TX) - 1994
Ortiz, Solomon P. (TX) - 1982, 1984, 1986, 1988, 1990, 1992, 1994, 1996, 1998, 2000
Ortmeyer, D. H. (IN) - 1912
Orton (MO) - 1894, 1896
Orton (WI) - 1876
Orton, Bill (UT) - 1990, 1992, 1994, 1996
Orton, Duane (IA) - 1960
Orvis, E. E. (PA) - 1878
Orwig, Samuel H. (PA) - 1882
Osborn (NJ) - 1854
Osborn, Michael (TN) - 1970
Osborn, Robert A. (NY) - 1922
Osborne (NJ) - 1856
Osborne, A. B. (PA) - 1902
Osborne, Bartley P. (PA) - 1960
Osborne, Charles (NY) - 1942
Osborne, Edwin S. (PA) - 1884, 1886, 1888
Osborne, George (KY) - 1924
Osborne, Henry Z. (CA) - 1914, 1916, 1918, 1920, 1922
Osborne, James W. (NC) - 1853
Osborne, John (NY) - 1994
Osborne, John E. (WY) - 1896
Osborne, Lithgow (NY) - 1932
Osborne, Michael D. "Oz" (VA) - 2000
Osborne, Thomas B. (CT) - 1839, 1841, 1843
Osborne, Thomas C. (NE) - 1926
Osborne, Tom (NE) - 2000
Osborne, W. Ted (OH) - 1958, 1960
Osburn, Frank C. (PA) - 1892
O'Scannlain, Diarmuid (OR) - 1974
Ose, Doug (CA) - 1998, 2000
Osgood (IL) - 1856
Osgood B. L. (TX) - 1904
Osgood, Charles (MA) - 1858
Osgood, Gayton P. (MA) - 1830, 1833, 1834, 1836, 1838, 1840, 1842
Osgood, Jason C. (NY) - 1868
Osgood, Jim (CA) - 1974
Osgood, William N. (MA) - 1912, 1914
O'Shaughnessy, Maryellen (OH) - 2000
O'Shaunessy, George F. (RI) - 1910, 1912, 1914, 1916, 1922
O'Shea, Bernard (VT) - 1970
O'Shea, Bernard G. (VT) - 1964
O'Shea, George J. (MA) - 1962
O'Shea, Robert S. (IL) - 1972
Osheal, Shaemas (NY) - 1940
Oshel, Val (IL) - 1968, 1974
O'Shinskie, John (PA) - 1948
Oshlo, Richard (IA) - 1968
Osmer, James H. (PA) - 1878
Osmers, Frank C. Jr. (NJ) - 1938, 1940, 1952, 1954, 1956, 1958, 1960, 1962, 1964, 1966
Osser, Maurice S. (PA) - 1948, 1950
Osserman, Stanley (NY) - 1937
Osteen, William L. (NC) - 1968
Osterhaut, J. P. (TX) - 1876, 1884
Ostertag, Harold C. (NY) - 1950, 1952, 1954, 1956, 1958, 1960, 1962
Ostrander (NY) - 1874
Ostrom, Robert B. (MD) - 1998
O'Sullivan, Daniel E. (VT) - 1914
O'Sullivan, Daniel F. Jr. (MO) - 1996

O'Sullivan, Eugene D. (NE) - 1948, 1950
O'Sullivan, Frank P. (CA) - 1954
O'Sullivan, Humphrey (MA) - 1912, 1924
O'Sullivan, Jeremiah J. (MA) - 1934
O'Sullivan, Jerry (IA) - 1968
O'Sullivan, Kevin (MA) - 1994
O'Sullivan, Patrick B. (CT) - 1922, 1924
O'Sullivan, William Jr. (NJ) - 1980
Oswald, Louis William (IL) - 1946
Otero-Warren, Adelina (NM) - 1922
Otey, John (VA) - 1996
Otey, Peter (VA) - 1894, 1896, 1898, 1900
Otgen, Theobald (WI) - 1893
Otii, Joseph (OK) - 1916
Otis (MO) - 1914
Otis (NJ) - 1904
Otis (NY) - 1878
Otis, John (ME) - 1848
Otis, John G. (KS) - 1890
Otis, Lusien B. (IL) - 1872
Otis, Norton P. (NY) - 1900, 1902
Otjen, Theobald (WI) - 1892, 1894, 1896, 1898, 1900, 1902, 1904
O'Toole, Donald L. (NY) - 1936, 1938, 1940, 1942, 1944, 1946, 1948, 1950, 1952, 1954, 1956
O'Toole, Phelim (MO) - 1944
O'Toole, Thomas J. (PA) - 1952
O'Toole, Thomas P. (CA) - 1964
Otrich, Charles L. (IL) - 1904
Ott, Ed A. (IA) - 1892
Ottenberg, Irving (NY) - 1916
Otter, C. L. "Butch" (ID) - 2000
Ottinger, Albert (NY) - 1914
Ottinger, Richard L. (NY) - 1964, 1966, 1968, 1972, 1974, 1976, 1978, 1980, 1982
Otto, Carl (MO) - 1932
Outhwaite, Joseph H. (OH) - 1884, 1886, 1888, 1890, 1892, 1894
Outland, George E. (CA) - 1942, 1944, 1946, 1948
Outlaw, David (NC) - 1845, 1847, 1849, 1851, 1853
Outlaw, George Sr. (NC) - 1825
Overby, Fred (GA) - 1994
Overby, W. A. (KY) - 1904
Overcarsh, Orville G. (IN) - 1910
Overmeyer, Arthur W. (OH) - 1914, 1916, 1918, 1922
Overmeyer, D. (KS) - 1888
Overstreet, E. K. Jr. (GA) - 1932
Overstreet, James W. (GA) - 1916, 1918, 1920
Overstreet, Jesse (IN) - 1894, 1896, 1898, 1900, 1902, 1904, 1906, 1908
Overstreet, Russell (OK) - 1944, 1948
Overton, Archibald W. (TN) - 1833
Overton, Edward Jr. (PA) - 1876, 1878, 1882
Overton, John H. (LA) - 1931
Overton, Walter H. (LA) - 1828
Owen (MO) - 1912
Owen (RI) - 1944
Owen, Alfred Dale (IN) - 1900
Owen, Allen F. (GA) - 1848
Owen, Emmett M. (GA) - 1932, 1934, 1936, 1938
Owen, Frank V. (OH) - 1908
Owen, George (AL) - 1825, 1827
Owen, John L. (MI) - 1970
Owen, Marion R. (NJ) - 1902
Owen, Robert Dale (IN) - 1839, 1843, 1845, 1847
Owen, Ruth Bryan (FL) - 1928, 1930
Owen, S. M. (MN) - 1896
Owen, William D. (IN) - 1884, 1886, 1888, 1890
Owen, William E. (WI) - 1954
Owen, William L. (VA) - 1870
Owens (GA) - 1832
Owens (KY) - 1827, 1916
Owens, A. W. (SC) - 1853
Owens, Bill (IL) - 1994
Owens, David M. (MA) - 1940
Owens, Dusty (FL) - 1976
Owens, E. S. (IA) - 1892
Owens, George C. (NY) - 1936, 1938
Owens, George W. (GA) - 1834, 1836

Owens, J. Henry (MI) - 1954
Owens, James W. (OH) - 1888, 1890
Owens, John J. (PA) - 1936
Owens, John M. (NY) - 1980
Owens, Leon (VA) - 1962
Owens, Major R. (NY) - 1982, 1984, 1986, 1988, 1990, 1992, 1994, 1996, 1998, 2000
Owens, Marv (OR) - 1960
Owens, Millard M. (FL) - 1920
Owens, Steve (AZ) - 1996, 1998
Owens, Thomas A. (PA) - 1946
Owens, Thomas L. (IL) - 1946
Owens, Wayne (UT) - 1972, 1986, 1988, 1990
Owens, William (KY) - 1829
Owens, William C. (KY) - 1894, 1904, 1906
Owensby, Don W. (MO) - 1958
Owings, Theodore R. (CA) - 1954
Ownbey, James A. (CO) - 1924
Owsley, Bryan Y. (KY) - 1841, 1843
Oxley, Michael G. (OH) - 1981, 1982, 1984, 1986, 1988, 1990, 1992, 1994, 1996, 1998, 2000
Oyster, Daniel C. (PA) - 1890
Ozols, Gunars (NY) - 1980
Ozols, Gunars M. (NY) - 1978

P

Pace, Stephen (GA) - 1936, 1938, 1940, 1942, 1944, 1946, 1948
Pacheco, Romualdo (CA) - 1876, 1879, 1880
Pachios, Harold C. (ME) - 1980
Pacht, Jerry (CA) - 1960
Packard, Eliot L. (MA) - 1908
Packard, Jasper (IN) - 1868, 1870, 1872, 1886
Packard, L. C. (AR) - 1914
Packard, Ron (CA) - 1982, 1984, 1986, 1988, 1990, 1992, 1994, 1996, 1998
Packard, William B. (PA) - 1900
Packer (PA) - 1834
Packer, Asa (PA) - 1852, 1854
Packer, Horace B. (PA) - 1896, 1898
Packer, John B. (PA) - 1868, 1870, 1872, 1874
Packer, Robert H. (PA) - 1880
Paczkowski, John M. (IL) - 1984
Padden, Frank M. (IL) - 1918, 1922
Padden, John W. (MN) - 1942
Paddock, A. S. (NE) - 1866
Paddock, Charles A. (IN) - 1920
Paddock, George A. (IL) - 1940
Paddock, Porter (IL) - 1914
Padgett, Lemuel P. (TN) - 1900, 1902, 1904, 1906, 1908, 1910, 1912, 1914, 1916, 1918, 1920
Padgett, William L. (NY) - 1931
Padrutt, Arthur L. (WI) - 1953
Padway, Joseph A. (WI) - 1932
Paecht (CT) - 1910
Paeirs, Herbert (TX) - 1922
Page (MO) - 1888
Page, Charles H. (RI) - 1876, 1884, 1887, 1890, 1891, 1892, 1893
Page, Dan (NC) - 1998
Page, Demerville (NY) - 1890
Page, Douglas R. (CA) - 1960
Page, Heber (TX) - 1922
Page, Henry (MD) - 1890
Page, Horace F. (CA) - 1872, 1875, 1876, 1879, 1880, 1882
Page, J. L. (ND) - 1926, 1928
Page, Jay W. (WI) - 1916
Page, Mann (VA) - 1886
Page, Marguerite A. (NJ) - 1984
Page, Oliver J. (MO) - 1934
Page, Robert N. (NC) - 1902, 1904, 1906, 1908, 1910, 1912, 1914
Page, Ronnie (TN) - 1968
Page, Sherman (NY) - 1832, 1834
Page, William T. (MD) - 1902
Page, Winfield E. (MT) - 1954
Pagett, Alfred (MI) - 1892
Paige (OH) - 1862
Paige, Alonzo C. (NY) - 1864
Paige, Calvin D. (MA) - 1914, 1916, 1918, 1920, 1922
Paige, David R. (OH) - 1882, 1884
Paine (NY) - 1856

Russell (MA) - 1880
Russell (MN) - 1918
Russell (NY) - 1882
Russell (VA) - 1849
Russell, A. J. (AR) - 1916
Russell, Allen (OH) - 1952
Russell, Aubrey (KY) - 1984
Russell, Benjamin E. (GA) - 1892, 1894
Russell, Carl D. (MO) - 1984
Russell, Charles A. (CT) - 1886, 1888, 1890, 1892, 1894, 1896, 1898, 1900
Russell, Charles H. (NV) - 1946, 1948
Russell, Charles P. (NY) - 1938
Russell, Charles W. (KY) - 1892
Russell, Chauncey S. (PA) - 1898
Russell, Daniel L. (NC) - 1878
Russell, David (NY) - 1834, 1836, 1838
Russell, Edward A. (IL) - 1924
Russell, Elbert (IN) - 1914
Russell, Frank B. (KY) - 1932
Russell, George (OH) - 1902
Russell, George B. (NV) - 1934
Russell, Gordon J. (TX) - 1902, 1904, 1906, 1908
Russell, Howard E. Jr. (RI) - 1968
Russell, J. C. (AR) - 1920
Russell, J. E. (OH) - 1914, 1916, 1918
Russell, J. Ward (NY) - 1920
Russell, James (MA) - 1830, 1834
Russell, James (TX) - 1972
Russell, James M. (PA) - 1842
Russell, Jeremiah (NY) - 1842, 1846
Russell, Jim (MO) - 1982
Russell, Joe W. (IL) - 1950
Russell, John B. (TN) - 1986
Russell, John C. (NY) - 1920
Russell, John E. (MA) - 1886
Russell, John R. (SD) - 1924
Russell, Joseph (NY) - 1844, 1850
Russell, Joseph J. (MO) - 1902, 1904, 1906, 1908, 1910, 1912, 1914, 1916, 1918
Russell, Lemuel A. (OH) - 1896, 1898
Russell, Leslie W. (NY) - 1890
Russell, Otis H. (VA) - 1898
Russell, P. J. (MN) - 1930
Russell, Rayburn L. (IL) - 1934
Russell, Reb (KS) - 1964
Russell, Reece L. (OK) - 1954
Russell, Richard M. (MA) - 1934, 1936, 1950
Russell, S. H. (TX) - 1876, 1882
Russell, S. M. (KY) - 1926
Russell, Sam (TX) - 1940, 1942, 1944
Russell, Samuel L. (PA) - 1852
Russell, T. H. (SC) - 1882
Russell, T. J. (TX) - 1898
Russell, W. M. (AL) - 1920, 1922
Russell, Walter G. (NY) - 1926
Russell, William (NC) - 1841
Russell, William (OH) - 1826, 1828, 1830, 1832, 1840
Russell, William A. (MA) - 1878, 1880, 1882
Russell, William F. (NY) - 1856
Russo, Gaetano A. Jr. (CT) - 1968
Russo, Lawrence P. (NY) - 1972
Russo, Martin A. (IL) - 1974, 1976
Russo, Marty (IL) - 1978, 1980, 1982, 1984, 1986, 1988, 1990
Russo, Peter J. (NJ) - 1990, 1994
Russum, George M. (MD) - 1866, 1884, 1890, 1892
Rust, Albert (AR) - 1846, 1854, 1858
Rust, Clarence E. (CA) - 1936
Rust, Gary (MO) - 1970
Rust, Robert W. (FL) - 1968
Rutan, Dick (CA) - 1992
Ruth, Earl B. (NC) - 1968, 1970, 1972, 1974
Ruthenberg, C. E. (OH) - 1914, 1918
Rutherford (PA) - 1872
Rutherford, Albert G. (PA) - 1936, 1938, 1940
Rutherford, Frank M. (CA) - 1912
Rutherford, Gideon L. (MI) - 1894
Rutherford, J. T. (TX) - 1954, 1956, 1958, 1960, 1962
Rutherford, Samuel (GA) - 1924, 1926, 1928, 1930
Rutherford, W. F. (OH) - 1924

Rutlard, Vernon A. (VT) - 1894
Rutledge, Henry B. (MN) - 1922
Rutledge, Howard (OK) - 1980, 1982
Rutshaw, Arthur Joseph (IL) - 1942
Rutta, Philip Robert (CA) - 1972
Rutter, Carroll L. (PA) - 1938
Ruyers (RI) - 1835
Ryall, Daniel B. (NJ) - 1838, 1840
Ryan (PA) - 1858, 1886
Ryan, Aileen B. (NY) - 1966
Ryan, Bob (NV) - 1986
Ryan, C. A. (MN) - 1936
Ryan, Charles J. (NY) - 1912
Ryan, Dan J. P. (IA) - 1946, 1948
Ryan, Donald P. (RI) - 1972
Ryan, E. G. (IL) - 1850
Ryan, Edward A. (MA) - 1936, 1938
Ryan, Edward J. (MD) - 1954
Ryan, Elmer J. (MN) - 1934, 1936, 1938, 1940
Ryan, Fran (OH) - 1974, 1976
Ryan, Frank D. (CA) - 1898
Ryan, Frank S. (IL) - 1909
Ryan, Harold M. (MI) - 1962
Ryan, Herbert F. (NY) - 1966
Ryan, Hewitt Fitts (CA) - 1986
Ryan, J. J. (IA) - 1892
Ryan, James W. (PA) - 1898, 1900, 1902
Ryan, Jim (TX) - 1982
Ryan, John A. (MA) - 1896
Ryan, John F. (MI) - 1906
Ryan, John F. Jr. (NY) - 1972
Ryan, John Michael (OH) - 1972, 1990
Ryan, Leo J. (CA) - 1972, 1974, 1976, 1978
Ryan, Lewis (PA) - 1918
Ryan, Matthew (IL) - 1976
Ryan, Michael (LA) - 1868, 1870
Ryan, Paul D. (WI) - 1998 2000
Ryan, Priscilla M. (NY) - 1972
Ryan, T. E. (IL) - 1894
Ryan, Thomas (KS) - 1876, 1878, 1880, 1882, 1884, 1886, 1888
Ryan, Thomas A. (WI) - 1924
Ryan, Thomas Jefferson (NY) - 1920, 1922
Ryan, Thomas P. (MN) - 1942
Ryan, Thomas Q. (NY) - 1942
Ryan, Timothy E. (NJ) - 1992
Ryan, William E. (NY) - 1892, 1894, 1896
Ryan, William F. (NY) - 1960, 1962, 1964, 1966, 1968, 1970
Ryan, William H. (KS) - 1940
Ryan, William H. (NY) - 1898, 1900, 1902, 1904, 1906
Ryan, William J. (VT) - 1966
Rybacki, Ray J. (IL) - 1964, 1966
Ryckman, James H. (CA) - 1916, 1918
Ryder, Percy C. (NY) - 1938
Ryder, Richard R. (VA) - 1958
Ryerson (NJ) - 1850
Ryland, J. W. (CA) - 1892
Rylander, Carole Keeton (TX) - 1986
Ryle (NJ) - 1882
Ryler, Joseph F. (CT) - 1944, 1946
Rynder (PA) - 1888
Ryon, John W. (PA) - 1878, 1880
Ryun, Jim (KS) - 1996, 1998, 2000

S

Saad, Paul A. (FL) - 1968
Saar, T. D. Jr. (KS) - 1970
Saari, Gene A. (MI) - 1948
Sabath, Adolph J. (IL) - 1906, 1908, 1910, 1912, 1914, 1916, 1918, 1920, 1922, 1924, 1926, 1928, 1930, 1932, 1934, 1936, 1938, 1940, 1942, 1944, 1946, 1948, 1950, 1952
Sabin, Alvah (VT) - 1852, 1854
Sabo, Martin Olav (MN) - 1978, 1980, 1982, 1984, 1986, 1988, 1990, 1992, 1994, 1996, 1998, 2000
Sabol, John (MI) - 1950
Sabol, Joseph Jr. (PA) - 1966, 1968
Sachs, Leon (PA) - 1938
Sacia, David (NY) - 1938
Sacia, Paul (WI) - 1992
Sackett (NY) - 1886
Sackett, G. L. (OH) - 1890
Sackett, William A. (NY) - 1848, 1850

Sacks, Alexander (NY) - 1968
Sacks, Leon (PA) - 1936, 1940, 1942
Saddler (OH) - 1852
Sadlak, Anton N. (CT) - 1946, 1948, 1950, 1952, 1954, 1956, 1958, 1960
Sadler, Claude E. (MI) - 1964
Sadler, Gareth W. (CA) - 1960
Sadler, Reinhold (NV) - 1904
Sadler, Thomas W. (AL) - 1884
Sadoff, Louis (NY) - 1932
Sadovy, Leo (TX) - 1988
Sadowski, George G. (MI) - 1932, 1934, 1936, 1942, 1944, 1946, 1948
Sadowski, Jeannie (TX) - 1992
Safford (GA) - 1853
Safford, Nathaniel F. (MA) - 1854
Safranek, Frank A. (CO) - 1946
Sage (NJ) - 1912
Sage, Russell (NY) - 1850, 1852, 1854
Sageng (MN) - 1908
Sageng, Ole O. (MN) - 1934, 1938
Sague, John K. (NY) - 1912, 1930
Saiki, Patricia (HI) - 1986, 1988
Sailor, Stephanie (IL) - 2000
Saintamour, Camille E. (VT) - 1956
Sajna, Michael (OH) - 1988
Saks, Carl (NY) - 1970
Salazar, Cecilia M. (NM) - 1988
Saldana, Gilbert R. (CA) - 1986
Sale, Irvin (MO) - 1926
Sale, W. W. (KY) - 1859
Salem, Robert J. (IA) - 1956
Salerno, Joseph A. (IL) - 1962
Salisbery (PA) - 1850
Salisbury, D. L. (WV) - 1948
Salisbury, William (MD) - 1976
Saliterman, Joel (MN) - 1980, 1982
Sallade, George Wahr (MI) - 1982
Sallah, Donald R. (NY) - 1974
Salley, Robert L. (CA) - 1976
Salloum, Robert J. (MI) - 1978
Salmon, Joshua S. (NJ) - 1898, 1900
Salmon, Matt (AZ) - 1994, 1996, 1998
Salmon, R. J. (KY) - 1910
Salmon, William C. (TN) - 1922
Salmona, Stelio (CT) - 1966, 1968
Salomon, Jim (CA) - 1988, 1990
Salsbury, Lester H. (MI) - 1886
Salter, James M. (WA) - 1918
Salter, Leslie E. (IL) - 1948
Saltonstall, John L. (MA) - 1958
Saltonstall, Leverett (MA) - 1828, 1838, 1840, 1860, 1866, 1868, 1869
Saltonstall, William (MA) - 1969
Salts (MO) - 1918
Saltus, Freeman M. (MA) - 1928
Saltzgaber, Gaylard M. (OH) - 1888
Salvi, Al (IL) - 1986
Salvi, Albert S. (IL) - 1968
Salyer, C. A. (WA) - 1896
Salyers, Willis Earl (MO) - 1966
Salzman, Jacob A. (NY) - 1944
Sam (OH) - 1852
Sam, Geraldine (TX) - 1996
Samford, William J. (AL) - 1878
Sammartino, Everett C. (RI) - 1966
Samons (NY) - 1848
Samp (PA) - 1852
Sample, Ed P. (CA) - 1936
Sample, Frank L. (NJ) - 1928
Sample, Samuel C. (IN) - 1843, 1845
Sampol, William (NY) - 1970, 1972, 1990
Sampson (NY) - 1842
Sampson, Ezekiel Silas (IA) - 1874, 1876, 1878
Sampson, Floyd G. (CA) - 1986
Sampson, J. E. (KY) - 1920
Sampson, Warner J. (MI) - 1902
Sams, W. Harold (NC) - 1958
Samuel, Edmund W. (PA) - 1904, 1906, 1908
Samuel, Ralph O. (PA) - 1964
Samuels (MO) - 1840
Samuels, Ben M. (IA) - 1860
Samuels, David L. (NY) - 1950
Samuels, Green B. (VA) - 1839
Samuelson, Bob (SD) - 1978
Sanborn (ME) - 1856

Sanborn (NH) - 1880
Sanborn, John C. (ID) - 1946, 1948
Sanborn, John P. (MI) - 1886
Sanbury, J. William (NY) - 1910
Sanbury, William J. (NY) - 1898
Sanchez, John (TX) - 1998
Sanchez, John M. (TX) - 1996
Sanchez, Loretta (CA) - 1996, 1998, 2000
Sanchez, Phillip V. (CA) - 1970
Sanchez, Stephanie (CT) - 2000
Sand, H. A. (OH) - 1960, 1962, 1964
Sandager, Harry (RI) - 1936, 1938, 1940, 1942
Sandberg, Gus C. (IL) - 1924
Sandberg, William C. (OH) - 1936
Sandegren, Andrew Sandy (MO) - 1952
Sander, Fred (NY) - 1932
Sander, Richard W. (OH) - 1978
Sanders (MN) - 1910
Sanders (NY) - 1874
Sanders (TN) - 1880
Sanders, Archie D. (NY) - 1916, 1918, 1920, 1922, 1924, 1926, 1928, 1930
Sanders, Barefoot (TX) - 1958
Sanders, Bernard (VT) - 1988, 1990, 1992, 1994, 1996, 1998, 2000
Sanders, Calvin (KY) - 1852
Sanders, Charles W. (OH) - 1998, 2000
Sanders, Claiborne "Clay" (CA) - 1998
Sanders, Claiborne "Clay" (TN) - 1990
Sanders, Emma (MS) - 1966
Sanders, Everett (IN) - 1916, 1918, 1920, 1922
Sanders, G. E. (OR) - 1908
Sanders, Gregory J. (UT) - 1996
Sanders, Hartley (WV) - 1938, 1940, 1944, 1946, 1948
Sanders, Herman (NY) - 1960, 1964
Sanders, J. M. (AZ) - 1974
Sanders, Jared Y. (LA) - 1916, 1918
Sanders, Jared Y. Jr. (LA) - 1934, 1940
Sanders, Jeff (PA) - 2000
Sanders, Jessie E. (SD) - 1948
Sanders, Leon (NY) - 1916
Sanders, Linn B. (NC) - 1859
Sanders, Marion K. (NY) - 1952
Sanders, Morgan G. (TX) - 1920, 1922, 1924, 1926, 1928, 1930, 1932, 1934, 1936
Sanders, William H. (WV) - 1956
Sanderson (PA) - 1852
Sanderson, George (OH) - 1840
Sanderson, H. S. (TX) - 1894
Sandford (KY) - 1827
Sandford, Alfred (KY) - 1826
Sandford, F. C. (MA) - 1860
Sandford, Reuben (NY) - 1836
Sandidge, John M. (LA) - 1855, 1857
Sandlin, John N. (LA) - 1920, 1922, 1924, 1926, 1928, 1930, 1932, 1934
Sandlin, Max (TX) - 1996, 1998, 2000
Sandman, Charles W. Jr. (NJ) - 1966, 1968, 1970, 1972, 1974
Sando, M. F. (PA) - 1898
Sands (NY) - 1858
Sands (TN) - 1865
Sands, A. P. "Sandy" (NC) - 1994
Sands, George (IN) - 1940
Sands, John (OH) - 1868
Sands, Joshua (NY) - 1824
Sanford (AL) - 1894
Sanford (GA) - 1844
Sanford (NY) - 1844, 1852, 1888
Sanford, Allen T. (UT) - 1910
Sanford, Henry (AL) - 1857
Sanford, James (TN) - 1825
Sanford, John (NY) - 1840
Sanford, John (NY) - 1888, 1890
Sanford, John W. A. (GA) - 1834, 1836
Sanford, Mark (SC) - 1994, 1996, 1998
Sanford, Mitchell (NY) - 1838
Sanford, Rollin B. (NY) - 1914, 1916, 1918
Sanford, Stephen (NY) - 1868
Sanford, W. S. (MO) - 1940
Sanford, William K. (NY) - 1946
Sanger (WI) - 1880
Sangmeister, George E. (IL) - 1988, 1990, 1992
Sanial, Lucien (NY) - 1898
Sanson, Albert W. (PA) - 1910

Stanley, Frank B. (TX) - 1904
Stanley, George S. (MI) - 1904
Stanley, John V. (ID) - 1916
Stanley, M. C. (OK) - 1976
Stanley, Thomas B. (VA) - 1946, 1948, 1950, 1952
Stanley, Thornton (AL) - 1970
Stanley, Winifred C. (NY) - 1942
Stanly, Edward (NC) - 1837, 1839, 1841, 1843, 1849, 1851
Stannard, Sarah (AZ) - 1992
Stant, Frederick T. Jr. (VA) - 1968
Stanton (KY) - 1849, 1916
Stanton, Benjamin (OH) - 1850, 1854, 1856, 1858
Stanton, Charles (NY) - 1928, 1932
Stanton, Elsie (OH) - 1938, 1944
Stanton, Frederick P. (TN) - 1845, 1847, 1849, 1851, 1853
Stanton, J. William (OH) - 1964, 1966, 1968, 1970, 1972, 1974, 1976, 1978, 1980
Stanton, James V. (OH) - 1968, 1970, 1972, 1974
Stanton, Richard H. (KY) - 1849, 1851, 1853, 1855
Stanton, W. H. (PA) - 1876
Staplekamp, Judson W. (WI) - 1934
Staples (TN) - 1904
Staples (VA) - 1855
Staples, David H. (ME) - 1944
Staples, E. W. (ME) - 1896
Starbird, C. R. (AR) - 1948
Starbird, Charles M. (ME) - 1926
Starbuck (NY) - 1860
Starin, John H. (NY) - 1876, 1878
Staring, George B. (NY) - 1908
Stark, Albert G. (CT) - 1853
Stark, Fortney H. (Pete) (CA) - 1972, 1974, 1976, 1978, 1980, 1982, 1984, 1986
Stark, James H. (GA) - 1843
Stark, John Paul (CA) - 1980, 1982, 1984, 1988
Stark, Judson L. (IN) - 1944
Stark, Pete (CA) - 1988, 1990, 1992, 1994, 1996, 1998, 2000
Stark, William L. (NE) - 1894, 1896, 1898, 1900, 1902, 1916
Starke (MS) - 1845
Starke, Jay (VA) - 1990
Starkey, Frank T. (MN) - 1944, 1946
Starkey, Hiram E. (OH) - 1912
Starkloff, Carl E. (MO) - 1942
Starkweather (OH) - 1860
Starkweather, David A. (OH) - 1838, 1844, 1846
Starkweather, George (NY) - 1846
Starkweather, Harvey G. (OR) - 1928, 1932
Starkweather, Henry H. (CT) - 1867, 1869, 1871, 1873, 1875
Starkweather, Samuel (OH) - 1844
Starky, Stuart Marc (AZ) - 1998
Starling, Alton H. (Bill) (FL) - 1984
Starnes, Joe (AL) - 1934, 1936, 1938, 1940, 1942
Starr, Charles (OR) - 2000
Starr, George (NY) - 1868
Starr, John F. (NJ) - 1862, 1864
Starr, Julius S. (IL) - 1884
Starr, Mark (NY) - 1950, 1962
Starr, Mike (IL) - 1992
Starr, Western (IL) - 1908
Staskiewicz, Ronald L. (NE) - 1992
Stassen, Harold (MN) - 1986
States, Michael A. (AK) - 1992
Staton, David M. (WV) - 1978
Staton, David Michael (WV) - 1982
Staton, Mick (WV) - 1980
Staton, R. Hilliard (NC) - 1912
Staton, Robert H. (IN) - 1966
Stauffer, John K. (PA) - 1914
Stauffer, Randolph (PA) - 1944
Stauffer, S. Walter (PA) - 1952, 1954, 1956, 1958
Staum, John R. M. (MD) - 1924
Staunton (TN) - 1843
Staver, Daniel (OR) - 1908
Stayart, L. W. (TX) - 1946

Stayles (NY) - 1844
Steadman, Martin J. (NY) - 1966
Steagall, Henry B. (AL) - 1918, 1920, 1922, 1926, 1928, 1930, 1932, 1934, 1936, 1938, 1940, 1942
Stearn, Mrs. Edith Shaffer (FL) - 1944
Stearns, Cliff (FL) - 1988, 1990, 1992, 1994, 1996, 1998, 2000
Stearns, Darrel H. (VA) - 1970
Stearns, Elisha (CT) - 1835
Stearns, Foster (NH) - 1938, 1940, 1942
Stearns, J. Thomas (NY) - 1890
Stearns, Willard (MI) - 1888
Stebbins (NY) - 1874
Stebbins, C. E. (IL) - 1906
Stebbins, Charles Jr. (NY) - 1868
Stebbins, Henry G. (NY) - 1862, 1864
Stebbins, Homer A. (NY) - 1934, 1936, 1938, 1940
Stebbins, Lucien (NE) - 1920
Stecher, Jack E. (OH) - 1980
Steck (PA) - 1888
Steck, A. C. (IA) - 1900
Steckler, Ferne M. (NY) - 1972
Stedem, Michael (FL) - 2000
Stedman (CT) - 1871
Stedman, Charles M. (NC) - 1910, 1912, 1914, 1916, 1918, 1920, 1922, 1924, 1926, 1928
Stedman, Seymorse (IL) - 1923
Steed, Tom (OK) - 1948, 1950, 1952, 1954, 1956, 1958, 1960, 1962, 1964, 1966, 1968, 1970, 1972, 1974, 1976, 1978
Steedman (OH) - 1860
Steeholm, Hardy (NY) - 1940
Steel (MO) - 1896
Steele (IN) - 1860
Steele (NJ) - 1908
Steele (TN) - 1872
Steele (VA) - 1833, 1839
Steele (VT) - 1872
Steele (WI) - 1878
Steele, Bill (CA) - 1986
Steele, David (VA) - 1837
Steele, David F. III (IN) - 1998
Steele, G. Fred Jr. (NC) - 1966, 1968
Steele, George W. (IN) - 1880, 1882, 1884, 1886, 1888, 1894, 1896, 1898, 1900
Steele, Henry J. (PA) - 1914, 1916, 1918
Steele, John B. (NY) - 1860, 1862
Steele, John D. (FL) - 1964
Steele, John N. (MD) - 1835
Steele, Leslie J. (GA) - 1926, 1928
Steele, Mark (MA) - 1996
Steele, Philip L. (CT) - 1992
Steele, Robert H. (CT) - 1970, 1972
Steele, Thomas J. (IA) - 1914, 1916, 1918
Steele, Tim (MI) - 2000
Steele, Walter L. (NC) - 1876, 1878
Steele, William G. (NJ) - 1860, 1862
Steelman, Alan (TX) - 1972, 1974
Steelman, Dorman L. (MO) - 1954
Steely, Marcus H. (CA) - 1922
Steenberger (VA) - 1825
Steenburg, Leon Ray (NY) - 1932
Steenerson, Halvor (MN) - 1902, 1904, 1906, 1908, 1910, 1912, 1914, 1916, 1918, 1920, 1922
Steenrod, Lewis (VA) - 1839, 1841, 1843
Steensland, A. O. (SD) - 1928
Steers, Newton (MD) - 1962, 1976
Steers, Newton I. Jr. (MD) - 1978, 1980
Steers, Schuyler B. (MS) - 1869
Stefan, Karl (NE) - 1934, 1936, 1938, 1940, 1942, 1944, 1946, 1948, 1950
Stefanic, William F. (PA) - 1964
Steffen, Frederick J. (IL) - 1978
Steffes, Robert J. (WI) - 1978
Stegall, Henry B. (AL) - 1914, 1916, 1924
Steger, William (TX) - 1962
Steiger, Herbert O. (MI) - 1974
Steiger, Sam (AZ) - 1964, 1966, 1968, 1970, 1972, 1974
Steiger, William A. (WI) - 1966, 1968, 1970, 1972, 1974, 1976, 1978
Steigerwalt, Wardell F. (PA) - 1972
Stein, Andrew J. (NY) - 1984

Stein, Michael (NY) - 1916
Steinbacher, Harold E. (MI) - 1942
Steinbeck, A. H. (MO) - 1928
Steinberg, Cathey (GA) - 1992
Steinberg, Henry (NY) - 1932
Steinbrenner, George F. (NY) - 1866
Steineman, G. C. (OH) - 1926
Steinemann, George C. (OH) - 1952, 1954
Steinhardt, David (NY) - 1928
Steinhice, Laural (TN) - 1982
Steinman, A. J. (PA) - 1898
Steinmetz, J. L. (PA) - 1880
Steinmetz, William (CA) - 1988
Steinn (PA) - 1862
Stell (GA) - 1851
Stell, Johannes (NY) - 1946
Stelle, John P. (IL) - 1889
Stelzel, Charles F. (IL) - 1914
Stempien, Marvin R. (MI) - 1972
Stender, John (WA) - 1960
Stenger, William S. (PA) - 1874, 1876, 1878
Stengle, Charles I. (NY) - 1916, 1922
Stenholm, Charles W. (TX) - 1978, 1980, 1982, 1984, 1986, 1988, 1990, 1992, 1994, 1996, 1998, 2000
Stennis, John Hampton (MS) - 1978
Stepanek, Paul (CA) - 1994, 1996
Stephanis, James T. (FL) - 1972
Stephen, Charles (KS) - 1922, 1924
Stephens (GA) - 1855
Stephens (NY) - 1858
Stephens, Alexander H. (GA) - 1843, 1844, 1846, 1848, 1851, 1853, 1855, 1857, 1874, 1876, 1878, 1880
Stephens, Ambrose E. B. (OH) - 1918, 1920, 1922, 1924, 1926
Stephens, Charles J. (NY) - 1974
Stephens, Craig C. (PA) - 2000
Stephens, Dana R. (PA) - 1914
Stephens, Daniel V. (NE) - 1912, 1914, 1916, 1918
Stephens, G. Douglas (IL) - 1982, 1988, 1994
Stephens, G. Frank (PA) - 1906
Stephens, Harold (IA) - 1962
Stephens, Hubert D. (MS) - 1910, 1912, 1914, 1916, 1918
Stephens, John H. (TX) - 1896, 1898, 1900, 1902, 1904, 1906, 1908, 1910, 1912, 1914
Stephens, John J. (AL) - 1912, 1926
Stephens, Joseph L. (OH) - 1894
Stephens, L. (GA) - 1857
Stephens, O. P. (TX) - 1944
Stephens, Paul A. (PA) - 1964
Stephens, Philander (PA) - 1828, 1830
Stephens, R. Clarence (IN) - 1912
Stephens, R. S. (IN) - 1914
Stephens, Richard "Even" (FL) - 1992
Stephens, Richard E. (TX) - 1928
Stephens, Robert G. Jr. (GA) - 1960, 1962, 1964, 1966, 1968, 1970, 1972, 1974
Stephens, Roderick (NY) - 1944
Stephens, S. E. (TN) - 1928
Stephens, Thomas H. (AL) - 1914
Stephens, U. S. (PA) - 1878
Stephens, Walter C. (OK) - 1928
Stephens, William D. (CA) - 1910, 1912, 1914
Stephens, Z. M. (MS) - 1898
Stephenson, G. C. (TN) - 1932
Stephenson, Isaac (WI) - 1882, 1884, 1886
Stephenson, J. B. (TX) - 1892
Stephenson, Percy S. (VA) - 1922
Stephenson, Samuel M. (MI) - 1888, 1890, 1892, 1894
Stephenson, Tommy (GA) - 1996
Stephenson, Wilson H. (PA) - 1952
Stepnowski, Edward L. (IL) - 1972
Sterigere, John B. (PA) - 1826, 1828
Sterling, Ansel (CT) - 1827
Sterling, Bruce F. (PA) - 1916, 1918, 1920
Sterling, John A. (IL) - 1902, 1904, 1906, 1908, 1910, 1912, 1914, 1916
Stern, Alfred K. (NY) - 1940
Stern, Herbert L. (IL) - 1966
Sternberger, J. B. (MS) - 1918
Sternfeld, Julius (AL) - 1902
Sterngass, Jack (NY) - 1968

Sterrett (MO) - 1894
Sterrett (VA) - 1853
Sterrett, Robert J. (PA) - 1922
Stethem, W. C. (CA) - 1956
Stetson, Charles (ME) - 1848, 1850
Stetson, Lemuel (NY) - 1842
Stevens (AL) - 1880
Stevens (MA) - 1878
Stevens (ME) - 1916
Stevens (MN) - 1914
Stevens (NH) - 1916
Stevens (NJ) - 1894, 1904
Stevens (NY) - 1844, 1850, 1888
Stevens (TN) - 1857
Stevens, Aaron F. (NH) - 1867, 1869, 1871
Stevens, Abraham P. (NY) - 1850
Stevens, Augustus C. (NY) - 1928
Stevens, Bradford N. (IL) - 1870
Stevens, Bryan W. (CA) - 1964
Stevens, Chandler Harrison (MA) - 1968
Stevens, Charles A. (MA) - 1874, 1875
Stevens, Charles S. (NJ) - 1922, 1924
Stevens, Christian B. (IN) - 1898
Stevens, Clinton C. (ME) - 1924, 1928, 1930
Stevens, Dana N. (FL) - 1982
Stevens, Donald E. (CA) - 1988
Stevens, Frederick C. (MN) - 1896, 1898, 1900, 1902, 1904, 1906, 1908, 1910, 1912
Stevens, George (MA) - 1872
Stevens, George D. (MI) - 1948
Stevens, Henry H. (MA) - 1868
Stevens, Hestor L. (MI) - 1852
Stevens, Isaac H. (CO) - 1910
Stevens, Joe (TX) - 1968
Stevens, John S. (KS) - 1972, 1975
Stevens, John S. (NC) - 1992
Stevens, Moses T. (MA) - 1890, 1892
Stevens, Paul E. (OH) - 1960
Stevens, Raymond B. (NH) - 1912
Stevens, Raymond H. (OH) - 1970
Stevens, Robert S. (NY) - 1880, 1882, 1884
Stevens, Roy E. (IA) - 1940
Stevens, Samuel (NY) - 1832
Stevens, Thaddeus (PA) - 1848, 1850, 1858, 1860, 1862, 1864, 1866
Stevens, Theodore Jr. (ME) - 1847
Stevens, W. B. (OH) - 1902
Stevens, William E. Jr. (NC) - 1954
Stevens, William Kerper (PA) - 1900
Stevenson (NJ) - 1884
Stevenson (NY) - 1842
Stevenson, A. Walter (UT) - 1960
Stevenson, Adlai E. (IL) - 1874, 1876, 1878, 1880, 1882
Stevenson, Andrew (VA) - 1825, 1827, 1829, 1831, 1833
Stevenson, Guy (OH) - 1926
Stevenson, James P. (IL) - 2000
Stevenson, James S. (PA) - 1824, 1826, 1828, 1829
Stevenson, Job E. (OH) - 1864, 1868, 1870, 1874
Stevenson, John H. (PA) - 1898
Stevenson, John W. (KY) - 1857, 1859
Stevenson, Maxwell (PA) - 1878, 1886
Stevenson, Noel C. (CA) - 1956
Stevenson, Thomas (MA) - 1898
Stevenson, William F. (SC) - 1918, 1920, 1922, 1924, 1926, 1928, 1930
Stevenson, William H. (WI) - 1940, 1942, 1944, 1946
Stevn (MD) - 1853
Stevson (MO) - 1856
Steward (PA) - 1862
Steward, Ewell (KS) - 1950
Steward, Julian R. (IL) - 1902
Steward, Lewis (IL) - 1890, 1892, 1894
Stewart (GA) - 1832
Stewart (LA) - 1849
Stewart (MD) - 1833
Stewart (NH) - 1849
Stewart (OH) - 1854
Stewart (WI) - 1918
Stewart, A. Charles (MD) - 1938
Stewart, Alexander (CT) - 1827, 1829
Stewart, Alexander (WI) - 1894, 1896, 1898

Urban, Stephen A. (PA) - 1996, 1998, 2000
Urbaszewski, John F. (IL) - 1976
Urner (NJ) - 1882
Urner, Milton G. (MD) - 1878, 1880
Urquehart (VA) - 1825, 1835
Usher (IN) - 1856
Usher (MA) - 1888
Utech, Franklin R. (WI) - 1970
Uthlaut, Ralph Jr. (MO) - 1986
Utley, Hamilton (WI) - 1894
Utley, W. H. (KS) - 1888
Utt, James B. (CA) - 1952, 1954, 1956, 1958, 1960, 1962, 1964, 1966, 1968
Utter, George H. (RI) - 1910
Utterback, Hubert (IA) - 1934, 1938
Utterback, John G. (ME) - 1932, 1934

V

Vail (NY) - 1854
Vail, Edmund G. (OH) - 1902
Vail, Fred (TN) - 1986
Vail, George (NJ) - 1850, 1852, 1854
Vail, Harry L. (OH) - 1914, 1918
Vail, Henry (NY) - 1836, 1838
Vail, John M. (IL) - 1906
Vail, Richard B. (IL) - 1946, 1948, 1950, 1952, 1954
Vaile, William N. (CO) - 1916, 1918, 1920, 1922, 1924, 1926
Valencia, Tony (CA) - 1992
Valenti, Paul Vincent (CT) - 2000
Valentine, Ben (CA) - 1972
Valentine, Carl H. (OH) - 1928
Valentine, Edward K. (NE) - 1878, 1880, 1882
Valentine, George M. (MI) - 1912
Valentine, H. E. (IA) - 1914
Valentine, H. Sage (OH) - 1922
Valentine, I. T. (Tim) (NC) - 1982, 1984
Valentine, J. M. (NY) - 1874
Valentine, Tim (NC) - 1986, 1988, 1990, 1992
Valez, Ramon S. (NY) - 1978
Valk, William W. (NY) - 1854
Vallandigham, Clement L. (OH) - 1852, 1856, 1858, 1860, 1862, 1868
Vallatt, Jules (IL) - 1928
Vallely, Paul E. (CA) - 1982
Vallettee, Henry (IL) - 1875
Valm (OH) - 1854
Valtierra, Steven (IL) - 1994
Valverde, Paz (NM) - 1911
Vambell, Clarence C. (NY) - 1952
Van Aernam, Henry (NY) - 1864, 1866, 1878, 1880
Van Allen, G. J. (MO) - 1870
Van Alstine, Abraham (NY) - 1846
Van Alstyne, Thomas J. (NY) - 1882, 1884
Van Alstyne, William A. (NY) - 1864
Van Artsdalen, Christopher (PA) - 1900
Van Auken (NY) - 1876
Van Auken, D. J. (NY) - 1904
Van Auken, Daniel M. (PA) - 1866, 1868
Van Auken, P. H. (NY) - 1880
Van Blarcom (NJ) - 1886
Van Brocklin, Loren E. (OH) - 1958
Van Brocklin, William W. (NY) - 1906
Van Brunt, D. C. (WI) - 1890
Van Brunt, James A. (NY) - 1866
Van Buren, John (NY) - 1840
Van Buskirk, S. A. (CO) - 1912
Van Camp, Oliver F. (NJ) - 1934
Van Campen (NY) - 1880
Van Cleave, Dorn E. III (IL) - 1998
Van de Brooke, John (CA) - 1986
Van de Graaf, A. S. (AL) - 1896
Van de Kamp, John K. (CA) - 1969
Van de Water, Charles F. (CA) - 1920
Van Deerlin, Lionel (CA) - 1952, 1958, 1962, 1964, 1966, 1968, 1970, 1972, 1974, 1976, 1978, 1980
Van Doren, Kenneth P. (WI) - 1982
Van Duzer, Clarence D. (NV) - 1902, 1904
Van Duzer, Isaac (NY) - 1830
Van Duzer, Jonas S. (NY) - 1914
Van Dyck (NY) - 1856
Van Dyke (MN) - 1904
Van Dyke (PA) - 1848

Van Dyke (TN) - 1853
Van Dyke, Carl C. (MN) - 1914, 1916, 1918
Van Dyke, Fredrick S. (CA) - 1958
Van Dyke, John (NJ) - 1846, 1848
Van Horn (MO) - 1902
Van Horn, Burt (NY) - 1860, 1864, 1866
Van Horn, Daniel (NY) - 1826
Van Horn, Espy (PA) - 1826
Van Horn, George (NY) - 1890, 1894
Van Horn, M. A. (PA) - 1910
Van Horn, Robert T. (MO) - 1864, 1866, 1868, 1880, 1894
Van Horne, Espy (PA) - 1824
Van Horne, Terry (PA) - 2000
Van Houten, Isaac (NY) - 1832
Van Middlesworth, H. (IL) - 1904
Van Natta, Ralph W. (IN) - 1982
Van Ness (VT) - 1834
Van Ness, C. P. (VT) - 1836
Van Patton, J. C. (WA) - 1892, 1894
Van Pelt, William K. (WI) - 1950, 1952, 1954, 1956, 1958, 1960, 1962, 1964
Van Rensselaer, Cortlandt S. (NY) - 1890
Van Rensselaer, Henry (NY) - 1838, 1840
Van Rensselaer, Stephen (NY) - 1824, 1826
Van Sandt, Hiram Gilmore (IL) - 1902
Van Sant, Joshua (MD) - 1853, 1855
Van Schaick, Isaac W. (WI) - 1884, 1888
Van Slyke, Jim (KS) - 1984, 1992
Van Trump, P. (OH) - 1850
Van Trump, Philadelph (OH) - 1866, 1868, 1870
Van Valkenburg, Robert B. (NY) - 1860, 1862
Van Vlear, Edwin F. (CA) - 1914
Van Voorhes, Nelson H. (OH) - 1858, 1874, 1876, 1878
Van Voorhis, Henry C. (OH) - 1892, 1894, 1896, 1898, 1900, 1902
Van Voorhis, John (NY) - 1878, 1880, 1882, 1890, 1892
Van Winkle, Marshall (NJ) - 1900, 1904
Van Winkle, William (TX) - 1964
Van Zandt, James E. (PA) - 1938, 1940, 1942, 1946, 1948, 1950, 1952, 1954, 1956, 1958, 1960
Van, Steven Grack (MD) - 1994
Van, Vernon (CA) - 2000
Vance (CT) - 1898
Vance (OH) - 1852
Vance, Chris (WA) - 2000
Vance, E. H. Jr. (AR) - 1900
Vance, Elijah (OH) - 1846, 1850
Vance, George L. (IL) - 1896
Vance, John L. (OH) - 1874, 1876, 1884
Vance, Johnstone (CT) - 1924
Vance, Joseph (OH) - 1824, 1826, 1828, 1830, 1832, 1843, 1844
Vance, Robert B. (NC) - 1825, 1827, 1872, 1874, 1876, 1878, 1880, 1882
Vance, Robert J. (CT) - 1886, 1888
Vance, Wilson (OH) - 1888
Vance, Zebulon B. (NC) - 1858, 1859
Vancott, Richard (NY) - 1900
Vandegrift, Charles S. (PA) - 1896
Vandenberge, John (MD) - 1986
Vandenheuvel, William J. (NY) - 1960
Vander Jagt, Guy A. (MI) - 1966, 1968, 1970, 1972, 1974, 1976, 1978, 1980, 1982, 1984
Vander Laan, Robert (MI) - 1974
Vander Veen, Richard F. (MI) - 1958, 1974, 1976
Vanderbilt (NJ) - 1918
Vanderbilt (NY) - 1888
Vanderbilt, Andrew N. (NY) - 1890
Vanderbilt, Samuel "Mark" (CA) - 1988
Vanderburg, W. S. (OR) - 1896
Vandergriff, James (TN) - 1992
Vandergriff, Tom (TX) - 1982, 1984
Vanderlin, Joseph C. (PA) - 1894
Vanderploeg, Jan B. (MI) - 1958
Vanderpoel, Aaron (NY) - 1832, 1834, 1838
Vanderpoel, James (NY) - 1828
Vanderpoel, W. Irving (NY) - 1926
Vanderpool, S. O. (NY) - 1880
Vanderslice, Kathryn Z. (PA) - 1961
Vanderveer, Abraham (NY) - 1836

Vanderventer, Isaac (IL) - 1846
Vandervoort, Robert (PA) - 1942
Vandeventer, Judson W. (PA) - 1892
Vandever, William (CA) - 1886, 1888
Vandever, William (IA) - 1858, 1860
Vandillen, H. C. (MO) - 1878
Vandiver, Willard D. (MO) - 1896, 1898, 1900, 1902
Vandusen, W. W. (WA) - 1894
Vandyken, Sam (CA) - 1966, 1968, 1970
Vaneaton, Henry S. (MS) - 1882, 1884
Vaneschen, John E. (IA) - 1968
Vanet, Randall (MO) - 1970
Vanguilder, Harry P. (WI) - 1944
Vanhecke, Frederick (WI) - 1972
Vanheusen (NY) - 1882
Vanheyde, Robert L. (OH) - 1964, 1966
Vanhoesen, Walter H. (NJ) - 1944, 1946
Vanhoose, Walter Clay (KY) - 1964
Vanik, Charles A. (OH) - 1954, 1956, 1958, 1960, 1962, 1964, 1966, 1968, 1970, 1972, 1974, 1976, 1978
Vankennen, John D. (NY) - 1944
Vanlear (MN) - 1914
Vanmatre, Nelson B. (CA) - 1936
Vanmeter, John I. (OH) - 1843, 1844
Vanmetre (KY) - 1837
Vann, W. A. (CA) - 1894
Vannatto, J. L. (TX) - 1916
Vannes, Dale R. (WI) - 1992
Vannoort, Frank J. (NJ) - 1934
Vannortwick, John (IL) - 1856
Vannostrand, Peter (WI) - 1940
Vanoosterhaut, P. D. (IA) - 1904
Vanpetten, H. O. (CA) - 1964
Vanrenr (NY) - 1852
Vanslyck (RI) - 1870
Vantassel, A. T. (OH) - 1896
Vantuys, Ben (TX) - 1906
Vanwagenan, Gerret (NY) - 1846
Vanwagenen, A. (IA) - 1912
Vanwagenen, Hubert (NY) - 1832
Vanwagner, H. (IA) - 1896
Vanwagner, Karl D. (NJ) - 1950
Vanwinder (LA) - 1851
VanWinkle, John (AR) - 1992
Vanwormer, A. (MO) - 1870
Vanworner, Clements H. (WI) - 1894
Vanwych (NY) - 1826
Vanwyck, Charles H. (NY) - 1858, 1860, 1866, 1868
Vanzandt, C. C. (RI) - 1881
Vare, William S. (PA) - 1912, 1914, 1916, 1918, 1920, 1922, 1924
Varian, Isaac (NY) - 1838
Varn, Wilfred C. (FL) - 1962
Varnadoe (GA) - 1855
Varnes, Blair L. (IL) - 1948
Varnum (NY) - 1852
Varnum, Charles W. (CO) - 1934
Varnum, John (MA) - 1824, 1826, 1828
Varon, Joe (FL) - 1966
Vatcher, William H. Jr. (CA) - 1956
Vaughan, Harry J. (WA) - 1922
Vaughan, Horace W. (TX) - 1912
Vaughan, John Charles (IL) - 1910, 1912, 1914
Vaughan, R. T. (VA) - 1902
Vaughan, Taylor G. (VA) - 1928, 1936
Vaughan, William W. (TN) - 1870
Vaughen, Daniel (FL) - 2000
Vaughey, Alex (IL) - 1904
Vaughn, Albert C. (PA) - 1950
Vaughn, Frank B. (TX) - 1932
Vaughn, Harry T. (PA) - 1918
Vaughn, John L. (TX) - 1916
Vaughn, M. H. (Mike) (NC) - 1976
Vaux (PA) - 1928
Vaux, Richard (PA) - 1872, 1890
Vawter, W. R. (VA) - 1910
Veach (IN) - 1856
Veal, Don-Terry (LA) - 1998
Veatch (IN) - 1868
Veatch, R. M. (OR) - 1892, 1898, 1904
Veazie, Samuel (ME) - 1848
Veeder, William D. (NY) - 1876
Veghte (NJ) - 1876

Vehslage, John H. G. (NY) - 1896
Veile, P. (IA) - 1852
Velasquez, Waldo (CA) - 1968
Velazquez, Manuel (NY) - 1958
Velázquez, Nydia M. (NY) - 1992, 1994, 1996, 1998, 2000
Velde, Harold H. (IL) - 1948, 1950, 1952, 1954
Veltre, Philip J. (PA) - 1984
Venable, Abraham W. (NC) - 1847, 1849, 1851, 1853
Venable, Edward C. (VA) - 1888
Venable, William W. (MS) - 1916, 1918
Vendsel, Raymond G. (ND) - 1954, 1960
Vener, Samuel S. (CA) - 1966
Vennard, George H. (LA) - 1904
Venner, Frank (OH) - 1984
Vento, Bruce F. (MN) - 1976, 1978, 1980, 1982, 1984, 1986, 1988, 1990, 1992, 1994, 1996, 1998
Venuti, Joseph E. (NY) - 1944
Ver Ploeg, C. (IA) - 1928
Verbofsky, Harry L. (PA) - 1958
Verga, Robert J. (NY) - 1996
Vergari, Carl A. (NY) - 1972
Verges, Frank G. (CA) - 1982
Verk (NY) - 1852
Vermilya, James I. (MN) - 1892
Vermorel, Dorothea M. B. (FL) - 1952
Vernon (TN) - 1898
Vernon, Thomas O. P. (SC) - 1858
Verplanck, Gulian (NY) - 1824, 1826, 1828, 1830, 1834
Verplanck, Isaac A. (NY) - 1868
Verree, John P. (PA) - 1858, 1860
Verreos, Nick A. (CA) - 1960, 1964
Verry (MA) - 1876
Verry, George F. (MA) - 1872
Verticchio, Rick (IL) - 1998
Vertrees (MO) - 1890
Vest, David D. (CA) - 1986
Vest, S. A. (TN) - 1922
Vesta, Vinton A. (WI) - 1978
Vestal, Albert H. (IN) - 1914, 1916, 1918, 1920, 1922, 1924, 1926, 1928, 1930
Vetter, V. Stephen (IL) - 1988
Vetterli, Reed E. (UT) - 1942
Veysey, Victor V. (CA) - 1970, 1972, 1974
Vibbard, Chauncey (NY) - 1860
Vick, M. R. (NC) - 1924
Vickerman, John (SD) - 1972
Vickers, David (NY) - 1998, 2000
Vickers, Robert L. (CA) - 1976
Vickers, Tom (NE) - 1984
Vickery, Charles R. (MA) - 1854, 1856
Vickery, Raymond E. (VA) - 1992
Victor, Eugene (NY) - 1980
Victora, William (WI) - 1924, 1928
Vidal, Gore (NY) - 1960
Viele, Egbert L. (NY) - 1884, 1886
Vifquain, Victor (NE) - 1892
Vigelius, Anton (NY) - 1894
Vigil-Giron, Rebecca (NM) - 1990
Vigil, Charles S. (CO) - 1988
Vigilante, Kevin (RI) - 1994
Vigorito, Joseph P. (PA) - 1964, 1966, 1968, 1970, 1972, 1974, 1976, 1978
Vilas (WI) - 1868
Vilas, Levi B. (VT) - 1844
Villiers (LA) - 1857
Vilt, Thomas E. (OH) - 1972
Vincent (CT) - 1912
Vincent, Beverly M. (KY) - 1938, 1940, 1942
Vincent, Bird J. (MI) - 1922, 1924, 1926, 1928, 1930
Vincent, Bobby Ray (CA) - 1974
Vincent, Charles C. (MI) - 1992
Vincent, Lena Duell (IL) - 1940
Vincent, Merle D. (CO) - 1920, 1922
Vincent, William D. (KS) - 1896, 1898, 1900
Vinich, John P. (WY) - 1989
Vinje, Syver (ND) - 1986
Vinson, Carl (GA) - 1914, 1916, 1918, 1920, 1922, 1924, 1926, 1928, 1930, 1932, 1934,

Worth, Jacob (NY) - 1900
Worth, Jonathan (NC) - 1841, 1845
Worth, Joseph S. (NC) - 1885
Worthington, Henry G. (NV) - 1864
Worthington, John I. (AR) - 1920
Worthington, John T. H. (MD) - 1831, 1833, 1837, 1839
Worthington, N. C. (IL) - 1872
Worthington, Nicholas E. (IL) - 1882, 1884, 1886, 1888, 1896
Worthington, Thomas (IL) - 1900
Worthington, Thomas C. (MD) - 1824
Worthy, A. N. (AL) - 1869
Wortley, George C. (NY) - 1976, 1980, 1982, 1984, 1986
Worton, Joseph Edward (FL) - 1950
Worzel, Harold W. (NY) - 1948
Woskow, Herman (NY) - 1950, 1952
Wozniak, Theodore (IL) - 1958
Wren, G. Louie (OH) - 1954
Wren, Thomas (NV) - 1876, 1898
Wrenn, George H. (MA) - 1902, 1904, 1906
Wrenn, Lossing L. (NC) - 1928
Wrenn, Thomas (AL) - 1968
Wright (DE) - 1872
Wright (GA) - 1859, 1884
Wright (MD) - 1845
Wright (NJ) - 1832
Wright (OH) - 1862
Wright (PA) - 1848, 1850
Wright, Alan D. (OH) - 1968
Wright, Ambrose R. (GA) - 1872
Wright, Anna C. (NY) - 1914
Wright, Ashley B. (MA) - 1892, 1894, 1896
Wright, Augustus R. (GA) - 1842, 1857
Wright, B. F. (TX) - 1914
Wright, Branson (IL) - 1954
Wright, Bryndan (TX) - 2000
Wright, C. P. (CA) - 1934
Wright, Carl E. Jr. (IL) - 1946
Wright, Charles Frederick (PA) - 1898, 1900, 1902
Wright, Chester M. (CA) - 1970
Wright, Crispus (CA) - 1958
Wright, Cullen N. (NE) - 1936
Wright, Daniel B. (MS) - 1853, 1855
Wright, Deborah (CA) - 1994, 1996
Wright, Donald (MN) - 1972
Wright, E. B. (PA) - 1872
Wright, E. N. (OK) - 1912
Wright, Edwin C. (OH) - 1900
Wright, Edwin R. V. (NJ) - 1864
Wright, Frank A. (IL) - 1924
Wright, Frank D. (PA) - 1896, 1898
Wright, Frederick K. (PA) - 1892
Wright, G. J. (GA) - 1872
Wright, George (KY) - 1878, 1880
Wright, George G. (IA) - 1850
Wright, George W. (CA) - 1849
Wright, Hendrick B. (PA) - 1852, 1854, 1874, 1876, 1878, 1880
Wright, Herbert William Jr. (OK) - 1958, 1962
Wright, Isaac H. (MA) - 1844, 1846, 1856
Wright, Jabez (OH) - 1836
Wright, James A. (PA) - 1940, 1942, 1944
Wright, James A. (WI) - 1978, 1980
Wright, James S. (IN) - 1890
Wright, Jim (TX) - 1954, 1956, 1958, 1960, 1962, 1964, 1966, 1968, 1970, 1972, 1974, 1976, 1978, 1980, 1982, 1984, 1986, 1988
Wright, Joe (KY) - 1996
Wright, John C. (OH) - 1824, 1826, 1828
Wright, John H. (TX) - 1980
Wright, John T. (NJ) - 1896
Wright, John V. (TN) - 1855, 1857, 1859
Wright, Joseph A. (IN) - 1843, 1845, 1847
Wright, Myron B. (PA) - 1888, 1890, 1892, 1894
Wright, N. Jackson (CA) - 1926
Wright, Nelson F. (MA) - 1936
Wright, O. H. (IL) - 1910
Wright, Oliver W. H. (OH) - 1906
Wright, Orestes H. (IL) - 1932
Wright, Robert H. (MI) - 1926
Wright, Sam H. (TX) - 1976
Wright, Samuel G. (NJ) - 1844

Wright, Silas (NY) - 1826, 1828
Wright, Theo (PA) - 1864, 1866
Wright, Uriel (MO) - 1846
Wright, Victor O. (IL) - 1956
Wright, Vivian S. (NC) - 1980
Wright, W. Clyde (NY) - 1960
Wright, W. J. (PA) - 1910
Wright, Warren W. (IL) - 1934
Wright, William (NJ) - 1843, 1844
Wright, William A. (VA) - 1950
Wright, William C. (GA) - 1918, 1920, 1922, 1924, 1926, 1928, 1930
Wright, William F. (GA) - 1870
Wright, Williamson (IN) - 1849
Wrightson, Thomas (KY) - 1870
Wrucke, Ernest C. (WI) - 1924, 1926
Wu, David (OR) - 1998, 2000
Wulster, Emil M. (NJ) - 1942, 1950
Wurst, Henry E. (MO) - 1964
Wurts (IL) - 1830
Wurts, John (PA) - 1824
Wurzbach, Harry M. (TX) - 1920, 1922, 1924, 1926, 1928, 1930
Wyant, Adam M. (PA) - 1920, 1922, 1924, 1926, 1928, 1930, 1932
Wyatt, Cecil (AL) - 1980
Wyatt, Joe (TX) - 1978
Wyatt, Joe Jr. (TX) - 1982
Wyatt, John M. (MD) - 1942
Wyatt, Wendell (OR) - 1964, 1966, 1968, 1970, 1972
Wyche, James (NC) - 1831
Wyckoff, John (NY) - 1830
Wyckoff, Ted (AZ) - 1972
Wyden, Ron (OR) - 1980, 1982, 1984, 1986, 1988, 1990, 1992, 1994
Wydler, John W. (NY) - 1962, 1964, 1966, 1968, 1970, 1972, 1974, 1976, 1978
Wydra, John (NJ) - 1986
Wykoff (MO) - 1890
Wyler, Arthur A. (NY) - 1936, 1940
Wylie, Chalmers P. (OH) - 1966, 1968, 1970, 1972, 1974, 1976, 1978, 1980, 1982, 1984, 1986, 1988, 1990
Wyman, Louis C. (NH) - 1962, 1964, 1966, 1968, 1970, 1972
Wynell, Dorothy (TX) - 1958, 1960
Wynn, Albert R. (MD) - 1992, 1994, 1996, 1998, 2000
Wynn, William J. (CA) - 1902, 1904
Wynne, Peter (NY) - 1912, 1946
Wyrick, James Douglas (TN) - 1946
Wyrick, Jim (WA) - 1994
Wyrick, Phil (AR) - 1998
Wysor, J. C. (VA) - 1904
Wyvell, Manton M. (NY) - 1912, 1914

Y

Yabs, Michael (WI) - 1910
Yaffe, Bertram A. (MA) - 1970
Yager, Arthur (KY) - 1928
Yambrek, Leopold (AL) - 1982
Yancey, Joel (KY) - 1827, 1829
Yancey, William L. (AL) - 1844, 1845
Yancy, Billy (TN) - 2000
Yandell, Argus W. Jr. (OK) - 2000
Yantis, John W. (IL) - 1906
Yaple, George L. (MI) - 1880, 1882, 1884, 1890, 1892
Yarbrough, Willard V. (TN) - 1964
Yardley, Robert M. (PA) - 1886, 1888
Yarling, William A. (IN) - 1920
Yarnall, George S. (CA) - 1912
Yarnall, J. (CA) - 1882
Yatar (IN) - 1860
Yates, Charles B. (NJ) - 1970, 1974
Yates, Comer (GA) - 1994
Yates, John O. (OH) - 1894
Yates, Joy (TX) - 1978
Yates, Richard (IL) - 1850, 1852, 1892, 1918, 1920, 1922, 1924, 1926, 1928, 1930, 1932
Yates, Sidney R. (IL) - 1948, 1950, 1952, 1954, 1956, 1958, 1960, 1964, 1966, 1968, 1970, 1972, 1974, 1976, 1978, 1980, 1982, 1984, 1986, 1988, 1990, 1992, 1994, 1996
Yates, Thomas S. (KY) - 1944

Yates, Tyrone K. (OH) - 1990
Yatron, Gus (PA) - 1968, 1970, 1972, 1974, 1976, 1978, 1980, 1982, 1984, 1986, 1988, 1990
Yauch, Michael B. (CA) - 1984
Yawger, Peter (NY) - 1840
Yazell, W. S. (KY) - 1924
Yeager, Charles E. (PA) - 1920
Yeager, Jim (PA) - 1994
Yeaman, George H. (KY) - 1862, 1863, 1865
Yeates, Jesse J. (NC) - 1876, 1878
Yeats, Jesse J. (NC) - 1874
Yell, Archibald (AR) - 1836, 1844
Yell, Pleasant M. (TX) - 1874
Yellowley (MS) - 1884
Yellowtail, Bill (MT) - 1996
Yellowtail, Robert (MT) - 1945
Yemen, Arpo (MI) - 1966
Yeoman, J. A. (IA) - 1888
Yeosock, Michael A. (PA) - 1938
Yerger (TN) - 1853
Yerger, Brower B. (PA) - 1972
Yerington, J. A. (NV) - 1904
Yoakum, Charles H. (TX) - 1894
Yob, Chuck (MI) - 2000
Yocum, Seth H. (PA) - 1878
Yoder (PA) - 1856
Yoder, Daniel B. (PA) - 1878
Yoder, Fred (WA) - 1954
Yoder, John A. (ND) - 1912
Yoder, Samuel S. (OH) - 1886, 1888
Yoist, John (LA) - 1887
Yon, Tom A. (FL) - 1926, 1928, 1930
Yonavick, Peter (PA) - 1968
Yorczyk, Robert S. (PA) - 1998, 2000
York, Charles I. (OH) - 1902
York, O. S. (TX) - 1908
York, Peter R. (NM) - 1984
York, Tyre (NC) - 1882
Yorke, Thomas Jones (NJ) - 1836, 1838, 1840
Yorty, Samuel William (CA) - 1950, 1952
Yost, Eric R. (KS) - 1992
Yost, G. A. (TN) - 1916
Yost, Jacob (VA) - 1884, 1886, 1888, 1894, 1896
Yost, Jacob S. (PA) - 1843, 1844
Yost, Z. F. (IL) - 1902, 1904
You, Adolph J. (IN) - 1892
Youhanaie, Stephen (IL) - 1988
Youmans, F. A. (AR) - 1902
Youmans, Henry M. (MI) - 1890, 1892, 1902
Young (AL) - 1843
Young (MO) - 1914
Young (OH) - 1832, 1852
Young (PA) - 1888
Young (TN) - 1888
Young, Alexander C. (NJ) - 1896
Young, Andrew (GA) - 1970, 1972, 1974, 1976
Young, Anna C. (AK) - 2000
Young, Archibald B. (CA) - 1944
Young, Arthur L. (CA) - 1962
Young, Augustus (VT) - 1840
Young, Boston G. (OH) - 1894
Young, Bryan R. (KY) - 1845, 1857
Young, C. W. Bill (FL) - 1970, 1972, 1974, 1976, 1978, 1980, 1982, 1984, 1986, 1988, 1990, 1992, 1994, 1996, 1998, 2000
Young, Charles L. (IL) - 1906
Young, Clair A. (OH) - 1940
Young, Clifford O. (CA) - 1976
Young, Clifton (NV) - 1952, 1954
Young, David (NC) - 1998
Young, Don (AK) - 1972, 1973, 1974, 1976, 1978, 1980, 1982, 1984, 1986, 1988, 1990, 1992, 1994, 1996, 1998, 2000
Young, Donald C. (IA) - 1980
Young, Ebenezer (CT) - 1829, 1831, 1833, 1835
Young, Edward L. (SC) - 1972, 1974, 1976
Young, Elisha (AL) - 1833
Young, Francis E. (OH) - 1954
Young, George E. (OK) - 1932, 1934, 1948, 1954
Young, George M. (ND) - 1912, 1914, 1916, 1918, 1920, 1922
Young, George R. (OH) - 1910
Young, Glenn O. (OK) - 1950

Young, H. Casey (TN) - 1874, 1876, 1878, 1880, 1882
Young, H. Olin (MI) - 1902, 1904, 1906, 1908, 1910, 1912
Young, Herman F. (KY) - 1922
Young, Houston G. (WV) - 1942
Young, Isaac D. (KS) - 1910, 1912
Young, Isaac J. (NC) - 1876
Young, J. B. (OH) - 1866
Young, J. H. (OH) - 1882
Young, James (TX) - 1910, 1912, 1914, 1916, 1918
Young, James A. (PA) - 1984
Young, James Rankin (PA) - 1896, 1898, 1900
Young, John (NY) - 1840
Young, John (TX) - 1956, 1958, 1960, 1962, 1964, 1968, 1970, 1972, 1974, 1976
Young, John A. (PA) - 1964
Young, John D. (KY) - 1867, 1872
Young, John H. (NY) - 1898
Young, John H. (OH) - 1844
Young, Ken (MO) - 1980, 1984, 1986
Young, LeRoy B. (UT) - 1938, 1940
Young, Lewis E. (VT) - 1992
Young, Martin J. (WI) - 1946, 1948
Young, Matthew P. (NY) - 1918
Young, Paul (CA) - 1994
Young, Paul R. (ME) - 1996
Young, Pierce M. B. (GA) - 1868, 1870, 1872
Young, Richard (NY) - 1908
Young, Robert A. (MO) - 1976, 1978, 1980, 1982, 1984, 1986
Young, Ronald E. (OH) - 1994
Young, S. R. (AR) - 1908
Young, Samuel (NY) - 1830
Young, Samuel H. (IL) - 1972, 1974, 1976
Young, Stephen M. (OH) - 1916, 1932, 1934, 1938, 1940, 1942, 1948, 1950
Young, Thomas H. (PA) - 1968, 1972
Young, Thomas L. (OH) - 1878, 1880
Young, Timothy R. (IL) - 1848
Young, Truman R. (CA) - 1946
Young, W. Hall (NC) - 1964, 1966
Young, Willard V. (WA) - 1938
Young, William A. (IL) - 1974
Young, William A. (VA) - 1896, 1898
Young, William S. (KY) - 1824, 1827
Youngblood, Francis M. (IL) - 1894
Youngblood, George S. (AL) - 1896
Youngblood, Harold F. (MI) - 1946, 1948, 1956
Youngdahl, Oscar (MN) - 1938, 1940
Youngdale, James M. (MN) - 1948, 1952
Younger, J. Arthur (CA) - 1952, 1954, 1956, 1958, 1960, 1962, 1964, 1966
Youssouf, Joseph D. (NJ) - 1994
Yowell, Randy D. (KS) - 1976
Yudelson, Jerry (CA) - 1988
Yunker, Donald E. (OH) - 1980
Yurkovsky, Michael E. (PA) - 1942

Z

Zablocki, Clement J. (WI) - 1948, 1950, 1952, 1954, 1956, 1958, 1960, 1962, 1964, 1966, 1968, 1970, 1972, 1974, 1976, 1978, 1980, 1982
Zablotny, John J. (NY) - 1954
Zabriskie, Andrew C. (NY) - 1908
Zabriskie, Elmer I. (NJ) - 1944
Zabrosky, Alex J. (IL) - 1970
Zachary, Billy Wayne (TX) - 2000
Zadrozny, Mitchell G. (IL) - 1974
Zafris, James G. Jr. (MA) - 1964
Zakas, Joe (IN) - 1996
Zamos, Jerome (CA) - 1978
Zampino, Thomas P. (NJ) - 1986
Zanillo, Michael R. (IL) - 1980
Zapp, R. (TX) - 1882
Zartman, Jim (CO) - 1988
Zartman, Joseph V. (IN) - 1912
Zatkovich, Gregory (PA) - 1944
Zbur, Rick (CA) - 1996
Zealor, Murray P. (PA) - 1952, 1978
Zeferetti, Leo C. (NY) - 1974, 1976, 1978, 1980, 1982
Zeigler (MO) - 1858
Zeigler, Fred (SC) - 1986

Senate General Election Candidates Index

The Senate General Election Candidates Index includes all candidates appearing in Chapter 26, Senate General Election Returns, 1913–2000. The index includes candidates' names followed by state abbreviations and the years of candidacy. To locate a candidate's returns, turn to pages 1268–1304 where the returns are arranged alphabetically by state and in chronological order by class of senator for each state. *(See "Senate's Three Classes," p. 1231; box, State Abbreviations, this page.)* For other references to Senate candidates in the *Guide to U. S. Elections*, fourth edition, see the General Index, pages I-153 to I-208.

A

Aandahl, Fred G. (ND) - 1952
Abdnor, James (SD) - 1980, 1986
Abel, Hazel H. (NE) - 1954
Abourezk, James (SD) - 1972
Abraham, Spencer (MI) - 1994, 2000
Abrams, Robert (NY) - 1992
Adams, Alva B. (CO) - 1924, 1932, 1938
Adams, Brock (WA) - 1986
Adams, Wilbur L. (DE) - 1934
Aiken, George D. (VT) - 1940, 1944, 1950, 1956, 1962, 1968
Aiken, Paul (KS) - 1950
Akaka, Daniel K. (HI) - 1990, 1994, 2000
Akins, Thomas J. (MO) - 1914
Alexander, Archibald S. (NJ) - 1948, 1952
Alexander, John G. (MN) - 1936
Alexander, Morton (CO) - 1924
Alexander, W. H. Bill (OK) - 1950
Allard, Wayne (CO) - 1996
Allen, George F. (VA) - 2000
Allen, Henry J. (KS) - 1930
Allen, Jim (AL) - 1968, 1974
Allott, Gordon (CO) - 1954, 1960, 1966, 1972
Anaya, Toney (NM) - 1978
Andersen, Bill (TN) - 1988
Anderson, Clinton P. (NM) - 1948, 1954, 1960, 1966
Anderson, Wendell R. (MN) - 1978
Andrews, Charles O. (FL) - 1936, 1940
Andrews, Jackson M. (KY) - 1986
Andrews, Lloyd J. (WA) - 1964
Andrews, Mark (ND) - 1980, 1986
Andrews, Thomas H. (ME) - 1994
Archambault, Raoul (RI) - 1960
Arndt, Raymond W. (NE) - 1964
Arnold, James W. (GA) - 1932
Ashcroft, John (MO) - 1994, 2000
Ashe, Victor (TN) - 1984
Ashurst, Henry F. (AZ) - 1916, 1922, 1928, 1934
Atcheson, Alex W. (TX) - 1916
Atchley, Forrest S. (NM) - 1958

Atkins, Hobart F. (TN) - 1952, 1958
Atkinson, C. D. (AR) - 1938
AuCoin, Les (OR) - 1992
Austin, Warren R. (VT) - 1931, 1934, 1940
Aylward Paul L. (KS) - 1962
Ayres, Tom (SD) - 1920, 1924

B

Babbitt, Wayne H. (AR) - 1972
Babcock, Howard C. (FL) - 1936
Babcock, Tim (MT) - 1966
Bachman, Nathan L. (TN) - 1934, 1936
Backus, Jan (VT) - 1994
Baesler, Scotty (KY) - 1998
Bailey, Carl E. (AR) - 1937
Bailey, John W. (MI) - 1928
Bailey, Josiah W. (ND) - 1930, 1936, 1942
Baird, David (NJ) - 1918
Baker, Howard (TN) - 1940
Baker, Howard H. Jr. (TN) - 1964, 1966, 1972, 1978
Baker, Ray T. (NV) - 1926
Baker, Stuart D. (VA) - 1960
Baldwin, Raymond E. (CT) - 1946
Baldwin, Simeon (CT) - 1914
Ball, Joseph H. (MN) - 1942, 1948
Ball, Lewis Heisler (DE) - 1918
Bamberger, Ernest (UT) - 1922, 1928
Bancroft, Philip (CA) - 1938
Bankhead, John H. (AL) - 1918, 1930, 1936, 1942
Banks, L. A. (OR) - 1930
Bantz, William B. (WA) - 1958
Barbour, Haley (MS) - 1982
Barbour, W. Warren (NJ) - 1932, 1936, 1938, 1940
Bard, Guy Kurtz (PA) - 1952
Barkley, Alben W. (KY) - 1926, 1932, 1938, 1944, 1954
Barkley, Dean M. (MN) - 1994, 1996
Barnett, Don (SD) - 1978
Barrett, Frank A. (WY) - 1952, 1958
Barry, Alex G. (OR) - 1938

Barth, Adam H. (WA) - 1914
Bartlett, Dewey F. (OK) - 1972
Bartlett, E. L. (AK) - 1958, 1960, 1966
Barton, Bruce (NY) - 1940
Barton, Joe L. (TX) - 1993
Bass, Perkins (NH) - 1962
Bass, Ross (TN) - 1964
Baucus, Max (MT) - 1978, 1984, 1990, 1996
Bauman, Rick (OR) - 1986
Baxter, James H. (DE) - 1978
Bayard, A. I. du Pont (DE) - 1952
Bayard, Thomas F. (DE) - 1922, 1928, 1930
Bayh, Birch (IN) - 1962, 1968, 1974, 1980
Bayh, Evan (IN) - 1998
Beall, J. Glenn (MD) - 1952, 1958, 1964
Beall, J. Glenn Jr. (MD) - 1970, 1976
Bean, Martha E. (OR) - 1918
Beard, Robin L. (TN) - 1976
Beasley, Michael (AK) - 1990
Beckham, John C. W. (KY) - 1914, 1920
Bedford, Roger (AL) - 1996
Beeckman, R. Livingston (RI) - 1922
Bell, Jeffrey (NJ) - 1978
Bellmon, Henry (OK) - 1968, 1974
Benavides, Tom R. (NM) - 1990
Bender, George H. (OH) - 1954, 1956
Benedict, Cleveland K. (WV) - 1982
Benedict, Cooper P. (WV) - 1964
Bennett, Robert F. (UT) - 1992, 1998
Bennett, Wallace F. (UT) - 1950, 1956, 1962, 1968
Bennion, Adams S. (UT) - 1944
Benson, Elmer A. (MN) - 1940, 1942
Bentley, Alvin M. (MI) - 1960
Benton, William (CT) - 1950, 1952
Bentsen, Lloyd (TX) - 1970, 1976, 1982, 1988
Berger, Victor L. (WI) - 1918
Berkstresser, H. E. (AL) - 1936
Berl, E. Ennalls (DE) - 1942
Berman, Dan (UT) - 1980
Bernard, Charles (AR) - 1968
Bernstein, Ed (NV) - 2000
Berry, Tom (SD) - 1938, 1942

Beshear, Steven L. (KY) - 1996
Bethune, Ed (AR) - 1984
Betley, Joseph J. (NH) - 1944
Betley, Stanley J. (NH) - 1954
Bettman, Gilbert (OH) - 1932
Betts, James E. (OH) - 1980
Beveridge, Albert J. (IN) - 1914, 1922
Bible, Alan (NV) - 1954, 1956, 1962, 1968
Biden, Joseph R. Jr. (DE) - 1972, 1978, 1984, 1990, 1996
Bigelow, James E. (VT) - 1950
Bilbo, Theodore G. (MS) - 1934, 1940, 1946
Bingaman, Jeff (NM) - 1982, 1988, 1994, 2000
Bingham, Hiram (CT) - 1924, 1926, 1932
Birch, Alex C. (AL) - 1914
Bishop, Neil S. (ME) - 1970
Bjornson, Val (MN) - 1954
Black, Hugo L. (AL) - 1926, 1932
Black, John G. (AR) - 1978
Black, W. W. (WA) - 1914
Blaine, John J. (WI) - 1926
Blakley, William A. (TX) - 1961
Blanton, Ray (TN) - 1972
Blatt, Genevieve (PA) - 1964
Blease, Cole L. (SC) - 1924
Blewett, Alex (MT) - 1964
Blount, Winton M. "Red" (AL) - 1972
Boggs, J. Caleb (DE) - 1960, 1966, 1972
Bond, Christopher S. (MO) - 1986, 1992, 1998
Bone, Homer T. (WA) - 1932, 1938
Bontrager, D. Russell (IN) - 1964
Boole, Ella A. (NY) - 1920
Booth, John P. (FL) - 1950
Booth, R. A. (OR) - 1914
Boozman, Fay (AR) - 1998
Borah, William E. (ID) - 1918, 1924, 1930, 1936
Boren, David L. (OK) - 1978, 1984, 1990
Boren, Jim (OK) - 1996
Borough, Reuben W. (CA) - 1952
Boschwitz, Rudy (MN) - 1978, 1984, 1990, 1996
Bottolfsen, C. A. (ID) - 1944

State Abbreviations

Alabama	AL	Indiana	IN	Nebraska	NE	South Carolina	SC
Alaska	AK	Iowa	IA	Nevada	NV	South Dakota	SD
Arizona	AZ	Kansas	KS	New Hampshire	NH	Tennessee	TN
Arkansas	AR	Kentucky	KY	New Jersey	NJ	Texas	TX
California	CA	Louisiana	LA	New Mexico	NM	Utah	UT
Colorado	CO	Maine	ME	New York	NY	Vermont	VT
Connecticut	CT	Maryland	MD	North Carolina	NC	Virginia	VA
Delaware	DE	Massachusetts	MA	North Dakota	ND	Washington	WA
Florida	FL	Michigan	MI	Ohio	OH	West Virginia	WV
Georgia	GA	Minnesota	MN	Oklahoma	OK	Wisconsin	WI
Hawaii	HI	Mississippi	MS	Oregon	OR	Wyoming	WY
Idaho	ID	Missouri	MO	Pennsylvania	PA		
Illinois	IL	Montana	MT	Rhode Island	RI		

Stone, William J. (MO) - 1914
Stoney, Jan (NE) - 1994
Strickland, Tom (CO) - 1996
Strinden, Earl (ND) - 1988
Stroup, Richard (ND) - 1976
Stubbs, W. R. (KS) - 1912
Stump, Albert (IN) - 1926, 1928
Sullivan, Florence M. (NY) - 1982
Sullivan, Mike (WY) - 1994
Sullivan, Roger C. (IL) - 1914
Summerfield, S. (NV) - 1912
Sundlun, Walter I. (RI) - 1954
Sutherland, George (UT) - 1916
Sutherland, Howard (WV) - 1916, 1922
Swanson, Claude A. (VA) - 1916, 1922, 1928
Swanson, Thomas E. (FL) - 1938
Sweeney, Thomas (WV) - 1940, 1946, 1954
Sweet, William E. (CO) - 1926
Swett, Dick (NH) - 1996
Sydness, Steve (ND) - 1992
Symington, Stuart (MO) - 1952, 1958, 1964, 1970
Symms, Steven D. (ID) - 1980, 1986

T

Taft, Kingsley A. (OH) - 1946
Taft, Robert A. (OH) - 1938, 1944, 1950
Taft, Robert A. Jr. (OH) - 1964, 1970, 1976
Taggart, Thomas (IN) - 1916, 1920
Talbot, Joseph E. (CT) - 1950
Talmadge, Herman E. (GA) - 1956, 1962, 1968, 1974, 1980
Tauke, Tom (IA) - 1990
Taylor, Glen H. (ID) - 1940, 1942, 1944, 1954, 1956
Tetzlaff, Arch MD (KS) - 1972
Thatcher, M. H. (KY) - 1932
Theis, Frank (KS) - 1960
Thiessen, Wayne C. (HI) - 1968
Thomas, Charles S. (CO) - 1912, 1914
Thomas, Craig (WY) - 1994, 2000
Thomas, Elbert D. (UT) - 1932, 1938, 1944, 1950
Thomas, Elmer (OK) - 1926, 1932, 1938, 1944
Thomas, J. J. (NE) - 1924
Thomas, John (ID) - 1928, 1932, 1940, 1942
Thomas, Norman (NY) - 1934
Thompson, Arthur E. (ND) - 1946
Thompson, Fletcher (GA) - 1972
Thompson, Fred (TN) - 1994, 1996
Thompson, J. E. (AZ) - 1934
Thompson, James (WI) - 1920
Thompson, Sally (KS) - 1996
Thompson, William H. (KS) - 1912, 1918
Thompson, William R. (MS) - 1970
Thomson, Keith (WY) - 1960
Thornburgh, Dick (PA) - 1991
Thornton, Dan (CO) - 1956
Thorsness, Leo K. (SD) - 1974
Thurmond, Strom (SC) - 1954, 1958, 1960, 1966, 1972, 1978, 1984, 1990, 1996
Thye, Edward J. (MN) - 1946, 1952, 1958
Thyng, Harrison R. (NH) - 1966
Tobey, Charles W. (NY) - 1938, 1944, 1950
Toel, William (AR) - 2000
Toledano, Ben C. (LA) - 1972
Tone, Joseph M. (CT) - 1946
Torricelli, Robert G. (NJ) - 1996
Towell, David (NV) - 1976

Tower, John (TX) - 1960, 1961, 1966, 1972, 1978
Townsend, Charles E. (MI) - 1916, 1922
Townsend, John G. Jr. (DE) - 1928, 1934, 1940
Townsend, M. Clifford (IN) - 1946
Trammell, Park (FL) - 1916, 1922, 1928, 1934
Traylor, Lawrence M. (VA) - 1966
Trible, Paul S. Jr. (VA) - 1982
Trombley, Bellani (CT) - 1938
Truax, Charles V. (OH) - 1928
Trujillo, Art (NM) - 1996
Truman, Harry S. (MO) - 1934, 1940
Tsongas, Paul E. (MA) - 1978
Tsukiyama, Wilfred C. (HI) - 1959
Tubbs, Tallant (CA) - 1932
Tucker, R. Walter (AR) - 1948
Tunnell, James M. (DE) - 1924, 1940, 1946
Tunnell, James M. Jr. (DE) - 1966
Tunney, John V. (CA) - 1970, 1976
Turner, George (WA) - 1916
Tuttle, Fred H. (VT) - 1998
Twilegar, Ron J. (ID) - 1990
Tydings, Joseph D. (MD) - 1964, 1970
Tydings, Millard E. (MD) - 1926, 1932, 1938, 1944, 1950
Tyler, Joseph M. (ID) - 1930
Tyler, Rollin U. (CT) - 1926
Tyson, Lawrence D. (TN) - 1924

U

Unander, Sig (OR) - 1962
Underwood, Cecil H. (WV) - 1960
Underwood, Oscar W. (AL) - 1914, 1920
Underwood, Thomas R. (KY) - 1952
Untermann, Ernest (CA) - 1914

V

Valentine, Bill (NM) - 1988
Vandenberg, Arthur H. (MI) - 1928, 1934, 1940, 1946
Van Essen, William J. (PA) - 1922
Van Nuys, Frederick (IN) - 1932, 1938
Van Zandt, James E. (PA) - 1962
Vare, William S. (PA) - 1926
Vaught, J. S. (NM) - 1928
Vendsel, Raymond (ND) - 1958
Vigil, Juan N. (NM) - 1928
Vignola, Joseph C. (PA) - 1988
Vinich, John (WY) - 1988
Vinich, Mike (WY) - 1972
Violette, Elmer H. (ME) - 1966
Vise, H. M. Sr. (VA) - 1952
Vogel, Charles J. (ND) - 1940
Voinovich, George V. (OH) - 1988, 1998

W

Wade, Victor M. (AR) - 1944
Wadsworth, James W. Jr. (NY) - 1914, 1920, 1926
Wagner, Robert F. (NY) - 1926, 1932, 1938, 1944, 1956
Walcott, Frederic C. (CT) - 1928, 1934
Walker, Harry C. (NY) - 1920
Walker, Prentiss (MS) - 1966
Walker, Walter (CO) - 1932
Wall, Tom (TN) - 1954
Wallace, Harold E. (MT) - 1970
Waller, Peter A. (IL) - 1920
Wallgren, Mon C. (WA) - 1940

Wallop, Malcolm (WY) - 1976, 1982, 1988
Walsh, David I. (MA) - 1918, 1924, 1926, 1928, 1934, 1940, 1946
Walsh, Thomas J. (MT) - 1912, 1918, 1924, 1930
Walton, John Calloway (OK) - 1924
Walton, W. B. (NM) - 1918
Warburton, Barclay H. (FL) - 1928
Warburton, Herbert B. (DE) - 1954
Warner, John W. (VA) - 1978, 1984, 1990, 1996
Warner, Mark (VA) - 1996
Warren, Francis E. (WY) - 1918, 1924
Washburn, Robert M. (MA) - 1934
Waterman, Charles W. (CO) - 1912, 1926
Watkins, Arthur V. (UT) - 1946, 1952, 1958
Watkins, Elton (OR) - 1930
Watson, Carlos G. (TX) - 1936, 1954
Watson, Clarence W. (WV) - 1918
Watson, James E. (IN) - 1916, 1920, 1926, 1932
Watson, Thomas (GA) - 1920
Weadock, Thomas A. E. (MI) - 1930
Webber, Henry P. (OH) - 1946
Weber, Frank J. (WI) - 1920
Wecht, Cyril H. (PA) - 1982
Weeks, John W. (MA) - 1918
Weicker, Lowell P. Jr. (CT) - 1970, 1976, 1982, 1988
Weilenmann, Milton L. (UT) - 1968
Welch, Lou W. (MT) - 1958
Welch, Robert T. (WI) - 1994
Weld, William F. (MA) - 1996
Welker, Herman (ID) - 1950, 1956
Weller, Ovington E. (MD) - 1920, 1926
Welling, Milton H. (UT) - 1920
Wellstone, Paul (MN) - 1990, 1996
Wene, Elmer H. (NJ) - 1944
Wensel, Louise (VA) - 1958
West, Oswald (OR) - 1918
West, Paul C. (NC) - 1954
Wetherby, Lawrence W. (KY) - 1956
Weygand, Bob (RI) - 2000
Whatley, Barney L. (CO) - 1944
Wheat, Alan (MO) - 1994
Wheeler, Burton K. (MT) - 1922, 1928, 1934, 1940
Wherry, Kenneth S. (NE) - 1942, 1948
Whitaker, Raymond B. (WY) - 1960, 1978
Whitbeck, Walter W. (OR) - 1942
White, Frank S. (AL) - 1914
White, John W. (AR) - 1932
White, Wallace H. Jr. (ME) - 1930, 1936, 1942
Whitener, A. A. (NC) - 1914, 1924
Whitley, Clifton R. (MS) - 1966
Whitman, Christine Todd (NJ) - 1990
Whitmore, Howard Jr. (MA) - 1964
Whitney, Wheelock (MN) - 1964
Whittaker, Jed (AK) - 1996
Whittenburg, Roy (TX) - 1958
Wickard, Claude R. (IN) - 1956
Wickes, Jack (IN) - 1988
Wilentz, Warren W. (NJ) - 1966
Wiley, Alexander (WI) - 1938, 1944, 1950, 1956, 1962
Wilkes, Lawrence S. (VA) - 1942
Wilkinson, Bud (OK) - 1964
Wilkinson, Ernest L. (UT) - 1964
Wilkinson, John A. (NC) - 1948
Williams (GA) - 1918

Williams, David L. (KY) - 1992
Williams, Dick (KS) - 1990
Williams, G. Mennen (MI) - 1966
Williams, George H. (MO) - 1926
Williams, Harrison A. Jr. (NJ) - 1958, 1964, 1970, 1976
Williams, John J. (DE) - 1946, 1952, 1958, 1964
Williams, John Sharp (MS) - 1916
Williams, Larry (MT) - 1978, 1982
Williams, Wallace (MD) - 1932
Williams, Walter (WA) - 1950
Williamson, Richard S. (IL) - 1992
Willis, Frank B. (OH) - 1920, 1926
Willis, Raymond E. (IN) - 1938, 1940
Willson (KY) - 1914
Wilson, George A. (IA) - 1942, 1948
Wilson, Manley J. (OR) - 1948
Wilson, Pete (CA) - 1982, 1988
Wilson, Ted (UT) - 1982
Wilson, Will (TX) - 1961
Wilson, William B. (PA) - 1926
Winter, Charles E. (WY) - 1928
Winter, William D. (MS) - 1984
Wirth, Timothy E. (CO) - 1986
Wise, Henry A. (VA) - 1933
Witters, Harry W. (VT) - 1934, 1944
Witwer, Samuel W. (IL) - 1960
Wofford, Harris (PA) - 1991, 1994
Wolcott, Josiah O. (DE) - 1916
Wold, John S. (WY) - 1964, 1970
Wolfe, M. Jay (WV) - 1988
Wolfe, William F. (WI) - 1916
Woo, S. B. (DE) - 1988
Woods, Harriett (MO) - 1982, 1986
Woods, Robert H. (VA) - 1946, 1948
Woollen, Evans (IN) - 1926
Work, Hubert (CO) - 1914
Workman, W. D. Jr. (SC) - 1962
Wright, Donn H. (SD) - 1966
Wright, Jim (TX) - 1961
Wright, William B. (NV) - 1962
Wyatt, Wilson W. (KY) - 1962
Wyden, Ron (OR) - 1996, 1998
Wyman, Jasper S. (ME) - 1988
Wyman, Louis C. (NH) - 1974, 1975
Wynia, Ann (MN) - 1994

Y

Yarborough, Ralph (TX) - 1957, 1958, 1964
Yates, Sidney R. (IL) - 1962
Yeakel, Lynn (PA) - 1992
Yoder, John (WV) - 1990
York, Stanley (WI) - 1976
Yorty, Samuel William (CA) - 1954
Young, Benjamin Loring (MA) - 1928
Young, Cliff (NV) - 1956
Young, Crystal (HI) - 1998
Young, Milton R. (ND) - 1946, 1950, 1956, 1962, 1968, 1974
Young, Stephen M. (OH) - 1958, 1964

Z

Zeigler, Eugene N. (SC) - 1972
Zimmer, Dick (NJ) - 1996
Zimmerman, Jacob (DE) - 1970
Zorinsky, Edward (NE) - 1976, 1982
Zschau, Ed (CA) - 1986
Zumwalt, Elmo (VA) - 1976

Senate Primary Candidates Index

The Senate Primary Candidates Index includes all candidates appearing in Chapter 27, Senate Primary Returns. The index includes candidates' names followed by state abbreviations and the years of candidacy. To locate a candidate's returns, turn to pages 1306–1374 where the returns are arranged alphabetically by state and in chronological order by class of senator for each state. *(See "Senate's Three Classes, p. 1231; box, State Abbreviations, this page.)* For other references to Senate candidates in the *Guide to U. S. Elections*, fourth edition, see the General Index, pages I-153 to I-208.

A

Abbott, John H. (CA) - 1986, 1988
Abdnor, James (SD) - 1980, 1986
Abercrombie, Neil (HI) - 1970
Abourezk, James (SD) - 1972
Abraham, Spencer (MI) - 1994, 2000
Abrams, Robert (NY) - 1992
Abzug, Bella (NY) - 1976
Accardo, Nick J. (LA) - 1992
Adams, Brock (WA) - 1986
Adams, Thomas B. (MA) - 1966
Addington, W. H. (KS) - 1986
Adefope, John O. (NY) - 2000
Adkins, Garry P. (WV) - 2000
Adkins, Homer M. (AR) - 1944
Aiken, George D. (VT) - 1956, 1962, 1968
Airy, Frederic W. (NJ) - 1960
Akaka, Daniel K. (HI) - 1990, 1994, 2000
Aker, Alan (SD) - 1998
Albough, William A. (MD) - 1964, 1982
Albright, Ernest G. (OK) - 1956
Alderson, Fleming N. (WV) - 1958
Alexander, Lee (NY) - 1974
Algood, Alice W. (TN) - 1988
Alioto, Kathleen Sullivan (MA) - 1978
Allard, Wayne (CO) - 1996
Allen, Frank Tunney (LA) - 1972
Allen, James B. Jr. (AL) - 1986
Allen, Jim (AL) - 1968, 1974
Allen, Maryon Pittman (AL) - 1978
Allen, Melba T. (AL) - 1972
Allen, Oscar K. (LA) - 1936
Allen, William B. (CA) - 1992
Allison, Clinton (MS) - 2000
Allott, Gordon (CO) - 1960, 1966, 1972
Allred, James (TX) - 1942
Allred, Thomas L. (NC) - 1984
Altman, Sidney (MD) - 2000
Altvater, George (OR) - 1960
Amen, Randolph John (HI) - 1998
Anaya, Toney (NM) - 1978
Anderson, Andy (NV) - 1992

Anderson, Anson (ND) - 1958
Anderson, Ava A. (KS) - 1966
Anderson, Bill (TN) - 1988
Anderson, Blanche (MT) - 1958
Anderson, Clinton P. (NM) - 1960, 1966
Anderson, Doug (UT) - 1992
Anderson, Fred (NV) - 1958
Anderson, Henry L. (AL) - 1932, 1936
Anderson, Le Roy (MT) - 1960
Anderson, Mark E. (UT) - 1968
Anderson, Steve (OR) - 1978, 1986, 1990
Anderson, Tom (PA) - 1980
Anderson, Wendell R. (MN) - 1978
Andrews, Charles O. (FL) - 1936, 1940
Andrews, Jackson M. (KY) - 1980, 1986
Andrews, Lloyd J. (WA) - 1964
Andrews, Mark (ND) - 1980, 1986
Andrews, Michael A. (TX) - 1994
Andrews, Thomas H. (ME) - 1994
Andromidas, Ted J. (CA) - 1994
Angell, Wayne (KS) - 1978
Annanders, David Louis (OK) - 1996
Antonovich, Michael D. (CA) - 1986
Apodaca, Jerry (NM) - 1982
Applegate, Ralph A. (OH) - 1988, 1994
Aragona, Xavier A. (MD) - 1974
Archambault, Raoul (RI) - 1960
Armstrong, Hepburn T. (WY) - 1958
Armstrong, William L. (CO) - 1978, 1984
Arn, Edward F. (KS) - 1962
Arndt, Raymond W. (NE) - 1964, 1966
Arnold, Burleigh (MO) - 1982
Aron, Ruthann (MD) - 1994
Arvidson, Gene (OR) - 1980
Asbury, Barry Steve (MD) - 1998
Ashcroft, John (MO) - 1994, 2000
Ashe, Victor (TN) - 1984
Askew, James J. (MO) - 1986, 1998
Atchley, Forrest S. (NM) - 1958
Atkins, Hobart F. (TN) - 1958
AuCoin, Les (OR) - 1992
Austin, Richard H. (MI) - 1976
Auvil, Ken (WV) - 1984

Avery, William (KS) - 1968
Aylward, Paul (KS) - 1956, 1962

B

Babb, Leslie R. (NH) - 1974
Babbitt, Wayne H. (AR) - 1972
Babcock, C. H. (NC) - 1962
Babcock, Tim M. (MT) - 1966
Bacaloff, James (OR) - 1966
Bachman, Nathan L. (TN) - 1924, 1934, 1936
Backus, Jan (VT) - 1994, 2000
Baesler, Scotty (KY) - 1998
Bagley, E. J. (GA) - 1980
Bailey, Carl E. (AR) - 1937
Bailey, Don (PA) - 1986
Bailey, J. W. (TX) - 1934
Bailey, Josiah W. (NC) - 1930, 1936, 1942
Bailey, Nan (WA) - 1998
Baker, Albert J. (NE) - 1960
Baker, Deane (MI) - 1976, 1982
Baker, Gerald (IA) - 1978
Baker, Howard H. Jr. (TN) - 1964, 1966, 1972, 1978
Baker, John (AL) - 1978
Baker, John (TN) - 1994
Ball, Albert T. (OH) - 1962
Ballard, John S. (OH) - 1962
Ballenger, William S. (MI) - 1982
Bangerter, Bruce (UT) - 1974
Bankhead, John H. II (AL) - 1926, 1930, 1936, 1942
Bantz, William B. (WA) - 1958
Banuelos, Robert J. (CA) - 1988
Barbour, Haley (MS) - 1982
Barilla, Bruce (WV) - 1996
Barkley, Dean (MN) - 1996
Barlow, Tom (KY) - 1996
Barnes, Bill (AK) - 1986
Barnes, John (KS) - 1980
Barnes, Michael D. (MD) - 1986
Barnett, Don (SD) - 1978
Baron, Murray (NY) - 1968
Barr, Bob (GA) - 1992

Barrasso, John (WY) - 1996
Barrett, Frank A. (WY) - 1958, 1960
Barron, Elizabeth Cervantes (CA) - 1994
Barrows, Gordon H. (WY) - 1978
Bartlett, Dewey F. (OK) - 1972
Bartlett, E. L. (AK) - 1958, 1960, 1966
Bartlett, Hamilton A. S. (FL) - 2000
Bartlett, Roscoe G. (MD) - 1980
Bartley, David M. (MA) - 1984
Barton, T. H. (AR) - 1944
Bass, Doris M. (MO) - 1970
Bass, Perkins (NH) - 1962
Bass, Ross (TN) - 1964, 1966
Batchelor, George M. (UT) - 1980
Bates, Joe B. (KY) - 1956
Battle, Laurie C. (AL) - 1954
Baucom, John D. (MN) - 1970
Baucus, Max S. (MT) - 1978, 1984, 1990, 1996
Bauman, Rick (OR) - 1986
Baxter, James H. (DE) - 1978
Bayh, Birch (IN) - 1980
Bayh, Evan (IN) - 1998
Bayley, Chris (WA) - 1998
Beall, Forest W. (OK) - 1964
Beall, J. Glenn (MD) - 1958, 1964, 1970, 1976
Beals, Manny (NV) - 1986
Beard, Robin L. (TN) - 1982
Beard, Samuel S. (DE) - 1988
Beasley, Michael (AK) - 1984, 1990, 1996
Beck, Paul V. (OK) - 1956
Beck, Rodney W. (ID) - 1992
Beckjord, Walter E. (OH) - 1982
Beckworth, Lindley (TX) - 1952
Bedford, Roger (AL) - 1996
Beilenson, Anthony C. (CA) - 1968
Belcher, A. P. (TX) - 1940
Belk, William I. (NC) - 1986
Bell, Alphonzo E. (CA) - 1976
Bell, Bob (OR) - 1992
Bell, Dale (SD) - 1980
Bell, Jeffrey (NJ) - 1978, 1982
Bellmon, Henry (OK) - 1968, 1974
Belluso, Nick M. (GA) - 1980

Gubernatorial General Election Candidates Index

The Gubernatorial General Election Candidates Index includes all candidates appearing in Chapter 30, Gubernatorial General Election Returns, 1776–2000. The index includes candidates' names followed by state abbreviations and the years of candidacy. *(See box, State Abbreviations, this page.)* To locate a candidate's returns, turn to pages 1416 to 1477 where the returns are arranged alphabetically by state and in chronological order of election for each state. For other references to gubernatorial candidates in the *Guide to U. S. Elections*, fourth edition, see the General Index, pages I-153 to I-208.

A

Aandahl, Fred G. (ND) - 1944, 1946, 1948
Abbett, Leon (NJ) - 1883, 1889
Abbott, Martha (VT) - 1974
Abernethy, Tom (AL) - 1954
Acker, Bert Lee (FL) - 1944, 1948
Ackerman, Lee (AZ) - 1960
Acuff, Roy (TN) - 1948
Adair, John (KY) - 1820
Adair, John A. M. (IN) - 1916
Adam, Andrew (ME) - 1990
Adams, Alva (CO) - 1884, 1886, 1896, 1904, 1906
Adams, Charles Francis (MA) - 1876
Adams, Jewett W. (NV) - 1882, 1886
Adams, John Quincy (MA) - 1833, 1867, 1868, 1869, 1870, 1871
Adams, Paul L. (NY) - 1966, 1970
Adams, Samuel (MA) - 1794, 1795, 1796
Adams, Sherman (NH) - 1948, 1950
Adams, Spencer B. (NC) - 1900
Adams, Tod R. (TX) - 1954
Adams, William H. (CO) - 1926, 1928, 1930
Adkins, Homer M. (AR) - 1940, 1942
Agnew, Spiro T. (MD) - 1966
Aiken, George D. (VT) - 1936, 1938
Akin, Warren (GA) - 1859
Alcorn, Hugh Meade (CT) - 1934
Alcorn, James L. (MS) - 1869, 1873
Aldrich, Chester H. (NE) - 1910, 1912
Aldrich, Walter J. (VT) - 1914
Alexander, Archibald (DE) - 1795
Alexander, Lamar (TN) - 1974, 1978, 1982
Alexander, Moses (ID) - 1908, 1914, 1916, 1922
Alexander, William C. (NJ) - 1856
Alfange, Dean (NY) - 1942
Alger, Fred M. Jr. (MI) - 1952
Alger, Horace C. (WY) - 1898
Alger, Russell A. (MI) - 1884
Allain, Bill (MS) - 1983
Allen, Byron G. (MN) - 1944
Allen, Charles H. (MA) - 1891

Allen, Charles H. (MO) - 1844
Allen, Frank G. (MA) - 1928, 1930
Allen, George F. (VA) - 1993
Allen, George H. (CO) - 1896
Allen, George W. (FL) - 1916
Allen, Heman (VT) - 1829, 1831
Allen, Henry J. (KS) - 1914, 1918, 1920
Allen, Henry W. (LA) - 1864, 1865
Allen, James C. (IL) - 1860
Allen, John (KY) - 1808
Allen, Oscar K. (LA) - 1932
Allen, Philip (RI) - 1851, 1852, 1853
Allen, Samuel L. (MA) - 1833
Allen, William (OH) - 1873, 1875
Allen, William C. (SD) - 1934
Allin, Roger (ND) - 1894
Allis, Edward P. (WI) - 1877
Allred, James V. (TX) - 1934, 1936
Almond, J. Lindsay Jr. (VA) - 1957
Almond, Lincoln (RI) - 1978, 1994, 1998
Alschuler, Samuel (IL) - 1900
Alsop, John P. (IL) - 1892, 1896
Altgeld, John P. (IL) - 1892, 1896
Ameringer, Oscar (WI) - 1914
Ames, Adelbert (MS) - 1873
Ames, Albert A. (MN) - 1886
Ames, Alfred K. (ME) - 1934
Ames, Oliver (MA) - 1886, 1887, 1888
Ammons, Elias M. (CO) - 1912
Ammons, Teller (CO) - 1936, 1938
Amsden, Charles H. (NH) - 1888, 1890
Anaya, Toney (NM) - 1982
Andersen, Elmer L. (MN) - 1960, 1962
Anderson, C. Elmer (MN) - 1952, 1954
Anderson, D. G. "Andy" (HI) - 1982, 1986
Anderson, Emmett T. (WA) - 1956
Anderson, Forrest H. (MT) - 1968
Anderson, Henry W. (VA) - 1921
Anderson, Hugh J. (ME) - 1843, 1844, 1845
Anderson, J. H. (ID) - 1898
Anderson, John Jr. (KS) - 1960, 1962
Anderson, Kenneth T. (KS) - 1950
Anderson, Sigurd (SD) - 1950, 1952

Anderson, T. J. (IA) - 1887
Anderson, Thomas J. (MN) - 1916
Anderson, Victor E. (NE) - 1954, 1956, 1958
Anderson, Wendell R. (MN) - 1970, 1974
Anderson, William R. (TN) - 1962
Andrew, John A. (MA) - 1860, 1861, 1862, 1863, 1864
Andrew, John F. (MA) - 1886
Andrews, Charles B. (CT) - 1878
Andrews, Garnett (GA) - 1855
Andrews, John (CO) - 1990
Andrews, Lloyd (WA) - 1960
Andrews, Mark (ND) - 1962
Andrews, Reddin (TX) - 1910, 1912
Andrus, Cecil D. (ID) - 1966, 1970, 1974, 1986, 1990
Ansel, Martin F. (SC) - 1906, 1908
Anthony, George T. (KS) - 1876
Anthony, Henry B. (RI) - 1849, 1850
Apodaca, Jerry (NM) - 1974
Appleton, James (ME) - 1842, 1843, 1844
Archambault, Alberic A. (RI) - 1918, 1928
Archambault, Raoul Jr. (RI) - 1952
Ariyoshi, George R. (HI) - 1974, 1978, 1982
Armstrong, Alexander (MD) - 1923
Armstrong, Charles M. (CO) - 1936
Armstrong, Robert (TN) - 1837
Arn, Edward F. (KS) - 1950, 1952
Arnall, Ellis (GA) - 1942
Arnesen, Deborah Arnie (NH) - 1992
Arnold, Lemuel H. (RI) - 1831, 1832, 1833
Arnold, Louis A. (WI) - 1922
Arnold, Olney (RI) - 1872, 1908, 1909
Arnold, Peleg (RI) - 1806, 1815
Arnold, William A. (WI) - 1904
Aronson, John Hugo (MT) - 1952, 1956
Ashcroft, John (MO) - 1984, 1988
Ashe, Thomas S. (NC) - 1868
Ashelstrom, Charles A. (CO) - 1912
Ashley, William H. (MO) - 1824, 1836
Askew, Reubin (FL) - 1970, 1974
Atiyeh, Victor G. (OR) - 1974, 1978, 1982
Atkinson, George (NH) - 1785

Atkinson, George W. (WV) - 1896
Atkinson, John M. (MO) - 1920
Atkinson, W. P. (OK) - 1962
Atkinson, William Y. (GA) - 1894, 1896
Atwater, Charles (CT) - 1878
Atwell, W. H. (TX) - 1922
Atwood, John (NH) - 1851, 1852
Austin, Horace (MN) - 1869, 1871
Austin, Richard B. (IL) - 1956
Auten, H. F. (AR) - 1898
Avenson, Donald D. (IA) - 1990
Avery, Carlos (MN) - 1924
Avery, William H. (KS) - 1964, 1966
Aycock, Charles B. (NC) - 1900
Ayers, Roy E. (MT) - 1936, 1940
Aylward, John A. (WI) - 1906, 1908
Ayres, Tom (SD) - 1926

B

Babb, W. I. (IA) - 1895
Babbitt, Bruce (AZ) - 1978, 1980
Babcock, Tim (MT) - 1964, 1968
Bachelder, Nahum J. (NH) - 1902
Bacon, Gaspar G. (MA) - 1934
Bacon, Waler W. (DE) - 1940, 1944
Badger, William (NH) - 1834, 1835
Bafalis, L. A. "Skip" (FL) - 1982
Bagby, Arthur P. (AL) - 1837, 1839
Bagley, John J. (MI) - 1872, 1874
Bagwell, Paul D. (MI) - 1958, 1960
Bailey, Carl E. (AR) - 1936, 1938
Bailey, Ed F. (OR) - 1930
Bailey, Ernest H. (VT) - 1944
Bailey, John (MA) - 1834
Bailey, John W. (MI) - 1918
Bailey, M. S. (CO) - 1896
Bailey, Thomas L. (MS) - 1943
Bailey, William J. (KS) - 1902
Bailey, William (FL) - 1848
Baird, David Jr. (NJ) - 1931
Baird, Henry S. (WI) - 1853
Bakalis, Michael (IL) - 1978
Baker, Conrad (IN) - 1868

State Abbreviations

Alabama	AL	Indiana	IN	Nebraska	NE	South Carolina	SC
Alaska	AK	Iowa	IA	Nevada	NV	South Dakota	SD
Arizona	AZ	Kansas	KS	New Hampshire	NH	Tennessee	TN
Arkansas	AR	Kentucky	KY	New Jersey	NJ	Texas	TX
California	CA	Louisiana	LA	New Mexico	NM	Utah	UT
Colorado	CO	Maine	ME	New York	NY	Vermont	VT
Connecticut	CT	Maryland	MD	North Carolina	NC	Virginia	VA
Delaware	DE	Massachusetts	MA	North Dakota	ND	Washington	WA
Florida	FL	Michigan	MI	Ohio	OH	West Virginia	WV
Georgia	GA	Minnesota	MN	Oklahoma	OK	Wisconsin	WI
Hawaii	HI	Mississippi	MS	Oregon	OR	Wyoming	WY
Idaho	ID	Missouri	MO	Pennsylvania	PA		
Illinois	IL	Montana	MT	Rhode Island	RI		

Baker, Davis S. Jr. (RI) - 1893, 1894
Baker, Howard H. (TN) - 1938
Baker, John I. (MA) - 1875
Baker, Nathaniel B. (NH) - 1854, 1855
Baker, R. Tarvin (KY) - 1868
Baker, Samuel Aaron (MO) - 1924
Baldridge, H. C. (ID) - 1926, 1928
Baldwin, Eli (OH) - 1836
Baldwin, Henry P. (MI) - 1868, 1870
Baldwin, Raymond E. (CT) - 1938, 1940, 1942, 1944
Baldwin, Roger S. (CT) - 1843, 1844, 1845
Baldwin, Simeon E. (CT) - 1910, 1912
Baliles, Gerald L. (VA) - 1985
Ballantine, James W. (ID) - 1894
Ballou, Olney (RI) - 1847
Balzar, Fred B. (NV) - 1926, 1930
Bamberger, Simon (UT) - 1916
Bancroft, George (MA) - 1844
Bancroft, Joseph (DE) - 1924
Bangerter, Norman H. (UT) - 1984, 1988
Banks, John (PA) - 1841
Banks, Nathaniel P. (MA) - 1857, 1858, 1859
Banning, William L. (MN) - 1877
Barker, D. E. (AR) - 1894
Barker, Harold H. (MN) - 1946
Barlocker, William A. (UT) - 1960
Barnaby, Jerothmul B. (RI) - 1877
Barnes, Orlando M. (MI) - 1878
Barnes, Roy E. (GA) - 1998
Barnes, Sidney M. (KY) - 1867
Barnett, Ross R. (MS) - 1959
Barnette, J. R. (AZ) - 1914
Barnum, E. M. (OR) - 1858
Barrere, Nelson (OH) - 1853
Barrett, Frank A. (WY) - 1950
Barrett, Jesse W. (MO) - 1936
Barron, William W. (WV) - 1960
Barrows, Lewis O. (ME) - 1936, 1938
Barry, John S. (MI) - 1841, 1843, 1849, 1854, 1860
Barry, William T. (KY) - 1828
Barstow, Amos C. (RI) - 1864
Barstow, John L. (VT) - 1882
Barstow, William Augustus (WI) - 1853, 1855
Bartlett, Charles W. (MA) - 1905
Bartlett, Dewey F. (OK) - 1966, 1970
Bartlett, Ichabod (NH) - 1831, 1832
Bartlett, John H. (NH) - 1918
Bartlett, Josiah (NH) - 1785, 1787, 1789, 1790, 1791, 1792, 1793
Bartlett, Washington (CA) - 1886
Bartley, Mordecai (OH) - 1844
Barton, Ara (MN) - 1873
Barzee, C. W. (OR) - 1906
Basha, Eddie (AZ) - 1994
Bashford, Coles (WI) - 1855
Baskin, Alonzo P. (FL) - 1892
Bass, Robert P. (NH) - 1910
Bassett, Richard (DE) - 1798
Bate, William B. (TN) - 1882, 1884
Bateman, Raymond H. (NJ) - 1977
Bates, Curtis (IA) - 1854
Bates, Frederick (MO) - 1824
Bates, John L. (MA) - 1902, 1903, 1904
Bates, Mark P. (SD) - 1918, 1920
Batt, Philip (ID) - 1982, 1994
Battle, John S. (VA) - 1949
Battle, William C. (VA) - 1969
Baxley, Bill (AL) - 1986
Baxter, Elisha (AR) - 1872
Baxter, George W. (WY) - 1890
Baxter, Lewis T. (TN) - 1890
Baxter, Percival P. (ME) - 1922
Bayh, Evan (IN) - 1988, 1992
Beach, Erasmus D. (MA) - 1855, 1856, 1857, 1858, 1860
Beach, William B. (RI) - 1876
Beall, J. Glenn (MD) - 1978
Beardsley, Morris (CT) - 1916
Beardsley, Samuel E. (CT) - 1912
Beardsley, William (IA) - 1948, 1950, 1952
Beasley, David (SC) - 1994, 1998
Beattie, Taylor (LA) - 1879
Beauvais, Arnaud (LA) - 1831
Beaver, James A. (PA) - 1882, 1886

Bebb, William (OH) - 1846
Beck, George T. (WY) - 1902
Becker, George L. (MN) - 1859, 1894
Beckham, John C. W. (KY) - 1900, 1903, 1927
Beddow, Jim (SD) - 1994
Bedell, John (NH) - 1869, 1870
Bedford, Gunning Jr. (DE) - 1795
Bedford, Homer F. (CO) - 1942
Bedle, Joseph D. (NJ) - 1874
Beeckman, R. Livingston (RI) - 1914, 1916, 1918
Beekman, C. C. (OR) - 1878
Beers, Seth P. (CT) - 1838
Begole, Josiah W. (MI) - 1882, 1884
Behan, W. J. (LA) - 1904
Belaga, Julie D. (CT) - 1986
Belknap, Morris B. (KY) - 1903
Bell, Bob (GA) - 1982
Bell, Charles H. (NH) - 1880
Bell, Charles J. (VT) - 1904
Bell, James (NH) - 1853, 1854, 1855
Bell, John (NH) - 1828, 1829
Bell, Joshua F. (KY) - 1859
Bell, P. Hansbrough (TX) - 1849, 1851
Bell, Samuel (NH) - 1819, 1820, 1821, 1822
Bell, Theodore A. (CA) - 1906, 1910, 1918
Bellmon, Henry L. (OK) - 1962, 1986
Bellotti, Francis X. (MA) - 1964
Benedict, Cleve (WV) - 1992
Benedict, Omer K. (OK) - 1926
Bennett, Louis (WV) - 1908
Bennett, Caleb P. (DE) - 1832
Bennett, John J. Jr. (NY) - 1942
Bennett, Robert F. (KS) - 1974, 1978
Benson, Bruce (CO) - 1994
Benson, Elmer A. (MN) - 1936, 1938
Bentall, J. O. (MN) - 1916
Bentley, Arthur A. (WI) - 1922
Benton, Thomas H. (IA) - 1865
Benton, Thomas Hart (MO) - 1856
Benz, Alexander O. (WI) - 1944
Berge, George W. (NE) - 1904
Bernhardt, Michael (VT) - 1988
Berry, James H. (AR) - 1882
Berry, Nathaniel S. (NH) - 1846, 1847, 1848, 1849, 1850, 1861, 1862
Berry, Tom (SD) - 1932, 1934, 1936
Berry, William H. (PA) - 1910
Best, Roy (CT) - 1944
Beveridge, Albert J. (IN) - 1912
Bibb, William Wyatt (AL) - 1819
Bickett, Thomas W. (NC) - 1916
Bicknell, Lewis W. (SD) - 1940, 1942
Biddle, John (MI) - 1835
Bidwell, John (CA) - 1875
Bierman, Adolph (MN) - 1883
Bigelow, Hobart B. (CT) - 1880
Bigger, Samuel (IN) - 1840, 1843
Biggs, Benjamin T. (DE) - 1886
Bigler, John (CA) - 1851, 1853, 1855
Bigler, William (PA) - 1851, 1854
Bilbo, Theodore G. (MS) - 1915, 1927
Billard, J. B. (KS) - 1914
Billings, Franklin S. (VT) - 1924
Bingham, Arthur (AL) - 1886
Bingham, Hiram (CT) - 1924
Bingham, J. A. (AL) - 1926
Bingham, Kinsley S. (MI) - 1854, 1856
Bingham, Robert P. (NH) - 1950
Bingham, W. H. H. (VT) - 1874, 1876, 1878
Bird, Charles Sumner (MA) - 1912, 1913
Bird, Francis W. (MA) - 1872
Bird, James B. (SD) - 1918
Birney, James G. (MI) - 1843, 1845
Bishop, A. (AR) - 1876
Bishop, Henry W. (MA) - 1852, 1853, 1854
Bishop, Neil (ME) - 1952
Bishop, Richard M. (OH) - 1877
Bishop, Robert R. (MA) - 1882
Bissell, Clark (CT) - 1846, 1847, 1848
Bissell, William H. (IL) - 1856
Black, Charles C. (NJ) - 1904
Black, Charles R. (AR) - 1948
Black, Chauncey F. (PA) - 1886
Black, Frank S. (NY) - 1896
Black, James D. (KY) - 1919

Black, W. W. (WA) - 1920
Blackburn, Luke P. (KY) - 1879
Blackford, Isaac (IN) - 1825
Blackmer, John (MA) - 1889
Blackwood, Ibra C. (SC) - 1930
Blaine, John J. (WI) - 1914, 1920, 1922, 1924
Blair, Austin (MI) - 1860, 1862, 1872
Blair, C. Stanley (MD) - 1970
Blair, James T. Jr. (MO) - 1956
Blair, John I. (NJ) - 1868
Blanchard, James J. (MI) - 1982, 1986, 1990
Blanchard, Newton C. (LA) - 1904
Blandin, Amos (NH) - 1936
Blanton, Ray (TN) - 1974
Blasdel, Henry G. (NV) - 1864, 1866
Blaylock, Len E. (AR) - 1972
Bleakley, William F. (NY) - 1936
Blease, Coleman L. (SC) - 1910, 1912
Blewett, Pierce (ND) - 1930
Bliss, Aaron T. (MI) - 1900, 1902
Blood, Henry H. (UT) - 1932, 1936
Blood, Robert O. (NH) - 1940, 1942
Blount, J. H. (AR) - 1920
Blount, William (TN) - 1809, 1811, 1813
Bloxham, William D. (FL) - 1872, 1880, 1896
Blue, Robert D. (IA) - 1944, 1946
Boardman, Elijah (CT) - 1812, 1813, 1814, 1815
Boatright, William L. (CO) - 1928
Bodwell, Joseph R. (ME) - 1886
Boe, Nils A. (SD) - 1964, 1966
Boggs, J. Caleb (DE) - 1952, 1956
Boggs, Lilburn W. (MO) - 1836
Bolens, Harry W. (WI) - 1938
Boles, Horace (IA) - 1889, 1891, 1893
Boles, Thomas (AR) - 1884
Bomrich, Louis G. (WI) - 1900
Bond, Christopher S. (MO) - 1972, 1976, 1980
Bond, Frank M. (NM) - 1990
Bond, Hugh L. (MD) - 1867
Bond, Shadrach (IL) - 1818
Bonner, John W. (MT) - 1948, 1952
Bonniwell, Eugene C. (PA) - 1918, 1926
Bookwalter, John W. (OH) - 1881
Boosalis, Helen (NE) - 1986
Booth, Gardner (WA) - 1988
Booth, James (DE) - 1822
Booth, Newton (CA) - 1871
Bordelon, Louis (LA) - 1852
Boreman, Arthur I. (WV) - 1863, 1864, 1866
Boreman, Herbert S. (WV) - 1948
Boren, David L. (OK) - 1974
Botkin, Alexander C. (MT) - 1896
Botkin, Jeremiah D. (KS) - 1908
Bottolfsen, C. A. (ID) - 1938, 1940, 1942
Botts, Clarence M. (NM) - 1930
Bouck, William C. (NY) - 1840, 1842
Bourn, Augustus O. (RI) - 1883, 1884
Boutin, Bernard L. (NH) - 1958, 1960
Boutwell, George S. (MA) - 1849, 1850, 1851
Bowdoin, James (MA) - 1780, 1785, 1786, 1787, 1789, 1790
Bowen, A. E. Jr. (ND) - 1912
Bowen, Otis R. (IN) - 1972, 1976
Bowerman, Jay (OR) - 1910
Bowers, M. D. (AR) - 1926, 1928
Bowie, George W. (CA) - 1857
Bowie, Oden (MD) - 1867
Bowie, Richard J. (MD) - 1853
Bowles, Chester (CT) - 1948, 1950
Bowles, Hargrove Jr. (NC) - 1972
Boyce, D. A. Jelly (OK) - 1958
Boyd, James E. (NE) - 1890
Boyd, Laura (OK) - 1998
Boyle, Emmet D. (NV) - 1914, 1918
Boynton, Charles A. (TX) - 1918
Brackett, John Q. A. (MA) - 1889, 1890
Bradbury, Bion (ME) - 1862, 1863
Bradford, Alexander B. (MS) - 1847
Bradford, Augustus W. (MD) - 1861
Bradford, Robert F. (MA) - 1946, 1948
Bradish, Luther (NY) - 1842
Bradley, Dorothy (MT) - 1992
Bradley, Jim (UT) - 1996
Bradley, Lewis R. (NV) - 1870, 1874, 1878
Bradley, Tom (CA) - 1982, 1986

Bradley, William C. (VT) - 1819, 1834, 1835, 1836, 1837, 1838
Bradley, William O. (KY) - 1887, 1895
Bradshaw, John Paul (MO) - 1944
Brady, James H. (ID) - 1908, 1910
Bragg, Thomas (NC) - 1854, 1856
Brainard, Lawrence (VT) - 1846, 1847, 1852, 1853
Bramlett, Leon (MS) - 1983
Bramlette, Thomas E. (KY) - 1863
Branch, John (NC) - 1838
Brandon, Gerald C. (MS) - 1827, 1829
Brandon, William W. (AL) - 1922
Branigin, Roger D. (IN) - 1964
Brann, Louis J. (ME) - 1932, 1934, 1938
Branon, E. Frank (VT) - 1954, 1956
Branson, L. C. (NV) - 1934
Branstad, Terry E. (IA) - 1982, 1986, 1990, 1994
Breathitt, Edward T. (KY) - 1963
Breathitt, John (KY) - 1832
Breaux, John E. (LA) - 1892
Bredesen, Phil (TN) - 1994
Breidenthal, John W. (KS) - 1900
Brennan, Joseph E. (ME) - 1978, 1982, 1990, 1994
Brewer, Earl (MS) - 1911
Brewster, Ralph O. (ME) - 1924, 1926
Breyer, Donald. S. (VA) - 1997
Bricker, John W. (OH) - 1936, 1938, 1940, 1942
Bridges, H. Styles (NH) - 1934
Bridges, Robert (WA) - 1920
Bridgham, Samuel W. (RI) - 1821
Briggs, Ansel (IA) - 1846
Briggs, Frank A. (ND) - 1896
Briggs, George N. (MA) - 1843, 1844, 1845, 1846, 1847, 1848, 1849, 1850, 1859
Brigham, Herbert F. (VT) - 1890
Brinkley, John R. (KS) - 1930, 1932
Briscoe, Dolph (TX) - 1972, 1974
Bristow, Bill (AR) - 1998
Britt, Henry M. (AR) - 1960
Brockett, Bruce D. (AZ) - 1946, 1948
Broderick, Raymond J. (PA) - 1970
Broening, William F. (MD) - 1930
Bronson, David (ME) - 1846, 1847
Bronson, Greene C. (NY) - 1854
Bronson, Samuel L. (CT) - 1900
Brooks, Bryant B. (WY) - 1904, 1906
Brooks, C. Wayland (IL) - 1936
Brooks, Erastus (NY) - 1856
Brooks, John (MA) - 1816, 1817, 1818, 1819, 1820, 1821, 1822
Brooks, Joseph (AR) - 1872
Brooks, Ralph G. (NE) - 1958
Brooks, Walter B. (MD) - 1887
Broome, James E. (FL) - 1852
Brotzman, Donald G. (CO) - 1954, 1956
Brough, Charles H. (AR) - 1916, 1918
Brough, John (OH) - 1863
Broughton, J. Melville (NC) - 1940
Broward, Napoleon Bonaparte (FL) - 1904
Brown, Aaron V. (TN) - 1845, 1847
Brown, Albert G. (MS) - 1843, 1845
Brown, Albert O. (NH) - 1920
Brown, Arthur M. (CT) - 1936
Brown, Benjamin Gratz (MO) - 1870
Brown, Clarence J. (OH) - 1934
Brown, Clarence Jr. (OH) - 1982
Brown, D. Russell (RI) - 1892, 1893, 1894
Brown, Earl (MN) - 1932
Brown, Edmund G. "Jerry" Jr. (CA) - 1974, 1978
Brown, Edmund G. (CA) - 1958, 1962, 1966
Brown, Ethan A. (OH) - 1816, 1818, 1820
Brown, Frank (MD) - 1891
Brown, Fred H. (NH) - 1922, 1924
Brown, Harvey D. (WI) - 1908
Brown, Jerry (OK) - 1986
Brown, John C. (TN) - 1870, 1872
Brown, John Y. Jr. (KY) - 1979
Brown, John Young (KY) - 1891
Brown, Joseph Emerson (GA) - 1857, 1859
Brown, Joseph M. (GA) - 1908, 1910, 1912
Brown, Kathleen (CA) - 1994

Durbin, Winfield T. (IN) - 1900, 1912
Durrette, Wyatt B. (VA) - 1985
Duryea, Perry B. (NY) - 1978
Dutton, Henry (CT) - 1853, 1854, 1855
Dwinell, Lane (NH) - 1954, 1956
Dwyer, Ruth (VT) - 1998, 2000
Dwyer, Thomas P. (MN) - 1916
Dyer, D. P. (MO) - 1880
Dyer, Charles V. (IL) - 1848
Dyer, Elisha (RI) - 1857, 1858, 1897, 1898, 1899
Dyke, William D. (WI) - 1974

E

Eagle, James P. (AR) - 1888, 1890
Earl, Anthony S. (WI) - 1982, 1986
Earle, George H. (PA) - 1934
Earnest, William S. (AL) - 1853
Easley, Mike (NC) - 2000
Eastman, Ira A. (NH) - 1863
Easton, John (VT) - 1984
Eaton, A. E. (OR) - 1910
Eaton, Benjamin H. (CO) - 1884
Eaton, George E. (VT) - 1882
Eaton, Horace (VT) - 1846, 1847
Eberhart, Adolph O. (MN) - 1910, 1912
Ebright, Don H. (OH) - 1950
EchoHawk, Larry (ID) - 1994
Eckerd, Jack M. (FL) - 1978
Eden, John R. (IL) - 1868
Edgar, Jim (IL) - 1990, 1994
Edge, Walter E. (NJ) - 1916, 1943
Edgerly, Martin V. B. (NH) - 1882
Edison, Charles (NJ) - 1940
Edmisten, Rufus (NC) - 1984
Edmondson, J. Howard (OK) - 1958
Edmunds, James M. (MI) - 1847
Edwards, Clark S. (ME) - 1886
Edwards, Cyrus (IL) - 1838
Edwards, Edward I. (NJ) - 1919
Edwards, Edwin W. (LA) - 1972, 1975, 1983, 1991
Edwards, Frank J. (MT) - 1912, 1916, 1924
Edwards, Henry W. (CT) - 1833, 1834, 1835, 1836, 1837
Edwards, James B. (SC) - 1974
Edwards, John Cummins (MO) - 1844
Edwards, John L. (VT) - 1867, 1868
Edwards, Ninian (IL) - 1826
Edwards, R. M. (TN) - 1878
Eels, Richard (IL) - 1846
Egan, William A. (AK) - 1958, 1962, 1966, 1970, 1974
Eggers, Paul (TX) - 1968, 1970
Eggleston, Beriah B. (MS) - 1868
Ehringhaus, J. C. B. (NC) - 1932
Eikenberry, Ken (WA) - 1992
Elder, Peter P. (KS) - 1888
Elkin, Richard (ND) - 1976
Ellerbe, William H. (SC) - 1896, 1898
Ellington, Buford (TN) - 1958, 1966
Elliott, Howard (MO) - 1952
Ellis, John W. (NC) - 1858, 1860
Ellsworth, Oliver (CT) - 1796
Ellsworth, William W. (CT) - 1837, 1838, 1839, 1840, 1841, 1842
Elrod, Samuel H. (SD) - 1904
Ely, Joseph B. (MA) - 1930, 1932
Emberton, Tom (KY) - 1971
Emerson, Frank C. (WY) - 1926, 1930
Emerson, Lee E. (VT) - 1950, 1952
Emery, Lewis Jr. (PA) - 1906
Emmerson, Louis L. (IL) - 1928
Endicott, William C. (MA) - 1884
England, Paren (NE) - 1876
Engler, John (MI) - 1990, 1994, 1998
English, James E. (CT) - 1866, 1867, 1868, 1869, 1870, 1871, 1880
Epperson, Benjamin H. (TX) - 1851
Erbe, Norman A. (IA) - 1960, 1962
Erickson, John E. (MT) - 1924, 1928, 1932
Erickson, Leif (MT) - 1944
Ertel, Allen E. (PA) - 1982
Ervin, Charles W. (NY) - 1918
Erwin, James S. (ME) - 1970, 1974
Erwin, S. B. (KY) - 1891

Estee, Morris M. (CA) - 1882, 1894
Etheridge, Emerson (TN) - 1867
Eustis, William (MA) - 1820, 1821, 1822, 1823, 1824
Eustis, William H. (MN) - 1898
Evans, Daniel J. (WA) - 1964, 1968, 1972
Evans, David H. (MN) - 1918
Evans, H. Clay (TN) - 1894, 1906
Evans, John Gary (SC) - 1894
Evans, John V. (ID) - 1978, 1982
Evans, L. D. (TX) - 1853
Evans, Walter (KY) - 1879
Everett, Edward (MA) - 1835, 1836, 1837, 1838, 1839
Everett, William (MA) - 1897
Evers, James Charles (MS) - 1971
Ewing, Robert C. (MO) - 1856
Ewing, Thomas (OH) - 1879
Ewing, W. T. (AL) - 1888
Exon, J. James (NE) - 1970, 1974
Exum, Wyatt P. (NC) - 1892

F

Fairbanks, Erastus (VT) - 1852, 1853, 1860
Fairbanks, Horace (VT) - 1876
Fairchild, Lucius (WI) - 1865, 1867, 1869
Fairchild, Roger (ID) - 1990
Fairchild, Sherman D. (ID) - 1920
Fairfield, John (ME) - 1838, 1839, 1840, 1841, 1842
Fancher, F. B. (ND) - 1898
Fannin, Paul (AZ) - 1958, 1960, 1962
Farmer, Edward G. (MO) - 1960
Farnham, Roswell (VT) - 1880
Farnsworth, Elon (MI) - 1839
Farrar, Frank L. (SD) - 1968, 1970
Farrar, Timothy (NH) - 1806
Farwell, Leonard J. (WI) - 1851
Fasi, Frank F. (HI) - 1982, 1994
Fassett, Jacob Sloat (NY) - 1891
Faubus, Orval E. (AR) - 1954, 1956, 1958, 1960, 1962, 1964
Feinstein, Dianne (CA) - 1990
Felch, Alpheus (MI) - 1845, 1856
Felker, Samuel D. (NH) - 1912
Fellows, J. Q. (LA) - 1864
Fellows, Lynn (SD) - 1944
Fenner, Arthur (RI) - 1790, 1791, 1792, 1793, 1794, 1795, 1796, 1797, 1798, 1799, 1800, 1801, 1802, 1803, 1804, 1805
Fenner, James (RI) - 1807, 1808, 1809, 1810, 1811, 1812, 1824, 1825, 1826, 1827, 1828, 1829, 1830, 1831, 1832, 1843, 1844, 1845
Fenton, Reuben E. (NY) - 1864, 1886
Fenton, William H. (MI) - 1864
Ferency, Zolton A. (MI) - 1966
Ferguson, Benjamin (WI) - 1861
Ferguson, James E. (TX) - 1914, 1916
Ferguson, Jo O. (OK) - 1950
Ferguson, Miriam A. (TX) - 1924, 1932
Ferguson, Phil (OK) - 1958
Fernald, Bert M. (ME) - 1908, 1910
Ferris, Woodbridge N. (MI) - 1904, 1912, 1914, 1920
Ferry, Elisha P. (WA) - 1889
Ferry, William M. (UT) - 1904
Fessenden, Samuel (ME) - 1845, 1846, 1847, 1848
Fieger, Geoffrey (MI) - 1998
Fielder, James F. (NJ) - 1913
Fields, Cleo (LA) - 1995
Fields, John (OK) - 1914, 1922
Fields, William J. (KY) - 1923
Fife, Symington (AZ) - 1990
Fifer, Joseph W. (IL) - 1888, 1892
Fike, Ed (NV) - 1970
Files, A. W. (AR) - 1896
Files, J. R. (IA) - 1922
Fillmore, Millard (NY) - 1844
Finch, Cliff (MS) - 1975
Findlay, James (OH) - 1834
Findlay, William (PA) - 1817, 1820
Fine, John S. (PA) - 1950
Fink, Tom (AK) - 1982
Finkelnburg, Gustavus A. (MO) - 1876
Finney, Joan (KS) - 1990

Fish, Hamilton (NY) - 1848
Fishback, William M. (AR) - 1892
Fisher, E. S. (MS) - 1865
Fisher, Jake (WV) - 1924
Fisher, John S. (PA) - 1926
Fisher, Lee (OH) - 1998
Fisher, Spencer O. (MI) - 1894
Fisk, Clinton B. (NJ) - 1886
Fitzgerald, David (CT) - 1922
Fitzgerald, Frank D. (MI) - 1934, 1936, 1938
Fitzgerald, Jerome D. (IA) - 1978
Fitzgerald, John F. (MA) - 1922
Fitzgerald, William (MI) - 1978
Fitzpatrick, Benjamin (AL) - 1841, 1843
Fizer, N. B. (AR) - 1890
Flaherty, David T. (NC) - 1976
Flaherty, Peter (PA) - 1978
Flanagan, Webster (TX) - 1890
Flanders, Benjamin (LA) - 1864
Flandrau, Charles E. (MN) - 1867
Flegel, Austin F. (OR) - 1950
Fleming, A. Brooks (WV) - 1888
Fleming, Francis P. (FL) - 1888
Fletcher, Allen M. (VT) - 1912
Fletcher, Ryland (VT) - 1856, 1857
Fletcher, Thomas C. (MO) - 1864
Flint, Samuel (NH) - 1870
Florio, James J. (NJ) - 1981, 1989, 1993
Flory, Joseph (MO) - 1900
Flournoy, Houston I. (CA) - 1974
Flournoy, Martin (KY) - 1836
Flournoy, Thomas S. (VA) - 1855, 1863
Flower, Roswell P. (NY) - 1891
Floyd, Charles M. (NH) - 1906
Flynn, Olney R. (OK) - 1946
Flynn, William S. (RI) - 1922
Folger, Charles J. (NY) - 1882
Folk, Joseph Wingate (MO) - 1904
Folmar, Emory (AL) - 1982
Folsom, David S. (MT) - 1900
Folsom, James E. (AL) - 1946, 1954
Folsom, James E. Jr. (AL) - 1994
Fontaine, Charles D. (MS) - 1855
Foot, Samuel A. (CT) - 1834, 1835
Foote, Henry S. (MS) - 1851
Foote, Ralph A. (VT) - 1964
Foraker, Joseph B. (OH) - 1883, 1885, 1887, 1889
Forbes, Malcolm S. (NJ) - 1957
Ford, Nicholas (MO) - 1884
Ford, Peter J. (DE) - 1900
Ford, Samuel C. (MT) - 1940, 1944, 1948
Ford, Seabury (OH) - 1848
Ford, Thomas (IL) - 1842
Ford, Wendell H. (KY) - 1971
Fordice, Kirk (MS) - 1991, 1995
Forgy, Larry E. (KY) - 1995
Forsyth, John (GA) - 1827
Fort, George F. (NJ) - 1850
Fort, John Franklin (NJ) - 1907
Fosheim, Oscar (SD) - 1938
Foss, Eugene N. (MA) - 1910, 1911, 1912
Foss, Joe (SD) - 1954, 1956
Foster, Ephraim H. (TN) - 1845
Foster, Charles (OH) - 1879, 1881
Foster, Henry D. (PA) - 1860
Foster, Lafayette S. (CT) - 1850, 1851
Foster, M. J. "Mike" (LA) - 1995, 1999
Foster, Murphy J. (LA) - 1892, 1896
Foster, Robert C. (TN) - 1815, 1817
Fowle, Daniel G. (NC) - 1888
Fowler (TN) - 1898
Fowler, Absalom (AR) - 1836
Francis, David Rowland (MO) - 1888
Francis, John Brown (RI) - 1833, 1834, 1835, 1836, 1837, 1838
Frank, Melvin P. (ME) - 1896
Frankland, Herman C. (ME) - 1978
Frantz, Frank (OK) - 1907
Franzenburg, Paul (IA) - 1968, 1972
Fratt, Nicholas D. (WI) - 1881, 1884
Frazier, C. N. (TN) - 1942
Frazier, Clifford (NC) - 1932
Frazier, James B. (TN) - 1902, 1904
Frazier, Lynn J. (ND) - 1916, 1918, 1920, 1921
Fredericks, John D. (CA) - 1914

Freehafer, A. L. (ID) - 1924
Freeman, A. A. (TN) - 1872
Freeman, Orville L. (MN) - 1952, 1954, 1956, 1958, 1960
Freeman, Woody (AR) - 1984
French, Augustus C. (IL) - 1846, 1848
French, N. B. (WV) - 1880
French, Richard (KY) - 1840
Frensdorf, Edward (MI) - 1924
Frink, J. M. (WA) - 1900
Frizzell, Kent (KS) - 1970
Frohmiller, Ana (AZ) - 1950
Frohnmayer, Dave (OR) - 1990
Frothingham, Louis A. (MA) - 1911
Fry, Edward J. (MI) - 1944
Fuhr, John D. (CO) - 1982
Fulks, Clay (AR) - 1918
Fuller, Alvan T. (MA) - 1924, 1926
Fuller, Levi K. (VT) - 1892
Fuller, Philo C. (MI) - 1841
Fulton, John A. (NV) - 1938
Fulton, Robert D. (IA) - 1970
Funk, Frank H. (IL) - 1912
Fuqua, Henry L. (LA) - 1924
Furches, David M. (NC) - 1892
Furcolo, Foster (MA) - 1956, 1958
Furnas, Robert W. (NE) - 1872
Furnish, W. J. (OR) - 1902
Futrell, Julius M. (AR) - 1932, 1934

G

Gable, Robert E. (KY) - 1975
Gage, Henry T. (CA) - 1898
Gage, Jack R. (WY) - 1962
Gainer, Joseph H. (RI) - 1926
Gaither, George A. (MD) - 1907
Galbraith, Gatewood (KY) - 1999
Gallagher, Thomas (MN) - 1938
Gallaway, Jim (NV) - 1990
Gallen, Hugh J. (NH) - 1978, 1980, 1982
Gallentine, P. W. (AZ) - 1911
Gallogly, Edward P. (RI) - 1964
Galloway, William (OR) - 1894
Galusha, Jonas (VT) - 1809, 1810, 1811, 1812, 1813, 1814, 1815, 1816, 1817, 1818, 1819
Garber, Silas (NE) - 1874, 1876
Garcelon, Alonzo (ME) - 1878, 1879
Garcia, Felix (NM) - 1918
Gardiner, William Tudor (ME) - 1928, 1930
Gardner, A. B. (VT) - 1872
Gardner, Augustus P. (MA) - 1913
Gardner, Booth (WA) - 1984
Gardner, Frederick Dozier (MO) - 1916
Gardner, Halbert P. (ME) - 1914
Gardner, Henry J. (MA) - 1854, 1855, 1856, 1857
Gardner, J. F. (NE) - 1874, 1876
Gardner, James C. (NC) - 1968
Gardner, Jim (NC) - 1992
Gardner, O. Max (NC) - 1928
Gardner, Obadiah (ME) - 1908
Garfield, James R. (OH) - 1914
Garford, Arthur L. (OH) - 1912
Garland, Augustus H. (AR) - 1874
Garland, R. K. (AR) - 1882
Garrahy, Joseph J. (RI) - 1976, 1978, 1980, 1982
Garrard, James (KY) - 1800
Gartrell, Lucius (GA) - 1882
Garvey, Dan E. (AZ) - 1948
Garvey, Edward R. (WI) - 1998
Garvin, Lucius F. C. (RI) - 1901, 1902, 1903, 1904, 1905
Gary, Raymond (OK) - 1954
Gaston, William (MA) - 1873, 1874, 1875, 1877
Gaston, William A. (MA) - 1902, 1903, 1926
Gates, Charles W. (VT) - 1914
Gates, Ralph F. (IN) - 1944
Gavin, Robert L. (NC) - 1960, 1964
Gay, George E. (FL) - 1920
Gayle, John (AL) - 1831, 1833
Gaylord, Winfield R. (WI) - 1906
Gear, John Henry (IA) - 1877, 1879
Geary, John W . (CA) - 1849
Geary, John White (PA) - 1866, 1869

Geer, Theodore Thurston (OR) - 1898
Gegax, Henry F. (NV) - 1910
Gellatly, John A. (WA) - 1932
Gengras, E. Clayton (CT) - 1966
Gentry, Meredith P. (TN) - 1855
Gentry, William (MO) - 1874
George, Hyland P. (DE) - 1948
Geringer, Jim (WY) - 1994, 1998
Gerry, Elbridge (MA) - 1788, 1800, 1801, 1802, 1803, 1810, 1811, 1812
Gibbons, Charles (MA) - 1958
Gibbons, Jim (NV) - 1994
Gibbs, Addison C. (OR) - 1862
Gibbs, Barnett (TX) - 1898
Gibbs, William C. (RI) - 1821, 1822, 1823
Gibson, Ernest W. (VT) - 1946, 1948
Gibson, Lorenzo (AR) - 1844
Gidley, Townsend E. (MI) - 1851
Gilchrist, Albert W. (FL) - 1908
Gill, Moses (MA) - 1797, 1800
Gillaspie, George (IA) - 1869
Gillett, James N. (CA) - 1906
Gillette, Francis (CT) - 1853
Gillette, Lester S. (IA) - 1950
Gilligan, John J. (OH) - 1970, 1974
Gilman, Benjamin (OH) - 1803
Gilman, John T. (NH) - 1793, 1794, 1795, 1796, 1797, 1798, 1799, 1800, 1801, 1802, 1803, 1804, 1805, 1806, 1808, 1812, 1813, 1814, 1815
Gilmer, George R. (GA) - 1829, 1831, 1837
Gilmer, John A. (NC) - 1856
Gilmore, James S. (VA) - 1997
Gilmore, Joseph A. (NH) - 1863, 1864
Glade, Earl J. (UT) - 1952
Glasscock, William E. (WV) - 1908
Glendening, Parris N. (MD) - 1994, 1998
Glenn, Hugh J. (CA) - 1879
Glenn, Robert B. (NC) - 1904
Glick, George W. (KS) - 1868, 1882, 1884
Glynn, Martin H. (NY) - 1914
Goddard, Sam (AZ) - 1962, 1964, 1966, 1968
Goddard, Terry (AZ) - 1990
Godwin, Mills E. Jr. (VA) - 1965, 1973
Goebel, William (KY) - 1899
Goff, Nathan (WV) - 1876, 1888
Goggin, William L. (VA) - 1859
Goldberg, Arthur J. (NY) - 1970
Goldsborough, Phillips Lee (MD) - 1911
Goldsborough, William T. (MD) - 1847
Goldschmidt, Neil (OR) - 1986
Goldsmith, Stephen (IN) - 1996
Golisano, Tom (NY) - 1998
Goodell, David H. (NH) - 1888
Goodenow, Daniel (ME) - 1831, 1832, 1833
Goodin, John R. (KS) - 1878
Gooding, Frank R. (ID) - 1904, 1906
Goodland, Walter S. (WI) - 1944, 1946
Goodnow, Windsor H. (NH) - 1922
Goodover, Pat M. (MT) - 1984
Goodrich, James P. (IN) - 1916
Goodwin, Charles A. (CT) - 1910
Goodwin, Frank A. (MA) - 1934
Goodwin, Ichabod (NH) - 1859, 1860
Goodwyn, Albert T. (AL) - 1896
Gordon, George W. (MA) - 1856
Gordon, John B. (GA) - 1868, 1886, 1888
Gordy, William J. (DE) - 1980
Gore, Christopher (MA) - 1808, 1809, 1810, 1811
Gore, Howard M. (WV) - 1924
Gore, Louise (MD) - 1974
Gorman, Arthur Pue (MD) - 1911
Gossett, Charles C. (ID) - 1944
Goudy, Frank C. (CO) - 1900
Gould, Samuel W. (ME) - 1902
Gould, Vick (WA) - 1972
Grabiel, John W. (AR) - 1922, 1924
Gragson, Oran K. (NV) - 1962
Graham, Bob (FL) - 1978, 1982
Graham, Horace F. (VT) - 1916
Graham, William A. (NC) - 1844, 1846
Granai, Edwin C. (VT) - 1978
Granberry, Jim (TX) - 1974
Grandmaison, J. Joseph (NH) - 1990
Granger, Francis (NY) - 1830, 1832

Grant, Earle S. (ME) - 1950
Grant, James B. (CO) - 1882
Grantham, Everett (NM) - 1952
Grasso, Ella T. (CT) - 1974, 1978
Graves, Bibb (AL) - 1926, 1934
Graves, Bill (KS) - 1994, 1998
Graves, Richard Perrin (CA) - 1954
Gray, C. A. (TX) - 1906
Gray, Isaac P. (IN) - 1884
Gray, James (MN) - 1910
Grayson, Beverly R. (MS) - 1827
Grayson, William (MD) - 1838
Greaves, Charles D. (AR) - 1902
Green, Charles B. (MS) - 1821
Green, Dwight H. (IL) - 1940, 1944, 1948
Green, Fred W. (MI) - 1926, 1928
Green, Jesse (DE) - 1820
Green, John T. (SC) - 1874
Green, Robert S. (NJ) - 1886
Green, Theodore Francis (RI) - 1912, 1930, 1932, 1934
Green, Warren E. (SD) - 1930, 1932
Greene, George W. (RI) - 1899
Greene, Howard T. (WI) - 1934
Greene, James L. (CT) - 1875
Greene, William (RI) - 1778, 1779, 1780, 1781, 1782, 1783, 1784, 1785, 1802
Greenhalge, Frederic T. (MA) - 1893, 1894, 1895
Greenup, Christopher (KY) - 1800, 1804
Greer, John A. (TX) - 1851
Gregg, Andrew (PA) - 1823
Gregg, Hugh (NH) - 1952, 1966
Gregg, S. (AR) - 1886
Gregory, William (RI) - 1900, 1901
Grevemberg, F. C. (LA) - 1960
Griffen, Horace B. (AZ) - 1956
Griffin, S. Marvin (GA) - 1954
Griffith, Benjamin (CO) - 1922
Griffith, Leon (AR) - 1976
Griggs, John W. (NJ) - 1895
Grim, Webster (PA) - 1910
Grimball, John A. (MS) - 1837
Grimes, James W. (IA) - 1854
Grissom, Gilliam (NC) - 1936
Griswold, Dwight (NE) - 1932, 1934, 1936, 1940, 1942, 1944
Griswold, John A. (NY) - 1868
Griswold, Matthew (CT) - 1781, 1784, 1785
Griswold, Morley (NV) - 1934
Griswold, Roger (CT) - 1810, 1811, 1812
Groark, Eunice Strong (CT) - 1994
Groesbeck, Alexander J. (MI) - 1920, 1922, 1924
Groome, John C. (MD) - 1857
Gropper, John L. (VT) - 1996
Gross, Harold J. (RI) - 1922
Grout, Josiah (VT) - 1896
Grover, Hank C. (TX) - 1972
Grover, LaFayette F. (OR) - 1870, 1874
Grubb, Edward B. (NJ) - 1889
Gubbrud, Archie M. (SD) - 1960, 1962
Guild, Curtis Jr. (MA) - 1905, 1906, 1907
Guinn, Kenny (NV) - 1998
Gunby, Edward R. (FL) - 1896
Gunderson, Carl (SD) - 1924, 1926
Gunderson, Carroll G. (NM) - 1944
Gunter, Julius C. (CO) - 1916
Gurham, George C. (CA) - 1867
Gurney, Chester (MI) - 1847
Guthrie, William A. (NC) - 1896
Guy, William L. (ND) - 1960, 1962, 1964, 1968

H

Hackel, Stella B. (VT) - 1976
Hackett, Luther F. (VT) - 1972
Hadley, Herbert Spencer (MO) - 1908
Haeder, Richard (SD) - 1946
Hafer, Barbara (PA) - 1990
Hagan, John N. (ND) - 1938
Hageman, Fred P. (IA) - 1930
Hagen, Oscar W. (ND) - 1942
Hager, Samuel W. (KY) - 1907
Hagood, Johnson (SC) - 1880
Hahn, Michael (LA) - 1864
Haight, Henry H. (CA) - 1867, 1871

Haight, Raymond L. (CA) - 1934
Haigis, John W. (MA) - 1936
Haile, William (NH) - 1857, 1858
Haile, William H. (MA) - 1892
Haines, Daniel (NJ) - 1847
Haines, H. H. (TX) - 1926
Haines, John M. (ID) - 1912, 1914
Haines, William T. (ME) - 1912, 1914
Halcrow, Don (ND) - 1964
Haldiman, Joe C. (AZ) - 1952
Hale, Samuel W. (NH) - 1882
Hale, William (NH) - 1817, 1818, 1819
Hall, David (DE) - 1798, 1801
Hall, David (OK) - 1970
Hall, Fred (KS) - 1954
Hall, Hiland (VT) - 1858, 1859
Hall, John W. (DE) - 1878
Hall, Luther E. (LA) - 1912
Hall, W. Scott (ID) - 1926
Halsey, George A. (NJ) - 1874
Halsted, Charles L. (MN) - 1948
Halvorson, Halvor L. (ND) - 1924
Hamil, David A. (CO) - 1948
Hamilton, Andrew J. (TX) - 1869
Hamilton, Clark (ID) - 1954
Hamilton, John T. (IA) - 1914
Hamilton, William S. (LA) - 1831
Hamilton, William T. (MD) - 1879
Hamlin, Edward O. (MN) - 1861
Hamlin, Elijah L. (ME) - 1848, 1849
Hamlin, Hannibal (ME) - 1856
Hamman, William H. (TX) - 1878, 1880
Hammersley, Charles E. (WI) - 1930
Hammill, John (IA) - 1924, 1926, 1928
Hammond, Jay S. (AK) - 1974, 1978
Hammond, Winfield S. (MN) - 1914
Hampton, Wade (SC) - 1865, 1876, 1878
Hancock, John (MA) - 1780, 1781, 1782, 1783, 1784, 1786, 1787, 1789, 1790, 1791, 1792, 1793
Handley, Harold W. (IN) - 1956
Hanly, J. Frank (IN) - 1904
Hanna, Louis B. (ND) - 1912, 1914
Hanna, Richard H. (NM) - 1920
Hannay, R. E. (TX) - 1900
Hannett, Arthur T. (NM) - 1924, 1926
Hansen, Clifford P. (WY) - 1962
Hansen, Lewis G. (NJ) - 1946
Hanson, Stewart (UT) - 1992
Hardace, Sam (KS) - 1982
Hardee, Cary A. (FL) - 1920
Hardin, Charles H. (MO) - 1874
Hardin, P. Watt (KY) - 1895
Harding, Warren G. (OH) - 1910
Harding, William L. (IA) - 1916, 1918
Hardman, Lamartine Griffin (GA) - 1926, 1928
Hardwick, Thomas W. (GA) - 1920
Hardy, H. W. (NE) - 1886
Harlan, John M. (KY) - 1875
Harman, Rick (KS) - 1968
Harmon, Judson (OH) - 1908, 1910
Harper, John (KY) - 1987
Harriman, Averell (NY) - 1954, 1958
Harriman, Walter (NH) - 1863, 1867, 1868
Harrington, Edward W. (NH) - 1864, 1865
Harrington, Emerson C. (MD) - 1915
Harris (CT) - 1874
Harris, Andrew L. (OH) - 1908
Harris, C. J. (NC) - 1904
Harris, C. O. (TX) - 1936
Harris, Edward (RI) - 1849, 1850
Harris, Elisha (RI) - 1847, 1848, 1852
Harris, Isham G. (TN) - 1857, 1859, 1861
Harris, J. Morrison (MD) - 1875
Harris, Joe Frank (GA) - 1982, 1986
Harris, Nathaniel E. (GA) - 1914
Harris, Wiley (MS) - 1831
Harris, William A. (KS) - 1906
Harrison, Albertis S. Jr. (VA) - 1961
Harrison, Benjamin (IN) - 1876
Harrison, Carter H. (IL) - 1884
Harrison, Christopher (IN) - 1819
Harrison, Henry B. (CT) - 1874, 1884
Harrison, Hugh (MN) - 1888
Harrison, William H. (OH) - 1820

Harrison, William B. (KY) - 1931
Harshbarger, Scott (MA) - 1998
Hart, Louis F. (WA) - 1920
Hart, Ossian B. (FL) - 1872
Hart, William (CT) - 1804, 1805, 1806, 1807, 1808
Hartigan, Neil F. (IL) - 1990
Hartley, Roland H. (WA) - 1924, 1928, 1936
Hartness, James (VT) - 1920
Hartranft, John Frederick (PA) - 1872, 1875
Harvey, James M. (KS) - 1868, 1870
Harvey, Louis (WI) - 1861
Harvey, Matthew (NH) - 1830
Haskell, A. C. (SC) - 1890
Haskell, C. N. (OK) - 1907
Hastings, Daniel H. (PA) - 1894
Hatch, Francis W. (MA) - 1978
Hatfield, Harry D. (WV) - 1912
Hatfield, Mark O. (OR) - 1958, 1962
Hathaway, Stanley K. (WY) - 1966, 1970
Hatton, Robert (TN) - 1857
Haucke, Frank (KS) - 1930
Haven, Henry P. (CT) - 1873
Hawkins, Alvin (TN) - 1880, 1882
Hawkins, Samuel W. (TN) - 1888
Hawley, James H. (ID) - 1910, 1912
Hawley, Joseph R. (CT) - 1866, 1867
Hay, John W. (WY) - 1922
Hay, M. E. (WA) - 1912
Hayden, Mike (KS) - 1986, 1990
Hayes, Kyle (NC) - 1956
Hayes, Robin (NC) - 1996
Hayes, Rutherford B. (OH) - 1867, 1869, 1875
Hays, George W. (AR) - 1913, 1914
Hayward, M. L. (NE) - 1898
Haywood, Joel (NY) - 1853
Haywood, William D. (CO) - 1906
Hazard, Rowland (RI) - 1875
Hazelbaker, Frank A. (MT) - 1932, 1936
Hazelton, Harry (MT) - 1908
Hazlehurst, Isaac (PA) - 1857
Hazlett, J. C. (NV) - 1874
Hazlett, Joseph (DE) - 1804, 1807, 1810, 1822
Hazzard, Daniel (DE) - 1823
Hazzard, David (DE) - 1826, 1829
Head, Douglas M. (MN) - 1970
Head, Natt (NH) - 1879
Headlee, Richard H. (MI) - 1982
Healey, James (NH) - 1836
Healey, Robert J. Jr. (RI) - 1994, 1998
Healy, Joseph (NH) - 1835
Heard, Dwight B. (AZ) - 1924
Heard, William Wright (LA) - 1900
Hearnes, Betty (MO) - 1988
Hearnes, Warren E. (MO) - 1964, 1968
Hearst, William R. (NY) - 1906
Heath, William (NH) - 1799
Heaton, Homer W. (VT) - 1869, 1870
Hebert, Paul O. (LA) - 1852
Hedges, Job E. (NY) - 1912
Hegge, M. F. (ND) - 1904
Heil, Julius P. (WI) - 1938, 1940, 1942
Heininger, Alfred H. (VT) - 1936
Heitfeld, Henry (ID) - 1904
Heitkamp, Heidi (ND) - 2000
Hellstrom, F. O. (ND) - 1912, 1914
Helm, John Larue (KY) - 1867
Helm, Joseph C. (CO) - 1892
Hemans, Lawton T. (MI) - 1908, 1910
Hemmings, Fred (HI) - 1990
Hemphill, John M. (PA) - 1930
Hempstead, Stephen (IA) - 1850
Henderson, Charles (LA) - 1914
Henderson, John B. (MO) - 1872
Hendricks, Thomas Andrews (IN) - 1860, 1868, 1872
Hendricks, William (IN) - 1822
Hendrickson, Robert C. (NJ) - 1940
Henry, Dwight (TN) - 1990
Henry, Gustavus H. (TN) - 1853
Henry, Howard (ND) - 1948
Henry, Louis D. (NC) - 1842
Herbert, Thomas J. (OH) - 1946, 1948
Herndon, Thomas H. (AL) - 1872
Herreid, Charles N. (SD) - 1900, 1902
Herrick, D. Cady (NY) - 1904

Herrick, Myron T. (OH) - 1903, 1905
Herrick, Thomas F. (RI) - 1899
Herring, Clyde E. (IA) - 1954
Herring, Clyde L. (IA) - 1920, 1932, 1934
Herschler, Ed (WY) - 1974, 1978, 1982
Herseth, R. Lars (SD) - 1986
Herseth, Ralph (SD) - 1956, 1958, 1960, 1962
Hershey, Harry B. (IL) - 1940
Herter, Christian A. (MA) - 1952, 1954
Hess, Henry L. (OR) - 1938
Heyward, Duncan C. (SC) - 1902, 1904
Hichborn, N. G. (ME) - 1869
Hickel, Walter J. (AK) - 1966, 1978, 1990
Hickenlooper, Bourke B. (IA) - 1942
Hickey, John J. (WY) - 1958
Hicks, L. C. (WA) - 1932
Hicks, Thomas Holliday (MD) - 1857
Hiester, Joseph (PA) - 1817, 1820
Higgins, Frank W. (NY) - 1904
Higgins, James H. (RI) - 1906, 1907
Higgins, John C. (DE) - 1896
High, Robert King (FL) - 1966
Hildreth, Horace A. (ME) - 1944, 1946, 1958
Hill, Ben F. (WA) - 1924
Hill, Benjamin H. (GA) - 1857
Hill, Charles I. (NM) - 1922
Hill, David B. (NY) - 1885, 1888, 1894
Hill, Edward Y. (GA) - 1849
Hill, George (NH) - 1884
Hill, Herbert W. (NH) - 1948
Hill, Ira A. (OK) - 1930
Hill, Isaac (NY) - 1836, 1837, 1838
Hill, John (TX) - 1978
Hill, John F. (ME) - 1900, 1902
Hillenbrand, John A. (IN) - 1980
Hills, Glenn R. (IN) - 1940
Hilton, Walter B. (WV) - 1912
Hinds, Thomas (MS) - 1819
Hines, James K. (GA) - 1894, 1902
Hinkle, James F. (NM) - 1922
Hipple, John E. (SD) - 1926
Hisgen, Thomas L. (MA) - 1907
Hoadly, George (OH) - 1883, 1885
Hoan, Daniel W. (WI) - 1944, 1946
Hoard, William D. (WI) - 1888, 1890
Hobart, Harrison C. (WI) - 1859, 1865
Hobbs, Horace E. (RI) - 1966
Hobby, William P. (TX) - 1918
Hoch, Edward W. (KS) - 1904, 1906
Hocker, Lon (MO) - 1956
Hodge, Robert T. (WA) - 1912
Hodges, George H. (KS) - 1910, 1912, 1914
Hodges, James H. (SC) - 1998
Hodges, Luther H. (NC) - 1956
Hodgson, L. C. (MN) - 1920
Hoegh, Leo A. (IA) - 1954, 1956
Hoeven, John (ND) - 2000
Hoey, Clyde R. (NC) - 1936
Hoff, Phillip H. (VT) - 1962, 1964, 1966
Hoffecker, James R. (DE) - 1886
Hoffecker, John H. (DE) - 1896
Hoffman, Harold G. (NJ) - 1934
Hoffman, John T. (NY) - 1866, 1868, 1870
Hogan, Dan (AR) - 1910, 1914
Hogan, J. R. (GA) - 1898
Hogan, Mark (CO) - 1970
Hogan, Thomas S. (MT) - 1900
Hoge, J. Hampton (VA) - 1901
Hoge, S. Harris (VA) - 1925
Hogg, James S. (TX) - 1890, 1892
Hoit, Daniel (NH) - 1843, 1844
Hoke, Michael (NC) - 1844
Holbrook, Frederick (VT) - 1861, 1862
Holcomb, Marcus H. (CT) - 1914, 1916, 1918
Holcomb, Silas A. (NE) - 1894, 1896
Holden, Bob (MO) - 2000
Holden, William W. (NC) - 1864, 1865, 1868
Holland, Spessard L. (FL) - 1940
Holley, Alexander H. (CT) - 1857
Holley, Charles R. (FL) - 1964
Holliday, Frederick W. M. (VA) - 1877
Holliday, William H. (WY) - 1894
Hollings, Ernest F. (SC) - 1958
Hollis, Henry F. (NH) - 1902, 1904

Holloway, Frederick M. (MI) - 1880
Holmes (ND) - 1898
Holmes, D. M. (ND) - 1926
Holmes, David (MS) - 1817, 1825
Holmes, Ezekiel (ME) - 1853
Holmes, Robert D. (OR) - 1956, 1958
Holmes, W. H. (TX) - 1928
Holshouser, James E. Jr. (NC) - 1972
Holt, Fred W. (OK) - 1914
Holt, Homer A. (WV) - 1936
Holt, John H. (WV) - 1900
Holt, Rush D. (WV) - 1952
Holton, Edward D. (WI) - 1853
Holton, Hart B. (MD) - 1883
Holton, Linwood (VA) - 1965, 1969
Hooker, John J. (TN) - 1970, 1998
Hooper, Ben W. (TN) - 1910, 1912, 1914
Hopkins, Arthur F. (AL) - 1839
Hopkins, Edward (FL) - 1860
Hopkins, G. C. (TX) - 1940
Hopkins, Larry J. (KY) - 1991
Hopkins, Raleigh (TN) - 1928
Hoppin, William W. (RI) - 1853, 1854, 1855, 1856
Hoppner, Bill (NE) - 1998
Horner, Henry (IL) - 1932, 1936
Horton, Henry H. (TN) - 1928, 1930
Hough, John S. (CO) - 1880
Housel, L. W. (IA) - 1928
Houston, George S. (AL) - 1874, 1876
Houston, James Ray (NV) - 1974
Houston, Sam (TX) - 1857, 1859
Houston, Samuel (TN) - 1827
Houx, Frank L. (WY) - 1918
Hovey, Alvin P. (IN) - 1888
Howard, Albert C. (RI) - 1876, 1880
Howard, Benjamin C. (MD) - 1861
Howard, Dean (VT) - 1992
Howard, Henry (RI) - 1873, 1874
Howard, Joseph (ME) - 1864, 1865
Howard, Tilghman, A. (IN) - 1840
Howe, Harland B. (VT) - 1912, 1914
Howe, Isaac (SD) - 1894
Howell, Henry (VA) - 1973, 1977
Howell, R. B. (NE) - 1914
Howes, W. W. (SD) - 1920
Howey, Benjamin F. (NJ) - 1886
Howey, W. J. (FL) - 1928, 1932
Hoyt, Daniel (NH) - 1842, 1845
Hoyt, Henry Martyn (PA) - 1878
Hubbard, Henry (NH) - 1842, 1843
Hubbard, John (ME) - 1849, 1850, 1852
Hubbard, Lucius F. (MN) - 1881, 1883
Hubbard, Richard D. (CT) - 1872, 1876, 1878
Hubbard, Samuel (MA) - 1826
Hubbert, Paul (AL) - 1990
Huber, Sherry E. (ME) - 1986
Huckabee, Mike (AR) - 1998
Hughes, Bela M. (CO) - 1876
Hughes, Charles E. (NY) - 1906, 1908
Hughes, Harold E. (IA) - 1962, 1964, 1966
Hughes, Harry (MD) - 1978, 1982
Hughes, James H. (DE) - 1916
Hughes, Richard J. (NJ) - 1961, 1965
Hughes, Robert W. (VA) - 1873
Hughes, Simon P. (AR) - 1884, 1886
Hull, Jane Dee (AZ) - 1998
Hultman, Evan (IA) - 1964
Humes, Albert H. (RI) - 1912
Humphrey, Gordon (NH) - 2000
Humphrey, Hubert H. III (MN) - 1998
Humphrey, Lyman U. (KS) - 1888, 1890
Humphreys, Benjamin G. (MS) - 1865, 1868
Humphries, West H. (TN) - 1835
Hunhoff, Bernie (SD) - 1998
Hunn, John (DE) - 1900
Hunt, Frank W. (ID) - 1900, 1902
Hunt, George W. P. (AZ) - 1911, 1914, 1916, 1922, 1924, 1926, 1928, 1930
Hunt, Guy (AL) - 1978, 1986, 1990
Hunt, Guy (GA) - 1986
Hunt, James B. Jr. (NC) - 1976, 1980, 1992, 1996
Hunt, Lester C. (WY) - 1942, 1946
Hunt, Washington (NY) - 1850, 1852
Hunter, Robert (CT) - 1910

Huntington, Samuel (CT) - 1781, 1783, 1784, 1785, 1787, 1788, 1789, 1790, 1791, 1792, 1793, 1794, 1795
Huntington, Samuel (OH) - 1808
Huntley, Robert C. (ID) - 1998
Hunton, Jonathan G. (ME) - 1829, 1830
Hurley, Charles F. (MA) - 1936
Hurley, Robert A. (CT) - 1940, 1942, 1944
Hurst, John E. (MD) - 1895
Hutchins, John C. (NH) - 1916
Hutchinson, Joseph (IA) - 1889
Hutchinson, Titus (VT) - 1841
Huxman, Walter A. (KS) - 1936, 1938
Hyde, Arthur Mastick (MO) - 1920
Hynson, George B. (DE) - 1912

I

Indrehus, Edward (MN) - 1922
Ingalls, David S. (OH) - 1932
Ingersoll, Charles R. (CT) - 1873, 1874, 1875, 1876
Ingersoll, E. P. (NE) - 1882
Ingersoll, Jonathan (CT) - 1796
Ingham, Samuel (CT) - 1854, 1855, 1856, 1857
Inhofe, James M. (OK) - 1974
Ireland, John (TX) - 1882, 1884
Irick, John B. (NM) - 1982
Irish, John P. (IA) - 1877
Irwin, James (PA) - 1847
Irwin, William (CA) - 1875
Irwin, William W. (OH) - 1822
Isakson, Johnny (GA) - 1990
Itkin, Ivan (PA) - 1998
Iverson, Sherman A. (SD) - 1952
Ives, Irving M. (NY) - 1954
Ivinson, Edward (WY) - 1892

J

Jack, William (WY) - 1954
Jackson, Charles (RI) - 1845, 1846
Jackson, Claiborne Fox (MO) - 1860
Jackson, Ed (IN) - 1924
Jackson, Elihu E. (MD) - 1887
Jackson, Frank D. (IA) - 1893
Jackson, Frederick H. (RI) - 1907
Jackson, Hancock (MO) - 1860
Jackson, J. Henry (VT) - 1896
Jackson, J. Holmes (VT) - 1922
Jackson, Jacob B. (WV) - 1880
Jackson, Richard Jr. (RI) - 1806
Jackson, Samuel D. (IN) - 1944
Jacob, John J. (WV) - 1870, 1872
Jacobs, William A. (WI) - 1910
Jacobson, Jacob F. (MN) - 1908
Jacobson, Judy (MT) - 1996
Jacques, Alfred (MN) - 1926
James, Arthur H. (PA) - 1938
James, Forrest H. "Fob" Jr. (AL) - 1978, 1994, 1998
Jameson, Charles D. (ME) - 1861, 1862
Jameson, Nathan C. (NH) - 1906
Janklow, William J. (SD) - 1978, 1982, 1994, 1998
Jarvis, Thomas J. (NC) - 1880
Jarvis, William C. (MA) - 1827
Jay, John (NY) - 1792, 1795, 1798
Jefferson, Samuel L. (DE) - 1862
Jefferson, Warren (DE) - 1840
Jefferson, William J. (LA) - 1999
Jelks, William D. (AL) - 1902
Jenkins, Charles (GA) - 1853, 1865
Jenkins, James G. (WI) - 1879
Jenks, George A. (PA) - 1898
Jennings, Jonathan (IN) - 1816, 1819
Jennings, William S. (FL) - 1900
Jennison, Silas H. (VT) - 1836, 1837, 1838, 1839, 1840
Jensen, Leslie (SD) - 1936
Jepson, Melvin E. (NV) - 1946
Jerome, David H. (MI) - 1880, 1882
Jester, Beauford H. (TX) - 1946, 1948
Jewell, Marshall (CT) - 1868, 1869, 1870, 1871, 1872
Jewett, Hugh J. (OH) - 1861
Johanns, Mike (NE) - 1998

Johnson, Andrew (TN) - 1853, 1855
Johnson, C. A. (ND) - 1908, 1910
Johnson, C. W. (TX) - 1912
Johnson, Charles F. (ME) - 1892, 1894
Johnson, Edwin C. (CO) - 1932, 1934, 1954
Johnson, Edwin S. (SD) - 1912
Johnson, Gary E. (NM) - 1994, 1998
Johnson, George W. (AR) - 1958
Johnson, Henry (LA) - 1824, 1842
Johnson, Hershel Vespasian (GA) - 1853, 1855
Johnson, Hiram W. (CA) - 1910, 1914
Johnson, Isaac (LA) - 1846
Johnson, J. Neeley (CA) - 1855
Johnson, James (AR) - 1966
Johnson, John A. (MN) - 1904, 1906, 1908
Johnson, John W. (MN) - 1974
Johnson, Joseph (VA) - 1851
Johnson, Joseph B. (VT) - 1954, 1956
Johnson, Keen (KY) - 1939
Johnson, Magnus (MN) - 1922, 1926
Johnson, Middletown T. (TX) - 1851
Johnson, Ole S. (ND) - 1952
Johnson, Paul (AZ) - 1998
Johnson, Paul B. (MS) - 1939, 1963
Johnson, Richard H. (AR) - 1860
Johnson, Richard W. (MN) - 1881
Johnson, Thomas (TN) - 1815
Johnson, Tom L. (OH) - 1903
Johnson, Walter (VA) - 1949
Johnson, Walter W. (CO) - 1950
Johnson, William C. (MD) - 1841
Johnston, Henry S. (OK) - 1926
Johnston, Joseph F. (AL) - 1896, 1898
Johnston, Olin D. (SC) - 1934, 1942
Johnston, William (OH) - 1850
Johnston, William F. (PA) - 1849, 1851
Johnston, William J. (NC) - 1862
Jones, Brereton C. (KY) - 1991
Jones, Buell F. (SD) - 1928
Jones, Charles Alvin (PA) - 1938
Jones, Daniel Webster (AR) - 1896, 1898
Jones, Dick (WY) - 1974
Jones, Frank (NY) - 1880
Jones, George W. (TX) - 1882, 1884
Jones, James C. (TN) - 1841, 1843
Jones, Jan Laverty (NV) - 1998
Jones, John E. (NV) - 1894
Jones, Norman L. (IL) - 1924
Jones, Robert T. (AZ) - 1938
Jones, Sam H. (LA) - 1940
Jones, Samuel M. (OH) - 1899
Jones, Thomas G. (AL) - 1890, 1892
Jones, William (RI) - 1811, 1812, 1813, 1814, 1815, 1816, 1817
Jordan, Chester B. (NH) - 1900
Jordan, Len B. (ID) - 1950
Jordan, Robert B. III (NC) - 1988
Joseph, J. M. (IA) - 1893
Judd, Gregg (NH) - 1988, 1990
Judge, Thomas L. (MT) - 1972, 1976, 1988
Jullien, Paul J. (ME) - 1944
Jump, Isaac (DE) - 1874
Jungert, Philip W. (ID) - 1966
Junkins, Lowell L. (IA) - 1986

K

Kaldor, Lee (ND) - 1996
Kanouse, Theodore D. (WI) - 1881
Karel, John C. (WI) - 1912, 1914
Kariotis, George (MA) - 1986
Karpan, Kathy (WY) - 1994
Katterfeld, L. E. (WA) - 1916
Katzenbach, Frank (NJ) - 1907
Kavanaugh, Edward (ME) - 1843
Kay, Morris (KS) - 1972
Kean, John Jr. (NJ) - 1892
Kean, Thomas H. (NJ) - 1981, 1985
Kearby, Jerome C. (TX) - 1896
Keating, Frank (OK) - 1994, 1998
Keefe, F. Clyde (NH) - 1940, 1946
Keister, Stephen A. D. (WY) - 1906
Kelley, David (VT) - 1906
Kelley, Thomas F. (ID) - 1906
Kellogg, Daniel (VT) - 1843, 1844, 1845
Kellogg, William Pitt (LA) - 1872
Kelly, David C. (TN) - 1890

Marks, Albert S. (TN) - 1878
Marland, Ernest W. (OK) - 1934
Marland, William C. (WV) - 1952
Marmaduke, John Sappington (MO) - 1884
Marshall, Joseph G. (IN) - 1846
Marshall, Thomas R. (IN) - 1908
Marshall, William R. (MN) - 1865, 1867
Martin, Burleigh (ME) - 1932
Martin, Charles H. (OR) - 1934
Martin, Clarence D. (WA) - 1932, 1936
Martin, Ed C. (SD) - 1954
Martin, Edward (PA) - 1942
Martin, Fred C. (VT) - 1920, 1924, 1938
Martin, G. H. (ID) - 1912
Martin, J. (FL) - 1924
Martin, James (AL) - 1966
Martin, James G. (NC) - 1984, 1988
Martin, John (KS) - 1876, 1888
Martin, John A. (KS) - 1884, 1886
Martin, John W. (FL) - 1924
Martin, John W. (SD) - 1902
Martin, Joshua L. (AL) - 1845
Martin, Marion (TX) - 1888
Martin, Nathaniel E. (NH) - 1918
Martin, Noah (NH) - 1852, 1853
Martin, Peppy (KY) - 1999
Martin, Wheeler (RI) - 1824
Martineau, John E. (AR) - 1926
Martinez, Bob (FL) - 1986, 1990
Marty, John (MN) - 1994
Martz, Judy (MT) - 2000
Marvel, Joshua H. (DE) - 1894
Marvel, Josiah Jr. (DE) - 1940
Marvel, Richard D. (NE) - 1974
Mason, Charles (IA) - 1867
Mason, Jeremiah (NH) - 1817, 1818
Mason, Samuel R. (PA) - 1878
Mason, Stevens T. (MI) - 1835, 1837
Massie, Nathanael (OH) - 1807
Matheson, Scott M. (UT) - 1976, 1980
Mathews, Henry M. (WV) - 1876
Matson, Courtland C. (IN) - 1888
Matson, John A. (IN) - 1849
Matteson, Joel A. (IL) - 1852
Matthews, Claude (IN) - 1892
Matthews, Joseph W. (MS) - 1847
Mattocks, John (VT) - 1843
Maupin, Joseph H. (CO) - 1892
Mauro, Gary (TX) - 1998
Maw, Herbert B. (UT) - 1940, 1944, 1948
Maxwell, Edwin (WV) - 1884
May, Reuben (WI) - 1879
Maybank, Burnet R. (SC) - 1938
Maybury, William C. (MI) - 1900
Mayer, Edwin S. (TX) - 1958
Maynard, Horace (TN) - 1874
Mayo, William B. (VT) - 1916, 1918
Mazullo, Vincent (RI) - 1982
McAlister, Hill (TN) - 1932, 1934
McAllister, Matthew (GA) - 1845
McArthur, D. H. (ND) - 1916
McArthur, Duncan (OH) - 1830
McBride, Henry (WA) - 1916
McCafferty, Matthew J. (MA) - 1884
McCall, John E. (TN) - 1900, 1932
McCall, Richard K. (FL) - 1845
McCall, Samuel W. (MA) - 1914, 1915, 1916, 1917
McCall, Tom (OR) - 1966, 1970
McCarney, Robert P. (ND) - 1968
McCarter, J. W. (SD) - 1914
McCarty, Daniel T. (FL) - 1952
McCarty, Nicholas (IN) - 1852
McCary, Elvin (AL) - 1974
McCaull, Patrick H. (VA) - 1897
McClaughry, John (VT) - 1992
McClellan, George B. (NJ) - 1878
McClelland, Robert (MI) - 1851, 1852
McClung, James W. (AL) - 1841
McClure, P. F. (SD) - 1889
McClurg, Joseph W. (MO) - 1868, 1870
McColl, J. H. (NE) - 1896
McConaughy, James L. (CT) - 1946
McConnell, J. H. Tyler (DE) - 1956
McConnell, John R. (CA) - 1861
McConnell, William J. (ID) - 1892, 1894

McCook, George W. (OH) - 1871
McCord, James N. (TN) - 1944, 1946, 1958
McCormack, Edward J. (MA) - 1966
McCormick, Vance C. (PA) - 1914
McCoy (WI) - 1920
McCrae, Duncan K. (NC) - 1858
McCray, Warren T. (IN) - 1920
McCreary, James B. (KY) - 1875, 1911
McCulloch, Carleton B. (IN) - 1920, 1924
McCullough, D. A. (SD) - 1930
McCullough, J. B. (NV) - 1898
McCullough, John G. (VT) - 1902
McCutchins, Luther (NH) - 1874
McDaniel, Henry D. (GA) - 1883, 1884
McDaniel, Larry (MO) - 1940
McDermott, James A. (WA) - 1980
McDonald, Charles James (GA) - 1839, 1841, 1851
McDonald, Jesse F. (CO) - 1908
McDonald, Joseph E. (IN) - 1864
McDonald, William C. (NM) - 1911
McDowell, J. L. (KS) - 1866
McEachern, Paul (NH) - 1986, 1988
McElroy, Hugh E. (ID) - 1914
McEnery, John (LA) - 1872
McEnery, Samuel D. (LA) - 1884, 1892
McEniry, Hugh (AL) - 1942
McFarland, Ernest W. (AZ) - 1954, 1956
McGettrick, Felix W. (VT) - 1902
McGill, Alexander T. (NJ) - 1895
McGill, Andrew R. (MN) - 1886
McGonigle, Arthur T. (PA) - 1958
McGovern (WI) - 1940
McGovern, Francis E. (WI) - 1910, 1912
McGrath, J. Howard (RI) - 1940, 1942, 1944
McGrath, John (VT) - 1940
McGraw, John H. (WA) - 1892
McGreevey, James (NJ) - 1997
McGregor, T. H. (TX) - 1920
McIntire, Albert W. (CO) - 1894
McIntire, Bertrand G. (ME) - 1918, 1920
McIntosh, David M. (IN) - 2000
McIntyre, John J. (WY) - 1950
McKay, Douglas (OR) - 1948, 1950
McKean, Frank (NH) - 1878
McKean, Thomas (PA) - 1799, 1802, 1805
McKeever, Horace G. (OK) - 1918
McKeithen, John J. (LA) - 1964, 1968
McKeldin, Theodore R. (MD) - 1942, 1946, 1950, 1954
McKellips, Roger (SD) - 1978
McKelvie, Samuel R. (NE) - 1918, 1920
McKernan, John R. Jr. (ME) - 1986, 1990
McKinley, John C. (MO) - 1912
McKinley, William Jr. (OH) - 1891, 1893
McKinney, Luther F. (NH) - 1892
McKinney, Philip W. (VA) - 1889
McKnight, Thomas (IA) - 1846
McLane, J. (SC) - 1882
McLane, John (NH) - 1904
McLane, Malcolm (NH) - 1972
McLane, Robert M. (MD) - 1883
McLaughlin, Robert H. (IL) - 1834
McLaurin, Anselm J. (MS) - 1895
McLean, Angus Wilton (NC) - 1924
McLean, Ernest L. (ME) - 1926
McLean, George P. (CT) - 1900
McLean, John R. (OH) - 1899
McLeod, Thomas G. (SC) - 1922, 1924
McLevy, Jasper (CT) - 1934, 1936, 1938, 1942
McManus, E. J. (IA) - 1960
McManus, James O. (RI) - 1942
McMaster, William H. (SD) - 1920, 1922
McMath, Sidney S. (AR) - 1948, 1950
McMillan, William (NV) - 1898
McMillin, Benton (TN) - 1898, 1900, 1912
McMinn, Joseph (TN) - 1815, 1817, 1819
McMinn, T. J. (TX) - 1900
McMullen, Adam (NE) - 1924, 1926
McMullen, Richard C. (DE) - 1936
McMurray, John (ID) - 1930
McNair, Alexander (MO) - 1820
McNair, Robert E. (SC) - 1966
McNeal, J. W. (OK) - 1910
McNeill, Robert H. (NC) - 1948

McNichols, Stephen L. R. (CO) - 1956, 1958, 1962
McNutt, Alexander G. (MS) - 1837, 1839
McNutt, Paul V. (IN) - 1932
McRae, Duncan K. (NC) - 1858
McRae, John J. (MS) - 1853, 1855
McRae, Thomas C. (AR) - 1920, 1922
McShane, J. A. (NE) - 1888
McSparran, John A. (PA) - 1922
McSweeney, John (OH) - 1942
McSweeney, Miles B. (SC) - 1900
McWane, Fred W. (VA) - 1933
McWherter, Ned R. (TN) - 1986, 1990
McWillie, William (MS) - 1857
Mead, Albert E. (WA) - 1904
Mead, Cowles (MS) - 1825
Mead, James M. (NY) - 1946
Mead, John A. (VT) - 1910
Mead, Mary (WY) - 1990
Meadows, Clarence W. (WV) - 1944
Meares, Iredell (NC) - 1912
Mecham, Evan (AZ) - 1978, 1986
Mechem, Edwin L. (NM) - 1950, 1952, 1956, 1958, 1960, 1962
Mechem, Merritt C. (NM) - 1920
Medary, Samuel (KS) - 1859
Medill, William (OH) - 1853, 1855
Meech, Ezra (VT) - 1830, 1831, 1832, 1833
Meekins, I. M. (NC) - 1924
Meier, Julius L. (OR) - 1930
Meigs, Return J. Jr. (OH) - 1807, 1810, 1812
Meitzen, E. R. (TX) - 1914, 1916
Melich, Mitchell (UT) - 1964
Mellette, Arthur C. (SD) - 1889, 1890
Menario, John E. (ME) - 1986
Meredith, E. T. (IA) - 1916
Merriam, Frank F. (CA) - 1934, 1938
Merriam, William R. (MN) - 1888, 1890
Merrill, Samuel (IA) - 1867, 1869
Merrill, Steve (NH) - 1992, 1994
Merrimon, Augustus S. (NC) - 1872
Merritt, William H. (IA) - 1861
Merwin, Samuel E. (CT) - 1890, 1892
Meskill, Thomas J. (CT) - 1970
Messer, Asa (RI) - 1830
Metcalf (RI) - 1893
Metcalf, Ralph (NH) - 1855, 1856
Metcalfe, Frank B. (WI) - 1932
Metcalfe, Ray (AK) - 1998
Metcalfe, Thomas (KY) - 1828
Metschan, Phil (OR) - 1930
Metzger, Frazer (VT) - 1912
Metzger, John W. (CO) - 1952
Meyer, William H. (CO) - 1886
Meyers, Harry H. (AR) - 1902, 1913
Meyner, Robert B. (NJ) - 1953, 1957, 1969
Mickelson, George S. (SD) - 1986, 1990
Mickelson, George T. (SD) - 1946, 1948
Mickey, John H. (NE) - 1902, 1904
Miera, Maurice (NM) - 1940
Mifflin, Thomas (PA) - 1790, 1793, 1796
Mikel, G. E. (AR) - 1912
Mildren, Jack (OK) - 1994
Miles, Frank (IA) - 1946
Miles, John E. (NM) - 1938, 1940, 1950
Miller, Alex R. (IA) - 1926
Miller, B. M. (AL) - 1930
Miller, Bob J. (NV) - 1990, 1994
Miller, Charles R. (DE) - 1912
Miller, Jaffa (NM) - 1934, 1936
Miller, James B. (TX) - 1847
Miller, John (MO) - 1825, 1828
Miller, John (ND) - 1889
Miller, John F. (OR) - 1862
Miller, John H. (NV) - 1922
Miller, Keith H. (AK) - 1970
Miller, Leslie A. (WY) - 1930, 1932, 1934, 1938
Miller, Nathan L. (NY) - 1920, 1922
Miller, Stephen (MN) - 1863
Miller, Vern (KS) - 1974
Miller, Warner (NY) - 1888
Miller, William R. (AR) - 1876, 1878
Miller, Zell (GA) - 1990, 1994
Milliken, Carl E. (ME) - 1916, 1918
Milliken, William G. (MI) - 1970, 1974, 1978

Millner, Guy (GA) - 1994, 1998
Mills, A. L. (TN) - 1894
Mills, John T. (TX) - 1849
Mills, Ogden L. (NY) - 1926
Mills, W. T. (AR) - 1946
Milton, John (FL) - 1860
Minner, Ruth Ann (DE) - 2000
Minor, William T. (CT) - 1855, 1856
Mitchell, Albert K. (NM) - 1938
Mitchell, D. P. (KS) - 1878
Mitchell, George (DE) - 1792
Mitchell, George J. (ME) - 1974
Mitchell, Henry L. (FL) - 1892
Mitchell, Hugh B. (WA) - 1952
Mitchell, James F. (NV) - 1906
Mitchell, James P. (NJ) - 1961
Mitchell, Nathanael (DE) - 1801, 1804
Mitchell, R. F. (IA) - 1944
Mitchell, Roy (AR) - 1956
Mitchell, Theo (SC) - 1990
Mobley, Al (OR) - 1990
Moehlenpah, Henry A. (WI) - 1918
Moeur, Benjamin B. (AZ) - 1932, 1934
Moffett, Charles (TN) - 1966
Molleston, Henry (DE) - 1819
Mollohan, Robert H. (WV) - 1956
Moloney, Thomas W. (VT) - 1898
Molpus, Dick (MS) - 1995
Monaghan, Thomas M. (DE) - 1912
Mondragon, Roberto (NM) - 1994
Montague, Andrew J. (VA) - 1901
Montgomery, Samuel B. (WV) - 1920
Montgomery, Thomas (DE) - 1792
Moodie, Thomas H. (ND) - 1934
Moody, Dan (TX) - 1926, 1928
Moody, Zenas F. (OR) - 1882
Mooney, Thomas J. (MD) - 1986
Moonlight, Thomas (KS) - 1886
Moore, Andrew B. (AL) - 1857, 1859
Moore, Arch A. Jr. (WV) - 1968, 1972, 1980, 1984, 1988
Moore, Arthur Harry (NJ) - 1925, 1931, 1937
Moore, Charles C. (ID) - 1922, 1924
Moore, Dan K. (NC) - 1964
Moore, Gabriel (AL) - 1829
Moore, Harbin H. (IN) - 1828
Moore, James B. (IL) - 1822
Moore, John (MI) - 1868
Moore, Preston J. (OK) - 1966
Moore, Samuel B. (AL) - 1831
Moore, Thomas O. (LA) - 1859
Moran, Edward C. Jr. (ME) - 1928, 1930
Moran, J. Edward (VT) - 1950
Moran, John B. (MA) - 1906
Morehead, Charles S. (KY) - 1855
Morehead, John H. (NE) - 1912, 1914, 1920
Morehead, John M. (NC) - 1840, 1842
Morgan, Daniel A. (CT) - 1898
Morgan, David (MN) - 1912
Morgan, Edwin D. (NY) - 1858, 1860, 1876
Morgan, Ephraim F. (WV) - 1920
Morgan, George W. (OH) - 1865
Morgan, J. B. (MS) - 1837
Morgan, James (WI) - 1888
Morgan, W. A. (NV) - 1914
Morgan, W. S. (AR) - 1898
Morgan, W. Y. (KS) - 1922
Morgenthau, Robert M. (NY) - 1962
Morison, W. S. D. (IL) - 1848
Morley, Clarence J. (CO) - 1924
Morrill, Ansen P. (ME) - 1853, 1854, 1855
Morrill, David L. (NH) - 1824, 1825, 1826, 1827
Morrill, Edmund N. (KS) - 1894, 1896
Morrill, Lot M. (ME) - 1857, 1858, 1859
Morris, Buckner S. (IL) - 1856
Morris, Charles (CT) - 1924, 1926, 1928
Morris, George L. (NE) - 1956
Morris, Luzon B. (CT) - 1888, 1890, 1892
Morris, Nephi L. (UT) - 1912, 1916
Morrison, Bruce A. (CT) - 1990
Morrison, Cameron (NC) - 1920
Morrison, Frank B. (NE) - 1960, 1962, 1964
Morrison, John T. (ID) - 1902
Morrison, Robert (AZ) - 1958
Morrow, Edwin P. (KY) - 1915, 1919

West, William H. (OH) - 1877
Weston, Harry R. (WY) - 1932
Weston, James A. (NH) - 1871, 1872, 1873, 1874
Wetherby, Lawrence W. (KY) - 1951
Wetmore, George Peabody (RI) - 1885, 1886, 1887
Wharton, Charles M. (DE) - 1928
Wharton, Jesse (TN) - 1815
Wheaton, Fred E. (MN) - 1918
Wheaton, Seth (RI) - 1807
Wheeler, Burton K. (MT) - 1920
Wheeler, Herman C. (IA) - 1891
Whelan, Gerald T. (NE) - 1978
Whipple, William G. (AR) - 1892
Whitcomb, Edgar D. (IN) - 1968
Whitcomb, James (IN) - 1843, 1846
White, Albert B. (WV) - 1900
White, Edward D. (LA) - 1834
White, Frank (AR) - 1986
White, Frank (ND) - 1900, 1902
White, Frank D. (AR) - 1980, 1982
White, Fred E. (IA) - 1897, 1899, 1908
White, George (OH) - 1930, 1932
White, Hugh L. (MS) - 1935, 1951
White, John H. (NH) - 1842, 1843, 1853
White, Kevin H. (MA) - 1970
White, Mark (TX) - 1982, 1986
White, Walter (TN) - 1926
White, William Allen (KS) - 1924
White, William F. (CA) - 1879
Whiteaker, John (OR) - 1858
Whitfield, Henry L. (MS) - 1923
Whiting, Charles (IA) - 1885
Whiting, Justin R. (MI) - 1898
Whitman, Charles S. (NY) - 1914, 1916, 1918
Whitman, Christine Todd (NJ) - 1993, 1997
Whitman, Ezekiel (ME) - 1821, 1822
Whitney, Arthur (NJ) - 1925
Whitney, Henry M. (MA) - 1907
Whitney, Wheelock (MN) - 1982
Whittier, Sumner G. (MA) - 1956
Whittlesey (CT) - 1847
Whyte, William P. (MD) - 1871
Wickliffe, Charles A. (KY) - 1863
Wickliffe, Robert C. (LA) - 1855
Wicks, William A. (FL) - 1896
Wight, E. M. (TN) - 1878
Wilder, L. Douglas (VA) - 1989
Wiles, Harry G. (KS) - 1964
Wiley, Alexander (WI) - 1936

Wiley, Calvin (CT) - 1832
Wilkerson, Ernest (WY) - 1966
Wilkinson, Wallace G. (KY) - 1987
Willard, Ashbel P. (IN) - 1856
Williams, Alpheus S. (MI) - 1866
Williams, Arnold (ID) - 1946
Williams, Bob (WA) - 1988
Williams, Burt (WI) - 1916
Williams, Charles K. (VT) - 1843, 1850, 1851
Williams, Clayton (TX) - 1990
Williams, Daniel (MS) - 1827
Williams, G. Mennen (MI) - 1948, 1950, 1952, 1954, 1956, 1958
Williams, George Fred (MA) - 1895, 1896, 1897
Williams, J. A. (ND) - 1914
Williams, Jack (AZ) - 1966, 1968, 1970
Williams, James Douglas (IN) - 1876
Williams, Jared W. (NH) - 1846, 1847, 1848
Williams, John Bell (MS) - 1967
Williams, Joseph H. (ME) - 1877
Williams, Robert L. (OK) - 1914
Williams, Russell (AZ) - 1974
Williams, Stephenson A. (MD) - 1903
Williams, W. D. (AL) - 1819
Willis, Frank B. (OH) - 1914, 1916, 1918
Willis, Simeon S. (KY) - 1943
Willits, J. F. (KS) - 1890
Wills, William H. (VT) - 1940, 1942
Willson, August E. (KY) - 1907
Wilmot, David (PA) - 1857
Wilson (ID) - 1891
Wilson (TN) - 1880
Wilson, Asher B. (ID) - 1926
Wilson, C. (AR) - 1849
Wilson, E. Willis (WV) - 1884
Wilson, Eugene M. (MN) - 1888
Wilson, Francis M. (MO) - 1928
Wilson, George (IA) - 1936, 1938, 1940
Wilson, Harry L. (MT) - 1912
Wilson, Henry (MA) - 1853, 1854
Wilson, J. Stitt (CA) - 1910
Wilson, James (NH) - 1838, 1839
Wilson, Malcolm (NY) - 1974
Wilson, Pete (CA) - 1990, 1994
Wilson, Stanley C. (VT) - 1930, 1932
Wilson, Ted (UT) - 1988
Wilson, Thomas (MN) - 1890
Wilson, Woodrow (NJ) - 1910
Wiltz, Louis A. (LA) - 1879

Winans, Edward B. (MI) - 1890
Winant, John G. (NH) - 1924, 1930, 1932
Winchester, George W. (MS) - 1829
Wingate, Joshua Jr. (ME) - 1821
Winsted, George W. (TN) - 1892
Winston, James (MO) - 1852
Winston, John A. (AL) - 1853, 1855
Winter, Edward H. (MO) - 1932
Winter, William (MS) - 1979
Winters, John D. (NV) - 1866
Winters, Theodore (NV) - 1894
Winters, Thomas (NV) - 1890
Winthrop, Robert C. (MA) - 1851
Wipperman, M. A. (ND) - 1900
Wise, Bob (WV) - 2000
Wise, Henry A. (VA) - 1855
Wise, John S. (VA) - 1885
Wisener, William H. (TN) - 1870
Wisner, Moses (MI) - 1858
Withycombe, James (OR) - 1906, 1914, 1918
Witt, R. Beecher (TN) - 1952
Wittpenn, H. Otto (NJ) - 1916
Wolcott, Henry R. (CO) - 1898
Wolcott, Oliver (CT) - 1781, 1783, 1784, 1796, 1797
Wolcott, Oliver Jr. (CT) - 1816, 1817, 1818, 1819, 1820, 1821, 1822, 1823, 1824, 1825, 1826, 1827
Wolcott, Roger (MA) - 1896, 1897, 1898
Wolf, George (PA) - 1829, 1832, 1835
Wolpe, Howard (MI) - 1994
Wood, Andrew T. (KY) - 1891
Wood, Chauncey L. (SD) - 1910
Wood, George T. (TX) - 1847, 1849, 1853
Wood, Lloyd H. (PA) - 1954
Wood, Reuben (OH) - 1850, 1851
Woodahl, Robert (MT) - 1976
Woodbridge, William (MI) - 1839
Woodbury, Levi (NH) - 1823, 1824
Woodbury, Urban A. (VT) - 1894
Woodford, Stewart L. (NY) - 1870
Woodman, David (MI) - 1880
Woodring, Harry H. (KS) - 1930, 1932, 1946
Woodruff, Noadiah (AL) - 1876
Woodruff, Rollin S. (CT) - 1906
Woods, George L. (OR) - 1866
Woodson, Silas (MO) - 1872
Woodward, George W. (PA) - 1863
Woodward, Gilbert M. (WI) - 1886

Woolwine, Thomas Lee (CA) - 1922
Worcester, Franklin (NY) - 1912
Workman, W. D. (SC) - 1982
Worth, Jonathan (NC) - 1865, 1866
Worthington, John I. (AR) - 1906, 1908
Worthington, Thomas (OH) - 1808, 1810, 1814, 1816
Wray, Arthur G. (NE) - 1920
Wright (TN) - 1880
Wright, Bob (UT) - 1980
Wright, Calvin E. (ID) - 1950
Wright, Earl (WY) - 1946
Wright, Fielding L. (MS) - 1947
Wright, Joseph A. (IN) - 1849, 1852
Wright, Seaborn (GA) - 1896
Wright, Silas (NY) - 1844, 1846
Wright, Edwin V. (NJ) - 1859
Wright, William (NJ) - 1847

Y

Yaple, George L. (MI) - 1886
Yates, Joseph C. (NY) - 1822
Yates, Richard (IL) - 1860, 1900
Yates, Robert (NY) - 1789, 1795
Yeaman, Caldwell (CO) - 1890
Yell, Archibald (AR) - 1840
Yell, James (AR) - 1856
Yerger, William (MS) - 1857
Yerkes, John W. (KY) - 1900
York, Myrth (RI) - 1994, 1998
York, Tyre (NC) - 1884
Young, C. W. (WA) - 1892
Young, Clement C. (CA) - 1926
Young, Edward L. (SC) - 1978
Young, George U. (AZ) - 1914
Young, John (NY) - 1846
Young, Milton K. (CA) - 1930
Young, Samuel (NY) - 1824
Young, Winthrop (MN) - 1871
Youngdahl, Luther W. (MN) - 1946, 1948, 1950
Younger, Evelle J. (CA) - 1978
Youngman, William Sterling (MA) - 1932

Z

Zeller, Fred R. (CT) - 1958
Zimmerman, Fred R. (WI) - 1926
Zimmerman, Peter (OR) - 1934

Gubernatorial Primary Candidates Index

The Gubernatorial Primary Candidates Index includes all candidates appearing in Chapter 31, Gubernatorial Primary Election Returns. The index includes candidates' names followed by state abbreviations and the years of candidacy. *(See box, State Abbreviations, this page.)* To locate a candidate's returns, turn to pages 1480 to 1542 where the returns are arranged alphabetically by state and in chronological order of election for each state. For other references to gubernatorial candidates in the *Guide to U. S. Elections*, fourth edition, see the General Index, page I-153 to I-208.

A

Abel, Hazel (NE) - 1960
Abernathy, Lee Roy (GA) - 1958
Able, William "Bill" (SC) - 1998
Acker, Bert L. (FL) - 1944, 1948, 1952
Ackerman, Lee (AZ) - 1960
Ackermann, Barbara (MA) - 1978
Acuff, Roy (TN) - 1948
Adams (SC) - 1938
Adams, Alto (FL) - 1952
Adams, Mary (ME) - 1994
Adams, Paul L. (NY) - 1970
Adams, Roy C. (MS) - 1971
Adams, Tom (FL) - 1974
Addington, William H. (KS) - 1960
Adkins, Homer M. (AR) - 1940, 1942
Agnew, Spiro T. (MD) - 1966
Albertazzie, Ralph D. (WV) - 1976
Albright, R. Mayne (NC) - 1948
Alexander, J. F. (NC) - 1976
Alexander, Lamar (TN) - 1974, 1978, 1982
Alford, Dale (AR) - 1962, 1966
Alioto, Joseph L. (CA) - 1974
Allain, William A. (MS) - 1983
Allen, Carrol V. "Red" (SD) - 1994
Allen, Clifford R. (TN) - 1950, 1952, 1958
Allen, Jim (AL) - 1954
Allen, Oscar K. (LA) - 1932
Allen, Thomas H. (ME) - 1994
Allen, William C. (NV) - 1978
Allensworth, Don (MD) - 1994
Allred, James V. (TX) - 1934, 1936
Almond, J. Lindsay Jr. (VA) - 1957
Almond, Lincoln C. (RI) - 1978, 1994, 1998
Altofer, John H. (IL) - 1968
Altvater, George (OR) - 1962
Amaimo, Morgan L. (MD) - 1958
Anaya, Toney (NM) - 1982
Andersen, Elmer L. (MN) - 1960, 1962
Anderson, A. C. (MS) - 1927

Anderson, Bob (IA) - 1986
Anderson, Bruce (NH) - 1986
Anderson, D. G. (HI) - 1982, 1986
Anderson, Emmett T. (WA) - 1956
Anderson, Forrest H. (MT) - 1968
Anderson, John (KS) - 1960, 1962, 1972
Anderson, LeRoy (MT) - 1968
Anderson, Nels Jr. (AK) - 1998
Anderson, Sigurd (SD) - 1964
Anderson, Victor E. (NE) - 1956, 1958
Anderson, Wendell R. (MN) - 1970, 1974
Andrews, John (CO) - 1990
Andrews, Lloyd J. (WA) - 1960
Andrews, Mark (ND) - 1962
Andrews, Robert E. (NJ) - 1997
Andrus, Cecil D. (ID) - 1966, 1970, 1974, 1986, 1990
Annable, Robert W. (OH) - 1970
Apodaca, Jerry (NM) - 1974, 1998
Ariyoshi, George R. (HI) - 1974, 1978, 1982
Armstrong, Bob (TX) - 1982
Arnall, Ellis (GA) - 1942, 1966
Arnesen, Deborah A. (NH) - 1992
Arnold, Remmie L. (VA) - 1949
Aronson, J. Hugo (MT) - 1956
Artinian, Gary (MI) - 1998
Ashcroft, John (MO) - 1984, 1988
Ashworth, Emily (OR) - 1978
Askew, Reubin (FL) - 1970, 1974
Atiyeh, Victor G. (OR) - 1974, 1978, 1982
Atkinson, David (VT) - 1990
Atkinson, W. P. (OK) - 1958
Austin, Gene (NV) - 1962
Avenson, Donald D. (IA) - 1990
Avery, William H. (KS) - 1964, 1966
Aycock, A. A. (LA) - 1971

B

Babbage, Bob (KY) - 1995
Babbitt, Bruce (AZ) - 1978, 1982
Babcock, Robert S. (VT) - 1960, 1964

Babcock, Tim M. (MT) - 1964, 1968
Baca, Jim (NM) - 1994
Bachrach, George A. (MA) - 1994
Badgett, Joseph M. (MO) - 1964
Baer, Steven (IL) - 1990
Baesler, Scott (KY) - 1991
Bafalis, L. A. "Skip" (FL) - 1970, 1982
Baggett, Bryce (OK) - 1970
Bagley, Hugh G. (CA) - 1986
Bagwell, Paul D. (MI) - 1958, 1960
Bailey, Carl E. (AR) - 1936, 1938, 1940
Bailey, Don (PA) - 1998
Bailey, Joseph W. (TX) - 1920
Bailey, Josiah W. (NC) - 1924
Bailey, Thomas L. (MS) - 1939, 1943
Bailey, Wendell (MO) - 1992
Bakalis, Michael (IL) - 1978
Baker, J. Edwin (FL) - 1944
Balentine, Karla (MD) - 1962
Bangerter, Norman H. (UT) - 1984
Barbee, James (FL) - 1940
Bardacke, Paul (NM) - 1990
Barlocker, W. A. (UT) - 1960
Barnes, Ben (TX) - 1972
Barnes, Clarence E. (OK) - 1958
Barnes, Roy E. (GA) - 1990, 1998
Barnes, Wallace (CT) - 1970
Barnes, Wilson K. (MD) - 1974
Barnett, Ross R. (MS) - 1951, 1955, 1959, 1967
Barr, Burton S. (AZ) - 1986
Barrett, Barbara (AZ) - 1994
Barrett, Michael J. (MA) - 1994
Barrett, Richard (MS) - 1999
Barringer, Richard E. (ME) - 1994
Barron, W. W. (WV) - 1960
Barry, James J. (NH) - 1966
Barry, Jonathan B. (WI) - 1986
Bartlett, Dewey F. (OK) - 1966, 1970
Basha, Eddie (AZ) - 1994
Batchelder, Clifton B. (NE) - 1970
Bateman, Raymond H. (NJ) - 1977

Bates (SC) - 1950, 1954
Bates, Charles A. (NE) - 1960, 1964
Batt, Phillip (ID) - 1982, 1994
Battle, John S. (VA) - 1949
Battle, Laurie C. (AL) - 1958
Battle, William C. (VA) - 1969
Baum, Ted (NE) - 1956
Baxley, Bill (AL) - 1978, 1986
Bayh, Evan (IN) - 1988, 1992
Beall, Carlton (MD) - 1978
Beall, J. Glenn Jr. (MD) - 1978
Beasely, Jere (AL) - 1978
Beasley, David (SC) - 1994, 1998
Beasley, Leonard W. (KY) - 1987
Beaulieu, Emile D. (NH) - 1998
Becht, Paul F. (NM) - 1986
Beck, Robert K. (IA) - 1966, 1968
Beck-Vosse, Shirley (TN) - 1998
Beddow, Jim (SD) - 1994
Bedsole, Ann (AL) - 1994
Begley, Elmer (KY) - 1975
Beitelspacher, Ron (ID) - 1994
Belaga, Julie D. (CT) - 1986
Beliveau, Severin M. (ME) - 1986
Bell, Bob (GA) - 1982
Bell, Howard L. (OK) - 1982
Bell, Percey (MS) - 1923
Bell, Robert K. "Buster" (AL) - 1950
Bell, Samuel (LA) - 1971
Bellmon, Henry L. (OK) - 1962, 1986
Bellotti, Francis X. (MA) - 1964, 1970, 1990
Benedict, Cleveland K. (WV) - 1992
Bennett (SC) - 1938
Bennett, Andrea (MT) - 1992
Bennett, Bruce (AR) - 1960, 1968
Bennett, Robert F. (KS) - 1974, 1978
Benson, Bruce (CO) - 1994
Bentley, Helen D. (MD) - 1994
Bentley, James L. (GA) - 1970
Berentson, Duane (WA) - 1980
Berg, Philip J. (PA) - 1990

State Abbreviations

Alabama	AL	Indiana	IN	Nebraska	NE	South Carolina	SC
Alaska	AK	Iowa	IA	Nevada	NV	South Dakota	SD
Arizona	AZ	Kansas	KS	New Hampshire	NH	Tennessee	TN
Arkansas	AR	Kentucky	KY	New Jersey	NJ	Texas	TX
California	CA	Louisiana	LA	New Mexico	NM	Utah	UT
Colorado	CO	Maine	ME	New York	NY	Vermont	VT
Connecticut	CT	Maryland	MD	North Carolina	NC	Virginia	VA
Delaware	DE	Massachusetts	MA	North Dakota	ND	Washington	WA
Florida	FL	Michigan	MI	Ohio	OH	West Virginia	WV
Georgia	GA	Minnesota	MN	Oklahoma	OK	Wisconsin	WI
Hawaii	HI	Mississippi	MS	Oregon	OR	Wyoming	WY
Idaho	ID	Missouri	MO	Pennsylvania	PA		
Illinois	IL	Montana	MT	Rhode Island	RI		

Gargan, Jack (FL) - 1994
Garrahy, J. Joseph (RI) - 1976, 1978, 1982
Garrison, Denzil D. (OK) - 1974
Gartin, Carroll (MS) - 1959
Garvey, Ed (WI) - 1998
Gary, Raymond (OK) - 1962, 1966
Gavin, Robert L. (NC) - 1960, 1964
Geisinger, Harry (GA) - 1974
George, Gary R. (WI) - 1998
Geringer, Jim (WY) - 1994, 1998
Geving, Herb (ND) - 1976
Gibbons, Charles (MA) - 1958
Gibbons, Jim (NV) - 1994
Gibson, Dan M. (MS) - 1999
Gibson, Kenneth A. (NJ) - 1981, 1985
Gigler, Andrew R. (OR) - 1970
Gigler, Roger (AK) - 1998
Gilbert, Andrew J. (AZ) - 1966
Gilbert, Rachel S. (ID) - 1990
Gilchrist, Bob (AL) - 1966
Gill, Thomas P. (HI) - 1970, 1974
Gill, Warren (OR) - 1958
Gilligan, John J. (OH) - 1970, 1974
Gillmor, Paul E. (OH) - 1986
Gilmore, Thomas O. (NC) - 1984
Ginn, Bo (GA) - 1982
Glasby, John (ID) - 1958
Glendening, Parris N. (MD) - 1994, 1998
Goddard, Sam (AZ) - 1962, 1964, 1966, 1968
Goddard, Terry (AZ) - 1990, 1994
Goetz, Phyllis (OH) - 1982
Goldberg, Arthur J. (NY) - 1970
Goldsby, Dean (AR) - 1986
Goldschmidt, Neil (OR) - 1986
Goldsmith, Stephen (IN) - 1996
Goldstein, Mark K. (FL) - 1986
Gonzalez, Henry B. (TX) - 1958
Goode, R. J. (AL) - 1938
Goodenough, Keith B. (WY) - 1986, 1998
Goodover, Pat M. (MT) - 1984
Goodwin, Gregory (HI) - 1994
Gordy, William J. (DE) - 1980
Gore, Louise (MD) - 1974, 1978
Gorman, Robert N. (OH) - 1958
Gormley, Bill (NJ) - 1989
Gottlieb, Richard F. (VT) - 1982, 1984, 1986,
    1988, 1990, 1992, 1994, 1998
Gowen, Charlie (GA) - 1954
Graddick, Charles (AL) - 1986
Gragson, Oran K. (NV) - 1962
Graham, A. H. (NC) - 1936
Graham, Bob (FL) - 1978
Graham, E. R. (FL) - 1944
Graham, Milton H. (AZ) - 1974
Granai, Edwin C. (VT) - 1978
Granberry, Jim (TX) - 1974
Grandmaison, J. Joseph (NH) - 1990
Grandy, Fred (IA) - 1994
Grant, John F. (TX) - 1930
Grant, Philip R. (NM) - 1978
Grass, Calvin F. (ME) - 1970
Grasso, Ella T. (CT) - 1978
Gravely, Lee (NC) - 1940
Graves, Bibb (AL) - 1922, 1926, 1934
Graves, Bill (KS) - 1994, 1998
Gray, James H. (GA) - 1966
Greely, Mike (MT) - 1988
Green, James C. (NC) - 1984
Green, Norman (AZ) - 1966
Green, Robert A. "Lex" (FL) - 1944
Greene, Keith H. (CA) - 1970
Greenspan, Elliot (NJ) - 1984
Greenspun, H. M. (NV) - 1962
Greenstein, Hyman (HI) - 1962
Gregg, Hugh (NH) - 1958, 1960, 1966
Gregg, Judd (NH) - 1988, 1990
Grevemberg, Francis C. (LA) - 1956, 1959
Griffen, Horace B. (AZ) - 1956
Griffin, Ben Hill (FL) - 1974
Griffin, James C. (CA) - 1982
Griffin, S. Marvin (GA) - 1954, 1962
Griffith, Leon (AR) - 1976
Griisser, Frederick M. (MD) - 1990
Gropper, John L. (VT) - 1994, 1996
Groszer, Andrew J. (MD) - 1966
Grover, Henry C. (TX) - 1972

Grunseth, Jon (MN) - 1990
Gubbrud, Archie M. (SD) - 1960, 1962
Guinn, Kenny (NV) - 1998
Guion, George Seth (LA) - 1932
Gundersen, Lamont B. (UT) - 1960
Guy, William L. (ND) - 1960, 1962, 1964, 1968
Gwin, William (VT) - 1990
Gwinn, L. E. (TN) - 1922, 1930

H

Hackel, Stella B. (VT) - 1976
Hackett, Luther F. (VT) - 1972
Haegen, Florence (MT) - 1980
Hafer, Barbara (PA) - 1990
Hagemeister, Bruce (NE) - 1966
Hagen, Orville W. (ND) - 1980
Hagen, Oscar W. (SD) - 1974
Hager, Elizabeth (NH) - 1992
Hager, Henry (PA) - 1978
Hager, James (OK) - 1998
Haines, H. H. (TX) - 1926
Halcrow, Donald M. (ND) - 1964
Haldane, Harold (AK) - 1998
Haldiman, Joe (AZ) - 1962
Hale, Virginia (OK) - 1994
Haley, J. Evetts (TX) - 1956
Halford, Rick (AK) - 1990
Hall, Chuck (FL) - 1970
Hall, David (OK) - 1966, 1970, 1974
Hall, Fred (KS) - 1956, 1958
Hall, John (TX) - 1972
Hamburg, Al (WY) - 1986
Hamburg, Dan (CA) - 1998
Hamil, David A. (CO) - 1962
Hamlin, Thurman J. (KY) - 1959, 1971, 1987
Hamm, Philip J. (AL) - 1950
Hammargren, Lonnie (NV) - 1998
Hammond, Jay S. (AK) - 1974, 1978
Hance, Kent (TX) - 1986, 1990
Hand, Fred (GA) - 1954
Haney, Franklin (TN) - 1974
Hannah, Harvey (TN) - 1922
Hansen, Clifford P. (WY) - 1962
Hansen, Gracie (OR) - 1970
Hansen, Lowell (SD) - 1986
Hansen, Robert V. (NE) - 1978
Hanson, H. Max (ID) - 1958
Hanson, Stewart (UT) - 1992
Hao, Joseph K. (HI) - 1974
Harbour, Mack (AR) - 1972
Hardage, Sam (KS) - 1982
Hardee, Cary A. (FL) - 1920, 1932
Hardin, Joe C. (AR) - 1960
Hardman, Lamartine G. (GA) - 1926, 1928
Hardwick, Chuck (NJ) - 1989
Hardwick, Thomas W. (GA) - 1920, 1922,
    1932
Hardy, Paul (LA) - 1979
Hare, James M. (MI) - 1960
Hargis, Burns (OK) - 1990
Harman, Jane (CA) - 1998
Harman, Rick (KS) - 1968, 1970
Harmon, David S. (WI) - 1994
Harper, John (KY) - 1987
Harris, Bill (NE) - 1990
Harris, Carmon C. (OK) - 1958
Harris, Fred R. (OK) - 1962
Harris, Joe Frank (GA) - 1982, 1986
Harrison, Albertis S. Jr. (VA) - 1961
Harshbarger, Scott (MA) - 1998
Hart, Edwin L. (NE) - 1956
Hart, George (KS) - 1962, 1964, 1966
Hartigan, Neil F. (IL) - 1990
Hartman, Edward M. (NM) - 1970
Hartnett, Thomas F. (SC) - 1994
Harvey, W. Brantley (SC) - 1978
Hatch, Francis W. (MA) - 1978
Hatch, Mike (MN) - 1990, 1994
Hatfield, Mark O. (OR) - 1958, 1962
Hathaway, Fons A. (FL) - 1928
Hathaway, Stan (WY) - 1966, 1970
Haugh, John (AZ) - 1966
Hawkins, Reginald A. (NC) - 1968, 1972
Hawley, Clifford J. (NM) - 1966, 1968
Hayden, Mike (KS) - 1986, 1990
Hayden, Tom (CA) - 1994

Hayes, Bert (AL) - 1978
Hayes, Joe L. (AK) - 1986
Hayes, Kyle (NC) - 1956
Hayes, Robin (NC) - 1996
Hayes, Thomas L. (VT) - 1966, 1970
Haynie, G. R. (AR) - 1920
Hays, Brooks (AR) - 1928, 1930, 1966
Head, Douglas M. (MN) - 1970
Head, Jim (OK) - 1978
Headlee, Richard H. (MI) - 1982
Heard, Paul (GA) - 1994
Hearnes, Betty C. (MO) - 1988
Hearnes, Warren E. (MO) - 1964, 1968
Hechler, Ken (WV) - 1976
Hechtner, Howard D. (ID) - 1962
Hector, Louis H. (NE) - 1958
Heftel, Cecil (HI) - 1986
Heigaard, Bill (ND) - 1992
Heitkamp, Heidi (ND) - 2000
Helbing, Stephen C. (NM) - 1970
Hellstoski, Henry (NJ) - 1969
Helms, Ned (NH) - 1992
Hemmings, Fred (HI) - 1990
Henderson, Frank E. (SD) - 1970
Henderson, J. Bruce (AL) - 1950, 1954
Henkle, Joseph W. (KS) - 1964
Henry, Dwight (TN) - 1990
Henry, E. L. (LA) - 1979
Henzler, Leo A. (AK) - 1994
Herbert (SC) - 1930
Herbert, Mary Alice (VT) - 1996
Herndon, Charles (ID) - 1962, 1966
Herrin, Bud (GA) - 1978
Herring, Jim (MS) - 1979
Herschler, Ed (WY) - 1974, 1978, 1982
Herseth, R. Lars (SD) - 1986
Herseth, Ralph (SD) - 1956, 1958, 1960, 1962
Hewlett, Steve (TN) - 1994
Hickel, Walter J. (AK) - 1966, 1974, 1978, 1986
Hickey, J. J. (WY) - 1958
Higby, Lester H. (CA) - 1974
Higgins, George N. (MI) - 1964
High, Robert King (FL) - 1964, 1966
Hildreth, Horace (ME) - 1958
Hill, John (TX) - 1968, 1978
Hillenbrand, John A. (IN) - 1980
Hines, Harry (TX) - 1940
Hitchcock, E. D. (HI) - 1959
Hobbs, Horace, E. (RI) - 1966
Hobby, Wilbur (NC) - 1972
Hoch, Ed (AK) - 1986
Hoch, Nancy (NE) - 1986
Hochstatter, Harold (WA) - 2000
Hocker, Lon (MO) - 1956
Hodges, James H. (SC) - 1998
Hodges, Luther H. (NC) - 1956
Hodges, William C. (FL) - 1936
Hoegh, Leo A. (IA) - 1956
Hoeven, John (ND) - 2000
Hoey, Clyde R. (NC) - 1936
Hoff, Philip H. (VT) - 1962, 1964, 1966
Hoffman (NC) - 1940
Hoffman, Joseph A. (NJ) - 1977
Hoffman, LeRoy G. (SD) - 1978
Hogan, Lawrence J. (MD) - 1974
Hogan, Mark (CA) - 1970
Hogan, Mark (CO) - 1970
Holden, Bob (MO) - 2000
Holder, John N. (GA) - 1920, 1926, 1930, 1932
Holdiman, Al (OR) - 1970
Holland, Spessard L. (FL) - 1940
Holland, Thomas E. (NM) - 1960
Hollenbach, Todd (KY) - 1975
Holley, Charles R. (FL) - 1964
Hollings, Ernest F. (SC) - 1958
Hollingsworth, Marvin J. (OR) - 1978
Hollis, Ray (TX) - 1994
Holloway, Clyde C. (LA) - 1991
Hollis, Robert D. (OR) - 1956, 1958
Holshouser, James E. (NC) - 1972
Holt, Frank (AR) - 1966
Holt, Jack (AR) - 1948, 1952
Hooker, John J. (TN) - 1966, 1970, 1998
Hooper, Ruby T. (NC) - 1984, 1992
Hopkins, Larry J. (KY) - 1991
Hoppe, Harley (WA) - 1976

Hoppner, Bill (NE) - 1990, 1998
Horn, Calvin (NM) - 1968
Horton, Henry H. (TN) - 1928, 1930
Horton, W. P. (NC) - 1940
Hou-Seye, Edmond E. (WI) - 1974, 1986
Houck, L. R. (SD) - 1958
Houston, Les (NM) - 1990
Howald, Edwin W. (MO) - 1996
Howard, Jeffrey (NH) - 2000
Howard, Marlene (FL) - 1990
Howell, Henry (VA) - 1969, 1977
Howell, Hugh (GA) - 1938
Howl, Jim (AZ) - 1998
Howlett, Michael J. (IL) - 1976
Hubbard, Carroll (KY) - 1979
Hubbard, Joe (AR) - 1964
Hubbert, Paul R. (AL) - 1990, 1994
Huber, Sherry F. (ME) - 1982
Huckabee, Mike (AR) - 1998
Huggins, Ira A. (UT) - 1960
Hughes, Harold E. (IA) - 1960, 1962, 1964,
    1966
Hughes, Harry R. (MD) - 1978, 1982
Hughes, James L. (NM) - 1974
Hughes, Maury (TX) - 1934
Hughes, Richard J. (NJ) - 1961, 1965
Hull, Jane Dee (AZ) - 1998
Hulley, Lincoln (FL) - 1920
Hultman, Evan (IA) - 1964
Hume, David (MD) - 1962
Humphrey, Gordon (NH) - 2000
Humphrey, Hubert H. "Skip" III (MN) - 1998
Hunhoff, Bernie (SD) - 1998
Hunt, Guy (AL) - 1978, 1986, 1990, 1998
Hunt, James B. "Jim" Jr. (NC) - 1976, 1980,
    1992, 1996
Hunter, Tom F. (TX) - 1932, 1934, 1936, 1938
Huntley, Robert C. (ID) - 1998
Hurst, Q. Byrum (AR) - 1972
Huss, Walter (OR) - 1982, 1998
Hutchinson, John G. (WV) - 1976
Hutchison, Ray (TX) - 1982
Hyatt, Gregory S. (MA) - 1986
Hynes, Charles J. (NY) - 1998
Hyslop, Jeffrey A. (WI) - 1998

I

Ingram, John (NC) - 1984
Inhofe, James M. (OK) - 1974
Inslee, Jay (WA) - 1996
Irick, John B. (NM) - 1982
Isakson, Johnny (GA) - 1990
Itkin, Ivan (PA) - 1998

J

Jaccaci, August (VT) - 1994
Jack, William (WY) - 1962
Jackson, Clingan (OH) - 1958
Jackson, Donald (TN) - 1998
Jackson, Edmund B. (SC) - 1926
Jackson, Larry (ID) - 1978
Jackson, Lowell B. (WI) - 1982
Jackson, Shelby M. (LA) - 1963
Jackvony, Louis (RI) - 1962
Jacobsen, Alan (NE) - 1994
Jacobson, Alvin J. (PA) - 1974
Jacquin, William C. (AZ) - 1974
James, Forrest H. "Fob" Jr. (AL) - 1978, 1986,
    1990, 1994, 1998
James, Peter (MD) - 1970
James, Ted (MT) - 1968
Jancek, Steve (AZ) - 1982
Janklow, William J. (SD) - 1978, 1982, 1994,
    1998
Jarman, Maxey (TN) - 1970
Jeffords, James M. (VT) - 1972
Jenkins, William (TN) - 1970
Jennings, Frank E. (FL) - 1924
Jester, Beauford H. (TX) - 1946, 1948
Johanns, Mike (NE) - 1998
Johns, Charley E. (FL) - 1954
Johnson, Carl A. (WY) - 1982
Johnson, Charles M. (NC) - 1948
Johnson, Donald E. (IA) - 1968
Johnson, Doug (MN) - 1998
Johnson, Gary E. (NM) - 1994, 1998

General Index

The General Index includes page references to all sections of the *Guide to U.S. Elections*, fourth edition, except the congrssional and gubernatorial popular vote returns, which are indexed separately in candidate indexes. The six candidate indexes are: Presidential Candidates Index, pp. I-1 to I-2, Vol. I; House Candidates Index,

pp. I-1 to I-111, Vol. II; Senate General Election Candidates Index, pp. I-113 to I-119, Vol. II; Senate Primary Candidates Index, pp. I-120 to I-128, Vol. II; Gubernatorial General Election Candidates Index, pp. I-129 to I-142, Vol. II; Gubernatorial Primary Candidates Index, pp. I-143 to I-151, Vol. II.

Liberty Party nominee, (1840, 1844)
66, 429, 446
popular vote, (1840) 648, (1844)
649
Birrenbach, John
presidential candidate
Independent Grassroots Party nominee, (1996) 439
popular vote, (1996) 699
Bishop, Richard M.
governor, Ohio, 1404
Bissell, Clark
governor, Connecticut, 1387
Bissell, William H.
governor, Illinois, 1390
Bixler, ——
presidential primary votes, (1948) 340
Black, Frank S.
governor, New York, 1403
Black, Hugo
senator, Alabama, 1236
Supreme Court justice, 818, 822
Black, James
presidential candidate
popular vote, (1872) 690
Prohibition Party nominee, (1872)
430
Black, James D.
governor, Kentucky, 1393
Black, Jeremiah S.
Democratic convention ballots, (1872)
585, (1880) 589
Black, John
senator, Mississippi, 1250
Black, John C., 472
"Black Codes," 26
Black Panther Party, 68
Blackburn, Joseph C. S.
Democratic convention ballots, (1896)
595
senator, Kentucky, 1245
Blackburn, Luke P.
governor, Kentucky, 1393
Blacks. See African Americans
Blackwood, Ibra C.
governor, South Carolina, 1408
Blaine, James G.
biography, 775
presidential candidate
electoral vote, (1884) 742
popular vote, (1884) 659
Republican contender, (1876) 465,
(1880) 249, 468, (1888) 251, 473,
(1892) 252, 474
Republican convention ballots,
(1876) 586, (1880) 588, (1884) 590,
(1888) 592, (1892) 593
Republican nominee, (1884) 222,
250–251, 431, 470
Republican leadership, 247
senator, Maine, 1247
Blaine, John J.
governor, Wisconsin, 1413
senator, Wisconsin, 1266
Blaine, John R.
Republican convention ballots, (1932)
610
Blair, Austin
governor, Michigan, 1397
Blair, Francis P. Jr.
biography, 776
Democratic convention ballots, (1868)
584
senator, Missouri, 1251
vice-presidential candidate
Democratic nominee, (1868) 246,
430, 462
electoral vote, (1868) 772
Blair, Henry W.
senator, New Hampshire, 1253
Blair, James T. Jr.
governor, Missouri, 1399
Blakley, William A.
senator, Texas, 132, 1262
Blanchard, James J.
governor, Michigan, 193, 1397

Blanchard, Newton C.
governor, Louisiana, 1393
senator, Louisiana, 1246
Bland, Richard P. "Silver Dick"
Democratic presidential contender,
(1896) 254, 478
convention ballots, (1896) 595
Blanton, Ray
governor, Tennessee, 1409
Blasdel, H. G.
governor, Nevada, 1400
Blease, Coleman L.
governor, South Carolina, 1408
senator, South Carolina, 1260
Bledsoe, Jesse
senator, Kentucky, 1245
Bliss, Aaron T.
governor, Michigan, 1397
Bliss, Ray C.
Republican National Committee chair,
417 (table), 426 (table)
Blodgett, Rufus
senator, New Jersey, 1254
Blomen, Constance
vice-presidential candidate
Socialist Labor nominee, (1976) 437
Blomen, Henning A.
presidential candidate
popular vote, (1968) 680
Socialist Labor nominee, (1968) 436
vice-presidential candidate
Socialist Labor nominee, (1964) 435
Blood, Henry H.
governor, Utah, 1410
Blood, Robert O.
governor, New Hampshire, 1401
Bloodworth, Timothy
senator, North Carolina, 1256
Bloomfield, Joseph
governor, New Jersey, 1401
Blount, William
governor, South Dakota, 1409
senator, Tennessee, 1261
Bloxham, William D.
governor, Florida, 1388
Blue, Robert D.
governor, Iowa, 1392
Blue Dogs (Democrats), 564
Blumenthal, Sidney, 289
Boardman, Elijah
senator, Connecticut, 1238
Bocock, Thomas, 580
Bodwell, Joseph R.
governor, Maine, 1394
Boe, Nils A.
governor, South Dakota, 1409
Boehner, John A., 820–821 (box)
Boggs, Hale, 13 (box)
Boggs, J. Caleb
governor, Delaware, 145, 1388
senator, Delaware, 172, 1240
Boggs, Lilburn W.
governor, Missouri, 1398
Boggs, Lindy
Democratic convention officers, 415
(table)
election anomalies, 13 (box)
Bogue, ——
presidential primary votes,
(1932) 332
Bogy, Lewis V.
senator, Missouri, 1251
Boies, David, 300
Boies, Horace
governor, Iowa, 1392
presidential candidate
Democratic contender, (1892) 475
Democratic convention ballots,
(1892) 593, (1896) 595
Bolack, Tom
governor, New Mexico, 1402
Bolin, Wesley
governor, Arizona, 1385
Bona, Frank
presidential primary votes, (1976) 364,
(1992) 394

Bond, Christopher S. "Kit"
governor, Missouri, 179, 1399
senator, Missouri, 188, 1251
Bond, Julian, 422, 531
Bond, Richard N.
Republican National Committee chair,
417 (table), 426 (table)
Bond, Shadrach
governor, Illinois, 1390
Bone, Homer T.
senator, Washington, 1265
Bonham, Milledge L.
governor, South Carolina, 1408
Bonner, John W.
governor, Montana, 1399
Bono, Mary, 788
Bono, Sonny, 788
"Bonus Army" protest, 261, 262
Bonus system, of convention delegate
selection, 412–413
Boon, Ratliff
governor, Indiana, 1391
Booth, Newton
governor, California, 1386
senator, California, 1237
Booth, John Wilkes, 15
Borah, William E.
presidential candidate
primary votes, (1936) 333–334
Republican contender, (1936) 504
Republican convention ballots,
(1916) 602, (1920) 604, (1936) 612
at Republican convention, (1912) 486
senator, Idaho, 1242
Boreman, Arthur I.
governor, West Virginia, 1412
senator, West Virginia, 1265
Boren, David L.
governor, Oklahoma, 176, 1405
senator, Oklahoma, 181, 1257
Boren, Jim
presidential candidate
Apathy Party nominee, (1992) 438
popular vote, (1992) 698
Borglum, Gutzon, 262
Bork, Robert
Republican convention ballots, (1996)
638
"Saturday night massacre," 281
Supreme Court nomination, 190
Borland, Solon
senator, Arkansas, 1237
Bosa, Richard P.
presidential primary votes, (1992) 393,
(1996) 403
Boschwitz, Rudy
senator, Minnesota, 181, 187, 193, 1250
Bottolfsen, Clarence A.
governor, Idaho, 1390
Bottum, Joe H.
presidential primary votes, (1944) 338
senator, South Dakota, 1261
Bouck, William
vice-presidential candidate
Farmer Labor nominee,
(1924) 433
Bouck, William C.
governor, New York, 1402
Bouligny, Dominique
senator, Louisiana, 1246
Bourn, Augustus O.
governor, Rhode Island, 1407
Bourne, Jonathan Jr.
presidential primary law, 310
senator, Oregon, 1258
Boutelle, Paul
vice-presidential candidate
Socialist Worker nominee,
(1968) 436
Boutwell, George S.
governor, Massachusetts, 1396
senator, Massachusetts, 1248
Bowden, Lemuel J.
senator, Virginia, 1264
Bowdoin, James
governor, Massachusetts, 1396

Bowen, Otis R.
governor, Indiana, 1391
Bowen, Thomas M.
senator, Colorado, 1238
Bowerman, Jay
governor, Oregon, 1405
Bowers, Claude G.
Democratic convention officers, 415
(table), 499
Bowie, Oden
governor, Maryland, 1395
Bowie, Robert
governor, Maryland, 1395
Bowles, Chester
governor, Connecticut, 141, 1387
Bowring, Eva
senator, Nebraska, 1252
Boxer, Barbara
Democratic convention officers, 415
(table)
senator, California, 18, 787, 789, 1238
Boyd, James E.
governor, Nebraska, 1399
Boyd, Linn, 577
Boyle, Emmet D.
governor, Nevada, 1400
Boyle, William M. Jr.
Democratic National Committee chair,
426 (table)
Boynton, James H.
governor, Georgia, 1389
Brackett, John Q. A.
governor, Massachusetts, 1396
Bradbury, James W.
senator, Maine, 1247
Braden, Tom, 280
Bradford, Augustus W.
governor, Maryland, 1395
Bradford, Drew
independent presidential candidate,
(1992) 438
popular vote, (1992) 698
Bradford, Robert F.
governor, Massachusetts, 138, 1396
Bradford, William
senator, Rhode Island, 1259
Bradley, Bill
at Democratic convention, (1992)
557
keynote speaker, 415 (table)
presidential candidate
Democratic contender, (2000) 204,
212, 296, 297, 568
no-run decision, (1992) 289
primary votes, (2000) 305, 318,
404–410
senator, New Jersey, 181, 1254
on TV ad expense, 99
Bradley, Joseph P., 711
Bradley, Lewis R.
governor, Nevada, 1400
Bradley, Stephen R.
Democratic-Republican caucus, (1808)
230
senator, Vermont, 1263
Bradley, Tom, 185
Bradley, William O.
governor, Kentucky, 1393
Republican vice-presidential contender,
(1888) 473
senator, Kentucky, 1245
Brady, James H.
governor, Idaho, 1390
senator, Idaho, 1242
Brady, James S., 564
Brady, Nicholas F.
senator, New Jersey, 1254
Brady, Sarah, 564
Bragg, Thomas
governor, North Carolina, 1403
senator, North Carolina, 1256
Brainerd, Lawrence
senator, Vermont, 1263
Bramlette, Thomas E.
biography, 776
governor, Kentucky, 1393

Deneen, Charles S.
    governor, Illinois, 1391
    senator, Illinois, 1242
Dennerl, Norbert G.
    presidential primary votes, (1988)
        378–385
Denney, William D.
    governor, Delaware, 1388
Dennis, David W., 175
Dennis, Delmar
    presidential candidate
        American Party nominee, (1984) 52,
        437, (1988) 52, 438
        popular vote, (1984, 1988) 697
Dennis, George R.
    senator, Maryland, 1247
Dennison, William
    governor, Ohio, 1404
    Republican convention officers, 417
        (table)
Denton, Jeremiah
    senator, Alabama, 188–189, 1236
Depew, Chauncey M.
    Republican presidential contender,
        (1888) 473
        convention ballots, (1888) 592
    senator, New York, 1255
Derbigny, Pierre
    governor, Louisiana, 1393
Dern, George H.
    governor, Utah, 1410
DeSarno, James, 118 (box)
Desha, Joseph
    governor, Kentucky, 1392
Destrehan, John N.
    senator, Louisiana, 1246
Deukmejian, George
    governor, California, 185, 189, 1386
Deutsch, Barry J.
    presidential primary votes, (1992) 394
Dever, Paul A.
    Democratic convention officers, speakers,
        415 (table)
    governor, Massachusetts, 1396
    presidential contender, (1952) 517
        Democratic convention ballots,
        (1952) 618
Devine, Annie, 803
Devine, Joseph M.
    governor, North Dakota, 1404
Dewey, Nelson
    governor, Wisconsin, 1413
Dewey, Thomas E.
    biography, 777
    governor, New York, 138, 1403
    political party development, 76
    presidential candidate
        "Dewey Defeats Truman" headline,
        17, 270
        election evolution, 8
        electoral vote, (1944) 757, (1948) 758
        as former governor, 223
        New York background, 222
        politics and issues, (1948) 139–141
        popular vote, (1944) 674, (1948) 675
        primary votes, (1940) 335–336,
        (1944) 337–338, (1948) 313,
        339–340
        Republican contender, (1940) 267,
        506
        Republican convention ballots,
        (1940) 613, (1944) 614, (1948) 615
        Republican nominee, (1944) 266,
        268, 434, 508–509, (1948)
        270–271, 434, 511
        at Republican convention, (1944) 427
DeWine, Mike
    senator, Ohio, 1257
Dexter, Samuel
    senator, Massachusetts, 1248
Dial, Nathaniel
    senator, South Carolina, 1260
Dick, Charles W. F.
    senator, Ohio, 1257
Dickerson, Denver S.
    governor, Nevada, 1400

Dickerson, Mahlon
    governor, New Jersey, 1401
    House redistricting, 817
    senator, New Jersey, 1253, 1254
Dickerson, Philemon
    governor, New Jersey, 1401
Dickinson, Daniel S.
    Democratic convention ballots, (1852)
        577, (1860) 580
    Republican (Union) vice-presidential con-
        tender, (1864) 459
    senator, New York, 1255
Dickinson, John
    governor, Delaware, 1387
Dickinson, John
    governor, Pennsylvania, 1406
Dickinson, L. J.
    Republican convention officers, 417
        (table)
    senator, Iowa, 1243
Dickinson, Luren D.
    governor, Michigan, 1397
Dickinson, Philemon
    senator, New Jersey, 1254
DiDonato, Florenzo
    presidential primary votes, (1988)
        378–385
Dietrich, Charles H.
    governor, Nebraska, 1399
    senator, Nebraska, 1252
Dietrich, William H.
    senator, Illinois, 1242
DiFrancesco, Donald T.
    governor, New Jersey, 1402
Diggs, Charles C. Jr., 791
Dill, Clarence C.
    senator, Washington, 1265
Dillingham, Paul
    governor, Vermont, 1410
Dillingham, William P.
    governor, Vermont, 1411
    senator, Vermont, 1263
Dillon, Richard C.
    governor, New Mexico, 1402
Diman, Byron
    governor, Rhode Island, 1406
Dimond, Francis M.
    governor, Rhode Island, 1407
Dingell, John D.
    length of service in Congress, 795 (table)
Dingley, Nelson Jr.
    governor, Maine, 1394
Dinkins, David, 552
Dinsmoor, Samuel
    governor, New Hampshire, 1400
Dinsmoor, Samuel Jr.
    governor, New Hampshire, 1400
DiPrete, Edward
    governor, Rhode Island, 189, 192, 1407
Direct election of senators
    Republican platform issue (1908) 423
        (box), 599
    Seventeenth Amendment, 14, 16, 1231,
        1232
Direct recording electronic (DRE) voting sys-
    tems, 218
Dirksen, Everett McKinley
    presidential primary votes, (1944)
        337–338
    Republican convention ballots, (1948)
        615
    senator, Illinois, 143, 1242
        Senate leadership, 158, 164
Disabled persons
    at Democratic convention, (1996) 564
    Republican platform issue, (1988) 555
DiSalle, Michael
    governor, Ohio, 152, 158, 1405
    presidential primary votes, (1960)
        346–347
Disarmament. See Arms control
District of Columbia
    platform issues
        Democrats, (1964) 527
        Republicans, (1996) 562
    presidential voting rights, 17, 21, 162, 220

"Divided government," 3, 10
Dix, John A.
    governor, New York, 1403
    senator, New York, 1255
Dixiecrats. See States' Rights Party
Dixon, Alan J.
    senator, Illinois, 1242
Dixon, Archibald
    senator, Kentucky, 1245
Dixon, Frank M.
    at Dixiecrat convention, (1948) 513
    governor, Alabama, 1384
Dixon, James
    senator, Connecticut, 1238
Dixon, Joseph M.
    governor, Montana, 1399
    senator, Montana, 1251
Dixon, Julian, 791
Dixon, Nathan F.
    senator, Rhode Island, 1259
Dixon, Nathan F. III
    senator, Rhode Island, 1259
DNC. See Democratic National Committee
Dobbs, Farrell
    presidential candidate
        popular vote, (1948) 693 (1952,
        1956, 1960) 694
        Socialist Workers nominee, (1948,
        1952) 434, (1956, 1960) 435
Dockery, Alexander M.
    governor, Missouri, 1399
Docking, George
    governor, Kansas, 149, 152, 1392
Docking, Robert B.
    governor, Kansas, 1392
Dodd, Christopher J.
    at Democratic convention, (1996) 564
    Democratic National Committee chair,
        426 (table)
    senator, Connecticut, 1239
Dodd, Thomas J.
    Democratic vice-presidential contender,
        (1964) 527
    senator, Connecticut, 152, 170, 1239
Dodge, Augustus C.
    senator, Iowa, 1244
Dodge, Earl F.
    presidential candidate
        popular vote, (1984, 1988) 697,
        (1992) 698, (1996, 2000) 699
        primary votes, (1992) 393
        Prohibition Party nominee,
        (1984–2000) 72, 437–439
    vice-presidential candidate
        Prohibition Party nominee, (1976)
        437
        Statesman Party nominee, (1980)
        437
Dodge, Henry
    Democratic convention ballots, (1852)
        577
    senator, Wisconsin, 1265
Doerschuck, Georgiana
    presidential primary votes, (1992) 393,
        (1996) 403
Dole, Elizabeth Hanford
    Bob Dole campaign, (1988) 287
    presidential candidate
        campaign funding, (2000) 91
        Republican contender, (2000) 204, 210,
        296
    at Republican convention, (1996) 561
        officers, 417 (table)
Dole, Robert
    biography, 777
    presidential candidate
        campaign finance, (1996) 94
        "character" issues, (1996) 210
        electoral vote, (1996) 770
        as former vice-presidential nominee,
        224
        politics and issues, (1996) 200
        popular vote, (1996) 687
        primary votes, (1980) 365–371,
        (1988) 311 (box), 315, 378–385,
        (1996) 311 (box), 318, 395–402

Republican contender, (1980) 182,
        (1988) 190, 286, 287
    Republican convention ballots,
        (1996) 638
    Republican nominee, (1996)
        293–295, 315, 439, 561–562
    Republican convention officers, 417
        (table)
    Republican National Committee chair,
        417 (table), 426 (table)
    senator, Kansas, 169, 175, 1244
        Senate leadership, 188, 191
        successor, 788
    vice-presidential candidate
        election milestones, 18
        electoral vote, (1976) 773
        Republican nominee, (1976) 178,
        282, 436, 540
        televised debates, (1976) 216
Dolliver, Jonathan P.
    senator, Iowa, 1243
Dolph, Joseph N.
    senator, Oregon, 1258
Dominici, Pete V.
    senator, New Mexico, 1255
Dominick, Peter H.
    senator, Colorado, 175, 1238
Donaghey, George W.
    governor, Arkansas, 1385
Donahey, Gertrude W.
    presidential primary votes, (1976) 364
Donahey, Victor
    Democratic convention ballots, (1928)
        609
    governor, Ohio, 1405
    presidential primary votes, (1928)
        329–330
    senator, Ohio, 1257
Donelson, Andrew Jackson
    biography, 777
    vice-presidential candidate
        American Party nominee, (1856) 430,
        454, 455
        electoral vote, (1856) 772
        Whig nominee, (1856) 430
Donnell, Forrest C.
    governor, Missouri, 1399
    senator, Missouri, 1251
Donnelly, Ignatius
    vice-presidential candidate
        Populist nominee, (1900) 69, 431
Donnelly, Phil M.
    governor, Missouri, 1399
Donnelly, James R.
    Democratic convention ballots, (1868)
        584
    Democratic convention officers, 415
        (table)
    senator, Wisconsin, 1265
Dorgan, Byron L.
    senator, North Dakota, 1256
Dornan, Robert K.
    contested House election, 804
    presidential candidate
        primary votes, (1996) 395–402
        Republican contender, (1996) 293,
        315
Dorsey, Hugh M.
    governor, Georgia, 1389
Dorsey, Stephen W.
    senator, Arkansas, 1237
Doty, Charles R.
    presidential primary votes, (1988)
        378–385, (1992) 393
Douglas, Emily Taft, 788
Douglas, Helen Gahagan, 143
Douglas, Paul H.
    Democratic convention ballots, (1952)
        618
    senator, Illinois, 141, 788, 1242
        civil rights, 148
Douglas, Stephen A.
    biography, 777
    on Kansas-Nebraska Act, 240
    as moderate, 239
    presidential candidate

governor, Maryland, 1395
McLauren, Anselm J.
   governor, Mississippi, 1398
   senator, Mississippi, 1250
McLaurin, John L.
   senator, South Carolina, 1260
McLean, Angus Wilton
   governor, North Carolina, 1403
McLean, George P.
   governor, Connecticut, 1387
   senator, Connecticut, 1239
McLean, John
   presidential candidate
      Anti-Mason nomination refused, (1832) 442
      Republican contender, (1856) 453
      Republican convention ballots, (1856) 579, (1860) 581
      Whig convention ballots, (1848) 576
   senator, Illinois, 1242
McLean, John R., 478
   Democratic convention ballots, (1896) 595
McLeod, Thomas G.
   governor, South Carolina, 1408
McMahon, Brien
   senator, Connecticut, 1239
McMahon, George
   vice-presidential candidate
      Independent Grassroots Party nominee, (1996) 439
McManus, Gerald J.
   presidential primary votes, (1996) 403
McMaster, William H.
   governor, South Dakota, 1408
   senator, South Dakota, 1261
McMath, Sidney S.
   governor, Arkansas, 1385
McMichael, Morton
   Republican convention officers, 417 (table)
McMillan, James
   senator, Michigan, 1249
McMillan, Samuel J. R.
   senator, Minnesota, 1249
McMillin, Benton
   governor, Tennessee, 1409
McMinn, Joseph
   governor, Tennessee, 1409
McMullen, Adam
   governor, Nebraska, 1399
McMullen, Richard C.
   governor, Delaware, 1388
McNair, Alexander
   governor, Missouri, 1398
McNair, Robert E.
   governor, South Carolina, 1408
McNamara, Patrick V.
   senator, Michigan, 1249
McNary, Charles L.
   biography, 779
   presidential candidate
      primary votes, (1940) 336
      Republican contender, (1936) 265, (1940) 267
      Republican convention ballots, (1940) 613
   senator, Oregon, 1258
   vice-presidential candidate
      electoral vote, (1940) 773
      Republican nominee, (1940) 267, 434, 506
McNichols, Stephen L. R.
   governor, Colorado, 1386
McNutt, Alexander G.
   governor, Mississippi, 1398
McNutt, Paul V.
   Democratic convention ballots, (1948) 616
   governor, Indiana, 1391
McPherson, Edward
   Republican convention officers, 417 (table)
McPherson, John R.
   senator, New Jersey, 1254

McRae, John J.
   governor, Mississippi, 1398
   senator, Mississippi, 1250
McRae, Thomas C.
   governor, Arkansas, 1385
McReynolds, David
   presidential candidate
      popular vote, (1980) 696, (2000) 699
      Socialist nominee, (1980) 437, (2000) 439
McRoberts, Samuel
   senator, Illinois, 1242
McSweeney, Miles B.
   governor, South Carolina, 1408
McVay, Hugh
   governor, Alabama, 1384
McWherter, Ned R.
   governor, Tennessee, 1409
McWillie, William
   governor, Mississippi, 1398
Mead, Albert E.
   governor, Washington, 1412
Mead, James M.
   senator, New York, 1255
Mead, John A.
   governor, Vermont, 1411
Meador, Edward Kirby
   vice-presidential candidate
      Greenback Party nominee, (1956, 1960) 435
Meadows, Clarence W.
   governor, West Virginia, 1412
Means, John Hugh
   governor, South Carolina, 1408
Means, Rice W.
   senator, Colorado, 1238
Mecham, Edwin L.
   governor, New Mexico, 149, 162, 1402
      impeachment, 1381 (box)
   senator, New Mexico, 1254
Mecham, Evan
   governor, Arizona, 189, 1385
Mecham, Merritt C.
   governor, New Mexico, 1402
Mechanical lever voting machines, 218
Medary, Samuel
   Democratic convention officers, 415 (table)
Medicare
   Democratic platform, (2000) 569
   enactment, 164
   Republican platform, (1964) 527, (1996) 563, (2000) 567
Medill, William
   governor, Ohio, 1404
Meehan, Martin T., 93
   campaign finance reform, 124 (box)
Meese, Edwin, 543
Meier, Julius L.
   governor, Oregon, 1405
Meigs, Return J.
   governor, Ohio, 1404
   senator, Ohio, 1257
Melcher, John
   senator, Montana, 179, 191, 1251
Melette, Arthur C.
   governor, South Dakota, 1408
Mellen, Prentiss
   senator, Massachusetts, 1248
Mellman, Mark, 22
Mellon, Andrew, 258
Menard, John W., 790
Mercer, John Francis
   governor, Maryland, 1395
Meredith, Edwin T.
   Democratic convention ballots, (1920) 605, (1924) 606–607
Meriwether, David
   senator, Kentucky, 1245
Merriam, Frank F.
   governor, California, 1386
Merriam, William R.
   governor, Minnesota, 1397
Merrick, William D.
   senator, Maryland, 1247

Merrill, Samuel
   governor, Iowa, 1391
Merrill, Steve
   governor, New Hampshire, 1401
Merrimon, Augustus S.
   senator, North Carolina, 1256
Merwin, John D.
   presidential primary votes, (1992) 386–393
Meskill, Thomas J.
   governor, Connecticut, 1387
Metcalf, Henry Brewer
   vice-presidential candidate
      Prohibition Party nominee, (1900) 431
Metcalf, Jesse H.
   senator, Rhode Island, 1260
Metcalf, Lee
   senator, Montana, 1251
Metcalf, Ralph
   governor, New Hampshire, 1400
Metcalfe, Thomas
   governor, Kentucky, 1392
   senator, Kentucky, 1245
Metzenbaum, Howard M.
   senator, Ohio, 179, 1257
      campaign finance, 112
Mexican War, 238, 448, 449
Meyers, Jan, 18, 789
Meyner, Robert B.
   Democratic convention ballots, (1960) 620
   governor, New Jersey, 146, 151, 1402
Michael, Stephen D.
   independent presidential candidate, 439
      popular vote, (1996) 699
      primary votes, (1992) 386–393, (1996) 403
Michel, Robert H.
   House leadership, 198
   Republican convention officers, 417 (table)
Michelson, George S.
   governor, South Dakota, 189
Michigan
   House redistricting, 823
Mickells, Kathleen
   vice-presidential candidate
      Socialist Workers nominee, (1988) 438
Mickelson, George S.
   governor, South Dakota, 1409
Mickelson, George T.
   governor, South Dakota, 1409
Mickey, John H.
   governor, Nebraska, 1399
Middle Class Party
   nominees, (1980) 437
Middle East
   Camp David accords, 180
   platform issue
      Democrats, (1944) 510, (1948) 513, (1984) 550, (1992) 558, (1996) 565, (2000) 570
      Republicans, (1944) 509, (1948) 512, (1956) 521, (1988) 556, (1992) 560, (1996) 563, (2000) 568
   Suez crisis, 147
Middleton, Henry
   governor, South Carolina, 1407
Mifflin, Thomas
   governor, Pennsylvania, 1406
Mikulski, Barbara A.
   Democratic rules reform, 418 (box)
   senator, Maryland, 188, 787, 789, 1247
   Senate leadership, 789
Miles, John E.
   governor, New Mexico, 1402
Miles, Nelson A.
   Democratic convention ballots, (1904) 597
Military service
   absentee voting, 37–38, 39
   census, 821 (box)
   members of Congress, 787

platform issues
   Democrats, (2000) 570
   Republicans, (1980) 544, (1996) 563, (2000) 566, 568
   presidential candidates, 221–222, 223
Milko, Hilary Michael
   presidential primary votes, (1996) 403
Millard, Joseph H.
   senator, Nebraska, 1252
Milledge, John
   governor, Georgia, 1389
   senator, Georgia, 1241
Miller, B. N.
   vice-presidential candidate
      Constitutional Party (Washington) nominee, (1960) 435
Miller, Benjamin M.
   governor, Alabama, 1384
Miller, Bert H.
   senator, Idaho, 1242
Miller, Bob J.
   governor, Nevada, 1400
Miller, Charles R.
   governor, Delaware, 1388
Miller, Dan, 821 (box)
Miller, Ernest L.
   presidential candidate
      popular vote, (1976) 696
      Restoration Party nominee, (1976) 437
Miller, Homer V. M.
   senator, Georgia, 1241
Miller, Jack
   senator, Iowa, 172, 1244
Miller, Jacob W.
   senator, New Jersey, 1254
Miller, John
   governor, Missouri, 1398
Miller, John
   governor, North Dakota, 1404
Miller, John E.
   senator, Arkansas, 131, 1237
Miller, John F.
   senator, California, 1237
Miller, Keith H.
   governor, Alaska, 1384
Miller, Leslie A.
   governor, Wyoming, 1413
Miller, Nathan L.
   governor, New York, 1403
Miller, Stephen
   governor, Minnesota, 1397
Miller, Stephen D.
   governor, South Carolina, 1407
   senator, South Carolina, 1260
Miller, Walter D.
   governor, South Dakota, 1409
Miller, Ward M., 803
Miller, Warner
   senator, New York, 1255
Miller, William
   governor, North Carolina, 1403
Miller, William E.
   biography, 779
   Republican National Committee chair, 161, 417 (table), 426 (table)
   vice-presidential candidate
      electoral vote, (1964) 773
      New York background, 222
      Republican nominee, (1964) 161–162, 276–277, 435, 525
Miller, William R.
   governor, Arkansas, 1385
Miller, Zell
   at Democratic convention, (1992) 557
      keynote speaker, 415 (table)
   governor, Georgia, 1390
   senator, Georgia, 1241
Milliken, Carl E.
   governor, Maine, 1394
Milliken, William G.
   governor, Michigan, 1397
Millikin, Eugene D.
   senator, Colorado, 1238
Mills, Elijah H.
   senator, Massachusetts, 1248

Democratic convention officers, 415
(table)
governor, New York, 1402, 1403
presidential candidate
black voters, 24
Democratic convention ballots,
(1860) 580, (1864) 582, (1868) 584,
(1880) 589
Democratic nominee, (1868) 246,
430, 462
electoral vote, (1868) 738
New York background, 222
popular vote, (1868) 655
Seymour, Horatio
senator, Vermont, 1263
Seymour, John
senator, California, 1237
Seymour, Thomas H.
governor, Connecticut, 1387
presidential candidate
Democratic contender, (1864) 460
Democratic convention ballots, 582
Shackleford, Rufus
vice-presidential candidate
American Party nominee, (1976) 51,
436
Shafer, George F.
governor, North Dakota, 1404
Shafer, Raymond P.
governor, Pennsylvania, 1406
presidential primary votes, (1968)
351–353
Shafroth, John F.
governor, Colorado, 1386
senator, Colorado, 1238
Shaheen, Jeanne
governor, New Hampshire, 1401
Shallenberger, Ashton C.
governor, Nebraska, 1399
Shannon, James C.
governor, Connecticut, 1387
Shannon, Wilson
governor, Ohio, 1404
Shapiro, Samuel H.
governor, Illinois, 1391
Shapp, Milton J.
governor, Pennsylvania, 1406
presidential candidate
Democratic convention ballots,
(1976) 627
primary votes, (1976) 359–364
Sharkey, William L.
governor, Mississippi, 1398
Sharon, William
senator, Nevada, 1252
Sharpe, Merrill Q.
governor, South Dakota, 1409
Shaver, Clem
Democratic National Committee chair,
415 (table), 426 (table)
Shaw, ——
presidential primary votes, (1952) 343
Shaw, Edward
vice-presidential candidate
Socialist Workers nominee, (1964)
435
Shaw, Leslie M.
governor, Iowa, 1392
Shaw, Mark
vice-presidential candidate
Prohibition nominee, (1964) 435
Shays, Christopher, 93
campaign finance reform, 124 (box)
Sheafe, James
senator, New Hampshire, 1253
Shearer, Eileen M.
vice-presidential candidate
American Independent Party nomi-
nee, (1980) 437
Shearer, William K., 51
Sheffield, Bill
governor, Alaska, 1384
Sheffield, William P.
senator, Rhode Island, 1259
Shelby, Isaac
governor, Kentucky, 1392

Shelby, Richard C.
senator, Alabama, 188–189, 1236
party switch, 796
Sheldon, Charles H.
governor, South Dakota, 1408
Sheldon, George L.
governor, Nebraska, 1399
Shelley, John F., 161
Shelton, Frank W.
presidential candidate
American Party nominee, (1980) 437
popular vote, (1980) 696
Shelton, Herbert M.
presidential candidate
American Vegetarian Party nominee,
(1956) 435
Shepley, Ether
senator, Maine, 1246
Shepley, George F.
governor, Louisiana, 1393
Sheppard, John C.
governor, South Carolina, 1408
Sheppard, Morris
senator, Texas, 1262
Sheridan, Philip, 244, 246
Sherman Anti-Trust Act, 488, 255
Sherman, Buren R.
governor, Iowa, 1391
Sherman, James S.
biography, 780
vice-presidential candidate
effect of death, 12–13 (box), 206, 425,
709
electoral vote, (1908) 773
Republican nominee, (1908) 255,
432, 484, (1912) 432, 486
Sherman, John
presidential contender, (1880) 249, 468,
(1888) 251, 473
Republican convention ballots,
(1880) 588, (1884) 590, (1888) 592
senator, Ohio, 1257
Sherman, Lawrence Y.
presidential candidate
primary votes, (1916) 322
Republican contender, (1916) 258
Republican convention ballots, (1916)
602
senator, Illinois, 1242
Sherman, Roger
on House elections, 799
senator, Connecticut, 1239
Sherman Silver Purchase Act, 251
Sherman, William T.
Civil War victories, 244
Grant campaign, (1868) 246
Johnson cabinet possibility, 246
Republican convention ballots, (1884)
590
Shiekman, Tom
presidential primary votes, (1992)
386–393
Shields, James
senator, Illinois, 1242
senator, Minnesota, 1249
senator, Missouri, 1251
Shields, John K.
senator, Tennessee, 1262
Ships and shipping
platform issue
Democrats, (1904) 482
Republicans, (1904) 482, (1916)
491
Shipstead, Henrik
senator, Minnesota, 1249
Shively, Benjamin F.
senator, Indiana, 1243
Shivers, Allan
governor, Texas, 1410
Sholtz, David
governor, Florida, 1388
Short, Dewey, 506
Shorter, John Gill
governor, Alabama, 1384
Shortridge, Eli C. D.
governor, North Dakota, 1404

Shortridge, Samuel M.
senator, California, 1238
Shott, Hugh Ike
senator, West Virginia, 1265
Shoup, George L.
governor, Idaho, 1390
senator, Idaho, 1242
Shouse, Jouett, 502
Shriver, R. Sargent
biography, 780
presidential candidate
Democratic contender, (1976) 177
as former vice-presidential nominee,
224
primary votes, (1976) 359–364
vice-presidential candidate
Democratic nominee, (1972) 172,
280, 425, 436, 535
electoral vote, (1972) 773
Shulze, John A.
governor, Pennsylvania, 1406
Shunk, Francis R.
governor, Pennsylvania, 1406
Sibley, Henry H.
governor, Minnesota, 1397
Sibley, John C., 478
Sick, Gary, 284
Sickles, Donald, 246
Siegelman, Don
governor, Alabama, 1384
Sigler, Kim
governor, Michigan, 138, 1397
Silsbee, Nathaniel
senator, Massachusetts, 1248
Silver. See Monetary policy
"Silver Gray" faction (Whigs)
nominees, (1856) 430
Silver Republican Party
nominees, (1900) 432
Silverman, Edward M.
vice-presidential candidate
Conservative Party of Virginia nomi-
nee, (1960) 435
Silzer, George S.
Democratic convention ballots, (1924)
606
governor, New Jersey, 1402
Simmons, Furnifold M.
Democratic convention ballots, (1920)
605
senator, North Carolina, 1256
Simmons, James F.
senator, Rhode Island, 1259
Simms, John F.
governor, New Mexico, 1402
Simon, Donald, 119 (box)
Simon, Joseph
senator, Oregon, 1258
Simon, Paul M.
presidential candidate
Democratic contender, (1988) 190,
287
primary votes, (1988) 378–385
senator, Illinois, 187, 1242
Simonetti, Joseph
Democratic convention ballots, (1992)
636
Simpson, Alan K.
senator, Wyoming, 181, 1266
Simpson, Milward L.
governor, Wyoming, 1413
senator, Wyoming, 1266
Simpson, Oramel H.
governor, Louisiana, 1393
Simpson, William D.
governor, South Carolina, 1408
Simpson, William O.
presidential primary votes, (1916) 322
Sinclair, Upton
California gubernatorial campaign,
265
presidential primary votes, (1936)
333–334
Singer, William, 534
Single Tax Party
nominees, (1920) 433

Sinner, George
governor, North Dakota, 1404
Sirhan, Sirhan, 17
Sirica, John J., 173
Skillen, Richard D.
presidential primary votes, (1996)
403
Skinner, Richard
governor, Vermont, 1410
Skok, Michael
presidential primary votes, (2000)
404–410
Skow, Philip
presidential primary votes, (1992)
386–393
Slade, William
governor, Vermont, 1410
Slater, James H.
senator, Oregon, 1258
Slaton, John M.
governor, Georgia, 1389
Slattery, James M.
senator, Illinois, 1242
Slaughter, Gabriel
governor, Kentucky, 1392
Slavery
in party development, 57, 63, 64, 66, 74,
81, 238, 239–240, 241
platform issue
Democrats, (1840) 445, (1852)
450–451, (1856) 455, (1860) 423
(box), 456–457
Free Soilers, (1848) 449, (1852)
452
Know-Nothings, (1856) 454
Liberty Party, (1844) 446
Republicans, (1856) 453–454, (1860)
458
population formula for House apportionment, 13 (box), 802
in sectional tension, 231–232
Sleeper, Albert E.
governor, Michigan, 1397
Slettandahl, ——
presidential primary votes, (1952) 343
Slidell, John
senator, Louisiana, 1246
Slizer, George S.
presidential primary votes, (1924)
327–328
Slocomb, Whitney Hart
presidential candidate
Greenback Party nominee, (1960)
435
Small, Len
governor, Illinois, 1391
Smalley, David A.
Democratic National Committee chair,
415 (table), 426 (table)
Smallwood, William
governor, Maryland, 1395
Smathers, George A.
Democratic convention ballots, (1960)
620
presidential primary votes, (1960)
346–347, (1968) 351–353
senator, Florida, 143, 1240
Smathers, William H.
senator, New Jersey, 1254
Smith, Alfred E.
biography, 780
governor, New York, 1403
New Deal opposition, 265
presidential candidate
Democratic contender, (1920) 494,
(1924) 260, 496–497, (1932) 262,
502
Democratic convention ballots,
(1920) 605, (1924) 606–607, (1928)
609, (1932) 611
Democratic nominee, (1928) 58, 261,
264, 433, 499–500
election evolution, 6, 16
electoral vote, (1928) 753
former governors, 222
popular vote, (1928) 670

primary votes, (1924) 327–328,
(1928) 329–330, (1932) 331–332,
(1936) 333–334
Prohibition repeal, 72
Smith, Benjamin
governor, North Carolina, 1403
Smith, Benjamin A. II
senator, Massachusetts, 1248
Smith, Charles A.
governor, South Carolina, 1408
Smith, Charles M.
governor, Vermont, 1411
Smith, Daniel
senator, Tennessee, 1261
Smith, Delazon
senator, Oregon, 1258
Smith, Edward C.
governor, Vermont, 1411
Smith, Ellison D.
senator, South Carolina, 1260
Smith, Elmo
governor, Oregon, 1406
Smith, Forrest
governor, Missouri, 1399
Smith, Frank L.
senator, Illinois, 1242
campaign finance, 110
Smith, George William
governor, Virginia, 1411
Smith, Gerald L. K.
presidential candidate
America First Party nominee, (1944)
434
Christian National Party nominee,
(1956) 435
Christian Nationalist Party nominee,
(1948) 434
popular vote, (1944) 693, (1956) 694
Union Party history, 79
Smith, Gerrit
presidential candidate
National Liberty Party nominee,
(1848) 430
popular vote, (1848, 1860) 690
Smith, Gordon H.
senator, Oregon, 200, 1258
Smith, Green Clay
presidential candidate
popular vote, (1876) 690
Prohibition Party nominee, (1876)
430
Smith, H. Alexander
senator, New Jersey, 1254
Smith, Henry
governor, Rhode Island, 1406
Smith, Hoke
governor, Georgia, 1389
senator, Georgia, 1241
Smith, Hulett C.
governor, West Virginia, 1412
Smith, Israel
governor, Vermont, 1410
senator, Vermont, 1263
Smith, James Jr.
senator, New Jersey, 1254
Smith, James M.
governor, Georgia, 1389
Smith, James Y.
governor, Rhode Island, 1407
Smith, Jeremiah
governor, New Hampshire, 1400
Smith, John
senator, New York, 1255
Smith, John
senator, Ohio, 1257
Smith, John B.
governor, New Hampshire, 1401
Smith, John Cotton
governor, Connecticut, 1387
Smith, John Gregory
governor, Vermont, 1410
Smith, John Walter
governor, Maryland, 1395
senator, Maryland, 1247
Smith, L. Neil
presidential candidate

Libertarian nominee, (2000) 439
popular vote, (2000) 699
Smith, Lonnie E., 26
Smith, Marcus A.
senator, Arizona, 1237
Smith, Margaret Chase
presidential primary votes, (1964)
348–350
Republican convention ballots, (1964)
621
senator, Maine, 141, 172, 787, 1247
widow's mandate, 788
Smith, Mary Louise
Republican National Committee chair,
417 (table), 426 (table)
Smith, Maureen
presidential candidate
Peace and Freedom Party nominee,
(1980) 68, 437
popular vote, (1980) 696
Smith, Nathan
senator, Connecticut, 1238
Smith, Nels H.
governor, Wyoming, 1413
Smith, Oliver H.
senator, Indiana, 1243
Smith, Perry
senator, Connecticut, 1239
Smith, Preston
governor, Texas, 1410
Smith, Ralph Tyler
senator, Illinois, 1242
Smith, Robert B.
governor, Montana, 1399
Smith, Robert C.
Constitution Party nomination feelers, 80
senator, New Hampshire, 1253
Smith, Robert J.
presidential candidate
American Party nominee, (1992) 52,
438
popular vote, (1992) 698
primary votes, (1992) 393
Smith, Samuel
senator, Maryland, 1247
appointment, 1232
Smith, Samuel E.
governor, Maine, 1394
Smith, Truman
senator, Connecticut, 1239
Smith, Tucker Powell
vice-presidential candidate
Socialist nominee, (1948) 434
Smith, William
biography, 780
senator, South Carolina, 1260
vice-presidential electoral vote, (1828,
1836) 772
Smith, William
governor, Virginia, 1411
Smith, William Alden
presidential primary votes, (1916)
322–323
senator, Michigan, 1249
Smith, William E.
governor, Wisconsin, 1413
Smith, William Hugh
governor, Alabama, 1384
Smith, William L., 713
Smith, Willis
senator, North Carolina, 143,
1256
Smith-Connally Act of 1943, 110
Smith-Lever Act of 1914, 257
Smoot, Reed
senator, Utah, 1263
Smoot-Hawley Tariff Act of 1930, 261
Smylie, Robert E.
governor, Idaho, 1390
Smyth, Frederick
governor, New Hampshire, 1400
Snell, Bertrand H.
Republican convention officers, 417
(table)
Snell, Earl
governor, Oregon, 1405

Snelling, Richard A.
governor, Vermont, 185, 1411
Snow, Wilbert
governor, Connecticut, 1387
Snowe, Olympia J.
senator, Maine, 199, 787, 789, 1246
marriage, 788
Snyder, Simon
Democratic-Republican vice-presidential
contender, (1816) 231
governor, Pennsylvania, 1406
Social Democratic Federation, 78, 79
Social Democratic Party
nominees, (1900) 431, 481
Socialist Party history, 78
Social Democratic Workingmen's Party, 79
Social Security
New Deal, 264, 265
platform issue
Democrats, (1948) 513, 518, (2000)
569
Green Party, (2000) 571
Progressives, (1912) 489
Republicans, (1936) 265, (1988) 555,
(1992) 559, (2000) 567
Socialists, (1912) 485
presidential campaign issue, (1948) 270,
(1964) 277, (1976) 178, (2000) 298
Socialist Equality Party
nominees, (1996) 439
Socialist International, 79
Socialist Labor Party
Debs candidacy (1900), 481
Greenback Party convention, (1880) 468
historical development, 46, 78
profile, 79
timeline, 47
nominees, (1892–1976) 431–437
Socialist Party
convention, platform, (1904) 481, (1908)
483, (1912) 485–486, (1916) 492, (1920)
492–493, (1932) 501
historical development, 46, 49
profile, 78–79
timeline, 47
nominees, (1904–56) 432–435,
(1976–2000) 437–439
Progressive ticket supporters, (1924) 70,
498
vote percentages, 424 (box)
Socialist Workers Party
historical development, 81
profile, 79
timeline, 47
nominees, (1948–2000) 434–439
Soeters, Kent M.
presidential popular vote, (1968 695
Soft money
as campaign finance issue, 104–105
overhaul legislation, 124 (box), 125
congressional campaigns, 97–98
definition, 83–84, 85 (box)
issue advocacy ads, 106
presidential campaigns, 92
Soldiers and Sailors Convention (1868), 246
Solidarity Party
presidential primary votes, (1988) 385
Solis, Hilda, 793
Sorauf, Frank J., 83, 96, 97, 101, 104
Sorlie, Arthur G.
governor, North Dakota, 1404
Soule, Pierre
senator, Louisiana, 1246
Souter, David, 301
South Carolina
Democratic convention credentials dispute, (1952), 422, (1972) 422, 534, 624
electoral vote contest, (1876) 248
South Carolinians for Independent Electors
nominee, (1956) 435
Southard, Samuel L.
governor, New Jersey, 1401
senator, New Jersey, 1253
Southern Alliance, 69
Southern Democratic Party
convention, (1860) 457

historical development
profile, 53–54
timeline, 47
nominees, (1860) 430
officers, 425 (box)
vote percentage, 424 (box)
Southern primaries, 129–132
Southgate, James Haywood
vice-presidential candidate
National Party nominee, (1896) 431
Soviet Union. *See also* Communism
collapse, 134, 192, 289
Kennedy policies, 156, 160
platform issue
Progressives, (1948) 514
Republicans, (1984) 551, (1988)
555–556
Reagan policies, 176–177, 185, 286
Sputnik, 149
U-2 flights, 152
Spaight, Richard D.
governor, North Carolina, 1403
Spaight, Richard D. Jr.
governor, North Carolina, 1403
Spangler, Harrison E.
Republican National Committee chair,
417 (table), 426 (table)
Spangler, Ronald W.
presidential primary votes, (1996) 403
Spanish-American War, 254
Spannous, Warren
Democratic convention ballots, (1980)
630
Sparkman, John J.
biography, 781
senator, Alabama, 1236
vice-presidential candidate
Democratic nominee, (1952) 434,
517
electoral vote, (1952) 773
politics and issues, (1952) 144–145
Sparks, Chauncey M.
governor, Alabama, 1384
Sparks, John
governor, Nevada, 1400
Sparrow, Cleveland
vice-presidential candidate
Third World Assembly nominee,
(1988) 438
Spaulding, Huntley N.
governor, New Hampshire, 1401
Spaulding, Rolland H.
governor, New Hampshire, 1401
Speakers of the House, 1588–1589
Special elections
electoral anomalies, 13 (box)
House, 803
removal of governors, 1381 (box)
Senate, 1232
southern primaries, 131–132
Specter, Arlen
senator, Pennsylvania, 183, 188, 1259
Speight, Jesse
senator, Mississippi, 1250
Spelbring, Ralph
presidential primary votes, (1992)
386–393
Spellman, John D.
governor, Washington, 1412
Spence, John S.
senator, Maryland, 1247
Spencer, Ambrose
Whig convention officers, 425 (box)
Spencer, George E.
senator, Alabama, 1236
Spencer, John C.
Anti-Mason convention officers, 425
(box)
Spencer, Lloyd
senator, Arkansas, 1237
Spencer, Selden P.
senator, Missouri, 1251
Spock, Benjamin M.
presidential candidate
Peace and Freedom Party nominee,
(1972) 68

Tomlinson, Homer Aubrey
  presidential candidate
    Church of God Party nominee, (1952) 434
    Theocratic Party nominee, (1960) 435, (1964) 436
Tompkins, Daniel D.
  biography, 781
  governor, New York, 1402
  vice-presidential candidate
    Democratic-Republican nominee, (1816) 231, (1820) 232
    electoral vote, (1816, 1820) 772
Tompkins, Mike
  vice-presidential candidate
    Natural Law Party nominee, (1992) 68, 438, (1996) 439
Tompkins, Rick
  presidential primary votes, (1996) 402
Tonkin Gulf resolution, 170, 277, 278
Toole, Joseph K.
  governor, Montana, 1399
Toombs, Robert
  senator, Georgia, 1241
Torricelli, Robert
  senator, New Jersey, 201, 1254
Toucey, Isaac
  Democratic convention ballots, (1860) 580
  governor, Connecticut, 1387
  senator, Connecticut, 1238
Tower, John G.
  Bush cabinet nomination, 290
  at Republican convention, (1972) 536
  senator, Texas, 155, 157, 187, 1262
  special election, 129, 132
Towne, Charles A.
  Democratic convention ballots, (1904) 597
  senator, Minnesota, 1249
Towns, George W.
  governor, Georgia, 1389
Townsend, Charles E.
  senator, Michigan, 1249
Townsend, Francis, 79, 265
Townsend, John G. Jr.
  governor, Delaware, 1388
  senator, Delaware, 1239
Townsend, M. Clifford
  governor, Indiana, 1391
Tracy, Uriah
  senator, Connecticut, 1239
Traficant, James A.
  presidential primary votes, (1988) 378–385
Trammell, Park
  governor, Florida, 1388
  senator, Florida, 1240
Transcontinental railroad
  Credit Mobilier scandal, 247
  platform issue
    Democrats, (1856) 455, (1860) 457
    Republicans, (1856) 454, (1860) 458
Transportation policy
  Republican platform issue, (1992) 560
Trapp, Martin E.
  governor, Oklahoma, 1405
Traylor, Melvin A.
  Democratic convention ballots, (1932) 611
Treadwell, John
  governor, Connecticut, 1387
Treaty of Versailles, 258
Treen, David C.
  governor, Louisiana, 1394
  at Republican convention, (1976) 541
Treutlen, John Adam
  governor, Georgia, 1389
Trevellick, Richard
  Greenback Party convention officers, 425 (box)
Tribbitt, Sherman W.
  governor, Delaware, 1388
Tribe, Laurence, 300
Trible, Paul S. Jr.
  senator, Virginia, 191, 1264

Trimble, Allen
  governor, Ohio, 1404
Trimble, William A.
  senator, Ohio, 1257
Trinkle, E. Lee
  governor, Virginia, 1411
Trinsey, Jack
  presidential primary votes, (1992) 393
Tripp, Alice
  Democratic convention ballots, (1980) 630
Trotskyite parties, 79
Trotter, James F.
  senator, Mississippi, 1250
Troup, George M.
  governor, Georgia, 1389
  presidential popular vote, (1852) 690
  senator, Georgia, 1241
Trousdale, William
  governor, Tennessee, 1409
Troutt, Arlin
  vice-presidential candidate
    Grassroots Party nominee, (1996) 439
Trowe, Margaret
  vice-presidential candidate
    Socialist Workers nominee, (2000) 439
Troxell, Richard K.
  presidential candidate
    Constitution Party nominee, (1968) 436
  popular vote, (1968) 695
Truitt, George
  governor, Delaware, 1388
Truman, Bess, 269
Truman, Harry S.
  biography, 781
  as Democratic leader, 59
  at convention, (1956) 518
    Harriman support, (1956) 148, 273
    on Kennedy, 273
    Stevenson support, (1952) 143–144
    Symington support, 273
  political party development, 46, 49–50, 61, 71
  as president, 271
    congressional relations, 137–139
    "Do-Nothing Eightieth Congress" (box), 141
    foreign policy, 138, 141–143
    House redistricting, 826
    politics and issues, 136–145
    succession, 268–269
  presidential candidate
    Democratic convention ballots, (1948) 616, (1952) 618
    Democratic nominee, (1948) 269–271, 423, 434, 512–513
    election evolution, 8, 17
    electoral vote, (1948) 703 (box), 758
    former members of Congress, 155 (box)
    as former vice president, 314 (box)
    as "minority" president, 223 (table)
    no-run decision, (1952) 143, 272
    politics and issues, (1948) 139–141
    popular vote, (1948) 675
    primary votes, (1948) 339–340, (1952) 313, 341–343
    public offices, 215
    reelection chances, (1948) 313 (box)
  senator, Missouri, 1251
  vice-presidential candidate
    Democratic nominee, (1944) 268, 434, 510
    electoral vote, (1944) 773
Trumbull, John H.
  governor, Connecticut, 1387
Trumbull, Jonathan
  governor, Connecticut, 1387
  senator, Connecticut, 1239
Trumbull, Joseph
  governor, Connecticut, 1387

Trumbull, Lyman
  Liberal Republican presidential contender, (1872) 247, 463
  senator, Illinois, 1242
Trump, Donald
  Reform Party contender, (2000) 73
Tsongas, Paul E.
  Democratic platform, (1992) 423 (box)
  presidential candidate
    Democratic contender, (1992) 195–196, 289, 557
    Democratic convention ballots, (1992) 636
    primary votes, (1992) 309, 386–393
  senator, Massachusetts, 181, 1248
Tuck, William M.
  governor, Virginia, 1412
Tucker, Jan
  presidential primary votes, (1996) 402
Tucker, Jim Guy Jr.
  governor, Arkansas, 1385
  resignation, 1381 (box)
Tucker, Tilgham M.
  governor, Mississippi, 1398
Tugwell, Rexford G., 263, 514
Tunnell, Ebe W.
  governor, Delaware, 1388
Tunnell, James M.
  senator, Delaware, 1239
Tunney, John V.
  senator, California, 179, 284, 1237
Tupahache, Asiba
  vice-presidential candidate
    Peace and Freedom Party nominee, (1992) 69, 438
Turley, Thomas B.
  senator, Tennessee, 1262
Turner, Daniel W.
  governor, Iowa, 1392
Turner, George
  senator, Washington, 1265
Turner, James
  governor, North Carolina, 1403
  senator, North Carolina, 1255
Turner, Roy J.
  governor, Oklahoma, 1405
Turner, Thomas G.
  governor, Rhode Island, 1407
Turner, W. F., 703 (box)
Turney, Daniel Braxton
  presidential candidate
    popular vote, (1908) 691
    United Christian Party nominee, (1908) 432
Turney, Hopkins L.
  senator, Tennessee, 1261
Turney, Peter
  governor, Tennessee, 1409
Turpie, David
  Democratic convention ballots, (1896) 595
  senator, Indiana, 1243
Tuttle, Hiram A.
  governor, New Hampshire, 1401
Twelfth Amendment, 14, 43–44, 225, 228, 229, 312, 542–543, 701, 702–703, 706 (box), 707, 709, 713
Twentieth Amendment, 16, 220, 1232
Twenty-fifth Amendment, 17, 18, 174, 281, 707, 714–715
Twenty-fourth Amendment, 17, 25, 132, 220
Twenty-second Amendment, 17, 139, 153–154, 194, 209
Twenty-sixth Amendment, 18, 21, 33, 220
Twenty-third Amendment, 17, 21, 162, 220
Tydings, Joseph D.
  senator, Maryland, 162, 1247
Tydings, Millard E.
  Democratic convention ballots, (1940) 612
  senator, Maryland, 143, 1247
Tyler, James Hoge
  governor, Virginia, 1411
Tyler, John
  governor, Virginia, 1411

Tyler, John
  biography, 781
  governor, Virginia, 1411
  presidential candidate
    as former governor, 176 (box)
    former members of Congress, 155 (box)
    as former vice president, 314 (box)
    National Democratic nominee, (1844) 429, 446, 447
    public offices, 214
    Whig rejection, 81
  senator, Virginia, 1264
    resignation, 1229
  succession to presidency, 15
  vice-presidential candidate
    electoral vote, (1836, 1840) 772
    Whig nominee, (1836) 429, 444, (1840) 237, 429, 444
Tyner, Jarvis
  vice-presidential candidate
    Communist nominee, (1972, 1976) 436
Tyson, Lawrence D.
  senator, Tennessee, 1262

U

U.S. Labor Party
  historical profile, 80
  nominees, (1976) 436
U.S. Taxpayers Party
  historical development
    profile, 80
    timeline, 47
  nominees, (1992) 438, (1996) 439
Udall, Morris K.
  Democratic convention speakers, 415 (table)
  presidential candidate
    Democratic contender, (1976) 177–178, 282, 538
    Democratic convention ballots, (1976) 627
    primary votes, (1976) 359–364
Ullmann, Daniel, 64
Umstead, William B.
  governor, North Carolina, 1404
  senator, North Carolina, 1256
Un-American Activities Committee, House, 272
Uncapher, Marshall
  vice-presidential candidate
    Prohibition Party nominee, (1972) 436
Underwood, Cecil H.
  governor, West Virginia, 149, 201, 206, 1412
  Republican convention officers, 417 (table)
Underwood, Joseph R.
  senator, Kentucky, 1245
Underwood, Oscar W.
  senator, Alabama, 1236
  presidential candidate
    Democratic contender, (1912) 257, 487, (1924) 497
    Democratic convention ballots, (1912) 601, (1920) 605, (1924) 606–607
Underwood, Thomas R.
  senator, Kentucky, 1245
Union Labor Party
  nominees, (1888) 431
Union Pacific Railroad Co., 247
Union Party (1864), 243, 459–460
Union Party (1936)
  convention, platform, 505–506
  historical development
    profile, 79–80
    timeline, 47
  nominees, 433
Union Reform Party
  nominees, (1900) 432
United American Party
  nominees, (1976) 437
United Auto Workers, 80

Wakefield, William H. T.
  vice-presidential candidate
    United Labor Party nominee, (1888)
      431
Walcott, Frederic
  senator, Connecticut, 1239
Wales, John
  senator, Delaware, 1239
Walker, Clifford M.
  governor, Georgia, 1389
Walker, Daniel
  governor, Illinois, 1391
Walker, David S.
  governor, Florida, 1388
Walker, Frank C.
  Democratic National Committee chair,
    426 (table)
Walker, Freeman
  senator, Georgia, 1241
Walker, George
  senator, Kentucky, 1244
Walker, Gilbert C.
  governor, Virginia, 1411
Walker, Isaac P.
  senator, Wisconsin, 1266
Walker, James B.
  presidential candidate
    American National Party nominee,
      (1876) 430
    popular vote, (1876) 690
Walker, James D.
  senator, Arkansas, 1237
Walker, John
  senator, Virginia, 1264
Walker, John W.
  senator, Alabama, 1236
Walker, Joseph M.
  governor, Louisiana, 1393
Walker, Prentiss, 803
Walker, Robert J.
  senator, Mississippi, 1250
Walker, Walter
  senator, Colorado, 1238
Wall, Edward C.
  Democratic convention ballots, (1904)
    597
Wall, Garrett D.
  senator, New Jersey, 1254
Wall, James W.
  senator, New Jersey, 1254
Wallace, David
  governor, Indiana, 1391
Wallace, George C.
  biography, 781
  effect on Democratic convention, (1968)
    531
  governor, Alabama, 1384
  presidential candidate
    American Independent Party nomi-
      nee, (1968) 51, 278, 279–280, 424
      (box), 436, 532
    Democratic contender, (1964) 276,
      (1972) 280, 535, (1976) 282, 538
    Democratic convention ballots,
      (1968) 623, (1972) 625, (1976) 177,
      627
    election evolution, 9, 18
    electoral college issues, (1968) 703
      (box), 706, 709–710, 711–712
    electoral vote, (1968) 763
    Patriotic Party nominee, (1968) 436
    political party development, 46, 50
    politics and issues, (1964) 160,
      (1968), 163, 166, 168, (1972) 171
    popular vote, (1968) 680
    primary votes, (1964) 348–350,
      (1968) 351–353, (1972) 354–358,
      (1976) 359–364
    third-party challenges, 4
Wallace, Henry A.
  biography, 781
  at Democratic convention, (1944) 509
  presidential candidate
    Communist Party support, 54
    election evolution, 8
    as former vice president, 314 (box)

political party development, 46,
  49–50, 59
politics and issues, (1948) 139,
  140–141
popular vote, (1948) 675
primary votes, (1948) 339–340
Progressive nominee, (1948) 71, 269,
  271, 434, 514
Truman cabinet, 137–138, 269
vice-presidential candidate
  Democratic contender, (1944) 268,
    510
  Democratic nominee, (1940) 267,
    312, 434, 507
  electoral vote, (1940) 773
Wallace, Lurleen
  governor, Alabama, 166, 1384
Wallace, William A.
  senator, Pennsylvania, 1258
Wallace, William J.
  presidential candidate
    Commonwealth Land Party nominee,
      (1924) 433
    popular vote, (1924) 692
Wallas, Graham, 277
Waller, Thomas M
  governor, Connecticut, 1387
Waller, William Lowe
  governor, Mississippi, 1398
Wallgren, Monrad C.
  governor, Washington, 1412
  senator, Washington, 1265
Wallop, Malcolm
  senator, Wyoming, 179, 1266
Walsh, Arthur
  senator, New Jersey, 1254
Walsh, David I.
  governor, Massachusetts, 1396
  senator, Massachusetts, 1248
Walsh, Patrick
  senator, Georgia, 1241
Walsh, Thomas J.
  Democratic convention officers, 415
    (table), (1932) 502
  presidential candidate
    Democratic convention ballots,
      (1924) 606–607
    primary votes, (1928) 329–330
  senator, Montana, 1251
Walters, David
  governor, Oklahoma, 1405
Walters, Herbert S.
  senator, Tennessee, 1262
Walthall, Edward C.
  senator, Mississippi, 1250
Walton, George
  governor, Georgia, 1389
  senator, Georgia, 1240
Walton, John C.
  governor, Oklahoma, 1405
Walton, Richard
  vice-presidential candidate
    Citizens Party nominee, (1984) 54,
      437
Wanamaker, John
  postal patronage, 252
  Republican convention ballots, (1916)
    602
War Labor Disputes Act of 1943, 110
War of 1812, 230, 231
"War on poverty," 160
Ward, John E.
  Democratic convention officers, 415
    (table)
Ward, Marcus L.
  governor, New Jersey, 1401
  Republican National Committee chair,
    417 (table), 426 (table)
Ward, Matthias
  senator, Texas, 1262
Ware, Nicholas
  senator, Georgia, 1241
Warfield, Edwin
  governor, Maryland, 1395
Warmouth, Henry C.
  governor, Louisiana, 1393

Warner, Fred M.
  governor, Michigan, 1397
Warner, John
  senator, Virginia, 181, 1264
Warner, Willard
  senator, Alabama, 1236
Warner, William
  senator, Missouri, 1251
Warren, Charles B.
  Republican convention ballots, (1920)
    604
Warren, Earl
  biography, 781
  governor, California, 138, 1386
  Kennedy assassination commission, 159
  presidential candidate
    primary votes, (1936) 333–334,
      (1948) 339–340, (1952) 144,
      341–343
    Republican contender, (1948) 140,
      272, (1952), 271
    Republican convention ballots,
      (1948) 615, (1952) 617
  Republican convention officers, speakers,
    417 (table)
  Supreme Court justice
    African American voting rights, 29
    House redistricting, 822
    school desegregation, 145–146
  vice-presidential candidate
    electoral vote, (1948) 773
    Republican bid declined, (1944) 268
    Republican nominee, (1948) 141,
      270, 434, 511
Warren, Francis E.
  governor, Wyoming, 1413
  senator, Wyoming, 1266
Warren, Fuller
  governor, Florida, 1389
Warren, James
  presidential candidate
    popular vote, (1988) 697, (1992) 698
    Socialist Workers nominee, (1988,
      1992) 79, 438
Washburn, Cadwallader C.
  governor, Wisconsin, 1413
Washburn, Emory
  governor, Massachusetts, 1396
Washburn, Israel Jr.
  governor, Maine, 1394
Washburn, Peter T.
  governor, Vermont, 1410
Washburn, William B.
  governor, Massachusetts, 1396
  senator, Massachusetts, 1248
Washburn, William D.
  senator, Minnesota, 1249
Washburne, Elihu B.
  Republican convention ballots, (1876)
    586, (1880) 588
  Republican vice-presidential contender,
    (1880) 468
Washington, George
  biography, 781
  as president
    Farewell Address, 227
    House reapportionment veto, 811
    political party development, 43–44,
      55, 62, 225
  presidential candidate
    electoral vote, (1789) 14, 702 (box),
      718, (1792) 719, (1796) 720
    former members of Congress, 155
      (box)
    public offices, 214
    third-term issue, 194
    uncontested elections, (1789, 1792)
      225–227
    Virginia House campaign, (1757) 108
Washington, Walter E.
  presidential primary votes, (1976)
    359–364
Washington Post
  Dole affair coverage, 295
Watergate scandal, 134, 163, 171, 172,
  173–174, 281

campaign finance reform, 83, 86, 114
Democratic convention, (1976) 539
election milestones, 18
Republican convention, (1976) 541
turnover in Congress, 793
Waterman, Charles W.
  senator, Colorado, 1238
Waterman, Robert W.
  governor, California, 1386
Waters, Maxine, 791
Watkins, Aaron Sherman
  presidential candidate
    popular vote, (1920) 692
    Prohibition Party nominee, (1920)
      433
  vice-presidential candidate
    Prohibition Party nominee, (1908,
      1912) 432
Watkins, Arthur V.
  senator, Utah, 138, 1263
Watkins, W. Dean
  vice-presidential candidate
    Prohibition Party nominee, (2000)
      439
Watson, Clarence W.
  senator, West Virginia, 1265
Watson, Claude A.
  presidential candidate
    popular vote, (1944) 674, (1948) 693
    Prohibition Party nominee, (1944,
      1948) 434
Watson, Diane, 791
Watson, James
  senator, New York, 1255
Watson, James E.
  presidential primary votes, (1928) 330
  Republican convention ballots, (1920)
    604, (1928) 609
  senator, Indiana, 1243
Watson, Thomas E.
  biography, 781
  political party development, 69
  presidential candidate
    popular vote, (1904, 1908) 691
    Populist nominee, (1904, 1908) 432
  senator, Georgia, 1241
    successor, 788
  vice-presidential candidate
    electoral vote, (1896) 773
    Populist nominee, (1896) 431
Watson, William T.
  governor, Delaware, 1388
Wattenberg, Ben, 219
Watterson, Henry M.
  Democratic convention officers, 415
    (table)
Watts, J. C., 791
Watts, Richard C.
  Democratic convention ballots, (1928)
    609
Watts, Thomas H.
  governor, Alabama, 1384
Watumull, David
  presidential primary votes, (1968) 353
Wayne, Stephen J., 713
Wealth and Poverty (Gilder), 284
Weare, Meshesh
  governor, New Hampshire, 1400
Weaver, Arthur J.
  governor, Nebraska, 1399
Weaver, James B.
  biography, 781
  presidential candidate
    electoral vote, (1892) 702 (box),
      744
    Greenback Party nominee, (1880) 64,
      431, 468
    political party development, 46
    popular vote, (1880) 658, (1892) 661
    Populist nominee, (1892) 69, 252,
      424 (box), 431, 476
Weber, Max, 246
Webb, Frank Elbridge
  presidential candidate
    Farmer Labor nominee, (1928) 433
    popular vote, (1928) 692

For Reference

Not to be taken from this room